Baldwin's Ohio Handbook Series

OHIO DOMESTIC VIOLENCE LAW

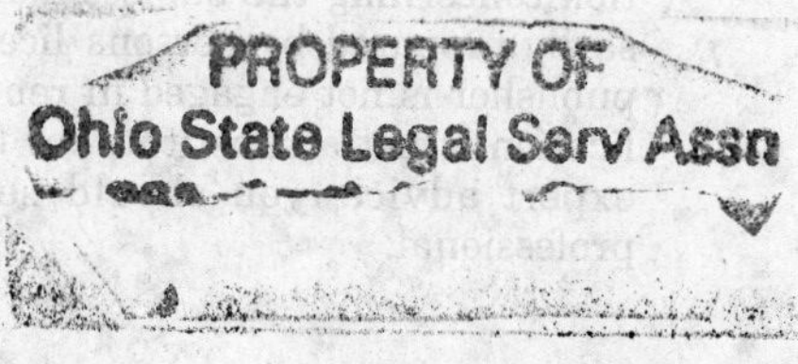

by

Ronald B. Adrine

Alexandria M. Ruden

Sherrie M. Miday

2018-2019 Edition
Issued in December 2018

For Customer Assistance Call 1-800-328-4880

Mat #42065815

This publication was created to provide you with accurate and authoritative information concerning the subject matter covered; however, this publication was not necessarily prepared by persons licensed to practice law in a particular jurisdiction. The publisher is not engaged in rendering legal or other professional advice and this publication is not a substitute for the advice of an attorney. If you require legal or other expert advice, you should seek the services of a competent attorney or other professional.

ISBN # 978-1-539-22827-1

Introduction to the 2018-2019 Edition

Ohio Domestic Violence Law, 2018-2019 ed. (Baldwin's Ohio Handbook Series) is a practical guide for law enforcement officials, family practitioners, social workers, judges, prosecutors, police, and defense attorneys. Ohio Domestic Violence Law covers Ohio civil and criminal laws governing domestic violence. It discusses current issues and emerging trends, with references to applicable state and federal statutes, rules and caselaw.

Highlights

- Effect of juvenile adjudications on subsequent offenses (Chapter 3)
- Hearsay evidence and Confrontation Clause (Chapter 7)
- Appeal of consent agreement (Chapter 9)
- Appeal of stalking civil protection order (Chapter 9)
- Dating relationships covered under domestic violence statute (Chapter 10)
- Address Confidentiality Act (Chapter 12)
- Collateral consequences exception to mootness (Chapter 12)
- Immigration and domestic violence (Chapter 18)

Thank you for subscribing to *Ohio Domestic Violence Law*, 2018-2019 ed. (Baldwin's Ohio Handbook Series). We hope you find this book an invaluable tool for your practice.

THE PUBLISHER

Preface to the 2018-2019 Edition

Domestic violence as a discrete area of the law has existed in America for little more than thirty years. The heightened attention focused on this issue, particularly in the last seven years, is the result of a belated national recognition that such violence has a wide-ranging negative impact on multiple facets of our social fabric. Homicide, suicide, child abuse, substance abuse, delinquency, homelessness, loss of economic productivity, among other social ills, all have major roots in the problem of domestic violence.

In Ohio, this area of the law has shown a particular dynamism. In 1994, Ohio's civil and criminal domestic violence laws both underwent radical revision. Since that time, the State has enacted no fewer than nine additional major pieces of legislation on this subject.

The rapid and constant modification of Ohio's domestic violence laws makes it hard for practitioners to remain current. Emerging trends and innovations to enhance the safety of victims and to protect the rights of those accused appear with great regularity, not just in Ohio but around the country. The purpose of this book, then, is to help those interested in this area of the law make sense of the dizzying array of developments and to put them in proper perspective.

This book provides comprehensive coverage of both the civil and criminal laws on domestic violence now in force in Ohio. It thoroughly analyzes the nature and variety of the relationships covered by those laws, the relief those laws afford to victims, and the rights of those accused of their violation. In addition, throughout the book, we have attempted to anticipate, hypothetically pose, and then concisely answer questions that those who are likely to use this reference might be expected to ask. However, as with any legal text, we consider this a work in progress, and we encourage readers to contact us with any questions we failed to address so that we might include them in future editions of this book.

The book includes checklists, interview formats, charts, sample questions, a brief and other aids that should serve as excellent starting points for police officers, prosecutors, defense attorneys, victim advocates, and others who desire to develop their own protocols for dealing with the intricacies of this area of the law.

Due to the dearth of civil case law on the subject of domestic violence when we began writing this book, where necessary, we drew from criminal and out-of-state case law. While such cases may not deal directly with the questions posed, they often provided useful and inventive arguments for Ohio practitioners to use in civil matters involving domestic violence. We still resort to these authorities but are pleased to note that, over the years, the volume of material on this subject produced by the courts of Ohio has expanded exponentially.

We also drew heavily from our colleagues in the domestic violence community. If we have borrowed your ideas without proper attribution, we did so unintentionally and we apologize.

Ronald B. Adrine
Alexandria M. Ruden
Sherrie M. Miday

Cleveland, Ohio
September, 2018

About the Authors

Ronald B. Adrine was first elected to the bench of Cleveland Municipal Court in 1981, serving over 36 years on the bench before retiring in January 2018.

Over the years, Judge Adrine was appointed to serve as a member of the Ohio Governor's Task Force on Family Violence, the Ohio Attorney General's Victim Assistance Advisory Board, the Ohio Supreme Court's Domestic Violence Task Force and the Board of Directors of the National Center for State Courts. He co-chaired the Advisory Board of the National Judicial Institute on Domestic Violence. He chaired the National Board of Directors of Futures Without Violence (formerly known as the Family Violence Prevention Fund), the Cleveland Domestic Violence Coordinating Committee, as well as the Cuyahoga County Domestic Violence Collaboration Task Force. Additionally, he initiated the successful effort to bring a Family Justice Center to Greater Cleveland.

Judge Adrine has lectured extensively on domestic violence issues for a wide variety of organizations, associations, and governmental agencies. Those entities include, the National Center for Disease Control, the Federal Bureau of Investigation, the National College of District Attorneys, the National Council of Juvenile and Family Court Judges, the National League of Cities, the National Governors Association, and the U.S. Department of Justice.

He received his B.A. from Fisk University in 1969 and his J.D. from Cleveland State University's Cleveland-Marshall College of Law in 1973.

Alexandria M. Ruden is a senior attorney with the Legal Aid Society of Cleveland where she established a domestic violence practice. Prior to her work at Legal Aid, Ms. Ruden was both Legal Director and a staff attorney for the Free Medical Clinic of Greater Cleveland, representing clients in their legal program and a small claims referee (magistrate) for Cleveland Heights Municipal Court.

She is a member of the Supreme Court of Ohio's Advisory Committee on Domestic Violence and a former member of the Supreme Court's Advisory Committee on Children & Families. She serves on the Supreme Court's Subcommittee on Responding to Child Abuse, Neglect and Dependency. She is an advisory board member of the Family Violence Prevention Center, through the Ohio Office of Criminal Justice Services. She is a member of the Cuyahoga County Domestic Violence Shelter Advisory Board and the Violence against Women Act Allocations Committee (Cuyahoga County). Ms. Ruden is a member of the Cuyahoga County Domestic Violence Collaboration Task Force. She is also a member of the Community of Partners through NIWAP.

She is a member of the Cleveland Metropolitan Bar Association, the Ohio Bar Association and the American Bar Association.

She is a national and statewide lecturer and trainer on domestic violence and the law and a consultant to various professionals including law enforcement, judges, attorneys and legislators and on Ohio domestic violence law and legislation.

Ms. Ruden was appointed by Governor Voinovich to the Ohio Children's Trust Fund and served from 1993-1997. She received her Juris Doctor form the Cleveland-Marshall College of Law in 1980 and her B.A from the Ohio State University.

Judge Sherrie M. Miday is a judge in the Court of Common Pleas in Cuyahoga County. As a Common Pleas judge, she is responsible for both general civil cases and felony criminal cases. She was first elected in November 8, 2016. Judge Miday received her undergraduate degree from John Carroll University in 1998 and her J.D. from the Case Western Reserve University School of Law in 2001. Prior to taking the bench, Judge Miday practiced law with the firm of Manley Deas Kochalski, LLC, specializing in foreclosure litigation and creditor's rights law. She previously served as an associate attorney with the law firm of Duvin, Cahn & Hutton, as an assistant prosecutor for the City of Cleveland, as a specialized domestic violence prosecutor, and as a judicial staff attorney for Judge Ann Mannen.

Acknowledgments

We wish to thank and acknowledge the contributions of all of those who contributed to the publication of this effort over the years. We extend special thanks to Ms. Ruden's husband, Sam Amata, who urged us to undertake this task in the first place and encouraged us to stay with it when we really did not want to. We also extend special thanks to Ms. Janice Hagwood, who showed great forbearance and patience during the original production of this title. She continually reminded us of the need and importance of this work and sacrificed much to assure that it got done. In addition, we never would have completed this work without the encouragement and prodding of Judge Adrine's late father, Attorney Russell T. Adrine, and the understanding of Ms. Ruden's children, Joshua and Jessica. Judge Miday's family deserves much recognition in giving of their time to allow Judge Miday to focus on this edition. Many thanks to Ryan, Athanasius, Mikhaila, and Helena.

We would also like to acknowledge Nancy Neylon, Executive Director of the Ohio Domestic Violence Network and Diana Ramos-Reardon, Program Manager for the Supreme Court of Ohio's Domestic Violence Program for all the time and effort they took in reviewing and critiquing our original work-in-progress and our subsequent updates.

Special thanks goes to Attorney Keevin Berman of the Cuyahoga County Public Defender's Office for his assistance with and critique of the original final draft of Chapter 7 and his insights into the intersection between domestic violence and immigration law.

Additionally, we would like to thank Joanne Wu, Katherine Mullin, Kimberly Baga and Joan Bascone, who worked with us, for their diligent research and analytical skills, without which the criminal sections of this volume would have been impossible.

We also owe a debt of gratitude to the entire community of domestic violence commentators and researchers, whose analyses, insights, and ideas prove invaluable to the on-going production of this book.

Lastly, we need to acknowledge the support and understanding, as well as the gentle pressure, relentlessly applied, of our editors at West, with whom it has been a joy to work while creating this work.

Table of Abbreviations

A.2d	Atlantic Reporter, Second Series
Ala. Crim. App.	Alabama Court of Criminal Appeals
A.L.R. Fed.	American Law Reports, Federal Series
Am. J. Pub. Health	American Journal of Public Health
Am. Psychol.	American Psychologist
Ariz. Rev. Stat. Ann.	Arizona Revised Statutes Annotated
Art.	Article
ASPO	Anti-stalking protection order
B.C. L. Rev.	Boston College Law Review
BYU J. Pub. L.	BYU Journal of Public Law
Cal. App.4th	California Appellate Reports, Fourth Series
Cal. Fam. Code	West's Annotated California Code, Family
Cal. Rptr.	West's California Reporter
Cal. Rptr.2d	West's California Reporter, Second Series
Case W. Res. L. Rev.	Case Western Reserve Law Review
cert. denied	certiorari denied
Civ. R.	Ohio Rules of Civil Procedure
Cong.	Congress
C.P.	Common Pleas Court
CPO	Civil protection order
Crim. R.	Ohio Rules of Criminal Procedure
D.C. Intrafamily R.	District of Columbia Superior Court Rules of the Family Division, Intrafamily Proceedings
Dist. Ct. App.	District Court of Appeals
D.R.	Disciplinary Rules, Code of Professional Responsibility
D.R. R.	Domestic Relations Court Rule
DSM	Diagnostic and Statistical Manual
Evid. R.	Ohio Rules of Evidence
F.2d	Federal Reporter, Second Series
F.3d	Federal Reporter, Third Series
Fam. Advoc.	Family Advocate
Fam. L. Q.	Family Law Quarterly
Fed.	Federal Reporter
Fla. B. J.	Florida Bar Journal
Fla. Stat. Ann.	Florida Statutes Annotated
F.Supp.	Federal Supplement
FVPSA	Family Violence Prevention and Services Act
Ham.	Hamilton County
Haw.	Hawaii Reports
H.B.	House Bill
H. Con. Res.	U.S. House of Representatives Congressional Resolution
Int'l J. Health Servs.	International Journal of Health Services

JAMA	Journal of the American Medical Association
J. Clin. Psychol.	Journal of Clinical Psychology
Judges' J.	The Judges' Journal
Just.	Justice
Juv. & Fam. Ct. J.	Juvenile and Family Court Journal
LEADS	Law Enforcement Automation Data System
L.Ed.	United States Supreme Court Reports, Lawyers' Edition
L.Ed.2d	United States Supreme Court Reports, Lawyers' Edition, Second Series
Loc. R.	Local Rule
Mass. Gen. L. Ann.	Massachusetts General Laws Annotated
Mich. App.	Michigan Appeals Reports
Mich. L. Rev.	Michigan Law Review
MMPI	Minnesota Multiphasic Personality Inventory
Mo. Ann. Stat.	Vernon's Annotated Missouri Statutes
Mont.	Montgomery County
Muni.	Municipal Court
N.C. App.	North Carolina Court of Appeals Reports
NCIC	National Crime Information Center database
N.D. Cent. Code	North Dakota Century Code
N.E.	North Eastern Reporter
N.E.2d	North Eastern Reporter, Second Series
N.H.	New Hampshire Reports
N.J. Stat. Ann.	New Jersey Statutes Annotated
N.J. Super.	New Jersey Superior Court Reports
N.M.	New Mexico Reports
N.W.2d	North Western Reporter, Second Series
N.Y.2d	New York Reports, Second Series
N.Y. Misc.2d	New York Miscellaneous Reports, Second Series
N.Y.S.2d	West's New York Supplement, Second Series
O.A.G.	Ohio Opinions of the Attorney General
O. Const.	Ohio Constitution
Ohio App.	Ohio Appellate Reports
Ohio App.2d	Ohio Appellate Reports, Second Series
Ohio App.3d	Ohio Appellate Reports, Third Series
Ohio Jur.2d	Ohio Jurisprudence, Second Series
Ohio Jur.3d	Ohio Jurisprudence, Third Series
Ohio Misc.	Ohio Miscellaneous Reports
Ohio Misc.2d	Ohio Miscellaneous Reports, Second Series
Ohio N.U. L. Rev.	Ohio Northern University Law Review
Ohio St.	Ohio State Reports
Ohio St.2d	Ohio State Reports, Second Series
Ohio St.3d	Ohio State Reports, Third Series
Ohio St. L. J.	Ohio State Law Journal
OJI	Ohio Jury Instructions
P.2d	Pacific Reporter, Second Series
Pa.	Pennsylvania State Reports

Pa. D. & C.4th	Pennsylvania District and County Reports, Fourth Series
Pa. Stat. Ann.	Purdon's Pennsylvania Statutes Annotated
Pa. Super.	Pennsylvania Superior Court Reports
Phila.	Philadelphia County Reporter
PKPA	Parental Kidnapping Prevention Act
Pub. L.	Public Law
Q.	Quarterly
RC	Revised Code of Ohio
Rts.	Rights
S.B.	Senate Bill
SCPO	Stalking civil protection order
S. Cal. Rev. L. & Women's Stud.	Southern California Review of Law & Women's Studies
S.C. L. Rev.	South Carolina Law Review
S.Ct.	United States Supreme Court Reporter
S.D.	South Dakota Reports
S.E.2d	South Eastern Reporter, Second Series
Servs.	Services
So.2d	Southern Reporter, Second Series
Soc. Work Res. & Abstracts	Social Work Research and Abstracts
SSN	Social security number
Stat.	Statutes
Sub.	Substitute
Summ.	Summit County
Supp.	Supplement
Sup. R.	Rules of Superintendence for the Courts of Ohio
S.W.2d	South Western Reporter, Second Series
Tex. Fam. Code Ann.	Vernon's Texas Codes Annotated, Family
tit.	Title
TPO	Temporary protection order
TRO	Temporary restraining order
UCCJA	Uniform Child Custody Jurisdiction Act
UCCJEA	Uniform Child Custody Jurisdiction and Enforcement Act
U.C. Davis L. Rev.	University of California at Davis Law Review
U.S.	United States Supreme Court Reports
U.S.C.A.	United States Code, Annotated
U.S. Const.	United States Constitution
Vand. L. Rev.	Vanderbilt Law Review
VAWA	Violence Against Women Act of 1994
Vt.	Vermont Reports
Vt. L. Rev.	Vermont Law Review
Wis.2d	Wisconsin Reports, Second Series
Wis. L. Rev.	Wisconsin Law Review
WL	Westlaw
Women & Pol.	Women and Politics
Women's Rts. L. Rep.	Women's Rights Law Reporter

Yale L.J. .... Yale Law Journal

THOMSON REUTERS PROVIEW™

This title is one of many now available on your tablet as an eBook.

Take your research mobile. Powered by the Thomson Reuters ProView™ app, our eBooks deliver the same trusted content as your print resources, but in a compact, on-the-go format.

ProView eBooks are designed for the way you work. You can add your own notes and highlights to the text, and all of your annotations will transfer electronically to every new edition of your eBook.

You can also instantly verify primary authority with built-in links to WestlawNext® and KeyCite®, so you can be confident that you're accessing the most current and accurate information.

To find out more about ProView eBooks and available discounts, call 1-800-344-5009.

RELATED PRODUCTS

STATUTES, CONSTITUTIONS, AND COURT RULES

Baldwin's Ohio Revised Code Annotated
Baldwin's Ohio Legislative Service Annotated

Ohio Constitution Handbook

Ohio Rules of Court, State and Federal

United States Code Annotated

CASE LAW, REPORTERS, DIGESTS, ATTORNEY GENERAL OPINIONS

Ohio Official Reports

West's Ohio Digest

Ohio Attorney General Opinions

SERB Official Reporter

Federal Reporter

Federal Supplement

West's Supreme Court Reporter

ADMINISTRATIVE LAW

Baldwin's Ohio Administrative Code

Ohio Administrative Law Handbook and Agency Directory
Lepp and McNeil

Baldwin's Ohio Monthly Record

Administrative Law and Practice 2d

Administrative Law: Practice and Procedure

GENERAL LEGAL REFERENCES

Ohio Jurisprudence 3d

American Jurisprudence 2d

American Law Reports

Corpus Juris Secundum

OHIO DATABASES ON WESTLAW

Cases, General & Topical

Statutes & Court Rules
Legislative Service, Bills & Bill Tracking

Administrative & Executive Materials

Public Information, Records & Filings

Baldwin's Ohio Practice Series

Ohio Jurisprudence 3d

Ohio Forms, Legal & Business

Law Reviews, Bar Journals & Legal Periodicals

Newspapers & Periodicals

Miscellany

CD-ROM

Baldwin's Ohio Revised Code Annotated with Ohio Administrative Code, and SERB Official Reporter

Ohio Reports

Ohio Unreported Appellate Decisions

Baldwin's Ohio Practice Library

West's Ohio Digest

Ohio Jurisprudence 3d

United States Code Annotated

West's Sixth Circuit Reporter

West's Federal District Court Reporter—Sixth Circuit

West's Supreme Court Reporter

Federal Reporter, 1st, 2d, and 3d Series

Federal Supplement

Federal Rules Decisions

Wright & Miller, Federal Practice and Procedure

Topical CD-ROM Libraries

Ohio Jurisprudence Pleading and Practice Forms

Ohio Criminal Defense Motions
Hennenberg and Reinhart

CIVIL PRACTICE AND PROCEDURE

Baldwin's Ohio Practice, Civil Practice 2d
Klein, Darling, and Terez

Baldwin's Ohio Practice, Civil Practice Laws & Rules Annotated

Ohio Personal Injury Practice
Nelson

Baldwin's Ohio Practice, Tort Law
Ernst

Ohio Trial Practice
Markus and Dickinson

CRIMINAL LAW AND PRACTICE

Baldwin's Ohio Practice, Criminal Law 3d
Katz and Martin

Baldwin's Ohio Practice, Statutory Charges

Ohio Arrest, Search and Seizure
Katz

Baldwin's Ohio Practice, Ohio Criminal Laws and Rules
Katz and Giannelli (Eds.)

Ohio Domestic Violence Law
Adrine and Ruden

Ohio Driving Under the Influence Law
Weiler and Weiler

Ohio Felony Sentencing Law
Griffin and Katz

Ohio Trial Practice
Markus and Dickinson

TRIAL AND APPELLATE PRACTICE

Baldwin's Ohio Practice, Evidence 3d
Giannelli

Baldwin's Ohio Practice, Rules of Evidence Handbook
Giannelli

Ohio Appellate Practice
Painter and Pollis

Ohio Trial Objections
Giannelli and Snyder

Ohio Trial Practice
Markus and Dickinson

DOMESTIC RELATIONS AND FAMILY LAW

Baldwin's Ohio Practice, Domestic Relations Law 4th
Sowald and Morganstern

Baldwin's Ohio Practice, Domestic Relations Laws and Rules Annotated

Ohio Domestic Violence Law
Adrine and Ruden

Ohio Elder Law
Kreiner

Domestic Relations Journal of Ohio
Morganstern

PROBATE AND JUVENILE LAW

Baldwin's Ohio Practice, Merrick-Rippner Probate Law 7th

Ohio Probate Code Annotated

Probate Law Journal of Ohio
Brucken

Ohio Juvenile Law
Yeomans Salvador

REAL ESTATE

Ohio Landlord Tenant Law
White

Baldwin's Ohio Practice, Ohio Real Estate Law 3d
Kuehnle and Levey

Ohio Condominium Law
Kuehnle and Williams

BUSINESS AND LEGAL

Baldwin's Ohio Practice, Business Organizations 2d
Blackford

Baldwin's Ohio Practice, Business Organizations Laws & Rules
Ekonomon and Heinle (Eds.)

Ohio Consumer Law
Legal Aid Society of Cleveland

LEGAL FORMS

Ohio Forms Legal and Business

Ohio Forms and Transactions

Ohio Jurisprudence Pleading and Practice Forms

West's Legal Forms, 2d

TAX LAW

Baldwin's Ohio Tax Law and Rules
Ebersole

LABOR LAW

Ohio Civil Service & Collective Bargaining Laws & Rules Annotated

Ohio Employment Practices Law

Workers' Compensation Journal of Ohio
Harris

GOVERNMENT

Baldwin's Ohio Practice, Local Government Law—Township
Princehorn

Baldwin's Ohio Practice, Local Government Law—Municipal
Gotherman, Babbit and Lang

Baldwin's Ohio Practice, Local Government Law—County
Conard II

Rutter's Ohio Municipal Service
Khouzam

Ohio Election Laws Annotated

Ohio Planning and Zoning Law
Meck and Pearlman

SCHOOL LAW

Baldwin's Ohio School Law
Hastings, Manoloff, Sharb, Sheeran and Jaffe

Ohio School Law Handbook
Hastings, Manoloff, Sharb, Sheeran and Jaffe

Baldwin's Ohio School Law Journal
Lentz

Lentz School Security
Lentz

United States School Laws and Rules

BUILDING CONSTRUCTION AND CODE ENFORCEMENT

Ohio Building Code and Related Codes

Know Your Code: A Guide to the OBC

Ohio Construction Law Manual

Code News

Thomson Reuters thanks you for subscribing to this product. Should you have any questions regarding this product please contact Customer Service at 1-800-328-4880 or by fax at 1-800-340-9378. If you would like to inquire about related publications or place an order, please contact us at 1-800-344-5009.

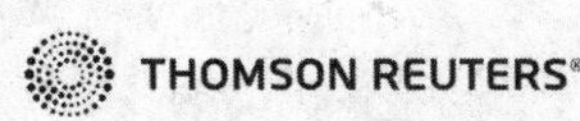

Thomson Reuters
610 Opperman Drive
Eagan, MN 55123

https://legal.thomsonreuters.com/

Summary of Contents

Summary of Contents

Table of Contents

CHAPTER 1. INTRODUCTION

CHAPTER 2. CRIMINAL DOMESTIC VIOLENCE IN OHIO

CHAPTER 3. RELATED OFFENSES AND THE EFFECT OF PRIOR CONVICTIONS UNDER OHIO'S DOMESTIC VIOLENCE LAW

CHAPTER 4. PROTECTION ORDERS IN CRIMINAL CASES

CHAPTER 5. DOMESTIC VIOLENCE PROSECUTION—INITIATION AND INITIAL CASE PREPARATION

CHAPTER 6. DOMESTIC VIOLENCE PROSECUTION—TRIAL PRESENTATION

CHAPTER 7. DOMESTIC VIOLENCE DEFENSE—TRIAL PREPARATION AND PRESENTATION ISSUES

CHAPTER 8. THE NATURE OF A CIVIL PROTECTION ORDER

CHAPTER 9. STALKING AND TRESPASS

CHAPTER 10. NATURE OF THE DOMESTIC VIOLENCE RELATIONSHIP

CHAPTER 11. ISSUANCE OF A CIVIL PROTECTION ORDER

CHAPTER 12. FULL HEARING ON CIVIL PROTECTION ORDERS

CHAPTER 13. COURT ENFORCEMENT OF CIVIL PROTECTION ORDERS AND RELATED ISSUES

CHAPTER 14. POLICE ENFORCEMENT OF PROTECTION ORDERS AND OTHER RELEVANT ISSUES

CHAPTER 15. DOMESTIC VIOLENCE AND CUSTODY AND VISITATION ISSUES

CHAPTER 16. DOMESTIC VIOLENCE CASE STRATEGY AND EVIDENTIARY CONSIDERATIONS

CHAPTER 17. ROLE OF THE VICTIM ADVOCATE

CHAPTER 18. FEDERAL REMEDIES

CHAPTER 19. TORT REMEDIES AVAILABLE

CHAPTER 20. JUVENILE PROTECTION ORDERS

APPENDICES

Chapter 1

Introduction

By Nancy Neylon[1]

> **KeyCite®**: Cases and other legal materials listed in KeyCite Scope can be researched through the KeyCite service on Westlaw®. Use KeyCite to check citations for form, parallel references, prior and later history, and comprehensive citator information, including citations to other decisions and secondary materials.

§ 1:1 General

Domestic violence is now recognized as a serious and widespread problem. It has a devastating and negative impact not only on its immediate victims but on all family members and the community. In addition to a thorough understanding of the available legal remedies and their application it is necessary to comprehend the complexity of domestic violence to effectively respond to the problem. Those involved in the justice system must be aware of the historical responses to domestic violence and must understand the dynamics particular to violence that occurs in the context of intimate relationships, and finally, they must acknowledge that effective intervention in domestic violence requires that both the community and the individual take responsibility for addressing the problem.

For those individuals who have been abused by their intimate partners, the past 40 years have seen both radical change and no change at all. The lives of some have been touched and empowered by the ever-expanding worldwide movement to support victims of violence, while others remain trapped in a nexus of traditional tolerance of family violence and indifference to those who suffer from such violence. This has been a time marked by social change and resistance to change, by innovation and reassertion of the status quo.

The domestic violence movement began with a vision of a world transformed, where everyone participated fully in all facets of society. This transformation cannot be achieved without major social changes in all aspects of cultural, political, economic, and spiritual life. The movement grew out of the women's movement and anti-rape movement of the 1960s and early 1970s and built on earlier movements including abolitionist, temperance, victims' rights, socialism, and unionism. While there is considerable diversity in the specific programs and larger ideological perspectives within the domestic violence movement, providing assistance for victims of domestic

---

[1]Executive Director, Ohio Domestic Violence Network. Although this chapter has not changed since the inception of the book, the information is still historically accurate and currently relevant.

violence and changing the attitudes, belief systems, policies, and procedures of institutions that serve to keep victims in violent relationships are universally endorsed goals. Thus, many such efforts have been directed at the justice system.

Domestic violence is not a new problem, nor is it a newly identified problem; however, it is new in its identification as a crime. In Great Britain, citizens used an informal justice system of processions and the banging of pots and pans to condemn excessive chastisement of wives.[1] However, in the late eighteenth century, Judge Blackstone, a prominent English legal authority, reaffirmed the right of moderate chastisement of wives by their husbands in his commentary on English common law.[2] This lack of a legal response continued. In 1874, a British parliamentary committee collected evidence on violence against children and wives. There was discussion, but ultimate rejection, of flogging as an appropriate sanction for "ordinary assaults." In the United States, flogging as a sanction for "wife beaters" was debated in several state legislatures in the 1880s.[3] President Theodore Roosevelt referred to the problem of wife abuse in his fourth annual address to Congress in 1904 and recommended corporal punishment for the perpetrators of such abuse.[4] The public debate that ensued in the late 1880s and early 1900s originated from the need for public order and focused on the alleged violence of the lower and working classes rather than on the increased safety of women. At the same time, the growth of the new behavioral sciences created novel ideas on how to address family problems in the public domain.

The growth of a family court system in the early 1900s was fueled by the advent of these new behavioral sciences. Family courts attempted to solve domestic disputes and family problems through timely intervention and social remedies. This succeeded in diverting the issue of violence against wives from the attention of the criminal courts.

The ideals of early intervention and social remedies were extended into police work to address overburdened police and courts. Arrest was considered inappropriate for solving family squabbles and dangerous for police officers. It was believed that police intervention inflamed conflicts and that police mediation would help promote a family's functioning where communication had broken down. By 1977, seventy percent of police departments were using crisis intervention in domestic violence incidents. Research showed that crisis intervention failed,

[Section 1:1]

[1] R. Emerson Dobash & Russell P. Dobash, Community Response to Violence Against Wives, Charivari, Abstract Justice and Patriarchy, 28 Social Problems 563–81 (1981).

[2] R. Emerson Dobash & Russell P. Dobash, Community Response to Violence Against Wives, Charivari, Abstract Justice and Patriarchy, 28 Social Problems 563–81 (1981).

[3] R. Emerson Dobash & Russell P. Dobash, Community Response to Violence Against Wives, Charivari, Abstract Justice and Patriarchy, 28 Social Problems 563–81 (1981).

[4] R. Emerson Dobash & Russell P. Dobash, Community Response to Violence Against Wives, Charivari, Abstract Justice and Patriarchy, 28 Social Problems 563–81 (1981).

resulting in more repeat calls and an increase in family homicides.[5] Crisis intervention only succeeded in moving the abuser away from the criminal justice system while appeasing the growing concern for victims and maintaining the status quo.

Lawsuits against the police departments in New York City in 1978 and Oakland, California in 1976 initiated changes in law enforcement's response to domestic violence. Both suits helped to raise public awareness of law enforcement inattention and began a precedent for changing the arrest requirements for domestic violence.[6] Additionally, in 1977, the Law Enforcement Assistance and Administrative Initiative (LEAA) established the Family Violence Program. This first federal response to domestic violence required not just a criminal justice system response but a comprehensive approach using both social and legal remedies.[7]

The first national hearing on domestic violence was held by the United States Commission on Civil Rights to consider whether battered women were receiving equal protection under the law. In January 1978, a hearing was held that set the stage for very interactive forms of discourse between the government and the public. Many advocates suggested that a wider analysis than one of personal interaction was necessary to understand the problem. Most of the presentations focused on legal responses and the importance of shelters.[8] Bills to support local efforts emerged very quickly; however, the Family Violence Prevention and Services Act (FVPSA) did not pass until October 1984 as an amendment to the Child Abuse Prevention and Treatment Act. The legislation took no specific legal actions but simply created some minimal funding for domestic violence shelters and related services.[9]

Legislators and advocates began work almost immediately on the Violence Against Women Act (VAWA), with bills being introduced by 1989. Again, work toward passage of this bill was slow, and passage ultimately was linked to the Violent Crime Control and Law Enforcement Act of 1994.

The intended scope of VAWA was much larger than that of FVPSA. It included, for the first time, federal legal remedies for victims, created new funding streams not only for service providers but also the criminal justice system, and created public policy that required collaboration between the social service/advocacy community and the justice system. VAWA was to provide a national response to the problem of domestic and sexual violence that would continue to evolve in response to emerging issues and challenges. The reauthorization of VAWA in 2000 highlighted the role of courts by making state and lo-

---

[5] J. Driscoll et al., Training Police in Family Crisis Intervention, 9 Journal of Applied Behavioral Services 62–82 (1973).

[6] Susan Schechter, Women and Male Violence: The Visions and Struggles of the Battered Women's Movement (1982).

[7] United States Commission on Civil Rights, Battered Women: Issues of Public Policy (1978).

[8] United States Commission on Civil Rights, Battered Women: Issues of Public Policy (1978).

[9] Susan Schechter, Women and Male Violence: The Visions and Struggles of the Battered Women's Movement (South End Press 1982).

cal courts expressly eligible for funding including 5% set aside in the state STOP grants. VAWA 2000 also created a specific program for civil legal services for victims of domestic violence, stalking and sexual assault and established a new program to provide training and technical assistance to better meet the needs of victims with disabilities. VAWA 2000 also expanded the provision for immigrant victims by creating protection for victims of serious crime (U Visas) and trafficking (T Visas) when they assist with the investigation and prosecution of the crime. The reauthorization of VAWA in 2005 included recognition of the impact of domestic violence on children and dating violence as emerging areas of concern. Sexual and dating violence among young people ages 16 to 24 occur at high rates than, with one out of five teen girls reporting violence in their dating relationship and one quarter of teen girls report being pressured to engage in sexual behavior when they did not want to. VAWA 2005 also created specific programs for prevention, recognizing that exposure to violence can have negative consequences on children. The Sexual Assault Services Program provided funding for advocacy through the medical and criminal justice system for sexual assault survivors and training relating to sexual assault to law enforcement, courts and hospitals. The reauthorization process allows VAWA to continue to bolster the remarkable gains made to address domestic and sexual violence, stalking and dating violence in states and local communities across the country.

From 1976 to the early 1980s was the initial period of legal reform on the state level. Legal changes required the introduction of legislation in all fifty states. The new laws, in general, decided who was eligible for protection, what behavior legitimately constituted a crime, and what relief was to be made available, with the notion of protection orders being made available to victims as a form of immediate relief. Changes in federal law were reflected in state law. Ohio passed two pieces of legislation to address violence in teen relationships. H.B. 19, effective March 29, 2012 mandated prevention programs in health classes, grades seven through 12 in dating violence prevention education. The legislation also required school personnel to receive training in the prevention of dating violence. H.B. 10, effective June 17, 2010 allowed juveniles to obtain civil protections orders through juvenile court.

Survivor autonomy, confidentiality and abuser accountability are core principles which guide response to domestic violence. Working with teen survivors and teen perpetrators presents unique challenges. Survivors must be informed of the limits of confidentiality in their particular circumstances. We are still learning what accountability looks like for teen perpetrators but building a coordinated community response that includes using school and court authority, along with universal prevention programs that model health relationships is essential.

In understanding and applying domestic violence laws, it is critical to note, how difficult it is to consistently and appropriately implement the intent of the legislation, and how resistance is inherent in any attempt to change public policy. How successful a victim may be in accessing legal remedies depends on each local jurisdiction's application of the law and on whether legal intervention is entirely safe in any victim's particular circumstances.

The United States has undergone significant changes in the way its justice system responds to battered women. The success is the result of alliances and productive working relationships between police, prosecutors, courts, and advocacy organizations.

Domestic violence, as it is most commonly called, has many different names: family violence, wife abuse, spouse abuse, battering, and partner abuse. The social or behavioral definition of the problem is different from the legal definition. Both behavioral and legal definitions include the relationship between the victim and the offender, and both include specific behaviors. However, the behavioral definition is broader and is also defined by the function the abusive behavior serves. Thus, under the behavioral definition, domestic violence is a pattern of on-going assaultive and coercive behaviors including physical, sexual, and psychological attacks and economic coercion used to achieve compliance and maintain control over an intimate partner. Domestic violence is not an out-of-control or impulsive act but rather is purposeful behavior. Control tactics are chosen selectively to limit the independence of the victim.

The relationship between the victim and the abuser is one where both are adults, peers with equal rights and responsibilities within the relationship. Neither has a legitimate role of controlling the other. The abuser in a domestic violence situation has on-going access to the victim. Thus, domestic violence is not an isolated event, but a pattern of repeated events and multiple tactics. The single incident of physical harm, which may bring a victim to the attention of the justice system, is only one small part of the arsenal of abusive tactics used by the perpetrator. Actual physical assaults may occur only infrequently, but the coercive tactics occur on a daily basis. The tactics that are not a part of a state's domestic violence law are those most frequently experienced by victims: emotional abuse, denying a victim's perception of reality, isolating a victim from family and friends, refusing to allow a victim to attend school, and controlling access to family resources including money, transportation, clothing, and food. Psychological battering is an effective weapon in controlling victims when it is reinforced with the use of physical force. The reality of past violence gives additional power to the abuser by establishing fear in the victim. At times, the physical abuse, threats of harm, and psychological abuse are marked by seemingly loving behavior (e.g., sending flowers after an assault, promising it will never happen again). This behavior is a part of the overall tactics of coercion. Should the victim refuse to respond to this apparent contrition on the part of the abuser, the most violent and damaging forms of control will be employed.

Domestic violence is behavior learned through observation and experience and is reinforced not only by the family but by society. Domestic violence is not anger-based behavior or out-of-control behavior. Current research indicates a wide variety of anger patterns among identified perpetrators of domestic violence, as well as among individuals not identified as perpetrators of domestic violence. Abusers in one study actually reduced their heart rate during observed domestic violence.[10]

Patterns observed in abusers, such as not being physically abusive in public, not destroying their own property, or hitting only certain parts of the body, suggest decision-making that indicates that they are in control when they are abusive. While research has demonstrated a high correlation between domestic violence and substance abuse, there is no data to prove a cause-and-effect relationship. It may be that the alcohol and/or drugs have a disinhibiting effect on the abuser. Certain drugs, such as crack cocaine, may in fact produce chemical reactions in the brain that cause violent behavior or psychosis that is accompanied by violent behavior.[11] Much more research is needed in this area to actually determine the effects of controlled substances on an individual's violent behavior.

Victims of domestic violence have in common only that they have been abused by an intimate partner. They may be of any age, racial or cultural group, economic status, or personality profile. The majority of victims are female, although domestic violence may be perpetrated by women against men or in same-sex partnerships. The research does not indicate that victims of domestic violence were necessarily previous victims of childhood abuse or witnesses to violence.

Victims of domestic violence are survivors of trauma. Trauma is a word that is used frequently, but it is important to understand the context and the impact of trauma on an individual. It is essential to understand that traumatic reactions are normal responses to abnormal situations. There is a direct relationship between the severity of the trauma and its psychological impact. Severity is often defined by experiences that are chronic and that are deliberate human cause. For a victim of domestic violence the perpetrator is a loved one. The violation of trust and disruption to interpersonal connection is more severe due to trauma occurring in the context of an intimate relationship.

The experience of trauma actually changes the structure and function of the brain. When the experience of trauma is chronic the brain continually responds as if under stress by preparing the body for "fight, flight or freeze." This hyper-arousal manifests itself in physical symptoms that can include panic, exhaustion, concentration problems, and sleep disturbance. These reactions are especially noticeable in children. Our brain is designed to remember dangers, so that if the same thing happens again we can respond quickly and efficiently. Sometimes something will happen that will remind a person of a past event and makes him or her feel as if he or she is in danger when they are not. This is a trauma trigger and it can be as simple as a sound, a smell, a color, a tone of voice. These triggers will make the survivors respond as if they are in danger, even if they are not.

There is evidence that traumatic memories are encoded into the

---

[10]Neil S. Jacobson et al., Affect, Verbal Content, and Psychophysiology in the Arguments of Couples With a Violent Husband, 62 Journal of Consulting and Clinical Psychology (1994).

[11]Anne L. Ganley, Domestic Violence: A National Curriculum for Family Preservation Practitioners, Understanding Domestic Violence: Preparatory Reading for Participants, Family Violence Prevention Fund, 1995.

brain differently due to the high levels of adrenaline and stress hormones that are circulating through the body during the traumatic event. They are encoded as vivid sensations and images rather than a verbal narrative or logical story. It is no wonder that survivors have difficulty remembering traumatic events in a way that allows them to describe events in a logical verbal manner.

In addition to hyper arousal or the flight, fight or freeze reaction, trauma victims frequently experience intrusion or re-experiencing events in the form of nightmares or flashbacks. These flashbacks are not perceived as memories but the survivor feels as though the trauma is actually occurring. Survivors also frequently experience constriction or avoidance, meaning the narrowing of consciousness or numbing of feeling or thoughts associated with the traumatic situation. The numbing is adaptive and protective but can produce in a survivors, denial and detachment.

It is the experience of trauma that causes reactions in survivors that can seem abnormal to helping professionals and to the survivors themselves. Psychological and cognitive reactions include difficulty concentrating, difficulty making decisions, confusion, poor attention span, memory difficulties. Emotional reactions include depression, anger or irritability, mood swings, panic, fear, disbelief, hopelessness and physical reactions include sleep or appetite disturbance, rapid heartbeat, nausea, dizziness, chronic pain, headaches.

There are a number of factors that help to guide survivors as they overcome their traumatic experiences. The first stage is establishing safety and sustaining a safe environment. The experience or trauma includes disempowerment and disconnections. Therefore survivors need to be empowered, and in control of their own decisions and future. A survivor will need to reconnect and establish stability in housing and employment and other daily living needs as necessary to individual circumstances.

Victims of domestic violence use many different strategies to cope with trauma and resist the abuse. Victims frequently seek to improve or terminate the relationship with outside intervention such as counseling, consulting with clergy, or seeking civil or criminal justice system intervention. If these strategies are not effective in stopping the violence and tactics of control, victims may believe that nothing can protect them. The primary reasons victims give for staying in violent situations are fear and the lack of appropriate interventions. This fear is very real, as abusers escalate their tactics of coercive control when they are threatened. Thus, for a victim of domestic violence, attempting to leave a violent situation is potentially very dangerous. For if the tactics of isolation and psychological abuse fail to control the victim, the tactic of physical abuse will most likely be employed by the abuser to regain control.

Appropriate follow-through may be hampered by inadequate resources for both the court and other social services. Victims may have various trauma reactions, especially in a courtroom setting. Furthermore, the behaviors that are exhibited by a victim may really be a "cover" for another reaction. For example, a victim who recants or is reluctant or refuses to testify may believe that cooperation or testimony would put him/her at greater risk from the perpetrator and may hope that recanting will be seen by the abuser as compliance. This same rationale may be applied to a victim who continues to have contact with the perpetrator.

A courtroom may be the first time a victim has had a safe place to express anger about the abuse, and he/she may be responding to support and encouragement to "stand up for himself/herself." A victim who insists on limited or no visitation for the abuser with the children may fear the abuser's capacity to endanger the children or recognize the abuser's use of custody or visitation demands as a means of continuing control. Victims focused on infidelity, property matters, or emotional abuse may be unable to address or deal with the physical abuse. Additionally, the emotional abuse may be the most demeaning to them. A highly articulate victim who can describe the abuse in precise detail may be further into the healing process or may find it important to get all the facts out.

Mistrust of the court process and attorneys may be a result of revictimization experienced with other professionals. Victims who wait a long time between the last abusive incident and seeking help may only recently have received information about legal remedies or may have concluded that now is the "safest" time to go forward.

As with victims, perpetrators of domestic violence do not belong to a specific age, racial, cultural, or economic group. Perpetrators minimize their violence and coercive control and deny its impact on the victim, the family, and others. If the abusive behavior is acknowledged, it is frequently intensified by blaming the victim or some other external factor. This denial and external blame may be used to avoid consequences, as perpetrators believe they have the right to control their intimate partners and family; or this denial may be used as a way for perpetrators to avoid their own discomfort with the use of coercive control and violence. Perpetrators tend to be very controlling of their children and are often unwilling or unable to consider the best interests of their children apart from their own needs and issues.

Perpetrators may appear calm, reasonable, and willing to compromise. Domestic violence offenders frequently present a facade to the outside world, especially when they believe that they have control; and many believe that they maintain control over their victims even in a courtroom. Even today, many perpetrators of domestic violence do not come to the attention of the criminal or civil justice system. Further, many jurisdictions do not have adequate or appropriate treatment options for offenders or intensive monitoring by probation. Lack of follow-up suggests to offenders that their behavior is not a serious problem.

The response to perpetrators of domestic violence has changed significantly over the past thirty years, and this response continues to evolve. The use of risk assessments has grown to help identify the most dangerous offenders as well as those most likely to recidivate. Risk assessment can have different goals and outcomes depending on who performs the assessment and how they are used. For example the court may use the results to determine provisions of release or sentencing, a batterer's intervention program for counseling strategies or other service referral or an advocate for safety planning with the survivor. The limitations of risk assessment include the potential for inadvertently placing victims in danger or overstating their validity or reliability. The best risk assessment is not a rote exercise but rather draws from a variety of sources including external sources such as police reports and victim statements. Good risk assessment does promote communication across systems.

The first programs specifically for batterers were founded in the 1970's. Research finding on the effectiveness of batterer intervention programs vary widely from little effect to reductions in violence behavior by participants who complete a program. However randomized control trails have failed to take into account the context of the broader community responses to domestic violence, including law enforcement, probation the courts, and mental health and substance abuse agencies. Research has to be designed to account for more than just re arrest and practice based evidence must be incorporated into research. What is emerging as best practice includes working closely with courts and probation to monitor court ordered referrals, partnering with other social services to enhance accountability and offer a range of services from substance abuse to job training, engaging offenders early in their role as parents and partners, using assessment and risk management to address the high risk offenders and developing coordinated community responses beyond the legal system.

Children who witness domestic violence are profoundly affected by it, and the ultimate effects are both short-term and long-term. The consequences of the abuse vary according to the age and developmental stage of the child. The immediate impact on children can be seen in such cognitive, physical, and psychological symptoms as eating or sleeping problems, over-compliance, aggressive acting out, detachment, language delays, stuttering, somatic complaints (e.g., stomach aches and headaches), and suicidal ideation. Children may view themselves as the cause of the violence and learn violence and coercion as appropriate skills in problem solving and relationship building. Development tasks are made more difficult by living with these circumstances. Infants who must make attachments for healthy development, grammar school children learning role development, and adolescents learning autonomy carry the long-term effects of violence into adulthood.

Research also indicates that each child's experiences and the impact of those experiences are unique. The impact is based on the various risk and protective factors present in a child's life. Intervention must be tailored to each child's individual circumstances. After experiencing trauma children need to experience a sense of normalcy, including educational stability, support of their peer group and stability in the structure of their daily life.

Due to the impact of domestic violence on children, the intersection between children's protective services and domestic violence requires effective interventions across systems. In 2008, 10 Ohio county children's services agencies began to implement an 18-month Alternative Response child protection model. The Alternative Response model recognizes the broad variation that exists among child maltreatment reports and the need for responding differently based on individual family need. Central to the alternative response model is the focus on child safety through partnership with families, assessment of strengths and the provision of services without a formal disposition that maltreatment has occurred. Through the process of the pilot program counties found a significant number of alternative response cases were experiencing domestic violence. In response the Ohio Intimate Partner Violence Collaborative was established to build competency within the children's protective services system on domestic violence and to foster enhanced relationships between child welfare, courts, domestic violence services providers, and other critical stakeholders. A capacity building initiative, Safe and Together was launched in four counties. The key principle of Safe and Together is that the safety and well-being of children exposed to batterer behaviors is ideally achieved through keeping then safe and together with the non-offending parent/domestic violence survivor. The skill based trainings improve capacity to conduct risk assessment, interview family members, accurately document domestic violence dynamics and develop safety plans. Wrap around training for community stakeholders enhance a community's ability to collaborate to families experiencing domestic violence. Evaluations indicated that the training built concrete strategies for working with children survivors and perpetrators and that the shift in practice fit with the work they were doing in alternative response. While children's services secured new partners in serving families they noted that developing more effective communication and referral processes across systems was essential in moving forward. The Safe and Together training has begun to roll out across the state with a plan to complete the training process in every county by the end of 2014.

The last three decades have brought great changes in the way Ohio responds to the problem of domestic violence. Many people have worked tirelessly to create safe, confidential shelters for victims and their children and to develop services such as legal advocacy, court accompaniment, twenty-four-hour hotlines, support groups, children's services, school prevention programs, and intervention services for batterers. Many have also worked for legislative changes and the system changes necessary to implement those legislative changes. Ohio has enjoyed many successes in intervention in the problem of domestic violence: greater visibility of the problem, creation of funding for essential services, and the passage of very good laws. And yet, Ohio cannot afford even one moment of complacency about our accomplishments. The Supreme Court of Ohio Domestic Violence Task Force convened in March 1995 released findings and recommendations in October 1996. The findings concluded that domestic violence laws are inconsistently applied throughout Ohio; that domestic violence services are often insufficient, unavailable, and inadequately funded; that Ohio laws and services provide inadequate safety for victims of domestic violence; that the collection of statistical data reflecting the prevalence of domestic violence is inadequate; and that those entities responsible for addressing domestic violence do not adequately coordinate their efforts.[12] Subsequent needs assessments conducted by the Ohio Department of Public Safety, Office of Criminal Justice Services, found the same conclusions.

A study completed by the Health Policy Institute of Ohio in 2006,

[12]Supreme Court of Ohio Domestic Violence Task Force, October 1996.

reported that an estimated 166,000 people were physically assaulted by an intimate partner in Ohio each year. The report found that 64,000 children were abused or neglected and 29,000 elderly were abused or neglected. Based on these finding the researchers surmised that domestic violence costs Ohio more than 1.1 billion dollars in health care, and social services each year. The costs and impacts on the justice system and the workplace are not included in these estimates or no doubt the costs would be much higher. (White Paper on Improving Family Violence Prevention in Ohio, Health Policy Institute of Ohio, 2008).

There can no longer be any doubt that domestic violence is an extremely prevalent problem; one that affects not only its immediate victims, but the entire community. Domestic violence is linked to a range of problems, and its costs have an impact on our justice system, health system, and workplace. It is clear that every community must develop a multidisciplinary collaborative response whose purpose is to coordinate the work of all relevant agencies by assuring that evidence based practices, policies, protocols, and procedures are used to address domestic violence in their community. Effective intervention in domestic violence requires on-going collaboration through regular meeting of all service providers, including law enforcement, courts, shelters and domestic violence service providers, medical service providers, child welfare agencies, mental health services, faith communities, business and community leaders, educational institutions, survivors of family violence, and service recipients. To be successful, these efforts must attend to the specific characteristics and cultural make-up of their communities. These coordinated efforts should create a shared vision in the community and provide on-going needs assessment and planning, resource development, on-going information sharing and training, policy and procedure development, data collection, collaboration on specific projects, and monitoring and evaluation of services and intervention. In addition, this coordinated community response must address primary prevention efforts that support emerging social norms and cultural systems that reflect a commitment to healthy relationships.

The monitoring and evaluations developed to measure the effectiveness of a coordinated community response must, first and foremost, evaluate the impact of an intervention on the victims of domestic violence in terms of safety, autonomy, quality of life, and efficacy of safety planning. The evaluation should also consider accountability through statistics and death review panels and the impact on perpetrators and the issues of recidivism, not only involvement with the justice system but methods to measure behavior that is coercive and exploitative. The evaluation process should also document changes in policies and procedures, the interface and communication between the various court systems and service providers, and the impact of on-going training.

The success of a community's coordinated response to family violence may be met through a variety of methods, goals, and objectives. Coordination across agencies requires flexibility, informed communication, and the voluntary exchange of information and resources. Many barriers and challenges may make this difficult, including differences in intervention goals and methods, cultural beliefs, "turf" issues, engrained practices, and political motivations. What is crucial is the commitment of core members of a local coordinating council or advisory group and the community to the principles of safety for victims, accountability for perpetrators, collaboration in the provision of services, and engagement of the community in education and prevention.

Chapter 2

Criminal Domestic Violence in Ohio

§ 2:1 Introduction

In Ohio, the primary distinction between the crime of domestic violence and other assaults or threats is one additional element. That additional element requires that the harm which the offender causes, attempts to cause, or threatens to cause be directed against a family or household member.

Ohio's domestic violence laws[1] generally recognize the unique problems of both proof and safety which exist when intimate and family relationships become violent. Under RC 2919.25 et seq., the courts have the authority to issue special orders to protect alleged victims and maintain the status quo until the equities in the situation can be weighed and analyzed.

Criminal violence between "family and household members" is not, however, always charged under the domestic violence laws. The crimes charged may also fall under one of several other related offenses which do not specifically require the element of "family or household member." Prohibitions and protections provided under these other laws, although inclusive of both the perpetrators and the victims of domestic violence, are not limited to those who fit the narrow definitions contained in the state's domestic violence enactments.

RC 2919.25 is divided into three subsections:

[Section 2:1]

[1]RC 2919.25 (Effective: September 17, 2010); RC 2919.26 (Effective: July 6, 2018); RC 2919.27 (Effective: September 27, 2017); see also all substantially similar municipal ordinances.

(1) an intentional effort to injure,
(2) reckless injury, and
(3) a threat to injure.

§ 2:2 Intentional domestic violence under RC 2919.25(A)

To commit a violation under RC 2919.25(A) an offender must:

(1) knowingly
(2) cause or attempt to cause
(3) physical harm
(4) to a family or household member
(5) within the state of Ohio.

An offender must act knowingly to be held criminally liable for committing a violation under RC 2919.25(A). Thus, he/she must have conscious knowledge of the actions which result in the charge. The definition of "knowingly" found in RC 2901.22(B) provides that "A person acts knowingly, regardless of his purpose, when he is aware that his conduct will probably cause a certain result or will probably be of a certain nature. A person has knowledge of circumstances when he is aware that such circumstances probably exist."

A criminal "attempt" is defined as an act that is a substantial step in a course of conduct planned to culminate in the commission of a crime.[1]

"Cause" is defined in the criminal volume of Ohio Jury Instructions as "an act or failure to act which in a natural and continuous sequence directly produces the physical harm to person, and without which it would not have occurred."[2]

Any injury, illness, or other damage to another's physical well-being will constitute "physical harm to persons" as defined in RC 2901.01(C). This definition results in criminal liability under RC 2919.25 for any person who purposely tries to hurt a family or household member, as defined in RC 2919.25(E), or who knowingly engages in conduct which the offender knows or should know is likely to result in injury to a family or household member. However, in *State v. Suchomski*,[3] the issue was whether a father who had previously been convicted of do-

---

[Section 2:2]

[1]See RC 2923.02(A) (Effective: April 4, 2007). Note that this statement is highly paraphrased from the language of the statute which reads: "No person, purposely or knowingly, and when purpose or knowledge is sufficient culpability for the commission of an offense, shall engage in conduct that, if successful, would constitute or result in the offense.".

[2]Ohio Jury Instructions, Volume IV, Criminal, Section 409.55.

[3]State v. Suchomski, 58 Ohio St. 3d 74, 567 N.E.2d 1304 (1991); see also, State v. Hauenstein, 121 Ohio App. 3d 511, 700 N.E.2d 378 (3d Dist. Putnam County 1997); State v. Adaranijo, 153 Ohio App. 3d 266, 2003-Ohio-3822, 792 N.E.2d 1138 (1st Dist. Hamilton County 2003); State v. Thompson, 2006-Ohio-582, 2006 WL 307715 (Ohio Ct. App. 2d Dist. Miami County 2006); Lumley v. Lumley, 2009-Ohio-6992, 2009 WL 5174121 (Ohio Ct. App. 10th Dist. Franklin County 2009); State v. Snyder, 2011-Ohio-1062, 2011 WL 826292 (Ohio Ct. App. 8th Dist. Cuyahoga County 2011); State v. Cordle, 2010-Ohio-5919, 2010 WL 4926590 (Ohio Ct. App. 5th Dist. Delaware County 2010); State v. Zielinski, 2011-Ohio-6535, 2011 WL 6382541 (Ohio Ct. App. 12th Dist. Warren County 2011); State v. Luke, 2011-Ohio-4330, 2011 WL 3813588 (Ohio Ct.

mestic violence against his son was precluded, by operation of the domestic violence statute, from using any corporal punishment to discipline that child. The defendant argued that, under RC 2919.22, he had the right to administer reasonable corporal punishment, so long as serious physical harm to the child did not result, but that he was prevented from doing so by the provisions of RC 2919.25(A) which prohibit the infliction of physical harm no matter how slight. The Ohio Supreme Court disagreed and noted that RC 2901.01(C) defined "physical harm" as "any injury." It then went on to note that *Black's Law Dictionary* defines "injury" as " '[t]he invasion of any legally protected interest of another.' "[4] The Court thereafter reasoned and held that a child does not have any legally protected interest which is invaded by proper and reasonable parental discipline; however, where the harm inflicted by a parent exceeds that which could be considered proper or reasonable, the parent commits the crime of domestic violence. In *State v. Hicks*,[5] the court stated, "We do not believe that the legislature of Ohio intended to outlaw corporal punishment when it enacted R.C. 2919.25(A)."[6] Criminal liability may attach regardless of how slight the injury may be, whether the injury suffered is an

---

App. 3d Dist. Union County 2011); State v. Clark, 2015-Ohio-2978, 2015 WL 4510693 (Ohio Ct. App. 9th Dist. Wayne County 2015); State v. Litton, 2016-Ohio-7913, 2016 WL 6948332 (Ohio Ct. App. 12th Dist. Preble County 2016).

[4]State v. Suchomski, 58 Ohio St. 3d 74, 567 N.E.2d 1304 (1991) (quoting Black's Law Dictionary (6th ed.) p 785); State v. Thompson, 2006-Ohio-582, 2006 WL 307715 (Ohio Ct. App. 2d Dist. Miami County 2006); In re J.L., 176 Ohio App. 3d 186, 2008-Ohio-1488, 891 N.E.2d 778 (3d Dist. Allen County 2008); State v. Cantwell, 2008-Ohio-3928, 2008 WL 2971386 (Ohio Ct. App. 5th Dist. Licking County 2008); In re Kristen V., 2008-Ohio-2994, 2008 WL 2468839 (Ohio Ct. App. 6th Dist. Ottawa County 2008); Lumley v. Lumley, 2009-Ohio-6992, 2009 WL 5174121 (Ohio Ct. App. 10th Dist. Franklin County 2009); State v. Snyder, 2011-Ohio-1062, 2011 WL 826292 (Ohio Ct. App. 8th Dist. Cuyahoga County 2011); State v. Zielinski, 2011-Ohio-6535, 2011 WL 6382541 (Ohio Ct. App. 12th Dist. Warren County 2011); State v. Habo, 2013-Ohio-2142, 2013 WL 2308483 (Ohio Ct. App. 11th Dist. Portage County 2013); State v. McKinney, 2012-Ohio-4521, 2012 WL 4482035 (Ohio Ct. App. 12th Dist. Butler County 2012); State v. Clark, 2015-Ohio-2978, 2015 WL 4510693 (Ohio Ct. App. 9th Dist. Wayne County 2015); State v. Behlke, 2017-Ohio-7910, ¶ 16, 2017 WL 4334342 (Ohio Ct. App. 9th Dist. Wayne County 2017); State v. Davis, 2017-Ohio-8535, ¶ 25, 2017 WL 5256348 (Ohio Ct. App. 12th Dist. Butler County 2017); State /City of Toledo v. Kinnebrew, 2018-Ohio-129, ¶ 17, 2018 WL 388852 (Ohio Ct. App. 6th Dist. Lucas County 2018); In re S.L., 2018-Ohio-1111, ¶ 17, 2018 WL 1470688 (Ohio Ct. App. 3d Dist. Logan County 2018).

[5]State v. Hicks, 88 Ohio App. 3d 515, 624 N.E.2d 332 (10th Dist. Franklin County 1993); State v. Thompson, 2006-Ohio-582, 2006 WL 307715 (Ohio Ct. App. 2d Dist. Miami County 2006); In re J.L., 176 Ohio App. 3d 186, 2008-Ohio-1488, 891 N.E.2d 778 (3d Dist. Allen County 2008); Lumley v. Lumley, 2009-Ohio-6992, 2009 WL 5174121 (Ohio Ct. App. 10th Dist. Franklin County 2009); State v. Zielinski, 2011-Ohio-6535, 2011 WL 6382541 (Ohio Ct. App. 12th Dist. Warren County 2011); State v. McKinney, 2012-Ohio-4521, 2012 WL 4482035 (Ohio Ct. App. 12th Dist. Butler County 2012); State v. Litton, 2016-Ohio-7913, 2016 WL 6948332 (Ohio Ct. App. 12th Dist. Preble County 2016); State v. Cunningham, 2017-Ohio-4363, ¶ 23, 93 N.E.3d 25 (Ohio Ct. App. 12th Dist. Butler County 2017).

[6]State v. Hicks, 88 Ohio App. 3d 515, 517, 624 N.E.2d 332 (10th Dist. Franklin County 1993); State v. Thompson, 2006-Ohio-582, 2006 WL 307715 (Ohio Ct. App. 2d Dist. Miami County 2006); In re J.L., 176 Ohio App. 3d 186, 2008-Ohio-1488, 891 N.E.2d 778 (3d Dist. Allen County 2008); State v. Cantwell, 2008-Ohio-3928, 2008 WL 2971386 (Ohio Ct. App. 5th Dist. Licking County 2008); In re Kristen V., 2008-Ohio-2994, 2008 WL 2468839 (Ohio Ct. App. 6th Dist. Ottawa County 2008); State v. Snyder, 2011-Ohio-1062, 2011 WL 826292 (Ohio Ct. App. 8th Dist. Cuyahoga County

actual physical injury or a psychological one, and regardless of how long the effects of the injury or attempted injury may last.[7] As long as there is competent, credible evidence before the trier of fact that the defendant *attempted* to cause physical harm to a family or household member, there is sufficient evidence to sustain a conviction for domestic violence. Accordingly, the prosecution is not required to establish the existence of actual physical injury.[8] However, a parent may use corporal punishment if it is not excessive under the circumstances and does not create a substantial risk of harm to the child.[9] The test to employ is whether, under the circumstances and after weighing all of the relevant factors, the corporal punishment inflicted by the defendant/parent was reasonable or unreasonable.[10] The encounter

---

2011); State v. Zielinski, 2011-Ohio-6535, 2011 WL 6382541 (Ohio Ct. App. 12th Dist. Warren County 2011); State v. Luke, 2011-Ohio-4330, 2011 WL 3813588 (Ohio Ct. App. 3d Dist. Union County 2011).

[7]State v. Howard, 1999 WL 1313691 (Ohio Ct. App. 11th Dist. Lake County 1999); State v. Zielinski, 2011-Ohio-6535, 2011 WL 6382541 (Ohio Ct. App. 12th Dist. Warren County 2011); State v. Litton, 2016-Ohio-7913, 2016 WL 6948332 (Ohio Ct. App. 12th Dist. Preble County 2016); State v. Davis, 2017-Ohio-8535, ¶ 25, 2017 WL 5256348 (Ohio Ct. App. 12th Dist. Butler County 2017); State v. Cunningham, 2017-Ohio-4363, ¶ 23, 93 N.E.3d 25 (Ohio Ct. App. 12th Dist. Butler County 2017).

[8]City of Niles v. Cadwallader, 2004-Ohio-6336, 2004 WL 2697274 (Ohio Ct. App. 11th Dist. Trumbull County 2004); State v. Habo, 2013-Ohio-2142, 2013 WL 2308483 (Ohio Ct. App. 11th Dist. Portage County 2013).

[9]State v. Howard, 1999 WL 1313691 (Ohio Ct. App. 11th Dist. Lake County 1999), citing State v. Hart, 110 Ohio App. 3d 250, 673 N.E.2d 992 (3d Dist. Defiance County 1996); see also Text § 8:6, Statutory elements of domestic violence under RC 3113.31(A)(1)(c); State v. Jones, 140 Ohio App. 3d 422, 747 N.E.2d 891 (8th Dist. Cuyahoga County 2000); State v. Holzwart, 151 Ohio App. 3d 417, 2003-Ohio-345, 784 N.E.2d 192 (3d Dist. Seneca County 2003). See also dissenting opinion in State v. Vandergriff, 2001-Ohio-4327, 2001 WL 1117182, *9 (Ohio Ct. App. 11th Dist. Ashtabula County 2001). See also State v. Craun, 158 Ohio App. 3d 389, 2004-Ohio-4403, 815 N.E.2d 1141 (3d Dist. Shelby County 2004); City of Niles v. Cadwallader, 2004-Ohio-6336, 2004 WL 2697274 (Ohio Ct. App. 11th Dist. Trumbull County 2004); State v. Whitfield, 2002-Ohio-5984, 2002 WL 31431840 (Ohio Ct. App. 1st Dist. Hamilton County 2002); In re J.L., 176 Ohio App. 3d 186, 2008-Ohio-1488, 891 N.E.2d 778 (3d Dist. Allen County 2008); Lumley v. Lumley, 2009-Ohio-6992, 2009 WL 5174121 (Ohio Ct. App. 10th Dist. Franklin County 2009); State v. Snyder, 2011-Ohio-1062, 2011 WL 826292 (Ohio Ct. App. 8th Dist. Cuyahoga County 2011); State v. Cordle, 2010-Ohio-5919, 2010 WL 4926590 (Ohio Ct. App. 5th Dist. Delaware County 2010); City of Cleveland v. Calhoun, 2018-Ohio-1758, ¶ 14–15, 2018 WL 2084929, *3 (Ohio Ct. App. 8th Dist. Cuyahoga County 2018) (The word "abuse" is not statutorily defined but this court has defined child abuse as **"an act which inflicts serious physical harm or creates a substantial risk of serious harm to the physical health or safety of the child."**); State v. Snyder, 2011-Ohio-1062, ¶ 17, 2011 WL 826292 (Ohio Ct. App. 8th Dist. Cuyahoga County 2011), quoting State v. Ivey, 98 Ohio App. 3d 249, 257, 648 N.E.2d 519 (8th Dist. Cuyahoga County 1994).

[10]State v. Hause, 1999 WL 959184 (Ohio Ct. App. 2d Dist. Montgomery County 1999); State v. Thompson, 2006-Ohio-582, 2006 WL 307715 (Ohio Ct. App. 2d Dist. Miami County 2006); In re J.L., 176 Ohio App. 3d 186, 2008-Ohio-1488, 891 N.E.2d 778 (3d Dist. Allen County 2008); Lumley v. Lumley, 2009-Ohio-6992, 2009 WL 5174121 (Ohio Ct. App. 10th Dist. Franklin County 2009); State v. Snyder, 2011-Ohio-1062, 2011 WL 826292 (Ohio Ct. App. 8th Dist. Cuyahoga County 2011); State v. Cordle, 2010-Ohio-5919, 2010 WL 4926590 (Ohio Ct. App. 5th Dist. Delaware County 2010); State v. Luke, 2011-Ohio-4330, 2011 WL 3813588 (Ohio Ct. App. 3d Dist. Union County 2011); State v. Habo, 2013-Ohio-2142, 2013 WL 2308483 (Ohio Ct. App. 11th Dist. Portage County 2013); State v. McKinney, 2012-Ohio-4521, 2012 WL 4482035 (Ohio Ct. App. 12th Dist. Butler County 2012); State v. Litton, 2016-Ohio-7913, 2016

must be weighed in light of such factors as the child's age, behavior, response to non-corporal punishment, the parent's state of mind at the time of the event, and the location and severity of the punishment.[11]

A charge of domestic violence under RC 2919.25(A) is brought in a proper venue when:

(1) the court in which the charge is brought has jurisdiction over the subject matter; and
(2) the court in which the charge is brought has jurisdiction over the geographical area where the event is alleged to have occurred.

As with all crimes, the presence of all of the elements is required for successful prosecution.

Q & A: If a man initiates a physical struggle with his wife and, in the process, accidentally knocks her to the floor, can he still be charged with domestic violence?

Yes. The issue was raised in *State v. Purvis*.[12] In affirming the defendant's conviction, the court said "the statute is quite clear that the [defendant's] underlying purpose is irrelevant in determining whether someone acted knowingly" where the evidence established that the defendant acted consciously and intentionally, and that "these

---

WL 6948332 (Ohio Ct. App. 12th Dist. Preble County 2016); State v. Cunningham, 2017-Ohio-4363, ¶ 23, 93 N.E.3d 25 (Ohio Ct. App. 12th Dist. Butler County 2017).

[11]State v. Hart, 110 Ohio App. 3d 250, 673 N.E.2d 992 (3d Dist. Defiance County 1996); State v. Hauenstein, 121 Ohio App. 3d 511, 700 N.E.2d 378 (3d Dist. Putnam County 1997); State v. Thompson, 2006-Ohio-582, 2006 WL 307715 (Ohio Ct. App. 2d Dist. Miami County 2006); In re J.L., 176 Ohio App. 3d 186, 2008-Ohio-1488, 891 N.E.2d 778 (3d Dist. Allen County 2008); Lumley v. Lumley, 2009-Ohio-6992, 2009 WL 5174121 (Ohio Ct. App. 10th Dist. Franklin County 2009); State v. Snyder, 2011-Ohio-1062, 2011 WL 826292 (Ohio Ct. App. 8th Dist. Cuyahoga County 2011); State v. Luke, 2011-Ohio-4330, 2011 WL 3813588 (Ohio Ct. App. 3d Dist. Union County 2011); State v. McKinney, 2012-Ohio-4521, 2012 WL 4482035 (Ohio Ct. App. 12th Dist. Butler County 2012); State v. Zielinski, 2011-Ohio-6535, 2011 WL 6382541 (Ohio Ct. App. 12th Dist. Warren County 2011); State v. Phillips, 2012-Ohio-6023, 2012 WL 6651822 (Ohio Ct. App. 10th Dist. Franklin County 2012); In re S.L., 2018-Ohio-1111, ¶ 19, 2018 WL 1470688 (Ohio Ct. App. 3d Dist. Logan County 2018). Whether parental discipline is "extreme or excessive" is determined in light of the totality of the circumstances. State v. Hauenstein, 121 Ohio App. 3d 511, 700 N.E.2d 378 (3d Dist. Putnam County 1997), citing State v. Hart, 110 Ohio App. 3d 250, 673 N.E.2d 992 (3d Dist. Defiance County 1996): **"In analyzing the totality of the circumstances, a court should consider the following factors: (1) the child's age; (2) the child's behavior leading up to the discipline; (3) the child's response to prior non-corporal punishment; (4) the location and severity of the punishment; and (5) the parent's state of mind while administering the punishment."** State v. Luke, 2011-Ohio–4330, ¶ 22, 2011 WL 3813588 (Ohio Ct. App. 3d Dist. Union County 2011), citing In re J.L., 176 Ohio App. 3d 186, 199, 2008–Ohio–1488, 891 N.E.2d 778 (3d Dist. Allen County 2008) (citations omitted). This inquiry is necessary to protect and balance a parents' fundamental right to raise and control their children and the state's interest in the protection and safety of children and in the reporting of child abuse. In re Horton, 2004-Ohio–6249, 2004 WL 2674562 (Ohio Ct. App. 10th Dist. Franklin County 2004); State v. Davis, 2017-Ohio-8535, ¶ 25, 2017 WL 5256348 (Ohio Ct. App. 12th Dist. Butler County 2017).

[12]State v. Purvis, 1989 WL 126298 (Ohio Ct. App. 9th Dist. Medina County 1989).

actions were such that a reasonable person should know" that his actions "would probably bring about certain results."[13]

Q & A: Where a defendant maintains that he was not attempting to harm his wife but merely attempting to protect himself from her attack, what would his lawyer have to do at trial to have the case thrown out of court?

The goal of the defense in any trial of a criminal case is to obtain a Criminal Rule 29(A) directed verdict of acquittal at the end of prosecution's case, or at the end of the presentation of all of the evidence, without having to present the case to a trier of fact for deliberation.

To obtain a directed verdict of acquittal in a domestic violence prosecution, the defense must convince the trial court that the prosecution presented no credible evidence in its case-in-chief that the defendant acted knowingly or recklessly in committing the alleged physical contact between himself and his wife.

If the prosecution adduces evidence from which reasonable minds could reach different conclusions as to whether each material element of the offense of domestic violence has been proven beyond a reasonable doubt, including the culpable mental state, a motion for a judgment of acquittal at the conclusion of the state's case, or at the conclusion of all of the evidence, will be denied.[14]

Q & A: If an offender never actually injured anyone, but merely tried to get at the alleged victim, could that offender still be charged under RC 2919.25(A)?

---

[13]State v. Purvis, 1989 WL 126298, *2 (Ohio Ct. App. 9th Dist. Medina County 1989).

[14]See State v. Bridgeman, 55 Ohio St. 2d 261, 9 Ohio Op. 3d 401, 381 N.E.2d 184 (1978); State v. Euton, 2007-Ohio-6704, 2007 WL 4374293 (Ohio Ct. App. 3d Dist. Auglaize County 2007); State v. McKinney, 2007-Ohio-3389, 2007 WL 1884647 (Ohio Ct. App. 11th Dist. Lake County 2007); State v. Reed, 2010-Ohio-1866, 2010 WL 1713024 (Ohio Ct. App. 8th Dist. Cuyahoga County 2010); State v. Moore, 2010-Ohio-509, 2010 WL 547707 (Ohio Ct. App. 8th Dist. Cuyahoga County 2010); State v. Maple, 2011-Ohio-1516, 2011 WL 1138387 (Ohio Ct. App. 9th Dist. Summit County 2011); State v. Wenker, 2011-Ohio-786, 2011 WL 646376 (Ohio Ct. App. 9th Dist. Summit County 2011). But see State v. Pepin-McCaffrey, 186 Ohio App. 3d 548, 2010-Ohio-617, 929 N.E.2d 476 (7th Dist. Mahoning County 2010); State v. Miller, 2012-Ohio-6115, 2012 WL 6726698 (Ohio Ct. App. 3d Dist. Henry County 2012); State v. Clouse, 2012-Ohio-3471, 2012 WL 3133059 (Ohio Ct. App. 10th Dist. Franklin County 2012); State v. Dirmeyer, 2014-Ohio-759, 9 N.E.3d 464 (Ohio Ct. App. 3d Dist. Seneca County 2014); State v. Flanagan, 2015-Ohio-5528, 2015 WL 9594509 (Ohio Ct. App. 11th Dist. Ashtabula County 2015); State v. Costell, 2016-Ohio-3386, 2016 WL 3223905 (Ohio Ct. App. 3d Dist. Union County 2016), appeal not allowed, 147 Ohio St. 3d 1505, 2017-Ohio-261, 67 N.E.3d 823 (2017), State v. Winton, 2017-Ohio-6908, 2017 WL 3098591 (Ohio Ct. App. 2d Dist. Montgomery County 2017); State v. Race, 2017-Ohio-612, 2017 WL 678814 (Ohio Ct. App. 6th Dist. Sandusky County 2017); State v. McAdams, 2016-Ohio-8225, 2016 WL 7427149 (Ohio Ct. App. 11th Dist. Lake County 2016); State v. Wynn, 2017-Ohio-8045, ¶ 12–13, 2017 WL 4417756 (Ohio Ct. App. 1st Dist. Hamilton County 2017); State v. Winton, 2017-Ohio-6908, ¶ 35, 2017 WL 3098591 (Ohio Ct. App. 2d Dist. Montgomery County 2017); State v. Hughes, 2018-Ohio-1237, ¶ 55, 2018 WL 1578822 (Ohio Ct. App. 6th Dist. Wood County 2018) (**"An entry of acquittal is improper 'if the evidence is such that reasonable minds can reach different conclusions as to whether each material element of a crime has been proved beyond a reasonable doubt.' "**).

While every case is unique on its own facts, generally speaking, the answer is yes.[15] To incur criminal sanctions under the statute, the offender need only *attempt* to do "physical harm" to a family or household member.

Q & A: If the only evidence of domestic violence is the victim's statement that the defendant struck a single blow that left no objective evidence of injury, should the trial court grant a defense motion for a directed verdict of acquittal?

No. The scenario you describe presents a factual issue, properly resolved by the trier of fact. Keep in mind, the testimony of one witness believed by the trier of fact is enough to to prove the fact in question. This is true even if the injury claimed resulted in only momentary pain.[16]

Q & A: In a proper case, where evidence has been presented which would entitle a defendant to an instruction on the right to employ "proper and reasonable parental discipline," does the failure of defense counsel to request such an instruction constitute ineffective assistance?

While each case must be examined carefully on its own merits, generally in a jury trial where some evidence is presented to establish the defense of parental discipline, the trier of fact must be placed in the position to weigh whether the actions of the defendant constituted proper and reasonable discipline, or whether those actions resulted in injury prohibited under the domestic violence laws.[17]

A defendant has the burden of going forward with evidence sufficient to raise the affirmative defense of reasonable and proper

---

[15]See State v. Powell, 49 Ohio St. 3d 255, 552 N.E.2d 191 (1990). But see City of Xenia v. Harris, 1998 WL 769838 (Ohio Ct. App. 2d Dist. Greene County 1998); State v. Powell, 49 Ohio St. 3d 255, 552 N.E.2d 191 (1990) (Superseded by Constitutional Amendment on other grounds).

[16]See State v. Amos, 1988 WL 4622 (Ohio Ct. App. 11th Dist. Lake County 1988).

[17]State v. Mills, 1997 WL 133430 (Ohio Ct. App. 1st Dist. Hamilton County 1997); State v. Hart, 110 Ohio App. 3d 250, 673 N.E.2d 992 (3d Dist. Defiance County 1996); State v. Craun, 158 Ohio App. 3d 389, 2004-Ohio-4403, 815 N.E.2d 1141 (3d Dist. Shelby County 2004); State v. Thompson, 2006-Ohio-582, 2006 WL 307715 (Ohio Ct. App. 2d Dist. Miami County 2006); In re J.L., 176 Ohio App. 3d 186, 2008-Ohio-1488, 891 N.E.2d 778 (3d Dist. Allen County 2008); Lumley v. Lumley, 2009-Ohio-6992, 2009 WL 5174121 (Ohio Ct. App. 10th Dist. Franklin County 2009); State v. Cordle, 2010-Ohio-5919, 2010 WL 4926590 (Ohio Ct. App. 5th Dist. Delaware County 2010); State v. Phillips, 2012-Ohio-6023, 2012 WL 6651822 (Ohio Ct. App. 10th Dist. Franklin County 2012); Royster v. Jenkins, 2016 WL 3765339 (S.D. Ohio 2016), supplemented, 2016 WL 4035516 (S.D. Ohio 2016), report and recommendation adopted, 2017 WL 663556 (S.D. Ohio 2017), certificate of appealability denied, 2017 WL 8218911 (6th Cir. 2017), cert. denied, 138 S. Ct. 1705, 200 L. Ed. 2d 960 (2018) and report and recommendation adopted, 2017 WL 663556 (S.D. Ohio 2017); State /City of Toledo v. Kinnebrew, 2018-Ohio-129, ¶ 19, 2018 WL 388852 (Ohio Ct. App. 6th Dist. Lucas County 2018) citing State v. Suchomski, 58 Ohio St. 3d 74, 567 N.E.2d 1304 (1991) ("[Defendant] presented some evidence that the child in this case was a discipline problem and that he was permitted by the child's mother to discipline her when appropriate. [Defendant] also presented evidence that the child acted in a manner that cried out for some discipline. * * * 'Once a defendant has presented evidence on the defense of parental discipline, the [trier of fact] must weigh whether the actions constituted proper and reasonable discipline, or whether they constituted an injury within the meaning set forth in Suchomski, *supra* . . .' ").

parental discipline, by a preponderance of the evidence, when charged with domestic violence against a minor child.[18]

The failure of a defendant's lawyer to request an instruction on this issue, under such circumstances, would require the jury to apply the general jury instruction defining physical harm, in part, "as any injury."[19] A jury so instructed could reach only one conclusion, that the defendant was guilty and, thus, an attorney's failure in this regard would fall below the objective standard of reasonable representation, requiring that any conviction obtained be reversed.[20]

However, if the evidence presented or developed by the defendant raises only a mere speculation or possible doubt, and is, therefore, insufficient to raise the affirmative defense, the submission of the issue to a jury is unwarranted and constitutes error on the part of the trial court.[21]

Q & A: I'm charged with domestic violence because I backhanded my child for back-talking to me. I thought that a parent was allowed to discipline a child.

Under Ohio law a parent is allowed to discipline a child within reason. Proper and reasonable parental discipline can be employed by a parent as an affirmative defense to the charge of domestic violence for physical harm to his or her child; however, the parent has the burden of proving such defense by a preponderance of evidence.[22]

A determination as to whether any particular conduct constitutes

---

[18]State v. Suchomski, 58 Ohio St. 3d 74, 567 N.E.2d 1304 (1991); State v. Hart, 110 Ohio App. 3d 250, 673 N.E.2d 992 (3d Dist. Defiance County 1996); State v. Vandergriff, 2001-Ohio-4327, 2001 WL 1117182, *9 (Ohio Ct. App. 11th Dist. Ashtabula County 2001); State v. Adaranijo, 153 Ohio App. 3d 266, 2003-Ohio-3822, 792 N.E.2d 1138 (1st Dist. Hamilton County 2003); State v. Craun, 158 Ohio App. 3d 389, 2004-Ohio-4403, 815 N.E.2d 1141 (3d Dist. Shelby County 2004); City of Niles v. Cadwallader, 2004-Ohio-6336, 2004 WL 2697274 (Ohio Ct. App. 11th Dist. Trumbull County 2004); State v. Thompson, 2006-Ohio-582, 2006 WL 307715 (Ohio Ct. App. 2d Dist. Miami County 2006); In re J.L., 176 Ohio App. 3d 186, 2008-Ohio-1488, 891 N.E.2d 778 (3d Dist. Allen County 2008); Lumley v. Lumley, 2009-Ohio-6992, 2009 WL 5174121 (Ohio Ct. App. 10th Dist. Franklin County 2009); State v. Cordle, 2010-Ohio-5919, 2010 WL 4926590 (Ohio Ct. App. 5th Dist. Delaware County 2010); State v. Snyder, 2011-Ohio-1062, 2011 WL 826292 (Ohio Ct. App. 8th Dist. Cuyahoga County 2011); State v. Habo, 2013-Ohio-2142, 2013 WL 2308483 (Ohio Ct. App. 11th Dist. Portage County 2013); State v. Phillips, 2012-Ohio-6023, 2012 WL 6651822 (Ohio Ct. App. 10th Dist. Franklin County 2012); State v. Clark, 2015-Ohio-2978, 2015 WL 4510693 (Ohio Ct. App. 9th Dist. Wayne County 2015); State v. Behlke, 2017-Ohio-7910, ¶ 16, 2017 WL 4334342 (Ohio Ct. App. 9th Dist. Wayne County 2017).

[19]RC 2901.01(A)(5)(c).

[20]State v. Vandergriff, 2001-Ohio-4327, 2001 WL 1117182 (Ohio Ct. App. 11th Dist. Ashtabula County 2001); State /City of Toledo v. Kinnebrew, 2018-Ohio-129, ¶ 19-20, 2018 WL 388852 (Ohio Ct. App. 6th Dist. Lucas County 2018) (the court makes a distinction from the *Vandergriff* case. Here, the appellant failed to introduce any evidence, directly or by virtue of cross-examination, that could lead a trier of fact to conclude that the injuries were the result of reasonable parental discipline. Appellant insisted at trial that he never hit the child. Therefore, this case focuses on the credibility of the witnesses).

[21]See dissenting opinion in State v. Vandergriff, 2001-Ohio-4327, 2001 WL 1117182 (Ohio Ct. App. 11th Dist. Ashtabula County 2001); State /City of Toledo v. Kinnebrew, 2018-Ohio-129, ¶ 19–20, 2018 WL 388852 (Ohio Ct. App. 6th Dist. Lucas County 2018).

[22]State v. Cordle, 2010-Ohio-5919, 2010 WL 4926590 (Ohio Ct. App. 5th Dist.

proper and reasonable parental discipline is a question that must be determined from the totality of the circumstances from all the relevant facts.[23]

A child's age, behavior, and response to non-corporal punishment, as well as the location and severity of the punishment, are factors to be examined in determining whether a parent's acts are proper and reasonable parental discipline.[24]

Q & A: Is the exercise of proper parental discipline an affirmative defense?

There is a split of authority pertaining to whether the State must disprove proper parental discipline as an element of domestic violence, or whether the exercise of proper parental discipline is an affirmative defense to domestic violence.[25] If it is an element of the offense, then the State bears the burden of proof, but if it is an affirmative defense, then the defendant bears the burden of proof.[26]

§ 2:3 Reckless domestic violence under RC 2919.25(B)

To violate RC 2919.25(B), an offender must:

(1) recklessly
(2) cause
(3) serious physical injury
(4) to a family or household member
(5) within the state of Ohio.

Delaware County 2010); State v. Hart, 110 Ohio App. 3d 250, 673 N.E.2d 992 (3d Dist. Defiance County 1996); State v. Adaranijo, 153 Ohio App. 3d 266, 2003-Ohio-3822, 792 N.E.2d 1138 (1st Dist. Hamilton County 2003); State v. Phillips, 2012-Ohio-6023, 2012 WL 6651822 (Ohio Ct. App. 10th Dist. Franklin County 2012); State v. Habo, 2013-Ohio-2142, 2013 WL 2308483 (Ohio Ct. App. 11th Dist. Portage County 2013).

[23] State v. Cordle, 2010-Ohio-5919, 2010 WL 4926590 (Ohio Ct. App. 5th Dist. Delaware County 2010); State v. Adaranijo, 153 Ohio App. 3d 266, 2003-Ohio-3822, 792 N.E.2d 1138 (1st Dist. Hamilton County 2003); State v. Behlke, 2017-Ohio-7910, ¶ 17-18, 2017 WL 4334342 (Ohio Ct. App. 9th Dist. Wayne County 2017).

[24] State v. Cordle, 2010-Ohio-5919, 2010 WL 4926590 (Ohio Ct. App. 5th Dist. Delaware County 2010); State v. Adaranijo, 153 Ohio App. 3d 266, 2003-Ohio-3822, 792 N.E.2d 1138 (1st Dist. Hamilton County 2003); State v. Phillips, 2012-Ohio-6023, 2012 WL 6651822 (Ohio Ct. App. 10th Dist. Franklin County 2012); State v. Behlke, 2017-Ohio-7910, ¶ 17-18, 2017 WL 4334342 (Ohio Ct. App. 9th Dist. Wayne County 2017).

[25] See State v. Rosa, 2013-Ohio-5867, 6 N.E.3d 57 (Ohio Ct. App. 7th Dist. Mahoning County 2013); State v. Clark, 2015-Ohio-2978, 2015 WL 4510693 (Ohio Ct. App. 9th Dist. Wayne County 2015); State v. Behlke, 2017-Ohio-7910, 2017 WL 4334342 (Ohio Ct. App. 9th Dist. Wayne County 2017) citing to State v. Rosa, 2013-Ohio-5867, 6 N.E.3d 57 (Ohio Ct. App. 7th Dist. Mahoning County 2013) (acknowledged the split among the district courts of Ohio as to whether proper and reasonable parental discipline must be raised as an affirmative defense, or if the prosecution must establish that it was not proper and reasonable within the physical harm element of the offense of domestic violence. In *Clark*, [State v. Clark, 2015-Ohio-2978, 2015 WL 4510693 (Ohio Ct. App. 9th Dist. Wayne County 2015)] we declined to consider the issue because it was not raised on appeal, and so our district has yet to take a position.).

[26] See R.C. 2901.05(A) and State v. Hancock, 108 Ohio St. 3d 57, ¶ 37, 2006-Ohio-160, 840 N.E.2d 1032 (2006); State v. Clark, 2015-Ohio-2978, 2015 WL 4510693 (Ohio Ct. App. 9th Dist. Wayne County 2015); State v. Behlke, 2017-Ohio-7910, ¶ 16, 2017 WL 4334342 (Ohio Ct. App. 9th Dist. Wayne County 2017).

Rather than the intentions of the offender, the extent of the injury caused is the controlling element in a violation of RC 2919.25(B).[1] An offender in Ohio, who, while engaged in some act, heedlessly ignores a known risk, and whose actions result in serious physical harm to a member of his/her family or household, has committed a violation under RC 2919.25(B), regardless of whether it can be shown that it was the intent of the offender to cause the injury.

"Serious physical harm to persons" is defined in RC 2901.01(E) as:

(1) Any mental illness or condition of such gravity as would normally require hospitalization or prolonged psychiatric treatment;
(2) Any physical harm that carries a substantial risk of death;
(3) Any physical harm that involves some permanent incapacity, whether partial or total, or which involves some temporary, substantial incapacity;
(4) Any physical harm that involves some permanent disfigurement, or involves some serious temporary disfigurement; or
(5) Any physical harm that involves acute pain of such duration as to result in substantial suffering, or that involves any degree of prolonged or intractable pain.

As with a violation under RC 2919.25(A), the prosecution must prove that the court has jurisdiction over the subject matter of the complaint and that the offense was committed within the boundaries of the court's geographical jurisdiction.

§ 2:4 Threats of domestic violence under RC 2919.25(C)

RC 2919.25(C) is violated when the offender:

(1) knowingly
(2) by threat of force
(3) causes
(4) a family or household member to believe
(5) that the offender will cause
(6) imminent physical harm
(7) to the family or household member
(8) within the state of Ohio.

The gravamen of a charge under RC 2919.25(C) is the statement or action of the offender. It must be directed toward a family or household member to constitute a violation. The statement or action must cause the person perceiving it to believe that the offender is on the verge of using force against him/her, at or near the point in time when the statement is made or the action complained of is taken.

The true intentions of the offender are not at issue. All that is

---

[Section 2:3]

[1]State v. Johnson, 1989 WL 43040 (Ohio Ct. App. 2d Dist. Greene County 1989); State v. Daniels, 2018-Ohio-1701, ¶ 35, 2018 WL 2058731 (Ohio Ct. App. 1st Dist. Hamilton County 2018) ("R.C. 2919.25(A) provides that 'No person shall knowingly cause or attempt to cause physical harm to a family or household member.' 'Physical harm' is defined as 'any injury, illness, or other physiological impairment, regardless of its gravity or duration.' R.C. 2901.01(A)(3). The slightest injury is sufficient proof of physical harm.").

required for conviction is that the prosecution show that the offender's words or actions caused the family or household member to fear *imminent* physical harm at the hands of the offender.

The phrase "threat of force," as used in RC 2919.25(B), is not defined in the Revised Code.[1] By reference to two other sources, a working definition for the phrase may be pieced together. A definition for the term "force" is found in RC 2901.01(A), which provides " 'Force' means any violence, compulsion, or constraint physically exerted by any means upon or against a person or thing." The word "threat" is defined in *Black's Law Dictionary* as "a declaration of intention or determination to inflict punishment, loss, or pain on another, or to injure another . . . by the commission of some unlawful act."[2]

Thus, in this context, "threat of force" appears to mean a declaration of an intention to injure another by using violence exerted by any means against that person.

Whether a case is established under RC 2919.25(C) is an extremely subjective proposition. Depending on the prior interactions between the parties, what would under normal circumstances be judged by most people to be innocent conduct or statements could reasonably be perceived by an RC 2919.25(C) victim as a terrorist act.

For an offender to be found guilty of a violation under RC 2919.25(C), the prosecution must establish that the complainant believed the offender's execution of the threat in question was "imminent." The issue of just what constitutes "imminent" is often hotly contested. *Black's Law Dictionary* defines "imminent" as "on the point of happening."[3] The standard used in judging the state of mind of a complainant under RC 2919.25(C) is one of reasonableness. Was it reasonable for the allegedly threatened family or household member to believe, under the circumstances then existing, that the offender was preparing to cause him/her imminent physical harm?

It is impossible to establish an objective standard to determine at what point an individual is justified in believing that an offender's threat is real and imminent. Each case must be judged on its own facts. Certainly, if the prosecution proves that an accused was able to carry out the threat and/or made any movement toward carrying it out, that would constitute strong evidence of the reasonableness of the intended victim's belief in its viability. However, it is well-established that the prosecution does not need to prove either the accused's ability or movement to carry out the threat to establish the elements of a threat offense.[4]

As with RC 2919.25(A) and RC 2919.25(B), venue is also an element

---

[Section 2:4]

[1]But see State v. Harvey, 1986 WL 7468 (Ohio Ct. App. 3d Dist. Marion County 1986).

[2]Black's Law Dictionary (10th ed. 2014). See also State v. Alvey, 2003-Ohio-7006, 2003 WL 22997277 (Ohio Ct. App. 7th Dist. Belmont County 2003).

[3]Black's Law Dictionary (10th ed. 2014); State v. Clay, 181 Ohio App. 3d 563, 2009-Ohio-1235, 910 N.E.2d 14 (8th Dist. Cuyahoga County 2009).

[4]State v. Schwartz, 77 Ohio App. 3d 484, 602 N.E.2d 671 (12th Dist. Butler County 1991); State v. McClelland, 2002-Ohio-1007, 2002 WL 356306 (Ohio Ct. App. 10th Dist. Franklin County 2002); State v. Goodwin, 2006-Ohio-66, 2006 WL 45897

of an RC 2919.25(C) prosecution. Determining the appropriate venue for a prosecution under RC 2919.25(C), however, can be somewhat more interesting.

Threats do not have to be made face-to-face. The question arises: If the offender is in one jurisdiction and makes a threat by mail, telephone, fax, or otherwise to the complainant, who is in another jurisdiction, which jurisdiction is the appropriate one for the initiation of the criminal complaint?

RC 2901.11(A)(1) provides that a person is subject to criminal prosecution and punishment in Ohio if that person commits an offense under Ohio law, any element of which takes place within the boundaries of the state. Accordingly, a person who is in one Ohio jurisdiction and who makes a threat in violation of RC 2919.25(C) to someone who lives in another Ohio jurisdiction is subject to criminal prosecution in either one of those jurisdictions. An individual who is outside the state of Ohio and who forwards an RC 2919.25(C) threat to someone in the state is subject to prosecution in the Ohio jurisdiction where the threat is received.

Q & A: Can an abuser who uses demeaning and belittling profanity and invectives at a family or household member be charged with domestic violence?

No. Unless the language used constitutes or can be construed to constitute a threat of imminent physical harm to the family or household member at whom it is directed, no crime is committed when one member of a family or household argues with or is verbally abusive toward another member of the family or household.[5]

Q & A: A victim testifies that a defendant called and said, "You will be sorry that you ever took this matter to the police." There is a past history of violence in the relationship, and the victim took the defendant's statement as a threat that he

---

(Ohio Ct. App. 10th Dist. Franklin County 2006); State v. Taylor, 79 Ohio Misc. 2d 82, 671 N.E.2d 343 (Mun. Ct. 1996); State v. Tackett, 2005-Ohio-1437, 2005 WL 697411 (Ohio Ct. App. 4th Dist. Jackson County 2005); State v. Walker, 2007-Ohio-4047, 2007 WL 2269467 (Ohio Ct. App. 8th Dist. Cuyahoga County 2007); E. Cleveland v. Perkins, 2009-Ohio-2131, 2009 WL 1244154 (Ohio Ct. App. 8th Dist. Cuyahoga County 2009); State v. Pash, 2010-Ohio-1267, 2010 WL 1175616 (Ohio Ct. App. 3d Dist. Mercer County 2010); State v. McKinney, 2009-Ohio-2225, 2009 WL 1314871 (Ohio Ct. App. 9th Dist. Summit County 2009); Morris v. Morris, 2009-Ohio-5164, 2009 WL 3119658 (Ohio Ct. App. 9th Dist. Summit County 2009); State v. Brandon, 2011-Ohio-1349, 2011 WL 1005554 (Ohio Ct. App. 9th Dist. Summit County 2011); Chafin v. Chafin, 2010-Ohio-3939, 2010 WL 3294288 (Ohio Ct. App. 9th Dist. Lorain County 2010). But see State v. Miles, 2012-Ohio-2607, 2012 WL 2128035 (Ohio Ct. App. 9th Dist. Summit County 2012); State v. Schweitzer, 2015-Ohio-925, 30 N.E.3d 190 (Ohio Ct. App. 3d Dist. Auglaize County 2015), but see the dissent, State v. Tomassetti, 2015-Ohio-3092, 2015 WL 4611373 (Ohio Ct. App. 9th Dist. Wayne County 2015), R.T. v. J.T., 2015-Ohio-4418, 2015 WL 6449294 (Ohio Ct. App. 9th Dist. Medina County 2015); Lewis v. Gravely, 2016-Ohio-1502, 2016 WL 1404159 (Ohio Ct. App. 4th Dist. Adams County 2016); M.K. v. J.K., 2015-Ohio-434, 2015 WL 557990 (Ohio Ct. App. 9th Dist. Medina County 2015).

[5]State v. Samarghandi, 84 Ohio Misc. 2d 6, 680 N.E.2d 738 (Mun. Ct. 1997); State v. Alvey, 2003-Ohio-7006, 2003 WL 22997277 (Ohio Ct. App. 7th Dist. Belmont County 2003); State v. Phillips, 2012-Ohio-6023, 2012 WL 6651822 (Ohio Ct. App. 10th Dist. Franklin County 2012); State v. McKinney, 2012-Ohio-4521, 2012 WL 4482035 (Ohio Ct. App. 12th Dist. Butler County 2012); A.D. v. B.D., 2017-Ohio-229, 2017 WL 277481 (Ohio Ct. App. 9th Dist. Medina County 2017).

would hurt her if he ever got the chance. Is the defendant's statement to the victim, in and of itself, enough to support a charge of domestic violence?

Probably not. In order for the charge to be maintained, the prosecution must prove that the victim feared the imminence of the defendant's threat. The facts presented suggest that the victim did not fear that the defendant would carry out the threat imminently.[6]

Q & A: A husband reports to the police that at the end of a heated argument about his infidelity, his wife said, "If I had a gun, I'd kill you!" and then stormed from their home. The husband claims that his wife appeared so enraged that he is very afraid she will try to carry out her threat. There is no history of violence, mental illness or substance abuse, and to his knowledge, his wife does not have access to any firearms. Can the husband file a complaint for domestic violence against his wife?

Probably not, without more. The husband's belief that the physical harm flowing from the threat is imminent is an essential element of the offense of domestic violence threats.[7] The utterance of a conditional threat to a family or household member is not legally sufficient to

[6]See State v. Strunk, 1999 WL 12743 (Ohio Ct. App. 1st Dist. Hamilton County 1999); Henry v. Henry, 2005-Ohio-67, 2005 WL 43888 (Ohio Ct. App. 4th Dist. Ross County 2005); Morris v. Morris, 2009-Ohio-5164, 2009 WL 3119658 (Ohio Ct. App. 9th Dist. Summit County 2009); Wohleber v. Wohleber, 2011-Ohio-6696, 2011 WL 6880736 (Ohio Ct. App. 9th Dist. Lorain County 2011); State v. McKinney, 2012-Ohio-4521, 2012 WL 4482035 (Ohio Ct. App. 12th Dist. Butler County 2012); M.K. v. J.K., 2015-Ohio-434, 2015 WL 557990 (Ohio Ct. App. 9th Dist. Medina County 2015); R.T. v. J.T., 2015-Ohio-4418, 2015 WL 6449294 (Ohio Ct. App. 9th Dist. Medina County 2015); Lewis v. Gravely, 2016-Ohio-1502, 2016 WL 1404159 (Ohio Ct. App. 4th Dist. Adams County 2016); A.M. v. D.L., 2017-Ohio-5621, 2017 WL 2870214 (Ohio Ct. App. 9th Dist. Medina County 2017); J.M. v. M.M., 2016-Ohio-5368, 2016 WL 4272340 (Ohio Ct. App. 9th Dist. Medina County 2016); Henry v. Henry, 2005-Ohio-67, 2005 WL 43888 (Ohio Ct. App. 4th Dist. Ross County 2005).

[7]State v. Denis, 117 Ohio App. 3d 442, 690 N.E.2d 955 (6th Dist. Ottawa County 1997); Hamilton v. Cameron, 121 Ohio App. 3d 445, 700 N.E.2d 336 (12th Dist. Butler County 1997); In re Jenkins, 2004-Ohio-2657, 2004 WL 1152853 (Ohio Ct. App. 5th Dist. Stark County 2004); State v. Shahan, 2006-Ohio-402, 2006 WL 234859 (Ohio Ct. App. 5th Dist. Tuscarawas County 2006); State v. Diroll, 2007-Ohio-6930, 2007 WL 4481430 (Ohio Ct. App. 11th Dist. Portage County 2007); State v. Clay, 181 Ohio App. 3d 563, 2009-Ohio-1235, 910 N.E.2d 14 (8th Dist. Cuyahoga County 2009); Youngstown v. Dixon, 2009-Ohio-1013, 2009 WL 581637 (Ohio Ct. App. 7th Dist. Mahoning County 2009); State v. Barnes, 2008-Ohio-5997, 2008 WL 4949833 (Ohio Ct. App. 8th Dist. Cuyahoga County 2008); Morris v. Morris, 2009-Ohio-5164, 2009 WL 3119658 (Ohio Ct. App. 9th Dist. Summit County 2009); Chafin v. Chafin, 2010-Ohio-3939, 2010 WL 3294288 (Ohio Ct. App. 9th Dist. Lorain County 2010); State v. Fisher, 197 Ohio App. 3d 591, 2011-Ohio-5965, 968 N.E.2d 510 (2d Dist. Miami County 2011); State v. Schweitzer, 2015-Ohio-925, 30 N.E.3d 190 (Ohio Ct. App. 3d Dist. Auglaize County 2015), but see the dissent; Cleveland Hts. v. Kleinhenz, 2015-Ohio-1540, 2015 WL 1851386 (Ohio Ct. App. 8th Dist. Cuyahoga County 2015); State v. Hilton, 2015-Ohio-5198, 2015 WL 8732667 (Ohio Ct. App. 12th Dist. Butler County 2015); State v. Race, 2017-Ohio-612, 2017 WL 678814 (Ohio Ct. App. 6th Dist. Sandusky County 2017); State v. McNeil, 2016-Ohio-4669, 2016 WL 3573123 (Ohio Ct. App. 9th Dist. Summit County 2016); A.M. v. D.L., 2017-Ohio-5621, 2017 WL 2870214 (Ohio Ct. App. 9th Dist. Medina County 2017); J.M. v. M.M., 2016-Ohio-5368, 2016 WL 4272340 (Ohio Ct. App. 9th Dist. Medina County 2016); M.R. v. T.R., 2016-Ohio-3493, 2016 WL 3384940 (Ohio Ct. App. 9th Dist. Wayne County 2016); Lewis v. Gravely, 2016-Ohio-1502, 2016 WL 1404159 (Ohio Ct. App. 4th Dist. Adams County 2016); Wootten v.

support a conviction.[8] The threat made here is conditional—that is, before the wife could make good on her threat she would have to perform another act first. In this case, that other act would be to obtain a firearm. Under the facts set forth, reasonable minds could only conclude that the wife did not have the means at hand to carry out her the threat to shoot the husband immediately. Thus, the element of imminence necessary for this charge is missing.[9]

§ 2:5 Nature of the relationships covered

The definition of the term "family or household member" has been refined over the years and now includes a wide range of individuals who currently reside or who formerly resided with the alleged

---

Culp, 2017-Ohio-665, ¶ 25, 85 N.E.3d 198, 204 (Ohio Ct. App. 4th Dist. Adams County 2017). Culp also argues that there was insufficient evidence that Wootten was in fear of "imminent" serious physical harm because his purported threats to her in April 2016 did not prevent her from spending time with him thereafter on Mother's Day in early May 2016. But **"a domestic violence victim's subjective belief that serious physical harm was imminent constitutes evidence of imminence."** Lewis v. Gravely, 2016-Ohio-1502, 2016 WL 1404159, ¶ 28 (Ohio Ct. App. 4th Dist. Adams County 2016). Wootten testified that Culp's threats made her fearful of imminent serious physical harm. In addition, **"a victim's actions following the incident may also help establish that the victim believed serious physical harm was imminent."** Lewis v. Gravely, 2016-Ohio-1502, 2016 WL 1404159, ¶ 28 (Ohio Ct. App. 4th Dist. Adams County 2016).

[8]State v. Collie, 108 Ohio App. 3d 580, 671 N.E.2d 338 (1st Dist. Hamilton County 1996); Cleveland v. Earnhart, 110 Ohio Misc. 2d 41, 743 N.E.2d 1000 (Mun. Ct. 2000). But see State v. Brown, 2003-Ohio-710, 2003 WL 352460 (Ohio Ct. App. 12th Dist. Butler County 2003); State v. McClelland, 2002-Ohio-1007, 2002 WL 356306 (Ohio Ct. App. 10th Dist. Franklin County 2002). See also State v. Perkins, 2006-Ohio-3678, 2006 WL 2023558 (Ohio Ct. App. 8th Dist. Cuyahoga County 2006); In re Fugate, 2002-Ohio-2771, 2002 WL 1067284 (Ohio Ct. App. 10th Dist. Franklin County 2002); Portsmouth v. Wrage, 2009-Ohio-3390, 2009 WL 2003386 (Ohio Ct. App. 4th Dist. Scioto County 2009); E. Cleveland v. Perkins, 2009-Ohio-2131, 2009 WL 1244154 (Ohio Ct. App. 8th Dist. Cuyahoga County 2009); State v. Pash, 2010-Ohio-1267, 2010 WL 1175616 (Ohio Ct. App. 3d Dist. Mercer County 2010); Smith v. Burroughs, 2010-Ohio-4806, 2010 WL 3861068 (Ohio Ct. App. 3d Dist. Wyandot County 2010); Wohleber v. Wohleber, 2011-Ohio-6696, 2011 WL 6880736 (Ohio Ct. App. 9th Dist. Lorain County 2011); State v. Habo, 2013-Ohio-2142, 2013 WL 2308483 (Ohio Ct. App. 11th Dist. Portage County 2013); State v. Schweitzer, 2015-Ohio-925, 30 N.E.3d 190 (Ohio Ct. App. 3d Dist. Auglaize County 2015); R.T. v. J.T., 2015-Ohio-4418, 2015 WL 6449294 (Ohio Ct. App. 9th Dist. Medina County 2015); State v. Race, 2017-Ohio-612, 2017 WL 678814 (Ohio Ct. App. 6th Dist. Sandusky County 2017); State v. Binks, 2018-Ohio-1570, ¶ 50, 2018 WL 1907302 (Ohio Ct. App. 12th Dist. Butler County 2018). With respect to the first and second parts of the test, this court has previously recognized that within the context of a trial for domestic violence, "prior acts of violence between a defendant and the victim are highly probative in establishing the victim's belief of impending harm." State v. Rhoads, 2013-Ohio-152, ¶ 29, 2013 WL 221512 (Ohio Ct. App. 12th Dist. Clermont County 2013).

[9]City of Cincinnati v. Baarlaer, 115 Ohio App. 3d 521, 526–527, 685 N.E.2d 836, 840 (1st Dist. Hamilton County 1996); In re Jenkins, 2004-Ohio-2657, 2004 WL 1152853 (Ohio Ct. App. 5th Dist. Stark County 2004); State v. Diroll, 2007-Ohio-6930, 2007 WL 4481430 (Ohio Ct. App. 11th Dist. Portage County 2007); E. Cleveland v. Perkins, 2009-Ohio-2131, 2009 WL 1244154 (Ohio Ct. App. 8th Dist. Cuyahoga County 2009); State v. Schweitzer, 2015-Ohio-925, 30 N.E.3d 190 (Ohio Ct. App. 3d Dist. Auglaize County 2015); State v. Race, 2017-Ohio-612, 2017 WL 678814 (Ohio Ct. App. 6th Dist. Sandusky County 2017).

offender.[1] The exception to this statement is the natural parent of a child of an alleged offender. RC 2919.25(F)(1)(b) covers individuals in this class to provide protection for those victims who have never lived with, but who have a child in common with, the offender.

The phrases "is residing [with]" and "has resided with" are central to the definition of "family or household member" found in RC 2919.25(F)(1). *Black's Law Dictionary* defines "reside" as "to dwell [in a place] permanently or continuously."[2] Thus, unless the parties intend or intended to permanently dwell with one another, they cannot be said to reside with, or to have resided with, each other. Periodic visits with one another, no matter how frequent, generally will not rise to the level necessary to meet the statute's residency requirements.[3]

At least one court also found that where, because of the non-

---

[Section 2:5]

[1]RC 2919.25(F).

[2]Black's Law Dictionary (10th ed). See also State v. Alvey, 2003-Ohio-7006, 2003 WL 22997277 (Ohio Ct. App. 7th Dist. Belmont County 2003); E. Cleveland v. Perkins, 2009-Ohio-2131, 2009 WL 1244154 (Ohio Ct. App. 8th Dist. Cuyahoga County 2009); State v. Burkhart, 2009-Ohio-1142, 2009 WL 653038 (Ohio Ct. App. 11th Dist. Ashtabula County 2009); State v. Turner, 2016-Ohio-813, 2016 WL 860301 (Ohio Ct. App. 8th Dist. Cuyahoga County 2016).

[3]But see State v. Williams, 79 Ohio St. 3d 459, 1997-Ohio-79, 683 N.E.2d 1126 (1997); State v. Colter, 2000 WL 282301 (Ohio Ct. App. 2d Dist. Montgomery County 2000); State v. Wallace, 2006-Ohio-5819, 2006 WL 3183386 (Ohio Ct. App. 9th Dist. Lorain County 2006); State v. Jenson, 2006-Ohio-5169, 2006 WL 2796284 (Ohio Ct. App. 11th Dist. Lake County 2006), judgment aff'd, 114 Ohio St. 3d 430, 2007-Ohio-4552, 872 N.E.2d 1212 (2007); State v. Rodriguez, 2006-Ohio-3378, 2006 WL 1793688 (Ohio Ct. App. 6th Dist. Huron County 2006), judgment aff'd, 114 Ohio St. 3d 430, 2007-Ohio-4552, 872 N.E.2d 1212 (2007); State v. Carswell, 114 Ohio St. 3d 210, 2007-Ohio-3723, 871 N.E.2d 547 (2007); Austin v. Austin, 170 Ohio App. 3d 132, 2007-Ohio-676, 866 N.E.2d 74 (9th Dist. Medina County 2007); Edwards v. Reser, 2007-Ohio-6520, 2007 WL 4277861 (Ohio Ct. App. 6th Dist. Ottawa County 2007); State v. McGrath, 2007-Ohio-4682, 2007 WL 2671267 (Ohio Ct. App. 8th Dist. Cuyahoga County 2007); State v. Pash, 2010-Ohio-1267, 2010 WL 1175616 (Ohio Ct. App. 3d Dist. Mercer County 2010); State v. Messenger, 2010-Ohio-479, 2010 WL 530087 (Ohio Ct. App. 3d Dist. Marion County 2010); State v. Jones, 2010-Ohio-351, 2010 WL 364469 (Ohio Ct. App. 9th Dist. Summit County 2010); State v. Freeman, 2010-Ohio-220, 2010 WL 302787 (Ohio Ct. App. 9th Dist. Summit County 2010); State v. Clay, 181 Ohio App. 3d 563, 2009-Ohio-1235, 910 N.E.2d 14 (8th Dist. Cuyahoga County 2009); State v. Moore, 2010-Ohio-509, 2010 WL 547707 (Ohio Ct. App. 8th Dist. Cuyahoga County 2010); State v. McQueen, 2009-Ohio-6272, 2009 WL 4308654 (Ohio Ct. App. 10th Dist. Franklin County 2009); State v. Barnes, 2009-Ohio-4874, 2009 WL 2963761 (Ohio Ct. App. 8th Dist. Cuyahoga County 2009); State v. Sudderth, 2009-Ohio-3363, 2009 WL 1941345 (Ohio Ct. App. 9th Dist. Summit County 2009); State v. Mauldin, 2010-Ohio-4192, 2010 WL 3482689 (Ohio Ct. App. 7th Dist. Mahoning County 2010); State v. Maple, 2011-Ohio-1516, 2011 WL 1138387 (Ohio Ct. App. 9th Dist. Summit County 2011); State v. Long, 2011-Ohio-1050, 2011 WL 806839 (Ohio Ct. App. 9th Dist. Summit County 2011); State v. Edwards, 2010-Ohio-6496, 2010 WL 5551002 (Ohio Ct. App. 9th Dist. Summit County 2010); State v. Travlus, 2010-Ohio-4046, 2010 WL 3366195 (Ohio Ct. App. 2d Dist. Montgomery County 2010); State v. Perkins, 2010-Ohio-2968, 2010 WL 2573770 (Ohio Ct. App. 12th Dist. Fayette County 2010); State v. Gomez, 2011-Ohio-5475, 2011 WL 5067230 (Ohio Ct. App. 9th Dist. Summit County 2011); State v. Walburg, 2011-Ohio-4762, 2011 WL 4362748 (Ohio Ct. App. 10th Dist. Franklin County 2011); State v. Simmons, 2011-Ohio-6074, 2011 WL 5869794 (Ohio Ct. App. 8th Dist. Cuyahoga County 2011); State v. Smith, 2011-Ohio-4409, 2011 WL 3860572 (Ohio Ct. App. 8th Dist. Cuyahoga County 2011); State v. Hawkins, 2012-Ohio-4622, 2012 WL 4762031 (Ohio Ct. App. 2d

participation of the victim or other failure of proof, the prosecution was unable to prove that a child ever resided with its allegedly abusive parent; the family or household relationship was not established, even though a blood relationship was not denied.[4]

The terms "consanguinity" and "affinity" also appear in the definition of "family and household member" under RC 2919.25(F)(1). These terms are not defined in RC Ch. 29. They are defined, however, in *Ohio Jurisprudence*. The definition given for "affinity" is "a relationship by marriage."[5] "Consanguinity" requires "blood relationship through some common ancestor, regardless of amount."[6]

Another term used to determine the status of one who seeks to obtain or avoid coverage under the statute is "cohabitation." The Ohio Supreme Court, in *State v. Williams*,[7] defined the elements of "cohabitation" as follows:

Dist. Montgomery County 2012); State v. Fernandez, 2012-Ohio-2538, 2012 WL 2061589 (Ohio Ct. App. 2d Dist. Montgomery County 2012); State v. Slevin, 2012-Ohio-2043, 2012 WL 1647115 (Ohio Ct. App. 9th Dist. Summit County 2012); State v. Rubes, 2012-Ohio-4100, 975 N.E.2d 1054 (Ohio Ct. App. 11th Dist. Portage County 2012); State v. Clouse, 2012-Ohio-3471, 2012 WL 3133059 (Ohio Ct. App. 10th Dist. Franklin County 2012); State v. Cornwell, 2015-Ohio-4617, 48 N.E.3d 169 (Ohio Ct. App. 9th Dist. Wayne County 2015); State v. Martin, 2016-Ohio-225, 57 N.E.3d 411 (Ohio Ct. App. 5th Dist. Tuscarawas County 2016); State v. Roberts, 2015-Ohio-5044, 2015 WL 8154018 (Ohio Ct. App. 9th Dist. Wayne County 2015); State v. Perander, 2015-Ohio-1752, 2015 WL 2169235 (Ohio Ct. App. 2d Dist. Montgomery County 2015); State v. Gipson, 2016-Ohio-994, 2016 WL 962400 (Ohio Ct. App. 3d Dist. Allen County 2016); Cleveland v. Merritt, 2016-Ohio-4693, 69 N.E.3d 102 (Ohio Ct. App. 8th Dist. Cuyahoga County 2016), appeal not allowed, 147 Ohio St. 3d 1506, 2017-Ohio-261, 67 N.E.3d 824 (2017); State v. Williams, 2017-Ohio-803, 2017 WL 900070 (Ohio Ct. App. 5th Dist. Stark County 2017); State v. Gipson, 2016-Ohio-994, 2016 WL 962400 (Ohio Ct. App. 3d Dist. Allen County 2016); Foster v. Foster, 2017-Ohio-4311, ¶ 26, 92 N.E.3d 333, 339–40 (Ohio Ct. App. 10th Dist. Franklin County 2017); State v. Riedel, 2017-Ohio-8865, ¶ 83, 100 N.E.3d 1155 (Ohio Ct. App. 8th Dist. Cuyahoga County 2017) (addresses the essential elements of "cohabitation").

[4]State v. Jorden, 134 Ohio App. 3d 131, 730 N.E.2d 447 (1st Dist. Hamilton County 1999); State v. Gibson, 2005-Ohio-1495, 2005 WL 730059 (Ohio Ct. App. 8th Dist. Cuyahoga County 2005); State v. Hannon, 2005-Ohio-874, 2005 WL 477858 (Ohio Ct. App. 4th Dist. Lawrence County 2005); State v. Sims, 169 Ohio App. 3d 579, 2006-Ohio-6285, 863 N.E.2d 1110 (1st Dist. Hamilton County 2006); State v. Jenson, 2006-Ohio-5169, 2006 WL 2796284 (Ohio Ct. App. 11th Dist. Lake County 2006), judgment aff'd, 114 Ohio St. 3d 430, 2007-Ohio-4552, 872 N.E.2d 1212 (2007); State v. Rodriguez, 2006-Ohio-3378, 2006 WL 1793688 (Ohio Ct. App. 6th Dist. Huron County 2006), judgment aff'd, 114 Ohio St. 3d 430, 2007-Ohio-4552, 872 N.E.2d 1212 (2007); State v. Koons, 2007-Ohio-5242, 2007 WL 2851882 (Ohio Ct. App. 7th Dist. Columbiana County 2007); E. Cleveland v. Perkins, 2009-Ohio-2131, 2009 WL 1244154 (Ohio Ct. App. 8th Dist. Cuyahoga County 2009); State v. Clay, 181 Ohio App. 3d 563, 2009-Ohio-1235, 910 N.E.2d 14 (8th Dist. Cuyahoga County 2009).

[5]Ohio Jur. 3d, Decedents' Estates § 84. See also State v. Youst, 74 Ohio App. 381, 29 Ohio Op. 578, 59 N.E.2d 167 (7th Dist. Belmont County 1943); State v. Harris, 109 Ohio App. 3d 873, 673 N.E.2d 237 (1st Dist. Hamilton County 1996).

[6]Ohio Jur. 3d, Decedents' Estates § 84. See also Buchert v. Newman, 90 Ohio App. 3d 382, 629 N.E.2d 489 (1st Dist. Hamilton County 1993).

[7]State v. Williams, 79 Ohio St. 3d 459, 1997-Ohio-79, 683 N.E.2d 1126 (1997); State v. Church, 2005-Ohio-5198, 2005 WL 2401487 (Ohio Ct. App. 8th Dist. Cuyahoga County 2005); State v. Jenson, 2006-Ohio-5169, 2006 WL 2796284 (Ohio Ct. App. 11th Dist. Lake County 2006), judgment aff'd, 114 Ohio St. 3d 430, 2007-Ohio-4552, 872 N.E.2d 1212 (2007); State v. Rodriguez, 2006-Ohio-3378, 2006 WL 1793688 (Ohio Ct. App. 6th Dist. Huron County 2006), judgment aff'd, 114 Ohio St. 3d 430, 2007-Ohio-4552, 872 N.E.2d 1212 (2007); State v. Pash, 2010-Ohio-1267, 2010 WL 1175616 (Ohio

(1) sharing of familial or financial responsibilities, and
(2) consortium.

Possible factors that a court might consider in determining whether or not a particular couple was cohabiting at the time that the act of domestic violence is said to have occurred include:

(1) Relating to shared familial or financial responsibilities, these factors include, but are not limited to:
   (a) provisions for shelter,
   (b) provisions for food,
   (c) provisions for utilities, and
   (d) provisions for the commingling of assets.
(2) Relating to consortium, these factors include, but are not limited to:
   (a) mutual respect,
   (b) fidelity,
   (c) affection,
   (d) society,
   (e) cooperation,
   (f) solace,
   (g) comfort,
   (h) aid to each other,
   (i) friendship, and
   (j) conjugal relations.

This set of factors broadens considerably the class of individuals who potentially qualify as family or household members. Thus, under the Ohio Supreme Court's current interpretation of the term "cohabita-

---

Ct. App. 3d Dist. Mercer County 2010); State v. Messenger, 2010-Ohio-479, 2010 WL 530087 (Ohio Ct. App. 3d Dist. Marion County 2010); State v. Jones, 2010-Ohio-351, 2010 WL 364469 (Ohio Ct. App. 9th Dist. Summit County 2010); State v. Freeman, 2010-Ohio-220, 2010 WL 302787 (Ohio Ct. App. 9th Dist. Summit County 2010); State v. Clay, 181 Ohio App. 3d 563, 2009-Ohio-1235, 910 N.E.2d 14 (8th Dist. Cuyahoga County 2009); State v. Moore, 2010-Ohio-509, 2010 WL 547707 (Ohio Ct. App. 8th Dist. Cuyahoga County 2010); State v. Bell, 2009-Ohio-6302, 2009 WL 4406068 (Ohio Ct. App. 8th Dist. Cuyahoga County 2009); State v. McQueen, 2009-Ohio-6272, 2009 WL 4308654 (Ohio Ct. App. 10th Dist. Franklin County 2009); State v. Barnes, 2009-Ohio-4874, 2009 WL 2963761 (Ohio Ct. App. 8th Dist. Cuyahoga County 2009); State v. Sudderth, 2009-Ohio-3363, 2009 WL 1941345 (Ohio Ct. App. 9th Dist. Summit County 2009); State v. Mauldin, 2010-Ohio-4192, 2010 WL 3482689 (Ohio Ct. App. 7th Dist. Mahoning County 2010); State v. Maple, 2011-Ohio-1516, 2011 WL 1138387 (Ohio Ct. App. 9th Dist. Summit County 2011); State v. Long, 2011-Ohio-1050, 2011 WL 806839 (Ohio Ct. App. 9th Dist. Summit County 2011); State v. Edwards, 2010-Ohio-6496, 2010 WL 5551002 (Ohio Ct. App. 9th Dist. Summit County 2010); State v. Travlus, 2010-Ohio-4046, 2010 WL 3366195 (Ohio Ct. App. 2d Dist. Montgomery County 2010); State v. Perkins, 2010-Ohio-2968, 2010 WL 2573770 (Ohio Ct. App. 12th Dist. Fayette County 2010); State v. Ward, 2010-Ohio-4614, 2010 WL 3782643 (Ohio Ct. App. 10th Dist. Franklin County 2010); State v. Hawkins, 2012-Ohio-4622, 2012 WL 4762031 (Ohio Ct. App. 2d Dist. Montgomery County 2012); State v. Fernandez, 2012-Ohio-2538, 2012 WL 2061589 (Ohio Ct. App. 2d Dist. Montgomery County 2012); State v. Clouse, 2012-Ohio-3471, 2012 WL 3133059 (Ohio Ct. App. 10th Dist. Franklin County 2012); State v. Blackmon, 2012-Ohio-5854, 2012 WL 6139910 (Ohio Ct. App. 5th Dist. Stark County 2012); Foster v. Foster, 2017-Ohio-4311, ¶ 26, 92 N.E.3d 333, 339–40 (Ohio Ct. App. 10th Dist. Franklin County 2017); State v. Riedel, 2017-Ohio-8865, ¶ 83, 100 N.E.3d 1155 (Ohio Ct. App. 8th Dist. Cuyahoga County 2017).

tion," it is foreseeable that courts will find that certain individuals who have never lived together and who have no children in common are, nonetheless, family or household members. At least one court has already made such a finding.[8] It is not, however, necessary that the prosecution establish all of these factors in order to prove a case of domestic violence beyond a reasonable doubt.[9] Each court should consider ordinary human experience, the unique facts of the individual case before it, and common sense.[10] Various Ohio appellate courts have held that "to cohabit" refers to the status of persons living together in the same household and behaving as would a husband and a wife. The courts are in accord that there need not be an actual assertion of marriage and that cohabitation can be based entirely on acts of living together without sexual relations.[11] In fact, at least two courts have held that the burden of establishing cohabitation is not substantial.[12] Other courts have held that the term cohabitation, as used in the statute, provides sufficient warning to potential offenders

---

[8]State v. Combs, 1998 WL 226375 (Ohio Ct. App. 2d Dist. Montgomery County 1998); State v. Young, 1998 WL 801498 (Ohio Ct. App. 2d Dist. Montgomery County 1998); State v. Rubes, 2012-Ohio-4100, 975 N.E.2d 1054 (Ohio Ct. App. 11th Dist. Portage County 2012). See State v. White, 2014-Ohio-1446, 2014 WL 1384082 (Ohio Ct. App. 2d Dist. Montgomery County 2014); State v. McGlothan, 138 Ohio St. 3d 146, 146, 2014-Ohio-85, 4 N.E.3d 1021, 1022 (2014) (reversing the judgment of the court of appeals and reinstating the judgment of the trial court finding defendant guilty of domestic violence. This reversal is based on the state having established that the victim was a family or household member because her testimony demonstrated that she was a person living as a spouse who resided with defendant at the time of the incident.).

[9]State v. Cohagen, 2000 WL 1357938 (Ohio Ct. App. 10th Dist. Franklin County 2000); Heflin v. Dunson, 2005-Ohio-304, 2005 WL 187435 (Ohio Ct. App. 2d Dist. Montgomery County 2005).

[10]State v. Combs, 1998 WL 226375 (Ohio Ct. App. 2d Dist. Montgomery County 1998); State v. Young, 1998 WL 801498 (Ohio Ct. App. 2d Dist. Montgomery County 1998). See also State v. Miller, 105 Ohio App. 3d 679, 664 N.E.2d 1309 (4th Dist. Washington County 1995); State v. Pash, 2010-Ohio-1267, 2010 WL 1175616 (Ohio Ct. App. 3d Dist. Mercer County 2010); State v. McQueen, 2009-Ohio-6272, 2009 WL 4308654 (Ohio Ct. App. 10th Dist. Franklin County 2009); State v. Long, 2011-Ohio-1050, 2011 WL 806839 (Ohio Ct. App. 9th Dist. Summit County 2011); State v. Ward, 2010-Ohio-4614, 2010 WL 3782643 (Ohio Ct. App. 10th Dist. Franklin County 2010); State v. Walburg, 2011-Ohio-4762, 2011 WL 4362748 (Ohio Ct. App. 10th Dist. Franklin County 2011); State v. McGlothan, 138 Ohio St. 3d 146, 146, 2014-Ohio-85, 4 N.E.3d 1021, 1022 (2014) (reversing the judgment of the court of appeals and reinstating the judgment of the trial court finding defendant guilty of domestic violence. This reversal is based on the state having established that the victim was a family or household member because her testimony demonstrated that she was a person living as a spouse who resided with defendant at the time of the incident.).

[11]State v. Miller, 105 Ohio App. 3d 679, 664 N.E.2d 1309 (4th Dist. Washington County 1995); State v. Van Hoose, 1993 WL 386314 (Ohio Ct. App. 2d Dist. Clark County 1993); State v. Ward, 2010-Ohio-4614, 2010 WL 3782643 (Ohio Ct. App. 10th Dist. Franklin County 2010); State v. Clouse, 2012-Ohio-3471, 2012 WL 3133059 (Ohio Ct. App. 10th Dist. Franklin County 2012). See State v. White, 2014-Ohio-1446, 2014 WL 1384082 (Ohio Ct. App. 2d Dist. Montgomery County 2014).

[12]Dyke v. Price, 2000 WL 1546555 (Ohio Ct. App. 2d Dist. Montgomery County 2000); State v. Williams, 2000 WL 1475585 (Ohio Ct. App. 2d Dist. Clark County 2000). For a good discussion of some of the thornier issues that judicial attempts to define cohabitation raise, see U.S. v. Costigan, 2000 WL 898455 (D. Me. 2000), judgment aff'd, 18 Fed. Appx. 2 (1st Cir. 2001). See State v. White, 2014-Ohio-1446, 2014 WL 1384082 (Ohio Ct. App. 2d Dist. Montgomery County 2014); State v. McGlothan, 138 Ohio St. 3d 146, 146, 2014-Ohio-85, 4 N.E.3d 1021, 1022 (2014) (reversing the judgment of the court of appeals and reinstating the judgment of the trial court

as to the types of relationships that are covered, and that the term is not so vague as to fail to meet the requirements of due process under the Constitution.[13]

Following the adoption of the so-called "Defense of Marriage" amendment to the Ohio Constitution in 2004, the concept of cohabitation was the subject of considerable controversy. The Amendment to Article XV, Section 11 was primarily promoted as a means of preserving the traditional concept of valid marriage, i.e., as an institution involving one man and one woman. However, the sweeping language contained in the second sentence of the Amendment was interpreted by many lawyers and some judges as having the unintended effect of calling into question the constitutionality of the state's domestic violence laws.[14] As amended, Ohio's Constitution prohibited the state and all of its political subdivisions from creating or recognizing any

---

finding defendant guilty of domestic violence. This reversal is based on the state having established that the victim was a family or household member because her testimony demonstrated that she was a person living as a spouse who resided with defendant at the time of the incident.).

[13]Cleveland v. Schill, 147 Ohio App. 3d 239, 2002-Ohio-1263, 769 N.E.2d 907 (8th Dist. Cuyahoga County 2002); Cleveland v. Bergman, 111 Ohio Misc. 2d 16, 748 N.E.2d 1214 (Mun. Ct. 2001); State v. Moore, 2010-Ohio-509, 2010 WL 547707 (Ohio Ct. App. 8th Dist. Cuyahoga County 2010).

[14]See, e.g., State v. Burk, 164 Ohio App. 3d 740, 2005-Ohio-6727, 843 N.E.2d 1254 (8th Dist. Cuyahoga County 2005), judgment aff'd, 114 Ohio St. 3d 430, 2007-Ohio-4552, 872 N.E.2d 1212 (2007) (Table); State v. Goshorn, 2006-Ohio-2755, 2006 WL 1495256 (Ohio Ct. App. 4th Dist. Ross County 2006); State v. Newell, 2005-Ohio-2848, 2005 WL 1364937 (Ohio Ct. App. 5th Dist. Stark County 2005); State v. Adams, 2005-Ohio-6333, 2005 WL 3196850 (Ohio Ct. App. 5th Dist. Stark County 2005); State v. Brown, 166 Ohio App. 3d 32, 2006-Ohio-1181, 849 N.E.2d 44 (5th Dist. Stark County 2006); State v. Edwards, 2005-Ohio-7064, 2005 WL 3642716 (Ohio Ct. App. 5th Dist. Stark County 2005); Uhrichsville v. Losey, 2005-Ohio-6564, 2005 WL 3361100 (Ohio Ct. App. 5th Dist. Tuscarawas County 2005); State v. Rodriguez, 2006-Ohio-3378, 2006 WL 1793688 (Ohio Ct. App. 6th Dist. Huron County 2006), judgment aff'd, 114 Ohio St. 3d 430, 2007-Ohio-4552, 872 N.E.2d 1212 (2007); State v. Rexroad, 2005-Ohio-6790, 2005 WL 3489726 (Ohio Ct. App. 7th Dist. Columbiana County 2005); Gough v. Triner, 2006-Ohio-3522, 2006 WL 1868330 (Ohio Ct. App. 7th Dist. Columbiana County 2006); Cleveland v. Voies, 2006-Ohio-815, 2006 WL 440341 (Ohio Ct. App. 8th Dist. Cuyahoga County 2006), judgment aff'd, 114 Ohio St. 3d 430, 2007-Ohio-4552, 872 N.E.2d 1212 (2007); State v. Douglas, 2006-Ohio-2343, 2006 WL 1304860 (Ohio Ct. App. 8th Dist. Cuyahoga County 2006), judgment aff'd, 114 Ohio St. 3d 430, 2007-Ohio-4552, 872 N.E.2d 1212 (2007); State v. Nixon, 165 Ohio App. 3d 178, 2006-Ohio-72, 845 N.E.2d 544 (9th Dist. Summit County 2006); State v. Rodgers, 166 Ohio App. 3d 218, 2006-Ohio-1528, 850 N.E.2d 90 (10th Dist. Franklin County 2006); State v. Carswell, 2005-Ohio-6547, 2005 WL 3358882 (Ohio Ct. App. 12th Dist. Warren County 2005), judgment aff'd, 114 Ohio St. 3d 210, 2007-Ohio-3723, 871 N.E.2d 547 (2007); State v. McCaslin, 2006-Ohio-891, 2006 WL 459261 (Ohio Ct. App. 7th Dist. Columbiana County 2006); State v. Jenson, 2006-Ohio-5169, 2006 WL 2796284 (Ohio Ct. App. 11th Dist. Lake County 2006), judgment aff'd, 114 Ohio St. 3d 430, 2007-Ohio-4552, 872 N.E.2d 1212 (2007); State v. Kvasne, 169 Ohio App. 3d 167, 2006-Ohio-5235, 862 N.E.2d 171 (8th Dist. Cuyahoga County 2006), judgment aff'd, 114 Ohio St. 3d 430, 2007-Ohio-4552, 872 N.E.2d 1212 (2007); State v. Carnes, 2007-Ohio-604, 2007 WL 446019 (Ohio Ct. App. 7th Dist. Mahoning County 2007); State v. Hampton, 2006-Ohio-5995, 2006 WL 3290799 (Ohio Ct. App. 5th Dist. Stark County 2006); State v. Hare, 2006-Ohio-3926, 2006 WL 2141587 (Ohio Ct. App. 5th Dist. Delaware County 2006); State v. Williams, 2006-Ohio-6281, 2006 WL 3446187 (Ohio Ct. App. 8th Dist. Cuyahoga County 2006). See In re Ohio Domestic-Violence Statute Cases, 114 Ohio St. 3d 430, 2007-Ohio-4552, 872 N.E.2d 1212 (2007).

legal status in unmarried couples that approximate the design, qualities, significance or effect of marriage.[15] However, the U.S. Supreme Court's most recent decisions on the issue of same-sex unions[16] caused Ohio's prohibition to face strong challenges.

Arguments were presented to trial courts across the state asserting that, as amended, Ohio's Constitution prohibited unmarried individuals who cohabit, i.e., live together, from enjoying the protection afforded to married couples under the state's domestic violence laws.[17] These arguments maintained that the extension of domestic violence law protections to unmarried cohabitants created or recognized for them a prohibited "legal status intended to approximate the design, qualities, significance or effect of marriage."[18] Accordingly, they

---

[15]O. Const. Art. XV § 11, as amended effective December 1, 2004; Ohio Const. Art. XV § 11 was found unconstitutional by Obergefell v. Hodges, 135 S. Ct. 2584, 192 L. Ed. 2d 609, 99 Empl. Prac. Dec. (CCH) P 45341, 2015-1 U.S. Tax Cas. (CCH) P 50357, 115 A.F.T.R.2d 2015-2309 (2015).

[16]U.S. v. Windsor, 570 U.S. 744, 133 S. Ct. 2675, 186 L. Ed. 2d 808, 57 Employee Benefits Cas. (BNA) 1577, 118 Fair Empl. Prac. Cas. (BNA) 1417, 2013-2 U.S. Tax Cas. (CCH) P 50400, 111 A.F.T.R.2d 2013-2385 (2013); Hollingsworth v. Perry, 570 U.S. 693, 133 S. Ct. 2652, 186 L. Ed. 2d 768, 57 Employee Benefits Cas. (BNA) 1605, 118 Fair Empl. Prac. Cas. (BNA) 1446 (2013); Ohio Const. Art. XV § 11 was found unconstitutional by Obergefell v. Hodges, 135 S. Ct. 2584, 192 L. Ed. 2d 609, 99 Empl. Prac. Dec. (CCH) P 45341, 2015-1 U.S. Tax Cas. (CCH) P 50357, 115 A.F.T.R.2d 2015-2309 (2015).

[17]State v. Burk, 164 Ohio App. 3d 740, 2005-Ohio-6727, 843 N.E.2d 1254 (8th Dist. Cuyahoga County 2005), judgment aff'd, 114 Ohio St. 3d 430, 2007-Ohio-4552, 872 N.E.2d 1212 (2007); State v. Goshorn, 2006-Ohio-2755, 2006 WL 1495256 (Ohio Ct. App. 4th Dist. Ross County 2006); State v. Newell, 2005-Ohio-2848, 2005 WL 1364937 (Ohio Ct. App. 5th Dist. Stark County 2005); State v. Adams, 2005-Ohio-6333, 2005 WL 3196850 (Ohio Ct. App. 5th Dist. Stark County 2005); State v. Brown, 166 Ohio App. 3d 32, 2006-Ohio-1181, 849 N.E.2d 44 (5th Dist. Stark County 2006); State v. Edwards, 2005-Ohio-7064, 2005 WL 3642716 (Ohio Ct. App. 5th Dist. Stark County 2005); Uhrichsville v. Losey, 2005-Ohio-6564, 2005 WL 3361100 (Ohio Ct. App. 5th Dist. Tuscarawas County 2005); State v. Rodriguez, 2006-Ohio-3378, 2006 WL 1793688 (Ohio Ct. App. 6th Dist. Huron County 2006), judgment aff'd, 114 Ohio St. 3d 430, 2007-Ohio-4552, 872 N.E.2d 1212 (2007); State v. Rexroad, 2005-Ohio-6790, 2005 WL 3489726 (Ohio Ct. App. 7th Dist. Columbiana County 2005); Gough v. Triner, 2006-Ohio-3522, 2006 WL 1868330 (Ohio Ct. App. 7th Dist. Columbiana County 2006); Cleveland v. Voies, 2006-Ohio-815, 2006 WL 440341 (Ohio Ct. App. 8th Dist. Cuyahoga County 2006), judgment aff'd, 114 Ohio St. 3d 430, 2007-Ohio-4552, 872 N.E.2d 1212 (2007); State v. Douglas, 2006-Ohio-2343, 2006 WL 1304860 (Ohio Ct. App. 8th Dist. Cuyahoga County 2006), judgment aff'd, 114 Ohio St. 3d 430, 2007-Ohio-4552, 872 N.E.2d 1212 (2007); State v. Nixon, 165 Ohio App. 3d 178, 2006-Ohio-72, 845 N.E.2d 544 (9th Dist. Summit County 2006); State v. Rodgers, 166 Ohio App. 3d 218, 2006-Ohio-1528, 850 N.E.2d 90 (10th Dist. Franklin County 2006); State v. Carswell, 2005-Ohio-6547, 2005 WL 3358882 (Ohio Ct. App. 12th Dist. Warren County 2005), judgment aff'd, 114 Ohio St. 3d 210, 2007-Ohio-3723, 871 N.E.2d 547 (2007). State v. Kvasne, 169 Ohio App. 3d 167, 2006-Ohio-5235, 862 N.E.2d 171 (8th Dist. Cuyahoga County 2006), judgment aff'd, 114 Ohio St. 3d 430, 2007-Ohio-4552, 872 N.E.2d 1212 (2007); State v. Lawrence, 2008-Ohio-1354, 2008 WL 757529 (Ohio Ct. App. 12th Dist. Butler County 2008), cause dismissed, 121 Ohio St. 3d 1224, 2009-Ohio-1112, 903 N.E.2d 643 (2009). Note that the cases cited in this footnote are for historical context and decided before the landmark decision of Obergefell v. Hodges, 135 S. Ct. 2584, 192 L. Ed. 2d 609, 99 Empl. Prac. Dec. (CCH) P 45341, 2015-1 U.S. Tax Cas. (CCH) P 50357, 115 A.F.T.R.2d 2015-2309 (2015), which rendered Ohio Const. Art. XV § 11 unconstitutional.

[18]O. Const. Art. XV § 11. Found unconstitutional by landmark decision of Obergefell v. Hodges, 135 S. Ct. 2584, 192 L. Ed. 2d 609, 99 Empl. Prac. Dec. (CCH) P 45341,

reasoned that an unmarried individual living with another in Ohio could never be legally, "living as spouse," without violating the state's Constitution.[19]

The counterargument, advanced by many prosecutors and victims' advocates, was that the backers and drafters of the Amendment did not intend to impact the domestic violence laws at all when they introduced this initiative.[20] In fact, there was evidence that the initiative's backers specifically denied any such intent.[21]

Additionally, some analysts maintained that the term, "living as spouse," contained in the state's domestic violence laws is merely descriptive and does not create or recognize a prohibited legal status outlawed by the Amendment.[22]

Yet a third analysis found that the domestic violence laws did confer upon unmarried cohabitants a legal status, but that the domestic violence laws' imposition of legal rights and liabilities neither intended to "approximate marriage" nor did that legal status approximate marriage in fact.[23]

Constitutional arguments regarding alleged due process and equal protection violations were also presented to and considered by the

---

2015-1 U.S. Tax Cas. (CCH) P 50357, 115 A.F.T.R.2d 2015-2309 (2015).

[19]Ohio Constitution, Article XV, Section 11. Found unconstitutional by landmark decision of Obergefell v. Hodges, 135 S. Ct. 2584, 192 L. Ed. 2d 609, 99 Empl. Prac. Dec. (CCH) P 45341, 2015-1 U.S. Tax Cas. (CCH) P 50357, 115 A.F.T.R.2d 2015-2309 (2015).

[20]See, e.g., State v. Newell, 2005-Ohio-2848, 2005 WL 1364937 (Ohio Ct. App. 5th Dist. Stark County 2005); State v. Rodgers, 131 Ohio Misc. 2d 1, 2005-Ohio-1730, 827 N.E.2d 872 (C.P. 2005); State v. Watson, 2005-Ohio-1729, 2005 WL 845228 (Ohio Ct. App. 5th Dist. Stark County 2005); City of Shaker Heights v. Mosely, 2005-Ohio-5433, 2005 WL 2562915 (Ohio Ct. App. 8th Dist. Cuyahoga County 2005), judgment aff'd, 113 Ohio St. 3d 329, 2007-Ohio-2072, 865 N.E.2d 859 (2007); State v. Rodriguez, 2006-Ohio-3378, 2006 WL 1793688 (Ohio Ct. App. 6th Dist. Huron County 2006), judgment aff'd, 114 Ohio St. 3d 430, 2007-Ohio-4552, 872 N.E.2d 1212 (2007). Note that the cases cited in this footnote are for historical context and decided before the landmark decision of Obergefell v. Hodges, 135 S. Ct. 2584, 192 L. Ed. 2d 609, 99 Empl. Prac. Dec. (CCH) P 45341, 2015-1 U.S. Tax Cas. (CCH) P 50357, 115 A.F.T.R.2d 2015-2309 (2015), which rendered Ohio Const. Art. XV § 11 unconstitutional.

[21]City of Cleveland v. Knipp, 2005 WL 1017620 (Ohio Mun. Ct. 2005). All cases cited are for historical context and decided before the landmark decision of Obergefell v. Hodges, 135 S. Ct. 2584, 192 L. Ed. 2d 609, 99 Empl. Prac. Dec. (CCH) P 45341, 2015-1 U.S. Tax Cas. (CCH) P 50357, 115 A.F.T.R.2d 2015-2309 (2015), which rendered Ohio Const. Art. XV § 11 unconstitutional.

[22]City of Cleveland v. Knipp, 2005 WL 1017620 (Ohio Mun. Ct. 2005). Note that the cases cited in this footnote are for historical context and decided before the landmark decision of Obergefell v. Hodges, 135 S. Ct. 2584, 192 L. Ed. 2d 609, 99 Empl. Prac. Dec. (CCH) P 45341, 2015-1 U.S. Tax Cas. (CCH) P 50357, 115 A.F.T.R.2d 2015-2309 (2015), which rendered Ohio Const. Art. XV § 11 unconstitutional.

[23]State v. Rodriguez, 2006-Ohio-3378, 2006 WL 1793688 (Ohio Ct. App. 6th Dist. Huron County 2006), judgment aff'd, 114 Ohio St. 3d 430, 2007-Ohio-4552, 872 N.E.2d 1212 (2007); State v. Jenson, 2006-Ohio-5169, 2006 WL 2796284 (Ohio Ct. App. 11th Dist. Lake County 2006), judgment aff'd, 114 Ohio St. 3d 430, 2007-Ohio-4552, 872 N.E.2d 1212 (2007). Note that the cases cited in this footnote are for historical context and decided before the landmark decision of Obergefell v. Hodges, 135 S. Ct. 2584, 192 L. Ed. 2d 609, 99 Empl. Prac. Dec. (CCH) P 45341, 2015-1 U.S. Tax Cas. (CCH) P 50357, 115 A.F.T.R.2d 2015-2309 (2015), which rendered Ohio Const. Art. XV § 11 unconstitutional.

trial courts.[24] A clear majority of Ohio's appellate jurisdictions that spoke to the issue, although not all, held that the domestic violence laws were constitutional. The lack of unanimity set up a conflict of authority, which was ultimately presented to the Supreme Court of Ohio for resolution.[25] That Court held that "the term 'person living as a spouse' as defined in R.C. 2919.25 merely identifies a particular class of persons for the purposes of the domestic-violence statutes. It does not create or recognize a legal relationship that approximates the designs, qualities, or significance of marriage as prohibited by Section 11, Article XV of the Ohio Constitution. Persons who satisfy the 'living as a spouse' category are not provided any of the rights, benefits, or duties of marriage. A 'person living as a spouse' is simply a classification with significance to only domestic-violence statutes. Thus, R.C. 2919.25 is not unconstitutional and does not create a quasi-

[24]See, e.g., City of Cleveland v. Knipp, 2005 WL 1017620 (Ohio Mun. Ct. 2005); State v. Abdellahi, 2005 WL 4651078 (Ohio C.P. 2005). Note that the cases cited in this footnote are for historical context and decided before the landmark decision of Obergefell v. Hodges, 135 S. Ct. 2584, 192 L. Ed. 2d 609, 99 Empl. Prac. Dec. (CCH) P 45341, 2015-1 U.S. Tax Cas. (CCH) P 50357, 115 A.F.T.R.2d 2015-2309 (2015), which rendered Ohio Const. Art. XV § 11 unconstitutional.

[25]State v. Burk, 164 Ohio App. 3d 740, 2005-Ohio-6727, 843 N.E.2d 1254 (8th Dist. Cuyahoga County 2005), judgment aff'd, 114 Ohio St. 3d 430, 2007-Ohio-4552, 872 N.E.2d 1212 (2007); State v. Goshorn, 2006-Ohio-2755, 2006 WL 1495256 (Ohio Ct. App. 4th Dist. Ross County 2006); State v. Newell, 2005-Ohio-2848, 2005 WL 1364937 (Ohio Ct. App. 5th Dist. Stark County 2005); State v. Adams, 2005-Ohio-6333, 2005 WL 3196850 (Ohio Ct. App. 5th Dist. Stark County 2005); State v. Brown, 166 Ohio App. 3d 32, 2006-Ohio-1181, 849 N.E.2d 44 (5th Dist. Stark County 2006); State v. Edwards, 2005-Ohio-7064, 2005 WL 3642716 (Ohio Ct. App. 5th Dist. Stark County 2005); Uhrichsville v. Losey, 2005-Ohio-6564, 2005 WL 3361100 (Ohio Ct. App. 5th Dist. Tuscarawas County 2005); State v. Rodriguez, 2006-Ohio-3378, 2006 WL 1793688 (Ohio Ct. App. 6th Dist. Huron County 2006), judgment aff'd, 114 Ohio St. 3d 430, 2007-Ohio-4552, 872 N.E.2d 1212 (2007); State v. Rexroad, 2005-Ohio-6790, 2005 WL 3489726 (Ohio Ct. App. 7th Dist. Columbiana County 2005); Gough v. Triner, 2006-Ohio-3522, 2006 WL 1868330 (Ohio Ct. App. 7th Dist. Columbiana County 2006); Cleveland v. Voies, 2006-Ohio-815, 2006 WL 440341 (Ohio Ct. App. 8th Dist. Cuyahoga County 2006), judgment aff'd, 114 Ohio St. 3d 430, 2007-Ohio-4552, 872 N.E.2d 1212 (2007); State v. Douglas, 2006-Ohio-2343, 2006 WL 1304860 (Ohio Ct. App. 8th Dist. Cuyahoga County 2006), judgment aff'd, 114 Ohio St. 3d 430, 2007-Ohio-4552, 872 N.E.2d 1212 (2007); State v. Nixon, 165 Ohio App. 3d 178, 2006-Ohio-72, 845 N.E.2d 544 (9th Dist. Summit County 2006); State v. Rodgers, 166 Ohio App. 3d 218, 2006-Ohio-1528, 850 N.E.2d 90 (10th Dist. Franklin County 2006); State v. Carswell, 2005-Ohio-6547, 2005 WL 3358882 (Ohio Ct. App. 12th Dist. Warren County 2005), judgment aff'd, 114 Ohio St. 3d 210, 2007-Ohio-3723, 871 N.E.2d 547 (2007); State v. McCaslin, 2006-Ohio-891, 2006 WL 459261 (Ohio Ct. App. 7th Dist. Columbiana County 2006); State v. Jenson, 2006-Ohio-5169, 2006 WL 2796284 (Ohio Ct. App. 11th Dist. Lake County 2006), judgment aff'd, 114 Ohio St. 3d 430, 2007-Ohio-4552, 872 N.E.2d 1212 (2007); State v. Kvasne, 169 Ohio App. 3d 167, 2006-Ohio-5235, 862 N.E.2d 171 (8th Dist. Cuyahoga County 2006), judgment aff'd, 114 Ohio St. 3d 430, 2007-Ohio-4552, 872 N.E.2d 1212 (2007); State v. Carnes, 2007-Ohio-604, 2007 WL 446019 (Ohio Ct. App. 7th Dist. Mahoning County 2007); State v. Hampton, 2006-Ohio-5995, 2006 WL 3290799 (Ohio Ct. App. 5th Dist. Stark County 2006); State v. Hare, 2006-Ohio-3926, 2006 WL 2141587 (Ohio Ct. App. 5th Dist. Delaware County 2006); State v. Williams, 2006-Ohio-6281, 2006 WL 3446187 (Ohio Ct. App. 8th Dist. Cuyahoga County 2006). See also State v. Terry, 2006-Ohio-4320, 2006 WL 2390284 (Ohio Ct. App. 3d Dist. Crawford County 2006). Note that the cases cited in this footnote are for historical context and decided before the landmark decision of Obergefell v. Hodges, 135 S. Ct. 2584, 192 L. Ed. 2d 609, 99 Empl. Prac. Dec. (CCH) P 45341, 2015-1 U.S. Tax Cas. (CCH) P 50357, 115 A.F.T.R.2d 2015-2309 (2015), which rendered Ohio Const. Art. XV § 11 unconstitutional.

marital relationship in violation of Section 11, Article XV of the Ohio Constitution."[26]

In a landmark decision the highest Court held same-sex couples may exercise the right to marry in all states.[27] In doing so, the US Supreme Court articulated four principles and traditions that illustrate the reasons marriage is fundamental under the Constitution and that these principles apply with equal force to same-sex marriages. This decision thus makes the prohibitions found in the the Defense of Marriage Act unconstitutional. The four principles for protecting the right to marry are:

1. The right to personal choice regarding marriage is inherent in the concept of individual autonomy;
2. The right to marry is fundamental because it supports a two-person union unlike any other in its importance to the committed individuals;
3. Safeguards children and families and draws meaning from related rights of childrearing procreation and education; and
4. Marriage is the keystone of our social order.

It then goes to reason that same-sex couples are afforded the same rights as heterosexual partners for the purposes of RC 2919.25(F).

The various classes of individuals who are covered under RC 2919.25(F) are as follows:

(1) The spouse of an alleged offender.
(2) A former spouse of the alleged offender.
(3) Any person who is living with the alleged offender in a common law marital relationship at the time of the offense.
(4) A person who has previously lived with the alleged offender in a common law marital relationship.
(5) A person who is otherwise cohabiting with the alleged offender.
(6) A person who has otherwise cohabited with the alleged offender within five years prior to the date of the alleged commission of the act.
(7) A person who is the natural parent of the alleged offender's child, or is alleged to be the parent of said child.[28]
(8) A person who is a parent of the alleged offender.
(9) A person who is a child, or alleged child, of the alleged offender.

---

[26]State v. Carswell, 114 Ohio St. 3d 210, 2007-Ohio-3723, 871 N.E.2d 547 (2007); Kvasne v. Collins, 2010 WL 3210949 (N.D. Ohio 2010); State v. Long, 2011-Ohio-1050, 2011 WL 806839 (Ohio Ct. App. 9th Dist. Summit County 2011); State v. Riedel, 2017-Ohio-8865, ¶ 84–85, 100 N.E.3d 1155 (Ohio Ct. App. 8th Dist. Cuyahoga County 2017); State v. Gipson, 2016-Ohio-994, ¶ 37, 2016 WL 962400 (Ohio Ct. App. 3d Dist. Allen County 2016); State v. Brown, 2015-Ohio-950, ¶ 33, 2015 WL 1138651 (Ohio Ct. App. 11th Dist. Lake County 2015).

[27]Obergefell v. Hodges, 135 S. Ct. 2584, 192 L. Ed. 2d 609, 99 Empl. Prac. Dec. (CCH) P 45341, 2015-1 U.S. Tax Cas. (CCH) P 50357, 115 A.F.T.R.2d 2015-2309 (2015).

[28]State v. Stringfield, 124 Ohio App. 3d 665, 707 N.E.2d 43 (9th Dist. Medina County 1998); State v. Johnston, 2004-Ohio-282, ¶ 13, 2004 WL 111642 (Ohio Ct. App. 12th Dist. Butler County 2004).

(10) An unborn, alleged to be that of the alleged offender and the pregnant woman who is victimized.[29]
(11) The mother of an unborn, alleged to be that of the alleged offender and the mother.[30]
(12) A person related to the alleged offender by either blood or marriage.
(13) A parent of the spouse of the alleged offender.
(14) A parent of a former spouse of the alleged offender.
(15) A parent of a person who is living with the alleged offender in a common law marital relationship.
(16) A parent of a person who has previously lived with the alleged offender in a common law marital relationship.
(17) A parent of a person who is otherwise cohabiting with the alleged offender.
(18) A parent of a person who has otherwise cohabited with the offender within five years prior to the date of the alleged commission of the act in question.
(19) A child of the spouse of the alleged offender (i.e., stepchild).
(20) A child of a former spouse of the alleged offender.
(21) A child of a person who is living with the alleged offender in a common law marital relationship.
(22) A child of a person who has previously lived with the alleged offender in a common law marital relationship.
(23) A child of a person who is otherwise cohabiting with the alleged offender.
(24) A child of a person who has otherwise cohabited with the alleged offender within five years prior to the date of the alleged commission of the act in question.
(25) A person who is related by blood or marriage to the spouse of the offender.
(26) A person who is related by blood or marriage to a former spouse of the alleged offender.
(27) A person who is related by blood or marriage to a person living in a common law relationship with the alleged offender.
(28) A person who is related by blood or marriage to a person who previously lived in a common law relationship with the alleged offender.
(29) A person who is related by blood or marriage to a person who is otherwise cohabiting with the offender.
(30) A person who is related by blood or marriage to a person who has otherwise cohabited with the offender within five years from the date of the alleged commission of the act in question.

In many instances, those injured by the actions of a violent, intimate partner do not fit the definition of "family or household member" currently found in the Ohio Revised Code. Falling outside the definition, for example, are a man and a woman who have enjoyed an intimate relationship for many years, but who have no children together and

---

[29]See Am. Sub. H.B. 280, eff. 1-6-2009.

[30]See Am. Sub. H.B. 280, eff. 1-6-2009. See also 2008 Ohio Laws File 155 (Am. Sub. H.B. 280).

who have never stayed together under the same roof for more than a few days at a time.[31] In a number of other states, the domestic violence laws have been expanded to cover such dating relationships.[32]

---

[31]See, e.g., State v. Rinehart, 2002-Ohio-6143, 2002 WL 31520346 (Ohio Ct. App. 4th Dist. Ross County 2002); State v. Douglas, 2006-Ohio-2343, 2006 WL 1304860 (Ohio Ct. App. 8th Dist. Cuyahoga County 2006), judgment aff'd, 114 Ohio St. 3d 430, 2007-Ohio-4552, 872 N.E.2d 1212 (2007); State v. Kvasne, 169 Ohio App. 3d 167, 2006-Ohio-5235, 862 N.E.2d 171 (8th Dist. Cuyahoga County 2006), judgment aff'd, 114 Ohio St. 3d 430, 2007-Ohio-4552, 872 N.E.2d 1212 (2007); see also State v. Carswell, 114 Ohio St. 3d 210, 2007-Ohio-3723, 871 N.E.2d 547 (2007); State v. Brown, 119 Ohio St. 3d 447, 2008-Ohio-4569, 895 N.E.2d 149 (2008); Kvasne v. Collins, 2010 WL 3210949 (N.D. Ohio 2010); State v. Long, 2011-Ohio-1050, 2011 WL 806839 (Ohio Ct. App. 9th Dist. Summit County 2011); State v. Rubes, 2012-Ohio-4100, 975 N.E.2d 1054 (Ohio Ct. App. 11th Dist. Portage County 2012); State v. McGlothan, 138 Ohio St. 3d 146, 146, 2014-Ohio-85, 4 N.E.3d 1021, 1022 (2014) (reversing judgment of the court of appeals and reinstating the judgment of the trial court finding defendant guilty of domestic violence); State v. Rodriguez, 2006-Ohio-3378, ¶ 25, 2006 WL 1793688 (Ohio Ct. App. 6th Dist. Huron County 2006), judgment aff'd, 114 Ohio St. 3d 430, 2007-Ohio-4552, 872 N.E.2d 1212 (2007); In re Ohio Domestic-Violence Statute Cases, 114 Ohio St. 3d 430, 2007-Ohio-4552, ¶ 25, 872 N.E.2d 1212 (2007).

[32]See survey reported in State v. Williams, 79 Ohio St. 3d 459, 1997-Ohio-79, 683 N.E.2d 1126 (1997); State v. Carswell, 114 Ohio St. 3d 210, 2007-Ohio-3723, 871 N.E.2d 547 (2007); Austin v. Austin, 170 Ohio App. 3d 132, 2007-Ohio-676, 866 N.E.2d 74 (9th Dist. Medina County 2007); State v. Boldin, 2008-Ohio-6408, 2008 WL 5147450 (Ohio Ct. App. 11th Dist. Geauga County 2008); State v. Barnes, 2008-Ohio-5997, 2008 WL 4949833 (Ohio Ct. App. 8th Dist. Cuyahoga County 2008); Youngstown v. Dixon, 2009-Ohio-1013, 2009 WL 581637 (Ohio Ct. App. 7th Dist. Mahoning County 2009); State v. Pash, 2010-Ohio-1267, 2010 WL 1175616 (Ohio Ct. App. 3d Dist. Mercer County 2010); State v. Messenger, 2010-Ohio-479, 2010 WL 530087 (Ohio Ct. App. 3d Dist. Marion County 2010); State v. Jones, 2010-Ohio-351, 2010 WL 364469 (Ohio Ct. App. 9th Dist. Summit County 2010); State v. Freeman, 2010-Ohio-220, 2010 WL 302787 (Ohio Ct. App. 9th Dist. Summit County 2010); State v. Clay, 181 Ohio App. 3d 563, 2009-Ohio-1235, 910 N.E.2d 14 (8th Dist. Cuyahoga County 2009); State v. Moore, 2010-Ohio-509, 2010 WL 547707 (Ohio Ct. App. 8th Dist. Cuyahoga County 2010); State v. Bell, 2009-Ohio-6302, 2009 WL 4406068 (Ohio Ct. App. 8th Dist. Cuyahoga County 2009); State v. McQueen, 2009-Ohio-6272, 2009 WL 4308654 (Ohio Ct. App. 10th Dist. Franklin County 2009); State v. Barnes, 2009-Ohio-4874, 2009 WL 2963761 (Ohio Ct. App. 8th Dist. Cuyahoga County 2009); State v. Sudderth, 2009-Ohio-3363, 2009 WL 1941345 (Ohio Ct. App. 9th Dist. Summit County 2009); State v. Walburg, 2011-Ohio-4762, 2011 WL 4362748 (Ohio Ct. App. 10th Dist. Franklin County 2011); State v. Smith, 2011-Ohio-4409, 2011 WL 3860572 (Ohio Ct. App. 8th Dist. Cuyahoga County 2011); State v. Fernandez, 2012-Ohio-2538, 2012 WL 2061589 (Ohio Ct. App. 2d Dist. Montgomery County 2012); State v. Ross, 2012-Ohio-1389, 2012 WL 1076253 (Ohio Ct. App. 9th Dist. Summit County 2012); State v. Hunter, 2012-Ohio-1121, 2012 WL 929696 (Ohio Ct. App. 9th Dist. Lorain County 2012); State v. Short, 2011-Ohio-5744, 2011 WL 5353078 (Ohio Ct. App. 12th Dist. Butler County 2011); State v. Corbin, 194 Ohio App. 3d 720, 2011-Ohio-3491, 957 N.E.2d 849 (6th Dist. Wood County 2011); State v. Gomez, 2011-Ohio-5475, 2011 WL 5067230 (Ohio Ct. App. 9th Dist. Summit County 2011); State v. Brown, 2015-Ohio-950, 2015 WL 1138651 (Ohio Ct. App. 11th Dist. Lake County 2015); State v. Gipson, 2016-Ohio-994, 2016 WL 962400 (Ohio Ct. App. 3d Dist. Allen County 2016); State v. Cornwell, 2015-Ohio-4617, 48 N.E.3d 169 (Ohio Ct. App. 9th Dist. Wayne County 2015); State v. Martin, 2016-Ohio-225, 57 N.E.3d 411 (Ohio Ct. App. 5th Dist. Tuscarawas County 2016); State v. Roberts, 2015-Ohio-5044, 2015 WL 8154018 (Ohio Ct. App. 9th Dist. Wayne County 2015); State v. Perander, 2015-Ohio-1752, 2015 WL 2169235 (Ohio Ct. App. 2d Dist. Montgomery County 2015); State v. Hughes, 2015-Ohio-1173, 2015 WL 1403276 (Ohio Ct. App. 5th Dist. Tuscarawas County 2015); State v. Matthews, 2015-Ohio-3297, 2015 WL 4880984 (Ohio Ct. App. 6th Dist. Ottawa County 2015); Foster v. Foster, 2017-Ohio-4311, ¶ 26, 92 N.E.3d 333, 339–40 (Ohio Ct. App. 10th Dist. Franklin County 2017); State v. Riedel, 2017-Ohio-8865,

Meanwhile, recent amendments to the definitions contained in Ohio's domestic violence statute extend additional protection to pregnant women who are family or household members of their abusers at the time of the offense and to the fetuses that they carry. Those amendments also require greater sanctions for the offenders who injure such women and/or their fetuses, including mandatory periods of incarceration of anywhere from six months to a year or more, while carefully avoiding declaring that those fetuses are human persons.[33]

Additionally, a "family or household member" is defined for purposes of Ohio's domestic violence laws as someone related by affinity or consanguinity to the offender and who is "residing or has resided with the offender."[34] The concept of residency is not defined anywhere in either statute or municipal ordinance. However, the intent of the parties is crucial to any definition of the term. Unless the parties intended at some point to permanently dwell with one another, they cannot be said to reside with or to have resided with each other at the time of the incident. Periodic visits with one another, whether or not they are overnight, and no matter how frequent, will not rise to the level necessary to meet the statutory requirements, without more.[35]

Q & A: If a victim is beaten by her boyfriend, with whom she has never lived and by whom she has no children, is she able to seek the issuance of a domestic violence complaint? Would it make a difference if the parties stay with each other three or four times each week in their respective homes?

Under the facts presented, the answer to both questions is "no." These parties clearly had no intention of establishing a residence with one another.[36] Visits to each other's homes, regardless of how frequent, are not sufficient, without more, to find that the parties are "family or household members."

The absence of children in this relationship requires the complainant to establish the existence of cohabitation and consortium between the parties as a prerequisite to bringing a charge of domestic violence against her boyfriend.[37]

Intent is the primary consideration in any determination of the residential status of the parties.

¶ 83, 100 N.E.3d 1155 (Ohio Ct. App. 8th Dist. Cuyahoga County 2017).

[33]See RC 2919.25(D)(6)(a) to (e), as well as RC 2919.25(F)(3) and RC 2919.25(F)(4). See also RC 2903.09(C).

[34]RC 2919.25(F)(1)(a)(ii).

[35]Text § 10:4, Nature of the relationships covered—Terminology—"Is residing with" and "has resided with"; State v. Toles, 1999 WL 1232092 (Ohio Ct. App. 4th Dist. Gallia County 1999); City of Cleveland v. Johnson, 2014-Ohio-4083, 19 N.E.3d 604 (Ohio Ct. App. 8th Dist. Cuyahoga County 2014), as corrected, (Sept. 23, 2014); State v. Perander, 2015-Ohio-1752, 2015 WL 2169235 (Ohio Ct. App. 2d Dist. Montgomery County 2015); State v. Riedel, 2017-Ohio-8865, 100 N.E.3d 1155 (Ohio Ct. App. 8th Dist. Cuyahoga County 2017).

[36]Black's Law Dictionary (6th ed.) p 1139 defines "permanent abode" as a home "which the party may leave as his interest or whim may dictate, but which he has no present intention of abandoning."

[37]See State v. Williams, 79 Ohio St. 3d 459, 1997-Ohio-79, 683 N.E.2d 1126 (1997); State v. Boldin, 2008-Ohio-6408, 2008 WL 5147450 (Ohio Ct. App. 11th Dist. Geauga County 2008); State v. Clay, 181 Ohio App. 3d 563, 2009-Ohio-1235, 910 N.E.2d 14 (8th Dist. Cuyahoga County 2009); Youngstown v. Dixon, 2009-Ohio-1013, 2009 WL 581637 (Ohio Ct. App. 7th Dist. Mahoning County 2009); State v. Barnes,

Q & A: The victim of a charge of domestic violence alleges that the parties were married by "common law" in 1993, after that concept had been abolished in Ohio. Does the fact that the parties were mistaken in their belief that they were "married" prevent them from being "family or household members" for purposes of the statute?

Not necessarily. Even though "common law" marriage was abolished in Ohio in 1991,[38] if the prosecution is able to establish that the couple has "otherwise cohabited" under the terms of the statute, regardless of what they believed their marital status to be, they will still be covered by RC 2919.25.[39]

2008-Ohio-5997, 2008 WL 4949833 (Ohio Ct. App. 8th Dist. Cuyahoga County 2008); State v. Pash, 2010-Ohio-1267, 2010 WL 1175616 (Ohio Ct. App. 3d Dist. Mercer County 2010); State v. Messenger, 2010-Ohio-479, 2010 WL 530087 (Ohio Ct. App. 3d Dist. Marion County 2010); State v. Jones, 2010-Ohio-351, 2010 WL 364469 (Ohio Ct. App. 9th Dist. Summit County 2010); State v. Freeman, 2010-Ohio-220, 2010 WL 302787 (Ohio Ct. App. 9th Dist. Summit County 2010); State v. Clay, 181 Ohio App. 3d 563, 2009-Ohio-1235, 910 N.E.2d 14 (8th Dist. Cuyahoga County 2009); State v. Moore, 2010-Ohio-509, 2010 WL 547707 (Ohio Ct. App. 8th Dist. Cuyahoga County 2010); State v. Bell, 2009-Ohio-6302, 2009 WL 4406068 (Ohio Ct. App. 8th Dist. Cuyahoga County 2009); State v. McQueen, 2009-Ohio-6272, 2009 WL 4308654 (Ohio Ct. App. 10th Dist. Franklin County 2009); State v. Barnes, 2009-Ohio-4874, 2009 WL 2963761 (Ohio Ct. App. 8th Dist. Cuyahoga County 2009); State v. Sudderth, 2009-Ohio-3363, 2009 WL 1941345 (Ohio Ct. App. 9th Dist. Summit County 2009); State v. Mauldin, 2010-Ohio-4192, 2010 WL 3482689 (Ohio Ct. App. 7th Dist. Mahoning County 2010); State v. Maple, 2011-Ohio-1516, 2011 WL 1138387 (Ohio Ct. App. 9th Dist. Summit County 2011); State v. Long, 2011-Ohio-1050, 2011 WL 806839 (Ohio Ct. App. 9th Dist. Summit County 2011); State v. Edwards, 2010-Ohio-6496, 2010 WL 5551002 (Ohio Ct. App. 9th Dist. Summit County 2010); State v. Travlus, 2010-Ohio-4046, 2010 WL 3366195 (Ohio Ct. App. 2d Dist. Montgomery County 2010); State v. Perkins, 2010-Ohio-2968, 2010 WL 2573770 (Ohio Ct. App. 12th Dist. Fayette County 2010); State v. Ward, 2010-Ohio-4614, 2010 WL 3782643 (Ohio Ct. App. 10th Dist. Franklin County 2010); State v. Gomez, 2011-Ohio-5475, 2011 WL 5067230 (Ohio Ct. App. 9th Dist. Summit County 2011); State v. Walburg, 2011-Ohio-4762, 2011 WL 4362748 (Ohio Ct. App. 10th Dist. Franklin County 2011); State v. Simmons, 2011-Ohio-6074, 2011 WL 5869794 (Ohio Ct. App. 8th Dist. Cuyahoga County 2011); State v. Smith, 2011-Ohio-4409, 2011 WL 3860572 (Ohio Ct. App. 8th Dist. Cuyahoga County 2011); State v. Hazel, 2012-Ohio-835, 2012 WL 690312 (Ohio Ct. App. 2d Dist. Clark County 2012); State v. Short, 2011-Ohio-5744, 2011 WL 5353078 (Ohio Ct. App. 12th Dist. Butler County 2011); Bickham v. Bickham, 2011-Ohio-4213, 2011 WL 3672097 (Ohio Ct. App. 5th Dist. Fairfield County 2011); State v. Corbin, 194 Ohio App. 3d 720, 2011-Ohio-3491, 957 N.E.2d 849 (6th Dist. Wood County 2011); State v. Hawkins, 2012-Ohio-4622, 2012 WL 4762031 (Ohio Ct. App. 2d Dist. Montgomery County 2012); State v. Fernandez, 2012-Ohio-2538, 2012 WL 2061589 (Ohio Ct. App. 2d Dist. Montgomery County 2012); State v. Slevin, 2012-Ohio-2043, 2012 WL 1647115 (Ohio Ct. App. 9th Dist. Summit County 2012); State v. Rubes, 2012-Ohio-4100, 975 N.E.2d 1054 (Ohio Ct. App. 11th Dist. Portage County 2012); State v. Perander, 2015-Ohio-1752, 2015 WL 2169235 (Ohio Ct. App. 2d Dist. Montgomery County 2015); State v. McGlothan, 138 Ohio St. 3d 146, 146, 2014-Ohio-85, 4 N.E.3d 1021, 1022 (2014) (reversing judgment of the court of appeals and reinstating the conviction of domestic violence); Foster v. Foster, 2017-Ohio-4311, ¶ 26, 92 N.E.3d 333, 339–40 (Ohio Ct. App. 10th Dist. Franklin County 2017); State v. Riedel, 2017-Ohio-8865, ¶ 83, 100 N.E.3d 1155 (Ohio Ct. App. 8th Dist. Cuyahoga County 2017).

[38]RC 3105.12(B)(1), as amended by 1991 H.B. 32, eff. 10-10-91, abolished "common law" marriage entered into in Ohio after that date.

[39]State v. Pertee, 1995 WL 688800 (Ohio Ct. App. 9th Dist. Wayne County 1995).

Q & A: Can same-sex couples qualify as "family and household members" under RC 2919.25?

Nothing in the statute specifically restricts its application based on the sexual preferences of the parties.[40] Therefore, if the couple otherwise qualifies, the protections afforded to a heterosexual relationship are equally available to a couple who is engaged in a same-sex relationship.

Coverage is provided under the section of the law that defines "family or household members" to include "persons living as spouses." Although incapable of either ceremonial or common law marriage, these couples are persons who are "otherwise cohabiting," as that term has been interpreted by the case law. In *State v. Hadinger*,[41] a case of first impression, the Tenth District Court of Appeals held that "the legislature intended that the domestic violence statute provide protection to persons who are cohabiting regardless of their sex. We believe that to read the domestic violence statute otherwise would eviscerate the efforts of the legislature to safeguard, regardless of gender, the rights of victims of domestic violence."

Q & A: What is the effect of the length of time that a couple has lived together on the establishment of a "family or household member" relationship for purposes of the statute?

The length of time that the parties have lived together is not as important as the degree of commitment that they have made to one another, for purposes of establishing the necessary relationship under the statute. At least one court has held that as little as one month is sufficient to establish the existence of the necessary components of a relationship.[42] The court held that the evidence was sufficient to establish that the complainant was a "person living as a spouse" of the defendant where it was shown that the couple had lived together for approximately one month, had gone places together, had been intimate on more than one occasion, shared closet space in their joint residence, and that the complainant cooked for the defendant and did the defendant's laundry.[43]

Q & A: If the parties have an on-going sexual relationship,

---

[40]State v. Linner, 77 Ohio Misc. 2d 22, 665 N.E.2d 1180 (Mun. Ct. 1996); State v. Yaden, 118 Ohio App. 3d 410, 692 N.E.2d 1097, 71 A.L.R.5th 749 (1st Dist. Hamilton County 1997); State v. Hadinger, 61 Ohio App. 3d 820, 573 N.E.2d 1191 (10th Dist. Franklin County 1991); State v. Rodgers, 131 Ohio Misc. 2d 1, 2005-Ohio-1730, 827 N.E.2d 872 (C.P. 2005); City of Cleveland v. Knipp, 2005 WL 1017620 (Ohio Mun. Ct. 2005); State v. Goshorn, 2006-Ohio-2755, ¶ 6-22, 2006 WL 1495256 (Ohio Ct. App. 4th Dist. Ross County 2006).

[41]State v. Hadinger, 61 Ohio App. 3d 820, 823, 573 N.E.2d 1191 (10th Dist. Franklin County 1991); State v. Rodgers, 131 Ohio Misc. 2d 1, 2005-Ohio-1730, 827 N.E.2d 872 (C.P. 2005); State v. Jenson, 2006-Ohio-5169, ¶ 30, 2006 WL 2796284 (Ohio Ct. App. 11th Dist. Lake County 2006), judgment aff'd, 114 Ohio St. 3d 430, 2007-Ohio-4552, 872 N.E.2d 1212 (2007); In re Ohio Domestic-Violence Statute Cases, 114 Ohio St. 3d 430, 2007-Ohio-4552, ¶ 30, 872 N.E.2d 1212 (2007); State v. Hampton, 2006-Ohio-5995, ¶ 16, 2006 WL 3290799 (Ohio Ct. App. 5th Dist. Stark County 2006).

[42]City of Cleveland v. Crawford, 1989 WL 113070 (Ohio Ct. App. 8th Dist. Cuyahoga County 1989).

[43]See also State v. Wagner, 1993 WL 303255 (Ohio Ct. App. 9th Dist. Medina County 1993) where the court found that the defendant and the complainant had cohabited in compliance with the statute after a period of joint residency that lasted only two weeks.

which has existed for some time, but have never lived together, are they still covered by the statute?

It depends. If the parties have never lived together, they may not qualify as family or household members, regardless of their sexual relationship. There is an exception to this rule, however. If the parties have a child in common, regardless of whether they have ever lived together, they are covered by the statute.[44]

Q & A: Does a child who lives with a natural parent and only periodically visits its non-custodial other parent and that parent's children by another union, qualify as a family or household member of those other children?

One court says no. The Fourth District Court of Appeals reasoned that where no evidence is presented to prove that the defendant and the victim ever resided together as that term is defined,[45] they could not be deemed to qualify as family and household members under the definition found in RC 2919.25.[46]

Q & A: The defendant is charged with domestic violence for threatening to kill his teenaged daughter. The defense makes a Motion for a Directed Verdict of Acquittal based upon the fact that the child was illegitimate and the defendant never lived with either the child or the mother. How should the court rule?

The legitimacy or illegitimacy of the defendant's child is irrelevant to a determination of whether or not the charge of domestic violence in this case should stand. However, whether the defendant and his daughter ever lived together is a crucial finding. The domestic violence statute defines "family or household member" to include a child of the offender, only if the child "is residing or has resided with the offender."[47] Notwithstanding a father-daughter relationship, a daughter must have resided with her father for the father to be convicted of domestic violence against her.[48]

The same residency requirement is required of certain other relationships described in the domestic violence statute.[49] The motion should be granted.

Q & A: The defendant is on trial before a jury on a charge of domestic violence. The defendant and the alleged victim live together, but are not married. Is the trial court required to give a specific instruction on "cohabitation"?

---

[44] RC 2919.25(F)(1)(b).

[45] Citing Black's Law Dictionary (5th ed.) p 1176.

[46] State v. Toles, 1999 WL 1232092 (Ohio Ct. App. 4th Dist. Gallia County 1999); State v. Gibson, 2005-Ohio-1495, 2005 WL 730059 (Ohio Ct. App. 8th Dist. Cuyahoga County 2005); State v. Sims, 169 Ohio App. 3d 579, 2006-Ohio-6285, 863 N.E.2d 1110 (1st Dist. Hamilton County 2006); E. Cleveland v. Perkins, 2009-Ohio-2131, 2009 WL 1244154 (Ohio Ct. App. 8th Dist. Cuyahoga County 2009); State v. Turner, 2016-Ohio-813, 2016 WL 860301 (Ohio Ct. App. 8th Dist. Cuyahoga County 2016).

[47] RC 2919.25(F)(1)(a)(ii).

[48] State v. Sims, 169 Ohio App. 3d 579, 2006-Ohio-6285, 863 N.E.2d 1110 (1st Dist. Hamilton County 2006); State v. Wynn, 2017-Ohio-8045, ¶ 14, 2017 WL 4417756 (Ohio Ct. App. 1st Dist. Hamilton County 2017).

[49] RC 2919.25(F)(1)(a).

The general rule requires the trial court to instruct the jury on all the elements that the prosecution must prove.[50] There are two essential elements of domestic violence: (1) appellant knowingly "caused or attempted to cause physical harm to the victim" and (2) "the victim was a family or household member." Cohabitation is not an essential element of domestic violence. Therefore, cohabiting is just one way in which the victim can be qualified as a "person living as a spouse." The trial court may instruct the jury on domestic violence, including the definitions of family or household member and person living as a spouse by reading the language of the statute. A specific instruction on cohabitation is not required.[51]

Q & A: My client is facing domestic violence charges brought against him by his daughter. He raised her from birth. She lived with him her entire life, but a recent paternity test established that another man was her natural father. Can he still be convicted of domestic violence?

No. The domestic-violence statute is specifically designed to protect two people who are more than merely roommates, enabling such a victim of assault additional protection. Domestic violence is a crime quite different from a general assault, precisely because of the special intimacy of the parties. The Revised Code requires that sections defining offenses or penalties shall be strictly construed against the state, and liberally construed in favor of the accused.[52] In strictly construing the domestic violence statute, we find that the statute does not provide that a person who was once thought to be a blood relative remains a family or household member after such blood relationship is determined to have been mistaken.[53]

Q & A: Are pregnant victims who have not cohabitated with and who do not already have other children with their alleged abusers considered "family or household members" under Ohio's domestic violence laws? Should the prosecutor bring these charges as assaults rather than domestic violence?

Most of the wide range of individuals that Ohio's domestic violence law protects must currently reside or must have formerly resided with the alleged offender.[54] The sole exception made is for an alleged victim

[50]State v. Adams, 62 Ohio St. 2d 151, 153, 16 Ohio Op. 3d 169, 404 N.E.2d 144, 16 A.L.R.4th 344 (1980); State v. Frazier, 2011-Ohio-3189, 2011 WL 2572157 (Ohio Ct. App. 9th Dist. Summit County 2011); State v. Chapman, 2011-Ohio-2695, 2011 WL 2174963 (Ohio Ct. App. 6th Dist. Sandusky County 2011); State v. Walburg, 2011-Ohio-4762, 2011 WL 4362748 (Ohio Ct. App. 10th Dist. Franklin County 2011); State v. Meinke, 2017-Ohio-7787, ¶ 15, 97 N.E.3d 1184, 1188–89 (Ohio Ct. App. 9th Dist. Lorain County 2017).

[51]State v. Wallace, 2006-Ohio-5819, 2006 WL 3183386 (Ohio Ct. App. 9th Dist. Lorain County 2006); State v. Long, 2011-Ohio-1050, 2011 WL 806839 (Ohio Ct. App. 9th Dist. Summit County 2011); State v. Walburg, 2011-Ohio-4762, 2011 WL 4362748 (Ohio Ct. App. 10th Dist. Franklin County 2011).

[52]R.C. 2901.04(A); State v. Jordan, 89 Ohio St. 3d 488, 492, 2000-Ohio-225, 733 N.E.2d 601 (2000); State v. Blackmon, 2012-Ohio-5854, ¶ 30, 2012 WL 6139910 (Ohio Ct. App. 5th Dist. Stark County 2012).

[53]R.C. 2919.25; State v. Blackmon, 2012-Ohio-5854, 2012 WL 6139910 (Ohio Ct. App. 5th Dist. Stark County 2012).

[54]R.C. 2919.25(F)(1)(a).

and a natural child or children parented with an alleged abuser.[55] In Ohio, if the fetus of the alleged victim and the alleged abuser is still in vitro, the couple are NOT "family or household members" as defined by the domestic violence law and the protections extended under the exception will not pertain, unless the couple has at least one other natural child in common; is cohabiting; or has cohabitated.[56]

In answer to your second question, the prosecutor should bring these charges as assaults. If cohabitation cannot be established between the alleged victim and the alleged abuser, and if they are not the natural parents of any other children, the mere fact that they are expecting an unborn, in and of itself, will not qualify them as "family or household members," subject to the current provisions of the domestic violence laws.[57]

Q & A: Doesn't the prosecution have to prove something more than the fact that the offender and the alleged victim lived together in the same residence for a significant period of time to establish that they have cohabited?

Not in Ohio. The Ohio Supreme Court holds that where the state demonstrates that the defendant and the alleged victim are or were involved in a romantic relationship and that they lived together for a significant period of time, the state has no obligation to demonstrate the sharing of familial or financial responsibilities and consortium to prove cohabitation.[58]

§ 2:6 Domestic violence under municipal ordinances in Ohio

Under Ohio law, so-called "home rule" communities have been empowered to exercise their police power locally, so long as their enactments do not conflict with laws promulgated by the state.[1]

As a result, a number of municipalities in Ohio have passed their own domestic violence laws. In Cuyahoga County, alone, over forty communities have exercised this right in enacting their own domestic violence laws. In most instances, these laws basically restate provi-

[55]R.C. 2919.25(F)(1)(b).

[56]R.C. 2919.25(F)(1)(b); R.C. 2919.25(F)(1)(a)(i); R.C. 2919.25(F)(2). See also Text § 10:7 and Text § 10:8.

[57]See Text § 10:7 and Text § 10:8.

[58]State v. McGlothan, 138 Ohio St. 3d 146, 2014-Ohio-85, 4 N.E.3d 1021 (2014); State v. Martin, 2016-Ohio-225, 57 N.E.3d 411 (Ohio Ct. App. 5th Dist. Tuscarawas County 2016); State v. Cornwell, 2015-Ohio-4617, 48 N.E.3d 169 (Ohio Ct. App. 9th Dist. Wayne County 2015), State v. Hughes, 2015-Ohio-1173, 2015 WL 1403276 (Ohio Ct. App. 5th Dist. Tuscarawas County 2015); State v. Matthews, 2015-Ohio-3297, 2015 WL 4880984 (Ohio Ct. App. 6th Dist. Ottawa County 2015); State v. Brown, 2015-Ohio-950, 2015 WL 1138651 (Ohio Ct. App. 11th Dist. Lake County 2015); State v. McGlothan, 138 Ohio St. 3d 146, 149, 2014-Ohio-85, 4 N.E.3d 1021, 1024 (2014) (reversing the judgment of the court of appeals and reaffirming the defendant's conviction of domestic violence finding that evidence was sufficient to support conclusion that victim was a "person living as a spouse" who resided with defendant at time he assaulted her).

[Section 2:6]

[1]O. Const. Art. XVIII § 3 reads,

"Powers. . . Municipalities shall have authority to exercise all powers of local self-government and to adopt and enforce within their limits such local police, sanitary and other similar regulations, as are not in conflict with general laws."

sions of the statute. Charging the offense under municipal ordinance allows the municipality to retain any revenue that might be derived from the fines imposed on those convicted of violation. A typical ordinance is the one enacted by Westlake, Ohio. It reads:

537.14 DOMESTIC VIOLENCE

(a) No person shall knowingly cause or attempt to cause physical harm to a family or household member.

(b) No person shall recklessly cause serious physical harm to a family or household member.

(c) No person, by threat of force shall knowingly cause a family or household member to believe that the offender will cause imminent physical harm to the family or household member.

(d) As used in this section: (1) "Family or household member" means any of the following, who is residing or has resided with the offender:

A. A spouse, a person living as a spouse or a former spouse of the offender;

B. A parent or a child of the offender, or of another person related by consanguinity to the offender;

C. A parent, or a child of a spouse, person living as a spouse, or former spouse of the offender; or another person related by consanguinity or affinity to a spouse, person living as a spouse or former spouse of the offender.

2. "Person living as spouse" means a person who is living or who has lived with the offender in a common law marital relationship with the offender, who is otherwise cohabiting with the offender, or who has otherwise cohabited with the offender within one year prior to the date of the alleged commission of the act in question, or who is the natural parent of the offender's child.

(e) Whoever violates this section is guilty of domestic violence.

(1) A violation of subsection (a) or (b) hereof is a misdemeanor of the first degree, if the offender has not previously been convicted of domestic violence, or a violation of Ohio RC 2903.11, 2903.12, 2903.13, 2903.211 or 2911.211 or Sections 537.03, 537.051 or 541.051 of the General Offense Code involving a person who was a family or household member at the time of such violation.

(2) A violation of subsection (c) hereof is a misdemeanor of the fourth degree. If the offender has been previously convicted of a violation of Ohio RC 2903.11, 2903.12, 2903.13, 2903.211 or 2911.211 or sections 537.03, 537.051 or 541.051 of this General Offense Code involving a person who was a family or household member at the time of such violation, a violation of subsection (c) hereof is a misdemeanor of the third degree.

(ORC 2919.25)

§ 2:7 Felony violations

In Ohio, proof of a prior conviction of any one of the several criminal violations listed in the statute,[1] i.e., domestic violence,[2] felonious assault,[3] aggravated assault,[4] simple assault,[5] negligent assault,[6] ag-

[Section 2:7]

[1]RC 2919.25(D).

[2]RC 2919.25.

[3]RC 2903.11.

gravated menacing,[7] menacing by stalking,[8] menacing,[9] aggravated trespass,[10] endangering children,[11] is most often required before domestic violence is charged as a felony. The domestic violence statutes call for enhancement of a new charge where the original conviction was obtained under a substantially similar domestic violence ordinance enacted pursuant to the home rule provisions of Ohio's Constitution.[12] The domestic violence statute also includes felony enhancement for a new charge where a previous domestic violence conviction was obtained in a foreign jurisdiction.[13] Because a prior criminal conviction is generally necessary to enhance a domestic violence charge from a misdemeanor to a felony, when required, an offender's prior conviction is an essential element of most felony charges of domestic violence that must be alleged and proven.[14]

The exceptions to this requirement are charges containing pregnancy specifications recently added to the domestic violence statute by Ohio's General Assembly during its 2008-2009 Session. These specifications were added in an attempt to provide additional protections for pregnant women and the fetuses that they carry.[15] Under the newly enacted penalty provisions, trial courts are required to impose mandatory sentences on offenders convicted of committing felony domestic violence, where it is proven that the offender caused or attempted to cause physical harm to a woman that the offender knew was pregnant at the time of the offense or to her fetus.[16] Under the law, the mandatory periods of incarceration called for range from six months, for intentionally or recklessly causing or attempting to cause physical harm to a pregnant woman or her fetus, up to one year, if the assault caused serious physical harm to the pregnant woman's fetus or caused the termination of the pregnant woman's pregnancy.[17] Interestingly, there is no mandatory period of incarceration provided in the specification if the offender inflicts serious physical harm on the pregnant woman.

If an offender, ***previously convicted of one of the enumerated offenses contained in the domestic violence statute***, faces a new charge of intentional or reckless domestic violence, the new violation

[4]RC 2903.12; State v. Johnson, 2007-Ohio-2225, 2007 WL 1365919 (Ohio Ct. App. 8th Dist. Cuyahoga County 2007), judgment rev'd on other grounds, 120 Ohio St. 3d 320, 2008-Ohio-6247, 898 N.E.2d 959 (2008).

[5]RC 2903.13.

[6]RC 2903.14.

[7]RC 2903.21.

[8]RC 2903.211.

[9]RC 2903.22.

[10]RC 2911.211.

[11]RC 2919.22.

[12]O. Const. Art. XVIII § 3.

[13]2003 S.B. 50; RC 2919.25(D)(3).

[14]See RC 2945.75; State v. Flora, 1995 WL 32716 (Ohio Ct. App. 8th Dist. Cuyahoga County 1995); 1997 H.B. 238, eff. 11-5-97; 2003 S.B. 50, eff. 1-8-04.

[15]Am. Sub. H.B. 280, eff. Apr. 7, 2009.

[16]RC 2919.25(D)(3) to (D)(6).

[17]RC 2919.25(D)(3) to (D)(6).

may be charged as a fourth degree felony.[18] If the offender was ***previously convicted of two or more of the enumerated offenses***, the new violation may be brought as a felony of the third degree.[19]

The penalties provided in the statute for domestic violence threats, upon initial conviction, are usually those of a fourth degree misdemeanor.[20] However, if the offender was ***previously convicted of one of the enhancing offenses found in the domestic violence statute***, the penalties on conviction are those of a second degree misdemeanor.[21] If the offender has ***previously been convicted of more than one of the enhancing offenses found in the domestic violence statute***, the penalties upon conviction are those of a first degree misdemeanor.[22] Even a first offender's penalties are enhanced, if the offender knew that the victim was pregnant at the time of the offense. If ***a first offender knew that the victim was pregnant***, the pregnancy specification enhances the penalty for a domestic violence threat to a misdemeanor of the third degree.[23]

If the offender knew that the victim was pregnant at the time that current incident took place, the penalties faced if previously convicted of one or more of the enhancing offenses enumerated in the domestic violence statute are more severe.[24] If an offender previously-convicted of ***one*** of the enhancing offenses enumerated in the statute knew that the victim was pregnant at the time of the offense, conviction of the new charge brings mandatory incarceration of not less than six months, although the sentencing court is free to impose a greater term of incarceration within the range set forth for fourth degree felonies.[25] If an offender previously convicted of ***two or more*** of the enhancing offenses enumerated in the statute knew that the victim was pregnant at the time of the offense, conviction of the new charge brings mandatory incarceration of not less than twelve months, although, again, the sentencing court, in its discretion, is free to impose a greater term of incarceration within the range set forth for third degree felonies.[26]

If a ***first-time*** offender knew that the victim of the pending offense was pregnant at the time of the incident, domestic violence may be charged as a felony of the fifth degree, rather than a misdemeanor of the first degree.[27] This is true, even if the offender was never previously convicted of one of the enhancing offenses enumerated in the domestic violence statute, upon conviction, the law requires that the

[18]RC 2919.25(D)(3); RC 2929.14.

[19]RC 2919.25(D)(4); RC 2929.14.

[20]RC 2919.25(C); RC 2929.24(A)(4).

[21]RC 2919.25(D)(3); RC 2929.24(A)(4).

[22]RC 2919.25(D)(4); RC 2929.24(A)(1).

[23]RC 2919.25(D)(5); RC 2929.24(A)(3).

[24]RC 2919.25(D)(3) to (D)(5).

[25]RC 2919.25(D)(3); RC 2929.14(A)(4).

[26]RC 2919.25(D)(3); RC 2929.14(A)(3).

[27]RC 2919.25(D)(5); RC 2929.24(A)(1).

court impose a mandatory period of incarceration of not less than six months on the offender.[28]

If the first-time offender, in committing the violation, caused serious physical harm to the "pregnant woman's unborn"[29] **or** caused the "termination of the pregnant woman's pregnancy,"[30] upon conviction, the law requires that the court impose a mandatory period of incarceration of not less than twelve months on the offender.[31] For first time offenders these additional sanctions represent a sharp change and departure from prior policy. Until these amendments were enacted, one could not be charged with felony domestic violence without a prior criminal conviction.

The addition of pregnancy specifications to the domestic violence law raises procedural due process questions, to wit: (1) Does the addition of the pregnancy specification fundamentally change the nature of the offense charged, when the defendant has never been convicted of another enhancing offense, or (2) Is the pregnancy specification just a sentencing factor, to be considered along with others by the court?

The U.S. Supreme Court holds that, "[o]ther than the fact of a prior conviction, any fact that increases the penalty for a crime beyond the prescribed statutory maximum must be submitted to a jury, and proved beyond a reasonable doubt. With that exception, we endorse the statement of the rule set forth in the concurring opinions in [Jones v. U.S., 526 U.S. 227 (1999)]: '[I]t is unconstitutional for a legislature to remove from the jury the assessment of facts that increase the prescribed range of penalties to which a criminal defendant is exposed. It is equally clear that such facts must be established by proof beyond a reasonable doubt.' "[32]

It is also clear that if a specification only enhances the penalty and not the degree of the offense, the prosecution is not required to allege the specification in the indictment nor prove it as a matter of law.[33] However, when a specification is a degree-enhancing element versus a sentence-enhancing element, the state is required to prove its existence beyond a reasonable doubt.[34]

The addition of the pregnancy specification to that portion of the do-

---

[28]RC 2919.25(D)(5).

[29]RC 2919.25(F)(3).

[30]RC 2919.25(F)(4).

[31]RC 2919.25(D)(5).

[32]Apprendi v. New Jersey, 530 U.S. 466, 490, 120 S. Ct. 2348, 147 L. Ed. 2d 435 (2000), citing Jones v. U.S., 526 U.S. 227, 119 S. Ct. 1215, 143 L. Ed. 2d 311 (1999).

[33]State v. Allen, 29 Ohio St. 3d 53, 55, 506 N.E.2d 199 (1987); State v. Baer, 2009-Ohio-3248, 2009 WL 1914394 (Ohio Ct. App. 7th Dist. Harrison County 2009); State v. Wagers, 2010-Ohio-2311, 2010 WL 2026779 (Ohio Ct. App. 12th Dist. Preble County 2010); State v. McCallum, 2009-Ohio-1424, 2009 WL 805805 (Ohio Ct. App. 9th Dist. Medina County 2009); State v. Miller, 2012-Ohio-997, 2012 WL 764907 (Ohio Ct. App. 12th Dist. Warren County 2012); State v. Bankston, 2011-Ohio-6486, 2011 WL 6351929 (Ohio Ct. App. 2d Dist. Montgomery County 2011); In re R.B., III, 2011-Ohio-5042, 2011 WL 4536969 (Ohio Ct. App. 6th Dist. Huron County 2011); State v. Bibler, 2014-Ohio-3375, 17 N.E.3d 1154 (Ohio Ct. App. 3d Dist. Marion County 2014); State v. Abernathy, 2015-Ohio-1363, 2015 WL 1530810 (Ohio Ct. App. 5th Dist. Stark County 2015).

[34]State v. Allen, 29 Ohio St. 3d 53, 54, 506 N.E.2d 199 (1987). See State v. Stevenson, 1996 WL 596452 (Ohio Ct. App. 8th Dist. Cuyahoga County 1996); State v.

mestic violence law that deals with first time offenders is a degree-enhancer. When applied, it moves what would otherwise be a first degree misdemeanor to a fifth degree felony. As such, the specification must appear in the charging document and must be proven to the trier of fact beyond a reasonable doubt before an offender may be found guilty of the charge.[35]

Thus, the pregnancy specification amendments, as originally drafted, were inserted into Ohio's domestic violence law for the sole purpose of enhancing the penalties when an act of domestic violence was committed against a family or household member that the offender knew was pregnant at the time of the act.[36] As enacted, however, the original pregnancy specifications contained drafting errors. The errors made reference to a non-existent division of the statute and, thereby, masked the clear intent of the drafters to connect the pregnancy specifications to the enhanced penalty section of the domestic violence law.[37] The adoption of new language corrected the errors and removed any confusion that those errors might have caused.[38]

In any case where the degree of the offense charged is elevated by a prior conviction, the conviction of the prior charge becomes an element of the new offense. As such, it must be set forth in the charging document and must be proven beyond a reasonable doubt, along with

---

Henderson, 58 Ohio St. 2d 171, 173, 12 Ohio Op. 3d 177, 389 N.E.2d 494 (1979), partially quoting State v. Gordon, 28 Ohio St. 2d 45, 57 Ohio Op. 2d 180, 276 N.E.2d 243 (1971); see also State v. Fittro, 66 Ohio St. 3d 16, 1993-Ohio-172, 607 N.E.2d 447 (1993); State v. Ireson, 72 Ohio App. 3d 235, 594 N.E.2d 165 (4th Dist. Ross County 1991); State v. Swiger, 34 Ohio App. 3d 371, 518 N.E.2d 972 (3d Dist. Shelby County 1987); State v. Baer, 2009-Ohio-3248, 2009 WL 1914394 (Ohio Ct. App. 7th Dist. Harrison County 2009); State v. Wagers, 2010-Ohio-2311, 2010 WL 2026779 (Ohio Ct. App. 12th Dist. Preble County 2010); State v. McCallum, 2009-Ohio-1424, 2009 WL 805805 (Ohio Ct. App. 9th Dist. Medina County 2009); State v. Nadock, 2010-Ohio-1161, 2010 WL 1058356 (Ohio Ct. App. 11th Dist. Lake County 2010); State v. Miller, 2012-Ohio-997, 2012 WL 764907 (Ohio Ct. App. 12th Dist. Warren County 2012); State v. Bankston, 2011-Ohio-6486, 2011 WL 6351929 (Ohio Ct. App. 2d Dist. Montgomery County 2011); In re R.B., III, 2011-Ohio-5042, 2011 WL 4536969 (Ohio Ct. App. 6th Dist. Huron County 2011); State v. Quinn, 2016-Ohio-139, 57 N.E.3d 379 (Ohio Ct. App. 2d Dist. Clark County 2016), appeal not allowed, 145 Ohio St. 3d 1447, 2016-Ohio-1596, 48 N.E.3d 585 (2016) and appeal reopened, 2017-Ohio-7000, 95 N.E.3d 664 (Ohio Ct. App. 2d Dist. Clark County 2017), appeal not allowed, 151Ohio St. 3d1457, 2017-Ohio-8842, 87 N.E.3d 224 (2017).

[35]State v. Allen, 29 Ohio St. 3d 53, 54, 506 N.E.2d 199 (1987). See State v. Stevenson, 1996 WL 596452 (Ohio Ct. App. 8th Dist. Cuyahoga County 1996); State v. Henderson, 58 Ohio St. 2d 171, 173, 12 Ohio Op. 3d 177, 389 N.E.2d 494 (1979); State v. Fittro, 66 Ohio St. 3d 16, 1993-Ohio-172, 607 N.E.2d 447 (1993); State v. Ireson, 72 Ohio App. 3d 235, 594 N.E.2d 165 (4th Dist. Ross County 1991); State v. Swiger, 34 Ohio App. 3d 371, 518 N.E.2d 972 (3d Dist. Shelby County 1987); State v. Clay, 181 Ohio App. 3d 563, 2009-Ohio-1235, 910 N.E.2d 14 (8th Dist. Cuyahoga County 2009); State v. Miller, 2012-Ohio-997, 2012 WL 764907 (Ohio Ct. App. 12th Dist. Warren County 2012); State v. Bankston, 2011-Ohio-6486, 2011 WL 6351929 (Ohio Ct. App. 2d Dist. Montgomery County 2011); In re R.B., III, 2011-Ohio-5042, 2011 WL 4536969 (Ohio Ct. App. 6th Dist. Huron County 2011); State v. Abernathy, 2015-Ohio-1363, 2015 WL 1530810 (Ohio Ct. App. 5th Dist. Stark County 2015).

[36]See 2008 HB 280, eff. 4-7-09.

[37]See 2008 HB 280, eff. 4-7-09.

[38]See 2010 SB 58, eff. 9-17-10.

all of the other elements of the felony offense charged.[39] To that end, the prosecution is entitled to present evidence of the defendant's prior convictions for domestic violence at a jury trial on a new charge of domestic violence, even in light of the defendant's desire to stipulate to the existence of the former convictions.[40] Verdict forms that reflect enhancement must also include reference to the prior conviction to be effective.[41]

A defendant currently charged in an enhanced domestic violence complaint offense due to a prior conviction may collaterally attack the prior conviction within the proceedings of the current offense only if the collateral attack concerns a violation of the defendant's right to counsel.[42]

Additionally, in the prosecution of an enhanced charge of domestic violence, a court may not establish the element of prior conviction by taking judicial notice of a defendant's prior criminal history.[43]

The fact that a defendant was not represented by counsel at the time of a prior conviction will not prevent the use of the prior conviction to enhance a current charge, unless actual imprisonment was imposed as a result of the prior conviction, and the record indicates that the defendant was indigent or financially unable to obtain counsel

---

[39] Crim. R. 3, Crim. R. 7; RC 2941.11 (This is a current statute, but its validity was called into question in State v. Jenkins, 2003-Ohio-1058, 2003 WL 894807 (Ohio Ct. App. 4th Dist. Lawrence County 2003).), RC 2945.75(B), RC 2941.143; see also State v. Allen, 29 Ohio St. 3d 53, 506 N.E.2d 199 (1987); State v. Fittro, 66 Ohio St. 3d 16, 1993-Ohio-172, 607 N.E.2d 447 (1993); State v. Baer, 2009-Ohio-3248, 2009 WL 1914394 (Ohio Ct. App. 7th Dist. Harrison County 2009); State v. Wagers, 2010-Ohio-2311, 2010 WL 2026779 (Ohio Ct. App. 12th Dist. Preble County 2010); State v. McCallum, 2009-Ohio-1424, 2009 WL 805805 (Ohio Ct. App. 9th Dist. Medina County 2009); State v. Nadock, 2010-Ohio-1161, 2010 WL 1058356 (Ohio Ct. App. 11th Dist. Lake County 2010); State v. Miller, 2012-Ohio-997, 2012 WL 764907 (Ohio Ct. App. 12th Dist. Warren County 2012); State v. Bankston, 2011-Ohio-6486, 2011 WL 6351929 (Ohio Ct. App. 2d Dist. Montgomery County 2011); In re R.B., III, 2011-Ohio-5042, 2011 WL 4536969 (Ohio Ct. App. 6th Dist. Huron County 2011); State v. Abernathy, 2015-Ohio-1363, 2015 WL 1530810 (Ohio Ct. App. 5th Dist. Stark County 2015).

[40] State v. Arnold, 2002 WL 93423 (Ohio Ct. App. 8th Dist. Cuyahoga County 2002); State v. Ganelli, 2005-Ohio-770, 2005 WL 433439 (Ohio Ct. App. 8th Dist. Cuyahoga County 2005); State v. Clark, 2010-Ohio-1746, 2010 WL 1610493 (Ohio Ct. App. 8th Dist. Cuyahoga County 2010); State v. Nadock, 2010-Ohio-1161, 2010 WL 1058356 (Ohio Ct. App. 11th Dist. Lake County 2010); State v. Ward, 2010-Ohio-4614, 2010 WL 3782643 (Ohio Ct. App. 10th Dist. Franklin County 2010); State v. Bibler, 2014-Ohio-3375, 17 N.E.3d 1154 (Ohio Ct. App. 3d Dist. Marion County 2014); State v. Abernathy, 2015-Ohio-1363, 2015 WL 1530810 (Ohio Ct. App. 5th Dist. Stark County 2015).

[41] State v. Bost, 2000 WL 1742104 (Ohio Ct. App. 10th Dist. Franklin County 2000).

[42] State v. O'Neill, 140 Ohio App. 3d 48, 2000-Ohio-2656, 746 N.E.2d 654 (7th Dist. Jefferson County 2000), citing Custis v. U.S., 511 U.S. 485, 487, 114 S. Ct. 1732, 128 L. Ed. 2d 517 (1994); State v. Nadock, 2010-Ohio-1161, 2010 WL 1058356 (Ohio Ct. App. 11th Dist. Lake County 2010); State v. Phillips, 2010-Ohio-1941, 2010 WL 1757943 (Ohio Ct. App. 12th Dist. Butler County 2010); State v. Kauffer, 2011-Ohio-676, 2011 WL 531725 (Ohio Ct. App. 10th Dist. Franklin County 2011).

[43] State v. Langford, 2003-Ohio-159, 2003 WL 125069, *5 (Ohio Ct. App. 8th Dist. Cuyahoga County 2003); see also State v. Wesley, 2002-Ohio-4429, 2002 WL 1986545, *6 (Ohio Ct. App. 8th Dist. Cuyahoga County 2002); State v. Clay, 181 Ohio App. 3d 563, 2009-Ohio-1235, 910 N.E.2d 14 (8th Dist. Cuyahoga County 2009).

at the time of the prior conviction.[44] It is the defendant's burden to challenge an apparently constitutional prior conviction with prima facie evidence that he or she was not afforded the right to counsel.[45] Once the defendant raises the issue with prima facie evidence, the state has the burden of proving the constitutional validity of the prior conviction. A silent record will not satisfy the state's burden of proof.[46]

If the state shows that the defendant knowingly, voluntarily and intelligently waived his right to counsel, the defendant's conviction will not be deemed an uncounseled conviction.[47]

The new violation of RC 2919.25(A) or RC 2919.25(B) may also be charged as a felony if the accused has been previously convicted of a violation of domestic violence under the threat provisions of RC 2919.25(C).[48] As with the enhancement provisions that accompany prior convictions under RC 2919.25(A) or RC 2919.25(B), enhance-

[44] State v. Gerwin, 69 Ohio St. 2d 488, 491, 23 Ohio Op. 3d 420, 432 N.E.2d 828 (1982), citing Scott v. Illinois, 440 U.S. 367, 99 S. Ct. 1158, 59 L. Ed. 2d 383 (1979), and Baldasar v. Illinois, 446 U.S. 222, 100 S. Ct. 1585, 64 L. Ed. 2d 169 (1980) (overruled by, Nichols v. U.S., 511 U.S. 738, 114 S. Ct. 1921, 128 L. Ed. 2d 745 (1994)) (overruling court finding uncounseled misdemeanor conviction, valid due to absence of imposition of prison term, is also valid when used to enhance punishment at subsequent conviction); State v. Colon, 2008-Ohio-4940, 2008 WL 4377446 (Ohio Ct. App. 9th Dist. Lorain County 2008); State v. Volpe, 2008-Ohio-1678, 2008 WL 928342 (Ohio Ct. App. 10th Dist. Franklin County 2008); State v. Thompson, 121 Ohio St. 3d 250, 2009-Ohio-314, 903 N.E.2d 618 (2009); State v. Nadock, 2010-Ohio-1161, 2010 WL 1058356 (Ohio Ct. App. 11th Dist. Lake County 2010); State v. Tanner, 2009-Ohio-3867, 2009 WL 2382970 (Ohio Ct. App. 9th Dist. Summit County 2009).

[45] Robards v. Rees, 789 F.2d 379, 385–86 (6th Cir. 1986); State v. Wang, 1984 WL 13997 (Ohio Ct. App. 1st Dist. Hamilton County 1984); State v. Roundtree, 1983 WL 5484, *14–16 (Ohio Ct. App. 8th Dist. Cuyahoga County 1983); State v. Brandon, 45 Ohio St. 3d 85, 86, 543 N.E.2d 501, 503 (1989). See also State v. Adams, 37 Ohio St. 3d 295, 297, 525 N.E.2d 1361, 1363 (1988); State v. Vales, 2000 WL 217802 (Ohio Ct. App. 8th Dist. Cuyahoga County 2000); State v. Brooke, 113 Ohio St. 3d 199, 2007-Ohio-1533, 863 N.E.2d 1024 (2007); State v. Maynez, 2008-Ohio-3054, 2008 WL 2485367 (Ohio Ct. App. 3d Dist. Defiance County 2008); State v. Clay, 181 Ohio App. 3d 563, 2009-Ohio-1235, 910 N.E.2d 14 (8th Dist. Cuyahoga County 2009); State v. Smith, 2008-Ohio-5985, 2008 WL 4951646 (Ohio Ct. App. 8th Dist. Cuyahoga County 2008); State v. Starett, 2009-Ohio-744, 2009 WL 405908 (Ohio Ct. App. 4th Dist. Athens County 2009); State v. Hupp, 2009-Ohio-1441, 2009 WL 806901 (Ohio Ct. App. 11th Dist. Lake County 2009); State v. Esner, 2008-Ohio-6654, 2008 WL 5259725 (Ohio Ct. App. 8th Dist. Cuyahoga County 2008); State v. Sartain, 2008-Ohio-2124, 2008 WL 1933447 (Ohio Ct. App. 11th Dist. Lake County 2008); State v. Nadock, 2010-Ohio-1161, 2010 WL 1058356 (Ohio Ct. App. 11th Dist. Lake County 2010); State v. Mariano, 2009-Ohio-5426, 2009 WL 3255304 (Ohio Ct. App. 11th Dist. Lake County 2009); State v. Tanner, 2009-Ohio-3867, 2009 WL 2382970 (Ohio Ct. App. 9th Dist. Summit County 2009); State v. Martin, 2010-Ohio-244, 2010 WL 320475 (Ohio Ct. App. 8th Dist. Cuyahoga County 2010); McCullough v. Warden, Allen Corr. Inst., 2011 WL 488710 (N.D. Ohio 2011), report and recommendation adopted, 2011 WL 486221 (N.D. Ohio 2011); State v. Caskey, 2010-Ohio-4697, 2010 WL 3794000 (Ohio Ct. App. 11th Dist. Lake County 2010); State v. Kauffer, 2011-Ohio-676, 2011 WL 531725 (Ohio Ct. App. 10th Dist. Franklin County 2011); State v. Bibler, 2014-Ohio-3375, 17 N.E.3d 1154 (Ohio Ct. App. 3d Dist. Marion County 2014).

[46] State v. Maynard, 38 Ohio App. 3d 50, 52–53, 526 N.E.2d 316 (8th Dist. Cuyahoga County 1987); State v. Mariano, 2009-Ohio-5426, 2009 WL 3255304 (Ohio Ct. App. 11th Dist. Lake County 2009).

[47] State v. Carrion, 84 Ohio App. 3d 27, 31, 616 N.E.2d 261, 264 (9th Dist. Lorain County 1992); State v. Hupp, 2009-Ohio-1441, 2009 WL 806901 (Ohio Ct. App. 11th Dist. Lake County 2009).

[48] State v. Canitia, 1993 WL 215389 (Ohio Ct. App. 8th Dist. Cuyahoga County

ment is also available if a previous charge was brought under RC 2925.19(C), a substantially similar municipal ordinance or the domestic violence laws of a foreign jurisdiction, where the offender is now subsequently accused of either purposeful or reckless assault, under RC 2919.25(A) or RC 2919.25(B). The reverse, however, is not true. If the offender was previously convicted of either purposeful or reckless assault under RC 2919.25(A) or RC 2919.25(B), then RC 2919.25(D) specifically provides that the penalty upon conviction of a new violation of RC 2919.25(C) can only enhance from a fourth degree misdemeanor to a second degree misdemeanor.[49]

If a second threats charge under RC 2919.25(C) results in a conviction, and the offender is charged on yet a third occasion under the threat section of RC 2919.25(C), RC 2919.25(D) provides that the third charge may enhance to carry the penalties of a first degree misdemeanor.[50]

As with the more serious offenses, the allegation that there has been a prior conviction for a violation of the threats section of RC 2919.25 also has to be contained in the charging document and proven beyond a reasonable doubt at trial to result in a felony conviction for a subsequent offense.

Q & A: If a defendant is arrested, charged and convicted of a misdemeanor domestic violence offense, can he later be charged with felony domestic violence arising out of the same facts, if the prosecution finds out about a prior domestic violence conviction in the defendant's criminal history?

Generally, the answer is no. The Fifth Amendment to the U.S. Constitution bars successive prosecutions for the same criminal act, unless each offense requires proof of an element that the other does not.[51]

In *State v. Tolbert*, the Supreme Court of Ohio held that a no contest plea, once filed and accepted under the court's discretion, constitutes the attachment of jeopardy.[52] A defendant is placed in jeopardy, therefore, at the time the trial court exercises its discretion to accept a no contest plea.[53] An exception to Tolbert, however, can occur where the state is unable to proceed on the more serious charge at the outset

1993).

[49] 2003 S.B. 50; RC 2919.25(D)(3).

[50] 2003 S.B. 50; RC 2919.25(D)(3).

[51] State v. Goodman, 2002-Ohio-818, 2002 WL 274639 (Ohio Ct. App. 9th Dist. Medina County 2002), citing Blockburger v. U.S., 284 U.S. 299, 304, 52 S. Ct. 180, 76 L. Ed. 306, 309 (1932); State v. Kimble, 123 Ohio Misc. 2d 67, 2003-Ohio-2779, 789 N.E.2d 1195 (C.P. 2003); McKitrick v. Smith, 2009 WL 1067321 (N.D. Ohio 2009); State v. Toth, 2017-Ohio-5481, ¶ 7–8, 2017 WL 2766248 (Ohio Ct. App. 9th Dist. Medina County 2017); State /City of Toledo v. Lear, 2018-Ohio-1874, ¶ 13, 2018 WL 2174378 (Ohio Ct. App. 6th Dist. Lucas County 2018); Saxton v. Warden, Trumbull Correctional Institution, 2018 WL 1014920, *7 (S.D. Ohio 2018), report and recommendation adopted, 2018 WL 1472528 (S.D. Ohio 2018).

[52] State v. Tolbert, 60 Ohio St. 3d 89, 90, 573 N.E.2d 617 (1991); State v. Kimble, 123 Ohio Misc. 2d 67, 2003-Ohio-2779, 789 N.E.2d 1195 (C.P. 2003); State v. Fairbanks, 117 Ohio St. 3d 543, 2008-Ohio-1470, 885 N.E.2d 888 (2008).

[53] State ex rel. Sawyer v. O'Connor, 54 Ohio St. 2d 380, 382, 8 Ohio Op. 3d 393, 377 N.E.2d 494 (1978); State v. Goodman, 2002-Ohio-818, 2002 WL 274639 (Ohio Ct. App. 9th Dist. Medina County 2002); State v. Kimble, 123 Ohio Misc. 2d 67,

because additional facts necessary to sustain that charge have not yet occurred or have not yet been discovered, despite due diligence. Whether jeopardy attaches, then, is dependent on the circumstances existing at the time of the first trial or dispositive plea.[54]

Thus, for example, an individual charged with, and convicted of, felonious assault may subsequently be prosecuted for murder if the victim expires after the felonious assault conviction is entered, since an additional fact, to wit: the death of the victim, was not in existence at the time of the first trial or plea. However, where the prosecution fails to determine that a defendant was previously convicted of a misdemeanor domestic violence offense until after a plea to a subsequent domestic violence misdemeanor is accepted by the court, even though information about the prior conviction was readily available at the time that the current plea was accepted, the prosecution is not privileged to pursue the defendant on the greater charge.[55]

Diagram of Domestic Violence Penalties

Conviction	Penalty
RC 2919.25(A)	M1
RC 2919.25(B)	M1
RC 2919.25(C)	M4

Diagram of Domestic Violence Penalties—Enhanced by One Prior Conviction

Original Conviction of	New Conviction of	New Penalty
RC 2919.25(A)	RC 2919.25(A)/(B)	F4
RC 2919.25(B)	RC 2919.25(A)/(B)	F4
RC 2919.25(C)	RC 2919.25(A)/(B)	F4
RC 2903.14	RC 2919.25(A)/(B)	F4
RC 2903.211	RC 2919.25(A)/(B)	F4
RC 2911.211	RC 2919.25(A)/(B)	F4
Muni. DV Ord.	RC 2919.25(A)/(B)	F4
Foreign DV Law	RC 2919.25(A)/(B)	F4
RC 2919.25(A)/(B)/(C)	RC 2919.25(C)	M2
RC 2903.14	RC 2919.25(C)	M2
RC 2911.211	RC 2919.25(C)	M2

2003-Ohio-2779, 789 N.E.2d 1195 (C.P. 2003).

[54]Diaz v. U.S., 223 U.S. 442, 449, 32 S. Ct. 250, 56 L. Ed. 500 (1912); State v. Cameron, 2004-Ohio-974, 2004 WL 396283 (Ohio Ct. App. 5th Dist. Tuscarawas County 2004); State v. Sturgell, 2009-Ohio-5628, 2009 WL 3403984 (Ohio Ct. App. 2d Dist. Darke County 2009).

[55]Diaz v. U.S., 223 U.S. 442, 449, 32 S. Ct. 250, 56 L. Ed. 500 (1912); State v. Cameron, 2004-Ohio-974, 2004 WL 396283 (Ohio Ct. App. 5th Dist. Tuscarawas County 2004).

Original Conviction of	New Conviction of	New Penalty
Mun. DV Ord.	RC 2919.25(C)	M2
Foreign DV Law	RC 2919.25(C)	M2
Any offense of violence defined in RC 2901.01(I)(1) to (4)[56]	RC 2919.25(A)/(B)	F4

Definitions—Offense of Violence

A violation of an existing or former municipal ordinance or law of the State of Ohio or any other state of the United States, substantially equivalent to any section listed in division (I)(1) of RC 2901.01(I) is also considered an offense of violence.[57]

An offense, other than a traffic offense, under an existing or former municipal ordinance or law of the State of Ohio or any other state of the United States, committed purposely or knowingly, and involving physical harm to persons or a risk of serious physical harm to persons likewise qualifies as an offense of violence.[58]

A conspiracy or attempt to commit, or complicity in committing, any offense under division RC 2901.01(I)(1), (2), or (3) is also defined as an offense of violence.[59]

◆ **NOTE:** The following thirty-three sections of the Ohio Revised Code are all designated Offenses of Violence: RC 2903.01 (Aggravated Murder), 2903.02 (Murder), 2903.03 (Voluntary Manslaughter), 2903.04 (Involuntary Manslaughter), 2903.11 (Felonious Assault), 2903.12 (Aggravated. Assault), 2903.13 (Assault), 2903.21 (Aggravated Menacing), 2903.22 (Menacing), 2905.01 (Kidnapping), 2905.02 (Abduction), 2905.11 (Extortion), 2907.02 (Rape), 2907.03 (Sexual Battery), 2907.12 (Felonious Sexual Penetration), 2909.02 (Aggravated Arson), 2909.03 (Arson), 2909.04 (Disrupting Public Services), 2909.05 (Vandalism), 2911.01 (Aggravated Robbery), 2911.02 (Robbery), 2911.11 (Aggravated Burglary), 2911.12 (Burglary), 2917.01 (Inciting to Violence), 2917.02 (Aggravated Riot), 2917.03 (Riot), 2917.31 (Inducing Panic), 2919.25 (Domestic Violence), 2921.03 (Intimidation), 2921.34 (Escape), 2921.35 (Aiding Escape or Resistance to Authority), 2923.12 (Carrying a Concealed Weapon), and 2923.13 (Having a Weapon While Under Disability).

Diagram of Domestic Violence Penalties Enhanced by Two or More Prior Convictions

Original Conviction of	New Conviction of	New Penalty
RC 2919.25(A)	RC 2919.25(A)/(B)	F3

[56] RC 2901.01(I).

[57] RC 2901.01(2).

[58] RC 2901.01(3).

[59] RC 2901.01(4).

Original Conviction of	New Conviction of	New Penalty
RC 2919.25(B)	RC 2919.25(A)/(B)	F3
RC 2919.25(C)	RC 2919.25(A)/(B)	F3
RC 2903.14[60]	RC 2919.25(A)/(B)	F3
RC 2911.211[61]	RC 2919.25(A)/(B)	F3
Muni. DV Ord.	RC 2919.25(A)/(B)	F3
Foreign DV Law	RC 2919.25(A)/(B)	F3
Any offense of violence defined in RC 2901.01(I)(1) to (4)[62]	RC 2919.25(A)/(B)	F3
RC 2919.25(A)	RC 2919.25(C)	M1
RC 2919.25(B)	RC 2919.25(C)	M1
RC 2919.25(C)	RC 2919.25(C)	M1
RC 2903.14[63]	RC 2919.25(C)	M1
RC 2911.211[64]	RC 2919.25(C)	M1
Mun. DV Ord.	RC 2919.25(C)	M1
Foreign DV Law	RC 2919.25(C)	M1

Diagram of Penalty Enhancement Provisions Where There is a Pregnancy Specification

If the underlying violation is a **fifth degree** felony
and
the offender, in committing the violation, caused serious physical harm to the "pregnant woman's unborn,"[65]
or
caused the "termination of the pregnant woman's pregnancy,"[66]
then the court **must** impose a **mandatory** prison term of 12 months.

****

If the underlying violation is a **fourth degree** felony
and

[60]Negligent assault.

[61]Aggravated trespass.

[62]Aggravated trespass.

[63]Negligent assault.

[64]Aggravated trespass.

[65]RC 2919.25(F)(3).

[66]RC 2919.25(F)(4).

the offender, in committing the violation, caused serious physical harm to the "pregnant woman's unborn,"[67]

or

caused the "termination of the pregnant woman's pregnancy,"[68] then the court **must** impose a **mandatory** prison term of **at least 12 months**.

****

If the underlying violation is a **third degree** felony, except as otherwise provided the court **must** impose a **mandatory prison term** of **either a definite term of six months**

or

one of the prison terms prescribed in the Felony Sentencing Law for third degree felonies,

****

If the violation is a **third degree** felony

and

the offender, in committing the violation, caused serious physical harm to the pregnant woman's unborn[69] or caused the termination of the pregnant woman's pregnancy,[70] the court **must impose a mandatory prison term of either a definite term of one year**

or

one of the prison terms prescribed in the Felony Sentencing Law for third degree felonies.

The prosecution is not limited to the domestic violence laws when pursuing an offender. Regardless of whether the relationship involved is covered under RC 2919.25, if the violence results in "serious physical harm," other felony offenses that carry greater penalties, such as aggravated and felonious assault, as well as attempted and accomplished homicides of all classifications, are also available and are often charged.

Q & A: If a couple is married, but separated, and one spouse breaks into the current home of the other and commits an assault, can the offender be charged with burglary?

This issue was raised in the Fourth Appellate District in 1993. In *State v. Middleton*,[71] the defendant broke into his estranged wife's residence and assaulted her. He was subsequently charged with both domestic violence and burglary. The defendant filed a motion with the court to dismiss the burglary charge, arguing that, since the victim was his wife, RC 3103.04 prevented a finding that he had trespassed in her home. RC 3103.04 reads in pertinent part, "Neither husband nor wife has any interest in the property of the other . . . . Neither can be excluded from the other's dwelling, except upon a decree or order of injunction made by a court of competent jurisdiction."

---

[67] RC 2919.25(F)(3).

[68] RC 2919.25(F)(4).

[69] RC 2919.25(D)(6)(e).

[70] RC 2919.25(D)(6)(e).

[71] State v. Middleton, 85 Ohio App. 3d 403, 619 N.E.2d 1113 (4th Dist. Vinton County 1993); Machuca v. Bunting, 2018 WL 3012273, *2 (N.D. Ohio 2018).

The trial court disagreed. It reasoned that RC 3103.04 was a civil, rather than a criminal, statute and, therefore, had no application to the burglary charge against the defendant. The trial court further explained that the offense of burglary included more than a mere trespass and that, as a result, the provisions of RC 3103.04 were unavailable to the defendant for means of defense on the criminal charge. The defendant was convicted of the burglary.

In reversing that part of the trial court's decision, the appellate court said, "We note R.C. 3103.04 unequivocally states that neither spouse can 'be excluded from the other's dwelling' except upon court order. The statute does not limit itself to civil matters. We may not 'restrict, constrict, qualify, narrow, enlarge, or abridge' the clear meaning of a statute to suit the particular facts of a case at bar. Wachendorf v. Shaver, 149 Ohio St. 231, 36 Ohio Op. 554, 78 N.E.2d 370 (1948), paragraph five of the syllabus."[72]

Most recently, however, the Ohio Supreme Court negated the result reached in *Middleton*. In *State v. Lilly*,[73] the Supreme Court agreed with the reasoning of the trial court in *Middleton*. It, therefore, held that the statute addressing the privileges of a husband and wife with respect to the property of the other is, in fact, civil in nature and was not meant to be enforced criminally. It does not, as a result, affect criminal liabilities. The *Lilly* syllabus goes on to say that a spouse may be held criminally liable for trespass and/or burglary in the dwelling of the other spouse who is exercising custody or control over that dwelling.[74] It goes without saying that what is true for a spouse is equally true for a partner who lacks the legal standing of a spouse.[75]

[72]State v. Middleton, 85 Ohio App. 3d 403, 408, 619 N.E.2d 1113 (4th Dist. Vinton County 1993). See also State v. Herder, 65 Ohio App. 2d 70, 19 Ohio Op. 3d 47, 415 N.E.2d 1000 (10th Dist. Franklin County 1979) (overruling recognized by, State v. Shinn, 2000 WL 781106 (Ohio Ct. App. 4th Dist. Washington County 2000)). See also State v. Cabrales, 118 Ohio St. 3d 54, 2008-Ohio-1625, 886 N.E.2d 181 (2008); State v. Boldin, 2008-Ohio-6408, 2008 WL 5147450 (Ohio Ct. App. 11th Dist. Geauga County 2008); State v. Janson, 183 Ohio App. 3d 377, 2009-Ohio-3256, 917 N.E.2d 296 (1st Dist. Hamilton County 2009); O'Neal v. Bagley, 2010 WL 6423295 (S.D. Ohio 2010), report and recommendation adopted, 2011 WL 1288111 (S.D. Ohio 2011), aff'd, 728 F.3d 552 (6th Cir. 2013), amended and superseded, 743 F.3d 1010 (6th Cir. 2013) and aff'd, 743 F.3d 1010 (6th Cir. 2013); State v. Canada, 2015-Ohio-2167, 2015 WL 3540402 (Ohio Ct. App. 10th Dist. Franklin County 2015); Machuca v. Bunting, 2018 WL 3012273, *2 (N.D. Ohio 2018).

[73]State v. Lilly, 87 Ohio St. 3d 97, 1999-Ohio-251, 717 N.E.2d 322 (1999). See also O'Neal v. Bagley, 2011 WL 1288111 (S.D. Ohio 2011), aff'd, 728 F.3d 552 (6th Cir. 2013), amended and superseded, 743 F.3d 1010 (6th Cir. 2013) and aff'd, 743 F.3d 1010 (6th Cir. 2013); State v. Helm, 2016-Ohio-500, 56 N.E.3d 436 (Ohio Ct. App. 1st Dist. Hamilton County 2016), appeal not allowed, 146 Ohio St. 3d 1415, 2016-Ohio-3390, 51 N.E.3d 659 (2016), Al-Lamadani v. Lang, 624 Fed. Appx. 405, 410 (6th Cir. 2015); Machuca v. Bunting, 2018 WL 3012273, *2 (N.D. Ohio 2018).

In any event, Ohio law is clear that one spouse can be prosecuted for burglary committed in the residence of the other spouse. State v. Lilly, 87 Ohio St. 3d 97, 100, 1999-Ohio-251, 717 N.E.2d 322 (1999) (**"[A] spouse may be criminally liable for trespass and/or burglary in the dwelling of the other spouse who is exercising custody or control over that dwelling."**).

[74]See also Text § 8:4, Statutory elements of domestic violence under RC 3113.31(A)(1)(b); State v. Shinn, 2000 WL 781106 (Ohio Ct. App. 4th Dist. Washington County 2000); State v. O'Neal, 1997 WL 770162 (Ohio Ct. App. 1st Dist. Hamilton County 1997), judgment aff'd, 87 Ohio St. 3d 402, 2000-Ohio-449, 721 N.E.2d 73

Q & A: Aren't the charges of felonious assault and second-offense domestic violence really the same offense, or at least allied offenses of similar import?

It depends. Each of the two offenses contains at least one element that is distinct from the other. Therefore, they are not the same. At least one Ohio appellate court has held that they are not allied offenses of similar import.[76] Where the defendant's conduct constitutes two or more offenses of dissimilar import, or where his conduct results in two or more offenses of the same or similar kind committed separately or with a separate animus as to each, the indictment or information may contain counts for all such offenses, and the defendant may be convicted of all of them.[77]

However, where the same conduct by defendant can be construed to constitute two or more allied offenses of similar import, the indictment or information may contain counts for all such offenses, but the defendant may be convicted of only one.[78]

Therefore, if the facts in a particular case support charges brought for both domestic violence and felonious assault, but the trial court's analysis finds that the prosecution relies on the same conduct for each offense, the charges are allied offenses of similar import and they must be merged for sentencing.

Q & A: Can a court grant a defendant's request for a finding outside of the presence of a jury concerning an elevating prior conviction to avoid having evidence of the prior offense presented to the jury?

No. The prior conviction is an essential element of a felony charge of domestic violence. The defendant does not have the right to bifurcate that element from the others, having the jury decide the existence of some of the elements of the offense and the court the remainder.[79]

Q & A: If the court cannot grant a defendant's request for a

(2000).

[75]State v. Mason, 2001 WL 1771047 (Ohio Ct. App. 5th Dist. Stark County 2001).

[76]State v. Chitwood, 83 Ohio App. 3d 443, 615 N.E.2d 257 (1st Dist. Hamilton County 1992). See also State v. Sanchez, 2010-Ohio-6153, 2010 WL 5235932 (Ohio Ct. App. 8th Dist. Cuyahoga County 2010); State v. Simmons, 2011-Ohio-6074, 2011 WL 5869794 (Ohio Ct. App. 8th Dist. Cuyahoga County 2011). But see State v. Damron, 129 Ohio St. 3d 86, 89, 2011-Ohio-2268, 950 N.E.2d 512, 515 (2011).

[77]2941.25 (B).

[78]2941.25 (A).

[79]State v. Day, 99 Ohio App. 3d 514, 651 N.E.2d 52 (12th Dist. Clermont County 1994); State v. Lynch, 1999 WL 11244 (Ohio Ct. App. 9th Dist. Lorain County 1999); State v. Flasck, 2001 WL 20823 (Ohio Ct. App. 11th Dist. Trumbull County 2000); State v. Maynez, 2008-Ohio-3054, 2008 WL 2485367 (Ohio Ct. App. 3d Dist. Defiance County 2008); State v. Nadock, 2010-Ohio-1161, 2010 WL 1058356 (Ohio Ct. App. 11th Dist. Lake County 2010); State v. Jones, 2012-Ohio-1480, 2012 WL 1107745 (Ohio Ct. App. 12th Dist. Warren County 2012); State v. Abernathy, 2015-Ohio-1363, 2015 WL 1530810 (Ohio Ct. App. 5th Dist. Stark County 2015); State v. Bibler, 2014-Ohio-3375, 17 N.E.3d 1154 (Ohio Ct. App. 3d Dist. Marion County 2014); Jones v. Warden, Noble Correctional Inst., 2014 WL 6673615 (S.D. Ohio 2014), report and recommendation adopted, 2015 WL 248031 (S.D. Ohio 2015); State v. Leasure, 2015-Ohio-5327, 43 N.E.3d 477 (Ohio Ct. App. 4th Dist. Ross County 2015); Howell v. Miller, 2017 WL 9478420, *11 (N.D. Ohio 2017), report and recommendation adopted, 2017 WL 3698617 (N.D. Ohio 2017).

finding relative to a prior conviction, can the defendant require the prosecution to accept a stipulation to the prior offense?

No. Because the prior offense is an essential element of the new crime charged, Ohio courts have held that the prosecution is not required to accept a defendant's stipulation to a prior conviction.[80]

Q & A: The municipal court in our jurisdiction has a reputation for being extremely tough on domestic violence offenders. My client was convicted of domestic violence in the municipal court before and has now been arrested again for domestic violence. The prosecutor has decided not to bring the new charge as a felony because he believes the municipal judge will deliver a much tougher sentence than the common pleas judge if there is a conviction. Doesn't the law require this second allegation to be charged as a felony?

No. The prosecution has the discretion to charge subsequent allegations of domestic violence as misdemeanor violations and its decisions in this regard are generally not subject to review.[81]

Q & A: At the conclusion of the State's case the defendant moves the court for a directed verdict of acquittal on the charge of felonious domestic violence. The defense urges that, because the defendant's prior conviction was uncounseled, constitutionally it cannot form the predicate to enhance a subsequent prosecution to a felony. Is this argument sound?

Possibly. One of the elements that the prosecution is required to prove against an individual charged with felony domestic violence is the preexistence of a prior conviction of one of the offenses that bring about the penalty enhancement. If a defendant does not stipulate to a prior domestic violence conviction, the prosecution must present evidence of the existence of the prior conviction through a certified copy of the judgment entry and testimony that identifies the defendant as the individual who was convicted of the previous offense.

The Supreme Court held that consistent with the 6th and 14th Amendment, a sentencing court may consider a defendant's previous uncounseled misdemeanor conviction in sentencing him for a subsequent offense so long as the previous uncounseled misdemeanor conviction did not result in a sentence of imprisonment.[82] However, when a defendant raises a constitutional question concerning a prior conviction, he must lodge an objection to the use of the conviction and he must present sufficient evidence to establish a prima facie showing of the constitutional infirmity.[83]

Q & A: My client is on trial for felony domestic violence. I

---

[80]State v. Russell, 1998 WL 778312 (Ohio Ct. App. 12th Dist. Butler County 1998); see also Heard v. Hudson, 2008 WL 5188274 (N.D. Ohio 2008); State v. Abernathy, 2015-Ohio-1363, 2015 WL 1530810 (Ohio Ct. App. 5th Dist. Stark County 2015).

[81]City of Maple Heights v. Spearman, 1998 WL 355850 (Ohio Ct. App. 8th Dist. Cuyahoga County 1998).

[82]Nichols v. U.S., 511 U.S. 738, 114 S. Ct. 1921, 128 L. Ed. 2d 745 (1994).

[83]State v. Adams, 37 Ohio St. 3d 295, 525 N.E.2d 1361 (1988). See also State v. Brandon, 45 Ohio St. 3d 85, 543 N.E.2d 501 (1989); State v. Kelly, 154 Ohio App. 3d 285, 2003-Ohio-4783, 797 N.E.2d 104 (9th Dist. Medina County 2003); State v. Brooke,

believe the prosecutor has failed to prove the municipal ordinance that my client was previously convicted of violating is "substantially similar to domestic violence," as required by RC 2919.25(D), and that as a result my client should not be facing felony charges. What do I have to argue to prevail in my Crim. R. 29 Motion for Directed Verdict of Acquittal?

The criteria that the prosecution is required to prove to establish that the prior conviction met the statutory predicate for enhancement is straightforward: Did the prior conviction involve an event where the defendant was charged with causing or attempting to cause physical harm to a family or household member? The combination of a certified copy of the judgment entry of the prior conviction for the offense which included such elements and the testimony of a witness able to identify your client as the person who suffered that conviction will get the prosecution past your motion. If, however, the prosecution fails to present evidence on either part of this issue, your argument to the court concerning that fact should prevail.[84]

Q & A: The defendant was charged with domestic violence as a third degree felony, due to two prior convictions. In the present case the state alleged that the defendant put his hands around the victim's neck in an attempt to strangle her. Upon a finding of guilty, the court sentenced him to 3 years of incarceration. The defendant wants to appeal the severity of

---

113 Ohio St. 3d 199, 2007-Ohio-1533, 863 N.E.2d 1024 (2007); State v. Colon, 2008-Ohio-4940, 2008 WL 4377446 (Ohio Ct. App. 9th Dist. Lorain County 2008); State v. Mayor, 2008-Ohio-7011, 2008 WL 5451377 (Ohio Ct. App. 7th Dist. Mahoning County 2008); State v. Volpe, 2008-Ohio-1678, 2008 WL 928342 (Ohio Ct. App. 10th Dist. Franklin County 2008); State v. Baker, 2009-Ohio-111, 2009 WL 81279 (Ohio Ct. App. 9th Dist. Summit County 2009); State v. Nadock, 2010-Ohio-1161, 2010 WL 1058356 (Ohio Ct. App. 11th Dist. Lake County 2010); State v. Tanner, 2009-Ohio-3867, 2009 WL 2382970 (Ohio Ct. App. 9th Dist. Summit County 2009); State v. James, 2009-Ohio-4392, 2009 WL 2625838 (Ohio Ct. App. 7th Dist. Columbiana County 2009); McCullough v. Warden, Allen Corr. Inst., 2011 WL 488710 (N.D. Ohio 2011), report and recommendation adopted, 2011 WL 486221 (N.D. Ohio 2011); State v. Lewis, 2011-Ohio-911, 2011 WL 705147 (Ohio Ct. App. 4th Dist. Lawrence County 2011); State v. Lewis, 2010-Ohio-4288, 2010 WL 3528923 (Ohio Ct. App. 11th Dist. Lake County 2010); State v. Waheed, 2016-Ohio-2951, 2016 WL 2841926 (Ohio Ct. App. 1st Dist. Hamilton County 2016); State v. Troyer, 2016-Ohio-3090, 2016 WL 2944812 (Ohio Ct. App. 5th Dist. Holmes County 2016); State v. Wood, 2018-Ohio-875, ¶ 33, 2018 WL 1225738 (Ohio Ct. App. 2d Dist. Clark County 2018), appeal not allowed, 153 Ohio St. 3d 1403, 2018-Ohio-2380, 100 N.E.3d 422 (2018) (*Wood's* case is factually distinguishable from State v. Troyer, 2016-Ohio-3090, 2016 WL 2944812 (Ohio Ct. App. 5th Dist. Holmes County 2016), a case on which he relies. In *Troyer*, the trial and appellate courts had before them extensive evidence about the defendant's prior pleas to domestic violence, including transcripts of his arraignments and plea hearings and his signed waivers of counsel. The trial court rejected Troyer's argument that his prior convictions could not be used to enhance the charge and sentence in the current case because the pleas were uncounseled. But, after reviewing all of the evidence, the appellate court concluded that the plea colloquy in one of the prior cases **"was insufficient to establish the constitutionality of appellant's uncounseled plea"** for purposes of the enhancement of the charge then before it; it remanded for resentencing. Because Wood did not present any evidence about the circumstances under which he entered his prior pleas to OVI offenses, *Troyer* does not support Wood's argument that his prior convictions likewise should not have been relied upon to enhance his offense and sentence.).

[84]State v. Mullins, 1999 WL 668812 (Ohio Ct. App. 5th Dist. Richland County 1999).

the sentence on the basis that it is contrary to law, because his conduct was not more serious than conduct normally constituting the offense. Should the appeal prevail?

The trial court is not limited to the sentencing factors specifically stated in the Revised Code.[85] It can consider any other factor that is necessary to achieve the overriding purposes and principles of felony sentencing.[86] Therefore, the trial court not only can consider factors that suggest that a victim suffered harm,[87] but also factors that establish that a defendant previously served prison time for similar conduct,[88] or abused substances, or showed no remorse for the harm the conduct caused,[89] in the determining the length of the current prison term. The appeal should fail.

Q & A: The defendant moves the court to set aside his domestic violence conviction arguing that although he was cohabitating with the victim and although they were previously married, they were not married at the time of the incident. Therefore, he argues, to find him guilty of domestic violence elevates the status of his relationship with the victim to one of marriage, which is constitutionally not permitted. Should the motion be granted?

No. A former spouse who resides with an offender is in one of three separate, potentially non-parental, status categories that are included in the domestic violence law's definition of "family or household member."[90] Accordingly, "former spouse" is a victim-status category separate and distinct from "person living as a spouse."

Status as a *former* spouse does not intend to approximate marriage when it specifically defines a relationship that existed in the past, but does not exist anymore. Unmarried cohabitants, regardless of their former status as husband and wife, are still covered by the provisions of the domestic violence law.[91]

The relationship of "former spouse" does not intend to approximate a present marriage. To hold otherwise would be to ignore the meaning of the word "former."[92]

Q & A: Although a written waiver appears in the court file of

---

[85]RC 2929.12(A).

[86]State v. Fletcher, 2005-Ohio-5929, 2005 WL 2981646 (Ohio Ct. App. 7th Dist. Belmont County 2005).

[87]RC 2929.12(B)(2).

[88]RC 2929.13.

[89]RC 2929.14.

[90]RC 2919.25(F).

[91]O. Const. Art. XV, § 11. (This provision of the Ohio Constitution was rendered unconstitutional by the U.S. Supreme Court's decision in Obergefell v. Hodges, 135 S. Ct. 2584, 192 L. Ed. 2d 609, 99 Empl. Prac. Dec. (CCH) P 45341, 2015-1 U.S. Tax Cas. (CCH) P 50357, 115 A.F.T.R.2d 2015-2309 (2015)). See also, State v. Heffley, 2007-Ohio-904, 2007 WL 638453 (Ohio Ct. App. 3d Dist. Allen County 2007); State v. Carswell, 114 Ohio St. 3d 210, 2007-Ohio-3723, 871 N.E.2d 547 (2007). But see the dissents in State v. Carswell, 114 Ohio St. 3d 210, 2007-Ohio-3723, 871 N.E.2d 547 (2007), and State v. Clay, 181 Ohio App. 3d 563, 2009-Ohio-1235, 910 N.E.2d 14 (8th Dist. Cuyahoga County 2009); State v. Gipson, 2016-Ohio-994, 2016 WL 962400 (Ohio Ct. App. 3d Dist. Allen County 2016).

[92]State v. Heffley, 2007-Ohio-904, 2007 WL 638453 (Ohio Ct. App. 3d Dist. Allen

a prior conviction, the defendant maintains that he does not recall executing a waiver of his right to counsel at the time that he entered the prior plea of guilty to a charge of domestic violence. If the record is otherwise silent on the issue, can the penalty for the new charge still be enhanced to a felony?

There is a limited right to collaterally attack a conviction when the state attempts to use the past conviction to enhance the penalty of a later criminal offense. A conviction obtained against a defendant who was without counsel, or its corollary, an uncounseled conviction obtained without a valid waiver of the right to counsel, is recognized as constitutionally infirm.[93]

For purposes of penalty enhancement in later convictions, when the defendant presents a prima facie showing that prior convictions were unconstitutional because they were uncounseled and resulted in confinement, the burden shifts to the state to prove that the right to counsel was properly "waived."[94]

In the present example, the defendant's failure of memory does not rise to the level of a prima facie showing that the prior plea was uncounseled and, therefore, he can still face the new charge as a felony.[95]

Q & A: My daughter tells me that my wife went to Domestic Relations Court and got an order putting me out of the house. She says that if I come home, my wife will have me arrested and charged with trespass or burglary. Can she do that?

Answer: It depends. Ordinarily, if one party fears intrusion and physical danger, a civil protection order may be sought. Such an order serves as a preemptive measure to deter domestic violence by

---

County 2007).

[93]State v. Brandon, 45 Ohio St. 3d 85, 86, 543 N.E.2d 501 (1989); Nichols v. U.S., 511 U.S. 738, 114 S. Ct. 1921, 128 L. Ed. 2d 745 (1994); State v. Neely, 2007-Ohio-6243, 2007 WL 4148461, ¶ 12 (Ohio Ct. App. 11th Dist. Lake County 2007); State v. Nadock, 2010-Ohio-1161, 2010 WL 1058356 (Ohio Ct. App. 11th Dist. Lake County 2010); State v. Hupp, 2009-Ohio-1441, 2009 WL 806901 (Ohio Ct. App. 11th Dist. Lake County 2009); State v. Albert, 2010-Ohio-110, 2010 WL 169480 (Ohio Ct. App. 2d Dist. Montgomery County 2010); State v. Lewis, 2011-Ohio-911, 2011 WL 705147 (Ohio Ct. App. 4th Dist. Lawrence County 2011); State v. Kauffer, 2011-Ohio-676, 2011 WL 531725 (Ohio Ct. App. 10th Dist. Franklin County 2011); State v. Caskey, 2010-Ohio-4697, 2010 WL 3794000 (Ohio Ct. App. 11th Dist. Lake County 2010); Cleveland Hts. v. Roland, 197 Ohio App. 3d 661, 666, 2012-Ohio-170, 968 N.E.2d 564 (8th Dist. Cuyahoga County 2012); State v. Waheed, 2016-Ohio-2951, 2016 WL 2841926 (Ohio Ct. App. 1st Dist. Hamilton County 2016); State v. Troyer, 2016-Ohio-3090, 2016 WL 2944812 (Ohio Ct. App. 5th Dist. Holmes County 2016); U.S. v. Bryant, 136 S. Ct. 1954, 195 L. Ed. 2d 317 (2016), as revised, (July 7, 2016); State v. Wood, 2018-Ohio-875, ¶ 29, 2018 WL 1225738 (Ohio Ct. App. 2d Dist. Clark County 2018), appeal not allowed, 153 Ohio St. 3d 1403, 2018-Ohio-2380, 100 N.E.3d 422 (2018).

[94]State v. Brooke, 113 Ohio St. 3d 199, 2007-Ohio-1533, 863 N.E.2d 1024 (2007); State v. Hupp, 2009-Ohio-1441, 2009 WL 806901 (Ohio Ct. App. 11th Dist. Lake County 2009); State v. Tanner, 2009-Ohio-3867, 2009 WL 2382970 (Ohio Ct. App. 9th Dist. Summit County 2009); State v. Caskey, 2010-Ohio-4697, 2010 WL 3794000 (Ohio Ct. App. 11th Dist. Lake County 2010); State v. Green, 2018-Ohio-2729, 2018 WL 3410056 (Ohio Ct. App. 8th Dist. Cuyahoga County 2018).

[95]State v. Kelly, 154 Ohio App. 3d 285, 2003-Ohio-4783, 797 N.E.2d 104 (9th Dist. Medina County 2003).

criminalizing any violation of its terms.[96] Before imposing criminal sanctions, however, civil protection order proceedings include mandatory due-process safeguards to provide notice to the respondent of the specific terms of the order, penalties that may be imposed, and a hearing that permits him to defend against alleged violations.[97]

Actual notice requires more than general knowledge that an order has been issued. A court's order is an order only to the extent of its terms. To know an order, one must know its terms.[98] In your case, it appears that you may still have some rights in your home and the property within it, depending on the terms of the court order. Since you have not been formally served with an order removing you from the home, you cannot be charged with knowledge of the terms of any such order.[99] Common sense would dictate that keeping your distance until you can clarify your situation, however, is the wisest course of action.

Q & A: Even though I didn't have a lawyer, can my prior adjudication as a domestic violence offender as a juvenile be used to enhance the penalties of a new charge of domestic violence brought against me as an adult?

It depends. If the state cannot show a valid waiver of your right to counsel, then it may not use a prior, uncounseled delinquency adjudication to enhance a sentence for a later violation.[100]

Q & A: The defendant contends that his conviction on a domestic violence "furthermore" specification was not supported by sufficient evidence because there were no medical records to corroborate the alleged victim's testimony that she was pregnant. Is he correct?

No. Medical records were not required to prove that the defendant violated the pregnancy specification. As in many cases, credible witness testimony is sufficient to establish all the elements of a crime. Criminal liability is often established solely on the victim's testimony.[101] Therefore, all the elements of a specification may be established through credible witness testimony, and this evidence, by itself, is sufficient to sustain the pregnancy specification.

---

[96]Toledo v. Lyphout, 2009-Ohio-4596, 2009 WL 2855714 (Ohio Ct. App. 6th Dist. Lucas County 2009), citing Parrish v. Parrish, 95 Ohio St. 3d 1201, 1204, 2002-Ohio-1623, 765 N.E.2d 359 (2002); State v. Thomas, 2012-Ohio-2430, 2012 WL 1970459 (Ohio Ct. App. 12th Dist. Warren County 2012); Lewis v. Gravely, 2016-Ohio-1502, 2016 WL 1404159 (Ohio Ct. App. 4th Dist. Adams County 2016); Howard v. Howard, 2018-Ohio-2218, ¶ 9-10, 2018 WL 2903270 (Ohio Ct. App. 2d Dist. Montgomery County 2018); E.W. v. T.W., 2017-Ohio-8504, ¶ 38, 2017 WL 5192035 (Ohio Ct. App. 10th Dist. Franklin County 2017).

[97]Civ. R. 65(D).

[98]Midland Steel Prods. Co. v. U.A.W. Local 486, 61 Ohio St. 3d 121, 573 N.E.2d 98 (1991).

[99]State v. Conner, 192 Ohio App. 3d 166, 2011-Ohio-146, 948 N.E.2d 497 (6th Dist. Fulton County 2011).

[100]State v. Bode, 144 Ohio St. 3d 155, 2015-Ohio-1519, 41 N.E.3d 1156 (2015); State v. Ott, 2017-Ohio-521, ¶ 7, 2017 WL 659374 (Ohio Ct. App. 9th Dist. Summit County 2017).

[101]In re C.T., 2013-Ohio-2458, 991 N.E.2d 1171 (Ohio Ct. App. 8th Dist. Cuyahoga County 2013); State v. McComas, 2013-Ohio-3180, 2013 WL 3817851 (Ohio Ct. App. 5th Dist. Tuscarawas County 2013); State v. Crawley, 2014-Ohio-1949, 2014 WL 1877544 (Ohio Ct. App. 8th Dist. Cuyahoga County 2014).

Q & A: The court issued a restraining order that excluded the defendant from a residence where both the defendant and the alleged victim reside. An officer responding to the residence on an allegation of trespass, is presented with a copy of the restraining order. That order shows no evidence that the alleged offender was served. Does the officer have probable cause to arrest?

No. The Supreme Court of Ohio has held that "a spouse may be criminally liable for trespass and/or burglary in the dwelling of the other spouse who is exercising custody or control over that dwelling." State v. Lilly, 87 Ohio St. 3d 97, 1999-Ohio-251, 717 N.E.2d 322, 325 (1999). However, where there is no evidence that an alleged offender was *not* served with a restraining order, the officer has no probable cause to detain.[102]

Q & A: Does it make any difference that an offender's prior convictions were rendered by a tribal court?

No. At least in federal prosecutions, uncounseled convictions obtained before tribal courts are treated the same as those obtained in other courts. The U.S. Supreme Court resisted creating a "hybrid" category of tribal-court convictions, "good for the punishment actually imposed but not available for sentence enhancement in a later prosecution.[103] An uncounseled previous tribal-court conviction presented as part of an ongoing new federal prosecution does not transform the prior, otherwise valid, tribal court convictions into new, invalid, federal ones."[104] Some state courts other than Ohio have come to different conclusions as it relates to the uses of prior tribal court convictions in subsequent state prosecutions.[105]

Q & A: At trial, the prosecution seeks to present evidence that at the time of the alleged act of domestic violence, the victim was four month's pregnant and, therefore, the alleged offender should be subject to greater penalties. The only evidence that the prosecution has to establish that the alleged offender knew that the alleged victim was pregnant is her testimony. The alleged offender denies knowledge. Doesn't the prosecution need more to meet its burden of proof?

No. As in many cases, credible witness testimony is sufficient to establish all the elements of a crime.[106]

Q & A: My client was previously charged with assault. In that case, my client waived the right to counsel, entered a no contest plea to the charge and was found guilty. The victim was my client's spouse. Presently, because of the prior assault conviction, my client is charged with domestic violence against the same victim, as a fourth degree felony. The plea colloquy in the assault case did not include a warning that any future

---

[102]Al-Lamadani v. Lang, 624 Fed. Appx. 405, 410 (6th Cir. 2015).

[103]Nichols v. U.S., 511 U.S. 738, 114 S. Ct. 1921, 128 L. Ed. 2d 745 (1994).

[104]U.S. v. Bryant, 136 S. Ct. 1954, 195 L. Ed. 2d 317 (2016), as revised, (July 7, 2016).

[105]State v. Young, 863 N.W.2d 249 (Iowa 2015).

[106]State v. Crawley, 2014-Ohio-1949, 2014 WL 1877544 (Ohio Ct. App. 8th Dist. Cuyahoga County 2014).

allegation of assault on a family or household member could result in an enhancement of a domestic violence charge from a first degree misdemeanor to a fourth degree felony. Can I succeed if I challenge the enhancement?

Yes. The constitutional right of an accused to be represented by counsel invokes, of itself, the protection of a trial court, in which the accused—whose life or liberty is at stake—is without counsel. This protecting duty imposes the serious and weighty responsibility upon the trial judge of determining whether there is an intelligent and competent waiver by the accused. To discharge this duty properly in light of the strong presumption against waiver of the constitutional right to counsel, a judge must investigate as long and as thoroughly as the circumstances of the case before him demand. The fact that an accused may tell him that he is informed of his right to counsel and desires to waive this right does not automatically end the judge's responsibility. To be valid, such waiver must be made with an apprehension of the nature of the charges, the statutory offenses included within them, the range of allowable punishments thereunder, possible defenses to the charges and circumstances in mitigation thereof, and all other facts essential to a broad understanding of the whole matter. A judge can make certain that an accused's professed waiver of counsel is understandingly and wisely made only from a penetrating and comprehensive examination of all the circumstances under which such a plea is tendered.[107] In the assault case, because the defendant waived the right to counsel, the trial court was required as part of its inquiry into that waiver, to inform the defendant of the possibility that a future assault on a family or household member was enhance-able. The court's failure to do so made that conviction unavailable for use to enhance the current charge.

§ 2:8 Lesser included, dissimilar, and allied offenses of similar import

Trial courts have, in some instances, treated related crimes either as lesser offenses contained in a charge of domestic violence[1] or as greater crimes in which the charge of domestic violence is the lesser included offense.[2]

When reviewed closely, these attempts to align similar offenses often fail to meet the tests for establishing the presence of a lesser

[107]Von Moltke v. Gillies, 332 U.S. 708, 723–724, 68 S. Ct. 316, 92 L. Ed. 309 (1948); State v. Troyer, 2016-Ohio-3090, 2016 WL 2944812 (Ohio Ct. App. 5th Dist. Holmes County 2016); State v. Ott, 2017-Ohio-521, ¶ 5-6, 2017 WL 659374 (Ohio Ct. App. 9th Dist. Summit County 2017); State v. Wood, 2018-Ohio-875, ¶ 33, 2018 WL 1225738 (Ohio Ct. App. 2d Dist. Clark County 2018), appeal not allowed, 153 Ohio St. 3d 1403, 2018-Ohio-2380, 100 N.E.3d 422 (2018).

[Section 2:8]

[1]See State v. Thomas, 1989 WL 147652 (Ohio Ct. App. 8th Dist. Cuyahoga County 1989), dismissed, 52 Ohio St. 3d 702, 556 N.E.2d 526 (1990).

[2]State v. Land, 1995 WL 1049591 (Ohio Ct. App. 11th Dist. Lake County 1995). See also State v. Corrill, 133 Ohio App. 3d 550, 729 N.E.2d 403 (12th Dist. Butler County 1999).

included offense, set forth in Criminal Rule 31(C) and the rulings of the Ohio Supreme Court.[3]

To meet that test, it must be shown:

(1) that the lesser included offense carries a lesser penalty than the greater offense;

(2) generally, that the greater offense cannot, as statutorily defined, ever be committed without also committing the lesser included offense.[4] However, in statutes like domestic violence, in which one element of the offense can be satisfied by proving either that the defendant actually committed the offense or, alternatively, attempted to commit it, the court should look at each alternative separately.[5] The theory is that a criminal statute written in the alternative creates a separate offense for each

[3]See State v. Brown, 119 Ohio St. 3d 447, 2008-Ohio-4569, 895 N.E.2d 149 (2008); State v. Gibson, 2009-Ohio-4984, 2009 WL 3043980 (Ohio Ct. App. 8th Dist. Cuyahoga County 2009); State v. Thomas, 1989 WL 147652 (Ohio Ct. App. 8th Dist. Cuyahoga County 1989), dismissed, 52 Ohio St. 3d 702, 556 N.E.2d 526 (1990); State v. Land, 1995 WL 1049591 (Ohio Ct. App. 11th Dist. Lake County 1995); State v. Journey, 2010-Ohio-2555, 2010 WL 2280735 (Ohio Ct. App. 4th Dist. Scioto County 2010); State v. Johnson, 128 Ohio St. 3d 153, 2010-Ohio-6314, 942 N.E.2d 1061 (2010); State v. LaPrairie, 2011-Ohio-2184, 2011 WL 1753195 (Ohio Ct. App. 2d Dist. Greene County 2011); State v. Blanda, 2011-Ohio-411, 2011 WL 332725 (Ohio Ct. App. 12th Dist. Butler County 2011); State v. Craycraft, 193 Ohio App. 3d 594, 2011-Ohio-413, 953 N.E.2d 337 (12th Dist. Clermont County 2011); State v. Damron, 129 Ohio St. 3d 86, 89, 2011-Ohio-2268, 950 N.E.2d 512, 515 (2011); State v. Brautigam, 2012-Ohio-2599, 2012 WL 2128013, *2 (Ohio Ct. App. 9th Dist. Summit County 2012); State v. Caudill, 2012-Ohio-2230, 2012 WL 1810189, *2 (Ohio Ct. App. 2d Dist. Montgomery County 2012); State v. Ross, 2012-Ohio-1389, 2012 WL 1076253, *5 (Ohio Ct. App. 9th Dist. Summit County 2012); State v. Carner, 2012-Ohio-1190, 2012 WL 985906, *8 (Ohio Ct. App. 8th Dist. Cuyahoga County 2012); State v. Sutphin, 2011-Ohio-5157, 2011 WL 4600412, *8 (Ohio Ct. App. 8th Dist. Cuyahoga County 2011); State v. Waltzer, 2011-Ohio-5147, 2011 WL 4599828, *3 (Ohio Ct. App. 8th Dist. Cuyahoga County 2011); State v. Hight, 2011-Ohio-5013, 2011 WL 4529356, *2 (Ohio Ct. App. 5th Dist. Licking County 2011); State v. Gulley, 2011-Ohio-4123, 2011 WL 3652761, *2 (Ohio Ct. App. 8th Dist. Cuyahoga County 2011); State v. Johnson, 2011-Ohio-2825, 2011 WL 2410054 (Ohio Ct. App. 2d Dist. Montgomery County 2011); State v. Johnson, 196 Ohio App. 3d 338, 2011-Ohio-2653, 963 N.E.2d 828, 834 (5th Dist. Richland County 2011); State v. Simmons, 2011-Ohio-6074, 2011 WL 5869794 (Ohio Ct. App. 8th Dist. Cuyahoga County 2011); State v. Parsons, 2015-Ohio-5103, 2015 WL 8467417 (Ohio Ct. App. 5th Dist. Fairfield County 2015); State v. Bridges, 2015-Ohio-4480, 2015 WL 6522860 (Ohio Ct. App. 10th Dist. Franklin County 2015); State v. Clark, 2016-Ohio-2825, 2016 WL 2586638 (Ohio Ct. App. 8th Dist. Cuyahoga County 2016), appeal not allowed, 147 Ohio St. 3d 1474, 2016-Ohio-8438, 65 N.E.3d 778 (2016); see Kilby v. Court of Common Pleas of Montgomery County, Ohio, Juvenile Div., 2015 WL 1729881 (S.D. Ohio 2015) (USDC, Southern Dist. Of Ohio West Div); State v. Earley, 145 Ohio St. 3d 281, 2015-Ohio-4615, 49 N.E.3d 266 (2015); State v. Clark, 2016-Ohio-2825, 2016 WL 2586638 (Ohio Ct. App. 8th Dist. Cuyahoga County 2016), appeal not allowed, 147 Ohio St. 3d 1474, 2016-Ohio-8438, 65 N.E.3d 778 (2016); State v. Craig, 2017-Ohio-4342, ¶ 42, 2017 WL 2616900 (Ohio Ct. App. 4th Dist. Athens County 2017), appeal not allowed, 151 Ohio St. 3d 1428, 2017-Ohio-8371, 84 N.E.3d 1065 (2017) and appeal not allowed, 152 Ohio St. 3d 1425, 2018-Ohio-923, 93 N.E.3d 1005 (2018); State v. Roberson, 2018-Ohio-1955, ¶ 17, 2018 WL 2277130 (Ohio Ct. App. 6th Dist. Lucas County 2018); State v. Povroznik, 2018-Ohio-1516, ¶ 26-27, 2018 WL 1882896 (Ohio Ct. App. 8th Dist. Cuyahoga County 2018).

[4]In re S.W., 2011-Ohio-5291, 2011 WL 4863972 (Ohio Ct. App. 2d Dist. Montgomery County 2011); State v. Houston, 2017-Ohio-1122, 87 N.E.3d 797 (Ohio Ct. App. 10th Dist. Franklin County 2017).

[5]See Whalen v. U.S., 445 U.S. 684, 694, 100 S. Ct. 1432, 63 L. Ed. 2d 715 (1980);

alternative and, therefore, when looking at a statute containing alternative elements, each statutory alternative should be construed as constituting a separate offense and analyzed accordingly as separate statutes would;[6] and

(3) that some element of the greater offense is not required to prove the commission of the lesser included offense.[7]

R.C. 2941.25(B) sets forth three categories in which there can be multiple punishments: (1) offenses that are dissimilar in import, (2) offenses similar in import but committed separately, and (3) offenses similar in import but committed with separate animus.[8]

---

see also Pandelli v. U.S., 635 F.2d 533, 537 (6th Cir. 1980); State v. Brown, 119 Ohio St. 3d 447, 2008-Ohio-4569, 895 N.E.2d 149 (2008); State v. Houston, 2017-Ohio-1122, 87 N.E.3d 797 (Ohio Ct. App. 10th Dist. Franklin County 2017).

[6]State v. Smith, 117 Ohio St. 3d 447, 2008-Ohio-1260, 884 N.E.2d 595 (2008), on reconsideration, 121 Ohio St. 3d 409, 2009-Ohio-787, 905 N.E.2d 151 (2009); State v. Zima, 102 Ohio St. 3d 61, 2004-Ohio-1807, 806 N.E.2d 542 (2004), State v. Hornbuckle, 2015-Ohio-3962, 2015 WL 5691911 (Ohio Ct. App. 7th Dist. Mahoning County 2015), appeal not allowed, 144 Ohio St. 3d 1506, 2016-Ohio-652, 45 N.E.3d 1051 (2016); State v. Toth, 2017-Ohio-5481, ¶ 7-8, 2017 WL 2766248, *2 (Ohio Ct. App. 9th Dist. Medina County 2017) ("[D]etermining whether an accused is being successively prosecuted for the 'same offense' requires courts to apply the 'same elements' test articulated in *Blockburger v. United States*, 284 U.S. 299, 304 (1932) * * *."

[7]State v. Deem, 40 Ohio St. 3d 205, 533 N.E.2d 294 (1988) (holding modified by, State v. Smith, 117 Ohio St. 3d 447, 2008-Ohio-1260, 884 N.E.2d 595 (2008)); State v. Ocasio, 2003-Ohio-6240, 2003 WL 22764145 (Ohio Ct. App. 2d Dist. Montgomery County 2003); State v. Evans, 153 Ohio App. 3d 226, 2003-Ohio-3475, 792 N.E.2d 757 (7th Dist. Jefferson County 2003), cause dismissed, 99 Ohio St. 3d 1534, 2003-Ohio-4677, 795 N.E.2d 55 (2003); State v. Poppe, 2006-Ohio-1994, 2006 WL 1062023 (Ohio Ct. App. 3d Dist. Auglaize County 2006). But see State v. Kvasne, 169 Ohio App. 3d 167, 2006-Ohio-5235, 862 N.E.2d 171 (8th Dist. Cuyahoga County 2006), judgment aff'd, 114 Ohio St. 3d 430, 2007-Ohio-4552, 872 N.E.2d 1212 (2007); State v. Smith, 2008-Ohio-6998, 2008 WL 5429204 (Ohio Ct. App. 11th Dist. Trumbull County 2008). See also State v. Nguyen, 165 Wash. 2d 428, 197 P.3d 673 (2008); State v. Keith, 2008-Ohio-6122, 2008 WL 5049753 (Ohio Ct. App. 10th Dist. Franklin County 2008); State v. Lawrence, 2008-Ohio-1354, 2008 WL 757529 (Ohio Ct. App. 12th Dist. Butler County 2008), cause dismissed, 121 Ohio St. 3d 1224, 2009-Ohio-1112, 903 N.E.2d 643 (2009); State v. Evans, 122 Ohio St. 3d 381, 2009-Ohio-2974, 911 N.E.2d 889 (2009); State v. Darling, 2009-Ohio-4198, 2009 WL 2579524 (Ohio Ct. App. 8th Dist. Cuyahoga County 2009); State v. Wilson, 182 Ohio App. 3d 171, 2009-Ohio-1681, 912 N.E.2d 133 (8th Dist. Cuyahoga County 2009), cause dismissed, 124 Ohio St. 3d 1424, 2010-Ohio-20, 919 N.E.2d 748 (2010); State v. Turks, 2010-Ohio-5944, 2010 WL 5050549 (Ohio Ct. App. 3d Dist. Allen County 2010); In re S.W., 2011-Ohio-5291, 2011 WL 4863972 (Ohio Ct. App. 2d Dist. Montgomery County 2011); State v. Rogers, 2018-Ohio-1356, ¶ 15, 2018 WL 1721854 (Ohio Ct. App. 12th Dist. Butler County 2018); State v. Short, 2018-Ohio-2429, ¶ 87, 2018 WL 3090038 (Ohio Ct. App. 2d Dist. Montgomery County 2018).

[8]State v. Ruff, 143 Ohio St. 3d 114, 2015-Ohio-995, 34 N.E.3d 892 (2015); State v. Studgions, 2016-Ohio-5236, 2016 WL 4141347 (Ohio Ct. App. 8th Dist. Cuyahoga County 2016); State v. Black, 2016-Ohio-383, 58 N.E.3d 561 (Ohio Ct. App. 8th Dist. Cuyahoga County 2016), appeal not allowed, 145 Ohio St. 3d 1461, 2016-Ohio-2807, 49 N.E.3d 322 (2016); State v. Harris, 2015-Ohio-5400, 2015 WL 9435183 (Ohio Ct. App. 5th Dist. Richland County 2015); State v. Jenkins, 2018-Ohio-2397, ¶ 61-62, 2018 WL 3088800 (Ohio Ct. App. 8th Dist. Cuyahoga County 2018); State v. Povroznik, 2018-Ohio-1516, ¶ 22, 2018 WL 1882896 (Ohio Ct. App. 8th Dist. Cuyahoga County 2018); State v. Roberson, 2018-Ohio-1955, ¶ 14-16, 2018 WL 2277130 (Ohio Ct. App. 6th Dist. Lucas County 2018); State v. Dean, 2018-Ohio-1740, ¶ 52-54, 2018 WL 2085103 (Ohio Ct. App. 6th Dist. Lucas County 2018), appeal not allowed, 2018-Ohio-3450, 2018 WL 4144533 (Ohio 2018); State v. Hornsby, 2018-Ohio-1457, ¶ 26-29, 2018

A defendant's conduct is but one factor to consider when determining whether multiple offenses are allied offenses of similar import pursuant to R.C. 2941.25(B). In practice, allied offenses of similar import are simply multiple offenses that arise out of the same criminal conduct and are similar but not identical in the significance of the criminal wrongs committed and the resulting harm.[9] In other words, offenses are not allied offenses of similar import if they are not alike in their significance and their resulting harm.[10]

The Supreme Court previously cautioned that the inquiry should not be limited to whether there is separate animus or whether there is separate conduct. Courts must also consider whether the offenses have similar import.[11]

A trial court and the reviewing court on appeal when considering whether there are allied offenses that merge into a single conviction[12] must first take into account the conduct of the defendant. In other words, how were the offenses committed? If any of the following is

WL 1791928 (Ohio Ct. App. 12th Dist. Clermont County 2018); State v. Flenner, 2018-Ohio-1027, ¶ 45, 2018 WL 1382365 (Ohio Ct. App. 11th Dist. Trumbull County 2018); State v. Randle, 2018-Ohio-207, ¶ 14-15, 104 N.E.3d 202 (Ohio Ct. App. 3d Dist. Marion County 2018), appeal not allowed, 152 Ohio St. 3d 1490, 2018-Ohio-2155, 99 N.E.3d 426 (2018); State v. Brumley, 2017-Ohio-8803, ¶ 29, 2017 WL 5997928 (Ohio Ct. App. 11th Dist. Portage County 2017); State v. Pichardo-Reyes, 2017-Ohio-8534, ¶ 62-63, 2017 WL 5290871 (Ohio Ct. App. 12th Dist. Butler County 2017); State v. Clarke, 2017-Ohio-8226, ¶ 26, 2017 WL 4711959 (Ohio Ct. App. 8th Dist. Cuyahoga County 2017); State v. Conyer, 2017-Ohio-7506, ¶ 40, 2017 WL 3971689 (Ohio Ct. App. 7th Dist. Mahoning County 2017), appeal not allowed, 152 Ohio St. 3d 1478, 2018-Ohio-1990, 98 N.E.3d 294 (2018); Long v. Sloan, 2017 WL 3088038, *4 (N.D. Ohio 2017), certificate of appealability denied, 2018 WL 841588 (6th Cir. 2018); State v. Love, 2017-Ohio-5688, ¶ 27, 2017 WL 2841683 (Ohio Ct. App. 6th Dist. Erie County 2017), appeal not allowed, 151 Ohio St. 3d 1457, 2017-Ohio-8842, 87 N.E.3d 223 (2017); State v. Dasen, 2017-Ohio-5556, ¶ 67, 2017 WL 2802235 (Ohio Ct. App. 9th Dist. Summit County 2017); State v. Toth, 2017-Ohio-5481, ¶ 10, 2017 WL 2766248 (Ohio Ct. App. 9th Dist. Medina County 2017); State v. Armengau, 2017-Ohio-4452, ¶ 123-124, 93 N.E.3d 284, 317–18 (Ohio Ct. App. 10th Dist. Franklin County 2017), appeal not allowed, 151 Ohio St. 3d 1511, 2018-Ohio-365, 90 N.E.3d 950 (2018); State v. Craig, 2017-Ohio-4342, ¶ 14-15, 2017 WL 2616900 (Ohio Ct. App. 4th Dist. Athens County 2017), appeal not allowed, 151 Ohio St. 3d 1428, 2017-Ohio-8371, 84 N.E.3d 1065 (2017) and appeal not allowed, 152 Ohio St. 3d 1425, 2018-Ohio-923, 93 N.E.3d 1005 (2018).

[9]State v. Johnson, 128 Ohio St. 3d 153, 2010-Ohio-6314, 942 N.E.2d 1061 (2010) (O'Connor, J., concurring in judgment); State v. Ruff, 143 Ohio St. 3d 114, 2015-Ohio-995, 34 N.E.3d 892 (2015); State v. Craig, 2017-Ohio-4342, ¶ 13-14, 2017 WL 2616900 (Ohio Ct. App. 4th Dist. Athens County 2017), appeal not allowed, 151 Ohio St. 3d 1428, 2017-Ohio-8371, 84 N.E.3d 1065 (2017) and appeal not allowed, 152 Ohio St. 3d 1425, 2018-Ohio-923, 93 N.E.3d 1005 (2018); State v. Conyer, 2017-Ohio-7506, ¶ 42-44, 2017 WL 3971689 (Ohio Ct. App. 7th Dist. Mahoning County 2017), appeal not allowed, 152 Ohio St. 3d 1478, 2018-Ohio-1990, 98 N.E.3d 294 (2018); State v. Roberson, 2018-Ohio-1955, ¶ 16, 2018 WL 2277130 (Ohio Ct. App. 6th Dist. Lucas County 2018); State v. Flenner, 2018-Ohio-1027, ¶ 45, 2018 WL 1382365 (Ohio Ct. App. 11th Dist. Trumbull County 2018); State v. Randle, 2018-Ohio-207, ¶ 14, 104 N.E.3d 202 (Ohio Ct. App. 3d Dist. Marion County 2018), appeal not allowed, 152 Ohio St. 3d 1490, 2018-Ohio-2155, 99 N.E.3d 426 (2018); State v. Brown, 2017-Ohio-9259, ¶ 71, 103 N.E.3d 32 (Ohio Ct. App. 11th Dist. Ashtabula County 2017).

[10]State v. Ruff, 143 Ohio St. 3d 114, 2015-Ohio-995, 34 N.E.3d 892 (2015).

[11]State v. Baer, 67 Ohio St. 2d 220, 226, 21 Ohio Op. 3d 138, 423 N.E.2d 432 (1981); State v. Ruff, 143 Ohio St. 3d 114, 2015-Ohio-995, 34 N.E.3d 892 (2015).

[12]R.C. 2941.25(A).

true, the offenses cannot merge and the defendant may be convicted and sentenced for multiple offenses: (1) the offenses are dissimilar in import or significance—in other words, each offense caused separate, identifiable harm, (2) the offenses were committed separately, and (3) the offenses were committed with separate animus or motivation.[13]

At its heart, the allied-offense analysis is dependent upon the facts of a case because the statute[14] focuses on the defendant's conduct. The evidence at trial or during a plea or sentencing hearing will reveal whether the offenses have similar import. When a defendant's conduct victimizes more than one person, the harm for each person is separate and distinct, and therefore, the defendant can be convicted of multiple counts. Also, a defendant's conduct that constitutes two or more offenses against a single victim can support multiple convictions if the harm that results from each offense is separate and identifiable from the harm of the other offense. Therefore, two or more offenses of dissimilar import exist when the defendant's conduct constitutes offenses involving separate victims or if the harm that results from each offense is separate and identifiable.[15]

Rather than compare the elements of two offenses to determine whether they are allied offenses of similar import, the analysis must focus on the defendant's conduct to determine whether one or more convictions may result because an offense may be committed in a variety of ways and the offenses committed may have different import. No bright-line rule can govern every situation.[16]

As a practical matter, when determining whether offenses are allied offenses of similar import, courts must ask three questions when a defendant's conduct supports multiple offenses: (1) Were the offenses dissimilar in import or significance? (2) Were they committed separately? and (3) Were they committed with separate animus or motivation? An affirmative answer to any of the above will permit separate convictions. The conduct, the animus, and the import must all be considered.[17]

While Criminal Rule 7(D) permits a trial court to amend a complaint even after trial with respect to, among other things, any variance with the evidence, "provided that there is no change in the name or identity of the crime charged," amending a complaint so that it charges domestic violence as a violation under RC 2919.25(C), rather than RC 2919.25(A), does change the identity of the offense charged in contravention of Criminal Rule 7(D).[18] In such a case, the defendant need not demonstrate prejudice to obtain a dismissal of the charges.[19]

---

[13] State v. Ruff, 143 Ohio St. 3d 114, 2015-Ohio-995, 34 N.E.3d 892 (2015).

[14] R.C. 2941.25.

[15] State v. Ruff, 143 Ohio St. 3d 114, 2015-Ohio-995, 34 N.E.3d 892 (2015).

[16] State v. Ruff, 143 Ohio St. 3d 114, 2015-Ohio-995, 34 N.E.3d 892 (2015).

[17] State v. Ruff, 143 Ohio St. 3d 114, 2015-Ohio-995, 34 N.E.3d 892 (2015); State v. Gay, 2015-Ohio-1832, 2015 WL 2254985 (Ohio Ct. App. 8th Dist. Cuyahoga County 2015).

[18] State v. Rihm, 101 Ohio App. 3d 626, 628, 656 N.E.2d 372 (2d Dist. Clark County 1995); City of Toledo v. Montgomery, 2002-Ohio-1872, 2002 WL 597360 (Ohio Ct. App. 6th Dist. Lucas County 2002).

[19] City of Toledo v. Montgomery, 2002-Ohio-1872, 2002 WL 597360 (Ohio Ct. App.

Q & A: If, after trial, a court finds no assault in violation of RC 2919.25(A) but finds that the offender did make threats which qualify as violations of RC 2919.25(C), can the offender be convicted of making the threat?

No. This fact pattern fails to meet the second prong of the *Deem* test. A violation of RC 2919.25(A) can be committed without also violating RC 2919.25(C). *State v. Rihm*[20] describes just such a situation:

> For example, a defendant who knowingly causes or attempts to cause physical harm to a family or household member by 'blind-siding' her or attacking her while she is asleep, and then leaves immediately thereafter, has not caused the victim to believe that he will cause her imminent physical harm.

For the same reasons, a charge of menacing is likewise not a lesser included offense of domestic violence.[21]

One court has, however, identified a situation where an individual who is charged with a violation of one of the assault sections of the domestic violence law might be found not guilty of that conduct, but found guilty of domestic violence under the threats section. The possibility can arise where the prosecution employs a boilerplate complaint form as the charging document. Such forms include sections (A), (B) and (C) of the state's domestic violence law, or of substantially similar municipal ordinances.[22]

It is true that a defendant cannot be convicted of a charge that is not contained in a complaint or indictment.[23] However, a "criminal complaint need not designate a specific statutory subsection by number, as long as its language is sufficient to specify the subsection."[24] Thus, when the prosecution's charging document references all sections of the statute or ordinance, and tracks the statutory or ordinance language precisely, the defendant may be required to defend as against each section contained in the complaint, unless a request is made for a bill of particulars, to clarify the specifics of the allegations charged.[25]

Q & A: Where an offender is originally charged with domestic violence under RC 2919.25(A), can a court find the defendant not guilty of that charge, but guilty of disorderly conduct under RC 2917.11, as a lesser included offense?

6th Dist. Lucas County 2002).

[20]State v. Rihm, 101 Ohio App. 3d 626, 629-30, 656 N.E.2d 372 (2d Dist. Clark County 1995).

[21]State v. Rose, 2000 WL 1643577 (Ohio Ct. App. 1st Dist. Hamilton County 2000).

[22]City of Cleveland v. Jenkins, 2002-Ohio-6046, 2002 WL 31492631 (Ohio Ct. App. 8th Dist. Cuyahoga County 2002).

[23]State v. Broughton, 51 Ohio App. 3d 10, 553 N.E.2d 1380 (12th Dist. Clermont County 1988); State v. Mitchell, 2011-Ohio-2465, 2011 WL 2112619 (Ohio Ct. App. 12th Dist. Butler County 2011).

[24]State v. Broughton, 51 Ohio App. 3d 10, 553 N.E.2d 1380 (12th Dist. Clermont County 1988).

[25]City of Cleveland v. Jenkins, 2002-Ohio-6046, 2002 WL 31492631 (Ohio Ct. App. 8th Dist. Cuyahoga County 2002).

Yes. In the past, several of Ohio's appellate jurisdictions held that disorderly conduct, when charged as a minor misdemeanor under state law, was a lesser included offense of domestic violence.[26] However, other appellate courts found that it did not.[27]

The Supreme Court of Ohio weighed in definitively to resolve the conflict of authority. The court held that minor misdemeanor disorderly conduct, which is an offense under state statute, is a lesser included offense of domestic violence under state statute and under a city ordinance that uses language identical to the state's domestic violence statute.[28]

A fourth degree misdemeanor charge of disorderly conduct under RC 2917.11(E) fails to meet the third prong of the *Deem* test. That charge requires proof of an additional element not required for a conviction of domestic violence. The additional element is either the offender's failure to desist from the disorderly conduct after reasonable warning or request to do so, or the commission of the offense in the vicinity of a school.

The greater offense, domestic violence, can be committed without also committing the fourth degree misdemeanor of disorderly conduct. Thus, disorderly conduct as a fourth degree misdemeanor under the

[26]State v. Stuber, 71 Ohio App. 3d 86, 593 N.E.2d 48 (3d Dist. Allen County 1990); State v. Burgess, 79 Ohio App. 3d 584, 607 N.E.2d 918 (12th Dist. Warren County 1992); State v. Amos, 1988 WL 4622 (Ohio Ct. App. 11th Dist. Lake County 1988); State v. Kutnar, 1999 WL 960943 (Ohio Ct. App. 11th Dist. Lake County 1999); State v. Stewart, 2003-Ohio-214, 2003 WL 139971, *1 (Ohio Ct. App. 2d Dist. Montgomery County 2003); Shaker Hts. v. Mosely, 113 Ohio St. 3d 329, 2007-Ohio-2072, 865 N.E.2d 859 (2007); State v. Golding, 2009-Ohio-1437, 2009 WL 806915 (Ohio Ct. App. 11th Dist. Lake County 2009). See also State v. Boldin, 2008-Ohio-6408, 2008 WL 5147450 (Ohio Ct. App. 11th Dist. Geauga County 2008); State v. Ward, 2009-Ohio-3145, 2009 WL 1844486 (Ohio Ct. App. 11th Dist. Geauga County 2009); State v. Tolbert, 2010-Ohio-2864, 2010 WL 2512584 (Ohio Ct. App. 9th Dist. Summit County 2010); In re S.W., 2011-Ohio-5291, 2011 WL 4863972 (Ohio Ct. App. 2d Dist. Montgomery County 2011); State v. Evans, 122 Ohio St. 3d 381, 2009-Ohio-2974, 911 N.E.2d 889 (2009); Cleveland Hts. v. Cohen, 2015-Ohio-1636, 31 N.E.3d 695 (Ohio Ct. App. 8th Dist. Cuyahoga County 2015); Cleveland v. Hall, 2015-Ohio-2698, 2015 WL 4043005 (Ohio Ct. App. 8th Dist. Cuyahoga County 2015).

[27]State v. Schaefer, 2000 WL 492094 (Ohio Ct. App. 2d Dist. Greene County 2000); State v. Neal, 1998 WL 614628 (Ohio Ct. App. 10th Dist. Franklin County 1998); State v. Blasdell, 155 Ohio App. 3d 423, 2003-Ohio-6392, 801 N.E.2d 853 (7th Dist. Mahoning County 2003); State v. Alvey, 2003-Ohio-7006, 2003 WL 22997277 (Ohio Ct. App. 7th Dist. Belmont County 2003); State v. Poppe, 2006-Ohio-1994, 2006 WL 1062023 (Ohio Ct. App. 3d Dist. Auglaize County 2006); Shaker Hts. v. Mosely, 113 Ohio St. 3d 329, 2007-Ohio-2072, 865 N.E.2d 859 (2007); State v. Evans, 122 Ohio St. 3d 381, 2009-Ohio-2974, 911 N.E.2d 889 (2009); Cleveland Hts. v. Cohen, 2015-Ohio-1636, 31 N.E.3d 695 (Ohio Ct. App. 8th Dist. Cuyahoga County 2015); Cleveland v. Hall, 2015-Ohio-2698, 2015 WL 4043005 (Ohio Ct. App. 8th Dist. Cuyahoga County 2015).

[28]Shaker Hts. v. Mosely, 113 Ohio St. 3d 329, 2007-Ohio-2072, 865 N.E.2d 859 (2007); State v. Evans, 122 Ohio St. 3d 381, 2009-Ohio-2974, 911 N.E.2d 889 (2009); Cleveland Hts. v. Cohen, 2015-Ohio-1636, 31 N.E.3d 695 (Ohio Ct. App. 8th Dist. Cuyahoga County 2015); Cleveland v. Hall, 2015-Ohio-2698, 2015 WL 4043005 (Ohio Ct. App. 8th Dist. Cuyahoga County 2015); State v. Powell, 2017-Ohio-5629, ¶ 48, 2017 WL 2857221 (Ohio Ct. App. 9th Dist. Summit County 2017), appeal not allowed, 152 Ohio St. 3d 1462, 2018-Ohio-1795, 97 N.E.3d 499 (2018).

Revised Code is not a lesser included offense of domestic violence.[29] Logic would suggest that substantially similar disorderly conduct ordinances which contain the same additional element found in RC 2917.11(E) do not meet the *Deem* test and, likewise, do not qualify as lesser included offenses of domestic violence.

Q & A: During trial, the defendant presents evidence that (1) the act was reflexive and was not intended to do physical harm, and (2) alternatively, any response made was in self-defense or justified to expel the victim who was a trespasser. At the conclusion of trial, the defendant requests that the court instruct the jury on the lesser-included offense of disorderly conduct. Is the court required to give the requested instruction?

No. A trial court is required to instruct a jury on a lesser included offense only where the facts presented could support a finding of guilt on the lesser included offense, but not on the greater offense.[30] Where the defendant puts forth alternate defenses, any one of which could constitute a complete defense to the crime charged, whether or not to give the requested instruction is within the sound discretion of the trial court.[31]

Q & A: Does a defendant have a right to prevent a trial court from giving a jury instruction on a lesser included offense?

No. A criminal defendant does not have the right to prevent a trial court from giving lesser-included-offense jury instructions. Whether to include such jury instructions lies within the discretion of the trial court and depends on whether the evidence presented could reasonably support a jury finding of guilt on a particular charge.[32]

Q & A: Can a defendant be tried and convicted of both the attempt to commit domestic violence and the act of domestic violence itself coming out of the same event?

No. Where a statue sets forth two means of committing the same of-

---

[29]State v. Reynolds, 25 Ohio App. 3d 59, 495 N.E.2d 971 (1st Dist. Hamilton County 1985); State v. Jewell, 1997 WL 779088 (Ohio Ct. App. 12th Dist. Butler County 1997); State v. Blasdell, 155 Ohio App. 3d 423, 2003-Ohio-6392, 801 N.E.2d 853 (7th Dist. Mahoning County 2003); State v. Alvey, 2003-Ohio-7006, 2003 WL 22997277 (Ohio Ct. App. 7th Dist. Belmont County 2003); State v. Watson, 2005-Ohio-1729, 2005 WL 845228 (Ohio Ct. App. 5th Dist. Stark County 2005); City of Shaker Heights v. Mosely, 2005-Ohio-5433, 2005 WL 2562915 (Ohio Ct. App. 8th Dist. Cuyahoga County 2005), judgment aff'd, 113 Ohio St. 3d 329, 2007-Ohio-2072, 865 N.E.2d 859 (2007); State v. Evans, 122 Ohio St. 3d 381, 2009-Ohio-2974, 911 N.E.2d 889 (2009); Cleveland Hts. v. Cohen, 2015-Ohio-1636, 31 N.E.3d 695 (Ohio Ct. App. 8th Dist. Cuyahoga County 2015); Cleveland v. Hall, 2015-Ohio-2698, 2015 WL 4043005 (Ohio Ct. App. 8th Dist. Cuyahoga County 2015).

[30]State v. Nolton, 19 Ohio St. 2d 133, 48 Ohio Op. 2d 119, 249 N.E.2d 797 (1969); State v. Garrett, 2003-Ohio-5000, 2003 WL 22170186 (Ohio Ct. App. 12th Dist. Butler County 2003); State v. Gooden, 2003-Ohio-905, 2003 WL 565823 (Ohio Ct. App. 2d Dist. Montgomery County 2003); State v. Barker, 2012-Ohio-522, 2012 WL 439658 (Ohio Ct. App. 11th Dist. Portage County 2012).

[31]State v. Milano-Tavella, 1999 WL 668562 (Ohio Ct. App. 5th Dist. Delaware County 1999); see also State v. Wright, 2000 WL 652542 (Ohio Ct. App. 7th Dist. Jefferson County 2000).

[32]State v. Wine, 140 Ohio St. 3d 409, 2014-Ohio-3948, 18 N.E.3d 1207 (2014); State v. Ryan, 2018-Ohio-2600, 2018 WL 3207162 (Ohio Ct. App. 11th Dist. Ashtabula County 2018).

fense both of which serve the same purpose—doing physical harm to persons—it is evident that the General Assembly did not intend them to be separately punishable when the offenses result from a single act.[33]

Q & A: The defendant is charged with domestic violence in violation of R.C. 2919.25(B). Just prior to the start of the trial, the prosecution moves the court to amend the complaint to change the charged subsection to R.C. 2919.25(A). Can the court grant that motion?

It depends. The amendment itself does not present a substantive change in the nature of the offense. At worst, the amendment results in an increase in the possible penalties that the defendant is exposed to. Unless the defense objects and is able to establish that the amendment will result in undue prejudice to its case, the court, in its discretion, can grant the motion.[34]

Q & A: Can a defendant who is convicted of felonious assault, felony domestic violence, and felonious violation of a protection order, all growing out of the same act of punching his victim, be sentenced separately for each of those convictions?

According to two of Ohio's Courts of Appeals, the answer is "no."[35] Where the defendant's conduct constitutes two or more offenses of dissimilar import, or where his conduct results in two or more offenses of the same or similar kind committed separately or with a separate animus as to each, the indictment or information may contain counts for all such offenses, and the defendant may be convicted of all of them.[36]

However, where the same conduct by defendant can be construed to constitute two or more allied offenses of similar import, the indictment or information may contain counts for all such offenses, but the defendant may be convicted of only one.[37]

Therefore, offenses that are allied offenses of similar import must be merged for sentencing where the prosecution relies on the same conduct for each offense.

---

[33]State v. Brown, 119 Ohio St. 3d 447, 2008-Ohio-4569, 895 N.E.2d 149 (2008). State v. Wright, 2010-Ohio-243, 2010 WL 320476 (Ohio Ct. App. 8th Dist. Cuyahoga County 2010); State v. Ruff, 143 Ohio St. 3d 114, 2015-Ohio-995, 34 N.E.3d 892 (2015); State v. Cherryholmes, 2015-Ohio-3063, 2015 WL 4600546 (Ohio Ct. App. 5th Dist. Fairfield County 2015), appeal not allowed, 144 Ohio St. 3d 1460, 2016-Ohio-172, 44 N.E.3d 288 (2016) and cert. denied, 136 S. Ct. 2493, 195 L. Ed. 2d 824 (2016); State v. Craig, 2017-Ohio-4342, ¶ 42, 2017 WL 2616900 (Ohio Ct. App. 4th Dist. Athens County 2017), appeal not allowed, 151 Ohio St. 3d 1428, 2017-Ohio-8371, 84 N.E.3d 1065 (2017) and appeal not allowed, 152 Ohio St. 3d 1425, 2018-Ohio-923, 93 N.E.3d 1005 (2018).

[34]State v. Cameron, 2011-Ohio-4602, 2011 WL 4048162 (Ohio Ct. App. 5th Dist. Tuscarawas County 2011).

[35]State v. Weathers, 2011-Ohio-6793, 2011 WL 6921088 (Ohio Ct. App. 12th Dist. Butler County 2011); State v. Williams, 2012-Ohio-3384, 2012 WL 3061172 (Ohio Ct. App. 2d Dist. Greene County 2012).

[36]2941.25 (B). State v. Warren, 2015-Ohio-604, 2015 WL 759145 (Ohio Ct. App. 8th Dist. Cuyahoga County 2015); State v. Thomas, 2014-Ohio-2666, 2014 WL 2810643 (Ohio Ct. App. 2d Dist. Darke County 2014).

[37]2941.25 (A).

Q & A: Can a defendant who is tried and found guilty of violations of both RC 2919.25(A) and RC 2919.25(C) be convicted and sentenced for both offenses?

Once again the answer is, it depends. Once the defendant is found guilty of both charges, the court must conduct an analysis to determine if the offenses are allied and of similar import. Ohio's allied offense statute is codified at R.C. 2941.25. It provides that

> "(A) Where the same conduct by defendant can be construed to constitute two or more allied offenses of similar import, the indictment or information may contain counts for all such offenses, but the defendant may be convicted of only one.
> (B) Where the defendant's conduct constitutes two or more offenses of dissimilar import, or where his conduct results in two or more offenses of the same or similar kind committed separately or with a separate animus as to each, the indictment or information may contain counts for all such offenses, and the defendant may be convicted of all of them."

To ensure compliance with R.C. 2941.25, the Double Jeopardy Clause of the Fifth Amendment to the United States Constitution and Section 10, Article I of the Ohio Constitution, a trial court is required to merge allied offenses of similar import at sentencing.[38] However, because R.C. 2941.25(A) protects a defendant only from being punished for allied offenses, the determination of the defendant's guilt for committing allied offenses remains intact, both before and after the merger of allied offenses for sentencing.[39] The defendant bears the burden to prove entitlement to merger.[40]

To determine whether offenses are allied offenses of similar import,

---

[38]State v. Williams, 134 Ohio St. 3d 482, 2012-Ohio-5699, 983 N.E.2d 1245 (2012); State v. Patterson, 2012-Ohio-5511, 2012 WL 5987118 (Ohio Ct. App. 8th Dist. Cuyahoga County 2012); State v. Warren, 2015-Ohio-604, 2015 WL 759145 (Ohio Ct. App. 8th Dist. Cuyahoga County 2015); State v. Cherryholmes, 2015-Ohio-3063, 2015 WL 4600546 (Ohio Ct. App. 5th Dist. Fairfield County 2015), appeal not allowed, 144 Ohio St. 3d 1460, 2016-Ohio-172, 44 N.E.3d 288 (2016) and cert. denied, 136 S. Ct. 2493, 195 L. Ed. 2d 824 (2016); State v. Jenkins, 2018-Ohio-2397, ¶ 62-63, 2018 WL 3088800 (Ohio Ct. App. 8th Dist. Cuyahoga County 2018); State v. Brumley, 2017-Ohio-8803, ¶ 27, 2017 WL 5997928 (Ohio Ct. App. 11th Dist. Portage County 2017); State v. Pichardo-Reyes, 2017-Ohio-8534, ¶ 63, 2017 WL 5290871 (Ohio Ct. App. 12th Dist. Butler County 2017); State v. Conyer, 2017-Ohio-7506, ¶ 37, 2017 WL 3971689 (Ohio Ct. App. 7th Dist. Mahoning County 2017), appeal not allowed, 152 Ohio St. 3d 1478, 2018-Ohio-1990, 98 N.E.3d 294 (2018); State v. Love, 2017-Ohio-5688, ¶ 27, 2017 WL 2841683 (Ohio Ct. App. 6th Dist. Erie County 2017), appeal not allowed, 151 Ohio St. 3d 1457, 2017-Ohio-8842, 87 N.E.3d 223 (2017); State v. Dasen, 2017-Ohio-5556, ¶ 67, 2017 WL 2802235 (Ohio Ct. App. 9th Dist. Summit County 2017); State v. Armengau, 2017-Ohio-4452, ¶ 123, 93 N.E.3d 284, 317 (Ohio Ct. App. 10th Dist. Franklin County 2017), appeal not allowed, 151 Ohio St. 3d 1511, 2018-Ohio-365, 90 N.E.3d 950 (2018); State v. Craig, 2017-Ohio-4342, ¶ 9, 2017 WL 2616900 (Ohio Ct. App. 4th Dist. Athens County 2017), appeal not allowed, 151 Ohio St. 3d 1428, 2017-Ohio-8371, 84 N.E.3d 1065 (2017) and appeal not allowed, 152 Ohio St. 3d 1425, 2018-Ohio-923, 93 N.E.3d 1005 (2018).

[39]State v. Williams, 134 Ohio St. 3d 482, 2012-Ohio-5699, 983 N.E.2d 1245 (2012); State v. Whitfield, 124 Ohio St. 3d 319, 2010-Ohio-2, 922 N.E.2d 182 (2010) paragraph three of the syllabus; State v. Harmon, 2013-Ohio-1769, 2013 WL 1820895 (Ohio Ct. App. 9th Dist. Summit County 2013); State v. Ruff, 143 Ohio St. 3d 114, 2015-Ohio-995, 34 N.E.3d 892 (2015).

[40]State v. Thomas, 2011-Ohio-1191, ¶ 16, 2011 WL 882644 (Ohio Ct. App. 10th Dist. Franklin County 2011); State v. Taylor, 2014-Ohio-3647, 2014 WL 4176135 (Ohio Ct. App. 2d Dist. Montgomery County 2014); State v. Kerby, 2014-Ohio-3358, 2014

the question is whether it is possible to commit one offense and commit the other with the same conduct, not whether it is possible to commit one ***without*** committing the other.[41] If the offenses correspond to such a degree that the conduct of the defendant constituting commission of one offense constitutes commission of the other, then the offenses are of similar import.[42] If the offenses can be committed by the same conduct, then the court must determine whether the offenses ***were*** committed by the same conduct, i.e., a single act, committed with a single state of mind.[43] If the answer to both questions is yes, then the offenses are allied offenses of similar import and merge.[44] Conversely, if the court determines that the commission of one offense will ***never*** result in the commission of the other, or if the offenses are committed separately, or if the defendant has separate animus for each offense,[45] the offenses will not merge, and upon a finding of guilt, each may be independently sentenced.[46]

The court should utilize the same analysis if the defendant is found guilty of multiple charges of domestic violence[47] or multiple charges

WL 3809050 (Ohio Ct. App. 2d Dist. Clark County 2014).

[41]State v. Johnson, 128 Ohio St. 3d 153, 2010-Ohio-6314, 942 N.E.2d 1061 (2010); State v. Brautigam, 2012-Ohio-2599, 2012 WL 2128013 (Ohio Ct. App. 9th Dist. Summit County 2012); State v. Caudill, 2012-Ohio-2230, 2012 WL 1810189 (Ohio Ct. App. 2d Dist. Montgomery County 2012); State v. Ruff, 143 Ohio St. 3d 114, 2015-Ohio-995, 34 N.E.3d 892 (2015); State v. Cherryholmes, 2015-Ohio-3063, 2015 WL 4600546 (Ohio Ct. App. 5th Dist. Fairfield County 2015), appeal not allowed, 144 Ohio St. 3d 1460, 2016-Ohio-172, 44 N.E.3d 288 (2016) and cert. denied, 136 S. Ct. 2493, 195 L. Ed. 2d 824 (2016); State v. Warren, 2015-Ohio-604, 2015 WL 759145 (Ohio Ct. App. 8th Dist. Cuyahoga County 2015).

[42]R.C. 2941.25(A), State v. Johnson, 128 Ohio St. 3d 153, 2010-Ohio-6314, 942 N.E.2d 1061 (2010); State v. Brautigam, 2012-Ohio-2599, 2012 WL 2128013 (Ohio Ct. App. 9th Dist. Summit County 2012); State v. Caudill, 2012-Ohio-2230, 2012 WL 1810189 (Ohio Ct. App. 2d Dist. Montgomery County 2012).

[43]State v. Johnson, 128 Ohio St. 3d 153, 2010-Ohio-6314, 942 N.E.2d 1061 (2010); State v. Brautigam, 2012-Ohio-2599, 2012 WL 2128013 (Ohio Ct. App. 9th Dist. Summit County 2012); State v. Brown, 119 Ohio St. 3d 447, 2008-Ohio-4569, 895 N.E.2d 149 (2008); State v. Caudill, 2012-Ohio-2230, 2012 WL 1810189 (Ohio Ct. App. 2d Dist. Montgomery County 2012); State v. Asefi, 2012-Ohio-6101, 2012 WL 6697391 (Ohio Ct. App. 9th Dist. Summit County 2012); State v. Chisholm, 2012-Ohio-3932, 2012 WL 3731608 (Ohio Ct. App. 9th Dist. Summit County 2012); State v. Damron, 2012-Ohio-5977, 2012 WL 6632786 (Ohio Ct. App. 10th Dist. Franklin County 2012).

[44]State v. Johnson, 128 Ohio St. 3d 153, 2010-Ohio-6314, 942 N.E.2d 1061 (2010); State v. Brautigam, 2012-Ohio-2599, 2012 WL 2128013 (Ohio Ct. App. 9th Dist. Summit County 2012); State v. Caudill, 2012-Ohio-2230, 2012 WL 1810189 (Ohio Ct. App. 2d Dist. Montgomery County 2012); State v. Chisholm, 2012-Ohio-3932, 2012 WL 3731608 (Ohio Ct. App. 9th Dist. Summit County 2012); State v. Damron, 2012-Ohio-5977, 2012 WL 6632786 (Ohio Ct. App. 10th Dist. Franklin County 2012).

[45]R.C. 2941.25(B).

[46]State v. Johnson, 128 Ohio St. 3d 153, 2010-Ohio-6314, 942 N.E.2d 1061 (2010); State v. Brautigam, 2012-Ohio-2599, 2012 WL 2128013 (Ohio Ct. App. 9th Dist. Summit County 2012); State v. Ruff, 143 Ohio St. 3d 114, 2015-Ohio-995, 34 N.E.3d 892 (2015); State v. Cherryholmes, 2015-Ohio-3063, 2015 WL 4600546 (Ohio Ct. App. 5th Dist. Fairfield County 2015), appeal not allowed, 144 Ohio St. 3d 1460, 2016-Ohio-172, 44 N.E.3d 288 (2016) and cert. denied, 136 S. Ct. 2493, 195 L. Ed. 2d 824 (2016).

[47]State v. Slevin, 2012-Ohio-2043, 2012 WL 1647115 (Ohio Ct. App. 9th Dist. Summit County 2012); State v. Ross, 2012-Ohio-1389, 2012 WL 1076253 (Ohio Ct. App. 9th Dist. Summit County 2012).

involving domestic violence and assault,[48] or domestic violence and menacing by stalking,[49] or any combination of charges involving domestic violence and other offenses arising from the same set of facts. A trial court's judgment that fails to make such a determination is reversible, as it constitutes plain error.[50] Plain error exists where there is an obvious deviation from a legal rule that affected the outcome of the proceeding.[51] In regard to sentencing, the imposition of multiple sentences for allied offenses of similar import amounts to plain error, whether ordered to be served consecutively or concurrently.[52]

Q & A: The defendant was charged with domestic violence and felonious assault. The defendant was found not guilty on the felonious assault charge. He argues that the domestic violence charge should be dismissed on a theory of "reverse merger." Should the defendant's argument prevail?

No. It may be true that the charges of felonious assault and domestic violence would have merged had the jury found defendant guilty on each count. However, it does not follow, that an acquittal on the felonious assault charge necessitates an acquittal on the domestic violence charge. The elements of the felonious assault and the domestic violence charge against appellant were not the same such that an acquittal on one charge would necessarily lead to an acquittal on the other."[53]

Q & A: The defendant was convicted of domestic violence and felonious assault, involving the same facts and the same victim. Shouldn't the court be required to merge the two convictions?

No. Domestic violence and felonious assault are not allied offenses that require merger. Their elements do not correspond to such a degree that the commission of domestic violence necessarily results in the commission of felonious assault. Domestic violence may occur without a felonious assault, where the harm does not rise to the level of serious physical harm. Likewise, felonious assault may occur without domestic violence, where the victim is not a family or household member.[54]

---

[48]State v. Carner, 2012-Ohio-1190, 2012 WL 985906 (Ohio Ct. App. 8th Dist. Cuyahoga County 2012); State v. Waltzer, 2011-Ohio-5147, 2011 WL 4599828 (Ohio Ct. App. 8th Dist. Cuyahoga County 2011)

[49]State v. Lawson, 2012-Ohio-1050, 2012 WL 907913 (Ohio Ct. App. 8th Dist. Cuyahoga County 2012).

[50]State v. Carner, 2012-Ohio-1190, 2012 WL 985906 (Ohio Ct. App. 8th Dist. Cuyahoga County 2012); State v. Blakely, 2012-Ohio-3841, 2012 WL 3637371 (Ohio Ct. App. 2d Dist. Montgomery County 2012).

[51]Crim. R. 52(B); State v. Seymore, 2012-Ohio-3125, 2012 WL 2707965 (Ohio Ct. App. 12th Dist. Butler County 2012).

[52]State v. Seymore, 2012-Ohio-3125, 2012 WL 2707965 (Ohio Ct. App. 12th Dist. Butler County 2012).

[53]State v. Brown, 2015-Ohio-950, 2015 WL 1138651 (Ohio Ct. App. 11th Dist. Lake County 2015).

[54]R.C. 2941.25; State v. Sandridge, 2006-Ohio-5243, 2006 WL 2831024 (Ohio Ct. App. 8th Dist. Cuyahoga County 2006); State v. Clark, 2016-Ohio-2825, 2016 WL 2586638 (Ohio Ct. App. 8th Dist. Cuyahoga County 2016), appeal not allowed, 147 Ohio St. 3d 1474, 2016-Ohio-8438, 65 N.E.3d 778 (2016); State v. Povroznik,

Q & A: Aren't domestic violence and aggravated meaning allied offenses of similar import?

The Supreme Court of Ohio redefined "separate animus" in *State v. Ruff*.[55] The court currently holds that two or more offenses of dissimilar import exist within the meaning of R.C. 2941.25(B) when the defendant's conduct constitutes offenses involving separate victims or if the harm that results from each offense is separate and identifiable. Rather than compare the elements of two offenses to determine whether they are allied offenses of similar import, the analysis must focus on the defendant's conduct to determine whether one or more convictions may result because an offense may be committed in a variety of ways and the offenses committed may have different import. No bright-line rule can govern every situation.

As a practical matter, when determining whether offenses are allied offenses of similar import within the meaning of R.C. 2941.25, courts must ask three questions when defendant's conduct supports multiple offenses: (1) Were the offenses dissimilar in import or significance? (2) Were they committed separately? and (3) Were they committed with separate animus or motivation? An affirmative answer to any of the above will permit separate convictions. The conduct, the animus, and the import must all be considered.[56]

Q & A: At the conclusion of a trial for domestic violence where the defendant is charged with an assault on a stepfather, defendant contends that an instruction on the lesser included offense of disorderly conduct was warranted because there was no evidence that harm was caused or was attempted to be caused to the stepfather, since the stepfather did not testify at trial. Should the instruction be given?

It depends. If there is other sufficient evidence that establishes that the defendant caused or attempted to cause physical harm to the stepfather, such as testimony from an independent withness that establishes the elements of the offense, then the instruction should not be given.[57]

Additionally, the Supreme Court of Ohio holds that a charge on a lesser-included offense is required when the facts warrant it.[58] It is obviously difficult to reconcile these two concepts. On the one hand, an instruction is required if warranted by the evidence. Yet, on the other, the court has discretion to refuse to give it. Despite this apparent inconsistency, the Supreme Court made it clear that discretion remains a part of the standard of review. The Court holds that whether to give a jury instruction on a lesser-included offense lies within the discretion of the trial court and depends on whether the

---

2018-Ohio-1516, ¶ 26-27, 2018 WL 1882896 (Ohio Ct. App. 8th Dist. Cuyahoga County 2018).

[55]State v. Ruff, 143 Ohio St. 3d 114, 2015-Ohio-995, 34 N.E.3d 892 (2015), paragraph two of the syllabus and ¶ 30–31, respectively.

[56]State v. Ruff, 143 Ohio St. 3d 114, 2015-Ohio-995, 34 N.E.3d 892 (2015).

[57]State v. Jones, 2016-Ohio-2777, 2016 WL 1730646 (Ohio Ct. App. 12th Dist. Fayette County 2016).

[58]State v. Wine, 140 Ohio St. 3d 409, ¶ 20, 2014-Ohio-3948, 18 N.E.3d 1207 (2014).

evidence could reasonably support a jury finding of guilty on a lesser-included offense.[59]

In determining whether a particular offense should be submitted to the jury as a lesser included offense, the Ohio Supreme Court sets forth a two-tiered analysis.[60]

The first tier, also called the "statutory-elements step," is a purely legal question, wherein we determine whether one offense is generally a lesser included offense of the charged offense.[61]

The second tier looks to the evidence in a particular case and determines whether " 'a jury could reasonably find the defendant not guilty of the charged offense, but could convict the defendant of the lesser included offense.' " Only in the second tier of the analysis do the facts of a particular case become relevant.[62]

While the Supreme Court's two-tiered test for determining whether offenses constitute allied offenses of similar import is helpful in construing legislative intent it is not necessary to resort to that test when the legislature's intent is clear from the language of the statute.[63]

Q & A: Are domestic violence and intimidation of a witness allied offenses of similar import?

The Ohio Supreme Court holds that two or more offenses are of dissimilar import "when the defendant's conduct constitutes offenses involving separate victims or if the harm that results from each offense is separate and identifiable."[64] Therefore, offenses do not merge and a defendant may be convicted and sentenced for multiple offenses if any of the following are true: "(1) the offenses are dissimilar in import or significance * * *, (2) the offenses were committed separately, [or] (3) the offenses were committed with separate animus or motivation." This analysis may result in varying results for the same set of offenses in different cases. But different results are permissible, given that the statute instructs courts to examine a defendant's conduct—an inherently subjective determination.[65]

---

[59]State v. Bolden, 2016-Ohio-4727, 2016 WL 3573879 (Ohio Ct. App. 11th Dist. Lake County 2016), appeal not allowed, 147 Ohio St. 3d 1445, 2016-Ohio-7854, 63 N.E.3d 1215 (2016); State v. Hall, 2018-Ohio-1676, ¶ 28, 2018 WL 2028318 (Ohio Ct. App. 11th Dist. Trumbull County 2018).

[60]State v. Deanda, 136 Ohio St. 3d 18, 2013-Ohio-1722, 989 N.E.2d 986 (2013); State v. Powell, 2017-Ohio-5629, ¶ 48, 2017 WL 2857221 (Ohio Ct. App. 9th Dist. Summit County 2017), appeal not allowed, 152 Ohio St. 3d 1462, 2018-Ohio-1795, 97 N.E.3d 499 (2018); State v. Garrison, 2018-Ohio-1048, ¶ 34, 2018 WL 1433184 (Ohio Ct. App. 5th Dist. Muskingum County 2018), appeal not allowed, 153 Ohio St. 3d 1442, 2018-Ohio-2834, 102 N.E.3d 499 (2018); State v. Garrison, 2018-Ohio-463, ¶ 18, 2018 WL 704129 (Ohio Ct. App. 5th Dist. Muskingum County 2018), appeal denied, 153 Ohio St. 3d 1429, 2018-Ohio-2418, 100 N.E.3d 445 (2018).

[61]State v. Deanda, 136 Ohio St. 3d 18, 2013-Ohio-1722, 989 N.E.2d 986 (2013).

[62]State v. Deanda, 136 Ohio St. 3d 18, 2013-Ohio-1722, 989 N.E.2d 986 (2013).

[63]State v. Brown, 119 Ohio St. 3d 447, 2008-Ohio-4569, 895 N.E.2d 149, ¶ 37 (2008); State v. Craig, 2017-Ohio-4342, ¶ 42, 2017 WL 2616900 (Ohio Ct. App. 4th Dist. Athens County 2017), appeal not allowed, 151 Ohio St. 3d 1428, 2017-Ohio-8371, 84 N.E.3d 1065 (2017) and appeal not allowed, 152 Ohio St. 3d 1425, 2018-Ohio-923, 93 N.E.3d 1005 (2018).

[64]State v. Ruff, 143 Ohio St. 3d 114, 2015-Ohio-995, 34 N.E.3d 892, ¶ 23 (2015).

[65]State v. Ruff, 143 Ohio St. 3d 114, 2015-Ohio-995, 34 N.E.3d 892 (2015).

Most recently, the Ohio Supreme Court addressed the allied-offense issue.[66]

The *Earley* court considered a defendant's *conduct,* his *animus,* and the *import* or significance of his offenses. For purposes of analysis, it's noted that a defendant bears the burden of establishing entitlement to merger, and that an appellate court will review a trial court's ruling on the issue de novo.[67]

The Supreme Court of Ohio interprets the term 'animus' to mean 'purpose or, more properly, immediate motive.[68] The defendant must shoulder the burden of establishing that merger was required, because the offenses were committed with separate conduct and with a separate animus.[69]

§ 2:9 Penalties

Conviction of a first offense of domestic violence under either RC 2919.25(A) or RC 2919.25(B) carries the penalties of a first-degree misdemeanor. Maximum punishment under such a conviction is six months of incarceration and up to $1,000 in fines or both.[1]

Where there has been one prior conviction of domestic violence under RC 2919.25(A) or RC 2919.25(B), a substantially similar existing or former municipal ordinance or law of the state of Ohio or any other state of the United States, a new conviction under RC 2919.25(A) or RC 2919.25(B) carries fourth degree felony penalties of possible incarceration from six, seven, eight, nine, ten, 11, 12, 13, 14, 15, 16, 17, or 18 months.[2] Fines of up to $5,000.00, as well as other financial sanctions including restitution and reimbursements, may also be required.[3]

Where there have been two or more prior convictions of domestic violence under RC 2919.25(A) or RC 2919.25(B), a substantially simi-

---

[66]State v. Earley, 145 Ohio St. 3d 281, 2015-Ohio-4615, 49 N.E.3d 266 (2015); State v. Roberson, 2018-Ohio-1955, ¶ 17, 2018 WL 2277130 (Ohio Ct. App. 6th Dist. Lucas County 2018).

[67]State v. LeGrant, 2014-Ohio-5803, 2014 WL 7463132 (Ohio Ct. App. 2d Dist. Miami County 2014).).

[68]State v. Thomas, 2014-Ohio-2666, 2014 WL 2810643 (Ohio Ct. App. 2d Dist. Darke County 2014), quoting State v. Logan, 60 Ohio St. 2d 126, 131, 14 Ohio Op. 3d 373, 397 N.E.2d 1345 (1979).

[69]State v. Quinn, 2016-Ohio-139, 57 N.E.3d 379 (Ohio Ct. App. 2d Dist. Clark County 2016), appeal not allowed, 145 Ohio St. 3d 1447, 2016-Ohio-1596, 48 N.E.3d 585 (2016) and appeal reopened, 2017-Ohio-7000, 95 N.E.3d 664 (Ohio Ct. App. 2d Dist. Clark County 2017), appeal not allowed, 151Ohio St. 3d1457, 2017-Ohio-8842, 87 N.E.3d 224 (2017).

[Section 2:9]

[1]RC 2929.24(A)(1) and RC 2929.28(A)(1) to (2)(a)(i). See also 2003 S.B. 50.

[2]RC 2929.14(A)(4). See also 2003 S.B. 50. But, review State v. Montgomery, 159 Ohio App. 3d 752, 2005-Ohio-1018, 825 N.E.2d 250 (1st Dist. Hamilton County 2005), judgment aff'd in part, rev'd in part, 109 Ohio St. 3d 313, 2006-Ohio-2109, 847 N.E.2d 1174 (2006)(affirmed as to the holding regarding more than minimum sentences and reversed and remanded on the portion of the opinion regarding consecutive sentence); State v. Lowery, 160 Ohio App. 3d 138, 2005-Ohio-1181, 826 N.E.2d 340 (1st Dist. Hamilton County 2005).

[3]RC 2929.18(A)(3)(d). See also 2003 S.B. 50.

lar existing or former municipal ordinance or law of the state of Ohio or any other state of the United States, a new conviction under RC 2919.25(A) or RC 2919.25(B) carries third degree felony penalties of possible incarceration from one, two, three, four, up to five years and financial sanctions, including fines of up to $10,000, restitution and reimbursements.[4]

A first violation of RC 2919.25(C) carries the penalties of a fourth degree misdemeanor, to wit, up to 30 days in jail and up to $250 in fines, or both[5] as well as other financial sanctions, such as reparations.[6]

Where there has been one prior conviction of domestic violence under RC 2919.25(C), a substantially similar existing or former municipal ordinance or law of the state of Ohio or any other state of the United States, a subsequent conviction, when properly charged, carries the penalties of a second degree misdemeanor, to wit, up to 90 days in jail and up to $750 in fines, as well as other financial sanctions.[7]

Passage of Am. Sub. H.B. 280, effective January 6, 2009, resulted in significant changes in the sentencing of certain domestic violence offenders. As amended, the law now requires courts to impose a mandatory prison term on offenders who injure or attempt to injure qualifying family or household members or their unborn, who are pregnant at the time of the offense. If the offense is a fourth or fifth degree felony, the court must impose mandatory imprisonment of at least six months. If the violation is a fifth degree felony and the offender, in committing the violation, caused serious physical harm to the "pregnant woman's unborn"[8] or caused the "termination of the pregnant woman's pregnancy,"[9] the court must impose a mandatory prison term of 12 months. If the violation is a fourth degree felony and the offender, in committing the violation, caused serious physical harm to the "pregnant woman's unborn"[10] or caused the "termination of the pregnant woman's pregnancy,"[11] the court must impose a mandatory prison term of at least 12 months. If the violation is a third degree felony, except as otherwise described in the Felony Sentencing Law for a third degree felony, the court must impose a mandatory prison term of either a definite term of six months or one of the prison terms prescribed in the Felony Sentencing Law for third degree felonies, and if the violation is a third degree felony and the offender, in committing the violation, caused serious physical harm to the pregnant woman's unborn[12] or caused the termination of the pregnant woman's pregnancy,[13] notwithstanding the range of prison terms prescribed in the Felony Sentencing Law for a third degree

[4]RC 2929.14(A)(3), RC 2929.18(A)(3)(c). See also 2003 S.B. 50.

[5]RC 2929.21(B)(4).

[6]RC 2929.22.

[7]RC 2929.21(B)(2) and RC 2929.21(C)(2). See also 2003 S.B. 50.

[8]RC 2919.25(F)(3).

[9]RC 2919.25(F)(4).

[10]RC 2919.25(F)(3).

[11]RC 2919.25(F)(4).

[12]RC 2919.25(F)(3).

[13]RC 2919.25(F)(4).

felony, the court must impose a mandatory prison term of either a definite term of one year or one of the prison terms prescribed in the Felony Sentencing Law for third degree felonies.

If there have been two prior convictions of domestic violence under RC 2919.25(C), a substantially similar existing or former municipal ordinance or law of the state of Ohio or any other state of the United States, a subsequent conviction, when properly charged, carries the penalties of a first degree misdemeanor, to wit, up to 180 days in jail and up to $1000 in fines, in addition to possible other financial sanctions.[14]

Prosecutors charging offenders under the 1995 Senate Bill 2 sentencing matrix will find themselves challenged. An individual who is charged under the domestic violence statutes may or may not face stronger penalties for violations than an offender who is charged under some other section of the criminal code. Each charging decision, therefore, will ultimately be decided on its own facts and merits.

[14]RC 2929.21(B)(1) and RC 2929.22(C)(1). See also 2003 S.B. 50.

Chapter 3

Related Offenses and the Effect of Prior Convictions Under Ohio's Domestic Violence Law

§ 3:1 Why other crimes are mentioned in the domestic violence statutes

Accurately identifying just what constitutes domestic violence has always been a challenge. Many offenses that are actually outgrowths of domestic violence are reported as other crimes. A case involving a man who attempts to murder his wife and then to kill himself is not likely to be reported as domestic violence. The distraught boyfriend who kidnaps and beats his live-in lover when she indicates that their relationship is over is probably not going to be charged with domestic violence.

Nonetheless, these events are all inextricably intertwined in the web of domestic violence. The Ohio legislature recognized these interconnections, and, over the years, amended the state's domestic violence statutes to reflect the ubiquitous nature of violence in the home.

These amendments attempt to accomplish two primary purposes. First, they provide the victims of these related crimes, who are family or household members of an offender, access to protection orders. This access is the same access that these victims would have if the state charged the offender with domestic violence. Secondly, the amendments require the courts to recognize the special nature of the relationships between this class of offenders and this class of victims. Consideration of the relationship must figure prominently into any decision by the court. A court's failure to consider the relationship factors identified as crucial by the legislature potentially affects the safety and well-being of the parties, and of the public.

§ 3:2 Effect of certain prior convictions on new charges of domestic violence

When an offender previously convicted of committing certain crimes against a family or household member faces a new charge of domestic violence, the new charge will trigger special provisions of Ohio's domestic violence laws.[1] When invoked, these provisions serve three primary purposes:

(1) To require that courts undertake special consideration of, among other things, an offender's history of criminal assaults or threatening behavior against family or household members before setting bond and establishing other conditions of pretrial release.[2] This requirement supersedes the general preference for releasing most individuals accused of criminal acts on their own personal recognizance, or upon the execution of unsecured appearance bonds.[3]

(2) To provide the coverage of a protection order to the family or household members of an offender previously convicted of assaultive or threatening behavior against family or household members.[4]

(3) To provide a basis for enhancing the penalties which a court may impose upon an offender convicted of a new charge of domestic violence.[5]

Specifically, the other crimes that the domestic violence statutes reference are:

(1) simple assault (RC 2903.13),
(2) aggravated assault (RC 2903.12),
(3) felonious assault (RC 2903.11),
(4) aggravated trespass (RC 2911.211),
(5) menacing by stalking (RC 2903.211),
(6) negligent assault (RC 2903.14),
(7) aggravated menacing (RC 2903.21),
(8) menacing (RC 2903.22),
(9) endangering children (RC 2919.22), and
(10) violating a protection order or consent agreement (RC 2919.27, RC 2903.214).

Additionally, when the victim of the earlier offense was a family or

---

[Section 3:2]

[1]RC 2919.25, RC 2919.251, RC 2919.26, RC 2919.27.

[2]RC 2919.251(A), RC 2919.251(B).

[3]Crim. R. 46(C), Crim. R. 46(D); RC 2937.222(A).

[4]RC 2919.26(A)(1), RC 2919.27(B).

[5]RC 2919.25(D), RC 2919.27.

household member, a prior conviction for violation of an existing or former municipal ordinance or law of the state of Ohio or of any other state of the United States that is substantially similar to any of enhancing offenses referenced in Ohio's domestic violence statute,[6] will also activate these same provisions.

Q & A: My client has been charged with aggravated menacing against his wife. This is the first time that that he has ever had to appear in court in his life. The court has indicated that it is worried about the state of his mental health. Over my objection, the court ordered him to undergo a mental examination pursuant to RC 2919.271. Can the judge do that?

No. Under the facts that you present, i.e., that there was never a consent agreement or temporary protection order issued against your client, the court is without authority to refer your client for a mental health examination under RC 2917.271. The violation of a protection order is foundational to a mental health referral under RC 2925.271.[7]

Q & A: Several years ago, my client was convicted of an assault on the woman to whom he is now married. This occurred back when they first started dating. He called me from jail this morning. He and his wife got into a fight last night and he's been charged with domestic violence. What effect will the old conviction have on my ability to bail him out?

The answer to your question will probably depend as much on the judge that you and your client find yourselves before as any other factor. This is true because your client's wife apparently was not a family or household member at the time of the original conviction.

Since she did not fit the definition of a family or household member at the time of the prior conviction, the court is not *required* by the terms of RC 2919.251(A) to consider your client's previous conviction in setting bail in his new case. The key word in this analysis is *required*.

The court has the discretion to consider the factors found in RC 2919.251(A) in making its bail bond decision. It is not *required* to do so. Given your client's history, no prudent court is likely to exercise that discretion without conducting a thorough examination of the statutory factors.

Q & A: The domestic relations court issued a civil protection order against my client that prohibited him from entering the marital residence. I've just been notified that he was arrested there this morning as he attempted to get some tools from the garage. He has a conviction on his record for violating a civil protection order from about three years ago. That case involved a former girlfriend, not his current wife. What can I expect at the bail hearing this time?

Because your client has been convicted of violating a protection order in the past, the court must consider all of the following factors before bond can be set:

---

[6]RC 2919.25(D)(3). See 2003 S.B. 50.

[7]State v. Phillips, 1991 WL 2018 (Ohio Ct. App. 9th Dist. Lorain County 1991).

(1) Whether your client has a history of engaging in acts of domestic violence,[8]
(2) Whether your client has a history of engaging in other violent acts,[9]
(3) The current state of your client's mental health,[10]
(4) Whether your client has a history of violating court orders,[11]
(5) Whether your client has a history of violating the orders of any other governmental entity,[12]
(6) Whether your client is potentially a threat to any other person,[13] and
(7) Whether the setting of bond at a high level will interfere with any treatment or counseling that your client or a family or household member of your client is undergoing.[14]

Only after the court has weighed all of these factors, as well as any others that may be relevant, can it draw a conclusion as to what terms or conditions of release are reasonable under the circumstances.

It does not matter that the person covered by the current protection order is not the same person who was protected by the order that resulted in his other conviction. The fact that the prior conviction exists is enough to require the court to take into consideration the factors contained in RC 2919.251(A).

You should be aware that the nature of this charge may cause the court to require your client to undergo an evaluation of his current mental status. The mental health considerations contained in RC 2919.251(A)(2) must be read in conjunction with the provisions of RC 2919.271.

RC 2919.271 allows a court to order special evaluations of the mental condition of certain defendants charged with violating a protection order. The option of ordering a mental examination is available if the prosecution alleges that a protection order violation resulted in physical harm to the person or property of an offender's family or household member.

The option is also available to the court if it is alleged that a protection order violation caused a family or household member to believe that the offender would cause physical harm to his/her person or property. RC 2919.271 also outlines the procedures that the court must follow in obtaining the mental health evaluation.[15]

Q & A: It's Saturday morning and I've just learned that my son was arrested last night and charged today with domestic violence against his wife. I went to the jail to bail him out but the officer in charge of the jail said that my son can't be released, even though he's been charged, until he sees a judge on Monday morning. What's going on here?

---

[8] RC 2919.251(A)(1).

[9] RC 2919.251(A)(1).

[10] RC 2919.251(A)(2).

[11] RC 2919.251(B)(3).

[12] RC 2919.251(B)(3).

[13] RC 2919.251(B)(4).

[14] RC 2919.251(B)(6).

[15] RC 2919.271(C)(1), RC 2919.271(C)(2), RC 2919.271(D).

All individuals charged with violent offenses are now required to appear before a judge before they may be released on bail,[16] *if* the alleged offender and the alleged victim, at the time of the event, were family or household members *and* if one or more of the following circumstances applied:

(1) The alleged offender, at the time of the current charge, was already subject to the terms of a specified protection order or consent decree;[17]
(2) The alleged offender, at the time of the current charge, had previously pled guilty to or had been found guilty of a charge of domestic violence;[18]
(3) The alleged offender, at the time of the current charge, had previously pled guilty to violating a temporary protection order;[19]
(4) The alleged offender, at the time of the current charge, had previously pled guilty to or been found guilty of violating any substantially similar domestic violence or protection order statute or ordinance of Ohio, or any federal or other state entity, when such law had been enacted to prohibit domestic violence against, or to provide protection for, endangered family or household members;[20]
(5) The alleged offender, at the time of the current charge, had previously been convicted of criminal damaging or endangering, involving an individual who was a family or household member at that time;[21]
(6) The alleged offender, at the time of the current charge, had previously been convicted of criminal mischief, involving an individual who was a family or household member at that time;[22]
(7) The alleged offender, at the time of the current charge, had previously been convicted of burglary, involving an individual who was a family or household member at that time;[23]
(8) The alleged offender, at the time of the current charge, had previously been convicted of aggravated trespass, involving an individual who was a family or household member at that time;[24] or
(9) The alleged offender, at the time of the current charge, had previously been convicted of any other offense of violence, as that phrase is defined in the Ohio Revised Code, involving an individual who was a family or household member at that time.[25]

Even if none of the above applies to your son, he may still be

[16]RC 2919.251(A). See. 126 Ohio Am. Sub 2005 H.B. 29, eff. 8-26-2005.

[17]RC 2919.251(A)(1). See 126 Ohio Am. Sub 2005 H.B. 29, eff. 8-26-2005.

[18]RC 2919.251(A)(1). See 126 Ohio Am. Sub 2005 H.B. 29, eff. 8-26-2005.

[19]RC 2919.251(A)(1). See 126 Ohio Am. Sub 2005 H.B. 29, eff. 8-26-2005.

[20]RC 2919.251(A)(1). See 126 Ohio Am. Sub 2005 H.B. 29, eff. 8-26-2005.

[21]RC 2919.251(A)(1). See 126 Ohio Am. Sub 2005 H.B. 29, eff. 8-26-2005.

[22]RC 2919.251(A)(1). See 126 Ohio Am. Sub 2005 H.B. 29, eff. 8-26-2005.

[23]RC 2919.251(A)(1). See 126 Ohio Am. Sub 2005 H.B. 29, eff. 8-26-2005.

[24]RC 2919.251(A)(1). See 126 Ohio Am. Sub 2005 H.B. 29, eff. 8-26-2005.

[25]RC 2919.251(A)(1). See 126 Ohio Am. Sub 2005 H.B. 29, eff. 8-26-2005.

required to face a judicial officer before being released on bond, since the alleged victim of the offense is identified as a family or household member.[26]

Your son will be required to appear, if the arresting officer indicated any of the following in the complaint, or in any other document accompanying the complaint, that charges your son with the commission of an offense:[27]

(1) That the officer observed objective injury to the alleged victim of the offense.[28]

(2) That the officer believes that your son had a deadly weapon or dangerous ordnance on his person at the time of the offense.[29]

(3) That the officer believes that your son presents a credible threat of serious physical harm to the alleged victim or any other person, if he is released on bond before trial.[30]

If the court is presented with any of the foregoing factors, the law requires it to consider all of the items appearing in the earlier version of the domestic violence bail statute.[31]

In addition, the court is now also required to consider several additional factors that were not contained in the former law before making a decision setting the appropriate terms for pretrial release. These include:

(1) The defendant's access to and prior history of using deadly weapons.[32]

(2) Whether the defendant has a history of abusing alcohol or any controlled substance.[33]

(3) The severity of the alleged violence underlying the charge.[34]

(4) Whether the defendant and the alleged victim have recently separated or terminated a relationship, or whether such a separation or termination is pending.[35]

(5) Whether the defendant has exhibited excessive or controlling behaviors toward the alleged victim.[36]

(6) Whether the defendant has expressed suicidal or homicidal ideations.[37]

[26] RC 2919.251(A)(2). See 126 Ohio Am. Sub 2005 H.B. 29, eff. 8-26-2005.

[27] RC 2919.251(A)(2). See 126 Ohio Am. Sub 2005 H.B. 29, eff. 8-26-2005.

[28] RC 2919.251(A)(2)(a). See 126 Ohio Am. Sub 2005 H.B. 29, eff. 8-26-2005.

[29] RC 2919.251(A)(2)(b). See 126 Ohio Am. Sub 2005 H.B. 29, eff. 8-26-2005.

[30] RC 2919.251(A)(2)(c). See 126 Ohio Am. Sub 2005 H.B. 29, eff. 8-26-2005.

[31] RC 2919.251(B)(1) to RC 2919.251(B)(11). See 126 Ohio Am. Sub 2005 H.B. 29, eff. 8-26-2005.

[32] RC 2919.251(B)(5). See 126 Ohio Am. Sub 2005 H.B. 29, eff. 8-26-2005.

[33] RC 2919.251(B)(6). See 126 Ohio Am. Sub 2005 H.B. 29, eff. 8-26-2005.

[34] RC 2919.251(B)(7). See 126 Ohio Am. Sub 2005 H.B. 29, eff. 8-26-2005.

[35] RC 2919.251(B)(8). See 126 Ohio Am. Sub 2005 H.B. 29, eff. 8-26-2005.

[36] RC 2919.251(B)(9). See 126 Ohio Am. Sub 2005 H.B. 29, eff. 8-26-2005.

[37] RC 2919.251(B)(10). See 126 Ohio Am. Sub 2005 H.B. 29, eff. 8-26-2005.

Consideration of such information is, of course, dependent upon the information being made available to the court.[38]

The court is no longer required to consider whether setting bail at a high level will interfere with any treatment or counseling the alleged offender or the alleged offender's family might be undergoing.[39]

Since the jailer indicates that your son will have to await a hearing before the court on Monday, it would appear that the jurisdiction where your son is being held has not taken advantage of the statutory provisions allowing a court to establish a bail schedule for offenses of this type or the law's video conferencing option for handling these hearings.[40]

All of these new provisions notwithstanding, the law still invests great discretion in the courts in making decision concerning the appropriateness of bail. Thus, even as amended, the law allows a court the discretion to decide to admit an individual charged with a misdemeanor crime of violence against a family or household member to bail according to the terms of its bail schedule, without appearing before it, if the court concludes that it is not practicable for the individual to appear for a bail hearing.[41]

Even if the court has not established a bail schedule for these types of offenses, it may still, in its discretion, forego a bail hearing and have the defendant post either a 10% bail bond or a surety bond, at the defendant's option.[42]

Q & A: My girlfriend lives with me. Yesterday, she and I got into a fight. I hit her once and drew blood. Somebody called the police. The police have charged me with felony domestic violence. They say I'm being charged with a felony because I was convicted nine years ago of felonious assault on my sister. I've never been charged with domestic violence before. I thought the first time that you were charged with domestic violence it was a misdemeanor. How can they do this?

The enhancement provisions of RC 2919.25(D) require that the police charge you with a felony. Under the facts presented, you were previously convicted of committing one of the crimes enumerated in RC 2919.25(D) against an individual who was, at the time of the prior violation, a family or household member.

The crime of felony domestic violence is contained in the same section of the Revised Code as the crime of misdemeanor domestic violence.[43] Nonetheless, it is a distinct offense. It is the prior conviction or the pregnancy of the alleged family or household member victim[44] that transforms misdemeanor domestic violence into felony

---

[38]RC 2919.251(B)(5). See 126 Ohio Am. Sub 2005 H.B. 29, eff. 8-26-2005.

[39]See 126 Ohio Am. Sub 2005 H.B. 29, eff. 8-26-2005.

[40]RC 2919.251(C) and RC 2919.251 (D)(1). See 126 Ohio Am. Sub 2005 H.B. 29, eff. 8-26-2005.

[41]RC 2919.251(D)(2). See 126 Ohio Am. Sub 2005 H.B. 29, eff. 8-26-2005.

[42]RC 2919.251(D)(2)(a) and RC 2919.251(D)(2)(b). See 126 Ohio Am. Sub 2005 H.B. 29, eff. 8-26-2005.

[43]RC 2919.25(D).

[44]R.C. 2919.25(D)(5).

domestic violence.[45] As an essential element, the prior conviction or the pregnancy of the alleged family or household member victim[46] must appear in the information or indictment charging the felony offense. Failure to include this information in the charging document will result in the offense improperly retaining the character of a first degree misdemeanor. Such a lapse is a fatal flaw in the institution of the prosecution, since it changes the identity of the crime and is not capable of subsequent correction.[47]

This situation differs significantly from one where the existence of a prior conviction only has the effect of increasing the penalty which an offender will suffer if convicted of the new charge.[48] A comparison of the effect of a prior conviction for operating a motor vehicle while under the influence (DUI) on a subsequent charge for a similar violation illustrates this point. A violator previously convicted of DUI within the five years preceding a new charge alleging the same offense faces a mandatory increase in the penalty suffered, if convicted. However, the new charge remains a first degree misdemeanor and the maximum penalties which the court can impose remain the same.[49] The elements which the prosecution must prove to obtain a conviction are the same for both a first and a second offense. The prior conviction is not considered by the trier of fact to determine guilt or innocence, but, rather, is used by the court following conviction to determine the appropriate level of punishment, both required and allowed, within the range provided for crimes of that class.

In a felony charge, as part of its case in chief, the prosecution must prove the element of prior conviction or the pregnancy of the alleged family or household member victim[50], along with all others, beyond a reasonable doubt in order to obtain a conviction.[51]

Q & A: My client is charged with felony domestic violence based upon a prior conviction for assault against a live-in girlfriend two years ago. The victim this time is another woman with whom he is now staying. He tells me that he didn't have a lawyer when he entered the prior plea. Can I challenge the felony charge?

---

[45]State v. Allen, 29 Ohio St. 3d 53, 506 N.E.2d 199 (1987); State v. Waheed, 2016-Ohio-2951, 2016 WL 2841926 (Ohio Ct. App. 1st Dist. Hamilton County 2016); State v. Shaw, 2017-Ohio-1259, 2017 WL 1231741 (Ohio Ct. App. 7th Dist. Belmont County 2017); State v. Graham, 2016-Ohio-8503, 2016 WL 7626180 (Ohio Ct. App. 9th Dist. Medina County 2016); State v. Little, 2016-Ohio-8398, 78 N.E.3d 323 (Ohio Ct. App. 3d Dist. Allen County 2016); State v. Troyer, 2016-Ohio-3090, 2016 WL 2944812 (Ohio Ct. App. 5th Dist. Holmes County 2016); State v. Wood, 2018-Ohio-875, ¶ 33, 2018 WL 1225738 (Ohio Ct. App. 2d Dist. Clark County 2018), appeal not allowed, 153 Ohio St. 3d 1403, 2018-Ohio-2380, 100 N.E.3d 422 (2018) (*Wood's* case is factually distinguishable from State v. Troyer, 2016-Ohio-3090, 2016 WL 2944812 (Ohio Ct. App. 5th Dist. Holmes County 2016), a case on which he relies).

[46]R.C. 2919.25(D)(5).

[47]Crim. R. 7(B), Crim. R. 7(D).

[48]See State v. Smith, 2008-Ohio-4431, 2008 WL 4058121 (Ohio Ct. App. 12th Dist. Clermont County 2008).

[49]RC 4511.99(A)(1) to RC 4511.99(A)(4).

[50]R.C. 2919.25(D)(5).

[51]State v. Howell, 1995 WL 497638 (Ohio Ct. App. 5th Dist. Stark County 1995); State v. McArthur, 1987 WL 29400 (Ohio Ct. App. 8th Dist. Cuyahoga County 1987).

A charge of felony domestic violence based upon an uncounseled prior conviction may be collaterally attacked within the proceedings on the current offense *only* if the collateral attack concerns a violation of the defendant's right to counsel at the time that the prior conviction was obtained.[52]

The fact that a defendant was not represented by counsel at the time of a prior conviction, in and of itself, however, will not prevent the use of the prior conviction to enhance the current charge. The defendant must also show that actual imprisonment was imposed as a result of the prior conviction. It should be noted that suspended sentences amount to "actual imprisonment" where there is the possibility that there may be an actual deprivation of a person's liberty. Therefore, a suspended sentence constitutes a term of confinement in enhancement cases.[53]

The record also must indicate that the defendant was indigent or financially unable to obtain counsel at the time to void the use of the prior conviction for enhancement purposes in the present circumstances.[54] It is the defendant's burden to challenge an apparently constitutional prior conviction with prima facie evidence that he or she was not afforded the right to counsel previously.[55] Once a defendant raises the issue with prima facie evidence, the state has

[52]State v. O'Neill, 140 Ohio App. 3d 48, 2000-Ohio-2656, 746 N.E.2d 654 (7th Dist. Jefferson County 2000), citing Custis v. U.S., 511 U.S. 485, 487, 114 S. Ct. 1732, 128 L. Ed. 2d 517 (1994); State v. Brooke, 165 Ohio App. 3d 409, 2005-Ohio-6161, 846 N.E.2d 897 (11th Dist. Lake County 2005), judgment aff'd in part, rev'd in part on other grounds, 113 Ohio St. 3d 199, 2007-Ohio-1533, 863 N.E.2d 1024 (2007).

[53]See Alabama v. Shelton, 535 U.S. 654, 658, 122 S. Ct. 1764, 152 L. Ed. 2d 888 (2002); State v. Williams, 2002-Ohio-4244, 2002 WL 1902879 (Ohio Ct. App. 5th Dist. Licking County 2002); City of Parma v. Romain, 2006-Ohio-3952, 2006 WL 2170600 (Ohio Ct. App. 8th Dist. Cuyahoga County 2006); State v. Kelly, 154 Ohio App. 3d 285, 2003-Ohio-4783, 797 N.E.2d 104 (9th Dist. Medina County 2003).

[54]State v. Kelly, 154 Ohio App. 3d 285, 2003-Ohio-4783, 797 N.E.2d 104 (9th Dist. Medina County 2003). State v. Gerwin, 69 Ohio St. 2d 488, 491, 23 Ohio Op. 3d 420, 432 N.E.2d 828 (1982), citing Scott v. Illinois, 440 U.S. 367, 99 S. Ct. 1158, 59 L. Ed. 2d 383 (1979), and Baldasar v. Illinois, 446 U.S. 222, 100 S. Ct. 1585, 64 L. Ed. 2d 169 (1980) (overruled on other grounds by, Nichols v. U.S., 511 U.S. 738, 114 S. Ct. 1921, 128 L. Ed. 2d 745 (1994)); Cleveland v. Cooper-Hill, 2004-Ohio-6920, 2004 WL 2931001 (Ohio Ct. App. 8th Dist. Cuyahoga County 2004); State v. Noble, 2007-Ohio-7051, 2007 WL 4554247 (Ohio Ct. App. 9th Dist. Lorain County 2007).

[55]Robards v. Rees, 789 F.2d 379, 385–86 (6th Cir. 1986); State v. Wang, 1984 WL 13997, *6-7 (Ohio Ct. App. 1st Dist. Hamilton County 1984); State v. Roundtree, 1983 WL 5484, *14-16 (Ohio Ct. App. 8th Dist. Cuyahoga County 1983); State v. Brandon, 45 Ohio St. 3d 85, 86, 543 N.E.2d 501, 503 (1989). See also State v. Adams, 37 Ohio St. 3d 295, 297, 525 N.E.2d 1361, 1363 (1988); State v. Vales, 2000 WL 217802 (Ohio Ct. App. 8th Dist. Cuyahoga County 2000); State v. Johnson, 2005-Ohio-3997, 2005 WL 1845263 (Ohio Ct. App. 6th Dist. Huron County 2005); State v. Smith, 2011-Ohio-3206, 2011 WL 2557043 (Ohio Ct. App. 5th Dist. Stark County 2011); State v. Brooke, 113 Ohio St. 3d 199, 2007, 2007-Ohio-1533, 863 N.E.2d 1024 (2007); State v. Waheed, 2016-Ohio-2951, 2016 WL 2841926 (Ohio Ct. App. 1st Dist. Hamilton County 2016); State v. Troyer, 2016-Ohio-3090, 2016 WL 2944812 (Ohio Ct. App. 5th Dist. Holmes County 2016); State v. Wood, 2018-Ohio-875, ¶ 33, 2018 WL 1225738 (Ohio Ct. App. 2d Dist. Clark County 2018), appeal not allowed, 153 Ohio St. 3d 1403, 2018-Ohio-2380, 100 N.E.3d 422 (2018) (*Wood's* case is factually distinguishable from State v. Troyer, 2016-Ohio-3090, 2016 WL 2944812 (Ohio Ct. App. 5th Dist. Holmes County 2016), a case on which he relies).

the burden of proving the constitutional validity of the prior conviction. A silent record will not satisfy the state's burden of proof.[56]

Two important points need to be reiterated here: First, the United States Supreme Court's landmark decisions regarding criminal defendants' constitutional rights to counsel are directed only to those who are determined to be indigent.[57] Secondly, both the U.S. and Ohio Supreme Courts have held that an uncounseled misdemeanor conviction can still be used to enhance a subsequent misdemeanor into a felony, so long as no actual imprisonment was imposed as part of the sentence in the prior case.[58] It should be noted that one Ohio appellate court has held that even a suspended jail sentence constitutes the imposition of "actual imprisonment," so as to preclude the use of a prior conviction for enhancement purposes.[59]

The Ohio Supreme Court's ruling in *State v. Watkins*[60] may simplify or complicate the task of determining whether a defendant's prior plea was uncounseled, depending on one's point of view. Under the

---

[56]State v. Kelly, 154 Ohio App. 3d 285, 2003-Ohio-4783, 797 N.E.2d 104 (9th Dist. Medina County 2003). State v. Adams, 37 Ohio St. 3d 295, 525 N.E.2d 1361 (1988); State v. Brandon, 45 Ohio St. 3d 85, 543 N.E.2d 501 (1989); State v. Hopkins, 2000 WL 235539 (Ohio Ct. App. 9th Dist. Lorain County 2000); State v. Kiger, 2002-Ohio-7172, 2002 WL 31859444 (Ohio Ct. App. 7th Dist. Columbiana County 2002); State v. Maynard, 38 Ohio App. 3d 50, 52-53, 526 N.E.2d 316 (8th Dist. Cuyahoga County 1987); State v. Haas, 2010-Ohio-6249, 2010 WL 5289198 (Ohio Ct. App. 11th Dist. Portage County 2010); State v. Burkett, 2010-Ohio-6250, 2010 WL 5289260 (Ohio Ct. App. 11th Dist. Portage County 2010); State v. Waheed, 2016-Ohio-2951, 2016 WL 2841926 (Ohio Ct. App. 1st Dist. Hamilton County 2016).

[57]Gideon v. Wainwright, 372 U.S. 335, 83 S. Ct. 792, 9 L. Ed. 2d 799, 93 A.L.R.2d 733 (1963); Scott v. Illinois, 440 U.S. 367, 99 S. Ct. 1158, 59 L. Ed. 2d 383 (1979); Cleveland v. Cooper-Hill, 2004-Ohio-6920, 2004 WL 2931001 (Ohio Ct. App. 8th Dist. Cuyahoga County 2004); U.S. v. Vera-Garcia, 2011 WL 831174 (D.N.M. 2011); State v. Furr, 2018-Ohio-2205, ¶¶ 4-5, 2018 WL 2937866 (Ohio Ct. App. 1st Dist. Hamilton County 2018).

[58]State v. Kelly, 154 Ohio App. 3d 285, 2003-Ohio-4783, 797 N.E.2d 104 (9th Dist. Medina County 2003). State v. Gerwin, 69 Ohio St. 2d 488, 23 Ohio Op. 3d 420, 432 N.E.2d 828 (1982); State v. Williams, 2002-Ohio-4244, 2002 WL 1902879 (Ohio Ct. App. 5th Dist. Licking County 2002); Scott v. Illinois, 440 U.S. 367, 99 S. Ct. 1158, 59 L. Ed. 2d 383 (1979); Nichols v. U.S., 511 U.S. 738, 114 S. Ct. 1921, 128 L. Ed. 2d 745 (1994); U.S. v. Pollard 389 F.3d 101 (2004); Argersinger v. Hamlin, 407 U.S. 25, 37, 92 S. Ct. 2006, 32 L. Ed. 2d 530 (1972); Alabama v. Shelton, 535 U.S. 654, 122 S. Ct. 1764, 152 L. Ed. 2d 888 (2002); State v. Noble, 2007-Ohio-7051, 2007 WL 4554247 (Ohio Ct. App. 9th Dist. Lorain County 2007); Pittman v. U.S., 2011 WL 1085107 (S.D. Ga. 2011), report and recommendation adopted, 2011 WL 997018 (S.D. Ga. 2011); State v. Smith, 2011-Ohio-3206, 2011 WL 2557043 (Ohio Ct. App. 5th Dist. Stark County 2011); Cleveland v. Anderson, 2013-Ohio-165, 2013 WL 267088 (Ohio Ct. App. 8th Dist. Cuyahoga County 2013); State v. Waheed, 2016-Ohio-2951, 2016 WL 2841926 (Ohio Ct. App. 1st Dist. Hamilton County 2016).

[59]State v. Kelly, 154 Ohio App. 3d 285, 2003-Ohio-4783, 797 N.E.2d 104 (9th Dist. Medina County 2003). See also State v. Williams, 2002-Ohio-4244, 2002 WL 1902879 (Ohio Ct. App. 5th Dist. Licking County 2002), citing Alabama v. Shelton, 535 U.S. 654, 122 S. Ct. 1764, 152 L. Ed. 2d 888 (2002); U.S. v. Pollard 389 F.3d 101 (2004).

[60]State v. Watkins, 99 Ohio St. 3d 12, 2003-Ohio-2419, 788 N.E.2d 635 (2003). See also State v. Hull, 2003-Ohio-5306, 2003 WL 22284065 (Ohio Ct. App. 7th Dist. Mahoning County 2003); State v. Griffith, 2010-Ohio-5556, 2010 WL 4632607 (Ohio Ct. App. 10th Dist. Franklin County 2010); State v. Hill, 2016-Ohio-7524, 2016 WL 6393146 (Ohio Ct. App. 6th Dist. Wood County 2016); State, City of Twinsburg v. Milano, 2018-Ohio-1367, ¶ 10, 2018 WL 1750475 (Ohio Ct. App. 9th Dist. Summit County 2018).

reasoning announced in that case, "A judge's duty to a defendant before accepting his guilty or no contest plea is graduated according to the seriousness of the crime with which the defendant is charged. *** In all cases, the judge must inform the defendant of the effect of his plea.[61] In felony cases and misdemeanor cases involving serious offenses, a judge must also 'addres[s] the defendant personally' and 'determin[e] that the defendant is making the plea voluntarily.' "[62]

For felony defendants, and felony defendants only, therefore, the court must explain all the rights attendant to the trial that are relinquished by operation of the plea, including the right to counsel.[63]

The prior subsection of the rule that requires the court to explain the effect of the guilty or no contest plea to the defendant is not sufficient in felony prosecutions.[64]

The subsequent subsection of the rule is a separate part of the statute spelling out additional requirements in felony cases only that are not required in misdemeanor cases. In felony cases, the Ohio and United States Constitutions require that a defendant entering a guilty plea be "informed in a reasonable manner at the time of entering his guilty plea of his rights to a trial by jury and to confront his accusers, and his privilege against self-incrimination, and his right of compulsory process for obtaining witnesses on his behalf."[65] The Supreme Court of Ohio holds that courts must strictly comply with this rule.

---

[61]State v. Jones, 116 Ohio St. 3d 211, 2007-Ohio-6093, 877 N.E.2d 677 (2007); Cleveland v. Paramount Land Holdings, L.L.C., 2011-Ohio-3383, 2011 WL 2640236 (Ohio Ct. App. 8th Dist. Cuyahoga County 2011); State v. Guerriero, 2012-Ohio-5990, 2012 WL 6619273 (Ohio Ct. App. 7th Dist. Mahoning County 2012); State v. Crosby, 2012-Ohio-4130, 2012 WL 3939970 (Ohio Ct. App. 10th Dist. Franklin County 2012); State v. Jones, 2014-Ohio-5574, 2014 WL 7224690 (Ohio Ct. App. 2d Dist. Montgomery County 2014); State v. O'Rourke, 2015-Ohio-670, 2015 WL 782623 (Ohio Ct. App. 4th Dist. Athens County 2015); State v. Erdman, 2017-Ohio-1092, 2017 WL 1131929 (Ohio Ct. App. 12th Dist. Butler County 2017); State v. Cisler, 2016-Ohio-5016, 2016 WL 3919716 (Ohio Ct. App. 4th Dist. Washington County 2016); State, City of Twinsburg v. Milano, 2018-Ohio-1367, ¶ 8, 2018 WL 1750475 (Ohio Ct. App. 9th Dist. Summit County 2018); State v. Hill, 2018-Ohio-1345, ¶¶ 7-8, 2018 WL 1721859 (Ohio Ct. App. 3d Dist. Henry County 2018); State v. Moore, 2017-Ohio-8483, ¶¶ 14-15, 2017 WL 5197255 (Ohio Ct. App. 8th Dist. Cuyahoga County 2017), appeal not allowed, 152 Ohio St. 3d 1490, 2018-Ohio-2155, 99 N.E.3d 426 (2018); State v. Young, 2017-Ohio-8685, ¶¶ 10-11, 2017 WL 5664757 (Ohio Ct. App. 3d Dist. Henry County 2017); State v. Rieves, 2018-Ohio-955, ¶ 47, 2018 WL 1353213 (Ohio Ct. App. 8th Dist. Cuyahoga County 2018), cause dismissed, 2018-Ohio-3543, 2018 WL 4214842 (Ohio 2018).

[62]State v. Watkins, 99 Ohio St. 3d 12, 16, 2003-Ohio-2419, 788 N.E.2d 635, 638-39 (2003); Parma v. Buckwald, 2009-Ohio-4032, 2009 WL 2462626 (Ohio Ct. App. 8th Dist. Cuyahoga County 2009); State v. Griffith, 2010-Ohio-5556, 2010 WL 4632607 (Ohio Ct. App. 10th Dist. Franklin County 2010); State v. Hill, 2016-Ohio-7524, 2016 WL 6393146 (Ohio Ct. App. 6th Dist. Wood County 2016); State, City of Twinsburg v. Milano, 2018-Ohio-1367, ¶ 10, 2018 WL 1750475 (Ohio Ct. App. 9th Dist. Summit County 2018).

[63]Crim. R. 11(C)(2)(c).

[64]See Crim. R. 11(C)(2)(b). State v. McKenna, 2009-Ohio-6154, 2009 WL 4021197 (Ohio Ct. App. 11th Dist. Trumbull County 2009); State v. Battigaglia, 2010-Ohio-802, 2010 WL 746759 (Ohio Ct. App. 6th Dist. Ottawa County 2010); State v. Clarke, 2018-Ohio-176, 2018 WL 459831, ¶ 10 (Ohio Ct. App. 8th Dist. Cuyahoga County 2018), appeal not allowed, 152 Ohio St. 3d 1482, 2018-Ohio-1990, 98 N.E.3d 296 (2018).

[65]State v. Feckley, 2003-Ohio-3667, 2003 WL 21555109 (Ohio Ct. App. 8th Dist.

Although the trial court may vary slightly from the literal wording of the criminal rule governing the plea colloquy, the court cannot simply rely on other sources to convey the constitutional rights to the defendant. Therefore, substantial compliance will not suffice.[66] The

---

Cuyahoga County 2003); State v. Ballard, 66 Ohio St. 2d 473, 477, 20 Ohio Op. 3d 397, 423 N.E.2d 115, 118, 23 A.L.R.4th 241 (1981); State v. Veney, 120 Ohio St. 3d 176, 2008-Ohio-5200, 897 N.E.2d 621 (2008); State v. McKenna, 2009-Ohio-6154, 2009 WL 4021197 (Ohio Ct. App. 11th Dist. Trumbull County 2009); State v. Robinson, 2009-Ohio-2921, 2009 WL 1719359 (Ohio Ct. App. 6th Dist. Erie County 2009); State v. Martin, 2010-Ohio-244, 2010 WL 320475 (Ohio Ct. App. 8th Dist. Cuyahoga County 2010); State v. Truitt, 2011-Ohio-2271, 2011 WL 1842247 (Ohio Ct. App. 10th Dist. Franklin County 2011); State v. Pigge, 2010-Ohio-6541, 2010 WL 5621533 (Ohio Ct. App. 4th Dist. Ross County 2010); State v. Woods, 192 Ohio App. 3d 494, 2011-Ohio-727, 949 N.E.2d 574 (8th Dist. Cuyahoga County 2011); State v. Young, 2011-Ohio-4018, 2011 WL 3558105 (Ohio Ct. App. 11th Dist. Trumbull County 2011). But see also State v. Barker, 129 Ohio St. 3d 472, 2011-Ohio-4130, 953 N.E.2d 826 (2011); State v. Truitt, 2011-Ohio-2271, 2011 WL 1842247 (Ohio Ct. App. 10th Dist. Franklin County 2011); State v. Birch, 2012-Ohio-543, 2012 WL 441133 (Ohio Ct. App. 12th Dist. Butler County 2012); State v. Perry, 2012-Ohio-1566, 2012 WL 1154560 (Ohio Ct. App. 6th Dist. Lucas County 2012); State v. Bennett, 2012-Ohio-3664, 2012 WL 3517328 (Ohio Ct. App. 9th Dist. Summit County 2012); State v. Cline, 2014-Ohio-241, 2014 WL 279679 (Ohio Ct. App. 4th Dist. Pickaway County 2014); State v. Lewis, 2014-Ohio-4559, 2014 WL 5162885 (Ohio Ct. App. 9th Dist. Summit County 2014); State v. Stump, 2016-Ohio-2723, 2016 WL 1704760 (Ohio Ct. App. 8th Dist. Cuyahoga County 2016); State v. Davis, 2016-Ohio-1569, 2016 WL 1547066 (Ohio Ct. App. 6th Dist. Erie County 2016); State v. Sergent, 2015-Ohio-2603, 38 N.E.3d 461 (Ohio Ct. App. 11th Dist. Lake County 2015), judgment rev'd on other grounds, 148 Ohio St. 3d 94, 2016-Ohio-2696, 69 N.E.3d 627 (2016); State v. Shinn, 2015-Ohio-2994, 2015 WL 4528492 (Ohio Ct. App. 7th Dist. Mahoning County 2015); State v. Thomas, 2015-Ohio-2152, 2015 WL 3540469 (Ohio Ct. App. 8th Dist. Cuyahoga County 2015); State v. Hart, 2016-Ohio-1008, 2016 WL 962475 (Ohio Ct. App. 7th Dist. Belmont County 2016); State v. Studgions, 2016-Ohio-4701, 2016 WL 3571261 (Ohio Ct. App. 8th Dist. Cuyahoga County 2016); State v. Phillips, 2016-Ohio-4687, 69 N.E.3d 80 (Ohio Ct. App. 8th Dist. Summit County 2016); State v. McQuirt, 2016-Ohio-1095, 2016 WL 1071464 (Ohio Ct. App. 2d Dist. Montgomery County 2016); State v. Montgomery, 148 Ohio St. 3d 347, 2016-Ohio-5487, 71 N.E.3d 180 (2016), reconsideration granted in part, 147 Ohio St. 3d 1438, 2016-Ohio-7677, 63 N.E.3d 157 (2016); State v. Nierman, 2017-Ohio-672, 2017 WL 728358 (Ohio Ct. App. 6th Dist. Ottawa County 2017); State v. Studgions, 2016-Ohio-4701, 2016 WL 3571261 (Ohio Ct. App. 8th Dist. Cuyahoga County 2016); State v. Phillips, 2016-Ohio-4687, 69 N.E.3d 80 (Ohio Ct. App. 8th Dist. Summit County 2016); State v. Johnson, 2016-Ohio-7945, 2016 WL 6994318 (Ohio Ct. App. 10th Dist. Franklin County 2016), appeal not allowed, 150 Ohio St. 3d 1430, 2017-Ohio-7567, 81 N.E.3d 1271 (2017); State v. Sergent, 2015-Ohio-2603, 38 N.E.3d 461 (Ohio Ct. App. 11th Dist. Lake County 2015), judgment rev'd on other grounds, 148 Ohio St. 3d 94, 2016-Ohio-2696, 69 N.E.3d 627 (2016).

[66]State v. Veney, 120 Ohio St. 3d 176, 2008-Ohio-5200, 897 N.E.2d 621 (2008); State v. Rox, 2010-Ohio-5238, 2010 WL 4286182 (Ohio Ct. App. 8th Dist. Cuyahoga County 2010); State v. Young, 2011-Ohio-4018, 2011 WL 3558105 (Ohio Ct. App. 11th Dist. Trumbull County 2011); State v. Johnson, 2016-Ohio-7945, 2016 WL 6994318 (Ohio Ct. App. 10th Dist. Franklin County 2016), appeal not allowed, 150 Ohio St. 3d 1430, 2017-Ohio-7567, 81 N.E.3d 1271 (2017); State v. Rieves, 2018-Ohio-955, ¶ 42, 2018 WL 1353213 (Ohio Ct. App. 8th Dist. Cuyahoga County 2018), cause dismissed, 2018-Ohio-3543, 2018 WL 4214842 (Ohio 2018); State v. Moore, 2017-Ohio-8483, ¶¶ 14-17, 2017 WL 5197255 (Ohio Ct. App. 8th Dist. Cuyahoga County 2017), appeal not allowed, 152 Ohio St. 3d 1490, 2018-Ohio-2155, 99 N.E.3d 426 (2018); State v. Tribble, 2017-Ohio-4425, ¶¶ 7-8, 2017 WL 2665145 (Ohio Ct. App. 7th Dist. Mahoning County 2017); State v. Kennard, 2018-Ohio-2752, ¶ 15, 2018 WL 3414232 (Ohio Ct. App. 2d Dist. Montgomery County 2018); State v. Strimpel, 2018-Ohio-1628, ¶¶ 8-11, 2018 WL 1975769 (Ohio Ct. App. 8th Dist. Cuyahoga County 2018); State v. Bracey, 2018-Ohio-618, ¶¶ 14-16, 2018 WL 921962 (Ohio Ct. App. 6th Dist. Sandusky County

duties of the trial court under Crim.R. 11 have been distinguished as constitutional and non-constitutional rights.[67]

To comply with the constitutional requirements of Crim.R. 11, the court must explain to the defendant that he is waiving: (1) the Fifth Amendment privilege against self-incrimination, (2) the right to a trial by jury, (3) the right to confront one's accusers, (4) the right to compulsory process of witnesses, and (5) the right to be proven guilty beyond a reasonable doubt.[68] Failure to strictly comply with these constitutional requirements invalidates a guilty plea.[69] "Strict compliance" does not require a rote recitation of the exact language of the

---

2018); State v. Shannon, 2017-Ohio-9344, ¶ 20, 2017 WL 6729832 (Ohio Ct. App. 11th Dist. Trumbull County 2017), appeal not allowed, 152 Ohio St. 3d 1489, 2018-Ohio-2154, 99 N.E.3d 425 (2018); State v. Sheffey, 2017-Ohio-5634, ¶¶ 36-41, 2017 WL 2831258 (Ohio Ct. App. 11th Dist. Ashtabula County 2017).

[67]See State v. Parks, 2006-Ohio-1352, 2006 WL 726912 (Ohio Ct. App. 8th Dist. Cuyahoga County 2006), citing State v. Higgs, 123 Ohio App. 3d 400, 402, 704 N.E.2d 308 (11th Dist. Trumbull County 1997); State v. Gibson, 34 Ohio App. 3d 146, 147, 517 N.E.2d 990 (8th Dist. Cuyahoga County 1986); State v. Chandler, 2011-Ohio-590, 2011 WL 486471 (Ohio Ct. App. 8th Dist. Cuyahoga County 2011).

[68]State v. Nero, 56 Ohio St. 3d 106, 107-08, 564 N.E.2d 474 (1990), citing Boykin v. Alabama, 395 U.S. 238, 242-43, 89 S. Ct. 1709, 23 L. Ed. 2d 274 (1969); U.S. v. Diaz-Ramirez, 646 F.3d 653 (9th Cir. 2011); State v. Corpening, 2011-Ohio-6002, 2011 WL 5829679 (Ohio Ct. App. 11th Dist. Ashtabula County 2011); State v. Maggard, 2011-Ohio-4233, 2011 WL 3765523 (Ohio Ct. App. 1st Dist. Hamilton County 2011); State v. Davis, 2016-Ohio-1569, 2016 WL 1547066 (Ohio Ct. App. 6th Dist. Erie County 2016); State v. Studgions, 2016-Ohio-4701, 2016 WL 3571261 (Ohio Ct. App. 8th Dist. Cuyahoga County 2016); State v. McQuirt, 2016-Ohio-1095, 2016 WL 1071464 (Ohio Ct. App. 2d Dist. Montgomery County 2016); State v. DeJesus, 2015-Ohio-4111, 2015 WL 5782347 (Ohio Ct. App. 2d Dist. Greene County 2015); State v. Shinn, 2015-Ohio-2994, 2015 WL 4528492 (Ohio Ct. App. 7th Dist. Mahoning County 2015); State v. Nordstrom, 2015-Ohio-1454, 2015 WL 1737857 (Ohio Ct. App. 8th Dist. Cuyahoga County 2015), State v. Davis, 2016-Ohio-1569, 2016 WL 1547066 (Ohio Ct. App. 6th Dist. Erie County 2016); State v. Welch, 2017-Ohio-314, 81 N.E.3d 997 (Ohio Ct. App. 2d Dist. Clark County 2017); State v. Dean, 2016-Ohio-8422, 2016 WL 7626242 (Ohio Ct. App. 11th Dist. Trumbull County 2016); State v. Moore, 2017-Ohio-8483, ¶¶ 14-16, 2017 WL 5197255 (Ohio Ct. App. 8th Dist. Cuyahoga County 2017), appeal not allowed, 152 Ohio St. 3d 1490, 2018-Ohio-2155, 99 N.E.3d 426 (2018); State v. Tribble, 2017-Ohio-4425, ¶ 8, 2017 WL 2665145 (Ohio Ct. App. 7th Dist. Mahoning County 2017); State v. Kennard, 2018-Ohio-2752, ¶ 14, 2018 WL 3414232 (Ohio Ct. App. 2d Dist. Montgomery County 2018); State v. Strimpel, 2018-Ohio-1628, ¶ 10, 2018 WL 1975769 (Ohio Ct. App. 8th Dist. Cuyahoga County 2018); State, City of Twinsburg v. Milano, 2018-Ohio-1367, ¶ 11, 2018 WL 1750475 (Ohio Ct. App. 9th Dist. Summit County 2018); State v. Hill, 2018-Ohio-1345, ¶ 9, 2018 WL 1721859 (Ohio Ct. App. 3d Dist. Henry County 2018); State v. Rieves, 2018-Ohio-955, ¶ 42, 2018 WL 1353213 (Ohio Ct. App. 8th Dist. Cuyahoga County 2018), cause dismissed, 2018-Ohio-3543, 2018 WL 4214842 (Ohio 2018); State v. Royse, 2018-Ohio-352, ¶ 17, 2018 WL 582369 (Ohio Ct. App. 5th Dist. Ashland County 2018).

[69]See State v. Higgs, 123 Ohio App. 3d 400, 402, 704 N.E.2d 308 (11th Dist. Trumbull County 1997); State v. Stewart, 51 Ohio St. 2d 86, 88-89, 5 Ohio Op. 3d 52, 364 N.E.2d 1163 (1977); State v. Ballard, 66 Ohio St. 2d 473, 20 Ohio Op. 3d 397, 423 N.E.2d 115, 23 A.L.R.4th 241 (1981) (¶ 1 of syllabus); State v. Allen, 2009-Ohio-3799, 2009 WL 2374285 (Ohio Ct. App. 6th Dist. Sandusky County 2009); State v. Thayer, 2009-Ohio-5198, 2009 WL 3132946 (Ohio Ct. App. 6th Dist. Erie County 2009); Morrison v. Warden, Ross Correctional Inst., 2011 WL 2945838 (S.D. Ohio 2011), report and recommendation adopted, 2011 WL 2945836 (S.D. Ohio 2011); State v. Montgomery, 2014-Ohio-1789, 2014 WL 1692762 (Ohio Ct. App. 3d Dist. Putnam County 2014); State v. Stump, 2016-Ohio-2723, 2016 WL 1704760 (Ohio Ct. App. 8th Dist. Cuyahoga County 2016); State v. Davis, 2016-Ohio-1569, 2016 WL 1547066 (Ohio Ct. App. 6th

rule. Its focus instead is on whether the record shows that the judge explained the defendant's rights in a manner that was reasonably intelligible.[70]

Under the broader standard for the non-constitutional rights[71] reviewing courts consider whether the trial court substantially complied with the rule.[72] "Substantial compliance" means that under the totality of the circumstances the defendant subjectively understood the implications of his plea and the nature of the rights he was waiving.[73]

Criminal Rule 11(C) sets forth how a judge should explain those rights to a felony defendant. However, there are no such constitutionally mandated informational requirements for defendants charged with petty misdemeanors, which are defined as offenses for which the maximum punishment is no more than six months of imprisonment.[74]

Thus, the protections that the Criminal Rules provide to felony defendants do not shield those who are only charged with petty misdemeanor offenses. As a result, where a defendant is charged with a petty misdemeanor and pleads guilty or no contest, the trial court complies with Criminal Rule 11(E) by informing the defendant of the

Dist. Erie County 2016); State v. Studgions, 2016-Ohio-4701, 2016 WL 3571261 (Ohio Ct. App. 8th Dist. Cuyahoga County 2016); State v. DeJesus, 2015-Ohio-4111, 2015 WL 5782347 (Ohio Ct. App. 2d Dist. Greene County 2015); State v. Nierman, 2017-Ohio-672, 2017 WL 728358 (Ohio Ct. App. 6th Dist. Ottawa County 2017); State v. Studgions, 2016-Ohio-4701, 2016 WL 3571261 (Ohio Ct. App. 8th Dist. Cuyahoga County 2016); State v. Davis, 2016-Ohio-1569, 2016 WL 1547066 (Ohio Ct. App. 6th Dist. Erie County 2016); State v. Dean, 2016-Ohio-8422, 2016 WL 7626242 (Ohio Ct. App. 11th Dist. Trumbull County 2016); State v. Stump, 2016-Ohio-2723, 2016 WL 1704760 (Ohio Ct. App. 8th Dist. Cuyahoga County 2016).

[70]State v. Ballard, 66 Ohio St. 2d 473, 20 Ohio Op. 3d 397, 423 N.E.2d 115, 23 A.L.R.4th 241 (1981); State v. Bobbitt, 2013-Ohio-5067, 2013 WL 6056231 (Ohio Ct. App. 6th Dist. Erie County 2013); State v. Rieves, 2018-Ohio-955, ¶ 40, 2018 WL 1353213 (Ohio Ct. App. 8th Dist. Cuyahoga County 2018), cause dismissed, 2018-Ohio-3543, 2018 WL 4214842 (Ohio 2018); State v. Royse, 2018-Ohio-352, ¶¶ 14-15, 2018 WL 582369 (Ohio Ct. App. 5th Dist. Ashland County 2018); State v. Moore, 2017-Ohio-8483, ¶ 15, 2017 WL 5197255 (Ohio Ct. App. 8th Dist. Cuyahoga County 2017), appeal not allowed, 152 Ohio St. 3d 1490, 2018-Ohio-2155, 99 N.E.3d 426 (2018); State v. Sheffey, 2017-Ohio-5634, ¶¶ 40-41, 2017 WL 2831258 (Ohio Ct. App. 11th Dist. Ashtabula County 2017).

[71]Crim.R. 11(C)(2)(a), (b). State v. McKenna, 2009-Ohio-6154, 2009 WL 4021197 (Ohio Ct. App. 11th Dist. Trumbull County 2009).

[72]State v. Stewart, 51 Ohio St. 2d 86, 88-89, 5 Ohio Op. 3d 52, 364 N.E.2d 1163 (1977); State v. Nero, 56 Ohio St. 3d 106, 107-08, 564 N.E.2d 474 (1990); State v. Bocanegra, 2009-Ohio-3202, 2009 WL 1864037 (Ohio Ct. App. 6th Dist. Sandusky County 2009); State v. Rieves, 2018-Ohio-955, ¶ 39, 2018 WL 1353213 (Ohio Ct. App. 8th Dist. Cuyahoga County 2018), cause dismissed, 2018-Ohio-3543, 2018 WL 4214842 (Ohio 2018); State v. Royse, 2018-Ohio-352, ¶ 14, 2018 WL 582369 (Ohio Ct. App. 5th Dist. Ashland County 2018); State v. Moore, 2017-Ohio-8483, ¶¶ 27-28, 2017 WL 5197255 (Ohio Ct. App. 8th Dist. Cuyahoga County 2017), appeal not allowed, 152 Ohio St. 3d 1490, 2018-Ohio-2155, 99 N.E.3d 426 (2018); State v. Strimpel, 2018-Ohio-1628, ¶ 10, 2018 WL 1975769 (Ohio Ct. App. 8th Dist. Cuyahoga County 2018).

[73]State v. Stewart, 51 Ohio St. 2d 86, 88-89, 5 Ohio Op. 3d 52, 364 N.E.2d 1163 (1977); State v. Nero, 56 Ohio St. 3d 106, 107-08, 564 N.E.2d 474 (1990); State v. Wiley, 2008-Ohio-5266, 2008 WL 4519024 (Ohio Ct. App. 8th Dist. Cuyahoga County 2008).

[74]See Crim. R. 11(E).

effect of his or her plea, and nothing more. A defendant who receives this minimal information, and who thereafter waives the right to counsel will be deemed, under the Ohio Supreme Court's interpretation of the Criminal Rules, to have done so knowingly and intelligently.[75] A waiver under these circumstances renders the conviction available to the prosecution for use in enhancing a subsequent charge of domestic violence to a felony violation.

Finally, if the state is able to show that the defendant knowingly, voluntarily and intelligently waived his right to counsel at the time of the prior conviction, the defendant's conviction will not be deemed to be uncounseled and it is likewise available for felony enhancement purposes.[76]

Ohio's adoption of the Defense of Marriage Amendment to its Constitution temporarily effected the operation of the enhancement provisions of the state's domestic violence laws in at least one appellate district.[77] In that district, the court held that a motion to dismiss a complaint charging a defendant with felony domestic violence for assaulting her "live-in boyfriend" was properly granted by the trial court. The decision, however, was subsequently reversed by the Supreme Court of Ohio.[78]

Q & A: Can an adjudication of juvenile delinquency for domestic violence be used to enhance a defendant's sentence, following a subsequent conviction for domestic violence?

The simple answer is yes. Nonetheless, the question does raise several noteworthy issues. Prior to January 1, 1996, juvenile offenders' adjudications were not classified as convictions and could not be used to enhance the penalty of a subsequent adult conviction.[79] The Ohio statute treating prior juvenile adjudications as the equivalent of adult convictions to enhance either the degree of or the sentence for subsequent offenses committed as adults was held to violate due process.[80] The Ohio General Assembly changed the law with respect to

[75]State v. Watkins, 99 Ohio St. 3d 12, 2003-Ohio-2419, 788 N.E.2d 635 (2003).

[76]State v. Carrion, 84 Ohio App. 3d 27, 31, 616 N.E.2d 261, 264 (9th Dist. Lorain County 1992); State v. Vales, 2000 WL 217802 (Ohio Ct. App. 8th Dist. Cuyahoga County 2000); State v. Blasdell, 155 Ohio App. 3d 423, 2003-Ohio-6392, 801 N.E.2d 853 (7th Dist. Mahoning County 2003); State v. Ocasio, 2003-Ohio-6240, 2003 WL 22764145 (Ohio Ct. App. 2d Dist. Montgomery County 2003); State v. Johnson, 2005-Ohio-3997, 2005 WL 1845263 (Ohio Ct. App. 6th Dist. Huron County 2005); State v. Starett, 2009-Ohio-744, 2009 WL 405908 (Ohio Ct. App. 4th Dist. Athens County 2009); State v. Baker, 2009-Ohio-111, 2009 WL 81279 (Ohio Ct. App. 9th Dist. Summit County 2009).

[77]State v. Ward, 166 Ohio App. 3d 188, 2006, 2006-Ohio-1407, 849 N.E.2d 1076 (2d Dist. Greene County 2006), judgment rev'd, 114 Ohio St. 3d 430, 2007-Ohio-4552, 872 N.E.2d 1212 (2007).

[78]See In re Ohio Domestic-Violence Statute Cases, 114 Ohio St. 3d 430, 2007-Ohio-4552, 872 N.E.2d 1212 (2007).

[79]See, for instance, State v. Blogna, 60 Ohio App. 3d 141, 573 N.E.2d 1223 (5th Dist. Stark County 1990) (superseded by statute as stated in State v. Adkins, 129 Ohio St. 3d 287, 2011-Ohio-3141, 951 N.E.2d 766 (2011)) with *Adkins* holding that state constitutional prohibition on retroactive statutes did not preclude application of statute allowing a prior juvenile adjudication to be considered a prior criminal offense for purposes of enhancing OVI charge.

[80]State v. Hand, 149 Ohio St. 3d 94, 2016-Ohio-5504, 73 N.E.3d 448 (2016), cert.

the effect of juvenile adjudications on subsequent offenses to allow for enhancements on subsequent offenses. This statute, however, was found unconstitutional by the Ohio Supreme Court. The Ohio Supreme Court found that Ohio Revised code 2901.08(A) violates the Due Process Clauses of Article l, Section 16 of the Ohio Constitution and the Fourteenth Amendment to the United States Constitution because it is fundamentally unfair to treat a juvenile adjudication as a previous conviction that enhances wither the degree of or the sentence for a subsequent offense committed as an adult. Because a juvenile adjudication is not established through a procedure that provides the right to a jury trial, it cannot be used to increase a sentence beyond a statutory maximum or mandatory minimum.

However, in another section of the Revised Code any ambiguity is clarified. That section provides that juvenile courts may enhance penalties following a subsequent juvenile adjudication of an enhanceable offense.[81]

Under the additional section, following adjudication of a child's delinquency at the dispositional hearing and prior to making any disposition, the court must determine whether the delinquent child previously was adjudicated delinquent for a previous violation of a law or ordinance. If the child was previously adjudicated a delinquent, the court, for purposes of entering an order of disposition in the pending case is required to consider the previous adjudication as a conviction in determining the degree of the offense the current violation would be had it been committed by an adult.[82]

Thus, a juvenile court, during the dispositional phase of its hearing, is allowed to treat prior adjudications as convictions for purposes of determining the degree of offense a juvenile's current violation would be if committed by an adult.[83]

Generally, the law does not permit a criminal defendant to attack a previous conviction in a subsequent case. An adjudication of juvenile delinquency is no exception.[84] There is an exception, however, when the state proposes to use the past conviction to enhance the penalty of a later criminal offense.[85] In that situation, a defendant may attack the constitutionality of a prior conviction if it was obtained in violation of the defendant's Sixth Amendment right to counsel.[86]

An uncounseled conviction cannot be used to enhance the penalty

---

denied, 137 S. Ct. 1074, 197 L. Ed. 2d 179 (2017).

[81]RC 2152.16(C).

[82]RC 2152.16(C).

[83]See In re M.A.L., 2007-Ohio-2426, 2007 WL 1454164 (Ohio Ct. App. 2d Dist. Miami County 2007).

[84]State v. Baker, 2009-Ohio-111, 2009 WL 81279 (Ohio Ct. App. 9th Dist. Summit County 2009); State v. Bewley, 2007-Ohio-7026, 2007 WL 4554150 (Ohio Ct. App. 9th Dist. Summit County 2007); State v. Brooke, 113 Ohio St. 3d 199, 2007-Ohio-1533, 863 N.E.2d 1024 (2007); State v. Troyer, 2016-Ohio-3090, 2016 WL 2944812 (Ohio Ct. App. 5th Dist. Holmes County 2016); State v. Waheed, 2016-Ohio-2951, 2016 WL 2841926 (Ohio Ct. App. 1st Dist. Hamilton County 2016).

[85]State v. Baker, 2009-Ohio-111, 2009 WL 81279 (Ohio Ct. App. 9th Dist. Summit County 2009); State v. Brooke, 113 Ohio St. 3d 199, 2007-Ohio-1533, 863 N.E.2d 1024 (2007).

[86]State v. Baker, 2009-Ohio-111, 2009 WL 81279 (Ohio Ct. App. 9th Dist. Summit

for a later conviction if the earlier conviction resulted in a sentence of confinement.[87] The Supreme Court of Ohio has held that uncounseled convictions, obtained without a valid waiver of the Sixth Amendment right to counsel, are "constitutionally infirm."[88]

If a defendant questions the use of a prior conviction based on his having entered an uncounseled plea in the earlier case, the burden is on the defendant to make "a prima-facie showing of constitutional infirmity."[89] In order to meet that burden, the defendant must present evidence showing that his earlier plea was uncounseled and resulted in a sentence of confinement.[90] Then the burden shifts to the state to prove the defendant's right to counsel was properly waived.[91] In order to meet its burden, the state must prove there was a knowing, voluntary, and intelligent waiver of the defendant's Sixth Amendment right to counsel.[92]

The Supreme Court of Ohio has held that "any waiver of counsel must be made on the record in open court."[93] A knowing, voluntary, and intelligent waiver cannot be presumed from a silent record.[94] Accordingly, the record must show, or there must be an allegation and

---

County 2009); State v. Brooke, 113 Ohio St. 3d 199, 2007-Ohio-1533, 863 N.E.2d 1024 (2007); State v. Williams, 197 Ohio App. 3d 505, 2011-Ohio-6267, 968 N.E.2d 27 (1st Dist. Hamilton County 2011); State v. Waheed, 2016-Ohio-2951, 2016 WL 2841926 (Ohio Ct. App. 1st Dist. Hamilton County 2016); State v. Torman, 2016-Ohio-748, 2016 WL 770598 (Ohio Ct. App. 3d Dist. Putnam County 2016).

[87]State v. Baker, 2009-Ohio-111, 2009 WL 81279 (Ohio Ct. App. 9th Dist. Summit County 2009); State v. Brooke, 113 Ohio St. 3d 199, 2007-Ohio-1533, 863 N.E.2d 1024 (2007), citing Nichols v. U.S., 511 U.S. 738, 749, 114 S. Ct. 1921, 128 L. Ed. 2d 745 (1994); State v. Williams, 197 Ohio App. 3d 505, 2011-Ohio-6267, 968 N.E.2d 27 (1st Dist. Hamilton County 2011).

[88]State v. Baker, 2009-Ohio-111, 2009 WL 81279 (Ohio Ct. App. 9th Dist. Summit County 2009); State v. Brooke, 113 Ohio St. 3d 199, 2007-Ohio-1533, 863 N.E.2d 1024 (2007), citing State v. Brandon, 45 Ohio St. 3d 85, 86, 543 N.E.2d 501 (1989); Nichols v. U.S., 511 U.S. 738, 749, 114 S. Ct. 1921, 128 L. Ed. 2d 745 (1994); State v. Williams, 197 Ohio App. 3d 505, 2011-Ohio-6267, 968 N.E.2d 27 (1st Dist. Hamilton County 2011).

[89]State v. Baker, 2009-Ohio-111, 2009 WL 81279 (Ohio Ct. App. 9th Dist. Summit County 2009); State v. Brooke, 113 Ohio St. 3d 199, 2007-Ohio-1533, 863 N.E.2d 1024 (2007), citing State v. Brandon, 45 Ohio St. 3d 85, 543 N.E.2d 501(1989) (at syllabus); State v. Anderson, 2012-Ohio-4476, 2012 WL 4475345 (Ohio Ct. App. 5th Dist. Stark County 2012); State v. Drager, 2014-Ohio-3056, 2014 WL 3407874 (Ohio Ct. App. 2d Dist. Montgomery County 2014).

[90]State v. Baker, 2009-Ohio-111, 2009 WL 81279 (Ohio Ct. App. 9th Dist. Summit County 2009); State v. Brooke, 113 Ohio St. 3d 199, 2007-Ohio-1533, 863 N.E.2d 1024 (2007); State v. Troyer, 2016-Ohio-3090, 2016 WL 2944812 (Ohio Ct. App. 5th Dist. Holmes County 2016).

[91]State v. Baker, 2009-Ohio-111, 2009 WL 81279 (Ohio Ct. App. 9th Dist. Summit County 2009); State v. Brooke, 113 Ohio St. 3d 199, 2007-Ohio-1533, 863 N.E.2d 1024 (2007).

[92]State v. Baker, 2009-Ohio-111, 2009 WL 81279 (Ohio Ct. App. 9th Dist. Summit County 2009); State v. Brooke, 113 Ohio St. 3d 199, 2007-Ohio-1533, 863 N.E.2d 1024 (2007); State v. Bewley, 2007-Ohio-7026, 2007 WL 4554150 (Ohio Ct. App. 9th Dist. Summit County 2007); State v. Adkins, 2011-Ohio-5360, 2011 WL 4917042 (Ohio Ct. App. 4th Dist. Scioto County 2011).

[93]State v. Baker, 2009-Ohio-111, 2009 WL 81279 (Ohio Ct. App. 9th Dist. Summit County 2009); State v. Brooke, 113 Ohio St. 3d 199, 2007-Ohio-1533, 863 N.E.2d 1024 (2007).

[94]State v. Baker, 2009-Ohio-111, 2009 WL 81279 (Ohio Ct. App. 9th Dist. Summit

evidence which shows, that an accused was offered counsel but intelligently and understandingly rejected the offer. Anything less is not waiver.[95]

§ 3:3 Elements and penalties—Felonious assault under RC 2903.11

A confrontation between family or household members that results in major injury or the use of a potentially deadly instrument is likely to result in the more serious charge of felonious assault rather than the less serious charge of domestic violence. The elements of felonious assault are:

(1) knowingly
  (a) causing serious physical harm to another, or
  (b) causing or attempting to cause physical harm to another by use of a deadly weapon or dangerous ordnance,
(2) within an appropriate venue of the state of Ohio.

The penalties associated with a charge of felonious assault vary depending on two factors:

(1) whether the offender has previously been convicted of any of the assaultive behaviors set forth in the Revised Code, and
(2) whether the victim is a peace officer as defined in RC 2935.01.

The penalties associated with a charge of felonious assault are those of a second degree felony, to wit:

(1) a prison term of two, three, four, five, six, seven, or eight years[1] as well as
(2) up to $15,000 in fines.[2]

During its 2008-2009 Session, Ohio's General Assembly attempted to provide additional protections for pregnant women and the fetuses that they carry.[3] Under the penalty provisions contained in the bill, trial courts are required to impose mandatory sentences on certain offenders convicted of felonious assault. Thus, if the offender committed felonious assault against a women that he or she knew was pregnant at the time of the assault, the court is required to impose a definite mandatory prison term of at least six months or, in the alternative, mandate one of the higher prison terms prescribed by the Revised

---

County 2009); State v. Brooke, 113 Ohio St. 3d 199, 2007-Ohio-1533, 863 N.E.2d 1024 (2007), citing State v. Wellman, 37 Ohio St. 2d 162, 66 Ohio Op. 2d 353, 309 N.E.2d 915 (1974) (at ¶ 2 of syllabus); State v. Jackson, 2015-Ohio-1694, 2015 WL 1966236 (Ohio Ct. App. 3d Dist. Seneca County 2015).

[95]State v. Baker, 2009-Ohio-111, 2009 WL 81279 (Ohio Ct. App. 9th Dist. Summit County 2009); State v. Brooke, 113 Ohio St. 3d 199, 2007-Ohio-1533, 863 N.E.2d 1024 (2007), quoting State v. Wellman, 37 Ohio St. 2d 162, 66 Ohio Op. 2d 353, 309 N.E.2d 915 (1974) (paragraph 2 of syllabus), citing Carnley v. Cochran, 369 U.S. 506, 82 S. Ct. 884, 8 L. Ed. 2d 70 (1962); Berghuis v. Thompkins, 560 U.S. 370, 130 S. Ct. 2250, 176 L. Ed. 2d 1098 (2010).

[Section 3:3]

[1]RC 2929.14(A)(2).

[2]RC 2929.18(A)(3)(b).

[3]Am. Sub. H.B. 280, eff. Apr. 7, 2009.

Code for felonies of the same degree as the violation.[4] If a mandatory prison term is imposed upon an offender, the offender is required by law to serve the mandatory prison term consecutively to any other mandatory prison term imposed, either before, at the same time as or even after the imposition of the mandatory term resulting from the pregnancy specification.[5] These mandatory sentencing provisions are precluded unless the pregnancy specification appears at the end of the body of the charging document, substantially in the form provided by statute, and the offender is convicted of the pregnancy specification and the offense.[6]

Domestic violence arrests often result in charges that a peace officer has been assaulted.[7] The elements which must be proved when an assault, an aggravated assault, or a felonious assault is allegedly committed against a peace officer are the same as those for any other assault, aggravated assault, or felonious assault. The penalties for such conduct, however, are significantly more severe. If a peace officer or an investigator of the bureau of criminal identification and investigation[8] is the victim of a felonious assault, the offense may be charged as a felony of the first degree,[9] carrying possible penalties of

(1) three, four, five, six, seven, eight, nine, or ten years, and
(2) a fine, not to exceed $20,000.[10]

If the prosecution alleges and proves that a felonious assault committed against a peace officer or investigator of the bureau of criminal identification and investigation[11] resulted in serious physical harm to the victim, conviction of the offense also requires the court to impose a mandatory jail term of not less than three, nor more than ten years.[12]

There is no differentiation made between an officer who is on duty and one who is not.[13] This raises an interesting, and currently unresolved, question: What penalty should a court impose upon an offender convicted of assaultive behavior against a family or household member who also happens to be an off-duty peace officer or investigator for the bureau of criminal identification and investigation[14] at the time of the violation?

Q & A: The prosecutor has charged my client with felonious assault against his wife, instead of domestic violence. When we go to trial, can I get the court to charge the jury on the lesser included offense of domestic violence?

---

[4]RC 2929.14(D)(1) to (3).

[5]RC 2929.14(E)(1).

[6]RC 2941.1423.

[7]RC 2903.11, RC 2903.12, RC 2903.13.

[8]RC 2935.01(B); RC 2903.11(E)(6).

[9]RC 2903.11(D)(1)(a) reads, in pertinent part, "If the victim of (felonious assault) is a peace officer or an investigator for the bureau of criminal identification and investigation, felonious assault is a felony of the first degree."

[10]RC 2929.18(A)(3)(a).

[11]RC 2935.01(B); RC 2903.11(E)(6).

[12]RC 2903.11(D)(1)(b).

[13]See RC 2903.11(D)(1)(a), (b).

[14]RC 2935.01(B); RC 2903.11(E)(6).

Your question assumes that the crime of domestic violence is a lesser included offense of felonious assault.

In order for an offense to be a lesser included offense of another, it must:

(1) carry a penalty lesser than the greater offense;

(2) always be committed when the greater offense is committed, except, generally, in statutes like felonious assault, in which one element of the offense can be satisfied by proving either that the defendant actually committed the offense or, alternatively, attempted to commit it, in which case, the court should look at each alternative separately.[15] The theory is that a criminal statute written in the alternative creates a separate offense for each alternative and, therefore, when looking at a statute containing alternative elements, each statutory alternative should be construed as constituting a separate offense and analyzed accordingly as separate statutes would;[16] and

(3) lack some element necessary for the commission of the greater offense.[17]

A comparison of the felonious assault and the domestic violence statutes reveals that domestic violence is not a lesser included offense of felonious assault. Using the test employed by the Ohio Supreme Court,[18] the validity of this conclusion is illustrated as follows:

(1) Does the charge of domestic violence carry a penalty which is lesser than the penalty for felonious assault?

Yes. Depending on the facts and circumstances of the particular

---

[15]See Whalen v. U.S., 445 U.S. 684, 694, 100 S. Ct. 1432, 63 L. Ed. 2d 715 (1980). See also Pandelli v. U.S., 635 F.2d 533, 537 (6th Cir. 1980).

[16]State v. Smith, 117 Ohio St. 3d 447, 2008-Ohio-1260, 884 N.E.2d 595 (2008), on reconsideration, 121 Ohio St. 3d 409, 2009-Ohio-787, 905 N.E.2d 151 (2009); State v. Zima, 102 Ohio St. 3d 61, 2004-Ohio-1807, 806 N.E.2d 542 (2004); State v. Jackson, 2011-Ohio-3079, 2011 WL 2519512 (Ohio Ct. App. 10th Dist. Franklin County 2011); State v. Houston, 2017-Ohio-1122, 87 N.E.3d 797 (Ohio Ct. App. 10th Dist. Franklin County 2017).

[17]State v. Kidder, 32 Ohio St. 3d 279, 513 N.E.2d 311 (1987); State v. Barnes, 94 Ohio St. 3d 21, 2002-Ohio-68, 759 N.E.2d 1240 (2002); State v. Dotson, 2002-Ohio-1132, 2002 WL 391690, *3 (Ohio Ct. App. 5th Dist. Stark County 2002); State v. Blasdell, 155 Ohio App. 3d 423, 2003-Ohio-6392, 801 N.E.2d 853 (7th Dist. Mahoning County 2003); State v. Ocasio, 2003-Ohio-6240, 2003 WL 22764145 (Ohio Ct. App. 2d Dist. Montgomery County 2003); State v. Diles, 2004-Ohio-6368, 2004 WL 2715626 (Ohio Ct. App. 5th Dist. Morrow County 2004); Lynch v. Hudson, 2009 WL 483325 (S.D. Ohio 2009); State v. Underwood, 124 Ohio St. 3d 365, 2010-Ohio-1, 922 N.E.2d 923 (2010); State v. Deanda, 136 Ohio St. 3d 18, 2013-Ohio-1722, 989 N.E.2d 986 (2013); State v. English, 2014-Ohio-89, 2014 WL 117396 (Ohio Ct. App. 10th Dist. Franklin County 2014); Cleveland Hts. v. Cohen, 2015-Ohio-1636, 31 N.E.3d 695 (Ohio Ct. App. 8th Dist. Cuyahoga County 2015).

[18]State v. Kidder, 32 Ohio St. 3d 279, 513 N.E.2d 311 (1987); State v. Deem, 40 Ohio St. 3d 205, 533 N.E.2d 294 (1988) (holding modified by, State v. Smith, 117 Ohio St. 3d 447, 2008-Ohio-1260, 884 N.E.2d 595 (2008)); see also State v. McKinzie, 2001 WL 604212, *3 (Ohio Ct. App. 10th Dist. Franklin County 2001); see also State v. Dotson, 2002-Ohio-1132, 2002 WL 391690 (Ohio Ct. App. 5th Dist. Stark County 2002); State v. Compton, 153 Ohio App. 3d 512, 2003-Ohio-4080, 794 N.E.2d 771 (1st Dist. Hamilton County 2003); State v. Payton, 2003-Ohio-6860, 2003 WL 22966837 (Ohio Ct. App. 5th Dist. Stark County 2003); State v. Trimble, 122 Ohio St. 3d 297, 2009-Ohio-2961, 911 N.E.2d 242 (2009); State v. Andrews, 2010-Ohio-3864, 2010 WL 3260047 (Ohio Ct. App. 8th Dist. Cuyahoga County 2010).

case, domestic violence carries the penalties of either a first degree misdemeanor or, at a maximum, a fifth degree felony. Again, depending on the circumstances, felonious assault is charged as either a second degree felony or first degree felony. Thus, the first part of the Supreme Court's test is met.

(2) Can felonious assault, as defined by statute, ever be committed without committing domestic violence, as defined by statute?

Yes. For example, an offender can commit the offense of felonious assault against a total stranger. An act of domestic violence, on the other hand, can only be committed against a person who is a family or household member of the person who commits the act. Clearly, domestic violence does not qualify as a lesser included offense of felonious assault by this measure.[19]

(3) Does the offense of domestic violence lack some element necessary for the commission of the offense of felonious assault?

Yes. Both domestic violence and felonious assault involve acts which attempt to cause, or cause, some form of bodily injury. The distinguishing characteristic of felonious assault is its far greater likelihood of damaging effects on an intended victim.

Thus, the elements of causing or attempting to cause *serious* physical harm,[20] or of causing *any* physical harm to a victim by means of a *deadly weapon or dangerous ordnance*,[21] required to prove a charge of felonious assault are not required to prove either misdemeanor or felony domestic violence.[22]

It would be error for a trial court to charge a jury on domestic violence as a lesser included offense of felonious assault.[23]

Q & A: My husband and I got into a fight. During the fight, somehow, his arm was broken. I've been charged with both domestic violence and felonious assault. There was only one fight. How can they do that?

Prior to June 1999, the case law in Ohio established a two-part test that a court was required to resort to when faced with an allegation that two or more crimes charged subject to the multiple-count statute were allied offenses of similar import.[24] The first prong of the test was to compare the elements of the two offenses to determine whether

---

[19]State v. Daniel, 1996 WL 11268 (Ohio Ct. App. 10th Dist. Franklin County 1996).

[20]RC 2903.11(A)(1).

[21]RC 2903.11(A)(2).

[22]RC 2919.25(A), RC 2919.25(C).

[23]State v. Daniel, 1996 WL 11268 (Ohio Ct. App. 10th Dist. Franklin County 1996).

[24]City of Newark v. Vazirani, 48 Ohio St. 3d 81, 549 N.E.2d 520 (1990) (overruled by, State v. Rance, 85 Ohio St. 3d 632, 1999-Ohio-291, 710 N.E.2d 699 (1999)); State v. Jackson, 2011-Ohio-3079, 2011 WL 2519512 (Ohio Ct. App. 10th Dist. Franklin County 2011); State v. Hipshire, 2011-Ohio-3863, 2011 WL 3371496 (Ohio Ct. App. 2d Dist. Darke County 2011); State v. Carner, 2012-Ohio-1190, 2012 WL 985906 (Ohio Ct. App. 8th Dist. Cuyahoga County 2012); State v. Swiergosz, 197 Ohio App. 3d 40, 2012-Ohio-830, 965 N.E.2d 1070 (6th Dist. Lucas County 2012); State v. Worth, 2012-Ohio-666, 2012 WL 554457 (Ohio Ct. App. 10th Dist. Franklin County 2012);

they corresponded to such a degree that the commission of one resulted in the commission of the other. The court was then required to proceed to the second prong of the test and determine whether each of the crimes was committed separately or with a separate animus. If the two prongs of the test were met, the offenses were allied offenses of similar import, and the defendant could only be convicted of one of them.

On June 16, 1999, however, the Ohio Supreme Court overruled *Newark* in *State v. Rance*.[25] *Rance* established that the applicable test for determining whether two offenses are of similar import for purposes of the multiple-count statute is as follows: if the elements of the crimes correspond to such a degree that the commission of one crime will result in the commission of the other, the crimes are allied offenses of similar import, but if the elements do not so correspond, the offenses are of dissimilar import, the court's inquiry ends, and multiple convictions are permitted. The Ohio Supreme Court's decision in *Rance*[26] permitted trial courts to convict and impose cumulative sentences for two or more offenses that arose from the same incident, if the offenses (1) were of dissimilar import; or (2) were of similar import, but were committed separately or with separate animus.[27]

In 2010, however, the Ohio Supreme Court reversed field again,

State v. Carver, 2011-Ohio-5955, 2011 WL 5822719 (Ohio Ct. App. 2d Dist. Montgomery County 2011); State v. Sutphin, 2011-Ohio-5157, 2011 WL 4600412 (Ohio Ct. App. 8th Dist. Cuyahoga County 2011); State v. Murphy, 2011-Ohio-3686, 2011 WL 3210042 (Ohio Ct. App. 8th Dist. Cuyahoga County 2011); State v. Lemmons, 2011-Ohio-3322, 2011 WL 2586486 (Ohio Ct. App. 5th Dist. Delaware County 2011); State v. Dority, 2011-Ohio-2438, 2011 WL 1991758 (Ohio Ct. App. 6th Dist. Erie County 2011).

[25]State v. Rance, 85 Ohio St. 3d 632, 1999-Ohio-291, 710 N.E.2d 699 (1999) (overruled by, State v. Johnson, 128 Ohio St. 3d 153, 2010-Ohio-6314, 942 N.E.2d 1061 (2010)); State v. Palmer, 148 Ohio App. 3d 246, 2002-Ohio-3536, 772 N.E.2d 726 (1st Dist. Hamilton County 2002) (abrogated by, State v. Cabrales, 118 Ohio St. 3d 54, 2008-Ohio-1625, 886 N.E.2d 181 (2008)) and (overruled by, State v. Madaris, 2008-Ohio-2470, 2008 WL 2152691 (Ohio Ct. App. 1st Dist. Hamilton County 2008)) and on reconsideration, 178Ohio App. 3d192, 2008-Ohio-4604, 897 N.E.2d 224 (1st Dist. Hamilton County 2008), judgment vacated, 124Ohio St. 3d282, 2010-Ohio-224, 921 N.E.2d 649 (2010); State v. Cox, 2003-Ohio-1935, 2003 WL 1889479 (Ohio Ct. App. 4th Dist. Adams County 2003); State v. Bates, 2002-Ohio-5512, 2002 WL 31296867 (Ohio Ct. App. 12th Dist. Fayette County 2002); State v. Brown, 2002-Ohio-277, 2002 WL 91088 (Ohio Ct. App. 2d Dist. Montgomery County 2002); State v. Edwards, 2013-Ohio-1290, 2013 WL 1294635 (Ohio Ct. App. 11th Dist. Lake County 2013); State v. Craig, 2017-Ohio-4342, 2017 WL 2616900 (Ohio Ct. App. 4th Dist. Athens County 2017), appeal not allowed, 151 Ohio St. 3d 1428, 2017-Ohio-8371, 84 N.E.3d 1065 (2017) and appeal not allowed, 152 Ohio St. 3d 1425, 2018-Ohio-923, 93 N.E.3d 1005 (2018); State v. Taylor, 2016-Ohio-5912, 2016 WL 5118653 (Ohio Ct. App. 5th Dist. Richland County 2016); State v. Norris, 2016-Ohio-5381, 2016 WL 4362859 (Ohio Ct. App. 5th Dist. Licking County 2016), appeal not allowed, 148 Ohio St. 3d 1411, 2017-Ohio-573, 69 N.E.3d 751 (2017); State v. Clark, 2016-Ohio-2825, 2016 WL 2586638 (Ohio Ct. App. 8th Dist. Cuyahoga County 2016), appeal not allowed, 147 Ohio St. 3d 1474, 2016-Ohio-8438, 65 N.E.3d 778 (2016).

[26]State v. Rance, 85 Ohio St. 3d 632, 1999-Ohio-291, 710 N.E.2d 699 (1999) (overruled by, State v. Johnson, 128 Ohio St. 3d 153, 2010-Ohio-6314, 942 N.E.2d 1061 (2010)).

[27]State v. Rance, 85 Ohio St. 3d 632, 636, 1999-Ohio-291, 710 N.E.2d 699 (1999) (overruled by, State v. Johnson, 128 Ohio St. 3d 153, 2010-Ohio-6314, 942 N.E.2d 1061 (2010)); State v. Edwards, 2013-Ohio-1290, 2013 WL 1294635 (Ohio Ct. App.

holding that "In 1999, when we decided [State v. Rance], we intended to create a test of ready application that would produce clear, predictable results with regard to allied offenses. [Citation omitted.] Unfortunately, the standard announced in *Rance* has proven difficult to apply. We take this opportunity to overrule *Rance*. In doing so, we return to the mandate of R.C. 2941.25, which instructs courts to consider whether a defendant's conduct constituted two or more allied offenses of similar import."[28]

In Ohio, one court that addressed this issue found that domestic violence and felonious assault are not the same offense and that, since the elements of those crimes do not correspond, it was not necessary to reach the second tier of the *Newark* analysis.[29] That court also held that domestic violence and felonious assault are not allied offenses of similar import. The court based its conclusions upon a determination that each of the two offenses contains an element that is distinct from the elements contained in the other.

Under this reasoning, the prosecution is within its rights to bring charges against you for both domestic violence and felonious assault growing out of the same conduct.

Q & A: The evidence presented in a jury trial before my court appears insufficient. I'm inclined to amend the indictment from felonious assault to the lesser included offense of domestic violence, and to submit the case to the jury on the charge as amended. Can I do that?

No. The court has the right to amend an indictment, information, complaint, or bill of particulars with respect to any defect, imperfection, or omission in form or substance, or any variance with the evidence at any time before, during, or even after trial, as long as the amendment does not change the name or the identity of the offense as originally charged.[30] The action that you propose, however, does change the name of the offense charged, since domestic violence is neither a lesser included offense nor the same crime as felonious assault.[31] It would be erroneous for you to amend the charge before you in the manner that you are suggesting.

11th Dist. Lake County 2013).

[28]State v. Johnson, 128 Ohio St. 3d 153, 2010-Ohio-6314, 942 N.E.2d 1061 (2010). See also State v. Lee, 190 Ohio App. 3d 581, 2010-Ohio-5672, 943 N.E.2d 602 (3d Dist. Crawford County 2010), appeal allowed, judgment vacated, 128 Ohio St. 3d 501, 2011-Ohio-1960, 946 N.E.2d 756 (2011); State v. Marrero, 2011-Ohio-1390, 2011 WL 1049294 (Ohio Ct. App. 10th Dist. Franklin County 2011); State v. Small, 2011-Ohio-4086, 2011 WL 3612206 (Ohio Ct. App. 5th Dist. Delaware County 2011); State v. Overton, 2011-Ohio-4204, 2011 WL 3669374 (Ohio Ct. App. 10th Dist. Franklin County 2011); State v. S.S., 2014 WL 6851969 (Ohio Ct. App. 10th Dist. Franklin County 2014).

[29]State v. Chitwood, 83 Ohio App. 3d 443, 615 N.E.2d 257 (1st Dist. Hamilton County 1992); see also State v. Thomas, 1989 WL 147652 (Ohio Ct. App. 8th Dist. Cuyahoga County 1989), dismissed, 52 Ohio St. 3d 702, 556 N.E.2d 526 (1990).

[30]Crim. R. 7(D); State v. Rihm, 101 Ohio App. 3d 626, 656 N.E.2d 372 (2d Dist. Clark County 1995); City of Toledo v. Montgomery, 2002-Ohio-1872, 2002 WL 597360 (Ohio Ct. App. 6th Dist. Lucas County 2002). But see City of Cleveland v. Jenkins, 2002-Ohio-6046, 2002 WL 31492631 (Ohio Ct. App. 8th Dist. Cuyahoga County 2002).

[31]State v. Chitwood, 83 Ohio App. 3d 443, 615 N.E.2d 257 (1st Dist. Hamilton County 1992); State v. Thomas, 1989 WL 147652 (Ohio Ct. App. 8th Dist. Cuyahoga County 1989), dismissed, 52 Ohio St. 3d 702, 556 N.E.2d 526 (1990).

Q & A: In a trial where a common-law husband is charged with felonious assault against his common-law wife, the defense requests a charge to the jury on the lesser included offense of aggravated menacing. Assuming that there are some facts in evidence that would support the charge, should the court comply with the request?

No. Aggravated menacing is not a lesser included offense of felonious assault. Each offense contains an element that the other does not.[32]

To find an offender guilty of aggravated menacing, it must be shown that the offender caused the victim to believe that the offender would cause serious physical harm to the person or property of the victim, or a member of the victim's immediate family.[33]

To find an offender guilty of felonious assault, the prosecution must prove that the offender actually attempted to cause or caused the victim *serious* physical harm by any means,[34] or attempted to cause or caused the victim *any* physical harm by means of a *deadly weapon or dangerous ordnance*.[35]

Q & A: When a defendant has been found guilty of allied offenses of similar import, should a trial court impose concurrent sentences for each of the charges on which the defendant is found guilty?

No. The statute governing multiple counts prohibits the imposition of multiple sentences in such cases.[36] Therefore, a trial court must merge the crimes into a single conviction and impose a sentence that is appropriate for the offense chosen for sentencing.[37]

Q & A: I'm confused. Since the Supreme Court of Ohio has gone back and forth on the issue, how do I determine when allied offenses are of similar import and merge?

In determining whether offenses are allied offenses of similar import under R.C. 2941.25(A), the question is whether it is possible to commit one offense and commit the other with the same conduct, not whether it is possible to commit one without committing the other. If the offenses correspond to such a degree that the conduct of the defendant constituting commission of one offense constitutes commission of the other, then the offenses are of similar import.[38]

If the offenses can be committed by the same conduct, then it must

---

[32]State v. Brown, 1982 WL 5220 (Ohio Ct. App. 8th Dist. Cuyahoga County 1982); State v. Spires, 1983 WL 3577 (Ohio Ct. App. 10th Dist. Franklin County 1983).

[33]RC 2903.21.

[34]RC 2903.11(A)(1).

[35]RC 2903.11(A)(2).

[36]R.C. 2941.25.

[37]State v. Damron, 129 Ohio St. 3d 86, 2011-Ohio-2268, 950 N.E.2d 512 (2011); State v. Jones, 2012-Ohio-2694, 2012 WL 2236740 (Ohio Ct. App. 3d Dist. Allen County 2012); State v. Linzy, 2014-Ohio-1738, 2014 WL 1673123 (Ohio Ct. App. 5th Dist. Richland County 2014).

[38]State v. Johnson, 128 Ohio St. 3d 153, 2010-Ohio-6314, 942 N.E.2d 1061 (2010); State v. White, 2011-Ohio-2364, 2011 WL 1988324 (Ohio Ct. App. 10th Dist. Franklin County 2011).

be determined whether the offenses were committed by the same conduct, i.e., a single act, committed with a single state of mind. If the answer to both questions is yes, then the offenses are allied offenses of similar import and will be merged.[39] Conversely, if the court determines that the commission of one offense will never result in the commission of the other, or if the offenses are committed separately, or if the defendant has separate animus for each offense, then, according to R.C. 2941.25(B), the offenses will not merge.[40]

§ 3:4 Elements and penalties—Aggravated assault under RC 2903.12

In many instances of emotional confrontation, where one family or household member commits a more serious assault against another, charges of aggravated assault follow. Like domestic violence, aggravated assault *is not* a lesser included offense of felonious assault.[1]

The distinction between felonious assault and aggravated assault is that the latter offense contains the mitigating element of a serious provocation of the offender caused by some action of the victim.[2] The culpability of the victim in the injury which the offender inflicts, or attempts to inflict, is a factor considered by the law. The victim's provocation does not serve as a justification for the offender's assaultive actions. However, it does put any injury that the victim suffers in context and diminishes the harshness of the view that the law otherwise takes regarding such acts.

The elements of aggravated assault are:

(1) while under the influence of sudden passion or in a sudden fit of rage,

(2) brought on by serious provocation occasioned by the victim reasonably sufficient to incite the offender to use deadly force,

(3) knowingly,

  (a) cause serious harm to another or to another's unborn child, or

  (b) cause or attempt to cause physical harm to another or to

---

[39]State v. Johnson, 128 Ohio St. 3d 153, 2010-Ohio-6314, 942 N.E.2d 1061 (2010); State v. White, 2011-Ohio-2364, 2011 WL 1988324 (Ohio Ct. App. 10th Dist. Franklin County 2011).

[40]State v. Johnson, 128 Ohio St. 3d 153, 2010-Ohio-6314, 942 N.E.2d 1061 (2010); State v. White, 2011-Ohio-2364, 2011 WL 1988324 (Ohio Ct. App. 10th Dist. Franklin County 2011).

[Section 3:4]

[1]State v. Deem, 40 Ohio St. 3d 205, 533 N.E.2d 294 (1988) (holding modified by, State v. Smith, 117 Ohio St. 3d 447, 2008-Ohio-1260, 884 N.E.2d 595 (2008)) (modifying court holding when a statute sets forth mutually exclusive ways of committing the greater offense, a court is required to apply the second part of the test for determining whether an offense is a lesser included offense to each alternative method of committing the greater offense); see also State v. Thomas, 1989 WL 147652 (Ohio Ct. App. 8th Dist. Cuyahoga County 1989), dismissed, 52 Ohio St. 3d 702, 556 N.E.2d 526 (1990); State v. Alvey, 2003-Ohio-7006, 2003 WL 22997277 (Ohio Ct. App. 7th Dist. Belmont County 2003); State v. Evans, 122 Ohio St. 3d 381, 2009-Ohio-2974, 911 N.E.2d 889 (2009).

[2]State v. Daniel, 1996 WL 11268 (Ohio Ct. App. 10th Dist. Franklin County 1996).

another's unborn child by means of a deadly weapon or dangerous ordnance

(4) within an appropriate venue of the state of Ohio.[3]

A charge of aggravated assault carries the penalties of a fourth degree felony, which include, at the court's discretion:

(1) 6, 7, 8, 9, 10, 11, 12, 13, 14, 15, 16, 17, or 18 months in prison, and

(2) up to $5,000 in fines.[4]

The penalties associated with a charge of aggravated assault are those of a fourth degree felony, to wit, at the discretion of the court:

(1) a prison term of six, seven, eight, nine, ten, eleven, twelve, thirteen, fourteen, fifteen, sixteen, seventeen or eighteen months,[5] as well as

(2) not more than $5,000 in fines.[6]

If a peace officer or an investigator of the bureau of criminal identification and investigation is the victim of an aggravated assault, the offense may be charged as a felony of the third degree,[7] carrying possible penalties, at the discretion of the court, of:

(1) Two, three, four or five years, and

(2) A fine, not to exceed $10,000.[8]

If the prosecution alleges and proves that an aggravated assault committed against a peace officer or investigator of the bureau of criminal identification and investigation[9] resulted in serious physical harm to the victim, conviction of the offense also includes the imposition of a mandatory jail term of not less two, nor more than five years.[10]

As in the case of felonious assault, no differentiation is made between an officer who is on duty and one who is not.[11] This again raises the interesting and unresolved question of what penalty should a court impose upon an offender convicted of assaultive behavior against a family or household member who also happens to be an off-duty peace officer or investigator for the bureau of criminal identification and investigation[12] at the time of the violation?

Additionally, amendments made to the aggravated assault statute during the 2008-2009 Session of the Ohio's General Assembly attempted to provide greater protections for pregnant women and the fetuses that they carry.[13] Under the penalty provisions contained in the bill that the legislature passed, trial courts are required to impose

---

[3]RC 2903.12.

[4]RC 2929.14.

[5]RC 2929.14(A)(4).

[6]RC 2929.18(A)(3)(d).

[7]RC 2935.01(B); RC 2903.11(D)(1)(a).

[8]RC 2929.18(A)(3)(a).

[9]RC 2935.01(B); RC 2903.11(E)(6).

[10]RC 2903.11(D)(1)(b).

[11]RC 2929.14.

[12]RC 2935.01(B); RC 2903.11(E)(6).

[13]Am. Sub. H.B. 280, eff. Apr. 7, 2009.

mandatory sentences on certain offenders convicted of aggravated assault. Thus, if the offender committed aggravated assault against a women that he or she knew was pregnant at the time of the assault, the court is required to impose a definite mandatory prison term of at least six months or, in the alternative, mandate one of the higher prison terms prescribed by the Revised Code for felonies of the same degree as the violation.[14] If a mandatory prison term is imposed upon an offender, the offender is required by law to serve the mandatory prison term consecutively to any other mandatory prison term imposed, either before, at the same time as or even after the imposition of the mandatory term resulting from the pregnancy specification.[15] These mandatory sentencing provisions are precluded unless the pregnancy specification appears at the end of the body of the charging document, substantially in the form provided by statute, and the offender is convicted of the pregnancy specification and the offense.[16]

Peace officers are frequently injured while responding to emotionally charged domestic violence calls. These injuries often result in allegations of aggravated assault. When the conduct of an offender results in an accusation of aggravated assault on a peace officer, the elements which the government must prove are the same as they are in any other aggravated assault case. The penalties for such conduct, however, are significantly more severe. Again, there is no differentiation made between an officer who is on duty and one who is not.[17] This presents a question that has yet to be addressed: What penalty should the court impose upon an offender convicted of felonious or aggravated assault against a family or household member who happens to be an off-duty peace officer?

Q & A: My client is on trial for felonious assault on a police officer. She discovered that her husband had sexually abused their child and went after him with a knife. Unfortunately, she cut one of the police officers who responded to the disturbance call. I want a jury instruction on aggravated assault. Is the court likely to give it?

An act performed under the influence of sudden passion or in the heat of blood is one committed, without time and opportunity for reflection or for passions to cool.[18] Your client certainly is able to show that she was provoked by her husband into the actions that she attempted to take against him. However, the facts reveal no action on the part of the injured police officer that would qualify as the provocation necessary to explain his injury at her hands.[19] That notwithstanding, since no time for reflection had transpired between the revelation

---

[14]RC 2929.14(D)(8).

[15]RC 2929.14(E)(1)(d).

[16]RC 2941.1423.

[17]RC 2935.01(B).

[18]See State v. Muscatello, 55 Ohio St. 2d 201, 9 Ohio Op. 3d 148, 378 N.E.2d 738 (1978) (holding modified by, State v. Rhodes, 63 Ohio St. 3d 613, 590 N.E.2d 261 (1992)) (defining "under the influence of sudden passion"); State v. Bostick, 2012-Ohio-5048, 2012 WL 5354990 (Ohio Ct. App. 9th Dist. Summit County 2012).

[19]State v. Brown, 1982 WL 5220 (Ohio Ct. App. 8th Dist. Cuyahoga County 1982).

concerning her husband and the defendant's actions which resulted in the injury to the officer, a strong argument could be made that might make the court feel justified in giving the instruction.[20]

§ 3:5 Elements and penalties—Assault under RC 2903.13

The prohibition against simple assault is found in RC 2903.13. Most Ohio municipalities that have home rule authority have enacted their own ordinances criminalizing assault. With the exception of the specific application to family or household members, the language used in drafting the elements of the domestic violence law is nearly identical to that of the assault statute.[1]

The presence of the additional element, requiring that the victim be a family or household member of the offender, is a recognition of the uniqueness of situations involving the assault of family or household members. Frequently, though, the prosecution is called upon to determine the nature of relationships that are difficult, if not impossible, to discern. In those instances where probable cause exists to establish that an assault has taken place, but where the status of the parties is less clear, assault is a logical charging option.

The elements which the prosecution must prove to obtain a conviction under RC 2903.13(A), or a substantially similar municipal ordinance, are that the offender:

(1) knowingly
(2) caused or attempted to cause
(3) physical harm to another or another's unborn child
(4) within an appropriate venue of this state.

Under RC 2903.13(B), or a substantially similar municipal ordinance, a conviction will result if the prosecution succeeds in proving that the offender:

(1) recklessly
(2) caused serious physical harm to another or another's unborn child
(3) within an appropriate venue of this state.

The penalties generally associated with a charge of assault are those of a first degree misdemeanor. A number of exceptions to that general rule are set forth in the law.[2] The penalties for a first degree misdemeanor available for the court's use, at its discretion, are:

(1) up to 180 days in jail,[3] as well as
(2) not more than $1,000 in fines.[4]

---

[20]State v. Brown, 1982 WL 5220 (Ohio Ct. App. 8th Dist. Cuyahoga County 1982).

[Section 3:5]

[1]RC 2919.25(A), RC 2919.25(B).

[2]See RC 2903.13(C)(1) to (5).

[3]RC 2929.14(A)(4).

[4]RC 2929.18(A)(3)(d).

However, if a peace officer or an investigator of the bureau of criminal identification and investigation[5] is the victim of an aggravated assault, the offense may be charged as a felony of the fourth degree,[6] carrying possible penalties, at the discretion of the court, of:

(1) a prison term of six, seven, eight, nine, ten, eleven, twelve, thirteen, fourteen, fifteen, sixteen, seventeen or eighteen months[7], as well as

(2) not more than $5,000 in fines.[8]

If the prosecution alleges and proves that an assault committed against a peace officer or investigator of the bureau of criminal identification and investigation[9] resulted in serious physical harm to the victim, conviction of the offense also includes the imposition of a mandatory jail term of not less than twelve months.[10]

As is the case with aggravated and felonious assault, no differentiation is made between an officer who is on duty and one who is not.[11] Thus, once again the interesting and unresolved question raised is what penalty a court should impose upon an offender convicted of assaultive behavior against a family or household member who also happens to be an off-duty peace officer or investigator for the bureau of criminal identification and investigation[12] at the time of the violation?

Additionally, amendments made to the assault statute during the 2008-2009 Session of the Ohio's General Assembly attempted to provide greater protections for pregnant women and the fetuses that they carry.[13] Under the penalty provisions contained in the bill that the legislature passed, trial courts are required to impose mandatory sentences on certain offenders convicted of an assault. Thus, if the offender is charged with and convicted of committing an assault against a women that he or she knew was pregnant at the time of the incident,[14] the court is required to impose a definite mandatory jail term of at least thirty (30) days.[15] This mandatory sentencing provision is precluded unless the pregnancy specification appears at the end of the body of the charging document, substantially in the form provided by statute, and the offender is convicted of the pregnancy specification and the offense.[16]

---

[5]RC 2935.01(B); RC 2903.11(E)(5), (6).

[6]RC 2903.13(C)(4).

[7]RC 2929.14(A)(4).

[8]RC 2929.18(A)(3)(d).

[9]RC 2935.01(B); RC 2903.11(E)(5), (6).

[10]RC 2903.13(C)(4).

[11]RC 2903.13(C)(3).

[12]RC 2935.01(B); RC 2903.11(E)(5), (6).

[13]Am. Sub. H.B. 280, eff. Apr. 7, 2009.

[14]RC 2929.24(G).

[15]RC 2929.14(D)(8).

[16]RC 2941.1423.

§ 3:6 Elements and penalties—Menacing by stalking under RC 2903.211

The elements of menacing by stalking are:

(1) engaging in a pattern of behavior

(2) knowingly

  (a) causing another to believe that the offender will cause physical harm to the other person, or

  (b) causing mental distress to the other person

(3) within an appropriate venue in the state of Ohio

The charges of menacing,[1] aggravated menacing,[2] and menacing by stalking[3] all share a similar element. Each requires that the offender's actions cause another to believe that the offender will cause to such other, or to such other's property, some level of harm defined in the Revised Code.[4]

In the case of menacing, that level is *any* physical harm. In the case of aggravated menacing, the level is *serious physical harm*. In the case of menacing by stalking, the requisite level is the same as with the menacing statute, i.e., *any* physical harm.

Two of the elements of the menacing by stalking statute set it apart from charges of either menacing or aggravated menacing. The first provides that the charge may be brought upon an allegation that the offender's actions have constituted a pattern of conduct.[5] The statute defines a "pattern of conduct" as "two or more actions or incidents closely related in time, whether or not there has been a prior conviction based on any of those actions or incidents."[6] A "pattern of conduct" may also include any two or more acts or incidents closely related in time that have the effect of preventing, obstructing, or delaying the performance of a public official (defined as any elected or appointed officer, employee or agent of the state or any political subdivision, whether in a temporary or permanent capacity and includes but is not limited to legislators, judges, and law enforcement officers).[7] Just what constitutes "closely related in time" is not spelled out in the statute. Given the wide variety of possibilities, the legislature wisely left the answer to that question to the individual judges and juries that will hear these matters to decide on a case-by-case basis.[8]

The second element provides that the charge is appropriate when the

---

[Section 3:6]

[1]R.C. 2903.22.

[2]R.C. 2903.21.

[3]R.C. 2903.211.

[4]R.C. 2901.01(C).

[5]RC 2903.211(A).

[6]RC 2903.211(D)(1); Echemann v. Echemann, 2016-Ohio-3212, 2016 WL 3057979 (Ohio Ct. App. 3d Dist. Shelby County 2016).

[7]RC 2903.211(D)(1); see also 1999 H.B. 137, eff. 3-10-00; RC 2921.01 (defining "public official").

[8]State v. Dario, 106 Ohio App. 3d 232, 665 N.E.2d 759 (1st Dist. Hamilton County 1995); State v. Honeycutt, 2002-Ohio-3490, 2002 WL 1438648, *5 (Ohio Ct. App. 2d Dist. Montgomery County 2002); Ellet v. Falk, 2010-Ohio-6219, 2010 WL 5269870 (Ohio Ct. App. 6th Dist. Lucas County 2010); Retterer v. Little, 2012-Ohio-

offender's actions result in mental distress to the complainant.[9] The term "mental distress" is defined as "any mental illness or condition that involves some temporary substantial incapacity or mental illness or condition that would normally require psychiatric treatment."[10]

It is not necessary for the prosecution to offer expert testimony to establish that the complainant suffered mental distress as a result of the offender's alleged actions in order to prevail.[11] Lay witnesses who are acquainted with the complainant may testify as to any marked changes in the complainant's emotional or habitual makeup that they observed after the alleged incidents occurred. The trier of fact must then determine whether, and to what extent, the offender's conduct brought about the complainant's mental distress.[12]

With the exception of those provisions that relate to the inclusion of acts or incidents that impede the performance of public officials in performance of their duties[13] and those that enhance the penalties for menacing by stalking to a fourth-degree felony on conviction for a second violation, the menacing by stalking statutes were copied by most of Ohio's home rule municipalities when they enacted similar stalking ordinances. Those remaining provisions, therefore, appear to be incorporated verbatim into those local ordinances.

If a defendant is charged under the statute rather than under most current ordinances, the penalties associated with a charge of menacing by stalking may depend on a number of factors.

In 1999, following the daylight slaying of a Shaker Heights teenager as she walked to school by a man who had been stalking her for a protracted period of time, the General Assembly reexamined the state's stalking laws and enhanced the penalties.[14] As amended,

---

131, 2012 WL 134305 (Ohio Ct. App. 3d Dist. Marion County 2012). But see Echemann v. Echemann, 2016-Ohio-3212, 2016 WL 3057979 (Ohio Ct. App. 3d Dist. Shelby County 2016).

[9] RC 2903.211(A).

[10] RC 2903.211(C)(2).

[11] State v. Bilder, 99 Ohio App. 3d 653, 651 N.E.2d 502 (9th Dist. Summit County 1994); Noah v. Brillhart, 2003-Ohio-2421, 2003 WL 21078077, *3 (Ohio Ct. App. 9th Dist. Wayne County 2003); Bach v. Crawford, 2003-Ohio-1255, 2003 WL 1193783, *4 (Ohio Ct. App. 2d Dist. Montgomery County 2003); City of Toledo v. Emery, 2000 WL 864305, *3 (Ohio Ct. App. 6th Dist. Lucas County 2000); State v. Smith, 126 Ohio App. 3d 193, 203, 709 N.E.2d 1245, 1251 (7th Dist. Mahoning County 1998); State v. Bone, 2006-Ohio-3809, 2006 WL 2053398 (Ohio Ct. App. 10th Dist. Franklin County 2006); Middletown v. Jones, 167 Ohio App. 3d 679, 2006-Ohio-3465, 856 N.E.2d 1003 (12th Dist. Butler County 2006); Perry v. Joseph, 2008-Ohio-1107, 2008 WL 660317 (Ohio Ct. App. 10th Dist. Franklin County 2008); Stump v. Hoagland, 2015-Ohio-2434, 2015 WL 3822270 (Ohio Ct. App. 2d Dist. Miami County 2015).

[12] State v. Tichon, 102 Ohio App. 3d 758, 658 N.E.2d 16 (9th Dist. Summit County 1995). State v. Rucker, 2002-Ohio-172, 2002 WL 83731 (Ohio Ct. App. 12th Dist. Butler County 2002); State v. Horsley, 2006-Ohio-6217, 2006 WL 3411423 (Ohio Ct. App. 10th Dist. Franklin County 2006); State v. McCoy, 2006-Ohio-6333, 2006 WL 3478338 (Ohio Ct. App. 9th Dist. Lorain County 2006); Perry v. Joseph, 2008-Ohio-1107, 2008 WL 660317 (Ohio Ct. App. 10th Dist. Franklin County 2008); City of Toledo v. Emery, 2000 WL 864305 (Ohio Ct. App. 6th Dist. Lucas County 2000).

[13] RC 2903.211(D)(1).

[14] 1999 H.B. 137, eff. 3-10-00; RC 2903.211(C).

menacing by stalking generally remains a first-degree misdemeanor,[15] however, if any of the following circumstances pertain, the penalty is enhanced to a felony of the fourth degree:

(1) The offender previously has been convicted of menacing by stalking or aggravated trespass;[16]
(2) In committing the offense, the offender made a threat of physical harm to or against the victim;[17]
(3) In committing the offense, the offender trespassed on the land or premises where the victim lives, is employed, or attends school;[18]
(4) The victim of the offense is a minor;[19]
(5) The offender has a history of violence toward the victim or any other person or a history of other violent acts toward the victim or any other person;[20]
(6) While committing the offense, the offender had a deadly weapon on or about the offender's person or under the offender's control;[21]
(7) At the time of the commission of the offense, the offender was the subject of an anti-stalking temporary protection order or anti-stalking civil protection order, regardless of whether the person to be protected under the order is the victim of the offense or another person;[22]
(8) In committing the offense, the offender caused serious physical harm to the premises at which the victim resides, to the real property on which that premises is located, or to any personal property located on that premises;[23] or
(9) The offender previously had been found to be a mentally ill person subject to hospitalization by court order under the criteria set forth in RC 5122.01(B)(1) or RC 5122.01(B)(2), i.e., the person, because of his/her mental illness, represents a substantial risk of physical harm to self as manifested by evidence of threats of, or attempts at, suicide or serious self-inflicted bodily harm, or represents a substantial risk of physical harm to others as manifested by evidence of recent homicidal or other violent behavior, evidence of recent threats that place another in reasonable fear of violent behavior and serious physical harm, or other evidence of present dangerousness, or the offender previously had been voluntarily admitted to a mental health facility under RC 5122.02 and, as the basis for or subsequent to that voluntary admission, the offender was

[15] RC 2903.211(B)(1).
[16] RC 2903.211(B)(2)(a).
[17] RC 2903.211(B)(2)(b).
[18] RC 2903.211(B)(2)(c).
[19] RC 2903.211(B)(2)(d).
[20] RC 2903.211(B)(2)(e).
[21] RC 2903.211(B)(2)(f).
[22] RC 2903.211(B)(2)(g).
[23] RC 2903.211(B)(2)(h).

determined to represent a risk to self or others to the extent described in RC 5122.01(B)(1) or RC 5122.01(B)(2).[24]

As a first-degree misdemeanor, menacing by stalking carries penalties of up to six months in jail[25] and up to $1,000 in fines. As a fourth-degree felony, the penalty for menacing by stalking is enhanced[26] and carries between six and eighteen months of imprisonment[27] and up to $5,000 in fines, at the court's discretion, upon conviction. Sanctions other than jail and/or fines are also provided for under the statutory scheme.[28]

While not strictly speaking a penalty, amendments to the bail statute[29] allow the court, on its own motion or on motion of the prosecuting attorney, to order that an individual charged with felony menacing by stalking be held without bond in certain cases. In order for the court to appropriately order the defendant in a qualifying menacing by stalking case to be held without bail, the court must first conduct a hearing. At the hearing, the prosecuting authority has the burden of proving by clear and convincing evidence that:

(1) The proof of the defendant's guilt is evident or the presumption of the defendant's guilt is great; AND
(2) The defendant poses a substantial risk of serious physical harm to ANY person or to the community; AND
(3) No release conditions will reasonably assure the safety of the individual at risk and of the community.[30]

Q & A: I called my ex-wife about twenty times last week to talk with her about the new child support order. I kept telling her that if she didn't talk to me, she would be very sorry. She refused to budge. The last time I called I got mad and told her I was on my way over to break her face. I've been charged with both aggravated menacing and menacing by stalking against my ex-wife. My lawyer says that I can't be convicted of both because what I did was, at worst, only one crime, menacing by stalking. Is he right?

Not really. The crimes of aggravated menacing and menacing by stalking share some of the same elements, but they are not identical.[31] Both could have some application under your facts. Aggravated menacing occurs when a person "knowingly cause[s] another to believe that the offender will cause serious physical harm to the person or property" of another.[32] Menacing by stalking occurs when a person, *by engaging in a pattern of conduct*, knowingly cause(s) another to believe

[24] RC 2903.211(B)(2)(i).

[25] RC 2929.21(B)(1).

[26] RC 2903.211(B)(2).

[27] RC 2929.14(A)(4).

[28] See RC 2929.11 to RC 2929.13.

[29] RC 2937.222.

[30] RC 2937.222(A).

[31] State v. Hicks, 1995 WL 768588 (Ohio Ct. App. 5th Dist. Richland County 1995). See also State v. Starkey, 1998 WL 753257 (Ohio Ct. App. 5th Dist. Stark County 1998).

[32] RC 2903.21(A).

that the offender will cause physical harm or mental distress to the other person.[33] The elements of the two offenses do not correspond to such a degree that the commission of the one offense will result in the commission of the other. Thus, it cannot be said that they are allied offenses of similar import. If they were, your lawyer would be right, and a court would be precluded from convicting you of both.

A court hearing your case could reasonably conclude that your acts were a pattern of conduct, knowingly designed by you to cause your ex-wife to believe that you intended to cause her physical harm. That conduct appropriately resulted in the charge of menacing by stalking.

The prosecution had the option of including your verbal threat over the phone to your ex-wife in the "pattern of conduct" element of the menacing by stalking charge. However, your threat, standing alone, also contained all of the elements of aggravated menacing, justifying a decision by the prosecutor to file a separate complaint for that violation.

Q & A: Isn't the menacing by stalking statute's definition of any two acts as a pattern of conduct unconstitutional?

No challenge to the constitutionality of Ohio's menacing by stalking statute, or to any local ordinance similar to the menacing by stalking statute, has succeeded. The statute has faced constitutional challenges primarily based upon two theories.

The first unsuccessful argument raised is that these laws are impermissibly vague and do not provide an individual of ordinary intelligence fair warning of the conduct that is prohibited.[34] The second theory is that the menacing by stalking laws are overbroad and that, in their attempt to prohibit the illegal activities of stalkers, they impermissibly outlaw other innocent and constitutionally protected conduct.[35]

In rejecting these arguments, Ohio's courts have followed the precedent that has been established in other jurisdictions.[36]

Q & A: I'm prosecuting a really bad actor for menacing by stalking. This is not the first time that he's gone after my victim. She's had to prosecute him for assault on two prior occasions. Can I get those priors into evidence before the jury, even though she eventually dropped those other charges?

The crime of menacing by stalking requires that the prosecution establish, as one of the elements, the state of mind of the complainant.[37]

---

[33] RC 2903.211(A).

[34] See State v. Benner, 96 Ohio App. 3d 327, 644 N.E.2d 1130 (1st Dist. Hamilton County 1994); State of Ohio v. Francway, 1995 WL 491104 (Ohio Ct. App. 8th Dist. Cuyahoga County 1995); State v. Dario, 106 Ohio App. 3d 232, 665 N.E.2d 759 (1st Dist. Hamilton County 1995); State v. Horsley, 2006-Ohio-6217, 2006 WL 3411423 (Ohio Ct. App. 10th Dist. Franklin County 2006).

[35] See State v. Bilder, 99 Ohio App. 3d 653, 651 N.E.2d 502 (9th Dist. Summit County 1994); State v. Dario, 106 Ohio App. 3d 232, 665 N.E.2d 759 (1st Dist. Hamilton County 1995).

[36] See Dayton v. Smith, 68 Ohio Misc. 2d 20, 646 N.E.2d 917 (Mun. Ct. 1994); U.S. v. Smith, 685 A.2d 380, 383 (D.C. 1996).

[37] RC 2903.211(A).

More so than in most crimes, the use of "other act"[38] evidence that presents the past history between the parties is both relevant and probative. This is so even if the "other acts" did not result in criminal convictions. Such testimony effectively explains why the complainant might legitimately believe that the offender would do her harm. A trial court should allow it into evidence, under proper instruction.[39]

Q & A: My ex-girlfriend and I broke up after living together for two years. She now lives in Michigan. She is very angry with me because of the breakup. During the last month, on the average of ten times a day, she has called me from Michigan. She is threatening to do something to me or my property when she comes to visit her folks next week. I want to prosecute her for menacing by stalking. The prosecutor says that there is nothing he can do because all of the acts that make up her "pattern of behavior" were done outside of his jurisdiction. Is he right?

No. The Revised Code establishes the proper venue for the prosecution of criminal acts in Ohio.[40] Pursuant to its authority, venue is proper in any county where any element of the crime was committed. One of the elements of the charge of menacing by stalking has to do with the effect that the offender's actions have on the state of mind of the intended victim.

Your ex-girlfriend's actions over the last month have caused you to belief that she will cause you physical harm. That belief is an element of the charge of menacing by stalking which the prosecution could bring against her. You live within the jurisdiction of an Ohio prosecutor. Under your facts, the charge of menacing by stalking against your ex-girlfriend is properly venued in your prosecutor's jurisdiction.

Q & A: At a trial on a charge of menacing by stalking, the alleged victim testified that the defendant screamed obscenities and threats against his life on a Monday and on the following Wednesday sat parked in a car across from the victim's home for more than an hour. He further testified that these acts by the defendant caused him to fear for his safety. At the close of the evidence, the defendant's attorney argued that the State failed to prove those two acts were sufficient to establish his client engaged in a pattern of conduct that justified the victim's belief the defendant would cause the victim physical harm. Was counsel's argument valid?

Proof of two or more incidents involving explicit threats of physical harm against a complainant is not necessary to establish the statutory elements of menacing by stalking.[41] Unless adequately refuted,

---

[38]Evid. R. 404(C); RC 2945.59.

[39]State v. Woodgeard, 1994 WL 167928 (Ohio Ct. App. 5th Dist. Fairfield County 1994), dismissed, 70 Ohio St. 3d 1473, 640 N.E.2d 846 (1994).

[40]RC 2901.12(A).

[41]State v. Smith, 126 Ohio App. 3d 193, 709 N.E.2d 1245 (7th Dist. Mahoning County 1998); Dayton v. Davis, 136 Ohio App. 3d 26, 735 N.E.2d 939 (2d Dist. Montgomery County 1999); State v. Smith, 2002-Ohio-5095, 2002 WL 31127531, *4 (Ohio Ct. App. 3d Dist. Seneca County 2002); State v. Boden, 2002-Ohio-5043, 2002

the complainant's testimony in this case that the defendant's actions on these two occasions caused him to believe the defendant would physically harm him raises jury issues on the physical harm and mental distress elements of the charge of menacing by stalking.[42]

Q & A: I just found out that my recent "ex" was charged with, but acquitted of, stalking two prior intimate partners. Today my two best friends each received greeting cards from my "ex" which indicate I'm being watched and that I'll be sorry that we broke up. Given past history, I think that I'm being stalked and I fear for my safety! Can I prosecute for stalking?

Under these facts, the answer is probably not. Before an individual may be prosecuted for stalking, the law requires that the offender, by engaging in a pattern of conduct, shall knowingly cause another person to believe that the offender will cause physical harm to the other person or cause mental distress to the other person.[43] A "pattern of conduct" is defined as "two or more actions or incidents closely related in time, whether or not there has been a prior conviction based on any of those actions or incidents."[44]

The receipt of the greeting cards by your best friends, while meeting the definition of "two or more actions or incidents closely related in time, whether or not there has been a prior conviction based on any of those actions or incidents," are probably not enough to justify a prosecutor's finding that their receipt caused you to reasonably believe that your "ex" would cause you physical harm or mental distress. As such, it is unlikely that initiation of stalking charges against your "ex" will issue.[45] Nonetheless, any additional action by your "ex" that raises your threat perception is likely to provide the element that is now missing.

§ 3:7 Elements and penalties—Aggravated trespass under RC 2911.211

Ohio's aggravated trespass statute, RC 2911.211, became effective on November 5, 1992. It took effect on the same day as the state's menacing by stalking statute. Both measures attempt to provide some

---

WL 31114894, *2 (Ohio Ct. App. 7th Dist. Jefferson County 2002); Tuuri v. Snyder, 2002-Ohio-2107, 2002 WL 818427, *3 (Ohio Ct. App. 11th Dist. Geauga County 2002); Dayton v. Davis, 136 Ohio App. 3d 26, 31, 735 N.E.2d 939, 943 (2d Dist. Montgomery County 1999); Middletown v. Jones, 167 Ohio App. 3d 679, 2006-Ohio-3465, 856 N.E.2d 1003 (12th Dist. Butler County 2006); Perry v. Joseph, 2008-Ohio-1107, 2008 WL 660317 (Ohio Ct. App. 10th Dist. Franklin County 2008); Lias v. Beekman, 2007-Ohio-5737, 2007 WL 3108899 (Ohio Ct. App. 10th Dist. Franklin County 2007); Walker v. Edgington, 2008-Ohio-3478, 2008 WL 2699430 (Ohio Ct. App. 2d Dist. Clark County 2008). But see also Holloway v. Parker, 2013-Ohio-1940, 2013 WL 1944400 (Ohio Ct. App. 3d Dist. Marion County 2013); Echemann v. Echemann, 2016-Ohio-3212, 2016 WL 3057979 (Ohio Ct. App. 3d Dist. Shelby County 2016).

[42]State v. Smith, 126 Ohio App. 3d 193, 709 N.E.2d 1245 (7th Dist. Mahoning County 1998); Ellet v. Falk, 2010-Ohio-6219, 2010 WL 5269870 (Ohio Ct. App. 6th Dist. Lucas County 2010); Echemann v. Echemann, 2016-Ohio-3212, 2016 WL 3057979 (Ohio Ct. App. 3d Dist. Shelby County 2016).

[43]R.C. 2903.211(A)(1).

[44]R.C. 2903.211(D)(1).

[45]State v. Hersh, 2012-Ohio-3807, 974 N.E.2d 161 (Ohio Ct. App. 8th Dist. Cuyahoga County 2012), as amended nunc pro tunc, (Sept. 10, 2012).

degree of preventative protection to the potential victims of these offenses before they are actually injured. Individuals extended protection by these laws are at risk from others who have indicated an intention to do harm but who have not yet followed through.

Arguably a valuable prosecution tool, the aggravated trespass statute, to date, is little used in Ohio. Its key elements are:

(1)
   (a) enter, or
   (b) remain
(2) on the land or premises of another
(3) with purpose to commit
(4) on that land or premises
(5) a misdemeanor the elements of which involve:
   (a) causing physical harm to another person, or
   (b) causing another to believe that the offender will cause physical harm to the other person
(6) within an appropriate venue of the state of Ohio.[1]

A conviction of aggravated trespass carries the penalties of a first degree misdemeanor, to wit:

(1) up to 180 days in jail, as well as,
(2) up to $1,000 in fines.[2]

Q & A: My client was arrested on the strength of a written statement, given by his estranged wife, charging him with aggravated trespass. The arresting officers never saw my client at the scene. I thought that the police had to actually see the commission of a misdemeanor in order to make an arrest?

It is generally true that the police are supposed to see the commission of a misdemeanor before they are empowered to make a arrest.[3] However, there is an exception to the general rule that allows an officer to make a warrantless arrest for a misdemeanor not committed in his presence.[4] Under the law, an officer is empowered to make a warrantless arrest for certain enumerated crimes when provided with a written statement from the complainant that the offender has committed the offense.[5] One of the crimes enumerated is aggravated trespass.[6]

§ 3:8 Elements and penalties—Menacing under RC 2903.22

The menacing statute is similar in some respects to RC 2919.25(C), the domestic violence threats section, but it is considerably broader in scope. The application of RC 2919.25(C) is limited to verbal or other

[Section 3:7]

[1]RC 2911.211.

[2]RC 2911.211(B), RC 2929.21(B)(1), RC 2929.21(C)(1).

[3]RC 2935.03(A).

[4]RC 2935.03(B).

[5]RC 2935.03(B)(2).

[6]RC 2935.03(B)(2)(a); State v. Miller, 91 Ohio App. 3d 270, 632 N.E.2d 569 (3d Dist. Logan County 1993).

behaviors that cause a family or household member to believe that the offender will imminently cause him/her or some other family or household member physical harm.

The menacing statute, on the other hand, prohibits verbal or other behaviors that cause any other person, regardless of the existence of a family or household relationship, to believe that the offender will cause physical harm to such other person, such other person's property, an immediate family member of such other person, or the property of an immediate family member of such other person. Further, the menacing statute,[1] unlike the domestic violence statute, does not require that the threat of harm be imminent.[2]

The elements that must be established to maintain a charge of menacing under RC 2903.22 or a substantially similar municipal ordinance, include:

(1) knowingly
(2) causing another to believe
(3) that the offender will cause physical harm to:
 (a) the person of the threatened party,
 (b) the property of the threatened party,
 (c) the unborn child of the threatened party, or
 (d) a member of the immediate family of the threatened party.

"Immediate family" is defined as "a person's spouse residing in the person's household, brothers and sisters of the whole or of the half blood, and children, including adopted children."[3]

The menacing statute is available to sanction offenders whose crimes against family or household members do not qualify for the issuance of complaints under the domestic violence threats section, RC 2919.25(C). However, if menacing is the only charge, even if the victim is a family or household member, the benefits of a protection order are not available.[4]

Q & A: The Defendant was charged with menacing against a family or household member. While highly intoxicated at a bar somewhere in the City, the defendant called, texted, and left multiple threatening voicemails on the alleged victim's cell phone, including "I will kill you and your kids" and "You are dead." The alleged victim received these calls at home in a suburban jurisdiction. The alleged victim called the suburb's police department and, thereafter, swore out a complaint for the Defendant's arrest.

At pretrial, the defendant's attorney now questions the jurisdiction of the suburb to hear the case, due to the fact that his client was in the City "while committing the alleged criminal act." Does the lawyer have a point?

[Section 3:8]

[1]RC 2903.22.

[2]State v. Strunk, 1999 WL 12743 (Ohio Ct. App. 1st Dist. Hamilton County 1999).

[3]RC 2905.21(I).

[4]See RC 2919.26.

No. Courts in Ohio have noted that "the trial of a criminal case in this state shall be held in a court having jurisdiction of the subject matter, and *in the territory of which the offense or any element* of the offense *was committed.*"[5] The elements of menacing are: (1) knowingly, (2) causing another to believe, (3) that the offender will cause physical harm to the person or property of such other person or a member of his immediate family.[6]

Appellant "knowingly" made the threatening statements from the City. In turn, the threats were communicated to the alleged victim while the alleged victim was within the jurisdiction of the suburb. The offense could not have been completed until such time when the alleged victim was made aware of the threats, thereby causing the alleged victim's belief of impending physical harm. In the case at bar, this particular element was fulfilled in the suburb where the victim heard defendant's threatening statements. The elements of menacing having been satisfied, the proper venue, under R.C. 2901.12(A), would have been either the location from which defendant made the threatening statements or the place where the threats caused the victim to believe defendant would cause the alleged victim physical harm.[7] Therefore, it is immaterial whether the alleged victim and defendant were in separate venues when the conversation occurred. The charges could have been filed in either the City or the suburban municipal Court since elements of the offense occurred in both counties.[8]

R.C. 2901.12(A) provides "[t]he trial of a criminal case in this state shall be held in a court having jurisdiction of the subject matter, and in the territory of which the offense or any element of the offense was committed." Venue is not a material element of a criminal case.[9] However, "venue is a fact that must be proven beyond a reasonable doubt."[10]

In a menacing case that occurs over landline telephones, venue is proper in either the location the calls are made or the location the calls are received.[11] However the situation becomes more complicated when the alleged meancing call is received on the alleged victim's cel-

[5]R.C. 2901.12(A) (emphasis added).

[6]State v. Applegate, 1992 WL 236775 (Ohio Ct. App. 12th Dist. Butler County 1992), cause dismissed, 66 Ohio St. 3d 1432, 608 N.E.2d 761 (1993).

[7]Compare State v. Novel, 1986 WL 11348 (Ohio Ct. App. 5th Dist. Licking County 1986).

[8]Fairfield v. McRoberts, 100 Ohio App. 3d 476, 654 N.E.2d 370 (12th Dist. Butler County 1995); State v. Dengg, 2009-Ohio-4101, 2009 WL 2488048 (Ohio Ct. App. 11th Dist. Portage County 2009).

[9]State v. Shaw, 134 Ohio App. 3d 316, 318, 730 N.E.2d 1075 (2d Dist. Greene County 1999), quoting State v. Headley, 6 Ohio St. 3d 475, 477, 453 N.E.2d 716 (1983).

[10]State v. Lahmann, 2007-Ohio-1795, ¶ 17, 2007 WL 1121472 (Ohio Ct. App. 12th Dist. Butler County 2007), citing State v. Smith, 87 Ohio St. 3d 424, 435, 2000-Ohio-450, 721 N.E.2d 93 (2000), citing State v. Headley, 6 Ohio St.3d at 477, 453 N.E.2d 716; State v. Sylvester, 2016-Ohio-5710, 2016 WL 4701543 (Ohio Ct. App. 8th Dist. Cuyahoga County 2016), appeal not allowed, 149 Ohio St. 3d 1418, 2017, 2017-Ohio-4038, 75 N.E.3d 236 (2017).

[11]Fairfield v. McRoberts, 100 Ohio App. 3d 476, 478, 654 N.E.2d 370 (12th Dist. Butler County 1995).

lular telephone. This is because the fact that the alleged victim received the call does not, by itself, establish venue existed in a certain location at that time. There must be some other evidence, such as testimony or telephone records introduced to show that the phone call actually occurred and where the alleged victim was located when she received the alleged threat, and/or, conversely, where the alleged offender was at that time.[12]

§ 3:9 Elements and penalties—Endangering children under RC 2919.22

The endangering children statute and substantially similar municipal ordinances were enacted to deal primarily with three problems involving the mistreatment of minors and handicapped young adults by their parents, guardians, caregivers, and others, to wit:

(1) circumstances of neglect,
(2) affirmative acts of torture, abuse, and/or excessive corporal punishment or other disciplinary measures, and
(3) permitting, allowing, enticing, encouraging, employing, using, hiring, coercing, or compelling a minor child to engage in or perform acts of pornography or prostitution.

A conviction under RC 2919.22(A), which deals with circumstances of neglect, requires the prosecution to prove that:

(1) a parent, guardian, person with custody or control, or a person in loco parentis
(2) created a substantial risk to the health or safety of:
    (a) a child under the age of eighteen, or
    (b) a mentally or physically handicapped person under the age of twenty-one,
(3) by violating a duty of care, protection, or support,
(4) within an appropriate venue of this state.

A conviction under RC 2919.22(B), which deals with affirmative acts of abuse, including child pornography and prostitution, requires the prosecution to prove:

(1) the offender did any of the following:
    (a) abused a child, or
    (b) tortured or cruelly abused a child, or
    (c) administered corporal punishment or another physical disciplinary measure or physically restrained a child in a cruel manner or for prolonged periods in a manner excessive under the circumstances and which created a substantial risk of physical harm to the child, or
    (d) repeatedly administered unwarranted disciplinary measures to a child involving a substantial risk that such conduct, if continued, would seriously impair or retard the mental health or development of the child, or
    (e) enticed, coerced, permitted, encouraged, compelled, employed, hired, used, or allowed a child to act, model, or in

[12]State v. Dengg, 2009-Ohio-4101, 2009 WL 2488048 (Ohio Ct. App. 11th Dist. Portage County 2009).

any other way participate in, or be photographed for, the production, presentation, dissemination, or advertisement of any material or performance that the offender knows or reasonably should know is obscene, as defined in RC 2907.01, or any material or performance that is sexually or nudity-oriented,

(2) the child is:

(a) under the age of eighteen, or

(b) if mentally or physically handicapped, under the age of twenty-one,

(3) within an appropriate venue of this state.

A conviction under RC 2919.22(C), which deals with endangering a child while operating a vehicle, streetcar, or trackless trolley, requires the prosecution to prove:

(1) the offender operated a vehicle, streetcar, or trackless trolley anywhere within this state,

(2) while under the influence of alcohol, a drug or drugs of abuse, or a combination of alcohol and a drug or drugs of abuse, in violation of RC 4511.19(A),

(3) when one or more of the persons in the vehicle, streetcar, or trackless trolley was a child under the age of eighteen,

(4) within an appropriate venue of this state.

The penalties for violations of RC 2919.22 range from those of a misdemeanor of the first degree for a first offense to those of a felony of the second degree, which are imposed on an offender who has previously been convicted of any of the enumerated enhancing offenses[1] and who causes serious physical harm to a child as a result of the current conviction.[2] Other penalties for the various violations of RC 2919.22 are found in RC 2929.21 and RC 2929.31.

The domestic violence statute, RC 2919.25, does not discern between convictions for violations of RC 2919.22(A), RC 2919.22(B), and RC 2919.22(C) for purposes of penalty enhancement.[3] Thus, an offender who was previously convicted of child endangering for having a child in a car that the offender was operating under the influence of alcohol and who subsequently assaults a live-in intimate partner may be charged with felony domestic violence for the subsequent offense.

§ 3:10 Elements and penalties—Violating a protection order under RC 2919.27

The statutory scheme for the enforcement of civil and criminal protection orders involves both new criminal sanctions[1] and the courts'

[Section 3:9]

[1]RC 2919.22(E)(2)(b).

[2]RC 2919.22(E)(2)(c).

[3]RC 2919.25(D).

[Section 3:10]

[1]RC 2919.27.

inherent contempt powers.[2] Analysis of these enforcement provisions warrants the detailed discussions found elsewhere in this text.[3] For purposes of this section, it is sufficient to say that, in order to prove that an offender has failed to abide by the terms of a protection order or consent decree in violation of the statute, the prosecution must prove that the offender:

(1) recklessly
(2) violated the terms of:
    (a) a protection order issued pursuant to RC 2903.213, RC 2903.214, RC 2919.26, or RC 3113.31, or
    (b) a protection order issued by a court of another state of the union, U.S. territory or protectorate, Indian tribe, or the District of Columbia
(3) within an appropriate venue of this state.

The penalties for violation of RC 2919.27 are dependent on several variables:

(1) For a violation of RC 2919.27(A)(1):
    (a) If there are no prior convictions—M1[4]
    (b) If there is a prior conviction or if there are two or more violations of RC 2903.211 or RC 2911.211 against the same person who is the subject of the current protection order—F5[5]
(2) For a violation of RC 2919.27(A)(2):
    (a) If there are no prior convictions—M1
    (b) If there are two prior convictions for violation of an anti-stalking protection order under the prior RC 2919.27 or two or more violations of protection orders under RC 2903.21, RC 2903.211, RC 2903.22, or RC 2911.211 (the current stalking and aggravated trespass sections) involving the same person covered under the current order, or two or more violations of RC 2903.214 as it existed prior to July 1, 1996—F5

A court's enforcement of its order through its inherent contempt powers is limited only by the restrictions of due process. If a court chooses to enforce its order in this manner, an offender may still be criminally prosecuted for the same violation of a protection order without offending the Double Jeopardy Clause of the Constitution.[6] This is true as long as the offender, if convicted of the criminal charge, is given credit for any penalty imposed for the same acts resulting

[2]RC 2705.02(A).

[3]See Text Ch 13, Court Enforcement of Civil Protection Orders and Related Issues; Text Ch 14, Police Enforcement of Protection Orders and Other Relevant Issues.

[4]RC 2929.21, RC 2929.31.

[5]RC 2929.11, RC 2929.31.

[6]See U.S. v. Dixon, 509 U.S. 688, 113 S. Ct. 2849, 125 L. Ed. 2d 556 (1993); see also State v. Higgins, 1996 WL 363543 (Ohio Ct. App. 5th Dist. Licking County 1996); State v. Lugli, 1995 WL 458671 (Ohio Ct. App. 6th Dist. Huron County 1995); State v. Ohm, 107 Ohio Misc. 2d 19, 736 N.E.2d 121 (Mun. Ct. 2000); State v. Bridges, 2015-Ohio-4480, 2015 WL 6522860 (Ohio Ct. App. 10th Dist. Franklin County 2015).

from the contempt finding.[7] Likewise, if the offender is first convicted of the criminal charge, no subsequent punishment for contempt for the same acts may be imposed.[8]

Q & A: My "ex" filed a motion with the court requiring me to show cause why I should not be held in contempt of court. She's alleging that I repeatedly contacted and harassed her via telephone, fax, and e-mail in direct violation of the terms of a civil protection order issued against me. Since the order was civil, can't I purge myself of contempt and avoid jail by agreeing to stop contacting her?

No. The primary purpose of the contempt proceedings is to preserve the authority and proper functioning of the court. The actions that you describe are viewed by most courts as indirect criminal contempt. An indirect contempt is one which is "committed outside the presence of the court, but which also tends to obstruct the due and orderly administration of justice."[9] Courts distinguish civil and criminal contempt in several important respects. While both types of contempt contain an element of punishment, courts differentiate between criminal and civil contempt not on the basis of punishment, but rather, by the character and purpose of the punishment.[10]

If the sanctions are primarily for reasons benefiting the complainant and are remedial and coercive in nature, the contempt is civil in nature.[11] In the context of a civil contempt proceeding, prison sentences are conditionally imposed, and "the contemnor is said to carry the keys of his prison in his own pocket," and the sentence will be suspended or terminated if the contemnor complies with the court's order. Civil contempt is a sanction to enforce compliance with an order of the court or to compensate for losses or damages sustained by reason of noncompliance.[12]

Criminal contempt, on the other hand, implies a purely punitive

[7]RC 2903.214(K)(2).

[8]RC 2903.214(K)(2). See also State v. Vanselow, 61 Ohio Misc. 2d 1, 572 N.E.2d 269 (Mun. Ct. 1991) and Westlake v. Patrick, 2005-Ohio-4419, 2005 WL 2046415 (Ohio Ct. App. 8th Dist. Cuyahoga County 2005).

[9]In re Lands, Lots or Parts of Lots Omitted From Foreclosure Proceedings-1944, 146 Ohio St. 589, 595, 33 Ohio Op. 80, 67 N.E.2d 433 (1946); Lyons v. Bowers, 2007-Ohio-1548, 2007 WL 959916 (Ohio Ct. App. 11th Dist. Lake County 2007).

[10]Brown v. Executive 200, Inc., 64 Ohio St. 2d 250, 253, 18 Ohio Op. 3d 446, 416 N.E.2d 610 (1980); Lyons v. Bowers, 2007-Ohio-1548, 2007 WL 959916 (Ohio Ct. App. 11th Dist. Lake County 2007); Shillitani v. U.S., 384 U.S. 364, 369, 86 S. Ct. 1531, 16 L. Ed. 2d 622 (1966); Goe v. Goe, 2007-Ohio-6767, 2007 WL 4395135 (Ohio Ct. App. 5th Dist. Stark County 2007); Morehart v. Snider, 2009-Ohio-5674, 2009 WL 3465746 (Ohio Ct. App. 9th Dist. Summit County 2009); Estate of Harrold v. Collier, 2009-Ohio-2782, 2009 WL 1655070 (Ohio Ct. App. 9th Dist. Wayne County 2009); Liming v. Damos, 2011-Ohio-2726, 2011 WL 2225067 (Ohio Ct. App. 4th Dist. Athens County 2011), judgment aff'd, 133 Ohio St. 3d 509, 2012-Ohio-4783, 979 N.E.2d 297 (2012); Hamper v. Dobrski, 2015-Ohio-1381, 2015 WL 1593249 (Ohio Ct. App. 8th Dist. Cuyahoga County 2015).

[11]Brown v. Executive 200, Inc., 64 Ohio St. 2d 250, 253, 18 Ohio Op. 3d 446, 416 N.E.2d 610 (1980); Lyons v. Bowers, 2007-Ohio-1548, 2007 WL 959916 (Ohio Ct. App. 11th Dist. Lake County 2007); Wilson v. Jones, 2013-Ohio-4368, 2013 WL 5739778 (Ohio Ct. App. 3d Dist. Seneca County 2013).

[12]Brown v. Executive 200, Inc., 64 Ohio St. 2d 250, 253, 18 Ohio Op. 3d 446, 416 N.E.2d 610 (1980). See also McComb v. Jacksonville Paper Co., 336 U.S. 187, 191, 69

aspect. It is not a remedy coercive in its nature, but rather, is punishment for the completed act of disobedience to vindicate the authority of the law and the court.[13] Thus, a key aspect of a civil contempt as opposed to one that is purely criminal is the opportunity for the contemnor to purge himself of the contempt sanction, and the discontinuation of the sanction once compliance is achieved.[14]

A protection order, not void on its face, must be complied with. A party may be criminally punished for violating a protection order even though the order itself is determined to be invalid after the violation occurred.[15]

In your case, there are no damages or losses sustained by reason of noncompliance that are compensable. The specific terms of the civil protection order that you violated were clear. You were not to contact the petitioner or other protected persons. Since you don't deny your failure to comply, your actions appear to constitute a violation of the terms of the civil protection order. There is no practical opportunity for you to purge or cure your contempt, because the contemptuous act of disobedience is already completed. Thus, the court's punishment for your contempt is criminal in nature, i.e., purely punitive, and meant to vindicate the authority of the court.[16]

Q & A: The Domestic Relations Court wants to hold me in contempt for violating a protection order that was never served on me. Can they do that?

Yes. Although the Ohio Supreme Court ruled that criminal prosecution for violation of a protection order requires that the defendant be served as a predicate to conviction, your case concerns whether you can be held to be in indirect civil contempt of the court's protection order, where the burden of proof is that of "clear and convincing evidence." Therefore, it is at least possible that you could be held in contempt for violating the order if you knew of its terms and willfully violated them.[17]

S. Ct. 497, 93 L. Ed. 599 (1949); Lyons v. Bowers, 2007-Ohio-1548, 2007 WL 959916 (Ohio Ct. App. 11th Dist. Lake County 2007); Home S. & L. Co. v. Midway Marine, Inc., 2012-Ohio-2432, 2012 WL 1971134 (Ohio Ct. App. 7th Dist. Mahoning County 2012); Wilson v. Jones, 2013-Ohio-4368, 2013 WL 5739778 (Ohio Ct. App. 3d Dist. Seneca County 2013).

[13]Brown v. Executive 200, Inc., 64 Ohio St. 2d 250, 254, 18 Ohio Op. 3d 446, 416 N.E.2d 610 (1980); Jenkins v. Jenkins, 2012-Ohio-4182, 975 N.E.2d 1060 (Ohio Ct. App. 2d Dist. Clark County 2012); Wilson v. Jones, 2013-Ohio-4368, 2013 WL 5739778 (Ohio Ct. App. 3d Dist. Seneca County 2013).

[14]In re Purola, 73 Ohio App. 3d 306, 312, 596 N.E.2d 1140 (3d Dist. Auglaize County 1991).

[15]Westlake v. Patrick, 2007-Ohio-1307, 2007 WL 853235 (Ohio Ct. App. 8th Dist. Cuyahoga County 2007).

[16]Lyons v. Bowers, 2007-Ohio-1548, 2007 WL 959916 (Ohio Ct. App. 11th Dist. Lake County 2007).

[17]Hamper v. Dobrski, 2015-Ohio-1381, 2015 WL 1593249 (Ohio Ct. App. 8th Dist. Cuyahoga County 2015).

Chapter 4

Protection Orders in Criminal Cases

§ 4:1 Purpose and description of the protection order

Ohio's domestic violence laws provide the state's criminal trial courts with the authority to provide certain victims a form of equitable relief once a criminal complaint is filed.[1] The primary purpose of the criminal protection order is to prevent any further harm from coming to the victim or any member of the victim's family or household while the criminal matter is pending.[2] A protection order will issue if a court determines that a failure to act preemptively will impair the safety and protection of the complainant or other family or household member.[3]

By statute, the protection order is a pretrial condition of release. It is distinct from any bail required to secure the offender's release from pretrial detention.[4] Bail secures the offender's promise to appear at all scheduled hearings on the underlying complaint. The protection order, in essence, is an offender's additional court-mandated promise to

---

[Section 4:1]

[1]RC 2919.26, RC 2903.213.

[2]See City of Xenia v. Berry, 1994 WL 12494 (Ohio Ct. App. 2d Dist. Greene County 1994); N. Olmsted v. Bullington, 139 Ohio App. 3d 565, 568, 744 N.E.2d 1225 (8th Dist. Cuyahoga County 2000) (**The purpose was to protect the victim, which sometimes means protecting the victim from the victim's own actions or behavior.**).

[3]RC 2919.26(C) (Effective July 6, 2018).

[4]RC 2919.26(A)(1), RC 2903.213(A); see Crim. R. 46.

abide by its terms in exchange for being allowed to remain at liberty while the criminal case proceeds.[5]

The typical terms of a temporary protection order mandate, at a minimum, that the offender have no contact with the affected family or household members while the court attempts to sort out the facts of a given case. The statute specifically grants the court the authority to require the offender to refrain from entering the residence, school, business, or place of employment of the complainant or other affected family or household member while the criminal matter is before the court.[6]

The statute also gives the court wide discretion to craft an order designed to ensure the safety of the individual or individuals for whom protection is sought.[7]

Q & A: The same judge that granted my wife's motion for a temporary protection order is going to hear the trial on the domestic violence complaint that she brought against me. Isn't that double jeopardy?

No. The hearing on the motion for a temporary protection order is a special proceeding. It is equitable in nature. Its purpose is not to determine whether the offender did or did not commit the alleged act. Rather, the court's function in hearing the motion is to determine whether the alleged offender's continued presence impairs the safety of any family or household member.

The law states that the granting of a temporary protection order against an offender does not constitute a finding of guilt.[8] The judge's consideration of the temporary protection order never placed you in jeopardy. Therefore, the court's consideration of the domestic violence case on its merits does not place you in the position to claim the constitutional protection of either the state or federal double jeopardy provisions.

Q & A: I am presiding over a trial where the defendant is charged with felonious assault. The prosecutor has just asked me to accept into evidence a certified copy of the protection order which was issued in this case. The defense has objected. Since the temporary protection order is a court order, I am inclined to let it in. Should I?

No. The law prohibits the use of a protection order as evidence in any trial of the matter whose facts generated the order.[9] Another question is presented, however, if the order that the prosecution wishes to present was issued in another criminal case involving a family or household member of the defendant. In that case, the prior order might be allowed in as an exception to the hearsay rule and under the statutory provision which allows evidence of prior bad acts, if a proper foundation is laid.

---

[5]State ex rel. Mormile v. Garfield Hts. Mun. Court, 79 Ohio App. 3d 539, 607 N.E.2d 890 (8th Dist. Cuyahoga County 1992), cause dismissed, 65 Ohio St. 3d 1452, 602 N.E.2d 249 (1992).

[6]RC 2919.26(C) (Effective July 6, 2018), RC 2903.213(C)(1).

[7]RC 2919.26(C) (Effective July 6, 2018), RC 2903.213(C)(1).

[8]RC 2919.26(E)(3).

[9]RC 2919.26(E)(3), RC 2903.213(E)(3).

Q & A: I got arrested last night for domestic violence. My girlfriend came to court this morning to drop the charges, but the prosecutor and the judge would not let her. In fact, the judge took one look at the black eye she got while we were tussling and issued a temporary protection order ordering me to leave the house. How can the judge do that when my girlfriend does not want to prosecute or have me leave?

Under the law, the court has the authority, on its own, to issue a temporary protection order.[10] The court may exercise that authority if it feels, based upon the circumstances, that the offender might pose a threat to the safety or protection of the complainant or any family or household member. The General Assembly decided that the peculiar dangers associated with domestic violence matters made it appropriate to grant judges the power to impose such conditions, even if they are not requested and even if they are not necessary to insure the alleged offender's appearance in court.[11] The appropriateness of legislative enactment of this authority, and judicial deployment of its use, is the subject of some debate.

Q & A: I'm the prosecutor in a small town. Today, a young man came in to file an assault charge against his girlfriend. He says that he is afraid of her and wants to get a temporary protection order. They've known each other all their lives, but they only began dating two months ago. What are the chances of the court granting the motion?

That depends on whether or not the young man and his girlfriend meet any of the definitions of family or household member found in the domestic violence statute.[12] If, for instance, during the short period of time that this couple dated they set up house together, but were never intimate, they might still qualify as family or household members under the statute.[13] In the months that followed the passage of the so-called "Defense of Marriage Amendment" to Ohio's Constitu-

[10]RC 2919.26(D)(1).

[11]State ex rel. Mormile v. Garfield Hts. Mun. Court, 79 Ohio App. 3d 539, 607 N.E.2d 890 (8th Dist. Cuyahoga County 1992), cause dismissed, 65 Ohio St. 3d 1452, 602 N.E.2d 249 (1992). See also Christopher Frank, Criminal Protection Orders in Domestic Violence Cases: Getting Rid of Rats With Snakes, 50 U. Miami L. Rev. 919 (July 1996).

[12]RC 2919.25(F). See also Text § 2:5, Nature of the relationships covered, for a complete listing of those considered family or household members under current Ohio law; State v. Gomez, 2011-Ohio-5475, 2011 WL 5067230 (Ohio Ct. App. 9th Dist. Summit County 2011); State v. Walburg, 2011-Ohio-4762, 2011 WL 4362748 (Ohio Ct. App. 10th Dist. Franklin County 2011); Bickham v. Bickham, 2011-Ohio-4213, 2011 WL 3672097 (Ohio Ct. App. 5th Dist. Fairfield County 2011); State v. Smith, 2011-Ohio-4409, 2011 WL 3860572 (Ohio Ct. App. 8th Dist. Cuyahoga County 2011); State v. McGlothan, 2012-Ohio-4049, 2012 WL 3862138 (Ohio Ct. App. 8th Dist. Cuyahoga County 2012), judgment rev'd, 138 Ohio St. 3d 146, 2014-Ohio-85, 4 N.E.3d 1021 (2014) (reversing court finding evidence sufficient to support conclusion victim was a person living as a spouse); State v. Rubes, 2012-Ohio-4100, 975 N.E.2d 1054 (Ohio Ct. App. 11th Dist. Portage County 2012); State v. Clouse, 2012-Ohio-3471, 2012 WL 3133059 (Ohio Ct. App. 10th Dist. Franklin County 2012); Prokopchuk v. Prokopchuk, 2012-Ohio-4480, 2012 WL 4478424 (Ohio Ct. App. 5th Dist. Stark County 2012); State v. Roberts, 2015-Ohio-5044, 2015 WL 8154018 (Ohio Ct. App. 9th Dist. Wayne County 2015).

[13]RC 2919.25(F)(2); Sindel v. Sindel, 1975 WL 181946 (Ohio Ct. App. 10th Dist. Franklin County 1975); Birthelmer v. Birthelmer, 1983 WL 6869 (Ohio Ct. App. 6th

tion,[14] this couple's residence in one appellate district as opposed to another would have determined not only whether a protection order would issue but whether the young lady faced prosecution at all.

The Supreme Court of Ohio's decision in *State v. Carswell*[15] resolved the conflict of authority that developed concerning the effect of the "Defense of Marriage Amendment" on Ohio's domestic violence statutes and ordinances. Prior to the Supreme Court of Ohio's decision in *Carswell*,[16] the majority of Ohio's appellate jurisdictions, to wit: the 1st,[17] 4th,[18] 5th,[19] 7th,[20] 8th,[21] 9th,[22] 10th,[23] and 12th,[24] ruled

---

Dist. Lucas County 1983); Dickerson v. Dickerson, 87 Ohio App. 3d 848, 850, 623 N.E.2d 237 (6th Dist. Lucas County 1993); Harrell v. Harrell, 1996 WL 170379 (Ohio Ct. App. 9th Dist. Lorain County 1996); State v. Simmons, 2011-Ohio-6074, 2011 WL 5869794 (Ohio Ct. App. 8th Dist. Cuyahoga County 2011); Laveer v. Laveer, 2013-Ohio-3294, 2013 WL 3935880 (Ohio Ct. App. 5th Dist. Delaware County 2013); Foster v. Foster, 2017-Ohio-4311, 92 N.E.3d 333 (Ohio Ct. App. 10th Dist. Franklin County 2017) (shared day-to-day expenses supported cohabitation).

[14]Ohio Constitution, Article XV, Section 11.

[15]State v. Carswell, 114 Ohio St. 3d 210, 2007-Ohio-3723, 871 N.E.2d 547 (2007); State v. McGlothan, 2012-Ohio-4049, 2012 WL 3862138 (Ohio Ct. App. 8th Dist. Cuyahoga County 2012), judgment rev'd, 138 Ohio St. 3d 146, 2014-Ohio-85, 4 N.E.3d 1021 (2014) (reversing court finding conviction for domestic violence supported); State v. Rubes, 2012-Ohio-4100, 975 N.E.2d 1054 (Ohio Ct. App. 11th Dist. Portage County 2012); City of Cleveland v. Johnson, 2014-Ohio-4083, 19 N.E.3d 604, 607 (Ohio Ct. App. 8th Dist. Cuyahoga County 2014), as corrected, (Sept. 23, 2014); State v. Mays, 2014-Ohio-814, 2014 WL 888375 (Ohio Ct. App. 8th Dist. Cuyahoga County 2014); State v. Brown, 2015-Ohio-950, 2015 WL 1138651 (Ohio Ct. App. 11th Dist. Lake County 2015); State v. Riedel, 2017-Ohio-8865, 100 N.E.3d 1155 (Ohio Ct. App. 8th Dist. Cuyahoga County 2017) (citing to State v. Carswell, 114 Ohio St. 3d 210, 2007-Ohio-3723, 871 N.E.2d 547 (2007), and State v. McGlothan, 138 Ohio St. 3d 146, 2014-Ohio-85, 4 N.E.3d 1021 (2014), affirming a domestic violence conviction where the victim lived with the defendant within five years of the assault).

[16]State v. Carswell, 114 Ohio St. 3d 210, 2007-Ohio-3723, 871 N.E.2d 547 (2007).

[17]State v. Ramirez, 2006-Ohio-5600, 2006 WL 3040638 (Ohio Ct. App. 1st Dist. Hamilton County 2006).

[18]State v. Goshorn, 2006-Ohio-2755, 2006 WL 1495256 (Ohio Ct. App. 4th Dist. Ross County 2006).

[19]State v. Newell, 2005-Ohio-2848, 2005 WL 1364937 (Ohio Ct. App. 5th Dist. Stark County 2005); State v. Hampton, 2006-Ohio-5995, 2006 WL 3290799 (Ohio Ct. App. 5th Dist. Stark County 2006); State v. Hare, 2006-Ohio-3926, 2006 WL 2141587 (Ohio Ct. App. 5th Dist. Delaware County 2006); State v. Brown, 166 Ohio App. 3d 32, 2006-Ohio-1181, 849 N.E.2d 44 (5th Dist. Stark County 2006).

[20]State v. Rexroad, 2005-Ohio-6790, 2005 WL 3489726 (Ohio Ct. App. 7th Dist. Columbiana County 2005); State v. Carnes, 2007-Ohio-604, 2007 WL 446019 (Ohio Ct. App. 7th Dist. Mahoning County 2007).

[21]State v. Burk, 164 Ohio App. 3d 740, 2005-Ohio-6727, 843 N.E.2d 1254 (8th Dist. Cuyahoga County 2005), judgment aff'd, 114 Ohio St. 3d 430, 2007-Ohio-4552, 872 N.E.2d 1212 (2007); State v. Brown, 2006-Ohio-6267, 2006 WL 3446238 (Ohio Ct. App. 8th Dist. Cuyahoga County 2006), aff'd on other grounds, 119 Ohio St. 3d 447, 2008-Ohio-4569, 895 N.E.2d 149 (2008); State v. Douglas, 2006-Ohio-2343, 2006 WL 1304860 (Ohio Ct. App. 8th Dist. Cuyahoga County 2006), judgment aff'd, 114 Ohio St. 3d 430, 2007-Ohio-4552, 872 N.E.2d 1212 (2007); Cleveland v. Voies, 2006-Ohio-815, 2006 WL 440341 (Ohio Ct. App. 8th Dist. Cuyahoga County 2006), judgment aff'd, 114 Ohio St. 3d 430, 2007-Ohio-4552, 872 N.E.2d 1212 (2007).

[22]State v. Nixon, 165 Ohio App. 3d 178, 2006-Ohio-72, 845 N.E.2d 544 (9th Dist. Summit County 2006).

[23]State v. Rodgers, 166 Ohio App. 3d 218, 2006-Ohio-1528, 850 N.E.2d 90 (10th

that the amendment did not affect the application of the state's domestic violence laws.

The 2d Appellate District, however, held that RC 2919.25 was unconstitutional as applied to cohabitants. It found that the statute recognized a "legal status" approximating marriage in violation of the prohibitions set forth in the "Defense of Marriage" amendment.[25] The 3d Appellate District came to similar conclusions.[26]

The 6th Appellate District agreed that the domestic violence laws created a "legal status" for cohabitants,[27] as did the 11th Appellate District,[28] but each found that the status those laws created did not approximate the design, qualities, significance, or effect of marriage. They, therefore, concluded that those laws and the "Defense of Marriage" provisions of Ohio's constitution could coexist.[29]

In *Carswell*,[30] the Supreme Court held that "[T]he term 'person living as a spouse' as defined in RC 2919.25 merely identifies a particular class of persons for the purposes of the domestic-violence statutes. It does not create or recognize a legal relationship that approximates the designs, qualities, or significance of marriage as prohibited by Section 11, Article XV of the Ohio Constitution. Persons who satisfy the 'living as a spouse' category are not provided any of the rights, benefits, or duties of marriage. A 'person living as a spouse' is simply a classification with significance to only domestic-violence statutes. Thus, RC 2919.25 is not unconstitutional and does not create a quasi-marital relationship in violation of Section 11, Article XV of the Ohio Constitution."

If the couple qualifies as family or household members under RC 2919.25(E)(1), then the young man is eligible to obtain a temporary protection order. On the other hand, if the couple did not live together, even if they were intimate throughout the period that they dated,

Dist. Franklin County 2006).

[24]State v. Carswell, 2005-Ohio-6547, 2005 WL 3358882 (Ohio Ct. App. 12th Dist. Warren County 2005), judgment aff'd, 114 Ohio St. 3d 210, 2007-Ohio-3723, 871 N.E.2d 547 (2007).

[25]State v. Ward, 166 Ohio App. 3d 188, 2006-Ohio-1407, 849 N.E.2d 1076 (2d Dist. Greene County 2006), judgment rev'd, 114 Ohio St. 3d 430, 2007-Ohio-4552, 872 N.E.2d 1212 (2007).

[26]State v. McKinley, 2006-Ohio-2507, 2006 WL 1381635 (Ohio Ct. App. 3d Dist. Logan County 2006), judgment rev'd, 114 Ohio St. 3d 430, 2007-Ohio-4552, 872 N.E.2d 1212 (2007); State v. Logsdon, 2006-Ohio-2938, 2006 WL 1585447 (Ohio Ct. App. 3d Dist. Seneca County 2006), judgment rev'd, 114 Ohio St. 3d 430, 2007-Ohio-4552, 872 N.E.2d 1212 (2007); State v. Shaffer, 2006-Ohio-2662, 2006 WL 1459769 (Ohio Ct. App. 3d Dist. Union County 2006), judgment rev'd, 114 Ohio St. 3d 430, 2007-Ohio-4552, 872 N.E.2d 1212 (2007).

[27]State v. Rodriguez, 2006-Ohio-3378, 2006 WL 1793688 (Ohio Ct. App. 6th Dist. Huron County 2006), judgment aff'd, 114 Ohio St. 3d 430, 2007-Ohio-4552, 872 N.E.2d 1212 (2007).

[28]State v. Jenson, 2006-Ohio-5169, 2006 WL 2796284 (Ohio Ct. App. 11th Dist. Lake County 2006), judgment aff'd, 114 Ohio St. 3d 430, 2007-Ohio-4552, 872 N.E.2d 1212 (2007).

[29]See also In re Ohio Domestic-Violence Statute Cases, 114 Ohio St. 3d 430, 2007-Ohio-4552, 872 N.E.2d 1212 (2007); State v. Koons, 2007-Ohio-5242, 2007 WL 2851882 (Ohio Ct. App. 7th Dist. Columbiana County 2007).

[30]State v. Carswell, 114 Ohio St. 3d 210, 2007-Ohio-3723, 871 N.E.2d 547 (2007).

their failure to fall into one of the categories of family or household members found in the domestic violence statute may prevent the court from issuing the temporary protection order that the young man seeks. Depending on the circumstances, if the prosecution can show that the victim's relationship with the offender included cohabitation and consortium, the couple may still qualify.[31] However, under the circumstances outlined, a better course of action might be to seek a more generic protection order—one that covers this couple based on the

[31]State v. Williams, 79 Ohio St. 3d 459, 1997-Ohio-79, 683 N.E.2d 1126 (1997). See also, State v. Woullard, 158 Ohio App. 3d 31, 2004-Ohio-3395, 813 N.E.2d 964 (2d Dist. Greene County 2004); State v. Eberly, 2004-Ohio-3026, 2004 WL 1302320 (Ohio Ct. App. 3d Dist. Wyandot County 2004); State v. Rodgers, 131 Ohio Misc. 2d 1, 2005-Ohio-1730, 827 N.E.2d 872 (C.P. 2005); State v. Clay, 181 Ohio App. 3d 563, 2009-Ohio-1235, 910 N.E.2d 14 (8th Dist. Cuyahoga County 2009) (*in dissent*); Youngstown v. Dixon, 2009-Ohio-1013, 2009 WL 581637 (Ohio Ct. App. 7th Dist. Mahoning County 2009); State v. Boldin, 2008-Ohio-6408, 2008 WL 5147450 (Ohio Ct. App. 11th Dist. Geauga County 2008); State v. Barnes, 2008-Ohio-5997, 2008 WL 4949833 (Ohio Ct. App. 8th Dist. Cuyahoga County 2008); State v. Pallai, 2008-Ohio-6635, 2008 WL 5245576 (Ohio Ct. App. 7th Dist. Mahoning County 2008); State v. Long, 2011-Ohio-1050, 2011 WL 806839 (Ohio Ct. App. 9th Dist. Summit County 2011); State v. Hazel, 2012-Ohio-835, 2012 WL 690312 (Ohio Ct. App. 2d Dist. Clark County 2012); State v. Short, 2011-Ohio-5744, 2011 WL 5353078 (Ohio Ct. App. 12th Dist. Butler County 2011); State v. Rubes, 2012-Ohio-4100, 975 N.E.2d 1054 (Ohio Ct. App. 11th Dist. Portage County 2012); State v. McGlothan, 138 Ohio St. 3d 146, 2014-Ohio-85, 4 N.E.3d 1021 (2014); State v. Riedel, 2017-Ohio-8865, 100 N.E.3d 1155 (Ohio Ct. App. 8th Dist. Cuyahoga County 2017), (citing to *Carswell* and *McGlothan*, affirming a DV conviction where the victim lived with the defendant within five years of the assault); Foster v. Foster, 2017-Ohio-4311, 92 N.E.3d 333 (Ohio Ct. App. 10th Dist. Franklin County 2017) (shared day-to-day expenses supported cohabitation); State v. White, 2014-Ohio-1446, 2014 WL 1384082 (Ohio Ct. App. 2d Dist. Montgomery County 2014); State v. Brauer, 2013-Ohio-3319, 2013 WL 3946124 (Ohio Ct. App. 12th Dist. Warren County 2013); State v. Hughes, 2015-Ohio-1173, 2015 WL 1403276 (Ohio Ct. App. 5th Dist. Tuscarawas County 2015); State v. Brown, 2015-Ohio-950, 2015 WL 1138651 (Ohio Ct. App. 11th Dist. Lake County 2015); State v. Blymiller, 2014-Ohio-5176, 2014 WL 6601976 (Ohio Ct. App. 5th Dist. Stark County 2014); City of Cleveland v. Johnson, 2014-Ohio-4083, 19 N.E.3d 604 (Ohio Ct. App. 8th Dist. Cuyahoga County 2014), as corrected, (Sept. 23, 2014); State v. Riedel, 2017-Ohio-8865, 100 N.E.3d 1155 (Ohio Ct. App. 8th Dist. Cuyahoga County 2017), (citing to *Carswell* and *McGlothan*, affirming a DV conviction where the victim lived with the defendant within five years of the assault); State v. Perander, 2015-Ohio-1752, 2015 WL 2169235 (Ohio Ct. App. 2d Dist. Montgomery County 2015); State v. Dobson, 2014-Ohio-3710, 2014 WL 4245968 (Ohio Ct. App. 8th Dist. Cuyahoga County 2014); State v. Martin, 2016-Ohio-225, 57 N.E.3d 411 (Ohio Ct. App. 5th Dist. Tuscarawas County 2016); State v. Roberts, 2015-Ohio-5044, 2015 WL 8154018 (Ohio Ct. App. 9th Dist. Wayne County 2015); State v. Hughes, 2015-Ohio-1173, 2015 WL 1403276 (Ohio Ct. App. 5th Dist. Tuscarawas County 2015); State v. Williams, 2017-Ohio-803, 2017 WL 900070 (Ohio Ct. App. 5th Dist. Stark County 2017); State v. Plott, 2017-Ohio-38, 80 N.E.3d 1108 (Ohio Ct. App. 3d Dist. Seneca County 2017), appeal not allowed, 150 Ohio St. 3d 1452, 2017-Ohio-8136, 83 N.E.3d 938 (2017); State v. Walker, 2016-Ohio-398, 2016 WL 529920 (Ohio Ct. App. 8th Dist. Cuyahoga County 2016); State v. Riedel, 2017-Ohio-8865, 100 N.E.3d 1155 (Ohio Ct. App. 8th Dist. Cuyahoga County 2017), (citing to State v. Carswell, 114 Ohio St. 3d 210, 2007-Ohio-3723, 871 N.E.2d 547 (2007), and State v. McGlothan, 138 Ohio St. 3d 146, 2014-Ohio-85, 4 N.E.3d 1021 (2014), affirming a domestic violence conviction where the victim lived with the defendant within five years of the assault); Foster v. Foster, 2017-Ohio-4311, 92 N.E.3d 333 (Ohio Ct. App. 10th Dist. Franklin County 2017) (shared day- to-day expenses supported cohabitation).

young lady's assaultive conduct rather than on the couple's status as family or household members.[32]

Q & A: At trial, the only witness for the prosecution was the alleged victim. The testimony presented indicated that the alleged victim and the defendant were involved as boyfriend and girlfriend and that they were sharing the same house at the time that the incident occurred. The defense made a motion for a directed verdict of acquittal at the close of the state's case, maintaining that the prosecution failed to establish that the parties shared household expenses and such that they cohabitated as family or household members at the time of the offense. Should the court grant the motion?

The Ohio Supreme Court holds that evidence of shared living expenses is not necessary to establish cohabitation, where, as here, the prosecution is able to show that the parties were engaged in a boyfriend/girlfriend relationship, that they were living together at the time of the incident and that they had been living together for some time prior thereto. Under these circumstances, the state has no obligation to demonstrate the sharing of familial or financial responsibilities and consortium to prove cohabitation. Instead, based upon this evidence, a trial court can reasonably determine that the state has established cohabitation and that the defendant was a person living as a spouse when the incident occurred. There is no authority for the proposition that there is a minimum duration that a couple must live together before they are accorded the protection of the Domestic Violence laws.[33]

§ 4:2 Distinctions between a criminal protection order and a civil protection order

Both a criminal protection order and a civil protection order attempt to provide equitable relief to those who claim abuse by assault or threat of assault.[1] The primary differences between the two orders are:

(1) The criminal protection order must be filed in conjunction with the filing of a criminal complaint,[2] while a petition for a civil protection order may be filed independently of any other action.[3]

(2) The criminal protection order serves primarily to separate the parties during the pendency of the criminal action before the court. This means that its effective life, at a maximum in most misdemeanor complaints, is no longer than forty-five to ninety

---

[32]See RC 2903.213(A).

[33]State v. McGlothan, 138 Ohio St. 3d 146, 2014-Ohio-85, 4 N.E.3d 1021 (2014); State v. Hughes, 2015-Ohio-1173, 2015 WL 1403276 (Ohio Ct. App. 5th Dist. Tuscarawas County 2015); State v. Brown, 2015-Ohio-950, 2015 WL 1138651 (Ohio Ct. App. 11th Dist. Lake County 2015); State v. Blymiller, 2014-Ohio-5176, 2014 WL 6601976 (Ohio Ct. App. 5th Dist. Stark County 2014); City of Cleveland v. Johnson, 2014-Ohio-4083, 19 N.E.3d 604 (Ohio Ct. App. 8th Dist. Cuyahoga County 2014), as corrected, (Sept. 23, 2014); State v. White, 2014-Ohio-1446, 2014 WL 1384082 (Ohio Ct. App. 2d Dist. Montgomery County 2014).

[Section 4:2]

[1]RC 2919.26, RC 2903.213, RC 3113.31(E)(1).

[2]RC 2919.26(A)(1), RC 2903.213(A).

[3]RC 3113.31(E)(1). See also RC 2903.214(D)(1), which provides coverage to individuals who are the victims of menacing by stalking.

days. In most felony cases, the maximum effective period of the order generally will not exceed 270 days.

Ohio's speedy trial statutes establish these time parameters.[4] Those statutes require that a defendant be brought to trial within the period provided. Unless the prosecution brings the defendant to trial within that period, the complaint must be dismissed. Whether the complaint is tried, pleaded, or dismissed for failure to abide by the provisions of the speedy trial statutes, the relief afforded by the criminal protection order terminates at the conclusion of the criminal matter.[5]

(3) Unlike the criminal protection order, the civil protection order seeks to define the nature of the relationship that will exist between the alleged victim and the alleged offender during the life of the order. The civil protection order may remain in place for up to five years, at the court's discretion.[6] The five-year life span of the civil protection order became law on January 1, 1998, following an amendment to the statute. Prior to that time, the maximum effective period for civil protection orders was no more than two years.[7]

Another amendment to the civil protection order statute makes it possible to obtain protection orders against juvenile respondents.[8] However, the duration of civil protection orders in cases involving juvenile respondents is not the same as that provided for adults.[9] Under the law, a protection order obtained against a juvenile will automatically terminate and the court will automatically seal the record of the proceeding in which it was granted, upon the respondent reaching nineteen years of age, unless the court determines that the respondent did not comply with all of the terms of the order.[10] Even if the court determines that the respondent did not comply with all of the terms of the order, it still must consider sealing the record of the proceeding, either sua sponte or on the respondent's motion, at any point after two years have elapsed from the expiration of the order.[11]

(4) The civil protection order can provide for the temporary possession of real property, the provision of support, the temporary allocation of parental rights and responsibilities, the requirement of the offender and/or the victim to undergo counseling, the apportionment of the household and family personal property, as well as any other relief that the court deems fair and equitable.[12] The relief available pursuant to a criminal protection order does not include support, allocation of parental rights and responsi-

[4]RC 2945.71, RC 2945.72.

[5]RC 2919.26(E)(2), RC 2903.213(E)(2).

[6]RC 3113.31(E)(3)(a).

[7]See Am. Sub. S.B. 1, eff. 1-1-98.

[8]Am. Sub. H.B. 10 (eff. 6-17-2010).

[9]Am. Sub. H.B. 10 (eff. 6-17-2010).

[10]Am. Sub. H.B. 10 (eff. 6-17-2010).

[11]Am. Sub. H.B. 10 (eff. 6-17-2010).

[12]RC 3113.31(E)(1)(a) to RC 3113(E)(1)(k).

bilities, prejudgment counseling for either party, or the apportionment of personal property.[13] It is, therefore, a much more limited tool.

Q & A: I just filed a complaint for aggravated assault against my baby's father. I plan to get a temporary protection order against him. He still has my car keys, a lot of my clothes, and some of my jewelry at his house. Will the temporary protection order let me get my things back?

No. A temporary protection order serves as an extraordinary way to enhance your safety during a time when you might otherwise be particularly vulnerable. It will not authorize you to get your personal items back from the offender. The disposition of personal property still in the possession of your child's father requires the imposition of a civil protection order by a common pleas court or the domestic relations division of a common pleas court.[14]

Q & A: Is the State required to produce formal documentation of civil paternity establishment in order to meet the "family member" element in father/child criminal domestic violence prosecutions and is a putative father's testimony that he and the defendant shared the same residence sufficient to satisfy the domestic violence law's requirement that they live together for purposes of prosecution?

The State can utilize testimonial evidence going to the issue of paternity, subject to a credibility determination by the jurors or the finder of fact.[15] The admission or exclusion of evidence rests in the sound discretion of the trial court. Thus, the trial court is within its discretion to credit the testimony of the putative father relative to the fact that he and the defendant lived together.[16]

§ 4:3 Who may be protected by a criminal protection order

A temporary protection order may issue to protect: (1) any alleged victim of, and/or (2) another person who qualified as a family or household member of an alleged victim at the time of the alleged commission of any of the following criminal acts or substantially similar municipal ordinances:

- Aggravated murder[1]
- Murder[2]
- Voluntary manslaughter[3]

---

[13]See RC 2919.26.

[14]RC 3113.31(E)(1)(h).

[15]State v. Davis, 2014-Ohio-1197, 2014 WL 1340774 (Ohio Ct. App. 5th Dist. Licking County 2014).

[16]State v. Davis, 2014-Ohio-1197, 2014 WL 1340774 (Ohio Ct. App. 5th Dist. Licking County 2014).

[Section 4:3]

[1]RC 2903.01.

[2]RC 2903.02.

[3]RC 2903.03.

- Involuntary manslaughter[4]
- Felonious assault[5]
- Aggravated assault[6]
- Assault[7]
- Permitting child abuse[8]
- Aggravated menacing[9]
- Menacing by stalking[10]
- Menacing[11]
- Kidnapping[12]
- Abduction[13]
- Extortion[14]
- Rape[15]
- Sexual battery[16]
- Gross sexual imposition[17]
- Aggravated arson[18]
- Arson[19]
- Criminal damaging and endangering[20]
- Criminal mischief[21]
- Aggravated robbery[22]
- Robbery[23]
- Aggravated burglary[24]
- Burglary[25]
- Aggravated trespass[26]

---

[4]RC 2903.04.

[5]RC 2903.11.

[6]RC 2903.12.

[7]RC 2903.13.

[8]RC 2903.15.

[9]RC 2903.21.

[10]RC 2903.211.

[11]RC 2903.22.

[12]RC 2905.01.

[13]RC 2905.02.

[14]RC 2905.11.

[15]RC 2907.02.

[16]RC 2907.03.

[17]RC 2907.05.

[18]RC 2909.02.

[19]RC 2909.03.

[20]RC 2909.06.

[21]RC 2909.07.

[22]RC 2911.01.

[23]RC 2911.02.

[24]RC 2911.11.

[25]RC 2911.12.

[26]RC 2911.211.

- Inciting to violence[27]
- Aggravated riot[28]
- Riot[29]
- Inducing panic[30]
- Endangering children[31]
- Domestic violence[32]
- Intimidation[33]
- Intimidation of attorney, victim or witness in a criminal case[34]
- Escape[35]
- Improperly discharging a firearm at or into a habitation or in a school safety zone;[36] and
- Criminal trespass.[37]

Thus, orders may issue for those involved in traditional, as well as nontraditional, families and households.

Enhancements to the state's criminal protection order statutes expanded the list of people who are now able to seek coverage under their provisions.[38] The law now allows *any* family or household member of a *victim* of an act of domestic violence to seek a protection order. Depending on the nature of the family or household relationship of the movant to both the victim and the offender, the order sought may cover the individual seeking the order, the complainant, the victim, and/or any other family or household member of the alleged offender. In fact, Ohio's General Assembly potentially extended the coverage of the criminal protection order statute[39] to include every individual who alleges that they are the victim of any sexually oriented offense,[40] even in the absence of a family or household relationship.

If the individual who seeks the protection order is a family or household member of the *alleged offender and* the alleged victim (i.e., a parent, child, sibling, in-law, etc.), an order sought under the domestic violence law may also provide protection for the individual making the request.[41]

---

[27]RC 2917.01.

[28]RC 2917.02.

[29]RC 2917.03.

[30]RC 2917.31.

[31]RC 2919.22(B)(1), RC 2919.22(B)(2), RC 2919.22(B)(3), RC 2919.22(B)(4).

[32]RC 2919.25.

[33]RC 2921.03.

[34]RC 2921.04.

[35]RC 2921.34.

[36]RC 2923.161.

[37]RC 2911.21.

[38]RC 2919.26(A) to RC 2919.26(D), RC 2919.26(G), RC 2919.26(I) and RC 2903.213(A) to RC 2903.213(D), RC 2903.213(G). See also the definitions of family or household members found in RC 2919.25(F).

[39]RC 2919.26(A)(1).

[40]See 2005 S.B. 17, eff. 8/3/2006.

[41]RC 2919.26(A)(1), RC 2919.26(C)(1).

If the individual who seeks the protection order is a family or household member of the *alleged victim but not* of the alleged offender (i.e., a new husband, wife, boyfriend/girlfriend), an order sought under the domestic violence law will *not* provide protection for the one making the request. This is because the requester lacks the prerequisite relationship to the alleged offender required for special protection under the law.[42]

An individual who is a family or household member of the victim *but not* of the offender may nonetheless qualify for an order under the expanded protection order provisions of the menacing-by-stalking laws, which do not depend on a pre-existing relationship to trigger their operation.[43]

Criminal protection orders are also available to other individuals involved in violent interpersonal relationships who do not qualify as family or household members. If these individuals allege that they are the victims of qualifying criminal acts (including assault, aggravated assault, felonious assault, menacing by stalking, aggravated trespass, aggravated menacing, or menacing), they may seek to enhance their safety by obtaining criminal protection orders.[44] In situations where the relationship status of the parties is tenuous, the prosecuting authority is well advised to consider this alternative when seeking protection for a complainant or alleged victim.

Q & A: My boyfriend is very jealous. He apparently saw me talking to a male friend earlier today. Claiming that I disrespected him, he beat me up badly. We've been together for more than one year. We've never lived together, and we don't have children in common. I called the police, but I want to get a protection order because he has hurt me before. Am I eligible?

Yes. An amendment to RC 2903.213, which took effect on December 31, 1997, extended protection order coverage to situations such as yours.[45] Under the amendment, it is not necessary to establish the existence of some type of relationship to qualify for a protection order. All that is necessary is evidence that you were the victim of an assault and that it is more probable than not that the offender committed the assault against you.[46]

Q & A: My granddaughter is on crack cocaine. Two weeks ago, she was evicted from her apartment. I let her and my great-grandson stay with me until she can find somewhere else to live. Yesterday, she threatened to kill me, herself, and her child if I didn't give her my social security check so she could buy crack. I am afraid for myself and my great-grandson! What can I do?

---

[42]RC 2919.26(A)(1), RC 2919.26(C)(1).

[43]RC 2903.211(A).

[44]RC 2903.213.

[45]See 1997 H.B. 93.

[46]RC 2903.213.

Even though your granddaughter is only staying with you temporarily, she still presently qualifies as a family or household member.[47] It is, therefore, possible for you to obtain protection under the state's domestic violence laws. A temporary protection order is available to remove your granddaughter from your home and to prohibit any future acts or threats of violence against you and your great-grandson.

Your great-grandson's situation is more complicated. As his natural parent, your granddaughter retains custody of her son. Since her behavior appears to put him at risk, however, you are not required to wait until she hurts him before moving to protect him. As a family or household member, he qualifies for, and is technically subject to, the terms and conditions of any temporary protection order that you obtain.

Since your great-grandson's custody as well as his safety are implicated here, the better course of action is for you to pursue a civil protection order. The latter takes precedence over a temporary protection order,[48] is more flexible, and can address the issue of custody.

Q & A: My wife charged me with domestic violence and had a temporary protection order issued against me. She's the one that really started this fight, and I want to get a temporary protection order against her. Can I do that?

The law generally frowns upon and discourages the issuance of mutual temporary protection orders for conduct arising out of the same event.[49] Under certain extraordinary circumstances, however, both parties may obtain the benefits of a temporary protection order. The court may issue a temporary protection order to both parties only if it is convinced that:

(1) both parties have filed separate criminal complaints against one another, *and*

(2) both parties acted as primary physical aggressors,[50] *and*

(3) neither party acted in self-defense.[51]

If the court finds it necessary to issue mutual protection orders, the law further requires the court to determine that the criteria for the issuance of a protection order, as set forth in the statute, are met for each request.[52]

Q & A: My eighteen-year-old stepson still lives at home with his mother and me. He recently broke up with his girlfriend because of her violent temper. She has not taken it well. For the last two weeks, she has called him at all times of the day and night. Today, she just showed up at our door. When I told her that he refused to come to the door to speak with her, she screamed that she knew that I was keeping him away from her and that we would all "pay" for the pain we have caused her.

Although my stepson filed a criminal complaint against his

---

[47]RC 2919.25(F)(1)(a)(ii).

[48]RC 2919.26(E)(2).

[49]RC 2919.26(I)(2).

[50]RC 2919.26(I)(2)(b).

[51]RC 2919.26(I)(2)(b).

[52]RC 2919.26(I)(2)(b).

ex-girlfriend for menacing by stalking, he is reluctant to take the additional step of obtaining a protection order. I am afraid that she will try to do something to my family if something more is not done to stop her. What legal options do I have?

Even though you are not the primary target of the young lady's stalking behavior, your status as a qualifying family or household member affords you the right to seek a protection order from the court on your stepson's behalf.[53] If such an order issues, it will be effective while the criminal matter is pending before the court.[54] The law provides that the specific provisions of the order direct themselves to insuring the safety and protection of your stepson.[55] However, the court has wide latitude in drafting its order so that it may contain provisions that have the practical effect of limiting the offender's ability to come within proximity of your family.[56]

Q & A: My sister and I have not lived in the same household for over 30 years. Yesterday, at a family gathering, we got in to a big fight and she hit me with a baseball bat. I am really afraid of her and want to get a protection order. Does the amount of time that has passed since we last lived together make that impossible?

No. As natural siblings, your status as family or household members under Ohio's domestic violence statute is perpetual. Although the language of the statute speaks of being "a family or household member at the time of the violation," that reference refers to the definition of the party as one entitled to relief under the statute, not to the actual physical living arrangements at the time of the event.[57]

The only members of the protected class whose status is time delimited are those individuals who have not been married but, rather, have only lived together as spouses. Members of this group have eligibility to seek a temporary protection order under Ohio's domestic violence law only if it can be established that they cohabited with the offender within five years of the alleged commission of the act in question.[58]

§ 4:4 Procedure for obtaining a temporary protection order

The issuance of a temporary protection order is an adjunct to a criminal prosecution. The procedure for obtaining a temporary protection order is set forth in detail in RC 2919.26(B) to RC 2919.26(D) and in RC 2903.211(B) to RC 2903.211(D).

Once a prosecution is commenced by the filing of a complaint, where appropriate, either the victim, the complainant, a family or household

[53]RC 2903.213(A).

[54]RC 2903.213(E)(2).

[55]RC 2903.213(C)(1).

[56]RC 2903.213(C)(1).

[57]Read RC 2919.26(A)(1), in conjunction with RC 2919.25(F)(2).

[58]Read RC 2919.26(A)(1), in conjunction with RC 2919.25(F)(2).

member of the victim or the offender,[1] or, in an emergency, an arresting officer on the complainant's behalf,[2] may move the court for a temporary protection order. The motion is required to follow a specific format.[3] The language to be used in the motion is established by statute.[4] The clerk of each court that handles criminal matters requiring the issuance of temporary protection orders is required to maintain forms bearing language substantially similar to that which appears in the statute.[5]

The only additional information that needs to be added to the form before it can be filed with the court is the defendant's name, the assigned case number, and the complainant's address and signature (or the address and signature of the arresting officer filing on behalf of the complainant).[6] A complainant may file for a temporary protection order without the assistance of a prosecutor or other attorney. A sample of the required format is found in RC 2919.26(B).

Once the motion is filed the court is obligated to hold a hearing on it as soon as possible, but no later than 24 hours after it is filed, to determine whether it should issue. The requirement of holding the hearing within 24 for hours of filing reinforces the legislature's desire to have the courts consider such motions and act on them as expeditiously as possible.

Even if the defendant remains at large, the court is still obligated to hold a hearing, ex parte, within 24 hours of the time that a motion for a criminal protection order is filed with the court. The alleged victim, the complainant, or the arresting officer who filed the motion on the victim's behalf, as appropriate, is required to appear at the hearing.[7] The witness must provide the court with the information it needs to decide whether or not to grant the motion.

In some instances, the damage done to the health of the victim of a domestic assault may be so severe that the court is required to take action. The court may act to provide protection even without the victim's active involvement in the process. If the facts warrant it, the court may even act in the face of active opposition of the victim. The court is authorized, under RC 2919.26(C), to receive information at a temporary protection order hearing from persons other than the victim or arresting officer if they are in a position to provide it and:

(1) the person who requested the temporary protection order has been hospitalized or has suffered some other medical problem as a result of the events which gave rise to the underlying criminal complaint, and

(2) the hospitalization or other medical problems suffered by the

---

[Section 4:4]

[1] RC 2919.26(A)(1), RC 2903.213(A).

[2] RC 2919.26(A)(1).

[3] RC 2919.26(B), RC 2903.213(B).

[4] RC 2919.26(B), RC 2903.213(B).

[5] RC 2919.26(B), RC 2903.213(B).

[6] RC 2919.26(B), RC 2903.213(B).

[7] State v. Conkle, 2003-Ohio-2410, 2003 WL 21060822 (Ohio Ct. App. 5th Dist. Knox County 2003).

person who requested the temporary protection order render the person who requested it unable to appear at the motion hearing.

Under these circumstances, a third party with knowledge of the facts supporting the issuance of the temporary protection order may present information to the court, regardless of whether the individual who requested the order is the victim or the officer who filed on the victim's behalf.[8] No provision is made for a family or household member, an officer, or a third party to appear on behalf of a victim where a protection order is sought as a result of an allegation of a menacing by stalking. Injury serious enough to impair a victim's ability to come to court undoubtedly would give rise to other charges of assaultive behavior to which protection orders would attach.[9]

The court is also authorized to issue a temporary protection order on its own motion at any time after an appropriate criminal complaint has been filed.[10] The authority of the court to grant a motion for a temporary protection order on its own motion is not predicated upon the court receiving the testimony of the complainant or the arresting officer. Rather, it would appear to be based upon the court's own assessment of the totality of the circumstances and the need to protect the safety of any family or household member of the alleged offender.[11]

The law provides for the protection of the due process rights of a defendant who has not been apprehended by the time that the temporary protection order hearing is held. If the defendant is not present at the time that the temporary protection order is granted, the court is required to hold a second hearing on the court's next business day following the defendant's apprehension, surrender, or response to a summons.[12] The purpose of the second hearing is to give the defendant the right to contest the facts that were presented to obtain the temporary protection order and to contest the continuation of any order granted in the defendant's absence.

Although a defendant who was not present at the first hearing has the right to have a second hearing to challenge the continued application of the order, the defendant is not required to exercise that right. If the defendant is willing to abide by the terms of the temporary protection order, the second hearing may be waived.

Q & A: My office has issued a complaint for domestic violence. The victim is so frightened that she has gone into hiding. The defendant is still at large. I am going to request a temporary protection order on the victim's behalf. Her doctor is available to testify as to the injuries that she suffered, which were quite extensive. Is it likely that the court will grant the motion?

Since the victim in this case has voluntarily absented herself, technically speaking, the court will not have the witness required by statute at the hearing on the temporary protection order hearing.

---

[8]RC 2919.26(C)(1)

[9]Cf. RC 2919.26(C)(1), RC 2903.213(C)(1), and RC 2903.214.

[10]RC 2919.26(D)(1), RC 2903.213(D)(1).

[11]RC 2919.26(D)(1), RC 2903.213(D)(1).

[12]RC 2919.26(d)(2)(a), RC 2903.213(D)(2)(a).

That being the case, the court would certainly be within its rights to refuse to issue the order. The court does have the discretion to issue the order even without the victim, if it can be convinced that the continued safety of the victim or some other member of the offender's family or household is in danger if the order does not issue. The testimony of the arresting officer and of the attending physician might be enough to convince the court of the need for the order.

The Supreme Court of Ohio held that, until an order was actually delivered to the defendant, it would not be effective. Under that ruling, if the defendant violated any of its terms before service was delivered, criminal prosecution for a violation was not available.[13]

However, subsequent to the Supreme Court's ruling the Ohio General Assembly passed, and the Governor signed, legislation that amended the law that governs violation of protection orders.[14] As amended, the law overturns the Supreme Court's decision and provides that it is no longer necessary for the prosecution to prove that a protection order or consent agreement was actually served on the defendant for it to be effective[15] if the prosecution is able to prove either,1) that the defendant was shown the protection order, consent agreement, or a copy thereof, **or** 2) that a judge, magistrate or law enforcement officer informed the defendant that the order was issued ***and*** that the defendant recklessly violated the terms of the order, the defendant is accountable for any violation of its terms.[16]

§ 4:5 When, where, and how a protection order takes effect

A protection order takes effect immediately upon its journalization by the court. Once journalized, it is effective throughout the state of Ohio. It is also enforceable in other states under the provisions of the Omnibus Crime Bill passed by the federal government in 1994. The Violence Against Women Act of 1994,[1] which was enacted as a part of that legislation, requires all jurisdictions to provide full faith and credit to the protection orders issued by other jurisdictions of the United States. Obviously, those same provisions require Ohio to extend full faith and credit to the protection orders of other jurisdictions, when those orders are presented in Ohio for enforcement.

Ohio's protection order law provides a complainant the ability to

---

[13] State v. Smith, 136 Ohio St. 3d 1, 2013-Ohio-1698, 989 N.E.2d 972 (2013); Toledo v. Lewis, 2013-Ohio-3289, 2013 WL 3936455 (Ohio Ct. App. 6th Dist. Lucas County 2013); State v. Johnson, 2014-Ohio-2435, 2014 WL 2566260 (Ohio Ct. App. 6th Dist. Wood County 2014). But see State v. Hall, 2013-Ohio-5856, 2013 WL 6918863 (Ohio Ct. App. 5th Dist. Delaware County 2013); State v. Terrell, 2014-Ohio-4344, 2014 WL 4823870 (Ohio Ct. App. 2d Dist. Clark County 2014); State v. Verga, 2015-Ohio-2582, 2015 WL 3938069 (Ohio Ct. App. 12th Dist. Warren County 2015); State v. Meinke, 2017-Ohio-7787, 97 N.E.3d 1184 (Ohio Ct. App. 9th Dist. Lorain County 2017) (citing State v. Smith, 136 Ohio St. 3d 1, 2013-Ohio-1698, 989 N.E.2d 972 (2013), for the proposition that service is a necessary element and reversing for the conviction because the court failed to instruct the jury of that element).

[14] RC 2919.27.

[15] R.C. 2919.17(D).

[16] R.C. 2919.17(D).

[Section 4:5]

[1] 34 U.S.C.A. §§ 10441 to 10453.

give notice that a protection order has been granted to counties other than the one where the order was issued.[2] Notice is accomplished by registering the order with the courts of the remote county.[3] Additionally, the complainant may also provide notice to the law enforcement agencies of the remote county.[4] However, it is not necessary to register the protection order in order to give it effect.[5]

Registration of a protection order with a county, other than the one in which it was granted, is effected by:

(1) obtaining a certified copy of the order from the clerk of the court that granted it[6] and
(2) presenting the certified copy to the clerk of either the common pleas or municipal court in the county where the complainant desires registration.[7]

Registration with the law enforcement agencies of a county other than the one in which the order was granted is effected by:

(1) obtaining a certified copy of the order from the clerk of the court that granted it,[8]
(2) presenting the certified copy to the clerk of either the common pleas or municipal court of the county where the complainant desires registration,[9] and
(3) filing a copy of the registered, certified order, bearing proof of registration, with one of the law enforcement agencies of the county where the order is desired to be registered.[10]

Notice of the existence of an out-of-county protection order may be given to a court of any non-issuing county, without giving notice to any of the non-issuing county's law enforcement agencies.[11] The converse is not true since the order provided to a law enforcement agency must bear, on its face, proof that it was first registered with a court in that non-issuing county.[12]

The giving of notice of the existence of a protection order to a remote county is not required by Ohio law. Thus, the notice provision in the statute can only serve to facilitate the enforcement of these orders. It cannot serve as a prerequisite to that enforcement. All law enforcement agencies in the state are required by law to establish and maintain an index of all protection orders presented to them.[13] Additionally, all common pleas and municipal courts are required to

[2]R.C. 2919.26(G)(4).

[3]R.C. 2919.26(G)(4).

[4]R.C. 2919.26(G)(4).

[5]RC 3113.31(F)(4), 2919.26(G)(5), 2903.213(G)(3).

[6]RC 2919.26(G)(4), RC 3113.31(N)(2)(a).

[7]RC 2919.26(G)(4), RC 3113.31(N)(2)(a).

[8]RC 2919.26(G)(4), RC 3113.31(N)(2)(a).

[9]RC 2919.26(G)(4), RC 3113.31(N)(2)(a).

[10]RC 2919.19(G)(4), RC 3113.31(N)(1).

[11]State v. Cooper, 163 Ohio Misc. 2d 27, 2010-Ohio-6697, 950 N.E.2d 248 (Mun. Ct. 2010).

[12]RC 3113.31(N)(2)(b).

[13]R.C. 2919.26(G)(3), 3113.31(F)(3), 2903.231(G)(2).

maintain a similar registry of all protection orders that are presented to them and which they accept and endorse for registration.[14]

Notice of a court order is usually required before an individual is answerable for its breach.[15] For some time, the appellate courts of Ohio were divided as to the exact type of notice required before an offender could be held criminally answerable for violation of a protection order. Some held that the only requirement was that the offender had actual notice of the existence of the court's order.[16] These courts asserted that service was not an element of the offense of violating a protection order and, therefore, proof of service was not required to hold an offender liable.[17]

Another appellate court found service of a temporary protection order on the defendant is not an element of the offense of violation of the protection order.[18]

The Supreme Court of Ohio resolved this conflict, declaring that delivery of a protection order is synonymous with service. Therefore, until its ruling was overturned by an amendment to the law,[19] if the State failed to prove that a defendant was served with a protection order before the defendant allegedly violated it, the evidence was not sufficient for conviction.[20] As amended in September 27, 2017, the law overturns the Supreme Court's decision in *State v. Smith* and provides that it is no longer necessary for the prosecution to prove that a protection order or consent agreement was actually served on the defendant for it to be effective,[21]if the prosecution is able to prove either: 1) that the defendant was shown the protection order, consent agreement, or a copy thereof, **or** 2) that a judge, magistrate or law enforcement officer informed the defendant that the order was issued ***and*** that the defendant recklessly violated the terms of the order, the defendant is accountable for any violation of its terms.[22]

Therefore, Ohio's domestic violence and menacing-by-stalking laws[23] do allow the court to grant an injured family or household member a protection order with or without prior notice to the alleged offender. The court's authority to grant a protection order without notifying the alleged perpetrator that the court is considering taking action, or af-

[14]RC 3113.31(N)(3).

[15]State v. Cooper, 163 Ohio Misc. 2d 27, 2010-Ohio-6697, 950 N.E.2d 248 (Mun. Ct. 2010).

[16]State v. Rutherford, 2009-Ohio-2071, 2009 WL 1175050 (Ohio Ct. App. 2d Dist. Champaign County 2009); State v. Bunch, 2001 WL 39599 (Ohio Ct. App. 9th Dist. Summit County 2001); State v. Bombardiere, 2007-Ohio-1537, 2007 WL 959895 (Ohio Ct. App. 3d Dist. Union County 2007).

[17]State v. Hall, 2013-Ohio-660, 989 N.E.2d 111 (Ohio Ct. App. 5th Dist. Delaware County 2013), appeal allowed, cause remanded, 135 Ohio St. 3d 1456, 2013-Ohio-2285, 988 N.E.2d 576 (2013).

[18]State v. Hall, 2013-Ohio-660, 989 N.E.2d 111 (Ohio Ct. App. 5th Dist. Delaware County 2013), appeal allowed, cause remanded, 135 Ohio St. 3d 1456, 2013-Ohio-2285, 988 N.E.2d 576 (2013).

[19]See Sub. S.B. 7, eff. 9-27-2017 and R.C. 2919.27.

[20]State v. Smith, 136 Ohio St. 3d 1, 2013-Ohio-1698, 989 N.E.2d 972 (2013).

[21]R.C. 2919.27.

[22]R.C. 2919.27.

[23]RC 2919.26, RC 2903.213, RC 2903.214.

fording the offender an opportunity to be heard prior to taking that action, is an abrogation of the basic principles of due process. It is obvious that the legislature took this extreme step because of the potential for additional harm to the victims of domestic violence if such authority did not exist.

Several procedural safeguards are in place to reduce any impairment of the due process rights of those alleged offenders who are not present when the initial hearing on a motion for a protection order is held. These safeguards include:

(1) A requirement that a second hearing on the motion be held as soon as is possible in the presence of the offender. The offender is afforded full due process protections at the second hearing.[24]

The person who requested the protection order is required to appear again at the second hearing.[25] This oral hearing is required by the statute.[26] The requirement for an oral hearing is at variance with the Ohio Rules of Criminal Procedure. The criminal rules allow the court to require the submission of most motions on briefs in support and in opposition, without the necessity of an oral hearing.[27]

The hearing on the motion, therefore, is a special proceeding. It is a critical stage of the criminal proceedings which could affect the substantive rights of the offender. The offender, therefore, is afforded the right to cross-examine the person who requested the protection order and any other witness that might appear in support of the granting of the order. Due process also requires that the offender be allowed to present any evidence which would contraindicate the granting of the protection order.

(2) The hearing must be held no later than:

(a) the day that the defendant appears in response to a summons on the underlying criminal charge,[28] or, in the alternative,

(b) on the court's next business day following the defendant's apprehension on the underlying criminal charge.[29]

(3) If the offender is able to post bail following arrest or surrender, the pendency of a motion for a protection order cannot be used as a justification for retaining the offender in jail until the motion can be heard by the court.[30]

(4) The issuance of the order cannot be introduced as evidence of the commission of the underlying crime at the offender's trial on that matter.[31]

(5) The defendant cannot be held criminally liable for violations of an ex parte order unless the prosecuting authority can prove, be-

---

[24]RC 2919.26(D)(2)(a), RC 2903.213(D)(2)(a).

[25]Read RC 2919.26(D)(2)(a) in conjunction with RC 2919.26(C) and RC 2903.213(D)(2)(a) in conjunction with RC 2903.213(C).

[26]RC 2919.26(C)(1), RC 2903.213(C)(1).

[27]Crim. R. 47.

[28]R.C. 2903.213(D)(2)(a), 2919.26(D)(2)(a).

[29]R.C. 2903.213(D)(2)(a), 2919.26(D)(2)(a).

[30]RC 2919.26(F), RC 2903.213(F).

[31]RC 2919.26(E)(3), RC 2903.213(E)(3).

yond a reasonable doubt, that the defendant received personal service, i.e., delivery, of the order.[32]

Q & A: My girlfriend and I had a fight last night. I heard from my brother that she got a temporary protection order to keep me out of the house. I haven't been arrested, and I don't know for a fact that she got an order. Can't I just go to the house to get my work clothes if I don't cause any trouble?

In the past, if a temporary protection order was issued against you, even if you were not yet served, failure of service would not have prevented your arrest for violation of the protection order.[33] However, the Ohio Supreme Court ruled held that you could not be charged with violation of an active protection order unless the prosecution could prove that you were served with the order.[34]

However, subsequent to the Supreme Court's ruling, the Governor signed legislation passed by the Ohio General Assembly that amended the law in 2017[35] to provide that it is no longer necessary for the prosecution to prove that a protection order or consent agreement was actually served on the defendant. if the prosecution is able to prove either,1) that the defendant was shown the protection order, consent agreement, or a copy thereof, or 2) that a judge, magistrate or law enforcement officer informed the defendant that the order was issued ***and*** that the defendant recklessly violated the terms of the order, the defendant is accountable for any violation.[36]

Going to your girlfriend's house under the circumstances that you describe is not a good idea. Even though you have not seen and have not been served with a copy of the protection order, if there is an active warrant for your arrest, it is very likely that you will be arrested on that warrant. Any way you look at it, picking up your things should wait until you have a better idea of your current situation.

Q & A: My client obtained an ex parte civil protection order. However, at the hearing on the merits, the protection order was denied. My client also brought criminal charges against the respondent and obtained a criminal protection order. Does the issuance, and then subsequent denial, of the civil protection order involving the same facts as those in a criminal case automatically terminate the criminal order?

The law is not clear and no court has spoken directly to this issue. Once granted, a criminal protection order issued as a pretrial condition of release is effective only until:

(1) Disposition of the underlying case or the order in the court that issued it.[37]

---

[32]State v. Smith, 136 Ohio St. 3d 1,2013-Ohio-1698, 989 N.E.2d 972 (2013).

[33]City of Xenia v. Berry, 1994 WL 12494, *3 (Ohio Ct. App. 2d Dist. Greene County 1994).

[34]State v. Smith, 136 Ohio St. 3d 1, 2013-Ohio-1698, 989 N.E.2d 972 (2013).

[35]RC 2919.27.

[36]R.C. 2919.27.

[37]RC 2919.26(E)(2)(a).

(2) Issuance of a protection order or the approval of a consent agreement, arising out of the same activities as those that were the basis of the complaint upon which the order is based.[38]

(3) Disposition of an underlying case containing the order, subsequently bound over to the court of common pleas for prosecution of a felony arising out of the same activities as those that were the basis of the complaint upon which the order is based.[39]

The operative word here is *effective*. While the legislature could have drafted the language in this section in such a way as to clearly indicate an intent to have the operation of a criminal protection order terminate once a civil protection order issues or a criminal case is bound over to the common pleas court for felony prosecution, it chose instead only to render such orders ineffective. As such, it can be argued that once the civil protection order is no longer in force, the criminal order resumes its effectiveness, as long as the criminal matter that gave rise to the order is still pending before the court that issued it.

§ 4:6 Violation of a protection order

An offender's failure to adhere to any term or condition of a protection order constitutes a violation of that order. Ordinarily, when a party violates a court's order, the court vindicates the order by resorting to its inherent power to find the violator in contempt. Sanctions for contempt are available for violations of a protection order.[1] In the case of a protection order, however, the violation may also constitute a new criminal violation[2] or, if the offender is a juvenile an act of delinquency.[3]

Under RC 2919.27(B)(2), a violation of a protection order is a first-degree misdemeanor, punishable by a maximum penalty of up to $1,000 in fines and/or up to 180 days in jail.

Violations of certain protection orders carry higher potential penalties. The penalty for violation of a protection order is enhanced to a felony of the fifth degree when:

1. the offender previously was convicted of **violating another protection order** and issued in connection with a charge of either aggravated menacing, menacing by stalking, menacing or aggravated trespass.[4] or
2. the offender was **convicted of two or more allegations of offenses** that charged violations of either aggravated menacing, menacing by stalking, menacing or aggravated trespass, under the Revised Code, or of a qualifying foreign protection order, a

[38] RC 2919.26(E)(2)(b).

[39] RC 2919.26(D)(4).

[Section 4:6]

[1] Westlake v. Patrick, 2007-Ohio-1307, 2007 WL 853235 (Ohio Ct. App. 8th Dist. Cuyahoga County 2007).

[2] RC 2919.27. See also Berry v. Patrick, 2005-Ohio-3708, 2005 WL 1707005 (Ohio Ct. App. 8th Dist. Cuyahoga County 2005).

[3] R.C. 2151.34.

[4] 2919.27(B)(3)(a).

substantially similar ordinance or a combination of those offenses, that involve the same person.[5]

3. the offender previously was convicted of a violation of a criminal or civil **domestic violence protection order** issued under Ohio statute.[6]
4. the offender previously was convicted of a violation of any other protection order covered under Ohio's protection order violation statute.[7]

Additionally, violating a protection order may be charged as a felony of the third degree,[8] if it is alleged that the violation occurred while the alleged offender was engaged in the commission of a felony.[9]

Many of Ohio's local municipalities have ordinances which are basically patterned after RC 2919.27. These laws also prohibit the violation of protection orders. The primary difference between these ordinances and the statute is that the ordinances cannot provide for enhancement of penalties from misdemeanor to felony for subsequent protection order violations. Thus, offenders committing second and subsequent violations of the terms of protection orders ordinances enacted by home-rule communities must be charged under the statute, rather than the ordinance, if they are to face the more severe punishment of felony sanctions.

An offender who violates the terms of a protection order is subject to more than just the penalties associated with the new criminal offense. A violation also subjects the offender to potential modifications of the terms of the original order. If an offender violates a protection order and the order violated was a stalking/sex-offense related civil protection order, the court may require, in addition to any other sentence imposed, that the offender be electronically monitored for a period not to exceed five years. Monitoring is assigned to a law enforcement agency selected by the court.[10] When monitoring is ordered, the offender must bear the cost of installation and of maintaining the monitoring for the period ordered. The offender is relieved of responsibility for monitoring costs if the court determines that the offender is indigent. In that case, the costs are paid from the state's Reparations Fund.[11] Because the protection order issues as an additional pretrial condition of release,[12] a violation of the original protection order justifies a finding by the court which remands the offender to jail. The court may predicate its action upon the offender's failure to abide by the condition or conditions, contained in the original order for the safety of the victim, that allowed the offender to be released from custody.

In addition, when a violation of a protection order is alleged, RC

[5]RC 2919.27(B)(3)(b).

[6]RC 2919.26, 3113.31.

[7]RC 2919.27

[8]RC 2929.14(A)(3)(b).

[9]RC 2919.27(B)(4).

[10]RC 2919.27(B)(5).

[11]RC 2743.191(A)(1)(n).

[12]RC 2919.26(H).

2919.271 grants the court, under certain circumstances, the authority to evaluate the offender's mental condition. An individual may be subjected to the evaluation requirements of RC 2919.271 if the individual is alleged to have violated the terms of a temporary protection order by:

(1) committing or threatening any conduct which results in additional physical harm to the person or property of the family or household member protected by the order, or

(2) committing or threatening any conduct which causes the family or household member covered by the order to *believe* that the offender will cause physical harm to the person or property of the family or household member.

RC 2919.271(A) to RC 2919.271(F) set forth the procedures that the court is required to follow if it decides that it needs to evaluate an offender's mental condition. If, for whatever reason, the court is not satisfied with the results of an initial examination and evaluation, the statute allows the court the discretion to order as many as two additional evaluations.[13]

In the event that more than one examination is required to establish the mental condition of an individual charged with a violation of a protection order, the court must give both the prosecutor and the defendant's counsel the opportunity to make recommendations regarding the selection of any subsequent examiner.[14] The final decision concerning the selection, however, belongs to the court.

The report of the examiner must be submitted to the court within thirty days of the journal entry requesting it.[15] It is conceivable that the court could require three evaluations and not have a hearing on the defendant's mental status for more than ninety days. The mental condition evaluation process provided for by RC 2919.271 has the effect of tolling the speedy trial provisions imposed by RC 2945.72(G).

The defendant may be compelled to submit to the examination either at the detention facility or at the facility where the examiner is located.[16] If the defendant is out on bail and refuses to cooperate, the statute allows the court to remand the defendant to jail so that the evaluation may be conducted.[17]

The person appointed by the court to conduct the evaluation of the offender may request that any family or household member of the offender provide information to assist in the evaluation.[18] However, no family or household member may be compelled to provide the information requested.[19]

The report or reports that the court receives from the examiner or examiners are required to contain certain information as provided in RC 2919.271(D). The information required should assist the court in

[13]RC 2919.271(B).

[14]RC 2919.271(B).

[15]RC 2919.271(D).

[16]RC 2919.271(C)(1), RC 2919.271(C)(2).

[17]RC 2919.271(C)(1).

[18]RC 2919.271(F).

[19]RC 2919.271(F).

assessing the defendant's current mental status. It should also allow the court to determine the offender's present risk to the family or household member protected by the order and to the community at large. The items which by law must be included in the report are:

(1) the examiner's findings;
(2) a reasonably detailed outline of the facts which form the basis for the examiner's findings;
(3) the examiner's opinion as to the offender's mental condition;
(4) the examiner's opinion as to whether the offender represents a substantial risk of physical harm to others as manifested by:
    (a) evidence of recent homicidal or other violent behavior;
    (b) evidence of recent threats that put others in reasonable fear of violent behavior or serious physical harm at the hands of the offender; or
    (c) evidence of present dangerousness; and
(5) the examiner's opinion as to the types of treatment or counseling that the defendant needs.[20]

The court is required to provide copies of the examiner's report to both the prosecutor and defendant's counsel.[21] The costs of these evaluations are taxed as court costs in the underlying criminal case.[22]

The court is not bound by any provision of the statute to accept the results of any of these mental evaluations.

The conviction of an individual criminally charged with the violation of a protection order issued for that individual's benefit constitutes a fundamental error of law which results in a manifest injustice.[23]

Q & A: In the trial of a felony charge (second offense) of violating a protection order, is it permissible to have the victim testify as to why the prior order was sought?

Yes. The victim's statement provides the trier of fact with a reason why the victim believed the order was necessary. Additionally, the existence of the prior conviction for a violation of a protection order is an element of the new charge, and the victim is the most appropriate witness to establish that element. However, caution must be exercised in the presentation of such evidence. It is not necessary to go into detail about the circumstances of the prior order. Too much detail could be deemed prejudicial to the defendant's right to a fair trial.[24]

Q & A: Can a victim be prosecuted for complicity in the violation of a protection order issued specifically to enhance his or her safety?

Two courts of appeals considered this question and came to different conclusions as to its answer.[25] The court in *Bullington* held that a

[20]RC 2919.271(D).

[21]RC 2919.271(D).

[22]RC 2919.271(E).

[23]Crim. R 32.1; State v. Youngpeter, 2005-Ohio-329, 2005 WL 196754 (Ohio Ct. App. 3d Dist. Van Wert County 2005).

[24]See State v. Wright, 1998 WL 542697 (Ohio Ct. App. 10th Dist. Franklin County 1998).

[25]See N. Olmsted v. Bullington, 139 Ohio App. 3d 565, 744 N.E.2d 1225 (8th Dist.

member of a class that a criminal law is enacted to protect may not be charged with violating a provision of that criminal law. Hence, the court in *Bullington* reasoned that a person for whose benefit a temporary protection order issues is a member of a class of individuals designated for protection from violent abusers and, therefore, may not be charged with aiding and abetting another's violation of the protection order.[26]

Although the court in *Lucas* did not disagree with the *Bullington* court's recitation of the General Assembly's purpose in enacting temporary protection laws, it did disagree with that court's conclusion that an alleged victim could not be charged as an aider and a better in a violation of that order by an offender simply because the victim is a member of a protected class.

The decision in *Lucas* noted that the complicity statute,[27] provides that "*[n]o* person, acting with the kind of culpability required for the commission of an offense * * * shall aid or abet another in committing the offense." The statute that prohibits the violation of a protection order states that *no* person shall recklessly violate the terms of a protection order issued pursuant to RC 2919.26 or 3113.31.[28] Neither section specifically excludes the protect person from the blanket prohibition otherwise provided.

The Supreme Court of Ohio resolved this conflict of authority when it rendered its decision in *Lucas*, ruling on a motion to certify.[29] The court held that an individual who is the protected subject of a temporary protection order may not be prosecuted for aiding and abetting the restrainee under the protection order in violating said order.[30] Noting an analogous situation in the federal statutes,[31] the court found that Ohio's protection order statutes failed to criminalize a protected party's activities in inviting or acquiescing in a violation of the statutes.[32] The court further found that the Ohio General Assembly both recognized and addressed the potential problem of a protected party's acquiescence in the violation of a protection order by removing the excuse of an invitation, a perceived invitation, or a

---

Cuyahoga County 2000); State v. Lucas, 147 Ohio App. 3d 297, 2002-Ohio-2514, 770 N.E.2d 114 (5th Dist. Licking County 2002), judgment rev'd, 100 Ohio St. 3d 1, 2003–Ohio-4778, 795 N.E.2d 642 (2003). See also Crim. R 32.1 and State v. Youngpeter, 2005-Ohio-329, 2005 WL 196754 (Ohio Ct. App. 3d Dist. Van Wert County 2005).

[26]N. Olmsted v. Bullington, 139 Ohio App. 3d 565, 744 N.E.2d 1225 (8th Dist. Cuyahoga County 2000); State v. Youngpeter, 2005-Ohio-329, 2005 WL 196754 (Ohio Ct. App. 3d Dist. Van Wert County 2005).

[27]RC 2923.03(A)(2).

[28]RC 2919.27(A)(1); State v. Lucas, 147 Ohio App. 3d 297, 2002-Ohio-2514, 770 N.E.2d 114 (5th Dist. Licking County 2002), judgment rev'd, 100 Ohio St. 3d 1, 2003–Ohio-4778, 795 N.E.2d 642 (2003) (emphasis added).

[29]State v. Lucas, 100 Ohio St. 3d 1, 2003-Ohio-4778, 795 N.E.2d 642 (2003).

[30]State v. Lucas, 100 Ohio St. 3d 1, 2003-Ohio-4778, 795 N.E.2d 642 (2003) (syllabus). See also State v. Youngpeter, 2005-Ohio-329, 2005 WL 196754 (Ohio Ct. App. 3d Dist. Van Wert County 2005); and Disciplinary Counsel v. Campbell, 126 Ohio St. 3d 150, 2010-Ohio-3265, 931 N.E.2d 558 (2010).

[31]Gebardi v. U.S., 287 U.S. 112, 53 S. Ct. 35, 77 L. Ed. 206, 84 A.L.R. 370 (1932).

[32]State v. Lucas, 100 Ohio St. 3d 1, 2003-Ohio-4778, 795 N.E.2d 642 (2003). See also State v. Youngpeter, 2005-Ohio-329, 2005 WL 196754 (Ohio Ct. App. 3d Dist. Van Wert County 2005).

concocted invitation from affecting the power of a protection order. In essence, according to the court, the legislature made the issue of an invitation entirely irrelevant as to the culpability of a respondent's violation of a protection order.[33]

Thus, the conviction of an individual criminally charged with the violation of a protection order issued for that individual's benefit constitutes a fundamental error of law which results in a manifest injustice.[34]

Q & A: If a court issues a temporary protection order on its own, instead of at the request of the victim or the prosecutor, does it still have to hold a hearing before the order is issued?

The courts that have addressed this issue held that a protection order that is not issued in compliance with statutory requirements is invalid.[35] For the order to be effective the defendant must be afforded, at minimum, the due process safeguards of notice and a timely opportunity to be heard contained in the protection order statute.

One of the same courts[36] also held that this is true regardless of whether the protection order issues as a result of a motion filed by the victim,[37] on the victim's behalf by the prosecution, law enforcement or a member of the victim's family or household,[38] or whether the court issues the protection order on its own motion.[39]

The practical effect of not affording the defendant a hearing that complies with the statutory requirements is less clear and will depend on the particular circumstances surrounding the issuance of the order.[40] An individual who is subject to the terms of such an order has no right to willfully violate it, even if it is invalid, unless a court has declared its invalidity or rescinded it.[41]

Thus, if it can be shown that a defendant was aware of the terms of

---

[33]State v. Lucas, 100 Ohio St. 3d 1, 2003-Ohio-4778, 795 N.E.2d 642 (2003). See also State v. Youngpeter, 2005-Ohio-329, 2005 WL 196754 (Ohio Ct. App. 3d Dist. Van Wert County 2005).

[34]Crim. R 32.1; State v. Youngpeter, 2005-Ohio-329, 2005 WL 196754 (Ohio Ct. App. 3d Dist. Van Wert County 2005).

[35]State v. Franklin, 2001 WL 698107 (Ohio Ct. App. 1st Dist. Hamilton County 2001); see R.C. 2919.26(D)(3); State v. Conkle, 2003-Ohio-2410, 2003 WL 21060822 (Ohio Ct. App. 5th Dist. Knox County 2003); State v. Blaine, 2004-Ohio-1241, 2004 WL 524667 (Ohio Ct. App. 4th Dist. Highland County 2004); State v. Hall, 2013-Ohio-5855, 2013 WL 6918874 (Ohio Ct. App. 5th Dist. Delaware County 2013).

[36]State v. Franklin, 2001 WL 698107 (Ohio Ct. App. 1st Dist. Hamilton County 2001).

[37]RC 2919.26(A)(1).

[38]RC 2919.26(A)(1).

[39]RC 2919.26(D)(1); State v. Finley, 146 Ohio App. 3d 548, 2001-Ohio-4347, 767 N.E.2d 302 (1st Dist. Hamilton County 2001); State v. Sutts, 2004-Ohio-3541, 2004 WL 1485909, *2 (Ohio Ct. App. 12th Dist. Warren County 2004).

[40]City of Reynoldsburg v. Eichenberger, 1990 WL 52467 (Ohio Ct. App. 5th Dist. Licking County 1990); State v. Sutts, 2004-Ohio-3541, 2004 WL 1485909, *2 (Ohio Ct. App. 12th Dist. Warren County 2004); State v. Hall, 2013-Ohio-660, 989 N.E.2d 111 (Ohio Ct. App. 5th Dist. Delaware County 2013), appeal allowed, cause remanded, 135 Ohio St. 3d 1456, 2013-Ohio-2285, 988 N.E.2d 576 (2013).

[41]City of Reynoldsburg v. Eichenberger, 1990 WL 52467 (Ohio Ct. App. 5th Dist. Licking County 1990); In re Contempt of Court of White, 60 Ohio App. 2d 62, 14 Ohio Op. 3d 34, 395 N.E.2d 499 (5th Dist. Stark County 1978), citing U.S. v. United Mine

a protection order and still defied its provisions, under some circumstances the defendant may still be charged with a violation of the protection order, even if it is later determined to be invalid.[42] It should be noted that not all Ohio courts that addressed this issue agree with this proposition.[43]

Q & A: Some Ohio judges believe that the domestic violence laws permit them to issue, ex parte, Domestic Violence Temporary Protection Orders, even without a written motion filed with the court or the appearance of any prosecuting witnesses. Are they right?

Yes. The law does allow the court to act on its own to enter an ex parte domestic violence temporary protection order as a pretrial condition of release. This can be done if the court finds that the continued presence of the alleged offender poses a threat to the safety or protection of the alleged victim.[44] However, without an adversarial hearing or the defendant entering an effective waiver of such a hearing, the court may not finalize the order.[45]

Q & A: Doesn't the domestic violence statute require the person requesting the order to appear before a judicial officer and give testimony at a hearing 24 hours after a Motion for a domestic violence protection order is filed with the court?

Yes—but only if a formal written motion seeking the issuance of a domestic violence protection order is filed with the court.[46] In that instance, the court must hold a hearing on the motion within 24 hours of the time that the motion is filed.

Before the motion is granted and the order issues, the person requesting the order is required to appear at the hearing to present testimony in support of the motion.[47] Only if the alleged victim is the person who requested the order *and* (emphasis added) is incapacitated by the act of domestic violence that forms the basis for the mo-

---

Workers of America, 330 U.S. 258, 67 S. Ct. 677, 91 L. Ed. 884, 19 L.R.R.M. (BNA) 2346, 12 Lab. Cas. (CCH) P 51239 (1947); State v. Sutts, 2004-Ohio-3541, 2004 WL 1485909, *2 (Ohio Ct. App. 12th Dist. Warren County 2004); State v. Eschrich, 2008-Ohio-2984, 2008 WL 2468572 (Ohio Ct. App. 6th Dist. Ottawa County 2008); State v. Hall, 2013-Ohio-660, 989 N.E.2d 111 (Ohio Ct. App. 5th Dist. Delaware County 2013), appeal allowed, cause remanded, 135 Ohio St. 3d 1456, 2013-Ohio-2285, 988 N.E.2d 576 (2013); State v. Ybarra, 2016-Ohio-5761, 2016 WL 4724354 (Ohio Ct. App. 5th Dist. Licking County 2016).

[42]City of Reynoldsburg v. Eichenberger, 1990 WL 52467 (Ohio Ct. App. 5th Dist. Licking County 1990); State v. Sutts, 2004-Ohio-3541, 2004 WL 1485909, *2 (Ohio Ct. App. 12th Dist. Warren County 2004); State v. Eschrich, 2008-Ohio-2984, 2008 WL 2468572 (Ohio Ct. App. 6th Dist. Ottawa County 2008); State v. Hall, 2013-Ohio-660, 989 N.E.2d 111 (Ohio Ct. App. 5th Dist. Delaware County 2013), appeal allowed, cause remanded, 135 Ohio St. 3d 1456, 2013-Ohio-2285, 988 N.E.2d 576 (2013); State v. Ybarra, 2016-Ohio-5761, 2016 WL 4724354 (Ohio Ct. App. 5th Dist. Licking County 2016).

[43]State v. Franklin, 2001 WL 698107 (Ohio Ct. App. 1st Dist. Hamilton County 2001).

[44]RC 2919.26(D)(1).

[45]RC 2919.26(D)(2).

[46]RC 2919.26(C)(1).

[47]RC 2919.26(C)(1).

tion, can any other person appear instead and provide the court with the information that it needs to decide if the order should issue.[48]

Q & A: Can a judge issue a TPO on mere hearsay?

Theoretically, yes. A protection order issued by a judge, sua sponte, as a pretrial condition of release, does not require the same formality required of an order sought by a complainant, or an order sought on the complainant's behalf by a party authorized by the statute. The court must, however, make a finding that the safety and protection of the complainant, alleged victim, or other family or household member of the alleged offender may be impaired by the continued presence of the alleged offender, before the order can issue.[49]

Technically, since there is no proscription on what the court can rely on when it issues a domestic violence temporary protection order, sua sponte,[50] it appears that the court can rely on any information that comes to its attention in determining that the alleged victim's safety and protection may be impaired. Not only does the law fail to spell out what the court should consider before issuing a temporary protection order, sua sponte, it also fails to require that the court hold a hearing at all.[51] Thus, a court can, sua sponte, issue a domestic violence temporary protection order, ex parte, based entirely on an oral statement or a written statement, sworn or unsworn, made by any person with knowledge of the facts however obtained, without more, if the court is convinced by the statement of the alleged victim's danger, and makes a finding that the alleged victim is in peril if the court fails to act.[52] The word "finding," in this context, means a "decision upon a question of fact reached as the result of a judicial examination or investigation by a court . . . A recital of the facts as found."[53]

Q & A: Instead of holding a hearing on a motion for a temporary protection order within 24 hours of its filing, can't the court just wait to hold the hearing until after the defendant is arrested on the underlying domestic violence complaint?

No. The statute is clear. If a formal motion is filed with the court requesting the issuance of a temporary protection order, a hearing on the merits of that motion *must* be held as soon as possible, but in no case later than 24 hours after the motion is filed. The word "hearing" is defined, inter alia, as "a proceeding of relative formality (though generally less formal than a trial), generally public, with definite issues of fact or of law to be tried, in which witnesses are heard and evidence presented."[54] The statute specifically requires that, at a minimum, the person who requested the order must appear at this initial hearing and provide the court with information in support of the motion. The only exception to this appearance requirement is if the alleged victim is impaired by injuries suffered as a result of the act of

[48]RC 2919.26(C)(1).

[49]RC 2919.26(C)(1).

[50]RC 2919.26(D)(1).

[51]RC 2919.26(D)(1).

[52]RC 2919.26(D)(1).

[53]Black's Law Dictionary 632 (6th ed. 1990).

[54]Black's Law Dictionary 721 (6th ed. 1990).

domestic violence.[55] The implication is that direct testimony and documentary evidence presented through a victim or witnesses will provide the information required by the court to decide whether or not to issue the order.

The hearing on the motion must be held within the statutorily prescribed time regardless of whether the defendant is available to appear. Therefore, even if the defendant is still at large, once a written motion seeking the issuance of a protection order is filed, the court is obligated to hold a hearing to determine if the order should issue within the allotted 24 hours. If the defendant is still at large at the time the hearing takes place, *and* the person seeking the issuance of the order appears and provides the court with the information required to justify issuance, the order issues ex parte.

Under the statute, if a domestic violence protection order issues ex parte, then a second hearing must be held no later than the next business day of court following the defendant's arrest or surrender.[56] Whether the court took testimony on a formal motion before it issued the ex parte order or whether the ex parte order was issued sua sponte is irrelevant. If the initial order was issued ex parte, the defendant is entitled (unless there is an effective waiver) to attend a hearing where the basis for issuing the order is subject to contest.[57]

Q & A: Is it true that the court can issue a temporary protection order even when the alleged victim refuses to sign a probable cause determination form or a charging document, or doesn't want the protection order to issue or domestic violence charges to be filed?

Yes. The court may take this action at any time after the filing of a domestic violence complaint.[58] No written motion for a temporary protection order needs be filed with the court. The court is not required to hold an initial hearing before it acts, even if its proposed action is actively opposed by the party for whose benefit it is undertaken.

However, if the court does issue an order in this fashion, it is required to hold a hearing, as soon as possible with the defendant present.[59] That hearing must take place no later than the next business day of court after the defendant's surrender or arrest.[60] The hearing must afford the defendant the right to confront the evidence upon which issuance of the ex parte domestic violence temporary protection order was based. At the hearing, the individual who sought the issuance of the order (or other person authorized by statute) must appear and present evidence, subject to cross-examination, in support of the continuing necessity for the order.[61] The procedure for these hearings is set forth in the Revised Code.[62]

---

[55] RC 2919.26(C)(1).

[56] R.C. 2919.26(D)(2)(a).

[57] See State v. Finley, 146 Ohio App. 3d 548, 2001-Ohio-4347, 767 N.E.2d 302 (1st Dist. Hamilton County 2001).

[58] RC 2919.26(D)(1).

[59] R.C. 2919.26(D)(2)(a).

[60] RC 2919.26(D)(2).

[61] See State v. Finley, 146 Ohio App. 3d 548, 2001-Ohio-4347, 767 N.E.2d 302 (1st

Q & A: The police in our jurisdiction are instructed to file motions for temporary protection orders in every domestic violence case, even when the alleged victims do not want them. This is routinely done, even when the victim is not incapacitated by the injuries suffered from the domestic violence incident. The written motions are presented at initial appearances or arraignments. Neither the police officers who file the motions nor the alleged victims ever appear. Can the court still grant a domestic violence protection order under these circumstances?

If there is a formal written motion filed with the court, the court is required to take testimony from the alleged victim or other person authorized by the statute. If the victim is incapacitated, then, and only then, can a third party provide the necessary information needed to establish the basis for granting the motion. If, as you state here, no one appears before the court to present evidence, then there is nothing for the court to base a decision on, and the motion should be denied.[63]

However, under the provisions of the statute,[64] the court can, sua sponte, find that the safety and protection of an alleged victim or other person enumerated by the statute may be impaired by the continued presence of the defendant and issue a domestic violence temporary protection order as a pretrial condition of release. Once the defendant is arrested or surrenders, the person who requested the order (or another authorized by the statute, in the case of the alleged victim's incapacity resulting from the violence) must appear at a hearing where the defendant is present and present information to support the continuation of the order.[65]

The filing of motions for temporary protection orders by officers making domestic violence arrests is only authorized by the law in the case of an emergency.[66] Even in the case of an emergency, only the person who makes the arrest is authorized to file for an order on behalf of the victim.[67] In the absence of an emergency, domestic violence temporary protection orders filed by arresting or other officers on behalf of alleged victims are improperly before the court and susceptible to motions to strike.

Q & A: If the court fails to hold the hearing on the motion for a domestic violence temporary protection order within the allotted 24 hours set forth in the statute, or if no one appears to present evidence at the hearing, does that mean that the order must automatically be denied?

Holding a hearing on a formal motion for a domestic violence protec-

---

Dist. Hamilton County 2001); State v. Franklin, 2001 WL 698107 (Ohio Ct. App. 1st Dist. Hamilton County 2001).

[62] RC 2919.26(C)(1).

[63] RC 2919.26(C)(1).

[64] RC 2919.26(D)(1).

[65] RC 2919.26(D)(2)(a).

[66] RC 2919.26(A)(1).

[67] RC 2919.26(A)(1).

tion order within 24 hours of the filing is mandatory.[68] If the court fails to hold the hearing within the time set, any order entered thereafter is ineffective.[69] If no one appears at the hearing to present evidence in support of the motion, the court should deny the order.[70]

Q & A: Under the statute, can't the court just issue a final temporary protection order without holding a hearing, as long as the defendant is present?

No. Unless the defendant waives the right to a hearing that allows the information presented in favor of the order to be tested, the court must hold the hearing. Failure to conduct the hearing renders the order ineffective, even if the defendant is physically present when the court issues the final order.[71]

If no hearing is held or waiver submitted, the order remains ex parte, i.e., "done for, in behalf of, or on the application of, one party only,"[72] and denies the defendant's right to minimum due process.[73]

Q & A: Waivers of domestic violence protection order hearings in our court are generally handled perfunctorily. The defendant is handed a waiver form and required to sign, without time to read its language. The court does not conduct a colloquy with the defendant, and does not inform the defendant of the right to a hearing where the alleged victim may be questioned concerning the necessity for the requested order. Is this waiver process sufficient and, if not, what is required to make these waivers effective?

The answer to the first part of your question is, no, the process is not sufficient. As with any waiver, the defendant's waiver of the right to have a final hearing, before a domestic violence temporary protection order issues, should be knowingly and voluntarily made.[74] Nothing in the process that you've outlined ensures that these waivers meet that standard.

Best practices for clearly establishing the procedural adequacy of a waiver include making a record that reflects: (1) that the judge's inquiry was sufficient; (2) that the defendant's responses were clear and direct; (3) that the defendant executed the written waiver that appears on the standardized protection order form mandated by the Supreme Court; and (4) that the defendant was provided the opportunity (whether exercised or not) to consult with counsel before the waiver was accepted.[75]

Q & A: I'm charged with domestic violence. Today, the court ordered an evaluation of my mental health because it feels

[68] RC 2919.26(C)(1).

[69] RC 2919.26(C)(1); State v. Finley, 146 Ohio App. 3d 548, 2001-Ohio-4347, 767 N.E.2d 302 (1st Dist. Hamilton County 2001).

[70] RC 2919.26(C)(1).

[71] Read RC 2919.26(C)(1) and RC 2919.26(D)(1), in pari materia.

[72] Black's Law Dictionary 576 (6th ed. 1990).

[73] RC 2919.26(C)(1).

[74] Smith v. Anderson, 104 F. Supp. 2d 773 (S.D. Ohio 2000), aff'd, 348 F.3d 177, 2003 FED App. 0381P (6th Cir. 2003).

[75] Smith v. Anderson, 104 F. Supp. 2d 773 (S.D. Ohio 2000), aff'd, 348 F.3d 177, 2003 FED App. 0381P (6th Cir. 2003).

that some of the allegations contained in the probable cause statement suggest that I pose a physical risk to my wife. Can the court do that?

It depends. The law provides the court the specific ability to order pre-adjudication mental health examinations only in limited situations. A mental health exam may be ordered by the court (1) when there is an allegation that a defendant violated a temporary protection order associated with a pending case of domestic violence or menacing by stalking, and (2) that allegation results in the institution of a criminal charge for the violation.[76]

There is no other specific authority for the court to order a mental health exam pretrial, simply because a defendant is charged with domestic violence. That being said, the defendant's competency to stand trial,[77] sanity at the time of the crime charged,[78] and/or need for emergency hospitalization[79] are always relevant inquiries for the court to make, if and when issues of the defendant's mental health are raised. Those inquires are separate and distinct from the evaluation of the risk that the defendant poses of committing additional acts of domestic violence.[80]

Q & A: The provisions of the section of the Ohio Revised Code that enhance the penalties for violating a protection order, consent agreement or anti-stalking protection order are confusing. How should they be interpreted?

Some clarity comes with dividing the section into subsections and analyzing each of the provisions of the subsections in turn, i.e.:

"If the offender previously has been convicted of or pleaded guilty to a violation of a protection order issued pursuant to section 2903.213 or 2903.214, ..."[81]

Under this provision, if the offender was previously found guilty of violating a stalking protection order against **ANY** person, the current charge may and should be brought as a 5th degree felony.

"If the offender was previously found guilty of or pleaded guilty to a violation of ... two or more violations of 2903.21, 2903.211, 2903.22 or 2911.211 that involved the same person who is the subject of the protection order or consent agreement..."[82]

Under this provision, if the offender was previously found guilty of committing two or more violations of **ANY** of the offenses listed, or any combination of them,[83] **and** those prior violations were against the same person who is now covered by the protection order that the prosecution alleges the offender has violated, then the current violation may and should be brought as a 5th degree felony.

---

[76] RC 2945.371.

[77] RC 2945.371.

[78] RC 2945.39.

[79] RC 2945.38; RC 2945.39; RC 2945.40.

[80] RC 2919.271.

[81] RC 2919.27(B)(3).

[82] RC 2919.27(B)(3).

[83] Aggravated Menacing, Menacing by Stalking, Menacing or Aggravated Trespassing—RC 2903.21, RC 2903.211, RC 2903.22 or RC 2911.211.

Some of the language used in this subsection is potentially the source of confusion. Some have interpreted the provision to focus on the status of the offender, rather than the victim, because it refers to "... the same person who is the subject **OF** the protection order or consent agreement..." While such an interpretation is possible, it is illogical.

"If the offender was previously found guilty of or pleaded guilty to a violation ... of one or more violations of this section ..."[84]

Under this provision of the subsection, if the offender was previously found guilty of violating **ANY** of the qualifying protection orders contained in the section,[85] including civil or criminal protection orders[86] or a protection order issued by another state], issued against the offender in favor of **ANY** person, the current charge may and should be brought as a 5th Degree Felony.

Lastly, *"If the offender violates a protection order or consent agreement while committing a felony offense . . .";*

This subsection allows an offender to be charged with a third degree felony if while violating a protection order or consent agreement the offender is also alleged to commit **ANY** other felony violation. The section places no restrictions on the type of felony that the offender might be found to commit when a protection order violation is alleged. Thus, not only the offenses that immediately come to mind, such as aggravated burglary, arson, attempted murder, aggravated or felonious assault, etc., but also drug offenses or theft offenses, for example, under plain reading of the law qualify for purposes of penalty enhancement.[87]

§ 4:7 Enforcement of a protection order

The enforcement of protection orders is now mandatory on all law enforcement agents of the state of Ohio. This is true, regardless of where the order originated.[1] The enhancements to the domestic violence laws require that each law enforcement agency in Ohio with jurisdiction over domestic violence cases must develop a set of policies for handling domestic violence cases.[2]

The new provisions of the law are quite specific as to the areas to be addressed by each agency's policies. Regarding the enforcement of protection orders, those policies must require peace officers to:

(1) Respond without undue delay to complaints of domestic violence or violations of a protection order.[3]

(2) Document facts and circumstances where a violation of a

---

[84]RC 2919.27(B)(3).

[85]RC 2919.27.

[86]R.C. 2151.34, 2903.213, 2903.214, 2919.26 and 3113.31.

[87]R.C. 2919.27(B)(4).

[Section 4:7]

[1]R.C. 2919.26(G)(5); see also Violent Crime Control and Law Enforcement Act of 1994, 42 U.S.C.A. § 13701.

[2]RC 2935.032(E).

[3]RC 2935.032(A)(2)(a).

protection order is alleged against an offender who is free on bond for the underlying offense.[4]

(3) Separate investigative interviews for alleged domestic violence offenders and victims.[5] Written statements from victims should include indications of the frequency and severity of any prior violence in the relationship.

(4) Provide specific information to victims of domestic violence,[6] including:
  (a) the responding officer's name and badge number (if the officer has a badge number),
  (b) the report number to be assigned to the incident (if that information is available),
  (c) a telephone number the victim can call for information about the case,
  (d) the availability of domestic violence resources within the community, and
  (e) the availability of both civil and criminal protection orders.

(5) A commitment to prepare a report on every domestic violence complaint, whether or not an arrest is made.[7] RC 2935.032(D) mandates that these reports document the officer's on-site observations, including:
  (a) any visible injuries noted,
  (b) any weapons found at the scene,
  (c) the actions and statements of the alleged offender,
  (d) the actions and statements of the victim,
  (e) statements of other witnesses, and
  (f) any other significant facts or circumstances.

(6) Mandatory arrest, upon probable cause, for aggravated assault or felonious assault resulting from domestic violence situations.[8]

(7) Confiscation of any deadly weapon that an offender used or threatened to use while violating a protection order.[9]

(8) Networking with local domestic violence shelters and programs in the development of the required policies.[10]

(9) Enforcement of out-of-jurisdiction and unregistered protection orders.[11]

(10) Enforcement of protection orders that have not been issued by the agency's jurisdiction or under state code.[12]

(11) Although the law[13] states that arrest is the preferred enforcement policy in Ohio for offenses which involve domestic

[4]RC 2935.032(A)(2)(b).

[5]RC 2935.032(A)(2)(c).

[6]RC 2935.032(C)(1) to RC 2935.032(C)(3).

[7]RC 2935.032(D).

[8]RC 2935.032(A)(1)(a), RC 2935.032(A)(1)(b).

[9]RC 2935.03(B)(3)(h).

[10]RC 2935.032(E).

[11]RC 2919.26(G)(5).

[12]RC 2919.26(G)(4).

[13]RC 2935.03(A).

violence, police officers can use their discretion in deciding whether arrest is appropriate. However, RC 2935.032(B)(1)(a) allows individual agencies to implement policies that make arrest *mandatory* upon probable cause.[14]

(12) Sanctions that the agency will impose upon an officer for failing to implement the terms of the agency's domestic violence policies.[15]

The investigating officer on a domestic violence complaint also has the ability to arrest and detain any person reasonably believed to be guilty of violating a temporary protection order without first obtaining an arrest warrant.[16]

An agency does not have to receive prior notice of a protection order before it can enforce that order.[17] However, before a law enforcement officer can enforce a protection order, typically one of a number of problematic questions requires resolution. These questions include:

(1) Was the underlying case that generated the order already disposed of at the time that enforcement of the protection order was requested?[18]
Unlike a civil protection order, a criminal protection order does not survive the conclusion of the criminal case that caused its issuance. When the underlying criminal case is concluded, the effectiveness of the protection order is also concluded. This is true even if the defendant is found guilty of the underlying criminal violation.

(2) Does the order have a fixed expiration date? Has it passed?[19]
Again, unlike its civil counterpart, the protection order does not have a fixed expiration date. It is limited only by the life of the underlying criminal case.

(3) Has the order been modified since it was issued?[20]
Criminal protection orders, as a rule, are seldom modified once they are granted. The limited purposes for which protection orders are issued generally make their modification unnecessary. However, the court does have the discretion to modify the order if it finds that a modification is necessary in the interest of justice.

(4) Has a subsequent civil protection order or consent agreement, covering the same matters, issued from the court of common pleas?[21]
The criminal protection order is subordinate to civil protection orders and consent agreements that are issued in domestic relations cases handled by the common pleas courts of the state. A civil protection order has the power to modify or suspend the

[14] RC 2935.032(B)(1)(a).

[15] RC 2935.032(A)(3).

[16] RC 2935.03(B)(1).

[17] RC 2919.26(G)(5).

[18] RC 2919.26(E)(2).

[19] RC 3113.31(E)(3)(a).

[20] RC 3113.31(E).

[21] RC 2919.26(E)(2).

provisions of a previously issued criminal protection order.[22] The converse is not true.

(5) Can a law enforcement officer validate a temporary protection order if the issuing court is not open for business?

Currently, with very few exceptions, a police officer who is presented with a temporary protection order after the business hours of the issuing court is unable to determine if that order is valid. Since temporary protection orders have no fixed expiration dates, and since the possibility exists that an order might have been modified after it was issued, the only sure way to determine if the order presented is still in effect is to talk to someone in the clerk's office of the issuing court. If the clerk's office is unavailable, the officer must attempt to use other less effective means to establish the validity of the order.

(6) If the temporary protection order cannot be validated, what are the officer's options?

When presented with a temporary protection order that cannot be immediately validated, a responding officer must exercise one of several options to obtain some indication that it is more probable than not that the order is still in effect under the same conditions as those presented. Those options include:

(a) Accepting the order at face value. An order that has an official court certification embossed on it, has the signature of an appropriate issuing court official, and which is relatively recent in point of time is probably valid. The responding officer is probably safer accepting the order and enforcing it than refusing to do so, since any subsequent injury due to a failure to protect would be much more costly than an action brought by the offender for the inconvenience of detention, upon probable cause, until an order can be verified. To be on the safe side, the officer should make an attempt to contact the issuing court, even if the officer knows that the attempt is probably futile.

(b) Checking the temporary protection order information through the federal government's National Crime Information Center (NCIC) database. The Ohio Supreme Court has recently required all of the state's trial courts that have jurisdiction to issue protection orders of any kind to post notice of the issuance and deletion of such orders with NCIC.[23] Unfortunately, NCIC does not update its postings daily. As a result, all NCIC postings carry a disclaimer which advises the inquirer to check with the issuing court to determine the current validity of any protection order which appears in the system.

These methods notwithstanding, nothing short of confirmation from the issuing court can, or should, give an officer full confidence in the validity of temporary protection order presented for enforcement.

Q & A: I am a police officer in a small town. I just answered a

[22] RC 2919.26(E)(2)(b).

[23] Sup. R. 10.

call for a violation of a temporary protection order. When I got there, there was no evidence to support the allegation that the temporary protection order had been violated. Do I still have to make a report?

The law is very clear that the investigating officer in any domestic violence situation is required to make a report, whether or not an arrest is made.[24] The report serves to document the fact that domestic violence at the particular location was alleged, even if no arrest was made. The record of law enforcement intervention may assist an officer on a subsequent occasion in determining whether domestic violence occurred and the identity of the likely primary physical aggressor.

This provision of the law is really as much to protect the officer as it is to document the occurrence. The production of a report that sets forth the basis for an officer's decision *not* to arrest goes a long way toward protecting that officer, and the entity that the officer works for, from false allegations that the officer failed to protect a family or household member of an offender.

Q & A: I am prosecuting an individual for domestic violence. We obtained a Temporary Protection Order against the defendant and in favor of the alleged victim. The alleged victim also sought a civil protection order in the Domestic Relations Division of the Common Pleas Court. Although that order was granted ex parte, the Domestic Relations Court denied and vacated the order following the hearing on its merits. Can I revive the criminal order, now that the Civil order was dismissed?

The statutory language provides that a temporary protection order is "*effective only*" (emphasis added) until the issuance of a civil protection order or a consent agreement arising out of the same activities as those that were the basis of the complaint upon which the temporary protection order is based.[25] The legislature chose to use the words "effective only until," when it could have used the words, "terminated upon." It can be argued, therefore, that the effectiveness of the temporary protection order is suspended, not terminated, by the issuance of the civil protection order. Thus, once the civil protection order is dismissed, the restraint on the effectiveness of the temporary protection order is removed and its effectiveness resumes until the criminal case is disposed or the criminal court dismisses it or modifies its terms. Logically, no additional action is required to revive the temporary protection order.

Q & A: A court issues an ex parte civil protection order (CPO) against a respondent. Among other terms, the order requires that the respondent not come within 500 feet of the protected person named in the order. The respondent has not been served with the order. If the respondent goes to the protected person's home in violation of the order, can the respondent be arrested for violating the CPO?

It depends. The Supreme Court of Ohio holds that unless a respon-

[24] RC 2935.032(D).

[25] RC 2919.26(E)(2)(b).

dent is properly served with a protection order, it is not possible to obtain a *conviction* for a violation of its terms.[26] However, the Ohio General Assembly created an exception to this requirement.[27] It is no longer necessary for the prosecution to prove that a protection order or consent agreement was actually served on the defendant, if the prosecution is able to prove either,1) that the defendant was shown the protection order, consent agreement, or a copy thereof, or 2) that a judge, magistrate or law enforcement officer informed the defendant that the order was issued ***and*** that the defendant recklessly violated the terms of the order, the defendant is accountable for any violation.[28] If the defendant/respondent is unaware of the existence of the order or has not been served with it, shown a copy of it by anyone, or informed of it by a law enforcement officer, a judge or a magistrate, going to the home of the protected person named in the order is not a crime, unless another offense (e.g., aggravated trespassing, assault, aggravated menacing, stalking, obstruction of justice or obstruction of official business) is committed. However, even if a respondent has not been previously served, law enforcement does have the authority to arrest the alleged offender, when presented with a facially valid protection order. Enforcing or executing a court order is intrinsically associated with a judicial proceeding.[29] Absolute judicial immunity has been extended to non-judicial officers who perform "quasi-judicial" duties.[30] Quasi-judicial immunity extends to those persons performing tasks so integral or intertwined with the judicial process that these persons are considered an arm of the judicial officer who is immune.[31] Law enforcement officials executing a facially valid court order are protected by absolute quasi-judicial immunity.[32] Where an arrest is made absent a valid warrant, or pursuant to an invalid warrant, the question becomes whether the arresting officers were justified in their belief that the arrestee had probably committed or was committing a

---

[26]State v. Smith, 136 Ohio St. 3d 1, 2013-Ohio-1698, 989 N.E.2d 972 (2013); State v. Meinke, 2017-Ohio-7787, 97 N.E.3d 1184 (Ohio Ct. App. 9th Dist. Lorain County 2017) (citing State v. Smith, 136 Ohio St. 3d 1, 2013-Ohio-1698, 989 N.E.2d 972 (2013), for the proposition that service is a necessary element and reversing for the conviction because the court failed to instruct the jury of that element).

[27]See Sub. S. B. 7.

[28]Sub. S.B. 7.

[29]Bush v. Rauch, 38 F.3d 842, 847, 1994 FED App. 0362P (6th Cir. 1994).

[30]Joseph v. Patterson, 795 F.2d 549, 560 (6th Cir. 1986) (abrogated on other grounds by, Kalina v. Fletcher, 522 U.S. 118, 118 S. Ct. 502, 139 L. Ed. 2d 471 (1997)); Johnson v. Granholm, 662 F.2d 449 (6th Cir. 1981).

[31]Scruggs v. Moellering, 870 F.2d 376 (7th Cir. 1989) (abrogated by, Antoine v. Byers & Anderson, Inc., 508 U.S. 429, 113 S. Ct. 2167, 124 L. Ed. 2d 391 (1993)) (abrogating court finding court reporters are not absolutely immune from damages for failure to produce a transcript of a federal criminal trial).

[32]Webb v. Greene County Sheriff's Office, 494 F. Supp. 2d 779 (S.D. Ohio 2007); Pisani v. Village of Bentleyville, Ohio, 103 F.3d 130 (6th Cir. 1996) (Table); see also, Roland v. Phillips, 19 F.3d 552, 556-57 (11th Cir. 1994); Valdez v. City and County of Denver, 878 F.2d 1285 (10th Cir. 1989); Coverdell v. Department of Social and Health Services, State of Wash., 834 F.2d 758, 10 Fed. R. Serv. 3d 143 (9th Cir. 1987); Henry v. Farmer City State Bank, 808 F.2d 1228, R.I.C.O. Bus. Disp. Guide (CCH) P 6475, 6 Fed. R. Serv. 3d 971 (7th Cir. 1986); Tymiak v. Omodt, 676 F.2d 306 (8th Cir. 1982); Fowler v. Alexander, 478 F.2d 694 (4th Cir. 1973).

crime.[33] Therefore, a law enforcement officer who reasonably establishes probable cause to effect an arrest based upon the terms of what appears to be a violation of a protection order or consent agreement of this state or another state, valid on its face, is immune from liability in a civil action for damages for injury, death, or loss to person or property that allegedly was caused by or related to the arrest.[34]

Q & A: The Defendant was charged with first degree misdemeanor domestic violence—threats (due to a previous 1st degree misdemeanor conviction). While highly intoxicated at a bar somewhere in the City, the defendant called, texted, and left multiple threatening voicemails on the alleged victim's cell phone while she was located in a neighboring suburban municipal court's jurisdiction, including "I will kill you and your kids" and " You are dead." At the time she received these calls, she was at her home in a suburban jurisdiction. The alleged victim had a protection order that prohibited the defendant from having any contact with the alleged victim, who called the suburb's police department and swore out a warrant for the Defendant's arrest.

At pretrial, the defendant's attorney now questions the fact that the charge was brought in the jurisdiction of the suburb court, when in fact his client was in the City "while committing the alleged criminal act." Does the lawyer have a point?

No. In analogous situations, courts in Ohio have noted that "the trial of a criminal case in this state shall be held in a court having jurisdiction of the subject matter, and *in the territory of which the offense or any element* of the offense *was committed.*"[35] The elements of menacing are: (1) knowingly, (2) causing another to believe, (3) that the offender will cause physical harm to the person or property of such other person or a member of his immediate family.[36]

The defendant "knowingly" made his threatening statements from the City. In turn, the threats were communicated to the alleged victim while she was within the jurisdiction of the suburb. The offense could not have been completed until such time when the alleged victim was made aware of the threats, thereby causing the alleged victim a belief of impending physical harm. In the case at bar, this particular element was fulfilled in the suburban court's jurisdiction where the victim heard the defendant's threatening statements.

Thus, the proper venue, under R.C. 2901.12(A), would have been either the location from which defendant made the threatening statements or the place where the threats caused the victim to believe defendant would cause physical harm.[37] Therefore, it is immaterial whether the victim and defendant were in separate venues when the

[33]Webb v. Greene County Sheriff's Office, 494 F. Supp. 2d 779 (S.D. Ohio 2007).

[34]RC 9.86, 2744.03.

[35]R.C. 2901.12(A) (emphasis added).

[36]State v. Applegate, 1992 WL 236775 (Ohio Ct. App. 12th Dist. Butler County 1992), cause dismissed, 66 Ohio St. 3d 1432, 608 N.E.2d 761 (1993).

[37]Compare State v. Novel, 1986 WL 11348 (Ohio Ct. App. 5th Dist. Licking County 1986), State v. Cremeans, 5 Ohio App. 3d 8, 448 N.E.2d 837 (4th Dist. Meigs County 1982).

conversation occurred. Charges could be filed in either, since elements of the offense occurred in both jurisdictions.[38]

Venue is not a material element of a criminal case.[39] However, "venue is a fact that must be proven beyond a reasonable doubt."[40]

In a menacing case that occurs over landline telephones, venue is proper in either the location the calls are made or the location the calls are received.[41] However, the situation becomes more complicated when the alleged menacing call is received on the alleged victim's cellular telephone. The complication comes about because receipt of the call by the alleged victim, by itself, does not establish that venue existed in a certain location at that time. There must be some other evidence, such as testimony or telephone records, introduced to show that the phone call actually occurred and where the alleged victim was located when the alleged threat was received. Conversely, evidence might also be introduced to establish where the alleged offender was at that time.[42]

§ 4:8 Other protection orders available in criminal cases

The amendments to the domestic violence laws enacted by the state legislature in 1994[1] increased the authority of trial courts to extend protection to the apparent victims of this class of criminal acts.[2] In order to exercise this authority, certain prerequisites must be present.[3] Those prerequisites include:

(1) A previously filed criminal complaint must be before the court;
(2) The victim of the original complaint or other person authorized by statute must be before the court. The motion must allege either: (a) that the offender, or another in concert with the offender, has committed or is likely to commit some act which would constitute an offense against the victim's person or property, or (b) that the offender, or someone acting in concert with the offender, has committed or is likely to commit some act which would constitute an offense against the person or property of a ward or child of the victim;
(3) The court must hold a hearing on the motion; and

[38]State v. Dengg, 2009-Ohio-4101, 2009 WL 2488048 (Ohio Ct. App. 11th Dist. Portage County 2009).

[39]State v. Shaw, 134 Ohio App.3d at 318, 730 N.E.2d 1075; State v. Headley, 6 Ohio St. 3d 475, 477, 453 N.E.2d 716 (1983).

[40]State v. Lahmann, 2007-Ohio-1795, 2007 WL 1121472 (Ohio Ct. App. 12th Dist. Butler County 2007); State v. Smith, 87 Ohio St. 3d 424, 435, 2000-Ohio-450, 721 N.E.2d 93 (2000); State v. Headley, 6 Ohio St.3d at 477, 453 N.E.2d 716).

[41]Fairfield v. McRoberts, 100 Ohio App. 3d 476, 478, 654 N.E.2d 370 (12th Dist. Butler County 1995).

[42]State v. Dengg, 2009-Ohio-4101, 2009 WL 2488048 (Ohio Ct. App. 11th Dist. Portage County 2009).

[Section 4:8]

[1]1994 Am. Sub. H.B. 335.

[2]RC 2945.04(B).

[3]RC 2945.04.

(4) The court must determine that the allegations contained in the motion are true.[4]

Once the prerequisites are met, the court may order the defendant:

(1) not to commit the anticipated act or acts,[5]
(2) not to continue committing the complained of act or acts,[6] or
(3) both of the above,[7]
(4) to maintain a prescribed geographic distance from any other person who is before the court and who is specified by the order,[8]
(5) not to communicate with any other person who is before the court and who is specified by the order,[9]
(6) evicted from a residence that the defendant cohabits with the complainant, if the complainant and the defendant are not family or household members and the residence is solely owned or leased by the complainant,[10]
(7) to vacate the premises when the residence is jointly owned by the defendant and the complainant.[11]

The law also gives the court the authority to direct the actions of persons other than the defendant in criminal cases involving domestic violence. In order to exercise this authority, the court must first establish, to its satisfaction, that the person to whom the order is directed is:

(1) before the court in some respect, i.e., as a subpoenaed witness, a person that has entered the courtroom, etc., and
(2) acting in concert with the defendant, to the detriment of the complainant or a witness in a criminal case involving an allegation of domestic violence,[12] and
(3) attempting to do any of the following to a crime victim or witness, or the ward or child of a complainant in the criminal case:[13]
    (a) intimidate,
    (b) harm the person of,
    (c) harm the property of, or
    (d) any combination of the above.

Once these prerequisites are established, the court may issue an order against a person other than the defendant who engages in such conduct. The order may:

---

[4]RC 2945.04(B).

[5]RC 2945.04(B)(1).

[6]RC 2945.04(B)(1).

[7]RC 2945.04(B)(1).

[8]RC 2945.04(B)(3).

[9]RC 2945.04(B)(4).

[10]RC 2945.04(B)(6).

[11]RC 2945.04(B)(6).

[12]RC 2945.04(B)(3), RC 2945.04(B)(4).

[13]RC 2945.04(A), RC 2945.04(B); see also RC 2921.04.

(1) prohibit the subject of the order from committing the anticipated act or acts complained of,[14]

(2) prohibit the subject of the order from continuing to commit the act or acts complained of,[15] or

(3) direct the subject of the order not to communicate with any person who is before the court and specified by the order.[16]

In addition, the court may order a specified law enforcement agency within the court's jurisdiction to provide the protection which the court has ordered.[17]

The orders issued under these provisions of the law are not, technically speaking, designated as "protection orders." They do, however, accomplish the same purposes as those orders that do carry that designation. They also subject their violators to criminal penalties and/or contempt sanctions.[18]

§ 4:9 The effect of a felony bind-over on a protection order issued in a municipal or county court

Before the legislature changed the law,[1] protection orders associated with domestic violence felony offenses initially filed in a municipal or county court ceased to exist once that lower court relinquished jurisdiction. Upon a determination of probable cause and bind-over of the case to a court of common pleas, the consequent dismissal of the original charge, at the municipal or county level, effectively terminated all proceedings and orders of the lower court, including any outstanding protection orders.

Technically, the domestic violence charges and their attendant protection orders ceased to exist in either court until the common pleas court, through indictment or information filed against the defendant assumed jurisdiction of the same facts and activities that gave rise to the original municipal or county court charge. As a result, a defendant could not be convicted of a violation of a protection order associated with charges bound over from the lower court if the violation was alleged to have occurred during this interim period.

Amended Sub. S.B. 98, passed in 1997, was enacted specifically to cure this problem. As amended, the law provides for the survival of a protection order, when, as noted above, the accompanying felony is dismissed by the lower court and bound over to the court of common pleas.[2] The order remains in full force and effect, as though issued by the common pleas court that ultimately assumes jurisdiction and disposes of the subject matter.[3] Common pleas courts receiving these

---

[14] RC 2945.04(A)(1), RC 2945.04(B)(1).

[15] RC 2945.04(A)(1), RC 2945.04(B)(1).

[16] RC 2945.04(B)(4).

[17] RC 2945.04(B)(5).

[18] RC 2945.04(D)(1), RC 2945.04(D)(2).

[Section 4:9]

[1] 1997 S.B. 98, eff. 3-17-98.

[2] RC 2919.26(D)(4).

[3] RC 2919.26(D)(4).

protection orders are required to treat them as though they themselves had issued the orders.[4] It must be noted that, once these cases are bound over, the common pleas courts to whom they are referred have exclusive jurisdiction to modify any associated protection orders originally issued at the municipal or county court level.[5]

As with all other protection orders issued pursuant to the domestic violence statutes, these protection orders are only effective while the criminal charges are pending before the court exercising ultimate jurisdiction.[6]

Q & A: The prosecutor in a misdemeanor domestic violence case has just informed the municipal court that the police have discovered the defendant's previous conviction for an escalating misdemeanor. The state now intends to dismiss the misdemeanor charge and to file a felony against the defendant instead. The victim's advocate is concerned that dismissing the misdemeanor case will have the effect of voiding the victim's protection order. Is the advocate's concern justified?

Presently, no Ohio court has spoken to this issue. The law that governs the question, as written, is ambiguous and susceptible to at least two very different interpretations. Its provisions were passed to fill a specific gap in the law. That gap occurred during the interim period between the time that a domestic violence charge, originally brought as a felony before a municipal or county court, was dismissed and the time that a true bill indictment relating to the same facts and activities was issued or information was filed, conferring jurisdiction on a court of common pleas.[7]

The legislative fix for this problem[8] extended the effective coverage provided by a protection order issued by a municipal or county court, pursuant to the domestic violence statute. The statute, as amended, now provides that municipal and county court protection orders cover the interim period between dismissal of a felony in a lower court, following bind-over, and indictment by a court of common pleas for the same felonious activities. The orders issued by the municipal and county courts thus continue to be enforceable, just as if they were reissued by the common pleas courts at the moment of bind-over.[9]

The issue posed by this question presents an interesting application of the extended protection coverage period. A number of the trial courts in Ohio have expanded the use of the extended period since the law was amended. They have taken the position that the language of the statute is expansive enough to include any protection order issued pursuant to the domestic violence statutes. Their interpretation includes both misdemeanor and felony offenses where a defendant is subsequently bound over to a common pleas court on charges arising out of the same facts that gave rise to the original issuance of a protec-

[4]RC 2919.26(D)(4).

[5]RC 2919.26(D)(4).

[6]RC 2919.26(D)(4).

[7]See the Legislative Commission's Bill Analysis of Am. Sub. S.B. 98, eff. 3-18-98, at 5.

[8]RC 2919.26(D)(4).

[9]RC 2919.26(D)(4).

tion order. The courts who employ this process assume that the filing of a new and separate felony case not contemplated at the time of the original complaint, but based on the same facts, will have no impact on the continuing effectiveness of the protection order originally issued.[10]

This interpretation advances the proposition that once a valid protection order issues from a municipal or county court, dismissal of the predicate charge does not terminate the order, if the same facts serve as the basis of any subsequent indictment or information filed against the defendant in the common pleas court. Therefore, any action by the defendant that constitutes a violation of the terms of the protection order during a covered interim period may serve as the basis for a new criminal complaint alleging violation of the order, once an indictment is returned or an information is filed against the defendant based on the same underlying facts.

This open-ended approach is problematic. For example, let's assume that a defendant is currently charged with a first-degree misdemeanor domestic violence offense and that a protection order is issued in conjunction with that charge. Let's assume further that the defendant was previously convicted of one of the offenses that could cause the current charge to escalate to a felony.[11] Under these facts, the defendant is placed in limbo if the current misdemeanor charge is dismissed, because under this interpretation of the law the attendant protection order survives indefinitely. Therefore, at least theoretically, the defendant is obliged to abide by the terms of that protection order until the expiration of the statute of limitations of any potential felony charge that conceivably might be brought.

Otherwise constitutionally protected conduct by the defendant, e.g., visiting a friend who lives within the zone proscribed in the order, could result in a new criminal charge for violation of the protection order, if the prosecuting authority commences a felony prosecution based upon the same facts as those that formed the basis for the previously dismissed misdemeanor. This result is possible, regardless of any issue that might be raised concerning the remoteness in time between the commission of the alleged violation and the commencement of the felony prosecution in the common pleas court, as long as the protection order violation takes place during the interim period that the order is interpreted to cover.

Courts that favor this approach do so because it has the advantage of obviating the need for a second motion for a temporary protection order, the conduct of a second set of hearings, the removal of the first protection order from the respective registries where it was enrolled, the issuance of a new order, service of the new order on the defendant and re-registration of the new protection order with the proper authorities.

Until the legislature clarifies its purpose or the appellate courts provide an authoritative interpretation, both approaches will continue to have their adherents in Ohio.

Q & A: Although the Ohio General Assembly clearly intended

---

[10]See RC 2919.26(D)(4) and RC 2919.26(E)(2)(a).

[11]See Text § 2:7, Felony violations.

protection orders issued by municipal and county courts associated with felony cases to survive bind-over to courts of common pleas, how can that survival happen, when the jurisdiction of the municipal or county courts terminates once the case is bound over or indicted?

The statute that allows for a protection order to survive the dismissal of the predicate case in a municipal or county court is clear. It applies: 1) when the offender is bound over after waiving a preliminary hearing on the charge that resulted in the issuance of the protection order, 2) when a person is bound over, after a hearing is held, to the common pleas court on the charge that resulted in the issuance of the protection order, 3) when a person is indicted by a common pleas court on the charge that resulted in the issuance of the protection order, or 4) in any other manner.[12]

The logistics of implementing and enforcing the statute, in some respects, however, are less clear. For instance, if a case that generated a protection order in a municipal or county court is indicted by a court of common pleas before it is bound-over, the common pleas court and the county prosecutor may have no way of knowing that a protection order is associated with that case. A bind-over packet from the court of limited jurisdiction containing that information is not necessary for presentation to the Grand Jury. The municipal or county court is not immediately made aware of the direct indictment. Limited jurisdiction court are not, therefore put on notice of any need to inform the common pleas court of the existence of the protection order. Even after the municipal or county court is informed of the indictment, the court of limited jurisdiction may not feel compelled to provide notice to the common pleas court about the order, since it may feel that its obligation to take any action concerning the case ends when the common pleas court issues its indictment and assumes jurisdiction by operation of law.

There is no case law or statutory language that speaks to this apparent dichotomy. That leaves each judge to apply his or her own individual statutory interpretation of a limited jurisdiction court's continuing authority to transfer protection orders associated with cases terminated and sent to the court of common plea. The result is that some judges believe that the General Assembly was without power to enact a special jurisdictional exception allowing protection orders to survive the termination of the predicate case.

However, municipal and county courts and the jurisdiction that they exercise are entirely creations of statute.[13] The General Assembly's power to create a court necessarily includes the power to define its jurisdiction.[14] It follows, therefore, that the legislature has the power to extend extraordinary jurisdiction to municipal and county

[12]R.C. 2919.26(D)(4).

[13]State ex rel. Ramey v. Davis, 119 Ohio St. 596, 7 Ohio L. Abs. 109, 165 N.E. 298 (1929).

[14]State ex rel. Ramey v. Davis, 119 Ohio St. 596, 7 Ohio L. Abs. 109, 165 N.E. 298 (1929).

courts for a specific purpose,[15] such as extending the life of a protection order.[16]

Certainly, the most effective way to resolve any lingering confusion regarding its intent would be for the General Assembly to amend the statute and clarify its language. In the alternative, a simple fix, would be for common pleas courts to ask limited jurisdiction courts, in each case involving a direct indictment that contains charges that qualify for the issuance of a protection order, whether a protection order was, in fact, issued.

§ 4:10 Civil/criminal protection order remedies compared

TYPE	CRIMINAL (TPO)	CIVIL (CPO)	CIV.R.75 DIVORCE RESTRAINING ORDER
Where filed:	county; municipal; common pleas court	common pleas; domestic relations court	common pleas; domestic relations (in conjunction with divorce proceeding)
Duration:	while criminal case is pending	up to 5 years	while divorce is pending
Scope:	solely to ensure family safety	to ensure safety; determine property use, custody, support, and visitation, and counseling issues for the life of the order	to restrain violence; prohibit removal of property and/or children from jurisdiction; can provide exclusive use of residence to non-violent spouse, following separate hearing after divorce is filed
How enforced:	police (new crime); contempt	police (new crime); contempt	contempt
Who is covered:	all family and household members	all family and household members	spouses and those with interest in marital property
Hearings required:	one, on next court date after filing; one on the next court date after offender's arrest or surrender	two hearings, no more than 7 court days apart	no hearing needed; effective when served

[15]See, for instance, R.C. 1901.18 (B).

[16]R.C. 2919.26(D)(4).

TYPE	CRIMINAL (TPO)	CIVIL (CPO)	CIV.R.75 DIVORCE RESTRAINING ORDER
Costs:	none	none	divorce filing fee

Chapter 5

Domestic Violence Prosecution—Initiation and Initial Case Preparation

§ 5:1 Prosecution's challenge

The prosecution of domestic violence cases presents unique challenges. In the past, the subjective judgments of police officers, judges, prosecutors, and victims often combined to negatively impact the appropriate resolution of these complaints. Police officers, judges, and prosecutors frequently required victims to decide the course of a domestic violence prosecution. The victim decided whether the police arrested the offender. The victim decided whether the prosecutor pursued the charges brought or terminated them. In some cases, the victim decided whether the court convicted the offender. In some instances, the victim even had the last word on whether a convicted offender went to jail or received the privilege of probation.

Reliance on the victim to make these decisions unilaterally was, and is, misplaced. Victims of domestic violence often find themselves under emotional, financial, religious, cultural, physical, and other pressures to make such decisions. This is not to say that the desires of victims of domestic violence should be discounted or disregarded entirely. To the contrary, the victims of domestic violence are most often in the best position to assess the level of threat that they face at the hands of those who abuse them and the consequences of continuing to pursue the goal of criminal conviction. Increasingly, communities are pursuing comprehensive approaches to addressing these problems that value and incorporate victim input into the charging calculus, while simultaneously reserving the final decision on going forward to the prosecuting authority.

Successful domestic violence prosecution requires those representing the government to focus on all of the potential evidence available. This means that the evidence in a given case, and not the wishes of the victim/complainant, drives the charging decision and subsequent prosecution of a domestic violence offender. The use of objective standards allows the prosecution to filter out extraneous considerations and to focus resources on identifying and developing strong, complete fact patterns for presentation to the ultimate triers of fact.

This approach is both strategic and tactical. It requires an overall framework for the prosecutor to work within and close coordination of efforts of police, prosecutor, witness, and victim support and advocacy staffs.

Ohio's domestic violence laws[1] require all state police and law enforcement agencies dealing with this group of offenses to establish a number of written policies for handling the investigation of these crimes.[2] The policies required of each agency include:

(1) A commitment to respond without undue delay to complaints of domestic violence.[3]

(2) How the agency will document facts and circumstances where a violation of a temporary protection order or a pretrial condition of release is alleged.[4]

(3) How the separate interviews required for alleged domestic violence offenders and victims will be conducted.[5]

(4) What information the agency will provide to victims of domestic violence, including:

[Section 5:1]

[1]See 1994 H.B. 335, eff. 3-9-94.

[2]RC 2935.032.

[3]RC 2935.032(A)(2)(a).

[4]RC 2935.032(A)(2)(b).

[5]RC 2935.032(A)(2)(c).

(a) the responding officer's name and badge number (if the officer has a badge number),[6]
(b) the report number assigned to the incident (if that information is available),[7]
(c) a telephone number for the victim to call for information about the case,[8] and
(d) information concerning the availability of domestic violence shelters and victim advocacy programs or other similar resources within the community.[9]

(5) A commitment to prepare a report on *every* domestic violence complaint, whether or not an arrest is made.[10] Such reports are required to document the officer's observations, including:
(a) any visible injuries,[11]
(b) any weapons found at the scene,[12]
(c) the actions and statements of the alleged offender,[13]
(d) any statements made by the victim or other witness,[14] and
(e) any other significant facts or circumstances.[15]

(6) Mandatory arrest, upon probable cause, for felonies resulting from domestic situations.[16]

(7) Consultation with local domestic violence shelters and programs in the development of the required policies.[17]

(8) Enforcement of out-of-jurisdiction and unregistered protection orders.[18]

(9) Enforcement of protection orders that have not been issued by the agency's jurisdiction or under state code.[19]

(10) Although arrest is the preferred policy for those believed to have committed the offense of domestic violence, agency policies can make arrest *mandatory* upon probable cause.[20]

These requirements have the collective effect of forcing law enforcement to put more emphasis on looking for, documenting, and preserving the existence of evidence in addition to the statements of the victim of a domestic violence-related offense. The changes in the law

---

[6]RC 2935.032(C)(3).

[7]RC 2935.032(C)(3).

[8]RC 2935.032(C)(3).

[9]RC 2935.032(C)(3).

[10]RC 2935.032(C)(1), RC 2935.032(D).

[11]RC 2935.032(D).

[12]RC 2935.032(D).

[13]RC 2935.032(D).

[14]RC 2935.032(D).

[15]RC 2935.032(D).

[16]Felonious assault, RC 2935.032(A)(1)(a)(i), RC 2935.032(A)(1)(a)(ii); Aggravated assault, RC 2935.032(A)(1)(b)(i), RC 2935.032(A)(1)(b)(ii).

[17]RC 2935.032(E).

[18]RC 2919.26(G)(4).

[19]RC 2919.26(G)(4).

[20]RC 2935.032(B)(1)(a), RC 2935.032(B)(1)(b).

also increase the level of law enforcement accountability for processing domestic violence complaints correctly.[21]

The new requirements placed on law enforcement also provide the raw material necessary for the aggressive prosecution of domestic violence-related crimes. The expansion of the available evidence to include testimonial evidence from individuals other than the complainant, physical evidence from the scene and elsewhere, and evidence which qualifies under one or more of the exceptions to the hearsay rule frees the government from its previous reliance on the victim as the essential component for a successful prosecution.

The development of effective collaboration between law enforcement and prosecutorial staffs requires closer coordination than existed in the past. This coordination is most effective when the prosecution clearly defines those things that it considers important when deciding to charge an individual with a criminal act of domestic violence. It is also useful for the prosecution to assist in training law enforcement on the contents of the state and local domestic violence laws and on the minimum evidentiary requirements for successful prosecution.

§ 5:2 Initial consultations with those who allege domestic violence

Most acts of domestic violence are committed in private. There is little advance warning of the exact moment that the violence will erupt. It is generally too late when they begin to develop a safety strategy.

However, by its very nature, domestic violence is cyclical and repetitive. Once an act of domestic violence occurs in a relationship, it is both logical and prudent to anticipate that other such acts of violence will eventually follow. Those who counsel individuals involved in domestic violence situations can, therefore, provide in advance practical and useful information that will allow those counseled to avoid, escape, or minimize the impact of any future violent acts.

The information that counselors provide will assist those who have been, or believe they may soon be, the victims of either a verbal or physical assault in developing viable safety plans. Those plans should include, at a minimum, all of the following:

(1) An emergency escape route and a plan to avoid being cornered, not just for their home but also for their place of business and any other location where they might encounter the abuser;

(2) A safe place to escape to while plans for more extended shelter are arranged, if necessary;

(3) A place to secret money and credit cards outside of the home, including, where appropriate, a separate bank account in case other funds become frozen;

(4) A repository, outside of the home, for a complete set of extra keys;

(5) Copies of all vital or important records or documents (certified, where necessary), such as birth certificates, employment records, contracts, deeds, medical cards and/or records, immigra-

[21] See RC 2935.032(A)(3), RC 2935.32(B)(2).

tion documents, protection orders, custody determinations or other court records, important addresses and phone numbers, etc.;

(6) Extra clothing kept at the home of a friend or relative for all family or household members who may need to leave the residence in a hurry;

(7) Any prescriptions for drugs or other medical treatments;

(8) A cellular phone;

(9) A small, hand-held portable tape recorder or a videocassette recorder; and

(10) Removal of all dangerous or deadly weapons from the home or, in the alternative, their placement in storage areas that are difficult to access quickly, if violence occurs.[1]

If law enforcement is called, counselors should advise their clients that it is imperative that they comply with the officer's requests and that they avoid additional problems by immediately disengaging from the conflict once law enforcement is on the scene, regardless of any additional provocation from the other party.

Orders from law enforcement officers are to be obeyed, even if they seem unfair. The scene of the incident is not the proper forum to contest a law enforcement decision, and doing so may result in the client's unnecessary arrest.

The client can address issues such as unjust removal from the home, lack of visitation with the children, retrieval of items left behind, as well as other concerns at early stages in either the criminal or civil court process, i.e., at initial appearance, arraignment, or protection order hearing in the criminal cases or during the protection order hearing in the civil case.

§ 5:3 Prosecutorial discretion

The decision to prosecute an individual for criminal behavior is a function of the executive branch of government.[1] Charging decisions are rarely simple matters. The public prosecutor has broad discretion in making these decisions. Probable cause is generally only the first of a number of considerations taken into account. Other considerations include the strength of the case, the prosecution's general deterrence value, the government's enforcement priorities, and the case's relationship to the government's overall enforcement plan.

The United States Supreme Court found these decisions particularly ill-suited to judicial review.[2] The power of the public prosecutor to exercise this discretion is, therefore, nearly absolute.[3]

Nonetheless, the public prosecutor is an official who, arguably, is

---

[Section 5:2]

[1]See also Text § 16:5, Preventing domestic violence; safety plans and provisions.

[Section 5:3]

[1]O. Const. Art. IV § 20.

[2]Wayte v. U.S., 470 U.S. 598, 105 S. Ct. 1524, 84 L. Ed. 2d 547 (1985).

[3]Newman v. U.S., 382 F.2d 479 (D.C. Cir. 1967); Powell v. Katzenbach, 359 F.2d 234 (D.C. Cir. 1965).

also answerable for any failure to conform to statutory mandates. Additionally, the decisions that these officials make must not constitute violations of the constitutional rights of any individuals, or of any class of individuals. If prosecutorial power is exercised in a way that is abusive or biased against a class of victims, the courts have the authority to place limits on the exercise of prosecutors' discretion.[4] In particularly egregious cases, it is possible to hold prosecutors responsible for damage resulting from abuses of their discretion.[5]

It is generally well-settled in Ohio that mandamus[6] is not available to compel the initiation of a specific criminal case, except in those instances where the failure to prosecute constitutes an abuse of discretion.[7] Prohibition[8] is likewise unavailable to bring about the termination of criminal charges brought by a public prosecutor. The maintenance of prosecutors' independence from judicial or other interference allows for a dispassionate assessment of whether the evidence gathered is sufficient in quantity and quality to result in the state's objectives on presentation to the ultimate trier of fact.

In *State v. Busch*,[9] the Ohio Supreme Court placed some limits on the prosecution's near-absolute authority to unilaterally decide whether to proceed with a criminal case. In reviewing the facts of the Franklin County domestic violence prosecution, the Court held that Criminal Rule 48 gives Ohio's trial courts the discretion to dismiss criminal cases over the objection of the prosecution where the complaining witness does not wish for the case to proceed and the dismissal serves the interest of justice.

The Court's position in *Busch* broke with established precedent on the issue of a trial court's right and authority to override a prosecutor's

---

[4]Bordenkircher v. Hayes, 434 U.S. 357, 98 S. Ct. 663, 54 L. Ed. 2d 604 (1978); Cleveland v. Whitner, 119 Ohio Misc. 2d 100, 2002-Ohio-4220, 774 N.E.2d 788 (Mun. Ct. 2002).

[5]Wilkinson v. Ellis, 484 F. Supp. 1072 (E.D. Pa. 1980).

[6]"Mandamus" is an order from a superior court commanding a public official to perform a certain function.

[7]State ex rel. Master v. Cleveland, 75 Ohio St. 3d 23, 1996-Ohio-228, 661 N.E.2d 180 (1996); State ex rel. Squire v. Taft, 69 Ohio St. 3d 365, 368, 632 N.E.2d 883 (1994); Pengov v. White, 146 Ohio App. 3d 402, 406, 2001-Ohio-1668, 766 N.E.2d 228, 231 (9th Dist. Lorain County 2001); State ex rel. Drake v. Fuerst, 1999 WL 328725, *2 (Ohio Ct. App. 8th Dist. Cuyahoga County 1999).

[8]"Prohibition" is the process by which a superior court prevents an inferior court from exceeding its jurisdiction.

[9]State v. Busch, 76 Ohio St. 3d 613, 1996-Ohio-82, 669 N.E.2d 1125 (1996). See also State v. Landers, 188 Ohio App. 3d 786, 2010-Ohio-3709, 936 N.E.2d 1026 (4th Dist. Meigs County 2010); State v. Sanders, 2013-Ohio-5220, 3 N.E.3d 749 (Ohio Ct. App. 7th Dist. Columbiana County 2013); State v. Carabello, 2017-Ohio-4449, 93 N.E.3d 322 (Ohio Ct. App. 8th Dist. Cuyahoga County 2017), appeal not allowed, 151 Ohio St. 3d 1508, 2018-Ohio-365, 90 N.E.3d 949 (2018) (Court dismissed indictments without prejudice on first day of trial over State objection due to outstanding discovery.); State /City of Toledo v. Lear, 2018-Ohio-1874, 2018 WL 2174378 (Ohio Ct. App. 6th Dist. Lucas County 2018) (Toledo Municipal Court's dismissal of misdemeanor TPO violation was reversed. The appellate court found the trial court's explanation for exercising its discretion to dismiss the criminal complaint was based on incorrect interpretation of Criminal Rule 5(B)(1).).

decision to proceed with a criminal prosecution.[10] The Ohio Constitution,[11] criminal rules,[12] and statutes[13] all seem to reserve the power to dismiss a criminal complaint for the prosecuting authority, although some supervisory oversight is provided to the court. The Supreme Court's pronouncement, however, provided Ohio's trial courts with the power to *initiate* the termination of a criminal charge without either the request or the agreement of the prosecution.[14] The implications of this decision reached well beyond the confines of the domestic violence area of the criminal law.

The *Busch* interpretation raised a number of interesting and troubling issues. First, what were the implications for the doctrine of separation of powers? Although the Ohio Constitution does not specifically set forth a separation of powers doctrine, a review of the relevant case law reveals that the doctrine is part of Ohio's jurisprudence.[15] The additional power to initiate the termination of a criminal prosecution granted by *Busch* was at odds with the power that the General Assembly granted specifically to the prosecution to exercise that function[16] and was overturned by legislative action.[17]

Second, the decision involved important issues of public policy. It provided all victims of domestic violence with the ability to bypass a prosecutorial decision to proceed with criminal charges. Under *Busch*, if the court found that the "interests of justice" were served, a victim's request that a charge not go forward prevailed over all other considerations. This was true even in the face of compelling independent corroborating evidence that the prosecution might use to convince a trier of fact of the offender's guilt, such as visible injuries, prior inconsistent statements, and excited utterances.

---

[10]See, e.g., State ex rel. Nagle v. Olin, 64 Ohio St. 2d 341, 18 Ohio Op. 3d 503, 415 N.E.2d 279 (1980); State v. Sutton, 64 Ohio App. 2d 105, 18 Ohio Op. 3d 83, 411 N.E.2d 818 (9th Dist. Wayne County 1979); City of Cleveland v. Mosquito, 10 Ohio App. 3d 239, 461 N.E.2d 924 (8th Dist. Cuyahoga County 1983); Chenault v. McLean, 48 Ohio App. 284, 1 Ohio Op. 371, 15 Ohio L. Abs. 610, 193 N.E. 352 (2d Dist. Fayette County 1933); State ex rel. Master v. Cleveland, 75 Ohio St. 3d 23, 1996-Ohio-228, 661 N.E.2d 180 (1996); State v. Dixon, 14 Ohio App. 3d 396, 471 N.E.2d 864 (8th Dist. Cuyahoga County 1984); Cleveland v. Whitner, 119 Ohio Misc. 2d 100, 108, 2002-Ohio-4220, 774 N.E.2d 788, 794 (Mun. Ct. 2002); State v. Daniels, 2018-Ohio-1701, 2018 WL 2058731 (Ohio Ct. App. 1st Dist. Hamilton County 2018) (the trial court denying the prosecutor's motion to dismiss when the alleged victim indicated she no longer wished to pursue charges. The court found and the decision was upheld on appeal, that based in the allegations, the complaint was sufficient to charge a domestic violence offense, and the prosecuting witness was present to testify regarding the allegations).

[11]O. Const. Art. IV § 20.

[12]Crim. R. 48(A). See also State v. Walker, 2006-Ohio-917, 2006 WL 475789 (Ohio Ct. App. 9th Dist. Summit County 2006); State v. Grundy, 2006-Ohio-521, 2006 WL 288114 (Ohio Ct. App. 9th Dist. Summit County 2006).

[13]RC 2941.33.

[14]State v. Busch, 76 Ohio St. 3d 613, 1996-Ohio-82, 669 N.E.2d 1125 (1996); State /City of Toledo v. Lear, 2018-Ohio-1874, 2018 WL 2174378 (Ohio Ct. App. 6th Dist. Lucas County 2018).

[15]State v. Hochhausler, 76 Ohio St. 3d 455, 1996-Ohio-374, 668 N.E.2d 457 (1996); City of South Euclid v. Jemison, 28 Ohio St. 3d 157, 503 N.E.2d 136 (1986).

[16]See Crim. R. 48(A); RC 2941.33.

[17]See 1997 S.B. 98, eff. 3-17-98.

In crafting this new standard, the Court attempted to narrow the impact of its decision. According to the Supreme Court, a trial court was not free to dismiss every case where a victim refused to testify and was required to inform and restrict the exercise of its discretion to those cases where:

(1) The trial court follows the procedure set forth in Criminal Rule 48(B), requiring that it reduce its reasons for dismissal to writing; and
(2) It considers circumstances such as:
   (a) the seriousness of the injuries inflicted,
   (b) the presence of independent witnesses,
   (c) the status of counseling efforts between the parties,
   (d) whether the complainant's refusal to testify is coerced, and
   (e) whether the defendant is a first-time offender.[18]

It was not entirely clear from the language used by the Supreme Court whether a trial court should take one, some, or all of these considerations under advisement before making a decision to dismiss. It is highly unlikely that all of the factors mentioned would appear in every domestic violence case that came before the trial courts of Ohio. Thus, under *Busch*, each trial court was free to decide what consideration or considerations to employ in deciding if the "interests of justice" were served by the dismissal of a case over the objections of the prosecutor. Subsequent to the Supreme Court's pronouncement in *Busch*, one appellate court did undertake to set forth at least some of the circumstances that would constitute an abuse of a trial court's discretion in dismissing a domestic violence charge, sua sponte, over the objection of the prosecuting authority.[19]

Any attempt to restrict the application of the court's discretionary power to certain domestic violence victims was difficult at best. Under the Supreme Court's interpretation of Criminal Rule 48(B), a trial court was free to dismiss *any* criminal charge over the objection of the prosecution if it found that the "interests of justice" were served. The only predicate to a trial court's exercise of this authority was the requirement that it put its reasons for dismissing the charge in writing and that its reasons not be unreasonable, arbitrary, or unconscionable. A trial court's decision to dismiss a domestic violence case did not require that it first assess any tangible or intangible prosecutorial considerations, such as enforcement policies and the general deterrence value of taking such cases to trial.

Another public policy concern was the power that the *Busch* interpretation gave to the perpetrators of crime. This decision provided offenders with an incentive to use any means necessary to convince a victim to ask for a dismissal. Correctly or incorrectly, victims were likely to be perceived by offenders as the key to escaping legal accountability for their violent acts. The decision also provided an escape for judges and prosecutors who were uncomfortable handling domestic violence cases for other reasons.

---

[18]State v. Busch, 76 Ohio St. 3d 613, 1996-Ohio-82, 669 N.E.2d 1125 (1996).

[19]State v. Lewis, 125 Ohio App. 3d 352, 708 N.E.2d 745 (9th Dist. Lorain County 1998). See also State v. Moran, 1998 WL 831570 (Ohio Ct. App. 9th Dist. Lorain County 1998) and State v. Montiel, 185 Ohio App. 3d 362, 2009-Ohio-6589, 924 N.E.2d 375 (2d Dist. Montgomery County 2009).

The Supreme Court's interpretation of Criminal Rule 48(B) came in a case based on facts that occurred prior to the amendments to Ohio's arrest laws in 1994. Those amendments evince a plain intention by the General Assembly to provide the prosecution with the discretion to proceed with a domestic violence complaint without the active participation of the victim.[20] The General Assembly clarified its intentions with the enactment of 1997 Senate Bill 98, which effectively overturned *Busch*.[21] 1997 Senate Bill 98 specifically prohibits the trial courts from dismissing a complaint over the objection of the prosecution solely at the request of the victim. Whether, in light of these legislative developments, the Supreme Court will continue to apply the same interpretation of Criminal Rule 48(B) to domestic violence prosecutions as it did in *Busch* remains to be seen.

One appellate court has repeatedly examined and approved of a trial court's right to dismiss a domestic violence case over the objection of the prosecution where it can be shown objectively that the court's decision is not based solely upon the request of the complaining witness.[22] Thus, in at least one appellate district in Ohio, where a victim fails to comply with a local rule of court and the trial court makes specific findings of fact regarding the impact of that failure on the progress of the case or the rights of the defendant, the trial court is empowered to enter a dismissal on the record.[23] The sustainability of such a dismissal upon appeal may be dependant upon the trial court's articulation of the facts that support its decision.[24] The trial court's failure to articulate its reasons for dismissal under these circumstances in all probability constitutes reversible error.[25]

Q & A: I went to the prosecutor's office on three separate occasions to complain about the verbal abuse that my client is subjected to by her husband. The prosecutor refuses to take my client's complaint. Can I get the court to force the prosecutor to accept my client's complaint?

No. The decision to prosecute is discretionary and generally not

---

[20]RC 2935.03(B)(3)(e)(ii).

[21]1997 S.B. 98, eff. 3-17-98.

[22]State v. Lowe, 2001 WL 682292 (Ohio Ct. App. 10th Dist. Franklin County 2001) (interpreting RC 1901.20(A)(2)); State v. Noland, 2001 WL 710160 (Ohio Ct. App. 10th Dist. Franklin County 2001); State v. Taylor, 2001 WL 951728 (Ohio Ct. App. 10th Dist. Franklin County 2001); State v. Watkins, 2003-Ohio-668, 2003 WL 321541 (Ohio Ct. App. 10th Dist. Franklin County 2003); State v. Ferguson, 2003-Ohio-665, 2003 WL 321532 (Ohio Ct. App. 10th Dist. Franklin County 2003). See also State v. Landers, 188 Ohio App. 3d 786, 2010-Ohio-3709, 936 N.E.2d 1026 (4th Dist. Meigs County 2010).

[23]State v. Lowe, 2001 WL 682292 (Ohio Ct. App. 10th Dist. Franklin County 2001) (interpreting RC 1901.20(A)(2)); State v. Watkins, 2003-Ohio-668, 2003 WL 321541 (Ohio Ct. App. 10th Dist. Franklin County 2003); State v. Ferguson, 2003-Ohio-665, 2003 WL 321532 (Ohio Ct. App. 10th Dist. Franklin County 2003).

[24]State v. Lowe, 2001 WL 682292 (Ohio Ct. App. 10th Dist. Franklin County 2001); Crim. R. 48(B); State v. Watkins, 2003-Ohio-668, 2003 WL 321541 (Ohio Ct. App. 10th Dist. Franklin County 2003); State v. Ferguson, 2003-Ohio-665, 2003 WL 321532 (Ohio Ct. App. 10th Dist. Franklin County 2003).

[25]State v. Lowe, 2001 WL 682292 (Ohio Ct. App. 10th Dist. Franklin County 2001); State v. Watkins, 2003-Ohio-668, 2003 WL 321541 (Ohio Ct. App. 10th Dist. Franklin County 2003); State v. Ferguson, 2003-Ohio-665, 2003 WL 321532 (Ohio Ct. App. 10th Dist. Franklin County 2003).

subject to judicial review, absent an abuse of the prosecutor's discretion.[26] Unless the verbal abuse constitutes a threat of physical harm or mental distress that the law recognizes as a criminal act,[27] they are not actionable. Generally, a court will not second-guess the prosecutor's decision not to prosecute.

Q & A: I am the prosecutor for my municipal jurisdiction. I made a motion, in open court, that the judge enter a nolle prosequi in a domestic violence case. The victim refused to participate, and I had insufficient other evidence to obtain a conviction. The court insisted that I go forward. Was the court right to require that I proceed?

No. If a prosecutor's application for a *nolle prosequi* meets the "good cause" and "open court" requirements of RC 2941.33 and Criminal Rule 48(A), it should be granted. Insufficiency of proof has always been regarded as good cause for a *nolle.*[28] However, the prosecutor is required to do more than make a mere conclusory statement that the evidence is insufficient to meet the good cause test.[29]

Q & A: I am a victim of domestic violence. Yesterday, the city prosecutor moved the court to dismiss my case, even though I wanted the case to proceed to trial. Last night my spouse kicked in my door and jumped on me, just like I told the prosecutor he would. I was seriously injured. I am very bitter and believe my civil rights have been violated. I want to hold the prosecutor responsible. Can I sue the prosecutor?

No. A public official charged with the responsibility of investigating and prosecuting crimes has a general duty to perform that function. The official owes that duty to the public at large. However, the official does not owe that duty to any one member of the public. Therefore, no individual member of the public has the right to compel that official to initiate, or terminate, a prosecution simply because the individual desires it.[30] A public prosecutor has absolute immunity from civil suit under the Civil Rights Acts[31] for the initiation and conduct of prosecutions.[32]

Q & A: The victim in a domestic violence case on my docket

---

[26]State ex rel. Master v. Cleveland, 75 Ohio St. 3d 23, 1996-Ohio-228, 661 N.E.2d 180 (1996).

[27]See RC 2919.25(C), RC 2903.11, RC 2903.12, RC 2903.13, RC 2903.21, RC 2903.211, RC 2911.211.

[28]See State v. Sutton, 64 Ohio App. 2d 105, 18 Ohio Op. 3d 83, 411 N.E.2d 818 (9th Dist. Wayne County 1979); State v. Daniels, 2018-Ohio-1701, 2018 WL 2058731 (Ohio Ct. App. 1st Dist. Hamilton County 2018).

[29]Lakewood v. Pfeifer, 61 Ohio Misc. 2d 704, 583 N.E.2d 1133 (Mun. Ct. 1991), judgment aff'd, 83 Ohio App. 3d 47, 613 N.E.2d 1079 (8th Dist. Cuyahoga County 1992); see also State v. Monroe, 2000 WL 807228 (Ohio Ct. App. 4th Dist. Pike County 2000); State v. Landers, 188 Ohio App. 3d 786, 2010-Ohio-3709, 936 N.E.2d 1026 (4th Dist. Meigs County 2010).

[30]Fulson v. City of Columbus, 801 F. Supp. 1 (S.D. Ohio 1992).

[31]42 U.S.C.A. § 1983; see also When is prosecutor entitled to absolute immunity from civil suit for damages under 42 U.S.C.A. sec. 1983: post-Imbler cases, 67 A.L.R. Fed. 640 (sec. 16 superseded in part Absolute Immunity for Failing to Disclose Exculpatory Evidence Under 42 U.S.C.A. s1983 Following Imbler v. Pachtman, 424 U.S. 409, 96 S. Ct. 984, 47 L. Ed. 2d 128 (1976), 63 A.L.R.6th 255)..

[32]Imbler v. Pachtman, 424 U.S. 409, 96 S. Ct. 984, 47 L. Ed. 2d 128 (1976); Ross

failed to appear at a pretrial today. Over the objection of the prosecutor, I granted a defense motion to dismiss the case. Was my action proper?

No. At the pretrial stage of proceedings, only a defect in the initiation of the prosecution would justify the court in granting a procedural motion to dismiss over the objection of the prosecution.[33]

Q & A: I am the victim of domestic violence, and I told the court that I do not want to pursue my case. The prosecutor objected to a dismissal. My "ex" took care of the medical bills that came from this incident, and we are back on good terms. Can the court enter a dismissal anyway?

No. The only acceptable reason for a dismissal is a denial of the defendant's constitutional or statutory rights which, in itself, acts as a bar to prosecution.[34] A dismissal solely on the basis that you and the offender have mended your relationship and the offender paid the medical expenses you incurred from the offense is, at a minimum, technically improper.[35] Despite what you feel, the law only recognizes you as a witness and not as a party in the case brought against your ex-spouse.[36] The real party in interest is considered the community in whose name the charge is lodged. Your protest notwithstanding, the real party in interest is entitled to its day in court. It would constitute reversible error for the trial court to prevent the prosecution from proceeding by granting your request for dismissal under the facts that you present here.[37]

Q & A: Does the court have the authority to dismiss a domestic violence complaint, over the objection of the prosecution, based solely upon the victim's failure to appear at trial, where the complaining witness is a police officer?

No. The victim in these matters is not a party to the lawsuit and is not the prosecutor's client. If a victim signs a complaint and fails to appear, or is present and does not wish to proceed, but particularly in those cases where the victim is not the person who signed the complaint, the discretion to carry the case forward resides with the prosecutor. The court's inherent power to dismiss includes the right to

v. Meagan, 638 F.2d 646 (3d Cir. 1981); Iseley v. Bucks County, 549 F. Supp. 160 (E.D. Pa. 1982); Lucas v. Parish of Jefferson, 999 F. Supp. 839 (E.D. La. 1998); Rieger v. Marsh, 2011-Ohio-6808, 2011 WL 6930159 (Ohio Ct. App. 2d Dist. Montgomery County 2011); Moore v. Cleveland, 2014-Ohio-1426, 2014 WL 1327910 (Ohio Ct. App. 8th Dist. Cuyahoga County 2014); Henderson v. State, 2015-Ohio-1742, 2015 WL 2168359 (Ohio Ct. App. 8th Dist. Cuyahoga County 2015).

[33]RC 2941.33; Crim. R. 12(B)(1), Crim. R. 12(B)(2), Crim. R. 48; State v. Spitzer, 107 Ohio App. 3d 707, 669 N.E.2d 339 (10th Dist. Franklin County 1995). But see State v. Landers, 188 Ohio App. 3d 786, 2010-Ohio-3709, 936 N.E.2d 1026 (4th Dist. Meigs County 2010).

[34]City of Cincinnati v. Tate, 1995 WL 734050 (Ohio Ct. App. 1st Dist. Hamilton County 1995).

[35]City of Cincinnati v. Tate, 1995 WL 734050 (Ohio Ct. App. 1st Dist. Hamilton County 1995).

[36]Dayton v. Thomas, No. 6567 (2d Dist. Ct. App., Montgomery, 4-18-80), unreported.

[37]State v. Wise, 99 Ohio App. 3d 239, 650 N.E.2d 191 (10th Dist. Franklin County 1994); see also Ohio v. Johnson, 467 U.S. 493, 104 S. Ct. 2536, 81 L. Ed. 2d 425 (1984).

dismiss with prejudice only where it is apparent that the defendant has been denied a constitutional or statutory right, the violation of which would, in itself, bar prosecution, or that the dismissal serves the interest of justice.[38]

One appellate court has, on three occasions, examined and approved of a trial court's right to dismiss a domestic violence case over the objection of the prosecution where it can be shown objectively that the court's decision is not based solely upon the request of the complaining witness.[39] Thus, in at least one appellate district in Ohio, where a victim fails to comply with a local rule of court and the trial court makes specific findings of fact regarding the impact of that failure on the progress of the case or the rights of the defendant, the trial court is empowered to enter a dismissal on the record.[40] The sustainability of such a dismissal upon appeal may be dependent upon the trial court's articulation of the facts that support its decision.[41] The trial court's failure to articulate its reasons for dismissal under these circumstances, in all probability, constitutes reversible error.[42]

Q & A: The alleged victim in a domestic violence case fails to appear for a mandatory pretrial, as required by a local rule of a municipal court. Counsel for the defense moves to dismiss. The prosecution objects to the motion. Does the court have the authority to grant the motion to dismiss, over the objection of the prosecution?

If a private citizen initiates a complaint in a municipal court, alleging domestic violence, and thereafter requests that the court dismiss the charge, the court may not grant the request, if the prosecuting authority objects and if the only reason for granting the relief sought is the complaining witness' request. The Ohio General Assembly specifically barred the judges of the state's statutory courts from granting such requests.[43] However, the restriction applies only to those situations where there is a "request of the complaining witness" to dismiss.[44]

Thus, according to this line of cases, the restrictions on dismissal

---

[38]State v. Sutton, 64 Ohio App. 2d 105, 108, 18 Ohio Op. 3d 83, 411 N.E.2d 818 (9th Dist. Wayne County 1979); State v. Clipner, 1999 WL 715891 (Ohio Ct. App. 10th Dist. Franklin County 1999).

[39]State v. Lowe, 2001 WL 682292 (Ohio Ct. App. 10th Dist. Franklin County 2001) (interpreting RC 1901.20(A)(2)); State v. Noland, 2001 WL 710160 (Ohio Ct. App. 10th Dist. Franklin County 2001); State v. Taylor, 2001 WL 951728 (Ohio Ct. App. 10th Dist. Franklin County 2001); State v. Landers, 188 Ohio App. 3d 786, 2010-Ohio-3709, 936 N.E.2d 1026 (4th Dist. Meigs County 2010).

[40]State v. Lowe, 2001 WL 682292 (Ohio Ct. App. 10th Dist. Franklin County 2001) (interpreting RC 1901.20(A)(2)); State v. Landers, 188 Ohio App. 3d 786, 2010-Ohio-3709, 936 N.E.2d 1026 (4th Dist. Meigs County 2010).

[41]State v. Lowe, 2001 WL 682292 (Ohio Ct. App. 10th Dist. Franklin County 2001) (Crim. R. 48(B)); State v. Landers, 188 Ohio App. 3d 786, 2010-Ohio-3709, 936 N.E.2d 1026 (4th Dist. Meigs County 2010).

[42]State v. Lowe, 2001 WL 682292 (Ohio Ct. App. 10th Dist. Franklin County 2001); State v. Landers, 188 Ohio App. 3d 786, 2010-Ohio-3709, 936 N.E.2d 1026 (4th Dist. Meigs County 2010).

[43]RC 1901.20(A)(2).

[44]RC 1901.20(A)(2); State v. Noland, 2001 WL 710160 (Ohio Ct. App. 10th Dist. Franklin County 2001); State v. Landers, 188 Ohio App. 3d 786, 2010-Ohio-3709, 936

imposed on the courts by the General Assembly are inapplicable: 1) where a complaining witness fails to appear, or 2) where it is otherwise unclear as to whether or not the complaining witness desires to participate in the prosecution, or 3) where the complaining witness is an agent of the state, i.e., a peace officer.[45] The courts in such cases retain their full inherent authority to dismiss charges over the objection of the prosecuting authority if they can show that the defendant's constitutional or statutory rights have been violated or that the dismissal serves the interests of justice.[46]

Even in those instances where the statute is applicable, its terms still provide courts the ability to grant dismissals where specific findings of fact are made that establish that those dismissals are not being granted solely at the request of complaining witnesses, but because of other objective factors, e.g., the inappropriateness of other available remedies.[47]

Q & A: Is it ever possible for a court to dismiss a charge of domestic violence over the objection of the prosecutor?

Yes. It is possible, but only if the court finds that the dismissal serves the interests of justice.[48] In order to enter a dismissal over the objection of the prosecution, the court must follow the procedure set forth in the Ohio Rules of Criminal Procedure.[49] Pursuant to the rules, a trial court wishing to dismiss a case over the objection of the prosecution must state on the record its findings of fact and reasons for the dismissal. That requirement contemplates an evidentiary hearing from which findings of fact may be made, and which is necessary for subsequent appellate review of any error assigned by the state regarding an objection by the state that the court overruled.[50] The court's failure to hold such a hearing, upon proper objection, constitutes reversible error.[51]

Q & A: The alleged victim in the domestic violence case before my bench failed to appear for a pretrial. The prosecutor is asking for a continuance. I think that the case ought to be dismissed. Do I have the right to do so, *sua sponte*?

At least one appellate court holds that the answer is yes. That court

---

N.E.2d 1026 (4th Dist. Meigs County 2010).

[45]State v. Lowe, 2001 WL 682292 (Ohio Ct. App. 10th Dist. Franklin County 2001); State v. Landers, 188 Ohio App. 3d 786, 2010-Ohio-3709, 936 N.E.2d 1026 (4th Dist. Meigs County 2010).

[46]Crim. R. 48(B); State v. Lowe, 2001 WL 682292 (Ohio Ct. App. 10th Dist. Franklin County 2001); RC 1901.20(A)(2); State v. Noland, 2001 WL 710160 (Ohio Ct. App. 10th Dist. Franklin County 2001). See also State v. Landers, 188 Ohio App. 3d 786, 2010-Ohio-3709, 936 N.E.2d 1026 (4th Dist. Meigs County 2010).

[47]State v. Noland, 2001 WL 710160 (Ohio Ct. App. 10th Dist. Franklin County 2001); State v. Landers, 188 Ohio App. 3d 786, 2010-Ohio-3709, 936 N.E.2d 1026 (4th Dist. Meigs County 2010).

[48]State v. Busch, 76 Ohio St. 3d 613, 616, 1996-Ohio-82, 669 N.E.2d 1125 (1996). See also State v. Landers, 188 Ohio App. 3d 786, 2010-Ohio-3709, 936 N.E.2d 1026 (4th Dist. Meigs County 2010).

[49]Crim. R. 48(B).

[50]State v. Montiel, 185 Ohio App. 3d 362, 2009-Ohio-6589, 924 N.E.2d 375 (2d Dist. Montgomery County 2009).

[51]State v. Montiel, 185 Ohio App. 3d 362, 2009-Ohio-6589, 924 N.E.2d 375 (2d Dist. Montgomery County 2009).

states that a trial court has an inherent power to regulate the practice before it and to protect the integrity of its proceedings.[52] In *State v. Busch*,[53] the court exceeded that inherent power when it attempted to enter a nolle prosequi on the record over the objection of the prosecution which indicated that it was able to successfully proceed even in the absence of the complaining witness. Your case is different, in that, *sua sponte*, you are concluding that this case, because of the paucity of evidence, should be dismissed. If the prosecution fails to indicate what other evidence it would present besides the testimony of the alleged victim, and is unable to establish the availability of the victim for future proceedings, certainly you are under no compulsion to continue the case, although to do so might be the better course of action. You are, however, required to "state on the record [your] findings of fact and reasons for the dismissal" if you dismiss a complaint over the prosecutor's objection.[54] Without more, it is unlikely that your dismissal of this case under the circumstances would be viewed by an appellate court as an abuse of discretion, requiring reversal.[55] The power to dismiss, however, is not without its limits.[56]

§ 5:4 Case triage

In any Ohio jurisdiction, the number of cases where domestic violence is alleged is likely to be greater than the resources available to prosecute them. The prosecutor, then, must develop a method to prioritize the cases presented in order to maximize the possibility of success, if, and when it becomes necessary to take a case to trial.

Prosecutors' offices are well advised to specially train a number of the attorneys on their staffs on the nuances and dynamics of domestic violence complaints. The process works better if the attorneys selected for this training are the only attorneys in the office to evaluate the viability of domestic violence cases submitted for review.

The review process includes a number of variables. Chief among these, as with virtually all other criminal prosecutions, are the available resources for deployment and the quality and quantity of the evidence gathered.

Effective "triage," or ranking of priority for prosecution according to an agreed-upon set of criteria, requires the following considerations:

First Priority: Independent Corroboration/Full Cooperation

Cases where the victim is desirous of prosecuting and where photographed visible injuries or documented medical treatment exist are the top priority for prosecution.

---

[52] State v. Landers, 188 Ohio App. 3d 786, 2010-Ohio-3709, 936 N.E.2d 1026 (4th Dist. Meigs County 2010), citing Royal Indem. Co. v. J.C. Penney Co., Inc., 27 Ohio St. 3d 31, 501 N.E.2d 617, 64 A.L.R.4th 1207 (1986).

[53] State v. Busch, 76 Ohio St. 3d 613, 616, 1996-Ohio-82, 669 N.E.2d 1125 (1996).

[54] Crim. R. 48(B); State v. Landers, 188 Ohio App. 3d 786, 2010-Ohio-3709, 936 N.E.2d 1026 (4th Dist. Meigs County 2010).

[55] State v. Landers, 188 Ohio App. 3d 786, 2010-Ohio-3709, 936 N.E.2d 1026 (4th Dist. Meigs County 2010).

[56] See Cleveland v. Simpkins, 192 Ohio App. 3d 808, 2011-Ohio-1249, 950 N.E.2d 982 (8th Dist. Cuyahoga County 2011).

"Visible injuries" include, but are not limited to, abrasions, bites, bruises, contusions, cuts, dislocations, punctures, or other injuries inflicted during the course of the event under review. Such injuries are those readily visible to the investigating officers.

"Photographed" visible injuries include those photographed by the investigating officers at the scene of the incident, as well as those photographed subsequent to the initial investigation of the incident. Follow-up photographs must corroborate the observations of, and the investigation conducted by, the original responding officers.

"Documented medical treatment" includes all treatment rendered to any victim of domestic violence for physical harm that apparently resulted from the actions of a family or household member. Proper documentation includes reference in the report of the investigating law enforcement agency to the treatment rendered, including the name, address, and telephone number of any medical service personnel who dealt with the injured victim at the scene of the incident and a copy of any medical records, including any hospital admission slip, paramedic run sheet, or emergency room treatment sheet, which will corroborate the findings of the investigating officers.

Second Priority: Independent Corroboration Only

Cases which meet the independent corroboration standard. Domestic violence prosecutions may proceed, even in situations where the victim does not participate or is hostile to the prosecution, if there is sufficient independent corroborating evidence to inculpate the offender.

It is not unusual for victims to become reluctant to proceed with domestic violence prosecutions, particularly with the passage of time. In many jurisdictions, victim reluctance is the rule and not the exception. Additionally, the injuries that domestic violence victims suffer frequently are not visible to the naked eye.

Neither of these circumstances automatically precludes the initiation of a criminal complaint and prosecution. The reviewing prosecutor needs to consider the following as the first step in determining whether the facts of a particular case justify the issuance of a domestic violence complaint:

(1) Any history of violent behavior in the background of the alleged offender, either charged or uncharged.
(2) The extent and seriousness of the injuries suffered by the alleged victim.
(3) The use or threatened use of a firearm or other deadly weapon by the alleged offender during the incident.
(4) The victim's fear of the alleged offender, reasonably related to the offender's use, threatened use, or past use of force against the victim.
(5) The victim's cooperation with the prosecution.
(6) Credible allegations of self-defense by either party.

When the prosecutor employs an independent corroboration standard, criminal charges are appropriate in domestic violence cases, even in the face of passive or active opposition from the victim, where:

(1) The evidence includes photographed visible injuries or documented medical treatment resulting from the incident under review.
(2) There is sufficient independent corroborative evidence for the case to survive a motion for acquittal pursuant to Criminal Rule 29. Examples of such evidence include:

(a) Statements of the victim, offender, or witness on 911 tapes made contemporaneously with the commission of the offense under review.
(b) Available third-party witness(es) who saw the offense take place.
(c) Available third-party witness(es) who saw some aspect of the offense take place or heard noises indicative of a violent confrontation, e.g., breaking glass, threats of bodily harm, or cries of pain or fear.
(d) Available third-party witness(es) who observed the victim's injuries at or near the time they were inflicted.
(e) Admissions by the offender to the responding officers or to other third parties concerning the offense under review.
(f) Physical evidence, e.g., torn clothes, broken telephone, smashed furniture or dinnerware, or a weapon.

The participation of the victim, while in many cases desirable, is not always essential to the successful prosecution of a domestic violence case.[1]

Under the state's domestic violence laws, the victim does not have to sign a domestic violence complaint.[2] Instead, when the responding law enforcement officer has probable cause to believe that a violation occurred, the officer has the power to serve as the complainant.[3]

Once the prosecutor decides to charge, it is axiomatic that the criminal complaint issues in the name of the prosecuting political entity. The victim, in all criminal cases, has an obligation to attend proceedings when subpoenaed and to give truthful testimony, but the victim does not have the power to unilaterally discontinue the prosecution of an offender. Except under extraordinary circumstances,[4] the decision to proceed or to discontinue belongs exclusively to the prosecuting authority.

Third Priority: Full Victim Cooperation

Cases with little or no corroborative evidence, but with a victim who agrees to fully cooperate with the prosecution.

A domestic violence charge is not necessarily dependent on the existence of corroborative evidence. It goes without saying that the testimony of the victim, in a case where the only evidence is that testimony, must be exceedingly strong. It is the job of the reviewing prosecutor to weigh the quality of the victim's testimony against the lack of other evidence in determining whether to bring the charge.

[Section 5:4]

[1]See State v. Busch, 76 Ohio St. 3d 613, 1996-Ohio-82, 669 N.E.2d 1125 (1996). See also State v. Landers, 188 Ohio App. 3d 786, 2010-Ohio-3709, 936 N.E.2d 1026 (4th Dist. Meigs County 2010).

[2]RC 2935.03(B)(3)(e)(i).

[3]RC 2935.03(B)(3)(a) to RC 2935.03(B)(3)(e).

[4]See State v. Busch, 76 Ohio St. 3d 613, 1996-Ohio-82, 669 N.E.2d 1125 (1996). See also State v. Landers, 188 Ohio App. 3d 786, 2010-Ohio-3709, 936 N.E.2d 1026 (4th Dist. Meigs County 2010).

Fourth Priority: No Corroboration/No Cooperation

Cases with little or no independent corroboration and a reluctant or missing victim.

Cases falling into this category cannot be prosecuted successfully. They do, however, provide valuable information about the nature of the relationship of the parties. The cyclical nature of domestic violence means that the probability of future violence in any given domestic violence case is markedly higher than in any other type of criminal case. Even when there is no corroborative evidence and the victim is less than fully cooperative, it is important for the prosecutor to maintain records of contacts with the households in which a party or parties have alleged domestic violence.

§ 5:5 Domestic violence prosecutor's charging decision; checklist

DOMESTIC VIOLENCE PROSECUTOR'S
CHARGING DECISION CHECKLIST

The reviewing prosecutor must assess all of the items on the following checklist before making a decision to charge. It is *not* necessary that all of the items appearing on the checklist be present. In fact, prosecution may proceed in cases where only one or two of the items on the checklist are present (e.g., the victim's statement and photographed injuries or documented medical treatment). The checklist allows the prosecutor to consider the totality of the circumstances presented.

Source Materials:

A. Consultation with the responding officer ________
B. Review of the responding officer's report ________
C. Consultation with victim(s) ________
D. Other ________ ________

Determinatives:

A. Physical evidence
   1. Photographs of:
      a. injuries YES NO
      b. crime scene YES NO
      c. other ________ YES NO
   2. 911 tape YES NO
   3. Broken or destroyed personal property YES NO
B. Medical treatment information
   1. Injuries required medical attention YES NO
   2. Firearm or other deadly weapon used/ threatened YES NO
   3. Name, address, and telephone number of medical provider(s) YES NO
   4. Medical information release from victim YES NO
C. Offender's criminal history
   1. Prior convictions
   (Attach documentation where possible)

a. for domestic violence YES NO
b. for aggravated assault YES NO
c. for felonious assault YES NO
d. for aggravated trespass YES NO
e. for menacing by stalking YES NO
f. for assault on a family or household member YES NO

2. Prior law enforcement contacts
(Attach documentation where possible)
a. arrests for domestic violence
i. same victim
a. within last six months YES NO
b. within last two years YES NO
c. same jurisdiction YES NO
ii. different victim
a. within last six months YES NO
b. within last two years YES NO
c. same jurisdiction YES NO
b. arrests for other crimes of violence YES NO

3. Felony charge indicated this arrest YES NO

D. <u>Direct evidence from witnesses other than victim</u>
1. Members of the victim's immediate family
a. Children YES NO
b. Parents YES NO
c. Siblings YES NO
d. Other family or household member(s) YES NO
2. Members of the offender's immediate family
a. Children YES NO
b. Parents YES NO
c. Siblings YES NO
d. Other family or household member(s) YES NO
3. Responding law enforcement agent(s) YES NO
4. Independent third parties YES NO

E. <u>Statements that can be used at trial</u>
1. From the victim
a. written/signed/in police report YES NO
b. oral statement YES NO
2. From the responding officers YES NO
3. From independent third-party witnesses YES NO
a. written/signed/in police report YES NO
b. oral statement YES NO
4. From the alleged offender
a. written/signed/in police report YES NO
b. oral statement YES NO
5. Exceptions to the hearsay rule evident YES NO

F. <u>Availability of the victim</u>

1. Victim's fear of offender is:
   - minimal ___
   - moderate ___
   - extreme ___
2. Temporary Protection Order
   - a. requested by the victim ___
   - b. victim *does not* want ___
   - c. prosecution should request ___
   - d. unavailable; CPO is in force ___
3. Victim may be contacted:
   - a. at the numbers appearing in the file ___
   - b. through the witness/victim program ___
   - c. through the shelter program ___
   - d. through none of the above ___
   - e. other ______ ___
4. Victim does not wish to participate in this case YES NO
5. Victim is hostile to prosecution/will testify for the defense YES NO

DOMESTIC VIOLENCE PRIMARY AGGRESSOR PROTOCOL

Even with the guidance provided through use of the foregoing checklist, many law enforcement officers and prosecutors in domestic violence cases will still find that they are presented with questions as to which of the parties in an altercation was the primary aggressor. The San Diego (California) City Attorney's Office has been on the cutting edge of many domestic violence issues for more than a decade and has developed an advanced protocol for determining the identity of primary physical aggressors in domestic violence cases.

Gael Strack was the Assistant San Diego City Attorney charged with developing and training the prosecutors in that office who handle these issues. She indicates that her office experienced an alarming increase in the number of erroneous arrests of individuals who were later determined to be victims of domestic violence, rather than perpetrators. Recognition of the problem led to a reexamination of the way charging decisions were made.[1]

Based on the work done in San Diego, the following protocol is provided to assist law enforcement and prosecutors confronted with primary aggressor issues in their arrest and charging decisions. Prosecutors can use this protocol to work with law enforcement and to provide guidance with regard to arrest decisions.

<u>Primary Considerations:</u>

A. The primary aggressor is the person determined to be the most significant aggressor in the altercation.

[Section 5:5]

[1]Gael Strack, Esq., Assistant City Attorney, San Diego, California, Post to the SafeNetwork listserve, http://www.safenetwork.net February 14, 2003.

B. The primary aggressor may, or may not, be the first aggressor.

C. The intent of the domestic violence laws is to protect victims from continuing abuse, actual and threatened.

D. Self-defense is not criminal behavior, unless it exceeds what is necessary to hard off the attacker or assure the safety of the defender.

E. Consequences of, and messages sent by, arresting the wrong party.

1. Offenders are rewarded for manipulating the system.
2. Victims will fear the system, choice not to use it.
3. Real victims are not protected.
4. Collateral issues, such as dependency, child custody, housing, immigration are complicated for the real victim.
5. Law enforcement confusion and frustration is enhanced.
6. Children become distrustful of authorities and, in the case of dual arrest, associate police with the break up of the family.

<u>Determinatives:</u>

A. Respective Comparison

1. Age, height, weight of the parties
2. Criminal Histories of the parties
3. Domestic violence arrest histories of the parties
4. Parties objective manifestations of fear at time of the time of police intervention
5. Seriousness of injuries
6. Motives to lie

<u>Secondary Considerations:</u>

A. Relative strength of the parties

B. Special skills of the parties, i.e. military training, martial arts, etc.

C. Existence of protection orders

D. Detail of provided statement

<u>Questions for the Prosecutor to Contemplate:</u>

A. Who appears to be the most fearful of the other?

B. Who most appears to have the violence stop?

C. Who is looking to avoid punishment?

D. Whose story do the injuries and evidence corroborate?

E. Does there appear to be any consciousness of guilt?

F. Does either party have a history of perpetrating domestic violence?

G. Does either party have a history as a victim of domestic violence?

<u>Additional process for law enforcement to pursue with the parties:</u>

A. Ask each "What was the argument about?"

B. Ask each "What will your partner tell me?"

C. Ask the same questions, in turn, of both parties separately

D. Confront each party with the other's response

E. Document discrepancies and any obvious reasons for either party to lie

F. Use questions to rule out self-defense for each party, following interview

Assessment of self-defense by law enforcement and prosecutors:

A. Is there a documented history of violence in this relationship?

B. If there are visible injuries, are they offensive or defensive?

C. Is there an allegation and evidence of strangulation?

1. Recognize that in attempted strangulation, visible objective injury will be present in only 16% of the cases

2. Objective injuries include:

a. Tiny red spots on the face

b. Bloody red eyes

c. Red marks, scratches and bruising of the neck

d. Subtle injuries around the eyes, under the eyelids

e. Subtle injuries to the nose, behind the ears, inside the mouth, to the shoulders and chest regions of the body

3. Non-visible symptoms usually reported by victims of attempted strangulation include:

a. Hoarse or raspy voice

b. Loss of voice

c. Throat pain or difficulty swallowing

d. Difficulty breathing

e. Coughing

f. Nausea and/or vomiting

g. Mental disorientation

h. Lightheadedness

i. Involuntary urination or defecation

4. When attempted strangulation is reported the victim should be referred for an internal examination of the neck, even if no visible injury is present, particularly if a loss of consciousness is also reported. Such injuries can cause permanent damage and some can even be life-threatening.

5. When attempted strangulation is alleged, investigators should be even more diligent in looking for and alert to the possibility of defensive injuries to the assailant. In many such instances, the perpetrator will have visible, objective injury, while the victim's visible injury will be slight or non-existent.

Assessing Women as Primary Aggressors:

A. Relative sizes and strength of the parties to the altercation

B. Use of weapons—credible allegation of self-defense? Excessive force?

C. Presence of history of violence as a mitigating factor at sentencing, not a justification for failure to arrest or charge, where current evidence establishes that female was the primary aggressor

Q & A: A husband and wife are both charged with domestic violence for actions that grew out of the same incident. The husband was found guilty and the wife now moves the court to

dismiss the charges against her, arguing that it would be inconsistent to find them both guilty. Should the motion be granted?

No. Two participants in a domestic violence altercation may both be guilty of domestic violence. Occasions may arise in which each participant to a domestic violence altercation intends solely to inflict harm upon the other, without any purpose of self-defense.[2]

§ 5:6 Law enforcement domestic violence investigation; checklist

The change in focus from the victim to the offender that the 1994 amendments[1] require also mandates significant changes in the investigation of domestic violence cases. In turn, a tool similar to the checklist that appears here promises to assure that no crucial evidence is overlooked at the scene of the alleged crime.

SAMPLE DOMESTIC VIOLENCE INVESTIGATIVE CHECKLIST [2]

________________ ________

UNIT CASE #

I. VICTIM

_____ The report describes the location of the victim upon our arrival.

_____ I/We administered first aid to the victim.

_____ I/We recorded any spontaneous statements made by the victim.

_____ The report contains a description of the victim's emotional condition.

_____ The report contains a description of the victim's physical condition.

_____ The report contains detailed documentation of the victim's injuries.

_____ The report notes the victim's relationship to the suspect.

_____ The report documents the history of abuse in the relationship.

_____ The report notes the existence of any TPOs or CPOs.

_____ Provided victim with required written information on social service, legal, etc., resources.

_____ Obtained alternate means of reaching victim while case is pending.

_____ Results of interview with the victim are attached to report.

---

[2]State v. Johnson, 1989 WL 43040 (Ohio Ct. App. 2d Dist. Greene County 1989); Davis v. Washington, 547 U.S. 813, 126 S. Ct. 2266, 165 L. Ed. 2d 224, 70 Fed. R. Evid. Serv. 472, 30 A.L.R.6th 599 (2006); State v. Sanchez, 2010-Ohio-6153, 2010 WL 5235932 (Ohio Ct. App. 8th Dist. Cuyahoga County 2010); State v. Vanderhorst, 2010-Ohio-1856, 2010 WL 1712246 (Ohio Ct. App. 8th Dist. Cuyahoga County 2010); State v. Daniels, 2018-Ohio-1701, 2018 WL 2058731 (Ohio Ct. App. 1st Dist. Hamilton County 2018) (Defendant grabbing victim's face caused victim pain. The court found the victim's testimony honest and rejected defendant's argument that the face grab was a startled reaction and not a deliberate attempt to harm victim.).

[Section 5:6]

[1]1994 Am. Sub. H.B. 335, eff. 12-9-94.

II. SUSPECT

_____ The report describes the location of the suspect upon our arrival.

_____ I/We administered first aid to the suspect.

_____ I/We recorded spontaneous statements made by the suspect.

_____ The report describes the suspect's emotional condition.

_____ The report describes the suspect's physical condition.

_____ The report contains detailed documentation of the suspect's injuries.

_____ Results of interview with the suspect are attached to report.

III. WITNESSES

_____ Interview with the reporting party, if different from victim, included in report.

_____ Identified all witnesses and interviewed separately.

_____ Recorded the means of contacting all witnesses.

_____ Listed names and ages of children present during the event.

_____ Interviewed the children present.

_____ Recorded the names and a means of contacting all medical providers involved.

_____ Identified treating physician.

_____ Report identifies the 911 tape # (_____________) and other identifiers.

IV. EVIDENCE

_____ Photographed the crime scene.

_____ Took "full body" photograph of the suspect.

_____ Photographed the victim's injuries.

_____ Photographed the suspect's injuries.

_____ Impounded all weapons used during the event.

_____ Impounded other physical evidence/weapons for safekeeping.

_____ Attached related reports, photographs, and impound tag to investigator's copy of report.

[2] Mark all items not applicable "N/A"

_______________	_______________	_______________
REPORTING OFFICER(S)	APPROVED BY	REPORT DATE/ TIME

Q & A: Is a suspect who is questioned by the police during the investigation of a domestic violence complaint entitled to receive *Miranda* warnings before any question may be asked because of Ohio's preferred arrest policy in such cases?

The purpose of Ohio's preferred arrest policies in domestic violence cases is to ensure adequate police response. Officers responding to such calls are there to investigate, not to exact confessions from each person who might be suspected of committing the offense. As such, absent a specific initial intent to arrest, *Miranda* warnings[2] are not required before an investigating officer can ask questions at the site of a domestic violence call. Once suspicion focuses on a particular suspect and the tenor of the interaction turns from investigatory to accusatory, *Miranda* warnings are required to prevent involuntary confessions, wrung from suspects in the coercive environment of custodial interrogation.[3]

§ 5:7 Case preparation; interviewing the alleged victim

Victims of domestic violence frequently come under extraordinary pressure from multiple sources to discontinue criminal prosecutions. These pressures become more effective as the incident becomes more remote in time.

Obtaining a detailed statement from the victim as quickly as possible after the incident accomplishes several important prosecution objectives:

(1) Increases the likelihood of receiving an accurate recitation of the incident if the detailed statement can be obtained from the victim during the one to three days immediately following the event. This is true, in part, because recollections of the pain and embarrassment that event generated are still fresh in the victim's mind.

(2) Commits the victim to a version of the facts by having a written, signed, and, if possible, sworn statement of the facts which is then more difficult for the victim to recant at a later date.

(3) Allows the prosecution to evaluate the emotional condition of the victim and to determine the existence of threats and other forms of coercion that the prosecution must address to assure the victim's continued cooperation.

(4) Gives the prosecutor an opportunity to develop a rapport with the victim.

(5) Give the prosecutor an opportunity to educate the victim concerning the respective roles of the prosecutor and the victim in the proceeding. This process both empowers and disempowers the victim. The process empowers the victim because the information provided allows for intelligent decision making on issues of safety, such as the process for obtaining a protection order. The victim is disempowered because the decision of whether or not to proceed with the criminal case is not in the victim's hands.

---

[2]Miranda v. Arizona, 384 U.S. 436, 478–79, 86 S. Ct. 1602, 1629–31, 16 L. Ed. 2d 694, 725–27, 10 A.L.R.3d 974 (1966); State v. Hergesheimer, 2014 WL 4725365 (Idaho Ct. App. 2014); State v. Harris, 1 Wash. App. 2d 1057, 2017 WL 6606027 (Div. 2 2017), review denied, 190 Wash. 2d 1015, 415 P.3d 1201 (2018) (Def argued he wasn't Mirandized when officer asked him what happened. Court held that Miranda didn't apply because defendant was standing on the street, 4 blocks away from home (therefore not custodial interrogation). Harris's statements to Officer Beall prior to arrest were not the product of custodial interrogation. The trial court did not err in admitting defendant's pre-*Miranda* statements.).

[3]Akron v. Sutton, 106 Ohio Misc. 2d 46, 733 N.E.2d 690 (Mun. Ct. 2000); City of Cleveland v. Morales, 2002-Ohio-5862, 2002 WL 31402003 (Ohio Ct. App. 8th Dist. Cuyahoga County 2002).

(6) Gives the prosecutor an opportunity to educate the victim concerning the behaviors that the offender is likely to exhibit while the case is pending.

(7) Allows the prosecutor to determine the need for support services and counseling for the victim and to coordinate those services, if necessary. In a classic battering situation, following an acute battering incident, the victim will have few, if any, means to carry out even the most routine tasks.

Small acts of concern and assistance go a long way toward convincing a victim of the prosecutor's sincere desire and ability to help make things better. In many instances, victims lose their resolve to continue prosecution because the offender told them that no one cares about them or can help them and that the authorities cannot prevent these offenders from finding the victims and causing them additional harm.

If the prosecution succeeds in providing the victim with the ability to operate in relative safety while the case is pending, the victim becomes more confident that the decision to prosecute was the right choice. If the prosecution also succeeds in providing interim resources to a victim and a victim's family as they make their way through the legal process, the victim's confidence in surviving following the conclusion of the legal process is likely to increase. A confident victim is much more likely to be a cooperative witness.

Preparation for the interview of the alleged victim is crucial to its ultimate success. The interview must seek to accomplish several prosecution purposes, including:

(1) Clarifying the respective roles of the prosecuting authority and the alleged victim.

(2) Obtaining as much information from the victim as possible regarding:
   (a) the incident;
   (b) the victim;
   (c) the accused;
   (d) the victim's relationship with the accused;
   (e) the nature of any injuries or other harm suffered;
   (f) the existence of any witnesses to the incident, how they can be contacted, and what they have to contribute;
   (g) any current, prior, or threatened legal proceedings involving the parties;
   (h) any role substance abuse played in the incident;
   (i) the presence and/or use of weapons during the incident;
   (j) past acts of violence against the victim by the offender, and vice versa; and
   (k) the current level of the victim's fear of the offender.

(3) Assessing the potential for the situation to turn lethal.

(4) Assessing the viability of the victim as a trial witness.[1]

(5) Establishing initial rapport with the victim, including a determination of the victim's needs, offering assistance with any

---

[Section 5:7]

[1] See Text § 5:8, Domestic violence victim—Interview; form.

special problems, and providing answers to any unanswered questions.

(6) Determining that the victim has a formal safety plan in place.[2]

Someone other than the prosecutor who will present the case at trial should conduct the actual interview. This is true because it may become necessary for the interviewer to serve as a witness to the victim's statements. Calling the interviewer as a witness is useful if the victim later recants, becomes forgetful, or is otherwise unavailable.

Wherever possible, it is a good idea for the prosecutor assigned to try the case to either sit in on this initial interview or to conduct a separate follow-up interview. The trial prosecutor is thus able to separately form a connection with the victim and evaluate the credibility and usefulness of the victim as a witness.

Proper preparation for the interview of the alleged victim includes:

(1) Assembly and review of all available documentary information about the offense and the history between the parties involved in the offense. This information should include such items as:
   (a) charging documents,
   (b) police reports (past and present),
   (c) photographs,
   (d) 911 tapes,
   (e) medical records, and
   (f) civil and/or criminal protective orders.

(2) Development of an interview strategy. The interview should focus on obtaining information to forward the primary objectives identified by the prosecutor as essential to the successful presentation of the case at trial. To the degree that that is possible, the interviewer should adhere to the strategy throughout the meeting with the victim.

(3) Putting the victim at ease before the interview by expressing the state's gratitude for the victim's cooperation. The interviewer may also further the process of solidifying victim cooperation by ascertaining whether the victim has any areas of particular concern. The interviewer should assure the victim that the interviewer intends to address any outstanding questions in those areas before the conclusion of the interview. The interviewer should sympathize with the victim's situation and stress a desire to assist wherever possible.

The interviewer should emphasize the importance of the victim's input in the resolution of the case while, at the same time, stressing that the final decision on how the matter proceeds remains with the prosecutor.

A good interview will also include a thorough explanation of the various sentencing options, in addition to jail, that are available to the court if prosecution results in a conviction. Soliciting and recording the victim's thoughts and desires concerning appropriate sanctions provides the possibility for the prosecutor and the victim to reach accord on the penalty options that serve both of their objectives.

---

[2]See Text Ch 15, Domestic Violence and Custody and Visitation Issues.

This part of the interview process also allays some victims' fear of what will happen to their abusers if prosecution proves successful. It is this fear of the unknown sanction that often leads some victims to discontinue participation in criminal prosecutions.

§ 5:8 Domestic violence victim—Interview; form

DOMESTIC VIOLENCE VICTIM INTERVIEW FORM

Case Number: ________
Date of Incident: ________

The purpose of this interview is to help the prosecutor's office determine the best way to increase your safety and to prevent any recurrence of the violence which caused you to seek our help. The interview will give us the background information that we need to assess any safety risks that you now face and to counsel you on the most effective ways to reduce those risks. It is our desire to provide you with all of the information necessary for you to make informed judgments on the options that are available to you.

It is also our responsibility to do whatever we can to assure that the criminal behavior which you experienced does not continue. The information that you provide will help us determine what type of intervention will be most appropriate in accomplishing this goal. If you have any questions about the interview, please feel free to ask them either before or after the interview is completed. You may direct any additional questions to the prosecutor conducting the interview, or to the witness/victim advocate, by calling our office during office hours at any time while the case is pending before the court. The numbers where they may be reached are:

Prosecutor: ____________________
Advocate: ____________________

Please read each question carefully. You are requested to answer <u>only</u> those questions which apply to <u>your</u> situation.

<u>GENERAL INFORMATION—OFFENDER</u>

SUSPECT'S NAME: ____________________
SUSPECT'S DATE OF BIRTH: ____________________
SUSPECT'S HEIGHT: ________ SUSPECT'S WEIGHT: ________
SUSPECT'S SOCIAL SECURITY NUMBER: ____________________
SUSPECT'S CURRENT ADDRESS: ____________________
____
SUSPECT'S CURRENT EMPLOYMENT: ____________________
SUSPECT'S EMPLOYMENT ADDRESS: ____________________
____

<u>GENERAL INFORMATION—VICTIM</u>

YOUR NAME: ____________________
YOUR DATE OF BIRTH: ____________________
YOUR HEIGHT: ________ YOUR WEIGHT: ________
YOUR SOCIAL SECURITY NUMBER: ____________________
YOUR CURRENT ADDRESS: ____________________
____

YOUR TELEPHONE NUMBER: HOME: ______ WORK: ______
YOUR BUSINESS ADDRESS: ______

Please list the names, addresses, and telephone numbers of two of your closest friends or relatives who have regular contact with you, do not live with you, and will always know where to reach you:

NAME	ADDRESS	PHONE #	RELATION TO VICTIM
______	______	______	______
			______

GENERAL INFORMATION—LEGAL

CURRENT RELATIONSHIP WITH SUSPECT:
LIVING TOGETHER ______ MARRIED ______ SEPARATED ______
DIVORCED ______ CHILD IN COMMON ______ NONE NOW ______
FORMERLY LIVED WITH SUSPECT: YES ______ NO ______
If yes: FROM ______ TO ______

ANY DIVORCE OR CHILD CUSTODY PROCEEDINGS PENDING OR THREATENED? YES ______ NO ______

If the answer is YES, please answer the following questions about that lawsuit:

1. In what court is the matter pending? ______
2. When is the next hearing scheduled? ______
3. What is the name of the suspect's attorney? ______
4. What is the name, address, and telephone number of your attorney? ______
5. Has either party been granted a protection order against the other in a civil or criminal case currently pending? YES ______ NO ______

If yes, which party? YOU ______ THE SUSPECT ______
CIVIL? CRIMINAL?

ARE THERE ANY OTHER LAWSUITS PENDING BETWEEN YOU AND THE SUSPECT OR MEMBERS OF YOUR FAMILIES? YES ______ NO ______

Nature of the lawsuit: ______

INCIDENT DESCRIPTION:

1. Date of the incident: ______ Time: ______
2. Location of the incident: ______
3. Did the incident involve:

a. Threats of violence YES NO

b. Actual violence YES NO

4. If actual violence was involved, who committed the first violent act?

a. You YES NO
b. The offender YES NO

5. Describe the incident in detail: ______________________________
____
____
____
____
____
____
____
____
____

6. Were either you or the suspect drinking or using drugs at the time of the incident? YES ________ NO ________

7. If the answer to question 6 is YES, which of you was using?
YOU ________ SUSPECT ________

8. What drug or alcohol was used? ____________

9. How much of the drug or alcohol was used (approximately)? __

10. Did the suspect force you to have sex in any way during the incident?
YES ________ NO ________

11. If the answer to question 10 is YES, please explain. ________
____
____

12. Did you hit the suspect or use any violence yourself during the incident?
YES ________ NO ________

13. If the answer to question 12 is YES,

a. What kind of violence did you use (e.g., fists, scratching, weapon, etc.)? ______________________________
____

b. At what stage of the incident did you resort to violence? ___
____

c. Why did you resort to violence? ____________________
____
____

14. Were other members of your immediate family or household, including your minor children, present during this incident? YES ________ NO ________

15. If the answer to question 14 is YES, please provide the following information for all those present:

NAME ADDRESS PHONE # AGE

____

____

____

____

16. Did you have any injuries that were visible at the time of the incident? YES ______ NO ______

17. If the answer to question 16 is YES, please describe the type of injury and where it was located on your body (e.g., a large dark bruise on the back of the right thigh):

____

____

18. Did you have any injuries that became visible after your initial report of this incident that will not be noted in the police report of the event? YES ______ NO ______

19. If the answer to question 18 is YES, please describe the injury and when it first became visible: ______________________________

____

____

20. Are the injuries still visible? YES ______ NO ______

21. Was anyone other than you injured during this incident? YES ______ NO ______

22. If the answer to question 21 is YES, provide below the requested information for all those who were injured:

NAME ADDRESS PHONE #

____

____

23. If the answer to question 21 is YES, explain how others were injured during the event: ______________________________

____

____

____

____

____

24. Were photographs taken of your injuries? YES ______ NO ______

25. If the answer to question 24 is YES, by whom were the photos taken?

a. Police ______

b. Other ______

26. If the answer to question 25 is OTHER, provide the information regarding the person who took the photographs:

NAME	ADDRESS	PHONE #	DATE OF PHOTO

27. Were you treated by any medical professional (e.g., doctor, nurse, medical technician, EMS, dentist, etc.) for your injuries? YES ________ NO ________

28. If the answer to question 27 is YES, provide the following information regarding the medical professional(s) that provided the service:

NAME	ADDRESS	PHONE #

29. If the answer to question 27 is YES, **please sign the medical information release form attached to this questionnaire**.

30. Did you show or tell anyone else about your injuries? YES ________ NO ________

31. If the answer to question 30 is YES, please provide the following information about each person that you told:

NAME	PHONE #	DATE TOLD OF INCIDENT

32. Were any pets belonging to you or your immediate family injured during this event? YES ________ NO ________

33. Was any of your personal property damaged during the incident? YES ________ NO ________

34. If the answer to question 33 is YES, describe what property was damaged and how: ____
____
____
____
____

35. As a result of this incident, have you incurred any expenses for which you need to seek restitution? YES ________ NO ________

36. If the answer to question 35 is YES, please explain your answer in detail: ____________________
____
____
____
____

37. Has the suspect threatened you either directly or indirectly by word or action since this incident? YES ________ NO ________

38. If the answer to question 37 is YES, as accurately and as completely as possible, describe and relate the exact threat: ________
____
____
____

39. Are you presently afraid of the suspect? YES ________ NO ________

40. Has the suspect ever been violent to you in the past (e.g., choked, pushed, punched, stabbed, cut, slapped, sexually assaulted, or thrown things at you)?

YES ________ NO ________

41. If the answer to question 40 is YES, please indicate the following:

a. Approximately when did the event occur? ________
b. Was the event reported to the authorities? ________
c. Were you injured? ________
d. Did you receive medical treatment? ________
e. Who provided the medical treatment? ________
f. Were there witnesses? If so, please list the name, address, and
telephone number of each witness:
____
____
____

§ 5:9 Domestic violence victim—Medical records release; form

CASE NUMBER: ________

MEDICAL RECORDS RELEASE

PATIENT: ____________________
ADDRESS: ____________________
DATE OF BIRTH: ____________________
SSN#: ____________________
INITIAL DATE OF TREATMENT: ____________________
MEDICAL SERVICE PROVIDERS: ____________________
NAME: ____________________
ADDRESS: ____________________

NAME: ______________________________

ADDRESS: ______________________________

I, ________, hereby authorize and request the medical service providers listed above to release any and all medical records in their possession concerning the medical diagnosis and treatment which I received before, on, or after the date set forth in this release to:
The Office of the Prosecuting Attorney
County/City of ________
________, Ohio ________
() ________________

SIGNED: ______________________________
(PATIENT OR ATTORNEY-IN-FACT) DATE: ________

***NOTE: An executed copy of this form is as legally effective as the original.**

STATE OF OHIO
COUNTY OF ________

On the ________ day of ________, ________, the aforesigned personally appeared before me, a duly authorized Notary Public of the State of Ohio, and swore or affirmed that all of the information contained herein is true and accurate to the best of the affiant's knowledge and belief. In witness whereof, the affiant's signature was caused to be affixed hereto.

____
NOTARY PUBLIC

My commission expires ________

§ 5:10 Domestic violence victim—Telephone records release; form

TELEPHONE RECORDS RELEASE

CASE NUMBER: ________

The undersigned hereby authorizes and requests the release of the complete records for all incoming and outgoing calls relating to my telephone number, ________, for the period beginning ________ and ending ________, to Office of the Prosecuting Attorney for ________, Ohio.

I request that you send the records to:
The Office of the Prosecuting Attorney
County/City of ________
________, Ohio ________

Refer any questions regarding this request to:
Prosecuting Attorney ________________________ at () ________________________

SIGNED: ______________________ DATE: ______________________

STATE OF OHIO
COUNTY OF ______

On the ______ day of ______, ______, the aforesigned personally appeared before me, a duly authorized Notary Public of the State of Ohio, and swore or affirmed that all of the information contained herein is true and accurate to the best of the affiant's knowledge and belief. In witness whereof, the affiant's signature was caused to be affixed hereto.

____
NOTARY PUBLIC

My commission expires ______

§ 5:11 Domestic violence victim—Notification; form

PROSECUTING ATTORNEY'S VICTIM NOTIFICATION FORM

CASE #: ______ DATE: ______

The use of physical force by one person against another, except in self-defense, is against the law in the state of Ohio. This is true regardless of the relationship that exists between the individuals.

It is claimed that a family or household member has physically abused you or has threatened to do so. The people of the state of Ohio have the right to pursue criminal charges against this individual for these acts, if there is probable cause to believe that they took place. The Office of the Prosecuting Attorney for this jurisdiction is responsible for deciding whether or not charges are filed.

If criminal charges are filed, the person accused of committing these crimes will be required to appear in court to answer for the crimes specified. The decision to charge or not to charge belongs **solely** to the people of this jurisdiction. While you cannot "press" charges or "drop" them, your input is extremely important to us.

If the prosecutor's office files criminal charges against the person who abused you and that person denies those charges by pleading "not guilty," a trial may be required. In that case, your testimony would be important to our case. Would you come forward to testify truthfully at trial concerning the facts of this matter?

YES ______ NO ______

If this office successfully prosecutes this case, what would you like to see happen to the individual who abused you? (e.g., an order to stay away from you, domestic violence counseling, substance abuse counseling, public service work, jail, a combination of jail and counseling, etc.)

Please specify: ______________________

____

Depending on your needs, we can request that the court fashion a specific Temporary Protection Order to increase your safety during the pendency of this case. The order will require, at a minimum, that the person charged leave your home and/or have no contact with you and/or your family while this case is pending. Considering what you know about the person that abused you, do you want a judge to grant a Temporary Protection Order in this case?

YES _______ NO _______

Would you like to consult with a victim advocate or counselor?

YES _______ NO _______

The foregoing notification was given to me on this _______ day of _______, _______. I have read it and any questions I had about it were answered to my satisfaction.

____
Complaining Witness

Dated: _______
Witness: _______
Witness: _______

§ 5:12 Case preparation—Physical evidence

The decreased reliance on the testimony of domestic violence victims increases the importance of physical evidence to support the prosecution's assertion that the alleged offender committed a criminal act. Effective prosecution of domestic violence cases in which the victim is reluctant or hostile requires much greater emphasis on the physical evidence collected at the time of the event.

The General Assembly recognized that fact when it enacted the 1994 amendments to the Revised Code dealing with domestic violence.[1] Among other requirements, officers investigating domestic violence complaints are now required to record and report any significant fact or circumstance observed at the scene.[2]

Although frequently overlooked, physical evidence is often present in domestic violence cases and can be documented by the presentation of either the actual item or its photographic image. Some examples of physical evidence include:

(1) photographable injuries suffered by the victim, the perpetrator, or both,
(2) other contemporaneous photographs of the participants that convey a sense of the event, e.g., the fear of the victim, the intoxication of the perpetrator, etc.,
(3) broken window, door, furniture, or dishes or photographs of them,
(4) telephones torn from walls or photographs of them,
(5) torn or blood-stained clothing,

[Section 5:12]

[1] RC 2935.03(D).

[2] RC 2935.03(D).

(6) letter from perpetrator regarding the event, remorse for actions, etc.,
(7) videotapes of the incident or its aftermath, and
(8) 911 and other audiotapes.

Q & A: During trial, the prosecution attempts to introduce into evidence a photograph of injuries that the victim claims to have suffered at the defendant's hands. The defendant objects, contending that the victim's testimony that the picture was taken within minutes of the injury being inflicted and that it shows exactly what the injury looked like at the time fails to establish the proper foundation for the admission of the photograph into evidence since the victim was not the one who took the photograph. In the alternative, the defendant argues that, even if the photograph is admissible, its probative value is far outweighed by its prejudicial effect. Should the court exclude the photograph?

Unless the trial court finds that the photograph's probative value truly is substantially outweighed by its prejudicial effect on the defendant's case, the answer is no. The victim's testimony satisfies the general requirement that the proponent must present testimony that a photograph accurately reflects the condition of the matter depicted, based on the witness's personal observation, before it can be properly admitted into evidence.[3] The Ohio Supreme Court has held that trial judges have broad discretion in terms of the admission of such evidence.[4] That discretion is so broad that, absent a clear abuse of discretion and material prejudice to the defendant, the trial court's decision to admit this evidence should not be disturbed by an appellate court. Conversely, a trial court decision not to admit the evidence also should stand on appellate review.[5]

---

[3]Midland Steel Prods. Co. v. U.A.W. Local 486, 61 Ohio St. 3d 121, 129, 573 N.E.2d 98 (1991); State v. Slavens, 1999 WL 4895 (Ohio Ct. App. 4th Dist. Vinton County 1998); State v. Poling, 1998 WL 255574 (Ohio Ct. App. 3d Dist. Shelby County 1998); Stevens v. Provitt, 2003-Ohio-7226, 2003 WL 23097088 (Ohio Ct. App. 11th Dist. Trumbull County 2003); State v. Peeples, 2009-Ohio-1198, 2009 WL 737922 (Ohio Ct. App. 7th Dist. Mahoning County 2009); Toledo v. Sailes, 180 Ohio App. 3d 56, 2008-Ohio-6400, 904 N.E.2d 543 (6th Dist. Lucas County 2008); State v. Rufus, 2008-Ohio-5478, 2008 WL 4681392 (Ohio Ct. App. 8th Dist. Cuyahoga County 2008); State v. Moorer, 2009-Ohio-1494, 2009 WL 818945 (Ohio Ct. App. 9th Dist. Summit County 2009); State v. Smith, 2008-Ohio-5985, 2008 WL 4951646 (Ohio Ct. App. 8th Dist. Cuyahoga County 2008); State v. Kingery, 2010-Ohio-1813, 2010 WL 1660424 (Ohio Ct. App. 12th Dist. Fayette County 2010); State v. Martin, 2011-Ohio-1213, 2011 WL 899553 (Ohio Ct. App. 9th Dist. Summit County 2011).

[4]Rigby v. Lake County, 58 Ohio St. 3d 269, 569 N.E.2d 1056 (1991); State v. Presley, 2003-Ohio-6069, 2003 WL 22681425 (Ohio Ct. App. 10th Dist. Franklin County 2003).

[5]Evid.R. 403, Evid.R. 611(A), Evid.R. 901(A); State v. Maurer, 15 Ohio St. 3d 239, 265, 473 N.E.2d 768 (1984); State v. Shakoor, 2003-Ohio-5140, 2003 WL 22231582 (Ohio Ct. App. 7th Dist. Mahoning County 2003); State v. Marcum, 2006-Ohio-7068, 2006 WL 3849861 (Ohio Ct. App. 7th Dist. Columbiana County 2006); State v. Kingery, 2010-Ohio-1813, 2010 WL 1660424 (Ohio Ct. App. 12th Dist. Fayette County 2010); State v. Marrero, 2011-Ohio-1390, 2011 WL 1049294 (Ohio Ct. App. 10th Dist. Franklin County 2011); State v. Shouse, 2014-Ohio-4620, 2014 WL 5316489 (Ohio Ct. App. 12th Dist. Brown County 2014); State v. Quinn, 2016-Ohio-139, 57 N.E.3d 379 (Ohio Ct. App. 2d Dist. Clark County 2016), appeal not allowed, 145 Ohio St. 3d 1447,

Q & A: How does the prosecution go about authenticating a 911 tape so that it may be admitted into evidence?

The prosecution must comply with the evidentiary rules that govern the admission of audio recordings before the court may receive them into evidence.[6] A nonexclusive set of examples of acceptable methods of compliance is contained in the rule. The set includes:

(1) Identification of a voice by the opinion of a witness, based on having heard the voice in question at any time under circumstances connecting the voice to the speaker. It is not material whether the person identifying the voice originally heard it firsthand or through a mechanical or electronic transmission or recording.

(2) Where the item to be authenticated is a telephone conversation, evidence that the call was made to the number that the telephone company assigned to the particular person or business at the time in question. In the case of a person, the circumstances presented by the proponent at the hearing where the evidence is sought to be admitted must show that the person who received the call or engaged in the subject telephone conversation is the person that the proponent seeks to identify.[7]

Q & A: At trial for striking the mother of his child in the head during the course of an argument, the defense offers to stipulate to the victim's medical records, but moves the court to redact the following note contained in the record: "Patient was hit in head with metal can by boyfriend," as inadmissible hearsay. Should the trial court grant the motion?

"Absent some evidence that the identity of the perpetrator is necessary for medical purposes, statements identifying an assailant are not properly admitted."[8] Hearsay statements in medical records cannot come into evidence under the business records exception to the hearsay rule,[9] unless they had an independent basis for their admission.[10]

However, common sense dictates that when a doctor can determine the cause of one's injuries from the mouth of the injured one, this is preferable as it facilitates and expedites a patient's diagnosis and recovery.[11] In this case, the statement which the defense objects to

---

2016-Ohio-1596, 48 N.E.3d 585 (2016) and appeal reopened, 2017-Ohio-7000, 95 N.E.3d 664 (Ohio Ct. App. 2d Dist. Clark County 2017), appeal not allowed, 151Ohio St. 3d1457, 2017-Ohio-8842, 87 N.E.3d 224 (2017).

[6] Evid.R. 901(B)(5), Evid.R. 901(B)(6).

[7] State v. Newell, 1998 WL 667651 (Ohio Ct. App. 5th Dist. Stark County 1998).

[8] Evid. R. 803(4); State v. Kingery, 2010-Ohio-1813, 2010 WL 1660424 (Ohio Ct. App. 12th Dist. Fayette County 2010); State v. Shouse, 2014-Ohio-4620, 2014 WL 5316489 (Ohio Ct. App. 12th Dist. Brown County 2014).

[9] Evid. R. 803(6).

[10] Mastran v. Urichich, 37 Ohio St. 3d 44, 48, 523 N.E.2d 509 (1988); State v. Kingery, 2010-Ohio-1813, 2010 WL 1660424 (Ohio Ct. App. 12th Dist. Fayette County 2010); State v. Shouse, 2014-Ohio-4620, 2014 WL 5316489 (Ohio Ct. App. 12th Dist. Brown County 2014).

[11] State v. Dartt, 2008-Ohio-373, 2008 WL 303135 (Ohio Ct. App. 6th Dist. Lucas County 2008).

does not actually identify the defendant but simply indicates a "boyfriend" hit the patient. Therefore, the included statement does not offend the medical records exception to the hearsay rule and should be admitted into evidence.[12]

Q & A: At trial, medical records, including photographs not necessary for diagnosis or treatment, were admitted into evidence. Doesn't that constitute reversible error?

Perhaps. It depends of the nature of the other evidence presented against the defendant at trial. If the photographs were merely cumulative, then their admission is harmless, even if erroneous, and should not result in reversal.[13]

§ 5:13 Case preparation—Medical evidence

The recent trend toward preparation of domestic violence cases under the assumption that the victim will not be available for trial puts new emphasis on the importance of evaluating the strength of other objective evidence before making the decision to charge an alleged offender. Medical evidence is crucial in this regard.

Many domestic violence cases involve injuries to both the victim and the primary physical aggressor. An evaluation of the injuries suffered should reveal whether the injuries to each party were more likely suffered defensively or offensively. Photographs taken by the investigating officers are invaluable in helping the prosecution make these determinations. However, photographs are not the only evidence of physical trauma. Photographs taken immediately following a traumatic event do not always reveal the extent of the injury suffered. It is, therefore, prudent for the police and/or the prosecution to follow up with the victim in the days and weeks after the incident to capture additional visual evidence of the damage resulting from the assault.

The investigating officer should carefully detail the nature of the injuries claimed by the alleged victim of a domestic assault. Where possible, the officer should make a body diagram that identifies the areas where the victim claims injury.

§ 5:14 Case preparation—Hearsay exceptions—Generally

Until relatively recently, the trial of a domestic violence case consisted primarily of the testimony of the victim. The arresting officers might be called to testify regarding their observations of the crime scene, the victim, and the offender, but only if they noted something significantly out of the ordinary when they made their report.

---

[12]Mastran v. Urichich, 37 Ohio St. 3d 44, 48, 523 N.E.2d 509 (1988). But see State v. Kingery, 2010-Ohio-1813, 2010 WL 1660424 (Ohio Ct. App. 12th Dist. Fayette County 2010); State v. Shouse, 2014-Ohio-4620, 2014 WL 5316489 (Ohio Ct. App. 12th Dist. Brown County 2014).

[13]State v. Kingery, 2010-Ohio-1813, 2010 WL 1660424 (Ohio Ct. App. 12th Dist. Fayette County 2010); State v. Shouse, 2014-Ohio-4620, 2014 WL 5316489 (Ohio Ct. App. 12th Dist. Brown County 2014).

The enactment of the 1994 amendments to the state's domestic violence statutes[1] signaled the legislature's desire to shift the focus of domestic violence prosecution away from near-total dependence on victim testimony.[2] The new focus is on the identification, collection, and presentation of *all* relevant evidence capable of convincing a trier of fact that the offender committed the crime, regardless of the origin of the evidence.

These revisions to the law require significant changes in prosecution case preparation. Effective prosecution now includes identification and preparation of evidence that many courts are not used to seeing in domestic violence cases. The extensive use of certain exceptions to the hearsay rule will appear at the heart of aggressive domestic violence prosecutions.

The United States Supreme Court holds that the procedural protections afforded to criminal defendants by the Confrontation Clause of the Sixth Amendment to the U.S. Constitution constitute bedrock guarantees that apply to both federal and state prosecutions. Therefore, the right of criminal defendants to confront the statements of witnesses against them by means of cross examination, is not merely a sufficient condition, it is a dispositive requirement, at least so far as it applies to the admission of *testimonial* hearsay statements offered at criminal trials. The general rule is that the *testimonial* hearsay statements of some unavailable declarants may be admissible only where it is shown that: 1) the declarant is truly unavailable, and 2) the defendant had a prior opportunity to cross-examine the absent witnesses' statement.[3] The Court's earlier precedent allowed such testimonial hearsay evidence to be admitted based upon indicia of

---

[Section 5:14]

[1]1994 H.B. 335, eff. 12-9-94.

[2]See RC 2935.01 et seq.

[3]See Crawford v. Washington, 541 U.S. 36, 59, 124 S. Ct. 1354, 1369, 158 L. Ed. 2d 177, 63 Fed. R. Evid. Serv. 1077 (2004); State v. Harr, 158 Ohio App. 3d 704, 2004-Ohio-5771, 821 N.E.2d 1058 (2d Dist. Clark County 2004); Fowler v. State, 809 N.E.2d 960 (Ind. Ct. App. 2004), transfer granted, opinion vacated, IN RAP 58(A), (Dec. 9, 2004) and opinion vacated, 829 N.E.2d 459 (Ind. 2005) and (abrogated by, Hammon v. State, 829 N.E.2d 444 (Ind. 2005)); Akron v. Hutton, 2005-Ohio-3300, 2005 WL 1523880 (Ohio Ct. App. 9th Dist. Summit County 2005); Davis v. Washington, 547 U.S. 813, 126 S. Ct. 2266, 165 L. Ed. 2d 224, 70 Fed. R. Evid. Serv. 472, 30 A.L.R.6th 599 (2006); State v. Newell, 2005-Ohio-2848, 2005 WL 1364937 (Ohio Ct. App. 5th Dist. Stark County 2005); State v. Mitchell, 171 Ohio App. 3d 225, 2007-Ohio-1696, 870 N.E.2d 228 (8th Dist. Cuyahoga County 2007); Cleveland v. Colon, 2007-Ohio-269, 2007 WL 179082 (Ohio Ct. App. 8th Dist. Cuyahoga County 2007); State v. Stahl, 111 Ohio St. 3d 186, 2006-Ohio-5482, 855 N.E.2d 834 (2006); State v. Lewis, 2007-Ohio-1485, 2007 WL 936571 (Ohio Ct. App. 1st Dist. Hamilton County 2007). But see State v. Edinger, 2006-Ohio-1527, 2006 WL 827412 (Ohio Ct. App. 10th Dist. Franklin County 2006); State v. Turks, 2010-Ohio-5944, 2010 WL 5050549 (Ohio Ct. App. 3d Dist. Allen County 2010). See also § 5:17, Case preparation—Hearsay exceptions—Present sense impression; State v. Eicholtz, 2013-Ohio-302, 2013 WL 425820 (Ohio Ct. App. 2d Dist. Clark County 2013); State v. Arnold, 2014-Ohio-1134, 2014 WL 1339806 (Ohio Ct. App. 3d Dist. Seneca County 2014), judgment aff'd, 147 Ohio St. 3d 138, 2016-Ohio-1595, 62 N.E.3d 153 (2016); State v. McClain, 2014-Ohio-93, 2014 WL 117962 (Ohio Ct. App. 10th Dist. Franklin County 2014); State v. Doyle, 2014-Ohio-285, 2014 WL 313139 (Ohio Ct. App. 5th Dist. Fairfield County 2014); State v. King, 2013-Ohio-1694, 2013 WL 1798337 (Ohio Ct. App. 2d Dist. Montgomery County 2013); State v. Clark, 137 Ohio St. 3d 346,

reliability.[4] Those indicia of reliability were determined by findings that such evidence fell within a firmly rooted hearsay exception or bore some particularized guarantees of trustworthiness. *Crawford* specifically abrogates that theory and basis of admissibility for this category of hearsay.[5] The Supreme Court of Ohio has also spoken on this issue. That court has held that while the Sixth Amendment to the U.S. Constitution provides in pertinent part that "(i)n all criminal prosecutions, the accused shall enjoy the right. . . to be confronted with the witnesses against him,"[6] the federal Confrontation Clause "does not necessarily prohibit the admission of hearsay statements against a criminal defendant, even though the admission of such statements might be thought to violate the literal terms of the Clause." That court went on to say that the scope of the Confrontation Clause is more expansive than the general rule prohibiting hearsay, however, and that Ohio's Confrontation Clause bars the admission of some evidence that the U.S. Supreme Court's interpretation of the federal clause, which had drifted away from requiring face-to-face confrontation, would have permitted before the ruling that it handed down in

---

2013-Ohio-4731, 999 N.E.2d 592 (2013), rev'd and remanded, 135 S. Ct. 2173, 192 L. Ed. 2d 306 (2015). State v. Williams, 2013-Ohio-726, 987 N.E.2d 322 (Ohio Ct. App. 6th Dist. Lucas County 2013); State v. Norris, 2015-Ohio-624, 2015 WL 753346 (Ohio Ct. App. 2d Dist. Montgomery County 2015); State v. Kerr, 2016-Ohio-965, 2016 WL 936844 (Ohio Ct. App. 2d Dist. Montgomery County 2016); State v. Martin, 2016-Ohio-225, 57 N.E.3d 411 (Ohio Ct. App. 5th Dist. Tuscarawas County 2016).

[4]Davis v. Washington, 547 U.S. 813, 126 S. Ct. 2266, 165 L. Ed. 2d 224, 70 Fed. R. Evid. Serv. 472, 30 A.L.R.6th 599 (2006). See also Ohio v. Roberts, 448 U.S. 56, 65, 100 S. Ct. 2531, 65 L. Ed. 2d 597, 7 Fed. R. Evid. Serv. 1 (1980) (abrogated by, Crawford v. Washington, 541 U.S. 36, 124 S. Ct. 1354, 158 L. Ed. 2d 177, 63 Fed. R. Evid. Serv. 1077 (2004)); State v. Harr, 158 Ohio App. 3d 704, 2004-Ohio-5771, 821 N.E.2d 1058 (2d Dist. Clark County 2004); Fowler v. State, 809 N.E.2d 960 (Ind. Ct. App. 2004), transfer granted, opinion vacated, IN RAP 58(A), (Dec. 9, 2004) and opinion vacated, 829 N.E.2d 459 (Ind. 2005) and (abrogated by, Hammon v. State, 829 N.E.2d 444 (Ind. 2005)); Akron v. Hutton, 2005-Ohio-3300, 2005 WL 1523880 (Ohio Ct. App. 9th Dist. Summit County 2005); Cleveland v. Colon, 2007-Ohio-269, 2007 WL 179082 (Ohio Ct. App. 8th Dist. Cuyahoga County 2007); State v. Clark, 137 Ohio St. 3d 346, 2013-Ohio-4731, 999 N.E.2d 592 (2013), rev'd and remanded, 135 S. Ct. 2173, 192 L. Ed. 2d 306 (2015).

[5]Davis v. Washington, 547 U.S. 813, 126 S. Ct. 2266, 165 L. Ed. 2d 224, 70 Fed. R. Evid. Serv. 472, 30 A.L.R.6th 599 (2006). See also Crawford v. Washington, 541 U.S. 36, 124 S. Ct. 1354, 158 L. Ed. 2d 177, 63 Fed. R. Evid. Serv. 1077 (2004), overruling Ohio v. Roberts, 448 U.S. 56, 100 S. Ct. 2531, 65 L. Ed. 2d 597, 7 Fed. R. Evid. Serv. 1 (1980) (abrogated by, Crawford v. Washington, 541 U.S. 36, 124 S. Ct. 1354, 158 L. Ed. 2d 177, 63 Fed. R. Evid. Serv. 1077 (2004)); State v. Harr, 158 Ohio App. 3d 704, 2004-Ohio-5771, 821 N.E.2d 1058 (2d Dist. Clark County 2004); Fowler v. State, 809 N.E.2d 960 (Ind. Ct. App. 2004), transfer granted, opinion vacated, IN RAP 58(A), (Dec. 9, 2004) and opinion vacated, 829 N.E.2d 459 (Ind. 2005) and (abrogated by, Hammon v. State, 829 N.E.2d 444 (Ind. 2005)); Akron v. Hutton, 2005-Ohio-3300, 2005 WL 1523880 (Ohio Ct. App. 9th Dist. Summit County 2005); State v. Davis, 2007-Ohio-3419, 2007 WL 1934364 (Ohio Ct. App. 8th Dist. Cuyahoga County 2007); State v. McKenzie, 2006-Ohio-5725, 2006 WL 3095671 (Ohio Ct. App. 8th Dist. Cuyahoga County 2006); Cleveland v. Colon, 2007-Ohio-269, 2007 WL 179082 (Ohio Ct. App. 8th Dist. Cuyahoga County 2007); State v. Brown, 2006-Ohio-6267, 2006 WL 3446238 (Ohio Ct. App. 8th Dist. Cuyahoga County 2006), aff'd on other grounds, 119 Ohio St. 3d 447, 2008-Ohio-4569, 895 N.E.2d 149 (2008); State v. Waltzer, 2011-Ohio-594, 2011 WL 486945 (Ohio Ct. App. 8th Dist. Cuyahoga County 2011).

[6]United States Constitution, Sixth Amendment.

Crawford.[7] Thus where a defendant has the opportunity to cross-examine a witness who made out-of-court statements and the witnesses who testified to those out-of-court statements, the defendant's right to confrontation is not violated.[8] The U.S. Supreme Court explained that the Confrontation Clause "guarantees only an opportunity for effective cross-examination, not cross-examination that is effective in whatever way, and to whatever extent, the defense might wish."[9] According to the Supreme Court, it "is sufficient that the defendant has the opportunity to bring out such matters as the witness' bias, his lack of care and attentiveness, his poor eyesight, and even . . . the very fact that he has a bad memory."[10]

In *Delaware v. Fensterer*,[11] the U.S. Supreme Court explained that:

> The Confrontation Clause includes no guarantee that every witness called by the prosecution will refrain from giving testimony that is marred by forgetfulness, confusion, or evasion. To the contrary, the Confrontation Clause is generally satisfied when the defense is given a full and fair opportunity to probe and expose these infirmities through

[7]Bugh v. Mitchell, 329 F.3d 496, 506, 61 Fed. R. Evid. Serv. 399, 2003 FED App. 0138P (6th Cir. 2003), citing Idaho v. Wright, 497 U.S. 805, 813, 110 S. Ct. 3139, 111 L. Ed. 2d 638, 30 Fed. R. Evid. Serv. 24 (1990).

[8]U.S. v. Owens, 484 U.S. 554, 108 S. Ct. 838, 98 L. Ed. 2d 951, 24 Fed. R. Evid. Serv. 193 (1988); Bugh v. Mitchell, 329 F.3d 496, 61 Fed. R. Evid. Serv. 399, 2003 FED App. 0138P (6th Cir. 2003); State v. Harris, 2010-Ohio-1865, 2010 WL 1713023 (Ohio Ct. App. 8th Dist. Cuyahoga County 2010); State v. Fown, 2009-Ohio-5141, 2009 WL 3111841 (Ohio Ct. App. 5th Dist. Licking County 2009); State v. Bryant, 2008-Ohio-3078, 2008 WL 2487253 (Ohio Ct. App. 12th Dist. Warren County 2008); In re Kitzmiller, 2007-Ohio-4565, 2007 WL 2482618 (Ohio Ct. App. 5th Dist. Licking County 2007); State v. Turks, 2010-Ohio-5944, 2010 WL 5050549 (Ohio Ct. App. 3d Dist. Allen County 2010); State v. Arnold, 2014-Ohio-1134, 2014 WL 1339806 (Ohio Ct. App. 3d Dist. Seneca County 2014), judgment aff'd, 147 Ohio St. 3d 138, 2016-Ohio-1595, 62 N.E.3d 153 (2016); State v. Stoneham, 2017 WL 2644320 (Ariz. Ct. App. Div. 1 2017).

[9]Kentucky v. Stincer, 482 U.S. 730, 739, 107 S. Ct. 2658, 96 L. Ed. 2d 631, 22 Fed. R. Evid. Serv. 1164 (1987), citing Delaware v. Fensterer, 474 U.S. 15, 20, 106 S. Ct. 292, 294, 88 L. Ed. 2d 15, 18 Fed. R. Evid. Serv. 945 (1985); State v. Harris, 2010-Ohio-1865, 2010 WL 1713023 (Ohio Ct. App. 8th Dist. Cuyahoga County 2010); State v. Fown, 2009-Ohio-5141, 2009 WL 3111841 (Ohio Ct. App. 5th Dist. Licking County 2009); State v. Bryant, 2008-Ohio-3078, 2008 WL 2487253 (Ohio Ct. App. 12th Dist. Warren County 2008); In re Kitzmiller, 2007-Ohio-4565, 2007 WL 2482618 (Ohio Ct. App. 5th Dist. Licking County 2007); State v. Williams, 2010-Ohio-3279, 2010 WL 2749598 (Ohio Ct. App. 7th Dist. Mahoning County 2010); State v. Spivey, 2013-Ohio-851, 2013 WL 937754 (Ohio Ct. App. 3d Dist. Marion County 2013). But see State v. Clark, 137 Ohio St. 3d 346, 2013-Ohio-4731, 999 N.E.2d 592 (2013), rev'd and remanded, 135 S. Ct. 2173, 192 L. Ed. 2d 306 (2015) reversed and remanded by the U.S. Supreme Court in Ohio v. Clark, 135 S. Ct. 2173, 192 L. Ed. 2d 306 (2015).

[10]U.S. v. Owens, 484 U.S. 554, 559, 108 S. Ct. 838, 842, 98 L. Ed. 2d 951, 24 Fed. R. Evid. Serv. 193 (1988); see also Delaware v. Fensterer, 474 U.S. 15, 21–22, 106 S. Ct. 292, 88 L. Ed. 2d 15, 18 Fed. R. Evid. Serv. 945 (1985); State v. Williams, 2010-Ohio-3279, 2010 WL 2749598 (Ohio Ct. App. 7th Dist. Mahoning County 2010); State v. Blackshear, 2013-Ohio-77, 2013 WL 160453 (Ohio Ct. App. 5th Dist. Stark County 2013).

[11]Delaware v. Fensterer, 474 U.S. 15, 21–22, 106 S. Ct. 292, 88 L. Ed. 2d 15, 18 Fed. R. Evid. Serv. 945 (1985); People v. Soto, 2017 WL 4784392 (Cal. App. 2d Dist. 2017), unpublished/noncitable(Defendant could not cross examine ER nurse regarding any domestic violence she may have experienced in 2009, reasoning that defendant had other means to attack nurse's credibility. Trial court's ruling still allowed defendant to attack nurse's credibility. Defendant did question nurse regarding inconsistencies between her testimony and her written statements.).

cross-examination, thereby calling to the attention of the factfinder the reasons for giving scant weight to the witness' testimony.

The *Owens* Court found this principle applied equally in the case of out-of-court statements.[12]

"Where non-testimonial hearsay is at issue, it is wholly consistent with the Framers' design to afford the States flexibility in their development of hearsay law—as does consistent with the holding in *Roberts*[13], and as would an approach that exempted such statements from Confrontation Clause scrutiny altogether. Where *testimonial* evidence is at issue, however, the Sixth Amendment demands what the common law required: unavailability and a prior opportunity for cross-examination."[14]

Thus, the threshold determination becomes whether the hearsay statements in question are classified as testimonial.[15] In a well-reasoned opinion, distinguishing the *Crawford* decision, an Indiana court held that non-testimonial out of court statements could be admitted without the defendant having an opportunity to cross-examine the witness, if the statements fall within a hearsay exception.[16]

In *Davis v. Washington*,[17] the U.S. Supreme Court agreed, holding that, for instance, "[w]ithout attempting to produce an exhaustive classification of all conceivable statements . . . as either testimonial or non-testimonial, it suffices to . . . hold as follows: Statements are non-testimonial when made in the course of police interrogation under

---

[12]U.S. v. Owens, 484 U.S. 554, 108 S. Ct. 838, 98 L. Ed. 2d 951, 24 Fed. R. Evid. Serv. 193 (1988).

[13]Ohio v. Roberts, 448 U.S. 56, 100 S. Ct. 2531, 65 L. Ed. 2d 597, 7 Fed. R. Evid. Serv. 1 (1980) (abrogated by, Crawford v. Washington, 541 U.S. 36, 124 S. Ct. 1354, 158 L. Ed. 2d 177, 63 Fed. R. Evid. Serv. 1077 (2004)); State v. Barton, 2007-Ohio-1099, 2007 WL 731409 (Ohio Ct. App. 12th Dist. Warren County 2007); State v. McCree, 2007-Ohio-268, 2007 WL 178933 (Ohio Ct. App. 8th Dist. Cuyahoga County 2007); State v. Clark, 137 Ohio St. 3d 346, 2013-Ohio-4731, 999 N.E.2d 592 (2013), rev'd and remanded, 135 S. Ct. 2173, 192 L. Ed. 2d 306 (2015).

[14]Davis v. Washington, 547 U.S. 813, 126 S. Ct. 2266, 165 L. Ed. 2d 224, 70 Fed. R. Evid. Serv. 472, 30 A.L.R.6th 599 (2006). See also Crawford v. Washington, 541 U.S. 36, 68, 124 S. Ct. 1354, 158 L. Ed. 2d 177, 63 Fed. R. Evid. Serv. 1077 (2004); State v. Clark, 137 Ohio St. 3d 346, 2013-Ohio-4731, 999 N.E.2d 592 (2013), rev'd and remanded, 135 S. Ct. 2173, 192 L. Ed. 2d 306 (2015); State v. McClain, 2014-Ohio-93, 2014 WL 117962 (Ohio Ct. App. 10th Dist. Franklin County 2014); State v. Goshade, 2013-Ohio-4457, 2013 WL 5577906 (Ohio Ct. App. 1st Dist. Hamilton County 2013); State v. Doyle, 2014-Ohio-285, 2014 WL 313139 (Ohio Ct. App. 5th Dist. Fairfield County 2014); State v. Martin, 2016-Ohio-225, 57 N.E.3d 411 (Ohio Ct. App. 5th Dist. Tuscarawas County 2016).

[15]Akron v. Hutton, 2005-Ohio-3300, 2005 WL 1523880 (Ohio Ct. App. 9th Dist. Summit County 2005); State v. Gilfillan, 2009-Ohio-1104, 2009 WL 638264 (Ohio Ct. App. 10th Dist. Franklin County 2009), judgment rev'd, 130 Ohio St. 3d 254, 2011-Ohio-5348, 957 N.E.2d 289 (2011), judgment reversed, on other grounds by State v. Williams, 129 Ohio St. 3d 344, 2011-Ohio-3374, 952 N.E.2d 1108 (2011).

[16]Fowler v. State, 809 N.E.2d 960 (Ind. Ct. App. 2004), transfer granted, opinion vacated, IN RAP 58(A), (Dec. 9, 2004) and opinion vacated, 829 N.E.2d 459 (Ind. 2005) and (abrogated by, Hammon v. State, 829 N.E.2d 444 (Ind. 2005)); State v. Gilfillan, 2009-Ohio-1104, 2009 WL 638264 (Ohio Ct. App. 10th Dist. Franklin County 2009), judgment rev'd, 130 Ohio St. 3d 254, 2011-Ohio-5348, 957 N.E.2d 289 (2011).

[17]Davis v. Washington, 547 U.S. 813, 126 S. Ct. 2266, 165 L. Ed. 2d 224, 70 Fed. R. Evid. Serv. 472, 30 A.L.R.6th 599 (2006); Ohio v. Clark, 135 S. Ct. 2173, 192 L. Ed. 2d 306 (2015).

circumstances objectively indicating that the primary purpose of the interrogation is to enable police assistance to meet an ongoing emergency. They are testimonial when the circumstances objectively indicate that there is no such ongoing emergency, and that the primary purpose of the interrogation is to establish or prove past events potentially relevant to later criminal prosecution."[18]

The U.S. Supreme Court's decision in *Michigan v. Bryant*[19] sets forth a test for determining a statement's primary purpose. In the trial of that case, the court admitted statements that the victim made to police officers who discovered him mortally wounded in a gas station parking lot. In reversing the Michigan Supreme Court's holding that the victim's statements were inadmissible, the U.S. Supreme Court held that to make the "primary purpose" determination, the Court must objectively evaluate the circumstances in which the encounter between the individual and the police occurs and the parties' statements and actions.[20]

The primary purpose inquiry is objective. The circumstances in which an encounter occurs are clearly matters of objective fact. And the relevant inquiry into the parties' statements and actions is not the subjective or actual purpose of the particular parties, but the purpose that reasonable participants would have had, as ascertained from the parties' statements and actions and the circumstances in which the encounter occurred.[21]

The existence of an "ongoing emergency" at the time of the encounter is among the most important circumstances informing the interrogation's "primary purpose." An emergency focuses the participants not on proving past events potentially relevant to later criminal prosecution, but on ending a threatening situation. A court must appreciate that whether an emergency exists and is ongoing is a highly context-dependent inquiry. An assessment of whether an emergency threatening the police and public is ongoing cannot narrowly focus on whether the threat to the first victim has been neutralized, because the threat to the first responders and public may continue.[22] An emergency's duration and scope may depend in part on the type of weapon involved. A victim's medical condition is important to the primary purpose inquiry to the extent that it sheds light on the victim's ability to have any purpose at all in responding to police questions and on

[18] Davis v. Washington, 547 U.S. 813, 126 S. Ct. 2266, 2273-74, 165 L. Ed. 2d 224, 70 Fed. R. Evid. Serv. 472, 30 A.L.R.6th 599 (2006); Ohio v. Clark, 135 S. Ct. 2173, 192 L. Ed. 2d 306 (2015).

[19] Michigan v. Bryant, 562 U.S. 344, 131 S. Ct. 1143, 179 L. Ed. 2d 93, 84 Fed. R. Evid. Serv. 1033 (2011); State v. Goshade, 2013-Ohio-4457, 2013 WL 5577906 (Ohio Ct. App. 1st Dist. Hamilton County 2013). But see State v. Clark, 137 Ohio St. 3d 346, 2013-Ohio-4731, 999 N.E.2d 592 (2013), rev'd and remanded, 135 S. Ct. 2173, 192 L. Ed. 2d 306 (2015); Ohio v. Clark, 135 S. Ct. 2173, 192 L. Ed. 2d 306 (2015).

[20] Michigan v. Bryant, 562 U.S. 344, 131 S. Ct. 1143, 179 L. Ed. 2d 93, 84 Fed. R. Evid. Serv. 1033 (2011); Ohio v. Clark, 135 S. Ct. 2173, 192 L. Ed. 2d 306 (2015).

[21] Michigan v. Bryant, 562 U.S. 344, 131 S. Ct. 1143, 179 L. Ed. 2d 93, 84 Fed. R. Evid. Serv. 1033 (2011).

[22] Michigan v. Bryant, 562 U.S. 344, 131 S. Ct. 1143, 179 L. Ed. 2d 93, 84 Fed. R. Evid. Serv. 1033 (2011); Ohio v. Clark, 135 S. Ct. 2173, 192 L. Ed. 2d 306 (2015).

the likelihood that any such purpose would be a testimonial one.[23] It also provides important context for first responders to judge the existence and magnitude of a continuing threat to the victim, themselves, and the public.[24] This does not mean that an emergency lasts the entire time that a perpetrator is on the loose, but trial courts can determine in the first instance when an interrogation transitions from non-testimonial to testimonial. Finally, whether an ongoing emergency exists is simply one factor informing the ultimate inquiry regarding an interrogation's "primary purpose."[25] Another is the encounter's informality; formality suggests the absence of an emergency, but informality does not necessarily indicate the presence of an emergency or the lack of testimonial intent.[26]

The statements and actions of both the declarant and interrogators also provide objective evidence of the interrogation's primary purpose. Looking to the contents of both the questions and the answers ameliorates problems that could arise from looking solely to one participant, since both interrogators and declarants may have mixed motives.[27] Police officers' dual responsibilities as both first responders and criminal investigators may lead them to act with different motives simultaneously or in quick succession. And during an ongoing emergency, victims may want the threat to end, but may not envision prosecution. Alternatively, a severely injured victim may have no purpose at all in answering questions. Taking into account such injuries does not make the inquiry subjective. The inquiry still focuses on the understanding and purpose of a reasonable victim in the actual victim's circumstances, which prominently include the victim's physical state.[28]

Ohio's highest court has said that some attempts to admit hearsay statements into evidence pursuant to firmly rooted hearsay exceptions may be violative of a defendant's rights to confrontation under the provisions of the Ohio Constitution,[29] even if the admission of such evidence does not violate the defendant's federal confrontation rights.[30] This is so because the Ohio Constitution specifically requires a face-to-face confrontation between a defendant and a witness making criminal accusations, while the United States Supreme Court's most recent interpretations of the federal Confrontation Clause have drifted away

[23]Michigan v. Bryant, 562 U.S. 344, 131 S. Ct. 1143, 179 L. Ed. 2d 93, 84 Fed. R. Evid. Serv. 1033 (2011); Ohio v. Clark, 135 S. Ct. 2173, 192 L. Ed. 2d 306 (2015).

[24]Michigan v. Bryant, 562 U.S. 344, 131 S. Ct. 1143, 179 L. Ed. 2d 93, 84 Fed. R. Evid. Serv. 1033 (2011); Ohio v. Clark, 135 S. Ct. 2173, 192 L. Ed. 2d 306 (2015).

[25]Michigan v. Bryant, 562 U.S. 344, 131 S. Ct. 1143, 179 L. Ed. 2d 93, 84 Fed. R. Evid. Serv. 1033 (2011); Ohio v. Clark, 135 S. Ct. 2173, 192 L. Ed. 2d 306 (2015).

[26]Michigan v. Bryant, 562 U.S. 344, 131 S. Ct. 1143, 179 L. Ed. 2d 93, 84 Fed. R. Evid. Serv. 1033 (2011); Ohio v. Clark, 135 S. Ct. 2173, 192 L. Ed. 2d 306 (2015).

[27]Michigan v. Bryant, 562 U.S. 344, 131 S. Ct. 1143, 179 L. Ed. 2d 93, 84 Fed. R. Evid. Serv. 1033 (2011); Ohio v. Clark, 135 S. Ct. 2173, 192 L. Ed. 2d 306 (2015).

[28]Michigan v. Bryant, 562 U.S. 344, 131 S. Ct. 1143, 179 L. Ed. 2d 93, 84 Fed. R. Evid. Serv. 1033 (2011); Ohio v. Clark, 135 S. Ct. 2173, 192 L. Ed. 2d 306 (2015).

[29]O. Const. Art. I § 10; But see State v. Gilfillan, 2009-Ohio-1104, 2009 WL 638264 (Ohio Ct. App. 10th Dist. Franklin County 2009), judgment rev'd, 130 Ohio St. 3d 254, 2011-Ohio-5348, 957 N.E.2d 289 (2011).

[30]State v. Storch, 66 Ohio St. 3d 280, 1993-Ohio-38, 612 N.E.2d 305 (1993).

from a face-to-face requirement.[31] With the advent of *Crawford*[32] and its progeny, the U.S. Supreme Court's focus appears to have returned to the defendant's fundamental right to face those who make criminal accusations. Crawford would prevent the state's use of the most egregious testimonial accusations without affording a right to the accused to have those accusations tested via cross examination.

However, that court made clear that not all out-of-court statements made to those in positions of authority will qualify as testimonial. According to the U.S. Supreme Court, a statement cannot fall within the Confrontation Clause unless its primary purpose was testimonial. Where no such primary purpose exists, the admissibility of a statement is the concern of state and federal rules of evidence, not the Confrontation Clause.[33] The Confrontation Clause does not bar every statement that satisfies the "primary purpose" test. The Supreme court recognized that the Confrontation Clause does not prohibit the introduction of out-of-court statements that were admissible in a criminal case at the time of the founding.[34] Thus, the primary purpose test is a necessary, but not always sufficient, condition for the exclusion of out-of-court statements under the Confrontation Clause.

In *Ohio v. Clark*,[35] the Supreme Court was presented with the question it has repeatedly reserved: whether statements to persons other than law enforcement officers are subject to the Confrontation Clause. Because at least some statements to individuals who are not law enforcement officers could conceivably raise confrontation concerns, the Court declined to adopt a categorical rule excluding them from the Sixth Amendment's reach. Nevertheless, the court held that such statements are much less likely to be testimonial than statements to law enforcement officers, and, therefore, less likely to violate the Confrontation Clause.[36]

Therefore, where the immediate concern is to protect the vulnerable, the emergency is ongoing, the circumstances are not entirely clear, there is no indication that the primary purpose of the conversation is to gather evidence for prosecution, the setting is informal and nothing like the formalized station-house questioning in *Crawford* or

[31]State v. Storch, 66 Ohio St. 3d 280, 288, 1993-Ohio-38, 612 N.E.2d 305 (1993); Ohio v. Roberts, 448 U.S. 56, 100 S. Ct. 2531, 65 L. Ed. 2d 597, 7 Fed. R. Evid. Serv. 1 (1980) (abrogated by, Crawford v. Washington, 541 U.S. 36, 124 S. Ct. 1354, 158 L. Ed. 2d 177, 63 Fed. R. Evid. Serv. 1077 (2004)); State v. Dever, 64 Ohio St. 3d 401, 415-418, 1992-Ohio-41, 596 N.E.2d 436 (1992); White v. Illinois, 502 U.S. 346, 112 S. Ct. 736, 116 L. Ed. 2d 848, 33 Fed. R. Evid. Serv. 881 (1992). See also In re Dustin, 1999 WL 956880 (Ohio Ct. App. 11th Dist. Lake County 1999); State v. Dartt, 2008-Ohio-373, 2008 WL 303135 (Ohio Ct. App. 6th Dist. Lucas County 2008).

[32]Davis v. Washington, 547 U.S. 813, 126 S. Ct. 2266, 165 L. Ed. 2d 224, 70 Fed. R. Evid. Serv. 472, 30 A.L.R.6th 599 (2006). See also Crawford v. Washington, 541 U.S. 36, 124 S. Ct. 1354, 158 L. Ed. 2d 177, 63 Fed. R. Evid. Serv. 1077 (2004); Ohio v. Clark, 135 S. Ct. 2173, 192 L. Ed. 2d 306 (2015).

[33]Ohio v. Clark, 135 S. Ct. 2173, 192 L. Ed. 2d 306 (2015).

[34]See Giles v. California, 554 U.S. 353, 358–359, 128 S. Ct. 2678, 171 L. Ed. 2d 488 (2008); *Crawford,* 541 U.S., at 56, n. 6, 62, 124 S.Ct. 1354.

[35]Ohio v. Clark, 135 S. Ct. 2173, 192 L. Ed. 2d 306 (2015).

[36]Ohio v. Clark, 135 S. Ct. 2173, 192 L. Ed. 2d 306 (2015).

the police interrogation and battery affidavit in *Hammon,* the statements elicited are less likely to qualify as testimonial.[37]

Q & A: At trial the defendant challenges the admission of the complaining witnesses medical records, which contained unredacted hearsay statements by the doctor who treated the witness after the event on trial. Defendant contends these prejudicial statements violate his rights to due process and confrontation of witnesses. Specifically, defendant cites to and relies upon *Crawford v. Washington.* The state counters by reminding the court that the doctors made the records testified at trial. How should the court rule?

Defendant's reliance on *Crawford*[38] is misplaced. Unlike in Crawford, there is no indication in this case that the information contained in the medical records was testimonial in nature. Rather, the notes were made for purposes of medical diagnosis.[39] Since the witnesses who wrote the statements appeared and testified at defendant's trial, the defendant had the opportunity to cross-examine with respect to the statements they made. The records should be admitted.[40]

Q & A: Does the U.S. Supreme Court's ruling in *Crawford* apply retroactively?

No. *Crawford*[41] announced a new rule of criminal procedure that does not fall within the exception for watershed rules.[42]

Under the framework set forth by the Supreme Court,[43] an old rule applies both on direct and collateral review, but a new rule generally applies only to cases still on direct review and applies retroactively in a collateral proceeding only if it (1) is substantive or (2) is a watershed rule that implicates "the fundamental fairness and accuracy of the criminal proceeding."

Because *Crawford*[44] announced a new rule and because that rule is procedural and not substantive, it cannot be retroactively applied unless it is a "watershed rul[e]" that implicates "the fundamental fairness and accuracy of the criminal proceeding." This exception is

---

[37]Ohio v. Clark, 135 S. Ct. 2173, 192 L. Ed. 2d 306 (2015); Crawford v. Washington, 541 U.S. 36, 124 S. Ct. 1354, 158 L. Ed. 2d 177, 63 Fed. R. Evid. Serv. 1077 (2004).

[38]Crawford v. Washington, 541 U.S. 36, 124 S. Ct. 1354, 158 L. Ed. 2d 177, 63 Fed. R. Evid. Serv. 1077 (2004).

[39]Evid.R. 803(4).

[40]State v. Grimes, 2006-Ohio-4262, 2006 WL 2373382 (Ohio Ct. App. 8th Dist. Cuyahoga County 2006).

[41]Crawford v. Washington, 541 U.S. 36, 124 S. Ct. 1354, 158 L. Ed. 2d 177, 63 Fed. R. Evid. Serv. 1077 (2004).

[42]Teague v. Lane, 489 U.S. 288, 311, 109 S. Ct. 1060, 103 L. Ed. 2d 334 (1989); State v. Bishop, 2014-Ohio-173, 7 N.E.3d 605 (Ohio Ct. App. 1st Dist. Hamilton County 2014).

[43]Teague v. Lane, 489 U.S. 288, 311, 109 S. Ct. 1060, 103 L. Ed. 2d 334 (1989).

[44]Crawford v. Washington, 541 U.S. 36, 124 S. Ct. 1354, 158 L. Ed. 2d 177, 63 Fed. R. Evid. Serv. 1077 (2004).

"extremely narrow."[45] The *Crawford* rule does not meet those two requirements.[46]

Q & A: A DNA analyst is present during the conduct of a DNA test, performed by another analyst, observes and is familiar with the laboratory protocol and how the DNA test results. This same analyst reviewed the results of the test performed immediately after they were obtained and initialed the final report that contained those results.

At trial, the analyst who performed the test is unavailable and the prosecution offers the testimony of the analyst who observed the test. The defendant objects on the basis that he is denied his right to confrontation and cites *Crawford v. Washington* as authority. Should the objection be sustained?

There is a split of authority on this issue. The Eighth District Court of Appeals says, "no."[47] That court held that testimony under such circumstances does not constitute hearsay. Hearsay is defined as an out-of-court statement offered for the truth of the matter asserted. In this situation the analyst reviewed the defendant's DNA report, and thereby was qualified to offer testimony about it. In addition, the analyst also signed the report. Because the document bears the signature of the testifying analyst, the analyst's testimony regarding the documents does not constitute inadmissible hearsay.

The Sixth District Court of Appeals agreed.[48] That court found that scientific reports were not implicated by the U.S. Supreme Court's Crawford decision for two reasons: (1) First, they bear no similarities to the types of evidence the Supreme Court labeled as testimonial: "prior testimony at a preliminary hearing, before a grand jury, or at a former trial, and police interrogations", and (2) that the records are business records, which, at least according to dicta in *Crawford*, are not testimonial.[49]

However, another Ohio court of appeals says, "yes."[50] That court found that although the DNA lab report fell within the general parameters of the business records exception,[51] the lab reports and DNA reports in question were prepared wholly in anticipation of

---

[45]Schriro v. Summerlin, 542 U.S. 348, 351, 124 S. Ct. 2519, 159 L. Ed. 2d 442 (2004).

[46]Whorton v. Bockting, 549 U.S. 406, 127 S. Ct. 1173, 167 L. Ed. 2d 1, 72 Fed. R. Evid. Serv. 635, 44 A.L.R. Fed. 2d 777 (2007). See also State v. Cunningham, 2006-Ohio-4339, 2006 WL 2411539 (Ohio Ct. App. 10th Dist. Franklin County 2006).

[47]State v. Cosme, 2007-Ohio-1454, 2007 WL 926357 (Ohio Ct. App. 8th Dist. Cuyahoga County 2007), judgment aff'd, 117 Ohio St. 3d 74, 2008-Ohio-500, 881 N.E.2d 864 (2008).

[48]State v. Cook, 2005-Ohio-1550, 2005 WL 736671 (Ohio Ct. App. 6th Dist. Wood County 2005), motion to reopen granted, 2005-Ohio-4174, 2005 WL 1926517 (Ohio Ct. App. 6th Dist. Wood County 2005).

[49]State v. Cook, 2005-Ohio-1550, 2005 WL 736671 (Ohio Ct. App. 6th Dist. Wood County 2005), motion to reopen granted, 2005-Ohio-4174, 2005 WL 1926517 (Ohio Ct. App. 6th Dist. Wood County 2005).

[50]State v. Crager, 164 Ohio App. 3d 816, 2005-Ohio-6868, 844 N.E.2d 390 (3d Dist. Marion County 2005), judgment rev'd, 116 Ohio St. 3d 369, 2007-Ohio-6840, 879 N.E.2d 745 (2007), cert. granted, judgment vacated, 557 U.S. 930, 129 S. Ct. 2856, 174 L. Ed. 2d 598 (2009).

[51]Evid.R. 803(6).

litigation. Because the reports were prepared solely in anticipation of prosecution, the court found them to be testimonial. Thus, when the person who prepared the report failed to appear at trial, and the defendant was not given a prior opportunity to cross-examine the witness about the findings of the report, the court found the defendant's right to confrontation under the Sixth Amendment was violated.[52]

The Ohio Supreme Court, in *State v. Crager*,[53] held that records of scientific tests are not testimonial and rejected the approach of those courts that hold that laboratory reports are testimonial because their primary purpose was to establish a fact at trial regarding the defendant's guilt. The Court reasoned that the DNA records at issue in that case were admissible under the business records exception and that they have neutral as opposed to a prosecutorial purpose. However, the Supreme Court of Ohio's decision was vacated by the U.S. Supreme Court in *Crager v. Ohio*.[54] The U.S. Supreme Court vacated the Ohio Supreme Court decision and remanded *Crager* back to the Supreme Court of Ohio for further consideration in light of the U.S. Supreme Court's decision in *Melendez-Diaz v. Massachusetts*.[55]

In *Melendez-Diaz*, the U.S. Supreme Court held that the written affidavits of analysts attesting to their findings were no substitute for a defendant's opportunity to cross-examine those analysts regarding those findings. The majority in that case concluded that the argument that the experts should not be subject to confrontation because their statements result from neutral scientific testing is little more than an invitation to return to the court's prior position, which held that evidence with "particularized guarantees of trustworthiness" was admissible without confrontation.[56]

Q & A: If a domestic violence victim appears at trial and claims to have been too intoxicated to now remember the events that resulted in the charges, is the defendant denied a meaningful opportunity to confront the witness concerning statements made to officers at the time of arrest?

No. Previous decisions of the United States Supreme Court, explain that the U.S. Constitution's Confrontation Clause guarantees only an opportunity for effective cross-examination, not cross-examination

[52]State v. Crager, 164 Ohio App. 3d 816, 2005-Ohio-6868, 844 N.E.2d 390 (3d Dist. Marion County 2005), judgment rev'd, 116 Ohio St. 3d 369, 2007-Ohio-6840, 879 N.E.2d 745 (2007), cert. granted, judgment vacated, 557 U.S. 930, 129 S. Ct. 2856, 174 L. Ed. 2d 598 (2009).

[53]State v. Crager, 116 Ohio St. 3d 369, 2007-Ohio-6840, 879 N.E.2d 745 (2007), cert. granted, judgment vacated, 557 U.S. 930, 129 S. Ct. 2856, 174 L. Ed. 2d 598 (2009).

[54]Crager v. Ohio, 557 U.S. 930, 129 S. Ct. 2856, 174 L. Ed. 2d 598 (2009).

[55]Melendez-Diaz v. Massachusetts, 557 U.S. 305, 129 S. Ct. 2527, 174 L. Ed. 2d 314 (2009).

[56]Ohio v. Roberts, 448 U.S. 56, 66, 100 S. Ct. 2531, 65 L. Ed. 2d 597, 7 Fed. R. Evid. Serv. 1 (1980) (abrogated by, Crawford v. Washington, 541 U.S. 36, 124 S. Ct. 1354, 158 L. Ed. 2d 177, 63 Fed. R. Evid. Serv. 1077 (2004)); Melendez-Diaz v. Massachusetts, 557 U.S. 305, 129 S. Ct. 2527, 174 L. Ed. 2d 314 (2009).

that is effective in whatever way, and to whatever extent, the defense might wish.[57]

Q & A: During a trial where the victim fails to appear, an officer testifies that immediately upon entering the victim's apartment in response to a 911 call, they heard the victim, who was covered in blood and holding appellant at bay with a knife, say "I'm glad you guys came because he would have killed me." The defense objects, stating that the statement to the police is testimonial hearsay. Should the objection be sustained?

No. The statements made to police were not testimonial in nature, since they were made under circumstances that indicate their primary purpose was to obtain police assistance during an emergency situation. Out-of-court statements of an unavailable declarant, whether testimonial or non-testimonial, however, still constitute hearsay, because they are "statement[s], other than one[s] made by the declarant while testifying at the trial or hearing, offered in evidence to prove the truth of the matter asserted." Evid.R. 801(C). In cases where a hearsay statement is found to be non-testimonial in nature, it may not be admitted at trial unless it "falls within a firmly rooted hearsay exception,"[58] such as an excited utterance. The statement offered into evidence in this trial was made spontaneously, without any prompting by police, and without any time for thought or reflection on the part of the declarant. Under such circumstances, the statement has the requisite degree of trustworthiness to qualify as an excited utterance and as such is admissible into evidence.[59]

Q & A: The victim failed to appear at trial, however, the court allowed the victim's friend to testify concerning a telephone call they had on the morning of the alleged event. Specifically, the friend testified that the victim was crying and said that she'd been beat up, was scared, in a lot of pain and did not want defendant returning. The defense objected maintaining that the friend's statements were inadmissible testimonial hearsay. Is the defense correct and should the statements be stricken from the record?

No. Various Ohio appellate courts have found that statements such as these made to a friend are not testimonial. However, there can still

---

[57]U.S. v. Owens, 484 U.S. 554, 558–559, 108 S. Ct. 838, 98 L. Ed. 2d 951, 24 Fed. R. Evid. Serv. 193 (1988), State v. Harris, 2010-Ohio-1865, 2010 WL 1713023 (Ohio Ct. App. 8th Dist. Cuyahoga County 2010); State v. Fown, 2009-Ohio-5141, 2009 WL 3111841 (Ohio Ct. App. 5th Dist. Licking County 2009); State v. Bryant, 2008-Ohio-3078, 2008 WL 2487253 (Ohio Ct. App. 12th Dist. Warren County 2008); In re Kitzmiller, 2007-Ohio-4565, 2007 WL 2482618 (Ohio Ct. App. 5th Dist. Licking County 2007).

[58]Ohio v. Roberts, 448 U.S. 56, 100 S. Ct. 2531, 65 L. Ed. 2d 597, 7 Fed. R. Evid. Serv. 1 (1980) (abrogated by, Crawford v. Washington, 541 U.S. 36, 124 S. Ct. 1354, 158 L. Ed. 2d 177, 63 Fed. R. Evid. Serv. 1077 (2004)); Evid.R. 802.

[59]State v. Davis, 2007-Ohio-3419, 2007 WL 1934364 (Ohio Ct. App. 8th Dist. Cuyahoga County 2007); State v. McKenzie, 2006-Ohio-5725, 2006 WL 3095671 (Ohio Ct. App. 8th Dist. Cuyahoga County 2006); Cleveland v. Colon, 2007-Ohio-269, 2007 WL 179082 (Ohio Ct. App. 8th Dist. Cuyahoga County 2007); State v. Brown, 2006-Ohio-6267, 2006 WL 3446238 (Ohio Ct. App. 8th Dist. Cuyahoga County 2006), aff'd on other grounds, 119 Ohio St. 3d 447, 2008-Ohio-4569, 895 N.E.2d 149 (2008).

be a hearsay issue even if there is no Confrontation issue. It is well established that the admission or exclusion of evidence rests within the sound discretion of the trial court.[60] The Rules of Evidence[61] provide that certain statements are not excluded by the hearsay rule even though the declarant is available as a witness. The victim was upset, emotional and crying. She described her injuries and her pain. She was fearful as the incident had just occurred that morning and defendant was likely to return.

Considering the friend's description of victim's demeanor and injuries, the trial court's decision to permit the friend's testimony concerning the victim's statements was allowable under more than one exception to the hearsay rule and was not unreasonable, arbitrary or unconscionable.[62]

Q & A: Is a Defendant's right to confront his accuser violated when the trial court permits the state to introduce witness's former testimony from parole revocation hearing where the state knew days before trial that the sole witness against the defendant had received a subpoena and had no intention to appear for trial?

Yes. The court must require the state to demonstrate that the witness was unavailable and that the state made reasonable efforts to secure the witness's appearance for trial before such evidence is properly admissible.[63]

Q & A: I wanted to question the complainant about some physical abuse she suffered at the hands of her father a couple of years before she met my client, but the court sustained the prosecution's objection. Doesn't that impinge on my client's right to confront his accuser?

No. Pursuant to Evid. R. 611(B), "cross-examination shall be permitted on all relevant matters affecting credibility." Further, the Confrontation Clause of the Sixth Amendment to the United States Constitution guarantees the right of a criminal defendant to confront and cross-examine adverse witnesses.[64] However, "a criminal defendant's right to confront and cross-examine a witness is not

---

[60] State v. Robb, 88 Ohio St. 3d 59, 68, 2000-Ohio-275, 723 N.E.2d 1019 (2000); State v. Tolbert, 2010-Ohio-2864, 2010 WL 2512584 (Ohio Ct. App. 9th Dist. Summit County 2010); State v. Flowers, 2012-Ohio-3783, 2012 WL 3595090 (Ohio Ct. App. 9th Dist. Summit County 2012); State v. Martinez, 2013-Ohio-1025, 2013 WL 1183305 (Ohio Ct. App. 8th Dist. Cuyahoga County 2013); State v. Fread, 2013-Ohio-5206, 2013 WL 6199154 (Ohio Ct. App. 12th Dist. Butler County 2013); State v. Spivey, 2013-Ohio-851, 2013 WL 937754 (Ohio Ct. App. 3d Dist. Marion County 2013).

[61] Evid.R. 803.

[62] State v. Peeples, 2009-Ohio-1198, 2009 WL 737922 (Ohio Ct. App. 7th Dist. Mahoning County 2009).

[63] State v. Smith, 2010-Ohio-745, 2010 WL 703377 (Ohio Ct. App. 2d Dist. Montgomery County 2010); State v. Tabor, 2012-Ohio-4642, 2012 WL 4761741 (Ohio Ct. App. 12th Dist. Warren County 2012).

[64] State v. Freeman, 2008-Ohio-2925, 2008 WL 2425532 (Ohio Ct. App. 7th Dist. Jefferson County 2008); State v. McIntosh, 145 Ohio App. 3d 567, 578, 763 N.E.2d 704 (1st Dist. Hamilton County 2001); State v. Spivey, 2013-Ohio-851, 2013 WL 937754 (Ohio Ct. App. 3d Dist. Marion County 2013).

unlimited."[65] Rather, a trial court retains wide latitude under the Confrontation Clause to impose reasonable limits on cross-examination due to concerns regarding issues such as harassment, prejudice, confusion of issues, witness safety or interrogation that is repetitive or only marginally relevant.[66] Thus, "the Confrontation Clause guarantees an *opportunity* for effective cross-examination, not cross-examination that is effective in whatever way, and to whatever extent, the defense might wish." (Emphasis sic.) Delaware v. Fensterer, 474 U.S. 15, 20, 106 S. Ct. 292, 88 L. Ed. 2d 15, 18 Fed. R. Evid. Serv. 945 (1985). Evidentiary rulings lie within the sound discretion of the trial court, and as such will be upheld absent an abuse thereof.[67] Abuse of discretion "connotes more than an error of law or of judgment; it implies that the court's attitude is unreasonable, arbitrary or unconscionable."[68] In your situation the court did not abuse its discretion, since whether the complainant's father abused her a couple of year ago was not relevant to the current charges pending against your client.

Q & A: During the defendant's domestic violence trial, the prosecution offers a 911 recording into evidence. The defense objects, arguing that in order to use an out of court statement of a witness against a defendant at trial the Ohio Constitution requires a showing that the witness is unavailable to testify. Should the exception be sustained?

No. There is no blanket exclusion of all out of court statements made by a witness who fails to testify at trial. In those instances where the statements in question are of the type firmly rooted in hearsay exceptions recognized in Ohio that apply without regard to the declarant's availability, Section 10, Article I of Ohio's Constitution provides no greater right of confrontation than the U.S. Constitution's Sixth Amendment.[69]

---

[65]State v. Freeman, 2008-Ohio-2925, 2008 WL 2425532 (Ohio Ct. App. 7th Dist. Jefferson County 2008); State v. Spivey, 2013-Ohio-851, 2013 WL 937754 (Ohio Ct. App. 3d Dist. Marion County 2013); State v. McKelton, 148 Ohio St. 3d 261, 2016-Ohio-5735, 70 N.E.3d 508 (2016), cert. denied, 137 S. Ct. 1594, 197 L. Ed. 2d 720 (2017).

[66]Delaware v. Van Arsdall, 475 U.S. 673, 679, 106 S. Ct. 1431, 89 L. Ed. 2d 674, 20 Fed. R. Evid. Serv. 1 (1986); State v. Clark, 2011-Ohio-4109, 2011 WL 3630484 (Ohio Ct. App. 8th Dist. Cuyahoga County 2011); State v. Blackshear, 2013-Ohio-77, 2013 WL 160453 (Ohio Ct. App. 5th Dist. Stark County 2013); State v. Morales, 2014-Ohio-362, 2014 WL 467331 (Ohio Ct. App. 1st Dist. Hamilton County 2014); State v. Arnold, 147 Ohio St. 3d 138, 2016-Ohio-1595, 62 N.E.3d 153 (2016); State v. Canada, 2015-Ohio-2167, 2015 WL 3540402 (Ohio Ct. App. 10th Dist. Franklin County 2015); State v. Abbasov, 2015-Ohio-5379, 2015 WL 9393521 (Ohio Ct. App. 2d Dist. Montgomery County 2015); State v. Akers, 2016-Ohio-1373, 2016 WL 1291722 (Ohio Ct. App. 5th Dist. Fairfield County 2016); State v. Phillips, 2016-Ohio-1216, 2016 WL 1176067 (Ohio Ct. App. 5th Dist. Licking County 2016); State v. Dolby, 2015-Ohio-2424, 2015 WL 3820922 (Ohio Ct. App. 2d Dist. Champaign County 2015).

[67]State v. Bey, 85 Ohio St. 3d 487, 490, 1999-Ohio-283, 709 N.E.2d 484 (1999).

[68]State v. Adams, 62 Ohio St. 2d 151, 157, 16 Ohio Op. 3d 169, 404 N.E.2d 144, 16 A.L.R.4th 344 (1980); State v. Sutphin, 2011-Ohio-5157, 2011 WL 4600412 (Ohio Ct. App. 8th Dist. Cuyahoga County 2011).

[69]State v. Self, 56 Ohio St. 3d 73, 79, 564 N.E.2d 446 (1990); State v. Arnold, 126 Ohio St. 3d 290, 2010-Ohio-2742, 933 N.E.2d 775 (2010); State v. Williams, 2013-Ohio-726, 987 N.E.2d 322 (Ohio Ct. App. 6th Dist. Lucas County 2013); State v. Goshade,

Q & A: The Defendant is on trial for domestic violence. The Prosecution attempts to offer out-of-court statements made by the alleged three-year old child victim to a pre-school teacher regarding the child's abuse by the defendant. The defense objects, citing the U.S. Constitution's Confrontation Clause. Should the trial court sustain the objection?

Probably not. Statements made to persons other than law enforcement officers are less likely to be subject to the Confrontation Clause's prohibitions. The trial court should look to the primary purpose of the teacher's inquiry to determine whether the teacher was more interested in safeguarding the child's safety or in trying to develop evidence to be used later against a criminal defendant.[70] Where the primary purpose is not to develop evidence for a later prosecution, the admissibility of a child's out-of-court statement is the concern of state and federal rules of evidence, not the Confrontation Clause.[71] Additionally, statements made by very young children will rarely, if ever, implicate the Confrontation Clause and Ohio's mandatory reporting obligations do not convert a conversation between a concerned teacher and a student into a law enforcement mission aimed at gathering evidence for prosecution.[72]

§ 5:15 Case preparation—Hearsay exceptions—Excited utterance[1]

Statements made by a witness contemporaneous to or soon after a startling or exciting event are afforded a high degree of credibility. The theory is that these statements are made before the declarant has the opportunity to reflect or to fabricate.[2] Primarily due to the

2013-Ohio-4457, 2013 WL 5577906 (Ohio Ct. App. 1st Dist. Hamilton County 2013); State v. McClain, 2014-Ohio-93, 2014 WL 117962 (Ohio Ct. App. 10th Dist. Franklin County 2014). But see State v. Clark, 137 Ohio St. 3d 346, 2013-Ohio-4731, 999 N.E.2d 592 (2013), rev'd and remanded, 135 S. Ct. 2173, 192 L. Ed. 2d 306 (2015); State v. Canada, 2015-Ohio-2167, 2015 WL 3540402 (Ohio Ct. App. 10th Dist. Franklin County 2015); Toledo v. Green, 2015-Ohio-1864, 33 N.E.3d 581 (Ohio Ct. App. 6th Dist. Lucas County 2015).

[70] Ohio v. Clark, 135 S. Ct. 2173, 192 L. Ed. 2d 306 (2015), on remand, see State v. Clark, 2016-Ohio-2825, 2016 WL 2586638 (Ohio Ct. App. 8th Dist. Cuyahoga County 2016), appeal not allowed, 147 Ohio St. 3d 1474, 2016-Ohio-8438, 65 N.E.3d 778 (2016).

[71] *Clark*, supra., Michigan v. Bryant, 562 U.S. 344, 369, 131 S. Ct. 1143, 179 L. Ed. 2d 93, 84 Fed. R. Evid. Serv. 1033 (2011).

[72] *Clark*, supra.

[Section 5:15]

[1] Evid.R. 803(2).

[2] State v. Wallace, 37 Ohio St. 3d 87, 88, 524 N.E.2d 466 (1988); Cleveland v. Thomas, 2003-Ohio-30, 2003 WL 60981 (Ohio Ct. App. 8th Dist. Cuyahoga County 2003); State v. Abner, 2006-Ohio-4510, 2006 WL 2522384 (Ohio Ct. App. 2d Dist. Montgomery County 2006); State v. Turks, 2010-Ohio-5944, 2010 WL 5050549 (Ohio Ct. App. 3d Dist. Allen County 2010); State v. Sutphin, 2011-Ohio-5157, 2011 WL 4600412 (Ohio Ct. App. 8th Dist. Cuyahoga County 2011); State v. Cunningham, 2012-Ohio-2333, 2012 WL 1900149 (Ohio Ct. App. 2d Dist. Clark County 2012); State v. Matthews, 2011-Ohio-5066, 2011 WL 4529667 (Ohio Ct. App. 2d Dist. Montgomery County 2011); State v. Stover, 2014-Ohio-2572, 2014 WL 2701213 (Ohio Ct. App. 9th Dist. Wayne County 2014); State v. Auerswald, 2013-Ohio-742, 2013 WL 785061 (Ohio

emotional nature of domestic violence, many statements uttered during an incident of domestic violence qualify for this exception.

To qualify under this exception, a statement must meet a four-part test:

(1) There must be a startling or exciting occurrence that stills the reflective faculties,
(2) The statement or declaration must be made while the one making the statement is still affected by the excitement of the occurrence,
(3) The declaration must concern the startling or exciting occurrence, and
(4) The one making the statement must have first-hand knowledge of the subject of the statement.[3]

Ct. App. 9th Dist. Medina County 2013); State v. Goshade, 2013-Ohio-4457, 2013 WL 5577906 (Ohio Ct. App. 1st Dist. Hamilton County 2013).

[3]Potter v. Baker, 162 Ohio St. 488, 55 Ohio Op. 389, 124 N.E.2d 140, 53 A.L.R.2d 1234 (1955); see also State v. Lee, 73 Ohio Misc. 2d 9, 657 N.E.2d 604 (Mun. Ct. 1995); State v. Duncan, 53 Ohio St. 2d 215, 7 Ohio Op. 3d 380, 373 N.E.2d 1234 (1978); State v. Rohrer, 1998 WL 400768 (Ohio Ct. App. 5th Dist. Fairfield County 1998); Weissenberger, Ohio Evidence 1997 Courtroom Manual 353 (1996); State v. Braden, 98 Ohio St. 3d 354, 372, 2003-Ohio-1325, 785 N.E.2d 439, 460 (2003); State v. Huertas, 51 Ohio St. 3d 22, 32, 553 N.E.2d 1058 (1990); State v. Smith, 97 Ohio St. 3d 367, 375, 2002-Ohio-6659, 780 N.E.2d 221, 232 (2002); State v. Bealer, 2003-Ohio-2114, 2003 WL 1956089, *3 (Ohio Ct. App. 12th Dist. Butler County 2003); State v. Harr, 158 Ohio App. 3d 704, 2004-Ohio-5771, 821 N.E.2d 1058 (2d Dist. Clark County 2004); Fowler v. State, 809 N.E.2d 960 (Ind. Ct. App. 2004), transfer granted, opinion vacated, IN RAP 58(A), (Dec. 9, 2004) and opinion vacated, 829 N.E.2d 459 (Ind. 2005) and (abrogated by, Hammon v. State, 829 N.E.2d 444 (Ind. 2005)); Akron v. Hutton, 2005-Ohio-3300, 2005 WL 1523880 (Ohio Ct. App. 9th Dist. Summit County 2005); Mayfield v. Cuccarese, 2008-Ohio-1812, 2008 WL 1747439 (Ohio Ct. App. 8th Dist. Cuyahoga County 2008); State v. Bozarth, 2009-Ohio-2013, 2009 WL 1153246 (Ohio Ct. App. 5th Dist. Licking County 2009); State v. Peeples, 2009-Ohio-1198, 2009 WL 737922 (Ohio Ct. App. 7th Dist. Mahoning County 2009); State v. Boles, 190 Ohio App. 3d 431, 2010-Ohio-5503, 942 N.E.2d 417 (6th Dist. Lucas County 2010); State v. Mauldin, 2010-Ohio-4192, 2010 WL 3482689 (Ohio Ct. App. 7th Dist. Mahoning County 2010); State v. Bateman, 2011-Ohio-3028, 2011 WL 2463070 (Ohio Ct. App. 10th Dist. Franklin County 2011); State v. Gwen, 2011-Ohio-1512, 2011 WL 1226763 (Ohio Ct. App. 9th Dist. Summit County 2011), judgment aff'd, 134 Ohio St. 3d 284, 2012-Ohio-5046, 982 N.E.2d 626 (2012); State v. Ray, 189 Ohio App. 3d 292, 2010-Ohio-2348, 938 N.E.2d 378 (8th Dist. Cuyahoga County 2010); State v. Clark, 2011-Ohio-6623, 2011 WL 6780456 (Ohio Ct. App. 8th Dist. Cuyahoga County 2011), aff'd, 137 Ohio St. 3d 346, 2013-Ohio-4731, 999 N.E.2d 592 (2013), rev'd and remanded, 135 S. Ct. 2173, 192 L. Ed. 2d 306 (2015). See also State v. Clark, 2016-Ohio-2825, 2016 WL 2586638 (Ohio Ct. App. 8th Dist. Cuyahoga County 2016), appeal not allowed, 147 Ohio St. 3d 1474, 2016-Ohio-8438, 65 N.E.3d 778 (2016); State v. Butts, 2012-Ohio-571, 2012 WL 474030 (Ohio Ct. App. 4th Dist. Hocking County 2012); State v. Hall, 2012-Ohio-266, 2012 WL 253317 (Ohio Ct. App. 8th Dist. Cuyahoga County 2012); State v. Beauford, 2011-Ohio-5379, 2011 WL 4973731 (Ohio Ct. App. 5th Dist. Richland County 2011); Michigan v. Bryant, 562 U.S. 344, 131 S. Ct. 1143, 1157, 179 L. Ed. 2d 93, 84 Fed. R. Evid. Serv. 1033 (2011); State v. Parks, 2011-Ohio-3037, 2011 WL 2464198 (Ohio Ct. App. 5th Dist. Stark County 2011); State v. McDaniel, 2011-Ohio-6326, 2011 WL 6153697 (Ohio Ct. App. 2d Dist. Montgomery County 2011); State v. Auerswald, 2013-Ohio-742, 2013 WL 785061 (Ohio Ct. App. 9th Dist. Medina County 2013); Toledo v. Huggins, 2013-Ohio-3467, 2013 WL 4041572 (Ohio Ct. App. 6th Dist. Lucas County 2013); State v. Williams, 2013-Ohio-726, 987 N.E.2d 322 (Ohio Ct. App. 6th Dist. Lucas County 2013); State v. Doyle, 2014-Ohio-285, 2014 WL 313139 (Ohio Ct. App. 5th Dist. Fairfield County 2014); State v. Canada, 2015-Ohio-2167, 2015 WL 3540402 (Ohio Ct. App. 10th Dist. Franklin County 2015);

Additionally, the United States Supreme Court has held that the Confrontation Clause of the Sixth Amendment to the United States Constitution does not always require a showing of the declarant's unavailability before the admission into evidence of statements that qualify as excited utterances.[4] That Court has held, however, that in-court or out-of-court 'testimonial' statements of an unavailable declarant, offered at a criminal trial, are not admissible into evidence.[5]

State v. Mack, 2015-Ohio-5214, 2015 WL 8607454 (Ohio Ct. App. 11th Dist. Ashtabula County 2015); State v. Kerr, 2016-Ohio-965, 2016 WL 936844 (Ohio Ct. App. 2d Dist. Montgomery County 2016); Cleveland v. Williams, 2015-Ohio-1739, 2015 WL 2165564 (Ohio Ct. App. 8th Dist. Cuyahoga County 2015); State v. Martin, 2016-Ohio-225, 57 N.E.3d 411 (Ohio Ct. App. 5th Dist. Tuscarawas County 2016); State v. Knecht, 2015-Ohio-4316, 2015 WL 6125747 (Ohio Ct. App. 12th Dist. Warren County 2015), appeal not allowed, 144 Ohio St. 3d 1507, 2016-Ohio-652, 45 N.E.3d 1051 (2016); 2016 WL 936844 (Ohio Ct. App. 2d Dist. Montgomery County 2016).

[4]See Crawford v. Washington, 541 U.S. 36, 124 S. Ct. 1354, 158 L. Ed. 2d 177, 63 Fed. R. Evid. Serv. 1077 (2004); State v. Harr, 158 Ohio App. 3d 704, 2004-Ohio-5771, 821 N.E.2d 1058 (2d Dist. Clark County 2004); Fowler v. State, 809 N.E.2d 960 (Ind. Ct. App. 2004), transfer granted, opinion vacated, IN RAP 58(A), (Dec. 9, 2004) and opinion vacated, 829 N.E.2d 459 (Ind. 2005) and (abrogated by, Hammon v. State, 829 N.E.2d 444 (Ind. 2005)); Akron v. Hutton, 2005-Ohio-3300, 2005 WL 1523880 (Ohio Ct. App. 9th Dist. Summit County 2005); State v. Sanchez, 2010-Ohio-6153, 2010 WL 5235932 (Ohio Ct. App. 8th Dist. Cuyahoga County 2010); Michigan v. Bryant, 562 U.S. 344, 131 S. Ct. 1143, 179 L. Ed. 2d 93, 84 Fed. R. Evid. Serv. 1033 (2011) and § 5:17, Case preparation—Hearsay exceptions—Present sense impression; State v. Clark, 2011-Ohio-6623, 2011 WL 6780456 (Ohio Ct. App. 8th Dist. Cuyahoga County 2011), aff'd, 137 Ohio St. 3d 346, 2013-Ohio-4731, 999 N.E.2d 592 (2013), rev'd and remanded, 135 S. Ct. 2173, 192 L. Ed. 2d 306 (2015); State v. Jones, 135 Ohio St. 3d 10, 2012-Ohio-5677, 984 N.E.2d 948 (2012); State v. Flowers, 2012-Ohio-3783, 2012 WL 3595090 (Ohio Ct. App. 9th Dist. Summit County 2012); State v. Diggle, 2012-Ohio-1583, 2012 WL 1187970 (Ohio Ct. App. 3d Dist. Auglaize County 2012); State v. Auerswald, 2013-Ohio-742, 2013 WL 785061 (Ohio Ct. App. 9th Dist. Medina County 2013); State v. McClain, 2014-Ohio-93, 2014 WL 117962 (Ohio Ct. App. 10th Dist. Franklin County 2014); State v. Goshade, 2013-Ohio-4457, 2013 WL 5577906 (Ohio Ct. App. 1st Dist. Hamilton County 2013); State v. Spivey, 2013-Ohio-851, 2013 WL 937754 (Ohio Ct. App. 3d Dist. Marion County 2013); Toledo v. Green, 2015-Ohio-1864, 33 N.E.3d 581 (Ohio Ct. App. 6th Dist. Lucas County 2015); Cleveland v. Williams, 2015-Ohio-1739, 2015 WL 2165564 (Ohio Ct. App. 8th Dist. Cuyahoga County 2015); State v. Martin, 2016-Ohio-225, 57 N.E.3d 411 (Ohio Ct. App. 5th Dist. Tuscarawas County 2016); State v. Knecht, 2015-Ohio-4316, 2015 WL 6125747 (Ohio Ct. App. 12th Dist. Warren County 2015), appeal not allowed, 144 Ohio St. 3d 1507, 2016-Ohio-652, 45 N.E.3d 1051 (2016); State v. Kerr, 2016-Ohio-965, 2016 WL 936844 (Ohio Ct. App. 2d Dist. Montgomery County 2016).

[5]Davis v. Washington, 547 U.S. 813, 126 S. Ct. 2266, 165 L. Ed. 2d 224, 70 Fed. R. Evid. Serv. 472, 30 A.L.R.6th 599 (2006); State v. Harr, 158 Ohio App. 3d 704, 2004-Ohio-5771, 821 N.E.2d 1058 (2d Dist. Clark County 2004); Fowler v. State, 809 N.E.2d 960 (Ind. Ct. App. 2004), transfer granted, opinion vacated, IN RAP 58(A), (Dec. 9, 2004) and opinion vacated, 829 N.E.2d 459 (Ind. 2005) and (abrogated by, Hammon v. State, 829 N.E.2d 444 (Ind. 2005)); Akron v. Hutton, 2005-Ohio-3300, 2005 WL 1523880 (Ohio Ct. App. 9th Dist. Summit County 2005); Michigan v. Bryant, 562 U.S. 344, 131 S. Ct. 1143, 179 L. Ed. 2d 93, 84 Fed. R. Evid. Serv. 1033 (2011); State v. Arnold, 126 Ohio St. 3d 290, 2010-Ohio-2742, 933 N.E.2d 775 (2010); State v. Diggle, 2012-Ohio-1583, 2012 WL 1187970 (Ohio Ct. App. 3d Dist. Auglaize County 2012); § 5:17, Case preparation—Hearsay exceptions—Present sense impression; State v. McClain, 2014-Ohio-93, 2014 WL 117962 (Ohio Ct. App. 10th Dist. Franklin County 2014); State v. Goshade, 2013-Ohio-4457, 2013 WL 5577906 (Ohio Ct. App. 1st Dist. Hamilton County 2013); State v. Williams, 2013-Ohio-726, 987 N.E.2d 322 (Ohio Ct. App. 6th Dist. Lucas County 2013); State v. King, 2013-Ohio-1694, 2013 WL 1798337 (Ohio Ct. App. 2d Dist. Montgomery County 2013); State v. Arnold,

Crawford does not set forth definitively just what varieties of hearsay should be classed as 'testimonial.' However, the opinion specifically identifies a 'core class' of statements that fall within that category. The class includes: 1) ex parte in-court testimony or its functional equivalent-that is, material such as affidavits, custodial examinations, prior testimony that the defendant was unable to cross-examine, or similar pretrial statements that declarants would reasonably expect to be used prosecutorially, and 2) extrajudicial statements-contained in formalized testimonial materials such as affidavits, depositions, prior testimony or confessions, and statements that were made under circumstances which would lead an objective witness to reasonably believe that the statement would be available for use at a later trial.[6]

The U.S. Supreme court somewhat clarified its position on what constitutes "testimonial evidence" in its decision in *Davis v. Washington*.[7] In that case the court held that statements are non-testimonial when made in the course of police interrogations under

---

2014-Ohio-1134, 2014 WL 1339806 (Ohio Ct. App. 3d Dist. Seneca County 2014), judgment aff'd, 147 Ohio St. 3d 138, 2016-Ohio-1595, 62 N.E.3d 153 (2016); State v. Auerswald, 2013-Ohio-742, 2013 WL 785061 (Ohio Ct. App. 9th Dist. Medina County 2013); State v. Doyle, 2014-Ohio-285, 2014 WL 313139 (Ohio Ct. App. 5th Dist. Fairfield County 2014). But see State v. Clark, 137 Ohio St. 3d 346, 2013-Ohio-4731, 999 N.E.2d 592 (2013), rev'd and remanded, 135 S. Ct. 2173, 192 L. Ed. 2d 306 (2015), reversed and remanded by the U.S. Supreme Court in Ohio v. Clark, 135 S. Ct. 2173, 192 L. Ed. 2d 306 (2015); Crawford v. Washington, 541 U.S. 36, 124 S. Ct. 1354, 158 L. Ed. 2d 177, 63 Fed. R. Evid. Serv. 1077 (2004); State v. Canada, 2015-Ohio-2167, 2015 WL 3540402 (Ohio Ct. App. 10th Dist. Franklin County 2015); State v. Mack, 2015-Ohio-5214, 2015 WL 8607454 (Ohio Ct. App. 11th Dist. Ashtabula County 2015); State v. Kerr, 2016-Ohio-965, 2016 WL 936844 (Ohio Ct. App. 2d Dist. Montgomery County 2016); Cleveland v. Williams, 2015-Ohio-1739, 2015 WL 2165564 (Ohio Ct. App. 8th Dist. Cuyahoga County 2015); State v. Martin, 2016-Ohio-225, 57 N.E.3d 411 (Ohio Ct. App. 5th Dist. Tuscarawas County 2016); State v. Knecht, 2015-Ohio-4316, 2015 WL 6125747 (Ohio Ct. App. 12th Dist. Warren County 2015), appeal not allowed, 144 Ohio St. 3d 1507, 2016-Ohio-652, 45 N.E.3d 1051 (2016); Toledo v. Green, 2015-Ohio-1864, 33 N.E.3d 581 (Ohio Ct. App. 6th Dist. Lucas County 2015).

[6]Crawford v. Washington, 541 U.S. 36, 124 S. Ct. 1354, 158 L. Ed. 2d 177, 63 Fed. R. Evid. Serv. 1077 (2004) and § 5:17, Case preparation—Hearsay exceptions—Present sense impression; State v. Clark, 137 Ohio St. 3d 346, 2013-Ohio-4731, 999 N.E.2d 592 (2013), rev'd and remanded, 135 S. Ct. 2173, 192 L. Ed. 2d 306 (2015), reversed and remanded by the U.S. Supreme Court in Ohio v. Clark, 135 S. Ct. 2173, 192 L. Ed. 2d 306 (2015); State v. McClain, 2014-Ohio-93, 2014 WL 117962 (Ohio Ct. App. 10th Dist. Franklin County 2014); State v. Goshade, 2013-Ohio-4457, 2013 WL 5577906 (Ohio Ct. App. 1st Dist. Hamilton County 2013); State v. Williams, 2013-Ohio-726, 987 N.E.2d 322 (Ohio Ct. App. 6th Dist. Lucas County 2013); State v. King, 2013-Ohio-1694, 2013 WL 1798337 (Ohio Ct. App. 2d Dist. Montgomery County 2013); State v. Arnold, 2014-Ohio-1134, 2014 WL 1339806 (Ohio Ct. App. 3d Dist. Seneca County 2014), judgment aff'd, 147 Ohio St. 3d 138, 2016-Ohio-1595, 62 N.E.3d 153 (2016); State v. Doyle, 2014-Ohio-285, 2014 WL 313139 (Ohio Ct. App. 5th Dist. Fairfield County 2014).

[7]Davis v. Washington, 547 U.S. 813, 126 S. Ct. 2266, 165 L. Ed. 2d 224, 70 Fed. R. Evid. Serv. 472, 30 A.L.R.6th 599 (2006); State v. Snider, 2012-Ohio-2183, 2012 WL 1744657 (Ohio Ct. App. 5th Dist. Licking County 2012); State v. Clark, 137 Ohio St. 3d 346, 2013-Ohio-4731, 999 N.E.2d 592 (2013), rev'd and remanded, 135 S. Ct. 2173, 192 L. Ed. 2d 306 (2015), reversed and remanded by the U.S. Supreme Court in Ohio v. Clark, 135 S. Ct. 2173, 192 L. Ed. 2d 306 (2015); Crawford v. Washington, 541 U.S. 36, 124 S. Ct. 1354, 158 L. Ed. 2d 177, 63 Fed. R. Evid. Serv. 1077 (2004); State v. McClain, 2014-Ohio-93, 2014 WL 117962 (Ohio Ct. App. 10th Dist. Franklin County

circumstances objectively indicating that the primary purpose of interrogation is to enable police assistance to meet an ongoing emergency. They are testimonial when the circumstances objectively indicate that there is no such ongoing emergency, and that the primary purpose of the interrogation is to establish or prove past events potentially relevant to later criminal prosecution.

Crawford also includes under the category of 'testimonial' certain statements taken by police officers during the course of interrogations.[8] However, the court specifically declined to define when police questioning crosses from inquisitive to interrogative.[9] In *Hammon v. Indiana*, decided concurrently with *Davis v. Washington*,[10] the U.S. Supreme

---

2014); State v. Goshade, 2013-Ohio-4457, 2013 WL 5577906 (Ohio Ct. App. 1st Dist. Hamilton County 2013); State v. Williams, 2013-Ohio-726, 987 N.E.2d 322 (Ohio Ct. App. 6th Dist. Lucas County 2013); State v. King, 2013-Ohio-1694, 2013 WL 1798337 (Ohio Ct. App. 2d Dist. Montgomery County 2013); Toledo v. Green, 2015-Ohio-1864, 33 N.E.3d 581 (Ohio Ct. App. 6th Dist. Lucas County 2015).

[8]Davis v. Washington, 547 U.S. 813, 126 S. Ct. 2266, 165 L. Ed. 2d 224, 70 Fed. R. Evid. Serv. 472, 30 A.L.R.6th 599 (2006). See also Crawford v. Washington, 541 U.S. 36, 124 S. Ct. 1354, 158 L. Ed. 2d 177, 63 Fed. R. Evid. Serv. 1077 (2004); State v. Eicholtz, 2013-Ohio-302, 2013 WL 425820 (Ohio Ct. App. 2d Dist. Clark County 2013); § 5:17, Case preparation—Hearsay exceptions—Present sense impression; State v. Clark, 137 Ohio St. 3d 346, 2013-Ohio-4731, 999 N.E.2d 592 (2013), rev'd and remanded, 135 S. Ct. 2173, 192 L. Ed. 2d 306 (2015), reversed and remanded by the U.S. Supreme Court in Ohio v. Clark, 135 S. Ct. 2173, 192 L. Ed. 2d 306 (2015); State v. McClain, 2014-Ohio-93, 2014 WL 117962 (Ohio Ct. App. 10th Dist. Franklin County 2014); State v. Goshade, 2013-Ohio-4457, 2013 WL 5577906 (Ohio Ct. App. 1st Dist. Hamilton County 2013); State v. Williams, 2013-Ohio-726, 987 N.E.2d 322 (Ohio Ct. App. 6th Dist. Lucas County 2013); State v. King, 2013-Ohio-1694, 2013 WL 1798337 (Ohio Ct. App. 2d Dist. Montgomery County 2013); State v. Norris, 2015-Ohio-624, 2015 WL 753346 (Ohio Ct. App. 2d Dist. Montgomery County 2015); State v. Kerr, 2016-Ohio-965, 2016 WL 936844 (Ohio Ct. App. 2d Dist. Montgomery County 2016).

[9]Crawford v. Washington, 541 U.S. 36, 124 S. Ct. 1354, 158 L. Ed. 2d 177, 63 Fed. R. Evid. Serv. 1077 (2004) and § 5:17, Case preparation—Hearsay exceptions—Present sense impression; State v. Clark, 137 Ohio St. 3d 346, 2013-Ohio-4731, 999 N.E.2d 592 (2013), rev'd and remanded, 135 S. Ct. 2173, 192 L. Ed. 2d 306 (2015), reversed and remanded by the U.S. Supreme Court in Ohio v. Clark, 135 S. Ct. 2173, 192 L. Ed. 2d 306 (2015); State v. McClain, 2014-Ohio-93, 2014 WL 117962 (Ohio Ct. App. 10th Dist. Franklin County 2014); State v. Arnold, 2014-Ohio-1134, 2014 WL 1339806 (Ohio Ct. App. 3d Dist. Seneca County 2014), judgment aff'd, 147 Ohio St. 3d 138, 2016-Ohio-1595, 62 N.E.3d 153 (2016); State v. Goshade, 2013-Ohio-4457, 2013 WL 5577906 (Ohio Ct. App. 1st Dist. Hamilton County 2013); State v. Williams, 2013-Ohio-726, 987 N.E.2d 322 (Ohio Ct. App. 6th Dist. Lucas County 2013); State v. King, 2013-Ohio-1694, 2013 WL 1798337 (Ohio Ct. App. 2d Dist. Montgomery County 2013); State v. Doyle, 2014-Ohio-285, 2014 WL 313139 (Ohio Ct. App. 5th Dist. Fairfield County 2014).

[10]Davis v. Washington, 547 U.S. 813, 126 S. Ct. 2266, 165 L. Ed. 2d 224, 70 Fed. R. Evid. Serv. 472, 30 A.L.R.6th 599 (2006); State v. Eicholtz, 2013-Ohio-302, 2013 WL 425820 (Ohio Ct. App. 2d Dist. Clark County 2013); State v. Clark, 137 Ohio St. 3d 346, 2013-Ohio-4731, 999 N.E.2d 592 (2013), rev'd and remanded, 135 S. Ct. 2173, 192 L. Ed. 2d 306 (2015), reversed and remanded by the U.S. Supreme Court in Ohio v. Clark, 135 S. Ct. 2173, 192 L. Ed. 2d 306 (2015); Crawford v. Washington, 541 U.S. 36, 124 S. Ct. 1354, 158 L. Ed. 2d 177, 63 Fed. R. Evid. Serv. 1077 (2004); State v. McClain, 2014-Ohio-93, 2014 WL 117962 (Ohio Ct. App. 10th Dist. Franklin County 2014); State v. Arnold, 2014-Ohio-1134, 2014 WL 1339806 (Ohio Ct. App. 3d Dist. Seneca County 2014), judgment aff'd, 147 Ohio St. 3d 138, 2016-Ohio-1595, 62 N.E.3d 153 (2016); State v. Goshade, 2013-Ohio-4457, 2013 WL 5577906 (Ohio Ct. App. 1st Dist. Hamilton County 2013); State v. Williams, 2013-Ohio-726, 987 N.E.2d 322 (Ohio Ct. App. 6th Dist. Lucas County 2013); State v. King, 2013-Ohio-1694, 2013 WL

Court identified and differentiated two varieties of statements likely to be given to police officers responding to emergency calls. Statements taken by police officers in the course of an interrogation are "non-testimonial," and not subject to the Confrontation Clause, when they are made under circumstances objectively indicating that the primary purpose of the interrogation is to enable police assistance to meet an ongoing emergency. Statements taken by a police officer in the course of interrogation are "testimonial," and subject to the Confrontation Clause, when the circumstances objectively indicate that there is no ongoing emergency, and that the primary purpose of the interrogation is to establish or prove past events potentially relevant to later criminal prosecution.[11] The Court also held that it considered 911 operators to be, at least, agents of the police when they interrogate callers for 911 services. Their acts, therefore, were considered in *Davis* to be the acts of the police and potentially "testimonial." As such, interrogations conducted by these operators must meet the same standards imposed on the police themselves when judging whether the statements that they elicit from callers are "testimonial" or "non-testimonial." Additionally, *Davis* makes plain that interrogations by the police or their agents that initially aim at determining the need for emergency services, can change into interrogations aimed at eliciting testimonial evidence.[12] The Court stated its belief that the trial courts will recognize the point at which, for Sixth Amendment purposes, statements in response to interrogations

---

1798337 (Ohio Ct. App. 2d Dist. Montgomery County 2013); State v. Doyle, 2014-Ohio-285, 2014 WL 313139 (Ohio Ct. App. 5th Dist. Fairfield County 2014); State v. Norris, 2015-Ohio-624, 2015 WL 753346 (Ohio Ct. App. 2d Dist. Montgomery County 2015).

[11]Davis v. Washington, 547 U.S. 813, 126 S. Ct. 2266, 165 L. Ed. 2d 224, 70 Fed. R. Evid. Serv. 472, 30 A.L.R.6th 599 (2006); State v. Snider, 2012-Ohio-2183, 2012 WL 1744657 (Ohio Ct. App. 5th Dist. Licking County 2012); State v. Clark, 137 Ohio St. 3d 346, 2013-Ohio-4731, 999 N.E.2d 592 (2013), rev'd and remanded, 135 S. Ct. 2173, 192 L. Ed. 2d 306 (2015), reversed and remanded by the U.S. Supreme Court in Ohio v. Clark, 135 S. Ct. 2173, 192 L. Ed. 2d 306 (2015). Crawford v. Washington, 541 U.S. 36, 124 S. Ct. 1354, 158 L. Ed. 2d 177, 63 Fed. R. Evid. Serv. 1077 (2004); State v. McClain, 2014-Ohio-93, 2014 WL 117962 (Ohio Ct. App. 10th Dist. Franklin County 2014); State v. Arnold, 2014-Ohio-1134, 2014 WL 1339806 (Ohio Ct. App. 3d Dist. Seneca County 2014), judgment aff'd, 147 Ohio St. 3d 138, 2016-Ohio-1595, 62 N.E.3d 153 (2016); State v. Goshade, 2013-Ohio-4457, 2013 WL 5577906 (Ohio Ct. App. 1st Dist. Hamilton County 2013); State v. Williams, 2013-Ohio-726, 987 N.E.2d 322 (Ohio Ct. App. 6th Dist. Lucas County 2013); State v. King, 2013-Ohio-1694, 2013 WL 1798337 (Ohio Ct. App. 2d Dist. Montgomery County 2013); State v. Doyle, 2014-Ohio-285, 2014 WL 313139 (Ohio Ct. App. 5th Dist. Fairfield County 2014).

[12]Davis v. Washington, 547 U.S. 813, 126 S. Ct. 2266, 165 L. Ed. 2d 224, 70 Fed. R. Evid. Serv. 472, 30 A.L.R.6th 599 (2006); State v. Clark, 137 Ohio St. 3d 346, 2013-Ohio-4731, 999 N.E.2d 592 (2013), rev'd and remanded, 135 S. Ct. 2173, 192 L. Ed. 2d 306 (2015), reversed and remanded by the U.S. Supreme Court in Ohio v. Clark, 135 S. Ct. 2173, 192 L. Ed. 2d 306 (2015) Crawford v. Washington, 541 U.S. 36, 124 S. Ct. 1354, 158 L. Ed. 2d 177, 63 Fed. R. Evid. Serv. 1077 (2004); State v. McClain, 2014-Ohio-93, 2014 WL 117962 (Ohio Ct. App. 10th Dist. Franklin County 2014); State v. Arnold, 2014-Ohio-1134, 2014 WL 1339806 (Ohio Ct. App. 3d Dist. Seneca County 2014), judgment aff'd, 147 Ohio St. 3d 138, 2016-Ohio-1595, 62 N.E.3d 153 (2016); State v. Goshade, 2013-Ohio-4457, 2013 WL 5577906 (Ohio Ct. App. 1st Dist. Hamilton County 2013); State v. Williams, 2013-Ohio-726, 987 N.E.2d 322 (Ohio Ct. App. 6th Dist. Lucas County 2013); State v. King, 2013-Ohio-1694, 2013 WL 1798337 (Ohio Ct. App. 2d Dist. Montgomery County 2013); State v. Doyle, 2014-Ohio-285, 2014 WL 313139 (Ohio Ct. App. 5th Dist. Fairfield County 2014).

become testimonial and will redact and exclude those statements that fall into that category from evidence.[13]

The U.S. Supreme Court has recognized, however, that certain criminal defendants may forfeit their right to confront a witness whose absence the defendant, or someone acting with the defendant's explicit or implicit approval, wrongfully procured.[14]

The Supreme Court of Ohio has stated that the right to face-to-face confrontation afforded to a criminal defendant under the state's constitution may require the prosecution, in some instances, to establish that a witness is truly unavailable before the witness's extrajudicial statements may be properly admitted into evidence at trial. In this, the Ohio Supreme Court is in full accord with the U.S. Supreme Court.[15]

Whether or not a particular excited utterance should be admitted

---

[13]Davis v. Washington, 547 U.S. 813, 126 S. Ct. 2266, 165 L. Ed. 2d 224, 70 Fed. R. Evid. Serv. 472, 30 A.L.R.6th 599 (2006); State v. Clark, 137 Ohio St. 3d 346, 2013-Ohio-4731, 999 N.E.2d 592 (2013), rev'd and remanded, 135 S. Ct. 2173, 192 L. Ed. 2d 306 (2015), reversed and remanded by the U.S. Supreme Court in Ohio v. Clark, 135 S. Ct. 2173, 192 L. Ed. 2d 306 (2015). Crawford v. Washington, 541 U.S. 36, 124 S. Ct. 1354, 158 L. Ed. 2d 177, 63 Fed. R. Evid. Serv. 1077 (2004); State v. McClain, 2014-Ohio-93, 2014 WL 117962 (Ohio Ct. App. 10th Dist. Franklin County 2014); State v. Arnold, 2014-Ohio-1134, 2014 WL 1339806 (Ohio Ct. App. 3d Dist. Seneca County 2014), judgment aff'd, 147 Ohio St. 3d 138, 2016-Ohio-1595, 62 N.E.3d 153 (2016); State v. Goshade, 2013-Ohio-4457, 2013 WL 5577906 (Ohio Ct. App. 1st Dist. Hamilton County 2013); State v. Williams, 2013-Ohio-726, 987 N.E.2d 322 (Ohio Ct. App. 6th Dist. Lucas County 2013); State v. King, 2013-Ohio-1694, 2013 WL 1798337 (Ohio Ct. App. 2d Dist. Montgomery County 2013); State v. Doyle, 2014-Ohio-285, 2014 WL 313139 (Ohio Ct. App. 5th Dist. Fairfield County 2014).

[14]Davis v. Washington, 547 U.S. 813, 126 S. Ct. 2266, 165 L. Ed. 2d 224, 70 Fed. R. Evid. Serv. 472, 30 A.L.R.6th 599 (2006). See also Crawford v. Washington, 541 U.S. 36, 124 S. Ct. 1354, 158 L. Ed. 2d 177, 63 Fed. R. Evid. Serv. 1077 (2004), citing Reynolds v. U.S., 98 U.S. 145, 25 L. Ed. 244, 1878 WL 18416 (1878). See also Motes v. U.S., 178 U.S. 458, 20 S. Ct. 993, 44 L. Ed. 1150 (1900). But see Giles v. California, 554 U.S. 353, 361, 128 S. Ct. 2678, 171 L. Ed. 2d 488 (2008); Ervin v. U.S., 2011 WL 2312564 (N.D. Ohio 2011); State v. Clark, 137 Ohio St. 3d 346, 2013-Ohio-4731, 999 N.E.2d 592 (2013), rev'd and remanded, 135 S. Ct. 2173, 192 L. Ed. 2d 306 (2015), reversed and remanded by the U.S. Supreme Court in Ohio v. Clark, 135 S. Ct. 2173, 192 L. Ed. 2d 306 (2015). Crawford v. Washington, 541 U.S. 36, 124 S. Ct. 1354, 158 L. Ed. 2d 177, 63 Fed. R. Evid. Serv. 1077 (2004); State v. McClain, 2014-Ohio-93, 2014 WL 117962 (Ohio Ct. App. 10th Dist. Franklin County 2014); State v. Arnold, 2014-Ohio-1134, 2014 WL 1339806 (Ohio Ct. App. 3d Dist. Seneca County 2014), judgment aff'd, 147 Ohio St. 3d 138, 2016-Ohio-1595, 62 N.E.3d 153 (2016); State v. Goshade, 2013-Ohio-4457, 2013 WL 5577906 (Ohio Ct. App. 1st Dist. Hamilton County 2013); State v. Williams, 2013-Ohio-726, 987 N.E.2d 322 (Ohio Ct. App. 6th Dist. Lucas County 2013); State v. King, 2013-Ohio-1694, 2013 WL 1798337 (Ohio Ct. App. 2d Dist. Montgomery County 2013); State v. Doyle, 2014-Ohio-285, 2014 WL 313139 (Ohio Ct. App. 5th Dist. Fairfield County 2014); State v. Pickens, 141 Ohio St. 3d 462, 2014-Ohio-5445, 25 N.E.3d 1023 (2014); State v. Martin, 2016-Ohio-225, 57 N.E.3d 411 (Ohio Ct. App. 5th Dist. Tuscarawas County 2016).

[15]Evid.R. 804; State v. Storch, 66 Ohio St. 3d 280, 294, 1993-Ohio-38, 612 N.E.2d 305 (1993). But see Ohio v. Roberts, 448 U.S. 56, 100 S. Ct. 2531, 65 L. Ed. 2d 597, 7 Fed. R. Evid. Serv. 1 (1980) (abrogated by, Crawford v. Washington, 541 U.S. 36, 124 S. Ct. 1354, 158 L. Ed. 2d 177, 63 Fed. R. Evid. Serv. 1077 (2004)); State v. Muncey, 1999 WL 59675 (Ohio Ct. App. 12th Dist. Madison County 1999); State v. Tabor, 2012-Ohio-4642, 2012 WL 4761741 (Ohio Ct. App. 12th Dist. Warren County 2012). See also State v. Clark, 137 Ohio St. 3d 346, 2013-Ohio-4731, 999 N.E.2d 592 (2013), rev'd and remanded, 135 S. Ct. 2173, 192 L. Ed. 2d 306 (2015), reversed and remanded by the U.S. Supreme Court in Ohio v. Clark, 135 S. Ct. 2173, 192 L. Ed. 2d 306

into evidence is a decision appropriately left to the trial judge.[16] Unless the defendant can establish that the trial court's decision to admit the statement was unreasonable, the trial court's decision should stand, even if on appeal, the reviewing court concludes that it would have come to a different decision had it been sitting as the trier-of-fact.[17]

Q & A: If, ten minutes after an attack, a victim of domestic violence drives five miles to a police station to report the incident, will the statement made still qualify as an excited utterance, despite the intervening time?

Applying the test announced in *Davis*, probably not. The victim at the time that these statements were made was not facing an emergency situation and was in no imminent danger. The statements therefore were made primarily to report on past events and to provide information that might be used in the future prosecution of the alleged offender.[18]

(2015); Crawford v. Washington, 541 U.S. 36, 124 S. Ct. 1354, 158 L. Ed. 2d 177, 63 Fed. R. Evid. Serv. 1077 (2004); State v. Martin, 2016-Ohio-225, 57 N.E.3d 411 (Ohio Ct. App. 5th Dist. Tuscarawas County 2016); State v. Arnold, 147 Ohio St. 3d 138, 2016-Ohio-1595, 62 N.E.3d 153 (2016); State v. Clark, 2011-Ohio-6623, 2011 WL 6780456 (Ohio Ct. App. 8th Dist. Cuyahoga County 2011), aff'd, 137 Ohio St. 3d 346, 2013-Ohio-4731, 999 N.E.2d 592 (2013), rev'd and remanded, 135 S. Ct. 2173, 192 L. Ed. 2d 306 (2015). See also State v. Clark, 2016-Ohio-2825, 2016 WL 2586638 (Ohio Ct. App. 8th Dist. Cuyahoga County 2016), appeal not allowed, 147 Ohio St. 3d 1474, 2016-Ohio-8438, 65 N.E.3d 778 (2016).

[16]State v. Taylor, 66 Ohio St. 3d 295, 612 N.E.2d 316 (1993); State v. Cornell, 129 Ohio App. 3d 106, 717 N.E.2d 361 (10th Dist. Franklin County 1998); State v. Clifford, 2002-Ohio-4531, 2002 WL 2010639, *7 (Ohio Ct. App. 9th Dist. Summit County 2002); State v. Shaffer, 2002-Ohio-4167, 2002 WL 1873443, *3 (Ohio Ct. App. 4th Dist. Pickaway County 2002); State v. Cannaday, 2005-Ohio-1513, 2005 WL 736583 (Ohio Ct. App. 10th Dist. Franklin County 2005); Mayfield v. Cuccarese, 2008-Ohio-1812, 2008 WL 1747439 (Ohio Ct. App. 8th Dist. Cuyahoga County 2008); State v. Cunningham, 2012-Ohio-2333, 2012 WL 1900149 (Ohio Ct. App. 2d Dist. Clark County 2012); State v. Matthews, 2011-Ohio-5066, 2011 WL 4529667 (Ohio Ct. App. 2d Dist. Montgomery County 2011); State v. Sutphin, 2011-Ohio-5157, 2011 WL 4600412 (Ohio Ct. App. 8th Dist. Cuyahoga County 2011); Toledo v. Huggins, 2013-Ohio-3467, 2013 WL 4041572 (Ohio Ct. App. 6th Dist. Lucas County 2013); State v. Knecht, 2015-Ohio-4316, 2015 WL 6125747 (Ohio Ct. App. 12th Dist. Warren County 2015), appeal not allowed, 144 Ohio St. 3d 1507, 2016-Ohio-652, 45 N.E.3d 1051 (2016).

[17]State v. Taylor, 66 Ohio St. 3d 295, 612 N.E.2d 316 (1993); State v. Griffitts, 2002-Ohio-921, 2002 WL 252786, *4 (Ohio Ct. App. 2d Dist. Montgomery County 2002); State v. Dawson, 2001-Ohio-3977, 2001 WL 1568406, *6 (Ohio Ct. App. 10th Dist. Franklin County 2001); State v. Nixon, 2012-Ohio-1292, 2012 WL 1032891 (Ohio Ct. App. 12th Dist. Warren County 2012); Toledo v. Huggins, 2013-Ohio-3467, 2013 WL 4041572 (Ohio Ct. App. 6th Dist. Lucas County 2013). But see the dissent in State v. Arnold, 2014-Ohio-1134, 2014 WL 1339806 (Ohio Ct. App. 3d Dist. Seneca County 2014), judgment aff'd, 147 Ohio St. 3d 138, 2016-Ohio-1595, 62 N.E.3d 153 (2016).

[18]Davis v. Washington, 547 U.S. 813, 126 S. Ct. 2266, 165 L. Ed. 2d 224, 70 Fed. R. Evid. Serv. 472, 30 A.L.R.6th 599 (2006). See also the concurring opinion in State v. Harris, 163 Ohio App. 3d 286, 2005-Ohio-4696, 837 N.E.2d 830 (1st Dist. Hamilton County 2005); State v. Hall, 2012-Ohio-266, 2012 WL 253317 (Ohio Ct. App. 8th Dist. Cuyahoga County 2012); State v. Clark, 2011-Ohio-6623, 2011 WL 6780456 (Ohio Ct. App. 8th Dist. Cuyahoga County 2011), aff'd, 137 Ohio St. 3d 346, 2013-Ohio-4731, 999 N.E.2d 592 (2013), rev'd and remanded, 135 S. Ct. 2173, 192 L. Ed. 2d 306 (2015), reversed and remanded by the U.S. Supreme Court in Ohio v. Clark, 135 S. Ct. 2173, 192 L. Ed. 2d 306 (2015), Crawford v. Washington, 541 U.S. 36, 124 S. Ct.

Q & A: At trial, the prosecution asks the court to allow the admission of the written statement of the victim who drove to the police station. The prosecution contends that this document is just the memorialization of the victim's excited utterance. The defense objects. Should the court sustain the objection?

Yes. Generally, a written statement is more likely the product of reflective thought than an oral recitation of events and more likely prepared rather than spontaneous. It, therefore, lacks the necessary indicia for exclusion from the operation of the hearsay rule.[19]

Q & A: Is the spontaneity of a declarant's statement to the responding or investigating officer destroyed by the officer's questions to clarify the declarant's original pronouncements?

No. The key considerations which the trial court must ponder in deciding whether to allow a statement into evidence as an exception to the hearsay rule are:

(1) the lapse of time between the event and the declaration,
(2) the mental and physical condition of the declarant,
(3) the nature of the statement,
(4) the influence of intervening circumstances,[20] and
(5) is the statement "testimonial"?

Q & A: The victim of an alleged incident of domestic violence failed to appear for court. The prosecution attempted to admit the victim's tape-recorded statements from the 911 call that was placed at the time of the event. The prosecutor maintained that these statements were excited utterances and, therefore, qualified for exemption from the operation of the hearsay rule. The defense objected. Should the court sustain the objection?

1354, 158 L. Ed. 2d 177, 63 Fed. R. Evid. Serv. 1077 (2004); State v. Parks, 2011-Ohio-3037, 2011 WL 2464198 (Ohio Ct. App. 5th Dist. Stark County 2011).

[19]Davis v. Washington, 547 U.S. 813, 126 S. Ct. 2266, 165 L. Ed. 2d 224, 70 Fed. R. Evid. Serv. 472, 30 A.L.R.6th 599 (2006). See also State v. Justice, 92 Ohio App. 3d 740, 637 N.E.2d 85 (9th Dist. Wayne County 1994); State v. Conigliaro, 356 N.J. Super. 54, 65, 811 A.2d 491, 497 (App. Div. 2002). But see State v. Nixon, 2012-Ohio-1292, 2012 WL 1032891 (Ohio Ct. App. 12th Dist. Warren County 2012); State v. Clark, 137 Ohio St. 3d 346, 2013-Ohio-4731, 999 N.E.2d 592 (2013), rev'd and remanded, 135 S. Ct. 2173, 192 L. Ed. 2d 306 (2015), reversed and remanded by the U.S. Supreme Court in Ohio v. Clark, 135 S. Ct. 2173, 192 L. Ed. 2d 306 (2015), Crawford v. Washington, 541 U.S. 36, 124 S. Ct. 1354, 158 L. Ed. 2d 177, 63 Fed. R. Evid. Serv. 1077 (2004); State v. McClain, 2014-Ohio-93, 2014 WL 117962 (Ohio Ct. App. 10th Dist. Franklin County 2014); State v. Goshade, 2013-Ohio-4457, 2013 WL 5577906 (Ohio Ct. App. 1st Dist. Hamilton County 2013); State v. Williams, 2013-Ohio-726, 987 N.E.2d 322 (Ohio Ct. App. 6th Dist. Lucas County 2013). But see the dissent in State v. Arnold, 2014-Ohio-1134, 2014 WL 1339806 (Ohio Ct. App. 3d Dist. Seneca County 2014), judgment aff'd, 147 Ohio St. 3d 138, 2016-Ohio-1595, 62 N.E.3d 153 (2016).

[20]Miles v. General Tire & Rubber Co., 10 Ohio App. 3d 186, 460 N.E.2d 1377 (10th Dist. Franklin County 1983); State v. Ledbetter, 1989 WL 114314 (Ohio Ct. App. 12th Dist. Clermont County 1989), dismissed, 49 Ohio St. 3d 712, 552 N.E.2d 945 (1990), reversed sub nom. Ledbetter v. Edwards, 35 F.3d 1062, 1994 FED App. 0330P (6th Cir. 1994); State v. Perdue, 1993 WL 546609 (Ohio Ct. App. 7th Dist. Mahoning County 1993); State v. Louk, 2002-Ohio-988, 2002 WL 358639, *2 (Ohio Ct. App. 5th Dist. Delaware County 2002); State v. Hill, 2002-Ohio-227, 2002 WL 109297, *5 (Ohio Ct. App. 5th Dist. Fairfield County 2002); State v. Rocker, 1996 WL 490687, *5 (Ohio Ct. App. 5th Dist. Guernsey County 1996).

It depends. The court must first determine if the statement is admissible consistent with the requirements of the Confrontation Clause, according to the test established in *Davis*.[21] That is, is it "testimonial" or "non-testimonial"? If the court determines that the statement is non-testimonial, the court should move forward to determine whether the statement meets the four part test for the excited utterance exception to the hearsay rule: (1) was there a startling occurrence; (2) was the statement made before the declarant had time to reflect on it; (3) was the statement related to the startling occurrence; and (4) did the declarant have personal knowledge of the matters asserted in the declaration?

If the statement passes both tests, the objection should be overruled.

Q & A: Can the prosecution, in its case-in-chief, present, through the testimony of a responding officer, the statement of the victim that the defendant beat her unconscious if the victim now plans to testify on behalf of the defendant at trial?

Yes. Whether the victim testifies in the prosecution's case-in-chief, on rebuttal, or for the defense is immaterial. If the victim appears, and is subject to cross-examination relative to the out-of-court statements made, the Confrontation Clause is satisfied.[22]

Q & A: Can the court admit into evidence an unidentified caller's statement to a police dispatcher that "He's going to kill me!"?

Yes, if the prosecution lays a proper foundation to establish a nexus between the statement and its relevance to the matter on trial, the statement can be admitted.[23]

§ 5:16 Case preparation—Hearsay exceptions—Excited utterance—Inadmissibility of testimonial hearsay

The U.S. Supreme Court has identified testimonial hearsay as particularly offensive to the Confrontation Clause of the Sixth Amend-

[21]Davis v. Washington, 547 U.S. 813, 126 S. Ct. 2266, 165 L. Ed. 2d 224, 70 Fed. R. Evid. Serv. 472, 30 A.L.R.6th 599 (2006). See also Michigan v. Bryant, 562 U.S. 344, 131 S. Ct. 1143, 179 L. Ed. 2d 93, 84 Fed. R. Evid. Serv. 1033 (2011); State v. Peeples, 2009-Ohio-1198, 2009 WL 737922 (Ohio Ct. App. 7th Dist. Mahoning County 2009); Toledo v. Sailes, 180 Ohio App. 3d 56, 2008-Ohio-6400, 904 N.E.2d 543 (6th Dist. Lucas County 2008); State v. Rufus, 2008-Ohio-5478, 2008 WL 4681392 (Ohio Ct. App. 8th Dist. Cuyahoga County 2008); State v. Moorer, 2009-Ohio-1494, 2009 WL 818945 (Ohio Ct. App. 9th Dist. Summit County 2009); State v. McClain, 2014-Ohio-93, 2014 WL 117962 (Ohio Ct. App. 10th Dist. Franklin County 2014); Conley v. Warden, Ross Correctional Inst., 2013 WL 1787384 (S.D. Ohio 2013); State v. Clark, 137 Ohio St. 3d 346, 2013-Ohio-4731, 999 N.E.2d 592 (2013), rev'd and remanded, 135 S. Ct. 2173, 192 L. Ed. 2d 306 (2015); Toledo v. Green, 2015-Ohio-1864, 33 N.E.3d 581 (Ohio Ct. App. 6th Dist. Lucas County 2015); In re A.K., 2015-Ohio-30, 2015 WL 132426 (Ohio Ct. App. 2d Dist. Montgomery County 2015); State v. Norris, 2015-Ohio-624, 2015 WL 753346 (Ohio Ct. App. 2d Dist. Montgomery County 2015).

[22]U.S. Const., Amend. 6. See also State v. Jeffries, 2006-Ohio-828, 2006 WL 438701 (Ohio Ct. App. 5th Dist. Stark County 2006); State v. Burgess, 2006-Ohio-772, 2006 WL 401273 (Ohio Ct. App. 2d Dist. Montgomery County 2006); State v. Johnson, 2006-Ohio-5195, 2006 WL 2796826 (Ohio Ct. App. 12th Dist. Butler County 2006), judgment rev'd, 116 Ohio St. 3d 541, 2008-Ohio-69, 880 N.E.2d 896 (2008).

[23]State v. Stewart, 75 Ohio App. 3d 141, 598 N.E.2d 1275 (11th Dist. Ashtabula County 1991); State v. Lenoir, 2003-Ohio-2820, 2003 WL 21267227 (Ohio Ct. App. 2d Dist. Montgomery County 2003).

ment to the Constitution of the United States.[1] The Court points out that the principal evil that the Confrontation Clause was directed against was the civil-law mode of criminal procedure, and particularly the use of ex parte examinations as evidence against an accused.[2] The Court further points out that the Confrontation Clause applies not only to in-court testimony, but also to out-of-court statements offered at trial.

To leave the regulation of out-of-court statements to the law of evidence, the Court notes, would render the clause powerless to prevent even the most flagrant inquisitorial practices.[3] In rejecting its earlier holding in *Ohio v. Roberts*,[4] the Supreme Court pointed out that Roberts conditioned the admissibility of all hearsay evidence on whether it falls under a firmly rooted hearsay exception or bears particularized guarantees of trustworthiness, that is, its "reliability."[5] The Court went on to take the position that it is unlikely that the Founders meant the Sixth Amendment's protections to be left to the vagaries of rules of evidence, much less to amorphous notions of "reliability."[6]

The *Crawford* court declared that in the case of non-testimonial

---

[Section 5:16]

[1]Davis v. Washington, 547 U.S. 813, 126 S. Ct. 2266, 165 L. Ed. 2d 224, 70 Fed. R. Evid. Serv. 472, 30 A.L.R.6th 599 (2006) (decided concurrently with Hammon v. Indiana). See also Crawford v. Washington, 541 U.S. 36, 124 S. Ct. 1354, 158 L. Ed. 2d 177, 63 Fed. R. Evid. Serv. 1077 (2004); State v. Peeples, 2009-Ohio-1198, 2009 WL 737922 (Ohio Ct. App. 7th Dist. Mahoning County 2009); Toledo v. Sailes, 180 Ohio App. 3d 56, 2008-Ohio-6400, 904 N.E.2d 543 (6th Dist. Lucas County 2008); State v. Rufus, 2008-Ohio-5478, 2008 WL 4681392 (Ohio Ct. App. 8th Dist. Cuyahoga County 2008); State v. Moorer, 2009-Ohio-1494, 2009 WL 818945 (Ohio Ct. App. 9th Dist. Summit County 2009); State v. Smith, 2008-Ohio-5985, 2008 WL 4951646 (Ohio Ct. App. 8th Dist. Cuyahoga County 2008).

[2]Crawford v. Washington, 541 U.S. 36, 124 S. Ct. 1354, 158 L. Ed. 2d 177, 63 Fed. R. Evid. Serv. 1077 (2004).

[3]Crawford v. Washington, 541 U.S. 36, 124 S. Ct. 1354, 158 L. Ed. 2d 177, 63 Fed. R. Evid. Serv. 1077 (2004).

[4]Ohio v. Roberts, 448 U.S. 56, 100 S. Ct. 2531, 65 L. Ed. 2d 597, 7 Fed. R. Evid. Serv. 1 (1980) (abrogated by, Crawford v. Washington, 541 U.S. 36, 124 S. Ct. 1354, 158 L. Ed. 2d 177, 63 Fed. R. Evid. Serv. 1077 (2004)); Fields v. Birkett, 461 Fed. Appx. 454 (6th Cir. 2012); U.S. v. Alexander, 467 Fed. Appx. 355 (6th Cir. 2012); U.S. v. Kokoski, 435 Fed. Appx. 472 (6th Cir. 2011); Bullcoming v. New Mexico, 564 U.S. 647, 131 S. Ct. 2705, 180 L. Ed. 2d 610 (2011); Chinn v. Warden, Mansfield Correctional Inst., 2011 WL 5338973 (S.D. Ohio 2011); Robertson v. Warden, Southern Ohio Correctional Facility, 2011 WL 5999032 (S.D. Ohio 2011), report and recommendation adopted, 2011 WL 5999604 (S.D. Ohio 2011), aff'd, 517 Fed. Appx. 404 (6th Cir. 2013); Jordan v. Sheets, 2012 WL 553091 (S.D. Ohio 2012), report and recommendation adopted, 2012 WL 2562428 (S.D. Ohio 2012); State v. Love, 2011-Ohio-4147, 2011 WL 3654577 (Ohio Ct. App. 4th Dist. Gallia County 2011); State v. Clark, 137 Ohio St. 3d 346, 2013-Ohio-4731, 999 N.E.2d 592 (2013), rev'd and remanded, 135 S. Ct. 2173, 192 L. Ed. 2d 306 (2015), reversed and remanded by the U.S. Supreme Court in Ohio v. Clark, 135 S. Ct. 2173, 192 L. Ed. 2d 306 (2015), Crawford v. Washington, 541 U.S. 36, 124 S. Ct. 1354, 158 L. Ed. 2d 177, 63 Fed. R. Evid. Serv. 1077 (2004); Toledo v. Green, 2015-Ohio-1864, 33 N.E.3d 581 (Ohio Ct. App. 6th Dist. Lucas County 2015).

[5]Crawford v. Washington, 541 U.S. 36, 124 S. Ct. 1354, 158 L. Ed. 2d 177, 63 Fed. R. Evid. Serv. 1077 (2004).

[6]Crawford v. Washington, 541 U.S. 36, 124 S. Ct. 1354, 158 L. Ed. 2d 177, 63 Fed. R. Evid. Serv. 1077 (2004).

hearsay, it is wholly consistent with the Framers' design that the States be afforded flexibility in the development of their individual hearsay laws. Thus, a *Roberts*-type approach that exempts such nontestimonial hearsay statements from Confrontation Clause scrutiny altogether can still pass constitutional muster.[7]

The admission or exclusion of a hearsay statement that falls into this core class of proffered evidence turns upon the definition of the term, "testimonial." *Crawford* provides some guidance in this regard by holding that, at a minimum, the term applies to hearsay derived from prior testimony before a grand jury, or at a former trial, and to hearsay obtained from police interrogations, since these are the modern practices that have the closest kinship to the abuses that the Confrontation Clause was drafted to address.[8] In order to bring some clarity, *Crawford* also undertook a working definition of the term "interrogation," which it defined as in it colloquial, rather than any technical sense. As such it specifically referenced statements taken by police officers in the course of interrogations and recorded statements knowingly given in response to structured police questioning.[9]

The *Crawford* Court left open for another day any effort to spell out a comprehensive definition of the term, "testimonial."

Q & A: The alleged victim in a domestic violence complaint refuses to testify at trial. The prosecution offers as evidence so-called "excited utterances" made by the victim to the officer who responded to the scene and took the victim's statement. How should the court rule on the defendant's objection to the admissibility of this evidence?

An Ohio Appellate court ruled on this specific issue after the U.S. Supreme Court's decision in *Crawford v. Washington*.[10] That Ohio court held that such statements are clearly testimonial in nature and are of the type contemplated as inadmissible by *Crawford*.[11] The Byrd court reasoned that, since the witness did not testify at trial, the defendant was unable to cross-examine statements allegedly made to the investigating officer.[12] Further, the court held that the defendant was correct in asserting that a reasonable complaining witness would

[7]Crawford v. Washington, 541 U.S. 36, 124 S. Ct. 1354, 158 L. Ed. 2d 177, 63 Fed. R. Evid. Serv. 1077 (2004); Williams v. Illinois, 567 U.S. 50, 132 S. Ct. 2221, 183 L. Ed. 2d 89, 83 A.L.R. Fed. 2d 649 (2012); Thompson v. Warden, Warren Correctional Inst., 2014 WL 2515317 (S.D. Ohio 2014), report and recommendation adopted, 2014 WL 2931416 (S.D. Ohio 2014).

[8]Crawford v. Washington, 541 U.S. 36, 124 S. Ct. 1354, 158 L. Ed. 2d 177, 63 Fed. R. Evid. Serv. 1077 (2004).

[9]Crawford v. Washington, 541 U.S. 36, 124 S. Ct. 1354, 158 L. Ed. 2d 177, 63 Fed. R. Evid. Serv. 1077 (2004).

[10]Crawford v. Washington, 541 U.S. 36, 124 S. Ct. 1354, 158 L. Ed. 2d 177, 63 Fed. R. Evid. Serv. 1077 (2004).

[11]State v. Byrd, 160 Ohio App. 3d 538, 2005-Ohio-1902, 828 N.E.2d 133 (2d Dist. Montgomery County 2005); State v. Hill, 160 Ohio App. 3d 324, 2005-Ohio-1501, 827 N.E.2d 351 (8th Dist. Cuyahoga County 2005); State v. Byrd, 2012-Ohio-1849, 2012 WL 1484203 (Ohio Ct. App. 2d Dist. Montgomery County 2012).

[12]State v. Byrd, 160 Ohio App. 3d 538, 2005-Ohio-1902, 828 N.E.2d 133 (2d Dist. Montgomery County 2005).

anticipate that the statements made would be used against the defendant in an investigation and a prosecution.[13]

As a result, the court concluded that allowing the investigating officer to testify as to those hearsay statements was a denial of the defendant's right to face his accusers under the Confrontation Clause of the Sixth Amendment to the U.S. Constitution.[14] The court further found that the trial court's error constituted an abuse of discretion, requiring reversal and remand for further proceedings.[15]

Ohio courts have not been unanimous in this point of view. Other Ohio appellate courts, also considering the admission of excited utterances evidence, post-*Crawford*, held that in a criminal trial, the admission of excited utterances against a defendant doesn't violate Ohio's Confrontation Clause. Nor does admission of such statements, following *Crawford*, violate the Confrontation Clause of the U.S. Constitution's Sixth Amendment.[16] The U. S. Supreme Court's decision in *Ohio v. Roberts*[17] still controls. Therefore, non-testimonial hearsay statements made by a third party, who does not testify at trial, may be admitted into evidence, if such statements fall within a "firmly rooted" hearsay exception because the statements bear the requisite "indicia of reliability."[18]

Addressing facts that presented similar issues, but in a very different context, another Ohio court came to interestingly different

---

[13]State v. Byrd, 160 Ohio App. 3d 538, 2005-Ohio-1902, 828 N.E.2d 133 (2d Dist. Montgomery County 2005).

[14]State v. Byrd, 160 Ohio App. 3d 538, 2005-Ohio-1902, 828 N.E.2d 133 (2d Dist. Montgomery County 2005).

[15]State v. Byrd, 160 Ohio App. 3d 538, 2005-Ohio-1902, 828 N.E.2d 133 (2d Dist. Montgomery County 2005).

[16]State v. Williams, 2005-Ohio-213, 2005 WL 120054 (Ohio Ct. App. 2d Dist. Montgomery County 2005); Akron v. Hutton, 2005-Ohio-3300, 2005 WL 1523880 (Ohio Ct. App. 9th Dist. Summit County 2005); State v. Mills, 2005-Ohio-2128, 2006 WL 1132543 (Ohio Ct. App. 2d Dist. Montgomery County 2006); State v. Johnson, 2006-Ohio-1232, 2006 WL 664354 (Ohio Ct. App. 6th Dist. Lucas County 2006); State v. Auerswald, 2013-Ohio-742, 2013 WL 785061 (Ohio Ct. App. 9th Dist. Medina County 2013); State v. Flowers, 2012-Ohio-3783, 2012 WL 3595090 (Ohio Ct. App. 9th Dist. Summit County 2012).

[17]Ohio v. Roberts, 448 U.S. 56, 100 S. Ct. 2531, 65 L. Ed. 2d 597, 7 Fed. R. Evid. Serv. 1 (1980) (abrogated by, Crawford v. Washington, 541 U.S. 36, 124 S. Ct. 1354, 158 L. Ed. 2d 177, 63 Fed. R. Evid. Serv. 1077 (2004)); State v. Tabor, 2012-Ohio-4642, 2012 WL 4761741 (Ohio Ct. App. 12th Dist. Warren County 2012).

[18]Ohio v. Roberts, 448 U.S. 56, 100 S. Ct. 2531, 65 L. Ed. 2d 597, 7 Fed. R. Evid. Serv. 1 (1980) (abrogated by, Crawford v. Washington, 541 U.S. 36, 124 S. Ct. 1354, 158 L. Ed. 2d 177, 63 Fed. R. Evid. Serv. 1077 (2004)). See also State v. Banks, 2004-Ohio-6522, 2004 WL 2809070 (Ohio Ct. App. 10th Dist. Franklin County 2004); State v. Cannaday, 2005-Ohio-1513, 2005 WL 736583 (Ohio Ct. App. 10th Dist. Franklin County 2005); State v. Lee, 2005-Ohio-996, 2005 WL 544837 (Ohio Ct. App. 9th Dist. Summit County 2005), judgment aff'd, 111 Ohio St. 3d 361, 2006-Ohio-5849, 856 N.E.2d 921 (2006); State v. Primo, 2005-Ohio-3903, 2005 WL 1799314 (Ohio Ct. App. 12th Dist. Butler County 2005); State v. Gray, 2007-Ohio-1504, 2007 WL 949440 (Ohio Ct. App. 10th Dist. Franklin County 2007), cause dismissed, 113 Ohio St. 3d 1517, 2007-Ohio-2356, 866 N.E.2d 514 (2007); State v. Albert, 2006-Ohio-6902, 2006 WL 3775879 (Ohio Ct. App. 10th Dist. Franklin County 2006); State v. Mauldin, 2010-Ohio-4192, 2010 WL 3482689 (Ohio Ct. App. 7th Dist. Mahoning County 2010); State v. Norris, 2015-Ohio-624, 2015 WL 753346 (Ohio Ct. App. 2d Dist. Montgomery County 2015).

conclusions.[19] Thus, where a wounded witness who gave statements to a police officer in a hospital shortly after he was attacked subsequently died, it was held that those statements were not "testimonial," as contemplated by *Crawford*.[20] The court came to this conclusion because the declarant: (1) was not a suspect in any crime himself at the time the statements were made, (2) was not under any form of custody himself when the statements were made that would have called for him to be given *Miranda* warnings, and (3) the declarant was not subjected to any type of structured questioning that could reasonably be deemed a police interrogation, even in the colloquial sense of the word.[21]

The court noted that other courts had taken a very broad view of the holding in *Crawford*. It further noted that courts taking this broad view of *Crawford* suggested that the definitive test for determining whether a declarant's out-of-court statement to a government official is "testimonial" should be "the declarant's expectation that his or her statements may later be used at a trial."[22] Declining to adopt such reasoning, the court declared that to do so would render "testimonial" anything said to a police officer involved in investigating a crime.[23]

Q & A: Defendant is on trial, charged with domestic violence for striking a family or household member about the head and face with fists. A police officer offers testimony that, upon responding to the complaint at the defendant's home, he was approached by a neighbor, who pointed out the defendant's residence and said that the defendant was screaming and throwing things at the complainant again, "like every day." The defense has objected to this testimony, because the neighbor is not available for cross-examination. Is the officer's statement barred as "testimonial hearsay?"

No. Although the unidentified declarant spoke to police officers in the course of a police investigation, the statement was not made in response to any questioning by police, but was voluntarily given by one who approached the police and offered information.[24]

Moreover, even if the statement at issue was "testimonial," because

[19]State v. Nix, 2004-Ohio-5502, 2004 WL 2315035 (Ohio Ct. App. 1st Dist. Hamilton County 2004).

[20]Crawford v. Washington, 541 U.S. 36, 68, 124 S. Ct. 1354, 158 L. Ed. 2d 177, 63 Fed. R. Evid. Serv. 1077 (2004).

[21]State v. Nix, 2004-Ohio-5502, 2004 WL 2315035 (Ohio Ct. App. 1st Dist. Hamilton County 2004).

[22]State v. Nix, 2004-Ohio-5502, 2004 WL 2315035 (Ohio Ct. App. 1st Dist. Hamilton County 2004), citing U.S. v. Saget, 377 F.3d 223, 228-229, 64 Fed. R. Evid. Serv. 1195 (2d Cir. 2004), opinion supplemented, 108 Fed. Appx. 667 (2d Cir. 2004); State v. Mitchell, 171 Ohio App. 3d 225, 2007-Ohio-1696, 870 N.E.2d 228 (8th Dist. Cuyahoga County 2007); State v. McKenzie, 2006-Ohio-5725, 2006 WL 3095671 (Ohio Ct. App. 8th Dist. Cuyahoga County 2006).

[23]State v. Nix, 2004-Ohio-5502, 2004 WL 2315035 (Ohio Ct. App. 1st Dist. Hamilton County 2004); State v. Norris, 2015-Ohio-624, 2015 WL 753346 (Ohio Ct. App. 2d Dist. Montgomery County 2015).

[24]State v. McClanahan, 2005-Ohio-2975, 2005 WL 1398835 (Ohio Ct. App. 9th Dist. Summit County 2005), judgment rev'd in part, 109 Ohio St. 3d 313, 2006-Ohio-2109, 847 N.E.2d 1174 (2006); State v. Keene, 2006-Ohio-6676, 2006 WL 3702643 (Ohio Ct. App. 9th Dist. Lorain County 2006); State v. Norris, 2015-Ohio-624, 2015

it was made to police officers during their investigation at a crime scene, the statement would not fall within the holding in *Crawford v. Washington*[25] because it was not offered for the truth of the matter asserted, i.e., that the defendant was screaming and throwing things at the complainant, "just like every day."[26] *Crawford* made clear that "[t]he Confrontation Clause does not bar the use of testimonial statements for purposes other than establishing the truth of the matter asserted."[27] The evidence in this case was offered, along with other evidence, to explain why the police officers directed their investigation toward the defendant's residence.[28]

Q & A: My client was charged with domestic violence and was awaiting trial when the U.S Supreme Court decided *Crawford*. The prosecution is unable to get the victim in my client's case to testify at the trial. The state is offering statements that the victim made to the police who responded to the incident as "excited utterances." My objection to the admission of these statements by the trial court was overruled. Can I prevail on this point on appeal?

Yes. New rules of criminal procedure that expand the rights of the accused always have retroactive application to criminal cases pending direct appeal. Thus, *Crawford*'s holding concerning testimonial hearsay applies retroactively to this case.[29]

Q & A: The defendant is on trial for domestic violence. During the prosecution's case in chief it calls a witness who maintains that he cannot remember the substantive nature of what he had written in an earlier statement that he gave to the police about what he saw at the time of the incident.

The defendant objects, asserting that his right to confront witnesses under the Sixth Amendment will be violated if the trial court allows the witness to read his prior statement at trial. Should the trial court sustain the objection?

WL 753346 (Ohio Ct. App. 2d Dist. Montgomery County 2015).

[25]Crawford v. Washington, 541 U.S. 36, 124 S. Ct. 1354, 158 L. Ed. 2d 177, 63 Fed. R. Evid. Serv. 1077 (2004).

[26]State v. McClanahan, 2005-Ohio-2975, 2005 WL 1398835 (Ohio Ct. App. 9th Dist. Summit County 2005), judgment rev'd in part, 109 Ohio St. 3d 313, 2006-Ohio-2109, 847 N.E.2d 1174 (2006); State v. Keene, 2006-Ohio-6676, 2006 WL 3702643 (Ohio Ct. App. 9th Dist. Lorain County 2006).

[27]State v. McClanahan, 2005-Ohio-2975, 2005 WL 1398835 (Ohio Ct. App. 9th Dist. Summit County 2005), judgment rev'd in part, 109 Ohio St. 3d 313, 2006-Ohio-2109, 847 N.E.2d 1174 (2006), citing Tennessee v. Street, 471 U.S. 409, 414, 105 S. Ct. 2078, 85 L. Ed. 2d 425, 17 Fed. R. Evid. Serv. 817 (1985); State v. Keene, 2006-Ohio-6676, 2006 WL 3702643 (Ohio Ct. App. 9th Dist. Lorain County 2006).

[28]State v. McClanahan, 2005-Ohio-2975, 2005 WL 1398835 (Ohio Ct. App. 9th Dist. Summit County 2005), judgment rev'd in part, 109 Ohio St. 3d 313, 2006-Ohio-2109, 847 N.E.2d 1174 (2006).

[29]Griffith v. Kentucky, 479 U.S. 314, 320-328, 107 S. Ct. 708, 93 L. Ed. 2d 649 (1987); State v. Hill, 160 Ohio App. 3d 324, 2005-Ohio-1501, 827 N.E.2d 351 (8th Dist. Cuyahoga County 2005); State v. Cutlip, 2004-Ohio-2120, 2004 WL 895980 (Ohio Ct. App. 9th Dist. Medina County 2004); State v. Allen, 2004-Ohio-3111, 2004 WL 1353169 (Ohio Ct. App. 8th Dist. Cuyahoga County 2004); State v. Dillard, 2006-Ohio-3524, 2006 WL 1868318 (Ohio Ct. App. 7th Dist. Jefferson County 2006); Cowans v. Bagley, 624 F. Supp. 2d 709 (S.D. Ohio 2008), aff'd, 639 F.3d 241 (6th Cir. 2011); Davis v. U.S., 564 U.S. 229, 131 S. Ct. 2419, 180 L. Ed. 2d 285, 68 A.L.R. Fed. 2d 665 (2011).

No. The witness, is present in open court and, therefore, capable of being confronted about his prior statement by all concerned: the state, the court, and defense counsel.

When the declarant appears for cross-examination at trial, the Confrontation Clause places no constraints at all on the use of his prior testimonial statements.[30] The Clause does not bar admission of a statement so long as the declarant is present at trial to defend or explain it. The Clause also does not bar the use of testimonial statements for purposes other than establishing the truth of the matter asserted.[31]

Q & A: What factors are required to determine whether the primary purpose of law enforcement interrogation is to address an ongoing emergency?

The Washington State Supreme Court draws from U.S. Supreme Court precedent four factors to determine whether the "primary purpose" of police interrogation is to enable assistance to meet an ongoing emergency: (1) whether a "reasonable listener" would conclude that the speaker was facing an ongoing emergency that required help; (2) whether the person was speaking about current events as they were actually occurring, requiring police assistance, or describing past events; (3) the nature of what was asked and answered; and (4) the level of formality of the investigation.[32]

§ 5:17 Case preparation—Hearsay exceptions—Present sense impression[1]

A present sense impression is a statement describing or explaining an event or condition made while the declarant was perceiving the event or condition or immediately thereafter. Such statements are admissible as exceptions to the hearsay rule unless circumstances indicate a lack of trustworthiness.

A present sense impression bears a high degree of trustworthiness because the declarant described the event and/or uttered a statement about the event in close temporal proximity to the event.[2] The spontaneity of the statement is the key to its trustworthiness.[3]

---

[30] California v. Green, 399 U.S. 149, 162, 90 S. Ct. 1930, 26 L. Ed. 2d 489 (1970).

[31] Tennessee v. Street, 471 U.S. 409, 414, 105 S. Ct. 2078, 85 L. Ed. 2d 425, 17 Fed. R. Evid. Serv. 817 (1985).

[32] State v. Koslowski, 166 Wash. 2d 409, 418–19, 209 P.3d 479 (2009).

[Section 5:17]

[1] Evid.R. 803(1); State v. McNeal, 2002-Ohio-2981, 2002 WL 1376177, *4 (Ohio Ct. App. 3d Dist. Allen County 2002); State v. Rose, 2008-Ohio-1263, 2008 WL 740563 (Ohio Ct. App. 8th Dist. Cuyahoga County 2008); State v. Monroe, 2011-Ohio-3045, 2011 WL 2476280 (Ohio Ct. App. 8th Dist. Cuyahoga County 2011).

[2] State v. Wages, 87 Ohio App. 3d 780, 623 N.E.2d 193 (8th Dist. Cuyahoga County 1993); State v. Dixon, 152 Ohio App. 3d 760, 2003-Ohio-2550, 790 N.E.2d 349 (3d Dist. Logan County 2003); State v. Simmons, 2003-Ohio-721, 2003 WL 356281, *6 (Ohio Ct. App. 9th Dist. Summit County 2003); State v. Easterling, 1999 WL 74554, *3 (Ohio Ct. App. 12th Dist. Butler County 1999); State v. Foster, 1998 WL 684834, *4 (Ohio Ct. App. 11th Dist. Trumbull County 1998); Donald v. Bobby, 2008 WL 891981 (N.D. Ohio 2008); State v. Graves, 2009-Ohio-1133, 2009 WL 653091 (Ohio Ct. App. 9th Dist. Lorain County 2009), judgment vacated, 2011-Ohio-5997, 2011 WL 5829643

One of the guarantees of trustworthiness on which the present sense impression exception is based is verification. The statement is usually made to a third party, who subsequently testifies to it. The third party is usually present at the time of the declarant's observation and usually will have an opportunity to observe the situation himself/herself. The third party is, therefore, frequently in the position to provide an independent check on the accuracy of the declarant's observation.

If the third party who offers testimony about another's present sense impression was not present at the time that the declarant made the statement, the statement lacks this important safeguard, and the validity of such testimony is suspect. The third party's presence is not, however, an absolute prerequisite to the admission of the statement.[4] The trial court has wide discretion in determining whether such testimony should be allowed.[5]

Q & A: The prosecution offers testimony of the victim's brother that the victim told him that the defendant threatened to kill her three days before attacking and beating her. The defense objects to the admission of this evidence as hearsay. Should the court admit the brother's testimony?

No.[6] The lead cases in this area hold that hearsay statements regarding a victim's fearful state of mind are admissible into evidence. However, the courts limit the admissibility of such testimony to statements that reflect the victim's state of mind and not the reasons underlying that state of mind.[7] The statement offered here sets forth the reason why the victim was fearful of the defendant and, therefore,

---

(Ohio Ct. App. 9th Dist. Lorain County 2011); State v. Askew, 2012-Ohio-585, 2012 WL 504211 (Ohio Ct. App. 8th Dist. Cuyahoga County 2012); State v. May, 2012-Ohio-5128, 2012 WL 5397126 (Ohio Ct. App. 3d Dist. Logan County 2012); State v. Taylor, 2014-Ohio-3820, 2014 WL 4362406 (Ohio Ct. App. 8th Dist. Cuyahoga County 2014).

[3]Cox v. Oliver Machinery Co., 41 Ohio App. 3d 28, 534 N.E.2d 855 (12th Dist. Butler County 1987); State v. Foster, 1998 WL 684834, *4 (Ohio Ct. App. 11th Dist. Trumbull County 1998); State v. Dixon, 152 Ohio App. 3d 760, 2003-Ohio-2550, 790 N.E.2d 349 (3d Dist. Logan County 2003); State v. Graves, 2009-Ohio-1133, 2009 WL 653091 (Ohio Ct. App. 9th Dist. Lorain County 2009), judgment vacated, 2011-Ohio-5997, 2011 WL 5829643 (Ohio Ct. App. 9th Dist. Lorain County 2011); State v. May, 2012-Ohio-5128, 2012 WL 5397126 (Ohio Ct. App. 3d Dist. Logan County 2012).

[4]See State v. Wages, 87 Ohio App. 3d 780, 623 N.E.2d 193 (8th Dist. Cuyahoga County 1993).

[5]State v. Martin, 2000 WL 1145465 (Ohio Ct. App. 12th Dist. Brown County 2000); State v. Dixon, 152 Ohio App. 3d 760, 2003-Ohio-2550, 790 N.E.2d 349 (3d Dist. Logan County 2003).

[6]State v. Apanovitch, 33 Ohio St. 3d 19, 21, 514 N.E.2d 394 (1987); State v. Miller, 96 Ohio St. 3d 384, 2002-Ohio-4931, 775 N.E.2d 498 (2002).

[7]State v. Apanovitch, 33 Ohio St. 3d 19, 514 N.E.2d 394 (1987); State v. Watts, 1998 WL 906745 (Ohio Ct. App. 2d Dist. Montgomery County 1998); State v. Miller, 96 Ohio St. 3d 384, 2002-Ohio-4931, 775 N.E.2d 498 (2002); State v. Frazier, 73 Ohio St. 3d 323, 1995-Ohio-235, 652 N.E.2d 1000 (1995); State v. Reynolds, 80 Ohio St. 3d 670, 1998-Ohio-171, 687 N.E.2d 1358 (1998).; State v. Collymore, 2003-Ohio-3328, 2003 WL 21469121 (Ohio Ct. App. 8th Dist. Cuyahoga County 2003); State v. Brinkley, 105 Ohio St. 3d 231, 245, 2005-Ohio-1507, 824 N.E.2d 959, 977 (2005); State v. Ahmed, 103 Ohio St. 3d 27, 39, 2004-Ohio-4190, 813 N.E.2d 637, 654 (2004) **writ of habeas corpus DENIED,** Ahmed v. Houk, 2014 WL 2709765 (S.D. Ohio 2014). But see State v. Hawn, 138 Ohio App. 3d 449, 741 N.E.2d 594 (2d Dist. Montgomery County 2000); State v. Manley, 2004-Ohio-4930, 2004 WL 2245114 (Ohio Ct. App. 2d Dist.

does not qualify as an exception to the hearsay rule under Evidence Rule 803(3).[8]

Q & A: The victim testified for the defendant at trial, claiming that the defendant was not present when the injuries occurred. The victim's mother offers to testify on rebuttal for the prosecution. She says that the victim called her on the date of the alleged incident, that the victim was upset and crying and hastily stated a need to get off the phone because the defendant entered the room. The defense objects to the mother's testimony as hearsay. Does the mother's statement come into evidence?

Yes. The statement qualifies for exemption from the operation of the hearsay rule as a present sense impression. The victim made the statement while perceiving the act of the defendant entering the room. The statement was uttered as the event took place, and there are no circumstances that indicate that the statement is otherwise untrustworthy.[9]

Q & A: The defendant is charged with threatening domestic violence. The victim's neighbor testifies that the victim came over on the date in question about an hour after the neighbor observed the defendant leave. According to the neighbor, the victim said the defendant pulled a knife on the victim just before storming out of the house. The victim has not appeared at trial, and the defense objects to the neighbor's testimony as hearsay. Should the victim's statements to the neighbor come into evidence?

No. The statement does not qualify as a present sense impression for two reasons. First, the statement was made more than an hour after the event and not contemporaneous to it. Second, the neighbor was not in a position to independently verify the accuracy of the victim's statement concerning the defendant's actions because the neighbor was not also present.[10]

Montgomery County 2004); State v. Jeffries, 119 Ohio St. 3d 265, 2008-Ohio-3865, 893 N.E.2d 487 (2008); Brinkley v. Houk, 866 F. Supp. 2d 747 (N.D. Ohio 2011), amended in part on other grounds, 2012 WL 1537661 (N.D. Ohio 2012) and aff'd, 831 F.3d 356 (6th Cir. 2016), cert. denied, 137 S. Ct. 2118, 198 L. Ed. 2d 203 (2017).

[8]State v. Awkal, 76 Ohio St. 3d 324, 1996-Ohio-395, 667 N.E.2d 960 (1996); State v. Frazier, 73 Ohio St. 3d 323, 1995-Ohio-235, 652 N.E.2d 1000 (1995); State v. Reynolds, 80 Ohio St. 3d 670, 1998-Ohio-171, 687 N.E.2d 1358 (1998); State v. Butcher, 170 Ohio App. 3d 52, 2007-Ohio-118, 866 N.E.2d 13 (11th Dist. Ashtabula County 2007); Leonard v. Warden, Ohio State Penitentiary, 2013 WL 831727 (S.D. Ohio 2013), report and recommendation adopted, 2015 WL 2341094 (S.D. Ohio 2015), aff'd, 846 F.3d 832 (6th Cir. 2017).

[9]State v. Wages, 87 Ohio App. 3d 780, 623 N.E.2d 193 (8th Dist. Cuyahoga County 1993); State v. McNeal, 2002-Ohio-2981, 2002 WL 1376177, *4 (Ohio Ct. App. 3d Dist. Allen County 2002); State v. Rose, 2008-Ohio-1263, 2008 WL 740563 (Ohio Ct. App. 8th Dist. Cuyahoga County 2008); State v. Monroe, 2011-Ohio-3045, 2011 WL 2476280 (Ohio Ct. App. 8th Dist. Cuyahoga County 2011).

[10]State v. Williams, 1991 WL 156545 (Ohio Ct. App. 6th Dist. Lucas County 1991).

§ 5:18 Case preparation—Hearsay exceptions—Then existing mental, emotional, or physical condition[1]

Wherever the bodily or mental feelings of an individual are material, the usual expressions of those feelings are original and competent evidence.[2] To qualify as an exception to the hearsay rule, the statement:

(1) must relate to the declarant's intent, motive, design, mental feeling, pain, or bodily health,[3]
(2) generally may not refer to memory or belief to prove a fact,[4]
(3) must be directed toward the future and not the past,[5]
(4) must not include any explanation of why the declarant was of a certain state of mind,[6] and
(5) must be relevant to a material issue in the case.

The Ohio Supreme Court has noted that the federal rule and the Ohio rule dealing with state-of-mind witnesses are identical.[7] Both rules permit witnesses to relate out-of-court statements that reflect any then existing mental or emotional condition that the declarant experienced, such as fear or anxiety.[8]

Q & A: I'm prosecuting a woman for striking her ex-husband several times in the head with a broom handle. In preparing my case, I discovered that the victim told a police officer two days before the incident that he was afraid his ex-wife was going to try to hurt him. Can the officer testify at trial as to that statement?

Yes. The victim's statement to the officer, made just two days before the attack, is admissible as evidence of the victim's fear that the offender would do him serious physical injury.[9] Evidence Rule 803(3) permits the admission of any of the declarant's out-of-court statements that he was scared, anxious, or in any other state reflecting his then-existing mental or emotional condition. Whether the statement should be admitted is within the sound discretion of the trial court.

[Section 5:18]

[1]Evid.R. 803(3).

[2]Mutual Life Ins. Co. of New York v. Hillmon, 145 U.S. 285, 12 S. Ct. 909, 36 L. Ed. 706 (1892).

[3]Evid.R. 803(3).

[4]Evid.R. 803(3).

[5]State v. Stewart, 75 Ohio App. 3d 141, 598 N.E.2d 1275 (11th Dist. Ashtabula County 1991).

[6]State v. Stewart, 75 Ohio App. 3d 141, 598 N.E.2d 1275 (11th Dist. Ashtabula County 1991); State v. May, 2012-Ohio-5128, 2012 WL 5397126 (Ohio Ct. App. 3d Dist. Logan County 2012); In re Estate of Beverly, 2013-Ohio-1498, 2013 WL 1561477 (Ohio Ct. App. 3d Dist. Seneca County 2013).

[7]Evid.R. 803(3).

[8]State v. Apanovitch, 33 Ohio St. 3d 19, 21, 514 N.E.2d 394 (1987); U.S. v. Cohen, 631 F.2d 1223, 7 Fed. R. Evid. Serv. 257 (5th Cir. 1980); State v. Watts, 1998 WL 906745 (Ohio Ct. App. 2d Dist. Montgomery County 1998); State v. Newcomb, 2001-Ohio-2325, 2001 WL 1504260, *4 (Ohio Ct. App. 3d Dist. Logan County 2001).

[9]See State v. Sherrell, 1995 WL 497590 (Ohio Ct. App. 5th Dist. Tuscarawas County 1995); Evid.R. 803(3).

Q & A: The prosecution produces three witnesses at trial who testify that the victim of a domestic violence complaint expressed to them a fear that the defendant intended to hurt her when he arrived home from work on the day in question. In each instance, the defense objects to the out-of-court statements offered by the prosecution witnesses as inadmissible hearsay. The victim does not testify at trial. Is the court correct in overruling the objections?

Yes. The admission of these statements is allowed under the then existing mental condition exception to the hearsay rule and is within the sound discretion of the trial court. The appearance of the victim at trial is immaterial to the court's decision to admit the statements. Testimony that a victim is fearful is admissible under this exception to the hearsay rule provided the statement otherwise meets the requirements for this exception. The critical requirements are that the statement refers to a present and not a past condition and that it must point toward the future and not the past.[10]

§ 5:19 Case preparation—Hearsay exceptions—Statements for purposes of medical diagnosis or treatment[1]

To qualify for this exception to the hearsay rule, the statement:

(1) must be for medical diagnostic or treatment purposes, and
(2) must describe the declarant's medical history or past or present symptoms, pain, or sensations, or the inception or general character of the cause or external source thereof insofar as reasonably pertinent to the diagnosis or treatment.

The patient's belief that his or her statements will be used for medical diagnosis or treatment is the basis for concluding such statements are reliable and the underlying reason for allowing such an exception to the hearsay rule.[2] This exception to the hearsay rule is based upon the commonsense notion that an individual has a strong incentive to tell the truth when describing a medical condition to a doctor, considering the consequence to the declarant of providing false information.[3]

Q & A: The prosecution in a domestic violence case wants to admit as evidence a hospital record. Counsel for the defendant objects to the record's admission on the grounds that the hospital report contains the following hearsay statement, which the defense maintains is extremely prejudicial to its case:

Upon visual examination, patient observed to be extremely ani-

---

[10]State v. Apanovitch, 33 Ohio St. 3d 19, 514 N.E.2d 394 (1987); see also State v. Wages, 87 Ohio App. 3d 780, 623 N.E.2d 193 (8th Dist. Cuyahoga County 1993).

[Section 5:19]

[1]Evid.R. 803(4).

[2]State v. Demiduk, 1998 WL 355864 (Ohio Ct. App. 7th Dist. Columbiana County 1998); State v. Winterich, 2008-Ohio-1813, 2008 WL 1747433 (Ohio Ct. App. 8th Dist. Cuyahoga County 2008).

[3]State v. Clary, 73 Ohio App. 3d 42, 596 N.E.2d 554 (10th Dist. Franklin County 1991); State v. Schauer, 2000 WL 670304, *3 (Ohio Ct. App. 4th Dist. Pickaway County 2000); Meaney v. U.S., 112 F.2d 538, 130 A.L.R. 973 (C.C.A. 2d Cir. 1940).

mated and emotional; bruises and contusions to the trunk, back, and arms evident. Patient claims that injuries resulted from an assault by spouse. Patient says assaults have occurred periodically over the last five years. Patient exhibits symptoms of Post Traumatic Stress Syndrome. Referred to psychiatric department for evaluation. Recommended that patient not return home. Police called.

Is the statement in the record admissible?

Yes. Hospital records, when properly authenticated, are generally admissible into evidence.[4] However, any statement contained in those records which is not associated with an observation, occurrence, or event connected to the diagnosis or treatment of the patient or helpful in understanding the medical or surgical aspect of the matter under review is inadmissible. Thus, statements attributing fault are generally inadmissible under Evidence Rule 803(4).[5] However, if the prosecution can show that the statement was pertinent to the diagnosis or treatment described, the court may, in its discretion, allow the statement to be admitted into evidence.[6]

In *State v. Evans*,[7] which involved a sexual assault on a young child, the court admitted into evidence statements contained in certain medical records. The statements identified the defendant, who was related to the victim, as the perpetrator of the criminal acts. The court found that the statements were admissible as a hearsay exception under Evidence Rule 803(4). The court's rationale was that the identity of the offender was necessary for the physician-author of the report to help the victim and was integral to the victim's medical diagnosis and treatment. The *Evans* court cited other examples of admissible statements in child sexual assault cases.[8] Evidence Rule 803(4) exceptions include situations where:

(1) the fact that the abuse was perpetrated by a family member responsible for taking care of the victim is necessary for diagnosing *psychological* problems and for effecting appropriate treatment;

(2) the source and type of abuse are necessary to properly diagnosis the psychological effects of the child abuse syndrome.[9]

As with victims of child sexual abuse, victims of domestic violence

---

[4]State v. Self, 56 Ohio St. 3d 73, 79, 564 N.E.2d 446, 452 (1990).

[5]Green v. City of Cleveland, 150 Ohio St. 441, 38 Ohio Op. 311, 83 N.E.2d 63 (1948); McQueen v. Goldey, 20 Ohio App. 3d 41, 484 N.E.2d 712 (12th Dist. Butler County 1984); State v. Clary, 73 Ohio App. 3d 42, 52, 596 N.E.2d 554, 560 (10th Dist. Franklin County 1991); Dewey v. Olson, 2000 WL 1434138 (Ohio Ct. App. 6th Dist. Lucas County 2000); Johnoff v. Watson, 2004-Ohio-6882, 2004 WL 2924600 (Ohio Ct. App. 6th Dist. Lucas County 2004). But see Wise v. Meyer, 2006-Ohio-4654, 2006 WL 2578858 (Ohio Ct. App. 2d Dist. Greene County 2006).

[6]But see State v. Hazel, 2012-Ohio-835, 2012 WL 690312 (Ohio Ct. App. 2d Dist. Clark County 2012).

[7]State v. Evans, 1987 WL 10358 (Ohio Ct. App. 12th Dist. Butler County 1987).

[8]State v. Myers, 1985 WL 11020 (Ohio Ct. App. 9th Dist. Summit County 1985); State v. Reger, 1986 WL 5699 (Ohio Ct. App. 9th Dist. Summit County 1986); People v. Wilkins, 134 Mich. App. 39, 349 N.W.2d 815 (1984) (rejected by, Cassidy v. State, 74 Md. App. 1, 536 A.2d 666 (1988)); Goldade v. State, 674 P.2d 721 (Wyo. 1983) (rejected by, Cassidy v. State, 74 Md. App. 1, 536 A.2d 666 (1988)).

[9]See State v. Soltis, 1990 WL 136085, *3 (Ohio Ct. App. 9th Dist. Summit County

often suffer from psychological abuse at the hands of their abusers. Frequently, the perpetrator of domestic violence is also a caregiver to the victim. Thus, in this example, the argument is available that statements concerning the defendant's identity were necessary for the treating physician to diagnosis and treat this victim. The doctor's diagnosis of Post Traumatic Stress Syndrome and recommendations that the victim receive psychiatric treatment, as well as the recommendation that the victim not return home, were impossible without knowledge of the offender's identity.

Q & A: At trial, the defense moves in limine to prevent the prosecution from offering as evidence medical records containing the following information:

> **Patient presented at the emergency room following an assault by a male friend. She was punched multiple times and kicked all over the body with steel-toed boots. Patient states that a television was smashed over her head. She believes that she may have lost consciousness.**

The defense argues that the statements in the medical reports are inadmissible hearsay. Should the court grant the motion?

No. Identification of the objects used to commit the assault and the manner in which they were employed to inflict the patient's injuries are pertinent to the diagnosis and to any course of treatment. Additionally, Ohio courts that addressed this issue have held that, when domestic violence is alleged, a statement contained in a medical record that identifies the patient's assailant as a male friend is pertinent to treatment.[10]

§ 5:20 Case preparation—Hearsay exceptions—Recorded recollection[1]

The applicability of this exception to the hearsay rule requires that the evidence be:

(1) a memorandum or record,
(2) concerning a matter that the declarant once had knowledge of, but now has trouble accurately recalling during testimony, and
(3) which, the witness's other testimony establishes, was made or adopted by the witness when the matter was fresh and which accurately reflects the witness's prior knowledge.[2]

This exception to the common-law proscription against the admis-

---

1990); State v. Ridley, 2013-Ohio-1268, 2013 WL 1289533 (Ohio Ct. App. 6th Dist. Lucas County 2013).

[10]See, e.g., State v. Patterson, 1998 WL 655388 (Ohio Ct. App. 10th Dist. Franklin County 1998); State v. Soltis, 1990 WL 136085, *3 (Ohio Ct. App. 9th Dist. Summit County 1990).

[Section 5:20]

[1]Evid.R. 803(5).

[2]State v. Scott, 31 Ohio St. 2d 1, 60 Ohio Op. 2d 1, 285 N.E.2d 344 (1972); U.S. v. Williams, 571 F.2d 344, 2 Fed. R. Evid. Serv. 1014 (6th Cir. 1978); State v. McLean, 2000 WL 777858 (Ohio Ct. App. 11th Dist. Lake County 2000); In re Sherry S., 2008-Ohio-6401, 2008 WL 5147442 (Ohio Ct. App. 6th Dist. Erie County 2008).

sion of hearsay evidence is recognized when a witness has testified that his present recollection is absent or incomplete, but that his recollection was complete at the time that the memorandum sought to be introduced was made and that his recollection was accurately recorded at that time.[3] Under this exception to the hearsay rule,[4] the writing itself, whether read into the record or introduced into evidence by an adverse party, constitutes *substantive* evidence.[5]

Q & A: The alleged victim of a domestic violence complaint takes the stand. On direct examination, she claims she has forgotten certain critical elements of the prosecution's case. The prosecutor wants her to refresh her recollection by reading portions of a written document that summarizes a statement she gave during an interview with the investigating detective. Is the prosecution allowed to proceed in this manner?

Yes. The court has the discretion to allow the witness to use the written statement. However, the witness may read the memorandum into the record, but the memorandum itself cannot come into evidence unless the party against whom it was offered proffers it.[6]

§ 5:21 Case preparation—Hearsay exceptions—Judgment of previous conviction[1]

To qualify for an exemption from the operation of the hearsay rule, evidence of a previous conviction must:

(1) be evidence of a final judgment, entered after trial or on any plea other than a no contest or equivalent plea,
(2) find a person guilty of a crime punishable by death or imprisonment in excess of one year,
(3) be offered to prove any fact essential to sustain the judgment, and
(4) NOT be used by the government in a criminal prosecution, for purposes other than impeachment, against persons *other than* the accused.

The question of the applicability of Evid.R. 803(21) is particularly pertinent in felony domestic violence prosecutions in Ohio. To obtain a felony conviction for domestic violence in Ohio, the prosecution is required, by statute,[2] to establish as an element of the crime the existence of the defendant's prior conviction for one of an enumerated set

[3]State v. Woods, 48 Ohio App. 3d 1, 548 N.E.2d 954 (1st Dist. Hamilton County 1988), cause dismissed, 38 Ohio St. 3d 715, 533 N.E.2d 783 (1988).

[4]Evid. R. 803(5).

[5]Cleveland v. Schumann, 2011-Ohio-741, 2011 WL 553495 (Ohio Ct. App. 8th Dist. Cuyahoga County 2011). However, see State v. Durham, 2011-Ohio-2256, 2011 WL 1849409 (Ohio Ct. App. 8th Dist. Cuyahoga County 2011).

[6]State v. Aiken, 1993 WL 204646 (Ohio Ct. App. 8th Dist. Cuyahoga County 1993). However, see State v. Durham, 2011-Ohio-2256, 2011 WL 1849409 (Ohio Ct. App. 8th Dist. Cuyahoga County 2011).

[Section 5:21]

[1]Evid.R. 803(21).

[2]RC 2919.25(D).

of criminal acts. Since the United States Supreme Court has held that recidivism statutes are not unconstitutional per se,[3] resort to evidence presented pursuant to this exception to the hearsay rule is essential to most felony domestic violence prosecutions in Ohio.

Q & A: In a felony domestic violence case, the prosecution offers a certified copy of the defendant's prior conviction for a misdemeanor domestic violence offense in support of its burden of proof on the prior conviction element of the offense. The defense objects to the admission of this conviction on the grounds that it is hearsay and is being offered for a purpose other than impeachment. Should the court overrule the objection?

Yes. The defendant here conveniently ignores the fact that Evidence Rule 803(21) prohibits the introduction of judgments of conviction for purposes other than impeachment *only* against persons other than the accused.[4]

However, it should be noted that the U.S. Supreme Court has recognized a significant exception to this rule. That exception aims to limit the prejudice a defendant might suffer if the admission of evidence under the rule was unfettered. In *Old Chief v. United States*[5] the petitioner was charged under a federal statute prohibiting the possession of a firearm by anyone who has been convicted of "a crime punishable by imprisonment for a term exceeding one year."[6] The petitioner offered to stipulate that he had been convicted of a crime punishable by imprisonment exceeding one year, arguing that the danger of unfair prejudice from revealing the name and nature of his prior conviction would outweigh its probative value.[7] The United States attorney refused to join the stipulation and introduced at trial, over petitioner's objection, an order of judgment and conviction disclosing that the petitioner had been previously sentenced to five years' imprisonment for assaulting and causing serious bodily injury to another.[8]

The Supreme Court ruled that the lower court erred by admitting this evidence. The question was not one of relevance but rather "the scope of a trial judge's discretion under Fed. Evid. Rule 403, which authorizes exclusion of relevant evidence when its 'probative value is

[3]Spencer v. State of Tex., 385 U.S. 554, 565–66, 87 S. Ct. 648, 17 L. Ed. 2d 606 (1967). See also Griffin v. Berghuis, 298 F. Supp. 2d 663 (E.D. Mich. 2004); Norris v. Warden, NCI, 2010 WL 582623 (S.D. Ohio 2010), report and recommendation adopted, 2010 WL 883847 (S.D. Ohio 2010).

[4]State v. King, 1989 WL 113131 (Ohio Ct. App. 2d Dist. Clark County 1989), dismissed, 53 Ohio St. 3d 715, 560 N.E.2d 774 (1990) and cause dismissed, 71 Ohio St. 3d 1488, 646 N.E.2d 464 (1995).

[5]Old Chief v. U.S., 519 U.S. 172, 117 S. Ct. 644, 136 L. Ed. 2d 574, 45 Fed. R. Evid. Serv. 835 (1997).

[6]Old Chief v. U.S., 519 U.S. 172, 174, 117 S. Ct. 644, 136 L. Ed. 2d 574, 45 Fed. R. Evid. Serv. 835 (1997), citing 18 U.S.C.A. 922(g)(1).

[7]Old Chief v. U.S., 519 U.S. 172, 117 S. Ct. 644, 136 L. Ed. 2d 574, 45 Fed. R. Evid. Serv. 835 (1997); State v. Bibler, 2014-Ohio-3375, 17 N.E.3d 1154 (Ohio Ct. App. 3d Dist. Marion County 2014). But see State v. Woods, 2001 WL 1002233 (Ohio Ct. App. 8th Dist. Cuyahoga County 2001).

[8]Old Chief v. U.S., 519 U.S. 172, 117 S. Ct. 644, 136 L. Ed. 2d 574, 45 Fed. R. Evid. Serv. 835 (1997).

substantially outweighed by the danger of unfair prejudice.' "[9] By offering to stipulate, the petitioner presented the trial court "alternative, relevant, admissible evidence of the prior conviction" that was "seemingly conclusive" of the prior conviction element of the statute.[10] The court reasoned: "The issue is not whether concrete details of the prior crime should come to the juror's attention but whether the name or general character of that crime is to be disclosed. Congress * * * has made it plain that distinctions among generic felonies does not count for this purpose; the fact of the qualifying conviction is alone what matters under the statute. * * * The most the jury needs to know is that the conviction admitted by the defendant falls within the class of crimes that Congress thought should bar a convict from possessing a gun * * *."[11] Since the petitioner's proposed stipulation provided a suitable evidentiary alternative to the order of judgment for petitioner's conviction without the risk of unfair prejudice inherent in the evidence of prior convictions, the trial court abused its discretion by not accepting petitioner's proffered stipulation.[12]

Ohio Evid.R. 403(A) provides that evidence, although relevant, "is not admissible if its probative value is substantially outweighed by the danger of unfair prejudice." However, two Ohio Courts of Appeals hold that *Old Chief* is totally inapplicable to state court prosecutions, finding that it involves interpretation of federal statute and therefore does not establish binding precedent.[13]

When considering evidence under Evid.R. 403, the trial court is vested with broad discretion and an appellate court should not interfere absent a clear abuse of that discretion. A trial court abuses its discretion by admitting evidence of multiple convictions when only one conviction is necessary to satisfy the elements of the offense.[14] Distinctions among offenses of violence do not matter for the purpose of elevating the degree of an offense. The most that a trier of fact would need to know is that a defendant has stipulated to a conviction for a crime defined under the Revised Code as an "offense of violence."[15]

Q & A: The defendant is charged with felony domestic

---

[9]Old Chief v. U.S., 519 U.S. 172, 117 S. Ct. 644, 136 L. Ed. 2d 574, 45 Fed. R. Evid. Serv. 835 (1997).

[10]Old Chief v. U.S., 519 U.S. 172, 117 S. Ct. 644, 136 L. Ed. 2d 574, 45 Fed. R. Evid. Serv. 835 (1997).

[11]Old Chief v. U.S., 519 U.S. 172, 117 S. Ct. 644, 136 L. Ed. 2d 574, 45 Fed. R. Evid. Serv. 835 (1997).

[12]Old Chief v. U.S., 519 U.S. 172, 117 S. Ct. 644, 136 L. Ed. 2d 574, 45 Fed. R. Evid. Serv. 835 (1997).

[13]State v. Simmons, 2011-Ohio-916, 2011 WL 721322 (Ohio Ct. App. 9th Dist. Summit County 2011); State v. Carr, 1999 WL 1314672 (Ohio Ct. App. 11th Dist. Lake County 1999). But see State v. Woods, 2001 WL 1002233 (Ohio Ct. App. 8th Dist. Cuyahoga County 2001); State v. Bibler, 2014-Ohio-3375, 17 N.E.3d 1154 (Ohio Ct. App. 3d Dist. Marion County 2014).

[14]State v. Henton, 121 Ohio App. 3d 501, 507-508, 700 N.E.2d 371 (11th Dist. Ashtabula County 1997); State v. Page, 2005-Ohio-1493, 2005 WL 730057 (Ohio Ct. App. 8th Dist. Cuyahoga County 2005). But see State v. Russell, 2013-Ohio-1381, 2013 WL 1438000 (Ohio Ct. App. 12th Dist. Butler County 2013).

[15]Old Chief v. U.S., 519 U.S. 172, 117 S. Ct. 644, 136 L. Ed. 2d 574, 45 Fed. R. Evid. Serv. 835 (1997). See also State v. Godbolt, 1999 WL 254370 (Ohio Ct. App. 5th Dist. Licking County 1999); Jones v. Warden, Noble Correctional Inst., 2014 WL

violence. During the direct examination of the investigating detective, the prosecutor presents a certified copy of a judgment entry and elicits testimony that the victim filed a complaint against the defendant on a prior occasion and that another jury found him guilty of domestic violence. The defense objects to this line of questioning as hearsay and moves for a mistrial. Should the court grant the motion for a mistrial?

No. The existence of a prior offense is an essential element of a felony domestic violence charge in Ohio.[16] The state is required to prove that element to the trier of fact beyond a reasonable doubt to enhance the degree of the domestic violence charge and, therefore, the penalty associated with the higher charge. The officer's testimony and the admission of the certified copy of the judgment entry are both appropriate evidence to establish the state's burden of proof.[17]

Q & A: Can a defendant on trial for felony domestic violence have the court make a finding regarding the existence of a prior domestic violence conviction and thereby avoid having the issue submitted to the jury?

No. The existence of the prior conviction is an element of the offense. It must, therefore, be submitted to the jury and cannot be decided by the court without the jury's knowledge.[18]

Q & A: In a felony prosecution, can a defendant avoid having the name and nature of a prior qualifying conviction under RC 2919.25(D) brought to the jury's attention by stipulating to the prior conviction and moving the court to exclude any and all evidence of the prior conviction from the jury's consideration?

If the prosecution agrees, by stipulating to its existence, the defendant can minimize the possibility that the jury will be prejudiced by its knowledge of the prior conviction.[19] However, even if a stipulation is entered, the jury must still be told, minimally, of the name and

---

6673615 (S.D. Ohio 2014), report and recommendation adopted, 2015 WL 248031 (S.D. Ohio 2015); State v. Bibler, 2014-Ohio-3375, 17 N.E.3d 1154 (Ohio Ct. App. 3d Dist. Marion County 2014); State v. Rodriguez, 2014-Ohio-911, 2014 WL 1345415 (Ohio Ct. App. 9th Dist. Summit County 2014); State v. Inman, 2014-Ohio-3538, 2014 WL 4057720 (Ohio Ct. App. 9th Dist. Medina County 2014).

[16] RC 2919.25(D); State v. Day, 99 Ohio App. 3d 514, 651 N.E.2d 52 (12th Dist. Clermont County 1994); State v. Maynez, 2008-Ohio-3054, 2008 WL 2485367 (Ohio Ct. App. 3d Dist. Defiance County 2008); State v. Bibler, 2014-Ohio-3375, 17 N.E.3d 1154 (Ohio Ct. App. 3d Dist. Marion County 2014).

[17] State v. King, 1989 WL 113131 (Ohio Ct. App. 2d Dist. Clark County 1989), dismissed, 53 Ohio St. 3d 715, 560 N.E.2d 774 (1990) and cause dismissed, 71 Ohio St. 3d 1488, 646 N.E.2d 464 (1995); State v. Arnold, 2002 WL 93423 (Ohio Ct. App. 8th Dist. Cuyahoga County 2002); State v. Thomas, 2009-Ohio-1784, 2009 WL 1019855 (Ohio Ct. App. 8th Dist. Cuyahoga County 2009); State v. Rodriguez, 2014-Ohio-911, 2014 WL 1345415 (Ohio Ct. App. 9th Dist. Summit County 2014); State v. Bibler, 2014-Ohio-3375, 17 N.E.3d 1154 (Ohio Ct. App. 3d Dist. Marion County 2014); State v. Inman, 2014-Ohio-3538, 2014 WL 4057720 (Ohio Ct. App. 9th Dist. Medina County 2014).

[18] Spencer v. State of Tex., 385 U.S. 554, 565–66, 87 S. Ct. 648, 17 L. Ed. 2d 606 (1967); Day v. Walker, 142 F.3d 433 (6th Cir. 1998); State v. Gordon, 28 Ohio St. 2d 45, 57 Ohio Op. 2d 180, 276 N.E.2d 243 (1971); State v. Hairston, 2008-Ohio-891, 2008 WL 583787 (Ohio Ct. App. 9th Dist. Summit County 2008).

[19] Day v. Walker, 142 F.3d 433 (6th Cir. 1998).

nature of the prior conviction. Further, the prosecution is not required to accept the defendant's proffered stipulation to the prior conviction.[20] In a felony prosecution for domestic violence, the name and nature of the prior offense has substantial probative value because of the prosecution's burden of proving beyond a reasonable doubt the defendant's prior conviction for domestic violence or one of the other crimes set forth in RC 2919.25(D). In order for the jury to find the defendant guilty, it must know the name and nature of the prior offense to determine whether the prior is one of those offenses enumerated in the statute that causes the current charge to become a felony.[21]

Q & A: In a felony domestic violence trial, the prosecution presented a certified copy of a journal entry to establish that the defendant was previously convicted of domestic violence. No other evidence was submitted on the issue of the defendant's prior conviction. At the conclusion of the state's case, the defense moved to dismiss the indictment, citing the prosecution's failure to prove all of the elements of the offense. Should the court grant the motion?

Yes. Maintaining the burden of proof concerning this element of a felony domestic violence charge requires more than the presentation of a court record that states that someone with the defendant's name was convicted on a prior occasion of one of the crimes set forth in RC 2919.25(D). The prosecution must also present evidence that will establish that the individual convicted on that prior occasion was, in fact, the defendant.[22] Any documentary evidence must be supplemented by additional testimony from witnesses familiar with the facts and circumstances of the prior offense who can identify the defendant as the same person involved in both violations.[23] The prior-conviction evidence presented at trial must be limited to the certified copy of the judgment entry and just enough evidence to identify the defendant named in the judgment entry as the same defendant in the case before the court. In other words, the prosecution must bear its burden of proof without presenting so many details of the former offense that the defendant is convicted on the basis of those crimes and not on the

---

[20]State v. Plas, 1995 WL 500110 (Ohio Ct. App. 9th Dist. Lorain County 1995); State v. Smith, 68 Ohio App. 3d 692, 589 N.E.2d 454 (9th Dist. Summit County 1990); State v. Baker, 2008-Ohio-1909, 2008 WL 1808339 (Ohio Ct. App. 9th Dist. Summit County 2008), appeal dismissed, ordered not precedential, 121 Ohio St. 3d 1233, 2009-Ohio-1675, 905 N.E.2d 194 (2009); Alston v. Voorhies, 2010 WL 3895069 (N.D. Ohio 2010); State v. Inman, 2014-Ohio-3538, 2014 WL 4057720 (Ohio Ct. App. 9th Dist. Medina County 2014).

[21]State v. Russell, 1998 WL 778312 (Ohio Ct. App. 12th Dist. Butler County 1998); Heard v. Hudson, 2008 WL 5188274 (N.D. Ohio 2008); State v. Jones, 2012-Ohio-1480, 2012 WL 1107745 (Ohio Ct. App. 12th Dist. Warren County 2012); Jones v. Warden, Noble Correctional Inst., 2014 WL 6673615 (S.D. Ohio 2014), report and recommendation adopted, 2015 WL 248031 (S.D. Ohio 2015).

[22]State v. McCoy, 89 Ohio App. 3d 479, 483, 624 N.E.2d 1102 (10th Dist. Franklin County 1993); State v. Blonski, 125 Ohio App. 3d 103, 707 N.E.2d 1168 (9th Dist. Medina County 1997); State v. King, 2000 WL 330048 (Ohio Ct. App. 5th Dist. Stark County 2000); State v. Werfel, 2003-Ohio-6958, 2003 WL 22994981 (Ohio Ct. App. 11th Dist. Lake County 2003); State v. Kellum, 2009-Ohio-6743, 2009 WL 4896239 (Ohio Ct. App. 12th Dist. Butler County 2009).

[23]State v. Lynch, 1999 WL 11244 (Ohio Ct. App. 9th Dist. Lorain County 1999).

basis of the evidence presented on the crimes pending before the bench.[24]

Q & A: Where the defendant denies being present at the time the event occurred, is it permissible for the court to allow testimony concerning "other acts" as a means of identifying the defendant as the perpetrator of the act of domestic violence?

No. "Other act" testimony may be used to prove identity by establishing a modus operandi applicable to the crime with which the defendant is charged. Such acts may be introduced to establish the identity of a perpetrator by showing that the defendant has committed similar crimes and that a distinct, identifiable scheme, plan, or system was used. Such evidence is admissible because it provides a "behavioral fingerprint" which, when compared to the "behavioral fingerprint" in the case before the bench, can be used to identify the defendant as the perpetrator of the current offense. To be admissible to prove identity through modus operandi, the "other acts" testimony must be related to and share common features with the crime in question.[25]

Where the only plausible purpose of the "other acts" testimony is to draw an impermissible character inference that the defendant committed the act before and, therefore, did so in the current case, a jury should not be permitted to hear the evidence.[26]

Q & A: Can a court take judicial notice of the prior convic-

[24]RC 2945.75(B); State v. Day, 99 Ohio App. 3d 514, 517, 651 N.E.2d 52 (12th Dist. Clermont County 1994); State v. King, 2000 WL 330048 (Ohio Ct. App. 5th Dist. Stark County 2000); State v. Abernathy, 2015-Ohio-1363, 2015 WL 1530810 (Ohio Ct. App. 5th Dist. Stark County 2015); State v. Bibler, 2014-Ohio-3375, 17 N.E.3d 1154 (Ohio Ct. App. 3d Dist. Marion County 2014); State v. Scott, 2015-Ohio-5397, 2015 WL 9435159 (Ohio Ct. App. 5th Dist. Fairfield County 2015).

[25]State v. Lowe, 69 Ohio St. 3d 527, 1994-Ohio-345, 634 N.E.2d 616 (1994); State v. Bey, 85 Ohio St. 3d 487, 1999-Ohio-283, 709 N.E.2d 484 (1999); State v. Jones, 2008-Ohio-968, 2008 WL 613116 (Ohio Ct. App. 4th Dist. Scioto County 2008); State v. Brooks, 2008-Ohio-6600, 2008 WL 5228438 (Ohio Ct. App. 7th Dist. Mahoning County 2008); State v. Richardson, 2010-Ohio-471, 2010 WL 497343 (Ohio Ct. App. 6th Dist. Lucas County 2010); State v. Edwards, 2011-Ohio-1752, 2011 WL 1378927 (Ohio Ct. App. 1st Dist. Hamilton County 2011); State v. Thomas, 2011-Ohio-1629, 2011 WL 1233310 (Ohio Ct. App. 9th Dist. Lorain County 2011); State v. Belger, 2011-Ohio-980, 2011 WL 766654 (Ohio Ct. App. 5th Dist. Delaware County 2011); State v. Knuckles, 2011-Ohio-4242, 2011 WL 3793342 (Ohio Ct. App. 8th Dist. Cuyahoga County 2011); State v. Ridley, 2013-Ohio-1268, 2013 WL 1289533 (Ohio Ct. App. 6th Dist. Lucas County 2013); Richardson v. Smith, 2012 WL 5903986 (N.D. Ohio 2012), report and recommendation adopted, 2012 WL 5903896 (N.D. Ohio 2012); State v. Primeau, 2012-Ohio-5172, 2012 WL 5463019 (Ohio Ct. App. 8th Dist. Cuyahoga County 2012); State v. Sargent, 2015-Ohio-704, 29 N.E.3d 331 (Ohio Ct. App. 6th Dist. Lucas County 2015); State v. Short, 2015-Ohio-3183, 2015 WL 4720395 (Ohio Ct. App. 5th Dist. Richland County 2015).

[26]State v. Deyling, 1998 WL 46753 (Ohio Ct. App. 9th Dist. Medina County 1998). But see *Deyling* dissent, quoting State v. Jamison, 49 Ohio St. 3d 182, 552 N.E.2d 180 (1990); State v. Baldwin, 2009-Ohio-1836, 2009 WL 1036099 (Ohio Ct. App. 3d Dist. Putnam County 2009); State v. McKim, 2009-Ohio-5949, 2009 WL 3756729 (Ohio Ct. App. 5th Dist. Delaware County 2009); State v. Morris, 2012-Ohio-6151, 985 N.E.2d 274 (Ohio Ct. App. 9th Dist. Medina County 2012), judgment aff'd, 141 Ohio St. 3d 399, 2014-Ohio-5052, 24 N.E.3d 1153 (2014); State v. Sargent, 2015-Ohio-704, 29 N.E.3d 331 (Ohio Ct. App. 6th Dist. Lucas County 2015); State v. Jenkins, 2015-Ohio-1113, 2015 WL 1303094 (Ohio Ct. App. 5th Dist. Stark County

tion that forms the basis of a felony charge of domestic violence, if the defendant is willing to stipulate to it?

No. Because the prior conviction not only enhances the penalty but also enhances the degree of the offense, the existence of the prior conviction is an element of the present crime.[27] The state must prove not only the existence of the prior conviction but also the identity of the accused as the perpetrator in the prior offense beyond a reasonable doubt to establish this element.[28] The trier of fact must then find for the prosecution on that element, along with all of the others of the current offense, in order to convict the defendant of the second violation.[29]

The court cannot bifurcate the proof of this element of the offense and it cannot allow any part of it to be proven by judicial notice.[30] It is not enough for a defendant to stipulate the existence of a prior conviction to support a finding that a prior conviction for domestic violence or another crime specified in RC 2919.25(D) existed against him. A defendant must also be willing to stipulate that he was the person convicted in the prior proceeding. Therefore, without the presentation of some proof on the latter issue, the trial court does not have evidence before it that would satisfy the prior conviction element of the present offense.[31]

Stipulation to prior convictions is widely recognized as a practice that benefits defendants by precluding the state from introducing evidence concerning the details of the prior convictions.[32] A failure to stipulate, on the other hand, places the burden of proof back on the state. Absent a stipulation, the state can prove a prior conviction with

---

2015).

[27]State v. Allen, 29 Ohio St. 3d 53, 54, 506 N.E.2d 199, 200 (1987); Parma v. Benedict, 2015-Ohio-3340, 2015 WL 4978992 (Ohio Ct. App. 8th Dist. Cuyahoga County 2015); State v. Canada, 2015-Ohio-2167, 2015 WL 3540402 (Ohio Ct. App. 10th Dist. Franklin County 2015); State v. Bibler, 2014-Ohio-3375, 17 N.E.3d 1154 (Ohio Ct. App. 3d Dist. Marion County 2014); State v. Waheed, 2016-Ohio-2951, 2016 WL 2841926 (Ohio Ct. App. 1st Dist. Hamilton County 2016).

[28]State v. Twyford, 94 Ohio St. 3d 340, 359, 2002-Ohio-894, 763 N.E.2d 122, 143 (2002).

[29]State v. Gordon, 28 Ohio St. 2d 45, 49, 57 Ohio Op. 2d 180, 276 N.E.2d 243 (1971).

[30]State v. Fittro, 66 Ohio St. 3d 16, 1993-Ohio-172, 607 N.E.2d 447 (1993); State v. Sweeney, 131 Ohio App. 3d 765, 773, 723 N.E.2d 655 (2d Dist. Montgomery County 1999); State v. Hairston, 2008-Ohio-891, 2008 WL 583787 (Ohio Ct. App. 9th Dist. Summit County 2008); State v. Bibler, 2014-Ohio-3375, 17 N.E.3d 1154 (Ohio Ct. App. 3d Dist. Marion County 2014); State v. Ramsey, 2015-Ohio-4812, 2015 WL 7428725 (Ohio Ct. App. 5th Dist. Richland County 2015), appeal not allowed, 145 Ohio St. 3d 1424, 2016-Ohio-1173, 47 N.E.3d 168 (2016).

[31]State v. Mitchell, 1996 WL 695665 (Ohio Ct. App. 8th Dist. Cuyahoga County 1996); State v. Arnold, 2002 WL 93423 (Ohio Ct. App. 8th Dist. Cuyahoga County 2002); State v. Gordon, 28 Ohio St. 2d 45, 57 Ohio Op. 2d 180, 276 N.E.2d 243 (1971); State v. Wesley, 2002-Ohio-4429, 2002 WL 1986545 (Ohio Ct. App. 8th Dist. Cuyahoga County 2002); State v. Thomas, 2009-Ohio-1784, 2009 WL 1019855 (Ohio Ct. App. 8th Dist. Cuyahoga County 2009); State v. Hairston, 2008-Ohio-891, 2008 WL 583787 (Ohio Ct. App. 9th Dist. Summit County 2008); State v. Kilpatrick, 2009-Ohio-5555, 2009 WL 3389182 (Ohio Ct. App. 8th Dist. Cuyahoga County 2009).

[32]State v. Adams, 37 Ohio St. 3d 295, 297, 525 N.E.2d 1361 (1988); State v. Waheed, 2016-Ohio-2951, 2016 WL 2841926 (Ohio Ct. App. 1st Dist. Hamilton County 2016).

a certified copy of the judgment entry of that conviction.[33] Without proof of identity, however, establishment of this element remains incomplete.

Q & A: The defendant is charged with domestic violence, elevated to a third degree felony because of two alleged prior convictions. At trial, the defense not only refuses to stipulate to any alleged prior conviction, but also objects to the introduction of an alleged third prior conviction proferred by the prosecution, maintaining that it is unduly prejudicial. How should the trial court rule?

In such a case, the probative value of the third conviction substantially outweighes its prejudicial effect. Since the defendant refuses to stipulate to any of the prior domestic violence convictions, it is entirely possible that the trier of fact could reject one of the prior convictions and leaving the other two needed to elevate the offense to a third-degree felony. The trial court should, however,instruct any jury that evidence of the defendant's past convictions cannot be used to show that the defendant acted in conformity with those past acts.[34]

Q & A: At a trial where the defendant is accused of attempting to strangle a family or household member, the prosecution offers evidence that on a prior occasion the defendant attempted to strangle another family or household member in the exact same manner. The defense objects to the admission of this "other acts" testimony. Should the evidence be admitted?

No. Other acts may prove identity by establishing a *modus operandi* applicable to the crime with which a defendant is charged. Other acts forming a unique, identifiable plan of criminal activity are admissible to establish identity.[35] However, where, as here, evidence of identity is undisputed and a determination of guilt is not furthered by such evidence, no legitimate purpose is served by use of other acts evidence to prove identity, and the use of other acts evidence to prove identity is of no probative value on any material issue in dispute. Its use is substantially outweighed by the danger of unfair prejudice and it should not be admitted.[36]

---

[33] RC 2945.75(B).

[34] State v. Russell, 2013-Ohio-1381, 2013 WL 1438000 (Ohio Ct. App. 12th Dist. Butler County 2013).

[35] Evid. R. 404(B); State v. Jamison, 49 Ohio St. 3d 182, 552 N.E.2d 180 (1990).

[36] State v. Jamison, 49 Ohio St. 3d 182, 552 N.E.2d 180 (1990); State v. Curry, 43 Ohio St. 2d 66, 72 Ohio Op. 2d 37, 330 N.E.2d 720 (1975); Whiteman v. State, 119 Ohio St. 285, 6 Ohio L. Abs. 695, 164 N.E. 51, 63 A.L.R. 595 (1928); Barnett v. State, 104 Ohio St. 298, 135 N.E. 647, 27 A.L.R. 351 (1922); State v. Williams, 134 Ohio St. 3d 521, 2012-Ohio-5695, 983 N.E.2d 1278 (2012); State v. Sargent, 2015-Ohio-704, 29 N.E.3d 331 (Ohio Ct. App. 6th Dist. Lucas County 2015). But see also State v. Meeks, 2015-Ohio-1527, 34 N.E.3d 382 (Ohio Ct. App. 5th Dist. Stark County 2015); State v. Short, 2015-Ohio-3183, 2015 WL 4720395 (Ohio Ct. App. 5th Dist. Richland County 2015); Cleveland v. Brown, 2016-Ohio-5405, 2016 WL 4399506 (Ohio Ct. App. 8th Dist. Cuyahoga County 2016); State v. Costell, 2016-Ohio-3386, 2016 WL 3223905 (Ohio Ct. App. 3d Dist. Union County 2016), appeal not allowed, 147 Ohio St. 3d 1505, 2017-Ohio-261, 67 N.E.3d 823 (2017); State v. Jordan, 2016-Ohio-603, 2016 WL 685307 (Ohio Ct. App. 2d Dist. Montgomery County 2016), appeal not allowed, 146

§ 5:22 Case preparation—Review of the charging document in felony domestic violence cases

In Ohio, with one exception, an individual may not be charged with felony domestic violence unless previously convicted of a specified prior criminal act or acts against a family or household member.[1] The exception is if the alleged offender knew that the alleged victim of the violation was pregnant at the time of the violation. In those instances where the alleged offender is believed to have knowingly or recklessly caused or attempted to cause physical harm to an alleged pregnant victim, the offender may be charged with a felony of the fifth degree.[2]

In those instances where a prior conviction or convictions are alleged as an element of the offense, the existence of those prior convictions must appear in the charging document.[3] If no prior conviction is alleged in the charging document, the offense remains a misdemeanor violation.[4]

The addition of a pregnancy specification not only enhances a first degree misdemeanor domestic violence charge to a fifth degree felony, it also requires, upon conviction, mandatory imprisonment of not less than six months.[5]

Where an offender was previously convicted of one, two or more qualifying offenses, a new allegation that the offender has violated either division (A) or (B) of the domestic violence statute enhances the penalties imposed upon a new conviction.[6] Pregnancy specifications, alleging that the offender caused physical harm to either a pregnant family or household member or that family or household member's unborn, carry escalating mandatory terms of imprisonment upon conviction.[7]

Q & A: The defense counsel maintains that the state cannot try his client for felony domestic violence because the indictment against the defendant fails to aver that the offense charged is a second or subsequent offense. Is the defense correct?

Yes. Before the state may seek to inflict greater punishment for a second or subsequent offense, it is essential that the indictment or information aver that the offense charged is, in fact, a second or subsequent offense.[8]

Q & A: The defendant is charged with felony domestic

Ohio St. 3d 1428, 2016-Ohio-4606, 52 N.E.3d 1204 (2016).

[Section 5:22]

[1]R.C. 2919.25(D). See also Cleveland v. Cooper-Hill, 2004-Ohio-6920, 2004 WL 2931001 (Ohio Ct. App. 8th Dist. Cuyahoga County 2004).

[2]R.C. 2919.25 (D)(5).

[3]State v. Bewley, 2007-Ohio-7026, 2007 WL 4554150 (Ohio Ct. App. 9th Dist. Summit County 2007).

[4]State v. Bewley, 2007-Ohio-7026, 2007 WL 4554150 (Ohio Ct. App. 9th Dist. Summit County 2007).

[5]R.C. 2919.25 (D)(5).

[6]R.C. 2919.25 (D)(3), (4), (5).

[7]R.C. 2919.25 (D)(6).

[8]State v. McArthur, 1987 WL 29400 (Ohio Ct. App. 8th Dist. Cuyahoga County

violence. His attorney moves to have the charge reduced to a misdemeanor. He argues that his client's plea to the earlier charge of domestic violence was uncounseled and, therefore, cannot be used to enhance the penalty in the case presently pending before the bench. The prosecutor opposes the motion on the grounds that the record reflects the defendant's written waiver of his right to counsel at the time of the prior no contest plea and the defense failed to provide any evidence to support its claim that the prior plea was uncounseled. Should the court grant the motion?

No. The defendant's contention that an uncounseled conviction cannot serve as the basis for penalty enhancement is correct.[9] However, a defendant who is afforded the right to counsel and rejects that right by written waiver filed with the court is not considered uncounseled, provided that waiver is knowingly and intelligently made.[10]

Q & A: The defendant in a felony domestic violence case maintains that he was incorrectly charged. At a hearing, he presents a transcript of his guilty plea in a prior domestic violence case. The transcript appears to show that the defendant was not informed that he had the right to appointed counsel at the time he entered the plea which now serves to enhance the current charge to a felony. Should the court grant the defendant's motion to strike the prior conviction from the indictment?

Yes. If it is established that the defendant was indigent and not informed of his right to appointed counsel, the prior conviction may not serve as the basis for an enhancement of penalty.[11] Where questions arise concerning a prior conviction, a reviewing court must presume that all underlying proceedings were conducted in accordance with the law. The defendant is required to introduce evidence

---

1987); State v. Hiles, 2009-Ohio-6602, 2009 WL 4827654 (Ohio Ct. App. 4th Dist. Ross County 2009); State ex rel. Smith v. Smith, 69 Ohio St. 196, 68 N.E. 1044 (1903).

[9]State v. Brandon, 45 Ohio St. 3d 85, 543 N.E.2d 501 (1989); State v. Brooke, 113 Ohio St. 3d 199, 2007-Ohio-1533, 863 N.E.2d 1024 (2007); State v. Colon, 2008-Ohio-4940, 2008 WL 4377446 (Ohio Ct. App. 9th Dist. Lorain County 2008); State v. Volpe, 2008-Ohio-1678, 2008 WL 928342 (Ohio Ct. App. 10th Dist. Franklin County 2008). See also State v. Anderson, 2012-Ohio-4476, 2012 WL 4475345 (Ohio Ct. App. 5th Dist. Stark County 2012); State v. Bode, 144 Ohio St. 3d 155, 2015-Ohio-1519, 41 N.E.3d 1156 (2015); State v. Troyer, 2016-Ohio-3090, 2016 WL 2944812 (Ohio Ct. App. 5th Dist. Holmes County 2016); State v. Waheed, 2016-Ohio-2951, 2016 WL 2841926 (Ohio Ct. App. 1st Dist. Hamilton County 2016).

[10]State v. Carrion, 84 Ohio App. 3d 27, 616 N.E.2d 261 (9th Dist. Lorain County 1992); State v. Kiger, 2002-Ohio-7172, 2002 WL 31859444, *2 (Ohio Ct. App. 7th Dist. Columbiana County 2002); State v. Vales, 2000 WL 217802, *3 (Ohio Ct. App. 8th Dist. Cuyahoga County 2000). But see State v. Clevenger, 2002-Ohio-5515, 2002 WL 31341521 (Ohio Ct. App. 11th Dist. Lake County 2002); State v. Starett, 2009-Ohio-744, 2009 WL 405908 (Ohio Ct. App. 4th Dist. Athens County 2009); State v. Hernandez, 2017-Ohio-4157, 2017 WL 2442980 (Ohio Ct. App. 7th Dist. Belmont County 2017), appeal not allowed, 151 Ohio St. 3d 1455, 2017-Ohio-8842, 87 N.E.3d 222 (2017).

[11]State v. Adams, 37 Ohio St. 3d 295, 525 N.E.2d 1361 (1988); see also State v. Talbot, 45 Ohio Misc. 2d 2, 545 N.E.2d 102 (Mun. Ct. 1988); State v. Hobbs, 2000 WL 988758 (Ohio Ct. App. 9th Dist. Summit County 2000); State v. Goodman, 2002-Ohio-818, 2002 WL 274639 (Ohio Ct. App. 9th Dist. Medina County 2002); State v. Esner, 2008-Ohio-6654, 2008 WL 5259725 (Ohio Ct. App. 8th Dist. Cuyahoga County 2008).

to the contrary in order to establish a prima facie showing of unconstitutionality.[12] If the defendant presents some evidence demonstrating that he was not afforded his constitutional right to counsel, the state has the obligation of proving that the prior conviction was constitutionally valid.[13] Once the defendant establishes a prima facie case, a silent record cannot establish that the defendant waived his constitutional right to counsel.[14]

Q & A: A defendant who pleaded guilty to a misdemeanor domestic violence charge was subsequently charged with a felony after the state discovered the existence of a prior escalating misdemeanor in the defendant's criminal history. Neither the defendant nor her counsel informed the court of the prior conviction at the time of the misdemeanor sentencing, which occurred immediately following the defendant's plea. The defendant now moves the court to dismiss the felony, citing double jeopardy. Should the court grant the defendant's motion?

A defendant who pleads no contest or guilty to a misdemeanor charge of domestic violence, because she is aware that a prior conviction could be used by the prosecution to escalate that charge to a felony, is still covered by the protections of the constitution's Double Jeopardy Clause, if a two-part test can be met. First, is the prior conviction an essential element of the subsequent felony charge that must be alleged and proven by the state? Secondly, is there an absence of evidence that the defendant attempted to control or impede the criminal proceedings by manipulating the judicial system?[15] Applying this test to the instant question, it can be seen that the existence of the escalating prior offense is an essential element of the subsequent felony charge and that the defendant's silence about the earlier conviction cannot be interpreted as an attempt to manipulate the system, as the defendant is under no obligation to assist the prosecution in its determination as to the appropriate charge to bring against her. Having failed to uncover the existence of the prior conviction in a timely fashion, although the information was easily uncovered through the exercise of due diligence, the prosecution cannot avoid the operation

---

[12]State v. Brandon, 45 Ohio St. 3d 85, 543 N.E.2d 501 (1989); State v. Brooke, 113 Ohio St. 3d 199, 2007-Ohio-1533, 863 N.E.2d 1024 (2007); State v. Colon, 2008-Ohio-4940, 2008 WL 4377446 (Ohio Ct. App. 9th Dist. Lorain County 2008); State v. Volpe, 2008-Ohio-1678, 2008 WL 928342 (Ohio Ct. App. 10th Dist. Franklin County 2008).

[13]State v. Maynard, 38 Ohio App. 3d 50, 526 N.E.2d 316 (8th Dist. Cuyahoga County 1987); State v. Jackman, 2008-Ohio-1944, 2008 WL 1822391 (Ohio Ct. App. 8th Dist. Cuyahoga County 2008).

[14]State v. Wellman, 37 Ohio St. 2d 162, 66 Ohio Op. 2d 353, 309 N.E.2d 915 (1974); State v. Chiominto, 2008-Ohio-3393, 2008 WL 2635487 (Ohio Ct. App. 11th Dist. Lake County 2008), judgment rev'd, 121 Ohio St. 3d 606, 2009-Ohio-1905, 906 N.E.2d 1111 (2009); State v. Karnofel, 2017-Ohio-428, 2017 WL 486901 (Ohio Ct. App. 11th Dist. Trumbull County 2017).

[15]State v. Goodman, 2002-Ohio-818, 2002 WL 274639 (Ohio Ct. App. 9th Dist. Medina County 2002).

of the Double Jeopardy Clause, and the defendant's motion to dismiss should be granted.[16]

Q & A: A defendant, who pleaded guilty to a misdemeanor domestic violence charge, was subsequently charged with a felony after the state discovered the existence of a prior escalating misdemeanor in the defendant's criminal history. Neither the defendant nor her counsel informed the court of the prior conviction at the time of the misdemeanor sentencing, which occurred immediately following the defendant's plea. The defendant now moves the court to dismiss the felony, citing double jeopardy. Should the court grant the defendant's motion?

A defendant who pleads no contest or guilty to a misdemeanor charge of domestic violence, because she is aware that a prior conviction could be used by the prosecution to escalate that charge to a felony, is still covered by the protections of the Constitution's Double Jeopardy Clause, if a two part test can be met. First, is the prior conviction an essential element of the subsequent felony charge that must be alleged and proven by the state? Second, is there an absence of evidence that the defendant attempted to control or impede the criminal proceedings by manipulating the judicial system?[17] Applying this test to the instant question, it can be seen that the existence of the escalating prior offense is an essential element of the subsequent felony charge and that the defendant's silence about the earlier conviction cannot be interpreted as an attempt to manipulate the system, as the defendant is under no obligation to assist the prosecution in its determination as to the appropriate charge to bring against her. Having failed to uncover the existence of the prior conviction in a timely fashion, although the information was easily uncovered through the exercise of due diligence, the prosecution cannot avoid the operation of the Double Jeopardy Clause, and the defendant's motion to dismiss should be granted.[18]

Q & A: Is the court required to inform a defendant of the inherent dangers of self-representation in order for the defendant's waiver of the right to counsel to be effective?

No. The Ohio Supreme Court has found a waiver of counsel valid even though the trial court did not advise the defendant of the dangers inherent in self-representation.[19]

§ 5:23 Case preparation—Declarant unavailability

Under Evidence Rule 804(A), an individual is unavailable if he/she:

---

[16]State v. Goodman, 2002-Ohio-818, 2002 WL 274639 (Ohio Ct. App. 9th Dist. Medina County 2002).

[17]State v. Goodman, 2002-Ohio-818, 2002 WL 274639 (Ohio Ct. App. 9th Dist. Medina County 2002).

[18]State v. Goodman, 2002-Ohio-818, 2002 WL 274639 (Ohio Ct. App. 9th Dist. Medina County 2002).

[19]State v. Brooke, 113 Ohio St. 3d 199, 2007-Ohio-1533, ¶ 27-39, 863 N.E.2d 1024 (2007); State v. Wells, 2009-Ohio-6803, 2009 WL 4984066 (Ohio Ct. App. 7th Dist. Belmont County 2009); State v. Drager, 2014-Ohio-3056, 2014 WL 3407874 (Ohio Ct. App. 2d Dist. Montgomery County 2014).

(1) is exempted by ruling of the court on grounds of privilege concerning the subject matter,
(2) persists in refusing to testify on the subject matter, despite order of court to do so,
(3) testifies to a lack of memory concerning the subject matter,
(4) is unable to be present or testify at the hearing because of death or then-existing physical or mental illness or infirmity, or
(5) is absent from the proceedings despite the efforts of the proponent to secure the declarant's attendance.

The following statements of an unavailable declarant are exempted from the hearsay rule under Evidence Rule 803(B):
(1) former testimony,
(2) statements made under a belief of impending death,
(3) statements against interest,
(4) statements of personal or family history, and
(5) statements by a deceased or incompetent person.

Q & A: The defense objects to the prosecution's attempt to offer the preliminary hearing testimony of an alleged domestic violence victim who fails to appear for trial. The prosecutor represents that numerous attempts were made to secure the victim's attendance, including going to her home and contacting her parents. The prosecutor requests that the court find the declarant unavailable and admit the transcribed statements as exceptions to the hearsay rule. Should the court sustain the defense counsel's objection?

Yes. The rule in Ohio governing this exception to the hearsay rule is set forth in a two-part test.[1] First, a witness is not considered unavailable unless the prosecution makes reasonable efforts in good faith to secure the witness's presence at trial. The prosecution must exhibit its efforts to secure the witness through the testimony of witnesses, rather than through hearsay not under oath, unless the unavailability of the witness is conceded by the party against whom the statement is offered. Second, the out-of-court statement must bear sufficient indicia of reliability.[2]

§ 5:24 Case preparation—Prior bad acts

The inherently cyclical and recurring nature of domestic violence means that the admissibility of "other acts" evidence is an issue that the prosecution will frequently address. In Ohio, evidence of previous

[Section 5:23]

[1]State v. Keairns, 9 Ohio St. 3d 228, 460 N.E.2d 245 (1984); State v. Wolderufael, 2003-Ohio-3817, 2003 WL 21666400 (Ohio Ct. App. 10th Dist. Franklin County 2003); State v. Walenciej, 2009-Ohio-936, 2009 WL 501251 (Ohio Ct. App. 7th Dist. Jefferson County 2009); State v. Hairston, 2009-Ohio-2346, 2009 WL 1396434 (Ohio Ct. App. 10th Dist. Franklin County 2009); State v. Ford, 2008-Ohio-4373, 2008 WL 3970913 (Ohio Ct. App. 10th Dist. Franklin County 2008); State v. Hiles, 2009-Ohio-6602, 2009 WL 4827654 (Ohio Ct. App. 4th Dist. Ross County 2009).

[2]State v. Robinson, 1998 WL 404216 (Ohio Ct. App. 7th Dist. Mahoning County 1998).

or subsequent criminal acts, wholly independent of the offense for which the defendant is charged, is generally *not* admissible in criminal cases.[1]

However, "other acts" testimony *is* admissible in certain cases as a result of the codification of exceptions to the general rule.[2]

Exceptions under Evidence Rule 404(B) are limited to those instances where the probative value of the evidence is not outweighed by the prejudice that the defendant suffers from its admission.[3] Evidence of "other acts" is admissible if it tends to provide substantial proof of a specific element of the crime charged or one of the matters specifically enumerated in RC 2945.59.[4]

[Section 5:24]

[1]State v. Wilkinson, 64 Ohio St. 2d 308, 18 Ohio Op. 3d 482, 415 N.E.2d 261 (1980); see also State v. Smith, 49 Ohio St. 3d 137, 551 N.E.2d 190 (1990); State v. Williams, 38 Ohio St. 3d 346, 528 N.E.2d 910 (1988); State v. Bloomfield, 2004-Ohio-749, 2004 WL 307467 (Ohio Ct. App. 4th Dist. Ross County 2004). But see State v. Griffin, 142 Ohio App. 3d 65, 753 N.E.2d 967 (1st Dist. Hamilton County 2001); State v. Hernandez, 2009-Ohio-386, 2009 WL 223882 (Ohio Ct. App. 6th Dist. Lucas County 2009); State v. Adams, 2009-Ohio-6863, 2009 WL 5064297 (Ohio Ct. App. 3d Dist. Defiance County 2009); State v. Thomas, 2013-Ohio-5386, 2013 WL 6535216 (Ohio Ct. App. 1st Dist. Hamilton County 2013); State v. Sargent, 2015-Ohio-704, 29 N.E.3d 331 (Ohio Ct. App. 6th Dist. Lucas County 2015); State v. Inman, 2014-Ohio-3538, 2014 WL 4057720 (Ohio Ct. App. 9th Dist. Medina County 2014).

[2]RC 2945.59; Evid.R. 404(B); State v. Burson, 38 Ohio St. 2d 157, 67 Ohio Op. 2d 174, 311 N.E.2d 526 (1974); see also State v. Wright, 2001-Ohio-2473, 2001 WL 1627643 (Ohio Ct. App. 4th Dist. Washington County 2001); State v. Broom, 40 Ohio St. 3d 277, 277, 533 N.E.2d 682, 686 (1988); State v. Stephens, 2008-Ohio-890, 2008 WL 583789 (Ohio Ct. App. 9th Dist. Summit County 2008); State v. Fisher, 2009-Ohio-2915, 2009 WL 1719370 (Ohio Ct. App. 4th Dist. Washington County 2009); State v. Lewis, 2010-Ohio-130, 2010 WL 177758 (Ohio Ct. App. 4th Dist. Pickaway County 2010); State v. Workman, 2009-Ohio-2995, 2009 WL 1798871 (Ohio Ct. App. 9th Dist. Summit County 2009); State v. Short, 2015-Ohio-3183, 2015 WL 4720395 (Ohio Ct. App. 5th Dist. Richland County 2015); Williams v. Turner, 2014 WL 4441409 (N.D. Ohio 2014).

[3]RC 2945.59; State v. Smith, 49 Ohio St. 3d 137, 551 N.E.2d 190 (1990); State v. Kinney, 2008-Ohio-4612, 2008 WL 4183324 (Ohio Ct. App. 4th Dist. Ross County 2008); State v. Gillispie, 2012-Ohio-2942, 985 N.E.2d 145 (Ohio Ct. App. 2d Dist. Montgomery County 2012); State v. Sargent, 2015-Ohio-704, 29 N.E.3d 331 (Ohio Ct. App. 6th Dist. Lucas County 2015); State v. Inman, 2014-Ohio-3538, 2014 WL 4057720 (Ohio Ct. App. 9th Dist. Medina County 2014).

[4]Evid.R. 404(B); State v. Flonnory, 31 Ohio St. 2d 124, 60 Ohio Op. 2d 95, 285 N.E.2d 726 (1972); State v. Curry, 43 Ohio St. 2d 66, 72 Ohio Op. 2d 37, 330 N.E.2d 720 (1975); State v. Pearson, 1999-Ohio-792, 1999 WL 378349 (Ohio Ct. App. 3d Dist. Seneca County 1999); State v. Wright, 2001-Ohio-2473, 2001 WL 1627643, *5 (Ohio Ct. App. 4th Dist. Washington County 2001); State v. Jamison, 49 Ohio St. 3d 182, 182, 552 N.E.2d 180, 181 (1990); State v. Thompson, 66 Ohio St. 2d 496, 498, 20 Ohio Op. 3d 411, 422 N.E.2d 855, 856 (1981); State v. Hawn, 138 Ohio App. 3d 449, 462, 741 N.E.2d 594, 603 (2d Dist. Montgomery County 2000); State v. Kinney, 2008-Ohio-4612, 2008 WL 4183324 (Ohio Ct. App. 4th Dist. Ross County 2008); State v. Hart, 2009-Ohio-997, 2009 WL 580808 (Ohio Ct. App. 12th Dist. Warren County 2009); State v. Baldwin, 2009-Ohio-1836, 2009 WL 1036099 (Ohio Ct. App. 3d Dist. Putnam County 2009); State v. Gonzalez, 2008-Ohio-2749, 2008 WL 2331444 (Ohio Ct. App. 7th Dist. Mahoning County 2008); State v. Morrow, 2008-Ohio-3958, 2008 WL 3009683 (Ohio Ct. App. 9th Dist. Summit County 2008); State v. Vinson, 2008-Ohio-2523, 2008 WL 2192819 (Ohio Ct. App. 9th Dist. Summit County 2008); Wright v. Kerns, 2009 WL 5178307 (S.D. Ohio 2009); In re J.M., 2009-Ohio-4574, 2009 WL 2836452 (Ohio Ct. App. 4th Dist. Pike County 2009), judgment vacated in part, 127 Ohio St. 3d 8,

"Other acts" evidence may be admitted for reasons other than those listed in the Revised Code[5] or the Rules of Evidence,[6] provided that the evidence is not offered solely to show the defendant's propensity to commit the crime in question.[7] Evidence of other crimes may be presented when they are so blended and connected with the one on trial that proof of one incidentally involves the other or explains the circumstances thereof, or tends logically to prove any element of the crime charged.[8]

The threshold question in determining the admissibility of "other acts" evidence under Evidence Rule 404(B) is whether any of the matters of proof (motive, opportunity, scheme, etc.) are at issue in the case. If not, then "other acts" evidence is not admissible, no matter how telling, and regardless of whether an accused's past behavior constitutes a behaviorist fingerprint.[9]

The Supreme Court of Ohio noted that "[t]he other acts of the defendant must have such a temporal, modal and situational relationship with the acts constituting the crime charged that evidence of the other acts discloses purposeful action in the commission of the offense in question. The evidence is then admissible to the extent it may be relevant in showing the defendant acted in the absence of mistake or accident."[10]

The acts that qualify under this exception may or may not be simi-

---

2010-Ohio-4935, 935 N.E.2d 839 (2010); State v. McKim, 2009-Ohio-5949, 2009 WL 3756729 (Ohio Ct. App. 5th Dist. Delaware County 2009); State v. Richardson, 2010-Ohio-471, 2010 WL 497343 (Ohio Ct. App. 6th Dist. Lucas County 2010); State v. Perkins, 191 Ohio App. 3d 263, 2010-Ohio-5161, 945 N.E.2d 1083 (2d Dist. Miami County 2010); State v. Bradford, 2010-Ohio-6429, 2010 WL 5508718 (Ohio Ct. App. 12th Dist. Warren County 2010). But see also State v. Sargent, 2015-Ohio-704, 29 N.E.3d 331 (Ohio Ct. App. 6th Dist. Lucas County 2015); State v. Meeks, 2015-Ohio-1527, 34 N.E.3d 382 (Ohio Ct. App. 5th Dist. Stark County 2015); Williams v. Turner, 2014 WL 4441409 (N.D. Ohio 2014); State v. Kinsworthy, 2014-Ohio-1584, 2014 WL 1489250 (Ohio Ct. App. 12th Dist. Warren County 2014); State v. Williams, 2017-Ohio-803, 2017 WL 900070 (Ohio Ct. App. 5th Dist. Stark County 2017).

[5]RC 2945.59; State v. Williams, 134 Ohio St. 3d 521, 2012-Ohio-5695, 983 N.E.2d 1278 (2012); State v. Sargent, 2015-Ohio-704, 29 N.E.3d 331 (Ohio Ct. App. 6th Dist. Lucas County 2015); State v. Machuca, 2016-Ohio-254, 2016 WL 363448 (Ohio Ct. App. 3d Dist. Allen County 2016), appeal not allowed, 145 Ohio St. 3d 1472, 2016-Ohio-3028, 49 N.E.3d 1314 (2016).

[6]Evid.R. 404.

[7]State v. Wright, 2001-Ohio-2473, 2001 WL 1627643 (Ohio Ct. App. 4th Dist. Washington County 2001); State v. Crosby, 186 Ohio App. 3d 453, 2010-Ohio-1584, 928 N.E.2d 795 (8th Dist. Cuyahoga County 2010); State v. Wright, 2011-Ohio-3575, 2011 WL 2899217 (Ohio Ct. App. 8th Dist. Cuyahoga County 2011).

[8]State v. Wilkinson, 64 Ohio St. 2d 308, 18 Ohio Op. 3d 482, 415 N.E.2d 261 (1980); U.S. v. Turner, 423 F.2d 481, 483–84 (7th Cir. 1970); State v. Watson, 28 Ohio St. 2d 15, 57 Ohio Op. 2d 95, 275 N.E.2d 153 (1971); Wright v. Kerns, 2009 WL 5178307 (S.D. Ohio 2009); State v. Clouse, 2012-Ohio-3471, 2012 WL 3133059 (Ohio Ct. App. 10th Dist. Franklin County 2012); State v. Partlow, 2013-Ohio-2771, 2013 WL 3356575 (Ohio Ct. App. 10th Dist. Franklin County 2013); State v. Kennard, 2016-Ohio-2811, 2016 WL 2348330 (Ohio Ct. App. 10th Dist. Franklin County 2016).

[9]State v. Smith, 2002-Ohio-2886, 2002 WL 1299769 (Ohio Ct. App. 1st Dist. Hamilton County 2002).

[10]State v. Burson, 38 Ohio St. 2d 157, 67 Ohio Op. 2d 174, 311 N.E.2d 526 (1974); State v. Shah, 2014-Ohio-1449, 2014 WL 1384365 (Ohio Ct. App. 2d Dist. Montgomery County 2014); State v. Short, 2015-Ohio-3183, 2015 WL 4720395 (Ohio Ct. App. 5th Dist. Richland County 2015).

lar to the crime on trial. "Other acts" evidence is not admissible to establish the character of a person in order to show that he/she acted in conformity with that character at the time in question or that the person had a propensity to act in a certain manner.[11]

A request for a curative instruction from the court, defining the limits of the use of "other acts" evidence, should always accompany any request for admission of such evidence.

Q & A: When arrested, the defendant told the police that the victim was injured when she tripped over a stool and struck her head on the side of a door. At trial, the prosecution wants to present evidence from several witnesses that the defendant had committed prior acts of domestic violence against the victim. Counsel for the defense objects on the grounds that the prosecution is offering the evidence solely to convince the jury that the defendant intended to hurt his wife at the time in question. The prosecution contends the evidence is offered to counter the defendant's anticipated defense of accident. Should the court sustain the objection?

No. The threshold criterion for judging the admissibility of evidence of "other acts" is whether that evidence can show by substantial proof any of the things enumerated in Evidence Rule 404(B) and RC 2945.59, such as proof of motive, opportunity, preparation, plan, knowledge, identity, absence of mistake, or accident. In this case, the evidence offered meets that criterion in that it rebuts the defendant's contention that the current incident of violence was anomalous.

Q & A: In a felony prosecution for domestic violence, the prosecution attempts to prove the defendant's prior conviction of domestic violence. In addition to a certified copy of the judgment entry of conviction, the prosecution calls the probation officer who supervised the defendant's probation for that offense. Over defense objection, the prosecutor is allowed to question the probation officer as to the sentence the defendant received and the terms of that probation. Did the court err in allowing this testimony?

Yes. A certified copy of the judgment entry of conviction, together with evidence sufficient to identify the defendant referenced in the entry as the same defendant currently before the bench, is sufficient to prove the prior conviction. Additional testimony concerning the sentence the defendant previously received and the terms of probation is not relevant and could prove prejudicial.[12]

Q & A: At trial, the defendant offers evidence that he acted in self-defense at the time of the incident before the court and that the complainant was injured when she fell as she lunged at him. The defendant maintains that he never struck a woman in his life. On rebuttal, the prosecution attempts to offer the

[11]Evid.R. 404(B); State v. Smith, 49 Ohio St. 3d 137, 551 N.E.2d 190 (1990); State v. Baldwin, 2009-Ohio-1836, 2009 WL 1036099 (Ohio Ct. App. 3d Dist. Putnam County 2009); State v. Adams, 2009-Ohio-6863, 2009 WL 5064297 (Ohio Ct. App. 3d Dist. Defiance County 2009); State v. Greene, 2012-Ohio-5624, 983 N.E.2d 773 (Ohio Ct. App. 5th Dist. Tuscarawas County 2012); State v. Sargent, 2015-Ohio-704, 29 N.E.3d 331 (Ohio Ct. App. 6th Dist. Lucas County 2015).

[12]State v. Amos, 1988 WL 4622 (Ohio Ct. App. 11th Dist. Lake County 1988).

testimony of the defendant's former wife to establish that he assaulted her during their marriage. The defense objects. Should the court sustain the objection?

No. Where a defendant only asserts self-defense and does not otherwise contradict any essential element of the crime charged, at least one Ohio court questioned the ability of the state to utilize "other acts" evidence to establish the defendant's intent or to demonstrate that the injuries suffered by the complainant were not the result of an accident.[13] In that court's view such matters are uncontested and, therefore, simply not in issue. When, as in this example, the defendant's testimony raises both the issue of self-defense *and* whether the complainant's injuries were accidental and not the result of any intentional or knowing conduct on the part of the defendant, a different situation exists. In that case, "other acts" evidence is admissible to prove the defendant's culpable mental state and the lack of accident.

Q & A: The defendant in a domestic violence case denies striking the complainant and further denies even being present when the complainant was injured. The prosecution intends to offer evidence of other acts to refute the defendant's claims and to establish the defendant's identity as the perpetrator of the current offense. Should the evidence be admitted for the stated purposes?

Probably not. Other acts may be introduced to establish the identity of a perpetrator by showing the commission of similar crimes and that a distinct identifiable scheme, plan or system was used in the commission of the charged offense. Other acts evidence is admissible to prove identity through the characteristics of acts rather than through a person's character. To be admissible to prove identity through modus operandi, other acts evidence must be related to and share common features with the crime in question.[14]

Evidence that fails to meet this test is likely offered for only one reason, and that is to draw the impermissible inference that the defendant committed this kind of crime before and therefore did so again.[15]

Q & A: The defendant objects to being cross-examined about

---

[13]State v. Grubb, 111 Ohio App. 3d 277, 675 N.E.2d 1353 (2d Dist. Montgomery County 1996); State v. Kinney, 2008-Ohio-4612, 2008 WL 4183324 (Ohio Ct. App. 4th Dist. Ross County 2008).

[14]State v. Lowe, 69 Ohio St. 3d 527, 1994-Ohio-345, 634 N.E.2d 616 (1994); State v. Kinney, 2008-Ohio-4612, 2008 WL 4183324 (Ohio Ct. App. 4th Dist. Ross County 2008); State v. Jones, 2008-Ohio-968, 2008 WL 613116 (Ohio Ct. App. 4th Dist. Scioto County 2008); State v. Richardson, 2010-Ohio-471, 2010 WL 497343 (Ohio Ct. App. 6th Dist. Lucas County 2010); State v. Craig, 2010-Ohio-1857, 2010 WL 1712253 (Ohio Ct. App. 8th Dist. Cuyahoga County 2010); State v. Clark, 2016-Ohio-4561, 67 N.E.3d 182 (Ohio Ct. App. 8th Dist. Cuyahoga County 2016), appeal not allowed, 147 Ohio St. 3d 1474, 2016-Ohio-8438, 65 N.E.3d 778 (2016); State v. Neil, 2016-Ohio-4762, 2016 WL 3574549 (Ohio Ct. App. 10th Dist. Franklin County 2016), appeal not allowed, 147 Ohio St. 3d 1506, 2017-Ohio-261, 67 N.E.3d 823 (2017) and cert. denied, 138 S. Ct. 124, 199 L. Ed. 2d 76 (2017) and appeal not allowed, 151 Ohio St. 3d 1476, 2017-Ohio-9111, 87 N.E.3d 1273 (2017).

[15]State v. Deyling, 1998 WL 46753 (Ohio Ct. App. 9th Dist. Medina County 1998); State v. Sargent, 2015-Ohio-704, 29 N.E.3d 331 (Ohio Ct. App. 6th Dist. Lucas County 2015).

other acts mentioned on direct examination. He argues the subject matter relates to another arrest for domestic violence, pending at the time of the trial, and not a conviction. Should the objection be sustained?

No. The existence of a prior offense is generally so inflammatory that it should not be permitted except as allowed under statute or rule.[16] Ordinarily it is reversible error for the prosecutor to be permitted to ask the defendant or another witness about *arrests* for other crimes, as distinguished from convictions for violations of state or federal law unless the defense opens the subject first.[17] However, when other act testimony is opened by the defense on direct examination, and thereby becomes known to the court, regardless of whether the questions are first put to the defendant or another witness, the prosecution is free to explore the issue.[18]

Q & A: The prosecution wants to introduce evidence regarding four incidents of domestic violence against the same victim who is allegedly the victim in the case presently on trial. The defense objects. Can the court admit the evidence?

It depends. To be admissible, other acts evidence is required to be relevant to a matter at issue in the litigation. Therefore, the evidence must tend to show by substantial proof one or more of the allowable purposes such as motive, opportunity, intent, preparation, plan, knowledge, identity or absence of mistake or accident.[19] Other acts evidence is never admissible when its sole purpose is to establish that the defendant committed the act alleged in a criminal complaint, which in turn is relevant to prove the criminal offense alleged.[20] Because the rule allowing the admission of prior bad acts evidence codifies an exception to the common law, it must be strictly construed against admissibility.[21] If the evidence offered merely proves prior conforming conduct on the part of the defendant, it is inadmissible.[22]

Q & A: Does the inappropriate admission of Other Acts evidence always necessitate the granting of a new trial?

No. Even though other acts evidence is improperly admitted during a trial, it is possible that, after considering both the impact of the of-

---

[16]State v. Allen, 29 Ohio St. 3d 53, 55, 506 N.E.2d 199 (1987); State v. Smith, 2008-Ohio-4431, 2008 WL 4058121 (Ohio Ct. App. 12th Dist. Clermont County 2008); Parma v. Benedict, 2015-Ohio-3340, 2015 WL 4978992 (Ohio Ct. App. 8th Dist. Cuyahoga County 2015); State v. Canada, 2015-Ohio-2167, 2015 WL 3540402 (Ohio Ct. App. 10th Dist. Franklin County 2015); State v. Bibler, 2014-Ohio-3375, 17 N.E.3d 1154 (Ohio Ct. App. 3d Dist. Marion County 2014).

[17]State v. Pollard, 21 Ohio St. 2d 171, 50 Ohio Op. 2d 394, 256 N.E.2d 620 (1970).

[18]State v. Scott, 1999 WL 126933 (Ohio Ct. App. 7th Dist. Belmont County 1999) (overruled by, State v. Alvey, 2003-Ohio-7006, 2003 WL 22997277 (Ohio Ct. App. 7th Dist. Belmont County 2003)).

[19]Evid. R. 404(B); State v. Sims, 191 Ohio App. 3d 622, 2010-Ohio-6228, 947 N.E.2d 227 (2d Dist. Greene County 2010).

[20]Evid. R. 404(B); State v. Sims, 191 Ohio App. 3d 622, 2010-Ohio-6228, 947 N.E.2d 227 (2d Dist. Greene County 2010).

[21]Evid. R. 404(B); State v. Sims, 191 Ohio App. 3d 622, 2010-Ohio-6228, 947 N.E.2d 227 (2d Dist. Greene County 2010).

[22]Evid. R. 404(B); State v. Sims, 191 Ohio App. 3d 622, 2010-Ohio-6228, 947 N.E.2d 227 (2d Dist. Greene County 2010).

fending evidence on the verdict and the strength of the remaining evidence once the tainted evidence is removed from the record, a reviewing court might decide not to order a new trial.[23] The Ohio Supreme Court holds that an improper evidentiary admission under the Other Acts Evidence Rule[24] may be deemed harmless error on review when, after the tainted evidence is removed, the remaining evidence is overwhelming.[25]

Q& A: The defendant and the alleged victim were in a 9-year relationship. During that time the defendant was twice convicted of domestic violence against the alleged victim. The same alleged victim has now filed a new complaint against the defendant charging menacing by stalking. At trial, the prosecutor offers evidence of the the defendant's prior conduct. The defense objects. How should the court rule?

The court should allow the evidnce to come in. Other acts evidence can be particularly useful in prosecutions for menacing by stalking because it can assist the jury in understanding that a defendant's otherwise innocent appearing acts in the current trial, when put into the context of previous contacts with the victim, may be knowing attempts to cause mental distress.[26] In prosecutions for menacing by stalking, the victim's belief that the defendant will cause physical harm is an element of the offense which is often intertwined with their past interactions.[27]

§ 5:25 Case preparation—Criminal defendant's out-of-court statement

A criminal defendant's own out-of-court statement may be offered against the defendant by the state and may be admitted into evidence at trial.[1] The statements of a party are admitted upon a different principle from that which governs prior inconsistent statements. Such statements are admissions and provable by independent testimony; no foundation is necessary for their introduction as evidence, except some proof that they were made by the party/defendant.[2] If a defendant's statements are admissions, therefore, it is not necessary

---

[23]State v. Morris, 141 Ohio St. 3d 399, 2014-Ohio-5052, 24 N.E.3d 1153 (2014).

[24]Evid. R. 404(B).

[25]State v. Morris, 141 Ohio St. 3d 399, 2014-Ohio-5052, 24 N.E.3d 1153 (2014); State v. Tate, 2015 WL 6630184 (Ohio Ct. App. 8th Dist. Cuyahoga County 2015).

[26]State v. Bilder, 99 Ohio App. 3d 653, 651 N.E.2d 502 (9th Dist. Summit County 1994).

[27]State v. Hart, 2009-Ohio-997, 2009 WL 580808 (Ohio Ct. App. 12th Dist. Warren County 2009), See also, State v. Nunez, 2017-Ohio-4295, 92 N.E.3d 294 (Ohio Ct. App. 8th Dist. Cuyahoga County 2017), appeal not allowed, 150 Ohio St. 3d 1455, 2017-Ohio-8136, 83 N.E.3d 940 (2017).

[Section 5:25]

[1]Evid.R. 801(D)(2)(a).

[2]State v. Thompson, 87 Ohio App. 3d 570, 622 N.E.2d 735 (9th Dist. Medina County 1993); State v. Johnson, 2003-Ohio-2540, 2003 WL 21142519, *4 (Ohio Ct. App. 12th Dist. Butler County 2003); State v. Baker, 137 Ohio App. 3d 628, 652, 739 N.E.2d 819, 836 (12th Dist. Clinton County 2000); State v. Pryor, 2013-Ohio-5693, 2013 WL 6836255 (Ohio Ct. App. 5th Dist. Stark County 2013); State v. Littrell, 2014-Ohio-2130, 2014 WL 2106791 (Ohio Ct. App. 5th Dist. Licking County 2014);

either that they be inconsistent with his trial testimony or that the prosecution establish the time place or other person involved for them to be admissible.[3] Use of the term "admission" in relation to statements of parties may be misleading. The term "admission" appears to imply that the out-of-court statement must be a confession or statement against interest, in actuality, any prior statement of a party is admissible providing it is offered against the party at trial.[4] Evidence Rule 801(D)(2)(a) does not require that the statement to be introduced contradict the defendant's position. Rather, it only requires that the statement be offered against the defendant's interest, and in support of the state's case.[5]

Q & A: Does the rule regarding a defendant's out-of-court statements extend to audio and video taped statements?

Yes. Any such statement may be admitted, as long as: (1) there is proof to establish that the out-of-court statement was made by the defendant, (2) the statement is presented against the defendant's interest at trial, and (3) the statement's probative value outweighs its prejudicial effect.[6]

Q & A: The defendant is on trial before a jury for domestic violence. The prosecution offers calls that the defendant made to the alleged victim from jail, in which the defendant apologizes for the "wrong" that resulted in the defendant's arrest. The defense objects to the introduction of the calls, on the grounds that they are more prejudicial than probative. How should the court rule?

The evidence presented on the tapes is relevant because the jury can infer that the defendant's apologies to the alleged victim on the tapes indicate consciousness of guilt.[7] The court should allow the introduction of the evidence.

§ 5:26 Case preparation—Victim and/or witness unavailability; sample trial brief

It is prudent for the prosecution to anticipate some initial resistance from many courts to going forward to trial when the victim will

State v. Phillips, 2016-Ohio-1216, 2016 WL 1176067 (Ohio Ct. App. 5th Dist. Licking County 2016).

[3]State v. Thompson, 87 Ohio App. 3d 570, 622 N.E.2d 735 (9th Dist. Medina County 1993).

[4]1 Weissenberger, Ohio Evidence, 801.33 (1993).

[5]State v. Thompson, 87 Ohio App. 3d 570, 622 N.E.2d 735 (9th Dist. Medina County 1993); State v. Johnson, 2003-Ohio-2540, 2003 WL 21142519 (Ohio Ct. App. 12th Dist. Butler County 2003).

[6]State v. Thompson, 87 Ohio App. 3d 570, 622 N.E.2d 735 (9th Dist. Medina County 1993); State v. Johnson, 2003-Ohio-2540, 2003 WL 21142519, *4 (Ohio Ct. App. 12th Dist. Butler County 2003); State v. Baker, 137 Ohio App. 3d 628, 652, 739 N.E.2d 819, 836 (12th Dist. Clinton County 2000); State v. Kelly, 2002-Ohio-6246, 2002 WL 31528695, *4 (Ohio Ct. App. 1st Dist. Hamilton County 2002); State v. Long, 53 Ohio St. 2d 91, 98, 7 Ohio Op. 3d 178, 181, 372 N.E.2d 804, 808 (1978).

[7]State v. Tvaroch, 2012-Ohio-5836, 982 N.E.2d 751 (Ohio Ct. App. 11th Dist. Trumbull County 2012), citing State v. Tichaona, 2011-Ohio-6001, 2011 WL 5829668 (Ohio Ct. App. 11th Dist. Portage County 2011), State v. Sims, 2009-Ohio-550, 2009 WL 295402 (Ohio Ct. App. 12th Dist. Butler County 2009); State v. Littrell, 2014-Ohio-2130, 2014 WL 2106791 (Ohio Ct. App. 5th Dist. Licking County 2014).

not appear and the government's case-in-chief depends primarily on evidence derived from exceptions to the hearsay rule. This is particularly true since the introduction of such evidence is likely to do severe damage to the defense and is, therefore, likely to invoke vociferous objections. Trial briefs, which provide the court with the authority to accept the legitimacy of proffered hearsay evidence, maximize the possibility of the court allowing the proffered material.

Sample Trial Brief

IN THE *[name of court]* COURT *[name of county]* COUNTY, OHIO

[Caption]

JUDGE *[name of judge]*
CASE NO. *[docket number]*
PROSECUTION'S TRIAL BRIEF

I. INTRODUCTION

The prosecution intends to prove that on *[date]* and at *[time in question]*, and within the jurisdiction of this court, the defendant, *[Defendant's Name]*, did cause or attempt to cause physical harm to the victim of this offense, *[Victim's Name]*, a *[specify victim's relationship to defendant]* of the defendant. These facts will be proven to the satisfaction of the trier of fact, beyond a reasonable doubt, by the presentation of *[outline the relevant evidence to be presented, e.g., testimony of the investigating officers, medical records, physical evidence, victim's spontaneous statements as recorded on the 911 call, statements made by the defendant to the investigating officers at the time of the offense, and the eyewitness testimony of individuals who were in a position to see or hear events that occurred at the time in question]*. It is the state's position that this evidence is all admissible under Ohio law based on the theories discussed below.

II. STATEMENT OF FACTS

The State expects the evidence to show the following:

1. On *[date]* at approximately *[time]*, officers *[names of responding officers]* responded to *[specify manner in which police became involved]* at *[location of incident]*.

2. Upon arriving at the above address, *[set forth a description of the responding officers' initial encounters with witness(es) upon arrival, including the exact wording of any exclamations, threats, etc.]*.

3. *[Describe the initial actions of the responding officers upon arriving on the scene.]*

4. The officers observed *[describe in some detail the officers' initial observations of the victim, including emotional state, appearance, presence and nature of injuries, etc.]*.

5. *[Recount any statements made by the victim to the responding police officers that support the prosecution of this defendant.]*

6. *[Outline the evidence-gathering activities of the police, including interviews with victim and the defendant, impoundment of any physical evidence, audio or videotapes produced, photographs taken, medical evidence preserved, etc.]*

7. *[Describe statements obtained from the victim and other wit-*

nesses (including the children of the parties who were present) about the incident.]

8. *[Describe any inculpatory statements obtained from the defendant.]*

9. *[Describe any medical attention necessitated by the incident.]*

10. *[Describe any other relevant facts.]*

III. WITNESS LIST

1. *[List all of the witnesses to be called at trial. Include a brief description of the relevance of each witness's testimony.]*

Additionally, the State reserves the right to call such other witnesses as may be uncovered before or during the course of the trial or who may be required to rebut testimony offered by witnesses for the defense.

IV. DOCUMENTARY EVIDENCE

During the trial of this case, the State expects to offer the following exhibits into evidence:

[List the exhibits that the government intends to present at trial.]

Additionally, the State reserves the right to augment the evidence it will present with any additional relevant evidence that may come to its attention before or during the trial of the matter now before the court. The State also reserves the right to present any other evidence that may be required to rebut testimony or evidence presented by the defense.

V. LEGAL ISSUES AND AUTHORITY

A. THE PROSECUTION IS UNDER NO OBLIGATION TO PRODUCE ANY PARTICULAR WITNESS, INCLUDING THE VICTIM, TO SUSTAIN ITS BURDEN OF PROOF AT TRIAL.

The State intended to call the complainant and her children to testify in this case. However, numerous efforts to contact the complainant in the last seven days have been unsuccessful. The State has sufficient credible evidence independent of the testimony of the complainant and her children to establish the defendant's guilt beyond a reasonable doubt. Therefore, the State intends to take this matter to trial with or without the active participation of the complainant and/or her children. If the prosecution's efforts to contact the complainant continue to be unsuccessful, it is the State's intention to present certain oral statements that the complainant and her children made to the police dispatcher and the investigating police officers during their initial investigation of this crime.

The prosecution is not required by law or rule to produce the victim at the trial of a complaint alleging domestic violence. State v. Lee, 73 Ohio Misc. 2d 9, 657 N.E.2d 604 (Mun. Ct. 1995). The prosecution's failure to do so will not deprive the defendant of his constitutional right to confront his accusers. In White v. Illinois, 502 U.S. 346, 112 S. Ct. 736, 116 L. Ed. 2d 848, 33 Fed. R. Evid. Serv. 881 (1992), the United States Supreme Court held that the Confrontation Clause of the Sixth Amendment to the United States Constitution does not require that the proponent of an Evidence Rule 803 hearsay exception demonstrate the unavailability of the declarant as a predicate for the admission of such evidence.

If the prosecution's efforts to locate the victim and her children continue to bear no fruit, the State will move the court, in limine, to allow the testimony of the deputy bailiff who attempted service to explain the witnesses' absence and establish their unavailability as required under the Rules of Evidence in order to counter any speculation that might arise in regard to the absence of the witnesses.

In the matter currently pending before this court, the prosecution complied with its obligations under Criminal Rule 16 by providing the defendant with identifying information regarding its potential witnesses and the substance of the statements which it now proposes to present at the time of trial. The defendant, therefore, is foreclosed from arguing that his right to receive a fair trial was purposely denied by the prosecution's attempt to prevent the trier of fact from hearing the testimony of a material witness or witnesses. The fact that a material witness is not available for trial, despite the prosecution's diligent efforts to produce the witness, does not automatically mean that the defendant's due process rights, in general, and right to confrontation, in specific, have been violated. In State v. Dever, 64 Ohio St. 3d 401, 415, 1992-Ohio-41, 596 N.E.2d 436 (1992), the Court quoted from the United States Supreme Court's holding in Ohio v. Roberts, 448 U.S. 56, 100 S. Ct. 2531, 65 L. Ed. 2d 597, 7 Fed. R. Evid. Serv. 1 (1980) (abrogated by, Crawford v. Washington, 541 U.S. 36, 124 S. Ct. 1354, 158 L. Ed. 2d 177, 63 Fed. R. Evid. Serv. 1077 (2004)), and said, "the prosecution must make a good faith effort to produce the declarant, or demonstrate the declarant's unavailability. The prosecution continues its efforts to locate and produce the complainant and will continue to do so up to the time of trial. The prosecution argues, however, that the out-of-court statements made by the complainant and her children are non-testimonial, as that term is set forth under the tests announced in Crawford v. Washington, 541 U.S. 36, 124 S. Ct. 1354, 158 L. Ed. 2d 177, 63 Fed. R. Evid. Serv. 1077 (2004), and Davis v. Washington, 547 U.S. 813, 126 S. Ct. 2266, 165 L. Ed. 2d 224, 70 Fed. R. Evid. Serv. 472, 30 A.L.R.6th 599 (2006), and that it will demonstrate, as required, that such statements are admissible as exceptions to the hearsay rule under Evid.R. 803, regardless of whether the declarant's unavailability is ultimately established. Dutton v. Evans, 400 U.S. 74, 91 S. Ct. 210, 27 L. Ed. 2d 213 (1970).

The State is aware of the more recent dictum employed by the Ohio Supreme Court in State v. Storch, 66 Ohio St. 3d 280, 1993-Ohio-38, 612 N.E.2d 305 (1993), which suggests that the Ohio Constitution might provide greater protection for an accused than does the United States Constitution. See O. Const. Art. I § 10. The *Storch* Court dictum goes on to construe the right to confrontation contained in Article I, Section 10, of the Ohio Constitution to require the live testimony of witnesses against a criminal defendant whenever possible. It also reflects a preference for requiring the prosecution to establish the unavailability of a declarant before admitting the declarant's hearsay statement(s) into evidence.

However, the *Syllabus* in *Storch* makes no mention of the effect of the Ohio Constitution's Confrontation Clause on the admission of hearsay evidence at trial. Rule 1(B) of the Supreme Court Rules for the Reporting of Opinions provides that "[t]he syllabus of a Supreme Court opinion states the controlling point or points of law decided in and necessarily arising from the facts of the specific case before the Court for adjudication." Where the justice writing an opinion expresses matters or views not included in the syllabus, those matters are merely the personal opinions of the justice. Thus, the *Storch syllabus*, which does not impose an availability requirement on firmly rooted hearsay exceptions, states the controlling points of law arising out of that case. State ex rel. Donahey v. Edmondson, 89 Ohio St. 93, 105 N.E. 269 (1913). See also State v. Johnson, 1995 WL 764319 (Ohio Ct. App. 4th Dist. Ross County 1995).

B. <u>STATEMENTS MADE BY THE VICTIM, HER CHILDREN, AND *[NAMES OF WITNESSES]* MADE AT THE TIME OF THEIR INITIAL INTERVIEWS BY THE POLICE AT THE SCENE WERE EACH EXCITED UTTERANCES. AS SUCH, ALL ARE ADMISSIBLE IN EVIDENCE UNDER EVIDENCE RULE 803(2).</u>

The rule which governs the admission of excited utterances into evidence was first announced by the Ohio Supreme Court in the lead case of Potter v. Baker, 162 Ohio St. 488, 495–96, 55 Ohio Op. 389, 124 N.E.2d 140, 53 A.L.R.2d 1234 (1955). That Court held:

> The basic justification advanced for this exception to the hearsay rule is 'that in the stress of nervous excitement the reflective faculties may be stilled and the utterance may become the unreflecting and sincere expression of one's actual impressions and belief.' 6 Wigmore on Evidence (3 Ed.), 139, Section 1749. With respect to this exception, it is stated in 6 Wigmore on Evidence (3 Ed.), 142, 155, Section 1749:
>
> . . . the following limitations, and these only, may legitimately be deduced:
>
> (a) . . . There must be some occurrence, startling enough to produce this nervous excitement and render the utterance spontaneous and unreflecting. . . .
>
> (b) Time of the Utterance. The utterance must have been before there has been time to contrive and misrepresent, i.e., while the nervous excitement may be supposed still to dominate and the reflective powers to be yet in abeyance. . . .
>
> It is to be observed that the statements need not be strictly contemporaneous with the exciting cause; they may be subsequent to it, provided there has not been time for the exciting influence to lose its sway and to be dissipated. . . .
>
> . . .
>
> Furthermore, there can be no definite and fixed limit of time. Each case must depend upon its own circumstances . . . .
>
> . . .
>
> (c) . . . The utterance must relate to the circumstances of the occurrence preceding it. . . .
>
> It is also stated in 6 Wigmore on Evidence (3 Ed.), 155, Section 1751:
>
> Upon the ordinary principle applicable to all testimonial evidence . . . and therefore to hearsay statements offered under these exceptions . . . the declarant must appear to have had an opportunity to observe personally the matter of which he speaks.

See also State v. Lee, 73 Ohio Misc. 2d 9, 657 N.E.2d 604 (Mun. Ct. 1995).

Excited utterances are exempted from the operation of the

prohibitions imposed by the hearsay rule for two reasons. First, such statements are deemed trustworthy because the stimulus renders the declarant incapable of fabrication. Second, the impression on the declarant's memory at the time of the statement is still fresh and intense. State v. Taylor, 66 Ohio St. 3d 295, 612 N.E.2d 316 (1993).

Because these statements are *exceptions* to the hearsay rule, the availability of the declarant is not an issue. Evidence Rule 803; U.S. v. Inadi, 475 U.S. 387, 106 S. Ct. 1121, 89 L. Ed. 2d 390, 19 Fed. R. Evid. Serv. 1009 (1986). Therefore, the statements should be allowed into evidence, whether or not the declarant takes the witness stand during the course of the trial.

The tests set forth in *Potter*, *supra*, were codified with the enactment of Evidence Rule 803(2). Again, to qualify as an excited utterance, a statement must meet the four-part test set forth in the Rule and under *Potter*, *supra*:

(1) There must have been an occurrence, startling enough to produce the requisite nervous excitement.

(2) Although the statement does not have to coincide exactly with the occurrence, it must be made before the excitement of the event has worn off and the declarant has had time to regain dominion over his reflective faculties.

(3) The statement must relate to the exciting occurrence or the circumstances of the exciting occurrence.

(4) The declarant must have had an opportunity to observe personally the matters asserted in his statement.

See also State v. Taylor, 66 Ohio St. 3d 295, 612 N.E.2d 316 (1993); State v. Justice, 92 Ohio App. 3d 740, 637 N.E.2d 85 (9th Dist. Wayne County 1994); *State v. Lee, supra.*

Additionally, in determining whether a particular excited utterance meets the test, consideration must be given to (1) the lapse of time between the event and the declaration, (2) the mental and physical condition of the declarant, (3) the nature of the statement, and (4) the influence of intervening circumstances. State v. Montgomery, 1986 WL 15250 (Ohio Ct. App. 8th Dist. Cuyahoga County 1986).

In the case at bar, the State will establish that each of the statements made by the declarants to the investigating officers meets the prerequisite tests of Evidence Rule 803(2). Therefore, the Court should admit them into evidence under the provisions of that rule and consistent with the Supreme Court's holding in *Potter*.

1. The statements were made after an exciting event.

There can be no question that the events under discussion here meet the first test for the admission of statements as excited utterances. Even under the defendant's version of the facts before the court, the incident that resulted in his arrest was *[describe the incident]*. Such an event would be considered sufficiently startling to cause excitement in the average person. If the acts are viewed from the standpoint of the victim, there is the assertion that a crime has been committed. Certainly, the event was "startling enough to still the declarant's reflective faculties." State

v. Estepp, 1989 WL 2293 (Ohio Ct. App. 1st Dist. Hamilton County 1989).

2. <u>The statements were made, in each instance, before the declarant had an opportunity to regain control of his/her reflective faculties.</u>

In the case before the bench, *[describe in detail the amount of time that passed from the occurrence of the incident to the arrival of the police and their taking of witnesses' statements to establish the spontaneity of the statements]*.

The victim and her children were, of course, present during the incident and made their statements to the police as the incident continued. All were observed to be visibly upset and still directly affected by the traumatic nature of their recent experiences. *[Modify this paragraph to conform to facts of case.]*

The emotional and/or physical condition of each of these witnesses at the time they were interviewed by the police clearly meets the requirements of the second test for the admission of excited utterances into evidence. See Potter v. Baker, 162 Ohio St. 488, 55 Ohio Op. 389, 124 N.E.2d 140, 53 A.L.R.2d 1234 (1955); State v. Duncan, 53 Ohio St. 2d 215, 7 Ohio Op. 3d 380, 373 N.E.2d 1234 (1978).

3. <u>The statements made by each of the witnesses relate to defendant's violent attack on the victim of this offense</u>.

The statements that each of the witnesses made to police in this case related back to the startling event of the defendant's attack on the victim of this assault. These statements are incidental to the main fact and explanatory of it. They are so connected to the main event that their utterance is an expression of the circumstances under which they were made, rather than the narrative result of thought. State v. Montgomery, 1986 WL 15250 (Ohio Ct. App. 8th Dist. Cuyahoga County 1986). Therefore, these statements meet the third prong of the *Potter* test for their admission into evidence as exceptions to the hearsay rule.

4. <u>Each of the witnesses had first-hand knowledge of the subject of their statements</u>.

[Names of witnesses] observed the defendant *[describe the incident]*. The victim and her children were actually involved in the disturbance that was the subject of their statements. Each of the declarants in this case actually observed the events that gave rise to the statements that they ultimately made to the police. Therefore, the fourth prong of the *Potter* test is also met. State v. Perdue, 1993 WL 546609 (Ohio Ct. App. 7th Dist. Mahoning County 1993). The circumstances of the statements made by each of these witnesses are such that they are each free on their face of premeditation and design. No cause intervened to damage the trustworthiness of the circumstantial guarantees inherent in any of the statements made by these witnesses immediately following the exciting incident that brings us to court. State v. Brown, 1983 WL 6945 (Ohio Ct. App. 6th Dist. Lucas County 1983).

The State is prepared to show by a preponderance of the evidence that the statements made by each declarant identified herein meet the tests set forth in both *Potter* and *Crawford*, supra. Each statement is, therefore, excepted from the operation of the hearsay rule and does not offend the defendant's right to confront *[his/her]* accuser under the Sixth Amendment to the U.S. Constitution or Article I, Section 10 of Ohio's Constitution. The court should allow each of the proffered statements into evidence as part of the prosecution's case-in-chief.

VI. CONCLUSION

The State will establish to the satisfaction of the trier of fact, beyond a reasonable doubt, that Defendant committed domestic violence against *[Victim's Name]* at the time and place alleged in the complaint. The State hopes to present its case with the active participation of the victim in its case-in-chief. However, even if the victim is unavailable to the State at the time of trial, enough independent evidence exists to establish that Defendant committed the offense charged and to require this Court to find that the State has borne its burden of proof in establishing Defendant's guilt.

Chapter 6

Domestic Violence Prosecution—Trial Presentation

§ 6:1 Trial presentation—Special considerations for domestic violence

Preparation for a domestic violence trial requires the prosecutor to expect the unexpected. Reluctant, uncooperative, and even hostile victims, witnesses of very tender years, incomplete investigations, and skeptical triers of fact make the domestic violence trial a landscape littered with mines. Thorough, methodical review, analysis, and integration of all relevant evidence supporting conviction are necessary to compensate for these obstacles.

During initial case intake, both the investigating officer and the prosecutor must take great care to identify, develop, and preserve as much corroborative evidence as possible. It is true that, under the law, the victim's testimony alone, if it is believed, is sufficient to justify a conviction.[1] Frequently, however, prosecutions fail where there is no confirmation of the abuser's criminal acts by supplemental evidence beyond the statements of the victim.

Cases that involve recanting victims are the most likely to suffer this fate. The nature and dynamics of domestic violence make it highly likely that a significant minority, if not a majority, of the victims who go to trial will be less than stellar witnesses for the government. As a result, the prosecutor must come to trial prepared to deal with a variety of circumstances only infrequently encountered in other criminal cases.

The prosecutor should develop an overall strategy for the presentation of domestic violence cases in general. In developing that strategy, some items for the prosecutor to consider are:

(1) How can the public's interest in prosecuting domestic violence be emphasized?

(2) How can the prosecutor present the pursuit of domestic violence crimes as an opportunity to intervene in potentially lethal situations before the violence becomes fatal?

(3) Is it possible to recreate for the trier of fact the tenseness leading up to the domestic violence episode? Can the evidence tangibly exhibit the victim's fear at the time of the attack? Is there a way to graphically present the defendant's aggressive, dominating, and ultimately violent behavior? It is important for the prosecutor to make it possible for the trier of fact to visualize the anxiety and danger surrounding a domestic violence incident in order to overcome prevalent biases and stereotypes concerning this crime.

(4) The use of witnesses tactically as well as strategically. For instance, the order in which the witnesses are presented can shift the burden of prosecution away from victims and toward the government. If the prosecution presents the victim after the responding officers, medical providers, and investigating detective testify, it is more likely that the trier of fact will see the victim's testimony as something other than the keystone of the government's case.

(5) The best way to tell the story. True domestic violence seldom occurs in a vacuum. There is usually a significant history leading up to the violent criminal act before the court. Presenting the entire picture to the trier of fact is crucial to obtaining a conviction.

(6) How to explode domestic violence myths. Stereotypes about domestic violence perpetrators and victims abound. When the victim testifies for the defense, the judge or jury may become confused about what they are seeing. The facts of a particular case may require the use of expert testimony to help the trier of fact understand the dynamics of the irrational, unusual, and bizarre behaviors that the principals in a domestic violence incident exhibit on the street and in the courtroom.

[Section 6:1]

[1]See State v. Quisenberry, 1996 WL 65253 (Ohio Ct. App. 2d Dist. Montgomery County 1996); State v. Johnson, 1991 WL 274490 (Ohio Ct. App. 9th Dist. Lorain County 1991).

(7) How to present the defendant's true character to the trier of fact. Few defendants are evil people all of the time. Many batterers have a public persona that contradicts the charges that the government presents against them. It is a mistake to paint such people as one-dimensional. Instead, the prosecution should focus on a strategy that capitalizes on those aspects of the defendant's personality that are congruent with the prosecution's view and exploit any flaws in that personality that shore up the reliability of the testimony offered by the prosecution's witnesses.

The uniqueness of domestic violence cases requires a special set of tools to overcome the inherent difficulties that their circumstances routinely bring to the trial setting. Such tools include the means to counter the infirmities of reluctant or hostile witnesses. They also prepare the uninitiated trier of fact for witness behavior that might appear, at best, bizarre and, at worst, aberrant, disrespectful, or obnoxious. These tools are absolutely essential for the government's successful trial presentation of criminal assaults complicated by intimate relationships.

§ 6:2 Trial presentation—Jury voir dire—Generally

The prosecutor's primary function during jury selection in domestic violence cases is to focus the prospective members of the jury on the fact that the case is being brought on behalf of all the people in the jurisdiction and not just the victim in the particular case before the bench. The prosecution must make every effort to establish the fact that the jury is reviewing an allegation of criminal, and not private, behavior.

Some classes of potential jurors can be more troublesome than others in domestic violence cases. The prosecutor should identify males who view women as inferior or weaker, religious fundamentalists, professional women, survivors of domestic violence, and others who might have rigid or dogmatic views about women, for example, for close questioning. For different reasons, members of each of these groups might find objective service on a jury examining domestic violence to be uncomfortable, difficult, or impossible.

§ 6:3 Trial presentation—Jury voir dire—Sample general questions

The following list of questions is presented to demonstrate the variety of issues that the prosecutor may legitimately explore when selecting a jury in a domestic violence case. The list is not meant to be exhaustive. Whether or not a specific question or a particular series of questions is appropriate depends on the fact pattern of the particular case.

(1) Do you agree that domestic violence may take place even if the victim is not injured, depending on the facts of a particular case?

(2) If the evidence presented in this case convinces you beyond a reasonable doubt that the defendant is guilty of domestic violence, do you have any religious, moral, or philosophical

beliefs that would make it difficult for you to convict the defendant of the charge of domestic violence?

(3) Do you understand that reasonable doubt does not exist merely because the defendant's version of this case differs substantially from the State's (City's) version?

(4) Does anyone on the panel believe that the State has no business sticking its nose in a dispute between two people involved in an intimate relationship unless the dispute results in serious physical injury to one of the parties?

(5) Except in the case of self-defense, are there any other circumstances that you believe would justify an individual hitting his/her partner?

(6) Does anyone feel that the use of physical force is sometimes acceptable to resolve a verbal argument? When would you feel that force is justified?

(7) Does anyone disagree with this statement: "When there is a disagreement in an intimate relationship, someone has to have the power to resolve the dispute"?

(8) Has anyone ever heard what he/she believed was a physical fight taking place at a neighbor's home? Did you call the police? If not, why not?

(9) If you heard your next-door neighbor beating his/her spouse [insert appropriate combination, e.g., her husband, his girlfriend, her boyfriend, etc.], would you ever get involved to stop it? If not, why not?

(10) Does anyone believe that violence in an intimate relationship should be worked out by the parties and not dragged into criminal court?

(11) Does anyone believe that if a woman did something that made her spouse or boyfriend mad enough to hit her, she probably deserved what happened?

(12) Does anyone believe that if a man did something that made his spouse or girlfriend mad enough to hit him, he probably deserved what happened?

(13) Does anyone feel that domestic violence happens primarily in certain ethnic or socioeconomic groups?

(14) Does anyone feel that they can tell whether a person is a batterer just by looking at him/her?

(15) The victim in this case was not married to the defendant at the time that this event took place. If the court instructs you that the relationship of the victim and defendant is, nonetheless, covered by the domestic violence laws of this state, could you accept that instruction?

(16) The victim in this case did not live with the defendant at the time that this event took place. If the court instructs you that the relationship of the victim and defendant is covered, nonetheless, by the domestic violence laws of this state, could you accept that instruction?

(17) The victim and the defendant in this case never lived together, but it is alleged that they had a child in common when this event took place. If the court instructs you that the domestic violence laws of this state cover their relationship, could you accept that instruction?

(18) Does anyone feel that the victim's marital status should disqualify him/her from the protection of the domestic violence laws?

(19) Do you believe that most allegations of domestic violence are false or exaggerated?

(20) Do you believe that someone can be hurt and not have any injuries that you can see?

(21) Does anyone agree with this statement: "Men are presumed guilty until proven innocent under the domestic violence laws"?

(22) Does anyone believe that it is better for the State to fight crime in the streets than to get involved in the affairs of people who are arguing and fighting in the privacy of their own homes?

(23) Can you base your decision in this case solely on the evidence presented in this court and set aside any feelings of sympathy or bias for or against either the victim or the defendant in this case?

(24) If you represented the people of this State, would you feel comfortable having a person with your attitudes, background, and experiences hearing this case?

(25) Would you be able to follow the law as the judge gives it to you and apply it to the facts in this case, even if it differs from what you think the law should be?

§ 6:4 Trial presentation—Jury voir dire—Sample questions for victimless prosecution

(1) Do you agree that the State has the right to prosecute this case, even if the victim does not want the defendant prosecuted?

(2) Do you agree that the State has an obligation to prosecute people who are violent toward their family and/or household members?

(3) Do you agree that the State has an obligation to prosecute a charge of domestic violence if it has sufficient evidence, even if that evidence does not include the testimony of the victim?

(4) Do you believe that the State has the right to prosecute domestic violence even if the victim refuses to come to court to testify against the defendant?

(5) Do you believe that it is possible for the State to prove this case if the victim does not testify?

(6) Would you be able to find the defendant guilty if the State is able to produce enough evidence to convince you of the defendant's guilt beyond a reasonable doubt *without* the testimony of the victim?

(7) If the State bears its burden of proof and presents enough evidence to convince you of the defendant's guilt beyond a reasonable doubt, could you find the defendant guilty even if the victim testifies on the defendant's behalf?

(8) Do you believe that a victim of domestic violence is less likely to tell the truth than a victim of another crime?

(9) Do you think that a victim of domestic violence is more likely to cover up for the suspect who committed that crime than someone who was the victim of another crime?

(10) Do you believe that a victim of domestic violence is more likely to come under pressure from friends, family, or the suspect than are victims of other crimes?

(11) Do you believe that the victims of domestic violence are more likely to refuse to cooperate with a prosecutor than victims of other crimes?

(12) Do you believe that the victims of domestic violence are more likely than victims of other crimes to fear for their security, whether physical or financial?

§ 6:5 Trial presentation—Jury voir dire—Sample questions regarding domestic violence as a crime

(1) The case before the court involves an allegation that the defendant, who is the (define defendant's relationship to victim, e.g., husband, wife, boyfriend, girlfriend, etc.) of the victim, did (describe the violent act) to the victim. Is there anyone on the panel who does not believe that this charge, if proven, is a crime?

(2) We expect that evidence will be presented that the defendant had consumed a quantity of alcohol (drugs) just prior to this offense. Do you believe that the consumption of alcohol (drugs) excuses an individual from responsibility for his/her criminal behavior?

(3) Do you believe that the State has an obligation to prosecute persons who cause domestic violence in their homes, even if their victims refuse to cooperate out of love, loyalty, culture, persuasion, or economic considerations?

(4) Do you believe that the victim "brought" these charges against the defendant? Does anyone on the panel believe that the victim can "drop" the charges?

(5) Do you understand that in Ohio victims do not "bring" or "drop charges"? Do you understand that the prosecutor makes these decisions after a full review of the facts?

§ 6:6 Trial presentation—Jury voir dire—Sample questions regarding personal issues

(1) Have you or anyone close to you ever been the victim of, or a witness to, domestic violence? Who? If so, would that fact prevent you from being fair and impartial to both sides in this case?

(2) Have you or anyone close to you ever been the victim of, or witness to, a violent crime? Who? Was anyone hurt? How badly? Was medical attention required? Was time lost from work? Was that case prosecuted? Did the victim assist the prosecution? Were the parties related or involved with one another? Did the parties stay together? Is there anything about that situation that would make it hard for you to be fair and impartial to both sides in this case?

(3) Have you ever been accused of threatening to hurt, attempting to hurt, or hurting a family or household member or a person with whom you were intimately involved?

(4) Have you ever been accused of committing any other violent crime? What? How long ago? How was that matter resolved?

(5) Has anyone close to you ever been accused of threatening to hurt, attempting to hurt, or hurting a family or household member or a person with whom he/she was intimately involved?

(6) Have you or anyone close to you ever been involved in any other criminal case? If so, in what capacity?

(7) Have you or anyone close to you ever been stopped by the police? Did that case result in a criminal charge? Do you believe that the police acted properly in that case?

(8) Have you ever been involved in a dispute in which the police were called to intervene? Do you believe that the matter was handled fairly by the police? By the prosecutor? By the court?

(9) Since you have been an adult, have you ever been involved as a participant in a physical altercation of any kind where the police had to be called?

(10) Do you believe that you could objectively evaluate the testimony of police officers that will testify during this trial?

(11) Do you agree with the following statement: "Prosecuting one romantic partner who hurts another is a waste of time and taxpayer money because they are just going to get back together again"?

(12) Do you believe that prosecuting violence that occurs between two people that love each other will probably just make matters worse?

(13) Do you agree with this statement: "Putting a person who hit a spouse or lover in jail will probably just make that person more angry"?

(14) Do you think that a person is justified in striking an unfaithful romantic partner?

(15) Is it possible for someone to still care about the person who abused them?

(16) Is there anything in your history or background that would make it hard for you to be objective in this case?

(17) Knowing that this is a domestic violence case, would you feel comfortable having someone like you judging the facts if you were the defendant? If you were the prosecutor?

(18) (Question for female prosecutors to ask, when appropriate) Do you think that the fact that I am a female and the victim is a female means that I am pursuing some radical feminist agenda in prosecuting this man? Do you understand that this law is even-handed and that, if the tables were reversed, it would be my job to pursue a female charged with this crime just as aggressively as I intend to pursue this defendant?

§ 6:7 Trial presentation—Examination of the reluctant victim—Generally

It is appropriate to reiterate here that many factors impact the reluctant victim's decision not to cooperate with the domestic violence prosecutor. These factors range from fear of the defendant to fabrication of the original story. The prosecutor's decision to go forward in the face of a reluctant or hostile victim will depend on the strength of the remaining evidence assembled by the investigating officers.

Regardless of the strength of the other evidence, however, the decision of whether or not to call the reluctant victim as a witness is crucial. In most cases, the jury will expect to hear from the victim. However, the assembly of enough other evidence renders the victim's presence or absence irrelevant.

If the victim is hostile, a better prosecution trial strategy allows the victim to initially testify for the defense. The prosecutor is then in the position to test the witnesses credibility during cross-examination. Deliberate and thorough preparation for this cross-examination is central to its success. The examiner should not restrict the scope of inquiry to the specific event that resulted in the trial. Questions regarding the nature of the parties' past relationship, current living arrangements, who controls the finances, prior arguments, intimidation or influence imposed by the accused, family members, friends, and others, as well as the witnesses' own attitudes about testifying, are all fair game.

Questioning the reluctant victim is a delicate undertaking for the prosecutor. It is not desirable to "beat up on" an already vulnerable victim on the witness stand. In an appropriate case and if handled correctly, the prosecutor's examination of the victim can portray the lack of control and susceptibility to external pressure that traditionally accompanies domestic violence victimization.

The sample questions that follow provide some ideas for the construction of an effective cross- examination of a reluctant victim. The list is not all-inclusive. Areas of examination are grouped together. However, the questions reflect the fact that the answers will necessarily dictate the direction that the examination ultimately takes. Which questions the examiner asks, of course, depends on the facts and issues raised in the case on trial.

§ 6:8 Trial presentation—Examination of the reluctant victim—Sample questions regarding the nature of the past and present relationship

These questions aim to establish the dominant position of the defendant in the relationship. By so doing, the prosecutor may also establish that the victim' s decision not cooperate is not arrived at free from the defendant's influence.

(1) Are you related to the defendant in this case? If not, how would you characterize your relationship? Is he/she the father/mother of any of your children? How many children do you have in common?
(2) How long have the two of you been together?
(3) How did you meet?
(4) How long was it before the two of you became intimate?
(5) Did you move in with him/her or did he/she move in with you?
(6) Have you ever worked outside of your home? When? When you and the defendant got together, did he/she ask you to quit work and stay home?
(7) What is your current occupation? Do you, personally, have any other source of income?
(8) Would it be fair to say that the defendant is the sole breadwinner in your household?

(9) How much money do you contribute to the household's income?
(10) Who decides how the household income is spent?
(11) Do you have many close friends? How often do you go out with your friends?
(12) Do you need your spouse's permission before you go out? Do you have to inform your spouse when you plan to go out and when you will return?
(13) Does your household have any other rules?
(14) Who makes the rules in your house?
(15) How are those household rules enforced?
(16) Are you worried about what might happen to the defendant's job as a result of this case?
(17) Would it be fair to say that the defendant is the man of your house and has the last word on most of the important decisions?
(18) Would it be fair to say that you would find it difficult to survive financially if the defendant were not there to help you?
(19) Do you depend on the defendant to take care of your mortgage (rent)?
(20) Who pays for the groceries?
(21) Who pays the utilities?
(22) Does the defendant share any of the household chores with you? Which ones? How often?
(23) Who handles the finances?
(24) Do you get an allowance from the defendant? How much?
(25) Who decides how the money in your house gets spent?
(26) Who pays the bills?
(27) Do you have your own checking account?
(28) Do you have your own savings account?
(29) Do you have any assets of your own that do not also belong to the defendant?
(30) Do you have any credit cards or other credit in your own name?
(31) Who decides how your children are disciplined?
(32) Is it fair to say that the defendant is very possessive of your time and does not like it when you go places without him/her?
(33) Does the defendant ever complain about the amount of time that you spend with your family or friends?
(34) Do you have to get the defendant's permission if you want to get home later than usual when you do go out?
(35) Does the defendant decide what social affairs you and your children can attend?
(36) Do you have any male (female, if male victim) friends? How does the defendant feel about them?
(37) Would it be fair to say that the defendant is the dominant one in your relationship and that what he/she says pretty much goes?

§ 6:9 Trial presentation—Examination of the reluctant victim—Sample general questions regarding the case before the bench

(1) You have testified that on [specify date], at your home, you and

the defendant argued. Would you mind telling the jury again how that argument started?

(2) Besides yourself and the defendant (and your children), was anyone else in the house at the time that this event took place?

(3) Where exactly were your children when the problem started?

(4) Did you see your children while the incident was going on? So, would it be fair to say that they were also in a position to see what happened to you?

(5) What exactly was the argument about?

(6) How long did the argument last?

(7) Did you actually move out of your home immediately following this incident?

§ 6:10 Trial presentation—Examination of the recanting victim—Sample questions

The prosecutor should use great care in cross-examining a recanting victim. If your examination is too harsh, it may engender sympathy for the couple and make the prosecutor look like the "bad guy." However, if the examination is not probing enough, it is impossible to discredit the defense's fabricated version of the facts.

The following sample questions are designed to expose the victim's motives for changing or abandoning the original story recounted to the police, advocates, and the prosecutor, establish the reasons why the victim has to protect the defendant, and show which party is most likely to gain from the victim's recantation.

A. Questions to establish who exercises the most power in the relationship.

(1) It is your testimony today that you were the one who initiated this argument, and not the defendant?

(2) How tall are you?

(3) How much do you weigh? Are you approximately the same weight that you were on the date that these events took place?

(4) How tall is the defendant?

(5) How much does the defendant weigh? Is the defendant approximately the same size that he/she was on the date of these events?

(6) Would it be safe to say that the defendant is a lot bigger than you are?

(7) Would it also be safe to say that the defendant is stronger than you are?

B. Questions regarding impeachment—Prior inconsistent statements.

(1) The testimony that you gave today is not the same as the story you told the police on the night that this happened, is it?

(2) Tell the jury exactly what you told the police.

(3) In fact, you described in some detail how the defendant hurt you that night, did you not?

(4) You told them that he/she [specify each of defendant's actions, e.g., hit you, grabbed you by the hair, threw you to the ground, kicked you, shoved you against a wall, etc.], did you not?

(5) You told the police that the defendant cursed you and threatened to harm you, did you not?

(6) You told the police that you were very afraid of the defendant, did you not?

(7) You showed the police where you were injured by the defendant, did you not?

(8) Showing you what has been marked as State's Exhibit 1, can you identify that exhibit as the written statement that you gave to the police on the day of the incident? Is that your signature that appears at the bottom of that document?

(9) You never told the police officers that came to your house that you started the argument, did you?

(10) Did you not sign the probable cause statement before the officers arrested the defendant? And you never once told the police not to arrest the defendant, did you?

(11) Did you not repeat the same story that you told the police to the prosecutor who prepared the complaint in this case?

(12) Is it not a fact that the statement you gave to the police is accurate and your testimony today is not truthful?

(13) Showing you what have been marked as State's Exhibits 2, 3, 4, and 5, do you recognize these photographs? Do they fairly and accurately depict your condition immediately following this event?

(14) Is it not true that, contrary to your testimony today, the defendant struck you on that day and that is how you received the [describe injury, e.g., cut, bruise, black eye, etc.] that appears in that photograph?

(15) Is it not a fact that the defendant caused the other injuries that appear in those pictures?

(16) Is it your testimony today that the defendant did not cause the injuries that appear in these photographs?

(17) Do you remember telling [name of officer] that the defendant [specify defendant's actions]?

(18) So, it is your testimony that you do not remember what you told the officer?

(19) Is it your testimony that you lied to the officer at the time of the incident, but you are telling the truth now?

(20) If the officer testified that you did make those statements, did the officer lie?

(21) You also spoke with a victim's advocate about this case, did you not? When did you speak to the victim's advocate?

(22) What did you tell the victim's advocate about how you got the injuries shown in the photographs?

(23) So, it is your testimony today that you were not truthful with the victim's advocate either?

(24) When did you decide to tell this current version of your story?

(25) You did not decide to change your story until after the defendant was released from jail and returned home, did you?

C. Questions to establish the continuing nature of the parties' relationship and the defendant's influence over the victim.

(1) Is it not a fact that you are afraid of what might happen to the

defendant if this jury (court) convicts him/her for what he/she did to you and that that is the real reason why you changed the story that you gave to the police on the scene?

(2) You really do not believe that the defendant intended to hurt you, do you?

(3) Did you talk to the defendant after the police took him/her to jail?

(4) Did you and the defendant talk about the events of that night?

(5) Did you call the defendant, or did the defendant call you?

(6) Did the defendant ask you to get him/her out of jail?

(7) Did you get the defendant out of jail? Why?

(8) Since the date of the incident, have you talked with the defendant about what happened that night? How many times have you discussed the incident with the defendant?

(9) Did the defendant apologize for what happened to you?

(10) Did the defendant tell you that he/she did not mean to hurt you?

(11) Did the defendant promise you that it would never happen again?

(12) Is it not a fact that you are under a lot of pressure to drop these charges?

(13) Is it not a fact that the defendant pleaded with you to drop these charges?

(14) Is it not a fact that the defendant called you from jail on numerous occasions to ask you not to go forward with this case?

(15) The defendant was angry at you because he/she was arrested for this, was he/she not?

(16) Is it not a fact that the defendant told you to change your story to say that you threw the first blow?

(17) In fact, the defendant threatened to harm you if you did not change your story, did he/she not?

(18) The defendant promised to change his/her behavior if you dropped these charges, and you believed that promise, did you not?

(19) In fact, you were the one who bailed the defendant out of jail, were you not?

(20) The defendant asked you to bail him/her out, did he/she not?

(21) Was the defendant still angry with you when he/she asked you to get him/her out of jail?

(22) Is it not a fact that you and the defendant have made up and that you just want to forget that all of this happened and get on with your life?

(23) You still care about the defendant, do you not?

(24) And you still care about what happens to the defendant, do you not?

(25) You are afraid of what will happen to the defendant if he/she is found guilty of striking you, are you not? That is really what motivated you to change your original story, is it not?

(26) You are afraid of what the defendant will do if he/she is found guilty of domestic violence, are you not?

D. Questions to establish the defendant's threats and the victim's fear.

(1) Is it not a fact that the defendant threatened to hurt you even more if you went to the police about what he/she did to you?
(2) Were you afraid of the defendant after he/she injured you?
(3) In fact, you were so afraid of the defendant that you left your home and went to a shelter/stayed with a relative/stayed with a friend after this happened to you, did you not?
(4) In fact, you told the police/your family/your friends that you were afraid of what the defendant might do, did you not?
(5) In fact, you were afraid that the defendant might try to retaliate against you for having him arrested, were you not?
(6) In fact, you were afraid that the defendant would try to take your children from you, were you not?

E. Questions to connect the victim to the 911 call.

(1) Were you the one who made the call to 911?
(2) Why did you call 911?
(3) Did you tell the dispatcher that you needed the police right away?
(4) Did you tell the dispatcher that the defendant had just attacked you?

If the victim denies making the call to 911 or claims not to remember, offer to refresh the victim's recollection by playing the tape recording of the 911 call. The following questions serve that function:

(5) Is that your voice on the 911 tape?
(6) Does listening to this tape refresh your memory?
(7) So you did, in fact, make the call to 911, did you not?
(8) And that is your voice asking the dispatcher to send the police?
(9) You sound afraid/hysterical on that tape. Were you afraid when you called for the police?
(10) What were you afraid of when you called 911?
(11) Is it fair to say that you made this call to 911 right after the defendant struck you?
(12) Was the defendant still in the home when you placed the 911 call?
(13) Is that the defendant's voice in the background on the 911 tape?
(14) Is it not also a fact that the defendant yanked the telephone from the wall when you tried to call 911?
(15) How long after you placed the 911 call did the police arrive?
(16) Could it have been less time than that?

F. Questions to establish the facts of the incident.

(1) When the police arrived at your home, did you tell them what happened?
(2) Did you show the police your injuries?
(3) Did you give the police a written statement concerning what happened?
(4) Did you get any medical attention for your injuries?

(5) Was EMS called or did you go to a hospital or other health care provider?
(6) Did you not tell the medical provider that the defendant struck you?
(7) So, it is your testimony that you lied to the medical provider about what the defendant did to you?
(8) Is it not a fact that when you met the police you were very [describe victim's emotional state, e.g., upset, agitated, crying, fearful, hysterical, etc.]?
(9) Where was the defendant when the police questioned you about what happened?
(10) Did the police take any photographs while they were at your home? Of you? (Have the victim identify any photos that were taken.)
(11) What condition was your home in when the police arrived? Showing you what have been marked as Plaintiff's Exhibits 5, 6, and 7, do these photographs fairly and accurately depict the way your home looked immediately after this incident took place?
(12) How did your home get so disarrayed?
(13) Showing you what have been marked as Plaintiff's Exhibits 5, 6, and 7, do these photographs fairly and accurately depict the way you looked immediately after this incident took place?

§ 6:11 Trial presentation—Examination of the recanting victim—Sample questions for felony prosecution involving a victim of a prior assault

It is highly likely that a victim of domestic violence will remain with the offender, even after a conviction. Therefore, subsequent violence should be anticipated. These victims are also likely to recant. The prosecution should prepare special questions to address this situation. Some examples follow.

(1) Has the defendant ever been prosecuted for assaulting you in the past?
(2) What was the result of that prosecution?
(3) You continued to stay in this relationship after that incident, even though the defendant was convicted of committing domestic violence against you?
(4) Who called the police that time?
(5) Did the defendant promise that he/she would never strike you again after that happened? But it did happen again, did it not?
(6) Did the defendant claim that you were at fault that time too?

§ 6:12 Trial presentation—Cross-examination of the defendant

In any type of case, cross-examination is as much art as it is science. This is even more so when the subject of the cross-examination is an alleged batterer. The prosecuting attorney whose task it is to conduct these examinations is likely to find that these witnesses present difficult targets. They often present themselves as the aggrieved party and are quite frequently skilled in manipulating the facts of the incident on trial. Unless the prosecutor is able to hone in on the constants of battering behavior that separate it from other more innocent behavior, the trier of fact will find it difficult, if not impossible, to discover the truth.

In its most classic form, battering behavior includes elements of power and control by the dominant partner in the battering relationship.[1] Domestic violence is seldom a single isolated event.[2] Research suggests that the violence is the key element in a pattern of behaviors that allows the batterer to exert his/her will over the victim. As part of its theory of the case, the prosecution should attempt to establish the existence of the defendant's power and control of the relationship as evidence that the defendant likely engaged in the full pattern of classic battering behavior, including the assault.

Areas of inquiry that prosecution might wish to explore with the defendant include:

(1) Whether the victim works outside of the home.
(2) Who is in charge of the family finances.
(3) Whether the victim contributes monetarily to the household income.
(4) Who writes the checks and pays the bills.
(5) Whether the victim has any discretionary income of his/her own.
(6) Whether the defendant has any influence on who the victim can have as friends.
(7) Whether the defendant does any of the housework.
(8) Whether the defendant established any rules for his/her spouse/partner concerning what the defendant expects regarding the spouse's/partner's conduct, e.g., what time to come and go, whether the spouse can have friends of the opposite sex, when the spouse's relatives can visit, what clothes the spouse can wear, etc.
(9) What happens if those rules are not followed.
(10) Whether the victim ever makes the defendant angry.
(11) What kinds of things the defendant's spouse/partner does to make the defendant angry.
(12) How the defendant reacts when he/she is angry.
(13) Whether the defendant yells at the victim when the defendant is angry.
(14) How often the defendant gets angry with the victim.
(15) Whether the defendant calls the victim derogatory names when the defendant is angry.
(16) Whether the defendant demeans the victim when the defendant is angry.

[Section 6:12]

[1]See Ellen L. Pence & Michael Paymar, Power and Control: Tactics of Men Who Batter: An Educational Curriculum (Minnesota Program Devel., Inc. 1986).

[2]See Ellen L. Pence & Michael Paymar, Power and Control: Tactics of Men Who Batter: An Educational Curriculum (Minnesota Program Devel., Inc. 1986). State v. Trimble, 122 Ohio St. 3d 297, 2009-Ohio-2961, 911 N.E.2d 242 (2009), cert. denied, 130 S. Ct. 752, 175 L. Ed. 2d 526 (2009).

(17) Whether the defendant is trying to look like the real victim in this case.
(18) Whether there are significant discrepancies in the defendant's testimony and the testimony of the State's witnesses that can be exploited.

Recognition of the general nature of those who batter is an advantage for the cross-examiner. Prosecutors should avail themselves of every opportunity to learn and understand as much as possible about people who batter. Certain "givens" should guide the construction of an effective cross-examination of a battering suspect:

(1) Know where you want the examination to go and direct all questions at getting there.
(2) Maintain control of the examination.
(3) Guide the witness to where you want to go in small increments.
(4) Feel the witness out, and probe for the witness's hot spots and weaknesses.
(5) Focus on the unbelievable and the incredible in the defendant's testimony. Without getting overly dramatic, highlight those aspects of the defendant's presentation that simply do not make sense.

§ 6:13 Trial presentation—Physical evidence

De-emphasizing the importance of the victim's testimony in domestic violence prosecutions necessarily means increasing the emphasis on the other aspects of the prosecutor's case, such as physical evidence collected at the scene and subsequent to the offense. Law enforcement officials' thorough understanding of the prosecutor's courtroom needs is essential to the success of this new thrust away from reliance on victim testimony.

Many, if not most, domestic violence crime scenes are rife with tangible evidence that the prosecutor can enter into evidence against an alleged abuser, if it is known to exist. In the past, however, law enforcement training did not focus on the collection of this evidence. Instead, the emphasis of domestic violence training was on the separation of the parties and obtaining the victim's cooperation with regard to the prosecution of the offender.

This approach resulted in placing the burden of prosecution squarely on the shoulders of the victim. Since little or no other evidence beyond the victim's statement was preserved, the entire case rested on the victim's testimony. However, the dynamics of the classic domestic violence relationship render dependence on the victim's continuing cooperation precarious at best. By definition, a batterer controls the victim in the violent intimate relationship.[1] It is little wonder that, under this prior victim-centered approach, the vast majority of domestic violence cases were terminated at the request of victims before any sanctions were imposed on or assistance provided to the offender.

[Section 6:13]

[1]Janet Carter et al., Domestic Violence: The Crucial Role of the Judge in Criminal Court Cases: A National Model for Judicial Education 25 (1991).

Conviction ratios can increase if the prosecutor enlists the assistance of law enforcement in obtaining the types of items that will assist in the presentation of a domestic violence case at trial. Those items include, but are not limited to, the following:

(1) Photographs of the crime scene. Photographs of the damage done to the interior of the residence or other building where the incident occurred are the minimum requirement of an effective domestic violence prosecution. These photographs allow the trier of fact to visualize the extent of the rage and violence that are often a hallmark of domestic violence cases. In noncapital cases, the admission of potentially prejudicial photographs is determined under a balancing test: the probative value of the photographs must be substantially outweighed by the danger of unfair prejudice to warrant exclusion.[2] Such photographs may be used to corroborate the testimony of witnesses, to help establish the intent of the accused, or to show the nature and circumstances of the crime.[3]

(2) Photographs of the victim. These pictures transmit the condition that the victim presented when the responding officers made their initial observations. They document the level of the victim's injury and the degree of the victim's fear and other emotional distress. Such photographs often make it harder for a victim to recant later in the proceedings and may give the court better insight into whether a victim's decision not to pursue prosecution or a protection order is rational under the circumstances.

(3) Photographs of the offender. Pictures of the offender are often inconsistent with the picture presented by the defendant's appearance in a courtroom setting. Candid photographs of the offender's turbulent behavior at the time of arrest may assist the trier of fact in its determination of which party was the primary physical aggressor.

(4) Photographs of the children on the scene. At least one study found that children are present in approximately seventy percent of all domestic violence offenses. Taking the children's photograph captures the horror of domestic violence, showing its intergenerational aspects and giving it a human face.

(5) Follow-up photographs. Injuries suffered by the victim of an assault often take days or even weeks to manifest the full extent of the trauma suffered. Follow-up photographs, taken anywhere from two days to two weeks after the assault, often provide graphic evidence of the damage that the victim suffered as a result of the event on trial.

(6) 911 tapes and transcripts. These items often provide invaluable evidence about the intensity of the events before the court.

---

[2]Evid.R. 403; see also State v. Franklin, 62 Ohio St. 3d 118, 580 N.E.2d 1 (1991); State v. Waddy, 1989 WL 133508, * 19 (Ohio Ct. App. 10th Dist. Franklin County 1989), aff'd, 63 Ohio St. 3d 424, 588 N.E.2d 819 (1992), reh'g granted, opinion recalled, 71 Ohio St. 3d 1418, 642 N.E.2d 384 (1994).

[3]State v. Jalowiec, 91 Ohio St. 3d 220, 2001-Ohio-26, 744 N.E.2d 163 (2001); Jalowiec v. Bradshaw, 2008 WL 312655 (N.D. Ohio 2008), judgment aff'd, 657 F.3d 293 (6th Cir. 2011), as amended, (Nov. 23, 2011).

They provide a clear window into the event itself and actually place the judge or the jury on the scene as the events unfolded. The most important aspect of such evidence is the statements made by victims and other witnesses at the time of the incident. However, other important information is often gleaned from their presentation, such as corroboration of property destruction at the crime scene at the time of the incident and incriminating statements made by the defendant. Law enforcement officers should routinely preserve, and prosecutors should routinely review, all 911 tapes and transcripts as part of their investigative, preparatory, and presentation efforts.

(7) Torn clothing and items stained with blood. This evidence exhibits the outcome of the violent attack and stands as powerful proof of the defendant's intention to inflict physical harm on the victim.

(8) Emergency medical service (EMS) run sheets. Victims, and sometimes even defendants, make critical statements about the domestic violence incident to the EMS technicians that respond to their calls. Frequently, these statements are preserved in the "run sheets" prepared by the EMS technicians. These business records should routinely come under the scrutiny of both the police and the prosecutor. Where appropriate, both run sheets and their authors should be presented at trial.

(9) Telephone records. In general, batterers do not easily relinquish their control. Thus, even after arrest and the imposition of a protection or no contact order, they continue to make efforts to bend the victim to their will. Telephone records may often prove the extent of the continued contact. Telephone bills and, in extreme cases, wiretapping devices corroborate a victim's allegation of on-going harassment.

(10) Written correspondence from the defendant. It is not unusual for domestic violence offenders to send their victims letters, cards, or notes during the pendency of a criminal proceeding. These writings frequently contain threats, admissions, and other inculpatory information that is extremely helpful to the prosecution. If documents of this nature do exist, they should be obtained from the victim as soon as possible so that they will be available later, even if the victim becomes reluctant to proceed with the prosecution.

(11) Diagrams of the scene. Accurate drawings of the location where the domestic violence incident took place will help the prosecutor and the trier of fact comprehend the progression of the events that resulted in the criminal charge.

(12) Body diagram of the victim. A complete and accurate diagram of the victim's injuries can demonstrate the places where the victim was struck and experienced pain, even where the injury resulted in no visible wound at the time that photographs were taken or where the photographs failed to pick up the injuries suffered. These diagrams are also useful for purposes of cross-examination of the victim in those cases where the victim decides to testify on behalf of the defendant.

(13) Weapons. All weapons used during a domestic violence episode should be preserved as evidence by the police.

Q & A: At a domestic violence trial, the prosecution moves to admit photographs of the victim's injuries. The defense vehemently objects, claiming that the only purpose that the photographs serve is to inflame and prejudice the jury against the defendant. Should the court allow the photographs into evidence?

The admission of photographs into evidence is within the sound discretion of the trial court.[4] The only foundation that the prosecution must establish for admission of the photographs is that they fairly and accurately reflect the condition of the things depicted in them at the time that they were taken.[5]

§ 6:14 Trial presentation—911 tapes and transcripts

In many cases, the call placed to 911 or a similar emergency number will be the single most important piece of evidence that the prosecution presents. This oral record captures the anxiety, the fear, the desperation, and, sometimes, even the violence of the event on trial in a way that even the direct testimony of the victim often is unable to portray.

The prosecution is required to lay a proper foundation before the court will allow the use of an audiotape as an exhibit or allow an audiotape to be admitted into evidence at a court hearing. That foundation should include:

(1) Establishing, to the court's satisfaction, that the statements made on the audiotape are more probative of one or more of the issues before the court than they are prejudicial to the defendant's right to a fair trial.
(2) Establishing that the audiotape is relevant.
(3) Establishing the authenticity of what the audiotape purports to represent.
(4) Establishing the chain of custody of the audiotape and that the document is in its original unaltered condition.

---

[4]State v. Maurer, 15 Ohio St. 3d 239, 265, 473 N.E.2d 768 (1984); see also State v. Poling, 1998 WL 255574 (Ohio Ct. App. 3d Dist. Shelby County 1998); State v. Santiago, 2002-Ohio-1114, 2002 WL 388901 (Ohio Ct. App. 9th Dist. Lorain County 2002); State v. Gray, 2009-Ohio-3165, 2009 WL 1856999 (Ohio Ct. App. 9th Dist. Wayne County 2009); State v. Cross, 2011-Ohio-3250, 2011 WL 2571645 (Ohio Ct. App. 9th Dist. Summit County 2011); State v. Grossniklaus, 2012-Ohio-2560, 2012 WL 2087401 (Ohio Ct. App. 9th Dist. Wayne County 2012); State v. Costell, 2016-Ohio-3386, 2016 WL 3223905 (Ohio Ct. App. 3d Dist. Union County 2016), appeal not allowed, 147 Ohio St. 3d 1505, 2017-Ohio-261, 67 N.E.3d 823 (2017); State v. Kerr, 2016-Ohio-965, 2016 WL 936844 (Ohio Ct. App. 2d Dist. Montgomery County 2016); State v. Knecht, 2015-Ohio-4316, 2015 WL 6125747 (Ohio Ct. App. 12th Dist. Warren County 2015), appeal not allowed, 144 Ohio St. 3d 1507, 2016-Ohio-652, 45 N.E.3d 1051 (2016); State v. Martin, 2016-Ohio-225, 57 N.E.3d 411 (Ohio Ct. App. 5th Dist. Tuscarawas County 2016); State v. Clark, 2016-Ohio-2825, 2016 WL 2586638 (Ohio Ct. App. 8th Dist. Cuyahoga County 2016), appeal not allowed, 147 Ohio St. 3d 1474, 2016-Ohio-8438, 65 N.E.3d 778 (2016); Cleveland v. Merritt, 2016-Ohio-4693, 69 N.E.3d 102 (Ohio Ct. App. 8th Dist. Cuyahoga County 2016), appeal not allowed, 147 Ohio St. 3d 1506, 2017-Ohio-261, 67 N.E.3d 824 (2017).

[5]Evid.R. 901; State v. Slavens, 1999 WL 4895 (Ohio Ct. App. 4th Dist. Vinton County 1998); State v. Poling, 1998 WL 255574 (Ohio Ct. App. 3d Dist. Shelby County 1998); State v. Brown, 2009-Ohio-5390, 2009 WL 3236206 (Ohio Ct. App. 4th Dist. Athens County 2009).

Since the 911 tape is offered for the truth of the matter asserted and is not susceptible to cross-examination by the opposing party, it is hearsay.[1] In order to gain the tape's admission at a domestic violence court hearing, the prosecutor must show as a predicate that the document fits into one of the established exceptions to the evidence rule that prohibits the introduction of hearsay in court proceedings.[2] The prosecution must also be able to establish that statements made in the course of police questioning and/or interrogation were made under circumstances objectively indicating that the primary purpose of the questioning and/or interrogation was to enable police assistance to meet an ongoing emergency.

Statements made when the circumstances objectively indicate that there was no such ongoing emergency, and/or that the primary purpose of the interrogation was to establish or prove past events potentially relevant to later criminal prosecution, are testimonial. Such statements are inadmissible hearsay if the accused is unable to confront the individual who made them during the court proceeding.[3] To make the "primary purpose" determination, the Court must

---

[Section 6:14]

[1]Evid.R. 801(C).

[2]See, e.g., present sense impression (Evid.R. 803(1)), excited utterance (Evid.R. 803(2)), then-existing mental, emotional, or physical condition (Evid.R. 803(3)), recorded recollection (Evid.R. 803(5)), statement under belief of impending death (Evid.R. 804(2)).

[3]Davis v. Washington, 547 U.S. 813, 126 S. Ct. 2266, 165 L. Ed. 2d 224, 70 Fed. R. Evid. Serv. 472, 30 A.L.R.6th 599 (2006); State v. Stahl, 111 Ohio St. 3d 186, 2006-Ohio-5482, 855 N.E.2d 834 (2006); Michigan v. Bryant, 562 U.S. 344, 131 S. Ct. 1143, 179 L. Ed. 2d 93, 84 Fed. R. Evid. Serv. 1033 (2011); State v. Arnold, 126 Ohio St. 3d 290, 2010-Ohio-2742, 933 N.E.2d 775 (2010); State v. Arnold, 2010-Ohio-5622, 2010 WL 4681890 (Ohio Ct. App. 10th Dist. Franklin County 2010); State v. Fry, 125 Ohio St. 3d 163, 2010-Ohio-1017, 926 N.E.2d 1239 (2010); State v. Sanchez, 2010-Ohio-6153, 2010 WL 5235932 (Ohio Ct. App. 8th Dist. Cuyahoga County 2010); In re C.S., 2012-Ohio-2988, 2012 WL 2523966 (Ohio Ct. App. 10th Dist. Franklin County 2012); State v. Simms, 2012-Ohio-2321, 2012 WL 1894276 (Ohio Ct. App. 10th Dist. Franklin County 2012); State v. Love, 2011-Ohio-4147, 2011 WL 3654577 (Ohio Ct. App. 4th Dist. Gallia County 2011); State v. Hill, 2011-Ohio-5810, 2011 WL 5452038 (Ohio Ct. App. 2d Dist. Montgomery County 2011); In re J.M., 2011-Ohio-3377, 2011 WL 2650706 (Ohio Ct. App. 4th Dist. Pike County 2011); In re T.L., 2011-Ohio-4709, 2011 WL 4346334 (Ohio Ct. App. 9th Dist. Medina County 2011); State v. Malone, 2012-Ohio-449, 2012 WL 382801 (Ohio Ct. App. 4th Dist. Hocking County 2012); State v. Eicholtz, 2013-Ohio-302, 2013 WL 425820 (Ohio Ct. App. 2d Dist. Clark County 2013); State v. Snider, 2012-Ohio-2183, 2012 WL 1744657 (Ohio Ct. App. 5th Dist. Licking County 2012); Cleveland v. Williams, 2015-Ohio-1739, 2015 WL 2165564 (Ohio Ct. App. 8th Dist. Cuyahoga County 2015); Toledo v. Jenkins, 2015-Ohio-1270, 2015 WL 1510849 (Ohio Ct. App. 6th Dist. Lucas County 2015); State v. McClain, 2014-Ohio-93, 2014 WL 117962 (Ohio Ct. App. 10th Dist. Franklin County 2014); State v. Canada, 2015-Ohio-2167, 2015 WL 3540402 (Ohio Ct. App. 10th Dist. Franklin County 2015); Toledo v. Green, 2015-Ohio-1864, 33 N.E.3d 581 (Ohio Ct. App. 6th Dist. Lucas County 2015); Toledo v. Green, 2015-Ohio-386, 27 N.E.3d 1015 (Ohio Ct. App. 6th Dist. Lucas County 2015); State v. Arnold, 2014-Ohio-1134, 2014 WL 1339806 (Ohio Ct. App. 3d Dist. Seneca County 2014), judgment aff'd, 147 Ohio St. 3d 138, 2016-Ohio-1595, 62 N.E.3d 153 (2016); State v. Norris, 2015-Ohio-624, 2015 WL 753346 (Ohio Ct. App. 2d Dist. Montgomery County 2015); State v. Abernathy, 2015-Ohio-1363, 2015 WL 1530810 (Ohio Ct. App. 5th Dist. Stark County 2015); State v. Clark, 2011-Ohio-6623, 2011 WL 6780456 (Ohio Ct. App. 8th Dist. Cuyahoga County 2011), aff'd, 137 Ohio St. 3d 346, 2013-Ohio-4731, 999 N.E.2d 592 (2013), rev'd and remanded, 135 S. Ct. 2173, 192 L. Ed. 2d 306 (2015); Cody v.

objectively evaluate the circumstances in which the encounter between the individual and the police occurs and the parties' statements and actions.[4]

The primary purpose inquiry is objective. The circumstances in which an encounter occurs—*e.g.*, at or near a crime scene versus at a police station, during an ongoing emergency or afterwards—are clearly matters of objective fact. And the relevant inquiry into the parties' statements and actions is not the subjective or actual purpose of the particular parties, but the purpose that reasonable participants would have had, as ascertained from the parties' statements and actions and the circumstances in which the encounter occurred.[5]

The existence of an "ongoing emergency" at the time of the encounter is among the most important circumstances informing the interrogation's "primary purpose."[6] An emergency focuses the participants not on "prov[ing] past events potentially relevant to later criminal prosecution, but on end[ing] a threatening situation."[7] Whether an emergency exists and is ongoing is a highly context-dependent inquiry. An assessment of whether an emergency threatening the police and public is ongoing cannot narrowly focus on whether the threat to the first victim has been neutralized because the threat to the first responders and public may continue.[8]

An emergency's duration and scope may depend in part on the type of weapon involved.[9] A victim's medical condition is important to the primary purpose inquiry to the extent that it sheds light on the victim's ability to have any purpose at all in responding to police questions and on the likelihood that any such purpose would be a testimonial one. It also provides important context for first responders to judge the existence and magnitude of a continuing threat to the victim, themselves, and the public.[10]

This does not mean that an emergency lasts the entire time that a

---

Commonwealth, 68 Va. App. 638, 812 S.E.2d 466 (2018) (Statements made to 911 dispatcher admissible where Weingarten was primarily "describ[ing] current circumstances requiring police assistance" not past events for the purpose of prosecution).

[4]Michigan v. Bryant, 562 U.S. 344, 131 S. Ct. 1143, 179 L. Ed. 2d 93, 84 Fed. R. Evid. Serv. 1033 (2011); State v. Stage, 2012-Ohio-3300, 2012 WL 2979331 (Ohio Ct. App. 9th Dist. Medina County 2012).

[5]Michigan v. Bryant, 562 U.S. 344, 131 S. Ct. 1143, 179 L. Ed. 2d 93, 84 Fed. R. Evid. Serv. 1033 (2011).

[6]See Michigan v. Bryant, 562 U.S. 344, 131 S. Ct. 1143, 179 L. Ed. 2d 93, 84 Fed. R. Evid. Serv. 1033 (2011); State v. Inman, 2014-Ohio-3538, 2014 WL 4057720 (Ohio Ct. App. 9th Dist. Medina County 2014).

[7]Michigan v. Bryant, 562 U.S. 344, 131 S. Ct. 1143, 1148, 179 L. Ed. 2d 93, 84 Fed. R. Evid. Serv. 1033 (2011); State v. Inman, 2014-Ohio-3538, 2014 WL 4057720 (Ohio Ct. App. 9th Dist. Medina County 2014).

[8]Michigan v. Bryant, 562 U.S. 344, 131 S. Ct. 1143, 179 L. Ed. 2d 93, 84 Fed. R. Evid. Serv. 1033 (2011); State v. Bulger, 2011-Ohio-3828, 2011 WL 3359861 (Ohio Ct. App. 8th Dist. Cuyahoga County 2011); State v. Jones, 135 Ohio St. 3d 10, 2012-Ohio-5677, 984 N.E.2d 948 (2012); State v. Stage, 2012-Ohio-3300, 2012 WL 2979331 (Ohio Ct. App. 9th Dist. Medina County 2012); State v. McClain, 2014-Ohio-93, 2014 WL 117962 (Ohio Ct. App. 10th Dist. Franklin County 2014).

[9]Michigan v. Bryant, 562 U.S. 344, 131 S. Ct. 1143, 179 L. Ed. 2d 93, 84 Fed. R. Evid. Serv. 1033 (2011); State v. Stage, 2012-Ohio-3300, 2012 WL 2979331 (Ohio Ct. App. 9th Dist. Medina County 2012).

[10]Michigan v. Bryant, 562 U.S. 344, 131 S. Ct. 1143, 179 L. Ed. 2d 93, 84 Fed. R.

perpetrator is on the loose, but trial courts can determine in the first instance when an interrogation transitions from non-testimonial to testimonial. Finally, whether an ongoing emergency exists is simply one factor informing the ultimate inquiry regarding an interrogation's "primary purpose." Another is the encounter's *informality*. Formality suggests the absence of an emergency, but informality does not necessarily indicate the presence of an emergency or the lack of testimonial intent. The fact that questioning occurred in an exposed, public area, before emergency medical services arrived, and in a disorganized fashion may distinguish a case from *Crawford*'s formal station-house interrogation.[11]

The statements and actions of both the declarant and interrogators also provide objective evidence of the interrogation's primary purpose. Looking to the contents of both the questions and the answers ameliorates problems that could arise from looking solely to one participant, since both interrogators and declarants may have mixed motives. Police officers' dual responsibilities as both first responders and criminal investigators may lead them to act with different motives simultaneously or in quick succession. And during an ongoing emergency, victims may want the threat to end, but may not envision prosecution. Alternatively, a severely injured victim may have no purpose at all in answering questions. Taking into account such injuries does not make the inquiry subjective. The inquiry still focuses on the understanding and purpose of a reasonable victim in the actual victim's circumstances, which prominently include the victim's physical state.[12]

Samples of questions that the prosecutor might ask of the custodian of the records to gain admission of a police dispatch tape, or a transcript of such a tape, into evidence include:

(1) Please state your name for the record.
(2) Are you currently employed? By whom are you employed?
(3) What is your title?
(4) Is your office responsible for receiving calls for emergency assistance in your department?
(5) Are the calls recorded immediately upon their receipt?
(6) How are the calls recorded?
(7) What records are kept of the calls for assistance that your office receives?
(8) Why do you keep these records?
(9) Are these records kept and maintained in the regular course of business?
(10) How long do you keep the records and audiotapes?
(11) Is your department also responsible for dispatching officers to respond to these calls?

Evid. Serv. 1033 (2011); State v. Jones, 135 Ohio St. 3d 10, 2012-Ohio-5677, 984 N.E.2d 948 (2012); State v. Stage, 2012-Ohio-3300, 2012 WL 2979331 (Ohio Ct. App. 9th Dist. Medina County 2012).

[11]Michigan v. Bryant, 562 U.S. 344, 131 S. Ct. 1143, 179 L. Ed. 2d 93, 84 Fed. R. Evid. Serv. 1033 (2011). See also State v. Vanderhorst, 2010-Ohio-1856, 2010 WL 1712246 (Ohio Ct. App. 8th Dist. Cuyahoga County 2010); State v. Stage, 2012-Ohio-3300, 2012 WL 2979331 (Ohio Ct. App. 9th Dist. Medina County 2012).

[12]Michigan v. Bryant, 562 U.S. 344, 131 S. Ct. 1143, 179 L. Ed. 2d 93, 84 Fed. R. Evid. Serv. 1033 (2011).

(12) Who has access to these records?

(13) Who is the custodian of these records? Are these records maintained under your care, custody, and control?

(14) In your capacity as custodian of these records, did you receive a request to copy and produce a copy of a 911 (dispatch) tape for a call that your department received on the ______ day of ______, 20__, that concerned an event that occurred at approximately ______.m., in the city of ______, Ohio?

(15) Do you still have the original of the tape segment you brought with you today? Is that original tape segment still on file at your office?

(16) Why did you not bring the original tape segment to court? (Is the original too cumbersome or bulky?) Is the tape segment you brought with you today an exact duplicate of the one you have on file?

(17) Did you, or someone under your direct supervision, copy the original tape, and did you bring that copy with you today?

(18) How were you able to find the specific segment of tape requested?

(19) How did you, or someone under your direct supervision, prepare the copy of the tape segment for transport and presentation at court today?

(20) Showing you what has been marked as State's Exhibit [number of the audiotape exhibit], can you identify this exhibit?

(21) How can you recognize it?

(22) Is the official sounding voice at the beginning of the tape your voice?

(23) Why does your voice appear on this tape?

Q & A: If the victim takes the stand and denies placing a call to 911 for an incident that resulted in police response, is the prosecution foreclosed from introducing the 911 tape as evidence in a subsequent trial?

No. Where the victim of a domestic violence incident denies placing the 911 call that triggered the emergency response, the testimony of the custodian of record that the call came into the dispatch center from the location of the incident at the time that the incident is alleged to have occurred, coupled with the testimony of an individual or individuals who were present at the scene who can identify the voice on the tape as that of the victim, should be sufficient to have the 911 tape admitted. This is particularly true if there is other corroborating evidence that those who were present can provide to establish the victim as the caller.[13]

Q & A: My mother-in-law called 911 last week when my son ran to her house and told her that my wife and I were fighting. The police came, and I was arrested for domestic violence. Can the prosecutor admit the 911 call from my mother-in-law into evidence? All she knew was what my son told her. Isn't that hearsay?

---

[13] State v. Newell, 1998 WL 667651 (Ohio Ct. App. 5th Dist. Stark County 1998); see also State v. Issa, 1998 WL 80301 (Ohio Ct. App. 1st Dist. Hamilton County 1998).

Yes, that is hearsay. Since your mother-in-law was not present to see what took place, her statement captured on the 911 tape does not qualify as either an excited utterance or a present sense impression exception to the Hearsay Rule. However, unless your counsel raises an objection to the tape's admission, it will probably come into evidence, unless it so adversely affects one of your substantial rights as to undermine the fairness of the guilt-determining process.[14]

Q & A: Does the Sixth Amendment's Confrontation Clause bar the prosecution from introducing statements a non-testifying witness made to police during a 911 call under all circumstances?

No. The U.S. Supreme Court held that statements made during police "interrogations" are non-testimonial, and therefore, admissible, when they are made "under circumstances objectively indicating that the primary purpose of interrogation is to enable police assistance to meet an ongoing emergency."[15] Such statements are testimonial when "the circumstances objectively indicate" that there is no such ongoing emergency, and that the primary purpose of the interrogation is to establish or prove past events potentially relevant to later criminal prosecution.[16] Most 911 calls are, therefore, by their very nature "non-testimonial" under the test that the U.S. Supreme Court sets forth.

Q & A: On appeal, the defendant argues that the state violated his right to confront his accuser when the state did not play the tape of the 911 call at issue until after the victim testified and the opportunity to cross-examine her was past. Should his argument prevail?

Probably not. Even if the victim's statements were testimonial, the Confrontation Clause was not violated because the victim testified at trial.[17] Although the state did not play the 911 call at issue until after the victim testified, the victim mentioned the conversation during her testimony, and defendant could have cross-examined her regarding the 911 call. Indeed, defendant could have requested the opportunity to recall the witness for further testimony after evidence of the 911 call was presented.[18]

---

[14]State v. Swanson, 16 Ohio App. 3d 375, 476 N.E.2d 672 (8th Dist. Cuyahoga County 1984); State v. Esparza, 1999 WL 155955 (Ohio Ct. App. 3d Dist. Defiance County 1999); State v. Martin, 2009-Ohio-5223, 2009 WL 3154497 (Ohio Ct. App. 8th Dist. Cuyahoga County 2009); State v. Butts, 2012-Ohio-571, 2012 WL 474030 (Ohio Ct. App. 4th Dist. Hocking County 2012).

[15]State v. Hall, 2012-Ohio-266, 2012 WL 253317 (Ohio Ct. App. 8th Dist. Cuyahoga County 2012).

[16]Davis v. Washington, 547 U.S. 813, 126 S. Ct. 2266, 165 L. Ed. 2d 224, 70 Fed. R. Evid. Serv. 472, 30 A.L.R.6th 599 (2006); Colon v. Taskey, 414 Fed. Appx. 735 (6th Cir. 2010); State v. Butts, 2012-Ohio-571, 2012 WL 474030 (Ohio Ct. App. 4th Dist. Hocking County 2012); State v. Hall, 2012-Ohio-266, 2012 WL 253317 (Ohio Ct. App. 8th Dist. Cuyahoga County 2012).

[17]State v. Taylor, 2008-Ohio-1462, 2008 WL 834437 (Ohio Ct. App. 9th Dist. Lorain County 2008).

[18]State v. Marrero, 2011-Ohio-1390, 2011 WL 1049294 (Ohio Ct. App. 10th Dist. Franklin County 2011). See also State v. Simmons, 2011-Ohio-916, 2011 WL 721322 (Ohio Ct. App. 9th Dist. Summit County 2011); State v. McClain, 2014-Ohio-93, 2014 WL 117962 (Ohio Ct. App. 10th Dist. Franklin County 2014).

§ 6:15 Trial presentation—Child witnesses

Children are often present when domestic violence occurs. In initial trial preparation, the prosecutor should determine if any children were present when the incident occurred. If a child or children were present, the police and the prosecutor should gain their cooperation as soon as possible. Child witnesses are invaluable sources of information.

Statements made by even the youngest children may qualify as evidence under exceptions to the hearsay rule, even if the children, themselves, are too young to qualify as competent witnesses.[1] The prosecutor will need to determine in each case where a child is potentially a witness whether or not it is useful to call the child as a witness.

To the degree possible, a prosecuting attorney should determine a child's competency[2] before presenting the child to a court as a witness. The rules of evidence contemplate that the competent child witness will possess several characteristics. Among other things, those characteristics include three elements. First, the child must have the ability to receive accurate impressions of fact. Second, the individual must be able to accurately recollect those impressions. Third, the individual must be able to relate those impressions truthfully.[3]

In making that determination, the prosecutor should engage in a cost-benefit analysis with regard to the child's testimony. The following questions are germane to the ultimate conclusion:

(1) Is the information that the child has to offer important enough to risk the psychological damage that the child may suffer from testifying against a parent?
(2) Are the child's parents likely to remain together after the case is concluded, even if the defendant goes to jail?
(3) Is the child at risk of additional abuse if he/she testifies against his/her parent in this case?
(4) Are witness/victim advocacy services available for the child after testifying?
(5) Did the child make a statement to the police at the time of the domestic violence incident?
(6) How did the child happen to make this statement?
(7) Did the child make any additional statements to the police or the prosecutor after the event was over?
(8) Is the child a credible witness?
(9) Is the child competent to testify?
(10) Can the prosecutor acclimate the child to the role of witness?

[Section 6:15]

[1]Ohio v. Clark, 135 S. Ct. 2173, 192 L. Ed. 2d 306 (2015)(fact that Ohio law barred incompetent children from testifying did not make it fundamentally unfair for trial court to admit three year old domestic abuse victim's statements to his preschool teachers identifying defendant as the person who had caused his injuries).

[2]Evid.R. 601(A).

[3]State v. Said, 71 Ohio St. 3d 473, 1994-Ohio-402, 644 N.E.2d 337 (1994); State v. Silverman, 121 Ohio St. 3d 581, 2009-Ohio-1576, 906 N.E.2d 427 (2009), clarification granted, 123 Ohio St. 3d 1521, 2009-Ohio-6487, 918 N.E.2d 524 (2009); State v. Cameron, 2009-Ohio-3341, 2009 WL 1916894 (Ohio Ct. App. 5th Dist. Richland County 2009).

Children who are the victims of or witnesses to domestic violence present many of the same challenges as their adult counterparts. They are, in general, confused and conflicted about what they should do about what is happening to them.

On the one hand, the children are angry that someone so close to them could treat them or their other parent so poorly. On the other hand, they feel a certain loyalty to their family and to the abusing parent.

They generally do not wish to see anything bad happen to the abuser. They are uncertain how adverse consequences for the abuser will affect their own personal situation. In most instances, their primary wish is to have the violence end, and most children are ready to do what it takes to accomplish that goal.

Regardless, children who agree to testify need a lot of support when it comes to courtroom appearances. If possible, the person who provides that support should be someone other than the non-abusing parent. That parent will likely face pressures of his/her own to discontinue the prosecution and may be ill-equipped to support the decision of the child who wishes to testify. Support the child's decision to testify:

(1) Provide positive reinforcement regarding the decision. Let the child know that you believe his/her version of the facts. The child should understand that he/she is doing the right thing for the family and that it is not a betrayal to try to end the violence.

(2) Be absolutely honest with the child witness. The possibility of success and the vagaries of a criminal trial should be explained. Do not guarantee the outcome.

(3) Refrain from speaking ill of the defendant. Even if the defendant has done unspeakable things, he/she is still that child's parent. Even though the child is agreeing to testify, the child is not likely to respond well to anyone speaking against his/her parent. The child may change his/her mind about testifying if the child perceives that the prosecution is "out to get" the defendant.

(4) Be careful not to place too much emphasis on the value of the child's testimony. Remember that you are dealing with a child and that statements like "we are all depending on you" and "your testimony will guarantee that your father never hurts your mother again" would be oppressive, even if the witness were an adult. Make sure that the child knows that everyone is proud of him/her, just for being strong enough to take the stand and tell the truth.

(5) Allow the child witness to become familiar with the courtroom setting. If possible, bring the child in early to see where the trial will take place. Have the child sit on the witness stand. Explain the roles of the various participants in the trial, and explain where those participants will be on the day that the child testifies.

(6) Attempt to develop a rapport with the child. The better the relationship between the prosecutor and any witness, the more likely the witness will feel at ease when testifying. The prosecutor should avoid, however, allowing that relationship to become too personal by not becoming too involved with the child's parents or with other problems in their lives.

(7) Provide support for the child witness *after* the testimony is given. Children who testify will be traumatized by the experience. The prosecutor should not abandon the child once the child's testimony is complete. The prosecution should make every effort to secure appropriate advocacy services to help the child cope with the issues that surround participating in an event of this magnitude.

Q & A: My seven-year-old son saw my husband strike me repeatedly with a leather belt. Is my son too young to testify as to what he saw?

No. There is no blanket prohibition on the testimony of young children in legal proceedings. The Supreme Court of Ohio set forth five factors that the trial court "must take into consideration" when determining whether a child under the age of ten is competent to testify: (1) the child's ability to receive accurate impressions of fact or to observe acts about which he or she will testify, (2) the child's ability to recollect those impressions or observations, (3) the child's ability to communicate what was observed, (4) the child's understanding of truth and falsity, and (5) the child's appreciation of his or her responsibility to be truthful.[4] Whether a child under the age of 12 is competent to testify is left to the sound discretion of the trial court. The court should exercise that discretion following a voir dire examination of the minor who is to testify.[5]

The Supreme Court of Ohio has stated that the declarant of any out-of-court statement must satisfy the minimal requirements of testimonial competence for that statement to be admitted under an exception to the hearsay rule.[6]

That Court held that a hearing to determine the competency of a potential child witness must be held on the record.[7] Additionally, a trial court must find that a declarant under the age of 10 was

[4]State v. Frazier, 61 Ohio St. 3d 247, 574 N.E.2d 483 (1991); State v. Silverman, 121 Ohio St. 3d 581, 2009-Ohio-1576, 906 N.E.2d 427 (2009), clarification granted, 123 Ohio St. 3d 1521, 2009-Ohio-6487, 918 N.E.2d 524 (2009); State v. Tebelman, 2010-Ohio-481, 2010 WL 529496 (Ohio Ct. App. 3d Dist. Putnam County 2010); Wilson v. Wilson, 2009-Ohio-4978, 2009 WL 3043967 (Ohio Ct. App. 4th Dist. Lawrence County 2009); State v. Cameron, 2009-Ohio-3341, 2009 WL 1916894 (Ohio Ct. App. 5th Dist. Richland County 2009); State v. Rossbach, 2011-Ohio-281, 2011 WL 302814 (Ohio Ct. App. 6th Dist. Lucas County 2011); Prado v. Elsayed, 2012-Ohio-290, 2012 WL 259573 (Ohio Ct. App. 2d Dist. Montgomery County 2012); Jones v. Jones, 2011-Ohio-4393, 2011 WL 3847339 (Ohio Ct. App. 9th Dist. Summit County 2011).

[5]State v. Frazier, 61 Ohio St. 3d 247, 250-51, 574 N.E.2d 483 (1991); State v. Allard, 75 Ohio St. 3d 482, 496, 1996-Ohio-208, 663 N.E.2d 1277 (1996); In re Slone, 2000 WL 1867585 (Ohio Ct. App. 2d Dist. Montgomery County 2000); State v. Goins, 2001-Ohio-8647, 2001 WL 1525298 (Ohio Ct. App. 12th Dist. Butler County 2001); State v. Rusnak, 2002-Ohio-2143, 2002 WL 832474 (Ohio Ct. App. 8th Dist. Cuyahoga County 2002); State v. Petaway, 2009-Ohio-1304, 2009 WL 737772 (Ohio Ct. App. 3d Dist. Logan County 2009); State v. Molen, 2008-Ohio-6237, 2008 WL 5064887 (Ohio Ct. App. 2d Dist. Montgomery County 2008); State v. Manning, 2008-Ohio-3801, 2008 WL 2931593 (Ohio Ct. App. 8th Dist. Cuyahoga County 2008).; State v. Tebelman, 2010-Ohio-481, 2010 WL 529496 (Ohio Ct. App. 3d Dist. Putnam County 2010); Wilson v. Wilson, 2009-Ohio-4978, 2009 WL 3043967 (Ohio Ct. App. 4th Dist. Lawrence County 2009).

[6]State v. Said, 71 Ohio St. 3d 473, 1994-Ohio-402, 644 N.E.2d 337 (1994).

[7]Evid.R. 601; Crim.R. 22.

competent at the time the statement was made in order to admit that statement into evidence.[8] The Court reasoned that certain hearsay statements are admissible because surrounding circumstances indicate that the declarant truthfully related his or her impressions. However, those circumstances do not guarantee that the declarant accurately received or recollected those impressions, i.e., that the declarant was competent.[9]

§ 6:16 Trial presentation—Pre-sentence memoranda

In many jurisdictions, the court has the benefit of a pre-sentence report prepared by a probation department or probation officer to assist the court in crafting an appropriate sentence once a defendant is convicted of domestic violence. In other jurisdictions, however, no such resource is available. Even in those jurisdictions that do have the benefit of probation services, the prosecution should consider submitting a sentencing memorandum to the court which:

(1) outlines the defendant's past propensity for violence,
(2) identifies any existing substance abuse problems of the defendant,
(3) details any problems that the victim experienced with the defendant while the case was pending, and
(4) recommends an appropriate sentence, including conditions that the prosecutor feels will enhance the victim's safety during any probationary period.

---

[8]Evid.R. 807; State v. Said, 71 Ohio St. 3d 473, 1994-Ohio-402, 644 N.E.2d 337 (1994).

[9]Evid.R. 601; State v. Said, 71 Ohio St. 3d 473, 1994-Ohio-402, 644 N.E.2d 337 (1994). See also State v. Edinger, 2006-Ohio-1527, 2006 WL 827412 (Ohio Ct. App. 10th Dist. Franklin County 2006); State v. Meadows, 2001-Ohio-2510, 2001 WL 803822 (Ohio Ct. App. 4th Dist. Scioto County 2001); State v. Silverman, 121 Ohio St. 3d 581, 2009-Ohio-1576, 906 N.E.2d 427 (2009), clarification granted, 123 Ohio St. 3d 1521, 2009-Ohio-6487, 918 N.E.2d 524 (2009).

Chapter 7

Domestic Violence Defense—Trial Preparation and Presentation Issues

§ 7:1 Defense challenges

Criminal defense attorneys face a myriad of challenges in representing clients charged with domestic violence. To begin with, in today's environment, the focus of new legislation and of prosecution practice is to provide more tools to target the behavior of domestic violence offenders. This is a marked difference from the focus of just a few years ago. In those days, and in the hundreds of years that preceded them, domestic violence was treated as a private problem between intimate partners, more properly handled behind closed doors. When a victim did come forward to report abuse at the hands of a domestic partner, the system tended to focus on the actions of the victim and not on the actions of the alleged assailant.

This new focus on the actions of the assailant means that more attention is paid to thorough investigation of crime scenes and evidence collection. Arrests are more likely than in the past. Prosecution is more frequent and more tenacious. More attention is paid to the past history of the defendant by the court when bond decisions are made. Courts are less reluctant to exclude an individual from a marital dwelling while the merits of a criminal case are hashed out and are more likely to impose additional restrictions on those who face the charge of domestic violence, before, during, and after trial. This chapter focuses on some of the unique problems associated with representing domestic violence defendants.

§ 7:2 Minimizing the impact of a violent incident: Things to consider when contacted by a client from the scene

Most acts of domestic violence are committed in private. But occasionally, counsel may receive a call seeking advice while an event is still on-going. The advice that an attorney gives in such situations may prove to be determinative of the ultimate outcome for one charged with committing violence against a family or household member.

If the police were called, and have yet to arrive, inform your client of the most basic rule of criminal defense: "Exercise your constitutional right against self-incrimination and make no statement of any kind to law enforcement without the presence or advice of legal counsel."

Advise clients involved in violent altercations with family or household members, that, if it is possible to do so safely, their best option is to remain on the scene until the police arrive. Leaving may allow an inference of guilty knowledge or desire to avoid arrest for wrongdoing.

Counsel your clients that once the police arrive, compliance with orders and commands received from law enforcement and relating to on-scene conduct is required. This advice does not extend, however, to law enforcement requests for any information, solicited in the absence of counsel, particularly information relating to the incident under investigation.

Advise the client to comply with law enforcement orders to physically disengage from the dispute that resulted in law enforcement intervention and to cease any and all verbal confrontations at the scene, even when provoked by any other person on the scene.

Orders from law enforcement concerning behavior modification must be obeyed, even if they seem unfair. The scene of the incident is not the proper forum to contest a law enforcement officer's authority or decisions. Doing so generally results in the client's unnecessary arrest and, in some instances, injury.

Problems with law enforcement conduct, such as unjust removal from the home, removal of children, seizure of some items—such as evidence or contraband—refusing to allow the client to remove certain personal items from the scene, as well as other concerns, are often addressed at other times, in the early stages of the civil or criminal court process. Such matters are frequently reviewed and adjusted in proceedings such as initial appearances, arraignments, and temporary and civil (anti-stalking, etc.) protection order hearings in criminal cases, and in protection order hearings in civil cases.[1]

§ 7:3 Family or household member status under the domestic violence statute

Historically, if the parties to a domestic violence incident did not and had not lived together, an essential element of domestic violence was missing. The authorities were free to charge a defendant with other criminal acts, such as assault[1] or menacing.[2] Charges brought under one of those sections, however, do not provide the government with the additional tools to assess, monitor, and restrict the activities of a defendant that the domestic violence laws provide.

As a result, a determination of a defendant's status as a family or household member is an initial consideration in fashioning an effective defense. If the defense can show from the outset that the defendant does not fit the criteria required for a family or household member under the statute, the defendant can avoid major inconvenience and the significant disruption of lifestyle occasioned by criminal prosecution. Logically, the converse also pertains. For individuals involved in intimate personal relationships, however, recent pronouncements of the Ohio Supreme Court make avoiding the designation of family or household member more difficult.

In *State v. Williams*,[3] the Ohio Supreme Court expanded the definition of cohabitation to include parties that do not share the same

---

[Section 7:2]

[1]See also Text § 16:5, Preventing domestic violence; safety plans and provisions.

[Section 7:3]

[1]RC 2903.13.

[2]RC 2903.21, RC 2903.22. See also State v. Cobb, 153 Ohio App. 3d 541, 2003-Ohio-3821, 795 N.E.2d 73 (1st Dist. Hamilton County 2003); State v. Ramirez, 2006-Ohio-5600, 2006 WL 3040638 (Ohio Ct. App. 1st Dist. Hamilton County 2006); State v. Edwards, 2010-Ohio-6496, 2010 WL 5551002 (Ohio Ct. App. 9th Dist. Summit County 2010).

[3]State v. Williams, 79 Ohio St. 3d 459, 1997-Ohio-79, 683 N.E.2d 1126 (1997); State v. Rinehart, 2002-Ohio-6143, 2002 WL 31520346, *3 (Ohio Ct. App. 4th Dist. Ross County 2002); State v. Rodriguez, 2006-Ohio-3378, 2006 WL 1793688 (Ohio Ct. App. 6th Dist. Huron County 2006), judgment aff'd, 114 Ohio St. 3d 430, 2007-Ohio-4552, 872 N.E.2d 1212 (2007); State v. Moore, 2010-Ohio-509, 2010 WL 547707 (Ohio Ct. App. 8th Dist. Cuyahoga County 2010); State v. Jones, 2010-Ohio-351, 2010 WL 364469 (Ohio Ct. App. 9th Dist. Summit County 2010); State v. Freeman, 2010-Ohio-220, 2010 WL 302787 (Ohio Ct. App. 9th Dist. Summit County 2010); Youngstown v. Dixon, 2009-Ohio-1013, 2009 WL 581637 (Ohio Ct. App. 7th Dist. Mahoning County 2009); State v. Barnes, 2009-Ohio-4874, 2009 WL 2963761 (Ohio Ct. App. 8th Dist. Cuyahoga County 2009); State v. Sudderth, 2009-Ohio-3363, 2009 WL 1941345 (Ohio Ct. App. 9th Dist. Summit County 2009); State v. Long, 2011-Ohio-1050, 2011 WL 806839 (Ohio Ct. App. 9th Dist. Summit County 2011); State v. Mauldin, 2010-Ohio-4192, 2010 WL 3482689 (Ohio Ct. App. 7th Dist. Mahoning County 2010); State v. Perkins, 2010-Ohio-2968, 2010 WL 2573770 (Ohio Ct. App. 12th Dist. Fayette County

domicile. This expanded definition arose from the court's assessment that "domestic violence arises out of the relationship itself, not the fact that the parties happen to share one address."[4] The Court claimed authority for its ruling from the legislative history of the statute and found:

> Clearly, the General Assembly believed that an assault involving a family or household member deserves further protection than an assault on a stranger. Therefore, we hold that the offense of domestic violence, as expressed in RC 2919.25(E)(1)(a) and related statutes, arises out of the relationship of the parties rather than their exact living circumstances.[5]

2010); State v. Hawkins, 2012-Ohio-4622, 2012 WL 4762031 (Ohio Ct. App. 2d Dist. Montgomery County 2012); State v. Fernandez, 2012-Ohio-2538, 2012 WL 2061589 (Ohio Ct. App. 2d Dist. Montgomery County 2012); State v. Slevin, 2012-Ohio-2043, 2012 WL 1647115 (Ohio Ct. App. 9th Dist. Summit County 2012); State v. Rubes, 2012-Ohio-4100, 975 N.E.2d 1054 (Ohio Ct. App. 11th Dist. Portage County 2012); State v. Clouse, 2012-Ohio-3471, 2012 WL 3133059 (Ohio Ct. App. 10th Dist. Franklin County 2012); State v. Taylor, 2013-Ohio-4588, 2013 WL 5657956 (Ohio Ct. App. 5th Dist. Richland County 2013); State v. Davis, 2014-Ohio-1197, 2014 WL 1340774 (Ohio Ct. App. 5th Dist. Licking County 2014); State v. McGlothan, 138 Ohio St. 3d 146, 2014-Ohio-85, 4 N.E.3d 1021 (2014); State v. White, 2014-Ohio-1446, 2014 WL 1384082 (Ohio Ct. App. 2d Dist. Montgomery County 2014); State v. Brauer, 2013-Ohio-3319, 2013 WL 3946124 (Ohio Ct. App. 12th Dist. Warren County 2013); State v. Brown, 2015-Ohio-950, 2015 WL 1138651 (Ohio Ct. App. 11th Dist. Lake County 2015); City of Cleveland v. Johnson, 2014-Ohio-4083, 19 N.E.3d 604 (Ohio Ct. App. 8th Dist. Cuyahoga County 2014), as corrected, (Sept. 23, 2014); State v. Hughes, 2015-Ohio-1173, 2015 WL 1403276 (Ohio Ct. App. 5th Dist. Tuscarawas County 2015); State v. Blymiller, 2014-Ohio-5176, 2014 WL 6601976 (Ohio Ct. App. 5th Dist. Stark County 2014); State v. Dobson, 2014-Ohio-3710, 2014 WL 4245968 (Ohio Ct. App. 8th Dist. Cuyahoga County 2014); State v. Gipson, 2016-Ohio-994, 2016 WL 962400 (Ohio Ct. App. 3d Dist. Allen County 2016); State v. Cornwell, 2015-Ohio-4617, 48 N.E.3d 169 (Ohio Ct. App. 9th Dist. Wayne County 2015); State v. Williams, 2017-Ohio-803, 2017 WL 900070 (Ohio Ct. App. 5th Dist. Stark County 2017); Cleveland v. Merritt, 2016-Ohio-4693, 69 N.E.3d 102 (Ohio Ct. App. 8th Dist. Cuyahoga County 2016), appeal not allowed, 147 Ohio St. 3d 1506, 2017-Ohio-261, 67 N.E.3d 824 (2017), State v. Plott, 2017-Ohio-38, 80 N.E.3d 1108 (Ohio Ct. App. 3d Dist. Seneca County 2017), appeal not allowed, 150 Ohio St. 3d 1452, 2017-Ohio-8136, 83 N.E.3d 938 (2017), State v. Walker, 2016-Ohio-398, 2016 WL 529920 (Ohio Ct. App. 8th Dist. Cuyahoga County 2016); State v. Riedel, 2017-Ohio-8865, 100 N.E.3d 1155 (Ohio Ct. App. 8th Dist. Cuyahoga County 2017) (cited and applied in a domestic violence case).

[4]State v. Williams, 79 Ohio St. 3d 459, 463, 1997-Ohio-79, 683 N.E.2d 1126 (1997); State v. Rinehart, 2002-Ohio-6143, 2002 WL 31520346, *3 (Ohio Ct. App. 4th Dist. Ross County 2002); State v. Hawkins, 2012-Ohio-4622, 2012 WL 4762031 (Ohio Ct. App. 2d Dist. Montgomery County 2012); State v. Fernandez, 2012-Ohio-2538, 2012 WL 2061589 (Ohio Ct. App. 2d Dist. Montgomery County 2012); State v. Slevin, 2012-Ohio-2043, 2012 WL 1647115 (Ohio Ct. App. 9th Dist. Summit County 2012); State v. Rubes, 2012-Ohio-4100, 975 N.E.2d 1054 (Ohio Ct. App. 11th Dist. Portage County 2012); State v. McGlothan, 2012-Ohio-4049, 2012 WL 3862138 (Ohio Ct. App. 8th Dist. Cuyahoga County 2012), judgment rev'd, 138 Ohio St. 3d 146, 2014-Ohio-85, 4 N.E.3d 1021 (2014); State v. Clouse, 2012-Ohio-3471, 2012 WL 3133059 (Ohio Ct. App. 10th Dist. Franklin County 2012); State v. Davis, 2014-Ohio-1197, 2014 WL 1340774 (Ohio Ct. App. 5th Dist. Licking County 2014); State v. White, 2014-Ohio-1446, 2014 WL 1384082 (Ohio Ct. App. 2d Dist. Montgomery County 2014); State v. Brauer, 2013-Ohio-3319, 2013 WL 3946124 (Ohio Ct. App. 12th Dist. Warren County 2013); State v. Rivera, 2013-Ohio-3244, 2013 WL 3877817 (Ohio Ct. App. 8th Dist. Cuyahoga County 2013); State v. Partlow, 2013-Ohio-2771, 2013 WL 3356575 (Ohio Ct. App. 10th Dist. Franklin County 2013).

[5]State v. Williams, 79 Ohio St. 3d 459, 463, 1997-Ohio-79, 683 N.E.2d 1126 (1997). See also State v. Williams, 2000 WL 1475585 (Ohio Ct. App. 2d Dist. Clark County 2000); State v. Rinehart, 2002-Ohio-6143, 2002 WL 31520346, *3 (Ohio Ct.

The Court provided some guidance to trial courts in determining whether parties are "cohabiting" for the purpose of RC 2919.25(E)(2):

> Having considered the above definitions of "cohabitant" and "family or household member," we conclude that the essential elements of "cohabitation" are (1) sharing of familial or financial responsibilities and (2) consortium. RC 2919.25(E)(2) and related statutes. Possible factors establishing shared familial or financial responsibilities might include provisions for shelter, food, clothing, utilities, and/or commingled assets. Factors that might establish consortium include mutual respect, fidelity, affection, society, cooperation, solace, comfort, aid of each other, friendship, and conjugal relations. These factors are unique to each case and how much weight, if any, to give to each of these factors must be decided on a case-by-case basis by the trier of fact.[6]

The court pointed out the following factors as examples of items a court could consider:

> In the case sub judice, both Liggins and Williams testified that the inception of the violence was a fight over money problems. Based on this testimony, the court could have reasonably concluded that a relationship existed wherein the two commingled their assets, thus sharing certain familial or financial responsibilities. Liggins further testified that the two spent most of their nights together at Williams's residence, and that at one time she thought she might be pregnant with his child. Their relationship thus was based upon society and conjugal relations, and therefore included consortium. Accordingly, the trial court did not err in finding that Liggins and Williams were cohabitants.[7]

It should be noted that avoidance of the residency requirements of

---

App. 4th Dist. Ross County 2002); State v. Hawkins, 2012-Ohio-4622, 2012 WL 4762031 (Ohio Ct. App. 2d Dist. Montgomery County 2012); State v. Fernandez, 2012-Ohio-2538, 2012 WL 2061589 (Ohio Ct. App. 2d Dist. Montgomery County 2012); State v. Slevin, 2012-Ohio-2043, 2012 WL 1647115 (Ohio Ct. App. 9th Dist. Summit County 2012); State v. Rubes, 2012-Ohio-4100, 975 N.E.2d 1054 (Ohio Ct. App. 11th Dist. Portage County 2012); State v. Clouse, 2012-Ohio-3471, 2012 WL 3133059 (Ohio Ct. App. 10th Dist. Franklin County 2012).

[6]State v. Williams, 79 Ohio St. 3d 459, 465, 1997-Ohio-79, 683 N.E.2d 1126 (1997). See also State v. Williams, 2000 WL 1475585 (Ohio Ct. App. 2d Dist. Clark County 2000); Cleveland v. Schill, 147 Ohio App. 3d 239, 2002-Ohio-1263, 769 N.E.2d 907 (8th Dist. Cuyahoga County 2002); Cleveland v. Bergman, 111 Ohio Misc. 2d 16, 748 N.E.2d 1214 (Mun. Ct. 2001); City of Akron v. Taylor, 2001-Ohio-1947, 2001 WL 1626941 (Ohio Ct. App. 9th Dist. Summit County 2001); State v. Rinehart, 2002-Ohio-6143, 2002 WL 31520346, *3 (Ohio Ct. App. 4th Dist. Ross County 2002); State v. Church, 2005-Ohio-5198, 2005 WL 2401487 (Ohio Ct. App. 8th Dist. Cuyahoga County 2005). But see State v. Kvasne, 169 Ohio App. 3d 167, 2006-Ohio-5235, 862 N.E.2d 171 (8th Dist. Cuyahoga County 2006), judgment aff'd, 114 Ohio St. 3d 430, 2007-Ohio-4552, 872 N.E.2d 1212 (2007); State v. Hawkins, 2012-Ohio-4622, 2012 WL 4762031 (Ohio Ct. App. 2d Dist. Montgomery County 2012); State v. Fernandez, 2012-Ohio-2538, 2012 WL 2061589 (Ohio Ct. App. 2d Dist. Montgomery County 2012); State v. Slevin, 2012-Ohio-2043, 2012 WL 1647115 (Ohio Ct. App. 9th Dist. Summit County 2012); State v. Rubes, 2012-Ohio-4100, 975 N.E.2d 1054 (Ohio Ct. App. 11th Dist. Portage County 2012); State v. Clouse, 2012-Ohio-3471, 2012 WL 3133059 (Ohio Ct. App. 10th Dist. Franklin County 2012).

[7]State v. Williams, 79 Ohio St. 3d 459, 465, 1997-Ohio-79, 683 N.E.2d 1126 (1997). See also State v. Cohagen, 2000 WL 1357938 (Ohio Ct. App. 10th Dist. Franklin County 2000) and Heflin v. Dunson, 2005-Ohio-304, 2005 WL 187435 (Ohio Ct. App. 2d Dist. Montgomery County 2005); State v. Hawkins, 2012-Ohio-4622, 2012 WL 4762031 (Ohio Ct. App. 2d Dist. Montgomery County 2012); State v. Fernandez, 2012-Ohio-2538, 2012 WL 2061589 (Ohio Ct. App. 2d Dist. Montgomery County 2012); State v. Slevin, 2012-Ohio-2043, 2012 WL 1647115 (Ohio Ct. App. 9th Dist. Summit County 2012); State v. Rubes, 2012-Ohio-4100, 975 N.E.2d 1054 (Ohio Ct.

the domestic violence law is limited to those situations that involve individuals who are engaged in intimate partner relationships.[8] Other individuals who may be related to the offender are not deemed to be "family or household members," as that term is understood for purposes of Ohio's domestic violence laws, unless the statute's residency requirements are met.[9]

Determination of whether unmarried intimate couples are covered by the definition of "family or household member" found in Ohio's domestic violence laws, however, was complicated following amendment of the state's constitution. On November 2, 2004, the people of Ohio passed a ballot initiative which, ostensibly, was aimed at protecting the prevailing traditional view of marriage in the state from governmental modification.[10] Pursuant to the second sentence of that Amendment, the state of Ohio and "its political subdivisions, shall not create or recognize a legal status for relationships of unmarried couples that intends to approximate the design, qualities, significance or effect of marriage."

An apparently unintended consequence of the amendment was to place into question the continued constitutionality of the state's domestic violence law. Any question was resolved with the announcement by the Supreme Court of Ohio of its decision in *State v. Carswell*.[11] In that case, the court held that the state's domestic violence law[12] is not unconstitutional, does not conflict with, and does not create quasi-marital relationships in violation of the state's constitution.[13]

Q & A: I recently went over to visit my mother in the home where we grew up. I got into a fight with my sister who still lives there and she called the police. I've been charged with domestic violence. Since I don't live there now, can they do that?

Yes. Although you and your sister don't currently live together, the

---

App. 11th Dist. Portage County 2012); State v. Clouse, 2012-Ohio-3471, 2012 WL 3133059 (Ohio Ct. App. 10th Dist. Franklin County 2012).

[8]RC 2919.25(F)(1)(a).

[9]RC 2919.25(F)(1)(a). See also State v. Alvey, 2003-Ohio-7006, 2003 WL 22997277 (Ohio Ct. App. 7th Dist. Belmont County 2003); State v. Toles, 1999 WL 1232092 (Ohio Ct. App. 4th Dist. Gallia County 1999); State v. Sims, 169 Ohio App. 3d 579, 2006-Ohio-6285, 863 N.E.2d 1110 (1st Dist. Hamilton County 2006); State v. Mauldin, 2010-Ohio-4192, 2010 WL 3482689 (Ohio Ct. App. 7th Dist. Mahoning County 2010); State v. Wynn, 2017-Ohio-8045, 2017 WL 4417756 (Ohio Ct. App. 1st Dist. Hamilton County 2017).

[10]See 2004 ballot initiative, State Issue One, amending O. Const. Art. XV, Section 11.

[11]State v. Carswell, 114 Ohio St. 3d 210, 2007-Ohio-3723, 871 N.E.2d 547 (2007); State v. Mays, 2014-Ohio-814, 2014 WL 888375 (Ohio Ct. App. 8th Dist. Cuyahoga County 2014); State v. Gipson, 2016-Ohio-994, 2016 WL 962400 (Ohio Ct. App. 3d Dist. Allen County 2016); State v. Riedel, 2017-Ohio-8865, 100 N.E.3d 1155 (Ohio Ct. App. 8th Dist. Cuyahoga County 2017).

[12]RC 2919.25.

[13]Ohio Constitution, Article XV, Section 11 (Rendered unconstitutional by the U.S. Supreme Court's decision in Obergefell v. Hodges, 135 S. Ct. 2584, 192 L. Ed. 2d 609, 99 Empl. Prac. Dec. (CCH) P 45341, 2015-1 U.S. Tax Cas. (CCH) P 50357, 115 A.F.T.R.2d 2015-2309 (2015).

fact that you are biologically related and that you lived together in the past is sufficient to qualify you as family or household members for purposes of Ohio's domestic violence law.[14]

Q & A: I got into a fight with my spouse's father the last time we visited. He called the police and had me arrested for domestic violence. We haven't stayed at his house for more than a year and we only stayed there for a month while we were looking for a place of our own. Can I really be charged with domestic violence?

Yes. Residency is determined from the living circumstances of the parties. Residency requirements under RC 2919.25 envision something more permanent in nature than just periodic visits even if those visits are overnight or last several days. However, courts, when considering the notion of residency, exclude only a temporary or transient visitor. Where, as here, the facts suggest that the living circumstances involved more than periodic visits or overnight visits lasting several days residency for purposes of the domestic violence law is established.[15]

Q & A: My ex-girlfriend and I got into a fight. We only lived together for six months and we don't live together anymore. We broke up almost two years ago. Now the police say that we are family or household members and are charging me with domestic violence, because I used to help her out with the rent and bills back then! Can they do that?

Yes. It is not necessary for the offender and victim to live together at the time of the incident in order to determine that they qualify as family or household members subject to the domestic violence statutes. The relationship between the offender and victim is crucial, as domestic violence is not a crime between strangers.[16] It is enough to show that the parties cohabited' by establishing that they (1) shared familial or financial responsibilities and (2) that there was consortium.[17]

In this case, you lived with the alleged victim, as her boyfriend, for

---

[14]E. Cleveland v. Perkins, 2009-Ohio-2131, 2009 WL 1244154 (Ohio Ct. App. 8th Dist. Cuyahoga County 2009); State v. Gibson, 2005-Ohio-1495, 2005 WL 730059 (Ohio Ct. App. 8th Dist. Cuyahoga County 2005); State v. Jorden, 134 Ohio App. 3d 131, 730 N.E.2d 447 (1st Dist. Hamilton County 1999); State v. Turner, 2016-Ohio-813, 2016 WL 860301 (Ohio Ct. App. 8th Dist. Cuyahoga County 2016).

[15]State v. Burkhart, 2009-Ohio-1142, 2009 WL 653038 (Ohio Ct. App. 11th Dist. Ashtabula County 2009); State v. Toles, 1999 WL 1232092 (Ohio Ct. App. 4th Dist. Gallia County 1999); State v. Sims, 169 Ohio App. 3d 579, 583, 2006-Ohio-6285, 863 N.E.2d 1110, 1112 (1st Dist. Hamilton County 2006).

[16]State v. Williams, 79 Ohio St. 3d 459, 1997-Ohio-79, 683 N.E.2d 1126 (1997); Cleveland v. Schill, 147 Ohio App. 3d 239, 2002-Ohio-1263, 769 N.E.2d 907 (8th Dist. Cuyahoga County 2002); State v. Moore, 2010-Ohio-509, 2010 WL 547707 (Ohio Ct. App. 8th Dist. Cuyahoga County 2010); State v. Hawkins, 2012-Ohio-4622, 2012 WL 4762031 (Ohio Ct. App. 2d Dist. Montgomery County 2012); State v. Fernandez, 2012-Ohio-2538, 2012 WL 2061589 (Ohio Ct. App. 2d Dist. Montgomery County 2012); State v. Slevin, 2012-Ohio-2043, 2012 WL 1647115 (Ohio Ct. App. 9th Dist. Summit County 2012); State v. Rubes, 2012-Ohio-4100, 975 N.E.2d 1054 (Ohio Ct. App. 11th Dist. Portage County 2012); State v. Clouse, 2012-Ohio-3471, 2012 WL 3133059 (Ohio Ct. App. 10th Dist. Franklin County 2012).

[17]State v. Williams, 79 Ohio St. 3d 459, 1997-Ohio-79, 683 N.E.2d 1126 (1997); State v. Hawkins, 2012-Ohio-4622, 2012 WL 4762031 (Ohio Ct. App. 2d Dist. Montgomery County 2012); State v. Fernandez, 2012-Ohio-2538, 2012 WL 2061589

six months even though that was two years prior to the current incident. You periodically paid rent and contributed to the expenses of the household. The nature of the relationship at issue here was clearly one of cohabitation, and it did not fall outside of the five-year look-back period. Therefore, you qualify as her family of household member under the domestic violence statute and can be charged with domestic violence.

Q & A: During trial on a charge of domestic violence, the prosecution proves that the defendant struck the victim and that the defendant and victim lived together as boyfriend and girlfriend, well-before the incident on trial. The prosecution also proved that the couple was living together at the time that the complained-of event took place. However, the prosecution was unable to prove that the defendant contributed to maintenance of their household in any financial way. At the end of the prosecution's case, the defense moves for a directed verdict of acquittal, on the grounds that the prosecution failed to establish the element of cohabitation. How should the trial court rule?

The Ohio Supreme Court holds that where the prosecution is able to demonstrate that the defendant and the victim are, and have been for some time before the incident, boyfriend and girlfriend, and the evidence also demonstrates that the victim resided with the defendant at the time that the incident occurred, the trial court can reasonably concluded that the victim and the defendant are family or household members. Thus, the state has no obligation to demonstrate the sharing of familial or financial responsibilities and consortium to prove cohabitation. Instead, the trial court can reasonably determine that the prosecution has established that the defendant is a person living as a spouse with the victim.[18] Based on the Supreme Court's holding, it is now sufficient to establish that the victim and the defendant merely by living together in the same residence satisfy the element of cohabitation for purposes of the domestic-violence statute, even if there is no proof that the victim and the offender shared living expenses, such as rent and utilities.[19]

Q & A: The defendant and the victim are twin siblings, but they were separated at birth. At the conclusion of the state's case, the defense moves for a directed verdict of acquittal. Should the court grant the motion?

Yes. Unless there is evidence presented that the two siblings ever "resided" together, the motion should be granted. R.C. 2919.25(F)(1) defines "family member household member" as follows:

(1) "Family or household member" means any of the following:

(a) Any of the following who is residing or *has resided* with the offender:

(Ohio Ct. App. 2d Dist. Montgomery County 2012); State v. Slevin, 2012-Ohio-2043, 2012 WL 1647115 (Ohio Ct. App. 9th Dist. Summit County 2012); State v. Rubes, 2012-Ohio-4100, 975 N.E.2d 1054 (Ohio Ct. App. 11th Dist. Portage County 2012); State v. Clouse, 2012-Ohio-3471, 2012 WL 3133059 (Ohio Ct. App. 10th Dist. Franklin County 2012).

[18]State v. McGlothan, 138 Ohio St. 3d 146, 2014-Ohio-85, 4 N.E.3d 1021 (2014).

[19]State v. McGlothan, 138 Ohio St. 3d 146, 2014-Ohio-85, 4 N.E.3d 1021 (2014).

* * *

(ii) A parent, a foster parent, or a child of the offender, or another person related by consanguinity or affinity to the offender. * * *.

Thus, the state was required to prove as an element of the offense that the siblings resided together at some point in order for the defendant to be convicted of domestic violence.

There is no specific time frame in the statute as to when the "residing" had to occur. The statute just requires that they lived together at some point in time.[20]

Q & A: At the conclusion of the state's case the defense moves for a directed verdict of acquittal. The defense argues that the uncontroverted evidence presented at trial was that the defendant owned the house where the couple lived and paid all of the household bills. Therefore, the defense maintains that the state failed to present evidence of the shared financial or familial responsibilities and consortium required to establish the element of "cohabitation," required for a domestic violence conviction. Should the motion be granted?

No. The Ohio Supreme Court found that the state is not required to present evidence of shared financial or familial responsibilities and consortium in order to establish "cohabitation" if there is evidence that the victim and the defendant were living together at the time of the incident.[21] The Court noted that that kind of evidence is only required when the victim and the defendant do *not* share the same residence.[22]

§ 7:4 Arrest considerations; determining the primary physical aggressor

It is not unusual for officers who respond to complaints of domestic violence to find themselves confronted with conflicting claims as to who is really at fault. Ohio's domestic violence law requires that law enforcement officers determine the primary physical aggressor before making a domestic violence arrest. The law also provides investigat-

---

[20]See E. Cleveland v. Perkins, 2009-Ohio-2131, 2009 WL 1244154 (Ohio Ct. App. 8th Dist. Cuyahoga County 2009); State v. Mrus, 71 Ohio App. 3d 828, 831, 595 N.E.2d 460 (11th Dist. Trumbull County 1991) (overruled by, State v. James, 1997 WL 269139 (Ohio Ct. App. 11th Dist. Portage County 1997)) and (overruled by, State v. Fleming, 1997 WL 269141 (Ohio Ct. App. 11th Dist. Portage County 1997)) and (abrogated by, State v. Uher, 1997 WL 269407 (Ohio Ct. App. 11th Dist. Portage County 1997)) and (abrogated by, State v. Wyand, 1997 WL 269143 (Ohio Ct. App. 11th Dist. Portage County 1997)) and (overruled by, State v. Musick, 119 Ohio App. 3d 361, 695 N.E.2d 317 (11th Dist. Portage County 1997)), overruled on other grounds; State v. Burkhart, 2009-Ohio-1142, 2009 WL 653038 (Ohio Ct. App. 11th Dist. Ashtabula County 2009); State v. Turner, 2016-Ohio-813, 2016 WL 860301 (Ohio Ct. App. 8th Dist. Cuyahoga County 2016).

[21]State v. McGlothan, 138 Ohio St. 3d 146, 2014-Ohio-85, 4 N.E.3d 1021 (2014); State v. Riedel, 2017-Ohio-8865, 100 N.E.3d 1155 (Ohio Ct. App. 8th Dist. Cuyahoga County 2017).

[22]State v. McGlothan, 138 Ohio St. 3d 146, 2014-Ohio-85, 4 N.E.3d 1021 (2014); State v. Riedel, 2017-Ohio-8865, 100 N.E.3d 1155 (Ohio Ct. App. 8th Dist. Cuyahoga County 2017).

ing officers with both objective and subjective benchmarks to look for in making that determination.[1]

In determining which party is the primary physical aggressor, an officer is required to investigate and determine, in addition to any other relevant circumstances, the following:

(1) Any history of domestic violence or violent acts by either person involved in the alleged offense that the officer can ascertain;[2]

(2) If actual physical violence is alleged, whether someone who was acting in self-defense committed the violence;[3]

(3) The level of fear that each party to the violence displays, if any. If it appears to the officer that there is fear present, the officer is then required to make two further assessments. First, the officer should attempt to determine whether the fear displayed appears to result from the other party's threatened use of force, or a history of use of force, against the party who exhibits the fear.[4] Second, the officer must attempt to determine whether the fear displayed is reasonable under all of the circumstances;[5]

(4) The comparative severity of the injuries suffered or inflicted by the parties.[6]

As with each of the other factors, severity of injury is not definitive in determining the identity of the primary physical aggressor. It is a useful tool, however, when considered in light of the totality of the circumstances. The relative severity of injuries may provide investigating officers with strong clues concerning which party they should arrest when combined with such additional information as whose injuries appear to be offensive, whose injuries appear to be defensive, and the relative size and strength of the parties. If a weapon or other implement was used to inflict the injury, the circumstances under which the weapon came into play are crucial to a determination of whether its use was justified.

An analysis of the comparative severity of injury requires that the initial investigation conducted by law enforcement does not stop at a determination of who struck the first blow. The law provides for self-defense in the face of a perceived threat of bodily harm, but it does not allow a representation of "self-defense" to serve as cover for a retaliatory criminal assault. If the force employed in self-defense is grossly disproportionate to that required to repel the threat, the victim becomes the primary aggressor.[7]

§ 7:5 Pretrial detention and initial appearance issues

Arrests for domestic violence offenses tend to be swift and result in at least some pre-release jail time. This is because of two factors:

[Section 7:4]

[1]RC 2935.03(B)(3)(d)(i) to (iv).

[2]RC 2935.03(B)(3)(d)(i); see also Text § 14:3, Arrest of the perpetrator, Text § 14:4, Determination of primary physical aggressor.

[3]RC 2935.03(B)(3)(d)(ii); see also Text § 14:3, Arrest of the perpetrator.

[4]RC 2935.03(B)(3)(d)(iii).

[5]RC 2935.03(B)(3)(d)(iii); see also Text § 14:3, Arrest of the perpetrator.

[6]RC 2935.03(B)(3)(d)(iv).

[7]See 2 Criminal Ohio Jury Instructions 421.23(3).

(1) Statutory requirements that make arrest the preferred option for law enforcement intervention in domestic violence cases, and
(2) The fear that the complainant will suffer additional harm if the suspect is not detained.

Domestic violence is most often charged as a misdemeanor. The Revised Code,[1] however, allows broader powers and immunities for officers making domestic violence arrests than are traditionally allowed in other misdemeanor arrest situations. Along with these enhanced powers and immunities, state law now requires law enforcement agencies to develop protocols, policies, and procedures for responding to complaints of domestic violence.[2] These protocols require the immediate arrest of the "primary aggressor," even when the "victim" does not wish to prosecute or denies that domestic violence occurred. By statutory definition, domestic violence has a broad sweep. Nonetheless, when the public thinks of domestic violence, it thinks of "wife beating." Studies show that if the cycle of violence between intimate partners is not broken it typically aggravates.

Increasingly, courts are also using arrest as an effective method for stopping the violence. Although not a curative, studies done on domestic violence intervention alternatives, including counseling, removal, referral, and arrest, generally support the conclusion that arrest provides the best opportunity for a victim to safely assess the dangerousness of the situation and to seek help.

When representing a defendant charged with domestic violence, it is important to keep in mind that these two considerations govern most decisions made by police, prosecutors, and judges. It is also well to keep in mind that "wife beaters" do not have an organized constituency to rally to the support of their behavior.

The Ohio Rules of Criminal Procedure[3] govern the initial appearance of a domestic violence defendant once a formal charge is brought, just as they do with any other individual charged with a crime in this state. The domestic violence defendant receives a copy of the complaint and an opportunity to know the nature of the charge lodged by the government. The defendant is also entitled to have a reasonable bail bond set.[4] There is no requirement that the defendant enter a plea at an initial appearance if the charge is a felony. Even if the charge is a misdemeanor, the defendant may postpone the entry of a plea at initial appearance until such time as an attorney is consulted. In addition, the court, on its own motion, may decline to accept a defendant's plea at initial appearance if it believes that justice requires the defendant to wait.

An initial misdemeanor appearance may combine the function of setting bond, hearing preliminary motions, and the entry of a plea.

[Section 7:5]

[1]RC 2935.03(B)(1).

[2]RC 2935.032.

[3]Crim.R. 5.

[4]Crim.R. 5(A).

The combination of these functions, however, is not a practice guaranteed under the Criminal Rules.

A court may bifurcate the domestic violence misdemeanor arraignment procedure. It is permissible to arraign misdemeanants like felons, that is to say, allow the formal entry of the plea at a point subsequent to the initial appearance.

In jurisdictions that handle all functions at once, three procedural events occur simultaneously during the defendant's initial appearance:

(1) the motion for a temporary protection order is heard,
(2) the court sets bond, and
(3) the defendant enters a plea.

If a court provides for separate treatment of each of these procedures, an initial appearance will probably deal only with those functions that the court feels must, by law, take place, such as bail[5] and the final hearing on the merits of any ex parte temporary protection order previously granted.[6]

Regardless of the desires of the client or pressures from the court, the entry of a not guilty plea at the arraignment is the best strategy for defense counsel to effectively represent a client. Most defense attorneys agree that the time between arrest and arraignment does not provide adequate opportunity to investigate cases as complicated and involved as domestic violence cases tend to be. Additionally, once a case is assigned to a particular judge, an attorney may be in a better position to advise a client concerning options and the likely success of possible dispositive motions. More insight is possible concerning the potential risks inherent in taking a case to trial before the bench and the advisability of demanding a jury. Additionally, familiarity with the assigned judge's sentencing patterns may implicate the expediency of engaging in plea negotiations designed to tailor an outcome that provides a maximum benefit to the client.

§ 7:6 Temporary protection orders; hearing considerations

Counsel should make the decision whether to have a hearing on the merits of a temporary protection order only after weighing all factors. The criteria for the court to follow in granting a temporary protection order are set out in RC 2919.26(C).

In practice, the hearing on the merits of a temporary protection order is generally brief and usually consists of a recitation of the underlying facts of the case. The victim usually presents this recitation. The statement of facts includes an assessment of the victim's fear of future harm at the hands of the defendant.

There are a number of important considerations that defense counsel must weigh. Traditional criminal defense practice suggests that the hearing should take place. At a minimum, the hearing provides early, quick, and easy discovery. The primary witness against the defendant must submit to cross-examination on the key facts that constitute the heart of the prosecution's case. The prosecution gener-

[5]Crim.R. 5(A)(5).

[6]R.C. 2919.26(D)(2)(a).

ally has not had an opportunity to fully prepare the witness for that cross-examination. Finally, the hearing gives defense counsel, as well as the defendant, an early indication of the type of witness the victim will be and what the defense is up against if the case goes to trial.

Nonetheless, holding the hearing does present one major pitfall. Participating in the hearing may embolden the otherwise hesitant victim. The temporary protection order procedure outlined in RC 2919.26, by its very nature, tends to empower the victim of a domestic violence offense, if it is conducted as the legislature clearly envisioned that it should be. Perpetrators of domestic violence rely on their position of power in these relationships to maintain control. Arrest and detention is the first erosion of their power, but that erosion has little if anything to do with the power that they exercise over their victims. This is true when it comes to protection orders because, absent a victim's express statement that a temporary protection order is unnecessary, the orders are routinely granted in much of the state.

When the defendant requests the hearing on the merits of the protection order, the victim may frequently observe the transfer of power away from the defendant and to the victim. With the memory of the violence, not to mention actual emotions, wounds, and bruises, usually fresh, victims at temporary protection order hearings generally make convincing witnesses. Success in obtaining a temporary protection order, primarily as a result of their testimony, even after that testimony is tested by cross-examination by the defendant's lawyer, is a lesson for the victim in getting through court and in gaining control.

Thus, the defense must weigh the possible effect of holding a hearing on the defendant's ability to control the overall situation against the value of the testimony that the hearing will record. The testimony obtained during a temporary protection order hearing cannot be introduced as evidence of the commission of the offense at the trial of the alleged offender on the complaint on which the order is based.[1] Any further action taken by the court, either granting or denying the temporary protection order, cannot be construed as a finding that the individual charged with the offense did or did not commit the offense.

RC 2919.26(E)(3) is in derogation of the rules of evidence regulating the admission of hearsay that would ordinarily govern.[2] But for the operation of the statute, the rules of evidence would provide the court with authority to order the testimony of a declarant/victim who obtained a temporary protection order and then persisted in refusing to testify, even in the face of an order of the court[3] read into the record at trial. The statute strips the court of that option.[4]

If, however, the victim changes his/her testimony regarding the facts (e.g., adds to the account given since the temporary protection

[Section 7:6]

[1]R.C. 2919.26(E)(3).

[2]Evid.R. 804(A)(2), Evid.R. 804(B)(1).

[3]Evid.R. 804(A)(2).

[4]R.C. 2919.26(E)(3) renders such testimony inadmissible.

order was granted), the testimony is available to the defense for purposes of impeachment.[5]

The basis for the statutory exemption[6] is to prevent the information that a temporary protection order was granted in a given case from prejudicing a jury. Granting a temporary protection order confers great public policy benefits. The decision to grant the temporary protection order, however, is based on different evidentiary standards than the decision of whether a defendant is guilty of domestic violence. It is not necessarily subject to the same scrutiny. Protection from the potentially prejudicial introduction of evidence that a temporary protection order was granted in favor of the victim and against the defendant is a procedural right that the defendant enjoys. It does not logically follow that the defendant does not enjoy the right to use temporary protection order testimony when its introduction is beneficial to the defense of the case-in-chief.

A temporary protection order may be granted ex parte prior to the defendant's first appearance. Even when the order is granted in this manner, the defendant is not precluded from having a hearing on the merits of the continued application of the order.[7]

In fact, many temporary protection orders are granted ex parte. There are two interpretations of the practical operation of the protection order hearing provisions of RC 2919.26(D)(2). One is that a defendant is entitled to a hearing de novo if the temporary protection order was granted ex parte. Under this interpretation, the victim/petitioner must appear at both the ex parte and final hearings.[8]

This interpretation, however, may not be correct. Demanding a full hearing may not require that the petitioner/victim be present. The defense may determine that all that needs to happen at the hearing on the merits of the order is for the court, particularly if it is the same judge who took the evidence at the ex parte hearing and little time has elapsed, to merely question the defendant and *determine whether the order should remain in effect, be modified, or be revoked*. For the reasons set forth earlier, demanding a full hearing may be counterproductive for the defense in some cases.

The temporary protection order is not construed as a part of any bail that the court sets under Criminal Rule 46. It is issued in addition to any bail that the court requires.

In many, if not most, Ohio jurisdictions, bond is set following the determination of the appropriateness of a motion for a temporary protection order. In more and more jurisdictions, bonds set before an initial hearing on a motion for a temporary protection order are higher than those set after temporary protection order motion hearings. Where practicable and within the parameters of the rules, courts often delay establishing bond until the first hearing on the motion for temporary protection order is held in order to gather some factual justification for the level of bail ultimately established.

Under RC 2919.26 and Criminal Rule 5(A)(5), the issuance of a

---

[5]Evid.R. 801(D)(1)(a).

[6]R.C. 2919.26(E)(3).

[7]R.C. 2919.26(D)(2)(a).

[8]R.C. 2919.26(C)(1).

temporary protection order and the setting of bond are two separate functions. Bond may not be denied prior to the temporary protection order hearing. The court is prohibited from holding an individual in custody on a domestic violence related charge simply because there is a motion pending for a temporary protection order[9] if that individual meets the other criteria for release on bond.[10]

One final consideration that counsel should keep in mind when deciding whether to request a final hearing on the granting or continuation of a Temporary Protection Order: The effect that the order will have on the client's right to obtain, possess or use a firearm. Under federal law, following notice and opportunity to be heard, if a qualifying protection order is granted, an alleged offender is stripped of the right to possess a firearm while the order is in effect.[11] If the right to possess a firearm is important to the client, even if the likelihood of having the order denied or vacated is slim, the possibility of success might be enough to warrant the effort. Remember, once a qualifying order issues, the client's right to possess a firearm is prohibited under federal law, any action of the state court notwithstanding.[12]

The reality of the situation is that, in most courts in Ohio, Temporary Protection Orders are routinely granted. Thus, from the standpoint of the defendant's counsel, it is important to assess whether conducting a hearing on the merits of a requested Temporary Protection Order will serve the interests of the client later, at trial or in some other resolution of the case that favors those interests. If it does, the hearing should go forward.

§ 7:7 Temporary protection orders and initial felony appearances

The Rules of Criminal Procedure allow for preliminary hearings for defendants charged with felonies.[1] A preliminary hearing in a domestic violence case may be similar to a hearing on a temporary protection order. However, unlike the testimony at a temporary protection order hearing, the testimony at the preliminary hearing is not excludable at future hearings before the court on the underlying charge. Counsel, therefore, should not agree to combine the preliminary hearing and temporary protection order hearing into one proceeding.[2]

In order to charge domestic violence as a felony in Ohio, one of two conditions must exist:

1. The offender was previously convicted of domestic violence, or

---

[9]RC 2919.26(F).

[10]Crim.R. 46.

[11]18 U.S.C.A. § 922(g); 18 U.S.C.A. § 922(t). See also Text § 18:11, Firearms offenses under VAWA.

[12]See Text § 18:11, Firearms offenses under VAWA. See also Amended H.B. 562 (eff. June 24, 2008).

[Section 7:7]

[1]Crim.R. 5(B); see also RC 2937.01 et seq.

[2]Evid.R. 804(B)(1) controls the determination of admissibility of testimony from a preliminary hearing.

another criminal violation specified in Ohio's domestic violence statute, against a family or household member,[3] to wit:

- Violation of an existing municipal ordinance of the state of Ohio, substantially similar to Ohio's domestic violence statute.
- Violation of a former municipal ordinance of the state of Ohio, substantially similar to Ohio's domestic violence statute.
- Violation of an existing state law of another jurisdiction, substantially similar to Ohio's domestic violence statute.
- Violation of a former state law of another jurisdiction, substantially similar to Ohio's domestic violence statute.
- Violation of an existing municipal ordinance in another state's jurisdiction, substantially similar to Ohio's domestic violence statute.
- Violation of a former municipal ordinance in another state's jurisdiction, substantially similar to Ohio's domestic violence statute.
- Violation of RC 2903.14, if the victim was a family or household member of the offender at the time of the offense.
- Violation of any other existing law of the state of Ohio that is substantially similar to RC 2903.14, if the victim was a family or household member of the offender at the time of the offense.
- Violation of any former law of the state of Ohio that is substantially similar to RC 2903.14, if the victim was a family or household member of the offender at the time of the offense.
- Violation of any existing law of any other state that is substantially that is substantially similar to RC 2903.14, if the victim was a family or household member of the offender at the time of the offense.
- Violation of any existing municipal ordinance of any other state that is substantially similar to RC 2903.14, if the victim was a family or household member of the offender at the time of the offense.
- Violation of any former municipal ordinance of any other state that is substantially similar to RC 2903.14, if the victim was a family or household member at the time of the offense.
- Violation of RC 2909.06, if the victim was a family or household member of the offender at the time of the offense.
- Violation of any other existing law of the state of Ohio that is substantially similar to RC 2909.06, if the victim was a family or household member of the offender at the time of the offense.
- Violation of any former law of the state of Ohio that is substantially similar to RC 2909.06, if the victim was a family or household member of the offender at the time of the offense.
- Violation of any existing law of any other state that is

[3]RC 2919.25(D)(3).

substantially that is substantially similar to RC 2909.06, if the victim was a family or household member of the offender at the time of the offense.

- Violation of any existing municipal ordinance of any other state that is substantially similar to RC 2909.06, if the victim was a family or household member of the offender at the time of the offense.
- Violation of any former municipal ordinance of any other state that is substantially similar to RC 2909.06, if the victim was a family or household member at the time of the offense.
- Violation of RC 2909.07, if the victim was a family or household member of the offender at the time of the offense.
- Violation of any other existing law of the state of Ohio that is substantially similar to RC 2909.07, if the victim was a family or household member of the offender at the time of the offense.
- Violation of any former law of the state of Ohio that is substantially similar to RC 2909.07, if the victim was a family or household member of the offender at the time of the offense.
- Violation of any existing law of any other state that is substantially that is substantially similar to RC 2909.07, if the victim was a family or household member of the offender at the time of the offense.
- Violation of any existing municipal ordinance of any other state that is substantially similar to RC 2909.07, if the victim was a family or household member of the offender at the time of the offense.
- Violation of any former municipal ordinance of any other state that is substantially similar to RC 2909.07, if the victim was a family or household member at the time of the offense.
- Violation of RC 2911.12, if the victim was a family or household member of the offender at the time of the offense.
- Violation of any other existing law of the state of Ohio that is substantially similar to RC 2911.12, if the victim was a family or household member of the offender at the time of the offense.
- Violation of any former law of the state of Ohio that is substantially similar to RC 2911.12, if the victim was a family or household member of the offender at the time of the offense.
- Violation of any existing law of any other state that is substantially that is substantially similar to RC 2911.12, if the victim was a family or household member of the offender at the time of the offense.
- Violation of any existing municipal ordinance of any other state that is substantially similar to RC 2911.12, if the victim was a family or household member of the offender at the time of the offense.
- Violation of any former municipal ordinance of any other state that is substantially similar to RC 2911.12, if the victim was a family or household member at the time of the offense.

- Violation of RC 2911.211, if the victim was a family or household member of the offender at the time of the offense.
- Violation of any other existing law of the state of Ohio that is substantially similar to RC 2911.211, if the victim was a family or household member of the offender at the time of the offense.
- Violation of any former law of the state of Ohio that is substantially similar to RC 2911.211, if the victim was a family or household member of the offender at the time of the offense.
- Violation of any existing law of any other state that is substantially that is substantially similar to RC 2911.211, if the victim was a family or household member of the offender at the time of the offense.
- Violation of any existing municipal ordinance of any other state that is substantially similar to RC 2911.211, if the victim was a family or household member of the offender at the time of the offense.
- Violation of any former municipal ordinance of any other state that is substantially similar to RC 2911.211, if the victim was a family or household member at the time of the offense.
- Violation of RC 2919.22, if the victim was a family or household member of the offender at the time of the offense.
- Violation of any other existing law of the state of Ohio that is substantially similar to 2919.22, if the victim was a family or household member of the offender at the time of the offense.
- Violation of any former law of the state of Ohio that is substantially similar to RC 2919.22, if the victim was a family or household member of the offender at the time of the offense.
- Violation of any existing law of any other state that is substantially that is substantially similar to RC 2919.22, if the victim was a family or household member of the offender at the time of the offense.
- Violation of any existing municipal ordinance of any other state that is substantially similar to RC 2919.22, if the victim was a family or household member of the offender at the time of the offense.
- Violation of any former municipal ordinance of any other state that is substantially similar to RC 2919.22, if the victim was a family or household member at the time of the offense.
- Any other offense of violence, as defined in the Ohio Revised Code.[4]

or

2. An allegation that the offender either intentionally or recklessly caused, or attempted to cause, physical harm to a family or

[4]RC 2901.01(A)(9)(a) to (d), if the victim was a family or household member of the offender at the time of the offense.

household member who the offender knew at the time of the incident was pregnant.[5]

In both misdemeanor and felony cases, defendants charged with domestic violence enter pleas at an arraignment where the charges are read. This need not be at the same time as the arrest and initial appearance. Criminal Rule 5(a) permits pleading at the initial appearance or at a later date. Defendants are entitled to enter one of four pleas pursuant to Criminal Rule 11(A): not guilty, not guilty by reason of insanity, guilty, or, with the consent of the court, no contest.

Courts are not required to accept no contest pleas, and there is a growing sentiment that courts should not do so in domestic violence cases.

The many collateral consequences of a conviction for domestic violence make the entry of a guilty or no contest plea at the initial stages of a domestic violence prosecution an ill-considered course of action—perilous, at best, for both the lawyer and the client.[6]

§ 7:8 Violation of temporary protection orders

It is not unusual for a defendant charged with domestic violence to find additional charges brought for violation of the terms of a temporary protection order issued in conjunction with the underlying domestic violence charge. In many instances, these temporary protection order violations result from the willful acts of the accused. However, some violations result from the defendant's ignorance of the existence of the order, manipulation by the victim/complainant, or logistical problems caused by the way such orders are registered by and with law enforcement agencies and courts.

The current validity of a protection order is always an area of legitimate defense inquiry. The order takes effect at the point that it is journalized by the court that issued it. Due process requires, however, that an order not be effective until it is served on the individual who is subject to its terms. Thus, if an order is issued ex parte and a defendant has no notice of its issuance, the defendant may not be held responsible for any violation of the terms of the order.[1]

In addition, a defendant may not be charged with violation of a temporary protection order for acts committed after disposal of the underlying criminal act which generated the order.[2]

One question that is still open is what notice is sufficient to require a defendant to adhere to the terms of a temporary protection order issued ex parte. Is it enough, for instance, to show that the defendant had actual notice that an order existed in order to hold the defendant responsible for its terms? If not, must the prosecution establish that

---

[5]RC 2919.25(D)(5).

[6]See Text § 7:10, Collateral effects of a guilty plea or of being found guilty—Generally, regarding the collateral consequences of a domestic violence conviction.

[Section 7:8]

[1]See also Text Ch 13, Court Enforcement of Civil Protection Orders and Related Issues; Text Ch 14, Police Enforcement of Protection Orders and Other Relevant Issues.

[2]RC 2919.26(E)(2).

the defendant was formally served with a copy of the order before a violation of the order may be charged?

Currently, neither statutes nor case law provides any guidance. Communities across the state and across the country are attempting to construct registries that accurately record and track protection orders as they are issued, modified, and rescinded. These efforts will provide police officers with higher levels of comfort when they are called on to enforce protection orders presented outside of regular court hours. These efforts will not, however, solve the underlying problem of knowing when a defendant is deemed to have chargeable notice of the terms of the protection order.[3]

Two as yet unanswered questions immediately come to mind. First, does the statute[4] require, at the point of the dismissal of a misdemeanor domestic violence complaint, the termination of any protection order associated with the case if that self-same case is not bound over to a court of common pleas? Secondly, following dismissal of a domestic violence misdemeanor, does the mere possibility that a felony arising from the same facts might be filed at some point in the future put the defendant in jeopardy of prosecution for something done or said in the interim that could be deemed a violation if and when the felony indictment is ultimately returned?[5]

The statutory language is unclear. Thus, if a protection order is issued in conjunction with a misdemeanor domestic violence charge, and the misdemeanor is dismissed, the defendant has only one safe course of action open to avoid any possibility of violating the order: Observe the terms of the accompanying protection order until such time as the statute of limitations for any possible felony arising from the same facts has expired.[6]

Q & A: The provisions of the Ohio Revised Code that enhance the penalties for violating a protection order, consent agreement or anti-stalking protection order are confusing. How should they be interpreted?

Some clarity comes with dividing the enhancement section into subsections and analyzing each of the provisions of the subsections in turn, i.e.:

If an offender was previously found guilty of violating a stalking protection order against **ANY** person, the current charge may and should be brought as a 5th degree felony.[7]

If an offender was previously found guilty of committing two or more violations of **ANY** of the offenses listed, or any combination of them,[8] **and** those prior violations were against the same person who is now covered by the protection order that the prosecution alleges the offender has violated, then the current violation may and should be brought as a 5th degree felony.

---

[3]See 28 U.S.C.A. § 534.

[4]R.C. 2919.26(E)(2)(a).

[5]RC 2919.26(D)(4).

[6]See the second Q & A: following Text § 4:9, The effect of a felony bind-over on a protection order issued in a municipal or county court.

[7]RC 2903.213, RC 2903.214, RC 2919.27(B)(3).

[8]Aggravated Menacing, Menacing by Stalking, Menacing or Aggravated Trespassing—RC 2903.21, RC 2903.211, RC 2903.22 or RC 2911.211.

Some of the language used in this subsection is potentially the source of confusion.[9] Some have interpreted the provision to focus on the status of the offender, rather than the victim, because it refers to ". . . the same person who is the subject **OF** the protection order or consent agreement. . ."[10] While such an interpretation is possible, it is illogical.

If an offender was previously found guilty of violating ANY of the qualifying protection orders contained in the section,[11] including civil or criminal protection orders[12] that are issued against the offender in favor of **ANY** person, the current charge may and should be brought as a 5th Degree Felony. ..."[13]

Lastly, the law allows an offender to be charged with a third degree felony if, while violating a protection order or consent agreement, the offender is also alleged to commit **ANY** other felony violation. The section places no restrictions on the type of other felony that the offender is alleged to commit while violating the protection violation. Thus, not only offenses that immediately come to mind, such as aggravated burglary, arson, attempted murder, aggravated or felonious assault, etc., but also drug offenses or theft offenses, for example, qualify under a plain reading of the law for purposes of penalty enhancement.[14]

§ 7:9 Pretrial motions

Defense counsel should carefully attend to the standard pretrial motions for discovery and for a bill of particulars when trying an allegation of domestic violence. Because domestic violence is essentially a subcategory of assault, the careful defense attorney will thoroughly scrutinize every element and accusation to see if it fits within the codified definition of the crime. Counsel should determine immediately after entering the case whether there were any calls to the police or 911 and who made them. Any discovery motion should specifically request inspection of all records pertaining to the dispatch of law enforcement officers to the incident under review by the court. Additionally, the discovery motions should also request a copy of the tape requesting the assistance of the police for the defense. If the client initiated police contact, counsel should issue a subpoena at the earliest possible moment to the law enforcement agency's dispatch center to ensure that any records or recordings of that fact will be preserved.

Also, defense counsel should demand hospital reports as soon as possible after being retained. Photographs should also be sought.

Suppression of all reports should also be sought. The grounds for suppression should include that:

---

[9]RC 2919.27(B)(3).

[10]RC 2919.27(B)(3).

[11]RC 2919.27.

[12]RC 2903.213, RC 2903.214, RC 2919.26(A)(1), and RC 3113.31(D)(or E)) or a protection order issued by another state.

[13]RC 2919.27(B)(3).

[14]RC 2919.27(B)(4).

(1) the police protocol required by law was not followed,[1]
(2) the defendant was not apprised of the required constitutional rights before a statement was taken by the police,[2]
(3) the reports are hearsay, and
(4) the reports are more inflammatory than probative.

It is important to remember that a suppression motion must contain a fact-specific brief, or the court is not obligated to entertain it.[3]

When factual circumstances do not lend themselves to the successful pursuit of a motion to suppress, counsel should consider filing motions in limine instead. These motions are particularly useful for the exclusion of part or all of hospital or other medical records which support a victim's claim of injury. In many instances, these reports contain extraneous hearsay statements that are extremely damaging to the defendant and which have little or no bearing on the course of treatment the victim received. This information is usually contained in notes made by the attending physician or an intake worker or other health care professional in compiling the victim's medical history. They often reflect on the truth of the ultimate issues of fact before the court. Many of these statements are more prejudicial than they are probative. They are, as a result, often susceptible to a properly framed motion that seeks the redaction of the questionable statements, or if that is not possible without rendering the document incomprehensible, the total exclusion of the report itself.[4]

For instance, a victim's visit to a hospital is a fact. The injuries noted or not noted is a fact. Why the victim went to the hospital or medical provider is the ultimate issue to be tried. Thus, statements purporting to explain the victim's motivation should be excluded.

Where the defendant is charged with felony domestic violence because of one or more qualifying prior convictions,[5] a motion challenging the enhanced charge may be in order. An indigent defendant may not be sentenced to a term of imprisonment unless the government affords the defendant the right to assistance of counsel.[6] As a result, the U.S. Supreme Court holds that it follows that an uncoun-

[Section 7:9]

[1]RC 2935.032.

[2]U.S. Const. amend. 5; O. Const. Art. I § 10.

[3]Crim.R. 12(E); U.S. v. One 1965 Buick, 392 F.2d 672, 678, 68-1 U.S. Tax Cas. (CCH) P 15839 (6th Cir. 1968) (disapproved of by, U.S. v. U.S. Coin and Currency, 1971-1 C.B. 411, 401 U.S. 715, 91 S. Ct. 1041, 28 L. Ed. 2d 434, 71-1 U.S. Tax Cas. (CCH) P 15979, 27 A.F.T.R.2d 71-1026 (1971)) and judgment vacated, 402 U.S. 937, 91 S. Ct. 1602, 29 L. Ed. 2d 105, 27 A.F.T.R.2d 71-1918 (1971); City of Solon v. Mallion, 10 Ohio App. 3d 130, 460 N.E.2d 729 (8th Dist. Cuyahoga County 1983); Crim.R. 47.

[4]Crim.R. 47.

[5]See the diagram in Text § 2:7, Felony violations.

[6]Scott v. Illinois, 440 U.S. 367, 99 S. Ct. 1158, 59 L. Ed. 2d 383 (1979); Argersinger v. Hamlin, 407 U.S. 25, 92 S. Ct. 2006, 32 L. Ed. 2d 530 (1972); Gideon v. Wainwright, 372 U.S. 335, 83 S. Ct. 792, 9 L. Ed. 2d 799, 93 A.L.R.2d 733 (1963); State v. Wellman, 37 Ohio St. 2d 162, 66 Ohio Op. 2d 353, 309 N.E.2d 915 (1974), citing Argersinger v. Hamlin, 407 U.S. 25, 92 S. Ct. 2006, 32 L. Ed. 2d 530 (1972); State v. Tymcio, 42 Ohio St. 2d 39, 45, 71 Ohio Op. 2d 22, 325 N.E.2d 556 (1975); State v. McLean, 87 Ohio App. 3d 392, 395, 622 N.E.2d 402 (1st Dist. Hamilton County 1993); State v. Paulsen, 2008-Ohio-6907, 2008 WL 5404878 (Ohio Ct. App. 4th Dist. Hocking

seled prior conviction generally may not be used to enhance a later conviction and sentence.[7]

An objection to the use of a prior conviction must be lodged and sufficient evidence must be presented by the defense to establish a prima facie showing of a constitutional infirmity. This is consistent with the obligation of a defendant to bring evidentiary objections to the attention of the trial court so that they can be dealt with in a timely fashion. If a defendant does not object to the constitutional infirmity of using the prior convictions at any time before or during trial, the issue is waived and does not provide the basis for an appeal.[8]

A critical pretrial action that counsel must make in domestic violence cases is the jury demand. In a misdemeanor case in Ohio, if a demand for a jury is not made in writing within the time set forth in the criminal rules, the right to a jury trial is waived.[9]

If the defendant is in jail in lieu of bond, a motion for a bond reduction with oral hearing requested is advisable. Usually, this motion will be heard at a pretrial hearing, and the victim will frequently be present. At that hearing, if the victim wants to recant, he/she will usually indicate his/her position. These statements frequently prove useful at trial.

Finally, a motion to voir dire identification witnesses[10] may be a helpful strategy. Though it is unlikely to be granted, this motion does give the defense a chance to examine the witness and get a feel for the case.

Carefully crafted pretrial motion practice is very important to the successful defense of domestic violence cases. The intricacies of the relationships involved require a high percentage of these cases to be

---

County 2008); State v. Albert, 2010-Ohio-110, 2010 WL 169480 (Ohio Ct. App. 2d Dist. Montgomery County 2010); State v. Black, 2012-Ohio-110, 2012 WL 114181 (Ohio Ct. App. 2d Dist. Champaign County 2012); State v. Wills, 2011-Ohio-5580, 2011 WL 5143142 (Ohio Ct. App. 5th Dist. Morrow County 2011); State v. Taylor, 2013-Ohio-1300, 2013 WL 1288668 (Ohio Ct. App. 3d Dist. Seneca County 2013); State v. Dinka, 2013-Ohio-4646, 2013 WL 5741499 (Ohio Ct. App. 12th Dist. Warren County 2013); State v. Lawson, 2014-Ohio-879, 2014 WL 1325751 (Ohio Ct. App. 7th Dist. Mahoning County 2014); State v. Kievman, 2014-Ohio-3008, 2014 WL 3056848 (Ohio Ct. App. 12th Dist. Clermont County 2014); State v. Smith, 2016-Ohio-3203, 66 N.E.3d 164 (Ohio Ct. App. 6th Dist. Lucas County 2016).

[7]Baldasar v. Illinois, 446 U.S. 222, 100 S. Ct. 1585, 64 L. Ed. 2d 169 (1980) (overruled by, Nichols v. U.S., 511 U.S. 738, 114 S. Ct. 1921, 128 L. Ed. 2d 745 (1994)). See also Cleveland v. Anderson, 2013-Ohio-165, 2013 WL 267088 (Ohio Ct. App. 8th Dist. Cuyahoga County 2013); State v. Bode, 2013-Ohio-2134, 2013 WL 2299190 (Ohio Ct. App. 5th Dist. Fairfield County 2013), judgment rev'd, 144 Ohio St. 3d 155, 2015-Ohio-1519, 41 N.E.3d 1156 (2015).

[8]State v. Adams, 37 Ohio St. 3d 295, 525 N.E.2d 1361 (1988). See also Text § 2:7, Felony violations; Text § 3:2, Effect of certain prior convictions on new charges of domestic violence; Text § 5:21, Case preparation—Hearsay evidence—Judgment of previous conviction; and Text § 5:22, Case preparation—Review of the charging document in felony domestic violence cases; State v. Barnes, 2008-Ohio-5997, 2008 WL 4949833 (Ohio Ct. App. 8th Dist. Cuyahoga County 2008); State v. McCullough, 2008-Ohio-3055, 2008 WL 2485366 (Ohio Ct. App. 3d Dist. Putnam County 2008); State v. Montgomery, 2010-Ohio-4555, 2010 WL 3733844 (Ohio Ct. App. 11th Dist. Ashtabula County 2010).

[9]State v. White, 6 Ohio App. 3d 1, 451 N.E.2d 533 (8th Dist. Cuyahoga County 1982).

[10]Crim.R. 23(A).

proven circumstantially, particularly because of a lack of cooperation from the primary witness, the victim. This fact requires heightened vigilance on the part of the defense attorney to ensure that the prosecution conforms to the rules regarding the production and admission of evidence. A cavalier attitude can result in irrelevant and inflammatory evidence being introduced at trial that is difficult to counter and which may mean the difference between the client's acquittal or conviction.

Q & A: Can the denial of a civil protection order, following a full hearing on its merits, ever serve as the grounds for a motion to dismiss a criminal charge based upon the exact same facts?

The Fifth Amendment to the U.S. Constitution precludes a criminal defendant from being twice placed in jeopardy for the alleged commission of a single act. A civil protection order proceeding, however, does not place a respondent in jeopardy, as it is not a criminal hearing and the court may not order criminal sanctions if it determines that the civil protection order should issue. The relief provided by the grant of a civil protection order is remedial rather than punitive in nature. The protections afforded by the Double Jeopardy Clause are limited to criminal proceedings and do not have application based upon the decisions made in judgments entered in civil causes based upon the same facts where no penalty is exacted nor possible.[11] Likewise, the doctrine of collateral estoppel is unavailable in this situation. The doctrine of collateral estoppel is contained within the constitutional guarantee against double jeopardy and holds that when an issue of ultimate fact has once been determined by a valid and final judgment, the same parties cannot litigate the issue again. In this instance the parties are not the same. In the civil protection order proceeding the parties are the alleged victim and the alleged perpetrator. In the criminal proceeding the parties are the State or the municipality and the defendant. Because a civil protection order proceeding is distinct from a criminal action, the theory of collateral estoppel is not applicable.[12]

Q & A: The state seeks to use a defendant's prior juvenile adjudications of domestic violence to enhance an adult charge of domestic violence to a felony, where the defendant was not counseled and did not waive the right to representation at the time of the juvenile adjudication. Should the defendant's juvenile offenses be suppressed?

Yes. The prior adjudications cannot be used to enhance the charge. If the record established that the defendant was not counseled and the defendant cannot recall waiving the right to representation, or the record is silent in that regard, then the state fails to prove that the

[11]Cleveland v. Hogan, 92 Ohio Misc. 2d 34, 699 N.E.2d 1020 (Mun. Ct. 1998); Westlake v. Patrick, 2005-Ohio-4419, 2005 WL 2046415 (Ohio Ct. App. 8th Dist. Cuyahoga County 2005). But see Walker v. Walker, 2011-Ohio-3933, 2011 WL 3452362 (Ohio Ct. App. 5th Dist. Stark County 2011).

[12]Cleveland v. Hogan, 92 Ohio Misc. 2d 34, 699 N.E.2d 1020 (Mun. Ct. 1998); see also Text § 12:27, Conflicting protection orders.

defendant effectively waived the right to counsel, and the evidence should not be allowed.[13]

Q & A: Last year, my client was convicted of a violation of the domestic violence threats section.[14] Because he was not represented by counsel, the court fined him $250 and sentenced him to 30 days in jail, but suspended the days and did not place him under any community control sanction. Last week, he was arrested for physically assaulting his wife. Due to the prior conviction, the prosecutor is now charging him with a fourth degree felony.[15] Since he was unrepresented before, can that prior conviction be used to enhance the new charge?

Yes. The lack of assistance of counsel precludes the imposition of a penal sentence, but it does not bar the levying of a fine, nor does it affect the constitutionality of the underlying conviction.[16] An uncounseled conviction may be relied upon to enhance the sentence for a subsequent offense, even though that sentence entails imprisonment. Enhancement statutes are commonplace in state criminal laws and do not change the penalty imposed for the earlier conviction. Accordingly, the U.S. Supreme Court has held that, consistent with the Sixth and Fourteenth Amendments of the Constitution, an uncounseled misdemeanor conviction, valid because no sanction of imprisonment was imposed, is also valid when used to enhance punishment at a subsequent conviction.[17]

Q & A: My client insisted on representing himself at trial. The judge asked him if he was sure that he wanted to represent himself and my client said yes. The judge then said, "Alright then, you have that right." And held the trial. My client was found guilty of domestic violence. We have appealed on the grounds that my client did not make a knowing, voluntary, and intelligent waiver of his right to counsel. Should we prevail?

Yes. The Ohio Supreme Court holds that in order to establish an effective waiver of the right to counsel, the trial court must make sufficient inquiry to determine whether a defendant fully understands and intelligently relinquishes that right. If there is no indication that the trial court explained to your client the nature of the charges, the statutory offenses included within them, the range of allowable punishments, possible defenses, mitigation, or other facts essential to a broad understanding of the whole matter, then it cannot be said

---

[13]State v. Baker, 2009-Ohio-111, 2009 WL 81279 (Ohio Ct. App. 9th Dist. Summit County 2009); State v. Bode, 144 Ohio St. 3d 155, 2015-Ohio-1519, 41 N.E.3d 1156 (2015).

[14]RC § 2919.25(C).

[15]R.C. § 2919.25(A); RC § 2919.25(D)

[16]State v. Boughner, 1999 WL 1297606 (Ohio Ct. App. 11th Dist. Geauga County 1999); City of Lakewood v. McDonald, 2005-Ohio-394, 2005 WL 272992 (Ohio Ct. App. 8th Dist. Cuyahoga County 2005); State v. Rockburn, 2003-Ohio-3537, 2003 WL 21513054 (Ohio Ct. App. 8th Dist. Cuyahoga County 2003).

[17]Nichols v. U.S., 511 U.S. 738, 114 S. Ct. 1921, 128 L. Ed. 2d 745 (1994).

that your client knowingly and intelligently waived the right to counsel.[18]

§ 7:10 Collateral effects of a guilty plea or of being found guilty—Generally

Advising a client concerning the pitfalls of criminal prosecution for domestic violation involves more than just the obvious concerns for loss of liberty and the size of the fine that the court will impose. A plea or finding of guilty to a charge of domestic violence or to a domestic violence-related offense has the potential for devastating consequences in a number of other important sectors of the client's life, depending on the client's status. It is absolutely essential, therefore, that counsel conduct a thorough review with the client of the areas that are most likely to prove problematic before engaging in the formation of a plea negotiation or trial strategy. Some of the areas where the potential for collateral damage is most acute are discussed below.

§ 7:11 Collateral effects of a guilty plea or of being found guilty—Immigration

Ohio law[1] requires criminal courts, as part of the process of receiving a no contest or guilty plea in any criminal case, to advise defendants of the potential effect of their plea on their naturalization status.[2] Federal judges have no comparable statute or rule to follow in accepting pleas from non-citizen defendants. In the federal courts, as

[18]State v. Martin, 103 Ohio St. 3d 385, 2004-Ohio–5471, ¶ 43, 816 N.E.2d 227 (2004); State v. Gibson, 45 Ohio St. 2d 366, 377, 74 Ohio Op. 2d 525, 345 N.E.2d 399 (1976), quoting Von Moltke v. Gillies, 332 U.S. 708, 723, 68 S. Ct. 316, 92 L. Ed. 309 (1948); State v. Ott, 2017-Ohio-521, 2017 WL 659374 (Ohio Ct. App. 9th Dist. Summit County 2017).

[Section 7:11]

[1]RC 2943.031.

[2]See Crim.R. 11. See also State v. Francis, 104 Ohio St. 3d 490, 2004-Ohio-6894, 820 N.E.2d 355 (2004); State v. Sibai, 2005-Ohio-2730, 2005 WL 1303215 (Ohio Ct. App. 8th Dist. Cuyahoga County 2005); State v. Lucente, 2005-Ohio-1657, 2005 WL 775886 (Ohio Ct. App. 7th Dist. Mahoning County 2005); State v. Zuniga, 2005-Ohio-2078, 2005 WL 1007173 (Ohio Ct. App. 11th Dist. Lake County 2005); State v. Ayupov, 2007-Ohio-2347, 2007 WL 1429707 (Ohio Ct. App. 2d Dist. Montgomery County 2007). But see State v. Encarnacion, 168 Ohio App. 3d 577, 2006-Ohio-4425, 861 N.E.2d 152 (12th Dist. Butler County 2006); State v. Kiss, 2009-Ohio-739, 2009 WL 406452 (Ohio Ct. App. 8th Dist. Cuyahoga County 2009); State v. Feldman, 2009-Ohio-5765, 2009 WL 3526249 (Ohio Ct. App. 11th Dist. Lake County 2009); State v. Voskoboynikov, 2009-Ohio-4882, 2009 WL 2964369 (Ohio Ct. App. 8th Dist. Cuyahoga County 2009); State v. Naoum, 2009-Ohio-618, 2009 WL 344994 (Ohio Ct. App. 8th Dist. Cuyahoga County 2009); State v. Abouelhana, 2009-Ohio-5838, 2009 WL 3681193 (Ohio Ct. App. 8th Dist. Cuyahoga County 2009); State v. Butcher, 2010-Ohio-4877, 2010 WL 3902573 (Ohio Ct. App. 4th Dist. Athens County 2010); Cleveland v. Dobrowski, 2011-Ohio-6071, 2011 WL 5868014 (Ohio Ct. App. 8th Dist. Cuyahoga County 2011); State v. Huang, 2014-Ohio-1511, 2014 WL 1408122 (Ohio Ct. App. 8th Dist. Cuyahoga County 2014) appeal not accepted for review 140 Ohio St. 3d 1416; Mayfield Hts. v. Grigoryan, 2015-Ohio-607, 27 N.E.3d 578 (Ohio Ct. App. 8th Dist. Cuyahoga County 2015); State v. Walton, 2014-Ohio-618, 2014 WL 705418 (Ohio Ct. App. 4th Dist. Washington County 2014); State v. Velazquez, 2016-Ohio-875, 2016 WL 868890 (Ohio Ct. App. 12th Dist. Butler County 2016); State v. Ayesta, 2015-Ohio-1695, 2015 WL 2091679 (Ohio Ct. App. 8th Dist. Cuyahoga County 2015); State v. Walker, 2017-Ohio-511, 78 N.E.3d 922 (Ohio Ct. App. 10th Dist. Franklin County

well as in courts of those states that have no applicable statute or rule, a non-citizen's plea is generally not deemed involuntary solely because of the defendant's ignorance of the immigration consequences.[3] Thus, the provision of such information to a non-citizen defendant by a federal trial court judge is entirely discretionary.[4] The statute goes so far as to provide the exact language of the advisement that the courts must offer:

> If you are not a citizen of the United States, you are hereby advised that conviction of the offense to which you are pleading guilty (or no contest, when applicable) may have the consequences of deportation, exclusion from admission to the United States, or denial of naturalization pursuant to the laws of the United States.[5]

This section was enacted[6] because the legislature determined that aliens frequently pled guilty to charges that rendered them deportable under the federal Immigration Act without being aware that they were doing so. In many instances, not only were the clients unaware of the consequences of their action, but so were their legal representatives, who did not practice immigration law. Thus the Supreme Court of Ohio has determined that trial courts may not assume that any defendant is a citizen of the United States, but must give the warning contained in the statute, verbatim, to every person entering a dispositive plea in a criminal case.[7] The only exceptions are certain defendants entering pleas to minor misdemeanor.[8] The statutory warning is not required if a defendant has indicated affirmatively, either in writing or orally, on the record that he or she is a citizen of the United States.[9]

If the court fails to advise the defendant of the consequences associated with a no contest plea, the law provides a process whereby the non-citizen may withdraw the plea and have the judgment set aside.[10] The law is now settled in Ohio that resort to the process provides a

---

2017); State v. Rai, 2017-Ohio-8655, 2017 WL 5641245 (Ohio Ct. App. 9th Dist. Summit County 2017) (DV Case where defendant appealed ability to withdraw his plea on the basis of *Francis),* 104 Ohio St.3d 490).

[3]State v. Francis, 104 Ohio St. 3d 490, 2004-Ohio-6894, 820 N.E.2d 355 (2004), citing U.S. v. Russell, 686 F.2d 35 (D.C. Cir. 1982) (abrogated by, Padilla v. Kentucky, 559 U.S. 356, 130 S. Ct. 1473, 176 L. Ed. 2d 284 (2010)).

[4]State v. Francis, 104 Ohio St. 3d 490, 2004-Ohio-6894, 820 N.E.2d 355 (2004), citing U.S. v. Russell, 686 F.2d 35 (D.C. Cir. 1982) (abrogated by, Padilla v. Kentucky, 559 U.S. 356, 130 S. Ct. 1473, 176 L. Ed. 2d 284 (2010)).

[5]RC 2943.031(A). See also State v. Francis, 104 Ohio St. 3d 490, 2004-Ohio-6894, 820 N.E.2d 355 (2004).

[6]Eff. 10-2-89.

[7]RC 2943.031(A) and RC 2943.031(B); State v. Francis, 104 Ohio St. 3d 490, 2004-Ohio-6894, 820 N.E.2d 355 (2004).

[8]RC 2943.031(A) and RC 2943.031(B); State v. Francis, 104 Ohio St. 3d 490, 2004-Ohio-6894, 820 N.E.2d 355 (2004).

[9]State v. Francis, 104 Ohio St. 3d 490, 2004-Ohio-6894, 820 N.E.2d 355 (2004).

[10]RC 2943.031(D). State v. Villafuerte, 2008-Ohio-5587, 2008 WL 4750347 (Ohio Ct. App. 8th Dist. Cuyahoga County 2008); State v. Voskoboynikov, 2009-Ohio-4882, 2009 WL 2964369 (Ohio Ct. App. 8th Dist. Cuyahoga County 2009); State v. Naoum, 2009-Ohio-618, 2009 WL 344994 (Ohio Ct. App. 8th Dist. Cuyahoga County 2009); State v. Abouelhana, 2009-Ohio-5838, 2009 WL 3681193 (Ohio Ct. App. 8th Dist. Cuyahoga County 2009)

defendant's exclusive remedy at law for a trial court's failure to comply with the statutory requirement that a non-citizen defendant be advised of the consequences that might follow a criminal conviction.[11] In order to obtain relief, the defendant is required to establish four statutory criteria: (1) the court failed to provide the advisement described in the statute, verbatim; (2) the advisement was required to be given; (3) the defendant is not a citizen of the United States; and (4) the offense to which the defendant pleaded guilty may result in the defendant being subject to deportation, exclusion, or denial of naturalization.[12]

If a motion to withdraw is filed and the prongs of the test are met, the trial court is statutorily mandated to grant the motion and to set aside a judgment of conviction.[13]

If the client is not a citizen, a conviction for domestic violence is one of the criminal violations that will trigger an order for removal by the Bureau of Immigration and Customs Enforcement (BICE). There is no discretion as to whether INS will issue the Order of Removal once it becomes aware of the conviction, and there is no discretionary waiver available to keep the client in the country, other than a new alien petition.[14]

Any alien who, at any time after admission, is convicted of a crime of domestic violence, a crime of stalking, or a crime of child abuse, child neglect, or child abandonment is deportable.[15] Under some circumstances, a conviction, once obtained, even if it is later vacated and

---

[11]State ex rel. White v. Suster, 101 Ohio St. 3d 212, 2004-Ohio-719, 803 N.E.2d 813 (2004), State v. Garmendia, 2003-Ohio-3769, 2003 WL 21658528 (Ohio Ct. App. 2d Dist. Montgomery County 2003), State v. Rodriguez, 2002-Ohio-3978, 2002 WL 1791115 (Ohio Ct. App. 12th Dist. Butler County 2002); State v. Francis, 104 Ohio St. 3d 490, 2004-Ohio-6894, 820 N.E.2d 355 (2004). But see the discussion in State v. Yuen, 2002-Ohio-5083, 2002 WL 31124023 (Ohio Ct. App. 10th Dist. Franklin County 2002). See also State v. Pineda, 2005-Ohio-6386, 2005 WL 3219708 (Ohio Ct. App. 8th Dist. Cuyahoga County 2005); State v. Ikharo, 2005-Ohio-6616, 2005 WL 3416177 (Ohio Ct. App. 10th Dist. Franklin County 2005); State v. Castillo, 2005-Ohio-93, 2005 WL 77083 (Ohio Ct. App. 8th Dist. Cuyahoga County 2005); State ex rel. McDonald v. Mitrovich, 113 Ohio St. 3d 167, 2007-Ohio-1258, 863 N.E.2d 172 (2007); State v. Naoum, 2009-Ohio-618, 2009 WL 344994 (Ohio Ct. App. 8th Dist. Cuyahoga County 2009); State v. Voskoboynikov, 2009-Ohio-4882, 2009 WL 2964369 (Ohio Ct. App. 8th Dist. Cuyahoga County 2009); State v. Feldman, 2009-Ohio-5765, 2009 WL 3526249 (Ohio Ct. App. 11th Dist. Lake County 2009); State v. Ikharo, 2011-Ohio-2746, 2011 WL 2201193 (Ohio Ct. App. 10th Dist. Franklin County 2011).

[12]State v. Weber, 125 Ohio App. 3d 120, 707 N.E.2d 1178 (10th Dist. Franklin County 1997); State v. Francis, 104 Ohio St. 3d 490, 2004-Ohio-6894, 820 N.E.2d 355 (2004); State v. Ayupov, 2007-Ohio-2347, 2007 WL 1429707 (Ohio Ct. App. 2d Dist. Montgomery County 2007); State v. Villavicencio, 2014-Ohio-1522, 2014 WL 1408291 (Ohio Ct. App. 8th Dist. Cuyahoga County 2014); State v. Toyloy, 2015-Ohio-1618, 2015 WL 1913431 (Ohio Ct. App. 10th Dist. Franklin County 2015).

[13]RC 2943.031(A). See also State v. Yuen, 2002-Ohio-5083, 2002 WL 31124023 (Ohio Ct. App. 10th Dist. Franklin County 2002); Cisneros-Perez v. Gonzales, 465 F.3d 386 (9th Cir. 2006); Ortega-Mendez v. Gonzales, 450 F.3d 1010 (9th Cir. 2006). But see Tokatly v. Ashcroft, 371 F.3d 613 (9th Cir. 2004).

[14]8 U.S.C.A. § 1227(a)(2)(E). But see Tokatly v. Ashcroft, 371 F.3d 613 (9th Cir. 2004); Euclid v. Muller, 134 Ohio App. 3d 737, 732 N.E.2d 410 (8th Dist. Cuyahoga County 1999); State v. Butcher, 2010-Ohio-4877, 2010 WL 3902573 (Ohio Ct. App. 4th Dist. Athens County 2010); Cleveland Hts. v. Roland, 197 Ohio App. 3d 661, 2012-Ohio-170, 968 N.E.2d 564 (8th Dist. Cuyahoga County 2012).

[15]8 U.S.C.A. § 1227(a)(2)(E)(i), 8 U.S.C.A. § 1230. See also Euclid v. Muller, 134

made null and void, can still serve as the basis for federal proceedings, potentially leading to the defendant's removal from the United States.[16] For purposes of this clause, "crime of domestic violence" means any crime of violence (as defined in 18 U.S.C.A. § 16) against a person committed by a current or former spouse of the person, by an individual with whom the person shares a child in common, by an individual who is cohabiting with or has cohabited with the person as a spouse, by an individual similarly situated to a spouse of the person under the domestic or family violence laws of the jurisdiction where the offense occurs, or by any other individual against a person who is protected from that individual's acts under the domestic or family violence laws of the United States or any state, Indian tribal government, or unit of local government.[17] A "crime of violence" is defined by federal law as "an offense that has as an element the use, attempted use, or threatened use of physical force against the person or property of another."[18] An element of a crime is "a constituent part of the offense which must be proved by the prosecution *in every case* to sustain a conviction under a given statute."[19]

Any alien who, at any time after admission, is enjoined under a protection order issued by a court and who the court determines has engaged in conduct that violates the portion of a protection order that involves protection against credible threats of violence, repeated harassment, or bodily injury to the person or persons for whom the protection order was issued is deportable. For purposes of this clause, "protection order" means any injunction issued for the purpose of preventing violent or threatening acts of domestic violence, including temporary or final orders issued by civil or criminal courts (other than support or child custody orders or provisions), whether obtained by filing an independent action or as a pendent lite order in another proceeding.[20]

Q & A: My client is not a citizen of the United States. She was convicted of domestic violence in 1988. She was not advised at the time that taking the plea bargain could cause her to be deported from the U.S. Although there is no action pending now to deport her, she recently learned that the conviction could cause her to be deported someday. I've researched the law and it appears that I can motion the court to allow her to vacate her plea. Given the age of the case, can I still prevail?

Upon proper motion, the statute mandates that a plea that results in a criminal conviction must be vacated where the trial court fails to

Ohio App. 3d 737, 732 N.E.2d 410 (8th Dist. Cuyahoga County 1999).

[16]Willoughby Hills v. Qasim, 2007-Ohio-2860, 2007 WL 1662059 (Ohio Ct. App. 11th Dist. Lake County 2007); State v. Jukic, 2015-Ohio-2695, 2015 WL 4043002 (Ohio Ct. App. 8th Dist. Cuyahoga County 2015); State v. Velazquez, 2016-Ohio-875, 2016 WL 868890 (Ohio Ct. App. 12th Dist. Butler County 2016).

[17]8 U.S.C.A. § 1227(a)(2)(E)(i).

[18]18 U.S.C.A. § 16(a).

[19]Singh v. Ashcroft, 386 F.3d 1228 (9th Cir. 2004); U.S. v. Innie, 7 F.3d 840, 850 (9th Cir. 1993); Ortega-Mendez v. Gonzales, 450 F.3d 1010 (9th Cir. 2006); Fernandez-Ruiz v. Gonzales, 466 F.3d 1121 (9th Cir. 2006); U.S. v. Moya-Matute, 2008 WL 4104129 (D.N.M. 2008).

[20]8 U.S.C.A. § 1227(a)(2)(E)(ii).

advise an immigrant defendant of the consequence of that conviction on the defendant's immigration status. According to these authorities, the court has no discretion to determine whether such a plea should be vacated.[21]

The majority of the courts that have ruled on this question have decided that the right to withdraw a plea because of a court's failure to advise an immigrant of the consequences of a conviction, that is, in regards to the defendant's immigration status, differs from the right to withdraw a plea under Ohio's Criminal Rules.[22]

Specifically, courts have found that the statute recites no time limitations as it relates to filing a motion to vacate a plea entered in derogation of its mandate. Thus, the amount of time that elapses is not determinative of whether the plea can be withdrawn.[23]

Prior to the Supreme Court of Ohio's definitive statement on the issue, a minority of the courts held the contrary view and required that the defendant file motions to vacate in a timely fashion.[24]

Q & A: How precise does the court's advisement to a non-citizen need to be about the consequences that a guilty finding may have on immigration status?

Very. The Ohio General Assembly required, by the unambiguous terms of a statute,[25] that a trial court accepting a guilty or no-contest plea from a defendant who is not a citizen of the United States must give a **verbatim** warning, informing the defendant that conviction of the offense for which the plea is entered "may have the consequences of deportation, exclusion from admission to the United States, or denial of naturalization pursuant to the laws of the United States."[26] Furthermore, a trial court accepting a plea should never assume that any defendant is a United States citizen but must give the warning verbatim to every criminal defendant (other than certain defendants pleading to a minor misdemeanor) unless a defendant affirmatively indicates either in writing or orally on the record that he or she is a citizen of the United States.[27] This practice precludes a defendant who

[21] RC 2943.031, State v. Yuen, 2002-Ohio-5083, 2002 WL 31124023 (Ohio Ct. App. 10th Dist. Franklin County 2002), State v. Mason, 2002-Ohio-930, 2002 WL 242662 (Ohio Ct. App. 2d Dist. Greene County 2002), State v. Weber, 125 Ohio App. 3d 120, 707 N.E.2d 1178 (10th Dist. Franklin County 1997); see also Crim.R. 32.1.

[22] State v. Yuen, 2002-Ohio-5083, 2002 WL 31124023 (Ohio Ct. App. 10th Dist. Franklin County 2002), State v. Mason, 2002-Ohio-930, 2002 WL 242662 (Ohio Ct. App. 2d Dist. Greene County 2002), State v. Weber, 125 Ohio App. 3d 120, 707 N.E.2d 1178 (10th Dist. Franklin County 1997); see also Crim.R. 32.1.

[23] State v. Yuen, 2002-Ohio-5083, 2002 WL 31124023 (Ohio Ct. App. 10th Dist. Franklin County 2002). See also State v. Francis, 104 Ohio St. 3d 490, 2004-Ohio-6894, 820 N.E.2d 355 (2004).

[24] State v. Tabbaa, 151 Ohio App. 3d 353, 2003-Ohio-299, 784 N.E.2d 143 (8th Dist. Cuyahoga County 2003), cause dismissed, 100 Ohio St. 3d 1417, 2003-Ohio-5098, 796 N.E.2d 939 (2003) and (overruled by, State v. Kiss, 2009-Ohio-739, 2009 WL 406452 (Ohio Ct. App. 8th Dist. Cuyahoga County 2009)); see also State v. Francis, 104 Ohio St. 3d 490, 2004-Ohio-6894, 820 N.E.2d 355 (2004); State v. Feldman, 2009-Ohio-5765, 2009 WL 3526249 (Ohio Ct. App. 11th Dist. Lake County 2009).

[25] RC 2943.031.

[26] RC 2943.031(A).

[27] RC 2943.031(B).

later reveals that he or she was not a citizen at the time of the plea from invoking the statute as grounds for withdrawing the plea.[28]

In the absence of an affirmative record that the court provided the advisement required by the statute to the defendant, the law presumes that the defendant did not receive the advisement.[29] This is particularly an issue when the plea took place so long ago that the court's records of the hearing are no longer available.

In most circumstances, motions to withdraw guilty or no-contest pleas are subject to the standards set forth in the criminal rules.[30] Those standards require that after sentencing occurs, a defendant must demonstrate "manifest injustice" before a trial court should permit withdrawal of the plea.

However, a different standard applies for non-citizen defendants. The General Assembly determined that due to the serious consequences of a criminal conviction on a non-citizen's status in this country, a trial court generally must give the immigration warning[31] and that failure to do so, when required, should not be subject to the manifest-injustice standard even if sentencing has already occurred.[32]

Although the better practice is for trial courts to read the statute verbatim, strict compliance is not necessary to put every defendant on notice that a conviction can have implications beyond the state criminal justice system.[33] The Supreme Court of Ohio requires substantial compliance as the standard for review.[34]

Q & A: Is the court required to hold a hearing on every motion seeking to withdraw a plea, based upon the court's failure to advise a defendant of the consequences of a guilty finding on the immigration status of a non-citizen charged with domestic violence?

No. A hearing is not required on every plea withdrawal motion.[35] However, the Ohio Supreme Court set forth the standard for plea withdrawal motions under these circumstances.[36] If some warning of immigration-related consequences was given at the time a non-citizen defendant's plea was accepted, but the warning was not a verbatim

---

[28]RC 2943.031(D); State v. Francis, 104 Ohio St. 3d 490, 2004-Ohio-6894, 820 N.E.2d 355 (2004).

[29]RC 2943.031(E).

[30]Crim.R. 32.1.

[31]RC 2943.031(A).

[32]State v. Francis, 104 Ohio St. 3d 490, 2004-Ohio-6894, 820 N.E.2d 355 (2004); State v. Muhumed, 2012-Ohio-6155, 2012 WL 6738337 (Ohio Ct. App. 10th Dist. Franklin County 2012).

[33]State v. Francis, 104 Ohio St. 3d 490, 2004-Ohio-6894, 820 N.E.2d 355 (2004).

[34]State v. Francis, 104 Ohio St. 3d 490, 2004-Ohio-6894, 820 N.E.2d 355 (2004); State v. Ayupov, 2007-Ohio-2347, 2007 WL 1429707 (Ohio Ct. App. 2d Dist. Montgomery County 2007). But see State v. Encarnacion, 168 Ohio App. 3d 577, 2006-Ohio-4425, 861 N.E.2d 152 (12th Dist. Butler County 2006); State v. Feldman, 2009-Ohio-5765, 2009 WL 3526249 (Ohio Ct. App. 11th Dist. Lake County 2009).

[35]State v. Francis, 104 Ohio St. 3d 490, 2004-Ohio-6894, 820 N.E.2d 355 (2004).

[36]RC 2943.031.

recital of the required language,[37] a trial court considering the defendant's motion to withdraw the plea[38] must exercise its discretion in determining whether the trial court that accepted the plea substantially complied with the law.[39] Substantial compliance means that under the totality of the circumstances the proceedings provide the defendant the opportunity to subjectively understand the implications of his plea and the rights he is waiving. The test is whether the plea would have otherwise been made.[40]

Substantial compliance also requires a defendant to be informed not only of the possibility of deportation, but also of the possibilities of exclusion from admission into the United States and denial of naturalization pursuant to the laws of the United States.[41]

Ultimately, whether to hold a hearing is left to the sound discretion of the trial court. However, in some situations, the failure to hold a hearing may constitute an abuse of that discretion.[42]

Q & A: In accepting a plea of no contest or guilty, is it suf-

---

[37]RC 2943.031(A).

[38]RC 2943.031(D).

[39]RC 2943.031(A); State v. Francis, 104 Ohio St. 3d 490, 2004-Ohio-6894, 820 N.E.2d 355 (2004); State v. Muhumed, 2012-Ohio-6155, 2012 WL 6738337 (Ohio Ct. App. 10th Dist. Franklin County 2012).

[40]State v. Francis, 104 Ohio St. 3d 490, 2004-Ohio-6894, 820 N.E.2d 355 (2004), quoting State v. Nero, 56 Ohio St. 3d 106, 564 N.E.2d 474 (1990); State v. Soltis, 2009-Ohio-6636, 2009 WL 4861127 (Ohio Ct. App. 8th Dist. Cuyahoga County 2009); State v. Douglass, 2009-Ohio-3826, 2009 WL 2371866 (Ohio Ct. App. 12th Dist. Butler County 2009); State v. Gearig, 2010-Ohio-939, 2010 WL 877575 (Ohio Ct. App. 6th Dist. Williams County 2010); State v. Voskoboynikov, 2009-Ohio-4882, 2009 WL 2964369 (Ohio Ct. App. 8th Dist. Cuyahoga County 2009); State v. Kiss, 2009-Ohio-739, 2009 WL 406452 (Ohio Ct. App. 8th Dist. Cuyahoga County 2009); State v. Naoum, 2009-Ohio-618, 2009 WL 344994 (Ohio Ct. App. 8th Dist. Cuyahoga County 2009); State v. Abouelhana, 2009-Ohio-5838, 2009 WL 3681193 (Ohio Ct. App. 8th Dist. Cuyahoga County 2009); State v. Montgomery, 2010-Ohio-4555, 2010 WL 3733844 (Ohio Ct. App. 11th Dist. Ashtabula County 2010); State v. Dunaway, 2010-Ohio-2304, 2010 WL 2029051 (Ohio Ct. App. 12th Dist. Butler County 2010); State v. Gosnell, 2011-Ohio-4289, 2011 WL 3807789 (Ohio Ct. App. 2d Dist. Montgomery County 2011); State v. Muhumed, 2012-Ohio-6155, 2012 WL 6738337 (Ohio Ct. App. 10th Dist. Franklin County 2012); State v. Ramey, 2014-Ohio-2345, 2014 WL 2533829 (Ohio Ct. App. 7th Dist. Mahoning County 2014); State v. Bailey, 2014-Ohio-639, 2014 WL 755411 (Ohio Ct. App. 2d Dist. Clark County 2014); State v. Marcum, 2013-Ohio-2447, 994 N.E.2d 1 (Ohio Ct. App. 4th Dist. Hocking County 2013); Saur v. Robinson, 2014 WL 1922848 (S.D. Ohio 2014), report and recommendation adopted, 2014 WL 3105012 (S.D. Ohio 2014); State v. Mays, 2013-Ohio-4031, 2013 WL 5314558 (Ohio Ct. App. 8th Dist. Cuyahoga County 2013); State v. Studgions, 2016-Ohio-4701, 2016 WL 3571261 (Ohio Ct. App. 8th Dist. Cuyahoga County 2016); State v. Moore, 2015-Ohio-4182, 2015 WL 5864786 (Ohio Ct. App. 8th Dist. Cuyahoga County 2015); State v. Davis, 2016-Ohio-1569, 2016 WL 1547066 (Ohio Ct. App. 6th Dist. Erie County 2016); State v. McQuirt, 2016-Ohio-1095, 2016 WL 1071464 (Ohio Ct. App. 2d Dist. Montgomery County 2016); State v. DeJesus, 2015-Ohio-4111, 2015 WL 5782347 (Ohio Ct. App. 2d Dist. Greene County 2015).

[41]RC 2943.031(A); State v. Ouch, 2006-Ohio-6949, 2006 WL 3805676, ¶ 28 (Ohio Ct. App. 10th Dist. Franklin County 2006), citing State v. Batista, 2004-Ohio-5066, 2004 WL 2803421, ¶ 9 (Ohio Ct. App. 10th Dist. Franklin County 2004); State v. Oluoch, 2007-Ohio-5560, 2007 WL 3027074 (Ohio Ct. App. 10th Dist. Franklin County 2007); State v. Schlaf, 2008-Ohio-6151, 2008 WL 5049959 (Ohio Ct. App. 8th Dist. Cuyahoga County 2008); State v. Muhumed, 2012-Ohio-6155, 2012 WL 6738337 (Ohio Ct. App. 10th Dist. Franklin County 2012).

[42]State v. Francis, 104 Ohio St. 3d 490, 2004-Ohio-6894, 820 N.E.2d 355 (2004);

ficient for the court to inform a non-citizen accused of domestic violence that a conviction could result in deportation?

No. The court's failure to inform a non-citizen of the possibility of all three statutory sanctions, deportation, exclusion from admission to the United States and denial of naturalization, cause the plea received to have a fatal flaw that renders it invalid.[43] A defendant who receives a defective statutory warning has, in many cases, the right to withdraw the invalid plea.[44] The right to withdraw the invalid plea may even extend if the plea was entered in the distant past.[45]

Q & A: Is an alien defendant automatically entitled to relief when a trial court fails to provide advisement of the potential effect of a plea on that defendant's immigration and naturalization status?

No. To obtain relief pursuant to R.C. 2943.031(D), the defendant must show he or she is not a citizen of the United States and that the offense to which he or she pled guilty may result in deportation, exclusion from admission to the United States, or denial of naturalization. In other words, the defendant must show prejudice.[46] In a hearing on a Motion to Withdraw a guilty or no contest plea, the defendant may present evidence, such as a notice of deportation proceedings or an affidavit averring that he or she is facing deportation proceedings as a result of the subject conviction or that he or she is facing exclusion from admission to the United States or denial of naturalization as a result of the subject conviction. At the hearing, the defendant might also submit an affidavit averring that, if the full advisement had been received, such advisement would have impacted the defendant's decision to plead guilty or no contest (i.e., the defendant would not have entered the plea). Without some type of affidavit or other supporting documentation or evidence backing a defendant's claim of prejudice flowing from the subject plea, the defendant's Motion to Withdraw is likely to fail.[47]

Q & A: Is it necessary for a non-citizen defendant seeking to withdraw a no contest or guilty plea to establish that the trial court's failure to grant the motion would result in "a manifest injustice?"

No. A trial court after sentence may set aside the judgment of conviction and permit the defendant to withdraw his or her plea in or-

---

State v. Ouch, 2006-Ohio-6949, 2006 WL 3805676 (Ohio Ct. App. 10th Dist. Franklin County 2006); State v. Muhumed, 2012-Ohio-6155, 2012 WL 6738337 (Ohio Ct. App. 10th Dist. Franklin County 2012).

[43]State v. Feldman, 2009-Ohio-5765, 2009 WL 3526249 (Ohio Ct. App. 11th Dist. Lake County 2009).

[44]State v. Voskoboynikov, 2009-Ohio-4882, 2009 WL 2964369 (Ohio Ct. App. 8th Dist. Cuyahoga County 2009); State v. Naoum, 2009-Ohio-618, 2009 WL 344994 (Ohio Ct. App. 8th Dist. Cuyahoga County 2009).

[45]State v. Abouelhana, 2009-Ohio-5838, 2009 WL 3681193 (Ohio Ct. App. 8th Dist. Cuyahoga County 2009).

[46]State v. Garmendia, 2003-Ohio-3769, 2003 WL 21658528 (Ohio Ct. App. 2d Dist. Montgomery County 2003).

[47]State v. Muhumed, 2012-Ohio-6155, 2012 WL 6738337 (Ohio Ct. App. 10th Dist. Franklin County 2012).

der to correct a "manifest injustice."[48] However, the standard set forth in R.C. 2943.031(D) supplants the requirement that a defendant must demonstrate "manifest injustice" to justify withdrawal of a plea.[49] While the law clearly recognizes that R.C. 2943.031(D) enunciates a distinct standard to allow a non-citizen defendant to withdraw a plea where a trial court has failed to give the proper statutory advisement, the statute does not prohibit a non-citizen defendant from seeking to withdraw a plea via the more conventional standard enunciated in the criminal rules.[50]

Q & A: If a trial court properly advises a defendant as to the immigration consequences of a plea, doesn't that cure an attorney's failure to properly advise as to that subject?

The answer is not clear. Counsel breaches a duty by either providing affirmative misadvice about immigration consequences, or by not providing any advice at all when advice is warranted.[51]. However, recently more than one Ohio court has begun to back away from the principle that a trial court's R.C. 2943.031(A) advisement during the plea hearing constitutes an absolute cure for an attorney's failure to properly advise his client as to the immigration consequences of such a plea.[52] These courts hold that counsel's failure to advise a noncitizen defendant of the immigration consequences could, in some instances, constitute deficient performance and that a trial court's proper recitation of statutory advisement at plea hearing might not cure trial counsel's deficient performance. If a defendant is prejudiced by trial counsel's deficient performance, reversal is warranted.[53]

§ 7:12 Collateral effects of a guilty plea or of being found guilty—Immigration—Duty of attorney to advise client

The U.S. Supreme Court has found that a noncitizen criminal defendant receives deficient performance from a lawyer who fails to advise a client that a plea of guilty subjects the defendant to automatic deportation. Changes to immigration law have dramatically raised the stakes of a noncitizen's criminal conviction. While once there was only a narrow class of deportable offenses and judges wielded broad discretionary authority to prevent deportation, immigration reforms

---

[48]Crim.R. 32.1

[49]State v. Francis, 104 Ohio St. 3d 490, 2004-Ohio-6894, 820 N.E.2d 355 (2004), State v Bravo

[50]Crim.R. 32.1

[51]Padilla v. Kentucky, 559 U.S. 356, 370–371, 130 S. Ct. 1473, 176 L. Ed. 2d 284 (2010)

[52]See State v. Ayesta, 2015-Ohio-1695, 2015 WL 2091679 (Ohio Ct. App. 8th Dist. Cuyahoga County 2015); State v. Tapia-Cortes, 2016-Ohio-8101, 75 N.E.3d 878, 883 (Ohio Ct. App. 12th Dist. Butler County 2016)State v. Galdamez, 2015-Ohio-3681, 41 N.E.3d 467 (Ohio Ct. App. 10th Dist. Franklin County 2015), appeal not allowed, 147 Ohio St. 3d 1412, 2016-Ohio-7455, 62 N.E.3d 185 (2016); State v. Valdez, 2017-Ohio-4260, 2017 WL 2569810 (Ohio Ct. App. 1st Dist. Hamilton County 2017) (affirmed the denial of a motion to withdraw guilty plea because of immigration advice).

[53]State v. Ayesta, 2015-Ohio-1695, 2015 WL 2091679 (Ohio Ct. App. 8th Dist. Cuyahoga County 2015); State v. Tapia-Cortes, 2016-Ohio-8101, 75 N.E.3d 878, 883 (Ohio Ct. App. 12th Dist. Butler County 2016); State v. Galdamez, 2015-Ohio-3681, 41 N.E.3d 467 (Ohio Ct. App. 10th Dist. Franklin County 2015), appeal not allowed, 147 Ohio St. 3d 1412, 2016-Ohio-7455, 62 N.E.3d 185 (2016)

have expanded the class of deportable offenses and limited judges' authority to alleviate deportation's harsh consequences. Because the drastic measure of deportation or removal is now virtually inevitable for a vast number of non-citizens convicted of crimes, the importance of accurate legal advice for noncitizens accused of crimes has never been more important. Thus, as a matter of federal law, deportation is an integral part of the penalty that may be imposed on noncitizen defendants who plead guilty to specified crimes.[1]

In order for a client to obtain relief for his or her attorney's deficient representation, the representation must have fallen "below an objective standard of reasonableness,"[2] and there must be "a reasonable

---

[Section 7:12]

[1]Padilla v. Kentucky, 559 U.S. 356, 130 S. Ct. 1473, 176 L. Ed. 2d 284 (2010); State v. Graves, 2013-Ohio-2197, 2013 WL 2382613 (Ohio Ct. App. 8th Dist. Cuyahoga County 2013). But see State v. Huang, 2014-Ohio-1511, 2014 WL 1408122 (Ohio Ct. App. 8th Dist. Cuyahoga County 2014); State v. Thompson, 2014-Ohio-1225, 2014 WL 1326540 (Ohio Ct. App. 7th Dist. Columbiana County 2014); State v. Ayesta, 2015-Ohio-1695, 2015 WL 2091679 (Ohio Ct. App. 8th Dist. Cuyahoga County 2015); Bell v. United States, 2016 WL 7315326 (E.D. Tenn. 2016).

[2]Strickland v. Washington, 466 U.S. 668, 104 S. Ct. 2052, 80 L. Ed. 2d 674 (1984); State v. Graves, 2013-Ohio-2197, 2013 WL 2382613 (Ohio Ct. App. 8th Dist. Cuyahoga County 2013); State v. Thompson, 2014-Ohio-1225, 2014 WL 1326540 (Ohio Ct. App. 7th Dist. Columbiana County 2014); State v. Mays, 2014-Ohio-814, 2014 WL 888375 (Ohio Ct. App. 8th Dist. Cuyahoga County 2014); State v. D'Agostino, 2014-Ohio-551, 2014 WL 605527 (Ohio Ct. App. 9th Dist. Lorain County 2014); State v. Foster, 2014-Ohio-530, 2014 WL 604564 (Ohio Ct. App. 2d Dist. Montgomery County 2014); State v. Hanson, 2013-Ohio-3916, 2013 WL 5005810 (Ohio Ct. App. 8th Dist. Cuyahoga County 2013); State v. Jackson, 2013-Ohio-1390, 990 N.E.2d 184 (Ohio Ct. App. 3d Dist. Hancock County 2013); State v. Weathers, 2013-Ohio-1104, 988 N.E.2d 16 (Ohio Ct. App. 12th Dist. Butler County 2013); State v. Lewis, 2013-Ohio-892, 2013 WL 978899 (Ohio Ct. App. 7th Dist. Mahoning County 2013); State v. Dozier, 2014-Ohio-2925, 2014 WL 2993841 (Ohio Ct. App. 5th Dist. Stark County 2014); State v. Matthews, 2014-Ohio-2561, 2014 WL 2700915 (Ohio Ct. App. 6th Dist. Sandusky County 2014); State v. Burrell, 2014-Ohio-1356, 2014 WL 1356137 (Ohio Ct. App. 11th Dist. Lake County 2014); State v. Davis, 2014-Ohio-1197, 2014 WL 1340774 (Ohio Ct. App. 5th Dist. Licking County 2014); State v. Hall, 2014-Ohio-416, 2014 WL 523072 (Ohio Ct. App. 2d Dist. Montgomery County 2014); City of Toledo v. White, 2013-Ohio-5911, 2013 WL 7123151 (Ohio Ct. App. 6th Dist. Lucas County 2013); State v. Renner, 2013-Ohio-5463, 2013 WL 6576714 (Ohio Ct. App. 2d Dist. Montgomery County 2013); Cleveland v. Crutcher, 2013-Ohio-5240, 2013 WL 6221101 (Ohio Ct. App. 8th Dist. Cuyahoga County 2013); State v. Goshade, 2013-Ohio-4457, 2013 WL 5577906 (Ohio Ct. App. 1st Dist. Hamilton County 2013); State v. Dixon, 2013-Ohio-4149, 2013 WL 5407478 (Ohio Ct. App. 5th Dist. Stark County 2013); State v. Partlow, 2013-Ohio-2771, 2013 WL 3356575 (Ohio Ct. App. 10th Dist. Franklin County 2013); State v. Marcum, 2013-Ohio-2447, 994 N.E.2d 1 (Ohio Ct. App. 4th Dist. Hocking County 2013); State v. Habo, 2013-Ohio-2142, 2013 WL 2308483 (Ohio Ct. App. 11th Dist. Portage County 2013); State v. Kesting, 2014-Ohio-3058, 2014 WL 3407923 (Ohio Ct. App. 2d Dist. Montgomery County 2014); State v. Pittman, 2013-Ohio-962, 2013 WL 1092420 (Ohio Ct. App. 2d Dist. Montgomery County 2013); State v. Kelly, 2013-Ohio-4755, 2013 WL 5783710 (Ohio Ct. App. 11th Dist. Ashtabula County 2013); State v. Sturgell, 2013-Ohio-3518, 2013 WL 4130073 (Ohio Ct. App. 9th Dist. Summit County 2013); Cleveland v. Williams, 2015-Ohio-1739, 2015 WL 2165564 (Ohio Ct. App. 8th Dist. Cuyahoga County 2015); State v. Fuller, 2015-Ohio-1325, 2015 WL 1512371 (Ohio Ct. App. 2d Dist. Greene County 2015); Cleveland v. Alexander, 2014-Ohio-5282, 2014 WL 6679556 (Ohio Ct. App. 8th Dist. Cuyahoga County 2014); State v. McKinney, 2015-Ohio-2036, 2015 WL 3422030 (Ohio Ct. App. 8th Dist. Cuyahoga County 2015); State v. Martin, 2015-Ohio-1106, 2015 WL 1331818 (Ohio Ct. App. 5th Dist. Delaware County 2015); State v. Youssef, 2015-Ohio-766, 2015 WL

probability that, but for counsel's unprofessional errors, the result of the proceeding would have been different."[3] The constitutional deficiency is necessarily linked to the legal community's practice and expectations.[4]

929816 (Ohio Ct. App. 8th Dist. Cuyahoga County 2015); State v. Short, 2015-Ohio-3183, 2015 WL 4720395 (Ohio Ct. App. 5th Dist. Richland County 2015); State v. Abernathy, 2015-Ohio-1363, 2015 WL 1530810 (Ohio Ct. App. 5th Dist. Stark County 2015); State v. Woods, 2016-Ohio-4830, 2016 WL 3608724 (Ohio Ct. App. 5th Dist. Ashland County 2016); State v. Pringle, 2016-Ohio-1149, 2016 WL 1090961 (Ohio Ct. App. 12th Dist. Brown County 2016); State v. Lisius, 2016-Ohio-27, 2016 WL 102879 (Ohio Ct. App. 5th Dist. Ashland County 2016).

[3]Strickland v. Washington, 466 U.S. 668, 104 S. Ct. 2052, 2068, 80 L. Ed. 2d 674 (1984); State v. Graves, 2013-Ohio-2197, 2013 WL 2382613 (Ohio Ct. App. 8th Dist. Cuyahoga County 2013); State v. Thompson, 2014-Ohio-1225, 2014 WL 1326540 (Ohio Ct. App. 7th Dist. Columbiana County 2014); State v. Mays, 2014-Ohio-814, 2014 WL 888375 (Ohio Ct. App. 8th Dist. Cuyahoga County 2014); State v. D'Agostino, 2014-Ohio-551, 2014 WL 605527 (Ohio Ct. App. 9th Dist. Lorain County 2014); State v. Foster, 2014-Ohio-530, 2014 WL 604564 (Ohio Ct. App. 2d Dist. Montgomery County 2014); State v. Hanson, 2013-Ohio-3916, 2013 WL 5005810 (Ohio Ct. App. 8th Dist. Cuyahoga County 2013); State v. Jackson, 2013-Ohio-1390, 990 N.E.2d 184 (Ohio Ct. App. 3d Dist. Hancock County 2013); State v. Weathers, 2013-Ohio-1104, 988 N.E.2d 16 (Ohio Ct. App. 12th Dist. Butler County 2013); State v. Lewis, 2013-Ohio-892, 2013 WL 978899 (Ohio Ct. App. 7th Dist. Mahoning County 2013); State v. Dozier, 2014-Ohio-2925, 2014 WL 2993841 (Ohio Ct. App. 5th Dist. Stark County 2014); State v. Matthews, 2014-Ohio-2561, 2014 WL 2700915 (Ohio Ct. App. 6th Dist. Sandusky County 2014); State v. Burrell, 2014-Ohio-1356, 2014 WL 1356137 (Ohio Ct. App. 11th Dist. Lake County 2014); State v. Davis, 2014-Ohio-1197, 2014 WL 1340774 (Ohio Ct. App. 5th Dist. Licking County 2014); State v. Hall, 2014-Ohio-416, 2014 WL 523072 (Ohio Ct. App. 2d Dist. Montgomery County 2014); City of Toledo v. White, 2013-Ohio-5911, 2013 WL 7123151 (Ohio Ct. App. 6th Dist. Lucas County 2013); State v. Renner, 2013-Ohio-5463, 2013 WL 6576714 (Ohio Ct. App. 2d Dist. Montgomery County 2013); Cleveland v. Crutcher, 2013-Ohio-5240, 2013 WL 6221101 (Ohio Ct. App. 8th Dist. Cuyahoga County 2013); State v. Goshade, 2013-Ohio-4457, 2013 WL 5577906 (Ohio Ct. App. 1st Dist. Hamilton County 2013); State v. Dixon, 2013-Ohio-4149, 2013 WL 5407478 (Ohio Ct. App. 5th Dist. Stark County 2013); State v. Partlow, 2013-Ohio-2771, 2013 WL 3356575 (Ohio Ct. App. 10th Dist. Franklin County 2013); State v. Marcum, 2013-Ohio-2447, 994 N.E.2d 1 (Ohio Ct. App. 4th Dist. Hocking County 2013); State v. Habo, 2013-Ohio-2142, 2013 WL 2308483 (Ohio Ct. App. 11th Dist. Portage County 2013); State v. Kesting, 2014-Ohio-3058, 2014 WL 3407923 (Ohio Ct. App. 2d Dist. Montgomery County 2014); State v. Pittman, 2013-Ohio-962, 2013 WL 1092420 (Ohio Ct. App. 2d Dist. Montgomery County 2013); State v. Kelly, 2013-Ohio-4755, 2013 WL 5783710 (Ohio Ct. App. 11th Dist. Ashtabula County 2013); State v. Sturgell, 2013-Ohio-3518, 2013 WL 4130073 (Ohio Ct. App. 9th Dist. Summit County 2013); State v. Short, 2015-Ohio-3183, 2015 WL 4720395 (Ohio Ct. App. 5th Dist. Richland County 2015); State v. Abernathy, 2015-Ohio-1363, 2015 WL 1530810 (Ohio Ct. App. 5th Dist. Stark County 2015); State v. Woods, 2016-Ohio-4830, 2016 WL 3608724 (Ohio Ct. App. 5th Dist. Ashland County 2016); State v. Pringle, 2016-Ohio-1149, 2016 WL 1090961 (Ohio Ct. App. 12th Dist. Brown County 2016).

[4]Strickland v. Washington, 466 U.S. 668, 104 S. Ct. 2052, 80 L. Ed. 2d 674 (1984); State v. Graves, 2013-Ohio-2197, 2013 WL 2382613 (Ohio Ct. App. 8th Dist. Cuyahoga County 2013); State v. Thompson, 2014-Ohio-1225, 2014 WL 1326540 (Ohio Ct. App. 7th Dist. Columbiana County 2014); State v. Mays, 2014-Ohio-814, 2014 WL 888375 (Ohio Ct. App. 8th Dist. Cuyahoga County 2014); State v. D'Agostino, 2014-Ohio-551, 2014 WL 605527 (Ohio Ct. App. 9th Dist. Lorain County 2014); State v. Foster, 2014-Ohio-530, 2014 WL 604564 (Ohio Ct. App. 2d Dist. Montgomery County 2014); State v. Hanson, 2013-Ohio-3916, 2013 WL 5005810 (Ohio Ct. App. 8th Dist. Cuyahoga County 2013); State v. Jackson, 2013-Ohio-1390, 990 N.E.2d 184 (Ohio Ct. App. 3d Dist. Hancock County 2013); State v. Weathers, 2013-Ohio-1104, 988 N.E.2d 16 (Ohio Ct. App. 12th Dist. Butler County 2013); State v. Lewis, 2013-Ohio-892, 2013

The weight of prevailing professional norms supports the view that counsel must advise noncitizen clients regarding deportation risks. The U.S. Supreme Court has recognized the importance to the client of preserving the right to remain in the United States and preserving the possibility of discretionary relief from deportation.[5] In those cases where the possibility of deportation is unclear, a criminal defense attorney need do no more than advise a noncitizen client that pending criminal charges may carry adverse immigration consequences. But when the deportation consequence is truly clear, the duty to give correct advice is equally clear.[6]

Ohio courts applying *Padilla* have adopted a narrow interpretation. They hold that *Padilla* does not apply if the defendant was informed by the trial court of the high risk of deportation, or if the defendant was informed by trial counsel of the risk of deportation that a plea might create.[7] However, where federal immigration law expressly mandates the removal of an alien convicted of a crime of domestic

---

WL 978899 (Ohio Ct. App. 7th Dist. Mahoning County 2013); State v. Dozier, 2014-Ohio-2925, 2014 WL 2993841 (Ohio Ct. App. 5th Dist. Stark County 2014); State v. Matthews, 2014-Ohio-2561, 2014 WL 2700915 (Ohio Ct. App. 6th Dist. Sandusky County 2014); State v. Burrell, 2014-Ohio-1356, 2014 WL 1356137 (Ohio Ct. App. 11th Dist. Lake County 2014); State v. Davis, 2014-Ohio-1197, 2014 WL 1340774 (Ohio Ct. App. 5th Dist. Licking County 2014); State v. Hall, 2014-Ohio-416, 2014 WL 523072 (Ohio Ct. App. 2d Dist. Montgomery County 2014); City of Toledo v. White, 2013-Ohio-5911, 2013 WL 7123151 (Ohio Ct. App. 6th Dist. Lucas County 2013); State v. Renner, 2013-Ohio-5463, 2013 WL 6576714 (Ohio Ct. App. 2d Dist. Montgomery County 2013); Cleveland v. Crutcher, 2013-Ohio-5240, 2013 WL 6221101 (Ohio Ct. App. 8th Dist. Cuyahoga County 2013); State v. Goshade, 2013-Ohio-4457, 2013 WL 5577906 (Ohio Ct. App. 1st Dist. Hamilton County 2013); State v. Dixon, 2013-Ohio-4149, 2013 WL 5407478 (Ohio Ct. App. 5th Dist. Stark County 2013); State v. Partlow, 2013-Ohio-2771, 2013 WL 3356575 (Ohio Ct. App. 10th Dist. Franklin County 2013); State v. Marcum, 2013-Ohio-2447, 994 N.E.2d 1 (Ohio Ct. App. 4th Dist. Hocking County 2013); State v. Habo, 2013-Ohio-2142, 2013 WL 2308483 (Ohio Ct. App. 11th Dist. Portage County 2013); State v. Kesting, 2014-Ohio-3058, 2014 WL 3407923 (Ohio Ct. App. 2d Dist. Montgomery County 2014); State v. Pittman, 2013-Ohio-962, 2013 WL 1092420 (Ohio Ct. App. 2d Dist. Montgomery County 2013); State v. Kelly, 2013-Ohio-4755, 2013 WL 5783710 (Ohio Ct. App. 11th Dist. Ashtabula County 2013); State v. Sturgell, 2013-Ohio-3518, 2013 WL 4130073 (Ohio Ct. App. 9th Dist. Summit County 2013); State v. Short, 2015-Ohio-3183, 2015 WL 4720395 (Ohio Ct. App. 5th Dist. Richland County 2015); State v. Abernathy, 2015-Ohio-1363, 2015 WL 1530810 (Ohio Ct. App. 5th Dist. Stark County 2015); State v. Woods, 2016-Ohio-4830, 2016 WL 3608724 (Ohio Ct. App. 5th Dist. Ashland County 2016); State v. Pringle, 2016-Ohio-1149, 2016 WL 1090961 (Ohio Ct. App. 12th Dist. Brown County 2016).

[5]Padilla v. Kentucky, 559 U.S. 356, 130 S. Ct. 1473, 176 L. Ed. 2d 284 (2010); State v. Graves, 2013-Ohio-2197, 2013 WL 2382613 (Ohio Ct. App. 8th Dist. Cuyahoga County 2013). But see State v. Huang, 2014-Ohio-1511, 2014 WL 1408122 (Ohio Ct. App. 8th Dist. Cuyahoga County 2014); State v. Thompson, 2014-Ohio-1225, 2014 WL 1326540 (Ohio Ct. App. 7th Dist. Columbiana County 2014).

[6]Padilla v. Kentucky, 559 U.S. 356, 130 S. Ct. 1473, 176 L. Ed. 2d 284 (2010); State v. Graves, 2013-Ohio-2197, 2013 WL 2382613 (Ohio Ct. App. 8th Dist. Cuyahoga County 2013). But see State v. Huang, 2014-Ohio-1511, 2014 WL 1408122 (Ohio Ct. App. 8th Dist. Cuyahoga County 2014); State v. Thompson, 2014-Ohio-1225, 2014 WL 1326540 (Ohio Ct. App. 7th Dist. Columbiana County 2014).

[7]See State v. Yazici, 2011-Ohio-583, 2011 WL 441473 (Ohio Ct. App. 5th Dist. Stark County 2011); State v. Gallegos-Martinez, 2010-Ohio-6463, 2010 WL 5550237 (Ohio Ct. App. 5th Dist. Delaware County 2010); State v. Bains, 2010-Ohio-5143, 2010 WL 4286167 (Ohio Ct. App. 8th Dist. Cuyahoga County 2010); State v. Schmidt, 2010-Ohio-4809, 2010 WL 3836161 (Ohio Ct. App. 3d Dist. Mercer County 2010);

violence,[8] counsel is required to advise a defendant charged with domestic violence that deportation is mandatory. Counsel's failure to provide such advice renders the representation afforded the defendant constitutionally deficient.[9] Additionally, the fact that counsel failed to provide the appropriate advice regarding the mandatory requirement of deportation following a domestic violence conviction cannot be used retroactively to allow a defendant to withdraw a plea finalized before March 31, 2010.[10]

Q & A: The defendant in a domestic violence case that I decided more than two years ago filed a motion to withdraw his no contest plea. He maintains that his lawyer never advised him that he would likely be deported because of the plea. He's requesting that I hold a hearing. I know that I properly advised him about the possibility of deportation at the time of the plea. Do I have to hold a hearing?

A trial court's advisement does not necessarily foreclose the possibility of finding that an alien defendant was prejudiced by the actions or inaction of counsel. Therefore, it cannot be said that the mere fact that a trial court's properly gave the required statutory advisement, alone, is a valid reason for denying a hearing on a motion to withdraw the plea of an individual facing the possibility of immigration consequences, This is particularly true when that individual presents prima facie evidence of ineffective assistance of counsel.[11]

§ 7:13 Collateral effects of a guilty plea or of being found guilty—Employment

A conviction for domestic violence can restrict a client's future opportunity for employment. Ohio law[1] provides for criminal background checks for childcare workers and for adoptive and foster parents. RC 2151.86(B)(1) provides that, except for persons specifically exempted by operation of rules adopted by the Ohio Department of Human Services, no governmental entity shall employ a person as a person responsible for a child's care in out-of-home care or permit a person to

---

State v. Huang, 2014-Ohio-1511, 2014 WL 1408122 (Ohio Ct. App. 8th Dist. Cuyahoga County 2014); State v. Ayesta, 2015-Ohio-1695, 2015 WL 2091679 (Ohio Ct. App. 8th Dist. Cuyahoga County 2015).

[8] 8 U.S.C.A. § 1227(a)(2)(E)(i).

[9] State v. Bishop, 2014-Ohio-173, 7 N.E.3d 605 (Ohio Ct. App. 1st Dist. Hamilton County 2014); but see State v. Valdez, 2017-Ohio-4260, 2017 WL 2569810 (Ohio Ct. App. 1st Dist. Hamilton County 2017) (affirmed the denial of a motion to withdraw guilty plea because of immigration advice where there wasn't enough record to determine claim.).

[10] Chaidez v. U.S., 568 U.S. 342, 133 S. Ct. 1103, 185 L. Ed. 2d 149 (2013), applying the principles set forth in Teague v. Lane, 489 U.S. 288, 109 S. Ct. 1060, 103 L. Ed. 2d 334 (1989); State v. Bishop, 2014-Ohio-173, 7 N.E.3d 605 (Ohio Ct. App. 1st Dist. Hamilton County 2014).

[11] State v. Ayesta, 2015-Ohio-1695, 2015 WL 2091679 (Ohio Ct. App. 8th Dist. Cuyahoga County 2015); but see State v. Valdez, 2017-Ohio-4260, 2017 WL 2569810 (Ohio Ct. App. 1st Dist. Hamilton County 2017) (affirmed the denial of a motion to withdraw guilty plea because of immigration advice where there wasn't enough record to determine claim).

[Section 7:13]

[1] RC 2151.86(A)(1).

become an adoptive parent or foster parent if the person previously has been convicted of or pleaded guilty to a violation of the state domestic violence statute.

Additionally, under the Federal Gun Control Act,[2] a conviction for domestic violence makes a person ineligible to possess a firearm.[3] This results in the inability of the defendant to perform any work (law enforcement, security, etc.) where a firearm is required.

Q & A: I'm a security guard and I was recently convicted of domestic violence under the threats section of the statute.[4] My boss says that I can't have a gun now because of the domestic violence conviction. Is that true?

No. Federal law makes it unlawful for anyone who has been convicted of a misdemeanor crime of domestic violence to, inter alia, possess any firearm or ammunition that has been shipped or transported in interstate or foreign commerce.[5] A "misdemeanor crime of domestic violence" is defined as one that, "has, as an element, the use or attempted use of physical force, or the threatened use of a deadly weapon committed by a former or current spouse."[6] Your conviction of domestic violence threats under the Ohio statute, does not disqualify you from possessing a weapon under federal law, because it does not meet the definition of domestic violence set forth in the federal statute.[7]

§ 7:14 Collateral effects of a guilty plea or of being found guilty—Custody and visitation

A conviction for domestic violence may affect a defendant's parental rights.[1] State law mandates that courts determine appropriate visitation or companionship rights for a parent who is not the residential parent.[2] The court is also required, however, to determine whether that parent has been convicted of or pleaded guilty to a violation of RC 2919.25 involving a victim who, at the time of the commission of the offense, was a member of the family or household that is the subject of the proceeding, has been convicted of or pleaded guilty to any other offense involving a victim who, at the time of the commission of the offense, was a member of the family or household that is the subject of the proceeding and caused physical harm to the victim

---

[2]18 U.S.C.A. § 922. Snell v. Snell, 2010-Ohio-2245, 2010 WL 2010899 (Ohio Ct. App. 5th Dist. Richland County 2010); Rieger v. Montgomery Cty., 2009-Ohio-4125, 2009 WL 2489855 (Ohio Ct. App. 2d Dist. Montgomery County 2009); Wilhoit v. N. Olmsted, 151 Ohio Misc. 2d 21, 2009-Ohio-1702, 905 N.E.2d 723 (Mun. Ct. 2009).

[3]Snell v. Snell, 2010-Ohio-2245, 2010 WL 2010899 (Ohio Ct. App. 5th Dist. Richland County 2010).

[4]RC 2919.25(C).

[5]18 U.S.C.A. § 922(g)(9).

[6]18 U.S.C.A. § 921(a)(33)(A)(ii).

[7]18 U.S.C.A. § 921(a)(33)(A). See also Wilhoit v. N. Olmsted, 151 Ohio Misc. 2d 21, 2009-Ohio-1702, 905 N.E.2d 723 (Mun. Ct. 2009).

[Section 7:14]

[1]See RC 3109.04(C), RC 3109.051(D)(12); see also Ch 14, Domestic Violence and Custody and Visitation Issues.

[2]RC 3109.051(A).

in the commission of the offense, or has been determined to be the perpetrator of the abusive act that is the basis of an adjudication that a child is an abused child. If the court determines that the parent who is granted the visitation or companionship rights has been convicted of or pleaded guilty to a violation of RC 2919.25 involving a victim who, at the time of the commission of the offense, was a member of the family or household that is the subject of the proceeding, has been convicted of or pleaded guilty to any other offense involving a victim who, at the time of the commission of the offense, was a member of the family or household that is the subject of the proceeding and caused physical harm to the victim in the commission of the offense, or has been determined to be the perpetrator of the abusive act that is the basis of an adjudication that a child is an abused child, it must issue an order stating that that parent will not be given a copy of any notice of relocation that is filed with the court, unless the court determines that it is in the best interest of the children to give that parent a copy of the notice of relocation, issues an order stating that that parent will be given a copy of any notice, and issues specific written findings of fact in support of its determination.[3]

§ 7:15 Case preparation—Interviewing the defendant; checklist

Most charges of domestic violence are brought as misdemeanors. Nonetheless, the fact that these cases are among the most serious charges appearing on the dockets of the municipal and county courts, as well as the potential for enhanced penalties for subsequent offenses, requires thorough preparation. One of the single most important parts of that preparation is the interview that defense counsel conducts with the client.

Because of the intimate nature of the relationships involved, the often deeply rooted self-denials, and the intergenerational acculturation associated with domestic violence, counsel must know more about the background of defendants charged with domestic violence than about the background of defendants charged with most other crimes.

Preparation for the interview of the defendant is crucial to its ultimate success. The interview must seek to accomplish several defense goals, including, but not necessarily limited to:

(1) Obtaining as much information from the defendant as possible regarding:
   (a) the incident,
   (b) the defendant,
   (c) the victim,
   (d) the accused's relationship with the victim,
   (e) the nature of any injuries or other harm suffered by the parties,
   (f) the existence of any witnesses to the incident, how they can be contacted, and what they have to contribute,
   (g) prior, current, as well as threatened, legal proceedings involving the parties,

[3]RC 3109.051(G)(2).

(h) any role substance abuse played in the incident,
(i) the presence and/or use of weapons during the incident,
(j) past acts of violence against the victim by the offender, and vice versa.

(2) Assessing the viability of the victim as a trial witness. (See attached form.)
(3) Establishing initial rapport with the defendant.

Those defending against an allegation of domestic violence must decide quickly how to respond to a request for a protection order sought on behalf of a victim in any criminal or civil case. Time is of the essence, since, by statute,[1] protection orders are given priority and must be heard within days, if not hours, of the request for their issuance.[2]

A defendant who is subjected to the provisions of a protection order is deprived of important rights[3] and may wish to have those rights restored quickly if the order was granted erroneously. Removal from one's home,[4] restrictions on contact with one's children,[5] and restrictions on access to one's assets[6] are just some of the consequences of the imposition of a protection order issued under Ohio's domestic violence laws.

Proper preparation for the interview includes development of an interview strategy. The interview should focus on obtaining information to forward the primary objectives identified by counsel as essential to the successful presentation of the case at trial. The interviewer should adhere to the strategy throughout the meeting with the defendant to the degree that such adherence is possible.

A good interview will also include a thorough explanation and exploration of the case theories and plea negotiation options, as well as various sentencing options available to the court if prosecution results in conviction.

Counsel should take a complete narrative from the client of the alleged incident as well as any other similar events that may have occurred during the relationship. If the client denies culpability in the current event, a determination should be made relative to any underlying collateral reasons why the alleged victim would seek court action, such as a desire to remove the client from the marital home, divorce or custody considerations, revenge, another relationship, or to preempt the client from obtaining a protection order.

The following annotated checklist can help an attorney secure the information necessary to appropriately advise a domestic violence client.

[Section 7:15]

[1]RC 2919.26, RC 2903.213, RC 3113.31.

[2]RC 2919.26, RC 2903.213, RC 3113.31.

[3]RC 2919.26, RC 2903.213, RC 3113.31.

[4]RC 2919.26, RC 2903.213, RC 3113.31.

[5]RC 2919.26, RC 2903.213, RC 3113.31.

[6]RC 3113.31.

§ 7:16 Case preparation—Client interview preparation; checklist

The information that is revealed in a thorough interview will allow counsel to evaluate the strategic and/or tactical value of seeking an early hearing to contest a motion for a protection order. Thus, it is important for counsel to adequately prepare for a client interview. Proper preparation includes:

(1) Reviewing the complaint for defects and any probable cause determination made by the court for basic information about the factual allegations;
(2) Determining whether a motion for a protection order is pending or was granted;
(3) Preparing to review standard motions with the client, such as requests for discovery, bills of particulars, and, where appropriate, motions to dismiss;
(4) If an ex parte protection order was granted, obtaining a copy of the transcript; and
(5) Reviewing Domestic Violence Defendant Interview Form.[1]

§ 7:17 Case preparation—Interviewing the defendant—Defendant interview; form

The use of a detailed form to collect vital information from a client about the facts and circumstances surrounding a charge of domestic violence is a matter of counsel's personal preference. While some lawyers feel the need to gather detailed information as early as possible in the process, others feel as though doing so locks clients into a version of facts from which they are later unwilling to retreat, even in the face of evidence to the contrary. Others feel no need to determine a detailed version of their clients' positions at all, since they see the primary job of the defense as discrediting the version of the facts presented by the prosecution.

The form presented in this section is comprehensive. It incorporates topics that counsel needs to investigate with a client and should be aware of in mounting an effective defense, regardless of whether the from itself is employed.

Case Number: ______
Date of Incident: ______

DOMESTIC VIOLENCE DEFENDANT INTERVIEW FORM

The purpose of this interview is to help secure the information to provide you with the best possible defense to the charges that the prosecution has brought against you and to identify all of your options for dealing with the current situation that you find yourself in. The interview will provide the background information needed to assess your vulnerability to the outstanding charge or charges and to allow for the crafting of the defense that will be most effective under the

[Section 7:16]

[1]See Text § 7:17, Case preparation—Interviewing the defendant—Defendant interview; form.

circumstances. It is our desire to provide you with all of the information necessary for you to make informed judgments on the options that are available to you.

It is also our responsibility to do whatever we can to assure that the criminal behavior which you experienced does not continue. The information that you provide will help us determine what type of intervention will be most appropriate in accomplishing this goal. If you have any questions about the interview, please feel free to ask them, either before or after the interview is completed.

Please read each question carefully. You are requested to answer ONLY those questions which apply to your situation.

(A) GENERAL INFORMATION—DEFENDANT

NAME: ______________________________

DATE OF BIRTH: ______________________________

HEIGHT: ________ WEIGHT: ________

SOCIAL SECURITY NUMBER: ______________________________

CURRENT ADDRESS: ______________________________

____

TELEPHONE: HOME: ________ WORK: ________

MARITAL STATUS: ______________________________

SPOUSE'S NAME: ______________________________

CHILDREN:

NAME:	MOTHER'S NAME:

CURRENT EMPLOYMENT: ______________________________

EMPLOYER'S ADDRESS: ______________________________

____

EDUCATIONAL HISTORY: ______________________________

____

____

(B) **CRIMINAL HISTORY WITH CURRENT COMPLAINANT/ VICTIM**

Please list all instances in the past where your interactions with the complainant/victim required you to have contact with the criminal justice system.

(1) ARRESTS:

FOR WHAT? WHEN? WHERE?

______

______

______

______

______

______

(2) PRIOR FELONY CONVICTIONS:

FOR WHAT? WHEN? WHERE?

______

______

______

______

______

______

(3) PRIOR MISDEMEANOR CONVICTIONS:

FOR WHAT? WHEN? WHERE?

______

______

______

______

FOR WHAT? WHEN? WHERE?

(4) PRIOR DISPUTE MEDIATIONS:

FOR WHAT? WHEN? WHERE?

(5) PRIOR DIVERSION PROGRAMS:

FOR WHAT? WHEN? WHERE?

(6) PRIOR UNREPORTED PHYSICAL CONFRONTATIONS:

WHAT? WHEN? WHERE?

WHAT? WHEN? WHERE?

(C) **OTHER CRIMINAL HISTORY**

Please list all other instances in the past where your actions caused you to have contact with the criminal justice system.

(1) ARRESTS:

FOR WHAT? WHEN? WHERE?

---

(2) PRIOR FELONY CONVICTIONS:

FOR WHAT? WHEN? WHERE?

---

(3) PRIOR MISDEMEANOR CONVICTIONS:

FOR WHAT? WHEN? WHERE?

FOR WHAT? WHEN? WHERE?

____

____

____

(4) PRIOR DISPUTE MEDIATIONS:

FOR WHAT? WHEN? WHERE?

____

____

____

____

____

____

(5) PRIOR DIVERSION PROGRAMS:

FOR WHAT? WHEN? WHERE?

____

____

____

____

____

____

(D) **GENERAL INFORMATION—VICTIM**

NAME: ____________________

DATE OF BIRTH: ____________________

HEIGHT: ________ WEIGHT: ________

SOCIAL SECURITY NUMBER: ____________________

CURRENT ADDRESS: ____________________

____

TELEPHONE: HOME: ________ WORK: ________

EMPLOYER'S ADDRESS: ______________________

____

Please list the names, addresses, and telephone numbers of two of your closest friends or relatives who have regular contact with you, do not live with you, and will always know where to reach you:

NAME:	ADDRESS:	PHONE NUMBER:
________	________	________
________	________	________

(E) **GENERAL INFORMATION: LEGAL**

CURRENT RELATIONSHIP WITH VICTIM:

HOW LONG HAVE YOU KNOWN THE VICTIM? ______

LIVING TOGETHER ______ MARRIED ______ SEPARATED ______

DIVORCED ______ CHILD IN COMMON ______ NONE NOW ______

FORMERLY LIVED WITH VICTIM: YES ______ NO ______

If yes: FROM: ______ TO: ______

ANY DIVORCE OR CHILD CUSTODY PROCEEDINGS PENDING OR THREATENED? YES ______ NO ______

If the answer is yes, please answer the following questions about that lawsuit:

(1) In what court is the matter pending? ______

(2) When is the next hearing scheduled? ______

(3) What is the name of the victim's attorney? ______

(4) What is the name of your attorney? ______

(5) Has either party been granted a protection order against the other in a civil or criminal case currently pending?

YES ______ NO ______ If yes, CIVIL ______ CRIMINAL ______

If yes, against which party? YOU ______ THE VICTIM ______

ARE THERE ANY OTHER LAWSUITS PENDING BETWEEN YOU AND THE VICTIM OR MEMBERS OF YOUR FAMILIES?

YES ______ NO ______

Nature of the lawsuit: ______

(F) **INCIDENT DESCRIPTION**

(1) Date of the incident: ______ Time: ______

(2) Location of the incident: ______

(3) Did the incident involve:

(a) Threats of violence YES NO

(b) Actual violence YES NO

(4) If actual violence was involved, who committed the first violent act?

(a) You YES NO
(b) The victim YES NO

(5) Describe the incident in detail: ____________________

(6) Were either you or the victim drinking or using drugs at the time of the incident? YES ________ NO ________
(7) If the answer to question 6 is YES, which of you was using? YOU ________ VICTIM ________
(8) What drug(s) or alcohol was used? ________
(9) How much of the drug or alcohol was used (approximately)? ________

(10) Did you hit the victim or use any violence during the incident? YES ________ NO ________
(11) If the answer to question 10 is YES,
(a) What kind of violence did you use (e.g., open hand, fists, strangulation, scratching, a weapon, etc.)? ________
(b) At what stage of the incident did you resort to violence? ________
(c) Why did you resort to violence? ________

(12) Were other members of your immediate family or household, including your minor children, present during this incident?
YES ________ NO ________
(13) If the answer to question 12 is YES, please provide the information for all those present:

<u>NAME</u>: <u>ADDRESS</u>: <u>PHONE NUMBER</u>: <u>AGE</u>:

____

____

____

____

(14) Did you have any injuries that were visible at the time of the incident? YES ________ NO ________

(15) If the answer to question 14 is YES, please describe the type of injury and where it was located on your body (e.g., a large dark bruise on the back of the right thigh): ________________

____

____

____

(16) Did you have any injuries that became visible immediately after this incident that will not be noted in the police report of the event? YES ________ NO ________

(17) If the answer to question 16 is YES, please describe the injury and when it first became visible: ________________

____

____

(18) Are the injuries still visible? YES ________ NO ________

(19) Was anyone other than you injured during this incident? YES ________ NO ________

(20) If the answer to question 19 is YES, provide the requested information for all those who were injured:

<u>NAME</u>: <u>ADDRESS</u>: <u>PHONE NUMBER</u>: <u>AGE</u>:

____

____

____

(21) If the answer to question 19 is YES, explain how the others were injured during the event: ________________

____

____

____

____

____

____

(22) Were photographs taken of your injuries? YES ________ NO ________

(23) If the answer to question 22 is YES, by whom were the photos taken?

(a) Police: ________

(b) Other: ________

(24) If the answer to question 23 is Other, provide the requested information regarding the person who took the photographs:

NAME:	ADDRESS:	PHONE NUMBER:	DATE OF PHOTO:

(25) Were you treated by any medical professional (e.g., doctor, nurse, medical technician, EMS, dentist, etc.) for your injuries? YES ________ NO ________

(26) If the answer to question 25 is YES, provide the name(s) of the medical professional(s) or organization that provided the service:

NAME:	ADDRESS:	PHONE NUMBER:

(27) If the answer to question 25 is YES, **please sign the medical information release form attached to this questionnaire.**

(28) Did you show or tell anyone else about your injuries? YES ________ NO ________

(29) If the answer to question 28 is YES, please provide the following information about each person that you told:

NAME:	PHONE NUMBER:	DATE TOLD OF INCIDENT:

(30) Were any pets belonging to you or your immediate family injured during this event? YES ________ NO ________

(31) Was any of your personal property damaged during the incident? YES ________ NO ________

(32) If the answer to question 31 is YES, describe the property that was damaged and how it was damaged:

____

____

____

____

(33) Has the victim threatened you either directly or indirectly by word or action since this incident? YES ________ NO ________

(34) If the answer to question 33 is YES, as accurately and as completely as possible, describe and relate the exact threat:

____

____

____

____

(35) Are you presently afraid of the victim? YES ________ NO ________

(36) Has the victim ever been violent to you in the past (e.g., choked, pushed, punched, stabbed, cut, slapped, sexually assaulted, or thrown things at you)? YES ________ NO ________

(37) If the answer to question 36 is YES, please answer the following:

(a) Approximately when did the event occur? ________

(b) Was the event reported to the authorities? ________

(c) Were you injured? ________

(d) Did you receive medical treatment? ________

(e) Who provided the medical treatment? ________

(f) Were there witnesses? If so, please list the name, address and/or phone number of each witness:

____

____

(38) To your knowledge, what other motivation does the victim have for bringing this charge? What proof do you have? Be specific.

____

§ 7:18 Case preparation—Interviewing the defendant—Medical records release; form

CASE NUMBER: ________

MEDICAL RECORDS RELEASE

PATIENT: ____

ADDRESS: ____

DATE OF BIRTH: ____

SSN: ____

INITIAL DATE OF TREATMENT: ____

MEDICAL SERVICE PROVIDERS:

NAME: ____

ADDRESS: ____

NAME: ______________________________

ADDRESS: ___________________________

I, ________, hereby authorize and request the medical service providers listed above to release any and all medical records in their possession concerning the medical diagnosis and treatment received on and after the date set forth in this release to:

____

Attorney for ________

________, Ohio ________

() ________________

SIGNED: ____________ DATE: ________

____

(PATIENT OR ATTORNEY-IN-FACT)

STATE OF OHIO

COUNTY OF ________

On the ________ day of ________, ________, the aforesigned personally appeared before me, a duly authorized Notary Public of the State of Ohio, and swore or affirmed that all of the information contained herein is true and accurate to the best of the affiant's knowledge and belief. In witness whereof, the affiant's signature was caused to be affixed hereto.

____

NOTARY PUBLIC

My commission expires ________

◆ **NOTE: An executed copy of this form is as legally effective as the original.**

§ 7:19 Case preparation—Interviewing the alleged victim

It is important for defense counsel to keep in mind that a criminal case is a lawsuit between a governmental entity and the defendant. The victim is not a party. Rather, the victim's status is that of witness. As such, it is perfectly ethical and, it might be argued, ethically required for the defendant's attorney to attempt to obtain an interview with the victim, just as counsel would attempt to interview any other essential adverse witness.

In domestic violence cases, two frequent scenarios present occasions for defense counsel to dialogue with victims. In the first scenario, the attorney initiates contact with the victim to elicit information. Such conduct presents no problems, as long as the attorney identifies himself/herself and conducts himself/herself in a professional manner. An interview with the complaining witness may provide useful information that counsel can use during cross-examination at trial. Minimally, it will present an opportunity to gauge demeanor and to anticipate performance in court. Even a refusal to be interviewed may have value during cross-examination at trial.

Some caution must be exercised when seeking to interview complaining witnesses. In order to protect against allegations of witness intimidation or tampering, a second person should always be present at the time the interview is attempted or conducted. Taking this precaution also avoids the possibility of counsel becoming a fact witness if the subject of the interview changes stories or recants at trial. In some instances, where an interview with the complaining witness is crucial to the defense, using a private investigator to obtain the information, if the client can afford it, is the better practice.

The second and more perplexing event for the attorney representing the defendant charged with domestic violence is the situation which occurs when the victim makes contact with the defense counsel. This generally happens in one of two ways: (1) the victim, on his/her own, contacts the attorney, or (2) the defendant brings the victim to the attorney.

In the first instance, the defendant's attorney should exercise extreme caution and should assume, given the volatile nature of all domestic violence cases, that the victim's motive for making contact is not necessarily in the client's best interest. It is wise to treat any conversation initiated by the victim as though it was being tape-recorded and to act accordingly.

The victim may have questions or may express a desire to "drop" the charges. Again, defense counsel should approach any discussions along these lines with caution. It is not unusual for victims to ask the defendant's lawyer, in these circumstances, for advice on how they should proceed or what to expect from the proceedings. Frequently, victims will ask defense counsel what will happen if they simply do not appear. The Ohio Rules of Professional Conduct govern these contacts.[1] According to Rule 3.4(g), A lawyer shall not "advise or cause a person to hide or to leave the jurisdiction of a tribunal for the purpose of becoming unavailable as a witness."

This single line should be carefully attended to. Attorneys should never give even the slightest appearance that they would condone disobeying a subpoena. It is advisable to tell the witness to contact the issuer of the subpoena as you did not issue the subpoena and cannot comment on it.

Counsel's position is even more tenuous when the defendant and victim appear together. Frequently, a temporary protection order is in place, and the attorney becomes a witness to the violation of the court's order.

In this situation, the attorney must decide how to handle the presence of the victim. Should the victim be interviewed? Should the defendant be present? Does the attorney have an obligation to warn both the victim and the client about their responsibilities under the protection order? What is the lawyer's liability, if no action is taken, to the court and to the client?

[Section 7:19]

[1]Prof. Cond. Rule 3.4.

The first question that the lawyer should resolve is why the victim is present in the first place. In some instances, it will clearly appear that the victim is motivated to talk to the defendant's lawyer because of honest opposition to the continuation of the case before the court and a desire to be of assistance to the defense.

On other occasions, the victim wishes to express a concern about the ultimate resolution of the case, e.g., the defendant needs help not jail, I want him/her to get substance abuse counseling, etc. Here, the victim's motivation is to help craft a sentence and to help the attorney plan a strategy that takes into account the victim's desired outcome. Such contacts are useful and may help defense counsel and the prosecutor negotiate an acceptable compromise that accomplishes the goals of all interested parties.

The more perplexing situation is where the client presents a victim to counsel who ostensibly wishes to drop the domestic violence charges. In this context, it is wise for the lawyer to err on the side of caution and to view the victim's statements with a high level of skepticism. While the victim's statements might be free and voluntary, the control exercised by a batterer in a classic domestic violence situation requires the lawyer presented with this situation to initially proceed under the assumption that the victim was influenced by the defendant, or others at the defendant's direction, to seek the termination of the charges. An astute defense attorney will look for body language or other signs that indicate that the defendant is controlling the victim's decision to recant an earlier decision to prosecute.

If counsel has any concerns in this regard, the victim should be interviewed outside of the presence of the defendant. Preferably, the interview with the victim should be recorded on tape. This precaution is as much, if not more so, for the attorney's protection as it is for the preservation of any evidence that the victim's statement might provide. Counsel's primary purpose in conducting this interview is to discern whether or not the defendant threatened, coerced, or otherwise intimidated or improperly influenced the victim to obtain the recantation, and most particularly, whether there was any additional violence or threat of violence. If any of these circumstances becomes evident during the interview, counsel should immediately terminate all additional questioning and refer the victim back to the prosecuting attorney or the victim advocate, if one is involved. Counsel should assure the victim that he/she has an ethical duty not to knowingly enable the defendant to break the law.[2]

In these rare situations, the risk of additional violence is great, and counsel should proceed with great care so as not to make a bad situation even worse. If for no more noble purpose than to prevent the client from more serious charges, counsel needs to make every effort to see that court orders are obeyed, witnesses are not intimidated, and perjury is not suborned.

Whenever the defendant and the victim appear in circumstances described in the third scenario, regardless of whether counsel believes anything improper has transpired, the parties should be addressed together. Counsel should review with them the court's policy on do-

[2]Prof. Cond. Rule 1.2(d).

mestic violence and prosecution policies concerning the dismissal of charges, if any such policies exist. Additionally, counsel should review with the parties the requirements imposed on them by any temporary protection order then in effect and remind them of the penalties for violating the court's order.

The attorney who follows this course of action is not compromising his/her client's position. Counsel is protecting, in the purest sense of the word, the client's vital penal, proprietary, and social interests.

§ 7:20 Case preparation—Pretrial discovery

Under the Rules of Criminal Procedure, the defense is entitled to discover information concerning the prosecution's case in order to effectively defend the accused.[1] Just how much information the defense may obtain during discovery is dependent upon the philosophy of the prosecuting attorney who serves the district where the defense is mounted. For instance, in jurisdictions that do not believe in open discovery, a defense lawyer has a duty to investigate the charges against a client more thoroughly and as part of that duty, should, independent of the request for discovery, obtain the following: copies of 911 tapes, the underlying police report, EMS run report, issue a direct subpoena for the alleged victim's medical records, and obtain any other police reports filed by or against the alleged victim in an effort to establish any pattern of conduct that might benefit the client in defeating the charges. Counsel should avail themselves of this tool as quickly as possible to obtain a more complete picture of the client's predicament and to formulate a strategy and tactics to ameliorate it. In addition to a copy of any oral or written statements that the client may have made that are within the knowledge of the authorities, the defense is also entitled to see any medical records, photographs, physical evidence, 911 tapes, expert reports, exculpatory information, and names of witnesses that the prosecution intends to use. In many instances, the rules not only entitle you to see but also obtain copies of the documents that are discoverable.[2]

Interviews with all relevant witnesses are essential. These interviews can be conducted either in person or by telephone, depending on your need to observe the witness to gage his/her credibility and demeanor. Find out from the client what these witnesses are likely to have to offer. In many instances, nominally neutral witnesses, such as neighbors, medical personnel, and law enforcement officers, may provide crucial information essential for mounting an effective defense.

§ 7:21 Trial presentation—Jury trial considerations

Domestic violence jury trials present unique challenges for the defense attorney. Juries tend to be more skeptical of claims of physical assault in the context of intimate relationships. They are likely to require high levels of circumstantial evidence from prosecutions that

---

[Section 7:20]

[1]Crim.R. 16.

[2]See Crim.R. 16.

do not include a cooperating victim. In addition, juries are more willing to believe a victim who takes the stand and recants the original version of the incident presented to the police. These tendencies cause many lawyers to favor jury trials over bench trials in domestic violence cases. Remember, an alleged victim may be cross-examined using prior statements made. Counsel is entitled to witness statements prior to trial. The Criminal Rules require that the court conduct an in camera inspection of the witness' prior statement and that defense counsel participate in the inspection.

Counsel should exercise care in making such decisions, however. Juries may tend to be more skeptical, but they are also more likely than judges to respond to emotional presentations from victims that are supported by independent, extrinsic evidence which supports the prosecution's case. In many domestic violence cases, a trial to the bench is the better defense strategy because many of these cases turn on more technical, mixed questions of law and fact, such as whether the defendant and the victim qualify as family or household members. The decision to waive a jury in these cases, as in any other, must rest in the sound discretion of counsel following a thorough analysis of the facts, circumstances and law that apply, as well as an assessment of the established predilections of the particular jurist who will hear the case if the jury is waived.

If the decision to proceed to jury trial is made, preparation should include a thorough review of Ohio's pattern jury instructions.[1] The incidence of domestic violence is so high that counsel must anticipate that any number of those who serve on the juries that try these cases may have some first-hand knowledge of this type of criminal behavior. It is also likely that not everybody that has such first-hand knowledge is ready to candidly disclose that fact. In domestic violence trials, more so than in most other criminal trials, the defense must anticipate conscious or unconscious biases as a potential problem that must be neutralized. Therefore, jury instructions that anticipate and move to overcome some of the more damning aspects of the typical domestic violence trial, and the law that normally applies to it, are essential.

The goal of the defense attorney in a jury trial should be to show that the acts of the defendant were reasonable for the situation and that common sense dictates that the defendant's actions did not rise to the level of criminal activity. The ultimate goal of a sound defense strategy is to integrate into the questions put to the witnesses, as well as the arguments and statements made before the jury, some variation of the language the court employs in its final instructions. When done effectively, many of the court's final instructions to the jury appear to have come directly from the defendant's closing argument.

Q & A: In a jury trial on a charge of domestic violence threats—second offense, the prosecution attempts to offer evidence of the facts involved in the case that resulted in the first conviction. Can they do that?

Yes. In a case where the existence of a prior conviction enhances the penalty for a subsequent offense, the prior conviction is an es-

---

[Section 7:21]

[1]Ohio Judicial Conference, Ohio Jury Instructions, Volume 4, Criminal.

sential element of the subsequent offense and needs to be alleged in the complaint or proved as a matter of fact.[2]

The existence of a prior offense is such an inflammatory fact that ordinarily it is only revealed to a jury when specifically permitted under statute or rule.[3]

Q & A: When a defendant has a prior domestic violence conviction, can that information ever be withheld from a jury in a felony trial, if the defendant stipulates to it?

No. A prior conviction is an essential element of the felony offense if it enhances the penalty, and the jury must determine the existence of a prior conviction as a factual matter before the trial court can impose a greater punishment. The defendant might stipulate to the prior conviction and argue that by doing so the need to have the jury make factual findings on the issue no longer exists. However, the trial court is still required to inform the jury of the stipulation and their duty to make the required finding.[4]

§ 7:22 Trial presentation—Hearsay evidence and the Confrontation Clause

One issue that arises with great regularity in domestic violence prosecutions is the admissibility of out-of-court statements by the alleged victim and/or other witnesses. Regardless of whether these individuals testify at trial, their out-of-court statements may nonetheless be inadmissible hearsay and should be objected to on that basis. When an alleged victim or witness does *not* testify, the admission of their out-of-court statements at trial may violate the defendant's confrontation rights under the Sixth and Fourteenth Amendments of the United States Constitution and its Ohio constitutional counterparts. Because this area of constitutional law is still rapidly developing, criminal defense attorneys should not hesitate to raise a confrontation issue.

---

[2]State v. Allen, 29 Ohio St. 3d 53, 506 N.E.2d 199 (1987); State v. Kingery, 2010-Ohio-1813, 2010 WL 1660424 (Ohio Ct. App. 12th Dist. Fayette County 2010); State v. Clay, 181 Ohio App. 3d 563, 2009-Ohio-1235, 910 N.E.2d 14 (8th Dist. Cuyahoga County 2009); State v. Tatum, 2009-Ohio-453, 2009 WL 252361 (Ohio Ct. App. 5th Dist. Stark County 2009); State v. Smith, 2008-Ohio-5985, 2008 WL 4951646 (Ohio Ct. App. 8th Dist. Cuyahoga County 2008); State v. Maynez, 2008-Ohio-3054, 2008 WL 2485367 (Ohio Ct. App. 3d Dist. Defiance County 2008); State v. Tate, 138 Ohio St. 3d 139, 2014-Ohio-44, 4 N.E.3d 1016 (2014); State v. Bibler, 2014-Ohio-3375, 17 N.E.3d 1154 (Ohio Ct. App. 3d Dist. Marion County 2014); State v. Sargent, 2015-Ohio-704, 29 N.E.3d 331 (Ohio Ct. App. 6th Dist. Lucas County 2015); State v. Canada, 2015-Ohio-2167, 2015 WL 3540402 (Ohio Ct. App. 10th Dist. Franklin County 2015); State v. Waheed, 2016-Ohio-2951, 2016 WL 2841926 (Ohio Ct. App. 1st Dist. Hamilton County 2016).

[3]State v. Allen, 29 Ohio St. 3d 53, 506 N.E.2d 199 (1987); State v. Clay, 181 Ohio App. 3d 563, 2009-Ohio-1235, 910 N.E.2d 14 (8th Dist. Cuyahoga County 2009).

[4]State v. Smith, 2008-Ohio-5985, 2008 WL 4951646 (Ohio Ct. App. 8th Dist. Cuyahoga County 2008); State v. Nunez, 2017-Ohio-4295, 92 N.E.3d 294 (Ohio Ct. App. 8th Dist. Cuyahoga County 2017), appeal not allowed, 150 Ohio St. 3d 1455, 2017-Ohio-8136, 83 N.E.3d 940 (2017) (while *Nunez* is not directly on point for this proposition but does hold that the state may use the prior conviction not just to satisfy an element of the offense but also as Ohio Evid. R. 404(B) evidence and when that happens, the state does not have to accept a stipulation); State v. Creech, 150 Ohio St. 3d 540, 2016-Ohio-8440, 84 N.E.3d 981 (2016).

In 2004, the United States Supreme Court held that the U.S. Constitution's Confrontation Clause barred the prosecution from introducing "testimonial" statements unless the declarant was previously subjected to cross-examination under oath.[1] "Where testimonial statements are at issue, the only indicium of reliability sufficient to satisfy constitutional demands is the one the Constitution actually prescribes: confrontation."[2] The Supreme Court's decision established an absolute

[Section 7:22]

[1]Crawford v. Washington, 541 U.S. 36, 124 S. Ct. 1354, 158 L. Ed. 2d 177, 63 Fed. R. Evid. Serv. 1077 (2004); State v. Stahl, 111 Ohio St. 3d 186, 2006-Ohio-5482, 855 N.E.2d 834 (2006). See also Text §§ 5:14 to 5:21, Case preparation—Hearsay exceptions; State v. Peeples, 2009-Ohio-1198, 2009 WL 737922 (Ohio Ct. App. 7th Dist. Mahoning County 2009); Toledo v. Sailes, 180 Ohio App. 3d 56, 2008-Ohio-6400, 904 N.E.2d 543 (6th Dist. Lucas County 2008); State v. Rufus, 2008-Ohio-5478, 2008 WL 4681392 (Ohio Ct. App. 8th Dist. Cuyahoga County 2008); State v. Moorer, 2009-Ohio-1494, 2009 WL 818945 (Ohio Ct. App. 9th Dist. Summit County 2009); State v. Marrero, 2011-Ohio-1390, 2011 WL 1049294 (Ohio Ct. App. 10th Dist. Franklin County 2011); State v. Sanchez, 2010-Ohio-6153, 2010 WL 5235932 (Ohio Ct. App. 8th Dist. Cuyahoga County 2010); State v. Tolbert, 2010-Ohio-2864, 2010 WL 2512584 (Ohio Ct. App. 9th Dist. Summit County 2010); State v. Vanderhorst, 2010-Ohio-1856, 2010 WL 1712246 (Ohio Ct. App. 8th Dist. Cuyahoga County 2010); State v. Cotton, 2010-Ohio-804, 2010 WL 746756 (Ohio Ct. App. 6th Dist. Lucas County 2010); State v. Butts, 2012-Ohio-571, 2012 WL 474030 (Ohio Ct. App. 4th Dist. Hocking County 2012); State v. Hall, 2012-Ohio-266, 2012 WL 253317 (Ohio Ct. App. 8th Dist. Cuyahoga County 2012); State v. Beauford, 2011-Ohio-5379, 2011 WL 4973731 (Ohio Ct. App. 5th Dist. Richland County 2011); State v. Parks, 2011-Ohio-3037, 2011 WL 2464198 (Ohio Ct. App. 5th Dist. Stark County 2011); State v. McDaniel, 2011-Ohio-6326, 2011 WL 6153697 (Ohio Ct. App. 2d Dist. Montgomery County 2011); State v. Arnold, 2014-Ohio-1134, 2014 WL 1339806 (Ohio Ct. App. 3d Dist. Seneca County 2014), judgment aff'd, 147 Ohio St. 3d 138, 2016-Ohio-1595, 62 N.E.3d 153 (2016); State v. Goshade, 2013-Ohio-4457, 2013 WL 5577906 (Ohio Ct. App. 1st Dist. Hamilton County 2013); State v. Doyle, 2014-Ohio-285, 2014 WL 313139 (Ohio Ct. App. 5th Dist. Fairfield County 2014); State v. McClain, 2014-Ohio-93, 2014 WL 117962 (Ohio Ct. App. 10th Dist. Franklin County 2014); State v. Canada, 2015-Ohio-2167, 2015 WL 3540402 (Ohio Ct. App. 10th Dist. Franklin County 2015); State v. Durdin, 2014-Ohio-5759, 2014 WL 7462990 (Ohio Ct. App. 10th Dist. Franklin County 2014); Cleveland v. Williams, 2015-Ohio-1739, 2015 WL 2165564 (Ohio Ct. App. 8th Dist. Cuyahoga County 2015); Toledo v. Jenkins, 2015-Ohio-1270, 2015 WL 1510849 (Ohio Ct. App. 6th Dist. Lucas County 2015); Cleveland v. Amoroso, 2015-Ohio-95, 2015 WL 178418 (Ohio Ct. App. 8th Dist. Cuyahoga County 2015); State v. Norris, 2015-Ohio-624, 2015 WL 753346 (Ohio Ct. App. 2d Dist. Montgomery County 2015); State v. Martin, 2016-Ohio-225, 57 N.E.3d 411 (Ohio Ct. App. 5th Dist. Tuscarawas County 2016); State v. Kerr, 2016-Ohio-965, 2016 WL 936844 (Ohio Ct. App. 2d Dist. Montgomery County 2016); okState v. Knecht, 2015-Ohio-4316, 2015 WL 6125747 (Ohio Ct. App. 12th Dist. Warren County 2015), appeal not allowed, 144 Ohio St. 3d 1507, 2016-Ohio-652, 45 N.E.3d 1051 (2016); Toledo v. Green, 2015-Ohio-1864, 33 N.E.3d 581 (Ohio Ct. App. 6th Dist. Lucas County 2015); okState v. Arnold, 147 Ohio St. 3d 138, 2016-Ohio-1595, 62 N.E.3d 153 (2016); okCleveland v. Merritt, 2016-Ohio-4693, 69 N.E.3d 102 (Ohio Ct. App. 8th Dist. Cuyahoga County 2016), appeal not allowed, 147 Ohio St. 3d 1506, 2017-Ohio-261, 67 N.E.3d 824 (2017); State v. Remy, 2018-Ohio-2857, 2018 WL 3493129 (Ohio Ct. App. 2d Dist. Clark County 2018) (has recent discussion of Clark and other confrontation law cases in appeal from Domestic Violence conviction).

[2]Crawford v. Washington, 541 U.S. 36, 124 S. Ct. 1354, 158 L. Ed. 2d 177, 63 Fed. R. Evid. Serv. 1077 (2004); State v. Stahl, 111 Ohio St. 3d 186, 2006-Ohio-5482, 855 N.E.2d 834 (2006); State v. Peeples, 2009-Ohio-1198, 2009 WL 737922 (Ohio Ct. App. 7th Dist. Mahoning County 2009); Toledo v. Sailes, 180 Ohio App. 3d 56, 2008-Ohio-6400, 904 N.E.2d 543 (6th Dist. Lucas County 2008); State v. Rufus, 2008-Ohio-5478, 2008 WL 4681392 (Ohio Ct. App. 8th Dist. Cuyahoga County 2008);

bar to statements that are testimonial, absent the unavailability of the declarant and a prior opportunity to cross examine.[3] Notwithstanding any reliability determination under the Rules of Evidence, the Sixth Amendment's Confrontation Clause requires independent safeguards on the use of out-of-court testimony.[4] The admission of statements deemed reliable solely by a judge is fundamentally at odds with the right of confrontation. In other words, a statement may be barred by the Confrontation Clause despite its admissibility under the Rules of Evidence.[5]

Although the Supreme Court did not define what it meant by testimonial hearsay, it did offer some guidance in that respect. The term "testimonial" includes any statement that a declarant would rea-

---

State v. Moorer, 2009-Ohio-1494, 2009 WL 818945 (Ohio Ct. App. 9th Dist. Summit County 2009); State v. Butts, 2012-Ohio-571, 2012 WL 474030 (Ohio Ct. App. 4th Dist. Hocking County 2012); State v. Hall, 2012-Ohio-266, 2012 WL 253317 (Ohio Ct. App. 8th Dist. Cuyahoga County 2012); State v. Beauford, 2011-Ohio-5379, 2011 WL 4973731 (Ohio Ct. App. 5th Dist. Richland County 2011); State v. Canada, 2015-Ohio-2167, 2015 WL 3540402 (Ohio Ct. App. 10th Dist. Franklin County 2015); State v. Durdin, 2014-Ohio-5759, 2014 WL 7462990 (Ohio Ct. App. 10th Dist. Franklin County 2014); Cleveland v. Williams, 2015-Ohio-1739, 2015 WL 2165564 (Ohio Ct. App. 8th Dist. Cuyahoga County 2015); Toledo v. Jenkins, 2015-Ohio-1270, 2015 WL 1510849 (Ohio Ct. App. 6th Dist. Lucas County 2015); Toledo v. Green, 2015-Ohio-1864, 33 N.E.3d 581 (Ohio Ct. App. 6th Dist. Lucas County 2015); Cleveland v. Amoroso, 2015-Ohio-95, 2015 WL 178418 (Ohio Ct. App. 8th Dist. Cuyahoga County 2015); State v. Norris, 2015-Ohio-624, 2015 WL 753346 (Ohio Ct. App. 2d Dist. Montgomery County 2015).

[3]Crawford v. Washington, 541 U.S. 36, 124 S. Ct. 1354, 158 L. Ed. 2d 177, 63 Fed. R. Evid. Serv. 1077 (2004); State v. Stahl, 111 Ohio St. 3d 186, 2006-Ohio-5482, 855 N.E.2d 834 (2006); State v. Peeples, 2009-Ohio-1198, 2009 WL 737922 (Ohio Ct. App. 7th Dist. Mahoning County 2009); Toledo v. Sailes, 180 Ohio App. 3d 56, 2008-Ohio-6400, 904 N.E.2d 543 (6th Dist. Lucas County 2008); State v. Rufus, 2008-Ohio-5478, 2008 WL 4681392 (Ohio Ct. App. 8th Dist. Cuyahoga County 2008); State v. Moorer, 2009-Ohio-1494, 2009 WL 818945 (Ohio Ct. App. 9th Dist. Summit County 2009); State v. Canada, 2015-Ohio-2167, 2015 WL 3540402 (Ohio Ct. App. 10th Dist. Franklin County 2015); State v. Durdin, 2014-Ohio-5759, 2014 WL 7462990 (Ohio Ct. App. 10th Dist. Franklin County 2014); Cleveland v. Williams, 2015-Ohio-1739, 2015 WL 2165564 (Ohio Ct. App. 8th Dist. Cuyahoga County 2015); Toledo v. Jenkins, 2015-Ohio-1270, 2015 WL 1510849 (Ohio Ct. App. 6th Dist. Lucas County 2015); Toledo v. Green, 2015-Ohio-1864, 33 N.E.3d 581 (Ohio Ct. App. 6th Dist. Lucas County 2015); Cleveland v. Amoroso, 2015-Ohio-95, 2015 WL 178418 (Ohio Ct. App. 8th Dist. Cuyahoga County 2015); State v. Norris, 2015-Ohio-624, 2015 WL 753346 (Ohio Ct. App. 2d Dist. Montgomery County 2015).

[4]Crawford v. Washington, 541 U.S. 36, 124 S. Ct. 1354, 158 L. Ed. 2d 177, 63 Fed. R. Evid. Serv. 1077 (2004); State v. Stahl, 111 Ohio St. 3d 186, 2006-Ohio-5482, 855 N.E.2d 834 (2006); State v. Peeples, 2009-Ohio-1198, 2009 WL 737922 (Ohio Ct. App. 7th Dist. Mahoning County 2009); Toledo v. Sailes, 180 Ohio App. 3d 56, 2008-Ohio-6400, 904 N.E.2d 543 (6th Dist. Lucas County 2008); State v. Rufus, 2008-Ohio-5478, 2008 WL 4681392 (Ohio Ct. App. 8th Dist. Cuyahoga County 2008); State v. Moorer, 2009-Ohio-1494, 2009 WL 818945 (Ohio Ct. App. 9th Dist. Summit County 2009).

[5]Crawford v. Washington, 541 U.S. 36, 124 S. Ct. 1354, 158 L. Ed. 2d 177, 63 Fed. R. Evid. Serv. 1077 (2004); State v. Stahl, 111 Ohio St. 3d 186, 2006-Ohio-5482, 855 N.E.2d 834 (2006); State v. Peeples, 2009-Ohio-1198, 2009 WL 737922 (Ohio Ct. App. 7th Dist. Mahoning County 2009); Toledo v. Sailes, 180 Ohio App. 3d 56, 2008-Ohio-6400, 904 N.E.2d 543 (6th Dist. Lucas County 2008); State v. Rufus, 2008-Ohio-5478, 2008 WL 4681392 (Ohio Ct. App. 8th Dist. Cuyahoga County 2008); State v. Moorer, 2009-Ohio-1494, 2009 WL 818945 (Ohio Ct. App. 9th Dist. Summit County 2009).

sonably expect to be used for purposes of prosecution.[6] It noted that "whatever else the term "testimonial" covers, it applies at a minimum to police interrogations"[7] Many statements made to police during the course of their investigation of a suspected crime fall into this broad category.[8]

More recently, the United States Supreme Court offered further guidance on the distinction between testimonial and nontestimonial hearsay.[9] With respect to statements made to the police or their agents during questioning at the scene, the Court determined that such state-

[6]Crawford v. Washington, 541 U.S. 36, 124 S. Ct. 1354, 158 L. Ed. 2d 177, 63 Fed. R. Evid. Serv. 1077 (2004); State v. Stahl, 111 Ohio St. 3d 186, 2006-Ohio-5482, 855 N.E.2d 834 (2006); State v. Peeples, 2009-Ohio-1198, 2009 WL 737922 (Ohio Ct. App. 7th Dist. Mahoning County 2009); Toledo v. Sailes, 180 Ohio App. 3d 56, 2008-Ohio-6400, 904 N.E.2d 543 (6th Dist. Lucas County 2008); State v. Rufus, 2008-Ohio-5478, 2008 WL 4681392 (Ohio Ct. App. 8th Dist. Cuyahoga County 2008); State v. Moorer, 2009-Ohio-1494, 2009 WL 818945 (Ohio Ct. App. 9th Dist. Summit County 2009).

[7]Crawford v. Washington, 541 U.S. 36, 124 S. Ct. 1354, 158 L. Ed. 2d 177, 63 Fed. R. Evid. Serv. 1077 (2004); State v. Stahl, 111 Ohio St. 3d 186, 2006-Ohio-5482, 855 N.E.2d 834 (2006); State v. Peeples, 2009-Ohio-1198, 2009 WL 737922 (Ohio Ct. App. 7th Dist. Mahoning County 2009); Toledo v. Sailes, 180 Ohio App. 3d 56, 2008-Ohio-6400, 904 N.E.2d 543 (6th Dist. Lucas County 2008); State v. Rufus, 2008-Ohio-5478, 2008 WL 4681392 (Ohio Ct. App. 8th Dist. Cuyahoga County 2008); State v. Moorer, 2009-Ohio-1494, 2009 WL 818945 (Ohio Ct. App. 9th Dist. Summit County 2009).

[8]Crawford v. Washington, 541 U.S. 36, 124 S. Ct. 1354, 158 L. Ed. 2d 177, 63 Fed. R. Evid. Serv. 1077 (2004); State v. Stahl, 111 Ohio St. 3d 186, 2006-Ohio-5482, 855 N.E.2d 834 (2006); State v. Peeples, 2009-Ohio-1198, 2009 WL 737922 (Ohio Ct. App. 7th Dist. Mahoning County 2009); Toledo v. Sailes, 180 Ohio App. 3d 56, 2008-Ohio-6400, 904 N.E.2d 543 (6th Dist. Lucas County 2008); State v. Rufus, 2008-Ohio-5478, 2008 WL 4681392 (Ohio Ct. App. 8th Dist. Cuyahoga County 2008); State v. Moorer, 2009-Ohio-1494, 2009 WL 818945 (Ohio Ct. App. 9th Dist. Summit County 2009).

[9]Davis v. Washington, 547 U.S. 813, 126 S. Ct. 2266, 165 L. Ed. 2d 224, 70 Fed. R. Evid. Serv. 472, 30 A.L.R.6th 599 (2006); State v. Siler, 116 Ohio St. 3d 39, 2007-Ohio-5637, 876 N.E.2d 534 (2007); State v. Stahl, 111 Ohio St. 3d 186, 2006-Ohio-5482, 855 N.E.2d 834 (2006); State v. Florence, 2005-Ohio-4508, 2005 WL 2083079 (Ohio Ct. App. 2d Dist. Montgomery County 2005); State v. Riley, 2007-Ohio-879, 2007 WL 625898 (Ohio Ct. App. 6th Dist. Wood County 2007); State v. Davis, 2007-Ohio-3419, 2007 WL 1934364 (Ohio Ct. App. 8th Dist. Cuyahoga County 2007); State v. Rose, 2008-Ohio-1263, 2008 WL 740563 (Ohio Ct. App. 8th Dist. Cuyahoga County 2008); State v. Taylor, 2008-Ohio-1462, 2008 WL 834437 (Ohio Ct. App. 9th Dist. Lorain County 2008); Cleveland v. Colon, 2007-Ohio-269, 2007 WL 179082 (Ohio Ct. App. 8th Dist. Cuyahoga County 2007); Toledo v. Loggins, 2007-Ohio-5887, 2007 WL 3227385 (Ohio Ct. App. 6th Dist. Lucas County 2007). See § 5:5, footnote 2. See also Text §§ 5:14 to 5:21, Case preparation—Hearsay exceptions; Toledo v. Sailes, 180 Ohio App. 3d 56, 2008-Ohio-6400, 904 N.E.2d 543 (6th Dist. Lucas County 2008); State v. Rufus, 2008-Ohio-5478, 2008 WL 4681392 (Ohio Ct. App. 8th Dist. Cuyahoga County 2008); State v. Cotton, 2010-Ohio-804, 2010 WL 746756 (Ohio Ct. App. 6th Dist. Lucas County 2010); State v. Peeples, 2009-Ohio-1198, 2009 WL 737922 (Ohio Ct. App. 7th Dist. Mahoning County 2009); State v. Moorer, 2009-Ohio-1494, 2009 WL 818945 (Ohio Ct. App. 9th Dist. Summit County 2009); State v. Swaby, 2009-Ohio-3690, 2009 WL 2244693 (Ohio Ct. App. 9th Dist. Summit County 2009); State v. Snider, 2012-Ohio-2183, 2012 WL 1744657 (Ohio Ct. App. 5th Dist. Licking County 2012); State v. Butts, 2012-Ohio-571, 2012 WL 474030 (Ohio Ct. App. 4th Dist. Hocking County 2012); State v. Hall, 2012-Ohio-266, 2012 WL 253317 (Ohio Ct. App. 8th Dist. Cuyahoga County 2012); State v. Beauford, 2011-Ohio-5379, 2011 WL 4973731 (Ohio Ct. App. 5th Dist. Richland County 2011); State v. Parks, 2011-Ohio-3037, 2011 WL 2464198 (Ohio Ct. App. 5th Dist. Stark County 2011); State v. Eicholtz,

ments are testimonial unless made in order to address an immediate emergency.[10] Statements made in a 911 call are a little more complicated. Although the initial request for emergency assistance in a 911 call may be non-testimonial, it may evolve into testimonial statements after the operator has gained the information necessary to address the exigency of the moment, and begins to gather intelligence that will assist the prosecution in obtaining the conviction of a partic-

---

2013-Ohio-302, 2013 WL 425820 (Ohio Ct. App. 2d Dist. Clark County 2013); State v. Hood, 135 Ohio St. 3d 137, 2012-Ohio-6208, 984 N.E.2d 1057 (2012); State v. Diggle, 2012-Ohio-1583, 2012 WL 1187970 (Ohio Ct. App. 3d Dist. Auglaize County 2012); State v. Jones, 135 Ohio St. 3d 10, 2012-Ohio-5677, 984 N.E.2d 948 (2012); State v. McClain, 2014-Ohio-93, 2014 WL 117962 (Ohio Ct. App. 10th Dist. Franklin County 2014); State v. Goshade, 2013-Ohio-4457, 2013 WL 5577906 (Ohio Ct. App. 1st Dist. Hamilton County 2013); State v. Renner, 2013-Ohio-5463, 2013 WL 6576714 (Ohio Ct. App. 2d Dist. Montgomery County 2013); State v. Canada, 2015-Ohio-2167, 2015 WL 3540402 (Ohio Ct. App. 10th Dist. Franklin County 2015); State v. Durdin, 2014-Ohio-5759, 2014 WL 7462990 (Ohio Ct. App. 10th Dist. Franklin County 2014); Cleveland v. Williams, 2015-Ohio-1739, 2015 WL 2165564 (Ohio Ct. App. 8th Dist. Cuyahoga County 2015); Toledo v. Jenkins, 2015-Ohio-1270, 2015 WL 1510849 (Ohio Ct. App. 6th Dist. Lucas County 2015); Toledo v. Green, 2015-Ohio-1864, 33 N.E.3d 581 (Ohio Ct. App. 6th Dist. Lucas County 2015); Cleveland v. Amoroso, 2015-Ohio-95, 2015 WL 178418 (Ohio Ct. App. 8th Dist. Cuyahoga County 2015); State v. Norris, 2015-Ohio-624, 2015 WL 753346 (Ohio Ct. App. 2d Dist. Montgomery County 2015); State v. Martin, 2016-Ohio-225, 57 N.E.3d 411 (Ohio Ct. App. 5th Dist. Tuscarawas County 2016); State v. Kerr, 2016-Ohio-965, 2016 WL 936844 (Ohio Ct. App. 2d Dist. Montgomery County 2016); okState v. Knecht, 2015-Ohio-4316, 2015 WL 6125747 (Ohio Ct. App. 12th Dist. Warren County 2015), appeal not allowed, 144 Ohio St. 3d 1507, 2016-Ohio-652, 45 N.E.3d 1051 (2016); State v. Arnold, 147 Ohio St. 3d 138, 2016-Ohio-1595, 62 N.E.3d 153 (2016); Cleveland v. Merritt, 2016-Ohio-4693, 69 N.E.3d 102 (Ohio Ct. App. 8th Dist. Cuyahoga County 2016), appeal not allowed, 147 Ohio St. 3d 1506, 2017-Ohio-261, 67 N.E.3d 824 (2017); Cleveland Hts. v. Cohen, 2015-Ohio-1636, 31 N.E.3d 695 (Ohio Ct. App. 8th Dist. Cuyahoga County 2015); State v. Remy, 2018-Ohio-2857, 2018 WL 3493129 (Ohio Ct. App. 2d Dist. Clark County 2018) (has recent discussion of Clark and other confrontation law cases in appeal from Domestic Violence conviction).

[10]Davis v. Washington, 547 U.S. 813, 126 S. Ct. 2266, 165 L. Ed. 2d 224, 70 Fed. R. Evid. Serv. 472, 30 A.L.R.6th 599 (2006); State v. Stahl, 111 Ohio St. 3d 186, 2006-Ohio-5482, 855 N.E.2d 834 (2006); State v. Florence, 2005-Ohio-4508, 2005 WL 2083079 (Ohio Ct. App. 2d Dist. Montgomery County 2005); State v. Riley, 2007-Ohio-879, 2007 WL 625898 (Ohio Ct. App. 6th Dist. Wood County 2007); State v. Davis, 2007-Ohio-3419, 2007 WL 1934364 (Ohio Ct. App. 8th Dist. Cuyahoga County 2007); State v. Rose, 2008-Ohio-1263, 2008 WL 740563 (Ohio Ct. App. 8th Dist. Cuyahoga County 2008); State v. Taylor, 2008-Ohio-1462, 2008 WL 834437 (Ohio Ct. App. 9th Dist. Lorain County 2008); Cleveland v. Colon, 2007-Ohio-269, 2007 WL 179082 (Ohio Ct. App. 8th Dist. Cuyahoga County 2007); Toledo v. Loggins, 2007-Ohio-5887, 2007 WL 3227385 (Ohio Ct. App. 6th Dist. Lucas County 2007). See § 5:5, footnote 2. See also Text §§ 5:14 to 5:21, Case preparation—Hearsay exceptions; Toledo v. Sailes, 180 Ohio App. 3d 56, 2008-Ohio-6400, 904 N.E.2d 543 (6th Dist. Lucas County 2008); State v. Rufus, 2008-Ohio-5478, 2008 WL 4681392 (Ohio Ct. App. 8th Dist. Cuyahoga County 2008); State v. Cotton, 2010-Ohio-804, 2010 WL 746756 (Ohio Ct. App. 6th Dist. Lucas County 2010); State v. Peeples, 2009-Ohio-1198, 2009 WL 737922 (Ohio Ct. App. 7th Dist. Mahoning County 2009); State v. Moorer, 2009-Ohio-1494, 2009 WL 818945 (Ohio Ct. App. 9th Dist. Summit County 2009); Colon v. Taskey, 2009 WL 1616112 (N.D. Ohio 2009); State v. Williams, 2009-Ohio-6967, 2009 WL 5174155 (Ohio Ct. App. 6th Dist. Lucas County 2009); U.S. v. Arnold, 486 F.3d 177, 73 Fed. R. Evid. Serv. 583 (6th Cir. 2007); State v. Swaby, 2009-Ohio-3690, 2009 WL 2244693 (Ohio Ct. App. 9th Dist. Summit County 2009); State v. Snider, 2012-Ohio-2183, 2012 WL 1744657 (Ohio Ct. App. 5th Dist. Licking County 2012).

ular suspect.[11] It is for these reasons that it is vitally important for defense counsel to closely scrutinize every witness' proffered out-of-court statements through the lens of the Confrontation Clause.

Q & A: The prosecution attempts to admit the tape of a "911" call into evidence at the defendant's domestic violence trial. The call was placed at the time of the incident. On the call the caller tells the operator that the defendant is beating the alleged victim senseless, and goes on to say, "You better get here quick! She's a bloody mess! I think he's trying to kill her! They're leaving in his car! The license number is AQ 2000! Hurry! The witness failed to appear at trial. The defense objects to the statement on the grounds that it is testimonial hearsay and violates her client's Sixth Amendment right to confrontation. Should the objection be sustained?

No. Statements made in the course of an ongoing emergency are admissible as evidence during a trial resulting from events forming the foundation of the emergency call. The statements in question here were not made for the primary purpose of being used at a trial of the accused. Instead, they were made primarily for emergency assistance and hence are not testimonial in nature.[12]

Q & A: Immediately following the violent event that resulted in the defendant's arrest and trial on charges of domestic violence, the hysterical alleged victim told her mother, in detail, exactly what the defendant did to her. The victim failed to appear at trial and, following several failed attempts to secure her attendance the prosecutor now calls her mother to testify as to what her daughter told her about the event. The defense objects, citing the defendant's Sixth Amendment right to confrontation. Should the objection be sustained?

---

[11] Davis v. Washington, 547 U.S. 813, 126 S. Ct. 2266, 165 L. Ed. 2d 224, 70 Fed. R. Evid. Serv. 472, 30 A.L.R.6th 599 (2006); State v. Canada, 2015-Ohio-2167, 2015 WL 3540402 (Ohio Ct. App. 10th Dist. Franklin County 2015); State v. Durdin, 2014-Ohio-5759, 2014 WL 7462990 (Ohio Ct. App. 10th Dist. Franklin County 2014); Cleveland v. Williams, 2015-Ohio-1739, 2015 WL 2165564 (Ohio Ct. App. 8th Dist. Cuyahoga County 2015); Toledo v. Jenkins, 2015-Ohio-1270, 2015 WL 1510849 (Ohio Ct. App. 6th Dist. Lucas County 2015); Toledo v. Green, 2015-Ohio-1864, 33 N.E.3d 581 (Ohio Ct. App. 6th Dist. Lucas County 2015); Cleveland v. Amoroso, 2015-Ohio-95, 2015 WL 178418 (Ohio Ct. App. 8th Dist. Cuyahoga County 2015); State v. Norris, 2015-Ohio-624, 2015 WL 753346 (Ohio Ct. App. 2d Dist. Montgomery County 2015).

[12] Davis v. Washington, 547 U.S. 813, 126 S. Ct. 2266, 165 L. Ed. 2d 224, 70 Fed. R. Evid. Serv. 472, 30 A.L.R.6th 599 (2006); State v. McKenzie, 2006-Ohio-5725, 2006 WL 3095671 (Ohio Ct. App. 8th Dist. Cuyahoga County 2006); State v. Richardson, 2010-Ohio-471, 2010 WL 497343 (Ohio Ct. App. 6th Dist. Lucas County 2010); U.S. v. Arnold, 486 F.3d 177, 73 Fed. R. Evid. Serv. 583 (6th Cir. 2007); State v. Swaby, 2009-Ohio-3690, 2009 WL 2244693 (Ohio Ct. App. 9th Dist. Summit County 2009); State v. Snider, 2012-Ohio-2183, 2012 WL 1744657 (Ohio Ct. App. 5th Dist. Licking County 2012); State v. Canada, 2015-Ohio-2167, 2015 WL 3540402 (Ohio Ct. App. 10th Dist. Franklin County 2015); State v. Durdin, 2014-Ohio-5759, 2014 WL 7462990 (Ohio Ct. App. 10th Dist. Franklin County 2014); Cleveland v. Williams, 2015-Ohio-1739, 2015 WL 2165564 (Ohio Ct. App. 8th Dist. Cuyahoga County 2015); Toledo v. Jenkins, 2015-Ohio-1270, 2015 WL 1510849 (Ohio Ct. App. 6th Dist. Lucas County 2015); Toledo v. Green, 2015-Ohio-1864, 33 N.E.3d 581 (Ohio Ct. App. 6th Dist. Lucas County 2015); Cleveland v. Amoroso, 2015-Ohio-95, 2015 WL 178418 (Ohio Ct. App. 8th Dist. Cuyahoga County 2015); State v. Norris, 2015-Ohio-624, 2015 WL 753346 (Ohio Ct. App. 2d Dist. Montgomery County 2015).

No. An accuser who makes a formal statement to government officers bears testimony in a sense that a person who makes a casual remark to an acquaintance does not.[13] The U.S. Supreme Court's decision in *Crawford v. Washington*[14] includes three general formulations of the core class of testimonial statements. In the first, testimonial statements consist of ex parte in-court testimony or its functional equivalent-that is, material such as affidavits, custodial examinations, prior testimony that the defendant was unable to cross-examine or similar pretrial statements that declarants would reasonably expect to be used prosecutorially. The second formulation described testimonial statements as consisting of extrajudicial statements contained in formalized testimonial materials, such as affidavits, depositions, prior testimony, or confessions. Finally, the third explained that testimonial statements are those "made under circumstances which would lead an objective witness reasonably to believe that the statement would be available for use at a later trial."[15]

The victim's statements to her mother do not qualify as testimonial. They were not ex-parte in-court testimony or its equivalent; were not contained in formalized documents such as affidavits, depositions, or prior testimony transcripts; and were not made as part of a confession resulting from custodial examination. Rather, the statements were made during a private conversation with her mom. In short, she did not make the statements under circumstances in which an objective person would "reasonably believe that the statement would be available for use at a later trial.[16] Therefore, because her statements were nontestimonial, the question of their admission is outside of *Crawford*'s scope and the objection should be denied.

Q & A: An officer was flagged down by the victim, who ran

---

[13]U.S. v. Reyes, 362 F.3d 536, 540 n.4, 63 Fed. R. Evid. Serv. 1278 (8th Cir. 2004).

[14]Crawford v. Washington, 541 U.S. 36, 124 S. Ct. 1354, 158 L. Ed. 2d 177, 63 Fed. R. Evid. Serv. 1077 (2004); State v. Peeples, 2009-Ohio-1198, 2009 WL 737922 (Ohio Ct. App. 7th Dist. Mahoning County 2009); Toledo v. Sailes, 180 Ohio App. 3d 56, 2008-Ohio-6400, 904 N.E.2d 543 (6th Dist. Lucas County 2008); State v. Rufus, 2008-Ohio-5478, 2008 WL 4681392 (Ohio Ct. App. 8th Dist. Cuyahoga County 2008); State v. Moorer, 2009-Ohio-1494, 2009 WL 818945 (Ohio Ct. App. 9th Dist. Summit County 2009); State v. Canada, 2015-Ohio-2167, 2015 WL 3540402 (Ohio Ct. App. 10th Dist. Franklin County 2015); State v. Durdin, 2014-Ohio-5759, 2014 WL 7462990 (Ohio Ct. App. 10th Dist. Franklin County 2014); Cleveland v. Williams, 2015-Ohio-1739, 2015 WL 2165564 (Ohio Ct. App. 8th Dist. Cuyahoga County 2015); Toledo v. Jenkins, 2015-Ohio-1270, 2015 WL 1510849 (Ohio Ct. App. 6th Dist. Lucas County 2015); Toledo v. Green, 2015-Ohio-1864, 33 N.E.3d 581 (Ohio Ct. App. 6th Dist. Lucas County 2015); Cleveland v. Amoroso, 2015-Ohio-95, 2015 WL 178418 (Ohio Ct. App. 8th Dist. Cuyahoga County 2015); State v. Norris, 2015-Ohio-624, 2015 WL 753346 (Ohio Ct. App. 2d Dist. Montgomery County 2015).

[15]Horton v. Allen, 370 F.3d 75 (1st Cir. 2004), citing Crawford v. Washington, 541 U.S. 36, 124 S. Ct. 1354, 158 L. Ed. 2d 177, 63 Fed. R. Evid. Serv. 1077 (2004); State v. Peeples, 2009-Ohio-1198, 2009 WL 737922 (Ohio Ct. App. 7th Dist. Mahoning County 2009).

[16]Crawford v. Washington, 541 U.S. 36, 124 S. Ct. 1354, 158 L. Ed. 2d 177, 63 Fed. R. Evid. Serv. 1077 (2004); Horton v. Allen, 370 F.3d 75 (1st Cir. 2004); State v. Peeples, 2009-Ohio-1198, 2009 WL 737922 (Ohio Ct. App. 7th Dist. Mahoning County 2009); Toledo v. Sailes, 180 Ohio App. 3d 56, 2008-Ohio-6400, 904 N.E.2d 543 (6th Dist. Lucas County 2008); State v. Rufus, 2008-Ohio-5478, 2008 WL 4681392 (Ohio Ct. App. 8th Dist. Cuyahoga County 2008); State v. Moorer, 2009-Ohio-1494, 2009 WL 818945 (Ohio Ct. App. 9th Dist. Summit County 2009).

out of an apartment building pointing at the defendant and screaming, "That's him, that's him. He's the one that just hit me."

Thereafter, the officer approached the defendant, arrested him and placed him in the back of the police car. The officer noted the victim had a two-inch "swollen knot right in the middle of her forehead." While the defendant remained in the police car, the officer took the victim back into the building and questioned her about what happened. She gave a detailed statement outlining the defendant's violence against her. The victim failed to attend the defendant's trial, despite the prosecutor's best efforts. The prosecutor wishes to call the officer to testify about the statements that the victim made at the time of the event. The defense objects, citing the *Crawford v. Washington*[17] and the U.S. Constitution's Confrontation Clause. Should the objection be sustained?

Yes, and no. The victim's statements to the arresting officer were in two parts. The first part occurred when she ran out into the street, pointing toward the defendant, and yelling at the officer, "That's him, that's him. He's the one that just hit me." The second part occurred after the officer secured defendant in the police car and questioned the victim about what happened, taking details of the alleged attack.

When the officer first saw the victim, she was running out of the apartment and calling for police assistance. She did this for the purpose of having the defendant apprehended, not for purposes of a later prosecution. These facts objectively indicate that the victim's primary purpose in calling was to alert the officer to an ongoing emergency.

However, with the defendant safely ensconced in the police car, the ongoing emergency ended. Any further remarks by the victim were obviously intended for prosecution, not just apprehension or the cessation of the emergency. Undoubtedly, this statement was intended for prosecution and thus testimonial in nature.

The victim's first statement meets the criteria for excited utterance, and may be admitted because it "falls within a firmly rooted hearsay exception.[18] Once the officer secured the defendant and removed any threat of harm to the victim, he then questioned her, which permitted her to reflect on the alleged assault. At this point, the victim's statements became testimonial because the officer admittedly engaged in an investigation to determine whether a crime had been committed. Given the victim's absence from trial, the Confrontation Clause

[17]Crawford v. Washington, 541 U.S. 36, 124 S. Ct. 1354, 158 L. Ed. 2d 177, 63 Fed. R. Evid. Serv. 1077 (2004).

[18]Ohio v. Roberts, 448 U.S. 56, 100 S. Ct. 2531, 65 L. Ed. 2d 597, 7 Fed. R. Evid. Serv. 1 (1980) (abrogated by, Crawford v. Washington, 541 U.S. 36, 124 S. Ct. 1354, 158 L. Ed. 2d 177, 63 Fed. R. Evid. Serv. 1077 (2004)). See White v. Illinois, 502 U.S. 346, 356-57, 112 S. Ct. 736, 116 L. Ed. 2d 848, 33 Fed. R. Evid. Serv. 881 (1992); State v. Martin, 2016-Ohio-225, 57 N.E.3d 411 (Ohio Ct. App. 5th Dist. Tuscarawas County 2016); State v. Arnold, 147 Ohio St. 3d 138, 2016-Ohio-1595, 62 N.E.3d 153 (2016).

prohibits the admission of the latter statements made to the officer into evidence at the defendant's trial.[19]

Q & A: I'm prosecuting a defendant for domestic violence. I'm planning to offer a 911 recording of the victim's call to police dispatch. The victim will authenticate the call at the trial. Defense counsel is objecting to the statements as impermissible testimonial hearsay, because he can't cross-examine the recording. Should the court allow the recording over counsel's objection?

Yes. The victim's statements arguably were non-testimonial, since they were to ensure police were coming to the scene of an emergency to aid the victim. Even if the victim's statements were testimonial, the Confrontation Clause is not violated because the victim will testify at trial.[20]

Q & A: How does a court determine when the primary purpose for a law enforcement officer's interrogation of a witness transitions, making further statements obtained testimonial rather than non-testimonial?

The U.S. Supreme Court has held that, "To make the "primary purpose" determination, the Court must objectively evaluate the circumstances in which the encounter between the individual and the police occurs and the parties' statements and actions.[21]

(1) The primary purpose inquiry is objective. The circumstances in which an encounter occurs— e.g., at or near a crime scene versus at a police station, during an ongoing emergency or afterwards—are clearly matters of objective fact. And the relevant inquiry into the parties' statements and actions is not the subjective or actual purpose of the particular parties, but the purpose that reasonable participants would have had, as

[19]State v. McKenzie, 2006-Ohio-5725, 2006 WL 3095671 (Ohio Ct. App. 8th Dist. Cuyahoga County 2006).

[20]State v. Marrero, 2011-Ohio-1390, 2011 WL 1049294 (Ohio Ct. App. 10th Dist. Franklin County 2011); State v. McClain, 2014-Ohio-93, 2014 WL 117962 (Ohio Ct. App. 10th Dist. Franklin County 2014); State v. Goshade, 2013-Ohio-4457, 2013 WL 5577906 (Ohio Ct. App. 1st Dist. Hamilton County 2013).

[21]Michigan v. Bryant, 562 U.S. 344, 131 S. Ct. 1143, 179 L. Ed. 2d 93, 84 Fed. R. Evid. Serv. 1033 (2011); State v. Hall, 2012-Ohio-266, 2012 WL 253317 (Ohio Ct. App. 8th Dist. Cuyahoga County 2012); State v. Parks, 2011-Ohio-3037, 2011 WL 2464198 (Ohio Ct. App. 5th Dist. Stark County 2011); State v. Diggle, 2012-Ohio-1583, 2012 WL 1187970 (Ohio Ct. App. 3d Dist. Auglaize County 2012); State v. Jones, 135 Ohio St. 3d 10, 2012-Ohio-5677, 984 N.E.2d 948 (2012); State v. Martin, 2016-Ohio-225, 57 N.E.3d 411 (Ohio Ct. App. 5th Dist. Tuscarawas County 2016); State v. Knecht, 2015-Ohio-4316, 2015 WL 6125747 (Ohio Ct. App. 12th Dist. Warren County 2015), appeal not allowed, 144 Ohio St. 3d 1507, 2016-Ohio-652, 45 N.E.3d 1051 (2016); State v. Clark, 2016-Ohio-2825, 2016 WL 2586638 (Ohio Ct. App. 8th Dist. Cuyahoga County 2016), appeal not allowed, 147 Ohio St. 3d 1474, 2016-Ohio-8438, 65 N.E.3d 778 (2016); State v. Remy, 2018-Ohio-2857, 2018 WL 3493129 (Ohio Ct. App. 2d Dist. Clark County 2018) (has recent discussion of Clark and other confrontation law cases in appeal from Domestic Violence conviction); State v. Heard, 2017-Ohio-8796, 2017 WL 5988500 (Ohio Ct. App. 12th Dist. Warren County 2017) (has recent discussion of primary purpose citing Michigan v. Bryant, 562 U.S. 344, 131 S. Ct. 1143, 179 L. Ed. 2d 93, 84 Fed. R. Evid. Serv. 1033 (2011), in appeal from DV conviction).

ascertained from the parties' statements and actions and the circumstances in which the encounter occurred.[22]

(2) The existence of an "ongoing emergency" at the time of the encounter is among the most important circumstances informing the interrogation's "primary purpose."[23] An emergency focuses the participants not on "prov[ing] past events potentially relevant to later criminal prosecution,"[24] but on "end[ing] a threatening situation."[25] Whether an emergency exists and is ongoing is a highly context-dependent inquiry. An assessment of whether an emergency threatening the police and public is ongoing cannot narrowly focus on whether the threat to the first victim has been neutralized, because the threat to the first responders and public may continue. An emergency's duration and scope may depend in part on the type of weapon involved. A victim's medical condition is important to the primary purpose inquiry to the extent that it sheds light on the victim's ability to have any purpose at all in responding to police questions and on the likelihood that any such purpose would be a testimonial one. It also provides important context for first responders to judge the existence and magnitude of a continuing threat to the victim, themselves, and the public. This does not mean that an emergency lasts the entire time that a perpetrator is on the loose, but trial courts can determine in the first instance when an interrogation transitions from nontestimonial to testimonial. Finally, whether an ongoing emergency exists is simply one factor informing the ultimate inquiry regarding an interrogation's "primary purpose." Another is the encounter's informality. Formality suggests the absence of an emergency, but informality does not necessarily indicate the presence of an emergency or the lack of testimonial intent. The fact that questioning oc-

[22]Michigan v. Bryant, 562 U.S. 344, 131 S. Ct. 1143, 179 L. Ed. 2d 93, 84 Fed. R. Evid. Serv. 1033 (2011).

[23]See, e.g., Davis v. Washington, 547 U.S. 813, 828–830, 126 S. Ct. 2266, 165 L. Ed. 2d 224, 70 Fed. R. Evid. Serv. 472, 30 A.L.R.6th 599 (2006); State v. Canada, 2015-Ohio-2167, 2015 WL 3540402 (Ohio Ct. App. 10th Dist. Franklin County 2015); State v. Durdin, 2014-Ohio-5759, 2014 WL 7462990 (Ohio Ct. App. 10th Dist. Franklin County 2014); Cleveland v. Williams, 2015-Ohio-1739, 2015 WL 2165564 (Ohio Ct. App. 8th Dist. Cuyahoga County 2015); Toledo v. Jenkins, 2015-Ohio-1270, 2015 WL 1510849 (Ohio Ct. App. 6th Dist. Lucas County 2015); Toledo v. Green, 2015-Ohio-1864, 33 N.E.3d 581 (Ohio Ct. App. 6th Dist. Lucas County 2015); Cleveland v. Amoroso, 2015-Ohio-95, 2015 WL 178418 (Ohio Ct. App. 8th Dist. Cuyahoga County 2015); State v. Norris, 2015-Ohio-624, 2015 WL 753346 (Ohio Ct. App. 2d Dist. Montgomery County 2015).

[24]Davis v. Washington, 547 U.S. 813, at 822, 126 S. Ct. 2266, 165 L. Ed. 2d 224, 70 Fed. R. Evid. Serv. 472, 30 A.L.R.6th 599 (2006); State v. Canada, 2015-Ohio-2167, 2015 WL 3540402 (Ohio Ct. App. 10th Dist. Franklin County 2015); State v. Durdin, 2014-Ohio-5759, 2014 WL 7462990 (Ohio Ct. App. 10th Dist. Franklin County 2014); Cleveland v. Williams, 2015-Ohio-1739, 2015 WL 2165564 (Ohio Ct. App. 8th Dist. Cuyahoga County 2015); Toledo v. Jenkins, 2015-Ohio-1270, 2015 WL 1510849 (Ohio Ct. App. 6th Dist. Lucas County 2015); Toledo v. Green, 2015-Ohio-1864, 33 N.E.3d 581 (Ohio Ct. App. 6th Dist. Lucas County 2015); Cleveland v. Amoroso, 2015-Ohio-95, 2015 WL 178418 (Ohio Ct. App. 8th Dist. Cuyahoga County 2015); State v. Norris, 2015-Ohio-624, 2015 WL 753346 (Ohio Ct. App. 2d Dist. Montgomery County 2015).

[25]Davis v. Washington, 547 U.S. 813, at 832, 126 S. Ct. 2266, 165 L. Ed. 2d 224, 70 Fed. R. Evid. Serv. 472, 30 A.L.R.6th 599 (2006).

curred in an exposed, public area, before emergency medical services arrived, and in a disorganized fashion may—distinguish a case from one involving formal station-house interrogation.[26]

(3) The statements and actions of both the declarant and interrogators also provide objective evidence of the interrogation's primary purpose. Looking to the contents of both the questions and the answers ameliorates problems that could arise from looking solely to one participant, since both interrogators and declarants may have mixed motives. Police officers' dual responsibilities as both first responders and criminal investigators may lead them to act with different motives simultaneously or in quick succession. And during an ongoing emergency, victims may want the threat to end, but may not envision prosecution. Alternatively, a severely injured victim may have no purpose at all in answering questions. Taking into account such injuries does not make the inquiry subjective. The inquiry still focuses on the understanding and purpose of a reasonable victim in the actual victim's circumstances, which prominently include the victim's physical state. Objectively ascertaining the primary purpose of the interrogation by examining the statements and actions of all participants is also consistent with the U.S. Supreme Court's holdings.[27]

Q & A: The Lab technician who performed a crucial test is not available to present the results at trial. The defense objects to the certification of those results being presented by another technician from the same lab who took no part in the conduct of the test, even though he is otherwise qualified as an expert on the procedures conducted to produce the document. Should the objection be sustained?

Yes. The material contained in the report is both hearsay and testimonial. The Confrontation Clause of the Sixth Amendment to the U.S. Constitution does not permit the prosecution to introduce a forensic laboratory report containing a testimonial certification, made in order to prove a fact at a criminal trial, through the in-court testimony of an analyst who did not sign the certification or personally perform or observe the performance of the test reported in the certification. The accused's right is to be confronted with the analyst who made the certification, unless that analyst is unavailable at trial, and the accused had an opportunity, pretrial, to cross-examine that particular scientist.[28] Alternatively, an accused's right to confront the analyst who made the certification is not violated where the accused

[26]Michigan v. Bryant, 562 U.S. 344, 131 S. Ct. 1143, 179 L. Ed. 2d 93, 84 Fed. R. Evid. Serv. 1033 (2011).

[27]Michigan v. Bryant, 562 U.S. 344, 131 S. Ct. 1143, 1148, 179 L. Ed. 2d 93, 84 Fed. R. Evid. Serv. 1033 (2011), citing Davis v. Washington, 547 U.S. 813, 822–823, n.1, 126 S. Ct. 2266, 165 L. Ed. 2d 224, 70 Fed. R. Evid. Serv. 472, 30 A.L.R.6th 599 (2006).

[28]Bullcoming v. New Mexico, 564 U.S. 647, 131 S. Ct. 2705, 180 L. Ed. 2d 610 (2011); Melendez-Diaz v. Massachusetts, 557 U.S. 305, 129 S. Ct. 2527, 174 L. Ed. 2d 314 (2009). But see Williams v. Illinois, 567 U.S. 50, 132 S. Ct. 2221, 183 L. Ed. 2d 89, 83 A.L.R. Fed. 2d 649 (2012).

stipulates to the admissibility and content of non-testifying analyst's scientific report.[29]

Q & A: Can a DNA profile be entered into evidence and not face a successful Confrontation Clause challenge?

According to the U.S. Supreme Court the answer is "yes." The primary purpose of such reports, viewed objectively, is not to accuse a particular individual, or to create evidence for use at trial. Generally, those producing the profile have no possible way of knowing that the profile that they produce will turn out to inculpate anyone whose DNA profile is in a law enforcement database. Under such circumstances, there is no "prospect of fabrication" and no incentive to produce anything other than a scientifically sound and reliable profile.[30]

§ 7:23 Trial presentation—Self-defense

The domestic violence laws were passed to deal with a particular insidious form of interpersonal mayhem, i.e., battering behavior where the perpetrator attempts to use violence as a tool to enforce his or her will on an intimate partner or other members of the household. The definition of domestic violence contained in the state's domestic violence laws, however, implicate a much broader range of assaultive acts that take place between people who have interpersonal relationships.

The fact of the matter is that disagreements between people engaged in close relationships occur, and frequently turn violent. In some, if not many instances, in the course of defending oneself, injuries are inflicted on the original aggressor which may be more severe than those sustained by the party forced to mount a defense.

Self-defense requires that the defendant purposely have used force because of his or her belief of "imminent danger" of death or great bodily harm. As an affirmative defense, it is a justification for behavior which otherwise would be criminal.[1]

At best, defense counsel are often presented with facts that are ambiguous as to who was the primary aggressor and that easily give rise to reasonably doubt as to the guilt of the accused. These opportunities should be exploited.

§ 7:24 Trial presentation—The Battered Woman Syndrome

In some cases where self-defense is alleged as justification for the violent acts of an individual charged with domestic violence, expert

---

[29]State v. Keck, 137 Ohio St. 3d 550, 2013-Ohio-5160, 1 N.E.3d 403 (2013). See also State v. Dial, 2013-Ohio-3980, 998 N.E.2d 821 (Ohio Ct. App. 3d Dist. Allen County 2013); State v. Martynowski, 2017-Ohio-9299, 2017 WL 6722849 (Ohio Ct. App. 9th Dist. Lorain County 2017) (applies State v. Keck, 137 Ohio St. 3d 550, 2013-Ohio-5160, 1 N.E.3d 403 (2013), discussion of stipulation in appeal from Domestic Violence conviction).

[30]Williams v. Illinois, 567 U.S. 50, 132 S. Ct. 2221, 183 L. Ed. 2d 89, 83 A.L.R. Fed. 2d 649 (2012); Bullcoming v. New Mexico, 564 U.S. 647, 131 S. Ct. 2705, 180 L. Ed. 2d 610 (2011).

[Section 7:23]

[1]State v. Poling, 1991 WL 84229 (Ohio Ct. App. 11th Dist. Trumbull County 1991).

testimony on the components of the Battered Woman Syndrome might help explain acts of the defendant that could otherwise appear criminal. To establish self-defense, the following elements must be shown: (1) the defendant was not at fault in creating the situation giving rise to the event, (2) the defendant had a bona fide belief that he or she was in imminent danger of death or great bodily harm and that his or her only means of escape from such danger was in the use of deadly force[1] and (3) the defendant must not have violated any duty to retreat or avoid the danger.[2] The Battered Woman Syndrome is a psychological construct[3] and is relatively new in Ohio Law.[4] However, the syndrome is not really a new defense or justification. It is merely an extended application of the traditional claim of self-defense.[5]

Ohio has a subjective test to determine whether a defendant properly acted in self-defense. If the defendant honestly believed at the time of the event that death or great bodily harm was imminent and that the only means of escape from such danger was in the use of deadly force, then the defendant who used such force acted in self-defense.[6]

[Section 7:24]

[1]Marts v. State, 26 Ohio St. 162, 1875 WL 27 (1875), paragraph two of the syllabus; State v. Champion, 109 Ohio St. 281, 2 Ohio L. Abs. 68, 2 Ohio L. Abs. 87, 142 N.E. 141 (1924), paragraph one of the syllabus; State v. Sheets, 115 Ohio St. 308, 310, 152 N.E. 664 (1926); State v. Walker, 2005-Ohio-6365, 2005 WL 3220217 (Ohio Ct. App. 10th Dist. Franklin County 2005); State v. Bunch, 2010-Ohio-515, 2010 WL 547402 (Ohio Ct. App. 8th Dist. Cuyahoga County 2010). See also State v. Imondi, 2015-Ohio-2605, 2015 WL 3964244 (Ohio Ct. App. 11th Dist. Lake County 2015).

[2]State v. Peacock, 40 Ohio St. 333, 1883 WL 106 (1883) (abrogation on other grounds recognized by, State v. Catlin, 56 Ohio App. 3d 75, 564 N.E.2d 750 (2d Dist. Montgomery County 1990)); Graham v. State, 98 Ohio St. 77, 120 N.E. 232, 18 A.L.R. 1272 (1918).

[3]Victoria Mikesell Mather, The Skeleton in the Closet: The Battered Woman Syndrome, Self-Defense, and Expert Testimony, 39 Mercer L. Rev. 545 (1987).

[4]RC 2901.06. For a good discussion of the genesis of the Battered Woman Syndrome, see State v. Daws, 104 Ohio App. 3d 448, 662 N.E.2d 805 (2d Dist. Montgomery County 1994); State v. Dyson, 2000 WL 1597952 (Ohio Ct. App. 2d Dist. Champaign County 2000).

[5]State v. Manning, 74 Ohio App. 3d 19, 31, 598 N.E.2d 25 (9th Dist. Lorain County 1991). For an excellent general discussion of various considerations concerning the application of the Battered Woman Syndrome, see People v. Seeley, 186 Misc. 2d 715, 720 N.Y.S.2d 315 (Sup 2000).

[6]State v. Sallie, 81 Ohio St. 3d 673, 674, 1998-Ohio-343, 693 N.E.2d 267 (1998), citing State v. Koss, 49 Ohio St. 3d 213, 551 N.E.2d 970 (1990). See also Stewart v. State, 1 Ohio St. 66, 75, 1852 WL 10 (1852); State v. Doty, 94 Ohio St. 258, 113 N.E. 811 (1916); State v. Morgan, 100 Ohio St. 66, 72, 125 N.E. 109 (1919); State v. Richardson, 2010-Ohio-471, 2010 WL 497343 (Ohio Ct. App. 6th Dist. Lucas County 2010); State v. Fagan, 2009-Ohio-3760, 2009 WL 2351753 (Ohio Ct. App. 2d Dist. Clark County 2009); State v. Williams, 2011-Ohio-2463, 2011 WL 2112540 (Ohio Ct. App. 7th Dist. Mahoning County 2011); State v. Goff, 128 Ohio St. 3d 169, 2010-Ohio-6317, 942 N.E.2d 1075 (2010); State v. Matthews, 2012-Ohio-1154, 2012 WL 949827 (Ohio Ct. App. 10th Dist. Franklin County 2012); State v. Baughman, 2014-Ohio-1821, 2014 WL 1759189 (Ohio Ct. App. 5th Dist. Fairfield County 2014); State v. Hall, 2014-Ohio-2959, 2014 WL 2984992 (Ohio Ct. App. 4th Dist. Ross County 2014); State v. D'Agostino, 2014-Ohio-551, 2014 WL 605527 (Ohio Ct. App. 9th Dist. Lorain County 2014); State v. Cornwell, 2015-Ohio-4617, 48 N.E.3d 169 (Ohio Ct. App. 9th Dist. Wayne County 2015); State v. Osborne, 2016-Ohio-282, 2016 WL 515404 (Ohio Ct.

The Battered Woman Syndrome was codified in Ohio in 1990[7] and was first recognized by the Ohio Supreme Court as sufficiently developed as a matter of commonly accepted scientific knowledge to warrant recognition by the state's courts.[8] The Supreme Court had refused to allow such testimony during the preceding 10 years.[9] Recognition of the syndrome now allows defendants to whom it applies to present expert testimony in furtherance of their claims that they acted properly in self-defense.[10]

In enacting the statutory provisions, the General Assembly also specifically recognized that (1) the Battered Woman Syndrome is a matter of commonly accepted scientific knowledge,[11] and (2) the subject matter and details of the syndrome are not within the general understanding or experience of a person who is a member of the general populace and are not within the field of common knowledge.[12]

Under the law in Ohio, when persons charged with criminal assaultive behavior claim that their actions were taken in self-defense, expert testimony may be offered to show that they had a bona fide belief that they were in imminent danger of death or great bodily harm and that their only means of escape was in the use of potentially deadly force.[13] Whether particular defendants reasonably perceive that they are in imminent danger of death or great bodily harm, so as to justify the use of potentially deadly force necessarily calls for some subjective judgments on their parts.[14] As such, defendant's mens rea is at issue in the defense. However, this does not permit the introduc-

---

App. 9th Dist. Summit County 2016).

[7]See 143 Ohio Senate and House Journals (1989–1990), 1990 H.B. 484, eff. 11-5-90 (enacting RC 2901.06).

[8]State v. Koss, 49 Ohio St. 3d 213, 551 N.E.2d 970 (1990); State v. Haines, 2005-Ohio-1692, 2005 WL 820539 (Ohio Ct. App. 11th Dist. Lake County 2005), judgment aff'd in part, rev'd in part, 112 Ohio St. 3d 393, 2006-Ohio-6711, 860 N.E.2d 91 (2006).

[9]See State v. Thomas, 66 Ohio St. 2d 518, 20 Ohio Op. 3d 424, 423 N.E.2d 137 (1981) (overruled by, State v. Koss, 49 Ohio St. 3d 213, 551 N.E.2d 970 (1990)); State v. Kraus, 2007-Ohio-6027, 2007 WL 3348426 (Ohio Ct. App. 12th Dist. Warren County 2007).

[10]State v. Koss, 49 Ohio St. 3d 213, 551 N.E.2d 970 (1990); State v. Haines, 2005-Ohio-1692, 2005 WL 820539 (Ohio Ct. App. 11th Dist. Lake County 2005), judgment aff'd in part, rev'd in part, 112 Ohio St. 3d 393, 2006-Ohio-6711, 860 N.E.2d 91 (2006).

[11]RC 2901.06(A)(1).

[12]RC 2901.06(A)(2).

[13]RC 2901.06(B).

[14]See State v. Thomas, 77 Ohio St. 3d 323, 1997-Ohio-269, 673 N.E.2d 1339, 67 A.L.R.5th 775 (1997); State v. Shane, 63 Ohio St. 3d 630, 590 N.E.2d 272 (1992); State v. Smith, 2004-Ohio-6608, 2004 WL 2830784 (Ohio Ct. App. 10th Dist. Franklin County 2004); State v. Bunch, 2010-Ohio-515, 2010 WL 547402 (Ohio Ct. App. 8th Dist. Cuyahoga County 2010); State v. Radabaugh, 2010-Ohio-4711, 2010 WL 3820528 (Ohio Ct. App. 6th Dist. Fulton County 2010); State v. Dale, 2013-Ohio-2229, 2013 WL 2406261 (Ohio Ct. App. 2d Dist. Montgomery County 2013); State v. Hall, 2014-Ohio-2959, 2014 WL 2984992 (Ohio Ct. App. 4th Dist. Ross County 2014); State v. D'Agostino, 2014-Ohio-551, 2014 WL 605527 (Ohio Ct. App. 9th Dist. Lorain County 2014); State v. Cornwell, 2015-Ohio-4617, 48 N.E.3d 169 (Ohio Ct. App. 9th Dist. Wayne County 2015); State v. Adams, 2018-Ohio-604, 2018 WL 920023 (Ohio Ct. App. 2d Dist. Champaign County 2018) (discussion of State v. Thomas, 77 Ohio St. 3d 323, 1997-Ohio-269, 673 N.E.2d 1339, 67 A.L.R.5th 775 (1997), in appeal from domestic

tion of Battered Woman Syndrome expert testimony on defendant's mens rea in any other context besides the issue of the defendant's perception of the danger and the reasonableness of the defendant's determination that the use of potentially deadly force was the only option available to avoid the danger.[15]

Generally, the law in Ohio remains that expert testimony, unrelated to the insanity defense, is inadmissible to show that an accused lacked the necessary state of mind for the charged crime.[16]

Battered Woman Syndrome expert testimony is not available to further a defendant's claim that the actions complained of were an accident,[17] were committed because the defendant was under duress,[18] or where the defendant claims not to be the person who committed the crime.[19]

Expert testimony regarding the Battered Woman Syndrome is admissible, however, in connection with a plea of not guilty by reason of insanity.[20]

Expert opinion testimony regarding a defendant's inability to form the specific intent to kill is not admissible into evidence. Expert testimony on the Battered Woman Syndrome which relates to the defendant's mental state and the reasonableness of the defendant's belief that the use of potentially deadly force was required for self-defense does not in any way speak to the issue of the defendant's ability or lack thereof to form the necessary mens rea to commit the crime charged.[21]

For expert testimony to be admissible on the issue of the Battered Woman Syndrome, the defendant must present sufficient evidence for the trier of fact to find that the defendant was a battered person. The expert can only give general information about the syndrome and its possible effects on the behavior of a battered person. The expert can offer an opinion as to whether or not the defendant is a battered

---

violence conviction).

[15]Curington v. Moon, 2009-Ohio-3013, 2009 WL 1800373 (Ohio Ct. App. 2d Dist. Montgomery County 2009); State v. Werfel, 2003-Ohio-6958, 2003 WL 22994981 (Ohio Ct. App. 11th Dist. Lake County 2003); State v. Mariana, 1999 WL 1271022 (Ohio Ct. App. 12th Dist. Butler County 1999).

[16]State v. Wilcox, 70 Ohio St. 2d 182, 24 Ohio Op. 3d 284, 436 N.E.2d 523 (1982); State v. Turner, 2004-Ohio-6489, 2004 WL 2785954 (Ohio Ct. App. 3d Dist. Marion County 2004); State v. Coulter, 75 Ohio App. 3d 219, 229, 598 N.E.2d 1324 (12th Dist. Warren County 1992).

[17]State v. Sallie, 81 Ohio St. 3d 673, 1998-Ohio-343, 693 N.E.2d 267 (1998).

[18]State v. Lundgren, 1994 WL 171657 (Ohio Ct. App. 11th Dist. Lake County 1994) (holding modified by, State v. Haines, 2005-Ohio-1692, 2005 WL 820539 (Ohio Ct. App. 11th Dist. Lake County 2005)).

[19]State v. Redding, 1992 WL 41840 (Ohio Ct. App. 8th Dist. Cuyahoga County 1992).

[20]RC 2945.392; State v. Mariana, 1999 WL 1271022 (Ohio Ct. App. 12th Dist. Butler County 1999).

[21]State v. Daws, 104 Ohio App. 3d 448, 662 N.E.2d 805 (2d Dist. Montgomery County 1994); State v. Koss, 49 Ohio St. 3d 213, 217, 551 N.E.2d 970 (1990); State v. Wilcox, 70 Ohio St. 2d 182, 24 Ohio Op. 3d 284, 436 N.E.2d 523 (1982).

person but cannot testify as to whether or not, at the time of the act, the defendant believed that he/she was in imminent danger.[22]

The Battered Woman Syndrome is not limited just to women. Although the various psychological conditions which mimic it are referred to by many different names, males and even children who exhibit the psychological characteristics of what is commonly referred to as Post-Traumatic Stress Disorder qualify for the introduction of such expert evidence to help to explain behavior that they characterize as self-defense.[23]

An understanding of the defendant's state of mind is critical to this defense.[24] Expert testimony that may assist the trier of fact in understanding the effect that the syndrome had on the psychology of a defendant who is alleged to have been suffering from it at the time of the violent act is admissible.[25] A history of physical abuse alone will not justify the use of potentially deadly force.[26] Having been assaulted by the abuser in the past is pertinent only as it contributed to the defendant's state of mind at the time of the event now before the court.[27] Use of the Battered Woman Syndrome defense is most necessary and provides the trier of fact with the greatest assistance in those situations where the facts of the case would not cause the average, reasonable person not suffering from the syndrome to believe that danger of death or great bodily harm was imminent.[28]

Evidence of the syndrome is most commonly admitted in those cases where the defendant mistakenly believed that the circumstances warranted the use of deadly force in self defense but submits to the court that the mistaken belief was reasonable in light of the fact that the defendant was suffering from the syndrome. Conversely, if the reasonableness of the defendant's fear of imminent death or great bodily harm is not in question, i.e., if the defendant testifies that the victim threatened to kill him/her and advanced as if to carry out the threat, expert testimony on the Battered Woman Syndrome is unnec-

---

[22]State v. Poling, 1991 WL 84229 (Ohio Ct. App. 11th Dist. Trumbull County 1991); State v. Coulter, 75 Ohio App. 3d 219, 598 N.E.2d 1324 (12th Dist. Warren County 1992).

[23]State v. Nemeth, 82 Ohio St. 3d 202, 205, 1998-Ohio-376, 694 N.E.2d 1332 (1998); State v. Berenyi, 1997 WL 576357 (Ohio Ct. App. 3d Dist. Paulding County 1997), aff'd, 81 Ohio St. 3d 550, 1998-Ohio-335, 692 N.E.2d 614 (1998); State v. Dyson, 2000 WL 1597952 (Ohio Ct. App. 2d Dist. Champaign County 2000); State v. Hartman, 93 Ohio St. 3d 274, 2001-Ohio-1580, 754 N.E.2d 1150 (2001); State v. Vaughn, 2003-Ohio-7023, 2003 WL 22999297 (Ohio Ct. App. 7th Dist. Carroll County 2003).

[24]State v. Koss, 49 Ohio St. 3d 213, 216, 551 N.E.2d 970 (1990); State v. Haines, 2005-Ohio-1692, 2005 WL 820539 (Ohio Ct. App. 11th Dist. Lake County 2005), judgment aff'd in part, rev'd in part, 112 Ohio St. 3d 393, 2006-Ohio-6711, 860 N.E.2d 91 (2006).

[25]State v. Koss, 49 Ohio St. 3d 213, 216, 551 N.E.2d 970 (1990); State v. McKelton, 148 Ohio St. 3d 261, 2016-Ohio-5735, 70 N.E.3d 508 (2016), cert. denied, 137 S. Ct. 1594, 197 L. Ed. 2d 720 (2017).

[26]State v. Sallie, 81 Ohio St. 3d 673, 674, 1998-Ohio-343, 693 N.E.2d 267 (1998) (citing *Koss*).

[27]State v. Sallie, 81 Ohio St. 3d 673, 674, 1998-Ohio-343, 693 N.E.2d 267 (1998).

[28]State v. Sallie, 81 Ohio St. 3d 673, 674, 1998-Ohio-343, 693 N.E.2d 267 (1998).

essary to show an honest belief in the imminent danger of death or great bodily harm.[29]

The expert testimony is aimed at an area where the purported common knowledge of the jury may be very much mistaken, to wit, the reasonableness of a person's fear of imminent serious danger.[30] The expert presentation is geared toward helping the jury disregard any prior conclusions they might have about the behavior of those who are battered and to treat those prior conclusions as being common myths rather than common knowledge.[31] The evidence is presented to assist the trier of fact in determining whether the defendant acted out of an honest belief that death or great bodily harm was imminent and that the use of potentially deadly force was the only means of escape.[32]

Testimony relative to the Battered Woman Syndrome is generally admitted when the affirmative defense of self-defense is raised. However, the Supreme Court of Ohio clarified that testimony relative to the Battered Woman Syndrome can also be admitted in the state's case-in-chief.[33] Relevancy to issues such as the credibility of a wavering alleged victim who gives inconsistent statements provide the basis for allowing expert testimony on the syndrome as rehabilitative evidence during the state's case-in-chief.[34] Even when Battered Woman Syndrome evidence is relevant, a court must carefully weigh whether its probative value is outweighed by the danger of unfair prejudice, confusion of the issues or of misleading the jury.[35]

The court can achieve an acceptable balance through placing limita-

[29]State v. Palmer, 2000 WL 311916 (Ohio Ct. App. 10th Dist. Franklin County 2000); State v. Sallie, 81 Ohio St. 3d 673, 674, 1998-Ohio-343, 693 N.E.2d 267 (1998).

[30]State v. Koss, 49 Ohio St. 3d 213, 217, 551 N.E.2d 970 (1990).

[31]State v. Koss, 49 Ohio St. 3d 213, 217, 551 N.E.2d 970 (1990); State v. Haines, 2005-Ohio-1692, 2005 WL 820539 (Ohio Ct. App. 11th Dist. Lake County 2005), judgment aff'd in part, rev'd in part, 112 Ohio St. 3d 393, 2006-Ohio-6711, 860 N.E.2d 91 (2006).

[32]RC 2901.06(B); State v. McKelton, 148 Ohio St. 3d 261, 2016-Ohio-5735, 70 N.E.3d 508 (2016), cert. denied, 137 S. Ct. 1594, 197 L. Ed. 2d 720 (2017).

[33]State v. Haines, 112 Ohio St. 3d 393, 2006-Ohio-6711, 860 N.E.2d 91 (2006); Evid.R. 702.

[34]State v. Haines, 112 Ohio St. 3d 393, 2006-Ohio-6711, 860 N.E.2d 91 (2006). See also Evid.R. 401; State v. Sorah, 2007-Ohio-5898, 2007 WL 3243536 (Ohio Ct. App. 12th Dist. Clermont County 2007); State v. Drew, 2008-Ohio-2797, 2008 WL 2349649 (Ohio Ct. App. 10th Dist. Franklin County 2008); State v. Stowers, 81 Ohio St. 3d 260, 1998-Ohio-632, 690 N.E.2d 881 (1998); State v. Kraus, 2007-Ohio-6027, 2007 WL 3348426 (Ohio Ct. App. 12th Dist. Warren County 2007); State v. Dyson, 2000 WL 1597952 (Ohio Ct. App. 2d Dist. Champaign County 2000); State v. Caudill, 2007-Ohio-1557, 2008 WL 852626 (Ohio Ct. App. 6th Dist. Wood County 2008); State v. Baughman, 2014-Ohio-1821, 2014 WL 1759189 (Ohio Ct. App. 5th Dist. Fairfield County 2014); State v. Myers, 2014-Ohio-3759, 2014 WL 4269104 (Ohio Ct. App. 6th Dist. Wood County 2014), appeal not allowed, 144 Ohio St. 3d 1507, 2016-Ohio-652, 45 N.E.3d 1051 (2016) and appeal not allowed, 145 Ohio St. 3d 1447, 2016-Ohio-1596, 48 N.E.3d 585 (2016); State v. Remy, 2018-Ohio-2857, 2018 WL 3493129 (Ohio Ct. App. 2d Dist. Clark County 2018) (discussion of State v. Stowers, 81 Ohio St. 3d 260, 1998-Ohio-632, 690 N.E.2d 881 (1998), in appeal from DV conviction).

[35]Evid.R. 403(A); State v. Haines, 112 Ohio St. 3d 393, 2006-Ohio-6711, 860 N.E.2d 91 (2006); State v. Sorah, 2007-Ohio-5898, 2007 WL 3243536 (Ohio Ct. App. 12th Dist. Clermont County 2007); State v. Drew, 2008-Ohio-2797, 2008 WL 2349649 (Ohio Ct. App. 10th Dist. Franklin County 2008); State v. Stowers, 81 Ohio St. 3d 260, 1998-Ohio-632, 690 N.E.2d 881 (1998); State v. Kraus, 2007-Ohio-6027, 2007 WL

tions on the expert's testimony that prohibit the expert from offering an opinion on whether the complainant was a battered person or that the defendant was a batterer; whether the defendant is guilty of the crime; whether the complainant is being truthful; whether the complainant suffers from the Battered Woman Syndrome; or as to which of the complainant's conflicting statements is more credible.[36]

Experts called to testify in regard to the Battered Woman Syndrome, therefore, must be limited in their testimony to the general characteristics of a victim suffering from the syndrome and hypothetical questions regarding specific abnormal behaviors generally exhibited by individuals suffering from the syndrome.[37] They should never offer an opinion relative to the specifics surrounding the condition of the alleged victim or the circumstances involving the specific behaviors of the alleged victim in the case on trial.[38]

A set of rigid foundational requirements for the admission of Bat-

---

3348426 (Ohio Ct. App. 12th Dist. Warren County 2007); State v. Dyson, 2000 WL 1597952 (Ohio Ct. App. 2d Dist. Champaign County 2000); State v. Caudill, 2007-Ohio-1557, 2008 WL 852626 (Ohio Ct. App. 6th Dist. Wood County 2008). See also State v. Goff, 128 Ohio St. 3d 169, 2010-Ohio-6317, 942 N.E.2d 1075 (2010); State v. Myers, 2014-Ohio-3759, 2014 WL 4269104 (Ohio Ct. App. 6th Dist. Wood County 2014), appeal not allowed, 144 Ohio St. 3d 1507, 2016-Ohio-652, 45 N.E.3d 1051 (2016) and appeal not allowed, 145 Ohio St. 3d 1447, 2016-Ohio-1596, 48 N.E.3d 585 (2016); State v. Remy, 2018-Ohio-2857, 2018 WL 3493129 (Ohio Ct. App. 2d Dist. Clark County 2018) (discussion of State v. Stowers, 81 Ohio St. 3d 260, 1998-Ohio-632, 690 N.E.2d 881 (1998), in appeal from DV conviction).

[36]State v. Haines, 112 Ohio St. 3d 393, 2006-Ohio-6711, 860 N.E.2d 91 (2006). Pay particular attention to Justice Lanzinger's dissent. State v. Sorah, 2007-Ohio-5898, 2007 WL 3243536 (Ohio Ct. App. 12th Dist. Clermont County 2007); State v. Drew, 2008-Ohio-2797, 2008 WL 2349649 (Ohio Ct. App. 10th Dist. Franklin County 2008); State v. Stowers, 81 Ohio St. 3d 260, 1998-Ohio-632, 690 N.E.2d 881 (1998); State v. Kraus, 2007-Ohio-6027, 2007 WL 3348426 (Ohio Ct. App. 12th Dist. Warren County 2007); State v. Dyson, 2000 WL 1597952 (Ohio Ct. App. 2d Dist. Champaign County 2000); State v. Caudill, 2007-Ohio-1557, 2008 WL 852626 (Ohio Ct. App. 6th Dist. Wood County 2008); State v. Remy, 2018-Ohio-2857, 2018 WL 3493129 (Ohio Ct. App. 2d Dist. Clark County 2018) (discussion of State v. Stowers, 81 Ohio St. 3d 260, 1998-Ohio-632, 690 N.E.2d 881 (1998), in appeal from DV conviction).

[37]State v. Haines, 112 Ohio St. 3d 393, 2006-Ohio-6711, 860 N.E.2d 91 (2006); Haws, Removing the Roadblocks to Successful Domestic Violence Prosecutions: Prosecutorial Use of Expert Testimony on the Battered Woman Syndrome in Ohio, 53 Clev. St. L. Rev. 133, 158 (2005); State v. Sorah, 2007-Ohio-5898, 2007 WL 3243536 (Ohio Ct. App. 12th Dist. Clermont County 2007); State v. Drew, 2008-Ohio-2797, 2008 WL 2349649 (Ohio Ct. App. 10th Dist. Franklin County 2008); State v. Stowers, 81 Ohio St. 3d 260, 1998-Ohio-632, 690 N.E.2d 881 (1998); State v. Kraus, 2007-Ohio-6027, 2007 WL 3348426 (Ohio Ct. App. 12th Dist. Warren County 2007); State v. Dyson, 2000 WL 1597952 (Ohio Ct. App. 2d Dist. Champaign County 2000); State v. Caudill, 2007-Ohio-1557, 2008 WL 852626 (Ohio Ct. App. 6th Dist. Wood County 2008); State v. Remy, 2018-Ohio-2857, 2018 WL 3493129 (Ohio Ct. App. 2d Dist. Clark County 2018) (discussion of State v. Stowers, 81 Ohio St. 3d 260, 1998-Ohio-632, 690 N.E.2d 881 (1998), in appeal from DV conviction).

[38]State v. Haines, 112 Ohio St. 3d 393, 2006-Ohio-6711, 860 N.E.2d 91 (2006); Haws, Removing the Roadblocks to Successful Domestic Violence Prosecutions: Prosecutorial Use of Expert Testimony on the Battered Woman Syndrome in Ohio, 53 Clev. St. L. Rev. 133, 158 (2005); State v. Sorah, 2007-Ohio-5898, 2007 WL 3243536 (Ohio Ct. App. 12th Dist. Clermont County 2007); State v. Drew, 2008-Ohio-2797, 2008 WL 2349649 (Ohio Ct. App. 10th Dist. Franklin County 2008); State v. Kraus, 2007-Ohio-6027, 2007 WL 3348426 (Ohio Ct. App. 12th Dist. Warren County 2007); State v. Dyson, 2000 WL 1597952 (Ohio Ct. App. 2d Dist. Champaign County 2000); State v. Caudill, 2007-Ohio-1557, 2008 WL 852626 (Ohio Ct. App. 6th Dist. Wood

tered Woman Syndrome testimony is not required, but the party seeking to introduce the evidence must lay an appropriate foundation substantiating that the conduct and behavior of the witness is consistent with the generally recognized symptoms of the syndrome and that the witness behaved in such a manner that a jury would be aided by expert testimony that provides a possible explanation for the behavior.[39] Expert testimony on the Battered Woman Syndrome is not admissible to prove anything about the defendant, but instead is offered only as background for understanding the alleged victim's behavior.[40] Juries should be instructed as to the limits of such expert testimony.[41]

Q & A: The defendant is charged with domestic violence. She testifies that she and her husband frequently argue but that he has never hit her, and that there has been no history of violence between them. She admits striking him on the day in question, but says she did so because he was yelling loudly and it scared her. She says that she did not fear for her safety when she hit him and that she did not think he was going to hit her. She said he has been controlling and emotionally abusive throughout their marriage and that she was fearful of his "control," which she had no way escaping.

She wants to invoke the Battered Woman Syndrome in her effort to establish self-defense. Should the court allow her to present the defense?

No. The defendant fails to establish that she was in fear of bodily harm when she struck her husband. Because she failed to establish this element of self-defense, there is no need to consider testimony regarding the "battered woman syndrome" and whether, based on that syndrome, she had an honest belief that she was in danger of im-

County 2008).

[39]State v. Haines, 112 Ohio St. 3d 393, 2006-Ohio-6711, 860 N.E.2d 91 (2006); State v. Sorah, 2007-Ohio-5898, 2007 WL 3243536 (Ohio Ct. App. 12th Dist. Clermont County 2007); State v. Drew, 2008-Ohio-2797, 2008 WL 2349649 (Ohio Ct. App. 10th Dist. Franklin County 2008); State v. Stowers, 81 Ohio St. 3d 260, 1998-Ohio-632, 690 N.E.2d 881 (1998); State v. Dyson, 2000 WL 1597952 (Ohio Ct. App. 2d Dist. Champaign County 2000); State v. Caudill, 2007-Ohio-1557, 2008 WL 852626 (Ohio Ct. App. 6th Dist. Wood County 2008); State v. Remy, 2018-Ohio-2857, 2018 WL 3493129 (Ohio Ct. App. 2d Dist. Clark County 2018) (discussion of State v. Stowers, 81 Ohio St. 3d 260, 1998-Ohio-632, 690 N.E.2d 881 (1998), in appeal from DV conviction).

[40]State v. Haines, 112 Ohio St. 3d 393, 2006-Ohio-6711, 860 N.E.2d 91 (2006); State v. Sorah, 2007-Ohio-5898, 2007 WL 3243536 (Ohio Ct. App. 12th Dist. Clermont County 2007); State v. Drew, 2008-Ohio-2797, 2008 WL 2349649 (Ohio Ct. App. 10th Dist. Franklin County 2008); State v. Stowers, 81 Ohio St. 3d 260, 1998-Ohio-632, 690 N.E.2d 881 (1998); State v. Kraus, 2007-Ohio-6027, 2007 WL 3348426 (Ohio Ct. App. 12th Dist. Warren County 2007); State v. Dyson, 2000 WL 1597952 (Ohio Ct. App. 2d Dist. Champaign County 2000); State v. Caudill, 2007-Ohio-1557, 2008 WL 852626 (Ohio Ct. App. 6th Dist. Wood County 2008); State v. Remy, 2018-Ohio-2857, 2018 WL 3493129 (Ohio Ct. App. 2d Dist. Clark County 2018) (discussion of State v. Stowers, 81 Ohio St. 3d 260, 1998-Ohio-632, 690 N.E.2d 881 (1998), in appeal from DV conviction).

[41]State v. Haines, 112 Ohio St. 3d 393, 2006-Ohio-6711, 860 N.E.2d 91 (2006); State v. Sorah, 2007-Ohio-5898, 2007 WL 3243536 (Ohio Ct. App. 12th Dist. Clermont County 2007); State v. Drew, 2008-Ohio-2797, 2008 WL 2349649 (Ohio Ct. App. 10th Dist. Franklin County 2008).

minent bodily harm. Based on her own testimony, she was not in danger of the imminent use of unlawful force, and the admission of evidence of the "battered woman syndrome" would not be warranted.[42]

Q & A: During closing arguments in a jury trial for domestic violence, the prosecution maintains that the defendant had a duty to retreat from her home when her abusive husband refused to leave her alone following a heated argument and advanced on her in a threatening manner, rather than striking him with a frying pan. The defense objects. How should the court rule?

The objection should be sustained. The Ohio Supreme Court holds that there is no duty to retreat when under attack in one's own home before resorting to the use of force, even if the attacker is someone who has an equal right to be there.[43]

Q & A: During a jury trial both the victim and the defendant claim that the other struck first. The defendant is requesting an instruction on self-defense. The prosecution objects, maintaining that the defendant's testimony on the issue was laughable! Should the court give the instruction?

It depends. When evidence of self-defense is forthcoming, the trial court must first, viewing that evidence in the light most favorable to the defendant, determine whether or not it is adequate to raise the issue, and, if believed, would under the legal tests applied to a claim of self-defense permit a reasonable doubt as to guilt, stemming from that claim, to arise; if the evidence adduced, so viewed, is legally insufficient to raise the issue, the trial court will have no occasion or obligation to instruct the jury on the elements essential to a valid claim of self-defense, but rather will remove the issue of self-defense from jury consideration.[44]

The Ohio Supreme Court's precedents conflict in the advice given trial courts that are requested by defendants to give jury instructions on inconsistent defenses arising from the presentation of the evidence. In one case, the court found that the appellant was not entitled a jury instruction for both accident and self-defense, explaining: "If the evidence warrants, the defendant has a right to one request or the other. By no manner of logic, law, or legerdemain is he entitled to both."[45]

In another, it considered whether "the state of Ohio may * * * place the burden of proving self-defense on a defendant if the truth of that defense would negate an essential element of the crime charged."[46] In that case, the court rejected the appellant's argument holding that

[42]State v. Fagan, 2009-Ohio-3760, 2009 WL 2351753 (Ohio Ct. App. 2d Dist. Clark County 2009).

[43]State v. Thomas, 77 Ohio St. 3d 323, 1997-Ohio-269, 673 N.E.2d 1339, 67 A.L.R.5th 775 (1997); State v. Williams, 2011-Ohio-2463, 2011 WL 2112540 (Ohio Ct. App. 7th Dist. Mahoning County 2011).

[44]State v. Belanger, 190 Ohio App. 3d 377, 2010-Ohio-5407, 941 N.E.2d 1265 (3d Dist. Allen County 2010); State v. Imondi, 2015-Ohio-2605, 2015 WL 3964244 (Ohio Ct. App. 11th Dist. Lake County 2015).

[45]State v. Champion, 109 Ohio St. 281, 286–87, 2 Ohio L. Abs. 68, 2 Ohio L. Abs. 87, 142 N.E. 141 (1924).

[46]State v. Martin, 21 Ohio St. 3d 91, 488 N.E.2d 166 (1986), judgment aff'd, 480 U.S. 228, 107 S. Ct. 1098, 94 L. Ed. 2d 267 (1987).

self-defense is an admission to "the facts claimed by the prosecution" that utilizes "independent facts or circumstances which the defendant claims exempt him from liability."[47]

However, in yet another case, the court noted that a lawyer's decision to present "inconsistent alternative [defense] theories is not per se deficient performance" as "the decision to advance two different theories of non-culpability is a trial tactic or strategy" that is not so unreasonable as to constitute ineffective assistance of counsel.[48]

One appellate court holds that, based upon the Supreme Court's mixed precedent, it cannot require a defendant to admit some part of the state's case in chief in order to argue self-defense.[49] That court maintains that "If arguing inconsistent defenses is a trial tactic that a competent trial attorney would utilize, then the jury should be instructed on the inconsistent defenses." That conclusion is in agreement with the federal standard, which permits a defendant to argue inconsistent theories before a jury.[50] Other courts have made similar findings when a self-defense instruction was requested when other inconsistent defenses were in evidence.[51]

§ 7:25 Trial presentation—Duress

Frequently, individuals who are subjected to abusive interpersonal or intimate relationships find themselves coerced into performing criminal acts that they would not perform but for the coercion of their abusive partner. In some instances, the defense of duress may be available to individuals who are charged with these other criminal activities.

Duress, an affirmative defense, has long been recognized as a legitimate defense to all crimes. At common law, the burden of proving duress, as with all other affirmative defenses, rests with the defendant.[1]

The rationale for a duress defense is that the defendant ought to be excused when he or she is the victim of a threat that a person of reasonable moral strength could not fairly be expected to resist.[2] Duress consists of any conduct which overpowers a person's will and coerces

---

[47]State v. Martin, 21 Ohio St. 3d 91, 488 N.E.2d 166 (1986), judgment aff'd, 480 U.S. 228, 107 S. Ct. 1098, 94 L. Ed. 2d 267 (1987).

[48]State v. Mundt, 115 Ohio St. 3d 22, 2007-Ohio-4836, 873 N.E.2d 828 (2007); State v. Kiehl, 2016-Ohio-8543, 78 N.E.3d 1226 (Ohio Ct. App. 11th Dist. Portage County 2016), appeal not allowed, 151 Ohio St. 3d 1453, 2017-Ohio-8842, 87 N.E.3d 221 (2017).

[49]State v. Imondi, 2015-Ohio-2605, 2015 WL 3964244 (Ohio Ct. App. 11th Dist. Lake County 2015).

[50]Mathews v. U.S., 485 U.S. 58, 62, 108 S. Ct. 883, 99 L. Ed. 2d 54 (1988) (rejected by, State v. Gray, 239 Ariz. 475, 372 P.3d 999 (2016)); State v. Imondi, 2015-Ohio-2605, 2015 WL 3964244 (Ohio Ct. App. 11th Dist. Lake County 2015).

[51]U.S. v. Goldson, 954 F.2d 51, 55 (2d Cir. 1992); U.S. v. Browner, 889 F.2d 549, 555 (5th Cir. 1989).

[Section 7:25]

[1]Patterson v. New York, 432 U.S. 197, 97 S. Ct. 2319, 53 L. Ed. 2d 281 (1977), State v. Sappienza, 84 Ohio St. 63, 73, 95 N.E. 381 (1911); State v. Getsy, 84 Ohio St. 3d 180, 198, 1998-Ohio-533, 702 N.E.2d 866 (1998).

[2]Dixon v. U.S., 548 U.S. 1, 126 S. Ct. 2437, 165 L. Ed. 2d 299 (2006); State v.

or constrains his performance of an act which he otherwise would not have performed. Consequently, one who, under the pressure of a threat from another person, commits what would otherwise be a crime may, under certain circumstances, be justified in committing the act and not be guilty of the crime.[3] The defense of duress requires a sense of immediate, imminent death or serious bodily injury if the actor does not commit the act as instructed.[4] The force that is used to compel the defendant's conduct must remain constant, controlling the will of the unwilling actor during the entire time he commits the act, and must be of such a nature that the actor cannot safely withdraw.[5]

The Supreme Court of Ohio has held that, in determining whether a course of conduct results in duress, the question is not what effect such conduct would have upon an ordinary man, but rather the effect upon the particular person toward whom such conduct is directed, and in determining such effect the age, sex, health and mental condition of the person affected, the relationship of the parties and all the surrounding circumstances may be considered.[6]

A defendant's subjective belief that he is in danger of imminent death or grave bodily injury must be objectively reasonable based upon the evidence presented.[7]

The Supreme Court of Ohio has also emphasized that the affirmative defense of duress is available only in rare circumstances. It must be understood that the defense of necessity or duress is strictly and extremely limited in application and will probably be effective in very rare occasions. It is a defense and not a conjured afterthought.[8]

All the conditions must be met, and the court must find as a matter of law that the evidence is sufficient to warrant an instruction on the affirmative defenses of necessity or duress, before such an instruction may be properly given. The court may refuse to give an instruction which is not applicable to the evidence governing the case, or which is incorrect.[9]

Q & A: The defendant's spouse was struck in the head by the defendant with a cast iron skillet, after the victim threatened to kill the defendant some night after the defendant went to sleep. The blow with the skillet left a wound that took five

---

Hall, 2014-Ohio-2959, 2014 WL 2984992 (Ohio Ct. App. 4th Dist. Ross County 2014).

[3]State v. Grinnell, 112 Ohio App. 3d 124, 144–45, 678 N.E.2d 231 (10th Dist. Franklin County 1996).

[4]State v. Cross, 58 Ohio St. 2d 482, 12 Ohio Op. 3d 396, 391 N.E.2d 319 (1979); State v. Hall, 2014-Ohio-2959, 2014 WL 2984992 (Ohio Ct. App. 4th Dist. Ross County 2014).

[5]State v. Good, 110 Ohio App. 415, 11 Ohio Op. 2d 459, 83 Ohio L. Abs. 65, 165 N.E.2d 28 (10th Dist. Franklin County 1960).

[6]Tallmadge v. Robinson, 158 Ohio St. 333, 49 Ohio Op. 206, 109 N.E.2d 496 (1952), paragraph two of the syllabus.

[7]State v. Elijah, 2000 WL 968781 (Ohio Ct. App. 2d Dist. Montgomery County 2000).

[8]State v. Cross, 58 Ohio St. 2d 482, 12 Ohio Op. 3d 396, 391 N.E.2d 319 (1979); State v. Thompson, 2009-Ohio-3552, 2009 WL 2159651 (Ohio Ct. App. 10th Dist. Franklin County 2009).

[9]State v. Thompson, 2009-Ohio-3552, 2009 WL 2159651 (Ohio Ct. App. 10th Dist. Franklin County 2009).

staples to close. The defendant is now on trial, charged with felonious assault. The defendant claims that the victim has a history of physically abusing the defendant, and asks the court to give a jury instruction on duress. Should the instruction be given?

No. The terms "necessity" and "duress" are distinct, yet are often used interchangeably and are often indistinguishable. They share in common the fact that they provide an excuse, justification or affirmative defense to a criminal charge. Running throughout their meanings is the theme that imminent, immediate danger or threat of danger prevents the actor from exercising his or her own will, and that there is no alternate path to take. Therefore, the actor is forced to choose between the lesser of two evils.

Given that there was no constant, imminent, immediate danger or threat of danger in this case, the fact that the victim was abusive in the past and might be so in the future is not enough to establish all of the conditions required for a duress instruction to be appropriate.[10]

§ 7:26 Post-conviction relief—Vacating pleas and sealing the record

Due to the immigration and other consequences, direct and collateral, that accompany domestic violence conviction, those convicted of these offenses occasionally desire to vacate judgments of conviction and/or to have the record of their arrests and convictions sealed. Taking such action is sometimes possible, but the law does not favor it.

A motion to withdraw a plea of guilty or no contest generally may be made only before sentence is imposed. However, to correct manifest injustice the court after sentence may set aside the judgment of conviction and permit the defendant to withdraw his or her plea.[1] When a defendant's request is made post-sentence, the standard by which the motion is considered, therefore, must, be "to correct manifest injustice."[2]

The accused has the burden of showing a manifest injustice warranting the withdrawal of a guilty plea.[3] A reviewing court will not disturb a trial court's decision whether to grant <u>or not to grant</u> a motion to withdraw a plea absent an abuse of discretion.[4] In order to conclude that a trial court abused its discretion, its decision must be

[10]State v. Cross, 58 Ohio St. 2d 482, 12 Ohio Op. 3d 396, 391 N.E.2d 319 (1979); State v. Simes, 2016-Ohio-7300, 2016 WL 5940204 (Ohio Ct. App. 8th Dist. Cuyahoga County 2016), appeal not allowed, 149 Ohio St. 3d 1420, 2017-Ohio-4038, 75 N.E.3d 237 (2017); State v. Good, 110 Ohio App. 415, 11 Ohio Op. 2d 459, 83 Ohio L. Abs. 65, 165 N.E.2d 28 (10th Dist. Franklin County 1960).

[Section 7:26]

[1]Crim. R. 32.1.

[2]State v. Rose, 2004-Ohio-4433, 2004 WL 1879673 (Ohio Ct. App. 5th Dist. Delaware County 2004).

[3]State v. Smith, 49 Ohio St. 2d 261, 3 Ohio Op. 3d 402, 361 N.E.2d 1324 (1977), paragraph one of the syllabus).

[4]State v. Xie, 62 Ohio St. 3d 521, 584 N.E.2d 715 (1992).

unreasonable, arbitrary or unconscionable and not merely an error of law or judgment.[5]

The Ohio Supreme Court holds that sealing a record of conviction is a post conviction remedy that is civil in nature.[6] An application to seal a record of conviction may not be filed until one year following the offender's final discharge if convicted of a misdemeanor or three years if convicted of a felony.[7] In this regard, an application to seal a record of conviction is a separate remedy, completely apart from the criminal action, and is sought after the criminal proceedings have concluded.[8]

However, the Revised Code was specifically amended to prohibit the sealing of records of first-degree misdemeanor convictions involving offenses of violence, including domestic violence.[9] The amendment is retroactive in its application and, therefore, also prohibits sealing records of those convicted of significant crimes of violence in cases that precede its effective date, March 23, 2000.[10]

Generally, Ohio's state legislature may not pass retroactive laws.[11]

Misdemeanor domestic violence convictions other than 1st degree misdemeanor convictions are unaffected by the amendment and, therefore, may be sealed.[12]

Generally, Ohio's state legislature may not pass retroactive laws.[13] However, this prohibition applies only to substantive and not to remedial laws.[14] It is well-settled in Ohio that the expungement laws found in the Revised Code are remedial in nature.[15] Therefore, the expungement statute can be applied retroactively.[16]

---

[5]Blakemore v. Blakemore, 5 Ohio St. 3d 217, 450 N.E.2d 1140 (1983), State v. Rose, 2004-Ohio-4433, 2004 WL 1879673 (Ohio Ct. App. 5th Dist. Delaware County 2004).

[6]R.C. 2953.32; State v. Bissantz, 30 Ohio St. 3d 120, 121, 507 N.E.2d 1117 (1987).

[7]R.C. 2953.32(A)(1).

[8]2001 WL 256326. (Ohio Court App. 2nd Dist Clark County 2001). See, generally, State v. Nichols, 11 Ohio St. 3d 40, 463 N.E.2d 375 (1984).

[9]R.C. 2953.36(A)(3).

[10]R.C. 2953.36(A)(3); State v. LaSalle, 96 Ohio St. 3d 178, 179, 2002-Ohio-4009, 772 N.E.2d 1172, 1174 (2002).

[11]Ohio Const. Art. II, § 28.

[12]R.C. 2953.36(A)(3).

[13]Ohio Const. Art. II, § 28.

[14]Kneisley v. Lattimer-Stevens Co., 40 Ohio St. 3d 354, 356, 533 N.E.2d 743 (1988).

[15]R.C. 2953.31 et seq.; State v. Bissantz, 30 Ohio St. 3d 120, 121, 507 N.E.2d 1117 (1987).

[16]State v. Heaton, 108 Ohio App. 3d 38, 40, 669 N.E.2d 885 (12th Dist. Clermont County 1995).

Chapter 8

The Nature of a Civil Protection Order

§ 8:1 Introduction

The purpose of the domestic civil protection order statutes is to protect the family or household members from domestic violence.[1] Over the past twenty years, civil protection orders have emerged as both accessible and effective responses to family violence.[2] This alternative approach[3] is in addition to the options available under the criminal law.[4]

The main distinction between the criminal protection order and the civil protection order is that one may obtain a criminal order only after an offender is charged with the crime of domestic violence or another crime of violence under RC 2919.25.[5] In contrast, a civil protection order may be obtained upon the commission of an act of violence,

---

[Section 8:1]

[1]Gaydash v. Gaydash, 168 Ohio App. 3d 418, 423, 2006-Ohio-4080, 860 N.E.2d 789 (9th Dist. Summit County 2006). See also State v. Bosley, 2010-Ohio-1570, 2010 WL 1406529 (Ohio Ct. App. 1st Dist. Hamilton County 2010).

[2]Hon. Hollis L. Webster, Enforcement in Domestic Violence Cases, 26 Loy. U. Chi. L.J. 663 (1995). But see Leigh Goodmark, The Legal Response to Domestic Violence: Problems and Possibilities, Law is the Answer? Do We Know That for Sure?, Questioning the Efficacy of Legal Interventions for Battered Women, 23 St. Louis U. Pub. L. Rev. 7 (2004).

[3]RC 3113.31.

[4]RC 2919.25 et seq.

[5]RC 2919.25, RC 2919.26.

no other underlying cause of action is required.[6] Nonetheless, both the criminal and civil protection orders are designed to deter further criminal activity.[7]

Civil protection orders offer judges a way to respond to the particular problems of domestic violence victims. They are effective in meeting the goals of court intervention by protecting victims from continuing acts of violence in the home.[8] Thus, evidence of an ongoing, continuous pattern of conduct that rises to the level of the acts set forth in RC 3113.31(A)(1)(a) to (c) should provide adequate grounds for obtaining a civil protection order.

When properly enforced, civil protection orders can reduce or eliminate further domestic violence,[9] but immediate enforcement is essential to their effectiveness. Research demonstrates that battering is reduced only when the perpetrator perceives that penalties for further violence will be both certain and severe.[10]

The effectiveness of civil protection orders also depends on whether they specifically detail the relief requested.[11] Comprehensive and precise conditions in the protection order make the perpetrator aware of the specific behavior prohibited. Explicit detail and exact terms in a civil protection order also make it easier for police officers and the court to determine whether a violation has occurred.[12]

§ 8:2 Authority and constitutionality

Ohio is one of the vast majority of jurisdictions allowing the filing of a civil protection action independent of any other family or criminal action. The authority to issue a civil protection order is set forth in RC 3113.31.

There have been several challenges to the constitutionality of Ohio's civil protection order statute; however, most courts have failed to address the issue. For example, in *Kelm v. Kelm*,[1] while declining to address the issues, the court noted "the issues raised by appellant should, at some time, be addressed." The same respondent then filed a

---

[6]RC 3113.31. But cf. RC 2919.26.

[7]But see Candela, Protecting the Invisible Victim: Incorporating Coercive Control in Domestic Violence Statutes, 54 Fam. Ct. Rev. 112 (2016) (discussion of the reasons to make this change to domestic violence statutes); Evan Stark, Coercive Control: How Men Entrap Women In Personal Life (Interpersonal Violence (2007)).

[8]RC 3113.31(E)(1). See also Felton v. Felton, 79 Ohio St. 3d 34, 37, 1997-Ohio-302, 679 N.E.2d 672 (1997); Martin v. Martin, 2013-Ohio-5703, 2013 WL 6843599 (Ohio Ct. App. 10th Dist. Franklin County 2013).

[9]Lenore E. Walker, The Battered Woman, 206–12 (1979); Grau et al., Restraining Orders for Battered Women: Issues of Access and Efficacy, 4 Women & Pol. 13–28 (1984); see also Damon Phillips, Civil Protection Orders: Issues in Obtainment, Enforcement and Effectiveness, 61 J. Mo. B. 29 (2005).

[10]Dianne C. Carmody & Kirk R. Williams, Wife Assault and Perceptions of Sanctions, 2 Violence & Victims 25 (1987); Barbara Hart, Violent No More: Intervention Against Women Abuse in Ohio (Ohio Domestic Violence Network 1990).

[11]RC 3113.31(E)(1)(a) to (h).

[12]RC 2919.27(A).

[Section 8:2]

[1]Kelm v. Kelm, 1993 WL 220881, *2 (Ohio Ct. App. 10th Dist. Franklin County 1993).

class action challenging the constitutionality of RC 3113.31 enabling victims to obtain ex parte civil protection orders.[2] In dismissing the due process challenge on abstention grounds, the Sixth Circuit Federal Court stated, "[W]e decline to rule on the constitutionality of the Ohio statutes at issue."[3]

When the issue was again raised in *Snyder v. Snyder*,[4] the court of appeals declined to address the constitutionality of the statute because the appellant failed to raise the argument in the trial court.

Finally, the Lake County Domestic Relations Court, in *Fusco v. Unger*,[5] the respondent argued to the court in an oral motion that RC 3113.31 is unconstitutional. The Ohio Attorney General only submitted an amicus brief and the Court overruled the respondent's oral motion.

These cases are important, not because the courts refused review, but because they left open the possibility that the constitutionality of RC 3113.31 may still be challenged. As observed above, the Franklin County Court of Appeals noted in *Kelm* that the constitutional issues should be addressed at a later time. Although domestic violence advocates may view this possibility as having frightening consequences, legal experts must consider future legislative enactments that may have harsh constitutional ramifications.

Recently, the Second District Court of Appeals addressed the constitutionality of the civil domestic violence statute. In *Calicoat v. Calicoat*,[6] appellant contended that the magistrate's decision granting the CPO should not have been adopted by the judge because it was based on an unconstitutional statute. He argued that the magistrate's decision resulted in an improper taking of his property in violation of the Fifth and Fourteenth amendments. He also alleged that the statute is void for vagueness.

The appellate court found that a CPO does not affect title to real property. However, depriving him of the use of his property for a period of time is a lawful exercise of police power. "The police power is the authority of the government to adopt and enforce measures to

[2]Black's Law Dictionary (6th ed.) p 576 defines an order that is ex parte as "granted at the instance and for the benefit of one party only, and without notice to, or contestation by, any person adversely interested."

[3]Kelm v. Hyatt, 44 F.3d 415, 419, 1995 FED App. 0025P (6th Cir. 1995).

[4]Snyder v. Snyder, 1995 WL 493998 (Ohio Ct. App. 4th Dist. Ross County 1995); see also Gooderham v. Patterson, 1999 WL 1034472, *4 (Ohio Ct. App. 4th Dist. Gallia County 1999) (noting that appellant failed to raise the constitutionality of RC 3113.31 in the trial court: "To the extent the appellant asks us to strike R.C. 3113.31 on the basis that it is bad public policy, his plea is directed at the wrong branch of government."); Devault v. Devault, 2004-Ohio-976, 2004 WL 397134 (Ohio Ct. App. 5th Dist. Ashland County 2004); Niepsuj v. Office of Administrative Judge, 2017 WL 4512483 (N.D. Ohio 2017) (where plaintiff claims the restrictions placed on him by a CPO violated his 1st Amendment right to free speech and his 14th Amendment right to due process, district court dismissed action *sua sponte* because complaint was "implausible, attenuated, unsubstantial, frivolous, devoid of merit or no longer open to discussion as to deprive the court of subject matter jurisdiction").

[5]*Fusco v. Unger, No. 96 DV 00028 (C.P., Lake, 10-2-96)* (wherein the amicus brief provides a legal analysis in support of the constitutionality of RC 3113.31).

[6]Calicoat v. Calicoat, 2009-Ohio-5869, 2009 WL 3683665 (Ohio Ct. App. 2d Dist. Miami County 2009).

protect the public health, safety, morals and general welfare and to the extent that the exercise of the police power is reasonable and has a real relationship to a legitimate governmental purpose, it has been held not to infringe constitutional rights, despite some incidental interference with individual rights."[7]

In applying this to RC 3113.31, the court stated that "[t]he protection of victims of domestic violence from further harm has as its purpose the protection of the public welfare which is a proper exercise of the police power conferred by the General Assembly. The provisions of RC 3113.31(E) authorizing exclusion of perpetrators from the residence of their victims is reasonable and it has a real relationship to the purpose of protecting victims of domestic violence from further harm. Orders issued pursuant to that section constitute valid exercise of the police power that supersede the constitutional protections against takings of private property. . . ."[8]

According to the appellant, the statute was void for vagueness because it failed to give fair notice of the conduct proscribed. He argued that because the focus was on the "reasonableness of another's subjective reactions," a court must determine each case not by a uniform standard but on a case by case basis.[9] The appellate court analyzed RC 3113.31(A)(1)(b) and held that the elements of domestic violence as defined in the statute are sufficiently definite to give a person of ordinary intelligence a reasonable opportunity to know what conduct is prohibited. That is, conduct which, by threat of force, is sufficient to place another in fear of imminent serious physical harm.

In overruling appellant's assignments of error, the court restated the obvious—that Ohio's civil domestic violence statute is constitutional.

On the other hand, the constitutionality of the *criminal* domestic violence statute[10] has been upheld. In *State v. Widdowson*,[11] the Ashland County Court of Appeals held that the criminal statute "is not unconstitutionally overbroad and vague. . . . Our review of the case law uncovered no instance where either the assault statute or the domestic violence statute was held unconstitutionally vague. We find that the statute is sufficiently definite to convey to a person of ordinary understanding what conduct is proscribed."[12]

Other state courts have repeatedly upheld the constitutionality of

---

[7]At *5, citing State v. Martin, 168 Ohio St. 37, 5 Ohio Op. 2d 293, 151 N.E.2d 7 (1958).

[8]At *5.

[9]At *5.

[10]RC 2919.25.

[11]State v. Widdowson, 1990 WL 79033 (Ohio Ct. App. 5th Dist. Ashland County 1990); see also State v. Sterling, 1998 WL 517867 (Ohio Ct. App. 5th Dist. Tuscarawas County 1998) (defendant unsuccessfully argued that court lacked subject matter jurisdiction because domestic violence statutes, including RC 3113.31, lack enacting clauses and are, therefore, void).

[12]State v. Widdowson, 1990 WL 79033, *2 (Ohio Ct. App. 5th Dist. Ashland County 1990). See also State v. Ealy, 2006-Ohio-414, 2006 WL 235043 (Ohio Ct. App. 2d Dist. Montgomery County 2006) (affirming trial court and holding that RC 2919.27 not unconstitutionally vague as applied in conjunction with RC 3113.31(E)(1)(d) and its parenting time provisions.).

their domestic violence statutes. They did so by balancing the government's interest in providing protection to victims of domestic violence against the risk of deprivation of a defendant's constitutional rights under existing procedures.[13]

The majority of the challenges involve the court's grant of an ex parte protection order, which can deprive a respondent of property and liberty interests without notice and an opportunity to be heard.[14] For example, potential due process concerns occur when a victim requests relief that provides for the ex parte eviction of a perpetrator from the home[15] or where temporary custody is awarded to the victim.[16]

Most courts have found, however, that the interest in aiding domestic violence victims justifies the temporary deprivation of respondent's interest. The shorter the period of deprivation, the more likely a court is to uphold a state statute on constitutional grounds.[17]

For example, in *State ex rel. Williams v. Marsh*,[18] the Missouri Court of Appeals held that the "provisions of the Adult Abuse Act permitting courts to issue ex parte orders of protection to exclude respondents from home or from contact with children for a 15-day period did not deprive respondent of due process." In this case, the court determined that the "Act was necessary to secure important governmental interests in protection of victims of abuse and prevention of further abuse."[19]

In *Pendleton v. Minichino*,[20] addressing a constitutional deprivation of rights challenge, the Connecticut Superior Court upheld the constitutionality of the Connecticut abuse statute allowing a court to grant an ex parte order for fear of physical abuse. Concluding that the order temporarily deprived the defendant of a significant constitutionally protected interest, the court then balanced this right against the petitioner's interest in being free from abuse and the government's

[13]Mathews v. Eldridge, 424 U.S. 319, 96 S. Ct. 893, 47 L. Ed. 2d 18 (1976).

[14]RC 3113.31(E)(4) (title to any real property shall not be affected by any protection order), RC 3113.31(E)(1)(b), RC 3113.31(E)(1)(c) (provides for the eviction of the respondent), RC 3113.31(E)(1)(d) (provides for an award of temporary allocation of parental rights).

[15]See, for example Devault v. Devault, 2004-Ohio-976, 2004 WL 397134 (Ohio Ct. App. 5th Dist. Ashland County 2004).

[16]RC 3113.31(E)(1)(b) to (d); see also Sanders v. Shephard, 185 Ill. App. 3d 719, 133 Ill. Dec. 712, 541 N.E.2d 1150 (1st Dist. 1989) (Illinois Appellate Court held that the provisions of the Domestic Violence Act regarding emergency protection orders were not unconstitutional for failing to provide notice to the respondent and that the emergency order of protection satisfied procedural due process. The court relied on the reasoning of the Supreme Court in Mitchell v. W. T. Grant Co., 416 U.S. 600, 94 S. Ct. 1895, 40 L. Ed. 2d 406, 15 U.C.C. Rep. Serv. 263 (1974), which sets forth the requirements for valid ex parte restraining orders); Kampf v. Kampf, 237 Mich. App. 377, 603 N.W.2d 295 (1999) (rejecting appellant's argument that issuance of ex parte protection order was unconstitutional).

[17]Cobb v. Cobb, 406 Mass. 21, 545 N.E.2d 1161 (1989).

[18]State ex rel. Williams v. Marsh, 626 S.W.2d 223, 223 (Mo. 1982).

[19]State ex rel. Williams v. Marsh, 626 S.W.2d 223, 229 (Mo. 1982); see also Schramek v. Bohren, 145 Wis. 2d 695, 429 N.W.2d 501 (Ct. App. 1988) (spousal abuse statute is not unconstitutional since it does not violate equal protection or due process).

[20]Pendleton v. Minichino, 6 Conn. L. Rptr. 241, 1992 WL 75920 (Conn. Super. Ct. 1992).

interest in the health, safety, and welfare of its citizens. The court noted that the statute provided several safeguards to the defendant because there must be a hearing within 14 days of the ex parte order, the applicant's affidavit must be given under oath, and only a court may issue the order.[21]

Ohio's statute provides for an opportunity to be heard within seven to ten days, a relatively short period of deprivation. RC 3113.31(D) provides for a full hearing within ten court days of the ex parte hearing except where the court evicted the alleged abuser from the home, in which case a full hearing must be held within seven days after the ex parte hearing. However, nothing in RC 3113.31 indicates that a full hearing cannot be held sooner than the stated seven or ten-day period.

An analogy may be drawn to ex parte temporary restraining orders which the United States Supreme Court held are permissible. In *Mitchell v. W.T. Grant Co.*,[22] the Supreme Court set forth the specific requirements necessary to find an ex parte restraining order valid. Specifically, the plaintiff must state facts rather than conclusory allegations by affidavit or testimony, a judge must participate in the decision, and there must be a provision for a post-seizure hearing where the plaintiff must present proof and defendant can present a defense.

Ohio's domestic violence statute, RC 3113.31 satisfies the United States Supreme Court's requirements for cases involving ex parte orders in that:

(1) Petition must allege "that the respondent engaged in domestic violence . . . . including a description of the nature and extent."[23]

(2) "Good cause" must be shown at an ex parte hearing before a judge.[24]

(3) Full hearing with notice to respondent and opportunity to be heard must be held within seven to ten days after the ex parte hearing.[25]

In other constitutional challenges, courts have also held that domestic violence statutes which proscribe physical abuse are not void since persons of ordinary intelligence would have reasonable opportunity to know that punching a person in the face or shoving them so they fall against a wall is illegal behavior.[26]

---

[21]Pendleton v. Minichino, 6 Conn. L. Rptr. 241, 1992 WL 75920 (Conn. Super. Ct. 1992); see also Connecticut v. Doehr, 501 U.S. 1, 111 S. Ct. 2105, 115 L. Ed. 2d 1 (1991); Dorothy Carl Quinn, Comment, Ex Parte Protection Orders: Is Due Process Locked Out? 58 Temp. L.Q. 843 (1985); Taub, Ex Parte Proceedings in Domestic Violence Situations: Alternative Frameworks for Constitutional Scrutiny, 9 Hofstra L. Rev. 95 (1980).

[22]Mitchell v. W. T. Grant Co., 416 U.S. 600, 94 S. Ct. 1895, 40 L. Ed. 2d 406, 15 U.C.C. Rep. Serv. 263 (1974); see also Fuentes v. Shevin, 407 U.S. 67, 92 S. Ct. 1983, 32 L. Ed. 2d 556, 10 U.C.C. Rep. Serv. 913 (1972); Sniadach v. Family Finance Corp. of Bay View, 395 U.S. 337, 89 S. Ct. 1820, 23 L. Ed. 2d 349, 19 Wage & Hour Cas. (BNA) 5 (1969).

[23]RC 3113.31(C)(1); RC 3113.31(A)(1)(d); RC 3113.31(A)(6).

[24]RC 3113.31(D).

[25]RC 3113.31(D).

[26]State v. Kameenui, 69 Haw. 620, 753 P.2d 1250 (1988). See also Calicoat v.

§ 8:3 Statutory elements of domestic violence under RC 3113.31(A)(1)(a)[1]

To commit an act of domestic violence under RC 3113.31(A)(1)(a), a respondent must:

(1) attempt
(2) to cause
(3) bodily injury
(4) to a family or household member; or
(1) recklessly
(2) cause
(3) bodily injury
(4) to a family or household member.

The civil domestic violence statute does not contain definitions of any of its statutory terms. As a matter of practice, in the absence of a specific definition under the civil statute, recourse to the criminal code is necessary to define similar terms. The civil and criminal components of the domestic violence act must necessarily be construed similarly as they both address "injury" and "physical harm." However, unlike RC 2919.25(A), RC 3113.31 does not require the perpetrator of domestic violence to knowingly cause or attempt to cause physical harm or bodily injury.[2]

In order to obtain a civil protection order pursuant to RC 3113.31(A)(1)(a), a petitioner must show that the respondent either "attempted to cause" bodily injury or "recklessly caused" bodily injury. The criminal statutory definitions are instructive for the family law practitioner who must determine whether certain actions rise to the level of domestic violence under RC 3113.31.

Q & A: How is "attempt" defined?

Pursuant to RC 2923.02(A), an attempt is defined as follows: [n]o

---

Calicoat, 2009-Ohio-5869, 2009 WL 3683665 (Ohio Ct. App. 2d Dist. Miami County 2009).

[Section 8:3]

[1]Recently, a new provision was added to RC 3113.31 permitting a CPO against another for "committing a sexually oriented offense" pursuant to RC 3113.31(A)(1)(d).

[2]See State v. Logan, 60 Ohio St. 2d 126, 14 Ohio Op. 3d 373, 397 N.E.2d 1345 (1979); State v. Wenger, 58 Ohio St. 2d 336, 339, 12 Ohio Op. 3d 309, 390 N.E.2d 801 (1979) (holding that to act knowingly, a person need not act with deliberate intent); State v. Knapp, 2001 WL 62519 (Ohio Ct. App. 2d Dist. Montgomery County 2001) (for a discussion of the definition of "knowingly"); see also State v. Zuber, 2001-Ohio-2427, 2001 WL 301408 (Ohio Ct. App. 4th Dist. Hocking County 2001) (defining "knowingly" as one who is aware that his/her conduct will probably cause a certain result, as opposed to possibly); State v. Taylor, 2003-Ohio-2025, 2003 WL 1916787 (Ohio Ct. App. 9th Dist. Summit County 2003) (noting that the state of mind of a defendant, in determining whether he acted knowingly, is made from the totality of the circumstances surrounding the alleged crime); State v. Amos, 1988 WL 4622 (Ohio Ct. App. 11th Dist. Lake County 1988) (for a discussion of physiological impairment and pain); State v. Terrell, 2008-Ohio-1863, 2008 WL 1759095, *3 (Ohio Ct. App. 2d Dist. Montgomery County 2008) (Court stated that "when knowledge suffices to establish an element of an offense, then purpose is also sufficient culpability for such an element." See also RC 2901.22(E); RC 2901.22(A). Purposeful conduct satisfies a requirement that defendant acted "knowingly." State v. Terrell, 2008-Ohio-1863, 2008 WL 1759095, *4 (Ohio Ct. App. 2d Dist. Montgomery County 2008)).

person purposely or knowingly, and when purpose or knowledge is sufficient culpability for the commission of an offense, shall engage in conduct that, if successful, would constitute or result in the offense. A criminal attempt is defined as "an act or omission constituting a substantial step in a course of conduct planned to culminate in [the] commission of the crime."[3] In *State v. Woods*,[4] the Ohio Supreme Court defined the term "criminal attempt" to mean "when one purposely does or omits to do anything which is an act or omission constituting a substantial step in a course of conduct planned to culminate in the commission of a crime. To constitute a substantial step, the conduct must be strongly corroborative of the actor's criminal purpose." The culpable mental state "purposely" is defined in RC 2901.22(A).

The *Woods* case presents a family law practitioner with a cogent argument that the intent to injure is at least as important as the intent to commit the act.[5] In the domestic violence context, even a punch that missed its intended target may be viewed as an attempt to cause injury or harm.[6] This is because of the difficulty in demonstrating intent to commit the act. For example, the respondent's actions and words may demonstrate that a respondent had the intent to injure and such actions are often sufficient to comply with the statutory language of RC 3113.31(A)(1)(a).[7] Additionally, evidence should be elicited as to the subjective intent of the respondent to determine intent as well as the subjective belief of the victim that the act caused him/her to fear further harm or injury.

As in Ohio, other states' decisions involved the criminal codes. However, analogies are necessarily made to the act of attempt for purposes of the civil protection order. For example, the construction of the term was also examined in *People v. Kinsey*,[8] where the defendant was convicted of attempting to cause injury to his girlfriend. The evidence showed that he had shoved, screamed and sworn at, and tried

---

[3]RC 2923.02(A).

[4]State v. Woods, 48 Ohio St. 2d 127, 2 Ohio Op. 3d 289, 357 N.E.2d 1059 (1976) (overruled by, State v. Downs, 51 Ohio St. 2d 47, 5 Ohio Op. 3d 30, 364 N.E.2d 1140 (1977)) and (disavowed by, State v. Barker, 53 Ohio St. 2d 135, 7 Ohio Op. 3d 213, 372 N.E.2d 1324 (1978)) and cert. granted, judgment vacated, 438 U.S. 910, 98 S. Ct. 3133, 57 L. Ed. 2d 1153 (1978); State v. Brooks, 44 Ohio St. 3d 185, 542 N.E.2d 636 (1989); State v. Curry, 43 Ohio St. 2d 66, 72 Ohio Op. 2d 37, 330 N.E.2d 720 (1975); see also City of Akron v. Morgan, 2000 WL 141065, *3 (Ohio Ct. App. 9th Dist. Summit County 2000) (discussing that the "state need only to prove that [the offender] caused the injury with an awareness that his conduct [would] probably cause a certain result or [would] probably be of a certain nature"); City of Warren v. Culver, 2004-Ohio-333, 2004 WL 144227 (Ohio Ct. App. 11th Dist. Trumbull County 2004).

[5]But see RC 2923.02(D), which provides that an action is not criminally punishable as attempt to commit a particular crime unless the accused had the intent to commit that crime.

[6]See Cauwenbergh v. Cauwenbergh, 2007-Ohio-1070, 2007 WL 726951, *3 (Ohio Ct. App. 11th Dist. Ashtabula County 2007) (holding that the act of pushing appellee, who had their child in her arms at the time, constituted domestic violence as far as it attempted to cause bodily injury to appellee. Thus her testimony that she was pushed, that she was concerned for her safety and that she feared that she was going to be injured supports the finding that she met her burden of proof).

[7]J.R. v. E.H., 2017-Ohio-516, 2017 WL 587314 (Ohio Ct. App. 10th Dist. Franklin County 2017).

[8]People v. Kinsey, 40 Cal. App. 4th 1621, 47 Cal. Rptr. 2d 769 (2d Dist. 1995).

to "get at her" for an hour.[9] Although he was restrained by a friend, the defendant did scratch his partner, causing a mark to her neck. The court construed an attempt to commit a crime as requiring a specific intent to commit the crime and an ineffectual act toward its commission. The court rejected the defendant's argument that attempted injury also requires a resultant traumatic condition.[10]

An attempt to harm a family or household member may demonstrate that the respondent is disposed to violence not only on that occasion, but on other occasions as well.[11] In fact, attempts to harm are strong indicators of a person's propensity for more serious and deadly violence in the future.[12] Attempts should be punishable by prosecution and conviction because, "in some circumstances, a person whose criminal scheme has miscarried on a particular occasion may present a greater continuing danger than the person who succeeded."[13]

Most Ohio courts will issue protection orders based on uncompleted acts or attempts that did not cause actual physical injury.[14] In *State v. Nielsen*,[15] the court held that "a defendant can be convicted of domestic violence for merely attempting to cause physical harm to a family member. The state was not required to prove actual injury."[16] Even if the petitioner is merely shoved or sustains minor injury or pain with

---

[9]But see City of Youngstown v. Osso, 115 Ohio App. 3d 416, 685 N.E.2d 593 (7th Dist. Mahoning County 1996) (overruling domestic violence conviction because, though defendant came to the victim's house, kicked the side door, and screamed, he left before victim came downstairs and holding that complete and voluntary renunciation of any criminal purpose is affirmative defense to attempt charge).

[10]See City of Youngstown v. Osso, 115 Ohio App. 3d 416, 685 N.E.2d 593 (7th Dist. Mahoning County 1996) (noting that RC 2919.25(A) does not require that actual physical harm be proven to sustain a conviction as the state may prove that an accused knowingly attempted to cause physical harm to a family or household member).

[11]LaFave and Scott, Handbook on Criminal Law (2d ed.) p 499.

[12]See Geraldine Butts Stahly, Victim Rights and Issues: Special Problems of Battered Woman as Victim/Witness in Partner Abuse Cases, paper presented at the Western Society of Criminology Conference, Las Vegas, Nevada (Feb. 27, 1978).

[13]LaFave and Scott, Handbook on Criminal Law (2d ed.) p 427.

[14]See also Dorsey v. Dorsey, 2009-Ohio-4894, 2009 WL 2973505 (Ohio Ct. App. 5th Dist. Richland County 2009).

[15]State v. Nielsen, 66 Ohio App. 3d 609, 612, 585 N.E.2d 906 (6th Dist. Huron County 1990); see also State v. Mossbarger, 2000 WL 303140 (Ohio Ct. App. 4th Dist. Pike County 2000); State v. Kartman, 2002-Ohio-5189, 2002 WL 31163739, *2 (Ohio Ct. App. 7th Dist. Belmont County 2002) (discussing attempt and noting that a defendant may be found guilty of domestic violence even if the victim sustains only minor injuries or no injury at all), citing State v. Blonski, 125 Ohio App. 3d 103, 707 N.E.2d 1168 (9th Dist. Medina County 1997); see State v. Ward, 2009-Ohio-3145, 2009 WL 1844486 (Ohio Ct. App. 11th Dist. Geauga County 2009); State v. Howell, 2017-Ohio-728, 86 N.E.3d 114 (Ohio Ct. App. 7th Dist. Mahoning County 2017) (defendant does not have to cause serious injury to be guilty of domestic violence; defendant may be found guilty even if victim sustains only minor injury or no injury at all).

[16]See Sroka v. Sroka, 121 Ohio App. 3d 728, 700 N.E.2d 916 (8th Dist. Cuyahoga County 1997) (grabbing victim by her neck and pushing her down to the floor was sufficient evidence to show an attempt to injure the victim; the fact that the victim was not injured was inconsequential to a finding); J.R. v. E.H., 2017-Ohio-516, 2017 WL 587314 (Ohio Ct. App. 10th Dist. Franklin County 2017) (no need for petitioner to demonstrate that he/she sustained a verifiable bodily injury).

no observable injuries, a defendant may be convicted for attempting to cause physical harm.[17]

For example, in *State v. Younker*,[18] the defendant was convicted of domestic violence when he threw an empty pop can at his wife from three or four feet. Although reversed on other grounds, the Darke County Court of Appeals found that there was legally sufficient evidence to warrant his conviction. The appellate court concluded that the statutory definition of physical harm was met by the victim's testimony that "when the cans struck her in the knee, the impacts caused her some pain for a short while."[19]

The fact that a respondent may have lacked the intent to cause physical harm or bodily injury is of no consequence because RC 3113.31(A)(1)(a) does not require this as relating to an "attempt."[20] Thus, the mere attempt to cause bodily injury is sufficient to constitute the act, whether or not actual injury or harm resulted from the act.

However, in *Stanzak v. Stanzak*,[21] the court of appeals reversed the granting of a civil protection order issued following an incident where the respondent backed up a car near the petitioner. The court found insufficient evidence to support a finding that the respondent attempted or threatened to injure the petitioner.

Civil protection orders should always be granted where a petitioner presents evidence of an attempt to harm or cause bodily injury. Unlike actual injury, an attempt often contains elements of a threat as defined in RC 3113.31 (A)(1)(b).

For example, in *J.R. v. E.H.*,[22] appellant appealed the denial of her petition for a civil protection order. The testimony indicated that appellee entered her home and pointed a gun at her and threatened to

---

[17]State v. Nielsen, 66 Ohio App. 3d 609, 613, 585 N.E.2d 906 (6th Dist. Huron County 1990); see also R.G. v. T.D., 448 Pa. Super. 525, 672 A.2d 341, 107 Ed. Law Rep. 876 (1996) (Despite neither actual nor attempted violence, the court found that evidence of unwanted telephone calls and electronic mail messages, including one that said "You're not answering me, you'll die," was sufficient to obtain a civil protection order). But see State v. Dotson, 2006-Ohio-1093, 2006 WL 562029, *2 (Ohio Ct. App. 7th Dist. Columbiana County 2006) (judgment reversing conviction for domestic violence because "pushing or pulling a person without evidence of anything more is simply not enough to justify a conviction for domestic violence"; there was no evidence that Dotson caused or attempted to cause physical harm to either victim or their children).

[18]State v. Younker, 2002-Ohio-5376, 2002 WL 31242238 (Ohio Ct. App. 2d Dist. Darke County 2002).

[19]State v. Younker, 2002-Ohio-5376, 2002 WL 31242238, *3 (Ohio Ct. App. 2d Dist. Darke County 2002).

[20]State v. Younker, 2002-Ohio-5376, 2002 WL 31242238, *3 (Ohio Ct. App. 2d Dist. Darke County 2002); State v. Howell, 2017-Ohio-728, 86 N.E.3d 114 (Ohio Ct. App. 7th Dist. Mahoning County 2017) (finding that it was irrelevant whether appellant could have anticipated degree of potential injury because he was generally aware that it was more likely than not that his actions would cause injury and in line with the established principle that a person who exposes another to danger is presumed to know the consequences of their actions).

[21]Stanzak v. Stanzak, 1990 WL 129456 (Ohio Ct. App. 12th Dist. Butler County 1990).

[22]J.R. v. E.H., 2017-Ohio-516, 2017 WL 587314 (Ohio Ct. App. 10th Dist. Franklin County 2017).

kill her, that 2 months earlier, the parties got into a shoving match and 2 months before that, appellee beat her and stole her truck. The trial court did not grant the CPO, holding that appellant failed to prove her allegations.

The appellate court began its analysis by reviewing the definition of "bodily injury" and "attempt." "Bodily injury was defined, for purposes of domestic violence, as the same as "physical harm" which is defined as "any injury, regardless of gravity or duration.[23]

The court then considered the statutory factors to determine whether a CPO should be issued or denied. The court relied on those cases that have determined that "the statutory criterion to determine whether or not to grant a civil protection order is the existence or threatened existence of domestic violence."[24] The court went on to say that "[w]here the evidence establishes that an act of domestic violence occurred, the mandates of RC 3113.31 for issuance of the order of protection are satisfied regardless of the fact that the petitioner no longer has contact with the respondent and, consequently, is no longer fearful of the respondent."[25] Since a petitioner need not testify that respondent placed her in fear of imminent harm when he actually harmed her,[26] the appellate court found that "RC 3113.31(A)(1)(a) requires the trial court to issue a CPO where the petitioner establishes by a preponderance of the evidence that respondent attempted to cause or recklessly cause bodily injury to petitioner."[27]

The court found that appellant had demonstrated that "beating each other in the truck" and appellee's biting of appellant requires the conclusion that appellee attempted to cause appellant bodily injury.[28] The court pointed out that RC 3113.31(A)(1)(a) does not require a finding of which party started the argument and why the argument escalated to the point of physical violence. In doing this, "the trial court imposed an additional burden of proof on appellant that is not required."[29] Nor is a determination of the identity of the primary physical aggressor an element of the offense.[30] In sustaining the assignment of error and reversing the judgment of the trial court, the admission that appellee bit appellant in the arm during the alterca-

---

[23] J.R. v. E.H., 2017-Ohio-516, ¶ 13, 2017 WL 587314 (Ohio Ct. App. 10th Dist. Franklin County 2017); RC 2901.01(A)(3).

[24] J.R. v. E.H., 2017-Ohio-516, ¶ 15, 2017 WL 587314 (Ohio Ct. App. 10th Dist. Franklin County 2017), quoting Thomas v. Thomas, 44 Ohio App. 3d 6, 8, 540 N.E.2d 745 (10th Dist. Franklin County 1988).

[25] J.R. v. E.H., 2017-Ohio-516, ¶ 15, 2017 WL 587314 (Ohio Ct. App. 10th Dist. Franklin County 2017), citing Duncan v. Duncan, 2010-Ohio-5334, 2010 WL 4345722 (Ohio Ct. App. 5th Dist. Muskingum County 2010).

[26] Zawrotuk v. Zawrotuk, 2014-Ohio-5225, ¶ 34, 2014 WL 6641772 (Ohio Ct. App. 7th Dist. Mahoning County 2014).

[27] J.R. v. E.H., 2017-Ohio-516, ¶ 15, 2017 WL 587314 (Ohio Ct. App. 10th Dist. Franklin County 2017), citing Zawrotuk at ¶ 34.

[28] J.R. v. E.H., 2017-Ohio-516, ¶ 17, 2017 WL 587314 (Ohio Ct. App. 10th Dist. Franklin County 2017).

[29] J.R. v. E.H., 2017-Ohio-516, ¶ 17, 2017 WL 587314 (Ohio Ct. App. 10th Dist. Franklin County 2017).

[30] J.R. v. E.H., 2017-Ohio-516, ¶ 17, 2017 WL 587314 (Ohio Ct. App. 10th Dist. Franklin County 2017).

tion demonstrates that he recklessly caused or attempted to cause bodily injury to appellant.[31]

Additionally, the court tangentially addressed appellee's argument that he acted in self defense and aptly noted that he failed to file his own petition for CPO as required under RC 3113.31(E)(4) or raise the defense of self defense at trial.[32]

Finally, the court also distinguished between the proof necessary to obtain an ex parte CPO as well as the proof necessary to obtain a CPO under RC 3113.31(A)(1)(b). As to an ex parte CPO, a petitioner must prove that the CPO was necessary to protect petitioner from domestic violence or that there was an "immediate and present danger" of domestic violence.[33] Regarding a threat under RC 3113.31(A)(1)(b), there must be proof that a petitioner was placed in fear of imminent serious physical harm.

It is important for the victim's attorney to consider the perception of the victim vis-a-vis the act in question and inquire as to the victim's subjective belief that the act put him/her in fear of physical harm. Further, testimony must be elicited from the victim that he/she is in danger of domestic violence.[34] A court's refusal to issue a civil protection order based on an attempt to injure may reinforce, in both parties' minds, the legitimacy of the batterer's behavior. More importantly, a judicial refusal may have serious or even deadly consequences.

Q & A: How is the term "cause" defined?

"Cause" is defined in the criminal volume of *Ohio Jury Instructions* as "an act or failure to act which in a natural and continuous sequence directly produces the (death) (physical harm to [person] [property]), and without which it would not have occurred."[35] The term has also been defined, in *State v. Fabritz*,[36] to mean "that person would in some manner have to be accountable for the 'condition that brings about an effect or that produces or calls forth a resultant action or state.' "

Q & A: How is the term "recklessly" defined?

A civil protection order may also be obtained if the respondent "recklessly caused bodily injury." The culpable mental state "recklessly" is defined in RC 2901.22(C), which provides that "[a] person acts recklessly when, with heedless indifference to the consequences, he perversely disregards a known risk that his conduct is likely to cause

[31]J.R. v. E.H., 2017-Ohio-516, ¶ 20, 2017 WL 587314 (Ohio Ct. App. 10th Dist. Franklin County 2017); see also McElroy v. McElroy, 2016-Ohio-5148, ¶ 33, 2016 WL 4039227 (Ohio Ct. App. 5th Dist. Guernsey County 2016) (entitling petitioner to a CPO even though the evidence established that the parties engaged in mutual combat).

[32]See also Burke v. Melton, 2003-Ohio-7054, 2003 WL 23009045 (Ohio Ct. App. 8th Dist. Cuyahoga County 2003).

[33]RC 3113.31(D).

[34]See Felton v. Felton, 79 Ohio St. 3d 34, 1997-Ohio-302, 679 N.E.2d 672 (1997).

[35]4 OJI 409.55 (1997).

[36]State v. Fabritz, 276 Md. 416, 424, 348 A.2d 275 (1975).

a certain result or is likely to be of a certain nature."[37] That said, the person must know there is a risk and then consciously disregard that risk.

In the context of a civil protection order, the reckless act causing "bodily injury" or "physical harm" to a petitioner is not as serious as under RC 2919.25(B), which discusses "recklessly" in terms of "serious physical harm." To prevail, the burden of proof is less stringent and the degree of actual harm is often less severe.

Q & A: How is the term "bodily injury" defined?

As an element of the act of domestic violence, the victim/petitioner must also prove that the respondent caused "bodily injury" to him/her. The Ohio legislature has not defined the term "bodily injury" in either the criminal or civil domestic violence statutes.[38] According to *Black's Law Dictionary*, "bodily injury" generally refers "only to injury to the body, or to sickness or disease contracted by the injured as a result of injury."[39] In *State v. Suchomski*,[40] the Ohio Supreme Court defined "injury" in the scope of RC 2919.25 as meaning an "invasion of any legally protected interest of another."

More and more cases are redefining "bodily injury" as "physical harm" under RC 2901.01(A)(3), the definition of domestic violence under the domestic violence criminal statute. For example, in *J.M. v. M.M.*,[41] the appellate court, in analyzing RC 3113.31 and its application to the facts at hand, defined "bodily injury" as that which would encompass "any injury, illness or other physiological impairment, regardless of gravity or duration, to wit: the definition of "physical harm" in the criminal code.[42]

Q & A: What is the definition of "physical harm" and can it be useful in the civil domestic violence context?

It may be useful to consider the definition of "physical harm" (an element of criminal domestic violence pursuant to RC 2919.25(A)[43] and RC 2919.25(B)) in order to understand the meaning of "bodily injury" under RC 3113.31(A)(1). Pursuant to RC 2901.01(A)(3), "physical harm to persons" is defined as "any injury,[44] illness, or other physi-

[37]RC 2901.22(C); see also State v. Edwards, 83 Ohio App. 3d 357, 614 N.E.2d 1123 (10th Dist. Franklin County 1992).

[38]R.T. v. J.T., 2015-Ohio-4418, 2015 WL 6449294 (Ohio Ct. App. 9th Dist. Medina County 2015) (Medina Court of Appeals defined bodily injury as "encompassing 'any injury, illness, or other physiological impairment, regardless of gravity or duration' " as set forth in RC 2901.01(A)(3) [at ¶ 14].

[39]Black's Law Dictionary (6th ed.) p 175.

[40]State v. Suchomski, 58 Ohio St. 3d 74, 75, 567 N.E.2d 1304 (1991).

[41]J.M. v. M.M., 2016-Ohio-5368, 2016 WL 4272340 (Ohio Ct. App. 9th Dist. Medina County 2016).

[42]J.R. v. E.H., 2017-Ohio-516, ¶ 13, 2017 WL 587314 (Ohio Ct. App. 10th Dist. Franklin County 2017).

[43]See, e.g., State v. Eberly, 2004-Ohio-3026, 2004 WL 1302320 (Ohio Ct. App. 3d Dist. Wyandot County 2004) (holding that bruises caused when appellant grabbed victim, bruises caused when he forced her head in mattress, and injuries sustained when he pushed her into a dresser were sufficient to constitute "physical harm").

[44]See State v. Tietge, 2006-Ohio-235, 2006 WL 164977, *5 (Ohio Ct. App. 2d Dist. Montgomery County 2006) (noting that defendant's act of slinging his wife around the

ological impairment,[45] regardless of its gravity or duration."[46] In *State v. Mills*,[47] the Hamilton County Court of Appeals applied this definition to the criminal domestic violence statute. In *State v. Gray*,[48] the Erie County Court of Appeals found that "[s]lapping, striking, and pushing, regardless of the gravity, do constitute physical harm to persons. R.C. 2901.01(C)."[49] The court rejected the appellant's argument that there must be a corroborating witness[50] or visual evidence such as bruises.[51] Arguably, "physical harm" may be an adequate way to evaluate "bodily injury" for the purpose of satisfying the statutory elements of RC 3113.31(A)(1).[52]

---

room, throwing her down on the couch and pinning her down with his arm would be likely to cause her physical harm; "The elbow blow to her eye was more a freakish accident, but a natural and probable outcome of the violence used in assaulting her.").

[45]State v. Amos, 1988 WL 4622 (Ohio Ct. App. 11th Dist. Lake County 1988) (finding a kick that caused momentary pain and injury constituted "physical harm" and noting that physiological impairment encompasses pain no matter how temporary in nature); see also State v. Johnson, 1989 WL 43040 (Ohio Ct. App. 2d Dist. Greene County 1989) (physical harm includes the infliction of pain by grabbing all or some portion of the male genital organ).

[46]But see State v. Younker, 2002-Ohio-5376, 2002 WL 31242238, *4 (Ohio Ct. App. 2d Dist. Darke County 2002) (noting that "physical harm" "encompasses almost anything that resulted in some harm. Further, lacking a specific intent requirement, whatever the accused did that caused [the harm] might qualify. This combination has produced a spate of domestic violence complaints on which law enforcement officers are required to act, made by persons engaged in dysfunctional relationships, over 'injuries' so negligible as to lack any sound reason to invoke the power of the state. Complaints then become tactical measures in an ongoing domestic dispute." The definitions of "knowingly" and "physical harm" are so broad, they have come to embrace situations their drafters probably never intended include. In this case, husband was convicted of domestic violence for throwing two empty pop cans at his wife from three to four feet away. Said conviction was reversed on appeal).

[47]State v. Mills, 1997 WL 133430 (Ohio Ct. App. 1st Dist. Hamilton County 1997); see also State v. Suchomski, 58 Ohio St. 3d 74, 567 N.E.2d 1304 (1991).

[48]State v. Gray, 1988 WL 51481, *3 (Ohio Ct. App. 6th Dist. Erie County 1988), cause dismissed, 38 Ohio St. 3d 722, 533 N.E.2d 1060 (1988).

[49]See State v. Mullins, 1999 WL 668812 (Ohio Ct. App. 5th Dist. Richland County 1999).

[50]See also Hoffman v. Hoffman, 1998 WL 469876 (Ohio Ct. App. 9th Dist. Summit County 1998); Maccabee v. Maccabee, 1999 WL 430943 (Ohio Ct. App. 10th Dist. Franklin County 1999) (relying on Felton v. Felton, 79 Ohio St. 3d 34, 44, 1997-Ohio-302, 679 N.E.2d 672 (1997)); State v. Parks, 2006-Ohio-2430, 2006 WL 1330930 (Ohio Ct. App. 5th Dist. Stark County 2006) (noting that evidence of visible injuries on victim is sufficient corroborative evidence of the uncontroverted statement of the victim).

[51]See also Visnich v. Visnich, 1999 WL 1299300 (Ohio Ct. App. 11th Dist. Trumbull County 1999) (upholding the issuance of a civil protection order even though the magistrate did not find that the victim suffered any direct physical harm at the hands of defendant); Bruns v. Bruns, 1999 WL 819344 (Ohio Ct. App. 6th Dist. Erie County 1999) (upholding the issuance of a civil protection order in the absence of visible marks or injuries). See also State v. Boldin, 2008-Ohio-6408, 2008 WL 5147450 (Ohio Ct. App. 11th Dist. Geauga County 2008) (noting that "physical harm" does not require evidence of visible injuries); State v. Mansour, 2011-Ohio-5438, 2011 WL 5028611 (Ohio Ct. App. 11th Dist. Trumbull County 2011).

[52]See also State v. Mabry, 1996 WL 577701 (Ohio Ct. App. 9th Dist. Medina County 1996); State v. Amos, 1988 WL 4622, *2 (Ohio Ct. App. 11th Dist. Lake County 1988) (determining that physiological impairment encompasses pain no matter how temporary in nature and finding "no indication that pain must be evidenced by an

Similarly, in *State v. Zuber*,[53] the court noted that infliction of significant pain can constitute "physical harm" as defined in RC 2901.01(C).[54] In this case, the appellate court found that "a reasonable fact-finder could infer that appellant kicked Zuber with enough force that she knew or should have known that it would cause him pain, and that he did in fact experience significant pain as a result."[55]

Q & A: Does emotional distress or mental anguish constitute "bodily injury"?[56]

It depends. Since the term "bodily injury" tends to imply physical harm to the human body, the courts have encountered great difficulty in determining whether mental anguish or emotional distress can be characterized as an injury to the body.

For example, the issue has been raised in several insurance coverage cases. Most courts, reluctant to hold that mental anguish or emotional distress constitutes the type of bodily injury which the insurer must indemnify, tend to adopt the general rule articulated in *Farm Bureau Mutual Insurance Co. v. Hoag*.[57] In that case, the court determined that "the term 'bodily injury' [was] unambiguous and understood to mean hurt or harm to the human body, contemplating actual physical harm or damage to a human body."[58] It further stated that bodily injury does not include humiliation and mental anguish.

Following the prevailing view espoused in *Hoag*, the Second District Court of Appeals, in *Reichard v. Nationwide Mutual Fire Insurance Co.*,[59] held that "emotional distress, in the absence of some physical harm, does not constitute 'bodily injury.'" The court then went on to say that it followed the reasoning of *Tomlinson v. Skolnik*[60] even though *Tomlinson* did not address the specific issue before the court.

---

outward physical manifestation in order to constitute 'physical harm' ").

[53]State v. Zuber, 2001-Ohio-2427, 2001 WL 301408 (Ohio Ct. App. 4th Dist. Hocking County 2001).

[54]But see State v. Gatson, 2009-Ohio-120, 2009 WL 94596, *4 (Ohio Ct. App. 8th Dist. Cuyahoga County 2009) (holding that significant injury is not an element of domestic violence; the state only needs to prove that Gatson caused or attempted to cause physical harm).

[55]State v. Zuber, 2001-Ohio-2427, 2001 WL 301408, *3 (Ohio Ct. App. 4th Dist. Hocking County 2001); see also State v. Wray, 2001-Ohio-2356, 2001 WL 243488 (Ohio Ct. App. 4th Dist. Gallia County 2001).

[56]See also Text § 9:8.

[57]Farm Bureau Mut. Ins. Co. of Michigan v. Hoag, 136 Mich. App. 326, 356 N.W.2d 630 (1984).

[58]Farm Bureau Mut. Ins. Co. of Michigan v. Hoag, 136 Mich. App. 326, 356 N.W.2d 630 (1984).

[59]Reichard v. Nationwide Mut. Fire Ins. Co., 1992 WL 361829, *2 (Ohio Ct. App. 2d Dist. Montgomery County 1992); Vance v. Sang Chong, Inc., 1990 WL 174121 (Ohio Ct. App. 11th Dist. Lake County 1990), dismissed, 60 Ohio St. 3d 702, 573 N.E.2d 118 (1991); see also E-Z Loader Boat Trailers, Inc. v. Travelers Indem. Co., 106 Wash. 2d 901, 726 P.2d 439, 45 Empl. Prac. Dec. (CCH) P 37772 (1986); State Farm Fire & Cas. Co. v. Hiermer, 720 F. Supp. 1310, 50 Fair Empl. Prac. Cas. (BNA) 1787, 53 Empl. Prac. Dec. (CCH) P 39789 (S.D. Ohio 1988), aff'd, 884 F.2d 580 (6th Cir. 1989).

[60]Tomlinson v. Skolnik, 44 Ohio St. 3d 11, 540 N.E.2d 716 (1989) (overruled by, Schaefer v. Allstate Ins. Co., 76 Ohio St. 3d 553, 1996-Ohio-368, 668 N.E.2d 913 (1996)).

In *Tomlinson v. Skolnik*, the Supreme Court of Ohio restricted the term "bodily injury" to "an injury caused by external violence."[61]

The impact of these decisions suggests a lack of recourse to a victim who is subjected to emotional trauma, however severe it may be. However, other courts, while acknowledging the rule enunciated in *Hoag*, have held that emotional or mental suffering and humiliation establish a bodily injury. For example, in *NPS Corp. v. Insurance Co. of North America*, the court stated that "[w]e are unable to separate a person's nerves and tensions from his body. Clearly, emotional trauma can be as disabling . . . as a visible physical wound."[62]

In the context of domestic violence, Ohio's civil domestic violence statute defines acts of domestic violence as either "bodily injury"[63] or "serious physical harm."[64] This distinction suggests a legislative recognition that the statute contemplates some emotional abuse or mental distress. The difference between "physical harm"[65] and "serious physical harm"[66] is a matter of degree and increased level of impairment. In order to rise to the level of "serious physical harm," the impairment to the victim must be protracted and of such severity that the victim's life, mental or physical health, function of a specific part of the body or bodily organ or mental condition is affected. RC 3113.31(A)(1)(b) defines an act of domestic violence as "[p]lacing another person by the threat of force in fear of imminent serious physical harm." "Serious physical harm to persons" is defined in RC 2901.01(E) as including "[a]ny mental illness or condition of such gravity as would normally require hospitalization or prolonged psychiatric treatment."[67]

It is important to note that, as more courts recognize stalking as domestic violence when it occurs against a family or household member, the elements of mental distress of RC 2903.211 must be considered when discussing emotional abuse and mental anguish.[68] For example,

---

[61]Tomlinson v. Skolnik, 44 Ohio St. 3d 11, 14, 540 N.E.2d 716 (1989) (overruled by, Schaefer v. Allstate Ins. Co., 76 Ohio St. 3d 553, 1996-Ohio-368, 668 N.E.2d 913 (1996)).

[62]NPS Corp. v. Insurance Co. of North America, 213 N.J. Super. 547, 517 A.2d 1211, 1214, 44 Fair Empl. Prac. Cas. (BNA) 224, 2 I.E.R. Cas. (BNA) 471, 43 Empl. Prac. Dec. (CCH) P 37014 (App. Div. 1986); Chemung County v. Hartford Cas. Ins. Co., 130 Misc. 2d 648, 496 N.Y.S.2d 933 (Sup 1985).

[63]RC 3113.31(A)(1)(a); Rosine v. Rosine, 2010-Ohio-613, 2010 WL 598642 (Ohio Ct. App. 7th Dist. Mahoning County 2010) (where respondent struck petitioner in head and buttocks and threw her to ground causing bruising, domestic violence occurred under RC 3113.31(A)(1)(a)).

[64]RC 3113.31(A)(1)(b). J.M. v. M.M., 2016-Ohio-5368, ¶ 13, 2016 WL 4272340 (Ohio Ct. App. 9th Dist. Medina County 2016) ("serious physical harm" must be considered in context of "fear of imminent serious physical harm").

[65]See RC 2901.01(A)(3).

[66]See RC 2901.01(A)(5).

[67]Eichenberger v. Eichenberger, 82 Ohio App. 3d 809, 613 N.E.2d 678 (10th Dist. Franklin County 1992); Merola v. Merola, 146 A.D.2d 611, 536 N.Y.S.2d 842 (2d Dep't 1989); Boniek v. Boniek, 443 N.W.2d 196 (Minn. Ct. App. 1989); Anne L. Ganley, Domestic Violence: The What, Why and Who, as Relevant to Civil Court Cases, in Domestic Violence in Civil Court Cases: A National Model for Judicial Education 23 (Jacqueline A. Agtuca et al. eds., 1992).

[68]See also Chapter 9 Stalking and Trespass; Text 11:10 and Text 12:11.

in Majeed v. Majeed,[69] appellee sought a CPO against her husband because of his mental abuse and controlling behavior. He had come to her separate residence, blocked her driveway and refused to allow her to go to her therapy appointments. "She stated that she was scared to come outside and for her life, and that he controlled her access to food and money."[70] She also testified that he controlled "how she drives," that he forbade her to work, that he paid for everything and that she suffered from anxiety. She also described that in the past he shoved her neck while they were driving causing her to suffer a cervical strain, that he had killed one of the puppies and that she was unable to open a day care at her home because he came into the backyard, took off his clothes and acted as if he was "ejaculating on me."[71]

Appellant claimed that the trial court erred when it issued the CPO, arguing that she had not proven her case by a preponderance of the evidence. However, the appellate court focused on stalking behaviors under RC 3113.31(A)(1)(b)[72] and determined that appellee had proven that she was in need of a CPO because of appellant's mental abuse of her, her fear and the anxiety she suffered.

In the context of children, domestic violence also includes acts with respect to a child that would result in the child being an abused child as defined in RC 2151.031.[73] Under RC 2151.031(C), child abuse is defined as an act that "exhibits evidence of any physical or mental injury or death, inflicted other than by accidental means."[74] Additionally, RC 2151.031(D) provides that an abused child is also one who, "Because of the acts of his parents . . . suffers physical or mental injury that harms or threatens to harm the child's health or welfare."[75]

At least two Ohio cases have contemplated mental injury as a basis for issuing a civil protection order. In *Kurincic v. Kurincic*,[76] the domestic violence incident occurred between the minor child and the appellant's new husband. The appellant mother had neither hit the child nor stopped the new husband from doing so.

In finding that there was competent, credible evidence to demonstrate that the appellant mother had committed acts of domestic violence against the minor child, the Eighth District Court of Appeals stated that "domestic violence includes acts of a parent which cause physical or mental injury that harms or threatens to harm the child's health or welfare."[77] The court relied on both RC 3113.31(A)(1)(c) and

---

[69]Majeed v. Majeed, 2016-Ohio-7243, 2016 WL 5887174 (Ohio Ct. App. 2d Dist. Montgomery County 2016).

[70]Majeed v. Majeed, 2016-Ohio-7243, ¶ 2, 2016 WL 5887174 (Ohio Ct. App. 2d Dist. Montgomery County 2016).

[71]Majeed v. Majeed, 2016-Ohio-7243, ¶ 6, 2016 WL 5887174 (Ohio Ct. App. 2d Dist. Montgomery County 2016).

[72]See also McElroy v. McElroy, 2016-Ohio-5148, 2016 WL 4039227 (Ohio Ct. App. 5th Dist. Guernsey County 2016).

[73]RC 3113.31(A)(1)(c).

[74]RC 2151.031(C).

[75]RC 2151.031(D).

[76]Kurincic v. Kurincic, 2000 WL 217808 (Ohio Ct. App. 8th Dist. Cuyahoga County 2000).

[77]Kurincic v. Kurincic, 2000 WL 217808, *3 (Ohio Ct. App. 8th Dist. Cuyahoga

RC 2151.031(D) to support its decision. It also noted that "serious physical harm" referred to in RC 3113.31(A)(1)(b) includes "'any mental illness or condition of such gravity as would normally require hospitalization or prolonged psychiatric treatment.' "[78]

Recognizing the seriousness of emotional abuse towards children, the Cuyahoga County Appellate Court upheld the issuance of the civil protection order against the mother even though there was no evidence that she had physically injured the child. The court relied on evidence that the child was "depressed and particularly susceptible to mental injury."[79] Moreover, the mother had yelled at her, called her names and failed to protect her from the violence of her new husband.

However, in *Vera v. Yellowrobe*,[80] the appellate court affirmed the trial court decision holding that the parties' children did not suffer mental distress after being in the care of appellee. The Court noted that for purposes of RC 2151.031(C), " 'mental injury' means any behavioral, cognitive, emotional or mental disorder that is described in [RC 2919.22] and is committed by the parent or other person responsible for the child's care. Further the acts or omissions a parent or caregiver may commit to cause such a disorder include abusing the child as well as administering corporal punishment . . . . or repeatedly administering unwarranted disciplinary measures to the child, when there is a substantial risk that such conduct, if continued, will seriously impair or retard the child's mental health or development."[81]

Thus, evidence that a parent or caregiver abused a child or administered discipline in such a manner as to create a substantial risk of serious physical harm or risk of impairment to a child's mental health is clearly relevant in determining whether a child has suffered a "mental injury," whether a child is an "abused child," and therefore, whether a CPO should be issued, pursuant to RC 3113.31 to protect against such domestic violence."[82]

The allegations of mental injury included the children's testimony that they saw appellee near the gas tank of their father's van with a bag of sugar, a tape reflecting a conversation whereby appellee allegedly threatened to kill appellant and an ongoing need for counseling.

The appellate court, however, determined that because appellee had

---

County 2000).

[78]Kurincic v. Kurincic, 2000 WL 217808, *3 (Ohio Ct. App. 8th Dist. Cuyahoga County 2000).

[79]Kurincic v. Kurincic, 2000 WL 217808, *3 (Ohio Ct. App. 8th Dist. Cuyahoga County 2000); see also Stark v. Stark, 2002-Ohio-90, 2002 WL 109281, *3 (Ohio Ct. App. 5th Dist. Delaware County 2002) (The appellate court upheld the issuance of a civil protection order based partially on testimony that the minor child, a protected party, was fearful of his father during visitation. Additionally, there was testimony that the child suffered from anxiety attacks, panic attacks, uncontrollable crying, nightmares, and hallucinations prior to visiting his father. "From these factors, the court could conclude that Brian Stark was in danger of commission of domestic violence, as defined by the statute.").

[80]Vera v. Yellowrobe, 2006-Ohio-3911, 2006 WL 2130726 (Ohio Ct. App. 10th Dist. Franklin County 2006).

[81]Vera v. Yellowrobe, 2006-Ohio-3911, 2006 WL 2130726, *3 (Ohio Ct. App. 10th Dist. Franklin County 2006).

[82]Vera v. Yellowrobe, 2006-Ohio-3911, 2006 WL 2130726, *3 (Ohio Ct. App. 10th Dist. Franklin County 2006).

not seen the children in the six months preceding the filing of the CPO, appellant's request for the CPO immediately upon his return to Ohio in order to avoid a pattern of abuse towards him and his daughters was not warranted. Absent evidence of recent threats or imminent violence or recent property damage, appellant did not present credible evidence that he and the children needed protection. In light of this and the fact that after one of the alleged incidents appellant permitted appellee supervised visitation with the children, the appellate court overruled the assignment of error and held that the trial court's denial of a CPO was not against the manifest weight of the evidence.

Hopefully, other courts may begin to apply this rationale to adult domestic violence victims. It is important that they not underestimate the nexus between physical abuse and mental injury in a domestic violence relationship. Courts that ignore this apparently require a victim to suffer at least one actual beating.[83]

Recently the Butler County Court of Appeals based its grant of a civil protection order on proof that the petitioner suffered mental distress. In *Carter v. Hooks*,[84] appellee obtained a civil protection order stating that she felt unsafe and scared and feared for her health due to threatening remarks made by appellant. The remarks were "rude and hurtful" and appellant's presence in the home was an emotional hardship for her.[85]

Appellant argued that appellee failed to present evidence of physical harm or threat of physical harm to support the granting of the CPO. Appellant also asserted that the trial court misstated the law when it determined that "mental distress" was sufficient to warrant issuing a civil protection order under the domestic violence statute.

The appellate court noted the definition of the domestic violence statute in its opinion and concluded that evidence of a pattern of rude, mean and hurtful comments causing appellee to suffer mental distress was sufficient for the issuance of the CPO under RC 3113.31(A)(1)(b) in that appellant committed a violation of section 2903.211 of the Revised Code. Appellee's testimony that her mental health suffered causing her to seek treatment from her doctor for her "nerves" and other witness testimony regarding the degree of distress she suffered as a result of appellant's conduct was sufficient evidence.

The Butler County Court of Appeals held that "[c]ontrary to appellant's assertion, appellee's failure to present evidence of physical harm or threat of physical harm in support of her petition is not dis-

[83] State v. Houston, 1992 WL 87449 (Ohio Ct. App. 2d Dist. Montgomery County 1992); Pendleton v. Minichino, 6 Conn. L. Rptr. 241, 1992 WL 75920 (Conn. Super. Ct. 1992).

[84] Carter v. Hooks, 2006-Ohio-5987, 2006 WL 3290733 (Ohio Ct. App. 12th Dist. Butler County 2006); see also Hoff v. Brown, 2001 WL 876228 (Ohio Ct. App. 5th Dist. Stark County 2001); M.C. v. B.K., 2015-Ohio-560, 2015 WL 628342 (Ohio Ct. App. 6th Dist. Sandusky County 2015) (judgment affirmed for issuance of CPO based on appellant's emotional and mental abuse and erratic behavior and texts such as "Hope you choke out on it in the worst way"; "Leave me to die in peace"; "I was fired thanks to you and your mother"; "F* * * off to both of you"; and "You will become pregnant in 2018 and dance on a pole just like your mother").

[85] Carter v. Hooks, 2006-Ohio-5987, 2006 WL 3290733, *1 (Ohio Ct. App. 12th Dist. Butler County 2006).

positive of the matter. Reviewing the record as a whole, there is evidence supporting the trial court's conclusion that appellant engaged in a pattern of conduct which caused appellee mental distress."[86]

Of significance is that the appellee is the 77-year-old aunt of appellant who was being treated for Alzheimer's. The appellant was her niece. It is possible that both the trial court and appellate court considered both appellee's age and infirmity in its decision.

Q & A: Where a person throws an object at the victim, but misses and hits the wall, can the victim obtain a civil protection order?

Under the facts presented, if the respondent attempted to injure the victim, the fact that he missed is not as important as the fact that he acted intentionally and consciously.[87] If the intent was to harm the victim, the victim should be able to obtain a civil protection order.

Q & A: Does a finding of domestic violence due to reckless behavior depend on evidence of physical injury?

In *R.T. v. J.T.*,[88] the appellate court specifically discussed and explained its reasoning as to why the father did not prove by a preponderance of the evidence that Mother had recklessly caused bodily injury. In the trial court, Father was granted a CPO against the mother, naming all three children as protected parties. Mother appealed, arguing that Father had not demonstrated that any of the children were victims of domestic violence.

In a methodical manner, the appellate court reviewed the elements of RC 3113.31(A)(1) regarding the acts that rise to the level of domestic violence from "attempting to cause or recklessly causing bodily injury." At the outset, the court detailed the allegations set forth in the petition and testimony, to wit: that mother threw a glass at L.T. that bounced off the wall and hit L.T. in the head.

The appellate court pointed out that none of the children testified, and that no evidence was presented by any professional who might have observed L.T. or the other children after the incident. There was

[86]Carter v. Hooks, 2006-Ohio-5987, 2006 WL 3290733, *3 (Ohio Ct. App. 12th Dist. Butler County 2006). But see Studer v. Studer, 2012-Ohio-2838, 2012 WL 2371452 (Ohio Ct. App. 3d Dist. Crawford County 2012) (petitioner's fragile medical condition alone cannot provide the basis for a CPO. Relying on the nexus between a restriction in a CPO and the conduct the court is attempting to prevent, the appellate court found that attempting to prevent conduct which causes another to experience adverse health consequences due to stress is contra to the purpose of the domestic violence statute which is to protect people from domestic violence).

[87]State v. Purvis, 1989 WL 126298 (Ohio Ct. App. 9th Dist. Medina County 1989); State v. Poppe, 2006-Ohio-1994, 2006 WL 1062023 (Ohio Ct. App. 3d Dist. Auglaize County 2006); but see State v. Younker, 2002-Ohio-5376, 2002 WL 31242238, *4 (Ohio Ct. App. 2d Dist. Darke County 2002), in which the appellate court stated that "the circumstances involved in this domestic violence prosecution are illustrative of problems that have come to vex law enforcement authorities and the courts." Because the term "physical harm" is defined so broadly and because there is no specific intent requirement, "[t]his combination has produced a spate of domestic violence complaints on which law enforcement officers are required to act, made by persons engaged in dysfunctional relationships, over "injuries" so negligible as to lack any sound reason to invoke the power of the state."

[88]R.T. v. J.T., 2015-Ohio-4418, 2015 WL 6449294 (Ohio Ct. App. 9th Dist. Medina County 2015).

no evidence of injury or physical pain to L.T. "Based on a review of the record, Father did not meet his burden of proving by a preponderance of the evidence that Mother caused any bodily injury to L.T. While throwing a cup across the room close to another person rises to the level of recklessness, in the absence of any evidence of injury to the children, the trial court's finding that Mother recklessly caused bodily injury to L.T. was against the manifest weight of the evidence."[89]

Of importance is that the 9th District appellate court appears to suggest a higher standard when one has "recklessly caused bodily harm." This Court has considered both intent and injury as a basis for granting a CPO. Not only must the act involve recklessness on the part of the actor, it must also involve injury to the alleged victim.

Q & A: Where a batterer smashes an object into the wall and a fragment of the object hits the victim who is in close proximity, causing injury to the victim, can the victim obtain a civil protection order?

Yes. Even though the perpetrator may not have intended to strike the victim, it must be assumed that he/she knew or should have known that his/her actions had the potential to cause bodily injury since the object was thrown in close proximity to the victim's location. Under such a fact pattern, the type of injuries suffered by the victim are inherently probable from the conduct. There is no need to inquire into the perpetrator's specific or subjective intent. The perpetrator's underlying purpose is irrelevant in determining whether he/she acted recklessly. The fact that he/she acted and that his/her conduct caused bodily injury to the victim is of primary importance. Additionally, the perpetrator's actions were such that "a reasonable person should know would probably bring about certain results."[90]

§ 8:4 Statutory elements of domestic violence under RC 3113.31(A)(1)(b)

To commit an act of domestic violence under RC 3113.31(A)(1)(b), a respondent must:

(1) place another family or household member
(2) by threat of force
(3) in fear
(4) of imminent serious physical harm, or
(5) commit a violation
(6) of RC 2903.211[1] or
(7) of RC 2911.211.

---

[89]R.T. v. J.T., 2015-Ohio-4418, 2015 WL 6449294, ¶ 35 (Ohio Ct. App. 9th Dist. Medina County 2015).

[90]State v. Purvis, 1989 WL 126298, *2 (Ohio Ct. App. 9th Dist. Medina County 1989); State v. Howell, 2017-Ohio-728, 86 N.E.3d 114 (Ohio Ct. App. 7th Dist. Mahoning County 2017).

[Section 8:4]

[1]See also §§ 9:1 et seq. Olson v. Olson, 2016-Ohio-149, 2016 WL 197117, ¶ 15 (Ohio Ct. App. 6th Dist. Wood County 2016) (explaining the level of proof necessary to satisfy the mental distress element of RC 2903.211 for purposes of domestic violence CPO and holding that "general allegations that appellant would get angry and yell without providing the context or content of the outburst provides no basis for us to

Unlike the actual physical act or an attempt as set forth in RC 3113.31(A)(1)(a), the primary focus of RC 3113.31(A)(1)(b) is the perception of the petitioner.[2] While it understood that the respondent intended his statement as a threat or, at least that he considered it substantially likely that it would be taken as a threat, its meaning must be assessed in light of the surrounding circumstances. The respondent's statement or action must cause the person perceiving it to believe that the respondent is on the verge of using force at or near the point in time when such statement is made.

This statement or action must be directed at a family or household member. Words or other actions must put a family or household member put in fear of "imminent serious physical harm." A threat to kill the petitioner or other family or household member is the most common threat for which a court will issue a civil protection order.[3]

Q & A: How is "threat of force" defined?

The phrase "threat of force" is not defined in the Revised Code. The term "force" is defined in RC 2901.01(A)(1) as "any violence, compulsion, or constraint physically exerted by any means against a person or thing."[4] A "threat" can be also defined as "a communicated intent to inflict physical or other harm on any person or on property or a men-

---

determine that appellee or the daughter feared mental distress or imminent physical harm." at ¶ 17); McElroy v. McElroy, 2016-Ohio-5148, 2016 WL 4039227 (Ohio Ct. App. 5th Dist. Guernsey County 2016).

[2]See State v. Rhoads, 2013-Ohio-152, 2013 WL 221512 (Ohio Ct. App. 12th Dist. Clermont County 2013) (noting that with a threat, the state of mind of the victim is an essential element), citing Hamilton v. Cameron, 121 Ohio App. 3d 445, 449, 700 N.E.2d 336 (12th Dist. Butler County 1997).

[3]See, e.g., Eichenberger v. Eichenberger, 82 Ohio App. 3d 809, 613 N.E.2d 678 (10th Dist. Franklin County 1992).

[4]See Sitton v. Sitton, 1999 WL 55717 (Ohio Ct. App. 2d Dist. Montgomery County 1999), and Siouffi v. Siouffi, 1998 WL 879255 (Ohio Ct. App. 2d Dist. Montgomery County 1998), wherein the court looked to the criminal statute (RC 2901.01) for a definition of "force" since it is not defined in RC 3113.31; Gaydash v. Gaydash, 168 Ohio App. 3d 418, 423, 2006-Ohio-4080, 860 N.E.2d 789 (9th Dist. Summit County 2006) (domestic violence requires fear inspired by a threat of force as defined in RC 2901. 01(A)(1). This court concludes that the act of driving a large sports utility vehicle directly at another vehicle constitutes a threat of force in that such conduct is a threat of violence against the occupants of the other vehicle. The fear that this particular threat of violence incites is domestic violence); State v. Rhoads, 2013-Ohio-152, 2013 WL 221512 (Ohio Ct. App. 12th Dist. Clermont County 2013) (discussing when a truck may be considered an instrument of violence). See also Markowitz v. Markowitz, 2006-Ohio-5932, 2006 WL 3234010, *2 (Ohio Ct. App. 8th Dist. Cuyahoga County 2006) (backing petitioner up against a wall and standing inches away and close enough to smell toothpaste while yelling obscenities at her is a threat of force that may be implied by respondent's physical and verbal intimidation of petitioner); but see Fleckner v. Fleckner, 177 Ohio App. 3d 706, 2008, 2008-Ohio-4000, 895 N.E.2d 896 (10th Dist. Franklin County 2008); Barton v. Barton, 2015-Ohio-3869, 2015 WL 5691887 (Ohio Ct. App. 2d Dist. Greene County 2015) (discussion of force and imminence; although a volatile and dysfunctional relationship, no evidence of a fear of imminent serious physical harm caused by a threat of force); Barton v. Barton, 2015-Ohio-3869, 2015 WL 5691887 (Ohio Ct. App. 2d Dist. Greene County 2015); Charles v. Peters, 2016-Ohio-1259, 2016 WL 1178776 (Ohio Ct. App. 2d Dist. Greene County 2016); J.M. v. M.M., 2016-Ohio-5368, 2016 WL 4272340 (Ohio Ct. App. 9th Dist. Medina County 2016); Wootten v. Culp, 2017-Ohio-665, 85 N.E.3d 198 (Ohio Ct. App. 4th Dist. Adams County 2017); Lundin v. Niepsuj, 2017-Ohio-7153, 2017 WL 3426957 (Ohio Ct. App. 9th Dist. Summit County 2017); Dodds on behalf of S.S. v. Stamper, 2018-Ohio-193, 2018 WL 481779 (Ohio Ct. App. 2d Dist. Champaign County

ace; especially, any menace of such a nature and extent as to unsettle the mind of the person on whom it operates, and to take away from his acts that free and voluntary action which alone constitute consent."[5] The word "threat" is defined in *Black's Law Dictionary* as "[a] declaration of intention or determination to inflict punishment, loss, or pain on another, or to injure another . . . by the commission of some unlawful act."[6]

In the context of RC 3113.31(A)(1)(b), "by threat of force" implies a declaration of an intention to injure another by means of violence exerted by any means against that person.[7]

" 'Threats of violence will constitute domestic violence if the fear resulting from those threats is reasonable.' "[8] " 'Reasonableness is determined by referencing the petitioner's history with the respondent.' "[9] " '[B]oth the totality of the circumstances, as well as

2018).

[5]Black's Law Dictionary (6th ed.) p. 1480; see also Blocker v. Carron, 2011-Ohio-3673, 2011 WL 3198261, ¶ 17 (Ohio Ct. App. 5th Dist. Tuscarawas County 2011) (upholding issuance of a CPO based on indirect written threats concerning petitioner's living past a certain date, not a publication of respondent's religious beliefs. "When the initial attack occurs, it will only be the start of things. Much more is coming. Regardless of what happens, please know I love you.").

[6]Black's Law Dictionary (6th ed.) p 1480; see also State v. Simcox, 2007-Ohio-1217, 2007 WL 789423, *2 (Ohio Ct. App. 9th Dist. Wayne County 2007) (discussing Ohio Supreme Court's approval of a definition of "threat"); State v. Young, 2013-Ohio-1247, 2013 WL 1303789 (Ohio Ct. App. 10th Dist. Franklin County 2013) (discussing "threat" and "force"); Zidan v. Zidan, 2015-Ohio-4021, 2015 WL 5723143 (Ohio Ct. App. 11th Dist. Lake County 2015).

[7]See also Mashburn v. Mashburn, 2000-Ohio-2606, 2000 WL 1726517 (Ohio Ct. App. 7th Dist. Mahoning County 2000) (threat of force, not actual force, is sufficient to establish an incident of domestic violence took place, even though police report did not set forth an incident of domestic violence); Tyler v. Tyler, 2004-Ohio-5784, 2004 WL 2436594 (Ohio Ct. App. 2d Dist. Montgomery County 2004) ("Regardless of whether the wife subjectively feared imminent serious physical harm, her evidence was lacking in any evidence of threats of force, an essential element of domestic violence under subsection (1)(b)"); Smith v. Mangan, 2007-Ohio-194, 2007 WL 127693, *2 (Ohio Ct. App. 2d Dist. Greene County 2007) (the fact that Smith may have been in fear of Mangan was not enough to warrant a CPO. Smith offered no evidence that Mangan had threatened her in any way, including through the use of force. The statute requires fear that arises from a threat of force and causes a fear of imminent serious physical harm); Calicoat v. Calicoat, 2009-Ohio-5869, 2009 WL 3683665 (Ohio Ct. App. 2d Dist. Miami County 2009) (per assignment of error alleging RC 3113.31 is void for vagueness, the conduct prohibited by statute is a threat of force that is by its nature reasonably sufficient to place another in fear of immediate and serious physical harm.); Charles v. Peters, 2016-Ohio-1259, 2016 WL 1178776 (Ohio Ct. App. 2d Dist. Greene County 2016); Lundin v. Niepsuj, 2017-Ohio-7153, 2017 WL 3426957 (Ohio Ct. App. 9th Dist. Summit County 2017).

[8]Donovan v. Donovan, 2012-Ohio-3521, 2012 WL 3156462, ¶ 6 (Ohio Ct. App. 9th Dist. Lorain County 2012), quoting Rhodes v. Gunter, 2003-Ohio-2342, 2003 WL 21040724, ¶ 4 (Ohio Ct. App. 9th Dist. Lorain County 2003); Burnett v. Burnett, 2012-Ohio-2673, 2012 WL 2196336 (Ohio Ct. App. 6th Dist. Sandusky County 2012); A.D. v. B.D., 2017-Ohio-229, 2017 WL 277481 (Ohio Ct. App. 9th Dist. Medina County 2017); J.M. v. M.M., 2016-Ohio-5368, ¶ 15, 2016 WL 4272340 (Ohio Ct. App. 9th Dist. Medina County 2016).

[9]Donovan v. Donovan, 2012-Ohio-3521, 2012 WL 3156462, ¶ 6 (Ohio Ct. App. 9th Dist. Lorain County 2012), quoting Rhodes v. Gunter, 2003-Ohio-2342, 2003 WL 21040724, ¶ 4 (Ohio Ct. App. 9th Dist. Lorain County 2003); see also Burnett v.

the victim's state of mind, are relevant to the determination that the threat of harm was imminent.' "[10]

Q & A: Does a threat of force need to be made verbally?

Not according to the Cuyahoga County Court of Appeals in *Markowitz v. Markowitz*.[11] In that case, the respondent argued that the act of pushing back on the door was not a threat of force. Petitioner's testimony indicated that "respondent backed her up against a wall and, standing just inches away, close enough that she could "smell his toothpaste," he yelled and screamed obscenities at her."[12]

The appellate court found that the evidence supported the issuance of the CPO and reasoned that "[w]hile the threat of violence may not be expressed in so many words, the trial court could have reasonably found that the threat of force was implied by respondent's physical and verbal intimidation of petitioner."[13]

Q & A: What kind of threat is not considered to be a "threat of force" for purposes of the civil domestic violence statute?

For example, in *Fleckner v. Fleckner*,[14] respondent emailed the petitioner to tell her that if she failed to accept his divorce settlement offer, he would take out all of his "anger and frustration" on her in court. In reversing the trial court, the Franklin County Court of Appeals determined that the trial court erred in applying only a subjective test. While acknowledging that the phrase "I'll get you," or severe physical or verbal intimidation, may be considered as a threat of force sufficient to constitute domestic violence, a threat to take legal action did not meet the definition of a threat of force under R.C.

Burnett, 2012-Ohio-2673, 2012 WL 2196336 (Ohio Ct. App. 6th Dist. Sandusky County 2012) (indicating that "past acts" are also considered in determining the reasonableness of a petitioner's fear).

[10]Donovan v. Donovan, 2012-Ohio-3521, ¶ 6, 2012 WL 3156462 (Ohio Ct. App. 9th Dist. Lorain County 2012), quoting Chafin v. Chafin, 2010-Ohio-3939, 2010 WL 3294288, ¶ 22 (Ohio Ct. App. 9th Dist. Lorain County 2010).

[11]Markowitz v. Markowitz, 2006-Ohio-5932, 2006 WL 3234010 (Ohio Ct. App. 8th Dist. Cuyahoga County 2006); Gaydash v. Gaydash, 168 Ohio App. 3d 418, 2006-Ohio-4080, ¶ 16, 860 N.E.2d 789 (9th Dist. Summit County 2006) (the offense of domestic violence requires fear inspired by the threat of force); State v. Bilyk, 2018-Ohio-1802, ¶ 15, 2018 WL 2113801 (Ohio Ct. App. 5th Dist. Licking County 2018) (noting that there is no logical support for a claim that a threat of force must be accompanied by a verbal statement; violent actions and a wordless scream in victim's face may suffice); see also Text § 8:4.

[12]Markowitz v. Markowitz, 2006-Ohio-5932, 2006 WL 3234010, *2 (Ohio Ct. App. 8th Dist. Cuyahoga County 2006).

[13]Markowitz v. Markowitz, 2006-Ohio-5932, 2006 WL 3234010, *2 (Ohio Ct. App. 8th Dist. Cuyahoga County 2006); see also Martauz v. Martauz, 2009-Ohio-2642, 2009 WL 1581185 (Ohio Ct. App. 7th Dist. Mahoning County 2009) (noting that threats do not have to be verbal in order to invoke the statute and upholding the grant of a CPO where respondent made 20 phone calls, 11 text messages and 15 minutes of knocking, ringing, pounding and calling which demonstrate how irrational his behavior had become and constituted a threat that would place a reasonable person in fear of imminent serious physical harm); Siouffi v. Siouffi, 1998 WL 879255 (Ohio Ct. App. 2d Dist. Montgomery County 1998); State v. McCord, 1998 WL 549266 (Ohio Ct. App. 5th Dist. Perry County 1998); Blocker v. Carron, 2011-Ohio-3673, 2011 WL 3198261 (Ohio Ct. App. 5th Dist. Tuscarawas County 2011).

[14]Fleckner v. Fleckner, 177 Ohio App. 3d 706, 2008-Ohio-4000, 895 N.E.2d 896 (10th Dist. Franklin County 2008).

3113.31(A)(1)(b).[15] It was not an explicit or implied threat of physical violence, compulsion or restraint under R.C. 2901.01(A)(1).

Similarly, in *A.D. v. B. D.*,[16] sister filed for a CPO against brother. The incident giving rise to the request was that after brother called her names, he said she "was good as nothing, good as dead." While there was testimony about past acts of domestic violence, the appellate court found that there were limited details about the events of the past.

The appellate held that "[c]onsidering the entirety of the circumstances, we cannot say that sufficient evidence was presented that she and her children were in danger of being placed in fear of imminent serious physical harm via a threat of force from Brother."[17] "Even if Brother's comment amounted to a veiled threat of force, we cannot conclude that such a comment would reasonably put Sister in fear of imminent serious physical harm."[18]

Q & A: How is the term "imminent" defined?

In order for a victim to prevail under this section, an attorney must be able to establish that the victim believed the respondent's execution of the threat in question was "imminent." Because the term imminent" is not defined in the statute, it must be construed according to its ordinary meaning.[19] *Black's Law Dictionary* defines "imminent" as "on the point of happening."[20]

" 'Imminent' has also been defined as the belief of the victim that

---

[15]Fleckner v. Fleckner, 177 Ohio App. 3d 706, 716, 2008-Ohio-4000, 895 N.E.2d 896 (10th Dist. Franklin County 2008). But see Donovan v. Donovan, 2012-Ohio-3521, 2012 WL 3156462, ¶ 15 (Ohio Ct. App. 9th Dist. Lorain County 2012) (distinguishing *Fleckner* and finding that a threat, by respondent, of suicide coupled with breaking down the door were considered recent threatening actions sufficient to grant a CPO; wife did not have to wait until a distinct act of domestic violence occurred).

[16]A.D. v. B.D., 2017-Ohio-229, 2017 WL 277481 (Ohio Ct. App. 9th Dist. Medina County 2017).

[17]A.D. v. B.D., 2017-Ohio-229, ¶ 28, 2017 WL 277481 (Ohio Ct. App. 9th Dist. Medina County 2017).

[18]A.D. v. B.D., 2017-Ohio-229, ¶ 28, 2017 WL 277481 (Ohio Ct. App. 9th Dist. Medina County 2017).

[19]Martauz v. Martauz, 2009-Ohio-2642, 2009 WL 1581185 (Ohio Ct. App. 7th Dist. Mahoning County 2009), citing State v. S.R., 63 Ohio St. 3d 590, 595, 589 N.E.2d 1319 (1992); Wootten v. Culp, 2017-Ohio-665, 85 N.E.3d 198 (Ohio Ct. App. 4th Dist. Adams County 2017) (defining "imminent" as ready to take place, near at hand, impending, hanging threateningly over one's head or menacingly near); A.D. v. B.D., 2017-Ohio-229, 2017 WL 277481 (Ohio Ct. App. 9th Dist. Medina County 2017).

[20]Black's Law Dictionary (6th ed.) p 750. See also State v. Collie, 108 Ohio App. 3d 580, 583, 671 N.E.2d 338 (1st Dist. Hamilton County 1996) (relying on Webster's Second International Dictionary to define "imminent" as "threatening to occur immediately"); see also Young v. Young, 2006-Ohio-978, 2006 WL 515522 (Ohio Ct. App. 2d Dist. Greene County 2006), citing Strong v. Bauman, 1999 WL 317432, *4 (Ohio Ct. App. 2d Dist. Montgomery County 1999) (holding that imminence does not require an offender to carry out a threat immediately or be in the process of carrying it out); Morris v. Morris, 2009-Ohio-5164, 2009 WL 3119658 (Ohio Ct. App. 9th Dist. Summit County 2009) (noting that a victim's state of mind is relevant in determining whether a threat is imminent); Smith v. Burroughs, 2010-Ohio-4806, 2010 WL 3861068 (Ohio Ct. App. 3d Dist. Wyandot County 2010) ("imminent" means threatening to occur immediately or at any moment, and is based on both the words of the person who threatens and the responses to the threat by the person against whom the threat was made).

harm would occur immediately or, in the alternative, that the defendant will cause immediate physical harm."[21] "Imminent" does not require that the offender carry out the threat immediately or be in the process of carrying it out. Rather, the critical inquiry is "whether a reasonable person would be placed in fear of imminent (in the sense of unconditional, non-contingent), serious physical harm" and which necessarily involves both subjective and objective elements.[22]

Several Ohio courts have attempted to define "imminent" for purposes of domestic violence. For example, in *State v. Collie*,[23] the defendant was charged with a violation of RC 2919.25(C) for stating that, if he had a gun, he would shoot the victim.[24] The Hamilton County Court of Appeals noted that the definition of "imminent" means "threatening to occur immediately."[25] The court determined that all that existed in the record was a conditional threat toward the victim that failed to rise to the level of domestic violence under RC 2919.25(C).[26] Without evidence of prior specific acts tying the defendant's drunkenness to violent behavior, there was no evidence in the record to prove the victim's belief that harm was imminent.[27] In *Collie*, the trial court had disallowed evidence of prior acts of domestic violence.

However, the appellate court stated that

> because of our recognition of the unique nature of domestic violence cases, and our concern for the victims thereof, we today announce a test which the state shall be permitted to use in the future in cases brought under RC 2919.25(C). We hold that in order to prove the element of the belief of a family member that the offender will cause imminent physical

---

[21]State v. Fisher, 197 Ohio App. 3d 591, 2011-Ohio-5965, 968 N.E.2d 510 (2d Dist. Miami County 2011); State v. Taylor, 79 Ohio Misc. 2d 82, 671 N.E.2d 343 (Mun. Ct. 1996).

[22]Strassell v. Chapman, 2010-Ohio-4376, 2010 WL 3610591 (Ohio Ct. App. 10th Dist. Franklin County 2010). See also Bargar v. Kirby, 2011-Ohio-4904, 2011 WL 4436634 (Ohio Ct. App. 12th Dist. Butler County 2011); State v. Taylor, 79 Ohio Misc. 2d 82, 671 N.E.2d 343 (Mun. Ct. 1996); Dodds on behalf of S.S. v. Stamper, 2018-Ohio-193, 2018 WL 481779 (Ohio Ct. App. 2d Dist. Champaign County 2018).

[23]State v. Collie, 108 Ohio App. 3d 580, 671 N.E.2d 338 (1st Dist. Hamilton County 1996).

[24]See also Steckler v. Steckler, 492 N.W.2d 76, 80 (N.D. 1992) (determining that "[i]mminent means close in point of time, but closeness is likewise a term of many degrees, according to the circumstances") (quoting State v. Kurle, 390 N.W.2d 48 (N.D. 1986), citing State Dept. of Human Services v. Northern, 563 S.W.2d 197 (Tenn. Ct. App. 1978)); Strong v. Bauman, 1999 WL 317432 (Ohio Ct. App. 2d Dist. Montgomery County 1999) (discussing the term "imminent").

[25]State v. Collie, 108 Ohio App. 3d 580, 583, 671 N.E.2d 338 (1st Dist. Hamilton County 1996); E. Cleveland v. Perkins, 2009-Ohio-2131, 2009 WL 1244154 (Ohio Ct. App. 8th Dist. Cuyahoga County 2009).

[26]See also Wohleber v. Wohleber, 2011-Ohio-6696, 2011 WL 6880736, *4 (Ohio Ct. App. 9th Dist. Lorain County 2011) (noting that a conditional threat is one where a prerequisite must occur before the actor intends to carry out the threat; citing Bargar v. Kirby, 2011-Ohio-4904, ¶ 21, 2011 WL 4436634 (Ohio Ct. App. 12th Dist. Butler County 2011); quoting In re Jenkins, 2004-Ohio-2657, 2004 WL 1152853, ¶ 26 (Ohio Ct. App. 5th Dist. Stark County 2004). But see State v. McClelland, 2002-Ohio-1007, 2002 WL 356306 (Ohio Ct. App. 10th Dist. Franklin County 2002).

[27]See also State v. Renner, 125 Ohio App. 3d 383, 708 N.E.2d 765 (2d Dist. Montgomery County 1998), for a discussion of the rationale for admitting evidence of prior acts of violence.

harm, evidence of "other acts" against the same victim will be admissible with appropriate safeguards.[28]

The *Collie* court not only set forth the test for admitting evidence of past acts of abuse, it indicated that even the conditional threat "If I had a gun, I would shoot you" might have been actionable had evidence of the victim's belief that harm was imminent been allowed.

Conversely, in *City of Cincinnati v. Baarlaer*,[29] the defendant was charged with domestic violence for pushing the victim up against the wall and threatening to kill her. The defendant appealed his conviction on the ground that the simple utterance of a conditional threat by a defendant who immediately left the premises and drove away from the alleged victim is not legally sufficient to support a conviction for domestic violence under RC 2919.25(C).

The Hamilton County Court of Appeals determined that the crux of the defendant's argument was that, because he separated from the victim immediately after he threatened to kill her, he could not have carried out the threat.[30] Therefore, his threat was merely conditional because he could not have caused the victim imminent physical harm. The court relied on the definition of "imminent" found in Webster's New International Dictionary as "near at hand, impending, threatening to occur immediately."[31] The court noted that the same source defined "immediate" as "not distant or separated in time, direct, continuous, occurring without delay."[32]

Further, the *Baarlaer* court stated that the defendant's reliance on *State v. Collie* was misplaced. The court distinguished the facts in *Collie* by noting that in that case the threat was not accompanied by an overt act of physical violence. In *Collie*, the defendant did not own a gun nor was there a gun in the house. The court reasoned that, in that case, "[u]nder such circumstances, reasonable minds could

---

[28]State v. Collie, 108 Ohio App. 3d 580, 583-84, 671 N.E.2d 338 (1st Dist. Hamilton County 1996); see also State v. Drake, 135 Ohio App. 3d 507, 734 N.E.2d 865 (12th Dist. Butler County 1999) (evidence that defendant told his wife "I'm going to burn you alive" was sufficient to support the conviction).

[29]City of Cincinnati v. Baarlaer, 115 Ohio App. 3d 521, 685 N.E.2d 836 (1st Dist. Hamilton County 1996); see also Cleveland v. Earnhart, 110 Ohio Misc. 2d 41, 743 N.E.2d 1000 (Mun. Ct. 2000) (in which the threat, "If I had a gun, I would kill you" is a conditional threat thereby lacking imminency; complainant had no reason to believe defendant had any intention to immediately complete the prerequisite (obtain the gun) and complete the threat (kill the complainant)); In re Jenkins, 2004-Ohio-2657, 2004 WL 1152853 (Ohio Ct. App. 5th Dist. Stark County 2004); State v. Race, 2017-Ohio-612, 2017 WL 678814 (Ohio Ct. App. 6th Dist. Sandusky County 2017) (since threat to kill victim was conditioned on victim returning home and fact that she wasn't afraid at that moment and since her concern was premised on what would happen upon her return, threat not imminent and conviction reversed).

[30]But see also Reynolds v. Reynolds, 2001 WL 62552 (Ohio Ct. App. 2d Dist. Montgomery County 2001) (upheld issuance of civil protection order and determined that threat to kill petitioner was "imminent" despite the distance between the parties' residences).

[31]City of Cincinnati v. Baarlaer, 115 Ohio App. 3d 521, 527, 685 N.E.2d 836 (1st Dist. Hamilton County 1996); Fleckner v. Fleckner, 177 Ohio App. 3d 706, 2008-Ohio-4000, 895 N.E.2d 896 (10th Dist. Franklin County 2008); Lundin v. Niepsuj, 2017-Ohio-7153, 2017 WL 3426957 (Ohio Ct. App. 9th Dist. Summit County 2017).

[32]City of Cincinnati v. Baarlaer, 115 Ohio App. 3d 521, 527, 685 N.E.2d 836 (1st Dist. Hamilton County 1996) (citation omitted).

conclude only that the accused had no means at hand to carry out the threat as made, viz., to shoot his wife, and that its realization depended on Collie's possession of a weapon capable of firing a projectile."[33]

In analyzing the facts, the court noted that witnesses described the victim as still upset several hours after the threat. The fact that the threat was in addition to a physical act of violence suggested that the victim could reasonably believe that the defendant would do that which he threatened. Accordingly, the court of appeals upheld the defendant's conviction.

In the civil protection order context, *Strong v. Bauman*[34] was one of the first cases to focus on the term "imminent." The Montgomery County Court of Appeals literally defined "imminent" as "ready to take place," "near at hand," "impending," "hanging threateningly over one's head," or "menacingly near."[35] "Based upon the ordinary definition of 'imminent,' we do not construe the imminence requirement as requiring that the offender carry out the threat immediately or be in the process of carrying it out."[36] Rather, the critical inquiry is "whether a reasonable person would be placed in fear of imminent (in the sense of unconditional, non-contingent),[37] serious physical harm . . . [which] necessarily involves both subjective and objective elements."[38]

---

[33]City of Cincinnati v. Baarlaer, 115 Ohio App. 3d 521, 527, 685 N.E.2d 836 (1st Dist. Hamilton County 1996).

[34]Strong v. Bauman, 1999 WL 317432 (Ohio Ct. App. 2d Dist. Montgomery County 1999) (citing Webster's Third New International Dictionary (1969)); see also Reynolds v. Reynolds, 2001 WL 62552 (Ohio Ct. App. 2d Dist. Montgomery County 2001) (Citing *Bauman* for its public policy considerations. "As we pointed out in *Bauman*, civil protection orders are intended to prevent domestic violence before it occurs and their purpose would be annulled if they could not be imposed in time to prevent the violence, rather than simply immediately after it occurs.").

[35]Lewis v. Gravely, 2016-Ohio-1502, 2016 WL 1404159 (Ohio Ct. App. 4th Dist. Adams County 2016); R.T. v. J.T., 2015-Ohio-4418, 2015 WL 6449294 (Ohio Ct. App. 9th Dist. Medina County 2015).

[36]Strong v. Bauman, 1999 WL 317432, *4 (Ohio Ct. App. 2d Dist. Montgomery County 1999); see also Reynolds v. Reynolds, 2001 WL 62552 (Ohio Ct. App. 2d Dist. Montgomery County 2001) (Defining imminent as "hanging threateningly over one's head." "As we pointed out in *Bauman*, civil protection orders are intended to prevent domestic violence before it occurs and their purpose would be annulled if they could not be imposed in time to prevent the violence, rather than simply immediately before it occurs."); Strassell v. Chapman, 2010-Ohio-4376, 2010 WL 3610591 (Ohio Ct. App. 10th Dist. Franklin County 2010) (the requirement of "imminent" fear addresses the reality of the threat rather than the timing of the threat); Nkurunziza v. Nyamusevya, 2010-Ohio-5966, 2010 WL 4968636 (Ohio Ct. App. 10th Dist. Franklin County 2010). But see Gatt v. Gatt, 2002-Ohio-1749, 2002 WL 570389 (Ohio Ct. App. 9th Dist. Medina County 2002) (Where petitioner testified that he did not feel the immediate need to call the police because Ms. Gatt was living in Florida with her parents at the time of the threat. Despite the lack of imminence, the appellate court affirmed the trial court's issuance of a CPO finding that "Mr. Gatt demonstrated a danger of domestic violence by showing that Ms. Gatt's threat to end his life placed him in fear of imminent serious physical harm." The threat was: "with the kind of money [Ms. Gatt's] mom and dad have, [Ms. Gatt] can make [Mr. Gatt] disappear.").

[37]See Fleckner v. Fleckner, 177 Ohio App. 3d 706, 2008-Ohio-4000, 895 N.E.2d 896 (10th Dist. Franklin County 2008) (construing imminence according to its ordinary meaning and pointing out that imminent is both unconditional and noncontingent); Martauz v. Martauz, 2009-Ohio-2642, 2009 WL 1581185 (Ohio Ct. App.

Likewise, in *Morris v. Morris*,[39] petitioner sought a protection order because respondent stated that he would kill her if he lost his nursing license as a result of an earlier domestic violence incident when he pulled her hair and pushed her.[40] Respondent appealed the issuance of the CPO, contending that she did not fear imminent serious physical harm because he only said that he would kill her if he lost his nursing license and that such a threat was conditional at best.

Considering the various definitions of "imminent," the appellate court reiterated that the focus of any inquiry should be on "whether a reasonable person would be placed in fear of imminent (in the sense of unconditional, non-contingent) serious physical harm."[41]

The Summit County appellate court also addressed a conditional threat, and stated that a conditional threat, standing alone, is generally not sufficient to satisfy the imminent physical harm element of the statute. However, in affirming the trial court decision to grant the CPO, the court relied on the analysis set forth in various court decisions that have held that a conditional threat may be considered by a court along with the totality of the circumstances.[42]

Q & A: Must the respondent be able to carry out the threat?[43]

Not according to several court decisions. Even though it must be

---

7th Dist. Mahoning County 2009); but see Richter v. Richter, 2009-Ohio-3828, 2009 WL 2371882 (Ohio Ct. App. 12th Dist. Butler County 2009) (differentiating *Fleckner* from the instant case, in which the type of threat found not to have placed the *Fleckner* petitioner in imminent fear of serious physical harm was a threat to take legal action). See also Strassell v. Chapman, 2010-Ohio-4376, 2010 WL 3610591 (Ohio Ct. App. 10th Dist. Franklin County 2010) (differentiating the facts in *Fleckner*).

[38]Strong v. Bauman, 1999 WL 317432, *4 (Ohio Ct. App. 2d Dist. Montgomery County 1999); see also Reynolds v. Reynolds, 2001 WL 62552 (Ohio Ct. App. 2d Dist. Montgomery County 2001); see also Henry v. Henry, 2005-Ohio-67, 2005 WL 43888 (Ohio Ct. App. 4th Dist. Ross County 2005) (Mr. Henry's threats were conditional).

[39]Morris v. Morris, 2009-Ohio-5164, 2009 WL 3119658 (Ohio Ct. App. 9th Dist. Summit County 2009).

[40]Morris v. Morris, 2009-Ohio-5164, 2009 WL 3119658, *2 (Ohio Ct. App. 9th Dist. Summit County 2009).

[41]Morris v. Morris, 2009-Ohio-5164, 2009 WL 3119658, *3 (Ohio Ct. App. 9th Dist. Summit County 2009); see also Henry v. Henry, 2005-Ohio-67, 2005 WL 43888 (Ohio Ct. App. 4th Dist. Ross County 2005); State v. Collie, 108 Ohio App. 3d 580, 671 N.E.2d 338 (1st Dist. Hamilton County 1996); B.C. v. A.S., 2014-Ohio-1326, 2014 WL 1345260 (Ohio Ct. App. 9th Dist. Medina County 2014).

[42]Wohleber v. Wohleber, 2011-Ohio-6696, 2011 WL 6880736 (Ohio Ct. App. 9th Dist. Lorain County 2011); Morris v. Morris, 2009-Ohio-5164, 2009 WL 3119658, *3 (Ohio Ct. App. 9th Dist. Summit County 2009); B.C. v. A.S., 2014-Ohio-1326, 2014 WL 1345260 (Ohio Ct. App. 9th Dist. Medina County 2014) (totality of circumstances and victim's state of mind relevant in determining that the threat of harm is imminent); Serdy v. Serdy, 2013-Ohio-5532, 2013 WL 6670830 (Ohio Ct. App. 7th Dist. Noble County 2013) (fact finder could find that wife's fears were reasonable under the totality of circumstances of the case).

[43]See also Text § 11:10. Lewis v. Gravely, 2016-Ohio-1502, 2016 WL 1404159 (Ohio Ct. App. 4th Dist. Adams County 2016) ("[i]mminence does not require an offender to be in the process of carrying out a threat of force at the time court considers decision; if that were the case, a man could threaten to kill his wife at some time in the near future; so long as the threat was coached in terms of a time span of more than a few minutes, the man would not be subject to a Civil Protection Order." *Strong* at *4. ¶ 30); Weber v. Forinash, 2015-Ohio-3187, 2015 WL 4720532 (Ohio Ct. App. 6th Dist. Sandusky County 2015); Young v. Young, 2006-Ohio-978, 2006 WL 515522 (Ohio Ct. App. 2d Dist. Greene County 2006); Charles v. Peters, 2016-Ohio-1259, 2016 WL

demonstrated that the threat is occurring immediately, there need not be a showing that the perpetrator was about to carry out the threat. For example, in *State v. Taylor*,[44] the Hamilton County Municipal Court held that

> [a] close analysis of the law, however, does not establish an absolute requirement that to sustain a domestic violence threat conviction, the State must prove the accused's ability to carry out the threat imminently and/or movement toward carrying it out. Instead, the critical inquiry is whether or not the proof fully evidences a reasonable belief by the victim that the accused will cause imminent physical harm.

Similarly, in *Nkurunziza v. Nyamusevya*,[45] the Franklin County appellate court affirmed the issuance of a CPO, finding that "imminence does not require an offender to carry out the threat immediately or be in the process of carrying it out."[46]

Q & A: So, is there a test to determine how to prove a "threat of force" and "imminent serious physical harm" for purposes of R.C. 3113.31(A)(1)(b)?

Since *Strong v. Baumann*, many recent decisions have adopted a two-tiered analysis. For example, the Franklin County Court of Appeals articulated the relevant case law and stated that "[c]ourts use both a subjective and an objective test in determining the reasonableness of the petitioner's fear. The subjective test 'inquires whether the respondent's threat of force actually caused the petitioner to fear imminent serious physical harm.' "[47]

The critical inquiry under R.C. 3113.31 is "whether a reasonable

---

1178776 (Ohio Ct. App. 2d Dist. Greene County 2016); Tyler v. Tyler, 2016-Ohio-7419, 2016 WL 6160139 (Ohio Ct. App. 2d Dist. Montgomery County 2016); Dodds on behalf of S.S. v. Stamper, 2018-Ohio-193, 2018 WL 481779 (Ohio Ct. App. 2d Dist. Champaign County 2018).

[44]State v. Taylor, 79 Ohio Misc. 2d 82, 671 N.E.2d 343 (Mun. Ct. 1996). But see State v. Fisher, 197 Ohio App. 3d 591, 2011-Ohio-5965, 968 N.E.2d 510 (2d Dist. Miami County 2011); see also State v. Schweitzer, 2015-Ohio-925, 30 N.E.3d 190 (Ohio Ct. App. 3d Dist. Auglaize County 2015) (dissent focused on fact that there was no past history; hence, no linkage between threat to a belief by victim that defendant would carry out threat; victim's declared "uncertainty" as to what might happen when he drinks would at most support a conditional fear of possible future harm, not an immediate threat of imminent harm. "[m]ere possibility is not imminent probability" ¶ 52).

[45]Nkurunziza v. Nyamusevya, 2010-Ohio-5966, 2010 WL 4968636 (Ohio Ct. App. 10th Dist. Franklin County 2010).

[46]Nkurunziza v. Nyamusevya, 2010-Ohio-5966, 2010 WL 4968636, *2 (Ohio Ct. App. 10th Dist. Franklin County 2010); quoting Young v. Young, 2006-Ohio-978, 2006 WL 515522, ¶ 105 (Ohio Ct. App. 2d Dist. Greene County 2006); Barton v. Barton, 2015-Ohio-3869, ¶ 8, 2015 WL 5691887 (Ohio Ct. App. 2d Dist. Greene County 2015) ("[w]ith regard to imminence, this court has previously held that because civil protection orders are intended to prevent domestic violence before it happens, imminence does not require an offender to carry out a threat or to be in the process of carrying it out.").

[47]Strassell v. Chapman, 2010-Ohio-4376, 2010 WL 3610591, *2 (Ohio Ct. App. 10th Dist. Franklin County 2010), quoting Fleckner v. Fleckner, 177 Ohio App. 3d 706, 2008-Ohio-4000, 895 N.E.2d 896, ¶ 23 (10th Dist. Franklin County 2008). By contrast, the objective test inquires whether the petitioner's fear is reasonable under the circumstances. Strassell v. Chapman, 2010-Ohio-4376, 2010 WL 3610591, *2 (Ohio Ct. App. 10th Dist. Franklin County 2010), quoting Fleckner v. Fleckner, 177 Ohio App. 3d 706, 2008-Ohio-4000, 895 N.E.2d 896, ¶ 23 (10th Dist. Franklin County

person would be placed in fear of imminent (in the sense of unconditional, non-contingent), serious physical harm."[48] In effect, the important questions must be whether the respondent's threat would cause a reasonable person to fear imminent serious physical harm and whether the petitioner's fear resulting from the threats is reasonable.[49]

In *Fleckner v. Fleckner*,[50] respondent sent petitioner an email threatening to "take out all of his anger and frustration in this family members'[sic] death sentence out on her in court."[51] In determining whether petitioner met her burden of proving fear of imminent serious physical harm, the appellate court reversed the judgment of the trial court and held that the evidence (showing a threat to take legal action) did not support findings of an unequivocal threat of force or a reasonable fear of imminent serious physical harm.[52]

Besides articulating the two-tiered test, the court also stressed that "the evidence must be clear and unequivocal that the petitioner was placed in fear of imminent physical harm. The evidence must reveal a nexus between the communication directed to a petitioner with subsequent actual fear of imminent, serious physical harm. While an objective standard is to be applied to the impact upon a victim's state of mind as it relates to threatening communications, the evidence must be unequivocal."[53]

In this decision, the Franklin County Court of Appeals appears to

---

2008).

[48]Strassell v. Chapman, 2010-Ohio-4376, 2010 WL 3610591, *2 (Ohio Ct. App. 10th Dist. Franklin County 2010), quoting Fleckner v. Fleckner, 177 Ohio App. 3d 706, 2008-Ohio-4000, 895 N.E.2d 896 (10th Dist. Franklin County 2008), in turn quoting Maccabee v. Maccabee, 1999 WL 430943 (Ohio Ct. App. 10th Dist. Franklin County 1999), in turn quoting Strong v. Bauman, 1999 WL 317432 (Ohio Ct. App. 2d Dist. Montgomery County 1999); Tyler v. Tyler, 2016-Ohio-7419, 2016 WL 6160139 (Ohio Ct. App. 2d Dist. Montgomery County 2016); Martindale v. Martindale, 2017-Ohio-9266, 102 N.E.3d 19 (Ohio Ct. App. 4th Dist. Athens County 2017) (discussion of what is considered sufficient evidence necessary to prove a fear of imminent serious physical harm and the test courts should apply to so determine).

[49]Strassell v. Chapman, 2010-Ohio-4376, 2010 WL 3610591, *2 (Ohio Ct. App. 10th Dist. Franklin County 2010); M.K. v. J.K., 2015-Ohio-434, 2015 WL 557990 (Ohio Ct. App. 9th Dist. Medina County 2015); A.D. v. B.D., 2017-Ohio-229, 2017 WL 277481 (Ohio Ct. App. 9th Dist. Medina County 2017) (finding that the statement, "you're as good as dead" when read in context, does not meet the threat of force test; for threats of violence to constitute domestic violence, the fear resulting from those threats must be reasonable); E.W. v. T.W., 2017-Ohio-8504, ¶ 16, 2017 WL 5192035 (Ohio Ct. App. 10th Dist. Franklin County 2017); Dodds on behalf of S.S. v. Stamper, 2018-Ohio-193, ¶ 32, 2018 WL 481779 (Ohio Ct. App. 2d Dist. Champaign County 2018); citing, Young v. Young, 2006-Ohio-978, ¶ 105, 2006 WL 515522 (Ohio Ct. App. 2d Dist. Greene County 2006) (noting that civil protection orders are intended to prevent violence before it happens).

[50]Fleckner v. Fleckner, 177 Ohio App. 3d 706, 2008-Ohio-4000, 895 N.E.2d 896 (10th Dist. Franklin County 2008).

[51]Fleckner v. Fleckner, 177 Ohio App. 3d 706, 710, 2008-Ohio-4000, 895 N.E.2d 896 (10th Dist. Franklin County 2008).

[52]Fleckner v. Fleckner, 177 Ohio App. 3d 706, 710, 2008-Ohio-4000, 895 N.E.2d 896 (10th Dist. Franklin County 2008) (syllabus).

[53]Fleckner v. Fleckner, 177 Ohio App. 3d 706, 715, 2008-Ohio-4000, 895 N.E.2d 896 (10th Dist. Franklin County 2008), quoting Coughlin v. Lancione, 1992 WL 40557 (Ohio Ct. App. 10th Dist. Franklin County 1992) (abrogated on other grounds by, Felton v. Felton, 79 Ohio St. 3d 34, 1997-Ohio-302, 679 N.E.2d 672 (1997)).

have moved the paradigm towards a more objective analysis, rather than balancing both the objective and subjective tests. In finding that the evidence must also be unequivocal, the court has articulated a more stringent test.

Likewise, in *Strassell v. Chapman*,[54] petitioner filed for a CPO based on threats of domestic violence. The 2008 incident included pushing her against the footboard of the bed, physically removing the phone from her hand and hitting and screaming at her. The 2009 incidents included acts of stalking and threatening words, to wit: "F*ck with my boat and I'll f*ck you like you have never been f*cked before."[55] These threats caused her to be fearful because respondent was "up in her face" when he said it. Further, she interpreted this threat as a physical threat, rather than a threat of a sexual nature.

The Franklin County Court of Appeals applied both the objective and subjective standard and pointed out that the reasonableness of a petitioner's fear should be determined with reference to the history between the parties.[56] The appellate court noted that petitioner had stated that she was in fear of serious physical harm on the date contained in the petition based on respondent's behavior in slamming the boat and his previous threat to "f*ck" her. In affirming the issuance of the CPO, the court held that a trial court could consider prior incidents of domestic violence to support its decision in determining the reasonableness of petitioner's fear.

The Ninth District Court of Appeals also adopted the legal analysis of the Tenth District, but with a twist. In *Chafin v. Chafin*,[57] the wife filed for a civil protection order against her husband, stating that he pounded on her door and told her that he'd never leave her alone. He also broke into her home while drunk and threatened her, saying, "If I can't have you-no one will have you."[58]

On appeal, respondent argued that petitioner's evidence did not establish her fear of imminent serious physical harm pursuant to the standard set out in *Fleckner*. The appellate court found that "[t]his Court has recognized that both the totality of the circumstances,[59] as well as the victim's state of mind, are relevant to the determinations that the threat of harm was imminent."[60]

---

[54]Strassell v. Chapman, 2010-Ohio-4376, 2010 WL 3610591 (Ohio Ct. App. 10th Dist. Franklin County 2010).

[55]Strassell v. Chapman, 2010-Ohio-4376, 2010 WL 3610591, *3 (Ohio Ct. App. 10th Dist. Franklin County 2010).

[56]Strassell v. Chapman, 2010-Ohio-4376, 2010 WL 3610591, *2 (Ohio Ct. App. 10th Dist. Franklin County 2010); see also McGuire v. Sprinkle, 2007-Ohio-2705, 2007 WL 1585100 (Ohio Ct. App. 12th Dist. Warren County 2007); Eichenberger v. Eichenberger, 82 Ohio App. 3d 809, 613 N.E.2d 678 (10th Dist. Franklin County 1992).

[57]Chafin v. Chafin, 2010-Ohio-3939, 2010 WL 3294288 (Ohio Ct. App. 9th Dist. Lorain County 2010).

[58]Chafin v. Chafin, 2010-Ohio-3939, 2010 WL 3294288, *2 (Ohio Ct. App. 9th Dist. Lorain County 2010).

[59]Cottrill v. Cottrill, 2017-Ohio-1422, 2017 WL 1376841 (Ohio Ct. App. 5th Dist. Fairfield County 2017); A.D. v. B.D., 2017-Ohio-229, 2017 WL 277481 (Ohio Ct. App. 9th Dist. Medina County 2017).

[60]Chafin v. Chafin, 2010-Ohio-3939, 2010 WL 3294288 (Ohio Ct. App. 9th Dist.

The Court went on to say that it further recognized that threats of violence constitute domestic violence if the victim's fear is reasonable, and that the reasonableness of the fear should be determined with reference to the history between the parties.[61] Consideration of the totality of the circumstances for context provided the rationale for affirming the trial court.

However, some courts have applied the *Fleckner* test and totality of the evidence standard but determined that there was a lack of sufficient evidence to find an actionable threat of force and fear of imminent serious physical harm. For example, in *M.H. v. J.H.*,[62] petitioner testified that the basis for her petition was that respondent came to her "confidential" residence in Ohio to take their daughter. She also stated that she did not feel safe knowing that J.H. could find her residence. She also testified about past domestic violence and a "controlling and angry marriage."

On appeal, the court reversed and remanded the case to the trial court, finding that there was insufficient evidence from which the trial court could have found that there was a recent threat of domestic violence upon which M.H. could reasonably infer fear of imminent harm to herself or the minor child and the recent incident did not involve any threat of violence or any contact between the parties.[63] "Rather, the record merely reflects that J.H. attempted to make contact with N.S. in the apartment complex's laundry room, told M.H.'s friend to not say anything, and asked N.S. to tell M.H. that he

---

Lorain County 2010), citing Morris v. Morris, 2009-Ohio-5164, 2009 WL 3119658 (Ohio Ct. App. 9th Dist. Summit County 2009); B.C. v. A.S., 2014-Ohio-1326, 2014 WL 1345260 (Ohio Ct. App. 9th Dist. Medina County 2014); Serdy v. Serdy, 2013-Ohio-5532, 2013 WL 6670830 (Ohio Ct. App. 7th Dist. Noble County 2013); M.H. v. J.H., 2015-Ohio-5178, 2015 WL 8553569 (Ohio Ct. App. 9th Dist. Medina County 2015) (noting that the purpose of the civil protection order is not to address past abuse); Lewis v. Gravely, 2016-Ohio-1502, 2016 WL 1404159 (Ohio Ct. App. 4th Dist. Adams County 2016) (victim's actions following the incident, such as going to the police, may help establish that the victim believed that serious physical harm was imminent and concluding that "a domestic violence victim's belief that serious physical harm was imminent constitutes evidence of imminence." at ¶ 28, citing State v. Tackett, 2005-Ohio-1437, 2005 WL 697411, ¶ 15 (Ohio Ct. App. 4th Dist. Jackson County 2005)); R.T. v. J.T., 2015-Ohio-4418, 2015 WL 6449294 (Ohio Ct. App. 9th Dist. Medina County 2015); J.M. v. M.M., 2016-Ohio-5368, 2016 WL 4272340 (Ohio Ct. App. 9th Dist. Medina County 2016); A.M. v. D.L., 2017-Ohio-5621, ¶ 6, 2017 WL 2870214 (Ohio Ct. App. 9th Dist. Medina County 2017); A.D. v. B.D., 2017-Ohio-229, 2017 WL 277481 (Ohio Ct. App. 9th Dist. Medina County 2017).

[61]Chafin v. Chafin, 2010-Ohio-3939, 2010 WL 3294288 (Ohio Ct. App. 9th Dist. Lorain County 2010), quoting Gatt v. Gatt, 2002-Ohio-1749, 2002 WL 570389 (Ohio Ct. App. 9th Dist. Medina County 2002), citing Eichenberger v. Eichenberger, 82 Ohio App. 3d 809, 816, 613 N.E.2d 678 (10th Dist. Franklin County 1992); M.R. v. T.R., 2016-Ohio-3493, 2016 WL 3384940 (Ohio Ct. App. 9th Dist. Wayne County 2016) (Noting that a court may consider evidence in light of the recent history between the parties in ruling on a CPO petition, citing Bowman v. Bowman, 2014-Ohio-2851, ¶ 10, 2014 WL 2957475 (Ohio Ct. App. 9th Dist. Medina County 2014), quoting State v. Payne, 178 Ohio App. 3d 617, 2008-Ohio-5447, ¶ 10, 899 N.E.2d 1011 (9th Dist. Summit County 2008)).

[62]M.H. v. J.H., 2015-Ohio-5178, 2015 WL 8553569 (Ohio Ct. App. 9th Dist. Medina County 2015).

[63]M.H. v. J.H., 2015-Ohio-5178, 2015 WL 8553569, ¶ 12 (Ohio Ct. App. 9th Dist. Medina County 2015).

wanted to speak with her."[64] No testimony was presented demonstrating that M.H. believed that J.H. would act violently towards her or the child. Without a threat of force that appellee faced serious physical harm or that she feared that his actions would cause her imminent harm, the civil protection order should be vacated. M.H.'s desire that J.H. not know where she was living or contact her is not the basis for the issuance of a civil protection order. "[I]t is inappropriate to use a protection order merely to create a buffer-zone around [the petitioner and her] children."[65]

Likewise, in *R.T. v. J.T.*,[66] the appellate court specifically discussed and explained its reasoning as to why the father did not prove that the mother had committed domestic violence. In that case, father was granted a CPO against the mother, naming all three children as protected parties.

Initially, the appellate court considered RC 3113.31(A)(1) regarding the acts that rise to the level of domestic violence from "attempting to cause or recklessly causing . . ." to "[p]lacing another by threat of force in fear of imminent serious physical harm." After defining all relevant terms, the court detailed the allegations set forth in the petition and testimony, to wit: that mother threw a glass at L.T. that bounced off the wall and hit L.T. As to T.T. and E.T., mother allegedly told the children that child protective services was coming to take them away.[67]

Father testified that several police reports had been made regarding Mother's actions towards the children and that the police had investigated some of these. However, the investigation indicated that the acts were considered discipline. Father testified that the children had told him of several incidents and that the children reported that they didn't feel safe at mother's home. Father also stated that he believed the children were in danger if they remained with Mother.[68]

However, he also testified that there had also been issues at his home that the children have disclosed to Mother, that E.T. had a confrontation with father's wife which did not involve violence and that he did not observe any violent behavior by mother during the time they lived together. Mother testified that she had never harmed L.T., the incident with the glass was an accident and that L.T. acts out with her.

At the end of the case, the magistrate advised Father that she did not have the authority to make an allocation of parental rights or supervised visitation. Father's attorney then asked that the children remain as protected parties on the CPO.

---

[64] M.H. v. J.H., 2015-Ohio-5178, 2015 WL 8553569, ¶ 12 (Ohio Ct. App. 9th Dist. Medina County 2015).

[65] M.H. v. J.H., 2015-Ohio-5178, 2015 WL 8553569, ¶ 13 (Ohio Ct. App. 9th Dist. Medina County 2015) quoting Williamson v. Williamson, 180 Ohio App. 3d 260, 2008-Ohio-6718, 905 N.E.2d 217, ¶ 60 (2d Dist. Greene County 2008).

[66] R.T. v. J.T., 2015-Ohio-4418, 2015 WL 6449294 (Ohio Ct. App. 9th Dist. Medina County 2015).

[67] R.T. v. J.T., 2015-Ohio-4418, 2015 WL 6449294, ¶ 17 (Ohio Ct. App. 9th Dist. Medina County 2015).

[68] R.T. v. J.T., 2015-Ohio-4418, 2015 WL 6449294, ¶ 21, 23-24 (Ohio Ct. App. 9th Dist. Medina County 2015).

The appellate court pointed out that none of the children testified, and that no evidence was presented by any professional who might have observed L.T. or the other children after the incident. There was no evidence of injury or physical pain to L.T. "Based on a review of the record, Father did not meet his burden of proving by a preponderance of the evidence that Mother caused any bodily injury to L.T. While throwing a cup across the room close to another person rises to the level of recklessness, in the absence of any evidence of injury to the children, the trial court's finding that Mother recklessly caused bodily injury to L.T. was against the manifest weight of the evidence."[69]

The appellate court also determined that Father failed to meet his burden of proving that Mother placed any of the children by threat of force in fear of imminent serious physical harm. Although Mother may have, in the past, thrown objects, none of the prior incidents rose to the level of "serious" harm. "Moreover, such past acts by Mother do not demonstrate a reasonable belief by the children that they were in danger of imminent serious physical harm, "absent an initial, explicit indication that [the children] w[ere] in fear of imminent serious physical harm on the date contained in the petition." "[70] Finally, there was no testimony that the other children either witnessed the incident or expressed fear on the date contained in the petition. In fact, L.T. did not express fear of imminent serious physical harm on the date of the incident, even though he told his school counselor. The Court reasoned that the fears were not significant enough that school personnel shielded the child from his mother, especially because the child indicated she felt safe going home with Mother and instead of expressing fear or running from Mother, the child continued yelling at Mother.[71] Therefore, the court sustained Mother's assignment of error.

Q & A: Is the meaning of "imminent" as used in R.C. 3113.31 restricted to the actual timing of the threat?

Not according to the Tenth District Court of Appeals. In *Strassell v. Chapman*,[72] petitioner filed for a CPO based on instances of threats of domestic violence pursuant to R.C. 3113.31. The appellate court indicated that the imminence requirement does not require that the offender carry out the threat immediately or be in the process of carrying out the threat, because "if that were the case, a man could

---

[69]R.T. v. J.T., 2015-Ohio-4418, 2015 WL 6449294, ¶ 35 (Ohio Ct. App. 9th Dist. Medina County 2015).

[70]R.T. v. J.T., 2015-Ohio-4418, 2015 WL 6449294, ¶ 36 (Ohio Ct. App. 9th Dist. Medina County 2015), citing *Chafin*at ¶ 22; J.M. v. M.M., 2016-Ohio-5368, 2016 WL 4272340 (Ohio Ct. App. 9th Dist. Medina County 2016); citing Chafin at ¶ 22).

[71]R.T. v. J.T., 2015-Ohio-4418, 2015 WL 6449294, ¶ 37 (Ohio Ct. App. 9th Dist. Medina County 2015).

[72]Strassell v. Chapman, 2010-Ohio-4376, 2010 WL 3610591 (Ohio Ct. App. 10th Dist. Franklin County 2010). But see Weber v. Forinash, 2015-Ohio-3187, 2015 WL 4720532 (Ohio Ct. App. 6th Dist. Sandusky County 2015) (in which the dissent argued that the acts forming the basis of the CPO occurred over 16-32 months before the full hearing was held and finding that no evidence existed to show that, at the time of the full hearing, appellee was in immediate and present danger as defined in RC 3113. 31(A)(1)); E.W. v. T.W., 2017-Ohio-8504, ¶ 43, 2017 WL 5192035 (Ohio Ct. App. 10th Dist. Franklin County 2017) (see Judge Brunner's concurring opinion in which the judge agreed that "[t]he requirement of imminent fear addresses the reality of the threat rather that the timing of the threat."; quoting *Strassel*).

threaten to kill his wife at sometime in the near future and not be subject to a CPO."[73] "Rather, since a CPO is intended to prevent domestic violence, courts construe the imminence requirement to ask whether a reasonable person would be placed in fear of unconditional, non-contingent serious physical harm."[74] Thus, the requirement of "imminent" fear addresses the reality of the threat rather than the timing of the threat.

Q & A: Must the threat be unequivocal or must the evidence that the victim was placed in fear be unequivocal?

Under the *Fleckner* test, it is unclear whether the threat or the evidence must be unequivocal.[75] The term "unequivocal" is defined in Webster's Dictionary as "admitting no doubt or misunderstanding."[76]

Inasmuch as the *Fleckner* appellate court skirted this issue and failed to provide adequate reasoning for its decision, it is unfortunately fraught with ambiguity. On the one hand, the court found that there was no evidence that appellant made an *unequivocal* threat of force. On the other hand, the court stated that the evidence must be clear and *unequivocal* that the petitioner was placed in fear of imminent serious physical harm.

If the threat must be unequivocal, it is then a matter of balancing both an objective and subjective standard in light of the history between the parties and a totality of the circumstances. If it is the evidence that must be unequivocal, the Franklin County Court of Appeals has transformed the standard of proof from preponderance of the evidence to a clear and convincing evidence standard.

Q & A: Is there a difference between "imminent" fear and fear related to potential future conduct?

The Hamilton County Court of Appeals has indicated as much. In *State v. Strunk*,[77] the victim testified that she had been frightened by defendant's telephone messages because she believed "the game is on" and "it's on now" were continuations of threats, made four days earlier during a telephone conversation, to physically injure her and to damage her car. The defendant argued that no evidence was presented to demonstrate that the victim believed she was in danger of imminent physical harm.

The Hamilton County Court of Appeals differentiated between fear believed to be imminent and fear related to potential future conduct.[78] Because the victim's own testimony failed to establish that she

---

[73]Strassell v. Chapman, 2010-Ohio-4376, 2010 WL 3610591, *6 (Ohio Ct. App. 10th Dist. Franklin County 2010), citing Strong v. Bauman, 1999 WL 317432 (Ohio Ct. App. 2d Dist. Montgomery County 1999).

[74]Strassell v. Chapman, 2010-Ohio-4376, 2010 WL 3610591, *6 (Ohio Ct. App. 10th Dist. Franklin County 2010), citing Siouffi v. Siouffi, 1998 WL 879255 (Ohio Ct. App. 2d Dist. Montgomery County 1998).

[75]See also Wohleber v. Wohleber, 2011-Ohio-6696, 2011 WL 6880736 (Ohio Ct. App. 9th Dist. Lorain County 2011) (magistrate focused on whether the threat was unequivocal, rather than the evidence being unequivocal and denied the CPO; trial court sustained objections and issued the CPO).

[76]Webster's II New Riverside University Dictionary (1984).

[77]State v. Strunk, 1999 WL 12743, *1 (Ohio Ct. App. 1st Dist. Hamilton County 1999).

[78]See also Henry v. Henry, 2005-Ohio-67, 2005 WL 43888 (Ohio Ct. App. 4th Dist.

believed the danger was imminent, as opposed to sometime in the future, the court sustained defendant's assignment of error.

Q & A: How is "serious physical harm" defined?

As with the term "force," RC 3113.31 does not define "serious physical harm." The Montgomery County Court of Appeals, in both *Sitton v. Sitton*[79] and *Siouffi v. Siouffi*,[80] looked to the criminal code sections of the Ohio Revised Code for guidance.[81]

"Serious physical harm to persons"[82] is defined in RC 2901.01(A)(5) as:

(a) Any mental illness or condition of such gravity as would normally require hospitalization or prolonged psychiatric treatment;
(b) Any physical harm that carries a substantial risk of death;
(c) Any physical harm that involves some permanent incapacity, whether partial or total, or that involves some temporary, substantial incapacity;
(d) Any physical harm that involves some permanent disfigurement, or that involves some temporary, serious disfigurement;
(e) Any physical harm that involves acute pain of such duration as to result in substantial suffering, or that involves any degree of prolonged or intractable pain.

Ross County 2005) (Court affirmed decision denying CPO because petitioner did not testify both about the act and the fear caused by the act. "Absent actual testimony about the fear of imminent serious physical harm caused by a particular threat, a trial court cannot imply and conclude the fear exists."). See also dissent, State v. Schweitzer, 2015-Ohio-925, 30 N.E.3d 190 (Ohio Ct. App. 3d Dist. Auglaize County 2015) (dissent focused on fact that there was no past history; hence, no linkage between threat to a belief by victim that defendant would carry out threat; victim's declared "uncertainty" as to what might happen when he drinks would at most support a conditional fear of possible future harm, not an immediate threat of imminent harm. "[m]ere possibility is not imminent probability" ¶ 52); M.J. v. L.P., 2016-Ohio-7080, 2016 WL 5723752 (Ohio Ct. App. 9th Dist. Medina County 2016); Dodds on behalf of S.S. v. Stamper, 2018-Ohio-193, 2018 WL 481779, ¶ 33 (Ohio Ct. App. 2d Dist. Champaign County 2018) ("It is important to distinguish between fear of potential future conduct and immediate physical conduct, and to remember that the petitioner must show sufficient evidence of the latter." quoting Williamson v. Williamson, 180 Ohio App. 3d 260, 2008-Ohio-6718, 905 N.E.2d 217, ¶ 47 (2d Dist. Greene County 2008)).

[79]Sitton v. Sitton, 1999 WL 55717 (Ohio Ct. App. 2d Dist. Montgomery County 1999).

[80]Siouffi v. Siouffi, 1998 WL 879255 (Ohio Ct. App. 2d Dist. Montgomery County 1998).

[81]See Fleckner v. Fleckner, 177 Ohio App. 3d 706, 2008-Ohio-4000, 895 N.E.2d 896 (10th Dist. Franklin County 2008).

[82]State v. Holsinger, 2017-Ohio-1378, 2017 WL 1365411 (Ohio Ct. App. 5th Dist. Richland County 2017), appeal not allowed, 150 Ohio St. 3d 1433, 2017-Ohio-7567, 81 N.E.3d 1272 (2017) ("[courts have held that "[t]he degree of harm that rises to the level of 'serious' physical harm is not an exact science "given the definition uses terms such as "substantial," "temporary," "acute" and "prolonged."" At ¶ 35, citing State v. Miller, 2013-Ohio-1651, ¶ 18, 2013 WL 1787565 (Ohio Ct. App. 8th Dist. Cuyahoga County 2013), quoting State v. Irwin, 2007-Ohio-4996, ¶ 37, 2007 WL 2758606 (Ohio Ct. App. 7th Dist. Mahoning County 2007)).

While RC 2919.25 requires an offender to "knowingly"[83] cause the family member to believe the offender will cause imminent "physical harm,"[84] there is no such mens rea requirement under RC 3113.31(A)(1)(b). Additionally, the threat must place the petitioner in fear of imminent "serious physical harm." The absence of "seriousness" as an element of the criminal offense under RC 2919.25(C) reflects a compromise between the onerous burden of proof necessary to sustain a criminal conviction and a less burdensome and more easily provable definition of "physical harm." In the civil context, the legislature sought to balance a lesser burden of proof with a greater showing of harm.[85]

The definition of "serious physical harm" may arguably encompass emotional harm or mental anguish under RC 3113.31(A)(1)(b).[86] The dissent in *Eichenberger v. Eichenberger*[87] notes that mental illness would have been considered as "serious physical harm" by the court had the issue been raised by the victim.

In *State v. Houston,*[88] however, the court found that mental illness or a psychological impairment is not sufficient for a finding of domestic violence. The court held that there was no evidence to indicate that the complainant sustained any physical injury, illness, or physiological impairment. Although the complainant did not attend work the day after the accident, the court held that "stress" is a psychological impairment. not a "physiological" one. The court reasoned that "while physical illness is included in the concept of physical harm to persons, mental illness is not."[89]

Q & A: What standard should be employed by a court to determine fear and the impact on a petitioner's state of mind?

RC 3113.31 is silent as to the standard to be applied by a court to determine fear and the impact on a petitioner's state of mind.[90]

---

[83]See State v. Knapp, 2001 WL 62519 (Ohio Ct. App. 2d Dist. Montgomery County 2001) (definition of knowingly); see also RC 2901.22(B) (for a definition of knowingly).

[84]RC 2919.25(C); see also State v. Robinette, 118 Ohio App. 3d 450, 693 N.E.2d 305 (4th Dist. Jackson County 1997); see State v. Brown, 2006-Ohio-6267, 2006 WL 3446238, *5 (Ohio Ct. App. 8th Dist. Cuyahoga County 2006), aff'd on other grounds, 119 Ohio St. 3d 447, 2008-Ohio-4569, 895 N.E.2d 149 (2008) (noting that "this Court has held that [g]enerally, a trial court does not err in finding serious physical harm where the evidence demonstrates the victim sustained injuries necessitating medical treatment.").

[85]See RC 2901.01(A)(5).

[86]RC 2901.01(E)(1).

[87]Eichenberger v. Eichenberger, 82 Ohio App. 3d 809, 613 N.E.2d 678 (10th Dist. Franklin County 1992); see also State v. Elliott, 104 Ohio App. 3d 812, 663 N.E.2d 412 (10th Dist. Franklin County 1995); State v. Edwards, 83 Ohio App. 3d 357, 614 N.E.2d 1123 (10th Dist. Franklin County 1992).

[88]State v. Houston, 1992 WL 87449 (Ohio Ct. App. 2d Dist. Montgomery County 1992).

[89]State v. Houston, 1992 WL 87449, *2-3 (Ohio Ct. App. 2d Dist. Montgomery County 1992). See also State v. Pennington, 1983 WL 2823 (Ohio Ct. App. 8th Dist. Cuyahoga County 1983), wherein the Cuyahoga County Appellate Court adopted the rationale of the Committee Commentary to RC 2901.01 which concludes that physiological impairment excludes mental distress, fright, or emotional disturbance.

[90]See Morris v. Morris, 2009-Ohio-5164, 2009 WL 3119658 (Ohio Ct. App. 9th

However, the essence of RC 3113.31(A)(1)(b) is the victim's fear.[91] Because the state of mind of the victim is essential to the threat provision of the statute,[92] the court must consider using a subjective standard. While the use of an objective standard permits a court to analyze the facts of the case in light of reasonableness, it is unlikely to establish at which point in time a particular individual is justified in believing that the respondent's threat is real and imminent.

Generally, an objective and subjective analysis have been applied by courts in attempting to find the right balance when assessing a threat pursuant to RC 3113.31(A)(1)(b). Ohio courts have considered either an objective or subjective analysis in determining fear and imminence at one time or another. Some courts have indicated the need for the objective component. Other courts have used a more subjective approach. More recent cases have considered a combined objective and subjective standard.

For example, in *State v. Lee*,[93] the Hamilton County Municipal Court stressed the objective component for purposes of the criminal domestic violence statute.[94] In that case, the brandishing of a knife to stab the door and bedroom mattress is "conduct which would reasonably lead any person to fear imminent physical harm from the accused."[95]

This issue has been raised repeatedly in the civil domestic violence arena. For example, in *West v. West*.[96] In that case, Mr. West had previously threatened Mrs. West with statements that included "all this pain and suffering will be taken care of later" and "wait till you see what I have got planned." These threats were the basis of a civil protection order obtained by the victim in November 1993. The issue was whether Mr. West's comments on the day in question caused Mrs. West to believe that he intended to carry out those threats of approximately five months earlier. The court relied on *City of Dayton v.*

Dist. Summit County 2009) (noting that a victim's state of mind is relevant in determining whether a threat of harm is imminent).

[91]See Bruns v. Bruns, 1999 WL 819344 (Ohio Ct. App. 6th Dist. Erie County 1999) (Past behavior may be used to establish that the petitioner's fear of imminent serious harm was reasonable.); see also Ankenbruck v. Ankenbruck, 2000 WL 1804360 (Ohio Ct. App. 11th Dist. Trumbull County 2000) (recognizing the subjective element of fear, but noting there was nothing to suggest appellee's fear was either irrational or unfounded; the court relied on evidence of past abuse); Hunter v. Hunter, 2006-Ohio-6307, 2006 WL 3462139, *2 (Ohio Ct. App. 2d Dist. Montgomery County 2006) (as correctly noted by the trial court in its judgment, "the primary focus of RC 3113.31(A)(1)(b) is the perception of the victim.").

[92]See State v. Sayres, 1997 WL 142361 (Ohio Ct. App. 4th Dist. Washington County 1997).

[93]State v. Lee, 73 Ohio Misc. 2d 9, 657 N.E.2d 604 (Mun. Ct. 1995).

[94]See RC 2919.25(C).

[95]State v. Lee, 73 Ohio Misc. 2d 9, 19, 657 N.E.2d 604 (Mun. Ct. 1995).

[96]West v. West, 1994 WL 680156, *3 (Ohio Ct. App. 2d Dist. Montgomery County 1994); see also Eichenberger v. Eichenberger, 82 Ohio App. 3d 809, 613 N.E.2d 678 (10th Dist. Franklin County 1992) (holding that, when the respondent threatened to kill the petitioner, causing her to fear that he would act on the threats, domestic violence had occurred); Conkle v. Wolfe, 131 Ohio App. 3d 375, 383, 722 N.E.2d 586 (4th Dist. Athens County 1998), citing Eichenberger v. Eichenberger, 82 Ohio App. 3d 809, 815, 613 N.E.2d 678 (10th Dist. Franklin County 1992) (threats of violence constitute domestic violence under RC 3113.31 provided the resulting fear from those threats is reasonable).

Waugh[97] in holding that "[t]he measure of whether Mr. West caused Mrs. West to believe that he would inflict physical harm is her subjective belief of the same. 'It is sufficient if the offender knowingly causes the victim to believe that the offender will carry his threat into execution. Hence, it is the victim's subjective belief which becomes the focal point for determining whether certain conduct violates the statute.' "[98] The court determined that these threats were sufficient to cause Mrs. West's subjective belief of physical harm. The court went on to say that "[t]he record does not reflect any direct evidence to show that Mr. West knowingly caused that belief; i.e., that he was aware that his statements would produce such a belief in the Appellee. However, a finder of fact may infer knowledge from 'surrounding facts and circumstances.' "[99] To that end, the statements of the respondent and his prior actions of pouring soap into his wife's coffee qualified as domestic violence under RC 3113.31.[100]

The issue was again raised in *Coughlin v. Lancione*[101] with a different result. In *Coughlin*, the respondent threatened "to take [her] down" and stated that she "was on his list." The appellant testified that "she was fearful of his conduct." The court held that:

> the evidence must be clear and unequivocal that the petitioner was placed in fear of imminent physical harm. The evidence must reveal a nexus between the communication directed to a petitioner with subsequent actual fear of imminent, serious physical harm. While an objective standard is to be applied to the impact upon a victim's state of mind as it relates to threatening communications, the evidence must be unequivocal.
>
> The record here is devoid of statements attributed to appellant that could reasonably lead one to be in fear of imminent serious physical harm.[102]

In this case, the court of appeals dismissed the civil protection order because it found that the evidence was not clear that respondent's conduct put petitioner in fear of "imminent serious physical harm." This case suggests that an objective standard should be employed to

[97] City of Dayton v. Waugh, No. 6965 (2d Dist. Ct. App., Montgomery, 1-2-81).

[98] West v. West, 1994 WL 680156, *3 (Ohio Ct. App. 2d Dist. Montgomery County 1994); Meyers v. Wimer, 2005-Ohio-3753, 2005 WL 1714194, *2 (Ohio Ct. App. 2d Dist. Montgomery County 2005) (relying on *West*, the court held that the test for fear of imminent serious physical harm is the victim's subjective belief that the threat of force will result in imminent serious physical harm).

[99] West v. West, 1994 WL 680156, *3 (Ohio Ct. App. 2d Dist. Montgomery County 1994).

[100] West v. West, 1994 WL 680156 (Ohio Ct. App. 2d Dist. Montgomery County 1994); see also Eichenberger v. Eichenberger, 82 Ohio App. 3d 809, 613 N.E.2d 678 (10th Dist. Franklin County 1992).

[101] Coughlin v. Lancione, 1992 WL 40557 (Ohio Ct. App. 10th Dist. Franklin County 1992) (abrogated by, Felton v. Felton, 79 Ohio St. 3d 34, 1997-Ohio-302, 679 N.E.2d 672 (1997)), abrogated by Felton v. Felton, 79 Ohio St. 3d 34, 1997-Ohio-302, 679 N.E.2d 672 (1997) (establishing preponderance-of-the-evidence standard).

[102] Coughlin v. Lancione, 1992 WL 40557, *1 (Ohio Ct. App. 10th Dist. Franklin County 1992) (abrogated by, Felton v. Felton, 79 Ohio St. 3d 34, 1997-Ohio-302, 679 N.E.2d 672 (1997)), abrogated by Felton v. Felton, 79 Ohio St. 3d 34, 1997-Ohio-302, 679 N.E.2d 672 (1997) (establishing preponderance-of-the-evidence standard).

measure fear and the impact on the petitioner's state of mind.[103] By requiring clear and unequivocal evidence to issue a protection order, the court of appeals sanctioned a clear and convincing standard. This higher burden of proof is more difficult for the petitioner to demonstrate, and it was not surprising that the petitioner failed to meet it.

West and *Coughlin* reflect the competing theories considered by various court jurisdictions.[104] The petitioner in *West* prevailed because the court employed a subjective standard of the victim's belief[105] rather than the more objective standard relied on by the court in *Coughlin*. Additionally, the *Coughlin* court applied a clear and convincing evidence burden, whereas the *West* court used a less stringent burden. Obviously, the lowered burden of proof enabled the petitioner in *West* to prevail.[106]

In any case, reasonableness is determined by introducing evidence that demonstrates behavior that would cause a reasonable person to experience fear of imminent serious physical harm.[107] In *Maglionico v. Maglionico*,[108] the appellant had threatened his brother and his brother's son by stating "I'm either gonna shoot you or stab you like a pig. It's your choice." The court considered the credibility of the testimony presented in deciding whether a civil protection order was necessary to ensure the petitioner's safety and would have granted

[103]See also Stevenson v. Stevenson, 314 N.J. Super. 350, 714 A.2d 986 (Ch. Div. 1998); Lundin v. Niepsuj, 2017-Ohio-7153, ¶ 28, 2017 WL 3426957 (Ohio Ct. App. 9th Dist. Summit County 2017) (in that appellee testified that the harm felt from respondent was emotional, that she relied on events occurring prior to initial CPO and that no dates were listed in her petition, appellate court found that appellee failed to present sufficient evidence to support finding that she was in fear of imminent serious physical harm as a result of appellant's force or threat of force. Fear "cannot be based on embarrassment in the community or some unspecified conduct that occurred at some unspecified time in the past." [at ¶ 28.]).

[104]See Tyler v. Tyler, 2004-Ohio-5784, 2004 WL 2436594 (Ohio Ct. App. 2d Dist. Montgomery County 2004) (Court held that magistrate's reliance on objective test for assessing wife's fear instead of relying on subjective test was harmless error; under either standard, wife failed to prove the essential elements of RC 3113.31(A)(1)(b).).

[105]See also Reynolds v. Reynolds, 2001 WL 62552 (Ohio Ct. App. 2d Dist. Montgomery County 2001) (noting that the standard for reviewing fear is subjective, that is, whether her fear was reasonable under the particular circumstances of her particular situation).

[106]In June 1997, the Ohio Supreme Court finally resolved the issue when it determined that the preponderance of the evidence is the appropriate standard to apply when issuing a civil protection order. See Felton v. Felton, 79 Ohio St. 3d 34, 1997-Ohio-302, 679 N.E.2d 672 (1997).

[107]Maglionico v. Maglionico, 2001-Ohio-8901, 2001 WL 1401978, *1 (Ohio Ct. App. 11th Dist. Portage County 2001); see also Katsenelenbogen v. Katsenelenbogen, 135 Md. App. 317, 762 A.2d 198 (2000), opinion vacated, 365 Md. 122, 775 A.2d 1249 (2001) (discussing whether actual fear is sufficient to prove imminent serious bodily injury and whether a subjective test is mandated by statute and holding that a trial court should consider whether there was a reasonable basis for the perceived imminent serious bodily harm. The court then defined "reasonable" as conduct that must cause a reasonable person under the same or similar circumstances to fear serious bodily injury. The circumstances include age, intelligence, gender, health and physical attributes of the parties); Newhouse v. Williams, 167 Ohio App. 3d 215, 2006-Ohio-3075, 854 N.E.2d 565 (3d Dist. Wyandot County 2006) (no evidence of reasonable fear of imminent serious physical harm was introduced).

[108]Maglionico v. Maglionico, 2001-Ohio-8901, 2001 WL 1401978, *3 (Ohio Ct. App. 11th Dist. Portage County 2001).

the order but for the lack of a family or household member relationship between the parties.

Q & A: When differentiating threats for purposes of domestic violence in the civil and criminal contexts, how are the above standards applied?

Family law attorneys would do well to review the case law involving Ohio's criminal domestic violence statute.[109] The threat provision of R.C. 3113.31 is substantially similar to that contained in R.C. 2919.25 and as such, the case law and legal analysis is instructive.[110]

Two Ohio cases clarified and refined the standard for conviction for a threat under R.C. 2919.25(C). Accordingly, the subjective belief of the victim is the appropriate standard to establish the elements of the domestic violence threat under R.C. 2919.25(C). In *State v. Collie*,[111] the Hamilton County Appellate Court first determined that R.C. 2919.25(C) has, as an element, the belief of a family member that the offender will cause imminent physical harm. The court also stated that evidence of past acts toward the same victim may be used to establish the basis of the victim's belief in the imminence of physical harm, if the evidence is specific to time and place.[112]

In *State v. Taylor*,[113] the Hamilton County Municipal Court applied the new test announced in Collie, holding that "[a] close analysis of the law, however, does not establish an absolute requirement that to sustain a domestic violence threat conviction, the state must prove

[109]R.C. 2919.25.

[110]But see the concurring opinion in Ankenbruck v. Ankenbruck, 2000 WL 1804360 (Ohio Ct. App. 11th Dist. Trumbull County 2000) (majority relied on State v. Blonski, 125 Ohio App. 3d 103, 707 N.E.2d 1168 (9th Dist. Medina County 1997), to support finding of domestic violence for purposes of civil protection order, in that a slap to the face was considered an attempt to cause bodily injury and constituted domestic violence in the criminal context; concurring judge cautioned that "the fact that certain conduct amounts to domestic violence in the context of a criminal case does not necessarily mean the same conduct, per se, warrants a civil protection order).

[111]State v. Collie, 108 Ohio App. 3d 580, 671 N.E.2d 338 (1st Dist. Hamilton County 1996). But see City of Cincinnati v. Baarlaer, 115 Ohio App. 3d 521, 685 N.E.2d 836 (1st Dist. Hamilton County 1996) (advancing a combination of the two standards by noting that the victim must believe the threat is imminent and further stating that reasonable minds could also conclude that the defendant's threat would cause her to believe he could kill her).

[112]See also Visnich v. Visnich, 1999 WL 1299300 (Ohio Ct. App. 11th Dist. Trumbull County 1999) (relying on Evid. R. 404(B) to support a finding of domestic violence where appellant's past use of firearms was admissible to prove that appellee was justified in her fear of imminent serious physical harm); State v. Drake, 135 Ohio App. 3d 507, 734 N.E.2d 865 (12th Dist. Butler County 1999). See also State v. Rhoads, 2013-Ohio-152, 2013 WL 221512, ¶ 29 (Ohio Ct. App. 12th Dist. Clermont County 2013) (noting that prior acts of violence between the parties is probative in establishing victim's belief of impending harm); B.C. v. A.S., 2014-Ohio-1326, 2014 WL 1345260 (Ohio Ct. App. 9th Dist. Medina County 2014).

[113]State v. Taylor, 79 Ohio Misc. 2d 82, 85, 671 N.E.2d 343 (Mun. Ct. 1996) (citations omitted). But see dissent in State v. Schweitzer, 2015-Ohio-925, 30 N.E.3d 190 (Ohio Ct. App. 3d Dist. Auglaize County 2015) (where defendant had never hurt her before and she only called police to stop the argument and in that she remained in the apt. after the argument, nothing she told police linked her fear to the threat; her declared "uncertainty" as to what might happen when he drinks would at most support a conditional fear of possible future harm, not an immediate threat of imminent harm).

the accused's ability to carry out the threat imminently . . ., [as] critical inquiry is whether or not the proof fully evidences a reasonable belief by the victim that the accused will cause imminent physical harm."

Some of the more recent appellate decisions regarding civil protection orders have applied a combined objective and subjective standard[114] in determining whether specific conduct put a particular victim in fear of imminent serious physical harm.[115]

In *Sitton v. Sitton*,[116] the Montgomery County Court of Appeals justified issuing of a civil protection order because the victim had a rational, objective basis for her fear. In that case, the defendant said, "I might as well just shoot both of us, you and me, because there's nothing that—nothing to lose anyway."[117] The trial court granted her a civil protection order. The defendant appealed on the ground that the trial court abused its discretion by granting the order.

In upholding the trial court's decision, the appellate court found that, although the defendant did not have a weapon with him on the day in question, he was a licensed gun dealer and had access to weapons in the basement.[118] Additionally, he had threatened to kill the victim the previous year. The court noted that the victim had testified as to her fear of defendant. The court rejected the defendant's argument that, because of the victim's mental history of multiple personalities, "any fear . . . was fictionalized, perceived fear based on irrationality."[119] In fact, the court held that "in view of Mr. Sitton's threats to kill his wife and his access to weapons, we cannot conclude that Mrs. Sitton lacked an objective basis to fear her husband."[120]

Moreover, the court made a factual finding that Mrs. Sitton was in fear of her husband, noting:

> [t]hat finding is supported not only by her own direct testimony of fear, but also by her actions in vacating the house on the day of the incident, hiding out from her husband, and returning to the residence only when

---

[114]See Young v. Young, 2006-Ohio-978, 2006 WL 515522 (Ohio Ct. App. 2d Dist. Greene County 2006) (noting that civil protection orders are intended to prevent violence before it happens).

[115]See also Ankenbruck v. Ankenbruck, 2000 WL 1804360 (Ohio Ct. App. 11th Dist. Trumbull County 2000); Reynolds v. Reynolds, 2001 WL 62552 (Ohio Ct. App. 2d Dist. Montgomery County 2001); Chapman v. Chapman, 2004-Ohio-2318, 2004 WL 1047577 (Ohio Ct. App. 2d Dist. Montgomery County 2004).

[116]Sitton v. Sitton, 1999 WL 55717 (Ohio Ct. App. 2d Dist. Montgomery County 1999). But see Reynolds v. Reynolds, 2001 WL 62552 (Ohio Ct. App. 2d Dist. Montgomery County 2001) (standard for reviewing victim's fear is subjective, that is whether her fear was reasonable under the circumstances of her particular situation).

[117]Sitton v. Sitton, 1999 WL 55717, *3 (Ohio Ct. App. 2d Dist. Montgomery County 1999).

[118]See also Lamont v. Lamont, 2005-Ohio-2256, 2005 WL 1075613, *2 (Ohio Ct. App. 11th Dist. Geauga County 2005) (In affirming conviction, court noted that appellant's threat to kill by "putting a bullet in his head" caused him fear, particularly because appellant also said she had the means to carry out threat because she owned a handgun.).

[119]Sitton v. Sitton, 1999 WL 55717, *4 (Ohio Ct. App. 2d Dist. Montgomery County 1999).

[120]Sitton v. Sitton, 1999 WL 55717, *4 (Ohio Ct. App. 2d Dist. Montgomery County 1999).

she was either accompanied by a police officer or at a time when she believed a protection order had been served on her husband.[121]

Similarly, in *Siouffi v. Siouffi*,[122] the Montgomery County Court of Appeals determined that "whether a person is placed in fear of imminent serious physical harm by particular threatening conduct also involves an element of objectivity."[123] Where the conduct involved the use of a 12-inch butcher knife, it was likely that a reasonable person would be placed in fear of imminent serious physical harm. The court also noted that any determination must be made on a case-by-case basis.

Recent case law has further refined the analysis. For example, in *Fleckner v. Fleckner*, the Franklin County Court of Appeals synthesized the analyses of the many earlier cases and stressed that the "critical inquiry under [R.C. 3113.31] 'is whether a reasonable person would be placed in fear of imminent (in the sense of unconditional, non-contingent), serious physical harm.' "[124] " 'This inquiry necessarily involves both subjective and objective elements.' "[125] In a case where there was no bodily injury or attempt to cause bodily injury, the ap-

---

[121]Sitton v. Sitton, 1999 WL 55717, *4 (Ohio Ct. App. 2d Dist. Montgomery County 1999); see also Strong v. Bauman, 1999 WL 317432 (Ohio Ct. App. 2d Dist. Montgomery County 1999) (relying on victim's actions to infer fear).

[122]Siouffi v. Siouffi, 1998 WL 879255 (Ohio Ct. App. 2d Dist. Montgomery County 1998).

[123]Siouffi v. Siouffi, 1998 WL 879255, *4 (Ohio Ct. App. 2d Dist. Montgomery County 1998); see also Maccabee v. Maccabee, 1999 WL 430943, *2 (Ohio Ct. App. 10th Dist. Franklin County 1999) (relying on the reasoning articulated in Strong v. Bauman in finding that "the critical inquiry under R.C. 3113.13 'is whether a reasonable person would be placed in fear of imminent (in the sense of unconditional, non-contingent), serious physical harm.' "); see also Markowitz v. Markowitz, 2006-Ohio-5932, 2006 WL 3234010, *2 (Ohio Ct. App. 8th Dist. Cuyahoga County 2006) ("Respondents resort to extreme physical violence—punching the car with sufficient force to dent it—to vent his anger or frustration with petitioner was ample evidence that petitioner had reasonable grounds to fear that serious physical harm was imminent in this similarly escalating situation." But see dissenting opinion, focusing on petitioner's not filing criminal charges against respondent to suggest petitioner did not fear respondent.).

[124]Fleckner v. Fleckner, 177 Ohio App. 3d 706, 714, 2008-Ohio-4000, 895 N.E.2d 896, 902 (10th Dist. Franklin County 2008), citing Maccabee v. Maccabee, 1999 WL 430943 (Ohio Ct. App. 10th Dist. Franklin County 1999), and quoting Strong v. Bauman, 1999 WL 317432, *4 (Ohio Ct. App. 2d Dist. Montgomery County 1999); Morris v. Morris, 2009-Ohio-5164, 2009 WL 3119658 (Ohio Ct. App. 9th Dist. Summit County 2009); Bargar v. Kirby, 2011-Ohio-4904, 2011 WL 4436634 (Ohio Ct. App. 12th Dist. Butler County 2011); Moore v. Guyton, 2013-Ohio-143, 2013 WL 221515, ¶ 14 (Ohio Ct. App. 3d Dist. Paulding County 2013) (when reviewing a trial court's issuance of a CPO, we assess "whether a reasonable person would be placed in fear of imminent (in the sense of unconditional, non-contingent) physical harm" but, also stressed that such an assessment involves both subjective and objective elements).

[125]Fleckner v. Fleckner, 177 Ohio App. 3d 706, 714, 2008-Ohio-4000, 895 N.E.2d 896, 902 (10th Dist. Franklin County 2008), citing Young v. Young, 2006-Ohio-978, 2006 WL 515522 (Ohio Ct. App. 2d Dist. Greene County 2006), and quoting Strong v. Bauman, 1999 WL 317432, *4 (Ohio Ct. App. 2d Dist. Montgomery County 1999); see also Williamson v. Williamson, 180 Ohio App. 3d 260, 2008-Ohio-6718, 905 N.E.2d 217 (2d Dist. Greene County 2008); Williams v. Hupp, 2011-Ohio-3403, 2011 WL 2670945 (Ohio Ct. App. 7th Dist. Mahoning County 2011); E.W. v. T.W., 2017-Ohio-8504, 2017 WL 5192035 (Ohio Ct. App. 10th Dist. Franklin County 2017); Dodds on behalf of S.S. v. Stamper, 2018-Ohio-193, 2018 WL 481779 (Ohio Ct. App. 2d Dist. Champaign County 2018).

pellate court found that the trial court erred in applying only a subjective test to the question of whether the wife met her burden to prove a fear of imminent serious physical harm under R.C. 3113.31(A)(1)(b).[126]

The Court also acknowledged a standard of reasonableness of the fear of a threat and that the reasonableness of the fear should be determined with reference to the history between the parties.[127] It then pointed out that in order to determine whether to grant a civil protection order, a court must inquire whether the respondent's threat of force actually caused the petitioner to fear imminent serious physical harm (a subjective test) and whether the petitioner's fear is reasonable under the circumstances, that is whether the respondent's threat would cause a reasonable person to fear imminent (unconditional, non-contingent) serious physical harm (an objective test).[128] Finally, there must be a nexus between the fear of harm and the communication directed to a petitioner.

In *Martauz v. Martauz*,[129] appellee sought a civil protection order because appellant called her 20 times, sent her 11 text messages, returned to the residence and repeatedly knocked on her door, pounded on the window, rang the door bell and called her on the telephone. Appellee contacted the police because appellant's obsessive behavior frightened her and she feared what might happen next.

Appellant appealed the issuance of the civil protection order, contending that his behavior did not constitute a threat that would place a reasonable person in fear of imminent physical harm. Despite the fact that appellant's conduct did not involve a verbal threat,[130] the appellate court determined that appellee's fear was reasonable. His behavior, including his refusal to leave the residence "when it would have been obvious to a rational person that Appellee had no intention of answering the door, combined with 15 minutes of relentless knocking, ringing, pounding and calling support the trial court's conclusion that Appellee's fear is reasonable. That conclusion is further supported by the fact that Appellant continued to call Appellee after the

---

[126]Fleckner v. Fleckner, 177 Ohio App. 3d 706, 2008-Ohio-4000, 895 N.E.2d 896 (10th Dist. Franklin County 2008) (at syllabus).

[127]See also Byron v. Byron, 2012-Ohio-1632, 2012 WL 1264486 (Ohio Ct. App. 1st Dist. Hamilton County 2012); Wohleber v. Wohleber, 2011-Ohio-6696, 2011 WL 6880736 (Ohio Ct. App. 9th Dist. Lorain County 2011); Gatt v. Gatt, 2002-Ohio-1749, 2002 WL 570389 (Ohio Ct. App. 9th Dist. Medina County 2002); Watts v. Watts, 2014-Ohio-1901, 2014 WL 1836326 (Ohio Ct. App. 5th Dist. Fairfield County 2014); Hyde v. Smith, 2015-Ohio-1701, 2015 WL 1976454 (Ohio Ct. App. 12th Dist. Butler County 2015).

[128]See also Jackson v. Jackson, 2011-Ohio-5529, 2011 WL 5135251 (Ohio Ct. App. 6th Dist. Lucas County 2011); Fleckner v. Fleckner, 177 Ohio App. 3d 706, 715, 2008-Ohio-4000, 895 N.E.2d 896, 902-03 (10th Dist. Franklin County 2008).

[129]Martauz v. Martauz, 2009-Ohio-2642, 2009 WL 1581185 (Ohio Ct. App. 7th Dist. Mahoning County 2009). See also Serdy v. Serdy, 2013-Ohio-5532, 2013 WL 6670830 (Ohio Ct. App. 7th Dist. Noble County 2013) (where threat is not explicit, the critical inquiry is whether a reasonable person would fear imminent serious physical harm).

[130]A.M. v. D.L., 2017-Ohio-5621, ¶ 10, 2017 WL 2870214 (Ohio Ct. App. 9th Dist. Medina County 2017) (citing *Williams v. Hupp*, and noting that threats do not have to be verbalized but threat can be apparent from conduct).

police had instructed him to stop."[131] The court also noted that Appellant was still on probation for a previous disorderly conduct conviction against Appellee.

Q & A: How does a petitioner prove that she/he had a reasonable basis to fear the respondent?[132]

The case law in this area has evolved. It is now accepted practice for courts to consider the history of abuse between the parties when evaluating fear and the reasonableness of that fear for purposes of determining whether a CPO should be granted.[133]

For example, in *McGuire v. Sprinkle*,[134] recent actions on the part of the petitioner's ex-wife giving rise to the CPO included a threat to kill the petitioner and kidnap the parties' daughter. The parties in this case had a volatile relationship. Appellee testified that, in the past, appellant had threatened to kill him and that he was afraid of her because she was crazy, that she had been ordered to undergo counseling and treatment and that she had previously kidnapped their daughter and was indicted for felony interference with custody. She had also been arrested for domestic violence with a previous husband.

In all cases, the seminal question is whether the offending act is one that places the alleged victim in fear of serious physical harm. In this case, the appellate court relied on the *Eichenberger* proposition in analyzing whether appellee had a reasonable basis to fear respondent. "Threats of violence constitute domestic violence for the purpose of granting a civil domestic violence protection order if the fear resulting

[131] Martauz v. Martauz, 2009-Ohio-2642, 2009 WL 1581185, *6 (Ohio Ct. App. 7th Dist. Mahoning County 2009).

[132] See also § 11:10; Thom v. Mulvin, 2009-Ohio-3797, 2009 WL 2365996 (Ohio Ct. App. 6th Dist. Erie County 2009); Martin v. Hanood, 2009-Ohio-1501, 2009 WL 825766 (Ohio Ct. App. 7th Dist. Jefferson County 2009); State v. Mayes, 2015-Ohio-1052, 2015 WL 1288118 (Ohio Ct. App. 7th Dist. Mahoning County 2015) (in order to establish fear in light of Jenny's decision to wait until the next day to report the incident, her mother's instruction that Jenny come home immediately because of her fear for Jenny's safety indicates Jenny's mental state and supported the conclusion that she feared for her imminent safety).

[133] See Eichenberger v. Eichenberger, 82 Ohio App. 3d 809, 816, 613 N.E.2d 678 (10th Dist. Franklin County 1992). See also Watts v. Watts, 2014-Ohio-1901, 2014 WL 1836326 (Ohio Ct. App. 5th Dist. Fairfield County 2014); Gatt v. Gatt, 2002-Ohio-1749, 2002 WL 570389 (Ohio Ct. App. 9th Dist. Medina County 2002); Hyde v. Smith, 2015-Ohio-1701, 2015 WL 1976454 (Ohio Ct. App. 12th Dist. Butler County 2015); Slepsky v. Slepsky, 2016-Ohio-8429, 2016 WL 7626260 (Ohio Ct. App. 11th Dist. Lake County 2016) (where there is a past history of being physically assaulted in 2000, a current threat of "Get out of my sight * * * you don't know what I'll do" must be considered with reference to the history in order to determine whether the threat constitutes domestic violence); A.M. v. D.L., 2017-Ohio-5621, ¶ 10, 2017 WL 2870214 (Ohio Ct. App. 9th Dist. Medina County 2017); Cottrill v. Cottrill, 2017-Ohio-1422, 2017 WL 1376841 (Ohio Ct. App. 5th Dist. Fairfield County 2017). But see Zidan v. Zidan, 2015-Ohio-4021, 2015 WL 5723143, ¶ 17 (Ohio Ct. App. 11th Dist. Lake County 2015) (determining that a history of domestic violence is not a necessary element for obtaining a CPO pursuant to RC 3113.31(A)(1)(b). Such evidence is relevant to the reasonableness of a petitioner's fear of domestic violence, but the lack of such evidence is not dispositive of whether a petitioner's fears are reasonable as a matter of law).

[134] McGuire v. Sprinkle, 2007-Ohio-2705, 2007 WL 1585100 (Ohio Ct. App. 12th Dist. Warren County 2007).

from those threats is reasonable."[135] The Warren County Court of Appeals then held that, based on the facts presented and the history of the parties, the appellee had a reasonable fear of serious physical harm from appellant when she threatened to kill him.[136]

However, this appellate court also pointed out that "as the domestic violence statute is designed to prevent future violence, the court looks at the danger of future violence, not whether there have been past acts of violence between the parties."[137] When assessing danger, a court need not rely on actual prior physical harm to find that a petitioner is in danger of future domestic violence.[138] In fact, the appellate court also noted that past acts do not have to include actual physical harm.

Of note in *McGuire* is that the fact that the appellant had limited means to carry out the threat was accorded no weight by the appellate court.

Q & A: Besides a history of past acts, are there other ways to prove fear?[139]

Besides evidence of a history of abuse,[140] courts tend to consider the actions of the victim in determining fear for purposes of R.C. 3113.31(A)(1)(b).[141] Petitioner's actions following the actual threat may help determine whether that petitioner/victim believed serious physical harm was imminent. After a threat, even filing for a CPO supports that conclusion.[142] For example, responsive actions on the part of the victim such as concealing one's location, changing a

---

[135]McGuire v. Sprinkle, 2007-Ohio-2705, 2007 WL 1585100, *4 (Ohio Ct. App. 12th Dist. Warren County 2007); see also Fleckner v. Fleckner, 177 Ohio App. 3d 706, 714, 2008-Ohio-4000, 895 N.E.2d 896, 902 (10th Dist. Franklin County 2008); Jackson v. Jackson, 2011-Ohio-5529, 2011 WL 5135251 (Ohio Ct. App. 6th Dist. Lucas County 2011); Partin v. Morrison, 2015-Ohio-4740, 2015 WL 7293332 (Ohio Ct. App. 12th Dist. Brown County 2015).

[136]McGuire v. Sprinkle, 2007-Ohio-2705, 2007 WL 1585100, *5 (Ohio Ct. App. 12th Dist. Warren County 2007). See also Johnson v. Burke, 2016-Ohio-2947, 2016 WL 2757891 (Ohio Ct. App. 8th Dist. Cuyahoga County 2016).

[137]McGuire v. Sprinkle, 2007-Ohio-2705, 2007 WL 1585100, *5 (Ohio Ct. App. 12th Dist. Warren County 2007), citing Gooderham v. Patterson, 1999 WL 1034472 (Ohio Ct. App. 4th Dist. Gallia County 1999); see also § 11:10. Martindale v. Martindale, 2017-Ohio-9266, ¶ 44, 102 N.E.3d 19 (Ohio Ct. App. 4th Dist. Athens County 2017).

[138]McGuire v. Sprinkle, 2007-Ohio-2705, 2007 WL 1585100, *5 (Ohio Ct. App. 12th Dist. Warren County 2007), citing *Gooderham*; see also Felton v. Felton, 79 Ohio St. 3d 34, 1997-Ohio-302, 679 N.E.2d 672 (1997); but see Rangel v. Woodbury, 2009-Ohio-4407, 2009 WL 2679675 (Ohio Ct. App. 6th Dist. Lucas County 2009) (dismissing petition for CPO finding no domestic violence because there was no physical contact between the parties at any time, two previous charges of domestic violence were dismissed and motions were pending in juvenile court regarding children).

[139]See also Text 9:8.

[140]See, e.g., Trent v. Trent, 1999 WL 298073 (Ohio Ct. App. 12th Dist. Preble County 1999); see also Osherow v. Osherow, 2003-Ohio-3927, 2003 WL 21697408 (Ohio Ct. App. 9th Dist. Summit County 2003).

[141]See Holland v. Garner, 2010-Ohio-2963, 2010 WL 2573927 (Ohio Ct. App. 12th Dist. Butler County 2010); Sitton v. Sitton, 1999 WL 55717 (Ohio Ct. App. 2d Dist. Montgomery County 1999); Smith v. Burroughs, 2010-Ohio-4806, 2010 WL 3861068 (Ohio Ct. App. 3d Dist. Wyandot County 2010).

[142]See Wootten v. Culp, 2017-Ohio-665, ¶ 25, 85 N.E.3d 198 (Ohio Ct. App. 4th Dist. Adams County 2017).

telephone number or a job, sleeping with the light on or with something in front of the door, or moving demonstrate fear on the part of the victim to the act or statement made by the offender. Even a victim's attempt to keep her address confidential may demonstrate fear.[143] The requisite intent to place a victim in fear of imminent serious physical harm may also be inferred from an abuser's words, acts and other conduct.[144]

Q & A: Is it necessary for the person threatened to be aware of the threat?

Several courts have tangentially addressed this issue. For example, in *Ngqakayi v. Ngqakayi*,[145] a grandmother petitioned the court for a civil protection order on behalf of her 10 year old granddaughter, alleging that her son (the child's father) had threatened to kill the child should she harm the new baby and that the father excessively spanked the child. The trial court denied the issuance of the order and grandmother appealed.

The appellate court held that "[a] threat made by one family member to another against a third family member, without evidence that the one at whom the threat was directed was even aware of the threat, let alone put in fear of imminent physical harm, is insufficient to warrant the issuance of a civil protection order."[146]

Conversely, the appellate court reached a different conclusion in

[143]Holland v. Garner, 2010-Ohio-2963, 2010 WL 2573927 (Ohio Ct. App. 12th Dist. Butler County 2010); Lewis v. Gravely, 2016-Ohio-1502, 2016 WL 1404159 (Ohio Ct. App. 4th Dist. Adams County 2016) (calling the police); M.H. v. J.H., 2015-Ohio-5178, 2015 WL 8553569 (Ohio Ct. App. 9th Dist. Medina County 2015) (petitioner testified that the basis for her petition was that respondent came to her "confidential" residence in Ohio to take their daughter. She also stated that she did not feel safe knowing that J.H. could find her residence).

[144]But see M.H. v. J.H., 2015-Ohio-5178, 2015 WL 8553569 (Ohio Ct. App. 9th Dist. Medina County 2015).

[145]Ngqakayi v. Ngqakayi, 2008-Ohio-4745, 2008 WL 4278334 (Ohio Ct. App. 2d Dist. Greene County 2008). But see Wohleber v. Wohleber, 2011-Ohio-6696, 2011 WL 6880736 (Ohio Ct. App. 9th Dist. Lorain County 2011) (upholding issuance of CPO and finding that although petitioner did not present evidence she was aware of the threat, she subsequently became aware of the threat to shoot her via her attorney before the filing of the CPO and distinguishing the facts from Ngqakayi v. Ngqakayi, 2008-Ohio-4745, 2008 WL 4278334 (Ohio Ct. App. 2d Dist. Greene County 2008)); Moore v. Guyton, 2013-Ohio-143, 2013 WL 221515 (Ohio Ct. App. 3d Dist. Paulding County 2013) (upholding CPO where petitioner testified that she neither personally heard Guyton's threats against her nor knew the individuals who allegedly did hear the threats. She stated that she heard the threats from her attorney); Kuhn v. Kuhn, 2013-Ohio-5807, 2013 WL 6869801 (Ohio Ct. App. 11th Dist. Lake County 2013) (noting that there is no requirement in the law that a threat be delivered directly from a potential aggressor to a potential victim).

[146]Ngqakayi v. Ngqakayi, 2008-Ohio-4745, 2008 WL 4278334, *1 (Ohio Ct. App. 2d Dist. Greene County 2008). See also Detrick v. Preece, 2013-Ohio-2499, 2013 WL 3089090 (Ohio Ct. App. 3d Dist. Logan County 2013) (reversing grant of CPO where Detrick testified that she did not know whether Preece made the alleged statement but if made and if true, she would be afraid); B.C. v. A.S., 2014-Ohio-1326, 2014 WL 1345260 (Ohio Ct. App. 9th Dist. Medina County 2014) (Noting that victims did not have personal knowledge of statements respondent allegedly made, court held that "testimony that recent statements made by A.S. to third parties were the 'last straw' cannot, without further evidence, support a finding that B.C. and her family were in danger of an imminent threat of serious physical harm.").

Zidan v. Zidan.[147] In that case, appellee sought a civil protection order based on a recording in which appellant stated he wished to kill appellee, threatened to stab her to death and kill himself to avoid prison. He then advised his daughter not to tell appellee about the threat "because [he] won't get the chance to kill her."[148] Appellee testified that she did not have enough time to review the recording until two days after the recording was made.

The appellate court stated that "[e]ven though this specific threat on appellee's life was not made directly to her,[149] appellee testified that the parties' relationship was tumultuous and volatile. Appellee further testified they frequently fight and are in the midst of divorce proceedings. Under the circumstances, we cannot conclude appellee's fears were unreasonable."[150]

Additionally, the court also stressed that although she did not adequately listen to the threat until two days later, this did not mean she had no basis to believe that threat was imminent. In fact, despite no evidence that appellant was planning to immediately carry out the threat, a reasonable person could conclude the threat was near at hand.[151]

Therefore, the appellate court reasoned that "[t]he recording, along with appellee's testimony, established that appellant articulated an intention to kill appellee by stabbing her with a knife."[152] This, coupled with appellee's testimony that she was "shaking in her boots" with fear, was sufficient for the court to conclude that appellant, by threat of force, placed appellee in imminent fear of serious physical harm.[153]

The takeaway is that there is no requirement in the law that a threat be delivered directly from a potential aggressor to a potential victim. The fact is that in these cases the victim became aware of the threat. Of importance is that one definition of "threat" is "a communicated intent to inflict physical or other harm on any person or on property."[154]

---

[147]Zidan v. Zidan, 2015-Ohio-4021, 2015 WL 5723143 (Ohio Ct. App. 11th Dist. Lake County 2015).

[148]Zidan v. Zidan, 2015-Ohio-4021, 2015 WL 5723143, ¶ 17 (Ohio Ct. App. 11th Dist. Lake County 2015).

[149]See also Wohleber v. Wohleber, 2011-Ohio-6696, 2011 WL 6880736 (Ohio Ct. App. 9th Dist. Lorain County 2011); Moore v. Guyton, 2013-Ohio-143, 2013 WL 221515 (Ohio Ct. App. 3d Dist. Paulding County 2013); Kuhn v. Kuhn, 2013-Ohio-5807, 2013 WL 6869801 (Ohio Ct. App. 11th Dist. Lake County 2013); Dunn v. Clark, 2016-Ohio-641, 2016 WL 698090 (Ohio Ct. App. 12th Dist. Warren County 2016) (in affirming issuance of CPO, appellate court noted that the plain language of RC 2903.214 does not require that the threats be made directly to the victim).

[150]Zidan v. Zidan, 2015-Ohio-4021, 2015 WL 5723143, ¶ 17 (Ohio Ct. App. 11th Dist. Lake County 2015).

[151]Zidan v. Zidan, 2015-Ohio-4021, 2015 WL 5723143, ¶ 18 (Ohio Ct. App. 11th Dist. Lake County 2015).

[152]Zidan v. Zidan, 2015-Ohio-4021, 2015 WL 5723143, ¶ 19 (Ohio Ct. App. 11th Dist. Lake County 2015).

[153]Zidan v. Zidan, 2015-Ohio-4021, 2015 WL 5723143, ¶ 19 (Ohio Ct. App. 11th Dist. Lake County 2015).

[154]Zidan v. Zidan, 2015-Ohio-4021, 2015 WL 5723143, ¶ 15 (Ohio Ct. App. 11th Dist. Lake County 2015), citing Blocker v. Carron, 2011-Ohio-3673, 2011 WL 3198261

Q & A: Is it any less imminent where a victim confronts an abuser?

At least one Ohio court has answered this in the negative. In *State v. Osterhaus*,[155] the defendant stated that he "would like to crack [her] head fucking wide open."[156] He was charged and convicted of domestic violence under the criminal threat section of Ohio's domestic violence statute.[157] The victim told him to "go right ahead and we'll send [you] to jail now and [you] won't have to wait any longer."[158]

On appeal, defendant argued that there was insufficient evidence that Mrs. Osterhaus had believed that he would cause her imminent physical harm based upon her response to his statement and upon the fact that she waited almost 24 hours to contact the police. (There was no other witness testimony presented at trial.) The Montgomery County Court of Appeals found that Mrs. Osterhaus's testimony was credible. Moreover, the court reasoned "[t]he fact that she may have confronted Mr. Osterhaus rather than cowering in response to his statement does not preclude the conclusion that she believed he meant to cause her harm."[159] The court also noted that it was reasonable to interpret Mrs. Osterhaus's response to defendant as to show that she thought an attack was inevitable.[160]

Q & A: Does it matter when the victim reports a threatening incident?

At least one case addressed this issue and chose not to consider it a problem. In *State v. Pate*,[161] the appellant threatened to kill the victim if he was forced to pay child support. The victim testified that the appellant had previously threatened her life and that he owned a gun. Appellant argued that the victim could not be in fear of imminent harm because she waited until the following morning to report the matter to the police.[162] "He further argued that this delay indicates

---

(Ohio Ct. App. 5th Dist. Tuscarawas County 2011); quoting Black's Law Dictionary (6th Ed. 1990) 1480).

[155]State v. Osterhaus, 2000 WL 1006573 (Ohio Ct. App. 2d Dist. Montgomery County 2000).

[156]State v. Osterhaus, 2000 WL 1006573, *1 (Ohio Ct. App. 2d Dist. Montgomery County 2000).

[157]See RC 2919.25(C).

[158]State v. Osterhaus, 2000 WL 1006573, *1 (Ohio Ct. App. 2d Dist. Montgomery County 2000).

[159]State v. Osterhaus, 2000 WL 1006573, *1 (Ohio Ct. App. 2d Dist. Montgomery County 2000).

[160]State v. Osterhaus, 2000 WL 1006573, *2 (Ohio Ct. App. 2d Dist. Montgomery County 2000).

[161]State v. Pate, 2001 WL 22485 (Ohio Ct. App. 9th Dist. Medina County 2001); see also State v. Parks, 2000 WL 221968 (Ohio Ct. App. 5th Dist. Licking County 2000); State v. Osterhaus, 2000 WL 1006573 (Ohio Ct. App. 2d Dist. Montgomery County 2000) (victim waited 24 hours before reporting incident to police); Rosine v. Rosine, 2010-Ohio-613, 2010 WL 598642 (Ohio Ct. App. 7th Dist. Mahoning County 2010) (affirming issuance of CPO despite fact that petitioner didn't notify police for several hours after the incident or seek medical attention); Bullard v. Alley, 2014-Ohio-1016, 2014 WL 1339719 (Ohio Ct. App. 4th Dist. Pike County 2014).

[162]See also Cable v. Cable, 2015-Ohio-4291, 2015 WL 6109531 (Ohio Ct. App. 2d Dist. Darke County 2015) (officer testified that it is not uncommon for a victim of do-

that she fabricated the story after having time to think about the matter."[163]

Because the victim testified that she was so fearful of defendant that she locked her doors and windows, hid in the house and stayed awake all night, and because the police officer testified that her appearance was consistent with one who had been awake all night and was fearful, the court found sufficient evidence to support the conviction. It was clear that the petitioner's response to the threatening conduct demonstrated a reasonable fear and justified the issuance of a CPO.[164]

Q & A: Are past acts of domestic violence alone sufficient to warrant the issuance of a civil protection order?[165]

Not according to the 7th District Court of Appeals. In *Solomon v. Solomon*,[166] the appellate court held that past acts of domestic violence may be relied upon to establish genuine fear *in the present situation*.[167] Although the court relied on the *Eichenberger* standard to evaluate the reasonableness of that fear, it emphasized that there must be an indication that the person was fearful in the present situation giving rise to the CPO.[168] "Merely finding that there were past acts of domes-

mestic violence to wait hours, even days, before involving the police and making a report).

[163]State v. Pate, 2001 WL 22485, *2 (Ohio Ct. App. 9th Dist. Medina County 2001).

[164]See also Smith v. Burroughs, 2010-Ohio-4806, 2010 WL 3861068 (Ohio Ct. App. 3d Dist. Wyandot County 2010).

[165]See also Text 11:2; Text 11:10 and Text 12:11.

[166]Solomon v. Solomon, 157 Ohio App. 3d 807, 2004-Ohio-2486, 813 N.E.2d 918 (7th Dist. Mahoning County 2004). See also Pinkney v. Salett, 2011-Ohio-4121, 2011 WL 3654420 (Ohio Ct. App. 8th Dist. Cuyahoga County 2011).

[167]Solomon v. Solomon, 157 Ohio App. 3d 807, 813, 2004-Ohio-2486, 813 N.E.2d 918 (7th Dist. Mahoning County 2004) (emphasis provided); Gannon v. Gannon, 2008-Ohio-4484, 2008 WL 4093687 (Ohio Ct. App. 6th Dist. Wood County 2008); Weber v. Weber, 2011-Ohio-2980, 2011 WL 2436963 (Ohio Ct. App. 2d Dist. Greene County 2011) (reversing the trial court grant of the CPO and finding that an act of domestic violence must have occurred on the date set forth on the petition for the civil protection order); Bargar v. Kirby, 2011-Ohio-4904, 2011 WL 4436634 (Ohio Ct. App. 12th Dist. Butler County 2011) (past domestic violence may be considered only if coupled with threats of present or future violence and must be considered in light of any current allegations requesting a CPO); Crabtree v. Dinsmoor, 2013-Ohio-5797, 2013 WL 6869957 (Ohio Ct. App. 10th Dist. Franklin County 2013); M.H. v. J.H., 2015-Ohio-5178, 2015 WL 8553569 (Ohio Ct. App. 9th Dist. Medina County 2015) (noting that the purpose of the civil protection order is not to address past abuse); Wetterman v. B.C., 2013-Ohio-57, ¶ 11, 2013 WL 141752 (Ohio Ct. App. 9th Dist. Medina County 2013); J.M. v. M.M., 2016-Ohio-5368, 2016 WL 4272340 (Ohio Ct. App. 9th Dist. Medina County 2016); Weber v. Forinash, 2015-Ohio-3187, 2015 WL 4720532 (Ohio Ct. App. 6th Dist. Sandusky County 2015); Partin v. Morrison, 2015-Ohio-4740, 2015 WL 7293332 (Ohio Ct. App. 12th Dist. Brown County 2015); Cottrill v. Cottrill, 2017-Ohio-1422, 2017 WL 1376841 (Ohio Ct. App. 5th Dist. Fairfield County 2017); Dodds on behalf of S.S. v. Stamper, 2018-Ohio-193, 2018 WL 481779 (Ohio Ct. App. 2d Dist. Champaign County 2018).

[168]See also Williams v. Hupp, 2011-Ohio-3403, 2011 WL 2670945 (Ohio Ct. App. 7th Dist. Mahoning County 2011); Holland v. Garner, 2010-Ohio-2963, 2010 WL 2573927 (Ohio Ct. App. 12th Dist. Butler County 2010); Wetterman v. B.C., 2013-Ohio-57, 2013 WL 141752 (Ohio Ct. App. 9th Dist. Medina County 2013); McElroy v. McElroy, 2016-Ohio-5148, ¶ 38, 2016 WL 4039227 (Ohio Ct. App. 5th Dist. Guernsey

tic violence, without anything more, is not enough to warrant a present civil protective order."[169]

While past acts of domestic violence are important to aid a court in determining whether a reasonable person would be placed in fear of imminent serious physical harm, most appellate courts agree that "there must also be evidence the petitioner has a reasonable belief of serious physical harm based on new threats of domestic violence."[170]

Apparently, the *Martindale* court seemed to conflate the proof necessary to grant a civil protection order issued after a full hearing with the proof needed to renew or extend a CPO.[171] These decisions appear to consider past domestic violence but require a present threat of future violence. This requirement of continued or new threats beyond those giving rise to the initial order is necessary because "the purpose of a CPO is not to address past violence."[172]

The significance of this reasoning is that this new paradigm presupposes that not only does a petitioner have to prove that an act of domestic violence was committed and/or that the person is in danger of future violence, but that there be a recent or present threat of future harm based on new or continued threats of domestic violence.

County 2016) (past abuse is relevant as a factor in determining whether there is a reasonable fear of future harm and even with past abuse, there must be some competent, credible evidence that there is a present fear of harm); A.M. v. S.M., 2018-Ohio-247, 2018 WL 542357 (Ohio Ct. App. 9th Dist. Summit County 2018).

[169]Woolum v. Woolum, 131 Ohio App. 3d 818, 822, 723 N.E.2d 1135 (12th Dist. Preble County 1999) (affirming extension of civil protection order "on the basis of past domestic violence coupled with present threat of future violence."); Solomon v. Solomon, 157 Ohio App. 3d 807, 814, 2004-Ohio-2486, 813 N.E.2d 918 (7th Dist. Mahoning County 2004); Bruner v. Bruner, 2000-Ohio-2554, 2000 WL 1486452 (Ohio Ct. App. 7th Dist. Mahoning County 2000); see also Martin v. Hanood, 2009-Ohio-1501, 2009 WL 825766 (Ohio Ct. App. 7th Dist. Jefferson County 2009) (affirming the trial court's refusal to grant the civil protection order, noting that the grant of a CPO cannot be based solely on previous acts of domestic violence but that a threat of violence may constitute domestic violence only if the resulting fear from the threats is reasonable); Thom v. Mulvin, 2009-Ohio-3797, 2009 WL 2365996 (Ohio Ct. App. 6th Dist. Erie County 2009); Martauz v. Martauz, 2009-Ohio-2642, 2009 WL 1581185 (Ohio Ct. App. 7th Dist. Mahoning County 2009); Hicks v. Barker, 2009-Ohio-2445, 2009 WL 1456532 (Ohio Ct. App. 12th Dist. Warren County 2009); Pinkney v. Salett, 2011-Ohio-4121, 2011 WL 3654420 (Ohio Ct. App. 8th Dist. Cuyahoga County 2011); Crabtree v. Dinsmoor, 2013-Ohio-5797, 2013 WL 6869957 (Ohio Ct. App. 10th Dist. Franklin County 2013) (past domestic violence alone not sufficient as basis for a CPO where there is no credible evidence of current danger of domestic violence); A.D. v. B.D., 2017-Ohio-229, 2017 WL 277481 (Ohio Ct. App. 9th Dist. Medina County 2017); Martindale v. Martindale, 2017-Ohio-9266, ¶ 44, 102 N.E.3d 19 (Ohio Ct. App. 4th Dist. Athens County 2017) (noting the importance of the petitioner's history with respondent but stating that "[t]here must also be evidence the petitioner had a reasonable belief of serious physical harm based on new threats of domestic violence." quoting Studer v. Studer, 2012-Ohio-2838, ¶ 23, 2012 WL 2371452 (Ohio Ct. App. 3d Dist. Crawford County 2012).

[170]Martindale v. Martindale, 2017-Ohio-9266, ¶ 44, 102 N.E.3d 19 (Ohio Ct. App. 4th Dist. Athens County 2017); quoting, Studer v. Studer, 2012-Ohio-2838, ¶ 23, 2012 WL 2371452 (Ohio Ct. App. 3d Dist. Crawford County 2012); see also Woolum v. Woolum, 131 Ohio App. 3d 818, 822, 723 N.E.2d 1135 (12th Dist. Preble County 1999).

[171]See R.C. 311.31(E)(3)(c).

[172]Martindale v. Martindale, 2017-Ohio-9266, ¶ 44, 102 N.E.3d 19 (Ohio Ct. App. 4th Dist. Athens County 2017) quoting Wetterman v. B.C., 2013-Ohio-57, ¶ 11, 2013 WL 141752 (Ohio Ct. App. 9th Dist. Medina County 2013).

Q & A: Must a civil protection order be based on a fear of serious physical harm on the date in the petition rather than on past acts of violence?

Some cases suggest a rather literal interpretation indicating that the act of domestic violence must have occurred on the date contained in the petition.[173]

Other cases have concluded that there must be evidence of current domestic violence but that the present act did not need to have necessarily occurred on the date contained in the petition. For example, in *McGuire v. Sprinkle*,[174] appellee obtained a civil protection order based on appellant's threats to kill him and kidnap their daughter. At the hearing, appellee testified that the threat that was the basis of the petition occurred in December 2005, although in his petition he alleged that the threat occurred in January 2006.

On appeal, appellant relied on the aforementioned cases to support his argument that for a CPO to be granted, the act of domestic violence (in this case a threat) must have occurred on the date contained in the petition. However, the appellate court held that "although the cases include language which, taken in isolation, would support this proposition, the statements must be viewed in the context of the entire decision. Instead, the cases stand for the proposition that in order to grant a civil protection order, past acts alone are not enough and there must be some evidence of current domestic violence[.]"[175]

The court also noted that Civ. R. 15 permits amending the plead-

---

[173]Bruner v. Bruner, 2000-Ohio-2554, 2000 WL 1486452 (Ohio Ct. App. 7th Dist. Mahoning County 2000); Solomon v. Solomon, 157 Ohio App. 3d 807, 2004-Ohio-2486, 813 N.E.2d 918 (7th Dist. Mahoning County 2004); Richter v. Richter, 2009-Ohio-3828, 2009 WL 2371882 (Ohio Ct. App. 12th Dist. Butler County 2009); Thom v. Mulvin, 2009-Ohio-3797, 2009 WL 2365996 (Ohio Ct. App. 6th Dist. Erie County 2009); Boals v. Miller, 2011-Ohio-1470, 2011 WL 1118464, *3 (Ohio Ct. App. 5th Dist. Ashland County 2011) (the reasonableness of a petitioner's fear of imminent serious physical harm may not be determined by incidents of prior domestic violence absent an initial, explicit indication that she was in fear of imminent serious physical harm on the date contained in the petition, quoting Bahr v. Bahr, 2003-Ohio-5024, 2003 WL 22176762, ¶ 29 (Ohio Ct. App. 5th Dist. Ashland County 2003)); Chafin v. Chafin, 2010-Ohio-3939, 2010 WL 3294288 (Ohio Ct. App. 9th Dist. Lorain County 2010); B.C. v. A.S., 2014-Ohio-1326, 2014 WL 1345260, ¶ 21 (Ohio Ct. App. 9th Dist. Medina County 2014); R.T. v. J.T., 2015-Ohio-4418, 2015 WL 6449294 (Ohio Ct. App. 9th Dist. Medina County 2015); Cottrill v. Cottrill, 2017-Ohio-1422, 2017 WL 1376841 (Ohio Ct. App. 5th Dist. Fairfield County 2017); J.M. v. M.M., 2016-Ohio-5368, 2016 WL 4272340 (Ohio Ct. App. 9th Dist. Medina County 2016); Dodds on behalf of S.S. v. Stamper, 2018-Ohio-193, 2018 WL 481779 (Ohio Ct. App. 2d Dist. Champaign County 2018).

[174]McGuire v. Sprinkle, 2007-Ohio-2705, 2007 WL 1585100 (Ohio Ct. App. 12th Dist. Warren County 2007); Clinage v. Smith, 2017-Ohio-1393, 2017 WL 1373612 (Ohio Ct. App. 6th Dist. Lucas County 2017) (fear was genuine and CPO was warranted even though the incident took place a few days before the filing, relying on Thom v. Mulvin, 2009-Ohio-3797, 2009 WL 2365996 (Ohio Ct. App. 6th Dist. Erie County 2009)).

[175]McGuire v. Sprinkle, 2007-Ohio-2705, 2007 WL 1585100, *3 (Ohio Ct. App. 12th Dist. Warren County 2007); see also Tabor v. Palacio, 2008-Ohio-349, 2008 WL 282127 (Ohio Ct. App. 12th Dist. Butler County 2008); see also Bargar v. Kirby, 2011-Ohio-4904, 2011 WL 4436634 (Ohio Ct. App. 12th Dist. Butler County 2011) (past domestic violence may be considered only if coupled with threats of present or future violence and must be considered in light of any current allegations requesting a CPO); Weber v. Forinash, 2015-Ohio-3187, 2015 WL 4720532 (Ohio Ct. App. 6th

ings to conform to the evidence presented at trial and that a trial court may sua sponte amend pleadings.[176] In this case, the trial court amended the petition to conform to the evidence as to the date in question. The Warren County Court of Appeals found no error in the lower court's determination that the date of the threat was December 2005, rather than January 2006 and that the appellant was not prejudiced by the change of date.

Q & A: Must past acts of physical abuse be accompanied by a recent threat or reason to place a petitioner in reasonable fear of imminent harm?

Not according to the Seventh District Court of Appeals. In *Zawrotuk v. Zawrotuk*,[177] the Mahoning County Court of Appeals addressed this issue by focusing on the fact that where the mainstay of the claimed domestic violence involved "an attempt to cause or recklessly causing physical harm," the petitioner need not strictly testify that the respondent placed her in fear of imminent physical harm.[178] "A victim's expressions of fear are valuable, but a court can find a danger of domestic violence from a prior attempt to cause or an actual reckless (or intentional) causing of physical harm and the totality of circumstances of a particular case."[179]

In the instant case, petitioner testified that she was fearful of appellant during the June 4 incident and afraid that he would return that night, that he was a current threat without a protection order due to the pending criminal case and divorce action and that a visitation schedule was in place. Taken together, these considerations all supported a finding of danger. In that future encounters were expected and because this was not an isolated incident, her testimony demonstrated a need for a civil protection order. "A rational fact-finder could also believe her testimony regarding the prior incidents and her fear of appellant as a result of this history and the current incident."[180]

Conversely, other appellate districts have focused on the necessity

---

Dist. Sandusky County 2015) (regarding the timing of acts of domestic violence, a finding of domestic violence may not be based solely on remote events but must be premised on conduct current enough that the fear engendered is current. Acts which instill fear of imminent harm need not happen on the same day as the petition. Rather, the acts must give rise to a fear that is "present on the day alleged, irrespective of when the acts precipitating the fear occurred" ¶ 18; quoting Gannon at ¶ 38.)

[176]See also Lane v. Brewster, 2012-Ohio-1290, 2012 WL 1029503 (Ohio Ct. App. 12th Dist. Clermont County 2012); McGuire v. Sprinkle, 2007-Ohio-2705, 2007 WL 1585100 (Ohio Ct. App. 12th Dist. Warren County 2007); Gannon v. Gannon, 2008-Ohio-4484, 2008 WL 4093687 (Ohio Ct. App. 6th Dist. Wood County 2008); Calicoat v. Calicoat, 2009-Ohio-5869, 2009 WL 3683665 (Ohio Ct. App. 2d Dist. Miami County 2009). See also text § 11:2.

[177]Zawrotuk v. Zawrotuk, 2014-Ohio-5225, 2014 WL 6641772 (Ohio Ct. App. 7th Dist. Mahoning County 2014).

[178]Zawrotuk v. Zawrotuk, 2014-Ohio-5225, 2014 WL 6641772, ¶ 34 (Ohio Ct. App. 7th Dist. Mahoning County 2014).

[179]Zawrotuk v. Zawrotuk, 2014-Ohio-5225, 2014 WL 6641772, ¶ 35 (Ohio Ct. App. 7th Dist. Mahoning County 2014); Cottrill v. Cottrill, 2017-Ohio-1422, 2017 WL 1376841 (Ohio Ct. App. 5th Dist. Fairfield County 2017) (grant of CPO based on totality of circumstances); A.M. v. D.L., 2017-Ohio-5621, ¶ 9, 2017 WL 2870214 (Ohio Ct. App. 9th Dist. Medina County 2017).

[180]Zawrotuk v. Zawrotuk, 2014-Ohio-5225, 2014 WL 6641772, ¶ 40 (Ohio Ct. App. 7th Dist. Mahoning County 2014).

to show both past abuse and a present threat of future violence. For example, in *Martindale v. Martindale,*[181] appellant argued on appeal that the evidence was not sufficient to demonstrate that petitioner was fearful of imminent serious physical harm. The appellate court explained that a petitioner's history with respondent is important but also acknowledged that [t]here must also be evidence that petitioner has a reasonable belief of serious physical harm based on new threats of domestic violence.[182] The court also relied on *Woolum v. Woolum,*[183] to explain that to affirm the extension of a CPO, consideration must be given to evidence of "past domestic violence coupled with the present threat of future violence." This requirement of continued threats beyond those that gave rise to the initial protection order is necessary because "[t]he purpose of the civil protection order is not to address past abuse."[184] In affirming the issuance of the civil protection order, the appellate court determined that given appellant's violent history, appellee's testimony that she was fearful and the evidence that he caused his wife to suffer a black eye in the past, the evidence justified the need for the issuance of the full hearing CPO.

It is important to point out that this court relied on cases that considered the extension (or renewal) of a CPO rather than a CPO granted in the first instance.

A review of most of the threat cases in Ohio indicate that a past history coupled with some new threat, a danger of future threats of violence based on a past history and/or the subjective fear of the petitioner based on the past history, each taken separately, may form the basis for the issuance of a CPO. Taken together, the totality of the circumstances may also form the basis for its issuance in the current situation. So long as the *Fleckner* test is applied, parsing out the examples appears to be an exercise of a distinction without a difference.

Q & A: Does it matter if the petition for civil protection is filed well after the incident giving rise to the petition?

It depends on the time between the incident alleged and the filing of the petition. For example, in Richter v. Richter,[185] the respondent challenged the grant of the CPO based on the fact that the incident

[181]Martindale v. Martindale, 2017-Ohio-9266, ¶ 44, 102 N.E.3d 19 (Ohio Ct. App. 4th Dist. Athens County 2017); see also Dodds on behalf of S.S. v. Stamper, 2018-Ohio-193, 2018 WL 481779 (Ohio Ct. App. 2d Dist. Champaign County 2018).

[182]Martindale, 2017-Ohio-9266, ¶ 44, 2017 WL 6616980, quoting, Studer v. Studer, 2012-Ohio-2838, ¶ 23, 2012 WL 2371452 (Ohio Ct. App. 3d Dist. Crawford County 2012).

[183]Woolum v. Woolum, 131 Ohio App. 3d 818, 823, 723 N.E.2d 1135, 1137 (12th Dist. Preble County 1999).

[184]Martindale v. Martindale, 2017-Ohio-9266, ¶ 44, 102 N.E.3d 19 (Ohio Ct. App. 4th Dist. Athens County 2017); quoting Wetterman v. B.C., 2013-Ohio-57, ¶ 11, 2013 WL 141752 (Ohio Ct. App. 9th Dist. Medina County 2013).

[185]Murral v. Thomson, 2004-Ohio-432, 2004 WL 193876 (Ohio Ct. App. 4th Dist. Hocking County 2004); Richter v. Richter, 2009-Ohio-3828, 2009 WL 2371882 (Ohio Ct. App. 12th Dist. Butler County 2009); see also Traut v. Leiby, 2010-Ohio-2563, 2010 WL 2298566 (Ohio Ct. App. 5th Dist. Richland County 2010); Serdy v. Serdy, 2013-Ohio-5532, 2013 WL 6670830 (Ohio Ct. App. 7th Dist. Noble County 2013) (that she sought the CPO six weeks after the incident doesn't preclude one from seeking a CPO); Zawrotuk v. Zawrotuk, 2014-Ohio-5225, 2014 WL 6641772 (Ohio Ct. App. 7th

where he woke her up and grabbed her ankle occurred three weeks before the filing of the petition.

In this case, the appellate court considered both the unwanted physical contact as well as the verbal attacks. In affirming the trial court, the appellate court also relied on evidence elicited by the petitioner indicating that after the incident, she immediately left the house and moved into a confidential residence. Only when he found her did she file the CPO. She filed the petition because "I don't feel safe with him knowing where I'm gonna be living if he has access to come near my home."[186]

Q & A: In granting a CPO based on a threat allegation, does it matter at what point in time a past incident of abuse occurred?

It depends. Courts are now beginning to assess context when it comes to threats of domestic violence. Obviously, a past history of domestic violence often provides context for a recent threat of harm. How remote in time the past history of abuse must be in relation to a recent threat and filing of a CPO is a determination made by a court and the time frame is clearly within a particular court's discretion. This could even mean that past acts of domestic violence in 2011 are not necessarily too remote in time to a 2016 petition for a CPO.[187]

What is clear is that a petitioner may rely on past acts of domestic violence to establish a genuine fear of violence in the present situation.[188] There must be evidence presented that the person was fearful in that present situation. Merely finding that there were past acts of domestic violence, without anything more, is not enough to warrant a present civil protection order.[189] Another way is saying this is that "[a] finding of statutory domestic violence may not be based solely on remote events, but must be premised on conduct current enough that the fear engendered is current."[190] To prevail, testimony

---

Dist. Mahoning County 2014) (wife waited one month to file her CPO after calling the police); Wootten v. Culp, 2017-Ohio-665, 85 N.E.3d 198 (Ohio Ct. App. 4th Dist. Adams County 2017) (RC 3113.31 provides no specific time limit for bringing allegations to the court in petitioning for a CPO and threats made a month before filing petition were not so remote in time to preclude issuance of CPO. at ¶ 27); but see Wagner v. Holland, 2016-Ohio-5028, 2016 WL 3920162 (Ohio Ct. App. 5th Dist. Fairfield County 2016) (pattern of conduct not proximate in time to the filing of petition and thus, there was no "immediate danger."); E.W. v. T.W., 2017-Ohio-8504, ¶ 18, 2017 WL 5192035 (Ohio Ct. App. 10th Dist. Franklin County 2017) (noting that the key determination is whether petitioner's CPO is supported by the evidence considering the several month time frame between the prior threats of force and when she filed the CPO petition and concluding that there were no findings for the court to make that determination).

[186] At *3.

[187] Cottrill v. Cottrill, 2017-Ohio-1422, 2017 WL 1376841 (Ohio Ct. App. 5th Dist. Fairfield County 2017).

[188] Solomon v. Solomon, 157 Ohio App. 3d 807, 813, 2004-Ohio-2486, 813 N.E.2d 918 (7th Dist. Mahoning County 2004); Pinkney v. Salett, 2011-Ohio-4121, 2011 WL 3654420 (Ohio Ct. App. 8th Dist. Cuyahoga County 2011).

[189] Solomon v. Solomon, 157 Ohio App. 3d 807, 814, 2004-Ohio-2486, 813 N.E.2d 918 (7th Dist. Mahoning County 2004).

[190] K.B. v. B.B., 2017-Ohio-71, ¶ 16, 80 N.E.3d 1173 (Ohio Ct. App. 9th Dist. Summit County 2017).

must be presented that there was a recent threat or a belief that the offending party would commit a future act of domestic violence.[191]

For example in *Zawrotuk v. Zawrotuk*,[192] appellant argued, on appeal, that appellee did not fear imminent harm because the most recent incident was more than a month before the filing of the petition. He relied on both *Bargar* and *Eichenberger* to justify his reasoning. He reasoned that because the most recent incident was a month before the filing of the petition, no threats were alleged during the month, no medical treatment was requested, past incidents were over four and five years prior, he was compliant with the ex parte order and had moved to another state were all reasons why a protection order was not needed.

The appellate court first stressed that a move to another state after the physical incident does not eliminate the need for protection. In fact, that the parties were married with children might increase the need for a protection order. Additionally, the court also acknowledged the statistics that indicate a greater risk of harm when a woman leaves the relationship.[193]

The court then differentiated the instant case from those cited by appellant, to wit: *Bargar* and *Eichenberger* which stand for the proposition that there must be some current abuse coupled with past acts of violence. Noting that a trial court could reasonably infer reasonable fear of one party even if the other party thinks it is not since that party never hurt the other party in the past, the court pointed out that that both of the cited cases proceeded under RC 3113.31(A)(1)(b), while the instant case proceeded under RC 3113.31(A)(1)(a). "Thus, a petitioner need not strictly testify that the respondent placed her in fear of imminent harm when he actually harmed her.[194] Rather, a court can find that there exists a danger of domestic violence based on the testimony presented.[195] "A victim's expressions of fear are valuable, but a court can find a danger of domestic violence from a prior attempt to cause or an actual reckless (or intentional) causing of physical harm and the totality of circumstances of a particular case."[196]

Appellee's testimony that she was fearful of appellant during the

[191]K.B. v. B.B., 2017-Ohio-71, ¶ 16, 80 N.E.3d 1173 (Ohio Ct. App. 9th Dist. Summit County 2017).

[192]Zawrotuk v. Zawrotuk, 2014-Ohio-5225, 2014 WL 6641772 (Ohio Ct. App. 7th Dist. Mahoning County 2014).

[193]Zawrotuk v. Zawrotuk, 2014-Ohio-5225, 2014 WL 6641772 (Ohio Ct. App. 7th Dist. Mahoning County 2014), citing Felton v. Felton, 79 Ohio St. 3d 34, 40, 1997-Ohio-302, 679 N.E.2d 672 (1997).

[194]Zawrotuk v. Zawrotuk, 2014-Ohio-5225, ¶ 34, 2014 WL 6641772 (Ohio Ct. App. 7th Dist. Mahoning County 2014).

[195]See Felton v. Felton, 79 Ohio St. 3d 34, ¶ 34, 1997-Ohio-302, 679 N.E.2d 672 (1997) (where testimony established physical harm, the Court merely mentioned a finding of a danger of domestic violence); J.M. v. M.M., 2016-Ohio-5368, 2016 WL 4272340 (Ohio Ct. App. 9th Dist. Medina County 2016); K.B. v. B.B., 2017-Ohio-71, 80 N.E.3d 1173 (Ohio Ct. App. 9th Dist. Summit County 2017); A.D. v. B.D., 2017-Ohio-229, 2017 WL 277481 (Ohio Ct. App. 9th Dist. Medina County 2017); Wootten v. Culp, 2017-Ohio-665, 85 N.E.3d 198 (Ohio Ct. App. 4th Dist. Adams County 2017).

[196]Zawrotuk v. Zawrotuk, 2014-Ohio-5225, ¶ 35, 2014 WL 6641772 (Ohio Ct. App. 7th Dist. Mahoning County 2014); J.R. v. E.H., 2017-Ohio-516, 2017 WL 587314 (Ohio Ct. App. 10th Dist. Franklin County 2017); Cottrill v. Cottrill, 2017-Ohio-1422, 2017

June 4 incident and afraid that he would return that night, that he was a current threat without a protection order; that a criminal case and divorce action were pending and that a visitation schedule was in place all supported a finding of danger. In that future encounters were expected and that this was not an isolated incident also were considerations supporting her need for protection.[197]

Of significance is that the timing of the threat was less important to the appellate court than the reality of the threat based on the evidence presented.[198] The court was less concerned about the timing of the incident of domestic violence relative to the filing of the CPO and agreed with wife that even after the pending criminal case, she might still need protection. "As appellee points out, the police filed charges against the husband after taking the wife's report the night of the incident and the criminal case was still pending at the time the wife filed her petition. A victim could reasonably feel a modicum of safety just after the charges are filed. Still, a criminal case has a much higher burden of proof, beyond a reasonable doubt, and the case was coming up for hearing on July 11."[199] The court also rejected the appellant's argument that the criminal case was a reason not to have granted the petition, reasoning that a civil protection order is in addition to, but not in lieu of other available remedies such as a criminal case or bond conditions.[200] "Where domestic violence taking the form of actual physical harm is found to have occurred in 2008, 2009 *and four weeks prior* to the petition, a reasonable trier of fact could find that the danger of domestic violence was not wholly eliminated by the passage of four weeks since the last incident and that the pending criminal case helped explain the delay in filing as well."[201]

Finally, the court also rejected appellant's compliance with the CPO argument as a reason not to grant the full hearing order. The court reasoned that appellant created the delay by continuing the full hearing; thus, his continuances cannot create a situation where a court can no longer issue a protection just because he complied with the ex parte order during the time since the precipitating incident.[202] "The need for protection is not erased due to compliance with the ex parte

WL 1376841 (Ohio Ct. App. 5th Dist. Fairfield County 2017).

[197]Zawrotuk v. Zawrotuk, 2014-Ohio-5225, ¶ 36, 2014 WL 6641772 (Ohio Ct. App. 7th Dist. Mahoning County 2014).

[198]See Weber v. Forinash, 2015-Ohio-3187, 2015 WL 4720532 (Ohio Ct. App. 6th Dist. Sandusky County 2015) (timing of the acts of domestic violence/threat not as important as evidence of current fear; thus, imminent danger of domestic violence existed at the time of filing the petition even though the parties had not lived together for over two months when the case was filed).

[199]Zawrotuk v. Zawrotuk, 2014-Ohio-5225, ¶ 42, 2014 WL 6641772 (Ohio Ct. App. 7th Dist. Mahoning County 2014).

[200]Zawrotuk v. Zawrotuk, 2014-Ohio-5225, ¶ 43, 2014 WL 6641772 (Ohio Ct. App. 7th Dist. Mahoning County 2014); RC 3113.31(G).

[201]Zawrotuk v. Zawrotuk, 2014-Ohio-5225, ¶ 43, 2014 WL 6641772 (Ohio Ct. App. 7th Dist. Mahoning County 2014).

[202]Zawrotuk v. Zawrotuk, 2014-Ohio-5225, ¶ 44, 2014 WL 6641772 (Ohio Ct. App. 7th Dist. Mahoning County 2014); Lutson v. Anderkin, 2013 WL 2150897 (Ohio C.P. 2013) (respondent made same argument that he had been in compliance with the CPO for the past five years; thus, the CPO should not be extended for another five years).

order; a lack of threatening contact may be the direct result of that order (and the criminal bond conditions)."[203]

Conversely, in *Newhouse v. Williams*,[204] the appellee was granted a CPO based on an alleged threat made stating, in pertinent part, "I'm not working nothing out. I'm not changing anything, we're going back to court over visitation." and "Well, things could get really, really bad for everybody involved. Things can get really really bad."[205] Appellee testified that she took this to be a physical threat based upon past incidents of domestic violence that occurred over nine years earlier. The trial court granted the CPO based on the threat and past events between the parties prior to their divorce.

On appeal, appellant argued that the evidence was insufficient to grant the CPO in the first instance. The Wyandot Court of Appeals first noted that, in order to grant a CPO in this case, the trial court was required to find that Williams threatened Newhouse with imminent serious physical harm and that Newhouse had a reasonable fear because of this threat. In analyzing the nature of the threat, the Court determined that Newhouse was not specific as to the nature of the threat. The Court then said that Newhouse admitted that the statement was made while discussing court action and a modification of custody. She also said she was fearful because she didn't know where he was or what he was doing.

However, the Court found that this fear was speculation and not reasonable. Even though Williams's wife heard Newhouse say that Williams had threatened Newhouse, the restatement of Newhouse's testimony is not specific nor does it provide the basis for a CPO. The Court of Appeals then held that "[t]his is not a threat of imminent serious physical harm, but rather a threat of the use of a legal process designed specifically to handle this type of dispute."[206]

Additionally, the Third District Court of Appeals addressed the issue of past conduct and its use in demonstrating reasonable fear. The Court noted that "incidents too remote in time with no intervening events to set up a pattern of behavior may not be the basis of a CPO."[207] The court also stated that besides past violence, there must be some

[203]Zawrotuk v. Zawrotuk, 2014-Ohio-5225, ¶ 44, 2014 WL 6641772 (Ohio Ct. App. 7th Dist. Mahoning County 2014); J.R. v. E.H., 2017-Ohio-516, 2017 WL 587314 (Ohio Ct. App. 10th Dist. Franklin County 2017); citing Duncan v. Duncan, 2010-Ohio-5334, 2010 WL 4345722 (Ohio Ct. App. 5th Dist. Muskingum County 2010).

[204]Newhouse v. Williams, 167 Ohio App. 3d 215, 2006-Ohio-3075, 854 N.E.2d 565 (3d Dist. Wyandot County 2006); see also Tabor v. Palacio, 2008-Ohio-349, 2008 WL 282127 (Ohio Ct. App. 12th Dist. Butler County 2008).

[205]Newhouse v. Williams, 167 Ohio App. 3d 215, 2006-Ohio-3075, 854 N.E.2d 565 (3d Dist. Wyandot County 2006).

[206]Newhouse v. Williams, 167 Ohio App. 3d 215, 222, 2006-Ohio-3075, 854 N.E.2d 565, 570 (3d Dist. Wyandot County 2006); see also Fleckner v. Fleckner, 177 Ohio App. 3d 706, 2008-Ohio-4000, 895 N.E.2d 896 (10th Dist. Franklin County 2008); Richter v. Richter, 2009-Ohio-3828, 2009 WL 2371882 (Ohio Ct. App. 12th Dist. Butler County 2009); M.J. v. L.P., 2016-Ohio-7080, 2016 WL 5723752 (Ohio Ct. App. 9th Dist. Medina County 2016) (threatening to take legal action is not domestic violence under RC 3113.31(A)(1)(b)).

[207]Newhouse v. Williams, 167 Ohio App. 3d 215, 222, 2006-Ohio-3075, 854 N.E.2d 565, 570 (3d Dist. Wyandot County 2006), citing Young v. Young, 2006-Ohio-978, 2006 WL 515522 (Ohio Ct. App. 2d Dist. Greene County 2006).

evidence of current abuse.[208] Finally, there must be some evidence of reasonable fear of imminent serious physical harm.[209]

Newhouse's testimony was that the alleged violence took place between 1993 and 1996, before the parties divorced. The appellate court reasoned that since no police report was made and no corroboration presented of the past violence, the fact that Newhouse supervised the visitation between father and daughter in her home and that no allegations of violence occurred in the intervening years, the evidence does not support the trial court's findings that Newhouse's current fear of imminent physical harm was reasonable due to Williams' alleged prior conduct.

Similarly, in *E.W. v. T. W.*,[210] respondent argued on appeal that the trial court erred in granting the protection order by determining that a threat received months earlier formed the basis for its issuance, there was no evidence presented of a present threat and petitioner was not in fear of imminent physical harm.[211]

The appellate court began its analysis by explaining that a petitioner must demonstrate a danger of domestic violence by showing a threat of force placing her in fear of imminent serious physical harm.[212] The second requirement involves both subjective and objective considerations meaning whether the petitioner was actually placed in fear of imminent serious physical harm and whether such

[208]See Gannon v. Gannon, 2008-Ohio-4484, 2008 WL 4093687, *4 (Ohio Ct. App. 6th Dist. Wood County 2008) (stressing that "a finding of statutory domestic violence may not be based solely on remote events, but must be premised on conduct current enough that the fear engendered is current"), citing Solomon v. Solomon, 157 Ohio App. 3d 807, 2004-Ohio-2486, 813 N.E.2d 918 (7th Dist. Mahoning County 2004); Bahr v. Bahr, 2003-Ohio-5024, 2003 WL 22176762 (Ohio Ct. App. 5th Dist. Ashland County 2003); Holland v. Garner, 2010-Ohio-2963, 2010 WL 2573927 (Ohio Ct. App. 12th Dist. Butler County 2010); Bargar v. Kirby, 2011-Ohio-4904, 2011 WL 4436634 (Ohio Ct. App. 12th Dist. Butler County 2011) (past domestic violence may be considered only if coupled with threats of present or future violence and must be considered in light of any current allegations requesting a CPO); Weber v. Forinash, 2015-Ohio-3187, 2015 WL 4720532 (Ohio Ct. App. 6th Dist. Sandusky County 2015).

[209]See also Martin v. Hanood, 2009-Ohio-1501, 2009 WL 825766 (Ohio Ct. App. 7th Dist. Jefferson County 2009); Weber v. Forinash, 2015-Ohio-3187, 2015 WL 4720532 (Ohio Ct. App. 6th Dist. Sandusky County 2015) (noting that evidence of pinning appellee against the wall while punching the wall next to her head and forcing her to have sex with him was sufficient to give rise to a fear of imminent serious physical harm on the day she filed her petition); A.M. v. D.L., 2017-Ohio-5621, ¶ 6, 2017 WL 2870214 (Ohio Ct. App. 9th Dist. Medina County 2017) (considering totality of the circumstances and petitioner's subjective state of mind and finding that past incidents and a "pattern of conduct" were not "too remote in time" where the recent threat was respondent coming to her apartment on a day that he was not scheduled to have the child causing her to move in with her grandmother because of the stress it caused her; "while Respondent's degrading comments to petitioner do not rise to the requisite level, the tumultuous history between the parties, together with the recent alleged sexual assault [four months before the filing of her petition], were sufficient to constitute reasonable fear of serious physical harm").

[210]E.W. v. T.W., 2017-Ohio-8504, 2017 WL 5192035 (Ohio Ct. App. 10th Dist. Franklin County 2017).

[211]E.W. v. T.W., 2017-Ohio-8504, ¶ 14, 2017 WL 5192035 (Ohio Ct. App. 10th Dist. Franklin County 2017).

[212]R.C. 3113.31(A)(1)(b).

fear was reasonable.[213] The court noted that a past history of domestic violence bears on the reasonableness of petitioner's fear of imminent physical harm.[214]

In this case, the message "I'll f**king kill you," respondent's communication to her that he'd break her face and his appearance at her condo in 2016 caused her to file a CPO four months later. "Petitioner testified that the impetus for filing the CPO was not only respondent's threats to take the child out of the state but because of their present custody issues and her belief and fear of him showing up at her condo in light of his prior threats to physically harm her."[215]

In that there was a gap of several months between the prior threats of force and the date of filing the petition, the question was whether petitioner, by a threat of force, was placed in fear of imminent serious physical harm under these circumstances.[216]

Based on the record, the appellate court determined that the trial court failed to assess the nature of the threat or address whether the threat was objectively reasonable under the circumstances. "As indicated above, the trial court makes no findings in this respect nor makes reference to the correct standard. Therefore, on the facts of this case, we find the trial court applied the incorrect legal standard under R.C. 3113.31(A)(1)(b) in issuing the CPO."[217] Without adequate findings of fact regarding whether petitioner was placed in fear of imminent serious physical harm by threat of force which occurred several months before the filing, the case was remanded back to the trial court for a new full hearing; thus, sustaining respondent's assignment of error.

While the concurring judge agreed with the conclusion, he advised the trial court, on remand, to first reinstate the ex parte CPO.

In her dissent, Judge Brunner concurred with the judgment of the appellate court but focused her dissent on which assignment of error was sustained. According to Brunner, the first assignment of error should have been sustained because the trial court failed to conduct a full hearing. The dissent also explained that at the new hearing the trial court is required to use both the subjective and objective tests in determining imminence. She then determined that "[f]ear from the threat may be reasonable, but fear that respondent will remove the

[213]E.W. v. T.W., 2017-Ohio-8504, ¶ 16, 2017 WL 5192035 (Ohio Ct. App. 10th Dist. Franklin County 2017).

[214]E.W. v. T.W., 2017-Ohio-8504, ¶ 16, 2017 WL 5192035 (Ohio Ct. App. 10th Dist. Franklin County 2017), citing Strassell v. Chapman, 2010-Ohio-4376, ¶ 20, 2010 WL 3610591 (Ohio Ct. App. 10th Dist. Franklin County 2010); Crabtree v. Dinsmoor, 2013-Ohio-5797, ¶ 13-14, 2013 WL 6869957 (Ohio Ct. App. 10th Dist. Franklin County 2013).

[215]E.W. v. T.W., 2017-Ohio-8504, ¶ 17, 2017 WL 5192035 (Ohio Ct. App. 10th Dist. Franklin County 2017).

[216]E.W. v. T.W., 2017-Ohio-8504, ¶ 18, 2017 WL 5192035 (Ohio Ct. App. 10th Dist. Franklin County 2017).

[217]E.W. v. T.W., 2017-Ohio-8504, ¶ 18, 2017 WL 5192035 (Ohio Ct. App. 10th Dist. Franklin County 2017).

child from the state may not necessarily be a threat of imminent danger of domestic violence."[218]

In her analysis, Judge Brunner noted that "[t]he requirement of imminent fear addresses the reality of the threat rather than the timing of the threat." Strassell v. Chapman, 2010-Ohio-4376, ¶ 27, 2010 WL 3610591 (Ohio Ct. App. 10th Dist. Franklin County 2010). "The 'staleness' of an incident is not dispositive of whether the incident should be considered because 'the language of RC 311.31(A) does not require evidence of "new" domestic violence before a civil protection order may be issued or continued.'"[219] Apparently, the dissent seemed to give less credence to the issue of timing, but focused on the requirement of using both the objective and subjective tests in its analysis.

Q & A: How important is the specificity of the recent threat?

According to the Ninth District Court of Appeals, the answer is "quite important." In *B.C. v. A.S.*,[220] petitioner sought a CPO against her former husband on behalf of her entire family which included her current husband and their child and the children she had with her former husband. Appellant appealed the grant of the CPO claiming the trial court's grant was against the manifest weight of the evidence.

The appellate court examined the nature of the threats which were "serious threats made by appellant while at the visitation center visiting with his children." Some of the threats were allegedly made to the staff and his children that he intended to beat up petitioner's current husband. Corroboration of these threats were in the notes from the staff at the visitation center indicating that appellant made "inappropriate comments" and was becoming more "belligerent." Other threats were alleged to have been made several years earlier and included a threat not to return the children after visitation and "mumbling" something to the current husband after the court hearing involving custody/visitation. Corroboration of these threats included a police call for service and a police escort from court.

In reversing and remanding the matter to the trial court, the appellate court indicated that 1) neither petitioner nor her current husband heard appellant making any threats of physical violence against the children; 2) petitioner could not provide any details as to the exact nature of the threats or when they specifically occurred; and 3) neither petitioner nor her current husband had personal knowledge of the statements made by appellant at the center.

The Medina appellate court found that "[t]estimony that recent statements made by A.S. to third parties or within earshot of third parties cannot, without further evidence, support a finding that B.C. and her family were in danger of an imminent threat of serious phys-

---

[218] E.W. v. T.W., 2017-Ohio-8504, ¶ 44, 2017 WL 5192035 (Ohio Ct. App. 10th Dist. Franklin County 2017).

[219] E.W. v. T.W., 2017-Ohio-8504, ¶ 43, 2017 WL 5192035 (Ohio Ct. App. 10th Dist. Franklin County 2017); citing Maccabee v. Maccabee, 10th Dist., No. 98AP-1213 (June 29, 1999), quoting Trent v. Trent, 12th Dist. No. CA 98-09-014 (May 10, 1999).

[220] B.C. v. A.S., 2014-Ohio-1326, 2014 WL 1345260 (Ohio Ct. App. 9th Dist. Medina County 2014); Partin v. Morrison, 2015-Ohio-4740, 2015 WL 7293332 (Ohio Ct. App. 12th Dist. Brown County 2015).

ical harm."[221] Noting that the trial court did not suggest an alleged threat of physical harm, the court explained that, even if the fear is reasonable and that threats of imminent physical harm were made, "the law requires the proffer of evidence sufficient upon which to base that fear at the time the petition was filed."[222] In that "[n]one of the witnesses who testified in support of the petition could provide any detail or time frame for the alleged threats which would allow the court to find that the statements were capable of producing a reasonable fear of imminent serious physical harm"[223] and because "[n]one of the witnesses could state with any particularity and on personal knowledge any recent incidents wherein A.S. threatened imminent physical harm to B.C., her husband, or her family,"[224] the appellate court sustained the assignment of error. It held that no evidence presented satisfied the burden placed on petitioner to show that appellant demonstrated a threat of force in order to produce a fear of imminent serious physical harm so as to constitute domestic violence under R.C. 3113.31(A)(1)(b).[225]

Of significance is the implication that in order to prevail on a claim where a threat is alleged under R.C. 311.31.31(A)(1)(b), it is crucial that the alleged threat be specific to time and place.[226]

Q & A: Have conditional threats been considered domestic violence for purposes of RC 3113.31(A)(1)(b)?

A "conditional threat" is one where a "prerequisite must occur before the actor intends or is empowered to carry out the threat."[227] Where the prerequisite to such a threat is one which cannot be fulfilled, a court cannot find that a fear of imminent serious physical harm resulting from such an impossibly conditioned threat is reasonable.[228]

In considering domestic violence threat cases, at least in the criminal context, Ohio's courts are able to apply the legal reasoning set

[221]B.C. v. A.S., 2014-Ohio-1326, 2014 WL 1345260, ¶ 23 (Ohio Ct. App. 9th Dist. Medina County 2014).

[222]B.C. v. A.S., 2014-Ohio-1326, 2014 WL 1345260, ¶ 23 (Ohio Ct. App. 9th Dist. Medina County 2014), citing Chafin v. Chafin, 2010-Ohio-3939, 2010 WL 3294288 (Ohio Ct. App. 9th Dist. Lorain County 2010).

[223]B.C. v. A.S., 2014-Ohio-1326, 2014 WL 1345260, ¶ 22 (Ohio Ct. App. 9th Dist. Medina County 2014).

[224]B.C. v. A.S., 2014-Ohio-1326, 2014 WL 1345260, ¶ 22 (Ohio Ct. App. 9th Dist. Medina County 2014).

[225]B.C. v. A.S., 2014-Ohio-1326, 2014 WL 1345260, ¶ 26 (Ohio Ct. App. 9th Dist. Medina County 2014).

[226]But see Hyde v. Smith, 2015-Ohio-1701, 2015 WL 1976454 (Ohio Ct. App. 12th Dist. Butler County 2015) (appellate court noted that while her testimony did not contain specific dates as to when the threatening behavior occurred, she presented evidence that the offending behavior was widespread and continuous over a period of several years up to and including when Hyde and her son moved into her parent's home, at ¶ 25).

[227]Bargar v. Kirby, 2011-Ohio-4904, 2011 WL 4436634, *3 (Ohio Ct. App. 12th Dist. Butler County 2011), quoting In re Jenkins, 2004-Ohio-2657, 2004 WL 1152853, *26 (Ohio Ct. App. 5th Dist. Stark County 2004).

[228]Bargar v. Kirby, 2011-Ohio-4904, 2011 WL 4436634, *3 (Ohio Ct. App. 12th Dist. Butler County 2011).

forth in *State v. Collie*.[229] In fact, the court in *State v. Taylor*[230] determined that the effect of the *Collie* decision "is to establish ground rules for the admission of a defendant's prior bad acts in domestic violence threat cases, *Collie* also instructs as to the threshold issue of conditional threats."

The Franklin County Court of Appeals defined the term "conditional threat" in *State v. McClelland*.[231] In that case, defendant was charged with domestic violence under RC 2919.25(C) and aggravated menacing for threatening his 70-year-old mother. The defendant argued that the state failed to establish that the victim believed she was in imminent danger of harm and that his threat was a conditional threat and nonactionable under *State v. Collie*.

The appellate court defined a "conditional threat" as a "threat conditioned on a separate set of circumstances," and quoted *Black's Law Dictionary*'s definition of conditional as "subject to or dependent on a condition."[232] Because defendant stated in no uncertain terms that he would kill her, the fact that she would not know the day, time or place that he would carry out his threat did not make the threat conditional. Relying on the definition in *Black's Law Dictionary*, the appellate court reasoned that defendant's threat was not conditioned on any other event.

Against this backdrop, the conditional threat "If I had a gun, I'd shoot you" might be actionable if coupled with sufficient evidence of the victim's belief that the harm was imminent. Prior bad acts by the defendant could be considered to prove the victim's belief that the harm was imminent. Applying the formula detailed in *Collie* and adopted by the municipal court in *Taylor*, threats such as "I'm going to fuck you up, bitch" and "You're going to jail, or I'm going to kill your ass" are examples of actionable conditional threats.[233]

Some Ohio courts have determined that conditional threats do not

[229]State v. Collie, 108 Ohio App. 3d 580, 671 N.E.2d 338 (1st Dist. Hamilton County 1996); State v. Schweitzer, 2015-Ohio-925, ¶ 40, 30 N.E.3d 190 (Ohio Ct. App. 3d Dist. Auglaize County 2015); State v. Race, 2017-Ohio-612, 2017 WL 678814 (Ohio Ct. App. 6th Dist. Sandusky County 2017).

[230]State v. Taylor, 79 Ohio Misc. 2d 82, 84, 671 N.E.2d 343 (Mun. Ct. 1996); but see Henry v. Henry, 2005-Ohio-67, 2005 WL 43888 (Ohio Ct. App. 4th Dist. Ross County 2005).

[231]State v. McClelland, 2002-Ohio-1007, 2002 WL 356306 (Ohio Ct. App. 10th Dist. Franklin County 2002).

[232]State v. McClelland, 2002-Ohio-1007, 2002 WL 356306, *5 (Ohio Ct. App. 10th Dist. Franklin County 2002).

[233]See State v. McClelland, 2002-Ohio-1007, 2002 WL 356306 (Ohio Ct. App. 10th Dist. Franklin County 2002); see also People v. Dias, 52 Cal. App. 4th 46, 53, 60 Cal. Rptr. 2d 443 (5th Dist. 1997) (concluding that a threat subject to an apparent condition may nonetheless be actionable as a "seemingly conditional threat contingent on an act highly likely to occur may convey to the victim a gravity of purpose and immediate prospect of execution"); People v. Martinez, 53 Cal. App. 4th 1212, 62 Cal. Rptr. 2d 303 (5th Dist. 1997) (holding that, although the threat "I'm going to get you" taken alone may not convey a threat to commit a crime that would result in injury or death, the meaning of the threat must be determined from the words used and the surrounding circumstances); but see Eatmon v. Safferman, 157 N.C. App. 141, 578 S.E.2d 328 (2003) (holding that the evidence presented only established that Safferman made the minor child feel afraid, but did not demonstrate that she was afraid of "serious imminent bodily injury." Of importance is that this court focused on the fear of

rise to the level of domestic violence for purposes of R.C. 2919.25 or 3113.31.[234]

For example, in *City of Cincinnati v. Baarlaer*,[235] the Hamilton County Court of Appeals determined that a threat made from jail is a conditional threat and does not rise to the level of an actionable threat under RC 2919.25(C). In that case, the defendant contacted the victim from jail, having been arrested for threatening her. While in jail and subject to a temporary protection order, the defendant said, "I'm making bond. I want my truck and my clothes or I'm going to kick your * * * ass."[236]

The court found the defendant's assignment of error to be well taken. The court reasoned that, when the defendant made the telephone call to his wife, he was in jail and not in proximity to her.[237] Additionally, the court concluded that his threat gave the victim an option to return the truck and clothes in order to avoid the beating he threatened to give her.

> When the totality of circumstances is considered,[238] a reasonable mind could conclude only that the threat was conditional to the degree that it

---

injury at the hands of the abuser. Although defendant may frighten or make another uncomfortable, the statute mandates that the defendant place the petitioner in fear of injury; the actions of the defendant, while scary and suspicious, do not rise to the level of domestic violence).

[234]See, for example, Henry v. Henry, 2005-Ohio-67, 2005 WL 43888 (Ohio Ct. App. 4th Dist. Ross County 2005) (Mr. Henry's threats were conditional, because appellee did not possess means to accomplish the threat.); see also Morris v. Morris, 2009-Ohio-5164, 2009 WL 3119658 (Ohio Ct. App. 9th Dist. Summit County 2009); Bargar v. Kirby, 2011-Ohio-4904, 2011 WL 4436634 (Ohio Ct. App. 12th Dist. Butler County 2011) (judgment granting the CPO reversed where the threat "if you were a man, I'd would whip your ass" is based on a condition that could not be met, because appellee was not a man; Rather, it was a generalized, conditional threat that could not have placed petitioner in fear of imminent serious physical harm).

[235]City of Cincinnati v. Baarlaer, 115 Ohio App. 3d 521, 685 N.E.2d 836 (1st Dist. Hamilton County 1996); see also Cleveland v. Earnhart, 110 Ohio Misc. 2d 41, 743 N.E.2d 1000 (Mun. Ct. 2000); In re Jenkins, 2004-Ohio-2657, 2004 WL 1152853 (Ohio Ct. App. 5th Dist. Stark County 2004). But see State v. Schweitzer, 2015-Ohio-925, 30 N.E.3d 190 (Ohio Ct. App. 3d Dist. Auglaize County 2015) ("a conditional threat standing alone, is insufficient to satisfy the element of imminent physical harm. * * *However, a conditional threat along with other circumstances, including the victim's state of mind, may sufficiently establish such element." at ¶ 40, quoting State v. Shahan, 2006-Ohio-402, 2006 WL 234859, ¶ 19 (Ohio Ct. App. 5th Dist. Tuscarawas County 2006).

[236]City of Cincinnati v. Baarlaer, 115 Ohio App. 3d 521, 526, 685 N.E.2d 836 (1st Dist. Hamilton County 1996); see also Hamilton v. Cameron, 121 Ohio App. 3d 445, 446, 700 N.E.2d 336 (12th Dist. Butler County 1997), where the court held that the defendant did not commit domestic violence by telling his wife, "I'd probably have to blow your head off to get you to shut up." Such a threat was determined to be conditional because there was no evidence that he attempted to carry out the threat or physically harm his wife. See dissent, State v. Schweitzer, 2015-Ohio-925, 30 N.E.3d 190 (Ohio Ct. App. 3d Dist. Auglaize County 2015).

[237]But see State v. Taylor, 79 Ohio Misc. 2d 82, 671 N.E.2d 343 (Mun. Ct. 1996); see also Strong v. Bauman, 1999 WL 317432 (Ohio Ct. App. 2d Dist. Montgomery County 1999).

[238]See Walker v. Lees, 2001 WL 197853 (Ohio Ct. App. 5th Dist. Licking County 2001) (court addressed totality of the evidence in order to grant civil protection order); Parrish v. Parrish, 146 Ohio App. 3d 640, 2000-Ohio-2693, 767 N.E.2d 1182 (4th Dist. Ross County 2000) (rejecting the petitioner's argument that the "totality of the cir-

> could not provide a basis, in law, upon which to predicate a violation of RC 2919.25(C) because the physical harm threatened was not imminent, and because the threat could not have caused the victim to believe that she stood in jeopardy of imminent harm.[239]

It is not clear whether the fact that he was in jail or the fact that he gave her an option was pivotal in the court's decision.

It is important to note that a conditional threat may constitute a violation of the menacing laws.[240] Unlike the domestic violence statute that contains the term "imminent," the menacing statute does not. However, it is not clear whether the state needs to prove the offender's ability to carry out the threat or any movement toward carrying it out.[241]

However, in the civil context, some courts have held that conditional threats do rise to the level of domestic violence under certain circumstances. For example, in *Strong v. Bauman*,[242] the appellant left a threatening letter in the victim's mailbox and placed about sixty telephone calls to her residence which were recorded on her answering machine. The appellate court first determined that the letter constituted a threat. The court then pointed out that the telephone messages constituted conditional threats. In one message, the defendant

---

cumstances" supported a finding of domestic violence).

[239] City of Cincinnati v. Baarlaer, 115 Ohio App. 3d 521, 528, 685 N.E.2d 836 (1st Dist. Hamilton County 1996); State v. Race, 2017-Ohio-612, 2017 WL 678814 (Ohio Ct. App. 6th Dist. Sandusky County 2017) (finding that a threat to kill victim if she returned home was conditioned on victim returning home and in that she did not testify she felt unsafe, such a threat was conditional and not imminent).

[240] State v. Collie, 108 Ohio App. 3d 580, 671 N.E.2d 338 (1st Dist. Hamilton County 1996); see also State v. Bayer, 102 Ohio App. 3d 172, 183, 656 N.E.2d 1314 (11th Dist. Geauga County 1995); see also State v. Keeney, 2009-Ohio-3094, 2009 WL 1819506 (Ohio Ct. App. 4th Dist. Lawrence County 2009).

[241] See State v. Collie, 108 Ohio App. 3d 580, 671 N.E.2d 338 (1st Dist. Hamilton County 1996); see also State v. Taylor, 79 Ohio Misc. 2d 82, 671 N.E.2d 343 (Mun. Ct. 1996); State v. McClelland, 2002-Ohio-1007, 2002 WL 356306, *4 (Ohio Ct. App. 10th Dist. Franklin County 2002) (where the Franklin County appellate court stated that "it is well established that the state does not need to prove the offender's ability to carry out a threat or any movement toward carrying it out," relying on State v. Schwartz, 77 Ohio App. 3d 484, 602 N.E.2d 671 (12th Dist. Butler County 1991)); Young v. Young, 2006-Ohio-978, 2006 WL 515522, *9 (Ohio Ct. App. 2d Dist. Greene County 2006) (holding that imminence does not require an offender to carry out a threat immediately or be in the process of carrying it out), relying on Strong v. Bauman, 1999 WL 317432 (Ohio Ct. App. 2d Dist. Montgomery County 1999); Walker v. Lees, 2001 WL 197853 (Ohio Ct. App. 5th Dist. Licking County 2001) (where appellant was obsessed with petitioner, telephoned her place of employment frequently, and sent her letters, the court looked at all the evidence taken together in order to support the issuance of a CPO).

[242] Strong v. Bauman, 1999 WL 317432 (Ohio Ct. App. 2d Dist. Montgomery County 1999); Reynolds v. Reynolds, 2001 WL 62552 (Ohio Ct. App. 2d Dist. Montgomery County 2001) (respondent's telephone threats were not conditional despite three-hour distance between the parties); but see State v. Schweitzer, 2015-Ohio-925, 30 N.E.3d 190 (Ohio Ct. App. 3d Dist. Auglaize County 2015) (dissent noting how the 2nd District Court of Appeals in *Strong v. Bauman* recognized a "close call" in a case where victim immediately called police, instituted criminal charges and subsequently sought a CPO, but failed to testify directly that she feared or believed defendant would cause her imminent harm and stressing that a 911 call alone (without seeking a CPO or instituting criminal charges) cannot be interpreted as evidence of the requisite belief that physical harm was imminent, at ¶ 50).

stated that, if he went to the victim's residence, he would give her an "ass whipping."[243]

In analyzing whether a reasonable person would be placed in fear of imminent serious physical harm, the court emphasized that imminent means "in the sense of unconditional, non-contingent."[244] The court then concluded, "there is no indication from the record that [the victim] believed that she was in danger of harm. . . . [and] given that the threats were of a conditional nature (i.e., if you come here, I will beat you), we cannot infer that a reasonable person would believe that she was in danger of imminent harm."[245] The Montgomery County Court of Appeals held that the trial court erred by finding that the calls constituted a threat of domestic violence. However, the court went on to say that "the conditional . . . calls, while insufficient in themselves to justify a civil protection order, do color the unconditional threats in the letter by making them more credible and frightening."[246] It is clear that this court looked to the totality of the circumstances to support the issuance of the civil protection order.[247]

Similarly, in *Morris v. Morris*,[248] respondent appealed the issuance of the CPO contending that appellee did not fear imminent serious physical harm because he said only that he would kill her if he lost his nursing license and that such a threat was conditional at best.

The appellate court first focused the inquiry on "whether a reasonable person would be placed in fear of imminent (in the sense of unconditional, non-contingent) serious physical harm."[249] Although a conditional threat, standing alone, is generally not sufficient to satisfy the imminent physical harm element of the statute, other courts have held that a conditional threat may be considered by a court along with the totality of the circumstances.[250]

It next determined that *this conditional threat differed from a typical conditional threat because the petitioner in this case did not have any control over the condition*, (emphasis added) that is, she had no

---

[243]Strong v. Bauman, 1999 WL 317432, *4 (Ohio Ct. App. 2d Dist. Montgomery County 1999).

[244]Strong v. Bauman, 1999 WL 317432, *4 (Ohio Ct. App. 2d Dist. Montgomery County 1999); see also Reynolds v. Reynolds, 2001 WL 62552 (Ohio Ct. App. 2d Dist. Montgomery County 2001).

[245]Strong v. Bauman, 1999 WL 317432, *5 (Ohio Ct. App. 2d Dist. Montgomery County 1999).

[246]Strong v. Bauman, 1999 WL 317432, *5 (Ohio Ct. App. 2d Dist. Montgomery County 1999).

[247]A.M. v. D.L., 2017-Ohio-5621, ¶ 9, ¶ 18, 2017 WL 2870214 (Ohio Ct. App. 9th Dist. Medina County 2017).

[248]Morris v. Morris, 2009-Ohio-5164, 2009 WL 3119658 (Ohio Ct. App. 9th Dist. Summit County 2009).

[249]At *3.

[250]At *3. See also B.C. v. A.S., 2014-Ohio-1326, 2014 WL 1345260 (Ohio Ct. App. 9th Dist. Medina County 2014) (totality of circumstances and victim's state of mind relevant in determining that the threat of harm is imminent); Serdy v. Serdy, 2013-Ohio-5532, 2013 WL 6670830 (Ohio Ct. App. 7th Dist. Noble County 2013) (fact finder could find that wife's fears were reasonable under the totality of circumstances of the case).

control over whether the respondent would lose his nursing license.[251] In light of surrounding circumstances, to wit: the previous domestic violence incidents, her call to the police and her belief that he was capable of killing her, competent credible evidence existed to show that appellee feared imminent serious physical harm.

In affirming the trial court, the Ninth District Court of Appeals stressed that "[c]ourts cannot look at incidents of domestic violence in a vacuum. Domestic violence is almost always a series of incidents that gradually escalate into increasing acts of brutality, repeating themselves in cycles."[252]

Moreover, in *State v. Johnson*,[253] the Hamilton County Municipal Court considered the totality of the circumstances to support a conviction under RC 2919.25(C), the threat provision of the criminal domestic violence statute. The court found that the defendant threatened the victim not to "let me have to kill you"; came to the victim's place of work, approaching her rapidly; addressed her forcefully; and punched her boyfriend when he attempted to intervene. These activities, in light of the surrounding circumstances, demonstrated a "rational fear of imminent bodily harm."[254]

Q & A: What actions do or do not constitute domestic violence for purposes of R.C. 31131.31(A)(1)(b)?[255]

In *Snyder v. Snyder*,[256] respondent threatened to "kick petitioner's butt" and burn her belongings; told his son in earshot of petitioner, that he might end up in jail for murdering his wife; and had loaded guns in the bedroom. This conduct was sufficient to cause the petitioner to believe that the respondent would shoot her. The court held that the actions of the respondent supported a finding that the respondent placed the petitioner by threat of force in fear of imminent serious physical harm.[257] It should be noted, however, that the trial court in *Snyder* considered the cumulative acts of the respondent. It is

---

[251]At *4.

[252]At *4; quoting the dissent in Parrish v. Parrish, 95 Ohio St. 3d 1201, 1207, 2002-Ohio-1623, 765 N.E.2d 359 (2002).

[253]State v. Johnson, 73 Ohio Misc. 2d 1, 657 N.E.2d 383 (Mun. Ct. 1994).

[254]State v. Johnson, 73 Ohio Misc. 2d 1, 2, 657 N.E.2d 383 (Mun. Ct. 1994); see also Sitton v. Sitton, 1999 WL 55717 (Ohio Ct. App. 2d Dist. Montgomery County 1999); State v. Shahan, 2006-Ohio-402, 2006 WL 234859 (Ohio Ct. App. 5th Dist. Tuscarawas County 2006) (a conditional threat along with other circumstances including victim's state of mind may sufficiently establish a fear of imminent physical harm); State v. Schweitzer, 2015-Ohio-925, 30 N.E.3d 190 (Ohio Ct. App. 3d Dist. Auglaize County 2015) (a direct threat to harm coupled with other circumstantial evidence established the element of imminent physical harm).

[255]See also § 11:10 and § 12:12.

[256]Snyder v. Snyder, 1995 WL 493998 (Ohio Ct. App. 4th Dist. Ross County 1995). See also Bradley v. Cox, 2004-Ohio-4840, 2004 WL 2035318 (Ohio Ct. App. 10th Dist. Franklin County 2004) (Court affirmed trial court where Respondent threatened to kill petitioner if he saw her with another man, that he was going to have friends beat her up and his friends had guns and were going "to spray everybody.").

[257]See also R.C. 2901.01(E). M.K. v. J.K., 2015-Ohio-434, 2015 WL 557990 (Ohio Ct. App. 9th Dist. Medina County 2015) (fear of imminent serious physical harm established by harassment, recent threats to harm, repeated contacts, hostile messages and history of domestic violence). But see Moore v. Bentley, 2004-Ohio-5060, 2004 WL 2804785 (Ohio Ct. App. 10th Dist. Franklin County 2004) (Appellate court affirmed denial of CPO even though appellant filed a police report stating that appel-

unclear, and highly doubtful, that a single act would have been sufficient to support a finding of domestic violence under R.C. 3113.31(A)(1)(b).[258]

The reasoning of *Snyder* was reinforced in *Eichenberger v. Eichenberger*.[259] That court held that where the respondent threatened to kill petitioner causing her to fear that he would follow up on the threats, domestic violence had occurred.[260] The court went on to say that "[f]ear always has a subjective element to it."[261] In this case, "Ms. Eichenberger's state of mind could very well have been the product, in part at least, of her past interactions with appellant. The fear she

lee pushed him, where the appellant continually brought appellee lunch up to the day he filed, they attended a public gathering together, and the appellant bought the appellee flowers the day prior to filing; "This behavior undermines a finding that appellant was in fear of imminent serious physical harm.").

[258]See also Baker v. Baker, 2005-Ohio-5770, 2005 WL 2840647 (Ohio Ct. App. 12th Dist. Butler County 2005) (appeals court mentioned the continuous pattern of domestic violence); Hunter v. Hunter, 2006-Ohio-6307, 2006 WL 3462139, *1 (Ohio Ct. App. 2d Dist. Montgomery County 2006) (Affirming judgment upholding CPO and stating appellee was placed in fear of imminent physical harm by the threat of force and by an actual act of domestic violence; he followed her, approached her car, and tried to open it and then attempted to intimidate her by saying "no one will believe you." Earlier that day, he forced her head into his groin and knelt on her lower leg until she screamed in pain.). But see State v. Ornellas, 79 Haw. 418, 903 P.2d 723 (Ct. App. 1995), where a single slap to the face constituted physical abuse within the meaning of the statute. In Ornellas, the wife slapped her husband in the face, leaving a red mark. There appeared to be no provocation for the slap, and the incident took place in the presence of police officers.

[259]Eichenberger v. Eichenberger, 82 Ohio App. 3d 809, 613 N.E.2d 678 (10th Dist. Franklin County 1992); see also Kreuzer v. Kreuzer, 2002-Ohio-105, 2002 WL 27392, *2 (Ohio Ct. App. 2d Dist. Greene County 2002) (The appellate court upheld the issuance of a CPO where the respondent picketed his daughter's school, asked for her school records, and, in the past, had climbed up a tree with binoculars and had also described where she slept. The court found that "even though the Respondent did not verbally or physically intimidate Petitioner, his continued ominous presence, first outside of her home and then continuously outside of her school, is dangerous and threatening."); Lavery v. Lavery, 2001-Ohio-1874, 2001 WL 1545663 (Ohio Ct. App. 9th Dist. Summit County 2001) (where physical abuse in the past and present threats and verbal harassment were sufficient for CPO); Spence v. Herbert, 2001 WL 876231 (Ohio Ct. App. 5th Dist. Licking County 2001); Steen v. Goad, 2001-Ohio-1771, 2001 WL 1421527 (Ohio Ct. App. 9th Dist. Wayne County 2001) (where appellant intimated "things could happen to her" while she was driving and there had been a past history of physical abuse).

[260]See Heflin v. Dunson, 2005-Ohio-304, 2005 WL 187435 (Ohio Ct. App. 2d Dist. Montgomery County 2005) ("If a petitioner testifies that the respondent threatened to kill her, this combined with her testimony that she is afraid is enough to prove domestic violence."); Noggle v. Smith, 2005-Ohio-5636, 2005 WL 2727128 (Ohio Ct. App. 5th Dist. Ashland County 2005) (male cohabitant's conduct such as a bear hug was violent and preventing female cohabitant from leaving house, causing her to exit through the window could justify finding of imminent fear).

[261]Eichenberger v. Eichenberger, 82 Ohio App. 3d 809, 815, 613 N.E.2d 678 (10th Dist. Franklin County 1992). See also Chapman v. Chapman, 2004-Ohio-2318, 2004 WL 1047577 (Ohio Ct. App. 2d Dist. Montgomery County 2004) (trial court decision won't be disturbed where there was evidence to support a finding that respondent knowingly caused petitioner to believe that he would cause her physical harm and calculated the threat to an extent to cause a person of reasonable sensibility to fear physical harm would occur).

claimed to have felt and the reasonableness of that fear could and should be determined with reference to her history with appellant."[262]

However, the dissent in *Eichenberger* approached the issue from the opposite viewpoint. The dissenting opinion reflects a very narrow and technical interpretation of both R.C. 2901.01(E) and 3113.31.[263] The dissent gave no credence to a particular petitioner's individual state of mind. The court held that, although the respondent engaged in improper and reprehensible conduct, such conduct did not give rise to the level of domestic violence. The dissent reasoned that "the standard for the granting of a civil protection order does not depend upon improper and reprehensible conduct no matter how crude, offensive, or vulgar it may be[.] Rather, domestic violence is defined in RC 3113. 31, to include . . . '[p]lacing another by the threat of force in fear of imminent serious physical harm.' "[264] The dissent concluded that "more than a demonstration of a fear of physical harm must be present."[265] "[T]he evidence presented . . . does not permit a finding of a threat of imminent serious physical harm."[266] Ms. Eichenberger did not testify she was injured by the actions of the respondent. Because she failed

[262]Eichenberger v. Eichenberger, 82 Ohio App. 3d 809, 816, 613 N.E.2d 678 (10th Dist. Franklin County 1992); see also Visnich v. Visnich, 1999 WL 1299300 (Ohio Ct. App. 11th Dist. Trumbull County 1999); Johnson v. Piorkowski, 2010-Ohio-4545, 2010 WL 3733559 (Ohio Ct. App. 9th Dist. Medina County 2010) (affirming grant of CPO where respondent made her sign a sex agreement; her fear was based on his threats to rape her and her daughter). But see Bruner v. Bruner, 2000-Ohio-2554, 2000 WL 1486452 (Ohio Ct. App. 7th Dist. Mahoning County 2000). But see Anderson v. Anderson, 2001-Ohio-3379, 2001 WL 1667875 (Ohio Ct. App. 7th Dist. Mahoning County 2001) (where the court found an insufficient nexus between appellant's violent behavior and appellee's fear of domestic violence; the evidence showed only that appellant had a reputation for violent behavior and that he threatened to do violence to himself); but see also Solomon v. Solomon, 157 Ohio App. 3d 807, 2004-Ohio-2486, 813 N.E.2d 918 (7th Dist. Mahoning County 2004) (while the court may consider past acts to determine whether the incident at issue constitutes domestic violence, the issuance of a CPO cannot be based solely on previous incidents of alleged domestic violence; rather, the petitioner must establish that an act of domestic violence occurred on the date set forth on the petition); Newhouse v. Williams, 167 Ohio App. 3d 215, 2006-Ohio-3075, 854 N.E.2d 565 (3d Dist. Wyandot County 2006), citing *Solomon*; Bahr v. Bahr, 2003-Ohio-5024, 2003 WL 22176762 (Ohio Ct. App. 5th Dist. Ashland County 2003), citing Bruner v. Bruner, 2000-Ohio-2554, 2000 WL 1486452 (Ohio Ct. App. 7th Dist. Mahoning County 2000); Tabor v. Palacio, 2008-Ohio-349, 2008 WL 282127, *4 (Ohio Ct. App. 12th Dist. Butler County 2008) (citing *Solomon* and stating that while the issuance of a CPO cannot be based solely on previous incidents of alleged domestic violence, a court may consider such past acts to determine *whether* the incident at issue constitutes domestic violence); Cottrill v. Cottrill, 2017-Ohio-1422, 2017 WL 1376841 (Ohio Ct. App. 5th Dist. Fairfield County 2017).

[263]See also dissenting opinion in Markowitz v. Markowitz, 2006-Ohio-5932, 2006 WL 3234010 (Ohio Ct. App. 8th Dist. Cuyahoga County 2006).

[264]Eichenberger v. Eichenberger, 82 Ohio App. 3d 809, 817, 613 N.E.2d 678 (10th Dist. Franklin County 1992) (Whiteside, J, dissenting); see also Young v. Young, 2006-Ohio-978, 2006 WL 515522 (Ohio Ct. App. 2d Dist. Greene County 2006).

[265]Eichenberger v. Eichenberger, 82 Ohio App. 3d 809, 818, 613 N.E.2d 678 (10th Dist. Franklin County 1992) (Whiteside, J, dissenting).

[266]Eichenberger v. Eichenberger, 82 Ohio App. 3d 809, 818, 613 N.E.2d 678 (10th Dist. Franklin County 1992) (Whiteside, J, dissenting); see Bruner v. Bruner, 2000-Ohio-2554, 2000 WL 1486452 (Ohio Ct. App. 7th Dist. Mahoning County 2000) (past acts may be used to establish a genuine fear of violence in the present situation of there must be an indication that the person was fearful in the present situation);

to suffer harm as defined in R.C. 2901.01(E), the standard was not met.[267]

Conversely, where a respondent, in an aggressive manner, unzipped his pants, pulled out his penis and told petitioner to put this "in your mouth," this was not considered to be threatening conduct justifying the issuance of a civil protection order. In *Beach v. Beach*,[268] the appellate court held that the evidence failed to meet the statutory definition of domestic violence under R.C. 3113.31(A)(1)(b).

Likewise, the threat "when I'm done with you, you will be begging for mercy" does not amount to domestic violence, at least according to the Butler County Court of Appeals. In *Stanzak v. Stanzak*,[269] appellee testified that she was afraid of defendant because he had assaulted her in the past. Nowhere in her testimony did she indicate that she was placed in fear of imminent serious physical harm. The court held that the threat did not fall under the domestic violence statute. "The statement is obviously a threat, but may well have been related to something else, such as custody or division of property. The relationship of the threat to appellant's subsequent conduct was tenuous at best."[270] "Very clearly, appellant did not threaten immediate force."[271]

However, the dissent in *Stanzak* noted that the term "threat"[272] should be given its common, accepted meaning. The dissent analyzed the threat made to appellee and determined that "[t]here is no requirement that threats be strictly oral. A threat can be made by word or deed or a combination of the two."[273] In referring to the statement of appellee that she feared appellant because of his past abusive actions

---

Newhouse v. Williams, 167 Ohio App. 3d 215, 2006-Ohio-3075, 854 N.E.2d 565 (3d Dist. Wyandot County 2006); Bahr v. Bahr, 2003-Ohio-5024, 2003 WL 22176762 (Ohio Ct. App. 5th Dist. Ashland County 2003).

[267]Eichenberger v. Eichenberger, 82 Ohio App. 3d 809, 613 N.E.2d 678 (10th Dist. Franklin County 1992).

[268]Beach v. Beach, 1992 WL 328642 (Ohio Ct. App. 10th Dist. Franklin County 1992).

[269]Stanzak v. Stanzak, 1990 WL 129456 (Ohio Ct. App. 12th Dist. Butler County 1990); see also Smith v. Mangan, 2007-Ohio-194, 2007 WL 127693 (Ohio Ct. App. 2d Dist. Greene County 2007) (cursing at her, saying "I'm glad you fucking bitches got to kiss and meet" and staring at her without saying anything did not rise to a threat of force causing a fear of imminent serious physical harm).

[270]Stanzak v. Stanzak, 1990 WL 129456, *2 (Ohio Ct. App. 12th Dist. Butler County 1990).

[271]Stanzak v. Stanzak, 1990 WL 129456, *3 (Ohio Ct. App. 12th Dist. Butler County 1990).

[272]See, for example, State v. McCornell, 2003-Ohio-2474, 2003 WL 21101258 (Ohio Ct. App. 8th Dist. Cuyahoga County 2003) (discussing a threat). See also Com. v. Baker, 722 A.2d 718, 722 (Pa. Super. Ct. 1998), order aff'd, 564 Pa. 192, 766 A.2d 328 (2001) (noting that a true threat is one which, on its face and in the circumstances in which it is made, is so unequivocal, unconditionally immediate, and specific as to the person threatened as to convey a gravity of purpose and imminent prospect of execution; defendant made statement while incarcerated and statement was not conveyed to plaintiff; order of protection not violated where defendant's statement did not occur in plaintiff's presence or place her in fear).

[273]Stanzak v. Stanzak, 1990 WL 129456, *4 (Ohio Ct. App. 12th Dist. Butler County 1990) (Young, J., dissenting).

toward her, it is clear that the dissent considered the subjective nature of fear and its relation to the past interactions between the parties.[274]

Beach and the majority opinion in *Stanzak* illustrate the tendency of some courts to find that verbal threats, without a further attempt to cause physical harm, do not constitute domestic violence within the meaning of R.C. 3113.31(A)(1)(b).[275] Such courts demand evidence of a present intent to inflict harm and require more than a showing of past acts.

On the other hand, *Snyder* and the majority opinion in *Eichenberger* demonstrate a growing trend by some courts to consider past abusive behavior[276] as a factor in determining whether there are grounds for a protection order, especially when recent threats are made and the victim testifies that she/he is in fear of "imminent serious physical harm."[277]

§ 8:5 Miscellaneous concerns involving RC 3113.31(A)(1)(a) and (b).

Q & A: Does operating a vehicle at a high rate of speed in an attempt to run his wife and a friend off the road constitute domestic violence?

In *Gaydash v. Gaydash*,[1] the appellate court found that there was competent, credible evidence that husband perpetrated domestic

[274]Stanzak v. Stanzak, 1990 WL 129456, *4 (Ohio Ct. App. 12th Dist. Butler County 1990) (Young, J., dissenting). See also Steen v. Goad, 2001-Ohio-1771, 2001 WL 1421527 (Ohio Ct. App. 9th Dist. Wayne County 2001) (appellee stated that appellant physically abused her and intimated that "things could happen to her" while she was driving).

[275]See also Tyler v. Tyler, 2004-Ohio-5784, 2004 WL 2436594 (Ohio Ct. App. 2d Dist. Montgomery County 2004) (angry and erratic driving; messages, often angry, to evict wife and daughter from house and "to take action" did not meet R.C. 3113.31(A)(1)(b) definition of domestic violence for want of threats of force); Wolf v. Rosson, 2005-Ohio-1174, 2005 WL 628235 (Ohio Ct. App. 8th Dist. Cuyahoga County 2005) (Verbal and emotional abuse of petitioner and in front of the child did not rise to level of a threat of physical harm where there was no evidence Respondent had ever been physically abusive to her or the child. Threats to "take you down" and a warning "to look over your shoulder" don't create a reasonable fear of imminent serious physical harm.).

[276]See, e.g., Pierce v. Pierce, 2001-Ohio-2312, 2001 WL 1432047 (Ohio Ct. App. 3d Dist. Marion County 2001); Gatt v. Gatt, 2002-Ohio-1749, 2002 WL 570389 (Ohio Ct. App. 9th Dist. Medina County 2002); Osherow v. Osherow, 2003-Ohio-3927, 2003 WL 21697408 (Ohio Ct. App. 9th Dist. Summit County 2003) (victim's testimony that she feared for her safety as a result of threat "I'll get you next time" was enhanced by defendant's past behavior).

[277]See also State v. Collie, 108 Ohio App. 3d 580, 671 N.E.2d 338 (1st Dist. Hamilton County 1996), and State v. Taylor, 79 Ohio Misc. 2d 82, 671 N.E.2d 343 (Mun. Ct. 1996), which encourage evidence of past acts. But see Anderson v. Anderson, 2001-Ohio-3379, 2001 WL 1667875, *4 (Ohio Ct. App. 7th Dist. Mahoning County 2001) (where the appellate court reversed the trial court's decision to grant a CPO, holding that appellant's reputation for violent behavior or his stated threat to do violence to himself does not equate to an overt act of violence or threat of violence to appellee). And see also § 11:10.

[Section 8:5]

[1]Gaydash v. Gaydash, 168 Ohio App. 3d 418, 2006-Ohio-4080, 860 N.E.2d 789 (9th Dist. Summit County 2006); Smith v. Strong, 2017-Ohio-6918, 2017 WL 3098601 (Ohio Ct. App. 6th Dist. Lucas County 2017) (action of driving his vehicle closely

violence on his wife and that wife established she was in danger of domestic violence. In this case, appellant drove his SUV at a high rate of speed straight at the vehicle driven by the appellee and her friend and causing the vehicle to go off the road. The appellant argued that he did not directly threaten or injure appellee and that it was impossible for appellee to have been in fear of imminent serious physical harm.

The appellate court considered the trial court ruling in light of facts that demonstrated that appellant had used his vehicle in an attempt to run the women's car off the road and had made threatening statements to both women.[2] It then found that such actions would place all occupants in fear of imminent serious physical harm, not just the driver. Thus, appellee's fear of imminent serious physical harm was reasonable given the history of violence and the incident in question. The court also noted that it had previously held that when used a certain way, a vehicle is an instrumentality of violence.[3]

Q & A: Can a person obtain a CPO against another who has been in prison and is about to be released?

The Second District Court of Appeals addressed this specific issue in *Williamson v. Williamson*.[4] In that case, the ex-wife sought a civil protection order (CPO) for herself and her minor children against her former husband who was about to be released from prison after serving a three year prison term. The appellate court reversed the trial court's issuance of the CPO because the former wife did not show reasonable fear of imminent serious physical harm.

The appellate court applied the same analysis set forth in *Fleckner*, stating that "[t]he critical inquiry, regarding threats to the person seeking a CPO is whether a reasonable person would be placed in fear of 'imminent,' in the sense of unconditional and non-contingent, serious physical harm, which necessarily involves both subjective and objective elements."[5] The court then stressed that "[i]t is important to distinguish between fear of potential future conduct and immediate physical conduct, and to remember that the petitioner must show sufficient evidence of the latter."[6]

The facts of this case indicate that the magistrate asked appellee if

---

behind petitioner placed her in reasonable fear of imminent serious physical harm where she called 911 and made a police report).

[2]Gaydash v. Gaydash, 168 Ohio App. 3d 418, 421-422, 2006-Ohio-4080, 860 N.E.2d 789 (9th Dist. Summit County 2006).

[3]Gaydash v. Gaydash, 168 Ohio App. 3d 418, 423, 2006-Ohio-4080, 860 N.E.2d 789 (9th Dist. Summit County 2006); see also State v. Brown, 2006-Ohio-6267, 2006 WL 3446238 (Ohio Ct. App. 8th Dist. Cuyahoga County 2006), aff'd on other grounds, 119 Ohio St. 3d 447, 2008-Ohio-4569, 895 N.E.2d 149 (2008) (holding that a steak knife can constitute a deadly weapon); State v. Rhoads, 2013-Ohio-152, 2013 WL 221512, ¶ 27 (Ohio Ct. App. 12th Dist. Clermont County 2013).

[4]Williamson v. Williamson, 180 Ohio App. 3d 260, 2008-Ohio-6718, 905 N.E.2d 217 (2d Dist. Greene County 2008). See also Text § 12:11.

[5]Williamson v. Williamson, 180 Ohio App. 3d 260, 2008-Ohio-6718, 905 N.E.2d 217 (2d Dist. Greene County 2008) (at syllabus); see also Williamson v. Williamson, 180 Ohio App. 3d 260, 2008-Ohio-6718, 905 N.E.2d 217 (2d Dist. Greene County 2008), quoting Strong v. Bauman, 1999 WL 317432 (Ohio Ct. App. 2d Dist. Montgomery County 1999).

[6]Williamson v. Williamson, 180 Ohio App. 3d 260, 2008-Ohio-6718, 905 N.E.2d

she was in fear of her safety, and she responded that she was. When asked if that was based on past events, she responded affirmatively. In her appellate brief, she argued that past acts are sufficient to warrant a protection order. But the appellate court disagreed, commenting that past domestic violence is only some evidence that more violence is imminent. "While it is true that past acts may be used to establish a genuine fear of violence in the present situation, there must be an indication that the person was fearful in the present situation. Merely finding that there were past acts of domestic violence, without anything more, is not enough to warrant a present civil protective order."[7]

To further illustrate this point, appellee relied on *Haynes-Soper v. Garrett*,[8] in which the appellate court affirmed the grant of the CPO for a petitioner who sought the CPO a month before respondent was to be released from prison. However, the appellate court distinguished the facts of *Haynes-Soper* from the instant case noting that the petitioner in *Haynes-Soper* suffered far more physical injury than appellee. "While Shawn did physically harm Mary, the nonserious nature of her injuries does not urge the same level of caution be taken in the absence of actual threats."[9] Additionally, in the case at hand, appellant was convicted and sentenced for aggravated burglary and violating a temporary protection order, not for domestic violence. Based on the foregoing, the appellate court found that there was an insufficient factual basis to support the issuance of a CPO.

In its reasoning, the appellate court addressed one particular fact considered by the lower court to support its grant of a CPO, that the appellant was diagnosed as bi-polar. In that he had been placed on medication for this condition, the appellate court viewed him as less of a threat.

In reversing the lower court, the Greene County Court of Appeals held that appellee failed to demonstrate a present fear of future domestic violence or establish the reasonable basis for such fear. Evidence of an actionable threat must connote more than the mere possibility of violence potentially occurring sometime in the future.[10]

Of significance is that the court also advised that "it is inappropriate to use a protection order merely to create a buffer-zone around Mary and the children while she decides whether contact with Shawn is a good idea. It is a means to prevent imminent physical harm, and

217 (2d Dist. Greene County 2008), citing State v. Strunk, 1999 WL 12743 (Ohio Ct. App. 1st Dist. Hamilton County 1999) (determining that the evidence established only the possibility of potential future conduct and therefore, the victim failed to show that the threat was imminent).

[7]Williamson v. Williamson, 180 Ohio App. 3d 260, 2008-Ohio-6718, 905 N.E.2d 217 (2d Dist. Greene County 2008), quoting Solomon v. Solomon, 157 Ohio App. 3d 807, 2004-Ohio-2486, 813 N.E.2d 918 (7th Dist. Mahoning County 2004).

[8]Haynes-Soper v. Garrett, 2000 WL 1289450 (Ohio Ct. App. 10th Dist. Franklin County 2000).

[9]Williamson v. Williamson, 180 Ohio App. 3d 260, 2008-Ohio-6718, 905 N.E.2d 217 (2d Dist. Greene County 2008).

[10]Williamson v. Williamson, 180 Ohio App. 3d 260, 2008-Ohio-6718, 905 N.E.2d 217 (2d Dist. Greene County 2008).

there is little evidence that Shawn is likely to harm her or his children."[11]

While Judge Fain concurred with the decision to vacate the CPO against the children, he would have kept the CPO in place for appellee. He focused on the presumption of regularity and stated that he would "presume that the trial court found that Shawn had committed an act of domestic violence against Mary, in the form of a violation of RC 2911.211, which would support the civil protection order as it pertains to Mary."[12] He reasoned that Shawn's entering and remaining on Mary's premises might have been an act of aggravated trespass under R.C. 2911.211 which is an act of domestic violence itself pursuant to R.C. 3113.31.

It is important to note that the Greene County Court of Appeals decision is heavily fact-based. In general, so long as petitioner can demonstrate a current threat and a reasonable basis for the fear, she or he should prevail in court. In the context of a respondent being released from prison, past violence causing significant physical injury should provide the basis for the issuance of a present CPO.

Q & A: When do rude or hurtful comments constitute a threat under RC 3113.31(A)(1)(b)?

In *Carter v. Hooks*,[13] the Butler County Court of Appeals considered mental distress as the rationale to grant a civil protection order. Appellee obtained a civil protection order stating that she felt unsafe and scared and feared for her health due to threatening remarks made by appellant. The remarks were "rude and hurtful" and appellant's presence in the home was an emotional hardship for her.[14]

On appeal, appellant argued that appellee failed to present evidence of physical harm or threat of physical harm to support the granting of the CPO. Appellant also asserted that the trial court misstated the law when it determined that "mental distress" was sufficient to warrant issuing a civil protection order under the domestic violence statute.

The appellate court first considered the definition of the domestic

---

[11]Williamson v. Williamson, 180 Ohio App. 3d 260, 2008-Ohio-6718, 905 N.E.2d 217 (2d Dist. Greene County 2008); M.H. v. J.H., 2015-Ohio-5178, 2015 WL 8553569 (Ohio Ct. App. 9th Dist. Medina County 2015).

[12]Williamson v. Williamson, 180 Ohio App. 3d 260, 2008-Ohio-6718, 905 N.E.2d 217 (2d Dist. Greene County 2008).

[13]Carter v. Hooks, 2006-Ohio-5987, 2006 WL 3290733 (Ohio Ct. App. 12th Dist. Butler County 2006). See also M.C. v. B.K., 2015-Ohio-560, 2015 WL 628342 (Ohio Ct. App. 6th Dist. Sandusky County 2015) (mental abuse was demonstrated based on text messages such as "Thanks for the no job.", "F* * *your Christmas and anything else." "I have nothing to overcome," and "You made your choice and I made mine." Trial court found that the texts were "emotionally, terribly abusive" and a past history that can be relieved by having no contact, and which decision was upheld by the appellate court).

[14]Carter v. Hooks, 2006-Ohio-5987, 2006 WL 3290733, *1 (Ohio Ct. App. 12th Dist. Butler County 2006); see also State v. Simcox, 2007-Ohio-1217, 2007 WL 789423 (Ohio Ct. App. 9th Dist. Wayne County 2007) (yelling, screaming, threatening to destroy property, stating, "Well, you remember the gun I showed you before" and threatening to take away victim's kidney medication provided examples of threatening the victim with imminent harm, which formed the basis of appellant's conviction for domestic violence).

violence statute and concluded that evidence of a pattern of rude, mean and hurtful comments causing appellee to suffer mental distress was sufficient for the issuance of the CPO under RC 3113.31(A)(1)(b) in that appellant committed a violation of section 2903.211 of the Revised Code. Appellee's testimony that her mental health suffered causing her to seek treatment from her doctor for her "nerves" and other witness testimony regarding the degree of distress she suffered as a result of appellant's conduct was sufficient evidence.

In affirming the trial court, the Butler County Court of Appeals held that "[c]ontrary to appellant's assertion, appellee's failure to present evidence of physical harm or threat of physical harm in support of her petition is not dispositive of the matter. Reviewing the record as a whole, there is evidence supporting the trial court's conclusion that appellant engaged in a pattern of conduct which caused appellee mental distress."[15]

The appellate court considered both a "pattern of conduct" and "mental distress" but did not relate the terms to an act of stalking as set forth in the statute or as illustrated by the case law on the matter.

Q & A: When do threatening texts not rise to the level of domestic violence?

In *Barton v. Barton*,[16] appellant appealed the trial court's issuance of a civil protection order. His wife filed for the CPO based on numerous test messages that caused her imminent fear. They included texts stating that "she better be ready for a s—t storm"; that he forced open the door to the marital residence with a crowbar and that he screamed obscenities at her and told her she better not go to sleep. Soon after that, appellant returned to the home. In mid 2012, appellant threw her around the living room, pushed and spit in her face and although she filed a CPO, she later dismissed it when he agreed to get counseling. Nothing further transpired until mid 2013, when appellee texted appellant 46 times for which she was arrested for domestic violence and convicted of disorderly conduct. Soon after that, appellant posted a picture on Facebook showing a picture of a woman bound with duct tape. In the months prior to her filing the CPO, appellant had been telling her to keep her mouth shut. In November 2013, wife filed the CPO,which was granted by the trial court.

On appeal, appellant claimed that there was insufficient evidence in the record that appellee was placed, by threat of force, in fear of imminent serious physical harm. After reiterating the facts of the case, the appellate court concluded that her testimony regarding her fear consisted of her generalized statement that she was afraid and that her safety was an imminent and continued risk.[17] The court found that appellee's actions of reconciling and residing together again did not support that claim. In fact, the record then indicated that the texts in June 2013 were initiated by her. Additionally, no evidence

[15]Carter v. Hooks, 2006-Ohio-5987, 2006 WL 3290733, *3 (Ohio Ct. App. 12th Dist. Butler County 2006).

[16]Barton v. Barton, 2015-Ohio-3869, 2015 WL 5691887 (Ohio Ct. App. 2d Dist. Greene County 2015).

[17]Barton v. Barton, 2015-Ohio-3869, ¶ 19, 2015 WL 5691887 (Ohio Ct. App. 2d Dist. Greene County 2015).

was presented that there had been any physical act of force or threat of force since November 2012. Relative to the allegation warning appellee to keep her mouth shut, no evidence was presented to show that the statements were made during face-to-face contact or via telephone or, text or email. While the Facebook post might have been distasteful, it was not transmitted to appellee and does not set forth any explicit there of force.[18] The appellate court reversed and held that ". . . the evidence regarding the contact between the parties in 2013 does not constitute sufficient, credible evidence to support a finding that Ms. Barton was placed, by force or threat of force, in fear of imminent serious physical harm."[19]

Of significance is that the parties' reconciliations and Ms. Barton's initiating numerous texts to appellant were important to the Court's analysis that she was not in fear of imminent serious physical harm. Additionally, the Court focused on specific, credible threats, rather than her generalized fear for her safety.[20]

Q & A: When do acts of harassment rise to the level of domestic violence?[21]

It is unclear whether RC 3113.31 contemplates acts of harassment. Although many petitioners testify to acts of harassment, most courts consider them acts of stalking behavior, which is specifically prohibited under RC 2903.211.[22] Neither the term nor the act of harassment is specifically included in RC 3113.31.[23] One Ohio court found that the act of putting a threatening letter in the victim's mailbox was considered domestic violence for the purpose of granting a civil protection order. In *Strong v. Bauman*,[24] the Montgomery County Court of Appeals affirmed the issuance of a civil protection or-

[18]Barton v. Barton, 2015-Ohio-3869, ¶ 20, 2015 WL 5691887 (Ohio Ct. App. 2d Dist. Greene County 2015). But see L.L. v. R.B., 2017-Ohio-7553, ¶ 23, 26, 2017 WL 3980553 (Ohio Ct. App. 5th Dist. Guernsey County 2017) (it is sufficient for LL to establish a fear of physical harm or mental distress based on the content of the Facebook posts).

[19]Barton v. Barton, 2015-Ohio-3869, ¶ 20, 2015 WL 5691887 (Ohio Ct. App. 2d Dist. Greene County 2015).

[20]See also Linda N. on behalf of Rebecca N. v. William N., 289 Neb. 607, 856 N.W.2d 436 (2014) (finding that father's conduct of sending crude and mean messages to daughter did not constitute abuse and a credible threat must include some threat of intentional physical injury or any other physical threat).

[21]See also Chapter 9, Stalking and Trespass.

[22]See Caramico v. Caramico, 2015-Ohio-4232, 2015 WL 5934194 (Ohio Ct. App. 12th Dist. Clermont County 2015) (affirming trial court based on an act of stalking committed by husband, where he engaged in a pattern of harassment through email, text message and postings on social media. The messages sent by Husband often referenced religious scripture focused on wrath, destruction and violence ¶ 28).

[23]See Gooderham v. Patterson, 1999 WL 1034472 (Ohio Ct. App. 4th Dist. Gallia County 1999) (finding that respondent engaged in domestic violence by stalking and menacing where the petitioner testified to numerous acts of harassment that made her fearful of respondent); see also Visnich v. Visnich, 1999 WL 1299300 (Ohio Ct. App. 11th Dist. Trumbull County 1999).

[24]Strong v. Bauman, 1999 WL 317432 (Ohio Ct. App. 2d Dist. Montgomery County 1999); see also Walker v. Lees, 2001 WL 197853 (Ohio Ct. App. 5th Dist. Licking County 2001) (upheld issuance of CPO based on totality of evidence including contacting victim's place of employment and sending her letters); Stark v. Stark, 2002-Ohio-90, 2002 WL 109281 (Ohio Ct. App. 5th Dist. Delaware County 2002).

der based on the contents of a letter addressed to the victim. In that case, the appellant placed a letter in the victim's mailbox addressed to "CunTuna." The letter provided that "With each day that passes since I last saw my daughter, the urge to kill something grows more and more overwhelming . . . Have you ever dreamed that one afternoon, you're all alone and just waking up from your daily dope nap and you look up and see the barrell [sic] of * * * shot gun?"[25] The court concluded that "the threats communicated in the letter are of a nature that they are calculated to cause a person of reasonable sensibility to fear that [the respondent] would harm her."[26]

In *Jeffers v. Jeffers*[27] the defendant argued that she was erroneously convicted of violating a consent agreement because the CPO was ambiguous and unenforceable as to the prohibition against harassment.

The Franklin County Court of Appeals held that the trial court erred in finding that the appellant harassed appellee. First the court noted that the CPO did not contain a definition of the term "harass." It then defined harass as "to disturb persistently; torment, as with troubles or cares; bother continually; pester; persecute *** to trouble by repeated attacks *** Webster's New Universal Unabridged Dictionary (1996) 870. Implicit in the word 'harass' is a continuing course of conduct."[28]

The court then stated that the appellant's actions of going to the Moose Lodge while appellee's party was taking place, driving once by appellee's house, and possessing the knowledge of the purchase price and address of appellee's new home, were not acts that rose to the level of harassment as defined. The court then reasoned that all parties agreed that appellant had no contact with appellee once the CPO went into effect. "While appellant may have gone to the Moose with the intent to bother appellee, appellee was not aware of appellant's presence and only became aware of it through other guests after appellant left."[29]

The Franklin County Court of Appeals reasoned that there wasn't a continuing course of conduct to legally constitute harassment. Of significance is that the court chose not to consider the intent of the appellant and instead, focused on whether the appellee knew of appellant's presence.

In other states, courts have determined that love letters, roses, and

[25]Strong v. Bauman, 1999 WL 317432, *1 (Ohio Ct. App. 2d Dist. Montgomery County 1999).

[26]Strong v. Bauman, 1999 WL 317432, *4 (Ohio Ct. App. 2d Dist. Montgomery County 1999); see also Hoff v. Brown, 2001 WL 876228, *2 (Ohio Ct. App. 5th Dist. Stark County 2001) ("While there has been no physical injury, he has engaged in verbal abuse, calling his wife an adulteress, in threatening behavior, telling her he can get nasty, and in physically intimidating behavior, blocking her way on several occasions. His attempts to control and to belittle her are abusive in nature and have resulted in Julia's fear of him.").

[27]Jeffers v. Jeffers, 2001 WL 118530 (Ohio Ct. App. 10th Dist. Franklin County 2001).

[28]Jeffers v. Jeffers, 2001 WL 118530, *3 (Ohio Ct. App. 10th Dist. Franklin County 2001).

[29]Jeffers v. Jeffers, 2001 WL 118530, *3 (Ohio Ct. App. 10th Dist. Franklin County 2001).

telephone messages declaring undying love to a former girlfriend may be abuse as defined in that state's domestic violence statute. For example, in *Shields v. Fry*,[30] the appellate court upheld the issuance of a civil protection order against the man and noted that the statute defines abuse as including harassment and that harassment results from intentional acts that cause someone to be worried, anxious, or uncomfortable. The court found that, because the victim made it clear that she wanted nothing to do with the man, his purpose of re-establishing their relationship was not reasonable and his actions constituted harassment under the act.

While abuse is not specifically defined as including acts of harassment under RC 3113.31(A)(1)(a) to (c), the provisions governing civil protection orders state that a court may grant a protection order to bring about a cessation of domestic violence against a family or household member.[31] RC 3113.31(E)(1)(h) also allows a court to grant other relief that it considers to be equitable and fair. The plain language of the statute demonstrates that the court, in granting a civil protection order, is not limited to prohibiting only acts of physical abuse or threats. It may prohibit any type of conduct that may lead to further acts of domestic violence as set forth in RC 3113.31(A)(1).[32]

Additionally, the domestic violence forms adopted by the Supreme Court do make mention of the term harassment.[33] In fact, both the ex parte civil protection order and the order issued after the full hearing specifically restrain the respondent from harassing the victim or any other family or household members. Although it does not appear that an individual may petition the court for a civil protection order based solely on harassment, harassment is clearly regarded as prohibited behavior under a civil protection order. Moreover, acts of harassment may be the basis for a violation of a civil protection order.[34]

---

[30]Shields v. Fry, 301 Ill. App. 3d 570, 234 Ill. Dec. 821, 703 N.E.2d 921 (4th Dist. 1998) (overruled by, Best v. Best, 223 Ill. 2d 342, 307 Ill. Dec. 586, 860 N.E.2d 240 (2006)); see also State v. Hoffman, 149 N.J. 564, 695 A.2d 236 (1997) (stating that the actions of a man who, while jailed on charges of breaking into his wife's home, mailed two packages of court documents to her, including torn-up copies of her support order, were sufficient to violate the domestic violence no-contact restraining order); Tribuzio v. Roder, 356 N.J. Super. 590, 813 A.2d 1210 (App. Div. 2003) (discussing harassment). But see Peranio v. Peranio, 280 N.J. Super. 47, 654 A.2d 495 (App. Div. 1995) (husband telling wife he would bury her upon discovering that she disposed of his property did not constitute harassment under New Jersey's domestic violence statute; court also noted that there was no history or pattern of threats or abusive acts); Witchell v. Witchell, 606 N.W.2d 730 (Minn. Ct. App. 2000) (holding that statements made in a visitation notebook used by the parties to communicate about children, was not harassment).

[31]See RC 3113.31(E)(1).

[32]See Spenner v. City of Sioux Falls, 1998 SD 56, 580 N.W.2d 606 (S.D. 1998), where the Supreme Court of South Dakota held that the domestic violence statute authorized the trial court to prohibit a husband from making telephone calls to his wife. Interestingly, the court noted that, before granting the ex parte order, there was a finding of domestic abuse as defined by statute. Because the order itself prohibits certain conduct, there need not be an act of domestic violence for there to be a violation of the existing protection order which, in turn, constitutes a violation of the statute.

[33]See Sup. R. Form 10.01-D, Sup. R. Form 10.01-H to Sup. R. Form 10.01-J.

[34]See RC 2919.27; see also State v. Mustaine, 2000 WL 966387 (Ohio Ct. App. 2d

Similarly, in *Partin v. Morrison*,[35] petitioner testified that respondent sent a threatening text to shoot her and called and texted her after being told not to do so.

On appeal, appellant argued that the grant of the CPO was against the manifest weight of the evidence. The appellate court presumed that the threat to shoot petitioner was relevant to the "placing another person, by threat of force in fear of imminent serious physical harm" under RC 3113.31.[36] The calls and texts appeared relevant to the trial court's finding of domestic violence based on the repeated and unwanted nature of the threats rather than the content of the communications.

However, to comply with statutory interpretation, any threat must place another in fear of both imminent and serious physical harm.[37] Moreover, such threats must be reasonable.

In this case, no evidence was presented that respondent ever texted petitioner with a threat to shoot her. Rather, the text message appeared to refer to a Facebook post made by respondent which stated: "[t]here is two bitches. One, Charles [Richey] or Liberty [petitioner], yeah, I guess I tried to shoot them the other night, when I worked nine 'til seven in the morning, laugh my ass off. People are crazy."[38]

The appellate court reasoned that "[t]his Facebook post does not appear to be a threat to shoot anyone, but rather appears to be a comment about a past event or claim, whether real or fabricated. Neither Richey nor petitioner testified respondent tried to shoot them. Nor did they testify that respondent directly and personally threatened to shoot them. There is no evidence, nor was it ever alleged that respondent had a gun in the presence of petitioner or Richey. While there was testimony about the Facebook post, there was none concerning the event referred to in the Facebook post."[39]

As to the repeated calls and texts, petitioner admitted that no threats were made against her in any of the text messages and the phone call her boyfriend received threatening to burn down his house and warning that he had a gun were not made to petitioner.

Asked whether she feared for her safety due to respondent's calls, texts and Facebook posts, petitioner indicated that she feared for her safety. However, the texts were not introduced into evidence and no

Dist. Montgomery County 2000) (defendant addressed an envelope with blank paper inside to his former wife at her former address, knowing the address to be correct, placed his return address on the envelope in order to obtain her address. He was charged with violating a civil protection order under RC 2919.27(A)); State v. Harley, 1999 WL 3933 (Ohio Ct. App. 5th Dist. Fairfield County 1998).

[35]Partin v. Morrison, 2015-Ohio-4740, 2015 WL 7293332 (Ohio Ct. App. 12th Dist. Brown County 2015).

[36]Partin v. Morrison, 2015-Ohio-4740, 2015 WL 7293332, ¶ 11 (Ohio Ct. App. 12th Dist. Brown County 2015).

[37]Partin v. Morrison, 2015-Ohio-4740, 2015 WL 7293332, ¶ 11 (Ohio Ct. App. 12th Dist. Brown County 2015), citingBargar v. Kirby, 2011-Ohio-4904, 2011 WL 4436634, ¶ 13 (Ohio Ct. App. 12th Dist. Butler County 2011).

[38]Partin v. Morrison, 2015-Ohio-4740, 2015 WL 7293332, ¶ 12 (Ohio Ct. App. 12th Dist. Brown County 2015).

[39]Partin v. Morrison, 2015-Ohio-4740, 2015 WL 7293332, ¶ 14` (Ohio Ct. App. 12th Dist. Brown County 2015).

testimony was presented as to the content of the texts and phone calls.

The appellate court determined that the trial court must have considered the calls as stalking behavior rather than a threat of force placing her in fear of imminent serious physical harm. However, petitioner failed to testify that "she is suffering from temporary substantial incapacity or sought or is in need of mental health treatment as a result of respondent's conduct."[40]

Recognizing that petitioner acted pro se, the court acknowledged that petitioner might have been helped by counsel. Nevertheless, it reversed the trial court, holding that the trial court could not reasonably find that petitioner was in danger of domestic violence as defined in RC 3113.31 and thus, the issuance of the CPO was against the weight of the evidence.[41]

Of importance is the appellate court's deliberate analysis in reaching its conclusions. It addressed the nature of the acts as defined in RC 3113.31 and set forth a template for attorneys to use in cases involving threats. To summarize, this court reviewed the elements RC 3113.31(A)(1)(b) and focused on statutory terminology. It reviewed past cases that have stressed that to find domestic violence based on a threat, one must detail the threat with some specificity and prove that the threat of force must place a party in fear of both imminent and serious physical harm. It noted that the fear must be reasonable and that past acts alone are not enough to establish fear without some evidence of current domestic violence. It then utilized the same analysis with the stalking prong of the statute. While the trial court was focused on the repeated and unwanted nature of the texts, the appellate court wanted evidence on the nature and content of the texts.

In finding that the evidence did not support the issuance of the CPO, the appellate court focused on the fact that petitioner 1) did not demonstrate an actual threat to harm; 2) did not detail any of the threats with specificity; 3) did not expound on her fear of imminent and serious physical harm or provide context for the same; and 4) failed to show that respondent's conduct caused her mental distress. Attorneys would be wise to review this case in order to adequately prepare a case when a threat is involved.

Q & A: Does choking a victim and pushing him/her to the floor constitute an attempt to commit domestic violence under RC 3113.31(A)?

Absolutely. Most Ohio courts would find the above-mentioned facts to rise to the level of domestic violence for purposes of a civil protection order. In *Sroka v. Sroka*,[42] the petitioner testified that the respondent choked and pushed her to the floor, causing injury to her head and arm. Although the respondent admitted grabbing her by the neck and pushing her down, he argued the petitioner was not injured.

[40]Partin v. Morrison, 2015-Ohio-4740, 2015 WL 7293332, ¶ 21 (Ohio Ct. App. 12th Dist. Brown County 2015).

[41]Partin v. Morrison, 2015-Ohio-4740, 2015 WL 7293332, ¶ 24 (Ohio Ct. App. 12th Dist. Brown County 2015).

[42]Sroka v. Sroka, 121 Ohio App. 3d 728, 700 N.E.2d 916 (8th Dist. Cuyahoga County 1997).

The Cuyahoga County Court of Appeals reversed the trial court's denial of a civil protection order. The court noted that "under the statute, an attempt to cause bodily injury can also constitute domestic violence."[43] Whether the victim was injured was inconsequential to such finding. The appellate court determined that, given the facts of the case, the trial court's decision was against the manifest weight of the evidence and an abuse of discretion. The court further acknowledged that the petitioner's testimony, as well as admissions made by the respondent, was credible evidence of domestic violence.

Q & A: Does the domestic violence statute require evidence of actual physical injury in order to obtain a civil protection order?

While it is clear that evidence of actual physical injury is not necessary to prevail under the threat provisions of the domestic violence statutes,[44] it is less clear when the statutory language defines domestic violence as physical harm or bodily injury.[45] Many court decisions seem to differentiate between an attempt to cause injury and actual physical injury for purposes of RC 2919.25(A) and RC 3113.31(A)(1)(a).[46]

For purposes of a civil protection order, the statutory language suggests that an intentional act to harm the victim is not required before a victim may petition the court for redress.[47] More importantly, the statute does not appear to require actual bodily injury.[48]

Because actual physical injury is still an ideal means to evaluate "physical harm" and/or "bodily injury," it is important to review some of the appellate cases that have considered the issue. However, many court decisions have either focused on the threat provisions[49] or the "attempt to cause harm" provisions[50] as a way of sustaining a finding of domestic violence without actual physical injury.[51]

Where granting the civil protection order is predicated on a threat

[43]Sroka v. Sroka, 121 Ohio App. 3d 728, 730, 700 N.E.2d 916 (8th Dist. Cuyahoga County 1997).

[44]RC 3113.31(A)(1)(b), RC 2919.25(C).

[45]RC 3113.31(A)(1)(a), RC 2919.25(A).

[46]See City of Youngstown v. Osso, 115 Ohio App. 3d 416, 685 N.E.2d 593 (7th Dist. Mahoning County 1996); see also Sroka v. Sroka, 121 Ohio App. 3d 728, 700 N.E.2d 916 (8th Dist. Cuyahoga County 1997).

[47]See RC 3113.31(A)(1)(a) to RC 3113.31(A)(1)(c).

[48]See Text § 8:3, Statutory elements of domestic violence under RC 3313.31(A)(1)(a), for a discussion of bodily injury and physical harm; J.R. v. E.H., 2017-Ohio-516, 2017 WL 587314 (Ohio Ct. App. 10th Dist. Franklin County 2017).

[49]See RC 2919.25(C); see also RC 3113.31(A)(1)(b); Kuhn v. Kuhn, 2013-Ohio-5807, 2013 WL 6869801 (Ohio Ct. App. 11th Dist. Lake County 2013) (noting that proof of actual violence is not required under RC 3113.31).

[50]See RC 2919.25(A); see also RC 3113.31(A)(1)(a).

[51]See Ankenbruck v. Ankenbruck, 2000 WL 1804360 (Ohio Ct. App. 11th Dist. Trumbull County 2000) (concurring opinion noted slap alone may satisfy either RC 3113.31(A)(1)(a) or RC 3113.31(A)(1)(b) when victim sustains no injury; judge disagreed with what he perceived to be establishment of per se rule indicating that). But see State v. Zuber, 2001-Ohio-2427, 2001 WL 301408 (Ohio Ct. App. 4th Dist. Hocking County 2001) (holding that the infliction of significant pain can constitute physical harm); State v. Wray, 2001-Ohio-2356, 2001 WL 243488 (Ohio Ct. App. 4th Dist. Gallia County 2001); State v. Younker, 2002-Ohio-5376, 2002 WL 31242238 (Ohio Ct.

under RC 3113.31(A)(1)(b), the history of domestic violence against the petitioner or other crimes, wrongs, or acts may be offered into evidence for the limited purpose of demonstrating motive, opportunity, intent, preparation, plan, knowledge, identity, or absence of mistake or accident.[52] Accordingly, the Trumbull County Court of Appeals, in *Visnich v. Visnich*,[53] determined that "testimony regarding appellant's past use of firearms in the context of domestic violence was clearly admissible to prove that appellee was justified in her fear of 'imminent serious physical harm.' "[54]

On the other hand, in *State v. Sanchez*,[55] the Medina Court of Appeals noted that the domestic violence statute[56] does require evidence of physical harm, however minimal.[57] In that case, the offender grabbed the victim's neck. He argued that the evidence concerning his alleged choking of her was insufficient because it did not indicate that she suffered any physical harm as a result of the alleged choking. "Ms. Redman testified that . . . her neck 'was red for a little bit.' This Court has previously held that red marks on a victim's neck are sufficient to satisfy the physical harm requirement of Section 2919.25(A)."[58]

However, the opposite was found in *State v. Nielsen*[59] where the Huron County Court of Appeals held that RC 2919.25(A) includes an attempt to cause physical harm. "We note that RC 2919.25 does not require the state to prove that a victim has sustained actual injury

App. 2d Dist. Darke County 2002).

[52]See Evid.R. 404(B); see also Visnich v. Visnich, 1999 WL 1299300 (Ohio Ct. App. 11th Dist. Trumbull County 1999).

[53]Visnich v. Visnich, 1999 WL 1299300 (Ohio Ct. App. 11th Dist. Trumbull County 1999).

[54]Visnich v. Visnich, 1999 WL 1299300, *3 (Ohio Ct. App. 11th Dist. Trumbull County 1999).

[55]State v. Sanchez, 1994 WL 619796 (Ohio Ct. App. 9th Dist. Medina County 1994); see also State v. Carbone, 1997 WL 799557 (Ohio Ct. App. 11th Dist. Trumbull County 1997) (finding that defendant knowingly attempted to cause physical harm to his wife based on testimony that he pushed his wife off the bed and positioned his elbow in the back of her neck, pinning her against a cedar chest).

[56]RC 2919.25.

[57]See also State v. Mitchell, 2007-Ohio-167, 2007 WL 118001, *2 (Ohio Ct. App. 10th Dist. Franklin County 2007) (noting the definition of physical harm under RC 2901.01(A)(3), "[one] does not have to cause serious injury to be guilty of domestic violence. A defendant may be found guilty of domestic violence if the victim sustains minor injuries or even no injuries at all."). But see Mashburn v. Mashburn, 2000-Ohio-2606, 2000 WL 1726517 (Ohio Ct. App. 7th Dist. Mahoning County 2000) (evidence of physical harm was unnecessary to support finding that domestic violence took place).

[58]State v. Sanchez, 1994 WL 619796, *2 (Ohio Ct. App. 9th Dist. Medina County 1994) (referring to State v. Purvis, 1989 WL 126298 (Ohio Ct. App. 9th Dist. Medina County 1989)); see also State v. Lee, 73 Ohio Misc. 2d 9, 657 N.E.2d 604 (Mun. Ct. 1995) (proof of assaultive domestic violence requires proof of injury or an attempt to cause injury).

[59]State v. Nielsen, 66 Ohio App. 3d 609, 585 N.E.2d 906 (6th Dist. Huron County 1990); see also State v. Blonski, 125 Ohio App. 3d 103, 707 N.E.2d 1168 (9th Dist. Medina County 1997); Ankenbruck v. Ankenbruck, 2000 WL 1804360, *2 (Ohio Ct. App. 11th Dist. Trumbull County 2000) ("While there was no testimony concerning the severity of the slap, that fact is ultimately immaterial to whether or not appellant committed domestic violence as that term is defined in RC 3113.31."); State v. Trefney, 2012-Ohio-869, 2012 WL 691630 (Ohio Ct. App. 11th Dist. Portage County 2012).

since a defendant can be convicted of domestic violence for merely attempting to cause physical harm to a family member."[60]

State v. Bolds[61] articulates the proposition that RC 2919.25(C) need not require acts of actual physical harm. In *Bolds*, the offender committed past acts of domestic violence when he held a match near the victim's face, burning her, and when he threw a brick through her window causing her to be cut by glass. When he threatened her, she was fearful he would harm her. The court reasoned that prior acts of violence and a recent threat are sufficient to qualify under RC 2919.25(C), whether or not there was actual physical harm:

> The State was required to prove . . . that the victim believed the offender would cause physical harm. The domestic violence statute does not require evidence of actual physical harm. It recognizes that the nature of domestic violence is most often a sequence of offensive acts. Thus, the event triggering prosecution is generally a conclusion to a series of events and is not always the most serious conduct. It is often, as here, the proverbial "straw that breaks the camel's back."[62]

Finally, in *Bruns v. Bruns*,[63] the appellant pushed his right elbow into appellee's left breast and threw silverware and plates at her, causing her to duck to avoid being hit. Appellee also testified that she truly feared for her safety at the time of the incident and that there had been prior incidents of abuse.

The appellant argued that there was no evidence that he attempted to cause or recklessly caused appellee bodily injury under RC 3113.31(A)(1)(a) because there were no visible marks or injuries. The Erie County Court of Appeals rejected his argument but noted that the fact that there was evidence that her left breast was sore for several days demonstrated that appellant had caused or attempted to cause her bodily injury.

Of significance is that the Ohio Supreme Court, in *Felton v. Felton*,[64] determined that, for a civil protection order to be granted after a full hearing, the petitioner need only show that the victim or the victim's family or household members are in danger of domestic violence. Many of Ohio's courts have articulated this standard in their

[60]State v. Nielsen, 66 Ohio App. 3d 609, 612, 585 N.E.2d 906 (6th Dist. Huron County 1990); see also City of Cincinnati v. Baarlaer, 115 Ohio App. 3d 521, 685 N.E.2d 836 (1st Dist. Hamilton County 1996); State v. Amos, 1988 WL 4622 (Ohio Ct. App. 11th Dist. Lake County 1988) (court held that pain need not be evidenced by an outward physical manifestation in order to constitute "physical harm"; here, the appellant's kick caused the victim momentary pain and injury); Ankenbruck v. Ankenbruck, 2000 WL 1804360 (Ohio Ct. App. 11th Dist. Trumbull County 2000) (affirming issuance of CPO over appellant's argument that appellee did not testify as to severity of slap or that she had suffered any injury as a result of the blow); State v. Mansour, 2011-Ohio-5438, 2011 WL 5028611 (Ohio Ct. App. 11th Dist. Trumbull County 2011); State v. Whitfield, 2002-Ohio-5984, 2002 WL 31431840 (Ohio Ct. App. 1st Dist. Hamilton County 2002).

[61]State v. Bolds, 1993 WL 35578 (Ohio Ct. App. 5th Dist. Stark County 1993); State v. Younker, 2002-Ohio-5376, 2002 WL 31242238 (Ohio Ct. App. 2d Dist. Darke County 2002); State v. Mansour, 2011-Ohio-5438, 2011 WL 5028611 (Ohio Ct. App. 11th Dist. Trumbull County 2011).

[62]State v. Bolds, 1993 WL 35578, *2 (Ohio Ct. App. 5th Dist. Stark County 1993).

[63]Bruns v. Bruns, 1999 WL 819344 (Ohio Ct. App. 6th Dist. Erie County 1999).

[64]Felton v. Felton, 79 Ohio St. 3d 34, 1997-Ohio-302, 679 N.E.2d 672 (1997).

opinions.[65] *Felton* supports the proposition that actual physical injury is not dispositive for the issuance of a civil protection order.[66] Nor is actual prior physical harm necessary for a finding that petitioner is in danger of domestic violence.[67]

These cases reveal the various legal arguments that can be used in either the civil or criminal context to demonstrate that domestic violence occurred without a showing of actual injury. Because the statutory acts are substantially similar, the reasoning applied by the courts relative to RC 2919.25 may be useful in interpreting RC 3113. 31, the civil domestic violence statute.[68]

Q & A: Absent actual physical injury, what evidence is needed to demonstrate "bodily injury" for purposes of RC 3113. 31(A)(1)(a)?

Absent a statutory definition for "bodily injury," the term "physical harm" may provide the practitioner with an adequate way to evaluate "bodily injury" for purposes of RC 3113.31. As noted earlier in this section, "physical harm" is defined as "any injury, illness or other physiological impairment, regardless of gravity or duration."[69] The criminal case law interpreting this term has indicated that pain is encompassed within the definition.[70]

Therefore, "bodily injury" may be established by evidence of actual physical injury, a showing that the injury complained of has had an adverse effect on the victim's ability to perform physical tasks, or evidence of the degree of pain the respondent caused the victim. For example, punching the victim in the eye and causing a black eye is ev-

---

[65]See Morris v. Stonewall, 1999 WL 1037507 (Ohio Ct. App. 12th Dist. Clinton County 1999); Strong v. Bauman, 1999 WL 317432 (Ohio Ct. App. 2d Dist. Montgomery County 1999); Visnich v. Visnich, 1999 WL 1299300 (Ohio Ct. App. 11th Dist. Trumbull County 1999).

[66]See also Mashburn v. Mashburn, 2000-Ohio-2606, 2000 WL 1726517 (Ohio Ct. App. 7th Dist. Mahoning County 2000).

[67]See Gooderham v. Patterson, 1999 WL 1034472, *4 (Ohio Ct. App. 4th Dist. Gallia County 1999); see also Pierce v. Pierce, 2001-Ohio-2312, 2001 WL 1432047 (Ohio Ct. App. 3d Dist. Marion County 2001); Visnich v. Visnich, 1999 WL 1299300 (Ohio Ct. App. 11th Dist. Trumbull County 1999).

[68]See Sroka v. Sroka, 121 Ohio App. 3d 728, 700 N.E.2d 916 (8th Dist. Cuyahoga County 1997) (rejecting argument that actual injury is required and finding that grabbing the victim by her neck and pushing her down to the floor was sufficient evidence to demonstrate an attempt to injure the victim). But see the concurring opinion in Ankenbruck v. Ankenbruck, 2000 WL 1804360, *4 (Ohio Ct. App. 11th Dist. Trumbull County 2000) ("[T]he fact that certain conduct amounts to domestic violence in the context of a criminal case does not mean the same conduct, per se, warrants a civil protection order.").

[69]RC 2901.01(A)(3); see also Text § 8:3, Statutory elements of domestic violence under RC 3113.31(A)(1)(a); State v. Zuber, 2001-Ohio-2427, 2001 WL 301408 (Ohio Ct. App. 4th Dist. Hocking County 2001); State v. Wray, 2001-Ohio-2356, 2001 WL 243488 (Ohio Ct. App. 4th Dist. Gallia County 2001); see also State v. Ward, 2009-Ohio-3145, 2009 WL 1844486 (Ohio Ct. App. 11th Dist. Geauga County 2009) (where victim said she was not injured, just attacked when defendant grabbed her, pulled her hair, and raised a fist to her. Court affirmed the conviction, holding that visible markings need not be observed); Dorsey v. Dorsey, 2009-Ohio-4894, 2009 WL 2973505 (Ohio Ct. App. 5th Dist. Richland County 2009) (upholding issuance of CPO where wife punched, pushed, and shoved husband is sufficient to support finding that she attempted to cause bodily injury, regardless of whether he sustained any bodily injury).

[70]See preceding paragraphs for pertinent case law.

idence of actual injury. Absent visible signs of injury, testimony by the victim that a punch to the eye caused her to suffer vision problems or swelling that limited her ability to see is sufficient to establish "bodily injury."[71] Finally, evidence of pain is usually sufficient to sustain a finding that the respondent committed an act of domestic violence.[72]

While it is helpful to have independent documentation of these injuries, such as medical records of treatment or emergency-room care, a police officer's report detailing the injury, or a photograph,[73] it is not necessary.[74]

A lack of actual physical injury does not mean that the civil protection order was erroneously granted. Appellate courts that have affirmed the lower court's issuance of a civil protection order have found sufficient credible evidence to prove by a preponderance of the evidence that the victim was in danger of domestic violence.[75] This analysis is used to affirm or reverse a lower court's ruling that the respondent committed acts of domestic violence against the victim.

In many cases, the attempt to cause bodily injury is sufficient to support a finding. For example, in *Bruns v. Bruns*,[76] appellant pinned appellee to the wall and pushed his elbow into her breast. The victim's testimony that her breast was sore for three or four days afterward was sufficient to support a finding that appellant caused or attempted to cause appellee bodily injury.[77]

According to RC 3113.31(A)(1)(b), domestic violence includes "[p]lacing another person by threat of force in fear of imminent serious physical harm or committing a violation of section 2903.211 or 2911.211 of the Revised Code."

---

[71]See, e.g., Sroka v. Sroka, 121 Ohio App. 3d 728, 729, 700 N.E.2d 916 (8th Dist. Cuyahoga County 1997) (victim testified that "her head, neck and arms were injured and as a result she had difficulty moving").

[72]See, e.g., Bruns v. Bruns, 1999 WL 819344 (Ohio Ct. App. 6th Dist. Erie County 1999); State v. Zuber, 2001-Ohio-2427, 2001 WL 301408 (Ohio Ct. App. 4th Dist. Hocking County 2001); State v. Younker, 2002-Ohio-5376, 2002 WL 31242238 (Ohio Ct. App. 2d Dist. Darke County 2002).

[73]State v. Wray, 2001-Ohio-2356, 2001 WL 243488 (Ohio Ct. App. 4th Dist. Gallia County 2001) (discussing admissibility of photographs).

[74]See Felton v. Felton, 79 Ohio St. 3d 34, 44, 1997-Ohio-302, 679 N.E.2d 672 (1997) (noting that "[g]enerally, the victim will not photograph bruises or share these episodes of abuse with others"). See also Text § 16:8, Documenting evidence of domestic violence. State v. Mansour, 2011-Ohio-5438, 2011 WL 5028611 (Ohio Ct. App. 11th Dist. Trumbull County 2011) ("[t]he testimony of a victim that she was injured is sufficient to support a domestic violence conviction, even when a victim 'failed to seek medical treatment, and no photographs were taken of her [injury]' "at*4; quoting State v. Summers, 2003-Ohio-5866, 2003 WL 22470865 (Ohio Ct. App. 11th Dist. Ashtabula County 2003).

[75]See, e.g., Reynolds v. White, 1999 WL 754496 (Ohio Ct. App. 8th Dist. Cuyahoga County 1999); Gooderham v. Patterson, 1999 WL 1034472 (Ohio Ct. App. 4th Dist. Gallia County 1999).

[76]Bruns v. Bruns, 1999 WL 819344 (Ohio Ct. App. 6th Dist. Erie County 1999).

[77]Bruns v. Bruns, 1999 WL 819344, *2 (Ohio Ct. App. 6th Dist. Erie County 1999); see also Sroka v. Sroka, 121 Ohio App. 3d 728, 700 N.E.2d 916 (8th Dist. Cuyahoga County 1997).

Q & A: Does domestic violence include acts of stalking?[78]

Pursuant to RC 3113.31(A)(1)(b), domestic violence, acts of stalking constitute domestic violence so long as there is a family or household member relationship between the petitioner and respondent. Every attorney representing a petitioner and a trial court hearing the testimony of the parties should consider the case law that has interpreted the elements of stalking as set forth in RC 2903.211.[79]

Each assessment must consider what it means to knowingly engage in a pattern of conduct that causes a person to believe that the offender will cause physical harm to the other person or cause mental distress to the other person.[80] A "pattern of conduct" is defined as two or more actions or incidents closely related in time, whether or not there has been a prior conviction based on any of those actions or incidents.[81] "Mental distress" means: a) any mental illness or condition that involves some temporary substantial incapacity; b) any mental illness or condition that would normally require psychiatric treatment, psychological treatment, or other mental health services, whether or not any person requested or received psychiatric treatment, psychological treatment or other mental health services.[82]

When reviewing the grounds for which a petitioner may seek a CPO, it is important to note that while a threat may form the basis for causing mental distress or causing a person to believe the other person will cause physical harm, an explicit threat of harm is not necessary under the stalking prong of the definition of domestic violence.[83]

---

[78]See §§ 9:1 et seq. See also A.M. v. S.M., 2018-Ohio-247, 2018 WL 542357 (Ohio Ct. App. 9th Dist. Summit County 2018) (findings that wife was afraid of husband, that he left nasty emails, screamed at her, called her names and showed up at her workplace uninvited were evidence of stalking behavior along with her testimony).

[79]See also R.C. 2903.213; R.C. 2903.214.

[80]R.C. 2903.211(A)(1); J.B. v. B.Y., 2016-Ohio-7918, 2016 WL 6948078 (Ohio Ct. App. 9th Dist. Medina County 2016) (relying on the stalking prong of RC 3113.31, the appellate court focused on the term "knowingly" as defined in RC 2903.211(A) and determined that taking a gun from the nightstand, sending threatening text messages and breaking the screen door to enter home caused petitioner to fear for his safety and that such fear was reasonable under the circumstances, especially in light of a specific threat to harm him).

[81]R.C. 2903.211(D)(1); McElroy v. McElroy, 2016-Ohio-5148, ¶ 28, 2016 WL 4039227 (Ohio Ct. App. 5th Dist. Guernsey County 2016) (when considering "closely related in time," case law suggests court consider the evidence in the context of all circumstances of the case and actions such as calling father on phone and threatening to fight him, kicking him in the arm and pointing a gun constitute a "pattern of conduct").

[82]R.C. 2903.211(D)(2); Tighe v. Kaiser, 2016-Ohio-1400, 2016 WL 1297407 (Ohio Ct. App. 6th Dist. Ottawa County 2016), appeal not allowed, 146 Ohio St. 3d 1491, 2016, 2016-Ohio-5585, 57 N.E.3d 1171 (2016) (which included trips to the emergency room because of chest pain and difficulty breathing); T.S. v. R.S., 2017-Ohio-281, ¶ 18, 81 N.E.3d 932 (Ohio Ct. App. 9th Dist. Summit County 2017) (where evidence demonstrated that son was unable to function at times and he was observed visibly shaking at hearing, court found mental distress noting that father's actions affected son's mental condition causing him temporary substantial incapacity).

[83]A.D. v. B.D., 2017-Ohio-229, ¶ 30, 2017 WL 277481 (Ohio Ct. App. 9th Dist. Medina County 2017); RC 3113.31(A)(1)(b). See also J.B. v. Harford, 2015-Ohio-13, ¶ 8, 2015 WL 82527 (Ohio Ct. App. 9th Dist. Summit County 2015).

For example, in *R.C. v. J.G.*,[84] respondent continued to contact petitioner despite the fact that the parties had ended their relationship. She contacted the police and obtained a CPO but withdrew it. After discovering that he had come to her business, she again sought a CPO.

On appeal, respondent alleged that the trial court erred in issuing the CPO because there was no proof that respondent knowingly engaged in a pattern of conduct that caused petitioner to believe that he would cause her physical harm. The appellate court relied on the trial court's factual analysis which found that that respondent had engaged in a pattern of conduct that caused the petitioner to fear he would physically harm her based on the breakup of the relationship, several notices for J.G. to stay away from her and a previous protection order.[85]

The appellate court overruled the assignment of error and explained that RC 2903.211 does not require explicit threats of physical harm.[86] That J.C. came to R.G.'s place of business despite cutting off all forms of communication with him and based on her testimony that his actions were designed to personally harass and intimidate her created an environment that caused her to believe he would physically harm her. The court explored "closely related in time" and found that the pattern of conduct could occur over a period of three years.[87]

Conversely, *Olson v. Olson*,[88] appellee sought a domestic violence civil protection order due to appellant's angry, violent outbursts and volatile behavior. She testified that he failed to take his medication for bipolar disorder and that she was concerned for her safety because he has not demonstrated regard for the dangers of firearms (he even

[84]R.C. v. J.G., 2013-Ohio-4265, 2013 WL 5437015 (Ohio Ct. App. 9th Dist. Medina County 2013). But see Olson v. Olson, 2016-Ohio-149, 2016 WL 197117 (Ohio Ct. App. 6th Dist. Wood County 2016) (reversing trial court and finding insufficient evidence showing a pattern of behavior that appellant knew would cause appellee to believe that appellant would cause her physical harm or mental distress. According to the appellate court, the act of pushing appellee on the couch 20 years ago, pushing appellee down to the floor six or seven years ago, firing a BB gun in the house at a target on the wall when no one else was present in the home a year ago and arguing with his son-in-law and yelling at his daughter did not rise to the level of stalking as the evidence failed to show that appellant had engaged in a pattern of conduct, closely related in time that caused appellee to be in fear of physical harm or mental distress. The testimony describes only one incident in the past several years that involved another person and in that situation appellant did not threaten or exert physical force. General allegations that appellant would get angry and yell without providing the context or content of the outburst provides no basis for us to determine that appellee or the daughter feared mental distress or imminent physical harm).

[85]R.C. v. J.G., 2013-Ohio-4265, 2013 WL 5437015, ¶ 10 (Ohio Ct. App. 9th Dist. Medina County 2013).

[86]R.C. v. J.G., 2013-Ohio-4265, 2013 WL 5437015, ¶ 11 (Ohio Ct. App. 9th Dist. Medina County 2013); citing State v. Honeycutt, 2002-Ohio-3490, 2002 WL 1438648 (Ohio Ct. App. 2d Dist. Montgomery County 2002).

[87]R.C. v. J.G., 2013-Ohio-4265, 2013 WL 5437015, ¶ 12 (Ohio Ct. App. 9th Dist. Medina County 2013).

[88]Olson v. Olson, 2016-Ohio-149, 2016 WL 197117 (Ohio Ct. App. 6th Dist. Wood County 2016); McElroy v. McElroy, 2016-Ohio-5148, 2016 WL 4039227 (Ohio Ct. App. 5th Dist. Guernsey County 2016); Tighe v. Kaiser, 2016-Ohio-1400, 2016 WL 1297407 (Ohio Ct. App. 6th Dist. Ottawa County 2016), appeal not allowed, 146 Ohio St. 3d 1491, 2016, 2016-Ohio-5585, 57 N.E.3d 1171 (2016).

admitted he had six long guns and five pistols in the home.) Although there was no evidence presented indicating physical violence directed towards appellee or their daughter and her family, testimony was presented regarding their fear for their safety. The trial court issued the protection order, finding that appellant had engaged in a pattern of behavior that caused mental distress to appellee, her daughter and family.

On appeal, appellant argued that the trial court had abused its discretion when it granted the protection order as there was no evidence of domestic violence. The appellate court first pointed out that a petitioner must show, by a preponderance of the evidence that petitioner and her family were in danger of domestic violence.[89] Focusing on the elements of stalking, " '[I]n determining what constitutes a pattern of conduct for purposes of RC 2903.211(D)(1), courts must take every action into consideration even if, * * * some of the person's actions may not, in isolation, seem particularly threatening.' "[90]

The Court then discussed the term "mental distress" and explained that the statute " 'does not require that the victim actually experience mental distress, but only that the victim believes the stalker would cause mental distress or physical harm.' *Ensley* at ¶ 13, quoting *Bloom v. McBeth*, 5th Dist. Ashland No. 2007-COA-050, 2008-Ohio-4564, ¶ 11. 'Moreover, the testimony of the victim herself as to her fear is sufficient to establish mental distress.' Id., citing *State v. Horsley,* 10th Dist. Franklin No. 05AP-350, 2006-Ohio-1208, ¶ 48. Notably, we recognize that 'mental distress for purposes of the menacing by stalking statute is not mere mental stress or annoyance.' Fonndessey v. Simon, 6th Dist. Ottawa No. OT-11-041, 2013-Ohio-3465, ¶ 19, quoting *Caban v. Ransome*, 7th Dist. Mahoning No. 08 MA 36, 2009-Ohio-1034, ¶ 29."[91]

After applying this analysis to the facts of the case, the Court found that the evidence was insufficient to support the issuance of a domestic violence CPO. It determined that there had only been one confrontational incident in the past several years in which there was no threat made or physical force exerted. "[General] allegations that appellant would get angry and yell without providing the context or content of the outburst provides no basis for us to determine that appellee or the daughter feared mental distress or imminent physical harm."[92]

This case serves as a warning to all attorneys who file petitions for civil protection orders in which a threat of harm or mental distress

---

[89] Olson v. Olson, 2016-Ohio-149, 2016 WL 197117 (Ohio Ct. App. 6th Dist. Wood County 2016).

[90] Olson v. Olson, 2016-Ohio-149, 2016 WL 197117 (Ohio Ct. App. 6th Dist. Wood County 2016); citing Ensley v. Glover, 2012-Ohio-4487, 2012 WL 4480734, ¶ 10 (Ohio Ct. App. 6th Dist. Lucas County 2012); quoting Middletown v. Jones, 167 Ohio App. 3d 679, 2006-Ohio-3465, 856 N.E.2d 1003, ¶ 10 (12th Dist. Butler County 2006).

[91] Olson v. Olson, 2016-Ohio-149, 2016 WL 197117, ¶ 15 (Ohio Ct. App. 6th Dist. Wood County 2016); Tighe v. Kaiser, 2016-Ohio-1400, 2016 WL 1297407 (Ohio Ct. App. 6th Dist. Ottawa County 2016), appeal not allowed, 146 Ohio St. 3d 1491, 2016, 2016-Ohio-5585, 57 N.E.3d 1171 (2016).

[92] Olson v. Olson, 2016-Ohio-149, 2016 WL 197117, ¶ 17 (Ohio Ct. App. 6th Dist. Wood County 2016).

forms the basis of the petition. The court focused its attention to the context and content of the action or incident, meaning that if a threat is alleged or if stalking is alleged, it is incumbent upon counsel to specifically describe the threat or conduct causing petitioner to believe that the stalker would cause mental distress or physical harm.

Additionally, appellate courts reviewing trial court decisions have focused their analyses of "threatening" conduct through the lens of stalking cases that have examined "pattern of conduct" and "mental distress" as well as those domestic violence cases that interpreted the concept of threat in context of fear and the reasonableness of that fear.[93]

Q & A: Are more petitioners seeking civil protection orders under RC 3113.31 based on acts of stalking?

Apparently so. For example, in *Johnson v. Komisarek*,[94] appellee sought a CPO because appellant pulled out a gun, pointed it at his chest and stated that he did not want to live if he couldn't have appellee. When she was able to escape him, she called her boyfriend and during the call, appellant grabbed the phone from her, took it back into the garage and smashed it with a sledgehammer. He then pushed her away from his motorcycle and into a toolbox causing bruising.

He appealed the granting of the CPO, arguing that the trial court abused its discretion when it found that appellee was in danger of domestic violence. The appellate court found that appellant's pulling the gun on himself and smashing the telephone were enough to establish that he had engaged in a pattern of conduct in which he knowingly caused appellee mental distress and a fear of physical harm which are prohibited under the stalking prong of the domestic violence statute. "Even excluding the injuries appellee sustained as a result of appellant pushing her into his toolbox, we find that the trial court's grant of the domestic violence civil protection order was appropriate and was not unreasonable, arbitrary, or unconscionable. The smashing of appellee's phone and brandishing of a firearm were sufficient to cause appellee to experience mental distress and to believe that she was in danger of physical harm under RC 2903.211(A)(1)."[95]

Likewise, in *Majeed v. Majeed*,[96] appellee sought a CPO against her husband because of his mental abuse and controlling behavior. He had come to her separate residence, blocked her driveway and refused to allow her to go to her therapy appointments. "She stated that she was scared to come outside and for her life, and that he controlled her access to food and money."[97] She also testified that he controlled how she drives, that he had forbidden her to work, that he pays for

[93] J.B. v. B.Y., 2016-Ohio-7918, 2016 WL 6948078 (Ohio Ct. App. 9th Dist. Medina County 2016).

[94] Johnson v. Komisarek, 2017-Ohio-2580, 2017 WL 1534901 (Ohio Ct. App. 6th Dist. Lucas County 2017).

[95] Johnson v. Komisarek, 2017-Ohio-2580, ¶ 10, 2017 WL 1534901 (Ohio Ct. App. 6th Dist. Lucas County 2017).

[96] Majeed v. Majeed, 2016-Ohio-7243, 2016 WL 5887174 (Ohio Ct. App. 2d Dist. Montgomery County 2016).

[97] Majeed v. Majeed, 2016-Ohio-7243, ¶ 2, 2016 WL 5887174 (Ohio Ct. App. 2d Dist. Montgomery County 2016).

everything and that she suffers from anxiety. She also described that in the past he shoved her neck while they were driving causing her to suffer a cervical strain, that he had killed one of the puppies and that she was unable to open a day care at her home because he came into the backyard took off his clothes and acted as if he was "ejaculating on me."[98]

Appellant claimed that the trial court erred when it issued the CPO, arguing that she had not proven her case by a preponderance of the evidence. The court focused on stalking behaviors under RC 3113. 31(A)(1)(b)[99] and determined that appellee had proven that she was in need of a CPO because of appellant's mental abuse of her, her fear and the anxiety she suffered.[100]

And in *Barrett v. Barrett*,[101] petitioner-appellee obtained a DVCPO based on a series of incidents- that she had been in hiding since the date of the separation when he told her he would "see her dead" before he would let her divorce him, that he showed her a gun when he returned to the home to retrieve some items, and that he appeared at the bank and the McDonald's lot causing her to believe that he had a tracking device put on her car. She testified that respondent-appellant's pattern of conduct was causing her mental distress.

Appellant appealed the decision granting a DVCPO on the ground that appellee had failed to prove any of the statutory elements of the domestic violence statute. Noting that domestic violence includes the commission of a violation of the stalking statute, the court examined the statutory factors and determined that she had proven that appellant had been stalking her. In that he had installed a tracking device in the car and appeared at various locations where she had been and his comments to her intimated a violent act that would necessitate police involvement,[102] appellee believed that he would hurt her and cause her mental distress. In fact, she testified that his behavior caused her to suffer a breakdown.

In this case, petitioner-appellee had presented evidence that appellant's behavior caused her to fear for her safety. Appellant had attempted to argue that she had not shown that he had threatened her and that she failed to show evidence of other temporary and substantial mental incapacity. "However, Beatrice presented evidence of Larry's stalking conduct and of mental distress she suffered that went beyond fearing for safety but culminated in a mental breakdown."[103] Therefore, there was competent and credible evidence to support the trial court's decision to grant the civil protection order.

---

[98]Majeed v. Majeed, 2016-Ohio-7243, ¶ 6, 2016 WL 5887174 (Ohio Ct. App. 2d Dist. Montgomery County 2016).

[99]See also McElroy v. McElroy, 2016-Ohio-5148, 2016 WL 4039227 (Ohio Ct. App. 5th Dist. Guernsey County 2016).

[100]T.S. v. R.S., 2017-Ohio-281, 81 N.E.3d 932 (Ohio Ct. App. 9th Dist. Summit County 2017).

[101]Barrett v. Barrett, 2017-Ohio-250, 2017 WL 283480 (Ohio Ct. App. 12th Dist. Warren County 2017).

[102]Barrett v. Barrett, 2017-Ohio-250, ¶ 22, 2017 WL 283480 (Ohio Ct. App. 12th Dist. Warren County 2017).

[103]Barrett v. Barrett, 2017-Ohio-250, ¶ 24, 2017 WL 283480 (Ohio Ct. App. 12th Dist. Warren County 2017).

Of importance is that the court considered the case law and legal analyses of the appellate courts that have issued decisions in the civil stalking protection order arena. For example, the court found that "a DVCPO petitioner is not required to prove that he or she actually suffered mental distress.[104] Instead, menacing by stalking only requires proof that the offender's pattern of conduct would cause the victim to believe that the offender *will cause* the victim mental distress."[105]

Q & A: Does it matter to a reviewing court whether the lower court identified a specific ground under RC 3113.31(A)(1) in determining that a respondent engaged in acts of domestic violence for purposes of issuing a civil protection order?[106]

Courts of appeals do not seem to predicate sustaining a trial court's issuance of a civil protection order on a specific ground. The Cuyahoga Court of Appeals aptly illustrated this point in *Reynolds v. White*.[107] In *Reynolds*, the petitioner requested a civil protection order. The trial court issued the order, but the judgment entry did not identify the precise ground on which the court determined that the defendant had engaged in acts or threats of domestic violence against his daughter.

On appeal, the appellant argued that his conduct did not cause the minor child to be an "abused child" as defined in RC 3113.31(A)(1)(c). Since there was no evidence to support that ground, he argued that the trial court erred when it found that he committed domestic violence. While the appellate court agreed that appellant's conduct did not permit a finding that the child was an "abused child," "the evidence was sufficient to permit a finding that [defendant] recklessly caused bodily injury under RC 3113.31(A)(1)(a) and/or placed [the child] in reasonable fear of imminent serious physical harm under RC 3113.31(A)(1)(b), either one of which provides independent grounds to affirm the judgment."[108]

In a footnote, the court added that "if the trial court had errone-

[104] Wulf v. Opp, 2015-Ohio-3285, ¶ 10, 2015 WL 4878495 (Ohio Ct. App. 12th Dist. Clermont County 2015); State v. Horsley, 2006-Ohio-1208, ¶ 47, 2006 WL 648849 (Ohio Ct. App. 10th Dist. Franklin County 2006).

[105] Barrett v. Barrett, 2017-Ohio-250, ¶ 18, 2017 WL 283480 (Ohio Ct. App. 12th Dist. Warren County 2017).

[106] A.M. v. S.M., 2018-Ohio-247, ¶ 17, 2018 WL 542357 (Ohio Ct. App. 9th Dist. Summit County 2018) (dissent pointed out that the trial court did not specify under which subsection of RC 3113.1(A)(1) husband was found to have committed domestic violence with respect to the children and noted that the wife's testimony that husband got physical with the son, left bruises over his body, that both children attempted suicide, that daughter cut herself when respondent's name was mentioned and that both children were fearful of husband did not demonstrate that the alleged domestic violence fit any of the four subsections of RC 3113.31(A)(1) or that the children had a reasonable fear of imminent future harm from their father).

[107] Reynolds v. White, 1999 WL 754496 (Ohio Ct. App. 8th Dist. Cuyahoga County 1999); see also Trent v. Trent, 1999 WL 298073 (Ohio Ct. App. 12th Dist. Preble County 1999); Myers v. Myers, 2005-Ohio-7040, 2005 WL 3610332 (Ohio Ct. App. 5th Dist. Muskingum County 2005) (holding that placing the petitioner by threat of force in fear of imminent serious physical harm is an alternative to committing an act of menacing by stalking and either of which may be the reason for which a CPO may be granted; a petitioner will be able to obtain a CPO based on an act of menacing by stalking even though no evidence is presented regarding a threat of imminent serious physical harm).

[108] Reynolds v. White, 1999 WL 754496, *6 (Ohio Ct. App. 8th Dist. Cuyahoga

ously found domestic violence under RC 3113.31(A)(1)(c), we would still be bound to affirm the judgment because a reviewing court may not reverse a correct judgment merely because erroneous reasons were assigned as a basis thereof."[109]

Similarly, in *Bruns v. Bruns*,[110] the appellant argued that the finding of domestic violence must be overturned because the court failed to specifically find that appellant had attempted to cause or caused appellee serious bodily injury. The court responded:

> We acknowledge that the particular statutory language was not used; however, the magistrate did state that appellant committed an act of "domestic violence" by restraining appellee against a wall with his elbow to her breast area. Thus, by using the term "domestic violence," and describing the incident, the magistrate substantially complied with the statute and made a proper finding under RC 3113.31.[111]

Obviously, the appellate courts appear to concentrate more on the acts in question rather than relying on a specific statutory provision to support the conclusion that there was sufficient credible evidence of domestic violence.[112] This should aid the family law practitioner who requests a civil protection order based on RC 3113.31(A)(1)(a) but is unable to prove the case. Using the *Reynolds* analysis, the court may still determine that the respondent committed acts of domestic violence and a finding of domestic violence may be predicated on other grounds.[113]

County 1999).

[109]Reynolds v. White, 1999 WL 754496, *6 (Ohio Ct. App. 8th Dist. Cuyahoga County 1999). See also Trent v. Trent, 1999 WL 298073 (Ohio Ct. App. 12th Dist. Preble County 1999); Halley v. Ashley, 1997 WL 760662 (Ohio Ct. App. 9th Dist. Summit County 1997).

[110]Bruns v. Bruns, 1999 WL 819344 (Ohio Ct. App. 6th Dist. Erie County 1999).

[111]Bruns v. Bruns, 1999 WL 819344, *2 (Ohio Ct. App. 6th Dist. Erie County 1999).

[112]See also Dickson v. Miller, 2012-Ohio-2142, 2012 WL 1664012 (Ohio Ct. App. 5th Dist. Fairfield County 2012). See for example, A.M. v. D.L., 2017-Ohio-5621, 2017 WL 2870214 (Ohio Ct. App. 9th Dist. Medina County 2017) (although the trial court noted that respondent engaged in a pattern of conduct under RC 3113.31(A)(1)(b), the appellate court found that the trial court did not rely on a "pattern of conduct" standard for domestic violence. Rather, the trial court noted that under RC 3113.31(A)(1), domestic violence is found when petitioners can prove that they are in fear of imminent serious physical harm and that the fear was reasonable. (at ¶ 6.) Appellant's claim that the incidents set forth in the protection order were too remote in time from one another to be considered a "pattern of conduct" was found to be meritless in that the court did not rely on a "pattern of conduct" standard in its analysis to find that domestic violence did occur.(at ¶ 7))

[113]See A.D. v. B.D., 2017-Ohio-229, 2017 WL 277481 (Ohio Ct. App. 9th Dist. Medina County 2017) (in order to grant a CPO, a trial court must find that petitioner established that petitioner was in danger of domestic violence. Absent a specific finding with respect to which prong of the definition under RC 3113.31 was satisfied, the appellate court sought to examine the testimony of the full hearing to determine if any prong was satisfied. at ¶ 10).

§ 8:6 Statutory elements of domestic violence under RC 3113.31(A)(1)(c)

To commit an act of domestic violence under RC 3113.31(A)(1)(c),[1] a respondent must:

(1) commit an act
(2) with respect to a child
(3) resulting in the child being an abused child, as defined in RC 2151.031.[2]

According to RC 2151.031, an abused child is defined as any child who:

(A) Is the victim of "sexual activity" as defined under Chapter 2907 . . .;[3]
(B) Is endangered as defined in [RC] 2919.22 . . .;[4]
(C) Exhibits evidence of any physical or mental injury[5] or death, inflicted other than by accidental means,[6] or an injury or death which is at variance with the history given of it. Except as provided in division (D) of this section, a child exhibiting evidence of corporal punishment or other physical disciplinary measure by a parent, guardian, custodian, person having custody or control, or person in loco parentis of a child is not an abused child under this division if the measure is not prohibited under [RC] 2919.22 . . .; [or]
(D) Because of the acts of his parents, guardian, or custodian, suffers physical or mental injury that harms or threatens to harm the child's health or welfare.[7]

RC 2919.22 defines endangering children as follows:

(A) No person, who is the parent, guardian, custodian, person hav-

[Section 8:6]

[1]See McBride v. McBride, 2012-Ohio-2146, 971 N.E.2d 1007 (Ohio Ct. App. 12th Dist. Butler County 2012) (discussion of relevant definitions encompassed within statutory language).

[2]See also M.C. v. B.K., 2015-Ohio-560, 2015 WL 628342 (Ohio Ct. App. 6th Dist. Sandusky County 2015) (discussing RC 2151.031(D)).

[3]Sanchez v. Sanchez, 2016-Ohio-4933, 2016 WL 3745699 (Ohio Ct. App. 1st Dist. Hamilton County 2016). But see K.B. v. B.B., 2017-Ohio-71, 80 N.E.3d 1173 (Ohio Ct. App. 9th Dist. Summit County 2017) ("defining sexual activity"; a clothed child sleeping with her naked father in the bed is not an abused child where no evidence was presented that father touched the child or committed any act with respect to the child that would cause child to be a victim of sexual activity and therefore an abused child).

[4]RC 2919.22 defines endangering a child as creating a substantial risk to the health or safety of the child by violating a duty of care, protection, or support.

[5]See also Vera v. Yellowrobe, 2006-Ohio-3911, 2006 WL 2130726 (Ohio Ct. App. 10th Dist. Franklin County 2006).

[6]Hynd v. Roesch, 2016-Ohio-7143, 2016 WL 5720642 (Ohio Ct. App. 11th Dist. Ashtabula County 2016) (finding that the child fell, was not abused and that the incident was of accidental means).

[7]See, e.g., Rielinger v. Rielinger, 2009-Ohio-1236, 2009 WL 714185 (Ohio Ct. App. 8th Dist. Cuyahoga County 2009) (finding that the cumulative effect of being tardy and absent from school can be domestic violence).

ing custody or control,[8] or person in loco parentis of a child under eighteen years of age[9] or a mentally or physically handicapped child under twenty-one years of age, shall create a substantial risk to the health or safety of the child,[10] by violating a duty of care,[11] protection,[12] or support.[13]

. . .

(B) No person shall do any of the following:

(1) Abuse the child;

(2) Torture or cruelly abuse the child;

(3) Administer corporal punishment[14] or other physical disciplinary measure, or physically restrain the child in a cruel manner or for a prolonged period, which punishment, discipline, or restraint is excessive under the circumstances and creates a substantial risk of serious physical harm to the child;[15]

---

[8]See also State v. Masterson, 2007-Ohio-1145, 2007 WL 764533 (Ohio Ct. App. 8th Dist. Cuyahoga County 2007).

[9]Glancy v. Spradley, 2012-Ohio-4224, 2012 WL 4074986 (Ohio Ct. App. 12th Dist. Butler County 2012) (discussing who has standing as a person "in loco parentis" and finding that live-in boyfriend who engaged in "switching" minor child with plastic for misbehaving was not prohibited by R.C. 2919.22).

[10]Ferris v. Ferris, 2006-Ohio-878, 2006 WL 456811, *4 (Ohio Ct. App. 12th Dist. Clermont County 2006) (placing children in an environment where there is a substantial risk to their health and safety constitutes one form or domestic violence); see also Hicks v. Barker, 2009-Ohio-2445, 2009 WL 1456532 (Ohio Ct. App. 12th Dist. Warren County 2009); Allan v. Allan, 2014-Ohio-5039, 2014 WL 6065710 (Ohio Ct. App. 8th Dist. Cuyahoga County 2014) (children were endangered because they were in the line of fire of their father's "rampage" and physical abuse against the mother); State v. Shannon, 2017-Ohio-31, 82 N.E.3d 493 (Ohio Ct. App. 5th Dist. Muskingum County 2017).

[11]Hynd v. Roesch, 2016-Ohio-7143, 2016 WL 5720642 (Ohio Ct. App. 11th Dist. Ashtabula County 2016) (Court determined that child not an abused child where child fell and mother argued that father violated his duty of care by not immediately providing child with medical care).

[12]J.M. v. M.M., 2016-Ohio-5368, ¶ 23, 2016 WL 4272340 (Ohio Ct. App. 9th Dist. Medina County 2016) (argument that father violated duty of protection by chasing mother and children through the parking lot at 20 miles per hour did not warrant issuance of a CPO as no evidence presented to suggest father intended to inflict serious bodily harm to children or that such injury was a strong probability as opposed to a remote or significant possibility).

[13]See, e.g., State v. Kamel, 12 Ohio St. 3d 306, 466 N.E.2d 860 (1984); State v. Elliott, 104 Ohio App. 3d 812, 663 N.E.2d 412 (10th Dist. Franklin County 1995); Couch v. Harrison, 2001-Ohio-4199, 2001 WL 121108 (Ohio Ct. App. 12th Dist. Clermont County 2001); Brubaker v. Farr, 2006-Ohio-2001, 2006 WL 1062102 (Ohio Ct. App. 3d Dist. Shelby County 2006) (noting that court need not find that any person has been convicted of child endangering in order to find that the child is abused per RC 2151.031(B)); State v. Hall, 2006-Ohio-1446, 2006 WL 763064 (Ohio Ct. App. 11th Dist. Ashtabula County 2006) (holding that the elements of child endangering have been proven even though there was not actual harm to the child).

[14]Judge Leonard P. Edwards, Corporal Punishment & the Legal System, 36 Santa Clara L. Rev. 983 (1996); see also David Orentlicher, Spanking and Other Corporal Punishment of Children by Parents: Overvaluing Pain, Undervaluing Children, 35 Houston L. Rev. 147 (1998).

[15]But see Rader v. Rader, 2007-Ohio-4288, 2007 WL 2390815, *3 (Ohio Ct. App. 5th Dist. Licking County 2007) (affirmed denial of CPO for 3 1/2 year old who was spanked, hit on the butt several times with a piece of wood trim; mother observed

(4) Repeatedly administer unwarranted disciplinary measures to the child, when there is a substantial risk that such conduct, if continued, will seriously impair or retard the child's mental health or development.[16]

"Substantial risk" is defined in RC 2901.01(A)(8) as "a strong possibility, as contrasted with a remote or significant possibility, that a certain result may occur or that certain circumstances may exist."[17] *Black's Law Dictionary* defines "corporal punishment" as "[p]hysical punishment; any kind of punishment of or inflicted on the body."[18] "An injury from corporal punishment will not result in child abuse unless the punishment is excessive under the circumstances and creates a substantial risk of harm to the child or the punishment is repeatedly administered, is unwarranted, and creates a substantial risk of seriously impairing the child's mental health or development."[19]

The culpable mental state of "recklessness" is an essential element of the crime of child endangering.[20] The state of mind in determining the culpability of recklessness still involves a subjective determination.

---

redness, swelling and bruising and lacerations. Court stated that ". . . while we share the trial court's overall concern that appellee used excessive punishment. . . we are unpersuaded the court abused its discretion in denying the issuance of a CPO.).

[16]See also Hicks v. Barker, 2009-Ohio-2445, 2009 WL 1456532 (Ohio Ct. App. 12th Dist. Warren County 2009); State v. Reeves, 2015-Ohio-363, 2015 WL 420015 (Ohio Ct. App. 12th Dist. Fayette County 2015).

[17]See also State v. Wright, 31 Ohio App. 3d 232, 510 N.E.2d 827 (10th Dist. Franklin County 1986) (discussing the concept of substantial risk and applying it to a specific fact pattern in a child endangering case); Ferris v. Ferris, 2006-Ohio-878, 2006 WL 456811, *2 (Ohio Ct. App. 12th Dist. Clermont County 2006) (holding that because one child was abused by her stepbrother, the respondent was endangering the two other children by bringing them around the stepbrother; "If Sarah was harmed or abused by Joseph, then in bringing her children around Joseph, appellant was creating a substantial risk to their health and safety and causing them to become abused children"); see also Clark v. Clark, 114 Ohio App. 3d 558, 683 N.E.2d 800 (12th Dist. Butler County 1996) (discussing the concepts of substantial risk of serious physical harm and abuse); Allan v. Allan, 2014-Ohio-5039, 2014 WL 6065710 (Ohio Ct. App. 8th Dist. Cuyahoga County 2014); Kohus v. Daly, 2016-Ohio-73, 2016 WL 116121 (Ohio Ct. App. 12th Dist. Clermont County 2016); J.M. v. M.M., 2016-Ohio-5368, 2016 WL 4272340 (Ohio Ct. App. 9th Dist. Medina County 2016).

[18]Black's Law Dictionary (6th ed.) p 339; see also State v. Ivey, 98 Ohio App. 3d 249, 648 N.E.2d 519 (8th Dist. Cuyahoga County 1994).

[19]McBride v. McBride, 2012-Ohio-2146, ¶ 12, 971 N.E.2d 1007, 1011 (Ohio Ct. App. 12th Dist. Butler County 2012), citing R.C. 2919.22(B)(3) and (4); Bowman v. Bowman, 2014-Ohio-2851, 2014 WL 2957475 (Ohio Ct. App. 9th Dist. Medina County 2014) (slapping 11 year old in the face with enough force to knock her to the ground, leaving a hand print and causing her lip to swell all because she would not hand over an iPod); Friedlander v. Friedlander, 2014-Ohio-2180, 2014 WL 2168238 (Ohio Ct. App. 8th Dist. Cuyahoga County 2014); Martindale v. Martindale, 2017-Ohio-9266, ¶ 55, 102 N.E.3d 19 (Ohio Ct. App. 4th Dist. Athens County 2017) (noting that the children were placed in substantial risk to their health and safety due to witnessing domestic violence (in an unsafe environment)).

[20]RC 2901.22(C); State v. Adams, 62 Ohio St. 2d 151, 16 Ohio Op. 3d 169, 404 N.E.2d 144, 16 A.L.R.4th 344 (1980); State v. O'Brien, 30 Ohio St. 3d 122, 508 N.E.2d 144 (1987); State v. Williams, 21 Ohio App. 3d 12, 486 N.E.2d 113 (9th Dist. Summit County 1984); see also State v. McGee, 79 Ohio St. 3d 193, 1997-Ohio-156, 680 N.E.2d 975 (1997); Newburgh Hts. v. Cole, 166 Ohio App. 3d 826, 828, 2006-Ohio-2463, ¶ 8, 853 N.E.2d 689, 690 (8th Dist. Cuyahoga County 2006) ("Because the statute does not specify the degree of culpability or indicate an intent to impose strict liability, the state must prove that the defendant acted recklessly"; the appellate court reversed

"[T]he court can consider the circumstances surrounding the act and determine the state of mind from inferences arising from those circumstances to determine whether criminal recklessness exists."[21]

Q & A: Must children be physically injured before they can be considered "abused children" under RC 2151.031(B)?

According to the Cuyahoga County Court of Appeals, the answer is no. In *Allan v. Allan*,[22] wife filed for a CPO against her husband. The children had "witnessed their father hit their mother, drag her by the hair and choke her to the point where she could not breathe and urinated on herself. Two of their sons even jumped on their father to get him off their mother. He then continued on a rampage while the children were on their parent's bed with their mother, smashing everything on the dresser, threatening to knock the 'dresser mirror' onto all of them, and pounding on the headboard of the bed when they were all on it to the point of breaking it."[23]

On appeal, husband claimed that the CPO should not have been granted with respect to the children. He argued that because the children were not injured, they could not be abused children because there was never any " 'substantial risk to the health or safety of [the] children sitting on the bed.' "[24]

The appellate court determined that "physical injury is not required to establish that a child is an abused child under RC 2151.031(B) when that child is an endangered child under RC 2919.22."[25]

The Court then found that the evidence demonstrated that the children were endangered because their father's reckless actions created a substantial risk of harm to their health and safety, thereby making them abused children as defined in RC 2151.031(B) and RC 2919.22(A).[26]

---

appellant's conviction for child endangering and domestic violence); City of Brooklyn v. Muniz, 2008-Ohio-54, 2008 WL 98200 (Ohio Ct. App. 8th Dist. Cuyahoga County 2008) (dissent's discussion of "substantial risk").

[21]State v. Voland, 99 Ohio Misc. 2d 61, 69, 716 N.E.2d 299 (C.P. 1999); see also State v. Wright, 31 Ohio App. 3d 232, 510 N.E.2d 827 (10th Dist. Franklin County 1986).

[22]Allan v. Allan, 2014-Ohio-5039, 2014 WL 6065710 (Ohio Ct. App. 8th Dist. Cuyahoga County 2014).

[23]Allan v. Allan, 2014-Ohio-5039, 2014 WL 6065710, ¶ 41 (Ohio Ct. App. 8th Dist. Cuyahoga County 2014).

[24]Allan v. Allan, 2014-Ohio-5039, 2014 WL 6065710, ¶ 40 (Ohio Ct. App. 8th Dist. Cuyahoga County 2014).

[25]Allan v. Allan, 2014-Ohio-5039, 2014 WL 6065710, ¶ 40 (Ohio Ct. App. 8th Dist. Cuyahoga County 2014); citing, State v. Griffin, 2014-Ohio-690, 2014 WL 795102 (Ohio Ct. App. 5th Dist. Stark County 2014) (where mother was convicted of child endangering after she allowed her ex boyfriend to come into her home when her two children were present; mother had previously obtained a CPO against him for holding a knife to her throat).

[26]See Kohus v. Daly, 2016-Ohio-73, 2016 WL 116121 (Ohio Ct. App. 12th Dist. Clermont County 2016) (grounds for issuance of CPO were that the children stayed in the car all night with mother's boyfriend while she worked; they lived in various hotels within the 1.5 months prior to her testimony; they moved around a lot; mother left them alone for periods of time and that mother's boyfriend beat mother).

Q & A: Does drinking beer while operating a motor vehicle while a minor child is in that vehicle create a substantial risk of harm in violation of R.C. 3113.31(A)(1)(c)?

Yes, according to *Hoyt v. Heindell*.[27] In that case, the father of a child requested a CPO for domestic violence on behalf of his child against the mother and her husband because the mother's husband would drink beer while driving with the minor child in the car. Sometimes, the mother would also drink in the car. The child testified that Richard Heindell (the mother's husband) often drank beer while operating the motor vehicle.

On appeal, appellants argued that the evidence was insufficient to support a finding of domestic violence by reason of child endangerment and that they could only be guilty of a violation of the open container law because they had not yet driven with the minor child when the police became involved. However, during a search of the car, four empty beer cans were discovered in the center console.

The appellate court found that there was ample evidence to suggest that appellant consumed more than one beer while driving and that appellant created a substantial risk to the health or safety of the minor child. "We note that not only were the Heindells placing E.H. in direct harm by their actions, they were also placing him in indirect harm, by implicitly telling a teenager that it is acceptable for someone to consume beer while driving a motor vehicle."[28]

The Court relied on R.C. 31113.31(A)(1)(C), which defines domestic violence as committing any act with respect to a child that would result in the child being an abused child, as defined in R.C. 2151.031. Pursuant to R.C. 2151.031(B), an abused child includes a child who is endangered under R.C. 2919.22. R.C. 2919.22(A) provides that no person who is the parent, guardian, custodian or person in loco parentis of a child under 18 years of age shall create a substantial risk to the health or safety of the child by violating a duty of care, protection or support.

Because evidence was presented that such behavior was condoned or allowed by the child's mother and that such actions occurred on several occasions, the appellate court determined that the Heindells acted recklessly by consuming beer and driving while the minor child was in the car.

Lastly, the Heindells also contended that there was no evidence presented that the child was in fear of their drinking while driving. However, the court's review of the record indicated that the minor child had warned appellants that consuming alcohol while driving could lead to a "car crash" and thus, evidence was presented that the child had a reasonable fear of the Heindells' actions.[29]

Based on the above, the Lake County Court of Appeals held that "the Heindells created a substantial risk to the health and safety of

---

[27]Hoyt v. Heindell, 191 Ohio App. 3d 373, 2010-Ohio-6058, 946 N.E.2d 258 (11th Dist. Lake County 2010).

[28]Hoyt v. Heindell, 191 Ohio App. 3d 373, 2010-Ohio-6058, 946 N.E.2d 258 (11th Dist. Lake County 2010).

[29]Hoyt v. Heindell, 191 Ohio App. 3d 373, 2010-Ohio-6058, 946 N.E.2d 258 (11th Dist. Lake County 2010).

the minor child by placing him in a motor vehicle in which the driver was consuming beer on multiple occasions."[30] "[W]e note that, as this matter concerns the issuance of civil protection orders, the petitioner needed only to show by a preponderance of the evidence that E.H. was in danger of domestic violence and our review is limited to whether the trial court abused its discretion."[31]

However, a judge who dissented in part focused on the fact that on the day in question, the Heindells had not driven with the minor child in the car while drinking beer. The judge found that "there is insufficient evidence, based on the elements of domestic violence, to justify a civil protection order, as the acts of appellant in this case do not satisfy the elements under RC 3113.31."[32] An open container violation is insufficient, standing alone, to justify a civil protection order as it does not rise to the level of recklessness necessary to sustain either domestic violence under R.C. 2919.22(A) or 3113.31(A). Without evidence that the child was in the car or that appellants had consumed alcohol on that date or that the minor child was harmed, the actions of the appellant did not rise to a level of domestic violence or child endangerment as defined by statute.

Q & A: Is an attorney limited to RC 3113.31(A)(1)(c) when filing for a protection order on behalf of a child?

No. Although it is useful for a practitioner to first consider RC 3113.31(A)(1)(c) as a ground for filing a civil protection order on behalf of a child because it specifically refers to child abuse, the language of the domestic violence statute does not preclude utilizing either RC 3113.31(A)(1)(a) or RC 3113.31(A)(1)(b).[33] A parent may obtain a civil protection order on behalf of a child because the other parent recklessly caused bodily injury to the child[34] or because the parent threatened the child with further bodily harm.[35] It is the attorney who must ultimately decide within which statutory provision the specific act of domestic violence committed by the respondent more readily fits.

The statutory language does not restrict domestic violence against a child to only those acts that result in the child being an abused child under RC 2151.031.[36] RC 3113.31(A)(1) defines "domestic violence" as:

---

[30] Hoyt v. Heindell, 191 Ohio App. 3d 373, 2010-Ohio-6058, 946 N.E.2d 258 (11th Dist. Lake County 2010).

[31] Hoyt v. Heindell, 191 Ohio App. 3d 373, 2010-Ohio-6058, 946 N.E.2d 258 (11th Dist. Lake County 2010).

[32] Hoyt v. Heindell, 191 Ohio App. 3d 373, 2010-Ohio-6058, 946 N.E.2d 258 (11th Dist. Lake County 2010) (O'Toole, J., concurring in part and dissenting in part).

[33] See Reynolds v. White, 1999 WL 754496 (Ohio Ct. App. 8th Dist. Cuyahoga County 1999).

[34] RC 3113.31(A)(1)(a). But see H.C. v. R.K., 2016-Ohio-1572, 2016 WL 1555594 (Ohio Ct. App. 9th Dist. Medina County 2016) (despite a Children and Family Services referral by the child's pediatrician and ample testimony of abuse towards the child by his father and fear of the father, the appellate court affirmed the trial court's denial of a CPO because none of the professional witnesses could definitely say that R.K. abused his son, committed an act of domestic violence against his son or posed an ongoing or future threat to the safety of his son).

[35] RC 3113.31(A)(1)(b).

[36] See Reynolds v. White, 1999 WL 754496 (Ohio Ct. App. 8th Dist. Cuyahoga

the occurrence of one *or more* [emphasis added] of the following acts against a family or household member:

(a) Attempting to cause or recklessly causing bodily injury;

(b) Placing another person by the threat of force in fear of imminent serious physical harm . . .;

(c) Committing any act with respect to a child that would result in the child being an abused child, as defined in section 2151.031 of the Revised Code.

The statute only requires one of the acts cited above as grounds for obtaining a protection order. Additionally, the statute specifically defines a family or household member to encompass a child of either the respondent or the victim.[37]

Clearly, the intent of the statute is to provide immediate protection for all family and household members who are subjected to acts of domestic violence, regardless of age. Any other interpretation would be illogical. RC 3113.31 contains no language that limits the protections available to children to RC 3113.31(A)(1)(c).[38] Conversely, RC 3113.31(A)(1)(c) applies only to children, and corporal punishment is inapplicable as a defense to a case involving adults.[39]

In September of 1999, the Cuyahoga County Court of Appeals decided such a case. In *Reynolds v. White*,[40] the defendant appealed the granting of a civil protection order on the ground that he committed domestic violence against his ten-year-old daughter by spanking her several times on her buttocks with his hand and causing bruising. He argued that he merely exercised his right as a parent to use corporal punishment as a form of discipline.

The Cuyahoga County Court of Appeals noted that, although the trial court did not identify the precise ground on which it determined that the appellant engaged in domestic violence against the child, his actions clearly caused bodily injury to the child and placed her in fear of imminent serious physical harm.[41] Although the court agreed that the evidence failed to support a finding of domestic violence under RC 3113.31(A)(1)(c) because the appellant's disciplining did not create a substantial risk of serious physical harm, the court held that "the evidence was sufficient to permit a finding that [defendant] recklessly caused bodily injury under RC 3113.31(A)(1)(a) and/or placed [the

County 1999).

[37]RC 3113.31(A)(3)(a)(ii), RC 3113.31(A)(3)(a)(iii).

[38]See Layman v. Layman, No. DR-92-79 (Lawrence 10-2-96); see also Beermann v. Beermann, 1997 SD 11, 559 N.W.2d 868 (S.D. 1997) (finding that a 14-year-old child was entitled to a protection order against her noncustodial parent to prevent him from abusing her during visits at his home).

[39]See State v. Blevins, 133 Ohio App. 3d 196, 727 N.E.2d 169 (12th Dist. Butler County 1999); see also State v. Miller, 134 Ohio App. 3d 649, 731 N.E.2d 1192 (1st Dist. Hamilton County 1999).

[40]Reynolds v. White, 1999 WL 754496 (Ohio Ct. App. 8th Dist. Cuyahoga County 1999).

[41]See Tabor v. Palacio, 2008-Ohio-349, 2008 WL 282127 (Ohio Ct. App. 12th Dist. Butler County 2008) (Court of appeals affirmed issuance of CPO based on both RC 3113.31(A)(1)(b) and RC 3113.31(A)(1)(c). Court determined that appellee presented credible evidence that she had a reasonable fear that the child faced imminent serious physical harm and that the spankings inflicted upon child amounted to physical abuse and, thus, domestic violence.).

child] in reasonable fear of imminent serious physical harm under RC 3113.31(A)(1)(b), either one of which provides independent grounds to affirm the judgment."[42]

The court acknowledged that a court may predicate the finding of domestic violence against a child on grounds other than that which would constitute a form of corporal punishment.[43] In doing so, the court sanctioned the use of the other statutory provisions as relating to domestic violence against children.[44] More importantly, the court effectively limited the argument raised by many appellants that, because corporal punishment is permissible, acts of corporal punishment as a form of parental discipline do not constitute domestic violence. While conceding that certain acts of corporal punishment may not be considered "abuse" for purposes of a finding of domestic violence pursuant to RC 3113.31(A)(1)(c), the court expanded the grounds for which a petitioner may seek protection on behalf of a child for acts of violence against the child.[45]

Importantly, the appellate court noted that the trial court's judgment entry failed to identify the precise ground on which it based its finding that appellant had engaged in acts of violence and threats to the child. In spite of this, and even "if the trial court had erroneously found domestic violence under RC 3113.31(A)(1)(c), we would still be bound to affirm the judgment because a reviewing court may not reverse a correct judgment merely because erroneous reasons were assigned as a basis thereof."[46]

§ 8:7 Parents and children

Americans have physically punished their children since the country was first settled, and corporal punishment of one's children is a clear parental right, which exists even today in 21st-century America. Because corporal punishment has been an American tradition, sanctioned by history, religion and the justice system, courts and legislatures have only recently become involved with the concerns expressed by the experts who question both the focus of the laws and their unintended consequences.

The debate is reflective of two extremes: that what goes on in the home is private and exempt from public scrutiny, and that even the slightest physical act constitutes abusive contact prohibited by law.

Ohio law has recognized that parents have the right of restraint

[42]Reynolds v. White, 1999 WL 754496, *6 (Ohio Ct. App. 8th Dist. Cuyahoga County 1999); Bullard v. Alley, 2014-Ohio-1016, 2014 WL 1339719 (Ohio Ct. App. 4th Dist. Pike County 2014) (noting that once domestic violence is shown under RC 3113. 31(A)(1)(a), a court needn't consider whether the evidence supports a finding under RC 3113.31(A)(1)(b)).

[43]See Fugate v. Fugate, 2008-Ohio-737, 2008 WL 483251 (Ohio Ct. App. 3d Dist. Auglaize County 2008) (appellate court reversed the issuance of a CPO on behalf of both children on RC 3113.31(A)(1)(a) to (b); apparently the appellate court chose not to focus on RC 3113.31(A)(1)(c) in reaching its conclusion).

[44]See RC 3113.31(A)(1)(a), RC 3113.31(A)(1)(b).

[45]See RC 3113.31(A)(1)(a), RC 3113.31(A)(1)(b).

[46]Reynolds v. White, 1999 WL 754496, *6 (Ohio Ct. App. 8th Dist. Cuyahoga County 1999); see also Halley v. Ashley, 1997 WL 760662 (Ohio Ct. App. 9th Dist. Summit County 1997).

over their children and the duty of correcting and punishing them for their misbehavior.[1] However, such punishment must be reasonable and not exceed the bounds of moderation or seek to inflict cruel or unusual punishment. Additionally, such punishment must not create a substantial risk of harm to the child.

Ohio law has sought to codify these principles in several statutes. For example, RC 2919.22 reflects the right of the parent to administer reasonable corporal punishment so long as serious physical harm does not result.[2] RC 2151.031(C) provides that where a child exhibits evidence of corporal punishment or other disciplinary measure by a parent, the child is not an abused child unless RC 2919.22 would also be violated.

On the other hand, RC 2919.25 provides that "no person shall knowingly[3] cause or attempt to cause physical harm" or "recklessly[4] cause serious physical harm to a family or household member." RC 3113.31 provides that no person may attempt to cause or recklessly cause bodily injury or threaten imminent serious physical harm[5] or commit any act with respect to a child that would result in the child being an abused child, as defined in RC 2151.031.

Many Ohio courts have sought to address the boundaries of permissible parental discipline within the confines of its statutory scheme.[6] Since the argument's premise is that corporal punishment is the parent's legal right of the parent,[7] reasonable parental discipline is neither domestic violence nor child abuse.[8]

In fact, since corporal punishment necessarily involves some physical harm, the harm required to constitute domestic violence must be

---

[Section 8:7]

[1]See, e.g., Richard Garner, Fundamentally Speaking: Application of Ohio's Domestic Violence Laws in Parental Discipline Cases — a Parental Perspective, 30 U. Toledo L. Rev. 1 (1998). But see David Orentlicher, Spanking and Other Corporal Punishment of Children by Parents: Overvaluing Pain, Undervaluing Children, 35 Houston L. Rev. 147 (1998).

[2]See RC 2901.01(A)(3), which defines physical harm as "any injury, illness or other psychological impairment regardless or gravity or duration." See also RC 2901. 01(A)(5), which defines serious physical harm as "[a]ny physical harm that carries a substantial risk of death or 'involves some permanent disfigurement' or 'acute pain' or 'prolonged, intractable pain' or 'some permanent incapacity,' " and Black's Law Dictionary, which defines injury as "the invasion of any legally protected interest of another."

[3]See RC 2901.22(B) for definition of "knowingly." See also State v. Masterson, 2007-Ohio-1145, 2007 WL 764533 (Ohio Ct. App. 8th Dist. Cuyahoga County 2007) (appellant's actions of grabbing cell phone from appellee as she carried a small child in her arms causing both to fall and injuring child shows that he knowingly caused physical harm).

[4]See RC 2901.22(C) for definition of "recklessly."

[5]See also Text § 8:3, Statutory elements of domestic violence under RC 3113. 31(A)(1)(a), and Text § 8:4, Statutory elements of domestic violence under RC 3113. 31(A)(1)(b).

[6]See generally Richard Garner, Fundamentally Speaking: Application of Ohio's Domestic Violence Laws in Parental Discipline Cases—A Parental Perspective, 30 U. Tol. L. Rev. 1 (1998).

[7]See RC 2901.01(A)(3).

[8]But see Gooderham v. Patterson, 1999 WL 1034472 (Ohio Ct. App. 4th Dist. Gallia County 1999) (acts of trespass committed by the respondent).

far greater.[9] Some courts have even held that to rise above parental discipline and become domestic violence, the parent's act must create "a risk of death, serious injury or substantial pain."[10] However, the criminal domestic violence statute[11] as written would arguably prohibit the use of corporal punishment because the level of harm needed to sustain a domestic violence conviction is less than under the child endangering statute.[12]

Q & A: Can a parent be charged with domestic violence for causing physical harm to his/her child?

The most significant case that attempts to balance the statutory dichotomies is *State v. Suchomski*.[13] In that case, a drunken parent dragged his eight-year-old child from bed, ordered him to stand at attention, punched him in the stomach with his fist, pushed him to the floor, and then pounded his head against the wall. The defendant argued that if he could be charged with domestic violence for attempting to cause physical harm to his child, RC 2919.25(A) effectively prohibited him from using corporal punishment to discipline his child. The defendant noted that, under RC 2919.22, he had the right to administer reasonable corporal punishment as long as serious physical harm did not result.

Both the trial court and the court of appeals granted the defendant's motion to dismiss. The State-appellant argued that a court errs when, as a matter of law, a defendant-parent cannot be charged with domestic violence where the victim is the defendant's child. The State's argument was that there is a significant difference between corporal punishment, which the statute does not intend to include, and causing physical harm, which the statute is designed to address. The Supreme Court of Ohio addressed the issue when it determined that:

> Nothing in RC 2919.25(A) prevents a parent from properly disciplining his or her child. The only prohibition is that a parent may not cause "physical harm" as that term is defined in RC 2901.01(C). "Physical harm" is defined as "any injury[.]" "Injury" is defined in Black's Law

---

[9]State v. Adaranijo, 153 Ohio App. 3d 266, 2003-Ohio-3822, 792 N.E.2d 1138 (1st Dist. Hamilton County 2003).

[10]State v. Adaranijo, 153 Ohio App. 3d 266, 2003-Ohio-3822, 792 N.E.2d 1138 (1st Dist. Hamilton County 2003), citing State v. Hause, 1999 WL 959184 (Ohio Ct. App. 2d Dist. Montgomery County 1999); see also Samples v. Cruz, 2001 WL 534165 (Ohio Ct. App. 8th Dist. Cuyahoga County 2001).

[11]RC 2919.25.

[12]See RC 2919.22; see also State v. Hicks, 88 Ohio App. 3d 515, 624 N.E.2d 332 (10th Dist. Franklin County 1993) (low standard required under definition of "physical harm" would subject parents to prosecution for domestic violence for many types of disciplinary acts).

[13]State v. Suchomski, 58 Ohio St. 3d 74, 567 N.E.2d 1304 (1991). See also State v. Mink, 2004-Ohio-2042, 2004 WL 869523 (Ohio Ct. App. 2d Dist. Montgomery County 2004) (19-month-old child with black eye, hand print to face, and defendant and child victim were only people present when victim was injured; court affirmed conviction. Concurring opinion noted injuries constitute physical harm; the only issue is whether defendant knowingly caused injuries and testimony that injuries were inconsistent with explanation given and the most common reason would be an abusive situation. "The physician's opinion, coupled with the undisputed fact of the injuries and that the child suffered them while he was alone with Defendant and in his care, is legally sufficient to prove the charge of domestic violence.").

> Dictionary (6th ed.) p 785, as ". . . [t]he invasion of any legally protected interest of another." . . . A child does not have any legally protected interest which is invaded by proper and reasonable parental discipline.[14]

The Supreme Court then promulgated a test for determining whether corporal punishment of a child is domestic violence within the meaning of RC 2919.25. If the discipline inflicted exceeded what was permissible as reasonable and proper under the circumstances, then it constituted actionable domestic violence.[15] Additionally, the court noted that there was no conflict between RC 2919.25 and RC 2919.22.

Several unreported cases buttress the position that child abuse for purposes of RC 2919.25 must exceed proper and reasonable discipline. For example, in *City of Galion v. Martin*,[16] the defendant struck his stepson on the face with an open hand so hard that the force of the blow knocked the child into an archway, cutting and bruising his face. In *State v. McClure*,[17] the defendant threw the child over a couch, hit and kicked her as she lay on the floor until she had difficulty breathing, chased her outside, threw her onto the ground, and dragged her back into the house. In *State v. Dickson*,[18] the defendant kicked a three-year-old child in the lower back hard enough to cause the child to fly through the air three to five feet and hit the child hard enough to leave welted hand prints and a bruise. In *City of Lorain v. Prudoff*,[19] the defendant struck a fourteen-year-old with a telephone and punched her.

Other courts have enumerated more specific factors that should be considered in determining whether corporal punishment rises to the level of domestic violence under the *Suchomski* test.[20] and explored

---

[14] State v. Suchomski, 58 Ohio St. 3d 74, 75, 567 N.E.2d 1304 (1991). See also State v. Luke, 2011-Ohio-4330, 2011 WL 3813588 (Ohio Ct. App. 3d Dist. Union County 2011); State v. Davis, 2017-Ohio-8535, 2017 WL 5256348 (Ohio Ct. App. 12th Dist. Butler County 2017) (where court found that striking 13 year old daughter in mouth with a closed fist was neither proper nor reasonable discipline).

[15] State v. Suchomski, 58 Ohio St. 3d 74, 75, 567 N.E.2d 1304 (1991).

[16] City of Galion v. Martin, 1991 WL 261835 (Ohio Ct. App. 3d Dist. Crawford County 1991).

[17] State v. McClure, 1993 WL 211663 (Ohio Ct. App. 2d Dist. Greene County 1993).

[18] State v. Dickson, 1993 WL 437738 (Ohio Ct. App. 5th Dist. Holmes County 1993).

[19] City of Lorain v. Prudoff, 1994 WL 709667 (Ohio Ct. App. 9th Dist. Lorain County 1994); see also State/City of Akron v. McGlaughlin, 1998 WL 801930 (Ohio Ct. App. 9th Dist. Summit County 1998) (upholding domestic violence conviction against father for hitting his 16-year-old child in chest where child's mother testified regarding fear in child's voice and police officer observed red mark on the child's chest); State v. Moser, 1999 WL 550272 (Ohio Ct. App. 6th Dist. Wood County 1999) (upholding domestic violence conviction against a father for hitting his son's arm several times with a closed fist, causing reddened area on the arm and temporarily rendering the son unable to move his arm).

[20] State v. Suchomski, 58 Ohio St. 3d 74, 567 N.E.2d 1304 (1991); see also Brooklyn v. Perna, 2012-Ohio-265, 2012 WL 253314 (Ohio Ct. App. 8th Dist. Cuyahoga County 2012); quoting State v. Ivey, 98 Ohio App. 3d 249, 648 N.E.2d 519 (8th Dist. Cuyahoga County 1994).

the use of affirmative defenses. For example, in *State v. Hicks*,[21] the defendant slapped the child on the back eight times, hard enough to leave marks which were still visible one week later.

The 10th District Court of Appeals determined that nothing in RC 2919.25(A) prevents a parent from properly disciplining a child and found that a parent cannot be found guilty of violating RC 2919.25 if the parent was engaged in proper and reasonable parental discipline. In reinforcing this principle, the court rejected any argument "that the legislature of Ohio intended to outlaw corporal punishment when it enacted RC 2919.25(A)."[22] In fact, the court also stated that "[t]he Supreme Court then seems to imply that 'proper and reasonable parental discipline' allows corporal punishment. The Supreme Court clearly indicated that proper and reasonable parental discipline stops well short of corporal punishment which creates a substantial risk of serious harm to a child."[23]

The court utilized the *Suchomski* test but cautioned that the low standard for what constitutes physical harm makes it easy for a parent to be charged and found guilty of domestic violence if he/she administers corporal punishment. In an effort to prevent parents from facing the prospect of criminal charges, the court noted that certain affirmative defenses for reasonable parental discipline should be raised.[24] It defined the terms "proper" and "reasonable." "'Proper' for this defense means suitable or appropriate. 'Reasonable' means not extreme or excessive."[25]

Finally, the court reasoned that it is not true that any parental discipline which involves physical harm is beyond the bounds of proper and reasonable discipline. The court distinguished its decision from *Suchomski* by noting that "the facts in the *Suchomski* case did not lend themselves to a careful analysis or finely crafted definition of the limits of 'proper and reasonable parental discipline.' "[26]

Similarly, *State v. Hart*,[27] the court held that the defendant's slapping his 14-year-old eight times and punching a hole in her bedroom wall did not rise to the level of domestic violence. In reversing the father's conviction, the court of appeals for Defiance County held that

---

[21] State v. Hicks, 88 Ohio App. 3d 515, 624 N.E.2d 332 (10th Dist. Franklin County 1993).

[22] State v. Hicks, 88 Ohio App. 3d 515, 517, 624 N.E.2d 332 (10th Dist. Franklin County 1993).

[23] State v. Hicks, 88 Ohio App. 3d 515, 518, 624 N.E.2d 332 (10th Dist. Franklin County 1993).

[24] But see State v. Esparza, 1999 WL 155955 (Ohio Ct. App. 3d Dist. Defiance County 1999) (trial court failed to instruct for parental discipline defense; reversed because it was unclear whether blow to child was for purpose of reasonable and proper parental discipline).

[25] State v. Hicks, 88 Ohio App. 3d 515, 520, 624 N.E.2d 332 (10th Dist. Franklin County 1993); State v. Zielinski, 2011-Ohio-6535, 2011 WL 6382541 (Ohio Ct. App. 12th Dist. Warren County 2011).

[26] State v. Hicks, 88 Ohio App. 3d 515, 519, 624 N.E.2d 332 (10th Dist. Franklin County 1993).

[27] State v. Hart, 110 Ohio App. 3d 250, 673 N.E.2d 992 (3d Dist. Defiance County 1996); see also Chronister ex rel. Morrison v. Brenneman, 1999 PA Super 284, 742 A.2d 190 (1999).

the discipline inflicted was both proper and reasonable. In *Hart*, the court determined that:

> [the] definition [of corporal punishment] would include extremities of the body . . .. It is clear . . . that the trial judge considered only spanking to qualify as corporal punishment and ignored the possibility that corporal punishment to other parts of the body may also be proper and reasonable. . . . The propriety and reasonableness of corporal punishment in each case must be judged in light of the totality of the circumstances. A child's age, behavior, and response to noncorporal punishment as well as the location and severity of the punishment are factors that should be examined. Without first recognizing slaps to the face or the head as a means of corporal punishment, the trial court never reached the issue of whether, under the circumstances, the corporal punishment was proper and reasonable.[28]

Additionally, the court explained that neither the legislature nor the Supreme Court chose to create the defense of corporal punishment provided for in RC 2919.22 for domestic violence cases under RC 2919. 25. Rather, the Supreme Court in *Suchomski* opted for a restrictive interpretation of the law by relying on the fact that a child has no legally protected interest which would be invaded by proper and reasonable parental discipline. The Defiance Court of Appeals relied on the *Hicks* decision and concluded that "proper" and "reasonable"[29] parental discipline can be employed by a parent as an affirmative defense to a charge of domestic violence.

The Hamilton County Court of Appeals also followed the reasoning of *Hart*. In *State v. Wagster*,[30] the defendant slapped the child with the back of the hand in an effort to calm her. The child's lip was injured when her lip was caught between two crooked teeth. The court held that the action was not domestic violence and that the discipline administered was both proper and reasonable.

In 1999, the pendulum moved yet again and the courts began to

---

[28]State v. Hart, 110 Ohio App. 3d 250, 255-56, 673 N.E.2d 992 (3d Dist. Defiance County 1996); see also State v. Hause, 1999 WL 959184 (Ohio Ct. App. 2d Dist. Montgomery County 1999); State v. Jones, 140 Ohio App. 3d 422, 747 N.E.2d 891 (8th Dist. Cuyahoga County 2000) (in which the court added another factor to the totality of the circumstances, to wit: the state of mind of the parent while administering discipline).

[29]See also State v. Stocker, 90 Haw. 85, 976 P.2d 399 (1999) (reversing domestic violence conviction, finding that noncustodial father was "parent" for purposes of parental discipline and that father's conduct of slapping child was reasonably proportionate to the child's misbehavior). See, e.g., State v. Vandergriff, 2001-Ohio-4327, 2001 WL 1117182 (Ohio Ct. App. 11th Dist. Ashtabula County 2001); see also State v. Mills, 1997 WL 133430 (Ohio Ct. App. 1st Dist. Hamilton County 1997); Samples v. Cruz, 2001 WL 534165 (Ohio Ct. App. 8th Dist. Cuyahoga County 2001) (in which the appellate court affirmed the trial court's decision and sanctioned the use of reasonable corporal punishment by a parent in disciplining an unruly child).

[30]State v. Wagster, 1996 WL 134538 (Ohio Ct. App. 1st Dist. Hamilton County 1996); see also State v. Hauenstein, 121 Ohio App. 3d 511, 700 N.E.2d 378 (3d Dist. Putnam County 1997) (slapping a child once in the face was appropriate in light of repeated attempts by child to take car keys and leave the house against her father's orders; defendant's conduct was neither drastic nor severe); State v. Hause, 1999 WL 959184 (Ohio Ct. App. 2d Dist. Montgomery County 1999) (overturning father's domestic violence conviction for punching his son in the face, deeming punishment reasonable because it did not cause serious harm and was in response to son's adamant refusal to follow his father's orders).

adopt a more liberal standard for defining abuse for purposes of a domestic violence conviction. In *State v. Howard*,[31] the defendant was charged with both domestic violence and child endangering for hitting his twelve-year-old son five or six times in the head, back, and legs with either a broomstick or mop handle, causing visible injury. On appeal, the defendant asserted that he should not have been convicted because he used reasonable corporal punishment to discipline his child.

Rather than focusing on what constitutes excessive corporal punishment, the trial court concentrated on the term "abuse." While acknowledging that the term is not defined in any criminal statute, the court, in its charge to the jury, defined abuse to mean "any act which causes physical or mental injury that harms or threatens to harm the child's health or welfare."[32] The definition was taken from the Ohio Jury Instructions that applied the definition of abuse as set forth in RC 2151.031(D), the juvenile court section of the Ohio Revised Code.

After reviewing the applicable case law, the Lake County Appellate Court affirmed defendant's conviction. The court stated that "[a]buse includes not only actual harm but actions which threaten to harm the child's health or welfare. Therefore, appellant's conduct was not proper or reasonable parental discipline and was sufficient to sustain the convictions for domestic violence and child endangerment."[33] While noting that the jury instructions may have been improper, defense counsel did not object and appellant's counsel failed to raise the issue on appeal.

Still, courts remain conflicted over the behavior that truly rises to actionable domestic violence. In fact, the Hamilton County Court of Appeals, in *State v. Adaranijo*,[34] recently noted that "[w]hile many people differ as to whether corporal discipline should be used, it is not the business of the courts unless the child is injured."[35]

In *Adaranijo*, the mother contacted the authorities when the father slapped the child and threatened to "beat the shit" out of her and then punched her in the leg. The father was charged with domestic violence under RC 2919.25 and was convicted. On appeal, the father argued that the conviction was against the manifest weight of the evidence.

[31]State v. Howard, 1999 WL 1313691 (Ohio Ct. App. 11th Dist. Lake County 1999).

[32]State v. Howard, 1999 WL 1313691, *4 (Ohio Ct. App. 11th Dist. Lake County 1999); see also Kurincic v. Kurincic, 2000 WL 217808 (Ohio Ct. App. 8th Dist. Cuyahoga County 2000) (where evidence indicated that minor child was depressed and particularly susceptible to mental injury, parent's yelling at her, calling her names, and failure to prevent husband from pinning child down in a violent manner amounted to domestic violence; court relied on RC 2901.01 for definition of "serious physical harm" and noted that domestic violence includes acts of a parent which cause physical or mental injury that harms or threatens to harm child's health or welfare pursuant to RC 3113.31(A)(1)(c) and RC 2151.03(D)).

[33]State v. Howard, 1999 WL 1313691, *5 (Ohio Ct. App. 11th Dist. Lake County 1999).

[34]State v. Adaranijo, 153 Ohio App. 3d 266, 2003-Ohio-3822, 792 N.E.2d 1138 (1st Dist. Hamilton County 2003).

[35]State v. Adaranijo, 153 Ohio App. 3d 266, 2003-Ohio-3822, 792 N.E.2d 1138 (1st Dist. Hamilton County 2003).

Initially, the court noted that the threat was rhetorical and then asked, "Should we jail every parent for such a threat? Were these words made criminal, who would be free? Ralph Kramden, who was never known to hit anyone, would be in jail forever."[36]

Balancing a parent's fundamental liberty interest in raising and controlling his or her children[37] against a state's interest in protecting children from harm, the appellate court reasoned that ". . . to rise above parental discipline and become domestic violence, the parent's act must create 'a risk of death, serious injury or substantial pain.' "[38] In reversing the conviction, the court held that without observable injury or a risk of serious physical harm, there can be no domestic violence as a result of striking a child.[39]

Q & A: Have corporal punishment issues been considered by the courts in the civil domestic violence context?

Many appellate districts have begun to address the issue of corporal punishment and parental discipline in relation to domestic violence in the civil protection order context.[40] For example, in Reynolds v. White,[41] the court tackled the issue of whether corporal punishment by a par-

---

[36]State v. Adaranijo, 153 Ohio App. 3d 266, 2003-Ohio-3822, 792 N.E.2d 1138 (1st Dist. Hamilton County 2003).

[37]See Santosky v. Kramer, 455 U.S. 745, 753, 102 S. Ct. 1388, 71 L. Ed. 2d 599 (1982).

[38]State v. Adaranijo, 153 Ohio App. 3d 266, 2003-Ohio-3822, 792 N.E.2d 1138 (1st Dist. Hamilton County 2003), citing State v. Hause, 1999 WL 959184 (Ohio Ct. App. 2d Dist. Montgomery County 1999). But see State v. Thompson, 2006-Ohio-582, 2006 WL 307715 (Ohio Ct. App. 2d Dist. Miami County 2006) (domestic violence conviction supported by a finding of the physical harm element, even though the physical harm was minimal in gravity or duration because the child did not experience any lasting physical effects into the next day, where parental discipline defense was not raised on appeal).

[39]State v. Adaranijo, 153 Ohio App. 3d 266, 2003-Ohio-3822, 792 N.E.2d 1138 (1st Dist. Hamilton County 2003); see also State v. Holzwart, 151 Ohio App. 3d 417, 420, 2003-Ohio-345, 784 N.E.2d 192 (3d Dist. Seneca County 2003); State v. Habo, 2013-Ohio-2142, 2013 WL 2308483 (Ohio Ct. App. 11th Dist. Portage County 2013) (finding that the domestic violence statute [R.C. 2919.25] does not require either observable injury or a risk of "serious physical harm"; it requires the perpetrator to either knowingly cause or attempt to cause physical harm to a family or household member). But see State v. Behlke, 2017-Ohio-7910, 2017 WL 4334342 (Ohio Ct. App. 9th Dist. Wayne County 2017) (where parental discipline defense was not raised on appeal, finding that the physical harm element was established, even though any physical harm was minimal in gravity or duration because child did not experience any lasting physical effects from the altercation into the next day, supported conviction for domestic violence).

[40]Tyler v. Tyler, 2016-Ohio-7419, ¶ 24, 2016 WL 6160139 (Ohio Ct. App. 2d Dist. Montgomery County 2016) (spanking constitutes reasonable corporal punishment, rather than domestic violence where there was no evidence presented of excessive frequency or severity. Not including the children within the scope of the protection order was not against the manifest weight of the evidence).

[41]Reynolds v. White, 1999 WL 754496 (Ohio Ct. App. 8th Dist. Cuyahoga County 1999); see also Text § 8:6, Statutory elements of domestic violence under RC 3113. 31(A)(1)(c); see also Tabor v. Palacio, 2008-Ohio-349, 2008 WL 282127 (Ohio Ct. App. 12th Dist. Butler County 2008) (affirmed judgment of CPO issued on behalf of minor child because there was ample evidence that the punishment inflicted by appellant on the parties' child went beyond any notions of legitimate corporal punishment and amounted to domestic violence).

ent of his minor child may constitute domestic violence where the alleged abuse did not constitute child endangering under RC 2919.22.

In that case, the father spanked his 11-year-old child several times on the buttocks. He also told her not to tell anyone. While the court stated that the evidence was neither sufficient to permit finding the child was abused under RC 2151.031 nor violative of RC 2919.22(B) so as to permit a finding under RC 3113.31(A)(1)(c), the court noted that one does not need to establish abuse in order to find domestic violence. The court held that the evidence was sufficient to permit a finding that the father recklessly caused bodily injury under RC 3113.31(A)(1)(a) or RC 3113.31(A)(1)(b) and that either one would provide independent grounds to affirm the judgment. The court then determined that it would be bound to affirm a judgment and not reverse a correct judgment merely because it was based upon erroneous reasons.

Additionally, the court noted that while it acknowledges that reasonable people may disagree as to the value and use of corporal punishment, Ohio law does not forbid such conduct so long as it does not exceed the prohibitions set forth in RC 2151.031 or RC 2919.22.

In a clarification of its analysis, the Eighth District Court of Appeals, in *Thompson v. Koontz*, appears to have retreated from its *Reynold* opinion.[42] In that case, the custodial mother had whipped her 10-year-old child, leaving welts and other marks. The trial court held that the conduct constituted corporal punishment and declined to issue a civil protection order, even though the Department of Children and Family Services substantiated abuse. The mother had testified that she whipped the child for failing to properly bathe himself.

The appellate court distinguished *Koontz* from *Reynolds* case by stating the recklessness element was met in *Reynolds* because the father attempted to prevent the child from reporting the violence.[43] Moreover, if the child had needed medical attention, such a cover-up might have prevented that help. It then held that "a reasonable corporal punishment defense may countervail RC 3113.31(A)(1)(a), (b) and (c) when a parent has been charged with domestic violence towards a child. Each case should be viewed on a case-by-case basis."[44]

In *Sepesi v. Goris*,[45] the stepmother tipped over the daughter's chair in an attempt to stop the child from sitting with her feet on the chair. The second time the child's head and chest hit a table. At trial, a social worker testified that the child had also reported being pulled down the stairs and slapped, which had been refuted by the father at the time of the incidents. After appellant presented her case, appellee moved to dismiss on the ground that appellant failed to sustain her burden of establishing domestic violence.

---

[42]Thompson v. Koontz, 2000 WL 1739291 (Ohio Ct. App. 8th Dist. Cuyahoga County 2000); see also Wilder v. Perna, 174 Ohio App. 3d 586, 2007-Ohio-6635, 883 N.E.2d 1095 (8th Dist. Cuyahoga County 2007) (abrogated by, Cyran v. Cyran, 152 Ohio St. 3d 484, 2018-Ohio-24, 97 N.E.3d 487 (2018)).

[43]See also State v. Jones, 140 Ohio App. 3d 422, 747 N.E.2d 891 (8th Dist. Cuyahoga County 2000) (mother's order to child to lie about origin of abuse-inflicted bruises indicated mother's awareness that beatings were excessive and unreasonable).

[44]Thompson v. Koontz, 2000 WL 1739291, *6 (Ohio Ct. App. 8th Dist. Cuyahoga County 2000).

[45]Sepesi v. Goris, 2003-Ohio-1622, 2003 WL 1702505 (Ohio Ct. App. 6th Dist. Wood County 2003).

On appeal, appellant challenged the trial court's dismissal of her CPO and argued that she had presented a prima facie case of domestic violence. The appellate court stated that "in dismissing appellant's petition below, the trial court found that appellee had at most performed a reasonable act of family discipline which had an unforeseen, accidental consequence of injury to Chelsea's chest. The court therefore concluded that appellant had not established an event of domestic violence as defined by R.C. 3113.31(A) and that Chelsea was not in any immediate or present danger of further domestic violence from appellee."[46]

In affirming the decision of the trial court, the Wood County Court of Appeals noted that the appellee did not raise the affirmative defense of reasonable corporal punishment and never presented any evidence as to the reasonableness of the punishment. The appellate court concluded that the trial court's finding that appellee engaged in a reasonable act of family discipline was against the manifest weight of the evidence; however, the court also relied on the conclusion of the trial court that the injury to the child was accidental as there was not any evidence to conclude that appellee's actions were either reckless or intentional. The Wood court held "that appellant failed to establish by a preponderance of the evidence that appellee had committed an act of domestic violence or that [the child] was in danger of further domestic violence."[47] Furthermore, there was no evidence to suggest that the Chelsea was an abused child under RC 2151.031.

In determining that appellant failed to sustain her burden of proof, the appellate court considered and analyzed each act of domestic violence as defined in RC 3113.31(A), relative to the facts presented. Additionally, it referred to the test set forth in *Felton v. Felton*[48] for the granting of a protection order. Appellant had failed to present evidence that appellee had committed an act of domestic violence or that the child was in danger of future domestic violence.

It is significant that the Wood County Court of Appeals considered both the acts as defined by statute and a danger of future domestic violence in its analysis. In doing so, the court has expanded the future role of courts, permitting them to examine either acts of domestic violence as defined or future danger to determine whether a prima facie case of domestic violence has been presented.

In *Rader v. Rader*,[49] the appellate court affirmed the denial of the issuance of a CPO. In this case, appellant (mother of minor child) sought a CPO on behalf of her 3½ year old daughter. Appellee spanked the child several times with his hand and then hit her several times on the butt with a piece of wood trim for refusing to pick up her book bag and bring it into the house despite being asked by appellee several times. Appellant testified that she observed redness, swelling and bruising and two lacerations near the small of the child's back.

[46]Sepesi v. Goris, 2003-Ohio-1622, 2003 WL 1702505, *3 (Ohio Ct. App. 6th Dist. Wood County 2003).

[47]Sepesi v. Goris, 2003-Ohio-1622, 2003 WL 1702505, *3 (Ohio Ct. App. 6th Dist. Wood County 2003).

[48]Felton v. Felton, 79 Ohio St. 3d 34, 1997-Ohio-302, 679 N.E.2d 672 (1997).

[49]Rader v. Rader, 2007-Ohio-4288, 2007 WL 2390815 (Ohio Ct. App. 5th Dist. Licking County 2007); but see Tabor v. Palacio, 2008-Ohio-349, 2008 WL 282127 (Ohio Ct. App. 12th Dist. Butler County 2008).

The trial court denied the issuance of the CPO, concluding that appellee's actions did not create a substantial risk of serious physical harm to the child and did not create physical harm to the child's health or welfare.

On review, the appellate court noted that RC 3113.31(A)(1)(c) was the pertinent statute and that the cross reference to corporal punishment was applicable where the "punishment, discipline or restraint is *excessive* under the circumstances and *creates a substantial risk of serious physical harm* to the child."[50] The court then acknowledged the trial court's reasoning that "appellee's actions fell within the area of excessive, but that the evidence did not show that appellee's punishment created a substantial risk of serious physical harm to the girl."[51] Additionally, the appellate court also pointed out that the trial court could not conclude which of appellee's actions created physical harm to the child's health or welfare.

The Licking County Court of Appeals then held that ". . .while we share the trial court's overall concern that appellee used excessive corporal punishment in this instance, we are unpersuaded the court abused its discretion in denying the issuance of a CPO. We further hold the trial court properly followed the requisite statutory scheme in reaching its decision."[52]

Of interest is that the appellate court noted that the Revised Code does not specifically define what actions constitutes abuse of a child and that a court has broad discretion to determine what actions are abuse. More importantly is that the court advanced a novel standard for use by a trial court when determining whether a CPO should be issued, being whether a CPO is actually necessary to ensure the family member's protection.[53] Inherent in this concept is the fear of future injury or harm. Under this analysis, a court is free to find that excessive punishment was used but conclude that 1) it did not create a substantial risk of serious physical harm to the child and that 2) it did not create a future risk of harm.

In *Hicks v. Barker*,[54] father was granted a CPO against mother because of an incident in which she repeatedly struck her child with a plastic spoon causing bruising and redness on the left side of the child's back.

On appeal, appellant mother argued that the trial court erred in

---

[50]Rader v. Rader, 2007-Ohio-4288, 2007 WL 2390815, *2 (Ohio Ct. App. 5th Dist. Licking County 2007); Bowman v. Bowman, 2014-Ohio-2851, 2014 WL 2957475 (Ohio Ct. App. 9th Dist. Medina County 2014); Friedlander v. Friedlander, 2014-Ohio-2180, 2014 WL 2168238 (Ohio Ct. App. 8th Dist. Cuyahoga County 2014).

[51]Rader v. Rader, 2007-Ohio-4288, 2007 WL 2390815, *3 (Ohio Ct. App. 5th Dist. Licking County 2007), citing the trial court opinion; Tyler v. Tyler, 2016-Ohio-7419, 2016 WL 6160139 (Ohio Ct. App. 2d Dist. Montgomery County 2016) (son suffered no serious physical harm when he was spanked).

[52]Rader v. Rader, 2007-Ohio-4288, 2007 WL 2390815, *3 (Ohio Ct. App. 5th Dist. Licking County 2007).

[53]Rader v. Rader, 2007-Ohio-4288, 2007 WL 2390815, *3 (Ohio Ct. App. 5th Dist. Licking County 2007), citing Lebeau v. Lebeau, 2001 WL 1339495 (Ohio Ct. App. 5th Dist. Stark County 2001).

[54]Hicks v. Barker, 2009-Ohio-2445, 2009 WL 1456532 (Ohio Ct. App. 12th Dist. Warren County 2009).

granting the civil protection order because the children were not in danger of or have been victims of domestic violence. The court considered the statutory language of RC 3113.31(A)(1)(c) and determined that the child might be considered an abused child. It then reviewed RC 2151.031(C) which defined an "abused" child as one who exhibits evidence of physical injury, excluding corporal punishment if such punishment is not prohibited by RC 2919.22.[55] Corporal punishment which is excessive under the circumstances and creates a substantial risk of serious physical harm to the child is child endangering under RC 2919.22.

Next, the court examined the relevant Ohio Revised Code definitions of "substantial risk" and "serious physical harm" and reasoned that "[a] significant factor in determining the risk of serious physical harm for purposes of RC 2919.22(B)(3) is the location of the injury. Injuries inflicted upon areas of the body which are in the immediate vicinity of vital organs create a substantial risk of serious physical harm to the child that is not present when the punishment is administered to a child's buttocks."[56]

The Warren Court of Appeals then concluded that in light of the totality of the circumstances and because the injury inflicted by the spoon was located close to the kidney, there is competent, credible evidence to support the issuance of the CPO.

Of interest is that the appellate court noted that the trial court's holding that the CPO should be granted was based more on the mental repercussions of the mother's actions. "The court cited RC 2151.031(D) which defines an "abused" child as one who suffers physical or mental injury that harms or threatens to harm the child's health or welfare due to the acts of his parents. The court also cited RC 2919.22(B)(4), which prohibits all persons from repeatedly administering unwarranted disciplinary measures when there is a substantial risk that such conduct, if continued, will seriously impair or slow the child's mental health or development."[57]

Finally, in *Mc Bride v. McBride*,[58] appellant father was alleged to have committed domestic violence against his son C.M., aged nine, by spanking and whipping him on several occasions during Christmas break. Besides the minor child, the mother testified that she had learned about the spankings from the school principal, saw some marks on the child and that she did not doubt the child's honesty about the incidents based on the children's behaviors after they returned from their father's. The trial court found C.M.'s testimony to be credible and granted the CPO, on behalf of both C.M. and his younger brother, E.M.

On appeal, father asserted that the trial court erred in relying on the testimony of C.M. for a finding that domestic violence occurred,

---

[55] At *2.

[56] At *5; see Clark v. Clark, 114 Ohio App. 3d 558, 683 N.E.2d 800 (12th Dist. Butler County 1996) (where the location of the injury was on the buttocks, there was no evidence that Clark's conduct created a substantial risk of serious physical harm).

[57] At *2.

[58] McBride v. McBride, 2012-Ohio-2146, 971 N.E.2d 1007 (Ohio Ct. App. 12th Dist. Butler County 2012).

because the discrepancies in his testimony (his description of the implements and with which ones he was spanked, his failure to mention the beatings until he was in trouble at school, that he was spanked twice daily and that no one witnessed the beatings except when his stepmother held him down on one occasion) diminished his credibility.

The question answered by the appellate court was whether there was sufficient credible evidence that father's acts caused the minor children to suffer a physical or mental injury that threaten their welfare or father's excessive corporal punishment created a strong possibility that either child would suffer acute pain and substantial suffering or prolonged pain.[59]

In finding that there was sufficient credible evidence to support the trial court's decision that father engaged in domestic violence, the appellate court determined that the trial court had the opportunity "to view the witnesses and observe their demeanor, gestures and voice inflections."[60] It then addressed evidence presented at trial that could have explained some of C.M.'s behavior regarding the abuse, such as father's threat to hurt C.M. if he told anyone about the beatings. Finally, it considered the grant of a CPO on behalf of E.M. and found that there was sufficient credible evidence to support a domestic violence finding for this child. First, E.M. was present in the home in which father had repeatedly beaten C.M., which placed the child in an unsafe environment. Relying on *Ferris v. Ferris*,[61] the court noted that "placing children in an environment where there is a substantial risk to their health and safety constitutes one form of domestic violence."[62] Further, the appellate court[63] considered the reasoning set forth in *Hicks v. Barker*.[64]

Of significance is that the dissenting judge found that there was a lack of competent, credible evidence and noting that while a trial court has discretion in determining credibility, "the law is also clear

---

[59]McBride v. McBride, 2012-Ohio-2146, 971 N.E.2d 1007 (Ohio Ct. App. 12th Dist. Butler County 2012).

[60]McBride v. McBride, 2012-Ohio-2146, ¶ 11, 971 N.E.2d 1007, 1010 (Ohio Ct. App. 12th Dist. Butler County 2012), quoting Seasons Coal Co., Inc. v. City of Cleveland, 10 Ohio St. 3d 77, 80, 461 N.E.2d 1273, 38 U.C.C. Rep. Serv. 469 (1984). See also Bullard v. Alley, 2014-Ohio-1016, 2014 WL 1339719 (Ohio Ct. App. 4th Dist. Pike County 2014) (holding that grabbing a 16 year old daughter's arm and squeezing it causing a bruise while upset and angry was domestic violence under RC 3113.31(A)(1)(a) and that the trial court was in the best position to evaluate fear and credibility); Rosine v. Rosine, 2010-Ohio-613, 2010 WL 598642 (Ohio Ct. App. 7th Dist. Mahoning County 2010) (trial court was in best position to determine credibility).

[61]Ferris v. Ferris, 2006-Ohio-878, 2006 WL 456811 (Ohio Ct. App. 12th Dist. Clermont County 2006).

[62]McBride v. McBride, 2012-Ohio-2146, ¶ 25, 971 N.E.2d 1007, 1014 (Ohio Ct. App. 12th Dist. Butler County 2012); Martindale v. Martindale, 2017-Ohio-9266, ¶ 55, 102 N.E.3d 19 (Ohio Ct. App. 4th Dist. Athens County 2017).

[63]McBride v. McBride, 2012-Ohio-2146, 971 N.E.2d 1007 (Ohio Ct. App. 12th Dist. Butler County 2012); see also Carpeno v. Carpeno, 2005-Ohio-7046, 2005 WL 3610425 (Ohio Ct. App. 11th Dist. Lake County 2005).

[64]Hicks v. Barker, 2009-Ohio-2445, 2009 WL 1456532 (Ohio Ct. App. 12th Dist. Warren County 2009) (where "in a case of child abuse against one child, the CPO should be extended to protect the other child because mother's actions put both children in an environment where there was a substantial risk to their health and safety").

that if the allegations are equally likely to have not occurred as they are to have occurred, the need for a civil protection order has not been sufficiently demonstrated by the required degree of proof."[65]

The dissenting judge discussed at great length the criteria for assessing credibility of witnesses. "While a trial court has the ability to hear and observe the testimony, seeing and hearing testimony is not the "stand-alone" or sole criteria for judging credibility.[66] He then pointed out that multiple factors must be considered when analyzing credibility: (1) seeing and hearing firsthand the demeanor of the witness; (2) consistency of the witness on direct, cross and as compared with others testifying about the facts; (3) motive; and (4) believability.[67] "Believability" is fundamentally rooted in common sense as to whether or not the nature of circumstances as a whole are likely within the range of known probabilities. When put into the context of all the other circumstances, even testimony that is delivered with sincerity may not have "believability."[68]

Q & A: What other behaviors are considered "child abuse" for purposes of RC 3113.31?

In *Ventura v. Ventura*, the court issued a civil protection order pursuant to RC 3113.31 based on incidents of sexual abuse towards the child.[69] In *Tischler v. Vahcic*,[70] one of the parents obtained a civil protection order because the other parent committed an act of domestic violence against the child under RC 3113.31(A)(1)(c). The evidence showed that the mother's apartment, in which the child lived, was filthy. Additionally, there was evidence presented that the child was physically injured while in the mother's care. Because the evidence was sufficient to sustain a finding that the child was abused under RC 31113.31, a civil protection order was granted.

---

[65]McBride v. McBride, 2012-Ohio-2146, ¶ 59, 971 N.E.2d 1007, 1021 (Ohio Ct. App. 12th Dist. Butler County 2012) (Piper, J., dissenting).

[66]McBride v. McBride, 2012-Ohio-2146, ¶ 37, 971 N.E.2d 1007, 1016 (Ohio Ct. App. 12th Dist. Butler County 2012) (Piper, J., dissenting).

[67]McBride v. McBride, 2012-Ohio-2146, ¶ 37, 971 N.E.2d 1007, 1016 (Ohio Ct. App. 12th Dist. Butler County 2012) (Piper, J., dissenting), and citing Martin v. Hanood, 2009-Ohio-1501, 2009 WL 825766 (Ohio Ct. App. 7th Dist. Jefferson County 2009); Evid. R. 404(B); R.C. 2945.59.

[68]McBride v. McBride, 2012-Ohio-2146, ¶ 37, 971 N.E.2d 1007, 1016 (Ohio Ct. App. 12th Dist. Butler County 2012) (Piper, J., dissenting).

[69]Ventura v. Ventura, 1986 WL 10595 (Ohio Ct. App. 11th Dist. Lake County 1986). See also Wardeh v. Altabchi, 158 Ohio App. 3d 325, 2004-Ohio-4423, 815 N.E.2d 712 (10th Dist. Franklin County 2004) (issuance of a CPO for protection of plaintiff and the child was affirmed based on RC 3113.31(A)(1)(c), and based partly on respondent's threats to abscond with child to Syria).

[70]Tischler v. Vahcic, 1995 WL 680928 (Ohio Ct. App. 8th Dist. Cuyahoga County 1995) (abrogated by, Felton v. Felton, 79 Ohio St. 3d 34, 1997-Ohio-302, 679 N.E.2d 672 (1997)) (applying clear-and-convincing standard; holding that lesser preponderance-of-the-evidence standard applies to petition for civil protection order); see also Text § 12:11, Standard of proof. But see Dybo v. Dybo, 1999 WL 1073781 (Ohio Ct. App. 11th Dist. Geauga County 1999) (affirming trial court's vacating of temporary protection order after full hearing, reasoning that, under the standard set forth in *Felton*, the children were not in danger of domestic violence; court noted that record was devoid of history of abuse or violence and that wife's testimony of what son told her was insufficient where son showed there were no problems between him and his father).

The foregoing cases illustrate various interpretations of the relationship between corporal punishment, child abuse, and discipline of children. All of the courts were quick to differentiate between punishable corporal punishment and proper and reasonable parental discipline.[71]

Q & A: Can a defendant raise an affirmative defense of applying proper and reasonable parental discipline?

Although this defense has not yet been codified in Ohio's laws, several appellate courts have permitted an affirmative defense to a charge of domestic violence.[72] "An essential part of raising the defense is getting a jury instruction that permits a finding it has been met."[73] In *State v. Hicks*, the Franklin County Court of Appeals considered the following instruction as appropriate in cases where the defense has been raised: " 'The defendant has asserted an affirmative defense that she (he) was engaged in properly disciplining her (his) child at the time alleged. Nothing in the domestic violence statute prevents a parent from properly disciplining her (his) child. If you find by a preponderance of the evidence that the defendant was engaged in proper and reasonable parental discipline at the time, then you shall find the defendant not guilty. "Proper" for purposes of this defense means suitable or appropriate. "Reasonable" for purposes of this defense means not extreme or excessive.' "[74] Several other appellate districts have considered a similar jury instruction when a defendant raised the defense.

Q & A: Who has the burden of going forward?

If a defendant raises an affirmative defense of reasonable parental

---

[71]But see Gomez v. Dyer, 2008-Ohio-1523, 2008 WL 850127, *7 (Ohio Ct. App. 7th Dist. Noble County 2008) (affirming trial court's denial of CPO on behalf of a child with an injury on her back and noting the conflicting evidence, the court held that "[a]lthough appellant's fear is understandable, we cannot substitute our judgment for that of the trial court on the topic of evidence weighing or credibility gauging").

[72]See, e.g., State v. Hicks, 88 Ohio App. 3d 515, 624 N.E.2d 332 (10th Dist. Franklin County 1993); State v. Hart, 110 Ohio App. 3d 250, 673 N.E.2d 992 (3d Dist. Defiance County 1996); State v. Jones, 140 Ohio App. 3d 422, 747 N.E.2d 891 (8th Dist. Cuyahoga County 2000); Samples v. Cruz, 2001 WL 534165 (Ohio Ct. App. 8th Dist. Cuyahoga County 2001); Sepesi v. Goris, 2003-Ohio-1622, 2003 WL 1702505 (Ohio Ct. App. 6th Dist. Wood County 2003) (reasonable corporal punishment is a recognized affirmative defense to a charge of domestic violence); State v. Thompson, 2006-Ohio-582, 2006 WL 307715 (Ohio Ct. App. 2d Dist. Miami County 2006) (appellate court acknowledged that the totality of the relevant facts and circumstances must be considered when deciding whether any particular conduct constitutes proper and reasonable parental discipline); State v. Davis, 2017-Ohio-8535, 2017 WL 5256348 (Ohio Ct. App. 12th Dist. Butler County 2017); Brooklyn v. Perna, 2012-Ohio-265, 2012 WL 253314 (Ohio Ct. App. 8th Dist. Cuyahoga County 2012) (noting that a determination as to whether particular conduct constitutes proper and reasonable parental discipline must be made from the totality of the circumstances in the case; citing State v. Snyder, 2011-Ohio-1062, 2011 WL 826292 (Ohio Ct. App. 8th Dist. Cuyahoga County 2011)); State v. Adaranijo, 153 Ohio App. 3d 266, 2003-Ohio-3822, 792 N.E.2d 1138 (1st Dist. Hamilton County 2003). But see State v. Rosa, 2013-Ohio-5867, 6 N.E.3d 57 (Ohio Ct. App. 7th Dist. Mahoning County 2013).

[73]State v. Vandergriff, 2001-Ohio-4327, 2001 WL 1117182, *6 (Ohio Ct. App. 11th Dist. Ashtabula County 2001).

[74]State v. Vandergriff, 2001-Ohio-4327, 2001 WL 1117182, *6 (Ohio Ct. App. 11th Dist. Ashtabula County 2001), quoting State v. Hicks, 88 Ohio App. 3d 515, 624 N.E.2d 332 (10th Dist. Franklin County 1993).

discipline, the burden of going forward with the evidence is on the defendant.[75] The burden of proof is by a preponderance of the evidence.[76]

Q & A: When should the court give the instruction?

Where the defendant has presented sufficient evidence that she or he was engaged in reasonably disciplining the child, the trier of fact must weigh whether the actions constituted domestic violence or whether they constituted reasonable and proper parental discipline.[77] In *State v. Vandergriff*,[78] the Ashtabula County Appellate Court noted that the defendant raised the issue in his testimony and further that counsel argued the defense in his closing. By not requesting a jury instruction on the issue, the defendant's attorney committed an error.[79]

Q & A: How is it determined that a parent may be absolved of domestic violence by invoking the parental discipline defense?

In *Samples v. Cruz*,[80] a 14-year-old child allegedly got into an altercation with her stepmother with whom she lives. The child's mother filed for a civil protection order. At the full hearing, the child told the court that her stepmother grabbed her arms and shook her and grabbed and pulled her hair. The social worker testified that she observed no bruises on the child. The father testified that he saw no bruises and that the child did not speak of any injuries. Several other witnesses stated that they saw no injuries or marks on the child.

The trial court denied the protection order, holding that "the respondent acted reasonably in disciplining the minor step-child without intent to inflict serious injury."[81] On appeal, the petitioner-appellant argued that the trial court erred by holding that intent to cause injury

---

[75]See State v. Habo, 2013-Ohio-2142, 2013 WL 2308483 (Ohio Ct. App. 11th Dist. Portage County 2013), citing State v. Phillips, 2012-Ohio-6023, 2012 WL 6651822 (Ohio Ct. App. 10th Dist. Franklin County 2012), citing State v. Zielinski, 2011-Ohio-6535, 2011 WL 6382541 (Ohio Ct. App. 12th Dist. Warren County 2011). But see State v. Rosa, 2013-Ohio-5867, 6 N.E.3d 57 (Ohio Ct. App. 7th Dist. Mahoning County 2013) (finding that the state bears the burden of proof that the parental discipline was improper); State v. Behlke, 2017-Ohio-7910, 2017 WL 4334342 (Ohio Ct. App. 9th Dist. Wayne County 2017) (explaining that the reasonable parental discipline defense must be raised or argued in the trial court and challenged on appeal in order to be considered by appellate court).

[76]See State v. Vandergriff, 2001-Ohio-4327, 2001 WL 1117182 (Ohio Ct. App. 11th Dist. Ashtabula County 2001).

[77]See, e.g., State v. Mills, 1997 WL 133430 (Ohio Ct. App. 1st Dist. Hamilton County 1997).

[78]State v. Vandergriff, 2001-Ohio-4327, 2001 WL 1117182, *7 (Ohio Ct. App. 11th Dist. Ashtabula County 2001).

[79]See State v. Adaranijo, 153 Ohio App. 3d 266, 2003-Ohio-3822, 792 N.E.2d 1138 (1st Dist. Hamilton County 2003) (where it is unclear whether the parental discipline defense was even raised. The court held that though reasonable parental discipline is an affirmative defense, here the evidence not only manifestly raised the defense, it proved it. "Therefore, we hold that, as a matter of law, Adaranijo's actions did not rise to a level exceeding reasonable parental discipline and, therefore the evidence to convict Adaranijo of domestic violence was insufficient.").

[80]Samples v. Cruz, 2001 WL 534165 (Ohio Ct. App. 8th Dist. Cuyahoga County 2001).

[81]Samples v. Cruz, 2001 WL 534165, *3 (Ohio Ct. App. 8th Dist. Cuyahoga County 2001). State v. Holzwart, 151 Ohio App. 3d 417, 2003-Ohio-345, 784 N.E.2d 192 (3d

was an essential element of civil domestic violence, despite overwhelming evidence of physical injury.

The appellate court stated that "when granting a protection order, the trial court must find that petitioner has shown by a preponderance of the evidence that petitioner or petitioner's family or household members are in danger of domestic violence."[82] The Cuyahoga County Court of Appeals then stated that respondent's intent to commit serious physical injury upon the child was irrelevant. The real question was whether the child was in danger of domestic violence in that whether the child was placed "by threat of force, in fear of imminent serious physical harm."

In affirming the trial court decision, the appellate court noted that there was no evidence of physical injury to the child. "Further, that Nakita was actually in fear of imminent serious physical injury that day is lessened by her not invoking the aid of her grandparent (who was in another room of the house watching television at the time of the incident), telling her father on the telephone within minutes of having received her punishment that she was okay, not showing the injuries later that evening to her father, brother, and step-sister, and not seeking medical attention for the claimed injuries."[83]

The court then discounted appellant's argument that the discipline was excessive. After noting that neither bruises nor scabbing or recent trauma to her bald spot were evident to a social worker that spoke to the child five days after the incident, the court determined that there was no imminent serious harm to the child. Additionally, the court reasoned that the child's punishment was the result of her hostile and disrespectful attitude to her stepmother. Even if the stepmother grabbed her arms in an attempt to get her to sit down and even if she did grab the child's hair as the child was running away, these responses were not unduly harsh or unreasonable.[84]

This decision focused on the level of conduct necessary to sustain the burden of proof. Moreover, the court apparently ascertained that the stepmother's motive for the physical conduct was punishment rather than domestic violence. Because her actions were reasonable and the physical conduct was not excessive under the circumstances, the parental discipline defense was properly invoked to absolve the stepmother of the charge of domestic violence.

On the other hand, the Hocking County Court of Appeals determined that a father's conduct rose to domestic violence and was not reason-

Dist. Seneca County 2003) (although appellant raised his voice at his stepdaughter for breaking house rules, without any physical harm, the discipline was reasonable and proper; appellant had threatened to bash in stepdaughter's head but stepdaughter said she was not fearful).

[82]Samples v. Cruz, 2001 WL 534165, *4 (Ohio Ct. App. 8th Dist. Cuyahoga County 2001), quoting Felton v. Felton, 79 Ohio St. 3d 34, 1997-Ohio-302, 679 N.E.2d 672 (1997).

[83]Samples v. Cruz, 2001 WL 534165, *4 (Ohio Ct. App. 8th Dist. Cuyahoga County 2001).

[84]Samples v. Cruz, 2001 WL 534165, *5 (Ohio Ct. App. 8th Dist. Cuyahoga County 2001); see also Thompson v. Koontz, 2000 WL 1739291 (Ohio Ct. App. 8th Dist. Cuyahoga County 2000).

able discipline of his daughter. In *State v. McNichols*,[85] defendant grabbed his 11-year-old daughter by the arm, shook her and pushed her to the floor because she refused to wear her slippers, go to her room, and because she argued with her parents. He also threatened to "kill somebody." Both the child and her mother testified that the child was not hurt and that she sustained no injury. Defendant argued that three eyewitnesses testified that there was no assault and that defendant was just a father exercising his parental control by grabbing his daughter's shoulder and directing her to her room.[86]

The Fourth District Court of Appeals analyzed the record and concluded that there was no evidence to indicate that an assault did not occur nor did anyone, besides the defendant, testify that they thought defendant was only trying to discipline his daughter.[87] The court reasoned that "a rational trier of fact could conclude that, an eleven year-old girl would probably be injured when she is shaken and pushed down by her father. Moreover, a reasonable trier of fact could conclude that because of his statement that he was going to kill somebody he was angry and intended to harm his daughter."[88] Therefore, the court affirmed the trial court and held that defendant's attempted discipline of his child was not reasonable.

Q & A: Are there cases that have addressed whether proof of unreasonable parental discipline is part of the analysis of the physical harm element of the domestic violence statute rather than as an affirmative defense?

Yes. In *State v. Rosa*,[89] appellant appealed his conviction for domestic violence. The appellate court determined that "[a] threshold issue of first impression in this district is whether unreasonable parental discipline is a component of the physical harm element of RC 2919.25(A) or whether reasonable parental discipline is an affirmative defense."[90]

Relying on *State v. Suchomski*,[91] the appellate court reasoned that *Suchomski* determined that the burden of proving the unreasonableness of parental discipline on the state as an element of the offense.[92] The appellate court noted that the fact pattern, coupled with the

[85]State v. McNichols, 2002-Ohio-6253, 2002 WL 31538788 (Ohio Ct. App. 4th Dist. Hocking County 2002); see also State v. Craun, 158 Ohio App. 3d 389, 2004-Ohio-4403, 815 N.E.2d 1141 (3d Dist. Shelby County 2004) (spanking 15 year old stepdaughter several times with a wooden paddle, forcing her to the ground, covering her mouth and causing her to suffer bruising and swelling was domestic violence and not reasonable parental discipline).

[86]State v. McNichols, 2002-Ohio-6253, 2002 WL 31538788, *1 (Ohio Ct. App. 4th Dist. Hocking County 2002).

[87]State v. McNichols, 2002-Ohio-6253, 2002 WL 31538788, *3 (Ohio Ct. App. 4th Dist. Hocking County 2002).

[88]State v. McNichols, 2002-Ohio-6253, 2002 WL 31538788, *3 (Ohio Ct. App. 4th Dist. Hocking County 2002).

[89]State v. Rosa, 2013-Ohio-5867, 6 N.E.3d 57 (Ohio Ct. App. 7th Dist. Mahoning County 2013).

[90]State v. Rosa, 2013-Ohio-5867, 6 N.E.3d 57, ¶ 2 (Ohio Ct. App. 7th Dist. Mahoning County 2013); see also State v. Clark, 2015-Ohio-2978, 2015 WL 4510693 (Ohio Ct. App. 9th Dist. Wayne County 2015) (declining to weigh in on the issue as defendant failed to challenge it in the trial court).

[91]State v. Suchomski, 58 Ohio St. 3d 74, 567 N.E.2d 1304 (1991).

[92]State v. Rosa, 2013-Ohio-5867, 6 N.E.3d 57, ¶ 2 (Ohio Ct. App. 7th Dist. Mahon-

limited analysis in *Suchomski*, made application of the holding difficult and in light of the lack of a resolution in the appellate districts, urged the Ohio Supreme Court to provide guidance.

Discussing the split within the appellate districts,[93] the Mahoning County Court of Appeals reasoned that unreasonable parental discipline was a component of a domestic violence charge pursuant to RC 2919.25(A) and that it was incumbent upon the state to prove. Additionally, the court found that since the nature of the parent's discipline was an element of the offense, then the state's burden of proof is beyond a reasonable doubt. Had the court decided that reasonable parental discipline was an affirmative defense, it would have been upon the defendant-parent to prove. That said, if it was an affirmative defense, the burden of proof would be on the defendant based on the preponderance of the evidence standard.

"Resolving a threshold issue of first impression in this district, we hold that in order to convict a parent of domestic violence pursuant to RC 2919.25, as part of the 'physical harm' element, the State bears the burden of proving the parent's discipline was improper and unreasonable given the circumstances. This is the better approach given the unique circumstances of the parent/child relationship; specifically the fundamental constitutional right of child-rearing, which includes the parent's right to discipline their child, including the use of reasonable corporal punishment. Placing the burden on the parent to prove the reasonableness of his or her discipline runs contrary to the Supreme Court of Ohio's *Suchomski* case and presents potential constitutional problems."[94]

Apparently, those courts that have held that the prosecutor must prove that the parental discipline was improper and unreasonable in a domestic violence case have found constitutional problems with forcing parents to prove their innocence especially because reasonable corporal punishment is legal in Ohio. This is because a child does not have any legally protected interest against proper and reasonable parental discipline.[95] So to, under RC 2919.22(B)(3), the state bears the burden of proving that parent administered excessive corporal punishment.

"In order to reconcile the general domestic violence statute, RC 2919.25(A), with the more specific child endangering statute, RC 2919. 22(B)(3), the burden of proof should remain with the state to prove unreasonable corporal punishment when the charge is brought against a parent under the domestic violence statute. Having this consistency will avoid the problem of the state using the domestic violence statute

ing County 2013).

[93]State v. Rosa, 2013-Ohio-5867, 6 N.E.3d 57, ¶ 26 (Ohio Ct. App. 7th Dist. Mahoning County 2013), but it is worth noting that the districts listed by *Rosa* to have treated the issue as an element of the offense with the state bearing the burden of proof have applied a sufficiency analysis and focused on the totality of the circumstances; but see State v. Zielinski, 2014-Ohio-5318, 2014 WL 6725663 (Ohio Ct. App. 12th Dist. Warren County 2014) noting that the 12th District is not obligated to follow the 7th District case or its reasoning).

[94]State v. Rosa, 2013-Ohio-5867, 6 N.E.3d 57, ¶ 52 (Ohio Ct. App. 7th Dist. Mahoning County 2013).

[95]See State v. Suchomski, 58 Ohio St. 3d 74, 567 N.E.2d 1304 (1991).

to avoid meeting part of its burden of proof in a situation that involves potential excessive or unreasonable corporal punishment by a parent."[96]

Q & A: May a parent who administers corporal punishment to a child be arrested and detained for the offense of domestic violence even though the punishment does not create a substantial risk of serious physical harm to the child for the purpose of charging the parent with endangering children under RC 2919.22?

Ohio's Attorney General has clarified that Ohio's preferred arrest policy in domestic violence cases applies to family or household members who administer corporal punishment to their children when the punishment exceeds that which is reasonable and proper under the circumstances even though the conduct falls short of that required to sustain an arrest for the offense of endangering children.[97] Thus, each case in which domestic violence against a child is alleged "should be viewed on a case-by-case basis by local law enforcement officers, prosecutors, and judges to determine whether the corporal punishment was reasonable and proper under the circumstances."[98]

The Attorney General then stressed that law enforcement officials should carefully evaluate the circumstances in which the corporal punishment was administered to determine whether the person acted with the requisite culpability for the offense of domestic violence and ensure discretion when they arrest in this circumstance.

Q & A: What are legally permissible reasons under RC 2935.03(B)(3)(c) for not making an arrest for domestic violence when a peace officer has reasonable grounds to believe that the offense of domestic violence has been committed and that the parent is guilty of committing domestic violence?

Ohio's Attorney General determined that RC 2935.03(B) does not identify in the statute the reasons a peace officer may consider for not arresting. Instead, RC 2935.032 requires that the agency adopt written policies that set forth examples of reasons a police officer may consider for not arresting in a specific situation.[99]

The Attorney General then advised that law enforcement policies may authorize an officer in such a situation to consider whether the corporal punishment is reasonable and proper under the circumstances. Factors such as the age, size, and conduct of the child, the nature of the child's misconduct, the influence of the child's misconduct upon other children in the same family or group, the mental and physical condition of the child, the child's response to the corporal punishment, the location, severity, frequency and duration of the punishment and the nature of the instrument used for administer-

---

[96]State v. Rosa, 2013-Ohio-5867, 6 N.E.3d 57, ¶ 34 (Ohio Ct. App. 7th Dist. Mahoning County 2013).

[97]2001 Ohio Op. Att'y Gen. No. 2-229, 2001 Ohio Op. Att'y. Gen. No. 2001-039, 2001 WL 1172828 (Ohio A.G.).

[98]2001 Ohio Op. Att'y Gen. No. 2-229, 2001 Ohio Op. Att'y. Gen. No. 2001-039, 2001 WL 1172828, at *4 (Ohio A.G.).

[99]2001 Ohio Op. Att'y Gen. No. 2-229, 2001 Ohio Op. Att'y. Gen. No. 2001-039, 2001 WL 1172828 (Ohio A.G.).

ing the punishment may be considered in order to aid peace officers in making a decision whether to arrest.[100]

Additionally, a peace officer should also consider a person's state of mind while administering the corporal punishment, a person's history of domestic violence or other violent acts, statements made to the officer by the person, the child or other witnesses, the officer's evaluation of the child's safety and any other facts or circumstances the officer considers relevant.[101] As each police report is required to document the officer's observations of the victim and the alleged perpetrator,[102] each agency policy must articulate its own reasons for not arresting in this situation.

Q & A: Can a parent invoke the parental discipline defense where the child is 18 years old?

Several cases have ruled in the negative. For example, in *State v. Miller*,[103] the defendant was charged with hitting his 18-year-old daughter with a belt, leaving welts. The father raised the parental discipline defense. The Hamilton County Appellate Court rejected the use of the defense and determined the defense is inapplicable when domestic violence is committed by a parent on a child already 18 years old. The court noted that the evidence was sufficient to support a conviction under RC 2919.25(A).

Similarly, in *State v. Blevins*,[104] the father was accused of using physical force against his 19-year-old daughter by slapping her twice across the side of her face, causing temporary hearing loss. The appellate court held that the parental discipline defense was inapplicable due to the child's age, and upheld the parent's domestic violence conviction. The court noted that even if the defense was applied, the evidence was sufficient to establish the defendant inflicted physical harm, which would overcome the defense.[105]

Of significance is that many courts appear to base their rulings on the child's age, rather than on the nature of the act; what may be considered domestic violence if committed against an adult child is reasonable parental discipline if committed against a minor.

Conclusion: Many of the court decisions demonstrate the level of conduct needed to sustain a conviction for domestic violence. Some courts are quick to explain that nothing in the domestic violence statute prevents a parent from properly disciplining his/her child. Others explain that the low standard of requiring only "physical harm" in the domestic violence statute does not ignore a parent's right to use corporal punishment.

---

[100] 2001 Ohio Op. Att'y Gen. No. 2-229, 2001 Ohio Op. Att'y. Gen. No. 2001-039, 2001 WL 1172828, at *7 (Ohio A.G.).

[101] 2001 Ohio Op. Att'y Gen. No. 2-229, 2001 Ohio Op. Att'y. Gen. No. 2001-039, 2001 WL 1172828, at *7 (Ohio A.G.).

[102] See RC 2935.032(D).

[103] State v. Miller, 134 Ohio App. 3d 649, 731 N.E.2d 1192 (1st Dist. Hamilton County 1999).

[104] State v. Blevins, 133 Ohio App. 3d 196, 727 N.E.2d 169 (12th Dist. Butler County 1999).

[105] See also the *Blevins* dissent, in which one justice stated that the daughter, although an adult, "was still appellant's child living in appellant's household, and thereby expected to conform her conduct to that determined by appellant." State v. Blevins, 133 Ohio App. 3d 196, 199, 727 N.E.2d 169 (12th Dist. Butler County 1999).

For example, striking a child in anger is not considered reasonable corporal punishment. Striking a child for purposes of parental discipline is reasonable and many of the more recent cases have overturned convictions for domestic violence where the court was able to ascertain that the motivation for the physical conduct in question was punishment.

However, each court was reluctant to overstep the boundaries created within the family structure relative to discipline of the children. It is quite clear that the courts did not intend to do more than seek to establish a healthy balance between corporal punishment and proper and reasonable parental discipline. Courts are unwilling to question a parent's personal disciplinary choice unless the child's welfare is jeopardized by the conduct. Underlying many of the court decisions is a fear of labeling a parent an abuser because he/she may use certain disciplinary measures that are not in accord with today's parental norms.

Q & A: How is excessive corporal punishment defined?

No Ohio court has specifically detailed those factors that constitute excessive corporal punishment.[106] However, an Illinois appeals court set forth factors that a court should consider in defining abusive behavior. In *In Interest of J.P.*,[107] the appellant used a wooden spoon to spank her child. Although this was done with some regularity, the court determined that the act did not by itself constitute abuse, even though a one-inch bruise resulted from one of the spankings. The court relied on the testimony of the child's baby-sitter that the child appeared happy and unaffected and the fact that the mother displayed a calm demeanor at the time of the spankings.

Because the court could draw no firm line between excessive and non-excessive corporal punishment, it looked to other court decisions for guidance. The Illinois appellate court applied factors set forth in *In re F. W.*[108] to evaluate the reasonableness of a parent's conduct. Those factors include (1) the degree of physical injury, (2) the likelihood of future, more serious injury, (3) the psychological effects on the child, and (4) the circumstances surrounding the discipline, including the parent's demeanor, whether the parent was calm or "lashing out" in anger.[109]

---

[106]See Bowman v. Bowman, 2014-Ohio-2851, 2014 WL 2957475 (Ohio Ct. App. 9th Dist. Medina County 2014) (holding that respondent's use of corporal punishment was excessive under the circumstances and created a substantial risk of harm to the child under RC 2919.22(B)(3) by slapping the child with enough force to knock her to the ground and leaving a handprint and causing her lip to swell all because she would not hand over the iPod). But see Rader v. Rader, 2007-Ohio-4288, 2007 WL 2390815 (Ohio Ct. App. 5th Dist. Licking County 2007) (despite excessive corporal punishment, court affirmed the denial of the issuance of CPO).

[107]In Interest of J.P., 294 Ill. App. 3d 991, 229 Ill. Dec. 565, 692 N.E.2d 338 (1st Dist. 1998).

[108]In re F.W., 261 Ill. App. 3d 894, 199 Ill. Dec. 769, 634 N.E.2d 1123 (4th Dist. 1994).

[109]In Interest of J.P., 294 Ill. App. 3d 991, 229 Ill. Dec. 565, 692 N.E.2d 338 (1st Dist. 1998); see also State v. Jones, 140 Ohio App. 3d 422, 747 N.E.2d 891 (8th Dist. Cuyahoga County 2000) (wherein the appellate court considered the parent's state of mind while administering the discipline as a factor to be considered in determining

In *State v. Hart*,[110] the court set forth several factors for determining the propriety and reasonableness of corporal punishment after analyzing the totality of the circumstances: 1) the child's age; 2) the child's behavior leading up to the discipline; 3) the child's response to prior non-corporal punishment; 4) the location and severity of the punishment; and 5) the parent's state of mind while administering the punishment.[111] With these factors and those applied in *In Interest of J.P.*, both attorneys and courts should now have a consistent and logical screening device for determining which cases rise to the level of domestic violence. Because it is apparent that the courts have been reluctant to encroach upon the family in the context of parental discipline, these particular factors may provide added guidance and direction to the courts.

Q & A: Can a parent be charged with a crime for failing to prevent the other parent from abusing the child?

It depends on the nature of the abusive act against the child and the level of inaction. Since there is an affirmative duty to protect children from harm, "an unexcusable failure to act in the discharge of [that] duty" constitutes an "act" under RC 2919.22.[112] Effective August 25, 1999, 1999 House Bill 162 created the new offense of permitting child abuse.[113] Specifically, RC 2903.15(A) provides that:

> [n]o parent, guardian, custodian, or person having custody of a child under eighteen years of age or of a mentally or physically handicapped child under twenty-one years of age shall cause serious physical harm to the child, or the death of the child, as a proximate result of permitting the child to be abused, to be tortured, to be administered corporal punishment or other physical disciplinary measure, or to be physically restrained in a cruel manner or for a prolonged period.[114]

Under RC 2903.15, the defendant is held to a strict liability standard. However, it is an affirmative defense that the defendant did not have readily available a means to prevent the harm to or death of

---

the reasonableness of a parent's conduct).

[110] State v. Hart, 110 Ohio App. 3d 250, 673 N.E.2d 992 (3d Dist. Defiance County 1996). See also Bowman v. Bowman, 2014-Ohio-2851, 2014 WL 2957475 (Ohio Ct. App. 9th Dist. Medina County 2014) (in determining whether the corporal punishment was excessive, a trial court must consider the totality of the circumstances including the age of the child, the child's response to non corporal punishment and the behavior being punished, at ¶ 11; citing In re K.B., 2003-Ohio-3784, 2003 WL 21658319, ¶ 9-15 (Ohio Ct. App. 9th Dist. Summit County 2003); quoting, Matter of Jandrew, 1997 WL 802848, *4 (Ohio Ct. App. 4th Dist. Washington County 1997).

[111] State v. Hart, 110 Ohio App. 3d 250, 256, 673 N.E.2d 992 (3d Dist. Defiance County 1996); State v. Sellers, 2012-Ohio-676, 2012 WL 562420 (Ohio Ct. App. 12th Dist. Butler County 2012); State v. Thompson, 2006-Ohio-582, 2006 WL 307715 (Ohio Ct. App. 2d Dist. Miami County 2006); State v. Zielinski, 2011-Ohio-6535, 2011 WL 6382541 (Ohio Ct. App. 12th Dist. Warren County 2011); State v. McKinney, 2012-Ohio-4521, 2012 WL 4482035 (Ohio Ct. App. 12th Dist. Butler County 2012); State v. Rosa, 2013-Ohio-5867, 6 N.E.3d 57 (Ohio Ct. App. 7th Dist. Mahoning County 2013).

[112] Couch v. Harrison, 2001-Ohio-4199, 2001 WL 121108, *2 (Ohio Ct. App. 12th Dist. Clermont County 2001).

[113] RC 2903.15.

[114] See also RC 2919.22.

the child[115] and that the defendant took timely and reasonable steps to summon aid.

These provisions may negatively and disproportionately impact victims of domestic violence who fail to leave the situation. Studies demonstrate that child abuse is domestic violence.[116] Child abuse exists in approximately sixty percent of families in which domestic violence is part of the family dynamic.[117] Therefore, children of mothers who are victims of domestic violence will be exposed, either directly or indirectly to that violence and may be at a greater risk of injury and/or death because of the exposure.

Sometimes, women stay in abusive relationships in order to ensure necessary financial support for their children. Sometimes they stay because of threats by violent partners to harm or further injure the children or launch lengthy custody battles if they leave.

Battered women may be charged with permitting child abuse if they fail to leave the battering relationship with the children or if they fail to protect the children from their abusive partner.[118] Such a strict liability standard for holding one parent liable for the acts of the other will only hurt victims of domestic violence who seek any kind of protection for themselves and their children.

RC 2903.15 fails to provide a definition for "permitting child abuse." Absent a concise and specific definition of the term "permitting," a victim of domestic violence may be charged with permitting child abuse simply for failing to leave the home in which the abuse is occurring. By creating a standard whereby both the perpetrator and the victim of domestic violence are culpable, the legislation reinforces the negative social stereotype that victims are to blame for not leaving their abusers.[119]

Besides being charged with criminal activity, victims of domestic violence have been found negligent or they may become respondents in civil protection order actions.[120] A New York appellate case, *In Re Lonell J.*,[121] illustrates the point that victims of domestic violence are often found culpable for the crimes committed by others towards their

[115]See, e.g., Couch v. Harrison, 2001-Ohio-4199, 2001 WL 121108 (Ohio Ct. App. 12th Dist. Clermont County 2001); see also Text § 15:24, Other issues that impact custody and visitation awards.

[116]See A. E. Appel & G. W. Holden, The Co-occurrence of Spouse and Physical Child Abuse: A Review and Appraisal, 12 J. of Fam. Psychol. 578–99 (1998); see also 5 Frazee, Noel and Brenneke, Violence Against Women pp 134–54; Howard A. Davidson, American Bar Association, A Report to the President of the American Bar Association, The Impact of Domestic Violence on Children (1994).

[117]See National Research Council, Understanding Child Abuse and Neglect (National Academy Press 1993).

[118]See Couch v. Harrison, 2001-Ohio-4199, 2001 WL 121108 (Ohio Ct. App. 12th Dist. Clermont County 2001); see also Laurel A. Kent, Addressing the Impact of Domestic Violence on Children: Alternatives to Laws Criminalizing the Commission of Domestic Violence in the Presence of a Child, 2001 Wis. L. Rev. 1337 (2001).

[119]See The "Failure to Protect" Working Group, Charging Battered Mothers With "Failure to Protect": Still Blaming the Victim, 27 Fordham Urb. L.J. 849 (Winter 2000).

[120]See, e.g., Couch v. Harrison, 2001-Ohio-4199, 2001 WL 121108 (Ohio Ct. App. 12th Dist. Clermont County 2001).

[121]In re Lonell J., 242 A.D.2d 58, 673 N.Y.S.2d 116 (1st Dep't 1998).

children. In that case, a parent was found to have neglected her children because of domestic violence committed by the other parent in the presence of the children. The court found sufficient evidence of neglect in the children's witnessing the abuse of their mother by their father. This case sends a chilling message to victims of domestic violence that they bear the responsibility for the violence created by the perpetrator and that they risk removal of their children by remaining in the home.

Q & A: Are there any cases that have determined the constitutionality of removing children from battered mothers?[122]

In a case of first impression, the United States Eastern District Court of New York issued a preliminary injunction prohibiting the Administration for Children's Services from removing children from battered mothers, not otherwise deemed to be unfit. In *In re Nicholson*,[123] a class action suit was filed in federal district court on behalf of women who were battered and who, through no fault of their own, had their children removed by the children's services agency. The judge focused his concern on the agency's practice of removing children of battered mothers for the reason that the mothers "engaged in" domestic violence by being victims of such violence and that the children had been witnesses. By granting the injunction, the court validated the plaintiffs' claim that this policy violated the constitutional right of parents and children not to be separated by the government unless the parent is unfit to care for the child. Additionally, the court required the children's services agency to improve its response to domestic violence in families.

Q & A: Do a parent's unpredictable actions, consumption of alcohol while taking prescription medications, and severe mental health problems create a danger to the other parent and the children such that the actions of the parent rise to the level of domestic violence for the purpose of obtaining a civil protection order?

This level of conduct was considered by the trial court in *Loeffler v.*

---

[122]See also Text § 15:24, Other issues that impact custody and visitation awards.

[123]In re Nicholson, 181 F. Supp. 2d 182 (E.D. N.Y. 2002), opinion supplemented, 203 F. Supp. 2d 153 (E.D. N.Y. 2002) and modified and superseded, 294 F. Supp. 2d 369 (E.D. N.Y. 2003) and modified and supplemented, 2004 WL 1304055 (E.D. N.Y. 2004); In re Nicholson, 2001 WL 1338834 (E.D. N.Y. 2001); see also Nicholson v. Williams, 202 F.R.D. 377 (E.D. N.Y. 2001), opinion corrected and superseded, 205 F.R.D. 92 (E.D. N.Y. 2001); question certified by Nicholson v. Scoppetta, 344 F.3d 154 (2d Cir. 2003), certified question accepted, 1 N.Y.3d 538, 775 N.Y.S.2d 233, 807 N.E.2d 283 (2003) and certified question answered, 3 N.Y.3d 357, 787 N.Y.S.2d 196, 820 N.E.2d 840 (2004); certified question accepted by Nicholson v. Scoppetta, 1 N.Y.3d 538, 775 N.Y.S.2d 233, 807 N.E.2d 283 (2003) (The questions presented for certification on appeal are: (1) Does the definition of a "neglected child" under N.Y. Fam. Ct. Act § 1012(f), (h) include instances in which the sole allegation of neglect is that the parent or other person legally responsible for the child's care allows the child to witness domestic abuse against the caretaker? (2) Can the injury or possible injury, if any, that results to a child who has witnessed domestic abuse against a parent or other caretaker constitute "danger" or "risk" to the child's "life or health" as those terms are defined in N.Y. Fam. Ct. Act § 1022, § 1024, §§ 1026 to 1028? (3) Does the fact that the child witnessed such abuse suffice to demonstrate that "removal is necessary" or that "removal was in the child's best interests" or must the child protective agency offer additional, particularized evidence to justify removal? Briefs by the respondents and appellants are pending).

Loeffler.[124] In that case, the victim had filed a petition in domestic violence alleging the respondent-wife committed acts of domestic violence under RC 3113.31. The respondent's severe mental health problems, alleged acts of domestic violence, and consumption of alcohol endangered his children. He requested that the respondent be evicted from the marital home and sought to restrict her visitation with the children. Evidence was presented at the hearing by the parties, a psychologist, and psychiatrist. The referee concluded that the respondent had committed an act of domestic violence and recommended that she vacate the marital home. The trial court appeared to consider the totality of appellee's actions, but did not find them extreme enough to create a danger to the children. The trial court then found that "appellee's actions constituted a single act of domestic violence but concluded that such act was not sufficient to require appellee to completely vacate the marital home."[125]

It is also significant that, even though the trial court determined that the cumulative actions of the parent did constitute an act of domestic violence under RC 3113.31, the court did not grant the petitioner the remedies he sought. Obviously, the totality of the respondent's actions did not rise to that level of conduct necessary for the court to justify evicting her from the marital home.

The Lucas County Court of Appeals failed to reverse the decision. The court stated that, absent an abuse of discretion, it would not reverse the trial court. In fact, it specifically found that the trial court did not abuse its discretion in determining that, though respondent's actions constituted a single act of domestic violence, she should only be required to partially vacate the residence.

Q & A: What persons are required by law to report suspected physical or sexual abuse of children?

RC 3113.31(H) specifically provides that "[w]hen a petition under this section alleges domestic violence against minor children, the court shall report the fact, or cause reports to be made, to a county, township, or municipal peace officer under section 2151.421 of the Revised Code." It is significant that the statute requires this reporting to be made by the court or by another at the insistence of the court. Furthermore, it should be noted that this directive is set into motion, not after the court has determined the truth of the allegations after a hearing, but merely when the petition alleges such fact.

Under RC 2151.421(A)(1),[126] an attorney who "knows or suspects that a child . . . has suffered or faces a threat of suffering any physical or mental wound, injury, disability, or condition of a nature that reasonably indicates abuse or neglect of the child" has a clear duty to report child abuse or neglect to the county department of human ser-

[124] Loeffler v. Loeffler, 1995 WL 628239 (Ohio Ct. App. 6th Dist. Lucas County 1995).

[125] Loeffler v. Loeffler, 1995 WL 628239, *1 (Ohio Ct. App. 6th Dist. Lucas County 1995).

[126] Am. Sub. S.B. 17, eff. 8-3-06, changes the term "suspect" in RC 2151.421(A)(1)(a) and other sections to: "has reasonable cause to suspect based on facts that would cause a reasonable person in a similar position to suspect . . . ."

vices or a municipal or county peace officer.[127] In civil protection order cases, an attorney who files for a protection order because of a known or suspected incident of child abuse must also report the suspected abuse to the appropriate agency. Filing the protection order does not excuse the attorney from reporting.[128]

Family law practitioners who routinely deal with domestic violence are encouraged to get to know their local department of human services staff. When domestic violence is known or suspected, the attorney could then let the parent know that he/she is familiar with the local human services staff who are available to assist the family members. Reporting of incidents of suspected abuse also serves child domestic violence victims by providing documentation which may be critical to pending or future litigation.

§ 8:8 Miscellaneous issues

Q & A: Can destruction of property be considered domestic violence under RC 3113.31(A)(1)(b)?

At least one Ohio court answered this in the affirmative. In *Siouffi v. Siouffi*,[1] the defendant slashed the tires on his wife's car with a twelve-inch-long knife, causing the victim to obtain a civil protection order. The evidence adduced at trial indicated that the victim saw him take the knife outside. However, she remained inside the home and did not actually witness the tire slashing. After he slashed her tires, he re-entered the residence and informed her of the act. The police officer testified that the victim seemed upset. The defendant testified that, when he attempted to re-enter the home, his wife would not let him in and that he had to push his way back inside.

On appeal, the defendant argued that, in slashing the tires on his wife's car, he only committed an act of property damage and that at no time did he threaten force against her. He also stated that, if tire slashing constitutes domestic violence, then breaking a plate or a glass during family discussions could also be considered domestic violence.

The Montgomery County Court of Appeals found that the defendant's conduct did not rise to the level of domestic violence under RC 3113.31(A)(1)(a) or RC 3113.31(A)(1)(c), but that it did rise to the level of a threat under RC 3113.31(A)(1)(b). That the victim did not expressly see the tire slashing did not make the defendant's conduct any less of a threat of force directed at her. The court noted that the question of "whether a person is placed in fear of imminent serious physical harm by particular threatening conduct also involves an ele-

[127]See Hite v. Brown, 100 Ohio App. 3d 606, 654 N.E.2d 452 (8th Dist. Cuyahoga County 1995) (discussing who should report child abuse); see also Fischer v. Metcalf, 543 So. 2d 785 (Fla. 3d DCA 1989).

[128]RC 3113.31(H). But see RC 2151.421(A)(2) for certain exceptions to attorney reporting, i.e., attorney-client privilege.

[Section 8:8]

[1]Siouffi v. Siouffi, 1998 WL 879255 (Ohio Ct. App. 2d Dist. Montgomery County 1998).

ment of objectivity."[2] In this case, it was reasonable for the victim to fear imminent serious physical harm from threatening conduct involving the use of a twelve-inch knife. "This is not a case where a person of unusual sensibilities was frightened by what might objectively be viewed as relatively innocuous conduct."[3]

The court also distinguished this situation from others involving destruction of property and reinforced that the use of the twelve-inch-long knife was crucial to the decision. The fact that the police officer testified to the victim's frightened demeanor was also a critical factor in the court's determination.[4]

Q & A: Does it matter whether the property destroyed was owned by both the victim and the defendant?

No Ohio court has addressed this specific issue. Other state courts have held that, for purposes of criminal prosecution, a person may be charged with destroying property that he/she co-owns with the victim. Although none of these cases specifically predicates prosecution on a violation of the domestic violence statutes, each discusses the facts in terms of domestic violence. Whether the charge was for malicious mischief or criminal damaging was not as significant as the fact that, in all of these cases, it was not a defense that the defendant had an interest in the property that he destroyed.[5]

Even in trespass cases, a spouse can be criminally liable for trespassing in his/her spouse's dwelling when the other spouse owns, has custody of, or has control over the property where the crime occurred.[6] The Supreme Court has determined in *O'Neal* and *Lilly* that custody and control, rather than legal title, is dispositive for purposes of criminal trespass and burglary.[7]

Although Ohio's domestic violence statutes[8] fail to specifically prohibit destruction of property, Ohio prosecutors may charge an offender with the crime of aggravated menacing under RC 2903.21 or

---

[2]Siouffi v. Siouffi, 1998 WL 879255, *4 (Ohio Ct. App. 2d Dist. Montgomery County 1998).

[3]Siouffi v. Siouffi, 1998 WL 879255, *4 (Ohio Ct. App. 2d Dist. Montgomery County 1998).

[4]See also City of Hamilton v. Roberson, 1998 WL 842754 (Ohio Ct. App. 12th Dist. Butler County 1998) (taking into consideration police officers' testimony that victim was shaken and appeared to be scared).

[5]See People v. Schneider, 139 Ill. App. 3d 222, 93 Ill. Dec. 712, 487 N.E.2d 379 (5th Dist. 1985); State v. Webb, 64 Wash. App. 480, 824 P.2d 1257 (Div. 1 1992), as amended on denial of reconsideration, (Mar. 31, 1992); State v. Superior Court In and For County of Maricopa, 188 Ariz. 372, 936 P.2d 558 (Ct. App. Div. 1 1997). But see People v. Kheyfets, 174 Misc. 2d 516, 665 N.Y.S.2d 802 (Sup 1997) (Court held that, because husband had equitable interest in the items he was charged with damaging, he could not be held liable under the criminal mischief statute. The court commented that the legislature should apply the domestic violence statute to the damage and destruction of marital or jointly owned property.).

[6]See State v. O'Neal, 87 Ohio St. 3d 402, 2000-Ohio-449, 721 N.E.2d 73 (2000); see also State v. Lilly, 87 Ohio St. 3d 97, 1999-Ohio-251, 717 N.E.2d 322 (1999); State v. Allen, 1999 WL 1101849 (Ohio Ct. App. 6th Dist. Lucas County 1999), cause dismissed, 88 Ohio St. 3d 1509, 728 N.E.2d 2 (2000).

[7]See State v. Crouse, 1999 WL 1123027 (Ohio Ct. App. 12th Dist. Fayette County 1999). See also Text § 2:7, Felony violations.

[8]See RC 3113.31, RC 2919.25.

menacing under RC 2903.22. The menacing statutes do not contemplate a specific relationship between the parties. However, the statutes provide that the offender must knowingly cause harm to the property of another, which suggests that the property is the victim's separate property.

Q & A: Is the defense of property a defense to domestic violence where both the defendant and the victim were joint owners of the property?

According to the majority opinion in *State v. Varney*,[9] the answer is no. In that case, defendant testified that his wife was damaging joint property and that the physical force used was to protect that property. On appeal, he argued that he should have been entitled to a jury instruction.

The Ashland County Court of Appeals acknowledged that the defense of property has been recognized if excessive force is not used, but that it was not applicable to the facts in *Varney*. The Court then pointed out that the legislative purpose in enacting the domestic violence statute was to protect family or household members. The Court reasoned that the "intent of the statute could be abrogated entirely by utilization of the defense of property unless clearly warranted as it is obvious that such would be claimed in virtually every case with the burden of establishing lack of ownership by the State often unlikely or impossible."[10] In affirming the trial court, the appellate court held that defense of property is not applicable to a charge of domestic violence under the facts as presented.

In contrast, the *Varney* dissent determined that if the property belonged to both, the wife did not have a right to destroy the property. By doing that, she would destroy appellant's property. Because defense of property was applicable to the facts in the case, a jury instruction should have been allowed. The dissent then noted that if the property clearly belonged to the wife or if it had minimal value, there would be no right to a jury instruction.

Q & A: Can threatening behavior, without an actual verbal threat, be sufficient for the issuance of a civil protection order?

The Montgomery County Court of Appeals answered this in the affirmative. In *Siouffi v. Siouffi*,[11] the defendant slashed the tires of his wife's car with a twelve-inch knife from the couple's kitchen and then forced his way back into the home. Although the defendant never threatened force against his wife, the appellate court upheld the issuance of a civil protection order. The court stated that "a threat of force need not be conveyed expressly; it may just as well be conveyed implicitly by conduct. Conduct which is threatening in nature is no

---

[9]State v. Varney, 2005-Ohio-1752, 2005 WL 859493 (Ohio Ct. App. 5th Dist. Ashland County 2005); see also Raynes v. Rogers, 183 Vt. 513, 2008 VT 52, 955 A.2d 1135 (2008) (holding that the defense of property defense is not a bar to the injunctive relief under the abuse prevention statute where the defendant uses reasonable force to protect personal property).

[10]State v. Varney, 2005-Ohio-1752, 2005 WL 859493, *1 (Ohio Ct. App. 5th Dist. Ashland County 2005).

[11]Siouffi v. Siouffi, 1998 WL 879255 (Ohio Ct. App. 2d Dist. Montgomery County 1998); see also Lefebvre v. Lefebvre, 165 Or. App. 297, 996 P.2d 518 (2000).

less threatening simply because it is unaccompanied by verbal expressions of the threat."[12]

Similarly, the Perry County Court of Appeals determined that a defendant's hitting of his palm with his fist was a threatening gesture that provided sufficient circumstantial evidence of a threat. In *State v. McCord*,[13] the victim testified that the appellant was facing her and repeatedly jamming his fist in the palm of his hand. Appellant admitted that he was hitting his palm with his fist but claimed that he was not threatening his wife but rather the person she went out with. The court found that, by appellant's own admission, his gestures were threatening and determined that there was "evidence of a threat which [the victim] could have believed was directed at her since she was alone in the apartment with appellant."[14]

It is clear that the courts have begun to define threatening conduct in terms other than words.[15] Because of these recent decisions, attorneys would do well to explore the totality of the circumstances of each incident. Even if there has been no verbal expression, the demeanor of a defendant may rise to an act of domestic violence.

Q & A: Do vague threats of fear, not specific to time and place, rise to the level of domestic violence for purposes of issuing a civil protection order?

Several appellate courts have answered in the negative. In *Rush v. Rush*,[16] the Cuyahoga County Court of Appeals reversed the trial court's issuance of a civil protection order, sustaining the husband's assignments of error. In that case, the petitioner testified in support of her civil protection order, " 'I have been stalked. I have been harassed. I was followed, watched, threatened—everything for the last—past four years, four years, and I can't get no help from nobody.' "[17]

The appellate court found that the evidence presented did not sustain a finding that the appellant had committed domestic violence under RC 3113.31(A)(1)(a) or RC 3113.31(A)(1)(b). The court reasoned that the wife failed to identify a single specific incident that would tend to suggest she was in reasonable fear of domestic violence. The "wife's evidence here was vague and wholly lacking in specific details. Standing alone, such a general summary of past unadjudicated events

---

[12] Siouffi v. Siouffi, 1998 WL 879255, *3 (Ohio Ct. App. 2d Dist. Montgomery County 1998).

[13] State v. McCord, 1998 WL 549266 (Ohio Ct. App. 5th Dist. Perry County 1998).

[14] State v. McCord, 1998 WL 549266, *3 (Ohio Ct. App. 5th Dist. Perry County 1998).

[15] See also State v. Harley, 1999 WL 3954 (Ohio Ct. App. 5th Dist. Fairfield County 1998); see also Martauz v. Martauz, 2009-Ohio-2642, 2009 WL 1581185 (Ohio Ct. App. 7th Dist. Mahoning County 2009).

[16] Rush v. Rush, 1999 WL 1044482 (Ohio Ct. App. 8th Dist. Cuyahoga County 1999); see also Bruner v. Bruner, 2000-Ohio-2554, 2000 WL 1486452 (Ohio Ct. App. 7th Dist. Mahoning County 2000); Anderson v. Anderson, 2001-Ohio-3379, 2001 WL 1667875 (Ohio Ct. App. 7th Dist. Mahoning County 2001); Newhouse v. Williams, 167 Ohio App. 3d 215, 2006-Ohio-3075, 854 N.E.2d 565 (3d Dist. Wyandot County 2006).

[17] Rush v. Rush, 1999 WL 1044482, *6 (Ohio Ct. App. 8th Dist. Cuyahoga County 1999).

is insufficient to show that the fear she claimed was objectively reasonable."[18]

Given the holding in *Rush*, it is important for a petitioner's attorney to have the victim describe each incident to the court. The description of each incident should be specific to time and place and should provide enough detail to enable a trial court and a reviewing court to conclude that the victim was in fear of imminent serious physical harm and that the fear was reasonable.[19] Vague allegations are insufficient to provide a court with credible evidence to sustain a finding under RC 3113.31(A)(1)(b).

It is equally important that victims of domestic violence appear credible when explaining to the court why they believed they could be killed or physically harmed by the perpetrator. Clearly, it is not only important that the uttered words demonstrate a reasonable and objective fear, but also that the victim actually believed the threat.

For example, in *State v. Keeney*,[20] the appellate court stated that whether the victim did or did not believe that the defendant intended to kill her is a matter for the trier of fact. The appellate court also noted that "[t]he victim's very demeanor and tone of voice in answering questions may have convinced the trial court that she believed the threat."[21]

Q & A: Must a petitioner prove each element of the act that constitutes domestic violence as set forth in RC 3113.31(A)(1)(b)?

Apparently so. The Hocking County Court of Appeals expects a petitioner to introduce evidence of each element of domestic violence pursuant to RC 3113.31(A)(1)(b). In *Murral v. Thomson*,[22] petitioner requested a CPO based on threats to cause her physical harm. She testified that the respondent threatened the minor child with physical harm on several occasions by calling her home and demanding that she come to pick up the child from her home or he would "go off" on the child. He also told her to watch her back, that she would get what was coming to her and that he would do whatever it took to get custody of the child.[23]

On appeal, respondent argued that petitioner offered no proof that the threats placed her in fear of imminent serious physical harm. Although petitioner articulated the threats and said that she feared for her daughter's safety and that she was afraid that his calls and visits

---

[18]Rush v. Rush, 1999 WL 1044482, *6 (Ohio Ct. App. 8th Dist. Cuyahoga County 1999); see also Lapsansky v. Lapsansky, 2000 WL 1114535 (Ohio Ct. App. 7th Dist. Columbiana County 2000) (upholding denial of civil protection order on grounds that appellant's accusations amounted to mere conjecture and suspicion).

[19]See also State v. Collie, 108 Ohio App. 3d 580, 671 N.E.2d 338 (1st Dist. Hamilton County 1996); B.C. v. A.S., 2014-Ohio-1326, 2014 WL 1345260 (Ohio Ct. App. 9th Dist. Medina County 2014).

[20]State v. Keeney, 2009-Ohio-3094, 2009 WL 1819506 (Ohio Ct. App. 4th Dist. Lawrence County 2009).

[21]At * 3.

[22]Murral v. Thomson, 2004-Ohio-432, 2004 WL 193876 (Ohio Ct. App. 4th Dist. Hocking County 2004).

[23]Murral v. Thomson, 2004-Ohio-432, 2004 WL 193876, *3 (Ohio Ct. App. 4th Dist. Hocking County 2004).

to her place of employment would cause her to lose her job, the appellate court stated that she failed to state that the threats placed her in fear of imminent physical harm as required by RC 3113.31(A)(1).[24]

The Hocking County Court of Appeals found that there was no competent, credible evidence to support the trial court's conclusion that the threats placed her in fear of imminent serious physical harm because she failed to specifically testify that they had. Additionally, the court of appeals apparently discounted the threat that caused petitioner to fear for the child's safety because her actions contradicted her testimony. In a footnote, the appellate court noted that petitioner continued to allow the child to visit with respondent, did not request supervised visitation and did not include the child as a protected party on the order.[25] However, the appellate court upheld the issuance of the CPO on other grounds.

The facts of this case illustrate what testimony a petitioner must provide where the act is a threat. It is important for a petitioner to testify both about the act and the fear caused by the act. Absent actual testimony about the fear of imminent serious physical harm caused by a particular threat, a trial court cannot imply and conclude that the fear exists.[26]

Q & A: Can the issuance of a CPO be based on restraint, notes of death and a threat of suicide without a physical incident or a direct or actual threat?

The Ashland County Court of Appeals answered this in the affirmative when it determined that the aforementioned acts amounted to a threat of domestic violence and potential danger to petitioner and her child. In *Harbaugh v. Jarrell*,[27] appellant argued that the issuance of a CPO was an abuse of discretion. The appellate court considered the testimony of the appellee, which included a time that he threatened suicide over the telephone, and a time when appellant placed himself between appellee and the door and refused to let her leave. She also testified that appellant would come home late at night and drunk and that he had written notes which caused her fear and concern for herself and the child and which included "I don't need nothing so if I disappear don't ask or wonder if I fell into the end of time" and "Now I feel real good things race through my mind Pain Murder Death Bad things I have not felt like that in so long* * *."[28]

Even though the appellate court noted that the appellee had testi-

---

[24]Murral v. Thomson, 2004-Ohio-432, 2004 WL 193876, *3 (Ohio Ct. App. 4th Dist. Hocking County 2004).

[25]Murral v. Thomson, 2004-Ohio-432, 2004 WL 193876, *3 (Ohio Ct. App. 4th Dist. Hocking County 2004).

[26]See Henry v. Henry, 2005-Ohio-67, 2005 WL 43888 (Ohio Ct. App. 4th Dist. Ross County 2005). But see State v. Schweitzer, 2015-Ohio-925, 30 N.E.3d 190 (Ohio Ct. App. 3d Dist. Auglaize County 2015) (holding that conviction was not against the manifest weight of the evidence, even though victim testified that she was not in fear of defendant where trial court found that victim "downplayed" the incident at trial and that the officers' statements that she was visually upset and that she wanted to press charges were more significant than her statement).

[27]Harbaugh v. Jarrell, 2005-Ohio-1753, 2005 WL 856927, *2 (Ohio Ct. App. 5th Dist. Ashland County 2005).

[28]Harbaugh v. Jarrell, 2005-Ohio-1753, 2005 WL 856927, *2 (Ohio Ct. App. 5th Dist. Ashland County 2005).

fied that appellant had never physically struck her or the child and the confrontations had never become physical, the court found that there was sufficient evidence to support the grant of the CPO based on "the threat of domestic violence and potential danger to appellee and the child, particularly in light of the ominous nature of appellee's notes when read in their entirety.[29]

Q & A: Is a batterer's threat of suicide enough for a petitioner to obtain a civil protection order?

Batterers often make threats of suicide as a means or method of exerting control over their battered partners.[30] These threats are often made in an effort to convince the partner that he/she should dismiss a civil protection order or recant previously given testimony. Most often, threats of suicide are a red flag that a batterer is desperate and has nothing left to lose.[31] Suicidal tendency is increased by depression from the failing relationship. Prior suicidal ideation is clearly a risk factor that must be considered by attorneys in assessing the need for a civil protection order.[32]

Social science studies reveal that threats and harassment, including threats of suicide, left unchecked, frequently escalate to greater violence or even death.[33] Unfortunately, recent threats of suicide by the respondent may not be sufficient to issue a civil protection order where there have been no concurrent acts of violence. There is one Ohio case that addressed this issue. In *Anderson v. Anderson*,[34] the trial court granted the CPO. On appeal, respondent argued that there was no evidence of any threat or any physical injury. The appellate court agreed with respondent and reversed the trial court's decision to grant the CPO as an abuse of discretion. The appellate court held that

---

[29]Harbaugh v. Jarrell, 2005-Ohio-1753, 2005 WL 856927, *2 (Ohio Ct. App. 5th Dist. Ashland County 2005). See also Donovan v. Donovan, 2012-Ohio-3521, 2012 WL 3156462 (Ohio Ct. App. 9th Dist. Lorain County 2012) (husband's threats to take his life, threats of suicide, diagnosis of bipolar and a statement that "the only way wife was getting divorced was if a judge shot him" coupled with the incident wherein husband allegedly broke down son's door to get to wife were considered by court in upholding issuance of CPO); Serdy v. Serdy, 2013-Ohio-5532, 2013 WL 6670830 (Ohio Ct. App. 7th Dist. Noble County 2013) (threat of suicide coupled with a shotgun and texts sufficient for grant of CPO); Kuhn v. Kuhn, 2013-Ohio-5807, 2013 WL 6869801 (Ohio Ct. App. 11th Dist. Lake County 2013) (consideration given to threat to kill oneself as one reason for upholding grant of CPO).

[30]Barbara J. Hart, Safety & Accountability: The Underpinnings of a Just Justice System, 42 Advoc. 12 (Idaho State Bar, March 1999).

[31]See Lisa Nolen Birmingham, Note, Closing the Loophole: Vermont's Legislative Response to Stalking, 18 Vt. L. Rev. 477, 486 (1994); Donna K. Coker, Women and Crime: Heat of Passion & Wife Killing: Men Who Batter/Men Who Kill, 2 S. Cal. Rev. L. & Women's Stud. 71, 88 (1992); Barbara J. Hart, Assessing Whether Batterers Will Kill (Pennsylvania Coalition Against Domestic Violence, 1990).

[32]See T.L. Stawar, Suicide & Homicidal Risk for Respondents, Petitioners & Family Members in an Injunction Program for Domestic Violence, 79 Psychol. Rep. 553–54 (1996).

[33]Cynthia Gillespie, Justifiable Homicide: Battered Women, Self-Defense and the Law, 52 (1989); Irene Hanson Frieze & Angela Brown, Violence in Marriage, in 11 Crime & Justice: A Review of the Research: Family Violence 163 (Lloyd Ohlin & Michael Tonry eds., 1989); Barbara J. Hart, Assessing Whether Batterers Will Kill (Pennsylvania Coalition Against Domestic Violence, 1990).

[34]Anderson v. Anderson, 2001-Ohio-3379, 2001 WL 1667875 (Ohio Ct. App. 7th Dist. Mahoning County 2001).

the petitioner's testimony was too vague to use as the basis for a CPO. Moreover, "[a]ppellant's overall reputation for violent behavior or his stated threat to do violence to himself which Appellee raised does not equate to an overt act of violence or threat of violence toward Appellee.[35] Therefore, there was no nexus between appellant's violent behavior and appellee's fear of domestic violence. Similarly, in *Bjergum v. Bjergum*,[36] the court reversed the entry of a civil protection order issued after a full hearing despite the petitioner's allegations that the respondent had threatened to commit suicide as recently as a week prior to the hearing. The respondent's threats of suicide did not influence the court's decision.

But in *State v. Rudd*,[37] the facts presented reinforce the finding with domestic violence that men who threaten suicide to their partners often kill those same partners.[38] Although *Rudd* does not involve domestic violence or the issuance of a civil protection order, it illustrates the connection between suicide and homicide in violent family relationships. In this case, the defendant threatened to kill himself on several occasions. After each suicide attempt, he begged the victim to forgive him. Each time she took him back. Ultimately, he killed her.

Q & A: Can a party's use of abusive and obscene language justify the issuance of a civil protection order?

One Ohio court has considered the issue in the criminal context of domestic violence. In *State v. White*,[39] the defendant threatened "to whip her ass."[40] On appeal, the defendant argued that there was insuf-

---

[35] Anderson v. Anderson, 2001-Ohio-3379, 2001 WL 1667875, *4 (Ohio Ct. App. 7th Dist. Mahoning County 2001). But see Serdy v. Serdy, 2013-Ohio-5532, 2013 WL 6670830 (Ohio Ct. App. 7th Dist. Noble County 2013) (Stressing that "[i]n today's world of escalating murder-suicide domestic events, a reasonable person could rationally fear her life in that same situation."); Kuhn v. Kuhn, 2013-Ohio-5807, 2013 WL 6869801 (Ohio Ct. App. 11th Dist. Lake County 2013) (consideration given to threat to kill oneself as one reason for upholding grant of CPO); Potter v. Johnson, 2016-Ohio-5652, 2016 WL 4594773 (Ohio Ct. App. 2d Dist. Clark County 2016) (threats to kill self if petitioner left him and a past history of assaultive behavior to her were sufficient reasons for the court to grant the CPO).

[36] Bjergum v. Bjergum, 392 N.W.2d 604 (Minn. Ct. App. 1986). But see Ternes v. Ternes, 555 N.W.2d 355 (N.D. 1996) (court chose not to consider whether husband's threats of suicide constituted domestic violence since the actions did not clearly fall within the statutory definition of domestic violence and the wife did not raise the issue in the lower court).

[37] State v. Rudd, 1986 WL 15286 (Ohio Ct. App. 12th Dist. Warren County 1986); see also Harbaugh v. Jarrell, 2005-Ohio-1753, 2005 WL 856927 (Ohio Ct. App. 5th Dist. Ashland County 2005) (notes written to appellee and appellant's threat of suicide warranted issuance of CPO).

[38] Y.A. Aderibigbe, Violence in America: A Survey of Suicide Linked to Homicides, 42 J. Forensic Sci. 662–65 (1997).

[39] State v. White, 2000 WL 799762 (Ohio Ct. App. 2d Dist. Montgomery County 2000). See also Wolf v. Rosson, 2005-Ohio-1174, 2005 WL 628235 (Ohio Ct. App. 8th Dist. Cuyahoga County 2005) (verbal and emotional abuse of petitioner did not rise to level of threat for purposes of domestic violence statute).

[40] State v. White, 2000 WL 799762, *4 (Ohio Ct. App. 2d Dist. Montgomery County 2000).

ficient evidence to establish a reasonable belief on the part of the victim that the defendant would cause her imminent physical harm.[41]

The Second District Court of Appeals upheld the conviction based on the victim's testimony that she was frightened and scared that defendant was going to attack her physically. The court held that "screaming obscenities and threatening at close proximity to 'whip your f—ing ass' have been held sufficient to support a conviction for domestic violence."[42]

Similarly, the North Dakota Supreme Court determined that such behavior is domestic violence. In *Lovcik v. Ellingson*,[43] the defendant's use of obscene and abusive language, including "cunt," "bitch," and "fucking liar," in telephone calls to his wife, though not threats per se, was domestic violence. Testimony that his wife feared for her safety after the calls and locked her windows and requested a police patrol car was found reasonable in light of the defendant's past conduct toward his wife.

Of significance was the fact that the wife had previously sought a protection order for the defendant's past abusive acts of physical violence. The Supreme Court rejected the defendant's argument that the past history should not be considered in the issuance of the current protection order. The Court held that, "[a]lthough past abusive behavior is not dispositive, it is relevant in determining whether domestic violence is actual or imminent."[44] The Court further stated, "Where . . . there exists a history of . . . allegations of abuse, the court may consider what happened [previously] as relevant evidence of what might occur in the future. It need not await a more tragic event to take action. The remoteness of the [previous] incident is a matter for the court to consider in weighing the evidence before it."[45]

Q & A: Do the acts of disabling the telephones and/or pushing warrant the issuance of a CPO?

Not according to the Montgomery County Court of Appeals. In *Rank v. Rank*,[46] the allegations for which petitioner requested a civil protection order were that her husband had used profanity and had shoved her. He was also alleged to have disabled the telephones (ripping the telephone from the wall).

The Second District Court of Appeals noted that there was "name-

[41]See also Hoff v. Brown, 2001 WL 876228 (Ohio Ct. App. 5th Dist. Stark County 2001); but see Rank v. Rank, 2003-Ohio-6524, 2003 WL 22880830 (Ohio Ct. App. 2d Dist. Montgomery County 2003) (history of profanity without other evidence that he ever threatened or caused physical harm not enough to warrant a CPO).

[42]State v. White, 2000 WL 799762, *4 (Ohio Ct. App. 2d Dist. Montgomery County 2000).

[43]Lovcik v. Ellingson, 1997 ND 201, 569 N.W.2d 697 (N.D. 1997). But see Gustafson v. Mauck, 743 So. 2d 614 (Fla. 1st DCA 1999); Grant v. Wright, 222 N.J. Super. 191, 536 A.2d 319 (App. Div. 1988).

[44]Lovcik v. Ellingson, 1997 ND 201, 569 N.W.2d 697, 700 (N.D. 1997).

[45]Lovcik v. Ellingson, 1997 ND 201, 569 N.W.2d 697, 700 (N.D. 1997) (quoting Steckler v. Steckler, 492 N.W.2d 76, 81 (N.D. 1992)). But see Gustafson v. Mauck, 743 So. 2d 614 (Fla. 1st DCA 1999); Grant v. Wright, 222 N.J. Super. 191, 536 A.2d 319 (App. Div. 1988).

[46]Rank v. Rank, 2003-Ohio-6524, 2003 WL 22880830 (Ohio Ct. App. 2d Dist. Montgomery County 2003).

calling" and "pushing" on the morning in question. Additionally, the record did not demonstrate that Mrs. Rank was harmed or injured or feared imminent serious physical harm even if Mr. Rank pushed her. The appellate court determined that the trial court did not abuse its discretion in failing to find that Mrs. Rank feared imminent serious physical harm by threat of force, particularly in light of her denial to a police officer that Mr. Rank had threatened her.

Q & A: Does it matter whether the standard upon which to base the issuance of a CPO is an actual act of domestic violence under RC 3113.31(A)(1) or whether the petitioner or the petitioner's family or household members are in danger of domestic violence?

It depends on the jurisdiction. Some jurisdictions rely on the literal wording of RC 3113.31(A)(1).[47] Other jurisdictions have determined that the danger standard set forth in *Felton v. Felton*[48] is the proper standard.[49] While few appellate jurisdictions have specifically considered this point or conceded its logic, several appellants have based their arguments on this seeming dichotomy.[50] In those jurisdictions that have relied on Felton, more petitioners appear to be granted more protection orders. Clearly, it is more difficult to prove that an act of domestic violence was committed than it is to demonstrate a danger of future violence.

For example, in *Jarvis v. Jarvis*,[51] the appellant argued that the evidence produced at the hearing did not show that he had ever attempted to cause the appellee bodily harm. The allegations were that he had blocked the driveway preventing her from leaving, that he threw a telephone at her and the children, that the children sleep with their clothes on in case they have to run in the middle of the night, that he threatened to kill her days before the hearing, that he has shoved her on the bed and that he has grabbed, pushed, shoved and kicked her.

The appellate court stated that while it may be questionable whether the appellee's testimony alone supported the issuance of a CPO, her testimony coupled with her children's testimony constituted competent, credible evidence that the children and/or appellee were in danger of domestic violence.[52]

---

[47]J.R. v. E.H., 2017-Ohio-516, 2017 WL 587314 (Ohio Ct. App. 10th Dist. Franklin County 2017) (relying on the existence or threatened existence of domestic violence).

[48]Felton v. Felton, 79 Ohio St. 3d 34, 1997-Ohio-302, 679 N.E.2d 672 (1997).

[49]See Text § 12:11, Standard of proof; Text § 11:10, Ex parte protection orders—Legal standard for issuance; Text § 8:6, Statutory elements of domestic violence under RC 3113.31(A)(1)(c).

[50]See Pierce v. Pierce, 2001-Ohio-2312, 2001 WL 1432047 (Ohio Ct. App. 3d Dist. Marion County 2001) (reasoning that appellant's argument was neither reasonable nor rational).

[51]Jarvis v. Jarvis, 2004-Ohio-1386, 2004 WL 549797 (Ohio Ct. App. 7th Dist. Jefferson County 2004).

[52]See Text § 12:11, Standard of proof; Text § 11:10, Ex parte protection orders—Legal standard for issuance; Text § 8:5, Statutory elements of domestic violence under RC 3113.31(A)(1)(c); Text § 8:4, Statutory elements of domestic violence under RC 3113.31(A)(1)(b) and Text § 8:3, Statutory elements of domestic violence under RC 3113.31(A)(1)(a).

Q & A: May a protection order be granted where the evidence demonstrates that the abuse was consensual?

At least one court has addressed this issue. In *Boldt v. Boldt*,[53] the alleged victim obtained a restraining order after being whipped on her buttocks with a belt. An Oregon court of appeals held that the woman was not entitled to a restraining order. The court found that the parties had practiced a dominant-submissive relationship throughout their marriage that included physical punishment by her husband with her consent. According to the court, even assuming such conduct constitutes abuse under the state's family protection statute, the woman failed to establish that she was in immediate and present danger of further abuse. The court noted that, at no time did the plaintiff suggest that she feared repetition of the conduct in question or that it was part of a cycle of abuse from which she was unable to extricate herself.

Q & A: Is the act of "goading" a defense in domestic violence cases?

The Fourth District Court of Appeals found that "goading" is not a defense to domestic violence. In *State v. Sayres*,[54] the appellant argued that his conviction for domestic violence under RC 2919.25(C) should be reversed because his mother was trying to goad him into violence with comments like "Hit me again" and "Do it."

The court rejected his argument, noting that

> [t]he provisions of RC 2919.25 neither provide an exception nor make a defense for "goading" by the victims of domestic violence. Appellant cites us to no authority where such a defense has been raised, let alone successfully asserted, and we have found none in our own research. It would also be unwise to allow such an excuse in the cause sub judice.[55]

The court declined to allow certain acts of domestic violence to be permissible merely because the victim supposedly invited them.[56]

Although this issue was raised in the criminal domestic violence context, the court's rationale may be useful for a civil protection order action.

Q & A: Does the intoxicated state of the alleged victim provide the defendant/respondent with a defense?

---

[53]Boldt v. Boldt, 155 Or. App. 244, 963 P.2d 719 (1998).

[54]State v. Sayres, 1997 WL 142361 (Ohio Ct. App. 4th Dist. Washington County 1997); see also Spence v. Herbert, 2001 WL 876231 (Ohio Ct. App. 5th Dist. Licking County 2001) (where provocation was not a defense or a reason to refuse to grant CPO); State v. Streight, 2002-Ohio-672, 2002 WL 235445 (Ohio Ct. App. 3d Dist. Auglaize County 2002) (the alleged need to protect the appellant's right to visitation with minor child does not justify the use of force as an affirmative defense to a charge of domestic violence, rather the conditions for the use of force in self-defense must be satisfied).

[55]State v. Sayres, 1997 WL 142361, *3 (Ohio Ct. App. 4th Dist. Washington County 1997).

[56]State v. Sayres, 1997 WL 142361, *3 (Ohio Ct. App. 4th Dist. Washington County 1997); see also State v. Carrion, 84 Ohio App. 3d 27, 616 N.E.2d 261 (9th Dist. Lorain County 1992). But see State v. Williams, 2014-Ohio-971, 2014 WL 1345431 (Ohio Ct. App. 9th Dist. Lorain County 2014) (dissent argued that conviction for domestic violence was against the manifest weight of the evidence because, among other reasons, wife did not flee scene; rather she remained on premises and verbally taunted defendant through open window).

At least one Ohio jurisdiction tangentially addressed the issue. In *State v. Agee*,[57] the appellate court upheld the conviction for domestic violence and determined that it was not against the manifest weight of the evidence. In this case, defendant punched victim in the eye. The police officer who responded to the incident testified that the victim appeared upset and that he saw swelling and redness around the eye. On cross examination, the victim admitted that she had been drinking but that her alcohol did not impact the subsequent events. Additionally, the responding officer testified that the victim's alcohol intake was not an issue.[58]

It remains unclear, however, whether the appellate court would have affirmed the trial court's decision if the victim's drinking had a greater disruptive effect or if the defendant had been able to make a case that her drinking had negatively impacted the subsequent events.

Q & A: Does it matter if the alleged victim continues a relationship with the alleged defendant/ respondent after the alleged incident of domestic violence?

The fact patterns of several Ohio cases suggest that a victim's continued involvement after the act of domestic violence or a failure to immediately separate from the perpetrator is considered by a trier of fact. For example, in *State v. Agee*,[59] the defendant punched victim in the eye. On appeal, defendant argued that the trial court erred in convicting him of domestic violence as it was against the manifest weight of the evidence.

In reviewing the verdict, the appellate court considered the victim's testimony that she had driven the defendant to a family reunion several weeks after the incident and that she had permitted him to live in the basement of her home for several weeks.[60] In affirming the trial court decision, the appellate court considered all the evidence and determined that the jury had not created a manifest miscarriage of justice.

Apparently, the Butler County Court of Appeals relied more heavily on evidence substantiating the actual act of domestic violence committed by defendant.

Similarly, in *Shimman v. Germano*,[61] the Lucas County Court of Appeals affirmed the decision of the trial court's issuance of the CPO but did not address the arguments raised by appellant because he failed to provide the trial court with a transcript of all the evidence. However, in the syllabus of its decision, the appellate court acknowledged the Magistrate's conclusions of law which stated that "[t]he Court is aware of Petitioner's voluntary engagement in sexual activity

[57] State v. Agee, 2007-Ohio-4972, 2007 WL 2758559 (Ohio Ct. App. 12th Dist. Butler County 2007).

[58] State v. Agee, 2007-Ohio-4972, 2007 WL 2758559, *2 (Ohio Ct. App. 12th Dist. Butler County 2007).

[59] State v. Agee, 2007-Ohio-4972, 2007 WL 2758559 (Ohio Ct. App. 12th Dist. Butler County 2007).

[60] State v. Agee, 2007-Ohio-4972, 2007 WL 2758559, *2 (Ohio Ct. App. 12th Dist. Butler County 2007).

[61] Shimman v. Germano, 2008-Ohio-717, 2008 WL 466787 (Ohio Ct. App. 6th Dist. Lucas County 2008).

with the Respondent subsequent to the February 11, 2006 incident. However, the Court believes that this activity does not nullify Petitioner's fear of the respondent. Petitioner's actions can be interpreted as an attempt to end the ongoing relationship in a manner to avoid further separation violence. Petitioner's activities viewed in the context of the entire case as presented to the Court is of no consequence as it relates to the Court's decision."[62]

On the other hand, in *Moore v. Bentley*,[63] the trial court denied the issuance of a CPO at the full hearing. The appellate court affirmed the judgment of the trial court and determined that the petitioner failed to provide sufficient evidence demonstrating a fear of imminent serious physical harm cause by a threat of force. The court relied on certain facts: petitioner continually brought his former partner to lunch up to the day before filing the petition; petitioner bought him flowers the day before he filed the petition and the parties had attended a public gathering together. "This behavior undermines a finding that appellant was in fear of imminent serious physical harm."[64]

In *Fugate v. Fugate*,[65] the appellate court reversed the trial court's decision granting a CPO to appellee which order granted her temporary parenting rights and prohibited appellant from having any contact with their son or her daughter. The basis of the CPO was that appellant's infliction of excessive corporal punishment (spanking) to her daughter caused her to fear that he would also commit an act of domestic violence against their son.

The court considered this issue when it stated, "[f]urthermore, this court is mindful that Nina stayed with Brian for several months after she alleges that the spanking incident with Deenah occurred which was the sole basis for concern with regard to Alexander."[66] While this was not the sole basis for the reversal, the appellate court took note of this fact.

---

[62]Shimman v. Germano, 2008-Ohio-717, 2008 WL 466787 (Ohio Ct. App. 6th Dist. Lucas County 2008); State v. Sims, 2018-Ohio-769, 2018 WL 1136587 (Ohio Ct. App. 2d Dist. Clark County 2018) (victim/petitioner's contact with defendant who was the subject of a CPO was not relevant for purposes of defendant's conviction for its violation).

[63]Moore v. Bentley, 2004-Ohio-5060, 2004 WL 2804785 (Ohio Ct. App. 10th Dist. Franklin County 2004).

[64]Moore v. Bentley, 2004-Ohio-5060, 2004 WL 2804785, *1 (Ohio Ct. App. 10th Dist. Franklin County 2004).

[65]Fugate v. Fugate, 2008-Ohio-737, 2008 WL 483251 (Ohio Ct. App. 3d Dist. Auglaize County 2008); see also Tabor v. Palacio, 2008-Ohio-349, 2008 WL 282127, *3 (Ohio Ct. App. 12th Dist. Butler County 2008) (affirming trial court decision granting CPO and noting that the fact that appellee had not mentioned that she had allowed appellant to visit with the parties' children on his birthday or failed to inform the police officers of her concerns when she denied appellant access to them were factors for the trial court to weigh and consider in determining whether appellee had met her burden of proof.

[66]Fugate v. Fugate, 2008-Ohio-737, 2008 WL 483251, *4 (Ohio Ct. App. 3d Dist. Auglaize County 2008).

Q & A: Can the defense of self-defense be used to exonerate an accused's admitted use of force in a domestic violence incident?[67]

Self-defense may be considered by a court in order to exonerate a defendant's admitted use of force against a partner.[68] In *State v. Wetherall*,[69] the defendant appealed his conviction for domestic violence against his wife arguing that the trial court erred in excluding evidence of his wife's violent character, by way of opinion testimony as to her reputation for violence and prior instances of violent conduct, in support of his claim that he acted in self-defense.

The Hamilton County Appellate Court reversed and remanded the case, holding that "the trial court materially prejudiced the defendant by improperly excluding opinion, reputation and specific-acts testimony concerning Mrs. Wetherall's violent character."[70] The trial court ruling restricted Mr. Wetherall's ability to prove, by a preponderance of the evidence, the affirmative defense of self-defense.

The court noted that a claim of self-defense may exonerate an accused's admitted use of force.[71] "To establish self-defense in the use of nondeadly force, the accused must show that (1) he was not at fault in creating the situation giving rise to the affray; (2) that he reasonably believed that he needed to use force to defend himself against the imminent use of unlawful force by the victim, and (3) that the force used was not likely to cause death or great bodily harm."[72] Therefore, character evidence of the victim's propensity for violence toward

[67]See Text § 14:4; Text § 12:29; Gooden v. City of Brunswick, 2014 WL 1379528 (N.D. Ohio 2014).

[68]But see Raynes v. Rogers, 183 Vt. 513, 2008 VT 52, 955 A.2d 1135 (2008) (Vermont Supreme Court held that the common law defense of property doctrine should not be imputed to the abuse prevention statute and that it is not a bar to injunctive relief under the statute where the defendant uses reasonable force to protect personal property).

[69]State v. Wetherall, 2002-Ohio-1613, 2002 WL 440700 (Ohio Ct. App. 1st Dist. Hamilton County 2002); State v. Williford, 49 Ohio St. 3d 247, 551 N.E.2d 1279 (1990); State v. Green, 2016-Ohio-8251, 2016 WL 7337967 (Ohio Ct. App. 5th Dist. Tuscarawas County 2016); but see State v. Roth, 2004-Ohio-374, 2004 WL 177151 (Ohio Ct. App. 1st Dist. Hamilton County 2004) (appellate court distinguished the facts in this case from the facts in *State v. Wetherall* because the prior behavior of the wife did not demonstrate violent aggressive behaviors and thus it was not admissible to prove self-defense); State v. Cobb, 153 Ohio App. 3d 541, 2003-Ohio-3821, 795 N.E.2d 73 (1st Dist. Hamilton County 2003); Burke v. Melton, 2003-Ohio-7054, 2003 WL 23009045 (Ohio Ct. App. 8th Dist. Cuyahoga County 2003) (appellate court acknowledged that the defense of self defense could be raised on appeal if raised in the trial court, and relied on record to show that appellant did not have a bona fide belief that he was in imminent danger of death or great bodily harm and that his only means of escape was the use of force); J.R. v. E.H., 2017-Ohio-516, 2017 WL 587314 (Ohio Ct. App. 10th Dist. Franklin County 2017).

[70]State v. Wetherall, 2002-Ohio-1613, 2002 WL 440700, *9 (Ohio Ct. App. 1st Dist. Hamilton County 2002).

[71]See State v. Boldin, 2008-Ohio-6408, 2008 WL 5147450, *8 (Ohio Ct. App. 11th Dist. Geauga County 2008) (stating that one cannot argue self-defense by both negating an element of the offense charged and at the same time seeking to be relieved from culpability).

[72]State v. Wetherall, 2002-Ohio-1613, 2002 WL 440700, *4 (Ohio Ct. App. 1st Dist. Hamilton County 2002), relying on In re Maupin, 1998 WL 852583 (Ohio Ct. App. 1st Dist. Hamilton County 1998); see also State v. Streight, 2002-Ohio-672, 2002

defendant was admissible to show that he did not create the situation giving rise to the affray (that he was not the aggressor)[73] and "that his state of mind was such that he was acting upon a reasonable belief that he needed to use force to defend himself against his wife's use of unlawful force."[74]

Although character evidence of the victim was admissible in the prosecution for domestic violence to support a defendant's claim for self-defense, the same arguments may be advanced by a defendant in a civil protection order proceeding where self-defense is raised.

Q & A: How does one prove that the incident was an accident rather than an intentional or reckless act?

In order to demonstrate that an incident was an accident rather than intentional or reckless, respondent must consider the nature of the incident giving rise to the protection order, the response and actions of each party, the past history of domestic violence between the parties and each prong of RC 3113.31, to wit: intentionally, recklessly or by threat of force. In viewing the incident through the lens of the statutory framework, it becomes easier to conclude whether an injury was accidental.

For example, in *Bullard v. Alley*,[75] a CPO was granted to respondent's 16 year old daughter. In that case, K.A. was visiting respondent when he asked her to move his truck. Because she ended up with a bruise on her arm, her mother filed for a CPO on her behalf. K.A.

WL 235445 (Ohio Ct. App. 3d Dist. Auglaize County 2002); State v. Williford, 49 Ohio St. 3d 247, 551 N.E.2d 1279 (1990); State v. Caudill, 2007-Ohio-1557, 2008 WL 852626 (Ohio Ct. App. 6th Dist. Wood County 2008) (discussing when evidence is insufficient to raise the issue of self-defense); State v. Williams, 2013-Ohio-1297, 2013 WL 1295405 (Ohio Ct. App. 11th Dist. Trumbull County 2013); State v. Batie, 2015-Ohio-762, 2015 WL 929478 (Ohio Ct. App. 8th Dist. Cuyahoga County 2015); State v. Malott, 2015-Ohio-2968, 2015 WL 4507537 (Ohio Ct. App. 2d Dist. Montgomery County 2015); State v. Cornwell, 2015-Ohio-4617, 48 N.E.3d 169 (Ohio Ct. App. 9th Dist. Wayne County 2015) (as the elements of self defense are cumulative, where one has failed to prove any one of the elements of self defense, s/he has failed to demonstrate that s/he acted in self defense); State v. Wagner, 2015-Ohio-5183, 2015 WL 8571092 (Ohio Ct. App. 3d Dist. Seneca County 2015); Cleveland v. Reese, 2016-Ohio-296, 2016 WL 515907 (Ohio Ct. App. 8th Dist. Cuyahoga County 2016); State v. Imondi, 2015-Ohio-2605, 2015 WL 3964244 (Ohio Ct. App. 11th Dist. Lake County 2015); State v. Adams, 2018-Ohio-604, 2018 WL 920023 (Ohio Ct. App. 2d Dist. Champaign County 2018); State v. Lipkins, 2017-Ohio-4085, 92 N.E.3d 82 (Ohio Ct. App. 10th Dist. Franklin County 2017) (discussing the Castle Doctrine and RC 2901.05(B)).

[73]See State v. Cobb, 153 Ohio App. 3d 541, 2003-Ohio-3821, 795 N.E.2d 73 (1st Dist. Hamilton County 2003) (evidence demonstrated that defendant was at fault by pushing his way into victim's apartment; thus he could not claim self-defense).

[74]State v. Wetherall, 2002-Ohio-1613, 2002 WL 440700, *4 (Ohio Ct. App. 1st Dist. Hamilton County 2002); State v. Smith, 2011-Ohio-1476, 2011 WL 1119716 (Ohio Ct. App. 12th Dist. Warren County 2011); In re D.N., 195 Ohio App. 3d 552, 2011-Ohio-5494, 960 N.E.2d 1063 (8th Dist. Cuyahoga County 2011) (noting that courts have held that a defendant arguing self defense may testify about his knowledge of specific instances of the victim's prior conduct in order to establish the defendant's state of mind at the time of the incident); see also Evid.R. 401, Evid.R. 402, Evid.R. 404(A)(2), Evid.R. 405(A); In re D.N., 195 Ohio App. 3d 552, 2011-Ohio-5494, 960 N.E.2d 1063 (8th Dist. Cuyahoga County 2011). But see State v. Demint, 2018-Ohio-2091, 2018 WL 2437253 (Ohio Ct. App. 4th Dist. Ross County 2018).

[75]Bullard v. Alley, 2014-Ohio-1016, 2014 WL 1339719 (Ohio Ct. App. 4th Dist. Pike County 2014).

provided testimony that respondent "grabbed her arm and squeezed."[76] K.A. stated that "she did not believe that appellant grabbed her arm to help her move the vehicle because if he had, he would not have squeezed her arm so hard."[77] Additionally K. A. testified that he had struck her in the past.

Respondent, on the other hand, testified that he grabbed her arm when he attempted to help her with the truck's stick shift and that the injury was accidental.

On appeal argued that the evidence was insufficient to show that he engaged in domestic violence or that he placed her in fear of imminent serious physical harm and although he may have caused K.A. injury, he did so accidently. In responding to appellant's assignment of error, the appellate court considered the statutory elements of RC 3113.31 in light of appellee's testimony and appellant's demeanor at the time of the incident.

Relying on *Rosine v. Roisine*,[78] the appellate court reasoned that because there was an actual injury and because K.A. testified that he was upset and "had his fists clenched and his face was all red like he was angry,"[79] there was enough credible evidence to demonstrate that domestic violence occurred and that the incident was not accidental.[80]

In this case, the court focused on the credibility of the victim based on her testimony, the past abuse she stated she suffered, her fear of appellant and his demeanor during the incident. In affirming the trial court, the appellate court stated that "the trial court is in a far better position than this court to evaluate K.A.'s fear and her credibility regarding the past incidents of alleged domestic violence."[81]

If a respondent asserts "accident" in his defense, a petitioner's counsel should be prepared to introduce evidence of prior acts of domestic violence to prove intent and lack of an accident. Additionally, prior acts of domestic violence may be admitted to prove intent or the absence of an accident.[82]

Q & A: Is a past history of domestic violence useful in provid-

---

[76]Bullard v. Alley, 2014-Ohio-1016, ¶ 5, 2014 WL 1339719 (Ohio Ct. App. 4th Dist. Pike County 2014).

[77]Bullard v. Alley, 2014-Ohio-1016, ¶ 5, 2014 WL 1339719 (Ohio Ct. App. 4th Dist. Pike County 2014).

[78]Rosine v. Rosine, 2010-Ohio-613, ¶ 13, 2010 WL 598642 (Ohio Ct. App. 7th Dist. Mahoning County 2010).

[79]Rosine v. Rosine, 2010-Ohio-613, ¶ 19, 2010 WL 598642 (Ohio Ct. App. 7th Dist. Mahoning County 2010).

[80]State v. Shannon, 2017-Ohio-31, ¶ 33, 82 N.E.3d 493 (Ohio Ct. App. 5th Dist. Muskingum County 2017) (sustaining assignment of error in a child endangerment case where appellate court determined defendant's actions might have been imprudent or even negligent but where there was no intent or conscious disregard of the consequences and noting that "the majority of parents in this country would be guilty of child endangering").

[81]Bullard v. Alley, 2014-Ohio-1016, ¶ 20, 2014 WL 1339719 (Ohio Ct. App. 4th Dist. Pike County 2014); but see Sepesi v. Goris, 2003-Ohio-1622, 2003 WL 1702505 (Ohio Ct. App. 6th Dist. Wood County 2003).

[82]Evid. R. 404(B); State v. Grubb, 111 Ohio App. 3d 277, 675 N.E.2d 1353 (2d Dist. Montgomery County 1996); State v. Blonski, 125 Ohio App. 3d 103, 707 N.E.2d 1168 (9th Dist. Medina County 1997); State v. Kinney, 2008-Ohio-4612, 2008 WL 4183324 (Ohio Ct. App. 4th Dist. Ross County 2008).

ing evidence to support a finding of domestic violence under RC 3113.31(A)(1)(a), RC 3113.31(A)(1)(b), or RC 3113.31(A)(1)(c) ?[83]

Absolutely. Ohio's courts rely on evidence of past acts of abuse in order to help them assess a victim's fear.[84] Attorneys should detail the history of domestic violence in order to prove by a preponderance of the evidence that the victim is in danger of domestic violence.[85]

RC 3113.31(D)(1) explicitly details that "immediate and present danger" includes, but is not limited to, "situations in which the respondent has threatened the family or household member with bodily harm or in which the respondent previously has been convicted of or pleaded guilty to an offense that constitutes domestic violence against the family or household member." Implicit in this definition is that past acts of abuse, a criminal conviction for domestic violence, or recent threats satisfy the evidentiary requirements for the issuance of an ex parte civil protection order.

Additionally, the legal practitioner should consider the use of any history of abusive acts committed by the respondent, especially towards the petitioner. These acts may be persuasive evidence to demonstrate why the petitioner is in danger of domestic violence and the reasonableness of the victim's fear. For example, in *Visnich v. Visnich*,[86] the Trumbull County Court of Appeals noted that "the language used in defining 'domestic violence' clearly contemplates prior acts being used as evidence to support a CPO."

Moreover, family law practitioners should also review the criminal cases that specifically state that prior bad acts are useful in establishing the basis of a victim's belief in the imminence of physical harm.[87] In *Collie*, the Hamilton County Court of Appeals clarified that a history of prior bad acts is sufficient to show a subjective belief by the victim of imminent harm, provided the acts are specific to time and

[83]See also Text § 8:3, Statutory elements of domestic violence under RC 3113. 31(A)(1)(a), and Text § 8:4, Statutory elements of domestic violence under RC 3113. 31(A)(1)(b).

[84]See, e.g., Gatt v. Gatt, 2002-Ohio-1749, 2002 WL 570389 (Ohio Ct. App. 9th Dist. Medina County 2002); see also Rhodes v. Gunter, 2003-Ohio-2342, 2003 WL 21040724 (Ohio Ct. App. 9th Dist. Lorain County 2003); Poth v. Poth, 2007-Ohio-5925, 2007 WL 3257367 (Ohio Ct. App. 10th Dist. Franklin County 2007); Hawkins v. Truss, 2007-Ohio-4415, 2007 WL 2422055 (Ohio Ct. App. 10th Dist. Franklin County 2007) (upholding issuance of CPO on grounds appellant slapped her and called her names. History of physical violence included hitting her, throwing water on her, kicking her and choking her. Her testimony was that she could not see going through such incidents again.).

[85]See Felton v. Felton, 79 Ohio St. 3d 34, 1997-Ohio-302, 679 N.E.2d 672 (1997).

[86]Visnich v. Visnich, 1999 WL 1299300, *3 (Ohio Ct. App. 11th Dist. Trumbull County 1999); see also Bruns v. Bruns, 1999 WL 819344 (Ohio Ct. App. 6th Dist. Erie County 1999) (relying on *Eichenberger* to demonstrate that reasonableness of petitioner's fear is determined with reference to petitioner's history with the respondent); Conkle v. Wolfe, 131 Ohio App. 3d 375, 722 N.E.2d 586 (4th Dist. Athens County 1998).

[87]See State v. Collie, 108 Ohio App. 3d 580, 671 N.E.2d 338 (1st Dist. Hamilton County 1996); State v. Taylor, 79 Ohio Misc. 2d 82, 671 N.E.2d 343 (Mun. Ct. 1996).

place.[88] Unfortunately vague threats do not provide evidence of the imminence of harm.[89]

Q & A: Does the domestic violence statute include sexually oriented offenses?

Yes. The domestic violence statue was amended in 2006 to add the commission of sexually oriented offenses as defined in RC 2950.01. This means that an individual or another filing on behalf of a family or household member may request and be granted a domestic violence civil protection order.[90] However, if the petitioner and respondent are not family or household members, the sexually oriented offense protection order would be brought in common pleas court under RC 2903.214.[91]

---

[88]Newhouse v. Williams, 167 Ohio App. 3d 215, 2006-Ohio-3075, 854 N.E.2d 565 (3d Dist. Wyandot County 2006) (holding that the past acts must not be so remote in time).

[89]See Rush v. Rush, 1999 WL 1044482 (Ohio Ct. App. 8th Dist. Cuyahoga County 1999); see also Bruner v. Bruner, 2000-Ohio-2554, 2000 WL 1486452 (Ohio Ct. App. 7th Dist. Mahoning County 2000); Anderson v. Anderson, 2001-Ohio-3379, 2001 WL 1667875 (Ohio Ct. App. 7th Dist. Mahoning County 2001); Newhouse v. Williams, 167 Ohio App. 3d 215, 2006-Ohio-3075, 854 N.E.2d 565 (3d Dist. Wyandot County 2006), citing Young v. Young, 2006-Ohio-978, 2006 WL 515522 (Ohio Ct. App. 2d Dist. Greene County 2006).

[90]Note that sexual abuse towards a child forms the basis of a sexually oriented offense protection order; see also Sanchez v. Sanchez, 2016-Ohio-4933, 2016 WL 3745699 (Ohio Ct. App. 1st Dist. Hamilton County 2016).

[91]Lutson v. Anderkin, 2013 WL 2150897 (Ohio C.P. 2013); Rehfus v. Smith, 2015-Ohio-2145, 2015 WL 3498686 (Ohio Ct. App. 7th Dist. Carroll County 2015); Rice v. Lewis, 2013-Ohio-5890, 2013 WL 6989772 (Ohio Ct. App. 4th Dist. Scioto County 2013) (a sexually oriented offense protection order (SOOPO) was requested in common pleas court, general division, where the relationship in an ongoing custody dispute was that of mother of child versus father and paternal grandmother).

Chapter 9

Stalking and Trespass

§ 9:1 Stalking[1]

Stalking is distinguishable from other types of criminal behaviors in two important ways. First, it entails repeat victimization of a person—it is, by its very nature, a series of acts, rather than a single incident. Second, it is partly defined by its impact on the victim.[2]

Stalking and domestic violence intersect in a variety of ways. Stalking, like domestic violence it is a crime of power and control.[3] If stalking is defined as a course of conduct that intimidates or frightens a victim, then relationships involving domestic violence also involve stalking. Research indicates that about 81% of women stalked by an intimate partner have also been physically assaulted by the same offender.[4] In fact, recent studies indicate that the best predictor of who would experience violations of CPOs was who had been stalked in the past six months prior to obtaining a CPO.[5]

[Section 9:1]

[1]SCPO is the same as CSPO.

[2]See also Katrina Baum, Shannon Catalano, Michael Rand and Kristina Rose, *Stalking Victimization in the United States* (January 2009, NCJ 224527); www.ojp.us doj.gov/bjs/pbub/pdf/svus.pdf.

[3]M. Brewster, Power and Control Dynamics in Prestalking and Stalking Situations, Journal of Family Violence 18(4) 207-217 (2003).

[4]Tjaden & Thoennes, Stalking in America: Findings From the National Violence Against Women Survey, Washington, DC: U.S. Department of Justice, National Institute of Justice and Centers for Disease Control and Prevention (1998).

[5]T.K. Logan, Robert Walker, William Hoyt and Teri Faragher, *The Kentucky*

Stalking precedes an exceedingly high proportion of homicides by intimates.[6] In fact, where both domestic violence and stalking exist in a relationship, there is a higher indicator of lethality than either behavior alone.[7]

The elements of the crime of menacing by stalking under R.C. 2903.211 are (1) engaging in a pattern of conduct[8] (2) to knowingly[9] (3) cause another to believe that the offender will cause physical harm[10] or (4) cause mental distress to the other person.[11]

§ 9:2 Constitutional challenges

R.C. 2903.211 has withstood various constitutional challenges on void for vagueness grounds. The argument supporting the unconstitutionality of the stalking statute is that the statute is vague and a person of ordinary intelligence cannot know what another person

Civil Protective Order Study: A Rural and Urban Multiple Perspective Study of Protective Order Protection Consequences, Responses and Costs, (Funded by NIJ 2009); www.ncjrs.gov/pdffiles1/nij/grants/228350.pdf.

[6]Bureau of Justice Statistics, Homicide Trends in the U. S. Intimate Partner Homicide, Washington, D.C.: U.S. Department of Justice, National Institute of Justice (2001).

[7]McFarlane, Campbell, Wilt, Sachs, Ulrich and Xu, Stalking and Intimate Partner Femicide, Homicide Studies 3 (4) (1999).

[8]See R.C. 2903.211(D)(1) which defines a pattern of conduct to include electronic communication and telecommunication; State v. Scruggs, 136 Ohio App. 3d 631, 737 N.E.2d 574 (2d Dist. Montgomery County 2000); see also State v. Smith, 126 Ohio App. 3d 193, 709 N.E.2d 1245 (7th Dist. Mahoning County 1998); State v. Dario, 106 Ohio App. 3d 232, 665 N.E.2d 759 (1st Dist. Hamilton County 1995) (defining two or more incidents closely related in time); State v. Honeycutt, 2002-Ohio-3490, 2002 WL 1438648 (Ohio Ct. App. 2d Dist. Montgomery County 2002); Myers v. Myers, 2005-Ohio-7040, 2005 WL 3610332, *4 (Ohio Ct. App. 5th Dist. Muskingum County 2005) (upheld trial court's granting of civil protection order based on a pattern of conduct).

[9]See, for example, Gilreath v. Kinderdine, 2004-Ohio-868, 2004 WL 362335 (Ohio Ct. App. 2d Dist. Miami County 2004); State v. Szloh, 189 Ohio App. 3d 13, 2010-Ohio-3777, 937 N.E.2d 168 (2d Dist. Greene County 2010) (defendant acted "knowingly" as evidenced by his repeated efforts to contact victim despite police warnings to desist and victim's repeated requests for him to leave and not contact her); Williams v. Flannery, 2015-Ohio-2040, 2015 WL 3421319, ¶ 22 (Ohio Ct. App. 8th Dist. Cuyahoga County 2015); Smith v. Hein, 2015-Ohio-2749, 2015 WL 4095636 (Ohio Ct. App. 1st Dist. Hamilton County 2015), appeal not allowed, 144 Ohio St. 3d 1458, 2016-Ohio-172, 44 N.E.3d 288 (2016); Joy v. Letostak, 2015-Ohio-2667, 2015 WL 3964179 (Ohio Ct. App. 10th Dist. Franklin County 2015).

[10]See, e.g., State v. Skeens, 1999 WL 1082658 (Ohio Ct. App. 2d Dist. Montgomery County 1999); State v. Smith, 126 Ohio App. 3d 193, 709 N.E.2d 1245 (7th Dist. Mahoning County 1998).

[11]See Dayton v. Davis, 136 Ohio App. 3d 26, 735 N.E.2d 939 (2d Dist. Montgomery County 1999) (where a showing of actual mental distress is not an element of menacing by stalking); State v. Davidson, 1995 WL 396455 (Ohio Ct. App. 2d Dist. Montgomery County 1995); see also State v. Tichon, 102 Ohio App. 3d 758, 658 N.E.2d 16 (9th Dist. Summit County 1995); State v. Honeycutt, 2002-Ohio-3490, 2002 WL 1438648, *6 (Ohio Ct. App. 2d Dist. Montgomery County 2002) (discussing that the statute does not require a victim to have suffered mental distress, just that she believed that he would cause her physical harm or distress, which she demonstrated by going to a motel, hiring body guards, installing a home security system and pressing charges three times); State v. Rucker, 2002-Ohio-172, 2002 WL 83731 (Ohio Ct. App. 12th Dist. Butler County 2002).

intended, thus, that person could not conform his or her behavior to the requirements of the statute. For example, in *Currington v. Moon*,[1] the respondent argued that R.C. 2903.211 was unconstitutional on vagueness grounds as it did not allow reasonable persons to know in advance what actions were prohibited, especially when the other person's intention was to cause mental distress.

The appellate court first examined what it meant for a statute to be unconstitutionally vague. "[A]n unconstitutionally vague statute is one which forbids or requires the doing of an act in terms so vague that individuals of common intelligence must necessarily guess at its meaning and differ as to its application. * * * The vagueness doctrine requires a statute to give fair notice of offending conduct. * * * Moreover, in order to be declared unconstitutionally vague, the statute must lack explicit standards such that it permits arbitrary and discriminatory enforcement."[2]

The court then applied a three part analysis in order to determine whether a statute was void for vagueness. First, did the wording of the statute provide fair warning to the ordinary citizen so that the citizen conformed his/her behavior to the requirements of the statute? Second, did the wording of the statute sufficiently prohibit arbitrary, capricious and discriminatory enforcement? Finally, did the wording of the statute unreasonably impinge or inhibit fundamental constitutionally protected freedoms?[3]

The Montgomery County Court of Appeals rejected respondent's argument and concluded that R.C. 2903.211 is not void for vagueness because the statute contains a scienter requirement.[4] Under R.C. 2903.211, the offender must "knowingly" cause another to believe that the offender will cause physical harm to the other person or cause mental distress to the other person. Therefore, a person of ordinary intelligence would be able to discern what conduct is prohibited. Moreover, the statute does not impinge of constitutionally guaranteed freedoms.[5]

Q & A: What is stalking?

[Section 9:2]

[1]Curington v. Moon, 2009-Ohio-3013, 2009 WL 1800373 (Ohio Ct. App. 2d Dist. Montgomery County 2009).

[2]*Moon, at *5*; quoting State v. Werfel, 2003-Ohio-6958, 2003 WL 22994981 (Ohio Ct. App. 11th Dist. Lake County 2003).

[3]At *5; quoting, State v. Barnhardt, 2006-Ohio-4531, 2006 WL 2528503 (Ohio Ct. App. 9th Dist. Lorain County 2006).

[4]See also State v. Benner, 96 Ohio App. 3d 327, 644 N.E.2d 1130 (1st Dist. Hamilton County 1994); State v. Schwab, 119 Ohio App. 3d 463, 695 N.E.2d 801 (12th Dist. Butler County 1997); State v. Dario, 106 Ohio App. 3d 232, 665 N.E.2d 759 (1st Dist. Hamilton County 1995).

[5]*Moon at *6*. State v. Farmer, 2015-Ohio-5434, 2015 WL 9438270, ¶ 82 (Ohio Ct. App. 5th Dist. Licking County 2015), appeal not allowed, 145 Ohio St. 3d 1459, 2016-Ohio-2807, 49 N.E.3d 321 (2016) (Court found that Appellant's pattern of conduct knowingly caused the victim mental distress. RC 2903.211 does not violate defendant 's right to free speech and "[a]ppellant's right to free speech is not absolute, and he can be punished when his speech is threatening or interferes with the rights of others" ¶ 82.).

Stalking,[6] by its very definition, requires an examination of the offender's past conduct involving the victim[7] and the victim's belief of impending physical harm.[8] Stalking includes (1) following the petitioner/victim;[9] (2) threatening the petitioner/victim;[10] and driving by petitioner/victim's house, place of employment or school.[11] It may also be committed by repeated e-mail[12] or other forms of communication[13] It may also include picketing outside the victim's home for over 13 years.[14]

---

[6]Clare Dalton & Elizabeth M. Schneider, Stalking and Domestic Violence, Battered Women and the Law, 668 (2001).

[7]State v. Woodgeard, 1994 WL 167928 (Ohio Ct. App. 5th Dist. Fairfield County 1994), dismissed, 70 Ohio St. 3d 1473, 640 N.E.2d 846 (1994); see also State v. Tichon, 102 Ohio App. 3d 758, 658 N.E.2d 16 (9th Dist. Summit County 1995); Wildi v. Wildi, 159 Ohio App. 3d 568, 571, 2005-Ohio-257, 824 N.E.2d 1011 (10th Dist. Franklin County 2005) (where court noted that "stalking, by definition, produces in the victim a sense of fear of physical harm or mental distress, appellant was capable of causing fear even if, as she claims, she was only doing the same tasks a private investigator would do"); see also Snell v. Snell, 2006-Ohio-2899, 2006 WL 1575159 (Ohio Ct. App. 5th Dist. Richland County 2006) (since R.C. 2903.214 specifically refers to a pattern of conduct, defined as two or more actions or incidents closely related in time, the court must consider the history of the parties in determining whether the circumstances require the issuance of the order).

[8]See, e.g., State v. Dario, 106 Ohio App. 3d 232, 665 N.E.2d 759 (1st Dist. Hamilton County 1995) (evidence of following, telephoning her at home and work, leaving unwanted flowers and notes, and showing up at her job was sufficient to establish that she feared for her life); see also Kreuzer v. Kreuzer, 144 Ohio App. 3d 610, 2001-Ohio-1542, 761 N.E.2d 77 (2d Dist. Greene County 2001).

[9]State v. Benner, 96 Ohio App. 3d 327, 644 N.E.2d 1130 (1st Dist. Hamilton County 1994).

[10]State v. Dario, 106 Ohio App. 3d 232, 665 N.E.2d 759 (1st Dist. Hamilton County 1995); see also H.E.S. v. J.C.S., 349 N.J. Super. 332, 793 A.2d 780 (App. Div. 2002), judgment aff'd in part, rev'd in part on other grounds, 175 N.J. 309, 815 A.2d 405 (2003) (installing surveillance system in wife's bedroom was stalking); Newsletter of the Stalking Resource Center, New Frontiers of Stalking-Video Voyeurism, Vol. 3, No. 1 (2003).

[11]State v. Woodgeard, 1994 WL 167928 (Ohio Ct. App. 5th Dist. Fairfield County 1994), dismissed, 70 Ohio St. 3d 1473, 640 N.E.2d 846 (1994); but see Curry v. State, 811 So. 2d 736 (Fla. 4th DCA 2002) (stalking does not include persistent harassment through governmental and court systems).

[12]See Dayton v. Davis, 136 Ohio App. 3d 26, 735 N.E.2d 939 (2d Dist. Montgomery County 1999) (where explicit threats are not an element of menacing by stalking); see also R.C. 2903.211(A)(2) which defines the definition of menacing by stalking to include no person, through the use of any electronic method by remotely transferring information, including but not limited to, any computer, computer network, computer program, or computer system, shall post a message with purpose to urge or incite another to commit a violation of division (A)(1)); State v. Hoying, 2005-Ohio-1366, 2005 WL 678989 (Ohio Ct. App. 2d Dist. Greene County 2005) (Defendant knew petitioner would consider the emails to be a threat to her physical safety and that the messages would cause her mental distress); Hangen v. McCaleb, 2006-Ohio-776, 2006 WL 400134 (Ohio Ct. App. 2d Dist. Greene County 2006) (repeated emails, some containing threats of violence, unsolicited gifts, interception her credit card statements, all constituted a pattern of conduct sufficient for the granting of a civil stalking protection order and upholding trial court).

[13]Miller v. Francisco, 2003-Ohio-1978, 2003 WL 1904066 (Ohio Ct. App. 11th Dist. Lake County 2003) (overruled on other grounds by, Davis v. DiNunzio, 2005-Ohio-2883, 2005 WL 1383975 (Ohio Ct. App. 11th Dist. Lake County 2005)).

[14]See Kreuzer v. Kreuzer, 144 Ohio App. 3d 610, 2001-Ohio-1542, 761 N.E.2d 77

"A person is not liable for a criminal violation unless he engages in a prohibited act or omission with the degree of culpability which the particular offense requires, when one is prescribed."[15] Menacing by stalking requires that an offender act "knowingly."[16] A person acts "knowingly," regardless of his purpose, when he is aware that his conduct will probably cause a certain result or will probably be of a certain nature. A person has knowledge of circumstances when he is aware that such circumstances probably exist.[17]

To commit an act of menacing by stalking, a person must, by a pattern of conduct, knowingly cause the victim to believe that the offender will cause a victim physical harm or knowingly cause the victim mental distress. Proof of those consequences is required, but it must also be shown that the offender knowingly caused the consequences to occur.[18] The culpable mental state of knowingly may be shown by circumstantial evidence as well as by direct evidence. For example, where the stalker is aware that the victim was disturbed and frightened by the stalking activity, the court could reasonably infer that the stalker knew this would cause the victim mental distress.[19]

"Physical harm to persons" is defined as "any injury, illness or other physiological impairment, regardless of its gravity or duration."[20]

Q & A: What is the legal definition of stalking?

Under RC 2903.211(A)(1), stalking is defined as "[n]o person by engaging in a pattern of conduct, shall knowingly cause another person to believe that the offender will cause physical harm to the other person or a family or household member of the other person or cause mental distress to the other person or a family or household member of the other person." Additionally, stalking under RC

(2d Dist. Greene County 2001).

[15]R.C. 2901.21(A).

[16]State v. Barnhardt, 2006-Ohio-4531, 2006 WL 2528503 (Ohio Ct. App. 9th Dist. Lorain County 2006).

[17]R.C. 2901.22(B). See also Curington v. Moon, 2009-Ohio-3013, 2009 WL 1800373 (Ohio Ct. App. 2d Dist. Montgomery County 2009); Barium & Chems., Inc. v. Miller, 2016-Ohio-5656, 2016 WL 4594277 (Ohio Ct. App. 7th Dist. Jefferson County 2016) (discussion of "knowingly" in denying the CSPO in that there was no evidence that "defendant was aware of any probability that his statements would get back to Plaintiff and because he had no reason to be aware that his statements would get back to Plaintiff or cause them to fear harm, it cannot be said that he "knowingly" "caused another to believe that the offender would cause physical harm."" at ¶ 30); Krzystan v. Bauer, 2017-Ohio-858, 2017 WL 945183 (Ohio Ct. App. 6th Dist. Ottawa County 2017) (calling appellee a "bitch," without more, does not suggest that appellant knowingly caused appellee to believe that he would cause her physical harm); Hudnell v. Blackshear, 2017-Ohio-2680, 2017 WL 1788691 (Ohio Ct. App. 2d Dist. Montgomery County 2017).

[18]Gilreath v. Kinderdine, 2004-Ohio-868, 2004 WL 362335 (Ohio Ct. App. 2d Dist. Miami County 2004).

[19]Kreuzer v. Kreuzer, 144 Ohio App. 3d 610, 2001-Ohio-1542, 761 N.E.2d 77 (2d Dist. Greene County 2001); see also Striff v. Striff, 2003-Ohio-794, 2003 WL 397869 (Ohio Ct. App. 6th Dist. Wood County 2003) (where there was an existing CPO in place, appellant would have known that his continuing contact with appellee would cause her mental distress); Gruber v. Hart, 2007-Ohio-873, 2007 WL 625818 (Ohio Ct. App. 6th Dist. Ottawa County 2007).

[20]R.C. 2901.01(A)(3); see also Text § 8:3, Statutory elements of domestic violence under R.C. 3113.31(A)(1)(a).

2903.211(A)(2) includes "[n]o person, through the use of any form of written communication or any electronic method of remotely transferring information, including, but not limited to, any computer, computer network, computer program, computer system, or telecommunication devise shall post a message or use any intentionally written or verbal or graphic gesture with purpose to do either of the following: a) violate division (A)(1) of this section or urge or incite another to commit a violation of division (A)(1) or (A)(2) of this section." Lastly, stalking under RC 2903.211(A)(3) provides that "[n]o person, with a sexual motivation, shall violate division (A)(1) or (2) of this section.

Q & A: What are the civil remedies available?

Under R.C. 3113.31(A)(1)(b), Ohio authorizes the issuance of a civil protection order for family or household members based on stalking behaviors intended to harass and intimidate the petitioner or other family or household members.[21] Specifically, R.C. 3113.31(A)(1)(b) defines domestic violence as "placing another person by the threat of force in fear of imminent serious physical harm or committing a violation of section R.C. 2903.211 or R.C. 2911.211 of the Revised Code.[22]

Additionally, under R.C. 2903.214, Ohio authorizes the issuance of a civil protection order for non-intimates and even possibly an additional forum for family or household members.[23] There not need be a prior conviction or charge based on any of the actions or incidents.

To obtain a civil protection order under R.C. 3113.31, the petitioner and the respondent must be family or household members as defined in the statute. To obtain a civil protection order under R.C. 2903.214, it is less clear. The statute appears to apply to non-family or household members. However, the statute also provides that a "family or household member" has the same meaning as in R.C. 3113.31. It

[21]Still v. Still, 1999 WL 236049 (Ohio Ct. App. 2d Dist. Montgomery County 1999); see also Gooderham v. Patterson, 1999 WL 1034472 (Ohio Ct. App. 4th Dist. Gallia County 1999); Rhodes v. Gunter, 2003-Ohio-2342, 2003 WL 21040724 (Ohio Ct. App. 9th Dist. Lorain County 2003) (competent credible evidence supported grant of a CPO where ex-husband repeatedly followed her in his car, drove past the house, stalked, and daughter stated her father always seems to be "right there" wherever she turned around); Myers v. Myers, 2005-Ohio-7040, 2005 WL 3610332, *4 (Ohio Ct. App. 5th Dist. Muskingum County 2005) (upheld judgment of trial court's granting of a CPO because Defendant had repeatedly driven past her home and work, called her, broke into her home, all causing her to be frightened; the appellate court noted that the trial court found a patter of conduct based on several incidents, stacked one on top of the other); Carter v. Hooks, 2006-Ohio-5987, 2006 WL 3290733 (Ohio Ct. App. 12th Dist. Butler County 2006) (where niece's mean, hurtful and rude comments caused 77 yr. old aunt mental distress); Lundin v. Niepsuj, 2014-Ohio-1212, 2014 WL 1478284 (Ohio Ct. App. 9th Dist. Summit County 2014) (applying those R.C. 2903.214 cases which interpreted a stalking violation in a R.C. 3113.31 case for its legal reasoning); R.C. v. J.G., 2013-Ohio-4265, 2013 WL 5437015 (Ohio Ct. App. 9th Dist. Medina County 2013) (issuance of CPO under RC 3113.31 based on a pattern of conduct in which respondent caused petitioner to believe that he would physically harm her); amended R.C. 2903.214, eff. 7-29-98, permitting common pleas courts to issue civil protection orders for nonfamily or nonhousehold-member victims when violations of R.C. 2903.211 occur.

[22]R.C. 3113.31(A)(1)(b); see also Stacey Casper Martinez, Utilizing the Tools: Successfully Implementing the Stalking Statutes, 35 Land & Water L. Rev. 521 (2000).

[23]See also Text § 9:3, Civil stalking protection orders.

would make perfect sense that, in the context of an R.C. 2903.214 civil protection order, the familial or household member relationship is between petitioner and her/his family or household members rather than between petitioner and respondent.

Civil domestic violence protection orders are filed in the Domestic Relations Court,[24] while civil stalking protection orders are filed in the common pleas court of the county in which the person to be protected by the protection order resides.[25]

The domestic violence protection order requires a relationship between the petitioner and respondent.[26] In effect, this relationship must be identified in the petition and is one of the elements that must be proven in court. The domestic violence petition must contain the relationship of the respondent to the petitioner and to the victim if other than the petitioner.[27] However, the civil stalking protection order does not require a relationship between the parties and no such requirement is set forth in the statute.[28]

The standard for the issuance of an *ex parte* domestic violence protection order is "immediate and present danger,"[29] while the test for a stalking protection order is "safety and protection" of the person to be protected.[30]

A domestic violence protection order full hearing must be heard within 7 or 10 days after the ex parte hearing, depending on whether the petitioner requests an order removing the respondent from the premises.[31] A stalking protection order full hearing must be heard in 10 days after the *ex parte* hearing.[32]

The statutory procedures are quite similar including those relating to the filing of continuances, protection orders that are not filed ex parte or ex parte protection orders denied[33] and the process of mutual protection orders and renewal.[34] Any proceeding under R.C. 2903.214 and R.C. 3113.31 shall be conducted in accordance with the civil rules and the remedies and procedures are in addition to and not in lieu of any other civil or criminal remedy.[35]

If an ex parte protection order is filed pursuant to R.C. 3113.31, the court shall hold a hearing on the same day that the petition is filed.[36] On the other hand, a court shall hold a hearing on an ex parte civil

---

[24]R.C. 3113.31(A)(2).

[25]R.C. 2903.214(A)(1).

[26]R.C. 3113.31(A)(3).

[27]R.C. 3113.31(C)(2).

[28]R.C. 2903.214(C); see also Nwosu v. Underwood, 2007-Ohio-1907, 2007 WL 1175230 (Ohio Ct. App. 3d Dist. Marion County 2007).

[29]R.C. 3113.31(D)(1).

[30]R.C. 2903.214(D)(1). Bower v. Long, 2013-Ohio-5467, ¶ 18, 2013 WL 6579075 (Ohio Ct. App. 6th Dist. Lucas County 2013).

[31]R.C. 3113.31(D)(2)(a).

[32]R.C. 2903.214(D)(2)(a).

[33]R.C. 2903.214(D); R.C. 3113.31(D).

[34]R.C. 2903.214(E); R.C. 3113.31(E).

[35]R.C. 3113.31(G); R.C. 2903.214(G).

[36]R.C. 3113.31(D)(1). On the other hand, a court shall hold a hearing on an ex

stalking protection order as soon as possible after the petition is filed, but not later than the next day that the court is in session after the petition is filed.[37]

Both protection orders restrain the respondent from certain behaviors and may prohibit the respondent from entering, the residence, school, business or place of employment of the petitioner.[38] However, a domestic violence protection order includes relief more focused on the nature of an intimate relationship and may include awarding possession of the residence to the petitioner, removing the respondent from the marital residence, support, custody and visitation, and apportioning personal property.

Finally a stalking civil protection order does not permit the issuance of a consent order or the modification or termination of the protection order. R.C. 3113.31 authorizes these remedies.

Q & A: Does a violation of R.C. 2903.211 depend on a reasonableness standard or the subjective perception of the victim?[39]

The Summit County Court of Appeals addressed this issue in *City of Akron v. Andrews*.[40] In that case, the appellant asserted that, in support of his vagueness argument, because the statute lacks a reasonableness standard, a violation of the statute depends on the subjective effect that an act has on an individual.[41] If a violation depends on the perception of an individual victim, an offender would not know what actions rise to the level of stalking.

The court of appeals reasoned that "[t]he determination of whether the statute was violated does not, as Defendant has asserted, depend on the subjective perception of the victim. Rather, in order to violate the statute, a defendant must act knowingly. Therefore, in order to show that a defendant violated R.C. 2903.211, the State must show that the defendant engaged in conduct that he knew would probably cause the complainant to believe that defendant would harm him or that he knew would cause the complainant to suffer from mental distress.[42] Accordingly, a defendant cannot be convicted based on the

---

parte civil stalking protection order as soon as possible after the petition is filed, but not later than the next day that the court is in session after the petition is filed. R.C. 2903.214(D)(1).

[37]R.C. 2903.214(D)(1).

[38]R.C. 2903.214(E); R.C. 3113.31(E).

[39]See also Text § 9:8.

[40]City of Akron v. Andrews, 2000 WL 108818 (Ohio Ct. App. 9th Dist. Summit County 2000).

[41]City of Akron v. Andrews, 2000 WL 108818, *7 (Ohio Ct. App. 9th Dist. Summit County 2000).

[42]Jenkins v. Jenkins, 2007-Ohio-422, 2007 WL 275700 (Ohio Ct. App. 10th Dist. Franklin County 2007); Hudnell v. Blackshear, 2017-Ohio-2680, 2017 WL 1788691 (Ohio Ct. App. 2d Dist. Montgomery County 2017) (where there is no evidence to establish that respondent took any actions to cause interference with the phone or that he was even aware of when petitioner used his phone in order to cause the interference, the court found no evidence of intent and no evidence indicating that respondent knowingly caused mental distress); Krzystan v. Bauer, 2017-Ohio-858, 2017 WL 945183 (Ohio Ct. App. 6th Dist. Ottawa County 2017) (although appellant considered being called a "bitch" a direct threat of physical harm, the comment did not support a finding of stalking without more, such as a physical gestures, body language or tone

subjective beliefs of a particular complainant.[43] If a defendant knows his behavior will cause the complainant distress, the defendant is not at the whim of the complainant to determine what behavior is prohibited. Therefore, the statute does not require a reasonableness standard."[44] A person acts "knowingly," regardless of his purpose, when he is aware that his conduct will probably cause a certain result or will probably be of a certain nature.[45] A person has knowledge of circumstances when he is aware that such circumstances probably exist.[46]

Q & A: Does R.C. 2903.214 contemplate a reasonable person standard or the subjective belief of the victim/petitioner?[47]

In *Lane v. Brewster*,[48] appellant asserted that the trial court is required to determine whether a reasonable person "in the same or similar circumstances" would suffer mental distress or fear of physical harm.

The Clermont County Court of Appeals overruled appellant's assignment of error and stated that the plain language of R.C. 2903.211(A)(1) simply refers to conduct that will "affect the other person, and

---

of voice. No facts were presented to suggest that appellant knowingly caused appellee to believe that he would cause her physical harm or that he intended for his statement to be taken as a physical threat).

[43]But see Caban v. Ransome, 2009-Ohio-1034, 2009 WL 582761 (Ohio Ct. App. 7th Dist. Mahoning County 2009) (noting that the element of causing her to believe has subjective requirements); Short v. Walker, 2001 WL 32808 (Ohio Ct. App. 12th Dist. Preble County 2001); Lane v. Brewster, 2012-Ohio-1290, 2012 WL 1029503 (Ohio Ct. App. 12th Dist. Clermont County 2012); Fortney v. Willhoite, 2012-Ohio-3024, 2012 WL 2522835 (Ohio Ct. App. 11th Dist. Lake County 2012); Cooper v. Manta, 2012-Ohio-867, 2012 WL 691547, ¶ 41 (Ohio Ct. App. 11th Dist. Lake County 2012).

[44]City of Akron v. Andrews, 2000 WL 108818, *7 (Ohio Ct. App. 9th Dist. Summit County 2000).

[45]See State v. Schwab, 119 Ohio App. 3d 463, 695 N.E.2d 801 (12th Dist. Butler County 1997); Nwosu v. Underwood, 2007-Ohio-1907, 2007 WL 1175230 (Ohio Ct. App. 3d Dist. Marion County 2007); McNaughton v. Cochenour, 2015-Ohio-4648, 2015 WL 6953983, ¶ 22 (Ohio Ct. App. 4th Dist. Ross County 2015) (noting that a petitioner is not required to prove either purpose or intent to cause physical harm or mental distress. It is enough that the offender knowingly performed an act that resulted in causing the victim mental distress. In other words, the offender's subjective intent does not appear relevant under RC 2903.211. Instead the issue is whether the offender acts when he is aware that his conduct will probably cause mental distress, regardless of whether it was his purpose to cause that result). But see Bright v. Lane, 2003-Ohio-225, 2003 WL 139755 (Ohio Ct. App. 5th Dist. Ashland County 2003).

[46]R.C. 2901.22(A); State v. Dario, 106 Ohio App. 3d 232, 665 N.E.2d 759 (1st Dist. Hamilton County 1995). See also Gilreath v. Kinderdine, 2004-Ohio-868, 2004 WL 362335 (Ohio Ct. App. 2d Dist. Miami County 2004); City of Akron v. Andrews, 2000 WL 108818 (Ohio Ct. App. 9th Dist. Summit County 2000) (a person acts knowingly, regardless of his purpose, when he is aware that his conduct will probably cause a certain result, as when a stalker is aware that his continued harassment caused the victim mental distress or caused the victim to believe that he would cause the victim physical harm); City of Toledo v. Emery, 2000 WL 864305, *3 (Ohio Ct. App. 6th Dist. Lucas County 2000) (sufficient evidence of a pattern of conduct is that "the accused exhibited a pattern of behavior with an awareness that his conduct will likely cause another to believe that the defendant will cause physical harm").

[47]See Text 9:8 for a more thorough discussion; Text § 9:2.

[48]Lane v. Brewster, 2012-Ohio-1290, 2012 WL 1029503 (Ohio Ct. App. 12th Dist. Clermont County 2012).

does not require a court to determine the respondent's effect on a "reasonable" person, only those specifically involved.[49] The court held that "the trial court was not required to use an objective 'reasonable person' test in determining whether Brewster's conduct caused mental distress or fear of physical harm under R.C. 2903.214(A)(1)."[50]

Q & A: Does a violation of RC 2903.211 depend on the subjective intent of the offender?

At least one court addressed this particular issue. In *McNaughton v. Cochenour,*[51] the appellate court, in determining whether to affirm the issuance of a CSPO, reasoned that a petitioner is not required to prove either purpose or intent to cause physical harm or mental distress. It is enough that the offender knowingly performed an act that resulted in causing the victim mental distress. In other words, the **offender's subjective intent** does not appear relevant under RC 2903.211.[52] To date, the Supreme Court of Ohio has yet to definitively answer this question.

Q & A: Is intent to carry out the threat required under the stalking statute?

The intent to carry out the threat is not required.[53] One needs only to prove that the stalking intended to place the victim in fear of her/his safety or cause her/him mental distress. Under the culpable mental state of "knowingly," it must be shown only that an offender intended to commit the actions he/she engaged in and that those actions were designed to put another in fear of physical harm or cause mental distress.[54] It need not be shown that the stalker specifically intended

[49] Lane v. Brewster, 2012-Ohio-1290, 2012 WL 1029503, *3 (Ohio Ct. App. 12th Dist. Clermont County 2012).

[50] Lane v. Brewster, 2012-Ohio-1290, 2012 WL 1029503, *3 (Ohio Ct. App. 12th Dist. Clermont County 2012), citing Short v. Walker, 2001 WL 32808 (Ohio Ct. App. 12th Dist. Preble County 2001); see also Fortney v. Willhoite, 2012-Ohio-3024, 2012 WL 2522835, *7 (Ohio Ct. App. 11th Dist. Lake County 2012) (stating that the trial court is required to determine the effect of the respondent's actions on the petitioner, not on an objective, "reasonable" person and further that the trial court may consider the petitioner's unequivocal expression of her fear of the respondent, and citing Cooper v. Manta, 2012-Ohio-867, 2012 WL 691547, ¶ 41 (Ohio Ct. App. 11th Dist. Lake County 2012)); Frenchko v. Frenchko-Nagy, 2015-Ohio-4546, 42 N.E.3d 829 (Ohio Ct. App. 11th Dist. Trumbull County 2015) ("[i]n determining whether petitioner suffered mental distress, the focus is on petitioner's fear, not that of an objective reasonable person. The court employs a subjective test, rather than an objective, reasonable person test." At ¶ 27, quoting Fortney v. Willhoite, 2012-Ohio-3024, 2012 WL 2522835, ¶ 43 (Ohio Ct. App. 11th Dist. Lake County 2012).

[51] McNaughton v. Cochenour, 2015-Ohio-4648, 2015 WL 6953983 (Ohio Ct. App. 4th Dist. Ross County 2015).

[52] McNaughton v. Cochenour, 2015-Ohio-4648, 2015 WL 6953983, ¶ 22 (Ohio Ct. App. 4th Dist. Ross County 2015); emphasis added; but see Elonis v. U.S., 135 S. Ct. 2001, 192 L. Ed. 2d 1, 43 Media L. Rep. (BNA) 1749 (2015) (holding that the reasonable person standard, an objective standard is not sufficient; there must be a subjective intent on the part of the offender).

[53] See Retterer v. Little, 2012-Ohio-131, 2012 WL 134305 (Ohio Ct. App. 3d Dist. Marion County 2012).

[54] See Jenkins v. Jenkins, 2007-Ohio-422, 2007 WL 275700 (Ohio Ct. App. 10th Dist. Franklin County 2007); Perry v. Joseph, 2008-Ohio-1107, 2008 WL 660317, *3 (Ohio Ct. App. 10th Dist. Franklin County 2008) ("Neither purpose nor intent to cause physical harm or mental distress is required," citing Guthrie v. Long, 2005-Ohio-

the cause the end result or intended the consequences of those actions.[55]

The stalker need only intend to place the victim in fear for her/his safety and that the victim was placed in that fear. Proof that the stalker actually caused physical harm or mental distress to the victim or made direct threats to the victim's safety is not required under the statute.[56] It is important to ask the victim why she/he believes that the stalker can hurt her or her immediate family.

Q & A: How does a court determine intent of the offender?

Assessing intent depends on whether an appellate court views RC 2903.214 as a general or specific intent statute. Where general intent is considered by a court, the stalker intends the actions in which he engages. In such a case, an attorney does not have to prove the consequences of his actions. The only question is whether the person intended to do the act.

On the other hand, where a court views RC 2903.214 as a specific intent statute, the stalker commits the offense with the subjective intent to cause the results of his actions, typically, the victim's fear. The question to be considered is whether the person actually intended to cause fear?

Q & A: So, what can attorneys learn from this?

In sum, some courts look to the subjective belief of the victim that an act resulted in the belief that the offender will cause physical harm or cause mental distress.[57]

These courts stand for the proposition that a petitioner seeking a civil stalking protection order is not required to prove either purpose or intent to cause physical harm or mental distress.

Other courts have determined that a violation of RC 2903.211 requires that there must be an objective test used to determine whether a particular victim suffered mental distress because of an act

---

1541, 2005 WL 737402 (Ohio Ct. App. 10th Dist. Franklin County 2005)).

[55]See also Szymanski v. Trendel, 2009-Ohio-992, 2009 WL 580457, *1 (Ohio Ct. App. 6th Dist. Lucas County 2009) ("[t]o obtain a SCPO, the petitioner is not required to prove either purpose or intent to cause physical harm or mental distress," citing Jenkins v. Jenkins, 2007-Ohio-422, 2007 WL 275700 (Ohio Ct. App. 10th Dist. Franklin County 2007). Text § 9:8, Text § 9:9; but see Elonis v. U.S., 135 S. Ct. 2001, 192 L. Ed. 2d 1, 43 Media L. Rep. (BNA) 1749 (2015) (holding that the reasonable person standard, an objective standard is not sufficient; there must be a subjective intent on the part of the offender); Curington v. Moon, 2009-Ohio-3013, 2009 WL 1800373 (Ohio Ct. App. 2d Dist. Montgomery County 2009) (noting that the menacing by stalking statute contains a scienter requirement of 'knowingly").

[56]See State v. Bone, 2006-Ohio-3809, 2006 WL 2053398 (Ohio Ct. App. 10th Dist. Franklin County 2006); but see Lemley v. Kirk, 2007-Ohio-1016, 2007 WL 701141 (Ohio Ct. App. 10th Dist. Franklin County 2007). Note that both decisions come from the same appellate district; see also Text § 9:3, Civil stalking protection orders.

[57]See Frenchko v. Frenchko-Nagy, 2015-Ohio-4546, 42 N.E.3d 829 (Ohio Ct. App. 11th Dist. Trumbull County 2015) ("[i]n determining whether petitioner suffered mental distress, the focus is on petitioner's fear, not that of an objective reasonable person. The court employs a subjective test, rather than an objective, reasonable person test." At ¶ 27, quoting Fortney v. Willhoite, 2012-Ohio-3024, 2012 WL 2522835, ¶ 43 (Ohio Ct. App. 11th Dist. Lake County 2012).

committed by the offender.[58] Still other courts focus on the subjective intent of the victim while considering both objective and subjective elements.[59]

Finally, other courts have indicated that the subjective intent of the offender is necessary when determining a pattern of conduct to cause another to believe that he/she will cause physical harm or causes mental distress.[60] Conversely, the Fourth District Court of Appeals has decided that the offender's subjective intent is not relevant to a determination of mental distress.

Q & A: How is a "pattern of conduct" defined?[61]

A "pattern of conduct" is defined in R.C.2903.211(D)(1) as two or more actions or incidents closely related in time, whether or not there has been a prior conviction based on any of those actions or incidents. Actions or incidents that prevent, obstruct or delay the performance of a public official, firefighter, rescuer, emergency medical services person, or emergency facility person of any authorized act within the public official's, firefighter's, rescuer's, emergency medical services person's, or emergency facility person's official capacity, or the posting of messages, or receipt of information or data through the use of an electronic method of remotely transferring information, including, but not limited to, a computer, computer network, computer program, computer system, or telecommunications devise, may constitute a "pattern of conduct."[62]

Ohio's statutory schema contemplates a course of conduct which is typically defined as a series of acts over a period of time.[63] There is a continuity of purpose to the offender's actions. Some courts have held that the pattern of conduct establishes how present behavior which is

---

[58]See also Text § 9:8.

[59]J.M. v. D.H., 2016-Ohio-8387, 2016 WL 7596244 (Ohio Ct. App. 9th Dist. Lorain County 2016) (no evidence presented to show that appellant had caused or that she believed would cause her physical harm or mental distress; although appellee was concerned that appellant commented that she thought about killing her soon-to-be ex-husband, appellee and then herself, appellee testified that she did not take the comment as a serious threat or that it caused mental distress).

[60]Elonis v. U.S., 135 S. Ct. 2001, 192 L. Ed. 2d 1, 43 Media L. Rep. (BNA) 1749 (2015); Hudnell v. Blackshear, 2017-Ohio-2680, 2017 WL 1788691 (Ohio Ct. App. 2d Dist. Montgomery County 2017); Krzystan v. Bauer, 2017-Ohio-858, 2017 WL 945183 (Ohio Ct. App. 6th Dist. Ottawa County 2017).

[61]See also Text § 9:3, Civil stalking protection orders. RC 2903.215 and RC 2903.211(A)(1) which has redefined "pattern of conduct" to include two or more actions or incidents closely related in time, whether or not there has been a prior conviction based on any of those actions or incidents, directed at one or more persons employed by or belonging to the same corporation, association or other organization. R.C. 2903.215, eff. 9-17-2014.

[62]See e.g., A.S. v. P.F., 2013-Ohio-4857, 2013 WL 5925968 (Ohio Ct. App. 9th Dist. Lorain County 2013); J.H. v. S.P., 2013-Ohio-3833, 2013 WL 4779047 (Ohio Ct. App. 10th Dist. Franklin County 2013).

[63]See, e.g., State v. Dario, 106 Ohio App. 3d 232, 665 N.E.2d 759 (1st Dist. Hamilton County 1995). See also State v. Payne, 178 Ohio App. 3d 617, 2008-Ohio-5447, 899 N.E.2d 1011 (9th Dist. Summit County 2008) (holding that defendant's driving around victim's neighborhood and past her house multiple times over the course of one day constituted a pattern of conduct sufficient for stalking based on the relatively short time between each incident and taken in the context of their prior abusive relationship and the belief that he may have intended to cause her physical harm).

apparently innocent can be deemed threatening based on prior encounters between the parties.[64] Clearly, more than one act is intended by the statute.[65] "A court must take everything into consideration when determining if a respondent's conduct constitutes a pattern of conduct,[66] even if some of the person's actions may not, in isolation, seem particularly threatening."[67]

Q & A: How is "mental distress" defined?[68]

"Mental distress" is defined in R.C. 2903.211(D)(2) as any mental illness or condition that involves some temporary substantial incapacity[69] or any mental illness or condition that would normally require psychiatric treatment,[70] psychological treatment, or other mental health services, whether or not any person requested or received psychiatric treatment, psychological treatment or other mental health services.

---

[64]State v. Bone, 2006-Ohio-3809, 2006 WL 2053398, *6 (Ohio Ct. App. 10th Dist. Franklin County 2006), quoting State v. Shue, 2004-Ohio-5021, 2004 WL 2340073 (Ohio Ct. App. 8th Dist. Cuyahoga County 2004), citing State v. Tichon, 102 Ohio App. 3d 758, 768, 658 N.E.2d 16 (9th Dist. Summit County 1995).

[65]R.C. 2903.211(D)(1) (in which a "pattern of conduct" is defined as two or more actions or incidents closely related in time, whether or not there has been a prior conviction based on any of those actions or incidents); State v. Benner, 96 Ohio App. 3d 327, 644 N.E.2d 1130 (1st Dist. Hamilton County 1994); see also State v. Scruggs, 136 Ohio App. 3d 631, 737 N.E.2d 574 (2d Dist. Montgomery County 2000); State v. Smith, 126 Ohio App. 3d 193, 709 N.E.2d 1245 (7th Dist. Mahoning County 1998); Luikart v. Shumate, 2003-Ohio-2130, 2003 WL 1961874 (Ohio Ct. App. 3d Dist. Marion County 2003) (holding that one incident is insufficient to establish a pattern of conduct); Tumblin v. Jackson, 2006-Ohio-3270, 2006 WL 1745055 (Ohio Ct. App. 5th Dist. Coshocton County 2006).

[66]See State v. Lawson, 2007-Ohio-2656, 2007 WL 1560266, *5 (Ohio Ct. App. 10th Dist. Franklin County 2007) (Whether the incidents in question were "closely related in time" should be resolved by the trier of fact "considering the evidence in the context of all the circumstance in the case."), quoting State v. Bone, 2006-Ohio-3809, 2006 WL 2053398 (Ohio Ct. App. 10th Dist. Franklin County 2006), quoting State v. Dario, 106 Ohio App. 3d 232, 238, 665 N.E.2d 759 (1st Dist. Hamilton County 1995).

[67]Guthrie v. Long, 2005-Ohio-1541, 2005 WL 737402 (Ohio Ct. App. 10th Dist. Franklin County 2005), quoting Miller v. Francisco, 2003-Ohio-1978, 2003 WL 1904066 (Ohio Ct. App. 11th Dist. Lake County 2003) (overruled on other grounds by, Davis v. DiNunzio, 2005-Ohio-2883, 2005 WL 1383975 (Ohio Ct. App. 11th Dist. Lake County 2005)); Myers v. Myers, 2005-Ohio-7040, 2005 WL 3610332, *4 (Ohio Ct. App. 5th Dist. Muskingum County 2005); Shockey v. Shockey, 2008-Ohio-6797, 2008 WL 5340554 (Ohio Ct. App. 5th Dist. Delaware County 2008).

[68]See also Text § 9:3, Civil stalking protection orders. See also RC 2903.215 and RC 2903.211(A)(1) which provides that "[i]n addition to any other basis for the other person's belief that the offender will cause physical harm or mental distress to the other person or the other person's mental distress, the other person's belief or mental distress may be based on words or conduct of the offender that are directed at or identify a corporation, association, or other organization that employs the other person or to which the other person belongs." R.C. 2903.211, eff. 9-17-2014.

[69]See State v. Payne, 178 Ohio App. 3d 617, 2008-Ohio-5447, ¶ 9, 899 N.E.2d 1011 (9th Dist. Summit County 2008) (determining that substantial incapacity sufficient to support a conviction for stalking does not mean that the victim must be hospitalized or totally unable to care for herself; rather, incapacity is substantial if it has a significant impact on the victim's daily life, such as the inability of the victim to leave her house).

[70]See Text § 9:3, Civil stalking protection orders.

Pursuant to R.C. 2903.211(E), the state does not need to prove in a prosecution that a person requested or received psychiatric treatment, psychological treatment, or other mental health services in order to show that the person was caused mental distress as described in R.C.2903.211(D)(2)(b).[71]

By the very terms of the statute, mental illness must be considered.[72] However, expert testimony is not required to establish the existence of mental distress of a victim.[73] The court noted that it is within the court's discretion to determine whether a victim suffered mental distress as a result of the offender's behavior and the court need not rely on expert testimony to establish this fact.[74] A trial court may rely

---

[71]See for e.g., State v. Bone, 2006-Ohio-3809, 2006 WL 2053398, *9 (Ohio Ct. App. 10th Dist. Franklin County 2006) (the trier of fact can refer to its own experiences in order to determine whether and to what extent, defendant's conduct caused the serious emotional distress), quoting State v. Bilder, 99 Ohio App. 3d 653, 651 N.E.2d 502 (9th Dist. Summit County 1994); Arruda v. Farmer, 2015-Ohio-5511, 55 N.E.3d 604 (Ohio Ct. App. 5th Dist. Licking County 2015), appeal not allowed, 145 Ohio St. 3d 1460, 2016-Ohio-2807, 49 N.E.3d 322 (2016) (treatment for mental distress is not determinative of whether one caused another mental distress; rather it is the duty of the trier of fact to determine whether the victim suffered mental distress as a result of offender's actions); R.G. v. R.M., 2017-Ohio-8918, 88 N.E.3d 1027 (Ohio Ct. App. 7th Dist. Mahoning County 2017) (a family physician can provide mental health services; citing, Frenchko v. Frenchko-Nagy, 2015-Ohio-4546, ¶ 28, 42 N.E.3d 829, 833–34 (Ohio Ct. App. 11th Dist. Trumbull County 2015).

[72]State v. Woodgeard, 1994 WL 167928 (Ohio Ct. App. 5th Dist. Fairfield County 1994), dismissed, 70 Ohio St. 3d 1473, 640 N.E.2d 846 (1994).

[73]See State v. Smith, 126 Ohio App. 3d 193, 709 N.E.2d 1245 (7th Dist. Mahoning County 1998); see also City of Toledo v. Emery, 2000 WL 864305 (Ohio Ct. App. 6th Dist. Lucas County 2000) (discussing that no expert testimony is required nor evidence that psychological treatment has been undertaken; Smith v. Wunsch, 162 Ohio App. 3d 21, 2005-Ohio-3498, 832 N.E.2d 757 (4th Dist. Hocking County 2005) ("The trier of fact does not need expert testimony on this issue (mental distress), but may rely on its knowledge and experience in determining if mental distress has been caused." at *4, citing Noah v. Brillhart, 2003-Ohio-2421, 2003 WL 21078077 (Ohio Ct. App. 9th Dist. Wayne County 2003); Strausser v. White, 2009-Ohio-3597, 2009 WL 2186620 (Ohio Ct. App. 8th Dist. Cuyahoga County 2009) (victim's testimony as to fear is sufficient to establish mental distress; citing State v. Horsley, 2006-Ohio-6217, 2006 WL 3411423 (Ohio Ct. App. 10th Dist. Franklin County 2006); see also Lane v. Brewster, 2012-Ohio-1290, 2012 WL 1029503 (Ohio Ct. App. 12th Dist. Clermont County 2012) (although petitioner did seek treatment for mental distress by asking her physician for additional anxiety medication); Mullen v. Hobbs, 2012-Ohio-6098, 2012 WL 6690114 (Ohio Ct. App. 1st Dist. Hamilton County 2012); Holloway v. Parker, 2013-Ohio-1940, 2013 WL 1944400 (Ohio Ct. App. 3d Dist. Marion County 2013); Sweet v. Hunt, 2014-Ohio-631, 2014 WL 707923, ¶ 14 (Ohio Ct. App. 2d Dist. Greene County 2014); N.P. v. T.N., 2018-Ohio-2647, 2018 WL 3302173 (Ohio Ct. App. 8th Dist. Cuyahoga County 2018).

[74]Short v. Walker, 2001 WL 32808, *3 (Ohio Ct. App. 12th Dist. Preble County 2001); see also State v. Schwab, 119 Ohio App. 3d 463, 695 N.E.2d 801 (12th Dist. Butler County 1997); State v. Rucker, 2002-Ohio-172, 2002 WL 83731 (Ohio Ct. App. 12th Dist. Butler County 2002); Palmer v. Abraham, 2013-Ohio-3062, 2013 WL 3776597 (Ohio Ct. App. 6th Dist. Ottawa County 2013); Taylor v. Taylor, 2012-Ohio-6190, 2012 WL 6738376, ¶ 16 (Ohio Ct. App. 2d Dist. Miami County 2012) ("[i]t is the duty of the trier of fact to determine whether a victim suffered mental distress as a result of the offender's actions"); Williams v. Flannery, 2015-Ohio-2040, 2015 WL 3421319 (Ohio Ct. App. 8th Dist. Cuyahoga County 2015).

on its knowledge and experience in determining whether mental distress has been caused.[75]

Additionally, the testimony of the victim as to her fear is sufficient to establish mental distress.[76] Further, "[t]he statute does not require that the victim actually experience mental distress, only that the victim believes the stalker would cause mental distress,"[77] In any case, the victim's testimony as to what constitutes mental distress and her fear are crucial to establishing that a victim suffered from mental distress in a given situation.

For example, in *Kreuzer v. Kreuzer*,[78] the trial court found that the victim's fear was reasonable and therefore the belief of impending harm was met despite the appellant's view that it was irrational in light of his lack of action causing physical harm in the past.

Likewise, in *Elkins v. Manley*,[79] respondent-appellant appealed the issuance of a CSPO on the grounds that the court failed to consider her story and which the appellate court interpreted as a challenge to the weight of the evidence in support of the order.

The petitioner-appellee testified in the trial court that appellant had harassed her and her family for years, repeatedly made disruptive phone calls and made false accusations against her with Children and Family Services "at least 180 times." Additionally, appellant canceled her bank account without permission and has made threatening statements, all of which caused her mental distress and depression.[80]

The appellate court articulated the definition of "mental distress" and relied on those cases that found that expert testimony was not

---

[75]Smith v. Wunsch, 162 Ohio App. 3d 21, 2005-Ohio-3498, 832 N.E.2d 757, ¶ 18 (4th Dist. Hocking County 2005); Middletown v. Jones, 167 Ohio App. 3d 679, 2006-Ohio-3465, 856 N.E.2d 1003, ¶ 7 (12th Dist. Butler County 2006); Smith v. Hein, 2015-Ohio-2749, 2015 WL 4095636 (Ohio Ct. App. 1st Dist. Hamilton County 2015), appeal not allowed, 144 Ohio St. 3d 1458, 2016-Ohio-172, 44 N.E.3d 288 (2016); Williams v. Flannery, 2015-Ohio-2040, 2015 WL 3421319, ¶ 22 (Ohio Ct. App. 8th Dist. Cuyahoga County 2015) (noting that the trial court understood that a person with PTSD may perceive threats even in a benign situation).

[76]Olson v. Olson, 2016-Ohio-149, 2016 WL 197117, ¶ 15 (Ohio Ct. App. 6th Dist. Wood County 2016), citingState v. Horsley, 2006-Ohio-1208, 2006 WL 648849, ¶ 48 (Ohio Ct. App. 10th Dist. Franklin County 2006); Tighe v. Kaiser, 2016-Ohio-1400, 2016 WL 1297407 (Ohio Ct. App. 6th Dist. Ottawa County 2016), appeal not allowed, 146 Ohio St. 3d 1491, 2016-Ohio-5585, 57 N.E.3d 1171 (2016).

[77]Olson at ¶ 15, quoting Ensley v. Glover, 2012-Ohio-4487, 2012 WL 4480734, ¶ 13 (Ohio Ct. App. 6th Dist. Lucas County 2012), quoting Bloom v. Macbeth, 2008-Ohio-4564, 2008 WL 4151319, ¶ 11 (Ohio Ct. App. 5th Dist. Ashland County 2008); but see § 9:8 for a discussion as to whether actual mental distress or a belief that the stalker would cause mental distress satisfies the mental distress element of the statute).

[78]Kreuzer v. Kreuzer, 144 Ohio App. 3d 610, 2001-Ohio-1542, 761 N.E.2d 77 (2d Dist. Greene County 2001).

[79]Elkins v. Manley, 2016-Ohio-8307, 2016 WL 7427267 (Ohio Ct. App. 8th Dist. Cuyahoga County 2016).

[80]Elkins v. Manley, 2016-Ohio-8307, ¶ 5, 2016 WL 7427267 (Ohio Ct. App. 8th Dist. Cuyahoga County 2016).

needed and that the testimony of the victim as to her fear was sufficient to establish mental distress.[81]

The court then weighed the evidence and determined that appellee presented sufficient evidence that appellant knowingly engaged in a pattern of conduct that caused appellee mental distress, which led to episodes of depression. "Under these circumstances, the trial court did not abuse its discretion in granting Elkin's petition for a CSPO."[82]

Conversely, in *State v. Beckworth,*[83] the Eighth District Court of Appeals reversed the judgment finding that menacing by stalking had occurred and indicated that "[w]hile expert testimony is not necessary to establish that a victim experienced mental distress as a result of the offender's behavior, mental distress must be proven by facts introduced at trial and the reasonable inferences springing from those facts."[84] The court pointed out that "RC 2903.211 was 'not enacted for the purpose of alleviating uncomfortable situations, but to prevent the type of persistent and threatening harassment that leaves victims in constant fear of physical danger.' "[85]

Q & A: What evidence is needed to prove a "pattern of conduct" for purposes of the stalking statute?[86]

In order to prove a stalking case, it is imperative to demonstrate a pattern of conduct. A pattern of conduct means more than one incident. This might be shown by phone logs, text messages or repeated saved telephone calls. It may be shown by a delivery receipt from the florist or stamped and dated envelopes from the stalker's letters.

Victims of stalkers should develop logs in order to create the history of the acts. A log should include the date, time and description of the incident, the location of the incident, witness names whether the police were called, the officer's badge number and whether a report was made.

---

[81]Elkins v. Manley, 2016-Ohio-8307, ¶ 15, 2016 WL 7427267 (Ohio Ct. App. 8th Dist. Cuyahoga County 2016), citing Strausser v. White, 2009-Ohio-3597, 2009 WL 2186620 (Ohio Ct. App. 8th Dist. Cuyahoga County 2009), citing State v. Horsley, 2006-Ohio-1208, 2006 WL 648849 (Ohio Ct. App. 10th Dist. Franklin County 2006).

[82]Elkins v. Manley, 2016-Ohio-8307, ¶ 17, 2016 WL 7427267 (Ohio Ct. App. 8th Dist. Cuyahoga County 2016).

[83]State v. Beckwith, 2013-Ohio-492, 2013 WL 588518 (Ohio Ct. App. 8th Dist. Cuyahoga County 2013).

[84]State v. Beckwith, 2013-Ohio-492, 2013 WL 588518, *3 (Ohio Ct. App. 8th Dist. Cuyahoga County 2013), citing City of Cleveland Heights v. Lewis, 2002-Ohio-2736, 2002 WL 1265580, ¶ 22 (Ohio Ct. App. 8th Dist. Cuyahoga County 2002); Rufener v. Hutson, 2012-Ohio-5061, 2012 WL 5364703, ¶ 17 (Ohio Ct. App. 8th Dist. Cuyahoga County 2012).

[85]State v. Beckwith, 2013-Ohio-492, 2013 WL 588518, *3 (Ohio Ct. App. 8th Dist. Cuyahoga County 2013), quoting McKinley v. Kuhn, 2011-Ohio-134, 2011 WL 281135 (Ohio Ct. App. 4th Dist. Hocking County 2011), citing Kramer v. Kramer, 2002-Ohio-4383, 2002 WL 1967104, ¶ 17 (Ohio Ct. App. 3d Dist. Seneca County 2002); Holloway v. Parker, 2013-Ohio-1940, 2013 WL 1944400 (Ohio Ct. App. 3d Dist. Marion County 2013); Krzystan v. Bauer, 2017-Ohio-858, 2017 WL 945183 (Ohio Ct. App. 6th Dist. Ottawa County 2017).

[86]See, for example, State v. Lawson, 2007-Ohio-2656, 2007 WL 1560266 (Ohio Ct. App. 10th Dist. Franklin County 2007); see also Walker v. Edgington, 2008-Ohio-3478, 2008 WL 2699430 (Ohio Ct. App. 2d Dist. Clark County 2008); see also Text § 9:8.

Q & A: If a family member follows another family member to work and back home on several occasions and stands outside of her house, does this constitute domestic violence?

Yes. Even absent a showing of actual harm or threat of imminent serious physical harm, a petitioner may still be able to obtain a civil protection order if the petitioner is able to convince the trier of fact that respondent's acts, such as following,[87] spying on, persistent calling, driving past the house, or tearing up clothes caused petitioner to believe that respondent would physically harm him/her. A past history of physical harm may be sufficient evidence from which it can be inferred that a petitioner's fear is reasonable and cause her/him to believe that he/she would be harmed.[88]

Actions such as those listed above as well as the reactions of the victim may also provide evidence of mental distress.[89] Reactions of the victim that demonstrate mental distress include changing the locks or putting locks on the windows of the home, changing route victim takes to work or school, leaving the home accompanied by friends or relatives, not leaving the house unless absolutely necessary, temporarily moving in with others, moving to another neighborhood, city or state, always carrying a gun, curtailing activities, and missing work. Additionally, suffering from crying spells and an inability to concentrate may also indicate mental distress and/or temporary substantial incapacity.

What is important to convey is not whether the stalker's conduct was threatening, but whether the stalker caused the victim to believe the stalker's conduct was threatening.[90] Therefore, either a belief of further harm or mental distress is sufficient for a petitioner to prevail.[91]

While some courts believe that evidence of mental distress is shown

---

[87]See, e.g., Rhodes v. Gunter, 2003-Ohio-2342, 2003 WL 21040724 (Ohio Ct. App. 9th Dist. Lorain County 2003); State v. McCoy, 2006-Ohio-6333, 2006 WL 3478338 (Ohio Ct. App. 9th Dist. Lorain County 2006) (holding that lay testimony as to one's mental condition—including testimony from the individual who is purportedly suffering from mental distress—can be sufficient to show the element of mental distress under R.C. 2903.211(A).

[88]See, for example, Short v. Walker, 2001 WL 32808 (Ohio Ct. App. 12th Dist. Preble County 2001); State v. Dario, 106 Ohio App. 3d 232, 665 N.E.2d 759 (1st Dist. Hamilton County 1995).

[89]See for example, Noah v. Brillhart, 2003-Ohio-2421, 2003 WL 21078077 (Ohio Ct. App. 9th Dist. Wayne County 2003); Ferdon v. Hoit, 2002-Ohio-4240, 2002 WL 1902872 (Ohio Ct. App. 5th Dist. Guernsey County 2002).

[90]See State v. Jones, 1996 WL 599428 (Ohio Ct. App. 12th Dist. Warren County 1996) (test is not whether the offender's conduct was threatening, but whether the offender, by engaging in a pattern of conduct, knowingly caused another to believe the offender's conduct was threatening); see also State v. Schwab, 119 Ohio App. 3d 463, 695 N.E.2d 801 (12th Dist. Butler County 1997); Myers v. Myers, 2005-Ohio-7040, 2005 WL 3610332, *4 (Ohio Ct. App. 5th Dist. Muskingum County 2005); Coleridge v. Tomsho, 2003-Ohio-650, 2003 WL 294356 (Ohio Ct. App. 5th Dist. Stark County 2003) (verbal threats unnecessary where it can be inferred that offender intended such a threat through his actions).

[91]See also State v. Smith, 2012-Ohio-335, 2012 WL 315315 (Ohio Ct. App. 9th Dist. Summit County 2012); State v. Honeycutt, 2002-Ohio-3490, 2002 WL 1438648 (Ohio Ct. App. 2d Dist. Montgomery County 2002); State v. Hart, 2000 WL 1824892 (Ohio Ct. App. 9th Dist. Lorain County 2000); State v. Hart, 2000 WL 1824892 (Ohio Ct. App. 9th Dist. Lorain County 2000); City of Middletown v. Hatt, 2001 WL 76317

by way of psychiatric treatment or psychological counseling,[92] it is now clear that such evidence is not a necessary requirement. R.C. 2903.211 was amended in 2003 to articulate that a petitioner need not prove that psychiatric treatment, psychological counseling or mental health services is necessary to demonstrate mental distress.[93] Neither a request for mental health services nor the receipt of actual mental health services is required under the law.[94] In fact, "[t]he mental distress required for a menacing-by-stalking violation need not always be incapacitating or debilitating."[95]

Q & A: Does it matter whether the victim mentions certain injuries or their cause to medical personnel and how long after an incident of domestic violence a victim must seek medical attention?

In *State v. Pruiett*,[96] the appellant argued that appellee's testimony was not credible because she provided several conflicting accounts of her injuries and because she failed to mention the burns or their cause to medical personnel. Additionally, she waited almost two weeks to seek medical attention for the burns.

The Summit County Court of Appeals reasoned that "[w]e are not in a position to speculate on the reasons for which the victim may not have sought medical treatment for the burns immediately, but a reasonable juror could find D.H.'s reasons for providing different explanations for her injuries credible and probable. We do note that many

(Ohio Ct. App. 12th Dist. Butler County 2001); Smith v. Wunsch, 162 Ohio App. 3d 21, 28, 2005-Ohio-3498, 832 N.E.2d 757 (4th Dist. Hocking County 2005) (noting that evidence of a changed routine corroborates a finding of mental distress; "the fact that appellant's unwanted attention influenced appellee to terminate her job indicates that she was under mental distress").

[92]See State v. Tichon, 102 Ohio App. 3d 758, 658 N.E.2d 16 (9th Dist. Summit County 1995) (counseling is sufficient to show that a person suffers from mental distress; expert medical testimony is not required to establish the existence of mental distress for the purpose of proving menacing by stalking); State v. Smith, 126 Ohio App. 3d 193, 709 N.E.2d 1245 (7th Dist. Mahoning County 1998); 2003 S.B. 8, eff. 8-29-03 (which clarifies the nature of "mental distress" to include psychological treatment or other mental health services whether or not the person requested or received the treatment or services); see also State v. Bilder, 99 Ohio App. 3d 653, 651 N.E.2d 502 (9th Dist. Summit County 1994); State v. Schwab, 119 Ohio App. 3d 463, 695 N.E.2d 801 (12th Dist. Butler County 1997). But see City of Toledo v. Emery, 2000 WL 864305 (Ohio Ct. App. 6th Dist. Lucas County 2000) (finding that evidence that psychological treatment has been undertaken is unnecessary).

[93]R.C. 2903.211(D)(2).

[94]See Lane v. Brewster, 2012-Ohio-1290, 2012 WL 1029503 (Ohio Ct. App. 12th Dist. Clermont County 2012); see also Fortney v. Willhoite, 2012-Ohio-3024, 2012 WL 2522835, *6 (Ohio Ct. App. 11th Dist. Lake County 2012) (citing *Lane* and noting that while actual treatment is not required by the statute to prove mental distress, where the petitioner seeks treatment for the stress the respondent caused, such circumstance is evidence of mental distress); Palmer v. Abraham, 2013-Ohio-3062, 2013 WL 3776597 (Ohio Ct. App. 6th Dist. Ottawa County 2013).

[95]Sweet v. Hunt, 2014-Ohio-631, 2014 WL 707923, ¶ 14 (Ohio Ct. App. 2d Dist. Greene County 2014), quoting Taylor v. Taylor, 2012-Ohio-6190, 2012 WL 6738376, ¶ 16 (Ohio Ct. App. 2d Dist. Miami County 2012); see also Howard v. Wilson, 186 Ohio App. 3d 521, 2010-Ohio-1125, 928 N.E.2d 1180 (2d Dist. Montgomery County 2010).

[96]State v. Pruiett, 2004-Ohio-4321, 2004 WL 1837036 (Ohio Ct. App. 9th Dist. Summit County 2004).

times in domestic violence and assault cases, the victims are hesitant to act against their attacker out of fear."[97]

Q & A: Have any courts addressed the issue of stalking for purposes of a civil protection order in a domestic violence context?[98]

In the civil domestic violence context, *Still v. Still*[99] is the first case where an appellate court addressed the issue of stalking for purposes of a civil protection order.[100] In that case, the victim obtained a civil protection order under R.C. 3113.31 because the respondent committed acts of stalking against her. She testified that the respondent called members of her family as well as the parents of her preschool students. He came uninvited to the parties' residence and appeared highly emotional. She went to a motel because of his banging on her door. He came to the motel and parked next to her car. He threatened her, and she believed he would hurt her.[101]

The appellate court found that her testimony provided the court with sufficient credible evidence of a "pattern of conduct" which satisfied the element of stalking under R.C. 2903.211.[102] The Montgomery County Court of Appeals affirmed the trial court decision that domestic violence occurred against the victim.

---

[97]State v. Pruiett, 2004-Ohio-4321, 2004 WL 1837036 (Ohio Ct. App. 9th Dist. Summit County 2004).

[98]See also Text § 8:4; McElroy v. McElroy, 2016-Ohio-5148, 2016 WL 4039227 (Ohio Ct. App. 5th Dist. Guernsey County 2016).

[99]Still v. Still, 1999 WL 236049 (Ohio Ct. App. 2d Dist. Montgomery County 1999); Patterson v. Gooderham, 1999 WL 1001108 (Ohio Ct. App. 4th Dist. Gallia County 1999) (involving alleged stalking by calling victim on the phone, following her to tanning salon, and photographing her); Gooderham v. Patterson, 1999 WL 1034472 (Ohio Ct. App. 4th Dist. Gallia County 1999); Visnich v. Visnich, 1999 WL 1299300 (Ohio Ct. App. 11th Dist. Trumbull County 1999); Reynolds v. Reynolds, 2001 WL 62552 (Ohio Ct. App. 2d Dist. Montgomery County 2001); Kreuzer v. Kreuzer, 144 Ohio App. 3d 610, 2001-Ohio-1542, 761 N.E.2d 77 (2d Dist. Greene County 2001); Rhodes v. Gunter, 2003-Ohio-2342, 2003 WL 21040724 (Ohio Ct. App. 9th Dist. Lorain County 2003) (noting that a CPO was appropriate as appellant's actions caused appellees to reasonably fear imminent serious physical harm). See also Barclay v. Haney, 2012-Ohio-5646, 2012 WL 6034070 (Ohio Ct. App. 9th Dist. Summit County 2012) (nature of communications included phone calls and texts, creating fictitious people to contact her, leaving messages with a computer generated voice, spoofing, emailing her mother regarding their relationship, stalking on Facebook and email accounts. That petitioner testified she doesn't sleep well, walks the parameters, installed security cameras, can't even park at the state park due to a fear respondent will find her, indicates a change in routine).

[100]Lapsansky v. Lapsansky, 2000 WL 1114535 (Ohio Ct. App. 7th Dist. Columbiana County 2000). See also Myers v. Myers, 2005-Ohio-7040, 2005 WL 3610332 (Ohio Ct. App. 5th Dist. Muskingum County 2005) (following petitioner, calling her, driving past her home and work, entering her residence without her consent, and publishing her phone number and derogatory comments about her in public places demonstrated a pattern of conduct that served as a basis for obtaining a CPO).

[101]See also Lefebvre v. Lefebvre, 165 Or. App. 297, 996 P.2d 518 (2000); Boyd v. Essin, 170 Or. App. 509, 12 P.3d 1003 (2000) (affirming issuance of protection order where ex-husband drove past ex-wife's house several times per day and watched her house through binoculars).

[102]See Saari v. Saari, 2000 WL 1729455, *3 (Ohio Ct. App. 9th Dist. Lorain County 2000) (pattern of conduct to harm petitioner "on two or more occasions close in time").

Similarly, in *Dunkin v. Ireland, III*,[103] the Tenth District Court of Appeals affirmed the trial court decision supporting the issuance of a CPO, partially based on acts of stalking behavior. The petitioner (the sister of respondent) alleged that respondent made threatening phone calls, followed her and tailgated with his car, loitered outside her home, took pictures of her and her property, looked through her trash, harassed a visitor to her house and threatened to take the children from her.

In light of the evidence, the appellate court found that, given his threats involving separating the children from her, her mental distress and fear was reasonable.

Since the passage of R.C. 2903.214 in 1998, advocates, victims and even some trial courts look to the civil stalking statute to provide protection against common stalking behaviors, such as following, spying, telephonic and cyber stalking and repeated unwanted contacts of any kind. These behaviors also include vandalism of victim's property, hurting pets or trespassing or burglarizing victim's home or business. There are no doubt many other types of conduct that could be used by a stalker to frighten or cause mental distress to a victim. Both family and non-family or household members have obtained protection orders under this statute.

On the other hand, where there are acts of stalking and the parties are family or household members, the stalking behaviors are often subsumed within the other acts of physical violence as described in R.C. 3113.31(A). It is less necessary for courts to accurately define specific acts of stalking when they occur in the context of domestic violence.

§ 9:3 Civil stalking and sexually oriented offense protection orders[1]

A civil stalking protection order is the same as an anti-stalking civil protection order. Additionally, the statute was recently amended to add the commission of a "sexually oriented offense"[2] to the actionable behaviors for which a victim may seek a protection order under R.C. 2903.214.[3] Of significance is that a civil stalking protection order is

---

[103]Dunkin v. Ireland, 2005-Ohio-3371, 2005 WL 1532425 (Ohio Ct. App. 10th Dist. Franklin County 2005); see also Everitt v. Everitt, 2010-Ohio-875, 2010 WL 816615 (Ohio Ct. App. 9th Dist. Summit County 2010).

[Section 9:3]

[1]See Sup. R. Form 10.03-D to 10.03-F.

[2]As defined in R.C. 2950.01. Wilson v. Lyons, 2014-Ohio-1665, 2014 WL 1561834 (Ohio Ct. App. 5th Dist. Fairfield County 2014); L.L.L. v. Junies, 2014-Ohio-141, 2014 WL 201640 (Ohio Ct. App. 2d Dist. Greene County 2014) ("RC 2903.214(C)(1) provides for the issuance of a protection order to protect those individuals who demonstrate that another has committed a sexually oriented offense against their person," at ¶ 13.).] See also Rehfus v. Smith, 2015-Ohio-2145, 2015 WL 3498686 (Ohio Ct. App. 7th Dist. Carroll County 2015) (denying the civil stalking protection order due to a lack of corroboration regarding sexual abuse of a child); Lutson v. Anderkin, 2013 WL 2150897 (Ohio C.P. 2013); D.R.B. by K.G.B. v. G.T.B., 2018-Ohio-2787, 2018 WL 3414261 (Ohio Ct. App. 7th Dist. Noble County 2018).

[3]R.C. 2903.214(C)(1); see also Gruber v. Hart, 2007-Ohio-873, 2007 WL 625818,

preventative in nature, allowing a court to act before the stalker causes harm.[4]

Q & A: What protection is available to parties who are not family or household members?

Ohio now permits non-family or household members to seek a civil protection order for acts of stalking[5] and the commission of sexually oriented offenses. Under R.C. 2903.214, common pleas courts have jurisdiction to issue protection orders when violations of R.C. 2903. 211[6] and sexually oriented offenses under R.C. 2950.01 occur.

At least one Ohio court acknowledged the importance of such protection orders. In *Lindsay v. Jackson*,[7] the Hamilton County Court of Appeals stated that "[t]hese orders are an important part of the overall legislative scheme that is designed to allow the police and the courts to act before a victim is harmed by a stalker."

Q & A: Does RC 2903.214 contemplate a conviction for stalking or for any of the sexually oriented offenses?

No. For purposes of a civil protection order, a violation of the stalking statute[8] or any of the sexually oriented offenses does not mean that the respondent was actually charged and convicted for the crime.[9] Rather, it only means that the respondent committed an act such that the behaviors necessary to prevail under RC 2903.214 rises to the level of stalking (or a sexually oriented offense) as defined in the criminal code.

The statute provides only that in order to obtain a civil protection order under this section, a respondent must have engaged in a violation of RC 2903.211 against the person to be protected by the protec-

---

*2 (Ohio Ct. App. 6th Dist. Ottawa County 2007) (stating that "[a] SCPO is preventative in nature, allowing a Court to act, before a stalker can harm his or her victim."), quoting Short v. Walker, 2001 WL 32808 (Ohio Ct. App. 12th Dist. Preble County 2001), citing Lindsay v. Jackson, 2000 WL 1268810 (Ohio Ct. App. 1st Dist. Hamilton County 2000); see also Hamlin-Scanlon v. Taylor, 2008-Ohio-411, 2008 WL 315458, *2 (Ohio Ct. App. 9th Dist. Summit County 2008) ("The goal of R.C. 2903.214 is to allow the police and the courts to act *before* (emphasis added in opinion) a victim is harmed by a stalker."), quoting Irwin v. Murray, 2006-Ohio-1633, 2006 WL 832830, *15 (Ohio Ct. App. 6th Dist. Lucas County 2006).

[4]Young v. Young, 2006-Ohio-978, ¶ 105, 2006 WL 515522 (Ohio Ct. App. 2d Dist. Greene County 2006) (noting that civil protection orders are intended to prevent violence before it happens); Bower v. Long, 2013-Ohio-5467, ¶ 9, 2013 WL 6579075 (Ohio Ct. App. 6th Dist. Lucas County 2013).

[5]But see Irwin v. Murray, 2006-Ohio-1633, 2006 WL 832830 (Ohio Ct. App. 6th Dist. Lucas County 2006) (in which appellate court affirmed lower court issuance of a civil stalking protection order in common pleas court, general division, even though the parties are family or household members as set forth in R.C. 3113.31). See also the following questions and answers.

[6]See Malone v. Lowry, 2007-Ohio-5665, 2007 WL 3076599 (Ohio Ct. App. 2d Dist. Greene County 2007) (appellate court noted that nothing in R.C. 2903.214 precludes a party—in this case the respondent—from filing other claims such as abuse of process, malicious prosecution, libel, slander, and intentional and negligent infliction of emotional distress).

[7]Lindsay v. Jackson, 2000 WL 1268810, *2 (Ohio Ct. App. 1st Dist. Hamilton County 2000).

[8]R.C. 2903.211.

[9]See Curington v. Moon, 2009-Ohio-3013, 2009 WL 1800373 (Ohio Ct. App. 2d Dist. Montgomery County 2009).

tion order[10] or committed any one of 29 sexually oriented offenses as described in RC 2950.01.[11]

However, to prevail in an action for a civil protection order, a petitioner must be able to prove each of the elements of the criminal offense.[12]

Q & A: Does R.C. 2903.214 require a court to find that a respondent committed a pattern of sexually oriented offenses?

Not according to the Richland County Court of Appeals in *Morris v. McQuillen*.[13] In that case, the trial court issued a civil protection order under R.C. 2903.214 filed by the mother on behalf of her 16 year old daughter.

On appeal respondent argued that the court should not have granted the protection order because the court misstated the evidence, to wit: that the sexual contact occurred twice although the appellee had testified about only one incident.

The appellate court found that "[t]he statute does not require the court to find a pattern of sexually oriented offenses. Thus, we find the court's misstatement of the evidence is not significant; there is evidence in the record that supports the court's conclusion the appellant had committed at least one sexually oriented offense. Based upon this evidence, the court found by a preponderance of the evidence J.D. had been a victim of a sexually oriented offense and the order was necessary to protect her from sexually oriented offenses."[14]

Similarly, in *L.L.L. v. Junies*,[15] appellant met the victim at the church that they both attended. They dated and after a few months, appellant moved out. A few days later, the victim returned some of appellant's clothing and went back to appellant's new apartment for a tour. After locking his apartment door, appellant hugged, fondled and had sexual intercourse with the victim, which was described as being non-consensual.

"When assessing whether a protection order should have been issued pursuant to R.C. 2903.214, a reviewing court must prove there was sufficient credible evidence to prove by a preponderance of the evidence that the petitioner was entitled to relief."[16] In the instant case, the victim testified that once inside appellant's apartment, he locked the door, preventing her from leaving. Although admitting that she gave him a goodbye hug, she did not consent to being fondled and

[10]See for example, Caban v. Ransome, 2009-Ohio-1034, 2009 WL 582761 (Ohio Ct. App. 7th Dist. Mahoning County 2009); Miller v. Shaw, 2009-Ohio-6753, 2009 WL 4895276 (Ohio Ct. App. 7th Dist. Carroll County 2009).

[11]R.C. 2903.214(C)(1).

[12]Saari v. Saari, 2000 WL 1729455 (Ohio Ct. App. 9th Dist. Lorain County 2000); see also Kreuzer v. Kreuzer, 144 Ohio App. 3d 610, 2001-Ohio-1542, 761 N.E.2d 77 (2d Dist. Greene County 2001); D.R.B. by K.G.B. v. G.T.B., 2018-Ohio-2787, 2018 WL 3414261 (Ohio Ct. App. 7th Dist. Noble County 2018).

[13]Morris v. McQuillen, 2009-Ohio-2848, 2009 WL 1677848 (Ohio Ct. App. 5th Dist. Richland County 2009).

[14]Morris at *3.

[15]L.L.L. v. Junies, 2014-Ohio-141, 2014 WL 201640 (Ohio Ct. App. 2d Dist. Greene County 2014).

[16]L.L.L. v. Junies, 2014-Ohio-141, 2014 WL 201640, ¶ 14 (Ohio Ct. App. 2d Dist. Greene County 2014).

groped. Nor did she consent to him pulling down her underwear and force himself on her. Despite her protests, he raped her.

R.C. 2950.01(A)(1) lists a number of charges, including rape, which fall under the definition of a "sexually oriented offense." R.C. 2907.02. "No person shall engage in sexual conduct with another when the offender purposely compels the other person to submit by force or threat of force. R.C. 2907.02(A)(2)."[17] The act of rape formed the basis for granting a sexually oriented offense civil protection order. At no point in the appellate court's opinion was it mentioned that a pattern of conduct or mental distress was a necessary component. Clearly, the issuance of a sexually oriented offense civil protection order need not be based on a pattern of conduct in order to fit within the statutory mandate.

Q & A: Are civil stalking protection orders and prosecutions for menacing by stalking mutually exclusive remedies?

No. R.C. 2903.214(G) specifically states that "the remedies and procedures provided in this section are, in addition to and not in lieu of, any other available civil or criminal remedies." Additionally, the definition of "pattern of conduct" is defined as 'two or more actions or incidents closely related in time, whether or not there has been a prior conviction based on any of those actions or incidents."[18] This language permits actions that may be the subject of prior convictions to be used in proving menacing by stalking for purposes of civil protection orders under R.C. 2903.214, but the actions forming the basis of a CPO do not have to be subject of prior convictions.[19]

Q & A: Have there been constitutional challenges to R.C. 2903.214?[20]

Yes. In *Lindsay v. Jackson*, the respondent raised due process concerns, arguing a lack of adequate notice and the opportunity to be heard.[21] However, the Hamilton County Court of Appeals did not specifically address the constitutionality of the statute.[22]

However, in *Snell v. Snell*,[23] appellant challenged the constitutionality of R.C. 2903.214, arguing that his due process rights were violated by the unconstitutional statute. The Richland County Court of Ap-

---

[17]L.L.L. v. Junies, 2014-Ohio-141, 2014 WL 201640, ¶ 13 (Ohio Ct. App. 2d Dist. Greene County 2014).

[18]R.C. 2903.211(D)(1).

[19]Curington v. Moon, 2009-Ohio-3013, 2009 WL 1800373, *4 (Ohio Ct. App. 2d Dist. Montgomery County 2009).

[20]See Text § 9:1.

[21]Lindsay v. Jackson, 2000 WL 1268810 (Ohio Ct. App. 1st Dist. Hamilton County 2000). See also Elliot v. Ball, 2004-Ohio-6300, 2004 WL 2677464 (Ohio Ct. App. 8th Dist. Cuyahoga County 2004); Kreuzer v. Kreuzer, 144 Ohio App. 3d 610, 2001-Ohio-1542, 761 N.E.2d 77 (2d Dist. Greene County 2001) (where the court found that the First Amendment does not protect speech that knowingly causes another to believe she/he faces physical harm or mental distress, even if the activity involves otherwise protected speech, such as picketing).

[22]See also Harris v. Miami Cty. Sheriff's Dept., 160 Ohio App. 3d 435, 2005-Ohio-1713, 827 N.E.2d 807 (2d Dist. Miami County 2005) (appellant waived argument as to unconstitutionality of R.C. 2903.214 by entering into a consent agreement).

[23]Snell v. Snell, 2006-Ohio-2899, 2006 WL 1575159 (Ohio Ct. App. 5th Dist. Richland County 2006).

peals noted that "[t]he civil protection statute has survived numerous constitutional challenges. A legislative enactment withstands a challenge on substantive due process grounds if it bears a real and substantial relationship to public health, safety, morals, or the general welfare of the public and if it is not unreasonable or arbitrary."[24] The Richland County appellate court held that R.C. 2903.214 does not violate appellant's constitutional rights to due process, free speech or association. "Nor does it violate his fundamental right to parent his children or his right to bear arms."[25]

Recently, the Montgomery County Court of Appeals considered a void for vagueness argument. In *Currington v. Moon*,[26] the respondent argued that R.C. 2903.211 was unconstitutional on vagueness grounds as it did not allow reasonable persons to know in advance what actions were prohibited, especially when the other person's intention was to cause mental distress. If the underlying statute was found to be unconstitutional, the civil stalking protection order statute allowing protection orders for the violation of an unconstitutional statue would also be void.

The Montgomery County Court of Appeals rejected respondent's argument and concluded that R.C. 2903.211 was not void for vagueness because the statute contains a scienter requirement.[27] Under R.C. 2903.211, the offender must "knowingly" cause another to believe that the offender will cause physical harm to the other person or cause mental distress to the other person. Therefore, a person of ordinary intelligence would be able to discern what conduct is prohibited. Moreover, the statute does not impinge on constitutionally guaranteed freedoms.[28]

For several years, victims of stalking were unable to bring civil actions against their stalkers in the Mahoning County Common Pleas Court.[29] In *State ex rel. Shannon Triplett v. Vivo*,[30] a writ of mandamus was filed against the County Clerk of Courts directing him to accept Ms. Triplett's petition for civil stalking protection order for filing. More importantly, the relator requested that the Supreme Court of Ohio determine whether the Mahoning County Common Pleas Court

---

[24]Snell v. Snell, 2006-Ohio-2899, 2006 WL 1575159, *4 (Ohio Ct. App. 5th Dist. Richland County 2006), citing Mottice v. Kirkpatrick, 2001-Ohio-7042, 2001 WL 1673733 (Ohio Ct. App. 5th Dist. Stark County 2001), which upheld the constitutionality of the statute on that basis.

[25]Snell v. Snell, 2006-Ohio-2899, 2006 WL 1575159, *4 (Ohio Ct. App. 5th Dist. Richland County 2006).

[26]Curington v. Moon, 2009-Ohio-3013, 2009 WL 1800373 (Ohio Ct. App. 2d Dist. Montgomery County 2009); see also Text § 9:1.

[27]See also State v. Benner, 96 Ohio App. 3d 327, 644 N.E.2d 1130 (1st Dist. Hamilton County 1994); State v. Schwab, 119 Ohio App. 3d 463, 695 N.E.2d 801 (12th Dist. Butler County 1997); State v. Dario, 106 Ohio App. 3d 232, 665 N.E.2d 759 (1st Dist. Hamilton County 1995).

[28]*Moon at *6.*

[29]See Holby v. Aurelio, 2000 WL 33908143 (Ohio C.P. 2000) (where the Mahoning County Common Pleas Court found R.C. 2903.214 unconstitutional on procedural grounds and ordered the Mahoning County Clerk of Court to cease accepting the filing of stalking civil protection orders).

[30]State ex rel. Shannon Triplett v. Vivo, Mahoning County Clerk of Courts, No. 02-565 (4-11-02).

had the authority to determine that R.C. 2903.214 was unconstitutional. In fact, the relator requested that the Supreme Court determine that the statute was and is constitutional. Before a hearing was held, the Ohio Attorney General intervened supporting the writ filed by the relator. The County Prosecutor issued an opinion advising the court to issue an order to the clerk of courts instructing him to follow the mandates of R.C. 2903.214, thereby vacating the ruling set forth in *Holby*. On April 22, 2002, the Mahoning County Court of Common Pleas filed a judgment entry vacating the prior ruling.

Similarly, a Montgomery County magistrate found portions of R.C. 2903.214 unconstitutional. In *Morgan v. Partridge*,[31] respondent filed a motion to dismiss prior to the full hearing, challenging the constitutionality of the statute on due process grounds. He argued that the statute was void for vagueness, as applied as it would deprive him of his right to freedom of association and freedom of movement or right to travel. The magistrate dismissed the petition for a stalking CPO on the grounds that R.C. 2903.214 was vague, lacked both substantive and procedural due process and failed to specify the appropriate standard of proof.

In ruling on the petitioner's objections to the magistrate's decision, the trial court found that the ex parte hearing provided for in R.C. 2903.214(D) (which is the same as that provided in R.C. 3113.31(D)) is unconstitutional. The court relied on the analysis found in *Goldberg v. Kelly*,[32] which set forth the test to be applied before taking a fundamental right without notice and an opportunity to be heard. In this case, the trial court pointed out that the forms promulgated by the Supreme Court Rules of Superintendence[33] proscribe conduct that may affect a party's fundamental right. The court held that "the ex parte hearing provided for in R.C. 2903.214, when conducted without an opportunity for the respondent to be heard, is too unreliable when used to deprive an individual of a fundamental right. At the ex parte stage, without testimony from the respondent, the Court does not usually have sufficient information to determine if terms in the standard CSPO will affect the respondent's fundamental rights. Therefore, to the extent that the statute directs the Court to take action by conducting an ex parte hearing, without notice and opportunity to be heard, the statute does not meet this *Goldberg* criteria."[34]

Additionally, the court discussed the standard of proof to be applied in establishing what must be proven to issue a CSPO after a full evidentiary hearing. Unlike the encompassing standard of a preponderance of the evidence set forth by the Supreme Court in *Felton v. Felton*,[35] the trial court suggested that a two-tiered standard be applied. Clear and convincing evidence must be established before depriving an individual of a fundamental right and the preponderance

[31]Morgan v. Partridge, No. 02-1848 (C.P., Montgomery, 2-25-03); Evans v. Riegle, 2004 WL 3469164 (Ohio C.P. 2004).

[32]Goldberg v. Kelly, 397 U.S. 254, 90 S. Ct. 1011, 25 L. Ed. 2d 287 (1970).

[33]See generally Sup. R. 10.01 et seq.

[34]Morgan v. Partridge, No. 02-1848 (C.P., Montgomery, 2-25-03).

[35]Felton v. Felton, 79 Ohio St. 3d 34, 1997-Ohio-302, 679 N.E.2d 672 (1997).

of the evidence standard may be applied when the CSPO does not include a deprivation of a fundamental right. Thus, under Form 10.01-E or 10.01-F, items 1, 3, 6 and 8 may be checked if the preponderance standard is met and items 2, 4, 5, 7 and 9 may be checked only if a respondent has had actual notice and an opportunity to be heard and if the petitioner proves all the elements of R.C. 2903.211 or a violation of a protection order under R.C. 2903.213 by clear and convincing evidence.[36] The court reasoned that, depending on the relief requested, different burdens of proof may be required.

Practically speaking, while this limited decision only affects petitioners who have been assigned to one common pleas trial court judge, the impact may be far greater. The court's rationale may be applied to protection orders issued under the domestic violence civil protection order statute in order to justify a finding that R.C. 3113.31 is unconstitutional.

Q & A: Is the "stay away" provision contained in the standardized civil stalking protection order form a violation of respondent's due process right because the civil protection order constitutionally denied deprived him of his right to intrastate travel?

Not according to the Miami County Court of Appeals in *Luttrell v. Younce*.[37] In that case, a respondent argued on appeal that the civil protection order provision contained in the mandated forms prohibited him from being within 500 yards or three blocks of the protected persons, wherever they might be found.[38] Such a restriction might make it impossible for the human eye to identify whether the alleged victim was within the restricted area, thereby making it difficult to determine what conduct was prohibited under the terms of the order.

The appellate court focused its analysis on the second sentence of Sup. R. Form 10.03-F, provision 5, which provides that "if respondent accidently comes in contact with protected persons in any public or private place, Respondent must depart *immediately*." "This sentence creates an exception to the geographical restriction placed on Younce. If he accidentally comes into prohibited contact with a person protected under the terms of the civil protection order, he can avoid a violation of the terms of the order if he departs immediately."

In overruling the assignments of error, the court also indicated that the culpable mental state for violation under R.C. 2919.27 is recklessness. Therefore, the "recklessly" language provided an additional safeguard that Younce would not be punished for an accidental violation of paragraph 5 of the civil protection order. The civil protection order against Younce was not issued because Younce was lawfully exercising his right to intrastate travel and minding his own business. Rather, Younce was engaging in activities that knowingly caused another person to believe that he would cause physical harm or mental distress. Such activities were not protected simply because Younce was exercising his right to intrastate travel at the time he

[36] Felton v. Felton, 79 Ohio St. 3d 34, 1997-Ohio-302, 679 N.E.2d 672 (1997).

[37] Luttrell v. Younce, 2011-Ohio-4458, 2011 WL 3890292 (Ohio Ct. App. 2d Dist. Miami County 2011).

[38] Sup. R. Form 10.03-F, provision 5.

engaged in those activities. Younce failed to show that the terms of the civil protection order were an unconstitutional restraint on his right to intrastate travel.[39]

Q & A: Is a civil stalking protection order pursuant to R.C. 2903.214 the same as a permanent injunction?

Not according to several appellate jurisdictions that have relied on the Ohio Supreme Court's opinion in *Felton v. Felton*[40] and in which the Supreme Court determined that a protection order is not the same as a restraining order or no-harassment order. "In Ohio, the domestic violence statutes grant police and courts great authority to enforce protection orders and violations of those protection orders incur harsh penalties. Therefore, protection orders. . . are the more appropriate and efficacious method to prevent future domestic violence . . . ."[41]

On the other hand, in *Prostejovsky v. Prostejovsky*,[42] the 5th District Court of Appeals reasoned that because a CSPO is analogous to a permanent injunction, any order made pursuant to R.C. 2903.214 is subject to modification or termination. The appellate court found that a protection order under this section is injunctive relief. "The design of an injunction is to prevent future injury and not to redress past wrongs."[43]

Of interest is that Justice Hoffman, in a concurring opinion, questioned whether a civil stalking protection order issued pursuant to R.C. 2903.214 is analogous to a permanent injunction "so as to render it always subject to modification or vacation."[44] Justice Hoffman pointed out that the court retained the authority to change the order and that it could do so without having pursued or satisfied the standard set forth in Civ. R. 60(B).[45]

[39]Luttrell v. Younce, 2011-Ohio-4458, 2011 WL 3890292, *6 (Ohio Ct. App. 2d Dist. Miami County 2011).

[40]Felton v. Felton, 79 Ohio St. 3d 34, 1997-Ohio-302, 679 N.E.2d 672 (1997).

[41]Felton v. Felton, 79 Ohio St. 3d 34, 1997-Ohio-302, 679 N.E.2d 672, 677 (1997); see also Niepsuj v. Niepsuj, 2004-Ohio-7179, 2004 WL 3017225 (Ohio Ct. App. 9th Dist. Summit County 2004); Wildi v. Wildi, 159 Ohio App. 3d 568, 2005-Ohio-257, 824 N.E.2d 1011 (10th Dist. Franklin County 2005); Irwin v. Murray, 2006-Ohio-1633, 2006 WL 832830 (Ohio Ct. App. 6th Dist. Lucas County 2006); Hamlin-Scanlon v. Taylor, 2008-Ohio-411, 2008 WL 315458 (Ohio Ct. App. 9th Dist. Summit County 2008).

[42]Prostejovsky v. Prostejovsky, 2007-Ohio-5743, 2007 WL 3119724 (Ohio Ct. App. 5th Dist. Ashland County 2007).

[43]Prostejovsky v. Prostejovsky, 2007-Ohio-5743, 2007 WL 3119724, *3 (Ohio Ct. App. 5th Dist. Ashland County 2007), quoting Athens Metropolitan Housing Authority v. Pierson, 2002-Ohio-2164, 2002 WL 851767 (Ohio Ct. App. 4th Dist. Athens County 2002). See also N.S. v. S.B., 2017-Ohio-1556, 2017 WL 1507322 (Ohio Ct. App. 8th Dist. Cuyahoga County 2017), as amended, (Aug. 22, 2017) (citing *Prostejovsky* for the proposition that a CSPO is like a permanent injunction and as such, the court had the authority to modify or vacate a CSPO).

[44]Prostejovsky v. Prostejovsky, 2007-Ohio-5743, 2007 WL 3119724, *5 (Ohio Ct. App. 5th Dist. Ashland County 2007).

[45]Prostejovsky v. Prostejovsky, 2007-Ohio-5743, 2007 WL 3119724, *5 (Ohio Ct. App. 5th Dist. Ashland County 2007).

§ 9:4 Persons covered under R.C. 2903.214[1]

Q & A: Who can be granted civil stalking protection orders under R.C. 2903.214?

The age limit for invoking the remedies set forth in R.C. 2903.214 has been clarified to permit only those individuals 18 years old and older to seek relief under this section of the Ohio Revised Code.[2] For example, in *Wilson v. Lyons*,[3] appellant appealed the issuance of a civil stalking protection order under R.C. 2903.214 on grounds that the petition should have been filed in juvenile court as the respondent was a juvenile at the time of the allegations.

The appellate court disagreed and found that because appellee was afraid of appellant and because the incidents occurred over the first semester during which appellant turned 18, the court of common pleas had jurisdiction for the offenses alleged in the petition.

The concurring opinion also supported the majority analysis but did so for a different reason. "I find the eighteen (18) year old age requirement found in R.C. 2903.214(C)(1) related to the age of the Respondent at the time the petition is filed and does not relate to the respondent's age at the time respondent engaged in the offensive conduct. The statute states the Respondent 'is' eighteen (18) years of age 'and' engaged in the violation of Section 2903.211, It does not require the Respondent 'was' eighteen (18) years of age at the time Respondent engaged in the violation."[4]

Of importance is that the concurring opinion focused on the statutory change in the law, acknowledging that R.C. 2903.214 applies only to persons that are 18 years of age or older.[5]

Non-family victims of domestic violence may seek relief under R.C. 2903.214 in the general division of common pleas courts.[6] While R.C. 2903.214 does not specifically prohibit intimate partners or family

---

[Section 9:4]

[1]Sub. HB 151, eff. August 16, 2016 amends the menacing by stalking statute (RC 2903.211) to prohibit a person from knowingly causing another person to believe that the offender will cause physical harm or mental distress to a family or household member of the other person).

[2]R.C. 2903.214(C)(1).

[3]Wilson v. Lyons, 2014-Ohio-1665, 2014 WL 1561834 (Ohio Ct. App. 5th Dist. Fairfield County 2014).

[4]Wilson v. Lyons, 2014-Ohio-1665, 2014 WL 1561834, ¶ 30 (Ohio Ct. App. 5th Dist. Fairfield County 2014).

[5]R.C. 2903.214(C)(1).

[6]See Spence v. Herbert, 2001 WL 876231 (Ohio Ct. App. 5th Dist. Licking County 2001) (where ex-spouse sought a stalking protection order for himself and his son against the boyfriend of his ex-wife); see also Mottice v. Kirkpatrick, 2001-Ohio-7042, 2001 WL 1673733 (Ohio Ct. App. 5th Dist. Stark County 2001) (where maternal grandmother sought a civil stalking protection order against the father of her daughter's children); Bright v. Lane, 2003-Ohio-225, 2003 WL 139755 (Ohio Ct. App. 5th Dist. Ashland County 2003) (brother filed a petition seeking a stalking order against sister who saw brother's children without brother's permission; court held that the situation was a long-standing family dispute that is not the kind of conduct which fits within the menacing by stalking statute, especially where appellant's brother repeatedly allowed his children to stay at their grandmother's nursery where he knew appellant was employed).

and household members from obtaining civil protection orders, stalking behavior between family or household members as defined in R.C. 3113.31(A)(3) is the type of behavior prohibited by R.C. 3113.31(A)(1)(b). Clearly, family or household members may seek relief under R.C. 3113.31 in the domestic relations courts.

While a petitioner and respondent must have a family or household member relationship for purposes of R.C. 3113.31, it is less clear how the family or household member relationship is or should be structured for purposes of R.C. 2903.214. It is quite possible that the family or household member relationship contemplated by R.C. 2903.214 is based on the relationship between petitioner and protected parties rather than on a relationship between the petitioner and the respondent.

Unfortunately, it is not certain whether family members can or should avail themselves of relief in common pleas courts as an additional forum or in lieu of domestic relations court. However, many courts have permitted spouses, former spouses and persons living as spouses to avail themselves of R.C. 2903.214. For example, in *Short v. Walker*,[7] a former spouse requested a stalking civil protection order. The court granted the former wife a protection order for herself and her new husband.[8]

Q & A: Have individuals obtained a civil stalking protection order where the relationship is a family or household member relationship as defined in R.C. 3113.31?

Yes. In *Irwin v. Murray*,[9] the parties' relationship was that of "persons living as spouses." Appellee was granted a CPO in Lucas County Domestic Relations Court. Subsequently, appellant filed an action for money judgment against appellee in Lucas County Common Pleas Court and a counter-petition for civil protection order in domestic relations court which was dismissed after a full hearing. Three months later, after appellant contacted appellee's customers and made disparaging remarks about her to them, appellee requested and was granted a stalking civil protection order (SCPO) in the General Division of the Lucas County Common Pleas Court.

---

[7]Short v. Walker, 2001 WL 32808 (Ohio Ct. App. 12th Dist. Preble County 2001); see also Tuuri v. Snyder, 2002-Ohio-2107, 2002 WL 818427 (Ohio Ct. App. 11th Dist. Geauga County 2002); Wildi v. Wildi, 159 Ohio App. 3d 568, 2005-Ohio-257, 824 N.E.2d 1011 (10th Dist. Franklin County 2005); Van Vorce v. Van Vorce, 2004-Ohio-5646, 2004 WL 2377839 (Ohio Ct. App. 3d Dist. Auglaize County 2004).

[8]See also B.C. v. A.S., 2014-Ohio-1326, 2014 WL 1345260 (Ohio Ct. App. 9th Dist. Medina County 2014) (where provable acts of domestic violence occurred against petitioner's current husband, the court stated that "a petition premised upon the alleged threat to B.C.'s husband would be more appropriate in the court of common pleas as a request for a civil stalking protection order issued under Section 2903.214 than the domestic relations court as a request for a DVCPO under Section 3113.31," at¶ 24).

[9]Irwin v. Murray, 2006-Ohio-1633, 2006 WL 832830 (Ohio Ct. App. 6th Dist. Lucas County 2006); see also Snell v. Snell, 2006-Ohio-2899, 2006 WL 1575159 (Ohio Ct. App. 5th Dist. Richland County 2006) (where the parties were spouses and the appellate court stated that R.C. 2903.214 was the statute in question); Jenkins v. Jenkins, 2007-Ohio-422, 2007 WL 275700 (Ohio Ct. App. 10th Dist. Franklin County 2007); Cooper v. Manta, 2012-Ohio-867, 2012 WL 691547 (Ohio Ct. App. 11th Dist. Lake County 2012) (relationship between the parties was that of father and adult daughter).

On appeal, appellant argued that the general division of the common pleas court lacked subject matter jurisdiction to issue the SCPO because the parties were family or household members pursuant to R.C. 3113.31(A)(4) and that only the domestic relations court had the authority to grant such an order against "persons living as spouses."

The Lucas County Court of Appeals stressed that, while R.C. 3113.31 authorizes the domestic relations court to hear domestic violence petitions, nothing in R.C. 3113.31 bars appellee from seeking relief through the general division of common pleas court. The Court reasoned that in *Felton v. Felton*, the Supreme Court noted "the remedies and procedures provided in this section[10] are *in addition to, and not in lieu of*, any other available civil or criminal remedies."[11]

Thus, the appellate court found that, because R.C. 2903.214(A)(3) defines the parties subject to the court's authority as having the same meaning as in R.C. 3113.31, "the parties fall within the statutory definition of 'family or household member.' "[12] Furthermore, the court noted that "R.C. 2903.214(B) states the court of common pleas has jurisdiction over all proceedings under this section." Therefore, the court of common pleas had the authority to issue the SCPO against appellant and the order is not void for lack of subject matter jurisdiction.[13]

However, the Lucas County Court of Appeals failed to address whether a petitioner could or should have two protection orders from two different courts in effect at the same time and the issue of forum shopping.

Q & A: Can a family or household member obtain a stalking civil protection order in common pleas court even though a divorce is pending in domestic relations court?

The Franklin County Court of Appeals held that the general division of the common pleas court had jurisdiction to issue wife an anti-stalking civil protection order. In *Wildi v. Wildi*,[14] the husband requested a stalking civil protection order against his wife even though the domestic relations court had issued a restraining order enjoining the wife from harassing him.

The Franklin County Court of Appeals held the common pleas court

---

[10]R.C. 3113.31.

[11]Irwin v. Murray, 2006-Ohio-1633, 2006 WL 832830, *2 (Ohio Ct. App. 6th Dist. Lucas County 2006), quoting *Felton*, emphasis in the original; see also Hamlin-Scanlon v. Taylor, 2008-Ohio-411, 2008 WL 315458 (Ohio Ct. App. 9th Dist. Summit County 2008).

[12]Irwin v. Murray, 2006-Ohio-1633, 2006 WL 832830, *2 (Ohio Ct. App. 6th Dist. Lucas County 2006).

[13]Irwin v. Murray, 2006-Ohio-1633, 2006 WL 832830, *2 (Ohio Ct. App. 6th Dist. Lucas County 2006).

[14]Wildi v. Wildi, 159 Ohio App. 3d 568, 2005-Ohio-257, 824 N.E.2d 1011 (10th Dist. Franklin County 2005); see also Hamlin-Scanlon v. Taylor, 2008-Ohio-411, 2008 WL 315458, *2 (Ohio Ct. App. 9th Dist. Summit County 2008) ("a party is not precluded from seeking a SCPO in the general division of a court while an action is pending in the domestic relations division"), quoting Irwin v. Murray, 2006-Ohio-1633, 2006 WL 832830 (Ohio Ct. App. 6th Dist. Lucas County 2006), citing Wildi v. Wildi, 159 Ohio App. 3d 568, 570, 2005-Ohio-257, ¶ 7824 N.E.2d 1011 (10th Dist. Franklin County 2005); Khan v. Hughes, 2015-Ohio-4502, 2015 WL 6550725 (Ohio Ct. App. 8th Dist. Cuyahoga County 2015).

did not lack subject matter jurisdiction to issue the husband a SCPO.[15] The court held that "a protective order from stalking is not tied to a divorce action, and its enforcement by police represents a more rapid, direct and punitive method of protecting a stalking victim than enforcing a domestic relations order."[16]

Unfortunately, the court of appeals missed an opportunity to discuss whether R.C. 2903.214 should apply to family or household members such as spouses in *Wildi* or whether R.C. 2903.214 is limited to persons who do not fit within the definition of family or household members as set forth in R.C. 3113.31, the domestic violence statute.[17]

Q & A: Can a person obtain a civil stalking protection order for herself and two children against a former spouse when visitation was already pending in domestic relations court?

The Summit County Court of Appeals answered this in the affirmative in *Hamlin-Scanlon v. Taylor*.[18] In this case, the parties were former spouses. Appellant was granted an ex parte civil stalking protection order pursuant to R.C. 2903.214 on behalf of herself and two children. The magistrate recommended the issuance of a full hearing protection order, permitting appellee to exercise visitation rights as set forth by the domestic relations court but prohibiting him from harming, threatening, stalking, harassing or annoying the appellant or the children. Appellee then objected to the magistrate's decision.

The trial court overruled the magistrate and reasoned that "case matters relating to visitation of the children were already pending before the domestic relations court. Specifically, 'the trial court determined that the resolution of the parties' difficulties rest with the Summit County Domestic Relations Court and this Court declines to participate in an action which the Court concludes it has no jurisdiction to hear.'"[19]

On appeal, appellant claimed that the trial court erred when it refused to issue a CSPO. The appellate court confined its analysis to whether the trial court erred when it concluded it lacked jurisdiction over the subject matter. In reversing the trial court decision, the ap-

---

[15]See also Irwin v. Murray, 2006-Ohio-1633, 2006 WL 832830 (Ohio Ct. App. 6th Dist. Lucas County 2006) (appellate court held that although domestic relations court could issue a CPO, the court of common pleas had the author to issue the SCPO and the order was not void for lack of subject matter jurisdiction); Hamlin-Scanlon v. Taylor, 2008-Ohio-411, 2008 WL 315458 (Ohio Ct. App. 9th Dist. Summit County 2008) (noting that former spouses may apply for civil stalking protection orders in Common Pleas Court and held that the trial court erred when it determined that it lacked subject matter jurisdiction).

[16]Wildi v. Wildi, 159 Ohio App. 3d 568, 5702005, 2005-Ohio-257, 824 N.E.2d 1011 (10th Dist. Franklin County 2005), citing Felton v. Felton, 79 Ohio St. 3d 34, 1997-Ohio-302, 679 N.E.2d 672 (1997) (interpreting R.C. 3113.31, an analogous statute; see also Niepsuj v. Niepsuj, 2004-Ohio-7179, 2004 WL 3017225 (Ohio Ct. App. 9th Dist. Summit County 2004) (discussing the difference between the standard of proof for an injunction (a cease and desist order) and a civil protection order).

[17]But see Irwin v. Murray, 2006-Ohio-1633, 2006 WL 832830 (Ohio Ct. App. 6th Dist. Lucas County 2006).

[18]Hamlin-Scanlon v. Taylor, 2008-Ohio-411, 2008 WL 315458 (Ohio Ct. App. 9th Dist. Summit County 2008).

[19]Hamlin-Scanlon v. Taylor, 2008-Ohio-411, 2008 WL 315458 (Ohio Ct. App. 9th Dist. Summit County 2008).

pellate court first pointed out that "[t]he goal of R.C. 2903.214 is to allow the police and the courts to act *before* a victim is harmed by a stalker." (Emphasis sic.)[20] The court relied on *Irwin v. Murray* and *Wildi v. Wildi* in concluding that the trial court erred when it concluded it had no subject matter jurisdiction. In fact, "a party is not precluded from seeking a SCPO in the general division of a court while an action is pending in the domestic relations division."[21]

Q & A: Who else may qualify as protected parties under R.C. 2903.214?

Clearly, this statute was enacted to protect those persons who are unable to seek relief under R.C. 3113.31.[22] For example, in *Mottice v. Kirkpatrick*,[23] a grandmother sought a civil protection order under R.C. 2903.214 on behalf of herself and her grandchildren and daughter who resided with her.[24]

It has also protected a new boyfriend from stalking behavior by his girlfriend's husband.[25] It has also protected an ex-spouse from stalking behavior by a new boyfriend. For example, in *Spence v. Herbert*,[26] the father sought a protection order on behalf of himself and his son against his ex-wife's boyfriend. The Licking County Court of Appeals reversed that part of the protection order relating to the son. In support of its reversal, the appellate court reasoned that the only time

---

[20]Hamlin-Scanlon v. Taylor, 2008-Ohio-411, 2008 WL 315458, *2 (Ohio Ct. App. 9th Dist. Summit County 2008), quoting Irwin v. Murray, 2006-Ohio-1633, 2006 WL 832830 (Ohio Ct. App. 6th Dist. Lucas County 2006).

[21]Hamlin-Scanlon v. Taylor, 2008-Ohio-411, 2008 WL 315458, *2 (Ohio Ct. App. 9th Dist. Summit County 2008), quoting Irwin v. Murray, 2006-Ohio-1633, 2006 WL 832830, *2 (Ohio Ct. App. 6th Dist. Lucas County 2006), citing Wildi v. Wildi, 159 Ohio App. 3d 568, 2005-Ohio-257, 824 N.E.2d 1011 (10th Dist. Franklin County 2005).

[22]But see *Dezarn v. Jordin, No. C-3-02-056 (F.D. Ohio 4-23-02)* (a Dayton federal district court judge ruled that neither state court nor federal court had authority to issue a stalking civil protection order against a Wright-Patterson Air Force Base employee on behalf of another employee for acts of menacing by stalking that occurred at the parties' workplace; the court further ruled that state court had no jurisdiction because federal court had exclusive jurisdiction; it then dismissed the petition because federal law did not authorize the issuance of a stalking civil protection order; this case suggests that federal government employees who are stalked by other federal employees at their workplace may not be able to obtain stalking CPOs. The key factor is whether the federal workplace is located in a "federal enclave" or "federal territory" and this falls within the exclusive legislative jurisdiction of Congress).

[23]Mottice v. Kirkpatrick, 2001-Ohio-7042, 2001 WL 1673733 (Ohio Ct. App. 5th Dist. Stark County 2001).

[24]But see Guthrie v. Long, 2005-Ohio-1541, 2005 WL 737402 (Ohio Ct. App. 10th Dist. Franklin County 2005) (Court reversed inclusion of petitioner's current boyfriend on SCPO where boyfriend was not a family or household member of petitioner.).

[25]See Huffer v. Chafin, 2002-Ohio-356, 2002 WL 144901 (Ohio Ct. App. 5th Dist. Licking County 2002); but see Miller v. Francisco, 2003-Ohio-1978, 2003 WL 1904066 (Ohio Ct. App. 11th Dist. Lake County 2003) (overruled on other grounds by, Davis v. DiNunzio, 2005-Ohio-2883, 2005 WL 1383975 (Ohio Ct. App. 11th Dist. Lake County 2005)) (boyfriend was not a family or household member as defined and where no evidence presented as to relationship of petitioner and her boyfriend, stalking CPO did not apply. Court determined that nature of relationship between petitioner and the protected party must be presented).

[26]Spence v. Herbert, 2001 WL 876231 (Ohio Ct. App. 5th Dist. Licking County 2001); Gilreath v. Kinderdine, 2004-Ohio-868, 2004 WL 362335 (Ohio Ct. App. 2d Dist. Miami County 2004) (sought by husband against wife's former husband).

there were problems between the son and the boyfriend was when the father was around.

Similarly, in *Bloom v. Macbeth*,[27] a son-in-law with custody of his children sought a protection order under R.C. 2903.214 against his mother-in-law, the children's grandmother. In affirming the issuance of the protection order, the appellate court indicated that appellant's interference with appellee's parenting, and the resulting physical harm and inappropriate behavior, was sufficient to establish that the grandmother had knowingly engaged in a pattern of conduct that caused her son-in-law and grandchildren to believe she might cause them physical harm or mental distress.[28]

Q & A: May a petitioner seek a civil stalking protection order on behalf of his/her child?[29]

RC 3113.31(A)(3)(iii) authorizes that parents may seek protection on behalf of their minor children. Because RC 2903.214(A)(3) provides that "family or household member" has the same meaning as in RC 3113.31, parents may seek protection on behalf of their children.

In *Henry v. Coogan*,[30] the appellee was granted a stalking CPO prohibiting appellant from having contact with her or her minor son. Appellant had been harassing and threatening the child because his friend had previously been convicted for beating the child. The pattern of conduct included fishing at the same lake as the minor child, driving slowly by appellee's house and revving the engine to get appellee's attention. In affirming the trial court, the appellate court concluded that there was enough evidence that appellee's conduct caused appellee mental distress and caused her to believe that her son would be physically injured. The court also pointed out that it was reasonable for appellee to fear appellant because he was present when his friend beat her minor child.

The Clermont County Court of Appeals rejected appellant's contention that no evidence was presented to establish that appellee's son suffered mental distress or that he believed that appellant would harm him. In affirming the issuance of the order, the appellate court held that "the stalking civil protection order statute allows a person to

---

[27] Bloom v. Macbeth, 2008-Ohio-4564, 2008 WL 4151319 (Ohio Ct. App. 5th Dist. Ashland County 2008).

[28] Bloom v. Macbeth, 2008-Ohio-4564, 2008 WL 4151319, *1 (Ohio Ct. App. 5th Dist. Ashland County 2008).

[29] Sub. HB 151, eff. August 16, 2016 amends the menacing by stalking statute to prohibit a person from knowingly causing another person to believe that the offender will cause physical harm or mental distress to a family or household member of the other person).

[30] Henry v. Coogan, 2002-Ohio-6519, 2002 WL 31682226 (Ohio Ct. App. 12th Dist. Clermont County 2002); Hamlin-Scanlon v. Taylor, 2008-Ohio-411, 2008 WL 315458 (Ohio Ct. App. 9th Dist. Summit County 2008); McMullen v. Baldwin, 2013-Ohio-2677, 2013 WL 3280031 (Ohio Ct. App. 5th Dist. Stark County 2013) (in which parents obtained a CSPO on behalf of their second grade child because appellant (the father of the child's classmate) caused the minor child mental distress by patting her on the back and knee, touching her food, standing outside of her classroom without reason, attending the child's softball practice and hugging the child); but see Luikart v. Shumate, 2003-Ohio-2130, 2003 WL 1961874 (Ohio Ct. App. 3d Dist. Marion County 2003) (here court reversed issuance of a CPO against appellee's wife and children because no evidence was presented showing a pattern of conduct against them).

seek relief for themselves or any other household member. R.C. 2903.214(C). In this case, Henry sought relief for her son, and the trial court found it appropriate to fashion an order protecting both Henry and her son."[31]

Q & A: Can a child be included in a civil stalking protection order as a protected party where the child was already the subject of a custody proceeding in another county?

Not according to the Jefferson County Court of Appeals. In *Kranek v. Richards*,[32] a father requested a civil stalking protection order against the mother of his child, who had allegedly threatened the father and his family over a dispute regarding the child (identified in the opinion as "J.K."). The mother subsequently appealed the grant of the civil stalking protection order asserting that J.K. should not have been included on the protection order as the trial court did not have jurisdiction over parental rights and responsibilities of the child.

The appellate court relied on case law in its determination that a trial court had no authority to issue orders regarding parental rights and responsibilities of a child where another court has made orders over parental rights and responsibilities. Additionally, the appellate court indicated that even if a child is only protected by the order and a parent is the respondent bound by the order, then most aspects of the CSPO will necessarily affect parental rights in some way.[33]

While the trial judge in this case had indicated at the civil stalking protection order hearing that J.K. would have to be removed from the order because the juvenile court of Madison County had issued custody orders regarding J.K., the trial court had failed to make the correction to the protection order. Thus, the case was remanded to the trial court to delete the child from the CSPO.

Q & A: What determines whether a family or household member is also a protected party?

According to the Third District Court of Appeals, evidence of stalking must be presented indicating a pattern of conduct towards a family or household member. In *Luikart v. Shumate*,[34] the boyfriend of the former wife engaged in a pattern of conduct that knowingly caused the husband to believe that the boyfriend would cause him physical harm or mental distress to warrant a civil stalking protection order. Husband included his wife and children as protected parties. Boyfriend appealed and then argued that no evidence was elicited at trial demonstrating a pattern of conduct against husband's wife and children. In reversing the trial court, the appellate court held that "[b]ecause no evidence was presented to establish the need for a CPO

[31]Henry v. Coogan, 2002-Ohio-6519, 2002 WL 31682226, *3 (Ohio Ct. App. 12th Dist. Clermont County 2002).

[32]Kranek v. Richards, 2011-Ohio-6374, 2011 WL 6164727 (Ohio Ct. App. 7th Dist. Jefferson County 2011).

[33]Kranek v. Richards, 2011-Ohio-6374, 2011 WL 6164727, *3 (Ohio Ct. App. 7th Dist. Jefferson County 2011).

[34]Luikart v. Shumate, 2003-Ohio-2130, 2003 WL 1961874 (Ohio Ct. App. 3d Dist. Marion County 2003); see also Miller v. Francisco, 2003-Ohio-1978, 2003 WL 1904066 (Ohio Ct. App. 11th Dist. Lake County 2003) (overruled on other grounds by, Davis v. DiNunzio, 2005-Ohio-2883, 2005 WL 1383975 (Ohio Ct. App. 11th Dist. Lake County 2005)).

protecting Appellee's wife and children, we sustain Shumate's assignment of error in this regard."[35] The court also stated that his wife and children were already protected because the CPO restrained Shumate from having contact with husband.

Q & A: Does a protected party need to be a family or household member of the petitioner in order to be listed on the protection order?

Yes. In *Guthrie v. Long*,[36] appellee obtained an anti-stalking civil protection order for herself and her boyfriend against her ex-boyfriend. On appeal, appellant argued that because appellee and the current boyfriend were not family or household members, the trial court erred when it granted the civil protection order.

The appellate court reversed the trial court decision as to the boyfriend on the grounds that the boyfriend is not a family or household member of the appellee. R.C. 2903.214(A) articulates the family or household members covered by the protection order and they include a spouse, former spouse, parent, child, person living as a spouse, persons related by consanguinity or affinity and certain other relatives.[37] Although included in the CPO, no evidence was presented that the boyfriend was a family or household member.

Clearly, the moral in this case is that each time a petitioner decides that other family or household members are in need of protection, evidence must be presented in the trial court relative to the listed protected parties and the reasons to include them on the protection order.[38]

Similarly, in *Griga v. DiBenedetto*,[39] the trial court issued a civil stalking protection order for himself as well as on behalf of his wife and children. On appeal, DiBenedetto argued that the trial court erred in granting the CSPO on behalf of a person not included in the definition of family or household member as defined in RC 2903.214(A)(3).

The appellate court first noted that "[u]nder RC 2903.214(C), a petitioner may seek relief for himself on behalf of a 'family or household member.' In the context of the CSPO statute, 'family or household member' is a legal term of art, as defined in RC 3113.31(A)

[35]Luikart v. Shumate, 2003-Ohio-2130, 2003 WL 1961874, *3 (Ohio Ct. App. 3d Dist. Marion County 2003).

[36]Guthrie v. Long, 2005-Ohio-1541, 2005 WL 737402 (Ohio Ct. App. 10th Dist. Franklin County 2005).

[37]But see dissenting opinion in Jenkins v. Douglas, 2007-Ohio-1909, 2007 WL 1175228, *4 (Ohio Ct. App. 3d Dist. Marion County 2007) (disagreeing with majority upholding extra clause in CPO regarding no contact between respondent and workers building a house on petitioner's property since workers are not protected parties as contemplated in R.C. 2903.214, citing *Guthrie*).

[38]See also Smith v. Hein, 2015-Ohio-2749, 2015 WL 4095636 (Ohio Ct. App. 1st Dist. Hamilton County 2015), appeal not allowed, 144 Ohio St. 3d 1458, 2016-Ohio-172, 44 N.E.3d 288 (2016) (a petitioner may seek relief on behalf of a family or household member; besides proof of domestic violence towards the family or household member, petitioner needed to prove that his wife and children lived or had lived with him in order to include them as protected parties on the protection order).

[39]Griga v. DiBenedetto, 2012-Ohio-6097, 988 N.E.2d 590 (Ohio Ct. App. 1st Dist. Hamilton County 2012).

(3). *See* RC 2903.214(A)(3)."[40] In reversing the CSPO against petitioner's family members, the court held that as with RC 3113.31, a petitioner was required to prove that each person he claimed as a "family member" lived or had lived with him. Griga had failed to establish that his wife and children met the legal definition of family or household member.[41]

Equally important is that some cases seem to suggest that protected parties must also reside or have resided with the petitioner, meaning that they are family or household members of the petitioner as set forth in RC 2903.214(C).[42]

Q & A: Does RC 2903.214 even suggest that a protected party must only be a "family or household member" of the respondent?

No. R.C. 2903.214(C) provides that "any parent or adult family or household member may seek relief under this section on behalf of any other family or household member." RC 2903.214(A)(3) states that for purposes of RC 2903.214, the phrase "family or household member" has the same meaning as in RC 3113.31.

It is clear that a "family or household member" relationship between petitioner and respondent is a prerequisite for protection under RC 3113.31. So long as there is a "family or household member" relationship between petitioner and respondent, RC 3113.31 specifically permits a petitioner to seek relief on behalf of any other "family or household member" of that petitioner.

Unlike RC 3113.31, any relationship between the petitioner and the respondent is inconsequential for obtaining a CSPO under RC 2903.214. But, because family or household member has the same meaning as in RC 3113.31, it should follow that a petitioner should be able to seek relief on behalf of another "family or household member." What is less clear, however, is whether there must be a family or household member relationship between the victim (if not petitioner) or protected party and the respondent.

At a minimum, the General Assembly failed to artfully craft RC 2903.214. Although case law appears to suggest that a protected person can be a "family or household member" of either the petitioner or the respondent, the only way the statute makes sense is if all categories of protected persons are meant to relate to the petitioner, not

[40] Griga v. DiBenedetto, 2012-Ohio-6097, ¶ 21, 988 N.E.2d 590 (Ohio Ct. App. 1st Dist. Hamilton County 2012).

[41] Griga v. DiBenedetto, 2012-Ohio-6097, ¶ 21, 988 N.E.2d 590 (Ohio Ct. App. 1st Dist. Hamilton County 2012); Smith v. Hein, 2015-Ohio-2749, 2015 WL 4095636 (Ohio Ct. App. 1st Dist. Hamilton County 2015), appeal not allowed, 144 Ohio St. 3d 1458, 2016-Ohio-172, 44 N.E.3d 288 (2016) (dissent focused on overruling the holding in *Griga*).

[42] See also J.S. v. D.E., 2017-Ohio-7507, 2017 WL 3971706 (Ohio Ct. App. 7th Dist. Mahoning County 2017); but see Cornell v. Hatfield, 2018-Ohio-549, 2018 WL 827136 (Ohio Ct. App. 12th Dist. Butler County 2018) (although this was in the context of a DVCPO, parents of the petitioner who Cornell v. Hatfield, 2018-Ohio-549, 2018 WL 827136 (Ohio Ct. App. 12th Dist. Fayette County 2018) are no longer residing with that petitioner may be protected parties on the order as they previously lived with petitioner and some of the threats were directed at them).

the respondent.[43] A well-reasoned analysis indicates that in order to obtain a civil stalking protection order, a family or household member relationship must exist only between the petitioner and the victim or petitioner and his/her family or household members. Further, the fact that the phrase "family or household member," for purposes of RC 2903.214, has the same meaning as it does in RC 3113.31 doesn't suggest its purpose; rather it merely provides an additional context for which protected relationships are covered vis-à-vis the petitioner.

In fact, it is illogical for the General Assembly to have meant that there must be a relationship between petitioner and respondent or between victim or other protected party and respondent under RC 2903.214. Since RC 3113.31 already permits the issuance of civil protection orders for family or household members of respondent, there was no reason to enact duplicative legislation; rather, it makes sense that the "family or household member" relationships covered under RC 2903.214 mean those protected persons who are "family or household members" of petitioner.

The fact that few judicial decisions have interpreted the "family or household member relationship" as meaning that the petitioner or protected party and the respondent must have the relationship, reinforces the intent of RC 2903.214, which is to protect petitioners and the family or household members of the petitioner from stalking acts committed by *non-family or household members.*[44]

On the other hand, one appellate court has determined that under RC 2903.214, those other "family or household members" must be "family or household members" of respondent.

In *Cook v. Bricker*,[45] respondent appealed the issuance of a civil stalking protection order on behalf of petitioner, petitioner's wife, son, father-in-law or brother-in-law. The appellate court held that the trial court lacked jurisdiction to enter a civil stalking protection order on behalf of the family or household members of petitioner as there was no evidence in the petition that the others were household or family members of the respondent.

While the Ashland Court of Appeals considered RC 3113.31(A) in defining who is a family or household member, it failed to acknowledge that both RC 3113.31(C) and RC 2903.214(C) provide protection for the petitioner who files on behalf of themselves as well as for the other family or household members of that petitioner.

Q & A: Does a court demand evidence of stalking behavior towards the protected parties?

More of the recent appellate decisions demand proof of acts of stalk-

---

[43]See Jenkins v. Douglas, 2007-Ohio-1909, 2007 WL 1175228 (Ohio Ct. App. 3d Dist. Marion County 2007); Spence v. Herbert, 2001 WL 876231(Ohio Ct. App. 5th Dist. Licking County 2001); Henry v. Coogan, 2002-Ohio-6519, 2002 WL 31682226 (Ohio Ct. App. 12th Dist. Clermont County 2002); Guthrie v. Long, 2005-Ohio-1541, 2005 WL 737402 (Ohio Ct. App. 10th Dist. Franklin County 2005).

[44]Emphasis added; see Guthrie v. Long, 2005-Ohio-1541, 2005 WL 737402 (Ohio Ct. App. 10th Dist. Franklin County 2005); Griga v. DiBenedetto, 2012-Ohio-6097, 988 N.E.2d 590 (Ohio Ct. App. 1st Dist. Hamilton County 2012).

[45]Cook v. Bricker, 2011-Ohio-4898, 2011 WL 4435945 (Ohio Ct. App. 5th Dist. Ashland County 2011).

ing directed to the protected parties.[46] In *Griga v. DiBenedetto*,[47] the appellate court determined that there must be evidence presented of a pattern of conduct constituting menacing by stalking as it pertained to the other protected parties. Absent that, the decision to grant a protection order to the protected parties was reversed.[48]

Q & A: Where a mother files for a protection order on behalf of another family or household member, can the respondent adequately present his case where the child was not available to be cross examined?

The respondent in *Morris v. McQuillen*,[49] raised this as an issue in his appellate brief and argued that he was not afforded an opportunity to fully present his objections to the issuance of the protection order because the declarants of the hearsay were not present for him to cross examine. However, he failed to raise this as an objection in the trial court. Nor did he cross examine the petitioner, the child's mother. In that he failed to do so, he failed preserve the issue for appeal. The appellate court determined that there was no prejudicial error and overruled his assignment of error.

The question, however, raises significant issues that, unfortunately, were not addressed in the decision. Under RC 2151.34, more parents will seek protection orders on behalf of their children. Some children will want their parents to seek this protection. Other children will not want to participate in the process. Some of the testimony will be considered inadmissible hearsay. Either a parent would be unable to provide admissible testimony to support the issuance of a protection order and which would withstand various evidentiary objections or ev-

---

[46]A.S. v. P.F., 2013-Ohio-4857, 2013 WL 5925968 (Ohio Ct. App. 9th Dist. Lorain County 2013) ("[g]iven the nature and tone of the threats and P.F.'s emphasis on the fact that she knew where to find A.S., it was not an abuse of discretion for the trial court to include A.S.'s children within the scope of the protection order").

[47]Griga v. DiBenedetto, 2012-Ohio-6097, 988 N.E.2d 590 (Ohio Ct. App. 1st Dist. Hamilton County 2012); Woodward v. Head, 2013-Ohio-1127, 2013 WL 1224910 (Ohio Ct. App. 1st Dist. Hamilton County 2013); Smith v. Hein, 2015-Ohio-2749, 2015 WL 4095636 (Ohio Ct. App. 1st Dist. Hamilton County 2015), appeal not allowed, 144 Ohio St. 3d 1458, 2016-Ohio-172, 44 N.E.3d 288 (2016); Doran v. Doran, 2015-Ohio-2369, 2015 WL 3765602, ¶ 29 (Ohio Ct. App. 5th Dist. Licking County 2015) (finding that appellant's actions caused mental distress to the child and focusing on trial judge's ability to view the witnesses and observe their demeanor and the implicit determination that appellee's testimony was more credible and thus, including the child as protected party not unreasonable, arbitrary or unconscionable).

[48]See also Woodward v. Head, 2013-Ohio-1127, 2013 WL 1224910 (Ohio Ct. App. 1st Dist. Hamilton County 2013); Luikart v. Shumate, 2003-Ohio-2130, 2003 WL 1961874 (Ohio Ct. App. 3d Dist. Marion County 2003); Holloway v. Parker, 2013-Ohio-1940, ¶ 18, 2013 WL 1944400 (Ohio Ct. App. 3d Dist. Marion County 2013); Prater v. Mullins, 2013-Ohio-3981, 2013 WL 5230272 (Ohio Ct. App. 3d Dist. Auglaize County 2013) (petitioner must present evidence that respondent engaged in a pattern of conduct that respondent knew would cause each person to be protected under the CSPO to believe that respondent would cause the person physical harm or mental distress); Wilson v. Lyon, 2016-Ohio-7734, 2016 WL 6678396 (Ohio Ct. App. 3d Dist. Marion County 2016) (reversing trial court judgment as to other family member included as protected party on CSPO because no evidence was presented to show that protected party believed that respondent would cause him physical harm or mental distress).

[49]Morris v. McQuillen, 2009-Ohio-2848, 2009 WL 1677848 (Ohio Ct. App. 5th Dist. Richland County 2009).

identiary exceptions would be created thereby, permitting the parent to prevail over objection.

In fact, this was the case in *Morris*. The child wanted to continue to see respondent and did not testify. Had the child not told her mother about one incident of sexual conduct, there might have been insufficient evidence to support the issuance of the civil protection order. As much of the testimony was hearsay, petitioner's case, which included statements made by her daughter, the police and her husband, depended on respondent's failure to object to the introduction of the testimony on the record and on his failure to cross examine the petitioner.

In that respondent presented a viable claim on appeal, the Richland County Court of Appeals left open that another person who followed the Rules of Evidence could raise the same concerns and prevail.

Of significance are the two interesting legal issues presented by this case: 1) where a parent files for a CPO on behalf of a child and the child refuses to participate, can that parent fully present a case without the testimony of the child and 2) whether parents should be permitted to file on behalf of children who don't want protection. So long as parents are permitted to seek protection orders for and on behalf of their children, the evidentiary framework will be forced to undergo changes to address the concerns presented here. For today's courts, these may become the issues of tomorrow.

Q & A: What unrelated persons can obtain a civil stalking protection order?

Interestingly, a guardian ad litem for children in a custody dispute sought a CSPO against the children's father on that guardian's his own behalf. In *Wallace v. Masten*,[50] the guardian ad litem presented evidence that the children's father, in over 40 to 45 encounters, drove his vehicle in an apparent attempt to run the guardian down, sat and watched the guardian with a hostile stare, yelled and called him vulgar names. However, he never threatened violence nor committed physical injury upon the guardian. Based on the evidence presented, the appellate court affirmed the trial court's grant of the civil stalking protection order, noting that the trial court could have inferred that the guardian was afraid appellant would cause him physical harm.

Appellant had also argued that, as it related to the most recent incident, appellee had crossed the street to confront appellant, suggesting that appellee could not have been afraid. The court noted that "it is not unheard of that a person might become so frustrated or angered that he or she might disregard his or her own fear and safety in order to confront the source of that agitation."[51]

Q & A: Can an unrelated person seek a protection order on behalf of an abused or stalked person?

In *Morton v. Pyles*,[52] the appointed guardian over a disabled female adult sought a civil stalking protection order on behalf of that dis-

---

[50]Wallace v. Masten, 2003-Ohio-1081, 2003 WL 927600 (Ohio Ct. App. 4th Dist. Hocking County 2003).

[51]Wallace v. Masten, 2003-Ohio-1081, 2003 WL 927600, *5 (Ohio Ct. App. 4th Dist. Hocking County 2003).

[52]Morton v. Pyles, 2012-Ohio-5343, 2012 WL 5842789 (Ohio Ct. App. 7th Dist.

abled adult against the church pastor.[53] "The petition alleged that there was a suspicion of sexual abuse and that numerous phone calls between Pyles and Hartman had occurred and those phone calls left Hartman physically and emotionally upset."[54] The magistrate issued a CSPO, but not a civil sexually oriented offense protection order. Despite objections, the trial court adopted the magistrate's decision.

On appeal, the appellant alleged that there was not enough evidence to support the issuance of the CSPO. The guardian's testimony was that Hartman cried a lot, and spent significant amount of time on the phone with Pyles. Hartman testified that she cried because she missed him. Whenever she returned from visits with Pyles, she is "difficult to deal with and is horrible." After she could no longer use her phone, she became less sad and "is happy and enjoys going places" with her caregiver.[55]

The appellate court reversed the trial court and found that the evidence did not demonstrate the requisite level of mental distress so as to warrant a civil protection order as there was no pattern of conduct. "[W]e do not have a typical civil protection stalking order case where the person claiming to be stalked by menacing is actually testifying that she feared for her physical or mental safety or that the contact with the perpetrator caused her mental anguish."[56] There was limited evidence of mental distress and there was no evidence presented regarding a change in routine. Recognizing that mental stress does not constitute mental distress, the court stated that, without more, a change in Hartman's behavior is not enough to show mental distress for purposes of a civil protection order.[57] The appellate court was unable to determine "whether Pyles is causing her mental distress or whether Hartman is merely missing Pyles and that is what is causing her change in behavior."[58]

Of significance is that the appellate court did not address the fact that the guardian (an unrelated person) sought the CSPO on behalf of the disabled adult, suggesting that given the right set of facts, a guardian has standing to file for a protection order on behalf of his or her ward.

Mahoning County 2012). See also J.S. v. D.E., 2017-Ohio-7507, 2017 WL 3971706 (Ohio Ct. App. 7th Dist. Mahoning County 2017) (appellant argued that petitioner, who sought the CSPO on behalf of a resident (of medical facility) who was the boyfriend of the respondent and who did not appear to have guardianship or legal custody over D.B. was not a family or household member of D.B. and thus, could not obtain a CSPO on his behalf. appellate court would not find that there was insufficient evidence of petitioner's authority to file the petition on behalf of D.B. or include him as a protected person and concluded that the face of the order does establish relationships).

[53]RC 2903.214(C).

[54]Morton v. Pyles, 2012-Ohio-5343, ¶ 3, 2012 WL 5842789 (Ohio Ct. App. 7th Dist. Mahoning County 2012).

[55]Morton v. Pyles, 2012-Ohio-5343, ¶ 16, 2012 WL 5842789 (Ohio Ct. App. 7th Dist. Mahoning County 2012).

[56]Morton v. Pyles, 2012-Ohio-5343, ¶ 20, 2012 WL 5842789 (Ohio Ct. App. 7th Dist. Mahoning County 2012).

[57]Morton v. Pyles, 2012-Ohio-5343, ¶ 24, 2012 WL 5842789 (Ohio Ct. App. 7th Dist. Mahoning County 2012).

[58]Morton v. Pyles, 2012-Ohio-5343, ¶ 24, 2012 WL 5842789 (Ohio Ct. App. 7th Dist. Mahoning County 2012).

Of interest is that the appellate court did consider the fact that Hartman testified she wanted to have contact with Pyles in reversing the grant of the protection order. The court then noted that the case at hand was similar to other cases in which courts reversed the grant of the protection order on the grounds that the person alleged to have been stalked consented to contact.[59]

Lastly, the appellate court focused on the mental disability of the alleged victim in this case. Because of her disability, "it is unclear whether her own perception that Pyles is not stalking her and not causing her mental distress is an accurate perception. It is true that, "stalkers engage in psychological warfare, which by its nature is devious, insidious and subtle. *State v. Werfel*, 11th Dist. No.2006-L-163, 2007-Ohio-5198, ¶ 34. Thus, in some instances a mentally disabled person may not be able to identify the subtle psychological manipulations that a stalker would engage in, and thus, would not fear his or her physical or mental safety or realize that the contact with the perpetrator caused him or her mental anguish."[60] "That said, we do not want to create a blanket holding that all mentally disabled persons who have a guardianship over their person would not be able to identify the subtle psychological manipulations that a stalker might engage in and would not fear their safety or realize their own mental anguish. Thus, in order to warrant a civil protection order there must be more in the record than the mere fact that the alleged victim has a mental disability and due to incompetence, a guardianship over his or her person has been granted. The evidence of the extent of the mental disability would be helpful to show that the mentally disabled person is unable to recognize the subtle psychological warfare of the alleged stalker."[61]

Q & A: Does a CSPO against a parent provide justifiable cause for not contacting his child such that an adoption of the child by another may be granted?

In *In re: Adoption of B.A.A.*,[62] the biological father of the child was subject to a CSPO which prohibited contact with mother and the child. Stepfather filed to adopt the child testifying that Father had not had contact with the child for at least one year preceding the filing of the adoption petition. The focus of the hearing was whether the CSPO provided justifiable cause for father's lack of contact with the child. The trial court determined that the CSPO did not constitute justifiable cause for father's lack of contact with B.A.A. and Father appealed.[63]

The appellate court sustained Father's assignment of error and held that under RC 3107, the term "justifiable cause" was not defined and

[59]See for example, Dupal v. Sommer, 2009-Ohio-5791, 2009 WL 3600358 (Ohio Ct. App. 5th Dist. Stark County 2009).

[60]Morton v. Pyles, 2012-Ohio-5343, ¶ 23, 2012 WL 5842789 (Ohio Ct. App. 7th Dist. Mahoning County 2012).

[61]Morton v. Pyles, 2012-Ohio-5343, ¶ 23, 2012 WL 5842789 (Ohio Ct. App. 7th Dist. Mahoning County 2012).

[62]In re Adoption of B.A.A., 2017-Ohio-8137, 2017 WL 4518670 (Ohio Ct. App. 9th Dist. Wayne County 2017).

[63]In re Adoption of B.A.A., 2017-Ohio-8137, ¶ 9, 2017 WL 4518670 (Ohio Ct. App. 9th Dist. Wayne County 2017).

because the trial court relied on case law from other appellate districts and that the case upon which it relied did not cover the one-year look back period, the trial court should not have concluded as a matter of law, that the CSPO did not constitute "justifiable cause."

Of significance is that the appellate court noted that Father had not been well represented at the trial court level because his attorney failed to explain that his parental rights could be terminated if he agreed to a consent entry that prohibited contact with his child.

Q & A: Does the civil stalking statute apply to nuisance suits between neighbors or road rage problems?[64]

Not unless the behavior complained of rises to the level of stalking as set forth in R.C. 2903.211.[65] However, unless there is a definitive legal opinion as to this issue, petitions will continue to be brought under R.C. 2903.214. For example, in *Williams v. McDougal*,[66] a neighbor was granted a stalking civil protection order against another neighbor. On appeal, the decision was reversed because the appellate court found there was insufficient evidence to establish that appellants engaged in a "pattern of conduct" as defined in R.C. 2903.211(D).[67] "Rather, the evidence adduced at the hearing reveals a one-time incident caused by a heated argument over a dog."[68] In this case, the relationship between the parties was not considered.

Q & A: For what other behaviors can one petition the court for a civil stalking protection order?

In *Sobieniak v. Chapdelaine*,[69] the appellate court affirmed the issuance of a civil stalking protection order for one neighbor against another. In that case, the pertinent incidents concerned several emails sent by appellant to an Ohio company connected to appellee alleging that appellee was engaged in acts of property theft to the detriment of the Ohio company.[70]

The appellate court reasoned that the allegations of theft in the

[64]See for example, Krlich v. Clemente, 2017-Ohio-7945, 98 N.E.3d 752 (Ohio Ct. App. 11th Dist. Trumbull County 2017); Martin v. Wills, 2017-Ohio-9382, 2017 WL 6804072 (Ohio Ct. App. 7th Dist. Mahoning County 2017), appeal not allowed, 152 Ohio St. 3d 1481, 2018-Ohio-1990, 98 N.E.3d 295 (2018).

[65]See, for example, Bucksbaum v. Mitchell, 2004-Ohio-2233, 2004 WL 943865 (Ohio Ct. App. 5th Dist. Richland County 2004) (where stalker attempted to run over petitioner, threatened to kill his dogs and engaged in surveillance of his house and following him); Davis v. DiNunzio, 2005-Ohio-2883, 2005 WL 1383975 (Ohio Ct. App. 11th Dist. Lake County 2005) (considered corroboration by police office and who observed one of the allegations in affirming issuance of CPO).

[66]Williams v. McDougal, 2001 WL 694591 (Ohio Ct. App. 4th Dist. Gallia County 2001); but see Meyers v. Sparrow, 2009-Ohio-945, 2009 WL 533057 (Ohio Ct. App. 5th Dist. Ashland County 2009) (affirming the issuance of the SCPO based on several incidents involving a dog).

[67]See also Lemley v. Kirk, 2007-Ohio-1016, 2007 WL 701141 (Ohio Ct. App. 10th Dist. Franklin County 2007).

[68]Williams v. McDougal, 2001 WL 694591, *2 (Ohio Ct. App. 4th Dist. Gallia County 2001).

[69]Sobieniak v. Chapdelaine, 2008-Ohio-6403, 2008 WL 5147439 (Ohio Ct. App. 6th Dist. Lucas County 2008); see also Retterer v. Little, 2012-Ohio-131, 2012 WL 134305 (Ohio Ct. App. 3d Dist. Marion County 2012).

[70]Sobieniak v. Chapdelaine, 2008-Ohio-6403, 2008 WL 5147439, *1 (Ohio Ct. App. 6th Dist. Lucas County 2008).

emails sent by appellant could undermine the business reputation and relationship appellee had with the company. In affirming the grant of the protection order, the court found that "this scenario [is] sufficient to cause appellee to believe appellant would cause him emotional distress."[71]

§ 9:5 Procedural issues

Q & A: Is the procedure set forth in R.C. 2903.214 similar to the procedure detailed in R.C. 3113.31?[1]

Yes. In fact, the Hamilton County Appellate Court considered the granting of a stalking civil protection order in light of R.C. 3113.31. In *Lindsay v. Jackson*,[2] the appellate court stated that "the procedure for the issuance of a domestic-violence protection order pursuant to R.C. 3113.31 is substantially similar to the procedure under R.C. 2903.214 and provides some guidance.[3]

The time frames for obtaining civil protection orders are similar.[4] The reasons to grant continuances are similar.[5] The procedures for mutual protection orders[6] and the renewal of the orders[7] are also similar as are the responsibilities of the court[8] and law enforcement.[9]

Additionally, the applicable standard of proof under both R.C. 2903.214 and R.C. 3113.31 is the preponderance of the evidence

---

[71]Sobieniak v. Chapdelaine, 2008-Ohio-6403, 2008 WL 5147439, *2 (Ohio Ct. App. 6th Dist. Lucas County 2008).

[Section 9:5]

[1]See Chapters 11 and 12; see also compliance with Civ. R. 53 cases: Butram v. Butram, 2005-Ohio-5469, 2005 WL 2622797 (Ohio Ct. App. 5th Dist. Ashland County 2005); Dickson v. Ball, 2006-Ohio-3436, 2006 WL 1817265 (Ohio Ct. App. 10th Dist. Franklin County 2006); Jenkins v. May, 2009-Ohio-1388, 2009 WL 791483 (Ohio Ct. App. 5th Dist. Ashland County 2009); Baldwin v. Remley, No. C-080007 (Ohio Ct. App. 1st Dist. Hamilton County Sept. 24, 2008) (unreported), available at www.hamilton-co.org/appealscourt/docs/decisions/C-080007_09242008.pdf. But see State v. Webley, 2013-Ohio-4598, 2013 WL 5676267 (Ohio Ct. App. 8th Dist. Cuyahoga County 2013) (discussing the similarities and differences between R.C. 2903.213 and R.C. 2919.26, the criminal protection order statutes).

[2]Lindsay v. Jackson, 2000 WL 1268810 (Ohio Ct. App. 1st Dist. Hamilton County 2000).

[3]Lindsay v. Jackson, 2000 WL 1268810, *2 (Ohio Ct. App. 1st Dist. Hamilton County 2000); see also Baddour v. Fox, 2000 WL 1719569 (Ohio Ct. App. 5th Dist. Licking County 2000) (applicability of Ohio Civ. R. 53 is discussed); Ch 11, Full Hearing on Civil Protection Orders, for a discussion of Civ. R. 53.

[4]R.C. 2903.214(D); R.C. 3113.31(D).

[5]R.C. 2903.214(D); R.C. 3113.31(D).

[6]R.C. 2903.214(E)(3); R.C. 3113.31(E)(4). See also Toledo v. Lewis, 2013-Ohio-3289, 2013 WL 3936455 (Ohio Ct. App. 6th Dist. Lucas County 2013) (applying *Smith* and finding that a conviction for violating the protection order under R.C. 2919.27 does not lie as the order was not properly issued because no separate petition for protection order was filed pursuant to R.C. 2903.214(E)(3)(a) and service was not perfected on respondent).

[7]R.C. 2903.214(E)(2); R.C. 3113.31(E)(3).

[8]R.C. 2903.214(K) & (M); R.C. 3113.31(K) & (M).

[9]R.C. 2903.214(F); R.C. 3113.31(F).

standard.[10] The burden is on the petitioner to prove that the respondent engaged in a pattern of conduct that caused mental distress or a belief of physical harm to the victim.[11]

The granting of a protection order as defined in R.C. 2903.214 requires a finding that the respondent engaged in a violation of R.C. 2903.211, menacing by stalking[12] or committed a sexually oriented offense as defined in R.C. 2950.01 while the granting of a domestic violence protection order requires a finding that the respondent committed an act of domestic violence as defined in R.C. 3113.31(A).

Recently, the General Assembly enacted legislation that requires the court to provide all parties to the civil protection order with the following notice, orally or in written form. R.C. 2903.214(F)(2) provides that the notice shall state:

NOTICE

> As a result of this order, it may be unlawful for you to possess or purchase a firearm, including a rifle, pistol, or revolver, or ammunition pursuant to federal law under 18 USC 922(g)(8) for the duration of this order. If you have any questions whether this law makes it illegal for

[10] Lindsay v. Jackson, 2000 WL 1268810, *4 (Ohio Ct. App. 1st Dist. Hamilton County 2000), relying on Felton v. Felton, 79 Ohio St. 3d 34, 1997-Ohio-302, 679 N.E.2d 672 (1997); see also Tuuri v. Snyder, 2002-Ohio-2107, 2002 WL 818427 (Ohio Ct. App. 11th Dist. Geauga County 2002); DeCarlo v. Schilla, 2002-Ohio-4186, 2002 WL 1879290 (Ohio Ct. App. 8th Dist. Cuyahoga County 2002); Huffer v. Chafin, 2002-Ohio-356, 2002 WL 144901 (Ohio Ct. App. 5th Dist. Licking County 2002); Olenik v. Huff, 2003-Ohio-4621, 2003 WL 22039490 (Ohio Ct. App. 5th Dist. Ashland County 2003); see also Caban v. Ransome, 2009-Ohio-1034, 2009 WL 582761 (Ohio Ct. App. 7th Dist. Mahoning County 2009); Miller v. Shaw, 2009-Ohio-6753, 2009 WL 4895276 (Ohio Ct. App. 7th Dist. Carroll County 2009); Strausser v. White, 2009-Ohio-3597, 2009 WL 2186620 (Ohio Ct. App. 8th Dist. Cuyahoga County 2009); Weismuller v. Polston, 2012-Ohio-1476, 2012 WL 1107717 (Ohio Ct. App. 12th Dist. Brown County 2012) (applying the preponderance of the evidence standard to the issuance of a sexually oriented offense protection order and indicating that a victim's testimony, if found credible, would be sufficient to meet that standard); Lerner v. Giolekas, 2016-Ohio-696, 2016 WL 762594 (Ohio Ct. App. 8th Dist. Cuyahoga County 2016), appeal not allowed, 146 Ohio St. 3d 1429, 2016-Ohio-4606, 52 N.E.3d 1204 (2016) (finding that the preponderance of the evidence standard was the appropriate standard where it was alleged that the CSPO unduly infringed on respondent's second amendment rights by restricting respondent's guns); Dunn v. Clark, 2016-Ohio-641, 2016 WL 698090 (Ohio Ct. App. 12th Dist. Warren County 2016) (preponderance of the evidence signifies that the existence of a contested fact is more probable than its nonexistence. At ¶ 9); Wulf v. Opp, 2015-Ohio-3285, 2015 WL 4878495 (Ohio Ct. App. 12th Dist. Clermont County 2015); Cole v. Tubbs, 2016-Ohio-8321, 2016 WL 7427345 (Ohio Ct. App. 8th Dist. Cuyahoga County 2016); Cipriani v. Ehlert, 2016-Ohio-5840, 2016 WL 4978558 (Ohio Ct. App. 8th Dist. Cuyahoga County 2016); J.M. v. D.H., 2016-Ohio-8387, 2016 WL 7596244 (Ohio Ct. App. 9th Dist. Lorain County 2016).

[11] Jenkins v. Jenkins, 2007-Ohio-422, 2007 WL 275700 (Ohio Ct. App. 10th Dist. Franklin County 2007).

[12] See Lindsay v. Jackson, 2000 WL 1268810, *4 (Ohio Ct. App. 1st Dist. Hamilton County 2000); see also R.C. 2903.214(C)(1); Irwin v. Murray, 2006-Ohio-1633, 2006 WL 832830 (Ohio Ct. App. 6th Dist. Lucas County 2006); Striff v. Striff, 2003-Ohio-794, 2003 WL 397869 (Ohio Ct. App. 6th Dist. Wood County 2003), citing Tuuri v. Snyder, 2002-Ohio-2107, 2002 WL 818427 (Ohio Ct. App. 11th Dist. Geauga County 2002).

you to possess or purchase a firearm or ammunition, you should consult an attorney.[13]

For purposes of both R.C. 2903.214 and R.C. 3113.31, the Warning Pages contain the required language.[14]

Finally, the issues regarding magistrate's orders and decisions and the Supreme Court forms are also similar.[15]

Q & A: What are the differences between R.C. 2903.214 and R.C. 3113.31?

There are several procedural differences, most of which are the result of the parties' relationship or lack thereof. For example, under R.C. 2903.214(D)(2)(a), a full hearing is held within ten court days after the ex parte hearing. The reason for this is that non-family members do not ordinarily evict individuals from the "marital" home. Therefore, there is no need for an earlier hearing date.

The nature of the relief is also different. Under R.C. 2903.214(E), relief includes a requirement that the respondent refrain from entering, the residence, school, business or place of employment of the petitioner. It may also include electronic monitoring of a respondent which is not included under R.C. 3113.31.

Under R.C. 3113.31(E), the relief is more expansive and includes support, the allocation of parental rights and responsibilities, apportionment of personal property, exclusive use of an automobile and possession of the marital home.

Both RC 3113.31 and RC 2903.214 have been recently amended to include protections for companion animals. Pursuant to a recent legislative amendment to RC 2903.214, "[t]he court may include within a protection order issued under this section, a term requiring that the respondent not remove, damage, hide, harm or dispose of any companion animal owned or possessed by the person to be protected by the order, and may include with the order a term authorizing the person to be protected by the order to remove a companion animal owned by the person to be protected by the order from the possession of the respondent."[16]

Under both statutory provisions, the petition must include allegations that the respondent engaged in the various prohibited acts, the nature and extent of the violence and a prayer for relief. However, the domestic violence petition also includes a provision requesting information about the relationship of the respondent to the petitioner and to the victim if other than the petitioner.

However, R.C. 2903.214 mandates an additional requirement. If the petitioner seeks relief in the form of electronic monitoring, the petition must also contain an allegation that at any time preceding the filing of the petition, the respondent engaged in conduct that would cause a reasonable person to believe that the health, welfare or safety

[13]See also R.C. 3113.31(F)(2).

[14]See Sup. R. Form 10.03-H and Sup. R. Form 10.01-G, respectively.

[15]See § 12:10; see also State v. Davis, 2008-Ohio-5281, 2008 WL 4531895 (Ohio Ct. App. 1st Dist. Hamilton County 2008); Rosen v. Chesler, 2009-Ohio-3163, 2009 WL 1900422 (Ohio Ct. App. 9th Dist. Lorain County 2009).

[16]See RC 2903.214(E)(1)(a).

of the person to be protected was at risk, a description of the nature and extent of that conduct and an allegation that the respondent presents a continuing danger to the person to be protected. R.C. 2903.214(C)(2).

Lastly, if a person files a petition under R.C. 2903.214 and requests an ex parte order, a hearing shall be held as soon as possible after the petition is filed but not later than the next day that the court is in session after the petition is filed.[17] On the other hand, an ex parte hearing under R.C. 3113.31 shall be held on the same day that the petition is filed.

Q & A: Must a petition for a civil stalking protection order be filed in the name of one person?

Yes. In *Darden v. Fambrough*,[18] petitioners Ford and Darden each filed a separate civil stalking protection order against Fambrough. Despite a lack of a consolidation order, the judge assigned to one of the cases, consolidated both cases under his jurisdiction.

The appellate court determined that, because there was no order consolidating Ford's case with Darden's, the trial court lacked jurisdiction over Ford's case. Absent compliance with the rules on consolidation, any orders made against Fambrough in the Ford case before the transfer was effected were void.[19]

Of importance is that the appellate court relied on R.C. 2903.214(C) as a basis for its legal opinion. R.C. 2903.214(C) provides that "[a]person may seek relief * * * for the person . . ." as meaning that only one person may file a petition for protection in any given case. The appellate court clearly stated that petitions for temporary protection orders can be filed in the name of one person only.[20]

However, that does not mean that a person cannot file for a protection order and include other family members as protected parties or that or that one parent or family or household member may not file on behalf of another family or household member or that one could not validly consolidate cases.

Q & A: Can a corporation or organization or business file for a civil stalking protection order against an individual?

Apparently the answer is yes. Recently the Ohio General Assembly enacted HB 129 which provides that the crimes of aggravated menacing, menacing by stalking and menacing would now include words or conduct or conduct directed at or identify a corporation, association or other organization that employs the victim or to which the victim belongs and authorizes the corporation, association or other organization that employs to or more victims or to which two or more victims belong to seek protection orders pursuant to RC 2903.215.

[17] R.C. 2903.214(D)(1); see also State v. Davis, 2008-Ohio-5281, 2008 WL 4531895 (Ohio Ct. App. 1st Dist. Hamilton County 2008) (discussing the procedures regarding ex parte and full hearings under R.C. 2903.214).

[18] Darden v. Fambrough, 2013-Ohio-5583, 5 N.E.3d 712, 37 I.E.R. Cas. (BNA) 730 (Ohio Ct. App. 8th Dist. Cuyahoga County 2013).

[19] Darden v. Fambrough, 2013-Ohio-5583, 5 N.E.3d 712, ¶ 7, 37 I.E.R. Cas. (BNA) 730 (Ohio Ct. App. 8th Dist. Cuyahoga County 2013).

[20] Darden v. Fambrough, 2013-Ohio-5583, 5 N.E.3d 712, ¶ 4, 37 I.E.R. Cas. (BNA) 730 (Ohio Ct. App. 8th Dist. Cuyahoga County 2013).

First, there must be two or more victims of the business or corporation or association that have been harmed under the aggravated menacing, menacing by stalking or menacing statutes. Second, the corporation may file for a protection order (either a civil stalking protection order per R.C. 2903.214 or a criminal stalking order under R.C. 2903.213) on behalf of the corporation if the violation is based on words or conduct of the offender that are directed at or identify the corporation, association or other organization. Third, an attorney licensed to practice law in the state on behalf of the corporation may file an affidavit to provide sufficient evidentiary support for the issuance of said protection order.

Q & A: Does the court have jurisdiction over a case brought under R.C. 2903.214 where appellant resides in one county and the abuse took place in that county, but the petitioner resides in another county?

In *Hayberg v. Tamburello*,[21] appellant argued that the Tuscarawas trial court did not have jurisdiction over the case because both the appellant and alleged actions took place in Cuyahoga County. In overruling the assignment of error, the appellate court explained that R.C. 2903.214(B) provides "[t]he court has jurisdiction over all proceedings under this section." Further, "Court" is defined as the court of common pleas of the county in which the person to be protected by the protection order resides.[22] Since appellee (the person to be protected) resided in Tuscarawas County, Tuscarawas County Common Pleas Court had jurisdiction over appellee's petition for civil protection order.[23] Clearly, that means that the party is not bound to file the protection order in the county where the cause of action arose.

Q & A: Do electronic communications sent to a petitioner in Ohio establish a basis for exercising personal jurisdiction over an out-of-state respondent?

In *M.W. v D.M.*,[24] respondent claimed on appeal that the Cuyahoga County Common Pleas Court lacked personal jurisdiction over him such that petitioner failed to satisfy the long arm statute for the purpose of establishing personal jurisdiction. The basis for this claim was that sending electronic communications to petitioner in Ohio, originating out of Ohio, was not sufficient to establish his connection with Ohio.[25]

Under R.C. 2307.382(A)(3), a court may exercise personal jurisdiction over a party who caused tortious injury by an act or omission in Ohio. It has been recognized that the existence of telephonic and

---

[21]Hayberg v. Tamburello, 2013-Ohio-3451, 2013 WL 4033623 (Ohio Ct. App. 5th Dist. Tuscarawas County 2013).

[22]R.C. 2903.214(A)(1). See also Vilk v. Dinardo, 2016-Ohio-5245, 2016 WL 4141673 (Ohio Ct. App. 8th Dist. Cuyahoga County 2016) (subject matter jurisdiction of a CSPO is in the county in which the protected person resides; absent that, the court does not have subject matter jurisdiction over the case).

[23]Hayberg v. Tamburello, 2013-Ohio-3451, 2013 WL 4033623, ¶ 20 (Ohio Ct. App. 5th Dist. Tuscarawas County 2013).

[24]M.W. v. D.M., 2018-Ohio-392, 2018 WL 660271 (Ohio Ct. App. 8th Dist. Cuyahoga County 2018).

[25]M.W. v. D.M., 2018-Ohio-392, ¶ 13, 2018 WL 660271 (Ohio Ct. App. 8th Dist. Cuyahoga County 2018).

electronic communications that originate from out-of-state respondents to in-state petitioners satisfies Ohio's long-arm statute for the purpose of protection orders as long as the content of the communication forms the basis of the alleged tortious conduct.[26]

Because the allegations stemmed from electronic communications attached to the petition and introduced at full hearing, and because the petition was based on the content of the electronic communications respondent sent to petitioner in Ohio, petitioner established a basis for exercising personal jurisdiction over respondent.[27]

Q & A: If a petitioner lists "safe address" on the petition for purposes of confidentiality, does the use of the safe address, rather than an actual address, divest the court of subject matter jurisdiction?

According to the 8th District Court of Appeals, the answer is no. In *M.W. v D.M.,*[28] respondent appealed the grant of a CSPO claiming that petitioner's failure to list her actual address on the petition should divest the trial court with subject matter jurisdiction. Respondent's argument was, that because she listed a "safe address" that was not her home address, the court had no subject matter jurisdiction.

Pursuant to RC 2903.214(A)(1), the civil stalking statute provides that "court" means the court of common pleas in which the person to be protected by the protection order resides. In this case, the court was located in Cuyahoga County. The argument advanced was that, without listing an actual address, there was no way for the court to determine whether petitioner resided in Cuyahoga County at the time of filing. The court found she established subject matter jurisdiction by her testimony and noted that "[u]sing a 'safe address' does not divest the trial court of subject-matter jurisdiction so long as the petitioner can establish a statutory basis for invoking jurisdiction when called upon."[29] In this case, petitioner wanted her address kept confidential from respondent.

On a more procedural ground, the court also addressed the fact that there is a legal distinction between the "state of things" at the time the action is brought and the allegations advanced in a pleading.[30] When considering the issue of subject matter jurisdiction, the court may consider affidavits and testimony for that purpose.[31] "Thus, the failure to allege facts in support of subject matter-jurisdiction is not fatal. Once challenged, however, the basis for subject-matter jurisdic-

[26]M.W. v. D.M., 2018-Ohio-392, ¶ 14, 2018 WL 660271 (Ohio Ct. App. 8th Dist. Cuyahoga County 2018); citing, Burnett v. Burnett, 2012-Ohio-2673, ¶ 21, 2012 WL 2196336 (Ohio Ct. App. 6th Dist. Sandusky County 2012); see also Chapter 10:13.

[27]M.W. v. D.M., 2018-Ohio-392, ¶ 15, 2018 WL 660271 (Ohio Ct. App. 8th Dist. Cuyahoga County 2018).

[28]M.W. v. D.M., 2018-Ohio-392, 2018 WL 660271 (Ohio Ct. App. 8th Dist. Cuyahoga County 2018).

[29]M.W. v. D.M., 2018-Ohio-392, ¶ 10, 2018 WL 660271 (Ohio Ct. App. 8th Dist. Cuyahoga County 2018).

[30]M.W. v. D.M., 2018-Ohio-392, ¶ 11, 2018 WL 660271 (Ohio Ct. App. 8th Dist. Cuyahoga County 2018).

[31]M.W. v. D.M., 2018-Ohio-392, ¶ 11, 2018 WL 660271 (Ohio Ct. App. 8th Dist. Cuyahoga County 2018).

tion must be supported with evidence."[32] In overruling the assignment of error, the court stressed that petitioner's testimony and an affidavit established sufficient proof of subject matter jurisdiction.

Unlike domestic violence protection orders issued under RC 3113.31, a court lacks subject matter jurisdiction if petitioner seeks a CSPO from a common pleas court in a county in which he/she does not reside.[33]

It is prudent for a petitioner to review the statute under which he/she would file noting that with a confidential or "safe address" they must understand that under RC 2903.214(A)(1), a petitioner must file in the court in the county in which the protected party resides. Moreover, a petitioner must also remember that a respondent might raise such a challenge.

Q & A: Can a person seek a protection order in one county and then move to another county before the full hearing and request that jurisdiction be transferred to petitioner's new county of residence for the full hearing?

There is currently no case law that has addressed this specific issue. However, because R.C. 2903.214(A)(1) provides that the court with jurisdiction over a CSPO case is the court in which the protected person resides,[34] an argument can be made that a petitioner is within his/her rights to request a transfer of jurisdiction to the new court. On the other hand, for court efficiency, it is unlikely that the second court would want to hear the full hearing when it was not the court that presided over the ex parte hearing. Moreover, it would mean that the second court would have to adopt the order of the first court in order to go forward with the full hearing. Thus, it would be more expedient for the first court to vacate the ex parte order and dismiss the petition and have the petitioner refile in the second court. Additionally, the first court may determine it no longer has jurisdiction to hear the case.

Q & A: Have any courts addressed rules for pro se litigants in the context of civil stalking protection orders?

Yes, in the context of an appeal of the denial of a civil protection order issued under R.C. 2903.214 by a pro se litigant. In *Rosen v. Chesler*,[35] appellant presented his oral argument before the court pro se. He argued that his actions did not constitute a pattern of conduct. However, he failed to present any case law to support his assertions.

The appellate court observed that:

"Pro se litigants should be granted reasonable leeway such that their motions and pleadings should be liberally construed so as to decide the

[32]M.W. v. D.M., 2018-Ohio-392, ¶ 11, 2018 WL 660271 (Ohio Ct. App. 8th Dist. Cuyahoga County 2018).

[33]M.W. v. D.M., 2018-Ohio-392, ¶ 9, 2018 WL 660271 (Ohio Ct. App. 8th Dist. Cuyahoga County 2018); see also Vilk v. Dinardo, 2016-Ohio-5245, ¶ 12, 2016 WL 4141673 (Ohio Ct. App. 8th Dist. Cuyahoga County 2016).

[34]See for example, Vilk v. Bridge, 2016-Ohio-4706, 2016 WL 3552151 (Ohio Ct. App. 8th Dist. Cuyahoga County 2016) (reinforcing that venue for a civil stalking protection order is where the protected party resides as set forth in Civ. R. 3(B)(10)).

[35]Rosen v. Chesler, 2009-Ohio-3163, 2009 WL 1900422 (Ohio Ct. App. 9th Dist. Lorain County 2009).

issues on the merits, as opposed to technicalities. However, a pro se litigant is presumed to have knowledge of the law and correct legal procedures so that he remains subject to the same rules and procedures to which represented litigants are bound. He is not given greater rights than represented parties, and must bear the consequences of his mistakes. This Court, therefore, must hold [pro se appellants] to the same standard as any represented party." (internal citations omitted.)[36]

Q & A: Is it reversible error to permit a petitioner to present evidence on incidents not specifically pled in the petition?

Not according to the appellate court in *Lane v. Brewster*.[37] In that case, petitioner alleged in her petition that respondent drove by her house in his work van on several occasions, that he removed the tags off her car and used his van to block her path. Respondent claimed the allegations were too broad, the allegations did not constitute violations of the statute and that her petition failed to comply with the directives of R.C. 2903.214(C) which states that the petition must contain a description of the nature and extent of the violation.

The appellate court first determined that the petition met the minimal requirements of R.C. 2903.214(C). While the pleadings did not specifically define each and every incident of stalking, the acts as set forth in her petition did in fact inform respondent that he was alleged to have engaged in a pattern of conduct that amounted to stalking. The court then found that the petitioner was entitled to offer evidence to further describe her allegations and the trial court did not err in relying on these incidents as a basis for finding that stalking had occurred.[38]

Q & A: In order to grant a petition for a civil stalking protection order, must there be a full hearing where evidence is pre-

---

[36] *Chesler at *3*; quoting Sherlock v. Myers, 2004-Ohio-5178, 2004 WL 2244102 (Ohio Ct. App. 9th Dist. Summit County 2004); see also Lukac v. Godfrey, 2011-Ohio-971, 2011 WL 766935 (Ohio Ct. App. 6th Dist. Ottawa County 2011); Preston v. Shutway, 2013-Ohio-185, 986 N.E.2d 584 (Ohio Ct. App. 2d Dist. Champaign County 2013); Pascual v. Pascual, 2012-Ohio-5819, 2012 WL 6104941 (Ohio Ct. App. 9th Dist. Medina County 2012); Brown v. Grauman, 2013-Ohio-4814, 2013 WL 5914961 (Ohio Ct. App. 2d Dist. Champaign County 2013); Vander Kam v. Brown, 2014-Ohio-632, 2014 WL 708089 (Ohio Ct. App. 2d Dist. Montgomery County 2014). But see, Hayberg v. Tamburello, 2013-Ohio-3451, 2013 WL 4033623 (Ohio Ct. App. 5th Dist. Tuscarawas County 2013) (explaining that "an appellate court will ordinarily indulge a pro se litigant where there is some semblance of compliance with the appellate rules" at ¶ 17, quoting State v. Richard, 2005-Ohio-6494, 2005 WL 3315308 (Ohio Ct. App. 8th Dist. Cuyahoga County 2005)); Joy v. Letostak, 2015-Ohio-2667, 2015 WL 3964179 (Ohio Ct. App. 10th Dist. Franklin County 2015); J.R. v. Pless, 2016-Ohio-14, 2016 WL 60000 (Ohio Ct. App. 9th Dist. Summit County 2016); Allen v. Thompson, 2017-Ohio-4234, 2017 WL 2542392 (Ohio Ct. App. 11th Dist. Lake County 2017); Williamson v. Caldwell, 2018-Ohio-311, 2018 WL 566470 (Ohio Ct. App. 2d Dist. Montgomery County 2018); Lloyd v. Thornsbery, 2018-Ohio-2893, 2018 WL 3536755 (Ohio Ct. App. 11th Dist. Portage County 2018).

[37] Lane v. Brewster, 2012-Ohio-1290, 2012 WL 1029503 (Ohio Ct. App. 12th Dist. Clermont County 2012). See also Doran v. Doran, 2015-Ohio-2369, 2015 WL 3765602 (Ohio Ct. App. 5th Dist. Licking County 2015) (suggesting that it was a notice problem and that appellant did have notice of the allegations).

[38] Lane v. Brewster, 2012-Ohio-1290, 2012 WL 1029503, *6 (Ohio Ct. App. 12th Dist. Clermont County 2012); McGuire v. Sprinkle, 2007-Ohio-2705, 2007 WL 1585100 (Ohio Ct. App. 12th Dist. Warren County 2007); Gannon v. Gannon, 2008-Ohio-4484, 2008 WL 4093687 (Ohio Ct. App. 6th Dist. Wood County 2008); Calicoat v. Calicoat, 2009-Ohio-5869, 2009 WL 3683665 (Ohio Ct. App. 2d Dist. Miami County 2009).

sented or can a judge order a petitioner to reiterate the allegations contained in the petition?

According to the Eighth District Court of Appeals, a trial court must hold a full hearing at which evidence is presented. In *Rufener v. Hutson*,[39] former boyfriend filed a petition seeking a CSPO against his former girlfriend. The protection order was granted as the trial court found, by a preponderance of the evidence that Hutson engaged in a pattern of stalking behaviors.

On appeal, *Hutson* argued that the trial court erred when it conducted a portion of the proceedings without applying the rules of evidence. The appellate court held that "[i]n order to grant a petitioner for a civil stalking protection order, a trial court must hold a full hearing; the petition itself is not evidence to be considered at the full hearing."[40] The trial court had instructed petitioner to reiterate the allegations contained in his petition in order to save time. "This resulted in an incorporation of the initial petition which the court considered during the ex-parte hearing, not the presentation of evidence as is required at a full hearing."[41]

Q & A: What is the effective date of the order for purposes of its duration?[42]

The statute is silent regarding the date to be considered by a court as to the start of the duration of the order, whether it be for a five year duration or a lesser time frame. In other words, does the time begin on the date of the issuance of the full hearing or does the time begin to run from the issuance of the ex parte order?

RC 2903.214(E)(2)(a) provides that "[a]ny protection order issued pursuant to this section shall be valid until a date certain but not later that five years from the date of its issuance." The wording of RC 2903.214 suggests that the date is discretionary for any particular court, meaning a court can interpret the term "date of issuance" as the date of the ex parte hearing (and/or filing) or the date of the final judgment.[43]

For example, in *Banfield v. Orazem*,[44] petitioner obtained an ex parte CSPO which was granted on March 22, 2016. At the full hearing the Magistrate determined that the CSPO would last until September 2017. Appellant objected to the magistrate's decision claiming that there was insufficient evidence to support "mental distress." The trial court overruled the objections and also modified the effective date of the order to the date of final judgment, (January 12, 2017)

---

[39] Rufener v. Hutson, 2012-Ohio-5061, 2012 WL 5364703 (Ohio Ct. App. 8th Dist. Cuyahoga County 2012).

[40] Rufener v. Hutson, 2012-Ohio-5061, 2012 WL 5364703, *3 (Ohio Ct. App. 8th Dist. Cuyahoga County 2012). See also Roxey v. Smallwood, 2016-Ohio-720, 2016 WL 763121 (Ohio Ct. App. 5th Dist. Fairfield County 2016) (right to a full hearing means the right to cross-examine witnesses, the right to look at evidence presented by appellee and the right to present witnesses and evidence on one's own behalf).

[41] Rufener v. Hutson, 2012-Ohio-5061, 2012 WL 5364703, *3 (Ohio Ct. App. 8th Dist. Cuyahoga County 2012).

[42] See also § 12:23.

[43] See also R.C. 3113.31(E)(3)(a).

[44] Banfield v. Orazem, 2017-Ohio-8438, 2017 WL 5151469 (Ohio Ct. App. 11th Dist. Geauga County 2017).

rather that the date of the ex parte order (March 22, 2016). On appeal, appellant argued that the trial court should have followed the recommendation of the magistrate regarding the effective date of the CSPO.

The appellate court determined that a trial court has discretion over the length of a CSPO, suggesting that a court can utilize the date of the final judgment rather that the date of the ex parte CSPO.

Q & A: Does a trial court lack jurisdiction to proceed with a civil stalking protection order case where it held a full hearing more than 10 days after the ex parte hearing?

According to RC 2903.214(D)(2), the court shall schedule a full hearing for a date that is within ten court days after the ex parte hearing.

In *Losey v. Diersing*,[45] the ex parte hearing was on June 10, 2010, and the full hearing was scheduled on July 13, 2010. Because more than 10 days had passed between the ex parte hearing and full hearing, appellant argued that the court was without jurisdiction to proceed with the case.

In this case, the appellate court overruled appellant's assignment of error because it determined that appellant had waived this argument because she failed to object to the magistrate's decision. However, the court noted that:

> There is nothing in RC 2903.214 that suggests that the failure to hold a full hearing within ten days of the ex parte hearing divests the trial court of jurisdiction to proceed, and therefore, objections to the time requirement may be waived. *Compare* Civ. R. 12(H)(3) ([w]henever it appears by suggestion of the parties or otherwise that the court lacks jurisdiction on the subject matter, the court shall dismiss the action). Because the time to object to non-jurisdictional defects stemming from the full hearing before the magistrate has passed, appellant has waived this argument on appeal.[46]

In that the time limitations were non-jurisdictional, appellant was bound to follow the civil rules of procedure and file objections to the magistrate's decision.[47]

Q & A: Can a trial court consider conduct occurring after the petition for protection order has been filed but before the full hearing on the petition?

At least one court has addressed the issue and answered in the affirmative. In *Shockey v. Shockey*,[48] appellant appealed the grant of a SCPO to his former wife on the grounds that some of the incidents testified to by former wife took place after the petition was filed but before the full hearing on the petition. These incidents were important to prove a "pattern of conduct" and without which appellee's petition should have been denied.

The appellate court disagreed with appellant that the trial court

[45] Losey v. Diersing, 2013-Ohio-1108, 2013 WL 1196674 (Ohio Ct. App. 12th Dist. Clermont County 2013).

[46] Losey v. Diersing, 2013-Ohio-1108, ¶ 22, 2013 WL 1196674 (Ohio Ct. App. 12th Dist. Clermont County 2013).

[47] But see newly adopted Civ. R. 65.1.

[48] Shockey v. Shockey, 2008-Ohio-6797, 2008 WL 5340554 (Ohio Ct. App. 5th Dist. Delaware County 2008).

was limited to consider only evidence relative to conduct occurring prior to the filing of the petition for protection order. "Rather, we find the legislative purpose best served by not restricting the trial court from considering relevant evidence occurring after the petition had been filed but prior to the full hearing on the petition."[49]

Of interest is that the appellate court disregarded appellant's claims that the parties engaged in sexual relations during the time between the filing of the petition and the date the magistrate granted the order.

Q & A: Does a respondent have the right to counsel for a civil stalking protection order full hearing?

No. The issue was addressed in *Walker v. Walker*,[50] wherein a respondent appealed the issuance of a civil stalking protection order, arguing that the trial court erred in failing to advise the pro se respondent of his right to counsel. He also contended that the court should have discussed with him the advisability of proceeding without counsel and determined whether he had made a knowingly and voluntary waiver.

The appellate court first reviewed the procedural provisions of R.C. 2903.214 and found that the grant of a civil protection order is not the equivalent of a finding the person against whom the order is granted has committed a criminal offense.[51] "Since proceedings involving the determination of whether to grant a protection order are civil, a defendant is generally not entitled to legal representation."[52]

The appellate court went even further in its legal analysis by considering Ohio case law that held that double jeopardy prohibitions do not attach to civil stalking protection order proceedings.[53]

Q & A: Does an incarcerated respondent have a right to be transported to the full hearing?

Not according to *Gaietto v. Noveck*.[54] In that case, respondent claimed on appeal that the Court erred in holding a full hearing

[49]Shockey v. Shockey, 2008-Ohio-6797, 2008 WL 5340554, *3 (Ohio Ct. App. 5th Dist. Delaware County 2008).

[50]Walker v. Walker, 2011-Ohio-3933, 2011 WL 3452362 (Ohio Ct. App. 5th Dist. Stark County 2011). See also Roxey v. Smallwood, 2016-Ohio-720, 2016 WL 763121 (Ohio Ct. App. 5th Dist. Fairfield County 2016).

[51]Walker v. Walker, 2011-Ohio-3933, 2011 WL 3452362, *2 (Ohio Ct. App. 5th Dist. Stark County 2011), citing Rieger v. Rieger, 165 Ohio App. 3d 454, 2006-Ohio-482, 847 N.E.2d 9 (2d Dist. Montgomery County 2006).

[52]Walker v. Walker, 2011-Ohio-3933, 2011 WL 3452362, *2 (Ohio Ct. App. 5th Dist. Stark County 2011), citing State ex rel. Jenkins v. Stern, 33 Ohio St. 3d 108, 110, 515 N.E.2d 928 (1987). See also Luttrell v. Younce, 2011-Ohio-4458, 2011 WL 3890292 (Ohio Ct. App. 2d Dist. Miami County 2011) (holding that in cases in which the issue is whether to grant a civil protection order, there is no entitlement to legal representation because they are civil proceedings, unlike a violation of a civil protection order which is a crime that may include criminal penalties including incarceration; citing Toledo v. Lyphout, 2009-Ohio-4596, 2009 WL 2855714 (Ohio Ct. App. 6th Dist. Lucas County 2009)); Lane v. Brewster, 2012-Ohio-1290, 2012 WL 1029503 (Ohio Ct. App. 12th Dist. Clermont County 2012).

[53]Walker v. Walker, 2011-Ohio-3933, 2011 WL 3452362, *2-3 (Ohio Ct. App. 5th Dist. Stark County 2011), quoting Westlake v. Patrick, 2005-Ohio-4419, 2005 WL 2046415 (Ohio Ct. App. 8th Dist. Cuyahoga County 2005).

[54]Gaietto v. Noveck, 2008-Ohio-519, 2008 WL 351460 (Ohio Ct. App. 3d Dist.

without him being present. The appellate court noted that respondent had failed to request a continuance from the full hearing or file a motion to transport him to the hearing. The Court then provided that "[i]ncarcerated individuals do "not have an absolute right to be present in a civil case" in which they are parties."[55] The Seneca County Court of Appeals then held that the trial court had no duty to sua sponte order the defendant to be transported to ensure his attendance at the full hearing.

The Court did not speak to the issue of whether transportation would have been provided at court expense if a defendant had filed a motion requesting transport.

Q & A: Is there a right to a trial by jury in a civil stalking protection order proceeding?

No. In *Welborn-Harlow v. Fuller*,[56] the appellant alleged that the trial court erred by not permitting him to file a jury demand and have a jury trial in a CSPO full hearing proceeding. The appellate court found that an action seeking a CSPO is a civil statutory action unknown at common law.[57] RC 2903.214 does not indicate that a jury be provided to a respondent in a civil stalking protection order proceeding. Thus, appellant had no right to a jury trial and the lower court did not err in denying his demand for a jury trial.

Q & A: Must the respondent receive reasonable notice of the full hearing?

Yes. In *Fahey v. Eschrich*,[58] appellant contends his constitutional due process rights were violated because he was not notified of the full hearing. He was served with the SCPO at his residence and requested a continuance of the full hearing. He was not notified of the new date and the record is devoid of any evidence that evidence of the new date was mailed or delivered to him.

The appellate court held that because appellant never received actual notice of the final hearing, and because such notice is required

---

Seneca County 2008).

[55]Gaietto v. Noveck, 2008-Ohio-519, 2008 WL 351460, *2 (Ohio Ct. App. 3d Dist. Seneca County 2008), quoting Waters v. Lattany, 2007-Ohio-1047, 2007 WL 707519 (Ohio Ct. App. 6th Dist. Lucas County 2007), citing In re Sprague, 113 Ohio App. 3d 274, 276, 680 N.E.2d 1041 (12th Dist. Butler County 1996); see also Trammell v. Powell, 2011-Ohio-2978, 2011 WL 2436915, *2 (Ohio Ct. App. 2d Dist. Montgomery County 2011) (discussing factors in determining whether a trial court can refuse to have a respondent brought from prison to a hearing, and determining that the expense and inconvenience of transporting respondent for the purpose of the hearing on petitioner's request for a protection order outweighed respondent's interest in being present; the court also noted that "as a practical matter, a 'No Contact Order' will be essentially the only real additional restriction that can be placed on the Respondent at this time, above and beyond the restrictions created by his incarceration").

[56]Welborn-Harlow v. Fuller, 2013-Ohio-54, 2013 WL 139592 (Ohio Ct. App. 6th Dist. Wood County 2013).

[57]Welborn-Harlow v. Fuller, 2013-Ohio-54, 2013 WL 139592, *4 (Ohio Ct. App. 6th Dist. Wood County 2013); see also Text 12:7.

[58]Fahey v. Eschrich, 2006-Ohio-5619, 2006 WL 3041193 (Ohio Ct. App. 6th Dist. Ottawa County 2006); but see Jenkins v. May, 2009-Ohio-1388, 2009 WL 791483 (Ohio Ct. App. 5th Dist. Ashland County 2009) (where continuance was denied because appellant had ample time to request an attorney).

under the local rules, he was denied his constitutional right to due process.[59]

Q & A: Is notice of a full hearing that is served on a respondent about one hour before the proceedings reasonable?

According to the Stark County Court of Appeals, the answer is qualified yes. Filing for or requesting a continuance may have led to a different response. In *Oddo v. Spencer*,[60] the respondent was served with the petition and ex parte protection order about an hour before the actual hearing. The magistrate proceeded with the hearing at the scheduled time.

On appeal, the respondent claimed that notice of the full hearing, served upon him about one hour before the actual full hearing commenced did not comply with the "[p]rior to the date scheduled" language of R.C. 2903.214(D)(2)(a)(i) because the magistrate failed to ask about his readiness to proceed or seek counsel.[61] However, the appellate court noted that R.C. 2903.214 permits court discretion regarding continuances and stated that there is nothing contained in the civil rules mandating full colloquy requirements. In overruling respondent's objection, the Court found that ". . . reasonable notice and opportunity to be heard were afforded to appellant under the facts and circumstances presented, and that the trial court did not err or abuse its discretion in declining to continue or reset the CPO hearing at a later date."[62]

However, the ruling may have been different had the respondent requested a continuance or asked for an opportunity to obtain an attorney.

Q & A: Who can request that a private process server be appointed to serve a civil stalking protection order?

In *Estel v. Catudal*,[63] respondent appealed the grant of a CSPO, contending that he was not properly served because the magistrate was not authorized to appoint a process server because appellee never filed a written motion such as required by Civ. R. 4.1(B). Although the appellee requested a private process server, it was the court that ordered the Clerk to re-issue service on appellant.

The appellate court reasoned that the civil rules do not apply to special statutory proceedings. Because a civil stalking protection order is a special statutory proceeding, appellee was not required to file a written request for the appointment of a private process server,

---

[59]See also Text § 11:11, Ex parte protection orders—Service and notice provisions; Beachler v. Beachler, 2007-Ohio-1220, 2007 WL 805526 (Ohio Ct. App. 12th Dist. Preble County 2007); but see State v. Eschrich, 2008-Ohio-2984, 2008 WL 2468572 (Ohio Ct. App. 6th Dist. Ottawa County 2008) (noting that the 12th District Court of Appeals concluded that the invalidity of a protection order does not provide a defense to a wilful violation of the order, citing State v. Sutts, 2004-Ohio-3541, 2004 WL 1485909 (Ohio Ct. App. 12th Dist. Warren County 2004)).

[60]Oddo v. Spencer, 2009-Ohio-4320, 2009 WL 2602210 (Ohio Ct. App. 5th Dist. Stark County 2009).

[61]*Oddo at *2.*

[62]*Oddo at *2.*

[63]Estel v. Catudal, 2014-Ohio-4719, 2014 WL 5420918 (Ohio Ct. App. 5th Dist. Licking County 2014).

Therefore, the court had the authority to appoint a process server to effectuate service as required by RC 2903.214.[64]

Q & A: Must the Court take sworn testimony at the ex parte hearing?

Yes. At least one appellate court suggests that, absent evidence that sworn testimony was provided at the ex parte hearing, the trial court must take evidence at the full hearing. In *Gaietto v. Noveck*,[65] the petitioner was granted an ex parte CSPO. The respondent was incarcerated at the time of the full hearing. On appeal, the respondent alleged that the trial court erred by relying on the petition and not taking any additional evidence at the full hearing and thus, the CSPO was against the manifest weight of the evidence.

The appellate court relied on R.C. 2903.214(E)(3)(d) which provides that "a full hearing must be held at which the respondent presents evidence in support of the request for a protection order and the petitioner is afforded an opportunity to defend against the evidence, the court determines that the petitioner has committed a violation of section R.C. 2903.211 . . ." Based on this section of the statute, (which details the requirements by which civil protection orders are issued against both parties) the appellate court found that R.C. 2903.214 requires evidence that the respondent violated R.C. 2903.211 and that under the facts of the case, such evidence was not presented.

The appellate court also reviewed the record indicating that the trial court asked whether the petitioner wished the CSPO to continue in effect. When she answered in the affirmative, the Court then stated that it would be granted for a period of 5 years, unless respondent were to request a hearing when he released from jail. In that event, a hearing would be granted.

The appellate court was concerned that the trial court did not know whether the magistrate had taken sworn testimony at the ex parte hearing. The record demonstrated that the trial court did not know whether the Magistrate had taken sworn testimony but only assumed that it had been taken. However, such an assumption suggested that the trial court did not review the testimony from the ex parte hearing. In light of the requirements under R.C. 2903.214(E)(3)(d), signing the CSPO in effect for 5 years based on the allegations in the petition was not within the meaning of a "full hearing."

Of significance is that the appellate court's reliance on R.C. 2903.214(E)(3)(d) was misplaced. That section applies to a respondent filing a petition in response to a petition filed by a petitioner. R.C. 2903.214(D) is the applicable provision and it does not articulate the requirements for a full hearing.

However, the analysis advanced by the appellate court does seem to suggest that sworn testimony must be taken by the court at the ex parte hearing and that a trial court must hold a full hearing which includes presenting evidence that respondent violated R.C. 2903.211, particularly if it is unclear whether sworn testimony was taken at the ex parte hearing.

---

[64]Estel v. Catudal, 2014-Ohio-4719, 2014 WL 5420918, ¶ 13 (Ohio Ct. App. 5th Dist. Licking County 2014).

[65]Gaietto v. Noveck, 2008-Ohio-519, 2008 WL 351460 (Ohio Ct. App. 3d Dist. Seneca County 2008).

Q & A: Does R.C. 2903.214 contain a jurisdictional requirement?

It appears so. In R.C. 2903.214(A)(1), a "court" is defined as the court of common pleas of the county in which the person to be protected by the protection order resides. Based on the wording of the statute, R.C. 2903.214 requires a petitioner to file for an anti-stalking civil protection order in the county in which the petitioner resides. No such requirement is included in R.C. 3113.31, the civil domestic violence statute.

Both "venue" and "jurisdiction" were addressed by the Franklin County Court of Appeals in *Reynolds v. Whitney*.[66] In that case, a former boyfriend filed, and was granted, a petition for an anti-stalking civil protection order against his former girlfriend. On appeal, the appellant argued that the court did not have subject matter jurisdiction over the petition because the appellee lived in another county, to wit: Fairfield, and thus, did not have the authority to issue the protection order.

The Tenth District Court of Appeals first discussed the concepts of "jurisdiction" and "venue." " 'Jurisdiction' connotes the power to hear and decide a case on its merits, while 'venue' connotes locality, the place where the suit should be heard."[67] It noted that if there was no subject matter jurisdiction over the petition for CPO, any judgment rendered is void and must be vacated.

The court then pointed out that R.C. 2903.214(B) provides that "the court has jurisdiction over all proceedings under this section." Court was then defined as provided in R.C. 2903.214(A)(1) to be the court of common pleas in the county in which the person to be protected resides.

In reversing the trial court judgment, the Franklin County Court of Appeals held that "[i]t is apparent from the plain language of R.C. 2903.214, and from the record, that the [Fairfield County] court of common pleas lacked jurisdiction to render the October 23, 2003 judgment in the present case. Thus the judgment was a nullity and must be vacated."[68]

Q & A: How is the doctrine of res judicata used in civil stalking protection order cases?[69]

"Res judicata is a doctrine of judicial preclusion. There are two theories on which res judicata operate: claim preclusion (estoppel by judgment) and issue preclusion (collateral estoppel)."[70] Under the doctrine of res judicata, "[a] valid final judgment rendered upon the

[66]Reynolds v. Whitney, 2004-Ohio-1628, 2004 WL 626872 (Ohio Ct. App. 10th Dist. Franklin County 2004); Vilk v. Dinardo, 2016-Ohio-5245, 2016 WL 4141673 (Ohio Ct. App. 8th Dist. Cuyahoga County 2016).

[67]Reynolds v. Whitney, 2004-Ohio-1628, 2004 WL 626872, *2 (Ohio Ct. App. 10th Dist. Franklin County 2004).

[68]Reynolds v. Whitney, 2004-Ohio-1628, 2004 WL 626872, *2 (Ohio Ct. App. 10th Dist. Franklin County 2004).

[69]See also Text § 12:27, Conflicting protection orders.

[70]J.P. v. T.H., 2017-Ohio-233, 2017 WL 277518 (Ohio Ct. App. 9th Dist. Lorain County 2017), citing Grava v. Parkman Twp., 73 Ohio St. 3d 379, 381, 1995-Ohio-331, 653 N.E.2d 226 (1995).

merits bars all subsequent actions based upon any claim arising out of the transaction or occurrence that was the subject matter of the previous action."[71] "Furthermore, res judicata operates to bar litigation of " 'all claims which were or might have been litigated in a first lawsuit.' "[72]

For example, in *Irwin v. Murray*,[73] the appellant raised the issue arguing that the doctrine of res judicata barred appellee from seeking an SCPO because the incidents presented in her testimony at the SCPO hearing were the same as those presented at the hearing on appellant's CPO, except for the incident regarding appellee's customers, but the Sixth District Court of Appeals upheld the trial court ruling.

The appellate court first determined that the doctrine of res judicata did not apply because appellee's petition for the SCPO was brought under R.C. 2903.214 which governs the issuance of SCPOs. "R.C. 2903.214 and R.C. 3113.31 are separate tools in Ohio's comprehensive protection legislation and offer distinct forms of relief. The goal of R.C. 2903.214 is to allow the police and the courts to act *before* a victim is harmed by a stalker. A party is not precluded from seeking a SCPO in the general division of a court while an action is pending in the domestic relations division."[74] The court then reasoned that, even if applicable, it would not bar appellee's petition because appellee raised additional allegations in her SCPO petition to those heard by the domestic relations court and "it was 'an expanded issue' presented in her petition."

In *Goldfuss v. Traxler*,[75] appellant appealed the issuance of a SCPO on the ground that one of the necessary incidents required to prove a pattern of conduct was barred by the doctrine of res judicata.

In that case, appellee was granted an ex parte SCPO based on an incident that appellant had followed her and her children in her car. The order was dismissed when she failed to appear at the full hearing. About 5 months later, appellee filed another SCPO alleging that appellant had made threats to family members and that she continued to follow her and her family. "[U]nder the doctrine of res judicata, ' "[w]hen a valid and final judgment rendered in an action extinguishes the plaintiff's claim * * *, the claim extinguished includes all rights of the plaintiff to remedies against the defendant with respect to all or any part of the transaction, or series of connected transactions, out of which the action arose." ' "[76]

The appellate court first dismissed appellant's assertion that the

[71] J.P. v. T.H., 2017-Ohio-233, ¶ 25, 2017 WL 277518 (Ohio Ct. App. 9th Dist. Lorain County 2017); Kelm v. Kelm, 92 Ohio St. 3d 223, 2001-Ohio-168, 749 N.E.2d 299 (2001), quoting Grava at syllabus).

[72] J.P. v. T.H., 2017-Ohio-233, ¶ 25, 2017 WL 277518 (Ohio Ct. App. 9th Dist. Lorain County 2017), quoting *Grava* at 382, quoting National Amusements, Inc. v. City of Springdale, 53 Ohio St. 3d 60, 62, 558 N.E.2d 1178 (1990).

[73] Irwin v. Murray, 2006-Ohio-1633, 2006 WL 832830 (Ohio Ct. App. 6th Dist. Lucas County 2006).

[74] Irwin v. Murray, 2006-Ohio-1633, 2006 WL 832830, *2 (Ohio Ct. App. 6th Dist. Lucas County 2006) (citation omitted), citing *Wildi v. Wildi*.

[75] Goldfuss v. Traxler, 2008-Ohio-6186, 2008 WL 5053451 (Ohio Ct. App. 3d Dist. Wyandot County 2008).

[76] Goldfuss v. Traxler, 2008-Ohio-6186, 2008 WL 5053451, *2 (Ohio Ct. App. 3d

first SCPO was dismissed with prejudice. A dismissal for the failure to prosecute does not equate to a dismissal after a hearing on the merits. The court then acknowledged that a separate criminal charge was filed based on the first incident whereby appellant was convicted after a plea to disorderly conduct.

In affirming the issuance of the SCPO, the court found that the doctrine of res judicata did not apply to the facts at hand because the appellee relied on subsequent incidents to the conduct that had been dismissed under the first SCPO petition.

In *Erdman v. Williams*,[77] a civil stalking protection order was granted to petitioner. After respondent's objections were denied, he filed a notice of appeal, but no appeal was then filed with the court. Subsequently, he filed a motion to dismiss with the trial court, which motion was overruled by the magistrate. After his motion to dismiss was denied, he again filed an appeal alleging that the trial court erroneously granted the CSPO.

The appellate court first noted that an order granting or refusing to grant a protection order, other than an ex parte order, is a final appealable order. "Accordingly, we find Appellant is barred from raising his arguments under the doctrine of res judicata. Appellant's arguments as presented herein could have or should have been raised on direct appeal of the trial court's December 6, 2011, Judgment Entry.[78] A motion to dismiss or a motion to vacate cannot be used as a substitute for a direct appeal."

Likewise, in *J.P. v. T.H.*,[79] J.P. sought and obtained an ex parte civil stalking protection order which was subsequently denied at full hearing. J.P. then filed a complaint for money damages in the Lorain County Common Pleas Court based on assault, battery, invasion of privacy and defamation stemming from T.H.'s alleged actions.

After much legal maneuvering, the court granted summary judgment to T.H. on the basis that all of J.P.'s claims were barred by the doctrine of res judicata as the matters had been fully litigated in the CSPO case.

The appellate court sustained J.P.'s assignment of error and determined that in a tort case and CSPO case, although derived from the same nucleus of operative facts, the issues litigated in a protection order were not the same as those litigated in a tort case.[80] Thus, J.P.'s tort case was not barred by the doctrine of res judicata.

The appellate court also noted that J.P. had no obligation to assert his tort claims at the same time he brought his petition for protection

---

Dist. Wyandot County 2008), quoting Grava v. Parkman Twp., 73 Ohio St. 3d 379, 1995-Ohio-331, 653 N.E.2d 226 (1995), and 1 Restatement of the Law 2d, Judgments, § 24(1) at 196 (1982).

[77]Erdman v. Williams, 2013-Ohio-980, 2013 WL 1092804 (Ohio Ct. App. 5th Dist. Tuscarawas County 2013).

[78]See also, Delaine v. Smith, 2016-Ohio-5250, 2016 WL 4141753 (Ohio Ct. App. 8th Dist. Cuyahoga County 2016).

[79]J.P. v. T.H., 2017-Ohio-233, 2017 WL 277518 (Ohio Ct. App. 9th Dist. Lorain County 2017).

[80]J.P. v. T.H., 2017-Ohio-233, ¶ 29, 2017 WL 277518 (Ohio Ct. App. 9th Dist. Lorain County 2017).

order because RC 2903.214(G) provided that the remedies available in a stalking case are "in addition to, and not in lieu of, any other available civil and criminal remedy." "To hold otherwise would punish petitioners seeking protection orders by forever depriving them of all legal remedies simply for prioritizing their own physical safety and/or the physical safety of their family members over their pecuniary damages."[81]

Conversely, in *Rice v. Lewis*,[82] appellant filed petitions for a civil SOOPO against appellees alleging that Rice committed a sexually oriented offense against the child and Kelly failed to protect the child from the abuse. Appellees then filed a motion to dismiss on the basis of res judicata because appellant raised the same allegations in the juvenile court proceeding years before and in various police reports through the ensuing years. The trial court agreed with appellees and dismissed the petition based on res judicata.

On appeal, appellant claimed that the trial court erred by finding that her petitions were barred by res judicata. She argued that the SOOPOs involved different issues than the issues in the juvenile court case. However, there were no new allegations of sexual abuse that occurred after the juvenile court's judgment. Since appellant's SOOPOs arose out of the same nucleus of operative facts as the abuse and neglect case, they were barred by the juvenile court's judgment under the doctrine of res judicata.[83] Thus, appellant's assignment of error was overruled.

Q & A: Does R.C. 2903.214 address the filing and granting of continuances of the full hearing?

Yes. Pursuant to R.C. 2903.214(D)(2)(a)(i) to R.C. 2903.214(D)(2)(a)(iv), the court may grant a continuance where respondent has not been served,[84] the parties consent to the continuance, the continuance is needed to allow a party to obtain counsel[85] or for other good cause.[86]

[81] J.P. v. T.H., 2017-Ohio-233, ¶ 28, 2017 WL 277518 (Ohio Ct. App. 9th Dist. Lorain County 2017).

[82] Rice v. Lewis, 2013-Ohio-5890, 2013 WL 6989772 (Ohio Ct. App. 4th Dist. Scioto County 2013).

[83] Rice v. Lewis, 2013-Ohio-5890, ¶ 30, 2013 WL 6989772 (Ohio Ct. App. 4th Dist. Scioto County 2013).

[84] See State v. Blaine, 2004-Ohio-1241, 2004 WL 524667 (Ohio Ct. App. 4th Dist. Highland County 2004) (where the appellate court found that continuing a full hearing in an SCPO case for two months and twelve days, after service was not perfected within the statutory 10 day time frame, was an abuse of discretion without just cause and not reasonable). See also Berry v. Patrick, 2005-Ohio-3708, 2005 WL 1707005 (Ohio Ct. App. 8th Dist. Cuyahoga County 2005) (reversing contempt because trial court's failure to conduct hearing and rule on motion for order in a timely manner was an abuse of discretion; a two-month delay between commencement and completion of the hearting without an explanation; eight months from time of filing of motion to issues ruling and 13 months before trial court issues its ruling from time Berry requested order was an abuse of discretion).

[85] Noah v. Brillhart, 2003-Ohio-2421, 2003 WL 21078077 (Ohio Ct. App. 9th Dist. Wayne County 2003) (appeals court held that trial court's denial of a continuance to obtain counsel where the parties had previously consented to a continuance and notice of the hearing was provided more than a month prior to the scheduled hearing was not an abuse of discretion).

[86] Gussler v. Morris, 2006-Ohio-6627, 2006 WL 3691200 (Ohio Ct. App. 4th Dist.

For example, in *Elliot v. Ball*,[87] the respondent was served with the stalking civil protection order a little more than a day before the full hearing. She called the court and then faxed a motion for continuance, which was denied by the trial court.

On appeal, respondent argued that the trial court abused its discretion by denying her a continuance. The Cuyahoga County Court of Appeals agreed and reasoned that "[a] fundamental requisite of procedural due process is notice and an opportunity to be heard. The notice must be reasonably calculated, under all the circumstances, to apprise interested parties of the pendency of the action and afford them an opportunity to present their objections. Moreover, the notice must also afford a reasonable time for interested parties to make their appearance."[88]

The court also relied on *Lindsay v. Jackson*,[89] in which the court found that one business day was not sufficient time to prepare a defense to a petition for a stalking civil protection order.

Q & A: Must a continuance be granted by the court every time a party requests a continuance?[90]

Not according to the statute or the Second District Appellate court

---

Ross County 2006); see also Roncone v. Bialkowski, 2007-Ohio-3326, 2007 WL 1874250 (Ohio Ct. App. 10th Dist. Franklin County 2007) (issuance of CSPO reversed because trial court abused its discretion in denying respondent's motion for continuance of the full hearing after counsel withdrew in the middle of hearing); Echemann v. Echemann, 2016-Ohio-3212, 2016 WL 3057979 (Ohio Ct. App. 3d Dist. Shelby County 2016) (finding that trial court's continuance for 60 days was not unreasonable when there was insufficient time to hear the case; where there is a scheduling conflict, it was not unreasonable to continue the hearing to a reasonable time thereafter).

[87]Elliot v. Ball, 2004-Ohio-6300, 2004 WL 2677464 (Ohio Ct. App. 8th Dist. Cuyahoga County 2004); compare State v. Blaine, 2004-Ohio-1241, 2004 WL 524667 (Ohio Ct. App. 4th Dist. Highland County 2004); Gussler v. Morris, 2006-Ohio-6627, 2006 WL 3691200 (Ohio Ct. App. 4th Dist. Ross County 2006); see also Vance v. Nichols, 2007-Ohio-3819, 2007 WL 2164162 (Ohio Ct. App. 2d Dist. Darke County 2007) (issuance of CSPO reversed by appellate court because respondent was denied reasonable opportunity to be heard after her request for continuance to obtain an attorney and request time off from her employer was denied by trial court).

[88]Elliot v. Ball, 2004-Ohio-6300, 2004 WL 2677464, *2 (Ohio Ct. App. 8th Dist. Cuyahoga County 2004); citing Mullane v. Central Hanover Bank & Trust Co., 339 U.S. 306, 314, 70 S. Ct. 652, 657, 94 L. Ed. 865 (1950).

[89]Lindsay v. Jackson, 2000 WL 1268810 (Ohio Ct. App. 1st Dist. Hamilton County 2000); but see Jenkins v. May, 2009-Ohio-1388, 2009 WL 791483 (Ohio Ct. App. 5th Dist. Ashland County 2009) (where continuance was denied and finding that 10 days was sufficient to obtain counsel); but see Oddo v. Spencer, 2009-Ohio-4320, 2009 WL 2602210 (Ohio Ct. App. 5th Dist. Stark County 2009) (court found that service of the protection order and notice of the full hearing only one hour before the hearing was reasonable. The respondent did not ask for a continuance or the opportunity to obtain counsel).

[90]See State v. Unger, 67 Ohio St. 2d 65, 67, 21 Ohio Op. 3d 41, 423 N.E.2d 1078 (1981); see also Osunde v. Ijeweme, 2013-Ohio-1207, 2013 WL 1286984 (Ohio Ct. App. 10th Dist. Franklin County 2013); McWilliam v. Dickey, 2013-Ohio-4036, 2013 WL 5310439 (Ohio Ct. App. 8th Dist. Cuyahoga County 2013) (trial court did not continue the hearing more than once due to the objection of petitioner and such action was not considered an abuse of discretion by appellate court); Roxey v. Smallwood, 2016-Ohio-720, 2016 WL 763121 (Ohio Ct. App. 5th Dist. Fairfield County 2016) (holding that where reasonable notice and an opportunity to be heard was afforded to respondent, the trial court did not abuse its discretion in proceeding with the full hearing).

in Luttrell v. Younce.[91] In *Luttrell*, a civil stalking protection order was granted by the court. Respondent appealed, contending that the trial court denied him his constitutionally guaranteed due process protections because he was not represented by counsel at the full hearing. Respondent relied on R.C. 2903.214(D)(2)(iii) which provides that the trial court *may* grant a continuance of a full hearing for a party to obtain counsel. (Emphasis added.) However, the record indicated that he had not requested a continuance to obtain counsel; he understood that petitioner was seeking a protection order; and he responded to the court that he was prepared to go forward without an attorney.

In finding that one must request a continuance if he or she wants additional time to obtain counsel, the appellate court stressed that while a trial court may grant a continuance to obtain an attorney, a trial court is not required to always continue a full hearing any time one or both of the parties appears at the hearing without counsel. "Otherwise, the legislature would have made a continuance mandatory in R.C. 2903.214(D)(2)(iii)."[92]

Q & A: Is respondent entitled to a continuance of the full hearing because of a pending criminal case when his testimony at the full hearing could be used against him in his upcoming criminal trial?

The Second District Court of Appeals answered in the negative. In *Sweet v. Hunt*,[93] appellee sought a civil stalking protection order against appellant for engaging in menacing by stalking actions. Appellant sought several continuances, for reasons that included his upcoming criminal trial for the same acts that formed the basis for the CSPO. After denying his continuance motion after granting a continuance on four other occasions, the trial court held the full hearing at which appellant appeared and renewed his objection to the denial of the continuance. After granting the CSPO, appellant appealed and challenged the denial of his continuance motion.

Appellant argued that the denial of his motion to continue because of the pending criminal case denied him a meaningful opportunity to defend himself.[94] At the outset, the appellate court reviewed the denial of the continuance for an abuse of discretion. Pursuant to R.C. 2903. 214(D)(2)(a)(iv), the court may grant a continuance "for other good cause." In that the trial court continued the case previously for the same reason and because it was unclear when the criminal case would resolve and because over three months had elapsed since the filing of the ex parte order and the full hearing, the appellate court did not find an abuse of discretion.

The appellate court also addressed Appellant's argument that the

---

[91]Luttrell v. Younce, 2011-Ohio-4458, 2011 WL 3890292 (Ohio Ct. App. 2d Dist. Miami County 2011).

[92]Luttrell v. Younce, 2011-Ohio-4458, ¶ 31, 2011 WL 3890292 (Ohio Ct. App. 2d Dist. Miami County 2011).

[93]Sweet v. Hunt, 2014-Ohio-631, 2014 WL 707923 (Ohio Ct. App. 2d Dist. Greene County 2014).

[94]Sweet v. Hunt, 2014-Ohio-631, 2014 WL 707923, ¶ 8 (Ohio Ct. App. 2d Dist. Greene County 2014).

denial of his right to defend himself violates the Fifth Amendment. "[T]he Fifth Amendment protection against compulsory, self incriminating testimony does not extend to prohibit civil litigation while the possibility of criminal prosecution exists."[95] In relying on *Wirtz v. Wirtz*,[96] the appellate court overruled appellant's assignment or error and commented that the Seventh District appellate court rejected a similar argument, finding no abuse of discretion in the denial of a motion to continue a CSPO hearing while related criminal charges were pending. "We reach the same conclusion here. The Fifth Amendment does not shield a party from appearing or defending in a civil action. *Tedeschi v. Grover*, 39 Ohio App. 3d 109, 111, 529 NE2d 480,482 (10th Dist. 1988). 'Accordingly, [a] defendant may not interpose whatever Fifth Amendment privilege he may enjoy as a witness to obtain a continuation of the litigation.' Id. '[M]erely because [a] defendant [may have] felt required to appear and defend does not, of itself, violate any Fifth Amendment guarantee.' "[97]

Of importance is that this case stands for the proposition that a respondent who refuses to testify at the full hearing on a civil protection order on the grounds of the Fifth Amendment should not be able to prevail in an appeal. Clearly, the Fifth Amendment's protection against compulsory, self-incriminating testimony does not extend to prohibit *civil* litigation while the possibility of criminal prosecution exists nor does the Fifth Amendment shield a party from appearing or defending in a *civil* action.[98]

Q & A: Does Civ. R. 65.1 apply to civil protection orders issued under RC 2903.214?[99]

Yes. According to Civ. R. 65.1(A), the provisions of the rule apply to special statutory proceedings under RC 2903.214, providing for civil stalking and sexually oriented offense protection orders. This includes service concerns, discovery concerns,[100] and orders issued by a magistrate. It also addresses appeals and objections.

---

[95]Sweet v. Hunt, 2014-Ohio-631, 2014 WL 707923, ¶ 11 (Ohio Ct. App. 2d Dist. Greene County 2014), quoting Walker v. State Medical Bd. of Ohio, 2002-Ohio-682, 2002 WL 243318, *4 (Ohio Ct. App. 10th Dist. Franklin County 2002); see also State ex rel. Verhovec v. Mascio, 81 Ohio St. 3d 334, 336, 1998-Ohio-431, 691 N.E.2d 282 (1998).

[96]Wirtz v. Wirtz, 2000-Ohio-2564, 2000 WL 1486652 (Ohio Ct. App. 7th Dist. Mahoning County 2000).

[97]Sweet v. Hunt, 2014-Ohio-631, 2014 WL 707923, ¶ 11 (Ohio Ct. App. 2d Dist. Greene County 2014).

[98]Sweet v. Hunt, 2014-Ohio-631, 2014 WL 707923, ¶ 11 (Ohio Ct. App. 2d Dist. Greene County 2014) (emphasis added).

[99]See also § 9:5; J.R. v. Pless, 2016-Ohio-14, 2016 WL 60000 (Ohio Ct. App. 9th Dist. Summit County 2016).

[100]Echemann v. Echemann, 2016-Ohio-3212, 2016 WL 3057979 (Ohio Ct. App. 3d Dist. Shelby County 2016) (noting, in dicta, that depositions were taken); M.W. v. D.M., 2018-Ohio-392, ¶ 17, 2018 WL 660271 (Ohio Ct. App. 8th Dist. Cuyahoga County 2018) (court found that while limited discovery is permitted under Civ. R. 65. 1(D), it must be completed before the time set for full hearing and under terms and conditions deemed necessary to assure the safety of petitioner and further, that there was no support to entitle respondent to petitioner's complete medical records).

Q & A: Under Civ. R. 65.1, must a court issue findings of fact and conclusions of law?[101]

Not according to the analysis set forth in *Wulf v. Opp*.[102] In that case, Opp filed an appeal alleging that she was denied her written request for findings of fact and conclusions of law, even though language was included within the original CSPO that required written findings of fact and conclusions of law prior to any objection being filed. She also argued that the inclusion of this language "effectively precluded her from having the ability to timely file objections to the magistrate's decision."[103] (While this appeal was brought relative to civil stalking protection order pursuant to RC 2903.214, the analysis is the same.).

Because all civil protection orders must comply with Civ. R. 65.1 and because the rule specifically states that the requirements of Civ. R. 53 do not apply, a request for findings of fact and conclusions of law provided by Civ. R. 53(D)(3)(a)(ii) was not mandatory. Thus, it was within the discretion of the trial court and not plain error to deny the request for written findings of fact and conclusions of law.

Q & A: Can a magistrate make orders in a civil protection order proceeding without judicial approval?

According to newly adopted Civ. R. 65.1(F)(2)(a), a magistrate now has written authority to conduct an ex parte hearing and, upon conclusion of the hearing, deny or grant an ex parte protection order.

A magistrate's denial or issuance of an ex parte protection order does not require judicial approval, shall otherwise comply with the statutory requirements relating to an ex parte protection order, shall be effective when signed by the magistrate and filed with the clerk and shall have the same effect as an ex parte protection order entered by the court without reference to a magistrate.[104]

A magistrate's denial or grant of an ex parte civil protection order without judicial approval under this division does not constitute a magistrate's order or a magistrate's decision under Civ. R. 53(D)(2) or (3) and is not subject to the requirements of those rules.[105] So too, the court's approval and signing of a magistrate's denial or grant of an ex parte protection order entered under this division does not constitute a judgment or interim order under Civ. R. 53(D)(4)(e) and is not subject to the requirements of that rule.[106]

Lastly, a magistrate is also permitted to grant or deny a protection order issued after a full hearing and that such grant or denial does not constitute a magistrate's order or magistrate's decision under Civ. R. 53 (D)(2) or (3) and is not subject to Rule 53.[107]

Q & A: Can objections be filed under Civ. R. 65.1?

---

[101]See also Text 12:10.

[102]Wulf v. Opp, 2015-Ohio-3285, 2015 WL 4878495 (Ohio Ct. App. 12th Dist. Clermont County 2015).

[103]Wulf v. Opp, 2015-Ohio-3285, 2015 WL 4878495, ¶ 15 (Ohio Ct. App. 12th Dist. Clermont County 2015).

[104]Civ. R. 65.1(F)(2)(b)(i).

[105]Civ. R. 65.1(F)(2)(b)(ii).

[106]Civ. R. 65.1(F)(2)(b)(ii).

[107]Civ. R. 65.1(F)(3)(b). See e.g., Keller v. Knight, 2014-Ohio-2432, 2014 WL

Civ. R. 65.1(F)(3)(d)(i) specifically states that "[a] party may file written objections to a court's adoption, modification, or rejection of a magistrate's denial or granting of a protection order after a full hearing, or any term of such order, within 14 days of the court's filing of the order."

Q & A: Must objections be filed before an appeal is filed?

Pursuant to Civ. R. 65.1, a party must file timely objections prior to filing an appeal.[108] If timely objections to the trial court order are not filed, an appellate court lacks jurisdiction to hear the appeal.[109]

Q & A: Is this mandate jurisdictional?

The requirement to file objections to the magistrate's decision under Civ. R. 65.1(F)(3)(d) is mandatory and any party who wants to object to the legal conclusions or wishing to demonstrate that the credible evidence is insufficient must file timely objections.[110]

However, the question that should be asked is whether such a failure to timely file objections is jurisdictional. According to *M.W. v. D.M.*, the failure to comply with Civ. R. 65.1(G) is not jurisdictional. Thus, any prevailing party must at least timely raise the procedural defect and a failure to challenge the scope of review based on respondent's failure to file objections forfeits any procedural error a petitioner may have.[111] "In this case, petitioner has not challenged the scope of our review based on respondent's failure to file objections to the magistrate's decision."[112] In effect, by not raising the procedural defect, any procedural error has been forfeited and the court was not obligated to address the issue beyond "determining that we possess jurisdiction to entertain the appeal."[113]

Q & A: Does a party object to the magistrate's decision or to the trial court's adoption, modification or rejection of a magistrate's decision?

[U]nlike Civ. R. 53 that permits a party to file objections to a magistrate's decision, Civ. R. 65.1 permits a party to file objections to

---

2566249 (Ohio Ct. App. 6th Dist. Wood County 2014).

[108]Civ. R. 65.1(G); see Martin v. Dockter, 2018-Ohio-858, ¶ 6, 2018 WL 1216633 (Ohio Ct. App. 10th Dist. Franklin County 2018); K.U. v. M.S., 2017-Ohio-8029, 2017 WL 4350999 (Ohio Ct. App. 7th Dist. Mahoning County 2017); M.W. v. D.M., 2018-Ohio-392, 2018 WL 660271 (Ohio Ct. App. 8th Dist. Cuyahoga County 2018); J.K. v. T.J., 2017-Ohio-9239, ¶ 6, 2017 WL 6550546 (Ohio Ct. App. 7th Dist. Mahoning County 2017); J.S. v. D.E., 2017-Ohio-7507, ¶ 21, 2017 WL 3971706 (Ohio Ct. App. 7th Dist. Mahoning County 2017); R.G. v. R.M., 2017-Ohio-8918, 88 N.E.3d 1027 (Ohio Ct. App. 7th Dist. Mahoning County 2017) (pointing out that former Civ. R. 65.1(G) which permitted either objections or an immediate appeal was amended in July 2016).

[109]Martin v. Dockter, 2018-Ohio-858, ¶ 6, 2018 WL 1216633 (Ohio Ct. App. 10th Dist. Franklin County 2018); K.R. v. T.B., 2017-Ohio-8647, ¶ 6, 2017 WL 5608198 (Ohio Ct. App. 10th Dist. Franklin County 2017).

[110]M.W. v. D.M., 2018-Ohio-392, ¶ 7, 2018 WL 660271 (Ohio Ct. App. 8th Dist. Cuyahoga County 2018).

[111]M.W. v. D.M., 2018-Ohio-392, ¶ 7, 2018 WL 660271 (Ohio Ct. App. 8th Dist. Cuyahoga County 2018).

[112]M.W. v. D.M., 2018-Ohio-392, ¶ 7, 2018 WL 660271 (Ohio Ct. App. 8th Dist. Cuyahoga County 2018).

[113]M.W. v. D.M., 2018-Ohio-392, ¶ 7, 2018 WL 660271 (Ohio Ct. App. 8th Dist. Cuyahoga County 2018).

the trial court's adoption, modification or rejection of a magistrate's grant or denial of a CSPO. Since a magistrate's decision is not effective unless adopted by the court, objections can only be filed to the trial court order, not the magistrate's decision.[114]

For example, in Martin v. *Doctker*,[115] the Martins filed a CSPO against Ms. Dockter which was denied at the ex parte level. Following the full hearing, the magistrate granted the order which was adopted by the court and filed on February 24, 2017 and served on respondent on March 10, 2017. (the same day that objections were due).

Dockter then filed her objections and a motion pursuant to Civ. R. 60(B)(2) seeking to file her objections to the trial court's adoption of the CPO outside of the 14 day timeframe due to a delay in service of the CPO, which motion was denied based on a finding that "it lacked jurisdiction 'to permit objections to a magistrate's decision when that decision was adopted and already made a final judgment.' "[116]

The appellate court pointed out that "[b]ased on this faulty premise, the trial court found that untimely objections are a nullity and Civ. R. 60(B) (2) is inapplicable."[117] It found that the trial court erred when it applied Civ. R. 53, instead of Civ. R. 65.1. It held that: "[t]he trial court's reasoning does not apply to a Civ. R. 65.1 order because the right to file objections is to the trial court's order, not to the magistrate's decision."[118] Because service of the CPO was delayed, the trial court had jurisdiction to rule on *Dockter's* motion requesting permission to file objections to the trial court's adoption of the CPO (out of rule) and her proposed objections.

Q & A: What are the steps in the process?

Pursuant to Civ. R. 65.1, a magistrate's grant of a protection order after a full hearing is not effective unless adopted by the trial court.[119] The court's adoption, modification or rejection of that order is effective when signed by the court and filed with the clerk.[120] The court may adopt the magistrate's grant or denial of the full hearing protection order "upon review of the order and a determination that there is no error of law or other defect evident on the face of the order."[121]

Q & A: What does such a review involve?

---

[114]See Insa v. Insa, 2016-Ohio-7425, 72 N.E.3d 1170, ¶ 26 (Ohio Ct. App. 2d Dist. Montgomery County 2016) (also pointing out that the rule does not provide for a request for findings of fact and conclusions of law like Civ. R. 53); Martin v. Dockter, 2018-Ohio-858, 2018 WL 1216633 (Ohio Ct. App. 10th Dist. Franklin County 2018); J.S. v. D.E., 2017-Ohio-7507, ¶ 13, 2017 WL 3971706 (Ohio Ct. App. 7th Dist. Mahoning County 2017).

[115]Martin v. Dockter, 2018-Ohio-858, 2018 WL 1216633 (Ohio Ct. App. 10th Dist. Franklin County 2018).

[116]Martin v. Dockter, 2018-Ohio-858, ¶ 9, 2018 WL 1216633 (Ohio Ct. App. 10th Dist. Franklin County 2018).

[117]Martin v. Dockter, 2018-Ohio-858, ¶ 9, 2018 WL 1216633 (Ohio Ct. App. 10th Dist. Franklin County 2018).

[118]Martin v. Dockter, 2018-Ohio-858, ¶ 9, 2018 WL 1216633 (Ohio Ct. App. 10th Dist. Franklin County 2018).

[119]Civ. R. 65.1(F)(3)(c)(i); see also J.S. v. D.E., 2017-Ohio-7507, 2017 WL 3971706 (Ohio Ct. App. 7th Dist. Mahoning County 2017).

[120]Civ. R. 65.1(F)(3)(c)(v).

[121]Civ. R. 65.1(F)(3)(c)(ii).

In order to make a determination regarding whether to adopt the magistrate's grant or denial of the CPO, the trial court must conduct a review to satisfy itself that there is no error of law or fact on the face of the order. According to *J.S. v D.E.*,[122] "[t]his review involves a review of the civil protection order signed by the magistrate after the full hearing, i.e., the petition, transcript of proceedings, or other documents are not reviewed by the trial court at this stage. We also note the petition is not evidence at the full hearing, and the court should not consider it in determining whether to grant the order."[123]

Q & A: What should an objection state?

According to *J.S. v D.E.*,[124], an objection should state the grounds for the objection. If a party proffers a general objection such as "I object to the protection order," they will have a difficult time meeting their burden of showing an error of law or other defect evident on the face of the order or that the evidence was insufficient to support the granting of the order or some other abuse of discretion. Additionally, the objections must be supported by a transcript of the evidence or an affidavit, if a transcript is not available.[125] Absent a transcript or affidavit, it is not the trial court's obligation to conduct a review of the items in the file such as the petition and ex parte order, where the objections do not refer the court to these items.[126]

Q & A: Must a trial court undertake a *de novo* review of a magistrate's decision under Civ. R. 65.1? (Although the protection order at issue was a CSPO, the same analysis clearly applies to DVCPOs)

In *J.P. v. T.H.*,[127] appellant assigned as error on appeal that the trial court failed to conduct a *de novo* review of the magistrate's decision denying the protection order issued after a full hearing. J.P. argued that the trial court adopted the magistrate's decision on the same day that the decision was issued and before the transcript was available. Since the trial court's decision to adopt the magistrate's decision could not have been based on any evidence, his due process rights were violated. [at ¶ 11.]

"Civ. R. 65.1(F)(3)(c)(ii) authorizes the trial court to adopt a magistrate's decision so long as there is "no error of law or other defect *on the face of the order*." (emphasis added). this language contemplates that pursuant to Civ. R. 65.1, the trial court need only review the order itself before deciding whether to adopt, reject or modify it. Nothing within the language of Civ. R. 65.1 prohibits a trial court from contemporaneously adopting a magistrate's decision." [at

[122] J.S. v. D.E., 2017-Ohio-7507, ¶ 14, 2017 WL 3971706 (Ohio Ct. App. 7th Dist. Mahoning County 2017).

[123] J.S. v. D.E., 2017-Ohio-7507, ¶ 14, 2017 WL 3971706 (Ohio Ct. App. 7th Dist. Mahoning County 2017) quoting Felton v. Felton, 79 Ohio St. 3d 34, 43, 1997-Ohio-302, 679 N.E.2d 672 (1997).

[124] J.S. v. D.E., 2017-Ohio-7507, 2017 WL 3971706 (Ohio Ct. App. 7th Dist. Mahoning County 2017).

[125] Civ. R. 65.1(F)(3)(d)(iv).

[126] J.S. v. D.E., 2017-Ohio-7507, ¶ 16, 2017 WL 3971706 (Ohio Ct. App. 7th Dist. Mahoning County 2017).

[127] J.P. v. T.H, 2016-Ohio-243, 2016 WL 363247 (Ohio Ct. App. 9th Dist. Lorain County 2016).

¶ 13.] In reliance on Civ. R. 65.1, the appellate court held that the trial court did not err in adopting the magistrate's decision on the same day and that a transcript was not necessary for that review. Implied in this decision is that a *de novo* review is not required. [see also C.Q. v. P.S., 2016-Ohio-4988, 2016 WL 3881115 (Ohio Ct. App. 9th Dist. Medina County 2016).]

Q & A: Can Civ. R. 53 ever be used by a court when considering any issues regarding a CSPO?

According to Civ. R. 65.1(A), "[t]he provisions of this rule apply to special statutory proceedings under RC 3113.31, RC 2151.34 and RC 2903.214 providing for domestic violence, stalking and sexually oriented offense civil protection orders, shall be interpreted and applied in a manner consistent with the intent and purposes of those protection order statutes, and supersede and make inapplicable in such proceedings the provisions of any other rules of civil procedure to the extent that such application is inconsistent with the provisions of this rule."[128]

In *Cutler o.b.o. Pavey v. Reed,*[129] the trial court issued a decision sustaining appellant's objections and remanding the case back to the magistrate for the purpose of making findings. Appellant then filed a motion to remove the magistrate from the proceedings due to the magistrate's alleged "bias and prejudice." After denying the motion, the magistrate issued an amended decision with findings and again appellant objected. This objection was denied and the trial court adopted the granting of the CSPO.

Appellant appealed on the ground that the court erred by denying appellant's motion to remove the magistrate. The appellate court first pointed out that "[c]ivil protection orders are generally governed by Civ. R. 65.1." Wulf v. Opp, 2015-Ohio-3285, ¶ 16, 2015 WL 4878495 (Ohio Ct. App. 12th Dist. Clermont County 2015). "That rule, however, does not affect the applicability of Civ. R. 53(D)(6) to the present matter." J.B. v. Harford, 2015-Ohio-13, ¶ 36, 2015 WL 82527 (Ohio Ct. App. 9th Dist. Summit County 2015). Pursuant to Civ. R. 53(D)(6), "disqualification of a magistrate for bias or other cause is within the discretion of the court and may be sought by motion filed with the court."[130] In affirming the trial court, the appellate court determined that, even under a Civ. R. 65.1(F)(3)(d)(iii) analysis, a trial court's review of a magistrate's decision to grant or deny a CSPO is based upon whether "the credible evidence of record is insufficient to support the grant or denial of the protection order. Our review on appeal of the granting or denial of a civil stalking protection order is 'whether there was sufficient credible evidence to prove by a preponderance of the evidence that the petitioner was entitled to relief.'" Fouch v.

[128]Martin v. Dockter, 2018-Ohio-858, 2018 WL 1216633 (Ohio Ct. App. 10th Dist. Franklin County 2018); but see L.L. v. R.B., 2017-Ohio-7553, 2017 WL 3980553 (Ohio Ct. App. 5th Dist. Guernsey County 2017) (in which court erroneously applied Civ. R. 53, rather than Civ. R. 65.1).]

[129]Cutler v. Reed, 2016-Ohio-1151, 2016 WL 1090783 (Ohio Ct. App. 12th Dist. Butler County 2016).

[130]Cutler v. Reed, 2016-Ohio-1151, 2016 WL 1090783, ¶ 19 (Ohio Ct. App. 12th Dist. Butler County 2016).

Pennington, 2012-Ohio-3536, 2012 WL 3158730, ¶ 9 (Ohio Ct. App. 12th Dist. Clermont County 2012)[131]

Although Civ. R. 65.1 applies to civil protection order proceedings, other civil rules may also be applicable.

Q & A: Is an appeal taken from the trial court's adoption or rejection of the magistrate's decision?

In *Justice v. Shell*,[132] the Summit County Court of Appeals held that "[w]hen appealing from a trial court's order adopting a magistrate's decision, 'any claim of trial court error must be based upon the actions of the trial court,' not the magistrate."[133]

The court further stated that "[t]he standards for appellate review do not apply to the trial court's acceptance or rejection of the magistrate's findings or proposed decision."[134] Instead, the proper inquiry [on appeal] is whether the trial court abused its discretion by overruling the objections to the magistrate's decision.[135] Because Shell did not argue that the trial court abused its discretion in adopting the magistrate's decision, the appellate court chose not to address the assignments of error.

Q & A: Can the trier of fact extend an ex parte civil stalking protection order an additional four months for a second fact hearing after it determined that there was insufficient evidence presented by the petitioner after a fact hearing to issue a permanent protection order?

Not according to the Hamilton County Court of Appeals. In *Jones v. Donaldson*,[136] petitioner sought a civil protection order under R.C. 2903.214. Despite finding that there was insufficient evidence to issue the CPO, the magistrate continued the case for four months for a second fact hearing and ordered the original ex parte order to remain in effect until then.

On appeal, appellant asserted that the magistrate had no authority to continue the ex parte CPO in effect for a second full hearing once it determined that there was insufficient evidence to grant the CPO after the first full hearing. Appellant argued that "once the magistrate had found that there was inadequate evidence to support a finding that he had engaged in conduct in violation of the civil stalking stat-

[131]Cutler v. Reed, 2016-Ohio-1151, 2016 WL 1090783, ¶ 22 n.1 (Ohio Ct. App. 12th Dist. Butler County 2016).

[132]Justice v. Schell, 2018-Ohio-1177, 2018 WL 1569809 (Ohio Ct. App. 9th Dist. Summit County 2018).

[133]Justice v. Schell, 2018-Ohio-1177, ¶ 6, 2018 WL 1569809 (Ohio Ct. App. 9th Dist. Summit County 2018); citing J.P. v. T.H, 2016-Ohio-243, ¶ 28, 2016 WL 363247 (Ohio Ct. App. 9th Dist. Lorain County 2016), quoting Citibank (South Dakota) v. Masters, 2008-Ohio-1323, ¶ 9, 2008 WL 754873 (Ohio Ct. App. 9th Dist. Medina County 2008.

[134]Justice v. Schell, 2018-Ohio-1177, ¶ 6, 2018 WL 1569809 (Ohio Ct. App. 9th Dist. Summit County 2018) citing Mealey v. Mealey, 1996 WL 233491 (Ohio Ct. App. 9th Dist. Wayne County 1996).

[135]Justice v. Schell, 2018-Ohio-1177, ¶ 6, 2018 WL 1569809 (Ohio Ct. App. 9th Dist. Summit County 2018).

[136]Jones v. Donaldson, 2010-Ohio-3961, 2010 WL 3328026 (Ohio Ct. App. 1st Dist. Hamilton County 2010).

ute, the magistrate had no option but to vacate the temporary ex parte CSPO and dismiss Jones's petition."[137]

The appellate court determined that while a protection order may be continued for service, counsel, by agreement or other good cause, the statute doesn't permit a court "to extend the life of an ex parte CSPO for an additional full hearing once a petitioner has been afforded an opportunity to put forth evidence and testimony at the first full hearing and the petitioner is unable to meet the burden of proof for granting a CSPO."[138] Because the magistrate did not vacate the ex parte order and dismiss the petition, the Hamilton County Court of Appeals sustained the assignment and reversed judgment.

Q & A: Must a civil stalking protection order issued under R.C. 2903.214 be requested ex parte?

No. R.C. 2903.214 does not require that a petitioner request an ex parte civil protection order. R.C. 2903.214(D)(3) provides that "[i]f a petitioner who files a petition pursuant to this section does not request an ex parte order, or if a person requests an ex parte order but the court does not issue an ex parte order after an ex parte hearing, the court shall proceed as in a normal civil action and grant a full hearing on the matter." Additionally, R.C. 2903.214(G) states that any proceeding under this section shall be conducted in accordance with the Rules of Civil Procedure.

However, service of the petition is a requirement. Absent service of the petition and an evidentiary hearing on the matter, there is no meaningful opportunity to be heard. Without a meaningful opportunity to be heard, a violation of due process results.[139]

Q & A: Can an ex parte temporary CSPO be appealed?

No. In *Preston v. Shutway*,[140] the respondent challenged the issuance of the temporary ex parte civil stalking protection order. The appellate court pointed to RC 2903.214(G) which articulates that "[a]n order issued under this section, other than an ex parte order, that grants a protection order or approves a consent agreement, that refuses to grant a protection order or approve a consent agreement . . . is a final appealable order." Thus, a temporary ex parte protection order is not a final appealable order.

However, in *Brown v. Grauman*,[141] the Second District Court of Appeals considered the concept of mootness as another legal rationale for determining whether an ex parte order can be appealed. The same appellate court considered an implied challenge by an appellant regarding the trial court's issuance of the ex parte civil protection order. In its ruling, the appellate court noted that the trial court had

---

[137] Jones v. Donaldson, 2010-Ohio-3961, 2010 WL 3328026, *1 (Ohio Ct. App. 1st Dist. Hamilton County 2010).

[138] Jones v. Donaldson, 2010-Ohio-3961, 2010 WL 3328026, *2 (Ohio Ct. App. 1st Dist. Hamilton County 2010).

[139] See Rauser v. Ghaster, 2011-Ohio-609, 2011 WL 486503 (Ohio Ct. App. 8th Dist. Cuyahoga County 2011).

[140] Preston v. Shutway, 2013-Ohio-185, 986 N.E.2d 584 (Ohio Ct. App. 2d Dist. Champaign County 2013).

[141] Brown v. Grauman, 2013-Ohio-4814, 2013 WL 5914961 (Ohio Ct. App. 2d Dist. Champaign County 2013).

issued a CPO after a full hearing. "In light of the court's finding, after a full hearing, that a civil protection order was warranted, Grauman's challenge to the ex parte order is moot."[142]

Of significance is that the Second District Court of Appeals has now considered two legal rationales for not appealing an ex parte order. The *Preston* court focused its reasoning on the concept of a final appealable order pursuant to R.C. 2903.214(G), while the *Brown* court, instead, focused on the concept of mootness. The question that appears to remain unanswered by the *Brown* court is whether the denial of a civil protection order issued after a full hearing also renders the ex parte order moot?

Q & A: Must the respondent be served before a full hearing civil stalking protection order can be granted?[143]

In a twist on the service theme, the Eighth District Court of Appeals addressed this issue in *Jones v. Jordan*.[144] In that case, the respondent was personally served four hours after the scheduled hearing. On appeal, the appellant alleged that the trial court erred when it granted appellee's CSPO without providing her proper notice of said hearing.

The appellate court agreed with appellant and reversed the trial court decision. The Court focused on personal jurisdiction and determined that the trial court did not have jurisdiction over the appellant. The court noted that unlike cases where one fails to object, in this case, the appellant challenged personal jurisdiction. Accordingly, it was then up to the trial court to resolve the matter of personal jurisdiction. Since the issue was not resolved by the trial court, there was no jurisdiction over appellant. Absent personal jurisdiction over appellant, the CSPO was void.

Q & A: Must the respondent be personally served with both the order and petition before a hearing may be had?[145]

In *Vance v. Nichols*,[146] the appellant was served with the protection order, but argued that she had not been served with the Petition for CSPO. She claimed that service of the order alone did not confer

---

[142] Brown v. Grauman, 2013-Ohio-4814, 2013 WL 5914961, ¶ 10 (Ohio Ct. App. 2d Dist. Champaign County 2013), citing Preston v. Shutway, 2013-Ohio-185, 986 N.E.2d 584 (Ohio Ct. App. 2d Dist. Champaign County 2013) (trial court's order after a full hearing superseded the ex parte order); Daugherty v. Daugherty, 2012-Ohio-1520, 2012 WL 1139129 (Ohio Ct. App. 4th Dist. Hocking County 2012) (trial court's final domestic violence civil protection order superseded prior ex parte order, rendering any claim regarding the ex parte order moot); Luttrell v. Younce, 2011-Ohio-4458, 2011 WL 3890292, ¶ 35 (Ohio Ct. App. 2d Dist. Miami County 2011) (ex parte CPO merges into final CPO); Zawrotuk v. Zawrotuk, 2014-Ohio-5225, 2014 WL 6641772 (Ohio Ct. App. 7th Dist. Mahoning County 2014) (noting that an issue with an ex parte order does not invalidate a protection order issued after a full hearing and the final protection order supersedes an ex parte order).

[143] See State v. Smith, 136 Ohio St. 3d 1, 2013-Ohio-1698, 989 N.E.2d 972 (2013); see also Text § 13:3; Civ. R. 65.1(C).

[144] Jones v. Jordan, 2007-Ohio-2519, 2007 WL 1508255 (Ohio Ct. App. 8th Dist. Cuyahoga County 2007).

[145] See Civ. R. 65.1(C) regarding service of both an ex parte CPO and a CPO issued after a full hearing; see also Text §§ 11:11, 12:8.

[146] Vance v. Nichols, 2007-Ohio-3819, 2007 WL 2164162 (Ohio Ct. App. 2d Dist. Darke County 2007).

personal jurisdiction over her. However, she did file a Motion to Continue the hearing.

The Court of Appeals held that because she had filed a continuance motion, she consented to the court's personal jurisdiction over her. This is important because the court also pointed out that "[l]itigants who choose to proceed pro se are presumed to know the law and correct procedure and are held to the same standard as other litigants."[147] "A litigant proceeding pro se 'cannot expect or demand special treatment from the judge, who is to sit as an impartial arbiter.' "[148]

The Court also mentioned that the file contained a Request for Service of both the petition and the order and that the return receipt indicated that the correspondence was signed by "other." However, the Court did not address that issue and reversed the trial court for failing to grant the continuance.

Q & A: Is discovery permitted in anticipation of a full hearing under R.C. 2903.214?[149]

In *Gussler v. Morris*,[150] the respondent propounded interrogatories and a request for admissions to the petitioner. Although she objected to a deposition, her objection was denied. The petitioner never appealed the issue of whether discovery is appropriate for a civil protection order. Because it was never addressed, the implication is that discovery is appropriate in Ross County.[151]

Q & A: Where the parties enter into a settlement agreement at the full hearing, thereby dismissing the SCPO, does the trial court retain jurisdiction to entertain a motion to show cause for contempt?

According to *Henneke v. Glisson*,[152] a trial court does not lose jurisdiction over the case, and as such, the finding of contempt was not error.

In that case, appellee sought a SCPO which was denied at the ex parte level. At the full hearing, the parties entered into a settlement agreement and the SCPO was dismissed. The agreement ordered both parties restrained from harassing or entering the premises of the

[147]Vance v. Nichols, 2007-Ohio-3819, 2007 WL 2164162, *2 (Ohio Ct. App. 2d Dist. Darke County 2007), quoting Yocum v. Means, 2002-Ohio-3803, 2002 WL 1729892 (Ohio Ct. App. 2d Dist. Darke County 2002); see also Dunina v. Stemple, 2007-Ohio-4719, 2007 WL 2684988 (Ohio Ct. App. 2d Dist. Miami County 2007).

[148]Gaietto v. Noveck, 2008-Ohio-519, 2008 WL 351460, *2 (Ohio Ct. App. 3d Dist. Seneca County 2008), quoting Yocum v. Means, 2002-Ohio-3803, 2002 WL 1729892, *3 (Ohio Ct. App. 2d Dist. Darke County 2002).

[149]See Civ. R. 65.1(D) regarding discovery; see also Text § 12:5. N.P. v. T.N., 2018-Ohio-2647, 2018 WL 3302173 (Ohio Ct. App. 8th Dist. Cuyahoga County 2018) (relying on RC 2903.214(G) to determine that discovery is permitted).

[150]Gussler v. Morris, 2006-Ohio-6627, 2006 WL 3691200 (Ohio Ct. App. 4th Dist. Ross County 2006).

[151]Text § 12:5, Full hearing—Discovery issues; see Civ. R. 65.1(D); Text § 12:5.

[152]Henneke v. Glisson, 2008-Ohio-6759, 2008 WL 5329993 (Ohio Ct. App. 12th Dist. Clermont County 2008) (abrogated by, Infinite Security Solutions, L.L.C. v. Karam Properties, II, Ltd., 143 Ohio St. 3d 346, 2015-Ohio-1101, 37 N.E.3d 1211 (2015)) (abrogating court finding trial court has jurisdiction to enforce settlement agreement after case has been dismissed only if the dismissal entry incorporated terms of the agreement or expressly stated that court retained jurisdiction to enforce the agreement).

other. The agreement also contained a provision that provided the trial court with continuing jurisdiction to entertain contempt violations of the agreement.[153]

In response to appellant's argument that the trial court lost its jurisdiction upon dismissing the SCPO, the appellate court found that because the parties clearly consented to the trial court's retaining jurisdiction over the issue of violations and enforcing the agreement, the agreement was a binding contract. This binding agreement between the parties specifically obligated the parties to refrain from violating its terms and gave the trial court continuing jurisdiction for the purpose of entertaining motions for contempt.[154]

Q & A: Can a court enforce an agreement entered into in a civil stalking protection order proceeding in which the CSPO has expired or is dismissed at the full hearing due to a signed agreement? What is the authority to enforce such an order?

No, a court has the discretion not to enforce an agreement where the terms or existence of the agreement is legitimately disputed. In *Wilson v. Rowe,*[155] appellant argued on appeal against the issuance of a civil stalking protection order which appellee had filed pro se. At the full hearing, the appellant's counsel presented the court with a signed agreement that allegedly resolved the matter without a hearing. By the time of the full hearing the ex parte order had expired.

The trial court pointed out that the agreement was unenforceable since there was no longer a valid protection order in place whereupon counsel argued that the parties could again file protections orders if the agreement was breached.[156] The trial court was concerned for appellees and would not accept the settlement agreement; rather it continued the case, extended the ex parte order and proceeded to full hearing, where it granted the CSPO.

On appeal, the appellant argued that the trial court erred when it rejected the settlement agreement. The appellate court affirmed the trial court and stated that ". . . substantively, we find that the trial court did not err in refusing to enforce the agreement."[157] While it is in the discretion of the trial court to encourage settlements to prevent litigation, a judge cannot force parties into settlement.[158] In this case,

[153]See also Infinite Security Solutions, L.L.C. v. Karam Properties, II, Ltd., 143 Ohio St. 3d 346, 354–55, 2015-Ohio-1101, ¶ 34, 37 N.E.3d 1211, 1220 (2015)(trial court had jurisdiction to enforce settlement agreement after case has been dismissed only if dismissal entry incorporated terms of agreement or expressly stated that court retained jurisdiction to enforce agreement).

[154]Henneke v. Glisson, 2008-Ohio-6759, 2008 WL 5329993, *3 (Ohio Ct. App. 12th Dist. Clermont County 2008) (abrogated by, Infinite Security Solutions, L.L.C. v. Karam Properties, II, Ltd., 143 Ohio St. 3d 346, 2015-Ohio-1101, 37 N.E.3d 1211 (2015)).

[155]Wilson v. Rowe, 2016-Ohio-523, 2016 WL 561527 (Ohio Ct. App. 5th Dist. Knox County 2016).

[156]Wilson v. Rowe, 2016-Ohio-523, 2016 WL 561527, ¶ 17 (Ohio Ct. App. 5th Dist. Knox County 2016).

[157]Wilson v. Rowe, 2016-Ohio-523, 2016 WL 561527, ¶ 38 (Ohio Ct. App. 5th Dist. Knox County 2016).

[158]Wilson v. Rowe, 2016-Ohio-523, 2016 WL 561527, ¶ 39 (Ohio Ct. App. 5th Dist. Knox County 2016).

the terms of the agreement were not certain or clear. Moreover, the trial court was uncomfortable with the terms of the settlement because it was unenforceable.

It is significant that the appellate court acknowledged that the only way to enforce the order would be for appellees to file a new petition for protection order. It is best practice for petitioners not to agree to a settlement agreement that, at its core, requires a dismissal of the protection order. Once the protection order is dismissed, the court has no jurisdiction to enforce the agreement; it is an unenforceable agreement and the remedy for its violation is the filing of a new protection order.

Q & A: Where the parties agree to the terms of the civil stalking protection order, can they also agree that the appropriate remedy for a violation is a motion for contempt?

No. In *State v. Myers*,[159] the defendant was convicted for violating a civil protection order issued pursuant to R.C. 2903.214. One of the terms ordered both parties not to contact each other and provided a procedure should they attend common classes or the same meetings of 3 mutual organizations. The order also provided that should the order be violated, contempt of court before the assigned judge would be the appropriate remedy. The defendant violated the civil protection order and a complaint was filed in Franklin County Municipal Court.

On appeal, defendant argued that the court lacked jurisdiction to hear the case because the parties previously agreed that contempt of court would be the remedy for a violation of the protection order. A reading of the applicable statutory provision, R.C. 2903.214(K)(1), indicates that a party is free to choose whether to impose criminal prosecution or contempt sanctions for the violation of the civil protection order. R.C. 2903.214(K)(2) provides that "[t]he punishment of a person for contempt of court for violation of a protection order issued under this section does not bar criminal prosecution of the person for a violation of section 2919.27 of the Revised Code." The remedies are not mutually exclusive. Inserting an impermissible "and" or an "or" would be contrary to the rules of statutory construction and to the intent of the General Assembly.[160]

In affirming the trial court, the appellate court held that the municipal court had subject matter jurisdiction over a defendant's prosecution for violating a protection order under R.C. 2919.27, notwithstanding any agreement between the respondent and the person who obtained the order.[161] Where the defendant commits a violation within a municipal court's territorial limits, "that municipal court has jurisdiction of * * * the violation of any misdemeanor committed within the limits of its territory."[162]

Q & A: For purposes of a stalking civil protection order under R.C. 2903.214, how does the court define a full hearing?

---

[159] State v. Myers, 2009-Ohio-4659, 2009 WL 2872977 (Ohio Ct. App. 10th Dist. Franklin County 2009).

[160] Myers at *3.

[161] At syllabus.

[162] At syllabus and *3.

At least one court has addressed this issue. In *Solon v. Geiger*,[163] appellant contends that the trial court committed error in failing to provide her an opportunity to cross-examine witnesses.[164] The appellate court relied on other court decisions, which have found that a full hearing grants to a defendant the right to present evidence as well as a reasonable opportunity to know the claims of an opposing party and meet them. "A full hearing is one where ample opportunity is afforded to all parties to make, by evidence and argument, a showing fairly adequate to establish the propriety or impropriety of the step asked to be taken."[165]

The Cuyahoga County Court of Appeals held that where a protection order is contested, evidence must be presented that includes both direct and rebuttal evidence as well as arguments.[166] In reversing the trial court, the appellate court pointed out that where a respondent is denied an opportunity to cross examine a party or present rebuttal evidence, he/she has been denied a full hearing and an opportunity to be heard consistent with due process.[167]

Q & A: Can a civil stalking protection order be modified or terminated?

Unlike RC 3113.31(E)(8), RC 2903.214 does not specifically provide for the modification or termination of a civil stalking protection order. When RC 3113.31 was amended to permit both modifications and terminations it was thought that since RC 2903.214 applied primarily to non-family or household member relationships (like strangers), requests for modifications or terminations of civil stalking protection orders might put a petitioner at a greater risk of harm especially when the modification or termination was sought by a respondent.

However, the Fifth District Court of Appeals in *Prostejovsky v. Prostejovsky*,[168] determined that there were several mechanisms to accomplish this.

---

[163] Solon v. Geiger, 2006-Ohio-6032, 2006 WL 3317920 (Ohio Ct. App. 8th Dist. Cuyahoga County 2006).

[164] See also Dupal v. Sommer, 2009-Ohio-5791, 2009 WL 3600358 (Ohio Ct. App. 5th Dist. Stark County 2009) (noting that a full hearing includes the right to cross examine witnesses).

[165] Solon v. Geiger, 2006-Ohio-6032, 2006 WL 3317920, *2 (Ohio Ct. App. 8th Dist. Cuyahoga County 2006); see also Gaietto v. Noveck, 2008-Ohio-519, 2008 WL 351460 (Ohio Ct. App. 3d Dist. Seneca County 2008).

[166] Solon v. Geiger, 2006-Ohio-6032, 2006 WL 3317920, *2 (Ohio Ct. App. 8th Dist. Cuyahoga County 2006), citing Deacon v. Landers, 68 Ohio App. 3d 26, 29-30, 587 N.E.2d 395, 398 (4th Dist. Ross County 1990) (referring to a CPO full hearing under R.C. 3113.31). See also Osunde v. Ijeweme, 2013-Ohio-1207, 2013 WL 1286984 (Ohio Ct. App. 10th Dist. Franklin County 2013) (in which magistrate reviewed proffered evidence, comprised of a CD and flash drive, and determined it wasn't relevant; thus, concluding that respondent was provided with a full hearing).

[167] M.H. v. J.P., 2017-Ohio-33, 2017 WL 74862 (Ohio Ct. App. 9th Dist. Lorain County 2017) (sustained objection of appellant where trial court prevented appellant from presenting a defense by stopping hearing because appellant was making "a mockery" out of the proceedings).

[168] Prostejovsky v. Prostejovsky, 2007-Ohio-5743, 2007 WL 3119724 (Ohio Ct. App. 5th Dist. Ashland County 2007); Hayberg v. Tamburello, 2013-Ohio-3451, 2013 WL 4033623 (Ohio Ct. App. 5th Dist. Tuscarawas County 2013) (noting that any motion for termination of a CSPO must be reviewed by an abuse of discretion standard). See also Delaine v. Smith, 2016-Ohio-5250, 2016 WL 4141753 (Ohio Ct. App. 8th Dist.

After the trial court granted appellee a civil stalking protection order, the appellant filed a Motion to Modify the Civil Protection Order asking that it be modified from 5 years to 3 years because the parties were getting along or in the alternative, terminating the order so that he could go hunting with his sons.

The magistrate, after an evidentiary hearing on the matter, recommended that appellant's motion be overruled because the appellee opposed the motion and because the order was issued due to his conduct before the order not his post-CPO behavior. The Magistrate, in his decision, stated that "[h]is good behavior subsequent to the issuance of the Order could be construed to be a conscious effort by Respondent to follow the Order of the Court. While the Court commends respondent for his lawful conduct, the Court cannot find that conduct alone as a reason to dismiss a Civil Protection Order before its termination date."[169]

Ruling on appellant's objections, the trial court denied the Motion to Modify on grounds that it did not have jurisdiction to modify the order and no section of RC 2903.214 provided such recourse. However, it also found that the CSPO could be modified or vacated pursuant to Civ. R. 60(B),[170] but not in this case as appellant had not established grounds under the rule.

On appeal, the appellant argued that the trial court erred in holding that it had no jurisdiction to modify the CSPO. The Ashland County Court of Appeals agreed that the trial court had jurisdiction to modify the order but that its reliance on Civ. R. 60(B) did not result in prejudicial error.[171]

Cuyahoga County 2016).

[169]Prostejovsky v. Prostejovsky, 2007-Ohio-5743, 2007 WL 3119724, *2 (Ohio Ct. App. 5th Dist. Ashland County 2007).

[170]See Jones v. Hunter, 2009-Ohio-917, 2009 WL 499319, *2 (Ohio Ct. App. 11th Dist. Portage County 2009) (holding that, absent an agreement to modify and acknowledging that R.C. 2903.214 does not provide for a modification, a mutual SCPO is still subject to modification or termination "if the movant shows that the original circumstances have materially changed and it is no longer equitable for the order to continue"; N.S. v. S.B., 2017-Ohio-1556, 2017 WL 1507322 (Ohio Ct. App. 8th Dist. Cuyahoga County 2017), as amended, (Aug. 22, 2017) (finding that "[i]n denying the motion, the trial court implicitly determined that the parties failed to establish any grounds for relief under Civ. R. 60(B), there was no material change in the original circumstances that caused the order to be issued, and prospective application of the protection order would not be inequitable."; quoting Prostejovsky v. Prostejovsky, 2007-Ohio-5743, 2007 WL 3119724 (Ohio Ct. App. 5th Dist. Ashland County 2007). See also Oddo v. Spencer, 2011-Ohio-4073, 2011 WL 3587436 (Ohio Ct. App. 5th Dist. Stark County 2011) (noting that a party cannot dismiss an already existing civil protection order under Civ. R. 41 and that only the court had the ability to terminate the protection order); Bowman v. Leisz, 2014-Ohio-4763, 2014 WL 5422556 (Ohio Ct. App. 12th Dist. Warren County 2014) (discussing the procedural aspects of Civ. R. 60(B)); Roxey v. Smallwood, 2016-Ohio-720, 2016 WL 763121 (Ohio Ct. App. 5th Dist. Fairfield County 2016); Delaine v. Smith, 2016-Ohio-5250, 2016 WL 4141753 (Ohio Ct. App. 8th Dist. Cuyahoga County 2016); T.D. v. C.N., 2018-Ohio-1840, ¶ 41, 2018 WL 2148447 (Ohio Ct. App. 8th Dist. Cuyahoga County 2018) (noting that, on appeal, "we review for an abuse of discretion.")..

[171]See also Dickson v. Ball, 2006-Ohio-3436, 2006 WL 1817265 (Ohio Ct. App. 10th Dist. Franklin County 2006).

The court also discussed the holding of *Signer v. Signer*,[172] wherein the Eighth District appellate court held the trial court had no authority to modify a civil protection order issued under R.C. 3113.31. It then stated that like the version of R.C. 3113.31 which was in effect at the time of *Signer*, R.C. 2903.214 does not provide the trial court with express statutory authority to modify or vacate a protection order.[173] However, despite its analysis of *Signer*, a civil protection order issued under R.C. 2903.214 could be modified or vacated, because such an order is a permanent injunction.

The Court then noted that "[g]enerally, the trial court has the authority to modify or vacate a permanent injunction if the original conditions have materially changed and it is no longer equitable for the injunction to continue."[174] It held that ". . . the trial court was incorrect in concluding that the civil protection stalking order may only be modified or vacated pursuant to Civ. R. 60(B).[175] We conclude that a court may modify or vacate a civil protection stalking order if the movant shows that the original circumstances have materially changed and it is no longer equitable for the order to continue."[176] "Civil. R. 60(B) provides an adequate and appropriate vehicle for the vacation of all or part of an R.C. 2903.214 civil stalking protection order upon a change of material circumstances that no longer makes the order equitable."[177]

In affirming the lower court decision, the Ashland appellate court held that there was no abuse of discretion or prejudicial error on the part of the trial court because appellant had not established or alleged any ground for vacating or modifying the protection order. Compliance with the CSPO as a reason for a modification or dismissal of the order did not fall within the provisions of Civ. R. 60(B). Moreover, because the CSPO was issued as a result of appellant's longstanding problem with anger management, compliance with the order was not sufficient to demonstrate a material change of circumstances.[178]

In a concurring opinion, Judge Hoffman questioned whether a CSPO is analogous to a permanent injunction so as to render it always subject to modification or vacation. "Nevertheless, I find the trial court had jurisdiction to modify or terminate the order without Appel-

[172]Signer v. Signer, 2006-Ohio-3580, 2006 WL 1918115 (Ohio Ct. App. 8th Dist. Cuyahoga County 2006).

[173]But see recently amended R.C. 3113.31(E)(3)(a) and R.C. 3113.31(E)(8), which now permits modifications and terminations of domestic violence civil protection orders; Text § 12:25.

[174]Signer v. Signer, 2006-Ohio-3580, 2006 WL 1918115, *4 (Ohio Ct. App. 8th Dist. Cuyahoga County 2006).

[175]See Leibold v. Hiddens, 2007-Ohio-2972, 2007 WL 1721347 (Ohio Ct. App. 2d Dist. Montgomery County 2007) (wherein the appellate court was not concerned with the trial court's reliance on Civ. R. 60(B) as a vehicle to vacate a CSPO.).

[176]Signer v. Signer, 2006-Ohio-3580, 2006 WL 1918115, *4 (Ohio Ct. App. 8th Dist. Cuyahoga County 2006); see also Prostejovsky v. Prostejovsky, 2007-Ohio-5743, 2007 WL 3119724 (Ohio Ct. App. 5th Dist. Ashland County 2007).

[177]Signer v. Signer, 2006-Ohio-3580, 2006 WL 1918115, *4 (Ohio Ct. App. 8th Dist. Cuyahoga County 2006), relying on Civ. R. 60(B)(4) and (5).

[178]Signer v. Signer, 2006-Ohio-3580, 2006 WL 1918115, *5 (Ohio Ct. App. 8th Dist. Cuyahoga County 2006).

lant having pursued and/or satisfied the standard set forth in Civ. R. 60(B). Within the four corners of the order, the court retained the authority to change the order. Appellee did not challenge whether the trial court could retain jurisdiction to change the order via appeal."[179]

Of significance is that the appellate court relied on the Supreme Court forms which provided that in both the body of the order and in the Warning Page, only a court can change the CSPO, and if there is a reason why an order must be changed, a person must petition the court.[180]

However, the importance of this decision cannot be understated. It first determined that a Motion for Relief from Judgment under Civ. R. 60(B) is merely one way to modify or terminate a CSPO. An alternate method is under the court's inherent authority to modify or terminate a CSPO because it is a permanent injunction necessitating the need for the movant to file a motion showing that the original circumstances have materially changed such that it is no longer equitable for the order to continue.[181]

Likewise, in *Cipriani v. Ehlert*,[182] petitioner-appellant obtained a CSPO against the boyfriend of his estranged wife. The minor child of the parties was added to the order as a protected party.

Approximately, 8 months later, respondent-appellee sought to modify the CSPO to remove the child from the order which request was granted. On appeal, appellant alleged that the trial court abused its discretion in granting the motion to modify to remove the minor child as a protected party.

The appellate court began its analysis by examining the grounds for which a person may seek a CSPO. The court then discussed that a person may modify a CSPO if they show, by a preponderance of the evidence, that the original circumstances have materially changed and it is no longer equitable for the order to remain in effect.[183] "[T]he court cannot be required to disregard significant changes in law or facts if it is 'satisfied that what it is has been doing has turned through changing circumstances into an instrument of wrong.' "[184]

At the hearing, the child's mother testified she has had to live with

[179]Signer v. Signer, 2006-Ohio-3580, 2006 WL 1918115, *5 (Ohio Ct. App. 8th Dist. Cuyahoga County 2006).

[180]See Sup. R. Form 10.03-F; 10.03-H.

[181]Reising v. Reising, 2017-Ohio-2859, 2017 WL 2241670 (Ohio Ct. App. 8th Dist. Cuyahoga County 2017); N.S. v. S.B., 2017-Ohio-1556, 2017 WL 1507322 (Ohio Ct. App. 8th Dist. Cuyahoga County 2017), as amended, (Aug. 22, 2017) (finding that although there is no section of RC 2903.214 that provides for a modification of a CSPO, a trial court may review an order made under this statute); T.D. v. C.N., 2018-Ohio-1840, ¶ 41, 2018 WL 2148447 (Ohio Ct. App. 8th Dist. Cuyahoga County 2018).

[182]Cipriani v. Ehlert, 2016-Ohio-5840, 2016 WL 4978558 (Ohio Ct. App. 8th Dist. Cuyahoga County 2016).

[183]Cipriani v. Ehlert, 2016-Ohio-5840, ¶ 7, 2016 WL 4978558 (Ohio Ct. App. 8th Dist. Cuyahoga County 2016), citing, Prostejovsky v. Prostejovsky, 2007-Ohio-5743, ¶ 26, 2007 WL 3119724 (Ohio Ct. App. 5th Dist. Ashland County 2007).

[184]Prostejovsky v. Prostejovsky, 2007-Ohio-5743, ¶ 25, 2007 WL 3119724 (Ohio Ct. App. 5th Dist. Ashland County 2007), quoting System Federation No. 91, Ry. Emp. Dept., AFL-CIO v. Wright, 364 U.S. 642, 647, 81 S. Ct. 368, 5 L. Ed. 2d 349, 47 L.R.R.M. (BNA) 2388, 41 Lab. Cas. (CCH) P 16718 (1961), quoting U.S. v. Swift & Co., 286 U.S. 106, 114–115, 52 S. Ct. 460, 76 L. Ed. 999 (1932).

the respondent and his mother, making compliance with the protection order difficult, to wit: she had to make various additional living accommodations so that the child would not be in the presence of respondent, that respondent's mother helped with the care of the child and she has had to remove the child from the home when respondent was expected, that respondent provided monetary support for her and the child and that she had no concerns that he would harm the child. "At the conclusion of the hearing, the trial court reminded the parties that the issue at hand is the CSPO, which is issued for the purposes of separating people before something happens; the issue is not "the big life or death issues of divorce court." The court also noted that protection orders should not be used as "new weapons in an ongoing family dispute." In that context, the court stated that the minor child was added to the protection order prior to a full hearing, and the court would have been within its rights to decline to issue the order as it related to the child."[185] The trial court further went on to say that the order was impracticable from the start as it had forced the wife and child to try to find a place to live and that the CSPO was a barrier to the mother and child living in the same house with respondent.[186]

Based on the standard of proof and the record, the appellate court determined that the trial court did not err in removing the child from the order as the current living accommodations had become a hardship in light of the effort to comply with the order. Thus, the circumstances had materially changed and it was no longer equitable for the child to continue to be named as a protected party on the CSPO.

Q & A: What is the standard of proof (burden of persuasion) for trial courts to apply when ruling on motions to modify or terminate civil stalking protection orders?

In *Reising v. Reising*,[187] appellant had filed a motion to terminate the CSPO arguing that the original circumstances that led up to the issuance of the CSPO had materially changed and that the order was no longer equitable. The trial court denied appellant's motion to terminate the CSPO indicating that appellant failed to show by "clear and convincing" evidence that the protection order should be terminated.

The appellate court considered other Eighth District appellate decisions which provided guidance on the standard of proof at the trial court level. For example, in *Delanie v. Smith*,[188] the trial court applied a preponderance of the evidence standard when it ruled on the motion to terminate the protection order. In *Schneider v. Razek*,[189] the trial court applied a preponderance of the evidence standard in determin-

[185] Cipriani v. Ehlert, 2016-Ohio-5840, ¶ 13, 2016 WL 4978558 (Ohio Ct. App. 8th Dist. Cuyahoga County 2016).

[186] Cipriani v. Ehlert, 2016-Ohio-5840, ¶ 14, 2016 WL 4978558 (Ohio Ct. App. 8th Dist. Cuyahoga County 2016) .

[187] Reising v. Reising, 2017-Ohio-2859, 2017 WL 2241670 (Ohio Ct. App. 8th Dist. Cuyahoga County 2017).

[188] Delaine v. Smith, 2016-Ohio-5250, 2016 WL 4141753 (Ohio Ct. App. 8th Dist. Cuyahoga County 2016).

[189] Schneider v. Razek, 2015-Ohio-410, 28 N.E.3d 591 (Ohio Ct. App. 8th Dist. Cuyahoga County 2015).

ing whether to modify or terminate a DVCPO issued under RC 3113. 31(E)(8), a statute similar to RC 2903.214.

"Here, the trial court did not apply the preponderance of the evidence standard of proof when it relied on Kelly's motion to terminate the CSPO. Rather, the trial court used the clear and convincing evidence standard. "Clear and convincing evidence" is a measure of proof that is more than a mere "preponderance of the evidence." *Cross v. Ledford*, 161 Ohio St. 469, 477, 120 NE2d 118 (1954). Because the trial court improperly applied a higher standard of proof than the law required in deciding Kelly's motion to terminate, we find that the trial court abused its discretion."[190]

The appellate court therefore remanded the case to the trial court to apply the "preponderance of the evidence" standard of proof in deciding whether the original circumstances changed such that the CSPO was no longer equitable for the order to continue.

Q & A: Can a trial court deny the parties' joint motion to modify or terminate the court's order issuing a CSPO, where the parties entered into an agreed no-contact order and requested that the CSPO be terminated?

In *N.S. v. S.B.*,[191] petitioner filed a CSPO against an ex boyfriend. The full hearing was continued in order for the parties to enter into a settlement. On the date of the full hearing, petitioner appeared in court with an agreed no-contact order entry and requested that the court adopt the agreement instead of the CSPO. In declining to adopt the agreement, the court stated that "the agreed no-contact order placed reciprocal obligations upon the petitioner and the respondent, and because there was no petition filed against N.S., the court lacked jurisdiction to impose any restrictions on N.S.."[192] Because the court declined to adopt the CSPO and because the ex parte order was to expire anyway, Sheerer chose to proceed with the full hearing at which time the court granted a five year CSPO.

Subsequent to the issuance of the order, the parties entered into another no-contact order agreement that eliminated the reciprocal obligations on petitioner and filed a joint Civ. R. 60(B) motion to modify or terminate the order. In the motion, the parties requested that the court dismiss the CSPO and adopt their proposed agreed entry, but the court again denied the joint motion under Civ. R. 60(B).

Respondent then appealed the decision of the court, claiming that the trial court erred when it failed to grant the joint motion to modify the CSPO and replace it with an agreed no-contact order.[193]

The appellate court affirmed the trial court and found that the trial court had not abused its discretion in denying the parties' joint motion to modify or terminate the CSPO having relied instead on the evidence and findings made during the full protection order hearing.

---

[190] Reising v. Reising, at ¶ 16.

[191] N.S. v. S.B., 2017-Ohio-1556, 2017 WL 1507322 (Ohio Ct. App. 8th Dist. Cuyahoga County 2017), as amended, (Aug. 22, 2017).

[192] N.S. v. S.B., 2017-Ohio-1556, ¶ 3, 2017 WL 1507322 (Ohio Ct. App. 8th Dist. Cuyahoga County 2017), as amended, (Aug. 22, 2017); see also RC 2903.214(E)(3).

[193] N.S. v. S.B., 2017-Ohio-1556, ¶ 8, 2017 WL 1507322 (Ohio Ct. App. 8th Dist. Cuyahoga County 2017), as amended, (Aug. 22, 2017).

The court also pointed out that Sheerer's testimony established the elements of menacing by stalking and therefore, the trial court was free to consider this evidence in making its determination.

However, the dissent reframed the issues on policy grounds, focusing on the fact that the parties were free to enter into a consent agreement before the full hearing. According to the dissent, "[p]arties should always be encouraged to work out their differences before requiring a trial court's intervention. The parties attempted to consent to an agreement that would accomplish the goals of any protection order but without the drain on court resources."[194]

Of interest is that the dissent also addressed the issue of reciprocal restrictions on both parties and noted that "RC 2903.214(E) does not preclude parties from entering a consent judgment that involves reciprocal burdens. Even if we considered the terms synonymous and if the parties' agreement to reciprocal burdens may not be authorized by statute, the statutory preclusion is not jurisdictional.[195] Parties are free to waive a statutory right by contract."[196]

Apparently the dissenting judge also differentiated between a motion to modify and a motion to terminate a CSPO relative to Civ. R. 60(B) and any alternatives. It noted that Civ. R. 60(B) applied to motions to terminate but that motions to modify were subject to the continuing jurisdiction of a court independent of a Civ. R. 60(B) motion. The dissent found that the majority's reliance on *Delaine* was misplaced as *Delaine* addressed a motion to terminate a CSPO and whether a hearing was required, not a motion to modify or a motion for relief from judgment under Civ. R. 60(B). The dissent suggested that *Delaine* stood for the proposition that Civ. R. 60(B) is applicable to motions to modify protection orders. In *Delaine*, "[t]he trial court did not determine whether the protection order could be modified; its sole consideration was the requirements of Civ. R. 60(B), which are not applicable in light of the trial court's continuing jurisdiction to consider modification of the protection order. The trial court thus erred in applying the Civ. R. 60(B) requirements to the motion to modify the protection order."[197]

While focusing on public policy grounds as reasons why the parties should have been permitted to terminate the CSPO and replace it with an agreed no-contact order entry, there was no discussion of the court's continuing jurisdiction to enforce the terms of the no-contact order if the CSPO was dismissed or terminated.

Q & A: Must the court actually hold a hearing on a party's motion to terminate a civil protection order?

---

[194]N.S. v. S.B., 2017-Ohio-1556, ¶ 21, 2017 WL 1507322 (Ohio Ct. App. 8th Dist. Cuyahoga County 2017), as amended, (Aug. 22, 2017).

[195]But see RC 2903.214(E)(3).

[196]N.S. v. S.B., 2017-Ohio-1556, ¶ 21, 2017 WL 1507322 (Ohio Ct. App. 8th Dist. Cuyahoga County 2017), as amended, (Aug. 22, 2017) citing Sanitary Commercial Services, Inc. v. Shank, 57 Ohio St. 3d 178, 566 N.E.2d 1215 (1991).

[197]N.S. v. S.B., 2017-Ohio-1556, ¶ 23, 2017 WL 1507322 (Ohio Ct. App. 8th Dist. Cuyahoga County 2017), as amended, (Aug. 22, 2017).

According to the 8th District Court of Appeals, the answer is no. In *Delaine v. Smith*,[198] petitioner-appellee sought a CSPO against her neighbor for verbally harassing her and physically abusing her husband, making verbal threats to her and her family and leaving a dead squirrel on her driveway.

On appeal, respondent appellant argued that the trial court failed to hold a full hearing on his motion to terminate the CSPO. The appellate court determined that "there are no provisions in RC 2903.214 mandating that a trial court must hold a hearing on a respondent's motion to terminate a CPO."[199] In affirming the trial court and finding no abuse of discretion, the appellate court held that ". . . since the court was not required to hold a hearing on Smith's request to terminate the CPO, the court was free to rely on the evidence and findings made during the August 2011 hearing."[200]

Q & A: So, can a person seek relief from judgment under Civ. R. 60(B)?

A 60(B) motion is available to a party who is denied relief in the trial court as an alternative to the filing of a motion to modify or terminate a CSPO. However, the only caveat is that the movant comply with the elements of Civ. R. 60(B).

In *Lerner v. Giolekas,*[201] the appellate court found that appellant was entitled to relief from judgment pursuant to Civ. R. 60(B).

In this case, appellant appealed the grant of a CSPO on the grounds of newly discovered evidence and under the catchall provision of Civ. R. 60(B). "In order to prevail on a Civ. R. 60(B) motion for relief from judgment, a movant must demonstrate that 1) the party has a meritorious defense or claim to present if relief is granted; 2) the party is entitled to relief under one of the grounds stated in Civ. R. 60(B)(1-5) and 3) the motion is made within a reasonable time."[202]

Here, appellant alleged a meritorious defense, to wit: he committed no wrongdoing and his motion was timely made. He also contended that he is entitled to relief under Civ. R. 60(B)(2) and (5), for newly discovered evidence and for any other reason justifying relief.[203] Per Civ. R. 60(B)(2), "newly discovered evidence" is that which by due diligence could not have been discovered in time to move for a new trial under Civ. R. 59. Evidence that appellee came by appellant's house

---

[198]Delaine v. Smith, 2016-Ohio-5250, 2016 WL 4141753 (Ohio Ct. App. 8th Dist. Cuyahoga County 2016).

[199]Delaine v. Smith, 2016-Ohio-5250, ¶ 16, 2016 WL 4141753 (Ohio Ct. App. 8th Dist. Cuyahoga County 2016).

[200]Delaine v. Smith, 2016-Ohio-5250, ¶ 23, 2016 WL 4141753 (Ohio Ct. App. 8th Dist. Cuyahoga County 2016).

[201]Lerner v. Giolekas, 2016-Ohio-696, 2016 WL 762594 (Ohio Ct. App. 8th Dist. Cuyahoga County 2016), appeal not allowed, 146 Ohio St. 3d 1429, 2016-Ohio-4606, 52 N.E.3d 1204 (2016); Roxey v. Smallwood, 2016-Ohio-720, 2016 WL 763121 (Ohio Ct. App. 5th Dist. Fairfield County 2016).

[202]Lerner v. Giolekas, 2016-Ohio-696, 2016 WL 762594, ¶ 39 (Ohio Ct. App. 8th Dist. Cuyahoga County 2016), appeal not allowed, 146 Ohio St. 3d 1429, 2016-Ohio-4606, 52 N.E.3d 1204 (2016); T.D. v. C.N., 2018-Ohio-1840, 2018 WL 2148447 (Ohio Ct. App. 8th Dist. Cuyahoga County 2018).

[203]But see J.P. v. T.H, 2016-Ohio-243, 2016 WL 363247 (Ohio Ct. App. 9th Dist. Lorain County 2016).

and then called the police on him was found to be newly discovered evidence, even though the incident took place after the final hearing and issuance of the order granting the CSPO.

In sustaining appellant's assignment of error, the court found that the "newly discovered evidence" was relevant to whether appellant engaged in stalking behavior under RC 2903.214. "Because the alleged incident occurred so close after the trial court granted the protection order, we find that constituted newly discovered evidence relative to this case."[204] Thus, the trial court had clearly abused its discretion in denying appellant's 60(B) motion.

Q & A: On what grounds may a petitioner withdraw or dismiss an ex parte civil protection order?

In *Guerrieri v. Brys*,[205] appellant alleged that appellee/petitioner had engaged in frivolous conduct because she withdrew her ex parte civil stalking protection order seven months after obtaining it. The trial court entered a judgment entry stating that appellee had filed to withdraw her petition for a CPO and ex parte order against appellant and then dismissed the case.

On appeal, appellant asserted that appellee's conduct in requesting the stalking civil protection order was frivolous conduct. In its ruling on the frivolous conduct, the appellate court found that "[g]iven the allegations set out in appellee's petition, her conduct in requesting a stalking CPO was not frivolous conduct. At the time she filed her petition, appellee believed appellant and Huff had threatened to abduct her against her will and had made their intentions known to the Warren City Law Director and appellant had shown up at her workplace and attempted to harass appellee and her co-workers. These actions caused appellee to fear for her safety."[206] "Furthermore, once appellee no longer considered appellant a threat, she moved to withdraw her petition."[207]

Of significance is that the Mahoning County Court of Appeals appeared to develop a new legal rationale against the various tort suits filed by respondents in cases in which petitioners seek to dismiss their civil protection orders, especially before the full hearing.[208] This legal reasoning may also be applied in cases in which respondents seek attorney fees against the petitioners if their orders are dismissed, withdrawn or denied.[209]

Q & A: Can a party dismiss an already existing civil protection order under Civ. R. 41(A)?

Not according to the Fifth District Court of Appeals. In *Oddo v.*

[204]Lerner v. Giolekas, 2016-Ohio-696, 2016 WL 762594, ¶ 42 (Ohio Ct. App. 8th Dist. Cuyahoga County 2016), appeal not allowed, 146 Ohio St. 3d 1429, 2016-Ohio-4606, 52 N.E.3d 1204 (2016).

[205]Guerrieri v. Brys, 2014-Ohio-1178, 2014 WL 1326098 (Ohio Ct. App. 7th Dist. Mahoning County 2014).

[206]Guerrieri v. Brys, 2014-Ohio-1178, 2014 WL 1326098, ¶ 17 (Ohio Ct. App. 7th Dist. Mahoning County 2014).

[207]Guerrieri v. Brys, 2014-Ohio-1178, 2014 WL 1326098, ¶ 18 (Ohio Ct. App. 7th Dist. Mahoning County 2014).

[208]See also Text § 19:10.

[209]See also Text § 12:21.

Spencer,[210] appellant requested that the civil protection order be terminated, which request was denied by the trial court. On appeal, he argued that the petitioner in the CPO has the right and/or ability to voluntarily dismiss such petition against appellant under Civ. R. 41(A).

In upholding the trial court, the appellate court held that "Mrs. Oddo was the Petitioner in the action for the civil protection order, not the plaintiff. While she may have been the person who initiated the proceedings, it was the trial court who issued the order, not Mrs. Oddo. As such, only the trial court has the ability to terminate, modify or renew the order."[211]

While it is clear that a civil protection order issued pursuant to R.C. 2903.214 is subject to modification or termination by a court, the court does not have to terminate or modify the order.[212] In the instant case, the Fifth District Court of Appeals determined that the trial court did not abuse its discretion in overruling the petitioner's motion to terminate the order. Relying on *Prostejovsky*, the court found that the evidence presented was insufficient to demonstrate that there had been a material change of circumstances to justify termination. In fact, while petitioner did not oppose termination, "it was clear from her testimony that it is still her desire that Appellant not have any contact with her family."[213]

Q & A: Can a stalking CPO ever be extended or renewed?

Yes. In *Striff v. Striff*,[214] the parties had entered into a consent agreement and stalking CPO, whereby the appellant agreed to have no contact with appellee. The order was to remain in seven months, unless extended, vacated, or modified. Appellee requested an extension because appellant had continually contacted her, criticized her regarding personal matters and threatened her with court action should she fail to comply with his requests, all despite the order.

On appeal, the respondent argued that appellee had failed to introduce evidence that she was threatened or in fear of being harassed or stalked. The Wood County Court of Appeals affirmed the trial court's extension of the order based on appellant's continual contact with appellee, despite an existing stalking order, appellant's past behavior and appellee's motion and testimony indicating a continual fear of appellant's harassing behavior.

Q & A: What does "In the same manner as the original ordered was issued" mean?

The Fourth District Court of Appeals determined that the same

[210]Oddo v. Spencer, 2011-Ohio-4073, 2011 WL 3587436 (Ohio Ct. App. 5th Dist. Stark County 2011).

[211]Oddo v. Spencer, 2011-Ohio-4073, 2011 WL 3587436, *2 (Ohio Ct. App. 5th Dist. Stark County 2011); Text § 12:25; but see also R.C. 3113.31(E)(8).

[212]See also N.S. v. S.B., 2017-Ohio-1556, 2017 WL 1507322 (Ohio Ct. App. 8th Dist. Cuyahoga County 2017), as amended, (Aug. 22, 2017).

[213]Oddo v. Spencer, 2011-Ohio-4073, 2011 WL 3587436, *3 (Ohio Ct. App. 5th Dist. Stark County 2011).

[214]Striff v. Striff, 2003-Ohio-794, 2003 WL 397869 (Ohio Ct. App. 6th Dist. Wood County 2003); see also Dennis v. Paulsen, 2009-Ohio-2916, 2009 WL 1719369 (Ohio Ct. App. 4th Dist. Hocking County 2009).

statutory framework must be followed when a civil protection order is renewed under R.C. 2903.214(E)(2)(b) as when the original civil protection order is issued. In *Dennis v. Paulson*,[215] respondent argued that he was not permitted a full hearing before the civil protection order was renewed. In that case, the trial court extended the protection order on petitioner's motion without holding a hearing.

In reversing the trial court, the appellate court held that the respondent must be given notice and an opportunity to be heard. Because R.C. 2903.214(D)(2)(a) requires a full hearing before a protection order can be granted in the first instance, the renewal of a protection order also requires that a full hearing be had.

Q & A: Can a civil protection order be extended past the time of the expiration of the original civil protection order?

It depends on the appellate district. For example, *Dennis v. Paulson*,[216] the trial court extended petitioner's stalking CPO for an additional three years. The original protection order was granted on September 20, 2005 and was to remain in effect for a period of three years. On September 10, 2008, petitioner filed a motion requesting that the CPO be extended an additional three years, which motion was granted.

In reversing the trial court and finding that it had abused its discretion, the Hocking County Court of Appeals relied on R.C. 2903.214(E)(2)(a) which limits a CSPO to a date certain, but not later than five years from the date of its issuance. The extension of the stalking CPO for an additional three years violated the maximum duration of a civil protection order imposed by R.C. 2903.214(E)(2)(a) by one year.[217]

In contrast, *Striff v. Striff*,[218] the parties had entered into a consent agreement and stalking CPO, whereby the appellant agreed to have no contact with appellee. The order was to remain in seven months, unless extended, vacated, or modified. Appellee requested an extension because appellant had continually contacted her, criticized her regarding personal matters and threatened her with court action should she fail to comply with his requests, all despite the order.

On appeal, the respondent argued that appellee had failed to introduce evidence that she was threatened or in fear of being harassed or stalked. The Wood County Court of Appeals affirmed the trial court's extension of the order based on appellant's continual contact with appellee, despite an existing stalking order, appellant's past behavior and appellee's motion and testimony indicating a continual fear of appellant's harassing behavior.

Interestingly, in *Banfield v. Orazem*,[219] appellant objected to the magistrate's decision, arguing that the mental distress finding was

---

[215] Dennis v. Paulsen, 2009-Ohio-2916, 2009 WL 1719369 (Ohio Ct. App. 4th Dist. Hocking County 2009).

[216] Dennis v. Paulsen, 2009-Ohio-2916, 2009 WL 1719369 (Ohio Ct. App. 4th Dist. Hocking County 2009).

[217] *Dennis at *2.*

[218] Striff v. Striff, 2003-Ohio-794, 2003 WL 397869 (Ohio Ct. App. 6th Dist. Wood County 2003); see also Dennis v. Paulsen, 2009-Ohio-2916, 2009 WL 1719369 (Ohio Ct. App. 4th Dist. Hocking County 2009).

[219] Banfield v. Orazem, 2017-Ohio-8438, 2017 WL 5151469 (Ohio Ct. App. 11th

not supported by the evidence. "In overruling the objections, the trial court concluded that appellant's repeated behavior over a sustained period constitutes mental distress."[220] In adopting the magistrate's decision, the trial court also made additional modifications, including extending the CPO an additional nine months even though no one had objected to the length of the order. The trial court used the date of final judgment, rather than the date of the ex parte temporary order.

On appeal, appellant claimed that it was reversible error for the trial court to extend the term of the CSPO rather than follow the magistrate's recommendation regarding the effective dates of the order as there was no evidence to support the change.

The appellate court reasoned that a trial court has discretion to determine the length of a civil stalking protection order. Changing the effective date from 18 months to 27 months was within the court's discretion. Moreover, such an enlargement was supported by the evidence presented. Therefore, "the decision to extend the length of the final protection order by nine months was sound and reasonable in light of the facts of this case."[221]

Q & A: What standard of proof (burden of persuasion) is to be applied in determining whether to extend a civil stalking protection order?

Like RC 3113.31, the "preponderance of the evidence" standard is applied when determining whether to issue a civil stalking protection order under RC 2903.214. The same standard should be considered when ruling on a motion to extend or renew a CSPO.

In *Striff v. Striff*,[222] the trial court applied a "preponderance of the evidence" standard when determining whether to extend the civil stalking protection order against appellant. The standard was never challenged on appeal. Therefore, it is presumed that the "preponderance of the evidence" standard is applicable to motions to extend civil stalking protection orders.

§ 9:6 Consent agreement civil stalking protection orders

Q & A: Does R.C. 2903.214 contemplate consent agreement civil stalking protection orders?

No. Unlike R.C. 2903.214, R.C. 3113.31 does not contemplate a consent agreement civil protection order. Comparing the statutes, R.C. 2903.214 does not permit the issuance of a consent civil protection order.[1] Even the Supreme Court of Ohio civil stalking order forms

Dist. Geauga County 2017).

[220]Banfield v. Orazem, 2017-Ohio-8438, ¶ 9, 2017 WL 5151469 (Ohio Ct. App. 11th Dist. Geauga County 2017).

[221]Banfield v. Orazem, 2017-Ohio-8438, ¶ 19, 2017 WL 5151469 (Ohio Ct. App. 11th Dist. Geauga County 2017).

[222]Striff v. Striff, 2003-Ohio-794, 2003 WL 397869 (Ohio Ct. App. 6th Dist. Wood County 2003).

[Section 9:6]

[1]See dissenting opinion in N.S. v. S.B., 2017-Ohio-1556, 2017 WL 1507322 (Ohio Ct. App. 8th Dist. Cuyahoga County 2017), as amended, (Aug. 22, 2017) (noting that

do not address consent civil protection orders.[2] However, the forms do contain waiver language as a way to avoid a full hearing with witnesses and testimony.

Q & A: Must the court make findings of fact as it would after any other full hearing?

Because R.C. 2903.214 does not contemplate consent agreement civil protection orders despite the waiver language contained in the forms, it is unclear whether a court that issues a CSPO by agreement with the required waivers is also required to make specific findings of fact.

The reason for any full hearing is to provide the respondent with a meaningful opportunity to be heard. On the other hand, the focus of a consent entry is the actual agreement by a respondent to be bound by the terms of the civil protection order. Where the parties can agree to the terms, a full hearing is unnecessary. Therefore, findings of fact are also not needed.

Public policy dictates that although not expressly provided by statute, orders similar to consent protection orders should continue to be issued and respondents who enter into these agreements with petitioners should not be subject to findings of fact where the main objective of a CSPO is for that respondent to abide by the terms of a protection order. For purposes of an order issued under R.C. 2903.214, waivers are akin to consent.

Q & A: Does the court have the authority to issue a consent agreement under R.C. 2903.214?

The Miami County Court of Appeals answered this in the affirmative in *Harris v. Miami County Sheriff's Dept.*[3] In that case, the petitioner was granted an ex parte anti-stalking civil protection order. At the full hearing, the parties entered into a consent agreement civil protection order. Subsequently, respondent was denied a license application to carry a concealed weapon due to the fact that he was the subject of a civil protection order. On appeal, appellant argued that R.C. 2903.214 does not authorize a trial court to issue a consent agreement. At issue was whether a consent agreement is a civil protection order such that a respondent is barred from obtaining a license to carry a weapon.

The Second District Court of Appeals reviewed R.C. 2903.214 and found that the statute permits the common pleas court to "issue any protection order, with or without bond, that contains terms designed to ensure the safety and protection of the person to be protected by the protection order. . ."[4] The court examined the protection order signed by respondent and determined that the order, entered into by

---

RC 2903.214 is merely silent as to consent agreements).

[2]See Sup. R. Form 10.03-E and 10.03-F.

[3]Harris v. Miami Cty. Sheriff's Dept., 160 Ohio App. 3d 435, 2005-Ohio-1713, 827 N.E.2d 807 (2d Dist. Miami County 2005); but see State v. Myers, 2009-Ohio-4659, 2009 WL 2872977 (Ohio Ct. App. 10th Dist. Franklin County 2009) (while the consent entry issue was not specifically addressed, the parties entered into an "agreed order of protection"). See also Text § 12:9.

[4]Harris v. Miami Cty. Sheriff's Dept., 160 Ohio App. 3d 435, 438, 2005-Ohio-1713, 827 N.E.2d 807 (2d Dist. Miami County 2005); R.C. 2903.214(E)(1).

way of an agreement, was designed to ensure the safety of the petitioner. "Therefore, we agree with the Sheriff that consent agreements, such as the one in this case, are within the jurisdiction and authority of the Greene County Common Pleas Court to issue under R.C. 2903.214. Since consent agreements can be issued under the authority of R.C. 2903.214, we cannot say the lower court abused its discretion in finding that this consent agreement was a civil protection order."[5]

Q & A: Can a party to a CSPO appeal a consent agreement?

According to the decision in *Windsor v. Bristow*,[6] the answer is no. In that case, appellant, a vexatious litigator against her, appealed the issuance of a CSPO by a consent agreement even though he had signed the last page of the standardized protection order form which contained waiver language.

On appeal, appellant claimed that the agreed signed consent order was unenforceable "because the trial court lacks jurisdiction to issue an order prohibiting his filing any legal action against appellee."[7]

The appellate court noted that consent orders are authorized in the context of protection orders issued pursuant to RC 2903.214.[8] The court stressed that "[w]e will not interfere with the clear and unambiguous agreement of the parties based upon the appellant's change of heart regarding the terms of the consent order. The Supreme Court of Ohio has noted that 'from early in this state's history, we have held that a party participating in a consent judgment will not be allowed to appeal errors from that judgment.' "[9]

This decision is instructive for all counsel who may be faced with a litigant who argues that they can appeal any agreement should they later determine that they no longer want to be bound by its terms.

Q & A: If a consent entry is permissible under R.C. 2903.214, can it be modified or terminated?

In *Leibold v. Hiddens*,[10] the petitioner was granted a civil stalking protection order issued under R.C. 2903.214. At the full hearing, the respondent agreed to be bound by a consent agreement that contained the same terms as the CSPO and the CSPO was vacated. Approximately 8 months later, respondent filed a Motion for Relief from Judgement pursuant to Civ. R. 60(B). Respondent appealed the denial of her motion for relief from the consent agreement.

[5]Harris v. Miami Cty. Sheriff's Dept., 160 Ohio App. 3d 435, 439, 2005-Ohio-1713, 827 N.E.2d 807 (2d Dist. Miami County 2005).

[6]Windsor v. Bristow, 2018-Ohio-1020, 2018 WL 1377850 (Ohio Ct. App. 5th Dist. Richland County 2018).

[7]Windsor v. Bristow, 2018-Ohio-1020, ¶ 19, 2018 WL 1377850 (Ohio Ct. App. 5th Dist. Richland County 2018).

[8]Windsor v. Bristow, 2018-Ohio-1020, ¶ 19, 2018 WL 1377850 (Ohio Ct. App. 5th Dist. Richland County 2018); citing, Harris v. Miami Cty. Sheriff's Dept., 160 Ohio App. 3d 435, 2005-Ohio-1713, 827 N.E.2d 807, ¶ 17 (2d Dist. Miami County 2005); State v. Myers, 2009-Ohio-4659, ¶ 2, 2009 WL 2872977 (Ohio Ct. App. 10th Dist. Franklin County 2009).

[9]Windsor v. Bristow, 2018-Ohio-1020, ¶ 22, 2018 WL 1377850 (Ohio Ct. App. 5th Dist. Richland County 2018).

[10]Leibold v. Hiddens, 2007-Ohio-2972, 2007 WL 1721347 (Ohio Ct. App. 2d Dist. Montgomery County 2007).

Although the appellate court acknowledged appellant's reasoning for agreeing to a Consent Agreement, which was to have the CSPO issued against her dismissed, it was silent as to the whether this process complied with the statute. In its silence, it remains unclear whether the Second District Court of Appeals viewed the parties' agreement as the only option permitted because a consent agreement/CSPO is statutorily unavailable. However, the court did stress that once voluntarily entered into, appellant was bound by the terms of the agreement.

The importance of this decision is that even if a Consent Agreement/CSPO is not expressly permitted by statute, similar orders appear to be available to the parties.[11] However, the court, in dicta, also stated that ". . . even if the CSPO was not vacated by the signing of the Consent Agreement, the trial court did not err when it found that Hiddens had failed to produce sufficient evidence to support a Civ. R. 60(B) motion for relief from judgment."[12]

In affirming the trial court, this court indicated that a consent agreement would not be set aside, pursuant to Civ. R. 60(B), if entered into voluntarily.

Q & A: Can a respondent be criminally charged with violating the protection order if it had been granted pursuant to a consent agreement?

Not according to the Miami County Court of Appeals in *Harris v. Miami County Sheriff's Dept.*[13] On appeal, appellant argued that R.C. 2903.214 does not authorize a trial court to issue a consent agreement. At issue was whether a consent agreement is a civil protection order such that a respondent is barred from obtaining a license to carry a weapon.

The Second District Court of Appeals reviewed the statute and found that it permits the common pleas court to "issue any protection order with or without bond, that contains terms designed to ensure the safety and protection of the person to be protected by the protection order. . ."[14] The court held that consent agreements, such as the one in this case, are within the jurisdiction and authority of the Greene County Common Pleas Court to issue under R.C. 2903.214.

However, the appellate court determined that, although the consent order states that a violation shall be prosecuted as a first degree misdemeanor, the trial court would not have the authority to criminally punish Harris for violating the order unless such authority had been specifically granted to it by R.C. 2903.214(K).[15]

[11]See also N.S. v. S.B., 2017-Ohio-1556, 2017 WL 1507322 (Ohio Ct. App. 8th Dist. Cuyahoga County 2017), as amended, (Aug. 22, 2017).

[12]Leibold v. Hiddens, 2007-Ohio-2972, 2007 WL 1721347, *3 (Ohio Ct. App. 2d Dist. Montgomery County 2007).

[13]Harris v. Miami Cty. Sheriff's Dept., 160 Ohio App. 3d 435, 2005-Ohio-1713, 827 N.E.2d 807 (2d Dist. Miami County 2005).

[14]Harris v. Miami Cty. Sheriff's Dept., 160 Ohio App. 3d 435, 438, 2005-Ohio-1713, 827 N.E.2d 807 (2d Dist. Miami County 2005); R.C. 2903.214(E)(1).

[15]But see State v. Myers, 2009-Ohio-4659, 2009 WL 2872977 (Ohio Ct. App. 10th Dist. Franklin County 2009) (although parties' agreement provided for contempt of court, R.C. 2903.214(K)(1) permits a party to decide whether to pursue a R.C. 2919.27

§ 9:7 Other procedural issues

Q & A: What is the standard on appeal of review of a stalking civil protection order?[1]

The decision whether or not to grant a civil stalking protection order (as with all protection orders) is within the discretion of the trial court. Some courts have held that the decision will only be reversed if there is an abuse of discretion.[2] An abuse of discretion connotes more than a mere error of law or judgment; rather, it implies that the court's attitude was unreasonable, arbitrary or unconscionable.[3] If there is some competent, credible evidence to support the trial court's decision, there is no abuse of discretion.[4]

Some of these same courts have also held that if the judgment of the trial court is supported by competent, credible evidence, the

---

violation or contempt of court. While the consent entry issue was not specifically addressed, the trial court journalized an agreed order of protection following an agreement between the parties).

[Section 9:7]

[1]See also 12:26; Denney v. Sanders, 2016-Ohio-5113, 2016 WL 4063898 (Ohio Ct. App. 1st Dist. Hamilton County 2016) (discussing the different standards for appellate review).

[2]See Bucksbaum v. Mitchell, 2004-Ohio-2233, 2004 WL 943865 (Ohio Ct. App. 5th Dist. Richland County 2004); Guthrie v. Long, 2005-Ohio-1541, 2005 WL 737402 (Ohio Ct. App. 10th Dist. Franklin County 2005); Parrish v. Parrish, 95 Ohio St. 3d 1201, 2002-Ohio-1623, 765 N.E.2d 359 (2002); Jenkins v. Jenkins, 2007-Ohio-422, 2007 WL 275700 (Ohio Ct. App. 10th Dist. Franklin County 2007); Felty v. Harper, 2009-Ohio-2855, 2009 WL 1700152 (Ohio Ct. App. 10th Dist. Franklin County 2009); Smith v. Wunsch, 162 Ohio App. 3d 21, 2005-Ohio-3498, 832 N.E.2d 757 (4th Dist. Hocking County 2005); Olenik v. Huff, 2003-Ohio-4621, 2003 WL 22039490 (Ohio Ct. App. 5th Dist. Ashland County 2003); Tupps v. Jansen, 2013-Ohio-1403, 2013 WL 1400949 (Ohio Ct. App. 5th Dist. Ashland County 2013); Holloway v. Parker, 2013-Ohio-1940, 2013 WL 1944400 (Ohio Ct. App. 3d Dist. Marion County 2013); Woodward v. Head, 2013-Ohio-1127, 2013 WL 1224910 (Ohio Ct. App. 1st Dist. Hamilton County 2013); Griga v. DiBenedetto, 2012-Ohio-6097, 988 N.E.2d 590 (Ohio Ct. App. 1st Dist. Hamilton County 2012); Mullen v. Hobbs, 2012-Ohio-6098, 2012 WL 6690114 (Ohio Ct. App. 1st Dist. Hamilton County 2012); Sweet v. Hunt, 2014-Ohio-631, 2014 WL 707923 (Ohio Ct. App. 2d Dist. Greene County 2014); Smith v. Hein, 2015-Ohio-2749, 2015 WL 4095636 (Ohio Ct. App. 1st Dist. Hamilton County 2015), appeal not allowed, 144 Ohio St. 3d 1458, 2016-Ohio-172, 44 N.E.3d 288 (2016); Stump v. Hoagland, 2015-Ohio-2434, 2015 WL 3822270 (Ohio Ct. App. 2d Dist. Miami County 2015); Echemann v. Echemann, 2016-Ohio-3212, ¶ 33, 2016 WL 3057979 (Ohio Ct. App. 3d Dist. Shelby County 2016); McNaughton v. Cochenour, 2015-Ohio-4648, 2015 WL 6953983 (Ohio Ct. App. 4th Dist. Ross County 2015); Wilson v. Rowe, 2016-Ohio-523, 2016 WL 561527 (Ohio Ct. App. 5th Dist. Knox County 2016); Masucci v. Burnbrier, 2015-Ohio-4102, 2015 WL 5781476 (Ohio Ct. App. 7th Dist. Mahoning County 2015); Theibert v. Anderson, 2017-Ohio-1029, 2017 WL 1075534 (Ohio Ct. App. 5th Dist. Knox County 2017); Delaine v. Smith, 2016-Ohio-5250, 2016 WL 4141753 (Ohio Ct. App. 8th Dist. Cuyahoga County 2016); N.S. v. S.B., 2017-Ohio-1556, 2017 WL 1507322 (Ohio Ct. App. 8th Dist. Cuyahoga County 2017), as amended, (Aug. 22, 2017); Hudnell v. Blackshear, 2017-Ohio-2680, 2017 WL 1788691 (Ohio Ct. App. 2d Dist. Montgomery County 2017) (indicates that an abuse of discretion standard should be applied but also considers the presumption in favor of the finder of fact in "weighing the evidence").

[3]Blakemore v. Blakemore, 5 Ohio St. 3d 217, 450 N.E.2d 1140 (1983).

[4]Ross v. Ross, 64 Ohio St. 2d 203, 18 Ohio Op. 3d 414, 414 N.E.2d 426 (1980).

reviewing court will not reverse the decision as being against the manifest weight of the evidence.[5]

"In applying the manifest weight of the evidence standard to civil cases, the appellate court should review the whole record, weigh the evidence and all reasonable inferences, consider the witnesses" credibility, and determine whether the trier of fact clearly lost its way and created such a miscarriage of justice that the court's order must be reversed.[6]

Some courts have made it quite simple. In *J.M. v. D.H.*,[7] appellant claimed that appellee did not present sufficient evidence to warrant the issuance of the civil stalking protection order. The Ninth District Court of Appeals was asked to "determine whether, viewing the evidence in the light most favorable to J.M., a reasonable trier of fact could find that J. M. demonstrated by a preponderance of the evidence that a civil stalking protection order should issue."[8] In that J.M. did not present any evidence to indicate that D.H. had caused or that she believed would cause her physical harm or mental distress, the appellate court reversed and held that the evidence was insufficient, when

---

[5]Derolph v. Cirillo, 2004-Ohio-5564, 2004 WL 2348509 (Ohio Ct. App. 5th Dist. Licking County 2004) quoting, C. E. Morris Co. v. Foley Const. Co., 54 Ohio St. 2d 279, 8 Ohio Op. 3d 261, 376 N.E.2d 578 (1978); Hayton v. White, 2004-Ohio-6640, 2004 WL 2847802 (Ohio Ct. App. 5th Dist. Ashland County 2004); Mann v. Sumser, 2002-Ohio-5103, 2002 WL 31151164 (Ohio Ct. App. 5th Dist. Stark County 2002); Olenik v. Huff, 2003-Ohio-4621, 2003 WL 22039490 (Ohio Ct. App. 5th Dist. Ashland County 2003); Tupps v. Jansen, 2013-Ohio-1403, 2013 WL 1400949 (Ohio Ct. App. 5th Dist. Ashland County 2013); Holloway v. Parker, 2013-Ohio-1940, 2013 WL 1944400 (Ohio Ct. App. 3d Dist. Marion County 2013); A.S. v. P.F., 2013-Ohio-4857, 2013 WL 5925968 (Ohio Ct. App. 9th Dist. Lorain County 2013); Wulf v. Opp, 2015-Ohio-3285, 2015 WL 4878495 (Ohio Ct. App. 12th Dist. Clermont County 2015); Cole v. Tubbs, 2016-Ohio-8321, 2016 WL 7427345 (Ohio Ct. App. 8th Dist. Cuyahoga County 2016) (standard of review of a trial court's denial of a petition for a civil protection order is whether there was "sufficient credible evidence); Krzystan v. Bauer, 2017-Ohio-858, 2017 WL 945183 (Ohio Ct. App. 6th Dist. Ottawa County 2017) (relying on the Third District, appellant claimed that an abuse of discretion standard should be applied when reviewing the issuance of a CSPO. However, the appellate court found that "[w]hile there is a split of authority on this issue, the Sixth District applies a manifest weight of the evidence standard for review."), at ¶ 13, citing Bullard v. Alley, 2014-Ohio-1016, 2014 WL 1339719 (Ohio Ct. App. 4th Dist. Pike County 2014) (applying the manifest weight standard of review but noting those districts that use an abuse of discretion standard).

[6]Ramsey v. Pellicioni, 2016-Ohio-558, 2016 WL 635212, ¶ 15 (Ohio Ct. App. 7th Dist. Mahoning County 2016); Vega v. Thomas, 2017-Ohio-298, 2017 WL 389911 (Ohio Ct. App. 8th Dist. Cuyahoga County 2017) (where the challenge is to the sufficiency of the evidence, appellate courts review the evidence in the light most favorable to appellee to determine whether there is some evidence going to every element in the petition and under a manifest weight of the evidence, appellate courts weigh the evidence and all reasonable inferences, consider the credibility of witnesses and determine whether the trial court lost its way and created such a miscarriage of justice that the judgment must be reversed).

[7]J.M. v. D.H., 2016-Ohio-8387, 2016 WL 7596244 (Ohio Ct. App. 9th Dist. Lorain County 2016).

[8]J.M. v. D.H., 2016-Ohio-8387, ¶ 7, 2016 WL 7596244 (Ohio Ct. App. 9th Dist. Lorain County 2016); relying on Bowman v. Bowman, 2014-Ohio-2851, 2014 WL 2957475 (Ohio Ct. App. 9th Dist. Medina County 2014).

viewed in the light most favorable to J.M., for the court to find that a civil stalking protection order should issue.[9]

In *R.G. v. R. M.*,[10] the appellate court explained when a party can raise both sufficiency of the evidence and weight of the evidence standards. In that case, the former girlfriend filed a civil stalking protection order against her former boyfriend. Once issued, the former boyfriend filed objections which were denied. Appellant's assignment of error on appeal was whether there was sufficient credible evidence for a trial court to make a decision to grant the CSPO because the elements of stalking were not established by the petitioner.

The appellate court first determined that appellant appeared to raise both sufficiency of the evidence and weight of the evidence as to the elements of mental distress. According to the court, "[b]oth standards can be applied when reviewing the issuance of a civil protection order if they are raised by the appellant."[11]

The court then pointed out that "[a]ppellate courts have often merged the review for civil protection orders because they assumed the concepts of weight and sufficiency merged in civil cases (and/or because only weight was raised). In 2012, the Supreme Court clarified that the concepts of weight and sufficiency do not merge in civil cases as the concepts are qualitatively and quantitatively different in civil cases just as they are in criminal cases."[12]

In differentiating the concepts, the court decided that "sufficiency of the evidence" "is a legal question evaluating the adequacy of the evidence. The question is whether the evidence, if believed, is sufficient proof of the elements. An evaluation of witness credibility is not involved in a sufficiency review. Sufficiency involves the burden of production rather than the burden of persuasion. The evidence and all rational inferences are evaluated in the light most favorable to the petitioner, and a judgment is not reversed on sufficiency grounds unless the reviewing court determines no rational fact-finder could find the existence of the elements by the relevant burden of proof."[13]

On the other hand, "[w]eight of the evidence concerns 'the inclination of the greater amount of credible evidence' supporting one side of an issue over the other as the fact-finder weighs the evidence in his mind . . . It is not a question of mathematics, but is a question of the persuasiveness of the evidence or the effect of the evidence in induc-

---

[9]J.M. v. D.H., 2016-Ohio-8387, ¶ 11, 2016 WL 7596244 (Ohio Ct. App. 9th Dist. Lorain County 2016).

[10]R.G. v. R.M., 2017-Ohio-8918, 88 N.E.3d 1027 (Ohio Ct. App. 7th Dist. Mahoning County 2017); see also Text § 12:26.

[11]R.G. v. R.M., 2017-Ohio-8918, 88 N.E.3d 1027, ¶ 8 (Ohio Ct. App. 7th Dist. Mahoning County 2017); citing Denney v. Sanders, 2016-Ohio-5113, 2016 WL 4063898 (Ohio Ct. App. 1st Dist. Hamilton County 2016); Vega v. Thomas, 2017-Ohio-298, 2017 WL 389911 (Ohio Ct. App. 8th Dist. Cuyahoga County 2017) and A.M. v. D.L., 2017-Ohio-5621, 2017 WL 2870214 (Ohio Ct. App. 9th Dist. Medina County 2017).

[12]R.G. v. R.M., 2017-Ohio-8918, 88 N.E.3d 1027, ¶ 8 (Ohio Ct. App. 7th Dist. Mahoning County 2017); citing, Eastley v. Volkman, 132 Ohio St. 3d 328, 2012-Ohio-2179, 972 N.E.2d 517, ¶ 9, 13-15, ¶ 23 (2012), applying State v. Thompkins, 78 Ohio St. 3d 380, 1997-Ohio-52, 678 N.E.2d 541 (1997).

[13]R.G. v. R.M., 2017-Ohio-8918, 88 N.E.3d 1027, ¶ 9 (Ohio Ct. App. 7th Dist. Mahoning County 2017).

ing belief . . .When evaluating whether a judgment is contrary to the manifest weight of the evidence, every reasonable presumption must be made in favor of the judgment . . . (and if the evidence is susceptible to more than one construction, the reviewing court is bound to interpret the evidence in a manner consistent with the judgment). The appellate court is to review the entire record, weigh the evidence and all reasonable inferences, consider the credibility of witnesses, and determine whether, in resolving conflicts in the evidence, the fact-finder clearly lost its way and created such a manifest miscarriage of justice that the conviction must be reversed and a new trial ordered."[14]

The appellate court then discussed the elements of stalking as defined in RC 2903.211 for purposes of a civil stalking protection order, considered both sufficiency and weight of the evidence and concluded that the CSPO was supported by sufficient evidence.

Other courts have blended the abuse of discretion standard and a manifest weight of the evidence standard of review when determining whether the issuance of the civil stalking protection order was proper.[15]

Still other courts have applied a standard based on the type of challenge presented on appeal.[16] Where the challenge is to the scope of the

[14]R.G. v. R.M., 2017-Ohio-8918, ¶ 10, 88 N.E.3d 1027, 1031 (Ohio Ct. App. 7th Dist. Mahoning County 2017).

[15]Wilson v. Rowe, 2016-Ohio-523, 2016 WL 561527 (Ohio Ct. App. 5th Dist. Knox County 2016); Williams v. Flannery, 2015-Ohio-2040, ¶ 5-7, 2015 WL 3421319 (Ohio Ct. App. 8th Dist. Cuyahoga County 2015); Rufener v. Hutson, 2012-Ohio-5061, 2012 WL 5364703 (Ohio Ct. App. 8th Dist. Cuyahoga County 2012); Wagner v. Holland, 2016-Ohio-5028, 2016 WL 3920162 (Ohio Ct. App. 5th Dist. Fairfield County 2016); Elkins v. Manley, 2016-Ohio-8307, 2016 WL 7427267 (Ohio Ct. App. 8th Dist. Cuyahoga County 2016) (appears to have considered both abuse of discretion and sufficiency of the evidence: where the challenge is to the weight of the evidence, the review is whether there is some competent, credible evidence and where the decision as to whether the CSPO should have been issued at all, the standard is an abuse of discretion; the court held that the trial court did not abuse its discretion in granting the CSPO); Wilson v. Lyon, 2016-Ohio-7734, 2016 WL 6678396 (Ohio Ct. App. 3d Dist. Marion County 2016) (whether the CSPO should have been issued at all calls for an abuse of discretion standard and when challenging the sufficiency of the evidence, the standard for review after viewing the evidence in a light most favorable to the prevailing party is whether the judgment is supported by some competent and credible evidence and when assessing the manifest weight of the evidence, the standard of review is whether the court's judgment is supported by the greater amount of credible evidence and whether the plaintiff met its burden of persuasion, which is the preponderance of the evidence. The appellate court held that trial court decision was not against the manifest weight of the evidence as the record contained competent, credible evidence).

[16]Corrao v. Corrao, 2016-Ohio-4862, 2016 WL 3632494 (Ohio Ct. App. 8th Dist. Cuyahoga County 2016), quoting Allan v. Allan, 2014-Ohio-5039, 2014 WL 6065710 (Ohio Ct. App. 8th Dist. Cuyahoga County 2014); citing Abuhamda-Sliman v. Sliman, 161 Ohio App. 3d 541, 2005-Ohio-2836, 831 N.E.2d 453 (8th Dist. Cuyahoga County 2005) (depends on the nature of the challenge, ie. Challenges to the scope of the order are reviewed for an abuse of discretion and when the issue is whether a protection order should have been issued at all, the question for review is whether there was sufficient credible evidence to support the trial court finding that petitioner was or was not entitled to the protection order. Although these cases are DVCPO cases, the same legal reasoning can be applied to CSPO cases. Because of the many similarities between RC 3113.31 and RC 2903.214, resulting court decisions rely on case law applicable to both statutes).

protection order, the court applies an abuse of discretion standard.[17] Where the challenge is to the issuance of the order itself, the court applies a manifest weight of the evidence standard.[18] Several appellate courts including the Second, Fourth, Tenth, Eighth and Sixth districts have applied this two tiered approach.[19]

A court will apply an abuse of discretion standard when the challenge is that the duration of a CSPO is excessive. For example, in *Lias v. Beekman*,[20] the appellant alleged that the trial court erred in granting the CSPO for five years. The appellate court affirmed the trial court and held that the duration of the CSPO did not constitute an abuse of discretion. The Court stated that "the duration of a civil stalking protection order is within the sound discretion of the trial court and will not be reversed on appeal absent a showing that the decision was arbitrary, unconscionable or unreasonable."[21]

---

[17]A.S. v. P.F., 2013-Ohio-4857, 2013 WL 5925968 (Ohio Ct. App. 9th Dist. Lorain County 2013) (the scope of the protection order does not reflect an abuse of discretion when it included the children); Joy v. Letostak, 2015-Ohio-2667, 2015 WL 3964179 (Ohio Ct. App. 10th Dist. Franklin County 2015) (duration of CSPO will not be reversed absent a showing that decision was arbitrary, unconscionable or unreasonable).

[18]See, for example, Cooper v. Manta, 2012-Ohio-867, 2012 WL 691547, *4 (Ohio Ct. App. 11th Dist. Lake County 2012) (noting that a manifest weight of the evidence standard applies when the court needs to determine whether the protection order should have been granted and thus, whether the elements of menacing by stalking were established by the preponderance of the evidence); Fortney v. Willhoite, 2012-Ohio-3024, 2012 WL 2522835, ¶ 33 (Ohio Ct. App. 11th Dist. Lake County 2012) (stating that generally, an appellate court considering whether a trial court properly issued a CPO reviews the record to determine whether there is some competent, credible evidence to support the trial court's determination); A.S. v. P.F., 2013-Ohio-4857, 2013 WL 5925968 (Ohio Ct. App. 9th Dist. Lorain County 2013); Williams v. Hupp, 2011-Ohio-3403, 2011 WL 2670945 (Ohio Ct. App. 7th Dist. Mahoning County 2011); Rehfus v. Smith, 2015-Ohio-2145, 2015 WL 3498686 (Ohio Ct. App. 7th Dist. Carroll County 2015) (applying manifest weight of the evidence standard when the challenge is whether the protection order should have been granted); Denney v. Sanders, 2016-Ohio-5113, 2016 WL 4063898 (Ohio Ct. App. 1st Dist. Hamilton County 2016) (finding that proper appellate review could entail a manifest weight of the evidence challenge, a sufficiency of the evidence challenge or both depending on the arguments raised when determining whether a CSPO should have been issued at all. At 20; citing, J.R. v. Pless, 2016-Ohio-14, 2016 WL 60000 (Ohio Ct. App. 9th Dist. Summit County 2016).

[19]See, e.g., Abuhamda-Sliman v. Sliman, 161 Ohio App. 3d 541, 2005-Ohio-2836, 831 N.E.2d 453 (8th Dist. Cuyahoga County 2005); Gruber v. Hart, 2007-Ohio-873, 2007 WL 625818 (Ohio Ct. App. 6th Dist. Ottawa County 2007) (noting the lack of uniformity with regard to the proper standard of review in appeals from SCPOs). See also Keller v. Knight, 2014-Ohio-2432, 2014 WL 2566249 (Ohio Ct. App. 6th Dist. Wood County 2014); Denney v. Sanders, 2016-Ohio-5113, 2016 WL 4063898 (Ohio Ct. App. 1st Dist. Hamilton County 2016).

[20]Lias v. Beekman, 2007-Ohio-5737, 2007 WL 3108899 (Ohio Ct. App. 10th Dist. Franklin County 2007); see also Text § 12:26, Appeal of a civil protection order; see also Caban v. Ransome, 2009-Ohio-1034, 2009 WL 582761 (Ohio Ct. App. 7th Dist. Mahoning County 2009) (abuse of discretion standard applies if there is a question as to the restrictions imposed by the court); Rauser v. Ghaster, 2009-Ohio-4027, 2009 WL 2462553 (Ohio Ct. App. 8th Dist. Cuyahoga County 2009), decision vacated and superseded on reconsideration on other grounds, 2009-Ohio-5698, 2009 WL 3490654 (Ohio Ct. App. 8th Dist. Cuyahoga County 2009) (later decision clarified that it was the directed verdict at the close of the evidence that was error; neither the decision nor the legal analysis changed).

[21]Lias v. Beekman, 2007-Ohio-5737, 2007 WL 3108899, *6 (Ohio Ct. App. 10th

The Court also relied on R.C. 2903.214(E)(2)(a) which provides that any protection order issued shall be valid until a date certain but no later that five years from the date of its issuance.

Interestingly, in *Fortney v Willhoite*,[22] the court differentiated between a trial court and a magistrate when determining the review on appeal. "Generally, an appellate court considering whether a trial court properly issued a civil protection order reviews the record to determine whether there is some competent, credible evidence to support the trial court's determination.[23] "However, when a magistrate issues a protection order and the trial court adopts the magistrate's decision, we review the trial court's adoption of the decision for an abuse of discretion."[24]

It is important to recognize that appellate courts reviewing civil protection orders in domestic violence cases have also focused on the same standards of review and applied them and analyzed them in much the same way.[25] Unfortunately, Ohio's appellate courts have not yet determined one consistent standard for all courts to use when reviewing challenges to all civil protection orders.

Q & A: What is the standard on appeal for reviewing a motion to terminate a CSPO?

In *Delaine v. Smith*,[26] appellant appealed the denial of his Motion to Terminate the CSPO, arguing that the trial court failed to hold a hearing on his motion.

After stating that trial courts have discretion in deciding whether or not to grant motions to terminate a CSPO under RC 2903.214, the court determined that their review would be limited to an abuse of that discretion.[27]

Dist. Franklin County 2007), quoting Jenkins v. Jenkins, 2007-Ohio-422, 2007 WL 275700, *19 (Ohio Ct. App. 10th Dist. Franklin County 2007), citing Mann v. Sumser, 2002-Ohio-5103, 2002 WL 31151164, *30-31 (Ohio Ct. App. 5th Dist. Stark County 2002). See also Taylor v. Taylor, 2012-Ohio-6190, 2012 WL 6738376 (Ohio Ct. App. 2d Dist. Miami County 2012).

[22] Fortney v. Willhoite, 2012-Ohio-3024, 2012 WL 2522835 (Ohio Ct. App. 11th Dist. Lake County 2012).

[23] Fortney v. Willhoite, 2012-Ohio-3024, ¶ 33, 2012 WL 2522835 (Ohio Ct. App. 11th Dist. Lake County 2012), citing J.L. v. M.D., 2011-Ohio-6208, 2011 WL 6016950, ¶ 56 (Ohio Ct. App. 11th Dist. Lake County 2011).

[24] Fortney v. Willhoite, 2012-Ohio-3024, ¶ 33, 2012 WL 2522835 (Ohio Ct. App. 11th Dist. Lake County 2012), citing J.L. v. M.D., 2011-Ohio-6208, 2011 WL 6016950, ¶ 56 (Ohio Ct. App. 11th Dist. Lake County 2011).

[25] See Text 12:26.

[26] Delaine v. Smith, 2016-Ohio-5250, 2016 WL 4141753 (Ohio Ct. App. 8th Dist. Cuyahoga County 2016).

[27] Delaine v. Smith, 2016-Ohio-5250, ¶ 16, 2016 WL 4141753 (Ohio Ct. App. 8th Dist. Cuyahoga County 2016); Hayberg v. Tamburello, 2013-Ohio-3451, 2013 WL 4033623 (Ohio Ct. App. 5th Dist. Tuscarawas County 2013); Jones v. Rose, 2009-Ohio-4347, 2009 WL 2607944 (Ohio Ct. App. 4th Dist. Hocking County 2009); Reising v. Reising, 2017-Ohio-2859, 2017 WL 2241670 (Ohio Ct. App. 8th Dist. Cuyahoga County 2017); N.S. v. S.B., 2017-Ohio-1556, 2017 WL 1507322 (Ohio Ct. App. 8th Dist. Cuyahoga County 2017), as amended, (Aug. 22, 2017).

Q & A: How important is credibility to the issuance of a civil stalking protection order?[28]

Credibility is extremely important. In virtually all instances, incidents of menacing by stalking do not take place in front of witnesses. Therefore it is often only the petitioner/victim that can testify as to the incidents in question. Civil stalking protection order cases most often turn on the credibility of the witnesses.[29]

A reviewing court will give great deference to the trial court decision and presume that the findings of the trial court are correct.[30] "Further, 'the weight to be given to the evidence and the credibility of the witnesses is primarily a matter for the trier of fact . . . because the trier of fact is in the best position to view the witnesses and consider their demeanor and truthfulness.' "[31] In fact, many appellate courts will not substitute its judgment for that of the trier of facts on the issue of witness credibility unless it is patently apparent that the trier of facts lost its way in arriving at its verdict.[32]

Q & A: Does the doctrine of mootness apply to civil stalking protection orders?[33]

Yes. In *Erbes v. Meyer*,[34] appellant sought relief under Civ. R. 60(B), requesting that the trial court vacate the CSPO. The appellate court first noted that the CSPO was set to expire on December 31, 2010, but that appellant had not sought to extend it. In taking judicial notice of

---

[28]See Didonato v. Stewart, 2015-Ohio-270, 2015 WL 329507 (Ohio Ct. App. 5th Dist. Tuscarawas County 2015); Stump v. Hoagland, 2015-Ohio-2434, 2015 WL 3822270 (Ohio Ct. App. 2d Dist. Miami County 2015); Lloyd v. Thornsbery, 2018-Ohio-2893, 2018 WL 3536755 (Ohio Ct. App. 11th Dist. Portage County 2018) (see majority opinion, noting that the test is subjective but that the evidence must be credible and concurring opinion, noting that while the trial court's determination of credibility should be given "substantial" deference, appellant's argument is sufficiently coherent as to merit acknowledgement from the court).

[29]Madison v. Wilborn, 2012-Ohio-2742, 2012 WL 2308618 (Ohio Ct. App. 5th Dist. Stark County 2012); see also Kruszynski v. Kruszynski, 2013-Ohio-3355, 2013 WL 3965465 (Ohio Ct. App. 5th Dist. Fairfield County 2013); Elkins v. Reed, 2014-Ohio-1217, 2014 WL 1350806 (Ohio Ct. App. 5th Dist. Stark County 2014); Text 12:26; Wilson v. Rowe, 2016-Ohio-523, 2016 WL 561527 (Ohio Ct. App. 5th Dist. Knox County 2016).

[30]Seasons Coal Co., Inc. v. City of Cleveland, 10 Ohio St. 3d 77, 80-81, 461 N.E.2d 1273, 38 U.C.C. Rep. Serv. 469 (1984).

[31]Seasons Coal Co., Inc. v. City of Cleveland, 10 Ohio St. 3d 77, ¶ 21, 461 N.E.2d 1273, 38 U.C.C. Rep. Serv. 469 (1984), quoting Jenkins v. Jenkins, 2007-Ohio-422, 2007 WL 275700 (Ohio Ct. App. 10th Dist. Franklin County 2007). See also Nichols v. Young, 2015-Ohio-1077, 2015 WL 1288148 (Ohio Ct. App. 3d Dist. Putnam County 2015) (holding that the fact-finder is in the best position to weigh the evidence and judge the credibility of witnesses by viewing the demeanor, voice inflections, eye movements, and gestures of the witnesses testifying before it. at ¶ 19); Dunn v. Clark, 2016-Ohio-641, 2016 WL 698090 (Ohio Ct. App. 12th Dist. Warren County 2016).

[32]Taylor v. Taylor, 2012-Ohio-6190, 2012 WL 6738376, ¶ 21 (Ohio Ct. App. 2d Dist. Miami County 2012), citing State v. Bradley, 1997 WL 691510, *4 (Ohio Ct. App. 2d Dist. Champaign County 1997); Weismuller v. Polston, 2012-Ohio-1476, 2012 WL 1107717, ¶ 24 (Ohio Ct. App. 12th Dist. Brown County 2012).

[33]See Text § 12:26. See also Brown v. Grauman, 2013-Ohio-4814, 2013 WL 5914961 (Ohio Ct. App. 2d Dist. Champaign County 2013).

[34]Erbes v. Meyer, 2011-Ohio-3274, 2011 WL 2586349 (Ohio Ct. App. 2d Dist. Montgomery County 2011).

the fact that the order was no longer in effect, the court held that the appeal was moot.[35]

Conversely, the Eleventh District Court of Appeals, in *Fortney v Willhoite*,[36] determined that the appeal was not moot. In that case, the duration of the civil was one year, but by the time the entry became a final, appealable order, the protection order was to be in effect for only seven more months, which was too short a period of time for the court of appeals to review the judgment entry. Relying on the legal reasoning articulated in *Cauwenbergh v. Cauwenbergh*,[37] the 11th District appellate court held "that appeals from entries granting civil protection orders are not rendered moot by the expiration of the protection order, either: 1) because they are capable of repetition, yet evading review or 2) because of the collateral consequences caused by such orders."[38] Therefore, the *Fortney* court determined that the appeal was not rendered moot.

Q & A: I was harassed by my neighbor. He also threatened my life in public and his behavior has affected my business. I have made several police reports documenting his behavior towards me and I have videos documenting my story. At the hearing, he testified that I was harassing him. Must the petitioner come to court with "clean hands?"

No. In *Denney v. Sanders,*[39] the trial court heard testimony about respondent's harassment towards petitioner, reviewed videos, and heard testimony from respondent that petitioner had harassed him by driving past his home and in his alley and took pictures of him and his family.

On appeal, respondent argued that the court abused its discretion in granting the CSPO because petitioner did not have "clean hands." The appellate court held that "[n]either RC 2903.214 or 2903.211 requires that a person seeking a CSPO must have 'clean hands' in order to pursue and obtain relief."[40] Further, the court also noted that

---

[35] Erbes v. Meyer, 2011-Ohio-3274, 2011 WL 2586349, *1 (Ohio Ct. App. 2d Dist. Montgomery County 2011), citing VanMeter v. VanMeter, 2004-Ohio-3390, 2004 WL 1446055 (Ohio Ct. App. 10th Dist. Franklin County 2004); Baldridge v. Baldridge, 2011-Ohio-2423, 2011 WL 1936056 (Ohio Ct. App. 2d Dist. Darke County 2011).

[36] Fortney v. Willhoite, 2012-Ohio-3024, 2012 WL 2522835 (Ohio Ct. App. 11th Dist. Lake County 2012). See also Tupps v. Jansen, 2013-Ohio-1403, 2013 WL 1400949 (Ohio Ct. App. 5th Dist. Ashland County 2013).

[37] Cauwenbergh v. Cauwenbergh, 2007-Ohio-1070, 2007 WL 726951 (Ohio Ct. App. 11th Dist. Ashtabula County 2007).

[38] Fortney v. Willhoite, 2012-Ohio-3024, 2012 WL 2522835, *5 (Ohio Ct. App. 11th Dist. Lake County 2012). See also Echemann v. Echemann, 2016-Ohio-3212, 2016 WL 3057979 (Ohio Ct. App. 3d Dist. Shelby County 2016); Masucci v. Burnbrier, 2015-Ohio-4102, 2015 WL 5781476 (Ohio Ct. App. 7th Dist. Mahoning County 2015) (although the CSPO had expired and once it was clear that it should not have been granted in the first instance, the appellate court determined that it should reverse and vacate the grant of the CSPO because appellant "is entitled to have it removed from his record." [at ¶ 19]).

[39] Denney v. Sanders, 2016-Ohio-5113, 2016 WL 4063898 (Ohio Ct. App. 1st Dist. Hamilton County 2016).

[40] Denney v. Sanders, 2016-Ohio-5113, 2016 WL 4063898, ¶ 30 (Ohio Ct. App. 1st Dist. Hamilton County 2016); citing Skiles v. Dearth, 2000 WL 1838747, *5 (Ohio Ct. App. 2d Dist. Clark County 2000).

respondent initiated many of the incidents and contributed to the ongoing feud.[41]

Q & A: How is a violation of the CSPO addressed?[42]

According to R.C. 2903.214(K)(1)(b), a person who violates a protection order issued under this section is subject to punishment for contempt of court. In *Chiles v. Brown*,[43] appellee was granted a SCPO in which appellant was ordered to stay away from her and not to be present within 500 feet. Appellee subsequently filed a Motion to Show Cause and appellant was found guilty of contempt and ordered to serve 30 days in jail. Appellant appealed the contempt finding on the ground that it was not supported by the evidence.

The appellate court began its analysis by assessing whether the contempt was civil or criminal. "In civil contempt, '[p]unishment is remedial or coercive and for the benefit of the complainant, and [p]rison sentences are conditional,' since the contemnor will be free if he agrees to do as ordered."[44] Whereas, criminal contempt is "usually characterized by an unconditional prison sentence," which "operates not as a remedy coercive in its nature but as punishment for the completed act of disobedience, and to vindicate the authority of the law and the court."[45]

The court reasoned that the contempt was civil because it was contingent upon appellant's abiding by the SCPO and committing no further violations. "Civil contempt requires a finding of guilt by clear and convincing evidence."[46] The court then applied an abuse of discretion standard of review of the trial court's finding of contempt and determined that the trial court did not abuse its discretion in finding appellant guilty of civil contempt.

Additionally, a person may be criminally charged with violating a civil stalking protection order. RC 2903.214(K)(1)(a) provides that a person who violates a protection order issued under this section is subject to criminal prosecution for a violation under sections 2919.27 of the Revised Code, if the violation of the protection order constitutes a violation of that section. Under RC 2919.27 (A)(2) states that "[n]o

[41]Denney v. Sanders, 2016-Ohio-5113, 2016 WL 4063898, ¶ 30 (Ohio Ct. App. 1st Dist. Hamilton County 2016).

[42]See also Text § 13:3; State v. Smith, 136 Ohio St. 3d 1, 2013-Ohio-1698, 989 N.E.2d 972 (2013).

[43]Chiles v. Brown, 2008-Ohio-4740, 2008 WL 4278173 (Ohio Ct. App. 6th Dist. Lucas County 2008).

[44]Chiles v. Brown, 2008-Ohio-4740, 2008 WL 4278173, *4 (Ohio Ct. App. 6th Dist. Lucas County 2008), quoting Brown v. Executive 200, Inc., 64 Ohio St. 2d 250, 253, 18 Ohio Op. 3d 446, 416 N.E.2d 610 (1980); see also Text § 13:4, Court enforcement of civil protection orders—Contempt—Generally defined.

[45]Chiles v. Brown, 2008-Ohio-4740, 2008 WL 4278173, *4 (Ohio Ct. App. 6th Dist. Lucas County 2008), quoting Brown v. Executive 200, Inc., 64 Ohio St. 2d 250, 254, 18 Ohio Op. 3d 446, 416 N.E.2d 610 (1980); Preston v. Shutway, 2013-Ohio-185, 986 N.E.2d 584 (Ohio Ct. App. 2d Dist. Champaign County 2013) (discussion of contempt and finding that respondent's conduct not sanctionable as direct criminal contempt).

[46]Chiles v. Brown, 2008-Ohio-4740, 2008 WL 4278173, *4 (Ohio Ct. App. 6th Dist. Lucas County 2008), quoting Brown v. Executive 200, Inc., 64 Ohio St. 2d 250, 253, 18 Ohio Op. 3d 446, 416 N.E.2d 610 (1980). See also Losey v. Diersing, 2013-Ohio-1108, 2013 WL 1196674 (Ohio Ct. App. 12th Dist. Clermont County 2013).

person shall recklessly violate the terms of * * *a protection order issued pursuant to.* * *section 2903.214 of the Revised Code.[47]

Furthermore, if a person was subject to electronic monitoring per RC 2903.214 and then violated a civil stalking protection order, "the court may require in addition to any other sentence imposed upon the offender that the offender be electronically monitored for a period not exceeding five years by a law enforcement agency designated by the court.[48]

Q & A: Does the Court of Common Pleas, General Division have jurisdiction to award possession of the marital home to the ex wife pursuant to a civil stalking protection order where the Domestic Relations Court had already addressed title to the real property?

In *Khan v. Hughes,*[49] Khan filed a CSPO requesting that Hughes keep away from her and the children. The parties' divorce decree ordered Hughes to refinance the home and transfer title into his name within 90 days and that if he failed to comply, the home was to be sold and the proceeds divided. The common pleas court, general division issued the CSPO and ordered Hughes to resolve the property issues within 45 days in Domestic Relations Court and revoked visitation until such matter was resolved. Several months later, Khan sought relief from the court because the property issues had not been resolved. After several continuances, the trial court granted Khan relief and ordered that she have exclusive possession of the residence and that Hughes vacate the property.

Hughes appealed and argued that the trial court did not have jurisdiction to award exclusive possession of the home to Khan because the Domestic Relations Court had already issued an order regarding the property.

The appellate court noted that the Ohio Constitution states that "[t]he courts of common pleas and divisions thereof shall have original jurisdiction over all justiciable matters . . . ."[50] According to RC 3105. 11, the courts of common pleas, including divisions of domestic relations, has full equitable powers and jurisdiction appropriate to the determination of all domestic relations matters. "Applying the above principles, this court in *Price v. Price*, 16 Ohio App.3d 93, 474 NE2d 662 (8th Dist. 1984), held as follows:

> [A]fter an action has been fully litigated in the Domestic Relations Court and a judgment entry has been filed granting a divorce and providing for the division of property, the exclusive jurisdiction is terminated. At that point, there exist[s] concurrent jurisdiction with the Common Pleas Court, General Division. The continuing jurisdiction of the Domestic Re-

---

[47]See for eg., State v. Sims, 2016-Ohio-7341, 2016 WL 6069093 (Ohio Ct. App. 6th Dist. Wood County 2016); see also Text ¶ 13:2 and Text ¶ 13:3.

[48]See RC 2919.27(B)(5).

[49]Khan v. Hughes, 2015-Ohio-4502, 2015 WL 6550725 (Ohio Ct. App. 8th Dist. Cuyahoga County 2015).

[50]Khan v. Hughes, 2015-Ohio-4502, 2015 WL 6550725, ¶ 11 (Ohio Ct. App. 8th Dist. Cuyahoga County 2015), citing Section 4(B), Article IV of the Ohio Constitution.

lations Court is concurrent with the General Division and not exclusive."[51]

In that Hughes refused to transfer title and the mortgage into his name and refused to allow the house to be sold in violation of the divorce decree, the common pleas court had jurisdiction to enforce the order of the domestic relations court. Additionally, the appellate court noted the court's concern was for Khan's safety when it issued the CSPO and the desire to prevent further unwanted contact between the parties which the trial court order accomplished.[52] Moreover, RC 2903.214(E)(1)(a) provides that the court may issue any protection order that contains terms to ensure the safety and protection of the persons to be protected, including a provision that restrains a respondent from entering the residence of the petitioner.

"Based on the facts of this case and Khan as the title holder of the home, the common pleas court had authority to order Hughes to vacate the home under the above provision."[53]

Q & A: Have any appellate courts addressed mutual protection orders in the context of civil stalking protection orders?[54]

Pursuant to RC 2903.214(E)(3), a court may not issue a protection order that requires a petitioner to do or to refrain from doing an act that the court may require a respondent to do or refrain from doing under division (E)(1) of this section unless all of the following apply:

(a) Respondent files a separate petition.

(a) Petitioner is served with notice of respondent's petition at least 48 hours before the court holds a hearing with respect to respondent's petition, or petitioner waives the right to receive this notice.

(a) If petitioner has requested an ex parte order pursuant to division (D) of this section, the court does not delay any hearing required by that division beyond the time specified in that division in order to consolidate the hearing with a hearing on the petition filed by respondent.

(a) After a full hearing at which the respondent presents evidence in support of the request for a protection order and the petitioner is afforded an opportunity to defend against that evidence, the court determines that petitioner has committed a violation of section 2903.211 against the person to be protected by the protection order issued pursuant to division (E)(3) of this section, has committed a sexually oriented offense or has violated a protection order issued pursuant to section 2903.213 relative to the person to be protected by the order.

In effect, mutual protection orders may be issued only in accordance with the above. They should never be issued based on the petition of

---

[51]Khan v. Hughes, 2015-Ohio-4502, 2015 WL 6550725, ¶ 13 (Ohio Ct. App. 8th Dist. Cuyahoga County 2015).

[52]Khan v. Hughes, 2015-Ohio-4502, 2015 WL 6550725, ¶ 15 (Ohio Ct. App. 8th Dist. Cuyahoga County 2015).

[53]Khan v. Hughes, 2015-Ohio-4502, 2015 WL 6550725, ¶ 16 (Ohio Ct. App. 8th Dist. Cuyahoga County 2015).

[54]See also § 12:29.

one party. Instead, any party seeking a protection order must file his or her own petition in accordance with the statute.

For example, in *N.S. v. S.B.*,[55] petitioner-appellee filed for a CSPO against appellant. The full hearing was continued to afford the parties a chance to enter into an agreement on the protection order. On the date set for the full hearing, appellee presented an agreement to the court which she asked the court to adopt because it provided for "no contact," in lieu of the CSPO. "The court declined to do so, stating that the agreed no-contact order placed reciprocal obligations upon the petitioner and the respondent, and because there was no petition filed against N.S., the court lacked jurisdiction to impose any restrictions on N.S..."[56] The court then went on to hold a full hearing and granted the CSPO. Subsequently, the parties drafted a new no-contact order eliminating the reciprocal provisions. They also filed a Civ. R. 60(B) motion to modify or terminate the CSPO, stating that the entry reflected the joint intentions of the parties and their desire to settle the matter upon the agreed terms.[57]

After the court denied the Civ. R. 60(B) motion, appellant filed an appeal arguing that the trial court erred when it failed to grant the joint motion to modify the prior court order granting the CSPO and replace it with an agreed no-contact order.

In affirming the trial court, the appellate court found that the trial court had not abused its discretion in denying the joint motion and reasoned that the trial court relied upon the evidence taken at the full hearing where appellee established the elements of stalking. It relied on *Delaine v. Smith*[58] wherein the same court found "that because a hearing is not required on a request to terminate, it was free to rely on evidence and findings established at the full protection order hearing."[59]

The dissenting judge provided an interesting twist in his opinion in which he noted that the statutory preclusions as to reciprocal burdens under RC 2903.214(E) were not jurisdictional and that this statutory right could be waived by contract. Moreover, he interpreted RC 2903.214(E) to apply to a protection order not a consent agreement, reasoning that those reciprocal burdens apply to a protection order but are silent as to a consent agreement. He also pointed out that "[p]arties should always be encouraged to work out their differences before requiring a trial court's intervention. The parties attempted to consent to an agreement that would accomplish the goals of any protection order but without the drain on court resources."[60] The judge also differentiated the facts of the case from those in *Delaine* and

---

[55]N.S. v. S.B., 2017-Ohio-1556, 2017 WL 1507322 (Ohio Ct. App. 8th Dist. Cuyahoga County 2017), as amended, (Aug. 22, 2017).

[56]N.S. v. S.B., 2017-Ohio-1556, ¶ 3, 2017 WL 1507322 (Ohio Ct. App. 8th Dist. Cuyahoga County 2017), as amended, (Aug. 22, 2017).

[57]N.S. v. S.B., 2017-Ohio-1556, ¶ 6, 2017 WL 1507322 (Ohio Ct. App. 8th Dist. Cuyahoga County 2017), as amended, (Aug. 22, 2017).

[58]Delaine v. Smith, 2016-Ohio-5250, 2016 WL 4141753 (Ohio Ct. App. 8th Dist. Cuyahoga County 2016)

[59]N.S. v. S.B., 2017-Ohio-1556, ¶ 19, 2017 WL 1507322 (Ohio Ct. App. 8th Dist. Cuyahoga County 2017), as amended, (Aug. 22, 2017) , citing *Delaine* at ¶ 23.

[60]N.S. v. S.B., 2017-Ohio-1556, ¶ 21, 2017 WL 1507322 (Ohio Ct. App. 8th Dist.

agreed with the parties that the court had jurisdiction to modify the CSPO, independent of a Civ. R. 60(B) motion.

§ 9:8 Mental distress, physical harm and pattern of conduct

Q & A: How is the term mental distress defined by way of the case law?[1]

In defining the term mental distress, the Hamilton County Appellate Court, in *Lindsay v. Jackson*,[2] noted that more than a simple statement of distress was required to meet the preponderance of the evidence standard. However, "expert testimony is not necessary to establish that a victim experienced mental distress as a result of defendant's behavior. . . . Rather, it is the function of the trier of fact to determine whether a victim suffered mental distress as a result of the offender's behavior."[3]

In *Tuuri v. Snyder*,[4] the Geauga County Court of Appeals reversed the trial court's denial of a stalking civil protection order. The trial court had noted that appellant's mental distress as described as having problems sleeping fell short of the definition of mental distress as defined by the statute. The appellate court stated that a showing of actual mental distress was not a required element of menacing by stalking.[5] All that had to be shown was that a defendant knowingly caused a victim to believe that defendant would cause the victim

---

Cuyahoga County 2017), as amended, (Aug. 22, 2017).

[Section 9:8]

[1]See R.C. 2903.211(D)(2). But see Gilreath v. Kinderdine, 2004-Ohio-868, 2004 WL 362335, *2 (Ohio Ct. App. 2d Dist. Miami County 2004) (mental distress was not demonstrated where anxiety (caused by appellant's behavior) is not a "substantial incapacity" and neither would it "normally require psychiatric treatment."); Berry v. Patrick, 2005-Ohio-3708, 2005 WL 1707005 (Ohio Ct. App. 8th Dist. Cuyahoga County 2005) (reversing trial court's finding that proof of multiple incidents occurring close in time and over a three-year period causing petitioner to miss work and seek mental health counseling was sufficient evidence to issue order).

[2]Lindsay v. Jackson, 2000 WL 1268810, *5 (Ohio Ct. App. 1st Dist. Hamilton County 2000); cf. State v. Schwab, 119 Ohio App. 3d 463, 695 N.E.2d 801 (12th Dist. Butler County 1997).

[3]Short v. Walker, 2001 WL 32808, *2 (Ohio Ct. App. 12th Dist. Preble County 2001); Jenkins v. Jenkins, 2007-Ohio-422, 2007 WL 275700, *4 (Ohio Ct. App. 10th Dist. Franklin County 2007) (stating that mental distress need not be incapacitating or debilitating. Lay testimony may be sufficient. A trial court "may rely on its knowledge and experience in determining whether mental distress has been caused," quoting Smith v. Wunsch, 162 Ohio App. 3d 21, 2005-Ohio-3498, 832 N.E.2d 757 (4th Dist. Hocking County 2005); Sweet v. Hunt, 2014-Ohio-631, 2014 WL 707923 (Ohio Ct. App. 2d Dist. Greene County 2014) (quoting *Smith v. Wunsch* and stating " 'In making this determination, (whether a victim suffered mental distress) the trial court may rely on its knowledge and experience in determining whether mental distress has been caused.' " at ¶ 14; quoting *Smith* at ¶ 18); Arruda v. Farmer, 2015-Ohio-5511, 55 N.E.3d 604 (Ohio Ct. App. 5th Dist. Licking County 2015), appeal not allowed, 145 Ohio St. 3d 1460, 2016-Ohio-2807, 49 N.E.3d 322 (2016); R.G. v. R.M., 2017-Ohio-8918, 88 N.E.3d 1027 (Ohio Ct. App. 7th Dist. Mahoning County 2017).

[4]Tuuri v. Snyder, 2002-Ohio-2107, 2002 WL 818427 (Ohio Ct. App. 11th Dist. Geauga County 2002); see Ferdon v. Hoit, 2002-Ohio-4240, 2002 WL 1902872 (Ohio Ct. App. 5th Dist. Guernsey County 2002) (victim's testimony that she became physically sick and afraid due to stalker's conduct sufficient to constitute a temporary substantial incapacity, meeting the definition of mental distress).

[5]See also Irwin v. Murray, 2006-Ohio-1633, 2006 WL 832830, *3 (Ohio Ct. App.

mental distress or physical harm.[6] It was the effect of the offender's behavior on the petitioner that was the important focus.[7]

In support of its reasoning, the appellate court stated that appellant had a reasonable belief that the appellee was going to cause her physical harm. The court relied on her request for an earlier restraining order and that she had filed several police reports because appellee had entered the home in violation of a valid restraining order.

Q & A: How is "pattern of conduct" shown?

A "pattern of conduct" is defined as "two or more actions or incidents, closely related in time, whether or not there has been a prior conviction based on any of those actions or incidents."[8] While the statute does not define "closely related in time," this fact is determined by the trial court in the context of all circumstances of the case.[9]

6th Dist. Lucas County 2006) (affirming trial court decision finding "appellant's actions were performed to 'harass, annoy, and cause emotional distress' to appellee. The trial court further found appellant 'acted with an understanding of the impact of his words and with the hope that his actions would result in appellee losing her job' ").

[6]Tuuri v. Snyder, 2002-Ohio-2107, 2002 WL 818427, *4 (Ohio Ct. App. 11th Dist. Geauga County 2002); see also Striff v. Striff, 2003-Ohio-794, 2003 WL 397869 (Ohio Ct. App. 6th Dist. Wood County 2003); Szymanski v. Trendel, 2009-Ohio-992, 2009 WL 580457, *1 (Ohio Ct. App. 6th Dist. Lucas County 2009) (stressing that a victim need not actually experience mental distress; "Furthermore, the testimony of the victim herself as to her fear is sufficient to establish mental distress."), citing State v. Horsley, 2006-Ohio-6217, 2006 WL 3411423, *1 (Ohio Ct. App. 10th Dist. Franklin County 2006).

[7]See also State v. Honeycutt, 2002-Ohio-3490, 2002 WL 1438648 (Ohio Ct. App. 2d Dist. Montgomery County 2002) (evidence sufficient to establish victim suffered mental distress shown by fact victim went to motel, hired body guards, installed a home security system, pressed charges three times, and feared for her safety); Luikart v. Shumate, 2003-Ohio-2130, 2003 WL 1961874 (Ohio Ct. App. 3d Dist. Marion County 2003); Striff v. Striff, 2003-Ohio-794, 2003 WL 397869 (Ohio Ct. App. 6th Dist. Wood County 2003); see also Noah v. Brillhart, 2003-Ohio-2421, 2003 WL 21078077 (Ohio Ct. App. 9th Dist. Wayne County 2003) (mental distress was evidenced by petitioner's change of routine and pattern of activities, fear of visiting friends at night, and request of deputy escort); Smith v. Wunsch, 162 Ohio App. 3d 21, 2005-Ohio-3498, 832 N.E.2d 757 (4th Dist. Hocking County 2005) (where evidence of a changed routine corroborates a finding of mental distress, such as quitting a job); State v. Horsley, 2006-Ohio-1208, 2006 WL 648849 (Ohio Ct. App. 10th Dist. Franklin County 2006) (victim's testimony was sufficient to meet statutory definition of mental distress in that she testified she was afraid of appellant and afraid of what he would do upon his release from jail; his conduct was scary, he made her nervous because she believed he would follow through with his threats and he caused her fear and anxiety which resulted in lack of sleep and an inability to concentrate); Strausser v. White, 2009-Ohio-3597, 2009 WL 2186620 (Ohio Ct. App. 8th Dist. Cuyahoga County 2009); Wilson v. Lyon, 2016-Ohio-7734, 2016 WL 6678396 (Ohio Ct. App. 3d Dist. Marion County 2016).

[8]R.C. 2903.211(D)(1).

[9]Nguyen v. Chaffee, 2009-Ohio-3352, 2009 WL 1929358 (Ohio Ct. App. 7th Dist. Columbiana County 2009); citing Middletown v. Jones, 167 Ohio App. 3d 679, 2006-Ohio-3465, 856 N.E.2d 1003 (12th Dist. Butler County 2006); Wilson v. Lyon, 2016-Ohio-7734, 2016 WL 6678396 (Ohio Ct. App. 3d Dist. Marion County 2016) ("Even though the phrase "closely related in time" is not defined, appellate districts have concluded that "[i]n failing to delimit the temporal period within which the two or more actions or incidents must occur, the statute leaves that matter to be determined by the trier of fact on a case-by-case basis."" at ¶ 14, citing Ellet v. Falk, 2010-Ohio-6219, ¶ 22, 2010 WL 5269870 (Ohio Ct. App. 6th Dist. Lucas County 2010), citing State v. Dario, 106 Ohio App. 3d 232, 238, 665 N.E.2d 759 (1st Dist. Hamilton

For example, in *Tuuri v. Snyder*,[10] the appellant ex-wife sought a stalking civil protection order against her ex-husband. The trial court denied the protection order, noting that she failed to prove that the appellee knowingly engaged in a pattern of conduct that led her to believe he would cause her mental distress or physical harm.[11]

The trial court determined that the incidents of appellee's entering her residence were not closely related in time, having occurred twice within a two-year period.[12] The Geauga County Court of Appeals disagreed, stated that those were not the only instances in which appellee acted inappropriately. The court held that "when looking at the pattern of conduct in this case, one must take into consideration everything: *i.e.*, the forcible entries, the phone calls, the thinly veiled threats, and the face-to-face meetings between the parties, 'even if some of his actions comprising this behavior, considered in isolation, might not appear to be particularly threatening.' "[13] In reversing the trial court's decision, the court of appeals stated that the record dem-

---

County 1995); Theibert v. Anderson, 2017-Ohio-1029, 2017 WL 1075534 (Ohio Ct. App. 5th Dist. Knox County 2017).

[10]Tuuri v. Snyder, 2002-Ohio-2107, 2002 WL 818427 (Ohio Ct. App. 11th Dist. Geauga County 2002); Fortney v. Willhoite, 2012-Ohio-3024, 2012 WL 2522835 (Ohio Ct. App. 11th Dist. Lake County 2012).

[11]Tuuri v. Snyder, 2002-Ohio-2107, 2002 WL 818427, *2 (Ohio Ct. App. 11th Dist. Geauga County 2002); see also Farris v. Kihm, 2002-Ohio-2277, 2002 WL 940178 (Ohio Ct. App. 2d Dist. Miami County 2002).

[12]See also Miller v. Shaw, 2009-Ohio-6753, 2009 WL 4895276 (Ohio Ct. App. 7th Dist. Carroll County 2009) (affirming judgment denying CSPO where appellate court determined that two mutual fist fights 20 months apart were not closely related in time so as to constitute a pattern of conduct); but see Williams v. McDougal, 2001 WL 694591 (Ohio Ct. App. 4th Dist. Gallia County 2001) (reversing trial court's dismissal of a stalking CPO as being against the manifest weight of the evidence because respondent's stated threat and menacing behavior over a two-year period constitutes a pattern of conduct meeting the definition of menacing by stalking); see also Jenkins v. Jenkins, 2007-Ohio-422, 2007 WL 275700, *4 (Ohio Ct. App. 10th Dist. Franklin County 2007) (stating that the incidents need not occur within any specific temporal period); Szymanski v. Trendel, 2009-Ohio-992, 2009 WL 580457 (Ohio Ct. App. 6th Dist. Lucas County 2009) (holding that the incidents do not need to occur within any specific temporal period); Garrigues v. Brown, 2008-Ohio-6705, 2008 WL 5265685 (Ohio Ct. App. 5th Dist. Ashland County 2008) (holding that two incidents over the course of one year was sufficient to constitute a pattern of conduct); Rosen v. Chesler, 2009-Ohio-3163, 2009 WL 1900422 (Ohio Ct. App. 9th Dist. Lorain County 2009) (respondent accosted petitioner several times within a two year period which is sufficient to cause petitioner to believe that the actions would cause physical harm).

[13]Tuuri v. Snyder, 2002-Ohio-2107, 2002 WL 818427, *3 (Ohio Ct. App. 11th Dist. Geauga County 2002), quoting Still v. Still, 1999 WL 236049 (Ohio Ct. App. 2d Dist. Montgomery County 1999); see also Miller v. Francisco, 2003-Ohio-1978, 2003 WL 1904066 (Ohio Ct. App. 11th Dist. Lake County 2003) (overruled on other grounds by, Davis v. DiNunzio, 2005-Ohio-2883, 2005 WL 1383975 (Ohio Ct. App. 11th Dist. Lake County 2005)); Derolph v. Cirillo, 2004-Ohio-5564, 2004 WL 2348509, *2 (Ohio Ct. App. 5th Dist. Licking County 2004) (appellate court affirmed trial court decision to grant stalking CPO, noting that "[t]he trial court found these incidents constituted threats of bodily harm which individually and collectively caused appellee mental distress and appellee's fear was reasonable in light of the same."); Smith v. Wunsch, 162 Ohio App. 3d 21, 2005-Ohio-3498, 832 N.E.2d 757 (4th Dist. Hocking County 2005); Needhamer v. Carlozzi, 2010-Ohio-4562, 2010 WL 3733866, *3 (Ohio Ct. App. 11th Dist. Lake County 2010) (the text message "hope you found better," sent several times, while not directly threatening, must be considered in light of a prior attack and threats and was sent in violation of the ex parte order); Clark v. Ellinwood, 2011-Ohio-145, 2011 WL 281146 (Ohio Ct. App. 6th Dist. Lucas County 2011); Lane v.

onstrated that appellant had a reasonable belief that appellee was going to cause her physical harm.

Further, the court indicated that a petitioner need only prove one of two prongs: either that the offender knowingly caused another to believe that he/she would cause physical harm[14] or that he/she knowingly caused mental distress mental distress.[15] Additionally, the court stressed that a petitioner has to prove this by a preponderance of the evidence. In this case, "even if appellant failed to prove that appellee's actions caused her to suffer mental distress, appellant's evidence still satisfied RC 2903.211(A)."[16]

Conversely, a single incident will not form the basis of a "pattern of conduct" for purposes of obtaining a stalking CPO.[17] In *Channing v. Perkins*,[18] the respondent appealed the grant of a stalking CPO on the ground that there was no pattern of conduct that caused the petitioner physical harm or mental distress.

In this case, the alleged stalker parked his truck near the victim and made an obscene gesture, which was witnessed by a bystander. The appellate court noted that this incident, while childish, "is not necessarily a threat of physical harm or intended to cause mental distress."[19] Without other evidence to indicate a pattern of conduct, a stalking CPO should not have been granted.

Brewster, 2012-Ohio-1290, 2012 WL 1029503 (Ohio Ct. App. 12th Dist. Clermont County 2012); Cooper v. Manta, 2012-Ohio-867, 2012 WL 691547 (Ohio Ct. App. 11th Dist. Lake County 2012); Fortney v. Willhoite, 2012-Ohio-3024, 2012 WL 2522835 (Ohio Ct. App. 11th Dist. Lake County 2012); Lewis v. Jacobs, 2013-Ohio-3461, 2013 WL 4041333 (Ohio Ct. App. 2d Dist. Montgomery County 2013); Sweet v. Hunt, 2014-Ohio-631, 2014 WL 707923 (Ohio Ct. App. 2d Dist. Greene County 2014); Masucci v. Burnbrier, 2015-Ohio-4102, 2015 WL 5781476 (Ohio Ct. App. 7th Dist. Mahoning County 2015) (determining that appellant's conduct did not rise to stalking based on the totality of the actions between the parties and because there were not two incidents).

[14]Wilson v. Lyon, 2016-Ohio-7734, 2016 WL 6678396 (Ohio Ct. App. 3d Dist. Marion County 2016).

[15]Tuuri v. Snyder, 2002-Ohio-2107, 2002 WL 818427, *4 (Ohio Ct. App. 11th Dist. Geauga County 2002); Kruszynski v. Kruszynski, 2013-Ohio-3355, 2013 WL 3965465 (Ohio Ct. App. 5th Dist. Fairfield County 2013); Echemann v. Echemann, 2016-Ohio-3212, 2016 WL 3057979 (Ohio Ct. App. 3d Dist. Shelby County 2016) (petitioner need only demonstrate that respondent knowingly caused petitioner to believe that the respondent would cause physical harm).

[16]Tuuri v. Snyder, 2002-Ohio-2107, 2002 WL 818427, *4 (Ohio Ct. App. 11th Dist. Geauga County 2002). But see dissent, Tuuri v. Snyder, 2002-Ohio-2107, 2002 WL 818427, *5 (Ohio Ct. App. 11th Dist. Geauga County 2002).

[17]See Liles v. Keith, 2009-Ohio-6874, 2009 WL 5064577 (Ohio Ct. App. 3d Dist. Auglaize County 2009); quoting, Kramer v. Kramer, 2002-Ohio-4383, 2002 WL 1967104 (Ohio Ct. App. 3d Dist. Seneca County 2002), citing State v. Scruggs, 136 Ohio App. 3d 631, 737 N.E.2d 574 (2d Dist. Montgomery County 2000). See also Ensley v. Glover, 2012-Ohio-4487, 2012 WL 4480734 (Ohio Ct. App. 6th Dist. Lucas County 2012) (one incident in which respondent indicated he was carrying a gun is not sufficient as a pattern of conduct); Bower v. Long, 2013-Ohio-5467, 2013 WL 6579075 (Ohio Ct. App. 6th Dist. Lucas County 2013).

[18]Channing v. Perkins, 2003-Ohio-4873, 2003 WL 22119575 (Ohio Ct. App. 3d Dist. Seneca County 2003); see also Lemley v. Kirk, 2007-Ohio-1016, 2007 WL 701141 (Ohio Ct. App. 10th Dist. Franklin County 2007) (single incident does not constitute a pattern of conduct).

[19]Channing v. Perkins, 2003-Ohio-4873, 2003 WL 22119575, *2 (Ohio Ct. App. 3d Dist. Seneca County 2003).

Q & A: Can a pattern of conduct (closely related in time) arise out of two or more incidents occurring on the same day, or may it consist of intermittent incidents occurring over a period of years?

Both are true. In *Ellet v. Falk*,[20] the uncle and aunt of two minor children appealed the issuance of a CSPO as being against the manifest weight of the evidence. In determining whether a CSPO should have been issued in this case, the Lucas County Court of Appeals reviewed the statutory elements. Recognizing that the statute fails to define "closely related in time" within which two or more incidents of stalking must occur, the appellate court determined that such a decision is within the discretion of the trier of fact on a case-by-case basis.[21] In order to constitute a "pattern of conduct," the incidents need not occur within any specific time frame.[22]

The appellate court then pointed out that a court should consider evidence in the context of all circumstances in the case. Depending upon those specific circumstances, two or more incidents occurring on the same day,[23] or intermittent incidents occurring over months[24] or years,[25] can constitute a pattern of conduct for purposes of R.C. 2903.211(D).[26]

Q & A: Can a petitioner testify as to a pattern of conduct in

---

[20]Ellet v. Falk, 2010-Ohio-6219, 2010 WL 5269870 (Ohio Ct. App. 6th Dist. Lucas County 2010); see also Retterer v. Little, 2012-Ohio-131, 2012 WL 134305 (Ohio Ct. App. 3d Dist. Marion County 2012).

[21]See also Fondessy v. Simon, 2013-Ohio-3465, 2013 WL 4041564 (Ohio Ct. App. 6th Dist. Ottawa County 2013).

[22]Ellet v. Falk, 2010-Ohio-6219, 2010 WL 5269870, *4 (Ohio Ct. App. 6th Dist. Lucas County 2010); Madison v. Wilborn, 2012-Ohio-2742, 2012 WL 2308618 (Ohio Ct. App. 5th Dist. Stark County 2012); Welborn-Harlow v. Fuller, 2013-Ohio-54, 2013 WL 139592 (Ohio Ct. App. 6th Dist. Wood County 2013); Rufener v. Hutson, 2012-Ohio-5061, 2012 WL 5364703 (Ohio Ct. App. 8th Dist. Cuyahoga County 2012); Williams v. Flannery, 2015-Ohio-2040, 2015 WL 3421319 (Ohio Ct. App. 8th Dist. Cuyahoga County 2015).

[23]See, for example, Warnecke v. Whitaker, 2011-Ohio-5442, 2011 WL 5028789 (Ohio Ct. App. 3d Dist. Putnam County 2011) (providing an example of two distinct acts of stalking occurring on the same day); Halton v. Crossley, 2012-Ohio-550, 2012 WL 440724 (Ohio Ct. App. 5th Dist. Coshocton County 2012); McWilliam v. Dickey, 2013-Ohio-4036, 2013 WL 5310439 (Ohio Ct. App. 8th Dist. Cuyahoga County 2013) (pushing her and then taking her keys and throwing them in a tree so that she could not leave the house formed the basis of a CSPO); Fouch v. Pennington, 2012-Ohio-3536, 2012 WL 3158730 (Ohio Ct. App. 12th Dist. Clermont County 2012); Shockey v. Shockey, 2008-Ohio-6797, 2008 WL 5340554 (Ohio Ct. App. 5th Dist. Delaware County 2008).

[24]See, for example, Kranek v. Richards, 2011-Ohio-6374, 2011 WL 6164727 (Ohio Ct. App. 7th Dist. Jefferson County 2011); Kruszynski v. Kruszynski, 2013-Ohio-3355, 2013 WL 3965465 (Ohio Ct. App. 5th Dist. Fairfield County 2013) (incidents occurring over the span of a few months constituted a pattern of conduct); Dunn v. Clark, 2016-Ohio-641, 2016 WL 698090 (Ohio Ct. App. 12th Dist. Warren County 2016) (Even though the two incidents occurred two months apart, the time span is not so remote as to defeat the existence of a pattern of conduct).

[25]Banfield v. Orazem, 2017-Ohio-8438, ¶ 18, 2017 WL 5151469 (Ohio Ct. App. 11th Dist. Geauga County 2017) (playing loud music making it difficult to hear the TV to upset petitioner and yelling obscenities over a three year period was sufficient proof of metal distress).

[26]Fortney v. Willhoite, 2012-Ohio-3024, 2012 WL 2522835 (Ohio Ct. App. 11th Dist. Lake County 2012); Cooper v. Manta, 2012-Ohio-867, 2012 WL 691547 (Ohio Ct.

which one of the incidents was about something she heard from another?

Not according to the Lucas County Court of Appeals. In *Ensley v. Glover,*[27] petitioner sought a civil stalking protection order. Petitioner testified about two incidents which formed a pattern of conduct and included an incident in which respondent indicated that he was carrying a gun. The other incident was one in which she heard from unnamed others that respondent was looking for her.

The appellate court determined that appellee's testimony that she heard from others that appellant was looking for her was inadmissible hearsay. In reversing judgment of the trial court, the Sixth District Court of Appeals found that "RC 2903.211(D)(1) refers to 'actions' or 'incidents' on the part of the respondent. In our view, the hearsay statements testified to by appellee do not suffice to establish an 'action' or 'incident' to support a finding of a 'pattern of conduct' as that phrase is used in RC 2903.211(D)(1)."[28]

Similarly, in *Masucci v. Burnbrier,*[29] the appellate court sustained appellant's assignment of error and vacated the civil stalking protection order. In *Masucci*, the appellant argued that much of the evidence presented was inadmissible hearsay under Evid. R. 801(C). The first incident that could form the pattern of conduct was an alleged threat that appellant made to Appellee's daughter, S.A., which appellee did not hear. S.A. did not testify. "Appellee testified about the alleged threat, and stated that his other daughter heard it in the background during a phone call between Appellee's daughter, SP, and one of her friends, neither of whom was called to testify about the phone call."[30] The alleged threatening message was that Appellant was heard to have said, he was going to "kick [her] ass."[31] However, no recording of the call was introduced into evidence.

Although appellant objected to the threat made to Appellant's daughter at the trial court level, the court overruled the objections. The appellate court concluded that "[t]he alleged threat does not qualify as non-hearsay under Evid. R. 801(D)(2) as an admission of a

---

App. 11th Dist. Lake County 2012) (even though two of the incidents had occurred two years prior to daughter's filing petition for stalking order and were not closely related in time for purposes of establishing a pattern of conduct, the incidents were relevant to providing context for understanding how subsequent seemingly innocent incidents could be deemed threatening by daughter); Ellet v. Falk, 2010-Ohio-6219, 2010 WL 5269870, *5 (Ohio Ct. App. 6th Dist. Lucas County 2010). But see Rufener v. Hutson, 2012-Ohio-5061, 2012 WL 5364703 (Ohio Ct. App. 8th Dist. Cuyahoga County 2012) (holding that where the threats stopped more than six months before the filing of the petition, the alleged activity was too remote from the petition to support issuance of CSPO).

[27] Ensley v. Glover, 2012-Ohio-4487, 2012 WL 4480734 (Ohio Ct. App. 6th Dist. Lucas County 2012).

[28] Ensley v. Glover, 2012-Ohio-4487, ¶ 15, 2012 WL 4480734 (Ohio Ct. App. 6th Dist. Lucas County 2012).

[29] Masucci v. Burnbrier, 2015-Ohio-4102, 2015 WL 5781476 (Ohio Ct. App. 7th Dist. Mahoning County 2015).

[30] Masucci v. Burnbrier, 2015-Ohio-4102, 2015 WL 5781476, ¶ 11 (Ohio Ct. App. 7th Dist. Mahoning County 2015).

[31] Masucci v. Burnbrier, 2015-Ohio-4102, 2015 WL 5781476, ¶ 11 (Ohio Ct. App. 7th Dist. Mahoning County 2015).

party opponent because it was introduced within hearsay statements. Even if the alleged threat would not be hearsay, the statements of the two daughters relating the threat are clearly hearsay. The statement was offered through Appellee, and not through the youngest daughter directly or even through the older daughter, who supposedly heard the threat in the background of a phone call."[32] Since no one who actually heard the threat was able to authenticate it since they didn't testify, the threat should not have been admitted and cannot be used to support the issuance of the protection order.

Based on the above analysis and because the other evidence presented was insufficient to issue a stalking protection order, the protection order was vacated.

Q & A: Does the statute require that a pattern of conduct be proved by events from at least two different days?

Not according to the Fifth District Court of Appeals in *Tumblin v. Jackson*.[33] In that case, petitioner's testimony that respondent got in her face and she feared physical harm and suffered emotional distress due to his continuous course of conduct was sufficient evidence to obtain a stalking civil protection order. There had been no previous incidents and the incident lasted approximately 20-25 minutes.

On appeal appellant argued, and the Coshocton County Court of Appeals agreed, that the issuance of the protection order was against the manifest weight of the evidence. In reversing the trial court, the appellate court determined that " 'R.C. 2903.211(D)(1) does not require that a pattern of conduct be proved by events from at least two different days. Arguably, a pattern of conduct could arise out of two or more events occurring on the same date, provided that there are sufficient intervals between them.'[34] One incident is insufficient to establish a 'pattern of conduct'."[35] Because the evidence reveals a one-time incident caused by a heated argument over the caring of the children, the record does not support that the appellant has, on more than one occasion, caused or threatened to cause appellee harm or mental distress.

Q & A: When determining if a respondent's conduct constitutes a pattern, is it important to look at the circumstances surrounding the conduct?

[32]Masucci v. Burnbrier, 2015-Ohio-4102, 2015 WL 5781476, ¶ 15 (Ohio Ct. App. 7th Dist. Mahoning County 2015).

[33]Tumblin v. Jackson, 2006-Ohio-3270, 2006 WL 1745055 (Ohio Ct. App. 5th Dist. Coshocton County 2006); see also Hosley v. Seaman, 2008-Ohio-1695, 2008 WL 946085 (Ohio Ct. App. 4th Dist. Ross County 2008).

[34]See also Shockey v. Shockey, 2008-Ohio-6797, 2008 WL 5340554 (Ohio Ct. App. 5th Dist. Delaware County 2008) (holding that the statute only requires actions closely related in time, which may occur on the same day provided that there is a sufficient interval between them); Halton v. Crossley, 2012-Ohio-550, 2012 WL 440724 (Ohio Ct. App. 5th Dist. Coshocton County 2012).

[35]Tumblin v. Jackson, 2006-Ohio-3270, 2006 WL 1745055, *2 (Ohio Ct. App. 5th Dist. Coshocton County 2006); see also Daugherty v. Cross, 2006-Ohio-5545, 2006 WL 3020258 (Ohio Ct. App. 5th Dist. Richland County 2006); Lemley v. Kirk, 2007-Ohio-1016, 2007 WL 701141 (Ohio Ct. App. 10th Dist. Franklin County 2007).

Yes. In *Guthrie v. Long*,[36] the court noted that "[a] court must take everything into consideration when determining if a respondent's conduct constitutes a pattern of conduct, even if some of the person's action's may not, in isolation, seem particularly threatening."[37] Since stalking is a series of acts over time, it is important to look at the totality of the circumstances.[38]

In fact, some courts have held that "the pattern of conduct establishes how present behavior which is apparently innocent can be deemed threatening based on prior encounters between the parties.[39]

On the other hand, an analysis of the "pattern of conduct" in an individual case may indicate that what is considered by the petitioner as threatening conduct is only innocent behavior. For example, in *Howard v. Wilson*,[40] ex-husband sought protection against the current husband under R.C. 2903.214. The basis of the SCPO were the follow-

---

[36]Guthrie v. Long, 2005-Ohio-1541, 2005 WL 737402 (Ohio Ct. App. 10th Dist. Franklin County 2005); see also State v. Lawson, 2007-Ohio-2656, 2007 WL 1560266 (Ohio Ct. App. 10th Dist. Franklin County 2007); see also Middletown v. Jones, 167 Ohio App. 3d 679, 2006-Ohio-3465, 856 N.E.2d 1003 (12th Dist. Butler County 2006); Nguyen v. Chaffee, 2009-Ohio-3352, 2009 WL 1929358 (Ohio Ct. App. 7th Dist. Columbiana County 2009); Krzystan v. Bauer, 2017-Ohio-858, 2017 WL 945183 (Ohio Ct. App. 6th Dist. Ottawa County 2017).

[37]Guthrie v. Long, 2005-Ohio-1541, 2005 WL 737402, *3 (Ohio Ct. App. 10th Dist. Franklin County 2005), quoting Miller v. Francisco, 2003-Ohio-1978, 2003 WL 1904066 (Ohio Ct. App. 11th Dist. Lake County 2003) (overruled on other grounds by, Davis v. DiNunzio, 2005-Ohio-2883, 2005 WL 1383975 (Ohio Ct. App. 11th Dist. Lake County 2005)); McKinley v. Kuhn, 2011-Ohio-134, 2011 WL 281135 (Ohio Ct. App. 4th Dist. Hocking County 2011); Needhamer v. Carlozzi, 2010-Ohio-4562, 2010 WL 3733866 (Ohio Ct. App. 11th Dist. Lake County 2010); Joy v. Letostak, 2015-Ohio-2667, 2015 WL 3964179 (Ohio Ct. App. 10th Dist. Franklin County 2015) (finding that sending angry accusatory emails and notes, threatening to go to petitioner's home uninvited and going to petitioner's home uninvited several times, and not leaving immediately when petitioner did not answer the door, taken together amounted to an implied threat of violence).

[38]See also Meyers v. Sparrow, 2009-Ohio-945, 2009 WL 533057 (Ohio Ct. App. 5th Dist. Ashland County 2009); Madison v. Wilborn, 2012-Ohio-2742, 2012 WL 2308618 (Ohio Ct. App. 5th Dist. Stark County 2012) (petitioner can establish a fear of physical harm or mental distress as a result of a culmination of incidents between himself and the respondent); Mullen v. Hobbs, 2012-Ohio-6098, 2012 WL 6690114 (Ohio Ct. App. 1st Dist. Hamilton County 2012) (court considered years of litigation between the parties); Fortney v. Willhoite, 2012-Ohio-3024, 2012 WL 2522835 (Ohio Ct. App. 11th Dist. Lake County 2012); Fouch v. Pennington, 2012-Ohio-3536, 2012 WL 3158730 (Ohio Ct. App. 12th Dist. Clermont County 2012); Welborn-Harlow v. Fuller, 2013-Ohio-54, 2013 WL 139592 (Ohio Ct. App. 6th Dist. Wood County 2013); Tupps v. Jansen, 2013-Ohio-1403, 2013 WL 1400949 (Ohio Ct. App. 5th Dist. Ashland County 2013).

[39]State v. Bone, 2006-Ohio-3809, 2006 WL 2053398, *6 (Ohio Ct. App. 10th Dist. Franklin County 2006), quoting State v. Shue, 2004-Ohio-5021, 2004 WL 2340073 (Ohio Ct. App. 8th Dist. Cuyahoga County 2004), citing State v. Tichon, 102 Ohio App. 3d 758, 768, 658 N.E.2d 16 (9th Dist. Summit County 1995); Cooper v. Manta, 2012-Ohio-867, 2012 WL 691547 (Ohio Ct. App. 11th Dist. Lake County 2012); Fortney v. Willhoite, 2012-Ohio-3024, 2012 WL 2522835 (Ohio Ct. App. 11th Dist. Lake County 2012).

[40]Howard v. Wilson, 186 Ohio App. 3d 521, 2010-Ohio-1125, 928 N.E.2d 1180 (2d Dist. Montgomery County 2010) See also Sweet v. Hunt, 2014-Ohio-631, 2014 WL 707923 (Ohio Ct. App. 2d Dist. Greene County 2014) (finding that the mental distress required for a menacing by stalking violation need not always be incapacitating or debilitating); Taylor v. Taylor, 2012-Ohio-6190, 2012 WL 6738376 (Ohio Ct. App. 2d Dist. Miami County 2012).

ing acts that caused petitioner to believe the respondent would physically harm him: making phone calls to the police and falsely alleged the children were missing, videotaping petitioner's home, honking the horn of his car, entering his property and leaving an envelope in the mailbox, and arriving early for his scheduled visitation and waiting outside of the petitioner's home. The trial court declined to issue the civil protection order stating that there was insufficient evidence to demonstrate a pattern of conduct "in which [Wilson] made precise threats, or took action to make Howard reasonably believe he was in danger of harm."[41] The trial court then held that "[Wilson's] actions all have a reasonable explanation and do not reasonably demonstrate intent by [Wilson] to harm or intimidate [Howard.]."[42]

The appellate court upheld the trial court denial of the SCPO and found no abuse of discretion. The court also adopted the rationale of the trial court that Wilson acted out of concern for his children and not to menace or stalk Howard. "In other words, as the trial court noted, Wilson's behavior has a logical explanation."[43] The court also relied on Howard's own statement that he had not spoken with Wilson for months and further, noted that Wilson's physical condition would realistically limit his ability to fight Howard.

Of significance is that the Second District Court of Appeals apparently looked at the totality of the circumstances and concluded that where Howard resided in the home with Wilson's wife and children, it was not a surprise that the relationship was less than cordial. That objective fact coupled with Wilson's physical disability and logical responses to Howard's assertions and the child's statement that her father's actions was not meant to be harassment were more significant than Howard's subjective belief that Wilson would physically harm him. Although the appellate court determined that there was insufficient evidence presented by Wilson to demonstrate a pattern of conduct, the more interesting point is that the court relied on the more objective factors relating to Wilson and the parties' relationship, rather than on whether there was an objective basis for Howard's belief that he would be physically harmed.

Q & A: Does it matter if a respondent ceases the conduct before the hearing?

No. In *Kruszynski v. Kruszynski*,[44] appellant appealed the issuance of a civil stalking protection order on the grounds that appellee failed to prove that appellant engaged in a pattern of conduct. In the instant case, appellant had verbally insulted appellee, drove erratically in tailgating her, and made inappropriate gestures at her.

Appellant argued that there was no "pattern of conduct" because the incidents of erratic driving and tailgating that appellee described had not occurred for at least a few months before appellee had filed her petition. Additionally, there was only one incident in the two months preceding the hearing.

---

[41] At *2.

[42] At *2.

[43] At *4.

[44] Kruszynski v. Kruszynski, 2013-Ohio-3355, 2013 WL 3965465 (Ohio Ct. App. 5th Dist. Fairfield County 2013).

The 5th District Court of Appeals first determined that incidents occurring within a few months of filing still constituted a pattern of conduct. Further, "[t]he fact that Appellant stopped or decreased the conduct following Appellee's filing of the petition and prior to the hearing does not negate the fact that he had engaged in a pattern of conduct."[45]

On the other hand, some courts consider whether the "pattern of conduct" is too remote in time to the filing of the petition. In *Wagner v. Holland*,[46] appellant sought a civil stalking protection order against her former paramour which petition was dismissed by the court after a full hearing. The facts of this case indicate that she and appellee engaged in a romantic relationship in May 2015. After exchanging texts, appellant testified that appellee would send numerous texts all the time and threatened to ruin her marriage, her life and her husband's job. He also threatened to kill himself. Appellant advised the court that his threats made her petrified. He also threatened to kill her. On cross-examination, appellant admitted that appellee had never physically assaulted her, that the last time they had contact was in early August 2015 and that she never changed her cell number or Facebook page. She filed for a civil stalking protection order in September 2015. At the time of the full hearing in October 2015, the parties had not had contact for about 2 months.

At the end of appellant's case, appellee requested that the trial court dismiss the case which motion was granted because there had been no pattern of conduct proven proximate in time to the filing of the CSPO and because there was no evidence of physical harm. The trial court found that there was not an "immediate and present danger" and that appellant "was equally culpable in sending text messages going the other way, encouraging the dust storm to continue just as much as the other way."[47]

The appellate court affirmed the trial court decision based on the fact that the parties had no contact in about a month, appellant did not change her phone number or her Facebook page and because she also sent text messages to him. The court also made mention of the trial court's findings that the pattern of conduct was not proximate in time to the filing of petition and that because there was no immediate and present danger.

It is important to note that the test for the granting of a protection order after a full hearing is whether the appellant believed that she was in continued danger.[48] The "immediate and present danger" test applies only to the ex parte protection order.[49] This is true whether it is a domestic violence civil protection order or a civil stalking protection order.

---

[45]Kruszynski v. Kruszynski, 2013-Ohio-3355, 2013 WL 3965465, ¶ 20 (Ohio Ct. App. 5th Dist. Fairfield County 2013).

[46]Wagner v. Holland, 2016-Ohio-5028, 2016 WL 3920162 (Ohio Ct. App. 5th Dist. Fairfield County 2016).

[47]Wagner v. Holland, 2016-Ohio-5028, ¶ 19, 2016 WL 3920162 (Ohio Ct. App. 5th Dist. Fairfield County 2016).

[48]See Felton v. Felton, 79 Ohio St. 3d 34, 1997-Ohio-302, 679 N.E.2d 672 (1997); see also Text 12:11; Text 8:3; Text 8:4.

[49]RC 2903.214(D)(1).

Q & A: What actions of a respondent constitute stalking for the purpose of obtaining a stalking civil protection order?

Pursuant to R.C. 2903.211, menacing by stalking is defined as "engaging in a pattern of conduct" which will knowingly cause another person to believe the offender will cause physical harm to the other person or cause mental distress to the other person. Whether a respondent's acts rise to the level of stalking is a factual determination made on a case by case basis.

For example, in *Guthrie v. Long*,[50] testimony was presented that appellant (appellee's former boyfriend) appeared uninvited to appellee's parents' home, which resulted in them calling the police and having him ordered to leave the premises. Appellee testified that appellant had sent e-mails regarding appellee to co-workers, had posted materials on bulletin boards at their place of employment, resulting in appellant being transferred to another location. Appellee testified that after appellant was transferred, she had seen his car at the office parking lot where she works.

In affirming the trial court, the Franklin County Court of Appeals agreed with the trial court's adoption of the magistrate conclusions that appellant's conduct caused appellee to fear for her safety.

Similarly, in *DeRolph v. Cirillo*,[51] the appellee obtained an anti-stalking civil protection order against appellant due to several threatening incidents. Evidence was presented indicating that appellant threatened to kill or beat her on several occasions. On one such occasion, appellant walked by appellee, "pointed at her and mouthed to her 'You're dead,' while sliding his right index finger across his throat and shaking his head 'yes' with a big smile on his face. Appellant and his wife were escorted out of the store."[52]

The appellate court affirmed the trial court decision, noting that appellee had provided a significant amount of evidence showing a

[50]Guthrie v. Long, 2005-Ohio-1541, 2005 WL 737402 (Ohio Ct. App. 10th Dist. Franklin County 2005). See also Jones v. Miley, 2003-Ohio-2939, 2003 WL 21321189 (Ohio Ct. App. 3d Dist. Marion County 2003) (where continuous harassment, driving by petitioner's residence, honking car horns, and making obscene gestures over a period of time constituted stalking for purposes of a civil talking protection order; in this case, however, the court had issues protection orders against both parties [each party filed a separate petition] because there was evidence of mutual harassment and each instigated the clashes at various times); Gruber v. Hart, 2007-Ohio-873, 2007 WL 625818, *4 (Ohio Ct. App. 6th Dist. Ottawa County 2007) (where appellant came to appellee's home, sought her out in public at least 5 times while in uniform, the contacts were unwanted, at least 1 contact resulted in physical injury to appellee and appellee was and remains in fear of appellant); Stout v. Bushong, 2008-Ohio-2223, 2008 WL 1991613 (Ohio Ct. App. 4th Dist. Adams County 2008) (affirming judgment of trial court upholding issuance of the CSPO for new husband against ex-spouse of wife who had recently obtained a CSPO against her ex-spouse; appellant had written three letters to appellee at the address shared by appellee and his wife in violation of wife's CSPO; such actions caused appellee and wife mental distress).

[51]Derolph v. Cirillo, 2004-Ohio-5564, 2004 WL 2348509 (Ohio Ct. App. 5th Dist. Licking County 2004); see also Hayton v. White, 2004-Ohio-6640, 2004 WL 2847802 (Ohio Ct. App. 5th Dist. Ashland County 2004); Bucksbaum v. Mitchell, 2004-Ohio-2233, 2004 WL 943865 (Ohio Ct. App. 5th Dist. Richland County 2004); Rosen v. Chesler, 2009-Ohio-3163, 2009 WL 1900422 (Ohio Ct. App. 9th Dist. Lorain County 2009).

[52]Derolph v. Cirillo, 2004-Ohio-5564, 2004 WL 2348509, *1 (Ohio Ct. App. 5th Dist. Licking County 2004).

number of threatening incidents which constituted threats of bodily harm[53] and which individually and collectively caused appellee mental distress and appellee's fear was reasonable in light of the same.[54]

Moreover, in *Jenkins v. Jenkins*,[55] appellee testified that appellant twice appeared in the late evening or early morning hours and banged loudly on her door, attempting to gain entry. In one of the incidents, he shouted, "I know where you live" before leaving in his car. The appellate court determined that [a] reasonable trier of fact could infer that the late night appearance and exclamation, "I know where you live," was an implied threat of violence. Therefore a reasonable trier of fact could conclude that appellant acted knowingly to cause appellee to believe that he would cause physical harm to her. A reasonable trier of fact could also conclude that appellant knowingly made the statement to cause mental distress to appellee."[56]

Likewise, in *Walker v. Edgington*,[57] appellant appealed the issuance of a civil stalking protection order. In that case, the parties had dated for two years. After their breakup, appellant continuously called and emailed her, followed her, pulled his car into her driveway, called her a "Bitch" and "Whore," and accused her of having sex. He even sent her emails after she filed the petition for protection order. He also called her and threatened suicide and left a rose and letter on the seat of her car which was located in her driveway. In the letter, he described a second suicide threat in graphic detail.

In her testimony, appellee stated that he was obsessed with her and that he "freaks her out."[58] She also testified that he had a gun collection and "always carries a gun."[59]

His actions caused her to change her telephone number and change her email account. His conduct caused her to have trouble sleeping and when she did sleep, she had nightmares.

In affirming the trial court, the Clark County Court of Appeals

---

[53]See also Daugherty v. Cross, 2006-Ohio-5545, 2006 WL 3020258 (Ohio Ct. App. 5th Dist. Richland County 2006).

[54]Derolph v. Cirillo, 2004-Ohio-5564, 2004 WL 2348509, *2 (Ohio Ct. App. 5th Dist. Licking County 2004).

[55]Jenkins v. Jenkins, 2007-Ohio-422, 2007 WL 275700 (Ohio Ct. App. 10th Dist. Franklin County 2007).

[56]Jenkins v. Jenkins, 2007-Ohio-422, 2007 WL 275700, *3-4 (Ohio Ct. App. 10th Dist. Franklin County 2007); see also Lias v. Beekman, 2007-Ohio-5737, 2007 WL 3108899, *3 (Ohio Ct. App. 10th Dist. Franklin County 2007) ("a trial court may rely on its knowledge and experience in determining whether mental distress has been caused").

[57]Walker v. Edgington, 2008-Ohio-3478, 2008 WL 2699430 (Ohio Ct. App. 2d Dist. Clark County 2008); Martin v. Popson, 2013-Ohio-3956, 2013 WL 5211329 (Ohio Ct. App. 6th Dist. Ottawa County 2013) (past act of physical abuse coupled with a "profanity laced order" not to take her horses out while appellant was present and to "get the f* * * away from her" were sufficient to constitute a pattern of behavior within the meaning of the law); Stump v. Hoagland, 2015-Ohio-2434, 2015 WL 3822270 (Ohio Ct. App. 2d Dist. Miami County 2015) (numerous calls, a block thrown through a car window and threats to "get out of my way" and "get out of my house f'n bitch" was enough to show mental distress).

[58]Walker v. Edgington, 2008-Ohio-3478, 2008 WL 2699430, *1(Ohio Ct. App. 2d Dist. Clark County 2008).

[59]Walker v. Edgington, 2008-Ohio-3478, 2008 WL 2699430, *2 (Ohio Ct. App. 2d Dist. Clark County 2008).

reasoned that the petitioner need not prove that the respondent intended to cause actual harm to her; instead, the evidence must show that the respondent knowingly engage in a pattern of conduct that caused the other person to believe that the respondent *will cause* physical harm or that *caused* mental distress to the other person.[60]

The "pattern of conduct" element of the statute was satisfied by the continuous calling and emailing, and by confronting her in the restaurant.[61] The "mental distress" element was established by appellee's testimony that she had trouble sleeping and her fear that appellant would cause her physical harm. "Indeed, Edgington acknowledged that Walker had cause to feel stress due to his actions."[62]

In *Rauser v. Ghaster*,[63] the respondent engaged in the following behaviors: yelling threats and gesturing obscenely as they walked in the neighborhood, standing on the street directly in front of their home for hours at a time yelling threats and taking photos of them, repeatedly calling on the phone saying that Laurie was "going to be sorry" if she did not testify and leaving a book in the bushes for their daughter.[64]

In reversing the trial court's grant of the directed verdict at the close of the Rausers' evidence, the appellate court found that although the threatening behaviors began in 2006, they persisted until the filing of the action in 2008. It determined that such behaviors created more than an uncomfortable situation or an annoyance; rather, it was persistent and threatening harassment that left the Rausers in constant fear of physical danger.[65] Additionally, the evidence of mental distress was a change in sleeping pattern; getting up every few hours

[60]Walker v. Edgington, 2008-Ohio-3478, 2008 WL 2699430, *3(Ohio Ct. App. 2d Dist. Clark County 2008) (emphasis added).

[61]See for example, Jones v. Bayer, 2014-Ohio-5326, 2014 WL 6758258 (Ohio Ct. App. 5th Dist. Tuscarawas County 2014) ("It ain't beneath me to deck you" and returning to petitioner's table three times, calling petitioner and her friends names, failing to leave when asked to, screaming at them and threatening them by saying "watch your back" met the definition of a pattern of conduct).

[62]Walker v. Edgington, 2008-Ohio-3478, 2008 WL 2699430, *4 (Ohio Ct. App. 2d Dist. Clark County 2008); R.G. v. R.M., 2017-Ohio-8918, ¶ 29, 88 N.E.3d 1027 (Ohio Ct. App. 7th Dist. Mahoning County 2017) (although petitioner did not mention lack of sleep, she expressed her alarm, concern and fear for her safety and her statement that her life changed completely by way of changed habits and behaviors caused a trier of fact to conclude that her daily life had been affected in a significant manner).

[63]Rauser v. Ghaster, 2009-Ohio-4027, 2009 WL 2462553 (Ohio Ct. App. 8th Dist. Cuyahoga County 2009), decision vacated and superseded on reconsideration on other grounds, 2009-Ohio-5698, 2009 WL 3490654 (Ohio Ct. App. 8th Dist. Cuyahoga County 2009) (later decision clarified that it was the directed verdict at the close of the evidence that was error; neither the decision nor the legal analysis changed).

[64]*Rauser at *3*; see also Needhamer v. Carlozzi, 2010-Ohio-4562, 2010 WL 3733866 (Ohio Ct. App. 11th Dist. Lake County 2010) (citing examples of behaviors from other cases including seemingly friendly encounters, indirect threats, text messages such as "hope you found better," hostile demeanor, intimidating hand gestures that, in light of prior indirect threats, could constitute a pattern of conduct for purposes of issuing a protection order and where some of the threats were made after the issuance of, and thus in violation of, the ex parte order).

[65]*Rauser at *4*, citing Kramer v. Kramer, 2002-Ohio-4383, 2002 WL 1967104 (Ohio Ct. App. 3d Dist. Seneca County 2002); see also Olenik v. Huff, 2003-Ohio-4621, 2003 WL 22039490 (Ohio Ct. App. 5th Dist. Ashland County 2003) but see Nwosu v. Underwood, 2007-Ohio-1907, 2007 WL 1175230 (Ohio Ct. App. 3d Dist. Marion County

to check the doors, even though they were checked and locked; and not letting their daughter out of their sight.[66]

Q & A: What actions do not rise to the level of stalking?

On the other hand, the trial court in *Gilreath v. Kinderdine*,[67] denied petitioner's request for an anti-stalking protection order on behalf of him and his wife, the former wife of respondent. In this case, evidence of the mental distress claim was that the current wife had been taking Paxil for several years for the anxiety disorder caused by the respondent. With respect to the physical harm claim, the petitioner testified that respondent used foul terms to describe him, that he sent a note to petitioner on which he drew a smiley face with a black eye, that he had rushed at his former wife's car, but then stopped and returned to his house when he saw petitioner waiting for her. Respondent had also threatened petitioner with legal action.[68]

The Miami County Court of Appeals affirmed the trial court's denial of the civil protection order and held that "R.C. 2903.211(A) comprehends conduct on the part of an offender that involves a direct threat of physical harm or conduct from which a victim reasonably would believe that a prospect of physical harm exists which is specific and real. None of Kinderdine's actions rise to that level. At most, they are a product of ongoing frictions and hostilities, many of them created by Gilreath himself, which portrays anger and frustration, but without the prospect that physical harm will be inflicted on him."[69]

In regard to the mental distress claim, the appellate court agreed with the trial court that anxiety is not a "substantial incapacity" and neither would it "normally require psychiatric treatment."[70]

2007).

[66]See also Needhamer v. Carlozzi, 2010-Ohio-4562, 2010 WL 3733866 (Ohio Ct. App. 11th Dist. Lake County 2010) (evidence of mental distress consisted of seeing a therapist soon after the incident and taking anti-anxiety medication); R.G. v. R.M., 2017-Ohio-8918, ¶ 30, 88 N.E.3d 1027 (Ohio Ct. App. 7th Dist. Mahoning County 2017) (testimony that petitioner felt as though she was required to be constantly aware of her surroundings due to a barrage of unanswered love letters caused court to conclude that "hypervigilance can be viewed by a reasonable fact-finder as a mental condition which would normally require mental health services or counselling").

[67]Gilreath v. Kinderdine, 2004-Ohio-868, 2004 WL 362335 (Ohio Ct. App. 2d Dist. Miami County 2004); see also Lemley v. Kirk, 2007-Ohio-1016, 2007 WL 701141, ¶ 4 (Ohio Ct. App. 10th Dist. Franklin County 2007) (because there was no pattern of threats of physical harm, only one incident, and no evidence of serious mental distress, these incidents could not have been part of a pattern of conduct, no matter when they occurred. There was one incident in 8/2004 when appellee threatened him by phone and another incident in 12/2005 when appellant overheard appellee say to another that "whomever subpoenaed him was going to have to pay him for it or they would be in serious trouble." Incidents of 2005 were not related in close proximity to the 2004 threat).

[68]Gilreath v. Kinderdine, 2004-Ohio-868, 2004 WL 362335, *2 (Ohio Ct. App. 2d Dist. Miami County 2004).

[69]Gilreath v. Kinderdine, 2004-Ohio-868, 2004 WL 362335, *2 (Ohio Ct. App. 2d Dist. Miami County 2004).

[70]Gilreath v. Kinderdine, 2004-Ohio-868, 2004 WL 362335, *2 (Ohio Ct. App. 2d Dist. Miami County 2004); see also R.C. 2903.211(D)(2); Beadnell v. McAdam, 2016-Ohio-8207, 2016 WL 7396476 (Ohio Ct. App. 7th Dist. Jefferson County 2016) (reversing the issuance of a CSPO and holding that anxiety alone, without more, does not rise to the statutory definition of mental distress because petitioner testified that

In *Dupal v. Sommer*,[71] the appellee filed for a SCPO in November 2008 based on numerous text messages and telephone calls and subtle threats. The appellant appealed claiming that the issuance of the order was against the manifest weight of the evidence and an abuse of discretion.

The appellate court reversed the issuance of the stalking civil protection order based on the fact that there were no timelines in the petition and no testimony to establish that there was any contact or threatening behavior between June 2008 and the filing of the petition in November 2008. The court held that "there is no evidence in the record to establish the mandates of R.C. 2903.211 and R.C. 2903.214. The allegations in the petition are very broad and allege 'stalking behavior' almost two years before the filing of the petition. Appellee consented to the relationship throughout 2007 and only testified to harassing text messages and telephone calls starting in January of 2008. However, appellee continued to reside in appellant's apartment rent free until May 2008 and retained possession of his truck until June 7, 2008. No evidence was presented to establish a "pattern of conduct" after June 2008."[72]

Q & A: In order to prevail on a motion for civil protection order, must the petitioner be able to identify the respondent as the person who committed the acts of stalking?

The Franklin County Court of Appeals tangentially addressed this issue and reversed the judgment supporting the issuance of a SCPO to Lee. In *Szymanski v. Trendel*,[73] appellee alleged that appellant made several late night/early morning telephone calls to her. In reversing the judgment, the appellate court considered the fact that appellee was unable to identify the caller because the calls were "blocked." Absent other relevant evidence supporting a pattern of conduct, the judgment supporting the issuance of the SCPO must be reversed.

Q & A: Does RC 2903.211 require that the victim actually experience mental distress or is it sufficient that a victim believes that the offender would cause the victim mental distress?

Unfortunately the law is unsettled in this area. RC 2903.211 is violated if an offender (respondent) knowingly causes another to believe that the offender will cause physical harm to the other person

---

the texts were not threatening and he was not afraid McAdam would hurt him); but see Wilson v. Lyon, 2016-Ohio-7734, 2016 WL 6678396 (Ohio Ct. App. 3d Dist. Marion County 2016) (considerable fear and anxiety can support a finding of mental distress).

[71]Dupal v. Sommer, 2009-Ohio-5791, 2009 WL 3600358 (Ohio Ct. App. 5th Dist. Stark County 2009)

[72]*Dupal at *5*; see also Miller v. Shaw, 2009-Ohio-6753, 2009 WL 4895276 (Ohio Ct. App. 7th Dist. Carroll County 2009) (denied SCPO based on insufficient evidence of a pattern of conduct).

[73]Szymanski v. Trendel, 2009-Ohio-992, 2009 WL 580457 (Ohio Ct. App. 6th Dist. Lucas County 2009); Charles v. Peters, 2016-Ohio-1259, 2016 WL 1178776 (Ohio Ct. App. 2d Dist. Greene County 2016); but see Frenchko v. Frenchko-Nagy, 2015-Ohio-4546, 42 N.E.3d 829 (Ohio Ct. App. 11th Dist. Trumbull County 2015).

or cause mental distress to the other person.[74] Implicit in the "physical harm" claim is the belief that one will cause another physical harm in the future. This is exactly the reason to request a protection order: to protect a person from future harm.[75] While Ohio courts agree that a petitioner only has to establish that the respondent caused a protected person to believe that the respondent will cause them physical harm, this is not the case for the "mental distress" claim.

Appellate courts are split concerning whether, to establish a violation of RC 2903.211(A)(1) based on mental distress, it is sufficient to show that the victim *believed* that the offender *would cause* mental distress or whether the offender must have *actually caused* mental distress.

Several appellate courts have indicated that to prevail on a claim of mental distress, the pattern of conduct must have *actually caused* mental distress.[76] For example, in *State v. Kent*, the appellate court found that the offender knowingly caused the victim to believe that he would cause her physical harm in the future, that her belief was reasonable and that he did cause her mental distress within the meaning of RC 2903.211.[77] However, the court also noted that "it was not necessary for Kent to have knowingly caused mental distress to the degree that Brandi Miller required counseling or to have actually caused her physical harm."[78]

The concurring opinion strongly advised the majority not to misinterpret the mental distress element of the statute. To violate RC 2903.211, the violator must cause the victim to believe that the action actually caused the victim mental distress.[79] "Mental distress is not used in the colloquial sense of 'discomfort,' but is specifically defined as any mental illness or condition that 1) involves some temporary substantial incapacity or 2) would normally require psychiatric treatment. Ms. Miller was obviously discomforted, but not to the extent of substantial incapacity or psychiatric treatment."[80]

---

[74]See, for example, Perry v. Joseph, 2008-Ohio-1107, 2008 WL 660317 (Ohio Ct. App. 10th Dist. Franklin County 2008).

[75]See for example, Mullen v. Hobbs, 2012-Ohio-6098, 2012 WL 6690114 (Ohio Ct. App. 1st Dist. Hamilton County 2012); Ensley v. Glover, 2012-Ohio-4487, 2012 WL 4480734 (Ohio Ct. App. 6th Dist. Lucas County 2012); Welborn-Harlow v. Fuller, 2013-Ohio-54, 2013 WL 139592 (Ohio Ct. App. 6th Dist. Wood County 2013).

[76]State v. Kent, 2000 WL 429612 (Ohio Ct. App. 1st Dist. Hamilton County 2000).

[77]State v. Kent, 2000 WL 429612, *6 (Ohio Ct. App. 1st Dist. Hamilton County 2000).

[78]State v. Kent, 2000 WL 429612, *6 (Ohio Ct. App. 1st Dist. Hamilton County 2000).

[79]But see State v. Smith, 126 Ohio App. 3d 193, 709 N.E.2d 1245 (7th Dist. Mahoning County 1998).

[80]State v. Kent, 2000 WL 429612, *6 (Ohio Ct. App. 1st Dist. Hamilton County 2000). But see Echemann v. Echemann, 2016-Ohio-3212, 2016 WL 3057979 (Ohio Ct. App. 3d Dist. Shelby County 2016) (to prove mental distress, petitioner must demonstrate that he/she suffered from a mental illness or condition that involved some temporary substantial incapacity or that would normally require mental health services. "Incapacity is substantial if it has a significant impact upon the victim's daily life." At ¶ 37; citing, *Retterer*, 2012-Ohio-131, ¶ 41, quoting State v. Horsley,

In *Baker v. Inman*,[81] the trial court found that appellee's testimony demonstrated that the victim suffered an elevated level of stress which reduced her productivity at work and affected her income. She had to increase her medication due to the aggravation of a pre-existing condition as a result of the stress caused by respondent. The trial court held that "the evidence taken in its entirety supported a finding that appellant "knowingly engaged in a pattern of conduct which *would* cause mental distress to appellee."[82]

However, the appellate court found that appellee had not shown that she suffered a "temporary substantial incapacity or mental illness or condition requiring psychiatric treatment," as set forth in RC 2903.211(D)(2). Her stress level did not cause her to fear leaving home to complete her daily tasks.[83] The fact that appellant was a law enforcement officer and carried a weapon was not enough, in and of itself, to support a finding that he knowingly engaged in a pattern of conduct to cause appellee to believe he would cause her harm, despite her subjective fear.[84] Repeated hang-up calls in the absence of demonstrated mental distress will not support the issuance of a civil stalking protection order.

Lastly, in *Darling v. Darling*,[85] appellee was granted a three year protection order against her mother-in-law and her sister-in-law because of confrontations occurring with both of them at school, church and other places. Additionally, appellee received threatening letters signed by "your loving family" and her car tires were slashed and her porch was set on fire.

The Jefferson County Court of Appeals reversed the trial court's issuance of the permanent civil stalking protection order because there was no concrete evidence that the appellants sent the threatening letters or caused the vandalism. "While the Court has held that explicit

---

2006-Ohio-1208, 2006 WL 648849 (Ohio Ct. App. 10th Dist. Franklin County 2006)); Ramsey v. Pellicioni, 2016-Ohio-558, 2016 WL 635212 (Ohio Ct. App. 7th Dist. Mahoning County 2016) (noting that had the Pellicionis' conduct been so distressing, it would seem that Mrs. Ramsey would have filed for the civil protection order much sooner. "While the Ramseys contacted the police on several occasions, they did not show they were at all incapacitated for any period of time or that their stress reached a level where one would normally require professional mental health services." at ¶ 34; but see Wulf v. Opp, 2015-Ohio-3285, 2015 WL 4878495 (Ohio Ct. App. 12th Dist. Clermont County 2015) (finding that mental distress need not be incapacitating.).

[81]Baker v. Inman, 2004-Ohio-6133, 2004 WL 2616419, *3 (Ohio Ct. App. 5th Dist. Delaware County 2004). But see J.B. v. Harford, 2015-Ohio-13, 2015 WL 82527, ¶ 30 (Ohio Ct. App. 9th Dist. Summit County 2015) (noting that it did not read the 5th District, in *Baker,* as standing for the proposition that petitioner's fear must be objectively reasonable, and explaining that some courts have held that petitioner's fear is judged by a subjective, rather than an objective test).

[82]Baker v. Inman, 2004-Ohio-6133, 2004 WL 2616419, *3 (Ohio Ct. App. 5th Dist. Delaware County 2004) (emphasis added).

[83]But see also Frenchko v. Frenchko-Nagy, 2015-Ohio-4546, 42 N.E.3d 829 (Ohio Ct. App. 11th Dist. Trumbull County 2015) (distinguishing *Baker* and finding that evidence that Natasha felt compelled to sleep on the floor, contact police and seek treatment from her doctor supported her testimony that she suffered mental distress).

[84]Baker v. Inman, 2004-Ohio-6133, 2004 WL 2616419, *4 (Ohio Ct. App. 5th Dist. Delaware County 2004).

[85]Darling v. Darling, 2007-Ohio-3151, 2007 WL 1806042 (Ohio Ct. App. 7th Dist. Jefferson County 2007).

threats are not necessary to establish the elements of menacing by stalking, and that stalking can be based, in part, on derogatory language and profane gestures, it is not at all clear that merely rude gestures or snide remarks to another person constitute menacing by stalking and by extension, justify issuing a civil stalking protection order."[86] Without some evidence to suggest that appellants **caused** appellee to suffer mental distress, there is no basis for the SCPO. Additionally, the Court found that there was no evidence to connect the incidents to the appellants.[87]

More recently, the Seventh District Court of Appeals refined the issue and asked whether a respondent must have actually caused the victim to suffer mental distress or whether he need have only caused the victim to believe he would cause her mental distress. What is different in this case is that the appellate court noted the various appellate district interpretations and analyses and formulated a test in order to determine whether mental distress must have actually been caused.

In *Caban v. Ransome,*[88] appellant appealed the grant of a SCPO issued against him on the ground that there was no competent, credible evidence against him as to the elements of menacing by stalking.

In first assessing whether appellant caused appellee to believe he would cause her physical harm, the appellate court noted that appellee did not testify that she feared for her safety; "[i]nstead, it seems as if what she feared was that appellant would confront her again and ask her again why she broke up with him after a fourteen year relationship."[89] The court next determined that "[l]abeling a call threatening does not express a belief that the caller would cause physical harm. That is, threatening to approach a person for conversation is not a threat of physical harm."[90]

The Court then analyzed whether actual mental distress is necessary to satisfy the statute. The Court acknowledged that both Lucas County and Montgomery County appellate courts have found that stalking can be found even if the defendant only caused the victim to believe that mental distress would be caused.[91]

---

[86]Darling v. Darling, 2007-Ohio-3151, 2007 WL 1806042, *4 (Ohio Ct. App. 7th Dist. Jefferson County 2007); Krzystan v. Bauer, 2017-Ohio-858, 2017 WL 945183 (Ohio Ct. App. 6th Dist. Ottawa County 2017) (calling someone a bitch may be rude or boorish but it is not stalking under RC 2903.211 or RC 2903.214).

[87]See also Szymanski v. Trendel, 2009-Ohio-992, 2009 WL 580457 (Ohio Ct. App. 6th Dist. Lucas County 2009); but see the dissent in *Darling v. Darling* in which the dissenting opinion stressed that it was reasonable to infer that the appellants sent the letters and caused the vandalism. Darling v. Darling, 2007-Ohio-3151, 2007 WL 1806042, *5 (Ohio Ct. App. 7th Dist. Jefferson County 2007).

[88]Caban v. Ransome, 2009-Ohio-1034, 2009 WL 582761 (Ohio Ct. App. 7th Dist. Mahoning County 2009). But see J.B. v. Harford, 2015-Ohio-13, 2015 WL 82527 (Ohio Ct. App. 9th Dist. Summit County 2015) (differentiating this case from *Caban* and stating that JB feared that Mr. Harford would cause her physical harm).

[89]Caban v. Ransome, 2009-Ohio-1034, 2009 WL 582761, *3 (Ohio Ct. App. 7th Dist. Mahoning County 2009).

[90]Caban v. Ransome, 2009-Ohio-1034, 2009 WL 582761, *3 (Ohio Ct. App. 7th Dist. Mahoning County 2009).

[91]Caban v. Ransome, 2009-Ohio-1034, 2009 WL 582761, *4 (Ohio Ct. App. 7th

However, in the Seventh,[92] Fourth, Ninth[93] and Twelfth[94] appellate districts, the test is whether mental distress was actually caused.[95] The question appears to be whether the behavior of the respondent causes mental distress to the victim or whether the respondent acted in such a way that would cause a reasonable person to feel threatened of physical harm and/or suffer mental distress. In concluding that mental distress must have actually been caused to the victim, the court further noted "that by repeating 'to the other person' after both physical harm and mental distress, rather than merely placing it at the end of the sentence, the legislature expressed that 'to believe' does not modify 'mental distress.' "[96]

In analyzing whether mental distress was caused to the victim in this case, the court acknowledged that, although the fact-finder can rely on its own experience and knowledge to determine if mental distress was caused, mental distress for purposes of menacing by stalking is not mere mental stress or annoyance.[97]

In reversing the grant of the SCPO, the appellate court found that

---

Dist. Mahoning County 2009), citing Irwin v. Murray, 2006-Ohio-1633, 2006 WL 832830 (Ohio Ct. App. 6th Dist. Lucas County 2006), and Dayton v. Davis, 136 Ohio App. 3d 26, 32, 735 N.E.2d 939 (2d Dist. Montgomery County 1999); see also Bloom v. Macbeth, 2008-Ohio-4564, 2008 WL 4151319 (Ohio Ct. App. 5th Dist. Ashland County 2008); Ellet v. Falk, 2010-Ohio-6219, 2010 WL 5269870 (Ohio Ct. App. 6th Dist. Lucas County 2010) (holding that victim must prove only that she/he believes mental distress would be caused); Gruber v. Hart, 2007-Ohio-873, 2007 WL 625818 (Ohio Ct. App. 6th Dist. Ottawa County 2007); Bower v. Long, 2013-Ohio-5467, 2013 WL 6579075 (Ohio Ct. App. 6th Dist. Lucas County 2013) (noting that the testimony of the victim as to his or her fear is sufficient to establish mental distress, at ¶ 14); Fondessy v. Simon, 2013-Ohio-3465, 2013 WL 4041564 (Ohio Ct. App. 6th Dist. Ottawa County 2013).

[92]R.G. v. R.M., 2017-Ohio-8918, ¶ 12-17, 88 N.E.3d 1027 (Ohio Ct. App. 7th Dist. Mahoning County 2017) (discussion of actual mental distress based on the relation of the phrases used, their construct and grammar and the stringent test used to determine whether mental distress exists in a case which requires more than mere stress or annoyance).

[93]See A.S. v. P.F., 2013-Ohio-4857, 2013 WL 5925968 (Ohio Ct. App. 9th Dist. Lorain County 2013) (relying on State v. Barnhardt, 2006-Ohio-4531, 2006 WL 2528503 (Ohio Ct. App. 9th Dist. Lorain County 2006), which found that in order to show that defendant violated R.C. 2903.213, the State must show that the defendant engaged in conduct that he knew would probably cause the complainant to believe that defendant would harm her or that he knew would probably cause the complainant to suffer from mental distress), cf. Holloway v. Parker, 2013-Ohio-1940, 2013 WL 1944400 (Ohio Ct. App. 3d Dist. Marion County 2013) (noting that a majority of appellate districts have concluded that the statute requires "only that the victim believes the stalker would cause mental distress," at ¶ 7).

[94]But see State v. Hart, 2009-Ohio-997, 2009 WL 580808 (Ohio Ct. App. 12th Dist. Warren County 2009); Fouch v. Pennington, 2012-Ohio-3536, 2012 WL 3158730 (Ohio Ct. App. 12th Dist. Clermont County 2012).

[95]See for example, Smith v. Wunsch, 162 Ohio App. 3d 21, 2005-Ohio-3498, 832 N.E.2d 757 (4th Dist. Hocking County 2005); State v. Payne, 178 Ohio App. 3d 617, 2008-Ohio-5447, 899 N.E.2d 1011 (9th Dist. Summit County 2008).

[96]Caban v. Ransome, 2009-Ohio-1034, 2009 WL 582761, *4 (Ohio Ct. App. 7th Dist. Mahoning County 2009).

[97]Caban v. Ransome, 2009-Ohio-1034, 2009 WL 582761, *5 (Ohio Ct. App. 7th Dist. Mahoning County 2009), citing Smith v. Wunsch, 162 Ohio App. 3d 21, ¶ 18, 2005-Ohio-3498, 832 N.E.2d 757 (4th Dist. Hocking County 2005); but see Walker v. Edgington, 2008-Ohio-3478, 2008 WL 2699430 (Ohio Ct. App. 2d Dist. Clark County 2008); see also Holloway v. Parker, 2013-Ohio-1940, 2013 WL 1944400 (Ohio Ct. App.

while the testimony demonstrated that appellee was sick of appellant and that he was annoyingly obsessed with why she left him and why she refused to speak with him and which incident may be telephone harassment, the calls did not establish that mental distress, as statutorily defined, was actually suffered by the appellee.[98]

On the other hand and as noted above, some of the appellate districts have held that ". . . a showing of actual mental distress is not a required element of menacing by stalking; a petitioner need only establish that the respondent knowingly caused him or her to believe that mental distress or physical harm would result in the future."[99]

For example, in *Jenkins v. Jenkins*,[100] the appellate court agreed with the decision of other courts that have held that a showing of actual mental distress is not a required element of menacing by stalking.[101] "Instead, it was only necessary to establish that appellant knowingly caused appellee to believe that he would cause her mental

---

3d Dist. Marion County 2013). But see Fondessy v. Simon, 2013-Ohio-3465, 2013 WL 4041564 (Ohio Ct. App. 6th Dist. Ottawa County 2013) (differentiating *Caban* and finding that a rational trier of fact could conclude that because appellant knew that the Fondessys were aging (both in their seventies) and that Wayne was in poor health, appellant knew that his actions and behavior (such as appellant's expressed wish that Wayne had another heart attack, his yelling profanities at them, blowing leaves and debris on their property) would cause the Fondessys mental distress); Echemann v. Echemann, 2016-Ohio-3212, 2016 WL 3057979 (Ohio Ct. App. 3d Dist. Shelby County 2016); Ramsey v. Pellicioni, 2016-Ohio-558, 2016 WL 635212 (Ohio Ct. App. 7th Dist. Mahoning County 2016); Wilson v. Lyon, 2016-Ohio-7734, 2016 WL 6678396 (Ohio Ct. App. 3d Dist. Marion County 2016).

[98]Caban v. Ransome, 2009-Ohio-1034, 2009 WL 582761, *5 (Ohio Ct. App. 7th Dist. Mahoning County 2009); but see Griga v. DiBenedetto, 2012-Ohio-6097, 988 N.E.2d 590 (Ohio Ct. App. 1st Dist. Hamilton County 2012).

[99]Van Vorce v. Van Vorce, 2004-Ohio-5646, 2004 WL 2377839, *4 (Ohio Ct. App. 3d Dist. Auglaize County 2004); quoting Luikart v. Shumate, 2003-Ohio-2130, 2003 WL 1961874 (Ohio Ct. App. 3d Dist. Marion County 2003); citing, Striff v. Striff, 2003-Ohio-794, 2003 WL 397869 (Ohio Ct. App. 6th Dist. Wood County 2003); but see State v. Horsley, 2006-Ohio-6217, 2006 WL 3411423 (Ohio Ct. App. 10th Dist. Franklin County 2006); Sobieniak v. Chapdelaine, 2008-Ohio-6403, 2008 WL 5147439 (Ohio Ct. App. 6th Dist. Lucas County 2008) (holding that the statute does not mandate that petitioner actually suffer mental distress); Dayton v. Davis, 136 Ohio App. 3d 26, 735 N.E.2d 939 (2d Dist. Montgomery County 1999); Bloom v. Macbeth, 2008-Ohio-4564, 2008 WL 4151319 (Ohio Ct. App. 5th Dist. Ashland County 2008); Cooper v. Manta, 2012-Ohio-867, 2012 WL 691547 (Ohio Ct. App. 11th Dist. Lake County 2012); Ensley v. Glover, 2012-Ohio-4487, 2012 WL 4480734 (Ohio Ct. App. 6th Dist. Lucas County 2012); Mullen v. Hobbs, 2012-Ohio-6098, 2012 WL 6690114 (Ohio Ct. App. 1st Dist. Hamilton County 2012); Welborn-Harlow v. Fuller, 2013-Ohio-54, 2013 WL 139592 (Ohio Ct. App. 6th Dist. Wood County 2013); Fouch v. Pennington, 2012-Ohio-3536, 2012 WL 3158730 (Ohio Ct. App. 12th Dist. Clermont County 2012); Rufener v. Hutson, 2012-Ohio-5061, 2012 WL 5364703 (Ohio Ct. App. 8th Dist. Cuyahoga County 2012); Fortney v. Willhoite, 2012-Ohio-3024, 2012 WL 2522835 (Ohio Ct. App. 11th Dist. Lake County 2012); Wulf v. Opp, 2015-Ohio-3285, 2015 WL 4878495 (Ohio Ct. App. 12th Dist. Clermont County 2015).

[100]Jenkins v. Jenkins, 2007-Ohio-422, 2007 WL 275700 (Ohio Ct. App. 10th Dist. Franklin County 2007); see also Retterer v. Little, 2012-Ohio-131, 2012 WL 134305 (Ohio Ct. App. 3d Dist. Marion County 2012); Warnecke v. Whitaker, 2011-Ohio-5442, 2011 WL 5028789 (Ohio Ct. App. 3d Dist. Putnam County 2011).

[101]Jenkins v. Jenkins, 2007-Ohio-422, 2007 WL 275700, *4 (Ohio Ct. App. 10th Dist. Franklin County 2007), citing Dayton v. Davis, 136 Ohio App. 3d 26, 32, 735 N.E.2d 939 (2d Dist. Montgomery County 1999).

distress or physical harm."[102] In fact, purpose or intent to cause physical harm or mental distress is not required. It is enough that the person acted knowingly.[103]

Similarly, in *Griga v. DiBenedetto*,[104] former husband sought a CSPO against former wife's boyfriend from having contact with him, his wife and his parents. The trial court granted the protection order naming everyone protected but the former husband's parents.

On appeal the boyfriend alleged that the trial court erred in granting the CSPO because it was based on insufficient evidence and was against the manifest weight of the evidence. In affirming the trial court, the appellate court found that telephone calls to victim, statements made to victim's father, visits to victim's place of employment and threats to financially ruin the victim support the trial court's judgment that DiBenedetto had engaged in a pattern of conduct that knowingly caused Griga to believe that DiBenedetto would cause him mental distress.[105]

Finally, in *Mullen v. Hobbs*,[106] petitioner filed a civil stalking protection order against her former same sex partner because Hobbs had insisted she had legal rights to Mullen's daughter and because she appeared unannounced at her daughter's school pacing outside, despite having been told by Mullen that she was unwelcome for the daughter's first day of school. Mullen also testified that Hobbs had told her that she, Hobbs had been arrested for aggravated menacing involving a firearm and had applied for a concealed carry permit, causing Mullen to be afraid that Hobbs would take the child or harm either Mullen or the child. The trial court granted a five year stalking protection order.

On appeal, Hobbs argued that, at most, Mullen's testimony showed

---

[102]Jenkins v. Jenkins, 2007-Ohio-422, 2007 WL 275700, *3 (Ohio Ct. App. 10th Dist. Franklin County 2007), citing Striff v. Striff, 2003-Ohio-794, 2003 WL 397869, ¶ 11 (Ohio Ct. App. 6th Dist. Wood County 2003); Gruber v. Hart, 2007-Ohio-873, 2007 WL 625818 (Ohio Ct. App. 6th Dist. Ottawa County 2007) (appellant's claim that appellee must show actual mental distress in order to meet her burden of proof is contrary to law. There is no requirement that a petitioner show actual mental distress to meet the elements of stalking); Holloway v. Parker, 2013-Ohio-1940, 2013 WL 1944400 (Ohio Ct. App. 3d Dist. Marion County 2013).

[103]Jenkins v. Jenkins, 2007-Ohio-422, 2007 WL 275700, ¶ 16 (Ohio Ct. App. 10th Dist. Franklin County 2007); see also McWilliam v. Dickey, 2013-Ohio-4036, 2013 WL 5310439 (Ohio Ct. App. 8th Dist. Cuyahoga County 2013); Williams v. Flannery, 2015-Ohio-2040, 2015 WL 3421319 (Ohio Ct. App. 8th Dist. Cuyahoga County 2015); Elkins v. Manley, 2016-Ohio-8307, 2016 WL 7427267 (Ohio Ct. App. 8th Dist. Cuyahoga County 2016).

[104]Griga v. DiBenedetto, 2012-Ohio-6097, 988 N.E.2d 590 (Ohio Ct. App. 1st Dist. Hamilton County 2012); State v. Szloh, 189 Ohio App. 3d 13, 2010-Ohio-3777, 937 N.E.2d 168 (2d Dist. Greene County 2010); Delaine v. Smith, 2016-Ohio-5250, 2016 WL 4141753 (Ohio Ct. App. 8th Dist. Cuyahoga County 2016).

[105]Griga v. DiBenedetto, 2012-Ohio-6097, ¶ 17, 988 N.E.2d 590 (Ohio Ct. App. 1st Dist. Hamilton County 2012). See also Smith v. Hein, 2015-Ohio-2749, 2015 WL 4095636 (Ohio Ct. App. 1st Dist. Hamilton County 2015), appeal not allowed, 144 Ohio St. 3d 1458, 2016-Ohio-172, 44 N.E.3d 288 (2016); Delaine v. Smith, 2016-Ohio-5250, 2016 WL 4141753 (Ohio Ct. App. 8th Dist. Cuyahoga County 2016) (the plain language of RC 2903.211(A)(1) simply refers to conduct that "will" affect the other person. at¶ 19).

[106]Mullen v. Hobbs, 2012-Ohio-6098, 2012 WL 6690114 (Ohio Ct. App. 1st Dist. Hamilton County 2012).

that Hobb's actions had bothered Mullen, embarrassed her and had made her uncomfortable, but that the evidence was insufficient to demonstrate that her actions had knowingly caused Mullen and her daughter mental distress.

Because the First District Court of Appeals had previously held in *Griga* that mental distress need not actually have been caused in order to show that an offender, by engaging in a pattern of conduct, knowingly caused the petitioner to believe that she or he would suffer mental distress or physical harm, the test the appellate court utilized was whether Hobb's actions caused Mullen and her daughter to believe that they would suffer mental distress.[107]

The appellate court found that "the escalation of Hobb's conduct toward Mullen and her daughter caused them to believe that they would suffer mental distress, especially in light of the years of litigation between Mullen and Hobbs. Therefore, the totality of the evidence presented to the trial court provides competent, credible evidence for the conclusion that Hobbs had caused Mullen and her daughter to believe that they would suffer mental distress."[108]

Q & A: How have the appellate courts reach their conclusions?

Interestingly, several of the appellate courts have reached their conclusions by applying either a "plain language" analysis or a "legislative intent" analysis. An interpretation of RC 2903.211(A)(1) often relies, either explicitly or implicitly, on the plain meaning of RC 2903.211(A)(1). Again, the statute provides that "[n]o person by engaging in a pattern of conduct shall knowingly cause another to believe that the offender will cause physical harm to the other person or cause mental distress to the other person."

For example, in *Griga v. DiBenedetto*,[109] the appellate court determined that "where the plain meaning is clear on its face, the statute must be applied as written and not construed."[110] "In this case, we find that the meaning of the statute is apparent on its face."[111]

It is unclear if the phrase "knowingly cause another person to believe" relates to causing both "physical harm" and causing "mental distress," or whether this phrase only modifies "physical harm."[112]

---

[107]Mullen v. Hobbs, 2012-Ohio-6098, ¶ 13, 2012 WL 6690114 (Ohio Ct. App. 1st Dist. Hamilton County 2012). See also Smith v. Hein, 2015-Ohio-2749, 2015 WL 4095636 (Ohio Ct. App. 1st Dist. Hamilton County 2015), appeal not allowed, 144 Ohio St. 3d 1458, 2016-Ohio-172, 44 N.E.3d 288 (2016).

[108]Mullen v. Hobbs, 2012-Ohio-6098, ¶ 23, 2012 WL 6690114 (Ohio Ct. App. 1st Dist. Hamilton County 2012).

[109]Griga v. DiBenedetto, 2012-Ohio-6097, 988 N.E.2d 590 (Ohio Ct. App. 1st Dist. Hamilton County 2012).

[110]Griga v. DiBenedetto, 2012-Ohio-6097, ¶ 9, 988 N.E.2d 590 (Ohio Ct. App. 1st Dist. Hamilton County 2012), citing Meeks v. Papadopulos, 62 Ohio St. 2d 187, 190, 16 Ohio Op. 3d 212, 404 N.E.2d 159, 92 Lab. Cas. (CCH) P 55308 (1980), citing Sears v. Weimer, 143 Ohio St. 312, 28 Ohio Op. 270, 55 N.E.2d 413 (1944).

[111]See also Retterer v. Little, 2012-Ohio-131, 2012 WL 134305, ¶ 39 (Ohio Ct. App. 3d Dist. Marion County 2012) (court determined that actual distress is not necessary based on the plain language of the statute without further analysis).

[112]See R.C. 2903.211(A)(1).

Since the statute is subject to more than one interpretation we must turn to rules of statutory construction for guidance."[113]

In turning its focus to "legislative intent," the *Griga* court found that "a 'common sense reading' of RC 2903.211(A)(1) along with the definition of "mental distress" in RC 2903.211(D)(2)(a) and (b) supports the majority view that proof of actual mental distress is not required."[114]

In contrast, in *Mullen v. Hobbs,*[115] the concurring opinion, while agreeing with the judgment upholding the grant of the protection order, disagreed with the majority view that mental distress need not actually have been suffered under RC 2903.211.[116]

The concurring opinion considered the statute itself and provided a plain language analysis. It first determined that of the appellate districts that have held that actual mental distress is not required under the menacing by stalking statute, at least one district has explained that the plain language of the statute dictates such an outcome, without any further analysis.[117]

It went on to point out that the *Griga* court did not reach its conclusion under the plain language analysis, but rather, the court examined the legislative intent of the statute.[118] "According to the court, the intent of the stalking statute is to allow a court to intervene before harm occurs- both physical and mental harm; therefore a petitioner or victim need only show that he or she believes that mental distress will occur."[119]

Relying on the reasoning set forth by the Seventh District Court of Appeals in *Caban v. Ransome*,[120] the *Mullen* concurring opinion determined that "the court need not resort to legislative intent in interpreting the mental distress prong of RC 2903.211 because the statute is not ambiguous, especially when read in context with the

---

[113]Griga v. DiBenedetto, 2012-Ohio-6097, ¶ 9, 988 N.E.2d 590 (Ohio Ct. App. 1st Dist. Hamilton County 2012).

[114]Griga v. DiBenedetto, 2012-Ohio-6097, ¶ 10, 988 N.E.2d 590 (Ohio Ct. App. 1st Dist. Hamilton County 2012).

[115]Mullen v. Hobbs, 2012-Ohio-6098, 2012 WL 6690114 (Ohio Ct. App. 1st Dist. Hamilton County 2012).

[116]See dissenting opinions in Smith v. Hein, 2015-Ohio-2749, 2015 WL 4095636 (Ohio Ct. App. 1st Dist. Hamilton County 2015), appeal not allowed, 144 Ohio St. 3d 1458, 2016-Ohio-172, 44 N.E.3d 288 (2016) (suggesting that the 1st District overturn its ruling in *Griga* and focusing on "knowingly caused mental distress" not a belief that the conduct would cause mental distress).

[117]Mullen v. Hobbs, 2012-Ohio-6098, ¶ 32, 2012 WL 6690114 (Ohio Ct. App. 1st Dist. Hamilton County 2012); see Retterer v. Little, 2012-Ohio-131, 2012 WL 134305, ¶ 39 (Ohio Ct. App. 3d Dist. Marion County 2012); see also Warnecke v. Whitaker, 2011-Ohio-5442, 2011 WL 5028789, ¶ 14 (Ohio Ct. App. 3d Dist. Putnam County 2011).

[118]Mullen v. Hobbs, 2012-Ohio-6098, ¶ 33, 2012 WL 6690114 (Ohio Ct. App. 1st Dist. Hamilton County 2012).

[119]Mullen v. Hobbs, 2012-Ohio-6098, ¶ 33, 2012 WL 6690114 (Ohio Ct. App. 1st Dist. Hamilton County 2012).

[120]Caban v. Ransome, 2009-Ohio-1034, 2009 WL 582761 (Ohio Ct. App. 7th Dist. Mahoning County 2009).

definition of mental distress under the statute."[121] "In reaching this conclusion, the *Caban* court determined that, by repeating 'to the other person' after both physical harm and mental distress, rather than merely placing it at the end of the sentence, the legislature expressed that 'to believe' does not modify 'mental distress.' "[122]

Additionally, it considered the statutory definition of mental distress in RC 2903.211(D)(2). "By using the phrase "normally require * * * treatment" in defining mental distress, the legislature created an objective inquiry. This objective test for mental distress is incompatible with an interpretation of the menacing by stalking statute requiring only that the victim or petitioner believe that mental distress will be caused—a subjective inquiry."[123] "Moreover, a subjective belief inquiry for mental distress, requiring only that a petitioner or victim believe that he or she will suffer mental distress, would render as superfluous the phrase 'whether or not any person requested or received * * * treatment or other mental health services [ ]' in the legislature's definition of mental distress under RC 2903.211(D)(2)(b) ."[124] Thus, the concurring opinion concluded that RC 2903.211 requires proof of mental distress or belief of physical harm.

Q & A: So, do all courts use an objective test?[125]

No. The Clermont County appellate court applied a subjective test and focused on petitioner's fear, not on that of an objective, reasonable person. In *Lane v. Brewster*,[126] the court of appeals overruled appellant's assignment of error stated that the plain language of RC 2903.211(A)(1) simply refers to conduct that will "affect the other person, and does not require a court to determine the respondent's ef-

---

[121]Mullen v. Hobbs, 2012-Ohio-6098, ¶ 34, 2012 WL 6690114 (Ohio Ct. App. 1st Dist. Hamilton County 2012).

[122]Mullen v. Hobbs, 2012-Ohio-6098, ¶ 35, 2012 WL 6690114 (Ohio Ct. App. 1st Dist. Hamilton County 2012), quoting Caban v. Ransome, 2009-Ohio-1034, ¶ 24, 2009 WL 582761 (Ohio Ct. App. 7th Dist. Mahoning County 2009).

[123]Mullen v. Hobbs, 2012-Ohio-6098, ¶ 37, 2012 WL 6690114 (Ohio Ct. App. 1st Dist. Hamilton County 2012); but see Lane v. Brewster, 2012-Ohio-1290, 2012 WL 1029503 (Ohio Ct. App. 12th Dist. Clermont County 2012); Fortney v. Willhoite, 2012-Ohio-3024, 2012 WL 2522835 (Ohio Ct. App. 11th Dist. Lake County 2012); Cooper v. Manta, 2012-Ohio-867, 2012 WL 691547, ¶ 41 (Ohio Ct. App. 11th Dist. Lake County 2012).

[124]Mullen v. Hobbs, 2012-Ohio-6098, ¶ 38, 2012 WL 6690114 (Ohio Ct. App. 1st Dist. Hamilton County 2012).

[125]See Text § 9:2; but see Elonis v. U.S., 135 S. Ct. 2001, 192 L. Ed. 2d 1, 43 Media L. Rep. (BNA) 1749 (2015) (holding that the subjective intent of the offender was necessary when determining the *mens rea*) of a specific criminal statute (18 U.S.C.A. section 875(c) where defendant communicated a threat to injure his wife and not an objective reasonable person standard).

[126]Lane v. Brewster, 2012-Ohio-1290, 2012 WL 1029503, *3 (Ohio Ct. App. 12th Dist. Clermont County 2012). See also J.B. v. Harford, 2015-Ohio-13, 2015 WL 82527 (Ohio Ct. App. 9th Dist. Summit County 2015). See Text § 9:2; Frenchko v. Frenchko-Nagy, 2015-Ohio-4546, 42 N.E.3d 829 (Ohio Ct. App. 11th Dist. Trumbull County 2015) ("[i]n determining whether petitioner suffered mental distress, the focus is on petitioner's fear, not that of an objective reasonable person. The court employs a subjective test, rather than an objective, reasonable person test." At ¶ 27, quoting Fortney v. Willhoite, 2012-Ohio-3024, 2012 WL 2522835, ¶ 43 (Ohio Ct. App. 11th Dist. Lake County 2012)).

fect on a 'reasonable' person, only those specifically involved."[127] The court held that "the trial court was not required to use an objective 'reasonable person' test in determining whether Brewster's conduct caused mental distress or fear of physical harm under RC 2903.211(A)(1)."[128]

Q & A: So what satisfies the mental distress element?

Apparently, courts that consider *actual* mental distress in the present and courts that consider a *belief* of mental distress in the future both appear to rely on the same behaviors of the victim. They often interchange fear of physical harm and mental distress, using a similar fear factor in order to substantiate mental distress. Additionally, the courts often utilize evidence of a change in routine to justify the issuance of the civil stalking protection order. While some courts may focus on a "temporary substantial incapacity,"[129] others focus on the "totality of the circumstances,"[130] as it relates to the pattern of conduct and which is designed to explain the reasons for mental distress.

What is clear is that evidence of prior acts and behavior is particularly important to prove menacing by stalking by way of providing a context to the trier of fact as to why such behavior, which might be considered innocent actions, causes a particular victim to be afraid and suffer mental distress. In effect, it can be used to explain why a victim might be afraid of what the offender might do.

In sum, most courts seem to consider the same evidence, usually a change in routine, to demonstrate either actual mental distress or a belief that mental distress would be caused in the future.[131] Thus, it appears that "actual mental distress" and "a belief that mental distress would be caused" is a distinction without a difference.

Finally, the Supreme Court of Ohio agreed to accept *certiorari* because of a conflict in appellate jurisdictions.[132] The question presented was whether RC 2903.211(A)(1) required a victim to actually

---

[127]Lane v. Brewster, 2012-Ohio-1290, 2012 WL 1029503, *3 (Ohio Ct. App. 12th Dist. Clermont County 2012).

[128]Lane v. Brewster, 2012-Ohio-1290, 2012 WL 1029503, *3 (Ohio Ct. App. 12th Dist. Clermont County 2012); Fortney v. Willhoite, 2012-Ohio-3024, 2012 WL 2522835, *7 (Ohio Ct. App. 11th Dist. Lake County 2012) (stating that the trial court is required to determine the effect of the respondent's actions on the petitioner, not on an objective, 'reasonable' person and further that the trial court may consider the petitioner's unequivocal expression of her fear of the respondent, and citing Cooper v. Manta, 2012-Ohio-867, 2012 WL 691547, ¶ 41 (Ohio Ct. App. 11th Dist. Lake County 2012)).

[129]See State v. Horsley, 2006-Ohio-1208, 2006 WL 648849, ¶ 49 (Ohio Ct. App. 10th Dist. Franklin County 2006) (Finding that substantial incapacity does not mean that the victim must be hospitalized, or totally unable to care for herself. Incapacity is substantial if it has a significant impact upon the victim's daily life. The inability to sleep or concentrate on one's work is substantially incapacitating to that person.); Retterer v. Little, 2012-Ohio-131, 2012 WL 134305, ¶ 16 (Ohio Ct. App. 3d Dist. Marion County 2012) (stressing that the statute does not require that the mental distress be totally or permanently incapacitating or debilitating; rather it merely has to be substantial; citing Lias v. Beekman, 2007-Ohio-5737, 2007 WL 3108899 (Ohio Ct. App. 10th Dist. Franklin County 2007)).

[130]Bartells v. Bertel, 2018-Ohio-21, ¶ 59, 2018 WL 265509 (Ohio Ct. App. 12th Dist. Butler County 2018).

[131]See State v. Horsley, 2006-Ohio-1208, 2006 WL 648849 (Ohio Ct. App. 10th Dist. Franklin County 2006).

[132]Fondessy v. Simon, 2013-Ohio-3465, 2013 WL 4041564 (Ohio Ct. App. 6th Dist.

experience mental distress or only believe that the stalker will cause the victim physical harm or mental distress in order for a court to issue a civil stalking protection order. The conflict case was *Caban v. Ransome*.[133]

In 2014, the Supreme Court of Ohio issued its opinion dismissing the certification of conflict *sua sponte*, as having been improvidently allowed.[134] In her dissent, Justice Kennedy reiterated the number of conflicting opinions. She admonished the majority for permitting the conflict in the appellate courts to continue.

Q & A: Does a "concern for one's safety" satisfy the mental distress element of R.C. 2903.214?

Yes. In *Clark v. Ellinwood*,[135] petitioner sought a civil protection order against respondent, who damaged the petitioner's personal property, telephoned her looking for the respondent's husband, tailgated too closely to petitioner's car, and stated that she "hoped that petitioner got run over like a dead raccoon."[136] Respondent appealed the issuance of the protection order, asserting that petitioner failed to meet her burden of proof by establishing that respondent acted with the requisite intent to prove menacing by stalking and by failing to prove that petitioner suffered mental distress or any risk of physical harm.

The Lucas County appellate court noted that a threat is not required for the issuance of a civil stalking protection order under R.C. 2903. 214. In affirming judgment, the court relied on petitioner's statement that she felt concerned for her safety and found that such a statement satisfied the mental distress requirement.[137]

Q & A: Must a petitioner demonstrate both mental distress and fear of physical harm?[138]

Ottawa County 2013).

[133]Caban v. Ransome, 2009-Ohio-1034, 2009 WL 582761 (Ohio Ct. App. 7th Dist. Mahoning County 2009).

[134]Fondessy v. Simon, 142 Ohio St. 3d 147, 2014-Ohio-4638, 28 N.E.3d 1202 (2014).

[135]Clark v. Ellinwood, 2011-Ohio-145, 2011 WL 281146 (Ohio Ct. App. 6th Dist. Lucas County 2011).

[136]Clark v. Ellinwood, 2011-Ohio-145, 2011 WL 281146, *1 (Ohio Ct. App. 6th Dist. Lucas County 2011). See also Wulf v. Opp, 2015-Ohio-3285, 2015 WL 4878495 (Ohio Ct. App. 12th Dist. Clermont County 2015) (repeated harassment of petitioner, in person and through prank calls, voice mail messages and social medial provided credible evidence of stalking).

[137]Clark v. Ellinwood, 2011-Ohio-145, 2011 WL 281146, *5 (Ohio Ct. App. 6th Dist. Lucas County 2011); citing Irwin v. Murray, 2006-Ohio-1633, 2006 WL 832830 (Ohio Ct. App. 6th Dist. Lucas County 2006). See also State v. Cannon, 2010-Ohio-2394, 2011 WL 1945718 (Ohio Ct. App. 8th Dist. Cuyahoga County 2011) (noting that a fear of one's safety coupled with testimony that the victim suffered a lot of anxiety was sufficient to sustain defendant's menacing by stalking conviction); but see State v. Schoeneman, 2012-Ohio-4710, 2012 WL 4831655 (Ohio Ct. App. 5th Dist. Stark County 2012) (finding that where appellee did not call the police or testify that he felt in fear or threatened, he did not prove that he suffered from mental distress. His testimony only established that he and his family were no longer happy as they had been in the past).

[138]See J.B. v. Harford, 2015-Ohio-13, 2015 WL 82527 (Ohio Ct. App. 9th Dist. Summit County 2015) (appellate court found that the court did not have to reach the issue of whether KB suffered mental distress because the court could have reasonably

In *Coleridge v. Tomsho*,[139] the Stark County Court of Appeals pointed out that it is not incumbent upon a petitioner to demonstrate mental distress when fear of physical harm is supported by the evidence presented. In that case, the appellee testified that she was relentlessly stalked and harassed for over one year, during which time stalker followed her to work and drove in circles around the block where she resided, causing her to change her telephone number and make several police reports. Clearly, there was sufficient evidence to establish that appellant's pattern of behavior constituted a violation of R.C. 2903.211, such that a stalking CPO was warranted to ensure the safety and protection of appellee.[140]

Q & A: What proof is necessary to establish a violation of R.C. 2903.211 for purposes of a stalking civil protection order under R.C. 2903.214?

To grant a civil protection order under R.C. 2903.214, some courts have held that a petitioner must show either that the respondent knowingly caused the petitioner to suffer mental distress or knowingly caused the petitioner to believe the respondent will cause physical harm to the petitioner.[141] Other courts have determined that R.C. 2903.211 requires only a pattern of conduct which causes the victim to believe that the offender will cause physical harm to the victim or will cause mental distress to the victim.[142] Still, other courts have framed the issue by stating that in order to show that a defendant violated R.C. 2903.211 and is subject to a civil protection order under R.C. 2903.214, it must be shown that the respondent engaged in conduct that he knew would probably cause the complainant to believe that he would cause her physical harm or cause her mental distress.[143]

Explicit or direct threats of physical harm are not necessary to es-

---

concluded that Mr. Harford acted knowingly, in that his actions would probably cause J.B. to fear physical harm, that she did in fact fear physical harm and that such a fear was reasonable in light of Harford's comments to her, inquiry about her by name and size difference between them). See also Frenchko v. Frenchko-Nagy, 2015-Ohio-4546, 42 N.E.3d 829 (Ohio Ct. App. 11th Dist. Trumbull County 2015) (noting that the statute requires that a respondent cause a belief of physical harm or cause mental distress).

[139] Coleridge v. Tomsho, 2003-Ohio-650, 2003 WL 294356, *2 (Ohio Ct. App. 5th Dist. Stark County 2003); see also Olenik v. Huff, 2003-Ohio-4621, 2003 WL 22039490 (Ohio Ct. App. 5th Dist. Ashland County 2003) (court noted that the threats of bodily harm individually and collectively caused Appellee mental distress); Madison v. Wilborn, 2012-Ohio-2742, 2012 WL 2308618 (Ohio Ct. App. 5th Dist. Stark County 2012) (RC 2903.211 was written in the disjunctive); Kruszynski v. Kruszynski, 2013-Ohio-3355, 2013 WL 3965465 (Ohio Ct. App. 5th Dist. Fairfield County 2013); Elkins v. Reed, 2014-Ohio-1217, 2014 WL 1350806 (Ohio Ct. App. 5th Dist. Stark County 2014) (a petitioner can establish physical harm *or* mental distress).

[140] Coleridge v. Tomsho, 2003-Ohio-650, 2003 WL 294356, *2 (Ohio Ct. App. 5th Dist. Stark County 2003).

[141] See R.C. 2903.211(A)(1); R.C. 2901.22(B) (for a definition of the term knowingly); R.C. 2903.211(A); see also Tuuri v. Snyder, 2002-Ohio-2107, 2002 WL 818427 (Ohio Ct. App. 11th Dist. Geauga County 2002); City of Akron v. Andrews, 2000 WL 108818 (Ohio Ct. App. 9th Dist. Summit County 2000); Lemley v. Kirk, 2007-Ohio-1016, 2007 WL 701141 (Ohio Ct. App. 10th Dist. Franklin County 2007); Text 9:2.

[142] See, for example, Gruber v. Hart, 2007-Ohio-873, 2007 WL 625818 (Ohio Ct. App. 6th Dist. Ottawa County 2007); State v. Bone, 2006-Ohio-3809, 2006 WL 2053398 (Ohio Ct. App. 10th Dist. Franklin County 2006).

[143] Jenkins v. Jenkins, 2007-Ohio-422, 2007 WL 275700, *4 (Ohio Ct. App. 10th

tablish a violation of R.C. 2903.211(A).[144] Implied threats of violence, if knowingly made, are sufficient to satisfy the statutory requirements.[145]

The petitioner need not prove that the respondent intended to cause actual harm to him/her.[146] Purpose or the intent to cause the physical harm or mental distress is not required.[147] The test is not whether the offender's conduct is threatening; instead, the evidence need only show that the respondent knowingly engaged in a pattern of conduct that causes the other person to believe that the respondent will cause physical harm or mental distress to the other person.

"Knowingly" is defined in R.C. 2901.22(B) which provides that a person acts knowingly, regardless of his purpose, when he is aware that his conduct will probably cause a certain result or will probably be of a certain nature. A person has knowledge of circumstances when he is aware that such circumstances probably exist. Therefore, it must be shown that the respondent engaged in conduct that he knew would

---

Dist. Franklin County 2007).

[144]See Nwosu v. Underwood, 2007-Ohio-1907, 2007 WL 1175230 (Ohio Ct. App. 3d Dist. Marion County 2007); State v. Neeley, 2013-Ohio-303, 2013 WL 425821 (Ohio Ct. App. 2d Dist. Montgomery County 2013) (evidenced by driving back and forth past her residence and following directly behind her in his vehicle); State v. Bone, 2006-Ohio-3809, 2006 WL 2053398 (Ohio Ct. App. 10th Dist. Franklin County 2006) (stating that "[p]roof that the accused actually caused physical harm or mental distress to the victim or made direct threats to the victim's safety is not required under the statute."); State v. Honeycutt, 2002-Ohio-3490, 2002 WL 1438648 (Ohio Ct. App. 2d Dist. Montgomery County 2002). But see Lemley v. Kirk, 2007-Ohio-1016, 2007 WL 701141 (Ohio Ct. App. 10th Dist. Franklin County 2007); Palmer v. Abraham, 2013-Ohio-3062, 2013 WL 3776597 (Ohio Ct. App. 6th Dist. Ottawa County 2013).

[145]Jenkins v. Jenkins, 2007-Ohio-422, 2007 WL 275700 (Ohio Ct. App. 10th Dist. Franklin County 2007). See also Joy v. Letostak, 2015-Ohio-2667, 2015 WL 3964179 (Ohio Ct. App. 10th Dist. Franklin County 2015) (finding that sending angry accusatory emails and notes, threatening to go to petitioner's home uninvited and going to petitioner's home uninvited several times, and not leaving immediately when petitioner did not answer the door, taken together amounted to an implied threat of violence). But see Krzystan v. Bauer, 2017-Ohio-858, 2017 WL 945183, ¶ 21 (Ohio Ct. App. 6th Dist. Ottawa County 2017) ("you are going to get what you deserve" might be considered an implied or veiled threat, that there were no physical gestures, body language or tone of voice to suggest that appellant intended for his statement to be taken as a physical threat).

[146]Gruber v. Hart, 2007-Ohio-873, 2007 WL 625818, *4 (Ohio Ct. App. 6th Dist. Ottawa County 2007) ("There is no requirement that a petitioner show actual mental distress to meet the elements of stalking."); see also Walker v. Edgington, 2008-Ohio-3478, 2008 WL 2699430 (Ohio Ct. App. 2d Dist. Clark County 2008) (stating that a petitioner need not have to prove that the respondent intended to cause her actual harm); Bryant v. Spear-Hardy, 2010-Ohio-1903, 2010 WL 1731763 (Ohio Ct. App. 2d Dist. Montgomery County 2010).

[147]Jenkins v. Jenkins, 2007-Ohio-422, 2007 WL 275700, *4 (Ohio Ct. App. 10th Dist. Franklin County 2007); see also Perry v. Joseph, 2008-Ohio-1107, 2008 WL 660317, *3 (Ohio Ct. App. 10th Dist. Franklin County 2008) (Interestingly, the 10th District Court of Appeals summerized the menacing by stalking statute and said that "menacing by stalking involves either behavior that causes the victim to believe that he or she *will be* physically harmed or behavior that *causes* mental distress to the victim."); Ellet v. Falk, 2010-Ohio-6219, 2010 WL 5269870 (Ohio Ct. App. 6th Dist. Lucas County 2010); Retterer v. Little, 2012-Ohio-131, 2012 WL 134305 (Ohio Ct. App. 3d Dist. Marion County 2012); Joy v. Letostak, 2015-Ohio-2667, 2015 WL 3964179 (Ohio Ct. App. 10th Dist. Franklin County 2015); Elkins v. Manley, 2016-Ohio-8307, 2016 WL 7427267 (Ohio Ct. App. 8th Dist. Cuyahoga County 2016).

probably cause the petitioner to believe that he would cause her physical harm or cause her to suffer mental distress.[148]

For example, in *Podeweltz v. Rieger*,[149] appellee testified that appellant had followed her to a local restaurant on a daily basis, that he telephoned her on a daily basis beginning as early as 5:30 am and that there was an occasion when he called her fifty times. The appellate court relied on the magistrate's findings to illustrate the culpable mental state of "knowingly." "In this case, given the volume of calls and following after numerous requests to stop, [Rieger] had a certain awareness. [Rieger] was rebuffed by [Podeweltz]. He attempted to enlist the aide of [Podeweltz's] family members. The rebuffed him. He persisted nonetheless. The conduct* * *was not occasional, it was constant. It was daily, not weekly. None of it resulted in any change in the position of [Podeweltz]. Given these circumstances, [Rieger] was aware that he was simply harassing [Podeweltz]. One would conclude that this harassment would result in [Podeweltz] becoming afraid. [Rieger] clearly had an awareness of all the circumstances."[150] The court of appeals agreed with the magistrate's conclusion that Rieger had knowledge that his conduct was of such a nature as to cause Podeweltz to believe that he would cause her physical harm.

Neither explicit nor direct threats of physical harm are necessary to establish a violation of R.C. 2903.211(A).[151] "The test is not whether the offender's conduct was threatening but whether the offender by engaging in a pattern of conduct knowingly caused another to believe the offender would cause physical harm to him or her."[152]

---

[148]Jenkins v. Jenkins, 2007-Ohio-422, 2007 WL 275700, *4 (Ohio Ct. App. 10th Dist. Franklin County 2007) (in which the statement "I know where you live" could have been made to cause mental distress to the petitioner); McNaughton v. Cochenour, 2015-Ohio-4648, 2015 WL 6953983 (Ohio Ct. App. 4th Dist. Ross County 2015) (noting that a petitioner is not required to prove either purpose or intent to cause physical harm or mental distress. It is enough that the offender knowingly performed an act that resulted in causing the victim mental distress. In other words, the offender's subjective intent is not relevant under RC 2903.211 at ¶ 22; but see Elonis v. U.S., 135 S. Ct. 2001, 192 L. Ed. 2d 1, 43 Media L. Rep. (BNA) 1749 (2015)) (emphasis added); Caban v. Ransome, 2009-Ohio-1034, 2009 WL 582761 (Ohio Ct. App. 7th Dist. Mahoning County 2009) (insufficient evidence to prove physical harm despite subjective requirement inherent in "causing her to believe," because labeling a call as threatening does not express a belief that the caller would cause physical harm and that threatening to approach a person for conversation is not a threat of physical harm. At ¶ 18); Wilson v. Lyon, 2016-Ohio-7734, 2016 WL 6678396 (Ohio Ct. App. 3d Dist. Marion County 2016).

[149]Podeweltz v. Rieger, 2007-Ohio-1513, 2007 WL 949482 (Ohio Ct. App. 2d Dist. Montgomery County 2007).

[150]Podeweltz v. Rieger, 2007-Ohio-1513, 2007 WL 949482, *5 (Ohio Ct. App. 2d Dist. Montgomery County 2007).

[151]See Short v. Walker, 2001 WL 32808 (Ohio Ct. App. 12th Dist. Preble County 2001); Kramer v. Kramer, 2002-Ohio-4383, 2002 WL 1967104 (Ohio Ct. App. 3d Dist. Seneca County 2002). But see Baddour v. Fox, 2000 WL 1719569 (Ohio Ct. App. 5th Dist. Licking County 2000).

[152]Short v. Walker, 2001 WL 32808, *3 (Ohio Ct. App. 12th Dist. Preble County 2001); see also Huffer v. Chafin, 2002-Ohio-356, 2002 WL 144901 (Ohio Ct. App. 5th Dist. Licking County 2002); Noah v. Brillhart, 2003-Ohio-2421, 2003 WL 21078077, *3 (Ohio Ct. App. 9th Dist. Wayne County 2003) (court noted that mental distress in this case was corroborated by the fact of her changed routine and pattern of doing things,

Q & A: How can a victim show mental distress?[153] Is the fear reasonable?

In order to demonstrate mental distress or her fear for her physical safety, the effect of the offender's behavior on the victim must be considered. It may be important to compare a day before and after the stalking began.[154] Mental distress may be shown by the victim moving, changing jobs,[155] changing her/his name or telephone number, or changing the child's school. It may be shown by behavioral changes as well. These behaviors may include absenteeism at work, a lack of focus, nervousness, canceling engagements and deliberate isolating behavior. The victim may have nightmares or be unable to sleep. The victim may have purchased a weapon, a dog, an alarm system[156] or pepper spray in order to find ways of keeping safe.[157] Mental distress can also be shown where the petitioner testifies that she now uses an anti-anxiety drug following the incident.[158]

In some cases, the focus is on "temporary substantial incapacity."[159]

---

her fear of visiting friends after dark, and requesting an escort by a Wayne County Sheriff's deputy to daytime meetings).

[153]Arruda v. Farmer, 2015-Ohio-5511, 55 N.E.3d 604 (Ohio Ct. App. 5th Dist. Licking County 2015), appeal not allowed, 145 Ohio St. 3d 1460, 2016-Ohio-2807, 49 N.E.3d 322 (2016) (mental distress was established where petitioner became afraid to be alone, was in a constant state of fear, installed an alarm system/security cameras, noticed neighbors and coworkers, was apprehensive and sought treatment for anxiety); J.R. v. Pless, 2016-Ohio-14, 2016 WL 60000 (Ohio Ct. App. 9th Dist. Summit County 2016) (concurring opinion discussing behavioral changes such as lack of focus, difficulty at school and inability to sleep); Cutler v. Reed, 2016-Ohio-1151, 2016 WL 1090783 (Ohio Ct. App. 12th Dist. Butler County 2016) (in determining whether the victim suffered mental distress, thoughts of suicide and seeking help from a school counselor support the issuance of the order. Egging her car, creating a fake Twitter account in her name, posting a picture of her on instagram calling her a skank, following her home from school, driving past her in a reckless manner, and making a false complaint against her at work "are behaviors that go well beyond the type of behavior that can simply be dismissed as typical teenage antics." At ¶ 30; Tighe v. Kaiser, 2016-Ohio-1400, 2016 WL 1297407 (Ohio Ct. App. 6th Dist. Ottawa County 2016), appeal not allowed, 146 Ohio St. 3d 1491, 2016-Ohio-5585, 57 N.E.3d 1171 (2016) (finding that after the encounters with appellant, appellee felt uncomfortable and resulted in several trips to the emergency room due to chest pain and breathing problems characteristic of panic attacks. at ¶ 18). See also Text 8:4.

[154]See Morton v. Pyles, 2012-Ohio-5343, 2012 WL 5842789, ¶ 25 (Ohio Ct. App. 7th Dist. Mahoning County 2012) (Reversing the trial court's grant of protection order and finding that "[m]ental stress does not constitute mental distress. A change in routine has been stated to constitute a showing of mental distress. However, a change in routine suggests going to work a different route to avoid having contact with the stalker or to change a lunch time or exercise time.").

[155]Guthrie v. Long, 2005-Ohio-1541, 2005 WL 737402 (Ohio Ct. App. 10th Dist. Franklin County 2005).

[156]See Podeweltz v. Rieger, 2007-Ohio-1513, 2007 WL 949482 (Ohio Ct. App. 2d Dist. Montgomery County 2007).

[157]Rhonda Saunders at http://www.stalkingalert.com; see also Stalking Resource Center.

[158]See Needhamer v. Carlozzi, 2010-Ohio-4562, 2010 WL 3733866 (Ohio Ct. App. 11th Dist. Lake County 2010). Kruszynski v. Kruszynski, 2013-Ohio-3355, 2013 WL 3965465 (Ohio Ct. App. 5th Dist. Fairfield County 2013) (testimony that petitioner was fearful of appellant and experienced anxiety as a result of his actions was sufficient to prove mental distress).

[159]See R.C. 2903.211(D)(2)(a).

According to *Retterer v. Little*,[160] the Marion County Court of Appeals noted that " 'incapacity is substantial if it has a significant impact upon the victim's daily life.' "[161] For example, a change in the protected person's daily routine can be evidence of mental distress.[162]

Similarly, in *Holloway v. Parker*,[163] the appellate court focused on substantial incapacity. " '[M]ere mental stress or annoyance' is generally not sufficient to constitute mental distress for purposes of menacing by stalking."[164]

For example, in *State v. Lawson*,[165] the court, in concluding that there was sufficient evidence to support the conviction, relied on the victim's testimony that she was "scared to death." Additionally, the court noted that the victim's own actions after she became aware of the stalker demonstrated her fear. Her brother had to be with her at her home during the time period after appellant left her the note. She was unable to sleep during this period of time. Moreover, her subsequent move from her home was illustrative of her fear.

---

[160] Retterer v. Little, 2012-Ohio-131, 2012 WL 134305 (Ohio Ct. App. 3d Dist. Marion County 2012).

[161] Retterer v. Little, 2012-Ohio-131, ¶ 41, 2012 WL 134305 (Ohio Ct. App. 3d Dist. Marion County 2012), quoting State v. Horsley, 2006-Ohio-6217, 2006 WL 3411423, ¶ 48 (Ohio Ct. App. 10th Dist. Franklin County 2006); see also Mullen v. Hobbs, 2012-Ohio-6098, 2012 WL 6690114 (Ohio Ct. App. 1st Dist. Hamilton County 2012); Morton v. Pyles, 2012-Ohio-5343, 2012 WL 5842789 (Ohio Ct. App. 7th Dist. Mahoning County 2012); State v. Payne, 178 Ohio App. 3d 617, 2008-Ohio-5447, 899 N.E.2d 1011 (9th Dist. Summit County 2008) (being so afraid as to be unable to leave one's house for 6 hours qualified as substantial incapacity); Smith v. Wunsch, 162 Ohio App. 3d 21, 2005-Ohio-3498, ¶ 20, 832 N.E.2d 757 (4th Dist. Hocking County 2005); McNaughton v. Cochenour, 2015-Ohio-4648, 2015 WL 6953983 (Ohio Ct. App. 4th Dist. Ross County 2015); Echemann v. Echemann, 2016-Ohio-3212, 2016 WL 3057979 (Ohio Ct. App. 3d Dist. Shelby County 2016) ("Incapacity is substantial if it has a significant impact upon the victim's daily life." at ¶ 37; citing, R*etterer*, 2012-Ohio-131, ¶ 41, quoting State v. Horsley, 2006-Ohio-1208, 2006 WL 648849 (Ohio Ct. App. 10th Dist. Franklin County 2006)); Wilson v. Lyon, 2016-Ohio-7734, 2016 WL 6678396 (Ohio Ct. App. 3d Dist. Marion County 2016).

[162] Retterer v. Little, 2012-Ohio-131, ¶ 41, 2012 WL 134305 (Ohio Ct. App. 3d Dist. Marion County 2012), citing Smith v. Wunsch, 162 Ohio App. 3d 21, 2005-Ohio-3498, 832 N.E.2d 757 (4th Dist. Hocking County 2005).

[163] Holloway v. Parker, 2013-Ohio-1940, 2013 WL 1944400, ¶ 25 (Ohio Ct. App. 3d Dist. Marion County 2013).

[164] Middletown v. Jones, 167 Ohio App. 3d 679, 683, 2006-Ohio-3465, 856 N.E.2d 1003, 1006, ¶ 8 (12th Dist. Butler County 2006) (testimony that petitioner felt "nervous," "frightened," "upset," "worried," and "scared" would support a finding of mental distress); Holloway v. Parker, 2013-Ohio-1940, 2013 WL 1944400, ¶ 25 (Ohio Ct. App. 3d Dist. Marion County 2013), citing, Retterer v. Little, 2012-Ohio-131, ¶ 41, 2012 WL 134305 (Ohio Ct. App. 3d Dist. Marion County 2012), quoting Caban v. Ransome, 2009-Ohio-1034, 2009 WL 582761, ¶ 29 (Ohio Ct. App. 7th Dist. Mahoning County 2009); Echemann v. Echemann, 2016-Ohio-3212, 2016 WL 3057979 (Ohio Ct. App. 3d Dist. Shelby County 2016) (noting that menacing by stalking requires more than hurt or humiliation); Ramsey v. Pellicioni, 2016-Ohio-558, 2016 WL 635212 (Ohio Ct. App. 7th Dist. Mahoning County 2016); L.L. v. R.B., 2017-Ohio-7553, ¶ 27, 2017 WL 3980553 (Ohio Ct. App. 5th Dist. Guernsey County 2017) (mental distress is more than annoyance or embarrassment. Testimony that the conduct caused the person considerable fear can support a finding of mental distress).

[165] State v. Lawson, 2007-Ohio-2656, 2007 WL 1560266 (Ohio Ct. App. 10th Dist. Franklin County 2007).

In *McWilliam v. Dickey*,[166] petitioner sought a CSPO on the grounds that respondent used drugs to excess, that he was high on heroin while in the hospital to visit his new born child and that such actions caused McWilliam mental distress. Besides the fear of physical harm based on the prior assault, mental distress was shown by his constant drug use and being under the influence of drugs which occurred both in her and in the baby's presence. In upholding the trial court's grant of the civil stalking protection order, the appellate court held that based on the facts of this case, McWilliam provided sufficient evidence of stalking behavior.

Q & A: Are proof of direct threats of physical harm necessary to establish stalking under R.C. 2903.214?

No.[167] For example, in *Kramer v. Kramer*,[168] a mother filed a stalking protection order on behalf of her minor child against her stepmother. The appellate court reversed the trial court's issuance of the stalking CPO and held that evidence that the stepmother went to the daughter's work only once was insufficient to establish a pattern of conduct or threat to the daughter's safety. While acknowledging that explicit or direct threats of physical harm are not necessary to establish a violation of R.C. 2903.211(A),[169] the court stated that "the test is whether the offender, by engaging in a pattern of conduct, knowingly caused another to believe the offender would cause physical harm to him or her."[170]

Of significance is that the Seneca County Court of Appeals noted

[166]McWilliam v. Dickey, 2013-Ohio-4036, 2013 WL 5310439 (Ohio Ct. App. 8th Dist. Cuyahoga County 2013).

[167]See e.g., State v. Horsley, 2006-Ohio-1208, 2006 WL 648849 (Ohio Ct. App. 10th Dist. Franklin County 2006).

[168]Kramer v. Kramer, 2002-Ohio-4383, 2002 WL 1967104 (Ohio Ct. App. 3d Dist. Seneca County 2002). See also Rauser v. Ghaster, 2009-Ohio-4027, 2009 WL 2462553 (Ohio Ct. App. 8th Dist. Cuyahoga County 2009), decision vacated and superseded on reconsideration on other grounds, 2009-Ohio-5698, 2009 WL 3490654 (Ohio Ct. App. 8th Dist. Cuyahoga County 2009) (later decision clarified that it was the directed verdict at the close of the evidence that was error, and neither the decision nor the legal analysis changed; appellate court reversed the directed verdict granted at the close of Rausers' evidence and noted that explicit or direct threats of physical harm are not necessary to establish a violation of R.C. 2903.211(A), quoting Kramer); Palmer v. Abraham, 2013-Ohio-3062, 2013 WL 3776597 (Ohio Ct. App. 6th Dist. Ottawa County 2013) (Direct threats are unnecessary to establish menacing by stalking. It is sufficient if the accused exhibits a pattern of behavior with an awareness that his conduct will likely cause another to become mentally distressed or believe the accused will cause physical harm, at ¶ 16; citing City of Toledo v. Emery, 2000 WL 864305 (Ohio Ct. App. 6th Dist. Lucas County 2000).). But see Lemley v. Kirk, 2007-Ohio-1016, 2007 WL 701141 (Ohio Ct. App. 10th Dist. Franklin County 2007) (court affirmed denial of a CSPO, suggesting the need for direct threats of physical harm).

[169]See Podeweltz v. Rieger, 2007-Ohio-1513, 2007 WL 949482, *5 (Ohio Ct. App. 2d Dist. Montgomery County 2007) (explicit threats are not necessary to establish the elements of stalking), citing State v. Smith, 126 Ohio App. 3d 193, 709 N.E.2d 1245 (7th Dist. Mahoning County 1998); see also Jenkins v. Jenkins, 2007-Ohio-422, 2007 WL 275700, *4 (Ohio Ct. App. 10th Dist. Franklin County 2007) ("I know where you live" is an implied threat of violence. Therefore the Court could conclude that appellant acted knowingly to cause appellee to believe that he would cause her physical harm); Nwosu v. Underwood, 2007-Ohio-1907, 2007 WL 1175230 (Ohio Ct. App. 3d Dist. Marion County 2007).

[170]Kramer v. Kramer, 2002-Ohio-4383, 2002 WL 1967104, *4 (Ohio Ct. App. 3d

that the statutory purpose for the enactment of the stalking statutes was "to prevent the type of persistent and threatening harassment that leaves victims in constant fear of physical danger," rather than alleviating uncomfortable situations.[171]

Q & A: Must a threat be made by direct and face to face contact?[172]

It depends. In *Paulus v. Rucker*,[173] the Eleventh District Court of Appeals reversed the grant of a stalking CPO because the supervisor was unable to establish that the employee knowingly engaged in a pattern of behavior sufficient to support a finding of menacing by stalking. In that case, the employee had made threatening comments to a co-worker about the supervisor, but had not communicated the threats directly to the supervisor. The employee also jokingly commented to others that ". . . * * * I wish we had the conceal law to carry in effect now. If we did, some of these people would have been blown away a long time ago."[174]

The appellate court noted that, while the supervisor learned of one comment ("somebody needed to be shot") through a co-worker, no effort was made to communicate other comments to the supervisor or even that the supervisor knew about subsequent comments.[175] The court then stated that, while inappropriate, the "joking" comment and the other comments were not actionable. The supervisor had failed to

---

Dist. Seneca County 2002); see also Coleridge v. Tomsho, 2003-Ohio-650, 2003 WL 294356 (Ohio Ct. App. 5th Dist. Stark County 2003) (stating that actual verbal threats are not necessary to establish a violation of the menacing by stalking statute; court may infer from the history between the parties that the accused intended a threat by his actions); Noah v. Brillhart, 2003-Ohio-2421, 2003 WL 21078077, *3 (Ohio Ct. App. 9th Dist. Wayne County 2003); Holloway v. Parker, 2013-Ohio-1940, 2013 WL 1944400 (Ohio Ct. App. 3d Dist. Marion County 2013).

[171]Kramer v. Kramer, 2002-Ohio-4383, 2002 WL 1967104, ¶ 17 (Ohio Ct. App. 3d Dist. Seneca County 2002); see also Nwosu v. Underwood, 2007-Ohio-1907, 2007 WL 1175230 (Ohio Ct. App. 3d Dist. Marion County 2007); McKinley v. Kuhn, 2011-Ohio-134, 2011 WL 281135 (Ohio Ct. App. 4th Dist. Hocking County 2011); State v. Beckwith, 2013-Ohio-492, 2013 WL 588518 (Ohio Ct. App. 8th Dist. Cuyahoga County 2013); Holloway v. Parker, 2013-Ohio-1940, 2013 WL 1944400 (Ohio Ct. App. 3d Dist. Marion County 2013) (differentiating between verbal and physical threats and reversing the trial court and holding that there was no evidence of a constant fear); Krzystan v. Bauer, 2017-Ohio-858, 2017 WL 945183 (Ohio Ct. App. 6th Dist. Ottawa County 2017).

[172]See Text § 8:4.

[173]Paulus v. Rucker, 2003-Ohio-2816, 20 I.E.R. Cas. (BNA) 1179, 2003 WL 21263203 (Ohio Ct. App. 11th Dist. Portage County 2003) (overruled by, Davis v. DiNunzio, 2005-Ohio-2883, 2005 WL 1383975 (Ohio Ct. App. 11th Dist. Lake County 2005)).

[174]Paulus v. Rucker, 2003-Ohio-2816, 20 I.E.R. Cas. (BNA) 1179, 2003 WL 21263203, *3 (Ohio Ct. App. 11th Dist. Portage County 2003) (overruled by, Davis v. DiNunzio, 2005-Ohio-2883, 2005 WL 1383975 (Ohio Ct. App. 11th Dist. Lake County 2005)); but see Noah v. Brillhart, 2003-Ohio-2421, 2003 WL 21078077 (Ohio Ct. App. 9th Dist. Wayne County 2003) (appellate court affirmed the trial court's issuance of the CPO where respondent's psychologist called petitioner to warn her that respondent threatened to "smash in" her face and made harassing calls to her family).

[175]Paulus v. Rucker, 2003-Ohio-2816, 20 I.E.R. Cas. (BNA) 1179, 2003 WL 21263203, *4 (Ohio Ct. App. 11th Dist. Portage County 2003) (overruled by, Davis v. DiNunzio, 2005-Ohio-2883, 2005 WL 1383975 (Ohio Ct. App. 11th Dist. Lake County 2005))(overruling court holding review of challenge to sufficiency and weight of evidence to support issuance of civil stalking protection order required separate analyses).

satisfy the "knowingly" requirement of R.C. 2903.211. The threat "somebody needs to be shot" became the only incident and, as such, the supervisor failed to satisfy the "pattern of conduct" requirement. Finally, the supervisor failed to meet the statutory standard of "mental distress." The supervisor's statement that she was upset failed to demonstrate a belief that the employee intended to cause her mental distress or fear of physical harm.

In reversing the trial court, the appellate court stated that it "could find no existing case law where menacing by stalking has been found to exist without some type of direct, face to face encounter between a petitioner and respondent. . . . Appellant made some inappropriate comments to third persons. Civil protection orders are not to be used to alleviate uncomfortable work situations, they are to be used in preventing individuals from being harassed and protect them from mental distress and physical harm."[176]

In a concurring opinion, Justice Christley disagreed with the majority that the comment did not rise to the level of stalking because there was no direct or face-to-face communication.[177] In noting that the stalking statute does not require proof of either direct or face-to-face communication, she concluded that "[s]talkers engage in psychological warfare, which by its nature is devious, insidious, and subtle.[178] Veiled references to third parties of dire consequences to the victim are stock-in-trade to such perpetrators. While such actions may be more difficult to prove than direct threats, the trial court should not be precluded from considering such third-party incidents, as appropriate evidence. . . To hold otherwise would defeat the purpose of R.C. 2903. 214. This civil statute was enacted to fill the void left by the menacing by stalking, menacing and aggravated menacing criminal statutes. With a stalking civil protection order, the court can now take proactive measures to immediately protect the victim instead of waiting until there are actual direct or face-to-face incidents or threatening behavior."[179]

---

[176]Paulus v. Rucker, 2003-Ohio-2816, 20 I.E.R. Cas. (BNA) 1179, 2003 WL 21263203, *5 (Ohio Ct. App. 11th Dist. Portage County 2003) (overruled by, Davis v. DiNunzio, 2005-Ohio-2883, 2005 WL 1383975 (Ohio Ct. App. 11th Dist. Lake County 2005)) (overruling court holding review of challenge to sufficiency and weight of evidence to support issuance of civil stalking protection order required separate analyses), quoting Kramer v. Kramer, 2002-Ohio-4383, 2002 WL 1967104 (Ohio Ct. App. 3d Dist. Seneca County 2002).

[177]See Dunn v. Clark, 2016-Ohio-641, 2016 WL 698090 (Ohio Ct. App. 12th Dist. Warren County 2016) (upholding issuance of protection order noting that the fact that Clark did not issue the threats directly to Dunn does not defeat the *mens rea* element of the offense. It can be inferred that Clark knew or reasonably should have known she would tell her boyfriend of the threats against his life. at ¶ 14).

[178]See also Fortney v. Willhoite, 2012-Ohio-3024, 2012 WL 2522835 (Ohio Ct. App. 11th Dist. Lake County 2012).

[179]Paulus v. Rucker, 2003-Ohio-2816, 20 I.E.R. Cas. (BNA) 1179, 2003 WL 21263203, *6 (Ohio Ct. App. 11th Dist. Portage County 2003) (overruled by, Davis v. DiNunzio, 2005-Ohio-2883, 2005 WL 1383975 (Ohio Ct. App. 11th Dist. Lake County 2005)) (overruling court holding review of challenge to sufficiency and weight of evidence to support issuance of civil stalking protection order required separate analyses), citing Lindsay v. Jackson, 2000 WL 1268810 (Ohio Ct. App. 1st Dist. Hamilton County 2000). See also Fortney v. Willhoite, 2012-Ohio-3024, 2012 WL

Q & A: Can the threatening behavior be in the form of text messages to the petitioner?

Yes. In *A.S. v. P.F.*[180] the nature of the acts were threats made through various text and social network messages. In this case, the appellant sent petitioner multiple text messages as well as comments on Facebook that were accusatory and hurtful towards petitioner.[181]

The appellate court determined that appellant caused petitioner to believe that he would cause her physical harm by way of his electronic messages. By threatening to reveal petitioner's criminal record to her employer and emphasizing that he knew where she lived, appellant had engaged in a pattern of conduct sufficient for the issuance of a civil stalking protection order.[182]

Q & A: Can a person obtain a civil protection order under R.C. 2903.214 based on verbal threats and other non-physical acts?

Of course. In *Miller v. Shaw*,[183] appellant appealed the denial of a protection order issued pursuant to R.C. 2903.214. In that there was only two actual fights in two years, appellant argued that the reason the trial court denied the CSPO was based on the fact that there were few physical acts. Appellant testified that appellee also threatened to kill him, slammed on his brakes in an attempt to have appellant hit him with his car from behind and made obscene gestures at him.[184]

2522835 (Ohio Ct. App. 11th Dist. Lake County 2012); Dunn v. Clark, 2016-Ohio-641, 2016 WL 698090 (Ohio Ct. App. 12th Dist. Warren County 2016) (noting that threats need not be made directly to the victim. In that Clark was aware Dunn was in an intimate relationship with Clark's wife, it can be inferred that Clark knew or reasonably should have known that the girlfriend would tell her boyfriend (Dunn) about threats against his life).

[180]A.S. v. P.F., 2013-Ohio-4857, 2013 WL 5925968 (Ohio Ct. App. 9th Dist. Lorain County 2013). See also Joy v. Letostak, 2015-Ohio-2667, 2015 WL 3964179 (Ohio Ct. App. 10th Dist. Franklin County 2015) (emails and facebook messages can form the basis of threatening behavior); Frenchko v. Frenchko-Nagy, 2015-Ohio-4546, 42 N.E.3d 829 (Ohio Ct. App. 11th Dist. Trumbull County 2015) (CSPO "pattern of conduct" established based on a phone call of a sexual nature, two Facebook posts linking to the page of a known criminal and a text message from a third party with a photograph of the respondent and the petitioner's boss); Wulf v. Opp, 2015-Ohio-3285, 2015 WL 4878495 (Ohio Ct. App. 12th Dist. Clermont County 2015) (repeated harassment of petitioner, in person and through prank calls, voice mail messages and social media provided credible evidence of stalking); Text § 16:20; L.L. v. R.B., 2017-Ohio-7553, 2017 WL 3980553 (Ohio Ct. App. 5th Dist. Guernsey County 2017) (Facebook posts can also cause a person mental distress where the posts demonstrated respondent was unstable and where petitioner feared for her job and reputation).

[181]See also Prater v. Mullins, 2013-Ohio-3981, 2013 WL 5230272 (Ohio Ct. App. 3d Dist. Auglaize County 2013).

[182]But see A.S. v. P.F., 2013-Ohio-4857, 2013 WL 5925968 (Ohio Ct. App. 9th Dist. Lorain County 2013) at dissent, ¶ 18.

[183]Miller v. Shaw, 2009-Ohio-6753, 2009 WL 4895276 (Ohio Ct. App. 7th Dist. Carroll County 2009).

[184]See Kruszynski v. Kruszynski, 2013-Ohio-3355, 2013 WL 3965465 (Ohio Ct. App. 5th Dist. Fairfield County 2013) (verbally insulting, driving erratically in tailgating, and making inappropriate hand gestures to appellee); Lewis v. Jacobs, 2013-Ohio-3461, 2013 WL 4041333 (Ohio Ct. App. 2d Dist. Montgomery County 2013) (making hand gestures that he would shoot petitioner on several occasions after threatening to take revenge on her where petitioner knew he owned several guns).

The appellant also cited several cases where civil protection orders were issued based on non-physical acts.[185]

In this case, however, the appellate court affirmed the denial of the CSPO based, in part, on appellant's own testimony that appellee had never stalked him at his home or his job or in the parking lot.[186] While there were two fights, 20 months apart, the fact that the acts were between a husband and the man with whom his wife was having an affair was an important consideration for the court. "This does not seem to be the type of situation that warrants a CSPO. While the two men clearly do not get along, that does not lead to the conclusion that the court must step in and issue a CSPO."[187] Additionally, the appellate court distinguished the cited cases from the instant case because, in those cases, the protection orders were granted. In light of the time frames between the incidents in the other cases and the fact that there was competent, credible evidence to uphold the denial of the CSPO in this case, the trial court's decision was not made in error.

§ 9:9 Other miscellaneous concerns

Q & A: What is the procedure if a respondent requests attorney fees as a sanction for petitioner's filing of a frivolous pleading?[1]

The Franklin County Court of Appeals considered this issue in *Donaldson v. Todd*.[2] In that case, petitioner requested a CSPO. An ex parte CSPO was granted to petitioner. When petitioner failed to appear at the full hearing, the trial court issued an order requiring petitioner to show cause why it should not dismiss her case for lack of prosecution. The trial court dismissed the case when petitioner failed to respond.

Subsequently, respondent filed a motion requesting attorney fees pursuant to R.C. 2323.51 and Civ. R. 11. In his affidavit in support, he disputed the facts set forth in petitioner's petition and also stated that *he was in jail* on one of the dates petitioner alleged he vandalized her car. (emphasis added.)

---

[185]See, for example, Szymanski v. Trendel, 2009-Ohio-992, 2009 WL 580457 (Ohio Ct. App. 6th Dist. Lucas County 2009); Sobieniak v. Chapdelaine, 2008-Ohio-6403, 2008 WL 5147439 (Ohio Ct. App. 6th Dist. Lucas County 2008).

[186]Beadnell v. McAdam, 2016-Ohio-8207, 2016 WL 7396476 (Ohio Ct. App. 7th Dist. Jefferson County 2016) (although the statute states "cause mental distress," the appellate court spoke in terms of "had caused mental distress, suggesting that mental distress must have actually been caused).

[187]*Miller at * 4.*

[Section 9:9]

[1]See also Text § 12:21.

[2]Donaldson v. Todd, 174 Ohio App. 3d 117, 2007-Ohio-6504, 881 N.E.2d 280 (10th Dist. Franklin County 2007); See also Bigelow v. Nguyen, 2009-Ohio-3325, 2009 WL 1915141 (Ohio Ct. App. 7th Dist. Columbiana County 2009) (protection order denied because petitioner had not testified that he believed Nguyen would harm him in any way and the denial of attorneys fees was reasonably based on the facts and circumstances); Lozada v. Lozada, 2014-Ohio-5700, 2014 WL 7357285 (Ohio Ct. App. 11th Dist. Geauga County 2014) (filed against a petitioner whose CPO was denied); Zielinski-Barnwell v. Prewitt, 2014-Ohio-3761, 2014 WL 4269111 (Ohio Ct. App. 6th Dist. Wood County 2014) (discussing the limitations of use of Civ. R. 11).

The appellate court reversed the trial court and remanded the case for a hearing on appellant's motion. (appellant's motion was denied without a hearing.) The court first discussed the definitional terms including 'frivolous conduct" under R.C. 2323.51.[3] It also noted that Civ. R. 11 "authorizes a trial court to award attorney fees if a pro se party willfully signs a document which the party knows is not supported by good ground."[4]

It acknowledged that a hearing is not necessary before denying a motion for attorney fees unless the motion demonstrates arguable merit. It reasoned that, pursuant to both statute and rule, a trial court may deny a hearing only when the motion, on its face, fails to demonstrate a triable issue. In this case, appellant was able to demonstrate arguable merit because he was incarcerated on one of the dates petitioner alleged he damaged her car.

Q & A: Does a trial court have discretion to place restrictions on a respondent's conduct as part of a civil stalking protection order?

The short answer is yes.[5]

As with civil protection orders issued under RC 3113.31, a trial court may issue a civil protection order under RC 2903.214 that contains various restrictions on a respondent's conduct. Under RC 2903.214, a trial court, after a hearing, may issue any protection order that contains terms designed to ensure the safety and protection of the person to be protected by the order.[6] For example, a court may order that the respondent be restrained from consuming alcohol or drugs while the protection order is in effect. A court may also restrain a respondent from possessing or using weapons during the duration of the protection order.

In *Lerner v. Giolekas,*[7] the appellate court balanced the right to bear arms with the right of a person to be safe and protected. "Restrictions on a person's second amendment rights have been upheld as valid

---

[3]See Guerrieri v. Brys, 2014-Ohio-1178, 2014 WL 1326098 (Ohio Ct. App. 7th Dist. Mahoning County 2014) (defining the term "frivolous conduct" in a case where respondent filed a suit alleging frivolous conduct against petitioner for misusing the CPO process when she then withdrew her petition and ex parte order and requesting expenses pursuant to R.C. 2323.51).

[4]Donaldson v. Todd, 174 Ohio App. 3d 117, 120, 2007-Ohio-6504, 881 N.E.2d 280 (10th Dist. Franklin County 2007), citing Neubauer v. Ohio Remcon, Inc., 2006-Ohio-1481, 2006 WL 772020, *29 (Ohio Ct. App. 10th Dist. Franklin County 2006).

[5]See also § 12:22.

[6]See Johnson v. Miller, 2018-Ohio-2113, ¶ 20, 2018 WL 2465137 (Ohio Ct. App. 2d Dist. Miami County 2018) (sustaining assignment of error with regard to the scope of the order and holding that respondent's being prevented from going to the homes of petitioner's relatives, even in petitioner's absence, was unreasonable in light of the purpose for seeking a CSPO-to protect the petitioner-which is not advanced by preventing Miller, even when Johnson is not present, from visiting the homes of her relatives).

[7]Lerner v. Giolekas, 2016-Ohio-696, 2016 WL 762594 (Ohio Ct. App. 8th Dist. Cuyahoga County 2016), appeal not allowed, 146 Ohio St. 3d 1429, 2016-Ohio-4606, 52 N.E.3d 1204 (2016).

exercises of police power as it related to civil stalking protection orders."[8]

Although the trial court has broad discretion when imposing restrictions under a protection order, such discretion is not limitless.[9] "Restrictions must bear a sufficient nexus to the conduct the trial court is attempting to prevent."[10]

According to the appellate court, the trial court, on remand, must find competent credible evidence that prohibiting appellant from possessing firearms bears a sufficient nexus to the conduct that the trial court is attempting to prevent.

Similarly, in *Arruda v. Farmer,*[11] Respondent contacted petitioner by way of an online dating website and when she didn't respond, he continued to contact her through the site. Once he discovered her name, birthdate and address which identifiers were not listed on the website, he began to contact her via her personal email. After learning of her work email, he began contacting her there and he also sent letters and packages to her at her place of employment and home. Such conduct caused her to fear physical harm and mental distress.[12]

On appeal he argued that the restrictions in the protection order, to wit: ordering him to stay 500 feet away from appellee, enjoining him from entering her residence, school, place of employment, etc., ordering him not to interfere with her right to occupy the residence or cancel utilities or insurance or disrupting mail service and ordering him causing/encouraging another to do an act prohibited by the order. Because of the emails sent to her work and packages to her home, "appellant demonstrates he was very sophisticated in his ability to

[8]Lerner v. Giolekas, 2016-Ohio-696, 2016 WL 762594, ¶ 50 (Ohio Ct. App. 8th Dist. Cuyahoga County 2016), appeal not allowed, 146 Ohio St. 3d 1429, 2016-Ohio-4606, 52 N.E.3d 1204 (2016); see also Arruda v. Farmer, 2015-Ohio-5511, 55 N.E.3d 604 (Ohio Ct. App. 5th Dist. Licking County 2015), appeal not allowed, 145 Ohio St. 3d 1460, 2016-Ohio-2807, 49 N.E.3d 322 (2016) (which includes the distance restriction of 500 feet); Elkins v. Reed, 2014-Ohio-1217, 2014 WL 1350806 (Ohio Ct. App. 5th Dist. Stark County 2014); Clementz-McBeth v. Craft, 2012-Ohio-985, 2012 WL 776851 (Ohio Ct. App. 3d Dist. Auglaize County 2012).

[9]Lerner v. Giolekas, 2016-Ohio-696, 2016 WL 762594, ¶ 51 (Ohio Ct. App. 8th Dist. Cuyahoga County 2016), appeal not allowed, 146 Ohio St. 3d 1429, 2016-Ohio-4606, 52 N.E.3d 1204 (2016), citing Newhouse v. Williams, 167 Ohio App. 3d 215, 223, 2006-Ohio-3075, 854 N.E.2d 565 (3d Dist. Wyandot County 2006), citing Maag v. Maag, 2002-Ohio-1401, 2002 WL 468585 (Ohio Ct. App. 3d Dist. Wyandot County 2002).

[10]Lerner v. Giolekas, 2016-Ohio-696, 2016 WL 762594, ¶ 51 (Ohio Ct. App. 8th Dist. Cuyahoga County 2016), appeal not allowed, 146 Ohio St. 3d 1429, 2016-Ohio-4606, 52 N.E.3d 1204 (2016), citing Newhouse v. Williams, 167 Ohio App. 3d 215, 223, 2006-Ohio-3075, 854 N.E.2d 565 (3d Dist. Wyandot County 2006), citing Maag v. Maag, 2002-Ohio-1401, 2002 WL 468585 (Ohio Ct. App. 3d Dist. Wyandot County 2002).

[11]Arruda v. Farmer, 2015-Ohio-5511, 55 N.E.3d 604 (Ohio Ct. App. 5th Dist. Licking County 2015), appeal not allowed, 145 Ohio St. 3d 1460, 2016-Ohio-2807, 49 N.E.3d 322 (2016).

[12]Arruda v. Farmer, 2015-Ohio-5511, 55 N.E.3d 604 (Ohio Ct. App. 5th Dist. Licking County 2015), appeal not allowed, 145 Ohio St. 3d 1460, 2016-Ohio-2807, 49 N.E.3d 322 (2016).

discern personal facts about appellee."[13] Based on the above, the appellate court found sufficient evidence of a nexus between the restrictions contained in the order and appellant's conduct.

Thus, the main take-a-way is that attorneys or litigants must not check all boxes without considering if the restriction bears a nexus to the conduct the court is trying to prevent. According to recent case law, there must be a sufficient nexus between appellant's pattern of conduct and the restrictions in the civil stalking protection order.[14]

Q & A: Where a stalking CPO is granted, must the court order all respondents to turn over their gun collection to the police?

Not necessarily. In *Wallace v. Masten*,[15] a guardian ad litem in a custody dispute was granted a stalking CPO against the children's father. As part of the order, appellant was prohibited from purchasing or possessing firearms. Appellant contended that the evidence did not support the prohibition against him possessing firearms.

The Hocking County Court of Appeals noted that there had been no evidence presented that appellant has used possessed firearms during any of the encounters he had with appellee. In modifying the trial court's judgment, the appellate court stated that "[a]ppellant's gun collection, which he maintains in his home, has had no impact in this ongoing dispute. Thus, this particular provision of the protection order is not reasonably tailored to, or designed for, this particular set of circumstances."[16]

On the other hand, the Stark County Court of Appeals determined that the required prohibition was necessary to ensure the safety and protection of the petitioner. In *Mann v. Sumser*,[17] the appellant had threatened to shoot petitioner and her family if she did not marry him. As a result of appellant's actions, appellee testified that she was terrified and felt that there was no safe place for her. Appellant had argued on appeal that the order requiring him to turn over weapons to the police and prohibiting him from using, carrying, purchasing or possessing them was not supported by the evidence.

The appellate court considered appellee's testimony and determined that R.C. 2903.214(E)(1) provides that a court is permitted to issue any protection order containing terms designed to ensure the safety and protection of the victim.

Of interest is that the appellate court pointed out that appellant failed to object to the prohibition of weapons provision in the stalking

---

[13]Arruda v. Farmer, 2015-Ohio-5511, 55 N.E.3d 604 (Ohio Ct. App. 5th Dist. Licking County 2015), appeal not allowed, 145 Ohio St. 3d 1460, 2016-Ohio-2807, 49 N.E.3d 322 (2016).

[14]See also § 12:22.

[15]Wallace v. Masten, 2003-Ohio-1081, 2003 WL 927600 (Ohio Ct. App. 4th Dist. Hocking County 2003).

[16]Wallace v. Masten, 2003-Ohio-1081, 2003 WL 927600, *6 (Ohio Ct. App. 4th Dist. Hocking County 2003).

[17]Mann v. Sumser, 2002-Ohio-5103, 2002 WL 31151164 (Ohio Ct. App. 5th Dist. Stark County 2002); see also Harris v. Miami Cty. Sheriff's Dept., 160 Ohio App. 3d 435, 2005-Ohio-1713, 827 N.E.2d 807 (2d Dist. Miami County 2005) (where appellate court held that a consent agreement is a protection order, thus sheriff did not err in refusing to grant respondent a license to carry a concealed weapon).

CPO as being unconstitutional or cite any authority documenting that such a requirement was unconstitutional. Had the appellant objected to the requirement as being unconstitutional, the appellate court may have considered the argument.

Q & A: Is the prohibition from possessing, using, carrying, or obtaining firearms for five years and requiring them to be turned over to police arbitrary, unreasonable, unconscionable and unconstitutional?

At least on appellate court answered this in the negative. In *Elkins v. Reed*,[18] appellant argued that the trial court's issuance of a CSPO with such a provision banning the use and possession of firearms was fundamentally wrong. In its analysis, the Stark appellate court noted that a court may issue any protection order that contains terms designed to ensure the safety and protection of the protected parties pursuant to R.C. 2903.214(E)(1) and stressed that the statute provides that the required terms *include but are not limited to* the articulated terms set forth in the statutory provision (emphasis added).

The Court then went on to explain that the right to bear arms is "not a right to keep and carry any weapon whatsoever in any manner and for whatever purpose."[19] It relied on the Second District Court of Appeals decision in *Calicoat v. Calicoat*[20] which considered the issue in the domestic violence context. The *Calicoat* court said:

> The protection of victims of domestic violence from further harm has as its purpose the protection of the public welfare, which is a proper exercise of the police power conferred on the General Assembly by Section 1, Article II of the Ohio Constitution. * * * Orders issued pursuant to that section constitute valid exercises of the police power that supersede the constitutional protections against takings of private property on which [appellant] relies.[21]

The recognition of protection orders as valid exercises of police power that may supersede constitutional protections has been applied to prohibitions against owning and possessing forearms and deadly weapons in other appellate districts. The Third District agreed with the Second District's finding that R.C. 3113.31 constitutes a valid exercise of police power that can supersede constitutional protections in the context of the Second Amendment, and we find the same public welfare analysis applicable here, in the context of a CSPO.[22] However, the appellate court also acknowledged that a restriction in a CPO

[18]Elkins v. Reed, 2014-Ohio-1217, 2014 WL 1350806 (Ohio Ct. App. 5th Dist. Stark County 2014).

[19]Elkins v. Reed, 2014-Ohio-1217, 2014 WL 1350806, ¶ 40 (Ohio Ct. App. 5th Dist. Stark County 2014), quoting District of Columbia v. Heller, 554 U.S. 570, 626, 128 S. Ct. 2783, 171 L. Ed. 2d 637 (2008). See also Binderup v. Attorney General United States of America, 836 F.3d 336 (3d Cir. 2016), cert. denied, 137 S. Ct. 2323, 198 L. Ed. 2d 746 (2017) and cert. denied, 137 S. Ct. 2323, 198 L. Ed. 2d 746 (2017).

[20]Calicoat v. Calicoat, 2009-Ohio-5869, 2009 WL 3683665, ¶ 38 (Ohio Ct. App. 2d Dist. Miami County 2009).

[21]Calicoat v. Calicoat, 2009-Ohio-5869, 2009 WL 3683665, ¶ 38 (Ohio Ct. App. 2d Dist. Miami County 2009).

[22]Elkins v. Reed, 2014-Ohio-1217, 2014 WL 1350806, ¶ 41 (Ohio Ct. App. 5th Dist. Stark County 2014), citing Clementz-McBeth v. Craft, 2012-Ohio-985, 2012 WL 776851 (Ohio Ct. App. 3d Dist. Auglaize County 2012); Lerner v. Giolekas, 2016-Ohio-

must be related to the conduct the restriction seeks to prevent and that a trial court has discretion in imposing restrictions.[23]

In overruling the assignment of error, the court applied the "nexus test" to analyze whether a condition in a CPO is unduly restrictive. In applying this test, appellate courts "look to the evidence in the record to find competent, credible evidence of the conduct the trial court is attempting to prevent."[24] The Court found that the Reeds fired their guns in frustration and intimidation, reacting to the dispute and, thus creating a valid reason why their guns were prohibited by the CSPO.

Q & A: Is the subject of a CSPO issued pursuant to R.C. 2903.214 Brady disqualified under federal firearms law (18 U.S.C.A. § 922)?

The Brady Act[25] restricts certain groups of persons from obtaining handguns or other firearms. In order to be Brady disqualified from possessing a firearm, there must be a domestic relationship between the petitioner and respondent such that the parties are intimate partners and the respondent must be subject to a qualifying protection order.

For purposes of a qualifying protection order, the parties must be intimate partners. Only intimate parties such as spouses, former spouses, present or former cohabitants and a parent of a common child or a child of the intimate partner are subject to Brady restrictions. Additionally, a qualifying protection order is one that is issued after a hearing with notice to the respondent who is provided a right to participate. There must also be a specific finding that the respondent either presents a credible threat to the victim or prohibits the use of physical force.

Therefore, not all protection orders issued pursuant to R.C. 2903.214 fall within the prohibitions of 18 U.S.C.A. § 922, are subject to disqualification under federal law or must be entered into NCIC. Dating relationships, siblings, strangers and others related by blood or marriage are not subject to Brady.[26]

Q & A: Is cyber stalking a crime in Ohio?[27]

Under R.C. 2903.211(A)(2), Ohio's menacing by stalking statute has

---

696, 2016 WL 762594 (Ohio Ct. App. 8th Dist. Cuyahoga County 2016), appeal not allowed, 146 Ohio St. 3d 1429, 2016-Ohio-4606, 52 N.E.3d 1204 (2016).

[23]See also Text § 12:22.

[24]Elkins v. Reed, 2014-Ohio-1217, 2014 WL 1350806, ¶ 45 (Ohio Ct. App. 5th Dist. Stark County 2014), citing Boals v. Miller, 2011-Ohio-1470, 2011 WL 1118464 (Ohio Ct. App. 5th Dist. Ashland County 2011).

[25]18 U.S.C.A. § 922.

[26]See also Chapter 18; Text § 18:11, Firearm offenses under VAWA.

[27]See, e.g., Nancy K.D. Lemon, "How New Technologies Are Changing Domestic Violence," Vol. 14, No. 3 Domestic Violence Report 33–48 (Feb./Mar. 2009). But see Young v. Young, 96 So. 3d 478 (Fla. 1st DCA 2012) (changing husband's email password, appropriating his emails and including them in a filing in their divorce proceeding do not amount to cyberstalking because they were not electronic communications by her of "words, images, or language directed at" Mr. Young. at *479); Horowitz v. Horowitz, 160 So. 3d 530 (Fla. 2d DCA 2015) (husband's two posts on his own social media webpage did not amount to cyberstalking); Christina M. Gagnier, Cyber Exploitation and Perpetration of Digital Abuse, 22 Domestic Violence Report 6, (August/September 2017).

been amended to prohibit persons, through the use of any electronic method of remotely transferring information, including, but not limited to, any computer, computer network, computer program, or computer system, from posting a message with purpose to urge or incite another to commit a violation of division (A)(1) of this section. Additionally, a "pattern of conduct" was amended to include the posting of messages or receipt of information or data through the use of an electronic method of remotely transferring information, including but not limited to, a computer, computer network, computer program, computer system, or telecommunications device.[28] Under this amended definition, cyber stalking is contemplated by Ohio's legislature.[29]

Q & A: Is a global positioning device considered a method of stalking?[30]

Yes. In a case of first impression, a Colorado court of appeals held that a defendant, who installed a GPS on his wife's car to document her movements, had engaged in harassment by stalking. In *People v. Sullivan*,[31] the appellate court reasoned that the statutory term " 'under surveillance' includes electronic surveillance that records a person's whereabouts as that person moves from one location to another and allows the stalker to access that information either simultaneously or shortly thereafter."[32] In affirming the defendant's conviction, the court pointed out that wife's testimony that her concern over being watched by defendant caused her to take alternate routes to her destinations and to be cautious that no one was following her, that she felt afraid and felt that she was constantly being watched and that these feelings made her uncomfortable and gave her stomach aches, that she had trouble falling asleep and would awaken with feelings of anxiety and that her concern for her safety caused her to take a leave of absence from work, was sufficient to demonstrate serious emotional distress caused by stalking.

Q & A: Can a petitioner request electronic monitoring as part of the relief requested in a civil protection order?

Yes. Recently, the Ohio General Assembly amended R.C. 2903.214

---

[28]2003 Sub. S.B. 8, eff. 8-29-03; see also Text § 18:6, Federal crimes under VAWA; 18 U.S.C.A. § 2261A(2). But see Elonis v. U.S., 135 S. Ct. 2001, 192 L. Ed. 2d 1, 43 Media L. Rep. (BNA) 1749 (2015) (Supreme Court overturned conviction of Elonis for making violent threats against his ex wife and others on Facebook. Court stressed that jury instructions were incorrect because they only required that a reasonable person would foresee that statements made by Elonis would be interpreted as a threat. Court held that defendant's crime required evidence that he intended to make the threats or knew that his communications would be viewed as threatening. Case failed to define standard for a threat to constitute a crime and ignored both objective belief and subjective fear of victim).

[29]See, e.g., Amy C. Radosevich, Thwarting the Stalker: Are Anti-Stalking Measures keeping Pace with Today's Stalker? 2000 U. Ill. L. Rev. 1371 (2000); Joseph C. Merschman, The Dark Side of the Web: Cyberstalking and the Need for Contemporary Legislation, 24 Harv. Women's L.J. 255 (2001).

[30]See Diane Rosenfeld, GPS Monitoring Systems for Batterers: Exploring a New Paradigm of Offender Accountability and Victiim/Survivor Safety, Vol. 12 No. 4 Domestic Violence Report 49 (April/May 2007) (using GPS monitoring as a method for victim safety).

[31]People v. Sullivan, 53 P.3d 1181 (Colo. App. 2002).

[32]People v. Sullivan, 53 P.3d 1181, 1184 (Colo. App. 2002).

to permit a petitioner to request electronic monitoring for respondent as a form of relief. A petitioner must allege that at any time preceding the filing of the petition, the respondent engaged in conduct that would cause a reasonable person to believe that the health, welfare or safety of the person to be protected was at risk.[33] The petitioner must also provide a description of the nature and extent of the conduct and an allegation that the respondent presents a continuing danger to the person to be protected.[34]

The statute also provides that, after the full hearing, if the court considering a petition that includes such a request or the court upon its own motion, finds upon clear and convincing evidence that the petitioner reasonably believed that the respondent's conduct at any time preceding the filing of the petition endangered the health, welfare or safety of the person to be protected and that the respondent presents a continuing danger to the person to be protected, the court may order that the respondent be electronically monitored for a period of time and under the terms and conditions that the court determines are appropriate. Electronic monitoring shall be in addition to any other relief granted to the petitioner.[35]

If electronic monitoring is ordered by the court, the court shall direct the sheriff's office or other appropriate law enforcement agency to install the electronic monitoring devise and to monitor the respondent.[36] If the respondent is able to pay the cost, the court shall order the respondent to pay the cost of installation and monitoring the electronic monitoring devise. If the court determines the respondent is indigent, the cost of installation and monitoring of the electronic monitoring devise shall be paid out of funds from the reparations fund created pursuant to section R.C. 2743.191.[37]

Lastly, if a respondent violates a civil stalking protection order under R.C. 2919.27 and electronic monitoring was required under the original order, the court may require in addition to any other sentence imposed upon the offender for violating the order, that the offender be electronically monitored for a period not to exceed five years by a law enforcement agency designated by the court.[38]

§ 9:10 Aggravated trespass

Q & A: What is aggravated trespass?

Aggravated trespass occurs when one enters or remains on the land or premises of another with the purpose to commit on that land or those premises a misdemeanor.[1] Besides the aforementioned, the other elements of R.C. 2911.211 are:

---

[33] R.C. 2903.214(C)(2).

[34] R.C. 2903.214(C)(2).

[35] R.C. 2903.214(E)(1)(b).

[36] R.C. 2903.214(N).

[37] R.C. 2903.214(N).

[38] R.C. 2919.27(B)(5).

[Section 9:10]

[1] See for example, State v. Blausey, 2006-Ohio-5536, 2006 WL 3020329 (Ohio Ct. App. 5th Dist. Licking County 2006) (discussing the elements of aggravated trespass

(1) causing physical harm,
(2) to another person,
(3) causing another person to believe the offender, or
(4) will cause physical harm to him/her.

The intent of the offender is considered because the offender must act "with purpose" to commit on the land or premises a misdemeanor. A person acts purposely when it is his specific intention to cause a certain result or, when the gist of the offense is a prohibition against conduct of a certain nature, regardless of what the offender intends to accomplish thereby, it is his specific intention to engage in conduct of that nature.

Besides the intent of a respondent, a victim must demonstrate that the respondent caused the victim physical harm or that the victim believed that the respondent will cause the victim physical harm. "Physical harm to persons" as defined in RC 2901.01(A)(3) means "any injury, illness or physiological impairment, regardless of gravity or duration." This definition should satisfy the statute.[2]

Clearly, the aggravated trespass statute encompasses both the specific intent of the respondent to commit on the land or premises of another, a misdemeanor causing physical harm to the victim and the subjective intent of the victim to believe that the respondent will cause physical harm to him or her. In effect, the victim must have feared physical harm or suffered from physical harm.

Q & A: What if respondent entered petitioner's house and said he wanted to hurt her, but did not touch her? Could petitioner obtain a civil protection order?

It is unlikely that the petitioner could prevail under that portion of R.C. 3113.31(A)(1)(b) that defines a threat of "imminent serious physical harm," unless it could be argued that this was part of a continuous course of conduct. A strict construction of the provision suggests that the type of threat considered must cause "serious physical harm" as defined in R.C. 2901.01(E). The threat must also appear to be imminent.

However, a petitioner should be able to prevail under that portion of R.C. 3113.31(A)(1)(b) which provides for the issuance of a civil protection order for committing a violation of R.C. 2911.211 (aggravated trespass).[3]

Because a violation of R.C. 2911.211 is one of the specific acts contemplated under R.C. 3113.31(A)(1)(b),[4] and because it has been previously suggested that a subjective standard should be used to

---

and its application to specific crimes); see also Williamson v. Williamson, 180 Ohio App. 3d 260, 2008-Ohio-6718, 905 N.E.2d 217 (2d Dist. Greene County 2008) (noting that the commission of aggravated trespass is itself an act of domestic violence justifying a civil protection order under R.C. 3113.31(A)(1)(b)). Toledo v. Wells, 2014-Ohio-4636, 2014 WL 5332877 (Ohio Ct. App. 6th Dist. Lucas County 2014).

[2]RC 2911.211(A).

[3]See Gooderham v. Patterson, 1999 WL 1034472 (Ohio Ct. App. 4th Dist. Gallia County 1999).

[4]See, e.g., Bach v. Crawford, 2003-Ohio-1255, 2003 WL 1193783 (Ohio Ct. App. 2d Dist. Montgomery County 2003) (noting that although R.C. 3113.31(A) does not

determine fear under this statutory provision, this same subjective standard and the impact on the victim's state of mind should be utilized in this context as well. The only caveat is that an attorney must first consider the specific statutory requirements of R.C. 2911.211, the aggravated trespass statute. R.C. 2911.211 mandates that a respondent must first enter or remain on the premises of the petitioner and that the actual harm or threat must be spoken or shown by acts or deeds while on the premises of the petitioner.

Unfortunately, there are few cases that define the statutory terms of R.C. 2911.211 in a domestic violence context or interpret the statute in any context.[5] One reason for this may be that prosecutors are more likely to charge under R.C. 2919.25, which is a more encompassing offense, or another available criminal provision.[6] Since so few defendants have been charged under R.C. 2911.211, it is not surprising that there are no reported appellate decisions. Additionally, the statute creating such a remedy is relatively recent.[7] What is even more apparent is that few family law attorneys, thus far, have sought civil protection orders on the grounds that acts of a respondent, while on the petitioner's property, caused the petitioner to believe that the respondent intended to cause physical harm to him/her.[8]

Q & A: Does a defendant's uninvited entry into the home or premises of a spouse give rise to criminal liability for trespass?

Although there are no Ohio cases that address the issue in the context of R.C. 2911.211, the issue has been raised in the context of criminal trespass and burglary.[9] The Ohio Supreme Court definitively decided the issue by holding that "a spouse can be convicted of trespass and aggravated burglary in the dwelling of the other spouse who owns, has custody of or has control over the property where the crime has occurred."[10] Sole possessory interest is often based on evidence showing that the parties made a conscious decision to live in separate places.

In both *O'Neal* and *Lilly*, a spouse entered the home of the estranged spouse with the intent to commit a crime. In neither case was there a court order barring the spouse from the premises. In *Lilly*, the evi-

---

require a conviction under R.C. 2911.211, sufficient facts must be presented to support a finding that the statute had been violated); Charles v. Peters, 2016-Ohio-1259, 2016 WL 1178776 (Ohio Ct. App. 2d Dist. Greene County 2016).

[5]See also Gooderham v. Patterson, 1999 WL 1034472 (Ohio Ct. App. 4th Dist. Gallia County 1999) (acts of trespass committed by the respondent); A.D. v. B.D., 2017-Ohio-229, 2017 WL 277481 (Ohio Ct. App. 9th Dist. Medina County 2017) (analyzing each aspect of RC 3113.31(A)(1)(b) relative to the facts presented).

[6]See, e.g., R.C. 2903.211.

[7]1992 H.B. 536, eff. 11-5-92.

[8]Gooderham v. Patterson, 1999 WL 1034472 (Ohio Ct. App. 4th Dist. Gallia County 1999) (granting of petitioner's protection order was based on stalking incidents as well as trespass).

[9]See R.C. 2911.21, R.C. 2911.11. See also State v. Shirley, 2002-Ohio-31, 2002 WL 5177 (Ohio Ct. App. 9th Dist. Summit County 2002); State v. Crouse, 1999 WL 1123027 (Ohio Ct. App. 12th Dist. Fayette County 1999); State v. Tompkins, 2000 WL 288650 (Ohio Ct. App. 7th Dist. Jefferson County 2000).

[10]State v. O'Neal, 87 Ohio St. 3d 402, 408, 2000-Ohio-449, 721 N.E.2d 73 (2000); see also State v. Lilly, 87 Ohio St. 3d 97, 1999-Ohio-251, 717 N.E.2d 322 (1999). See also State v. Parvilus, 2014-NMSC-028, 332 P.3d 281 (N.M. 2014).

dence demonstrated that the wife's apartment was leased solely in her name, that the husband did not pay any part of the rent, that the husband never lived in the apartment and did not have a key to it, and that he entered through a door he had previously unlocked with the purpose of committing a crime. In *O'Neal*, the marital residence was leased in the wife's name, the husband had moved out following an altercation, the wife had filed a motion for a temporary protection order, and the husband had shattered the glass in the front door to enter the residence and kill his wife.

The *O'Neal* Court effectively abrogated the application of R.C. 3103.04 in criminal cases. R.C. 3103.04 provides that "neither [spouse] can be excluded from the other's dwelling, except upon a decree or order of injunction made by a court of competent jurisdiction."[11] The Court noted that the statute was "intended to address property ownership rights of married persons which are matters of civil nature and was not meant to be enforced criminally and does not affect criminal liabilities."[12]

The *Lilly* Court reasoned that, because R.C. 3103.04 was set forth in the domestic relations chapter of the Ohio Revised Code, it was designed to address property rights as they relate to domestic relations issues and concerns of ejecting one spouse from the marital dwelling. The Court noted that R.C. 3103.04 deals with matters of civil nature. "Because we find that the General Assembly never intended for R.C. 3103.04 to apply in criminal contexts, we must turn to the Criminal Code to address the issue."[13]

The Court next determined that the burglary statute was designed to protect the dweller and that, because trespass is an element of burglary, "custody and control, rather than legal title, is dispositive."[14] "Thus, in Ohio, one can commit a trespass and burglary against property of which one is the legal owner if another has control or custody of that property."[15] Because each of the estranged spouses solely occupied the property in which they were residing, the residences were in their sole custody or control. Because the husbands entered on properties not within their control and without permission of the owner or occupant, a trespass occurred.

As in Ohio, other state courts have looked to the circumstances of the case and whether one spouse has sole possessory interest. For example, an Alabama Court of Appeals reached a similar result. In

---

[11]But see State v. Meeks, 1995 WL 1036642 (Ohio Ct. App. 11th Dist. Lake County 1995) (overruled in part by *State v. Lilly* and *State v. O'Neal*).

[12]State v. O'Neal, 87 Ohio St. 3d 402, 402, 2000-Ohio-449, 721 N.E.2d 73 (2000). See also State v. Lilly, 87 Ohio St. 3d 97, 1999-Ohio-251, 717 N.E.2d 322 (1999).

[13]State v. Lilly, 87 Ohio St. 3d 97, 102, 1999-Ohio-251, 717 N.E.2d 322 (1999).

[14]State v. Lilly, 87 Ohio St. 3d 97, 102, 1999-Ohio-251, 717 N.E.2d 322 (1999). But see State v. Conner, 192 Ohio App. 3d 166, 2011-Ohio-146, 948 N.E.2d 497 (6th Dist. Fulton County 2011) (a temporary ex parte civil order issued pursuant to a divorce filing, designating a party as having *exclusive use* of the marital home, was not sufficient to show such "custody and control" so as to allow for criminal trespass) (emphasis added).

[15]State v. Lilly, 87 Ohio St. 3d 97, 102, 1999-Ohio-251, 717 N.E.2d 322 (1999); see also State v. O'Neal, 87 Ohio St. 3d 402, 408, 2000-Ohio-449, 721 N.E.2d 73 (2000).

Folsom v. State,[16] the court upheld a burglary conviction where the defendant moved into his wife's house after their marriage. When he became abusive, she asked him to leave. He did so but kept returning to the house. On the burglary issue, the court found that, despite the fact that the parties were married and the defendant resided in the premises, nonconsensual entry was predicated on a showing that defendant had neither a possessory interest in that residence nor a right to be in the residence at the time he entered.

Other state courts have upheld burglary and trespass convictions based on evidence of a restraining order or protection order. Whether the victim obtained a restraining order or protection order against the defendant is often determinative of the right of defendant to enter the premises.[17]

---

[16]Folsom v. State, 668 So. 2d 114 (Ala. Crim. App. 1995).

[17]See Com. v. Majeed, 548 Pa. 48, 694 A.2d 336 (1997) (defendant's agreeing to protection order effectively terminated any privilege he may have had to enter the premises); see also State v. Robinson, 656 A.2d 744 (Me. 1995); State v. Steed, 140 N.H. 153, 665 A.2d 1072 (1995). But see Kamen v. Egan, 322 N.J. Super. 222, 730 A.2d 873 (App. Div. 1999) (holding that a single act of trespass unaccompanied by violence was insufficient to justify the issuance of a restraining order).

Chapter 10

Nature of the Domestic Violence Relationship

§ 10:1 Introduction

Ohio's domestic violence statutes, when enacted in 1979, were designed to offer protection to persons who had previously fallen through the cracks of the legal system. Most often, crimes that occurred within intimate family relationships were not treated as seriously as crimes between strangers. Redress was unavailable because of the justice system's reluctance to involve itself in the family dynamic.

Fortunately, this failing on the part of the system to protect certain individuals led to the enactment of statutes that addressed some of the inequities in the treatment of these victims. Statutes and subsequent case law defined the relationships necessary to be eligible for protection under domestic violence legislation. The significance of the relationship is that, "in contrast to stranger violence, domestic violence arises out of the relationship."[1]

Ohio's domestic violence statutes encompass both civil and criminal

---

[Section 10:1]

[1]State v. Williams, 79 Ohio St. 3d 459, 462, 1997-Ohio-79, 683 N.E.2d 1126 (1997).

remedies for victims who, in the past, had no relief. The same family or household members covered under RC 3113.31 (civil provision) are also covered under RC 2919.25 (criminal provision). Under RC 3113. 31, the victim is the "petitioner" and the perpetrator is the "respondent"; whereas, under RC 2919.25, the victim is the "complainant" and the perpetrator is the "offender."

§ 10:2 Nature of the relationships covered; generally

The classifications of covered individuals represent various intimate spousal-type relationships and other family and household members.[1] The classes of family and household member relationships covered under both the civil[2] and criminal[3] statutory provisions include:

(1) The spouse of the respondent.[4]
(2) Any former spouse of the respondent.[5]
(3) Any person who is currently living with the respondent in a common law marital relationship.[6]
(4) Any person who is otherwise cohabiting with the respondent.[7]
(5) Any person who has otherwise cohabited with the respondent within five years prior to the date of the alleged occurrence of the act in question.[8]
(6) Any person who has lived with the respondent in a common law marital relationship.[9]
(7) Any person who is the natural parent or the putative natural parent of the respondent's child.[10]
(8) Any person who is a parent of the respondent.[11]
(9) Any person who is a child of the respondent.[12]
(10) Any person who is a foster parent of the respondent.[13]
(11) Any person related to the respondent by either blood or marriage.[14]

[Section 10:2]

[1]See Storch v. Sauerhoff, 334 N.J. Super. 226, 757 A.2d 836 (Ch. Div. 2000) (definition of household member for purposes of domestic violence).

[2]See RC 3113.31(A)(3).

[3]See RC 2919.25(E).

[4]RC 3113.31(A)(3)(a)(i).

[5]RC 3113.31(A)(3)(a)(i); see also State v. Gee, 2000-Ohio-1963, 2000 WL 33226303, *4 (Ohio Ct. App. 4th Dist. Scioto County 2000) (noting that former spouses are protected under Ohio's domestic violence statute and that it made no difference that the parties had been divorced for four years and not living together for four years at the time of the incident).

[6]RC 3113.31(A)(3)(a)(ii).

[7]RC 3113.31(A)(3)(a)(ii).

[8]RC 3113.31(A)(3)(a)(ii).

[9]RC 3113.31(A)(3)(a)(ii).

[10]RC 3113.31(A)(3)(b).

[11]RC 3113.31(A)(3)(a)(ii).

[12]RC 3113.31(A)(3)(a)(ii).

[13]RC 3113.31(A)(3)(a)(ii).

[14]RC 3113.31(A)(3)(a)(ii).

(12) A parent of the spouse of the respondent.[15]
(13) A parent of a former spouse of the respondent.[16]
(14) A parent of a person who is living with the respondent in a common law marital relationship.[17]
(15) A parent of a person who has lived with the respondent in a common law marital relationship.[18]
(16) A parent of a person who is otherwise cohabiting with the respondent.[19]
(17) A parent of a person who has otherwise cohabited with the respondent within five years prior to the date of the alleged occurrence of the act in question.[20]
(18) A child of the spouse of the respondent (i.e., stepchild).[21]
(19) A child of a former spouse of the respondent.[22]
(20) A child of a person who is living with the respondent in a common law marital relationship.[23]
(21) A child of a person who has lived with the respondent in a common law marital relationship.[24]
(22) A child of a person who is otherwise cohabiting with the respondent.[25]
(23) A child of a person who has otherwise cohabited with the respondent within five years prior to the date of the alleged occurrence of the act in question.[26]
(24) A person who is related by blood or marriage to the spouse of the respondent.[27]
(25) A person who is related by blood or marriage to a former spouse of the respondent.[28]
(26) A person who is related by blood or marriage to a person who is living in a common law marital relationship with the respondent.[29]
(27) A person who is related by blood or marriage to a person who has lived in a common law relationship with the respondent.[30]

[15] RC 3113.31(A)(3)(a)(iii).
[16] RC 3113.31(A)(3)(a)(iii).
[17] RC 3113.31(A)(3)(a)(iii).
[18] RC 3113.31(A)(3)(a)(iii).
[19] RC 3113.31(A)(3)(a)(iii).
[20] RC 3113.31(A)(3)(a)(iii).
[21] RC 3113.31(A)(3)(a)(iii).
[22] RC 3113.31(A)(3)(a)(iii).
[23] RC 3113.31(A)(3)(a)(iii).
[24] RC 3113.31(A)(3)(a)(iii).
[25] RC 3113.31(A)(3)(a)(iii).
[26] RC 3113.31(A)(3)(a)(iii).
[27] RC 3113.31(A)(3)(a)(iii).
[28] RC 3113.31(A)(3)(a)(iii).
[29] RC 3113.31(A)(3)(a)(iii).
[30] RC 3113.31(A)(3)(a)(iii).

(28) A person who is related by blood or marriage to a person who is otherwise cohabiting with the respondent.[31]

(29) A person who is related by blood or marriage to a person who has otherwise cohabited with the respondent within five years prior to the date of the alleged occurrence of the act in question.[32]

The only other requirement is that victims that fall into any of the above-mentioned categories must either reside with or have resided with the respondent.[33] The one exception is the natural parent of any child of whom the respondent is the other natural parent or the putative natural parent.[34] The intent of RC 3113.31(A)(3)(b) is to extend protection to a victim of domestic violence who may have never lived with the respondent but who has a child in common with the respondent.

Ohio's General Assembly expanded coverage of both the civil and criminal domestic violence protection order statutes[FN 35] to protect family or household members who allege that they are victims of a sexually oriented offense as defined in RC 2951.01.

Although it is only listed as a specific act pursuant to RC 3113. 31(A)(3), it is contemplated that one can seek any of the protection orders against a family or household member if that person committed a sexually oriented offense.[35]

Additionally, the General Assembly expanded coverage to foster parents who have been abused by their foster children.[36]

§ 10:3 Nature of the relationships covered—Terminology—Generally

As stated, the categories of protected persons set forth in the statute are discrete classifications and if a person falls within one of these classifications, the statute applies. Obviously, spouses and former spouses are protected persons that fit within the ambit of RC 3113. 31(A)(3)(a)(i). Besides spouses or former spouses, RC 3113.31(A)(3)(a) (i) also includes "persons living as spouses."[1] This indicates that the intent of the statute was to include persons who are currently or were involved in committed romantic relationships. Protected status also extends to those romantic relationships that produced children, whether or not the parties ever resided together.[2] Clearly then, there is no question that these romantic relationships are the types of

---

[31] RC 3113.31(A)(3)(a)(iii).

[32] RC 3113.31(A)(3)(a)(iii).

[33] RC 3113.31(A)(3)(a).

[34] RC 3113.31(A)(3)(b); see also State v. Stringfield, 124 Ohio App. 3d 665, 707 N.E.2d 43 (9th Dist. Medina County 1998) (where neither disputed parentage).

[35] See R.C. 2903.214(C); see also RC 2919.26 and RC 2903.213 in which the term is strategically placed throughout the statutes.

[36] RC 3113.31(A)(3)(a)(ii) so long as the foster parent resides or has resided with the respondent.

[Section 10:3]

[1] See RC 3113.31(A)(4) for the definition of a "person living as a spouse."

[2] RC 3113.31(A)(3)(b).

protected domestic or familial relationship that the statute intended to cover.

A parent or child of a respondent or spouse is considered a domestic relationship that falls within the statutory mandate as set forth in RC 3113.31(A)(3)(a)(ii) and (iii). Further, persons related by blood or marriage to either the victim or the respondent fall within the ambit of the statutory framework as well.[3] These relationships are considered domestic relationships when the victims and the respondent either reside or have resided together at or before the time of the violent act. In fact, the exact relationship between the offender and the victim is less important than the fact that the parties resided together and have a domestic/familial-type relationship.

It is not as clear what other household members fit within the statutory framework. However, in light of the purpose of the statute and the fact that the common thread uniting the classifications is that they are "family or household members," it would seem logical that the domestic violence statute protects all domestic familial relationships.

The Ohio Legislature, the Ohio legislature amended RC 3113.31 to add to the circumstances under which family or household members may seek protection orders. The statute now permits a person on his or her own behalf or a parent or adult household member on behalf of any other family or household member to seek a CPO against a respondent who allegedly committed a sexually oriented offense against the petitioner or another victim. A list of sexually oriented offenses is set forth in RC 2950.01 and includes rape, sexual battery, gross sexual imposition, sexual imposition, voyeurism and importuning.

However, the statute is silent as to the definition of many of its terms. Much of the reported case law involves defining the requisite terms and applying them to the particular facts of each case. In doing so, other potential individuals may either be recognized or eliminated.

For example, the statute fails to specifically define the term "household member." "Household member" is such a broad term that it defies precise definition. It has been defined for purposes of insurance, tort, and zoning cases.[4] In failing to specifically define the term, it is possible that, as the nature of the family relationship evolves within a societal framework, groups of individuals not currently covered may fall within the ambit of "household member."

Q & A: Are dating relationships covered under the domestic violence statute?

In 2018, the Ohio General Assembly enacted HB 1, eff. 7/5/2018, which permits a person to obtain a civil protection order under RC 3113.31 so long as that person is in a "dating relationship" with the

---

[3]RC 3113.31(A)(3)(ii) and (iii).

[4]See, e.g., Moore v. City of East Cleveland, Ohio, 431 U.S. 494, 97 S. Ct. 1932, 52 L. Ed. 2d 531 (1977); Frierson v. Nationwide Ins. Co., 96 Ohio Misc. 2d 5, 707 N.E.2d 1221 (C.P. 1997); State Farm Fire & Cas. Co. v. Davidson, 87 Ohio App. 3d 101, 621 N.E.2d 887 (2d Dist. Montgomery County 1993); Farmers Ins. of Columbus, Inc. v. Taylor, 39 Ohio App. 3d 68, 528 N.E.2d 968 (10th Dist. Franklin County 1987); Mahoney v. Shaker Square Beverages, 46 Ohio Op. 250, 64 Ohio L. Abs. 200, 102 N.E.2d 281 (C.P. 1951); Carroll v. Washington Tp. Zoning Commission, 63 Ohio St. 2d 249, 17 Ohio Op. 3d 161, 408 N.E.2d 191 (1980).

respondent. RC 3113.31(A)(1)(b) provides that domestic violence also includes "the occurrence of one or more of the acts identified in divisions (A)(1)(a)(i) to (iv) of this section against a person with whom the respondent is or was in a dating relationship."

A "dating relationship" has been defined as a relationship between individuals who have, or have had, a relationship of a romantic or intimate nature. "Dating relationship" does not include a casual acquaintanceship or ordinary fraternization in a business or social context.[5]

A "person with whom the respondent is or was in a dating relationship" means an adult who, at the time of the conduct in question, is in a dating relationship with the respondent who is also an adult or who, within the 12 months preceding the conduct in question has had a dating relationship with the respondent who is also an adult.[6]

Based on the language of the statutory provisions, both petitioner and respondent must be adults. Clearly, juveniles are not intended to be included as protected persons or petitioners for purposes of a dating relationship.

Who exactly fits within the statute will be determined over the next five years as courts refine and clarify the language.

Q & A: Are persons who have annulled their marriage covered under Ohio's statutory framework?

Although no Ohio case has specifically answered this question, the Mercer County Court of Appeals touched on this concern in *Slusser v. Klosterman*.[7] The facts indicate that the parties were married but had annulled their marriage soon after. However, they remained business partners until both parties filed for civil protection orders against the other. The basis of the appeal was that the trial court erred in denying Klosterman's motion for continuance to obtain counsel.

On appeal, the court held that the trial court committed an abuse of discretion and reversed the judgment. In dicta, the appellate court introduced an additional issue for the trial court to resolve on remand. While the parties in their respective petitions for a CPO alleged they were former spouses, one of the parties acknowledged that they had annulled their marriage. Relying on Black's Law Dictionary, the court stated that "an annulment differs from a divorce in that a divorce terminates a legal status, whereas an annulment establishes that a marital status never existed."[8] The Mercer County Court of Appeals then concluded that "[i]f the marriage has been annulled, the stated relationship permitting the CPO, i.e. the status of former spouse, may not exist. Other permitted statuses may exist, but none are claimed. This court leaves the matter for the trial court to determine."[9]

Thus, it is pretty clear that a CPO under RC 3113.31 would not be

---

[5]R.C. 3113.31(A)(8).

[6]R.C. 3113.31(A)(9).

[7]Slusser v. Klosterman, 2008-Ohio-2608, 2008 WL 2229635 (Ohio Ct. App. 3d Dist. Mercer County 2008).

[8]Slusser v. Klosterman, 2008-Ohio-2608, 2008 WL 2229635, *3 (Ohio Ct. App. 3d Dist. Mercer County 2008), citing Black's Law Dictionary (6 Ed. Rev. 1990).

[9]Slusser v. Klosterman, 2008-Ohio-2608, 2008 WL 2229635, *3 (Ohio Ct. App. 3d Dist. Mercer County 2008).

available to the parties in this case unless another permitted status exists. The status of a former spouse is available only to one who is divorced from the other spouse.

§ 10:4 Nature of the relationships covered—Terminology—"Is residing with" and "has resided with"[1]

The phrases "is residing with" or "has resided with" are crucial to the definition of family or household member as set forth in RC 3113.31(A)(3)(a).[2] In fact, "is residing with or has resided with" is a condition precedent for coverage under the statute, except as to persons who have a child in common.[3]

Black's Law Dictionary defines "reside" as "to dwell in a place permanently or continuously."[4] In *State v. Morton*,[5] the Seneca County Court of Appeals instructed the jury that "reside" means to live in a place for an extended period of time.[6]

Accordingly, the intent of the parties is crucial to the definition. Unless the parties intended to permanently dwell with one another, they cannot be said to reside with each other. Under this definition, periodic visits with one another, whether or not they are overnight, and no matter how frequent, will not rise to the level necessary to meet the statutory requirements.[7] In *State v. Toles*,[8] an adult daughter was visiting her mother. During the visit, she struck her younger sister who lived in the household with her mother. The older sister admitted to "smacking" her younger sister in the face and was charged and convicted of domestic violence under a municipal ordinance very similar to RC 2919.25. On appeal, the Gallia County Court of Appeals determined that, while they were clearly related by consanguinity, the sisters did not meet the definition of family or household members for purposes of the domestic violence law. The court reasoned that they did not meet the "residing with" requirement since no evidence

---

[Section 10:4]

[1]See also § 10:2.

[2]See State v. Wynn, 2017-Ohio-8045, 2017 WL 4417756, ¶ 16 (Ohio Ct. App. 1st Dist. Hamilton County 2017) (while majority found that petitioner's testimony was sufficient to establish the "residing or has resided" requirement, dissent found that victim's testimony (after being asked whether she and Wynn had been separated on the date of the offense) that she was not living with Wynn on the date of the offense but that they were still together, was too ambivalent to reasonably suggest that they once lived together. In fact, the mere fact that Jennifer and Wynn were married and not legally separated does not mean that they had resided together at one point.").

[3]See RC 3113.31(A)(3)(a)(i) to (iii); RC 3113.31(A)(3)(b). Cornell v. Hatfield, 2018-Ohio-549, 2018 WL 827136 (Ohio Ct. App. 12th Dist. Fayette County 2018) (family or household members include parents who do not live with the respondent but who once lived with the petitioner).

[4]Black's Law Dictionary (6th ed.) p 1308. See also City of Xenia v. Berry, 1994 WL 12494, *2 (Ohio Ct. App. 2d Dist. Greene County 1994) (defines the term residence as "the place where one actually lives or has his home").

[5]State v. Morton, 1994 WL 49941 (Ohio Ct. App. 3d Dist. Seneca County 1994).

[6]See also Ark. Op. Att'y Gen 97-392 (2-23-98), 1998 WL 92215.

[7]See RC 3113.31(A)(3); see also Birthelmer v. Birthelmer, 1983 WL 6869 (Ohio Ct. App. 6th Dist. Lucas County 1983).

[8]State v. Toles, 1999 WL 1232092 (Ohio Ct. App. 4th Dist. Gallia County 1999).

demonstrated that the older sister was, or had been at one time, a permanent or continuous member of the household.[9]

It is important to note, however, that the Ohio Supreme Court in State v. Williams[10] concerned itself less with the parties' exact living arrangements and more with the relationship of the parties. In fact, the Court specifically declined to adopt a narrow definition of "reside" that would confine the statute's application to those family or household members who share one residential address.[11]

In interpreting RC 3113.31(A)(3)(a), one must be guided by common sense. Obviously, certain relationships do not fit within the parameters of the statutory language. However, the statute should be liberally construed to include those family relationships where there is an increased propensity for future violence.

Q & A: Will siblings always be considered family or household members for purposes of the domestic violence statute?

Not necessarily. RC 3113.31(A)(3) provides, in pertinent part, "'family or household member' means . . . any of the following who is residing with or has resided with the respondent." These persons include persons related by consanguinity or affinity to the offender. Where the complaining party and the respondent are related by consanguinity, such as siblings, the court must decide whether they ever lived together. If they lived together, even in the distant past, they are family or household members for purposes of the statute.[12] Residency is a requirement which must be proven to sustain a domestic violence conviction and is not found merely because the parties are related by consanguinity.[13]

On the other hand, if the siblings have never lived together, such as in *State v. Toles*,[14] an argument can be made that they are not family or household members under the statute. In *Toles*, the adult sibling lived with the father and only visited with her mother and sister.

Q & A: Is a boyfriend's ex-girlfriend a family or household member for purposes of the domestic violence statute?

---

[9]State v. Toles, 1999 WL 1232092, *2 (Ohio Ct. App. 4th Dist. Gallia County 1999). But see Maglionico v. Maglionico, 2001-Ohio-8901, 2001 WL 1401978, *3 (Ohio Ct. App. 11th Dist. Portage County 2001) (the court determined that "it is evident that R.C. 3113.31(A)(3)(a)(ii) requires some indication that, in addition to relation by consanguinity or affinity, the parties in dispute currently reside with each other or had resided with each other at some time in the past"); State v. Burkhart, 2009-Ohio-1142, 2009 WL 653038 (Ohio Ct. App. 11th Dist. Ashtabula County 2009) (differentiating the case at hand from *Toles*, indicating that when considering the notion of residency, some courts like *Toles* exclude only a temporary or transient visitor; other courts define residency to include a more permanent or continuous resident).

[10]State v. Williams, 79 Ohio St. 3d 459, 1997-Ohio-79, 683 N.E.2d 1126 (1997).

[11]State v. Williams, 79 Ohio St. 3d 459, 1997-Ohio-79, 683 N.E.2d 1126 (1997).

[12]See, e.g., Maglionico v. Maglionico, 2001-Ohio-8901, 2001 WL 1401978 (Ohio Ct. App. 11th Dist. Portage County 2001).

[13]See State v. Alvey, 2003-Ohio-7006, 2003 WL 22997277 (Ohio Ct. App. 7th Dist. Belmont County 2003).

[14]State v. Toles, 1999 WL 1232092 (Ohio Ct. App. 4th Dist. Gallia County 1999).

Although no Ohio court has addressed this specific issue, at least one court has considered the issue. For example, in *Smith v. Moore,*[15] the New Jersey Superior Court determined that harassing telephone calls made to the plaintiff from her boyfriend's ex-girlfriend are not contemplated by New Jersey's domestic violence statutes. The court found that the plaintiff and the ex-girlfriend were not related and had not lived together. Sharing a summer home with several other women several years before was inconsequential.

In Ohio, this concern may be addressed by way of a protection order issued under RC 2903.214.[16] Although the current boyfriend's ex girlfriend is not a family or household member to the current girlfriend, there is no mandate under RC 2903.214 that the petitioner and respondent be family or household members. Thus, the current girlfriend may be able to seek a protection order against her boyfriend's ex girlfriend.

Q & A: Can a sister-in-law obtain a protection order against her brother-in-law?

Probably not, unless the parties are currently residing together or had resided together.

Although no Ohio court has addressed this particular issue, Florida, which has a statute similar to Ohio's, has considered this. In *Sharpe v. Sharpe,*[17] a Florida appellate court reversed the granting of a domestic violence injunction on behalf of a sister-in-law against her brother-in-law. The Florida statute provides that protected individuals are those related by blood or marriage and requires that they reside or had resided together in the same dwelling unit. The appellate court reasoned that, despite the fact that the parties were related by marriage, they did not share a common living accommodation. Therefore, the sister-in-law failed to qualify as a protected party under the statute. It is important to note that, at that time Florida's statute was more narrowly drawn than Ohio's. Since *Sharpe* was decided, the Florida legislature eliminated the requirement that the parties reside in the same dwelling.

Q & A: What about brother and sister?

At least one Ohio court has applied the reasoning of *State v. Williams*[18] to include certain relationships within the statutory ambit by focusing on the nature of the relationship, rather than the parties' exact living arrangements.[19] In *State v. Scott,*[20] the Belmont County Court of Appeals affirmed the granting of a criminal protection order issued to a sister against her brother.

---

[15]Smith v. Moore, 298 N.J. Super. 121, 689 A.2d 145 (App. Div. 1997).

[16]See § 9:3.

[17]Sharpe v. Sharpe, 695 So. 2d 1302 (Fla. 5th DCA 1997); but see State v. Archuletta, 85 Haw. 512, 949 P.2d 620 (Ct. App. 1997).

[18]State v. Williams, 79 Ohio St. 3d 459, 1997-Ohio-79, 683 N.E.2d 1126 (1997).

[19]State v. Williams, 79 Ohio St. 3d 459, 462, 1997-Ohio-79, 683 N.E.2d 1126 (1997).

[20]State v. Scott, 1999 WL 126933 (Ohio Ct. App. 7th Dist. Belmont County 1999) (overruled by, State v. Alvey, 2003-Ohio-7006, 2003 WL 22997277 (Ohio Ct. App. 7th Dist. Belmont County 2003))(overruling court finding is no longer sufficient for the state to rely merely upon the fact that the victim and offender are related to prove domestic violence).

The appellate court rejected the brother's argument that, because the statutory provision required that certain family or household members "reside or have resided"[21] with the offender, the court should "adopt a narrow definition of 'reside' which would limit 'family or household members' to those who actually share one residential address."[22] The court adopted the rationale set forth in *Williams* and held that "since it is the appellant's sister who is the victim here, this is the type of relationship RC 2919.25 is aimed at preventing."[23]

In *Scott*, the appellate court noted that the statutory protections extended to the parties who were related by consanguinity. Thus, the state did not have to present additional evidence to show that the offender and his sister, the victim, had resided or were residing together at the time of the incident in order to prove domestic violence. Whether they were or were not residing together was less important than whether they had a familial relationship. Had their relationship been one of in-laws, it is unclear whether the court would have relied on *Williams* to support its reasoning.

Q & A: What about uncle and niece?

In *State v. Alvey*,[24] the appellate court reversed the trial court decision and held that the state failed to prove an essential element of domestic violence, residency. In that case, defendant was convicted of domestic violence against his niece, who lived next door. On appeal, he argued that the evidence presented at trial did not support the finding that his niece (the victim) was a family or household member as defined under RC 2919.25, even though they were related by consanguinity and the niece went to defendant's home each day and ate his food.

The Belmont County Court of Appeals reversed its prior holding in *State v. Scott* to the extent that "we now hold that the state must show under RC 2919.25(E)(1)(a) that the offender resides or had resided with the victim in order to sustain a domestic violence conviction. It is no longer sufficient for the state to rely merely upon the fact that the victim and offender are related to prove domestic violence under subsection (E)(1)(a)."[25]

The appellate court examined the reasoning of the Supreme Court in *State v. Williams*[26] and its application to both *Scott* and *Alvey*. Acknowledging the *Williams* court's explanation that "domestic violence arises out of the relationship of the parties rather than their

[21]RC 2919.25(E)(1)(a).

[22]State v. Scott, 1999 WL 126933 (Ohio Ct. App. 7th Dist. Belmont County 1999) (overruled by, State v. Alvey, 2003-Ohio-7006, 2003 WL 22997277 (Ohio Ct. App. 7th Dist. Belmont County 2003)).

[23]State v. Scott, 1999 WL 126933 (Ohio Ct. App. 7th Dist. Belmont County 1999) (overruled by, State v. Alvey, 2003-Ohio-7006, 2003 WL 22997277 (Ohio Ct. App. 7th Dist. Belmont County 2003))(overruling court finding it is no longer sufficient for the state to rely merely upon the fact that the victim and offender are related to prove domestic violence).

[24]State v. Alvey, 2003-Ohio-7006, 2003 WL 22997277 (Ohio Ct. App. 7th Dist. Belmont County 2003).

[25]State v. Alvey, 2003-Ohio-7006, 2003 WL 22997277, *3 (Ohio Ct. App. 7th Dist. Belmont County 2003).

[26]State v. Williams, 79 Ohio St. 3d 459, 1997-Ohio-79, 683 N.E.2d 1126 (1997).

exact living circumstances,"[27] the appellate court rejected the *Scott* interpretation, which was to focus on the relationship between the offender and the victim and ignore the residency requirement in the statute. "If the General Assembly intended for only the relationship to matter under subsection (a), it would have constructed that subsection the same way it constructed subsection (b) (i.e., leaving out the residency requirement)."[28] Concluding that its interpretation in *Scott* was flawed, the court held that the determination of whether sufficient evidence was presented to prove domestic violence under RC 2919.25(E)(1)(a) must include a discussion of whether the offender resides with or has resided with the victim instead of solely relying on the relationship between the offender and the victim.[29]

Finally, the Belmont County Court of Appeals noted that *Williams* should be read in the context in which it was decided.[30] In *Williams*, the query was whether the parties were living as spouses. The *Williams* court found that, because they were cohabiting, they were persons living as spouses. The *Alvey* court concluded that, in *Williams*, the residency requirement was not meant to be ignored; rather the residency element and the cohabitation element partially overlap. In the situation where it is claimed that the offender and the victim are living as spouses, domestic violence does arise out of the relationship, because given their relationship, they are residing together even though they may not have the same residential address. Nor do they need to share the same residential address to be considered residing together. However, in each case, the court must examine the particular living arrangement of the parties to determine whether they are currently residing or had resided together.[31]

In *State v. Blackmon*,[32] appellant punched his 20 year old niece several times and choked her, causing visible injuries. From birth to age 16, the child was presumed to be the natural child of his brother and his natural niece. When she turned 16, a blood test determined that appellant's brother was not the father. Regardless, she continued to live with the family. Appellant was charged with felony domestic violence against her.

He argued that the victim of the assault was not a family or household member. "He claimed that while the victim had been raised in his family since her birth, under the mistaken assumption that she was the natural daughter of appellant's brother, that assumption was

[27]State v. Alvey, 2003-Ohio-7006, 2003 WL 22997277, *2 (Ohio Ct. App. 7th Dist. Belmont County 2003), quoting State v. Williams, 79 Ohio St. 3d 459, 462, 1997-Ohio-79, 683 N.E.2d 1126 (1997).

[28]State v. Alvey, 2003-Ohio-7006, 2003 WL 22997277, *3 (Ohio Ct. App. 7th Dist. Belmont County 2003).

[29]State v. Alvey, 2003-Ohio-7006, 2003 WL 22997277, *3 (Ohio Ct. App. 7th Dist. Belmont County 2003).

[30]State v. Alvey, 2003-Ohio-7006, 2003 WL 22997277, *4 (Ohio Ct. App. 7th Dist. Belmont County 2003).

[31]State v. Alvey, 2003-Ohio-7006, 2003 WL 22997277, *4 (Ohio Ct. App. 7th Dist. Belmont County 2003).

[32]State v. Blackmon, 2012-Ohio-5854, 2012 WL 6139910 (Ohio Ct. App. 5th Dist. Stark County 2012).

dispelled by a subsequent blood test."[33] He was convicted of domestic violence.

On appeal, the question for the judges was whether the victim in this case was a family or household member within the meaning of the domestic violence statute. The appellate court first pointed out that a victim's status as a family or household member is a required element of the offense of domestic violence. The court reversed the conviction and held that "in strictly construing RC 2919.25, we find that such statute does not provide that a person who once thought to be a blood relative remains a family or household member after such blood relationship is determined to have been mistaken."[34]

Q & A: Is there a length of time that family members must have resided together to qualify under the statute?

No. Several cases have stated that persons related by consanguinity and/or affinity must have lived together at some time in the past. Besides satisfying the relation of consanguinity and affinity between petitioner and respondent, evidence must be presented to show that respondent had resided with the petitioner at some time in the past.

For example, in Maglionico v. Maglionico,[35] the Portage County Court of Appeals reversed the issuance of a civil protection order of one brother against the other. In that case, the trial court stated that "R.C. 3113.31(A)(iii) provides that a family member, among others, is a person related by consanguinity; therefore there is no requirement that they must live together." On appeal, appellant argued that more than proof of the relationship of consanguinity satisfies the statutory requirements for the issuance of a civil protection order.

The appellate court relied on *State v. Mrus*[36] in determining that "there is no specific timeframe as to when the residing had to occur." However, the parties must have resided together at some time in the past. Proof of both the relation and that they had resided together satisfies the statutory mandates of RC 3113.31(A)(3).[37]

Q & A: B.C. requests a domestic violence civil protection order for herself and her current husband against her former

[33] State v. Blackmon, 2012-Ohio-5854, 2012 WL 6139910, ¶ 8 (Ohio Ct. App. 5th Dist. Stark County 2012).

[34] State v. Blackmon, 2012-Ohio-5854, 2012 WL 6139910, ¶ 31 (Ohio Ct. App. 5th Dist. Stark County 2012).

[35] Maglionico v. Maglionico, 2001-Ohio-8901, 2001 WL 1401978, *1 (Ohio Ct. App. 11th Dist. Portage County 2001); Mansaray v. Sankoh, 2005-Ohio-1451, 2005 WL 704856 (Ohio Ct. App. 10th Dist. Franklin County 2005); State v. Burkhart, 2009-Ohio-1142, 2009 WL 653038 (Ohio Ct. App. 11th Dist. Ashtabula County 2009) (attempting to provide a definition for the term "residing").

[36] State v. Mrus, 71 Ohio App. 3d 828, 831, 595 N.E.2d 460 (11th Dist. Trumbull County 1991) (overruled by, State v. James, 1997 WL 269139 (Ohio Ct. App. 11th Dist. Portage County 1997)) and (overruled by, State v. Fleming, 1997 WL 269141 (Ohio Ct. App. 11th Dist. Portage County 1997)) and (abrogated by, State v. Uher, 1997 WL 269407 (Ohio Ct. App. 11th Dist. Portage County 1997)) and (abrogated by, State v. Wyand, 1997 WL 269143 (Ohio Ct. App. 11th Dist. Portage County 1997)) and (overruled by, State v. Musick, 119 Ohio App. 3d 361, 695 N.E.2d 317 (11th Dist. Portage County 1997)).

[37] See also State v. Saltsman, 1997 WL 779119 (Ohio Ct. App. 2d Dist. Montgomery County 1997); see also § 10:8, Relationships covered-Parents and children.

husband. Is the current spouse a covered family or household member such that the CPO will protect him?

In *B.C. v. A.S.*,[38] the 9th District Court of Appeals found that a current husband who is not related to the respondent cannot seek a domestic violence protection order against that respondent. B.C. sought a protection order for her entire family against A.S, the former husband of B.C. The trial court issued the ex parte CPO and also granted a CPO issued after the full hearing. A.S. appealed the issuance of the CPO on the grounds that the CPO was against the weight of the evidence.

Among the reasons for reversing the decision, the Medina Court of Appeals noted that the most specific incident was a 2011 telephone call in which A.S. allegedly threatened to kill the current husband of B.C. The court relied on RC 3113.31(A)(3) which provides that a "family or household member" includes any of the following, who is residing or has resided with the respondent, to wit: i) a spouse, person living as a spouse or former spouse of the respondent; ii) a parent, a foster parent or a child of the respondent or another person related by consanguinity or affinity to the respondent; iii) a parent or child of a spouse, person living as a spouse or another person related by consanguinity or affinity to a spouse, person living as a spouse, or former spouse of the respondent; or iv) the natural parent of any child of whom the respondent is the other natural parent.

In that the appellate court determined that B.C.'s current husband was not a family or household member as defined and because the only specific threat was made against B.C.'s current husband (who is not a covered person under the statute), "such an allegation could not form the sole basis of a DVCPO petition. Accordingly, a petition premised upon the alleged threat to B.C.'s husband would be more appropriate in the court of common pleas as a request for a civil stalking protection order under Section 2903.214 than the domestic relations court as a request for a DVCPO under Section 3113.31."[39]

As decided by the appellate court, the more logical reading of R.C. 3113.31(A)(3) suggests that the current spouse of B.C. would not be a "family or household member" of the respondent. However, if other recent and specific incidents of domestic violence towards B.C. had occurred, it is arguable that the current spouse of B.C. might have been considered a protected party covered by the DVCPO.

§ 10:5 Nature of the relationships covered—Terminology—"Consanguinity" and "affinity"

The terms "consanguinity" and "affinity" also appear in RC 3113.31(A)(3)(a)(iii) but remain undefined in the statute.[1] The *Morton*

[38] B.C. v. A.S., 2014-Ohio-1326, 2014 WL 1345260 (Ohio Ct. App. 9th Dist. Medina County 2014).

[39] B.C. v. A.S., 2014-Ohio-1326, 2014 WL 1345260, ¶ 24 (Ohio Ct. App. 9th Dist. Medina County 2014).

[Section 10:5]

[1] See Miss. Op. Att'y Gen. No. 2000-0588 (10–6–00), 2000 WL 1648390.

court defined "consanguinity" as a blood relationship.[2] In *Morton*, the defendant went to the home where his girlfriend, their daughter, and the girlfriend's half-sister lived. The defendant was charged with domestic violence for hitting his girlfriend's half-sister. The defendant argued that he and the half-sister were not family members. The court held that, because the girlfriend and the half-sister have the same mother and because the half-sister resided with the girlfriend and the defendant, the half-sister was related to the defendant by consanguinity to the girlfriend.[3]

In *Chinn v. State*,[4] the Ohio Supreme Court defined "affinity" as "the relationship which arises by marriage between one of the parties and the blood relations of the other."[5]

The Lake County Court of Appeals, in *State v. Peine*,[6] also sought to define these terms. In that case, the defendant moved into Mrs. Needham's home and had an intimate relationship with her. The defendant then committed a violation of RC 2919.25(A) against Mrs. Needham's daughter, who also lived in the home. The court found that the daughter was not a family or household member under RC 2919.25(D) because she was not related to the defendant by either blood or marriage. The court noted that "[e]ven the amended statute, however, did not go so far as to modify the word 'affinity' to include relationship by one who is cohabiting with another."[7] Even if affinity had been established between Mrs. Needham and the defendant, "this does not create a condition of consanguinity (blood relationship) between the defendant and the daughter so as to bring the defendant within the terms of the statute."[8] Therefore, the status of family or household member did not apply to the parties.

The *Peine* court relied on *Ohio Jurisprudence* in defining "affinity" as "related by marriage"[9] and "consanguinity" as "blood relationship."[10] *Peine* is relevant only as it defines the terminology used by Ohio's do-

---

[2]See also Maglionico v. Maglionico, 2001-Ohio-8901, 2001 WL 1401978 (Ohio Ct. App. 11th Dist. Portage County 2001).

[3]State v. Morton, 1994 WL 49941 (Ohio Ct. App. 3d Dist. Seneca County 1994); State v. Scott, 1999 WL 126933 (Ohio Ct. App. 7th Dist. Belmont County 1999) (overruled by, State v. Alvey, 2003-Ohio-7006, 2003 WL 22997277 (Ohio Ct. App. 7th Dist. Belmont County 2003))(overruling court finding it is no longer sufficient for the state to rely merely upon the fact that the victim and offender are related to prove domestic violence).

[4]Chinn v. State, 47 Ohio St. 575, 579, 26 N.E. 986, 987 (1890); see also Coma v. Kellogg, 1999 WL 135294, *2 (Ohio Ct. App. 7th Dist. Columbiana County 1999) (relying on Black's Law Dictionary definition of "affinity" as a "[r]elation which one spouse because of marriage has to blood relatives of the other. . . . The connection existing, in consequence of marriage, between each of the married persons and the kindred of the other").

[5]Chinn v. State, 47 Ohio St. 575, 579, 26 N.E. 986, 987 (1890); See also Mansaray v. Sankoh, 2005-Ohio-1451, ¶ 9, 2005 WL 704856, *2 (Ohio Ct. App. 10th Dist. Franklin County 2005) (where petitioner and respondent are related by affinity defined as "the relation that one spouse has to the blood relatives of the other spouse") .

[6]State v. Peine, 1982 WL 5837 (Ohio Ct. App. 11th Dist. Lake County 1982).

[7]State v. Peine, 1982 WL 5837, *1 (Ohio Ct. App. 11th Dist. Lake County 1982).

[8]State v. Peine, 1982 WL 5837, *1 (Ohio Ct. App. 11th Dist. Lake County 1982).

[9]See also Benjamin v. McKinnon, 379 Ill. App. 3d 1013, 320 Ill. Dec. 234, 887 N.E.2d 14 (4th Dist. 2008) (discussing degrees of affinity including "direct affinity"

mestic violence statutes.[11] Because the statutes have since been amended to cover persons who cohabit and their children, the legal analysis of *Peine* is no longer relevant.

Q & A: Is there an affinity between the blood relations of one spouse and the blood relations of the other?

Not according to *Geigep v. Progressive Preferred Insurance, Co.*[12] In that non-domestic violence case, the issue was whether a relative by marriage was covered under an insurance policy. The Summit County Court of Appeals held that the relationship between a husband's blood relatives and the wife's blood relatives is defined as collateral affinity.[13] Because the relationship between the husband's father and the wife's daughter was not a relationship of affinity, the insurance policy did not apply to them.

If this had been a domestic violence case, it is questionable whether those related by collateral affinity would be considered family or household members under RC 3113.31.

Q & A: Can the legal guardian of a child obtain a civil protection order on behalf of himself and his wife?

In *Rocky River v. Bakos*,[14] Bakos argued on appeal that his conviction for violating the civil protection order should be overturned because the trial court had no subject matter jurisdiction to issue a civil protection order for Mr. Funk and his wife. The basis of the relationship between Bakos and the Funks was that Funk and his wife were the legal guardians of Bakos's three children.

At the trial court level, the State argued that RC 3113.31(A)(3)(ii) provides that a family or household member is another person related by consanguinity or affinity to the respondent. It reasoned that Funk could get a civil protection order because, as legal guardian of the children, he was related by affinity to Bakos.[15]

The appellate court found that the trial court had no subject matter jurisdiction to issue the civil protection order in the first instance because RC 3113.31(A)(3)(ii) specifically provides that the petitioner and respondent be persons who are residing or have resided with the respondent. In that the parties were neighbors, and because they had never resided together, the court remanded the case to the trial court to vacate the conviction.

and "collateral affinity," which is the relationship of a spouse's relatives to the other spouse's blood relatives, such as a wife's brother and her husband's sister, citing Black's Law Dictionary 63 (8th ed. 2004)).

[10]State v. Peine, 1982 WL 5837 (Ohio Ct. App. 11th Dist. Lake County 1982) (citing Ohio Jur. 2d, Descent and Distribution § 97).

[11]RC 3113.31, RC 2919.25.

[12]Geigep v. Progressive Preferred Ins. Co., 2008 WL 5325462 (Ohio C.P. 2008).

[13]Black's Law Dictionary (8th ed. 2004).

[14]Rocky River v. Bakos, 2015-Ohio-4366, 45 N.E.3d 668 (Ohio Ct. App. 8th Dist. Cuyahoga County 2015).

[15]Rocky River v. Bakos, 2015-Ohio-4366, ¶ 12, 45 N.E.3d 668 (Ohio Ct. App. 8th Dist. Cuyahoga County 2015).

§ 10:6 Nature of the relationships covered—Terminology—"Cohabit"[1]

"Cohabiting"[2] is another common term used to determine the status of one who seeks to obtain coverage under RC 3113.31(A)(4).[3] Although the legislature has declined to specifically define this term in either RC 3113.31 or RC 2919.25, there are various definitions for this word in the case law.[4] Because there is no universally held definition of "cohabiting," the term must be initially examined in the broad context of divorce, separation, and spousal support.[5]

The most commonly held definition suggests that two adults living together in the same household, sharing certain obligations which are equivalent to a spousal-type relationship, provides the framework for the definition of "cohabiting."[6] In *Birthelmer v. Birthelmer*,[7] the Lucas County Court of Appeals interpreted the term "cohabitation" in the context of a post-dissolution decree property settlement. The court stated that "the key test of cohabitation is living together and that living together is a question of fact in each particular case."[8] Examples cited by the court to support the status of cohabiting include the shar-

---

[Section 10:6]

[1]See also Text § 10:9, Relationships covered—Person living as a spouse; Text § 10:10, Relationships covered—Same sex relationships.

[2]See "Cohabitation" for purposes of domestic violence statutes, 71 A.L.R.5th 285 (sec. 4 superseded in part Legal Protection Against Domestic Violence in Same-Sex Relationships, 19 A.L.R.7th Art. 1)..

[3]See U.S. v. Costigan, 2000 WL 898455 (D. Me. 2000), judgment aff'd, 18 Fed. Appx. 2 (1st Cir. 2001) (questions to ask when determining whether parties have cohabited); see also City of Cleveland v. Bergman, 1999 CRB 13867 (Cleve. Muni. Ct. 1-5-01).

[4]See State v. Williams, 79 Ohio St. 3d 459, 1997-Ohio-79, 683 N.E.2d 1126 (1997) (for the definition of cohabitation in the context of domestic violence).

[5]But see Cleveland v. Schill, 147 Ohio App. 3d 239, 2002-Ohio-1263, 769 N.E.2d 907 (8th Dist. Cuyahoga County 2002) (Cuyahoga County appeals court held that "the term 'cohabitating' as used by legislature in the domestic violence statute provides sufficient warning to offenders as to the type of relationships that are covered and that the term is not too vague to meet the requirements of due process under the Constitution.").

[6]See, e.g., Sindel v. Sindel, 1975 WL 181946 (Ohio Ct. App. 10th Dist. Franklin County 1975); Fuller v. Fuller, 10 Ohio App. 3d 253, 461 N.E.2d 1348 (10th Dist. Franklin County 1983); Taylor v. Taylor, 11 Ohio App. 3d 279, 465 N.E.2d 476 (1st Dist. Hamilton County 1983); State v. Taylor, 2013-Ohio-4588, 2013 WL 5657956 (Ohio Ct. App. 5th Dist. Richland County 2013) (reasoning that "cohabitation" depends on the acts of a man and a woman living together in the same household and behaving as would a husband and wife and finding that merely living together without a sharing of financial or other familial responsibilities, in addition to the provision of money and conjugal relations, does not rise to the level of cohabitation).

[7]Birthelmer v. Birthelmer, 1983 WL 6869 (Ohio Ct. App. 6th Dist. Lucas County 1983).

[8]Birthelmer v. Birthelmer, 1983 WL 6869, *3 (Ohio Ct. App. 6th Dist. Lucas County 1983), citing Bond v. Heebsh, 1982 WL 6579 (Ohio Ct. App. 6th Dist. Lucas County 1982); but see State v. Humbarger, 149 Ohio App. 3d 30, 2002-Ohio-4160, 775 N.E.2d 585 (3d Dist. Van Wert County 2002) (noting that a three-day visit between the victim and defendant was insufficient to show cohabitation).

ing of expenses and a spousal-type support obligation.[9] However, the *Birthelmer* court did not accord great weight to the "spousal-type support obligation," concluding that "[w]hile it is difficult to conceive what a 'spousal-type support obligation' might be in the context of a nonspousal nonmarital relationship, we conclude that this finding is superfluous since everything else in the record militates against concluding that appellee and [appellant] were cohabiting."[10] The *Birthelmer* court instead relied on the following factors:

> [T]here must be an actual living together, that is, the man and the woman must reside together in the same home or apartment. Secondly, such a living together must be of a sustained duration. Thirdly, shared expenses with respect to financing the residence (i.e. rent or mortgage payments) and incidental day-to-day expenses (e.g. groceries) are the principal relevant considerations.[11]

Only a few Ohio courts have addressed the problem of interpreting or defining the term "cohabiting" in the context of either RC 3113.31 or RC 2919.25.[12] Most of the cases address the term "cohabiting" in the context of family or household member coverage under RC 2919. 25. Additionally, many of the cases involve the concepts of same-sex relationships and cohabitation.

In both the domestic violence and domestic relations areas, most Ohio courts agree that there need not be an actual assertion of marriage and that cohabitation can be based entirely on acts of living together, even without sexual relations. For example, in *State v. Van Hoose*,[13] the court stated that "a sexual relationship is not required in order to find evidence of cohabitation." The court determined that living together for a period of two months, behaving as if they were married, and the fact that he moved into the residence with clothing, a television, and other personal belongings as sufficient to support a finding of cohabitation.[14]

Q & A: Are there differences between "reside" and "cohabitation"?

---

[9]See also Fuller v. Fuller, 10 Ohio App. 3d 253, 461 N.E.2d 1348 (10th Dist. Franklin County 1983).

[10]Birthelmer v. Birthelmer, 1983 WL 6869, *5 (Ohio Ct. App. 6th Dist. Lucas County 1983).

[11]Birthelmer v. Birthelmer, 1983 WL 6869, *5 (Ohio Ct. App. 6th Dist. Lucas County 1983).

[12]See, e.g., State v. Williams, 79 Ohio St. 3d 459, 1997-Ohio-79, 683 N.E.2d 1126 (1997); State v. Miller, 105 Ohio App. 3d 679, 664 N.E.2d 1309 (4th Dist. Washington County 1995); State v. Hadinger, 61 Ohio App. 3d 820, 573 N.E.2d 1191 (10th Dist. Franklin County 1991); State v. Linner, 77 Ohio Misc. 2d 22, 665 N.E.2d 1180 (Mun. Ct. 1996); State v. Yaden, 118 Ohio App. 3d 410, 692 N.E.2d 1097, 71 A.L.R.5th 749 (1st Dist. Hamilton County 1997). But see Cleveland v. Schill, 147 Ohio App. 3d 239, 2002-Ohio-1263, 769 N.E.2d 907 (8th Dist. Cuyahoga County 2002).

[13]State v. Van Hoose, 1993 WL 386314, *2 (Ohio Ct. App. 2d Dist. Clark County 1993).

[14]See also State v. Miller, 105 Ohio App. 3d 679, 664 N.E.2d 1309 (4th Dist. Washington County 1995) (evidence supported a finding that the victim was a family or household member even though both parties testified that their relationship was purely sexual and at no time did they share any living expenses); State v. Hadinger, 61 Ohio App. 3d 820, 573 N.E.2d 1191 (10th Dist. Franklin County 1991); Sindel v. Sindel, 1975 WL 181946 (Ohio Ct. App. 10th Dist. Franklin County 1975). But see State v. Hunt, 1996 WL 132268 (Ohio Ct. App. 5th Dist. Stark County 1996) (sustaining appellant's objection that parties were not family or household members where

The terms "to reside" and "cohabiting" are interrelated. Many of the cases often use and define these words interchangeably. For example, in *Hicks v. Hicks*,[15] the court discussed the meaning of cohabitation and determined that it means "a living together in one house . . . it carries with it the idea of a fixed residence." Other courts suggest that the term "cohabiting" implies a greater degree of commitment,[16] whereas "to reside" implies a permanency of place.[17]

Unfortunately, any interpretation that permits these terms to be used interchangeably creates a degree of confusion. That the legislature chose to consider both of these terms in differing contexts suggests that the intention of the legislature was to differentiate between the degree of commitment within the relationship and the actual living arrangements. Their placement within the statute indicates that "cohabiting" is used to reflect a class of individuals afforded the protection of the domestic violence statute. The placement of "reside" indicates a specific requirement that must be satisfied before an individual can be considered "a person living as a spouse."

An examination of the cases that have provided statutory constructions of these terms is relevant. The Franklin County Court of Appeals addressed issues of statutory construction in *State v. Allen.*[18] In that case, the court considered "whether RC 2919.25(E)(1) should be interpreted to provide that the clause 'who is residing or has resided with the offender' applies to 'a person living as a spouse.' "[19] The court reasoned that persons living as spouses are "subject to the domestic violence law only if they have resided or are residing with the offender. They do not become subject to the law merely by proof of the relationship itself."[20] Additionally, the court found that "RC 2919.25, does not provide that a person who once lived as a spouse remains a 'family or household member' after he no longer resides with the victim."[21]

The importance of Allen lies in the court's understanding of the placement of the phrase "is residing or has resided" and its relation to "cohabiting." The court did not use these terms interchangeably but considered each term as a separate factor to be considered in determining whether the parties were family or household members for purposes of RC 2919.25. It is noteworthy that the court's interpre-

---

trial court instructed jury that "cohabit" means to live together in a sexual relationship when not legally married and state had not asked the complaining witness whether they had a sexual relationship).

[15]Hicks v. Hicks, 1982 WL 2709, *1 (Ohio Ct. App. 9th Dist. Lorain County 1982).

[16]See Riddle v. Riddle, 1988 WL 94005 (Ohio Ct. App. 5th Dist. Richland County 1988).

[17]See State v. Morton, 1994 WL 49941 (Ohio Ct. App. 3d Dist. Seneca County 1994).

[18]State v. Allen, 42 Ohio App. 3d 116, 536 N.E.2d 1195 (10th Dist. Franklin County 1988).

[19]State v. Allen, 42 Ohio App. 3d 116, 117, 536 N.E.2d 1195 (10th Dist. Franklin County 1988).

[20]State v. Allen, 42 Ohio App. 3d 116, 117, 536 N.E.2d 1195 (10th Dist. Franklin County 1988). But see State v. Williams, 79 Ohio St. 3d 459, 1997-Ohio-79, 683 N.E.2d 1126 (1997) (concluding that the relationship was a more significant factor than the parties' exact living arrangements).

[21]State v. Allen, 42 Ohio App. 3d 116, 116, 536 N.E.2d 1195 (10th Dist. Franklin County 1988).

tation of the terms contained in RC 2919.25 was based on statutory language that has subsequently been amended.

Similarly, in *State v. Mrus*,[22] the Trumbull County Court of Appeals found that the phrase "residing or has resided with" merely qualifies what constitutes a family or household member and is not an element of the offense of domestic violence. The implication is that whether the parties were persons living as spouses or any other class of family or household members is a material element of the crime without which a conviction cannot be sustained.[23]

Q & A: Is there a common definition for the term "cohabitation"?

In 1997, the Supreme Court of Ohio advanced a common definition for cohabitation for domestic violence purposes. In *State v. Williams*,[24] the complaining witness testified that the parties did not live together but that they "were going together." She also stated that she spent more nights at his home than her own. The trial court found appellant guilty of domestic violence. On appeal, appellant argued that he couldn't be convicted of domestic violence because no evidence was presented to establish cohabitation by the parties. The appeals court reversed the conviction and the state appealed to the Supreme Court.

Appellant argued that the definition of family or household member included a person "who is residing" or "has resided" with the offender pursuant to RC 2919.25(E)(1)(a) and urged the Court to restrict the definition of "reside" to family or household members who actually share one residential address.[25]

At the outset, the Supreme Court declined to focus on the term "reside" or to restrict its decision to family or household members who share one address or residence; rather, it decided to examine the term "cohabitation" and develop a more expansive definition. It also noted that the various courts of appeals in Ohio adopted various definitions of cohabitation and that most courts, both in Ohio and outside the state, considered a more far-reaching definition of the term "cohabitation" in the context of domestic violence.

Besides addressing the public policy reasons for the enactment of the domestic violence statute, the Court also acknowledged the difference between "stranger" violence and domestic violence which arises out of the parties' relationship and concluded that "domestic violence

[22]State v. Mrus, 71 Ohio App. 3d 828, 595 N.E.2d 460 (11th Dist. Trumbull County 1991) (overruled by, State v. James, 1997 WL 269139 (Ohio Ct. App. 11th Dist. Portage County 1997)) and (overruled by, State v. Fleming, 1997 WL 269141 (Ohio Ct. App. 11th Dist. Portage County 1997)) and (abrogated by, State v. Uher, 1997 WL 269407 (Ohio Ct. App. 11th Dist. Portage County 1997)) and (abrogated by, State v. Wyand, 1997 WL 269143 (Ohio Ct. App. 11th Dist. Portage County 1997)) and (overruled by, State v. Musick, 119 Ohio App. 3d 361, 695 N.E.2d 317 (11th Dist. Portage County 1997)).

[23]See Maglionico v. Maglionico, 2001-Ohio-8901, 2001 WL 1401978 (Ohio Ct. App. 11th Dist. Portage County 2001).

[24]State v. Williams, 79 Ohio St. 3d 459, 1997-Ohio-79, 683 N.E.2d 1126 (1997).

[25]State v. Williams, 79 Ohio St. 3d 459, 1997-Ohio-79, 683 N.E.2d 1126 (1997).

arises out of the nature of the relationship itself, rather than the exact living circumstances of the victim and perpetrator."[26]

The Court then determined that the essential elements of cohabitation are 1) a sharing of financial or familial responsibilities and 2) consortium. "Possible factors establishing shared financial and familial responsibilities might include provisions for shelter, food, clothing, utilities, and/or commingled assets.[27] Factors that might establish consortium include mutual respect, fidelity, affection, society, cooperation, solace, comfort, aid of each other, friendship, and conjugal relations."[28]

It is important to stress that sexual relations appears to be a required factor to demonstrate consortium.[29] One can reach this conclusion by reviewing the placement of the word "and" which indicates that consortium includes several factors "and conjugal relations."

By applying this two-tiered approach to "dating relationships," roommates and other casual relationships do not appear to be covered.

In fact, case law interpreting RC 3113.31 reflected a reluctance to expand coverage of the statute beyond the enumerated categories.[30] For example, in *Middletown v. Walker*,[31] the appellate court found that persons who do not live together, have never cohabited, have no children and are not related by blood or marriage, do not qualify as family or household members. This was found to be true even if they had dated extensively over a period of time. Of significance is that without those factors, the parties apparently lacked a degree of commitment necessary.

Of significance is that in addressing dating relationships, the *Williams* Court also determined that dating relations are to be included

---

[26]State v. Williams, 79 Ohio St. 3d 459, 1997-Ohio-79, 683 N.E.2d 1126 (1997).

[27]See Dyke v. Price, 2000 WL 1546555 (Ohio Ct. App. 2d Dist. Montgomery County 2000) (examples of evidence satisfying familial and financial responsibility prong of cohabitation); see also State v. Ward, 2000 WL 33231613 (Ohio Ct. App. 10th Dist. Franklin County 2000); but see State v. Humbarger, 149 Ohio App. 3d 30, 2002-Ohio-4160, 775 N.E.2d 585 (3d Dist. Van Wert County 2002) (reversing trial court decision as to family or household member, holding that "no evidence was presented in this case to suggest the presence of either of these two essential elements between the parties," discussing the factors set forth in *State v. Williams*).

[28]State v. Williams, 79 Ohio St. 3d 459, 1997-Ohio-79, 683 N.E.2d 1126 (1997); see Dyke v. Price, 2000 WL 1546555 (Ohio Ct. App. 2d Dist. Montgomery County 2000) (evidence that satisfied the consortium prong of cohabitation); but see State v. Cobb, 153 Ohio App. 3d 541, 2003-Ohio-3821, 795 N.E.2d 73 (1st Dist. Hamilton County 2003) ("sporadic provision of money and conjugal relations" does not a cohabitation relationship make).

[29]State v. Williams, 79 Ohio St. 3d 459, 1997-Ohio-79, 683 N.E.2d 1126 (1997), Dyke v. Price, 2000 WL 1546555 (Ohio Ct. App. 2d Dist. Montgomery County 2000); but see, State v. Clay, 181 Ohio App. 3d 563, 2009-Ohio-1235, 910 N.E.2d 14 (8th Dist. Cuyahoga County 2009) (appellate court determined that state need not have to establish that the parties had a sexual relationship to support conviction for domestic violence. That they shared the same household and were cohabiting by sharing financial responsibilities was enough).

[30]R.C. 3113.31(A)(3).

[31]Middletown v. Walker, 107 Ohio App. 3d 516, 669 N.E.2d 69 (12th Dist. Butler County 1995).

within "persons living as spouses," suggesting that there was no need to specifically identify another class of protected persons.

However, the Ohio General Assembly's enactment of HB 1 specifically provides protections to dating relationships, not as family or household members but as a distinct protected class under RC 3113.31.[32]

How broadly a court may define dating relationships and the context within which they are protected under RC 3113.31 will be settled over the course of the next 5 to 10 years as case law is developed and refined.

The Court also noted that "[t]hese factors are unique to each case and how much weight, if any, to give to each of these factors must be decided on a case-by-case basis by the trier of fact."[33] The Court reversed the court of appeals and remanded the case for a new trial to determine whether, in light of the above-mentioned factors, there was sufficient evidence to prove that the parties were "family or household members."

The *Williams* Court appeared to narrow the definition of "dating" to "dating relationship." To have extended protection to those individuals who were merely "dating" would have left an undefined concept even more ambiguous. Not to have included the term "relationship" or provided the factors regarding financial or familial responsibilities for guidance may have led to the circumstance where two people meet for a casual lunch date on only one occasion and then one of the parties requested a CPO.

Q & A: Has the Supreme Court resolved the ambiguity between "cohabiting" and "residing?"

Unfortunately, the *Williams* Supreme Court of Ohio, did not adequately resolve the distinction between "cohabiting" and "residing," which continues to allow for ambiguity over these terms. The rationale given by the Court indicates an unwillingness to limit the application of "cohabiting" to individuals who only share an address. Throughout its opinion, the Supreme Court appears to use the terms "cohabiting" and "residing" interchangeably. At other times, the Court intimates that "cohabiting" implies a degree of commitment between the parties arising out of the relationship and "residing" describes only the status of their living arrangements. This would suggest that the Supreme Court accorded greater weight to the term "cohabiting" and did not consider the placement of the terms in the statute of any consequence.[34]

On the other hand, the Supreme Court may not have meant for

---

[32]R.C. 3113.31(A)(8); see also § 10:9.

[33]State v. Williams, 79 Ohio St. 3d 459, 1997-Ohio-79, 683 N.E.2d 1126 (1997). But see Cleveland v. Schill, 147 Ohio App. 3d 239, 2002-Ohio-1263, 769 N.E.2d 907 (8th Dist. Cuyahoga County 2002) (where the defendant argued "that the cohabitation factors set forth in *Williams* are too subjective and delve too deeply into the private lives of the offender and victim," and challenged the constitutionality of RC 2919.25 on the ground that the term "cohabitating" was too vague. The appellate court determined that "judges and juries are able to make the necessary determination as to whether the offender and victim are cohabitating and fairly administer the law.").

[34]See R.C. 2919.25(E)(1)(a).

lower courts to totally ignore whether the parties reside or have resided together. Rather, the residency element and cohabitation may partially overlap in the case of "persons living as spouses." In those situations, domestic violence arises out of the relationship, because given their relationship, they are considered to be residing together even though they may not have the same residential address.[35] Moreover, they do not even need to share the same residential address to be considered as residing together. However, even in those cases, a court must review the particular living arrangement in order to determine whether they are currently residing together or had resided together.[36]

Q & A: Does this decision only apply to the criminal domestic violence statute?

No. The same family and household members are covered in both the civil domestic violence statute[37] and the criminal domestic violence statute.[38] Therefore, the definitions contained in *State v. Williams*[39] are applicable to civil protection order cases.

Q & A: When do dating relationships rise to the level of cohabitation in the context of domestic violence?[40]

The most significant aspect of *Williams* is that it expands the categories of individuals who may seek protection under the domestic violence statutes. In effect, by expanding coverage to dating relationships in its written opinion, the Supreme Court amended the law without the benefit of statutory enactment. The Supreme Court specifically noted that "[s]ocial science studies show that the rate of violence in dating relationships is at least the same as, if not greater than, that of couples who maintain one address. . . . 'Social science research that documents violence in dating relationships supports offering broader civil protection order coverage to dating partners and adolescents.' "[41]

Q & A: How has *State v. Williams* been interpreted in the context of appellate decisions?[42]

An important consequence of the *Williams* decision is its interpretation by the appellate courts. Over the past one and one-half years, the courts have relied on *Williams* to support decisions that demonstrate

[35]See also Noggle v. Smith, 2005-Ohio-5636, 2005 WL 2727128 (Ohio Ct. App. 5th Dist. Ashland County 2005) (noting that cohabitation need not be continual); State v. McGrath, 2007-Ohio-4682, 2007 WL 2671267 (Ohio Ct. App. 8th Dist. Cuyahoga County 2007) (in spite of client's nomadic life style, cohabitation was established because she did not live anywhere but spent time with defendant at his house).

[36]State v. Alvey, 2003-Ohio-7006, 2003 WL 22997277, *4 (Ohio Ct. App. 7th Dist. Belmont County 2003).

[37]RC 3113.31.

[38]RC 2919.25.

[39]State v. Williams, 79 Ohio St. 3d 459, 1997-Ohio-79, 683 N.E.2d 1126 (1997).

[40]See also Text § 10:9, Relationships covered—Person living as a spouse.

[41]State v. Williams, 79 Ohio St. 3d 459, 462, 1997-Ohio-79, 683 N.E.2d 1126 (1997) (citing Catherine F. Klein & Leslye E. Orloff, Providing Legal Protection for Battered Women: An Analysis of State Statutes and Case Law, 21 Hofstra L. Rev. 801, 836–37 (1993)). But see Oriola v. Thaler, 84 Cal. App. 4th 397, 100 Cal. Rptr. 2d 822 (1st Dist. 2000) (in-depth discussion of what constitutes a dating relationship).

[42]See also Text § 10:9, Relationships covered-person living as a spouse.

a reluctance to limit family or household members to those who actually share a residential address.[43] For example, in *State v. Scott*,[44] the victim was the offender's sister. The offender argued that, because he and his sister did not reside together at the time of the incident, their relationship was outside the purview of the domestic violence statute. The court declined to narrowly define "family or household member."

Similarly, the Columbiana Court of Appeals, in *Coma v. Kellogg*,[45] reversed the trial court ruling that, where they had not resided together at the time of the incident, the stepchildren/stepparent relationship does not meet the elements of "family or household member." The appeals court relied on the Supreme Court's *Williams* decision to support its conclusion that this family dynamic falls within the scope of RC 3113.31.

There is no doubt that *Williams* has had far-reaching application. What is unclear at this time is how this decision will impact other areas of Ohio law. Nothing in this opinion specifically suggests that the definition of "cohabiting" is restricted to domestic violence cases. The application of this opinion and its use in other domestic relations matters is unknown; but, conceivably, the broad definition of "cohabiting" may be used by courts to terminate spousal support.[46]

The Montgomery County Court of Appeals considered the *Williams*[47] opinion in two recent decisions. In *State v. Combs*,[48] the defendant argued that he and the victim were not cohabitants. The court, relying on the factors set forth in *Williams*, found that the victim "shared her home with Combs on a frequent if not a constant basis, cooking for Combs and allowing him to sleep in her bedroom and spend the night."[49] The court of appeals concluded that the defendant and the victim were cohabitants as defined in *Williams* and that an element of RC 2919.25(A) was satisfied.[50] Additionally, and more importantly, the court determined that *Williams* does not "require evidence of all of the factors that are mentioned in the opinion as bearing on

[43]See also State v. Cohagen, 2000 WL 1357938 (Ohio Ct. App. 10th Dist. Franklin County 2000).

[44]State v. Scott, 1999 WL 126933 (Ohio Ct. App. 7th Dist. Belmont County 1999) (overruled by, State v. Alvey, 2003-Ohio-7006, 2003 WL 22997277 (Ohio Ct. App. 7th Dist. Belmont County 2003)) (overruling court finding that state must show that offender resides or had resided with the victim in order to sustain a domestic violence conviction).

[45]Coma v. Kellogg, 1999 WL 135294 (Ohio Ct. App. 7th Dist. Columbiana County 1999).

[46]See, e.g., Schmidt v. Schmidt, 2000 WL 1867396 (Ohio Ct. App. 8th Dist. Cuyahoga County 2000).

[47]State v. Williams, 79 Ohio St. 3d 459, 1997-Ohio-79, 683 N.E.2d 1126 (1997).

[48]State v. Combs, 1998 WL 226375 (Ohio Ct. App. 2d Dist. Montgomery County 1998).

[49]State v. Combs, 1998 WL 226375, *3 (Ohio Ct. App. 2d Dist. Montgomery County 1998).

[50]But see City of Akron v. Taylor, 2001-Ohio-1947, 2001 WL 1626941 (Ohio Ct. App. 9th Dist. Summit County 2001) (where testimony that the parties dated and that he sometimes stayed at her home for up to four days a week and that he took her daughter to a store to buy her clothes was insufficient to demonstrate the element of familial or financial responsibility required to demonstrate cohabitation).

cohabitation."[51] Cooking for the defendant and the description of the parties' relationship as "boyfriend and girlfriend" created an inference "that some of the consortium factors identified in *Williams*—society, aid of each other, and conjugal relations—existed in this relationship."[52]

In *State v. Young*,[53] the defendant's assignment of error was that the parties did not live together and the complainant was not a "person living as a spouse." The complainant testified that their relationship was that of boyfriend and girlfriend. The court of appeals determined that, under *Williams*, the burden of proving cohabitation is not substantial. To that end, testimony that indicated that the parties were boyfriend and girlfriend, were living at the same address, and were listening to music together on the night of the incident was determinative of cohabitation.[54]

Reiterating the holding set forth in *State v. Combs*,[55] the *Young* court concluded that the prosecution need not prove all of the factors listed in *Williams* and that "the factors listed in *Williams* are not the only way to prove cohabitation."[56] The court reasoned that the *Williams* Court provided only possible factors establishing familial or financial responsibilities and consortium and that, "in weighing these kinds of issues, courts should be guided by common sense and by ordinary human experience."[57] The *Young* holding suggests an ever-widening array of factors for determining cohabitation in domestic violence cases.[58]

Several newer cases are focused squarely on the sharing or financial

---

[51]State v. Combs, 1998 WL 226375, *3 (Ohio Ct. App. 2d Dist. Montgomery County 1998).

[52]State v. Combs, 1998 WL 226375, *3 (Ohio Ct. App. 2d Dist. Montgomery County 1998); see State v. Banks, 2005-Ohio-186, 2005 WL 110437 (Ohio Ct. App. 8th Dist. Cuyahoga County 2005) (where the parties were romantically involved for 6 years, fought over finances, both owned keys to the main door and commingled assets; moreover, appellant has clothes are her residence, and had slept there most of the time the elements of cohabitation were satisfied).

[53]State v. Young, 1998 WL 801498 (Ohio Ct. App. 2d Dist. Montgomery County 1998).

[54]See also Heflin v. Dunson, 2005-Ohio-304, 2005 WL 187435 (Ohio Ct. App. 2d Dist. Montgomery County 2005); State v. Wallace, 2006-Ohio-5819, 2006 WL 3183386 (Ohio Ct. App. 9th Dist. Lorain County 2006) (testimony that appellant lived with appellee because he was homeless, that he would cook, clean and help around the house while she was at work and because they were dating and she was 6 months pregnant with his child was sufficient to demonstrate cohabitation).

[55]State v. Combs, 1998 WL 226375 (Ohio Ct. App. 2d Dist. Montgomery County 1998).

[56]State v. Young, 1998 WL 801498, *3 (Ohio Ct. App. 2d Dist. Montgomery County 1998); see also State v. Hare, 2001 WL 46251 (Ohio Ct. App. 5th Dist. Delaware County 2001); State v. Woullard, 158 Ohio App. 3d 31, 2004-Ohio-3395, 813 N.E.2d 964 (2d Dist. Greene County 2004).

[57]State v. Young, 1998 WL 801498, *3 (Ohio Ct. App. 2d Dist. Montgomery County 1998). See also State v. Long, 2011-Ohio-1050, 2011 WL 806839 (Ohio Ct. App. 9th Dist. Summit County 2011) (noting that the burden of establishing cohabitation is not substantial).

[58]See also State v. Hare, 2001 WL 46251 (Ohio Ct. App. 5th Dist. Delaware County 2001); State v. Colter, 2000 WL 282301 (Ohio Ct. App. 2d Dist. Montgomery County 2000); State v. Ward, 2000 WL 33231613 (Ohio Ct. App. 10th Dist. Franklin County 2000); State v. Rinehart, 2002-Ohio-6143, 2002 WL 31520346 (Ohio Ct. App. 4th Dist. Ross County 2002); State v. Perkins, 2010-Ohio-2968, 2010 WL 2573770

and familial responsibilities element of the *Williams* factors. For example, in *State v. Rubes*,[59] the only issue to be decided was whether, for purposes of a domestic violence conviction, the defendant is cohabiting with the victim when he lives with her, she is his girlfriend, he gets mail at her home, sleeps in the same bed with her and spends every night with her. In this case, Kim and Rubes both lived with the victim's father who, along with his daughter, was a victim in the domestic violence case brought against the boyfriend.

On appeal, Defendant argued that the state had failed to prove the family or household element in regards to the charge involving the father or Kim. The appellate court first noted that O'Neal was Kim's father and that Rubes was living not only with Kim but with her father in the father's home. The only remaining question was whether Kim was a person living as a spouse with Rubes such that the statutory definition applies to include O'Neal as a family or household member. Unlike other appellate cases, neither Kim nor Rubes paid rent or utilities.[60] Rubes did not pay for groceries, although he did do some odd jobs around the house and Kim did purchase some food for the household.[61]

While it was clear that Kim and Rubes were in a relationship for about a year and that they slept in the same bed while living in her bedroom, the familial or financial responsibilities connection was wanting. However, the appellate court pointed out that Kim and Rubes were in unique circumstances and were not required to pay living expenses, "we cannot determine that their failure to jointly pay

---

(Ohio Ct. App. 12th Dist. Fayette County 2010) (parties were cohabiting where they shared a apartment for one month before the alleged incident and defendant watched victim's daughter when she was at work); State v. Travlus, 2010-Ohio-4046, 2010 WL 3366195 (Ohio Ct. App. 2d Dist. Montgomery County 2010) (parties cohabited where defendant stayed with the victim but was not on the lease, had a key to the apartment and received mail at the address and paid for some groceries); State v. Ward, 2010-Ohio-4614, 2010 WL 3782643 (Ohio Ct. App. 10th Dist. Franklin County 2010) (no requirement to introduce a marriage license or testimony of a minister of justice of the peace in order to find cohabitation); State v. Maple, 2011-Ohio-1516, 2011 WL 1138387 (Ohio Ct. App. 9th Dist. Summit County 2011) (where defendant frequently spent the night at victim's home, essentially stayed there for the month prior to the incident, slept, showered, changed clothes at her home and kept clothing and his dogs there, ate out and at home together, attended family gatherings, and used victim's car was evidence of cohabitation); State v. Gomez, 2011-Ohio-5475, 2011 WL 5067230 (Ohio Ct. App. 9th Dist. Summit County 2011) (evidence that victim accompanied defendant on some of his out of town trucking jobs, stayed at defendant's home on a regular basis, provided support for her during her pregnancy, and shared household duties such as cleaning and cooking supported elements of cohabitation for purposes of domestic violence); State v. Ross, 2012-Ohio-1389, 2012 WL 1076253 (Ohio Ct. App. 9th Dist. Summit County 2012); State v. Partlow, 2013-Ohio-2771, 2013 WL 3356575 (Ohio Ct. App. 10th Dist. Franklin County 2013) (cohabitation relationship satisfied by victim cooking, washing, cleaning and engaging in an intimate relationship with appellant as well as appellant providing victim money, all of which evidenced a sharing of financial responsibilities).

[59]State v. Rubes, 2012-Ohio-4100, 975 N.E.2d 1054 (Ohio Ct. App. 11th Dist. Portage County 2012).

[60]See also State v. Hawkins, 2012-Ohio-4622, 2012 WL 4762031 (Ohio Ct. App. 2d Dist. Montgomery County 2012).

[61]See also State v. Slevin, 2012-Ohio-2043, 2012 WL 1647115 (Ohio Ct. App. 9th Dist. Summit County 2012); State v. Walburg, 2011-Ohio-4762, 2011 WL 4362748 (Ohio Ct. App. 10th Dist. Franklin County 2011).

such expenses means that they were not cohabiting."[62] The court found that Kim's purchase of some food and Rubes doing odd jobs created at least some familial and financial relationship.

Additionally, while no evidence was provided of a conjugal or sexual relationship between Kim and Rubes, the fact that they lived in the same room and slept in the same bed established some level of consortium between them.[63] Once it was determined that Kim and Rubes satisfied the elements of cohabitation, the court determined that O'Neal and Rubes were family or household members because both Rubes and Kim lived in O'Neal's home. Thus, Rubes' assignment of error was without merit.

What is important about the appellate court's legal analysis is the in- depth level of specificity regarding each of the *Williams* factors. While the facts of this particular case are somewhat unique, it is clear that there is more structured legal analysis in applying the *Williams* factors to the facts of the individual case.

Of interest is that the *Rubes* court also reiterated an important point from the Ohio Supreme Court's decision in *State v. Carswell* when it noted that "[T]he Ohio Supreme Court has emphasized that 'it is a person's determination to share some measure of life's responsibilities with another that creates cohabitation.' "[64]

Q & A: Without mutual respect, aid of each other and comfort, can there be evidence of consortium under *Williams*?

In *Edwards v. Reser*,[65] the 6th District Court of Appeals considered whether mutual respect, comfort and mutual aid of each other are necessary for consortium. In this case, appellee was granted a CPO against her ex boyfriend. On appeal, appellant argued that appellee did not demonstrate that she and appellant were "living as spouses." Appellant relied on the *Williams* opinion which defined the elements of cohabitation, particularly consortium. Evidence of consortium might include mutual respect, fidelity, affection, society, cooperation, solace, comfort, aid of each other friendship and conjugal relations.[66]

Appellant argued that because the parties appeared not to respect, comfort or aid each other, there was no evidence of consortium. The

[62]State v. Rubes, 2012-Ohio-4100, ¶ 30, 975 N.E.2d 1054 (Ohio Ct. App. 11th Dist. Portage County 2012); see also State v. Williams, 79 Ohio St. 3d 459, 1997-Ohio-79, 683 N.E.2d 1126 (1997) (finding cohabitation where the defendant invited victim to live in a place where he was staying for free and the victim purchased food and that the parties shared familial and financial responsibilities to the extent that they had any such responsibilities); State v. McGlothan, 138 Ohio St. 3d 146, 2014-Ohio-85, 4 N.E.3d 1021 (2014).

[63]See also State v. Messenger, 2010-Ohio-479, 2010 WL 530087 (Ohio Ct. App. 3d Dist. Marion County 2010) (that victim testified defendant was her live-in boyfriend and slept with her in the same bedroom was sufficient evidence that the consortium element was met).

[64]State v. Rubes, 2012-Ohio-4100, ¶ 26, 975 N.E.2d 1054 (Ohio Ct. App. 11th Dist. Portage County 2012), quoting State v. Carswell, 114 Ohio St. 3d 210, 2007-Ohio-3723, 871 N.E.2d 547 (2007); see also State v. Long, 2011-Ohio-1050, 2011 WL 806839 (Ohio Ct. App. 9th Dist. Summit County 2011).

[65]Edwards v. Reser, 2007-Ohio-6520, 2007 WL 4277861 (Ohio Ct. App. 6th Dist. Ottawa County 2007).

[66]Edwards v. Reser, 2007-Ohio-6520, 2007 WL 4277861, *3 (Ohio Ct. App. 6th Dist. Ottawa County 2007).

6th District Court of Appeals stated that "[c]ertainly, in most domestic violence cases the parties have a volatile relationship; if this fact negated consortium, few domestic violence cases would be successful."[67]

Q & A: Without conjugal relations, can there be evidence of consortium?

The decision in Williams is not definitive in this regard, but placement of the factors suggests that conjugal relations are necessary.[68] According to *Williams*, factors establishing consortium might include mutual respect, fidelity, affection, society, cooperation, solace, comfort, aid of each other, friendship and conjugal relations.[69] That the Supreme Court separated conjugal relations from the other factors with "and," not "or," is significant.

According to the American Heritage Dictionary of the English Language, the word "and" means "in addition to" or "as well as."[70] The word "or" means "an alternative."[71] In the context of this case, the word "and" is used to separate the various consortium factors which may include several factors "as well as" or "in addition to" conjugal relations. The Supreme Court intended to include other factors *and* conjugal relations. Conversely, the use of the word "or" indicates that any of the included factors may prove that the parties shared familial or financial responsibilities.

Cohabitation may include various other factors, but it must include conjugal relations.[72] However, without conjugal relations, the parties are merely roommates.[73]

Q & A: Has the definition of cohabitation advanced by the Supreme Court of Ohio in *Williams* been considered by the Supreme Court since the late 1990's?

Apparently, the Supreme Court of Ohio decided to clarify its decision in *Williams* but appears to have developed a two tiered standard

[67]Edwards v. Reser, 2007-Ohio-6520, 2007 WL 4277861, *3 (Ohio Ct. App. 6th Dist. Ottawa County 2007).

[68]See also State v. Rubes, 2012-Ohio-4100, 975 N.E.2d 1054 (Ohio Ct. App. 11th Dist. Portage County 2012).

[69]State v. Williams, 79 Ohio St. 3d 459, 1997-Ohio-79, 683 N.E.2d 1126 (1997).

[70]The American Heritage Dictionary of the English Language, 49.

[71]The American Heritage Dictionary of the English Language, 923.

[72]See also State v. Mauldin, 2010-Ohio-4192, 2010 WL 3482689 (Ohio Ct. App. 7th Dist. Mahoning County 2010) (testimony of the victim that at one time she thought she was pregnant with defendant's child was evidence of consortium); State v. Maple, 2011-Ohio-1516, 2011 WL 1138387 (Ohio Ct. App. 9th Dist. Summit County 2011) (that victim was pregnant reinforced elements of cohabitation for purposes of domestic violence); State v. Gomez, 2011-Ohio-5475, 2011 WL 5067230 (Ohio Ct. App. 9th Dist. Summit County 2011) (pregnancy reinforced elements of cohabitation); but see State v. Clay, 181 Ohio App. 3d 563, 2009-Ohio-1235, 910 N.E.2d 14 (8th Dist. Cuyahoga County 2009) (court determined that state need not have to establish that the parties had a sexual relationship to support a domestic violence conviction; that they shared the same household and were cohabiting by sharing responsibilities was enough); State v. Brauer, 2013-Ohio-3319, 2013 WL 3946124 (Ohio Ct. App. 12th Dist. Warren County 2013) (finding that proof of conjugal relations not an essential element of domestic violence); State v. Taylor, 2013-Ohio-4588, 2013 WL 5657956 (Ohio Ct. App. 5th Dist. Richland County 2013) (noting that "cohabitation" can be based on acts of living together without, sexual relations).

[73]See also § 10:9.

for cohabitation. In *State v. McGlothan*,[74] the Supreme Court of Ohio accepted *certiorari* in an Eighth District Court of Appeals case and clarified what evidence was necessary to establish cohabitation for purposes of R.C. 2919.25. In that case, the victim testified that at the time of the incident, defendant was her boyfriend and had lived with her in her apartment for about one year. After pushing and grabbing the victim, defendant was charged with felonious assault and convicted by attempted felonious assault and domestic violence. On appeal, appellant/defendant claimed that the state had failed to present sufficient evidence to support the conviction for domestic violence based on the *Williams* definition.

At the appellate level, the Court found that while there was evidence that the parties were a couple and that defendant had slept at her apartment for over a year, no testimony was presented that the couple shared familial or financial responsibilities, such as rent and utilities which would demonstrate shared familial or financial responsibilities.[75] However, the dissenting judge found that it was not necessary for the State to prove that the couple shared living expenses when it established that the parties lived together.

On appeal to the Supreme Court, the state asserted that by requiring evidence of shared living expenses to demonstrate shared familial or financial responsibilities, the appellate court elevated one of the non-exhaustive factors set forth in *Williams* to an essential element of cohabitation.[76] Instead, it argued that shared living expenses is merely one factor that a court may consider in its cohabitation analysis.[77] "The state further maintains that the Eighth District's requirement of shared living expenses to establish cohabitation is contrary to decisions of the Second, Ninth, Tenth and Eleventh Districts."[78] The appellant claimed that the appellate court did not hold that the State needed to prove shared financial responsibilities, but rather ruled that the State had failed to establish the cohabitation factors of

[74]State v. McGlothan, 138 Ohio St. 3d 146, 2014-Ohio-85, 4 N.E.3d 1021 (2014); see also State v. White, 2014-Ohio-1446, 2014 WL 1384082 (Ohio Ct. App. 2d Dist. Montgomery County 2014) (relying on the analysis of *McGlothan* and noting that there is no minimum duration that a couple must live together before they are accorded the protections of the domestic violence statutes and finding that if there is a minimum, a two month duration exceeds it); Cleveland v. Merritt, 2016-Ohio-4693, 69 N.E.3d 102 (Ohio Ct. App. 8th Dist. Cuyahoga County 2016), appeal not allowed, 147 Ohio St. 3d 1506, 2017-Ohio-261, 67 N.E.3d 824 (2017) (state need not prove shared familial or financial responsibilities where victim stated that she lived at the address in question, where subpoena was sent to her at his address, and the booking sheet indicated the same address for the parties; however, the dissent admonished the majority because no actual evidence was presented that the victim and abuser lived together at that address).

[75]State v. McGlothan, 2012-Ohio-4049, 2012 WL 3862138 (Ohio Ct. App. 8th Dist. Cuyahoga County 2012), judgment rev'd, 138 Ohio St. 3d 146, 2014-Ohio-85, 4 N.E.3d 1021 (2014).

[76]State v. McGlothan, 138 Ohio St. 3d 146, 147, 2014-Ohio-85, 4 N.E.3d 1021 (2014).

[77]State v. McGlothan, 138 Ohio St. 3d 146, 147, 2014-Ohio-85, 4 N.E.3d 1021 (2014).

[78]State v. McGlothan, 138 Ohio St. 3d 146, 147, 2014-Ohio-85, 4 N.E.3d 1021 (2014).

Williams.[79] Further, the appellant stated that it was reasonable for the appellate court to conclude that the fact that appellant was her boyfriend and spent every night at her apartment was not by itself enough to prove cohabitation.[80]

The Supreme Court of Ohio noted "the court of appeals misread our decision in *Williams* as supporting the proposition that evidence of shared living expenses is necessary to establish cohabitation."[81] In distinguishing the decision in *McGlothan* from *Williams*, it found that *Williams* addressed living arrangements between a victim and defendant that were "markedly different from the circumstances here."[82] In *Williams*, the focus was on a couple who was going together but did not live together. "Thus, in order to prove cohabitation when the victim and the defendant did not share the same residence, evidence of shared financial or familial responsibilities and consortium are required."[83] In contrast, McGlothan and the victim were boyfriend and girlfriend and had lived together in her apartment. "Because the state demonstrated that the defendant was the victim's boyfriend and that they had lived together for about a year, the state had no obligation to demonstrate the sharing of familial or financial responsibilities and consortium to prove cohabitation in this case.[84] "[E]ven if the *Williams* factors did apply regarding the non-exhaustive list establishing shared familial or financial responsibilities, circumstantial evidence shows that McGlothan and Robinson, by sharing her apartment for about a year, did share shelter and utilities. In addition, the trial court could have reasonably concluded that Robinson's testimony demonstrated factors establishing consortium, such as affection, society and aid of each other."[85]

The Supreme Court also stated that the *Williams* court declined to

---

[79]State v. McGlothan, 138 Ohio St. 3d 146, 147-48, 2014-Ohio-85, 4 N.E.3d 1021 (2014).

[80]State v. McGlothan, 138 Ohio St. 3d 146, 148, 2014-Ohio-85, 4 N.E.3d 1021 (2014).

[81]State v. McGlothan, 138 Ohio St. 3d 146, 148, 2014-Ohio-85, 4 N.E.3d 1021 (2014).

[82]State v. McGlothan, 138 Ohio St. 3d 146, 148, 2014-Ohio-85, 4 N.E.3d 1021 (2014).

[83]State v. McGlothan, 138 Ohio St. 3d 146, 148, 2014-Ohio-85, 4 N.E.3d 1021 (2014), citing, *Williams* at 463–465; see also State v. White, 2014-Ohio-1446, 2014 WL 1384082 (Ohio Ct. App. 2d Dist. Montgomery County 2014) (interpreting *McGlothan* to mean that *Williams* only applied when the victim and defendant do not share the same residence).

[84]State v. McGlothan, 138 Ohio St. 3d 146, 149, 2014-Ohio-85, 4 N.E.3d 1021 (2014); Cleveland v. Merritt, 2016-Ohio-4693, 69 N.E.3d 102 (Ohio Ct. App. 8th Dist. Cuyahoga County 2016), appeal not allowed, 147 Ohio St. 3d 1506, 2017-Ohio-261, 67 N.E.3d 824 (2017) (see also, dissenting opinion); State v. Martin, 2016-Ohio-225, 57 N.E.3d 411 (Ohio Ct. App. 5th Dist. Tuscarawas County 2016) (family or household member relationship existed where parties had been in a relationship for 25 years on and off, that they were never married and had no children, that the victim had been staying with offender at his apartment and that he lived with victim at apartment on the date of the incident); State v. Plott, 2017-Ohio-38, 80 N.E.3d 1108 (Ohio Ct. App. 3d Dist. Seneca County 2017), appeal not allowed, 150 Ohio St. 3d 1452, 2017-Ohio-8136, 83 N.E.3d 938 (2017).

[85]State v. McGlothan, 138 Ohio St. 3d 146, 149, 2014-Ohio-85, 4 N.E.3d 1021 (2014), citing, *Williams* at 465.

adopt a narrow definition of "reside" which would have limited "family or household members" to those actually sharing one address.

In her dissent, Justice Lanzinger found that:

> [W]ithout expressly acknowledging the fact, the majority overrules a portion of *State v. Williams*. 79 Ohio St.3d 459, 683 NE2d 1126 (1997). It now decides that merely living in the same residence will satisfy the element of cohabitation for the domestic-violence statute, stating that '[b]ecause the state demonstrated that the defendant was victim's boyfriend and that they had lived together for about a year, the State had no obligation to demonstrate a sharing of familial or financial responsibilities and consortium to prove cohabitation in this case.' Majority opinion, ¶ 15. Rather than clarifying *Williams*, this statement repudiates one of the cohabitation requirements set forth in *Williams*:
>
> > [W]e conclude that the essential *elements* of "cohabitation" are 1) *sharing of familial or financial responsibilities and 2) consortium.*"[86]

The importance of this decision cannot be overstated. In this case, the Court looked to the General Assembly whose objective in enacting the domestic violence statutes was to protect persons from violence by close family members or residents of the same household and to offer protections to a wide class of persons.[87] In *Williams*, the analysis was based on the victim's relationship with the offender and focused on the fact that the offense of domestic violence "arises out of the relationship of the parties, rather than their exact living circumstances."[88] Similarly, *McGlothan* adopted a very broad definition as well but clarified *Williams* by differentiating situations in which persons are living together from those who do not in determining cohabitation in a given case. The sharing of familial or financial responsibilities does not require evidence of shared living expenses to establish cohabitation; rather it is merely one factor of among many that a court may consider in determining cohabitation, none of which are, by themselves, a necessary condition for cohabitation.[89] However, in doing so, the justices just might have broadened the domestic violence statutes to apply to roommates.

Since *McGlothan*, several appellate cases have been decided. In *State v. Roberts*,[90] appellant had been convicted under RC 2919.25, but argued that she and M.R. were not family or household members. The facts of this case are that the parties had a four year romantic relationship, she continued to support M.R. after their breakup by pay-

---

[86]State v. McGlothan, 138 Ohio St. 3d 146, 150, 2014-Ohio-85, 4 N.E.3d 1021 (2014).

[87]State v. McGlothan, 138 Ohio St.3d 146, 2014-Ohio-85, 4 N.E.3d 1021 (2014), quoting *Williams* at 463 and citing State v. Carswell, 114 Ohio St. 3d 210, 150, 2007-Ohio-3723, 871 N.E.2d 547 (2007).

[88]State v. McGlothan, 138 Ohio St. 3d 146, 148, 2014-Ohio-85, 4 N.E.3d 1021 (2014), quoting, *Williams* at 464.

[89]State v. McGlothan, 138 Ohio St.3d 146, 2014-Ohio-85, 4 N.E.3d 1021 (2014); State v. Brown, 2015-Ohio-950, 2015 WL 1138651, ¶ 33 (Ohio Ct. App. 11th Dist. Lake County 2015); State v. Hughes, 2015-Ohio-1173, 2015 WL 1403276 (Ohio Ct. App. 5th Dist. Tuscarawas County 2015); City of Cleveland v. Johnson, 2014-Ohio-4083, 19 N.E.3d 604 (Ohio Ct. App. 8th Dist. Cuyahoga County 2014), as corrected, (Sept. 23, 2014).

[90]State v. Roberts, 2015-Ohio-5044, 2015 WL 8154018 (Ohio Ct. App. 9th Dist. Wayne County 2015).

ing for gas and his car payment and that she had personal items at the home of M.R. Although the parties had separate residences, she stayed at M.R.'s residence, which was described as her "secondary residence."

The appellate court found that there was enough evidence to prove that the parties were family or household members under RC 2919.25.[91] Based on the observations of the police officer who determined that the parties lived together in that she described herself as M.R.'s live-in girlfriend and the parties' separate testimonies that she used M.R.'s residence even after the end of their relationship, sufficient evidence was provided to demonstrate proof of shared financial responsibilities.

Likewise, in *State v. Cornwell*,[92] the court found that the parties were family or household members for purposes of appellant's conviction under RC 2919.25. In this case, the parties did not live together as boyfriend and girlfriend at the time of the incident but had lived together at some point during the five year period. The victim testified that she often was an overnight guest at appellant's apartment and that she and appellant were engaged to be married. She also testified that she kept some personal belongings at appellant's apartment.

On appeal, appellant argued that the State had failed to prove that he and the victim had cohabited. He cited *State v. Williams* to support his position, noting the essential elements of cohabitation are 1) sharing of familial and financial responsibilities and 2) consortium. However, the appellate court stressed that the Supreme Court had clarified Williams "as strictly applying 'when the victim and defendant do *not* share the same residence[.]' "[93] It went on to say that, in *McGlothan,* "the Court held that the "sharing of familial and financial responsibilities does not *require* evidence of shared living expenses to establish cohabitation; rather, such conduct is but one of a non-exhaustive list of factors that a court may consider in determining cohabitation." *McGlothan* ¶ 13-14. The Supreme Court of Ohio further emphasized that the domestic violence statute was enacted because the General Assembly " 'believed that an assault involving a family or household member deserves further protection than an assault on a stranger.' "[94]

Noting that the parties had cohabited within five years prior to the act in question, the Court found that the parties were family or household members.

Q & A: Have any cases challenged the constitutionality of the term cohabiting for purposes of RC 3113.31(A)(3)(a)(i) and

---

[91]See also State v. Bump, 2016-Ohio-4717, 2016 WL 3573174 (Ohio Ct. App. 2d Dist. Champaign County 2016) (jury did not lose its way in finding that the parties were family or household members under RC 2919.25 in that they discussed fact that they were boyfriend and girlfriend and began a sexual relationship, that she stayed in defendant's apartment for a week, left and then left and returned to his apartment).

[92]State v. Cornwell, 2015-Ohio-4617, 48 N.E.3d 169 (Ohio Ct. App. 9th Dist. Wayne County 2015).

[93]Emphasis sic., at ¶ 15, quoting *McGlothan* ¶ 13.

[94]State v. Cornwell, 2015-Ohio-4617, 48 N.E.3d 169 (Ohio Ct. App. 9th Dist. Wayne County 2015) quoting *McGlothan*, at ¶ 17, quoting *Williams* at 463, 683 NE2d 1126.

(4) and RC 2919.25(E)(1)(i) and (2) or questioned the Supreme Court's definition of cohabitation as defined in *State v. Williams*?

At least one Ohio case challenged the constitutionality of the term "cohabiting" as used in RC 2919.25. In *City of Cleveland v. Schill*,[95] the appellate court upheld the constitutionality of the domestic violence statute.

In that case, defendant was the live-in boyfriend of the victim. The parties were not married, had no children together and were not otherwise related. The defendant did not dispute that he caused his girlfriend physical harm. His only argument was that the term "cohabiting" as used in RC 2919.25 was vague as to the definition of family or household member and that he should have been charged under the assault statute, not the domestic violence statute. Defendant argued that the plain language of the statute does not provide minimal guidelines for law enforcement to avoid arbitrary enforcement and that the factors set forth in *State vs. Williams* were too subjective and delve too deeply into the private lives of the offender and victim.[96] On the other hand, the city argued the constitutionality of RC 2919.25, and stated that a person of ordinary intelligence would know whether his relationship was encompassed within the term "cohabiting."[97]

The Cuyahoga County Court of Appeals relied on the United States Supreme Court's decision in *Grayned v. City of Rockford*[98] and the Ohio Supreme Court's decision in *State v. Dorso*[99] to determine whether a statute is vague.[100] Under the guidelines set forth in *Grayned* and *Dorso*, the Eighth District Court of Appeals found that the domestic violence statute was not unconstitutionally vague. The court held that "the ordinary person, including the defendant, is adequately warned that to assault the person he lives with, and with whom he is intimately involved, may be a violation of the domestic violence statute and that his or her conduct is therefore prohibited."[101]

Additionally, the court noted that because the legislature declined to define the term "cohabitation," it must be given a common, everyday meaning. It then pointed out that the Ohio Supreme Court defined the term for purposes of the domestic violence statute in *State v. Williams*,[102] and further provided courts with an understanding of the characteristics of the relationship. The court stated that "[a]s the Ohio Supreme Court has interpreted the elements of 'cohabitation'

---

[95] Cleveland v. Schill, 147 Ohio App. 3d 239, 2002-Ohio-1263, 769 N.E.2d 907 (8th Dist. Cuyahoga County 2002).

[96] Cleveland v. Schill, 147 Ohio App. 3d 239, 2002-Ohio-1263, 769 N.E.2d 907 (8th Dist. Cuyahoga County 2002).

[97] Cleveland v. Schill, 147 Ohio App. 3d 239, 2002, 2002-Ohio-1263, 769 N.E.2d 907 (8th Dist. Cuyahoga County 2002).

[98] Grayned v. City of Rockford, 408 U.S. 104, 92 S. Ct. 2294, 33 L. Ed. 2d 222 (1972).

[99] State v. Dorso, 4 Ohio St. 3d 60, 446 N.E.2d 449 (1983).

[100] Cleveland v. Schill, 147 Ohio App. 3d 239, 2002-Ohio-1263, 769 N.E.2d 907 (8th Dist. Cuyahoga County 2002).

[101] Cleveland v. Schill, 147 Ohio App. 3d 239, 2002-Ohio-1263, 769 N.E.2d 907 (8th Dist. Cuyahoga County 2002).

[102] State v. Williams, 79 Ohio St. 3d 459, 1997-Ohio-79, 683 N.E.2d 1126 (1997).

under RC 2919.25 and has given a constitutional construction to the statute, we follow *Williams*."[103]

Since the same family and household members are covered under the civil[104] and criminal[105] domestic violence statutes, the reasoning of the Eighth District Court of Appeals is applicable to a domestic violence proceeding under RC 3113.31.

§ 10:7 Relationships covered—Persons who have a child in common

Under RC 3113.31(A)(3)(b), covered individuals include those persons who have never lived together but who have a child in common.[1] This provision was recently amended in October 1997 to provide that the respondent need only be an alleged or putative parent.[2] The intent of the amendment was to provide continued coverage and protection by means of a protection order to a victim who alleges that the respondent is the natural parent of her child.[3] No proof of parentage is required for coverage under the statute to attach.

Q & A: How is the term "natural" parent defined?

The Third District Court of Appeals recently considered the issue in *State v. Hess*.[4] In that case, the defendant appealed his conviction for domestic violence on the ground that the state had failed to prove that he was a family or household member of the victim pursuant to RC 2919.25(E)(1)(b). While he admitted that he had impregnated the victim and that she had given birth to a child, he argued that he should no longer be considered the natural parent of the child because his parental rights had been terminated.

In affirming the trial court, the Seneca County Court of Appeals noted that the Ohio Revised Code did not define the term "natural parent." However, the court then looked to Black's Law Dictionary

---

[103]Cleveland v. Schill, 147 Ohio App. 3d 239, 2002-Ohio-1263, 769 N.E.2d 907 (8th Dist. Cuyahoga County 2002).

[104]RC 3113.31.

[105]RC 2919.25.

[Section 10:7]

[1]See also State v. Stringfield, 124 Ohio App. 3d 665, 707 N.E.2d 43 (9th Dist. Medina County 1998); State v. Johnston, 2004-Ohio-282, 2004 WL 111642 (Ohio Ct. App. 12th Dist. Butler County 2004).

[2]See RC 3113.31(A)(3)(b), as amended by 1997 S.B. 1, eff. 10-21-97; see also State v. Mills, 2005-Ohio-2128, 2006 WL 1132543 (Ohio Ct. App. 2d Dist. Montgomery County 2006) (the offender respondent's status as either a natural parent or a putative parent of the victim's child will establish the family or household member relationship).

[3]But see State v. Crawford, 2007-Ohio-2254, 2007 WL 1378390 (Ohio Ct. App. 6th Dist. Fulton County 2007) (where mother's husband is presumed to be and is legally designated as the child's father pursuant to RC 3111.03, the state can't prove the defendant's guilt by a mere allegation of mother that there was a possibility defendant might be the child's father. Since the husband is the undisputed natural father, defendant can't be a putative natural father. Thus, in light of the presumption created by RC 3111.03, appellee's status as a family or household member cannot be proven beyond a reasonable doubt).

[4]State v. Hess, 2004-Ohio-534, 2004 WL 231481 (Ohio Ct. App. 3d Dist. Seneca County 2004).

which defined natural father as, [t]he man who impregnated the child's natural mother."[5]

The appellate court stated that "[i]t is clear from this definition, and a common sense understanding of the terms, that a natural parent is a person who biologically causes a child to come into existence."[6] In refuting defendant's argument that a termination of rights terminates his status as biological parent, the court concluded that "[i]f the Ohio legislature had intended the outcome Hess proposes, it could have used the term 'legal parent'. But that was not the language chosen. Instead, the legislature used the adjective 'natural'."[7] Therefore, the intent of the legislature is to prohibit one biological parent from physically harming the other biological parent.

Q & A: What is a putative parent?

The issue was raised in *State v. Williams*.[8] In that case, appellant disputed parentage of the child and argued that evidence of the child's birth certificate that he is father of the victim's child was hearsay in hearsay and no exception applies.

In overruling appellant's objection, the appellate court relied on RC 3107.01(H) which provides that a '[p]utative father' means a man, including one under age eighteen, who may be a child's father and to whom all of the following apply:

1) He is not married to the child's mother at the time of the child's conception or birth;
2) He has not adopted the child;
3) He has not been determined, prior to the date of the petition to adopt the child is filed, to have a parent and child relationship with the child by a court proceeding pursuant to sections 3111.01 to 3111.18 of the Revised Code. A court proceeding of another state, an administrative agency proceeding * * * * *;
4) He has not acknowledged paternity of the child pursuant to section 3111.21 to 3111.35 of the Revised Code."

The court next reiterated that the statute mandates that the state in a domestic violence case only prove that appellant was the putative father of the victim's child.[9] "Thus, appellant's name on the birth certificate need only stand for the proposition that appellant may be the child's father; it does not need to be proof of the matter asserted. Further, even if we assume that appellant's name on the birth certificate was improperly admitted, appellant's brother testified that appellant is the father of victim's child, the child has appellant's last name, and

[5]Black's Law Dictionary (7th ed.) p 623.

[6]State v. Hess, 2004-Ohio-534, 2004 WL 231481, *1 (Ohio Ct. App. 3d Dist. Seneca County 2004). See also State v. Smith, 2011-Ohio-2346, 2011 WL 1938315 (Ohio Ct. App. 12th Dist. Warren County 2011) (elements of statute met where petitioner testified that appellant was biological father of two year old and appellant testified that he had previously gone to petitioner's residence to see his children).

[7]State v. Hess, 2004-Ohio-534, 2004 WL 231481, *1 (Ohio Ct. App. 3d Dist. Seneca County 2004).

[8]State v. Williams, 2009-Ohio-6967, 2009 WL 5174155 (Ohio Ct. App. 6th Dist. Lucas County 2009).

[9]See also State v. Woods, 2001 WL 1783086 (Ohio Ct. App. 5th Dist. Licking County 2001).

(as will be discussed, infra) appellant informed the 911 operator that she and appellant have a child together."[10]

Q & A: Is the quantum of proof the same for determining a natural parent versus a putative parent?

This issue was touched upon in *State v. Mills*.[11] In that case appellant asserted on appeal that his equal protection rights were violated because the quantum of proof necessary to establish Defendant's status as a putative parent is less than is required to prove that he is a natural parent. Thus, natural and putative parents, though similarly situated, are not treated alike under the statute.

The appellate court was not persuaded by his argument that a mere allegation that defendant is the father would satisfy the putative parent prong but that proof of paternity is needed to demonstrate that defendant is the natural father. The Ross County Court of Appeals held that the victim's testimony that the defendant was the father of her child was legally sufficient to establish that he was the natural father. Therefore, defendant cannot argue that he was treated differently as a putative father.

Q & A: My client wants a civil protection order. She tells me that the batterer and she have never lived together, but that the batterer is the father of her child. We have already obtained an ex parte order. His lawyer tells me that his client denies that he is the father. What proof do I present at the full hearing to show that he is the father?

RC 3113.31 does not indicate whether evidence may be required at the full hearing to demonstrate that the parties have a child in common or what that evidence should be. However, if a victim is unprepared to address the challenge, her status as a family or household member will be undermined. Under the amended statutory provision, however, it is unlikely that a victim would be denied a civil protection order if she could not prove parentage. More likely, if challenged by the respondent, a court would continue the order in effect and refer the matter to the juvenile court for paternity testing or order genetic testing in the domestic relations court.[12]

Under the provisions of RC 3111.02 and RC 3111.03, a male is presumed to be the natural father of a child under certain circumstances. These include:

(1) when the male has acknowledged paternity pursuant to RC 2105.18;[13] or

(2) when a parent-child relationship has been legally established in the juvenile court.

---

[10] *Williams at *3.*

[11] State v. Mills, 2005-Ohio-2128, 2006 WL 1132543 (Ohio Ct. App. 2d Dist. Montgomery County 2006).

[12] See, e.g., State v. Lynch, 1999 WL 11244, *2 (Ohio Ct. App. 9th Dist. Lorain County 1999) (wherein the court was satisfied with the relationship of the parties based on "uncontroverted testimony that appellant was not only the father of her child, but that he also had acknowledged paternity, thus placing her within the applicable statutory definition").

[13] State v. Hazel, 2018-Ohio-766, 2018 WL 1136978 (Ohio Ct. App. 2d Dist. Clark County 2018), appeal not allowed, 2018-Ohio-3450, 2018 WL 4144393 (Ohio 2018) (defendant used DNA report to show that he was not biological father to argue he was not a family or household member for purposes of enhancement).

Absent these specific court actions, other evidence of parenthood, although not as effective as the above-mentioned legal presumptions, may provide proof of parentage. This includes:

(1) the male has been named as the father of the child on the birth certificate;

(2) the male has signed the child's birth certificate;

(3) the male has volunteered, in writing, to financially support the child;

(4) the male has been court ordered to support the child;

(5) the male has been named as the father for purposes of welfare, Social Security, or the Internal Revenue Service.

Absent a genetic test result or a court order conclusively establishing parentage, these other methods of proof may or may not be sufficient to convince a hearing officer that the individual seeking the order is a family or household member entitled to protection. Counsel seeking to obtain a civil protection order should still attempt to obtain sufficient circumstantial evidence to satisfy the burden of proof on the issue of parentage should the issue be raised by the respondent or the court at the full hearing.

A similar issue was considered by the Medina County Court of Appeals. In *State v. Mabry*,[14] the defendant argued that he was not the father of the victim's child and, therefore, was not a family or household member for purposes of RC 2919.25. The victim testified on direct examination that the defendant was the father of her child. On cross-examination, however, she was less clear. The court found that the evidence was sufficient to support the conclusion that the parties were the parents of the child. The court also considered the testimony of witnesses that the defendant referred to the child as his son. This case is instructive because it demonstrates the type of evidence a court may consider in evaluating whether the parties have a child in common.

Q & A: Would the civil protection order remain in effect pending resolution of the paternity issue?

Under amended RC 3113.31, this should be the result. The petitioner need only show that the respondent is the natural parent or the putative natural parent of her child. The recent statutory amendment[15] refers only to the sufficiency of the evidence needed to bring a prima facie case. However, there is nothing in the statute that restricts a court from inquiring about the relationship. Therefore, it is incumbent on the petitioner's attorney to have sufficient evidence on hand, should it be needed.

---

[14]State v. Mabry, 1996 WL 577701 (Ohio Ct. App. 9th Dist. Medina County 1996). See also State v. Mills, 2005-Ohio-2128, 2006 WL 1132543 (Ohio Ct. App. 2d Dist. Montgomery County 2006) (affirming trial court's decision that appellant was the natural parent of victim's child; appellant argued that victim's testimony was a mere allegation and that the quantum of proof needed to establish his status as a putative parent is less than that required to proof that he is the natural parent; there, natural versus putative parents, although similarly situated, are not treated alike under the statute. The appellate court was not persuaded by his argument that mere allegation should not be sufficient to prove that appellant was putative father when proof that he was the natural parent required proof of paternity).

[15]1997 S.B. 1, eff. 10-21-97.

The determining factor for the court should always be the nature of the abuse. Rather than dismiss a protection order, the court should maintain the order in effect, at least pending the outcome of genetic testing. So long as provisions for safety are included in any protection order, the court need not grant the petitioner any other remedies if it is subsequently shown that the respondent is not the natural parent of the petitioner's child.

It is unclear whether the legislature intended coverage for individuals under newly amended RC 3113.31(A)(3)(b) for purposes of an ex parte order only or whether coverage continues for the duration of the order, even if the evidence presented at the full hearing suggests that the respondent is not the father.

Q & A: Must a party present formal documentation of paternity in order to meet the family or household member element of the father/child relationship for domestic violence purposes?

According to the Fifth District Court of Appeals, a party does not need to present formal documentation of paternity. In *State v. Davis*,[16] appellant argued that evidence was not presented that he was a family member, to wit: the son of the victim. He asserted that the state failed to present evidence that a father-son relationship between victim and himself had been formally established via Ohio's paternity statutes (see R.C. 3111.01 et seq.) or via a birth certificate.

The appellate court reasoned that the state did not need produce formal documentation of civil paternity in order to meet the family or household member requirement for purposes of the domestic violence statute. Instead, the state can utilize testimonial evidence of the father/son relationship regarding the issue of paternity. In overruling appellant's assignment of error, the appellate court held that "establishing the element of paternity for purposes of a criminal domestic violence prosecution would not impair the future consideration of paternity in a RC 3111 case should the issue duly arise."[17] Since the same family or household members are covered by the civil domestic violence statute, the same reasoning should apply to an R.C. 3113.31 civil protection order action.

In this case, the court also considered the challenge of appellant that no evidence established that father and son lived together. However, testimony established the fact that the victim and the appellant had lived with each other for some period of time, establishing the relationship element of R.C. 2919.25 by "residing or has resided with."

Q & A: Can one person be the putative natural parent of a child for purposes of the domestic violence statute if the mother of that child is already married to someone else?

In *State v. Parish*,[18] defendant and the victim were in a relationship and a child was born to them. The child was given defendant's last

---

[16]State v. Davis, 2014-Ohio-1197, 2014 WL 1340774 (Ohio Ct. App. 5th Dist. Licking County 2014).

[17]State v. Davis, 2014-Ohio-1197, 2014 WL 1340774, ¶ 36 (Ohio Ct. App. 5th Dist. Licking County 2014).

[18]State v. Parish, 2014-Ohio-1410, 2014 WL 1350961 (Ohio Ct. App. 5th Dist.

name and he was in the hospital room when the victim gave birth. However, the victim was married to another man who was incarcerated at the time at the time of the birth. Defendant was convicted and on appeal, he challenged that he was a family or household member of the victim.

At issue was whether the mother was a natural parent of any child of whom defendant was the other natural parent or was the putative other natural parent. Defendant claimed that because the mother was married to another man at the time of the child's birth, he cannot be considered the natural or putative natural parent of the child. The appellate court held that the evidence was sufficient to establish that the victim mother was Parish's family or household member.[19] Had Parish presented evidence that he wasn't the biological father of the child, the ruling may have been different.

Q & A: Is a petitioner eligible for a civil protection order when she is pregnant with respondent's child?[20]

Although no Ohio court has specifically answered this question, dicta in several cases suggests that a pregnant victim would be able to sustain her burden of proof as a family and household member for purposes of obtaining a protection order.[21] Some courts have held that a pregnant woman may obtain a civil protection order because she comes within the purpose and intent of the "child in common" provision of the domestic violence statute.[22] In *Gloria C. v. William C.*,[23] the court held that the mother of an unborn child could petition for and receive a protection order on the child's behalf after her husband punched her in the stomach and threw her to the floor. The child's birth was not a condition precedent to the order's enforcement. The court extended protection to the fetus where the husband was trying to force her to have a spontaneous abortion.

On the other hand, some courts have reluctantly denied standing to obtain civil protection orders to petitioners who were pregnant with the respondents' children. The courts concluded that an unborn child

Stark County 2014).

[19]State v. Parish, 2014-Ohio-1410, 2014 WL 1350961, ¶ 20 (Ohio Ct. App. 5th Dist. Stark County 2014), citing State v. Mills, 2005-Ohio-2128, 2006 WL 1132543 (Ohio Ct. App. 2d Dist. Montgomery County 2006).

[20]See also Text 2:5.

[21]See State v. Wallace, 2006-Ohio-5819, 2006 WL 3183386 (Ohio Ct. App. 9th Dist. Lorain County 2006) (referencing the appellee's pregnancy to support cohabitation for purposes of domestic violence); State v. Mauldin, 2010-Ohio-4192, 2010 WL 3482689 (Ohio Ct. App. 7th Dist. Mahoning County 2010) (noting that the victim's belief that she was pregnant with defendant's child was evidence of conjugal relations and suggesting that a pregnant victim of domestic violence clearly demonstrates consortium for purposes of cohabitation); see also Smith v. Martin, 2009-Ohio-3440, 2009 WL 2028403 (Ohio Ct. App. 10th Dist. Franklin County 2009) (that petitioner was pregnant by her boyfriend was not considered an issue by the courts for purposes of obtaining a CPO); State v. Maple, 2011-Ohio-1516, 2011 WL 1138387 (Ohio Ct. App. 9th Dist. Summit County 2011) (that victim was pregnant reinforced elements of cohabitation for purposes of domestic violence); State v. Gomez, 2011-Ohio-5475, 2011 WL 5067230 (Ohio Ct. App. 9th Dist. Summit County 2011) (pregnancy reinforced elements of cohabitation).

[22]RC 3113.31(A)(4).

[23]Gloria C. v. William C., 124 Misc. 2d 313, 476 N.Y.S.2d 991 (Fam. Ct. 1984).

was not a child within the meaning of the domestic violence statutes. However, in each case, the court recognized that this interpretation left a dangerous gap in the statute.[24]

Where there is a continuing relationship between the parents of an unborn child in common, there is a continuing risk of abuse. The most effective way to address this oversight is to amend the language of the statute. Such a statutory change would result in the ability to more fully reach the types of relationships where violence occurs and would prevent victims of abuse from falling through statutory cracks.[25]

In *Gallagher v. Staszewski*,[26] the Connecticut Superior Court dismissed a relief from abuse application. Because of threats of violence, the petitioner requested a protection order, claiming that the respondent was the father of petitioner's unborn child. Her claim that she and the respondent were persons with an unborn child in common and, therefore, that she was entitled to protection under the statute was rejected by the court. The court determined that the word "child" did not "encompass[] the fetus allegedly being carried by" petitioner and that the parties were not a family in any meaningful sense.[27]

This case is significant for legal practitioners in the state of Ohio because Connecticut's civil protection order statute is similar in scope to Ohio's. Moreover, it underscores the problem of providing sufficient proof of the family or household member relationship to the court.

Q & A: If the victim and the offender have a child in common but the victim is married to someone else at the time of the birth, are they still "family or household members" protected under RC 3113.31(A)(3)(b)?

One Ohio court summarily addressed this issue. In *State v. Wright*,[28] the defendant fathered the petitioner's child. He was subsequently found guilty of violating the protection order. On appeal, the defendant argued that he and the petitioner were not family members as defined by the statute. Although he is the biological father of the petitioner's child, she was married to another man at the time of the child's birth, and the child's birth certificate lists her husband, not the defendant, as the father.

Appellant's assignments of error did not address whether or not the parties should be considered family members under the domestic violence laws. His appeal focused in part on the petitioner's credibility. He claimed that, because the petitioner provided incorrect informa-

---

[24]Woodin v. Rasmussen, 455 N.W.2d 535 (Minn. Ct. App. 1990); Gina C v. Stephen F, 150 Misc. 2d 459, 576 N.Y.S.2d 776 (Fam. Ct. 1991).

[25]See Angela Brown, Violence Against Women: Relevance for Medical Practitioners, 267 JAMA 3184–89 (1992); Evan Stark & Anne E. Flitcraft, Women Battering, Child Abuse and Social Heredity: What is the Relationship? Marital Violence 147 (N. Johnson ed. 1985); A. Henton et al., Battered and Pregnant, 77 Am. J. Pub. Health 1337–39 (1987); Richard Gelles, Violence and Pregnancy: A Note on the Extent of the Problem and Needed Services, Family Coordinator 81–86 (1975).

[26]Gallagher v. Staszewski, 15 Conn. L. Rptr. 205, 1995 WL 500563 (Conn. Super. Ct. 1995).

[27]Gallagher v. Staszewski, 15 Conn. L. Rptr. 205, 1995 WL 500563, *2 (Conn. Super. Ct. 1995).

[28]State v. Wright, 1998 WL 542697 (Ohio Ct. App. 10th Dist. Franklin County 1998).

tion on the child's birth certificate, she was not a credible witness. Although the appellate court acknowledged the statutory presumption of parentage under RC 3111.03(A)(1) because of the petitioner's marriage to another, the court refused to reverse the defendant's conviction on that basis.

Where the respondent admits that he is the father of the petitioner's child, that admission should rebut the statutory presumption of paternity. Absent that, genetic testing and the establishment of paternity may be necessary to overcome the statutory presumption. If that is the case, it may be some time before a victim in this situation is able to request a civil protection order.

Q & A: Does a terminated pregnancy in common with the batterer qualify an individual for protection under the domestic violence statutes?

No Ohio court has addressed this issue. However, a New Jersey appellate court considered it in *Croswell v. Shenouda*.[29] In that case, the parties never resided together. The court determined that a prior terminated pregnancy does not qualify the parties as persons having a child in common, even though the defendant admitted paternity. The court added that "even if plaintiff were currently pregnant, this court would not be willing to hold, without clear evidence of such an intent, that by using the word 'child' the legislature intended to include a pregnancy."[30]

Based on case law in other jurisdictions and pending New Jersey legislation, the court determined that the legislature did not intend for persons who only share a common pregnancy to be included in the definition of "victim of domestic violence." "This means, a fortiori, and I so hold, that the Act does not cover persons who shared a pregnancy in the past which was never brought to term."[31]

§ 10:8 Relationships covered—Parents and children

Q & A: Does the statute contemplate a specific time frame within which parents and children must reside?[1]

Few Ohio courts have addressed the relationship between parents and children and the application of either RC 3113.31(A)(3)(a)(ii), RC 3113.31(A)(3)(a)(iii), RC 2919.25(E)(1)(a)(ii), or RC 2919.25(E)(1)(a)(iii) to that relationship. However, at least two Ohio jurisdictions have determined that the time frame provisions for "person living as a spouse" do not apply to parents and children.

For example, in *State v. Mrus*,[2] the Trumbull County Appellate

[29]Croswell v. Shenouda, 275 N.J. Super. 614, 646 A.2d 1140 (Ch. Div. 1994).

[30]Croswell v. Shenouda, 275 N.J. Super. 614, 620, 646 A.2d 1140 (Ch. Div. 1994). But see People v. Ward, 62 Cal. App. 4th 122, 72 Cal. Rptr. 2d 531 (4th Dist. 1998) (discussing application of domestic violence statute to a pregnant victim).

[31]Croswell v. Shenouda, 275 N.J. Super. 614, 622, 646 A.2d 1140 (Ch. Div. 1994).

[Section 10:8]

[1]See also § 10:4, Nature of the relationships covered—Terminology—"Is residing with" and "has resided with?"

[2]State v. Mrus, 71 Ohio App. 3d 828, 595 N.E.2d 460 (11th Dist. Trumbull County 1991) (overruled by, State v. James, 1997 WL 269139 (Ohio Ct. App. 11th

Court determined that a time requirement of "has resided" in the domestic violence statute was not a material element of the offense of domestic violence. In *Mrus*, the defendant had lived with a woman many years earlier and had a child with her. The defendant came to the home where the mother and daughter resided and physically abused the daughter when she would not permit him to speak with her mother. The daughter subsequently filed a criminal complaint.

The issue on appeal was whether the "has resided" requirement applied to the defendant. The court found that the defendant and his daughter had resided together years before and that "in the portion of the statute that applies to a child of the offender, RC 2919.25(E)(1)(b), there is no specification as to when the child must have resided in the household of the offender."[3] The court went on to differentiate between RC 2919.25(E)(1)(b) and RC 2919.25(E)(2), which does provide a duration date for cohabitation, concluding that "it is apparent that the legislature did not intend to specify a time period during which any other class of persons must have resided in the household of the offender in order to find the offender guilty of domestic violence involving a member of such a class."[4]

Likewise, in *State v. Saltsman*,[5] the defendant argued that the Ohio legislature did not intend to apply the offense of domestic violence to an act occurring between a parent and child merely because they had resided together in the past. The defendant relied on the definition of "person living as a spouse" to buttress his argument. The Montgomery County Court of Appeals determined that "this definitional section has no application to the relationship of parent and child for purposes of the Domestic Violence statute."[6] Even if the provision did apply, the

---

Dist. Portage County 1997)) and (overruled by, State v. Fleming, 1997 WL 269141 (Ohio Ct. App. 11th Dist. Portage County 1997)) and (abrogated by, State v. Uher, 1997 WL 269407 (Ohio Ct. App. 11th Dist. Portage County 1997)) and (abrogated by, State v. Wyand, 1997 WL 269143 (Ohio Ct. App. 11th Dist. Portage County 1997)) and (overruled by, State v. Musick, 119 Ohio App. 3d 361, 695 N.E.2d 317 (11th Dist. Portage County 1997)).

[3]State v. Mrus, 71 Ohio App. 3d 828, 831, 595 N.E.2d 460 (11th Dist. Trumbull County 1991) (overruled by, State v. James, 1997 WL 269139 (Ohio Ct. App. 11th Dist. Portage County 1997)) and (overruled by, State v. Fleming, 1997 WL 269141 (Ohio Ct. App. 11th Dist. Portage County 1997)) and (abrogated by, State v. Uher, 1997 WL 269407 (Ohio Ct. App. 11th Dist. Portage County 1997)) and (abrogated by, State v. Wyand, 1997 WL 269143 (Ohio Ct. App. 11th Dist. Portage County 1997)) and (overruled by, State v. Musick, 119 Ohio App. 3d 361, 695 N.E.2d 317 (11th Dist. Portage County 1997)).

[4]State v. Mrus, 71 Ohio App. 3d 828, 831, 595 N.E.2d 460 (11th Dist. Trumbull County 1991) (overruled by, State v. James, 1997 WL 269139 (Ohio Ct. App. 11th Dist. Portage County 1997)) and (overruled by, State v. Fleming, 1997 WL 269141 (Ohio Ct. App. 11th Dist. Portage County 1997)) and (abrogated by, State v. Uher, 1997 WL 269407 (Ohio Ct. App. 11th Dist. Portage County 1997)) and (abrogated by, State v. Wyand, 1997 WL 269143 (Ohio Ct. App. 11th Dist. Portage County 1997)) and (overruled by, State v. Musick, 119 Ohio App. 3d 361, 695 N.E.2d 317 (11th Dist. Portage County 1997)).

[5]State v. Saltsman, 1997 WL 779119 (Ohio Ct. App. 2d Dist. Montgomery County 1997); see also State v. Poling, 1998 WL 255574 (Ohio Ct. App. 3d Dist. Shelby County 1998).

[6]State v. Saltsman, 1997 WL 779119, *1 (Ohio Ct. App. 2d Dist. Montgomery County 1997).

parties lived together in the requisite time period, which, in effect, rendered the defendant's argument moot.

The legal reasoning of *Saltsman* can be applied to the civil domestic violence statute.[7] For example, where a respondent argues that he/she no longer lives with the child or is only a visiting parent, the petitioner can follow the legal reasoning of *Mrus* and *Saltsman* to support the position that the statute does not require a specific duration of time within which parents and children must have resided together in order for the statute to apply.[8] More importantly, the holding of *Saltsman* can be used to reinforce an attorney's argument that, except in the case of a "person living as a spouse," the legislature did not intend for there to be any time period for other classes of individuals who have resided with the offender/respondent in the past.

Q & A: In order for the domestic violence statutes to apply, must the parent and child reside together at some point in time?

Several Ohio courts have addressed this issue. For example, in *State v. Jorden*,[9] the defendant argued that because he and his daughter were not family or household members as set forth in the statute, his conviction for domestic violence must be reversed as it applied to his daughter. In that case, no evidence was presented to demonstrate that defendant had ever lived with either the mother of his child or his daughter, although evidence was presented regarding the fact that he and the child's mother were the minor child's natural parents. The Hamilton County Appellate Court noted that RC 2919.25(E)(1)(b) covers people who have never lived together but who have a child in common. Therefore, the child's mother was considered a protected family member under the domestic violence statute. However, the court stated that a different provision of the statute applied to a child of the parties. Pursuant to RC 2919.25(E)(1)(a)(ii), ". . . the child of an offender is a 'family or household member' only if the child and the offender currently reside together or have resided together in the past."[10] Accordingly, the judgment was reversed.

So long as the parent and child lived together at some point in time, the child is a family or household member of the relationship. To that

---

[7]See RC 3113.31(A)(3)(b).

[8]See also Maglionico v. Maglionico, 2001-Ohio-8901, 2001 WL 1401978 (Ohio Ct. App. 11th Dist. Portage County 2001); Ross v. Ross, 2006-Ohio-5274, 2006 WL 2846327 (Ohio Ct. App. 4th Dist. Ross County 2006) (noting that the child meets the definition of family or household member because she is appellant's daughter and although the child's mother was the residential parent, the child had resided with appellant in the past).

[9]State v. Jorden, 134 Ohio App. 3d 131, 730 N.E.2d 447 (1st Dist. Hamilton County 1999). See also State v. Gibson, 2005-Ohio-1495, 2005 WL 730059 (Ohio Ct. App. 8th Dist. Cuyahoga County 2005); State v. Sims, 169 Ohio App. 3d 579, 2006-Ohio-6285, 863 N.E.2d 1110 (1st Dist. Hamilton County 2006); E. Cleveland v. Perkins, 2009-Ohio-2131, 2009 WL 1244154 (Ohio Ct. App. 8th Dist. Cuyahoga County 2009) (differentiating between the everyday meaning of a biological child under which a child may qualify as a protected party and the narrower definition of family or household member set forth in RC 3113.31 as being a child who resides or has resided with the offender).

[10]State v. Jorden, 134 Ohio App. 3d 131, 137, 730 N.E.2d 447 (1st Dist. Hamilton County 1999).

end, the protections of the domestic violence law would extend to that relationship. Since both RC 2919.25 and RC 3113.31 contain identical provisions relative to protected individuals, a similar analysis would apply in the civil context. It is important to note that the court did not specify a time duration within which parents and their children are required to reside together.

Q & A: Who are parents for purposes of RC 3113.31(A)(3)?

There are no appellate decisions addressing this issue in the context of the civil domestic violence statute. Since the same family or household members are covered under the civil and criminal domestic violence statutes, decisions rendered under RC 2919.25 can be examined. Black's Law Dictionary defines "parent" as:

> The lawful father or mother of a person. In common and ordinary usage the word comprehends much more than mere fact of who was responsible for child's conception and birth and is commonly understood to describe and refer to . . . persons who share mutual love and affection with a child and who supply child support and maintenance, instruction, discipline and guidance.[11]

In the context of a statute, *Black's Law Dictionary* defines "parent" to include:

> (1) either the natural father or the natural mother . . . (2) either the adoptive father or the adoptive mother . . . (3) the natural mother of an illegitimate child . . . (4) a child's putative blood parent who has expressly acknowledged paternity . . . (5) any individual or agency whose status as guardian of the person of the child has been established by judicial decree.[12]

A person "in loco parentis" is defined as one who "undertakes care and control of another in absence of such supervision by latter's natural parents and in absence of formal legal approval, and is temporary in character and is not to be likened to an adoption which is permanent."[13]

Against this backdrop, an examination of the cases reveals that there must be some type of legal relationship of the parent toward the child. For example, in *State v. Harris*,[14] the defendant challenged his conviction for domestic violence under RC 2919.25.[15] The defendant argued that the person he was convicted of harming did not qualify as

---

[11]Black's Law Dictionary (6th ed.) p 1114 (citation omitted).

[12]Black's Law Dictionary (6th ed.) p 1114.

[13]Black's Law Dictionary (6th ed.) p 787 (citation omitted); see also State v. Noggle, 67 Ohio St. 3d 31, 1993-Ohio-189, 615 N.E.2d 1040, 83 Ed. Law Rep. 720 (1993); Evans v. Ohio State Univ., 112 Ohio App. 3d 724, 680 N.E.2d 161, 118 Ed. Law Rep. 1104 (10th Dist. Franklin County 1996); Glancy v. Spradley, 2012-Ohio-4224, 2012 WL 4074986 (Ohio Ct. App. 12th Dist. Butler County 2012) (Upholding denial of CPO and finding that mother's live-in boyfriend has standing as a parent because he assumed the same duties as a guardian or custodian. Testimony was presented that mother's boyfriend has raised the child as a co-primary caregiver and that they share primary duties of caring for child including bathing her, making sure she goes to school, feeding her and raising her to be a well adjusted young lady.).

[14]State v. Harris, 109 Ohio App. 3d 873, 673 N.E.2d 237 (1st Dist. Hamilton County 1996).

[15]The definition of "family or household member" is identical under RC 2919.25 and RC 3113.31.

a family or household member under the statute. The defendant had struck Marie Dodds, the woman who had raised him since the age of three days. The appellate court reasoned that:

> Although Dodds raised Harris, she was not his natural, or adoptive parent, or his parent through affinity, or related to him in any other legal manner. At most, Dodds was a person who had once stood in loco parentis to Harris. The legislature could certainly have included an in loco parentis relationship in the statute, as it did in RC 2919.22 (endangering children) and RC 2907.03 (sexual battery), though even if it had, the victim here still may not have qualified, since that particular relationship was over.[16]

However, the *Harris* court left open the question of whether a person who is related in a legal manner may be included within the purview of the statute. For example, individuals who act as legal guardians over others may be afforded protection under the domestic violence statutes. That the guardian relationship is a legal relationship under RC 2111.02, and is included within the definition of parent, would suggest that coverage may be extended to guardians in the context of domestic violence.[17] The court in *Harris* found that adoptive parents are covered within the statutory framework of the domestic violence statute.

Q & A: Are foster parents protected parties under Ohio's domestic violence statute?

The term "foster parent" is defined as "[o]ne who has performed the duties of a parent to the child of another by rearing the child as his own child."[18] A "foster child" is defined as a [c]hild whose care, comfort, education and upbringing has been left to persons other than his natural parents."[19]

Several courts have rejected arguments that foster parents qualify as "parents" for purposes of coverage under the domestic violence statute. For example, in *In re Whitley*,[20] a foster child was found delinquent by reason of felony domestic violence. The complaint was subsequently amended to alleged delinquency by reason of assault. The relevant trial court issue was whether the child was a member of the victim's family or household. The trial court found that a foster parent does not fall within the scope of the domestic violence statute. The case was appealed on other grounds. But it is significant that the Stark County Court of Appeals did not address the legal impact of this finding.

---

[16] State v. Harris, 109 Ohio App. 3d 873, 876, 673 N.E.2d 237 (1st Dist. Hamilton County 1996).

[17] But see City of Cleveland v. Cleveland Police Patrolman's Ass'n, 2000 WL 573195 (Ohio Ct. App. 8th Dist. Cuyahoga County 2000) (court of appeals declined to address issue of whether cohabitant may also act as parent or guardian or was similarly situated to parent or guardian when he abused girlfriend's children).

[18] Black's Law Dictionary, 5th Ed. 1979.

[19] Black's at 590; see also In re Adoption of Huitzil, 29 Ohio App. 3d 222, 504 N.E.2d 1173 (12th Dist. Butler County 1985).

[20] In Matter of Whitley, 1996 WL 488806 (Ohio Ct. App. 5th Dist. Stark County 1996).

In *State v. Wickard*,[21] appellant was convicted of assault for striking his "foster child." On appeal, he argued that he should have been charged with domestic violence and not assault. In affirming the trial court, the Hancock County Court of Appeals found that a "foster child" did not fit within the definition of "family or household member.

However, the Ohio General Assembly recently passed HB 10,[22] which broadened the definition of family and household member to include "foster parents."[23] Therefore the foster parent-child relationship is now a protected class of persons under Ohio's domestic violence law.

Q & A: Can a stepchild obtain a civil protection order against a stepparent?

At least one Ohio court answered this in the affirmative. In *Coma v. Kellogg*,[24] a stepchild requested a civil protection order because of an act of domestic violence committed against her by her stepfather. At the full hearing on the protection order, the magistrate dismissed the action, holding that the appellant was not a family or household member within the meaning of RC 3113.31. The stepdaughter appealed the decision of the trial court.

The evidence demonstrated that the parties are stepdaughter and stepfather. Although they had not resided together in nine years, they had previously resided in the same household. The Columbiana County Appellate Court relied on the Ohio Supreme Court's holdings in *Felton v. Felton*[25] and *State v. Williams*[26] for instruction and clarification of the intent of the domestic violence statute. The court stated that

> [t]he Ohio Supreme Court determined that the General Assembly clearly believed that an assault or attempted assault involving a family or household member deserved greater protection than an assault upon a stranger and concluded that "the offense of domestic violence . . . arises out of the relationship of the parties rather than their exact living circumstances."[27]

Holding that a civil protection order should have been granted, the appellate court reversed the trial court decision. The appellate court rejected the argument that, because the parties did not reside in the same household at the time of the incident, they were prohibited from being considered family or household members.[28] Moreover, the parties' relationship falls within the meaning of family or household

[21]State v. Wickard, 2006-Ohio-6088, 2006 WL 3350772 (Ohio Ct. App. 3d Dist. Hancock County 2006).

[22]HB 10, Ohio General Assembly, eff. 6-17-2010.

[23]See RC 3113.31(A)(3)(a)(ii).

[24]Coma v. Kellogg, 1999 WL 135294 (Ohio Ct. App. 7th Dist. Columbiana County 1999).

[25]Felton v. Felton, 79 Ohio St. 3d 34, 1997-Ohio-302, 679 N.E.2d 672 (1997).

[26]State v. Williams, 79 Ohio St. 3d 459, 1997-Ohio-79, 683 N.E.2d 1126 (1997).

[27]Coma v. Kellogg, 1999 WL 135294, *3 (Ohio Ct. App. 7th Dist. Columbiana County 1999) (quoting State v. Williams, 79 Ohio St. 3d 459, 464, 1997-Ohio-79, 683 N.E.2d 1126 (1997)).

[28]See also State v. Poling, 1998 WL 255574 (Ohio Ct. App. 3d Dist. Shelby County 1998) (Court found that son who no longer lived with his father (the offender) was a

member as defined in RC 3113.31(A)(3)(a)(ii)—they were related by affinity.[29] Of importance is that the parties resided together at some point in time.[30]

Q & A Does the death of a stepchild's natural parent extinguish the bond between the stepchild and his/her stepparent?

No court has addressed this issue. Those courts that have addressed the issue of stepfamilies[31] have not inquired as to whether the parents are divorced or deceased. However, the common thread in those cases is that the parties resided together or resided together at some point in time. The relationship should survive the death of the natural parent if that residence criterion is met.

The holding in *State v. Williams*[32] also bolsters this conclusion. That the legislature enacted the domestic violence statutes to authorize courts to issue protection orders designed to ensure safety and protection is pivotal to any analysis. Both *Williams* and *Felton*[33] suggest an expansion of the definition of "family and household member" contained in the domestic violence statutes. Under some circumstances, definitions must be broadened and protection must be accorded to these family or household members.

Q & A: Does the statute authorize a "foster child" to seek a civil protection order against his or her foster parent?

Cases such as *In Matter of Whitley*,[34] and *State v. Wickard*,[35] are illustrative of an apparent distinction made between a "parent" and a "foster parent" and "child" and "foster child" for purposes of determining coverage for those protected family or household members contemplated by Ohio's domestic violence statutes. In these cases, the courts of appeals determined that neither the "foster parent" nor the "foster child" qualifies as part of the protected relationship.

RC 3113.31 was recently expanded to provide protection to "foster

---

family member as contemplated by the domestic violence statute. The fact that they resided together in the past was crucial to the court's analysis.).

[29]See also State v. Wilhelm, 1996 WL 447957, *3 (Ohio Ct. App. 4th Dist. Ross County 1996) (holding that a family or household member includes a child of another person related by affinity to the offender and pointing out that "[the victim] is appellant's stepson and thus clearly constitutes a 'family or household member' for purposes of [the domestic violence] statute").

[30]See Evans v. Evans, 599 So. 2d 205 (Fla. 2d DCA 1992) (holding that stepmother lacked standing to bring action for protection order because the parties never lived together).

[31]See, e.g., State v. Scott, 1999 WL 126933 (Ohio Ct. App. 7th Dist. Belmont County 1999) (overruled by, State v. Alvey, 2003-Ohio-7006, 2003 WL 22997277 (Ohio Ct. App. 7th Dist. Belmont County 2003))(overruling court finding is no longer sufficient for the state to rely merely upon the fact that the victim and offender are related to prove domestic violence); Coma v. Kellogg, 1999 WL 135294 (Ohio Ct. App. 7th Dist. Columbiana County 1999).

[32]State v. Williams, 79 Ohio St. 3d 459, 1997-Ohio-79, 683 N.E.2d 1126 (1997).

[33]Felton v. Felton, 79 Ohio St. 3d 34, 1997-Ohio-302, 679 N.E.2d 672 (1997).

[34]In Matter of Whitley, 1996 WL 488806 (Ohio Ct. App. 5th Dist. Stark County 1996).

[35]State v. Wickard, 2006-Ohio-6088, 2006 WL 3350772 (Ohio Ct. App. 3d Dist. Hancock County 2006). See also In re N.M., 2018-Ohio-1099, 2018 WL 1445738 (Ohio Ct. App. 8th Dist. Cuyahoga County 2018) (noting that a foster parent obtained a civil protection order against her foster child).

parents."[36] As written, family or household members now include any of the following who is residing or has resided with the respondent, to wit: a parent, *foster parent* or child of the respondent or another person related by consanguinity or affinity. [emphasis added.] Clearly then, a "foster parent" may now seek protection from a respondent who is that "foster parent's" "foster child."

However, it is not as clear whether those same protections extend to "foster children." Does the inclusion of "foster parent" in the statute imply the inclusion of "foster child?" Can a "foster child" seek protection against the "foster parent?"

A review of the case law indicates a reliance on Black's Law Dictionary to provide an acceptable definition of both a "foster parent" and a "foster child." A "foster parent" is defined as "one who has preformed the duties of a parent to the child of another by rearing the child as his own child" and a "foster child" is defined as a "child whose care, comfort, education and upbringing has been left to persons other than his natural parents.[37]

Under this definition, a "foster child" is a "child" for purposes of the relationship between him/her and his/her foster parent. The nature of the child-foster parent relationship is similar to that of a child-parent relationship except for the biological fact that the foster parent did not physically beget the foster child.[38] Similarly, a "foster child" should be a "child" for purposes of his relationship vis a vis the domestic violence statute.

It is not logical to separate the interrelated nature of the child-foster parent relationship and find that the domestic violence statute only contemplated inclusion of a "foster parent." Ignoring the "child" severs that relationship. A "foster parent" does not have a relationship with a respondent. He/She has that relationship with a "child." Because that "foster child" is a "child" for purposes of the child-foster parent relationship, that "foster child" qualifies as a "child" for purposes of the domestic violence statute. As such, he or she may seek protection as a family or household member against his/her "foster parent."

Q & A: Can a petitioner seek protection for her unborn child?

One Ohio court has recently addressed this issue. In *Smith v. Martin*,[39] petitioner requested that her CPO be modified to protect her unborn child. The trial court denied extending coverage to an unborn child.

On appeal, the appellant argued that RC 3113.31 should be expanded to provide coverage to a viable fetus. Such an expansion of the family or household member definition would advance the safety and protection of family and household members.[40]

The Franklin County Court of Appeals determined that a CPO for a

---

[36]RC 3113.31(A)(1)(a)(ii).

[37]Black's Law Dictionary, page 590 (5th Ed. 1979).

[38]In re Adoption of Huitzil, 29 Ohio App. 3d 222, 504 N.E.2d 1173, 1175 (12th Dist. Butler County 1985).

[39]Smith v. Martin, 2009-Ohio-3440, 2009 WL 2028403 (Ohio Ct. App. 10th Dist. Franklin County 2009).

[40]*Smith at *2.*

respondent to stay away from a pregnant petitioner necessarily protects the unborn child to the same extent as it protects the petitioner. However, the appellate court declined to expand the statute to include the unborn child, holding that "[u]nder the plain language of RC 3113.31, a viable fetus is outside the statutory definition of persons entitled to seek relief."[41]

When it was argued that a newborn would be unprotected if separated from the mother and that it would be a hardship for a new mother to return to court to obtain a CPO soon after the birth, the appellate court stated that "[h]owever, until such time as the legislature sees fit to grant such protection to an unborn, we conclude that the court made an order that protected the child in the only effective way available, absent a request for prospective protection on the child's birth.[42] The refusal to grant additional relief by including the unborn child is not reversible error.

Q & A: May a parent obtain a civil protection order against his or her child?[43]

Over the past 25 years, many Ohio domestic relations courts have granted civil protection orders to parents against their children. This has often been in the context of parents seeking protection against their *adult*children. There is no question that parents can obtain protection orders against adult children.

Where the child is a minor under the age of 18, the juvenile court has exclusive jurisdiction to issue and enforce a civil protection order. [R.C. 3113.31(A)(2); see also §§ 20:1 et seq.] Attorneys requesting civil protection orders on behalf of parents against their minor children should consider several factors. First, the age of the child is important. The older the child is, the more likely it is that the court would be willing to issue such an order. Younger children and children who a court determines may not have an understanding of the proceedings would be unlikely respondents.

Second, the nature of the violent act is a significant factor. The more violent the incident, the more an act of violence is a repeated behavior by the child towards the parent and the more the violence has escalated in severity and frequency over time, the more likely a parent is to persuade a court to grant the protection order.

The relief requested will definitely have an impact on both the family and the court. A court will be more likely to grant a parent a protection order that is designed to prevent the child from abusing, threatening and beating that parent or other family members. On the other hand, "no contact" provisions and provisions ordering the offending child to vacate the residence such as are set forth in Sup. R. Form 10.05-B through 10.05-E are granted under more limited

---

[41]*Smith at *2*; but see Hofstetter and John, Shielding Ohio's Newborns: Defending a Broad Interpretation of "Child" within the Meaning of O.R.C. 3113.31, 58 Clev. St. L. Rev. 717 (2010) (arguing that "viable fetuses" should be viewed as children within the meaning of RC 3113.31).

[42]*Smith at *3.*

[43]See also RC 2903.214, RC 2903.213, RC 2903.211. RC 2903.211(B)(2)(d) contemplates the filing of stalking protection orders on behalf of minors and where the respondent is also a minor; the same logic should hold true.

circumstances. Because these more expansive provisions effectively terminate the parental bond, courts are reluctant to utilize such broad remedies unless it is clear that there are other living circumstances or placements available to the child.

Finally, the duration of the order must be considered. The shorter the duration of the order, the more likely it is that a court would issue the parent relief.

It is likely that judicial hearing officers would grant civil protection orders to parents whose children are over 14 years old, especially where the parent presents evidence that the parent fears the child or where the parent demonstrates that the child cannot be disciplined by reasonable means.

Q & A: Can a child obtain a civil protection order against a parent?[44]

In *Seibert v. Seibert*,[45] the Crawford County Court of Appeals reversed the trial court and held that a CPO should not have been granted to a 14 year old child against her mother where the child testified that she did not fear her mother. The appellate court disagreed with the magistrate's rationale that the child failed to appreciate the danger because she was a minor and should have been in fear. Although the magistrate found that the minor was not competent to know when to be afraid, there was no evidence presented that the minor was too young or immature to understand the situation. The appellate court held that ". . . without evidence from which to determine that Stephanie's judgment was impaired by her age, this finding is speculative and the judgment based on it is an abuse of discretion."[46]

However, the South Dakota Supreme Court also considered the issue in *Beermann v. Beermann*.[47] In that case, the 14-year-old daughter of divorced parents requested a civil protection order against her father to prevent him from physically abusing her during visits to his home. The trial court determined that the state's domestic abuse law did not apply and suggested that the child seek redress under the child abuse and neglect laws or have the mother modify the father's visitation.

On appeal, the South Dakota Supreme Court stated that the domestic abuse statute authorizes any family or household member to file a petition for a protection order against any other family or household member, noting that the law is not limited to adult family or household members and does not expressly exclude the parent-child relationship. The court then rejected the trial court's ruling that the child's age barred her from filing the action and pointed out that a

---

[44]See Text § 13:11, Court enforcement of civil protection orders—Related substantive concerns, regarding whether a court would enforce a protection order brought by a parent against a child; see also In re Lovell, 226 Mich. App. 84, 572 N.W.2d 44 (1997).

[45]Seibert v. Seibert, 2003-Ohio-3758, 2003 WL 21658309 (Ohio Ct. App. 3d Dist. Crawford County 2003).

[46]Seibert v. Seibert, 2003-Ohio-3758, 2003 WL 21658309, *3 (Ohio Ct. App. 3d Dist. Crawford County 2003).

[47]Beermann v. Beermann, 1997 SD 11, 559 N.W.2d 868 (S.D. 1997).

guardian ad litem could have been appointed, if needed. Rejecting the trial court's alternative options for relief because they lacked the immediacy provided by the domestic abuse law, the Supreme Court remanded the case to the trial court to determine whether abuse occurred and what action is appropriate to protect the child from further abuse.

Because South Dakota's domestic abuse law is similar to Ohio's, the same legal analysis should apply.[48] The South Dakota Supreme Court's decision in *Beermann* is instructive because it provides options such as the appointment of a guardian ad litem. There is no reason to suggest that a similar approach could not be taken in Ohio.

Q & A: Can a parent obtain a CPO on behalf of his/her child against another juvenile?[49]

The statutes clearly provide that parents may file protection orders on behalf of their children.[50] Parents often request protection on behalf of their child when that child is the victim of abuse or threatening behavior at the hands of another family or household member. Since the enactment of RC 2151.34, parents have been seeking protection orders on behalf of their children against other juvenile respondents.[51]

Whether that same parent may do so on behalf of a child who does not want the order depends on several factors such as the ages of the child and the perpetrator, the severity of the abuse and the relationship between the victim and the respondent.[52]

Where the child is young and the abuse is committed by an older family or household member, the court will grant the civil protection order. On the other hand, where the child is older and the perpetrator is a girl/boyfriend who is not liked by the parent, it is less clear, especially when the minor does not agree with his/her parent. If there has been documented evidence of abuse towards the minor it is more likely that the court would grant the CPO.

§ 10:9 Relationships covered—Person living as a spouse[1]

Since the enactment of the domestic violence statutes in 1979, various reviewing courts have grappled with the interpretation of who is a

[48]But see M.A. v. E.A., 388 N.J. Super. 612, 909 A.2d 1168 (App. Div. 2006) (Noting that the parent did not have standing as a guardian to seek a restraining order on behalf of a child because the daughter was not a victim eligible to seek an order under the Prevention of Domestic Violence Act. Definition of victim specifically applied to persons over 18 years or emancipated minors.).

[49]See also §§ 20:1 et seq.

[50]R.C. 3113.31(C); R.C. 2151.34(C).

[51]See §§ 20:1 et seq.

[52]See, e.g., People v. VanGlahn, 189 Misc. 2d 613, 734 N.Y.S.2d 820 (Dist. Ct. 2001) (court denied mother's application for a protection order on behalf of her daughter against her daughter's boyfriend where daughter did not want the order; court held that a criminal court is not the place to determine whether young people on the verge of adulthood should, because of their sexual activity, be banned from seeing each other) see also Text § 20:28.

[Section 10:9]

[1]See also Text § 10:6, Nature of the relationships covered—Terminology—"Cohabit"; Text § 10:10, Relationships covered—Same sex relationships.

covered individual under the statute. For example, in *City of Chillicothe v. Copp*,[2] the defendant argued that RC 2919.25 did not apply to ex-spouses who are not residing together. The Ross County Court of Appeals determined that the defendant's ex-wife was a family or household member because she was a person living as a spouse who "has resided with" the offender. In *City of Columbus v. Cleveland*,[3] the defendant had never been married to the victim, nor was he living with her at the time of the alleged violence. The Franklin County Court of Appeals found that RC 2919.25(E)(2) applies to persons who are presently cohabiting, not persons who have cohabited in the past. That they have children together does not make the parties present cohabitants.[4]

Some of these decisions have been rendered moot by statutory amendment; others are legal aberrations. Some of the legal arguments may be relevant to other cases not yet decided.

RC 3113.31(A)(3)(a)(ii) defines "person living as a spouse" as "a person who is living or has lived with the respondent in a common law marital relationship,[5] who otherwise is cohabiting with the respondent,[6] or who otherwise has cohabited with the respondent within five years prior to the date of the alleged occurrence of the act in question."[7]

Q & A: The victim alleges the parties have lived together for the past two years in a "common law" marital relationship. Can the victim obtain a civil protection order?

Pursuant to law, the status of "common law" marriage was abolished by the Ohio Legislature in 1991.[8] If the parties established their common law marriage prior to October 10, 1991, they would still be considered married by common law. After that date, if it can be established that the couple had "otherwise cohabited" under the terms

[2]City of Chillicothe v. Copp, 1981 WL 6025 (Ohio Ct. App. 4th Dist. Ross County 1981).

[3]City of Columbus v. Cleveland, 1988 WL 101988 (Ohio Ct. App. 10th Dist. Franklin County 1988).

[4]See also State v. Ruland, 1991 WL 70786 (Ohio Ct. App. 11th Dist. Ashtabula County 1991) (finding that "a heightened obligation of tolerance and respect must be placed upon persons who reside together" and noting that the domestic violence statute should extend to those co-occupants unrelated by blood or marriage).

[5]Common law marriage in Ohio was repealed effective 9-10-91. See also Noggle v. Smith, 2005-Ohio-5636, 2005 WL 2727128 (Ohio Ct. App. 5th Dist. Ashland County 2005) (holding oneself as married, while required under the prior legal common law marriage, is not a consideration when the relationship rather than a legal marriage is the determining factor).

[6]See State v. Mullins, 1999 WL 668812 (Ohio Ct. App. 5th Dist. Richland County 1999) (upholding conviction for domestic violence of defendant who shared a residence with his wife and the victim, his lover with whom he had a child and with whom he also lived). See also Noggle v. Smith, 2005-Ohio-5636, 2005 WL 2727128 (Ohio Ct. App. 5th Dist. Ashland County 2005) (evidence that parties acted as common law spouses and cohabited, though not continually, established relationship required for issuance of a CPO).

[7]See also City of Cleveland v. Johnson, 2014-Ohio-4083, 19 N.E.3d 604 (Ohio Ct. App. 8th Dist. Cuyahoga County 2014), as corrected, (Sept. 23, 2014) (finding that the parties need not have to live together at the time of the incident in order to qualify as cohabitants or former cohabitants under the domestic violence statute).

[8]RC 3105.12(B)(4), as amended by 1991 H.B. 32, eff. 10-10-91.

of the statute, regardless of what they believed their marital status to be, they will still be covered by RC 2919.25 and RC 3113.31.[9]

The elements of a valid common law marriage are set forth in RC 3105.12 and the applicable case law. The elements of a common law marriage include: (1) a mutual agreement to marry in praesenti made by parties competent to marry, (2) cohabitation, (3) the parties holding themselves out as husband and wife in the community in which they live, and (4) a reputation as husband and wife in the community in which they live.[10]

Q & A: Is there a length of time that a couple must have lived together to qualify as persons living as spouses?

There are no cases that have raised this issue in the context of a civil protection order. However, the issue has been raised in the criminal arena. Obviously, the length of time that the parties have lived together is not as important as the degree of commitment they share. At least one Ohio court has held that as little as one month is sufficient to establish the existence of the necessary components of a relationship.[11] The court held that the evidence was sufficient to establish that the complainant was a "person living as a spouse" of the defendant where it was shown that the couple had lived together for approximately one month, had gone places together, had been intimate on more than one occasion, shared closet space in their joint residence, and the complainant cooked for the defendant and did the defendant's laundry. Similarly, in *State v. Wagner*,[12] the court found that the defendant and the complainant had cohabited in compliance with the statute after a period of joint residency that lasted only two weeks.

The Ohio Supreme Court also reinforced this concept in *State v. Williams*.[13] In that case, the victim testified that she and the defendant were not living together, but that they were going together. She testified that she was staying more nights at his home than at hers. The court found that the parties were cohabitants and held that "the offense of domestic violence, as expressed in RC 2919.25(E)(1)(a) and related statutes, arises out of the relationship of the parties rather than their exact living circumstances."[14]

The Montgomery County Court of Appeals has also reinforced the proposition that there is no minimum duration that a couple must

[9]State v. Pertee, 1995 WL 688800 (Ohio Ct. App. 9th Dist. Wayne County 1995).

[10]Nestor v. Nestor, 15 Ohio St. 3d 143, 472 N.E.2d 1091 (1984); Jolley v. Jolley, 46 Ohio Misc. 40, 75 Ohio Op. 2d 350, 347 N.E.2d 557 (C.P. 1975); see also State v. Allen, 42 Ohio App. 3d 116, 536 N.E.2d 1195 (10th Dist. Franklin County 1988) (discussing common law marriage in the context of RC 2919.25).

[11]City of Cleveland v. Crawford, 1989 WL 113070 (Ohio Ct. App. 8th Dist. Cuyahoga County 1989).

[12]State v. Wagner, 1993 WL 303255 (Ohio Ct. App. 9th Dist. Medina County 1993).

[13]State v. Williams, 79 Ohio St. 3d 459, 1997-Ohio-79, 683 N.E.2d 1126 (1997); but see State v. Humbarger, 149 Ohio App. 3d 30, 2002-Ohio-4160, 775 N.E.2d 585 (3d Dist. Van Wert County 2002) (where three days was insufficient to establish cohabitation).

[14]State v. Williams, 79 Ohio St. 3d 459, 463-64, 1997-Ohio-79, 683 N.E.2d 1126 (1997).

live together before they may seek a protection order or file charges under the domestic violence statutes. In *State v. White*,[15] the defendant testified he did not live with victim and that she only slept at his apartment once or twice, but the victim testified she lived with him and cleaned his room and did his dishes and left some clothes at his home. On appeal the defendant alleged that the victim was not a family or household member under the domestic violence statute.

The appellate court held that based on evidence that the victim lived with defendant for two months when the incident occurred, a jury could reasonably infer that they resided together continuously from the time she moved in with him until the time of the offense.[16] No evidence was presented that the victim and offender maintained separate residences during this time. No authority exists for "the proposition that there is a minimum duration that a couple must live together before they are accorded protection of the domestic violence laws. If there is a minimum, we conclude that the two-month duration supported by Griffeth's testimony exceed it."[17]

Q & A: Is there a maximum amount of time that can pass between the end of the relationship and the occurrence of an alleged violent act for the parties' relationship to still be covered under RC 3113.31?

No Ohio court has specifically addressed this issue. RC 3113.31(A)(4) indicates that an act of domestic violence may occur any time within five years of the parties' cohabitation.[18]

In *Cleveland v. Johnson*,[19] the defendant, convicted of domestic violence, argued that he was not a family or household member within the meaning of the statute because he was not cohabiting with the victim at the time of the offense. He relied on *State v. Williams* and *State v. McGlothan* "to support his argument that, to find a defendant guilty of domestic violence, the prosecution must prove the defendant was living with the victim at the time of the offense."[20]

The appellate court found that the Supreme Court's decisions considered factors relevant to determining whether a couple cohabited

[15]State v. White, 2014-Ohio-1446, 2014 WL 1384082 (Ohio Ct. App. 2d Dist. Montgomery County 2014).

[16]State v. White, 2014-Ohio-1446, 2014 WL 1384082, ¶ 14 (Ohio Ct. App. 2d Dist. Montgomery County 2014); State v. Brown, 2015-Ohio-950, 2015 WL 1138651 (Ohio Ct. App. 11th Dist. Lake County 2015) (although victim lived with defendant for only eight days before the incident, she was a cohabitant as she was in a romantic, intimate relationship and she and defendant shared shelter, food and utilities during this time); State v. Hughes, 2015-Ohio-1173, 2015 WL 1403276 (Ohio Ct. App. 5th Dist. Tuscarawas County 2015) (where parties live together at the time of the incident, the state has no obligation to demonstrate a sharing of familial or financial responsibilities and consortium).

[17]State v. White, 2014-Ohio-1446, 2014 WL 1384082, ¶ 15 (Ohio Ct. App. 2d Dist. Montgomery County 2014).

[18]See State v. Vanderhorst, 2010-Ohio-1856, 2010 WL 1712246 (Ohio Ct. App. 8th Dist. Cuyahoga County 2010) (noting that the parties were still household member even though defendant was removing items from the home at the time of the incident).

[19]City of Cleveland v. Johnson, 2014-Ohio-4083, 19 N.E.3d 604 (Ohio Ct. App. 8th Dist. Cuyahoga County 2014), as corrected, (Sept. 23, 2014).

[20]City of Cleveland v. Johnson, 2014-Ohio-4083, 19 N.E.3d 604, ¶ 13 (Ohio Ct. App. 8th Dist. Cuyahoga County 2014), as corrected, (Sept. 23, 2014).

including evidence of "shared financial responsibilities." Such factor was merely one factor to be considered when deciding whether the victim qualified as a family or household member. The court also noted that the prosecution was only required to prove the elements set forth in the domestic violence statute.

Relying on *McGlothan,* the court acknowledged that the legislature intended "to protect persons from violence by close family members or residents of the same household" and "to offer protections to a wide class of persons."[21] "Accordingly, the legislature extended the protection to victims who have lived with the defendant 'within five years prior to the date of the commission of the act in question.' "[22] That the parties lived together as boyfriend and girlfriend for a year or two and broke up less than a year before the domestic violence incident was sufficient evidence to establish that they were "persons living as a spouse."

However, the New Jersey Superior Court, in *Sperling v. Teplitsky*,[23] determined that former cohabitants who had not lived together in four years were no longer family or household members for purposes of a protection order. In that case, the court held that, where there was a significant passage of time between the end of the parties' relationship and the alleged violent act and there was no evidence of continuing violence or ongoing controlling behavior by the alleged perpetrator, the domestic violence statute does not apply.

Q & A: Are dating relationships or engaged couples covered under RC 3113.31?[24]

Through *State v. Williams*[25] and *State v. McGlothan*,[26] the Supreme Court of Ohio indicated a willingness to expand coverage of the civil and criminal domestic violence statutes to dating relationships. Additionally, the Supreme Court, in *Williams*, noted that a trial court is to make a decision to extend this coverage on a case-by-case basis.

However, neither case suggested that another category of persons was to be included within the statute or that RC 3113.31 applied outside of the family or household member relationship.

In fact, the Supreme Court in *State v. Williams*,[27] focused on a definition of cohabitation and appeared to include certain "dating relationships" so long as it could be determined that there was some degree of commitment between the parties. If a court found this commitment, a petitioner would be able to seek a domestic violence protection order

---

[21]City of Cleveland v. Johnson, 2014-Ohio-4083, 19 N.E.3d 604, ¶ 14 (Ohio Ct. App. 8th Dist. Cuyahoga County 2014); as corrected, (Sept. 23, 2014), quoting State v. Carswell, 114 Ohio St. 3d 210, 2007-Ohio-3723, 871 N.E.2d 547, ¶ 32, ¶ 36 (2007); see also State v. Brown, 2015-Ohio-950, 2015 WL 1138651 (Ohio Ct. App. 11th Dist. Lake County 2015).

[22]City of Cleveland v. Johnson, 2014-Ohio-4083, 19 N.E.3d 604, ¶ 14 (Ohio Ct. App. 8th Dist. Cuyahoga County 2014), as corrected, (Sept. 23, 2014).

[23]Sperling v. Teplitsky, 294 N.J. Super. 312, 683 A.2d 244 (Ch. Div. 1996). But see South v. North, 304 N.J. Super. 104, 698 A.2d 553 (Ch. Div. 1997) (defendant became a de facto member of household because he was a constant presence in the household).

[24]See § 10:6, Cohabitation.

[25]State v. Williams, 79 Ohio St. 3d 459, 1997-Ohio-79, 683 N.E.2d 1126 (1997).

[26]State v. McGlothan, 138 Ohio St. 3d 146, 2014-Ohio-85, 4 N.E.3d 1021 (2014).

[27]State v. Williams, 79 Ohio St. 3d 459, 1997-Ohio-79, 683 N.E.2d 1126 (1997).

as a "person living as a spouse." Additionally, the Supreme Court provided guidance to local courts by suggesting factors that a court might consider regarding financial and familial responsibilities.[28]

Subsequently, the Supreme Court sought to clarify *Williams*[29] in *State v. McGlothan*.[30] by creating a two tiered standard for cohabitation.

Recently, the Ohio General Assembly enacted HB 1 in which the legislature expanded coverage under RC 3113.31 to specifically include dating relationships. A "dating relationship" is defined as a relationship between individuals who have, or have had, a relationship of a romantic or intimate nature. "Dating relationship" does not include a casual acquaintanceship or ordinary fraternization in a business or social context.[31] "Persons with whom the respondent is or was in a dating relationship" means an adult who, at the time of the conduct in question, is in a dating relationship with the respondent who also is an adult or who, within 12 months preceding the conduct in question, has had a dating relationship with the respondent, who is also an adult.[32]

It is clear that the legislature chose to narrow the definition of "dating" to "dating relationships." To have extended protection to those individuals who were merely "dating," would have left an undefined concept even more ambiguous. Not to have included the term "relationship" or specifically delineated that a casual acquaintanceship or ordinary fraternization in a business or social context is not to be included may lead to the circumstance where two people meet for a causal lunch date on only one occasion and then one requests a civil protection order.

In analyzing whether a "dating relationship" exists between the parties, the following questions could be asked: was there a minimal interpersonal bonding; how long did the dating activities continue prior to the acts of domestic violence; what were the nature and frequency of the parties' interactions; what were the parties' ongoing expectations with respect to the relationship, either individually or jointly; and did the parties demonstrate an affirmation of the relationship before others by statement or conduct.[33]

Q & A: Are there any specific procedural statutory mandates relative to dating relationships?

Any person seeking relief must include the following in the petition: an allegation that the respondent engaged in domestic violence against a family or household member or against a person with whom the respondent is or was in a dating relationship including a description of the nature and extent of the domestic violence; the relationship of the respondent to the petitioner and to the victim if other than the

---

[28] State v. Williams, 79 Ohio St. 3d 459, 465, 1997-Ohio-79, 683 N.E.2d 1126 (1997); Text § 10:6.

[29] State v. Williams, 79 Ohio St. 3d 459, 1997-Ohio-79, 683 N.E.2d 1126 (1997).

[30] State v. McGlothan, 138 Ohio St. 3d 146, 2014-Ohio-85, 4 N.E.3d 1021 (2014).

[31] R.C. 3113.31(A)(8).

[32] R.C. 3113.31(A)(9).

[33] See for e.g., Andrews v. Rutherford, 363 N.J. Super. 252, 260, 832 A.2d 379 (Ch. Div. 2003).

petitioner; and the relief requested. If the petitioner is seeking a CPO as a dating adult, that petitioner the petition must include the facts upon which the court may conclude that a dating relationship existed between the person to be protected and the respondent.[34]

This provision is important because a petitioner must include in the petition the specifics of the dating relationship which might and often does include a sexual relationship.

Q & A: What acts satisfy the statute relative to a dating relationship?

Pursuant to RC 3113.31(A)(1)(b), the same acts/conduct for which a CPO is issued for a family or household member is allowable for a person in a dating relationship. This means that a respondent may attempt to cause or recklessly cause bodily injury, place petitioner by threat of force in fear of imminent serious physical harm or commit an act of stalking or aggravated trespass or commit a sexually oriented offense against a family or household member.

Q & A: Can a person get a dating domestic violence temporary protection order (TPO) in the criminal context?

No. There is no criminal equivalency. However, if a respondent violates the dating violence protection order, he or she is subject to the same sanctions set forth in RC 2919.27.[35]

Q & A: Does the juvenile protection order statute permit the issuance of civil protection orders for persons in a dating relationship?

No, the statutory provisions only apply to adults.

Q & A: Is the relief the same as for a family or household member?

No. A petitioner in a dating relationship may only request the following relief: direct the respondent to refrain from abusing, or committing a sexually related offense against the person with whom he or she was in a dating relationship;[36] require either party to seek counseling;[37] require the respondent to refrain from entering the residence, school, business or place of employment of the petitioner;[38] grant other relief that the court considers equitable and fair including, but not limited to, ordering the respondent to permit the use of the motor vehicle by petitioner;[39] require the respondent not remove, damage, hide, harm or dispose of any companion animal owned or possessed by the petitioner;[40] authorize the petitioner to remove a companion animal owned by the petitioner from the possession of respondent;[41]

---

[34] R.C. 3113.31(C)(3).

[35] R.C. 3113.31(L).

[36] R.C. 3113.31(E)(1)(a).

[37] R.C. 3113.31(E)(1)(f).

[38] R.C. 3113.31(E)(1)(g).

[39] R.C. 3113.31(E)(1)(h).

[40] R.C. 3113.31(E)(1)(i).

[41] R.C. 3113.31(E)(1)(j).

and, require a wireless transfer in accordance with sections 3113.45 to 3113.459 of the Revised Code.[42]

Q & A: Are roommates covered under RC 3113.31?

No. Ohio courts have not interpreted RC 3113.31 to include roommates.[43] The intent of the statute is to protect family members and extended family household members from violence in the home. The concept of family relationships is the expected model. Roommates are not considered to be family members, are not related by blood or marriage, are not children or parents of each other, and are not persons living as spouses.[44] Even under *State v. Williams*,[45] roommates are not covered because conjugal relations is a required factor for cohabitation.

The Domestic Relations Court of Montgomery County addressed this issue in *Freeman v. DiFlora*.[46] In that case, the petitioner's husband had invited the respondent, Julie DiFlora, to stay at his and the petitioner's home. It was unclear whether the respondent resided with the petitioner and her husband for only a few days or as long as two weeks. The respondent moved the court to dismiss the petition on the grounds that the petitioner was not a family or household member of the respondent. The petitioner argued that she and the respondent were persons living as spouses.

The issue before the court was whether persons of the same sex who briefly live together without having a romantic relationship are family or household members subject to RC 3113.31. The court held that the parties were not household members within the meaning of RC 3113.31 and that the petitioner was stretching the statutory definition of household members too far. Additionally, the court stated that the parties were not "persons living as spouses," which include former romantic partners but do not include boarders and roomers as they are not cohabiting with each other.

A variety of intimate relationships are covered under RC 3113.31. They include parents, stepparents, grandparents, stepchildren, nieces, aunts, uncles, and other family members living in the household and related to either the victim or the alleged respondent. Those individuals not specifically included are thought to be excluded.[47] In *oore v.*

---

[42]R.C. 3113.31(E)(1)(k); see also § 12.

[43]See also State v. Blackmon, 2012-Ohio-5854, 2012 WL 6139910, ¶ 29 (Ohio Ct. App. 5th Dist. Stark County 2012) (noting that "[t]he domestic violence statute is specifically designed to protect two people who are more than merely roommates, enabling such a victim of assault additional protection. Domestic violence is a crime quite different from a general assault, precisely because of the special intimacy of the parties."). But see Hamilton v. Ali, 350 N.J. Super. 479, 795 A.2d 929 (Ch. Div. 2001) (court upheld order of protection for student who was a household member of college dormitory suitemate).

[44]RC 3113.31.

[45]State v. Williams, 79 Ohio St. 3d 459, 1997-Ohio-79, 683 N.E.2d 1126 (1997).

[46]Freeman v. DiFlora, No. DV-93-86 (C.P., Montgomery, 5-18-93).

[47]But see State v. Williams, 79 Ohio St. 3d 459, 1997-Ohio-79, 683 N.E.2d 1126 (1997), wherein the Court expanded the coverage of the domestic violence statute, at least in theory, to include persons involved in a dating relationship.

City of East Cleveland, Ohio,[48] the United States Supreme Court struck down an East Cleveland zoning ordinance that attempted to restrict extended family members from living together in the same household as unconstitutional under the Fourteenth Amendment Due Process Clause. The Court held that the constitution protects this larger concept of family and clarified that the state can neither lightly deny the choice of individuals to live with extended family members nor force people to live in certain narrowly defined family patterns.

Both the majority opinion and concurrence in *Moore* demonstrate the respect which the state must accord the extended family model. The legal analysis set forth in *Moore* explains why states should not arbitrarily preclude extended family relationships when considering which particular family or household members civil protection order statutes should safeguard. Arguably, the definition of family members embraced by all civil protection order statutes must be equally applicable to all concepts of family.

However, jurisdictions around the country have held that various other family or household relationships, although co-occupants of sorts, are not family or household members in the context of domestic violence. For example, in *O'Kane v. Irvine*,[49] the California Court of Appeals held that sublessees are not cohabitants within the meaning of the domestic violence statute. In that case, the plaintiff sublet a bedroom in a house in which the defendant also sublet a room. They shared some common areas, but there was no friendly or romantic relationship between them; nor were they acquainted with each other prior to subletting the rooms. Under California's statute, "cohabitant" includes the term "household" which has been interpreted to mean "'a collection of persons, whether related or not, who live together as a group or unit of permanent or domestic character . . . who direct their attention toward a common goal consisting of their mutual interests.' "[50]

Prison cellmates are not entitled to protection under Iowa's protection from abuse statute. In *Livingood v. Negrete*,[51] a prisoner sought relief under Iowa's Domestic Abuse Act based on his cellmate's physical abuse and threats. The prisoner argued that he and the cellmate were cohabitants. The Iowa Supreme Court refused to broadly define "cohabitants" as persons merely living together, including those in involuntary living arrangements.

Q & A: GF filed a civil stalking protection order in common pleas court pursuant to R.C. 2903.214. Although she and BF have dated, she doesn't think they are family or household members under the domestic violence statute. At the same time, BF files a domestic violence civil protection order in domestic relations court pursuant to R.C. 3113.31. BF claims the

[48]Moore v. City of East Cleveland, Ohio, 431 U.S. 494, 97 S. Ct. 1932, 52 L. Ed. 2d 531 (1977).

[49]O'Kane v. Irvine, 47 Cal. App. 4th 207, 54 Cal. Rptr. 2d 549 (1st Dist. 1996).

[50]O'Kane v. Irvine, 47 Cal. App. 4th 207, 211, 54 Cal. Rptr. 2d 549 (1st Dist. 1996).

[51]Livingood v. Negrete, 547 N.W.2d 196 (Iowa 1996); see also In re Lovell, 226 Mich. App. 84, 572 N.W.2d 44 (1997) (discussing whether college roommates were family or household members).

parties have lived together and fall within the ambit of the definition of family and household members. Can petitions for a civil stalking protection order and a domestic violence civil protection order be consolidated when the facts arise out of the same incident?

Both statutes are silent as to this specific issue and the provisions of the statutes are not instructive. Clearly, mutual protection order concerns do not apply under this fact scenario. The Rules of Civil Procedure regarding joinder are not instructive because they apply to the consolidation of claims, remedies and individuals, not courts.[52]

It appears that the only way to avoid conflicting civil protection orders is for one of the courts to dismiss the civil protection order for a lack of subject matter jurisdiction and the other court to permit the aggrieved party the opportunity to refile in that court. Then, the proceedings will be consolidated in the one court and the statutory provisions of R.C. 2903.214(E)(3) or 3113.31(E)(4).

Based on the statutory language contained in both statutes, only a family or household member may file a domestic violence civil protection order. Therefore, it would be wise to dismiss the civil protection order issued in domestic relations court so long as it permits that party to refile in common pleas court, where the grant of a civil protection order is not dependent on the parties' relationship. It is probable that the incidents of domestic violence can be subsumed within the definitions contained in R.C. 2903.214.

Q & A: Can a protection order be granted to a victim where the defendant is simultaneously cohabiting in a different location with another?

At least one state court has addressed this issue. In *People v. Moore*,[53] the defendant lived with the victim for several years during which time he abused her. At his trial for the alleged crimes, he alleged that he did not cohabit with her during several of the incidents. The appellate court held that "a defendant may cohabit simultaneously with two or more people in different locations, during the same time frame, if he maintains substantial ongoing relations with each and lives with each for significant periods."[54]

Q & A Can the reasoning of *Williams* be applied to a child abused by the offender, when the child does not reside with the offender for extended periods of time?

According to the Eighth District Court of Appeals, the answer is yes. In *State v. Rivera*,[55] the minor child and victim of the abuse resided with his mother but sometimes spent nights with Rivera, who

---

[52]Civ. R. 18, 19.

[53]People v. Moore, 44 Cal. App. 4th 1323, 52 Cal. Rptr. 2d 256 (1st Dist. 1996), as modified on denial of reh'g, (May 24, 1996); see also State v. Archuletta, 85 Haw. 512, 946 P.2d 620 (Ct. App. 1997).

[54]People v. Moore, 44 Cal. App. 4th 1323, 52 Cal. Rptr. 2d 256 (1st Dist. 1996), as modified on denial of reh'g, (May 24, 1996); see also Farmers Ins. of Columbus, Inc. v. Taylor, 39 Ohio App. 3d 68, 528 N.E.2d 968 (10th Dist. Franklin County 1987) (discussing the concept of dual residency and determining that dual residency is not precluded for insurance purposes).

[55]State v. Rivera, 2013-Ohio-3244, 2013 WL 3877817 (Ohio Ct. App. 8th Dist. Cuyahoga County 2013).

was the father of the child's half-brother. While the minor child did not permanently reside with Rivera, he testified that he stayed with Rivera for several nights at a time. Rivera was convicted of domestic violence against the minor child in the trial court.

On appeal, Rivera claimed that the state failed to prove that the minor victim was a family or household member under R.C. 2919.25 because there was no evidence presented that the child resided with Rivera.

The appellate court first discussed *Williams*[56] and noted that the offense of domestic violence arises out of the relationship of the parties rather than the exact living circumstances of the victim and the perpetrator. As relationships are unique, they must be decided on a case-by-case basis. In that the minor child victim stayed with Rivera, sometimes for extended periods of time, the child and his half brother shared the same biological mother, Rivera is like a father to the victim and calls Rivera "Poppy," and because the child's mother has been previously established as a family member for purposes of prior domestic violence convictions against Rivera, a reasonable trier of fact could conclude that the child is a family member in accordance with the statute.[57]

§ 10:10 Relationships covered—Same-sex relationships[1]

Q & A: Are civil protection orders available only to those involved in heterosexual relationships?

There is nothing in the statute which specifically restricts its application based on the sexual preferences of the parties. Therefore, the protections afforded to heterosexual relationships are equally available to same-sex relationships.[2]

Coverage is provided under that section of the law which defines "family or household member" as, among other things, "a person living as spouse."[3] Although incapable of either a ceremonial or common law marriage, same-sex couples who live together are persons who are "otherwise cohabiting." The legislature has declined to define the term "cohabiting," but numerous definitions for this word are found in the case law.

In determining how the protections of the domestic violence statute are applied to same-sex couples, judges and lawyers have consistently returned to a common theme. The majority of the cases on point suggest that two adults living together in the same household, sharing certain obligations which are equivalent to a spousal type of relation-

---

[56]State v. Williams, 79 Ohio St. 3d 459, 464, 1997-Ohio-79, 683 N.E.2d 1126 (1997).

[57]State v. Rivera, 2013-Ohio-3244, 2013 WL 3877817 (Ohio Ct. App. 8th Dist. Cuyahoga County 2013).

[Section 10:10]

[1]See also Text § 10:6, Nature of the relationships covered—Terminology—"Cohabit"; see also Text § 10:9, Relationships covered—Person living as a spouse.

[2]See, e.g., Moore v. Bentley, 2004-Ohio-5060, 2004 WL 2804785 (Ohio Ct. App. 10th Dist. Franklin County 2004); State v. Wood, 2007-Ohio-6380, 2007 WL 4216959 (Ohio Ct. App. 10th Dist. Franklin County 2007).

[3]RC 3113.31(A)(3)(a)(i), RC 3113.31(A)(4).

ship, is the legal definition of "cohabiting." The application of the definition of "persons living as spouses" to same-sex relationships brings them within the ambit of the protections provided by the statute and reflects the degree of commitment which RC 3113.31 requires.

In *State v. Hadinger*,[4] a case of first impression in Ohio, the court of appeals held that the domestic violence statute provided protection to same-sex couples. The Franklin County Municipal Court dismissed domestic violence charges on the basis that, under the Ohio law, two women cannot be married to one another. The state appealed on the grounds that the definition of "persons living as spouses" should include same-sex couples who are cohabiting.

The appellate court held that "cohabitation means the act of living together."[5] In its ruling, the court stated, "the legislature intended [to] protect[] persons who are cohabiting regardless of their sex. We believe that to read the domestic violence statute otherwise would eviscerate the efforts of the legislature to safeguard, regardless of gender, the rights of victims of domestic violence."[6]

Another court of appeals, in *State v. Linner*,[7] followed the reasoning and expanded the analysis of *Hadinger*. It determined that "cohabiting can generally be defined as living together and functioning as a husband and wife."[8] The most persuasive factors in evaluating the existence of cohabitation as a spouse include whether or not the parties are (1) living together under one roof, (2) sharing expenses and liabilities, (3) owning property together, (4) socializing together as a couple, (5) engaging in a sexual relationship, (6) exchanging vows of commitment, and (7) parenting a child together and/or raising children together. It is apparent from this and other case law definitions that "persons living as spouses" represents the degree of commitment required under the statute.[9]

The *Linner* court also determined that fundamental principles of constitutional law would preclude application of the domestic violence laws only to heterosexuals. A gender-based construction of the statute would render the statute unconstitutional on equal protection grounds. In analyzing this particular issue, the court "construes RC 2919.25(E) so as to avoid an equal protection challenge to the constitutionality of the statute."[10]

There are currently no cases in Ohio which have examined the application of the civil protection order provisions to same-sex relationships. However, the reasoning of the courts in *Hadinger* and

---

[4]State v. Hadinger, 61 Ohio App. 3d 820, 573 N.E.2d 1191 (10th Dist. Franklin County 1991).

[5]State v. Hadinger, 61 Ohio App. 3d 820, 823, 573 N.E.2d 1191 (10th Dist. Franklin County 1991).

[6]State v. Hadinger, 61 Ohio App. 3d 820, 823, 573 N.E.2d 1191 (10th Dist. Franklin County 1991).

[7]State v. Linner, 77 Ohio Misc. 2d 22, 665 N.E.2d 1180 (Mun. Ct. 1996).

[8]State v. Linner, 77 Ohio Misc. 2d 22, 28, 665 N.E.2d 1180 (Mun. Ct. 1996).

[9]See also State v. Yaden, 118 Ohio App. 3d 410, 692 N.E.2d 1097, 71 A.L.R.5th 749 (1st Dist. Hamilton County 1997) (adopting the *Linner* holding as it relates to same-sex couples and broadening the definition of "cohabiting").

[10]State v. Linner, 77 Ohio Misc. 2d 22, 28, 665 N.E.2d 1180 (Mun. Ct. 1996).

Linner establishes a precedent that other courts are likely to follow by extending the same protections found in RC 3113.31 to all of Ohio's citizens, regardless of sexual preference. In fact, *Linner* states that "[t]he statutory language of Ohio's civil domestic violence laws is virtually identical to that of Ohio's criminal domestic violence laws, and both must be applied in the same manner."[11]

Q & A: What does the Marriage Amendment[12] have to do with unmarried heterosexuals and homosexuals and domestic violence?[13]

In November 2004, the voters in Ohio passed Issue 1, a statewide initiative that amended the Ohio Constitution. Called the Marriage Amendment, it provided as follows:

> Only a union between one man and one woman may be a marriage valid in or recognized by this state and its political subdivisions. This state and its political subdivisions shall not create or recognize a legal status for relationships of unmarried individuals that intends to approximate the design, qualities, significance or effects of marriage.[14]

The domestic violence statute protects, among others, "persons living as spouses." "Persons living as spouses" is one of the protected groups of individual relationships covered under Ohio's Domestic Violence Act.[15] The term is further defined in both the civil and criminal statutes as a person who is living or has lived with the respondent/offender in a common law marital relationship, who otherwise is cohabiting with the respondent/offender or who otherwise has cohabited with the respondent/offender within five years prior to the date of the alleged occurrence/commission of the act in question.[16]

It is the second sentence of Ohio's Marriage Amendment that impacted victims of domestic violence. Soon after the Amendment took effect in December 2004, defendants charged with domestic violence in unmarried relationships filed motions to dismiss the domestic violence charges. Dozens of defendants challenged the constitutionality of Ohio's domestic violence laws as applied to unmarried couples. They allege that the use of the term "living as a spouse" violates the state constitution by creating a legal status for unmarried couples that approximates marriage.

The descriptive term "living as a spouse" is used to define cohabiting individuals who are not married or related by blood or marriage. The statute does not define cohabiting but the Ohio Supreme Court in *Williams* advanced a common definition of cohabitation and determined that cohabitation means a sharing of financial or familial responsibilities and consortium.[17] The Supreme Court held that domestic violence arises out of the relationship between the parties based on

---

[11]State v. Linner, 77 Ohio Misc. 2d 22, 25 n.1, 665 N.E.2d 1180 (Mun. Ct. 1996).

[12]Now codified in RC 3101.01(C).

[13]See also Text § 10:6, Nature of the relationships covered—Terminology—"Cohabit."

[14]O. Const. Art. XV, § 11; see also RC 3101.01(C) (clarifying which individuals may marry in this state).

[15]See RC 3113.31(A)(3)(a) and RC 2919.25(F)(1)(a).

[16]RC 3113.31(A)(4) and RC 2919.25(F)(2).

[17]See State v. Williams, 79 Ohio St. 3d 459, 465, 1997-Ohio-79, 683 N.E.2d 1126

these factors and that each case must be decided on a case by case basis.[18] This reinforces that the domestic violence laws are not premised on a legal marital status, but on the facts of a particular intimate relationship.

The question was whether the drafters of the amendment and the voters of Ohio intended the second sentence only to clarify the definition of marriage as between one man and one woman or whether and which unmarried relationships are included within the penumbra of the amendment's prohibition.

Simplistically speaking, it was unclear whether the drafters intended the second sentence to prohibit any legal status for relationships of unmarried individuals that intends to approximate the design, qualities, significance or effect of marriage such as domestic partnerships or civil unions or whether the amendment prohibited all unmarried couples from enjoying public benefits or legal protections for which married couples are eligible.

Q & A: On what legal grounds was the domestic violence statutes challenged?

Between 40 and 50 defendants challenged the constitutionality of the domestic violence statutes. Some trial courts upheld the constitutionality of the domestic violence statute and denied the motions to dismiss.[19] Other trial courts dismissed domestic violence charges after holding that the domestic violence laws were unconstitutional for "persons living as spouses" in light of the Amendment.[20] In those jurisdictions that granted motions to dismiss, some intimate partners were left without legal recourse; in others, the court either amended the charge to assault or prosecutors refiled assault charges.

For example, the trial court in *Burk* amended the charge to assault. The court considered the "plain meaning" of the language as written in both the Amendment and statute and concluded that the domestic violence laws recognized a legal status for the relationships of unmarried individuals that intends to approximate the design, qualities, significance, or effect of marriage by including the term "persons living as spouses." Since the Amendment prohibited the state from either creating or recognizing a legal status for unmarried relationships and,

---

(1997).

[18]State v. Williams, 79 Ohio St. 3d 459, 465, 1997-Ohio-79, 683 N.E.2d 1126 (1997).

[19]See, e.g., City of Cleveland v. Knipp, 2005 WL 1017620 (Ohio Mun. Ct. 2005); State v. Rodgers, 131 Ohio Misc. 2d 1, 2005-Ohio-1730, 827 N.E.2d 872 (C.P. 2005); see also State v. McIntosh, 2005 WL 1940099 (Ohio C.P. 2005), judgment rev'd on other grounds, 2006-Ohio-1815, 2006 WL 925179 (Ohio Ct. App. 2d Dist. Montgomery County 2006), judgment rev'd, 114Ohio St. 3d430, 2007-Ohio-4552, 872 N.E.2d 1212 (2007).

[20]See State v. Burk, 2005 WL 786212 (Ohio C.P. 2005), judgment rev'd, 164 Ohio App. 3d 740, 2005-Ohio-6727, 843 N.E.2d 1254 (8th Dist. Cuyahoga County 2005), judgment aff'd, 114 Ohio St. 3d 430, 2007-Ohio-4552, 872 N.E.2d 1212 (2007); see also City of Cleveland v. Voies, 2005 WL 1940135 (Ohio Mun. Ct. 2005), judgment rev'd on other grounds, 2006-Ohio-815, 2006 WL 440341 (Ohio Ct. App. 8th Dist. Cuyahoga County 2006), judgment aff'd, 114Ohio St. 3d430, 2007-Ohio-4552, 872 N.E.2d 1212 (2007); State v. Carswell, No. CA2005-04-047 (Ohio Ct. App. 12th Dist. Warren County 2005); State v. Dixon, 2005 WL 1940110 (Ohio C.P. 2005), judgment aff'd, 2006-Ohio-1584, 2006 WL 827395 (Ohio Ct. App. 2d Dist. Greene County 2006).

under the principles of statutory construction, the words of both the amendment and the statute must be construed to give effect to the plain meaning of the language therein, the Amendment prohibited the state from recognizing unmarried cohabitants who are living as spouses because cohabitation is a relationship that approximates a marriage.[21]

Other lower court decisions, such as *Carswell, Knipp, Nixon, Rodgers*, and *McIntosh*, concluded that the legislature's intent in enacting the domestic violence statute was to prosecute batterers and protect victims, not to establish a legal status approximating a marriage.

Still, other trial courts held that the domestic violence laws do not give unmarried individuals any special rights, especially those that mimic a legal marriage. An unmarried cohabiting individual does not suddenly find herself/himself able to access the privileges available to married couples by virtue of seeking protection from abuse. These couples may not inherit from each other, claim an entitlement to social security benefits, claim each other as tax exemptions, or file joint tax returns and their communications are not privileged nor are they excluded from testifying.

Q & A: How did Ohio's courts of appeals handle these cases?

Many of Ohio's appellate courts reversed several of these lower courts rulings. For example, the appellate court in *State v. Burk*[22] reversed the lower court and held that because the domestic violence statute is predicated upon a factual determination of cohabitation and not a legal status of marriage, both the amendment and the statute may stand.[23] In *State v. Nixon*[24] and *State v. Rodgers*,[25] the appellate courts affirmed the trial court decisions. In fact, there is unanimous agreement in the Fourth, Fifth, Sixth, Eighth, Ninth, Tenth, and Twelfth appellate districts that the Marriage Amendment does not render the domestic violence statutes unconstitutional.

On the other hand, the Second and Third District Courts of Appeals found that the domestic violence statute is unconstitutional as applied to "persons living as spouses." The trial court rulings in many of these cases, including *Ward, Dixon, Peterson*, and *Steinman* were affirmed. The rulings in *State v. McIntosh* and *State v. Maddox*, among others, were reversed.

For example, in the *Ward* case, the Second District Court of Ap-

---

[21]State v. Burk, 2005 WL 786212, *6 (Ohio C.P. 2005), judgment rev'd, 164 Ohio App. 3d 740, 2005-Ohio-6727, 843 N.E.2d 1254 (8th Dist. Cuyahoga County 2005), judgment aff'd, 114 Ohio St. 3d 430, 2007-Ohio-4552, 872 N.E.2d 1212 (2007).

[22]State v. Burk, 164 Ohio App. 3d 740, 2005-Ohio-6727, 843 N.E.2d 1254 (8th Dist. Cuyahoga County 2005), judgment aff'd, 114 Ohio St. 3d 430, 2007-Ohio-4552, 872 N.E.2d 1212 (2007).

[23]See also City of Cleveland v. Voies, 2005 WL 1940135 (Ohio Mun. Ct. 2005), judgment rev'd on other grounds, 2006-Ohio-815, 2006 WL 440341 (Ohio Ct. App. 8th Dist. Cuyahoga County 2006), judgment aff'd, 114Ohio St. 3d430, 2007-Ohio-4552, 872 N.E.2d 1212 (2007) and State v. Carswell, 2005-Ohio-6547, 2005 WL 3358882 (Ohio Ct. App. 12th Dist. Warren County 2005), judgment aff'd, 114 Ohio St. 3d 210, 2007-Ohio-3723, 871 N.E.2d 547 (2007).

[24]State v. Nixon, 2006-Ohio-72, 2006 WL 52251 (Ohio Ct. App. 9th Dist. Summit County 2006).

[25]State v. Rodgers, 166 Ohio App. 3d 218, 2006-Ohio-1528, 850 N.E.2d 90 (10th Dist. Franklin County 2006).

peals rejected the state construction argument, applied by several appellate districts and argued by the ACLU in its amicus brief, which asserted that where there is a potential conflict between a statute and the Ohio Constitution, not only must the statute be construed, if reasonably possible, so as to avoid a conflict—a familiar principle of statutory construction—but the Ohio Constitution also must, if reasonably possible to do so, be construed to avoid a conflict with the statute.[26]

The Second District noted that the Ohio Constitution is the supreme law of this state and the laws of the United States enacted consistently with the federal constitution. "The provisions of the Constitution of Ohio may not be required to defer to statutory law, whether directly or indirectly through mechanism of deferential construction."[27] "The Defense of Marriage Amendment is no less a part of the fundamental, organic law of Ohio by reason of its recent vintage; if anything, it is entitled to greater deference. By definition, an amendment to the Ohio Constitution, once adopted, supersedes any preexisting provisions of the Constitution. In stating this obvious fact, we make no observations concerning the wisdom of the electorate in having adopted the amendment. Our sworn obligation to uphold the Constitution of Ohio is not limited or qualified in any way based upon our assessment of its merits."[28]

Additionally, the appellate court determined that any decision to carve exceptions into the Amendment would be equivalent to causing a death of a thousand cuts. The court also wondered which of the potential exceptions would have found favor with the voters. Thus, the second sentence was designed to avoid exceptions by either the courts or the General Assembly. The court then concluded that amending the statute to expand its reach to all persons sharing residential quarters would present no constitutional problems because the person who lives as a cohabitant would be accorded protection not by being a quasi spouse, but by reason of sharing a residence.

In *State v. Douglas*,[29] the majority ruling issued by the Eighth District Court of Appeals found that the domestic violence laws were constitutional as applied to unmarried cohabitants. However, the dissenting judge stated that, while she agreed with a presumption of statutory constitutionality, she did not agree that in determining whether the statute and the amendment conflict, the next step is to give a reasonable construction so that both may stand. *Burk* and the majority applied the wrong rule of construction. The judge also noted the scholarly critique applied in *Ward*.

---

[26]State v. Ward, 166 Ohio App. 3d 188, 2006-Ohio-1407, 849 N.E.2d 1076 (2d Dist. Greene County 2006), judgment rev'd, 114 Ohio St. 3d 430, 2007-Ohio-4552, 872 N.E.2d 1212 (2007).

[27]State v. Ward, 166 Ohio App. 3d 188, 190, 2006-Ohio-1407, 849 N.E.2d 1076 (2d Dist. Greene County 2006), judgment rev'd, 114 Ohio St. 3d 430, 2007-Ohio-4552, 872 N.E.2d 1212 (2007).

[28]State v. Ward, 166 Ohio App. 3d 188, 192, 2006-Ohio-1407, 849 N.E.2d 1076 (2d Dist. Greene County 2006), judgment rev'd, 114 Ohio St. 3d 430, 2007-Ohio-4552, 872 N.E.2d 1212 (2007).

[29]State v. Douglas, 2006-Ohio-2343, 2006 WL 1304860 (Ohio Ct. App. 8th Dist. Cuyahoga County 2006), judgment aff'd, 114 Ohio St. 3d 430, 2007-Ohio-4552, 872 N.E.2d 1212 (2007).

In noting that *Williams* held that domestic violence arises out of the nature of the relationship rather than the exact living circumstances of the parties, it also underscores the purpose of the domestic violence statute to acknowledge that an assault on a family member is more serious than an assault on a stranger. By enacting domestic violence statutes, legislative bodies intend to protect persons who are in a certain type of relationship rather than persons who are strangers.

After noting the magnitude of legal authority defining cohabitation for domestic violence statutes, the dissenting judge said *Williams* stands for the proposition that people who share familial and financial responsibilities and engage in consortium are recognized as a being in a relationship that possesses the design, qualities, significance and effect of marriage. Cohabitants attain a legal status: each may prosecute the other for an act of violence. It is a crime quite different from general assault precisely because of the special intimacy of the parties. However, the dissent failed to explore the issue of "intent" as approximating the qualities, significance, design and effect of marriage.

Finally, the Third District Court of Appeals in *State v. McKinley*[30] also discussed the definition of a legal status, but determined that the domestic violence statutes do not create a status for unmarried relationships. Rather, it only creates a status for a class of victims, based on the relationship between offender and victim.

However, it then stated that the state and the courts recognize such a status in that the General Assembly recognized a legal status of cohabitation. Because cohabitation intended to approximate a marriage, a legal status is created that the courts recognize, even when no benefits or rights are conferred or are minimal. The court further stated that there was no need to address the intent behind the amendment. Thus, the Logan Court of Appeals held that the statutes are unconstitutional as applied.

Many courts requested that the Supreme Court of Ohio address the issue and conflicts between appellate districts. In *Douglas*, the appellate court itself noted the Second District's decision in *Ward* and the conflict. It sua sponte certified the following question to the Supreme Court: Is RC 2919.25 unconstitutional in light of the Amendment?

Q & A: Did any courts challenge the amendment on equal protection grounds?

Although no appellate court case advanced an equal protection argument, at least two lower courts concluded that by prohibiting unmarried cohabitants from seeking protection under the domestic violence laws, the Amendment may violate the Equal Protection Clause of the U.S. Constitution. For example, Judge James P. Celebrezze of the Cuyahoga County Domestic Relations Court in *Phelps v. Johnson*[31] held that, although the domestic violence statute creates a legal status, the Marriage Amendment violates the equal protection clause because it draws a distinction between married and unmarried victims

[30] State v. McKinley, 2006-Ohio-2507, 2006 WL 1381635 (Ohio Ct. App. 3d Dist. Logan County 2006), judgment rev'd, 114 Ohio St. 3d 430, 2007-Ohio-4552, 872 N.E.2d 1212 (2007).

[31] Phelps v. Johnson, 2005 WL 4651081 (Ohio C.P. 2005).

when the classification bears no rational relationship to the stated governmental interest.

Similarly, in *State v. Abdellahi*[32] the Franklin County Municipal Court reasoned that the amendment would arbitrarily subject certain victims to less protection based on their marital status or sexual orientation in violation of the equal protection clause.

Q & A: Did the Supreme Court of Ohio issue an opinion?

Yes, on July 25, 2007, the Ohio Supreme Court rejected the constitutional challenge to the state's domestic violence law. A 6-1 majority determined that the constitutional amendment does not conflict with the criminal domestic violence statute. The court determined that the term "person living as a spouse" merely identifies a particular class of persons protected by the statute. It does not create or recognize a legal relationship that intends to approximate the design, qualities significance or effect of marriage.[33]

§ 10:11 Parties authorized to file for civil protection orders[1]

Pursuant to RC 3113.31(C), a person may seek relief under this section for himself or herself, or a parent or adult household member may seek relief under this section on behalf of any other family or household member.

Clearly, an abused adult can petition the court for a civil protection order. A parent or other adult can also file for a civil protection order on behalf of a minor child[2] or other family or household member.[3] Unlike the criminal temporary protection order statute,[4] however, there is no provision in RC 3113.31 for law enforcement officials to file on behalf of an abused party.

Q & A: Can a related adult not living with the victim or batterer file on behalf of the victim?

---

[32]State v. Abdellahi, 2005 WL 4651078 (Ohio C.P. 2005).

[33]State v. Carswell, 114 Ohio St. 3d 210, 2007-Ohio-3723, 871 N.E.2d 547 (2007).

[Section 10:11]

[1]See also Text § 10:8, Relationships covered—Parents and children; juveniles.

[2]But see Spence v. Herbert, 2001 WL 876231 (Ohio Ct. App. 5th Dist. Licking County 2001) (while appellate court acknowledged that RC 2903.214(C) permits a parent to seek relief on behalf of a child, the court must find an immediate and present danger to the child. The wording of RC 2903.214 is identical to RC 3113.31(C)); Parrish v. Parrish, 95 Ohio St. 3d 1201, 2002-Ohio-1623, 765 N.E.2d 359 (2002) (where the dissenting opinion concludes that any evidence that respondent abused family or household members other than those for whom the protection order is sought is admissible to demonstrate a petitioner's fear that respondent may abuse her child and thus she should have been able to obtain a protection order for her child).

[3]See Farris v. Kihm, 2002-Ohio-2277, 2002 WL 940178 (Ohio Ct. App. 2d Dist. Miami County 2002) (where petitioner sought a protection order individually and on behalf of his wife and her child, the court held that the "statute permitted petitioner, who had previously been a victim of respondent's acts of domestic violence, to petition for an order of protection on behalf of his wife, petitioner and respondent were family and household members since they had a child together, and extension of an order of protection to members of the victim's household who were vulnerable to abuse was reasonable.").

[4]RC 2919.26(A)(1).

At least one court has raised this issue. In *Carney v. Pankey*,[5] the court of appeals held that the mother of an adult victim of domestic violence may petition the court for a civil protection order on the victim's behalf. The court determined that the statute does not require a petitioner to be a current household member of the person for whom relief is sought. Under this interpretation, the court intimated that the respondent need not be a family or household member of the petitioner so long as the victim and the respondent are family or household members pursuant to statute.

On the other hand, the Crawford County Court of Appeals determined that a paternal uncle lacked standing to request a civil protection order on behalf of his niece against her mother. In *Seibert v. Seibert*,[6] the appellate court reasoned that the uncle never resided in the household with either his niece or her mother. While evidence was presented that Christopher was Traci's brother-in-law, which satisfied the family relationship by affinity, they had never resided together,[7] nor had they shared either familial or financial responsibilities.[8] "In order to have standing to file on behalf of Stephanie, Christopher must have previously resided with Traci. R.C. 3113.31(C). Since he has not resided with the respondent, Christopher does not meet the statutory definition of family or household member set forth in RC 3113.31(A)(3). Thus, Christopher has no standing to bring the petition for CPO."[9]

In concluding that the CPO should not have been granted, the court then noted that Christopher had the option of reporting his concerns for Stephanie's safety to the county children service's agency whose job is to investigate such claims. In doing otherwise, the jurisdiction of juvenile court and the due process requirements set in place by statute for that court to protect both the rights of children and the custodial rights of parents were evaded.[10]

Q & A: Where the victim is reluctant to file, may another adult family member file the petition?

It depends on several factors. The civil domestic violence statute[11] is silent on this point, and there is no case law that addresses the issue. The statute states that an adult household member may seek relief on

---

[5]Carney v. Pankey, 1988 WL 34644 (Ohio Ct. App. 7th Dist. Mahoning County 1988); see also RC 3113.31(C); Martin v. Fisher, 2001 WL 370519 (Ohio Ct. App. 8th Dist. Cuyahoga County 2001) (wife's sister filed for and was granted civil protection order). But see J.M.R. v. S.T.R., 15 P.3d 253 (Alaska 2001) (trial court properly denied grandmother's request for visitation with grandchildren brought by her as part of a CPO she filed against her son and daughter-in-law).

[6]Seibert v. Seibert, 2003-Ohio-3758, 2003 WL 21658309 (Ohio Ct. App. 3d Dist. Crawford County 2003).

[7]See Maglionico v. Maglionico, 2001-Ohio-8901, 2001 WL 1401978 (Ohio Ct. App. 11th Dist. Portage County 2001).

[8]State v. Williams, 79 Ohio St. 3d 459, 1997-Ohio-79, 683 N.E.2d 1126 (1997) (in which the residency requirement is eliminated).

[9]Seibert v. Seibert, 2003-Ohio-3758, 2003 WL 21658309, *4 (Ohio Ct. App. 3d Dist. Crawford County 2003).

[10]Seibert v. Seibert, 2003-Ohio-3758, 2003 WL 21658309, *4 (Ohio Ct. App. 3d Dist. Crawford County 2003).

[11]RC 3113.31.

behalf of any other family or household member, whether that person is an adult or a child.[12] The state of mind of the victim is not addressed in RC 3113.31. The only limitation seems to be that the other adult member must also reside in the home with the victim and the respondent, unless the petitioner is the parent of the victim.[13]

In contrast, RC 2919.26(A)(1) provides that the officer who made the arrest for the alleged violation under RC 2935.03 may file a complaint on behalf of the complainant, if the complainant is unable to file. The officer may request that the court issue a protection order as well. Additionally, RC 2919.26(C) specifically creates an exception for another to appear in court on behalf of the victim for a hearing to determine whether to issue the protection order. If the person who requested the order is unable to appear and if the court finds that the failure to appear is because of the person's hospitalization or medical condition resulting from the offense alleged in the complaint, another person who is able to provide the court with the information it requests may appear in lieu of the person who requested the order.[14]

Because the civil statute[15] carves out no specific circumstances for filing by another unrelated adult, it is doubtful that just "any" adult who is not a household member may file on behalf of a reluctant victim.

Q & A: Does an unmarried father have standing to request a civil protection order on behalf of his minor child where he has not established paternity and the child is in the possession of the respondent-mother? Can the court grant petitioner-father custody of the child?

At least one Ohio court addressed a similar issue. In *Carney v. Pankey*,[16] the Mahoning County Court of Appeals held that the mother of an adult victim of domestic violence may petition the court for a civil protection order on the victim's behalf even though she did not reside with the victim or respondent. The court reasoned that the statute does not require that the petitioner be a member of the victim's household to the person for whom the relief is sought.[17]

Pursuant to the court's reasoning in *Carney v. Pankey* and in light of RC 3113.31(C), a father may petition the court for a civil protection order on behalf of his minor child if he resides with the minor child. Thus, he would be an adult household member. If paternity had been previously established, he would have had standing even if he had not lived with the child. He would then have been considered a parent.

On the other hand, the court cannot grant the petitioner-father an

[12]RC 3113.31(C).

[13]Carney v. Pankey, 1988 WL 34644 (Ohio Ct. App. 7th Dist. Mahoning County 1988).

[14]RC 2919.26(C).

[15]RC 3113.31.

[16]Carney v. Pankey, 1988 WL 34644 (Ohio Ct. App. 7th Dist. Mahoning County 1988).

[17]See also RC 3113.31(C) which states that a person may seek relief under this section for himself, or any parent or adult household member may seek relief under this section on behalf of any other family or household member, by filing a petition with the court.

allocation of parental rights and responsibilities under RC 3113.31(E)(1)(d) where he has not yet been determined to be the biological father. Although the domestic relations court has jurisdiction to determine whether or not domestic violence has been committed, the allocation of parental rights and responsibilities should be decided in the juvenile court after an establishment of paternity.[18]

Q & A: My parents are always fighting. My mother is bruised and has black eyes. I am afraid for her safety and mine, but she will not request a civil protection order. I am sixteen years old, can I file for one on her behalf?

There are no reported cases that address this issue. However, a minor who wishes to obtain a civil protection order under those circumstances may encounter several problems. An adult may file a legal action on a minor's behalf, and the adult will appear on the caption as "by and through next friend." However, as a minor, the child cannot file an action in court.

More significant is that RC 3113.31 specifically permits another adult household member to file a petition on behalf of the victim. If the legislature wanted to include a minor within the purview of RC 3113.31(C), it would have. It did not. Therefore, it is unlikely that a minor has standing to file for a protection order on behalf of a parent, even through a next friend. In this analysis, it does not matter that the parent does not want the protection.

There is a growing body of research that demonstrates the negative impact that domestic violence has on children.[19] A child who witnesses abuse between his/her parents is also a victim of domestic violence.[20] Recognition of this fact may establish a sufficient basis for a minor to file a petition for a civil protection order through a next friend. It may be easier to prevail in court since the minor would be both a victim and the petitioner. Any protection order so obtained should state that the abused parent is a protected family or household member.

Q & A: Do children have a right to protection orders on the basis that they witnessed the abuse of their parent?

Not according to the Iowa Supreme Court. In *D.M.H. by Hefel v. Thompson*,[21] the Iowa Supreme Court affirmed the dismissal of third-party petitions brought by fathers on behalf of their children who had witnessed abuse toward their mother by their stepfather. The Court reasoned that Iowa's domestic abuse statute did not contemplate a situation in which children witness abuse between family or household

---

[18]See also RC 3109.042 which states that "an unmarried female who gives birth to a child is the sole residential parent and legal custodian of the child until a court of competent jurisdiction issues an order designating another person as the residential parent and legal custodian." But see Horning v. Wolff, 2006-Ohio-6397, 2006 WL 3505864 (Ohio Ct. App. 5th Dist. Stark County 2006) (noting that neither parent is entitled to a strong presumption in his or her favor; RC 3109.042 requires a trial court to treat each parent as standing upon equal footing).

[19]See, e.g., Naomi R. Cahn, Civil Images of Battered Women: The Impact of Domestic Violence on Child Custody Decisions, 5 Vand. L. Rev. 1041 (1991); see also Text Ch 15, Domestic Violence and Custody and Visitation Issues.

[20]Mildred Pagelow, "Children in Violent Families: Direct and Indirect Victims," in Young Children and Their Families (Hill & Barnes, eds., 1982).

[21]D.M.H. by Hefel v. Thompson, 577 N.W.2d 643 (Iowa 1998).

members. The Court pointed out that domestic abuse can only occur between family and household members and the statute expressly excludes children from the definition of "family or household members." Accordingly, minors do not have a right of action for relief from domestic violence based on witnessing their mother's abuse at the hands of their stepfather. The Court chose not to expand the statutory framework to cover children who witness violence, noting that other statutory provisions exist to protect such children such as the custody statute and other relief set forth in the domestic abuse statute regarding custody and visitation. However, the Iowa Supreme Court made it quite clear that the protections under the domestic abuse statute depend "on the abused parent's right of action for relief against domestic abuse."[22]

Of significance is that Iowa's domestic abuse statute specifically excludes children under the age of eighteen as family or household members. As a result, this class of individuals is not entitled to bring a domestic violence action. Ohio's statute includes no such limitation and permits another adult or household member to file on behalf of any other family or household member.[23]

Q & A: May a juvenile file for a civil protection order on his/her own behalf against an intimate partner?[24]

It depends. Prior to the passage of HB 10, some courts issued civil protection orders under RC 3113.31 or RC 2903.214 to minors for abuse inflicted against them by an intimate partner. In most of these cases, the abusive partner was a minor. In most of these cases, courts have done so by issuing the order on behalf of the minor victim.[25] It has often been the parent who filed on behalf of the minor child.

However, many courts found that there was no statutory authority to do so and that enforcement of the protection order against the minor was problematic absent specific statutory guidance.

Recently, the Ohio General Assembly enacted HB 10 which authorized juvenile courts to both issue and enforce civil protection orders against minor respondents. Pursuant to statute, minors may file on their on behalf without a parent.[26]

Q & A: My boyfriend and I had a few drinks. He told me that he had an affair. I got angry and screamed at him. I slapped his face. He picked up a baseball bat and began hitting me in the head. I was all bruised and had to go to the hospital. I want to get a protection order, but I slapped him. Must the petitioner come to court with "clean hands"?[27]

No. Many domestic violence cases involve abuse or threats by each

---

[22] D.M.H. by Hefel v. Thompson, 577 N.W.2d 643, 647 (Iowa 1998).

[23] See RC 3113.31(C).

[24] See also Liza Siebel and Vicky Lin, Do State Restraining Order Laws Protect Youth?, Vol. 11, No. 1 Domestic Violence Report 6 (2005); see also Text § 10:8, Relationships covered—Parents and children; juveniles.

[25] See RC 3113.31(C) and RC 2903.214.

[26] RC 2151.34(C)(1)(a).

[27] See Skiles v. Dearth, 2000 WL 1838747, *5 (Ohio Ct. App. 2d Dist. Clark County 2000) ("the target of domestic violence is not required to have 'clean hands' in order to obtain relief under the statute"); Denney v. Sanders, 2016-Ohio-5113, 2016 WL

party against the other. RC 3113.31 does not require that, to have access to the courts for protection from abuse, the petitioner must not have committed an act of domestic violence against the respondent, must not have yelled or provoked the respondent by words or actions, or must not have said anything that may be construed as threatening. As the attorney for the petitioner, it is wiser to reframe the question to avoid focusing on who caused or provoked the fight or even who was more at fault. The only legal issue before the court is whether the respondent committed an act of domestic violence pursuant to RC 3113.31(A)(1)(a) to RC 3113.31(A)(1)(c).

Of course, these issues will most often be raised by a respondent at the full hearing when he/she has an opportunity to present evidence regarding any acts of the petitioner that could also constitute domestic violence. A court is not required to consider alleged acts committed by the petitioner if simply raised by the respondent at the full hearing. The respondent has the opportunity to file for a protection order, either prior to the petitioner's filing or in compliance with RC 3113.31(E)(4).[28] At this juncture, the court need only decide whether the petitioner has been able to meet the burden of proof needed to keep the protection order in effect or it if must dismiss the protection order for a lack of sufficient, credible evidence. The basis on which a judge should decide to issue or maintain a civil protection order is whether the petitioner is able to prove that the respondent committed the alleged act of domestic violence as set forth in RC 3113.31(A)(1).

It is important for the family law practitioner to have a working knowledge of the requirements for issuing a mutual protection order as the court has no legal authority to issue mutual protection orders to both parties at the full hearing on the petitioner's protection order.[29] Unless the respondent previously complied with the procedural provisions of RC 3113.31(E)(4), the respondent is without recourse to request a protection order at the full hearing on petitioner's petition. An argument presented by the respondent that the petitioner also committed domestic violence should not justify either a mutual protection order or the dismissal of the petitioner's protection order.

Q & A: May grandparents seek protection orders on behalf of their grandchildren?

While grandparents may, of course, file for protection orders on behalf of their grandchildren, no Ohio court has directly addressed the issue of whether grandparents have standing to request protection orders against their children on behalf of their grandchildren.[30]

4063898 (Ohio Ct. App. 1st Dist. Hamilton County 2016).

[28]See RC 3113.31(E)(4) for a discussion of mutual protection orders; see also Skiles v. Dearth, 2000 WL 1838747 (Ohio Ct. App. 2d Dist. Clark County 2000) (The court noted that "there is nothing inconsistent about one domestic partner obtaining a domestic violence civil protection order after the other has already obtained one.").

[29]See RC 3113.31(E)(4); Deacon v. Landers, 68 Ohio App. 3d 26, 587 N.E.2d 395 (4th Dist. Ross County 1990).

[30]See Ngqakayi v. Ngqakayi, 2008-Ohio-4745, 2008 WL 4278334 (Ohio Ct. App. 2d Dist. Greene County 2008) (upholding the denial of the petition for civil protection order brought by a grandmother on behalf of her grandchild against her son on the ground of insufficient evidence; the issue of whether a grandparent has standing to bring such an action was never addressed). See also Dodds on behalf of S.S. v.

However, the Missouri Court of Appeals peripherally considered this issue in *In re J.M.Z.*[31] In that case, the maternal grandparents filed a petition for a protection order on behalf of their grandchild, against the daughter who allegedly abused the child. The trial court dismissed the action, stating that there was no subject matter jurisdiction because the grandparents' exclusive remedy is a motion to modify custody where a prior order of custody already exists. The appeals court reversed that decision, noting that a motion to modify custody was not the only remedy and that protection orders are in addition to, and not in lieu of, other civil remedies. The court further stressed that, while both are available to litigants, the remedies afforded by each are different. The court cautioned that "[o]nly when an order of custody is pending or already exists can the court not make an award of custody additional to the full order of protection."[32] In this case, the grandparents were already custodians of the child and were merely seeking modifications to the mother's visitation.

Unfortunately, the Missouri Court of Appeals offered no guidance regarding whether grandparents are family or household members for purposes of the state's domestic violence statute. Had the grandparents not had legal custody of the child, the court may have reached a different result.

§ 10:12 Jurisdiction and venue—Generally

It is important that venue and jurisdiction be distinguished. Venue is the locality or geographic division where the lawsuit should be heard.[1] Jurisdiction refers to the power to adjudicate.[2]

Venue is procedural. Accordingly, venue does not affect the power of the court to render a valid judgment. Even if a case is not venued in the proper county, a judgment rendered by a court that proceeds to hear the matter is not void. On the other hand, subject matter jurisdiction defines the court's ability to hear the lawsuit. Without subject matter jurisdiction, the entire lawsuit must be dismissed.[3] Personal jurisdiction, by service of the particular papers and allegations, must

---

Stamper, 2018-Ohio-193, 2018 WL 481779 (Ohio Ct. App. 2d Dist. Champaign County 2018) (sustaining respondent's assignment of error, not based on the relationship or standing, but because the grandmother did not establish by sufficient evidence that the CPO should have been granted).

[31] In re J.M.Z., 983 S.W.2d 573 (Mo. Ct. App. E.D. 1998); see also J.M.R. v. S.T.R., 15 P.3d 253 (Alaska 2001) (where trial court properly denied grandmother's request for visitation with grandchildren brought by her as part of a CPO she filed against her son and daughter-in-law); but see Viruet ex rel. Velasquez v. Cancel, 1999 PA Super 53, 727 A.2d 591 (1999) (trial court erred in refusing to use Protection from Abuse Act when grandmother failed to protect granddaughter who had suffered from physical abuse at hands of mother).

[32] In re J.M.Z., 983 S.W.2d 573, 575 (Mo. Ct. App. E.D. 1998).

[Section 10:12]

[1] Sowald and Morganstern, Baldwin's Ohio Practice, Domestic Relations Law § 27:39 (4th ed.). See also Durrah v. Durrah, 2006-Ohio-2138, 2006 WL 1132851 (Ohio Ct. App. 12th Dist. Butler County 2006).

[2] Sowald and Morganstern, Baldwin's Ohio Practice, Domestic Relations Law § 27:39 (4th ed.).

[3] See In re J.M.Z., 983 S.W.2d 573 (Mo. Ct. App. E.D. 1998) (discussing subject matter jurisdiction for purposes of a protection order).

be perfected before the court can impose a personal obligation or duty or terminate a defendant's rights. While actual notice of the proceeding may not be a substitute for personal service, service of process is sufficient to ensure that a defendant/respondent has actual notice of the proceeding.[4]

In many instances, persons may obtain ex parte divorces. Although an ex parte decree may not impose orders of support where the court lacks personal jurisdiction over a nonresident, a valid unilateral ex parte divorce with proper jurisdictional requirements of residency can terminate the legal marital status.[5] It is possible that, under this legal fiction, victims of domestic violence may be granted ex parte protection orders designed to protect them from abusive partners where the court is unable to effect personal service on the defendant. Only those remedies that provide protection from abuse may be ordered.[6] Custody, visitation, support, and use of property cannot be awarded.

§ 10:13 Jurisdiction and venue—In domestic violence cases[1]

Q & A: What is subject matter jurisdiction?

Subject matter jurisdiction of a court is the court's power to hear and decide a case on its merits. A court's subject matter jurisdiction is invoked by the filing of a complaint. Subject matter jurisdiction over requests for civil protection orders in domestic violence cases can be obtained when an incident of domestic violence has occurred within the state or county.

As subject matter jurisdiction is conferred by statute in domestic violence cases, RC 3113.31(B) controls and states that the court has jurisdiction over all proceedings under this section. RC 3113.31(A)(2) defines "court" as the domestic relations division of the court of common pleas in counties that have a domestic relations division and the court of common pleas in counties that do not have a domestic relations court.

Q & A: What is personal jurisdiction?[2]

Personal jurisdiction is the authority of a court to enter a judgment

[4]See also Text § 11:11, Ex parte protection orders—Service and notice provisions; Text § 13:3, Court enforcement of civil protection orders—Criminal prosecution; Text § 13:8, Enforcement of civil protection orders; procedures for initiating contempt motions; McKnight v. Scott, 665 A.2d 973 (D.C. 1995); see also Beachler v. Beachler, 2007-Ohio-1220, 2007 WL 805526 (Ohio Ct. App. 12th Dist. Preble County 2007); Jones v. Jordan, 2007-Ohio-2519, 2007 WL 1508255 (Ohio Ct. App. 8th Dist. Cuyahoga County 2007) (in the context of RC 2903.214).

[5]Sowald and Morganstern, Baldwin's Ohio Practice, Domestic Relations Law § 27:33 (4th ed.).

[6]See RC 3113.31(E)(1)(a) to RC 3113.31(E)(1)(h).

[Section 10:13]

[1]See, e.g., Reynolds v. Whitney, 2004-Ohio-1628, 2004 WL 626872 (Ohio Ct. App. 10th Dist. Franklin County 2004) (distinguishing venue and subject matter jurisdiction for purposes of obtaining a stalking protection order).

[2]See also Jessica Miles, We Are Never Ever Getting Back Together: Domestic Violence Victims, Defendants, And Due Process, 35 Cardozo L. Rev. 141 (2013), http://ssrn.com/abstract=2375969. Jacobs, The Stream of Violence: A New Approach to Domestic Violence Personal Jurisdiction, 64 UCLA L. Rev. 684 (2017) (reframing the

constitutionally binding on a defendant in a case. The underlying foundation for asserting personal jurisdiction is the presence of the person involved in the litigation within the court's jurisdiction or territorial boundaries. Personal jurisdiction can be obtained through service of process, voluntary appearance or waiver.[3] If the person is not present within the jurisdiction, he or she must have certain minimum contacts with the jurisdiction in order to establish personal jurisdiction.

Q & A: How is personal jurisdiction effected in Ohio?

All states have enacted long-arm statutes or rules to establish personal jurisdiction over out-of-state defendants. Ohio's long -arm statute, RC 2307.382, authorizes the exercise of jurisdiction over defendants who are nonresidents. Civ. R. 4.3 provides for service of process on named individuals outside of Ohio and determines the "minimum contacts" necessary to effectuate personal jurisdiction. A transient presence in Ohio may be enough to confer personal jurisdiction. Causing tortious injury in this state to any person when the person to be served might reasonably have expected that some person would be injured by the act in this state may also confer personal jurisdiction.[4]

Additionally, in order to subject a defendant to personal jurisdiction if he or she is not within the state, he must have sufficient minimum contacts in the state so as not to offend traditional notions of fair play and substantial justice.[5] "Ordinarily, this requires that a person 'purposely* * *[avail] itself of the privilege of conducting activities within the forum state* * *.' "[6] The "purposeful availment" standard set forth in *Hanson v. Denckla* ensures that a defendant will not be randomly brought into another jurisdiction.

Finally, in determining minimum contacts, a court's primary focus should be on the relationship among the defendant, the forum and the litigation. Sufficient minimum contacts exist when a defendant should reasonably anticipate being brought into court in the state.[7]

Q & A: What is venue?

The proper forum is any county authorized under Civil Rule 3,

---

issue of personal jurisdiction in domestic violence cases by focusing on the knowledge of the defendant about the victim's likely destination if she is forced to flee to another state).

[3]See also Text § 11:11, Ex parte protection orders—Service and notice provisions; Text § 13:3, Court enforcement of civil protection orders—Criminal prosecution; Vance v. Nichols, 2007-Ohio-3819, 2007 WL 2164162 (Ohio Ct. App. 2d Dist. Darke County 2007).

[4]See RC 2307.382; see Civ.R. 4.3(A)(3), Civ.R. 4.3(A)(9), Civ.R. 4.3(A)(10).

[5]International Shoe Co. v. State of Wash., Office of Unemployment Compensation and Placement, 326 U.S. 310, 316, 66 S. Ct. 154, 90 L. Ed. 95, 161 A.L.R. 1057 (1945); Burger King Corp. v. Rudzewicz, 471 U.S. 462, 105 S. Ct. 2174, 85 L. Ed. 2d 528 (1985).

[6]Haas v. Semrad, 2007-Ohio-2828, 2007 WL 1653032 (Ohio Ct. App. 6th Dist. Lucas County 2007), citing Hanson v. Denckla, 357 U.S. 235, 253, 78 S. Ct. 1228, 2 L. Ed. 2d 1283 (1958). See also Dobos v. Dobos, 179 Ohio App. 3d 173, 2008-Ohio-5665, 901 N.E.2d 248 (12th Dist. Clermont County 2008).

[7]Haas v. Semrad, 2007-Ohio-2828, 2007 WL 1653032 (Ohio Ct. App. 6th Dist. Lucas County 2007), relying on World-Wide Volkswagen Corp. v. Woodson, 444 U.S. 286, 297, 100 S. Ct. 589, 62 L. Ed. 2d 490 (1980).

which specifies the various venue options.[8] The most commonly utilized venue provision is the county where both the victim and the respondent reside. Sometimes it is necessary to file a petition for a protection order where the respondent (but not the victim) resides[9] or where the cause of action arose.[10]

Civil Rule 3(B) was amended[11] to make venue proper in "the county in which the petitioner currently or temporarily resides" in actions for a civil protection order.[12] The Supreme Court noted that the term "reside" should be liberally construed and should not be confused with the requirement for domicile.[13] The respondent is still free to challenge venue under Civil Rule 3(D).[14]

This provision further provides victims with access to protection against domestic violence. Such an amendment recognizes that victims of domestic violence relocate for a variety of reasons, such as to obtain shelter or escape their abusers. To limit victims of domestic violence to legal protection only in the jurisdiction where the abuse occurred fails to provide victims with immediate access to the courts.

Over 30 states have addressed venue in their domestic violence statutes and have concluded that jurisdiction lies where the petitioner currently resides, including cases where the petitioner may be residing in a shelter. Unfortunately, the courts may or may not issue protection orders in the county where the petitioner resides if the act of domestic violence occurred in another county or if the respondent does not reside in that county.

The courts should consider the party's individual circumstances deciding where and whether to issue a civil protection order. The court should first determine whether there exists an immediate and present danger toward the victim.[15] If there is an immediate and present danger in the county in which the petitioner resides, or temporarily resides, the courts should grant the requested civil protection order. One problem for the petitioner may be perfecting service on the

---

[8]RC 3113.31(G); Durrah v. Durrah, 2006-Ohio-2138, 2006 WL 1132851 (Ohio Ct. App. 12th Dist. Butler County 2006) (defines venue as the geographic division, either by county or district, where a case should be tried). See also Wise v. Wise, 8 Ohio App. 3d 243, 456 N.E.2d 1317 (1st Dist. Hamilton County 1983); Johnson v. Warner, 2000 WL 1460079 (Ohio Ct. App. 5th Dist. Muskingum County 2000) (trial court transferred venue of civil protection order domestic relations court to be heard in conjunction with the divorce case; appeals court dismissed appeal for lack of final appealable order).

[9]Civ.R. 3(B)(1).

[10]Civ.R. 3(B)(6).

[11]Eff. 7-1-98.

[12]Durrah v. Durrah, 2006-Ohio-2138, 2006 WL 1132851 (Ohio Ct. App. 12th Dist. Butler County 2006) (discusses the 1998 amendment; the staff notes permitting a respondent in a CPO action to challenge venue and the time frame for challenging venue).

[13]See State ex rel. Saunders v. Court of Common Pleas of Allen County, 34 Ohio St. 3d 15, 17, 516 N.E.2d 232 (1987) (quoting John W. McCormac, Ohio Civil Rules Practice).

[14]See also Sperling v. Teplitsky, 294 N.J. Super. 312, 683 A.2d 244 (Ch. Div. 1996).

[15]RC 3113.31(D).

respondent if the respondent does not live within the county.[16] RC 3113.31(F)(1) requires that a copy of the order be delivered to the respondent on the same day that the order is entered. This may be difficult to achieve without the use of a private process server.

It may be necessary to consult the local domestic relations court and/or the county sheriff's department to determine how long it generally takes to serve the respondent with in-county protection orders. In many counties, the courts do not strictly adhere to the time restrictions imposed by RC 3113.31(F)(1). Reviewing the procedures for service will enable the petitioner's attorney to determine whether certified mail to the respondent or personal service on the respondent by way of that county's sheriff's department is appropriate given the time frame for service in that county.

Q & A: Does the domestic violence statute contain residency requirements?

RC 3113.31 contains no residency requirements.[17] Therefore, a petitioner need not reside within a particular state or county for any particular period of time before filing a petition for a civil protection order. The absence of residency limitations, coupled with the provisions of RC 3113.31(N)(1) and RC 3113.31(N)(2), suggests that protection orders may be issued anywhere in the state for domestic violence incidents occurring anywhere else in the state. RC 3113.31(F)(3) provides that protection orders shall be enforced anywhere in the state, regardless of whether they are registered in the enforcing county. Additionally, the Violence Against Women Act provides that states shall accord full faith and credit to protection orders issued by the courts of another state.[18]

Under the newer statutory provisions, there is a less rigid adherence to certain boundaries, territories, and judicial districts. Since civil protection orders are enforceable anywhere in the state and the country and because out-of-county protection orders can be registered in any county, the logical conclusion is that a petitioner who leaves the county of abuse and relocates to another county or state,[19] even temporarily, may file for a protection order.

---

[16]RC 3113.31(F)(1); see also Text § 12:27, Conflicting protection orders (discussing the particular problem of res judicata).

[17]Thomas v. Thomas, 44 Ohio App. 3d 6, 540 N.E.2d 745 (10th Dist. Franklin County 1988); see also O'Hara v. Dials, 1996 WL 38810, *4 (Ohio Ct. App. 6th Dist. Erie County 1996) (abrogated on other grounds by, Felton v. Felton, 79 Ohio St. 3d 34, 1997-Ohio-302, 679 N.E.2d 672 (1997)).

[18]See VAWA, 18 U.S.C.A. § 2265.

[19]See State v. Reyes, 172 N.J. 154, 796 A.2d 879 (2002) (repeated acts of harassment in N.J. formed basis for a domestic violence restraining order where wife sought physical shelter in that state; court noted that N.J. court has jurisdiction to issue a domestic violence restraining order where act of violence occurred in another state but where victim fled to N.J. for shelter). See also In re Marriage of Malwitz, 81 P.3d 1076, 1079 (Colo. App. 2003), judgment rev'd, 99 P.3d 56 (Colo. 2004). The Colorado Supreme Court reversed and remanded appellate court's ruling that trial court did not have personal jurisdiction over father to establish child support, and holding that the trial court's exercise of jurisdiction over defendant was consistent with due process protections; "By abusing and harassing Malwitz, effectively forcing his wife to Colorado where she and the Defendant's child became dependent on public assistance, the Defendant caused important consequences in Colorado and thereby created a substantial connection between himself and Colorado. Additionally, the Defendant

Q & A: Where the act of violence occurred in Michigan and where the parties subsequently moved to Ohio, can a victim request relief in Ohio?

It depends. Unless there is an immediate and present danger, which is the test for obtaining an ex parte civil protection order under RC 3113.31(D), or recent threats, the petitioner may not qualify for a protection order whether or not the respondent was in Ohio. Where there is no longer an emergency requiring immediate protection, the courts do not feel justified in granting the requested protection order.

On the other hand, some Ohio courts have issued civil protection orders for violence that occurred in other counties and even in other countries. For example, in *Davis v. Mendez*,[20] the trial court issued a civil protection order for petitioner based on an act of domestic violence occurring in Mexico City where she lived with the minor child and respondent, her husband. Upon her return to Ohio with the child, she filed for a civil protection order. Approximately 1 year later, the parties entered into a consent agreement. Subsequently, wife filed for a divorce.

While the appeal concerned a violation of the divorce decree, it is important to note that the appellate court did not question wife's preexisting CPO, issued by a Greene County, Ohio trial court based on an incident occurring in Mexico City.

Q & A: What if the victim moved to Ohio to escape the respondent and the violence occurred in Michigan?[21]

If there is an immediate and present danger to the victim in Ohio, the victim may petition the courts in Ohio for a civil protection order.[22] The only problem may be perfecting service on a respondent living in another state.

If recent threats to the victim occurred in Ohio since the victim's relocation, the victim should be able to obtain a civil protection order in an Ohio court.

This question underscores the problem regarding personal jurisdiction over a respondent living in another state.[23] Although a victim may be able to obtain a civil protection order against a respondent liv-

should have expected Malwitz to flee to Colorado in particular because he knew that Colorado was the only place where she had family ties and, therefore, should have foreseen the possibility of litigation in this forum. Finally, the exercise of personal jurisdiction comports with traditional notions of fair play and substantial justice, in light of the manifest interests of Malwitz and her child, the state of Colorado, and the interstate justice system as a whole." See In re Marriage of Malwitz, 99 P.3d 56, 63-64 (Colo. 2004).

[20]Davis v. Mendez, 2008-Ohio-5768, 2008 WL 4823367 (Ohio Ct. App. 2d Dist. Greene County 2008).

[21]See also Text § 15:24, Other issues that impact custody and visitation awards; see also RC 3127.18.

[22]See J.N. v. D.S., 300 N.J. Super. 647, 693 A.2d 571 (Ch. Div. 1996) (discussing venue and jurisdiction and public policy arguments in favor of victim leaving state to avoid abuse and obtaining protection order in new state for acts committed in old state); Dobos v. Dobos, 179 Ohio App. 3d 173, 2008-Ohio-5665, 901 N.E.2d 248 (12th Dist. Clermont County 2008) (regarding a defendant who resides out of the country).

[23]See also Hogue v. Hogue, 16 Cal. App. 5th 833, 224 Cal. Rptr. 3d 651 (3d Dist. 2017) (where husband videoed himself pretending to shoot himself in the mouth (especially in the context of alleged domestic violence in the past), appellate court noted

ing in another state, service on the respondent may be difficult to perfect.

Q & A: What are sufficient minimum contacts for purposes of obtaining jurisdiction over out-of-state defendants in civil protection order cases?[24]

In *Haas v. Semrad,*[25] the Lucas County appellate court affirmed the trial court's issuance of a civil protection order under RC 3113.31 against an out-of-state respondent. The respondent's two previous visits (both involving alleged domestic violence incidents) to petitioner in Ohio and his telephone threats to petitioner were sufficient to confer personal jurisdiction over appellant under Civ. R. 4.3(A)(9).

Although appellant argued that his physical contacts with Ohio were insufficient to confer personal jurisdiction, the Court noted that "a defendant's physical presence in the forum state is unnecessary when, in modern life, a substantial amount of interactions occur via telephone and electronic communication."[26] While a single contact in the forum state may not be sufficient to confer jurisdiction in a divorce action, in the context of civil protection orders, the relationship of the parties and Ohio weigh heavily in favor of the exercise of specific jurisdiction over appellant.[27]

Thus, the threatening telephone call, when viewed in the context of allegations of previous domestic violence in Ohio, constituted a sufficient minimum contact in Ohio. "While the burden on an out-of-state defendant who is forced to defend in Ohio is not insignificant, the interest in providing protection through local forums against defendants who purposely direct threatening communications into Ohio outweighs appellant's burden in this instance."[28]

Similarly, in *Dobos v. Dobos,*[29] the wife fled Hungary and her abusive husband, returned to Ohio and filed a petition for civil protection order for an incident that took place in Hungary as well as phone calls made by him into Ohio to threaten her. She alleged that her husband had been attempting to find her in Ohio via telephone calls, often threatening to force her and the children to return to Hungary. The trial court dismissed her petition for lack of subject matter and

---

that the domestic violence statute itself bespoke of California's concern with an exceptional type of conduct that is subject to special regulation and that the court's exercise of personal jurisdiction was not unreasonable); Parocha v. Parocha, 2018 CO 41, 418 P.3d 523 (Colo. 2018).

[24]Miles, We Are Never Getting Back Together: Domestic Violence Victims, Defendants, and Due Process, 35 Cardozo L. Rev. 141 (2013).

[25]Haas v. Semrad, 2007-Ohio-2828, 2007 WL 1653032 (Ohio Ct. App. 6th Dist. Lucas County 2007).

[26]Haas v. Semrad, 2007-Ohio-2828, 2007 WL 1653032, *3 (Ohio Ct. App. 6th Dist. Lucas County 2007). See also Sobieniak v. Chapdelaine, 2008-Ohio-6403, 2008 WL 5147439 (Ohio Ct. App. 6th Dist. Lucas County 2008) (a string of emails sent from appellant in Connecticut to appellee in Ohio establishes a sufficient Ohio connection for jurisdictional purposes for the issuance of a CPO in Ohio).

[27]Haas v. Semrad, 2007-Ohio-2828, 2007 WL 1653032, *4 (Ohio Ct. App. 6th Dist. Lucas County 2007).

[28]Haas v. Semrad, 2007-Ohio-2828, 2007 WL 1653032, *3 (Ohio Ct. App. 6th Dist. Lucas County 2007).

[29]Dobos v. Dobos, 179 Ohio App. 3d 173, 2008-Ohio-5665, 901 N.E.2d 248 (12th Dist. Clermont County 2008).

personal jurisdiction finding that, as her husband was six time zones and approximately 6,000 miles away, she was not in immediate and present danger.[30]

The appellate court reversed and found that the trial court erred by not holding an evidentiary hearing to establish what contact the husband's threatening calls created or to what degree the wife had suffered domestic violence while she lived in Ohio.[31] Besides, only an evidentiary hearing would enable a court to accurately determine minimum contacts and balance the competing interests.

It is worth noting that the defendant in this case had previously resided in the state of Ohio with his wife for several years and that he committed domestic violence in the state. In fact, during the time the parties previously lived in Ohio, the defendant "worked and carried on his life here, establishing contacts with the state and availing himself to Ohio."[32] It is unclear, however, how much weight the appellate court accorded this fact.

Explaining that the court should have analyzed how the phone calls or the possibility of husband's coming to Ohio could have reasonably placed the wife and children in fear of imminent physical harm, the appellate court ruled that an evidentiary hearing would offer the husband "an opportunity to prove that the contacts he has established with this state by living here have been eviscerated by some means. Or, the court could determine that the husband has added to these contacts and avails himself to Ohio by deliberately trying to find his wife and children, thereby engaging in activities directed towards this state."[33]

The appellate court observed that "[t]his distinction becomes important in an age where electronic communication eliminates the need for a defendant to physically appear in the state before establishing personal jurisdiction over him. Specifically, Ohio courts have found that purposeful availment exists where the non-resident uses the phone or email to establish minimum contacts."[34] If her assertions were substantiated that her husband caused either tortious injury or, in the alternative, an element of domestic violence, then the long arm statute would be satisfied.[35]

Secondly, an evidentiary hearing would determine if exercising

[30]Dobos v. Dobos, 179 Ohio App. 3d 173, 177, 2008-Ohio-5665, ¶ 16, 901 N.E.2d 248, 251 (12th Dist. Clermont County 2008).

[31]See Burnett v. Burnett, 2012-Ohio-2673, 2012 WL 2196336, *7 (Ohio Ct. App. 6th Dist. Sandusky County 2012) (reversing grant of CPO and holding that "[w]hen the issue is minimum contacts for the issuance of a domestic violence CPO, the content of those communications is an essential element. That is, it is the content that creates the threat and thereby establishes the minimum contacts necessary to effectuate [personal] jurisdiction under R.C. 2307.382.").

[32]Dobos v. Dobos, 179 Ohio App. 3d 173, 180, 2008-Ohio-5665, 901 N.E.2d 248, 253 (12th Dist. Clermont County 2008).

[33]Dobos v. Dobos, 179 Ohio App. 3d 173, 180, 2008-Ohio-5665, 901 N.E.2d 248, 253 (12th Dist. Clermont County 2008).

[34]Dobos v. Dobos, 179 Ohio App. 3d 173, 2008-Ohio-5665, 901 N.E.2d 248 (12th Dist. Clermont County 2008).

[35]Dobos v. Dobos, 179 Ohio App. 3d 173, 2008-Ohio-5665, 901 N.E.2d 248 (12th Dist. Clermont County 2008).

personal jurisdiction over the husband would violate due process by creating a burden on him to defend in Ohio. Such a burden would have to outweigh the state interests in protecting a victim from domestic violence.

Furthermore, in *In re Holbert*,[36] the juvenile court noted that appellant had some minimal contacts with the state of Ohio, having lived in Franklin County for one year. Additionally, the court mentioned that appellee and her son had been subjected to or threatened with physical abuse by the appellant within the meaning of RC 3109.22(A)(3). "To the extent that threats and/or physical abuse could constitute tortious conduct within the state of Ohio, such tortious conduct is sufficient for purposes of the long-arm statute."[37] It is arguable that acts of violence both within and outside the state are the type of tortious conduct contemplated by Civil Rule 4.3(A)(3), Civil Rule 4.3(A)(9), and Civil Rule 4.3(A)(10).

Additionally, the Iowa Supreme Court, in *Bartsch v. Bartsch*,[38] upheld the trial court decision to deny husband's motion to dismiss the wife's protection order due to the fact that he was a non-resident and wife did not have personal jurisdiction over him. The Supreme Court of Iowa agreed that there were insufficient contacts for personal jurisdiction, but held that personal jurisdiction was not required for a

[36]In re Holbert, 1997 WL 566191 (Ohio Ct. App. 10th Dist. Franklin County 1997); see also Bates v. Jarrett, 135 N.C. App. 594, 521 S.E.2d 735 (1999) (holding that husband's act of transferring car title in violation of protection order met sufficient minimum contacts test for exercising personal jurisdiction); A.R. v. M.R., 351 N.J. Super. 512, 799 A.2d 27 (App. Div. 2002) (holding that husband's threats to track down and kill her and repeated telephone calls to New Jersey satisfied minimum contacts test for asserting personal jurisdiction).

[37]In re Holbert, 1997 WL 566191, *3 (Ohio Ct. App. 10th Dist. Franklin County 1997); see also Hughs on Behalf of Praul v. Cole, 572 N.W.2d 747 (Minn. Ct. App. 1997) (noting that child suffered emotionally and physically in Minnesota even though abuse took place in Pennsylvania and reasoning that personal jurisdiction can be established by a single contact, in which case nature and quality of contact is dispositive; minimum contacts satisfied since father called his son in Minnesota and had continuing relationship with his son and it was foreseeable that consequences of abuse would arise in Minnesota); McNair v. McNair, 151 N.H. 343, 856 A.2d 5 (2004) (allegations in wife's domestic violence petitioner that husband made threatening telephone calls from out of state to wife in state alleged tortious conduct as would permit the use of long arm statute to exercise jurisdiction over husband). But see Anderson v. Deas, 273 Ga. App. 770, 615 S.E.2d 859 (2005), cert. granted, cause remanded, (Nov. 7, 2005) (in which the appellate court rejected the argument that long arm jurisdiction exists because the tort is a composite of both the act and the resulting injury).

[38]Bartsch v. Bartsch, 636 N.W.2d 3, 5 (Iowa 2001); see also Pierson v. Pierson, 147 Misc. 2d 209, 555 N.Y.S.2d 227 (Fam. Ct. 1990); Anthony T. v. Anthony J., 134 Misc. 2d 375, 510 N.Y.S.2d 810 (Fam. Ct. 1986); Shah v. Shah, 373 N.J. Super. 47, 860 A.2d 940 (App. Div. 2004), judgment aff'd as modified, 184 N.J. 125, 875 A.2d 931 (2005) (even though New Jersey lacked personal jurisdiction over husband, an Illinois resident, trial court had authority to issue a TRO for the protection of wife, a resident of New Jersey, but only to the extent the TRO afforded prohibitory relief; trial court had subject matter jurisdiction and wife was entitled to protection of New Jersey law and upon adequate notice of entry, husband was prohibited from violating the TRO within New Jersey). But see Spencer v. Spencer, 191 S.W.3d 14 (Ky. Ct. App. 2006) (husband lacked minimum contacts with state so as to confer personal jurisdiction over him in a domestic violence proceeding; discussion of prohibitory versus affirmative protection orders); Fox v. Fox, 197 Vt. 466, 2014 VT 100, 106 A.3d 919 (2014).

court to issue a protection order.[39] The court determined that the defendant's due process rights were not violated because he was served notice of the order in his home state and he had opportunity to appear.

The nature of the requested relief imposed no personal judgment against the defendant.[40] The Iowa Supreme Court's understanding of domestic violence was significant to the decision. Because of the interstate nature of most abusive relationships and the need to protect victims beyond the borders of a particular state, " '[f]uture violence ought to be constrained in any state in which the victim is located.' "[41]

Q & A: What is the test for determining minimum contacts?

In *Burnett v. Burnett*,[42] the trial court granted the CPO because of death threats expressed in the event appellee ever left appellant, and text message threats sent to appellee while she resided in Ohio. Appellant asserted that the grant of a CPO was erroneous where the record of the proceedings failed to establish sufficient minimum contacts necessary for the court to exercise personal jurisdiction over him.

The Sixth District Court of Appeals reviewed cases that addressed minimum contacts for purposes of civil protection orders and determined that "[w]here a plaintiff has been granted a domestic violence CPO against a defendant, and the only basis for the defendant's connection to the state is through phone calls and electronic communication, some evidence as to the content of those communications is essential to our affirmance of the trial court's order."[43] At the full hearing, no evidence was presented as to the threats appellant had made since appellee moved to Ohio; rather, the testimony dealt with appellant's history of threatening behavior while the parties lived in other states. In that the only evidence of content of these communications was submitted at the ex parte hearing and no record of the hearing was made, the evidence was insufficient to determine minimum contacts. "The lower court then essentially "tacked" the evidence from the ex parte hearing onto the evidence from the full hearing to find the minimum contacts necessary to grant the full CPO."[44]

The appellate court first determined that "tacking" was not contemplated by RC 3113.31. It then held that "[w]hen the issue is minimum contacts for the issuance of a domestic violence CPO, the content of those communications is an essential element. That is, it is the content that creates the threat and thereby establishes the minimum contacts necessary to effectuate [personal] jurisdiction under RC

[39] See also Caplan v. Donovan, 450 Mass. 463, 879 N.E.2d 117 (2008).

[40] Bartsch v. Bartsch, 636 N.W.2d 3, 10 (Iowa 2001).

[41] Bartsch v. Bartsch, 636 N.W.2d 3, 9 (Iowa 2001), quoting State v. Bellows, 596 N.W.2d 509 (Iowa 1999).

[42] Burnett v. Burnett, 2012-Ohio-2673, 2012 WL 2196336 (Ohio Ct. App. 6th Dist. Sandusky County 2012).

[43] Burnett v. Burnett, 2012-Ohio-2673, 2012 WL 2196336, *6 (Ohio Ct. App. 6th Dist. Sandusky County 2012).

[44] Burnett v. Burnett, 2012-Ohio-2673, 2012 WL 2196336, *7 (Ohio Ct. App. 6th Dist. Sandusky County 2012).

2307.382."[45] In reversing the trial court, the appellate court found that there were insufficient minimum contacts to confer personal jurisdiction over appellant.

However, the dissent admonished the majority and stated that "the majority's decision implies that to have the requisite minimum contacts with Ohio to gain personal jurisdiction over appellant, he had to have been either physically in the state of Ohio when the threats were made or that the history of violent acts must have occurred within the state of Ohio. I disagree."[46] "In an age where electronic communication eliminates the need for a defendant to physically appear in a state before establishing personal jurisdiction, Ohio courts have found the minimum contacts exist when a non-resident uses the phone or email to contact persons within the state."[47]

The dissent also determined that minimum contacts do not require such history of violent acts to have occurred in the same place in which a petitioner seeks the civil protection order. "The majority's decision would prevent the grant of a civil protection order based only on telephone, text or email threats to an abused spouse who flees in fear to Ohio from the abusive spouse in another state. Instead, the majority requires the abused spouse to remain in the jurisdiction where the history of violence has occurred, to take his or her chances of finding a place of safety while seeking the civil protection order. This view is both impractical and unsupported by law."[48]

In response to the "tacking" issue, the dissent noted that a court may rely on all evidence presented at either the ex parte or full hearing to justify issuing the CPO.

Q & A: What if the victim is in Ohio only temporarily to escape the violence or is an out-of-county resident who has moved into the forum to live with family or friends temporarily or to stay at a battered women's shelter?

The courts may accept the petition of a victim, even though the victim's residence may be temporary, to deter further violence in the forum county.[49] The test should be whether there is an "immediate and present danger" to the victim under RC 3113.31(D), whether there is a likelihood of future violence in the forum county or state, and whether due process protections are afforded to the respondent.

Recently, the Supreme Court of New Hampshire reiterated the analysis in *Bartsch* and *Caplan* when it held that a family court could issue a civil protection order absent personal jurisdiction so long as the order did not require affirmative action from the defendant. In *Hemen-*

---

[45]Burnett v. Burnett, 2012-Ohio-2673, 2012 WL 2196336, *7 (Ohio Ct. App. 6th Dist. Sandusky County 2012).

[46]Burnett v. Burnett, 2012-Ohio-2673, 2012 WL 2196336, ¶ 24 (Ohio Ct. App. 6th Dist. Sandusky County 2012).

[47]Burnett v. Burnett, 2012-Ohio-2673, 2012 WL 2196336, ¶ 25 (Ohio Ct. App. 6th Dist. Sandusky County 2012), citing Sobieniak v. Chapdelaine, 2008-Ohio-6403, 2008 WL 5147439 (Ohio Ct. App. 6th Dist. Lucas County 2008).

[48]Burnett v. Burnett, 2012-Ohio-2673, 2012 WL 2196336, ¶ 27 (Ohio Ct. App. 6th Dist. Sandusky County 2012).

[49]Civ.R. 3(B)(10).

way v. Hemenway,[50] the state Supreme Court held that so long as the protection order focused on the plaintiff's protected status by prohibiting abuse but does not impose any personal obligations on a defendant, the order is valid even without personal jurisdiction over the defendant.

The Court determined that "[a] protective order 'prohibit[s] acts of domestic violence,' providing 'the victim with the very protection the law specifically allows,' while preventing 'the defendant from engaging in behavior already specifically outlawed.' "[51] "A contrary ruling would present a domestic violence victim with two 'unpalatable choices. . .either to. . .return to the State in which the abuse occurred. . .or, alternatively, to wait for the abuser to follow the victim to [New Hampshire] and, in the event of a new incident of abuse, seek an order from a [New Hampshire] court.' "[52]

Interestingly, the affirmative action that may not be imposed upon defendant absent personal jurisdiction includes the relinquishment of all deadly weapons and weapons permits and hunting licenses and purchasing any firearms or ammunition.[53]

Q & A: What if the victim wants to obtain a civil protection order in the county where the respondent resides and the victim does not live in that county and has no intention of living there?

A petitioner should be able to obtain a civil protection order against a respondent living in another county.[54] The issue is not whether a petitioner can obtain a civil protection order. The issue is whether service over the respondent can be perfected.

Theoretically, a victim should also be able to obtain a protection order in the county in which the respondent resides, whether or not the victim also resides in that county.[55] The issues are twofold: whether a petitioner is able to obtain relief where the violence occurred in the other county and whether the protection order can be enforced in the county in which the victim lives should there be a violation.

Prior to December 1994, the prevailing view was that the county where the victim resided or where the incident occurred was the appropriate forum. There was no question that an order so issued could be enforced by the local police. Unfortunately, a protection order issued in the county where the respondent resided posed an enforcement problem for the petitioner when the violation took place in the county in which the petitioner resided. There were also enforcement problems when the protection order was issued in the county where the petitioner resided and the petitioner later moved to a different county.

In 1994, the statute was amended to require law enforcement agen-

[50]Hemenway v. Hemenway, 159 N.H. 680, 992 A.2d 575 (2010).

[51]*Hemenway at *6*, quoting Shah v. Shah, 184 N.J. 125, 875 A.2d 931 (2005).

[52]*Hemenway at *6*, quoting Caplan v. Donovan, 450 Mass. 463, 879 N.E.2d 117 (2008).

[53]See also Text 12:22.

[54]Civ.R. 3(B)(1); RC 3113.31(F)(3), RC 3113.31(N).

[55]See Reese v. Reese, 1997 WL 272368 (Ohio Ct. App. 8th Dist. Cuyahoga County 1997).

cies to enforce all civil protection orders issued anywhere in the state.[56] Additionally, the statute provides for a procedure for registering civil protection orders in other counties.[57]

Rather than requesting a protection order from the county in which the respondent resides, the petitioner should file for a protection order in the county in which he/she lives and register the protection order in the county where the respondent resides pursuant to RC 3113. 31(N). The petitioner should also request that the court serve a copy of the order on the respondent's local police department.

Q & A: A woman left the county and state to escape domestic abuse by her spouse. She then commenced divorce proceedings in the county she left. Are venue and jurisdiction proper?

According to the Cuyahoga County Court of Appeals, the answer is yes. In *Reese v. Reese*,[58] the victim vacated the marital home because of domestic violence. Several weeks after leaving the county and the state, she commenced divorce proceedings in Cuyahoga County. The defendant appealed, arguing that neither venue nor jurisdiction was proper. The appellate court reasoned that, since the plaintiff did not establish residency in Florida, she was still a resident of Ohio for purposes of filing a divorce. More importantly, the Cuyahoga County Court of Appeals rejected defendant's argument on public policy grounds, holding:

> To find that the trial court lacked jurisdiction would supersede the paramount issue of protecting individuals against domestic abuse. . . . To find that victims of domestic violence who seek temporary shelter in another state forfeit their rights as residents would deny such victims the protection available to them under RC Chapter 3113 during the period they would be required to re-establish residency.[59]

Q & A: In what court should a petitioner file?

This now depends on the relationship between the petitioner and respondent and in some circumstances, the age of the respondent.

Ohio law authorizes a family or household member to file for a civil protection order in the domestic relations division of the court of common pleas in counties that have a domestic relations division and in the court of common pleas in counties that do not have a domestic relations division.[60]

Where the parties are not family or household members as defined in RC 3113.31, the appropriate court is the court of common pleas of the county in which the person to be protected resides.[61] Most persons in adult dating relationships or the ex partner or in-law of a current partner are examples of relationships that must file for protection orders in common pleas courts. Even some family or household

---

[56]RC 3113.31(F)(3).

[57]RC 3113.31(N)(1) to RC 3113.31(N)(4).

[58]Reese v. Reese, 1997 WL 272368 (Ohio Ct. App. 8th Dist. Cuyahoga County 1997).

[59]Reese v. Reese, 1997 WL 272368, *2 (Ohio Ct. App. 8th Dist. Cuyahoga County 1997).

[60]RC 3113.31(A)(2).

[61]RC 2903.214(C)(1) indicating that the respondent must be 18 years or older.

members file for civil protection orders in common pleas courts.[62]

---

[62]RC 2903.214; see also § 9:3 Civil Stalking Protection Orders.

Chapter 11

Issuance of a Civil Protection Order

§ 11:1 Commencement of an action

An action for a civil protection order may be commenced by filing a petition with the clerk of courts of the domestic relations division of the court of common pleas or the court of common pleas in counties that do not have a separate domestic relations division.[1] The court has

---

[Section 11:1]

[1]RC 3113.31(A)(2); see for example Devault v. Devault, 2004-Ohio-976, 2004 WL 397134 (Ohio Ct. App. 5th Dist. Ashland County 2004).

jurisdiction over all proceedings under this section,[2] including motions for contempt brought under this section of the statute.[3]

Any proceeding under RC 3113.31 must be conducted in accordance with the Rules of Civil Procedure.[4] For example, issues related to commencement, venue, pleadings, and process must comport with the Ohio Rules of Civil Procedure. Any proceedings before the court must also follow the Rules of Procedure.[5]

For example, in *Snyder v. Snyder*,[6] the respondent appealed the granting of a protection order asserting that the trial court erred by failing to afford him an opportunity to utilize any discovery procedures and motion practice available under the Rules of Civil Procedure. He argued that RC 3113.31(G) afforded him additional time "'to prepare as provided by the Civil Rules . . . for the purpose of further developing the defenses made plain by the testimony' given at the [full] hearing."[7] The court of appeals noted that the respondent could have requested a continuance to further prepare, but failed to do so. The court pointed out that RC 3113.31 provides for only two hearings. RC 3113.31 does not provide for a third hearing.

Q & A: Is a Peace Bond the same as a protection order?

Bonds are often used by courts when injunctions are issued. Accordingly, a bond may be obtained for any protection order issued under RC 3113.31(G), which provides that "any proceeding under this section shall be conducted in accordance with the Rules of Civil Procedure, except that an order under this section may be obtained with or without bond."

Generally, a bond is an amount of money deposited to exact compliance with an act or event upon which it is conditioned. According to *Black's Law Dictionary*, a "peace bond" is defined as a "[t]ype of surety bond required by a judge or magistrate of one who has threatened to breach the peace or has a history of such misconduct."[8] In domestic violence actions, a bond may be granted in order to insure compliance with the law and the orders issued.

Pursuant to the Rules of Civil Procedure, however,

> the party obtaining [an ex parte order may give] a bond executed by sufficient surety, approved by the clerk of the court granting the order or injunction, in an amount fixed by the court or judge allowing it, to secure

[2]RC 3113.31(B).

[3]RC 3113.31(L)(1)(b); see also West v. West, 1994 WL 680156 (Ohio Ct. App. 2d Dist. Montgomery County 1994).

[4]RC 3113.31(G); see also Hoff v. Brown, 2001 WL 876228 (Ohio Ct. App. 5th Dist. Stark County 2001).

[5]See Stanton v. Guerrero, 1994 WL 472104 (Ohio Ct. App. 2d Dist. Montgomery County 1994).

[6]Snyder v. Snyder, 1995 WL 493998 (Ohio Ct. App. 4th Dist. Ross County 1995); see also Martinez v. Martinez, 52 S.W.3d 429 (Tex. App. Fort Worth 2001).

[7]Snyder v. Snyder, 1995 WL 493998, *3 (Ohio Ct. App. 4th Dist. Ross County 1995).

[8]Black's Law Dictionary (6th ed.) p 1130.

to the party enjoined the damages he may sustain, if it is finally decided that the order or injunction should not have been granted.[9]

The language of RC 3113.31 suggests that a bond may be secured against either the petitioner or the respondent in a domestic violence proceeding. If a bond is ordered against the petitioner, it is ordered prior to the petitioner obtaining an ex parte protection order. A bond may also be granted after a full hearing if it is necessary to obtain compliance with orders issued by the court under RC 3113.31(E)(1). If ordered after the full hearing, the bond will most likely be ordered against the respondent.

However, ordering bonds against either the petitioner or the respondent is rarely, if ever, considered by the court. In none of Ohio's eighty-eight counties are bonds routinely granted. Nevertheless, it is important for the family law practitioner to recognize that the statute clearly permits this additional security.

§ 11:2 Contents of the petition

The petition must contain or state the following information:

(1) an allegation that the respondent engaged in domestic violence[1] against a family or household member of the respondent, including a description of the nature and extent of the domestic violence.[2]

(2) the relationship of the respondent to the petitioner and to the victim if other than the petitioner.[3]

(3) a request for relief under this section.[4]

The petition must set forth the relationship between the parties.[5] This includes detailing the relationship between the petitioner and the respondent in those instances where the petitioner is not also the victim.[6] It must also contain a request for relief.[7] The types of relief available are enumerated in RC 3113.31(E)(1). The petition must be

[9]Civ.R. 65(C).

[Section 11:2]

[1]See also Bahr v. Bahr, 2003-Ohio-5024, 2003 WL 22176762 (Ohio Ct. App. 5th Dist. Ashland County 2003) (holding that one must be able to prove domestic violence on the date and time indicated in the petition).

[2]RC 3113.31(C)(1). See also Ferris v. Ferris, 2006-Ohio-878, 2006 WL 456811 (Ohio Ct. App. 12th Dist. Clermont County 2006) (discussing whether petition contained a sufficient description of domestic violence). RC 3113.31(A)(1)(c) has been added to provide that domestic violence includes committing a sexually oriented offenses as defined in RC 2950.01. Note that sexual abuse towards a child forms the basis of a sexually oriented offense protection order; see also Lutson v. Anderkin, 2013 WL 2150897 (Ohio C.P. 2013); Rehfus v. Smith, 2015-Ohio-2145, 2015 WL 3498686 (Ohio Ct. App. 7th Dist. Carroll County 2015).

[3]RC 3113.31(C)(2). But see RC 2903.214(C) which does not require that the petition include the parties' relationship.

[4]RC 3113.31(C)(3).

[5]RC 3113.31(C)(2); see also RC 3113.31(A)(3) and RC 3113.31(A)(4) for the relationships covered.

[6]See Carney v. Pankey, 1988 WL 34644 (Ohio Ct. App. 7th Dist. Mahoning County 1988) (petitioner was the parent of an unconscious and severely beaten adult daughter who did not reside with the respondent).

accompanied by a specific order providing for the relief as ordered by the court[8] and penalties for noncompliance.[9]

The nature and extent of the domestic violence directed at the victim or another family or household member must be described in detail.[10] The nature of the violence must fall under one of the acts enumerated in RC 3113.31(A)(1). An affidavit should be attached to the petition detailing the acts of domestic violence committed by the respondent against a family or household member, including a description of the extent of the injury. Although not required by statute, some courts have local rules requiring that a specific affidavit be filed with the petition.[11] Other courts do not have specific local rules regarding domestic violence but include procedures regarding ex parte orders generally.[12] It is good legal practice for the petitioner's attorney to prepare an affidavit and file it with the petition. An individualized affidavit projects an image of the abuse and sets forth a prima facie case of domestic violence. The petitioner can then testify to the specific allegations stated in the affidavit at the hearing.[13]

At the very least, a detailed description of the nature of the violence should be included with any petition filed. Each act should be set forth with particularity as to approximate date of occurrence. Past acts of domestic violence and/or stalking should be enumerated as well.[14] Besides stating a case for its issuance, a description of the acts of violence perpetrated by a specific respondent puts that individual on notice as to the specific allegations against him or her.[15]

Providing notice to a respondent of the specific allegations against

---

[7]RC 3113.31(C)(3).

[8]See RC 3113.31(E)(1).

[9]See RC 3113.31(L).

[10]RC 3113.31(C)(1); see also Martinez v. Martinez, 52 S.W.3d 429 (Tex. App. Fort Worth 2001) (The Texas statute does not require a detailed affidavit as to the description of facts and circumstances concerning domestic violence except when seeking an ex parte order. Ohio statute requires a description of the violence for either an ex parte or full hearing CPO); Podeweltz v. Rieger, 2007-Ohio-1513, ¶ 71, 2007 WL 949482 (Ohio Ct. App. 2d Dist. Montgomery County 2007) (noting that the Supreme Court standardized forms merely requires a petitioner to describe nature and extent of 2 or more threats or other pattern of conduct, but there is not requirement that petitioner file a statement that she/he feels threatened by the respondent. The form by its very language contains the appropriate allegations).

[11]See, e.g., Cuy. D.R. R. 26(A)(1).

[12]See, eg., Cuy. D.R.R. 26; Licking D.R.R. 7.0; Mahoning D.R.R. 38; Montgomery D.R.R. 4.46; Summit D.R.R. 15; Stark D.R.R. 20.

[13]But see Whitten v. Whitten, 292 Ill. App. 3d 780, 226 Ill. Dec. 670, 686 N.E.2d 19, 22 (3d Dist. 1997) (regarding affidavits); see H.E.S. v. J.C.S., 175 N.J. 309, 815 A.2d 405 (2003) (holding that due process rights of husband were violated by trial court's refusal to grant him a continuance after wife alleged an incident of domestic violence not alleged in her petition).

[14]But see Coburn v. Coburn, 342 Md. 244, 674 A.2d 951 (1996) (affirming trial court holding that past history of domestic violence admissible at a protection order hearing even if not pled in original petition).

[15]See, e.g., Henry v. Coogan, 2002-Ohio-6519, 2002 WL 31682226, *1 (Ohio Ct. App. 12th Dist. Clermont County 2002) (man had reasonable notice of stalking allegations by woman who brought action for civil protective order and thus his due process rights were not violated by trial court's reliance on incidents not specifically alleged in petition; man was given notice of the full hearing; pleadings were sufficient to

him may enhance his ability to defend against the allegations. However, general allegations may encourage a respondent to request discovery,[16] or may be grounds for the dismissal of the protection order at the full hearing.[17]

Q & A: Must the act of domestic violence occur on the date set forth in the petition?[18]

This issue becomes particularly important if the respondent has an alibi for the date that petitioner alleges the abuse occurred. It may also provide a respondent a due process argument.[19]

Several cases have addressed this issue. For example, in *Solomon v. Solomon*,[20] the trial court denied the CPO against the husband. The appellate court affirmed the trial court and held that the evidence did not establish that appellant was in fear of imminent serious physical harm.

In its reasoning, the court first acknowledged that no part of RC 3113.31 refers to the examination of past acts of domestic violence in present cases but then noted that courts have held that in certain circumstances, they may consider past behaviors when determining

inform him that he was alleged to have engaged in a pattern of conduct that amounted to stalking; man did not object to questioning regarding incidents not alleged in pleadings); Bateman v. Shipman, 2000 WL 1459721 (Ohio Ct. App. 11th Dist. Trumbull County 2000) (appellate court affirmed decision of trial court's granting of a protection order despite fact that evidence was presented of allegations that were not set forth in the original petition); Podeweltz v. Rieger, 2007-Ohio-1513, ¶ 71, 2007 WL 949482 (Ohio Ct. App. 2d Dist. Montgomery County 2007) ("The fact that Podeweitz set forth a description of the actions which caused her to believe Rieger would cause her physical harm serves to put him on notice of her allegations."); Chafin v. Chafin, 2010-Ohio-3939, 2010 WL 3294288 (Ohio Ct. App. 9th Dist. Lorain County 2010) (despite respondent's argument that the trial court erred by adopting the CPO because the only evidence that he actually physically assaulted petitioner was in her testimony at the hearing for the first time (and not in her affidavit), appellate court noted that trial court did not base its decision upon a finding of physical harm, but rather that respondent placed her in fear of imminent physical harm); but see Bahr v. Bahr, 2003-Ohio-5024, 2003 WL 22176762 (Ohio Ct. App. 5th Dist. Ashland County 2003) (where appellate court held wife failed to prove that domestic violence occurred on date and time alleged in her petition, citing Bruner v. Bruner, 2000-Ohio-2554, 2000 WL 1486452 (Ohio Ct. App. 7th Dist. Mahoning County 2000).

[16]Note that RC 3113.31(G) provides that any proceeding must be conducted in accordance with the Civil Rules of Procedure and discovery permitted under the Civil Rules; see also Text § 12:5, Full hearing—Discovery issues; Martinez v. Martinez, 52 S.W.3d 429 (Tex. App. Fort Worth 2001) (discussing reasons for discovery in protection order proceeding).

[17]Nicola v. Nicola, 2015-Ohio-4017, 2015 WL 5728577 (Ohio Ct. App. 11th Dist. Lake County 2015).

[18]See also Text § 8:4.

[19]See Bahr v. Bahr, 2003-Ohio-5024, 2003 WL 22176762 (Ohio Ct. App. 5th Dist. Ashland County 2003) (holding that the wife failed to prove that domestic violence occurred on date and time set forth in petition); but see Henry v. Coogan, 2002-Ohio-6519, 2002 WL 31682226 (Ohio Ct. App. 12th Dist. Clermont County 2002).

[20]Solomon v. Solomon, 157 Ohio App. 3d 807, 2004-Ohio-2486, 813 N.E.2d 918 (7th Dist. Mahoning County 2004). See also Pinkney v. Salett, 2011-Ohio-4121, 2011 WL 3654420 (Ohio Ct. App. 8th Dist. Cuyahoga County 2011); Weber v. Weber, 2011-Ohio-2980, 2011 WL 2436963 (Ohio Ct. App. 2d Dist. Greene County 2011) (reversing the trial court grant of the CPO and finding that an act of domestic violence must have occurred on the date set forth on the petition for the civil protection order).

whether there was an act of domestic violence.[21] "That is because in a situation such as this where the alleged offending act is one that places the assumed victim in fear of harm, '[t]he fear* * *and the reasonableness of that fear could and should be determined with reference to [a petitioner's] history with [the respondent].' "[22]

The appellate court then noted that while a court may consider past acts to determine whether the present incident constitutes domestic violence, the issuance of the CPO cannot be based on previous acts of domestic violence alone.[23] "Rather, the petitioner must establish by a preponderance of the evidence that an act of domestic violence occurred on the date set forth on the petition for a civil protection order."[24]

On the other hand, the 12th District Court of Appeals rejected this interpretation in *McGuire v. Sprinkle*.[25] In that case, appellant alleged that the trial court erred in finding that she threatened appellee on December 21, 2005. The petition alleged that the date of the threat was on January 7, 2006. Appellee testified that the date of the threat was December 21, 2005. Appellant supported this contention with language from *Solomon* and *Bruner* which held that a CPO must be based on a fear of serious physical harm that occurred on the date in the petition.

Although the *McGuire* appellate court acknowledged that *Solomon* and *Bruner* do include such language which, taken in isolation, would support this proposition, the statements must be viewed in the context

[21]Solomon v. Solomon, 157 Ohio App. 3d 807, 813, 2004-Ohio-2486, 813 N.E.2d 918 (7th Dist. Mahoning County 2004), citing Eichenberger v. Eichenberger, 82 Ohio App. 3d 809, 613 N.E.2d 678 (10th Dist. Franklin County 1992). See also Thom v. Mulvin, 2009-Ohio-3797, 2009 WL 2365996 (Ohio Ct. App. 6th Dist. Erie County 2009).

[22]Solomon v. Solomon, 157 Ohio App. 3d 807, 813, 2004-Ohio-2486, 813 N.E.2d 918 (7th Dist. Mahoning County 2004), quoting Eichenberger v. Eichenberger, 82 Ohio App. 3d 809, 816, 613 N.E.2d 678 (10th Dist. Franklin County 1992). See also Martauz v. Martauz, 2009-Ohio-2642, 2009 WL 1581185 (Ohio Ct. App. 7th Dist. Mahoning County 2009); Crabtree v. Dinsmoor, 2013-Ohio-5797, 2013 WL 6869957 (Ohio Ct. App. 10th Dist. Franklin County 2013); Strassell v. Chapman, 2010-Ohio-4376, 2010 WL 3610591 (Ohio Ct. App. 10th Dist. Franklin County 2010).

[23]Solomon v. Solomon, 157 Ohio App. 3d 807, 813, 2004-Ohio-2486, 813 N.E.2d 918 (7th Dist. Mahoning County 2004), citing Bruner v. Bruner, 2000-Ohio-2554, 2000 WL 1486452 (Ohio Ct. App. 7th Dist. Mahoning County 2000); see also Anderson v. Anderson, 2001-Ohio-3379, 2001 WL 1667875 (Ohio Ct. App. 7th Dist. Mahoning County 2001); Williamson v. Williamson, 180 Ohio App. 3d 260, 2008-Ohio-6718, 905 N.E.2d 217 (2d Dist. Greene County 2008); Pinkney v. Salett, 2011-Ohio-4121, 2011 WL 3654420 (Ohio Ct. App. 8th Dist. Cuyahoga County 2011); Weber v. Weber, 2011-Ohio-2980, 2011 WL 2436963 (Ohio Ct. App. 2d Dist. Greene County 2011); Cottrill v. Cottrill, 2017-Ohio-1422, 2017 WL 1376841 (Ohio Ct. App. 5th Dist. Fairfield County 2017).

[24]Solomon v. Solomon, 157 Ohio App. 3d 807, 813, 2004-Ohio-2486, 813 N.E.2d 918 (7th Dist. Mahoning County 2004); Weber v. Weber, 2011-Ohio-2980, 2011 WL 2436963 (Ohio Ct. App. 2d Dist. Greene County 2011); Williams v. Hupp, 2011-Ohio-3403, 2011 WL 2670945 (Ohio Ct. App. 7th Dist. Mahoning County 2011); but see Gannon v. Gannon, 2008-Ohio-4484, 2008 WL 4093687 (Ohio Ct. App. 6th Dist. Wood County 2008) (interpreting this holding differently); J.M. v. M.M., 2016-Ohio-5368, 2016 WL 4272340 (Ohio Ct. App. 9th Dist. Medina County 2016).

[25]McGuire v. Sprinkle, 2007-Ohio-2705, 2007 WL 1585100 (Ohio Ct. App. 12th Dist. Warren County 2007).

of the entire decision. "Instead, the cases stand for the proposition that in order to grant a civil protection order, past acts alone are not enough and there must be some evidence of current domestic violence, as set forth in statute."[26]

Additionally, the court relied on Civ. R. 15 which permits amending pleadings to conform to the evidence.[27] The court also stated that the rule does not prohibit a trial court from *sua sponte* amending a pleading.

Similarly, the Mahoning County Court of Appeals addressed this issue in *Zawrotuk v. Zawrotuk*.[28] In this case, appellee detailed several incidents of domestic violence in her petition for CPO against her husband. Appellee testified that on June 4, 2013, after appellant stated he could hurt her and lunged at her after an argument, she packed and threw his bags over a banister. She then stated that he aggressively put both hands around her head and pulled her towards him which frightened her because of a prior domestic violence incident. She responded by swinging her arm and hit him as he forcefully kissed her while he held her face with both hands.[29] He then threw her to the ground causing her head to hit the floor. Upon the arrival of the police, they saw a crying and visibly shaken woman and observed visible physical injuries.

The defense pointed out that wife waited a month before filing the CPO and argued that she was not under a threat at the time of the ex parte order, that the petition did not detail the June 4, 2013, date of the incident and that she did not testify about the date at the ex parte hearing.[30] Finally, the defense further stressed that "without knowing the timing of the alleged incident, it was impossible to apply the test for issuing an ex parte order. He concludes that the ex parte order

---

[26]McGuire v. Sprinkle, 2007-Ohio-2705, 2007 WL 1585100, *3 (Ohio Ct. App. 12th Dist. Warren County 2007); see also Gannon v. Gannon, 2008-Ohio-4484, 2008 WL 4093687 (Ohio Ct. App. 6th Dist. Wood County 2008) (while a finding of statutory domestic violence may not be based solely on remote events, it must be premised on conduct current enough that the fear engendered is current; thus, the fear must be present on the date alleged in the petition even though the act that precipitated the fear occurred earlier; although the incident of domestic violence occurred on July 1, this was sufficiently close to the date of filing the petition, which was July 11); Text §§ 8:4, 12:11. Lewis v. Gravely, 2016-Ohio-1502, 2016 WL 1404159 (Ohio Ct. App. 4th Dist. Adams County 2016) (noting that the relevant time frame for examining whether respondent caused another to fear imminent serious physical harm is the time frame alleged in the petition. At ¶ 30); Weber v. Forinash, 2015-Ohio-3187, 2015 WL 4720532 (Ohio Ct. App. 6th Dist. Sandusky County 2015) (relying on *Gannon* and explaining that the fear must still be present on the date alleged in the petition, irrespective of when the acts precipitating the fear occurred. ¶ 18); but see dissent in *Weber v. Forinash* (suggesting that majority's decision is flawed in that the full hearing took place over 13 months after appellee asserted her claim and finding no evidence to show appellee was in "immediate and present danger of domestic violence" at the time of the full hearing. At ¶ 34).

[27]See also Gannon v. Gannon, 2008-Ohio-4484, 2008 WL 4093687 (Ohio Ct. App. 6th Dist. Wood County 2008).

[28]Zawrotuk v. Zawrotuk, 2014-Ohio-5225, 2014 WL 6641772 (Ohio Ct. App. 7th Dist. Mahoning County 2014).

[29]Zawrotuk v. Zawrotuk, 2014-Ohio-5225, 2014 WL 6641772, ¶ 5 (Ohio Ct. App. 7th Dist. Mahoning County 2014).

[30]Zawrotuk v. Zawrotuk, 2014-Ohio-5225, 2014 WL 6641772, ¶ 9 (Ohio Ct. App. 7th Dist. Mahoning County 2014).

was based on an incomplete foundation and thus it should have been invalidated rather than extended after the full hearing."[31]

The appellate court noted that RC 3113.31(C)(1-3) does not require the petition to contain the date of the incident set forth in the petition. In fact, "[t]he petition is typically filed without counsel, and the process is designed for use even by the most unsophisticated of victims. A hearing is required before an ex parte petition can be granted, and this is where timing should be discussed."[32]

The court then pointed out that an issue with an ex parte order does not invalidate a protection order issued after a full hearing. Noting that in some cases a CPO is not requested or a CPO can be denied, a court is still permitted to issue a CPO after a full hearing. "Likewise, a questionable presentation of facts at the ex parte hearing does not preclude a court from granting a protection order after a full hearing."[33]

In finding that appellant's arguments lacked merit, the Seventh District Court of Appeals held that "[t]he final protection order comes with its owns protections and determinations and does not rely on whether an ex parte order was made or made properly."[34]

Q & A: What do the Supreme Court forms provide?

The Ohio Supreme Court drafted standardized civil, domestic violence and criminal protection order forms, and civil and criminal stalking protection order forms[35] for statewide dissemination.[36] These form packets include instructions for completing the forms so that the petitioner may file the forms without the assistance of an attorney.[37] Additionally, Superintendence Rule 10.01(B) and Superintendence Rule 10.01(C) authorizes the domestic relations division to use forms that are substantially similar to the standard forms.[38]

The standardized petition for a civil protection order does not require that a specific affidavit be attached. The petition contains several blank lines for describing the abuse. The instruction packet, however, requires that the petitioner sign the petition in the presence

[31]Zawrotuk v. Zawrotuk, 2014-Ohio-5225, 2014 WL 6641772, ¶ 23 (Ohio Ct. App. 7th Dist. Mahoning County 2014).

[32]Zawrotuk v. Zawrotuk, 2014-Ohio-5225, 2014 WL 6641772, ¶ 24 (Ohio Ct. App. 7th Dist. Mahoning County 2014).

[33]Zawrotuk v. Zawrotuk, 2014-Ohio-5225, 2014 WL 6641772, ¶ 27 (Ohio Ct. App. 7th Dist. Mahoning County 2014).

[34]Zawrotuk v. Zawrotuk, 2014-Ohio-5225, 2014 WL 6641772, ¶ 28 (Ohio Ct. App. 7th Dist. Mahoning County 2014).

[35]See Sup. R. Form 10.03-B and Sup. R. Form 10.03-E.

[36]See Sup. R. 10.01, Sup. R. Form 10.01-A to Sup. R. Form 10.01-J (civil), Sup. R. 10.02, Sup. R. Form 10.02-A (criminal), eff. 1-1-98.

[37]See Sup. R. 10.01(A), eff. 1-1-98.

[38]See also Cuy. D.R. R. 26(A)(1). Weber v. Forinash, 2015-Ohio-3187, 2015 WL 4720532 (Ohio Ct. App. 6th Dist. Sandusky County 2015) (dissent disagreed with majority opinion's silence in not acknowledging trial court's failure to complete a full hearing form (Sup. R.10.01-I) after the full hearing and failing to comply with the Rules of Superintendence for the Courts of Ohio, relying on Sup. R. 10.01(C); conversely, the majority reasoned that the law in the 6th Dist. suggests that " '[t]he rules of superintendence * * * are guidelines for judges only and are not intended to function as rules of practice and procedure.' Caudill v. Caudill, 6th Dist. Sandusky No. S-04-018, 2006-Ohio-1116, ¶ 5, citing State v. Mahoney, 34 Ohio App.3d 114, 517 NE2d 957 (1st Dist. 1986)." At *8).

of a notary. Since Superintendence Rule 10.01 requires only substantial compliance with the standard forms, petitions drafted by attorneys should comply with the statutory directives of RC 3113.31(C). A separate affidavit is preferable for describing the nature and extent of the violence.[39] Before an attorney chooses to disregard an affidavit, it is incumbent that he/she check the local court rules and/or practice.

Q & A: Why should protection order forms be standardized across the state of Ohio?

In 1994, the Ohio General Assembly enacted H.B. 335 that provided for statewide enforcement of protection orders.[40] Law enforcement agencies were directed to enforce both civil and criminal protection orders issued anywhere in the state of Ohio. In addition, the legislature requested that the Supreme Court, in consultation with the Ohio Department of Human Services, prescribe uniform protection order forms.[41]

The primary goal of standardized forms enabled police officers to better address the needs of all parties in an efficient and prompt manner.[42] A protection order that is familiar to an officer is more likely to be enforced in a swift manner.[43]

Q & A: Are there any other forms that must be filed in addition to the petition for civil protection order and the accompanying order?

When children are part of the family relationship, additional forms may be filed with the petition. Although the domestic violence statute does not require that the petitioner requesting to be named residential parent or temporary custodian include specific UCCJEA provisions, the standardized petition[44] includes a parenting proceeding affidavit which complies with the requirements of the Uniform Child Custody Jurisdiction and Enforcement Act ("UCCJEA").[45]

The family law practitioner is cautioned, however, that the inclusion of certain UCCJEA provisions relative to the most current address of the petitioner and children may create safety issues for the petitioner. Some experts in the area of domestic violence law have

[39]See also Ritter v. Ritter, 2004-Ohio-2550, 2004 WL 1120824 (Ohio Ct. App. 8th Dist. Cuyahoga County 2004) (petitioner admitted on cross-examination that his affidavit was inaccurate and that he had not even read the affidavit prior to signing).

[40]See RC 3113.31(F)(3), RC 2919.26(G)(4).

[41]See 1994 H.B. 335, § 4, eff. 12-9-94; see also Wilson v. Wilson, 134 N.C. App. 642, 518 S.E.2d 255 (1999), as to completeness of printed domestic violence forms; Price v. Price, 133 N.C. App. 440, 441, 514 S.E.2d 553 (1999) (court failed to check all boxes of the protective order form, including box marked "Findings & Conclusions"; "because of the large number of domestic violence cases filed each year in North Carolina, we appreciate the usefulness of form orders. The trial court, however, should not neglect its responsibility to make necessary findings and conclusions.").

[42]See commentary to Sup. R. 10.01, eff. 1-1-98, amended eff. 6-1-2000.

[43]Calzo v. Lynch, 2012-Ohio-1353, 2012 WL 1067921 (Ohio Ct. App. 5th Dist. Richland County 2012); Weber v. Forinash, 2015-Ohio-3187, 2015 WL 4720532 (Ohio Ct. App. 6th Dist. Sandusky County 2015) (see dissent).

[44]See Sup. R. Form 10.01-F.

[45]See RC 3109.21 to RC 3109.27; see also Cuy. D.R. R. 26(A)(2). Sub. S.B. 185 was recently enacted, eff. 4-11-05. The Uniform Child Custody Jurisdiction and Enforcement Act (UCCJEA) repealed UCCJA.

suggested that the address provided on a parenting affidavit remain confidential.[46]

Additionally, it is imperative that all litigants truthfully answer questions set forth in the parenting affidavit[47] as well as in the petition[48], especially because these documents must be notarized.[49] That means that a petitioner must truthfully disclose whether they have participated in other custody cases and provide requested information about the custody case; whether they or other members of their household have any criminal convictions involving acts that resulted in a child being abused or neglected, any offense that is a violation of RC 2919.25, any sexually oriented offense as defined in RC 2950.01 and any offense involving a victim who was a family or household member at the time of the offense and cause physical harm to the victim in the commission of the offense. Petitioners must also disclose whether another party, not a party to the case, has physical custody or visitation rights to a child subject to the case. Lastly, a petitioner is on notice that she or he has continuing duty to advise the court of any custody, visitation, parenting time, divorce, dissolution of marriage, separation, neglect, abuse, dependency, guardianship, parentage, termination of parenting time or protection from domestic violence case concerning the children in this state or any other state about which information is obtained during this case.

Similarly, all litigants must truthfully respond to any questions set forth in the petition for civil protection order and they also have a duty to list all present and past court cases including civil, criminal, juvenile, divorce, custody, visitation and bankruptcy cases that relate to the respondent, petitioner, children, family and household members.

Several commentators go one step further and suggest that civil protection order proceedings should be exempt from any UCCJEA requirements and that the domestic violence statutes and the UCCJEA should reflect this amendment.[50]

If a petitioner is requesting temporary child support or spousal support, the forms required by each county relative to support and health

[46]See RC 3127.23. See also Text § 15:24, Other issues that impact custody and visitation awards.

[47]Sup. R. Form 10.01-F.

[48]Sup R. Form 10.01-D which mandates a petitioner to "list all present court cases and pertinent past court cases (including civil, criminal, divorce, juvenile, custody, visitation and bankruptcy cases) that relate to the respondent, you, your children, your family, or your household members"; see also Lyons v. Schandel, 2015-Ohio-3960, 2015 WL 5691906 (Ohio Ct. App. 7th Dist. Carroll County 2015) (which also includes any family or household members in your household convicted of sex abuse).

[49]See, e.g., State v. Rodriguez, 2009-Ohio-549, 2009 WL 295403 (Ohio Ct. App. 12th Dist. Butler County 2009) (upholding a perjury conviction for a petitioner who knowingly falsified her parenting proceeding affidavit by failing to disclose that she had been involved in both a child neglect and domestic violence case).

[50]D. Edwards & J. Meier, Coordination of State and Federal Statutes Related to Family Violence, paper written for the National Council of Juvenile & Family Court Judges (1992). But see Text § 15:24, Other issues that impact custody and visitation awards; Text § 18:9, Other remedies under VAWA.

insurance should also be included with the petition.[51] A completed child support computation worksheet must be included and made a part of the court record.[52]

Additionally, all protection orders that are issued by a court must contain a cover sheet which is, in effect, a warning page.[53] This page contains several visible warnings to both the respondent and the petitioner: (1) that the protection order is enforceable in all fifty states, the District of Columbia, tribal lands, and U.S. territories pursuant to the federal Violence Against Women Act; (2) that the violation of the order is a crime; (3) that only the court may modify the terms of the order; and (4) that the petitioner's consent does not authorize the respondent to violate the order. It also notifies the petitioner that, if he/she invites the respondent to the residence, the respondent may be arrested. The cover sheet also serves to educate law enforcement officials that the protection order is enforceable in all jurisdictions and stresses that arrest is the preferred course of action for a violation.

Upon the issuance of the civil protection order, a 10-A form must be completed by the court or counsel for the petitioner if authorized by the court and filed with the local law enforcement agency for entry into the FBI's National Crime Information Center (NCIC), rather than the state's Law Enforcement Automated Data System (LEADS). This change reflects a national resolve to provide nationwide dissemination of civil and criminal protection orders.[54] The 10-A form must include the following: (1) the respondent's name and address, (2) the respondent's social security number, date of birth, and physical description, (3) the terms of the order, (4) the effective date and expiration date of the order, (5) whether the respondent is Brady Handgun disqualified under 18 U.S.C.A. § 922(d)(8),[55] and (6) the names of the protected persons and their dates of birth. Law enforcement officials will have 24-hour access to this information, which will enable them to identify a valid protection order and understand the pertinent provisions of the order.[56]

Even though the forms are now standardized, there are still variations in both the method and extent of compliance in each of Ohio's eighty-eight counties and in court practice and procedure.[57] Since local procedures vary, family law practitioners should consult the local rules and court personnel for the proper procedure for filing a petition for a civil protection order in that jurisdiction.

Local rules of court are procedural in nature, not substantive. Therefore, they may not be used to determine substantive rights.

---

[51]RC 3113.31(K), RC 3113.21; see also Frank. D.R. R. 24.

[52]See Halley v. Ashley, 1997 WL 760662 (Ohio Ct. App. 9th Dist. Summit County 1997).

[53]See Sup. R. 10.01(D), eff. 1-1-98.

[54]See VAWA, 18 U.S.C.A. § 2265.

[55]See also Text § 18:11, Firearm offenses under VAWA.

[56]See Commentary (1-1-98) to Sup. R. 10.01.

[57]Note, for example, that procedures for magistrates when hearing CPO cases are inconsistent across Ohio.

Where local rules are adopted in the civil protection order arena, it is urged that they address only procedural concerns.[58]

§ 11:3 Filing issues

A petitioner may file for a civil protection order as a single action or as a second count to a divorce action. Nothing in the statute prohibits the filing of a two-count complaint seeking both a divorce and civil protection order. However, victims of domestic violence need not file for divorce in order to obtain a civil protection order.

Civil Rule 75 was amended, effective July 1, 1998, to provide that "[a] claim for a civil protection order based upon an allegation of domestic violence shall be a separate claim from a claim for divorce, dissolution of marriage, annulment, or legal separation."[1] However, the Civil Rules do not specify whether a claim for a civil protection order must be set forth in a separate cause of action and a separate complaint. Practice demonstrates, however, that it is common for one complaint to contain several counts or claims. In fact, a party may join as many claims as he/she has against the opposing party.[2] Therefore, it is arguable that the Civil Rule modification was made only to reinforce that a civil protection order proceeding is a separate claim from a divorce, dissolution, or legal separation.

However, most domestic relations courts now encourage separate filings. More and more courts are utilizing separate case numbers for the petition for CPO and the divorce if filed at the same time. The rationale for separate filings is that courts are better able to track civil protection order actions if they are not combined with divorce actions.

Q & A: Do I need an attorney to obtain a civil protection order?[3]

There is nothing in RC 3113.31 prohibiting petitioners from filing for protection orders without an attorney, i.e., pro se. In fact, the Ohio Supreme Court established uniform civil protection order forms and instruction packets for completing the forms so that a petitioner may file without the assistance of an attorney.[4] Pro se litigants should familiarize themselves with local court rules and domestic relations court procedures before filing in order to comply with the law.[5]

All courts allow pro se litigants to file petitions for civil protection

[58]See, e.g., Patterson v. Loveless, 2001 WL 524372, *2(Ohio Ct. App. 2d Dist. Montgomery County 2001) (discussing the use of local rules and when a trial court may not rely on the terms of the rule alone).

[Section 11:3]

[1]Civ.R. 75(G); see also Lapsansky v. Lapsansky, 2000 WL 1114535 (Ohio Ct. App. 7th Dist. Columbiana County 2000) (stressing that a CPO is a separate claim from a claim for divorce).

[2]Civ.R. 18(A).

[3]See D.N. v. K.M., 216 N.J. 587, 83 A.3d 825 (2014) (no right to appointed counsel in a domestic violence case).

[4]See 1994 H.B. 335, § 4 (uncodified), eff. 12-9-94.

[5]See, e.g., Summit D.R.R. 15, which details the court procedure so that a pro se litigant is able to file a protection order with the court; Dyke v. Price, 2000 WL 1546555 (Ohio Ct. App. 2d Dist. Montgomery County 2000); see also Text § 12:3, Full hearing—Participation of the parties.

orders. In fact all courts and clerks of courts have the domestic violence packets readily available.

Each pro se litigant must weigh the benefits of proceeding without an attorney in a system that traditionally utilizes attorneys. Most often, problems arise for a petitioner at the second hearing if the respondent is represented by counsel or if children's issues surface.

Q & A: Can a respondent appear for the ex parte CPO?

While it is possible, the prudent course of action is that the respondent not be present. In fact, the definition of an ex parte hearing is one in which only one side appears at the hearing, to wit: the petitioner. The Fourth District Court of Appeals, in *Wheeler v. Wheeler,*[6] determined that RC 3113.31 allows for an ex parte hearing which does not require the presence of the abuser. "Indeed, when the abuser has engaged in repeated abuse and has often threatened a spouse, excluding the abuser from the courtroom while the abused spouse is testifying may be advisable. The need for immediate attention to the abusive relationship necessitates procedures such as that provided by the Ohio Legislature."[7]

Q & A: May court clerks and domestic violence advocates aid pro se litigants in the preparation of their protection orders?[8]

It depends. Currently, there is no specific statute, court rule, or policy that provides guidance for a clerk or advocate who chooses to aid pro se litigants in the preparation of the petition for protection order. Although the Supreme Court Domestic Violence Advisory Committee has recommended that court clerks and advocates be immune from liability, no immunity clause has been enacted or adopted by court rule.[9]

Q & A: Can a judge or magistrate advise a pro se litigant in a domestic violence proceeding?[10]

The Preble County Court of Appeals considered whether a trial court might advise a petitioner in a domestic violence action.[11] In *Lain*

---

[6]Wheeler v. Wheeler, 2015-Ohio-4206, 2015 WL 5918030 (Ohio Ct. App. 4th Dist. Scioto County 2015).

[7]Wheeler v. Wheeler, 2015-Ohio-4206, 2015 WL 5918030, ¶ 4 (Ohio Ct. App. 4th Dist. Scioto County 2015).

[8]See also Text § 17:3, The unauthorized practice of law; but see State v. Rodriguez, 2009-Ohio-549, 2009 WL 295403 (Ohio Ct. App. 12th Dist. Butler County 2009) (where the domestic relations court receptionist provided petitioner a packet of the documents with instructions and placed her in a private room to complete the documents without court assistance; the receptionist then notarized the pertinent documents).

[9]See In the Matter of Amendment of the Commission's Rules Regarding the 37.0-38.6 GHz and 38.6-40.0 GHz Bands, 11 F.C.C.R. 4930, 1995 WL 783585 (F.C.C. 1995), rule modification granted, 12 F.C.C.R. 18600, 1997 WL 679996 (F.C.C. 1997), review denied, order aff'd, 237 F.3d 683 (D.C. Cir. 2001) and review denied, order aff'd, 237 F.3d 683 (D.C. Cir. 2001); see also Ch. 16 Role of the Victim Advocate.

[10]See also Niepsuj v. Niepsuj, 2010-Ohio-638, 2010 WL 625837 (Ohio Ct. App. 9th Dist. Summit County 2010); Text § 9:3; Swartz v. Swartz, 2011-Ohio-6685, 2011 WL 6880733 (Ohio Ct. App. 9th Dist. Medina County 2011). See also Text 12:4.

[11]See also State v. Gordon, 2003-Ohio-6558, 2003 WL 22889573 (Ohio Ct. App. 10th Dist. Franklin County 2003); Vasile v. Marinescu, 2006-Ohio-1739, 2006 WL 891026, *1 (Ohio Ct. App. 8th Dist. Cuyahoga County 2006) (acknowledging that "pro

v. Ververis,[12] the appellant contended that the trial court abused its discretion by advising the appellee to file a new petition for a civil protection order. Thought it reversed the trial court ruling and deemed the assignment of error moot, the appellate court explained, "we feel comment is necessary because this issue may arise again in the future. A trial court is not precluded from advising a party of the proper procedure to be followed in a given case, especially where that party is represented pro se."[13]

Q & A: How should courts respond to pro se litigants who have language barriers?

The Cuyahoga County Court of Appeals addressed a similar issue in *Vasile v. Marinescu*.[14] In this case, the respondent appealed the granting of a CPO issued against him. As his assignment of error, appellant argued "that he misunderstood the court proceedings because of the language barrier and because he did not have an attorney representing him."[15]

Although both parties gave opening statements, appellant did not present evidence despite a request from the Magistrate as to calling any witnesses. The magistrate based her decision to grant the CPO on the appellee's testimony only after being informed by appellant that he had nothing further.

In reversing the decision and remanding for a new CPO hearing, the appellate court noted "that 'pro se litigants were bound by the same rules and procedures as those litigants with retained counsel.' "[16] It then held that "because Marinescu did not intend to waive his right to testify or to call witnesses on his behalf, the magistrate's finding was based on incomplete evidence."[17] The court relied on *State v. Pina*, which held that the "failure to ensure that non-English speaking defendants are given the same opportunities as others to be present, to speak in their defense and to understand what is taking place,

se litigants are bound by the same rules and procedures as those litigants who retain counsel"), quoting Meyers v. First Nat. Bank of Cincinnati, 3 Ohio App. 3d 209, 444 N.E.2d 412 (1st Dist. Hamilton County 1981); Gibson v. Gibson, 2006-Ohio-2880, 2006 WL 1555935 (Ohio Ct. App. 4th Dist. Washington County 2006) (discussing pro se issues); Butcher v. Stevens, 182 Ohio App. 3d 77, 2009-Ohio-1754, 911 N.E.2d 928 (4th Dist. Athens County 2009).

[12]Lain v. Ververis, 1999 WL 893611 (Ohio Ct. App. 12th Dist. Preble County 1999).

[13]Lain v. Ververis, 1999 WL 893611, *3 (Ohio Ct. App. 12th Dist. Preble County 1999); but see Vance v. Nichols, 2007-Ohio-3819, 2007 WL 2164162 (Ohio Ct. App. 2d Dist. Darke County 2007).

[14]Vasile v. Marinescu, 2006-Ohio-1739, 2006 WL 891026 (Ohio Ct. App. 8th Dist. Cuyahoga County 2006).

[15]Vasile v. Marinescu, 2006-Ohio-1739, 2006 WL 891026, *1 (Ohio Ct. App. 8th Dist. Cuyahoga County 2006).

[16]Vasile v. Marinescu, 2006-Ohio-1739, 2006 WL 891026, *1 (Ohio Ct. App. 8th Dist. Cuyahoga County 2006), quoting Meyers v. First Nat. Bank of Cincinnati, 3 Ohio App. 3d 209, 444 N.E.2d 412 (1st Dist. Hamilton County 1981).

[17]Vasile v. Marinescu, 2006-Ohio-1739, 2006 WL 891026, *2 (Ohio Ct. App. 8th Dist. Cuyahoga County 2006).

in whatever language they possess, reaches constitutional proportions."[18]

Of significance is that the Cuyahoga County Court of Appeals compared the case to *Pina*, which discussed constitutional concerns. That having been said, many courts, including the Cuyahoga County Domestic Relations Court, are beginning to look at the court's role in ensuring that interpreters are available for non-English-speaking litigants. Additionally, the Supreme Court of Ohio has an advisory committee addressing cultural competency and interpreter certification.[19]

Q & A: Must a court order an interpreter for a non-English speaking party?

In *Luna-Crona v. Esquivel-Parrales*,[20] the issue was raised by a respondent in a civil protection order case. On appeal, the respondent argued that the trial court abused its discretion for failing to appoint him a qualified interpreter for the CPO proceedings.

The appellate court relied on RC 2311.14(A)(1) which provides that '[w]henever, because of a hearing, speech, or other impairment of a party to or witness in a legal proceeding cannot readily understand or communicate, the court shall appoint a qualified interpreter to assist such a person." The decision regarding whether to appoint an interpreter depends on the trial court's assessment of the person's apparent ability to comprehend and communicate in English.[21] "An imperfect grasp of the English language may be sufficient as long as the defendant has the ability to understand and communicate in English."[22] If the trial court determines that the witness or party cannot effectively understand or communicate in English, the court may also consider whether the party's counsel is bilingual, whether the trier of fact is bilingual, and whether a timely request for an interpreter was made when deciding if an interpreter should be appointed.[23]

Because the decision to appoint an interpreter is discretionary with the court, an appellate court will not reverse the decision absent an abuse of discretion.[24] In this case, the record demonstrated that counsel could and did interpret for him and that the court offered to continue the final hearing. Additionally, because appellant responded to all questions directed at him, he did not demonstrate that he was unable to understand and communicate in English. Finally, counsel,

---

[18]Vasile v. Marinescu, 2006-Ohio-1739, 2006 WL 891026, *2 (Ohio Ct. App. 8th Dist. Cuyahoga County 2006), quoting State v. Pina, 49 Ohio App. 2d 394, 401, 3 Ohio Op. 3d 457, 361 N.E.2d 262 (2d Dist. Clark County 1975).

[19]See Interpreters in the Ohio Judicial System, A Handbook for Ohio Judges (Supreme Court of Ohio 2008) (email www.romerob@sconet.state.oh.us for more information).

[20]Luna-Corona v. Esquivel-Parrales, 2009-Ohio-2628, 2009 WL 1581133 (Ohio Ct. App. 12th Dist. Butler County 2009).

[21]At *2, citing State v. Castro, 1995 WL 558782, *4 (Ohio Ct. App. 2d Dist. Montgomery County 1995).

[22]At *2; quoting Castro.

[23]At*2, quoting *Castro at *4.*

[24]State v. Marquez, 2008-Ohio-5324, 2008 WL 4561147 (Ohio Ct. App. 11th Dist. Ashtabula County 2008).

at no time, communicated to the court that he was unable to understand the proceedings.[25] In that the evidence demonstrated appellant's understanding of the English language, his assignment of error was overruled.

Q & A: Is a filing fee or other cost associated with the filing or issuance of a civil protection order?

No. RC 3113.31(J) specifically states that "[n]otwithstanding any provision of law to the contrary and regardless of whether a protection order is issued or consent agreement is approved by a court of another state, no court or unit of state or local government shall charge any fee, cost, deposit, or money in connection with the filing of a petition pursuant to this section or in connection with the filing, issuance, registration, or service of a protection order or consent agreement, or for obtaining a certified copy of a protection order or consent agreement."[26] This recent statutory amendment finally resolved the question of whether a petitioner can be assessed costs, fees, or expenses following the disposition of the petition.[27]

The importance of this provision is in its scope. No cost or fee can be assessed to a petitioner for the filing, issuance, registration, modification, enforcement, dismissal, withdrawal or service of any civil or criminal stalking protection order or a protection order issued by the court of another state; nor are courts permitted to assess costs, fees, expenses, or other deposits at the conclusion of the domestic violence case. This also includes a witness subpoena and obtaining a

---

[25]At *3; see also State v. Marquez, 2008-Ohio-5324, 2008 WL 4561147 (Ohio Ct. App. 11th Dist. Ashtabula County 2008).

[26]This language was mandated by the federal Violence Against Women Act in 42 U.S.C.A. 3796(gg)-5(a)(1) as a condition of eligibility for certain domestic violence funding awards, which act was amended in Senate Bill 47 as recently as 2013 by the Violence Against Women Reauthorization Act of 2013 and now provides that: [a] State, Indian tribal government, or unit of local government shall not be entitled to funds under this subchapter unless the State, Indian tribal government or unit of local government certifies that victims of domestic violence, dating violence, sexual assault or stalking are not charged fees or any other costs related to the filing, petitioning, modifying, issuance, registration, enforcement, withdrawal, or dismissal of matters relating to the domestic violence, dating violence, sexual assault or stalking.

In effect, "[a] State, Indian tribal government, or unit of local government shall not be entitled to funds under this subchapter unless the State, Indian tribal government, or unit of local government—certifies that its laws, policies, and practices do not require, in connection with the prosecution of any misdemeanor or felony domestic violence offense, or in connection with the filing, issuance, registration, modification, enforcement, dismissal, withdrawal, or service of a protection order, or a petition for a protection order, to protect a victim of domestic violence, dating violence, stalking or sexual assault, that the victim bear fees or other costs associated with the filing of criminal charges against the offender, or the costs associated with the filing, issuance, registration, modification, enforcement, dismissal, withdrawal, or service of a warrant, protection order, or a petition for a protection order or witness subpoena, whether issued inside or outside the State, tribal or local jurisdiction." 42 U.S.C.A. 3796gg-5(a)(1), as amended by Sen. Bill 47 (2013).

[27]See 1996 Ohio Op. Att'y Gen. No. 2-219, 1996 Ohio Op. Att'y Gen. No. 96-058, 1996 WL 708353, (11-6-1996) in which the Ohio Attorney General concluded that the (previous) language set forth in RC 3113.31(J) did not limit or restrict the discretion of the court, following the disposition of the petition, to enter an order requiring a petitioner to pay whatever charges, costs, fees deposits or expenses that may result from its filing.

certified copy.[28] No longer may courts be able to charge filing fees, fees for the service of out of state or out of county protection orders, fees for the registration of protection orders issued in other counties or states, or fees associated with obtaining certified copies of protection orders or serving witness subpoenas. Courts may not charge fees when a petitioner dismisses or withdraws a protection order or seeks to modify a protection order. Finally, no fees or costs may be assessed to a petitioner for the enforcement of a protection order.

Of importance is that it is now within the court's discretion as to whether costs and fees may be assessed against respondent.[29] Unfortunately, the statutory amendments do not include a provision prohibiting the assessment of costs or fees to petitioners who failed to prevail with their appeals.[30]

§ 11:4 Duration of protection order

An ex parte protection order lasts only until the court, at the full hearing, issues another order.[1] Theoretically, an ex parte order should only last for seven or ten court days.[2] If the full hearing is continued, the ex parte order will remain in effect until the full hearing is rescheduled.[3] To avoid the problems associated with a failure of service or requests for continuances, attorneys should consider noting in the Domestic Violence Ex Parte Civil Protection Order (Sup. R. Form 10.01-H) and on the NCIC form (Sup. R. Form 10-A) that the expiration date of the ex parte protection order is five years from the date the order is issued. This is accomplished by setting forth a date certain, five years from the date the court issues the ex parte order. This allows the already existing ex parte protection order and NCIC form to remain undisturbed until the full hearing is held. If this is not done, attorneys risk termination of the order or removal of the order from the NCIC database until the ex parte order is modified and a new NCIC form is completed.[4]

Any protection order issued ex parte and not otherwise modified, vacated, or dismissed at the full hearing shall remain in effect for a date certain, but not later than five years from the date of its issuance or approval. Where the court maintains the terms of the ex parte protection order, it issues a new protection order possibly with a dif-

[28] R.C. 3113.31(J)(1). See also Sowders v. Sowders, 2012-Ohio-4786, 2012 WL 4882671 (Ohio Ct. App. 5th Dist. Ashland County 2012) (reversing trial court taxing costs to petitioner-appellant even though petition was dismissed by appellant prior to full hearing per RC 3113.31(J) and the Supreme Court forms 10.01-K and 10.01-L).

[29] R.C. 26.75 3113.31(J)(2), eff. 9/17/2014.

[30] See D.R. v. J.R., 2013-Ohio-2987, 2013 WL 3486845 (Ohio Ct. App. 9th Dist. Summit County 2013) (taxing costs to appellee/petitioner).

[Section 11:4]

[1] See Text § 11:20, Ex parte protection orders—Length of order.

[2] See RC 3113.31(D)(2)(a).

[3] See RC 3113.31(D)(2)(b).

[4] See also Text § 14:5, False arrest, warrantless arrests and searches, and weapons confiscation.

ferent expiration date[5] and submits the order to the clerk with a new NCIC form. It is important that the new NCIC form be checked as a "modification of previous form"[6] so as to inform requesting police officers that the order entered into the database is the protection order issued after the full hearing. The court may either modify the expiration date or reiterate the same five-year expiration date stated in the initial NCIC form.

Q & A: Do all terms of a civil protection order terminate in five years?

No. Pursuant to statute,[7] a civil protection order terminates no later than five years from the date the order is issued or approved. That is, a protection order may terminate before that, either by court order or pursuant to a modification[8] or dismissal. Any order that is issued must include a date certain for its termination or expiration. "Until further order of the court" does not comply with the statute and is too ambiguous a phrase to be effective for this purpose.[9] Custody, visitation, and support orders that are included in the civil protection order terminate on the date the domestic relations or juvenile court issues a custody, visitation, or support order, but no later than five years.[10] Unless another date certain is directed by the court, five years is the longest period of time a protection order will remain in effect.

If filed with a divorce, a protection order would appear to survive the final divorce decree unless specifically terminated by the final judgment of divorce and written into the entry. For example, in *Petrak v. Petrak*,[11] the trial court granted appellee an ex parte civil protection order. At the full hearing, the parties entered into an agreement. In that order, the parties continued the order in effect "until further Order of Court, and until the divorce action . . . is final."[12] The court of appeals determined that the language of the parties' agreed entry indicated that the "date certain" was the date when the divorce action was finalized.[13]

---

[5]See RC 3113.31(E)(3)(a) for the length of time a civil protection order is valid.

[6]Sup. R. Form 10-A.

[7]RC 3113.31(E)(3)(a).

[8]But see Signer v. Signer, 2006-Ohio-3580, 2006 WL 1918115, *5 (Ohio Ct. App. 8th Dist. Cuyahoga County 2006) (holding that RC 3113.31 does not "vest any authority in the court to modify the terms of the allocation of parental rights and responsibilities under the civil protection order"; the court also noted that, upon filing for divorce, a court could exercise its jurisdiction to issue a new order).

[9]See, e.g., State v. Myers, 2002-Ohio-253, 2002 WL 54753 (Ohio Ct. App. 5th Dist. Perry County 2002).

[10]RC 3113.31(E)(3)(b); see also Text § 12:16, Remedies—Protected party concerns.

[11]Petrak v. Petrak, 1994 WL 50386 (Ohio Ct. App. 12th Dist. Butler County 1994); see also State v. Havard, 2001 WL 1566932 (Ohio Ct. App. 12th Dist. Butler County 2001).

[12]Petrak v. Petrak, 1994 WL 50386, *1 (Ohio Ct. App. 12th Dist. Butler County 1994).

[13]See also Elkins v. Elkins, 1992 WL 180118 (Ohio Ct. App. 10th Dist. Franklin County 1992).

Q & A: Will a court dismiss an ex parte civil protection order if the respondent is not served and within what period of time?[14]

RC 3113.31(G) provides that any proceeding under this section shall be conducted in accordance with the Rules of Civil Procedure. Civil Rule 3(A) details that a civil action is commenced by filing a complaint with the court, if service is obtained within *one year* from such filing upon a named defendant. (Emphasis added.) Since a petition for civil protection order is similar to a complaint, it too must be served upon a respondent within one year from the date of filing.

Civ. R. 4(E) provides that "[i]f a service of summons and complaint is not made upon a defendant within six months after the filing of the complaint and the party on whose behalf such service was required cannot show good cause why such service was not made within that period, the action shall be dismissed as to that defendant."

Applying the operative phrase "good cause," domestic violence petitioners who have made good faith attempts to serve respondents may have valid grounds to request that their protection order actions and ex parte civil protection orders not be dismissed after six months. While it is within the discretion of a court to dismiss a civil protection order for a failure of service at the time the full hearing is set, most courts permit a petitioner to attempt service for at least six months.

Unfortunately, however, absent service, an ex parte CPO will eventually be dismissed for failure of service within that six-month period. While an argument can be made that service on an ex parte CPO should be attempted for a one year period in accordance with Civ. R. 3(A), it is unlikely that many courts will keep cases pending for one year unless repeated attempts are made during the one year period to perfect service and/or it becomes clear during that one year period that a respondent is deliberately evading service.

§ 11:5 Election of remedies

The remedies and procedures provided in RC 3113.31 are in addition to, and not in lieu of, any other available civil or criminal remedies.[1] The intent of the statute is to expand the alternatives already available to the victim, not to replace existing remedies. In effect, this section directs courts to issue civil protection orders regard-

---

[14]See also Text §§ 11:21, 12:4.

[Section 11:5]

[1]RC 3113.31(G); see also Thomas v. Thomas, 44 Ohio App. 3d 6, 540 N.E.2d 745 (10th Dist. Franklin County 1988); Felton v. Felton, 79 Ohio St. 3d 34, 1997-Ohio-302, 679 N.E.2d 672 (1997); Lebeau v. Lebeau, 2001 WL 1339495, *12 (Ohio Ct. App. 5th Dist. Stark County 2001); Hoff v. Brown, 2001 WL 876228, *4 (Ohio Ct. App. 5th Dist. Stark County 2001) (the court of appeals noted that "R.C. 3113.31(G) was intended in part to preclude alleged domestic violence perpetrators named in a C.P.O. petition from utilizing the doctrine of res judicata in this manner to defeat the legislative purpose of protecting domestic violence victims"); Irwin v. Murray, 2006-Ohio-1633, 2006 WL 832830 (Ohio Ct. App. 6th Dist. Lucas County 2006); Schultz v. Schultz, 2010-Ohio-3665, 2010 WL 3075758 (Ohio Ct. App. 9th Dist. Medina County 2010); Text Ch. 13, Court Enforcement of Civil Protection Orders and Related Issues.

less of other pending proceedings.[2] However, some courts have been reluctant to proceed with petitions for civil protection orders in cases in which other criminal or domestic relations proceedings are pending.[3]

One court in Ohio gave a different twist to this statutory provision. In *Ventura v. Ventura*,[4] the appellant sought a protection order alleging that the appellee had sexually abused the child. The trial court dismissed the action. Appellant then filed a motion to modify custody. The trial court dismissed her motion, stating that the appellant "was attempting to relitigate the identical facts between the same parties after the matters had already been finally determined in the previous domestic violence action."[5]

Although it mentioned RC 3113.31(G) in its opinion, the Eleventh District Court of Appeals determined that

> a judgment rendered pursuant to the act is subject to the same "rules of conclusiveness" which generally apply to all judgments. Public policy dictates that those who have contested an issue shall be bound by the result of the contest, and that matters once tried shall be forever settled between the parties.[6]

Moreover, the civil protection order is not intended to serve as an alternative to, or a substitute for, a divorce or criminal prosecution. In some cases, victims elect to pursue both civil and criminal remedies simultaneously. A victim may have domestic violence charges pending against the respondent in municipal court[7] and also request a civil protection order.[8] To fully protect the victim, an action must be available in both forums. The goal of each proceeding is different. The civil protection order proceeding is brought by the victim to safeguard himself/herself from further abuse; the criminal case is brought by the state to punish the batterer for his/her criminal conduct.

Q & A: What if a victim requests a CPO after first receiving a criminal protection order?

If a victim is the complainant in a pending criminal case and has obtained a criminal protection order, the issuance of a civil protection

---

[2]RC 3113.31(G).

[3]See Zawrotuk v. Zawrotuk, 2014-Ohio-5225, 2014 WL 6641772 (Ohio Ct. App. 7th Dist. Mahoning County 2014) (where defense argued that CPO should not have been granted because of the pending criminal case, appellate court stated that "a reasonable trier of fact could find that the danger of domestic violence was not wholly eliminated by the passage of four weeks since the last incident and that the pending criminal case helped explain the delay in filing as well" at ¶ 43).

[4]Ventura v. Ventura, 1986 WL 10595 (Ohio Ct. App. 11th Dist. Lake County 1986).

[5]Ventura v. Ventura, 1986 WL 10595, *1 (Ohio Ct. App. 11th Dist. Lake County 1986).

[6]Ventura v. Ventura, 1986 WL 10595, *1 (Ohio Ct. App. 11th Dist. Lake County 1986).

[7]RC 2919.25.

[8]RC 3113.31; see also Halley v. Ashley, 1997 WL 760662, *4 (Ohio Ct. App. 9th Dist. Summit County 1997) (rejecting argument that, for purposes of a civil protection order under RC 3113.31, domestic violence may only be found upon a violation of RC 2919.25, the criminal domestic violence statute, and finding that "[t]he plain language of the statute does not require that a violation of R.C. 2919.25 be proven before a civil protective order may issue").

order against the same batterer terminates the criminal protection order[9] if the civil protection order arose out of the same activities that were the basis of the criminal complaint.[10]

On the other hand, it is quite possible that a criminal protection order does not terminate upon the issuance of a civil protection order. The specific language of RC 2919.26(E)(2)(b) provides that "a temporary protection order that is issued as a pretrial condition of release under this section is effective only until the occurrence of the issuance of a protection order or the approval of a consent agreement, arising out of the same activities as those that were the basis of the complaint upon which the order is based under RC 3113.31." That said, the TPO might not terminate or "expire"; rather, "is effective until" might mean only that it is no longer functioning or operative during the time that a CPO is in effect. If so, it is arguable that the TPO is suspended during this time. If the CPO is dismissed, the original TPO could be reactivated by the filing of a motion to reinstate.[11]

Q & A: What if a victim first obtains a civil protection order and then presses charges against the same person under the criminal domestic violence statute and obtains a criminal protection order?

If the victim obtains a civil protection order and then criminal charges are filed against the same person and a criminal protection order is granted in municipal court, nothing in either statute reveals whether one of the orders would terminate or whether both would remain in effect until expiration pursuant to their respective statutes. Under this fact scenario, it appears that a petitioner could have two orders in effect simultaneously.[12]

§ 11:6 Disclosure issues[1]

Q & A: Must a petitioner's address be included on the petition?

Many state codes provide that the petitions and orders are valid and enforceable without explicitly noting the petitioner's address, separate residence, place of employment, or children's school. Other codes specify that, upon request, the address of the petitioner not be made public. Ohio's statute is silent, although a respondent may be restrained from entering or approaching the petitioner's residence, school, business, or place of employment.[2] Recently, the Supreme Court of Ohio adopted a new civil protection rule of civil procedure that addresses confidentiality in the context of service of a civil protection order. In Civ. R. 65.1(B)(4), "[u]pon request of the Petitioner, any

---

[9]RC 2919.26(E)(2).

[10]RC 2919.26(E)(2); see also State v. Copp, 2003-Ohio-5399, 2003 WL 22318519 (Ohio Ct. App. 2d Dist. Montgomery County 2003); State v. Frazier, 158 Ohio App. 3d 407, 2004-Ohio-4506, 815 N.E.2d 1155 (1st Dist. Hamilton County 2004).

[11]See also Text 4:7.

[12]See also Text § 12:27, Conflicting protection orders.

[Section 11:6]

[1]See also Text § 15:24, Other issues that impact custody and visitation awards; Text § 11:2, Contents of the petition.

[2]RC 3113.31(E)(1)(g).

method of service provided in Civ. R. 4 to 4.6 or by Civ. R. 5(B) may be limited or modified by the court to protect the confidentiality of the Petitioner's address in making service under this division."

The issue of confidentiality is addressed under Ohio's Standardized Protection Order forms. Although the Petition for Domestic Violence Civil Protection Order provides lines for the petitioner's address, there is a bolded instruction on the petition that states: "Do not write your address at left or below if you are requesting confidentiality."[3]

Victims should not be compelled to choose between requesting legal protection from the court and keeping their addresses confidential.[4] The courts in this state should permit nondisclosure of the victim's address. The goal of court intervention must be to protect a victim who has moved to a location unknown to the abuser, whether it be a shelter or a separate residence.[5] Oftentimes, however, a respondent may wish to gather this information in order to know where the children are residing. In such cases, the courts should have a policy in place which is designed to protect the victim, while at the same time, recognizing the rights of the respondent to have access to the children.

Of some importance is the fact that the Violence Against Women Act of 1994 requires the United States Postal Service to promulgate regulations to secure the confidentiality of domestic violence shelters, and abused persons' addresses.[6]

Q & A: Is there any requirement that a child's address be disclosed to the respondent?

RC 3113.31 neither requires disclosure of the children's address to the respondent nor prohibits disclosure of that information.[7] The goal of any protection order is to protect both the victims of domestic violence and their children. Absent a statutory requirement, the recommended practice in this area is nondisclosure of the address where safety is the paramount concern.[8]Many perpetrators merely use the children to continue to abuse their adult victims.

Perpetrators of abusive behavior often attempt to obtain the victim's address from the children's school records. If schools divulge this information where the victim and children are living in a shelter, the abusive parent would then be aware of the shelter's confidential

[3]See Sup. R. Form 10.01-D; see also Sup. R. Form 10.01-C.

[4]See also Wendy J. Murphy, Minimizing the Likelihood of Discovery of Victim's Counseling Records and Other Personal Information in Criminal Cases: Massachusetts Gives the Nod to a Constitutional Right to Confidentiality, 32 New Eng. L. Rev. 983 (1998); Joan Zorza, Recognizing and Protecting the Privacy and Confidentiality Needs of Battered Women, 29 Fam. L.Q. 273 (1995).

[5]See, e.g., Waldmann v. Waldmann, 48 Ohio St. 2d 176, 2 Ohio Op. 3d 373, 358 N.E.2d 521 (1976).

[6]42 U.S.C.A. § 40281; see also Text Ch. 15 Domestic Violence and Custody and Visitation Issues, Text Ch. 17, Role of the Victim Advocate, and Text Ch. 18, Federal Remedies. But see Sacharow v. Sacharow, 177 N.J. 62, 826 A.2d 710 (2003).

[7]See also Text § 15:10, Batterer access to the victim and children. But see Sup. R. Form 10.01-C and Sup. R. Form 10.01-D.

[8]See Casivant v. Greene County Community Action Agency, Inc., 234 A.D.2d 818, 652 N.Y.S.2d 115 (3d Dep't 1996), aff'd, 90 N.Y.2d 969, 665 N.Y.S.2d 952, 688 N.E.2d 1034 (1997); see also State ex rel. Hope House, Inc. v. Merrigan, 133 S.W.3d 44 (Mo. 2004) (discussing domestic violence and shelter confidentiality).

address. Both the victim and the shelter would be placed at a greater risk of harm. RC 3319.321(F) has resolved one of the more difficult problems for victims and shelters alike by providing that:

> No person shall release to a parent of a student who is not the student's residential parent or to any other person, or permit a parent of a student who is not the student's residential parent or permit any other person to have access to, any information about the location of any elementary or secondary school to which a student has transferred or information that would enable the parent who is not the student's residential parent or the other person to determine the location of that elementary or secondary school . . . if the student is under the care of a shelter for victims of domestic violence, as defined in section 3113.33 of the Revised Code.[9]

A similar issued was raised in *Waliser v. Tada.*[10] In *Waliser*, the defendant and the parties' minor child went into a domestic violence shelter. Plaintiff-appellant contacted the shelter in an attempt to communicate with his wife. The shelter would neither confirm nor deny the identity of any client. Plaintiff then filed for a divorce in Franklin County and service of process was returned by the shelter, "addressee unknown." The plaintiff then initiated a civil tort action for the negligent and intentional infliction of emotional distress against the shelter.

The Franklin County Court of Appeals held that "[s]ince the court prematurely granted summary judgment, the issue of whether [the shelter] owed a legal duty to plaintiff upon which a claim of negligence may be founded is not ripe for determination."[11] The appellate court reversed the trial court, stating that discovery had not been completed due to the trial court's granting the shelter a protective order barring discovery on the grounds of privilege. The appellate court then stated that "unjustifiably denying information to a parent, information as to the whereabouts and safety of his missing child and spouse, can constitute negligent infliction of emotional distress if such distress in fact occurred."[12]

Waliser is significant because it suggests that domestic violence shelters may not be immune from civil liability for failing to disclose the whereabouts of victims and their children. Until shelters are granted immunity for refusing to disclose the whereabouts of their residents by legislative enactment, disclosure issues and confidentiality concerns will continue to plague them. More importantly, victims of domestic violence and their children who seek shelter from abuse should not be thwarted in their attempts to leave for fear of disclosure.

Q & A: I filed a complaint for divorce for my client. Now my client is in need of a civil protection order. Must I notify the court of the pending divorce?

Many courts have a policy that a petitioner must notify the court of other pending actions at the time he/she files for a civil protection

---

[9]RC 3319.321(F); see also RC 3113.36(A)(5), RC 3113.40.

[10]Waliser v. Tada, 1990 WL 20080 (Ohio Ct. App. 10th Dist. Franklin County 1990), cause dismissed, 61 Ohio St. 3d 1405, 573 N.E.2d 1097 (1991).

[11]Waliser v. Tada, 1990 WL 20080, *4 (Ohio Ct. App. 10th Dist. Franklin County 1990), cause dismissed, 61 Ohio St. 3d 1405, 573 N.E.2d 1097 (1991).

[12]Waliser v. Tada, 1990 WL 20080, *5 (Ohio Ct. App. 10th Dist. Franklin County 1990), cause dismissed, 61 Ohio St. 3d 1405, 573 N.E.2d 1097 (1991).

order. This type of notification policy helps courts identify existing court orders and better assess what types of statutory provisions would best protect the petitioner. Once apprised of other pending proceedings, the court can make more informed decisions, resolve conflicts with pre-existing orders, and make appropriate changes to the order. A family's legal history, both current and past, enables the court to have a more complete understanding of the interrelationship between the parties.

Although the statute is silent, practical application of the statute necessitates that courts adopt a notification policy of a continuing nature, especially when a divorce or criminal domestic violence case is pending. Seventeen states have enacted statutory provisions requiring a petitioner to inform the court of other pending actions.[13]

The standard petition for a civil protection order under RC 3113.31 includes a provision that directs the petitioner to list all present and pertinent past court cases of which the petitioner has knowledge involving the petitioner, the respondent, or any of their family or household members.[14] This includes civil, criminal, divorce, juvenile, custody, visitation and bankruptcy cases. If known, the petitioner is to provide the case name, the case number, and the court and county in which the case was brought. Disclosure of this information prevents a court from issuing a conflicting order. Over time, consistent use of this provision will reduce the problems associated with conflicting custody orders issued in a divorce and in a protection order.[15]

§ 11:7 Specific domestic violence and divorce issues

Q & A: My client filed for divorce. While the divorce was pending, the client needed a civil protection order. I then filed for a protection order. It was denied because there was a divorce pending. Can the court deny the protection order?

According to *Thomas v. Thomas*,[1] the answer is no. In that case, a protection order was denied solely because there was an already pending divorce action. The court held that "the mere filing of an action for divorce is not a basis on which to deny a civil protection order."[2] The court based its decision on RC 3113.31(G), which provides that the remedies of RC 3113.31 are in addition to, and not in lieu of, any other civil and criminal remedies. The court reasoned that:

---

[13]See Ariz. Rev. Stat. Ann. § 13-3602B.4 (Supp. 1993); Fla. Stat. Ann. § 741.30(2)(b) (Supp. 1993); Mass. Gen. L. Ann. ch. 209A, § 3 (Supp. 1993); see also National Council of Juvenile & Family Court Judges, Model Code on Domestic and Family Violence § 304 (1994).

[14]See Sup. R. 10.01, Sup. R. Form 10.01-D.

[15]See also Text § 12:24, Renewal of a civil protection order.

[Section 11:7]

[1]Thomas v. Thomas, 44 Ohio App. 3d 6, 540 N.E.2d 745 (10th Dist. Franklin County 1988); see also Wildi v. Wildi, 159 Ohio App. 3d 568, 2005-Ohio-257, 824 N.E.2d 1011 (10th Dist. Franklin County 2005); Irwin v. Murray, 2006-Ohio-1633, 2006 WL 832830 (Ohio Ct. App. 6th Dist. Lucas County 2006); Felton v. Felton, 79 Ohio St. 3d 34, 1997-Ohio-302, 679 N.E.2d 672 (1997); Text § 11:22, Ex parte protection orders—Miscellaneous issues.

[2]Thomas v. Thomas, 44 Ohio App. 3d 6, 8, 540 N.E.2d 745 (10th Dist. Franklin County 1988).

A comparison of RC 3113.31 and Civ.R. 75 shows that while the relief available under both provisions is somewhat similar, it is directed to a different purpose. The purpose of a civil protection order issued pursuant to RC 3113.31 is to provide protection from domestic violence and, incidental to that relief, to provide for support and shelter; the relief is available to a broader range of petitioners; the scope of relief is broader; there is no residency requirement; and a violation of a civil protection order can form the basis of a criminal offense, RC 2919.27. Civ.R. 75, while providing for financial support and custody, does so only incidentally to a divorce or dissolution and is available only to parties to the action.[3]

However, the dissent in *Thomas* argued, that although the statute does not preclude relief under RC 3113.31 even though a divorce action is pending or is subsequently filed, the same issue should not be litigated in two different proceedings. The dissent went on to point out:

> The availability of such relief in the divorce proceedings vests authority in the trial court to deny RC 3113.31 relief where the parties are litigating, or could litigate, the same issue in the divorce proceedings. Ordinarily, it is appropriate to avoid multiple litigation where one action can encompass and determine all rights and controversies between the parties. There is no reason not to apply that principle here.[4]

If a court or attorney is concerned about joining both the divorce and protection order actions, they may consider consolidating the proceedings as suggested by the dissent in *Thomas*. Consolidation allows for each action to proceed on the merits without limiting the relief available under either option.

Q & A: My marriage ended by a dissolution. I subsequently filed for a protection order. Can the court deny the protection order because the dissolution decree already prohibits my ex-wife and me from harassing each other?

No. This specific issue was addressed by the Ohio Supreme Court in *Felton v. Felton*.[5] In that case, the parties dissolved their marriage. As part of the dissolution, the parties were prohibited from harassing each other. Subsequently, the wife filed for a civil protection order. The trial court granted the wife's petition for an ex parte order but dismissed the action after the full hearing. The court of appeals held that, because the parties' decree of dissolution contained a no-harassment provision, a protection order would be unnecessary.

The Supreme Court disagreed and compared the remedies available to the ex-wife under the no-harassment provision in the dissolution decree and under the civil protection order. The court determined that (1) the domestic violence provisions are more extensive in nature, (2) the police are obligated to enforce protection orders, (3) violations of

[3]Thomas v. Thomas, 44 Ohio App. 3d 6, 7-8, 540 N.E.2d 745 (10th Dist. Franklin County 1988); see also Eichenberger v. Eichenberger, 1993 WL 460570 (Ohio Ct. App. 10th Dist. Franklin County 1993); Felton v. Felton, 79 Ohio St. 3d 34, 1997-Ohio-302, 679 N.E.2d 672 (1997); but see Prostejovsky v. Prostejovsky, 2007-Ohio-5743, 2007 WL 3119724 (Ohio Ct. App. 5th Dist. Ashland County 2007) (holding that a CSPO is analogous to a permanent injunction).

[4]Thomas v. Thomas, 44 Ohio App. 3d 6, 9, 540 N.E.2d 745 (10th Dist. Franklin County 1988).

[5]Felton v. Felton, 79 Ohio St. 3d 34, 1997-Ohio-302, 679 N.E.2d 672 (1997).

protection orders are subject to the state's preferred arrest policies, (4) protection orders are easier to enforce, and (5) the consequence of violating a protection order is more immediate. Of significance is that the court recognized the strong public policy reasons for allowing a court to issue a protection order after a divorce or dissolution is final, noting that the violence against a former spouse does not necessarily stop with the divorce.

The Supreme Court also relied on RC 3113.31(G), which provides that a civil protection order is in addition to, and not in lieu of, any other available civil or criminal remedies.[6] Finally, the court concluded that "a court is not precluded by statute or public policy reasons from issuing a protection order pursuant to Ohio's civil domestic violence statute, RC 3113.31, where the parties' dissolution or divorce decree already prohibits the parties from harassing each other."[7]

Q & A: I filed for both a divorce and a protection order. The protection order was granted. I am about to go to court for the divorce. Will the divorce decree modify the protection order?

When several court proceedings involving the same issues and parties occur simultaneously, the resulting court orders may conflict. A subsequent order in the divorce action or juvenile court action may modify some forms of relief granted in the protection order (custody, support, visitation, and possibly possession of the marital premises), but will not negate the protection order provisions which protect the petitioner from continued abuse.[8]

The Ohio statute specifically provides for modifications in allocation of parental rights and responsibilities and support orders issued as part of a civil protection order. These orders will terminate on the date that a court, in an action for divorce, dissolution, or legal separation brought by the petitioner or respondent, issues an order allocating parental rights and responsibilities for the care of the children or for support or on the date that a juvenile court, in an action brought by the petitioner or respondent, issues an order awarding legal custody of the minor children or for support.[9]

Additionally, exclusive use of property may change pursuant to the parties' divorce. For example, where the protection order permitted use of an automobile or personal property such as furniture by one party, the divorce may resolve the issue by giving the other party

[6]See also Schultz v. Schultz, 2010-Ohio-3665, 2010 WL 3075758 (Ohio Ct. App. 9th Dist. Medina County 2010) (stressing that R.C. 3113.31(G) provides that the remedies and procedures provided in a CPO are in addition to and not in lieu of any other available civil or criminal remedies).

[7]Felton v. Felton, 79 Ohio St. 3d 34, 41, 1997-Ohio-302, 679 N.E.2d 672 (1997).

[8]See RC 3113.31(G), RC 3113.31(E)(3)(b); see also Elkins v. Elkins, 1992 WL 180118 (Ohio Ct. App. 10th Dist. Franklin County 1992).

[9]RC 3113.31(E)(3)(b). See also Signer v. Signer, 2006-Ohio-3580, 2006 WL 1918115 (Ohio Ct. App. 8th Dist. Cuyahoga County 2006) (holding that RC 3113.31 has no authority to modify an order of allocated parental rights and responsibilities; such modifications must be made in a subsequently filed divorce or juvenile court action).

ownership of that property. The same is true for exclusive possession of or ownership of real estate.[10]

It would be wise for family law practitioners to include a specific provision in clients' divorce decrees that states that "the civil protection order issued by the court in case number ______ on the ______ day of ______, should remain in effect subject to the modifications herein." By including such a provision, there is no doubt that the civil protection order will continue to remain in effect until its expiration. Ideally, a new NCIC form should be entered into the NCIC database that reflects any modifications to the civil protection order as included in the divorce decree.

Q & A: Is a trial court mandated to consolidate a pending divorce with a pending CPO in order or hear one case before the other?

No. In *Wheeler v. Wheeler,*[11] appellant argued that the trial court abused its discretion by failing to consolidate the civil protection order and the divorce proceedings. The appellate court stressed that a trial court is not required to consolidate the two actions. "CPO proceedings often require prompt action, Divorce cases can extend for years. A trial court does not abuse his or her discretion by refusing to consolidate the two."[12] The court also discounted appellant's reliance on another Fourth District case, to wit: *Yazdani-Isfehani v. Yazdani-Isfehani*[13] stating that the case addressed a different issue and did not stand for the proposition that the CPO proceeding and the divorce action must be consolidated into one singe action.

Additionally, the court also responded to appellant's argument that the trial court erred by including the children as protected parties in the protection order when a divorce case was already pending and had subject matter jurisdiction. The appellate court found that "[m]inors were present for at least some of the abuse. The trial court had every right to take steps to prevent them from witnessing future incidents. The trial court judge did not have to wait for the divorce case to proceed to the point of allocating parental rights and responsibilities before taking steps to protect the wife and children."[14]

Lastly, the two actions are separate relative to duration, remedies, procedure and enforcement. They cannot be merged into one at the end of a divorce. Even in those counties that permit consolidation under one case number, the actions are not the same. The CPO statute specifically states that "[t]he remedies and procedures provided in

[10]See Devault v. Devault, 2004-Ohio-976, 2004 WL 397134 (Ohio Ct. App. 5th Dist. Ashland County 2004) (noting that a divorce action may have some impact on the protection order).

[11]Wheeler v. Wheeler, 2015-Ohio-4206, 2015 WL 5918030 (Ohio Ct. App. 4th Dist. Scioto County 2015).

[12]Wheeler v. Wheeler, 2015-Ohio-4206, 2015 WL 5918030, ¶ 6 (Ohio Ct. App. 4th Dist. Scioto County 2015).

[13]Yazdani-Isfehani v. Yazdani-Isfehani, 170 Ohio App. 3d 1, 2006-Ohio-7105, 865 N.E.2d 924 (4th Dist. Athens County 2006).

[14]Wheeler v. Wheeler, 2015-Ohio-4206, 2015 WL 5918030, ¶ 5 (Ohio Ct. App. 4th Dist. Scioto County 2015).

this section are in addition to, and not in lieu of, any other available civil or criminal remedies."[15]

§ 11:8 Ex parte protection orders—Constitutional challenges to ex parte relief

To date, Ohio courts have rejected legal challenges to ex parte relief granted in protection orders.[1] Cases that have upheld the constitutionality of civil protection order statutes reflect the public's interest in preventing domestic violence and demonstrate a judicial acceptance of the immediate safety aspects of the protection order. By their very nature, ex parte protection orders raise serious due process concerns. Ordering a respondent out of his/her home or denying a respondent contact with his/her children, albeit temporarily, deprives a respondent of substantial and protected rights without notice, hearing, or a prior opportunity to be heard. Courts routinely balance the competing interests of protecting victims from continued abuse and avoiding erroneous deprivations of respondents' rights. So long as the deprivation is temporary and a hearing is promptly scheduled, courts have been reluctant to declare a domestic violence statute unconstitutional.

The significance of ex parte orders in the domestic violence context cannot be overstated. In *Baker v. Baker*,[2] the Minnesota Supreme Court emphasized that an ex parte order is "central to the substantive relief provided for under the [domestic violence] Act." The court noted that "notice, or extensive justification for lack thereof, [would impede a victim's ability to obtain the] immediate remedy [and extraordinary relief the statute] contemplates."[3] The court even pointed out that "such notice might, in fact, incite further domestic violence."[4]

§ 11:9 Ex parte protection orders—Hearing

The person filing the petition for a protection order may request an ex parte order. An ex parte order is one made by the court upon the application of one of the parties to an action without notice to the other.[1]

According to RC 3113.31(D), an ex parte hearing shall precede the issuance of an ex parte protection order. Because the intent of the

---

[15] R.C. 3113.31(G).

[Section 11:8]

[1] See generally Text § 8:2, Authority and constitutionality; see also Kelm v. Kelm, 1993 WL 220881 (Ohio Ct. App. 10th Dist. Franklin County 1993); but see Morgan v. Partridge, No. 02-1848 (C.P., Montgomery, 2-25-03) (the common pleas court judge sustained the magistrate's decision finding that RC 2903.214 is unconstitutionally vague as applied to ex parte protection orders; although the decision applies to civil stalking orders, RC 2903.214 mirrors RC 3113.31).

[2] Baker v. Baker, 494 N.W.2d 282, 286 (Minn. 1992); see also Nollet v. Justices of Trial Court of Com. of Mass., 83 F. Supp. 2d 204 (D. Mass. 2000), aff'd, 248 F.3d 1127 (1st Cir. 2000).

[3] Baker v. Baker, 494 N.W.2d 282, 286 (Minn. 1992).

[4] Baker v. Baker, 494 N.W.2d 282, 286 (Minn. 1992); see also Kampf v. Kampf, 237 Mich. App. 377, 603 N.W.2d 295 (1999).

[Section 11:9]

[1] Black's Law Dictionary (6th ed.) p 576.

statute is to provide immediate assistance to a victim of domestic violence, the court is required to hold a hearing on the same day the petition is filed if an ex parte order is requested.[2]

RC 3113.31 does not provide the method by which a court is to receive a petitioner's evidence, nor does it explicitly require a petitioner to personally appear at the ex parte hearing. The statute only provides that any proceeding shall be conducted in accordance with the Rules of Civil Procedure.[3] The absence of statutory guidance regarding the relevant and appropriate procedures at the ex parte hearing has encouraged courts to adopt their own local procedures for compliance. The Rules of Civil Procedure and the local rules permit courts to decide certain motions and ex parte orders based on testimony and/or affidavit or brief.[4] In domestic violence actions, the court may issue an order based on a petitioner's affidavit and/or testimony at the hearing. Most Ohio court jurisdictions do require that the petitioner testify under oath at the ex parte hearing. Prior to the actual hearing, courts usually review the affidavit for legal sufficiency. Various reported cases reflect this two-pronged approach.[5]

Q & A: Must the petitioner be present for the ex parte protection order?

At least one Ohio court determined that the petitioner need not be present at the ex parte hearing. In that case, the victim was hospitalized because of the domestic violence inflicted upon her by the respondent. Her mother filed for the petition and appeared at the hearing on her behalf.[6]

Q & A: Can an ex parte civil protection order be heard by a magistrate?

According to Civ. R. 65.1(F)(1), a court may refer the proceedings under these special statutory proceedings to a magistrate. Further, the magistrate has the authority to conduct an ex parte CPO hearing and at the conclusion of the hearing, deny or grant an ex parte protection order.[7] A magistrate's denial or granting of an ex parte protection order does not require judicial approval and shall be effective when signed by the magistrate and filed with the clerk and as such does not constitute a magistrate's order or decision under Civ. R. 53(D)(2) and (3).[8] Finally, the court's approval and signing of a magistrate's denial or granting of an ex parte CPO does not constitute a judgment or interim order under Civ. R. 53(D)(4)(3).[9]

Q & A: Can a magistrate's order be challenged?

Not according to the provisions set forth in the civil rules as pertain-

---

[2]RC 3113.31(D)(1).

[3]RC 3113.31(G).

[4]Civ. R. 7(B)(2). See, e.g., Cuy. D.R.R. 26; Licking D.R.R. 7.0; Mahoning D.R.R. 38; Montgomery D.R.R. 4.46; Summit D.R.R. 15; Stark D.R.R. 20.

[5]See, e.g., Eichenberger v. Eichenberger, 82 Ohio App. 3d 809, 613 N.E.2d 678 (10th Dist. Franklin County 1992).

[6]Carney v. Pankey, 1988 WL 34644 (Ohio Ct. App. 7th Dist. Mahoning County 1988).

[7]Civ. R. 65.1(F)(2)(a).

[8]Civ. R. 65.1(F)(2)(a)(i) and (ii).

[9]Civ. R. 65.1(F)(2)(a)(iii).

ing to civil protection orders. Civ. R. 65.1 expressly states that the granting of an ex parte civil protection order is not a magistrate's order. Pursuant to Civ. R. 65.1(F)(2)(b)(ii) provides that "[a] magistrate's denial or granting of an ex parte protection order without judicial approval under this division does not constitute a magistrate's order or a magistrate's decision under Civ. R. 53(D)(2) or (3) and is not subject to the requirements of those rules."

It would appear, then, that neither a respondent nor a petitioner has a legal mechanism to challenge, set aside or object to the issuance of an ex parte civil protection order if granted or denied by a magistrate.

Q & A: Can an ex parte protection order be issued at any hour, day or night?

There are no statutory provisions allowing for twenty-four-hour or weekend access to the courts for civil protection orders. However, local practice in some Ohio jurisdictions may allow for either after-business hours or weekend access through law enforcement officials who can communicate with the court by telephone and provide written documentation of the oral order issued by the court. Many jurisdictions allow for the issuance of criminal protection orders by this method.

Some courts, however, advise attorneys and others of their business hours in their local court rules. For example, Summit County Local Rule 8.04 indicates that a petition seeking an ex parte civil protection order that is filed after 3:00 p.m. will not be heard until the following business day.

Q & A: Can a respondent file a motion to modify the ex parte civil protection order?

The Sixth District Court of Appeals recently addressed this issue. In *Gorman v. Oates*,[10] the trial court granted petitioner's ex parte CPO ordering the respondent to vacate the residence. The respondent then filed a motion to modify the ex parte order as to the use of the property, however, the court did not rule on the motion.

The court of appeals noted that it was unfortunate that the respondent was forced to vacate the premises. "However, the trial court had the authority to issue such order until a full hearing could be held on the matter. RC 3113.31(E)(1)(b)."[11]

It is highly unlikely that a trial court would rule on a respondent's motion to modify an ex parte civil protection order prior to the full hearing. The requirements of RC 3113.31(D) set forth the time frame in which a full hearing must be held. That time frame is sufficiently short so as to make another court hearing unnecessary.

Civ. R. 65.1(F)(2)(b)(ii) provides that a magistrate's grant or denial of an ex parte civil protection order does not constitute a magistrate's order under Civ. R. 53(D)(2)(b). Since there is no articulated mechanism to challenge the grant or denial of an ex parte protection order

[10]Gorman v. Oates, 2002-Ohio-1511, 2002 WL 471716 (Ohio Ct. App. 6th Dist. Lucas County 2002).

[11]Gorman v. Oates, 2002-Ohio-1511, 2002 WL 471716, *3 (Ohio Ct. App. 6th Dist. Lucas County 2002).

under Civ. R. 65.1, it would appear that Civ. R. 65.1 does not contemplate a modification of an ex parte order.

Additionally, RC 3113.31(E)(8) specifically provides that only a protection order issued after a full hearing can be modified or terminated.[12]

§ 11:10 Ex parte protection orders—Legal standard for issuance[1]

In most jurisdictions, the standard of proof required for ex parte relief is reasonable or probable cause to believe that the petitioner or a member of his/her household is in present danger of being abused or threatened with future abuse by the respondent.[2] Beyond this, Ohio requires the petitioner to show, at the ex parte hearing, that he/she is in immediate and present danger.[3] The statutory language seems to imply that a subjective standard should be used to determine whether there is an "immediate and present danger."[4]

It is important to note that no Ohio appellate decision defines the term "danger" for purposes of the ex parte civil protection order versus the domestic violence full hearing protection order. While various appellate decisions reference the "immediate and present danger" standard for purposes of issuing an ex parte civil protection order, they merely note that, in order to grant a civil protection order, a trial court must find that a petitioner has shown by a preponderance of the evidence that the petitioner or the petitioner's family member is in danger of domestic violence.[5] Although some courts do acknowledge that there may be different standards for determining danger, they fail to articulate any difference for purposes of a standard for issuance.[6]

Because "immediate and present danger" is defined in RC 3113.31,[7] it does not appear necessary to further define the term. Similarly, in applying the standard for issuance as set forth by the Supreme Court

---

[12]R.C. 3113.31(E)(8)(a); Text § 12:25.

[Section 11:10]

[1]See also Text § 8:4, Statutory elements of domestic violence under RC 3113.31(A)(1)(b); see also Text § 12:11, Standard of proof.

[2]But see Am. Sub. S.B. 17, eff. 8-3-06, expanding RC 3113.31(D)(1) to include threatening the petitioner or victim with a sexually oriented offense.

[3]RC 3113.31(D)(1). J.R. v. E.H., 2017-Ohio-516, 2017 WL 587314 (Ohio Ct. App. 10th Dist. Franklin County 2017).

[4]See Text § 8:4, Statutory elements of domestic violence under RC 3113.31(A)(1)(b); see also Bruns v. Bruns, 1999 WL 819344 (Ohio Ct. App. 6th Dist. Erie County 1999); Reynolds v. White, 1999 WL 754496 (Ohio Ct. App. 8th Dist. Cuyahoga County 1999); Ferris v. Ferris, 2006-Ohio-878, 2006 WL 456811 (Ohio Ct. App. 12th Dist. Clermont County 2006), relying on Felton v. Felton, 79 Ohio St. 3d 34, 1997-Ohio-302, 679 N.E.2d 672 (1997).

[5]Felton v. Felton, 79 Ohio St. 3d 34, 1997-Ohio-302, 679 N.E.2d 672 (1997).

[6]See, e.g., Reynolds v. White, 1999 WL 754496 (Ohio Ct. App. 8th Dist. Cuyahoga County 1999); Morris v. Stonewall, 1999 WL 1037507 (Ohio Ct. App. 12th Dist. Clinton County 1999); Siouffi v. Siouffi, 1998 WL 879255 (Ohio Ct. App. 2d Dist. Montgomery County 1998). See also Wilburn v. Wilburn, 2006-Ohio-2553, 2006 WL 1409784 (Ohio Ct. App. 9th Dist. Lorain County 2006) (noting that the *Felton* decision drew no distinction between ex parte orders and orders following a full hearing).

[7]See RC 3113.31(D)(1).

in *Felton v. Felton*, Ohio's appellate courts have consciously declined to further clarify the term "danger." They have, instead, focused on the specific acts or threats of domestic violence.[8]

On the other hand, the Clinton County Court of Appeals applied the *Felton* standard of danger but based the issuance of the civil protection order on the fact that there remained "a present threat of future violence."[9] Implicit in this statement is a definition of "danger."

An ex parte order is granted if good cause can be shown at the hearing, good cause being defined as "immediate and present danger" to the family or household member.[10]

RC 3113.31(D)(1)[11] provides examples of "immediate and present danger" which include situations in which the respondent has threatened the family or household member with bodily harm[12] in which the respondent has threatened the family or household member with a sexually oriented offense[13] or in which the respondent previously has been convicted of or pleaded guilty to an offense that consti-

[8]See, e.g., Reynolds v. White, 1999 WL 754496 (Ohio Ct. App. 8th Dist. Cuyahoga County 1999); Thomas v. Thomas, 44 Ohio App. 3d 6, 8, 540 N.E.2d 745 (10th Dist. Franklin County 1988) (determining that "the statutory criterion to determine whether or not to grant a civil protection order pursuant to R.C. 3113.31 is the existence or threatened existence of domestic violence"); Singhaus v. Zumbar, 2015-Ohio-4755, 2015 WL 7300195 (Ohio Ct. App. 5th Dist. Tuscarawas County 2015); McElroy v. McElroy, 2016-Ohio-5148, 2016 WL 4039227 (Ohio Ct. App. 5th Dist. Guernsey County 2016) (focused on the existence or threatened existence of domestic violence); Weber v. Weber, 2011-Ohio-2980, 2011 WL 2436963 (Ohio Ct. App. 2d Dist. Greene County 2011); see also Gaydash v. Gaydash, 168 Ohio App. 3d 418, 2006-Ohio-4080, 860 N.E.2d 789 (9th Dist. Summit County 2006) (noting that to show danger, there must be an act of domestic violence as defined in R.C. 3113.31(A)(1)); J.R. v. E.H., 2017-Ohio-516, 2017 WL 587314 (Ohio Ct. App. 10th Dist. Franklin County 2017).

[9]Morris v. Stonewall, 1999 WL 1037507, *4 (Ohio Ct. App. 12th Dist. Clinton County 1999) (quoting Lain v. Ververis, 1999 WL 893611 (Ohio Ct. App. 12th Dist. Preble County 1999)); see also Traut v. Leiby, 2010-Ohio-2563, 2010 WL 2298566 (Ohio Ct. App. 5th Dist. Richland County 2010) (stressing that "the focus in a CPO proceeding should be on whether the "petitioner or petitioner's family or household members are *in danger of* domestic violence"") at *2, quoting Folmar v. Griffin, 2008-Ohio-2941, 2008 WL 2573279 (Ohio Ct. App. 5th Dist. Delaware County 2008).

[10]RC 3113.31(D)(1); see also Siouffi v. Siouffi, 1998 WL 879255 (Ohio Ct. App. 2d Dist. Montgomery County 1998); Haynes-Soper v. Garrett, 2000 WL 1289450 (Ohio Ct. App. 10th Dist. Franklin County 2000) ("R.C. 3113.31(D) adds an additional requirement that an immediate and present danger of harm exists before an ex parte order may be entered, but R.C. 3113.31 does not require proof of an immediate and present danger for a civil protection order to be issued after a full hearing."). But see Am. Sub. S.B. 17, eff. 8-3-06, adding to immediate and present danger situations in which the respondent has threatened the petitioner or victim with a sexually oriented offense or in which the respondent was previously convicted of a sexually oriented offense against the petitioner or victim. RC 3113.31(D)(1).

[11]See Gaydash v. Gaydash, 168 Ohio App. 3d 418, 423, 2006-Ohio-4080, 860 N.E.2d 789 (9th Dist. Summit County 2006) (noting that the purpose of the domestic civil protection statutes is to "protect the family or household member from Domestic Violence.").

[12]See also Sitton v. Sitton, 1999 WL 55717 (Ohio Ct. App. 2d Dist. Montgomery County 1999); Siouffi v. Siouffi, 1998 WL 879255 (Ohio Ct. App. 2d Dist. Montgomery County 1998).

[13]Sub. S.B. 260, eff. 1-2-07.

tutes domestic violence against the family or household member.[14] Additionally, a history of domestic violence may provide suitable evidence of an "immediate and present danger," especially where the respondent previously engaged in acts of domestic violence against a family or household member.[15]

This standard can usually be met by showing that the respondent has subjected the petitioner to recent physical abuse or threats. A past history of abuse may also satisfy the statutory burden of proof, especially where the victim reasonably fears abuse in the future.[16] A history of domestic violence may be a reliable indicator that further violence will occur.[17] One incident of abuse, no matter how remote in time, can be indicative of future and more severe violence.[18]

Past abuse instills in a victim a present fear and an impending belief that harm is just around the corner.[19] It can also signify the present intention of the batterer to commit further acts of harm.[20]

The act that precipitates the filing of a petition for a protection order is often a minor act. The Fifth District Court of Appeals, in *State v. Bolds*,[21] noted that "the nature of domestic violence is most often a sequence of offensive acts. Thus, the event triggering prosecution is generally a conclusion to a series of events and is not always the most serious conduct. It is often, as here, the proverbial 'straw that breaks the camel's back.' " However, it is the sequence of events, including both verbal and physical assaults, that causes a victim to fear further abuse in the future.[22]

---

[14]But see Henry v. Henry, 2005-Ohio-67, 2005 WL 43888 (Ohio Ct. App. 4th Dist. Ross County 2005) (where appellate court rejected appellant's argument that husband's death threats, standing alone, or his prior domestic violence conviction, standing alone, warrants a civil protection order pursuant to RC 3113.31(D)(1), noting that a different standard governs the ex parte hearing).

[15]See Morris v. Stonewall, 1999 WL 1037507 (Ohio Ct. App. 12th Dist. Clinton County 1999); see also Visnich v. Visnich, 1999 WL 1299300 (Ohio Ct. App. 11th Dist. Trumbull County 1999).

[16]See Bruns v. Bruns, 1999 WL 819344 (Ohio Ct. App. 6th Dist. Erie County 1999); see also Trent v. Trent, 1999 WL 298073 (Ohio Ct. App. 12th Dist. Preble County 1999); Reynolds v. White, 1999 WL 754496 (Ohio Ct. App. 8th Dist. Cuyahoga County 1999).

[17]See Anne L. Ganley, The Impact of Domestic Violence on the Defendant and the Victim in the Courtroom, in Domestic Violence: The Crucial Role of the Judge in Criminal Court Cases: A National Model for Judicial Education 71–74 (Janet Carter et al. eds., 1991); see also Conkle v. Wolfe, 131 Ohio App. 3d 375, 722 N.E.2d 586 (4th Dist. Athens County 1998).

[18]Janet Carter et al., Domestic Violence: The Crucial Role of the Judge in Criminal Court Cases: A National Model for Judicial Education (1991); see also Halley v. Ashley, 1997 WL 760662 (Ohio Ct. App. 9th Dist. Summit County 1997).

[19]See Visnich v. Visnich, 1999 WL 1299300 (Ohio Ct. App. 11th Dist. Trumbull County 1999).

[20]Diane R. Follingstad et al., The Role of Emotional Abuse in Physically Abusive Relationships, 5 J. Fam. Violence 107, 113 (1990); see also Eichenberger v. Eichenberger, 82 Ohio App. 3d 809, 613 N.E.2d 678 (10th Dist. Franklin County 1992).

[21]State v. Bolds, 1993 WL 35578, *2 (Ohio Ct. App. 5th Dist. Stark County 1993).

[22]See Mary Ann Dutton, The Dynamics of Domestic Violence: Understanding the Response from Battered Women, 68 Fla. B. J. 24 (1994).

The *Felton*[23] case established guidelines for the granting of civil protection orders. Besides validating a "preponderance of the evidence" burden of proof[24] required of a petitioner to obtain a civil protection order, the Court also states that the proof required is not that domestic violence has already been committed against the petitioner. Rather, "when granting a protection order, the trial court must find that petitioner has shown by a preponderance of the evidence that petitioner or petitioner's family or household members are in danger of domestic violence."[25] Since the statute is designed to prevent future violence,[26] the court looks for the danger of future violence, not proof of recent acts of domestic violence,[27] or an immediate and present danger.[28] Actual prior physical harm, while helpful, is not necessary for a finding that a petitioner is in danger of domestic violence.[29]

In fact, a petitioner's reaction to a perceived threat may be sufficient to support the issuance of a civil protection order. For example, in *Sitton v. Sitton*,[30] the petitioner testified regarding her fear of the defendant. She explained that she vacated the residence on the day of the incident and hid from him. When she returned to the apartment for her medicine, she made sure she was accompanied by a police officer. She also stated that she was even afraid to stay with relatives because they were afraid of the defendant. The trial court made a factual finding that the petitioner was very fearful of the defendant.

---

[23]Felton v. Felton, 79 Ohio St. 3d 34, 1997-Ohio-302, 679 N.E.2d 672 (1997); see also Lavery v. Lavery, 2001-Ohio-1874, 2001 WL 1545663 (Ohio Ct. App. 9th Dist. Summit County 2001). See also Text § 8:8, Miscellaneous issues and Text § 12:11, Standard of proof.

[24]But see Jarvis v. Jarvis, 2004-Ohio-1386, 2004 WL 549797 (Ohio Ct. App. 7th Dist. Jefferson County 2004) (appellate court chastised lower court for referring to matters outside the record, such as securing police reports, and reviewing a previously filed and dismissed protection order. While trial court exceeded its authority, error was harmless because sufficient competent and credible evidence existed on the record from which court could conclude a protection order was necessary.).

[25]Felton v. Felton, 79 Ohio St. 3d 34, 42, 1997-Ohio-302, 679 N.E.2d 672 (1997); see also Visnich v. Visnich, 1999 WL 1299300 (Ohio Ct. App. 11th Dist. Trumbull County 1999); Jarvis v. Jarvis, 2004-Ohio-1386, 2004 WL 549797 (Ohio Ct. App. 7th Dist. Jefferson County 2004); Schultz v. Schultz, 2010-Ohio-3665, 2010 WL 3075758 (Ohio Ct. App. 9th Dist. Medina County 2010).

[26]See Reynolds v. White, 1999 WL 754496 (Ohio Ct. App. 8th Dist. Cuyahoga County 1999); see also Gooderham v. Patterson, 1999 WL 1034472 (Ohio Ct. App. 4th Dist. Gallia County 1999); Strassell v. Chapman, 2010-Ohio-4376, 2010 WL 3610591, ¶ 7 (Ohio Ct. App. 10th Dist. Franklin County 2010); Donovan v. Donovan, 2012-Ohio-3521, 2012 WL 3156462, ¶ 16 (Ohio Ct. App. 9th Dist. Lorain County 2012) (noting that wife was not required to wait until a distinct act of domestic violence occurred. Where husband lost his temper, broke down son's door, followed wife around house and stated that they would not be divorced until a judge shot him, his actions caused her to fear for her safety and thus, was in danger of domestic violence).

[27]See Strong v. Bauman, 1999 WL 317432 (Ohio Ct. App. 2d Dist. Montgomery County 1999).

[28]Haynes-Soper v. Garrett, 2000 WL 1289450 (Ohio Ct. App. 10th Dist. Franklin County 2000).

[29]See Text § 8:4, Statutory elements of domestic violence under RC 3113.31(A)(1)(b); see also Gooderham v. Patterson, 1999 WL 1034472 (Ohio Ct. App. 4th Dist. Gallia County 1999).

[30]Sitton v. Sitton, 1999 WL 55717 (Ohio Ct. App. 2d Dist. Montgomery County 1999); see also Rhodes v. Gunter, 2003-Ohio-2342, 2003 WL 21040724 (Ohio Ct. App. 9th Dist. Lorain County 2003).

The court reasoned that the petitioner's reaction to the defendant's threat further supported the finding that she was in fear of imminent serious physical harm.[31]

The very nature of domestic violence emphasizes the need for courts to consider a past history of domestic violence[32] and to allow the admission of reliable testimony of past abuse to demonstrate the victim's present state of mind.[33]

Attorneys should elicit, and courts should consider: the degree of injury in the past as well as in the present,[34] whether the frequency and severity of the violence appears to be escalating, any threats of retaliation made by the respondent to the victim or another family or household member,[35] the use or threatened use of a weapon, the respondent's prior criminal history, the respondent's alleged use of drugs and/or alcohol, the respondent's access to the victim, the respondent's mental health, whether the respondent has threatened suicide,[36] and the specific past acts of physical abuse. The preceding fac-

[31]See Morris v. Morris, 2009-Ohio-5164, 2009 WL 3119658 (Ohio Ct. App. 9th Dist. Summit County 2009) (noting that the victim's state of mind is relevant in determining whether a threat of harm is imminent); see also Text 12:11. But see Anderson v. Anderson, 2001-Ohio-3379, 2001 WL 1667875 (Ohio Ct. App. 7th Dist. Mahoning County 2001) (where appellate court found insufficient nexus between appellant's violent behavior on a specific date and appellee's fear of domestic violence); Bruner v. Bruner, 2000-Ohio-2554, 2000 WL 1486452 (Ohio Ct. App. 7th Dist. Mahoning County 2000); Bahr v. Bahr, 2003-Ohio-5024, 2003 WL 22176762, *3 (Ohio Ct. App. 5th Dist. Ashland County 2003) (reversing judgment and adding that "the reasonableness of appellee's fear of imminent serious physical harm may not be determined by incidents of prior domestic violence absent an initial, explicit indication that she was in fear of imminent serious physical harm on the date contained in the petition").

[32]See, e.g., Visnich v. Visnich, 1999 WL 1299300, *3 (Ohio Ct. App. 11th Dist. Trumbull County 1999) (where the court of appeals stated that "nothing in R.C. 3113. 31, either explicitly or implicitly, precludes a court from considering a person's past violent acts when deciding whether or not to grant a CPO." The language used in defining domestic violence clearly provides that " 'domestic violence' means the occurrence of one or more of the following acts . . . ." RC 3113.31(A). Therefore the statute "contemplates prior acts being used as evidence to support a CPO. Otherwise it would be unnecessary to specify that multiple acts may be considered when an application for a CPO has been filed."). But see Bruner v. Bruner, 2000-Ohio-2554, 2000 WL 1486452 (Ohio Ct. App. 7th Dist. Mahoning County 2000); Bahr v. Bahr, 2003-Ohio-5024, 2003 WL 22176762, *3 (Ohio Ct. App. 5th Dist. Ashland County 2003).

[33]See Eichenberger v. Eichenberger, 82 Ohio App. 3d 809, 613 N.E.2d 678 (10th Dist. Franklin County 1992); see also Bruns v. Bruns, 1999 WL 819344 (Ohio Ct. App. 6th Dist. Erie County 1999); Visnich v. Visnich, 1999 WL 1299300 (Ohio Ct. App. 11th Dist. Trumbull County 1999); Conkle v. Wolfe, 131 Ohio App. 3d 375, 722 N.E.2d 586 (4th Dist. Athens County 1998); Ankenbruck v. Ankenbruck, 2000 WL 1804360 (Ohio Ct. App. 11th Dist. Trumbull County 2000); Morris v. Morris, 2009-Ohio-5164, 2009 WL 3119658 (Ohio Ct. App. 9th Dist. Summit County 2009).

[34]See State v. Dawson, 1979 WL 209389 (Ohio Ct. App. 10th Dist. Franklin County 1979).

[35]See Eichenberger v. Eichenberger, 1993 WL 460570 (Ohio Ct. App. 10th Dist. Franklin County 1993).

[36]But see Anderson v. Anderson, 2001-Ohio-3379, 2001 WL 1667875, *3 (Ohio Ct. App. 7th Dist. Mahoning County 2001) (where respondent's threat to do violence to himself "does not equate to an overt act of violence or a threat of violence toward Appellee").

tors indicate that courts should develop a lethality checklist[37] for assessing whether a respondent is likely to seriously injure or kill the victim in the future. Each of these factors indicates a likelihood of potential future abuse and helps to explain a victim's fear of continued abuse.[38]

A court should not summarily dismiss an ex parte protection order or summarily fail to grant one where the only action by the respondent is a threat of bodily harm.[39] Testimony evidencing both the threat and a subjective belief that the respondent's threat caused the victim to fear imminent serious physical harm may establish an "immediate and present danger" to that victim.[40] If a petitioner can demonstrate that an "immediate and present danger" exists, the petitioner should prevail at an ex parte proceeding. Since the standard of proof in ex parte proceedings is, generally, good cause to believe he/she is in immediate danger, a petitioner should be able to easily meet the burden of proof. For example, where the respondent threatens to kill the petitioner with a gun and the respondent has access to a gun, there is an immediate and present danger to that victim.[41] Even without the gun, the threat remains if the petitioner believes that the respondent would and could carry out the threat.[42]

From a psychological standpoint, whether a person responds to a statement as a threat depends on whether that person has been subjected to repeated physical assaults.[43] Obviously, not all verbal statements or insults are perceived as threats by intimate partners. A verbal attack by one who has never been physically abusive is not the same as a verbal attack by one who has been violent in the past. "It is the perpetrator's use of physical force that gives power to the psychological abuse. The psychological battering becomes an effective weapon in controlling victims because victims know through experi-

[37]See Text Ch. 15, Domestic Violence and Custody and Visitation Issues, for a discussion of lethality.

[38]See Patsy Klaus & Michael R. Rand, U.S. Department of Justice, Family Violence, Bureau of Justice Statistics Special Report 4 (1984); see also Anne L. Ganley, Domestic Violence: The What, Why and Who, as Relevant to Civil Court Cases, in Domestic Violence in Civil Court Cases: A National Model for Judicial Education 23, 33 (Jacqueline A. Agtuca et al. eds., 1992).

[39]See also Text 12:11; Text 8:4.

[40]RC 3113.31(D)(1). See Bruns v. Bruns, 1999 WL 819344 (Ohio Ct. App. 6th Dist. Erie County 1999); Visnich v. Visnich, 1999 WL 1299300 (Ohio Ct. App. 11th Dist. Trumbull County 1999).

[41]See Snyder v. Snyder, 1995 WL 493998 (Ohio Ct. App. 4th Dist. Ross County 1995); Maccabee v. Maccabee, 1999 WL 430943 (Ohio Ct. App. 10th Dist. Franklin County 1999); Morris v. Stonewall, 1999 WL 1037507 (Ohio Ct. App. 12th Dist. Clinton County 1999).

[42]See State v. Taylor, 79 Ohio Misc. 2d 82, 671 N.E.2d 343 (Mun. Ct. 1996); see also Eichenberger v. Eichenberger, 82 Ohio App. 3d 809, 815, 613 N.E.2d 678 (10th Dist. Franklin County 1992).

[43]See, e.g., Ankenbruck v. Ankenbruck, 2000 WL 1804360 (Ohio Ct. App. 11th Dist. Trumbull County 2000); see also Morris v. Morris, 2009-Ohio-5164, 2009 WL 3119658 (Ohio Ct. App. 9th Dist. Summit County 2009).

ence that perpetrators will at times back up the threats with physical assaults."[44]

In effect, to ascertain whether and to what extent an abuser poses a threat to the victim's safety for purposes of determining whether to grant a civil protection order, a court must consider the abuser's behavior within the context of the relationship and its history.[45]

Equally important is that petitioners must present evidence of specific acts or threats of domestic violence and that these specific acts or threats place them in fear of future violence.[46] Absent a record detailing a petitioner's fear in conjunction with specific acts, a trial court may be reluctant to issue a civil protection order or an appellate court may reverse the granting of a civil protection order.[47]

Q & A: What is the appropriate burden of proof required to issue an ex parte civil protection order?

Unlike many state domestic violence statutes, RC 3113.31 does not specifically detail the appropriate burden of proof to be applied by a court in evaluating whether a particular petitioner has met her or his burden of proof for the granting of a CPO. Ohio courts have applied the preponderance of the evidence standard,[48] the clear and convincing evidence standard,[49] a standard of proof based on the statutory language of RC 3113.31(A)(1),[50] and some evidence of immediate and present danger of domestic violence as set forth in RC 3113.31(D)(1).[51]

In *Wilburn v. Wilburn*,[52] an inquiry as to the correct burden of proof was raised by appellant who sought and was denied an ex parte civil protection order. On appeal, she alleged that the trial court erred by applying the criminal beyond a reasonable doubt burden of proof when

[44]Anne L. Ganley, The What, Why and Who of Domestic Violence, in Domestic Violence: The Crucial Role of the Judge in Criminal Court Cases: A National Model for Judicial Education 25 (Janet Carter et al. eds., 1991).

[45]See, for example, Osherow v. Osherow, 2003-Ohio-3927, 2003 WL 21697408 (Ohio Ct. App. 9th Dist. Summit County 2003).

[46]See State v. Collie, 108 Ohio App. 3d 580, 671 N.E.2d 338 (1st Dist. Hamilton County 1996).

[47]See, e.g., Anderson v. Anderson, 2001-Ohio-3379, 2001 WL 1667875 (Ohio Ct. App. 7th Dist. Mahoning County 2001); see also Bruner v. Bruner, 2000-Ohio-2554, 2000 WL 1486452 (Ohio Ct. App. 7th Dist. Mahoning County 2000); Newhouse v. Williams, 167 Ohio App. 3d 215, 2006-Ohio-3075, 854 N.E.2d 565 (3d Dist. Wyandot County 2006), citing Young v. Young, 2006-Ohio-978, 2006 WL 515522 (Ohio Ct. App. 2d Dist. Greene County 2006).

[48]See, e.g., Eichenberger v. Eichenberger, 82 Ohio App. 3d 809, 613 N.E.2d 678 (10th Dist. Franklin County 1992).

[49]See, e.g., O'Hara v. Dials, 1996 WL 38810 (Ohio Ct. App. 6th Dist. Erie County 1996) (abrogated by, Felton v. Felton, 79 Ohio St. 3d 34, 1997-Ohio-302, 679 N.E.2d 672 (1997)); Tischler v. Vahcic, 1995 WL 680928 (Ohio Ct. App. 8th Dist. Cuyahoga County 1995) (abrogated by, Felton v. Felton, 79 Ohio St. 3d 34, 1997-Ohio-302, 679 N.E.2d 672 (1997)).

[50]See, e.g., Thomas v. Thomas, 44 Ohio App. 3d 6, 540 N.E.2d 745 (10th Dist. Franklin County 1988).

[51]See also Ferris v. Ferris, 2006-Ohio-878, 2006 WL 456811 (Ohio Ct. App. 12th Dist. Clermont County 2006) (holding that the standard for issuing a temporary protection order is good cause to conclude there is an immediate and present danger to the person to be protected by the order).

[52]Wilburn v. Wilburn, 2006-Ohio-2553, 2006 WL 1409784 (Ohio Ct. App. 9th Dist. Lorain County 2006).

the correct standard should be *some* evidence of immediate and present danger of domestic violence. She also compared this standard in an uncontested ex parte civil protection order to a more stringent standard necessary to justify an order following a full adversarial hearing.

However, the Lorain County Court of Appeals disagreed with her reasoning, relying on *Felton v. Felton*.[53] The appellate court acknowledged the preponderance of the evidence standard applied in *Felton* and noted that "the *Felton* decision drew no distinction between ex parte orders and orders following a full hearing. We decline to do so here. Instead, we follow the *Felton* reasoning and conclude that had the General Assembly intended a burden of proof other than preponderance of the evidence, it could have so specified. It did not, nor will we. We hold that a petitioner's burden of proof in seeking an ex parte civil protection order under RC 3113.31 is a preponderance of the evidence."[54]

Q & A: Is there a difference between the burden of proof and the preponderance of the evidence standard?

It is important for attorneys to use correct terminology when describing the "burden of proof" and the "preponderance of the evidence" standard. As illustrated in the foregoing paragraphs, most courts use these terms interchangeably and to mean various things. Strictly speaking, the 'burden of proof' denotes "the duty of establishing by a fair preponderance of the evidence the truth of the operative facts upon which the issue at hand is made to turn by substantive law."[55] It should be distinguished from the 'standard of proof' which is the degree or level of proof demanded in a specific case, such as proof by a "preponderance of the evidence" meaning the weight of the evidence.[56]

In civil cases, an issue of fact is not proved unless the party having the burden of proof produces a preponderance of the evidence. A preponderance of the evidence standard is customarily used to prescribe one possible burden or standard of proof before a trier of fact.[57]

For purposes of a civil protection order the Supreme Court in *Felton* held that, in granting a civil protection order, "the trial court must find that petitioner has shown by a preponderance of the evidence that petitioner or petitioner's family or household members are in danger of domestic violence."[58]

---

[53]Felton v. Felton, 79 Ohio St. 3d 34, 1997-Ohio-302, 679 N.E.2d 672 (1997).

[54]Wilburn v. Wilburn, 2006-Ohio-2553, 2006 WL 1409784, *2 (Ohio Ct. App. 9th Dist. Lorain County 2006).

[55]Black's Law Dictionary (8th Ed. 2004).

[56]Black's Law Dictionary (8th Ed. 2004). See also Eckstein v. Colian, 2012-Ohio-4038, 2012 WL 3834883 (Ohio Ct. App. 7th Dist. Columbiana County 2012) (preponderance of the evidence means the greater weight of the evidence, or evidence that leads the trier of fact to find that the existence of the contested fact is more probable than its non existence), citing State v. Stumpf, 32 Ohio St. 3d 95, 102, 512 N.E.2d 598 (1987); Zawrotuk v. Zawrotuk, 2014-Ohio-5225, 2014 WL 6641772, ¶ 37 (Ohio Ct. App. 7th Dist. Mahoning County 2014).

[57]32A C.J.S. Evidence 1310.

[58]Felton v. Felton, 79 Ohio St. 3d 34, ¶ 2, 1997-Ohio-302, 679 N.E.2d 672 (1997).

Q & A: Is there a difference between burden of production and burden of proof?[59]

Apparently, a burden of proof is a rather ambiguous term that encompasses the burden of producing evidence and the burden of persuasion.

The burden of producing evidence (burden of going forward) tells a court which party must come forward with evidence to support a particular proposition, whereas the burden of persuasion determines which party must produce sufficient evidence to convince a judge that a fact has been established.

If a party fails to satisfy the burden of producing evidence, that party risks a directed verdict. The burden of producing evidence is usually allocated to the party that asserts the affirmative fact to be proved, which is usually carried by a plaintiff. Once such a burden is satisfied and plaintiff makes a prima facie case, the burden then shifts to the defendant who must produce evidence to support a defense or to rebut plaintiff's evidence.

The burden of persuasion is the responsibility of persuading the trier of fact that the fact at issue is true. The party that bears the burden of persuasion must satisfy that burden in order to prevent a decision against him or her. It is almost always allocated to the plaintiff who must persuade the trier of fact of the lack of any defense raised by defendant.

Q & A: My client was threatened by her spouse. Can she obtain an ex parte civil protection order?[60]

Most likely. Although RC 3113.31 does not define "threat of bodily harm," it must be assumed that such a threat must comport with RC 3113.31(A)(1)(b), which defines domestic violence as "[p]lacing another person by the threat of force in fear of imminent serious physical harm."[61] Threats of bodily harm, whether or not accompanied by previous acts of domestic violence, constitute good cause to obtain a civil protection order pursuant to RC 3113.31(D)(1).[62]

Much of the case law suggests that the threat must be of a nature to cause the victim to believe that the offender will carry out the threat.[63] However, that is different from whether there must be proof

---

[59]See R.G. v. R.M., 2017-Ohio-8918, 88 N.E.3d 1027 (Ohio Ct. App. 7th Dist. Mahoning County 2017); Text § 9:7.

[60]See also Text § 8:4; Text § 12:11.

[61]See also § 8:4. Gaydash v. Gaydash, 168 Ohio App. 3d 418, 2006-Ohio-4080, 860 N.E.2d 789 (9th Dist. Summit County 2006) (noting that domestic violence requires fear inspired by a threat of force as defined in RC 2901.01(A)(1)). But see Moore v. Bentley, 2004-Ohio-5060, 2004 WL 2804785 (Ohio Ct. App. 10th Dist. Franklin County 2004) (affirming judgment of the trial court in not granting CPO, holding that appellant's subsequent behavior undermined a finding that he was in fear of imminent serious physical harm).

[62]See Siouffi v. Siouffi, 1998 WL 879255 (Ohio Ct. App. 2d Dist. Montgomery County 1998).

[63]See West v. West, 1994 WL 680156 (Ohio Ct. App. 2d Dist. Montgomery County 1994); State v. Collie, 108 Ohio App. 3d 580, 671 N.E.2d 338 (1st Dist. Hamilton County 1996); Meyers v. Wimer, 2005-Ohio-3753, 2005 WL 1714194 (Ohio Ct. App. 2d Dist. Montgomery County 2005) (relying on *West* and stating that petitioner must

that the respondent intended to or was about to carry out the threat.[64] Case law also suggests that past acts of domestic violence often instill in the victim a fear of imminent serious physical harm.[65] Clearly, recent threats, accompanied by a past history of domestic violence, should satisfy the requirements set forth in the various cases.[66]

Even threatening behavior without verbal threats may be sufficient evidence for the issuance of a civil protection order. In *Siouffi v. Siouffi*,[67] the Montgomery County Court of Appeals found that a husband slashing the tires on his wife's car with a twelve-inch knife taken from the kitchen during an argument and forcing his way back into the home was sufficient to justify the issuance of a civil protection order. Though the defendant argued that he never verbally threatened his wife, the appellate court found that "a threat of force need not be conveyed expressly; it may just as well be conveyed implicitly by conduct. Conduct which is threatening in nature is no less threatening simply because it is unaccompanied by verbal expressions of the threat."[68]

Additionally, a petitioner must show that he/she is at risk of imminent harm in order to obtain an ex parte civil protection order.[69] Obviously, evidence of recent physical violence is sufficient proof of

---

first establish that a threat occurred before a court could assess and petitioner could demonstrate whether she subjectively believed that respondent would cause her and the children imminent serious physical harm). But see State v. Taylor, 79 Ohio Misc. 2d 82, 671 N.E.2d 343 (Mun. Ct. 1996); see also Strong v. Bauman, 1999 WL 317432 (Ohio Ct. App. 2d Dist. Montgomery County 1999).

[64]See Text § 8:4.

[65]See Reynolds v. White, 1999 WL 754496 (Ohio Ct. App. 8th Dist. Cuyahoga County 1999); Bruns v. Bruns, 1999 WL 819344 (Ohio Ct. App. 6th Dist. Erie County 1999); Visnich v. Visnich, 1999 WL 1299300 (Ohio Ct. App. 11th Dist. Trumbull County 1999).

[66]See also Bruns v. Bruns, 1999 WL 819344 (Ohio Ct. App. 6th Dist. Erie County 1999); Ankenbruck v. Ankenbruck, 2000 WL 1804360 (Ohio Ct. App. 11th Dist. Trumbull County 2000); Newhouse v. Williams, 167 Ohio App. 3d 215, 2006-Ohio-3075, 854 N.E.2d 565 (3d Dist. Wyandot County 2006) (concluding that past events, not too remote in time, evidence of current domestic violence and evidence of a reasonable fear of imminent serious physical harm is needed to prevail); Hamper v. Dobrski, 2015-Ohio-1381, 2015 WL 1593249 (Ohio Ct. App. 8th Dist. Cuyahoga County 2015) (comments such as he was "poisoning her food," "thought about cutting her brake lines," "make her life a living hell" and "wanted revenge" all put her in fear. Petitioner also testified that appellant refused to permit her to take their daughter for a walk without "silently" accompanying her and that he followed her in his car to "see where she went." The aforementioned coupled with past shoving of petitioner and their child supported the magistrate's decision to grant the CPO).

[67]Siouffi v. Siouffi, 1998 WL 879255 (Ohio Ct. App. 2d Dist. Montgomery County 1998); see also Markowitz v. Markowitz, 2006-Ohio-5932, 2006 WL 3234010 (Ohio Ct. App. 8th Dist. Cuyahoga County 2006) (respondent standing inches away from petitioner, close enough that she smelled his toothpaste and screaming obscenities at her constituted an implied threat of force); Williams v. Hupp, 2011-Ohio-3403, 2011 WL 2670945 (Ohio Ct. App. 7th Dist. Mahoning County 2011) (threats need not be verbalized).

[68]Siouffi v. Siouffi, 1998 WL 879255, *3 (Ohio Ct. App. 2d Dist. Montgomery County 1998).

[69]See RC 3113.31(A)(1)(b); see also Strong v. Bauman, 1999 WL 317432 (Ohio Ct. App. 2d Dist. Montgomery County 1999) (discussing of imminent); Reynolds v. Reynolds, 2001 WL 62552 (Ohio Ct. App. 2d Dist. Montgomery County 2001) (discussing the factors necessary to support a finding that petitioner was placed in imminent

imminent harm. However, visible evidence of physical harm is by no means required for a civil protection order to be issued.[70]

The case law illustrates the broad variety of acts, threats, and situations which are sufficient to constitute imminent harm, including the respondent's verbal threats against the petitioner[71] and the respondent's harassment of the petitioner.[72] In certain cases, a respondent's threat to kidnap the child may be sufficient.[73]

For example, in *Eichenberger v. Eichenberger*,[74] the Franklin County Court of Appeals affirmed the trial court's decision that a civil protection order was appropriate when the wife alleged that the husband had used extremely offensive and threatening language in front of the children, had attempted to cause serious bodily injury to her, had previously engaged in similar conduct, and had threatened to take their minor child and run. The court held that the relief requested under RC 3113.31 was necessary to protect her. The court went on to say that "[t]he fear she . . . felt and the reasonableness of that fear could and should be determined with reference to her history with appellant."[75] In *Eichenberger*, previous acts of domestic violence and recent threats were sufficient to demonstrate an immediate and present danger and to warrant a civil protection order.[76]

---

fear of harm).

[70]See State v. Bolds, 1993 WL 35578 (Ohio Ct. App. 5th Dist. Stark County 1993); see also Text § 8:4, Statutory elements of domestic violence under RC 3113.31(A)(1)(b).

[71]Eichenberger v. Eichenberger, 82 Ohio App. 3d 809, 613 N.E.2d 678 (10th Dist. Franklin County 1992); see also Diane R. Follingstad et al., The Role of Emotional Abuse in Physically Abusive Relationships, 5 J. Fam. Violence 107, 113 (1990); Sitton v. Sitton, 1999 WL 55717 (Ohio Ct. App. 2d Dist. Montgomery County 1999); State v. Brown, 2003-Ohio-710, 2003 WL 352460 (Ohio Ct. App. 12th Dist. Butler County 2003) (noting that evidence demonstrating that victim believed offender could cause imminent physical harm must be shown by victim's statements or other evidence where such harm could be inferred).

[72]West v. West, 1994 WL 680156 (Ohio Ct. App. 2d Dist. Montgomery County 1994); see also Gooderham v. Patterson, 1999 WL 1034472 (Ohio Ct. App. 4th Dist. Gallia County 1999).

[73]Sanders v. Shephard, 185 Ill. App. 3d 719, 133 Ill. Dec. 712, 541 N.E.2d 1150 (1st Dist. 1989); see also Maccabee v. Maccabee, 1999 WL 430943 (Ohio Ct. App. 10th Dist. Franklin County 1999).

[74]Eichenberger v. Eichenberger, 82 Ohio App. 3d 809, 613 N.E.2d 678 (10th Dist. Franklin County 1992).

[75]Eichenberger v. Eichenberger, 82 Ohio App. 3d 809, 816, 613 N.E.2d 678 (10th Dist. Franklin County 1992); see also *Eichenberger* dissent which focuses on whether the threat places a victim in fear of imminent serious physical harm rather than on the victim's subjective belief; Conkle v. Wolfe, 131 Ohio App. 3d 375, 722 N.E.2d 586 (4th Dist. Athens County 1998); Yoel v. Yoel, 1998 WL 1051779 (Ohio Ct. App. 11th Dist. Lake County 1998); Ankenbruck v. Ankenbruck, 2000 WL 1804360 (Ohio Ct. App. 11th Dist. Trumbull County 2000); Bruns v. Bruns, 1999 WL 819344 (Ohio Ct. App. 6th Dist. Erie County 1999); Text § 16:13, Hearsay exceptions; *Crawford* concerns; Johnson v. Burke, 2016-Ohio-2947, 2016 WL 2757891 (Ohio Ct. App. 8th Dist. Cuyahoga County 2016).

[76]But see Solomon v. Solomon, 157 Ohio App. 3d 807, 2004-Ohio-2486, 813 N.E.2d 918 (7th Dist. Mahoning County 2004). See also Martauz v. Martauz, 2009-Ohio-2642, 2009 WL 1581185 (Ohio Ct. App. 7th Dist. Mahoning County 2009); Thom v. Mulvin, 2009-Ohio-3797, 2009 WL 2365996 (Ohio Ct. App. 6th Dist. Erie County 2009); Martin v. Hanood, 2009-Ohio-1501, 2009 WL 825766 (Ohio Ct. App. 7th Dist. Jefferson County

Additionally, in *West v. West*,[77] the statements "all this pain and suffering will be taken care of later" and "wait till you see what I have got planned" were considered threats because they placed the victim "in fear of imminent serious physical harm." The court also relied on other past acts, such as pouring soap in the petitioner's coffee, to explain why the respondent's statements caused the petitioner to fear impending harm. The court concluded that "it is the victim's subjective belief which becomes the focal point for determining whether certain conduct violates the statute."[78]

In some cases, the fear of domestic violence is predicated on more than a past history with the respondent. For example, in *Sitton v. Sitton*,[79] the court relied both on the past history of threatening behavior and on the victim's actions on the day in question. On that day, she vacated the house, hid out from her husband, and returned to the residence only when she was accompanied by a police officer or at a time when she believed a protection order had been served on her husband.[80]

The *Sitton* court held that based on her actions on the date of the incident and "in view of [defendant's] threats to kill his wife and his access to weapons, we cannot conclude that [the victim] lacked an objective basis to fear her husband."[81] The Montgomery County Court of Appeals found there to be competent, credible evidence to support the trial court's finding that she was fearful of her husband. Of significance is that the appellate court used a combined subjective/objective approach in order to determine fear.[82]

In contrast, some courts in Ohio have been reluctant to issue protection orders based on a victim's subjective fear and threats where the words or statements do not show unequivocally that the victim was placed in fear of harm by force.[83] For example, in *Coughlin v.*

2009).

[77]West v. West, 1994 WL 680156, *3–4 (Ohio Ct. App. 2d Dist. Montgomery County 1994).

[78]West v. West, 1994 WL 680156, *3 (Ohio Ct. App. 2d Dist. Montgomery County 1994) (citing City of Dayton v. Waugh, No. 6965 (2d Dist. Ct. App., Montgomery, 1-2-81)). See also Meyers v. Wimer, 2005-Ohio-3753, 2005 WL 1714194 (Ohio Ct. App. 2d Dist. Montgomery County 2005); Chapman v. Chapman, 2006-Ohio-2328, 2006 WL 1284592 (Ohio Ct. App. 2d Dist. Montgomery County 2006); Hunter v. Hunter, 2006-Ohio-6307, 2006 WL 3462139, *2 (Ohio Ct. App. 2d Dist. Montgomery County 2006) (noting that "the primary focus of RC 3113.31(A)(1)(b) is the perception of the victim.").

[79]Sitton v. Sitton, 1999 WL 55717 (Ohio Ct. App. 2d Dist. Montgomery County 1999).

[80]Sitton v. Sitton, 1999 WL 55717, *4 (Ohio Ct. App. 2d Dist. Montgomery County 1999).

[81]Sitton v. Sitton, 1999 WL 55717, *4 (Ohio Ct. App. 2d Dist. Montgomery County 1999); see also Conkle v. Wolfe, 131 Ohio App. 3d 375, 722 N.E.2d 586 (4th Dist. Athens County 1998).

[82]See also Text Ch. 8, The Nature of a Civil Protection Order. See also Young v. Young, 2006-Ohio-978, 2006 WL 515522 (Ohio Ct. App. 2d Dist. Greene County 2006) (fear of imminent serious physical harm involves both subjective and objective elements).

[83]See Smith v. Mangan, 2007-Ohio-194, 2007 WL 127693, *2 (Ohio Ct. App. 2d Dist. Greene County 2007) (sustaining assignment of error and disagreeing with the

Lancione,[84] the Franklin County Court of Appeals found that the statement "I am going to take you down" did not rise to the level of fear of imminent serious physical harm. Likewise, the Tenth District Court of Appeals, in *Beach v. Beach*,[85] determined that the words "put this in your mouth," referring to the respondent's penis, after he unzipped his pants in an aggressive manner, did not comport with the minimum statutory requirements of RC 3113.31(A)(1)(b).

In *Fleckner v. Fleckner*,[86] the appellate court articulated the critical inquiry in determining whether a party seeking a CPO has been placed, by threat of force, in fear of imminent serious physical harm, which is whether a reasonable person would be placed in fear of imminent, i.e., unconditional and non-contingent, serious physical harm.[87] The court then pointed out that such an inquiry "necessarily involves both subjective and objective elements."[88] The subjective test

---

trial court which stated that "the tempestuous history between the parties proves that it is reasonable to conclude Petitioner would fear that any contact with the respondent could result in physical danger." But appellate court held that "the fact that appellee may have been in fear of Mangan however was not enough to warrant a CPO. The statute requires fear that arises from a "threat of force" and causes a fear of imminent serious physical harm." Smith offered no evidence). But see Markowitz v. Markowitz, 2006-Ohio-5932, 2006 WL 3234010 (Ohio Ct. App. 8th Dist. Cuyahoga County 2006) (threat of force may be implied).

[84]Coughlin v. Lancione, 1992 WL 40557, *1 (Ohio Ct. App. 10th Dist. Franklin County 1992) (abrogated by, Felton v. Felton, 79 Ohio St. 3d 34, 1997-Ohio-302, 679 N.E.2d 672 (1997)), abrogated by Felton v. Felton, 79 Ohio St. 3d 34, 1997-Ohio-302, 679 N.E.2d 672 (1997) (regarding requisite standard of proof); see also Text § 12:11, Standard of proof; Siouffi v. Siouffi, 1998 WL 879255 (Ohio Ct. App. 2d Dist. Montgomery County 1998); Anderson v. Anderson, 2001-Ohio-3379, 2001 WL 1667875 (Ohio Ct. App. 7th Dist. Mahoning County 2001); Bruner v. Bruner, 2000-Ohio-2554, 2000 WL 1486452 (Ohio Ct. App. 7th Dist. Mahoning County 2000).

[85]Beach v. Beach, 1992 WL 328642, *1 (Ohio Ct. App. 10th Dist. Franklin County 1992).

[86]Fleckner v. Fleckner, 177 Ohio App. 3d 706, 2008-Ohio-4000, 895 N.E.2d 896 (10th Dist. Franklin County 2008); see also Johnson v. Auls, 2008-Ohio-6123, 2008 WL 5049751 (Ohio Ct. App. 10th Dist. Franklin County 2008) (upholding grant of CPO and finding that respondent had actually committed acts of violence and also placed appellee in reasonable fear of harm by threat of force); Williamson v. Williamson, 180 Ohio App. 3d 260, 2008-Ohio-6718, 905 N.E.2d 217 (2d Dist. Greene County 2008); but see Strassell v. Chapman, 2010-Ohio-4376, 2010 WL 3610591 (Ohio Ct. App. 10th Dist. Franklin County 2010) (finding that respondent misapplied *Fleckner*; because petitioner explicitly indicated she was in fear of imminent serious physical harm on the date contained in the petition, the trial court could consider prior incidents of domestic violence and thus, could conclude that her fear of respondent was reasonable); Richter v. Richter, 2009-Ohio-3828, 2009 WL 2371882 (Ohio Ct. App. 12th Dist. Butler County 2009) (differentiating Fleckner); Donovan v. Donovan, 2012-Ohio-3521, 2012 WL 3156462 (Ohio Ct. App. 9th Dist. Lorain County 2012) (differentiating *Fleckner* and focusing on the fact that, in *Fleckner*, the wife did not identify a recent threatening action of Husband's in her petition and in her testimony).

[87]Fleckner v. Fleckner, 177 Ohio App. 3d 706, 714, 2008-Ohio-4000, 895 N.E.2d 896 (10th Dist. Franklin County 2008), citing Maccabee v. Maccabee, 1999 WL 430943 (Ohio Ct. App. 10th Dist. Franklin County 1999), and quoting Strong v. Bauman, 1999 WL 317432 (Ohio Ct. App. 2d Dist. Montgomery County 1999); Strassell v. Chapman, 2010-Ohio-4376, 2010 WL 3610591 (Ohio Ct. App. 10th Dist. Franklin County 2010).

[88]Fleckner v. Fleckner, 177 Ohio App. 3d 706, 714, 2008-Ohio-4000, 895 N.E.2d 896 (10th Dist. Franklin County 2008), citing Young v. Young, 2006-Ohio-978, 2006 WL 515522, ¶ 106 (Ohio Ct. App. 2d Dist. Greene County 2006), and quoting Strong v.

inquires whether a respondent's threat of force actually caused petitioner to fear imminent serious physical harm and the objective test inquires whether the petitioner's fear is reasonable under the circumstances. In this case, the threat *to take legal action* does not meet the requirements under RC 3113.31.[89]

Q & A: My client needs a protection order. The last incident of violence occurred three months ago. Will the court grant my client an ex parte protection order?

It depends. Generally, there is no statute of limitations within which a victim of domestic violence must file a petition for an ex parte protection order.[90] RC 3113.31(D) declines to include filing deadlines which state at what point in time a previous act of violence must have occurred in relation to a present request for a protection order. Such a provision would enable a court to accurately determine whether certain acts fit within the mandated time frame. Reported case law supports the position that a court should not deny a petition solely because it was not filed within a particular time in relation to the last incident of violence.[91]

Several Ohio courts have addressed this issue. For example, in *Halley v. Ashley*,[92] in the six months prior to the protection order hearing, the defendant harassed the petitioner, leaving obscene mes-

---

Bauman, 1999 WL 317432 (Ohio Ct. App. 2d Dist. Montgomery County 1999); Martauz v. Martauz, 2009-Ohio-2642, 2009 WL 1581185 (Ohio Ct. App. 7th Dist. Mahoning County 2009); Williams v. Hupp, 2011-Ohio-3403, 2011 WL 2670945 (Ohio Ct. App. 7th Dist. Mahoning County 2011).

[89]R.T. v. J.T., 2015-Ohio-4418, 2015 WL 6449294 (Ohio Ct. App. 9th Dist. Medina County 2015) (telling the children that a child protective agency was coming to take them away does not rise to the level of domestic violence under any section of RC 3113.31).

[90]See Harbaugh v. Jarrell, 2005-Ohio-1753, 2005 WL 856927 (Ohio Ct. App. 5th Dist. Ashland County 2005) (RC 3113.31 provides no time restrictions for bring allegations to the court in petitioning for a protective order); see also Hoff v. Brown, 2001 WL 876228 (Ohio Ct. App. 5th Dist. Stark County 2001); Oliver v. Johnson, 2007-Ohio-5880, 2007 WL 3227668 (Ohio Ct. App. 4th Dist. Jackson County 2007) (stating that there is no time bar for filing the motion, but that petitioner has the burden to establish that he/she is presently in fear of imminent serious physical harm).

[91]See Halley v. Ashley, 1997 WL 760662 (Ohio Ct. App. 9th Dist. Summit County 1997); see also Morris v. Stonewall, 1999 WL 1037507 (Ohio Ct. App. 12th Dist. Clinton County 1999); Trent v. Trent, 1999 WL 298073 (Ohio Ct. App. 12th Dist. Preble County 1999); Serdy v. Serdy, 2013-Ohio-5532, 2013 WL 6670830 (Ohio Ct. App. 7th Dist. Noble County 2013) (finding that 6 weeks between the act and the time petitioner requested CPO does not preclude her from seeking CPO, although if she had sought the order closer in time to the main event, the case would not be a close one). But see Lebeau v. Lebeau, 2001 WL 1339495 (Ohio Ct. App. 5th Dist. Stark County 2001).

[92]Halley v. Ashley, 1997 WL 760662 (Ohio Ct. App. 9th Dist. Summit County 1997); Murral v. Thomson, 2004-Ohio-432, 2004 WL 193876 (Ohio Ct. App. 4th Dist. Hocking County 2004); see also Hoff v. Brown, 2001 WL 876228 (Ohio Ct. App. 5th Dist. Stark County 2001); see also Chiarovano v. Chiarovano, Case No. CA2002-11-027 (Ohio Ct. App. 12th Dist. 2003) (whether an occurrence of domestic violence is recent enough to warrant a CPO is a matter left to the sound discretion of the trial court); Wardeh v. Altabchi, 158 Ohio App. 3d 325, 2004-Ohio-4423, 815 N.E.2d 712 (10th Dist. Franklin County 2004) (although the most recent incidents of physical violence occurred two years before the CPO petition was filed, trial court did not abuse its discretion in considering those incidents along with husband's continual and

sages on her answering machine and obscene notes on her door. He threw keys at her chest and pushed her. She even changed her residence in an attempt to get away from him. Shortly before she filed her petition for a protection order, her car was vandalized.

It must be reiterated that the incidents took place within six months preceding the filing of the victim's petition and the defendant argued that any incident of domestic violence must be close in time to the filing of the petition for a protection order. The Summit County Court of Appeals held that there was sufficient evidence to support a finding of domestic violence and noted, in a footnote, that "the statute does not place any outer limit on when the domestic violence must have occurred. Further, the Stark County Court of Appeals in *Lebeau v. Lebeau*,[93] agreed when it held that RC 3113.31 provides no time restrictions for bringing allegations to the court in petitioners for a protection order and that relief may be granted even if the victim merely cohabited with the perpetrator within five years prior to the date of the alleged acts. Whether an occurrence of domestic violence is recent enough to warrant a civil protective order is a matter committed to the sound discretion of the trial court."[94]

Similarly, in *Morris v. Stonewall*,[95] the petitioner testified that she suffered verbal, physical, and sexual abuse throughout her marriage. She also stated that her husband had followed, stalked, and threatened her. The trial court found that the physical and sexual abuse that occurred during the marriage constituted domestic violence even though it had took place at least nine months prior to her petition.[96] The appellate court noted that the trial court could find no applicable

---

increasing threats to abscond to Syria with their child); Richter v. Richter, 2009-Ohio-3828, 2009 WL 2371882 (Ohio Ct. App. 12th Dist. Butler County 2009) (petitioner filed the CPO three weeks after the incident and her fear of imminent serious physical harm shown by leaving the couple's residence with her children. After he discovered her new address, she immediately filed the CPO); Traut v. Leiby, 2010-Ohio-2563, 2010 WL 2298566 (Ohio Ct. App. 5th Dist. Richland County 2010) (holding that RC 3113.31 provides no specific time restrictions for bringing allegations to the court in petitioning for a protective order, but cautioning about the over application of the CPO remedy when there is an absence of direct threats against or actual violence towards petitioner. at *2); Zawrotuk v. Zawrotuk, 2014-Ohio-5225, 2014 WL 6641772, ¶ 37 (Ohio Ct. App. 7th Dist. Mahoning County 2014) (reasoning that trial court found that it was not dispositive that the most recent incident occurred a month before wife filed her petition, noting that incident was relatively new and criminal charges were pending regarding the incident at the time. The trial court pointed out that regardless of the ex parte order, wife had burden to prove domestic violence occurred at the full hearing. at ¶ 15).

[93] Lebeau v. Lebeau, 2001 WL 1339495 (Ohio Ct. App. 5th Dist. Stark County 2001).

[94] Halley v. Ashley, 1997 WL 760662, *4 (Ohio Ct. App. 9th Dist. Summit County 1997); see also Trent v. Trent, 1999 WL 298073 (Ohio Ct. App. 12th Dist. Preble County 1999). But see Lebeau v. Lebeau, 2001 WL 1339495, *2 (Ohio Ct. App. 5th Dist. Stark County 2001) (discussing that RC 3113.31 provides no time restrictions for bringing allegations to the court in petitioning for a protection order and that relief may be granted even if the victim merely cohabited with the perpetrator within five years prior to the date of the alleged acts).

[95] Morris v. Stonewall, 1999 WL 1037507 (Ohio Ct. App. 12th Dist. Clinton County 1999); see also Maccabee v. Maccabee, 1999 WL 430943 (Ohio Ct. App. 10th Dist. Franklin County 1999).

[96] Morris v. Stonewall, 1999 WL 1037507, *3 (Ohio Ct. App. 12th Dist. Clinton County 1999).

statute of limitations and thus issued the protection order.[97] The appellate court relied on the reasoning of *Trent v.Trent*,[98] which relied on *Halley v. Ashley*,[99] to uphold the issuance of the civil protection order.

Finally, in *Parkhurst v. Parkhurst*,[100] the court held that the last incident of abuse, which occurred two months prior to the civil protection order petition, was admissible when accompanied by the victim's present fear of violence by the respondent on his being served with divorce papers.[101]

Local procedure and practice may vary in Ohio's courts. Before filing for a protection order, attorneys should consider such local variations. For example, in Cuyahoga County Domestic Relations Court, ex parte petitions are scrutinized if the last act of violence took place several months earlier. Unless a petitioner can show that he/she is still in danger, the court will question the emergency nature of the petition.

It is important that family law practitioners understand that, for purposes of an ex parte civil protection order, an immediate and present danger must exist.[102] Regardless of when the act of violence occurred, it must be demonstrated to the court that the act complained of placed the petitioner in a situation such that an immediate and present danger exists at the time of filing.

Q & A: When the petitioner does not request an ex parte protection order, what standard does the court employ to find that domestic violence occurred?

When an ex parte protection order is requested, the statute requires that a petitioner demonstrate "an immediate and present danger."[103] On the other hand, where an ex parte order is not requested,[104] it has been argued that, in deciding whether to issue the civil protection or-

---

[97] Morris v. Stonewall, 1999 WL 1037507, *3 (Ohio Ct. App. 12th Dist. Clinton County 1999).

[98] Trent v. Trent, 1999 WL 298073 (Ohio Ct. App. 12th Dist. Preble County 1999).

[99] Halley v. Ashley, 1997 WL 760662 (Ohio Ct. App. 9th Dist. Summit County 1997).

[100] Parkhurst v. Parkhurst, 793 S.W.2d 634 (Mo. Ct. App. E.D. 1990).

[101] See also Coburn v. Coburn, 342 Md. 244, 674 A.2d 951 (1996) (holding that prior history of domestic violence admissible regardless of whether they were pled in original petition). But see Bruner v. Bruner, 2000-Ohio-2554, 2000 WL 1486452 (Ohio Ct. App. 7th Dist. Mahoning County 2000) (where testimony of fear consisted of a generalized, unsubstantiated statement); Young v. Young, 2006-Ohio-978, 2006 WL 515522 (Ohio Ct. App. 2d Dist. Greene County 2006); Newhouse v. Williams, 167 Ohio App. 3d 215, 222–23, 2006-Ohio-3075, ¶ 15, 854 N.E.2d 565, 570–71 (3d Dist. Wyandot County 2006) (a past incident five years earlier is too remote in time, when accompanied by a recent action that does not constitute a recent threat; distasteful and vulgar language, where petitioner said she does not fear for her safety, may be childish and inappropriate but is not the basis for the issuance of a CPO; however, the court also stressed that incidents too remote in time, with no intervening events to set up a pattern of behavior, cannot be the basis for a civil protection order).

[102] RC 3113.31(D)(1). See also Siouffi v. Siouffi, 1998 WL 879255 (Ohio Ct. App. 2d Dist. Montgomery County 1998); Reynolds v. White, 1999 WL 754496 (Ohio Ct. App. 8th Dist. Cuyahoga County 1999).

[103] RC 3113.31(D)(1).

[104] See RC 3113.31(D)(3); Genari v. Genari, 2001-Ohio-1524, 2001 WL 848569

der after a full hearing, the court must determine whether, in fact, domestic violence has occurred as defined in RC 3113.31(A). However, recent case law appears to have softened this standard. In *Felton v. Felton*,[105] the Ohio Supreme Court stated that "when granting a protection order, the trial court must find that petitioner has shown by a preponderance of the evidence that petitioner or petitioner's family or household members are in danger of domestic violence."[106]

The Montgomery County Court of Appeals adopted this criterion in *Siouffi v. Siouffi*.[107] There, the defendant slashed the petitioner's tires with a twelve-inch knife. The trial court issued an ex parte civil protection order. At the full hearing, the order was vacated by the magistrate who stated that the respondent did not cause, attempt to cause, or recklessly cause the petitioner any bodily injury, nor did he place her in fear of serious physical harm. The petitioner's objections to the magistrate's decision were sustained, and the trial court concluded that the respondent's admitted actions created an immediate and present danger of domestic violence against the petitioner.

On appeal, the respondent argued that the trial court employed an inappropriate and lesser standard for the issuance of the civil protection order after the full hearing. Relying on *Felton*, the appellate court rejected that argument, explaining that

> the standard to be used in determining whether a civil protection order is to be issued is whether the petitioner is in danger of domestic violence. Regardless of the language employed by the court, it is apparent from a reading of its decision that the court found [the petitioner] to be in danger of domestic violence.[108]

§ 11:11 Ex parte protection orders—Service and notice provisions[1]

Proper service is a requirement for a court's exercise of personal

(Ohio Ct. App. 2d Dist. Greene County 2001) (discussing RC 3113.31(D)(3)); see also § 11:1, Introduction.

[105]Felton v. Felton, 79 Ohio St. 3d 34, 42, 1997-Ohio-302, 679 N.E.2d 672 (1997).

[106]See also Pierce v. Pierce, 2001-Ohio-2312, 2001 WL 1432047, *3 (Ohio Ct. App. 3d Dist. Marion County 2001) (where appellant argued that a CPO can only be granted after the trial court determines that the petitioner is in danger of domestic violence. The entry in *Pierce* allowed a CPO to be issued based on actual occurrences of domestic violence. The appellate court held appellant misinterpreted *Felton*: "According to the appellant's interpretation of *Felton*, a court could not protect an actual victim of domestic violence, but it could only protect a person who is in danger of future domestic violence. The Court does not believe such an interpretation has any reasonable or rational basis."); Lavery v. Lavery, 2001-Ohio-1874, 2001 WL 1545663 (Ohio Ct. App. 9th Dist. Summit County 2001).

[107]Siouffi v. Siouffi, 1998 WL 879255 (Ohio Ct. App. 2d Dist. Montgomery County 1998) (relying on Thomas v. Thomas, 44 Ohio App. 3d 6, 540 N.E.2d 745 (10th Dist. Franklin County 1988)).

[108]Siouffi v. Siouffi, 1998 WL 879255, *2 (Ohio Ct. App. 2d Dist. Montgomery County 1998) (citations omitted); see also Sitton v. Sitton, 1999 WL 55717 (Ohio Ct. App. 2d Dist. Montgomery County 1999); Strong v. Bauman, 1999 WL 317432 (Ohio Ct. App. 2d Dist. Montgomery County 1999).

[Section 11:11]

[1]See also Text § 12:8, Service of the protection order issued after the full hearing, and Text Ch. 13, Court Enforcement of Civil Protection Orders and Related Issues; Parker v. Jamison, 2003-Ohio-7295, 2003 WL 24135688 (Ohio Ct. App. 4th Dist. Scioto County 2003).

jurisdiction.[2] Any order entered without having first obtained personal jurisdiction over the respondent is void.[3]

The respondent must be served with process providing notice of, and an opportunity to be heard at, a full hearing on the civil protection order.[4] In accordance with the requirements of due process, Ohio's statutory scheme provides that a respondent must be served with the petition and notice of the date of the full hearing prior to the full hearing. If an ex parte protection order is requested by the petitioner and issued by the court, a copy of the ex parte order must be included.[5] For reasons of efficiency, the ex parte order is served contemporaneously with written notice of the hearing date for the full hearing on the petition.

Conversely, if an ex parte order is not requested or is requested but not granted, the court shall proceed as in any civil action and grant a full hearing.[6] Unfortunately, both the domestic violence statute and the Civil Rules fail to provide a procedure or a date certain for the full hearing in these instances; and it is unclear whether the provisions set forth in RC 3113.31(D)(2)(a), as to the time frame of the full hearing, apply to these petitions.

If an ex parte order is not requested, the petition is considered a written motion, and notice of the hearing "shall be served not later than seven days before the time fixed for the hearing, unless a different period is fixed by these rules or by order of the court."[7] Where the petition for protection order is filed with the county clerk of courts, it proceeds as any other motion. Most courts do not schedule the full hearing earlier than 28 days after service of process. However, attorneys should request that the court set the full hearing within the same time frame as any other full hearing of a civil protection order—within seven or 10 court days.[8] In requesting the hearing within this shortened time frame, the intent and purpose of the civil protection order is preserved.

If an ex parte order is requested, but not granted by the court, most courts do schedule the full hearing within the seven- or 10-day time

[2]See, for example, Vance v. Nichols, 2007-Ohio-3819, 2007 WL 2164162 (Ohio Ct. App. 2d Dist. Darke County 2007).

[3]See Text § 10:13, Jurisdiction and venue—In domestic violence cases. See also Text § 14:15, Potential police liability in the enforcement of protection orders, for a discussion of the validity of an ex parte order; Text § 13:3, Court enforcement of civil protection orders—Criminal prosecution. See also Lucas v. Green, 1999 WL 961499 (Ohio Ct. App. 8th Dist. Cuyahoga County 1999), citing Maryhew v. Yova, 11 Ohio St. 3d 154, 464 N.E.2d 538 (1984); State ex rel. Ballard v. O'Donnell, 50 Ohio St. 3d 182, 553 N.E.2d 650 (1990); see also Beachler v. Beachler, 2007-Ohio-1220, 2007 WL 805526 (Ohio Ct. App. 12th Dist. Preble County 2007) (where appellant did not receive timely notice of the full hearing pursuant to RC 3113.31(D)(2), the CPO was void); Jones v. Jordan, 2007-Ohio-2519, 2007 WL 1508255 (Ohio Ct. App. 8th Dist. Cuyahoga County 2007) (objection to jurisdiction made via motion for relief from judgment).

[4]RC 3113.31(D)(2).

[5]RC 3113.31(F)(1).

[6]See RC 3113.31(D)(3); see also Text § 12:1, Introduction; Genari v. Genari, 2001-Ohio-1524, 2001 WL 848569 (Ohio Ct. App. 2d Dist. Greene County 2001).

[7]Civ.R. 6(D).

[8]RC 3113.31(D)(2)(a).

frame. It is incumbent upon the attorney to advocate for a shortened time frame in this instance because the petitioner expected an ex parte order and may, in fact, remain at risk without protection.

Q & A: How does Ohio's domestic violence statute address the issue of service?

Pursuant to RC 3113.31(G), any proceeding under this section shall be conducted in accordance with the Rules of Civil Procedure. Therefore all pleadings, processes and orders must be served upon a respondent in compliance with the civil rules. RC 3113.31(F)(1) directs the court to provide the procedure by which a copy of the protection order is given to the respondent.

Ohio's domestic violence statute provides that "[a] copy of any protection order, or consent agreement, that is issued or approved under this section shall be issued by the court to the petitioner, to the respondent, and to all law enforcement agencies that have jurisdiction to enforce the order or agreement. The court shall direct that a copy of an order be delivered to the respondent on the same day that the order is entered."[9]

Unfortunately, Ohio's domestic violence statute offers no clear direction as to how a respondent is to receive a copy of the protection order. Moreover, the terms "issue," "deliver," "serve," and "notice" have been used interchangeably by both the legislature and the courts.

Ohio's legislative history of Am. Sub. H.B. 835 demonstrates that in both the House and Senate Reports[10] as well as in the Legislative Analysis of enacted Am. Sub. H.B. 835,[11] a copy of the protection order was required "to be given" to the respondent and the court was required to direct that the respondent's copy be delivered the same day it is entered.

To "issue" means "to put forth or send out officially."[12] To "deliver" means "to give possession of something to another."[13] "Delivery" is the "formal act of transferring something or yielding possession or control of something to another."[14] To "serve" means to "present a person with a notice or process as required by law."[15] "Service" is defined as "[t]he formal delivery of a writ, summons, or other legal process."[16]

Q & A: What guidance do the Rules of Civil Procedure provide?

Civ.R. 4 governs civil jurisdiction and service of process. "Process"

---

[9] RC 3113.31(F)(1); see also RC 2919.26(G)(1).

[10] House and Senate Reports, Am. Sub. H.B. 835 (1978).

[11] Legislative Analysis, Am. Sub. H.B. 835 (1979).

[12] Black's Law Dictionary, 7th ed. (1999).

[13] Black's Law Dictionary, 7th ed. (1999).

[14] Black's Law Dictionary (9th ed.) (2009); see also State v. Smith, 136 Ohio St. 3d 1, 2013-Ohio-1698, 989 N.E.2d 972 (2013); but see Am. Sub. SB 7, which effectively superseded holding of *State v. Smith* regarding violations of civil protection orders under RC 2919.27(D), so that unperfected service of a protection order or consent agreement does not preclude a prosecution for a violation of division (A) of that section.

[15] Black's Law Dictionary, 7th ed. (1999).

[16] Black's Law Dictionary (9th ed.) (2009); see also State v. Smith, 136 Ohio St. 3d 1, 2013-Ohio-1698, 989 N.E.2d 972 (2013); Text § 13:3.

means a writ or summons issued in the course of judicial proceedings and used to inform the defendant of the institution of proceedings against him and to compel his appearance in either civil or criminal cases.[17] Because an ex parte civil protection order provides for notice and the opportunity to be heard and accompanies the petition for a civil protection order (complaint), service of process must be perfected.

In contrast, Civ.R. 5 applies to service of papers other than process and applies to every order required to be served. The civil protection order issued after the full hearing is neither a writ nor a summons. Therefore, it is not "process" and is governed by Civ.R. 5.

Civil Rule 5(B) provides that service shall be made upon the party by "delivering a copy" to the person served, transmitting it to the office of the person to be served by facsimile transmission, mailing it to the last known address of the person to be served, or if no address is known, leaving it with the clerk of courts. Within the rule, "delivering a copy" means handing it to the attorney or party; leaving it at the office of the person to be served with a clerk or other person in charge; if there is no one in charge, leaving it in a conspicuous place in the office; or if the office is closed or the person to be served has no office, leaving it at the dwelling house or usual abode of the person to be served with some person of suitable age and discretion then residing in the dwelling house or usual place of abode.

Q & A: Does the definition of "delivering a copy" imply personal service?

Although the definition of "delivering a copy" as used in the Civil Rules may be applicable in domestic violence cases, Civil Rule 5 applies to service and filing of pleadings subsequent to the original complaint. Moreover, Civil Rule 5(A) specifically excludes ex parte motions. However, it is arguable that, because the legislature chose the phrase "deliver a copy to respondent," it intended that service be perfected by any of the above methods.

That RC 3113.31(F) states that the order is required to be delivered to the respondent "on the same day that the order is entered" implies personal service.[18] Actual delivery of the notice or process to the person to whom it is directed is "personal service."[19] Personal service is effected by filing a written request with the clerk of courts.[20]

Personal service includes service on the respondent by handing the

---

[17]Black's Law Dictionary, 7th ed. (1999). See also Furniture Sales Specialists, Inc. v. Thomas, 82 Ohio App. 3d 759, 613 N.E.2d 259 (5th Dist. Knox County 1993); Elliott v. Elliott, 1982 WL 6669 (Ohio Ct. App. 6th Dist. Lucas County 1982).

[18]See also Sup. R. Form 10.01-H for a definition of "deliver" relative to service; Text § 14:5, False arrest, warrantless arrests and searches, and weapons confiscation. Personal service is effected by filing a written request with the clerk of courts. See also Civ.R. 4.1(B). See State v. Smith, 136 Ohio St. 3d 1, 2013-Ohio-1698, 989 N.E.2d 972 (2013) (holding that service and delivery to the respondent are synonymous in the context of civil protection orders and thus, when the statute requires delivery of the order, it is requiring service of the order); see Am. Sub. SB 7, which effectively superseded the holding of *State v. Smith* regarding violations of civil protection orders under RC 2919.27(D), so that unperfected service of a protection order or consent agreement does not preclude a prosecution for a violation of division (A) of that section. see also Text § 13:3.

[19]Black's Law Dictionary, 7th ed. (1999).

[20]Civ.R. 4.1(B).

respondent the papers.[21] In some counties, proper service may also include residence service, which is effected by delivering the documents to a person of suitable age or discretion residing at the respondent's home who is not a party to the action.[22]

Q & A: What guidance does Civ. R. 65.1 provide?

Civ. R. 65.1(C)(1) specifically addresses service of civil protection orders. The clerk of courts shall cause service to be made of a copy of the petition and all other documents required by the applicable protection order statute to be served on the respondent and, if applicable, on the parent, guardian or legal custodian of the Respondent.

Q & A: What type of service is contemplated by Civ. R. 65.1?

Because Ohio's domestic violence statute fails to clearly state that personal service is required[23] or specifies the methods of alternative service if any, Civ. R. 65.1 was needed to address this problem. Civ. R. 65.1(C)(2) provides that, initial service and service of any ex parte protection order that is entered shall be made in accordance with the provisions for personal service of process within the state under Civ. R. 4.1(B) or outside the state under Civ. R. 4.3(B)(2). Upon failure of such personal service, or in addition to such personal service, service may be made in accordance with any applicable provision of Civ. R. 4 to 4.6.

The Staff Notes have been replaced as of July 1, 2016 and have reinforced the provision of the decision set forth in *State v. Smith,*[24] wherein the Supreme Court stated that that [i]t is well established that all proceedings under RC 3113.31, RC 2151.34 and RC 2903.214 must follow the Rules of Civil Procedure. Accordingly, division (C) of this rule provides clear direction regarding the methods of service in civil protection order proceedings. Division (C)(2) of this rule directs the clerk of court to cause the first attempt at initial service in these proceedings, including service of a copy of the petition and an ex parte order, by personal service of process. This method of service provides the respondent expeditious notice consistent with the urgent nature of these proceedings. Notwithstanding, division (C)(2) of this rule also recognizes, only upon failure of personal service, the other methods of service of process in the Rules of Civil Procedure, i.e., Civ. R. 4 through 4.6, provide similar reliable form of notice for the initial service.

Service on a motion for modification, contempt, renewal or termination of the civil protection order shall be made in a manner consistent with Civ. R. 4 through 4.6.[25] Because a motion for modification, contempt, renewal or termination of the civil protection order is not part of the initial issuance of the order, an initial attempt by personal

[21] Civ.R. 4.1(B).

[22] Civ.R. 4.1(C).

[23] See, for example, State v. Bunch, 2001 WL 39599 (Ohio Ct. App. 9th Dist. Summit County 2001) (where service was attempted by certified mail and then followed by ordinary mail. Even though it is unclear whether appellant was actually served with the CPO, knowledge of the order was sufficient to find him guilty of violating the CPO); see also Text § 13:3, Court enforcement of civil protection orders—Criminal prosecution, and § 13:8, Enforcement of civil protection orders; procedures for initiating contempt motions.

[24] State v. Smith, 136 Ohio St. 3d 1, 2013-Ohio-1698, ¶ 21, 989 N.E.2d 972 (2013).

[25] Civ. R. 65.1(C)(4).

service is not required and any of the methods of service under Civ. R. 4 through 4.6 is appropriate for such a motion.

After service has been made in accordance with division (C)(4)(a) of this rule, any additional service required to be made on the respondent and, if applicable, on the parent, guardian or legal custodian of the respondent, shall be made in accordance with provisions of Civ. R. 5(B).

When a motion for modification, contempt, renewal or termination of the civil protection order is referred to a magistrate for determination, the provisions of this division (F)(3) of this rule relating to full hearing proceedings shall apply unless such provisions would by their nature be clearly inapplicable.[26] The Staff Notes noted that this division was adopted to address the issues raised in *Schneider v. Razek*[27]

Q & A: Does this mean certified mail, ordinary mail and service by publication or posting?

Yes. Certified mail service,[28] ordinary mail service[29] and service by publication[30] are alternative methods of service for serving civil protection orders contemplated by Civ. R. 65.1(C), should personal service fail.

Amendments to Civ. R. 4.4(A)(2) permitted the use of publication by posting as an appropriate method of service of process in civil protection order proceedings pursuant to Civ. R. 65.1(C)(2). Per the language of the civil rules, posting appeared to be reserved for persons with limited resources.

As soon as adopted, however, a contradiction was discovered between Civ. R. 4.4(A)(2), which provided that posting applied only to those filing with a poverty affidavit (indigent parties) and RC 3113.31(J)[31] which specifically prohibited all fees and costs associated with the issuance of a civil protection order including service.

In an effort to eliminate confusion, a recent amendment was adopted, effective July 1, 2018, which provided that service by posting

---

[26]Civ. R. 65.1(F)(3)(e).

[27]Schneider v. Razek, 2015-Ohio-410, 28 N.E.3d 591 (Ohio Ct. App. 8th Dist. Cuyahoga County 2015).

[28]Civ.R. 4.1(A).

[29]Civ. R. 4.6(D). Barrett v. Soltesz, 2015-Ohio-794, 2015 WL 995439 (Ohio Ct. App. 6th Dist. Erie County 2015) (discussion of an endorsement showing "wrong address"; noting that Civ. R. 4.6(D) states that service shall be deemed complete when the fact of mailing is entered of record, provided that the ordinary mail envelope is not returned by the postal authorities with an endorsement showing failure of delivery); see also Cervelli v. Cervelli, 1993 WL 130103 (Ohio Ct. App. 11th Dist. Geauga County 1993).

[30]Civ.R. 4.4. See also Dowers v. Krause, 2004-Ohio-1487, 2004 WL 595639 (Ohio Ct. App. 1st Dist. Hamilton County 2004) (discussing requirements for publication service including requirement of an affidavit that should not whether a party has concealed whereabouts to avoid service of process); Hamper v. Dobrski, 2015-Ohio-1381, 2015 WL 1593249 (Ohio Ct. App. 8th Dist. Cuyahoga County 2015) (while it appeared that service was perfected by personal service, counsel for appellee had also requested service by publication).

[31]See also R.C. 2903.214(J); R.C. 2151.34(J).

does apply to anyone filing a civil protection order where service of process is an issue, regardless of indigency.[32]

As stated in newly adopted division (A)(2)(b), service of a civil protection order may be served by posting or mail without the necessity of a poverty affidavit where the respondent's residence is unknown. Before service by posting or mail can be made, the petitioner must file an affidavit with the court containing the same averments required by division (A)(1) of the rule, i.e., that service of summons cannot be made because the residence of the defendant (respondent) is unknown to the affiant, all of the efforts made on behalf of the party to ascertain the residence of the defendant, and that the residence of the defendant cannot be ascertained with reasonable diligence. Petitioner shall also set forth the last known address of the party to be served.

Civ. R. 4.4(A)(2)(b) would then allow for publication by a clerk in a conspicuous place in the courthouse(s) within the county where Civ. R. 65.1 civil protection order proceedings may be filed and in two additional public places in the county that have been designated by local rule for the posting of notices pursuant to this rule. The postings under division (A)(2)(b) *shall not be made on the website* of the clerk of courts.[33] The notice shall contain the same information required by division (A)(1) of this rule that is contained in a newspaper publication. The notice shall be posted for six consecutive weeks.

Additionally, "when service by publication is sought by posting and mail under division (A)(2)(b), the clerk shall also cause the documents for service to be mailed by United States ordinary mail, address correction requested, to the last known address of the party to be served. The clerk shall obtain a certificate of mailing from the USPS. If the clerk is notified of a corrected or forwarded address of the party to be served within the six-week period that notice is posted pursuant to division (A)(2)(a) or division (A)(2)(b) of this rule, the clerk shall cause the documents for service to be mailed to the corrected forwarding address and note the name, address, and date of each mailing on the docket."[34]

After the last week of posting under either division (A)(2)(a) or (A)(2)(b) of this rule, the clerk shall note on the docket where and when notice was posted. Service shall be complete upon entry of posting.[35]

Q & A: Where personal service is utilized, who is authorized to serve the respondent with the petition and ex parte protection order?

The statute is silent as to who may effect service of the papers on the respondent. Each county has addressed this issue in its own way, taking into account its specific resources. For example, many counties provide that the county sheriff shall effect service on the respondent. The designation of the sheriff as process server is a reasonable choice because a civil protection order is granted by the county court of com-

[32]Civ. R. 4.4(A)(2)(b).

[33]Emphasis added; see also 18 U.S.C.A. § 2265(d)(3).

[34]Civ. R. 4.4(A)(2)(b).

[35]Civ. R. 4.4(A)(2)(d).

mon pleas or domestic relations court. Moreover, Civil Rule 4.1(B) specifically authorizes the county sheriff or another designated private process server to effect service of process.

In some jurisdictions, police officers are responsible for serving protection orders. Many officers charged with serving process read the key terms of the order to the respondent as part of service. By reading an order aloud, an officer may compensate for any literacy barriers a respondent may have and eliminate future claims by a respondent that he/she did not understand the terms of the order. Additionally, the officer may promptly evict a respondent from the residence if the order provides for such relief.

Q & A: How will the court know that the respondent has been served with an ex parte civil protection order?

Ohio's statute does not address the procedure to follow relative to return of service to the court. However, proof of service is necessary and shall note the date and manner of service. Civil Rule 4.1(B) requires that, when a copy of process has been served, the process server shall endorse that act on the process and return it to the clerk, who shall note that entry on the docket. Conversely, when the person serving process is unable to perfect service within twenty-eight days (or, in domestic violence actions, within the seven- or ten-day period prescribed for the full hearing), the person shall endorse that fact and the reasons therefor on the process and return the process and copies to the clerk who will then enter such fact on the docket.[36] General practice indicates, however, that proof of adequate service be filed with the court clerk. In many counties, the sheriff's department provides this verification to the court clerk.

Without proof of proper service,[37] the hearing cannot proceed. More importantly, without proof of service, police officers, charged with enforcement,[38] will be unable to act on a violation of a civil protection order.[39]

Q & A: The judge granted my client an ex parte protection order, but I have been unable to serve the respondent. Is the protection order enforceable?

Unfortunately, the statute fails to address this very significant issue. Service on the respondent and the enforcement of a civil protection order are often competing concerns. On the one hand, an ex parte civil protection order must be served on a respondent before a court may hold a full hearing. In fact, due process requires notice and an opportunity to be heard. A failure to serve the respondent results in a continuance of the full hearing,[40] and a lack of service will ultimately result in the termination of the ex parte protection order. However, it is important to remember that the ex parte civil protection order

[36]Civ.R. 4.1(B).

[37]Civ.R. 4.1(A) to Civ.R. 4.1(C).

[38]RC 3113.31(F)(1).

[39]But see Kampf v. Kampf, 237 Mich. App. 377, 603 N.W.2d 295 (1999); State v. Bunch, 2001 WL 39599 (Ohio Ct. App. 9th Dist. Summit County 2001).

[40]See RC 3113.31(D)(2)(a)(i).

automatically remains in effect until service is perfected or the order is eventually dismissed.[41]

On the other hand, a failure to enforce a protection order may subject a victim to further harm. Predicating enforcement of an ex parte order on service of the documents frustrates the intent and purpose of the domestic violence statute, which is to provide immediate protection to the victim.

Until a respondent is served with the civil protection order, a court will not enforce the order. It is also unclear whether the court will find a defendant guilty of violating the protection order.[42] This is because a respondent cannot violate an order of which he/she has no knowledge.[43] RC 2919.27 requires "reckless" violation of a protection order. "A person acts recklessly when, with headless indifference to the consequences, he perversely disregards a known risk that his conduct is likely to cause a certain result or is likely to be of a certain nature."[44]

However, a respondent may be aware of the terms of the order without being formally served.[45] In fact, some Ohio courts have held that a defendant's actual notice of a protection order is sufficient to enforce it, regardless of whether he was served.[46] "Actual notice"

---

[41]See RC 3113.31(D)(2)(b).

[42]R.C. 2919.27; Text § 13:3; Text § 13:8; State v. Smith, 136 Ohio St. 3d 1, 2013-Ohio-1698, 989 N.E.2d 972 (2013); but see State v. Bunch, 2001 WL 39599 (Ohio Ct. App. 9th Dist. Summit County 2001) ("[t]he Revised Code does not require that service of a CPO be accomplished upon the person against whom a CPO is issued before that person can be found to have violated the order. Rather, RC 2919.27 requires that the prosecution prove beyond a reasonable doubt that defendant acted in disregard of a known risk that a CPO was likely to have existed against him. The prosecution proffered sufficient evidence of this culpable mental state via Deborah's testimony that she had previously advised Bunch that a CPO had been issued and Bunch responded, 'I know.' ").

[43]See Sup. R. 10.01(D), Sup. R. Form 10.01-G.

[44]RC 2901.22(C).

[45]See Midland Steel Prods. Co. v. U.A.W. Local 486, 61 Ohio St. 3d 121, 573 N.E.2d 98 (1991); see also MacDonald v. State, 997 P.2d 1187 (Alaska Ct. App. 2000); State v. Bunch, 2001 WL 39599 (Ohio Ct. App. 9th Dist. Summit County 2001) (defendant response of "I know" was sufficient to show he knew of the CPO issued against him); see also Text § 13:3, Court enforcement of civil protection orders—Criminal prosecution, and § 13:8, Enforcement of civil protection orders; procedures for initiating contempt motions. Toledo v. Lyphout, 2009-Ohio-4596, 2009 WL 2855714 (Ohio Ct. App. 6th Dist. Lucas County 2009) (holding that absent proper service or actual notice of the terms contained in the order and the prohibited behavior, appellant cannot be held criminally liable for disobeying the order's terms); but see State v. Williams, 2009-Ohio-3162, 2009 WL 1856743 (Ohio Ct. App. 9th Dist. Summit County 2009) (needing mere "notice of the existence of the protection order").

[46]State v. Bunch, 2001 WL 39599 (Ohio Ct. App. 9th Dist. Summit County 2001); see also State v. Rutherford, 2009-Ohio-2071, 2009 WL 1175050 (Ohio Ct. App. 2d Dist. Champaign County 2009); Toledo v. Lanier, 2009-Ohio-5191, 2009 WL 3132601 (Ohio Ct. App. 6th Dist. Lucas County 2009); Alagha v. Cameron, 2009-Ohio-4886, 2009 WL 2974892 (Ohio Ct. App. 1st Dist. Hamilton County 2009); see also Text § 13.3. But see, State v. Smith, 136 Ohio St. 3d 1, 2013-Ohio-1698, 989 N.E.2d 972 (2013) (of importance is that no mention was made of the term "actual notice" in the majority's analysis); see Am. Sub. SB7, which effectively superseded the holding of *State v. Smith* regarding violations of civil protection orders under RC 2919.27(D), so that unperfected service of a protection order or consent agreement does not preclude

means notice given to, or received personally by, a party,[47] although the standard is cited by courts in Ohio and elsewhere,[48] it may be difficult for officers to determine. Because it is not provided for in the statute or civil rules, many courts refuse to consider it.

If court enforcement is assumed to depend on service of the papers, and police enforcement on notice, it is far easier to synthesize these competing concerns. An officer who gives the respondent a copy of the papers puts him on notice of the order and its terms[49] and can even arrest the respondent for any future violent acts. At the very least, the police should be able to enforce the order against the respondent to prevent future violence.[50]

Because it is unclear whether a civil protection order is enforceable absent service on the respondent, immediate perfection of service is crucial. Any intervening time without service can create a serious danger of further or increased violence to a petitioner or other household members.

Service can be expedited if the victim provides as much information as possible regarding the potential whereabouts of the respondent, including times when the respondent is likely to be at each location, a physical description of the respondent, including any identifying characteristics, and a description of the respondent's vehicle and license plate number, if known.

Q & A: What happens where a respondent refuses to accept service of an ex parte order?

Service is one of the larger problem areas, especially when the respondent refuses to accept service or eludes the process server. In such cases, other modes of adequate service of process could also be attempted. Leaving the papers on the door of the residence if it is known that the respondent lives there (even if the respondent refuses to accept the papers or throws them back at the process server), leaving the papers with a person of suitable age and discretion residing at the respondent's home, or leaving the papers at the respondent's place of employment may be adequate methods to effect service of process. Certified mail, ordinary mail or service by posting should also be attempted as a way to perfect service, should personal service fail.[51]

Additionally, other states have allowed some rather creative methods in unusual circumstances. For example, if the respondent is seen in the area, the petitioner should call the police and request that

a prosecution for a violation of division (A) of that section.

[47]Black's Law Dictionary (7th ed. 1999).

[48]See, e.g., U.S. v. Casciano, 124 F.3d 106 (2d Cir. 1997); MacDonald v. State, 997 P.2d 1187 (Alaska Ct. App. 2000); People v. Mandic, 325 Ill. App. 3d 544, 259 Ill. Dec. 658, 759 N.E.2d 138 (2d Dist. 2001); State v. Karas, 108 Wash. App. 692, 32 P.3d 1016 (Div. 2 2001); State v. Mernar, 345 N.J. Super. 591, 786 A.2d 141 (App. Div. 2001).

[49]See also State v. Cardinal, 2006-Ohio-5088, 2006 WL 2789903 (Ohio Ct. App. 10th Dist. Franklin County 2006).

[50]Kampf v. Kampf, 237 Mich. App. 377, 603 N.W.2d 295 (1999) (discussing validity of ex parte orders).

[51]See Civ. R. 65.1(C).

an officer serve the petition and order.[52] Service of process can also be effectuated at the courthouse if the respondent is there on an unrelated matter. However, this method should only be considered if not otherwise prohibited by law, local court rules, or court practice. In unusual cases, such as when there is reason to believe the respondent will leave the jurisdiction, where the respondent has failed to appear in the past, or where the safety of the petitioner and/or children so requires, some states provide that a warrant may be issued for the respondent's arrest.[53] However, such a method is not currently available in Ohio and would require legislative enactment.

In any situation where service of process is not perfected by the date scheduled for the full hearing, the attorney for the petitioner should require that the ex parte order remain in effect until service can be perfected on the respondent. RC 3113.31(D)(2) specifically provides that an ex parte civil protection order does not expire because of a failure to serve notice of the full hearing. Although an ex parte protection order may not be enforceable by law enforcement officials, when those same officials are called to the scene because a violation, they may still be able to enforce the order after informing the respondent of the order's terms at the scene.[54]

Q & A: What if am unable to serve the respondent on the same day that the order is entered?[55]

At least one Ohio court has addressed this issue. In *Stickel v. Pryor*,[56] the appellate court noted that the provision requiring the court to "direct that a copy of the protection order be delivered to respondent on the same day that the order is entered"[57] is directive, not mandatory. Pursuant to *Stickel v. Pryor*, a failure to comply would not invalidate the order. (*Stickel v. Pryor* related to a consent agreement.) Therefore, it is arguable that the statute does not mandate that service must be perfected on the same day the order is entered, only that the court must direct that it be done.

Practically speaking, as long as a respondent receives the pleadings prior to the date set for the full hearing and has complied with the civil rules, service of process is perfected. Of significance is that there have been no court challenges to this provision to date. Additionally, every court permits additional time to perfect service.[58]

This does not mean that the law enforcement agency or sheriff department directed to perfect service does not have to receive the paperwork on the day the order is issued by the court. It merely takes

---

[52]See, e.g., Neb. Att'y. Gen. Op. No. 00018 (2000) WL 263818 (3-9-00).

[53]See, e.g., N.Y. Fam. Ct. Act § 827(a).

[54]See Ch. 14, Police Enforcement of Protection Orders and Other Relevant Issues, for a discussion of service and enforcement.

[55]See State v. Smith, 136 Ohio St. 3d 1, 2013-Ohio-1698, 989 N.E.2d 972 (2013) (although not specifically addressed by the majority, the decision leaves open whether an ex parte CPO that is not served on the date that the order is entered, is an invalid order).

[56]Stickel v. Pryor, 2002-Ohio-3309, 2002 WL 1396077, *1 (Ohio Ct. App. 2d Dist. Miami County 2002).

[57]RC 3113.31(F)(1).

[58]RC 3113.31(D)(2)(a)(I).

into account that service on the respondent is not always perfected as quickly.

Q & A: My client has a copy of a civil protection order. Is a copy of the order sent to the law enforcement agency where my client lives?

The statute provides that a copy of a valid protection order is to be served on the police department(s) with jurisdiction to enforce the order.[59] Ordinarily, that means the jurisdiction in which the petitioner resides. Although the statute directs the court to facilitate the process relative to the respondent and the law enforcement agency,[60] nothing in the statute details the procedure by which a law enforcement agency is to obtain a copy of the order or within what time frame. Local practice and procedure would appear to dictate the policy followed in each county.

For example, in Cuyahoga County, the sheriff's department has been designated to serve both the respondent and the local law enforcement agency by personal service. In other jurisdictions, the clerk of court mails a copy of the ex parte order to the local police department. In still other jurisdictions, the attorney for the petitioner is responsible for delivering a copy of the order to the appropriate police department. Franklin County utilizes such a policy.

Q & A: What other law enforcement agencies should receive copies of the ex parte order?

Clearly, a copy of a valid ex parte protection order must be served on, or forwarded to, the local law enforcement agency with jurisdiction over the residence of the petitioner.[61] Additionally, a copy of the protection order should be sent to the law enforcement agency of any jurisdiction where it is determined that acts of domestic violence are likely to occur. This determination should be made by the petitioner with input from his/her attorney or victim advocate. Only the victim knows the places the respondent frequents and how likely it is that the petitioner will run into the respondent. For example, copies of the protection order may be delivered to the police department in the jurisdiction where the petitioner works, where the petitioner or children attend school, or where the petitioner's children's babysitter or daycare center is located. Although the court may direct the clerk to mail a copy of the order to other law enforcement agencies, the better practice is for the petitioner to personally deliver a certified copy of the order to these agencies.

Q & A: What law enforcement agency is directed to enforce the civil protection order?

The statute provides that any officer of a law enforcement agency shall enforce a protection order issued by any court in this state in accordance with the provisions of the order.[62] In short, all local law enforcement agencies in Ohio have the jurisdiction to enforce another jurisdiction's protection order.

---

[59] RC 3113.31(F)(1).

[60] RC 3113.31(F)(1).

[61] RC 3113.31(F)(1).

[62] RC 3113.31(F)(3).

Q & A: How is another city or county notified of a civil protection order?[63]

The statute also states that a petitioner who obtains a protection order may provide notice of the issuance of the order to the judicial or law enforcement officials in any county other than the county in which the order was issued.[64] The order can be registered by obtaining a certified copy of the order and presenting the copy to the clerk of court of common pleas in which the order is to be registered.[65] The clerk of court of common pleas shall then place an endorsement of registration on the order and give the petitioner a copy of the order that bears proof of registration.[66] A copy of the registered order can then be filed with a law enforcement agency in the other county.[67]

Regardless of whether the petitioner has registered the order in the county in which the officer's agency has jurisdiction, a protection order issued by any court in this state is enforceable by any local law enforcement agency anywhere else in the state.[68]

Additionally, protection orders issued by a court of another state are accorded full faith and credit by the courts of Ohio.[69] Accordingly, a person who obtains a protection order issued by a court of another state may provide notice of the issuance of the order to the judicial and law enforcement officials in any county of this state by registering the order in that county pursuant to RC 2919.272 and filing a copy of the registered order with a law enforcement agency in that county.[70]

§ 11:12 Ex parte protection orders—Available relief

Should an ex parte civil protection order be granted, the statute authorizes the court to enter any temporary orders, with or without bond, including, but not limited to, an order described in RC 3113.31(E)(1)(a), RC 3113.31(E)(1)(b), or RC 3113.31(E)(1)(c) that the court finds necessary to protect the family or household member from domestic violence.[1] The statutory language allows for judicial discretion in the wording and extent of the order.[2]

The civil relief available under RC 3113.31 is similar to, but broader in scope than, that provided under RC 2919.26. Because the statute empowers the court to grant any protection order that will bring about

[63]See also Text § 12:28, Enforcement of civil protection orders, and Text § 14:16, Enforcement of protection orders issued by the courts of Ohio.

[64]RC 3113.31(N)(1).

[65]RC 3113.31(N)(2)(a).

[66]RC 3113.31(N)(2)(b).

[67]RC 3113.31(N)(1).

[68]RC 3113.31(F)(3).

[69]RC 2919.27(D). See VAWA, 18 U.S.C.A. § 2265; see also RC 2919.272; Text § 14:17, Enforcement of out-of-state protection orders; and Text Ch. 18, Federal Remedies.

[70]See RC 3113.31(N)(1).

[Section 11:12]

[1]RC 3113.31(E)(1).

[2]See Reynolds v. White, 1999 WL 754496, *4 (Ohio Ct. App. 8th Dist. Cuyahoga County 1999).

a cessation of domestic violence against the family or household members, courts are permitted to craft their orders to the needs of the particular parties involved.[3]

At an ex parte hearing, the court may grant the following relief:

(1) direct the respondent to refrain from abusing the family or household members;[4]

(2) grant possession of the residence or household to the petitioner or other family or household member, to the exclusion of the respondent, by evicting the respondent, when the petitioner or other household member owns or leases the residence;[5]

(3) grant possession of the residence or household to the petitioner by ordering the respondent to vacate the residence when both the petitioner or other household member and respondent jointly own or lease the residence;[6]

(4) grant possession of the residence to the petitioner or other household member to the exclusion of the respondent by ordering the respondent to vacate the residence, where the respondent has a duty to support the petitioner or other family or household member and the respondent is the sole owner or lessee of the residence;[7]

(5) allocate, temporarily, parental rights and responsibilities (custody and visitation of minor children), provided no other court has jurisdiction over child issues for that child;[8]

(6) award support if the respondent has a duty to support the petitioner or household member or if the respondent customarily provides for, or contributes to, the support of the family or household member;[9]

(7) require the respondent, petitioner, victim of domestic violence, or any combination of those persons, to seek counseling;[10]

(8) require the respondent to refrain from entering the residence, school, business, or place of employment of the petitioner or family or household member;[11] or

(9) grant any other relief that the court considers equitable and fair, including, but not limited to, ordering the respondent to permit the use of a motor vehicle by the petitioner or other family or household member and dividing the household and family personal property;[12]

(10) Require that the respondent not remove, damage, hide, harm

---

[3]RC 3113.31(E)(1).

[4]RC 3113.31(E)(1)(a). See also Am. Sub. S.B. 17, eff. 8-3-06, directing respondent to refrain from committing a sexually oriented offense against petitioner or victim.

[5]RC 3113.31(E)(1)(b).

[6]RC 3113.31(E)(1)(b).

[7]RC 3113.31(E)(1)(c).

[8]RC 3113.31(E)(1)(d).

[9]RC 3113.31(E)(1)(e).

[10]RC 3113.31(E)(1)(f).

[11]RC 3113.31(E)(1)(g).

[12]RC 3113.31(E)(1)(h).

or dispose of any companion animal owned or possessed by the petitioner. R.C. 3113.31(E)(1)(i);

(11) Authorize the petitioner to remove a companion animal owned by the petitioner from the possession of the respondent. R.C. 3113.31(E)(1)(j).

Pursuant to a legislative amendment to RC 3113.31, the court may include within a protection order issued under this section terms necessary to protect companion animals belonging to a petitioner.

Where a protection order has previously been issued involving the respondent and the petitioner or one or more of the family or household members, the court may also include in a protection order a prohibition against the respondent returning to the residence or household.[13] Under recently amended RC 3113.31, if the court includes such a prohibition in the protection order, it must also include a provision of the type described in RC 3113.31(E)(7)(a). The court is also permitted to include in a protection order or consent agreement, in circumstances other than those described in RC 3113.31(E)(2), a requirement that the respondent be evicted from or vacate the residence or household or refrain from entering the residence, school, business, or place of employment of the petitioner or household member, providing that there is compliance with RC 3113.31(E)(7)(a).[14] In effect, all civil protection orders that include this type of restriction must also include in the order those provisions set forth in RC 3113.31(E)(7)(a).[15]

RC 3113.31(E)(7)(a) provides that, if a protection order or consent agreement includes a requirement that the respondent be evicted from or vacate the residence or household or refrain from entering the residence, school, business, or place of employment of the petitioner or household member, the order or agreement shall state clearly that the order or agreement cannot be waived or nullified by an invitation to the respondent from the petitioner or other household member to enter the designated areas or by the consent of the petitioner or other family or household member.

The amended provisions are designed to educate police officers that, even if the petitioner or other family or household member invites the respondent back to the residence, school, place of employment, or business, such action does not nullify the order or give the police officer reason to arrest the petitioner for violating the protection order. It also serves to advise the respondent that the order will not be rendered invalid because the petitioner invited the respondent back to the home. Of significance is that the Ohio legislature deleted the language that prohibited the petitioner from inviting or admitting the respondent into the residence while the order is in effect.[16] This language was eliminated because the legislature recognized that the order is against the respondent and that the petitioner should not be responsible for the respondent's actions.

RC 3113.31(E)(2) now contains specific language that grants the

---

[13]RC 3113.31(E)(2).

[14]See RC 3113.31(E)(2).

[15]RC 3113.31(E)(2).

[16]1997 S.B. 1, eff. 10-21-97.

court the authority to prohibit the respondent from returning to the residence or household where the order has either evicted the respondent or requested that the respondent vacate a residence or refrain from entering the school, home, or place of employment of the petitioner, whether or not the court had previously issued a protection order. The prohibitions against a respondent, as well as the mandate of RC 3113.31(E)(7)(a), are applicable in situations where a protection order has previously been issued involving the same family members and in all other situations where protection orders are requested.[17] In effect, the legislature clarified what had always been the directive of RC 3113.31.

In 1988, however, the language of RC 3113.31(E)(2) presented some statutory construction problems. In *Mallin v. Mallin*,[18] the defendant was ordered to vacate the marital residence pursuant to a civil protection order. He argued that, absent a prior protection order, RC 3113.31(E)(2) allowed him to return to the premises at any time. The Cuyahoga County Court of Appeals interpreted RC 3113.31(E)(2) to "allow[] the trial court to enter a greater sanction than was issued in a previous order."[19] The court disagreed with the defendant's interpretation that "only if a prior protection order has been granted may the court order him not to enter the marital residence."[20] In fact, the court relied on RC 3113.31(E)(1)(b) to support its position and clarify the intent of the statute, holding that "in an initial proceeding, the respondent may be ordered not to return to the marital premises."[21]

The court is both empowered and directed to include a provision similar to RC 3113.31(E)(7) in both the ex parte civil protection order and the order issued after the full hearing. The standard protection order forms provide that:

> if this order requires you to vacate a residence or refrain from entering the residence, school, business or place of employment of the family or household member named in the order, this order cannot be waived or nullified by an invitation to you to enter their residence, school, business or place of employment or your entry into one of those places otherwise upon their consent.[22]

The warning sheet contains a similar provision as well as a warning to the petitioner that inviting the respondent into the residence while the protection order is in effect can cause the respondent to be arrested. The warning sheet makes it clear that only the court can modify or dismiss a protection order.

These provisions further strengthen the protection order and decrease the likelihood that the petitioner will invite the respondent

---

[17]See RC 3113.31(E)(2).

[18]Mallin v. Mallin, 44 Ohio App. 3d 53, 541 N.E.2d 116 (8th Dist. Cuyahoga County 1988).

[19]Mallin v. Mallin, 44 Ohio App. 3d 53, 56, 541 N.E.2d 116 (8th Dist. Cuyahoga County 1988).

[20]Mallin v. Mallin, 44 Ohio App. 3d 53, 56, 541 N.E.2d 116 (8th Dist. Cuyahoga County 1988).

[21]Mallin v. Mallin, 44 Ohio App. 3d 53, 56, 541 N.E.2d 116 (8th Dist. Cuyahoga County 1988).

[22]Sup. R. Form 10.01-H to Sup. R. Form 10.01-J, Sup. R. Form 10.02-A.

back into the residence. They also advise both parties that the court takes these orders seriously and that they have a legal responsibility to do so as well.

Q & A: What if the petitioner invites the respondent back into the residence in spite of the court order?

If the respondent returns to the residence, he/she may be arrested for violating the protection order.[23] Only the court has the authority to modify the terms of a protection order or dismiss it entirely.[24] However, a petitioner who invites a respondent back to the residence is, in no way, in violation of the protection order.[25] Because the order is against the respondent, the petitioner should not be arrested or charged with a crime for inviting the respondent back to the residence.[26] Additionally, the order is not nullified should the petitioner invite the respondent to the residence.[27]

However, the statute specifically contains exculpatory language that provides that RC 3113.31(E)(7)(a) does not limit the court's discretion to determine that a respondent charged with violating a protection order under RC 2919.27 or with contempt of court, which charge is based on an alleged violation of a protection order or consent agreement issued under RC 3113.31, did not commit the violation or was not in contempt of court.[28] This provision was deliberately included to explicitly account for those situations in which a respondent is invited back to the residence for legitimate reasons such as caring for a sick child. It also provides the court with the discretion to find a respondent not guilty.

---

[23]See Ch. 13.

[24]See also RC 3113.31(E)(8).

[25]See Patterson v. Gooderham, 1999 WL 1001108 (Ohio Ct. App. 4th Dist. Gallia County 1999).

[26]See Text § 12:22, Remedies—Miscellaneous issues; State v. Lucas, 100 Ohio St. 3d 1, 2003-Ohio-4778, 795 N.E.2d 642 (2003) (where the Ohio Supreme Court held that a victim of domestic violence who is protected by a protection order may not be prosecuted for aiding and abetting in the violation of their own protection order); see also Ferguson v. Ferguson, 2000 WL 1724294 (Ohio Ct. App. 5th Dist. Knox County 2000) (Appeal from trial court's dismissal of contempt motion because petitioner put respondent in position of having to disobey protection order by agreeing to meet him to exchange belongings. The appellate court declined to address the issue but reversed because the trial court failed to provide findings of fact and conclusions of law.); State v. Bombardiere, 2007-Ohio-1537, 2007 WL 959895, *3 (Ohio Ct. App. 3d Dist. Union County 2007) (quoting Supreme Court in *Lucas* decision that protection orders are about the behavior by respondent and nothing else. How or why a respondent finds himself at the petitioner's doorstep is irrelevant.

[27]See RC 3113.31(E)(7)(a).

[28]RC 3113.31(E)(7)(b). But see State v. Dejarlais, 136 Wash. 2d 939, 969 P.2d 90 (1998) (rejecting the defendant's consent defense and holding that consent should not be a defense to violating a domestic violence protection order).

§ 11:13 Ex parte protection orders—Available relief—Orders to restrain

The purpose of any protection order is to provide immediate relief that leads to a cessation of domestic violence.[1] Incidental to that relief are orders regarding support and shelter.[2] A request that a respondent refrain from further abusing a family or household member is the most often utilized remedy. This type of relief directly relates to the protection and safety of the victim.

These provisions effectively prohibit many actions that respondents direct towards petitioners, petitioner's children, or other family or household members. They can order respondents not to act recklessly or to engage in conduct intended to cause physical or emotional harm and not to threaten, harass, intimidate, molest, interfere with, stalk, follow, annoy, contact, bother, assault, and/or physically abuse the protected persons.[3]

Q & A: The respondent has been following my client to work, following her to the bus stop, breaking into her house when she is not there, and sitting outside her house for hours at a time. Can she get a civil protection order?

The civil protection order statute provides protection for victims of domestic violence when the acts involve stalking behavior[4] or trespass.[5] Following a petitioner and sitting outside of a petitioner's house is considered stalking behavior if the pattern of conduct engaged in by the respondent causes the petitioner to believe the respondent will cause physical harm or cause mental distress.[6] Breaking into the victim's home when she is not there is an act of trespass that may serve as the basis of a civil protection order.[7]

[Section 11:13]

[1]RC 3113.31(E)(1); see also Jackson v. Jackson, 1993 WL 526704 (Ohio Ct. App. 8th Dist. Cuyahoga County 1993).

[2]Thomas v. Thomas, 44 Ohio App. 3d 6, 540 N.E.2d 745 (10th Dist. Franklin County 1988).

[3]See also Sup. R. Form 10.01-H to Sup. R. Form 10.01-J.

[4]RC 3113.31(A)(1)(b). See Text Ch. 8, The Nature of a Civil Protection Order; Reynolds v. Reynolds, 2001 WL 62552 (Ohio Ct. App. 2d Dist. Montgomery County 2001); Still v. Still, 1999 WL 236049 (Ohio Ct. App. 2d Dist. Montgomery County 1999); Steen v. Goad, 2001-Ohio-1771, 2001 WL 1421527 (Ohio Ct. App. 9th Dist. Wayne County 2001); Myers v. Myers, 2005-Ohio-7040, 2005 WL 3610332 (Ohio Ct. App. 5th Dist. Muskingum County 2005); Rhodes v. Gunter, 2003-Ohio-2342, 2003 WL 21040724 (Ohio Ct. App. 9th Dist. Lorain County 2003).

[5]See RC 3113.31(A)(1)(b), RC 2911.211; see also RC 2903.211; Text § 9:1, Stalking and trespass (for a discussion of stalking); Bach v. Crawford, 2003-Ohio-1255, 2003 WL 1193783 (Ohio Ct. App. 2d Dist. Montgomery County 2003).

[6]RC 2903.211; see also State v. Davidson, 1995 WL 396455 (Ohio Ct. App. 2d Dist. Montgomery County 1995); State v. Woodgeard, 1994 WL 167928 (Ohio Ct. App. 5th Dist. Fairfield County 1994), dismissed, 70 Ohio St. 3d 1473, 640 N.E.2d 846 (1994); Gooderham v. Patterson, 1999 WL 1034472 (Ohio Ct. App. 4th Dist. Gallia County 1999); Hoff v. Brown, 2001 WL 876228 (Ohio Ct. App. 5th Dist. Stark County 2001).

[7]See Gooderham v. Patterson, 1999 WL 1034472 (Ohio Ct. App. 4th Dist. Gallia County 1999).

§ 11:14 Ex parte protection orders—Available relief—Orders to vacate or evict

The purpose of an eviction in domestic violence cases is to remove the offender from the victim.[1] If the perpetrator of the violence has access to the victim, abuse is likely to continue. Therefore, vacate orders, which evict the respondent from the residence, have been regarded as one of the most effective ways of protecting a victim of domestic violence.[2] Safety concerns dictate that the respondent not be permitted to continue to live with the victim or other family or household members.

If the victim chooses to leave the residence, the statute clearly states that a petitioner's right to relief is not affected by his/her leaving the residence or household to avoid further acts of domestic violence.[3] The dissent in *Clum v. Searcy*[4] emphasizes that "the statute's purpose is one involving 'petitioner's right to relief,' not the respondents [sic]."

However, the most difficult decision for judges is not whether to evict the respondent as part of the order issued after the full hearing, but whether to include a provision evicting a respondent from the residence in an ex parte proceeding before the respondent has had a chance to present his/her side of the case.[5]

Although the statute provides for a full hearing within seven days after the ex parte hearing,[6] some courts believe that an ex parte eviction might violate the respondent's due process rights to proper notice and a hearing.[7] Most often, courts are concerned about respondents incurring the hardship of leaving the home under an ex parte order on the basis of a petitioner's claim which is not substantiated by the evidence later adduced at the full hearing. This becomes problematic in situations where a divorce is filed and one party is perceived as wanting leverage in the divorce action. However, ordering a respondent to vacate the residence on a showing of an "immediate and present danger" is necessary to comply with the intent of the domestic violence statute.[8]

The intent of the statute is to protect the victim and, if requested, remove the respondent to bring about a cessation of violence. Because the full hearing is scheduled within seven days, this temporary deprivation of the respondent's rights is outweighed by the need to provide

---

[Section 11:14]

[1]Mallin v. Mallin, 44 Ohio App. 3d 53, 541 N.E.2d 116 (8th Dist. Cuyahoga County 1988); see also RC 3113.31(E)(1)(b).

[2]See, e.g., Gorman v. Oates, 2002-Ohio-1511, 2002 WL 471716 (Ohio Ct. App. 6th Dist. Lucas County 2002).

[3]RC 3113.31(B).

[4]Clum v. Searcy, 1993 WL 535383, *2 (Ohio Ct. App. 5th Dist. Tuscarawas County 1993).

[5]See, e.g., State v. Myers, 2002-Ohio-253, 2002 WL 54753 (Ohio Ct. App. 5th Dist. Perry County 2002).

[6]RC 3113.31(D)(1).

[7]See Text Ch. 8, The Nature of a Civil Protection Order.

[8]See, e.g., State ex rel. Williams v. Marsh, 626 S.W.2d 223 (Mo. 1982).

adequate safety protections for the petitioner and other family or household members on an emergency basis.

Ex parte relief is part of the American civil law tradition of issuing temporary restraining orders as a means of preventing immediate and irreparable harm. Such orders enjoin one party from specific behavior that may occur in the interval between the time the court learns of the danger and the time a hearing can be held in the presence of both the respondent and the petitioner. As stated in Ch 8, ex parte relief is strongly supported by both case law and statute.[9]

RC 3113.31(E)(1)(b) permits a court to evict a respondent on an ex parte basis as long as the situation presents an emergency for which any delay might seriously endanger the petitioner's safety. Ohio's statute[10] requires that there be an "immediate and present danger." Factors that courts should consider in determining whether to grant an ex parte order to vacate are (1) the frequency and severity of the violence; (2) the history of abuse by each of the parties, not necessarily against the other (including prior violent acts against other parties and the respondent's criminal history); (3) the nature and extent of the injuries and any injuries to minor children; and (4) whether the petitioner fears physical harm from the respondent and the reasonableness of that fear.

Ohio's statute[11] also specifies that evicting a respondent from the residence shall not affect title to any real property.[12]

Pursuant to the statutory scheme, a respondent may be evicted or required to vacate the residence when the petitioner owns or leases the property or when it is jointly owned by both the respondent and the petitioner.[13] However, no order to vacate may issue against a respondent who owns or leases the property solely in his/her name unless the respondent also has a duty to support the petitioner or other family or household member.[14]

The new standard forms also include provisions that restrain the respondent from interfering with the petitioner's right to occupy the residence through actions such as canceling utilities or insurance and interrupting telephone service, mail delivery, or the delivery of any other documents or items.[15] The intent is to minimize contact between the parties and eliminate the respondent's control over the petitioner.

Q & A: My client lives with her boyfriend. They have a child together. The residence is leased to her boyfriend. Can he be

---

[9]See Mitchell v. W. T. Grant Co., 416 U.S. 600, 94 S. Ct. 1895, 40 L. Ed. 2d 406, 15 U.C.C. Rep. Serv. 263 (1974); Boyle v. Boyle, 12 Pa. D. & C.3d 767, 1979 WL 764 (C.P. 1979).

[10]RC 3113.31(D).

[11]RC 3113.31(E)(5).

[12]See also Ruedele v. Kiefer, 1993 WL 438787 (Ohio Ct. App. 5th Dist. Licking County 1993), cause dismissed, 68 Ohio St. 3d 1444, 626 N.E.2d 686 (1994).

[13]RC 3113.31(E)(1)(b).

[14]RC 3113.31(E)(1)(c); see also Gorman v. Oates, 2002-Ohio-1511, 2002 WL 471716 (Ohio Ct. App. 6th Dist. Lucas County 2002) (where appellant argued that he should have been able to present evidence showing petitioner's intent to remove her name from the lease. Appellate court stated that refusing to admit letter by woman seeking a CPO, to landlord, to remove her name from the lease, was harmless error.).

[15]Sup. R. Form 10.01-H to Sup. R. Form 10.01-J, Sup. R. Form 10.02-A.

ordered by the court to vacate the residence when there has not been a judicial determination of paternity?

It depends. RC 3113.31(E)(1)(c) provides that a respondent who is the sole owner or lessee of the premises and has a duty to support may be ordered to vacate the premises. The fact that the parties live together does not create a duty to support the petitioner. The duty to support arises by virtue of a marriage or a child in common. Since the parties are not married, there exists no statutory duty to support the petitioner.

However, the boyfriend has a duty to support his child. Theoretically, this duty attaches whether or not paternity has been established. As discussed in Ch 9, evidence of parentage may be established by the male's name as father on the birth certificate,[16] the male signing the birth certificate,[17] or the male having been named as the father for purposes of welfare, Social Security, or the Internal Revenue Service. Valid arguments can be made in those cases to find that there is a duty to support. Assuming a valid duty of support can be found, the boyfriend may be ordered to vacate the premises.

Q & A: How specific should the protection order be with regard to removing the respondent from the premises?

When a court grants an order to vacate, it is important that the court specifies in the civil protection order how the order to vacate will be implemented. RC 3113.31(F)(3) provides that law enforcement officials are responsible for removing a respondent from the premises, if appropriate. If the terms of the order specify sheriff or police involvement, the named law enforcement officials are authorized to evict or remove the respondent from the residence.

Family law practitioners should also include in the civil protection order the time frame in which the respondent must vacate and should instruct the law enforcement officer how, and in what time frame, the respondent must be removed.

Q & A: Does an order requiring a respondent to vacate the premises imply a prohibition against reentering the same residence?

Absolutely. An order to vacate the residence implies that the same respondent must also remain away from the residence for the duration of the protection order. An order to vacate the home grants the petitioner a refuge from future or continued abuse. Obviously, the only way to achieve this objective is to prohibit the respondent from reentering the home.[18] There is no doubt that the legislative intent of an order to vacate necessarily encompasses a requirement that the respondent remain away from the home. Specifically, RC 3113.31(E)(1)(b) contains the language granting possession of the residence to the petitioner "to the exclusion of the respondent."[19]

---

[16] RC 3111.03(A)(3)(b).

[17] RC 3111.03(A)(4).

[18] See RC 3113.31(E)(2).

[19] See also RC 3113.31(E)(2).

A similar issue was raised in *Mallin v. Mallin*.[20] The Eighth District Court of Appeals rejected the defendant's interpretation of RC 3113.31(E)(1)(b) that an eviction order, absent a prior protection order, allowed him to return to the premises at any time. The court dismissed this argument and noted that the purpose of eviction, to remove the offender from the victim, cannot be accomplished if the offender is allowed to return at any time.

§ 11:15 Ex parte protection orders—Available relief—Orders allocating parental rights and responsibilities

Although there has been no challenge to RC 3113.31 regarding custody and visitation, the ex parte award of temporary custody has created due process issues for other states. In *State ex rel. Williams v. Marsh*,[1] the Missouri Supreme Court upheld against a due process challenge a provision of the Missouri Adult Abuse Act authorizing an ex parte award of temporary custody of minor children to the petitioner. The court ruled that, although the liberty interest in the custody of one's children was a significant private interest, the governmental interest in preventing domestic violence outweighed the private interest because of the high incidence and severity of domestic violence. The court also based its decision on the statute's fifteen-day limitation on an ex parte order, after which a hearing must take place at which time the perpetrator may contest the custody provision of the temporary order.[2]

Custody questions arise in a variety of domestic violence contexts. An award of temporary custody is often requested by a petitioner when an ex parte civil protection order is sought.[3] Provided that no other court has made, or is in the process of making, a custody and/or visitation determination, the court has the authority to grant such relief. Awarding the victim custody at this juncture helps to protect the petitioner from unnecessary contact with the respondent which could lead to a resumption of violence. Such an award also protects the children from being abused by the respondent. Studies suggest that batterers who abuse their partners may also abuse their children.[4]

The court also has the authority to award visitation to the respondent at the ex parte hearing.[5] However, there seems little reason to do so since the maximum duration of the ex parte order is ten days, unless there are service problems. More importantly, since the purpose of protection orders is to prohibit immediate contact between the parties, visitation at this point may thwart the intent of the statute.

---

[20]Mallin v. Mallin, 44 Ohio App. 3d 53, 541 N.E.2d 116 (8th Dist. Cuyahoga County 1988); see also Text § 11:12, Ex parte protection orders—Available relief.

[Section 11:15]

[1]State ex rel. Williams v. Marsh, 626 S.W.2d 223 (Mo. 1982).

[2]See also Mathews v. Eldridge, 424 U.S. 319, 96 S. Ct. 893, 47 L. Ed. 2d 18 (1976).

[3]RC 3113.31(E)(1)(d).

[4]See Lenore E. Walker, The Battered Woman 35 (1979); National Woman Abuse Prevention Project, Understanding Domestic Violence: Fact Sheets 3 (1989); Peter G. Jaffe et al., Children of Battered Women 26 (1990).

[5]RC 3113.31(E)(1)(d).

Unfortunately, the intent of the abuser is to continue the abuse of the victim, with little regard for the damage this controlling behavior has on the children.[6]

The standardized civil protection order forms include various provisions for relief in the ex parte protection order form.[7] The form permits visitation rights to be established for a respondent. It also permits the suspension of the respondent's visitation rights until the full hearing. The protection order form specifically contains the provision that visitation orders do not permit the respondent to violate the terms of the ex parte order.

§ 11:16 Ex parte protection orders—Available relief—Support

Where the respondent has a legal duty to support, such as through marriage, courts may order the respondent to maintain support. Some courts award either child support, spousal support, or both at the ex parte hearing. Most courts award support only after the full hearing on the protection order. Franklin County awards temporary child support only if paternity has previously been established. Still other courts have decided not to award child support or spousal support to a married petitioner in a protection order where a divorce is pending.[1] The legal rationale is that support issues are more likely to be thoroughly litigated in the underlying divorce. Since the purpose of the statute is to provide protection, these seemingly extraneous issues are better left to the judge who hears the divorce. On the other hand, victims of domestic violence are in great need of financial support when they initially separate from their spouses. To restrict an award of support to the divorce punishes the victim who finally leaves an abusive marriage. Often, a lack of resources, including support, catapults the victim back into the abusive marriage. Additionally, in many jurisdictions, support hearings are not scheduled for several months after the filing of a motion for temporary support.

All payments of child or spousal support must be paid through the Child Support Enforcement Agency.[2] The obligor (respondent) is ordered to pay said sums from wages, if employed, or from other assets, in accordance with RC 3113.31(K) and RC 3113.21. RC 3113.21(B)(1) governs the procedural details regarding support. Any award of child support must be calculated according to the child support computation worksheet.[3] The Summit County Court of Appeals, in

[6]See E. A. Walker & G. Edwall, Domestic Violence and the Determination of Visitation and Custody in Divorce, in Domestic Violence on Trial: Psychological and Legal Dimensions of Family Violence (D. Sonkin ed., 1987).

[7]See Sup. R. Form 10.01-H.

[Section 11:16]

[1]See Hayes v. Gibbs, 2008-Ohio-1115, 2008 WL 682493 (Ohio Ct. App. 1st Dist. Hamilton County 2008) (reversed trial court that had stated "a divorce action is the more appropriate forum to establish a child support order" holding instead that trial court erred in refusing to consider request for child support).

[2]RC 3113.31; see also RC 2301.35.

[3]See, for example, Murral v. Thomson, 2004-Ohio-432, 2004 WL 193876 (Ohio Ct. App. 4th Dist. Hocking County 2004), citing Marker v. Grimm, 65 Ohio St. 3d 139, 601 N.E.2d 496 (1992).

Halley v. Ashley,[4] reversed that part of a civil protection order awarding child support where a completed child support worksheet was not included in the court's decision.

The statute also affords petitioners who are not legally entitled to support the opportunity to receive support pursuant to RC 3113.31(E)(1)(e). The petitioner may be awarded support where the respondent customarily provides for or contributes to the support or where the respondent has a duty to support the petitioner or other household member.[5] Such a duty arises by virtue of the parties' relationship.

If support has previously been provided to a petitioner or family member, the court may order the respondent to maintain it. Such a duty arises from the habits or usual customs of the parties rather than by law or contract. *Black's Law Dictionary* defines "customarily" as "usually, habitually, according to the customs."[6] For example, where the parties cohabit and the respondent has supported the petitioner's minor child from birth, the respondent may have a duty to maintain support for this child though he may not be the child's father, at least while the protection order is in effect. It can be argued that the respondent has customarily provided for or contributed to the support of the family or household member and should, therefore, be ordered to maintain it.

§ 11:17 Ex parte protection orders—Available relief—Counseling

Counseling is another remedy which may be included in a protection order.[1] The court may order the respondent, the petitioner, the victim of the domestic violence, or a combination of those persons to seek counseling. Although it may be requested at the ex parte hearing, counseling should only be considered after the full hearing. To order a respondent into counseling at the ex parte hearing is unreasonable because the respondent has not yet been served with the protection order and the duration of the ex parte order is only ten days. It would be rather difficult to order a respondent to comply with the terms of an order of which he/she has no knowledge.

§ 11:18 Ex parte protection orders—Available relief—Orders to refrain from entering the residence, school, business, or place of employment

The respondent may be ordered to stay away from certain places that the petitioner, the children, or other family or household members frequent. Such orders include restraining the respondent from approaching, entering, or attempting to enter a petitioner's separate

---

[4]Halley v. Ashley, 1997 WL 760662 (Ohio Ct. App. 9th Dist. Summit County 1997) See also Murral v. Thomson, 2004-Ohio-432, 2004 WL 193876 (Ohio Ct. App. 4th Dist. Hocking County 2004).

[5]RC 3113.31(E)(1)(e). See also Sup. R. Form 10.01-H to Sup. R. Form 10.01-J.

[6]Black's Law Dictionary (6th ed.) p 385.

[Section 11:17]

[1]RC 3113.31(E)(1)(f).

residence.[1] Since protection orders are specific to each petitioner and follow a person rather than a place, a respondent may also be restrained from entering a petitioner's residence, wherever that may be. This type of an order covers a petitioner who moves from place to place. The respondent may also be excluded from being around the petitioner's place of employment or business or the business or place of employment of a family or household member.[2]

Additionally, the respondent may be ordered to stay away from the petitioner's school and the children's school, day care center, or other type of child care facility.[3] In each instance, the goal of the court is to minimize contact between the petitioner and the respondent.

Where the petitioner is in hiding, the court may want to consider ordering the respondent to stay away from the petitioner's residence without revealing its location. The court may go so far as to order the respondent not to attempt to discover the location of the petitioner's residence nor enlist the help of others in locating the petitioner.

The standard protection order forms order the respondent to stay away from the family or household members named in the order.[4] The order specifically prohibits a respondent from being within a specific distance, usually in feet or yards, of the protected family or household members. The order restrains the respondent from entering any place where the protected persons may be found. This includes, but is not limited to, the buildings, grounds, and parking lots of their residences, schools, businesses, places of employment, day care centers, and babysitters. Additionally, the order advises the respondent, who may accidentally come in contact with the protected family or household members in any public or private place, to depart immediately.

The forms also prohibit the respondent from initiating contact with the family or household members or causing or encouraging any other person to do so.[5] Such contact includes contact by telephone, facsimile, e-mail, and voice mail. It also includes contact at their residences, businesses, places of employment, schools, daycare centers, and babysitters.

Carefully drafted, issue-specific protection orders may limit future violence because they leave no questions regarding the restrictions placed on the respondent's conduct. More importantly, orders that are very specific make enforcement of the order certain. Under RC 3113.31(E)(1), courts have broad authority to issue any form of relief that may prevent future violence. Orders need not be limited in scope to the relief provided for in RC 3113.31. It was within this framework

---

[Section 11:18]

[1]RC 3113.31(E)(1)(g); see City of Xenia v. Berry, 1994 WL 12494 (Ohio Ct. App. 2d Dist. Greene County 1994) (discussing the term "residence").

[2]RC 3113.31(E)(1)(g).

[3]RC 3113.31(E)(1)(g).

[4]See Sup. R. Form 10.01-H to Sup. R. Form 10.01-J.

[5]See Sup. R. Form 10.01-H to Sup. R. Form 10.01-J.

that the Supreme Court Task Force on Domestic Violence drafted the standard forms.[6]

Q & A: My client wants to obtain an ex parte protection order. Can she request that the court order the respondent to refrain from approaching her church or place of worship?

It depends. If the petitioner frequents a different church from the respondent, there should be no problem with an order enjoining the respondent from approaching the petitioner's place of worship. If the parties frequent the same church, an issue may be raised relative to infringing upon the respondent's due process rights to worship in a place of his choosing. Many courts may be concerned about restricting a person's freedom to worship. One way to avoid this problem is to restrict or limit the respondent's access to the petitioner while at church or to order the respondent to attend a different service.

There are no Ohio cases that have addressed this particular issue. However, other state courts have restrained a respondent from entering the petitioner's church. In *State ex rel. Emery v. Andisha*,[7] the Oregon Court of Appeals restrained the respondent from entering the petitioner's home, school, church, or day care center. Although dissimilar to the facts presented in the question, it is significant that the *Andisha* court included a prohibition against entering the petitioner's church in the protection order. At the very least, such a provision indicates a recognition of the problem.

Some courts have resolved this issue by specifying a minimum distance that a respondent must keep from a petitioner. Although the Ohio statute does not specifically address a minimum distance in its remedies, it can be argued that a court has the authority to grant this relief under RC 3113.31(E)(1). Under RC 3113.31(E)(1), a court may grant any protection order to bring about a cessation of domestic violence.[8] Additionally, a court may grant other relief that the court considers equitable and fair.[9] This catchall provision may be used to justify the type of relief requested if it is not specifically enumerated in the statute.

In *State v. Sutley*,[10] the court ordered the respondent to stay away from the petitioner, her family members, and the quadrant of the city where she resided. The Court of Appeals for Ashtabula County held that the order did not violate the respondent's freedom of association rights where the restrictions related to his offenses and would help ensure future compliance with the court order. The court imposed these restrictions for the purposes of rehabilitating the respondent and reducing the possibility of a reoccurrence of similar conduct.

---

[6]See also Catherine F. Klein & Leslye E. Orloff, Civil Protection Orders, in The Impact of Domestic Violence on your Legal Practice, A Lawyer's Handbook 4-1 (1996).

[7]State ex rel. Emery v. Andisha, 105 Or. App. 473, 805 P.2d 718 (1991).

[8]See Sup. R. Form 10.01-H to Sup. R. Form 10.01-J which include "minimum distance" requirements.

[9]RC 3113.31(E)(1)(h).

[10]State v. Sutley, 1990 WL 208811 (Ohio Ct. App. 11th Dist. Ashtabula County 1990).

The *Sutley* court relied on *People v. Mason*,[11] which held that a person, by reason of his conviction of a public offense, enjoys "a reduced expectation of privacy." Although *Mason* and *Sutley* both related to criminal domestic violence cases and protection orders, this same analysis may be applied to Ohio's civil protection order statute, RC 3113.31.

Q & A: Does a civil protection order prohibit a respondent from telephone contact with the petitioner while the order is in effect?

The statute does not specifically prohibit telephone contact by the respondent. The recently published standard civil protection order forms include a provision that the respondent not initiate any contact by telephone, facsimile, e-mail, and/or voice mail with the protected family or household members at their residences, schools, businesses, places of employment, day care centers, or babysitters. Even absent a specific provision, it is still arguable that, when an order prohibits harassing behavior, included in that provision is the implied prohibition against telephone contact.[12]

Q & A: Can a respondent use a third party to violate a protection order?

The statute is silent on this issue, and there are no reported Ohio cases addressing it. However, the Ohio Supreme Court standard protection order forms provide that a respondent shall not encourage another person to do any prohibited act.[13]

An Illinois court addressed this issue. In *Wood v. Wood*,[14] a wife obtained a civil protection order awarding her possession of the marital home. In order to thwart the protection order, the husband requested that his parents, who held title to the property, evict her. One purpose of the Illinois domestic violence statute is to help victims avoid further abuse by granting them accessible housing. The parents, by filing an eviction action against the wife, aided and abetted the husband's violation of the protection order. Thus, the Illinois appellate court found the husband's parents equally guilty of the violation. The court also noted that, even if they were acting independently of the husband, they might be barred by a "retaliatory eviction" defense.

Q & A: Can a court enforce all provisions of a civil protection order form?

When the Ohio Supreme Court adopted specific domestic violence forms, it assumed that the court had the authority to order all of the provisions set forth in the forms, including those not specifically set

[11] People v. Mason, 5 Cal. 3d 759, 764, 97 Cal. Rptr. 302, 488 P.2d 630 (1971) (disapproved of by, People v. Lent, 15 Cal. 3d 481, 124 Cal. Rptr. 905, 541 P.2d 545 (1975)).

[12] See State ex rel. Emery v. Andisha, 105 Or. App. 473, 805 P.2d 718 (1991).

[13] See also Sup. R. Form 10.01-H to Sup. R. Form 10.01-J, which include prohibitions on damaging property and initiating contact as well as requirements to stay away from the victim or household members and vacate the residence.

[14] Wood v. Wood, 284 Ill. App. 3d 718, 219 Ill. Dec. 877, 672 N.E.2d 385 (4th Dist. 1996); see also Nechay v. Nechay, 685 A.2d 377 (Del. Fam. Ct. 1995).

out in the statute.[15] These include surrendering all keys and garage door openers and prohibiting the respondent from interfering with the petitioner's right to occupy the residence through actions such as canceling utilities or insurance and interrupting phone service, mail delivery, or the delivery of any other documents or items.[16]

The court's authority to enforce these provisions is implied by the statutory language that a court may grant any protection order to bring about a cessation of domestic violence.[17] Additionally, a court may grant other relief that it considers equitable and fair.[18]

Q & A: Can a court order a respondent to pay the victim's utilities to avoid their being cancelled?

It is clear that the Supreme Court's standard protection order forms provide that a respondent shall not request a utility company to shut off a utility. That is an intentional action on the part of the respondent that is prohibited. However, it is less clear whether that also implies that a respondent must pay a utility bill so that the utility company does not shut off the utility. Absent language in the protection order requiring the respondent to maintain the utilities for a period of time, a shut-off by the utility company cannot be equated with an act by respondent. Attorneys should be cautioned that canceling the utilities and maintaining them are two different actions, and a failure to pay the debt, which in turn causes the cancellation by the utility company, may not be the same as intentionally asking that the utility be shut off. To avoid this potential problem, attorneys should specifically request that the respondent maintain the utilities.

§ 11:19 Ex parte protection orders—Available relief—Property division

The statute authorizes the court to "[g]rant other relief that the court considers equitable and fair, including, but not limited to, ordering the respondent to permit the use of a motor vehicle by the petitioner or other family or household member and the apportionment of household and family personal property."[1]

Necessary property, including clothing, medical equipment, personal papers, keys, and other personal effects may be awarded to the petitioner at the ex parte hearing. If the desired items are in the possession of the respondent at that time, the petitioner may still have to wait until the full hearing to enforce this provision. The respondent has to be served before he can be ordered to give up the items.

Even assuming proper service on the respondent, the petitioner must also consider how to effect such a transfer. If the items are

---

[15]But see Swenson v. Swenson, 490 N.W.2d 668 (Minn. Ct. App. 1992) (holding that the district court erred by ordering a remedy not available under the Minnesota statute).

[16]Sup. R. Form 10.01-H to Sup. R. Form 10.01-J.

[17]RC 3113.31(E)(1).

[18]RC 3113.31(E)(1)(h).

[Section 11:19]

[1]RC 3113.31(E)(1)(h). See also Downs v. Strouse, 2006-Ohio-505, 2006 WL 280417 (Ohio Ct. App. 10th Dist. Franklin County 2006) (suggesting that a party must request apportionment of personal property).

needed immediately, the police department should be authorized to aid the petitioner in the enforcement of the order, including helping the petitioner to obtain the desired items.[2] Such an authorization must be detailed within the protection order itself.

A division of limited personal property or the use of a motor vehicle should only be awarded after a full hearing on the protection order. Such a division of property should not be interpreted to mean the same as a general division of marital property under RC 3105.171. "A general division of marital property under RC 3105.171 presupposes that the parties have terminated their marriage. In a civil protection order hearing, there is no termination of a marriage. Thus, a thorough division of property is unwarranted."[3]

Even if personal property is not apportioned until the full hearing, every protection order should include a provision that restrains the respondent from removing, damaging, hiding, or disposing of any property owned or possessed by the family or household members named in the order. The standard forms contain such a provision.

The intent of RC 3113.31(E)(1)(h) is to provide petitioners or family or household members with items necessary and reasonable to maintain themselves during the duration of the order. It also is a useful tool to aid the petitioner in having his/her separate or personal property returned. The ultimate goal of this provision is to create an atmosphere whereby contact between the parties is unnecessary.

Additionally, the duration of the order is limited by statute to five years.[4] Any apportionment of property under RC 3113.31(E)(1)(h) is not meant to be considered a permanent property settlement, especially where the parties are married.[5]

The standard protection order forms adopted by the State of Ohio reflect a more expansive reading of RC 3113.31(E)(1)(h). The forms include provisions that order a respondent to surrender all keys and garage door openers to the law enforcement agency which serves the order on the respondent, to surrender possession of and all keys to a specific automobile of which petitioner is granted exclusive use, and to turn over all deadly weapons to the law enforcement agency which serves respondent with the order.

RC 3113.31(E)(1)(h) has also been interpreted to allow further restrictions on one party harassing or contacting the other. For example, in *Deacon v. Landers*,[6] the dissent construed RC 3113.31(E)(1)(h) to expand safety provisions to include ordering the petitioner to leave the respondent alone. In effect, the dissent sanctioned mutual

---

[2]RC 3113.31(F)(3).

[3]Hon. June Rose Galvin & Grace A. Kilbane, Ohio Domestic Relations Law, Text 5.06(E) (1992).

[4]RC 3113.31(E)(3)(a).

[5]See Cooley v. Cooley, 90 Ohio App. 3d 706, 630 N.E.2d 417 (2d Dist. Montgomery County 1993).

[6]Deacon v. Landers, 68 Ohio App. 3d 26, 587 N.E.2d 395 (4th Dist. Ross County 1990).

protection orders without first giving the petitioner an opportunity to be heard.[7]

The enactment of House Bill 335 in December 1994 specifically prohibited mutual orders of protection, except in compliance with the requirements of RC 3113.31(E)(4). The *Deacon* interpretation is no longer permitted by Ohio's courts. Because of the statutory directives regarding mutual protection orders, any court that attempts to issue a mutual protection order by relying on RC 3113.31(E)(1)(h) should be summarily reversed on appeal.

Q & A: Can a petitioner request that the court order the respondent to turn over a weapon to the police?[8]

RC 3113.31 does not include a specific prohibition against respondents possessing weapons. Where domestic violence has included the use or threatened use of weapons, the court may need to make an order regarding weapons, including a requirement that the respondent surrender weapons to police. The authority for such an order lies in the general relief provision of the statute.[9]

Additionally, a respondent may be ordered to refrain from possessing, using, carrying, or obtaining a deadly weapon.[10] In special circumstances, the court may also order police officers to search for and confiscate any weapons when they assist the petitioner with a vacate order.[11]

Q & A: How does the respondent retrieve his/her personal items after being ordered to vacate?

Each ex parte protection order should contain a specific provision detailing which items a respondent may retrieve as well as the manner in which he/she should retrieve those items. The standard protection order forms permit the respondent to pick up clothing and personal items from the residence. However, the respondent is obligated to provide the petitioner with reasonable notice, be accompanied by a uniformed officer, and pick up the desired items within seven days of the filing of the ex parte order.[12]

---

[7]See also Clum v. Searcy, 1993 WL 535383 (Ohio Ct. App. 5th Dist. Tuscarawas County 1993).

[8]See also Text § 14:5, False arrest, warrantless arrests and searches, and weapons confiscation; Text § 12:22, Remedies—Miscellaneous issues.

[9]RC 3113.31(E)(1)(h); see also standard protection order forms, Sup. R. Form 10.01-A to Sup. R. Form 10.01-J; Conkle v. Wolfe, 131 Ohio App. 3d 375, 722 N.E.2d 586 (4th Dist. Athens County 1998); Woolum v. Woolum, 131 Ohio App. 3d 818, 723 N.E.2d 1135 (12th Dist. Preble County 1999). See also Text § 12:22, Remedies—Miscellaneous issues; Text § 14:5, False arrest, warrantless arrests and searches, and weapons confiscation; Text § 18:11, Firearm offenses under VAWA.

[10]See Sup. R. Form 10.01-H and Sup. R. Form 10.01-J.

[11]See Text Ch. 14, Police Enforcement of Protection Orders and Other Relevant Issues, for a more thorough discussion of search and seizure; see also RC 2935.03(B)(3)(h).

[12]See Text § 14:6, Law enforcement policies and procedures.

§ 11:20 Ex parte protection orders—Length of order

An ex parte civil protection order lasts for a maximum of ten days.[1] If a petitioner requests that a respondent either vacate the premises or be evicted from the residence, the statute authorizes the court to schedule a full hearing within seven court days after the ex parte hearing.[2] Seven court days excludes the day that the ex parte hearing was held and excludes weekends and holidays.[3]

Of significance is that the ex parte order remains in effect past the 7 or 10 day time frame if there is a failure of service.[4] It does not automatically expire after the seven- or ten-day period. RC 3113.31(D)(2)(b) provides that "an ex parte order issued under this section does not expire because of a failure to serve notice of the full hearing upon the respondent before the date set for the full hearing under division (D)(2)(a) of this section or because the court grants a continuance under that division."

If any other type of protection order authorized under RC 3113.31(E) is issued, the court must schedule a full hearing within ten court days after the ex parte hearing. Similarly, ten court days excludes the day that the ex parte order was heard and also excludes weekends and holidays.[5]

The statute does not mandate that the full hearing be held only on the seventh or tenth day. It allows for a hearing within a shorter period of time so long as the full hearing is held within the prescribed seven- or ten-day period. Franklin County is among several counties which allow for a full hearing in three to five days after the ex parte hearing. Where the court fails to grant the ex parte protection order, the full hearing may also be held before the seven- or ten-day maximum time period.[6]

The wording of RC 3113.31(D)(2)(a) was changed from "shall be held" to "shall schedule."[7] This change was necessary to reflect the reality of continuances. In effect, the legislature recognized that not all ex parte protection orders are heard within the prescribed time period. RC 3113.31(D)(2)(a) further provides that the court shall hold the full hearing on the date scheduled, unless the court grants a continuance of the hearing.

[Section 11:20]

[1]See RC 3113.31(D)(2)(a).

[2]RC 3113.31(D)(2)(a).

[3]Civ.R. 6.

[4]See also Text § 11:4, Duration of protection order.

[5]See Civ.R. 6.

[6]See also Text § 11:22, Ex parte protection orders—Miscellaneous issues. But see Losey v. Diersing, 2013-Ohio-1108, 2013 WL 1196674 (Ohio Ct. App. 12th Dist. Clermont County 2013) (noting that there is nothing in RC 2903.214 that suggests that a failure to hold a full hearing with 10 days of the ex parte hearing divests the trial court of jurisdiction to proceed).

[7]See 1997 S.B. 1, eff. 10-21-97.

§ 11:21 Ex parte protection orders—Continuances[1]

Q & A: Can a petitioner continue the full hearing?

RC 3113.31(D)(2)(a) specifically enumerates the reasons for which a court may grant a continuance of the full hearing. Continuances may be granted to a reasonable time determined by the court. They include that (1) prior to the date scheduled for the full hearing, the respondent has not been served with the petition and notice of the full hearing; (2) the parties consented to the continuance; (3) the continuance is needed to allow a party to obtain counsel;[2] and (4) the continuance is needed for other good cause.[3]

Q & A: Can a respondent continue the full hearing?[4]

The statute contains several bases for continuing the full hearing. Specifically, if the respondent requests a continuance to obtain counsel, the court will grant the continuance.[5] If the respondent requests a continuance and the petitioner consents, the court will grant a continuance.[6]

Besides those reasons, a continuance may be granted for good cause.[7] In *Conkle v. Wolfe*,[8] the Preble County Court of Appeals denied a respondent's request for a continuance. In that case, the respondent requested a continuance of the full hearing pending completion of his trial on criminal charges. The petitioner did not agree to the continuance and further indicated that the criminal trial might be rescheduled. The appellate court determined that the trial court did not abuse its discretion in overruling the respondent's motion to continue the full hearing.

Q & A: If the court continues the full hearing, will the ex parte order remain in effect?

RC 3113.31 specifically addresses this question. According to RC

[Section 11:21]

[1]See also Text § 12:4, Full hearing—Continuances; Text § 12:2, Full hearing—Scheduling and filing issues. See generally State v. Unger, 67 Ohio St. 2d 65, 21 Ohio Op. 3d 41, 423 N.E.2d 1078 (1981); Ohio Valley Radiology Associates, Inc. v. Ohio Valley Hosp. Ass'n, 28 Ohio St. 3d 118, 502 N.E.2d 599 (1986).

[2]See Ferretti v. Graham, 2001 WL 118601 (Ohio Ct. App. 10th Dist. Franklin County 2001) (continuing ex parte stalking civil protection order to allow petitioner to obtain counsel).

[3]RC 3113.31(D)(2)(a)(i) to RC 3113.31(D)(2)(a)(iv).

[4]See also Text § 12:4, Full hearing—Continuances.

[5]RC 3113.31(D)(2)(a)(iii); but see Noah v. Brillhart, 2003-Ohio-2421, 2003 WL 21078077 (Ohio Ct. App. 9th Dist. Wayne County 2003).

[6]RC 3113.31(D)(2)(a)(ii).

[7]RC 3113.31(D)(2)(a)(iv); see also Sigler v. Arvay, 2002-Ohio-6762, 2002 WL 31761478 (Ohio Ct. App. 9th Dist. Summit County 2002) (where the appellate court reversed issuance of a CPO because respondent was incarcerated at the time of the fully hearing and he was unable to attend the hearing or request counsel or a continuance).

[8]Conkle v. Wolfe, 131 Ohio App. 3d 375, 722 N.E.2d 586 (4th Dist. Athens County 1998); see also Wirtz v. Wirtz, 2000-Ohio-2564, 2000 WL 1486652 (Ohio Ct. App. 7th Dist. Mahoning County 2000) in which the respondent appealed the denial of a continuance pending resolution of criminal domestic violence charges arising from the same facts. The appellate court affirmed and relied on the reasoning advanced by the magistrate that granting a continuance would result in unreasonable delay.

3113.31(D)(2)(b), even if a continuance is granted, the ex parte order does not expire.[9] Counsel should also check with the forum jurisdiction regarding local procedure and practice prior to commencing a petition for a civil protection order under RC 3113.31. If, for any reason, a full hearing is continued, counsel must verify how this provision is implemented by the court, i.e., is it an automatic action or is an interim order entered which is designed to address this issue.

Prior to the enactment of Senate Bill 1,[10] some courts kept the ex parte order in effect when a continuance was granted without the petitioner requesting that the order be extended. Cuyahoga County was among the counties providing for this.[11] Other courts required a consent agreement from the parties requesting that the ex parte order continue in effect.

Under newly enacted RC 3113.31(D)(2)(b), statutory enactment replaces local rules and practice. The intent of the legislation is to automatically extend the ex parte protection order so that a petitioner does not have to address this issue and so that law enforcement across the state would know that the ex parte protection order did not expire if the full hearing was continued. One way of avoiding this problem is to note on the ex parte protection order form and the 10-A form that the duration of the order is five years. The time frame should be written out. In this way, a petitioner is covered. If the terms are modified after the full hearing, whenever it is, a new protection order and 10-A form will be generated and a new expiration date will be provided.

Q & A: How long do ex parte orders remain in effect?

An ex parte civil protection order is effective until the issuance of a full hearing civil protection order.[12] It becomes an issue when the full hearing is continued for service or any other reason. While some courts have used the full hearing date as the expiration of the ex parte order, this creates problems because the date will have to be extended if service is not perfected or if the full hearing is continued for another reason.

Other courts have used the maximum five year duration date, but that may also be problematic because it might conflict with Civ. R. 3(A) which limits the time a civil action may remain pending, absent service of process. More recently, courts have determined that ex parte civil protection orders should expire one year from the date of issuance, which apparently complies with Civ. R. 3(A) and Civ. R. 4(E).[13]

---

[9]See also Barrett v. Soltesz, 2015-Ohio-794, 2015 WL 995439 (Ohio Ct. App. 6th Dist. Erie County 2015).

[10]1997 S.B. 1, eff. 10-21-97.

[11]See Cuy. D.R. R. 26(B)(5).

[12]See Preston v. Shutway, 2013-Ohio-185, 986 N.E.2d 584, ¶ 15 (Ohio Ct. App. 2d Dist. Champaign County 2013) (trial court's order after a full hearing superseded the ex parte order); Daugherty v. Daugherty, 2012-Ohio-1520, 2012 WL 1139129 (Ohio Ct. App. 4th Dist. Hocking County 2012) (trial court's final domestic violence civil protection order superseded prior ex parte order, rendering any claim regarding the ex parte order moot).

[13]See also Text 12:4.

However, in light of the cases decided after *State v. Smith*,[14] it might be wise to return to the five year date, in order to make sure that the ex parte order is still in effect for purposes of a R.C. 2919.27 violation, if the full hearing order has not been served.[15]

Q & A: Is it proper for a magistrate to maintain the ex parte CPO in effect for a definite period of time without holding the full hearing?

Some magistrates have determined that this strategy is useful to resolve cases. In applying such a strategy, these courts have found that by setting a date certain in the future and continuing the ex parte order, the parties are more likely to settle the cases. On that date certain, if neither party requests additional action, the order will expire at that time.

From the court's perspective, there is no finality of judgment. From the domestic violence expert perspective, such a strategy might render the CPO meaningless for purposes of full faith and credit. If such a method is utilized, it is unlikely that the respondent will be weapons banned.[16] Thus, while such a strategy might help in some cases, it leaves many survivors without adequate protections.

Q & A: How many times can a petitioner continue the full hearing for a failure of service?

RC 3113.31(D)(2)(a) states that "the court may grant a continuance of the full hearing to a reasonable time determined by the court." Local practice has dictated how a jurisdiction responds to this issue. Although the statute is silent regarding the number of continuances that may be granted, it is clear that a trial court has discretion when deciding to grant or deny a motion for a continuance.[17]

There are several Ohio courts that have addressed this issue. For example, in *Eichenberger v. Eichenberger*,[18] the Court of Appeals for Franklin County held that the trial court did not err in twice continuing a civil protection order hearing date, thereby failing to hold the hearing within seven days of issuance of the ex parte order. The court's rationale was that the limited delay was reasonable in light of the trial judge's heavy docket responsibilities, and neither the integrity nor the constitutionality of the proceedings were jeopardized.

Additionally, in *Deacon v. Landers*,[19] the court noted that the hearing was continued several times because of difficulties in obtaining service. The court of appeals did not even consider this a problem to be addressed.

---

[14] State v. Smith, 136 Ohio St. 3d 1, 2013-Ohio-1698, 989 N.E.2d 972 (2013); see also Text 13:3.

[15] See also State v. Johnson, 2014-Ohio-2435, 2014 WL 2566260 (Ohio Ct. App. 6th Dist. Wood County 2014); State v. Hall, 2013-Ohio-5855, 2013 WL 6918874 (Ohio Ct. App. 5th Dist. Delaware County 2013).

[16] See Text 18:13.

[17] Conkle v. Wolfe, 131 Ohio App. 3d 375, 722 N.E.2d 586 (4th Dist. Athens County 1998).

[18] Eichenberger v. Eichenberger, 82 Ohio App. 3d 809, 613 N.E.2d 678 (10th Dist. Franklin County 1992); see also Wirtz v. Wirtz, 2000-Ohio-2564, 2000 WL 1486652 (Ohio Ct. App. 7th Dist. Mahoning County 2000) (discussing rationale for granting or denying continuances, generally).

[19] Deacon v. Landers, 68 Ohio App. 3d 26, 587 N.E.2d 395 (4th Dist. Ross County 1990).

Other states have considered this issue and addressed it both by statute and in case law. For example, the Texas Abuse Statute provides for a maximum continuance of fourteen days for no service.[20] In *Nohner v. Anderson*,[21] the Minnesota Court of Appeals held that the trial court could not continue an ex parte order for more than fourteen days without a full hearing and findings of domestic violence.

Most courts will not allow the petitioner to continue the full hearing where the respondent has already been served. At this point, the petitioner must appear for the full hearing. A failure to appear will most often result in a dismissal of the petition and a termination of the order. Permitting the petitioner to continue the hearing could result in an infringement of the respondent's due process rights to a hearing.

For example, Cuyahoga County often refuses to grant a petitioner leave to continue a full hearing where it has been established that the respondent has been served. Unfortunately, RC 3113.31(D)(2)(a) does not address this particular issue. Unless both parties consent, a party needs to obtain counsel, or the petitioner can demonstrate good cause, a petitioner is not likely to prevail on a request to continue the full hearing.

On the other hand, many courts will allow the respondent to continue the full hearing. The courts' reasoning is that a full hearing is scheduled for the benefit of the respondent. The petitioner's attorney must be sure to request that the court advise the respondent that he/she is bound by the terms of the ex parte order until the rescheduled hearing date.

Q & A: Can a petitioner continue the full hearing for failure of service for five years, the statutory duration of the protection order?

RC 3113.31(D)(2)(a) does not address this issue. Theoretically, it is possible that service may not be perfected by any means within the five-year period. If it can be shown that the respondent is eluding the process server and continuing his/her abusive conduct, but not getting caught, it is reasonable to argue that the order should remain in effect for the five-year period while the petitioner continues to attempt service on the respondent.

Additionally, RC 3113.31(E)(3)(a) provides that a protection order shall be valid until a date certain, but not later than five years from the date of its issuance.[22] The date of its issuance, in this circumstance, is when the court grants the ex parte order. It is possible that this provision implies that, unlike other civil actions, a protection order may remain in effect for the entire five-year period if service is being attempted.[23]

Q & A: Do the Rules of Civil Procedure provide any guidance?

---

[20] Tex. Fam. Code Ann. § 84.003.

[21] Nohner v. Anderson, 446 N.W.2d 202 (Minn. Ct. App. 1989).

[22] See also Wirtz v. Wirtz, 2000-Ohio-2564, 2000 WL 1486652 (Ohio Ct. App. 7th Dist. Mahoning County 2000).

[23] See, for example, Wirtz v. Wirtz, 2000-Ohio-2564, 2000 WL 1486652 (Ohio Ct. App. 7th Dist. Mahoning County 2000) (discussing RC 3113.31(E)(3)(a)).

RC 3113.31(G) provides, however, that any proceeding under this section shall be conducted in accordance with the Rules of Civil Procedure. Civil Rule 3(A) details that a civil action is commenced by filing a complaint with the court, if service is obtained within one year from such filing upon a named defendant. Since a petition for civil protection order is a complaint, it too must be served upon a respondent within one year from the date of filing. Civil Rule 4(E) provides that, if service of summons and complaint is not made on a defendant within six months after the filing of the complaint and the party on whose behalf such service was required cannot show good cause why such service was not made within that period, the action shall be dismissed as to the defendant.

The operative phrase is "good cause," and in domestic violence cases, a showing that a petitioner is attempting to perfect service of process appears to be good cause for not dismissing the action after six months and attempting to perfect service for one full year. A petitioner's attorney should make a mental note of that fact and address it with the court if, there is no service after six months. Of course, that implies that service has been attempted during the six-month period. If service has been repeatedly attempted, it is arguable that the court should reset the full hearing several times during the one year period.

Q & A: Can my client obtain an ex parte civil protection order without knowing the respondent's address?

The domestic violence statute specifically provides that an ex parte order must be delivered to the respondent on the same day as the order is entered.[24] Unfortunately, without an address for a respondent, service cannot be perfected. Without service, a respondent will not know the terms of the CPO. Hence, there will be no full hearing in order to determine whether the ex parte protection order will remain in effect for up to five years.

While the intent of the statute is to provide immediate relief to a victim of domestic violence, the court must also take into account the statutory protections afforded any defendant. Without an address for a respondent, the provisions of RC 3113.31(F)(1) are not met. Eventually, the petition and CPO will be dismissed for a failure of service.

While the domestic violence statute permits the filing of a continuance for a failure to perfect service of process on a respondent, such implies that the petitioner had an address that she/he believed was valid upon filing.

Amendments to Civ. R. 4.4(A)(2) permitted the use of publication by posting as an appropriate method of service of process in civil protection order proceedings pursuant to Civ. R. 65.1(C)(2). Per the language of the civil rules, posting appeared to be reserved for persons with limited resources.

As soon as adopted, however, a contradiction was discovered between Civ. R. 4.4(A)(2), which provided that posting applied only to those filing with a poverty affidavit (indigent parties) and RC 3113.31(J)[25] which specifically prohibited all fees and costs associated with the issuance of a civil protection order including service.

[24] R.C. 3113.31(F)(1).

[25] See also R.C. 2903.214(J); R.C. 2151.34(J).

In an effort to eliminate confusion, a recent amendment was adopted, effective July 1, 2018, which provided that service by posting does apply to anyone filing a civil protection order where service of process is an issue, regardless of indigency.[26]

As stated in newly adopted division (A)(2)(b), service of a civil protection order may be served by posting or mail without the necessity of a poverty affidavit where the respondent's residence is unknown. Before service by posting or mail can be made, the petitioner must file an affidavit with the court containing the same averments required by division (A)(1) of the rule, i.e., that service of summons cannot be made because the residence of the defendant (respondent) is unknown to the affiant, all of the efforts made on behalf of the party to ascertain the residence of the defendant, and that the residence of the defendant cannot be ascertained with reasonable diligence. Petitioner shall also set forth the last known address of the party to be served.

Civ. R. 4.4(A)(2)(b) would then allow for publication by a clerk in a conspicuous place in the courthouse(s) within the county where Civ. R. 65.1 civil protection order proceedings may be filed and in two additional public places in the county that have been designated by local rule for the posting of notices pursuant to this rule. The postings under division (A)(2)(b) *shall not be made on the website* of the clerk of courts.[27] The notice shall contain the same information required by division (A)(1) of this rule that is contained in a newspaper publication. The notice shall be posted for six consecutive weeks.

Additionally, "when service by publication is sought by posting and mail under division (A)(2)(b), the clerk shall also cause the documents for service to be mailed by United States ordinary mail, address correction requested, to the last known address of the party to be served. The clerk shall obtain a certificate of mailing from the USPS. If the clerk is notified of a corrected or forwarded address of the party to be served within the six-week period that notice is posted pursuant to division (A)(2)(a) or division (A)(2)(b) of this rule, the clerk shall cause the documents for service to be mailed to the corrected forwarding address and note the name, address, and date of each mailing on the docket."[28]

After the last week of posting under either division (A)(2)(a) or (A)(2)(b) of this rule, the clerk shall note on the docket where and when notice was posted. Service shall be complete upon entry of posting.[29]

Q & A: Must the court grant a continuance without a request made by a party?

At least one jurisdiction has said no. In *Clementz-McBeth v. Craft*, appellant appealed the issuance of a CPO on several grounds, includ-

---

[26]Civ. R. 4.4(A)(2)(b).

[27]Emphasis added; see also 18 U.S.C.A. § 2265(d)(3).

[28]Civ. R. 4.4(A)(2)(b).

[29]Civ. R. 4.4(A)(2)(d).

ing that the trial court failed to grant a continuance on its own motion, without a request by respondent to do so.[30]

The appellate court found that courts are not required to sua sponte issue continuances.[31] If appellant had wanted a continuance, it was up to him to request one. "It is not the responsibility of the court to make sure parties are prepared or to grant a continuance where one was not requested. Though some leeway is often given to pro se litigants, 'ordinary civil litigants proceeding *pro se* * * * are not entitled to special treatment.' "[32]

§ 11:22 Ex parte protection orders—Miscellaneous issues

Under Ohio law, a petition for a protection order need not include a request for an ex parte order.[1] If a petitioner files a petition and does not request an ex parte order, the court shall proceed as it would in a normal civil action and schedule a full hearing on the matter.[2] In that case, the Rules of Civil Procedure apply as to service and time frames. Under this scenario, there may be no reason to schedule a full hearing within the seven- or ten-day time period. It is also more likely that service by certified mail, express mail, publication, or posting will be acceptable to the court.[3]

It is clear that RC 3113.31(D)(3) can be utilized when service has been a problem or where the petitioner does not know the address of the respondent. Rather than have the action dismissed for a failure of service, an attorney can dismiss or withdraw the petition and refile the petition without a request for ex parte relief.

It may be advisable to proceed as in an ordinary civil action when there is a scant history of violence and no recent acts or threats but the petitioner believes the potential for future abuse is likely. This may come up when the respondent has been in jail for an extended period of time or has not been able to act on any threat because of his/her proximity to the victim. Rather than have a court fail to issue an ex parte order or dismiss the petition because there is no emergency, the attorney can file the case as an ordinary civil action. The victim can still request the relief available under RC 3113.31(E)(1)(a) to (h).

Q & A: What happens if a court does not issue an ex parte order even though one was requested?

The statute provides that, if a person requests an ex parte order but

---

[30]Clementz-McBeth v. Craft, 2012-Ohio-985, 2012 WL 776851 (Ohio Ct. App. 3d Dist. Auglaize County 2012).

[31]Clementz-McBeth v. Craft, 2012-Ohio-985, 2012 WL 776851, *4 (Ohio Ct. App. 3d Dist. Auglaize County 2012), citing Gannon v. Gannon, 2008-Ohio-4484, 2008 WL 4093687 (Ohio Ct. App. 6th Dist. Wood County 2008).

[32]Clementz-McBeth v. Craft, 2012-Ohio-985, 2012 WL 776851, *4 (Ohio Ct. App. 3d Dist. Auglaize County 2012), quoting McKinnie v. Roadway Express, Inc., 341 F.3d 554, 558, 92 Fair Empl. Prac. Cas. (BNA) 741, 84 Empl. Prac. Dec. (CCH) P 41456, 2003 FED App. 0294P (6th Cir. 2003).

[Section 11:22]

[1]See Genari v. Genari, 2001-Ohio-1524, 2001 WL 848569 (Ohio Ct. App. 2d Dist. Greene County 2001).

[2]RC 3113.31(D).

[3]See Civ.R. 4.1, Civ.R. 4.4, Civ.R. 4.6.

the court fails to issue it after the ex parte hearing, the court shall proceed as in a normal civil action and grant a full hearing.[4] There is no time frame within which to schedule a hearing. Counsel should note that if an ex parte protection order is not issued by the court, a petitioner is not entitled to relief until after a full hearing is held. The action must then proceed as in a normal civil action.[5] Unfortunately, there is no guarantee that a full hearing will be provided quickly. Because an ex parte order was sought in this case scenario, it would appear that the court would schedule a full hearing within the seven- or ten-day period.

The reasons for a court not to grant an ex parte order after an ex parte hearing include (1) not finding that an emergency exists, (2) not finding an immediate and present danger, and (3) not finding the petitioner credible.[6] Since the purpose of any protection order is to eliminate violence between the parties, the statute still provides for a full hearing for the benefit of the petitioner.

If the court finds that the petitioner is not a credible witness, however, the court may dismiss the petition on the affidavit or testimony of the petitioner. The decision to grant a civil protection order is within the discretion of the court.[7]

Some courts may be reluctant to dismiss the petition without giving the petitioner a chance to present a case within a short period of time. Scheduling a full hearing within the seven- or ten-day time period allows the petitioner to present his/her case to the court at the full hearing while, at the same time, giving the respondent an opportunity to be heard without restricting or infringing on the respondent's rights.

Q & A: Is an ex parte protection order the same as an ex parte restraining order issued as part of a divorce?[8]

Absolutely not. An ex parte civil protection order is granted in a special statutory proceeding.[9] The authority of the court to issue specific orders, which are designed to ensure the safety and protection of the petitioner, is provided by RC 3113.31. An ex parte restraining order, in contrast, contains only general prohibitions. The court has the authority to grant such injunctive relief pursuant to Civil Rule 75(H).

---

[4]RC 3113.31(D)(3); see also Skiles v. Dearth, 2000 WL 1838747 (Ohio Ct. App. 2d Dist. Clark County 2000); Genari v. Genari, 2001-Ohio-1524, 2001 WL 848569 (Ohio Ct. App. 2d Dist. Greene County 2001); Text § 11:11, Ex parte protection orders—Service and notice provisions; Vance v. Nichols, 2007-Ohio-3819, 2007 WL 2164162 (Ohio Ct. App. 2d Dist. Darke County 2007) (magistrate noted in the record that respondent requested a second hearing). But see Wilburn v. Wilburn, 2006-Ohio-2553, 2006 WL 1409784 (Ohio Ct. App. 9th Dist. Lorain County 2006).

[5]See RC 3113.31(D)(3).

[6]See, e.g., Scott v. Chalk, 2002-Ohio-1980, 2002 WL 440783 (Ohio Ct. App. 1st Dist. Hamilton County 2002).

[7]Thomas v. Thomas, 44 Ohio App. 3d 6, 540 N.E.2d 745 (10th Dist. Franklin County 1988); see also Deacon v. Landers, 68 Ohio App. 3d 26, 587 N.E.2d 395 (4th Dist. Ross County 1990).

[8]See also Text § 11:7, Specific domestic violence and divorce issues.

[9]See also Skiles v. Dearth, 2000 WL 1838747 (Ohio Ct. App. 2d Dist. Clark County 2000); Oliver v. Johnson, 2007-Ohio-5880, 2007 WL 3227668 (Ohio Ct. App. 4th Dist. Jackson County 2007).

Additionally, an ex parte protection order contains several features not available to a party seeking an ex parte restraining order. For example, a violation of a protection order results in criminal sanctions under RC 2919.27 as well as in contempt pursuant to RC 3113.31(L)(1).[10] There is also an enhancement of penalties for subsequent violations of a protection order.[11] A violation of a restraining order in a divorce action subjects the violator only to contempt of court under RC 2705.02(A).

Most important is that violations of a civil protection order subject the violator to the state's preferred arrest policies.[12] No such policy extends to violators of restraining orders. Additionally, law enforcement officials are obligated to enforce protection orders.[13] Likewise, a protection order is more likely to be enforced because the police are required to enforce civil protection orders but not restraining orders.

Unlike a protection order, a restraining order remains in effect only until the divorce is final. A protection order remains in effect for a date certain, but not later than five years from the date of its issuance or approval.[14]

Q & A: What is the procedure if a petitioner wants to dismiss an ex parte protection order?[15]

There are no cases that have addressed this issue and the statute is silent.[16] Common sense dictates that there may be many reasons, some non-volitional, that lead a petitioner to dismiss an ex parte protection order. The petitioner may fail to appear or request a dismissal by telephone or in person.

At least one non-Ohio court has tackled this issue. In *Kelleher v. Galindo*,[17] the plaintiff had repeatedly requested and dismissed several protection orders over the past five years, either by a failure to appear or a request to dismiss. The plaintiff then requested another dismissal.

The Superior Court of New Jersey addressed this as a case of first impression and denied the plaintiff's motion to dismiss. In fact, the court issued the final order.

The court then stated that an actual appearance is necessary before the court would entertain a dismissal. Additionally, the domestic violence unit staff person must "ascertain that the plaintiff has not been coerced, understands the cycle of violence, is aware of the protec-

[10]See also Text Ch. 13, Court Enforcement of Civil Protection Orders and Related Issues.

[11]See RC 2919.27(B).

[12]See RC 2935.03(B)(3)(b).

[13]See RC 3113.31(F)(3).

[14]See RC 3113.31(E)(3)(a); see also Felton v. Felton, 79 Ohio St. 3d 34, 1997-Ohio-302, 679 N.E.2d 672 (1997) for a complete discussion by the Supreme Court regarding the differences between protection orders and restraining orders; Hershberger v. Hershberger, 2000-Ohio-1716, 2000 WL 1675568 (Ohio Ct. App. 3d Dist. Seneca County 2000).

[15]See also Text § 12:25, Modification and termination of civil protection orders; Text § 12:7.

[16]See also Text § 12:23, Duration of a civil protection order.

[17]Kelleher v. Galindo, 350 N.J. Super. 570, 796 A.2d 306 (Ch. Div. 2002).

tive resources available, understands that the dismissal of the TRO will eliminate the protections under same and is also aware that he/she can seek the protection of a TRO in the future should there be a future act of domestic violence."[18]

Q & A: Does compliance with the ex parte CPO eliminate the need to grant the full hearing order?

Of course not. In *Zawrotuk v. Zawrotuk*,[19] petitioner was granted an ex parte CPO. Four months passed before the court heard the matter. In the instant case, respondent argued that compliance with the ex parte order for these months precluded the grant of an order issued after a full hearing.

The appellate court relied on RC 3113.31(E)(8) which provides that compliance with a protection order is merely one factor to consider when determining whether to modify or terminate a CPO issued after a full hearing. The court further noted that the extensions of the full hearing were requested by appellant. "His extensions cannot create a situation where a court can no longer issue a protection order because time has passed since the precipitating incident and the respondent obeyed the ex parte order during that time. The need for protection is not erased due to compliance with the ex parte order; a lack of threatening contact may be the direct result of that order. . . ."[20]

§ 11:23 Ex parte protection orders—Appeal of an order

RC 3113.31 specifically states that an ex parte protection order is not a final appealable order.[1] This should pose no problem for petitioners because the statutory language also suggests that a protection order may not be dismissed at the ex parte hearing. RC 3113.31(D)(3) provides that an ex parte order, if requested but not issued after an ex parte hearing, shall be set for a full hearing.[2] In effect, the need for an appeal is unnecessary because a petitioner is still permitted an opportunity to present a case at the full hearing.

Additionally, Ohio is replete with case law providing that an ex parte order is temporary in nature, and temporary orders are not appealable.[3] Most reported case law involves ex parte orders for temporary custody. For example, in Lee v. Lee,[4] the court of appeals held that "[i]t is well-established in Ohio that the granting . . . of an

---

[18]Kelleher v. Galindo, 350 N.J. Super. 570, 796 A.2d 306 (Ch. Div. 2002).

[19]Zawrotuk v. Zawrotuk, 2014-Ohio-5225, 2014 WL 6641772 (Ohio Ct. App. 7th Dist. Mahoning County 2014).

[20]Zawrotuk v. Zawrotuk, 2014-Ohio-5225, 2014 WL 6641772, ¶ 44 (Ohio Ct. App. 7th Dist. Mahoning County 2014).

[Section 11:23]

[1]See RC 3113.31(G); Civ. R. 65.1; see also Palo v. Palo, 2004-Ohio-5638, 2004 WL 2376277 (Ohio Ct. App. 11th Dist. Ashtabula County 2004); Hanna v. Keszei, 2009-Ohio-4136, 2009 WL 2490035 (Ohio Ct. App. 12th Dist. Clermont County 2009).

[2]See Text § 12:1, Introduction.

[3]See Amalgamated Clothing Workers of America v. Richman Bros., 348 U.S. 511, 75 S. Ct. 452, 99 L. Ed. 600, 71 Ohio L. Abs. 177, 35 L.R.R.M. (BNA) 2682, 27 Lab. Cas. (CCH) P 69080 (1955); see also Rigsby v. Rigsby, 1987 WL 8853 (Ohio Ct. App. 4th Dist. Pickaway County 1987).

[4]Lee v. Lee, 1987 WL 16064, *2 (Ohio Ct. App. 12th Dist. Clermont County

ex parte custody order is interlocutory . . . subject to modification in a later final judgment, and thus is not a final appealable order within the contemplation of RC 2505.02."[5]

Kelm v. Kelm[6] is the one Ohio case where an appellate court considered the issue. The court dismissed the appeal because it determined that the protection order was not a final appealable order since it was filed in the pending divorce action. However, the court mentioned the problems inherent in attempting to appeal an ex parte protection order granted pursuant to RC 3113.31(D). The court further noted that "the issues raised by appellant should, at some time, be addressed."[7]

This case reveals one of the potential problems in filing a divorce and a request for a protection order simultaneously under the divorce case number. In *Kelm*, the court found that the ex parte order was interlocutory in nature only because it was filed in the divorce action. The court left open the question of whether an ex parte protection order filed in an independent action would also be interlocutory.

§ 11:24 Ex parte protection orders—Violation of an ex parte order

Q & A: Can a respondent violate an ex parte civil protection order?[1]

This issue is rarely raised in the domestic violence context because ex parte protection orders are not final appealable orders.[2] Generally, petitioners do not file specific contempt motions regarding ex parte violations. Without a specific motion in front of it, a court does not usually find a violation absent notice to the respondent of the contempt charge. Moreover, petitioners are often granted the final civil protection order and are advised that most future violations are subject to a contempt action.[3]

The Cuyahoga County Court of Appeals addressed this issue in Rush v. Rush.[4] In that case, the appellant had been granted an ex parte protection order by the court. After respondent-husband was

---

1987).

[5]See Spence v. Spence, 2 Ohio App. 3d 280, 441 N.E.2d 822 (10th Dist. Franklin County 1981); see also Chef Italiano Corp. v. Kent State University, 44 Ohio St. 3d 86, 541 N.E.2d 64, 54 Ed. Law Rep. 947 (1989).

[6]Kelm v. Kelm, 1993 WL 220881 (Ohio Ct. App. 10th Dist. Franklin County 1993).

[7]Kelm v. Kelm, 1993 WL 220881, *2 (Ohio Ct. App. 10th Dist. Franklin County 1993).

[Section 11:24]

[1]See Text Ch. 13, Court Enforcement of Civil Protection Orders and Related Issues; § 13:2, Court enforcement of civil protection orders—Generally, § 13:3, Court enforcement of civil protection orders—Criminal prosecution and § 13:4, Court enforcement of civil protection orders—Contempt—Generally defined.

[2]See Text § 11:23, Ex parte protection orders—Appeal of an order.

[3]See Text § 13:4, Court enforcement of civil protection orders—Contempt—Generally defined.

[4]Rush v. Rush, 1999 WL 1044482 (Ohio Ct. App. 8th Dist. Cuyahoga County 1999); see also Text § 11:11, Ex parte protection orders—Service and notice provisions.

served, but before the full hearing, respondent returned to appellant's apartment to pick up the child for visitation. A neighbor called police, but the respondent-husband left before they arrived.

At the full hearing, the trial court found that an incident of domestic violence had occurred and that respondent had violated the ex parte protection order. The court declined to fine him because it was a first offense but noted that any further violation would result in a thirty-day jail sentence. The respondent appealed, arguing that the trial court erred in finding him in indirect contempt because he was not provided with notice that he faced contempt charges and because the finding of domestic violence was against the manifest weight of the evidence.

Finding that the evidence adduced at trial failed to sustain a finding of domestic violence under RC 3113.31(A)(1)(a) to RC 3113.31(A)(1)(c), the Eighth District Court of Appeals reversed the judgment of the trial court granting the civil protection order. However, the appellate court upheld the finding that respondent had violated the ex parte civil protection order. After finding that the respondent was personally served prior to returning to his wife's apartment, the appellate court noted that the trial court had entered an ex parte protection order forbidding the respondent from being within 500 feet of the wife's residence. Moreover, the court pointed to the unambiguous warning to husband that the violation of the order is a crime and that it is punishable by imprisonment or fine or contempt. Because respondent admitted that he went to his wife's apartment, there was credible evidence that he violated the ex parte order.

The appellate court noted that "even after finding this violation, the court did not impose a fine and noted that this was a first offense. The court added that '[a]ny further violation will result in a 30 day jail sentence.' "[5]

Of significance is that the appellate court upheld the contempt violation against the respondent despite the fact that the evidence at trial failed to support a finding of domestic violence and even though respondent was not provided with notice that he faced contempt charges. In a footnote, the appellate court advanced an important public policy consideration that an ex parte protection order is a lawful court order. The court pointed out that "While we have concluded on the basis of the full hearing that wife did not show by a preponderance of the evidence that either she or [defendant] were in danger of domestic violence by husband, that does not negate the lawful effect of the ex parte order entered on May 20, 1998 and does not provide husband with any grounds to defy that lawful court order."[6]

---

[5]Rush v. Rush, 1999 WL 1044482 (Ohio Ct. App. 8th Dist. Cuyahoga County 1999).

[6]Rush v. Rush, 1999 WL 1044482 (Ohio Ct. App. 8th Dist. Cuyahoga County 1999) (footnote 2).

§ 11:25 Ex parte protection orders—Strategies for counsel at ex parte hearing

Due to the cyclical nature of domestic violence,[1] introduction of evidence of the relationship between the parties and the history of abuse is vital in allowing a court to fully comprehend the risk posed to a particular petitioner.[2] Attorneys should always elicit evidence of past abusive acts. Evidence of past abusive acts is relevant because it provides a context within which to evaluate the petitioner's present fear and danger.[3]

Attorneys should consider a history of violence in the relationship as evidence of the need for a current protection order. Protection orders are issued when the victim fears further violence based on abuse which may have occurred some time in the past.[4] Attorneys should also consider evidence of past physical harm[5] when the petitioner has a present fear of harm, to show a trend toward escalating the current violence, to evaluate present threats, and to defeat an abuser's claim of self-defense.[6] Courts should consider the history of abuse when deciding whether to extend a civil protection order and which remedies the order must contain to effectively stop the violence.

Although RC 3113.31 contains no statute of limitations, counsel should determine, before filing the petition, whether "an immediate and present danger" exists such that an ex parte order will be issued by the court.[7] Consideration should be given to the victim's safety and to when the most recent act of violence took place in relation to the time of filing of the petition.[8]

As previously stated, some courts are reluctant to grant an ex parte

---

[Section 11:25]

[1]See Cynthia Gillespie, Justifiable Homicide: Battered Women, Self Defense, and the Law 52 (1989); Angela Browne, Violence Against Women: Relevance for Medical Practitioners, 267 JAMA 3184, 3186 (1992).

[2]See Eichenberger v. Eichenberger, 82 Ohio App. 3d 809, 613 N.E.2d 678 (10th Dist. Franklin County 1992).

[3]See Visnich v. Visnich, 1999 WL 1299300 (Ohio Ct. App. 11th Dist. Trumbull County 1999).

[4]See Visnich v. Visnich, 1999 WL 1299300 (Ohio Ct. App. 11th Dist. Trumbull County 1999); see also Rhodes v. Gunter, 2003-Ohio-2342, 2003 WL 21040724 (Ohio Ct. App. 9th Dist. Lorain County 2003); Lavery v. Lavery, 2001-Ohio-1874, 2001 WL 1545663 (Ohio Ct. App. 9th Dist. Summit County 2001); Gatt v. Gatt, 2002-Ohio-1749, 2002 WL 570389 (Ohio Ct. App. 9th Dist. Medina County 2002); but see Solomon v. Solomon, 157 Ohio App. 3d 807, 2004-Ohio-2486, 813 N.E.2d 918 (7th Dist. Mahoning County 2004).

[5]See McGuire v. Sprinkle, 2007-Ohio-2705, 2007 WL 1585100 (Ohio Ct. App. 12th Dist. Warren County 2007) (holding that past acts do not have to include actual physical harm); see also Text § 8:4, Statutory elements of domestic violence under RC 3113.31(A)(1)(b).

[6]See Bruns v. Bruns, 1999 WL 819344 (Ohio Ct. App. 6th Dist. Erie County 1999). See also Text § 8:8; Text § 12:29; Text § 14:4.

[7]See Felton v. Felton, 79 Ohio St. 3d 34, 1997-Ohio-302, 679 N.E.2d 672 (1997); see also Siouffi v. Siouffi, 1998 WL 879255 (Ohio Ct. App. 2d Dist. Montgomery County 1998).

[8]But see Halley v. Ashley, 1997 WL 760662 (Ohio Ct. App. 9th Dist. Summit County 1997); see also Trent v. Trent, 1999 WL 298073 (Ohio Ct. App. 12th Dist. Preble County 1999); Morris v. Stonewall, 1999 WL 1037507 (Ohio Ct. App. 12th Dist.

order for a petitioner when the act of violence is remote in time. For example, if the violence took place several months before the filing of the petition, the court may not feel that an emergency still exists unless there have been new threats or other reasons for immediacy.

Counsel should assess the reasons for any delay in filing a petition. That the victim was in hiding and was discovered by the perpetrator, that the victim had previously obtained a criminal protection order under RC 2919.26, that the perpetrator had been incarcerated, and that the victim's criminal protection order had expired are examples of valid reasons why the petition for an ex parte protection order may be filed long after the incident of domestic violence which is the subject of the filing. None of these reasons suggests that the victim/petitioner is no longer in an immediate and present danger.

The delay may also be a result of the strategy of counsel. Many times an attorney will wait until the criminal protection order expires or is terminated before requesting an ex parte civil protection order. This strategy may account for the time lag between the last incident of violence and when the petitioner appears in court for the civil protection order.

Counsel must understand that the reason to request a civil protection order is to protect the victim from future domestic violence.[9] Each of the remedies enumerated in RC 3113.31(E)(1) are designed to effectuate that goal. Absent an immediate and present danger to the victim and other family or household members, a party will have a difficult time obtaining the civil protection order, particularly if requesting temporary custody and/or evicting the respondent from the premises.

Q & A: Is a civil stalking protection order a good alternative to a domestic violence CPO when the relationship between the parties is family or household members?

If an attorney is thinking of filing a CSPO rather than a domestic violence CPO when the parties are in a domestic violence relationship as defined in RC 3113.31, it is important to remember both statutory sections of the Revised Code.[10]

While there are many similarities in the statutes, the differences might become significant depending on the facts of a given case. If filing a CSPO, a petitioner must file in that county where the petitioner resides. If filing a DVCPO, a petitioner can file where he/she resides, where the respondent resides, where the cause of action arose or where the petitioner temporarily resides.[11]

In which court a protection order is filed should also depend on the relief sought. A CSPO doesn't address specific child issues like an allocation of parental rights and responsibilities and child support. It doesn't order a person to vacate the premises, award exclusive possession of property, award support, or apportion household property or

---

Clinton County 1999).

[9]See, e.g., Donovan v. Donovan, 2012-Ohio-3521, 2012 WL 3156462 (Ohio Ct. App. 9th Dist. Lorain County 2012).

[10]See also Text ¶ 9:5.

[11]See also Text ¶ 10:13.

award use of a car. It is clearly more like a no-contact or stay away order.[12]

Unlike a domestic violence civil protection order, a CSPO cannot be modified or terminated by statute.[13] Additionally, RC 2903.214 does not specifically allow for consent entries.

If the reasoning is that domestic relations courts don't know anything about stalking, it is important to push these courts to recognize that stalking is domestic violence when it occurs against a family or household member.

Some reasons for filing a CSPO when the parties are family or household members might be if an attorney believes that a common pleas jurist might grant the protection order more easily, understands stalking, or if electronic monitoring is sought.[14]

[12]RC 2903.214(E)(1); Text ¶ 9:5.

[13]See RC 3113.31(E)(8).

[14]RC 2903.214 (N).

Chapter 12

Full Hearing on Civil Protection Orders

§ 12:1 Introduction

Most civil protection orders are granted ex parte.[1] Some protection orders, however, are not granted ex parte, either because the order of

---

[Section 12:1]

[1]RC 3113.31(D)(1).

protection is not issued by the court at the ex parte hearing or because an ex parte order is not requested by the petitioner.[2]

In any case, the court is required to schedule a full hearing on the matter.[3] If the court issues an ex parte order, the primary purpose of the full hearing is to determine whether the ex parte order should be maintained, modified, or terminated. If the court schedules the full hearing without an initial ex parte order, the primary purpose of the full hearing is to convince the court that a protection order should be granted.

If a civil protection order is granted ex parte, the full hearing provides the respondent an opportunity to present a defense. Since due process safeguards mandate that the respondent be provided with notice and an opportunity to be heard, Ohio's statutory scheme provides a timely opportunity for a full hearing.[4]

For example, when the ex parte order seeks to evict the respondent from the residence or suspends access to the children, the full hearing is necessary to protect the defendant's due process rights. In effect, the purpose of an evidentiary hearing is to safeguard against situations where one party's rights may be denied for a potentially prolonged period of time.

If a civil protection order is not granted ex parte or if the petitioner does not request that the court issue the order ex parte, the full hearing is scheduled for the benefit of both parties. For the petitioner, it is the opportunity to present a case in order to obtain a protection order. For the respondent, it is the chance to respond to the petitioner's allegations.

Q & A: If granted at the full hearing, is the ex parte CPO merged into the CPO issued after the full hearing?

According to *Zawrotuk v. Zawrotuk*,[5] the answer is yes. In that case, appellant claimed that the petitioner neither provided the date of the incident on the petition nor discussed the date of the June 4 incident at the ex parte hearing and that the magistrate failed to inquire when the incident occurred.

The appellate court noted that an issue with an ex parte order does not invalidate a protection order issued after a full hearing. The court

[2]RC 3113.31(D)(3).

[3]RC 3113.31(D)(2), RC 3113.31(D)(3).

[4]See RC 3113.31(D)(2). See Butcher v. Stevens, 182 Ohio App. 3d 77, 2009-Ohio-1754, 911 N.E.2d 928 (4th Dist. Athens County 2009) (holding that based upon a plain reading of the statute, one day's notice of the full hearing is sufficient; statute doesn't require that *notice and an opportunity to be heard* (emphasis added) doesn't imply three or more days advance notice of the hearing); Oddo v. Spencer, 2009-Ohio-4320, 2009 WL 2602210 (Ohio Ct. App. 5th Dist. Stark County 2009) (holding that being served with the ex parte CPO 1 hour before the full hearing is reasonable notice and opportunity to be heard); Evans v. Evans, 2008-Ohio-5695, 2008 WL 4787582 (Ohio Ct. App. 10th Dist. Franklin County 2008) (holding that where party failed to seek a continuance or argue that failure to be served or noticed of the full hearing violated his due process rights, he waived his right to appeal the issue of a lack of notice); but see H.E.S. v. J.C.S., 175 N.J. 309, 815 A.2d 405 (2003) (holding that service of a domestic violence complaint on husband less than 24 hours before hearing violated due process).

[5]Zawrotuk v. Zawrotuk, 2014-Ohio-5225, 2014 WL 6641772 (Ohio Ct. App. 7th Dist. Mahoning County 2014).

explained that sometimes the court denies the ex parte order. However, that does not prevent the trial court from issuing a protection order after a full hearing. "Likewise, a questionable presentation of facts at an ex parte hearing does not preclude a court from granting a protection order after a full hearing."[6]

In finding that appellant's argument lacked merit, the appellate court reasoned that "[i]n a sense, the ex parte order 'merges' out of existence and 'into' the final order."[7] That is to say, a final protection order supersedes an ex parte order.[8] The final protection order comes with its own protections and determinations and does not rely on whether an ex parte order was made or made properly.[9]

Q & A: If the court declines to grant the ex parte civil protection order, does the petitioner have any recourse?

Yes. RC 3113.31(D)(3) specifically provides that "if a person who files a petition pursuant to this section does not request an ex parte order, or if a person requests an ex parte order but the court does not issue an ex parte order after an ex parte hearing, the court shall proceed as in a normal civil action and grant a full hearing on the matter."[10] Clearly, the term "shall proceed" indicates a legislative mandate.

The Greene County Court of Appeals reinforced this conclusion in *Genari v. Genari*.[11] In that case, the magistrate denied appellee's request for an ex parte civil protection order and scheduled a full hearing pursuant to RC 3113.31(D)(2)(a).

On appeal, the appellant argued that, because the trial court did not issue an ex parte order, RC 3113.31(D)(2)(a) did not apply. Therefore, the trial court abused its discretion in proceeding with the full hearing after the ex parte order was denied because it was without the authority to do so. However, the Greene County appellate court noted that RC 3113.31(D)(3) specifically applied to the facts of the case. It held that "where a petitioner for a domestic violence civil protection order has sought, but failed to obtain, an ex parte order, [R.C. 3113.31(D)(3)] expressly provides . . . that the trial court 'shall proceed as in a normal civil action and grant a full hearing on the

---

[6]Zawrotuk v. Zawrotuk, 2014-Ohio-5225, 2014 WL 6641772, ¶ 27 (Ohio Ct. App. 7th Dist. Mahoning County 2014); see also R.C. 3113.31(D)(3).

[7]See, e.g., Luttrell v. Younce, 2011-Ohio-4458, 2011 WL 3890292, ¶ 35 (Ohio Ct. App. 2d Dist. Miami County 2011).

[8]See Daugherty v. Daugherty, 2012-Ohio-1520, 2012 WL 1139129, ¶ 15 (Ohio Ct. App. 4th Dist. Hocking County 2012).

[9]Zawrotuk v. Zawrotuk, 2014-Ohio-5225, 2014 WL 6641772, ¶ 28 (Ohio Ct. App. 7th Dist. Mahoning County 2014).

[10]Caramico v. Caramico, 2015-Ohio-4232, 2015 WL 5934194 (Ohio Ct. App. 12th Dist. Clermont County 2015) (scheduled a full hearing date even though the ex parte CPO was denied).

[11]Genari v. Genari, 2001-Ohio-1524, 2001 WL 848569 (Ohio Ct. App. 2d Dist. Greene County 2001). But see Wilburn v. Wilburn, 2006-Ohio-2553, 2006 WL 1409784, *6 (Ohio Ct. App. 9th Dist. Lorain County 2006) (holding that, as a general rule, appellate courts will not rule on alleged errors that court have been raised to the trial court but were not; appellant was aware that the ex parte petitioner for civil protection order was denied, that there would be no further hearing on the matter, and that the court would be ordering mediation instead; since appellant made no objection, she has failed to preserve this issue for appeal).

matter.' Thus, when the trial court set a full hearing on [petitioner's] petition for a protection order, it was complying with the requirement of R.C. 3113.31(D)(3)."[12]

Where a civil protection order is granted ex parte, the seven or ten court day time frame controls, depending on the nature of the relief requested.[13] However, when a protection order is not filed ex parte, the statute provides that "the court shall proceed as in a normal civil action."[14] Unfortunately, the legislature offers no statutory guidance relative to whether a court must comply with the time frame set forth in RC 3113.31(D)(2)(a) or proceed in accordance with the Ohio Rules of Civil Procedure.[15] Without a statutory mandate, compliance may be effected by following either the dictates of RC 3113.31(D)(2)(a) or the Rules of Civil Procedure regarding service.

Where an ex parte protection order is either not requested or denied, there is little consistency around the state as to the time frame in which a full hearing is held. If the petitioner chooses not to file a civil protection order ex parte, it is likely that certified or express mail, ordinary mail, or even service by publication or posting would be acceptable to the court.[16] If certified or express mail or posting service is permitted, a full hearing is usually scheduled within a reasonable time and in compliance with the Ohio Rules of Civil Procedure.[17] However, if the court schedules the full hearing within the seven or ten court day time frame, personal service is often required.[18]

Whenever an ex parte civil protection order is denied, the full hearing should always be scheduled within the seven or ten court day time frame. If not, counsel should either request compliance with RC 3113.31(D)(2)(a) for an earlier date or ask that the court advance the hearing date,[19] especially when a petitioner may be at risk for future harm. Scheduling a full hearing within a short period of time is necessary because the nature of domestic violence demands swift and immediate action.

---

[12]Genari v. Genari, 2001-Ohio-1524, 2001 WL 848569, *3 (Ohio Ct. App. 2d Dist. Greene County 2001).

[13]RC 3113.31(D)(2)(a).

[14]RC 3113.31(D)(3). See also Skiles v. Dearth, 2000 WL 1838747 (Ohio Ct. App. 2d Dist. Clark County 2000) (noting that if an ex parte order was not issued in a RC 3113.31 proceeding, then a Civ. R. 13(A) would not be "clearly inapplicable" to an action brought under that section because in that circumstance, a respondent would have the full 28 days to respond with an answer and counterclaim as provided in the civil rules, since RC 3113.31(D)(3) provides that . . . if the court does not issue an ex parte order after an ex parte hearing, the court shall proceed as in a normal civil action and grant a full hearing on the matter." At *4).

[15]See Civ.R. 4.1, Civ.R. 4.4, Civ.R. 4.6.

[16]See Text § 11:22, Ex parte protection orders—Miscellaneous issues.

[17]See RC 3113.31(D)(3). See also Text § 11:10, Ex parte protection orders—Legal standard for issuance, Text § 11:11, Ex parte protection orders—Service and notice provisions, and Text § 11:21, Ex parte protection orders—Continuances.

[18]See RC 3113.31(F)(1).

[19]See Text § 11:11, Ex parte protection orders—Service and notice provisions, and Text § 11:21, Ex parte protection orders—Continuances.

Of importance is that even if the ex parte civil protection order is denied, this does not prohibit the court from issuing the protection order after the full hearing.[20]

For example, in *Genari v. Genari*,[21] the magistrate denied the ex parte hearing and scheduled the full hearing within 10 days as provided in RC 3113.31(D)(2)(a). Since neither party objected to the time frame, it is probable that the magistrate followed local court practice in adhering to the customary time limits set forth in RC 3113.31(D)(2)(a), rather than within a reasonable time or pursuant to the Ohio Rules of Civil Procedure.

Q & A: Does the expiration of an ex parte order affect the trial court's jurisdiction to grant a CPO after a full hearing?

In *Barrow v. Brown*,[22] petitioner sought a CPO on September 1, 2016. After several delays, she filed a motion to terminate the ex parte CPO on January 18, 2017. On February 7, 2017, the trial court held a full hearing on the petition as well as on her termination motion. On February 14, 2017, the trial court granted the CPO after the full hearing.

On appeal, respondent argued that the ex parte CPO should have expired, by its own terms, prior to the full hearing.

The appellate court determined that, even if true, the trial court retained jurisdiction to proceed with the hearing on the petition and to issue the final order that it did.[23] The court relied on *McDaniel v. McDaniel* in which the 12th District Court of Appeals held that "[t]he expiration of an ex parte order does not affect the trial court's jurisdiction to grant a CPO after a full hearing is held."[24]

While it is best practice to request an extension if the ex parte CPO is set to expire before the full hearing, at least two appellate courts appear to indicate that a trial court still retains jurisdiction to grant a full hearing order even though the ex parte order may have expired before the actual hearing.[25]

Q & A: How is the term "full hearing" defined?

Although the statute does not define "full hearing," it clearly sets forth the legislative intent that "[t]he court shall give the respondent notice of, and an opportunity to be heard at, the full hearing."[26]

---

[20]Zawrotuk v. Zawrotuk, 2014-Ohio-5225, 2014 WL 6641772 (Ohio Ct. App. 7th Dist. Mahoning County 2014).

[21]Genari v. Genari, 2001-Ohio-1524, 2001 WL 848569 (Ohio Ct. App. 2d Dist. Greene County 2001).

[22]Barrow v. Brown, 2017-Ohio-7926, 2017 WL 4329767 (Ohio Ct. App. 2d Dist. Greene County 2017).

[23]Barrow v. Brown, 2017-Ohio-7926, ¶ 4, 2017 WL 4329767 (Ohio Ct. App. 2d Dist. Greene County 2017).

[24]Barrow v. Brown, 2017-Ohio-7926, ¶ 4, 2017 WL 4329767 (Ohio Ct. App. 2d Dist. Greene County 2017); quoting, McDaniel v. McDaniel, 2002-Ohio-6111, ¶ 20, 2002 WL 31502097 (Ohio Ct. App. 12th Dist. Warren County 2002).

[25]See also Zawrotuk v. Zawrotuk, 2014-Ohio-5225, 2014 WL 6641772 (Ohio Ct. App. 7th Dist. Mahoning County 2014).

[26]RC 3113.31(D)(2)(a). See Evans v. Evans, 2008-Ohio-5695, 2008 WL 4787582 (Ohio Ct. App. 10th Dist. Franklin County 2008) (trial court did not have an affirmative duty to inquire whether appellant had received proper notice of the full hearing.

Many Ohio cases have interpreted the meaning of "full hearing." In *Stanton v. Guerrero*,[27] the Montgomery County Court of Appeals found that "It is reasonably clear to us that the term 'full hearing' is used in RC 3113.31 to distinguish the ultimate trial from the pretrial ex parte hearing. . . . the words 'full hearing' as used in RC 3113.31 mean the same thing as the word 'trial' as used in the Civil Rules."[28]

Other Ohio cases have analyzed the term "full hearing" in the constitutional context. In *Deacon v. Landers*,[29] the Ross County Court of Appeals held that "[a] 'full hearing' [for due process purposes] is one in which ample opportunity is afforded to all parties to make, by evidence and argument, a showing fairly adequate to establish the propriety or impropriety of the step asked to be taken." The court found that there were no reported cases that defined the parameters of a "full hearing."[30] When a case is contested, a full hearing contemplates the presentation of evidence, both direct and rebuttal arguments.[31] Other jurisdictions have determined that a "full hearing" embraces not only the right to present evidence, but also a reasonable opportunity to know the claims of an opposing party and to meet them.[32]

In *Terrell v. Terrell*,[33] the court conducted a full hearing in accordance with the directives set forth in RC 3113.31(D)(2)(a) regarding domestic violence and other relief in the nature of temporary support.

"Because Walter neither objected nor sought a continuance, we conclude that Walter failed to preserve any alleged error regarding the lack of notice." at *2); see also Butcher v. Stevens, 182 Ohio App. 3d 77, 2009-Ohio-1754, 911 N.E.2d 928 (4th Dist. Athens County 2009).

[27]Stanton v. Guerrero, 1994 WL 472104, *2 (Ohio Ct. App. 2d Dist. Montgomery County 1994); see also Black's Law Dictionary (5th ed.).

[28]See also Burnett v. Burnett, 2012-Ohio-2673, 2012 WL 2196336 (Ohio Ct. App. 6th Dist. Sandusky County 2012).

[29]Deacon v. Landers, 68 Ohio App. 3d 26, 30, 587 N.E.2d 395 (4th Dist. Ross County 1990).

[30]Deacon v. Landers, 68 Ohio App. 3d 26, 587 N.E.2d 395 (4th Dist. Ross County 1990); see also Lindsay v. Jackson, 2000 WL 1268810, *3 (Ohio Ct. App. 1st Dist. Hamilton County 2000) (stating that "where the issuance of a protection order is contested the court must, at the very least, allow for presentation of evidence, both direct and rebuttal, as well as arguments."). See also Spigos v. Spigos, 2004-Ohio-757, 2004 WL 308098, *3 (Ohio Ct. App. 10th Dist. Franklin County 2004) (reversing the trial court and holding that "where the issuance of a protection order is contested, the court must at the very least, allow for presentation of evidence, both direct and rebuttal, as well as arguments.").

[31]Deacon v. Landers, 68 Ohio App. 3d 26, 30, 587 N.E.2d 395 (4th Dist. Ross County 1990) (discussing whether a closing argument is warranted). See also Hamper v. Dobrski, 2015-Ohio-1381, 2015 WL 1593249 (Ohio Ct. App. 8th Dist. Cuyahoga County 2015) (including the opportunity to call witnesses and noting that while the magistrate had first relied on Local R. 12 in precluding the parties from calling witnesses, she reversed her decision after the matter had been continued and permitted the parties to present witnesses).

[32]Deacon v. Landers, 68 Ohio App. 3d 26, 587 N.E.2d 395 (4th Dist. Ross County 1990); see also Mechtel v. Mechtel, 528 N.W.2d 916 (Minn. Ct. App. 1995) (noting that the mere appearance of counsel, without acceptance of any evidence, is insufficient to satisfy the full hearing requirement); Morgan v. U.S., 304 U.S. 1, 18, 58 S. Ct. 773, 776, 82 L. Ed. 1129, 1 Lab. Cas. (CCH) P 17033, 1 Lab. Cas. (CCH) P 17037 (1938).

[33]Terrell v. Terrell, 2003-Ohio-150, 2003 WL 125013 (Ohio Ct. App. 8th Dist. Cuyahoga County 2003).

The trial court permitted the parties to inquire about the amount of money that came into the marriage and precluded both parties from inquiring as to of the spending habits of the other and of the wife's possible motives.[34] On appeal, the appellant argued that the trial court failed to allow the appellant the opportunity to introduce certain evidence at the full hearing.

The Cuyahoga County Court of Appeals affirmed the trial court decision and held that because the amount of money coming into the marriage on a monthly basis was the only relevant inquiry for a temporary support determination, the court did not abuse its discretion in precluding evidence of wife's spending habits or her possible financial motives for filing the action.[35]

In a dissenting opinion, Justice O'Donnell focused the issue on whether, by failing to permit appellant an opportunity to present evidence as to his wife's spending habits or her motives, "the trial court afforded Clarence a 'full hearing' as provided in R.C. 3113.31(D)(2)(a)."[36] He relied on *Deacon v. Landers*,[37] to buttress the argument that, "where the issuance of a protection order is contested, the court must, at the very least, allow for presentation of evidence, both direct and rebuttal, as well as arguments."[38] He believed that the trial court abused its discretion in denying the husband an opportunity to cross-examine the wife on her spending habits and finances that could have related to his claim that the wife had financial motives to accuse him of domestic violence.[39]

In *Tarini v. Tarini*,[40] the petitioner-appellant appealed the judgment of the trial court denying his request for a CPO. In this case, the issue was that the trial court denied petitioner-appellant the opportunity to complete his case. Midway through the direct examina-

---

[34]Terrell v. Terrell, 2003-Ohio-150, 2003 WL 125013, *3 (Ohio Ct. App. 8th Dist. Cuyahoga County 2003). See State v. Younker, 2002-Ohio-5376, 2002 WL 31242238 (Ohio Ct. App. 2d Dist. Darke County 2002) (reversing conviction because trial court failed to permit defendant to cross-examine complainant about the pending divorce action).

[35]Terrell v. Terrell, 2003-Ohio-150, 2003 WL 125013, *3 (Ohio Ct. App. 8th Dist. Cuyahoga County 2003).

[36]Terrell v. Terrell, 2003-Ohio-150, 2003 WL 125013, *5 (Ohio Ct. App. 8th Dist. Cuyahoga County 2003).

[37]Deacon v. Landers, 68 Ohio App. 3d 26, 29–30, 587 N.E.2d 395 (4th Dist. Ross County 1990) (where a "full hearing" for domestic violence purposes is defined as one in which ample opportunity is afforded to all parties to make, by evidence and argument, a showing fairly adequate to establish the propriety or impropriety of the step asked to be taken).

[38]Terrell v. Terrell, 2003-Ohio-150, 2003 WL 125013, *6 (Ohio Ct. App. 8th Dist. Cuyahoga County 2003), quoting Deacon v. Landers, 68 Ohio App. 3d 26, 29–30, 587 N.E.2d 395 (4th Dist. Ross County 1990); see also Solon v. Geiger, 2006-Ohio-6032, 2006 WL 3317920 (Ohio Ct. App. 8th Dist. Cuyahoga County 2006) (full hearing same under RC 2903.214 as if under RC 3113.31).

[39]Terrell v. Terrell, 2003-Ohio-150, 2003 WL 125013, *6 (Ohio Ct. App. 8th Dist. Cuyahoga County 2003).

[40]Tarini v. Tarini, 2012-Ohio-6165, 2012 WL 6738317 (Ohio Ct. App. 10th Dist. Franklin County 2012); E.W. v. T.W., 2017-Ohio-8504, ¶ 42, 2017 WL 5192035 (Ohio Ct. App. 10th Dist. Franklin County 2017) (dissent admonished majority for not sustaining respondent's error in that trial court did not allow him to question petitioner or present any evidence or defense or engaging in any argument).

tion of petitioner, "the court stated: 'All right. I'm going to stop you at this point. You have met the threshold and I'm going to turn it over to [respondent's counsel] to put on your case in chief and rebuttal. I'm doing this because this is going to go on forever. It's not necessary at this point.' (Tr. 116)."[41] Petitioner's attorney was assured by the court that he could call the petitioner back to the stand "to redirect based upon his cross."[42] However, after the respondent rested his case, petitioner's counsel was told that he had met his threshold and because of this, he only asked a few questions. Counsel for petitioner did not rest his case until the court admonished him that he had, in fact, rested his case. After denying petitioner's CPO, counsel for petitioner appealed, asserting that he was not able to complete his case in chief or his rebuttal evidence.

In sustaining the assignment of error, the appellate relied on *Deacon v. Landers*, holding that "a full hearing generally 'is one in which ample opportunity is afforded to all parties to make, by evidence and argument, a showing fairly adequate to establish the propriety or impropriety of the step to be taken.' "[43] " '[W]here the issuance of a protection order is contested, the court must, at the very least, allow for presentation of evidence, both direct and rebuttal, as well as arguments.' "[44]

Of significance is that the appellate court also stated that, "even if the trial court's refusal to allow petitioner to present direct and rebuttal evidence is in itself not sufficient to deprive petitioner of due process, the trial court's actions during the hearing, coupled with the judgment entry terminating the action, demonstrate a due process violation. During the hearing, the court assured petitioner he had met his threshold and then gave respondent the opportunity to present evidence. In using 'threshold,' the court can be understood only as informing petitioner he presented a prima facie case entitling him to a civil protection order; the court otherwise would have had no reason to allow respondent to proceed with his case-in-chief. Yet, in the judgment entry terminating the action, the court concluded petitioner failed to present a prima facie case. We, then, are left with the trial court's having denied petitioner the opportunity to present additional

[41]Tarini v. Tarini, 2012-Ohio-6165, ¶ 5, 2012 WL 6738317 (Ohio Ct. App. 10th Dist. Franklin County 2012).

[42]Tarini v. Tarini, 2012-Ohio-6165, ¶ 6, 2012 WL 6738317 (Ohio Ct. App. 10th Dist. Franklin County 2012).

[43]Tarini v. Tarini, 2012-Ohio-6165, ¶ 14, 2012 WL 6738317 (Ohio Ct. App. 10th Dist. Franklin County 2012), quoting Deacon v. Landers, 68 Ohio App. 3d 26, 30, 587 N.E.2d 395 (4th Dist. Ross County 1990); see also Burnett v. Burnett, 2012-Ohio-2673, 2012 WL 2196336 (Ohio Ct. App. 6th Dist. Sandusky County 2012); [D.M.W.] v. [E.W.], 2018-Ohio-821, ¶ 13, 2018 WL 1169656 (Ohio Ct. App. 10th Dist. Franklin County 2018) (the trial court's failure to conduct a full hearing as contemplated by RC 3113.31 constitutes reversible plain error).

[44]Tarini v. Tarini, 2012-Ohio-6165, ¶ 14, 2012 WL 6738317 (Ohio Ct. App. 10th Dist. Franklin County 2012), quoting Deacon v. Landers, 68 Ohio App. 3d 26, 30, 587 N.E.2d 395 (4th Dist. Ross County 1990); H.C. v. R.C., 2016-Ohio-668, 2016 WL 716253 (Ohio Ct. App. 10th Dist. Franklin County 2016) (sustaining assignment of error and holding that a full hearing is one in which a party is entitled to call witnesses and present a closing argument; the absence of which constitutes reversible plain error).

evidence but dismissing his request for civil protection order because his evidence did not establish a prima facie case for such an order."[45]

This focus on "threshold" and whether petitioner presented a prima facie case appears to be more important to the appellate court's reasoning than the fact that petitioner was denied the opportunity to adequately present his case, based on the representations of the trier of fact.

§ 12:2 Full hearing—Scheduling and filing issues[1]

The domestic violence statute specifies a time frame within which to schedule a full hearing after the issuance of an ex parte order. RC 3113.31(D)(2)(a)[2] provides in part:

> If the court, after an ex parte hearing, issues an order described in division (E)(1)(b) or (c) of this section, the court shall schedule a full hearing for a date that is within seven court days after the ex parte hearing.[3] If any other type of protection order that is authorized under division (E) of this section is issued by the court after an ex parte hearing, the court shall schedule a full hearing for a date that is within ten court days after the ex parte hearing.[4]

If an ex parte protection order ordered the respondent to vacate the residence,[5] the full hearing is scheduled within seven court days. If a respondent is out of the residence but has an interest in the property by way of a legal or equitable interest, a full hearing should be scheduled in seven days. If the ex parte order provided for any remedy other than eviction from the residence, the full hearing is scheduled within ten court days. Whether the hearing will be scheduled on the seventh or tenth day, or any time in between, will be determined by the local court jurisdiction.[6]

Q & A: Does the statute require the court to hold a full hearing on the issuance of a CPO within seven court days whenever a petitioner requests exclusive use of the marital residence?

---

[45]Tarini v. Tarini, 2012-Ohio-6165, ¶ 20, 2012 WL 6738317 (Ohio Ct. App. 10th Dist. Franklin County 2012).

[Section 12:2]

[1]See also Text § 12:4, Full hearing—Continuances; Text § 11:21, Ex parte protection orders—Continuances.

[2]See Glenn v. Glenn, 2009-Ohio-1345, 2009 WL 765480, *3 (Ohio Ct. App. 5th Dist. Stark County 2009) (finding that "within ten court days does not mean within ten calendar days" and "[w]e interpret the language 'court days' to mean the court's business days").

[3]But see Donoghue v. Donoghue, 2009-Ohio-3834, 2009 WL 2374416 (Ohio Ct. App. 5th Dist. Fairfield County 2009) (affirming trial court decision granting full hearing even though it was held eight days after ex parte hearing. Even with "shall" as the operative verb, a statutory time provision may be directory, especially where the statute fixes the time simply for convenience or orderly procedure. at *2).

[4]But see Yun v. Yun, 2003-Ohio-2644, 2003 WL 21185852 (Ohio Ct. App. 5th Dist. Stark County 2003) (indicating that the appellant could have pursued a Civ.R. 6(B) argument as part of his objections to the magistrate's decision, but failed to raise the issue).

[5]See RC 3113.31(E)(1)(b), RC 3113.31(E)(1)(c).

[6]See for example Sigler v. Arvay, 2002-Ohio-6762, 2002 WL 31761478 (Ohio Ct. App. 9th Dist. Summit County 2002).

Yes, according to *Lupica v. Lupica*.[7] In that case, the trial court awarded petitioner exclusive possession of the marital home and set a full hearing within ten court days. At the full hearing, respondent's attorney moved to dismiss the ex parte order, arguing that R.C. 3113.31(D)(2)(a) mandates that a hearing be set within seven court days when an individual is ordered away from the marital residence. Petitioner's attorney responded that under the terms of respondent's probation, he was already barred from the residence.

On appeal, respondent asserted that because he was not voluntarily vacated from the residence, the hearing should have been set within seven court days. The appellate court agreed and held that "[t]his seven-court day provision contemplates that a full hearing is necessary when the court grants the petitioner *sole* occupancy of the residence."[8]

Q & A: Must the full hearing be held on the date that it is scheduled?

RC 3113.31 specifically states that "[t]he court shall hold the full hearing on the date scheduled under this division unless the court grants a continuance of the hearing in accordance with this division."[9] However, the statute fails to define the term "hold" for purposes of a full hearing. *Black's Law Dictionary* defines "hold" as "to conduct or preside at."[10]

That the legislature emphasized that the full hearing shall be held on the day it is scheduled, unless continued, indicates a clear direction or mandate. This requirement is further reflected in the terminology used by the Ohio General Assembly. *Black's Law Dictionary* defines the word "shall" as "generally imperative or mandatory . . . a word of command."[11]

For example, in *Donoghue v. Donoghue*,[12] the appellant filed a Motion to Dismiss the full hearing civil protection order because it was issued on the 8th day after the ex parte order was granted. On ap-

[7]Lupica v. Lupica, 2011-Ohio-5664, 2011 WL 5320671 (Ohio Ct. App. 8th Dist. Cuyahoga County 2011).

[8]Lupica v. Lupica, 2011-Ohio-5664, 2011 WL 5320671, *3 (Ohio Ct. App. 8th Dist. Cuyahoga County 2011) (emphasis added).

[9]RC 3113.31(D)(2)(a). Wheeler v. Wheeler, 2015-Ohio-4206, 2015 WL 5918030 (Ohio Ct. App. 4th Dist. Scioto County 2015) (finding that while a full hearing should be conducted with seven days following the ex parte hearing, a trial court might need to extend the time in order to be fair to one or both of the parties and that a court has discretion to continue the case). But see State v. Blaine, 2004-Ohio-1241, 2004 WL 524667 (Ohio Ct. App. 4th Dist. Highland County 2004) (a continuance of full hearing for two months and 12 days is an abuse of discretion without a showing by the court of good cause); Berry v. Patrick, 2005-Ohio-3708, 2005 WL 1707005 (Ohio Ct. App. 8th Dist. Cuyahoga County 2005) (noting that an ex parte CPO may be continued to a "reasonable period of time determined by the court" for a lack of service; court held that the trial court's actions in conducting full hearing over two months after filing, in failing to rule on the motion for a CPO until six months after the conclusion of the hearing, and not journalizing the final ruling until 13 months after requesting the order is an abuse of discretion).

[10]Black's Law Dictionary (6th ed.) p 731.

[11]Black's Law Dictionary (6th ed.) p 1375.

[12]Donoghue v. Donoghue, 2009-Ohio-3834, 2009 WL 2374416 (Ohio Ct. App. 5th Dist. Fairfield County 2009). See also Doran v. Doran, 2015-Ohio-2369, 2015 WL 3765602 (Ohio Ct. App. 5th Dist. Licking County 2015).

peal, he argued that the trial court erred when it overruled his motion to dismiss the CPO because of the court's failure to conduct a full hearing within seven days as required by statute.[13] He also argued that the time frame within which to hold a full hearing was mandatory and the failure to conduct a full hearing within the prescribed time frame renders the five year protection order void.

The 5th District Court of Appeals noted that 'shall' will often be construed as mandatory.[14] "A mandatory statue may be defined as one where noncompliance * * * will render the proceedings to which it relates illegal and void."[15] However, when used in the context of a time frame, the time frame may be directory. "As a general rule, a statute providing a time for performance of an official duty will be construed as directory as far as time for performance is concerned, especially where the statute fixes the time simply for convenience or orderly procedure."[16] "This rule applies "unless the object or purpose of a statutory provision requiring some act to be performed within a specified period of time is discernible from the language employed.""[17] In effect, only where a time frame evinces a purpose to limit a court's authority will it be considered jurisdictional.[18]

The appellate court then held that because RC 3113.31(D) is a time restriction on a performance of an official duty and does not express an intent to restrict the jurisdiction of the court for untimeliness, the trial court's failure to follow time constraints does not render the CPO void.[19]

It must also be noted that that the court stressed that because appellant failed to timely file his appeal, he may not now collaterally attack the grant of the CPO by appealing the denial of his motion to dismiss the CPO.[20]

The importance of these cases cannot be ignored. The policy significance is that prompt hearing requirements do not mean a complete procedural bar to judicial access. As noted above, it may only represent a time limitation on the duration of the ex parte order. When a trial court fails to set the full hearing within the mandated time limits, it may only mean that the ex parte protection order expires

---

[13]See RC 3113.31(D).

[14]At *2; citing, Dorrian v. Scioto Conservancy Dist., 27 Ohio St. 2d 102, 56 Ohio Op. 2d 58, 271 N.E.2d 834 (1971).

[15]At *2; quoting State ex rel. Jones v. Farrar, 146 Ohio St. 467, 471–472, 32 Ohio Op. 542, 66 N.E.2d 531 (1946).

[16]At *2; quoting Farrar, at paragraph three of syllabus. See also Doran v. Doran, 2015-Ohio-2369, 2015 WL 3765602 (Ohio Ct. App. 5th Dist. Licking County 2015).

[17]At *2.

[18]At *2.

[19]At *2. Doran v. Doran, 2015-Ohio-2369, 2015 WL 3765602 (Ohio Ct. App. 5th Dist. Licking County 2015). See also dissent in Glenn v. Glenn, 2009-Ohio-1345, 2009 WL 765480 (Ohio Ct. App. 5th Dist. Stark County 2009) (noting that the trial court's failure to hold the full hearing within 10 court days does not divest it of subject matter jurisdiction).

[20]At *2.

and the case assumes the posture of a case in which no ex parte order has been issued.[21]

A plain reading of RC 3113.31 in no way suggests that the legislature intended for a court to lose its jurisdiction if it does not act on the matter within the seven-or-ten day time frame; that the protection order would lose its efficacy; or that the court would lose jurisdiction to issue the order subsequently.[22] Additionally, the fact that the legislature authorized a court to issue a non-ex parte protection order reinforces the notion that jurisdiction is retained even if a full hearing is not held within the requisite time frame.[23]

Q & A: Must the full hearing be concluded on the day it is set?

While it is clear that the full hearing is required to be held on the day that it is scheduled, unless otherwise continued,[24] the statute fails to indicate whether it must be concluded on the same day. Case law supports the position that, as long as some evidence is presented to the court, a court need not complete the hearing on the scheduled date. Local practice in the various courts suggests that this is the procedure most courts follow.

For example, in *O'Hara v. Dials*,[25] the Erie County Court of Appeals found that a continuance of thirty days was not an unreasonable delay where the parties agreed to a continuance because the full hearing could not be completed by the scheduled date. The court relied upon the rationale set forth in *Eichenberger v. Eichenberger*[26] when it stated: "Although in proceedings pursuant to RC 3113.31 the scheduling of 'hearings to determine the validity of . . . temporary orders should be given priority,' necessary continuances 'for reasonable, limited periods of time' do not jeopardize the integrity or constitutionality of the proceedings or constitute prejudicial error."[27] The *O'Hara* court concluded that the delay did not prejudice the respondent. However, the court indicated that the delay of the final hearing was due to the continuance agreed to by both parties. Had the respondent objected to a continuance of the full hearing, it is not clear whether the court would have delayed the hearing or allowed additional time to complete the hearing.

Similarly, one appellate court has recognized that a trial court may

---

[21]See Kite v. Kite, 22 S.W.3d 803 (Tenn. 1997).

[22]See Baugus v. Baugus, 1997 WL 207984, *1 (Tenn. Ct. App. 1997).

[23]See RC 3113.31(D)(3).

[24]See RC 3113.31(D)(2)(a).

[25]O'Hara v. Dials, 1996 WL 38810, *4 (Ohio Ct. App. 6th Dist. Erie County 1996) (abrogated by, Felton v. Felton, 79 Ohio St. 3d 34, 1997-Ohio-302, 679 N.E.2d 672 (1997)).

[26]Eichenberger v. Eichenberger, 82 Ohio App. 3d 809, 613 N.E.2d 678 (10th Dist. Franklin County 1992); see also Sterling v. Sterling, 2002-Ohio-4997, 2002 WL 31111778 (Ohio Ct. App. 5th Dist. Fairfield County 2002) (where the appellate court found no error in continuing the domestic violence full hearing beyond the statutory 10-day time period while awaiting the resolution of certain matters in another county given that similar issues were being litigated in that county).

[27]O'Hara v. Dials, 1996 WL 38810, *4 (Ohio Ct. App. 6th Dist. Erie County 1996) (abrogated by, Felton v. Felton, 79 Ohio St. 3d 34, 1997-Ohio-302, 679 N.E.2d 672 (1997)).

have a heavy docket, preventing it from concluding the hearing. In *Eichenberger v. Eichenberger*,[28] the court discussed this issue in depth when it said: "Given the present docket responsibilities of trial judges in a major metropolitan area, continuances for reasonable, limited periods of time are necessary. The trial court did, in fact, conduct extended proceedings on the seventh day after the action was filed but was unable to complete the hearing."

Both of these court opinions reveal a willingness to adapt the intricacies of procedure to the realities of a court docket. Provided that the rights of the parties are not unduly prejudiced, completing the full hearing on another day is allowable and, in some cases, both practical and necessary.

Q & A: Must a respondent be present for the full hearing?

Not according to the Eighth District Court of Appeals in *Rielinger v. Rielinger*.[29] In that case, the appellant claimed that the magistrate's decision not to grant her a continuance was in error. The court of appeals reviewed the statutory factors for a continuance in RC 3113.31(D)(2)(a)(i) to (iv) and determined that the only ground to grant a continuance under the facts presented was "for other good cause." The appellate court then applied the factors set forth in *State v. Unger*,[30] to the facts and found that appellant had already filed several continuances and that another continuance would have caused great inconvenience for the witnesses who included a school counselor and the minor child.

In affirming the trial court, the appellate court reasoned that "there is no statutory right to be present at the full hearing, although preferable in circumstances such as these."[31] Moreover, her counsel was still able to cross-examine witnesses and had the opportunity to present witnesses herself should she have chosen to do so. Finally, the parties had set the date for the hearing together.

Q & A: I represent the respondent in a protection order hearing. Must I file an answer?

There is no statutory requirement that a responsive pleading or answer be filed. In fact, the time constraints of the domestic violence statute are such that the filing of an answer would hinder the immediacy of the order and the full hearing.[32] However, some jurisdictions permit the filing of an answer.[33]

Even if an answer is permitted, the Ohio Supreme Court, in *Felton*

[28]Eichenberger v. Eichenberger, 82 Ohio App. 3d 809, 816, 613 N.E.2d 678 (10th Dist. Franklin County 1992).

[29]Rielinger v. Rielinger, 2009-Ohio-1236, 2009 WL 714185 (Ohio Ct. App. 8th Dist. Cuyahoga County 2009).

[30]State v. Unger, 67 Ohio St. 2d 65, 21 Ohio Op. 3d 41, 423 N.E.2d 1078 (1981).

[31]Rielinger v. Rielinger, 2009-Ohio-1236, 2009 WL 714185, *4 (Ohio Ct. App. 8th Dist. Cuyahoga County 2009).

[32]See Skiles v. Dearth, 2000 WL 1838747 (Ohio Ct. App. 2d Dist. Clark County 2000) (court held that the compulsory counterclaim rule is clearly inapplicable to proceedings governing petitions for ex parte civil protection orders, suggesting that a party may file an answer and counterclaim but is not obligated to do so and stating that if an ex parte CPO was not issued, a party would have time to file an answer and counterclaim because he/she would have the full 28 days).

[33]Snyder v. Snyder, 1995 WL 493998 (Ohio Ct. App. 4th Dist. Ross County 1995).

v. Felton,[34] determined that the court may not rely on a pleading as evidence to controvert the petitioner's testimony.[35] The Court held that "a pleading is not admissible into evidence at a hearing to prove a party's allegations and must not be considered as evidence by the court."[36]

Q & A: Can a hearing officer base the decision to grant a civil protection order partly on the petition, despite the fact that the petitioner failed to testify to certain facts?

The Seventh District Court of Appeals considered this issue in *Caban v. Ransome*.[37] In that case, the petitioner-appellee was granted a civil stalking protection order. The call in question gave petitioner "a deadline to contact him, opined that he would find her wherever she was, warned that 'all bets are off' and seemed confident that she would talk to him this time."[38] The issue on appeal was whether the call combined with appellant's previous conduct actually caused petitioner the kind of mental distress required by the statutory definition.

On appeal, the respondent argued that there was no competent, credible evidence on the elements of menacing by stalking, which is a prerequisite for granting a civil stalking protection order. While the magistrate heard evidence from the petitioner who testified that she had received messages from appellant asking why their long-term relationship ended, she never testified that these calls caused her stress "[n]or did she mention any stress reactions that could qualify as temporary substantial incapacity or that would lead one to seek mental health services."[39]

The appellate court considered that petitioner failed to present testimony that she suffered actual mental distress or that she suffered any stress reactions that would lead her to seek mental health counseling and determined only that petitioner was sick of appellant's annoyingly obsessive behavior.[40] The court then reasoned that although the calls may constitute telephone harassment, they do not by themselves establish mental distress was actually suffered."[41]

Additionally, the appellate court pointed out that the magistrate

---

[34]Felton v. Felton, 79 Ohio St. 3d 34, 1997-Ohio-302, 679 N.E.2d 672 (1997).

[35]See also Caban v. Ransome, 2009-Ohio-1034, 2009 WL 582761 (Ohio Ct. App. 7th Dist. Mahoning County 2009).

[36]Felton v. Felton, 79 Ohio St. 3d 34, 43, 1997-Ohio-302, 679 N.E.2d 672 (1997). See also McIntyre v. Johnson-Estes, 2011-Ohio-1696, 2011 WL 1327392 (Ohio Ct. App. 8th Dist. Cuyahoga County 2011) (where petitioner did not testify, the petition is not evidence and there was no evidence for the court to consider; thus, trial court abused its discretion when it granted McIntyre the CPO without an evidentiary basis); Partin v. Morrison, 2015-Ohio-4740, 2015 WL 7293332 (Ohio Ct. App. 12th Dist. Brown County 2015).

[37]Caban v. Ransome, 2009-Ohio-1034, 2009 WL 582761 (Ohio Ct. App. 7th Dist. Mahoning County 2009).

[38]Caban v. Ransome, 2009-Ohio-1034, 2009 WL 582761, *4 (Ohio Ct. App. 7th Dist. Mahoning County 2009).

[39]Caban v. Ransome, 2009-Ohio-1034, 2009 WL 582761, *5 (Ohio Ct. App. 7th Dist. Mahoning County 2009).

[40]Caban v. Ransome, 2009-Ohio-1034, 2009 WL 582761, *5 (Ohio Ct. App. 7th Dist. Mahoning County 2009).

[41]Caban v. Ransome, 2009-Ohio-1034, 2009 WL 582761, *5 (Ohio Ct. App. 7th Dist. Mahoning County 2009).

read the petition into the record. Of importance is that the appellate court stressed that a trial court cannot base a decision to grant a civil stalking protection order at the full hearing on evidence gleaned from the petition. The court then cited *Felton*[42] for the proposition that "the petition is not evidence and its contents cannot be considered by the court in granting a petition."[43] Without sufficient testimony by petitioner at the full hearing evidencing mental distress, the appellate court reversed the granting of the CSPO and vacated the order. "In conclusion, without any mention of or allusion to her mental state in the evidence presented to the court, the fairly stringent test of mental distress has not been met under the particular facts and circumstances of this case."[44]

Q & A: Will a court dismiss a petition for a CPO at the full hearing pursuant to a Civ. R. 12(B)(6) motion to dismiss where evidence was presented that was not pled in the petition, or will the pleadings be amended to conform to the evidence presented at trial in accordance with Civ. R. 15(B)?

The issue was addressed in *Gannon v. Gannon*,[45] but a 12(B)(6) motion did not lie under this fact pattern. In this case, appellant argued that the trial court erred by failing to grant its Civ. R. 12(B)(6) motion to dismiss the CPO filed by his wife which was raised by respondent at the conclusion of the full hearing. He argued that because the language used by appellee in her petition did not state that appellant had attempted or recklessly caused bodily injury or by threat of force caused her fear of serious physical harm, the CPO should have been dismissed.

Appellee relied on Civ. R. 15(B), which provides for amendment of the pleadings to conform to the evidence on issues not pled, but tried with the express or implied consent of the parties and that her testimony at the final hearing on the petition was undisputed and clearly established acts of violence or threatened violence sufficient to demonstrate behavior by appellant within the statute. Because appellant did not object to this testimony, he impliedly consented to trial of those issues.[46]

The appellate court found appellant's error not well taken and held that, because appellant had neither objected to appellee's testimony

---

[42]Felton v. Felton, 79 Ohio St. 3d 34, 1997-Ohio-302, 679 N.E.2d 672 (1997).

[43]Caban v. Ransome, 2009-Ohio-1034, 2009 WL 582761, *5 (Ohio Ct. App. 7th Dist. Mahoning County 2009), quoting Felton v. Felton, 79 Ohio St. 3d 34, 42, 1997-Ohio-302, 679 N.E.2d 672 (1997).

[44]Caban v. Ransome, 2009-Ohio-1034, 2009 WL 582761, *6 (Ohio Ct. App. 7th Dist. Mahoning County 2009).

[45]Gannon v. Gannon, 2008-Ohio-4484, 2008 WL 4093687 (Ohio Ct. App. 6th Dist. Wood County 2008).

[46]Gannon v. Gannon, 2008-Ohio-4484, 2008 WL 4093687, *3 (Ohio Ct. App. 6th Dist. Wood County 2008); Calicoat v. Calicoat, 2009-Ohio-5869, 2009 WL 3683665 (Ohio Ct. App. 2d Dist. Miami County 2009) (service on amended CPO before full hearing provided appellant with notice and an opportunity to be heard in relation to the car chase allegations as well as past abuse. Because appellant didn't object at the time to the evidence presented concerning matters outside the petition, he may not now object on appeal).

nor sought a continuance to respond to the issues presented, he had impliedly consented to trial of the issues as set forth in Civ. R. 15(B).[47]

While the appellate court did not find that appellee's failure to use specific language in her petition was reversible error since her testimony clearly established acts of domestic violence, it is interesting that the appellate court did note that her testimony was manifestly beyond the allegations contained in her petition.[48]

Q & A: May a trial court may properly exclude testimony regarding acts of domestic violence not alleged in the petition?[49]

Several courts have held that petitioners are limited in their testimony to only the facts alleged in their petitions. For example, in *Nicola v. Nicola,*[50] In *Nicola*, the appellant filed a petition for domestic violence against respondent-appellee on behalf of her children, alleging that respondent twisted the child's arm, gave him knuckles on his head and is rough with the children, especially when he drinks. An ex parte order was granted.

At the full hearing, an officer testified that a detective was investigating the incident for criminal charges. Petitioner-appellant testified about the incident as did a day care worker who spoke with the child when his arm was in a sling. The child testified that respondent had grabbed him and pulled and twisted his arm. The child admitted he pushed respondent when respondent made comments about his weight but testified that respondent "purposely tries to hurt him because there is an incident every time he visits him."[51] Respondent testified that the child had complained about his elbow hurting when he picked him up. He also stated that the child began punching him, causing him to give a "knuckle head." He also testified that he did not know what motivated the child as he did not notice anything wrong with the arm at the end of his visitation.

The magistrate explained that, as a preliminary manner, petitioner was limited to the specific allegation of domestic violence raised in her petition and went on to say that "* * * Mr. Nicola is entitled to have notice of what he has to defend and I just want to bring that up prior to testimony being presented, because in my review of the allegations, there are specific allegations over a relatively small period of time and that's what Mr. Nicola is going to have to defend."[52] In fact, the magistrate sustained an objection when appellee began to testify about

---

[47]Gannon v. Gannon, 2008-Ohio-4484, 2008 WL 4093687, *3 (Ohio Ct. App. 6th Dist. Wood County 2008).

[48]Gannon v. Gannon, 2008-Ohio-4484, 2008 WL 4093687, *3 (Ohio Ct. App. 6th Dist. Wood County 2008). See also Lane v. Brewster, 2012-Ohio-1290, 2012 WL 1029503 (Ohio Ct. App. 12th Dist. Clermont County 2012); McGuire v. Sprinkle, 2007-Ohio-2705, 2007 WL 1585100 (Ohio Ct. App. 12th Dist. Warren County 2007); Calicoat v. Calicoat, 2009-Ohio-5869, 2009 WL 3683665 (Ohio Ct. App. 2d Dist. Miami County 2009).

[49]See Text 11:2.

[50]Nicola v. Nicola, 2015-Ohio-4017, 2015 WL 5728577 (Ohio Ct. App. 11th Dist. Lake County 2015); see also § 11:2.

[51]Nicola v. Nicola, 2015-Ohio-4017, 2015 WL 5728577, ¶ 10 (Ohio Ct. App. 11th Dist. Lake County 2015).

[52]Nicola v. Nicola, 2015-Ohio-4017, 2015 WL 5728577, ¶ 25 (Ohio Ct. App. 11th

other facts not alleged in her petition which caused petitioner to file the divorce as well as comments made by petitioner about her fear. After all relevant testimony was elicited, the magistrate issued an order dismissing the Ex Parte CPO which was then signed by the judge.

On appeal, Petitioner-appellant argued that the magistrate refused to allow both her and her son from testifying as to past acts of domestic violence or the fear of respondent. She alleged that the trial court abused its discretion because it excluded relevant and admissible evidence of past acts of domestic violence not alleged in the petition and because the evidence as presented demonstrated that the child's arm was broken by respondent-appellant, an act which constitutes domestic violence as defined by law.[53]

However, the magistrate did permit the minor child to testify without a limitation on the scope of his testimony.

The appellate court first reiterated settled law that the decision to issue a CPO lies within the discretion of the trial court[54] and that the "trial court is vested with broad discretion in determining the admissibility of evidence in any particular case, so long as such discretion is exercised in line with the rules of procedure and evidence."[55]

The Court then affirmed the trial court's decision that respondent's actions did not rise to purposeful or reckless conduct.[56] In that the trial court found respondent's testimony to be credible, the court held that there was no abuse of discretion.

The cautionary warning contained in this opinion is that it is best practice to be as thorough in detailing the nature and extent of the violence in CPO petitions.[57] Additionally, if litigants or their attorneys fail to do this, a motion to amend the petition and amended petition should be filed before the full hearing.[58] Absent that, it is quite possible that a petitioner's testimony may be limited in scope to what was alleged in the petition.

In her dissent, Judge O'Toole stressed that petitioner-appellant should not have been prevented from presenting testimony about past acts of domestic violence directed at her or the children. In that case law has found that threats of violence will constitute domestic violence if the resulting fear is reasonable, the reasonableness of that fear can be determined by the history between the parties. "And the legislative

---

Dist. Lake County 2015).

[53]Nicola v. Nicola, 2015-Ohio-4017, 2015 WL 5728577, ¶ 19 (Ohio Ct. App. 11th Dist. Lake County 2015).

[54]Hoyt v. Heindell, 191 Ohio App. 3d 373, 2010-Ohio-6058, 946 N.E.2d 258, ¶ 39 (11th Dist. Lake County 2010).

[55]Nicola v. Nicola, 2015-Ohio-4017, 2015 WL 5728577, ¶ 23 (Ohio Ct. App. 11th Dist. Lake County 2015), citing Rigby v. Lake County, 58 Ohio St. 3d 269, 271, 569 N.E.2d 1056 (1991).

[56]Nicola v. Nicola, 2015-Ohio-4017, 2015 WL 5728577, ¶ 31 (Ohio Ct. App. 11th Dist. Lake County 2015).

[57]See R.C. 3113.31(C)(1); see also Text § 11:2.

[58]See Civ. R. 15.

purpose of the domestic violence statute is best served when the trial court considers all of the relevant evidence."[59]

The dissent then pointed out that the petition was filed on behalf of both children. "If, in fact there was some evidence of prior acts of domestic violence, it was relevant, and that evidence should have been elicited."[60] Therefore, "evidence of prior acts of violence toward a petitioner or other family members is admissible to prove that a petitioner and his or her children are at risk of harm."[61]

Q & A: What options would have been available if a petitioner had been prevented from testifying or if the scope of the testimony had been limited?

"It is well established that the admission of or exclusion of relevant evidence is within the discretion of the trial court, Further, a trial court is given great deference in controlling its docket."[62]

That said, where a trial court excludes evidence sought to be presented in a party's case-in-chief, that party is required to make an offer of proof. "Specifically, Evid. R. 103(A)(2) provides that error may not be predicated upon a ruling excluding evidence unless a substantial right of the party is thereby affected and the substance of the excluded evidence was made known to the court by proffer or was apparent from the context within which questions were asked."[63]

"A proffer generally consists of two elements. "First, the offering party must inform the trial court as to the legal theory upon which admissibility is proposed. Second, an offering party must show what a witness was expected to testify to and what that evidence would have proven or tended to have proven.""[64] "While the proffer of the expected testimony need not be as specific as the testimony itself would have been[,] it must nonetheless be sufficient to enable the reviewing court to determine roughly what, if any, impact the testimony may have had upon the final disposition of the case."[65]

The intent of a proffer is to assist the reviewing court in determining whether the trial court's exclusion of certain evidence affected a substantial right of the offering party.[66] Thus, it is an important tool for an attorney to have in their tool box as it has proven useful in a given case.

---

[59]Nicola v. Nicola, 2015-Ohio-4017, 2015 WL 5728577, ¶ 35 (Ohio Ct. App. 11th Dist. Lake County 2015), quoting Shockey v. Shockey, 2008-Ohio-6797, ¶ 20, 2008 WL 5340554 (Ohio Ct. App. 5th Dist. Delaware County 2008).

[60]Nicola v. Nicola, 2015-Ohio-4017, 2015 WL 5728577, ¶ 36(Ohio Ct. App. 11th Dist. Lake County 2015).

[61]Nicola v. Nicola, 2015-Ohio-4017, 2015 WL 5728577, ¶ 36 (Ohio Ct. App. 11th Dist. Lake County 2015), citing Parrish v. Parrish, 95 Ohio St. 3d 1201, 1207–1208, 2002-Ohio-1623, 765 N.E.2d 359 (2002).

[62]Heath v. Heath, 2017-Ohio-5506, ¶ 24-25, 2017 WL 2730298 (Ohio Ct. App. 12th Dist. Fayette County 2017); Evid. R. 611(A).

[63]Heath v. Heath, 2017-Ohio-5506, ¶ 26, 2017 WL 2730298 (Ohio Ct. App. 12th Dist. Fayette County 2017).

[64]Heath v. Heath, 2017-Ohio-5506, ¶ 27, 2017 WL 2730298 (Ohio Ct. App. 12th Dist. Fayette County 2017), quoting, Moser v. Moser, 72 Ohio App. 3d 575, 580, 595 N.E.2d 518 (3d Dist. Allen County 1991).

[65]Heath v. Heath, 2017-Ohio-5506, ¶ 27, 2017 WL 2730298 (Ohio Ct. App. 12th Dist. Fayette County 2017), quoting *Moser* at 580.

[66]Heath v. Heath, 2017-Ohio-5506, ¶ 28, 2017 WL 2730298 (Ohio Ct. App. 12th

§ 12:3 Full hearing—Participation of the parties

If the respondent appears at the full hearing, the parties may negotiate a settlement. If that happens, the parties enter into what is called a consent agreement. In effect, this means that they have agreed to certain terms.[1] By statute, a consent agreement is a protection order and is enforced in the same manner as any other civil protection order.[2] The respondent may agree to be bound by the terms of the original ex parte order. The parties may agree to modify or delete certain terms or may even consider additional terms. Whatever the terms agreed to by the parties and reduced to writing, both parties must understand that they are bound by the terms as written.

If the parties fail to reach an agreement, the judge or magistrate will conduct a full hearing at which the petitioner will present her/his case and the respondent will defend against the allegations. The court will ultimately decide whether the evidence presented supports the issuance of the protection order. If the court determines that petitioner has proven his/her case, it will incorporate the terms of the initial ex parte order into a new protection order. Based on the testimony presented, it is within the court's discretion to modify any or all of the existing terms of the initial order. A court may also dismiss the protection order if it concludes that the protection order should not have been granted or that petitioner has failed to prove her/his case.

Oftentimes, a respondent fails to appear at the full hearing. Provided that there is service on the respondent, the court will usually grant to the petitioner the relief sought. Sometimes, the court summarily maintains the order without requiring any additional testimony. Some judges demand that evidence of the acts of domestic violence be elicited by the petitioner before granting a new order or maintaining the ex parte order in effect in accordance with RC 3113.31(E)(3)(a). It should be cautioned that the court always has the authority to dismiss the petition and terminate the protection order if it finds that there were no grounds for its issuance.

Family law practitioners must advise their clients that the court will not go forward on the full hearing unless and until the respondent has been served with the pleadings. All respondents must have notice of the petition and order and an opportunity to be heard at a hearing. Rather than dismiss the protection order for lack of service, a failure to serve the respondent is good cause to grant a continuance of the full hearing in order to perfect service.[3]

Q & A: If I don't have an attorney at the full hearing, will the court treat me the same as if I had an attorney?[4]

Yes. Most courts "continue to hold that *pro se* civil litigants are bound by the same rules and procedures as litigants who retain

---

Dist. Fayette County 2017), citing Carter v. Carter, 62 Ohio App. 3d 167, 171, 574 N.E.2d 1154 (12th Dist. Clermont County 1989).

[Section 12:3]

[1] See RC 3113.31(E)(1).

[2] See RC 3113.31(L), RC 2919.27(A)(1). See also RC 2935.03.

[3] RC 3113.31(D)(2)(i).

[4] See also Text § 11:3, Filing issues.

counsel.[5] When parties choose to represent themselves they are bound just as attorneys are, by the rules of evidence and civil procedure."[6]

Although this is a general rule, courts may still grant some latitude toward pro se litigants. Some judges and magistrates have aided the pro se litigant by not strictly adhering to the rules of evidence or by advising a party of the proper procedure to be followed.[7]

Q & A: Is it important to advise all litigants to truthfully complete the documents?

It is always wise to make sure that all litigants, including pro se litigants, read all instructions before completing the protection order forms. A failure to do so may be the difference between obtaining the CPO and being denied the CPO at either the ex parte or full hearing. Just as importantly, a litigant must fill out all questions truthfully. A failure to do so may mean a conviction for perjury. For example, in *State v. Rodriguez*,[8] appellant sought a CPO against the father of her daughter for alleged abuse to the child. The father had been previously awarded custody of the child. The child was removed from the father and awarded to appellant based on the appellant's answers in the petition for the ex parte protection order and parenting affidavit. At the full hearing on the CPO, it was made known to the court that there was a pending case in juvenile court and the child was returned to the father. The CPO was dismissed and appellant was charged with perjury. The basis of the perjury case was that appellant had falsely answered questions set forth in the petition and the parenting proceeding affidavit. The appellant's answers were then notarized by the domestic relations court receptionist.

On appeal, appellant argued that she did not knowingly provide false information on her parenting proceeding affidavit. However, the appellate court disagreed and relied, in part, on the testimony of the

[5]See also Yocum v. Means, 2002-Ohio-3803, 2002 WL 1729892 (Ohio Ct. App. 2d Dist. Darke County 2002); Vance v. Nichols, 2007-Ohio-3819, 2007 WL 2164162 (Ohio Ct. App. 2d Dist. Darke County 2007); Lias v. Beekman, 2007-Ohio-5737, 2007 WL 3108899 (Ohio Ct. App. 10th Dist. Franklin County 2007); Gomez v. Dyer, 2008-Ohio-1523, 2008 WL 850127 (Ohio Ct. App. 7th Dist. Noble County 2008); Lukac v. Godfrey, 2011-Ohio-971, 2011 WL 766935 (Ohio Ct. App. 6th Dist. Ottawa County 2011); Barton v. Barton, 2016-Ohio-5264, 2016 WL 4168857 (Ohio Ct. App. 2d Dist. Greene County 2016), appeal not allowed, 148 Ohio St. 3d 1411, 2017-Ohio-573, 69 N.E.3d 751 (2017); Howard v. Howard, 2018-Ohio-2218, 2018 WL 2903270 (Ohio Ct. App. 2d Dist. Montgomery County 2018) (following the rules includes compliance with appellate rules).

[6]Shaughnessy v. Shaughnessy, 1999 WL 159211, *6 (Ohio Ct. App. 7th Dist. Mahoning County 1999) (citation omitted); see also Blinsky v. Protain, 2001-Ohio-3321, 2001 WL 772244 (Ohio Ct. App. 7th Dist. Mahoning County 2001); Gibson v. Gibson, 2006-Ohio-2880, 2006 WL 1555935 (Ohio Ct. App. 4th Dist. Washington County 2006); Text § 11:3, Filing issues; Butcher v. Stevens, 182 Ohio App. 3d 77, 2009-Ohio-1754, 911 N.E.2d 928 (4th Dist. Athens County 2009); Niepsuj v. Niepsuj, 2010-Ohio-638, 2010 WL 625837 (Ohio Ct. App. 9th Dist. Summit County 2010); Rosen v. Chesler, 2009-Ohio-3163, 2009 WL 1900422 (Ohio Ct. App. 9th Dist. Lorain County 2009); Allen v. Thompson, 2017-Ohio-4234, 2017 WL 2542392 (Ohio Ct. App. 11th Dist. Lake County 2017).

[7]See Lain v. Ververis, 1999 WL 893611, *3 (Ohio Ct. App. 12th Dist. Preble County 1999). See also Vasile v. Marinescu, 2006-Ohio-1739, 2006 WL 891026 (Ohio Ct. App. 8th Dist. Cuyahoga County 2006).

[8]State v. Rodriguez, 2009-Ohio-549, 2009 WL 295403 (Ohio Ct. App. 12th Dist. Butler County 2009).

trial court judge who testified that she relied on appellant's answers in the parenting affidavit in granting the CPO and would have asked additional questions had the answers been different. She also testified that had she been aware of the pending court order, she would have contacted juvenile court before granting the ex parte CPO.

Of interest is that the appellate court apparently disregarded the appellant's testimony that she did not understand the questions. The case underscores the importance of truthful litigant responses, especially because courts often rely on their sworn answers in issuing the civil protection orders.

§ 12:4 Full hearing—Continuances[1]

Generally, a court may grant or deny a continuance filed by either party. A trial court is accorded broad discretion to do so.[2] An appellate court will not reverse denial of a continuance absent an abuse of discretion. [State v. Unger, 67 Ohio St. 2d 65, 21 Ohio Op. 3d 41, 423 N.E.2d 1078 (1981).] "In determining whether a trial court abused its discretion in denying a motion for continuance an appellate court should consider the following factors: 1) the length of the delay requested; 2) whether other continuances have been requested and received; 3) the inconvenience to the witnesses, opposing counsel and the court; 4) whether there is a legitimate reason for the continuance; 5) whether the defendant contributed to the circumstances giving rise to the need for the continuance; and other relevant factors depending on the unique facts of each case."[3]

Q & A: Can a petitioner continue the full hearing?

The Ohio legislature has provided several statutory reasons for granting continuances of the full hearing. RC 3113.31(D)(2)(a) provides that the court shall hold the full hearing on the date scheduled unless a court grants a continuance of the hearing. The reasons for granting a continuance include: (1) prior to the date scheduled for the full hearing, the respondent has not been served with the petition and notice of the full hearing;[4] (2) the parties consent

---

[Section 12:4]

[1]See also Text § 11:21, Ex parte protection orders—Continuances; Text § 12:2, Full hearing—Scheduling and filing issues, and Text § 9:1, Civil stalking protection orders. Kohus v. Daly, 2016-Ohio-73, 2016 WL 116121, ¶ 15 (Ohio Ct. App. 12th Dist. Clermont County 2016), citing Gomez v. Dyer, 2008-Ohio-1523, 2008 WL 850127, ¶ 20 (Ohio Ct. App. 7th Dist. Noble County 2008) (noting that a trial court has the discretion not to continue a full hearing anytime a party appears at the hearing without counsel, nor does such a situation require court inquiry and it is incumbent upon the party to request a continuance if she or he needs additional time to obtain counsel. at ¶ 15, citing Evans v. Evans, 2008-Ohio-5695, 2008 WL 4787582 (Ohio Ct. App. 10th Dist. Franklin County 2008); Lane v. Brewster, 2012-Ohio-1290, 2012 WL 1029503 (Ohio Ct. App. 12th Dist. Clermont County 2012)).

[2]Caramico v. Caramico, 2015-Ohio-4232, 2015 WL 5934194 (Ohio Ct. App. 12th Dist. Clermont County 2015), citing, Black v. Black, 2009-Ohio-92, 2009 WL 57638, ¶ 11 (Ohio Ct. App. 12th Dist. Clinton County 2009); citing, State v. Unger, 67 Ohio St. 2d 65, 67, 21 Ohio Op. 3d 41, 423 N.E.2d 1078 (1981).

[3]Caramico at ¶ 10, citing Black at ¶ 12, Kirkpatrick v. Kirkpatrick, 2015-Ohio-427, 2015 WL 668976, ¶ 22 (Ohio Ct. App. 5th Dist. Tuscarawas County 2015).

[4]See RC 3113.31(D)(2)(a)(i).

to a continuance;[5] (3) the continuance is needed to allow a party to obtain counsel;[6] and (4) the continuance is needed for other good cause.[7] For the stated reasons, a court may grant a continuance of the full hearing to a reasonable time determined by the court.[8]

The most common ground for granting a continuance is failure of service on the respondent. Many jurisdictions have implemented local rules that dictate the procedure for filing a continuance. For example, in Cuyahoga County, the local rules of the domestic relations division state that "requests for continuances must be made prior to the expiration of the time set for the first full hearing."[9] It should be noted that, where the respondent has not been served, most judges will grant a continuance even if the request is made on the scheduled date of the full hearing.[10] Additionally, continuances of the full hearing are most often made orally without the filing of a written continuance.

Finally, "good cause" includes any other reason for granting a continuance.[11] It may be particular to an individual case, or it may have broader appeal. For example, Lucas County local practice dictates that "continuances should be granted consistent with due process considerations where good cause is shown, e.g., respondent has entered an alcohol rehabilitation program."[12]

Q & A: When should a petitioner request a continuance to obtain counsel?

---

[5]See RC 3113.31(D)(2)(a)(ii).

[6]See RC 3113.31(D)(2)(a)(iii); see also Ferretti v. Graham, 2001 WL 118601 (Ohio Ct. App. 10th Dist. Franklin County 2001) (continuing ex parte stalking civil protection order to permit petitioner to obtain counsel); D.N. v. K.M., 216 N.J. 587, 83 A.3d 825 (2014) (see dissenting opinion on the right to appointed counsel in a domestic violence case); Wheeler v. Wheeler, 2015-Ohio-4206, 2015 WL 5918030 (Ohio Ct. App. 4th Dist. Scioto County 2015) (explaining that a trial court has the discretion to continue the case in order for petitioner to obtain counsel).

[7]See RC 3113.31(D)(2)(a)(iv). Martin v. Martin, 2013-Ohio-5703, 2013 WL 6843599 (Ohio Ct. App. 10th Dist. Franklin County 2013) (pending criminal case against appellant was good cause to continue full hearing). But see Wirtz v. Wirtz, 2000-Ohio-2564, 2000 WL 1486652 (Ohio Ct. App. 7th Dist. Mahoning County 2000) (respondent's intended assertion of his 5th Amendment privilege was not good cause to continue proceedings).

[8]See RC 3113.31(D)(2)(a); see also Abriani v. Abriani, 2007-Ohio-3534, 2007 WL 2008887 (Ohio Ct. App. 8th Dist. Cuyahoga County 2007).

[9]Cuy. D.R. R. 26(B)(5).

[10]But see Oddo v. Spencer, 2009-Ohio-4320, 2009 WL 2602210 (Ohio Ct. App. 5th Dist. Stark County 2009) (where defendant argued on appeal that the full hearing did not comply with the statutory language in RC 2903.214 (D)(2)(a)(i) (mirroring RC 3113.31(D)(2)(a)(i)) which provided that the court may grant a continuance "prior to the date scheduled for a full hearing" under this division, if the respondent has not been served with the petition filed pursuant to this section and notice of the full hearing. Because he had not been served "prior to the date of the full hearing" (he was served 1 hour before the hearing), he believed that 1) he was entitled to a continuance because the court failed to comply with the plain wording of the statute; and, 2) the court should have inquired about his readiness to proceed. In overruling his objection, the appellate court noted that he failed to request a continuance at the hearing).

[11]But see Coleman v. Coleman, 1996 WL 199165 (Ohio Ct. App. 6th Dist. Lucas County 1996), cause dismissed, 77 Ohio St. 3d 1432, 671 N.E.2d 264 (1996) (denial of a continuance upheld for a respondent who failed to file a motion for continuance).

[12]June Rose Galvin & Grace A. Kilbane, Baldwin's Ohio Practice, Domestic Relations Law T. 5.05 (1992).

A pro se petitioner should request a continuance to obtain counsel for the full hearing if the respondent is represented by an attorney, especially if removal from the premises or custody or visitation are main issues. If petitioner knows that respondent will have counsel present, she/he should seek an attorney as well. Even the Supreme Court's standard forms and instructions stress that legal representation in these situations is advised.[13]

The National Council of Juvenile and Family Court Judges, in Improving Court Practice, noted that victims of domestic violence are not in an equal position of power vis-a-vis the batterer. It cautioned that:

> determination of custody and visitation of children are ways in which batterers frequently continue their harassment and other abuse. Because of his control and her fear, the battered spouse may agree to custody provisions which are not really desirable for herself or the children. Alternatively, the battered spouse may trade financial support or equitable distribution of assets for more protective custody or visitation.[14]

Legal counsel is in the best position to readjust the balance of power for purposes of negotiating a settlement or trying the case. Procedurally speaking, a petitioner should file a motion to continue the full hearing in order to obtain counsel as soon as it becomes known to him/her that the respondent has obtained counsel. If she/he is made aware that a respondent has obtained counsel but is uncertain whether the court will receive her motion before the full hearing, a petitioner should take a filed copy of the motion to the full hearing. It is unwise to expect that a court will have the original or a copy of the filed motion before or on the hearing date. If a motion to continue is not filed, a pro se petitioner should orally request a continuance to obtain counsel at the full hearing.

Q & A: How many times can a petitioner continue the full hearing?

Although the legislature now permits continuances of full hearings in civil protection order actions to a reasonable time determined by the court,[15] there is no statutory direction regarding the number of times a party may continue the full hearing for any reason.[16] Rarely do courts continue the full hearing more than once for any reason other than a failure of service. However, most courts will allow more than one continuance for a failure of service, especially if there are difficulties in obtaining service on the respondent. Since the purpose of civil protection orders is to provide safety for victims of domestic violence, many judges grant repeated requests for continuances so that petitioners remain protected until service is obtained.

---

[13]See Sup. R. 10.01, Standard Civil Protection Order Forms—Domestic Relations Division; Sup. R. Form 10.01-A, General Information About Domestic Violence Protection Orders.

[14]National Council of Juvenile & Family Court Judges, Family Violence: Improving Court Practice 26 (1990).

[15]RC 3113.31(D)(2)(a).

[16]See Berry v. Patrick, 2005-Ohio-3708, 2005 WL 1707005, *3 (Ohio Ct. App. 8th Dist. Cuyahoga County 2005) (court noted that an ex parte CPO may be continued to a "reasonable period of time").

Additionally, two cases in Ohio have touched on similar issues. In *Eichenberger v. Eichenberger*,[17] the Court of Appeals for Franklin County held that the trial court did not err in twice continuing a civil protection hearing date, thereby failing to hold the hearing within seven days of issuance. The court's rationale was that the limited delay was reasonable in light of the trial judge's heavy docket responsibilities and neither the integrity nor the constitutionality of the proceedings were jeopardized. In effect, the court sanctioned the continuance of the full hearing for a variety of reasons.

Similarly, in *Deacon v. Landers*,[18] the court simply noted that the hearing was continued several times because of difficulties in obtaining service. The court of appeals did not even consider this a problem needing to be addressed.

Other states have considered this issue and addressed it both by statute and in case law. For example, the Texas Abuse Statute provides for a maximum continuance of fourteen days for no service.[19] In *Nohner v. Anderson*,[20] the Minnesota Court of Appeals held that the trial court could not continue an ex parte order for more than fourteen days without a full hearing and findings of domestic violence.

Q & A: Is there a time frame within which service must be perfected or the petition will be dismissed and the ex parte order terminated?[21]

The domestic violence statute is silent as to this issue. RC 3113.31(D)(2)(a)(i) provides only that the full hearing may be continued for a failure of service.[22] Local practices and procedures dictate how a particular jurisdiction might respond to the question presented. In most jurisdictions, the ex parte order expires when the respondent is not served after the petitioner makes repeated attempts at service. Absent service on the respondent within a reasonable time, most courts will dismiss the petition and terminate the order.

Many courts continue the full hearing for six to eight months, scheduling periodic full hearings in order to verify that service is being attempted.[23] Other courts may not even reschedule the full hearing until service is perfected and the petitioner so informs the court.

[17]Eichenberger v. Eichenberger, 82 Ohio App. 3d 809, 613 N.E.2d 678 (10th Dist. Franklin County 1992); see also Sterling v. Sterling, 2002-Ohio-4997, 2002 WL 31111778 (Ohio Ct. App. 5th Dist. Fairfield County 2002); but see State v. Blaine, 2004-Ohio-1241, 2004 WL 524667, *5 (Ohio Ct. App. 4th Dist. Highland County 2004) (holding that a continuance for two months and 12 days for the full hearing is an abuse of discretion without good cause given the intent of the legislature to set the full hearing within ten days or as soon thereafter as is reasonable).

[18]Deacon v. Landers, 68 Ohio App. 3d 26, 587 N.E.2d 395 (4th Dist. Ross County 1990).

[19]Tex. Fam. Code Ann. § 84.003(b).

[20]Nohner v. Anderson, 446 N.W.2d 202 (Minn. Ct. App. 1989).

[21]See also Text §§ 11:4, 11:21.

[22]But see Berry v. Patrick, 2005-Ohio-3708, 2005 WL 1707005, *3 (Ohio Ct. App. 8th Dist. Cuyahoga County 2005) (where a respondent has not been served, the full hearing may be continued for a "reasonable time determined by the court").

[23]Cuyahoga County utilizes this method.

Unfortunately, other jurisdictions dismiss the petition and order if the full hearing is not perfected at the time the full hearing is scheduled.[24]

It is arguable, however, that the full hearing may be continued repeatedly for the duration of the order—five years. At least one Ohio jurist relied on RC 3113.31(E)(3)(a), which provides that "[a]ny protection order . . . or consent agreement approved . . . shall be valid until a date certain, but not later than five years from the date of its issuance or approval," and reasoned that all protection orders, including ex parte orders, remain in effect for this five-year period. Therefore, continuances for failure of service are permitted and encouraged for the duration of the protection order.[25]

The problem with this approach is threefold. First, most courts have interpreted RC 3113.31(E)(3)(a) to apply only to the protection order issued after the full hearing.

Second, to repeatedly continue the full hearing for the duration of the protection order, which is now five years, might conflict with the Rules of Civil Procedure. At the outset, any proceedings under RC 3113.31 shall be conducted in accordance with the Rules of Civil Procedure.[26] Civil Rule 4(E) provides a specific time limit for perfecting service: "If a service of the summons and complaint is not made upon a defendant within six months after the filing of the complaint and the party on whose behalf such service was required cannot show good cause why such service was not made within that period, the action shall be dismissed as to that defendant." If read together, these provisions indicate a clear legislative intent to limit the time frame within which service of the petition and CPO must be completed.

Of significance is Civil Rule 3(A) which provides that "[a]civil action is commenced by filing a complaint with the court, if service is obtained within one year from such filing upon a named defendant[.]" In that Civil Rule 4(E) permits a "good cause" exception to the six-month period, it can be argued that in civil protection order proceedings, more so than in other actions, continuing the hearing for a longer period of time to perfect service is necessary in order to provide protection to the petitioner and other family or household members. It may be unfair to dismiss the civil protection order in certain situations, especially where the respondent cannot be found, where he/she is still harassing the petitioner, or where he/she has eluded the process server. It is important that the family law practitioner demonstrate that "good cause" exists and be mindful of a potential conflict so as to provide well-reasoned arguments to the court, should that become necessary. In any case, five years is not contemplated by the Rules of Civil Procedure.

Third, there is a problem in continuing the full hearing for the five-year duration of a civil protection order, in that a potentially

---

[24]See, e.g., Licking D.R. R. 7.3.

[25]See R.C. 3113.31(E)(3)(a). See also Wirtz v. Wirtz, 2000-Ohio-2564, 2000 WL 1486652 (Ohio Ct. App. 7th Dist. Mahoning County 2000) (in dicta, appeals court suggests that an ex parte order may be in effect for five years).

[26]R.C. 3113.31(G).

unenforceable ex parte CPO would be in effect for this period of time.[27] While it is far better that the ex parte order not terminate, it is unclear whether an ex parte protection order can be enforced by either the courts or law enforcement officials if service on the respondent has not been perfected.[28] A civil protection order that is potentially unenforceable by the courts and law enforcement provides a petitioner with a false sense of security. Counsel has an obligation to inform the petitioner of this potential problem in order to consider other safety measures until service is perfected.

Q & A: If the court continues the full hearing, will the ex parte order remain in effect until the new full hearing?

RC 3113.31 specifically provides that an ex parte protection order does not expire because of a failure to serve notice of the full hearing on the respondent before the date set for the full hearing or because the court grants a continuance.[29] Provided that the court permits the continuance of the full hearing, the ex parte order will not expire during a period of time that is determined by the court.[30]

Prior to the enactment of 1997 Senate Bill 1, most courts that allowed for continuances of the full hearing also created a procedure for extending the effectiveness of the ex parte order for a period of time. In some jurisdictions, local practice allowed for an automatic extension of the ex parte order.[31] For others, a separate order provided for the extension,[32] or a consent entry of the parties was required.[33]

Statewide police enforcement of a civil protection order[34] provided the impetus for this clarification to the statute. Without jurisdictional uniformity, there was a lack of consistent law enforcement of civil protection orders in Ohio. Ohio's law enforcement agencies did not know whether a specific order was still valid and were reluctant to enforce ex parte orders beyond a specific expiration date, which was often the date of the first full hearing.

Q & A: Are there any procedural problems associated with an automatic extension of an ex parte order?

The Rules of Superintendence provide in part:

> Upon issuance of a civil or criminal protection order by a court pursuant

[27]See R.C. 3113.31(D)(2)(b); see also Text § 11:11, Ex parte protection orders—Service and notice provisions.

[28]See Text § 11:11, Ex parte protection orders—Service and notice provisions; Text § 14:7, Police liability for failing to protect victims of domestic violence—Introduction.

[29]See RC 3113.31(D)(2)(b). Barrett v. Soltesz, 2015-Ohio-794, 2015 WL 995439 (Ohio Ct. App. 6th Dist. Erie County 2015).

[30]See State v. Davis, 2008-Ohio-5281, 2008 WL 4531895 (Ohio Ct. App. 1st Dist. Hamilton County 2008).

[31]In Cuyahoga County, the court permits an automatic extension of the order. See also Snyder v. Snyder, 1995 WL 493998 (Ohio Ct. App. 4th Dist. Ross County 1995) (indicating on the record that the ex parte order would remain in effect with no separate order required).

[32]Monroe, Morgan, Noble, and Washington counties required that separate orders be entered.

[33]Franklin County followed this approach.

[34]See RC 3113.31(F)(3).

to section 2919.26(E)(2) or 3113.31 of the Revised Code, the court shall complete Form 10-A. Form 10-A and a copy of the order shall be filed by the court with the local enforcement agency for entry in the National Crime Information Center database and nationwide dissemination.[35]

This rule instructs both the municipal court and domestic relations court to provide an expiration date of the ex parte order on the form. That date is most often the full hearing date in civil protection orders. In criminal protection order cases under RC 2919.26, the National Crime Information Center (NCIC) form includes a provision that permits courts to write in "NONEXP."[36] Such detail is necessary for NCIC database input.

As stated above, RC 3113.31(D)(2)(b) provides that an ex parte order does not expire because of a failure of service or because the court granted a continuance for other reasons. However, the statute does not provide guidance as to how this is to be accomplished.

Each jurisdiction must develop a procedure that determines how and for how long an ex parte protection order is to be extended because of a continuance for a failure of service or other reason. Each extension must have an expiration date. Each new expiration date must be sent to NCIC by way of a new 10-A form. Unfortunately, law enforcement officials will not have this crucial piece of information if it has not been entered into the NCIC database.

Rather than risk confusion among the various jurisdictions, one procedural option is to request that a new 10-A form be issued extending the ex parte order at the same time a continuance is requested. This additional information would then be entered into the NCIC database for access by law enforcement officials across the state of Ohio.

An alternative option, at least in the jurisdictions that permit civil protection orders to remain in effect for the full five years without periodic renewal, would be to note on form 10-A that the expiration of the protection order is five years from the date of the issuance of the ex parte order.[37] If the order is later dismissed or modified, any new expiration date will be noted on any subsequent order and accompanying form 10-A.[38]

Q & A: Can a petitioner continue the full hearing more than once for a reason other than a failure of service or to obtain counsel?

Many courts refuse to grant the petitioner leave to continue a full hearing even once where it has been established that the respondent has been served,[39] unless both parties consent[40] or a continuance is needed to obtain counsel.[41]

Since the purpose of a full hearing is to provide the respondent with

---

[35] Sup. R. 10, eff. 3-24-98.

[36] See Sup. R. Form 10-A.

[37] See RC 3113.31(E)(3)(a).

[38] Sup. R. 10, Sup. R. Form 10-A.

[39] Cuyahoga County Domestic Relations Court practice.

[40] RC 3113.31(D)(2)(a)(ii).

[41] RC 3113.31(D)(2)(a)(iii); see also Ferretti v. Graham, 2001 WL 118601 (Ohio Ct.

his day in court, petitioner's continuance could result in an infringement of respondent's due process rights. A petitioner must show "good cause" to justify the issuance of a continuance, particularly when the respondent has already been served and appears at the hearing.

Q & A: What if the petitioner fails to appear at the hearing?

Since petitioners must present evidence demonstrating fear of continued danger[42] or an act of domestic violence,[43] they must appear for the full hearing. Nothing in the statute or case law permits the issuance of a civil protection after the full hearing without the testimony of the petitioner. A failure of the petitioner to appear, especially if the respondent has been served, will often result in a dismissal and termination of the order.

However, there may be valid reasons for a petitioner's lack of appearance in court. These reasons include the victim being physically unable to appear for the hearing due to injuries suffered at the hands of the respondent and the victim being intimidated by threats of greater violence from the respondent as a result of pursuing court action.[44]

The likelihood that one of these situations may exist makes the dismissal of the civil protection order petition based solely on the petitioner's failure to appear, without further inquiry, potentially dangerous to the petitioner.[45] Courts and attorneys should not agree to automatically dismiss the proceeding. Rather, the hearing should be continued to another date, if possible, or delayed until counsel is able to communicate with the petitioner.

If local practice in the jurisdiction provides for a dismissal of the petition and a termination of the order, any dismissal for a petitioner's failure to appear should be without prejudice. When the court and the petitioner's attorney are uncertain of the reason for the petitioner's failure to appear and the respondent appears and requests a dismissal, the court should take adequate steps to ascertain the petitioner's desires.

Q & A: Under what conditions can the respondent continue the full hearing?[46]

App. 10th Dist. Franklin County 2001).

[42]Felton v. Felton, 79 Ohio St. 3d 34, 1997-Ohio-302, 679 N.E.2d 672 (1997); see also Text § 12:11, Standard of Proof, Text § 11:10, Ex parte protection orders—Legal standard for issuance, Text § 8:4, Statutory elements of domestic violence under RC 3113.31(A)(1)(b), Text § 8:8, Miscellaneous issues.

[43]RC 3113.31(A)(1).

[44]Catherine F. Klein & Leslye E. Orloff, Providing Legal Protection for Battered Women: An Analysis of State Statutes and Case Law, 21 Hofstra L. Rev. 801, 1065 (1993).

[45]Catherine F. Klein & Leslye E. Orloff, Providing Legal Protection for Battered Women: An Analysis of State Statutes and Case Law, 21 Hofstra L. Rev. 801, 1065 (1993).

[46]See, e.g., H.E.S. v. J.C.S., 175 N.J. 309, 815 A.2d 405 (2003) (holding that due process was violated by trial court's refusal to grant continuance to husband after wife alleged an incident of domestic violence not contained in her petition).

RC 3113.31(D)(2)(a) specifically permits a respondent to continue the full hearing in order to obtain counsel.[47] Ordinarily, the court will only allow one continuance to obtain counsel unless good cause is shown.[48] It should be noted that a respondent need not have received the papers within any specific time frame in order to take advantage of this provision. This is the case whether a respondent has had nine days to obtain counsel after service or one day.[49]

Besides the above, many courts grant the respondent permission to continue the full hearing at least once. Most courts reason that a full hearing is scheduled for the benefit of the respondent.[50] So long as a respondent understands that he/she is to remain bound by the terms of the ex parte order until the hearing is reset,[51] the courts have determined that neither party is prejudiced by the continuance.[52]

That may not be the sentiment, however, if the respondent continues a full hearing where the petitioner has not yet been granted the protection order.[53] In this circumstance, repeated continuances

[47]See Roncone v. Bialkowski, 2007-Ohio-3326, 2007 WL 1874250 (Ohio Ct. App. 10th Dist. Franklin County 2007) (reversing trial court decision denying continuance). But see Dyke v. Price, 2000 WL 1546555 (Ohio Ct. App. 2d Dist. Montgomery County 2000); Conkle v. Wolfe, 131 Ohio App. 3d 375, 722 N.E.2d 586 (4th Dist. Athens County 1998) (Noting that the court has discretion when deciding to grant or deny a continuance, the appellate court upheld the denial of defendant's motion for continuance due to his pending criminal trial where the defendant failed to raise the issue of his need to consult with counsel with the trial court.); Abriani v. Abriani, 2007-Ohio-3534, 2007 WL 2008887, *4 (Ohio Ct. App. 8th Dist. Cuyahoga County 2007) (holding that trial court did not err or abuse its discretion in proceeding to a full hearing on petitioner's CPO where respondent's attorney filed a motion to withdraw as counsel and a motion to continue the hearing 50 minutes before the full hearing. Court also noted that respondent was previously granted a continuance. The court also stressed that the domestic violence statute uses the term "may" not "shall." "It does not require the granting of a motion to continue a civil protection order when counsel files an untimely motion to withdraw immediately prior to a hearing."); Caramico v. Caramico, 2015-Ohio-4232, 2015 WL 5934194 (Ohio Ct. App. 12th Dist. Clermont County 2015) (where respondent failed to timely retain substitute counsel just prior to the date of trial, a subsequent request for a continuance based on a substitution of counsel is not an adequate ground for a continuance. At ¶ 14).

[48]See also Slusser v. Klosterman, 2008-Ohio-2608, 2008 WL 2229635 (Ohio Ct. App. 3d Dist. Mercer County 2008) (good cause includes a continuance to have retained counsel given time to prepare the case). But see Wirtz v. Wirtz, 2000-Ohio-2564, 2000 WL 1486652, *3 (Ohio Ct. App. 7th Dist. Mahoning County 2000) (where the appellate court found that appellant's intended assertion of his Fifth Amendment privilege was insufficient "good cause" to continue the proceedings. "Permitting appellant to delay a full hearing could well tread upon the limitations imposed by statute.")

[49]See, for example, Vance v. Nichols, 2007-Ohio-3819, 2007 WL 2164162 (Ohio Ct. App. 2d Dist. Darke County 2007) (respondent received notice on July 5, 2006 that a full hearing was set for July 10, 2006, providing respondent with three working days notice.).

[50]See, e.g., Snyder v. Snyder, 1995 WL 493998 (Ohio Ct. App. 4th Dist. Ross County 1995); Eichenberger v. Eichenberger, 82 Ohio App. 3d 809, 613 N.E.2d 678 (10th Dist. Franklin County 1992).

[51]See RC 3113.31(D)(2)(b). But see Wirtz v. Wirtz, 2000-Ohio-2564, 2000 WL 1486652 (Ohio Ct. App. 7th Dist. Mahoning County 2000).

[52]But see Wirtz v. Wirtz, 2000-Ohio-2564, 2000 WL 1486652, *3 (Ohio Ct. App. 7th Dist. Mahoning County 2000); Klosterman v. Klosterman, 2000-Ohio-1807, 2000 WL 1752235 (Ohio Ct. App. 3d Dist. Mercer County 2000).

[53]See RC 3113.31(D)(3).

will clearly prejudice a petitioner who has yet to acquire a protection order.

At least one Ohio court suggests that the respondent may request a continuance of the full hearing for discovery purposes.[54] In *Snyder v. Snyder*,[55] the court of appeals noted that the appellant "did not request a continuance to enable him to utilize any discovery procedures or other proceedings available under the civil rules." Implicit in this is that the need for discovery may be a valid reason for a continuance.[56]

Q & A: Can a respondent continue the full hearing on Fifth Amendment grounds?

In *Sweet v. Hunt*,[57] appellant appealed the denial of his continuance motion based on his pending related criminal case. In this case, appellant was a respondent in a civil stalking protection order action. His concern was that his testimony in the civil case could be used against him in the criminal case. After being granted a continuance, he again requested a continuance which was denied by the court.

In reviewing the trial court's denial of the continuance for an abuse of discretion, the appellate court considered the reason for the motion under RC 2903.214(D)(2)(a) which provides for a continuance for "other good cause." In that the trial court granted another continuance due to the pending criminal action, "the trial court had no way of knowing when the charges would be resolved because Hunt had waived a speedy trial. Ultimately, more than 100 days elapsed between the trial court's issuance of the ex parte order and the full CSPO hearing."[58] Under the circumstances, the appellate court overruled the assignment of error, having found no abuse of discretion in the trial court's denial of another continuance.

It is important to note that the same analysis would apply to a civil protection order issued under RC 3113.31 due to the similar statutory schema.

Q & A: What if a respondent appears at the hearing but has not been served with the papers or notice of the hearing? Does the trial court have an affirmative duty to ask whether a respondent has received notice and a copy of the ex parte civil protection order?

The Franklin County Court of Appeals has responded in the negative. In *Evans v. Evans*,[59] respondent appealed the issuance of the CPO. He alleged that the Clerk of Court had failed to serve him with a copy of the ex arte civil protection order. While searching the court website two days before the hearing, he discovered the existence

[54]But see Martinez v. Martinez, 52 S.W.3d 429 (Tex. App. Fort Worth 2001).

[55]Snyder v. Snyder, 1995 WL 493998, *2 (Ohio Ct. App. 4th Dist. Ross County 1995).

[56]See also Patterson v. Loveless, 2001 WL 524372 (Ohio Ct. App. 2d Dist. Montgomery County 2001).

[57]Sweet v. Hunt, 2014-Ohio-631, 2014 WL 707923 (Ohio Ct. App. 2d Dist. Greene County 2014).

[58]Sweet v. Hunt, 2014-Ohio-631, 2014 WL 707923, ¶ 10 (Ohio Ct. App. 2d Dist. Greene County 2014).

[59]Evans v. Evans, 2008-Ohio-5695, 2008 WL 4787582 (Ohio Ct. App. 10th Dist. Franklin County 2008).

of the order.[60] At the full hearing, he testified that he did not receive notice of the full hearing.

Appellant argued that he was denied due process when the court held the full hearing because he had not received notice of the hearing from the Clerk of Courts. The appellate court noted that appellant never objected to the lack of notice, argued that it violated the domestic violence statute or that it infringed on his due process rights. Moreover, appellant never requested a continuance. "Because Walter neither objected nor sought a continuance, we conclude that Walter failed to preserve any alleged error regarding the lack of notice."[61]

Appellant also argued that the trial court had an affirmative duty, imposed by RC 3113.31(D)(2)(a)(i), to inquire whether he had received proper notice and to grant a continuance if he had not.[62] While acknowledging that a court may grant a continuance if a respondent has not been served with the petition and notice of the full hearing, the appellate court considered the language broad enough to permit a court to grant a continuance if a respondent has not received the petition and notice of the full hearing. In affirming the issuance of the order, the Franklin County Court of Appeals stated that "[c]ontrary to Walter's argument, the provision does not require the trial court to affirmatively take any action. Necessarily then, the respondent bears the burden of asserting the lack of notice and seeking a continuance. Therefore, when Walter failed to object to the lack of notice or to ask for a continuance to remedy the situation, he foreclosed any potential appeal based upon the lack of notice."[63]

Of significance is that the appellate court did not consider appellant's motion to dismiss to be equivalent to a continuance. In fact, the court equated his motion to dismiss to a pretrial motion and stated that "[w]hen a trial court fails to rule upon a pretrial motion, an appellate court presumes that the trial court overruled it."[64]

Q & A: Does the denial of a continuance because of the incarceration of the respondent constitute a lack of a fair hearing as contemplated by RC 3113.31(D)(2)(a)?

No. In *Haynes-Soper v. Soper*,[65] the defendant appealed the civil protection order issued against him on the grounds that the court's

---

[60] Evans v. Evans, 2008-Ohio-5695, 2008 WL 4787582, *1 (Ohio Ct. App. 10th Dist. Franklin County 2008).

[61] Evans v. Evans, 2008-Ohio-5695, 2008 WL 4787582, *2 (Ohio Ct. App. 10th Dist. Franklin County 2008).

[62] Evans v. Evans, 2008-Ohio-5695, 2008 WL 4787582, *2 (Ohio Ct. App. 10th Dist. Franklin County 2008); see also Oddo v. Spencer, 2009-Ohio-4320, 2009 WL 2602210 (Ohio Ct. App. 5th Dist. Stark County 2009) (holding that the domestic violence statute indicates that the granting of continuances are within the court's discretion and that full colloquy requirements (as required in criminal proceedings), are not required in a CPO proceeding); Butcher v. Stevens, 182 Ohio App. 3d 77, 2009-Ohio-1754, 911 N.E.2d 928 (4th Dist. Athens County 2009).

[63] Evans v. Evans, 2008-Ohio-5695, 2008 WL 4787582, *3 (Ohio Ct. App. 10th Dist. Franklin County 2008).

[64] Evans v. Evans, 2008-Ohio-5695, 2008 WL 4787582, *3 (Ohio Ct. App. 10th Dist. Franklin County 2008), citing State ex rel. The V Cos. v. Marshall, 81 Ohio St. 3d 467, 469, 1998-Ohio-329, 692 N.E.2d 198 (1998).

[65] Haynes-Soper v. Garrett, 2000 WL 1289450 (Ohio Ct. App. 10th Dist. Franklin County 2000).

denial of a continuance for the full hearing prevented him from a full and fair hearing under RC 3113.31(D)(2)(a). In this case, the defendant was incarcerated at the time of the full hearing and the court summarily noted he could not appear in person unless the court arranged for his presence.[66]

The Tenth District Court of Appeals did not think this reason enough to reverse the trial court decision. It focused on the facts that the defendant had admitted to domestic violence in his brief, that he was sentenced to a jail term for the domestic violence and that the defendant's presence at a full hearing could result in unnecessary personal conduct between the parties. Therefore, the trial court's refusal to continue the full hearing was not prejudicial error.[67]

On the other hand, the Summit County Court of Appeals, in *Sigler v. Arvay*,[68] reversed the trial court and held that the appellant was not afforded due process protections when the court granted the protection order even though the appellant was incarcerated. In this case, Mr. Arvay did not request a continuance in the trial court. He appealed the trial court's granting of the protection order.[69]

On appeal, Ms. Sigler "argued that the requirements of both R.C. 3113.31 and due process of law were complied with because Mr. Arvay was served with notice of the hearing prior to its commencement. According to Ms. Sigler, Mr. Arvay's incarceration did not prevent him from requesting either permission to attend or a continuance of the hearing, and he therefore failed to take advantage of his 'opportunity to appear.' "[70]

The Ninth District Court of Appeals disagreed with appellee and held that Mr. Arvay did not have adequate notice or a reasonable opportunity to be heard. The court reasoned that because he was served with notice of the hearing one day before the actual full hearing and that he was in jail, he did not have a reasonable opportunity to attend the hearing, secure counsel or file a continuance. The court noted that he had no prior convictions and was not familiar with the procedures in jail. In effect, the Summit County Court of Appeals accepted that his lack of familiarity with jail procedures hindered his ability to request a continuance or permission to attend the hearing.[71] Had Mr. Arvay not been in jail or been provided adequate notice of the hearing, it is quite possible the court would have affirmed the trial court.

---

[66]Parker v. Jamison, 2003-Ohio-7295, 2003 WL 24135688 (Ohio Ct. App. 4th Dist. Scioto County 2003) (holding that a person who is incarcerated has no absolute right to appear at a civil action and motion to continue pending release from jail or a motion to transport could have been filed in this case and may have enabled appellant's attendance at the CPO hearing).

[67]Haynes-Soper v. Garrett, 2000 WL 1289450, *28 (Ohio Ct. App. 10th Dist. Franklin County 2000).

[68]Sigler v. Arvay, 2002-Ohio-6762, 2002 WL 31761478 (Ohio Ct. App. 9th Dist. Summit County 2002).

[69]In *Haynes-Soper v. Soper*, the appellant requested a continuance, which was denied and it was from this denial that he appealed.

[70]Sigler v. Arvay, 2002-Ohio-6762, 2002 WL 31761478, *2 (Ohio Ct. App. 9th Dist. Summit County 2002). See also Text § 12:7, Full hearing—Other procedural concerns.

[71]But see State v. Gordon, 2003-Ohio-6558, 2003 WL 22889573 (Ohio Ct. App. 10th Dist. Franklin County 2003).

Of importance is that the appellate court noted that its ruling was specific to the facts and circumstances of the case. One should not assume that this ruling is an instruction from the Summit County Court of Appeals to other petitioners to either request continuances due to the incarceration of respondents or provide a mechanism to permit respondents to leave jail to attend the full hearing.

Q & A: What is adequate notice of the full hearing date?

Several courts have addressed the issue. In *Puls v. Puls*,[72] the parties each filed petitions for protection orders against the other. Following several continuances, the full hearing was rescheduled to February 19, 2002. Appellant argued on appeal that his due process rights were violated, as he was not provided with adequate notice that the hearing on the protection orders was to be held on February 19, 2002.

The Montgomery County Court of Appeals overruled his assignment of error and stated that the record contained an order of court continuing the full hearing to February 19, 2002. Appellant's attorney signed the order. Nothing in the record suggests that the hearing was further continued. "Therefore, it appears that Mr. Puls did receive notice that the hearing on the parties' petition was to be held on February 19, 2002."[73] In effect, notice to the attorney is notice to his/her client.

§ 12:5 Full hearing—Discovery issues

Pursuant to Civ.R. 26(B)(1), a party may obtain discovery regarding non-privileged information relevant to the claim or defense of a proceeding. A party may depose witnesses,[1] gather documents,[2] or request relevant information by way of written interrogatories.[3]

Q & A: Is discovery permitted in a civil protection order proceeding?

Yes. RC 3113.31(G) provides that civil domestic violence actions "shall be conducted in accordance with the Rules of Civil Procedure. Recently adopted Civ. R. 65.1 applies only to civil protection order proceedings and specifically provides for a procedure for discovery."[4]

---

[72]Puls v. Puls, 2003-Ohio-211, 2003 WL 139966 (Ohio Ct. App. 2d Dist. Montgomery County 2003). See also Prichard v. Crago, 2003-Ohio-4603, 2003 WL 22038703 (Ohio Ct. App. 11th Dist. Portage County 2003); Butcher v. Stevens, 182 Ohio App. 3d 77, 2009-Ohio-1754, 911 N.E.2d 928 (4th Dist. Athens County 2009) (holding that notice of one day is sufficient notice of full hearing).

[73]Puls v. Puls, 2003-Ohio-211, 2003 WL 139966, *1 (Ohio Ct. App. 2d Dist. Montgomery County 2003).

[Section 12:5]

[1]See Civ.R. 30.

[2]See Civ.R. 34.

[3]Civ.R. 33.

[4]Civ. R. 65.1(D); see also Snyder v. Snyder, 1995 WL 493998 (Ohio Ct. App. 4th Dist. Ross County 1995); see also Patterson v. Loveless, 2001 WL 524372 (Ohio Ct. App. 2d Dist. Montgomery County 2001); Martinez v. Martinez, 52 S.W.3d 429 (Tex. App. Fort Worth 2001), (discussing discovery requests in a protection order proceeding); Caito v. Zucallo, 2001-Ohio-8881, 2001 WL 1388377 (Ohio Ct. App. 11th Dist. Portage County 2001); but see Skiles v. Dearth, 2000 WL 1838747 (Ohio Ct. App. 2d Dist. Clark County 2000).

Q & A: What is the procedure for discovery under Civ. R. 65. 1(D)?

First and foremost, a civil protection order proceeding is a "special statutory proceeding."[5] As a special statutory proceeding, the provisions of Civ. R. 65.1 apply to special statutory proceedings under RC 3113.31, RC 2151.34 and RC 2903.214 and "shall be interpreted and applied in a manner consistent with the intent and purposes of those protection order statutes and supersede and make inapplicable in such proceedings the provisions of any other rules of civil procedure to the extent that such application is inconsistent with the provisions of this rule."

Under Civ. R. 65.1(D)(2), whether to grant discovery in a particular civil protection order action is within the discretion of the court[6] and may be had only upon entry of an order. It shall contain the following to the extent applicable:

(1) The time and place of the discovery;[7]
(2) The identities of the persons permitted to be present, which shall include any victim advocate;[8]
(3) Such terms and conditions deemed by the court to be necessary to assure the safety of the Petitioner, including if applicable, maintaining the confidentiality of the Petitioner's address.[9]

Finally, any discovery under the rule must be completed prior to the time set for the full hearing.[10] Although the rule does not contemplate a continuance process in order to address discovery, the Staff Notes indicate that, because there is a shortened time frame between the ex parte order and the full hearing, a statutory request for a continuance might be appropriate.

Q & A: Is there any internal inconsistency between the nature of a civil protection order action and the discovery process?

Despite the mandates of Civ. R. 65(D), there still appears to be an inherent conflict between the discovery procedure contemplated by the Rules of Civil Procedure and the mandatory seven and ten day full hearing dates set forth in the domestic violence statute.[11] Because the domestic violence statute provides an expedited time frame and includes no specific provision for discovery, it is quite possible that the

---

[5]Civ. R. 65.1(A); see also Scheib v. Crosby, 160 Wash. App. 345, 249 P.3d 184 (Div. 3 2011).

[6]See also Scheib v. Crosby, 160 Wash. App. 345, 249 P.3d 184 (Div. 3 2011) (denying defendant's request for discovery and holding that because protection order proceedings are special statutory proceedings, "the trial court retained the inherent authority and discretion to decide the nature and extent of any discovery"); at Syllabus.

[7]Civ. R. 65.1(D)(2)(a).

[8]Civ. R. 65.1(D)(2)(b).

[9]Civ. R. 65.1(D)(2)(c).

[10]Civ. R. 65.1(D)(1). But see Crawford v. Brandon, 2014-Ohio-3659, 2014 WL 4180286 (Ohio Ct. App. 12th Dist. Butler County 2014) (noting that court had some concerns about strict enforcement of discovery deadline).

[11]R.C. 3113.31(D)(2)(a).

legislature intended that there be no or limited discovery prior to the full hearing.[12]

Moreover, the need to conduct discovery is not one of the statutory grounds to continue a full hearing.[13] Arguably, its omission in the statute can be viewed as a deliberate action, which if permitted, could delay the full hearing for significant periods of time, contravene the purpose of the domestic violence statute and hamper judicial efficiency.

Since the goal of the domestic violence statute is to create a quick and easy mechanism to stop the violence and protect the petitioner, discovery in civil protection order cases must be formulated in light of the summary nature of the proceedings and the need to avoid delays in the issuance of protection orders.[14]

Therefore, family law practitioners should have a clear understanding of the limits of the discovery rules in civil protection order proceedings that must be consistent with the safety concerns of the petitioner.[15] Discovery should be limited to that information which is relevant to the subject matter involved in the pending action[16] and which is appropriate to the particular pleadings involved. In fact, discovery may be restricted where necessary to "protect a party . . . from annoyance, embarrassment oppression, or undue burden or expense."[17]

Much like other the rules of other jurisdictions, Ohio's rule attempts to advance the need to both assure victim safety and define the scope of discovery. For example, the District of Columbia's Rules Governing Intrafamily Proceedings provides that "[u]nless otherwise directed by the Court, the scope of discovery is limited to matters directly relating to the incident or incidents of abuse alleged in the petition. . . .and to medical treatment obtained as a result of those incidents."[18]

Q & A: Are there any reasons not to permit discovery requests?

Absolutely.[19] Neither depositions[20] nor interrogatories should be permitted if their use may further endanger the victim or be

---

[12]See Skiles v. Dearth, 2000 WL 1838747 (Ohio Ct. App. 2d Dist. Clark County 2000) (analysis of R.C. 3113.31 in light of certain rules of civil procedure and why the rules may not apply even though R.C. 3113.31(G) provides that "any proceeding under this section shall be conducted in accordance with the Rules of Civil Procedure").

[13]See R.C. 3113.31(D)(2)(a)(i) to (iv); see also Skiles v. Dearth, 2000 WL 1838747 (Ohio Ct. App. 2d Dist. Clark County 2000). But see the Staff Notes, which provide that, although discovery must be completed prior to the date set for full hearing, there may not be sufficient time for meaningful discovery in such cases and a statutory request for a continuance of the full hearing would be appropriate.

[14]*Catherine F. Klein & Leslye E. Orloff, Providing Legal Protection for Battered Women: An Analysis of State Statutes and Case Law, 21 Hofstra L. Rev. 801, 1054 (1993).*

[15]Civ. R. 65.1(D).

[16]See Civ.R. 26(B)(1).

[17]Civ.R. 26(C).

[18]D.C. Intrafamily R. 8(b).

[19]Martinez v. Martinez, 52 S.W.3d 429 (Tex. App. Fort Worth 2001), (discussing discovery for purposes of a protection order proceeding); Mugrage v. Mugrage, 335 N.J. Super. 653, 763 A.2d 347 (Ch. Div. 2000).

interposed only for delay. "Long delays before trials not only leave victims vulnerable to more violence, but decrease the likelihood that they will be supportive witnesses during trial."[21] Production of documents should not be used to gather privileged information or information that could aid the batterer in locating the victim's confidential whereabouts.[22]

Discovery may be requested by a respondent as a way to get information for use in a criminal domestic violence case arising from the same incident.[23] If counsel for the petitioner suspects that this is the case, he/she should request either that a protective order be granted pursuant to Civil Rule 26(C) or that the court continue the full hearing until final disposition of the criminal case and postpone discovery until that time. Counsel should, at least, anticipate a discovery request for this purpose.

Courts, attorneys, and advocates must guard against the use of discovery as a means of intimidating petitioners, locating petitioners, or discovering information about petitioners' current lives.[24] "Discovery which requires any direct contact between the parties should not be used or enforced. Minimizing contact between the parties in domestic violence cases reduces friction between the parties, and reduces the danger to the petitioner posed by each renewed contact."[25]

Discovery can never be used by a batterer to gain access to the victim's journal. In *Roe v. Roe*,[26] the court found that the wife's diary about specific events occurring between herself and her husband, kept at her lawyer's direction, was a work product and not subject to discovery.

Sometimes, a respondent may request discovery to gain insight into the allegations brought by the petitioner against him. In this particular instance, a respondent's argument that failing to permit discovery would violate his due process rights or hinder his ability to adequately prepare a defense is without merit.

---

[20]See Depos v. Depos, 307 N.J. Super. 396, 704 A.2d 1049 (Ch. Div. 1997) (denying defendant's motion to depose plaintiff in domestic violence action and holding that questioning of victims must be done in presence of judge at a hearing to insure that it is done fairly and that victims are not further victimized by the process to which they turn for protection).

[21]The National Council of Juvenile & Family Court Judges, Family Violence: Improving Court Practice 43 (1990).

[22]But see People v. Ramsey, 174 Misc. 2d 304, 307, 665 N.Y.S.2d 501 (Sup 1997) (rejecting the argument that "the addresses and phone numbers of domestic violence victims are protected by a common-law privilege" and finding that "no privilege exists between a battered woman and her counselor").

[23]See Com. v. Tripolone, 425 Mass. 487, 681 N.E.2d 1216 (1997) (discussing when domestic violence shelters and counselors have to comply with defendant's discovery requests regarding particular victim). But see Waliser v. Tada, 1990 WL 20080 (Ohio Ct. App. 10th Dist. Franklin County 1990), cause dismissed, 61 Ohio St. 3d 1405, 573 N.E.2d 1097 (1991).

[24]Catherine F. Klein & Leslye E. Orloff, Providing Legal Protection for Battered Women: An Analysis of State Statutes and Case Law, 21 Hofstra L. Rev. 801, 1054 (1993).

[25]Catherine F. Klein & Leslye E. Orloff, Providing Legal Protection for Battered Women: An Analysis of State Statutes and Case Law, 21 Hofstra L. Rev. 801, 1054 (1993).

[26]Roe v. Roe, 253 N.J. Super. 418, 601 A.2d 1201 (App. Div. 1992).

Discovery is often not needed to properly prepare for the full hearing. Ohio's statutory framework directs that detailed facts of violence be alleged in the petition. RC 3113.31(C)(1) states that the petition shall contain an allegation that the respondent engaged in domestic violence, including a description of the nature and extent of the violence.[27] Since Ohio mandates more than a general allegation of abusive conduct, there are no arguable grounds to support the request.[28]

Because the full hearing must be scheduled within a short period of time,[29] due process rights are more likely to be violated if discovery is requested and the full hearing is delayed. Moreover, respondent's due process rights are protected because notice and an opportunity to be heard are mandated by statute.

Lastly, it should be noted that several states have enacted statutes which prohibit discovery requests of communications between domestic violence counselors and victims, including a disclosure of records.[30] Although Ohio is not yet one of these states, it is incumbent on petitioner's counsel to argue that communications between the victim and the battered women's shelter staff and volunteers and/or the victim witness assistance staff and volunteers are not subject to discovery or subpoena without the permission of the victim.

Petitioner's counsel, or an advocate for a pro se petitioner, has a duty to request that the scope of discovery in the civil protection order proceeding be restricted.[31] It should be stressed that the "dangers inherent in the examination and discovery procedures outweigh the importance of the respondent's right to acquire certain information."[32]

Q & A: What types of discovery are best suited to civil protection order actions?[33]

Whatever the discovery mechanism, it should not further endanger the petitioner. Face-to-face contact between the parties prior to the full hearing is not advised. Any deposition should take place in the courthouse where security is present. Respondent should be excluded from the courthouse during the deposition.

A deposition may be an intimidating experience for a victim of domestic violence. In certain instances, depositions may perpetrate the cycle of power and control seen in a domestic violence relationship. Moreover, the deposition itself may cause victims to question their

[27]See, for example, Whitten v. Whitten, 292 Ill. App. 3d 780, 226 Ill. Dec. 670, 686 N.E.2d 19 (3d Dist. 1997); H.E.S. v. J.C.S., 175 N.J. 309, 815 A.2d 405 (2003).

[28]Martinez v. Martinez, 52 S.W.3d 429 (Tex. App. Fort Worth 2001).

[29]RC 3113.31(D)(2)(a).

[30]See, e.g., Calif. Evid. Code §§ 1037 to 1037.7, Calif. Evid. Code § 912(b); State v. J.G., 261 N.J. Super. 409, 619 A.2d 232 (App. Div. 1993); see also Com. v. Tripolone, 425 Mass. 487, 681 N.E.2d 1216 (1997).

[31]Catherine F. Klein & Leslye E. Orloff, Providing Legal Protection for Battered Women: An Analysis of State Statutes and Case Law, 21 Hofstra L. Rev. 801, 1055 (1993).

[32]Catherine F. Klein & Leslye E. Orloff, Providing Legal Protection for Battered Women: An Analysis of State Statutes and Case Law, 21 Hofstra L. Rev. 801, 1055 (1993).

[33]See, e.g., Martinez v. Martinez, 52 S.W.3d 429 (Tex. App. Fort Worth 2001).

resolve to proceed at the full hearing. Because of potential delays, increase in expenses for the victims and further intimidation, it is possible that a deposition could quickly become the strategy of choice for some respondents. Therefore, a petitioner's attorney should argue that depositions not be used absent unusual circumstances.[34]

Interrogatories[35] and requests for production of documents[36] may be considered provided they are not interposed for delay. Furthermore, any information solicited by the respondent should not be privileged information, other information not subject to the rules of discovery, or information that may endanger the petitioner if obtained, such as the petitioner's address and telephone number, child's school or day care provider, or the shelter's address.

If the court permits a respondent's discovery request, counsel for the petitioner must make sure the court and the respondent understand that the ex parte protection order stays in effect pending the full hearing.[37] If the petitioner has not requested an ex parte protection order, discovery requests of any kind should not be granted. Any continuance permitted at this time may endanger a petitioner who does not have a protection order in place.

Q & A: What is the procedure for obtaining discovery?

Some Ohio jurisdictions permit discovery if requested by the respondent by continuance prior to the full hearing. If requested by the respondent at the full hearing, many courts will deny the respondent the opportunity for discovery.

At least one Ohio court has addressed this issue. In *Snyder v. Snyder*,[38] the Ross County Court of Appeals stated that the "[a]ppellant . . . did not request a continuance to enable him to utilize any discovery procedures or other proceedings available under the civil rules."

The *Snyder* court reasoned that because appellant failed to continue the case, and because he attended the full hearing with witnesses, he could not request an additional hearing in order to prepare his defense and respond to the testimony at the full hearing. The court determined that what appellant wanted was a third hearing and that a third hearing was not contemplated by the statute.[39]

The court of appeals overruled appellant's assignment of error only because appellant failed to request a continuance to enable him to utilize discovery procedures. Had he requested a continuance to obtain discovery, it is intimated that the court would have granted a continuance for this reason.

Q & A: When should a protective order be considered?

Pursuant to Civ.R. 26(C), a protective order may issue for any rea-

---

[34]Civ.R. 33.

[35]Civ.R. 33.

[36]Civ.R. 34.

[37]See RC 3113.31(D)(2)(b).

[38]Snyder v. Snyder, 1995 WL 493998, *2 (Ohio Ct. App. 4th Dist. Ross County 1995).

[39]Snyder v. Snyder, 1995 WL 493998 (Ohio Ct. App. 4th Dist. Ross County 1995); see also RC 3113.31.

son which justice requires in order to protect a party from annoyance, embarrassment, oppression, or undue burden or expense. If it can be shown by good cause that it is needed, a judge will usually grant the litigant's motion.[40]

If discovery is not prohibited, the protective order should be requested to limit discovery to that which is appropriate to the proceedings and preclude any discovery that would unnecessarily intimidate the petitioner.[41] In any event, the scope of the discovery must be limited to the incidents contained in the petitioner's petition.

Q & A: Can a petitioner request discovery of the respondent's records from a batterers' treatment program or communications from the respondent's counselor from such a program?

There is no statutory prohibition preventing discovery of these items. It has been suggested that a privilege should exist for respondents regarding information obtained by a counselor during such batterers' treatment. However, statements by a counselor that a respondent failed to complete a batterers' program or threatened further violence to the petitioner should not be considered confidential information and should be made available to the court.

Additionally, the Ohio Supreme Court's standard forms permit a court to request a batterers' counseling program to provide the court with written notice if the respondent fails to attend the initial appointment and a written report when the respondent completes the program.[42] In fact, all program reports will be accepted into evidence by the court at the next scheduled hearing as the direct examination of the author of each report, subject to cross-examination by the parties.[43]

While this requirement in the civil protection order eliminates the need to request discovery for those who are required to enter a program as part of the order issued by the court, discovery issues may still exist where a respondent had been ordered into a counseling program prior to the issuance of the civil protection order.

§ 12:6 Full hearing—Evidentiary issues[1]

Q & A: Is an answer or other pleading considered evidence for purposes of prevailing at a full hearing?

No. The Supreme Court of Ohio has determined that an answer filed by the respondent is not adequate evidence to prove a party's allegations. In *Felton v. Felton*,[2] the appellee-respondent filed an answer in response to appellant's petition for a protection order. The trial court then considered this answer as evidence in deciding

---

[40]See Civ.R. 26(C).

[41]See Alpha Benefits Agency, Inc. v. King Ins. Agency, Inc., 134 Ohio App. 3d 673, 731 N.E.2d 1209, 1213 (8th Dist. Cuyahoga County 1999).

[42]Sup. R. Form 10.01-I, Sup. R. Form 10.01-J.

[43]See Sup. R. Form 10.01-I, Sup. R. Form 10.01-J.

[Section 12:6]

[1]See also Ch 15, Domestic Violence Case Strategy and Evidentiary Considerations.

[2]Felton v. Felton, 79 Ohio St. 3d 34, 1997-Ohio-302, 679 N.E.2d 672 (1997).

whether to grant the petition for a protection order. In fact, the trial court found that appellee's answer was sufficient enough to controvert the appellant's testimony. On appeal, the Supreme Court held that "[a] pleading is not admissible into evidence at a hearing to prove a party's allegations and must not be considered as evidence by the court."[3]

Q & A: Must the parties present evidence at the full hearing?

Each party to a civil protection order proceeding is entitled to present evidence at the full hearing. In *Deacon v. Landers*,[4] the Ross County Court discussed the issue of whether evidence must be presented to sustain the issuance of the protection order. The court stated that "in an unrelated context, a mere 'hearing' has been held to include the introduction of testimony and documents."[5] Applying this reasoning to full hearings, the court wrote that, in both contested and noncontested cases, evidence must be presented to maintain a civil protection order in effect.[6] The court held that "where the issuance of a protection order is contested, the court must, at the very least, allow for presentation of evidence, both direct and rebuttal, as well as arguments."[7]

What is apparent from the case law is that to hold a "full hearing" means to present evidence and take testimony. It may also include

[3]Felton v. Felton, 79 Ohio St. 3d 34, 43, 1997-Ohio-302, 679 N.E.2d 672 (1997); see also McIntyre v. Johnson-Estes, 2011-Ohio-1696, 2011 WL 1327392 (Ohio Ct. App. 8th Dist. Cuyahoga County 2011) (reversing judgment issuing a CPO and finding that a petition itself is not evidence that an individual committed domestic violence, and that testimony is necessary to show that an individual committed domestic violence or that the individual placed another in any danger).

[4]Deacon v. Landers, 68 Ohio App. 3d 26, 587 N.E.2d 395 (4th Dist. Ross County 1990); see also Lindsay v. Jackson, 2000 WL 1268810 (Ohio Ct. App. 1st Dist. Hamilton County 2000); Terrell v. Terrell, 2003-Ohio-150, 2003 WL 125013 (Ohio Ct. App. 8th Dist. Cuyahoga County 2003).

[5]Deacon v. Landers, 68 Ohio App. 3d 26, 29 n.4, 587 N.E.2d 395 (4th Dist. Ross County 1990); see also Bateman v. Shipman, 2000 WL 1459721 (Ohio Ct. App. 11th Dist. Trumbull County 2000) (CPO upheld over respondent's argument the trial court improperly considered evidence and allegations not included in the petition).

[6]See Gaietto v. Noveck, 2008-Ohio-519, 2008 WL 351460, *4 (Ohio Ct. App. 3d Dist. Seneca County 2008) (Reversing and remanding to trial court for a full hearing, appellate court held that trial court cannot sign a CSPO into effect for a period of 5 years while noting that if Noveck subsequently requested a hearing, the trial court would probably grant it. "Such action is not within the meaning of 'full hearing' provided by RC 2903.214(E)(3)(d).").

[7]Deacon v. Landers, 68 Ohio App. 3d 26, 30, 587 N.E.2d 395 (4th Dist. Ross County 1990); see also Spigos v. Spigos, 2004-Ohio-757, 2004 WL 308098 (Ohio Ct. App. 10th Dist. Franklin County 2004). But see Wirtz v. Wirtz, 2000-Ohio-2564, 2000 WL 1486652 (Ohio Ct. App. 7th Dist. Mahoning County 2000) (appellant who chooses not to testify at a CPO hearing suffers no more penalty than he faces in choosing not to testify in his criminal proceeding); Klosterman v. Klosterman, 2000-Ohio-1807, 2000 WL 1752235 (Ohio Ct. App. 3d Dist. Mercer County 2000) (Appellant contended that his due process rights were violated when he was forced to assert his Fifth Amendment rights because of a pending criminal case against him. In finding that the appellant's arguments were without merit, the court of appeals stated that he had the opportunity to testify and that invoking his Fifth Amendment rights was his choice).

opening statements, legal arguments, testimony, and closing statements,[8] all in accordance with the Rules of Civil Procedure.[9]

Q & A: Does that mean that a petitioner should be allowed to finish her testimony and present witnesses?

Yes, according to the Tenth District Court of Appeals in *Spigos v. Spigos*.[10] During petitioner's testimony at the full hearing, the trial court judge terminated the hearing and did not allow her to finish her testimony.[11] By court entry, the judge held that the petitioner had failed to prove, by a preponderance of the evidence, that domestic violence occurred. On appeal, she argued that the trial court only permitted her to call one witness (herself) and did not let her finish her testimony. Moreover, it failed to allow her to call additional witnesses although her counsel had informed the court that their professional witnesses were on the way to court.[12]

In reversing the trial court's denial of petitioner's civil protection order, the Franklin County Court of Appeals held that "[w]ithout attempting to set definitive guidelines for the manner in which to conduct a "full hearing" under RC 3113.31, we hold that where the issuance of a protection order is contested, the court must, at the very least, allow for presentation of evidence, both direct and rebuttal as well as arguments."[13] The appellate court reasoned that appellant was denied a full hearing when the trial court rendered its decision before permitting her to conclude her testimony, offer other evidence and present arguments.

Q & A: Can a magistrate limit the duration of a full hearing?

In *J.J. v. J.A.*,[14] appellant raised this issue on appeal when he argued that the manner in which the magistrate conducted the full hearing violated his due process rights, particularly because he had no notice that there was a time limitation on the length of the hearing and that he was not able to present evidence in his defense.

The appellate court determined that balance was necessary. It noted that "a trial court has broad discretion to control the proceedings to enable it to exercise its jurisdiction in an orderly and efficient manner."[15] However, "the proceedings must be managed in a manner that fulfills the court's duty to promote accuracy and fairness of the

---

[8]But see Bradley v. Cox, 2004-Ohio-4840, 2004 WL 2035318 (Ohio Ct. App. 10th Dist. Franklin County 2004) (discussing closing arguments).

[9]RC 3113.31(G); see also Jackson v. Jackson, 1993 WL 526704 (Ohio Ct. App. 8th Dist. Cuyahoga County 1993); Mechtel v. Mechtel, 528 N.W.2d 916 (Minn. Ct. App. 1995).

[10]Spigos v. Spigos, 2004-Ohio-757, 2004 WL 308098 (Ohio Ct. App. 10th Dist. Franklin County 2004).

[11]But see Clementz-McBeth v. Craft, 2012-Ohio-985, 2012 WL 776851 (Ohio Ct. App. 3d Dist. Auglaize County 2012) (differentiating the facts and holding from Spigos).

[12]Spigos v. Spigos, 2004-Ohio-757, 2004 WL 308098, *2 (Ohio Ct. App. 10th Dist. Franklin County 2004).

[13]Spigos v. Spigos, 2004-Ohio-757, 2004 WL 308098, *3 (Ohio Ct. App. 10th Dist. Franklin County 2004).

[14]J.J. v. J.A., 2013-Ohio-5729, 2013 WL 6843592 (Ohio Ct. App. 9th Dist. Summit County 2013).

[15]J.J. v. J.A., 2013-Ohio-5729, 2013 WL 6843592, ¶ 9 (Ohio Ct. App. 9th Dist.

hearing."[16] Absent a local rule to the contrary or notice to a party that the hearing would be of limited duration, the appellant was deprived of an opportunity to present his case, once appellee rested. In reversing judgment, the appellate court held that "under the facts of this case, it was unreasonable for the magistrate and the trial court to refuse to grant J.A. additional time to present his case and therefore, his right to due process was violated."[17]

Q & A: Can a respondent refuse to present evidence at a full hearing?

A respondent may always choose not to testify at the full hearing. Usually a respondent voices this issue where there is also a pending companion criminal case.[18] However, it would be difficult for a respondent to rebut petitioner's arguments without presenting a defense.

In fact, many courts have been unsympathetic to respondents who request continuances until after the conclusion of the pending criminal case. For example, in *Wirtz v. Wirtz*,[19] respondent appealed the denial of a continuance of the full hearing pending disposition of his criminal case arising from the same facts. He asserted that his testimony at the full hearing, if he was made to testify, could be used against him at the later criminal trial. He also argued "that he was compelled to choose between protecting his privilege against self-incrimination at the later criminal trial and protecting his parental rights and property interests at the domestic relations hearing."[20]

The appellate court rejected his argument and held that "appellant suffers no more of a penalty in choosing not to testify in his domestic violence hearing than he faces in choosing not to testify in his criminal proceeding. In order to find that Appellant has committed an act of domestic violence, the complainant must show by a preponderance of the evidence that she is entitled to a protective order. Thus, the burden on the complainant is basically the same as that carried by the state in a criminal trial and Appellant, in deciding whether or not to testify at either proceeding, faces no greater danger if he does not

Summit County 2013), quoting Loewen v. Newsome, 2012-Ohio-566, 2012 WL 473850 (Ohio Ct. App. 9th Dist. Summit County 2012), citing State ex rel. Butler v. Demis, 66 Ohio St. 2d 123, 128-129, 20 Ohio Op. 3d 121, 420 N.E.2d 116 (1981).

[16]J.J. v. J.A., 2013-Ohio-5729, 2013 WL 6843592, ¶ 9 (Ohio Ct. App. 9th Dist. Summit County 2013), quoting *Loewen*, at ¶ 15.

[17]J.J. v. J.A., 2013-Ohio-5729, 2013 WL 6843592, ¶ 11 (Ohio Ct. App. 9th Dist. Summit County 2013).

[18]See also C.Q. v. P.S., 2016-Ohio-4988, 2016 WL 3881115 (Ohio Ct. App. 9th Dist. Medina County 2016).

[19]Wirtz v. Wirtz, 2000-Ohio-2564, 2000 WL 1486652 (Ohio Ct. App. 7th Dist. Mahoning County 2000); see also Klosterman v. Klosterman, 2000-Ohio-1807, 2000 WL 1752235 (Ohio Ct. App. 3d Dist. Mercer County 2000) (appellate court rejected appellant's argument that the presence of the prosecutor at his civil protection order hearing violated his due process rights where he was not free to defend himself and thus, forced to invoke his Fifth Amendment rights).

[20]Wirtz v. Wirtz, 2000-Ohio-2564, 2000 WL 1486652, *1 (Ohio Ct. App. 7th Dist. Mahoning County 2000). See also Sweet v. Hunt, 2014-Ohio-631, 2014 WL 707923 (Ohio Ct. App. 2d Dist. Greene County 2014) (holding that the Fifth Amendment's protection against compulsory, self-incriminating testimony does not extend to prohibit civil litigation while the possibility of criminal prosecution exists and that the Fifth Amendment does not shield a party from appearing or defending in a civil action).

testify at the domestic violence hearing than he faces in making that same determination at his criminal trial. He is not, as he argues, penalized for failing to testify at the domestic violence hearing, either explicitly or implicitly."[21]

Q & A: Is a court required to draw a negative inference from a respondent's refusal to testify?

Not according to the Cuyahoga County Court of Appeals in *Wolf v. Rosson*.[22] In that case, the appellant asserted on appeal that the trial court erred by failing to draw a negative inference from appellee's refusal to testify based upon the Fifth Amendment. The Eighth District Court of Appeals stated that "[w]hile we agree that the court could have drawn a negative inference from appellee's refusal to testify, the court was not required to do so."[23]

While not required to do so, a court may draw a negative inference from a respondent's refusal to testify. In *Zawrotuk v. Zawrotuk*,[24] the appellant appealed the issuance of a CPO on several grounds, among them, that the trial court improperly drew a negative inference from appellant's refusal to testify at the full protection order hearing. It is important to note that appellant did not specifically invoke his right against self-incrimination as he was not called to testify; nonetheless, he did not testify in his defense.[25] Appellant argued that the grant of the CPO was an abuse of discretion as he was not required to testify on his own behalf and pursuant to the Fifth Amendment to the U.S. Constitution, a court should not draw any negative inference based on this refusal to testify.

While it is clear that drawing inferences from a defendant's failure to testify violates the Fifth Amendment, "the Fifth Amendment does not prohibit the ability of the factfinder to make adverse inferences against parties in a civil action when they refuse to testify in response to probative evidence offered against them."[26] "Thus, a defendant's failure to testify may be commented upon to a jury in a civil trial."[27]

Since a civil protection order proceeding is conducted in accordance

---

[21] Wirtz v. Wirtz, 2000-Ohio-2564, 2000 WL 1486652, *4 (Ohio Ct. App. 7th Dist. Mahoning County 2000).

[22] Wolf v. Rosson, 2005-Ohio-1174, 2005 WL 628235 (Ohio Ct. App. 8th Dist. Cuyahoga County 2005).

[23] Wolf v. Rosson, 2005-Ohio-1174, 2005 WL 628235, *3 (Ohio Ct. App. 8th Dist. Cuyahoga County 2005), citing Baxter v. Palmigiano, 425 U.S. 308, 309, 96 S. Ct. 1551, 47 L. Ed. 2d 810 (1976).

[24] Zawrotuk v. Zawrotuk, 2014-Ohio-5225, 2014 WL 6641772 (Ohio Ct. App. 7th Dist. Mahoning County 2014).

[25] Zawrotuk v. Zawrotuk, 2014-Ohio-5225, 2014 WL 6641772, ¶ 45 (Ohio Ct. App. 7th Dist. Mahoning County 2014).

[26] Zawrotuk v. Zawrotuk, 2014-Ohio-5225, 2014 WL 6641772, ¶ 48 (Ohio Ct. App. 7th Dist. Mahoning County 2014), citing Baxter v. Palmigiano, 425 U.S. 308, 318–319, 96 S. Ct. 1551, 47 L. Ed. 2d 810 (1976) (silence is often evidence of the most persuasive character).

[27] Zawrotuk v. Zawrotuk, 2014-Ohio-5225, 2014 WL 6641772, ¶ 48 (Ohio Ct. App. 7th Dist. Mahoning County 2014), citing Burns v. Adams, 2014-Ohio-1917, 2014 WL 1853038, ¶ 72 (Ohio Ct. App. 4th Dist. Scioto County 2014); Bigler v. Personal Serv. Ins. Co., 2014-Ohio-1467, 2014 WL 1384572, ¶ 105-108 (Ohio Ct. App. 7th Dist. Belmont County 2014) (also stating that the court may disallow comments to jury due to an explanation, besides fear of exposure, as to why the defendant is absent, e.g.

with the Rules of Civil Procedure, the constitutional rights applicable in a criminal case are not applicable in a civil protection order proceeding.[28] This does not change just because the criminal proceedings are pending. Therefore, the appellate court upheld the decision of the trial court.

Q & A: After the parties rested their cases at the trial court level, respondent requested that the case against him be dismissed because the petitioner failed to present evidence of the family or household member relationship. Can the trial court re-open the case to permit petitioner's counsel to present this evidence?

Yes. In *Nichols v. Young*,[29] the parties each presented testimony at the full hearing. When the respondent rested its case, the trial court asked both counsel whether they would waive closing argument. At that time, respondent asked that the case against him be dismissed because petitioner failed to demonstrate that the family or household member relationship existed between the parties. Petitioner's counsel stated that the relationship between the parties was that of siblings and then noted that the mother also testified about the relationship. The trial judge then asked whether petitioner's counsel was asking the court to reopen the case to establish that fact, to which petitioner's counsel answered in the affirmative.

On appeal, appellant argued that the trial court's actions amounted to a *sua sponte* reopening of petitioner's case. The appellate court focused on the trial court record which sought only to clarify whether petitioner's counsel was making a request to reopen the case, "which was within the trial court's discretion to grant."[30] Since no legal authority was presented to controvert this and because petitioner presented evidence that demonstrated the fact that the parties were siblings, the court's decision to reopen the case was not an abuse of discretion.

Q & A: Can a party file a motion for new trial as a way to reopen proceedings and present newly discovered evidence?

In *Insa v. Insa*,[31] appellant appealed the trial court decision overruling her objections to the magistrate's decision and vacating the ex

medical reasons due to the accident for which he was sued); Smith v. Lautenslager, 15 Ohio App. 2d 212, 214, 44 Ohio Op. 2d 371, 240 N.E.2d 109 (1st Dist. Hamilton County 1968); Cincinnati Traction Co. v. Reis, 17 Ohio App. 198, 1922 WL 1758 (1st Dist. Hamilton County 1922); citing Wigmore on Evidence, Sec. 285 (inferences on civil party's failure to testify can be made except upon certain conditions and are open to explanation that a different hypothesis is more natural than *a party's fear of exposure*).

[28]Zawrotuk v. Zawrotuk, 2014-Ohio-5225, 2014 WL 6641772, ¶ 49 (Ohio Ct. App. 7th Dist. Mahoning County 2014).

[29]Nichols v. Young, 2015-Ohio-1077, 2015 WL 1288148 (Ohio Ct. App. 3d Dist. Putnam County 2015).

[30]Nichols v. Young, 2015-Ohio-1077, 2015 WL 1288148, ¶ 28 (Ohio Ct. App. 3d Dist. Putnam County 2015).

[31]Insa v. Insa, 2016-Ohio-7425, 72 N.E.3d 1170 (Ohio Ct. App. 2d Dist. Montgomery County 2016).

parte CPO against her husband and dismissing the petition for CPO.[32] Among her assignments of error, she claimed the trial court erred in refusing to reopen the proceedings after a hearing on her petition to address newly discovered evidence related to the potential abduction of the child.[33] The facts in this case demonstrate that she filed a motion for new trial under Civ. R. 59(A)(8) one day before the magistrate's ruling.

The appellate court reviewed the denial of the motion for new trial under Civ. R. 59 for an abuse of discretion and determined that there was no abuse of discretion because 1) a fear of abduction was not a ground for a domestic violence CPO under the facts of the case and 2) no allegations concerning a fear of abduction were raised in her petition for protection order. "With proper supporting evidence, fears of abduction might be relevant to the issuance of a domestic violence civil protection order, especially in conjunction with a finding that a defendant is engaging in acts of physical or sexual abuse that are likely to continue in the new location. On the record before us, however, we are unconvinced that the newly discovered evidence at issue-Mahamadou's request for his own daughter's passport after his wife's death-probably would have changed the result with regard to dismissal of the petition for protection order. Absent that showing, denial of the Civ. R. 59 motion was not an abuse of discretion."[34]

Clearly then, a party may consider filing a motion for a new trial to present additional evidence so long as such evidence is newly discovered and only if that evidence would probably change the result.[35]

§ 12:7 Full hearing—Other procedural concerns

Q & A: Is the trial court required to make a finding of domestic violence?

Except where a civil protection order is issued by consent entry,[1] a trial court must make a finding that domestic violence occurred.[2]

---

[32]Insa v. Insa, 2016-Ohio-7425, ¶ 1, 72 N.E.3d 1170 (Ohio Ct. App. 2d Dist. Montgomery County 2016).

[33]Insa v. Insa, 2016-Ohio-7425, ¶ 2, 72 N.E.3d 1170 (Ohio Ct. App. 2d Dist. Montgomery County 2016).

[34]Insa v. Insa, 2016-Ohio-7425, ¶ 43, 72 N.E.3d 1170 (Ohio Ct. App. 2d Dist. Montgomery County 2016).

[35]But see Besman v. Leventhal, 2017-Ohio-464, ¶ 4, 2017 WL 526288 (Ohio Ct. App. 8th Dist. Cuyahoga County 2017), appeal not allowed, 151 Ohio St. 3d 1503, 2018-Ohio-365, 90 N.E.3d 946 (2018) (finding that a new trial motion is inapplicable to Civ. R. 65.1 proceedings because it would not expedite the process).

[Section 12:7]

[1]See Lain v. Ververis, 1999 WL 893611 (Ohio Ct. App. 12th Dist. Preble County 1999).

[2]See, for example, Mechtel v. Mechtel, 528 N.W.2d 916 (Minn. Ct. App. 1995); Basden v. Basden, 154 N.C. App. 520, 572 S.E.2d 442 (2002) (appellate court cautioned the trial court relative to completing standard forms and making sufficient findings of fact); see also Price v. Price, 133 N.C. App. 440, 514 S.E.2d 553 (1999) (appellate court admonished trial court to make findings of fact and conclusions of law on form orders and noted it could have remanded case to trial court to enter new order with necessary findings).

Ohio's pre-printed forms have blank spaces for findings that domestic violence occurred.[3] Of importance is that these blank spaces for findings are omitted from the consent entry civil protection order form.[4]

Q & A: Where a respondent commits domestic violence in a civil protection order proceeding, is such a finding equivalent to a finding of guilt?

No. In *Elkins v. Elkins*,[5] the appellant argued that the trial court's finding that she committed domestic violence, when no jury found her guilty, violated her inherent constitutional right to a trial by jury. The Franklin County Court of Appeals held that a finding that a party committed domestic violence as set forth in RC 3113.31(A) is not the same as a finding of guilt for the crime of domestic violence. The court pointed out that the respondent's actions constituted domestic violence as defined pursuant to statute. An occurrence of act that constitutes domestic violence is significant only because it permits a court to grant a civil protection order.

Q & A: Is the respondent entitled to a jury trial?

In no jurisdiction is there a right to a jury trial in civil protection order cases for the issuance, modification, or extension of a civil protection order.[6] Civil protection orders are civil in nature, and the possibility of a criminal penalty upon violation does not create the right to a trial by jury.[7]

It is well settled that there is no constitutional right to a trial by jury in civil actions or proceedings.[8] Article I, Section 5 of the Ohio Constitution only guarantees the right to a trial by jury in actions that were in existence before the adoption of the Ohio Constitution.[9] For civil trials and proceedings that did not exist at common law, jury trials can be provided only by legislative enactment.[10]

Ohio's civil protection order statute, RC 3113.31, was enacted by the General Assembly on March 23, 1979, well after the adoption of the Ohio Constitution. The statute does not indicate that a jury be provided to a respondent in any civil protection order proceedings. The statute, however, does specifically indicate that any proceeding be conducted in accordance with the Rules of Civil Procedure.[11] Therefore, any proceeding initiated pursuant to RC 3113.31, including the full

---

[3]Sup. R. Form 10.01-I.

[4]See Sup. R. Form 10.01-J. But see Text Ch. 18, Federal Remedies, as to the Brady disqualifiers.

[5]Elkins v. Elkins, 1992 WL 180118 (Ohio Ct. App. 10th Dist. Franklin County 1992).

[6]See Cooke v. Naylor, 573 A.2d 376 (Me. 1990).

[7]Catherine F. Klein & Leslye E. Orloff, Providing Legal Protection for Battered Women: An Analysis of State Statutes and Case Law, 21 Hofstra L. Rev. 801, 1070 (1993).

[8]See Hagany v. Cohnen, 29 Ohio St. 82, 1876 WL 44 (1876); Belding v. State, 121 Ohio St. 393, 8 Ohio L. Abs. 28, 169 N.E. 301 (1929).

[9]See City of Cincinnati v. Cincinnati Dist. Council 51, Am. Federation of State, County and Municipal Emp., AFL-CIO, 35 Ohio St. 2d 197, 64 Ohio Op. 2d 129, 299 N.E.2d 686, 84 L.R.R.M. (BNA) 2241, 72 Lab. Cas. (CCH) P 53136 (1973); Renee v. Sanders, 160 Ohio St. 279, 52 Ohio Op. 175, 116 N.E.2d 420 (1953).

[10]See Gunsaullus v. Pettit, 46 Ohio St. 27, 17 N.E. 231 (1888).

[11]See RC 3113.31(G).

hearing, is a civil action where the right to a trial by jury is not accorded a respondent.

In *State ex rel. Miller v. Anthony*,[12] the Ohio Supreme Court followed this approach in a similar type of equitable action. In that case, the defendant argued that he had a right to a trial by jury in a nuisance abatement proceeding initiated by the state. The Ohio Supreme Court determined that nuisance abatement is essentially an equitable action for injunctive relief. The Court then held that jury trials are not required or guaranteed in such actions.

Ohio domestic violence case law further supports this conclusion. In *Snyder v. Snyder*,[13] the Ross County Court of Appeals upheld the trial court's decision that an appellant is not entitled to a trial by jury in a civil protection order proceeding.[14]

Q & A: Is a respondent entitled to be transported to the full hearing?

Not according to the Franklin County Court of Appeals. In *State v. Gordon*,[15] the appellant claimed that the domestic relations court failed to provide him with proper notice and an opportunity to be heard at the full hearing. The court concluded that the trial court had complied with the statute and then stated that "[c]ontrary to appellant's claims, we find no requirement in that statute and appellant provides no other authority that the trial court must transport the defendant in a CPO action to the hearing[16] or appoint counsel to rep-

---

[12]State ex rel. Miller v. Anthony, 72 Ohio St. 3d 132, 1995-Ohio-39, 647 N.E.2d 1368 (1995).

[13]Snyder v. Snyder, 1995 WL 493998 (Ohio Ct. App. 4th Dist. Ross County 1995).

[14]But see Felton v. Felton, 79 Ohio St. 3d 34, 1997-Ohio-302, 679 N.E.2d 672 (1997), wherein the Court merely noted that there was no jury. Of significance is that the Court did not strongly state a position regarding whether a respondent has the right to a trial by jury in a civil protection order proceeding. The issue may still be open.

[15]State v. Gordon, 2003-Ohio-6558, 2003 WL 22889573 (Ohio Ct. App. 10th Dist. Franklin County 2003). See also Text § 12:4, Full hearings—Continuances; Parker v. Jamison, 2003-Ohio-7295, 2003 WL 24135688 (Ohio Ct. App. 4th Dist. Scioto County 2003); Waters v. Lattany, 2007-Ohio-1047, 2007 WL 707519 (Ohio Ct. App. 6th Dist. Lucas County 2007) (appellant failed to file either a continuance pending his release from incarceration or a motion to transport); Gaietto v. Noveck, 2008-Ohio-519, 2008 WL 351460 (Ohio Ct. App. 3d Dist. Seneca County 2008); Barrow v. Brown, 2017-Ohio-7926, 2017 WL 4329767 (Ohio Ct. App. 2d Dist. Greene County 2017) (noting that the record contained no motion to continue or motion to transport, and suggesting that the decision could have been different had a motion been filed, but that as an incarcerated person, he had no absolute right to be present). But see Sigler v. Arvay, 2002-Ohio-6762, 2002 WL 31761478 (Ohio Ct. App. 9th Dist. Summit County 2002).

[16]See also Parker v. Jamison, 2003-Ohio-7295, 2003 WL 24135688, *5 (Ohio Ct. App. 4th Dist. Scioto County 2003) (Noting that "Ohio courts have repeatedly recognized that a person who is incarcerated has no absolute right to appear at a civil action." Further, that the trial court did not have a duty to sua sponte order respondent's transport from the jail to secure his attendance at the full CPO hearing.); Allen v. Thompson, 2017-Ohio-4234, 2017 WL 2542392 (Ohio Ct. App. 11th Dist. Lake County 2017) (intimating that a respondent may motion the court to transport him from jail); Mancino v. City of Lakewood, 36 Ohio App. 3d 219, 523 N.E.2d 332 (8th Dist. Cuyahoga County 1987); Leflore v. Leflore, 2014-Ohio-5327, 2014 WL 6758522 (Ohio Ct. App. 5th Dist. Richland County 2014) (prisoners have no constitutional right to be personally present at any stage of the judicial proceedings, citing *Mancino*

resent his interests."[17] The appellate court also noted that appellant failed to take any action upon receipt of the CPO. "Appellant presented no testimonial or documentary evidence that he was precluded from contacting the court or an attorney on his own in order to make some sort of arrangement. There is no substantive evidence in the record demonstrating that appellant was prohibited from using the telephone, contacting an attorney or contacting the domestic relations court."[18]

Q & A: Is a respondent entitled to appointed counsel?

No. Civil protection orders are civil in nature[19] and the possibility of a criminal penalty upon violation does not create a right to the appointment of counsel.[20] Therefore, a respondent will not be appointed counsel for a full hearing and may not continue a full hearing on the grounds that counsel will be appointed for him/her.[21] However, a court may continue a case should a respondent advise the court that he/she seeks a continuance to obtain counsel for him/herself.[22]

---

at 221); Price v. Johnston, 334 U.S. 266, 68 S. Ct. 1049, 92 L. Ed. 1356 (1948) (abrogation on other grounds recognized by, McCleskey v. Zant, 499 U.S. 467, 111 S. Ct. 1454, 113 L. Ed. 2d 517 (1991)).

[17]State v. Gordon, 2003-Ohio-6558, 2003 WL 22889573, *3 (Ohio Ct. App. 10th Dist. Franklin County 2003).

[18]State v. Gordon, 2003-Ohio-6558, 2003 WL 22889573, *3 (Ohio Ct. App. 10th Dist. Franklin County 2003).

[19]See State v. Gordon, 2003-Ohio-6558, 2003 WL 22889573 (Ohio Ct. App. 10th Dist. Franklin County 2003); see also Butcher v. Stevens, 182 Ohio App. 3d 77, 2009-Ohio-1754, 911 N.E.2d 928 (4th Dist. Athens County 2009); Schumaker v. Schumaker, 2010-Ohio-3490, 2010 WL 2914347 (Ohio Ct. App. 5th Dist. Licking County 2010).

[20]See Catherine F. Klein & Leslye E. Orloff, Providing Legal Protection for Battered Women: An Analysis of State Statutes and Case Law, 21 Hofstra L. Rev. 801 (1993); see also Waters v. Lattany, 2007-Ohio-1047, 2007 WL 707519 (Ohio Ct. App. 6th Dist. Lucas County 2007); Gomez v. Dyer, 2008-Ohio-1523, 2008 WL 850127 (Ohio Ct. App. 7th Dist. Noble County 2008); Slusser v. Klosterman, 2008-Ohio-2608, 2008 WL 2229635 (Ohio Ct. App. 3d Dist. Mercer County 2008) (noting that respondent had no constitutional right to appointed counsel); Caramico v. Caramico, 2015-Ohio-4232, 2015 WL 5934194 (Ohio Ct. App. 12th Dist. Clermont County 2015) (a respondent has no right to counsel in a civil action); Butcher v. Stevens, 182 Ohio App. 3d 77, 2009-Ohio-1754, 911 N.E.2d 928, ¶ 13 (4th Dist. Athens County 2009).

[21]See Noah v. Brillhart, 2003-Ohio-2421, 2003 WL 21078077 (Ohio Ct. App. 9th Dist. Wayne County 2003); State v. Gordon, 2003-Ohio-6558, 2003 WL 22889573 (Ohio Ct. App. 10th Dist. Franklin County 2003) (holding that there is no constitutional right to appointment of counsel in a civil action), citing Schottenstein v. Schottenstein, 2003-Ohio-5032, 2003 WL 22176786 (Ohio Ct. App. 10th Dist. Franklin County 2003). See also Waters v. Lattany, 2007-Ohio-1047, 2007 WL 707519 (Ohio Ct. App. 6th Dist. Lucas County 2007); Butcher v. Stevens, 182 Ohio App. 3d 77, 2009-Ohio-1754, 911 N.E.2d 928 (4th Dist. Athens County 2009) (although parties do not have a right to appointed counsel, they have a right to appear with retained counsel); see also Patton v. Patton, 2010-Ohio-2096, 2010 WL 1918793 (Ohio Ct. App. 5th Dist. Muskingum County 2010).

[22]Leflore v. Leflore, 2014-Ohio-5327, 2014 WL 6758522 (Ohio Ct. App. 5th Dist. Richland County 2014) (where appellant was in jail at the time he was served with a CPO, he failed to take any actions such as contacting an attorney to prepare a defense, or requesting a continuance or filing a direct appeal. Thus his Motion to Vacate the original CPO was not well taken based on the claim that he was not allowed to be present at any of the relevant hearings).

Q & A: Is a petitioner entitled to appointed counsel in a civil protection order proceeding?

No Ohio court has addressed this issue. However, an Illinois appellate court determined that a petitioner was entitled to appointed counsel. In *Scroggins v. Scroggins*,[23] the petitioner sought a civil protection order under the Illinois Domestic Violence Act. At the plenary hearing (Ohio's full hearing) petitioner appeared pro se and the respondent appeared with an attorney. The trial court appointed the petitioner counsel and rescheduled the full hearing. On appeal, the respondent argued that the trial court did not have the authority to appoint the domestic violence attorney under the Illinois Domestic Violence Act.

The appellate court relied on the fact that a civil domestic violence proceeding is a domestic relations matter and that "[t]rial courts are in fact encouraged to appoint counsel to the indigent in 'domestic relations matters.' "[24] Further, the appellate court noted that the legislature has sanctioned the policy of providing legal representation to the indigent party in domestic relations cases in order to reduce an over-burdened system.[25] Therefore, appointment of counsel in this instance was within the trial court's authority. Clearly, under Illinois law, a respondent should be entitled to an appointed counsel as well.[26]

Q & A: Can a respondent in a civil protection order proceeding argue ineffective assistance of trial counsel?

A respondent would not prevail if such a claim was made to the court. According to *Moore v. Moore*,[27] the granting of a civil protection order is a civil proceeding, which does not result in incarceration in its application.[28] Therefore, a claim of ineffective assistance of counsel is inappropriate.[29]

Q & A: Besides motions for continuances for discovery, what other types of motions are often made during civil protection order proceedings?

---

[23]Scroggins v. Scroggins, 327 Ill. App. 3d 333, 261 Ill. Dec. 268, 272, 762 N.E.2d 1195 (4th Dist. 2002). But see D.N. v. K.M., 216 N.J. 587, 83 A.3d 825 (2014) (see dissenting opinion on the right to appointed counsel in a domestic violence case).

[24]Scroggins v. Scroggins, 327 Ill. App. 3d 333, 337, 261 Ill. Dec. 268, 272, 762 N.E.2d 1195, 1199, (4th Dist. 2002).

[25]Scroggins v. Scroggins, 327 Ill. App. 3d 333, 337, 261 Ill. Dec. 268, 272, 762 N.E.2d 1195, 1199, (4th Dist. 2002).

[26]But see Cloutterbuck v. Cloutterbuck, 556 A.2d 1082 (D.C. 1989) (discussing that the possibility of imprisonment as a punishment for eventual violation of a CPO is too remote as of the time the order is entered to trigger a right to counsel).

[27]Moore v. Moore, 2003-Ohio-1382, 2003 WL 1422447 (Ohio Ct. App. 5th Dist. Licking County 2003); see also Luna-Corona v. Esquivel-Parrales, 2009-Ohio-2628, 2009 WL 1581133 (Ohio Ct. App. 12th Dist. Butler County 2009).

[28]Moore v. Moore, 2003-Ohio-1382, 2003 WL 1422447, *3 (Ohio Ct. App. 5th Dist. Licking County 2003); see also Mottice v. Kirkpatrick, 2001-Ohio-7042, 2001 WL 1673733 (Ohio Ct. App. 5th Dist. Stark County 2001).

[29]Moore v. Moore, 2003-Ohio-1382, 2003 WL 1422447, *3 (Ohio Ct. App. 5th Dist. Licking County 2003). See also Chapman v. Chapman, 2006-Ohio-2328, 2006 WL 1284592 (Ohio Ct. App. 2d Dist. Montgomery County 2006) (stating that if the attorney neglected to perform the basic duties of his representation, the client's remedy is against the attorney in a suit for malpractice); Luna-Corona v. Esquivel-Parrales, 2009-Ohio-2628, 2009 WL 1581133 (Ohio Ct. App. 12th Dist. Butler County 2009).

At the full hearings, many attorneys for respondents will strategically make oral motions to dismiss the petition for a protection order on the basis that the petitioner failed to prove the case. Civil Rule 41(B)(2) provides:

> After the plaintiff, in an action tried by the court without a jury, has completed the presentation of his evidence, the defendant, without waiving his right to offer evidence in the event the motion is not granted, may move for a dismissal on the ground that upon the facts and the law the plaintiff has shown no right to relief. The court as trier of the facts may then determine them and render judgment against the plaintiff or may decline to render any judgment until the close of all the evidence. If the court renders judgment on the merits against the plaintiff, the court shall make findings as provided in Rule 52 if requested to do so by any party.

Because civil protection order actions are conducted in accordance with the Rules of Civil Procedure,[30] dismissal motions are permitted.[31] However, if the court chooses to dismiss the protection order on its own, and outside of the hearing, the petitioner must be given notice of any impending dismissal of a CPO.[32]

In *Shutway v. Shutway*,[33] the trial court granted the respondent's motion to dismiss the petition for a protection order on the basis that the petitioner failed to prove her case. On appeal, the petitioner argued that it was reversible error for the trial court to grant the respondent's motion.

The Cuyahoga County Court of Appeals first provided the framework under which a party may proceed with a motion to dismiss. The court noted that a motion to dismiss, without a jury, is governed by Civ.R. 41(B)(2). Additionally, "in considering a Civ.R. 41(B)(2), a trial court is not required to construe the evidence in favor of the nonmoving party. The decision to dismiss must be guided by the evidence in the case and the pertinent case law."[34] Since the trial court may consider both the law and facts of the case, "the trial judge . . . actually determines whether the plaintiff proved the necessary facts by the necessary quantum of proof."[35]

In reversing the trial court decision, the appellate court determined that the trial court erred as a matter of law in granting appellee's mo-

---

[30]See RC 3113.31(G).

[31]See Shutway v. Shutway, 2000 WL 146533, *3 (Ohio Ct. App. 8th Dist. Cuyahoga County 2000) (noting that dismissal may be appropriate where "the trial court determines that the necessary quantum of proof makes it clear that plaintiff will not prevail"); see also Maccabee v. Maccabee, 1999 WL 430943 (Ohio Ct. App. 10th Dist. Franklin County 1999); Ferguson v. Ferguson, 2000 WL 1724294 (Ohio Ct. App. 5th Dist. Knox County 2000).

[32]See Sterling v. Sterling, 2002-Ohio-4997, 2002 WL 31111778 (Ohio Ct. App. 5th Dist. Fairfield County 2002); see also Text § 12:25, Modification and termination of civil protection orders.

[33]Shutway v. Shutway, 2000 WL 146533 (Ohio Ct. App. 8th Dist. Cuyahoga County 2000).

[34]Shutway v. Shutway, 2000 WL 146533, *3 (Ohio Ct. App. 8th Dist. Cuyahoga County 2000).

[35]Shutway v. Shutway, 2000 WL 146533, *3 (Ohio Ct. App. 8th Dist. Cuyahoga County 2000).

tion to dismiss the petition for civil protection order where the evidence presented at hearing was sufficient to establish her case. In recognizing that an erroneous standard of proof was applied to the facts of the case at hand, the court indicated that, in order to defeat a motion to dismiss, a petitioner must prove that domestic violence occurred by a preponderance of the evidence.[36]

Family law practitioners should be prepared to present their cases by a preponderance of the evidence, and they should object or appeal if it becomes apparent that a trial court has applied an incorrect standard of proof. The Ohio Supreme Court articulated the correct standard in *Felton v. Felton*.[37] "[W]hen granting a protection order, the trial court must find that petitioner or has shown by a preponderance of the evidence that petitioner or petioner's family or household members are in danger of domestic violence."[38] The *Shutway* court also noted that "[t]he statutory criteria for determining whether to grant a civil protection order pursuant to RC 3113.31 is the existence or the threatened existence of domestic violence."[39] An attorney who relies on the aforementioned principles should be able to effectively withstand a motion to dismiss the petition for a civil protection order.

Although answers and other responsive pleadings cannot be admitted as evidence in a civil protection order proceeding to prove a party's allegation,[40] these pleadings may raise an affirmative defense to be considered on appeal.[41] Failing to plead these affirmative defenses at the trial court level waives them on appeal.[42]

Sometimes it may become necessary to withdraw the petition for protection order and terminate the ex parte civil protection order. A petitioner who already has a pending criminal domestic violence case arising from the same facts may consider this. If a petitioner institutes a civil protection order proceeding, the respondent (who is also the defendant in the criminal case) may request discovery in the civil case in order to obtain information for the criminal case. Besides requesting information, a respondent may proceed to a full hearing in order to view the petitioner's court demeanor. Moreover, respondent may attempt to impeach petitioner's credibility if testimony at the civil hearing contradicts that presented in the criminal case.

An attorney should review the options at various points during the case in order to decide whether the risk to a petitioner who presents testimony at the full hearing outweighs the issuance of a civil protection order at a specific point in time. For a petitioner who is a confused witness but already has a criminal protection order, the prudent

[36]See Felton v. Felton, 79 Ohio St. 3d 34, 1997-Ohio-302, 679 N.E.2d 672 (1997).

[37]Felton v. Felton, 79 Ohio St. 3d 34, 1997-Ohio-302, 679 N.E.2d 672 (1997).

[38]Felton v. Felton, 79 Ohio St. 3d 34, 42, 1997-Ohio-302, 679 N.E.2d 672 (1997).

[39]Shutway v. Shutway, 2000 WL 146533, *4 (Ohio Ct. App. 8th Dist. Cuyahoga County 2000).

[40]See Felton v. Felton, 79 Ohio St. 3d 34, 1997-Ohio-302, 679 N.E.2d 672 (1997).

[41]See Genari v. Genari, 2001-Ohio-1524, 2001 WL 848569 (Ohio Ct. App. 2d Dist. Greene County 2001).

[42]Genari v. Genari, 2001-Ohio-1524, 2001 WL 848569 (Ohio Ct. App. 2d Dist. Greene County 2001) (discussing the failure of appellant to waive the issue of res judicata).

course of action may be to withdraw the petition and terminate the ex parte order. A civil protection order can always be requested after disposition of the criminal case.

Q & A: Must the full hearing be recorded?

Not according to the 10th District Court of Appeals. In *Nkurunziza v. Nyamusevya*,[43] the husband threatened to kill his wife, printed reports of men who killed their wives and stated that he agreed with the killings, and hit her, giving her a black eye. Wife testified that she was afraid to call the police because husband threatened to rape her, abandon her and the children, divorce her and interfere with her ability to become a citizen. Based on this testimony, the trial court granted the CPO.

On appeal, respondent contended that his due process rights were violated because the full hearing was not recorded. While acknowledging that App. R. 9(C) permitted him to file a proposed statement, he asserted that a statement was not as accurate as a transcript. He also argued that "a hearing of this nature should be recorded because violation of a DVCPO may subject him to serious criminal consequences."[44]

The appellate court first pointed out that appellant could point to no rule or statute supporting his argument that a recording of a full hearing was required. The court then reasoned that "[t]he statute itself does not require it, nor do the rules of the trial court." Appellant's reliance on Crim. R. 22, which provides that "in serious offense cases all proceedings shall be recorded," was misplaced because the full hearing was not a criminal proceeding and no criminal charges were pending. Therefore, the due process principles at work in a criminal proceeding did not apply.[45] Finally, the court also noted that appellant never requested that the hearing be recorded.

Q & A: When can a petitioner dismiss a CPO?[46]

Under Civ. R. 41(A)(1)(a), a plaintiff may dismiss an action without order of the court by filing a notice of dismissal at any time before commencement of trial. In the context of a civil protection order, a petitioner may file a Notice of Dismissal of her petition and civil protection order at any time before commencement of the full hearing.[47] Unless otherwise stated in the notice of dismissal or by stipulation,

---

[43]Nkurunziza v. Nyamusevya, 2010-Ohio-5966, 2010 WL 4968636 (Ohio Ct. App. 10th Dist. Franklin County 2010).

[44]Nkurunziza v. Nyamusevya, 2010-Ohio-5966, 2010 WL 4968636, *3 (Ohio Ct. App. 10th Dist. Franklin County 2010).

[45]Nkurunziza v. Nyamusevya, 2010-Ohio-5966, 2010 WL 4968636, *3 (Ohio Ct. App. 10th Dist. Franklin County 2010).

[46]See also Text § 12:25, Modification and termination of civil protection orders.

[47]See Edwards v. Reser, 2007-Ohio-6520, 2007 WL 4277861 (Ohio Ct. App. 6th Dist. Ottawa County 2007); see also Vistula Management Co. v. Shoemake, 2008-Ohio-365, 2008 WL 300292 (Ohio Ct. App. 6th Dist. Lucas County 2008) (discussing Civ. R. 41(A)); Crawford v. Mack, 929 A.2d 250 (Pa. Super. Ct. 2007) (discussing whether a petitioner may withdraw a protection order). But see Oddo v. Spencer, 2011-Ohio-4073, 2011 WL 3587436, *2 (Ohio Ct. App. 5th Dist. Stark County 2011) (Holding that rule providing for voluntary dismissal of action by a plaintiff did not authorize dismissal of existing protection order by protected party. "Mrs. Oddo was the Petitioner in the action for the civil protection order, not the plaintiff. While she may have been the person who initiated the proceedings, it was the trial court who issued the order,

the dismissal is without prejudice, except that a notice of dismissal operates as an adjudication upon the merits of any claim that the plaintiff has once dismissed in any court.[48] In effect, this raises the issue of when a "dismissal without prejudice" implicates the doctrine of res judicata, which " 'bars all subsequent action based upon any claim arising out of a transaction or occurrence that was previously decided as a final and valid judgment in a prior action.' "[49]

Civ. R. 41(A)(2) states that a court, on its own motion, may also dismiss an action upon such terms and conditions as the court deems proper. Unless otherwise specified in the order, a dismissal under division (A)(2) of this rule is without prejudice.[50]

For attorneys who represent domestic violence petitioners, such dismissals should always be without prejudice. To that end, if the court dismisses the action after a notice of dismissal is filed, such dismissal is without prejudice and the action should be able to be brought again by a petitioner. It is important for counsel to advise the jurist that a dismissal is not a denial of the CPO. It should be argued that any CPO that is dismissed before a full hearing is not a final, appealable order and, thus, is not a valid judgment such that the doctrine of res judicata applies or bars further filings based on the same facts.[51]

Of importance is that attorneys for petitioners make sure that any dismissal is without prejudice and that such judgment entry specifically enters this in its judgment entry. On the other hand, because a civil protection order proceeding is a special statutory proceeding under Civ. R. 65.1, Civ. R. 41(A) may not even apply to these proceedings.

Sometimes, however, if children are involved and an affidavit describes serious abuse towards minor children, the court may choose not to dismiss the civil protection order. In some instances, the court might only dismiss the action as it relates to the petitioner but maintain the CPO for the benefit of the minor children.

It is clear, however, that a civil protection order issued after a full hearing cannot be dismissed pursuant to Civ. R. 41. If issued after a full hearing, a CPO can only be terminated in compliance with RC 3113.31(E)(8). If, however, such an order is denied after the full hearing, res judicata does apply.

Q & A: Can a trial court dismiss a CPO?[52]

Yes. Under Civ. R. 41(B)(1), a court can, on its own motion, dismiss

---

not Mrs. Oddo. As such, only the trial court has the ability to terminate, modify or renew the order.").

[48]Civ. R. 41(A).

[49]Barclay v. Haney, 2012-Ohio-5646, ¶ 9, 2012 WL 6034070 (Ohio Ct. App. 9th Dist. Summit County 2012), quoting Moore v. Moore, 2003-Ohio-3789, ¶ 7, 2003 WL 21658466 (Ohio Ct. App. 9th Dist. Wayne County 2003) (noting that it is not clear whether a temporary or ex parte protection order, if dismissed without prejudice, is a final and valid judgment).

[50]Civ. R. 41(A)(2).

[51]Barclay v. Haney, 2012-Ohio-5646, ¶ 10, 2012 WL 6034070 (Ohio Ct. App. 9th Dist. Summit County 2012).

[52]See also Text § 12:25, Modification and termination of civil protection orders; Sterling v. Sterling, 2002-Ohio-4997, 2002 WL 31111778 (Ohio Ct. App. 5th Dist. Fairfield County 2002). See also Smith v. Smith, 2013-Ohio-3551, 2013 WL 4401326

an action when the plaintiff fails to prosecute[53] and that, pursuant to Civ. R. 41(B)(3), such a dismissal under Civ. R. 41(B)(1) operates as an adjudication on the merits unless the court in its order of dismissal otherwise specifies.[54]

Q & A: May a trial court dismiss a CPO after petitioner has presented evidence to the court? May a petitioner move for a directed verdict?

Additionally, a court may also dismiss a CPO after the action is tried before the court and plaintiff (petitioner) has presented the evidence pursuant to Civ. R. 41(B)(2). The defendant (respondent), without waiving the right to offer evidence in the event that the motion is not granted, may move for a dismissal on the ground that upon the facts and the law, the plaintiff has shown no right to relief. The court may render judgment against the Plaintiff at that time or decline to render judgment until the close of all the evidence. If the court renders judgment on the merits against the Plaintiff, the court shall make findings as provided in Civ. R. 52 if requested to do so by any party.[55] The trial court is not required to construe the evidence in favor of the nonmoving party.[56]

A petitioner may also move for a directed verdict.[57] Pursuant to Civ. R. 50(A), a motion for a directed verdict may be made on the opening statement of the opponent's case, at the close of the opponent's evidence or at the close of all the evidence.[58] When a motion for directed verdict has been properly made, and the trial court, after construing the evidence most strongly in favor of the party against whom the motion is directed, finds that . . . reasonable minds could come to but

(Ohio Ct. App. 5th Dist. Muskingum County 2013) (upholding dismissal of the CPO for failing to file a witness list as set forth in the pretrial order); Speakman v. Crabtree, 2014-Ohio-2152, 2014 WL 2155355 (Ohio Ct. App. 10th Dist. Franklin County 2014).

[53]E.H. v. T.S., 2015-Ohio-5444, 2015 WL 9461788 (Ohio Ct. App. 3d Dist. Hardin County 2015) (where trial court dismissed CPO petition for failing to attend full hearing, court did not have jurisdiction to reopen the case, sua sponte reverse the dismissal, and hold a full hearing).

[54]Howard v. Howard, 2009-Ohio-155, 2009 WL 105684, *1 (Ohio Ct. App. 2d Dist. Greene County 2009).

[55]Civ. R. 41(B)(2); see also Zidan v. Zidan, 2015-Ohio-4021, 2015 WL 5723143 (Ohio Ct. App. 11th Dist. Lake County 2015) (noting that a trial court's ruling on a Civ. R. 41(B)(2) motion will be set aside on appeal only if it is erroneous as a matter of law or against the manifest weight of the evidence. ¶ 9).

[56]Zidan v. Zidan, 2015-Ohio-4021, 2015 WL 5723143, ¶ 9 (Ohio Ct. App. 11th Dist. Lake County 2015).

[57]While a directed verdict is often used when a case is tried to a jury and Civ. R. 41(B)(2) is used to dismiss a case tried before a judge, "a moving party is not prejudiced if the trial court erroneously applies Civ. R. 50(A) standard for a directed verdict rather that the less rigorous standard for a dismissal under Civ. R. 41(B)(2). Satisfaction of the Civ. R. 50(A) standard implies satisfaction of the Civ. R. 41(B)(2) standard." Heath v. Heath, 2017-Ohio-5506, 2017 WL 2730298, ¶ 34 (Ohio Ct. App. 12th Dist. Fayette County 2017); quoting Aztec Internatl. Foods, Inc. v. Duenas, 2013-Ohio-450, 2013 WL 501734, ¶ 14 n.6 (Ohio Ct. App. 12th Dist. Clermont County 2013).

[58]Civ. R. 50(A)(1).

one conclusion . . . the court shall sustain the motion and direct a verdict for the moving party as to that issue.[59]

Q & A: Can the court require one or both parties to take a polygraph test?

In *Toohill v. Toohill*,[60] the husband filed for a civil protection order alleging that his wife had engaged in domestic violence by kicking, slapping, pinching and restraining him. At the full hearing, the petitioner-husband testified to the incidents described in his petition, and said that two months earlier, his wife threatened him with a knife. The wife denied the allegations. Because the knife incident was crucial to his determination, the trial judge asked the wife to undergo a polygraph test and granted the civil protection order pending the results.

In noting that the trial court was unable to resolve the conflicting evidence or reconcile the different versions of the events, the appellate court stated that "[t]his fact evinces Mr. Toohill's failure to prove, by a preponderance of the evidence, that he was entitled to a domestic violence civil protection order."[61] In sustaining the respondent's assignment of error, the court admonished the trial court that unsubstantiated concerns for safety are not enough to justify the issuance of protection orders.[62]

The Greene County Court of Appeals addressed the polygraph issue by stating that "polygraph test results generally may not be admitted as evidence without a stipulation between the parties."[63]

Q & A: Can a court dismiss a CPO stating that the case had not been completed within the appropriate time frame?

According to the Fifth District Court of Appeals, the answer is no. In *Duff v. Duff*,[64] appellant filed a DVCPO against appellee. After the hearing, the magistrate issued an order indicating that testimony and evidence was received, but that the case had not been completed. The magistrate then ordered the ex parte CPO to remain in effect until a date certain or until a divorce is filed by either party and noted on the record that there was no time to complete the case.[65] During this time, both parties filed motions which the trial court addressed by way of scheduling hearing date to which appellee filed a motion to continue.

A week before the hearing, the trial court entered an order *sua sponte* "stating that the case 'had not been completed within the appropriate time frame (30 days) and, therefore, the court lacks

[59]Civ. R. 50(A)(4).

[60]Toohill v. Toohill, 2000 WL 1162049 (Ohio Ct. App. 2d Dist. Greene County 2000).

[61]Toohill v. Toohill, 2000 WL 1162049, *2 (Ohio Ct. App. 2d Dist. Greene County 2000).

[62]Toohill v. Toohill, 2000 WL 1162049, *2 (Ohio Ct. App. 2d Dist. Greene County 2000).

[63]Toohill v. Toohill, 2000 WL 1162049, *2 (Ohio Ct. App. 2d Dist. Greene County 2000).

[64]Duff v. Duff, 2014-Ohio-1040, 2014 WL 1340025 (Ohio Ct. App. 5th Dist. Guernsey County 2014).

[65]Duff v. Duff, 2014-Ohio-1040, 2014 WL 1340025, ¶ 19 (Ohio Ct. App. 5th Dist. Guernsey County 2014).

jurisdiction.' "[66] Thus, the trial court had dismissed the DVCPO without further hearing. On appeal, appellant claimed that the trial court's dismissal was in error and that the dismissal left her without protection.

The appellate court noted that the trial court had relied on the Supreme Court of Ohio's Rules of Superintendence Rules 37 and 39, "which appear to set forth a one-month guideline for the disposition of domestic violence cases in the domestic relations division of common pleas court. Certainly, '[t]he Rules of Superintendence were designed to secure the prompt and efficient disposition of cases.' "[67] But it is important to recognize that the Rules of Superintendence are general guidelines for the court to follow at its discretion.[68] In *Daniels*, the Fifth District appellate court determined that "[t]o dismiss a case because the guideline for disposition has been exceeded and advising the parties it can be refiled-thereby beginning anew the start of the clock-does not serve [the purpose of the Superintendence Rules], but rather thwarts it."[69] Relying on its rationale in *Daniels v. Daniels*, the appellate court decided that the trial court erred in dismissing the case and failing to finalize a decision on the DVCPO petition.

§ 12:8 Service of the protection order issued after the full hearing[1]

Q & A: Does the domestic violence statute mandate that a respondent be served with a copy of a civil protection order issued after the full hearing?

RC 3113.31(F)(1) provides some direction for service of a protection order, whether the order is granted ex parte or issued after a full hearing.[2] A copy of both the ex parte civil protection order and the civil protection order issued after the full hearing shall be delivered to the respondent on the same day that the order is entered.

To "serve" means to present a person with a notice or process as required by law.[3] To "deliver" means to give possession of something to another[4] and is further defined in Civ.R. 5(B).[5] Absent a specified method of service, recourse has been to rely on the Rules of Civil

[66]Duff v. Duff, 2014-Ohio-1040, 2014 WL 1340025, ¶ 10 (Ohio Ct. App. 5th Dist. Guernsey County 2014).

[67]Duff v. Duff, 2014-Ohio-1040, 2014 WL 1340025, ¶ 17 (Ohio Ct. App. 5th Dist. Guernsey County 2014), quoting Daniels v. Daniels, 2014-Ohio-83, 2014 WL 108792 (Ohio Ct. App. 5th Dist. Licking County 2014).

[68]Duff v. Duff, 2014-Ohio-1040, 2014 WL 1340025, ¶ 17 (Ohio Ct. App. 5th Dist. Guernsey County 2014).

[69]Duff v. Duff, 2014-Ohio-1040, 2014 WL 1340025, ¶ 18 (Ohio Ct. App. 5th Dist. Guernsey County 2014), quoting *Daniels* at ¶ 13.

[Section 12:8]

[1]See also Text § 11:11, Ex parte protection orders—Service and notice provisions.

[2]See also Text § 11:11, Ex parte protection orders—Service and notice provisions; Text § 14:15, Potential police liability in the enforcement of protection orders.

[3]Black's Law Dictionary (7th ed. 1999).

[4]Black's Law Dictionary (7th ed. 1999).

[5]See also Text Ch. 11, Issuance of a Civil Protection Order; Text § 11:11, Ex parte protection orders—Service and notice provisions.

Procedure. Rule 4 governs civil jurisdiction and service of process. Process means a writ or summons issued in the course of judicial proceedings and used to inform the defendant of the institution of proceedings against him and to compel his appearance in either civil or criminal cases.[6] Because an ex parte civil protection order accompanies the petition for a civil protection order, a summons is issued and its service is governed by Rule 4.[7]

In contrast, Civ. R. 65.1(C)(3)[8] provides that after service has been made in accordance with division (C)(2) of this rule, any additional service required to be made during the course of the proceedings on Respondent and, if applicable, on the parent, guardian or legal custodian of Respondent, shall be made in accordance with the provisions of Civ. R. 5(B). Civ. R. 5 applies to the service of papers other than process and specifically applies to every order required by its terms to be served, including civil protection orders issued after a full hearing. Service by mail is complete upon mailing.[9] Since the civil protection order issued after a full hearing is neither a writ nor a summons, it is not process. Hence, its service is governed by Civ. R. 5(B).

However, Civ. R. 65.1(C) appears to conflict with the Supreme Court of Ohio in *State v. Smith*.[10] This is because the opinion in *Smith* implies same day service where the issue is the proof necessary to sustain a conviction for a violation under RC 2919.27. In *Smith*, the state must prove, beyond a reasonable doubt, that the order was delivered to defendant. Under the service provisions of both Civ. R. 5(B) and Civ. R. 65.1(C)(3), service by mail is complete upon mailing. Unfortunately, there is usually no proof beyond a reasonable doubt that a CPO issued after a full hearing has been delivered/served on a defendant/respondent. Rather, completion of service is presumed.

In *Smith*, defendant was charged with violating a civil protection order after breaking into the victim's home and attempting to strangle her. The victims had previously advised defendant that she had obtained a CSPO requiring him to stay at least 500 feet away from her. Defendant had not been served with the CSPO until after the incident occurred. The trial court found Smith guilty of violating the CSPO, which decision was affirmed by the Franklin County appellate court.

In his merit brief to the Ohio Supreme Court, Smith argued that he was not lawfully convicted of violating RC 2919.27 because he was never served with the order before the alleged offense. The State as-

---

[6] Black's Law Dictionary (7th ed. 1999).

[7] See Staff Notes to amended Civ. R. 65.1 (effective July 1, 2016) addressing the *Smith* rationale that suggests an adherence to the service requirements in accordance with the Ohio Rules of Civil Procedure; hence, utilizing alternative methods of service is proper when personal service fails.

[8] See also Amendment and Staff Notes to Civ. R. 65.1.

[9] Civ. R. 5(b).

[10] State v. Smith, 136 Ohio St. 3d 1, 2013-Ohio-1698, 989 N.E.2d 972 (2013). But see Am. Sub. SB7, eff. 9/27/2017 superseding the holding in *Smith* relative to service and violations of protection orders under RC 2919.27, so that unperfected service of a protection order or consent agreement does not preclude a prosecution for a violation of division (A) of that section.

serted that the plain language of RC 2919.27 requires only proof that the defendant recklessly violated a protection order issued pursuant to RC 2919.27, not proof of service. (RC 2919.27(A)(2) provides that no person shall recklessly violate the terms of a protection order issued pursuant to section * * * 2903.214 of the Revised Code). The State also claimed that protection orders are enforceable upon issuance, not service.

The majority stated that to prove a violation of RC 2919.27(A)(2), the state must prove, beyond a reasonable doubt, all requirements of RC 2903.214, including that the order be delivered to the defendant. Similarly, that same element is part of RC 3113.31. The pivotal question for any civil protection order is whether delivery implies service. According to the majority, "delivery" means that a court is mandated to bring about a transfer of possession of a copy of the protection order to the respondent. "The statute requires more than just the court's issuing the protection order and ordering its delivery to respondent. It requires that the order actually be delivered."[11] The only manner by which the court is able to fulfill this mandate is to serve the SSOOPO.[12]

In reversing the appellate court, the Supreme Court held that "service" and "delivery" are synonymous in this context and therefore, the State must establish beyond a reasonable doubt, that it served defendant with the order. Thus, when RC 2903.214(F)(1) requires "delivery" of the order, it is requiring "service" on the respondent.[13]

However, the decision also raises many other concerns. Since it is unclear whether this decision applies equally to both ex parte protection orders and protection orders issued after a full hearing, one wonders about the enforceability of a full hearing protection order not served[14] or not served on the day the order is entered. If the majority's analysis applies equally to both ex parte and protection orders issued after a full hearing, then Civ. R. 65.1 is implicated. Civ. R. 65.1(C)(3) provides that delivery/service of a protection order issued after a full hearing is accomplished in accordance with Civ. R. 5(B), which is by ordinary mail.

Both RC 2903.214(F)(1) and RC 3113.13(F)(1) state that "the court shall cause a copy of any protection order that is issued under this section to the petitioner, to the respondent, and to all law enforcement agencies that have jurisdiction to enforce the order. The court shall direct that a copy of the order be delivered to the respondent on the same day that the order is entered." Since "service" is synonymous with "delivery," it appears from the opinion that a civil protection or-

[11]State v. Smith, 136 Ohio St. 3d 1, 2013-Ohio-1698, ¶ 19, 989 N.E.2d 972 (2013).

[12]State v. Smith, 136 Ohio St. 3d 1, 2013-Ohio-1698, ¶ 28, 989 N.E.2d 972 (2013).

[13]State v. Smith, 136 Ohio St. 3d 1, 2013-Ohio-1698, ¶ 20, 989 N.E.2d 972 (2013).

[14]But see State v. Hall, 2013-Ohio-660, 989 N.E.2d 111 (Ohio Ct. App. 5th Dist. Delaware County 2013), appeal allowed, cause remanded, 135 Ohio St. 3d 1456, 2013-Ohio-2285, 988 N.E.2d 576 (2013) (where appellate court upheld conviction for violating CPO, defendant appealed to the Supreme Court of Ohio on ground that he wasn't served with CPO issued after full hearing and Supreme Court remanded case to lower court ordering the court to comply with decision in *State v. Smith*); State v. Hall, 2013-Ohio-5855, 2013 WL 6918874 (Ohio Ct. App. 5th Dist. Delaware County 2013) (on remand, appellate court distinguished the decision in *Smith* and affirmed the decision of *Hall* 1).

der must be served on a respondent on the same day that the order is entered. If this is truly the Supreme Court's interpretation of the statutes, it must mean that a protection order not served on the day that the order is filed is, at the very least, unenforceable.

Q & A: Is there a proper procedure for serving civil protection orders issued after the full hearing?

No. Some counties instruct clerks of court or attorneys for the petitioner to serve respondents with orders issued after the full hearing by personal service.[15] In other counties, mailing a copy of the order to respondent by ordinary mail is sufficient.[16] Still other counties require that respondents be served by certified mail. Some counties require only that a petitioner or counsel perfect service of the civil protection issued after the full hearing on respondent and appropriate law enforcement agencies.[17]

Where the respondent appears at the full hearing and enters into a consent entry, he or she is hand-delivered a copy of the order. If there is a full hearing on the matter, the court often will mail a copy of its decision to both parties.[18]

Q & A: Is there a time frame within which a respondent must be delivered a copy of the CPO issued after a full hearing?

Although the statute requires that the order must be delivered to a respondent on the same day the order is entered,[19] this does not usually happen. It is unlikely for a respondent to actually receive a copy of the CPO issued after a full hearing on the same day the order is entered.

Where personal service is required, a copy of the order issued after a full hearing is delivered to a respondent within a day or two. In some jurisdictions and pursuant to local practice, a respondent is mailed a copy of the order, either by ordinary or certified mail.

Civ. R. 65.1 has addressed service of a CPO issued after a full hearing. Civ. R. 65.1(C)(3) provides that "[a]fter service has been made in accordance with division (C)(2) of this rule, any additional service required to be made during the course of the proceedings on Respondent, and if applicable, on the parent, guardian, or legal custodian of Respondent, shall be made in accordance with the provisions of Civ. R. 5(B)." Pursuant to Civ. R. 5(B), service by ordinary mail is complete upon mailing and service by fax is complete upon transmission of the fax. Generally, a respondent is presumed to have received a copy of the order when the papers are mailed or faxed, unless a respondent is provided an opportunity to dispute this presumption.

---

[15]See State v. Cardinal, 2006-Ohio-5088, 2006 WL 2789903 (Ohio Ct. App. 10th Dist. Franklin County 2006).

[16]Barrett v. Soltesz, 2015-Ohio-794, 2015 WL 995439 (Ohio Ct. App. 6th Dist. Erie County 2015) (discussion of an endorsement showing "wrong address"; noting that Civ. R. 4.6(D) states that service shall be deemed complete when the fact of mailing is entered of record, provided that the ordinary mail envelope is not returned by the postal authorities with an endorsement showing failure of delivery).

[17]See Cuy. County. DR Loc. R. 26(B)(4).

[18]See Sup. R. Form 10.01-I and Sup. R. Form 10.01-J (defining delivery of the protection order issued after a full hearing as service in accordance with Civ.R. 5).

[19]RC 3113.31(F)(1).

Proof of service under Civ. R. 5(B) is not limited to what is allowed under Civ. R. 4. Per Civ. R. 5(D), the proof of service shall state the date and manner of service and shall be signed in accordance with Civ. R. 11. Unlike Civ. R. 4, a signed receipt is not necessary for Civ. R. 5 service. Although Civ. R. 5 allows for Civ. R. 4 service, it does not require Civ. R. 4 service for things other than service of process.

Q & A: What does it matter if a respondent has not been served a copy of the protection order issued after the full hearing?[20]

If a respondent has not been served with a protection order issued after the full hearing, law enforcement officials may not enforce the order if it is violated. Prosecutors may be reluctant to file charges against a respondent for violating the protection order under RC 2919.27.[21] Domestic Relations Courts may not be able to find respondents in contempt for failing to abide by the terms of the civil protection order.

It has been argued that once a respondent has been served with the ex parte order, he or she is on notice of the terms of the civil protection order. Thus, service of the order issued after the full hearing is unnecessary. While this reasoning may apply when the terms of the order issued after the full hearing are the same as the ex parte order, all too often the terms and conditions are modified at the full hearing. The better practice is to make sure the civil protection order issued after the full hearing is served on the respondent.

§ 12:9 Consent agreement concerns[1]

A consent agreement is a civil protection order in which the parties agree upon the terms of the order. As long as the parties agree to be bound by the terms of the order, a finding of domestic violence is not necessary.[2] In fact, Ohio's standardized Consent Agreement form does not provide space to include findings of fact.[3]

Q & A: What evidence is needed to sustain a consent entry?

In Ohio, no court has considered this issue. By its very definition, a consent entry is one in which the terms of the order are agreed to by

[20]See also § 11:11; § 13:3; § 14:15.

[21]See State v. Smith, 136 Ohio St. 3d 1, 2013-Ohio-1698, 989 N.E.2d 972 (2013) (holding that, without service, a conviction for a violation of a CPO cannot not stand). But see Am. Sub. SB7, eff. 9/27/2017 superseding the holding in *Smith* relative to service and violations of protection orders under RC 2919.27, so that unperfected service of a protection order or consent agreement does not preclude a prosecution for a violation of division (A) of that section.

[Section 12:9]

[1]See also Text § 18:9, Other remedies under VAWA.

[2]See also Durrstein v. Cox, 2003-Ohio-4585, 2003 WL 22026056 (Ohio Ct. App. 2d Dist. Montgomery County 2003) (appellate court accepted fact that the parties entered into a consent entry and no finding was made that respondent had committed an act of domestic violence); Ashburn v. Roth, 2007-Ohio-2995, 2007 WL 1731426 (Ohio Ct. App. 12th Dist. Butler County 2007) (noting that no finding of domestic violence was made in a consent entry).

[3]See Sup. R. Form 10.01-J.

the parties.[4] So long as the parties have agreed to the terms of the order, most Ohio courts have determined that no evidence needs to be presented. Since no evidence is adduced at the hearing, a finding of domestic violence is unnecessary.

For example, in *Lain v. Ververis*,[5] the parties entered into a consent entry. In its decision, the Preble County Appellate Court noted, "[b]ecause the CPO was issued under a consent agreement, a finding of domestic violence was unnecessary."[6]

In other states, courts have held that evidence is needed to sustain the issuance of even a consent entry. In *Ehrhart v. Ehrhart*,[7] a Missouri county court of appeals reversed a protection order issued by the trial court. Both parties entered into an agreement by which the ex parte order would remain in effect. The court of appeals determined that the trial court failed to conduct a hearing complete with witnesses, documents, and the opportunity to cross-examine. The court remanded the case for an evidentiary hearing and held that there had been no evidence presented in a proper adversarial proceeding.[8]

Q & A: Is the court permitted to change the terms of a consent entry already signed by the parties?

At least two trial courts did just that. In Fry v. Fry,[9] the parties entered into a consent agreement in a civil protection order proceeding in which they agreed that the protection order should remain in effect for three years. The magistrate then commented that the custody and/or companionship part of the order would expire in 60 days, and that to extend the order beyond that would require the filing of a divorce action. The court queried whether it was bound by the parties' consent agreement.

Although the petitioner chose not to appeal the court's decision, the case raises an interesting issue. Clearly, the intent of a consent agreement is that the parties agree to the order's terms. As with other agreements, the court usually adopts the agreement unless it is not fair, just or equitable.

Similarly, the trial court included additional language to a consent entry. In Gibson v. Redman,[10] the parties entered into a consent entry as to the terms of the order. Over objections, the trial court added the following: "Petitioner shall not encourage nor permit any violation and shall report all violations within 60 seconds of notice to her."[11] The Jefferson County Court of Appeals reversed that portion of the

[4]Margaret Martin Barry, The Downside of Benign Intent, 5 Am. U.J. Gender and L. 433 (1997).

[5]Lain v. Ververis, 1999 WL 893611 (Ohio Ct. App. 12th Dist. Preble County 1999).

[6]Lain v. Ververis, 1999 WL 893611, *1 (Ohio Ct. App. 12th Dist. Preble County 1999).

[7]*Ehrhart v. Ehrhart, 776 S.W.2d 450 (Mo. Ct. App. E.D. 1989).*

[8]*Ehrhart v. Ehrhart, 776 S.W.2d 450 (Mo. Ct. App. E.D. 1989).*

[9]Fry v. Fry, No. 00-DV-34, Richland County.

[10]Gibson v. Redman, 2001-Ohio-3449, 2001 WL 1497085 (Ohio Ct. App. 7th Dist. Jefferson County 2001).

[11]Gibson v. Redman, 2001-Ohio-3449, 2001 WL 1497085, *1 (Ohio Ct. App. 7th Dist. Jefferson County 2001).

trial court's decision and found that it was unreasonable for the trial court to require that the petitioner report a violation within 60 seconds of the occurrence of the violation. Moreover, the court found that such a prohibition was a mutual protection order and the procedural requirements of RC 3113.31(E)(4) must be met before a court may issue a mutual protection order.[12]

However, RC 3113.31(E)(1) provides that the court may grant any protection order or approve any consent entry to bring about a cessation of violence. Because the statute specifically states that the court must approve the consent entry, it appears that a court is permitted to change its terms.

Q & A: Must the consent entry be signed by a respondent and counsel if represented?

Not according to the Butler County Court of Appeals in *Luna-Corona v. Esquivel-Parrales*.[13] In that case, the consent agreement was only signed by appellee and her attorney. Neither appellant nor his counsel signed the entry.

While not raised as an assignment of error in the case, the appellate court addressed this at the outset. In defining a consent entry as a contract founded upon the agreement of the parties, there is no requirement that it be signed by the parties. What is required is an offer, an acceptance, contractual capacity, a manifestation of mutual asset and legality of object and consideration.[14] Besides this, a meeting of the minds is also essential. Finally, while it is preferable that any settlement be reduced to writing, the Stark County Court of Appeals held that an agreement entered into in the presence of the court is a legally binding contract, whether or not it is reduced to writing.

In this case, appellant's counsel informed the court that his client had no problem with the terms of the ex parte protection order except as to parenting provisions. On the record, the trial court discussed the terms of the order with appellant and his counsel. In that the record was replete with evidence of that discussion, the appellate court found that the appellant had understood and agreed to the terms of the consent entry, making a written signature unnecessary.

Q & A: Must a consent agreement/civil protection order be served on respondent in accordance with the requirements of RC 3113.31(F)(1)?

The Second District Court of Appeals addressed the issue in *Stickel v. Pryor*.[15] In that case, the parties entered into a consent agreement/ civil protection order. Appellant then requested that the court nullify the consent agreement, which said motion was denied. On appeal, the appellant argued that a copy of the consent agreement had not been

[12]Gibson v. Redman, 2001-Ohio-3449, 2001 WL 1497085, *3 (Ohio Ct. App. 7th Dist. Jefferson County 2001).

[13]Luna-Corona v. Esquivel-Parrales, 2009-Ohio-2628, 2009 WL 1581133 (Ohio Ct. App. 12th Dist. Butler County 2009).

[14]*Luna-Corona at *3*; citing Eckliff v. Walters, 168 Ohio App. 3d 727, 2006-Ohio-4817, 861 N.E.2d 843 (11th Dist. Lake County 2006), quoting Phillips v. Phillips, 2005-Ohio-231, 2005 WL 121657 (Ohio Ct. App. 5th Dist. Stark County 2005).

[15]Stickel v. Pryor, 2002-Ohio-3309, 2002 WL 1396077 (Ohio Ct. App. 2d Dist. Miami County 2002).

served on him on the same day that the agreement was entered as required by statute.

RC 3113.31(F)(1) requires that the court shall direct that a copy of an order be delivered to the respondent on the same day the ordered in entered. The appellate court held that "[to] the extent that R.C. 3113.31 distinguishes between protection orders and consent agreements as it does, and because the service requirements of Paragraph (F)(1) should apply only to 'an order,' the requirement should not be read to likewise extend to consent agreements. . . . Indeed, to hold that the court should have caused a copy to be served on Pryor would require a superfluous act because, as the magistrate found in his September 5, 2001 decision, Pryor had actual notice of the consent agreement and its terms when he signed it."[16] The court also noted that Mr. Pryor subsequently received a copy of the consent agreement from the clerk of courts.

Of significance is that the Second District Court of Appeals also indicated that the provisions of RC 3113.31(F)(1) are directive, not mandatory.[17] In this case, at least, the failure to comply with the statutory directives of RC 3113.31(F)(1) did not invalidate the agreement. This analysis could be used to buttress the argument that the failure to comply with directives of RC 3113.31(F)(1) does not invalidate any civil protection order.

Q & A: On what date does a consent agreement become effective?

It depends on whether the consent agreement was obtained before a judge or magistrate and whether one of the parties objects or motions the court. Where the agreement was obtained before a magistrate, the provisions of Civil Rule 53 must be followed. For example, in *Stickel v. Pryor*, the Second District Court of Appeals suggested the proper procedure to be followed by courts where magistrates recommend that the trial judge approve and adopt consent agreements.[18] In this case, a consent agreement was obtained before a magistrate on July 10, 2001. On September 5, 2001, the magistrate heard Mr. Pryor's motion to invalidate the agreement. After the magistrate denied his motion, Mr. Pryor appealed on the ground that the consent agreement lacked an effective date.

The appellate court disagreed and reasoned that the consent agreement, obtained before a magistrate, was actually submitted to the court as the magistrate's decision. In this case, it appears that the court adopted the decision as the court's interim order on July 10, 2001, in accordance with Civil Rule 53(E)(4)(a) and (c) and that was the date it became effective.[19] Despite the absence of an effective date

[16]Stickel v. Pryor, 2002-Ohio-3309, 2002 WL 1396077, *1 (Ohio Ct. App. 2d Dist. Miami County 2002).

[17]Stickel v. Pryor, 2002-Ohio-3309, 2002 WL 1396077, *1 (Ohio Ct. App. 2d Dist. Miami County 2002).

[18]Stickel v. Pryor, 2002-Ohio-3309, 2002 WL 1396077 (Ohio Ct. App. 2d Dist. Miami County 2002).

[19]Stickel v. Pryor, 2002-Ohio-3309, 2002 WL 1396077, *2 (Ohio Ct. App. 2d Dist. Miami County 2002).

in the agreement, the consent agreement was effective on the date the court adopted the agreement, submitted as the magistrate's decision.[20]

In *State v. Hamlett*,[21] defendant appealed his conviction of violating a domestic violence CPO, arguing that because the consent CPO was not journalized by the court at the time of the alleged offense, it was not valid and therefore, the evidence was insufficient that he violated the CPO.

The appellate court couched the issue as whether the CPO was effective on the date the parties had notice of its terms and signed it or when it was journalized in accordance with Civ. R. 58(A). The Mahoning Court of Appeals first summarized the civil rule which provides that a judgment is effective only when entered by the clerk upon the journal. "To journalize a decision means that certain formal requirements have been met, i.e., the decision is reduced to writing, signed by a judge, and filed with the clerk so that it may become part of the permanent record of the court."[22] The court then pointed out that "the time-stamp on the date of an entry is proof of journalization."[23] It further stressed that "[i]t is well established that a 'court of record speaks only through its journal and not by oral pronouncement.' "[24]

The State argued that because the CPO was set to expire on a date certain which was five years from the date of the full hearing CPO, the effective date was five years from issuance which was the true intended effective date.[25] At oral argument the State argued for the first time that because the case involved a consent agreement, the effective date of the CPO was prior to jounalization. Relying on the language of RC 2919.27 which prohibited a person from recklessly violating the terms of a protection order or consent agreement approved, the State noted that the word 'approved' demonstrated a legislative exception to the established principle that a judgment becomes effective only upon journalization by the clerk pursuant to Civ. R. 58 and asserted that a consent CPO becomes effective on the date that it is signed by the parties and approved by the magistrate at the conclusion of the hearing.[26]

In reversing the trial court, the Seventh District Court of Appeals

[20]Stickel v. Pryor, 2002-Ohio-3309, 2002 WL 1396077 (Ohio Ct. App. 2d Dist. Miami County 2002). See also Text § 12:23, Duration of a civil protection order; Holderman v. Hagner, 2000 PA Super 292, 760 A.2d 1189 (2000) (maximum duration period of protection order ran from date of final hearing, not from date of ex parte hearing).

[21]State v. Hamlett, 191 Ohio App. 3d 397, 2010-Ohio-6605, 946 N.E.2d 277 (7th Dist. Mahoning County 2010).

[22]State v. Hamlett, 191 Ohio App. 3d 397, 401-402, 2010-Ohio-6605, 946 N.E.2d 277 (7th Dist. Mahoning County 2010), quoting San Filipo v. San Filipo, 81 Ohio App. 3d 111, 112, 610 N.E.2d 493 (9th Dist. Summit County 1991).

[23]State v. Hamlett, 191 Ohio App. 3d 397, 402, 2010-Ohio-6605, 946 N.E.2d 277 (7th Dist. Mahoning County 2010), Hrina v. Segall, 2001-Ohio-3281, 2001 WL 641509 (Ohio Ct. App. 7th Dist. Mahoning County 2001).

[24]State v. Hamlett, 191 Ohio App. 3d 397, 402, 2010-Ohio-6605, 946 N.E.2d 277 (7th Dist. Mahoning County 2010), quoting Schenley v. Kauth, 160 Ohio St. 109, 51, 51 Ohio Op. 30, 113 N.E.2d 625 (1953).

[25]State v. Hamlett, 191 Ohio App. 3d 397, 402, 2010-Ohio-6605, 946 N.E.2d 277 (7th Dist. Mahoning County 2010).

[26]State v. Hamlett, 191 Ohio App. 3d 397, 402, 2010-Ohio-6605, 946 N.E.2d 277

determined that consent entry CPO was effective on the date that the order was journalized, rather than on the date that the consent agreement was signed by both parties and approved by magistrate. Since the order was not effective on the date of the alleged violation, his conviction for violating the CPO was vacated. The court adopted the reasoning of *Stickel*, in which the consent order was found to be fully effective from the date the court signed and filed it, to support its holding in *Hamlett*.[27]

On another note, neither the State nor the defendant requested that the ex parte civil protection order be entered into evidence. The only evidence in the record was that the officer testified that when the victim presented the ex parte CPO to him, he noted that it had expired. "Thus, that order cannot serve as a basis for Hamlett's conviction for violating a CPO."[28] What is clear from this decision is that an ex parte CPO can expire before the CPO is granted at the full hearing.[29] It is important that attorneys representing petitioners always check to make sure that the ex parte order has not expired, or does not expire, until the consent entry CPO is signed by the court, filed with the clerk and journalized.

Q & A: Is a consent agreement a civil protection order for purposes of prohibiting the offending party from being issued a concealed weapon license?[30]

According to the Greene County Court of Appeals in *Harris v. Miami County Sheriff's Department*,[31] a consent agreement entered into by a respondent is a civil protection order for purposes of prohibiting him from obtaining a license to carry a concealed weapon.

Appellant was the subject of a stalking civil protection order issued against him pursuant to RC 2903.214. Subsequently, appellant applied for a license to carry a concealed weapon. The applications asked whether he was currently the subject of a protection order issued in this or any other state. Although he indicated that he was not, a background check indicated that he was the subject of a protection order issued by the Greene County Common Pleas Court.

On appeal, appellant argued that the consent agreement is not a civil protection order because RC 2903.214 does not authorize a trial court to issue a consent agreement. The appellate court disagreed and

---

(7th Dist. Mahoning County 2010).

[27]State v. Hamlett, 191 Ohio App. 3d 397, 403, 2010-Ohio-6605, 946 N.E.2d 277 (7th Dist. Mahoning County 2010).

[28]State v. Hamlett, 191 Ohio App. 3d 397, 401, 2010-Ohio-6605, 946 N.E.2d 277 (7th Dist. Mahoning County 2010).

[29]See McDaniel v. McDaniel, 2002-Ohio-6111, 2002 WL 31502097 (Ohio Ct. App. 12th Dist. Warren County 2002) (finding that the trial court retained jurisdiction to issue a full hearing order despite fact that the ex parte order may have expired before the full hearing ¶ 20); Barrow v. Brown, 2017-Ohio-7926, ¶ 4, 2017 WL 4329767 (Ohio Ct. App. 2d Dist. Greene County 2017) (trial court retained jurisdiction to proceed with the full hearing and issue a full hearing protection order even if the ex parte order expired before the full hearing).

[30]See also Text § 12:22, Remedies—Miscellaneous issues; Text § 18:11, Firearm offenses under VAWA.

[31]Harris v. Miami Cty. Sheriff's Dept., 160 Ohio App. 3d 435, 2005-Ohio-1713, 827 N.E.2d 807 (2d Dist. Miami County 2005) (appellant recently filed for certiorari to the Ohio Supreme Court). See also Text § 9:6.

affirmed the trial court decision. In its opinion, the Second District Court of Appeals noted that RC 2903.214(E)(1) allows the court to issue any protection order that is designed to protect the person named in the order. An examination of the order demonstrated that the elements in the order and agreed to by appellant were designed to ensure the safety and protection of the petitioner. "Therefore, we agree with the Sheriff that consent agreements, such as the one in this case, are within the jurisdiction and authority of the Greene County Common Pleas Court to issue under RC 2903.214. Since consent agreements can be issued under the authority of RC 2903.214, we cannot say that the lower court abused its discretion in finding that this consent agreement was a civil protection order."[32]

The statutory language of RC 2903.214 mirrors that of RC 3113.31. The procedure for issuing a domestic violence civil protection order is substantially similar to the procedure under RC 2903.214.[33]

However, there are a few differences. Unlike RC 2903.214, RC 3113.31 specifically provides for the issuance of a consent agreement civil protection order. Additionally, the relief available to family or household members is more expansive. There are no statutory equivalents in RC 2903.214. It can be argued that, because stalking civil protection orders are designed to protect persons who are not considered to be family or household members, it is less likely that petitioners would find a need to enter into agreements as to the terms, such as might be desirable in domestic violence civil protection orders.

Although the Greene County Court of Appeals couched the question in more general terms, the more specific question in *Harris* should have been whether the trial court had jurisdiction to issue a consent agreement where the statute does not specifically allow its issuance. The appellate court's reasoning was sound, however, as a trial court has wide discretion under RC 2903.214(E)(1) to issue any protection order that is designed to protect the person named in the order, including the issuance of a consent agreement.

Q & A: Can a consent agreement be appealed?

Yes. RC 3113.31(G) specifically provides that an order issued under this section, other than an ex parte order, that grants a protection order or approves a consent agreement, or that refuses to grant a protection order or refuses to approve a consent agreement, is a final appealable order.

Q & A: Is a consent agreement a final appealable order if it is a second count in a complaint for divorce?

Pursuant to Rule 75(G) of the Ohio Rules of Civil Procedure, a claim for a civil protection order based upon an allegation of domestic violence, shall be a separate claim from a claim for divorce, dissolution of marriage, annulment or legal separation. Although a consent agreement may be filed as a second count in a divorce action, it is a

---

[32]Harris v. Miami Cty. Sheriff's Dept., 160 Ohio App. 3d 435, 439, 2005-Ohio-1713, ¶ 17, 827 N.E.2d 807, 810 (2d Dist. Miami County 2005).

[33]See Lindsay v. Jackson, 2000 WL 1268810, *2 (Ohio Ct. App. 1st Dist. Hamilton County 2000).

separate claim. As a final appealable order,[34] it may be appealed even though the underlying divorce has not been concluded.

Q & A: A CPO was granted pursuant to a consent agreement and there was a specific finding written into the agreement that states "This is not an admission of domestic violence" or "There is no finding of domestic violence." Can the issue of the domestic violence be litigated in the underlying divorce proceeding?

Parties agree to a "no finding" of domestic violence finding for their own strategic reasons. For a petitioner, an agreement eliminates the need for a full hearing and the confrontation that may ensue. For a respondent, a finding of domestic violence may prejudice him in another proceeding; he may believe that a "no finding" finding may insulate him or her from future liability. A "no finding" of domestic violence does not mean that the domestic violence did not occur.

Arguably, it is similar to a no contest plea. It permits a respondent to subject himself or herself to the terms of a civil protection order without an admission of guilt. Because the respondent has agreed to the terms of the protection order, any violation of the terms subjects the respondent to the same penalties as with any civil protection order.

RC 3113.31(G) states that the remedies and procedures provided in this section are in addition to, and not in lieu of, any other available civil or criminal remedies. So long as the domestic violence statute provides a petitioner with multiple remedies, it is unlikely that res judicata or collateral estoppel would apply. If the parties have entered into a consent agreement that indicates a "no finding" of domestic violence, it is clear that the issue of domestic violence has not been litigated. Thus, it is reasonable to conclude that the parties are not precluded from litigating the issue of domestic violence at a subsequent divorce hearing.

Additionally, in *Felton v. Felton*,[35] the Supreme Court of Ohio held that "a court is not precluded by statute or public policy reasons from issuing a protection order pursuant to Ohio's civil domestic violence statute where the parties' dissolution decree already prohibits the parties from harassing each other."

Q & A: What are the advantages and disadvantages in negotiating a consent agreement versus having an actual full hearing?

The benefits of consent orders cannot be understated. The process may be less painful for a petitioner who suffered trauma as a result of the incident and does not want to testify in open court. Sometimes the evidence might be weak and a negotiated consent entry might adequately address the situation. Lastly, some courts have refused to grant certain remedies absent an agreement, such as those remedies

---

[34]See RC 3113.31(G).

[35]Felton v. Felton, 79 Ohio St. 3d 34, 1997-Ohio-302, 679 N.E.2d 672 (1997); see also Walton v. Walton, 2004-Ohio-7151, 2004 WL 3017265 (Ohio Ct. App. 6th Dist. Wood County 2004); Text § 12:27, Conflicting protection orders; but see Text § 11:5, Election of remedies; Ventura v. Ventura, 1986 WL 10595 (Ohio Ct. App. 11th Dist. Lake County 1986).

regarding the allocation of parental rights and responsibilities. Thus, a consent agreement might enable a petitioner to achieve by agreement that which she/he would not be available if the case had gone to full hearing.

On the other hand, law enforcement has been known not to enforce consent agreements, even though they are protection orders. A consent agreement negotiated by way of mediation might cause problems for some victims. A court may be less likely to take judicial notice of a consent agreement in a subsequent case (custody, divorce) as the consent agreement does not contain findings. Additionally, it has been argued that a consent entry might create unwanted res judicata concerns. For example, if a consent entry is issued, can the petitioner litigate the domestic violence in a subsequently filed divorce action?

Moreover, without a specific finding of "credible threat," weapons may not be restricted under Brady. So too, full faith and credit issues might be raised.

Finally, without admissions of guilt or specific findings of domestic violence made, a respondent might not be held accountable. Additionally, without findings, a petitioner might find it more difficult to renew a CPO.

However, on balance, a consent agreement CPO is usually an effective way to achieve the goal of safety.

§ 12:10 Magistrate hearings[1]

The Supreme Court of Ohio adopted a civil rule of procedure regarding civil protection orders, effective July 1, 2012. Civ. R. 65.1 applies to civil protection order proceedings under RC 3113.31, RC 2903.214 and RC 2151.34 for domestic violence, stalking and sexually oriented offense civil protection orders. The rule recognizes that a civil protection order proceeding is a special statutory proceeding and that the provisions of Civ. Rule 65.1 shall be interpreted and applied in a manner consistent with the intent and purposes of those protection order statutes, and supersede and make inapplicable the provisions of any other rules of civil procedure that are inconsistent with Civ. R. 65.1.[2] When first adopted, Civ. R. 65.1 was intended to apply to civil protection order proceedings. However, recent case law has demonstrated

---

[Section 12:10]

[1]Civ. R. 65.1 has replaced Civ. R. 53. See also §§ 9:5, 11:9, 11:11.

[2]Civ. R. 65.1(A). See also R.C. v. J.G., 2013-Ohio-4265, 2013 WL 5437015 (Ohio Ct. App. 9th Dist. Medina County 2013) (discussing the 2012 Staff Note to Civ. R. 65. 1); Besman v. Leventhal, 2017-Ohio-464, ¶ 4-5, 2017 WL 526288 (Ohio Ct. App. 8th Dist. Cuyahoga County 2017), appeal not allowed, 151 Ohio St. 3d 1503, 2018-Ohio-365, 90 N.E.3d 946 (2018) (indicating that Civ. R. 65.1 does not provide for a request for findings of fact and conclusions of law, (as it would delay the proceedings) suggesting a more streamlined process for protection orders. At ¶ 5, quoting Insa v. Insa, 2016-Ohio-7425, ¶ 27, 72 N.E.3d 1170 (Ohio Ct. App. 2d Dist. Montgomery County 2016); but see Lundin v. Niepsuj, 2017-Ohio-7153, 2017 WL 3426957 (Ohio Ct. App. 9th Dist. Summit County 2017) (court permitted findings of fact and conclusions of law under Civ. R. 52).

that courts still consider aspects of Civ. R. 53 when reviewing a magistrate's decision.[3]

Q & A: Why was Civ. R. 53 replaced with Civ. R. 65.1?[4]

Several courts have questioned the procedures suggested in the forms.[5] For example, the forms provide for a judge to transform a document prepared by a magistrate after a hearing conducted by a magistrate into an order without complying with the procedural mandates of Civ.R. 53.[6] The forms also include a box that states, "Notice of Final Appealable Order."[7]

In *McCown v. McCown*,[8] the ex-wife filed a petition for a protection order against her former husband and his mother. A magistrate granted the orders and the respondents filed objections to the decision and appealed.

In this case, the civil protection orders issued after the full hearing were signed by both the magistrate and the judge and were marked "Final Appealable Order." The respondents filed objections and appealed on the same day.

The Fayette County Court of Appeals dismissed the appeal and held that "[b]ecause a trial court judge has not yet independently reviewed the magistrate's decision and ruled upon the appellants' objections as required by Civ.R. 53, there is no final order before us to consider in this case and this appeal is premature."[9] The court also noted that "[o]nly a judge, not a magistrate, may terminate a claim or action by entering judgment."[10] It may be argued that the Supreme Court forms provided this ambiguity.

The holding in *McCown* is consistent with holdings in other appellate cases regarding magistrates' decisions. In *Sabrina J. v. Robbin*

---

[3]See also Text 9:5; Cutler v. Reed, 2016-Ohio-1151, 2016 WL 1090783 (Ohio Ct. App. 12th Dist. Butler County 2016); M.H. v. J.H., 2017-Ohio-8679, 2017 WL 5706128 (Ohio Ct. App. 9th Dist. Medina County 2017) (where appellate court utilized Civ. R. 53 in its analysis); L.L. v. R.B., 2017-Ohio-7553, 2017 WL 3980553 (Ohio Ct. App. 5th Dist. Guernsey County 2017) (concluding correctly despite applying Civ. R. 53).

[4]See e.g., Mills v. Mills, 2008-Ohio-3774, 2008 WL 2906524 (Ohio Ct. App. 9th Dist. Summit County 2008) (overruled by, Tabatabai v. Tabatabai, 2009-Ohio-3139, 2009 WL 1844353 (Ohio Ct. App. 9th Dist. Medina County 2009)).

[5]See Sup. R. Form 10.01-H to Sup. R. Form 10.01-J.

[6]See Larson v. Larson, 2011-Ohio-6013, 2011 WL 5829788 (Ohio Ct. App. 3d Dist. Seneca County 2011) (reconciling the civil protection order forms and Civ. R. 53 by relying on Sup. R. 10.01(C) to avoid the procedural problem by adding the necessary Civ. R. 53 language to the forms because the Superintendence Rule does not require the domestic relations courts to use the exact forms found in 10.01-H to 10.01-J but rather that the court forms only be *substantially similar* to the Supreme Court forms.); see also Calzo v. Lynch, 2012-Ohio-1353, 2012 WL 1067921 (Ohio Ct. App. 5th Dist. Richland County 2012).

[7]See Sup. R. Form 10.01-I and Sup. R. Form 10.01-J.

[8]McCown v. McCown, 145 Ohio App. 3d 170, 762 N.E.2d 398 (12th Dist. Fayette County 2001).

[9]McCown v. McCown, 145 Ohio App. 3d 170, 172, 762 N.E.2d 398, 400 (12th Dist. Fayette County 2001).

[10]McCown v. McCown, 145 Ohio App. 3d 170, 172, 762 N.E.2d 398, 400 (12th Dist. Fayette County 2001) (quoting Harkai v. Scherba Industries, Inc., 136 Ohio App. 3d 211, 218, 736 N.E.2d 101, 106 (9th Dist. Medina County 2000)).

C.,[11] the Lucas County Court of Appeals held that "an order of a trial court which merely adopts a magistrate's decision and enters it as the judgment of the court is not a final appealable order."[12]

The appellate court determined that to be a final appealable order, a judgment entry by the trial court pursuant to Civ.R. 53(D)(4)(e) must:

> (1) adopt, reject, or modify the magistrate's decision and should state, for identification purposes, the date the magistrate's decision was signed by the magistrate; (2) state the outcome and contain an order which states the relief granted so that the parties are able to determine their rights and obligations by referring solely to the judgment entry; and (3) be a document separate from the magistrate's decision.[13]

The holding of this case appears to conflict with the Supreme Court standardized civil protection order forms because the forms contain both a judge's signature line and a magistrate's signature line in the same order.[14] Clearly, a magistrate's decision cannot be a part of or attached to a court's order.

Additionally, a magistrate issues a decision; a judge issues an order. The standardized forms put a signature line for the magistrate under the words, "It Is So Ordered." As written, the standardized protection order forms may be confusing to litigants who may think that a magistrate's decision is a final appealable order.

"Civ. R. 65.1 was enacted, in part, to expedite the process for obtaining rulings on matters related to protection orders. Schneider v. Razek, 2015-Ohio-410, 28 N.E.3d 591 (Ohio Ct. App. 8th Dist. Cuyahoga County 2015). As such, it "uniquely applies to special statutory proceedings set forth in RC 3113.3, which provides the requirements for the entry of a CPO against adults for the protection of victims of domestic violence."""[15]

Q & A: Who can preside over civil protection order proceedings?

It depends on the trial court. Clearly judges of the state's domestic relations courts have the power to hear both ex parte petitions for protection orders and the full hearing. Whether a judge of a particular court actually hears the case or refers it to a magistrate is entirely up to the judge in a particular county.

Under Civ. R. 65.1(F)(1), a court may refer the proceedings under these special statutory proceedings to a magistrate. The civil rules now permit a magistrate to conduct both the ex parte hearing and the full hearing.

---

[11]Sabrina J. v. Robbin C., 2001 WL 85157 (Ohio Ct. App. 6th Dist. Lucas County 2001).

[12]Sabrina J. v. Robbin C., 2001 WL 85157, *3 (Ohio Ct. App. 6th Dist. Lucas County 2001).

[13]Sabrina J. v. Robbin C., 2001 WL 85157 (Ohio Ct. App. 6th Dist. Lucas County 2001).

[14]See Sup. R. Form 10.01-H to Sup. R. Form 10.01-J.

[15]Besman v. Leventhal, 2017-Ohio-464, ¶ 4, 2017 WL 526288 (Ohio Ct. App. 8th Dist. Cuyahoga County 2017), appeal not allowed, 151 Ohio St. 3d 1503, 2018-Ohio-365, 90 N.E.3d 946 (2018); quoting, Heimann v. Heekin, 2014-Ohio-4276, ¶ 5, 2014 WL 4816258 (Ohio Ct. App. 1st Dist. Hamilton County 2014).

Q & A: Can magistrates conduct ex parte hearings?

In many county domestic relations courts, judges grant or deny the relief requested at the ex parte hearing. In other courts, magistrates have and will continue to conduct ex parte hearings. According to Civ. R. 65.1(F)(2)(a), the magistrate now has the written authority to conduct the ex parte hearing and, upon conclusion of the hearing, deny or grant an ex parte protection order.

A magistrate's denial or granting of an ex parte protection order does not require judicial approval, shall otherwise comply with the statutory requirements relating to an ex parte protection order, shall be effective when signed by the magistrate and filed with the clerk, and shall have the same effect as an ex parte protection order entered by the court without reference to a magistrate.[16]

A magistrate's denial or granting of an ex parte protection order without judicial approval under this division does not constitute a magistrate's order or a magistrate's decision under Civ. R. 53(D)(2) or (3) and is not subject to the requirements of those rules.[17]

The court's approval and signing of a magistrate's denial or granting of an ex parte protection order entered under this division does not constitute a judgment or interim order under Civ. R. 53(D)(4)(e) and is not subject to the requirements of that rule.[18]

Q & A: Can a magistrate conduct the full hearing?

According to Civ. R. 65.1(F)(3)(a), a magistrate is permitted to conduct the full hearing and upon conclusion of the hearing deny or grant a protection order.

A magistrate's denial or granting of a protection order after full hearing under this division does not constitute a magistrate's order or a magistrate's decision under Civ. R. 53(D)(2) or (3) and is not subject to the requirements of those rules.[19]

Q & A: Must a trial court/magistrate issue a full hearing order that comports with Sup. R. 10.01(C)?

In *Weber v. Forinash,*[20] the magistrate conducted a full hearing on a Civil Protection Order but never entered a full hearing order per Form 10.01-I entitled Domestic Violence Civil Protection Order (CPO) Full Hearing. Instead the magistrate issued a decision recommending that the Court grant the petition for CPO and advising the Court which provisions to check. However, there was no evidence to support that a full hearing order was ever issued.

[16] Civ. R. 65.1(F)(2)(b)(i).

[17] Civ. R. 65.1(F)(2)(b)(ii); see also Baldwin v. Remley, No. C-080007 (Ohio Ct. App. 1st Dist. Hamilton County Sept. 24, 2008) (unreported; available at www.hamilton-co.org/appealscourt/docs/decisions/C-080007_09242008.pdf); Bressler v. Nunemaker, 2017-Ohio-5804, 2017 WL 2964199 (Ohio Ct. App. 5th Dist. Licking County 2017).

[18] Civ. R. 65.1(F)(2)(b)(ii).

[19] Civ. R. 65.1(F)(3)(b). See also A.S. v. P.F., 2013-Ohio-4857, 2013 WL 5925968 (Ohio Ct. App. 9th Dist. Lorain County 2013); R.C. v. J.G., 2013-Ohio-4265, 2013 WL 5437015 (Ohio Ct. App. 9th Dist. Medina County 2013); M.K. v. J.K., 2015-Ohio-434, 2015 WL 557990 (Ohio Ct. App. 9th Dist. Medina County 2015).

[20] Weber v. Forinash, 2015-Ohio-3187, 2015 WL 4720532 (Ohio Ct. App. 6th Dist. Sandusky County 2015).

The appellate court began by addressing the issue as raised by the dissent and concluding that the judgment entry of the Sandusky County trial court which stated that "[t]he Decision/Recommendation of the Magistrate is correct and approved" constitutes an order under Civ. R. 65.1(F)(3)(c) and thus, is a final appealable order under Civ. R. 65.1(G).[21] 'Thus, we must disagree with the dissent's conclusion that the entry does not constitute a final appealable order. Consequently, we will proceed to address the merits of appellant's assignment of error.'[22]

On the other hand, the dissent argued that, according to Sup. R. 10. 01(C), "the court shall use, as applicable, forms that are substantially similar to Forms 10.01-H through 10.01-J. Thus, the Court's approving the decision of the magistrate on an ex parte form without utilizing Form 10.01-I or a form substantially similar to it, failed to comply with the Rules of Superintendence for the Courts of Ohio."[23] Additionally, the fact that the ex parte CPO expired well before the judgment entry approving the magistrate's decision and ordering the CPO to remain in full force and effect suggested that it had no legal effect at the time the judgment was entered.[24]

The dissent's point must be considered in the future so as to avoid potential procedural missteps that might cause reversible error. Further, every practicing attorney should be concerned if a trial court fails to actually issue a full hearing CPO (Sup. R. Form 10.01-I) and must request that a full hearing order be issued indicating when the order is to expire.

Q & A: What is the procedure for issuing the full hearing order?

According to Civ. R. 65.1(F)(3)(c)(i), a magistrate's denial or granting of a protection order after a full hearing shall comply with the statutory requirements relating to such orders and is not effective until adopted by the court.

When a magistrate has denied or granted a protection order after a full hearing, the court may adopt the magistrate's denial or granting of the protection order upon review of the order and a determination that there is no error of law or other defect evident on the face of the order.[25]

Upon a review of a magistrate's denial or granting of a protection order after a full hearing, the court may modify or reject the magistrate's order.[26]

---

[21] Weber v. Forinash, 2015-Ohio-3187, 2015 WL 4720532, ¶ 13-14 (Ohio Ct. App. 6th Dist. Sandusky County 2015).

[22] Weber v. Forinash, 2015-Ohio-3187, 2015 WL 4720532, ¶ 14 (Ohio Ct. App. 6th Dist. Sandusky County 2015).

[23] Weber v. Forinash, 2015-Ohio-3187, 2015 WL 4720532, ¶ 25 (Ohio Ct. App. 6th Dist. Sandusky County 2015).

[24] Weber v. Forinash, 2015-Ohio-3187, 2015 WL 4720532, ¶ 26 (Ohio Ct. App. 6th Dist. Sandusky County 2015).

[25] Civ. R. 65.1(F)(3)(c)(ii). C.Q. v. P.S., 2016-Ohio-4988, 2016 WL 3881115 (Ohio Ct. App. 9th Dist. Medina County 2016).

[26] Civ. R. 65.1(F)(3)(c)(iii). J.B. v. Harford, 2015-Ohio-13, 2015 WL 82527 (Ohio Ct. App. 9th Dist. Summit County 2015).

A court's adoption, modification or rejection of a magistrate's denial or granting of a protection order after a full hearing under this division does not constitute a judgment or interim order under Civ. R. 53(D)(4)(e) and is not subject to the requirements of that rule.[27]

A court's adoption, modification or rejection of a magistrate's denial or granting of a protection order after a full hearing shall be effective when signed by the court and filed with the clerk.[28] It is important to note that the full hearing protection order is not final and enforceable when signed by the parties; rather it becomes final and enforceable when the court signs the order and it is filed and journalized by the clerk.[29]

Q & A: Must a trial court conduct an independent review of the facts and conclusions contained in the order?

There exists no requirement that the trial court conduct a de novo or independent review of the magistrate's denial or granting of a protection order after a full hearing.[30] The rule states only that the court may adopt, modify or reject the magistrate's order.[31]

In fact, the 9th District Court of Appeals stressed that "[a] civil protection order issued by a magistrate must still be adopted by the trial court, but only upon a review to determine whether there is an error of law or another defect evident on the face of the order," per Civ. R. 65.1(F)(3)(c).[32] Clearly, that does not mean a de novo review.

Rather, the 9th District has concluded that it is up to the appellate court to conduct a full review based on the challenge to the order.[33]

Similarly, in *J.P. v. T.H.*,[34] appellant assigned as error on appeal that the trial court failed to conduct a *de novo* review of the

---

[27]Civ. R. 65.1(F)(3)(c)(iv).

[28]Civ. R. 65.1(F)(3)(c)(v).

[29]See also State v. Hamlett, 191 Ohio App. 3d 397, 2010-Ohio-6605, 946 N.E.2d 277 (7th Dist. Mahoning County 2010).

[30]See A.S. v. P.F., 2013-Ohio-4857, 2013 WL 5925968 (Ohio Ct. App. 9th Dist. Lorain County 2013) (court of appeals stating that the trial court's review [of a magistrate's decision] is limited and a protection order is a final appealable order that may be fully reviewed on appeal with or without objections being filed in the trial court)]; see also J.P. v. T.H, 2016-Ohio-243, 2016 WL 363247 (Ohio Ct. App. 9th Dist. Lorain County 2016); C.Q. v. P.S., 2016-Ohio-4988, 2016 WL 3881115 (Ohio Ct. App. 9th Dist. Medina County 2016); but see Friedlander v. Friedlander, 2014-Ohio-2180, 2014 WL 2168238 (Ohio Ct. App. 8th Dist. Cuyahoga County 2014) (considering an independent review while not specifically addressing Civ. R. 65.1).

[31]Insa v. Insa, 2016-Ohio-7425, 72 N.E.3d 1170, ¶ 27 n.3 (Ohio Ct. App. 2d Dist. Montgomery County 2016)(noting that no standard of review is designated, the rule does not indicate whether the trial court has the inherent authority to take additional evidence or return a matter upon objection under Civ. R. 65.1).

[32]R.C. v. J.G., 2013-Ohio-4265, 2013 WL 5437015, ¶ 5 (Ohio Ct. App. 9th Dist. Medina County 2013); A.S. v. P.F., 2013-Ohio-4857, 2013 WL 5925968 (Ohio Ct. App. 9th Dist. Lorain County 2013); J.J. v. J.A., 2013-Ohio-5729, 2013 WL 6843592 (Ohio Ct. App. 9th Dist. Summit County 2013); B.C. v. A.S., 2014-Ohio-1326, 2014 WL 1345260 (Ohio Ct. App. 9th Dist. Medina County 2014).

[33]J.J. v. J.A., 2013-Ohio-5729, 2013 WL 6843592, ¶ 7 (Ohio Ct. App. 9th Dist. Summit County 2013); see also Martin v. Martin, 2013-Ohio-5703, 2013 WL 6843599 (Ohio Ct. App. 10th Dist. Franklin County 2013) (discussing when an appellate court must conduct a de novo standard of review).

[34]J.P. v. T.H, 2016-Ohio-243, 2016 WL 363247 (Ohio Ct. App. 9th Dist. Lorain County 2016).

magistrate's decision denying the civil stalking protection order issued after a full hearing. (note that the same analysis would apply to a DVCPO). J.P. argued that the trial court adopted the magistrate's decision on the same day that the decision was issued and before the transcript was available. Since the trial court's decision to adopt the magistrate's decision could not have been based on any evidence, his due process rights were violated.[35]

"Civ. R. 65.1(F)(3)(c)(ii) authorizes the trial court to adopt a magistrate's decision so long as there is 'no error of law or other defect *on the face of the order*.' (emphasis added). This language contemplates that pursuant to Civ. R. 65.1, the trial court need only review the order itself before deciding whether to adopt, reject or modify it. Nothing within the language of Civ. R. 65.1 prohibits a trial court from contemporaneously adopting a magistrate's decision."[36] In reliance on Civ. R. 65.1, the appellate court held that the trial court did not err in adopting the magistrate's decision on the same day and that a transcript was not necessary for that review. Implied in this decision is that a *de novo* review is not required.

On the other hand, in *Cottrell v. Cottrell*[37] appellant appealed the grant of a civil protection order claiming that the trial court failed to make a *de novo,* independent review of the magistrate's decision.

In its decision, the appellate court first noted that Civ. R. 53(D)(4) governs magistrate's decisions and when ruling on objections, a court shall undertake an independent review. The court also relied on decisions from the Fourth Appellate District wherein an independent analysis is presumed.[38] The court then focused on the trial court's conclusion that there was no error or law or other defect in the granting of the domestic violence CPO and therefore, respondent had not met his burden under Civ. R. 65.1(F).

Finally, the appellate court reviewed *Williams v. Tumblin nka Volk,*[39] in which the court also considered the same argument and held that "[a]ppellant's argument that the court failed to exercise independent judgment rests on the fact that the court failed to specifically mention certain factors, and also on the fact that the trial court overruled her objections. However, the trial court's failure to agree with appellant or to specifically discuss every factor weighing into the decision does not rebut the presumption that the trial court conducted an independent analysis in accordance with Civ. R. 53(D)(4)(d)."[40]

---

[35]J.P. v. T.H, 2016-Ohio-243, 2016 WL 363247, ¶ 11 (Ohio Ct. App. 9th Dist. Lorain County 2016).

[36]J.P. v. T.H, 2016-Ohio-243, 2016 WL 363247, ¶ 13 (Ohio Ct. App. 9th Dist. Lorain County 2016).

[37]Cottrill v. Cottrill, 2017-Ohio-1422, 2017 WL 1376841 (Ohio Ct. App. 5th Dist. Fairfield County 2017).

[38]Martindale v. Martindale, 2017-Ohio-9266, ¶ 41, 102 N.E.3d 19 (Ohio Ct. App. 4th Dist. Athens County 2017) (referring to the trial court's statement that it had made its own independent analysis in its review of the record).

[39]Williams v. Tumblin, 2014-Ohio-4365, ¶ 37, 2014 WL 4907048 (Ohio Ct. App. 5th Dist. Coshocton County 2014).

[40]Cottrill v. Cottrill, 2017-Ohio-1422, ¶ 18, 2017 WL 1376841 (Ohio Ct. App. 5th Dist. Fairfield County 2017).

Based on this analysis, the appellate court found that, in this case, "the trial court did conduct a *de novo*, independent review."[41]

Of significance is that the Fifth District Court of Appeals has implied that a *de novo* review is required. However, the court appears to have utilized both Civ. 53 and Civ. R. 65.1 interchangeably so it is unclear whether the analysis is based on Civ. R. 65.1 or a rule that no longer applies to magistrates in civil protection order actions.

Q & A: Must a trial court defer to the magistrate's determinations as to witness credibility?

According to *Bressler v. Nunemaker*,[42] the answer is no. In that case, petitioner testified in support of the CPO that the parties were separated by the time she filed the CPO. The full hearing was held by a magistrate who denied the protection order on the grounds that petitioner "did not prove by a preponderance of the evidence that appellant committed a recent act of domestic violence as defined in RC 311.31(A)(1)."[43] Additionally, the magistrate found that "appellee's alleged fear that appellant would harm her now that the relationship had ended was not credible."[44]

However, after objections were filed, the trial court issued an opinion rejecting the magistrate's decision and concluding that the CPO should have been issued as there was no requirement that a petitioner prove a recent act of domestic violence.[45]

On appeal, appellant claimed that the decision was against the manifest weight of the evidence and argued that the trial court erred in rejecting the magistrate's denial of the CPO because the magistrate found that appellee's testimony was not credible and that the magistrate was in the best position to determine credibility of witnesses.[46]

The appellate court held that nothing in Civ. R. 65.1 suggests that upon objections, the court is required to defer to the magistrate's determination of credibility.[47] In fact, "Civ. R. 65.1(F)(3)(c)(iii) gives the court the authority to modify or reject the magistrate's order, without any restrictions on the court's ability to reach its own conclusions concerning credibility."[48]

The court affirmed the trial court's decision based on the testimony of physical abuse and threatening behavior. In addition, the appellate

[41]Cottrill v. Cottrill, 2017-Ohio-1422, ¶ 19, 2017 WL 1376841 (Ohio Ct. App. 5th Dist. Fairfield County 2017).

[42]Bressler v. Nunemaker, 2017-Ohio-5804, 2017 WL 2964199 (Ohio Ct. App. 5th Dist. Licking County 2017).

[43]Bressler v. Nunemaker, 2017-Ohio-5804, ¶ 3, 2017 WL 2964199 (Ohio Ct. App. 5th Dist. Licking County 2017).

[44]Bressler v. Nunemaker, 2017-Ohio-5804, ¶ 3, 2017 WL 2964199 (Ohio Ct. App. 5th Dist. Licking County 2017).

[45]Bressler v. Nunemaker, 2017-Ohio-5804, ¶ 4, 2017 WL 2964199 (Ohio Ct. App. 5th Dist. Licking County 2017).

[46]Bressler v. Nunemaker, 2017-Ohio-5804, ¶ 9, 2017 WL 2964199 (Ohio Ct. App. 5th Dist. Licking County 2017).

[47]Bressler v. Nunemaker, 2017-Ohio-5804, ¶ 9, 2017 WL 2964199 (Ohio Ct. App. 5th Dist. Licking County 2017), citing In re A.M., 2010-Ohio-948, 2010 WL 890940 (Ohio Ct. App. 2d Dist. Greene County 2010).

[48]Bressler v. Nunemaker, 2017-Ohio-5804, ¶ 9, 2017 WL 2964199 (Ohio Ct. App. 5th Dist. Licking County 2017).

court quoted from the decision of *Rader v. Rader*, in which the court determined that "[t]he parameters of a trial court's discretion must also encompass the determination of whether a CPO is actually necessary to ensure the family member's protection."[49]

Q & A: Must the trial court issue specific findings to support the adoption or denial of the civil protection order?

Not according to the Medina County Court of Appeals. In *R.C. v J.G.*[50] appellant argued on appeal that the trial court erred by adopting the civil protection order without making a specific finding that the magistrate's order did not contain an error or other defect on its face.[51] The appellate court noted that the role of a trial court under Civ. R. 65.1(F)(3)(c) is more limited. It found that, while Civ. R. 65.1 does require that the trial court examine an order to determine if there is an error of law or defect on the face of the order, the rule does not require specific findings in the judgment, regardless of whether objections had been filed.[52] "Given that the purpose of Civ. R. 65.1 is to expedite the process of obtaining a civil protection order, it would be incongruous to require more of the trial court by way of specific findings. We therefore decline to imply what Civ. R. 65.1 does not require."

Similarly, in *Wulf v. Opp*,[53] Opp filed an appeal alleging that she was denied her written request for findings of fact and conclusions of law, even though language was included within the original CSPO that required written findings of fact and conclusions of law prior to any objection being filed. She also argued that the inclusion of this language "effectively precluded her from having the ability to timely file objections to the magistrate's decision"[54] (While this appeal was brought relative to civil stalking protection order pursuant to RC 2903.214, the analysis is the same.).

Because all civil protection orders must comply with Civ. R. 65.1 and because the rule specifically states that the requirements of Civ. R. 53 do not apply, a request for findings of fact and conclusions of law provided by Civ. R. 53(D)(3)(a)(ii) was not mandatory. Thus, it was within the discretion of the trial court and not plain error to deny the request for written findings of fact and conclusions of law.[55]

---

[49] Bressler v. Nunemaker, 2017-Ohio-5804, ¶ 10, 2017 WL 2964199 (Ohio Ct. App. 5th Dist. Licking County 2017), quoting Rader v. Rader, 2007-Ohio-4288, ¶ 19, 2007 WL 2390815 (Ohio Ct. App. 5th Dist. Licking County 2007).

[50] R.C. v. J.G., 2013-Ohio-4265, 2013 WL 5437015 (Ohio Ct. App. 9th Dist. Medina County 2013); Wulf v. Opp, 2015-Ohio-3285, 2015 WL 4878495, ¶ 16 (Ohio Ct. App. 12th Dist. Clermont County 2015); but see Bullard v. Alley, 2014-Ohio-1016, 2014 WL 1339719 (Ohio Ct. App. 4th Dist. Pike County 2014) (noting that an appellate review is more limited if specific findings are not made by a trial court).

[51] R.C. v. J.G., 2013-Ohio-4265, 2013 WL 5437015 (Ohio Ct. App. 9th Dist. Medina County 2013).

[52] See also B.C. v. A.S., 2014-Ohio-1326, 2014 WL 1345260 (Ohio Ct. App. 9th Dist. Medina County 2014).

[53] Wulf v. Opp, 2015-Ohio-3285, 2015 WL 4878495 (Ohio Ct. App. 12th Dist. Clermont County 2015).

[54] Wulf v. Opp, 2015-Ohio-3285, 2015 WL 4878495, ¶ 15 (Ohio Ct. App. 12th Dist. Clermont County 2015).

[55] But see Rehfus v. Smith, 2015-Ohio-2145, 2015 WL 3498686 (Ohio Ct. App. 7th

Q & A: Is a movant prohibited from requesting findings of fact and conclusions of law and/or new trial?[56]

In *Besman v. Leventhal*,[57] appellant filed a request for findings of fact and conclusions of law after a CPO was issued against him. "When the [trial] court denied that request as inapplicable to CPO proceedings, he filed a motion for a new trial and/or a motion for relief from judgment."[58]

He argued that nothing in the language of Civ. R. 65.1 prohibits a party from filing a motion requesting findings of fact and conclusions of law.[59] However, the appellate court relied on Civ. R. 65.1(A) which provides that the rule "supersedes and makes inapplicable in such proceedings and provisions of any other rules of civil procedure *to the extent that such application is inconsistent with the provisions of this rule.*"[60] In effect, to allow findings of fact and conclusions of law would be inconsistent with the Rule because it would delay the proceedings, rather than streamlining such proceedings.

The appellate court also disagreed with appellant's claim that the purpose of the rule was to avoid delay in the enforcement of the CPO and that such a request would not affect the immediate enforceability of a CPO. Instead, the court chose to rely on precedent that held that "[w]hile avoiding delay in the enforcement of a protection order may be a consequence of the rule, we abide by precedent stating that the rule is intended to "expedite" the process for obtaining rulings on matters related to protection orders."[61]

Even if Civ. R. 65.1 had permitted a request for findings of fact and conclusions of law, the record in this case shows that the court issued findings of fact when it issued the CPO. The court considered that the use of Form 10.01-G, a provision of which provides that "The Court hereby makes the following findings of fact[.]"[62] While admittedly not comprehensive, these findings were adequate to fulfill the purpose of

Dist. Carroll County 2015) (an absence of findings of fact and conclusions of law narrows the standard of review).

[56]See also Text 9:5.

[57]Besman v. Leventhal, 2017-Ohio-464, 2017 WL 526288 (Ohio Ct. App. 8th Dist. Cuyahoga County 2017), appeal not allowed, 151 Ohio St. 3d 1503, 2018-Ohio-365, 90 N.E.3d 946 (2018).

[58]Besman v. Leventhal, 2017-Ohio-464, ¶ 1, 2017 WL 526288 (Ohio Ct. App. 8th Dist. Cuyahoga County 2017), appeal not allowed, 151 Ohio St. 3d 1503, 2018-Ohio-365, 90 N.E.3d 946 (2018).

[59]But see Lundin v. Niepsuj, 2017-Ohio-7153, 2017 WL 3426957 (Ohio Ct. App. 9th Dist. Summit County 2017) (appellate court pointed out that "[w]hen a timely motion for findings of fact and conclusions of law has been filed in accordance with Civ. R. 52, the time period for filing a notice of appeal does not commence to run until the trial court files its findings of fact and conclusions of law." at ¶ 8).

[60]Besman v. Leventhal, 2017-Ohio-464, ¶ 5, 2017 WL 526288 (Ohio Ct. App. 8th Dist. Cuyahoga County 2017), appeal not allowed, 151 Ohio St. 3d 1503, 2018-Ohio-365, 90 N.E.3d 946 (2018).

[61]Besman v. Leventhal, 2017-Ohio-464, ¶ 6, 2017 WL 526288 (Ohio Ct. App. 8th Dist. Cuyahoga County 2017), appeal not allowed, 151 Ohio St. 3d 1503, 2018-Ohio-365, 90 N.E.3d 946 (2018), citing Schneider v. Razek, 2015-Ohio-410, ¶ 29, 28 N.E.3d 591 (Ohio Ct. App. 8th Dist. Cuyahoga County 2015); see also Insa v. Insa, 2016-Ohio-7425, 72 N.E.3d 1170 (Ohio Ct. App. 2d Dist. Montgomery County 2016).

[62]Besman v. Leventhal, 2017-Ohio-464, ¶ 7, 2017 WL 526288 (Ohio Ct. App. 8th

separately stated findings of fact and conclusions of law to enable a reviewing court to determine the existence of assigned error.[63]

The same analysis was applied to appellant's request for a motion for a new trial. Additionally, such a request would be superfluous in that the objections already contained in the Civ. R. 65.1(F)(3)(d) were identical to the grounds asserted in a Civ. R. 59 motion for a new trial.[64]

Conversely, in *Martindale v. Martindale*,[65] appellant appealed the trial court decision granting the CPO. The appellate court pointed out that appellant's failure to request findings of fact and conclusions of law limited the ability of the court in its review. The court noted the purpose of Civ. R. findings of fact and conclusions of law are "to aid the appellate court in reviewing the record and determining the validity of the basis of the trial court's judgment."[66] Without findings of fact and conclusions of law, an appellate court must presume that the trial court applied the law correctly and would affirm the trial court if the evidence supports it. Therefore, a party may request findings of fact and conclusions of law pursuant to Civ. R. 52 "in order to ensure the fullest possible review."[67]

The court reasoned that when findings of fact and conclusions of law are not requested, "the challenger is not entitled to be elevated to a position superior than if he made such a request."[68] The court then issued a cautionary warning: "If a party wishes to challenge the ***judgment as being against the manifest weight of the evidence he had best secure separate findings of fact and conclusions of law. Otherwise, his already 'uphill' burden of demonstrating error becomes an almost insurmountable 'mountain.' "[69]

After the trial court dismissed the CPO in the first instance, appellee requested a new trial based on newly discovered evidence. Based on that hearing, the trial court granted the CPO. This is important because the *Martindale* court granted a new trial which was rejected by the appellate court and is contrary to the *Besman v. Leventhal*

Dist. Cuyahoga County 2017), appeal not allowed, 151 Ohio St. 3d 1503, 2018-Ohio-365, 90 N.E.3d 946 (2018).

[63] Besman v. Leventhal, 2017-Ohio-464, ¶ 9, 2017 WL 526288 (Ohio Ct. App. 8th Dist. Cuyahoga County 2017), appeal not allowed, 151 Ohio St. 3d 1503, 2018-Ohio-365, 90 N.E.3d 946 (2018).

[64] Besman v. Leventhal, 2017-Ohio-464, ¶ 11, 2017 WL 526288 (Ohio Ct. App. 8th Dist. Cuyahoga County 2017), appeal not allowed, 151 Ohio St. 3d 1503, 2018-Ohio-365, 90 N.E.3d 946 (2018); see also Insa v. Insa, 2016-Ohio-7425, 72 N.E.3d 1170 (Ohio Ct. App. 2d Dist. Montgomery County 2016).

[65] Martindale v. Martindale, 2017-Ohio-9266, 102 N.E.3d 19 (Ohio Ct. App. 4th Dist. Athens County 2017).

[66] Martindale v. Martindale, 2017-Ohio-9266, ¶ 23, 102 N.E.3d 19, 25, (Ohio Ct. App. 4th Dist. Athens County 2017).

[67] Martindale v. Martindale, 2017-Ohio-9266, ¶ 23, 102 N.E.3d 19, 25, (Ohio Ct. App. 4th Dist. Athens County 2017).

[68] Martindale v. Martindale, 2017-Ohio-9266, ¶ 25, 102 N.E.3d 19, 25, (Ohio Ct. App. 4th Dist. Athens County 2017).

[69] Martindale v. Martindale, 2017-Ohio-9266, ¶ 25, 102 N.E.3d 19, 25, (Ohio Ct. App. 4th Dist. Athens County 2017)., quoting Harper v. Neal, 2016-Ohio-7179, ¶ 19, 2016 WL 5874628 (Ohio Ct. App. 4th Dist. Hocking County 2016).

court of appeals which determined that a new trial would be superfluous.

Q & A: Must objections be filed before an appeal is filed?[70]

Pursuant to Civ. R. 65.1, a party must file timely objections prior to filing an appeal.[71] However, if timely objections to the trial court order are not filed, an appellate court lacks jurisdiction to hear the appeal.[72]

In *Frith v. Frith,*[73] the appellate court even addressed the reason for filing objections before filing an appeal. "As the staff notes for division (G) indicate, the purpose of requiring that objections be filed prior to the filing of an appeal is to provide the trial court an opportunity to review the transcript and address any insufficiency of evidence or abuse of discretion, and to create a more robust record for the appeal."[74]

Q & A: Is the requirement to file objections to the magistrate's decision mandatory? Is that mandate to do so jurisdictional?

All jurisdictions have determined that the requirement to file objections under Civ. R. 65.1(F)(3)(d) is mandatory, meaning that any party wishing to object to the legal conclusions or wishing to demonstrate that the credible evidence is insufficient bears the burden of demonstrating such in timely filed objections.[75]

However, some appellate jurisdictions have determined that the failure to comply with Civ. R. 65.1(G) is not a jurisdictional bar, creating a split of authority with respect to the effect of a failure to file *timely* objections. (Emphasis added.)

For example, in *M.W. v. D. M.*,[76] appellee sought a civil stalking protection order because of numerous emails sent by respondent. In light of the unwanted, persistent and increasingly hostile contact, ap-

[70]See also Text § 9:5.

[71]Civ. R. 65.1(G); Hetrick v. Lockwood, 2018-Ohio-118, 2018 WL 388965 (Ohio Ct. App. 6th Dist. Sandusky County 2018) (noting that several other appellate districts have addressed the same issue); K.R. v. T.B., 2017-Ohio-8647, 2017 WL 5608198 (Ohio Ct. App. 10th Dist. Franklin County 2017); J.S. v. D.E., 2017-Ohio-7507, 2017 WL 3971706 (Ohio Ct. App. 7th Dist. Mahoning County 2017); J.K. v. T.J., 2017-Ohio-9239, 2017 WL 6550546 (Ohio Ct. App. 7th Dist. Mahoning County 2017); R.G. v. R.M., 2017-Ohio-8918, 88 N.E.3d 1027 (Ohio Ct. App. 7th Dist. Mahoning County 2017) (pointing out that former Civ. R. 65.1(G) which permitted either objections or an immediate appeal was amended in July 2016); A. S. v. D. S., 2017-Ohio-7782, 2017 WL 4242009 (Ohio Ct. App. 9th Dist. Medina County 2017).

[72]Martin v. Dockter, 2018-Ohio-858, 2018 WL 1216633 (Ohio Ct. App. 10th Dist. Franklin County 2018); Frith v. Frith, 2017-Ohio-7848, ¶ 5, 2017 WL 4287925 (Ohio Ct. App. 9th Dist. Summit County 2017) (noting that objections must be both timely filed and ruled upon or resolved by the trial court prior to filing an appeal and dismissing objections due to trial court not ruling on appellant's timely filed objections prior to appeal as required by Civ. R. 65.1(G)).

[73]Frith v. Frith, 2017-Ohio-7848, 2017 WL 4287925 (Ohio Ct. App. 9th Dist. Summit County 2017).

[74]Frith v. Frith, 2017-Ohio-7848, ¶ 4, 2017 WL 4287925 (Ohio Ct. App. 9th Dist. Summit County 2017).

[75]M.W. v. D.M., 2018-Ohio-392, ¶ 7, 2018 WL 660271 (Ohio Ct. App. 8th Dist. Cuyahoga County 2018); Martin v. Dockter, 2018-Ohio-858, ¶ 6, 2018 WL 1216633 (Ohio Ct. App. 10th Dist. Franklin County 2018); K.R. v. T.B., 2017-Ohio-8647, ¶ 5, 2017 WL 5608198 (Ohio Ct. App. 10th Dist. Franklin County 2017).

[76]M.W. v. D.M., 2018-Ohio-392, 2018 WL 660271 (Ohio Ct. App. 8th Dist. Cuyahoga County 2018).

pellee alleged respondent's conduct caused her mental distress. At the full hearing, the magistrate issued a CSPO. Respondent failed to appear at the full hearing and did not file objections.

The appellate court first noted Civ. R. 65.1 procedurally changed the scope of appellate review. The court then reiterated that Civ. R. 65.1(G) was applicable to the case at hand and pointed out that "any order entered by the court under Civ. R. 65.1(F)(3)(c) is a final appealable order" suggesting that the appellate court had jurisdiction over the appeal.[77]

The appellate court then reviewed opinions from other appellate districts regarding the issue of jurisdiction when an appellant fails to file objections. Some appellate districts held that an appellate court lacks jurisdiction over the appeal.[78]

The 8th District Court of Appeals then determined that the failure to comply with Civ. R. 65.1(G) is not jurisdictional, meaning that the procedural defect must be raised by the prevailing party. Since it was not, the procedural error had been forfeited and the court did not need to address the issue beyond determining that it possessed jurisdiction to entertain the appeal.[79]

While achieving the same result, the 1st District Court of Appeals reasoned that providing notice of the right to file objections changed the narrative. In *Saqr v. Naji*,[80] appellant claimed that the trial court erred in denying his motion to terminate the CPO; however he failed to file objections before appealing the denial.

The appellate court then pointed out that the trial court had failed to even notify respondent that objections could be filed. Absent notice that objections could be filed, the failure to file objections before the appeal, pursuant to Civ. R. 65.1(G), did not create a jurisdictional bar. Thus, the court found that it had jurisdiction to hear the appeal.

Q & A: Must a notice of filing objections be provided to a litigant?

According to *Saqr v. Naji*,[81] the court allowed the appeal despite no objections having been filed because the appellant was not provided with notice that he could file objections. Clearly, the absence of such notice to file objections created an exception to the mandates of the civil rules.

---

[77]M.W. v. D.M., 2018-Ohio-392, ¶ 4, 2018 WL 660271 (Ohio Ct. App. 8th Dist. Cuyahoga County 2018); but see A. S. v. D. S., 2017-Ohio-7782, ¶ 6, 2017 WL 4242009 (Ohio Ct. App. 9th Dist. Medina County 2017) (although mindful of the fact that the CPO was a final appealable order, D.S. still had an obligation to follow the mandates of Civ. R. 65.1(G). Absent that, the appellate court could not address the merits of the appeal).

[78]See J.S. v. D.E., 2017-Ohio-7507, 2017 WL 3971706 (Ohio Ct. App. 7th Dist. Mahoning County 2017); J.K. v. T.J., 2017-Ohio-9239, 2017 WL 6550546 (Ohio Ct. App. 7th Dist. Mahoning County 2017); K.U. v. M.S., 2017-Ohio-8029, 2017 WL 4350999 (Ohio Ct. App. 7th Dist. Mahoning County 2017); Hetrick v. Lockwood, 2018-Ohio-118, 2018 WL 388965 (Ohio Ct. App. 6th Dist. Sandusky County 2018).

[79]M.W. v. D.M., 2018-Ohio-392, ¶ 7, 2018 WL 660271 (Ohio Ct. App. 8th Dist. Cuyahoga County 2018).

[80]Saqr v. Naji, 2017-Ohio-8142, 2017 WL 4538886 (Ohio Ct. App. 1st Dist. Hamilton County 2017).

[81]Saqr v. Naji, 2017-Ohio-8142, 2017 WL 4538886 (Ohio Ct. App. 1st Dist. Hamilton County 2017).

The take-away is that under certain circumstances, appellate courts will allow an appeal to move forward even though objections were not filed.[82]

Q & A: Does a party object to a magistrate's order or to the trial court's adoption, modification or rejection of a magistrate's order?

Under Civ. R. 53 a party is permitted to file objections to a magistrate's grant or denial of a civil protection order.[83]

However, a civil protection order proceeding is a special statutory proceeding and other civil rules, including Civ. R. 53, apply only when they are not inconsistent with Civ. R. 65.1.[84] As a special statutory proceeding, there is no magistrate's decision issued. Technically, the order is neither a magistrate's decision nor magistrate's order; however, most courts use the terms interchangeably. Once a magistrate grants or denies either a CPO[85] or a CSPO,[86] the trial court may adopt, modify, or reject the magistrate's grant or denial of the protection order.[87] A court's adoption, modification or rejection of a magistrate's denial or granting of a protection order after a full hearing does not constitute a judgment or interim order under Civ. R. 539D)(4)(e) and is not subject to the requirements of that rule.[88]

Since the magistrate's denial or granting of a protection order is adopted, modified or rejected immediately, a party receives the actual court order. In that the magistrate's decision is not effective unless adopted by the court, objections can only be filed to the trial court order, not the magistrate's decision.[89]

According to Civ. R. 65.1(F)(3)(d)(i), a party may file objections to the trial court's adoption, modification or rejection of a magistrate's grant or denial of a civil protection order issued after a full hearing or any of the terms of the order, within 14 days of the trial court's filing of the order.

If any party timely files objections, any other party may also file objections not later than 10 days after the first objections are filed.[90]

For example, in Martin v. *Dockter*,[91] the Martins filed a CSPO against Ms. Dockter which was denied at the ex parte level, but granted after a full hearing. It was adopted by the court and filed on February 24, 2017 and served on respondent on March 10, 2017.

---

[82]See also M.W. v. D.M., 2018-Ohio-392, 2018 WL 660271 (Ohio Ct. App. 8th Dist. Cuyahoga County 2018).

[83]See Heimann v. Heekin, 2014-Ohio-4276, ¶ 7, 2014 WL 4816258 (Ohio Ct. App. 1st Dist. Hamilton County 2014); Insa v. Insa, 2016-Ohio-7425, ¶ 26, 72 N.E.3d 1170 (Ohio Ct. App. 2d Dist. Montgomery County 2016).

[84]Civ. R. 65.1(A).

[85]R.C. 3113.31.

[86]R.C. 2903.214; see also § 9:5.

[87]Civ. R. 65.1(F)(3)c)(ii), (iii).

[88]Civ. R. 65.1(F)(3)(c)(iv).

[89]See Martin v. Dockter, 2018-Ohio-858, 2018 WL 1216633 (Ohio Ct. App. 10th Dist. Franklin County 2018); J.S. v. D.E., 2017-Ohio-7507, 2017 WL 3971706 (Ohio Ct. App. 7th Dist. Mahoning County 2017).

[90]Civ. R. 65.1(F)(3)(d)(i).

[91]Martin v. Dockter, 2018-Ohio-858, 2018 WL 1216633 (Ohio Ct. App. 10th Dist. Franklin County 2018).

Dockter then filed her objections and a motion pursuant to Civ. R. 60(B)(2) seeking to file her objections to the trial court's adoption of the CPO outside of the 14 day timeframe, which motion was denied based on a finding that it lacked jurisdiction. From this denial, she appealed.

On appeal, the appellate court agreed with Dockter that the trial court erred when it denied her 60(B)(2) motion. The trial court based its decision on a faulty premise that that Civ. R. 53 still applied to CPOs. The court pointed out that the trial court erred when it applied Civ. R. 53, instead of Civ. R. 65.1. It held that "[t]he trial court's reasoning does not apply to a Civ. R. 65.1 order because the right to file objections is to the trial court's order, not to the magistrate's decision."[92] In that the objections were due on the date Dockter filed both her motion and objections, the trial court had jurisdiction to decide the 60(B)(2) motion.

Q & A: Do objections stay the execution of the order?

No. The timely filing of objections under this division shall not stay the execution of the order.[93]

Q & A: What does the objecting party have to show to the court?

A party filing objections under this division has the burden of showing that an error of law or other defect is evident on the face of the order, or that the credible evidence of record is insufficient to support the granting or denial of the protection order, or that the magistrate abused the magistrate's discretion in including or failing to include specific terms in the protection order.[94]

Q & A: Is a transcript a requirement?

Objections based upon evidence of record shall be supported by a transcript of all the evidence submitted to the magistrate or an affidavit of that evidence if a transcript is not available. With leave of court, alternative technology or manner of reviewing the relevant evidence may be considered. The objecting party shall file the transcript or affidavit with the court within 30 days after filing objections unless the court extends the time in writing for preparation of the transcript or other good cause. If a party files timely objections prior to the date on which a transcript is prepared, the party may seek leave of court to supplement the objections.[95]

Q & A: When is the order a final appealable order?

According the recent amendment to Civ. R. 65.1(G), notwithstanding the provisions of any other rule, an order entered by the court under division (F)(3)(c) or division (F)(3)(e) of this rule is a final appealable order. *However, a party must timely file objections to such an order under (F)(3)(d) of this rule prior to filing an appeal, and the*

[92]Martin v. Dockter, 2018-Ohio-858, ¶ 9, 2018 WL 1216633 (Ohio Ct. App. 10th Dist. Franklin County 2018).

[93]Civ. R. 65.1(F)(3)(d)(ii). Collins v. Clancy, 2014 WL 1653103 (S.D. Ohio 2014) (noting that the timely filing of objections under (F)(3)(d) shall stay the running of the time for appeal until the objections are ruled upon but does not stay enforcement of the order).

[94]Civ. R. 65.1(F)(3)(d)(iii).

[95]Civ. R. 65.1(F)(3)(d)(iv).

timely filing of such objections shall stay the running of the time for appeal until the filing of the court's ruling on the objections.[96]

The Staff Notes, adopted in July 1, 2016, indicate that the reason for the amendment was to inform a party that objections must be filed prior to filing an appeal from a trial court's otherwise appealable adoption, modification or rejection of a magistrate's ruling. The amendment was grounded on two principles. First, it promotes the fair administration of justice, including affording the trial court an opportunity to review the transcript and address any insufficiency of evidence or abuse of discretion that would render the order or term of the order unjust. Second, it creates a more robust record upon which the appeal may proceed.

In fact, a lack of a record makes it more difficult for appellate courts to review a given case. A review of the case law supports this claim.[97] Thus, the need for objections before an appeal is filed.

Q & A: Since the adoption of Civ. R. 65.1, have there been any cases that have discussed this rule?

As of July 1, 2016, the Supreme Court of Ohio has adopted new provisions to Civ. R. 65.1 which require objections to be filed *before* an appeal of a civil protection order. All case law decisions that have addressed this provision of the civil rules will no longer be effective for this point of law.

Besides the aforementioned cases that have been decided since the adoption of the amendment in 2016, the appellate court has also decided other cases since the adoption of Civ. R. 65.1 in 2012 which were instructive for other points of law. For example, in *Heimann v. Heekin*,[98] petitioner/appellant appealed the trial court's denial of her CPO.

In August 2012, Heimann filed for a CPO and a full hearing was had on November 1, 2012. After Heimann rested, Heekin requested a continuance to bring in witnesses to rebut Heimann's testimony. The court denied the continuance, believing it it to be a fishing expedition, and ordered the CPO to remain in effect until November 1, 2017.

Heekin then objected to the magistrate's grant of the CPO claiming that it was against the weight of the evidence. In January 2013, Heekin moved the court to take additional evidence and rehear the case. In March 2013, the trial court granted the objections and set the matter for a full hearing. However, after repeated joint requests to continue, the trial court dismissed the petition on August 22, 2013.

On September 19, 2013, Heimann filed her notice of appeal which was deemed untimely. Under Civ. R. 65.1, Heimann should have appealed the trial court's decision, journalized March 18, 2013, which rejected the magistrate's granting of the protection order. "From a review of the record, it appears that Heimann may have been misled

[96]Emphasis added.

[97]See for eg., Heimann v. Heekin, 2014-Ohio-4276, 2014 WL 4816258 (Ohio Ct. App. 1st Dist. Hamilton County 2014).

[98]Heimann v. Heekin, 2014-Ohio-4276, 2014 WL 4816258 (Ohio Ct. App. 1st Dist. Hamilton County 2014).

by the trial court's misunderstanding of which civil rule governed petitions for protection orders brought under RC 3113.31."[99]

The appellate court reviewed Civ. R. 65.1 and noted that under Civ. R. 65.1(F)(3)(c), the magistrate's grant or denial of a protection order after a full hearing is not effective until adopted by the court. The court may adopt a magistrate's grant or denial of a CPO so long as there is no error or law or other defect evident on the face of the order. Once signed by the court and filed with the clerk, the judgment becomes a final appealable order.

The record demonstrated that the trial court failed to follow the procedure for magistrate's orders set forth in Civ. R. 65.1; rather it followed the dictates of Civ. R. 53. Clearly, many courts are still unfamiliar with Civ. R. 65.1.[100]

More problematic, Civ. R. 65.1 permitted a moving party both options-to appeal or object and each must apply a different time line. That said, the decision itself was confusing and indicated a lack of understanding regarding Civ. R. 65.1. In one provision, the appellate court states that "[n]otably, unlike Civ. R. 53, a party may not object to the magistrate's grant or denial of a protection order under Civ. R. 65.1."[101] In another provision, the court recognizes alternative remedies. To eliminate this confusion, the Civil Rules were amended in 2016.

Apparently, the appellate court had reasoned that the trial court had rejected the magistrate's order and that the journalized rejection of magistrate's order was a final appealable order under Civ. R. 65.1, and the time for appeal began to run from date of entry. Had the magistrate adopted the magistrate's order, it too would have become a final appealable order.

In this case, the appellate court's reading of the rule seems to suggest that a party could object only to the adoption, modification or rejection of the magistrate's order and not to the magistrate's grant or denial of the CPO. While that might not be problematic to attorneys and judges who have not been versed in Civ. R. 53, it is confusing to those who have a more thorough understanding of Civ. R. 53.

---

[99]Heimann v. Heekin, 2014-Ohio-4276, ¶ 4, 2014 WL 4816258 (Ohio Ct. App. 1st Dist. Hamilton County 2014).

[100]M.L. v. E.M., 2015-Ohio-4004, 2015 WL 5728282 (Ohio Ct. App. 9th Dist. Medina County 2015) (discussing differences between proceedings under Civ. R. 53 and 65.1); see also Ramsey v. Pellicioni, 2016-Ohio-558, 2016 WL 635212 (Ohio Ct. App. 7th Dist. Mahoning County 2016) (applying Civ. R. 53 to resolve a Civ. R. 65.1 matter); J.B. v. R.B., 2015-Ohio-3808, 2015 WL 5517797 (Ohio Ct. App. 9th Dist. Medina County 2015) (in a consent entry where petitioner failed to make monthly payments for the jeep, trial court found that respondent should not have been able to file a contempt motion as the court did not have the ability to require a petitioner to perform particular acts; appeal dismissed based on a misapplied Civ. R. 53 analysis regarding objections); Weber v. Forinash, 2015-Ohio-3187, 2015 WL 4720532 (Ohio Ct. App. 6th Dist. Sandusky County 2015) (the dissent admonished the majority for ignoring the trial court's procedural missteps in using Civ. R. 53 rather than 65.1); M.H. v. J.H., 2017-Ohio-8679, 2017 WL 5706128 (Ohio Ct. App. 9th Dist. Medina County 2017) (where appellate court utilized Civ. R. 53 in its analysis); L.L. v. R.B., 2017-Ohio-7553, 2017 WL 3980553 (Ohio Ct. App. 5th Dist. Guernsey County 2017) (concluding correctly despite applying Civ. R. 53).

[101]Heimann v. Heekin, 2014-Ohio-4276, ¶ 7, 2014 WL 4816258 (Ohio Ct. App. 1st Dist. Hamilton County 2014).

Unfortunately, under Civ. R. 53, a further hearing was permissible. The appellate court appeared to punish Heimann for the ignorance of the trial court both in its misunderstanding of the civil rules and not knowing that it had no authority to reset the matter for a hearing before the court as was permissible under Civ. R. 53. Of concern is that the appellate court and the trial court employed a Civ. R. 53 analysis and applied it to R. 65.1 and the facts of the case.[102] Lawyers and parties need to understand that R. 65.1 does not provide for another hearing after a journalized rejection of the magistrate's order. A lawyer or a party must appeal or lose the chance to do so.[103]

On another note, the Civil Rule provides for a trial court to review to determine that there is no error of law or other defect evident on the face of the order.[104] However, once a party objects to the adoption, modification or rejection of the magistrate's order, the court shall do a more thorough review to determine whether there is an error of law or other defect evident on the face of the order, or that the credible evidence of record is insufficient to support the granting or denial of the order or that the magistrate abused its discretion in including or failing to include specific terms in the protection order.[105] Thus, the nature of the review depends on whether a party objects. Of course, it remains unclear as to whether one is objecting to the grant or denial or the order or to the adoption, modification or rejection of that order.

In *Schneider v. Razek*,[106] the ex wife appealed from two orders entered by the trial court relating to a CPO entered by the court five years earlier, regarding the ex husband's grant of a motion to terminate the order and the denial of ex wife's motion to extend the CPO.

Relying on Civ. R. 65(G), the appellate court reiterated that the court's adoption, modification or rejection of a magistrate's denial or granting of a protection order, with or without the subsequent filing of objections, is a final appealable order that can be appealed upon the issuance of the order. The timely filing of objections under Civ. R. 65(F)(3)(d) shall stay the running of the time for appeal until the filing of the court's ruling on the objections.[107] The appellate court noted that the filing of objections to the orders does not preclude the immediate appeal of those orders. It then reasoned that, based on the Staff

[102]See, for example, Miller v. Tye, 2015-Ohio-199, 2015 WL 302833 (Ohio Ct. App. 2d Dist. Montgomery County 2015).

[103]See M.L. v. E.M., 2015-Ohio-4004, 2015 WL 5728282 (Ohio Ct. App. 9th Dist. Medina County 2015) (where appellant argued that the trial court erred in granting appellee a new hearing after determining that the objections were well taken, the appellate court sustained the assignment of error. The appellate court held that "[b]ecause we conclude that it appears from reviewing the record that the trial court failed to apply Civ. R. 65.1 in resolving the matter, we decline to address the merits of M.L.'s arguments, but nonetheless sustain her assignment of error to the extent that she asserts the trial court's grant of a new hearing was not in compliance with Civ. R. 65.1." at ¶ 7).

[104]Civ. R. 65.1(F)(3)(c)(ii).

[105]Civ. R 65.1(F)(3)(d)(ii).

[106]Schneider v. Razek, 2015-Ohio-410, 28 N.E.3d 591 (Ohio Ct. App. 8th Dist. Cuyahoga County 2015).

[107]Schneider v. Razek, 2015-Ohio-410, ¶ 29, 28 N.E.3d 591 (Ohio Ct. App. 8th Dist. Cuyahoga County 2015).

Note to the rule, while the filing of objections stays the running of the time for appeal, that provision only extends the time for appeal when the parties elect to have the trial court consider their objections first and do not immediately appeal the court's order.[108]

The question before the appellate court was whether, the pending objections trump the notice of appeal, where a party files both objections to the court's adoption, modification or rejection of a magistrate's decision relating to a CPO and at the same time, appeals that court order. In the instant case the majority found that "[w]e believe the better course–one that is more consistent with the language and objectives of Civ. R. 65.1—is to find that the filing of a valid notice of appeal trumps objections, i.e., a valid notice of appeal renders the objections that were previously filed under Civ. R. 65.1(F)(3)(d)(i) moot."[109] Noting that under Civil R. 53, when timely objections to a magistrate's decision are pending, the appellate court must remand the matter to the trial court to rule on the objections. Under Civ. R. 65.1, there is no such provision. Thus, the court found that the appeal was not premature due to the pending objections to the trial court's adoption of the magistrate's orders terminating the CPO and denying her motion to extend the CPO.

"The impact of a ruling precluding the immediate hearing of an appeal when objections are timely filed under Civ. R. 65.1(F)(3)(d), prior to the filing of a notice of appeal, would perhaps be less of a concern where, as here, one party chooses to file both objections to, and a notice of appeal from, a court order adopting, modifying, or rejecting a magistrate's decision relating to a protection order. However, there are circumstances—such as where a protection order is entered that is more limited in scope than the protection order sought—where more than one party may seek to challenge the court order adopting, modifying or rejecting the magistrate's decision. Given the purposes of Civ. R. 65.1, we do not believe it was intended that one party should lose the right he or she would otherwise have to immediately appeal that court order (and to have that appeal then heard) simply because another party has filed objections to that order."[110] Interestingly, it appears that the decision addresses a problem that doesn't exist in this case-one in which one of the parties' appeals and one objects.

The dissent argued that although the right to appeal existed, the notice of that appeal did not vitiate the appellant's objections to the court's adoption of the magistrate's decision. In fact, Civ. R. 65.1 permits a party the right to file objections. Noting that an aggrieved party has two options, the dissent believed that ruling on the appeal would be improvident in light of the objections filed.[111] Additionally, the court adopted the magistrate's decision without giving the parties an opportunity to object and provide a record of the claimed errors

[108]Schneider v. Razek, 2015-Ohio-410, 28 N.E.3d 591, ¶ 31 (Ohio Ct. App. 8th Dist. Cuyahoga County 2015).

[109]Schneider v. Razek, 2015-Ohio-410, 28 N.E.3d 591, ¶ 32 (Ohio Ct. App. 8th Dist. Cuyahoga County 2015).

[110]Schneider v. Razek, 2015-Ohio-410, 28 N.E.3d 591, ¶ 34 (Ohio Ct. App. 8th Dist. Cuyahoga County 2015).

[111]Schneider v. Razek, 2015-Ohio-410, 28 N.E.3d 591, ¶ 78 (Ohio Ct. App. 8th Dist. Cuyahoga County 2015).

depriving the appellate court of the ability to consider evidentiary objections.[112] Finally, the dissent considered Civ. R. 65.1(G) and noted that an order adopting a magistrate's decision is a final appealable order that *can* be appealed.

"The court correctly believed it lacked jurisdiction to rule on Schneider's objections while her appeal was pending. See Special Prosecutors v. Judges Court of Common Pleas, 55 Ohio St.2d 94, 97, 378 NE2d 162 (1978). Nevertheless, those objections were filed before a notice of appeal was filed and should be ruled upon by the court in the first instance. If the goal behind Civ. R. 65.1 is to provide an 'expedited process' for obtaining protection orders, see Staff Notes Division (F), the fastest way to accomplish this goal is to let the court rule on the objections and cure any potential defects in its order."[113]

Of importance is that the orders objected to and appealed from are not the magistrate's denial or granting or a protection order after a full hearing. Rather they are orders adopting the magistrate's decisions to terminate the CPO and to deny a motion to extend or renew the order. Nevertheless, they are part of the special statutory proceedings under RC 3113.31 and have similar impact as a decision denying or granting a protection order.[114] Thus, the orders at issue are within the scope of Civ. R. 65.1(G).[115]

The dissent also admonished the court for not ruling on the objections more quickly and stated that "[w]hen objections remain pending as the 30-day time period for filing a notice of appeal runs, it is not surprising that counsel would, in an abundance of caution, file a notice of appeal in order to preserve the right to appeal even though, as previously mentioned, the timely filing of an appeal stays the running of the time for appeal until the court rules on the objections. Filing a notice of appeal as the 30-day time period approaches cannot reasonably be considered as abandoning those objections."[116]

Of significance is the dissent's rationale as to why a ruling on objections should be made before a notice of appeal is filed. The sound reasoning of the dissent in *Razek* was reinforced in the Staff Notes when the Civil Rules were amended in 2016.

§ 12:11 Standard of proof[1]

RC 3113.31 is one of a handful of state statutes that does not address the acceptable standard of proof to be used by a court in evaluating whether a particular petitioner has met the burden of proof for

[112] Schneider v. Razek, 2015-Ohio-410, 28 N.E.3d 591, ¶ 78 (Ohio Ct. App. 8th Dist. Cuyahoga County 2015).

[113] Schneider v. Razek, 2015-Ohio-410, 28 N.E.3d 591, ¶ 81 (Ohio Ct. App. 8th Dist. Cuyahoga County 2015).

[114] Schneider v. Razek, 2015-Ohio-410, 28 N.E.3d 591, ¶ 20 (Ohio Ct. App. 8th Dist. Cuyahoga County 2015).

[115] Schneider v. Razek, 2015-Ohio-410, 28 N.E.3d 591, ¶ 20 (Ohio Ct. App. 8th Dist. Cuyahoga County 2015).

[116] Schneider v. Razek, 2015-Ohio-410, 28 N.E.3d 591, ¶ 20 (Ohio Ct. App. 8th Dist. Cuyahoga County 2015).

[Section 12:11]

[1] See also Text § 11:10, Ex parte protection orders—Legal standard for issuance.

granting a civil protection order. In states where the statute leaves the question open, most individual courts have rejected imposing a higher burden of proof than a preponderance of the evidence.[2]

Prior to 1997, Ohio courts utilized a preponderance of the evidence standard,[3] a stricter clear and convincing evidentiary standard,[4] and a lesser standard of proof based only on the statutory language.[5] The beyond-a-reasonable doubt standard has never been applied in civil protection order actions; it is reserved for criminal cases.

In 1997, the Ohio Supreme Court decided *Felton v. Felton*.[6] The Supreme Court established an evidentiary standard for use in civil protection order proceedings. In that case, the Court first determined that trial courts utilized several evidentiary standards. It also noted that, in the instant case, the trial court found that the petitioner had failed to prove her case by a preponderance of the evidence.

The Supreme Court held that "when granting a protection order, the trial court must find that petitioner has shown by a preponderance of the evidence that petitioner or petitioner's family or household members are in danger of domestic violence."[7] The Court reasoned that "[h]ad the General Assembly intended that the clear-and-

---

[2]See, e.g., In re Marriage of Hagaman, 123 Ill. App. 3d 549, 78 Ill. Dec. 922, 462 N.E.2d 1276 (4th Dist. 1984) (holding that by the plain language of the Act, "a trial court must use a preponderance-of-the-evidence standard in deciding whether an order of protection should issue"); Marquette v. Marquette, 1984 OK CIV APP 25, 686 P.2d 990 (Ct. App. Div. 1 1984).

[3]See Eichenberger v. Eichenberger, 82 Ohio App. 3d 809, 613 N.E.2d 678 (10th Dist. Franklin County 1992); Ventura v. Ventura, 1986 WL 10595 (Ohio Ct. App. 11th Dist. Lake County 1986).

[4]See O'Hara v. Dials, 1996 WL 38810, *4 (Ohio Ct. App. 6th Dist. Erie County 1996) (abrogated by, Felton v. Felton, 79 Ohio St. 3d 34, 1997-Ohio-302, 679 N.E.2d 672 (1997)); Tischler v. Vahcic, 1995 WL 680928 (Ohio Ct. App. 8th Dist. Cuyahoga County 1995) (abrogated by, Felton v. Felton, 79 Ohio St. 3d 34, 1997-Ohio-302, 679 N.E.2d 672 (1997)); Coughlin v. Lancione, 1992 WL 40557 (Ohio Ct. App. 10th Dist. Franklin County 1992) (abrogated by, Felton v. Felton, 79 Ohio St. 3d 34, 1997-Ohio-302, 679 N.E.2d 672 (1997)); Moman v. Smith, 1996 WL 586771 (Ohio Ct. App. 12th Dist. Clermont County 1996) (abrogated by, Felton v. Felton, 79 Ohio St. 3d 34, 1997-Ohio-302, 679 N.E.2d 672 (1997)).

[5]See Thomas v. Thomas, 44 Ohio App. 3d 6, 540 N.E.2d 745 (10th Dist. Franklin County 1988) (holding that the statutory criterion for determining whether or not to grant a civil protection order is the existence or threatened existence of domestic violence); Beach v. Beach, 1992 WL 328642 (Ohio Ct. App. 10th Dist. Franklin County 1992) (determining that the evidence used as a basis for issuance must meet the minimal requirement of the statute defining domestic violence); Prado v. Elsayed, 2012-Ohio-290, 2012 WL 259573 (Ohio Ct. App. 2d Dist. Montgomery County 2012); see also Deacon v. Landers, 68 Ohio App. 3d 26, 587 N.E.2d 395 (4th Dist. Ross County 1990).

[6]Felton v. Felton, 79 Ohio St. 3d 34, 1997-Ohio-302, 679 N.E.2d 672 (1997).

[7]Felton v. Felton, 79 Ohio St. 3d 34, 42, 1997-Ohio-302, 679 N.E.2d 672 (1997); see also Siouffi v. Siouffi, 1998 WL 879255 (Ohio Ct. App. 2d Dist. Montgomery County 1998); Sitton v. Sitton, 1999 WL 55717 (Ohio Ct. App. 2d Dist. Montgomery County 1999); Wolf v. Rosson, 2005-Ohio-1174, 2005 WL 628235 (Ohio Ct. App. 8th Dist. Cuyahoga County 2005); Noggle v. Smith, 2005-Ohio-5636, 2005 WL 2727128 (Ohio Ct. App. 5th Dist. Ashland County 2005); Eckstein v. Colian, 2012-Ohio-4038, 2012 WL 3834883 (Ohio Ct. App. 7th Dist. Columbiana County 2012) (preponderance of the evidence means the greater weight of the evidence, or evidence that leads the trier of fact to find that the existence of the contested fact is more probable than its non existence); Bush v. Bush, 2015-Ohio-2017, 2015 WL 3385649 (Ohio Ct. App. 5th Dist.

convincing standard apply, it certainly knew how to specify that standard."[8]

Q & A: Does the granting of a civil protection order based on a danger of domestic violence indicate that a civil protection order may not be granted based upon actual occurrences of domestic violence?[9]

This issue was raised by a respondent in *Pierce v. Pierce*.[10] In that case, the respondent noted that the Supreme Court in *Felton* held that "[w]hen granting a protection order, the trial court must find that petitioner has shown by a preponderance of the evidence that petitioner or petitioner's family or household members are in danger of domestic violence."[11] Appellant argued that the trial court did not comply with *Felton* because "it allows a CPO to be issued based upon actual occurrences of domestic violence while *Felton* permits the issuance of a CPO only when there is a danger of domestic violence."[12]

However, the Marion County Court of Appeals found that appellant misinterpreted the *Felton* decision. The court reasoned that "[a]ccording to the appellant's interpretation of *Felton*, a court could not protect an actual victim of domestic violence, but it could only protect a person who is in danger of future domestic violence. This Court does not believe such an interpretation has any reasonable or rational basis."[13] Clearly, the Marion County Appellate Court suggested an either/or approach. In order to prevail on a petition for a protection order, a petitioner must show by a preponderance of the evidence either that he/she is in danger of future domestic violence or an actual act of domestic violence has been perpetrated against him/her.[14]

The court's analysis appears to broaden the scope for the type of evidence needed to demonstrate domestic violence for purposes of a full hearing. The court relied on past acts of threats, vandalism, harassment, and actual acts of abuse over the parties' 20-year marriage

---

Licking County 2015) (preponderance of the evidence is defined as the greater weight of the evidence and "[t]he greater weight may be infinitesimal, and it is only necessary that it be sufficient to destroy the equilibrium," at ¶ 19, quoting Travelers' Ins. Co. of Hartford, Conn., v. Gath, 118 Ohio St. 257, 261, 6 Ohio L. Abs. 190, 160 N.E. 710 (1928)); Zawrotuk v. Zawrotuk, 2014-Ohio-5225, 2014 WL 6641772 (Ohio Ct. App. 7th Dist. Mahoning County 2014).

[8]Felton v. Felton, 79 Ohio St. 3d 34, 42, 1997-Ohio-302, 679 N.E.2d 672 (1997); Baker v. Baker, 2005-Ohio-5770, 2005 WL 2840647, *5 (Ohio Ct. App. 12th Dist. Butler County 2005), citing *Felton*.

[9]See also Text § 11:10, Ex parte protection orders—Legal standard for issuance, Text § 8:4, Statutory elements of domestic violence under RC 3113.31(A)(1)(b), Text § 8:8, Miscellaneous issues.

[10]Pierce v. Pierce, 2001-Ohio-2312, 2001 WL 1432047 (Ohio Ct. App. 3d Dist. Marion County 2001); see also Jarvis v. Jarvis, 2004-Ohio-1386, 2004 WL 549797 (Ohio Ct. App. 7th Dist. Jefferson County 2004).

[11]Pierce v. Pierce, 2001-Ohio-2312, 2001 WL 1432047, *3 (Ohio Ct. App. 3d Dist. Marion County 2001) (quoting *Felton*).

[12]Pierce v. Pierce, 2001-Ohio-2312, 2001 WL 1432047, *3 (Ohio Ct. App. 3d Dist. Marion County 2001).

[13]Pierce v. Pierce, 2001-Ohio-2312, 2001 WL 1432047, *3 (Ohio Ct. App. 3d Dist. Marion County 2001).

[14]Johnson v. Komisarek, 2017-Ohio-2580, 2017 WL 1534901 (Ohio Ct. App. 6th Dist. Lucas County 2017).

evidencing a pattern of abuse to justify granting the permanent civil protection order.

Over time, many courts have considered a two tiered approach. These courts have used both actual acts of domestic violence and future danger in order to determine whether a CPO should be granted after a full hearing. While a petitioner must present evidence of an actual act of domestic violence as set forth in RC 3113.31(A)(1), there must also be evidence of danger of future domestic violence to the petitioner and/or the protected parties.[15] For example, in *Burkholder v. Carter*,[16] the appellate court found that "[i]n order to grant a CPO against an individual, a trial court must find that the proponent has demonstrated by a preponderance of the evidence that the individual's family or household members are in danger of domestic violence."[17] In that case, the court also considered evidence showing actual acts of domestic violence which included pointing a gun at the petitioner, striking her in the side of her head with the gun, and pushing her up against a wall.

Similarly, in *Folmar v. Griffin*,[18] the appellate court found that "the Licking County CPO proceedings appear to have inordinately focused on the issue of whether a particular incident of domestic violence had or had not occurred; the broader focus should have been whether the 'petitioner or petitioner's family or household members are in *danger of* domestic violence.' "[19]

Q & A: Who bears the burden of proof, and what evidence satisfies that burden?[20]

It is clear that the person seeking the protection order bears the

---

[15]See In Re: C.B., (C.L., Appellant)., 2017-Ohio-4413, ¶ 3, 2017 WL 2645621 (Ohio Ct. App. 10th Dist. Franklin County 2017) (noting that the court considered proof of actual acts of domestic violence as set forth in RC 3113.31(A)(1) as well as evidence that a civil protection order is necessary[,] fair and/or equitable); see also J.M. v. M.M., 2016-Ohio-5368, 2016 WL 4272340 (Ohio Ct. App. 9th Dist. Medina County 2016) (issuance of the CPO is equitable, fair, and necessary to protect); K.B. v. B.B., 2017-Ohio-71, 80 N.E.3d 1173 (Ohio Ct. App. 9th Dist. Summit County 2017).

[16]Burkholder v. Carter, 2008-Ohio-4644, 2008 WL 4193260 (Ohio Ct. App. 3d Dist. Allen County 2008).

[17]Burkholder v. Carter, 2008-Ohio-4644, 2008 WL 4193260, *4 (Ohio Ct. App. 3d Dist. Allen County 2008), quoting Brubaker v. Farr, 2006-Ohio-2001, 2006 WL 1062102 (Ohio Ct. App. 3d Dist. Shelby County 2006), and citing Felton v. Felton, 79 Ohio St. 3d 34, 41-42, 1997-Ohio-302, 679 N.E.2d 672 (1997); but see Snell v. Snell, 2010-Ohio-2245, 2010 WL 2010899 (Ohio Ct. App. 5th Dist. Richland County 2010) (apparently finding that an "either" "or" standard may be applied to support issuance of CPO and stating there was sufficient credible evidence to determine that appellee is in danger of **or** has been the victim of domestic violence **and** that the orders are equitable, fair and necessary to bring about the cessation or prevention of domestic violence against her (emphasis added)).

[18]Folmar v. Griffin, 2008-Ohio-2941, 2008 WL 2573279 (Ohio Ct. App. 5th Dist. Delaware County 2008). See also In re E.P., 2011-Ohio-5829, 2011 WL 5507221 (Ohio Ct. App. 8th Dist. Cuyahoga County 2011) (focusing on danger of future domestic violence and a pattern of conduct rather than just an incident of domestic violence).

[19]Folmar v. Griffin, 2008-Ohio-2941, 2008 WL 2573279, *3 (Ohio Ct. App. 5th Dist. Delaware County 2008), quoting Felton v. Felton, 79 Ohio St. 3d 34, 42, 1997-Ohio-302, 679 N.E.2d 672 (1997), and citing RC 3113.31(D) (emphasis added); Traut v. Leiby, 2010-Ohio-2563, 2010 WL 2298566 (Ohio Ct. App. 5th Dist. Richland County 2010).

[20]See also Text Ch. 8, The Nature of a Civil Protection Order; Text § 11:10, Ex

burden of establishing that the other party committed an act of domestic violence[21] in effect, justifying continuation of the order.

The petitioner can usually meet the burden of proof by showing that the respondent subjected the petitioner to recent physical abuse in accordance with the statutory definition under RC 3113.31.[22] For example, in *Thomas v. Thomas*,[23] the appellate court held that "[t]he statutory criterion to determine whether or not to grant a civil protection order pursuant to RC 3113.31 is the existence or threatened existence of domestic violence."[24] This suggests that an actual act of violence or verbal threat is necessary for the issuance of a CPO.

Recent case law has demonstrated that the burden of proof may also be met by establishing that the victim is in fear of harm from the respondent.[25] A past history of violence perpetrated on the victim by the same respondent is often a reliable indicator of future violence.[26] Evidence that a victim believes the respondent's threats will cause him/her harm or even death should satisfy the requisite burden of proof.[27] For example, the Erie County Court of Appeals, in *Bruns v. Bruns*,[28] set forth the test for determining whether a victim is "in fear of imminent serious physical harm."[29] The court held that "threats of violence constitute domestic violence if the fear resulting from those threats is reasonable."[30] "Whether the fear felt by the petitioner is

---

parte protection orders—Legal standard for issuance; Text § 16:13, Hearsay exceptions; *Crawford* concerns.

[21]See Felton v. Felton, 79 Ohio St. 3d 34, 44, 1997-Ohio-302, 679 N.E.2d 672 (1997); see also Ventura v. Ventura, 1986 WL 10595 (Ohio Ct. App. 11th Dist. Lake County 1986); Stanzak v. Stanzak, 1990 WL 129456 (Ohio Ct. App. 12th Dist. Butler County 1990); Lapsansky v. Lapsansky, 2000 WL 1114535 (Ohio Ct. App. 7th Dist. Columbiana County 2000).

[22]See, e.g., Bruns v. Bruns, 1999 WL 819344 (Ohio Ct. App. 6th Dist. Erie County 1999); Reynolds v. White, 1999 WL 754496 (Ohio Ct. App. 8th Dist. Cuyahoga County 1999).

[23]Thomas v. Thomas, 44 Ohio App. 3d 6, 540 N.E.2d 745 (10th Dist. Franklin County 1988).

[24]Thomas v. Thomas, 44 Ohio App. 3d 6, 540 N.E.2d 745, 746 (10th Dist. Franklin County 1988); see also Prado v. Elsayed, 2012-Ohio-290, 2012 WL 259573 (Ohio Ct. App. 2d Dist. Montgomery County 2012); Weber v. Weber, 2011-Ohio-2980, 2011 WL 2436963 (Ohio Ct. App. 2d Dist. Greene County 2011).

[25]But see Moore v. Bentley, 2004-Ohio-5060, 2004 WL 2804785, *1 (Ohio Ct. App. 10th Dist. Franklin County 2004) (in affirming denial of CPO, court concluded appellant failed to demonstrate fear of imminent serious physical harm caused by threat of force in that appellant continually brought appellee lunch, up to the day before the filing of this matter, attended a public gathering together, and brought him flowers the day prior to filing the action).

[26]See, e.g., Visnich v. Visnich, 1999 WL 1299300 (Ohio Ct. App. 11th Dist. Trumbull County 1999); see also Ankenbruck v. Ankenbruck, 2000 WL 1804360 (Ohio Ct. App. 11th Dist. Trumbull County 2000).

[27]See also State v. Brown, 2003-Ohio-710, 2003 WL 352460, *1 (Ohio Ct. App. 12th Dist. Butler County 2003) (noting that evidence that the victim believed the accused would cause imminent harm may be stated by victim or inferred from other evidence).

[28]Bruns v. Bruns, 1999 WL 819344 (Ohio Ct. App. 6th Dist. Erie County 1999).

[29]See RC 3113.31(A)(1)(b).

[30]Bruns v. Bruns, 1999 WL 819344 (Ohio Ct. App. 6th Dist. Erie County 1999) (citing *Eichenberger*); see also Conkle v. Wolfe, 131 Ohio App. 3d 375, 722 N.E.2d 586

reasonable is determined with reference to the petitioner's history with the respondent."[31]

Interestingly, the Ohio Supreme Court appears to have framed the issue somewhat differently. The basis of the *Felton* standard is whether a particular victim believes the respondent's acts of domestic violence have put him/her in danger of future harm.[32] Proof of past violence, while helpful, is not necessary for a finding that a petitioner is danger of domestic violence.[33] For example, in *Sitton v. Sitton*,[34] the appellate court adopted the *Felton* standard of danger by upholding the issuance of the civil protection order based on the victim's testimony of fear and her actions on the day of the incident, which included hiding out from her husband and returning to the residence only when she was accompanied by a police officer or after she received a protection order.[35]

Many Ohio court decisions have relied on, further interpreted, or clarified the *Felton* standard of proof with regard to what types of acts rise to the level of domestic violence for purposes of a civil protection

(4th Dist. Athens County 1998); Anderson v. Anderson, 2001-Ohio-3379, 2001 WL 1667875 (Ohio Ct. App. 7th Dist. Mahoning County 2001); Fleckner v. Fleckner, 177 Ohio App. 3d 706, 2008-Ohio-4000, 895 N.E.2d 896 (10th Dist. Franklin County 2008); Williamson v. Williamson, 180 Ohio App. 3d 260, 2008-Ohio-6718, 905 N.E.2d 217 (2d Dist. Greene County 2008) (finding that for a CPO to be issued, the evidence must show more than the mere possibility of violence potentially occurring sometime in the future).

[31]Bruns v. Bruns, 1999 WL 819344, *2 (Ohio Ct. App. 6th Dist. Erie County 1999) (citing *Eichenberger*); Reynolds v. Reynolds, 2001 WL 62552 (Ohio Ct. App. 2d Dist. Montgomery County 2001); Chapman v. Chapman, 2004-Ohio-2318, 2004 WL 1047577 (Ohio Ct. App. 2d Dist. Montgomery County 2004). But see Bruner v. Bruner, 2000-Ohio-2554, 2000 WL 1486452 (Ohio Ct. App. 7th Dist. Mahoning County 2000); Solomon v. Solomon, 157 Ohio App. 3d 807, 814, 2004-Ohio-2486, ¶ 27, 813 N.E.2d 918, 923 (7th Dist. Mahoning County 2004) (although past acts may be used to establish a genuine fear of violence in the present situation, there must be an indication that the person was fearful in that present situation; merely finding that there were past acts of domestic violence, without anything more, is not enough to warrant a present civil protection order); Young v. Young, 2006-Ohio-978, 2006 WL 515522 (Ohio Ct. App. 2d Dist. Greene County 2006) (holding that events occurring five years ago with no other events since were too remote to support a CPO); Newhouse v. Williams, 167 Ohio App. 3d 215, 2006-Ohio-3075, 854 N.E.2d 565 (3d Dist. Wyandot County 2006); Pinkney v. Salett, 2011-Ohio-4121, 2011 WL 3654420 (Ohio Ct. App. 8th Dist. Cuyahoga County 2011).

[32]Felton v. Felton, 79 Ohio St. 3d 34, 42, 1997-Ohio-302, 679 N.E.2d 672 (1997); Lavery v. Lavery, 2001-Ohio-1874, 2001 WL 1545663 (Ohio Ct. App. 9th Dist. Summit County 2001). See also B.C. v. A.S., 2014-Ohio-1326, 2014 WL 1345260 (Ohio Ct. App. 9th Dist. Medina County 2014); M.K. v. J.K., 2015-Ohio-434, 2015 WL 557990 (Ohio Ct. App. 9th Dist. Medina County 2015).

[33]See Text § 11:10, Ex parte protection orders—Legal standard for issuance; see also Gooderham v. Patterson, 1999 WL 1034472 (Ohio Ct. App. 4th Dist. Gallia County 1999). But see Pierce v. Pierce, 2001-Ohio-2312, 2001 WL 1432047 (Ohio Ct. App. 3d Dist. Marion County 2001) (court of appeals stated that "as *Felton* noted, the past abuse of a person is often quite indicative of a danger of future domestic violence").

[34]Sitton v. Sitton, 1999 WL 55717 (Ohio Ct. App. 2d Dist. Montgomery County 1999).

[35]Sitton v. Sitton, 1999 WL 55717, *4 (Ohio Ct. App. 2d Dist. Montgomery County 1999).

order. For example, in *Reynolds v. White*,[36] the Cuyahoga County Court of Appeals held that "when a respondent contends that it was error to issue a protection order, the question on review is whether there was sufficient credible evidence to support a finding that the respondent had engaged in acts or threats of domestic violence." The appellate court relied on the language in RC 3113.31(A)(1) for the acts that constitute domestic violence and found that the testimony of the victim and the photographs presented to the trial court demonstrated that the respondent recklessly caused her bodily injury. Additionally, there was evidence that the respondent placed the petitioner in fear of imminent serious physical harm. "A victim's history with the perpetrator may cause the victim to experience reasonable fear of the perpetrator's threats of domestic violence."[37] For example, the respondent's threat that she would "get it twice as bad" if she informed anyone, was sufficient evidence to place the victim in reasonable fear of domestic violence.[38]

Moreover, in *Visnich v. Visnich*,[39] the Trumbull County Court of Appeals relied on the *Felton* standard of proof in determining whether the magistrate's decision contained sufficient findings of fact to sustain appellee's request for a civil protection order. "When granting a protection order, the trial court must find that petitioner has shown by a preponderance of the evidence that petitioner or petitioner's family or household members are in danger of domestic violence."[40] In *Visnich*, past acts of domestic violence involving weapons, coupled with recent acts of harassment and stalking, were sufficient evidence for granting and upholding the issuance of a civil protection order.[41] This pattern of abuse provides evidence that petitioner was in danger of domestic violence and a victim of domestic violence.

---

[36]Reynolds v. White, 1999 WL 754496, *4 (Ohio Ct. App. 8th Dist. Cuyahoga County 1999) (relying on *Felton*).

[37]Reynolds v. White, 1999 WL 754496, *4 (Ohio Ct. App. 8th Dist. Cuyahoga County 1999). But see Bruner v. Bruner, 2000-Ohio-2554, 2000 WL 1486452 (Ohio Ct. App. 7th Dist. Mahoning County 2000); Murral v. Thomson, 2004-Ohio-432, 2004 WL 193876 (Ohio Ct. App. 4th Dist. Hocking County 2004).

[38]Reynolds v. White, 1999 WL 754496, *4 (Ohio Ct. App. 8th Dist. Cuyahoga County 1999).

[39]Visnich v. Visnich, 1999 WL 1299300 (Ohio Ct. App. 11th Dist. Trumbull County 1999); see also Rhodes v. Gunter, 2003-Ohio-2342, 2003 WL 21040724 (Ohio Ct. App. 9th Dist. Lorain County 2003).

[40]Visnich v. Visnich, 1999 WL 1299300, *2 (Ohio Ct. App. 11th Dist. Trumbull County 1999) (quoting *Felton*). But see Dybo v. Dybo, 1999 WL 1073781 (Ohio Ct. App. 11th Dist. Geauga County 1999) (determining that neither appellant nor her children were in danger of domestic violence); see also Haynes-Soper v. Garrett, 2000 WL 1289450 (Ohio Ct. App. 10th Dist. Franklin County 2000) (Franklin County Court of Appeals stated that "RC 3113.31 does not require proof of an immediate and present danger for a civil protection order to be issued after a final hearing").

[41]See also Saari v. Saari, 2000 WL 1729455 (Ohio Ct. App. 9th Dist. Lorain County 2000); Ankenbruck v. Ankenbruck, 2000 WL 1804360 (Ohio Ct. App. 11th Dist. Trumbull County 2000); Lundin v. Niepsuj, 2014-Ohio-1212, 2014 WL 1478284 (Ohio Ct. App. 9th Dist. Summit County 2014); Johnson v. Komisarek, 2017-Ohio-2580, 2017 WL 1534901 (Ohio Ct. App. 6th Dist. Lucas County 2017); Majeed v. Majeed, 2016-Ohio-7243, 2016 WL 5887174 (Ohio Ct. App. 2d Dist. Montgomery County 2016).

Similarly, in *Siouffi v. Siouffi*,[42] the Montgomery County Court of Appeals noted that the "question of whether a person is placed in fear of imminent serious physical harm by particular threatening conduct also involves an element of objectivity." There, the respondent slashed the tires on the victim's car. The evidence demonstrated that the victim believed she was in fear of imminent physical harm. The court also determined that it was not unlikely for a reasonable person to be in fear of imminent harm based on that conduct or to believe that the particular victim would be placed in fear. Moreover, the court held that "it was not unreasonable for [the victim] to fear imminent serious physical harm from threatening conduct that involved the use of a twelve-inch long knife. This is not a case where a person of unusual sensibilities was frightened by what might objectively be viewed as relatively innocuous conduct."[43]

On the other hand, the 7th District Court of Appeals has held that while past acts may be used to establish a fear of violence in the present situation, previous incidents cannot provide the sole basis for the issuance of a CPO.[44] For example, in *Martauz v. Martauz*,[45] appellee became fearful of appellant's "obsessive and abnormal behavior" in repeatedly texting her and banging on her windows and door. However, she admitted that he hadn't threatened to hurt her. In fact, the only actual physical violence occurred five months before.

The appellate court applied the standard used by many courts and which permits a trial court to "consider past acts of domestic violence in order to determine whether the petitioner's fear in the present situation is reasonable."[46] "However, the issuance of a civil protection order cannot be based solely on previous incidents of alleged domestic violence."[47] "[A]bsent an initial, explicit indication that appellee [petitioner] was in fear of imminent serious physical harm from ap-

---

[42]Siouffi v. Siouffi, 1998 WL 879255, *4 (Ohio Ct. App. 2d Dist. Montgomery County 1998); see also Martauz v. Martauz, 2009-Ohio-2642, 2009 WL 1581185 (Ohio Ct. App. 7th Dist. Mahoning County 2009).

[43]Siouffi v. Siouffi, 1998 WL 879255, *4 (Ohio Ct. App. 2d Dist. Montgomery County 1998).

[44]Cottrill v. Cottrill, 2017-Ohio-1422, 2017 WL 1376841 (Ohio Ct. App. 5th Dist. Fairfield County 2017).

[45]Martauz v. Martauz, 2009-Ohio-2642, 2009 WL 1581185 (Ohio Ct. App. 7th Dist. Mahoning County 2009); see also Martin v. Hanood, 2009-Ohio-1501, 2009 WL 825766 (Ohio Ct. App. 7th Dist. Jefferson County 2009); Solomon v. Solomon, 157 Ohio App. 3d 807, 2004-Ohio-2486, 813 N.E.2d 918 (7th Dist. Mahoning County 2004); Thom v. Mulvin, 2009-Ohio-3797, 2009 WL 2365996 (Ohio Ct. App. 6th Dist. Erie County 2009); Weber v. Weber, 2011-Ohio-2980, 2011 WL 2436963 (Ohio Ct. App. 2d Dist. Greene County 2011).

[46]*Martauz at *3*; citing Eichenberger v. Eichenberger, 82 Ohio App. 3d 809, 816, 613 N.E.2d 678 (10th Dist. Franklin County 1992). See also Jackson v. Jackson, 2011-Ohio-5529, 2011 WL 5135251 (Ohio Ct. App. 6th Dist. Lucas County 2011); Solomon v. Solomon, 157 Ohio App. 3d 807, 2004-Ohio-2486, 813 N.E.2d 918 (7th Dist. Mahoning County 2004); Dague v. Dague, 2012-Ohio-1582, 2012 WL 1187920 (Ohio Ct. App. 11th Dist. Lake County 2012); Baltes v. Baltes, 2012-Ohio-4890, 2012 WL 5195824 (Ohio Ct. App. 11th Dist. Trumbull County 2012) (substantiated evidence of a history of violence punctuated by photos of bruises all over her body and ongoing instances of intimidation (acts of aggressively honking) and threats including a threat to "bury her," all produced a genuine fear that was sufficient to establish the need for a civil protection order).

[47]*Martauz at *3*; citing Bruner v. Bruner, 2000-Ohio-2554, 2000 WL 1486452

pellant [respondent], on* * *[the date set forth in the petition for civil protection order], the reasonableness of her alleged fear cannot be determined by reference to her past history with appellant."[48]

In this case, however, the appellate court determined that the appellee's fear was reasonable and affirmed the trial court.

Q & A: Can a party prevail in obtaining a CPO where the respondent is about to be released from prison and the last domestic violence was committed before the respondent was imprisoned?[49]

At least one Ohio appellate court addressed this specific issue. In *Williamson v. Williamson*,[50] the respondent appealed the grant of the CPO against him. In this case, there was evidence that the former husband had broken into her house, threatened her, pushed her down, pulled her hair and scratched her. He was convicted for domestic violence. He also violated a criminal TPO and was arrested, charged and convicted of violating the temporary protection order and for aggravated burglary. Before his release from prison, former wife requested and was granted a civil protection order for herself and the minor children.

The appellate court reversed the judgment of the trial court and vacated the CPO because each of the incidents took place before former husband's release from prison. The court relied on cases that held that the occurrence of past domestic violence is only some evidence supporting the issuance of a CPO. "While it is true that past acts may be used to establish a genuine fear of violence in the present situation, there must be an indication that the person was fearful in that present situation."[51] Despite the past acts of violence, the former wife did not demonstrate a present fear of future domestic violence or establish a reasonable basis for that fear.[52]

Additionally, the court relied upon a letter from the prison acknowledging that appellant had addressed his mental health (bipolar condition) problems in prison. Besides this, the court noted that "it is inappropriate to use a protection order merely to create a

---

(Ohio Ct. App. 7th Dist. Mahoning County 2000); Crabtree v. Dinsmoor, 2013-Ohio-5797, 2013 WL 6869957 (Ohio Ct. App. 10th Dist. Franklin County 2013) (past domestic violence alone not sufficient as basis for a CPO where there is no credible evidence of current danger of domestic violence).

[48]*Martauz at *3*; quoting *Bruner at *3*.

[49]See also Text § 8.4.

[50]Williamson v. Williamson, 180 Ohio App. 3d 260, 2008-Ohio-6718, 905 N.E.2d 217 (2d Dist. Greene County 2008).

[51]Williamson v. Williamson, 180 Ohio App. 3d 260, 268, 2008-Ohio-6718, ¶ 50, 905 N.E.2d 217, 223 (2d Dist. Greene County 2008), citing Solomon v. Solomon, 157 Ohio App. 3d 807, 814, 2004-Ohio-2486, ¶ 27, 813 N.E.2d 918, 923 (7th Dist. Mahoning County 2004); Pinkney v. Salett, 2011-Ohio-4121, 2011 WL 3654420 (Ohio Ct. App. 8th Dist. Cuyahoga County 2011).

[52]Williamson v. Williamson, 180 Ohio App. 3d 260, 269, 2008-Ohio-6718, ¶ 51, 905 N.E.2d 217, 224 (2d Dist. Greene County 2008). But see Cottrill v. Cottrill, 2017-Ohio-1422, 2017 WL 1376841 (Ohio Ct. App. 5th Dist. Fairfield County 2017) (finding that the *Williamson* and *Solomon* cases illustrate that the fear a petitioner has felt and the reasonableness of that fear could and should be determined with reference to her history with respondent and thus, the court did not err in permitting testimony on past acts).

buffer-zone around Mary and the children while she decides whether contact with Shawn is a good idea. It is a means to prevent imminent physical harm, and there is little evidence that Shawn is likely to harm her or his children."[53]

What is evident is that the majority did not view past violence as a predictor of future violence, nor did they focus on the fact that appellant also had a significant history of violating court orders. Because the majority focused on whether the former wife established a reasonable fear of imminent serious physical harm, they found that there were not enough facts upon which to base the issuance of the CPO. In fact, the majority missed that other acts were committed that did not involve as an element, a fear of imminent serious physical harm.

The dissent acknowledged as much and would have granted the CPO for Mary. "There is evidence in the record from which the trial court could find that Shawn entered or remained on Mary's premises with purpose to commit on . . . those premises a misdemeanor, the elements of which involve causing physical harm to another person to believe that the offender will cause physical harm to him.' This is aggravated trespass, a violation of RC 2911.211. Significantly, there is no 'serious' component to the physical harm element in aggravated trespass. The commission of aggravated trespass is, in itself, an act of domestic violence justifying a civil protection order."[54]

Q & A: Must one prove each element of the family or household member relationship?

The Portage County Court of Appeals has considered this issue in *Maglionico v. Maglionico*.[55] The parties were brothers who did not live together. Appellant challenged the issuance of the civil protection order on the ground that the trial court erred in determining that, because individuals are related by consanguinity, they are not required to live together. In fact, the trial court's judgment entry specifically stated that, pursuant to RC 3113.31(A)(3), there is no requirement that they live together since they are related by consanguinity.

In reversing the trial court, the Portage County Court of Appeals determined that RC 3113.31(A)(3)(a)(ii) requires some indication that a petitioner demonstrate both a relationship based on consanguinity or affinity and that the parties reside or have resided together. The court reasoned that the appellee had the burden to prove that they were family or household members and that he was in danger of domestic violence. In order to prove the relationship necessary for a protection order, appellee was required to show that he and his brother were related by consanguinity and that they had resided together at some time in the past.

This case illustrates the importance of proving by a preponderance of the evidence the nature of the parties' relationship as well as acts

---

[53]Williamson v. Williamson, 180 Ohio App. 3d 260, 270, 2008-Ohio-6718, ¶ 60, 905 N.E.2d 217, 225 (2d Dist. Greene County 2008).

[54]Williamson v. Williamson, 180 Ohio App. 3d 260, 271, 2008-Ohio-6718, ¶ 67, 905 N.E.2d 217, 225 (2d Dist. Greene County 2008).

[55]Maglionico v. Maglionico, 2001-Ohio-8901, 2001 WL 1401978 (Ohio Ct. App. 11th Dist. Portage County 2001).

of domestic violence as defined by statute. Each element of the act and the relationship must be identified and presented as evidence in court.[56]

Q & A: Is the victim's testimony sufficient to satisfy the preponderance of the evidence standard?

The *Felton* Court addressed this issue. In *Felton*, the victim testified that:

> appellee's assaults upon her increased during her marriage, and continued after the divorce, culminating in a violent episode . . . in which appellee attempted to strangle her. Moreover, she stated that appellee would harass her on the phone. She also testified that she was afraid that if she did anything to anger appellee, he would actually try to kill her.[57]

A friend also testified that, over one year earlier, he had witnessed a bruise on her shoulder.

The Supreme Court determined that this uncontroverted testimony was sufficient, credible evidence to prove by a preponderance of the evidence that appellee committed acts of domestic violence. The Court pointed out that, based on the comments of the trial court, the victim's testimony alone would never be sufficient to establish proof by a preponderance of the evidence. The Court reasoned that "[d]omestic violence is seldom committed in the presence of eyewitnesses. Moreover, in many cases medical evidence is absent. Often the only evidence of domestic violence is the testimony of the victim."[58] This includes evidence that the victim believed the respondent would cause her imminent serious physical harm. The Court noted the realities of domestic violence and then reinforced the position that the testimony of the victim was sufficient to prove by a preponderance of the evidence that the appellee committed acts of domestic violence and that a protection order should have been granted.[59] It is difficult to assess whether the victim's testimony would have satisfied the burden of

[56]Murral v. Thomson, 2004-Ohio-432, 2004 WL 193876 (Ohio Ct. App. 4th Dist. Hocking County 2004).

[57]Felton v. Felton, 79 Ohio St. 3d 34, 43-44, 1997-Ohio-302, 679 N.E.2d 672 (1997).

[58]Felton v. Felton, 79 Ohio St. 3d 34, 44, 1997-Ohio-302, 679 N.E.2d 672 (1997); see also Hoffman v. Hoffman, 1998 WL 469876 (Ohio Ct. App. 9th Dist. Summit County 1998); Maccabee v. Maccabee, 1999 WL 430943 (Ohio Ct. App. 10th Dist. Franklin County 1999); Terrell v. Terrell, 2003-Ohio-150, 2003 WL 125013, *4 (Ohio Ct. App. 8th Dist. Cuyahoga County 2003) (where the appellate court noted that although RC 3113.31 establishes jurisdiction and hearing guidelines, it does not delineate the type of evidence to be considered by a trial court; "specifically, it does not require any corroboration of the victim's own testimony"); A.M. v. S.M., 2018-Ohio-247, 2018 WL 542357 (Ohio Ct. App. 9th Dist. Summit County 2018).

[59]See also Stanley v. Stanley, 2001-Ohio-3375, 2001 WL 1128835 (Ohio Ct. App. 7th Dist. Mahoning County 2001) (appellate court upheld the trial court's finding that the victim's testimony was sufficient to prove the act of domestic violence in spite of the contradictory evidence provided by the respondent. The court noted the trial court relied on *Felton*. Additionally, the Mahoning County Court of Appeals stated that "the testimony in *Felton* did provide that court with more corroborating evidence of past abuse than the case at bar, and there was no witness in *Felton* to the act that precipitated the petition of domestic violence and civil protection order." Stanley v. Stanley, 2001-Ohio-3375, 2001 WL 1128835, *2 (Ohio Ct. App. 7th Dist. Mahoning County 2001). Because the magistrate specifically noted the credibility and demeanor of the

proof if the respondent had also provided testimony at the full hearing. Of primary significance is that the *Felton* Court set forth a public policy rationale for justifying why corroborating eyewitness testimony, police documentation, and/or medical evidence is not required to satisfy the standard of proof. The court also considered the dynamics of domestic violence in crafting its decision.

However, in *Hoffman v. Hoffman*,[60] the victim testified to several incidents of abusive and assaultive behavior which caused her to fear for her life and safety. Her mother testified that she only saw the results of the abuse and observed that her daughter appeared to be a nervous wreck and scared. In his testimony, the defendant denied abusing his wife and explained that, given his wife's timid demeanor, "what is yelling to her does not constitute yelling to me."[61] Although the police were not eyewitnesses to the abuse, they did testify as to prior complaints from the wife.

The defendant in *Hoffman* appealed, alleging that there was a lack of reliable corroborative evidence.[62] The appellate court relied on *Felton* to affirm the trial court's decision. The Summit County Court of Appeals noted that the Supreme Court found that "[d]omestic violence is seldom committed in the presence of eyewitnesses. . . Often the only evidence of domestic violence is the testimony of the victim."[63] As in *Felton*, the court found that the evidence presented was sufficient to meet the burden of proof and justify the protection order.

As in all cases, the court must weigh the credibility of the testimony of the parties and any other witnesses. Absent other corroborative

---

witnesses in making his decision and because these types of determinations are best left to the trial court, the court of appeals affirmed the trial court decision granting petitioner the civil protection order).

[60] Hoffman v. Hoffman, 1998 WL 469876 (Ohio Ct. App. 9th Dist. Summit County 1998); see also Johnson v. Auls, 2008-Ohio-6123, 2008 WL 5049751 (Ohio Ct. App. 10th Dist. Franklin County 2008).

[61] Hoffman v. Hoffman, 1998 WL 469876, *1 (Ohio Ct. App. 9th Dist. Summit County 1998).

[62] See also Cunningham v. Morgan, 2004-Ohio-6007, 2004 WL 2578873 (Ohio Ct. App. 8th Dist. Cuyahoga County 2004); Bradley v. Cox, 2004-Ohio-4840, 2004 WL 2035318 (Ohio Ct. App. 10th Dist. Franklin County 2004); Eckstein v. Colian, 2012-Ohio-4038, 2012 WL 3834883 (Ohio Ct. App. 7th Dist. Columbiana County 2012) (although none of the other witnesses saw the incident happen, they were able to testify as to the effects of the concussion on petitioner. The appellate court found that such an "observation disregards the extensive circumstantial evidence that supports Kathryn's testimony and circumstantial evidence has the same probative value as direct evidence." Eckstein v. Colian, 2012-Ohio-4038, ¶ 16, 2012 WL 3834883 (Ohio Ct. App. 7th Dist. Columbiana County 2012), citing, State v. Treesh, 90 Ohio St. 3d 460, 485, 2001-Ohio-4, 739 N.E.2d 749 (2001). "Furthermore, 'the mere number of witnesses, who may support a claim of one or the other of the parties to an action, is not to be taken as a basis for resolving disputed facts. The degree of proof required is determined by the impression which the testimony of the witnesses makes upon the trier of facts, and the character of the testimony itself.' " Eckstein v. Colian, 2012-Ohio-4038, ¶ 16, 2012 WL 3834883 (Ohio Ct. App. 7th Dist. Columbiana County 2012), quoting Cross v. Ledford, 161 Ohio St. 469, 477–478, 53 Ohio Op. 361, 120 N.E.2d 118 (1954)).

[63] Hoffman v. Hoffman, 1998 WL 469876, *1 (Ohio Ct. App. 9th Dist. Summit County 1998) (quoting Felton v. Felton, 79 Ohio St. 3d 34, 44, 1997-Ohio-302, 679 N.E.2d 672 (1997).

testimony, the parties' testimony and demeanor is of great importance to a trier of fact.[64]

Q & A: Can a trial court rely on an inference of domestic violence rather than proof that the person who is the alleged subject of the order is the perpetrator of the act in question?

According to the Second District Court of Appeals, the answer is no. In *Charles v. Peters,*[65] the trial court determined that that there was no sufficient credible evidence to support the issuance of the CPO.

On appeal, the appellant admitted that while she had no direct evidence that Peters was responsible for any of the incidents that caused her to fear him, she argued that the evidence presented created an assumption that it is more likely than not that Peters perpetrated the act.[66] The appellate court then stressed that "[w]e recognize that the trial court, as the trier of fact, is entitled to make reasonable inferences, not assumption, from the facts shown with direct proof, but an 'inference cannot be based upon evidence that is too uncertain or speculative or which raises merely a conjecture or possibility.' " Haughey v. Twins Group, Inc., 2005-Ohio-1371, ¶ 30, 2005 WL 678919 (Ohio Ct. App. 2d Dist. Champaign County 2005), citing 20 American Jurisprudence, 169, Section 165.[67]

Although appellant contended that her testimony regarding the missing key, an open back door an anonymous note and a drawing was sufficient to give rise to an inference that Peters committed the acts and that he engaged in a pattern of conduct causing a reasonable belief that he would cause her physical harm or mental distress, the appellate court found that, although the above may have given rise to an inference, a trial court is not required to draw inferences from proven facts.[68]

Of particular importance is that "gut feelings" or beliefs that a respondent may have stalked, broken in to a home, damaged property or trespassed, and that because a respondent had done this before, h/she committed a specific act on the date in question, such assumptions must be supported by sufficient credible evidence. Mere assumptions will not meet the test.

§ 12:12 Remedies—Generally

As stated in Issuance of a Civil Protection Order Ch 10, the statute authorizes that the court award certain relief to the petitioner upon granting or extending a protection order after a full hearing on the

---

[64]See M.R. v. T.R., 2016-Ohio-3493, 2016 WL 3384940 (Ohio Ct. App. 9th Dist. Wayne County 2016) (in sustaining appellant's objection the appellate court noted that appellee lacked adequate corroboration to withstand a manifest weight of the evidence challenge).

[65]Charles v. Peters, 2016-Ohio-1259, 2016 WL 1178776 (Ohio Ct. App. 2d Dist. Greene County 2016).

[66]Charles v. Peters, 2016-Ohio-1259, 2016 WL 1178776, ¶ 18 (Ohio Ct. App. 2d Dist. Greene County 2016).

[67]Charles v. Peters, 2016-Ohio-1259, 2016 WL 1178776, ¶ 18 (Ohio Ct. App. 2d Dist. Greene County 2016).

[68]Charles v. Peters, 2016-Ohio-1259, ¶ 24, 2016 WL 1178776 (Ohio Ct. App. 2d Dist. Greene County 2016).

matter.[1] Additionally, the court has the discretion to grant a protection order with or without bond. Most importantly, the court has the authority to enter any order that is designed to bring about a cessation of domestic violence against a family or household member.[2]

The court may grant the following relief:

(1) Direct the respondent to refrain from abusing or committing sexually oriented offenses[3] against the family or household members;[4]

(2) Grant possession of the residence or household to the petitioner or other family or household member, to the exclusion of the respondent, by evicting the respondent, when the petitioner or other household member owns or leases the residence;[5]

(3) Grant possession of the residence or household to the petitioner by ordering the respondent to vacate the residence when both the petitioner or other household member and respondent jointly own or lease the residence;[6]

(4) Grant possession of the residence to the petitioner or other household member, to the exclusion of the respondent, by ordering the respondent to vacate the residence, where the respondent has a duty to support the petitioner or other family or household member and the respondent is the sole owner or lessee of the residence, or, in the case of a consent agreement, allow the respondent to provide alternative suitable housing;[7]

(5) Allocate, temporarily, parental rights and responsibilities (custody and visitation of minor children), provided no other court has jurisdiction over child issues for that child;[8]

(6) Award support if the respondent has a duty to support the petitioner or household member or if the respondent customarily provides for, or contributes to, the support of the family or household member;[9]

(7) Require the respondent, petitioner, victim of domestic violence, or any combination of those persons to seek counseling;[10]

(8) Require the respondent to refrain from entering the residence,

[Section 12:12]

[1]RC 3113.31(E)(1).

[2]RC 3113.31(E)(1). But see Snyder v. Snyder, 1995 WL 493998 (Ohio Ct. App. 4th Dist. Ross County 1995) (raising the issue of whether each remedy requested must be necessarily linked to protecting the petitioner from domestic violence or necessary to end the domestic violence).

[3]See Sub. S.B. 260, eff. 1-2-07.

[4]RC 3113.31(E)(1)(a).

[5]RC 3113.31(E)(1)(b).

[6]RC 3113.31(E)(1)(b).

[7]RC 3113.31(E)(1)(c).

[8]RC 3113.31(E)(1)(d).

[9]RC 3113.31(E)(1)(e).

[10]RC 3113.31(E)(1)(f).

school, business, or place of employment of the petitioner or family or household member;[11] or

(9) Grant any other relief that the court considers equitable and fair, including, but not limited to, ordering the respondent to permit the use of a motor vehicle by the petitioner or other family or household member and dividing the household and family personal property;[12]

(10) Require that the respondent not remove, damage, hide, harm or dispose of any companion animal owned or possessed by the petitioner. R.C. 3113.31(E)(1)(i);

(11) Authorize the petitioner to remove a companion animal owned by the petitioner from the possession of the respondent. R.C. 3113.31(E)(1)(j).

Pursuant to a recent legislative amendment to RC 3113.31, the court may now include within a protection order issued under this section terms necessary to protect companion animals belonging to a petitioner.

§ 12:13 Remedies—Orders to restrain from abuse

The main purpose of any civil protection order is to provide safety and protection to a petitioner or other family or household member. Any protection order that is issued after a full hearing is designed to bring about a cessation of domestic violence.[1] A court is authorized to order any of the provisions set forth in the Supreme Court forms.[2] This authority is implied in both RC 3113.31(E)(1) and RC 3113.31(E)(1)(h).

Orders that restrain a respondent from beating, threatening, harassing, or abusing the petitioner or other family or household member carry out this most important mandate of the statute.[3] The Supreme Court standard forms include a thorough itemization of actions that a respondent is prohibited from doing to the petitioner, such as harming, attempting to harm, molesting, stalking, following, bothering, annoying, contacting, or forcing sexual relations upon the petitioner or a family or household member.[4] The standard forms also articulate the type of contact that is prohibited by a respondent: telephone, fax, e-mail and voice mail.[5] Such clearly worded clauses specifically inform a respondent of which types of conduct are forbid-

---

[11]RC 3113.31(E)(1)(g).

[12]RC 3113.31(E)(1)(h).

[Section 12:13]

[1]RC 3113.31(E)(1).

[2]Sup. R. Form 10.01-H to Sup. R. Form 10.01-J.

[3]RC 3113.31(E)(1). Note that Am. Sub. S.B. 17, eff. 8-3-06, will expand this section to restrain a respondent from committing a sexually oriented offense against the petitioner or victim.

[4]See Sup. R. 10.01(C), Sup. R. Form 10.01-H to Sup. R. Form 10.01-J. See also Text § 11:18, Ex parte protection orders—Available relief—Orders to refrain from entering the residence, school, business, or place of employment.

[5]State v. Putman-Albright, 2016-Ohio-319, 2016 WL 525863 (Ohio Ct. App. 2d Dist. Montgomery County 2016) (where CPO terms allowed respondent to have contact with the petitioner by phone, text or email and said communication only be

den, and a respondent would have a difficult time arguing that the restrictive language was ambiguous.[6]

Since the primary purpose of the protection order is to provide for the safety and protection of the victim, the "no further abuse" provision is essential relief. Without this specific relief, it would be very difficult to enforce a protection order through either contempt or criminal prosecution.[7]

Since a protection order issued under RC 3113.31(E)(1) prohibits any contact between the respondent and the protected party, acts that may not rise to the level of domestic violence for the purpose of issuing the order may become the basis for a contempt action under RC 3113.31(L) or a criminal prosecution for the violation of the order. Ohio's standard forms enumerate prohibited conduct, which includes acts of domestic violence pursuant to RC 3113.31. Several other types of conduct are also prohibited in the order. Performance of any of the prohibited acts contained in the order would violate the order. The petitioner or the state need not show an act of domestic violence to find that there has been a violation of the existing protection order.

For example, in *South Dakota v. Scott*,[8] the defendant was convicted of violating a protection order by making numerous telephone calls to his wife.[9] Similarly, in *Rush v. Rush*,[10] the respondent was found to have violated the ex parte civil protection order by appearing at his wife's residence to pick up the child for visitation.

§ 12:14 Remedies—Orders to vacate or evict

Ohio is one of over 28 states that requires police to assist in the removal of the respondent from the residence. RC 3113.31 specifically states that law enforcement agencies shall enforce protection orders "including removing the respondent from the premises, if appropriate."[1]

Since service of process of the protection order on a respondent is the catalyst to enforcement, law enforcement officials have been reluctant to enforce civil protection orders if service has not been

---

regarding their child and respondent was subsequently convicted of violating the CPO, the court found that respondent was not permitted to speak to petitioner about matters beyond parental concerns; thus, affirming conviction under RC 2919.27).

[6]See also Text § 11:18, Ex parte protection orders—Available relief—Orders to refrain from entering the residence, school, business, or place of employment.

[7]See RC 3113.31(L).

[8]State v. Scott, 1998 SD 2, 574 N.W.2d 595 (S.D. 1998).

[9]See also State v. Hauge, 1996 SD 48, 547 N.W.2d 173 (S.D. 1996) (where protection order prohibited verbal contact, defendant was convicted of violating order for sending his ex-wife a letter); State v. Hoffman, 149 N.J. 564, 695 A.2d 236 (1997) (defendant's mailing of torn-up copies of support order to his ex-wife constituted a violation of protection order prohibiting contact with ex-wife); Strong v. Bauman, 1999 WL 317432 (Ohio Ct. App. 2d Dist. Montgomery County 1999).

[10]Rush v. Rush, 1999 WL 1044482 (Ohio Ct. App. 8th Dist. Cuyahoga County 1999).

[Section 12:14]

[1]RC 3113.31(F)(3).

perfected or verified.[2] In many jurisdictions, law enforcement officials will not remove the respondent from the premises until they have ascertained whether service has been perfected on the ex parte order or until after the full hearing.

Unfortunately, many police officers are hesitant to arrest a respondent who will not vacate the residence even when service has been perfected, although RC 3113.31(F)(3) directs police officers to enforce a protection order in accordance with its terms, including removing the respondent from the premises if appropriate. Officers may still comply with the statutory directive to "remove a respondent from the residence" by requesting that the respondent leave. Only if the respondent adamantly refuses will the issue of arrest and adequate service even arise. If service has been perfected, the police officer should arrest the respondent for violating the protection order. If there is no evidence that service has been perfected, the police officer should provide the respondent with a copy of the order or read the terms of the order to the respondent. If the police are again contacted by the petitioner, they should arrest the respondent. The rationale for this is that the police have put the respondent on notice of the terms of the order.[3]

Where a respondent is ordered to vacate or be evicted from the residence, the petitioner and other family or household members are granted exclusive possession of the residence.[4] The respondent may be evicted from the residence or household when the residence or household is owned or leased solely by the petitioner or other family or household member.[5] The respondent may be ordered to vacate the premises or household when the residence is jointly owned or leased by the respondent and the petitioner or other household member.[6] Lastly, a petitioner may be granted sole occupancy of the residence even though the residence is solely owned or leased by the respondent only if the respondent has a duty to support petitioner or other family or household member.[7]

As important as exclusive possession is to the petitioner, any protection order should also include a provision requiring the respondent to refrain from interfering with the petitioner's right to occupy the resi-

[2]But see RC 2935.032(F) which provides that an officer who arrests an offender for the offense of violating a protection order that on its face is valid is immune from liability. See also Text § 11:11, Ex parte protection orders—Service and notice provisions.

[3]See Text Ch. 13, Court Enforcement of Civil Protection Orders and Related Issues, and Text Ch. 14, Police Enforcement of Protection Orders and Other Relevant Issues, for further discussion of notice; Text § 11:11, Ex parte protection orders—Service and notice provisions, for a discussion of service and notice.

[4]RC 3113.31(E)(1)(b); Devault v. Devault, 2004-Ohio-976, 2004 WL 397134, *2 (Ohio Ct. App. 5th Dist. Ashland County 2004) (Affirming trial court decision upholding CPO and holding that trial court did not abuse discretion in awarding wife exclusive possession of residence for 5 year period despite pendency of divorce. Court also said trial court specifically indicated the divorce action may have some impact on the protection order.).

[5]RC 3113.31(E)(1)(c).

[6]RC 3113.31(E)(1)(c).

[7]R.C. 31113.31(E)(1)(c); see also Judd v. Meszaros, 2011-Ohio-4983, 2011 WL 4489049 (Ohio Ct. App. 10th Dist. Franklin County 2011).

dence through actions such as canceling utilities or insurance and interrupting telephone service, mail delivery, or the delivery of any other documents or items.[8]

When vacate orders are entered by the court, counsel should also request that the civil protection order specify how the removal of respondent will be implemented. Much specificity should go into this order. Terms to include are the date and time of removal, which items of personal property the respondent will retrieve from the residence, whether the respondent will be allowed back to the residence for any reason, which law enforcement agency will remove the respondent from the residence, and whether the police will obtain keys and garage door openers to the residence from the respondent. Ohio's standard forms provide for this remedy and details how and when the keys are to be turned over and how the respondent may retrieve personal belongings.[9]

For example, in *Smart v. Smart*,[10] a North Carolina court fashioned an order that created a safe means of accomplishing a vacate order. The court of appeals upheld the temporary protection order in which the court gave the wife exclusive possession of the marital home and ordered the husband to remove his personal belongings and turn over the house keys to the police.

In *Mallin v. Mallin*,[11] the Cuyahoga County trial court issued a protection order that ordered the eviction of the respondent for the duration of the civil protection order and further provided that the defendant shall be permitted access to the premises "only for purposes of picking up and returning the minor children for periods of visitation, and shall, under no circumstances, enter the marital residence." In that case, the trial court crafted a specific protection order, which was subsequently upheld by the court of appeals.

An ideal order would require the respondent to vacate immediately and would order the police to accompany the petitioner to the residence, serve the respondent with a copy of the civil protection order, stand by while the respondent removes his/her personal belongings, obtain all keys to the premises from the respondent, verify that the keys are the real set of keys and then have the police turn them over to petitioner, and escort the respondent elsewhere.[12]

Q & A: Can the court permit the respondent to provide other housing to the petitioner rather than vacate the premises that he/she owns?

The statute is quite clear on this point. If the respondent has a duty to support the petitioner or other family or household member living in the residence and the respondent is the sole owner or lessee of the residence or household, the court has two options. It can require that

[8]Sup. R. 10.01(C), Sup. R. Form 10.01-H to Sup. R. Form 10.01-J. See also Text § 11:18, Ex parte protection orders—Available relief—Orders to refrain from entering the residence, school, business, or place of employment.

[9]See Sup. R. Forms 10.01-I and 10.01-J.

[10]Smart v. Smart, 59 N.C. App. 533, 297 S.E.2d 135 (1982).

[11]Mallin v. Mallin, 44 Ohio App. 3d 53, 55, 541 N.E.2d 116 (8th Dist. Cuyahoga County 1988).

[12]See Sup. R. Forms 10.01-I and 10.01-J.

the respondent vacate the premises or, in the case of a consent agreement, the respondent may provide the petitioner with alternative, suitable housing.[13]

A respondent who is the sole owner or lessee of the residence is not obligated to vacate the premises where there is a domestic violence incident under RC 3113.31 unless he/she also has a duty to support the petitioner or other family or household member. A duty to support attaches if the parties have a legally binding relationship such as marriage. This duty may also attach where the respondent is the parent of a child living in the home of the petitioner.

Once the duty to support is established, the parties must also enter into a consent agreement at the full hearing. That means that the parties agree to the terms of the civil protection order and sign the written agreement. Counsel, the court, or even the respondent may suggest that he/she provide alternative, suitable housing rather than vacate the residence. If the petitioner agrees, an order will be drafted indicating the terms of the "alternative, suitable housing."

Even if the duty to support has been established, if the parties cannot agree to the concept, terms, or type of alternative suitable housing, the court cannot order the respondent to provide the relief available pursuant to this option.[14] The discretion of the court is not limited, and the court may still order that the respondent vacate the premises.

Of significance is that the alternative housing must be of a "suitable" nature. The housing must be commensurate with the type of housing given up by petitioner. Should the housing not be appropriate or adequate, the court still has the option to evict the respondent.

Many times this option will appear attractive to a respondent who does not want to give up possession of the home he owns or rents. This option may also be advantageous for a petitioner who would rather not maintain any contact with the respondent. If the respondent owns the premises, it is very likely that he/she will be on or about the premises, in spite of the order, for the reason that the respondent has a need to protect the property he/she owns. Additionally, a respondent who is responsible for the rent or mortgage payment may have a vested interest in the property such that he/she may believe that he/she has a right to access the property.

Q & A: If the respondent is ordered to vacate the residence, who is legally required to pay the rent or mortgage?

The statute does not address who will pay the rent or mortgage, utilities, and maintenance costs of the property during the period of time that the civil protection order is in effect, should the petitioner be allowed to remain in the residence. If the respondent owns the residence and is ordered to vacate, counsel for one or both of the parties must be sure that the issue of payment has been specifically resolved in the protection order.[15]

Although the statute does not address who will pay utilities while a

---

[13] RC 3113.31(E)(1)(c).

[14] See RC 3113.31(E)(1)(c).

[15] See Ruedele v. Kiefer, 1993 WL 438787 (Ohio Ct. App. 5th Dist. Licking County 1993), cause dismissed, 68 Ohio St. 3d 1444, 626 N.E.2d 686 (1994).

civil protection order is in effect, the Supreme Court standard forms require that a respondent not request the utility company to shut off the utility.[16] This is an intentional act on the part of the respondent that is prohibited.

An attorney should make sure that, where the petitioner is granted exclusive possession of the residence, the attorney knows (1) which party customarily paid the utilities and (2) in which party's name the utilities are listed. This will allow the attorney to craft an order that will further protect the victim by setting forth the obligations and expectations of each party.[17]

Q & A: If the respondent is evicted from the residence, is the respondent in danger of losing title to the property?

Absolutely not. It is clear from the statute that no order or agreement shall in any manner affect title to any real property.[18] The order may only affect possession of the premises for a period of time, not to exceed five years.[19]

This position has been reinforced by the Ohio courts. For example, in *State v. Mueller*,[20] the Hamilton County Court of Appeals determined that a man convicted of domestic violence should not have been ordered as a special condition of his probation to execute a quitclaim deed transferring to the victim (with whom he cohabited) his interest in their jointly owned home. While the court acknowledged that the domestic relations court has the authority to grant exclusive possession of a residence to a victim of domestic violence for a period of time and order the respondent to vacate the residence, RC 3113.31(E)(5) states that no order or consent agreement shall affect title to any real property. In addition, the court held that the trial court exceeded its authority by ordering the actual transfer of ownership to the house as a condition of probation. The court reasoned that such an order was equivalent to a taking without due process and released the man from the condition of probation, finding the order to quitclaim the property to the victim to be "void and of no lawful effect."[21]

Family law practitioners should explain to their clients that any protection order term regarding property, including real property, may be modified by a subsequent divorce or legal separation. In those situations, the provisions regarding property rendered in a divorce,

---

[16]See Sup. R. Form 10.01-H to Sup. R. Form 10.01-J. See also Judd v. Meszaros, 2011-Ohio-4983, 2011 WL 4489049 (Ohio Ct. App. 10th Dist. Franklin County 2011).

[17]See Drake v. Drake, 1985 WL 7861 (Ohio Ct. App. 2d Dist. Montgomery County 1985) (respondent ordered to pay utilities); see also Text § 12:17, Remedies—Orders of support.

[18]R.C. 3113.31(E)(5); see also Calicoat v. Calicoat, 2009-Ohio-5869, 2009 WL 3683665 (Ohio Ct. App. 2d Dist. Miami County 2009) (upholding grant of CPO awarding wife exclusive use of the residence subject to modification by pending divorce decree and further noting that a CPO does not affect title to real property). See also Judd v. Meszaros, 2011-Ohio-4983, 2011 WL 4489049 (Ohio Ct. App. 10th Dist. Franklin County 2011).

[19]R.C. 3113.31(E)(3)(a). See also R.C. 3113.31(E)(1)(c).

[20]State v. Mueller, 122 Ohio App. 3d 483, 702 N.E.2d 139 (1st Dist. Hamilton County 1997).

[21]State v. Mueller, 122 Ohio App. 3d 483, 702 N.E.2d 139 (1st Dist. Hamilton County 1997).

dissolution, or legal separation will take precedence over the civil protection order and its time restrictions.[22]

For example, in *Cooley v. Cooley*,[23] the parties entered into a consent entry in a civil protection order proceeding pursuant to RC 3113.31. The parties subsequently divorced, and the issue on appeal was whether a consent agreement was enforceable as a final property settlement of parties to a divorce action. The Montgomery County Court of Appeals stated that "it is extremely doubtful that the legislature contemplated permanent property settlements when it alluded to protection orders or consent agreements in the domestic violence statutes, and this observation is clearly borne out by the time restrictions imposed by RC 3113.31(E)(3)."[24] The appellate court interpreted this provision of the statute to demonstrate that the terms of a protection order regarding property do not survive a subsequent divorce. However, because a genuine issue of fact precluded summary judgment, the court of appeals sustained appellant's assigned error.

Q & A: Can a trial court issue a CPO that grants possession of the home to a petitioner where the respondent is sole owner of the real property?

Yes, under certain conditions. Pursuant to R.C. 3113.31(E)(1)(c) permits a court to grant petitioner exclusive possession of real estate even though respondent is sole owner or lessee of the residence where the respondent has a duty to support petitioner or other family or household member living in the residence or household.

In *Judd v. Meszaros*,[25] the parties were an unmarried couple with one child together. The parties resided in a home owned by the Meszaros (respondent), although all monies used to purchase the home and to construct the property were provided by Judd (petitioner). Judd admitted that he arranged for the property to put in Meszaros's name to avoid creditors. After Meszaros vacated the property, Judd filed for and was granted a CPO because Meszaros shut off the water to the marital home, kicked the dining room window and verbally threatened Judd. A CPO was issued whereby he was granted exclusive possession of the property for one year and Meszaros was enjoined from interfering with Judd's right to occupy the residence, including cancelling utilities during that one year time period.[26]

After the issuance of the order, Meszaros sold the home and the new purchaser attempted to evict petitioner from the home. Petitioner filed a contempt motion against the purchaser and purchaser filed a motion for frivolous conduct against petitioner. The appellate court upheld the trial court decision dismissing purchaser's motion for sanctions because petitioner had a good faith argument that the purchaser, although not a party to the CPO, was bound by the terms of the order so as to prevent him from evicting petitioner.

---

[22]See RC 3113.31(E)(3)(b).

[23]Cooley v. Cooley, 90 Ohio App. 3d 706, 630 N.E.2d 417 (2d Dist. Montgomery County 1993).

[24]Cooley v. Cooley, 90 Ohio App. 3d 706, 707, 630 N.E.2d 417 (2d Dist. Montgomery County 1993).

[25]Judd v. Meszaros, 2011-Ohio-4983, 2011 WL 4489049 (Ohio Ct. App. 10th Dist. Franklin County 2011).

[26]See R.C. 3113.31(E)(1)(c).

The salient findings in this case for purposes of the CPO are that, while nothing in the CPO affected title to the real estate, petitioner was a victim of domestic violence, the domestic violence statute should not be applied to allow respondent to profit at his expense, especially since he paid for the property and he was granted possession of the property for a period of time in accordance with the statute.[27] Thus, Judd's right of possession did not end when Meszaros's ownership interest in the property ended by virtue of a sale.

Of interest is that the purchaser complained that the ruling "means a CPO can create property rights in a victim of domestic violence and in effect establishes 'a requirement that such purchasers (and title companies) must now search the domestic relations court records in all of Ohio's 88 counties to determine if such CPO rights exist.' "[28]

Q & A: Is a provision in a CPO requiring the respondent to vacate the residence, made contingent upon refinancing the property and removing respondent's name from the mortgage, a valid provision?

Not according to the Delaware County Court of Appeals in *Harris v. Ross*.[29] In *Harris*, appellant was granted a CPO requiring that appellee vacate the residence. That directive, however, was predicated upon appellant's being able to secure refinancing and removing appellee's name from the mortgage within 90 days. Subsequently, appellee filed a Motion for Relief from Protection Order because appellant had failed to secure refinancing within the requisite period of time. The trial court then ordered appellant to vacate the premises and awarded appellee exclusive possession of the residence.

On appeal, appellant argued that the trial court had erred by ordering him out of the residence and that it had exceeded its jurisdiction in granting a CPO which affected title to real property. The appellate court relied on the domestic violence statute, which provides in part that a CPO may include the granting of "possession of the residence . . . to the petitioner . . . to the exclusion of the respondent, by evicting the respondent . . . or by ordering the respondent to vacate the premises[.]"[30] It also cited R.C. 3113.31(E)(5), which provides that "No protection order issued or consent agreement approved under this section shall in any manner affect title to real property."

The provision of the consent entry stating that appellee had to vacate the property on condition that appellant refinance the mortgage to remove appellee's name from the mortgage was a provision that would affect title to the property, "because no lending institution would permit appellant to assume the entire obligation for the note, and pledge the subject property as security for the same, if appellant

[27] Judd v. Meszaros, 2011-Ohio-4983, 2011 WL 4489049, *7 (Ohio Ct. App. 10th Dist. Franklin County 2011).

[28] Judd v. Meszaros, 2011-Ohio-4983, 2011 WL 4489049, *8 (Ohio Ct. App. 10th Dist. Franklin County 2011), quoting appellant's brief.

[29] Harris v. Ross, 2011-Ohio-1075, 2011 WL 825739 (Ohio Ct. App. 5th Dist. Delaware County 2011).

[30] R.C. 3113.31(E)(1)(b).

were not sole owner of such property."[31] The appellate court also admonished the trial court for subsequently awarding the property to appellee when appellant could not refinance it, because "[i]n doing so, the trial court sanctioned appellant for violation of the portion of the consent agreement which the trial court had no authority to issue because such order violated RC 3113.31(E)(5) and affected title to property."[32]

In reversing the trial court judgment and remanding the case for further proceedings based on the fact that the trial court had exceeded its jurisdiction, the ruling admonishes a trial court for its failure to adequately review all consent agreements. In this case, the trial court merely approved a consent agreement agreed upon by the parties without reviewing it.

Underlying this decision is an unaddressed concern for family law practitioners and advocates: If the terms of a CPO consent agreement can be appealed for any or no reason, a petitioner should be made aware that, despite the parties' agreement, either party may still appeal a consent CPO.

Q & A: Can a party file for a partition of real estate or a breach of contract or unjust enrichment in a civil protection order action in domestic relations court, rather than filing those claims in a specific civil action in common pleas court?

No. The domestic violence statute is very specific as to the relief available to the petitioner.[33] In *Ruedele v. Kiefer*,[34] a protection order was granted to appellee ordering appellant to pay one-half of the monthly mortgage payment. Appellant failed to pay and the sum was reduced to judgment. Appellant filed another action seeking partition of the property in common pleas court. Appellee counterclaimed for partition, breach of contract, and unjust enrichment. Appellant contended that appellee's counterclaim was barred by res judicata, as the claims could have been raised in the action for a civil protection order. The Licking County Court of Appeals held that:

> In determining the civil protection action, the trial court was without authority to determine the claims raised by appellee in her counterclaim. RC 3113.31(E)(1) specifies the types of relief a court may grant in making a civil protection order, and does not give the court the authority to award damages in a civil action for breach of contract or unjust enrichment, or to partition real estate. In fact, RC 3113.31(E)(4) specifically states that a civil protection order may not affect title to real property.[35]

The *Ruedele* court also pointed out that the remedies provided by the domestic violence statute were in addition to any other available

---

[31]Harris v. Ross, 2011-Ohio-1075, 2011 WL 825739, *2 (Ohio Ct. App. 5th Dist. Delaware County 2011).

[32]Harris v. Ross, 2011-Ohio-1075, 2011 WL 825739, *2 (Ohio Ct. App. 5th Dist. Delaware County 2011).

[33]RC 3113.31(E)(1)(a) to RC 3113.31(E)(1)(h).

[34]Ruedele v. Kiefer, 1993 WL 438787 (Ohio Ct. App. 5th Dist. Licking County 1993), cause dismissed, 68 Ohio St. 3d 1444, 626 N.E.2d 686 (1994).

[35]Ruedele v. Kiefer, 1993 WL 438787 (Ohio Ct. App. 5th Dist. Licking County 1993), cause dismissed, 68 Ohio St. 3d 1444, 626 N.E.2d 686 (1994).

civil remedies.[36] Because the remedies available under RC 3113.31 were not in lieu of other civil remedies, a party to a civil protection order has the right to bring other civil actions, even though the issues may overlap. These other actions are not barred by res judicata.[37]

Q & A: Can a party be ordered to vacate the marital residence pursuant to RC 3113.31 if a divorce action is pending?

This particular issue was raised by the appellant in *Eichenberger v. Eichenberger*.[38] In that case, during the pendency of the parties' divorce, the wife filed for and was granted a civil protection order. On appeal, the husband alleged that the parties' pending divorce prevented the trial court from issuing a civil protection order or, at least, issuing an order which required the appellant to vacate the marital residence. The Franklin County Court of Appeals held that:

> A person who perceives himself or herself as being the victim of domestic violence does not forfeit the right to proceed under RC 3113.31 simply because the person files or has filed a divorce case. The pressure of crowded dockets in many courts does not allow motions to vacate to be heard rapidly, so a means of addressing the emergencies which true domestic violence situations present has to be available. The only other alternative is to force more criminal filings which allege domestic violence.[39]

The court relied on the rationale expressed in *Thomas v. Thomas*,[40] which also dealt with the issuance of a civil protection order during the pendency of a divorce, and determined that the *Thomas* decision was dispositive of the assignment of error.

§ 12:15 Remedies—Orders allocating parental rights and responsibilities

The court has the authority to award temporary custody and visitation to either of the parties.[1] The only requirement is that "no other court has determined, or is determining, the allocation of parental rights and responsibilities for the minor children or visitation rights."[2]

To that end, if the children are under the jurisdiction of the juvenile

---

[36] RC 3113.31(G).

[37] Ruedele v. Kiefer, 1993 WL 438787 (Ohio Ct. App. 5th Dist. Licking County 1993), cause dismissed, 68 Ohio St. 3d 1444, 626 N.E.2d 686 (1994).

[38] Eichenberger v. Eichenberger, 1993 WL 460570 (Ohio Ct. App. 10th Dist. Franklin County 1993); see also Champagne v. Champagne, 429 Mass. 324, 708 N.E.2d 100 (1999) (stating that protection orders may be granted during the pendency of a divorce proceeding).

[39] Eichenberger v. Eichenberger, 1993 WL 460570, *3 (Ohio Ct. App. 10th Dist. Franklin County 1993).

[40] Thomas v. Thomas, 44 Ohio App. 3d 6, 540 N.E.2d 745 (10th Dist. Franklin County 1988).

[Section 12:15]

[1] See Trent v. Trent, 1999 WL 298073 (Ohio Ct. App. 12th Dist. Preble County 1999); see also Couch v. Harrison, 2001-Ohio-4199, 2001 WL 121108 (Ohio Ct. App. 12th Dist. Clermont County 2001).

[2] RC 3113.31(E)(1)(d); see also Parker v. Jamison, 2003-Ohio-7295, 2003 WL 24135688, *5 (Ohio Ct. App. 4th Dist. Scioto County 2003) ("interpreting limitation of the court's authority as a means to prevent forum shopping when another court has already issued a custody order").

court, then the domestic relations court is without authority to make any custody or parenting time orders regarding the children. Similarly, if the probate court has granted guardianship of the children to another, then the domestic relations court is without authority to make custody or parenting time orders regarding the children by way of a civil protection order.[3]

For example, in *Tischler v. Vahcic*,[4] the mother was granted a custody order in juvenile court. The father was granted visitation; and, during his period of visitation, the father noticed a bump on the child's forehead. Additionally, the father observed a bruise and scuff marks on the child's arm. Approximately one month after the juvenile court awarded the mother custody, the father filed for a civil protection order in domestic relations court. Among the other orders granted by the court, the court awarded the father temporary allocation of parental rights and responsibilities of the child. The mother appealed.

The Cuyahoga County Court of Appeals determined that the child was abused pursuant to statute and overruled the mother's assignments of error. The court then stated that "[a]lthough not raised as an issue in this case, RC 3113.31(E)(1)(d) indicates that the Domestic Relations Court was without jurisdiction to give custody . . . to the father due to the fact that the Cuyahoga County Juvenile Court had previously made a custody determination."[5] The court relied on *Stanton v. Guerrero*,[6] which held:

> Because the visitation rights which this petition sought to modify

---

[3]See Stella v. Platz, 1999 WL 427672 (Ohio Ct. App. 4th Dist. Washington County 1999) (CPO may not prohibit respondent from removing child from area where prior juvenile court visitation order concerned no such restriction); Kiedrowicz v. Kiedrowicz, 1999 WL 197793 (Ohio Ct. App. 6th Dist. Huron County 1999) (magistrate lacked authority to enter order regarding child issues in civil protection order where those same child issues were already covered by orders entered in the parties' divorce action). See also Rush v. Rush, 1999 WL 1044482 (Ohio Ct. App. 8th Dist. Cuyahoga County 1999) (determining that Cuyahoga County Domestic Relations Court was without authority to modify husband's visitation rights because Lake County Domestic Relations Court had determined or was determining the visitation rights relating to the minor child). But see Couch v. Harrison, 2001-Ohio-4199, 2001 WL 121108 (Ohio Ct. App. 12th Dist. Clermont County 2001) (trial court has jurisdiction under RC 3113.31(E)(1)(d) to allocate parental rights and responsibilities in a CPO where same court allocated parental rights and responsibilities); Kitchen v. Kitchen, 2001 WL 279026 (Ohio Ct. App. 12th Dist. Madison County 2001); McCue v. Marlin, 187 Ohio App. 3d 1, 2010-Ohio-1298, 930 N.E.2d 855 (7th Dist. Mahoning County 2010).

[4]Tischler v. Vahcic, 1995 WL 680928 (Ohio Ct. App. 8th Dist. Cuyahoga County 1995) (abrogated by, Felton v. Felton, 79 Ohio St. 3d 34, 1997-Ohio-302, 679 N.E.2d 672 (1997)).

[5]Tischler v. Vahcic, 1995 WL 680928 (Ohio Ct. App. 8th Dist. Cuyahoga County 1995) (abrogated by, Felton v. Felton, 79 Ohio St. 3d 34, 1997-Ohio-302, 679 N.E.2d 672 (1997)).

[6]Stanton v. Guerrero, 1994 WL 472104, *3 (Ohio Ct. App. 2d Dist. Montgomery County 1994); see also Stella v. Platz, 1999 WL 427672 (Ohio Ct. App. 4th Dist. Washington County 1999) in which the court of appeals held that the (trial court exceeded its jurisdiction by issuing civil protection order that modified respondent's visitation rights from those contained in previous juvenile court order; the court relied on *Stanton* when it noted the relief requested is "readily available" in juvenile court); Rush v. Rush, 1999 WL 1044482 (Ohio Ct. App. 8th Dist. Cuyahoga County 1999); McCue v. Marlin, 187 Ohio App. 3d 1, 2010-Ohio-1298, 930 N.E.2d 855 (7th Dist. Mahoning County 2010).

resulted from the prior determination and orders of the Juvenile Division, the Domestic Relations Division could not grant the relief requested in the petition, which would constitute orders creating temporary visitation rights, albeit diminished ones.

The relief requested in this petition was readily available through the Juvenile Division, which is authorized in Juv. R. 13 to make temporary orders 'as the child's interest and welfare may require' and to do so through ex parte proceedings when necessary.

The *Tischler* court reasoned that the aforementioned interpretation is necessary "[t]o prevent judge and forum shopping between the Juvenile Division and Domestic Relations Division where the Juvenile Division has previously issued a custody order."[7]

Similarly, in *McCue v. Marlin*,[8] the parties had a previously issued parenting order from juvenile court awarding custody and visitation. Appellee filed a CPO because of appellant's committing domestic violence to the child. Appellant objected to the CPO arguing that the domestic relations court had no jurisdiction to issue temporary orders as to parental rights and visitation because juvenile court had previously determined. The trial court agreed with appellant and struck the provisions dealing with parental rights. However, the remainder of the CPO would remain effective until 2013.

On appeal, appellant claimed that because the juvenile court already had jurisdiction over the minor child, the entire CPO should be vacated. The appellate court first determined that the custody/visitation portions of a CPO are temporary orders that last only until the matter is litigated in a subsequent divorce or juvenile court proceeding.[9] "A court in a DVCPO proceeding cannot issue a permanent decree allocating parental rights and responsibilities, nor can it modify an existing decree."[10]

The Court of Appeals then reasoned that other portions of the CPO affected the parental rights and visitation provisions such as contact, prohibiting from coming within 500 feet, or entering schools etc. Those provisions should also be stricken from the CPO. However, provisions relating to prohibitions against abuse, use of weapons and possession of alcohol or drugs may remain untouched. In vacating certain portions of the CPO, the appellate court held that only the portions of the CPO that infringed upon prior jurisdiction of the juvenile court over parental rights and visitation matters were invalidated.

The same is true when a civil protection order is filed in one county while another matter addressing the allocation of parental rights and

---

[7]Tischler v. Vahcic, 1995 WL 680928 (Ohio Ct. App. 8th Dist. Cuyahoga County 1995) (abrogated on other grounds by, Felton v. Felton, 79 Ohio St. 3d 34, 1997-Ohio-302, 679 N.E.2d 672 (1997)). But see Kurincic v. Kurincic, 2000 WL 217808, *6 (Ohio Ct. App. 8th Dist. Cuyahoga County 2000) (Cuyahoga County Domestic Relations Court had jurisdiction to issue temporary protection order on minor's behalf even though complaint was filed against minor in juvenile court; appellate court reasoned that "the Juvenile Court had not made any custody determination and agreed to hold the domestic violence issue in abeyance").

[8]McCue v. Marlin, 187 Ohio App. 3d 1, 2010-Ohio-1298, 930 N.E.2d 855 (7th Dist. Mahoning County 2010).

[9]At *4; RC 3113.31(E)(1)(d).

[10]At *4; citing Couch v. Harrison, 2001-Ohio-4199, 2001 WL 121108 (Ohio Ct. App. 12th Dist. Clermont County 2001).

responsibilities is pending or has been decided in another county. For example, in *Yannitell v. Oaks*,[11] the parties had been previously divorced in Washington County in 2005. Appellant was designated residential parent of the minor children and Appellee was granted standard visitation. Appellee relocated to Texas and Appellant moved to Franklin County, Ohio.

In 2007, Appellant filed several motions including a motion to transfer jurisdiction to Franklin County and an emergency motion to terminate or suspend visitation and a motion to reallocate parental rights and responsibilities. The trial court ordered that Appellee have supervised visitation with the children pending further hearing. Appellant also filed a motion for a civil protection order in the Franklin County Court of Common Pleas which resulted in the granting of a CPO against Appellee with respect to the minor children. At a subsequent hearing in Washington County, the trial court denied Appellant's motions and ordered that Appellee continue to have standard visitation. Appellant appealed on the ground that the Washington County trial court abused its discretion in failing to defer to the Franklin County CPO determination and that by hearing evidence on issues previously litigated in the CPO, the action was barred by collateral estoppel.[12]

The Washington County appellate court first addressed the statutory process set forth in RC 3113.31(E)(3)(b) and noted the temporary nature of a court's order allocating parental rights and responsibilities in the context of a CPO. The appellate court relied on *Signer v. Signer*[13] in reasoning that while RC 3113.31(E)(3)(b) permits a trial court to issue temporary orders allocating parental rights and responsibilities, "*it does not vest the court with authority to modify the allocation of parental rights and responsibilities*. Instead, the only modification of those orders expressly contemplated by the General Assembly is in the context of a separate divorce, dissolution, legal separation or juvenile court proceeding."[14] However, this reliance on *Signer* is misplaced in light of recently amended RC 3113.31(E)(8) which permits the modification and termination of a CPO.

Despite this, the appellate court affirmed the judgment of the lower court and correctly determined that the Franklin County Court lacked jurisdiction. "[B]ecause the motion for reallocation of parental rights and responsibilities or motion for modification of parenting time was pending in the Washington County Court of Common Pleas, the Franklin County Court did not have jurisdiction to consider the motion. Rather, the motion should have been brought in the Washing-

[11]Yannitell v. Oaks, 2008-Ohio-6271, 2008 WL 5077646 (Ohio Ct. App. 4th Dist. Washington County 2008); see also Text § 12:27, Conflicting protection orders.

[12]Yannitell v. Oaks, 2008-Ohio-6271, 2008 WL 5077646, *4 (Ohio Ct. App. 4th Dist. Washington County 2008).

[13]Signer v. Signer, 2006-Ohio-3580, 2006 WL 1918115 (Ohio Ct. App. 8th Dist. Cuyahoga County 2006).

[14]Yannitell v. Oaks, 2008-Ohio-6271, 2008 WL 5077646, *8 (Ohio Ct. App. 4th Dist. Washington County 2008).

ton County Court and should have been consolidated with the already pending motion of modification of parenting time."[15]

Finally it is worth noting that the Fourth District Court of Appeals generally discussed the doctrines of res judicata and collateral estoppel,[16] but did not address Appellant's collateral estoppel argument because he failed to make the CPO order a part of the appellate record.

To prevent the inequities that would result from allocating parental rights and responsibilities to a parent in one court when another court has already determined the issues, the Supreme Court's domestic violence standard forms specifically request that the petitioner state whether any present or past court cases exist involving the petitioner, the respondent, or any of their family or household members.[17] Several experts in the area of domestic violence have approved this approach. "It is critical that family, criminal, civil, and juvenile court judges avail themselves of information regarding pending legal processes and current court orders involving the same parties so as to avoid issuing conflicting orders."[18] Additionally, knowledge of other cases and court orders aids the issuing judge in both crafting a protection order that is designed to protect the petitioner and other family members and determining appropriate sentencing dispositions.

Q & A: Can a court temporarily allocate parental rights to one of the parties as part of a CPO where a juvenile court is determining the allocation of parental rights and responsibilities?[19]

Yes and no. According to *Hoyt v. Heindell*,[20] the father requested a CPO on behalf of a child against the mother and her husband where the husband apparently drove with the child in his motor vehicle after having consumed beer, and the mother permitted such conduct. The CPO designated the father as the temporary residential parent and awarded mother visitation. However, there had been a prior juvenile court decision designating the mother as residential parent and awarding the father visitation rights.

On appeal, the mother argued that the domestic relations court had no jurisdiction to make a custody determination because there was a custody proceeding pending in juvenile court. The appellate court relied on R.C. 3113.31(E)(1)(d), which provides that a CPO may "temporarily allocate parental rights and responsibilities for the care of, or establish temporary parenting time rights with regard to, minor children, *if no other court has determined, or is determining, the allocation of parental rights and responsibilities for the minor children*

---

[15]Yannitell v. Oaks, 2008-Ohio-6271, 2008 WL 5077646, *8 (Ohio Ct. App. 4th Dist. Washington County 2008).

[16]See also Text § 12:27, Conflicting protection orders.

[17]See Sup. R. 10.01(B), Sup. R. Form 10.01-D.

[18]Leslye Orloff, Domestic Violence in Civil Court Cases, A National Model for Judicial Education, Family Violence Prevention Fund 157 (1992).

[19]See also Text § 12:16; Text § 15:12.

[20]Hoyt v. Heindell, 191 Ohio App. 3d 373, 2010-Ohio-6058, 946 N.E.2d 258 (11th Dist. Lake County 2010).

or parenting time rights."[21] In reversing the CPO regarding the allocation of parental rights and responsibilities, the appellate court held that the domestic relations court did not have the authority to make an allocation of parental rights and responsibilities since the juvenile court had previously determined the custody issues pertaining to the child.[22]

Of interest is that, in *dicta*, the court also stated that "[o]ur decision should not be construed to eliminate all authority of domestic relations courts. A domestic relations court is permitted to make emergency decisions, on an interim basis, to protect children from imminently dangerous situations. However, such determinations should remain in effect only until such time as the court that originally exercised jurisdiction over the custody issues can property review the matter."[23] Unfortunately, the majority did not set forth in detail how this is to be accomplished.

A separate opinion, concurring in part and dissenting in part, offered a more scathing view and stated that the domestic relations court was mandated to transfer incidents of alleged child abuse to the juvenile court for determination and adjudication.[24] Moreover, the dissenting judge would not have granted the CPO at all, stating that the father's CPO was another way to get custody during a contentious custody battle. "The movant chose not to file an emergency motion to suspend visitation in the court that had jurisdiction over the custody of the minor child and the court most familiar with the family's issues, which is the purpose of original jurisdiction in custody disputes. The primary and exclusive jurisdiction is in juvenile court. The effect was an erroneous decision that has the effect of prolonging the custody battle at the minor child's expense."[25]

Of significance is that the appellate court acknowledged that a domestic relations court still has jurisdiction to deal with safety concerns of minor children of unmarried parents, even where custody is pending in juvenile court. The court then indicated that a civil protection order can be issued and will remain in effect until such time as the court of original jurisdiction can properly review the matter.

Q & A: A mother was awarded custody pursuant to a divorce decree. Several years later, the father filed a petition for a protection order alleging that the minor child has been abused. Does the domestic relations court that entered the divorce decree become another court for purposes of RC 3113.31(E)(1)(d) jurisdictional issues?

The statute is silent on this issue. Relying upon the reasoning set

---

[21]Hoyt v. Heindell, 191 Ohio App. 3d 373, 2010-Ohio-6058, 946 N.E.2d 258 (11th Dist. Lake County 2010) (emphasis added by the court).

[22]Hoyt v. Heindell, 191 Ohio App. 3d 373, 2010-Ohio-6058, 946 N.E.2d 258 (11th Dist. Lake County 2010).

[23]Hoyt v. Heindell, 191 Ohio App. 3d 373, 2010-Ohio-6058, 946 N.E.2d 258 (11th Dist. Lake County 2010); Hyde v. Smith, 2015-Ohio-1701, 2015 WL 1976454 (Ohio Ct. App. 12th Dist. Butler County 2015).

[24]See R.C. 2151.23, 3109.06.

[25]Hoyt v. Heindell, 191 Ohio App. 3d 373, 2010-Ohio-6058, 946 N.E.2d 258 (11th Dist. Lake County 2010).

forth in *Tischler v. Vahcic*,[26] it would appear that a jurisdictional issue might arise only between the domestic relations division and juvenile division.

On the other hand, it may be logical to consider the domestic relations division as "another court" for purposes of reallocating parental rights and responsibilities under this fact pattern. Applying the same logic as in *Tischler*, the domestic relations court may be without jurisdiction to award custody to the other parent or withhold visitation from a parent in the protection order proceeding if the domestic relations court previously entered orders allocating parental rights and responsibilities in a prior divorce action or dissolution decree. The reasoning would be the same: to prevent forum and judge shopping, as well as to prohibit the advantage that may be gained from a temporary modification of parental rights and responsibilities in a protection order proceeding.

Q & A: Can the juvenile court modify the no-contact provisions in a CPO issued in domestic relations court to effectuate the visitation provisions?

According to the 9th District Court of Appeals the answer is no. In *In re K.C.*,[27] mother obtained a CPO prohibiting father from having any contact with Mother or the children. Subsequently, juvenile court became involved to address parental rights pursuant to a dependency action. The parents returned to domestic relations court to request a modification of the CPO to permit father to visit with the children. The domestic relations court transferred all child issues to juvenile court and juvenile court issued a limited order of visitation. The domestic relations court issued a modified CPO and continued the no contact order for the mother.

Father appealed claiming that the trial court abused its discretion by failing to expand his parenting time with the children to the standard order of parenting time and asserting that the trial court acted unreasonably by conditioning his right to increased parenting time upon him obtaining a modification of the existing CPO to permit the parties to communicate. The appellate court overruled Father's assignment of error and found that, although the trial court (juvenile court) believed that communication and contact was necessary to effectuate visitation, it had no ability to modify the CPO to allow the parties to communicate as that authority was vested solely with the domestic relations court and implying that only the same court is able to modify the CPO.[28]

---

[26]Tischler v. Vahcic, 1995 WL 680928 (Ohio Ct. App. 8th Dist. Cuyahoga County 1995) (abrogated on other grounds by, Felton v. Felton, 79 Ohio St. 3d 34, 1997-Ohio-302, 679 N.E.2d 672 (1997)).

[27]In re K.C., 2014-Ohio-372, 2014 WL 467476 (Ohio Ct. App. 9th Dist. Summit County 2014).

[28]In re K.C., 2014-Ohio-372, 2014 WL 467476, ¶ 31 (Ohio Ct. App. 9th Dist. Summit County 2014); see also State v. Price, 118 Ohio St. 3d 144, 2008-Ohio-1974, 886 N.E.2d 852 (2008).

Q & A: Is the domestic relations court that allocated parental rights and responsibilities the same court for purposes of a subsequent civil protection order?[29]

For example, in *Kiedrowicz v. Kiedrowicz*,[30] the defendant appealed the granting of a civil protection order. In that case, the allocation of parental rights and responsibilities, by way of a shared parenting plan, had previously been agreed to in the parties' divorce action. The magistrate modified defendant's visitation rights in the CPO.[31]

The appellate court noted that RC 3113.31(E)(1)(d) authorizes the court to make these orders only if no other court has determined or is determining the allocation of parental rights. The court found that "the magistrate lacked the authority . . . to enter any temporary orders concerning those issues in the civil protection order. Consequently, the trial court should have sustained appellant's objection to that portion of the magistrate's decision."[32] In response to the trial court taking judicial notice of its own shared parenting determination in the divorce proceeding, the Huron County Court of Appeals held that "[a] court may not take judicial notice of proceedings in other cases even in those instances where the cases are between the same parties before the same court."[33]

On the other hand, the Franklin County Court of Appeals addressed a similar issue in Wardeh v. Altabchi.[34] In *Wardeh*, the allocation of parental rights and responsibilities had been established in the

---

[29]See also State v. Price, 118 Ohio St. 3d 144, 2008-Ohio-1974, 886 N.E.2d 852 (2008).

[30]Kiedrowicz v. Kiedrowicz, 1999 WL 197793 (Ohio Ct. App. 6th Dist. Huron County 1999). But see Kurincic v. Kurincic, 2000 WL 217808 (Ohio Ct. App. 8th Dist. Cuyahoga County 2000).

[31]See also Steckler v. Steckler, 492 N.W.2d 76 (N.D. 1992) (protection order altered visitation pick-up and delivery points (but did not modify the substance of the divorce decree visitation rights) and stayed the shared parenting plan entered into by agreement in the parties' divorce proceeding for so long as the civil protection order was in effect).

[32]Kiedrowicz v. Kiedrowicz, 1999 WL 197793, *3 (Ohio Ct. App. 6th Dist. Huron County 1999). But see Couch v. Harrison, 2001-Ohio-4199, 2001 WL 121108 (Ohio Ct. App. 12th Dist. Clermont County 2001); see also Kitchen v. Kitchen, 2001 WL 279026 (Ohio Ct. App. 12th Dist. Madison County 2001); Parker v. Jamison, 2003-Ohio-7295, 2003 WL 24135688 (Ohio Ct. App. 4th Dist. Scioto County 2003) (holding that when the court issuing the civil protection order is the same court that previously allocated the parental rights and responsibilities of the parties, the trial court has jurisdiction under RC 3113.31(E)(1)(d) to allocate parental rights and responsibilities in the context of a civil protection order proceeding; here the same trial court presided over the divorce and the civil protection order proceedings, and therefore the trial court had subject matter jurisdiction to temporarily allocate parental rights and responsibilities); Waters v. Lattany, 2007-Ohio-1047, 2007 WL 707519, *4 (Ohio Ct. App. 6th Dist. Lucas County 2007) ("when the court issuing the CPO is the same court that previously allocated the parental rights and responsibilities of the parties, the trial court has jurisdiction under RC 3113.31(E)(1)(d) to allocate parental rights and responsibilities in the context of the CPO proceeding").

[33]Kiedrowicz v. Kiedrowicz, 1999 WL 197793, *3 (Ohio Ct. App. 6th Dist. Huron County 1999).

[34]Wardeh v. Altabchi, 158 Ohio App. 3d 325, 2004-Ohio-4423, 815 N.E.2d 712 (10th Dist. Franklin County 2004); Couch v. Harrison, 2001-Ohio-4199, 2001 WL 121108 (Ohio Ct. App. 12th Dist. Clermont County 2001); see also Kitchen v. Kitchen, 2001 WL 279026 (Ohio Ct. App. 12th Dist. Madison County 2001); Parker v. Jamison, 2003-Ohio-7295, 2003 WL 24135688 (Ohio Ct. App. 4th Dist. Scioto County 2003)

underlying divorce action. While the divorce was pending, the wife filed a separate petition for a civil protection order against her husband. In the divorce action, the father was awarded supervised visitation with the minor child. In the civil protection order, he was also awarded supervised visitation.

On appeal, the father asserted that the trial court in the civil protection order action had no authority to determine any matters affecting his parental rights because the trial court in the divorce action had previously determined this matter. Under RC 3113.31(E)(1)(d), a civil protection order granted by a court may temporarily allocate parental rights and responsibilities if no other court has determined or is determining the allocation of parental rights and responsibilities or parenting time rights. Because the judge assigned to the divorce case was not the same judge as the one assigned to the civil protection order action, the judge in the civil protection order action was precluded from addressing the allocation in the civil protection order. He argued that the definition of "court" means an individual judge of a county common pleas court, not a division of a county common pleas court.

However, the appellate court first determined that RC 3113.31(A)(2) defines "court" as the domestic relations division of the court of common pleas in counties that have a domestic relations division, and the court of common pleas in counties that do not have a domestic relations division. "The term "court" in RC 3113.31 does not refer to a specific judge, but rather the common pleas court's domestic relations division as a whole."[35] Because the Franklin County Domestic Relations Court in the divorce action is the same court that had jurisdiction to grant the civil protection order, the trial court in the civil protection order did not intrude on another court's jurisdiction with regard to the allocation of parental rights and responsibilities.[36] In overruling the father's assignment of error, the appellate court relied on RC 3113.31(G) and *Felton v. Felton* which held that "a court is not precluded by statute or public policy from issuing a CPO pursuant to

(holding that when the court issuing the civil protection order is the same court that previously allocated the parental rights and responsibilities of the parties, the trial court has jurisdiction under RC 3113.31(E)(1)(d) to allocate parental rights and responsibilities in the context of a civil protection order proceedings; here the same trial court presided over the divorce and the civil protection order proceedings, and therefore the trial court had subject matter jurisdiction to temporarily allocate parental rights and responsibilities); Dowhan v. Dowhan, 2013-Ohio-4097, 2013 WL 5346465 (Ohio Ct. App. 11th Dist. Lake County 2013); Sanchez v. Sanchez, 2016-Ohio-4933, 2016 WL 3745699 (Ohio Ct. App. 1st Dist. Hamilton County 2016) (noting that RC 3113.31(E)(1)(d) is to prevent forum shopping where another court has previously issued a custody order. Where both the divorce proceedings and the CPO were filed in the same court and presided over by the same judge, there was no issue of forum shopping and the trial court had jurisdiction over the matter. At ¶ 14; see also Waters v. Lattany, 2007-Ohio-1047, 2007 WL 707519 (Ohio Ct. App. 6th Dist. Lucas County 2007)).

[35]Wardeh v. Altabchi, 158 Ohio App. 3d 325, 332, 2004-Ohio-4423, 815 N.E.2d 712 (10th Dist. Franklin County 2004).

[36]Wardeh v. Altabchi, 158 Ohio App. 3d 325, 2004-Ohio-4423, 815 N.E.2d 712 (10th Dist. Franklin County 2004).

RC 3113.31 even though a divorce decree already addresses similar matters."[37]

Counsel should be aware that this issue could be asserted by one of the parties or the court. Until this issue is resolved by way of a Supreme Court decision or statutory change, a petitioner should continue to request a protection order with all its remedies on behalf of a child who meets the statutory definition of an abused child, even where there has already been a prior allocation of parental rights and responsibilities pursuant to a divorce decree.[38]

Q & A: Is a civil protection order regarded as a custody proceeding?

Not according to *Tabler v. Myers*.[39] In *Tabler*, the appellate court determined that the custody determination arising from the CPO was only a temporary order that lasts until the issue is litigated in a domestic relations or juvenile court.[40] An allocation of parental rights entered pursuant to a subsequent divorce action or juvenile court action must be treated as an initial custody determination rather than a change of custody case. Because an award of custody arising from a CPO is merely a temporary order, it is not an initial custody determination.

Q & A: Is a court's allocation of parental rights and responsibilities in the context of a civil protection order always a temporary order?

Generally, the provisions relating to the allocation of parental rights and responsibilities shall be effective for a date certain, but not to exceed 5 years.[41] However, these provisions may also expire when a court in a divorce, dissolution, legal separation or juvenile court proceeding issues subsequent orders.

In *Delmatto v. Hamed*,[42] the appellate court specifically addressed the issue of whether orders regarding the allocation of parental rights and responsibilities are temporary in the context of civil protection orders. In that case, petitioner-appellant appealed the judgment of Fairfield County Domestic Relations Court which sustained a motion filed by respondent to modify its previously issued CPO. The focus of respondent's motion was to remove the child as a protected party from the order because the Franklin County Domestic Relations Court issued temporary orders in the divorce, which among other things granted respondent supervised visitation rights.

---

[37]Wardeh v. Altabchi, 158 Ohio App. 3d 325, 333, 2004-Ohio-4423, 815 N.E.2d 712 (10th Dist. Franklin County 2004), citing Felton v. Felton, 79 Ohio St. 3d 34, 1997-Ohio-302, 679 N.E.2d 672 (1997); see also Kandel v. Kandel, 2004-Ohio-4548, 2004 WL 1925690 (Ohio Ct. App. 5th Dist. Ashland County 2004).

[38]RC 3113.31(A)(1)(c); see also RC 2151.031, RC 2919.22.

[39]Tabler v. Myers, 173 Ohio App. 3d 657, 2007-Ohio-6219, 880 N.E.2d 103 (7th Dist. Noble County 2007); see also Text § 15:12, Other issues that impact custody and visitation awards. See also McCue v. Marlin, 187 Ohio App. 3d 1, 2010-Ohio-1298, 930 N.E.2d 855 (7th Dist. Mahoning County 2010).

[40]Tabler v. Myers, 173 Ohio App. 3d 657, 2007-Ohio-6219, 880 N.E.2d 103, 106 (7th Dist. Noble County 2007).

[41]RC 3113.31(E)(3)(b).

[42]Delmatto v. Hamed, 2008-Ohio-6375, 2008 WL 5124388 (Ohio Ct. App. 5th Dist. Fairfield County 2008).

The appellate court found that the statute expressly contemplates that orders regarding the allocation of parental rights and responsibilities in a divorce shall supersede a civil protection order as it applies to minor children.[43] Thus, any orders entered by a court in a civil protection order regarding the allocation of parental rights and responsibilities are temporary.

Q & A: Is a trial court required to make a best interest determination when resolving a request for a civil protection order?

Not according to the Second District Court of Appeals. In *Insa v. Insa*,[44] appellant wife appealed the denial of her civil protection order claiming that the trial court failed to conduct an in camera interview of the child who was a protected party on the CPO.

She argued that, under RC 3109.04(A), her petition for a CPO was a "proceeding pertaining to the allocation of parental rights and responsibilities" because her petition sought a temporary custody order which was permitted under RC 311.31.(E)(1)(d). However, the appellate court indicated that her reliance on RC 3109.04 was misplaced because RC 3113.31 was not designed to address the designation of residential parent status as the options available in a custody proceeding exceed the scope of the temporary allocation that occurs in the context of a protection order.[45] The appellate court differentiated between the "temporary custody" order of a protection order and the designation of a residential parent. Further, no other rights and responsibilities were considered. Moreover, the requirement to interview a child in camera at the request of a party (as set forth in RC 3109. 04(A)) did not apply to a protection order petition.

More importantly, because RC 3109.04 directs a court to consider the best interest of the children when allocating parental rights and responsibilities under that section and in furtherance of a best interest analysis, the court is required to permit an in camera interview of the child if it is requested.[46] "Notably, however, the protection order statute, RC 311.31, does not "specifically require the trial court to consider the 'best interest factors' [in RC 3109.04(F)(1)] used for creating or modifying a shared parenting plan, or determining companionship rights."[47] "Had the legislature intended to have trial courts weigh the best interest factors in RC 3109.04(F)(1) before allocating parental rights and responsibilities in a civil protection order, it would have expressly so declared."[48] "Instead, RC 3113.31 demonstrates a clear and unambiguous legislative intent to enable the trial court to im-

[43]Delmatto v. Hamed, 2008-Ohio-6375, 2008 WL 5124388, *3 (Ohio Ct. App. 5th Dist. Fairfield County 2008), citing Yazdani-Isfehani v. Yazdani-Isfehani, 170 Ohio App. 3d 1, 2006-Ohio-7105, 865 N.E.2d 924, ¶ 23 (4th Dist. Athens County 2006).

[44]Insa v. Insa, 2016-Ohio-7425, 72 N.E.3d 1170 (Ohio Ct. App. 2d Dist. Montgomery County 2016).

[45]Insa v. Insa, 2016-Ohio-7425, ¶ 33, 72 N.E.3d 1170 (Ohio Ct. App. 2d Dist. Montgomery County 2016).

[46]RC 3109.04(B)(1).

[47]Insa v. Insa, 2016-Ohio-7425, ¶ 34, 72 N.E.3d 1170 (Ohio Ct. App. 2d Dist. Montgomery County 2016), quoting Couch v. Harrison, 2001-Ohio-4199, 2001 WL 121108, *3 (Ohio Ct. App. 12th Dist. Clermont County 2001).

[48]Insa v. Insa, 2016-Ohio-7425, ¶ 34, 72 N.E.3d 1170 (Ohio Ct. App. 2d Dist.

mediately provide for the temporary safety and protection of minor children."[49]

"Because a trial court is not required to consider the RC 3109.04 best interest factors, or even to make an explicit best interest determination, when resolving a request for a civil protection order, RC 3109.04(B)(1)'s requirement for a trial court to conduct an in camera interview to determine a child's best interest does not apply."[50]

Q & A: Is a temporary allocation of parental rights in the context of a civil protection order a prior decree allocating parental rights and responsibilities?

It does not appear so. In *Insa v. Insa*,[51] the appellate court considered whether a temporary allocation of parental rights and responsibilities in the context of a CPO constitutes a prior decree such that there must be a change of circumstances before such order can be modified pursuant to RC 3109(E)(1)(a).[52]

The appellate court reasoned that a protection order is not a custody proceeding. It is only a temporary order that lasts until the domestic relations or juvenile court issues another order.[53] "[A] temporary allocation of parental rights in a protection order proceeding falls outside of the scope of RC 3109.04 because such a proceeding is not a custody proceeding under that statute."[54]

Q & A: Can visitation issues be addressed in a civil protection order proceeding?

Yes. Ohio is one of a majority of states that permits courts to include temporary visitation provisions as a term of a civil protection order.[55] Each order awarding visitation to a respondent should be crafted to secure the safety of the victim and other family or household members.

There is growing recognition in this country of the risks posed to victims and their children by unsupervised visitation in domestic violence cases.[56]

Ohio's civil protection order statute[57] was amended in August 1996

Montgomery County 2016) quoting *Couch* at *3.

[49]Insa at 34.

[50]Insa v. Insa, 2016-Ohio-7425, ¶ 34, 72 N.E.3d 1170 (Ohio Ct. App. 2d Dist. Montgomery County 2016).

[51]Insa v. Insa, 2016-Ohio-7425, 72 N.E.3d 1170 (Ohio Ct. App. 2d Dist. Montgomery County 2016).

[52]Insa v. Insa, 2016-Ohio-7425, ¶ 35, 72 N.E.3d 1170 (Ohio Ct. App. 2d Dist. Montgomery County 2016).

[53]Insa v. Insa, 2016-Ohio-7425, ¶ 35, 72 N.E.3d 1170 (Ohio Ct. App. 2d Dist. Montgomery County 2016); see Tabler v. Myers, 173 Ohio App. 3d 657, 2007-Ohio-6219, 880 N.E.2d 103 (7th Dist. Noble County 2007).

[54]Insa v. Insa, 2016-Ohio-7425, ¶ 35, 72 N.E.3d 1170 (Ohio Ct. App. 2d Dist. Montgomery County 2016); see also State ex rel. Thompson v. Spon, 83 Ohio St. 3d 551, 1998-Ohio-298, 700 N.E.2d 1281 (1998) (wherein the Ohio Supreme Court ruled that RC 3109.04(C) applies only to final decrees or subsequent modifications, rather than temporary orders allocating parental rights).

[55]RC 3113.31(E)(1)(d).

[56]Robert B. Straus, Supervised Visitation and Family Violence, 29 Fam. L. Q. 229 (1995).

[57]RC 3113.31.

to include a provision which authorizes the Department of Human Services to provide supervised visitation if the following conditions are met pursuant to RC 3113.31(E)(6)(a):

> If a petitioner, or the child of a petitioner, who obtains a protection order. . . and is the subject of a visitation or companionship order . . ., the court may require the public children services agency of the county in which the court is located to provide supervision of the respondent's exercise of visitation or companionship rights with respect to the child for a period not to exceed nine months, if the court makes the following findings of fact:
>
> (i) The child is in danger from the respondent;
>
> (ii) No other person or agency is available to provide the supervision or other services.

This statutory provision suggests an understanding by the Ohio legislature that safety of children is of paramount concern and that few centers dedicated to supervision exist in the state of Ohio. As written, the statute provides for the local children services agency (local counterpart of the Ohio Department of Human Services) to supervise visitation for a period of nine months or less. This is the case in a situation in which a party is granted visitation in a civil protection order in the first instance[58] or where a petitioner obtains a protection order in an action pursuant to RC 3113.31 or RC 2919.26 and the child is already subject of a prior visitation order, by way of a divorce, legal separation or annulment,[59] or pursuant to RC 3109.11 or RC 3109.12, the trial court may require the local agency to supervise visitation (parenting time).[60]

Since there is no mandate attached to RC 3113.31(E)(6)(a), a court may decline to order the local children services agency to provide supervised visitation. If the court wants the local agency to supervise the visitation, it must make certain findings in its order. The child must be in danger from the respondent. Moreover, a finding that the petitioner parent is in danger from the respondent will not necessarily invoke the protections of this provision.

It is important to note that the safety to the child, not the victim, is the primary concern. However, danger to the child need not only be physical. Children who witness domestic violence are at great risk.[61] Additionally, studies have shown that there is a consistent and disturbing correlation between spouse abuse and child abuse.[62]

Counsel for the petitioner should elicit certain information from the petitioner. A petitioner must show that the child has, at the very least, witnessed the domestic violence between the parents. The petitioner must testify that witnessing violence caused the child to

[58]R.C. 3113.31(E)(1)(d).

[59]RC 3109.051.

[60]See In re J.H.P., 2015-Ohio-548, 2015 WL 627638 (Ohio Ct. App. 2d Dist. Montgomery County 2015) (acknowledging that the court may order public children's services agency to provide such supervision).

[61]"Research on the Effects of Witnessing Parental Battering: Clinical and Legal Policy Implications," in Woman Battering: Policy Responses 237 (Michael Steinman ed., 1991); see also Lenore E. Walker, The Battered Woman Syndrome 59 (1984).

[62]See Peter G. Jaffe et al., Children of Battered Women (1990).

suffer emotional trauma. Such activity is dangerous to a child's mental and physical development.[63]

Additionally, the court must determine that no other agency or person is available to provide the supervised visitation. The statute also provides that the court shall order the respondent to reimburse the agency for the cost of providing the supervision, if it determines that the respondent has sufficient income or resources to pay that cost.[64]

Q & A: What type of visitation can be awarded to a respondent at the full hearing?[65]

It depends on the individual court as well as on whether the respondent appears at the hearing. If the respondent fails to appear at the full hearing, most courts do not even address the respondent's visitation rights. Local practice in Cuyahoga, Franklin, Monroe, Morgan, Noble, and Washington counties dictates such a policy.

On the other hand, if a respondent appears for the hearing and requests visitation, most courts establish some type of visitation privileges for the respondent.[66] Whether the visitation accorded to the respondent is unsupervised or supervised depends on the type of contact the respondent had previously enjoyed, the danger to the petitioner and the child, and the degree of domestic violence inflicted upon the victim.[67]

Any visitation order must be specific as it relates to dates, times, and places. In families where there has been domestic violence, it is unlikely that the parents can effectively establish or follow through with a nonspecific visitation schedule. Where there is a high probability of future violence, an order should be crafted to afford the victim a high degree of protection such as supervised visitation at a neutral location[68] or setting forth a neutral pick-up and drop-off point.[69]

Recently, the Montgomery County Domestic Violence Protocol was adopted by the criminal justice system and the domestic relations court in that county. In making visitation orders in a domestic violence

[63]See Mildred Pagelow, Children in Violent Families: Direct and Indirect Victims, in Young Children and Their Families 47–73 (Shirley Hill & B.J. Barnes eds., 1982).

[64]RC 3113.31(E)(6)(b).

[65]See also Text Ch. 15, Domestic Violence and Custody and Visitation Issues.

[66]See Trent v. Trent, 1999 WL 298073 (Ohio Ct. App. 12th Dist. Preble County 1999) (affirming trial court's grant of visitation provided respondent does not consume alcohol during visitation).

[67]See, e.g., Brown v. Brown, 2000 WL 271769 (Ohio Ct. App. 10th Dist. Franklin County 2000) (supervised visitation did not violate father's constitutional right to due process or legislature's intent regarding RC 3113.31).

[68]RC 3113.31(E)(6).

[69]See Goode v. Goode, 89 Ohio App. 3d 405, 624 N.E.2d 788 (10th Dist. Franklin County 1993); see also Heckel v. Heckel, 2000 WL 1279171 (Ohio Ct. App. 12th Dist. Butler County 2000) (trial court properly ordered pick up/drop off site to be Hamilton Police Department due to prior domestic violence incident arising out of exchange for visitation); a police station provides "safe harbor" and "provides an extra incentive for the parties to refrain from hostilities."); Shimman v. Germano, 2008-Ohio-717, 2008 WL 466787 (Ohio Ct. App. 6th Dist. Lucas County 2008) (appellant was permitted to visit with his son at stated time with the exchange to occur at the police department or at appellee's apartment with a police officer present).

proceeding, the Montgomery County Protocol has determined that the Montgomery County Domestic Relations Court will consider whether to do the following:

(1) order the exchange of the child to occur in a protected setting;
(2) order supervised visitation by another person or agency (not under the control of the respondent);
(3) order the respondent to attend and complete, to the satisfaction of the court, a program of batterer's intervention or other designated counseling as a condition of the visitation;
(4) order the respondent to abstain from possession or consumption of alcohol or controlled substances during the visitation and for 24 hours preceding the visitation;
(5) order the respondent to pay a fee to defray the costs of the supervision;
(6) prohibit overnight visitation;
(7) require a bond from respondent for the return and safety of the child;
(8) suspend visitation if there is a likelihood that the respondent will flee with the child based upon prior, credible threats.[70]

Q & A: Does the court have the authority to suspend the respondent's visitation?

Ohio's domestic violence statute[71] is silent as to whether a court may entirely suspend a respondent's visitation. However, local practice in several Ohio jurisdictions allows for the suspension of the respondent's visitation under certain circumstances.

For example, in Montgomery County, one of the terms of the civil protection order provides that a respondent's visitation may be suspended[72] or held in abeyance until such time as the judge issues another order in a divorce,[73] legal separation, or dissolution action, until the respondent completes counseling, or until a juvenile court issues an order.

The Supreme Court has adopted the approach taken in Montgomery County and has established forms that permit all Ohio courts to suspend a respondent's visitation rights or order that a respondent's visitation be supervised.[74]

---

[70]Montgomery County Domestic Violence Protocol, Civil Judicial Response (1996).

[71]RC 3113.31.

[72]See, for example, State v. Price, 118 Ohio St. 3d 144, 2008-Ohio-1974, 886 N.E.2d 852 (2008) (CPO suspended visitation until respondent engages in regular counseling for his bipolar disorder and takes his medication).

[73]See for example, Waters v. Lattany, 2007-Ohio-1047, 2007 WL 707519 (Ohio Ct. App. 6th Dist. Lucas County 2007) (reasoning that suspension of visitation in the CPO can be revisited upon action in the pending divorce case or upon motion of either party; RC 3113.31(E)(8)).

[74]Sup. R. 10.01(B), Sup. R. Form 10.01-D; see Walker v. Lees, 2001 WL 197853 (Ohio Ct. App. 5th Dist. Licking County 2001) (court of appeals affirmed trial court decision ordering that respondent have supervised visitation pending a psychological evaluation).

Several Ohio courts have addressed this issue. In *Eichenberger v. Eichenberger*,[75] the trial court issued a civil protection order that included a provision that no visitation was to occur between the respondent and the children until a guardian ad litem was appointed and had an opportunity to investigate and make a recommendation as to appropriate visitation. The court of appeals upheld the trial court's decision regarding this issue, finding that "[t]he trial court's temporary suspension of visitation was not an abuse of discretion."[76]

In *Rush v. Rush*,[77] the Cuyahoga County Domestic Relations Court issued a protection order against petitioner's former husband and suspended his visitation with the minor child pending a case plan by the Cuyahoga County Department of Children and Family Services. The court further ordered the Cuyahoga County Department of Children and Family Services to make arrangements to have visitation supervised by a caseworker. The husband appealed the issuance of the civil protection order, arguing, among other things, that the trial court lacked jurisdiction to modify his visitation rights because the Lake County Domestic Relations Court had already made a visitation order.

The Eight District Court of Appeals held that "because the Lake County Domestic Relations Court had determined or was determining husband's visitation rights, the Cuyahoga County Domestic Relations Court lacked the authority under RC 3113.31(E)(1)(d) to modify husband's visitation rights."[78] The court then pointed out that, had the petitioner sustained her burden in order to obtain a civil protection order, "the court below would have had discretion to order husband to stay away from the family or household members named in the temporary protection order and this order would have necessarily restricted visitation by implication."[79]

However, there is no guarantee that a trial court would have considered the child a protected family or household member under that circumstance. Oftentimes, the court will deliberately not include the minor child as a protected family member and will specifically note in the order that the stay-away provisions do not apply where visitation is ordered. On the other hand, where the abuse is directed at the child, a court may choose to include the child as a protected member on the protection order so that visitation is restricted by implication as it could not be by court order.[80]

Other state statutes and case law have recognized that, under

[75] Eichenberger v. Eichenberger, 1993 WL 460570 (Ohio Ct. App. 10th Dist. Franklin County 1993).

[76] Eichenberger v. Eichenberger, 1993 WL 460570, *3 (Ohio Ct. App. 10th Dist. Franklin County 1993); Sanchez v. Sanchez, 2016-Ohio-4933, 2016 WL 3745699 (Ohio Ct. App. 1st Dist. Hamilton County 2016).

[77] Rush v. Rush, 1999 WL 1044482 (Ohio Ct. App. 8th Dist. Cuyahoga County 1999).

[78] Rush v. Rush, 1999 WL 1044482, *8 (Ohio Ct. App. 8th Dist. Cuyahoga County 1999).

[79] Rush v. Rush, 1999 WL 1044482, *8 (Ohio Ct. App. 8th Dist. Cuyahoga County 1999). See also Kranek v. Richards, 2011-Ohio-6374, 2011 WL 6164727 (Ohio Ct. App. 7th Dist. Jefferson County 2011).

[80] See also State v. Harley, 1999 WL 3933 (Ohio Ct. App. 5th Dist. Fairfield County

certain circumstances, a court may suspend a respondent's visitation rights.[81] Several states have authorized courts to suspend visitation to protect the safety of the victim and the children. For example, the Minnesota statute states that the court will suspend visitation "as needed to guard the safety of the victim and children."[82]

Appellate courts that have addressed this question have been willing to suspend or limit visitation in protection order cases to protect the petitioner or the children from further abuse. In *Campbell v. Campbell*,[83] a Florida court suspended respondent's visitation because of petitioner's fear of future domestic violence and the respondent's prior arrest for sexual battery of their three-year-old daughter. The court found that the children "like their mother, had reasonable cause to believe that they were about to become the victims of an act of domestic violence. Surely, fear that a custodial parent will be assaulted or battered by a non custodial parent constitutes an act of domestic violence as to their child."[84]

In *Hughes v. Hughes*,[85] the court found the father's history of violence towards the mother, which included holding the mother and child hostage for eight hours while threatening to kill the mother and himself and later breaking into the mother's home and shooting her while she held the child, so egregious that the court suspended visitation entirely, finding contact with the father to be against the child's best interests. The court held that, while parents should seldom lose visitation, in this case the father's reckless endangerment of the child and abuse of the mother confirmed a moral deficiency which threatened the child.

Q & A: Can a parent's intention to take the minor children to Israel over spring break provide the basis for issuing a CPO and suspending father's visitation?

In *Hanna v. Keszei*,[86] father informed his ex wife that he intended to take his children on a vacation to Israel. Although both parents were designated residential parents and legal custodian, mother filed for and was granted an ex parte CPO, alleging that the locality was "war-torn and unsafe." Before a full hearing was held, father turned over his passports and the court restored his parenting time rights,

---

1998) (raising interesting issue of whether a parent who is allocated temporary visitation rights with his children but who is subject to a protection order can initiate contact with his children where the order specifically orders defendant to have no contact with the victim; though the appeal in *Harley* was ultimately dismissed for lack of jurisdiction, the issue it raised underscores the importance of making any protection order specific enough that both parties are protected, either from future violence or from charges for violating the protection order); Walker v. Lees, 2001 WL 197853 (Ohio Ct. App. 5th Dist. Licking County 2001).

[81]But see Cosme v. Figueroa, 258 N.J. Super. 333, 609 A.2d 523 (Ch. Div. 1992).

[82]Minn. Stat. Ann. § 518B.01.6(a)(3) (Supp. 1993).

[83]Campbell v. Campbell, 584 So. 2d 125 (Fla. 4th DCA 1991).

[84]Campbell v. Campbell, 584 So. 2d 125, 126–27 (Fla. 4th DCA 1991).

[85]Hughes v. Hughes, 316 Pa. Super. 505, 463 A.2d 478 (1983); see also Bender v. Kramer, 1992 WL 435693 (Del. Fam. Ct. 1992). But see State v. Brillhart, 129 Ohio App. 3d 180, 717 N.E.2d 413 (9th Dist. Wayne County 1998) (holding "no contact" order against a man with children as a condition of his probation to be invalid).

[86]Hanna v. Keszei, 2009-Ohio-4136, 2009 WL 2490035 (Ohio Ct. App. 12th Dist. Clermont County 2009).

pending the full hearing. Father filed a writ of prohibition barring the trial court from exercising jurisdiction over the matter. Mother then dismissed the CPO.

In dismissing the appeal for lack of a final, appealable order, the appellate court also stated that it had ". . . serious doubts regarding whether a parent's expressed intention to vacation with his children in Israel is sufficient to constitute 'domestic violence' within the meaning of RC 3113.31(A)(1) . . .." Of significance is that the Clermont County Court of Appeals even chose to address this issue in light of its intention to dismiss the appeal. Clearly, attorneys and advocates should be mindful of the use of these special statutory orders. (writ of prohibition).

Q & A: Does it matter at what point in time the respondent requests visitation?

It depends on the mature of the parties' relationship and the nature of the legal proceedings. Where the parties are not yet divorced, many Ohio courts accord a respondent some access to the children upon request. However, if the violence is severe or directed at the child, however, the court may decide not to grant visitation and direct that the respondent request visitation in an underlying divorce action. Alternatively, the court may order supervised visitation.[87]

If the parties are already divorced at the time the protection order is sought and the reason for the protection order is violence directed at the child, the court may suspend visitation privileges for a period of time or until another court order is made in the underlying divorce action. This practice is followed in Montgomery County as well as Monroe, Morgan, Noble, and Washington counties.

If the parties are not married but have a child in common, the court may decide that juvenile court is the appropriate forum in which to make the custody/visitation determination. However, the court should maintain the civil protection order in effect as it relates to safety issues.

Where a respondent contests paternity, courts often decline to allocate parental rights and responsibilities and refer the parties to juvenile court. Most jurisdictions, however, will award custody to the petitioner but refer the respondent to juvenile court for genetic testing and a paternity determination. Visitation issues are held in abeyance. Once again, the court should keep the provisions of the protection order in effect to protect the petitioner pending any paternity determination.

In Cuyahoga County, for example, the court will grant a custody order to the petitioner, but often declines to establish visitation for the respondent if the petitioner is concerned about safety issues or if paternity is questioned. Since juvenile court also offers a long-term solution to custody and visitation, the domestic relations court is very likely to defer to the juvenile court.

Q & A: How long does a custody/visitation order granted in a protection order last?

Although a civil protection order stays in effect for a period of no

---

[87]See RC 3113.31(E)(6). See also Eichenberger v. Eichenberger, 1993 WL 460570 (Ohio Ct. App. 10th Dist. Franklin County 1993).

more than five years,[88] any custody or visitation order that is established by a court in a civil protection order shall terminate on the date that a court in an action for divorce, dissolution of marriage, or legal separation brought by the petitioner or respondent issues an order allocating parental rights and responsibilities for the care of the children or on the date that a juvenile court issues an order awarding legal custody of minor children.[89]

For example, a married petitioner who is awarded custody in a protection order is granted this for a period of five years or until the domestic relations court awards one of the parties custody in a subsequent divorce, dissolution, or legal separation action. The same is true for visitation issues.

If the parties are not married, however, any custody, visitation, or child support orders entered by the court pursuant to the civil protection order remain in effect for the five-year period unless otherwise modified by the juvenile court.[90] This modification is usually accomplished by one of the parties filing a parentage complaint or a motion to determine custody in juvenile court.

Q & A: A custody order was entered in a divorce decree granting Party A custody. Subsequent to the divorce, Party B obtains a CPO designating Party B custody of the same child. How long does the custody provision of the CPO last?

The statutory language in RC 3113.31(E)(3)(b) does not address this specific concern and it doesn't happen very often. As stated earlier, pursuant to RC 3113.31(E)(3)(a), any custody order contained in a civil protection order will remain valid until a date certain, but not later than five years from the date of its issuance or approval, or it will expire on the date that the court enters another order regarding the children pursuant to a divorce, dissolution, legal separation, or juvenile court action.[91] Since RC 3113.31(E)(3)(b) appears to apply only to protection orders issued before a divorce or during a pending divorce proceeding, it is unclear whether the legislature intended to apply RC 3113.31(E)(3)(a) to other situations. Where the divorce was finalized well before the filing of the petition for protection order, it depends on who was granted custody in the original divorce action. If a trial court decides that the domestic relations court becomes another court for

[88]RC 3113.31(E)(3)(a); see also Brown v. Brown, 2000 WL 271769 (Ohio Ct. App. 10th Dist. Franklin County 2000) (because a CPO expires by its own terms, defendant's argument that he was permanently deprived of custody or unrestricted visitation with his son was without merit); see also Couch v. Harrison, 2001-Ohio-4199, 2001 WL 121108 (Ohio Ct. App. 12th Dist. Clermont County 2001).

[89]R.C. 3113.31(E)(3)(b); see also Hershberger v. Hershberger, 2000-Ohio-1716, 2000 WL 1675568 (Ohio Ct. App. 3d Dist. Seneca County 2000). See also Baldridge v. Baldridge, 2011-Ohio-2423, 2011 WL 1936056 (Ohio Ct. App. 2d Dist. Darke County 2011) (finding that the custody and visitation portions of the CPO terminated by operation of law after a decree of divorce was obtained). See also Allan v. Allan, 2014-Ohio-5039, 2014 WL 6065710, ¶ 46 (Ohio Ct. App. 8th Dist. Cuyahoga County 2014).

[90]See R.C. 3113.31(E)(3)(b).

[91]See R.C. 3113.31(E)(3)(b). See also Signer v. Signer, 2006-Ohio-3580, 2006 WL 1918115 (Ohio Ct. App. 8th Dist. Cuyahoga County 2006) (holding that R.C. 3113.31 doesn't vest the court with authority to modify the allocation of parental rights and responsibilities in a CPO).

purposes of the civil protection order action, then it may choose not to issue a conflicting custody order. Rather, the court may instruct a petitioner to file a motion to modify parental rights and responsibilities.[92]

The court may also grant temporary custody to the noncustodial party in the civil protection order proceeding pending resolution of an underlying motion to modify parental rights. The custody relief granted pursuant to the protection order will then expire when the court in the underlying divorce action reallocates parental rights and responsibilities.

Counsel for petitioner should note that any orders issued pursuant to a CPO will only be valid for five years. After that, custody will revert back to the terms as set forth in the original decree, unless otherwise modified by a motion to modify parental rights and responsibilities. However, the court has the authority to determine that the order terminate on another date certain which is shorter than the five-year statutory period.[93]

Q & A: How does the trial court determine which parent should be granted custody after the full hearing in a civil protection order proceeding?

Although no Ohio court has articulated a specific standard, the Preble County Court of Appeals noted in *Trent v. Trent*[94] that a domestic relations court looks to RC 3109.04(B)(1) in deciding to whom the care, custody, and control of a minor child shall be awarded, giving primary consideration to the best interests of the child.[95]

In *Trent*, the court held an in camera hearing with the parties' children at which the children testified that their parents fought, that the respondent gets angry when he drinks too much, and that he has damaged property when he gets angry. Testimony was also presented as to the mother's substance abuse. However, the court noted that the children were not aware of their mother's marijuana use and, to that end, her abuse of drugs has not had an adverse impact on the children. Additionally, the mother testified that she was the primary caregiver of the children.

The appellate court noted that, while the record is devoid of information connecting the children with knowledge of their mother's marijuana use, they were aware of their father's drinking problem. In light of this, the Preble County Court of Appeals held that there was competent, credible evidence to support the trial court's finding that "For the time being the best interests [sic] of the children are served in continuing their placement with [appellee]."[96]

Q & A: Must a court include the minor child in a civil protec-

---

[92]See, e.g., Cuy. D.R. R. 26(A); see also Kiedrowicz v. Kiedrowicz, 1999 WL 197793 (Ohio Ct. App. 6th Dist. Huron County 1999); R.T. v. J.T., 2015-Ohio-4418, 2015 WL 6449294 (Ohio Ct. App. 9th Dist. Medina County 2015).

[93]See RC 3113.31(E)(3)(a).

[94]Trent v. Trent, 1999 WL 298073, *4 (Ohio Ct. App. 12th Dist. Preble County 1999); see also RC 3109.04(F)(1) for the best interest factors.

[95]But see Couch v. Harrison, 2001-Ohio-4199, 2001 WL 121108 (Ohio Ct. App. 12th Dist. Clermont County 2001).

[96]Trent v. Trent, 1999 WL 298073, *6 (Ohio Ct. App. 12th Dist. Preble County

tion order? Where a protection order is granted, must the court award only supervised visitation?

There is nothing in the statute or in the standard protection order forms that requires a court to include the minor child in the protection order granted to the petitioner. Where a court awards the respondent unsupervised visitation, it is unlikely that the court will impose safety precautions or restrictions on that visitation.

At least one Ohio court considered this issue. In *Sabur v. El-Zant*,[97] the petitioner appealed the granting of a protection order on the ground that the trial court failed to include the minor child in the protection order and awarded the respondent unsupervised visitation with his daughter. The appellate court reviewed the history between the parties and stated that, although there were two verbal incidents against the petitioner, she subsequently consented to a temporary visitation arrangement.

In light of the principle that a noncustodial parent's right of visitation is a natural right and should be denied only under extraordinary circumstances, and because the incidents of violence were not directed at the child, the Eighth District Court of Appeals concluded that the trial court did not abuse its discretion in failing to include the child in the protection order, in failing to impose any safety precautions for visitation, or in ordering unsupervised visitation.[98]

However, the dissent in *Sabur* would have terminated the father's visitation in order to protect the best interests of the child.[99] The dissenting justice reframed the issue, noting that, while there was no evidence that the father harmed his daughter, "I cannot agree that visitation with [father] would not be harmful to her."[100] The dissent reasoned that emotional abuse negatively impacts a child, relying on *Reese v. Reese*,[101] in which the Cuyahoga County Court of Appeals held that "[I]f there is clear and convincing evidence to show that visitation may present a significant risk of serious emotional or physical harm to the child, the court may deny visitation."[102] Clearly, one appellate justice has recognized that abuse to the other parent, even if verbal, directly and negatively impacts the child.[103]

1999).

[97]Sabur v. El-Zant, 1999 WL 652042 (Ohio Ct. App. 8th Dist. Cuyahoga County 1999).

[98]Sabur v. El-Zant, 1999 WL 652042, *2 (Ohio Ct. App. 8th Dist. Cuyahoga County 1999).

[99]Sabur v. El-Zant, 1999 WL 652042, *5 (Ohio Ct. App. 8th Dist. Cuyahoga County 1999).

[100]Sabur v. El-Zant, 1999 WL 652042, *4 (Ohio Ct. App. 8th Dist. Cuyahoga County 1999) (Blackmon, J., dissenting).

[101]Reese v. Reese, 1997 WL 272368 (Ohio Ct. App. 8th Dist. Cuyahoga County 1997).

[102]Sabur v. El-Zant, 1999 WL 652042, *4 (Ohio Ct. App. 8th Dist. Cuyahoga County 1999) (Blackmon, J., dissenting) (quoting Reese).

[103]See Text § 15:11, Impact of domestic violence on children; see also Jeffrey L. Edleson, Children's Witnessing of Adult Domestic Violence, 14 J. of Interpersonal Violence 839–70 (1999); see also 1999 S.B. 9, eff. 3-8-00, requiring the court to consider as an aggravating factor in determining the sentence of an offender convicted of domestic violence the fact that the offender committed the offense in the vicinity of the

Q & A: If placement of the children pursuant to RC 3113.31(E)(1)(d) is requested as part of a civil protection order, must the court show that the children's placement into the custody of one of the parties was in their best interests?

At least one Ohio court has answered this question in the negative. In *Couch v. Harrison*,[104] the respondent appealed the civil protection order and the court's award of the children's custody to the petitioner because the petitioner failed to present evidence showing such a placement was in the children's best interest pursuant to RC 3109.04.

The appellate court said the Legislature intended for civil protection orders to ensure the safety and protection of family and household members. "When faced with the reality of domestic violence, the trial court has an obligation to exercise its discretionary authority to respond to the immediate needs of the victim(s) and influence the behavior of the abuser."[105]

The court then determined that while an allocation of parental rights and responsibilities for children pursuant to a civil protection order "necessarily involves considerations of the best interest of the children, the statute does not specifically require the trial court to consider the 'best interest factors' used for creating or modifying a shared parenting plan, or determining companionship rights."[106] The court said that if the legislature wanted a court to consider the "best interest" factors of RC 3109.04(F)(1) or RC 3109.51(D), it would have said so explicitly. The Twelfth District Court of Appeals held that the civil domestic violence statute "demonstrates a clear and unambiguous legislative intent to enable the trial court to immediately provide for the temporary safety and protection of minor children."[107]

However, it is important to note that the court may have suggested a standard to be applied to cases where the children's placement is at issue. In *Harrison*, the court noted that where the minor child had been a victim of domestic violence, it was obvious that removal to the other parent's custody was in the best interest of the child. What is not as clear is whether the court would have taken the same stand as to the temporary safety and protection of the child if the child was not the victim of domestic violence.

Q & A: Must the court award visitation privileges to a respondent at the full hearing?

An Ohio court is not obligated to establish visitation rights for the respondent during the duration of the protection order; nor, for that matter, is the court obligated to award custody to one of the parties. Allocation of parental rights and responsibilities is just one of the

---

victim's child.

[104]Couch v. Harrison, 2001-Ohio-4199, 2001 WL 121108 (Ohio Ct. App. 12th Dist. Clermont County 2001).

[105]Couch v. Harrison, 2001-Ohio-4199, 2001 WL 121108, *3 (Ohio Ct. App. 12th Dist. Clermont County 2001) (citation omitted).

[106]Couch v. Harrison, 2001-Ohio-4199, 2001 WL 121108, *3 (Ohio Ct. App. 12th Dist. Clermont County 2001).

[107]See also Ashburn v. Roth, 2007-Ohio-2995, 2007 WL 1731426 (Ohio Ct. App. 12th Dist. Butler County 2007).

many remedies afforded the court to prevent violence within families.[108]

However, at least one Ohio court has determined that, since the trial court was vested with the authority to establish temporary custody and visitation, it must do so. In *Elkins v. Elkins*,[109] the Franklin County Court of Appeals found that the trial court failed to establish visitation privileges for the respondent-wife in a protection order action, but instead

> relegat[ed] that task to the Franklin County Children Services. In effect, the trial court's order places respondent at the mercy of Franklin County Children Services, requiring her first to request visitation rights from Franklin County Children Services and then, on failing to achieve the desired result with that entity, to approach the trial court for relief.

The court held that "[s]uch a procedure not only is convoluted, but fails to comply with the spirit of RC 3113.31(E)(1)(d), which authorizes the trial court to 'establish temporary visitation rights.' "[110]

In *Elkins*, the appellant also suggested that the court consider certain factors when deciding temporary custody in protection order cases. These factors include a history of the parties' physical custody of the children, status as homemaker, the young age of the children, and the children's need for a parent's care and attention. Although the appellate court determined that, absent a transcript, no error was evident on the record, these points or similar ones may be factored into a temporary custody determination.[111]

Q & A: Can an Ohio domestic relations court award visitation or restrict a parent's parenting time with a child by the issuance of a CPO where visitation was already decided in a prior court order issued by a court of another state?[112]

In *Ashburn v. Roth*,[113] the appellate court upheld the issuance of the CPO. The parties had separated and Appellee moved to Ohio where she resides and where she gave birth to the child and appellant remained in Illinois. Appellant had been abusive to her in Illinois and in Ohio where he has stalked appellee and threatened to kill her and kidnap the child. In 2003, appellant filed a paternity action in Illinois and the parties entered into a shared parenting agreement. Despite later motions to restrict appellant's access to the child, the Illinois court upheld the parties' shared parenting agreement and even provided him with more visitation.

In 2005, appellee filed for a CPO in Ohio because of appellant's intimidating behavior which had escalated since he has visited the

---

[108] RC 3113.31(E)(1)(d).

[109] Elkins v. Elkins, 1992 WL 180118, *3 (Ohio Ct. App. 10th Dist. Franklin County 1992).

[110] Elkins v. Elkins, 1992 WL 180118, *3 (Ohio Ct. App. 10th Dist. Franklin County 1992).

[111] See Elkins v. Elkins, 1992 WL 180118 (Ohio Ct. App. 10th Dist. Franklin County 1992).

[112] See also Text § 15:24, Other issues that impact custody and visitation awards.

[113] Ashburn v. Roth, 2007-Ohio-2995, 2007 WL 1731426 (Ohio Ct. App. 12th Dist. Butler County 2007).

child. The parties entered into a consent entry whereby appellee was named as a protected party and a visitation schedule was put in place. Appellant then filed a motion to set aside the CPO arguing that the court had no jurisdiction to modify his visitation with his daughter. The trial court overruled his motion and in a later decision amended the CPO to include the minor child as a protected party.

On appeal, appellant claimed that the Butler County Domestic Relations Court was without jurisdiction to modify his previously existing visitation order issued by an Illinois court. The Butler County Court of Appeals first determined that it did not have to rely on the previously existing Illinois court order because the UCCJEA[114] states that Ohio is the child's home state and has been so since her birth. The court also pointed out that even if the Illinois court orders were proper, the Ohio domestic relations court had the authority to issue an ex parte CPO. "The mere existence of visitation orders in another state does not form the basis upon which to deny a CPO when the petitioner is subject to a threat of violence."[115]

The Court then advanced public policy in its decision when it stated that "[n]ot only was it within the trial court's discretion to address Ashburn and Sophia's immediate need for protection, but it was the court's responsibility to issue an order ensuring their protection. While the CPO effectively restricted Roth's visitation with Sophia, the chief purpose in of the order was to protect the child. In fashioning such an order, the court acted within its discretion and fulfilled its duty to protect the citizens of the state. To hold that a domestic relations court cannot issue an order to protect its citizens when there is an existing visitation order from a foreign state is nonsensical. Such a holding would defeat the purpose of the domestic relations statute, which is to protect people from the harm."[116]

§ 12:16 Remedies—Protected party concerns[1]

Q & A: How can a child be protected from domestic violence?

A child may be joined as a party and named as the petitioner in the Petition for Protection Order.[2] Where a child is named as a petitioner in a domestic violence proceeding, proof of domestic violence must be presented to demonstrate that the child has been harmed by an act of domestic violence by the respondent.[3]

A child may also be named as a protected party in the petition and

---

[114]RC 3127.01 et seq.

[115]Ashburn v. Roth, 2007-Ohio-2995, 2007 WL 1731426, *3 (Ohio Ct. App. 12th Dist. Butler County 2007).

[116]Ashburn v. Roth, 2007-Ohio-2995, 2007 WL 1731426, *3 (Ohio Ct. App. 12th Dist. Butler County 2007).

[Section 12:16]

[1]See Text § 12:27, Conflicting protection orders; Text § 15:24, Other issues that impact custody and visitation awards.

[2]See Parrish v. Parrish, 146 Ohio App. 3d 640, 2000-Ohio-2693, 767 N.E.2d 1182 (4th Dist. Ross County 2000).

[3]See Parrish v. Parrish, 146 Ohio App. 3d 640, 2000-Ohio-2693, 767 N.E.2d 1182 (4th Dist. Ross County 2000); see also Text § 15:24, Other issues that impact custody and visitations awards; Carpeno v. Carpeno, 2005-Ohio-7046, 2005 WL 3610425 (Ohio

is protected by the terms of the civil protection order.[4] Where a child is included as a protected family member, he or she is protected from future domestic violence of the respondent.[5]

Additionally, a child may be named a protected party because a parent has filed a protection order for that child who was abused by the respondent and because that parent filed for the CPO, included him or herself as well. Unless proof of that abuse was found against the petitioner who filed for the order, the adult petitioner may be removed from the CPO, although the minor child will remain as a protected party.[6]

Q & A: Does Ohio's domestic violence statute permit a child to be a protected party on a civil protection order?

Ohio law permits victims of domestic violence to obtain protection orders for themselves. As petitioners, they may obtain protection orders on behalf of other family or household members.[7] The Supreme Court of Ohio's domestic violence forms allow for the inclusion of additional protected parties.[8] Most often, these protected parties are children in the household. In fact, RC 3113.31(O) specifically provides that "[n]othing in this section prohibits the domestic relations division of a court of common pleas in counties that have a domestic relations division or a court of common pleas in counties that do not have a domestic relations division from designating a minor child as a protected party on a protection order or consent agreement."

Q & A: Must a protected party be a recipient of an act of domestic violence by the respondent in order for that person to be included on a CPO as a protected party?

It depends. Some jurisdictions do not demand independent proof of domestic violence for a child to be included as a protected party. Other courts have determined that independent evidence of domestic violence towards a family or household member, other than a child of the relationship is necessary. Still other courts expect that evidence of domestic violence towards any protected party is necessary before inclusion of a family or household member is permitted as a protected party on a civil protection order.

Ct. App. 11th Dist. Lake County 2005); Dowhan v. Dowhan, 2012-Ohio-5830, 2012 WL 6114935 (Ohio Ct. App. 11th Dist. Lake County 2012).

[4]See Rush v. Rush, 1999 WL 1044482 (Ohio Ct. App. 8th Dist. Cuyahoga County 1999); see also Ashburn v. Roth, 2007-Ohio-2995, 2007 WL 1731426 (Ohio Ct. App. 12th Dist. Butler County 2007).

[5]See RC 3113.31(C).

[6]Bush v. Bush, 2015-Ohio-2017, 2015 WL 3385649 (Ohio Ct. App. 5th Dist. Licking County 2015); Albers v. Albers, 2012-Ohio-3838, 2012 WL 3637366 (Ohio Ct. App. 2d Dist. Greene County 2012) (where respondent was convicted of a sexually oriented offense against his daughter, court held that the other two minor children should be protected parties on the CPO, but that the mother who brought the action presented no evidence that she was in danger of domestic violence and thus, the court sustained the assignment of error to the extent that the CPO was modified to exclude her on the CPO).

[7]RC 3113.31(C).

[8]See Sup. R. Form 10.01-H to Sup. R. Form 10.01-J.

For example, in *Stark v. Stark*,[9] the petitioner obtained a protection order because of violence directed at her. At the full hearing, she also presented evidence that the minor child was fearful of his father. The trial court issued a protection order against appellant, protecting both appellee and the minor child. On appeal, the appellant challenged the issuance of the civil protection order as to the protected party. The appellate court did not differentiate between the victim and the protected party for purposes of the order, but it did determine that there was independent evidence to conclude that the minor child was a victim of domestic violence.

The underlying issue is whether the petitioner must present independent proof of domestic violence by the respondent against the protected party. Most experts in this area agree that the petitioner need only show, by a preponderance of the evidence, that she is in danger of future domestic violence or that the respondent committed acts of domestic violence against her. The child is a protected party because of his relationship to her. No independent proof of domestic violence toward the child need be presented.[10]

Similarly, in *Farris v. Kihm*,[11] the issue on appeal was whether the petitioner's wife was entitled to a civil protection order when she had not previously been a victim of an act of domestic violence by respondent and was not a family or household member of respondent. Pursuant to RC 3113.31(C), a petitioner may seek relief on his own behalf and on behalf of any other family or household member.

In that case, the petitioner and respondent were persons who had a child in common. Respondent had committed acts of domestic violence against the petitioner. Appellant argued that petitioner's wife did not qualify for relief under RC 3113.31, because she and petitioner's wife were not family or household members.

The appellate court rejected his argument, noting that petitioner had reason to fear for the safety of his wife. It reasoned that the petitioner and respondent were family or household members by virtue of their child in common. The court then stated that the petitioner proved that the respondent engaged in acts of domestic violence against the petitioner. Although the wife was not a petitioner, she was a party and RC 3113.31(C) permitted this petitioner to seek a protection order on behalf of his wife. Therefore, a party may benefit from a civil protection order even though she is not a family or household member of the named respondent.

The other issue presented was whether independent proof of acts of abuse committed towards the protected party by respondent was required. In this case, the court acknowledged that threats such as "I will kill you, bitch" while pounding on the door demonstrated acts of domestic violence against the protected party and justified the civil protection order.

---

[9]Stark v. Stark, 2002-Ohio-90, 2002 WL 109281 (Ohio Ct. App. 5th Dist. Delaware County 2002).

[10]But see Kandel v. Kandel, 2004-Ohio-4548, 2004 WL 1925690 (Ohio Ct. App. 5th Dist. Ashland County 2004).

[11]Farris v. Kihm, 2002-Ohio-2277, 2002 WL 940178 (Ohio Ct. App. 2d Dist. Miami County 2002).

The court concluded that "[t]he fact that a person who benefits from the coverage of a domestic violence civil protection order was not a victim of a predicate act of domestic violence which that relief requires, or even a family or household member of the named respondent, may seem to some to be overreaching. We are not of that view. When, as here, a third person is a family or household member of both, albeit for different reasons, and that third person was also a victim of domestic violence the respondent committed, extending the coverage of the resulting civil protection order to other members of the victim's household who are also vulnerable to abuse at the respondent's hands, and likely targets of such abuse, makes good sense."[12]

This court focused on the family or household relationships between the petitioner, the protected party, and the respondent, rather than on whether independent proof of domestic violence towards the protected party was required. In this case, the wife was accorded relief as a third party because the respondent had committed acts of domestic violence against the petitioner and because she was a victim of domestic violence committed by respondent. The court stated that when the victim and respondent are not members of the same family or household, "there is no right to relief under the statute unless the respondent has also committed an act of domestic violence against the petitioner."[13] Had petitioner's wife not been a victim of domestic violence committed by respondent, it is unclear whether the court would have extended relief to her, even if the petitioner had demonstrated domestic violence committed by the respondent. Had only the wife been victimized, no right to relief would exist.

On the other hand, more and more Ohio courts have determined that for a child or any other family member to be included as a protected party on a civil protection order, there must be proof of some actual abuse or some anticipated danger to that child by the respondent.[14] In *Kandel v. Kandel*,[15] the Ashland County Court of Appeals sustained appellant's assignment of error in which appellant

[12]Farris v. Kihm, 2002-Ohio-2277, 2002 WL 940178, *5 (Ohio Ct. App. 2d Dist. Miami County 2002). See also Wolfe v. Wolfe, 2014-Ohio-2159, 2014 WL 2156778 (Ohio Ct. App. 5th Dist. Stark County 2014) (since numerous acts of violence and threatening behavior (such as acts of seeing one's grandmother being choked or one's father pushed and assaulted) occurred when the children were present and caused a fear of imminent serious physical harm, it was not against the manifest weight of the evidence that the children should be included on the CPO).

[13]Farris v. Kihm, 2002-Ohio-2277, 2002 WL 940178, *3 (Ohio Ct. App. 2d Dist. Miami County 2002).

[14]See for example, M.C. v. B.K., 2015-Ohio-560, 2015 WL 628342 (Ohio Ct. App. 6th Dist. Sandusky County 2015) (reasoning that the child should remain as a protected party on the CPO because the child is an abused child under RC 2151.031(D) which includes any child who, because of the acts of his parents, guardian or custodian, suffers physical or mental injury that harms or threatens to harm the child's health or welfare). See also R.T. v. J.T., 2015-Ohio-4418, 2015 WL 6449294 (Ohio Ct. App. 9th Dist. Medina County 2015) (where father requested that the children be placed on the CPO as protected parties as a precautionary measure based on his belief that the anger could be directed at them if the other child was not in the home, the appellate court stated that the other children, not victims of the incident, would have had to witness the tea cup incident involving L.T. or expressed some fear of serious physical harm).

[15]Kandel v. Kandel, 2004-Ohio-4548, 2004 WL 1925690 (Ohio Ct. App. 5th Dist. Ashland County 2004). See also Albers v. Albers, 2012-Ohio-3838, 2012 WL 3637366

argued that the evidence did not support the inclusion of the minor son as a protected person to the civil protection order, noting that the son was not home at the time of the incident. The only testimony presented as to the child was by the mother who indicated that the child wished to be included on the civil protection order. Absent proof of some anticipated danger towards the child,[16] there was insufficient evidence presented to warrant the child being included as a protected person on the civil protection order.[17]

In *Lillard v. Allen*,[18] appellee sought a CPO for herself and the minor children because appellant slammed a car door on her foot, pushed her and threatened to bash her skull in. The appellate court reversed the CPO regarding the children, finding that the CPO was too broad by including the children in the order. The court reasoned that "[w]hile RC 3113.31 allows the trial court to extend coverage to household members who are not victims of a predicate act of domestic violence but instead may be 'vulnerable' to such abuse, we find no immediate or present danger to Ray's two children and find no evidence that the two children are in danger when they are with him. Because no evidence was presented to establish the need for a CPO protecting Ray's two minor children, we sustain Ray's second assignment of error."[19]

(Ohio Ct. App. 2d Dist. Greene County 2012) (see dissenting opinion comparing this case to Kandel); Luikart v. Shumate, 2003-Ohio-2130, 2003 WL 1961874 (Ohio Ct. App. 3d Dist. Marion County 2003) (where no evidence was presented to establish a need for the civil protection order protecting appellee's wife and children, the judgment as it relates to the protected parties must be reversed); Miller v. Francisco, 2003-Ohio-1978, 2003 WL 1904066 (Ohio Ct. App. 11th Dist. Lake County 2003) (overruled by, Davis v. DiNunzio, 2005-Ohio-2883, 2005 WL 1383975 (Ohio Ct. App. 11th Dist. Lake County 2005)); Osunde v. Ijeweme, 2013-Ohio-1207, 2013 WL 1286984 (Ohio Ct. App. 10th Dist. Franklin County 2013) (CPO extended to minor child where appellant was holding baby when he struck appellee.).

[16]See also Parrish v. Parrish, 146 Ohio App. 3d 640, 2000-Ohio-2693, 767 N.E.2d 1182 (4th Dist. Ross County 2000), citing Felton v. Felton, 79 Ohio St. 3d 34, 1997-Ohio-302, 679 N.E.2d 672 (1997) (the trial court must find that petitioner has shown, by a preponderance of the evidence, that the petitioner or the petitioner's family or household members are in danger of domestic violence).

[17]See also Wootten v. Culp, 2017-Ohio-665, 85 N.E.3d 198 (Ohio Ct. App. 4th Dist. Adams County 2017) (where there was no evidence presented that father ever harmed or threatened children and because appellee also testified that the children needed to see him, the trial court committed an abuse of discretion to include them on the CPO); Tyler v. Tyler, 2016-Ohio-7419, 2016 WL 6160139 (Ohio Ct. App. 2d Dist. Montgomery County 2016) (where there was no evidence presented that father committed acts of domestic violence against the children, the children should not have been included within the scope of the CPO).

[18]Lillard v. Allen, 2008-Ohio-3664, 2008 WL 2836879 (Ohio Ct. App. 8th Dist. Cuyahoga County 2008); Miller v. Francisco, 2003-Ohio-1978, 2003 WL 1904066 (Ohio Ct. App. 11th Dist. Lake County 2003) (overruled by, Davis v. DiNunzio, 2005-Ohio-2883, 2005 WL 1383975 (Ohio Ct. App. 11th Dist. Lake County 2005)).

[19]Lillard v. Allen, 2008-Ohio-3664, 2008 WL 2836879, *2 (Ohio Ct. App. 8th Dist. Cuyahoga County 2008); Moore v. Guyton, 2013-Ohio-143, 2013 WL 221515 (Ohio Ct. App. 3d Dist. Paulding County 2013) (no evidence presented to show that the children were in danger of domestic violence or that he made a threat of imminent physical harm against children). But see Wolfe v. Wolfe, 2014-Ohio-2159, 2014 WL 2156778 (Ohio Ct. App. 5th Dist. Stark County 2014) (sufficient evidence to establish that the children had a fear of imminent serious physical harm and should be protected parties on CPO where children were present during the incident and saw grandmother

Of interest is that one of the appellate judges dissented in part to the majority's modifying the CPO to exclude the two minor children. The judge found the reliance on *Luikart v. Shumate*,[20] to be misplaced. "The majority relies on the *Luikart* case to support its position that a failure to present evidence showing the need for a CPO for the children is dispositive. However, in *Luikart*, the children were not present during the violent incident involving the children's father and the mother's boyfriend. This is far different than the facts in the instant case where the children witnessed the violent act toward their mother, and their mother seeks a protective order for herself and the children. As the majority correctly notes, RC 3113.31 allows the trial court to extend coverage to household members who may be 'vulnerable' to such abuse. I would find no abuse of discretion in the trial court's including the children in the CPO."[21]

Similarly, in *Smith v. Burroughs*,[22] petitioner sought a protection order against her live-in boyfriend, based on a threat that "the only way that you are going to leave this house and going to leave me is going to be in a body bag." Petitioner's children were also included on the protection order.

In reversing that part of the CPO listing the children as protected parties, the Wyandot Court of Appeals held that "because a trial court cannot include a family member in a CPO when no direct evidence was presented indicating the family member was placed in fear of imminent, serious physical harm, it was plain error for the trial court to have included the children in the order when no evidence was even presented as to the children."[23] Therefore, the appellate court remanded the case to the trial court to exclude the minor children from the CPO.

However, there was a scathing dissent in this case. The dissenting judge stated that "[w]hile the evidence does not indicate that the minor children were actually present during the specific threats to

choked and father assaulted and where respondent stalked children at school and counseling provides); Martindale v. Martindale, 2017-Ohio-9266, ¶ 54, 102 N.E.3d 19 (Ohio Ct. App. 4th Dist. Athens County 2017) (while no evidence was presented as to direct violence towards the children, they were present and observed the physical injury and the altercation between the parties; relying on McBride v. McBride, 2012-Ohio-2146, 971 N.E.2d 1007 (Ohio Ct. App. 12th Dist. Butler County 2012), this decision is instructive for attorneys because it suggests that direct violence to a protected party may not be necessary when deciding whether to include them as protected parties as exposure to the violence may be, and often is, sufficient); Hyde v. Smith, 2015-Ohio-1701, 2015 WL 1976454 (Ohio Ct. App. 12th Dist. Butler County 2015) (finding that son should be included in CPO where petitioner testified that respondent had warned her that "if he wants to come to the house because I live there his son lives there and he wants to see us, he'll come," ¶ 31, and where he made threats to burn down the home in which son lived).

[20]Luikart v. Shumate, 2003-Ohio-2130, 2003 WL 1961874 (Ohio Ct. App. 3d Dist. Marion County 2003).

[21]Luikart v. Shumate, 2003-Ohio-2130, 2003 WL 1961874, *3 (Ohio Ct. App. 3d Dist. Marion County 2003); see also Carpeno v. Carpeno, 2005-Ohio-7046, 2005 WL 3610425 (Ohio Ct. App. 11th Dist. Lake County 2005).

[22]Smith v. Burroughs, 2010-Ohio-4806, 2010 WL 3861068 (Ohio Ct. App. 3d Dist. Wyandot County 2010).

[23]Smith v. Burroughs, 2010-Ohio-4806, 2010 WL 3861068, *5 (Ohio Ct. App. 3d Dist. Wyandot County 2010).

Alysha, the children did reside in the home where the threats took place and were commonly exposed to Richard's actions in general both at home and at school. It is also important to note that the specific threats by Richard in this case referred to Alysha's attempts to leave him at any time now or in the *future* and thereby posed an ongoing threat of physical harm or death subject to implementation at any time in the future when the children might be present."[24]

The dissent also stressed that the trial court was well within its discretion to determine that the children's safety was put at risk by Richard's threats against Alysha. "This determination by the trial court, again unobjected to by anyone, was entirely reasonable based on the record. In any event, it does not constitute an abuse of discretion and certainly does not in any way pose a 'challenge to the legitimacy of the judicial process' as required to support any application of the so-called 'civil plain error doctrine' by this court."[25] Indeed, in my view, the decision of the majority on this issue is itself an abuse of discretion."[26]

Unfortunately, these decisions still leave unresolved the issue of whether a child listed on a CPO as a protected party must be an actual victim of domestic violence as defined in R.C. 3113.31, or whether general exposure to the domestic violence in the household is reason enough to grant that child protected party status. Even if general exposure to domestic violence is sufficient, the type of direct evidence necessary to prevail is still unclear. The dissenting opinion in *Smith* underscores the importance of risk of potential harm to a child because of the other party's abusive behaviors to the non-offending parent.

Q & A: What if a civil protection order names a child as a protected party, but custody or visitation of that child was previously awarded by another court?

Pursuant to RC 3113.31(E)(1)(d), parental rights and responsibilities may be allocated to the petitioner unless another court has determined or is determining the allocation of parental rights and responsibilities for that child. Therefore, if juvenile court has already determined which parent has been designated the residential parent and legal custodian or if the court has granted a parent parenting time rights (visitation), the court with jurisdiction to issue civil protection orders has no jurisdiction to allocate parental rights and responsibilities.[27]

Adding a child as a protected party to a civil protection order and

---

[24]Smith v. Burroughs, 2010-Ohio-4806, 2010 WL 3861068, *5 (Ohio Ct. App. 3d Dist. Wyandot County 2010) (Shaw, J., dissenting).

[25]Smith v. Burroughs, 2010-Ohio-4806, 2010 WL 3861068, *5 (Ohio Ct. App. 3d Dist. Wyandot County 2010) (Shaw, J., dissenting); citing Ordean v. Ordean, 2007-Ohio-3979, 2007 WL 2231453, *14 (Ohio Ct. App. 3d Dist. Shelby County 2007), which in turn quoted the syllabus in Goldfuss v. Davidson, 79 Ohio St. 3d 116, 1997-Ohio-401, 679 N.E.2d 1099 (1997).

[26]Smith v. Burroughs, 2010-Ohio-4806, 2010 WL 3861068, *5 (Ohio Ct. App. 3d Dist. Wyandot County 2010) (Shaw, J., dissenting).

[27]Tischler v. Vahcic, 1995 WL 680928 (Ohio Ct. App. 8th Dist. Cuyahoga County 1995) (abrogated by, Felton v. Felton, 79 Ohio St. 3d 34, 1997-Ohio-302, 679 N.E.2d 672 (1997)); Stanton v. Guerrero, 1994 WL 472104 (Ohio Ct. App. 2d Dist. Montgomery County 1994); Stella v. Platz, 1999 WL 427672 (Ohio Ct. App. 4th Dist. Washington

restricting contact with the respondent and with whom the child has a court-ordered relationship, may limit the respondent's rights to visit with the parent or may effectively modify custody rights. In *Rush v. Rush*,[28] the Cuyahoga County Domestic Relations Court issued a civil protection order against petitioner's former husband and suspended his visitation with the minor children pending a case plan by Children and Family Services. The court further ordered the Department of Children and Family Services to make arrangements to have visitation supervised by a caseworker. The husband appealed the issuance of the civil protection order arguing, among other things, that the trial court lacked jurisdiction to modify his visitation rights because the Lake County Domestic Relations Court had already made a visitation order.

The Cuyahoga County Court of Appeals held that "because the Lake County Domestic Relations Court had determined or was determining husband's visitation rights, the Cuyahoga County Domestic Relations Court lacked the authority under RC 3113.31(E)(1)(d) to modify husband's visitation rights."[29] The court then pointed out that, had petitioner sustained her burden in order to obtain a civil protection order, "the court below would have had discretion to order husband to stay away from the family or household members named in the temporary order and this order would have necessarily restricted visitation by implication."[30]

The issue is whether a civil protection order that restricts contact between a respondent and the protected parties modifies the respondent's visitation or custody rights. Clearly, naming a child as a protected party for purposes of contact does not reallocate parental rights and responsibilities. The *Rush* case suggests that a court is permitted to exercise its discretion to include a child as a protected party on a civil protection order although it may restrict contact between the respondent and the protected party.

To suggest that a court lacks the authority to protect a protected party from future domestic violence is overly simplistic and bad public policy. Rather, in jurisdictions concerned with naming children as protected parties where the allocation of parental rights has been previously determined should consider options other than a blanket prohibition. Courts may require the moving party to file a motion to modify the allocation of parental rights and responsibilities at the

County 1999); but see Parker v. Jamison, 2003-Ohio-7295, 2003 WL 24135688 (Ohio Ct. App. 4th Dist. Scioto County 2003).

[28]Rush v. Rush, 1999 WL 1044482 (Ohio Ct. App. 8th Dist. Cuyahoga County 1999).

[29]Rush v. Rush, 1999 WL 1044482, *8 (Ohio Ct. App. 8th Dist. Cuyahoga County 1999).

[30]Rush v. Rush, 1999 WL 1044482, *8 (Ohio Ct. App. 8th Dist. Cuyahoga County 1999); but see McCue v. Marlin, 187 Ohio App. 3d 1, 2010-Ohio-1298, 930 N.E.2d 855 (7th Dist. Mahoning County 2010) (sustaining assignment of error deleting portions of a CPO such as contact, stay away orders, entering the residence, school etc., as infringing on the prior jurisdiction of juvenile court over parental rights and responsibilities under RC 3113.31(E)(1)(d)); see also State v. Price, 118 Ohio St. 3d 144, 2008-Ohio-1974, 886 N.E.2d 852 (2008) (holding that a divorce decree, allocating parental rights and responsibilities, may modify multiple aspects of the CPO beyond those provisions dealing with parental rights and visitation).

same time he or she files for the civil protection order. They may also permit the inclusion of a protected party and restrain a respondent from beating, threatening and abusing the protected party. They may name the protected party in the ex parte order and request independent proof of danger towards the protected party in order to include them in the final order. Finally, courts may also choose to restrict contact with a protected party for a short period of time.

Q & A: Can a trial court *sua sponte* amend a CPO to add a minor child as a protected party?

The Butler County Court of Appeals answered this is the affirmative in *Ashburn v. Roth*.[31] In that case, the appellant appealed the trial court decision to amend the CPO sua sponte to include the minor child as a protected party on the order on the ground that the amended CPO was issued in violation of Civ. R. 60(A). Civ. R. 60(A) provides that a court may correct clerical mistakes in its decisions either on its own initiative or by a motion filed by one of the parties. The appellate court held that the trial court did not abuse its discretion in amending the CPO and determined that, after reviewing the evidence and facts and circumstances of the case, the failure to initially include the minor child as a protected party on the order was a clerical mistake.

Q & A: Can a court include a child as a protected party in a CPO when another court is determining parental rights and responsibilities?[32]

Yes. In *Hyde v. Smith*,[33] petitioner sought a protection order on behalf of herself and named her parents and son as protected parties on the order. On appeal, appellee conceded that her parents should be removed from the CPO because no evidence was presented that they were family or household members. Their son was included within the ambit of the order. Appellant also claimed that the domestic relations courts erred by designating appellee as sole residential parent and legal custodian and awarding him supervised visitation when his motion for legal custody was pending in juvenile court.

The appellate court first noted that RC 3113.31(E)(1)(d) states that a domestic relations court has no jurisdiction to make such an award, including divisions of the same county court, if another court has determined or is determining parental rights and responsibilities.[34] That statute, however, has been limited to allow a domestic relations court "to make emergency decision, on an interim basis, to protect

---

[31]Ashburn v. Roth, 2007-Ohio-2995, 2007 WL 1731426 (Ohio Ct. App. 12th Dist. Butler County 2007).

[32]See also Text § 12:15; Text § 15:12.

[33]Hyde v. Smith, 2015-Ohio-1701, 2015 WL 1976454 (Ohio Ct. App. 12th Dist. Butler County 2015).

[34]Hyde v. Smith, 2015-Ohio-1701, 2015 WL 1976454, ¶ 36 (Ohio Ct. App. 12th Dist. Butler County 2015), quoting Couch v. Harrison, 2001-Ohio-4199, 2001 WL 121108 (Ohio Ct. App. 12th Dist. Clermont County 2001).

children from imminently dangerous situations."[35] That is exactly what the domestic relations court did here."[36]

The court reasoned that the CPO remained in effect for a date certain and that appellant's supervised visitation "was to continue until further order of court but not to extend past the Final CPO expiration date."[37] The court also noted that, 'in ruling on Smith's objections to the magistrate's decision, the domestic relations court found it was "not prohibited from making parenting orders at least until such time that the Juvenile Court initiates orders concerning [the child.]' "[38]

In that there were recent threats to break in and burn down the house in which appellee resided with her son, the trial court's decision was not unreasonable. In fact, the court also pointed out that appellant had only recently filed his motion in juvenile court and the court had yet to hold a hearing on the matter and questioned whether the "juvenile court was even in the process of 'determining the allocation' of such rights and responsibilities as that phrase is used in RC 3113. 31(E)(1)(d)."[39]

"Regardless, as the Ohio Supreme Court previously stated, the domestic relations court has extensive authority under RC 3113.31(E) 'to tailor the domestic violence protection order to the exact situation before it at the time' in order to carry out the legislative goals of protecting victims of domestic violence."[40] In overruling the assignment of error, the appellate court held that, based on the facts and circumstances of this case, "we find no error in the domestic relations court's decision to temporarily provide for the care of the parties' son until the juvenile court could initiate its own orders concerning the child."[41]

Of interest is that the appellate court did not set a specific expiration to be at the end of the five year period. Rather, the trial court determined that the CPO "was to continue* * *until further order of court, but not to extend past the Final CPO expiration date."[42] In doing so, the trial court acknowledged that the juvenile court had the final authority.

[35]Hyde v. Smith, 2015-Ohio-1701, 2015 WL 1976454, ¶ 36 (Ohio Ct. App. 12th Dist. Butler County 2015), quoting Hoyt v. Heindell, 191 Ohio App. 3d 373, 2010-Ohio-6058, ¶ 31, 946 N.E.2d 258 (11th Dist. Lake County 2010).

[36]Hyde v. Smith, 2015-Ohio-1701, 2015 WL 1976454, ¶ 36 (Ohio Ct. App. 12th Dist. Butler County 2015).

[37]Hyde v. Smith, 2015-Ohio-1701, 2015 WL 1976454, ¶ 37 (Ohio Ct. App. 12th Dist. Butler County 2015).

[38]Hyde v. Smith, 2015-Ohio-1701, 2015 WL 1976454, ¶ 37 (Ohio Ct. App. 12th Dist. Butler County 2015).

[39]Hyde v. Smith, 2015-Ohio-1701, 2015 WL 1976454, ¶ 38 (Ohio Ct. App. 12th Dist. Butler County 2015).

[40]Hyde v. Smith, 2015-Ohio-1701, 2015 WL 1976454, ¶ 39 (Ohio Ct. App. 12th Dist. Butler County 2015), quoting Felton v. Felton, 79 Ohio St. 3d 34, 38, 44-45, 1997-Ohio-302, 679 N.E.2d 672 (1997).

[41]Hyde v. Smith, 2015-Ohio-1701, 2015 WL 1976454, ¶ 39 (Ohio Ct. App. 12th Dist. Butler County 2015).

[42]Hyde v. Smith, 2015-Ohio-1701, 2015 WL 1976454, ¶ 42 (Ohio Ct. App. 12th Dist. Butler County 2015).

Additionally, it is worth noting that the Supreme Court of Ohio has adopted a Rule of Superintendence that encourages court to adopt a local rule to address conflicting orders and orders issued in both domestic relations and juvenile court when addressing parental rights and responsibilities.[43] At the very least, domestic relations courts and juvenile courts within a county should adopt policies and procedures to address the allocation of parental rights and responsibilities when both courts are involved; such as, where a CPO is issued and one of the parties seeks an order allocating parental rights and responsibilities.

Q & A: Where one party obtains a CPO from an ex-boyfriend, can that party include her new fiancé, his children and her parents who no longer resides with her in the house on the order?

According to *Cornell v. Hatfield*,[44] a "family or household member" is a term of art defined in RC 3113.31(A)(3). The operative question is whether the persons reside in the same house or have resided together in the past. In that Cornell was engaged and residing with Mallow, he may be considered a protected party on a CPO. Mallow's children who also reside in the house may be included as well. Lastly, Cornell's parents, who resided with Cornell in the past, can also be included in the order.

However, there is a second part to the question which is whether there was any abuse towards the protected parties. In this case, the court reasoned that Hatfield threatened to take out anyone in his way, which included Mallow and his children. Finally, Hatfield also made specific threats to Cornell's parents including a "graphic and disturbing" threat against her mother.[45] Since Cornell resides with Mallow and his children currently and lived with the others in the past, they are considered "family or household members."

The appellate court also relied on the reasoning set forth in *Woolum v. Woolum* in which the court stated "when issuing a civil protection order where domestic violence exists, the court is prompted to consider not only the petitioner but also the petitioner's family or household members."[46] Thus, the court overruled Hatfield's assignment of error.

§ 12:17 Remedies—Orders of support

Besides fear, one of the major reasons why abuse victims remain with or return to the abuser is economic dependence on the abuser.[1] Lack of economic resources fosters a feeling of financial stress on

---

[43]See Sup. R. 10.06.

[44]Cornell v. Hatfield, 2018-Ohio-549, 2018 WL 827136 (Ohio Ct. App. 12th Dist. Fayette County 2018).

[45]Cornell v. Hatfield, 2018-Ohio-549, 2018 WL 827136, ¶ 14 (Ohio Ct. App. 12th Dist. Fayette County 2018).

[46]Cornell v. Hatfield, 2018-Ohio-549, 2018 WL 827136, ¶ 14 (Ohio Ct. App. 12th Dist. Fayette County 2018), quoting Woolum v. Woolum, 131 Ohio App. 3d 818, 824, 723 N.E.2d 1135 (12th Dist. Preble County 1999).

[Section 12:17]

[1]Anne L. Ganley, Domestic Violence: The What, Why and Who, as Relevant to Civil Court Cases, in Domestic Violence in Civil Court Cases: A National Model for

abused victims which creates an untenable situation that often forces victims to return to their batterers.[2]

Ohio is one of a majority of states that has included both child support and spousal support relief as part of a civil protection order.[3]

In most instances, this relief is granted after the full hearing. It is unlikely that the court will grant support as part of the ex parte order because the respondent has not even been served at that point. Whenever it is granted, the respondent must be found to either have a duty to support the petitioner or family or household member or to customarily provide for or contribute to the support of the family or household member.[4]

Any child support order must comply with the procedural statutory provisions such as the child support guidelines,[5] health insurance,[6] and other procedural withholding or deduction requirements.[7] Counsel should check with the local jurisdiction for the inclusion of the appropriate forms.

An award of spousal support must comport with the statutory guidelines of RC 3105.18. It must be stressed that spousal support will not be granted if the respondent has no duty to support the petitioner.[8]

If the petition for a protection order is filed as a second count to a divorce complaint, the court may require that the petitioner file for temporary support in the divorce and limit the relief in the protection order to other issues. However, counsel for the petitioner should argue that spousal support must necessarily be awarded at the full hearing in order to provide financial alternatives to the petitioner so that he/she does not return to the abuser. It should also be noted that, in many jurisdictions, support hearings are not even scheduled until several months after the filing of the initial complaint.

Actual child support and spousal support payments must be made through the Child Support Enforcement Agency[9] and are governed by

---

Judicial Education 23, 33 (Jacqueline A. Agtuca et al. eds., 1992).

[2]Del Martin, Battered Wives 232 (1977); see also Lewis Okun, "Termination or Resumption of Cohabitation," in Women Battering Relationships: A Statistical Study in Coping with Family Violence, Research and Policy Perspectives 107, 116 (Gerald Hotaling et al. eds., 1988).

[3]RC 3113.31(E)(1)(e).

[4]RC 3113.31(E)(1)(e). But see Hayes v. Hayes, 251 N.J. Super. 160, 597 A.2d 567 (Ch. Div. 1991) (support provision in a domestic violence order is an emergency measure not intended as a substitute for an order issued in a more orderly and deliberative support proceeding where the court fully explores all factors).

[5]See RC 3113.215, RC 3113.31(K); see also Halley v. Ashley, 1997 WL 760662 (Ohio Ct. App. 9th Dist. Summit County 1997) (stressing that an award of child support is governed by the general child support statute).

[6]See RC 3113.217.

[7]See RC 3113.21.

[8]See RC 3113.31(E)(1)(e); see Coleman v. Coleman, 1996 WL 199165 (Ohio Ct. App. 6th Dist. Lucas County 1996), cause dismissed, 77 Ohio St. 3d 1432, 671 N.E.2d 264 (1996) (court awarded spousal support without documentation of financial demonstrating her financial need).

[9]See RC 3113.31(K).

the general child support statute.[10] All orders of support must be accompanied by a completed child support computation worksheet. The failure to include a completed worksheet may result in a reversal by an appellate court of that portion of the civil protection order.[11] However, counsel for the petitioner may also suggest creative options such as requiring the respondent to pay the current rent or mortgage, utilities, and/or other expenses in lieu of support. Clearly, if a respondent fails to comply, besides the filing of a motion to show cause, support can always be ordered or modified at a temporary support hearing in the underlying divorce, if applicable.

Q & A: Must the parties be married in order to take advantage of the support provisions?

No. RC 3113.31(E)(1)(e) clearly entitles married petitioners to both child support and spousal support, if they otherwise qualify. Obviously, there is a legal duty to support one's spouse. However, the statute also affords petitioners who are not married the opportunity to be granted support. The petitioner may be awarded support where the respondent customarily provides for or contributes to the support of the petitioner or family or household member. This arises from the habits or customs of the parties rather than by law or contract.

Q & A: Can support be ordered for the children of unmarried parties?

The same reasoning extends to the children of unmarried partners. Where the court has entered an order that a particular respondent is the father of the petitioner's child, that respondent has a legal duty to support the child. Where the parties cohabit and the respondent has provided support for the family, the respondent may have a duty to maintain this support, at least for the duration of the protection order.[12]

Q & A: When does an order of support terminate?

If support is awarded by the court in a protection order, the order shall terminate on the date that a court in an action for divorce, dissolution, or legal separation brought by either party issues a support order or on the date that a juvenile court issues a subsequent support order.[13] This order may be either a temporary or permanent support order issued pursuant to a motion in the divorce action or in an action for support in juvenile court.

Q & A: Is the child support enforcement agency considered "another court" for purposes of issuing a support order?

No. Even though the child support enforcement agency is authorized to issue both child support and spousal support orders under certain circumstances,[14] the agency is not a court. Any decision made by the administrative agency in regard to support does not affect the

---

[10]RC 3113.21.

[11]See Halley v. Ashley, 1997 WL 760662 (Ohio Ct. App. 9th Dist. Summit County 1997); see also Brown v. Brown, 2000 WL 271769 (Ohio Ct. App. 10th Dist. Franklin County 2000); Murral v. Thomson, 2004-Ohio-432, 2004 WL 193876 (Ohio Ct. App. 4th Dist. Hocking County 2004).

[12]See RC 3113.31(E)(1)(e).

[13]See RC 3113.31(E)(3)(b).

[14]RC 3113.21(B)(1)(a); see also RC 3113.212.

support awarded in a protection order until a judge in either domestic or juvenile court signs and journalizes the order.

Q & A: Can the court order the respondent to pay rent, mortgage, or housing costs as support?

Several state protection order statutes specifically authorize the payment of mortgage or rent costs as part of the civil protection order.[15]

Although Ohio's statute is silent on this issue, nothing in the statute prohibits a court from awarding this relief. It can be argued that rent and mortgage payments[16] may be considered maintenance and financial support for the victim of domestic violence. Such payments may be ordered in lieu of monetary support. It may also be considered as other relief under the statute's catchall provision.[17]

Case law in Ohio has authorized rent and mortgage payments as part of a civil protection order. In *Ruedele v. Kiefer*,[18] the court awarded mortgage payments to the petitioner for property jointly owned by the unmarried couple.

Q & A: Can the court order respondent to make utility payments?

Although not specifically authorized by statute, the same analysis as utilized above can be applied to the payment of utilities. The court may order a respondent to make utility payments under RC 3113.31(E)(1)(h). Such relief is considered "equitable and fair."

For example, in *Drake v. Drake*,[19] the court ordered the respondent to pay utilities. Similarly, in *Mugan v. Mugan*,[20] the New Jersey Superior Court awarded monetary relief which included the payment of utilities, reasoning that "the Legislature did not intend victims of domestic violence to be discouraged by a threat of financial distress."

Unfortunately, provisions in protection orders that require the respondent to pay the rent or utilities may also make the petitioner dependent on the respondent. This reliance on the respondent/batterer for the payment of bills makes the petitioner/victim "vulnerable to continued contact with the batterer, or hesitant to seek the batterer's removal from the residence in the first place."[21]

A failure by the respondent to pay the rent or utilities as ordered

[15] See, e.g., Mo. Ann. Stat. § 455.050(4) (Supp. 1993); N.J. Stat. Ann. § 2C:25-29(b)(8) (1993); see also National Council of Juvenile & Family Court Judges, Model Code on Domestic Violence § 306 (1994).

[16] See also Combs v. Combs, 2009-Ohio-1683, 2009 WL 943965 (Ohio Ct. App. 5th Dist. Stark County 2009) (noting that the CPO included a provision ordering respondent to pay the mortgage); Dilley v. Dilley, 2011-Ohio-2093, 2011 WL 1662359 (Ohio Ct. App. 11th Dist. Geauga County 2011) (noting that appellant agreed to make mortgage and insurance payments as a consequence of the CPO; however, any violation of that order must be resolved in the CPO case, not in the divorce).

[17] RC 3113.31(E)(1)(h).

[18] Ruedele v. Kiefer, 1993 WL 438787 (Ohio Ct. App. 5th Dist. Licking County 1993), cause dismissed, 68 Ohio St. 3d 1444, 626 N.E.2d 686 (1994).

[19] Drake v. Drake, 1985 WL 7861 (Ohio Ct. App. 2d Dist. Montgomery County 1985).

[20] Mugan v. Mugan, 231 N.J. Super. 31, 33, 555 A.2d 2 (App. Div. 1989).

[21] Catherine F. Klein & Leslye E. Orloff, Providing Legal Protection for Battered Women: An Analysis of State Statutes and Case Law, 21 Hofstra L. Rev. 801, 1002 (1993).

may also force contact between the parties. The petitioner may have to continually request payment from the respondent. The petitioner may also continue to seek redress from the court. Worse yet, the respondent may use the leverage of payment to control the petitioner. For example, if the petitioner does not do what the respondent wants, the respondent will withhold payment. Many petitioners will choose to give in rather than risk being evicted or having the utilities turned off.

Many of Ohio's 88 counties order a respondent to make rent and mortgage payments as well as utility payments in the civil protection order in lieu of monetary support or in addition to monetary support. Such relief should be requested by counsel for the petitioner at the full hearing. Counsel should have the petitioner prepared to testify as to his/her monthly expenses. An itemization of the amounts owed, as well as the name of each creditor and the process by which the creditor receives payment, must be addressed by the court.

In many cases, the actual procedure for payment of monthly bills should not be left up to the parties, especially where the violence has been severe and the petitioner has expressed fear of the respondent. Any order drafted in these cases must restrict contact between the parties. The respondent may be ordered to make the payment directly to the creditor or to mail the payment to the petitioner in advance of when the payment is due the creditor.

The Supreme Court standard forms specifically require that the respondent shall not interfere with the petitioner's right to occupy the residence through actions such as canceling the utilities[22] or insurance and interrupting telephone service, mail delivery, or the delivery of any other documents or items.[23] This mandate against such interference is provided for in both the ex parte orders and protection orders issued after the full hearing.

Q & A: Must the court award support at the full hearing?

Although the statute is silent as to this issue, practice in Ohio's eighty-eight counties suggests that child support will be awarded if requested by the petitioner. Unfortunately, that is not the case with spousal support, where local practice varies widely.

In Cuyahoga County, child support and spousal support are established at the full hearing unless the protection order is filed as a second count to a divorce. If there is a pending divorce, support will most often be set and determined in the underlying divorce action. The court's reasoning is that any support order in the protection order will terminate when the court makes another order in the divorce. Generally, the court would rather award support at a temporary hearing in the divorce, where the court has the ability to fully explore all

---

[22]But see Hamper v. Dobrski, 2015-Ohio-1381, 2015 WL 1593249 (Ohio Ct. App. 8th Dist. Cuyahoga County 2015) (finding respondent in contempt for turning off the utilities and mail service to the home but not expressly requiring him to make the payments); Lapsansky v. Lapsansky, 2000 WL 1114535 (Ohio Ct. App. 7th Dist. Columbiana County 2000) (respondent "had no obligation to pay appellant's bills at that time").

[23]See Sup. R. 10.01(C), Sup. R. Form 10.01-H to Sup. R. Form 10.01-J.

relevant factors affecting the calculation of a support obligation.[24] Counsel for the petitioner should always request that child support be granted at the full hearing, whether or not the protection order is a second count to a divorce action.

In many other counties, the court will grant both child and spousal support at the full hearing. In some counties, the court will only award child support if the parties are married. If the parties have a child in common and are living together, but paternity has not yet been established, no support will be awarded.[25] On the other hand, if evidence of paternity is presented to the court at the full hearing, the court may more readily award support. Arguably, a legal duty to support the child has been established.

Q & A: Can a trial court refuse to award child support at the full hearing if it has been requested by a petitioner?

The Hamilton County Court of Appeals addressed this issue in *Hayes v. Gibbs.*[26] The wife requested that her husband be required to pay child support as part of a CPO. The trial court granted the civil protection order but denied petitioner's request for child support stating that " 'a divorce action is the more appropriate forum to establish a child support order.' "[27]

On appeal, the wife argued that the trial court erred when it refused to entertain her request for child support on the merits. The appellate court reviewed the language of in RC 3113.31(E)(1)(e) which provides that a protection order may require a respondent to maintain support, if the respondent customarily provides for or contributes to the support of the family or household member, or if the respondent has a duty to support petitioner or the family or household member. Thus, a trial court has the authority to award child support as part of a civil protection order.

The appellate court noted that "[a]lthough the relief available under RC 3113.31 is somewhat similar to the relief available in a divorce action, 'it is directed to a different purpose.' . . . The purpose of a civil protection order issued pursuant to RC 3113.31 is to provide protection from domestic violence and, incidental to that relief, to provide for support and shelter. . . The relief available in an action for divorce provides for financial support in the context of that divorce."[28]

The Hamilton County Court of Appeals then reasoned that because RC 3113.31 explicitly provides that child support is one of the remedies available to a petitioner when a CPO is issued, "[t]he refusal of a trial court in this case to consider an award of child support on the basis that another forum, was "more appropriate" constituted an error. We hold that RC 3113.31 required the trial court to consider

[24]See also Hayes v. Hayes, 251 N.J. Super. 160, 597 A.2d 567 (Ch. Div. 1991).

[25]Franklin County has followed this approach.

[26]Hayes v. Gibbs, 2008-Ohio-1115, 2008 WL 682493 (Ohio Ct. App. 1st Dist. Hamilton County 2008).

[27]Hayes v. Gibbs, 2008-Ohio-1115, 2008 WL 682493 (Ohio Ct. App. 1st Dist. Hamilton County 2008).

[28]Hayes v. Gibbs, 2008-Ohio-1115, 2008 WL 682493, *1 (Ohio Ct. App. 1st Dist. Hamilton County 2008), quoting Thomas v. Thomas, 44 Ohio App. 3d 6, 8, 540 N.E.2d 745 (10th Dist. Franklin County 1988).

the merits of Hayes's request for child support. We point out that the trial court was not required to issue an order for child support because the statute is permissive, stating that support may be awarded. But the court was required to consider the merits of Hayes's request."[29]

Q & A: Does a parties' reconciliation after the issuance of a civil protection order invalidate the support order contained therein?

Although no Ohio court has addressed this issue, a Maryland court held that the parties' reconciliation nullified the support provision of the protective order. In *Torboli v. Torboli*,[30] the wife obtained the equivalent of an Ohio civil protection order. The defendant was ordered to pay support for his wife and daughter. Subsequently, the parties reconciled. About ten months after the order had expired, the wife petitioned the court to enforce the support provision. The court declined to enforce the provision, and the wife appealed.

In a case of first impression, the Maryland Court of Special Appeals held that the parties reconciliation nullified the requirement that the husband make support payments for his family. The court reasoned that the purpose of such an order is to provide financial support to those eligible for relief while the parties are separated. Since support is provided for food, clothing, and housing, "[i]t follows that if the parties reconcile during the period of the protective order they are no longer separated and this provision for financial support is no longer necessary."[31]

Q & A: Is a conviction for domestic violence and subsequent termination from employment considered a voluntary underemployment for purposes of a child support award?

In *Heropulos v. Heropulos*,[32] the trial court awarded the wife child support in the parties' divorce action. In his appeal, the husband argued that his termination as a police officer as a result of his domestic violence conviction did not constitute voluntary underemployment, and therefore the child support award was an abuse of discretion.

The Fifth District Court of Appeals affirmed and held that criminal conviction and subsequent incarceration are voluntary acts and are not beyond the control of a child support obligor.[33] Relying on unreported cases from the same appellate district, the court held the defendant's conviction for domestic violence, jail sentence, and termination from his employment due to his conviction were voluntary acts. Therefore, imputing income to the defendant for the purposes of child support because of his voluntary underemployment was not an abuse of discretion.

---

[29]Hayes v. Gibbs, 2008-Ohio-1115, 2008 WL 682493, *1 (Ohio Ct. App. 1st Dist. Hamilton County 2008).

[30]Torboli v. Torboli, 127 Md. App. 666, 736 A.2d 400 (1999), aff'd on other grounds, 365 Md. 52, 775 A.2d 1207 (2001).

[31]Torboli v. Torboli, 127 Md. App. 666, 677, 736 A.2d 400 (1999), aff'd on other grounds, 365 Md. 52, 775 A.2d 1207 (2001).

[32]Heropulos v. Heropulos, 2000 WL 700285 (Ohio Ct. App. 5th Dist. Stark County 2000).

[33]Heropulos v. Heropulos, 2000 WL 700285, *2 (Ohio Ct. App. 5th Dist. Stark County 2000).

§ 12:18 Remedies—Counseling

Counseling is another remedy that may be considered by the court after the full hearing. By statute, the court may require the respondent,[1] petitioner, victim of domestic violence (if different from the petitioner), or any combination of those persons to seek counseling.[2]

The court should not order general counseling for the respondent and/or marriage or family counseling for the parties because such relief does not ameliorate the domestic violence. In fact, recent studies have found that the civil protection order contempt rate is twice as high when the parties are ordered into family counseling as opposed to individual counseling for the batterer.[3]

Only counseling specific to the issue of domestic violence offers the respondent a chance at rehabilitation. The National Institute of Justice instituted a study which demonstrated that "mandatory counseling that is specifically designed to treat domestic violence can teach some batterers non-abusive ways of relating to their partner."[4]

It should be noted that batterers' treatment is not expected to work with all who attend. To that end, courts need to recognize that batterers' treatment programs are but one of the many options available to the court to deter domestic violence.

The primary problems with court-ordered counseling for the respondent are compliance by the respondent and the respondent's unwillingness to seek counseling. Although a contempt action is available to enforce the court order,[5] batterers are hardly willing candidates for therapy. "Practically speaking, the success of such an order is dependent upon the party's voluntary cooperation with the therapist."[6]

Additionally, court-ordered programs that are devoid of monitoring systems are ineffective tools for intervention. Absent a structured monitoring system, the courts should, for example, require written notification by the counselor that the respondent is attending the counseling appointments.

It is well settled that substance abuse counseling may complement batterers' treatment but should not be ordered in lieu of batterers' treatment.[7] However, there is sufficient research that indicates that

---

[Section 12:18]

[1]See Siouffi v. Siouffi, 1998 WL 879255 (Ohio Ct. App. 2d Dist. Montgomery County 1998); Strong v. Bauman, 1999 WL 317432 (Ohio Ct. App. 2d Dist. Montgomery County 1999).

[2]RC 3113.31(E)(1)(f).

[3]Catherine F. Klein & Leslye E. Orloff, Providing Legal Protection for Battered Women: An Analysis of State Statutes and Case Law, 21 Hofstra L. Rev. 801, 948 (1993); see also Task Force on Racial and Ethnic Bias and Task Force on Gender Bias in the Courts, District of Columbia Courts, Final Report, 146, app. H at 20 (May 1992).

[4]Peter Finn & Sarah Colson, National Institute of Justice, Civil Protection Orders: Legislation, Current Court Practice and Enforcement 44 (1990).

[5]See RC 3113.31(L).

[6]Michael A. Partlow, Baldwin's Ohio Practice, Domestic Relations Law § 5.13 (1997).

[7]See National Council of Juvenile & Family Court Judges, Courts and Communi-

substance abuse does not cause domestic violence.[8] If the substance abuse is eliminated, the result is still a batterer, only a sober batterer. Stopping the alcohol or drugs does not necessarily stop the abuse.[9] It must be understood that the battering is a separate problem from the alcohol or drug abuse.

State v. Sutley[10] is an example of an Ohio case in which the appellate court determined that the substance abuse treatment ordered as a condition of bail was inappropriate and unreasonable as it was only "remotely related" to the domestic violence crime with which the defendant was charged. The court found that this treatment would not be effective in the rehabilitation of the defendant.

This case highlights the need for any counseling or treatment ordered by the court for the batterer to meet appropriate criteria and standards. The Ohio Domestic Violence Network introduced certain criteria and certification standards for batterers' programs. Certified programs for batterers' intervention must be set up across Ohio. Sadly, there is a dearth of such programs in most Ohio counties.[11]

However, it is widely agreed by the domestic violence experts and courts alike that all court-ordered programs should share the following goals:

(1) to increase the offender's responsibility for the behavior;
(2) to develop behavioral alternatives to battering;
(3) to increase constructive expression of emotions and enhance listening skills and anger control;
(4) to decrease isolation and develop personal support systems;
(5) to decrease dependency on and control of the relationship; and
(6) to increase the batterer's understanding of the family and the dynamics of domestic violence.[12]

Case law around the country reflects this trend toward court-ordered batterers' treatment. Courts have ordered that batterers obtain domestic violence counseling.[13] Other courts have used batterers' treatment programs to elicit information about the batterers such as risk assessments regarding lethality and the probability of future

---

ties: Confronting Violence in the Family, State Justice Institute Conference, 31 (1993).

[8]Anne L. Ganley, Domestic Violence: The What, Why and Who, as Relevant to Civil Court Cases in Domestic Violence in Civil Court Cases: A National Model for Judicial Education 32 (Jacqueline A. Agtuca et al. eds., 1992).

[9]See National Council of Juvenile & Family Court Judges, Courts and Communities: Confronting Violence in the Family, State Justice Institute Conference, 18 (1993).

[10]State v. Sutley, 1990 WL 208811 (Ohio Ct. App. 11th Dist. Ashtabula County 1990).

[11]Contact Ohio Domestic Violence Network, 4041 North High St., Ste 400, Columbus, OH 43214, 1-800-934-9840, for a listing of certified batters' intervention programs and certification standards.

[12]National Council of Juvenile & Family Court Judges, Courts and Communities: Confronting Violence in the Family, State Justice Institute Conference, 31 (1993).

[13]See, e.g., West v. West, 1994 WL 680156 (Ohio Ct. App. 2d Dist. Montgomery County 1994); Cosme v. Figueroa, 258 N.J. Super. 333, 609 A.2d 523 (Ch. Div. 1992).

violence.[14] Still other courts have ordered batterers into treatment in order to obtain psychiatric examinations.[15]

Q & A: Are all batterers good candidates for batterers' intervention and treatment?

Absolutely not. Just as batterers' treatment will not work for all who attend, it is not an option for all batterers. Before ordering batterers into treatment for domestic violence, the court should do the following:

(1) assess the respondent's suitability for domestic violence treatment including the respondent's dangerous propensities, the motivation for change, and the safety needs of the victim;
(2) ensure that the victim's safety is addressed by developing a safety plan;
(3) determine whether an appropriate batterers' treatment program exists in the community;
(4) ensure that there will be adequate monitoring of the respondent's progress in the counseling program; and
(5) verify that the criminal contempt mechanism is in place for a violation of a civil protection order if there is a new incident of battering or the respondent is not performing satisfactorily in the program.[16]

Q & A: How effective is batterers' treatment?

Very little is really known about the effectiveness of the various treatment programs in preventing future domestic violence. Both attorneys and courts should be aware that domestic violence experts stress that domestic violence represents a long-standing behavioral pattern that is not readily changed.[17] In fact, studies suggest that counseling programs for batterers have a thirty-three to fifty percent dropout rate.[18]

Some studies demonstrate, however, that most men who complete treatment are nonviolent during the following year.[19] Men who drop out of treatment are significantly more likely to continue their violence than men who complete treatment.[20]

The most interesting results come from a Duluth study which indicates that "abusers who have been involved with the courts were

---

[14]See Cosme v. Figueroa, 258 N.J. Super. 333, 609 A.2d 523 (Ch. Div. 1992).

[15]See Agnew v. Campbell, 1990 WL 188723 (Minn. Ct. App. 1990); Katz v. Katz, 97 A.D.2d 398, 467 N.Y.S.2d 223 (2d Dep't 1983).

[16]Catherine F. Klein & Leslye E. Orloff, Providing Legal Protection for Battered Women: An Analysis of State Statutes and Case Law, 21 Hofstra L. Rev. 801, 947 (1993).

[17]See Lenore E. Walker & Angela Browne, Gender and Victimization by Inmates, 53 J. Personality 179, 192 (1988).

[18]See Edward Gondolf, Evaluating Programs for Men Who Batter: Problems and Prospects, 2 J. Fam. Violence 95, 98 (1978); L. Kevin Hamberger & James Hastings, Characteristics of Spouse Abuse: Predictors of Treatment Acceptance, 1 J. Interpersonal Violence 363–73 (1986).

[19]R. M. Tolman & L. W. Bennett, A Review of Quantitative Research on Men Who Batter, 1 J. Interpersonal Violence 87–110 (1990).

[20]L. Kevin Hamberger & James Hastings, Characteristics of Spouse Abuse: Predictors of Treatment Acceptance, 1 J. Interpersonal Violence 363–73 (1986).

significantly less likely to have been violent than other abusers, leading the researchers to conclude that 'over a longer period of time the possibility of new court involvement becomes the strongest deterrent to further violence.' "[21]

Q & A: How have Ohio courts approached batterers' treatment?

In most court jurisdictions, court-ordered batterers' intervention is mandated in criminal domestic violence cases. Completion of batterers' treatment is one of the most utilized sentencing alternatives.

Unfortunately, the same cannot be said in the civil protection order context. Although batterers' treatment is permitted by statute, it is rarely used as an option by the court.[22] When it is used as a remedy by the court, the order should contain the name of the agency or therapist that is to provide the counseling. Additionally, the court must provide both a mechanism to review compliance and consistent sanctions for noncompliance.

The Supreme Court standard forms now provide specific provisions regarding the nature of this relief. The standard petition includes a provision for the petitioner to request that the respondent be required to complete batterer counseling, substance abuse counseling, or other counseling as determined necessary by the court.[23]

Additionally, the standard forms indicate that each protection order issued after the full hearing contains a provision that requires the respondent to complete a specific program. The standard order further requires the respondent to initiate this contact. It requests the counseling program to report back to the court if the respondent fails to attend the initial appointment. It also requests that the program complete a written report when the respondent completes the program. The most important provision is the monitoring provision that establishes a specific date for the court to review the respondent's compliance with the counseling order.[24]

The Supreme Court committee which introduced the standard forms recognized the importance of noting the relief available to the petitioner with specificity. Rather than generalizing, the committee believed that a thorough explanation of the relief available would serve as an educational tool for the parties, the attorneys, and the court.

Q & A: Is treatment available for the victim of domestic violence?

Victims of domestic violence can achieve success from counseling designed at helping them both understand and break the cycle of violence. Such treatment should be done outside of the courtroom and away from the batterer. Treatment for victims should not be manda-

---

[21]National Council of Juvenile & Family Court Judges, Courts and Communities: Confronting Violence in the Family, State Justice Institute Conference, 32 (1993).

[22]But see Siouffi v. Siouffi, 1998 WL 879255 (Ohio Ct. App. 2d Dist. Montgomery County 1998). See also Strong v. Bauman, 1999 WL 317432 (Ohio Ct. App. 2d Dist. Montgomery County 1999) (ordering defendant to attend "The Batterer's Group" program).

[23]See Sup. R. 10.01(B), Sup. R. Form 10.01-D.

[24]See Sup. R. 10.01(C), Sup. R. Form 10.01-I, Sup. R. Form 10.01-J.

tory, and they should never be ordered into treatment programs against their wishes. The National Institute of Justice Civil Protection Order study states:

> Requiring the victim to enter counseling may put her in increased jeopardy by suggesting to the batterer that he is not responsible for his violence and thereby giving him an excuse to continue his abuse. Couples' counseling improperly conducted may have the same effect; furthermore, it may create a setting in which the victim is at an inherent disadvantage given her fear of the batterer.[25]

§ 12:19 Remedies—Orders to refrain from entering separate residence, school, or place of employment

A petitioner may also be granted a specific order for the respondent to refrain from entering the victim's residence,[1] school, place of employment, or business.[2] Because the legislature has also authorized the court to issue or approve any order designed to bring about a cessation of violence,[3] the court also has the authority to order the respondent not to contact or communicate with the petitioner.

The Supreme Court standard civil protection order forms provide specific detail, which strengthens the intent and substance of the order. For example, the protection orders contain provisions specifically requiring the respondent to stay away from the petitioner or family or household member. In fact, the protection order forms specify a distance within which a respondent must not be present[4] and further provide that the respondent refrain from entering any place where the family member may be found, including the buildings, grounds, and parking lots of their residences, schools, businesses, places of employment, day care centers, and baby sitters.[5] The standard protection order forms also instruct the respondent that, if he/she accidentally comes in contact with the family or household member in any public or private place, he/she must depart immediately.[6]

Moreover, the recently adopted standard forms include specific types of contact or communication that are forbidden. For example, the respondent shall not initiate any contact, including telephone, e-mail, fax, and voice mail at any of the locations stated in the order.[7]

This approach offers the petitioner the best protection because it

---

[25]Peter Finn & Sarah Colson, National Institute of Justice, Civil Protection Orders: Legislation, Current Court Practice and Enforcement 44 (1990).

[Section 12:19]

[1]See City of Xenia v. Berry, 1994 WL 12494 (Ohio Ct. App. 2d Dist. Greene County 1994) (discussing the term "residence" for purposes of protection order).

[2]RC 3113.31(E)(1)(g).

[3]RC 3113.31(E)(1).

[4]See, e.g., State v. Ball, 2001 WL 468383 (Ohio Ct. App. 2d Dist. Montgomery County 2001) (discussing how to prove that a person subject to a protection order violated the order by being within the proscribed distance).

[5]See also Jenkins v. Douglas, 2007-Ohio-1909, 2007 WL 1175228 (Ohio Ct. App. 3d Dist. Marion County 2007) (SCPO restraining respondent from contacting petitioner and the workers on the property owned by petitioner was upheld).

[6]See Sup. R. 10.01(C), Sup. R. Form 10.01-H to Sup. R. Form 10.01-J.

[7]Sup. R. 10.01(C), Sup. R. Form 10.01-H to Sup. R. Form 10.01-J; see also State

clearly and explicitly precludes all communication between the parties. Each order should be specifically tailored to fit the individual victim's circumstances. All options must be left open to afford the victim the greatest possible protection from the respondent.

If the protection order leaves open any avenue for contact and/or communication, the respondent may often use it to exert control over the petitioner and avoid compliance with the order.[8] Specific terms in a civil protection order instruct respondents that they may best avoid future court proceedings for contempt if they have absolutely no contact with the petitioner.

On the other hand, protection orders that provide exceptions for contact regarding the children may create problems. For example, in *State v. Lundberg*,[9] the court granted each party a protection order but provided an exception permitting the parties to communicate regarding their children.[10] Each provided contradictory testimony. The appellate court affirmed the trial court decision noting that it was in the best position to assess the credibility of the parties.

Also, police may be reluctant to protect petitioners when an order is too vague. It is far too easy for law enforcement officials to argue that they are unable to enforce the order if the specific behavior is not proscribed in the protection order. The more specific the order, the more effectively it will be enforced by law enforcement agencies. Respondents will have a clearer understanding of what is expected of them. Petitioners will be further protected from future abuse, threats, and harassment.

Q & A: Where a CPO prohibits a respondent from coming within 100 feet of his wife, does a subsequent visitation order modify the prior CPO?

At least one Ohio court considered this issue in the negative. In *City of Toledo v. Eissa*,[11] the domestic relations court granted appellant a visitation order, which set forth conditions for when appellant picked up the children. A previously issued CPO prohibited the appellant from coming within 100 feet of his wife. In a subsequent divorce action, the trial court granted visitation and ordered the wife to stay in the residence when appellant picked up the children. The appellant was subsequently charged with violating a CPO by being within 100 feet of his wife when he exercised his visitation.

v. Calhoun, 2008-Ohio-265, 2008 WL 204674 (Ohio Ct. App. 2d Dist. Montgomery County 2008).

[8] Catherine F. Klein & Leslye E. Orloff, Providing Legal Protection for Battered Women: An Analysis of State Statutes and Case Law, 21 Hofstra L. Rev. 801, 928 (1993).

[9] State v. Lundberg, 2002-Ohio-1811, 2002 WL 506439 (Ohio Ct. App. 2d Dist. Montgomery County 2002).

[10] See Text § 12:27, Conflicting protection orders; see State v. Price, 2006-Ohio-3856, 2006 WL 2105855 (Ohio Ct. App. 2d Dist. Montgomery County 2006), judgment rev'd, 118 Ohio St. 3d 144, 2008-Ohio-1974, 886 N.E.2d 852 (2008) (dissenting opinion and domestic relations courts' conflicting orders); Markowitz v. Markowitz, 2006-Ohio-5932, 2006 WL 3234010 (Ohio Ct. App. 8th Dist. Cuyahoga County 2006) (discussion on inconsistent court orders).

[11] City of Toledo v. Eissa, 2003-Ohio-3425, 2003 WL 21489426 (Ohio Ct. App. 6th Dist. Lucas County 2003); see also State v. Price, 118 Ohio St. 3d 144, 2008-Ohio-1974, 886 N.E.2d 852 (2008); Text § 12:23, Duration of a civil protection order; Text § 12:27, Conflicting protection orders.

On appeal from his conviction, appellant argued that the visitation order entered in the divorce modified the previously issued CPO. The Lucas County Court of Appeals noted that the CPO contained language providing that visitation orders do not permit a violation of the requirement that appellant stay 100 feet away from the wife on the grounds of her premises. In affirming his conviction, the appellate court first determined that the subsequent visitation order did not modify the prior CPO. The court then held that appellant knew of the terms of the CPO and he knew of his risk of arrest if he disregarded the terms of the order. When he entered on the grounds of his wife's apartment within 100 feet of his wife, he displayed a heedless indifference to the consequences of his actions.[12]

Q & A: How should courts address the issues raised in the standard protection order forms?[13]

The goal of the protection order forms is to provide uniformity among Ohio's eighty-eight counties regarding the nature of the relief available. Although it is always important to check local practice in the given jurisdiction, the relief available should not vary from jurisdiction to jurisdiction, and all courts should craft substantially similar orders. Of significance is that the forms, as adopted, encourage the protection order to follow the victim rather than be restricted to a specific residence.

Since the adoption of the domestic violence forms, courts have begun to realize the authority they have in crafting orders that provide protection[14] and increase enforcement. For example, many courts now grant orders that prohibit others, acting on behalf of the respondent, from contacting the petitioner.[15] Where this type of order is drafted, the names of the individuals should be included in the order. The standard protection orders also contain a provision restraining a respondent from causing or encouraging any person to do any act prohibited by the order.[16]

Where the petitioner is residing at a confidential location, an order should be crafted that prohibits a respondent from attempting to discover the petitioner's whereabouts and from enlisting others in

[12]City of Toledo v. Eissa, 2003-Ohio-3425, 2003 WL 21489426 (Ohio Ct. App. 6th Dist. Lucas County 2003); see also State v. Stoner, 2009-Ohio-2073, 2009 WL 1174942 (Ohio Ct. App. 2d Dist. Clark County 2009) (discussing measurements and distance of 500 feet); but see State v. Ealy, 2006-Ohio-414, 2006 WL 235043 (Ohio Ct. App. 2d Dist. Montgomery County 2006) (holding that a protection order issued under RC 2919.26 or RC 3113.31 that prohibits contact does not necessarily conflict with a protection order that also permits contact for purposes of parenting time provisions under RC 3113.31(E)(1)(d)).

[13]See Wilson v. Wilson, 134 N.C. App. 642, 518 S.E.2d 255 (1999) (cautions judges in completing the standard domestic violence forms).

[14]See also Markowitz v. Markowitz, 2006-Ohio-5932, 2006 WL 3234010 (Ohio Ct. App. 8th Dist. Cuyahoga County 2006).

[15]See also Nechay v. Nechay, 685 A.2d 377 (Del. Fam. Ct. 1995).

[16]See Sup. R. 10.01(C), Sup. R. Form 10.01-H to Sup. R. Form 10.01-J. See also Nechay v. Nechay, 685 A.2d 377 (Del. Fam. Ct. 1995); Wood v. Wood, 284 Ill. App. 3d 718, 219 Ill. Dec. 877, 672 N.E.2d 385 (4th Dist. 1996). See also State v. Kidder, 150 N.H. 600, 843 A.2d 312 (2004), as modified on denial of reconsideration, (Mar. 24, 2004) (defendant was found to have violated a protection order where he knowingly contacted the unrepresented complainant through his attorney).

locating the petitioner. Orders are routinely granted that prohibit a respondent from being around the petitioner and that provide a minimum distance within which a respondent must not intrude.[17] Definition of the distance in yards and feet enables the police to effectively enforce such orders.[18]

In *State v. Sutley*,[19] the trial court ordered the respondent to stay away from the petitioner, her family members, and the quadrant of the city where the petitioner resided. The appellate court held that this type of order did not violate the respondent's freedom of association rights where the restrictions related to his offenses and would help ensure future compliance with the court order.

Q & A: Do the terms of a CPO prohibiting a respondent from being within a certain distance of petitioner's premises mean that a respondent may violate the order for being around her premises even if she is not home?

This issue was raised in *State v. Ball*.[20] In that case, appellant was stopped by a police officer after driving by petitioner's house where the CPO prohibited respondent from being within 500 yards of petitioner or from entering any place where petitioner could be found. At the time respondent drove by, petitioner was not home and respondent did not enter her residence or come within 500 yards of her. The officer measured the distance and found she was within 374 feet of petitioner's residence. Respondent was then charged with violating the CPO under RC 2919.27 and subsequently convicted.

On appeal, he argued that the CPO (condition number six as set forth in Sup. R. Form 10.01-I) did not state that he was prohibited from driving his car within 500 yards of petitioner's residence when she was not home. The State responded that the plain language of the condition required him to stay 500 yards away from petitioner's residence regardless of whether she was home.

The appellate court found the appellant's reading of the disputed language contained in the CPO to be the most reasonable. The court reasoned that the first sentence requires respondent to stay away from the family members named in this order. The second sentence of the "stay away" requirement states that "respondent shall not be present within 500 yards (distance) of them, and shall refrain from entering any place where they may be found." This imposed two specific obligations on respondent: (1) not to come within 500 yards of petitioner; and (2) not to enter any place where she may be found.[21]

It is the third sentence that creates some ambiguity. The third sentence may provide specific places that a respondent may not enter.

[17]City of Toledo v. Eissa, 2003-Ohio-3425, 2003 WL 21489426 (Ohio Ct. App. 6th Dist. Lucas County 2003).

[18]See, e.g., State v. Ball, 2001 WL 468383 (Ohio Ct. App. 2d Dist. Montgomery County 2001). But see State v. Ball, 2006-Ohio-980, 2006 WL 515514 (Ohio Ct. App. 2d Dist. Montgomery County 2006).

[19]State v. Sutley, 1990 WL 208811 (Ohio Ct. App. 11th Dist. Ashtabula County 1990); see also Benson v. Muscari, 172 Vt. 1, 769 A.2d 1291 (2001).

[20]State v. Ball, 2006-Ohio-980, 2006 WL 515514 (Ohio Ct. App. 2d Dist. Montgomery County 2006).

[21]State v. Ball, 2006-Ohio-980, 2006 WL 515514, *2 (Ohio Ct. App. 2d Dist. Montgomery County 2006).

On the other hand, the third sentence could also clarify "the first half of sentence two, which requires Ball to stay away from Estelle by prohibiting him from coming within 500 yards of her."[22] Or the third sentence may be intended to identify places respondent must stay 500 yards away from regardless of whether petitioner is present.

The Court reasoned that the second sentence could have included the following: that "Respondent shall not be present within 500 yards of them *or any place where they may be found* and shall refrain from entering any place where they may be found," which if added, would have clearly obligated the respondent to stay 500 yards away from petitioner even when she was not home. Because this language was not added to the forms or to the order, the Court concluded that appellant's act of driving within the vicinity of the petitioner when she was not home did not violate the terms of the CPO. The court reversed his conviction and discharged him from any criminal liability.

The Montgomery County Court of Appeals also responded to the State's argument that, by allowing appellant to come within 500 yards of her residence when she is not present will "enable him to 'harass' her by lurking in front of her house every day and fleeing immediately upon her return home."[23] However, the Court noted that appellant's conduct would then violate the first condition of the order. Thus, no loophole was created by their interpretation, but if there was a problem, "it would lie not in our interpretation, but in the drafting of the fifth [it is the sixth condition in Sup. R. Form 10.01-I] condition."[24]

Q & A: When the CPO contains a restriction restraining a respondent from being within 500 feet of the petitioner, must the court also craft other terms to ensure that the respondent not violate the order where the parties live 6 houses apart?

Yes. In *Sistek v. Grendence*,[25] appellant appealed the issuance of the CPO, contending, among other things that there was no nexus between his conduct and some of the restrictions. In addressing the restrictions, the appellate court discussed the restriction, restraining appellant from being within 500 feet of petitioner in light of the fact that the parties live only 6 houses apart.

The appellate court first noted that the restriction was a boilerplate form restriction. Because the evidence at the hearing established that the parties lived in such close proximity to each other, the trial court, on remand, was instructed to revisit the restriction to ensure that ap-

[22]State v. Ball, 2006-Ohio-980, 2006 WL 515514, *2 (Ohio Ct. App. 2d Dist. Montgomery County 2006).

[23]State v. Ball, 2006-Ohio-980, 2006 WL 515514, *3 (Ohio Ct. App. 2d Dist. Montgomery County 2006); see also Gevedon v. Gevedon, 167 Ohio App. 3d 450, 2006-Ohio-3195, 855 N.E.2d 548 (2d Dist. Greene County 2006) (noting that a contempt would not lie where petitioner was not at the businesses when respondent drove by).

[24]State v. Ball, 2006-Ohio-980, 2006 WL 515514, *3 (Ohio Ct. App. 2d Dist. Montgomery County 2006).

[25]Sistek v. Grendence, 2006-Ohio-4169, 2006 WL 2337189 (Ohio Ct. App. 11th Dist. Lake County 2006). See also Rosen v. Chesler, 2009-Ohio-3163, 2009 WL 1900422 (Ohio Ct. App. 9th Dist. Lorain County 2009) (noting that the court modified the 500 feet distance requirement to 50 feet for a specific purpose-to permit the parties to attend public hearings at the same time without violating the CPO).

pellant is not violating the CPO when he is on his own property or when he is traveling past petitioner's home as a means of ingress or egress to his home. "If necessary, the trial court is to modify the distance so it does not apply to Grendence when his is on his own property. Also, the trial court is to ensure the provision does not interfere with Grendence's ability to travel as part of his normal activities. The trial court may place restrictions on Grendence's conduct during the times it permits him to travel past Sistek's house. Thus, while we anticipate an order from the trial court permitting Grendence to travel past Sistek's residence, we in no way intend for Grendence to harass, intimidate, threaten or attempt to contact Sistek as a result."[26]

Q & A: Can the appellate court instruct a trial court to modify the restrictions of a CPO in order to eliminate confusion or clarify terms?[27]

Several appellate courts have done just that. In *Sistek v. Grendence*,[28] the appellate court reviewed the CPO as issued by the trial court in its entirety and determined that several terms needed clarification. The appellate court considered the trial court's provision for appellant to have limited visitation with the minor child, only to the extent provided by the juvenile court. The Court then instructed the trial court, on remand, to modify this provision to reflect the current status of the visitation as set forth in the juvenile court order and to continue to allow any court-ordered visitation between appellant and the child in a manner consistent with the juvenile order.

Similarly, in *Markowitz v. Markowitz*,[29] appellant contends that the CPO was overly broad because it restricted him from attending school functions at which petitioner may also be present. The Cuyahoga County Court of Appeals noted that while courts are authorized to craft protection orders that are tailored to the particular circumstances, it follows that the trial court has discretion to establish the scope of a protection order. However, the appellate court also reasoned that there was an inconsistency between the CPO restriction that orders the appellant to stay away from the children's school and the previously issued shared parenting plan that encourages him to attend the children's school functions. The appellate court stressed that while there was no abuse of discretion for the court to limit appellant's attendance at school functions, it is inconsistent to state that the shared parenting plan continues in full force and effect despite the order requiring him from staying away from the school.[30]

Additionally, the appellate court found the orders to be internally

---

[26]Sistek v. Grendence, 2006-Ohio-4169, 2006 WL 2337189, *5 (Ohio Ct. App. 11th Dist. Lake County 2006).

[27]See also Text § 12:27, Conflicting protection orders.

[28]Sistek v. Grendence, 2006-Ohio-4169, 2006 WL 2337189 (Ohio Ct. App. 11th Dist. Lake County 2006).

[29]Markowitz v. Markowitz, 2006-Ohio-5932, 2006 WL 3234010 (Ohio Ct. App. 8th Dist. Cuyahoga County 2006).

[30]See also State v. Price, 2006-Ohio-3856, 2006 WL 2105855 (Ohio Ct. App. 2d Dist. Montgomery County 2006), judgment rev'd, 118 Ohio St. 3d 144, 2008-Ohio-1974, 886 N.E.2d 852 (2008) (the dissenting opinion stated that "as a result of clearly conflicting orders issued by the Domestic Relations Court, Price's legal rights and

inconsistent because while the order protects the petitioner only, it also restrains appellant from various actions toward the other family or household members and limits appellant's activities with the children and family and household members. The order also indicated that appellant may email petitioner about the children not more than every other day and may telephone the children on alternating days. The court then found that there were no exceptions clearly incorporated into the CPO.

Because of the inconsistencies in the terms of the CPO making it unenforceable as written, the appellate court vacated the order in part and remanded it to the trial court for reconsideration of the terms. The court also instructed the trial court to consider whether its restrictions on the possession of weapons and on the consumption of alcohol were warranted by the evidence.

Q & A: Does a protection order permit a perpetrator of domestic violence to collect his personal property from the residence he shared with his victim? Is immunity extended to the officer who escorts the perpetrator back to the family residence?

As to the first question, the statute is silent as to whether the court may include such a provision in a protection order. In effect, the law neither explicitly permits nor specifically prohibits the inclusion of such a provision. However, the civil protection order itself contains a provision explicitly allowing a perpetrator to retrieve his personal belongings from the family residence within seven days if accompanied by a uniformed law enforcement officer and only upon reasonable notice to the petitioner.[31]

As to an officer's immunity should he or she accompany a perpetrator to the family residence in order to pick up personal items, the relevant statutes are silent. RC 3113.31 contains no good faith immunity provisions. RC 2935.032(F) provides for immunity only in the circumstances where the officer arrests an individual based on a protection order that appears valid on its face.

Clearly, the Ohio code sections set forth in the domestic violence statutes provide little assistance. Therefore, it is important for law enforcement agencies to review general tort law and the doctrine of official immunity under Ohio law.[32]

§ 12:20 Address Confidentiality Act

As a provision in the Address Confidentiality Act of 2016, RC 3113.31 was amended to "require a wireless service transfer in accordance with sections 3113.45 to 3113.49 of the Ohio Revised Code.[1]

"Wireless service" means a federally licensed commercial mobile service as defined in 47 USC 332(d) and further defined as commercial

duties were not clearly defined."); Text § 12:27, Conflicting protection orders.

[31]See Sup. R. Form 10.01-H to Sup. R. Form 10.01-J.

[32]See Tex. Atty. Gen. Op. JC-0289, 2000 WL 1478990 (10-3-00) for an analysis of the issues.

[Section 12:20]

[1]R.C. 3113.31(E)(1)(k).

mobile radio service in 47 CFR 20.3, and includes service provided by any wireless, two-way communications devise, including a radio-telephone communications line used in cellular telephone service or personal communications service, a network radio access line, or any functional or competitive equivalent of such radio-telephone communications or network radio access line.[2] A wireless service provider is defined as a facilities-based provider of wireless service to one or more end-users in this state.[3]

Q & A: Who make seek this relief?

Petitioners may seek relief pursuant to a civil protection order that requires a wireless service provider to transfer wireless service to a petitioner or other protected parties. "After an ex parte or full hearing under section 3113.31 of the Revised Code, a court may issue an order directing a wireless service provider or reseller to transfer the rights to, and billing responsibility for, the wireless service number or numbers in use by petitioner or any minor children in the care of the petitioner when the petitioner is not the account holder."[4]

Q & A: What must a petitioner provide to the court in order to obtain such an order?

Compliance with the statute includes the name and billing telephone number of the account holder, which for this purpose is presumed to be the respondent. Additionally, petitioners must provide their name and contact information to whom the wireless number or numbers shall be transferred. Lastly, the petitioner must indicate each wireless service number to be transferred.[5]

Q & A: What can a petitioner do to make sure that the contact information remains confidential?

A court shall ensure that any contact information of a petitioner be kept confidential from the account holder.[6]

Q & A: On a procedural level, how is service perfected on a wireless service provider?

Pursuant to RC 3113.454, an order issued by a court shall be served on the wireless service provider's or reseller's agent for service of process as listed with the Secretary of State. Since the statute is silent as to the type of service, it can be assumed service is made on the statutory agent by certified mail.

Q & A: Is this order a mandate on a wireless service provider or reseller?

A wireless service provider or reseller shall notify the petitioner within 72 hours of receipt of the order if the order cannot be complied with because the wireless service provider or reseller *cannot* (emphasis added) operationally or technically effectuate the order due to certain circumstances. These conditions include: 1) the account holder has already terminated the account; 2) differences in network technology prevent the functionality of a devise on the network; 3) geographic or

[2]R.C. 128.01(F)(1); R.C. 3113.45.

[3]R.C. 128.01(2)(j); R.C. 3113.45.

[4]R.C. 3113.451.

[5]R.C. 3113.452.

[6]R.C. 3113.453.

other limitations on network or service availability; and 4) any other operational or technical issue that would prevent or impair the use of the wireless service number if the transfer occurs.[7]

Q & A: Who would assume financial responsibility upon transfer?

According to statute, upon transfer of the wireless service number to a petitioner, the petitioner shall assume all financial responsibility for any costs associated with the wireless service number and any costs for the devise associated with the wireless service number.[8]

It is unclear whether the petitioner is also responsible for any outstanding debt owed by a respondent at the time of transfer.

Q & A: What is the process for account establishment to a petitioner?

Noting that a petitioner assumes financial responsibility of billing upon transfer, a wireless service provider or reseller is not precluded from applying to the petitioner any routine and customary requirements for account establishment as part of the transfer, including identification, financial information and customer preference.[9]

Q & A: Does the transfer of the wireless service number suggest an apportionment of assets or debt?

Nothing in sections 3113.45 to 3113.459 of the Revised Code shall affect the ability of the court to apportion the assets or debts of the parties as provided for in the revised Code, or the ability to determine temporary use, possession, and control of personal property pursuant to division (E)(1)(h) of section 3113.31 of the Revised Code.[10]

Q & A: Does the wireless service provider or reseller enjoy immunity from any law suit?

No cause of action shall arise against any wireless service provider or reseller, its officers, employees, or agents, for any action taken in accordance with sections 3113.45 to 3113.459 of the Revised Code or with the terms of a court order issued in compliance with section 3113.451 of the Revised Code.

Therefore, by the very terms of the statute, neither a respondent nor a petitioner can bring suit against the wireless service provider.

§ 12:21 Remedies—Orders that grant other relief

A court has the authority to grant any constitutionally defensible relief necessary to cause the cessation of violence against the family or household member.[1] Besides this provision, RC 3113.31(E)(1)(h) specifically allows the court to grant other relief that it considers equitable and fair, including, but not limited to, ordering the respondent to permit the use of a motor vehicle by the petitioner or other family

---

[7]R.C. 3113.455.

[8]R.C. 3113.456.

[9]R.C. 3113.457.

[10]R.C. 3113.458.

[Section 12:21]

[1]RC 3113.31(E)(1); see also Snyder v. Snyder, 1995 WL 493998 (Ohio Ct. App. 4th Dist. Ross County 1995).

or household member and the apportionment of household and family personal property.[2] If the relief is necessary to protect the safety of the victim or other household members or the relief is equitable and fair under the circumstances of the case, the court does not need specific statutory authority to grant the requested relief.[3]

At least one Ohio court interpreted the legislative intent of RC 3113.31(E)(1)(h). In *Clum v. Searcy*,[4] the court of appeals of Tuscarawas County stated that "[w]e read this section as a legislative grant of broad authority to the trial court to issue orders that best serve the parties involved in domestic violence." Based upon this interpretation, the safety of the victim may not always be the overriding factor for a court in awarding relief under this section. In this particular case, the court granted the respondent a protection order against the petitioner.[5]

On the other hand, most courts that have fashioned orders under this provision have done so with the safety of the victim as the paramount concern. For example, the court has the authority to keep the victim's address secret if the measure is designed to protect the victim from future harm. In some counties, the address of the victim

---

[2]RC 3113.31(E)(1)(h). But see Howard v. Pharis-Rine, 2009-Ohio-3981, 2009 WL 2457775 (Ohio Ct. App. 5th Dist. Licking County 2009) (holding that awarding monetary damages to appellee was like litigating a tort claim and beyond the authority of the domestic relations court in a civil protection order proceeding under RC 3113.31(E)(1)(h); Basile v. Basile, 255 N.J. Super. 181, 604 A.2d 693 (Ch. Div. 1992) (holding that, under N.J. domestic violence statute, the authority of court to handle issues pertaining to domestic violence under that state's Domestic Violence statute is not broad enough to include a change of name proceeding).

[3]Gaydash v. Gaydash, 168 Ohio App. 3d 418, 423, 2006-Ohio-4080, 860 N.E.2d 789 (9th Dist. Summit County 2006). See Mann v. Sumser, 2002-Ohio-5103, 2002 WL 31151164 (Ohio Ct. App. 5th Dist. Stark County 2002) (upholding a restriction prohibiting weapons where evidence showed respondent threatened to shoot petitioner and thus restrictions were based on the evidence of the case). But see Newhouse v. Williams, 167 Ohio App. 3d 215, 223, 2006-Ohio-3075, ¶ 16, 854 N.E.2d 565, 571 (3d Dist. Wyandot County 2006) (holding that a trial court has broad discretion when imposing restrictions pursuant to a CPO, this direction is not limitless; "[R]estrictions must bear a sufficient nexus to the conduct the trial court was attempting to prevent"; in sustaining appellant's assignment of error, the court held that no evidence was presented that appellant had ever used or threatened appellee with a gun; no evidence was presented that appellant even owned a deadly weapon; those, restricting appellant in this manner was an abuse of discretion), citing Maag v. Maag, 2002-Ohio-1401, 2002 WL 468585 (Ohio Ct. App. 3d Dist. Wyandot County 2002); see also Sistek v. Grendence, 2006-Ohio-4169, 2006 WL 2337189 (Ohio Ct. App. 11th Dist. Lake County 2006); T.S. v. R.S., 2017-Ohio-281, 81 N.E.3d 932 (Ohio Ct. App. 9th Dist. Summit County 2017) (noting that a court may grant other relief as is equitable and fair and that may include ordering respondent to permit the use of a motor vehicle by petitioner and that the trial court retains statutory authority to "craft protection orders that are tailored to the particular circumstances." [at ¶ 20; quoting R.C. v. J.G., 2013-Ohio-4265, ¶ 15, 2013 WL 5437015 (Ohio Ct. App. 9th Dist. Medina County 2013), citing RC 3113.31 and Abuhamda-Sliman v. Sliman, 161 Ohio App. 3d 541, 2005-Ohio-2836, ¶ 9, 831 N.E.2d 453 (8th Dist. Cuyahoga County 2005). In crafting the parameters of the order, the restrictions must bear a sufficient nexus to the conduct the trial court is attempting to prevent." [at ¶ 20 citing *Pacek* at ¶ 16) quoting Boals v. Miller, 2011-Ohio-1470, ¶ 37, 2011 WL 1118464 (Ohio Ct. App. 5th Dist. Ashland County 2011).

[4]Clum v. Searcy, 1993 WL 535383, *2 (Ohio Ct. App. 5th Dist. Tuscarawas County 1993).

[5]See Text § 12:29, Mutual protection orders, for a discussion of mutual protection orders.

will remain confidential unless the parties have a child in common. In other counties, the address of the victim will remain confidential even where the parties have a child in common.

Some courts may order the respondent to maintain the utilities. The Supreme Court forms also authorize a court to prohibit the respondent from cancelling insurance or health benefits or from interfering with the petitioner's phone service, mail delivery, or the delivery of any other papers to the petitioner during the time the protection order is in effect.[6]

As county systems begin to develop policies in the area of domestic violence, more courts will afford attorneys greater latitude in creatively structuring protection orders. In addition, the Supreme Court standard forms go a long way in encouraging both creativity and latitude.

Q & A: Can the court apportion household and family personal property?

RC 3113.31(E)(1)(h) specifically grants the court authority to apportion household or family personal property as relief in a civil protection order action.[7] Household or family personal property includes furniture, appliances, tools, clothing, children's items, and other household goods, possessions, or personal effects.[8] *Black's Law Dictionary* has defined the term "apportion" to mean "to divide and distribute proportionally."[9] "To divide" means "to cut into parts, disunite, separate."[10]

The statute is silent as to whether this allocation represents a permanent division of property for the petitioner and respondent or whether it represents only exclusive possession or use for the duration of the order. The statute also fails to indicate whether the status of marriage impacts the property division.

A liberal interpretation of the terms seems to suggest a permanent division of property. However, the temporary nature of a protection order suggests otherwise. At the very least, the legislature seems to have provided the parties with an additional arena in which to retrieve their possessions separate from small claims or another civil action.

The statute recognizes that the parties need not be married in order for the court to apportion the property between the parties. It is also not necessary to construe this provision as being the same as a general division of marital property under RC 3105.18.

In order to be awarded the items of property requested, the

[6]Sup. R. 10.01(C), Sup. R. Form 10.01-H to Sup. R. Form 10.01-J.

[7]See Downs v. Strouse, 2006-Ohio-505, 2006 WL 280417 (Ohio Ct. App. 10th Dist. Franklin County 2006) (concluding that appellant failed to request apportionment of personal property).

[8]But see Grant v. Wright, 222 N.J. Super. 191, 201, 536 A.2d 319 (App. Div. 1988) (reversing granting of civil protection order, stating that the domestic violence statute "was never intended to provide a jurisdictional basis for property disputes, unsupported by the jurisdictionally required fact finding, and unrelated to its purpose").

[9]Black's Law Dictionary (6th ed.) p 99.

[10]Black's Law Dictionary (6th ed.) p 478.

petitioner must first present evidence that she/he is in need of a protection order for safety reasons. Once this has been established, the court may divide personal property between the petitioner and respondent.

Without such a division of property as a term of the civil protection order, conflict between the parties may continue until the personal property issues are resolved. Reducing the conflict between the parties over the retrieval of personal property can help prevent future violence.

Q & A: Is the division of property contemplated by statute considered to be permanent?

Only one Ohio court has analyzed this issue. In *Cooley v. Cooley*,[11] the Montgomery County Court of Appeals interpreted RC 3113.31 regarding property division. In that case, the parties had entered into a consent entry granting one party exclusive occupancy of the marital property in exchange for paying the other party $7,000 as a total property settlement. The court determined that "it is extremely doubtful that the legislature contemplated permanent property settlements when it alluded to protection orders or consent agreements in the domestic violence statutes, and this observation is clearly borne out by the time restrictions imposed by RC 3113.31(E)(3)."[12]

This decision is important for two reasons. First, it provides an analysis of one appellate court's interpretation of the permanency of property settlements pursuant to RC 3113.31. Under this interpretation, property settlements are not permanent, whether the distributions are in personalty or cash. All settlements expire when the protection order terminates. Second, the court has determined that, where the parties are married, a protection order cannot provide for a permanent property division.

On the other hand, as it relates to unmarried individuals, the division or allocation of personal property should be permanent. It would seem foolish to require the party to return those items awarded to him/her as soon as the protection order expired.

The *Cooley* analysis has been followed in many of Ohio's courts. Local practice suggests that this provision merely provides the parties with exclusive use for the duration of the order. This is the case in Franklin, Monroe, Morgan, Noble, and Washington counties. Practically speaking, there is no permanent division of property in these counties.

In other counties, however, the courts appear to make a permanent division of personal property. The courts in these counties in no way indicate that such an apportionment is temporary in nature. For example, Cuyahoga County courts have divided certain items of personal property, and there have been few contempt motions, if any, for the return of that personal property. Until someone files a motion with the court for a return of that property, the issue will remain open.

---

[11]Cooley v. Cooley, 90 Ohio App. 3d 706, 630 N.E.2d 417 (2d Dist. Montgomery County 1993).

[12]Cooley v. Cooley, 90 Ohio App. 3d 706, 707, 630 N.E.2d 417 (2d Dist. Montgomery County 1993).

Q & A: Pursuant to a civil protection order, petitioner was awarded certain items of personal property, which were in respondent's possession. When petitioner did not receive these items, he filed a motion to enforce the provision in the order that ordered respondent to return his personal property. Could petitioner have filed a small claims action seeking monetary relief for the property he had not received?

RC 3113.31(E)(1)(h) specifically permits a court to grant other relief that the court considers equitable and fair, including, but not limited to, the apportionment of household and family personal property. Therefore, any failure to turn over the personal property itemized in the civil protection order would become the basis of a motion to show cause to enforce the order.[13] Clearly, domestic relations courts have jurisdiction to enforce civil protection orders and their provisions.

However, a party is not precluded from bringing an action in small claims court. A failure to return personal property under a civil protection order may give rise to a small claims filing seeking money damages for the value of the items of personal property not returned. While a small claims court does not have jurisdiction to enforce the terms of the civil protection order, it clearly has the authority to award monetary damages.[14]

Q & A: What items of personalty are subject to division?

If the parties are married, several types of property are subject to division. The court should award clothing, children's items, and the respondent's tools of trade at the ex parte hearing if possible. Such specific items may be necessary for the maintenance of the parties during this time period.

These items should definitely be allocated at the full hearing. Personal property that is needed for each party to maintain a similar standard of living should also be allocated at the full hearing. Items such as refrigerator, stove, and washer and dryer are among the necessary items that should be divided at this time, especially in cases involving children.

If the parties are cohabiting, or have cohabited in the recent past, the court should return separate property to the owner. Additionally, the court has the authority to divide between the parties all other items of personal property. Such a division is necessary to preclude contact between the parties. Without contact, future violence between the parties is reduced.

Q & A: Will the court award personal property to one or both of the parties pursuant to the protection order where a divorce is pending?

It depends on the court jurisdiction. Some Ohio courts do not divide personal property at the full hearing if there is also a divorce pending. Some courts will grant the parties only certain necessary items, especially in cases where there are children. Still other courts will award exclusive possession of any items to one or the other party for the entire duration of the civil protection order or until the divorce action is resolved.

---

[13] See RC 3113.31(L).

[14] See also LaPlume v. Lavallee, 177 Vt. 526, 2004 VT 78, 858 A.2d 255 (2004).

Most Ohio courts will award the parties only their personal belongings at the full hearing. Contested or disputed items may not be addressed until the divorce is final. Such is the case in Cuyahoga County. It should also be noted that in many of Ohio's counties, a two-count divorce/civil protection order action is discouraged.

On the other hand, other states allow for the petitioner to obtain personal property from the respondent in a civil protection order proceeding even if a divorce has already addressed property issues.[15]

Q & A: Can the court restrain a respondent from damaging personal and real property during the pendency of the protection order?

Many court jurisdictions have begun to fashion civil protection orders that restrain a respondent from removing, damaging, hiding, or disposing of any of the property owned or possessed by the family or household member named in the order.[16] This applies to personal as well as real property.

Because there is growing recognition that batterers often destroy personal property as a way of maintaining control over their victims,[17] protection orders are designed to protect a victim of domestic violence from increased contact with the batterer. Specific orders about usage and damage during the duration of the order reduce potential avenues for conflict and controversy between the parties and can help prevent future violence.

Q & A: Can a respondent retrieve personal possessions?

Absolutely. The trend in the country is to allow for an award and transfer of personal property.[18] In fact, the Supreme Court standard forms permit the respondent to pick up clothing and personal items from the residence upon reasonable notice to the petitioner and in the company of a uniformed law enforcement official within seven days of the filing of the order.[19]

Rather than risk future conflict over these items, many courts will include a specific time, date, and list of the exact items to be exchanged in the civil protection order. During the exchange, a police officer should accompany the respondent in order to ensure the safety of the victim and compliance with the order.[20]

Prior to the adoption of the Supreme Court standard forms, one Ohio court determined that, where the protection order restrains a party from entering the marital home, the court should grant the respondent the right to recover personal possessions from the residence.

---

[15]See FitzGerald v. FitzGerald, 406 N.W.2d 52 (Minn. Ct. App. 1987).

[16]See also Sup. R. 10.01(C), Sup. R. Form 10.01-H to Sup. R. Form 10.01-J.

[17]See Diane R. Follingstad et al., The Role of Emotional Abuse in Physically Abusive Relationships, 5 J. Fam. Violence 107 (1990); see also Elkins v. Elkins, 1992 WL 180118 (Ohio Ct. App. 10th Dist. Franklin County 1992); Parkhurst v. Parkhurst, 793 S.W.2d 634 (Mo. Ct. App. E.D. 1990).

[18]See Elkins v. Elkins, 1992 WL 180118 (Ohio Ct. App. 10th Dist. Franklin County 1992).

[19]See Sup. R. 10.01(C), Sup. R. Form 10.01-H to Sup. R. Form 10.01-J.

[20]See State v. Wiltse, 386 N.W.2d 315 (Minn. Ct. App. 1986); see also Smart v. Smart, 59 N.C. App. 533, 297 S.E.2d 135 (1982); State v. Lewis, 179 Wis. 2d 503, 508 N.W.2d 75 (Ct. App. 1993).

In *Elkins v. Elkins*,[21] the Franklin County Court of Appeals found that the trial court erred in failing to grant the respondent the opportunity to recover personal possessions from the marital residence and in failing to grant the respondent rights concerning those possessions. The appellate court held that "[i]nasmuch as the civil protection order restrains respondent from entering the marital residence, respondent should have the opportunity to recover her personal possessions from that residence in order to continue an existence elsewhere."[22]

Although the Franklin County Court of Appeals determined that the respondent had a right to recover personal possessions and that this right should have been written into the court order, of significance is that the residence from which the respondent was restrained was the marital residence. It is unclear whether the court would have ruled the same if the parties merely cohabited.

Q & A: Can the court determine exclusive use of the parties' automobile?

The statute specifically states that the court may order the respondent to permit use of a motor vehicle by the petitioner or other family or household member.[23] Note that the legislature did not specifically use the term "divide" or "apportion" in relation to automobiles. Clearly, the legislature intended the court to only authorize exclusive possession for a period of time. Under this catchall provision,[24] a petitioner should also request that the court order the respondent to turn over the keys to the vehicle. In fact, the newly adopted Supreme Court standard forms also require a respondent to immediately surrender possession of any and all keys to a specific motor vehicle to the petitioner who is awarded exclusive use of the motor vehicle.[25]

The Ross County Court of Appeals addressed an interesting issue with ramifications that extend beyond the issue of exclusive use of an automobile. In *Snyder v. Snyder*,[26] the appellant was ordered to provide an automobile for the appellee's use. The appellant appealed the trial court's decision and argued that the evidence failed to show that the automobile was essential to protect the appellee from domestic violence. In effect, the appellant contended that the purpose of any protection order was limited to the protection of the petitioner from domestic violence and that all relief should be in furtherance of that purpose.

---

[21]Elkins v. Elkins, 1992 WL 180118 (Ohio Ct. App. 10th Dist. Franklin County 1992).

[22]Elkins v. Elkins, 1992 WL 180118, *3 (Ohio Ct. App. 10th Dist. Franklin County 1992). See also Marshall v. Marshall, 2016-Ohio-3405, 2016 WL 3384312 (Ohio Ct. App. 11th Dist. Portage County 2016) (finding that where there was no prohibition in a CPO preventing appellant from retrieving his personal property, "the fact that a protection order was put in place making it more difficult for Robert to retrieve his possessions cannot be blamed on petitioner nor should she be held financially responsible for personal property where there is no evidence she disposed of the property or destroyed it." ¶ 32.).

[23]RC 3113.31(E)(1)(h).

[24]RC 3113.31(E)(1)(h).

[25]Sup. R. 10.01(C), Sup. R. Form 10.01-H to Sup. R. Form 10.01-J.

[26]Snyder v. Snyder, 1995 WL 493998 (Ohio Ct. App. 4th Dist. Ross County 1995).

In this particular case, the trial court deleted the provision requiring the appellant to provide the appellee with an automobile before the case was heard on appeal. Although the appellate court found the issue to be moot, it is unclear how the court would have ruled if it had to decide the issue.

It is hoped that the Ross County Court of Appeals would reject the argument advanced by the appellant in this case. Although the intent of the domestic violence statute is to protect the petitioner from further violence through a civil protection order, the relief contained in the order is designed to both bring about a cessation of violence[27] and award other relief which is equitable and fair.[28] Taken together, these two provisions increase the protection afforded a petitioner. The legislature, recognizing that decisions about personal property can create tension and conflict in the relationship, permitted courts to craft orders to avoid and/or lessen the conflict.

Q & A: Can the court order the respondent to pay attorney fees and litigation costs of the petitioner?[29]

The statute does not address this issue. Case law in Ohio has only tangentially addressed this issue.[30] However, the standardized civil protection order forms indicate that court costs may be assessed to the respondent.[31]

In *Gannon v. Gannon*,[32] appellant argued that the court had no authority under RC 3113.31 to award attorney fees.

In affirming the judgment of the trial court supporting the award of attorneys fees, the Fourth District Court of Appeals reasoned that "RC 3113.31(E)(1)(e) expressly permits the court to order a respondent to maintain the support of the petitioner if the respondent customarily provides or has a duty to provide support. It was as a support order that the court directed appellant to reimburse the cost of appellee's attorney in obtaining her protection order."[33]

However, over 25 states, the District of Columbia, and Puerto Rico

---

[27]See RC 3113.31(E)(1).

[28]See RC 3113.31(E)(1)(h).

[29]See Suttle v. Suttle, 2015-Ohio-5398, 2015 WL 9435160 (Ohio Ct. App. 5th Dist. Fairfield County 2015) (noting that RC 3105.73 did not apply to civil protection orders and finding that it was not appropriate to award attorneys fees for a separate CPO proceeding).

[30]See Strong v. Bauman, 1999 WL 317432 (Ohio Ct. App. 2d Dist. Montgomery County 1999) (ordering respondent to pay court costs and interim attorney's fees for litigating a contempt motion for violating a protection order); see also Patterson v. Loveless, 2001 WL 524372, *3 (Ohio Ct. App. 2d Dist. Montgomery County 2001) (appellate court agreed that attorney fees may be ordered on a contempt motion, but not when petitioner appeared pro se). But see Lapsansky v. Lapsansky, 2000 WL 1114535 (Ohio Ct. App. 7th Dist. Columbiana County 2000) (Appellate court denied an award of attorney fees to a petitioner whose protection order was denied. The court held that "[b]ecause a CPO is not a stage in divorce proceedings, attorneys' fees were not available under RC 3105.18(H).").

[31]Sup. R. Form 10.01-I and Sup. R. Form 10.01-J; see also Stella v. Platz, 1999 WL 427672 (Ohio Ct. App. 4th Dist. Washington County 1999).

[32]Gannon v. Gannon, 2008-Ohio-4484, 2008 WL 4093687 (Ohio Ct. App. 6th Dist. Wood County 2008).

[33]Gannon v. Gannon, 2008-Ohio-4484, 2008 WL 4093687, *4 (Ohio Ct. App. 6th Dist. Wood County 2008).

authorize the payment of attorney fees in a civil protection order.[34] Many states also include court costs as a civil protection order remedy.[35]

Courts in other states have also sanctioned an award of attorney fees. In *Parkhurst v. Parkhurst*,[36] the court awarded attorney fees in a civil protection order. Many cases provide for an award of attorney fees only when a petitioner testifies as to the nature and extent of the legal services provided.[37] Across the country, courts have also awarded attorney fees when the respondent's subsequent misconduct warrants such an award.[38] At least one court awarded attorney fees to a publicly funded legal services agency after the court issued a civil protection order.[39]

An attorney in Ohio may prevail by arguing that an award of attorney fees is both fair and equitable.[40] Much will depend on the nature and extent of the injuries, the victim's ability to pay, and whether sufficient evidence was advanced at trial as to the nature and extent of the legal services provided.

Q & A: Will a court award attorney fees against a petitioner when a civil protection order is denied?

Several Ohio cases have addressed this issue. For example, in *Lapsansky v. Lapsansky*,[41] the trial court denied petitioner's civil protection order. The court then granted the respondent the sum of $300 for attorney fees, stating the motion for CPO was frivolous because there was insufficient evidence connecting respondent to the acts of domestic violence.

The Seventh District Court of Appeals noted that because the trial court did not state that the petition was willfully frivolous and because the petitioner could have been rightfully fearful, it was unwilling to infer willful conduct. Additionally, the trial court awarded attorneys' fees on its own motion without notice to the parties.

The appellate court then reversed the trial court decision, holding that the attorneys' fees on the motion for a CPO were improper under

[34]See, e.g., Pa. Stat. Ann. tit. 23, § 6108(a)(8) (1991); but see Baumgartner v. Baumgartner, 693 So. 2d 84 (Fla. 2d DCA 1997) (holding that where attorney fees are not provided for in statute, the court cannot imply a right to attorney fees given the legislature's sanctioned use of pro se procedures).

[35]See, e.g., Mo. Ann. Stat. § 455.050(3)10 (Vernon Supp. 1993).

[36]Parkhurst v. Parkhurst, 793 S.W.2d 634 (Mo. Ct. App. E.D. 1990); see also Rogers v. Rogers, 161 A.D.2d 766, 556 N.Y.S.2d 114 (2d Dep't 1990).

[37]See Todd v. Todd, 772 S.W.2d 14 (Mo. Ct. App. E.D. 1989).

[38]See Agnew v. Campbell, 1990 WL 188723 (Minn. Ct. App. 1990); Linda D. v. Peter D., 152 Misc. 2d 564, 577 N.Y.S.2d 354 (Fam. Ct. 1991).

[39]Spoto v. McCarroll, 250 N.J. Super. 66, 593 A.2d 375 (App. Div. 1991); see also Krassnoski v. Rosey, 454 Pa. Super. 78, 684 A.2d 635 (1996).

[40]See RC 3113.31(E)(1)(h).

[41]Lapsansky v. Lapsansky, 2000 WL 1114535 (Ohio Ct. App. 7th Dist. Columbiana County 2000); see also A.L.K. v. A.K., 2014-Ohio-2284, 2014 WL 2465314 (Ohio Ct. App. 10th Dist. Franklin County 2014) (holding that the minor child on whose behalf mother filed the CPO did not engage in frivolous conduct or was responsible for the litigation initiated on her behalf; thus, the award of $2,948 in attorney fees against the child was against the manifest weight of the evidence).

Civ.R. 11.[42] Moreover, "[b]ecause a CPO is not a stage in divorce proceedings, attorneys' fees were not available under RC 3105.18(H) ."[43]

Similarly, in *Kass v. Kass*,[44] the Minnesota Court of Appeals determined that, absent clear evidence of the petitioner's bad faith in bringing the action or intent to assert a frivolous claim, the court will not award attorney fees or reimburse costs against the petitioner when a civil protection order is denied.

In *Lozada v. Lozada*,[45] petitioner sought a protection order, which was denied at the full hearing. The magistrate found that the petitioner had made materially false statements in her affidavit with the intent of causing the court to believe that her husband had been harassing her. The magistrate also found that the petitioner was not credible and all of her claims were unsupported generalizations. Since neither objected, the trial court entered judgment adopting the magistrate's decision. Finally, the magistrate recommended that the court make an express finding that husband did not commit any acts of domestic violence on wife or the parties' child because wife's case

---

[42]But see Donaldson v. Todd, 174 Ohio App. 3d 117, 2007-Ohio-6504, 881 N.E.2d 280 (10th Dist. Franklin County 2007) (reversing judgment and holding respondent entitled to a hearing on his motion for attorney's fees); see also Bigelow v. Nguyen, 2009-Ohio-3325, 2009 WL 1915141 (Ohio Ct. App. 7th Dist. Columbiana County 2009) (affirming denial of attorney fees requested by appellant pursuant to RC 2323.51(A)(2)(a) and Civ. R. 11 where trial court denied stalking civil protection order. Appellant's failure to request attorney's fees under Civ. R. 11 during trial court proceedings waived review of issue on appeal); Zielinski-Barnwell v. Prewitt, 2014-Ohio-3761, 2014 WL 4269111 (Ohio Ct. App. 6th Dist. Wood County 2014) (denying appellant's assignment of error and noting that Rule 11 sanctions may only be imposed upon attorneys or, in some circumstances, pro se litigants, suggesting that they are not imposed on litigants who were or are represented by counsel, ¶ 10).

[43]Lapsansky v. Lapsansky, 2000 WL 1114535 (Ohio Ct. App. 7th Dist. Columbiana County 2000).

[44]Kass v. Kass, 355 N.W.2d 335 (Minn. Ct. App. 1984) (overruled on other grounds by, Thompson o/b/o Minor Child v. Schrimsher, 906 N.W.2d 495 (Minn. 2018)); see also M.W. v. R.L., 286 N.J. Super. 408, 669 A.2d 817 (App. Div. 1995) (party who filed a domestic violence complaint in bad faith required to pay other party's attorney fees); Lasater v. Vidahl, 2013-Ohio-5558, 2013 WL 6711191 (Ohio Ct. App. 9th Dist. Summit County 2013) (in which one party requested attorney fees for the other's frivolous appeal).

[45]Lozada v. Lozada, 2014-Ohio-5700, 2014 WL 7357285 (Ohio Ct. App. 11th Dist. Geauga County 2014); Winn v. Wilson, 2016-Ohio-7545, 2016 WL 6462463 (Ohio Ct. App. 12th Dist. Butler County 2016) (affirming denial of attorney fees where CPO was denied and examining the use of RC 2323.51(B)(1) which provides that a court may award attorney fees in connection with a civil action to a party adversely affected by "frivolous conduct," reviewing that conduct which rises to the level of "frivolous" and holding that sanctions were not warranted just because petitioner was unable to persuade the trial court to grant her a CPO); Tredanary v. Fritz, 2018-Ohio-2374, n.2, 2018 WL 3045730 (Ohio Ct. App. 11th Dist. Lake County 2018) (trial court erred in awarding attorney fees when it failed to hold a hearing on the issue and petitioner did not respond to respondent's motion. Since the decision to hold the hearing when granting motion for sanctions for frivolous conduct is discretionary, the court applied the *de novo* standard of review appropriate "when reviewing legal conclusions"); but see Oliver v. Johnson, 2007-Ohio-5880, 2007 WL 3227668 (Ohio Ct. App. 4th Dist. Jackson County 2007) (finding that a CPO did not create a civil action).

was "so utterly devoid of merit and the contrary evidence against her case is so strong."[46]

Four days after the trial court adopted the decision, respondent filed a Motion for Attorney Fees per RC 2324.51 and Civ. R. 11. After a hearing, the same magistrate concluded that petitioner engaged in frivolous conduct in both filing and prosecuting the CPO petition as defined under RC 2323.51(A)(2)(a)(i), (ii) and (iii) and awarded respondent attorneys fees in the amount of $22,852.52 as well as litigation expenses in the sum of $1,045.16. The trial court ruled on petitioner's objections and reduced the attorney fee award to $15,000.

On appeal, petitioner/appellant argued that the trial court's finding of a sanction of attorney fees was against the manifest weight of the evidence. Generally, an award of attorney fees is within the trial court's discretion where the court has determined that a party has engaged in frivolous conduct. She also argued that "her conduct only becomes frivolous when the expectation of finding evidence in support of an action is unreasonable. Because she had a concern for her safety that prompted her to seek the CPO, she provided reasonable evidence for the petition. Given our conclusion that the trial court did not err in finding frivolous conduct pursuant to RC 2323.51(A)(2)(a)(i), evaluating wife's argument would be an advisory exercise."[47] In the instant case, petitioner did not object to the trial court's decision that she engaged in frivolous conduct. "Because the trial court's findings and conclusions in the instant matter were based upon its conclusive determinations in the judgment denying wife's petition for a CPO, we conclude the trial court's judgment that wife engaged in frivolous conduct is consistent with the manifest weight of the evidence."[48]

Next, appellant argued that assessing attorney fees pursuant to RC 2323.51 does not apply to civil protection order proceedings because RC 3113.31 is not an ordinary civil action. "Wife notes that such a proceeding does not seek redress of a legal wrong, enforcement of a legal right or punishment of a public offense; rather, a petition for a domestic violence civil protection order, by definition, seeks protection, not civil gain. Thus, she concludes, the mechanisms set forth under RC 2323.51 are not available to parties litigating an RC 3113.31 petition."[49]

The appellate court reasoned that courts have found that a domestic violence civil protection order is a civil proceeding and noted that Civil R. 2 provides that there shall be one form of action and it shall be known as a civil action. It further stressed that the purpose of RC 2323.51 is to provide a remedy for those harmed by frivolous conduct. If RC 2323.51 could not apply to a RC 3113.31 proceeding, an aggrieved respondent would have no right to relief.

---

[46]Lozada v. Lozada, 2014-Ohio-5700, 2014 WL 7357285, ¶ 3 (Ohio Ct. App. 11th Dist. Geauga County 2014).

[47]Lozada v. Lozada, 2014-Ohio-5700, 2014 WL 7357285, ¶ 22 (Ohio Ct. App. 11th Dist. Geauga County 2014).

[48]Lozada v. Lozada, 2014-Ohio-5700, 2014 WL 7357285, ¶ 21 (Ohio Ct. App. 11th Dist. Geauga County 2014); Tredanary v. Fritz, 2018-Ohio-2374, n.2, 2018 WL 3045730 (Ohio Ct. App. 11th Dist. Lake County 2018).

[49]Lozada v. Lozada, 2014-Ohio-5700, 2014 WL 7357285, ¶ 35 (Ohio Ct. App. 11th Dist. Geauga County 2014).

The court also addressed the dissenting opinion which determined that a RC 3113.31 proceeding is a special statutory proceeding, which falls outside of the parameters of RC 2323.51. The consequence of removing civil protection order proceedings from the ambit of RC 2323.51 "would be problematic insofar as it would permit a party to file a petition based upon false allegations or merely an intention to harass without concern that his or her conduct might be sanctionable as frivolous. Moreover, would-be respondents would be without a powerful mechanism to deter such abuses of the legal process."[50] While the majority recognized the dissent's point, it held that the remedial purpose behind RC 2323.51 contemplates its application to all civil proceedings, both "ordinary" and "special." "This will not have a chilling effect discouraging actual victims to come forward; quite the contrary, it merely discourages using the legal system as a forum for gamesmanship or harassment. We therefore disagree that RC 3113.31 proceedings are beyond the reach of RC 2323.51."[51]

The appellate court then disputed the dissent's assertion that RC 2323.51 is inapplicable to the instant matter because RC 3113.31(J) provides that no court shall charge any fee in connection with filing a petition. The majority stated that "a judgment imposing a sanction for frivolous conduct is not a 'charge' by the court."[52]

Conversely, in *Winn v. Wilson*,[53] the appellate court determined that father was not entitled to attorney fees when mother's CPO was denied.

In *Winn,* mother filed for a CPO against father in which the children testified at the ex parte hearing regarding their fear of father. At the full hearing, the children again testified about their fear of father because of an incident between father and his brother in which father "lifted Jimmy from the couch, placed him in a chokehold and punched him. Father testified that he merely placed Jimmy in a "fireman's hold to get him downstairs due to his intoxication.

The magistrate found there was insufficient evidence to support the issuance of the CPO which denial was supported by the trial court. Father subsequently filed a motion for attorney fees in which the magistrate awarded father $9727.50 and mother filed objections. The trial court overruled the magistrate's decision and denied father's award of attorney fees. It is from this order that father appealed arguing that the trial court erred by finding that petitioner did not engage in frivolous conduct when she provided no evidence to support her claim that the children suffered mental injury.[54]

The appellate court first examined the statute that provides for at-

---

[50]Lozada v. Lozada, 2014-Ohio-5700, 2014 WL 7357285, ¶ 39 (Ohio Ct. App. 11th Dist. Geauga County 2014).

[51]Lozada v. Lozada, 2014-Ohio-5700, 2014 WL 7357285, ¶ 40 (Ohio Ct. App. 11th Dist. Geauga County 2014).

[52]Lozada v. Lozada, 2014-Ohio-5700, 2014 WL 7357285, ¶ 41 (Ohio Ct. App. 11th Dist. Geauga County 2014).

[53]Winn v. Wilson, 2016-Ohio-7545, 2016 WL 6462463 (Ohio Ct. App. 12th Dist. Butler County 2016).

[54]Winn v. Wilson, 2016-Ohio-7545, 2016 WL 6462463, ¶ 8 (Ohio Ct. App. 12th Dist. Butler County 2016).

torney fees when frivolous conduct is alleged.[55] In reviewing the transcript, the court found that "the insufficiency of the evidence does not rise to the level of frivolous conduct as no evidence was presented to suggest that mother's motives or conduct were designed to harass or maliciously injure father.[56] The court then found that even though mother did not meet her burden of proof required to grant the CPO, father was not entitled to attorney fees. "It is well-established that " '[s]anctions are not warranted under RC 2323.51 merely because Mother was unable to persuade the trial court to grant her motion after it weighed the evidence.' "[57]

Q & A: Can a court order one party to pay attorney fees to the other party on a contempt motion when both parties are pro se?

At least one Ohio court addressed this issue regarding a contempt motion filed by the petitioner. In *Patterson v. Loveless*,[58] the petitioner filed a contempt motion from her civil protection order ordering appellant to return her keys. The trial court awarded her attorney fees. The Montgomery County Court of Appeals reversed the decision as to attorney fees because the appellee was pro se. However, the court recognized that "[a]ttorneys fees may be awarded as costs of the action to a party who successfully prosecutes charges in contempt."[59]

Q & A: Can a domestic relations court charge a party to a divorce action with dissipation of funds for using marital money to defend his/her own domestic violence charge?

At least one Ohio court answered this in the affirmative. In *Schindler v. Schindler*,[60] the defendant in a divorce action removed funds from the parties' joint account. He admitted that he used the money to defend himself against a charge of domestic violence. The trial court determined that he had committed financial misconduct with regard to the monies in the savings account in that he had wrongfully dissipated the money by using it to his own benefit.

Noting the defendant's admission, the Summit County Court of Appeals found

> nothing unreasonable, arbitrary or unconscionable in the court's refusal to charge appellee with half of such an expense. Whether labeled financial misconduct or not, whether there was a restraining order on

---

[55] RC 2323.51(B)(1).

[56] Winn v. Wilson, 2016-Ohio-7545, ¶ 12, 2016 WL 6462463 (Ohio Ct. App. 12th Dist. Butler County 2016).

[57] Winn v. Wilson, 2016-Ohio-7545, ¶ 13, 2016 WL 6462463 (Ohio Ct. App. 12th Dist. Butler County 2016), quoting Eastwood v. Eastwood, 2010-Ohio-6492, ¶ 15, 2010 WL 5550706 (Ohio Ct. App. 9th Dist. Summit County 2010), citing Callahan v. Akron Gen. Med. Ctr., 2009-Ohio-5148, ¶ 45, 2009 WL 3119626 (Ohio Ct. App. 9th Dist. Summit County 2009).

[58] Patterson v. Loveless, 2001 WL 524372 (Ohio Ct. App. 2d Dist. Montgomery County 2001).

[59] Patterson v. Loveless, 2001 WL 524372, *3 (Ohio Ct. App. 2d Dist. Montgomery County 2001).

[60] Schindler v. Schindler, 1998 WL 46764 (Ohio Ct. App. 9th Dist. Summit County 1998).

the account or not, we find no abuse of discretion in the court charging appellant with the full amount of his domestic violence defense.[61]

§ 12:22 Remedies—Miscellaneous issues

Q & A: Is the physical abuse of one spouse by the other relevant for purposes of dividing the marital assets in a divorce action?

One Ohio court touched on this issue. In *Fraley v. Fraley*,[1] the defendant appealed the divorce, arguing that the court abused its discretion in awarding all marital property to his wife. At the time of the divorce hearing, defendant was incarcerated for a domestic violence and vandalism conviction.

The Second District court of Appeals reversed, holding the trial court failed to justify granting the wife an unequal division of marital property. The court then held that "[c]riminal convictions are not one of the factors that RC 3105.171(F) requires the court to consider. Sandra was not the victim of Richard's acts of domestic violence, [his stepdaughter was the victim] though she may have suffered losses as a result of his acts of vandalism. If so, the award to her may be reasonable compensation for her loss."[2]

The appeals court left open the issue of whether, under a different fact pattern, a spouse may be awarded the marital property because of domestic violence. The court suggests that the argument might be made in the right circumstance.

In other states, the courts have squarely considered the issue. For example, the Nevada Supreme Court determined that physical abuse during the marriage does not justify an unequal property division. In *Wheeler v. Upton-Wheeler*,[3] a divorcing wife alleged physical abuse by her husband. The trial court found that physical abuse was a compelling reason to make an unequal disposition of the parties' joint property. The Nevada Supreme Court noted that the legislature mandated an equal division of joint property unless there is a compelling reason for an unequal division. Emphasizing the legislative desire to keep Nevada a no-fault divorce state, the Supreme Court held that spousal abuse is not a compelling reason unless the conduct at issue had an adverse financial impact on the victimized spouse.

Conversely, in *Murtha v. Murtha*,[4] a New York appellate court held that a victim of domestic violence during the marriage was entitled to more than sixty percent of the marital assets in her divorce case due

---

[61]Schindler v. Schindler, 1998 WL 46764, *5 (Ohio Ct. App. 9th Dist. Summit County 1998).

[Section 12:22]

[1]Fraley v. Fraley, 1999 WL 960963 (Ohio Ct. App. 2d Dist. Montgomery County 1999).

[2]Fraley v. Fraley, 1999 WL 960963, *2 (Ohio Ct. App. 2d Dist. Montgomery County 1999).

[3]Wheeler v. Upton-Wheeler, 113 Nev. 1185, 946 P.2d 200 (1997); see also In re Petition of Fenzau, 2002 MT 197, 311 Mont. 163, 54 P.3d 43 (2002); In re Letendre, 149 N.H. 31, 815 A.2d 938 (2002); Havell v. Islam, 301 A.D.2d 339, 751 N.Y.S.2d 449 (1st Dep't 2002).

[4]Murtha v. Murtha, No. 301457/99 (N.Y. App. Div., 5-15-98).

to her husband's "egregious behavior," which included physical and emotional abuse.[5]

Q & A: Does spousal abuse in a relationship impair the abused spouse's ability to validly execute an agreement in a divorce?

This issue was addressed by a New York court in *Reich v. Reich*.[6] In that case, the wife sought money damages for fraud on the basis that a post-nuptial agreement signed by her in 1995 was not validly executed due to her mental disability resulting from the defendant's physical abuse. In this agreement, the parties had resolved all issues, including support, maintenance, and property division. In permitting the wife to present this argument, the court stated that, while such marital agreements may be valid, they are subject to great scrutiny, especially where the parties have been married a long time and spousal abuse was alleged. The court refused to permit the husband to dismiss the wife's claims, noting that she raised sufficient factual issues. Moreover, a ten-and-one-half-month delay in repudiating the agreement was not unreasonable under the circumstances.

The fact that the court even allowed her to argue the issue is significant for battered spouses. Such a decision opens the door for future litigation involving parties who wish to invalidate separation agreements based on allegations of domestic violence in the relationship.

Q & A: Does a court have discretion to issue a CPO that includes various restrictions on the respondent's conduct?[7]

Yes, but the discretion of a court is not without certain limits. In *Maag v. Maag*,[8] appellee had sought a five year civil protection order. Among other restrictions, appellant was prohibited from consuming alcohol or drugs for the five-year duration.

On appeal, appellant contended that the trial court abused its discretion by ordering him to refrain from possessing or consuming alcoholic beverages or illegal drugs for the duration of the order. The appellate court noted that R.C. 3113.31(E)(1)(h) affords trial courts discretion to grant relief in protection orders that the court considers "equitable and fair." However, the record must indicate a nexus between the act of violence and the consumption of alcohol or illegal drugs.[9] Absent evidence that the substance abuse precipitated appellant's conduct or would exacerbate the risk of future harm, the court should not have ordered the restriction.

---

[5]See also In re Marriage of Severino, 298 Ill. App. 3d 224, 226, 232 Ill. Dec. 355, 698 N.E.2d 193 (2d Dist. 1998) (finding husband's physical abuse of his wife to be a relevant factor in determining whether a permanent alimony award was appropriate and noting that consideration of the wife's emotional state in making a support award does not constitute punishment of husband for bad behavior).

[6]Reich v. Reich, 239 A.D.2d 246, 657 N.Y.S.2d 671 (1st Dep't 1997); see also Quebodeaux v. Quebodeaux, 102 Ohio App. 3d 502, 657 N.E.2d 539 (9th Dist. Lorain County 1995) (court affirmed trial court decision in granting the wife's motion for relief from judgment and invalidating the signed separation agreement as having been signed under duress, based in part on the repeated acts of domestic violence during the marriage).

[7]See also Text § 9:9.

[8]Maag v. Maag, 2002-Ohio-1401, 2002 WL 468585 (Ohio Ct. App. 3d Dist. Wyandot County 2002).

[9]See also Markowitz v. Markowitz, 2006-Ohio-5932, 2006 WL 3234010 (Ohio Ct.

In sustaining appellant's assignment of error, the Wyandot Court of Appeals reasoned that while the statute permits trial courts the discretion to impose restrictions in a CPO on an appellant, this discretion is not limitless. "We find the restriction barring Appellant's consumption or possession of alcohol analogous to those cases discussing unduly restrictive conditions placed on individuals subject to probation."[10] The court then articulated the test to determine whether a restriction set forth in a CPO can be imposed, and held that "restrictions must bear a sufficient nexus to the conduct that the trial court is attempting to prevent."[11] Because the evidence did not demonstrate the connection between the appellant's behavior and the restriction imposed by the trial court, the appellate court found that the trial court abused its discretion by imposing such a restriction.[12]

Similarly, in *Hoyt v. Heindell*,[13] the father of a minor child requested a CPO for domestic violence on behalf of his child against the mother and her husband, because the mother's husband would drink beer while driving with the child in the car. Sometimes, the mother would also drink in the car.

The terms of the civil protection order included provisions that restricted the mother and her husband from transporting the child. But the CPO also prohibited them from entering the child's school or school grounds or from being within 500 feet of the child or from having contact with the child (except during the exercise of their visitation).

On appeal, the court chose to address the restrictions placed on the Heindells in light of their contention that the trial court erred in making a custody determination as part of the CPO. The appellate court first looked at R.C. 3113.31(E)(1)(h), which provides that a court may grant other relief or may add restrictions so long as they are equitable and fair. "While RC 3113.31 affords trial courts discretion in imposing

App. 8th Dist. Cuyahoga County 2006) (asking court on remand to consider whether its restrictions on the possession of weapons and on the consumption of alcohol were warranted by the evidence); F.-S. v. Pacek, 2015-Ohio-4310, 2015 WL 6128507 (Ohio Ct. App. 9th Dist. Medina County 2015) (need for a nexus between alcohol use and respondent's behavior).

[10]Maag v. Maag, 2002-Ohio-1401, 2002 WL 468585, *3 (Ohio Ct. App. 3d Dist. Wyandot County 2002).

[11]Maag v. Maag, 2002-Ohio-1401, 2002 WL 468585, *3 (Ohio Ct. App. 3d Dist. Wyandot County 2002).

[12]See Boals v. Miller, 2011-Ohio-1470, 2011 WL 1118464 (Ohio Ct. App. 5th Dist. Ashland County 2011) (restriction against use of alcohol/drugs did not bear a sufficient nexus to the conduct the court was attempting to prevent, as no evidence was presented that respondent's alcohol and drug use contributed to the violence); T.S. v. R.S., 2017-Ohio-281, 81 N.E.3d 932 (Ohio Ct. App. 9th Dist. Summit County 2017) (finding that trial court abused its discretion when it imposed restrictions on father's use of his own car by ordering father to sign over title to his son or grant son power of attorney to register the car and maintain exclusive use of it and noting that a determination of a sufficient nexus is dependent on a finding of competent, credible evidence of the conduct the trial court seeks to prevent).

[13]Hoyt v. Heindell, 191 Ohio App. 3d 373, 2010-Ohio-6058, 946 N.E.2d 258 (11th Dist. Lake County 2010).

restrictions corresponding to a [civil protection order], this discretion is not limitless."[14]

The court then adopted the standard used by other appellate courts which found that in determining the reasonableness of a restriction in a civil protection order, the restriction must bear a sufficient nexus to the conduct that the trial court is attempting to prevent.[15] The court found that the behavior to be prevented was driving a motor vehicle and drinking while the minor child was a passenger. Thus, the restrictions had to be limited to the Heindells' conduct. Since these restrictions did not have a significant nexus to the conduct the court was trying to prevent, they were unreasonable. Of importance is that the court acknowledged that there was no evidence in the record indicating that the child was not safe with the mother or his stepfather, or that the child was physically abused or otherwise harmed.

Likewise, the 5th District Court of Appeals also addressed this issue in *Boals v. Miller*,[16] in which the magistrate issued a CPO based on a physical confrontation in which petitioner was taken to the hospital. The magistrate stated that the prohibition against consuming alcohol was standard for every CPO the court issued because the incidents were typically because of drugs or alcohol. The trial court modified the CPO to permit respondent's use of alcohol for religious purposes.

On appeal, appellant argued that the trial court abused its discretion when it prohibited appellant from consuming alcohol and from using, possessing, carrying or obtaining any firearm or deadly weapon for the duration of the CPO, and the appellate court agreed. The test set forth in *Mann v. Sumser*[17] focused on whether the CPO contained terms designed to insure the safety and protection of the petitioner, and the *Maag* test[18] articulated the need for a nexus between the respondent's behavior and the restriction imposed.

In light of these tests, the appellate court in *Boals* reasoned that "[i]n analyzing whether a sufficient nexus exists to warrant the prohibition of the conduct, the courts look to the evidence in the record to find competent, credible evidence of the conduct the trial court is attempting to prevent. This is the method this Court utilized in *Mann*, supra, to determine that a prohibition on possessing firearms was supported by the evidence in the record."[19] Because the appellate court did not find evidence in the record in this case to indicate that

---

[14]Hoyt v. Heindell, 191 Ohio App. 3d 373, 2010-Ohio-6058, 946 N.E.2d 258 (11th Dist. Lake County 2010), quoting Maag v. Maag, 2002-Ohio-1401, 2002 WL 468585, *3 (Ohio Ct. App. 3d Dist. Wyandot County 2002).

[15]Hoyt v. Heindell, 191 Ohio App. 3d 373, 2010-Ohio-6058, 946 N.E.2d 258 (11th Dist. Lake County 2010), quoting Maag v. Maag, 2002-Ohio-1401, 2002 WL 468585, *9 (Ohio Ct. App. 3d Dist. Wyandot County 2002), and citing Sistek v. Grendence, 2006-Ohio-4169, 2006 WL 2337189 (Ohio Ct. App. 11th Dist. Lake County 2006).

[16]Boals v. Miller, 2011-Ohio-1470, 2011 WL 1118464 (Ohio Ct. App. 5th Dist. Ashland County 2011).

[17]Mann v. Sumser, 2002-Ohio-5103, 2002 WL 31151164 (Ohio Ct. App. 5th Dist. Stark County 2002).

[18]Maag v. Maag, 2002-Ohio-1401, 2002 WL 468585, *3 (Ohio Ct. App. 3d Dist. Wyandot County 2002).

[19]Boals v. Miller, 2011-Ohio-1470, 2011 WL 1118464, *4 (Ohio Ct. App. 5th Dist.

appellant threatened appellee with a deadly weapon, the trial court abused its discretion when it prohibited appellant from possessing firearms.

The appellate court next determined that while the parties did engage in drug and alcohol use, there was an insufficient nexus between appellant's use of alcohol and the resulting restriction supporting a five year prohibition on alcohol. In fact, the evidence presented focused on appellee's use, rather than appellant's use. Therefore, the appellate court sustained appellant's assignment of error.

It is important to note that the Supreme Court's standardized forms offer many options for trial courts to consider when crafting appropriate civil protection orders. However, specific provisions must be based on the facts of a particular case.

Q & A: Can a court prohibit a respondent from possessing guns or other weapons for the duration of the civil protection order?

As with alcohol or drugs, the question related to all remedies permitted to a petitioner by statute or the standard forms should be whether the evidence warrants the restrictions.

In *Sistek v. Grendence*,[20] appellant appealed the issuance of the CPO because the CPO prohibited him from possessing, using, carrying or obtaining any deadly weapon and from consuming alcohol. The appellate court remanded the case to the trial court to remove the restriction regarding the alcohol.

The Eleventh District Court of Appeals framed the issue by initially noting that a trial court, in issuing a CPO, may add restrictions provided they are both equitable and fair.[21] "While RC 3113.31 affords trial courts discretion in imposing restrictions corresponding to a [civil protection order], this discretion is not limitless."[22] In determining the reasonableness of a restriction of a civil protection order, the Third Appellate District has adopted a standard similar to that used in determining whether a condition of probation is unduly restrictive. Thus, "restrictions must bear a sufficient nexus to the conduct that the trial court is attempting to prevent."[23]

In the instant case, appellant contends that there was no nexus between his conduct and the restriction prohibiting him from possessing deadly weapons or from him consuming alcohol during the duration of the CPO.

Ashland County 2011).

[20]Sistek v. Grendence, 2006-Ohio-4169, 2006 WL 2337189 (Ohio Ct. App. 11th Dist. Lake County 2006).

[21]RC 3113.31(E)(1)(h).

[22]Sistek v. Grendence, 2006-Ohio-4169, 2006 WL 2337189, *4 (Ohio Ct. App. 11th Dist. Lake County 2006), citing Maag v. Maag, 2002-Ohio-1401, 2002 WL 468585, *9 (Ohio Ct. App. 3d Dist. Wyandot County 2002).

[23]Sistek v. Grendence, 2006-Ohio-4169, 2006 WL 2337189, *4 (Ohio Ct. App. 11th Dist. Lake County 2006), citing Maag v. Maag, 2002-Ohio-1401, 2002 WL 468585, *9 (Ohio Ct. App. 3d Dist. Wyandot County 2002); see Markowitz v. Markowitz, 2006-Ohio-5932, 2006 WL 3234010 (Ohio Ct. App. 8th Dist. Cuyahoga County 2006); see also Mann v. Sumser, 2002-Ohio-5103, 2002 WL 31151164 (Ohio Ct. App. 5th Dist. Stark County 2002); Newhouse v. Williams, 167 Ohio App. 3d 215, 2006-Ohio-3075, 854 N.E.2d 565 (3d Dist. Wyandot County 2006).

The appellate court determined that there was sufficient evidence presented to demonstrate that there was a nexus between appellant's conduct and the prohibition against deadly weapons.[24] This was based on threats to kill the protected parties by slitting their throats and a past history of threatening petitioner while holding a knife.

On the other hand, the court determined there was no nexus between appellant's conduct and the alcohol prohibition. Appellant had not been under the influence on the day in question and there was no evidence that he was intoxicated during any of the other incidents. Moreover, there was no evidence that appellant had an alcohol or drug problem. The appellate court held that the trial court had abused its discretion by imposing a restriction against using alcohol or drugs during the duration of the order.

Q & A: Must each term of a civil protection order be supported by independent evidence presented at the full hearing?

In *Butcher v. Stevens*,[25] the respondent appealed the granting of a CPO which prohibited respondent from possessing, using, carrying or obtaining any deadly weapon.

The appellate court reversed, in part, the trial court's judgment regarding the weapons terms. The court relied on the reasoning set forth in *Sistek v. Grendence*,[26] in which the Eleventh District Court of Appeals held that in issuing a civil protection order, the trial court may add restrictions that are "equitable and fair." " 'While RC 3113.31 affords trial courts discretion in imposing restrictions corresponding to a [civil protection order], this discretion is not limitless.' "[27] "As further noted by the *Sistek* court, '[i]n determining the reasonableness of a restriction of a civil protection order, the Third Appellate District has adopted a standard similar to that used in determining whether a condition of probation is unduly restrictive.' "[28] "Thus, 'restrictions must bear a sufficient nexus to the conduct that the trial court is attempting to prevent.' "[29]

Neither weapons nor the threat to use weapons played a role in the commission of the acts that formed the basis of the CPO. Because weapons were not involved in the acts of domestic violence, the appellate court held that the weapons restrictions imposed upon appellant

---

[24]See also Mann v. Sumser, 2002-Ohio-5103, 2002 WL 31151164 (Ohio Ct. App. 5th Dist. Stark County 2002); Gaydash v. Gaydash, 168 Ohio App. 3d 418, 2006-Ohio-4080, 860 N.E.2d 789 (9th Dist. Summit County 2006) (noting that appellant had failed to develop his argument that the CPO infringed on his right to bear arms).

[25]Butcher v. Stevens, 182 Ohio App. 3d 77, 2009-Ohio-1754, 911 N.E.2d 928 (4th Dist. Athens County 2009).

[26]Sistek v. Grendence, 2006-Ohio-4169, 2006 WL 2337189 (Ohio Ct. App. 11th Dist. Lake County 2006).

[27]Butcher v. Stevens, 182 Ohio App. 3d 77, 83, 2009-Ohio-1754, ¶ 15, 911 N.E.2d 928, 933 (4th Dist. Athens County 2009), quoting Sistek v. Grendence, 2006-Ohio-4169, 2006 WL 2337189, *4 (Ohio Ct. App. 11th Dist. Lake County 2006), and citing Maag v. Maag, 2002-Ohio-1401, 2002 WL 468585 (Ohio Ct. App. 3d Dist. Wyandot County 2002).

[28]Butcher v. Stevens, 182 Ohio App. 3d 77, 83–84, 2009-Ohio-1754, ¶ 15, 911 N.E.2d 928, 933 (4th Dist. Athens County 2009).

[29]Butcher v. Stevens, 182 Ohio App. 3d 77, 84, 2009-Ohio-1754, ¶ 15, 911 N.E.2d 928, 933 (4th Dist. Athens County 2009), quoting Sistek v. Grendence, 2006-Ohio-4169, 2006 WL 2337189, *4 (Ohio Ct. App. 11th Dist. Lake County 2006).

in the CPO lacked the sufficient nexus to the conduct at issue and is therefore, unreasonable.[30] As such, the term is not supported by the evidence presented.

Q & A: Can a party use joint funds to file a complaint for divorce and a domestic violence petition?

Yes, according to one Ohio court. In *Petrusch v. Petrusch*,[31] the wife filed a divorce complaint and a domestic violence petition. She had no income of her own because of her husband's insistence that she not work outside the home. In order to file the divorce and domestic violence claims, she withdrew $5,000 out of the parties' joint funds. The court awarded her spousal support and attorney fees which were partially satisfied by permitting her to keep her husband's share of the joint funds she had withdrawn. The husband appealed the decision, and the court of appeals found that her use of the funds was justified.

The Montgomery County Court of Appeals noted that "[i]t would be poor public policy to require a spouse to remain in an abusive relationship because she is not allowed to spend the only money to which she has access, a joint marital bank account, to retain an attorney for the purpose of filing for divorce."[32] The court held that the money withdrawn by the wife was properly spent by her and was not subject to distribution.

Law Enforcement Concerns:[33]

Q & A: Can the court order the police to provide assistance to the petitioner?

The police play a vital role in preventing domestic violence. Law enforcement acts as the gatekeeper between the victim, the respondent, the criminal justice system, the legal system, and the social service system. Oftentimes, victims first hear about their legal rights from the local police officer.[34]

Ohio's civil protection order statute specifically articulates that it is a police officer's proper role to provide both information[35] and assistance.[36] Law enforcement must provide a victim of domestic violence with information regarding the relief available by obtaining either a civil or criminal protection order.[37] Additionally, police are required to give victims the officer's name and badge number, the

---

[30]Butcher v. Stevens, 182 Ohio App. 3d 77, 84, 2009-Ohio-1754, ¶ 17, 911 N.E.2d 928, 933 (4th Dist. Athens County 2009).

[31]Petrusch v. Petrusch, 1997 WL 102014 (Ohio Ct. App. 2d Dist. Montgomery County 1997).

[32]Petrusch v. Petrusch, 1997 WL 102014, *2 (Ohio Ct. App. 2d Dist. Montgomery County 1997). But see Schindler v. Schindler, 1998 WL 46764 (Ohio Ct. App. 9th Dist. Summit County 1998) (stating that the abuser must pay his own attorney fees in defending against a charge of domestic violence).

[33]See Text Ch. 13, Court Enforcement of Civil Protection Orders and Related Issues, and Text Ch. 14, Police Enforcement of Protection Orders and Other Relevant Issues.

[34]See RC 2935.032(C)(2), RC 2935.032(C)(3).

[35]RC 2935.032(C), RC 3113.31(I).

[36]RC 3113.31(F)(3).

[37]RC 2935.032(C)(2), RC 3113.31(I).

report number for the incident if available, a telephone number that the victim can call for information about the case, the telephone number of a domestic violence shelter in the area, and information on any local victim advocate program.[38]

Significantly, the law also requires that law enforcement officers make a written report of the domestic violence incident documenting the officer's observations of the victim and alleged offender, any visible injuries of the victim or alleged offender, any weapons at the scene, the actions of the alleged offender, any statements made by the victim or witnesses, and any other significant facts or circumstances.[39] Sometimes, this written report is the most important piece of information a victim may have. It will aid the victim in documenting the history of abuse for the future.

Besides information, a police officer must provide assistance to the petitioner and other family or household members. The law provides that "any officer of a law enforcement agency shall enforce a protection order issued or consent agreement approved by any court in this state in accordance with the provisions of the order or agreement, including removing the respondent from the premises, if appropriate."[40]

Police officers are also obligated to perform certain acts if written into a civil protection order. The law requires officers to enforce a protection order in accordance with its terms.[41]

Attorneys and the court can direct officers to enforce other provisions as well. For example, law enforcement officers can be directed to accompany the victim or respondent to retrieve personal property, obtain house keys, garage door openers, or motor vehicle keys from the respondent, confiscate weapons, retrieve the children from the batterer, and serve process on the respondent.[42] Such provisions may be included by the court in a protection order to secure safety for the victim.

Weapons Concerns:[43]

Q & A: Do state trial courts have the authority to order respondents to turn over weapons, and do the police have the authority to seize these weapons?[44]

Under the catchall provisions inherent in the statute, courts have

---

[38]RC 2935.032(C)(3).

[39]RC 2935.032(C)(1), RC 2935.032(D).

[40]RC 3113.31(F)(3); see also Md. Op. Att'y Gen. 99-012 (8-10-99), 1999 WL 636670 (stating that a trial court in a domestic violence matter that involves the violation of a custody order may have the authority to direct law enforcement officers to forcibly return a minor child to the custodial parent).

[41]RC 3113.31(F)(3).

[42]See, for example, Sup. R. Forms 10.01-I and 10.01-J.

[43]See Text § 18:11, Firearms offenses under VAWA; see also Podeweltz v. Rieger, 2007-Ohio-1513, 2007 WL 949482 (Ohio Ct. App. 2d Dist. Montgomery County 2007) (magistrate informed respondent that despite SCPO he did not think Rieger would have to turn in his hunting firearms and that he thought Rieger might "have difficulty" purchasing new firearms if found guilty).

[44]See Text § 14:5, False arrest, warrantless arrests and searches, and weapons confiscation. See also Text § 18:11, Firearm offenses under VAWA. See also City of

the authority to write into civil protection orders terms designed to bring about a cessation of violence.[45] Given the danger weapons pose in abusive relationships, courts often prohibit a respondent from possessing, using, carrying, or obtaining any weapon during the duration of the civil protection order. The Supreme Court's standard protection order forms also require a respondent to turn over all deadly weapons to law enforcement officials to hold in protective custody until further order of court.[46] Additionally, the Supreme Court's forms also include language ordering a respondent to turn over to law enforcement any concealed carry license.[47]

Several states have also codified these provisions. For example, California prohibits a respondent who has a protection order issued against him from purchasing, receiving, or attempting to purchase or receive a firearm.[48]

In addition, the Violence Against Women Act,[49] enacted on September 13, 1994, contains a provision that includes individuals who are the subject of final protection orders in the list of persons prohibited from purchasing, receiving, and possessing firearms or ammunition. It also makes it a federal crime to knowingly transfer or sell these items to someone subject to such an order. An exception is made for members of the military and law enforcement.[50]

It is important to note that, under the Violence Against Women Act, where there is a prohibition against firearms in the protection order, the victim is entitled to state law enforcement in addition to federal law enforcement. However, if the prohibition is not written into the protection order, the petitioner will only be entitled to federal enforcement.

Recently, the Bureau of Alcohol, Tobacco and Firearms informed all state and local law enforcement agencies that it is unlawful for any person convicted of a misdemeanor crime of domestic violence to ship, transport, possess, or receive firearms or ammunition. This prohibi-

---

Cleveland v. Carpenter, 2003-Ohio-6923, 2003 WL 22976619 (Ohio Ct. App. 8th Dist. Cuyahoga County 2003).

[45]RC 3113.31(E)(1); see also RC 3113.31(E)(1)(h).

[46]See Sup. R. 10.01(C), Sup. R. Form 10.01-H to Sup. R. Form 10.01-J; Golden v. Bay Village Police Dept., 2002-Ohio-673, 2002 WL 253878 (Ohio Ct. App. 8th Dist. Cuyahoga County 2002); State v. Majka, 2002-Ohio-1378, 2002 WL 462858 (Ohio Ct. App. 9th Dist. Summit County 2002); see also Text § 14:5, False arrest, warrantless arrests and searches, and weapons confiscation.

[47]Sup. R. 10.01-H-J; Sup. R. 10.02-A; Sup. R. 10.03-B; Sup. R. 10.03-E-G; see also RC 2923.125 which provides that an applicant for a concealed carry license must not be the subject of a civil protection order.

[48]See Cal. Fam. Code § 6304. See also Cal. Fam. Code § 6389. See recently introduced HB 494 (2015-2016).

[49]18 U.S.C.A. § 922; see also Text § 18:11, Firearm offenses under VAWA (discussing firearms while a civil protection order is in place); Text § 14:6, Law enforcement policies and procedures.

[50]See 18 U.S.C.A. § 922(d)(8), 18 U.S.C.A. § 922(g)(8); see also Text § 18:11, Firearm offenses under VAWA; Text § 14:6, Law enforcement policies and procedures. Sup. R. 10.01-H-J; Sup. R. 10.02-A; Sup. R. 10.03-B; and Sup. R. 10.03-E-G all provide that a respondent will not be permitted to possess, use, carry or obtain any weapon at any time while the order remains in effect, unless excepted for official use pursuant to 18 U.S.C. 925(a)(1).

tion applies to law enforcement officers.[51] For most police officers, not being able to possess a firearm means they will be discharged.[52] This law applies to persons convicted of such misdemeanors at any time, even if the conviction occurred prior to the new law's effective date of September 30, 1996. As one commentator noted:

> The [Act] recognizes the escalating nature of domestic violence which tends to increase in severity. A 1993 study in the New England Journal of Medicine revealed that homes that had experienced domestic violence were close to five times more likely to be the scene of a homicide than other homes. It also showed that a handgun in the home is 43 times more likely to kill a family member or an acquaintance than an intruder.[53]

Courts should inquire at the full hearing whether respondents in domestic violence cases own weapons and, if so, order their confiscation by police in the civil protection order. Attorneys for victims of domestic violence should request this relief whenever a victim raises concerns over weapons. Research data on batterers who ultimately kill their victims underscores the importance of retrieving weapons.[54]

Since law enforcement officials are mandated to enforce protection orders according to the terms of the order,[55] a police officer is obligated and authorized to confiscate weapons if so ordered.

Furthermore, the domestic violence statute specifically grants law enforcement officials the authority to seize weapons in domestic violence cases even where the protection order does not provide for such seizure.[56] Police officers shall seize weapons under the following circumstances:

> If a peace officer . . . responds to a report of an alleged incident of the offense of domestic violence or an alleged incident of the offense of violating a protection order and if the circumstances of the incident involved the use or threatened use of a deadly weapon or any person . . . brandished a deadly weapon during or in relation to the incident, the deadly weapon that was used, threatened to be used, or brandished constitutes contraband, and, to the extent possible, the officer shall seize the deadly weapon as contraband pursuant to [RC] 2933.43.[57]

Q & A: What exactly is a deadly weapon?

Pursuant to RC 2923.11(A), a deadly weapon includes "any instrument, device, or thing capable of inflicting death, and designed or specially adapted for use as a weapon, or possessed, carried, or used

[51]See Omnibus Consolidated Appropriations Act of 1997; 18 U.S.C.A. § 922(d)(8), 18 U.S.C.A. § 922(g)(8). See also U.S. v. Smith, 964 F. Supp. 286 (N.D. Iowa 1997), judgment aff'd, 171 F.3d 617 (8th Cir. 1999); U.S. v. Meade, 986 F. Supp. 66 (D. Mass. 1997), aff'd, 175 F.3d 215 (1st Cir. 1999).

[52]See Fraternal Order of Police v. U.S., 152 F.3d 998 (D.C. Cir. 1998), on reh'g, 173 F.3d 898 (D.C. Cir. 1999).

[53]Ohio Domestic Violence Network, Network News, Vol. 4 Issue 2 Fall 1996 at 2.

[54]Daniel G. Saunders & Angela Browne, Domestic Homicide, in Case Studies in Family Violence 379, 381 (Robert Ammerman & Michel Hersen eds., 1991).

[55]RC 3113.31(F)(3).

[56]RC 2935.03(B)(3)(h); see also City of Cleveland v. Carpenter, 2003-Ohio-6923, 2003 WL 22976619 (Ohio Ct. App. 8th Dist. Cuyahoga County 2003).

[57]RC 2935.03(B)(3)(h).

as a weapon."[58] For example, in *State v. Taylor*,[59] the appellant argued on appeal that a pitchfork does not constitute a deadly weapon within the meaning of RC 2923.11(A) in a felonious assault case for domestic violence. The Summit County Court of Appeals upheld the jury verdict against appellant and reasoned that "[t]his Court has held that the description of a deadly weapon is in the disjunctive, and hence an item is a deadly weapon if it is capable of inflicting death and used as a weapon."[60] The appellant had conceded that the pitchfork was capable of inflicting death, but argued that it was not a weapon because it was not possessed, carried, or used as a weapon as required in RC 2923.11(A). However, witness testimony corroborated that appellant had entered victim's house carrying a pitchfork and that the victim "was crying and appeared to be hurt."[61] The court concluded that it was reasonable to infer that appellant used the pitchfork as a weapon after he carried it in to victim's house.

Q & A: What is a qualifying civil protection order?[62]

A qualifying protection order is one that was issued after a hearing of which the person subject to the order has had actual notice and an opportunity to be heard. It must restrain the person from harassing, stalking or threatening an intimate partner of the person, or child of the person or intimate partner or engage in other conduct that would place an intimate partner in reasonable fear of bodily injury to the partner or child. It must also include either a finding that the person subject to the order represents a credible threat to the physical safety of an intimate partner or child, or an explicit prohibition against the use, attempted use, or threatened use of physical force against an intimate partner or child which would reasonably be expected to cause bodily injury.[63]

An intimate partner is a current or former spouse, co-parent, or one who cohabits or has cohabited with the subject of the order.[64]

Clearly then, Ohio cases that rely on the "nexus" argument appear to misunderstand or choose to ignore federal law and its relation to state law. Moreover, the nexus argument could be applied in state CPO cases to expand rather than limit firearms prohibitions. It is arguable that the nexus claim may be made if a respondent's criminal history is considered by the court as well as the statistics evidencing the public health impact of firearms and its nexus to domestic violence.

---

[58]RC 2923.11(A); see also RC 2903.11(E)(1); Gaydash v. Gaydash, 168 Ohio App. 3d 418, 2006-Ohio-4080, 860 N.E.2d 789 (9th Dist. Summit County 2006) (a vehicle may be an instrumentality of violence).

[59]State v. Taylor, 2003-Ohio-2025, 2003 WL 1916787 (Ohio Ct. App. 9th Dist. Summit County 2003).

[60]State v. Taylor, 2003-Ohio-2025, 2003 WL 1916787, *2 (Ohio Ct. App. 9th Dist. Summit County 2003), quoting State v. Flowers, 2000 WL 296081 (Ohio Ct. App. 9th Dist. Summit County 2000).

[61]State v. Taylor, 2003-Ohio-2025, 2003 WL 1916787, *2 (Ohio Ct. App. 9th Dist. Summit County 2003).

[62]See also Text § 18:11 and Text § 18:13).

[63]18 U.S.C.A. § 922(g)(8); see also § 18:13.

[64]18 U.S.C.A. § 921(a)(32).

Q & A: Does a state trial court have the legal authority to issue a protection order that restrains a defendant from possessing weapons or firearms?

In *Woolum v. Woolum*,[65] the Preble County Court of Appeals determined that the Gun Control Act of 1968 was intended by Congress "to assist the states effectively to regulate firearms traffic within their borders." Specifically, the court relied on a provision which stated that it is unlawful for a person to possess a firearm or weapon when that person is subject to a court order that restrains that person from harassing, stalking, or threatening an intimate partner.[66] Since the appellant was subject to a civil protection order, the trial court had the discretion to include the remedy provided by Congress in the Gun Control Act of 1968.[67] The appellate court concluded that a civil protection order that contains a provision restraining a defendant from possessing a weapon or firearm was well within the authority of the trial court.

The Seventh Circuit Court of Appeals recently upheld the constitutionality of 18 U.S.C.A. § 922(g)(8) in *United States v. Wilson*.[68] In that case, the defendant was subject to a protection order stemming from divorce proceedings instituted by his wife. He was arrested on an outstanding warrant unrelated to the case at hand. The police officer discovered several firearms in the defendant's truck and on his person. He was convicted of possessing a firearm and affecting interstate commerce while subject to a protection order. On appeal, he argued that the statute exceeds the authority granted to Congress. The Seventh Circuit upheld the constitutionality of the statute, noting that a minimal connection with interstate commerce is all that is required to satisfy the Commerce Clause.

Additionally, in light of the fact that 18 U.S.C.A. § 922(g)(8) was lawfully enacted pursuant to Congress' Commerce Clause authority, the court also ruled that the statute does not violate the Tenth Amendment's reservation of power to the states. The court added that, contrary to the defendant's assertions, 18 U.S.C.A. § 922(g)(8) does not interfere with a state judge's ability to enforce state domestic relations law.

Q & A: What guidance do the Supreme Court forms provide?

Pursuant to the Ohio Supreme Court's standard forms, a respondent "shall not possess, use, carry or obtain any deadly weapon at any time while the Order remains in effect."

What is most important is that there is no check box for this provision. This means that the provision is a directive. It is neither ambiguous nor unclear.

---

[65]Woolum v. Woolum, 131 Ohio App. 3d 818, 824, 723 N.E.2d 1135 (12th Dist. Preble County 1999); see also Benson v. Muscari, 172 Vt. 1, 769 A.2d 1291 (2001) (citing *Woodlum*).

[66]Gun Control Act of 1968, 18 U.S.C.A. § 922(g)(8).

[67]See also Conkle v. Wolfe, 131 Ohio App. 3d 375, 722 N.E.2d 586 (4th Dist. Athens County 1998).

[68]U.S. v. Wilson, 159 F.3d 280 (7th Cir. 1998); see also U.S. v. Pierson, 139 F.3d 501 (5th Cir. 1998); Text § 18:11, Firearm offenses under VAWA (discussing cases that address firearm access); Text § 14:5, False arrest, warrantless arrests and searches, and weapons confiscation.

Q & A: Does federal preemption apply and is the state's prohibition barring possession of fireman as a term of a CPO a violation of the Supremacy Clause of the United States Constitution?

Federal preemption is not applicable to this area of the law. Moreover, terms such as these in a CPO do not violate the U.S. Supremacy Clause. For example, in *Conkle v. Wolfe*,[69] defendant argued that the court had to first find him a "credible threat" to the physical safety of his partner before applying the prohibition and that the order, as written, excessively restricted his right to possess firearms. The Athens County Court of Appeals noted that the trial court was not required to make such a finding because it did not issue the protection order pursuant to federal law.[70] In fact, the court depended on the catch all provision in RC 3113.31(E)(1)(h) which provides that a court can grant other relief that the court considers equitable and fair. . .and which has been used to regulate weapons of respondents. Because the decision was based on state law, there was no need to satisfy the federal "credible threat" standard under 18 U.S.C. § 922(g)(8). The court reasoned that the trial court had complied with the provisions of RC 3113.31 by first determining that the defendant committed domestic violence and then retraining him from possessing weapons, which was both fair and equitable.

The appellate court held that "[t]he federal scheme to regulate interstate traffic in firearms does not displace the state's power to restrict certain individuals from possessing weapons. Ohio law does not stand as an obstacle to the accomplishment and execution of the full purposes and objectives of Congress that are reflected in the Gun Control Act. Congress designed the Gun Control Act to assist states in regulating firearms within their own borders, not to prevent states from regulating firearms within their borders."[71]

State firearms laws do not have to be identical to federal laws for them to apply. The federal firearms prohibitions apply even if they are inconsistent with state law.

Although it is possible that such a prohibition may be constitutionally challenged as being outside the purview of the state domestic violence statue, the legal analysis suggests that a state court has the discretion to issue a protection order that incorporates the federal remedy provided in the Gun Control Act of 1968.

However, because state law is silent as to the application of § 922(g)(8), some Ohio courts have advanced the concept of "nexus" to place limits and restrictions on firearms in domestic violence cases when civil protection orders are sought.

Q & A: Can a CPO containing a restriction against possessing firearms be modified to permit the possession of firearms?[72]

While no Ohio court has specifically addressed this issue, the Iowa

[69]Conkle v. Wolfe, 131 Ohio App. 3d 375, 722 N.E.2d 586 (4th Dist. Athens County 1998).

[70]See 18 U.S.C.A. § 922.

[71]Conkle v. Wolfe, 131 Ohio App. 3d 375, 386, 722 N.E.2d 586, 594 (4th Dist. Athens County 1998).

[72]See for eg., Benjamin Thomas Greer & Jeffrey G. Purvis, *Judges Going Rogue:*

Supreme Court has considered the issue in *Weissenburger v. Iowa District Court of Warren County*.[73] in that case, a defendant was the subject of a criminal no-contact order (similar to Ohio's protection orders) containing the language that "defendant shall not possess firearms while this order is in effect." Subsequently, defendant requested that the order be modified to permit him to possess firearms for hunting. Former wife appealed the ruling and argued that the amended order violated 18 U.S.C.A. § 922(G)(8).

The court framed the issue as whether the district court properly allowed the defendant to possess a firearm for hunting notwithstanding the prohibitions of federal law? The court relied on the Supremacy Clause of the U.S. Constitution stating that "state courts cannot refuse to apply federal law."[74] The court held that "[i]n view of these governing principles, we conclude the district court had no power to authorize Joseph to possess firearms in violation of federal law. Once the court determined the no-contact order should continue in effect, Joseph was prohibited under federal law from possessing firearms regardless of whether this prohibition was included in the court's no-contact order."[75]

The Iowa court's reasoning can be applied to Ohio's protection orders. Once a protection order is entered, a respondent does not have the right to possess weapons for the time period that the protection order is in effect, regardless of whether the order specifically prohibits possession of weapons.

Q & A: Can a court prohibit a respondent, who is subject to a CPO, from possessing, using, carrying or obtaining weapons where no evidence was presented that the respondent used or threatened to use the weapon in the commission of the act of domestic violence?[76]

Not according to several recent appellate districts. For example, in *Butcher v. Stevens*,[77] the appellant appealed a term of a civil protection order that the order prohibited him from obtaining or possessing a deadly weapon. His major objection was that he wanted to use a weapon to hunt or protect the animals on his property.

The Athens County Court of Appeals first noted that the domestic violence statute permits a court to add restrictions so long as they are equitable and fair.[78] However, the discretion of the trial court is not limitless and the restriction must be reasonable and bear a sufficient

Constitutional Implications When Mandatory Firearm Restrictions Are Removed From Domestic Violence Restraining Orders, 26 Wis. J.L. Gender & Soc'y 275 (Fall 2011).

[73]Weissenburger v. Iowa Dist. Court for Warren County, 740 N.W.2d 431 (Iowa 2007).

[74]Weissenburger v. Iowa Dist. Court for Warren County, 740 N.W.2d 431, 436 (Iowa 2007), quoting Printz v. U.S., 521 U.S. 898, 928, 117 S. Ct. 2365, 2381, 138 L. Ed. 2d 914, 940 (1997).

[75]Weissenburger v. Iowa Dist. Court for Warren County, 740 N.W.2d 431, 436 (Iowa 2007).

[76]See also § 9:9.

[77]Butcher v. Stevens, 182 Ohio App. 3d 77, 2009-Ohio-1754, 911 N.E.2d 928 (4th Dist. Athens County 2009).

[78]At *5; citing Sistek v. Grendence, 2006-Ohio-4169, 2006 WL 2337189 (Ohio Ct. App. 11th Dist. Lake County 2006); see also RC 3113.31(E)(1)(h).

nexus to the conduct being prevented by the order.[79] In that weapons played no part in the domestic violence incidents that were the basis of the CPO, the restrictions prohibiting weapons lacked a sufficient nexus to the conduct at issue and are unreasonable.[80] Therefore, the appellate court reversed the trial court's imposition of the weapons restriction in the civil protection order.

Similarly, in *Doran v. Doran*,[81] the CPO prohibited respondent from possessing, using, carrying or obtaining deadly weapons. On appeal, he argued that the trial court erred by including this restriction in the CPO.

The court of appeals noted that RC 3113.31(E)(1)(h) permits a court to impose restrictions on an individual to a CPO provided the restrictions are equitable and fair. "While RC 3113.31 affords a trial court discretion in imposing restrictions as part of a civil protection order, such discretion is not without limit."[82] "In determining the reasonableness of a restriction, some appellate districts have adopted a standard similar to that used in determining whether a condition of probation is unduly restrictive."[83] "Under this standard, the restriction must bear a sufficient nexus to the conduct that the trial court is attempting to prevent."[84]

The court of appeals held that a trial court abuses its discretion in imposing a weapons restriction as part of a civil protection order where no evidence is presented that the respondent used or threatened to use a deadly weapon to harm the petitioner.[85] Even where evidence is presented that a physical altercation occurred between the petitioner and respondent, some courts have found the imposition of a weapons restriction is unreasonable, absent evidence that weapons or a threat to use weapons were involved.[86]

---

[79]At *5; citing Sistek, quoting Maag v. Maag, 2002-Ohio-1401, 2002 WL 468585, *3 (Ohio Ct. App. 3d Dist. Wyandot County 2002); see also Newhouse v. Williams, 167 Ohio App. 3d 215, 2006-Ohio-3075, 854 N.E.2d 565 (3d Dist. Wyandot County 2006); Lerner v. Giolekas, 2016-Ohio-696, 2016 WL 762594 (Ohio Ct. App. 8th Dist. Cuyahoga County 2016), appeal not allowed, 146 Ohio St. 3d 1429, 2016-Ohio-4606, 52 N.E.3d 1204 (2016).

[80]At *5.

[81]Doran v. Doran, 2009-Ohio-5521, 2009 WL 3350841 (Ohio Ct. App. 12th Dist. Warren County 2009).

[82]At *4; citing, Butcher v. Stevens, 182 Ohio App. 3d 77, 2009-Ohio-1754, 911 N.E.2d 928 (4th Dist. Athens County 2009); citing Sistek v. Grendence, 2006-Ohio-4169, 2006 WL 2337189 (Ohio Ct. App. 11th Dist. Lake County 2006).

[83]At *4; citing Sistek, quoting Maag v. Maag, 2002-Ohio-1401, 2002 WL 468585, *3 (Ohio Ct. App. 3d Dist. Wyandot County 2002).

[84]At *4, citing, *Butcher at *5*; citing, *Sistek* at section 36, quoting *Maag at *3*.

[85]At *4; citing Newhouse v. Williams, 167 Ohio App. 3d 215, 2006-Ohio-3075, ¶ 16, 854 N.E.2d 565 (3d Dist. Wyandot County 2006); Boals v. Miller, 2011-Ohio-1470, 2011 WL 1118464 (Ohio Ct. App. 5th Dist. Ashland County 2011) (no evidence was presented that respondent threatened to shoot petitioner and no evidence presented that respondent's use of alcohol/drugs contributed to the violence; thus, restrictions in the CPO were not supported); F.-S. v. Pacek, 2015-Ohio-4310, 2015 WL 6128507 (Ohio Ct. App. 9th Dist. Medina County 2015).

[86]At *4; citing Butcher; but see Thom v. Mulvin, 2009-Ohio-3797, 2009 WL 2365996 (Ohio Ct. App. 6th Dist. Erie County 2009) (holding that the imposition of weapons restrictions was justified where appellant acted unnecessarily violent and

In *Cee v. Stone*,[87] the appellate court reasoned once again that, without a nexus, one cannot impose additional restrictions in a CPO. Where there is no nexus between the conduct and the restriction, the restriction will not be upheld. In this case, no evidence was ever presented that Stone ever owned a gun or threatened petitioner with a firearm. Thus, the firearms restriction violated the respondent's right to bear arms. Further, the court said that "[t]he only reason that the restriction was present was because it was on the preprinted form."[88]

Although the Court acknowledged the notice requirement regarding weapons in the statute,[89] it commented that "[t]he Ohio legislature has not made it a requirement that any respondent who is subject to a CPO be restricted from possessing a firearm.[90] In that federal law had not been codified into the state code, there was, apparently, no need to abide by federal law. Moreover, the court also noted (in footnote one of the opinion) that ". . . 18 U.S.C. 922(g) has been recognized as unconstitutional as applied (referencing 922(G)(4)) and is currently the subject of proposed legislation in the United States House and United States Senate."[91]

Unfortunately, the 3rd District Court of Appeals relied on a federal case from the 3rd Circuit Court of Appeals[92] that was not on point and further, misapplied the case holding in that case as well as the intents and purposes of Congressional H.R. 4142.

While it is true that the Ohio legislature has yet to codify federal law regarding firearms and domestic violence, it is also true that pursuant to federal law,[93] a person who is subject to a qualifying protection order is prohibited from possessing any firearm or ammunition in or affecting commerce, . . .or receiving any such firearm or ammunition, while the protection order is in effect.

Utilizing the same nexus analysis, some courts have determined that weapon restrictions are justified so long as the restrictions bear a sufficient nexus to the conduct the court is attempting to prevent.[94] Applying a nexus standard, these courts focused on the reasonable-

---

combative towards other people and animals, where he failed to turn over all of his weapons pursuant to a criminal TPO and where he had several guns kept in his car to scare people).

[87]Cee v. Stone, 2017-Ohio-8687, 2017 WL 5664759 (Ohio Ct. App. 3d Dist. Union County 2017).

[88]Cee v. Stone, 2017-Ohio-8687, ¶ 8, 2017 WL 5664759 (Ohio Ct. App. 3d Dist. Union County 2017).

[89]R.C. 3113.31(F)(2).

[90]Cee v. Stone, 2017-Ohio-8687, ¶ 6, 2017 WL 5664759 (Ohio Ct. App. 3d Dist. Union County 2017).

[91]Cee v. Stone, 2017-Ohio-8687, 2017 WL 5664759 (Ohio Ct. App. 3d Dist. Union County 2017).

[92]Binderup v. Attorney General United States of America, 836 F.3d 336 (3d Cir. 2016), cert. denied, 137 S. Ct. 2323, 198 L. Ed. 2d 746 (2017) and cert. denied, 137 S. Ct. 2323, 198 L. Ed. 2d 746 (2017).

[93]See Gun Control Act, 18 U.S.C. § 922(g)(8).

[94]Dague v. Dague, 2012-Ohio-1582, 2012 WL 1187920 (Ohio Ct. App. 11th Dist. Lake County 2012) (upholding issuance of restriction as bearing a sufficient nexus to conduct court was attempting to prevent and that bringing out weapon and cleaning it just as petitioner told husband she wanted to leave, although innocent, was considered another method of intimidation); Clementz-McBeth v. Craft, 2012-Ohio-

ness of the restriction and whether a particular restriction is fair and designed to bring about a cessation of violence. For example, in *Snell v. Snell*,[95] the appellant argued that the weapons restriction in the CPO was unfair and inequitable and violated his due process rights.

The appellate court relied on *Woolum v. Woolum*[96] in applying an abuse of discretion standard. It then held that "[a] trial court can include a prohibition about firearms in an order if it finds, after a full hearing, that the order is equitable, fair and necessary to bring about a cessation or prevention of domestic violence.[97] **Even if it does not specifically order restrictions on a respondent's possession of firearms, federal law prohibits it."** (emphasis added)[98]

Q & A: If a person is subject to a civil protection order, how long does the gun ban last?[99]

Although the Supreme Court's standard forms[100] do not provide a specific length of time during which a respondent is prohibited from purchasing, receiving or possessing firearms or ammunition, federal law[101] indicates that one is prohibited while the protection order is in effect. Under federal law, a violation of this prohibition while the order remains in effect is a federal offense punishable by up to 10 years imprisonment.[102] Upon expiration of the CPO,[103] or when criminal charges are dismissed[104] all restrictions terminate and all firearms are to be returned to a respondent.[105] However, neither federal nor state law provides a process by which this may occur.

Under the aforementioned analysis, it is likely that even where a state court does not find a nexus, a respondent who purchases a weapon, may still be in contravention of federal law.

985, 2012 WL 776851 (Ohio Ct. App. 3d Dist. Auglaize County 2012).

[95]Snell v. Snell, 2010-Ohio-2245, 2010 WL 2010899 (Ohio Ct. App. 5th Dist. Richland County 2010).

[96]Woolum v. Woolum, 131 Ohio App. 3d 818, 723 N.E.2d 1135 (12th Dist. Preble County 1999); see also Prostejovsky v. Prostejovsky, 2007-Ohio-5743, 2007 WL 3119724 (Ohio Ct. App. 5th Dist. Ashland County 2007).

[97]See also Thom v. Mulvin, 2009-Ohio-3797, 2009 WL 2365996 (Ohio Ct. App. 6th Dist. Erie County 2009).

[98]*Snell at *5.*

[99]See also Text § 18:11, Firearm offenses under VAWA, Text § 14:5, False arrest, warrantless arrests and searches, and weapons confiscation.

[100]Sup. R. Form 10.01-G to Sup. R. Form 10.01-J.

[101]See 18 U.S.C.A. § 922(d)(8), 18 U.S.C.A. § 922(g)(8).

[102]18 U.S.C.A. §§ 922(g)(8); 924(a)(2).

[103]See RC 3113.31(E)(3) for the duration of a civil protection order; see also Wilson v. Wilson, 134 N.C. App. 642, 518 S.E.2d 255 (1999).

[104]See State v. Solomon, 262 N.J. Super. 618, 621 A.2d 559 (Ch. Div. 1993) (discussing "complaint" and when guns may be returned to the alleged abuser).

[105]See, e.g., U.S. v. Wilson, 159 F.3d 280 (7th Cir. 1998); see also State v. S.A., 290 N.J. Super. 240, 675 A.2d 678 (App. Div. 1996) (prohibiting return of firearm under federal law where order of protection was pending). But see State v. Solomon, 262 N.J. Super. 618, 621 A.2d 559 (Ch. Div. 1993) (holding that a court might continue to hold an alleged perpetrator's guns even if the charges and domestic violence complaint are dismissed where, after a hearing, the court determines there still exists some underlying reason to seize the weapons to protect the victim of domestic violence).

Q & A: Within what period of time must a respondent/ defendant turn over weapons to the law enforcement agency?

Neither the CPO nor the TPO forms provide a time frame in which a respondent/defendant must turn over weapons to the police department.[106] The forms state that "a respondent/defendant, if ordered not to use, carry, obtain or possess any deadly weapon, must turn over all deadly weapons in his possession to the law enforcement agency that serves respondent/defendant with the Order or as follows." Unless a hearing officer adds a specific time frame, the forms are silent.

However, in *State v. King*,[107] the appellate court held that, if the protection order fails to specify the time frame within which a weapon is to be turned over to law enforcement, a reasonable amount of time to do so will be presumed. In that case, the defendant was released from jail on March 5 and on March 7, he still had not complied with the Order, although he had ample time to do so. Thus, his conviction for violating the terms of the TPO was upheld.

Q & A: What is the procedure for the return of firearms?[108]

However, the issue was recently raised in an Ohio case. In *Golden v. Bay Village Police Department*,[109] the defendant was the subject of a criminal protection order issued in connection with an allegation of domestic violence. The police confiscated several guns from the defendant's home pursuant to the order. Subsequently, the charge of domestic violence was dismissed and the protection order was dissolved.

The defendant requested the return of his guns and he was advised that he would need a court order for the release of the weapons and further advised to file a replevin action. He was then informed that if he failed to secure a replevin order, the weapons would be destroyed. After receiving the replevin order, he then requested attorney fees. From the denial of fees, he appealed.

The Eighth District Court of Appeals stated that the trial court did not err in denying Golden's request for fees. The appellate court reasoned that since the police confiscated the weapons pursuant to a

[106] See Sup. R. Forms 10.01H to J and 10.02-A.

[107] State v. King, 2005-Ohio-863, 2005 WL 469270 (Ohio Ct. App. 5th Dist. Tuscarawas County 2005).

[108] See Text 14:5; Text 18:11; see also Henderson v. U.S., 135 S. Ct. 1780, 191 L. Ed. 2d 874 (2015) (U.S. Supreme Court addressed the issue of property rights to certain surrendered firearms not involved in the underlying criminal case when the individual is a prohibited person under 18 U.S.C. 922(g) which could have consequences in domestic violence firearm surrender cases when that same firearm is transferred to a third party friend for purchase); see also Weisberg and Kelly, U.S. Supreme Court to Decide *Henderson* case: Scope of felon's Ownership Rights to Firearms, 20 Domestic Violence Reports 49 (April/May 2015).

[109] Golden v. Bay Village Police Dept., 2002-Ohio-673, 2002 WL 253878 (Ohio Ct. App. 8th Dist. Cuyahoga County 2002). See also Text § 14:15, Potential police liability in the enforcement of protection orders. But see In re Expungements, 2007 PA Super 377, 938 A.2d 1075 (2007); Fisher v. Kealoha, 2012 WL 2526923 (D. Haw. 2012); State v. Pessetto, 160 N.H. 813, 8 A.3d 75 (2010); Johnson v. Johnson, 1997 WL 906024 (Del. Fam. Ct. 1997); Ritchie v. Konrad, 115 Cal. App. 4th 1275, 10 Cal. Rptr. 3d 387 (2d Dist. 2004).

court order, the defendant was on notice that it would take a court order to release his weapons.[110]

The appellate court then noted that "[t]he fact that the protection order was dissolved is of no consequence. The police department confiscated the weapons pursuant to court order; thus, it was reasonable for the police not to return the property unless instructed to do so by the court."[111]

The appellate court then held that the police recommendation of a replevin action[112] was reasonable in light of the fact that the defendant failed to request the return of his property when the charges against him were dismissed and because of the delay of several months. Consequently, the police did not exercise bad faith, warranting an award of attorney fees.

Q & A: What guidance do the standardized Supreme Court forms provide?

Recently, the Supreme Court revised the domestic violence forms to address the issue of weapons return. The forms provide that: "Any law enforcement officer is authorized to take possession of deadly weapons pursuant to this paragraph and hold them in protective custody until further Court order." "Upon the expiration of this order, any deadly weapons, including firearms and ammunition, held in protective custody by law enforcement pursuant to this Order shall be disposed of as unclaimed property pursuant to RC 2981.12 unless the Respondent files a motion for return with this Court within 30 days before the Expiration of this Order."[113]

The protection order forms adopted by the Supreme Court also include the following language: "Respondent shall turn over all deadly weapons and **conceal carry weapon license** in Respondent's possession to the law enforcement agency that serves Respondent with the order . . . ."[114]

Of importance is that the Supreme Court Forms also track current

[110]SeeSup. R. Form 10.01-H to Sup. R. Form 10.01-J and Sup. R. Form 10.02-A10.02–a. Note that Ohio's standardized forms provide that law enforcement agencies shall hold weapons in protective custody until further court order.

[111]Golden v. Bay Village Police Dept., 2002-Ohio-673, 2002 WL 253878, *2 (Ohio Ct. App. 8th Dist. Cuyahoga County 2002). But see State v. Solomon, 262 N.J. Super. 618, 621 A.2d 559 (Ch. Div. 1993); see also City of Cleveland v. Carpenter, 2003-Ohio-6923, 2003 WL 22976619 (Ohio Ct. App. 8th Dist. Cuyahoga County 2003) (where appellant was convicted of misdemeanor assault, a crime of violence under 18 U.S.C.A. 922(g), the trial court did not err in denying appellant's request for the return of his firearms); Kise v. Barber, 2005-Ohio-6438, 2005 WL 3293763 (Ohio Ct. App. 5th Dist. Knox County 2005) (sustaining error and holding that a respondent can seek the return of his weapons in replevin in a municipal court and that the sheriff is entitled to defend against the return of the weapon under RC 2923.13(A) or argue that the weapon is contraband); Wilhoit v. N. Olmsted, 151 Ohio Misc. 2d 21, 2009-Ohio-1702, 905 N.E.2d 723 (Mun. Ct. 2009) (person convicted of threat of domestic violence not precluded from seeking the return of weapons).

[112]See Wysocki v. Oberlin Police Dept., 2014-Ohio-2869, 2014 WL 2957713 (Ohio Ct. App. 9th Dist. Lorain County 2014) (because the prosecution had not sought either a criminal or civil forfeiture of the firearms, it did not have authority to release the weapons to defendant unless he filed a replevin action).

[113]Sup. R. Form 10.01-I; 10.01-J.

[114]See Sup. R. Form 10.01-H, 10.01-I; 10.01-J; 10.02-A; 10.03-B; 10.03-E; and 10.03-F.

law. RC 2923.125(D)(1)(e) provides that, among the requirements, the sheriff must issue a concealed carry license within 45 days of applying for such license if the applicant is not subject to a civil protection order.

Q & A: Does a consent agreement entered into by the parties waive the Brady Disqualifiers?[115]

It depends. This issue has been raised in several Ohio counties where respondents want to use their guns for recreational purposes, such as hunting.

The federal statute provides that a person, who is the subject of a civil protection order, is prohibited from purchasing a firearm if the protection order protects an intimate partner or child and only if the subject was given an opportunity to participate at a hearing regarding the order. Additionally, the qualifying order must restrain the respondent from harassing, stalking or threatening the intimate partner or child or engaging in other conduct that would place an intimate partner in reasonable fear of bodily injury to the partner or child. Finally, the order must either include a finding that the subject presents a credible threat to the physical safety of such intimate partner or child or, by its terms, explicitly prohibits physical force against such intimate partner or child that would reasonably be expected to cause bodily injury.[116] Unless all three qualifying factors are met, a person is not Brady disqualified.

The Brady Handgun disqualifiers are predicated on *either* a finding of a credible threat *or* where the order explicitly prohibits certain conduct. Nowhere does the statute require a specific finding of abuse. Consent agreements do not contain findings that the subject committed domestic violence or presents a threat. However, consent agreements do prohibit certain conduct. It is unclear whether an absence of specific judicial findings may be a way to avoid federal firearm disqualifications or if eliminating the phrase "physical force" or other similar terms from the list of prohibitive conduct contained in the consent entry may be sufficient to avoid the Brady ban.

Federal authorities suggest that the intent of the Gun Control Act contemplated a ban on the purchase and possession of firearms whenever a civil protection is issued. Since the objective for the issuance of any civil protection order is to prevent future violence, prohibitions against firearm purchases and possession are often necessary to effectuate that result.

Q & A: By entering into a consent agreement, a hearing was avoided. How can the Brady ban apply when federal law requires a hearing?

The federal law does not require an evidentiary hearing. In fact, the term "hearing" is not defined in the Gun Control Act. However, the term is generally interpreted as an opportunity to present one's side

[115]See also Text § 18:11, Firearm offenses under VAWA; Text § 12:9, Consent agreement concerns; see also Harris v. Miami Cty. Sheriff's Dept., 160 Ohio App. 3d 435, 2005-Ohio-1713, 827 N.E.2d 807 (2d Dist. Miami County 2005) (where appellate court determine that a consent agreement is a civil protection order for purposes of prohibiting respondent from obtaining a license to carry a concealed weapon).

[116]18 U.S.C.A. 922(g)(8).

of the case.[117] If the court has met with the parties or their counsel and the consent agreement is based upon the representations made and agreed upon by the parties involved, that constitutes a hearing as defined in the case law, whether or not the parties testify. Thus, the consent agreement would subject the respondent to the federal firearm ban so long as the order met the other criteria contained in 18 U.S.C.A. 922(g)(8).[118]

Q & A: May an applicant for a license to carry a concealed weapon be barred even when the CPO does not say so?

According to the Fifth District Court of Appeals, a respondent may not obtain a license for a concealed weapon when he is subject to a CPO even when the CPO does not prohibit him. In *Masten v. Phalen*,[119] the applicant for a license to carry a concealed weapon was subject to a civil protection order. The CPO specifically stated that it did not affect applicant's right to possess, carry, or use firearms. His application was denied. He appealed, arguing that the trial court erred by upholding the Sheriff's denial of his application.

In affirming the trial court, the Fairfield County Court of Appeals noted that the statute governing concealed weapons clearly provides that an applicant not be subject to a civil protection order. Because the applicant in question was the subject of a CPO, the trial court's decision was in accordance with law. Of significance is that the appellate court also found that "[t]he denial does not prohibit appellant from purchasing and possessing handguns, just concealed ones, which in effect are the same rights appellant had under the civil protection order. Therefore, there has been no violation of appellant's rights under the Second Amendment."[120]

RC 2923.125(D)(1)(e) provides that, among the requirements, the sheriff must issue a concealed carry license within 45 days of applying for such license so long as the applicant is not subject to a civil protection order.[121] The Supreme Court Forms were revised to specifically include that a respondent/defendant must turn over any concealed carry license when turning over to law enforcement all deadly weapons.[122]

Invitations and Violation Issues:

Q & A: What if the petitioner invites the respondent back into the home while the protection order is in effect?

As stated in the previous chapter, the court now has the discretion

[117]U.S. v. Wilson, 159 F.3d 280 (7th Cir. 1998).

[118]See also Fanny L. Haslebacher, Esq., Firearms and Domestic Violence: Important Considerations for Judges, presented to the National College of District Attorneys, Thirteenth Annual National Conference on Domestic Violence 2003.

[119]Masten v. Phalen, 2005-Ohio-4076, 2005 WL 1871190 (Ohio Ct. App. 5th Dist. Fairfield County 2005).

[120]Masten v. Phalen, 2005-Ohio-4076, 2005 WL 1871190, *2 (Ohio Ct. App. 5th Dist. Fairfield County 2005).

[121]See also Salgado v. Montgomery Cty. Sheriff, 2015-Ohio-3387, 2015 WL 5000131 (Ohio Ct. App. 2d Dist. Montgomery County 2015); Runions v. Burchett, 2018-Ohio-2754, 2018 WL 3414235 (Ohio Ct. App. 2d Dist. Clark County 2018).

[122]See Sup. R. Form 10.01-H, 10.01-I; 10.01-J; 10.02-A; 10.03-B; 10.03-E; and 10.03-F.

to include in a protection order a prohibition against the respondent returning to the residence or household.[123] RC 3113.31(E)(2) provides that:

> If it includes a prohibition against the respondent returning to the residence or household in the order, it also shall include in the order provisions of the type described in division (E)(7) of this section. This division does not preclude the court from including in a protection order or consent agreement, in circumstances other than those described in this division, a requirement that the respondent be evicted from or vacate the residence or household or refrain from entering the residence, school, business, or place of employment of the petitioner or a family or household member, and . . . also shall include in the order provisions of the type described in division (E)(7) of this section.

RC 3113.31(E)(7)(a) states that any protection order issued must note that the order is not invalidated by the return of the respondent to the premises when invited by the petitioner. Specifically, the statute provides that, if a protection order or consent agreement includes a requirement that the respondent be evicted from or vacate the residence or household or refrain from entering the residence, school, business, or place of employment of the petitioner or household member, the order shall state clearly that the order cannot be waived or nullified by an invitation to the respondent from the petitioner.[124]

The legislative intent of RC 3113.31(E)(2) and RC 3113.31(E)(7), as amended in October 1997, was to educate police officers that, in spite of the petitioner's invitation back to the home, the protection order is not nullified or negated.[125] These statutory provisions are necessary to communicate to law enforcement officials the importance of enforcing a civil protection order according to its terms. Additionally, an order that contains this language advises the respondent that the order will remain valid, subjecting him/her to arrest for its violation.

It is significant that the Ohio legislature deleted language specifically prohibiting the petitioner from inviting or admitting the respondent to the residence while the order is in effect. Such an omission specifically demonstrates the legislative intent that a protection order is effective only against the party who is alleged to have committed acts of domestic violence. In fact, a petitioner cannot be arrested for violating a protection order by inviting the respondent back to the home because there is no order requiring the petitioner to respond in a certain way. It is now very clear that the order is only against the respondent and that the petitioner is not responsible for the respondent's actions. Even with the consent of the petitioner or at the insistence of the petitioner, a respondent who returns to the residence disobeys a court order.

---

[123] See RC 3113.31(E)(2); see also Text Ch. 11, Issuance of a Civil Protection Order.

[124] See also State v. Washington, 319 N.J. Super. 681, 726 A.2d 326 (Law Div. 1998); State v. Blaylock, 2000 WL 706797 (Ohio Ct. App. 2d Dist. Montgomery County 2000); City of Xenia v. Berry, 1994 WL 12494, *3 (Ohio Ct. App. 2d Dist. Greene County 1994) (the appellate court held that "[t]he enforcement of these orders cannot be undermined by any change in relationships between the two spouses or else their enforcement and the very authority of the court that issues them would be a nullity").

[125] See, e.g., Stella v. Platz, 1999 WL 427672 (Ohio Ct. App. 4th Dist. Washington County 1999) (court summarily rejected respondent's argument that a 5-year protection order was too lengthy, especially if the petitioner "invites him to break it").

Apparently, RC 3113.31(E)(2) was amended to include two distinct prohibitions. The provisions set forth in RC 3113.31(E)(7) must be included in a protection order if a protection order has been issued in a prior action between the same parties and the subsequent protection order issued by the court contains a provision prohibiting the respondent from returning to the residence.[126] The statute also provides that the relief available under RC 3113.31(E)(7) must be included in a protection order where the respondent is evicted from or ordered to vacate the residence or household, etc. Any ambiguity in RC 3113.31(E)(2) should be resolved in favor of the petitioner. Each and every protection order issued by a court should contain the statutory prohibitions set forth in RC 3113.31(E)(7)(a).

In fact, Ohio's courts are both empowered and directed to include a provision similar to that contained in RC 3113.31(E)(7) in both ex parte civil protection orders and those issued after the full hearing. Additionally, the standard protection order forms provide that:

> If this order requires you to vacate a residence or refrain from entering the residence, school, business, or place of employment of the family or household member(s) named in this order, this order cannot be waived or nullified by an invitation to you to enter their residence, school, business, or place of employment or your entry into one of those places otherwise upon their consent.[127]

The mandatory warning sheet that accompanies each and every protection order and consent agreement also contains a similar provision warning the respondent that only the court can modify or dismiss a protection order. It also advises the petitioner that inviting the respondent into the residence while the protection order is in effect can cause the respondent to be arrested.[128] Of significance is that there is no similar provision for the petitioner.[129]

Q & A: Will a respondent necessarily be found in contempt for violating a protection order where the respondent returns to the residence at the invitation of the petitioner?

No. RC 3113.31(E)(7)(a) states that any protection order that includes a requirement that the respondent be evicted or vacate the residence, school, business, or place of employment or refrain from entering these places must also contain a provision that the protection order is not nullified or waived by an invitation to return to the residence by the petitioner. However, RC 3113.31(E)(7)(b) specifically provides that the court has the discretion to determine that a respondent charged with either contempt of court or criminal prosecution under RC 2919.27 did not commit the violation or was not in contempt of court.

Although the respondent may initially be arrested for violating a protection order, he/she may prevail in court. The statutory language

[126] But see Mallin v. Mallin, 44 Ohio App. 3d 53, 56, 541 N.E.2d 116 (8th Dist. Cuyahoga County 1988) (clarifying the statutory intent and holding that "in an initial proceeding the respondent may be ordered not to return to the marital premises").

[127] Sup. R. Form 10.01-H to Sup. R. Form 10.01-J.

[128] See Sup. R. 10.01(D), Sup. R. Form 10.01-G.

[129] See, e.g., N. Olmsted v. Bullington, 139 Ohio App. 3d 565, 744 N.E.2d 1225 (8th Dist. Cuyahoga County 2000).

reiterates the authority of the court to find a respondent not guilty of violating the protection order under these circumstances.[130]

For example, in *Ferguson v. Ferguson*,[131] the Knox County Common Pleas Court denied a motion to show cause which was filed because the respondent violated a protection order by physically assaulting the petitioner and threatening to kill her. The respondent argued in defense of his admitted violation that the petitioner initiated contact with him and that she went to the storage facility knowing that he would be there. Based on the transcript presented, it was apparent that the trial court relied on this defense to summarily dismiss the petitioner's contempt motion.[132]

Q & A: Can a petitioner be charged with violating his/her own protection order?[133]

The Ohio Supreme Court finally resolved this issue in *State v. Lucas*.[134] The Supreme Court of Ohio accepted certification because of the conflicting law in two Ohio jurisdictions.

In *N. Olmsted v. Bullington*,[135] the city prosecutor charged the victim, who had a criminal protection order issued on her behalf, with willfully aiding and abetting the intentional violation of her own order. The victim had been seen in a vehicle with her husband, the subject of the criminal order. On appeal, the City of North Olmsted challenged the trial court's dismissal of the complicity charges brought against the original victim. The Eighth District Court of Appeals held that, as a matter of law, the trial court's decision to dismiss the complicity charges against the victim was proper. The appellate court considered whether "a victim of a crime in a protected class of a criminal law may be punished for its criminal violation."[136] The court relied on legislative intent and noted that the law "focused absolutely on the behavior of the offender with intent to punish the offender's

---

[130]See RC 3113.31(E)(7)(b). But see State v. Dejarlais, 136 Wash. 2d 939, 969 P.2d 90 (1998) (holding that consent is not a defense to violating a domestic violence protection order). See also State v. Washington, 319 N.J. Super. 681, 726 A.2d 326 (Law Div. 1998) (holding that the conduct of the parties to a domestic violence order cannot serve as a defense to a contempt charge).

[131]Ferguson v. Ferguson, 2000 WL 1724294 (Ohio Ct. App. 5th Dist. Knox County 2000) (reversed on other grounds); see also Text § 13:11, Court enforcement of civil protection orders—Related substantive concerns.

[132]See State v. Justice, 2001 WL 1769925 (Ohio Ct. App. 5th Dist. Fairfield County 2001) (appellant argued that because wife initiated conversation with husband, husband did not violate TPO; court held there was enough evidence to conclude husband had initiated call; court failed to state any policy argument as set forth in *State v. Lucas*).

[133]Lucas, An Invitation to Liability?: Attempts at Holding Victims of Domestic Violence Liable as Accomplices When They Invite Violations of Their Own Protective Orders, 5 Geo. J. Gender & L. 763 (Spring 2004).

[134]State v. Lucas, 147 Ohio App. 3d 297, 2002-Ohio-2514, 770 N.E.2d 114 (5th Dist. Licking County 2002), judgment rev'd, 100 Ohio St. 3d 1, 2003-Ohio-4778, 795 N.E.2d 642 (2003); but see Henley v. Iowa Dist. Court for Emmet County, 533 N.W.2d 199 (Iowa 1995).

[135]N. Olmsted v. Bullington, 139 Ohio App. 3d 565, 744 N.E.2d 1225 (8th Dist. Cuyahoga County 2000).

[136]N. Olmsted v. Bullington, 139 Ohio App. 3d 565, 568, 744 N.E.2d 1225, 1227 (8th Dist. Cuyahoga County 2000).

behavior and not the behavior of the victim, whom the order is designed to protect."[137]

On the other hand, the Licking County Court of Appeals concluded the opposite in *State v. Lucas*.[138] The original victim was charged and convicted of complicity to aid and abet in the violation of her own protection order. In rejecting the reasoning in *N. Olmsted v. Bullington*, the Licking County Court of Appeals relied on the literal language of RC 2919.27(A)(1) which provides that "no person shall recklessly violate the terms of a protection order issued pursuant to R.C. 2919.26 or 3113.31."[139] The appellate court held that ". . .we find that appellant's mental state went beyond "reckless" to the point of intentional. Unlike the victim of a statutory rape, who is automatically protected as a result of his or her age, the victim of a protection order asks for the protection. A victim is not a protected person under the laws authorizing the issuance of protective orders merely by his or her existence, but rather the status is achieved through a formal request to the trial court. We cannot agree with the *Bullington* court's public-policy rationale, as it becomes overreaching when the victim, such as appellant herein, requested the protection order and then recklessly exposed herself to the offender from whom she had sought protection."[140]

In a unanimous decision, the Supreme Court of Ohio declined to assign accomplice liability to the victim. The court considered legislative intent, the warning page of Ohio's standardized protection order forms and the instructive analysis of *Gebardi v. United States* relating to the Mann Act.[141] The court stated, "[p]rotection orders are about the behavior of the respondent and nothing else. How or why a respondent finds himself at the petitioner's doorstep is irrelevant. To find appellant guilty of complicity would be to criminalize an irrelevancy."[142] Therefore, "an individual who is the protected subject of a temporary protection order may not be prosecuted for aiding and abetting the restrainee under the protection order in violating said order."[143]

---

[137]N. Olmsted v. Bullington, 139 Ohio App. 3d 565, 568, 744 N.E.2d 1225, 1227 (8th Dist. Cuyahoga County 2000).

[138]State v. Lucas, 147 Ohio App. 3d 297, 2002-Ohio-2514, 770 N.E.2d 114 (5th Dist. Licking County 2002), judgment rev'd, 100 Ohio St. 3d 1, 2003-Ohio-4778, 795 N.E.2d 642 (2003).

[139]State v. Lucas, 147 Ohio App. 3d 297, 300, 2002-Ohio-2514, 770 N.E.2d 114 (5th Dist. Licking County 2002), judgment rev'd, 100 Ohio St. 3d 1, 2003-Ohio-4778, 795 N.E.2d 642 (2003).

[140]State v. Lucas, 147 Ohio App. 3d 297, 301, 2002-Ohio-2514, 770 N.E.2d 114 (5th Dist. Licking County 2002), judgment rev'd, 100 Ohio St. 3d 1, 2003-Ohio-4778, 795 N.E.2d 642 (2003).

[141]Gebardi v. U.S., 287 U.S. 112, 53 S. Ct. 35, 77 L. Ed. 206, 84 A.L.R. 370 (1932).

[142]State v. Lucas, 100 Ohio St. 3d 1, 2003-Ohio-4778, 795 N.E.2d 642 (2003).

[143]State v. Lucas, 100 Ohio St. 3d 1, 2003-Ohio-4778, 795 N.E.2d 642 (2003); see also State v. Bombardiere, 2007-Ohio-1537, 2007 WL 959895, *4 (Ohio Ct. App. 3d Dist. Union County 2007) (The Supreme Court of Ohio in *Lucas* held that "the General Assembly has made issue of an invitation entirely irrelevant as to the culpability of a respondents' violation of a protection order." Furthermore "the General Assembly has made an invitation by the petitioner for the respondent to violate the terms of a

Other Miscellaneous Concerns:

Q & A: Can a trial court take judicial notice of a civil protection order proceeding?

This issue was raised in the dissent in *Dowhan v. Dowhan.*[144] In this case, the issue was whether a court may adjudicate a Motion to Modify Custody and Establish Visitation based on the outcome of a related proceeding to establish a civil protection order. At the time of the parties' divorce, appellant was incarcerated and thus, no visitation was established. Because of a threatening letter written to petitioner from jail, she was granted a CPO by the same judge in the same court, ordering appellant to maintain a distance of 1000 feet from her and the children. Approximately three months after issuance of the CPO, appellant filed a Motion to Modify Custody and Establish Visitation and subsequently filed a Motion to Modify the CPO, which motion was denied. The domestic relations court then denied the Motion to Modify Custody and Establish Visitation and acknowledged that, in the "companion case," the same judge held a trial on appellant's Motion to Modify CPO and found that petitioner and the children were in fear of imminent physical harm from appellant.

On appeal, appellant asserted that the domestic relations court's refusal to consider his Motion to Modify Custody based on the CPO proceeding violated the statutory provisions governing protection orders. Under these provisions, a protection order may temporarily allocate parental rights and responsibilities for children if no other court has determined or is determining the allocation of parental rights and responsibilities for the children. R.C. 3113.31(E)(1)(d).

The appellate court first differentiated the facts of the current case from the case in which a CPO is issued pending final allocation of parental rights and responsibilities in a divorce. Further, the appellate court noted that R.C. 3113.31(E)(1)(d) contemplates the prior situation, not the situation in the instant case. In *Dowhan*, the custody determination was made almost two years before appellee applied for the CPO. The Court then held that because the same judge and court conducted a hearing on the Motion to Modify the CPO filed four months after the Motion to Modify Custody and found that appellant could not come within 1000 feet of appellee, a hearing on the Motion to Modify Custody was unnecessary. "We need not notice the underlying factual basis for the protection order and its terms which preclude the possibility of Terrance exercising visitation with his children. The failure to hold a hearing on the Motion to Modify [Custody] did not deprive Terrance of an opportunity to be heard, as Terrance had fully exercised that right in the proceedings to modify the protection order and the appeal thereof. Modification of the protection order is a necessary prerequisite to the establishment of parenting time with the children."[145]

However, in a dissenting opinion, Judge Wright focused on the

---

protection order irrelevant to a respondent's guilt. Protection orders are about the behavior of the respondent and nothing else. How or why a respondent finds himself at the petitioner's doorstep is irrelevant.").

[144]Dowhan v. Dowhan, 2013-Ohio-4097, 2013 WL 5346465, ¶ 24 (Ohio Ct. App. 11th Dist. Lake County 2013).

[145]Dowhan v. Dowhan, 2013-Ohio-4097, 2013 WL 5346465, ¶ 19 (Ohio Ct. App.

concept of judicial notice. "Evid. 201(B) provides that judicial notice may be taken of any fact which is not in dispute and which is capable of ready determination by resort to certain sources. In applying this rule, the courts of this state have consistently held that a trial court cannot take judicial notice of proceedings in a separate action, even if the prior action was between the same parties and was tried before the same trial judge."[146] *"The rationale for this holding is that, if a trial court tries to take notice of a prior proceeding, the appellate court cannot review the propriety of the trial court's reliance on the prior case because the record of the prior case is not before the appellate court."*[147]

Apparently, where a party fails to make the CPO order part of the record in a motion for reallocation of parental rights and responsibilities or a motion to modify parenting time, the trial court would rely on improper evidence in making its ruling because the evidence was not part of the record in the underlying matter involving custody and visitation.[148] Further, it would bind the trial court to another court's determinations regarding credibility of witnesses.[149]

Q & A: Can a hearing officer contemplate the list of lethality factors as findings to support the issuance of a civil protection order? Is the use of these factors considered inappropriate judicial notice?

Although no Ohio court has actually addressed this concept, the Supreme Court of Kentucky recently addressed this exact concern. In *Pettingill v. Pettingill*,[150] the trial court found there was sufficient evidence and testimony to support the issuance of the civil protection order. On the docket sheet in the court file, the trial court noted additional findings of fact including the presence of 9 of 12 top lethality factors and listed the nine factual findings identified as risk factors, including respondent's cyberstalking of the victim, his possessive and jealous behavior towards the victims, his recent purchase of a firearm (despite a prior felony conviction) and the recent separation of the

---

11th Dist. Lake County 2013).

[146]Dowhan v. Dowhan, 2013-Ohio-4097, 2013 WL 5346465, ¶ 24 (Ohio Ct. App. 11th Dist. Lake County 2013); see also Kiedrowicz v. Kiedrowicz, 1999 WL 197793 (Ohio Ct. App. 6th Dist. Huron County 1999).

[147]Dowhan v. Dowhan, 2013-Ohio-4097, 2013 WL 5346465, ¶ 24 (Ohio Ct. App. 11th Dist. Lake County 2013) (emphasis added), citing Deli Table, Inc. v. Great Lakes Mall, 1996 WL 761984 (Ohio Ct. App. 11th Dist. Lake County 1996).

[148]See also City of Cleveland v. Boone, 2018-Ohio-849, 2018 WL 1217716 (Ohio Ct. App. 8th Dist. Cuyahoga County 2018) (in appeal for violating a TPO, court reversed and rejected trial court's reliance on testimony that TPO existed on date in question and held that trial court could not take judicial notice of the content of TPO without having it be introduced as evidence and admitted as an exhibit or be stipulated to by appellant).

[149]Dowhan v. Dowhan, 2013-Ohio-4097, 2013 WL 5346465, ¶ 24 (Ohio Ct. App. 11th Dist. Lake County 2013), citing Yannitell v. Oaks, 2008-Ohio-6271, 2008 WL 5077646 (Ohio Ct. App. 4th Dist. Washington County 2008); see also Sherman v. Sherman, 2013-Ohio-3501, 2013 WL 4106674 (Ohio Ct. App. 1st Dist. Hamilton County 2013) (the trial court erroneously took judicial notice of a CPO entered against appellant in another case because the CPO was not issued in conjunction with the instant case and was not admitted into evidence).

[150]Pettingill v. Pettingill, 480 S.W.3d 920 (Ky. 2015).

parties. The court also concluded that the petitioner was placed at extreme risk of physical harm.

The respondent appealed the issuance of the order, arguing that the trial court erred when it took "judicial notice" of the lethality factors, and basing its decision on these factors rather that the statutory standard.[151]

In denying respondent's petition for rehearing, the appellate court found that the court had applied the appropriate standard and that "the additional findings noted on the docket sheet could not be seen to indicate the family court's disregard of the correct standard nor did the reference to lethality factors render the decision infirm. Furthermore, the Court found no inference by the family court that it was taking judicial notice of any fact and that comparing its findings to the lethality factors did not change the nature or character of the adjudicated facts adduced during the hearing."[152]

In affirming the appellate court, the Kentucky Supreme Court found that the trial court committed no error. In its ruling, the Kentucky Supreme Court discussed "judicial notice" and whether it was utilized by the trial court. Judicial notice is defined as an act by a court, on its own or at a party's request and recognized the truth of certain facts that are generally acknowledged such as historical events or dates. However, supporting evidence is not required.[153]

In this case, the Court concluded that the "lethality factors" are not generally facts, but risk factors used by courts, law enforcement and social scientists to evaluate the threat of domestic violence between partners. Louise E. Graham and James E. Keller, 15 Kentucky Practice: Domestic Relations Law § 5:13 (West 2014); Symposium, Death by Intimacy: Risk factors for Domestic Violence, 20 Pace L. Rev. 263 (2000).[154]

Noting that the factors were not taken by judicial notice, the Court determined that "[t]he family court's reorganization of facts elicited during the hearing was not done according to judicial notice; all the adjudicative facts were proven through testimony, The list of lethality factors—presumably contained in the court's mind—was judicial knowledge rather than judicial notice. This Court has previously held that judicial knowledge and notice are inherently different and that '[while a resident judge's background knowledge of an area may "inform the judge's assessment of historical facts,' the judge may not actually testify in the proceeding or interject facts (excluding facts for which proper judicial notice is taken." Com. v. Howlett, 328 S.W.3d 191, 193 (Ky. 2010) (quotingU.S. v. Berber-Tinoco, 510 F.3d 1083, 1091, 75 Fed. R. Evid. Serv. 399 (9th Cir. 2007)). The family court had permissible judicial knowledge of the lethality factors. In other words, the court employed its background knowledge of domestic violence

[151] Pettingill v. Pettingill, 480 S.W.3d 920 (Ky. 2015).

[152] Pettingill v. Pettingill, 480 S.W.3d 920, 922 (Ky. 2015).

[153] Pettingill v. Pettingill, 480 S.W.3d 920 (Ky. 2015).

[154] Pettingill v. Pettingill, 480 S.W.3d 920 (Ky. 2015); see also 21 Domestic Violence Report 69 (June/July 2016) (articles addressing the use of risk assessments/lethality factors in judicial decision-making in domestic violence cases).

risk factors to inform its judgment as to whether the facts of this case indicated that domestic violence may occur again.[155]

§ 12:23 Duration of a civil protection order

Pursuant to statute, civil protection orders or consent agreements may remain valid for a date certain, but not later than five years from the date of issuance or approval.[1] All provisions related to safety terminate no later than the end of the five-year period. Provisions related to the allocation of parental rights and responsibilities and support expire on the date that a domestic relations court or juvenile court issues another order awarding custody and/or visitation or ordering support.[2]

Nothing in the statute requires that a civil protection order be granted for the full five-year period. In fact, a protection order may be granted for a period of less than five years provided that the expiration date be a date certain.

In *Walters v. Walters*,[3] the trial court issued a civil protection order for one year, rather than the five-year period. The trial court determined that a one-year protection order was sufficient under the circumstances given the fact that the victim was able to obtain a divorce within the year and that the respondent had been charged with felony domestic violence. On appeal, the petitioner asserted that the trial court erred in issuing only a one-year order in light of the fact that RC 3113.31(E) permitted the issuance of a five-year order, especially where the respondent committed serious acts of domestic violence.

The appellate court acknowledged that "public policy supports granting or extending a CPO beyond the divorce or separation because '[t]he risk of assault is greatest when a woman leaves or threatens to leave an abusive relationship.' "[4] However, it then considered the reasoning of the trial court and determined that the court's decision to

---

[155] Pettingill v. Pettingill, 480 S.W.3d 920 (Ky. 2015).

[Section 12:23]

[1] RC 3113.31(E)(3)(a); see also Stella v. Platz, 1999 WL 427672 (Ohio Ct. App. 4th Dist. Washington County 1999) (validating existence of 5-year civil protection order); Maag v. Maag, 2002-Ohio-1401, 2002 WL 468585 (Ohio Ct. App. 3d Dist. Wyandot County 2002); Jenkins v. Jenkins, 2007-Ohio-422, 2007 WL 275700 (Ohio Ct. App. 10th Dist. Franklin County 2007) (five year period was appropriate even though magistrate recommended 3 years).

[2] RC 3113.31(E)(3)(b); see also Delmatto v. Hamed, 2008-Ohio-6375, 2008 WL 5124388 (Ohio Ct. App. 5th Dist. Fairfield County 2008). See also Allan v. Allan, 2014-Ohio-5039, 2014 WL 6065710, ¶ 46 (Ohio Ct. App. 8th Dist. Cuyahoga County 2014) (granting temporary custody of children in a CPO pursuant to RC 3113.31(E)(3)(b) for duration of five years not an abuse of discretion where a modification pursuant to RC 3113.31(E)(8) or a subsequent order in a divorce action may be available and noting that issue of visitation would be handled in parties' divorce).

[3] Walters v. Walters, 150 Ohio App. 3d 287, 2002-Ohio-6455, 780 N.E.2d 1032 (4th Dist. Gallia County 2002); but see Sinclair v. Sinclair, Nos. 08CA16, 08CA25 (Ohio Ct. App. 4th Dist. Athens County May 18, 2009) (unreported) (reversing trial court and holding that the trial court improperly limited duration of the CPO on the basis that a divorce proceeding automatically alleviates the need for a CPO), docket available at http://coc.athenscountygovernment.com/pa.

[4] Walters v. Walters, 150 Ohio App. 3d 287, 290, 2002-Ohio-6455, 780 N.E.2d

limit the CPO to one year was not unreasonable, arbitrary or unconscionable. In its decision, the court noted that the trial court had considered the probability that the respondent would incur jail time in light of the felony domestic violence charge against him and that the appellant would file a divorce within the year. The appellate court then reasoned that "[u]nder the circumstances in this case, a one-year separation of the parties seems likely to prevent further domestic violence. The parties dated for only two months before marrying, the violence began less than a week after the marriage, and the parties separated less than two months after the marriage. Thus, a one-year CPO will be effective for three times the length of the parties' relationship. Additionally, the court considered the fact that the parties live in a small community, where Samuel is likely to need to actively avoid inadvertently violating the restrictions of the CPO. Extending such a restriction upon Samuel, beyond what is necessary to prevent further violence and beyond any criminal sanctions Samuel receives, is not called for under the statute."[5]

The upside of this decision is that the appellate court intimated that a trial court must justify its decision in writing if it decides to issue a CPO that expires before the five-year period. On the downside, the court seems more focused on the infringement of respondent's rights if contact would occur than on the continued safety of the victim of domestic violence.

Q & A: Can a CPO be limited in duration despite the statutory language indicating a five year maximum?

A civil protection order can be granted for a period of time so long that it is valid until a date certain, but not later than five years from the date of its issuance.[6] Arbitrary policies that seek to limit the duration of a civil protection order should always be challenged.

In *Sinclair v. Sinclair*,[7] appellant appealed the trial court's limitation of the duration of a CPO to 1 year because of the seriousness of the domestic violence. The appellate court held that the trial court improperly limited the duration of the CPO based on a policy that the divorce proceedings automatically alleviated the need for a CPO. In finding reversible error, the court relied on RC 3113.31(G) which states that the CPO remedy is in addition to and not in lieu of other available civil or criminal remedies.

While the trial court relied on the pending divorce case in making its decision, the file did not indicate whether appellant even sought a temporary order that would supersede the civil protection order. Since the trial court could only take judicial notice from the prior proceed-

---

1032 (4th Dist. Gallia County 2002), citing Felton v. Felton, 79 Ohio St. 3d 34, 40, 1997-Ohio-302, 679 N.E.2d 672 (1997).

[5]Walters v. Walters, 150 Ohio App. 3d 287, 291, 2002-Ohio-6455, 780 N.E.2d 1032 (4th Dist. Gallia County 2002).

[6]RC 3113.31(E)(3)(a).

[7]Sinclair v. Sinclair, 182 Ohio App. 3d 691, 2009-Ohio-3106, 914 N.E.2d 1084 (4th Dist. Athens County 2009); see also Parker v. Parker, 2014-Ohio-5516, 2014 WL 7177914 (Ohio Ct. App. 1st Dist. Hamilton County 2014) (divorce proceedings did not automatically limit the duration of requested CPO from five years to one where petitioner sought a divorce to remove herself from the danger of domestic violence in accordance with RC 3113.31(G)).

ings in the CPO case and not the divorce case and because evidence of the divorce case was not entered into the record, the trial court abused its discretion. Obviously, the Fourth District Court of Appeals determined that a trial court could not take judicial notice of a different case between the same parties and issue a decision, the basis of which was the pending divorce case, not entered in evidence. "Because that evidence was not presented at the hearing, appellant did not have an opportunity to question, examine, or clarify it."[8]

What is of concern, however, is that the appellate court appeared to leave open whether the result might have been any different had actual evidence of the divorce case been presented at the CPO hearing.

Some courts routinely issue protection orders that remain in effect for the entire five-year duration. Cuyahoga County Domestic Relations Court grants protection orders for five years in all cases, except in exceptional circumstances. Other courts issue protection orders for a lesser period of time but may then reissue the protection order several times within the five-year period, if requested by the petitioner. Sometimes, the protection orders are reissued within the five-year period only if the petitioner presents evidence of a new act or incident of domestic violence. Still other courts issue the protection order for a date certain, the expiration of which is contingent on the occurrence of a significant event within the five-year period.

For example, in *Petrak v. Petrak*,[9] the parties entered into a consent agreement providing that the civil protection order would remain in effect only until the divorce action was final. The Hamilton County Court of Appeals determined that "[t]he plain language of the statute provides that a protection order is only valid until a date certain. The language of the parties' Agreed Entry indicates that this 'date certain' was the date when the parties' divorce action was finalized."[10]

Q & A: Do the restrictions on contact in a CPO relative to children also terminate when a court in a subsequent action for divorce issues an order for the allocation of parental rights and responsibilities?

The Supreme Court of Ohio considered this issue in *State v. Price*.[11] In that case, the mother obtained a CPO prohibiting father from having any contact with the minor child. Subsequent to the issuance of the CPO, the parties divorced and an order was entered providing him with visitation at the mother's discretion. Appellant was convicted of violating the CPO because he left four telephone messages.

On appeal, the appellant presented the following question for review: whether an allocation of parental rights and responsibilities in a divorce decree can modify a CPO beyond the sections of the CPO concerning parental rights and responsibilities.

According to RC 3113.31(E)(3)(b) provides that any order under division (E)(1)(d) of this section (involving the allocation of parental

[8]At *694.

[9]Petrak v. Petrak, 1994 WL 50386 (Ohio Ct. App. 12th Dist. Butler County 1994).

[10]Petrak v. Petrak, 1994 WL 50386, *2 (Ohio Ct. App. 12th Dist. Butler County 1994).

[11]State v. Price, 118 Ohio St. 3d 144, 2008-Ohio-1974, 886 N.E.2d 852 (2008).

rights and responsibilities and support) shall terminate on the date that a court in an action for divorce* * * issues an order allocating parental rights and responsibilities for the care of children* * *.

Additionally, the CPO forms state that "[e]xcept for paragraphs 11, 12, 13, 14, and 15 above, this order survives a divorce, dissolution of marriage or legal separation"[12]

In considering both the statutory language of RC 3113.31 and the actual CPO, the Supreme Court determined that "* * *as an order from the same court that issued the CPO, a divorce decree may modify the terms of a CPO. Depending upon how a divorce decree allocates parental rights and responsibilities, it may modify multiple aspects of the CPO beyond the paragraphs dealing with parental rights and visitation."[13] Thus, the contact provisions may also be modified by a subsequent divorce.

The Court pointed out that the CPO prohibited appellant from abusing the protected parties, from being around the same parties or from having contact with them. It also noted that the divorce decree was unclear as to how visitation was to be achieved. "The divorce decree in this case left the protected parties and the respondent without clear boundaries regarding nonabusive contact."[14]

The Court stated that it could not affirm appellant's conviction because to do so "would be giving this court's imprimatur to Item V of the divorce decree, which sets forth that "visitation would be at the discretion of the mother," and we would encourage its use in future cases where a divorce is granted while a CPO is still active. We cannot."[15] It went on to say that [t]he terms of the CPO itself allowed the court to modify the CPO and that the Court had the power to allow contact which it did by permitting contact to effectuate visitation.[16]

In reversing appellant's conviction, the Supreme Court held that "* * * the divorce decree, which sets forth that visitation was to be at the mother's discretion, created a limited exception to paragraph 6 of the CPO, which forbids contact between a respondent and protected parties."[17]

Had the divorce decree been more deliberately and unambiguously crafted, it is unlikely that the Court would have ruled this way. Pursuant to RC 3113.31(E)(3)(b), modifications to the allocation of parental rights in a divorce decree often result in contact between the parties in order to effectuate parenting access.

In many cases, petitioners are ready to provide contact to respondents by the time a divorce entry is entered so as to permit parenting access and no further action is necessary. It is a rather intrinsic exception to the CPO needing no formal modifications. However, some clients do not want contact for any purpose, even for purposes of effectuating parenting access. In those cases, divorce provisions must be

---

[12]See Sup. R. Form 10.01-H; Sup. R. Form 10.01-I; Sup. R. Form 10.01-J.

[13]State v. Price, 118 Ohio St. 3d 144, 147, 2008-Ohio-1974, 886 N.E.2d 852 (2008).

[14]State v. Price, 118 Ohio St. 3d 144, 150, 2008-Ohio-1974, 886 N.E.2d 852 (2008).

[15]State v. Price, 118 Ohio St. 3d 144, 150, 2008-Ohio-1974, 886 N.E.2d 852 (2008).

[16]State v. Price, 118 Ohio St. 3d 144, 150, 2008-Ohio-1974, 886 N.E.2d 852 (2008).

[17]State v. Price, 118 Ohio St. 3d 144, 150, 2008-Ohio-1974, 886 N.E.2d 852 (2008).

specifically tailored to address how parenting access is to be achieved while adhering to the no contact provisions of the CPO.

Of significance is that the Court stressed that whatever the modifications the court had the authority to make, the CPO remained in effect to prohibit any abuse. "* * *Paragraph 1 of the CPO, forbidding abuse of the protected parties, cannot be modified by a divorce decree's allocation of parental rights. One cannot imagine an instance where abuse would be necessary to achieve visitation."[18]

Q & A: On what date does the five-year period begin to run?

The statute is silent regarding the date to be considered by the court as the start of the five-year period. The wording of the statute seems to suggest that the date is discretionary for any particular court. A court may use either the date of "issuance" or "approval."[19]

The date is of some significance, especially where it has been difficult to serve the respondent. If it takes several months to perfect service, a petitioner will lose several months of protection if the date of filing of the ex parte civil protection order is used rather than the date of issuance or approval of the protection order after the full hearing.

Since the statute provides a five-year time frame for both a protection order and a consent agreement and since the consent entry would not be approved until after the full hearing, it seems logical that the legislature intended that a civil protection order remain in effect for five years from the date of the full hearing.[20]

Unfortunately, there is no consistent practice in Ohio's eighty-eight counties. Some courts utilize the date of filing the ex parte order to begin the running of the five-year period. Most courts, however, consider the date on which the order was issued or approved by the court after a full hearing.[21]

Q & A: After filing for and obtaining a civil protection order, the petitioner files a complaint for divorce. Does the protection order merge into the decree of divorce such that the protection order expires upon the divorce of the parties?

---

[18]State v. Price, 118 Ohio St. 3d 144, 148, 2008-Ohio-1974, 886 N.E.2d 852 (2008). See also R.C. 3113.31(O), which provides that "[n]othing in this section prohibits the domestic relations division of a common pleas . . . from designating a minor child as a protected party on a protection order or consent agreement."

[19]See also Perry v. Joseph, 2008-Ohio-1107, 2008 WL 660317 (Ohio Ct. App. 10th Dist. Franklin County 2008) (suggesting that either date is correct); Banfield v. Orazem, 2017-Ohio-8438, 2017 WL 5151469 (Ohio Ct. App. 11th Dist. Geauga County 2017) (utilizing date of the final judgment rather that the date of the ex parte CSPO).

[20]See Holderman v. Hagner, 2000 PA Super 292, 760 A.2d 1189 (2000) (in a case of first impression Superior Court held that the maximum duration period of protection order ran from date of final hearing, not from date of ex parte hearing); see also Mary Ann Fenicato, Protection from Abuse Orders Reviewed, 2 No. 22, Lawyers J. 2 (2000); Perry v. Joseph, 2008-Ohio-1107, 2008 WL 660317 (Ohio Ct. App. 10th Dist. Franklin County 2008) (dicta suggested that appellate court had no problem with date of order beginning to run from either date of magistrate's order or from date of ex parte order). But see Wirtz v. Wirtz, 2000-Ohio-2564, 2000 WL 1486652 (Ohio Ct. App. 7th Dist. Mahoning County 2000) (dicta suggested time begins to run from issuance of ex parte order); Stickel v. Pryor, 2002-Ohio-3309, 2002 WL 1396077 (Ohio Ct. App. 2d Dist. Miami County 2002). See also Text § 12:10, Magistrate hearings.

[21]See Franklin, Monroe, Morgan, Noble, and Washington counties.

At least one Ohio case addressed this issue. In *Petrak v. Petrak*,[22] the parties filed a separate divorce action and protection order action. Each action had a separate case number. The court reasoned that:

> orders from each respective case apply only to that case and a divorce decree entered in one case would have no effect on the validity of a temporary protection order issued in a separate case, regardless of whether the divorce decree expressly released all prior restraining orders. This is because the merger doctrine, which provides that all prior temporary orders entered in a divorce case are merged and extinguished into the final divorce decree, applies only to orders within a single case and not to orders in separate cases.[23]

Besides the reasons given by the Butler County Court of Appeals, there are other strong public policy and legal rationales for a civil protection order to survive the final divorce decree. Unlike other temporary orders, a civil protection order exists for a finite period of time, which, in many cases, extends past the final divorce. Likewise, the grant or denial of a protection order issued after a full hearing is a final, appealable order.[24]

Even the Supreme Court noted that "the overwhelming benefits to the victim of domestic violence that the protection order offers far outweigh any concerns about the temporary nature of the protection order, which can be renewed at the end of the effective period."[25] The Supreme Court also stressed that, because the violence against a spouse does not stop with a separation or divorce, "[s]tate statutes need to protect women and children during and after the break-up of relationships because of their continuing, and often heightened, vulnerability to violence."[26]

For these reasons, a protection order should never be merged nor extinguished into a final decree of divorce. To suggest that merger is applicable to civil protection orders is to thwart the intent and purpose of the domestic violence statute.

Q & A: Does the court have the authority to extend the effective date of a protection order under Civil Rule 60(A)?[27]

Not according to the Montgomery Court of Appeals in *Harlett v. Harlett*.[28] In January 1995, the trial court entered a protection order which provided that the order was to remain in effect for one year.

---

[22]Petrak v. Petrak, 1994 WL 50386 (Ohio Ct. App. 12th Dist. Butler County 1994); see also Champagne v. Champagne, 429 Mass. 324, 708 N.E.2d 100 (1999) (ruling that a divorce decree does not bar the issuance of a permanent protection order which may be incorporated into the divorce decree); State v. Havard, 2001 WL 1566932, *3 (Ohio Ct. App. 12th Dist. Butler County 2001) (the court held that, in the absence of an agreed entry to the contrary and where the divorce decree itself does not explicitly abrogate the prior protection order, the issuance of a decree of divorce did not terminate or modify the prior protection order).

[23]Petrak v. Petrak, 1994 WL 50386, *2 n.1 (Ohio Ct. App. 12th Dist. Butler County 1994).

[24]See RC 3113.31(G).

[25]Felton v. Felton, 79 Ohio St. 3d 34, 40, 1997-Ohio-302, 679 N.E.2d 672 (1997).

[26]Felton v. Felton, 79 Ohio St. 3d 34, 41, 1997-Ohio-302, 679 N.E.2d 672 (1997).

[27]See also Text § 12:25, Modification and termination of civil protection orders.

[28]Harlett v. Harlett, 1996 WL 629510 (Ohio Ct. App. 2d Dist. Montgomery County 1996); but see Ashburn v. Roth, 2007-Ohio-2995, 2007 WL 1731426 (Ohio Ct. App.

Subsequent to its order, the court noted that the law had been amended in December 1994 and corrected the judgment entry nunc pro tunc to reflect the new two-year duration.[29] The entry noted that the court had corrected a clerical mistake on its own motion pursuant to Civil Rule 60(A).

The appellant challenged the trial court order and questioned whether a trial court could extend the effective term of a protection order. The appellate court held that "the failure to notice the amendment to a statute is not the type of 'oversight or omission' contemplated by Civ.R. 60(A)."[30] The court reasoned that the one-year effective date of the order was within the two-year limit of the initial protection order and that the trial court's unawareness of the amendment amounted to something other than a clerical mistake. The court considered the new entry a substantial change beyond the scope of Civil Rule 60(A).

Q & A: Does the doctrine of merger apply when a protection order is filed as a second count to a divorce action?

While the issue of merger was addressed by one Ohio court in the context of separate cases,[31] no court has examined the merger doctrine with regard to a protection order filed as a second count to a divorce complaint. Even though a divorce and protection order may have the same case number, protection orders are, by nature, separate and distinct from divorce actions.[32] Each action grants different remedies and relief.

The merger doctrine addresses prior temporary orders that are entered in divorce cases. Although filed under the same case number, a civil protection order is neither obtained nor entered by virtue of the divorce. It is a special statutory proceeding established by special legislation. Unlike other claims contained in a complaint, a protection order is a separate claim, included in the same pleading for convenience and only where allowable by local rule.[33] Because a protection order is a separate claim that is not entered pursuant to the divorce, it should survive the granting of the divorce. Sometimes, however, the terms of a protection order may be incorporated into a decree of divorce.[34]

Many jurisdictions prohibit or discourage the filing of a protection order as a second count to a complaint for divorce. Policy and procedure is implemented either by local rule or local practice. Thus, it is

---

12th Dist. Butler County 2007) (trial court's decision to amend the CPO to include the minor child as a protected party under Civ.R. 60(A) was not an abuse of discretion); see also Text § 12:25, Modification and termination of civil protection orders.

[29]Effective 10-27-97, the duration of a civil protection order was increased from two to five years. See RC 3113.31(E)(3)(a) as amended by 1997 S.B. 1.

[30]Harlett v. Harlett, 1996 WL 629510, *1 (Ohio Ct. App. 2d Dist. Montgomery County 1996).

[31]See Petrak v. Petrak, 1994 WL 50386 (Ohio Ct. App. 12th Dist. Butler County 1994); see also State v. Havard, 2001 WL 1566932 (Ohio Ct. App. 12th Dist. Butler County 2001).

[32]Civ.R. 75(G); see also Lapsansky v. Lapsansky, 2000 WL 1114535 (Ohio Ct. App. 7th Dist. Columbiana County 2000).

[33]See, e.g., Cuy. D.R. R. 26(A).

[34]See Champagne v. Champagne, 429 Mass. 324, 708 N.E.2d 100 (1999).

important to check with the local jurisdiction before filing a two-count action.

To prevent merger issues, it is prudent to write into both the protection order and the final divorce decree that the protection order shall survive the final divorce. Any provision should also contain the effective expiration date of the protection order.

However, certain provisions contained in the protection order may be modified by a divorce decree. Besides custody and support that are statutorily modified at the time of divorce,[35] title to real property, title to an automobile, and a permanent division of personal property may be modified by a subsequent divorce decree. If a civil protection order was previously issued by the court, all safety provisions survive the decree of divorce.

With that in mind, an attorney should add a provision in the divorce decree that states that "the civil protection order, issued by this court on ________ shall survive the decree of divorce, except as modified herein. Said protection order shall expire on ________, unless renewed in the same manner in which it was entered." It is also important to provide a new NCIC 10-A form[36] if any modifications are made.

Q & A: Can the record of a CPO proceeding be expunged or sealed?[37]

It is arguable that the grant of a civil protection order is not a criminal offense. No charges are filed against a respondent, and if the CPO is granted, a respondent is not found guilty of a crime. A civil protection order proceeding is not a criminal proceeding and the grant of the CPO is not a criminal conviction. Therefore, there is nothing to expunge or seal.[38]

While Ohio's appellate courts have acknowledged that there is no statutory authority to expunge or seal a civil protection order proceeding,[39] they have considered the doctrine of judicial expungement.[40] Many courts have stressed the need to weigh the competing interests of the government and the individual's privacy rights.

---

[35]See RC 3113.31(E)(3)(b).

[36]Sup. R. Form 10-A.

[37]Text § 13:15; R.C. 2151.358(D) (permitting the sealing of protection orders issued against juvenile respondents). See also H.B. 49, eff. 9/29/2017, which directs a court to expunge the record of the CPO including the petition and ex parte order if the court refuses to issue the CPO at the full hearing and after the time for the appeal has run or all appellate remedies have been exhausted).

[38]Rieger v. Rieger, 165 Ohio App. 3d 454, 463, 2006-Ohio-482, 847 N.E.2d 9 (2d Dist. Montgomery County 2006) (Grady, P.J., dissenting; noting that, although the protection order was issued pursuant to RC 3113.31, "an allegation of domestic violence and a finding that domestic violence occurred are necessary predicates to the issuance of a protective order. And domestic violence is a criminal offense, Therefore, under the extraordinary-circumstances standard of *Pepper Pike v. Doe*, expungement of the protection order and sealing of the record of the proceeding in which it was issued may be proper.").

[39]Bemis v. Oblak, 2006-Ohio-403, 2006 WL 234862, *2 (Ohio Ct. App. 2d Dist. Champaign County 2006); Vaccaro v. Vaccaro, 425 Mass. 153, 680 N.E.2d 55 (1997).

[40]Bemis v. Oblak, 2006-Ohio-403, 2006 WL 234862, *2 (Ohio Ct. App. 2d Dist. Champaign County 2006).

For example, in *Rieger v. Rieger*,[41] appellant agreed to be bound by the terms of a consent entry civil protection order, One year after its expiration, appellant sought to have the CPO sealed on the ground that its accessibility on the Internet prevented him from obtaining a better job. The trial court denied his motion and he appealed.

While noting that the legislature was the proper vehicle to provide such a remedy, the court of appeals concluded that the trial court erred in finding that it required statutory authorization to seal records of a CPO proceeding. In applying the doctrine of judicial expungement[42] to a motion to seal the record of a CPO, the appellate court reversed and remanded the case to the trial court, instructing the lower court to engage in weighing the various interests involved to determine whether the circumstances were unusual and exceptional such that sealing the record was required.[43]

In *Schussheim v. Schussheim*,[44] respondent appealed the trial court's decision denying his motion to expunge and seal the record of an ex parte CPO issued by the trial court against him and later dismissed by the petitioner. The trial court found that respondent failed to present evidence that his employment had been directly affected or directly harmed by the record of the CPO and/or would be hindered or terminated under company policy as a result.

On appeal, respondent/appellant argued that the trial court had the authority to expunge and seal, both under the constitution and the Ohio Supreme Court's *Pepper Pike* decision.[45] The appellate court stressed that there is no statutory or judicial authority to expunge and seal the records of a CPO and declined to extend the *Pepper Pike* holding (*Pepper Pike* dealt with whether a criminal defendant charged but not convicted had the right to judicial expungement) to include non-criminal cases or proceedings.[46]

Of significance is the dissenting opinion in *Schussheim*, which maintained that, while the majority opinion acknowledged the holding in *Pepper Pike*—establishing that, absent statutory authority, a judge has the authority to expunge once a balancing test is performed to determine whether the individual's privacy interest outweighs the government's legitimate need to maintain the records—the majority

---

[41]Rieger v. Rieger, 165 Ohio App. 3d 454, 2006-Ohio-482, 847 N.E.2d 9 (2d Dist. Montgomery County 2006).

[42]City of Pepper Pike v. Doe, 66 Ohio St. 2d 374, 20 Ohio Op. 3d 334, 421 N.E.2d 1303 (1981).

[43]Rieger v. Rieger, 165 Ohio App. 3d 454, 2006-Ohio-482, 847 N.E.2d 9 (2d Dist. Montgomery County 2006).

[44]Schussheim v. Schussheim, 2012-Ohio-2573, 2012 WL 2087406 (Ohio Ct. App. 12th Dist. Warren County 2012), judgment rev'd, 137 Ohio St. 3d 133, 2013-Ohio-4529, 998 N.E.2d 446 (2013). But note that the Supreme Court accepted an appeal in this case to determine whether and when the record of a CPO can be expunged or sealed. Appeal allowed by, 133 Ohio St.3d 1422, 976 NE2d 913, 2012-Ohio-4902 (2012).

[45]City of Pepper Pike v. Doe, 66 Ohio St. 2d 374, 20 Ohio Op. 3d 334, 421 N.E.2d 1303 (1981).

[46]Schussheim v. Schussheim, 2012-Ohio-2573, 2012 WL 2087406, *4 (Ohio Ct. App. 12th Dist. Warren County 2012), judgment rev'd, 137 Ohio St. 3d 133, 2013-Ohio-4529, 998 N.E.2d 446 (2013); see also R.C. 2953.32; R.C. 2953.52.

erroneously found that because *Pepper Pike* was a criminal proceeding, such judicial authority is not applicable to a civil proceeding.[47]

In finding that judicial expungement may apply, the dissenting judge concluded that the allegation in this case is one of domestic violence, which is a criminal accusation, regardless of whether the proceeding is labeled criminal, civil or quasi-criminal. Therefore, a judicial remedy springing from constitutional principles should be applicable to a CPO. "The accused in an ex parte civil protection order which is dismissed, or unsubstantiated, should at least have the due process of having his privacy interest weighed by the court, particularly where the allegations arose from a domestic quarrel where the parties subsequently divorced and are currently raising their children together and the party who originally initiated the ex parte proceedings supports the sealing of the records. The inherent authority of the trial court to administer justice should be permitted to operate, particularly where the legislature has failed to act."[48]

Subsequent to the appellate decision, appellant appealed the decision to the Supreme Court of Ohio. Of note is that no brief by appellee was filed. On October 16, 2013, the Supreme Court of Ohio issued its decision.[49] The majority held that a "court has inherent authority to order expungement and sealing of records that relate to a dissolved civil protection order in an adult proceeding when "unusual and exceptional circumstances" exist."[50] To determine whether "unusual and exceptional circumstances" exist that would grant a court the inherent authority to order the sealing and expungement of records would depend on a balancing test-whether the interest of the accused in his/her right to be free from unwarranted punishment outweighs the legitimate need of government to maintain the records. "Where there is no compelling state interest to retain the records, the expungement applicant is entitled to his remedy."[51] Of note is that the majority relied on the reasoning set forth in *Pepper Pike v. Doe* to support its decision.

The majority explained that the fact that the original complainant who petitioned for the CPO in the first instance moved to dissolve the CPO and provided an affidavit stating that she believed the expungement to be in the best interests of the minor children demonstrated the "unusual and exceptional circumstances" in this case. Additionally, the Supreme Court stressed that the trial court, on remand, should consider that no related criminal charges were filed.

However, the Chief Justice issued a separate dissent in which she

---

[47]Schussheim v. Schussheim, 2012-Ohio-2573, 2012 WL 2087406, *5 (Ohio Ct. App. 12th Dist. Warren County 2012), judgment rev'd, 137 Ohio St. 3d 133, 2013-Ohio-4529, 998 N.E.2d 446 (2013) (Piper, J., dissenting).

[48]Schussheim v. Schussheim, 2012-Ohio-2573, 2012 WL 2087406, *7 (Ohio Ct. App. 12th Dist. Warren County 2012), judgment rev'd, 137 Ohio St. 3d 133, 2013-Ohio-4529, 998 N.E.2d 446 (2013) (Piper, J., dissenting).

[49]Schussheim v. Schussheim, 137 Ohio St. 3d 133, 2013-Ohio-4529, 998 N.E.2d 446 (2013).

[50]Schussheim v. Schussheim, 137 Ohio St. 3d 133, 2013-Ohio-4529, ¶ 14, 998 N.E.2d 446 (2013).

[51]Schussheim v. Schussheim, 137 Ohio St. 3d 133, 2013-Ohio-4529, ¶ 14, 998 N.E.2d 446 (2013).

noted her concern for the majority's "disturbing judicial activism."[52] She reasoned that "[b]y asserting that there is no statute that precludes sealing of records in adult proceedings and therefore the court may rule to allow it, the majority fails to acknowledge the significance of the General Assembly's enactment of a comprehensive statutory scheme that permits the sealing of records related to CPOs but limits the applicability of the sealing provision to juvenile proceedings. If the legislature had wanted to afford adults the same sealing provision, it would have done so."[53]

The dissent also admonished the majority for expanding the holding in *Pepper Pike v. Doe*, noting that the case at hand was not a criminal case, a fact that distinguished it from *Pepper Pike*. While the right to expunge and seal, in *Pepper Pike*, was based on the fact that the case arose from "a person's use of the court as a vindictive tool to harass,"[54] the contrary was true in *Schussheim*. In *Schussheim*, the fact that Henneman requested that the CPO be dismissed did not change the fact that she needed the CPO in the first instance. "And that she shortly thereafter notified the court that the CPO should be dissolved gives rise to the inference that she had responsibly, rather than vindictively, used the courts to secure only that protection that she needed for only that time that she needed it."[55] In that Henneman never claimed the domestic violence allegations were untrue when she requested that the CPO be dissolved, this case is ordinary and usual; there is nothing to indicate that this CPO was not issued for valid reasons.[56] A balancing test would demonstrate only that the underlying CPO was dismissed, there were no further acts of domestic violence and no criminal charges pending and Schussheim's fear that the record could inhibit future employment. Nothing in the record provides the requisite "unusual and exceptional circumstances."

Concluding that the majority extended *Pepper Pike*, redefined "unusual and exceptional circumstances" and legislated from the bench, the Chief Justice found that, with the limited information presented to the court, "we cannot know whether the majority's new law is good public policy for Ohio. As a practical matter, there is great potential for unintended consequences in the majority's decision. Most obviously, it increases the risk that respondents will use fear, intimidation, false promises, or threats to procure favorable affidavits from domestic violence victims."[57]

---

[52]Schussheim v. Schussheim, 137 Ohio St. 3d 133, 2013-Ohio-4529, ¶ 18, 998 N.E.2d 446 (2013).

[53]Schussheim v. Schussheim, 137 Ohio St. 3d 133, 2013-Ohio-4529, ¶ 20, 998 N.E.2d 446 (2013); see also Text § 13:15.

[54]Schussheim v. Schussheim, 137 Ohio St. 3d 133, 2013-Ohio-4529, ¶ 34, 998 N.E.2d 446 (2013).

[55]Schussheim v. Schussheim, 137 Ohio St. 3d 133, 2013-Ohio-4529, ¶ 42, 998 N.E.2d 446 (2013).

[56]Schussheim v. Schussheim, 137 Ohio St. 3d 133, 2013-Ohio-4529, ¶ 41, 998 N.E.2d 446 (2013).

[57]Schussheim v. Schussheim, 137 Ohio St. 3d 133, 2013-Ohio-4529, ¶ 60, 998 N.E.2d 446 (2013).

In *Henneman v. Schussheim*,[58] the case was remanded to the trial court to again address appellant's request of expungement.[59] The trial court again denied the request finding that "there was a legitimate need of the government to maintain its record of the CPO, at least until the parties' minor child was emancipated."[60]

On appeal, the appellate court first noted that there had been another incident between father and daughter and that the mother, in light of the recent incident, no longer approved of the expungement. The court then found such evidence relevant despite no criminal charges having been filed and reiterated the trial court's statement that the state had interest in maintaining the record where there are repeated acts of conduct.[61] In affirming the original judgment, the court held that "[w]hile we recognize that the Ohio Supreme Court has found that unusual and exceptional circumstances may exist in the present case, we cannot find that the trial court abused its discretion in determining that the state's interest in maintaining the record outweighs appellant's interest in 'clearing his name.' "[62]

Q & A: Can a party to a civil protection order request that the record of the CPO not be made publicly available on the Internet?

According to 18 U.S.C.A. § 2265, the government shall not make available publicly on the Internet any information regarding the registration, filing of a petition for or issuance of a protection order, restraining order or injunction if such publication would be likely to reveal the identity or location of the party protection under such order.

Since 2007, several jurisdictions have since redacted identifying information from the Internet. In fact some counties have instituted sweeping blanket prohibitions on the posting of such orders on the Internet. For example, the Cuyahoga County docket page now has language that states "Pursuant to federal law and at the discretion of the Domestic relations Court, domestic violence case information is no longer available via internet access. Such information can be obtained in person at the Clerk of Court's office or by contacting the Clerk's

[58]Henneman v. Schussheim, 2015-Ohio-829, 2015 WL 1005340, *3 (Ohio Ct. App. 12th Dist. Warren County 2015).

[59]See also Capital One Bank, USA, N.A. v. Essex, 2014-Ohio-4247, 2014 WL 4792583 (Ohio Ct. App. 2d Dist. Montgomery County 2014) (discussing difference between expungement and sealing).

[60]Henneman v. Schussheim, 2015-Ohio-829, 2015 WL 1005340, ¶ 7 (Ohio Ct. App. 12th Dist. Warren County 2015).

[61]Henneman v. Schussheim, 2015-Ohio-829, 2015 WL 1005340, ¶ 18 (Ohio Ct. App. 12th Dist. Warren County 2015).

[62]Henneman v. Schussheim, 2015-Ohio-829, 2015 WL 1005340, ¶ 20 (Ohio Ct. App. 12th Dist. Warren County 2015); see also Ward v. Balsley, 2014-Ohio-4050, 2014 WL 4629607 (Ohio Ct. App. 5th Dist. Muskingum County 2014) (and its companion cases); Wetz v. Pomeroy, 2014-Ohio-5085, 2014 WL 6158910 (Ohio Ct. App. 12th Dist. Warren County 2014) (no unusual and exceptional circumstances to expunge and seal such that respondent's interest in clearing his name from "scandalous accusations" was outweighed by state's interest in maintaining public records, despite petitioner having filed and dismissed repeated petitions).

docket information line. There is a similar policy in Montgomery County.[63]

At least one Ohio court has tangentially addressed this issue. In *Rieger v. Montgomery County Clerk of Courts*,[64] respondent of a civil protection order sued the clerk of court for maintaining information about an expired CPO on its Website, alleging that he was defamed by the clerk who violated federal law prohibiting a governmental unit from publishing on the internet certain information regarding the issuance of a protection order.

Previously, respondent had consented to the issuance of a CPO against him for five years. At the expiration of the CPO, he requested that the CPO be sealed. In a previous appeal, the appellate court affirmed the trial court's denial of respondent's motion to seal the record on the ground that there were no compelling and extraordinary reasons to justify sealing the consensual order.[65]

In the instant case, respondent "claimed that the Website led the public to believe that he was "guilty of domestic violence and basically just a bad person." Rieger maintained throughout these proceedings that the Clerk of Courts' website prevented him from obtaining employment at his full potential because the CPO could be discovered in a background check.[66]

In affirming the trial court's dismissal of respondent's action, the appellate court stated that 18 U.S.C.A. § 2265 "does not contain a sweeping prohibition on the posting of such orders on the Internet. Rieger was not protected by the order, did not allege facts to establish that the section was violated, and did not state any legitimate basis under the section to object to the Clerk's posting of the CPO on the Internet. Thus, the trial court properly concluded that Rieger had not stated a claim that the Clerk of Courts had violated section 2265, Title 18, U.S. Code."[67] Had this lawsuit been brought by the protected party, the court might have decided differently.

In an earlier *Rieger* opinion,[68] the dissenting opinion pointed out that the real complaint of this appellant "is not that the record of the CPO and the proceeding that produced it is maintained, but that the clerk of courts publishes the record on its Internet web site, making it

[63]See also Sup. R. 45(C).

[64]Rieger v. Montgomery Cty. Clerk of Courts, 2009-Ohio-426, 2009 WL 242668 (Ohio Ct. App. 2d Dist. Montgomery County 2009).

[65]Rieger v. Montgomery Cty. Clerk of Courts, 2009-Ohio-426, 2009 WL 242668, *1 (Ohio Ct. App. 2d Dist. Montgomery County 2009), citing Rieger v. Rieger, 2007-Ohio-2366, 2007 WL 1430191 (Ohio Ct. App. 2d Dist. Montgomery County 2007); see also Text § 13:15, Court enforcement of civil protection orders—Sentencing civil protection order violators; generally.

[66]Rieger v. Montgomery Cty. Clerk of Courts, 2009-Ohio-426, 2009 WL 242668, *1 (Ohio Ct. App. 2d Dist. Montgomery County 2009).

[67]Rieger v. Montgomery Cty. Clerk of Courts, 2009-Ohio-426, 2009 WL 242668, *2 (Ohio Ct. App. 2d Dist. Montgomery County 2009); see also Vaccaro v. Vaccaro, 425 Mass. 153, 680 N.E.2d 55 (1997) (holding that trial court had no statutory authority to direct expungement of husband's record from statewide domestic violence recordkeeping system); but see P.E.S. v. K.L., 720 A.2d 487 (Pa. Super. Ct. 1998).

[68]Rieger v. Rieger, 165 Ohio App. 3d 454, 2006-Ohio-482, 847 N.E.2d 9 (2d Dist. Montgomery County 2006).

available to Rieger's prospective employers. That undertaking on the part of clerks is wholly voluntary, being required neither by statute nor rule of the Supreme Court. It implicates an issue of public policy, not a claim subject to judicial relief. Because of that fact, and because clerks are public officials whose positions are created by statute, Rieger's proper avenue of relief is not through an application to the courts for expungement but with the General Assembly, through legislation limiting the clerk's Internet publication of court records. A more appropriate alternative to the practice generally may be a Rule of Superintendence governing the practice promulgated by the Supreme Court, a form of enactment authorized by section 5(A), Article IV of the Ohio Constitution and more specifically by Section 5(B) of the same Article, which authorizes the Supreme Court to 'make rules to require uniform record keeping for all courts of the state.' "[69]

§ 12:24 Renewal of a civil protection order

It is important to note that some courts use the term "extend," others use the term "renew" and still others use the term "modify" when discussing a renewal of the CPO.[1] The reason some courts may modify the order is that the extension of the duration of the order for another period of time suggests a modification. However, the statute differentiates between the procedure for modification[2] and renewal[3] of the civil protection order.

Since the statute mandates different considerations depending on whether a CPO is to be renewed or modified, courts must utilize the correct language when determining what was meant by an extension, renewal or modification and termination and applying the correct legal analyses.

Q & A: What does it mean "to renew" a civil protection order?

A survey of many Ohio courts indicates that most courts do not routinely renew civil protection orders. *Black's Law Dictionary* defines "renew" as "to make new again; to resume; to reestablish; to restore to existence; to grant or obtain an extension of."[4] Based on the dictionary definition, the term "renew" indicates either a continuation of the original protection order or a starting over.

One statutory interpretation follows the practice in some courts of

---

[69]Rieger v. Rieger, 165 Ohio App. 3d 454, 2006-Ohio-482, 847 N.E.2d 9 (2d Dist. Montgomery County 2006) (Grady, P.J., dissenting).

[Section 12:24]

[1]See for eg., Lundin v. Niepsuj, 2017-Ohio-7153, 2017 WL 3426957 (Ohio Ct. App. 9th Dist. Summit County 2017) (extending a CPO in this case means renewing the order).

[2]R.C. 3113.31(E)(8).

[3]R.C. 3113.3(E)(3)(c).

[4]Black's Law Dictionary (6th ed.) p 1296. Martin v. Martin, 2013-Ohio-5703, 2013 WL 6843599 (Ohio Ct. App. 10th Dist. Franklin County 2013) (noting that the term to "extend" a protection order has been used interchangeably with to "renew" a protection order and discussing when to differentiate; if one was to extend the consent CPO (rather than renew it), then the final CPO would have exceeded the maximum term permitted by law).

periodically renewing a protection order within the five-year period. As stated in previous sections, some Ohio courts do not automatically grant protection orders for the five-year period. Instead, orders are granted for finite incremental periods. These orders may then be reissued within the five-year period. When this approach is utilized by the court, it is not pursuant to any defined local policy. Rather, it is based on local practice in that particular jurisdiction.

For example, in *Dennis v. Paulson*,[5] the trial court granted appellee a civil stalking protection order pursuant to RC 2903.214 for a period of three years. A few days before the order was to expire, she requested that the order be continued (renewed) for an additional three years, which the court granted without a hearing.

Appellant appealed the decision granting the renewal on due process grounds and argued that RC 2903.214(E)(2)(b) states that "[a]ny protection order issued pursuant to this section may be renewed in the same manner as the original order was issued.[6] The Court sustained his assignment of error and remanded the case to the trial court. Of significance was that the court held that extending the civil protection order an additional three years violated the maximum duration of a civil protection order of five years as imposed by RC 2903.214(E)(2)(a).[7] By granting the motion to renew the order for an additional three years, "the trial court extended the CSPO beyond the five-year maximum" imposed by statute.[8]

Other courts renew protection orders at the end of the five-year period. The Supreme Court expressed this opinion in dicta in *Felton v. Felton*.[9] In discussing the public policy reasons why a civil protection order is more effective than a restraining order, the Court explained that the benefits of a protection order outweigh any concerns about the temporary nature of the order. The Court then pointed out that civil protection orders can be renewed at the end of the effective period. As with other documents that may be renewed, the better practice is to have the order renewed before its expiration date.[10]

Finally, in Lundin v. Niepsuj,[11] the court noted that "[t]he statute does not explicitly set forth when a renewal is permitted, but use of

[5]Dennis v. Paulsen, 2009-Ohio-2916, 2009 WL 1719369 (Ohio Ct. App. 4th Dist. Hocking County 2009).

[6]See also RC 3113.31(E)(3)(c).

[7]See also RC 3113.31(E)(3)(a).

[8]*Dennis at *2.*

[9]Felton v. Felton, 79 Ohio St. 3d 34, 1997-Ohio-302, 679 N.E.2d 672 (1997); see also Harlett v. Harlett, 1996 WL 629510 (Ohio Ct. App. 2d Dist. Montgomery County 1996); Martin v. Martin, 2013-Ohio-5703, 2013 WL 6843599 (Ohio Ct. App. 10th Dist. Franklin County 2013).

[10]But see Woolum v. Woolum, 131 Ohio App. 3d 818, 723 N.E.2d 1135 (12th Dist. Preble County 1999) (renewal of the civil protection order granted where requested almost one month after expiration of the prior order); see also Hershberger v. Hershberger, 2000-Ohio-1716, 2000 WL 1675568 (Ohio Ct. App. 3d Dist. Seneca County 2000) (petitioner may renew protection order once specified time limit has expired).

[11]Lundin v. Niepsuj, 2017-Ohio-7153, 2017 WL 3426957 (Ohio Ct. App. 9th Dist. Summit County 2017).

the term "renew" suggests the issuance of an additional CPO after the expiration of an original order."[12]

Q & A: What is the procedure for renewal?

The statute fails to address the procedural aspects of a renewal. "In the same manner" suggests that the same type of procedure used in the initial filing of the petition should be adopted.[13]

The Ashland County Court of Appeals interpreted the provision "in the same manner as the original order or agreement was originally issued or approved" in *Workman v. Workman*.[14] In *Workman*, the civil protection order was granted pursuant to a consent entry. Prior to its expiration date, appellee requested that the order be renewed, which said order was granted without an evidentiary hearing and over the objection of the appellant. In reversing the trial court decision, the 5th District Court of Appeals held that "[s]ince subsection (c) provides for renewal in the same manner as the originally approved, which in this case was by consent, now absent, the court could not automatically extend the expiration date."[15]

The Ashland County appellate court did not interpret RC 3113.31(E)(3)(c) as applying either to the content of the petition that formed the basis of the original order or the procedure used for the initial filing. Rather, the court focused on how the order was originally issued and the fact that the order was agreed upon by the parties without an evidentiary hearing. This decision suggests that persons who obtain protection orders by entering into consent entries would not be able to renew their orders unless both parties agree to the extension or renewal.

[12]Lundin v. Niepsuj, 2017-Ohio-7153, ¶ 15, 2017 WL 3426957 (Ohio Ct. App. 9th Dist. Summit County 2017); quoting Martin v. Martin, 2013-Ohio-5703, ¶ 8, 2013 WL 6843599 (Ohio Ct. App. 10th Dist. Franklin County 2013); citing Felton v. Felton, 79 Ohio St. 3d 34, 1997-Ohio-302, 679 N.E.2d 672 (1997)(noting that a CPO can be renewed at the end of the effective period); also citing Little v. Little, 2011-Ohio-318, ¶ 6, 2011 WL 303823 (Ohio Ct. App. 10th Dist. Franklin County 2011); Patton v. Patton, 2010-Ohio-2096, ¶ 3, 2010 WL 1918793 (Ohio Ct. App. 5th Dist. Muskingum County 2010); Hershberger v. Hershberger, 2000-Ohio-1716, 2000 WL 1675568, *2 (Ohio Ct. App. 3d Dist. Seneca County 2000); Woolum v. Woolum, 131 Ohio App. 3d 818, 821, 723 N.E.2d 1135 (12th Dist. Preble County 1999).

[13]See Woolum v. Woolum, 131 Ohio App. 3d 818, 723 N.E.2d 1135 (12th Dist. Preble County 1999); see also Saari v. Saari, 2000 WL 1729455 (Ohio Ct. App. 9th Dist. Lorain County 2000) (CPO may be renewed only after full hearing and not sua sponte); Bennett v. Bennett, 2006-Ohio-681, 2006 WL 337372 (Ohio Ct. App. 5th Dist. Stark County 2006) (although appellant argued that a CPO may be renewed only after a full hearing and not sua sponte, the court held that he failed to raise the issue at the trial court level); Little v. Little, 2011-Ohio-318, 2011 WL 303823 (Ohio Ct. App. 10th Dist. Franklin County 2011) (noting that the procedure for issuing a renewal order must go forward in the same manner as that for issuing the original protection order, and indicating that service of the motion to extend/renew was necessary); Martin v. Martin, 2013-Ohio-5703, 2013 WL 6843599 (Ohio Ct. App. 10th Dist. Franklin County 2013); M.J. v. L.P., 2016-Ohio-7080, 2016 WL 5723752 (Ohio Ct. App. 9th Dist. Medina County 2016).

[14]Workman v. Workman, 2005-Ohio-1232, 2005 WL 635040 (Ohio Ct. App. 5th Dist. Ashland County 2005).

[15]Workman v. Workman, 2005-Ohio-1232, 2005 WL 635040, *1 (Ohio Ct. App. 5th Dist. Ashland County 2005).

Q & A: Where a party files a motion to renew a CPO and the CPO is set to expire, is the court obligated to extend the CPO to avoid a lapse in the order?

No. In *Schneider v. Razek*,[16] the appellant argued that the court was obligated to hold an ex parte hearing on the motion to extend the CPO, to avoid a lapse in the CPO. The appellate court found that "[t]here is, however, no such requirement under RC 3113.31. Only if a party requests an ex parte order is the court required, under RC 3113. 31(D)(1), to hold an ex parte hearing. Where no ex parte hearing is requested, RC 3113.31(D)(3) provides that "the court shall proceed as in a normal civil action and grant a full hearing on the matter."[17]

However, it is always a good idea for an attorney to file the Motion to Renew well in advance of the expiration date of the CPO *or* request an ex parte CPO if time is getting short.[18]

Q & A: Can a protection order be renewed when the order expires?

In light of the continuing nature of domestic violence, it may be necessary to renew a civil protection order under certain circumstances.[19] RC 3113.31(E)(3)(c) permits a court to renew any protection order or consent agreement in the same manner as the original order or agreement was issued or approved.[20]

While it is clear that judges across the state may renew protection orders, three issues present themselves. The first issue involves the statutory interpretation of the term "renew." The second issue relates to the procedure employed by a petitioner who desires to renew a protection order for an additional period of time, and the third issue involves the type of evidence required and the standard of proof for renewing a protection order.

The statutory language is ambiguous in that it is unclear whether a protection order must be renewed within the five-year period or whether it may be renewed only after the five year period expires.[21] Some courts suggest that a renewal motion must be filed prior to the

[16]Schneider v. Razek, 2015-Ohio-410, 28 N.E.3d 591 (Ohio Ct. App. 8th Dist. Cuyahoga County 2015).

[17]Schneider v. Razek, 2015-Ohio-410, 28 N.E.3d 591, ¶ 71 (Ohio Ct. App. 8th Dist. Cuyahoga County 2015).

[18]See Martin v. Martin, 2013-Ohio-5703, 2013 WL 6843599 (Ohio Ct. App. 10th Dist. Franklin County 2013) (noting that the trial court had authority to grant a temporary ex parte CPO and finding that to avoid a lapse of the CPO was to construe the motion to extend as a request for an ex parte order pending a hearing on renewal of the order).

[19]See Cherry Henault, The Reissuance of Domestic Violence Orders Under Kentucky Law: A Due Process Analysis, 40 Brandeis L.J. 575 (2001) (a constitutional analysis).

[20]R.C. 3113.31(E)(3)(c). See also Little v. Little, 2011-Ohio-318, 2011 WL 303823 (Ohio Ct. App. 10th Dist. Franklin County 2011) (stating that "the procedure for issuing a renewal order must go forward in the same manner as that for issuing an original protection order," and citing Woolum v. Woolum, 131 Ohio App. 3d 818, 823, 723 N.E.2d 1135 (12th Dist. Preble County 1999)); Martin v. Martin, 2013-Ohio-5703, 2013 WL 6843599 (Ohio Ct. App. 10th Dist. Franklin County 2013) ("in the same manner" means that the procedure for issuing a renewal order must go forward in the same manner as that for issuing the original CPO).

[21]See also Frisk v. Frisk, 2006 ND 165, 719 N.W.2d 332, 336 (N.D. 2006) (point-

expiration of the full hearing CPO.[22] Other courts have determined that a motion to renew may be filed after expiration of the full hearing CPO.[23]

In *Martin v. Martin*,[24] appellee filed a motion to extend the consent entry from its effective duration of six months almost three weeks before the CPO was set to expire. In that appellee filed a continuance to perfect service of the motion, the court issued an ex parte CPO. After continuing the hearing again and ordering that the ex parte CPO would remain in effect, the court issued a domestic violence full hearing CPO containing the same terms as the consent CPO and ordering the CPO to remain in effect for five years.

On appeal, appellant argued, among other reasons, that the trial court should not have granted another ex parte CPO and that the court lacked authority to conduct the full hearing because the consent CPO had expired two months before. The appellate court first considered R.C. 3113.31(D)(1) which authorizes a trial court to issue an ex parte civil protection order based on a showing of immediate and present danger. "Under the principle that a trial court may renew a civil protection order following the same procedural requirements as an original order, the trial court in this case had authority to grant a temporary ex parte civil protection order."[25]

The court then reasoned that "[t]he civil domestic violence statute does not explicitly provide for extension of an expired civil protection order; however, as explained above, it authorizes a trial court to renew a civil protection order, subject to the same procedural requirements that apply to the issuance of an original order."[26] Under the statute a full hearing is required before the trial court may enter a final civil protection order.[27] "Therefore, a full hearing is also required before the trial court may enter a final order on a renewed civil protection order. Thus, the trial court had authority under the statute to conduct the February 5, 2013, hearing before entering the final CPO in this case."[28]

Because the CPO was set to expire on 12/13/2012, the only way to avoid a lapse in the protection afforded under the original order was to construe the request to renew as a request for an ex parte order pending a hearing on the renewal of the order. Thus, the appellate

---

ing out that RC 3113.31 does not state that a renewal must occur before an original order expires).

[22]Patton v. Patton, 2010-Ohio-2096, 2010 WL 1918793 (Ohio Ct. App. 5th Dist. Muskingum County 2010).

[23]Woolum v. Woolum, 131 Ohio App. 3d 818, 723 N.E.2d 1135 (12th Dist. Preble County 1999); Hershberger v. Hershberger, 2000-Ohio-1716, 2000 WL 1675568 (Ohio Ct. App. 3d Dist. Seneca County 2000); Little v. Little, 2011-Ohio-318, 2011 WL 303823 (Ohio Ct. App. 10th Dist. Franklin County 2011).

[24]Martin v. Martin, 2013-Ohio-5703, 2013 WL 6843599 (Ohio Ct. App. 10th Dist. Franklin County 2013).

[25]Martin v. Martin, 2013-Ohio-5703, 2013 WL 6843599, ¶ 14 (Ohio Ct. App. 10th Dist. Franklin County 2013).

[26]See R.C. 3113.31(E)(3)(c).

[27]R.C. 3113.31(D)(2) to (3).

[28]Martin v. Martin, 2013-Ohio-5703, 2013 WL 6843599, ¶ 21 (Ohio Ct. App. 10th Dist. Franklin County 2013).

court found a way to avoid an unprotected period of time due to the expiration of the consent CPO.

Interestingly, the appellate court interpreted the statute to mean that all procedural requirements must be followed when filing a motion to renew. In effect, that means new violence or at least a showing of an immediate and present danger for the issuance of an ex parte CPO, an ex parte hearing and a full hearing after service and notice.

Q & A: Does the statute address service or notice of the motion to renew or the grant or denial of the renewed protection order?

No reference to service or notice to the respondent is set forth in the statute. The term, "in the same manner" could imply that personal service be utilized by a petitioner who seeks to renew the CPO, especially because personal service must be attempted when a civil protection order is requested in the first instance.

For example, in *Dennis v. Paulson*,[29] appellant appealed the trial court's decision extending the final protection order an additional three years without providing him notice and an opportunity to be heard.

The appellate court agreed and found that "in order to renew a CSPO, the respondent must be given notice and an opportunity to be heard. RC 2903.214(E)(2)(b) states that a protection order can be renewed "in the same manner as the original." Under RC 29031. 214(D)(2)(a), the original imposition of a CSPO requires a full hearing. "Accordingly, we find that a renewal of a CSPO also requires a full hearing."[30] It goes without saying that a full hearing mandates service.

However, the Civil Rules of Procedure have recently provided guidance to courts. The civil rules were amended to provide that "[s]ervice of a motion for modification, contempt, renewal or termination of a civil protection order issued after a full hearing or an approved consent agreement shall be made in the manner provided for service of process under Civ. R. 4 through 4.6."[31]

Pursuant to Civ. R. 65.1(C)(4)(b), "[a]fter service has been made in accordance with division (C)(4)(a) of this rule, any additional service required to be made on the Respondent, and, if applicable, on the parent, guardian, or legal custodian, shall be made in accordance with provisions of Civ. R. 5(B)."

Q & A: Does the statute require that a new act of violence is needed in order to renew a civil protection order?

Unfortunately, there is little informative case law on the matter.[32] In some Ohio courts, a new act of domestic violence[33] is required for an extension of the civil protection order. In other courts, a CPO is

[29]Dennis v. Paulsen, 2009-Ohio-2916, 2009 WL 1719369 (Ohio Ct. App. 4th Dist. Hocking County 2009).

[30]At *2; see also RC 3113.31(3)(c); RC 3113.31(D)(2)(a).

[31]Civ. R. 65.1(C)(4)(a).

[32]Studer v. Studer, 2012-Ohio-2838, 2012 WL 2371452 (Ohio Ct. App. 3d Dist. Crawford County 2012).

[33]See RC 3113.31(A)(1) for a definition of the acts that constitute domestic violence for purposes of the issuance of a CPO. Charles v. Peters, 2016-Ohio-1259, 2016 WL 1178776 (Ohio Ct. App. 2d Dist. Greene County 2016) (request for renewal

renewed based on petitioner's testimony of continued fear of the respondent. In most jurisdictions, however, a renewal is based on a past history and a present threat of future violence.

In several court decisions, an actual and new act of domestic violence is not necessary in order to renew the civil protection order. For example, in *Woolum v. Woolum*,[34] the Preble County Court of Appeals utilized a two-tier approach by which past history of domestic violence and present threats of future violence formed the basis of the court's decision to renew the civil protection order.[35] In that case, the appellee had sought a renewal of a civil protection order on the basis that the appellant had acted in a threatening manner. The trial court granted her request because the evidence indicated that appellant had placed appellee in fear of imminent serious physical harm and that the order was needed to prevent irreparable harm. The appellant argued that a civil protection order should be based on a present danger of domestic violence. The court interpreted appellant's argument to suggest that "there must be new evidence of domestic violence to support the renewal of the civil protection order, not merely that evidence which supported the original order."[36]

In rejecting the appellant's argument, the Preble County Court of Appeals noted that the trial court did not find that the evidence sup-

---

based on continued fear of respondent due to ongoing stalking, harassment threatening notes and verbal threats was denied because petitioner did not meet the requirements of RC 3113.31(A)(1) in that there was no evidence of any physical contact between the parties for more than three years, no evidence of a past or present history of domestic violence and no threat of physical harm. At ¶ 26).

[34]Woolum v. Woolum, 131 Ohio App. 3d 818, 723 N.E.2d 1135 (12th Dist. Preble County 1999); see also Trent v. Trent, 1999 WL 298073 (Ohio Ct. App. 12th Dist. Preble County 1999); Ritchie v. Konrad, 115 Cal. App. 4th 1275, 10 Cal. Rptr. 3d 387 (2d Dist. 2004) (citing *Woolum v. Woolum* for its holding that a renewal of a domestic violence protection order is predicated on finding that protected party has a reasonable apprehension of future abuse); Patton v. Patton, 2010-Ohio-2096, 2010 WL 1918793 (Ohio Ct. App. 5th Dist. Muskingum County 2010) (reiterated the holding in *Woolum* that a civil protection order could be renewed even if no new acts of violence had been committed since the original CPO was issued. Rather, testimony by a petitioner that he/she continues to fear the respondent would support the renewal of the order); Studer v. Studer, 2012-Ohio-2838, 2012 WL 2371452 (Ohio Ct. App. 3d Dist. Crawford County 2012) (stating that past acts of domestic violence coupled with new threats of domestic violence and a reasonable fear of serious physical harm based on new threats of domestic violence are sufficient to provide the court grounds for renewing the CPO; also noting that "change in circumstances and the severity of the physical injury or the nature of the domestic violence have also been considered in determining the propriety of granting a CPO"; citing Williamson v. Williamson, 180 Ohio App. 3d 260, 2008-Ohio-6718, 905 N.E.2d 217 (2d Dist. Greene County 2008)).

[35]See also Anderson v. Anderson, 2001-Ohio-3379, 2001 WL 1667875 (Ohio Ct. App. 7th Dist. Mahoning County 2001); Bruner v. Bruner, 2000-Ohio-2554, 2000 WL 1486452 (Ohio Ct. App. 7th Dist. Mahoning County 2000); but see Welch v. Staggs, 2009-Ohio-379, 2009 WL 223414 (Ohio Ct. App. 4th Dist. Scioto County 2009) (trial court did not abuse its discretion in denying a renewal of a CPO as petitioner failed to report any alleged incidents of domestic violence or alleged violations of the initial CPO to law enforcement or to the court); Weber v. Weber, 2011-Ohio-2980, 2011 WL 2436963 (Ohio Ct. App. 2d Dist. Greene County 2011) (reversing trial court and holding that no evidence was presented to demonstrate that former wife was in danger of domestic violence; the last domestic violence had occurred 11 years ago and the recent letter she received from her former husband contained no threatening language).

[36]Woolum v. Woolum, 131 Ohio App. 3d 818, 822, 723 N.E.2d 1135 (12th Dist. Preble County 1999).

ported a finding that the appellant had committed an act of domestic violence subsequent to the expiration of the prior protection order. However, the court renewed the protection order and predicated its ruling on a finding that RC 3113.31 "did not preclude the court from considering domestic violence that may have occurred two or more years prior, nor did the language of RC 3113.31 require evidence of 'new' domestic violence before the civil protection order may be renewed."[37]

While acknowledging the appellant's concern of possible future protection orders if appellee was allowed to request a new protection order upon expiration of the prior order, the Preble County Court of Appeals determined that the renewal of the civil protection order in this case was based on past domestic violence as well as present threats of future violence, even if the threats did not rise to the level of domestic violence as set forth in RC 3113.31(A)(1).[38] The court held that a civil protection order that expired due to the passage of time might be renewed if there is a past history of domestic violence coupled with a present threat of future violence.

The legal analysis in *Woolum* demonstrates an awareness by the court that past domestic violence may potentially escalate to new domestic violence if the safety of the victim is not assured. Although the court noted that renewal of a civil protection order should be considered on a case-by-case basis, the *Woolum* decision signals a significant step in offering continuing and long-term protection for victims of domestic violence.

However, the Preble County Court of Appeals reversed the trial court's renewal of a civil protection order in *Lain v. Ververis*.[39] In that case, the petitioner filed a motion to renew the civil protection order. The only evidence of threats or other domestic violence was petitioner's testimony about the threat which was the basis for the 1996 protection order. Since that time, there were no threats or actions suggesting that the defendant was likely to commit domestic violence in the future.

The court distinguished its opinion in *Lain* from its prior holding in *Woolum*.

> The holding above should not be construed as saying that a threat or violent act from the past can never be the basis for renewing a CPO or issuing a new CPO. Rather, we adhere to our holding in Woolum, as stated above, which requires some evidence that there remains a "present threat of future violence" before the trial court may renew or issue a CPO.[40]

The Twelfth District Court of Appeals further refined its reasoning

[37]Woolum v. Woolum, 131 Ohio App. 3d 818, 822, 723 N.E.2d 1135 (12th Dist. Preble County 1999); Lutson v. Anderkin, 2013 WL 2150897 (Ohio C.P. 2013) (discussing the standard for renewal based on the analysis in *Woolum* and *Lain*).

[38]See also Striff v. Striff, 2003-Ohio-794, 2003 WL 397869 (Ohio Ct. App. 6th Dist. Wood County 2003) (holding that appellant's continual contact with appellee despite an existing stalking CPO, appellant's past behavior and appellee's continual fear of appellant's harassment justified need to extend order).

[39]Lain v. Ververis, 1999 WL 893611 (Ohio Ct. App. 12th Dist. Preble County 1999).

[40]Lain v. Ververis, 1999 WL 893611, *3 (Ohio Ct. App. 12th Dist. Preble County

in *Morris v. Stonewall.*[41] In *Morris*, the respondent appealed the issuance of a civil protection order as an abuse of discretion based on the holding in *Woolum.*[42] The Clinton County Court of Appeals distinguished *Woolum* by noting that it involved a renewal of a civil protection order whereas the instant case involves the original issuance of a civil protection order.

The *Morris* court then differentiated the present case from Lain by stating that the protection order in *Lain*:

> was based on a single verbal threat made at a public place, whereas the CPO in this case is based upon verbal, physical and sexual abuse sustained over a period of years in a marriage. . . . That the perpetrator of the abuse is a member of the law enforcement community who frequents some of the same places Morris does further increases the need for a CPO, even if a recent threat or harm has not been shown. Under these facts, there is a basis for finding that there remains "a present threat of future violence."[43]

In this case, evidence was presented that indicated that the respondent had stalked the petitioner on several occasions during the fall and winter of 1998.

The Fourth District Court of Appeals also weighed in on the issue. In *Welch v. Staggs*,[44] the appellant appealed the denial of the renewal of her CPO. Since the original CPO was issued, appellee-respondent had repeatedly driven by her home honking, yelling, making obscene gestures and throwing items out of his car as he drove past. He also shot a gun up the hill aiming at her Aunt's house, but it was unclear whether that incident took place after the original order was entered.

In its opinion, the appellate court noted that the weight to be accorded to a past incident of domestic violence is within the court's discretion.[45]

The appellate court noted that the trial court had accorded no weight to incidents occurring in or before 2002. In failing to report recent incidents or alleged violations to law enforcement officials or the court, the appellate court surmised that the trial court found ap-

---

1999); see also Owens v. Owens, 2008-Ohio-7036, 2008 WL 5456353 (Ohio Ct. App. 5th Dist. Richland County 2008) (renewal of the CPO was upheld on appeal; while the original CPO permitted appellant visitation, his unannounced visits to the child's preschool where appellee worked and his stalking behaviors amounted to threats necessitating the renewal of the order; appellant had argued that the fact that he had been permitted visitation with the child evidenced a lack of a "present threat," the articulated test for renewal under *Lain v Ververis*).

[41]Morris v. Stonewall, 1999 WL 1037507 (Ohio Ct. App. 12th Dist. Clinton County 1999).

[42]Woolum v. Woolum, 131 Ohio App. 3d 818, 723 N.E.2d 1135 (12th Dist. Preble County 1999) (holding that past domestic violence must be coupled with the present threat of future violence in order for a protection order to be issued).

[43]Morris v. Stonewall, 1999 WL 1037507, *4 (Ohio Ct. App. 12th Dist. Clinton County 1999) (quoting *Lain*).

[44]Welch v. Staggs, 2009-Ohio-379, 2009 WL 223414 (Ohio Ct. App. 4th Dist. Scioto County 2009).

[45]Welch v. Staggs, 2009-Ohio-379, 2009 WL 223414, *4 (Ohio Ct. App. 4th Dist. Scioto County 2009), quoting Henry v. Henry, 2005-Ohio-67, 2005 WL 43888 (Ohio Ct. App. 4th Dist. Ross County 2005), and citing Murral v. Thomson, 2004-Ohio-432, 2004 WL 193876 (Ohio Ct. App. 4th Dist. Hocking County 2004).

pellant either not credible or that she demonstrated a lack of fear of imminent physical harm. In either case, it was not an abuse of discretion for the trial court to deny the renewal of her order.

Likewise, in M.J. v. L.P.,[46] the Ninth District Court of Appeals reversed the trial court's grant of the CPO and held that the continuation of a CPO cannot be based on 1) continued litigation of the original protection order including an appeal and a subsequently filed Motion for Relief from Judgment, 2) the filing of a civil lawsuit against petitioner, and 3) the fear that as soon as the CPO terminates, respondent will begin stalking her again. In this case, the trial court had renewed/extended the CPO because of petitioner's testimony that she continued to fear for her safety based upon the trauma she suffered by the acts of L.P. which led to the original filing.[47]

The appellate court first pointed out that the trial court's findings involved RC 3113.31(A)(1)(b) which defines domestic violence for purposes of a CPO proceeding as "[p]lacing another person by threat of force in fear of imminent serious physical harm." "In reviewing whether there is sufficient evidence that the petitioner was under fear of imminent serious physical harm, "the critical inquiry is "whether a reasonable person would be placed in fear of imminent (in the sense of unconditional, non-contingent) serious physical harm." State v. McKinney, 2009-Ohio-2225, ¶ 11, 2009 WL 1314871 (Ohio Ct. App. 9th Dist. Summit County 2009), quoting State v. Tackett, 2005-Ohio-1437, ¶ 14, 2005 WL 697411 (Ohio Ct. App. 4th Dist. Jackson County 2005). Although "we refer to the petitioner's history with respondent" when carrying out this inquiry, M.H. v. J.H., 2015-Ohio-5178, ¶ 7, 2015 WL 8553569 (Ohio Ct. App. 9th Dist. Medina County 2015), to support the extension of a civil protection order, "[t]here must also be evidence the petitioner has a reasonable belief of serious physical harm based on new threats of domestic violence." Studer v. Studer, 2012-Ohio-2838, ¶ 23, 2012 WL 2371452 (Ohio Ct. App. 3d Dist. Crawford County 2012); see also Woolum v. Woolum, 131 Ohio App. 3d 818, 822, 723 N.E.2d 1135 (12th Dist. Preble County 1999) (affirming extension of civil protection order "on the basis of past domestic abuse *coupled with present threat of future violence*") (Emphasis added).This requirement of continued threats beyond those that gave rise to the initial civil protection order is necessary because "[t]he purpose of the civil protection order is not to address past abuse."[48] In effect, the events giving rise to the original CPO are not enough, without more, to support the extension of the order.[49]

Because appellee only testified that she had seen appellant at court

---

[46]M.J. v. L.P., 2016-Ohio-7080, 2016 WL 5723752 (Ohio Ct. App. 9th Dist. Medina County 2016).

[47]M.J. v. L.P., 2016-Ohio-7080, ¶ 10, 2016 WL 5723752 (Ohio Ct. App. 9th Dist. Medina County 2016).

[48]M.J. v. L.P., 2016-Ohio-7080, ¶ 11, 2016 WL 5723752 (Ohio Ct. App. 9th Dist. Medina County 2016); quoting Wetterman v. B.C., 2013-Ohio-57, ¶ 11, 2013 WL 141752 (Ohio Ct. App. 9th Dist. Medina County 2013).

[49]M.J. v. L.P., 2016-Ohio-7080, ¶ 12, 2016 WL 5723752 (Ohio Ct. App. 9th Dist. Medina County 2016); Solomon v. Solomon, 157 Ohio App. 3d 807, 2004-Ohio-2486, ¶ 27, 813 N.E.2d 918 (7th Dist. Mahoning County 2004); see also Lundin v. Niepsuj, 2017-Ohio-7153, 2017 WL 3426957 (Ohio Ct. App. 9th Dist. Summit County 2017) (noting that a renewal "would require a new finding of domestic violence, or threat

hearings and that he had not harassed her in any other way and no evidence was presented that there had been any threats since the issuance of the original order, the court found that appellee did not demonstrate that she was under a reasonable fear of imminent serious physical harm. Additionally, the possibility of potential problems does not demonstrate fear of imminent serious physical harm. The mere fear of potential future conduct does not rise to the level of imminent fear such that such that the CPO should be extended or renewed. The desire to remain free of contact with appellant is not enough to satisfy the requisite elements.[50]

Of significance is that the concurring opinion raised an interesting legal question which is whether a CPO can be renewed or extended when the parties are no longer family or household members at the time of the filing of the motion to extend the CPO. In this case, the parties were former cohabitants having lived together within five years prior to the alleged occurrence of the act in question. At the time of the filing of the motion, more than five years had passed and the parties ceased to be family or household members. "L.P. ceased to be a "household member," before the protection order was granted and therefore incapable of committing future acts of domestic violence pursuant to Section 3113.31."[51] The only remedy available to M.J would have been to file a civil stalking CPO under 2903.211 which does not require a family or household member relationship.

Since the enactment of RC 3113.31, this is the first written appellate decision to address this particular issue, suggesting that the relationship developed during the original CPO must survive a motion to renew or extend. In any case, such an analysis might be useful for a party in a given case.

In a dissenting opinion, Judge Carr commented that M.J. had established a continued pattern of conduct that placed her in fear. Had this been an initial CPO, she would not have demonstrated the need for the CPO; however, as a renewal situation, "this Court need not examine the evidence in a vacuum."[52] Because she had obtained the original order based on degrading sexual acts in exchange for a place to live and because she testified at the renewal hearing that he is still intruding into her life by filing baseless court actions, "[t]his conduct coupled with his prior egregious behavior that formed the basis of the initial CPO is sufficient to support a renewal of the CPO."[53]

In other states, the case law demonstrates a growing trend toward renewing or extending protection orders based on the petitioner's

---

thereof, under the law set forth below, to justify the issuance of what amounted to an effectively new order." at¶ 18).

[50]M.J. v. L.P., 2016-Ohio-7080, ¶ 12, 2016 WL 5723752 (Ohio Ct. App. 9th Dist. Medina County 2016).

[51]M.J. v. L.P., 2016-Ohio-7080, ¶ 21, 2016 WL 5723752 (Ohio Ct. App. 9th Dist. Medina County 2016).

[52]M.J. v. L.P., 2016-Ohio-7080, ¶ 23, 2016 WL 5723752 (Ohio Ct. App. 9th Dist. Medina County 2016).

[53]M.J. v. L.P., 2016-Ohio-7080, ¶ 23, 2016 WL 5723752 (Ohio Ct. App. 9th Dist. Medina County 2016).

testimony that he/she is still in fear. For example, in *Barry v. Iverson*,[54] the Minnesota Court of Appeals found that the extension of the protection order was based on a finding that the appellant's actions in the last one and one-half years made the appellee's fear of imminent harm reasonable.

In determining whether or not to extend a civil protection order, other courts have considered the entire history of abuse between the parties, the totality of the present circumstances of the relationship and actions between the parties, and whether the balance of harm favors the granting of an extension.[55] In *Capps v. Capps*,[56] the Missouri Court of Appeals held that the renewal of a civil protection order did not require that the petitioner allege new acts of abuse so long as the circumstances which formed the basis for the initial order continued unabated. The court determined that the standard of proof was by a preponderance of the evidence.

Likewise, in *Knuth v. Knuth*,[57] the Minnesota Court of Appeals upheld the extension of a civil protection order based on the respondent's continued and frequent presence in the petitioner's vicinity, including moving within two blocks of the family residence, following the petitioner, and loitering around the family home and domestic violence shelter where the petitioner stayed. The court held that such behavior placed the petitioner in fear of imminent bodily harm sufficient to extend the protection order.

These cases illustrate that evidence must be presented to the court by way of the petitioner's testimony. The only difference between the original hearing and the renewal hearing is that, in light of the history of abuse, a petitioner need only show that he/she continues to fear the respondent based on certain behaviors of the respondent, whether or not those behaviors rise to the level of domestic violence pursuant to the statutory definition.[58]

In light of the *Felton* decision and the Supreme Court's determination that preponderance of the evidence is the correct standard of proof for purposes of obtaining an original protection order, the preponderance of the evidence standard should also be the standard of proof for determining whether to renew a protection order.[59] The evidence need not be a new act of violence but, rather, that the expiration of the order will place the petitioner in immediate and present

---

[54]Barry v. Iverson, 1990 WL 119349 (Minn. Ct. App. 1990); see also Gaab v. Ochsner, 2001 ND 195, 636 N.W.2d 669 (N.D. 2001) (court stated that once a petitioner obtains a protection order, there is no requirement to prove actual or imminent domestic violence in order to prevail on a motion to extend that order).

[55]See, e.g., Cruz-Foster v. Foster, 597 A.2d 927 (D.C. 1991); Rybolt v. Riley, 20 Cal. App. 5th 864, 229 Cal. Rptr. 3d 576 (3d Dist. 2018).

[56]Capps v. Capps, 715 S.W.2d 547 (Mo. Ct. App. E.D. 1986).

[57]Knuth v. Knuth, 1992 WL 145387 (Minn. Ct. App. 1992).

[58]See Woolum v. Woolum, 131 Ohio App. 3d 818, 723 N.E.2d 1135 (12th Dist. Preble County 1999) (renewing protection order even though the recent threats, in and of themselves, did not rise to the level of domestic violence as defined in RC 3113.31(A)(1)).

[59]See Woolum v. Woolum, 131 Ohio App. 3d 818, 723 N.E.2d 1135 (12th Dist. Preble County 1999) (relying on *Felton* and using the "preponderance of the evidence" standard).

danger. However, each order renewing a civil protection order must be based on sufficient findings of fact and conclusions of law.[60]

Q & A: If a civil protection order is renewed, can it be more expansive in scope than the original order?

According to *Woolum v. Woolum*,[61] it is within the court's discretion to determine the scope of a civil protection order. In that case, the appellant argued that the new protection order included the parties' children as protected persons and included a provision ordering appellant to surrender his firearms and weapons.

The appellate court relied on the legal analysis and public policy arguments advanced by the Supreme Court in *Felton v. Felton*.[62] Additionally, the court noted that the language contained in RC 3113.31(E)(1) permits a court to tailor any number of specific remedies to the circumstances of a particular case as well as to "'grant any other relief that the court considers equitable and fair.' "[63] Finally, the court determined that the trial court did not abuse its discretion by incorporating into its protection order a remedy provided by Congress.[64]

Additionally, in overruling the appellant's second assignment of error, the Preble County Court of Appeals noted that, because the original protection order granted custody of the minor children to appellee and visitation to the appellant and because the order was fashioned to effectuate appellant's visitation, the children were "implicitly included within the ambit of the original order."[65] It can be anticipated that the court would have reached the same conclusion even if custody and visitation provisions were not contained in the original order. Citing *Felton*, the court acknowledged the importance of considering not only the petitioner but the petitioner's family or household members when issuing civil protection orders.

Q & A: Is the standard different when the underlying act is a sexually oriented offense?

According to the trial court decision in *Lutson v. Anderkin*,[66] petitioner was granted a CPO in 2007 for herself and minor child for a five year duration based on acts of sexual abuse under RC 2950.01 towards the minor child by the paternal grandfather. Prior to its expiration, petitioner requested that the order be renewed for an additional five year period. Respondent filed objections to its issuance, arguing that the protection order was not necessary to protect

[60]See, e.g., Basden v. Basden, 154 N.C. App. 520, 572 S.E.2d 442 (2002).

[61]Woolum v. Woolum, 131 Ohio App. 3d 818, 723 N.E.2d 1135 (12th Dist. Preble County 1999).

[62]Felton v. Felton, 79 Ohio St. 3d 34, 1997-Ohio-302, 679 N.E.2d 672 (1997).

[63]Woolum v. Woolum, 131 Ohio App. 3d 818, 823-24, 723 N.E.2d 1135 (12th Dist. Preble County 1999).

[64]See Gun Control Act of 1968, 18 U.S.C.A. § 922(g)(8), which states that it is unlawful for a person to possess a weapon or firearm when that person is subject to a court order that restrains such person from harassing, stalking, or threatening an intimate partner.

[65]Woolum v. Woolum, 131 Ohio App. 3d 818, 824, 723 N.E.2d 1135 (12th Dist. Preble County 1999).

[66]Lutson v. Anderkin, 2013 WL 2150897 (Ohio C.P. 2013).

petitioner and her minor daughter and that testimony of his son (the child's father) and the paternal grandfather's wife indicated that the respondent did not pose a threat to the child's well being. Besides this fact, respondent argued that he has complied with the original protection order and would not repeat the offense if given an opportunity and that the child is eight years old (having been abused when the child was three).

While acknowledging the analysis of *Woolum*, the trial court stated that the renewal of a sexually oriented offense protection orders involves different considerations. "Specifically, to be entitled to a sexually oriented offense protection order, one must establish that they were or are in danger or being the victim of a sexually oriented offense committed by the respondent and that the orders are equitable, fair and necessary to protect them from sexually oriented offenses."[67]

"Additionally, a sexually oriented offense protection order is unique in that once an individual is the victim of a sexually oriented offense, that status does not change. Thus, a court must determine whether a protection order is still equitable, fair and necessary to protect the victim of the sexually oriented offense when determining whether to renew the order of protection."[68]

The trial court found that there was evidence to support that the minor child was a victim of a sexually oriented offense at age 3 by the paternal grandfather in the original CPO and that the protection order was still equitable, fair and necessary to protect the child and upheld the magistrate's renewal of the CPO. The court also pointed out that because the son (father of the child) did not believe the allegations against his father, it could be inferred that he would let his child be around the respondent if not for the protection order. "A sexually oriented offense by a relative against a child is an offense of opportunity and access. At eight years old, C.P. is still vulnerable to being the victim of another similar offense by the respondent."[69]

Of note, the trial court also determined that there was no evidence to support a finding that the renewal of the order should extend to the mother.

Q & A: Can a CPO be renewed where the only evidence presented is the adverse health effects on the petitioner by the continued presence of the respondent?

Not according to the Crawford County Court of Appeals. In *Studer v Studer*,[70] petitioner was granted an extension of the CPO for an additional term of years following respondent's filing of a motion to terminate the CPO. The basis for the extension was petitioner's fragile medical condition, the conflict-ridden nature of his relationship with respondent and the risk that his medical conditions could worsen

[67]Lutson v. Anderkin, 2013 WL 2150897 (Ohio C.P. 2013).

[68]Lutson v. Anderkin, 2013 WL 2150897 (Ohio C.P. 2013).

[69]Lutson v. Anderkin, 2013 WL 2150897 (Ohio C.P. 2013).

[70]Studer v. Studer, 2012-Ohio-2838, 2012 WL 2371452, *4 (Ohio Ct. App. 3d Dist. Crawford County 2012).

if triggered by stress with contact with respondent.[71] Respondent appealed, arguing that petitioner failed to meet his burden of proof by a preponderance of the evidence.

The appellate court first determined that the purpose of a CPO is to provide a petitioner with protection from domestic violence.[72] The court then pointed out that a court must find that a petitioner has shown by a preponderance of the evidence that petitioner is in danger of domestic violence.[73] Finally, the court considered the cases that have attempted to determine the standard for renewal of a CPO, relying on cases that held that past acts of domestic violence may serve as the basis for an extension of a CPO when coupled with new threats of domestic violence, that there must be evidence that petitioner had a reasonable fear of serious physical harm based on new threats of domestic violence and reasonable or those that have considered a change in circumstances and the severity of the physical injury or the nature of the domestic violence.

In the instant case, the appellate court noted that a past act of domestic violence had occurred, but that no evidence was presented as to respondent's current threats of domestic violence occurring since the initial CPO was granted. Additionally, there was no evidence of petitioner's current fear of serious physical harm. Although petitioner failed to appear at the hearing, his witnesses did not possess firsthand knowledge of his fear. Rather, they only testified as to their subjective fear that petitioner would be unable to defend himself against an attack or that the stress caused by such a confrontation with respondent would kill him.

In reversing the trial court and vacating the CPO, the appellate court found that the trial court failed to apply any of the relevant factors, instead, choosing to protect petitioner due to his medical condition. While the restrictions must bear a sufficient nexus to the conduct that the trial court is attempting to prevent, the trial court in this case is attempting to prevent conduct which may cause petitioner to experience adverse health consequences due to stress. "The purpose of a civil protection order, however, is not to protect people from adverse health effects; the purpose is to protect people from domestic violence."[74] Therefore, a petitioner's fragile medical condition cannot provide the basis for a CPO under RC 3113.31. "Without evidence of Petitioner's reasonable fear of and Respondent's ongoing threats of future violence, especially in light of the weak evidence regarding past domestic violence, the extension of the domestic violence civil

[71] Studer v. Studer, 2012-Ohio-2838, 2012 WL 2371452, *4 (Ohio Ct. App. 3d Dist. Crawford County 2012).

[72] Studer v. Studer, 2012-Ohio-2838, 2012 WL 2371452, *4 (Ohio Ct. App. 3d Dist. Crawford County 2012), citing Thomas v. Thomas, 44 Ohio App. 3d 6, 7, 540 N.E.2d 745 (10th Dist. Franklin County 1988).

[73] Studer v. Studer, 2012-Ohio-2838, 2012 WL 2371452, *4 (Ohio Ct. App. 3d Dist. Crawford County 2012), quoting Felton v. Felton, 79 Ohio St. 3d 34, 1997-Ohio-302, 679 N.E.2d 672 (1997).

[74] Studer v. Studer, 2012-Ohio-2838, 2012 WL 2371452, *6 (Ohio Ct. App. 3d Dist. Crawford County 2012), citing Thomas v. Thomas, 44 Ohio App. 3d 6, 7, 540 N.E.2d 745 (10th Dist. Franklin County 1988).

protection order, in this case, is not the proper means to protect Petitioner."[75]

Of interest is that the appellate court appeared to stress the narrowness of its holding and left open a different result had more testimony going to the relevant factors been presented.

Q & A: What is the standard on appeal for reviewing a renewal of a CPO?

According to Lundin v. Niepsuj,[76] the appellate court determined that the decision to renew a CPO is within the discretion of the trial court. When the trial court exercises its discretion it must find that a petitioner has shown, by a preponderance of the evidence, that petitioner or petitioner's family are victims of, or in danger of, domestic violence.[77] "Consequently, as in other civil cases, we review the evidence underlying protection orders to determine whether sufficient evidence was presented or whether the protection order is against the manifest weight of the evidence."[78] Noting a presumption in favor of the trier of fact, a renewal should only be reviewed to determine whether the trier court clearly lost its way and created such a manifest weight of the evidence that the decision must be reversed.[79]

§ 12:25 Modification and termination of civil protection orders[1]

Until January 2007, Ohio's domestic violence civil protection order statute[2] did not contemplate either the modification or termination of civil protection orders. Only two appellate districts had specifically addressed whether courts have continuing jurisdiction to either modify or dismiss civil protection orders without specific statutory authorization. Both appellate courts held that RC 3113.31 did not vest jurisdiction in the trial court to modify a civil protection order except as stated in RC 3113.31(E)(3)(b).[3]

On the other hand, some appellate courts have seemingly ignored

---

[75]Studer v. Studer, 2012-Ohio-2838, 2012 WL 2371452, *7 (Ohio Ct. App. 3d Dist. Crawford County 2012).

[76]Lundin v. Niepsuj, 2017-Ohio-7153, 2017 WL 3426957 (Ohio Ct. App. 9th Dist. Summit County 2017)

[77]Lundin v. Niepsuj, 2017-Ohio-7153, ¶ 19, 2017 WL 3426957 (Ohio Ct. App. 9th Dist. Summit County 2017), Felton v. Felton at 42, citing RC 3113.31(D).

[78]Lundin v. Niepsuj, 2017-Ohio-7153, ¶ 19, 2017 WL 3426957 (Ohio Ct. App. 9th Dist. Summit County 2017); citing Charles v. Peters, 2016-Ohio-1259, ¶ 10, 2016 WL 1178776 (Ohio Ct. App. 2d Dist. Greene County 2016) ("a protection order, or an order extending a protection order, requires sufficient evidence.").

[79]Lundin v. Niepsuj, 2017-Ohio-7153, ¶ 20, 2017 WL 3426957 (Ohio Ct. App. 9th Dist. Summit County 2017).

[Section 12:25]

[1]See also Tamara L. Kuennen, "No-Drop" Civil Protection Orders: Exploring the Bounds of Judicial Intervention in the Lives of Domestic Violence Victims, 16 UCLA Women's L.J. 39 (2007); see also Text § 12:8, Service of the protection order issued after the full hearing.

[2]RC 3113.31.

[3]Signer v. Signer, 2006-Ohio-3580, 2006 WL 1918115 (Ohio Ct. App. 8th Dist. Cuyahoga County 2006); see also Yazdani-Isfehani v. Yazdani-Isfehani, 170 Ohio App. 3d 1, 2006-Ohio-7105, 865 N.E.2d 924 (4th Dist. Athens County 2006); Prostejovsky v.

the issue, suggesting that a modification or dismissal of a civil protection order is permitted.[4] For example, in *State v. McLean*,[5] appellee filed a motion to modify or suspend a civil protection order requesting that the order be modified to include a 1999 Plymouth Neon. Service on the motion was perfected by certified mail. The case was subsequently dismissed for lack of prosecution. However, neither the appellant in his objections nor the appellate court in its opinion raised the issue of whether the courts are statutorily authorized to modify or dismiss civil protection orders.

Q & A: Can a party vacate or modify a civil protection order under Civ. R. 60(B)?[6]

As a general rule, courts have inherent power to correct, modify or vacate their own judgments.[7] The procedure to do so is contained in Civ. R. 60 of the Rules of Civil Procedure.[8] For example, Civ. R. 60(A) provides for corrections of clerical mistakes.[9] An order may be partially vacated if certain parts of the order are found to be no longer equitable for the order to continue and the movant shows that the original circumstances have changed.[10] Civ. R. 60(B)(4) allows relief from a final order "if it is no longer equitable that it should have prospective

---

Prostejovsky, 2007-Ohio-5743, 2007 WL 3119724 (Ohio Ct. App. 5th Dist. Ashland County 2007).

[4]See Eble v. Emery, 2007-Ohio-4857, 2007 WL 2729462 (Ohio Ct. App. 10th Dist. Franklin County 2007) (affirming trial court dismissal of a CPO because petitioner placed over 100 calls to respondent over a 2 day period).

[5]State v. McLean, 2005-Ohio-1562, 2005 WL 737412 (Ohio Ct. App. 11th Dist. Trumbull County 2005).

[6]See generally, Patty Hopper, Memorandum on Modifications of CPOs (2003). See also Nkurunziza v. Nyamusevya, 2011-Ohio-6133, 2011 WL 5924448 (Ohio Ct. App. 10th Dist. Franklin County 2011) (discussing the requirements for a Civ. R. 60(B) motion and implying that it may be used in a civil protection order proceeding); but see Jackson v. Jackson, 2011-Ohio-5529, 2011 WL 5135251 (Ohio Ct. App. 6th Dist. Lucas County 2011) (noting that a Motion to Vacate was construed by the trial court as a Motion for Relief from Judgment under Civ. R. 60(B) and by the appellate court as objections to the magistrate's decision under Civ. R. 53).

[7]See, e.g., Yun v. Yun, 2003-Ohio-2644, 2003 WL 21185852 (Ohio Ct. App. 5th Dist. Stark County 2003); Chapman v. Chapman, 2006-Ohio-2328, 2006 WL 1284592 (Ohio Ct. App. 2d Dist. Montgomery County 2006); Bowman v. Leisz, 2014-Ohio-4763, 2014 WL 5422556 (Ohio Ct. App. 12th Dist. Warren County 2014) (applicable to civil stalking protection orders under RC 2903.214).

[8]See Lundin v. Niepsuj, 2014-Ohio-1212, 2014 WL 1478284 (Ohio Ct. App. 9th Dist. Summit County 2014) (noting that filing objections by way of a Civ. R. 60(B) motion for relief of an ex parte CPO is untimely and said motion was overruled); Moore v. Higgins, 2015-Ohio-1751, 2015 WL 2169232 (Ohio Ct. App. 2d Dist. Montgomery County 2015) (appellant failed to satisfy the three prong test necessary to support grounds for her motion for relief); J.P. v. T.H, 2016-Ohio-243, 2016 WL 363247 (Ohio Ct. App. 9th Dist. Lorain County 2016) (discussing the test set forth in GTE Automatic Elec., Inc. v. ARC Industries, Inc., 47 Ohio St. 2d 146, 1 Ohio Op. 3d 86, 351 N.E.2d 113 (1976) to prevail on a 60(B) motion and focusing on Civ. R. 60(B)(2)-"newly discovered evidence" and holding that the incidents noted by appellant occurred after the full hearing and were not facts in existence at the time of trial).

[9]Harlett v. Harlett, 1996 WL 629510 (Ohio Ct. App. 2d Dist. Montgomery County 1996); Londrico v. Delores C. Knowlton, Inc., 88 Ohio App. 3d 282, 623 N.E.2d 723 (9th Dist. Summit County 1993); see also Ashburn v. Roth, 2007-Ohio-2995, 2007 WL 1731426 (Ohio Ct. App. 12th Dist. Butler County 2007); Text § 12:16.

[10]See Prostejovsky v. Prostejovsky, 2007-Ohio-5743, 2007 WL 3119724 (Ohio Ct. App. 5th Dist. Ashland County 2007). See also Oddo v. Spencer, 2011-Ohio-4073, 2011

application."[11] The staff commentary to this provision advises that Civ. R. 60(B)(4) may be used to afford relief from the prospective operation of an injunction. Some have likened civil protection orders as being analogous to injunctions.[12]

On the one hand, RC 3113.31 is a special statutory proceeding.[13] A civil protection order is a final appealable order,[14] which expires on a date certain[15] unless it is renewed.[16] Because a CPO is not a judgment in the true sense of the word, but rather a temporary order, it can be argued that dismissals are not contemplated or authorized by statute.

On the other hand, any proceeding under RC 3113.31 is to be conducted in accordance with the Rules of Civil Procedure.[17] Therefore, it is also arguable that the Civil Rules may permit the vacation or dismissal of a CPO under Civ. R. 60.[18]

In any case, it is clear that the Civil Rules do not contemplate nor authorize modifications.[19] The term "modification" is used in RC 3113.

WL 3587436, *3 (Ohio Ct. App. 5th Dist. Stark County 2011) (utilizing the test set forth in *Prostejovsky* to uphold trial court decision and also finding that compliance with the order, in the context of this case, is insufficient to demonstrate that there has been a material change in circumstances such that the order be terminated and noting that while petitioner does not oppose termination, it is clear from her testimony that she still desires that appellant not have any contact with her family. "Further, the protection order in this case was issued primarily for the safety of Ms. Oddo's son Justin, and while he is now two years older than her was when the CPO was initially issued, he is still a minor. Further, due to the fact that his parents have since divorced, he is now arguably in a more vulnerable position than he was when the CPO was granted in 2008." It is notable that R.C. 3113.31(E)(8) does not apply to civil protection orders issued pursuant to R.C. 2903.214).

[11]See also Risner v. Cline, 2004-Ohio-3786, 2004 WL 1588086 (Ohio Ct. App. 2d Dist. Champaign County 2004) (appellant requested relief from the stalking civil protection order issued against him by way of a Civ.R. 60(B) relief from judgment); Chapman v. Chapman, 2006-Ohio-2328, 2006 WL 1284592 (Ohio Ct. App. 2d Dist. Montgomery County 2006) (appellant sought a dismissal of a CPO on Civ.R. 60(B)(4) grounds).

[12]Felton v. Felton, 79 Ohio St. 3d 34, 41, 1997-Ohio-302, 679 N.E.2d 672 (1997); see also Mitchell v. Mitchell, 62 Mass. App. Ct. 769, 821 N.E.2d 79 (2005) (appellate court analyzed Civ.R. 60(B) in relation to modifications of civil protection orders and the standard for determining whether and when prospective relief from a protection order is warranted); see also Prostejovsky v. Prostejovsky, 2007-Ohio-5743, 2007 WL 3119724 (Ohio Ct. App. 5th Dist. Ashland County 2007).

[13]See Civ. R. 65.1(A). See Oliver v. Johnson, 2007-Ohio-5880, 2007 WL 3227668 (Ohio Ct. App. 4th Dist. Jackson County 2007); Skiles v. Dearth, 2000 WL 1838747 (Ohio Ct. App. 2d Dist. Clark County 2000).

[14]RC 3113.31(G).

[15]RC 3113.31(E)(3)(a) and (b).

[16]RC 3113.31(E)(3)(c).

[17]RC 3113.31(G).

[18]See also Glenn v. Glenn, 2009-Ohio-1345, 2009 WL 765480 (Ohio Ct. App. 5th Dist. Stark County 2009); Dickson v. Ball, 2006-Ohio-3436, 2006 WL 1817265 (Ohio Ct. App. 10th Dist. Franklin County 2006); Studebaker v. Studebaker, 2008-Ohio-5356, 2008 WL 4598745 (Ohio Ct. App. 2d Dist. Miami County 2008). But see Staats v. Finkel, 2011-Ohio-4063, 2011 WL 3611464 (Ohio Ct. App. 9th Dist. Summit County 2011) (holding that girlfriend was not entitled to vacate her consent protection order under Civ. R. 60(B) based on her hearing difficulties and assertion that she was unable to fully understand substance of the CPO proceedings).

[19]See Signer v. Signer, 2006-Ohio-3580, 2006 WL 1918115 (Ohio Ct. App. 8th

31(K), citing Chapters 3119, 3121, 3123, and 3125 of the Revised Code regarding a modification of child support.

Q & A: What if a respondent fails to identify the motion under which he/she seeks relief?

In *Saqr v. Naji*,[20] appellant argued that the trial court erred by not granting him relief from judgment. "At the outset, we note that Naji never explicitly identified his motion to terminate the CPO as a motion for relief from judgment under Civ. R. 60(B), yet he claims that the trial court erred by failing to grant him relief from judgment under that rule."[21]

The appellate court pointed out that to allow Naji's motion for relief from judgment would have meant that the magistrate erred by failing to construe his motion to terminate as a motion for relief from judgment.

The court then determined that a failure to identify a motion is not fatal. "When a motion is ambiguous or unclear, the name given to the motion is not controlling, but instead the substance, not the caption, determines the operative effect of the motion."[22]

In reviewing the actual motion, the appellate court reasoned that it was not unreasonable for the magistrate to construe the motion as a motion to terminate in that his motion stated, "the civil protection order should be terminated." However, even if the motion should have been brought as a Civ. R. 60(B), Naji would not be entitled to relief from judgment as he was not in compliance with the civil rule.

Because of the ambiguity, attorneys and litigants who want to terminate a CPO must caption and identity their motions as such. If one does intend to file a Motion for Relief from Judgment under Civ. R. 60(B), they must follow the mandates of that rule as well as relevant case law interpreting the rule and indicating what one has to prove to succeed on a 60(B) motion.

Q & A: Why was special legislation needed?

A Motion for Relief from Judgment is complex and may be difficult for pro se litigants. Because petitioners have often requested that courts dismiss or modify their orders, a process permitting this option was needed. Absent specific statutory procedure, courts have been inconsistent in their process. Some have granted dismissals of CPOs based on letters requesting the same. Others have required the filing of Motions for Relief from Judgment under Civ. R. 60 and held

Dist. Cuyahoga County 2006); but see Parker v. Jamison, 2003-Ohio-7295, 2003 WL 24135688 (Ohio Ct. App. 4th Dist. Scioto County 2003) (construing father's motion to set aside or modify the judgment to be a motion to vacate for lack of jurisdiction and/or a Motion for Relief from Judgment pursuant to Civ. R. 60(B)).

[20]Saqr v. Naji, 2017-Ohio-8142, 2017 WL 4538886 (Ohio Ct. App. 1st Dist. Hamilton County 2017).

[21]Saqr v. Naji, 2017-Ohio-8142, ¶ 25, 2017 WL 4538886 (Ohio Ct. App. 1st Dist. Hamilton County 2017).

[22]Saqr v. Naji, 2017-Ohio-8142, ¶ 26, 2017 WL 4538886 (Ohio Ct. App. 1st Dist. Hamilton County 2017), quoting Jackson v. Jackson, 188 Ohio App. 3d 493, 2010-Ohio-3531, ¶ 17, 935 N.E.2d 937 (6th Dist. Lucas County 2010). See State v. Smith, 2016-Ohio-3521, ¶ 16, 68 N.E.3d 114 (Ohio Ct. App. 1st Dist. Hamilton County 2016) quoting State v. Schlee, 117 Ohio St. 3d 153, 2008-Ohio-545, ¶ 12, 882 N.E.2d 431 (2008).

hearings. Still others have denied parties the right to either dismiss or modify stating that the statute does not provide for such a remedy. All the while, petitioners have repeatedly requested that their orders be dismissed or modified.

A logical resolution to this dilemma was to amend RC 3113.31[23] to specifically provide for the dismissal and modification of civil protection orders, a procedure to follow and a consistent standard to be applied by all courts in deciding whether to grant the dismissal or modification of a CPO.

Q & A: Are Ohio's courts now authorized to either modify or terminate civil protection orders?

Effective January 2007, RC 3113.31 was amended to authorize Ohio courts to both modify and terminate civil protection orders.[24] Pursuant to statute, courts may modify or terminate civil protection orders issued after a full hearing. The court that issued the original order has jurisdiction to hear a modification or termination of a protection order or consent agreement.[25]

Q & A: Who can terminate or modify a civil protection order under RC 3113.31?

According to RC 3113.31(E)(8)(b), a petitioner or a respondent may seek a modification or termination of a civil protection order.[26]

Q & A: What is the procedure for modifying or terminating a civil protection order?

Either party may file a motion with the court requesting a modification or termination of a civil protection order or a consent agreement issued or approved after a full hearing. The court shall require notice of the motion to be made as provided by the Ohio Rules of Civil Procedure.[27]

If the petitioner for the original civil protection order had requested that the petitioner's address be kept confidential, the court shall not disclose the address to the respondent or any other person, except as otherwise required by law.

Q & A: Who has the burden of proof and what is the standard?

The moving party has the burden of proof to show, by a preponderance of the evidence, that modification or termination of the protection order or consent agreement is appropriate because either the protection order or consent agreement is no longer needed or because

[23]RC 3113.31(E)(8).

[24]Sub. S.B. 260, eff. January 2, 2007; RC 3113.31(E)(8).

[25]RC 3113.31(E)(1)(a).

[26]See In re K.C., 2014-Ohio-372, 2014 WL 467476 (Ohio Ct. App. 9th Dist. Summit County 2014) (affirming decision of trial court and finding that it was not unreasonable for the trial court to require father to modify the CPO before his parenting time with the children would be expanded); Dowhan v. Dowhan, 2013-Ohio-4097, 2013 WL 5346465, ¶ 24 (Ohio Ct. App. 11th Dist. Lake County 2013).

[27]Delaine v. Smith, 2016-Ohio-5250, 2016 WL 4141753 (Ohio Ct. App. 8th Dist. Cuyahoga County 2016) (appellate court determined that RC 2903.214 does not mandate that a trial court must hold a hearing on a respondent's motion to terminate a civil protection order).

the terms of the original protection order or consent agreement are no longer appropriate.[28]

Q & A: Does RC 3113.31(E)(8) require a court to modify or terminate the civil protection order upon a motion filed by either party?

No. The statute authorizes a court to modify or terminate a CPO if certain factors are met. However, RC 3113.31(E)(8)(a) provides in part: "A court may modify or terminate as provided in division (E)(8) of this section a protection order or consent agreement that was issued after a full hearing under this section." The operative word is "may." The issue was addressed by the Franklin County Court of Appeals in *Twitty v. Bowe*.[29] In that case, appellant argued that the trial court erred when it denied his motion to terminate the CPO under RC 3113.31(E)(8).

The appellate court reasoned that "[t]he word "may" in a statute usually connotes an intent on the part of the Ohio General Assembly to vest the court with discretion in those matters."[30] For purposes of RC 3113.31(E)(8), it is within the court's discretion whether or not to modify or terminate the CPO. Because of the discretion permitted a trial court in such a matter, the Court determined that a ruling on a motion to modify or terminate would not be disturbed absent an abuse of discretion.[31]

After reviewing the evidence and applying the doctrine of res judicata, the court overruled appellant's assignment of error. The court found that appellant's second motion to terminate was dismissed based on res judicata grounds, finding that the matter had been successfully litigated in a hearing on his first motion; doctrine of res judicata prevents endless litigation of an issue on which appellant already received a full and fair opportunity to be heard.[32]

Q & A: What specific criteria must a court consider in deciding whether to grant or deny a request to modify or terminate a civil protection order?

In considering whether to modify or terminate a protection order or consent agreement issued or approved, the court shall consider all relevant factors, including, but not limited to the following:

(1) whether the petitioner consent to the modification or termination of the protection order or consent agreement;

[28]See also Snell v. Snell, 2012-Ohio-2159, 2012 WL 1685850 (Ohio Ct. App. 5th Dist. Richland County 2012); Jones v. Rose, 2009-Ohio-4347, 2009 WL 2607944 (Ohio Ct. App. 4th Dist. Hocking County 2009); Dowhan v. Dowhan, 2012-Ohio-5830, 2012 WL 6114935 (Ohio Ct. App. 11th Dist. Lake County 2012).

[29]Twitty v. Bowe, 2010-Ohio-1391, 2010 WL 1254601 (Ohio Ct. App. 10th Dist. Franklin County 2010)

[30]At *1; citing Kuptz v. Youngstown City School Dist. Bd. of Edn., 175 Ohio App. 3d 738, 2008-Ohio-1676, 889 N.E.2d 166, 233 Ed. Law Rep. 895 (7th Dist. Mahoning County 2008); Dowhan v. Dowhan, 2012-Ohio-5830, 2012 WL 6114935, ¶ 39 (Ohio Ct. App. 11th Dist. Lake County 2012) (noting that the term "may" connotes an intent on the part of the General Assembly to vest the court with discretion in those matters).

[31]At *1; citing Jones v. Rose, 2009-Ohio-4347, 2009 WL 2607944 (Ohio Ct. App. 4th Dist. Hocking County 2009); Dowhan v. Dowhan, 2012-Ohio-5830, 2012 WL 6114935 (Ohio Ct. App. 11th Dist. Lake County 2012).

[32]At *3.

(2) whether the petitioner fears the respondent;[33]
(3) the current nature of the parties' relationship;
(4) the circumstances of the petitioner and the respondent, including the relative proximity of their workplaces and residences and whether they have minor children together;
(5) whether the respondent has complied with the terms and conditions of the original protection order or consent agreement;[34]
(6) whether the respondent has a continuing involvement with illegal drugs or alcohol;
(7) whether the respondent has been convicted of or pleaded guilty to an offense of violence since the issuance of the protection order or approval of the consent agreement;
(8) whether any other protection orders, consent agreements, restraining orders or no-contact orders have been issued against the respondent pursuant to this section, RC 2919.26, any other provision of state law or the law of any other state;
(9) whether the respondent has participated in any domestic violence treatment, intervention program, or other counseling addressing domestic violence and whether the respondent has completed the treatment, program or counseling;
(10) the time that has elapsed since the protection order was issue or since the consent agreement was approved;
(11) the age and health of the respondent; and
(12) when the last incident of abuse, threat of harm or commission of a sexually oriented offense occurred or other relevant information concerning the safety and protection of the petitioner or other protected parties.[35]

Q & A: How should courts make such a determination?[36]

Since courts now have the discretion to modify or terminate civil protection orders, it is important that a court evaluate any request to do so in light of the aforementioned criteria. A court must explore the circumstances giving rise to the request including which party is requesting the modification or termination.[37] A failure to explore the relationship in light of these factors may subject the victim/petitioner

[33]See Brown v. Naff, 2012-Ohio-1770, 2012 WL 1383262 (Ohio Ct. App. 2d Dist. Miami County 2012) (noting that trial court has the discretion to disbelieve the testimony given at hearing about petitioner not needing or wanting the CPO and about not fearing respondent).

[34]Speakman v. Crabtree, 2014-Ohio-2152, 2014 WL 2155355 (Ohio Ct. App. 10th Dist. Franklin County 2014) (appellant's argument that he has complied with the order so far, he is unlikely to violate the order given his current imprisonment and the order's existence negatively impacts his prison life and rehabilitation were not persuasive reasons for appellate court to terminate the CPO).

[35]RC 3113.31(E)(8)(c).

[36]See Barton v. Barton, 2017-Ohio-980, 86 N.E.3d 937 (Ohio Ct. App. 2d Dist. Greene County 2017), appeal not allowed, 150 Ohio St. 3d 1410, 2017-Ohio-6964, 78 N.E.3d 910 (2017) (stating that, on a motion to modify or terminate a CPO under RC 3113.31(E)(8), findings based on the enumerated factors are required).

[37]See also Powell v. Becher, 2011-Ohio-267, 2011 WL 303209 (Ohio Ct. App. 5th Dist. Stark County 2011) (upholding denial of mother's motion to terminate CPO based on wanting father to be a part of the child's life where trial denied CPO and

to future violence or even death. Whenever a termination or modification is requested, it is important for the court to inquire about the terms of any modification, the safeguards that are in place if the order is modified or terminated, and whether there have been any violations of the original order since the date of issuance. Without exploring the totality of the circumstances, victims may lose the legal protections that are designed to keep them safe.

It is crucial that a court inquire about the factors during a hearing and specifically consider whether the petitioner consents to the termination of the order and whether she/he still *fears* the respondent.[38] At the hearing, it important for a trial court to independently review each factor and determine the credibility of the parties, especially when considering consent and fear.[39]

Attorneys should always request that a court not summarily terminate a civil protection order, particularly if the moving party is the respondent. Even requiring a client to sign a form that he/she no longer fears the respondent or no longer needs or wants the order does little to preserve the legislative intent of the statute relative to safety.

If the respondent requests the termination or modification, it is essential that a full hearing be held in order to determine the reasons for the termination or modification,[40] whether the respondent has complied with the terms and conditions associated with the civil protection order, the petitioner's response, and whether the potential for future violence exists.[41] Particular consideration should be given to the last incident of abuse or threat of harm and when it occurred, whether the respondent has been convicted of or pleaded guilty to a crime of violence since the issuance of the protection order and whether any other restraining orders, no contact orders or protection orders have been subsequently issued against the respondent. Such a thorough examination is likely to elicit whether the petitioner still fears the respondent, the reasonableness of that fear and the need to maintain the civil protection order.

If requested by a petitioner, a history of the violence in the parties' relationship should also be assessed, even prior acts of domestic violence, stalking or sexual violence that may not have been testified to at the full hearing should now be considered.

---

noting that father was undergoing counseling and stating that parties are advised to seek counsel if desired in future).

[38]See Highfield v. Highfield, 2013-Ohio-3466, 2013 WL 4041568 (Ohio Ct. App. 6th Dist. Ottawa County 2013) (in denying respondent's motion to modify CPO, appellate court focused on petitioner's consent and continued fear; of interest is that the appellate court also commented on the Ohio Legal Service CPO brochure which formed basis of appellant's arguments about termination of CPO).

[39]Brown v. Naff, 2012-Ohio-1770, 2012 WL 1383262 (Ohio Ct. App. 2d Dist. Miami County 2012) (noting that trial court has the discretion to disbelieve the testimony given at hearing about petitioner not needing or wanting the CPO and about not fearing respondent).

[40]But see Delaine v. Smith, 2016-Ohio-5250, 2016 WL 4141753 (Ohio Ct. App. 8th Dist. Cuyahoga County 2016) (appellate court determined that RC 2903.214 does not mandate that a trial court must hold a hearing on a respondent's motion to terminate a civil protection order).

[41]See also Pickering v. Pickering, 253 Mich. App. 694, 659 N.W.2d 649 (2002) (discussing who has the burden of proof in a hearing to rescind the order).

If the victim/petitioner is requesting that the protection order be terminated, any termination should depend on a showing of "good cause" and be based on the facts of the particular case. In *Stevenson v. Stevenson*,[42] the victim requested that the final protection order be dismissed (terminated). The court decided that dissolving a protection order is not mandatory but is at the judge's discretion, with an independent finding in each case based on the facts presented. After considering the husband's prior history of wife-beating and alcohol abuse, the court found that good cause was not established and denied the victim's application to dissolve the order.[43]

The court then pointed out that good cause must be shown before a protection order can be dissolved. In deciding whether good cause exists, the court must determine whether objective fear can be said to continue to exist and whether there is real danger of future domestic violence if the order is dismissed. Even where the parties reconcile, the court must still make an independent finding that continued protection is unnecessary.

Finally, the *Stevenson* court stated that, where a judge fails to make such a finding based on objective evidence, a judge does not meet the state statute's public policy dictates. These policy considerations include:

(1) that victims of domestic violence must be assured the maximum protection from abuse the law can provide;
(2) that the official response to domestic violence, including that of the courts, shall communicate the attitude that domestic violent behavior will not be excused or tolerated; and
(3) that it is the responsibility of the courts to protect victims of domestic violence by ordering those remedies and sanctions that are available to assure the safety of the victims and the public.[44]

Q & A: What are the other procedures?

If a protection order is modified or terminated, the court shall issue copies of the modified or terminated order to the parties and to the law enforcement agencies that have jurisdiction to enforce the order or agreement.[45] The court shall direct that a copy of the order be delivered to the respondent (or non-moving party) on the same day that the order is entered, thus suggesting personal service of the modified or terminated order.[46]

A modified order may be registered in the same manner as provided in RC 311.31(N).

---

[42]Stevenson v. Stevenson, 314 N.J. Super. 350, 714 A.2d 986 (Ch. Div. 1998) (petitioner requested reinstatement of a dismissed protection order in which the dismissal was predicated on defendant's participation in counseling and court held that the abuser's breach of promise to obtain counseling justified reinstatement of the order).

[43]See also Brown v. Naff, 2012-Ohio-1770, 2012 WL 1383262 (Ohio Ct. App. 2d Dist. Miami County 2012).

[44]Stevenson v. Stevenson, 314 N.J. Super. 350, 361, 714 A.2d 986 (Ch. Div. 1998).

[45]RC 3113.31(E)(8)(d); RC 3113.31(F).

[46]RC 3113.31(F)(1); but see State v. McLean, 2005-Ohio-1562, 2005 WL 737412 (Ohio Ct. App. 11th Dist. Trumbull County 2005) (affirming trial court decision convicting respondent of violating a CPO where motion to modify CPO filed by petitioner was dismissed for failure to prosecute and that respondent-appellant was served the magistrate's decision regarding the dismissal of the motion to modify the

If the respondent moves for the modification or termination of a protection order or consent agreement, the court may assess costs against the respondent for the filing of the motion.[47]

Q & A: Must notice be given to the non-moving party of the impending dismissal (termination) of a civil protection order?

According to Fairfield County Court of Appeals, the petitioner should have been provided notice of the impending dismissal of her civil protection order where the court dismissed the protection order on its own motion or at the request of the other party. In *Sterling v. Sterling*,[48] the ex-wife filed a petition for a civil protection order in Fairfield County on January 19, 2001. The order was dismissed on March 5, 2001, for "good cause shown" and reinstated on March 8, 2001. In a footnote, the appellate court noted that the matter was probably dismissed because of the ongoing proceedings in Muskingum County. (Appellant had filed for a civil protection order against his ex-wife in Muskingum County on February 6, 2001.) The Fairfield County order had been reinstated on the motion of the ex-wife, claiming that she did not approve of the dismissal and was not afforded notice.

In his appeal, appellant challenged the reinstatement of the civil protection order. The Fifth District Court of Appeals held that, pursuant to Civil Rule 41(B)(1), appellee should have been given notice of the dismissal.[49]

Q & A: Can a civil protection order be modified on the court's own motion and without notice to one or both of the parties?

It depends on the nature of the modification. In *Wardeh v. Altabchi*,[50] the trial court granted the wife a civil protection order and then amended the civil protection order sua sponte and pursuant to Civ.R. 60(A). The original order had stated in paragraph 13, that "as a limited exception to paragraph 6 [which prohibits defendant from being present within 500 yards of petitioner or the child] temporary visitation rights are established as follows: any visitation of the child by defendant will be supervised at all times. Paragraph 18 stated that "[t]he child shall not be removed from the United States by his

---

CPO by regular mail. The trial court's judgment entry adopting the Magistrate's decision was also sent to respondent by regular mail. Respondent had argued that he did not receive the judgment entry and/or decisions that would have put him on notice that the CPO was still in effect).

[47]RC 3113.31(E)(8)(e).

[48]Sterling v. Sterling, 2002-Ohio-4997, 2002 WL 31111778 (Ohio Ct. App. 5th Dist. Fairfield County 2002).

[49]Sterling v. Sterling, 2002-Ohio-4997, 2002 WL 31111778, *3 (Ohio Ct. App. 5th Dist. Fairfield County 2002); see also Text § 12:18, Remedies—Counseling; Text § 12:7, Full hearing—Other procedural concerns; see also Howard v. Howard, 2009-Ohio-155, 2009 WL 105684, *1 (Ohio Ct. App. 2d Dist. Greene County 2009) (reversing the trial court's issuance of the civil protection order on the ground that the trial court should not have reset full hearing without providing respondent with an opportunity to respond to petitioner's motion to reset the hearing; the trial court previously dismissed the action pursuant to Civ. R. 41(B) because Petitioner failed to appear at the full hearing; she filed a motion to reset the hearing arguing that she had not been noticed for the full hearing; the court reset the full hearing and granted the CPO).

[50]Wardeh v. Altabchi, 158 Ohio App. 3d 325, 2004-Ohio-4423, 815 N.E.2d 712 (10th Dist. Franklin County 2004).

father."[51] The amended civil protection order deleted paragraph 13 and amended paragraph 18 to state that "[t]he child shall not be removed from the United States by his father and that his father have only supervised visitation/parenting time with the child."[52]

On appeal, the defendant asserted that the trial court did not have the authority to modify the terms of the civil protection order because the changes made were substantive rather than clerical in nature. Thus, the court exceeded the scope of authority pursuant to Civ.R. 60(A).[53] Because the modified civil protection order deleted the phrase "[a]s a limited exception to paragraph six's prohibition against defendant being within 500 yards," substantive changes to the original civil protection order were made, which were not within the purview of Civ.R. 60(A).[54]

The appellate court found that "[t]he basic distinction between clerical mistakes that can be corrected under Civ.R. 60(A) and substantive mistakes that cannot be corrected is that the former consists of 'blunders in execution' whereas the latter consists of instances where the court changes its mind, either because it made a legal or factual mistake in making its original determination, or because, on second thought, it has decided to exercise its discretion in a different manner."[55] Therefore, the deletion of paragraph 13 in the civil protection order was a substantive change and thus, not a permissible modification under Civ.R. 60(A).

Q & A: If certified or ordinary mail service is utilized, how can it be shown that a respondent has actually received the papers?

In *State v. McLean*,[56] a motion to modify the civil protection order was served on respondent by certified mail. When the petitioner failed to appear at the hearing, the magistrate dismissed the motion for lack of prosecution. Service of the magistrate's decision and the dismissal entry were made by regular mail to respondent.

Subsequently, respondent was charged with violating the civil protection order. He argued that, because he had not received the relevant documents, he could not be charged with violating the civil protection order.

---

[51] Wardeh v. Altabchi, 158 Ohio App. 3d 325, 332, 2004-Ohio-4423, 815 N.E.2d 712 (10th Dist. Franklin County 2004).

[52] Wardeh v. Altabchi, 158 Ohio App. 3d 325, 332, 2004-Ohio-4423, 815 N.E.2d 712 (10th Dist. Franklin County 2004).

[53] See Harlett v. Harlett, 1996 WL 629510 (Ohio Ct. App. 2d Dist. Montgomery County 1996); see also Text § 12:23, Duration of a civil protection order.

[54] Wardeh v. Altabchi, 158 Ohio App. 3d 325, 332, 2004-Ohio-4423, 815 N.E.2d 712 (10th Dist. Franklin County 2004); but see Ashburn v. Roth, 2007-Ohio-2995, 2007 WL 1731426 (Ohio Ct. App. 12th Dist. Butler County 2007) (adding a child to a CPO as a protected party may be made sua sponte to correct a clerical mistake under Civ.R. 60(A)). See also Text § 12:23, Duration of a civil protection order.

[55] Wardeh v. Altabchi, 158 Ohio App. 3d 325, 332, 2004-Ohio-4423, 815 N.E.2d 712 (10th Dist. Franklin County 2004), quoting Kuehn v. Kuehn, 55 Ohio App. 3d 245, 247, 564 N.E.2d 97 (12th Dist. Clinton County 1988).

[56] State v. McLean, 2005-Ohio-1562, 2005 WL 737412 (Ohio Ct. App. 11th Dist. Trumbull County 2005). But see State v. Bunch, 2001 WL 39599 (Ohio Ct. App. 9th Dist. Summit County 2001) (where certified mail was attempted but not perfected, the violation was based on actual notice, not service).

In affirming McLean's conviction for violating the civil protection order, the appellate court noted that ample circumstantial evidence was presented demonstrating that he was aware of the amended magistrate's decision and that the protection order was still in effect. Despite the lack of direct evidence showing that the documents had been mailed to respondent or that he actually received the documents, the prosecution had established that the trial court had instructed the clerk of courts to mail copies of the documents to respondent at his address. Other circumstantial evidence indicated that McLean received notice that the order was still in effect, that he acted as if the protection order was still in effect and that he knew that his former wife had filed a motion to modify not a motion to dismiss the original order.

It is important to note that the *McLean* appellate court discussed the violation in terms of notice of the existence of the civil protection order, rather than service of relevant documents. So long as evidence existed to demonstrate that respondent was aware of the civil protection order, the conviction against him for its violation was upheld.

Q & A: By what method of service should a motion to modify or terminate a civil protection order be served on the opposing party?

Nothing in the domestic violence statute specifically addresses the appropriate method of service of motions to modify or terminate civil protection orders. RC 3113.31(E)(8) provides that "[t]he court shall require notice of the motion to be made as provided by the Rules of Procedure." The civil rules were recently amended to provide that "[s]ervice of a motion for modification, contempt, renewal or termination of a civil protection order issued after a full hearing or an approved consent agreement shall be made in the manner provided for service of process under Civ. R. 4 through 4.6."[57]

While that could mean personal service, residence service, certified or express mail, ordinary mail or publication when the residence of the party is unknown, best practice dictates that motions to modify or terminate civil protection orders should be served on the non-moving party by either personal service or certified mail service in accordance with Civ. R. 4.

Because of the possibility that a civil protection order may terminated, it is important that both parties are provided the right to notice and an opportunity to participate in a hearing.[58] This is especially true when the respondent seeks to modify or terminate a civil protection order.

Clearly then, the most responsible method of service of a modification or termination motion should be attempted first by personal service and, if that fails, alternate methods of service should be considered. Besides personal service, certified mail is the most effec-

---

[57]Civ. R. 65.1(C)(4)(a).

[58]See also State v. McLean, 2005-Ohio-1562, 2005 WL 737412 (Ohio Ct. App. 11th Dist. Trumbull County 2005) (where the motion to modify a CPO was served by certified mail); Leflore v. Leflore, 2014-Ohio-5327, 2014 WL 6758522 (Ohio Ct. App. 5th Dist. Richland County 2014) (noting that notice of the hearing on the motion to Modify CPO may be mailed by ordinary mail).

tive way to achieve this. Ordinary mail to the non moving party does nothing to guarantee service. Service on that party's previous attorney is not proper under Civ. R. 4. In fact, attorneys should communicate to the court, after a protection order is issued, that they are not to be served with subsequent motions to terminate or modify civil protection orders.[59]

Of course, the court should have discretion to permit alternate methods of service under Civ. R. 4 so long as the victim safety is contemplated.

Q & A: What method of service is appropriate for decisions issued on motions to modify or terminate protection orders?

While the domestic violence statute does not address the appropriate method of service of a court entry/decision on a motion to modify or terminate a civil protection order, the civil rules were recently amended to address this. Pursuant to Civ. R. 65.1(C)(4)(b), "[a]fter service has been made in accordance with division (C)(4)(a) of this rule, any additional service required to be made on the Respondent, and, if applicable, on the parent, guardian, or legal custodian, shall be made in accordance with provisions of Civ. R. 5(B)."

The only statutory provision that speaks to service of an actual decision of a court is contained in RC 31331.31(E)(8) which provides that "[i]f a protection order or consent agreement is modified or terminated . . . the court shall issue copies of the modified or terminated order or consent agreement as provided in division (F) of this section." RC 3113.31(F)(1) provides that "[t]he court shall direct that a copy of an order be delivered to the respondent on the same day that the order is entered." While, it can be argued that, based on the statutory language, personal service is contemplated, case law and Civil Rule 65.1 indicate that ordinary mail service is appropriate.

For example, in *State v. McLean*,[60] appellee had filed a motion to modify a civil protection order to include a 1989 Plymouth Neon. Respondent was served by certified mail. When petitioner failed to appear at the hearing, the magistrate dismissed the motion for lack of prosecution. Service of the magistrate's decision and the dismissal entry was made by regular mail to respondent.

Subsequently, the respondent was charged with violating protection order. At trial, he argued that he could not have recklessly violated the civil protection order because he reasonably believed that the magistrate had dismissed the CPO.[61] He also argued that he had never received the documents. However, respondent never argued

[59]See Delmatto v. Hamed, 2008-Ohio-6375, 2008 WL 5124388 (Ohio Ct. App. 5th Dist. Fairfield County 2008) (overruling appellant's assignment of error and finding that Civ. R. 5 applied to service of the motion to modify a CPO, where appellant argued that service of the motion must be made in accordance with Civ. R. 4.1 and Civ. R. 75 and appellee argued that Civ. R. 5 was sufficient for service on opposing counsel when a party is represented by counsel).

[60]State v. McLean, 2005-Ohio-1562, 2005 WL 737412 (Ohio Ct. App. 11th Dist. Trumbull County 2005); see also State v. Wolff, 512 N.W.2d 670 (N.D. 1994) (discussing the meaning of "serve" and determining that service of process is governed by Civ.R. 4, but that Civ.R. 5 governs all other papers).

[61]State v. McLean, 2005-Ohio-1562, 2005 WL 737412, *3 (Ohio Ct. App. 11th Dist. Trumbull County 2005).

that either certified mail or regular mail service was inadequate. In its opinion, the Trumbull County Court of Appeals chose not to address or challenge the use of either certified or ordinary mail to effect service of subsequent court entries.

Q & A: Are there special procedures under Civ. R. 65.1 that must be followed when a motion to modify or terminate a civil protection order is referred to a magistrate?

According to Civ. R. 65.1(F)(3)(e), "[w]hen a motion for modification, contempt, renewal or termination of a civil protection order is referred to a magistrate for determination, the provisions of this division (F)(3) of this rule relating to full hearing proceedings shall apply unless such provisions would by their nature be clearly inapplicable." These procedures include a determination of the nature of the order, court adoption, modification or rejection of the order and objections to the order. According to the Staff Notes, (F)(3)(e) of this rule had been added to address issues discussed in *Schneider v. Razek,*[62] relating to proceedings on motions for renewal, contempt, modification or termination of civil protection orders.

Q & A: Does RC 3113.31(E)(8) contemplate ex parte civil protection orders?[63]

No. RC 3113.31(E)(8)(a) specifically excludes the modification or termination of an ex parte civil protection order.

Q & A: Can the court modify a civil protection order and grant an order of spousal support, where no spousal support was ordered in the original CPO?

Yes. In *Schumaker v. Schumaker,*[64] petitioner was granted a CPO for a term of five years. Several months later, respondent filed a motion to modify or suspend the CPO, claiming that he had learned that his wife was no longer residing at the marital residence and that he should be able to return to the home if it was no longer occupied by petitioner. Petitioner then filed a motion to modify the CPO, requesting that respondent be ordered to pay her spousal support. The trial court awarded petitioner spousal support, retroactive to the date on which she filed her motion.

On appeal, respondent argued that the trial court erred in ordering him to pay spousal support because petitioner had not asked for spousal support in her original petition for CPO.

The Licking County Court of Appeals acknowledged that the domestic violence statute "gives the trial court extensive authority to tailor the domestic violence protection order to the exact situation before it at the time. RC 3113.31(E) permits a court to modify its previous civil protection order, and notice of the motion to modify must be made in accordance with the Rules of Civil Procedure."[65]

It then reasoned that "[a]lthough RC 3113.31 does not expressly

[62] Schneider v. Razek, 2015-Ohio-410, 28 N.E.3d 591 (Ohio Ct. App. 8th Dist. Cuyahoga County 2015).

[63] See also Text § 12:23, Duration of a civil protection order.

[64] Schumaker v. Schumaker, 2010-Ohio-3490, 2010 WL 2914347 (Ohio Ct. App. 5th Dist. Licking County 2010).

[65] Schumaker v. Schumaker, 2010-Ohio-3490, 2010 WL 2914347, *2 (Ohio Ct. App. 5th Dist. Licking County 2010).

provide for the modification of spousal support when no spousal support has been ordered initially in the protection order, it does not expressly prohibit a modification under those circumstances. A contrary holding would require a trial court to award spousal support in a nominal amount to act as a predicate for its reservation of jurisdiction to modify the award in the event of changed circumstances. In the alternative, the petitioner would be required to dismiss the civil protection order and to immediately re-file a second request for a protection order in which he or she expressly requests the court award spousal support. In light of the fact that appellant in the case at bar was given notice and a full evidentiary hearing to contest the appellee's request for spousal support, we find little will be gained by either procedure. In the case at bar, we find that the trial court did not err in granting spousal support."[66]

Q & A: Does the petitioner have the burden to prove once again that domestic violence occurred as part of respondent's motion to modify or terminate the protection order?

No. In *Dowhan v. Dowhan*,[67] respondent appealed the denial of his motion to modify the CPO issued against him in order to remove the minor children from the order. On appeal respondent argued that the trial court erred in failing to modify the CPO because there was no current incident of domestic violence between the parties or children sufficient to support a finding that the children were in imminent danger of domestic violence at the time of the filing of the original petition for protection order.[68] In effect, respondent has argued that petitioner (ex wife) failed to prove she was entitled to the CPO in the first instance.

The appellate court specifically concentrated on respondent's burden to prove that the CPO is no longer needed or its terms no longer appropriate. Arguments challenging the validity of the CPO are res judicata. "Sharon did not have the burden to prove domestic violence because she had already met that burden when the trial court issued the CPO. Since appellant failed to appeal the CPO, it is res judicata."[69]

Q & A: How does a respondent meet the burden of proof that a CPO is no longer needed or its terms no longer appropriate?

For example, in *Dowhan v. Dowhan*,[70] appellant challenged the trial court's denial of his motion to modify the terms of a civil protection order granted to his ex wife and the parties' children on the grounds that the children are not in danger and that appellee's fear regarding the children was not reasonable.

In this case, evidence at the original CPO hearing demonstrated a

[66]Schumaker v. Schumaker, 2010-Ohio-3490, 2010 WL 2914347, *3 (Ohio Ct. App. 5th Dist. Licking County 2010).

[67]Dowhan v. Dowhan, 2012-Ohio-5830, 2012 WL 6114935 (Ohio Ct. App. 11th Dist. Lake County 2012).

[68]Dowhan v. Dowhan, 2012-Ohio-5830, ¶ 31, 2012 WL 6114935 (Ohio Ct. App. 11th Dist. Lake County 2012).

[69]Dowhan v. Dowhan, 2012-Ohio-5830, ¶ 41, 2012 WL 6114935 (Ohio Ct. App. 11th Dist. Lake County 2012).

[70]Dowhan v. Dowhan, 2012-Ohio-5830, 2012 WL 6114935 (Ohio Ct. App. 11th Dist. Lake County 2012).

significant history of domestic violence, several criminal convictions, domestic violence exacerbated by alcohol, convictions for OVI and a letter he wrote before his release from NEOCAP to his ex-wife threatening her with serious physical injury. In granting the original petition for protection order, the trial court concluded that the multiple letters written to petitioner placed her in fear of imminent serious physical harm. Appellant did not appeal the issuance of the CPO; rather, he waited seven months and then sought to modify the terms of the CPO to remove the children from the order.

Initially, the appellate court noted that the trial court granted the CPO based on the fact that appellant placed his ex-wife in fear of imminent serious harm for the children.[71] If the basis of appellant's argument was that the children are no longer exposed to the danger of domestic violence, entitling him to modification, he had the burden of proof.[72] He also had the burden to prove that his ex-wife's fear of imminent serious physical harm was no longer reasonable.

The 11th District Court of Appeals found that, in determining whether appellee's fear for her children stemming from appellant's letter was reasonable, the trial court was entitled to consider history between the parties. There is no doubt that appellee was the victim of physical abuse for 15 years and there was undisputed evidence that abuse was committed against A.P. (his step-child) and T.D. (his child). Since these children would have been entitled to a civil protection order, " 'it follows that any remaining children of the family would also properly fall within the ambit of the CPO.' "[73] "In light of appellant's history of domestic violence against his children, the trial court was entitled to find, as it did, that appellant failed to prove Sharon's fear for her children was no longer reasonable."[74]

Because the appellate court reviewed the decision of the trial court on an "abuse of discretion" standard, it focused on the trial court's judgment and whether it comported with reason or the record.[75] In determining that the trial court's reasoning was sound, the appellate court examined how the trial court reached its decision.[76] Of interest is that the appellant court focused less on whether the CPO was no longer needed or its terms no longer appropriate[77] and more on appellant's challenge that the CPO is no longer reasonable for the ex-wife to consider the letter to her a threat to his children.

Of interest to practitioners is that appellant argued that the trial

[71]See R.C. 3113.31(A)(1)(b).

[72]Dowhan v. Dowhan, 2012-Ohio-5830, ¶ 42, 2012 WL 6114935 (Ohio Ct. App. 11th Dist. Lake County 2012).

[73]Dowhan v. Dowhan, 2012-Ohio-5830, ¶ 49, 2012 WL 6114935 (Ohio Ct. App. 11th Dist. Lake County 2012), quoting Carpeno v. Carpeno, 2005-Ohio-7046, 2005 WL 3610425 (Ohio Ct. App. 11th Dist. Lake County 2005).

[74]Dowhan v. Dowhan, 2012-Ohio-5830, ¶ 49, 2012 WL 6114935 (Ohio Ct. App. 11th Dist. Lake County 2012). But see Schneider v. Razek, 2015-Ohio-410, 28 N.E.3d 591 (Ohio Ct. App. 8th Dist. Cuyahoga County 2015).

[75]Dowhan v. Dowhan, 2012-Ohio-5830, ¶ 39, 2012 WL 6114935 (Ohio Ct. App. 11th Dist. Lake County 2012).

[76]Dowhan v. Dowhan, 2012-Ohio-5830, ¶ 48, 2012 WL 6114935 (Ohio Ct. App. 11th Dist. Lake County 2012).

[77]See R.C. 3113.31(E)(8)(b).

court erred in denying the motion because the acts which formed the basis of the original CPO took place before he went to prison, and which were too remote to support the CPO. The Lake County appellate court found that "[t]o the extent this argument challenges the CPO, it is barred by res judicata. To the extent appellant is arguing there were no current acts of domestic violence so the CPO should have been modified, he had the burden of proof."[78] While RC 3113.31(E)(8) does not require a petitioner to prove recent acts of domestic violence, this Court implied that recent acts of abuse might be relevant to its legal analysis. Because there was a threat communicated to petitioner by letter while appellant was still imprisoned, the CPO was not based solely on acts committed before he went to prison; hence, the trial court was entitled to find that the appellant had failed to meet his burden of proof.[79]

Appellant also argued he was entitled to a modification of the CPO because his prior acts of domestic violence involved alcohol and he had addressed the problem. Since there was evidence that appellant's violence was not limited to his alcohol abuse and that he was violent even without drinking, he had the burden of proving that the CPO was no longer needed. Instead, the appellate court concentrated on the fact that he did not call his AA sponsor as a witness. In holding that the trial court did not abuse its discretion in finding that appellant failed to meet his burden of proof, the appellate court stated that "in these circumstances, the trial court was entitled to discount appellant's protestations of sobriety and reform and, instead, to give credit to the eloquent and heartbreaking testimony of Sharon, A.P. and T.D."[80]

Q & A: Must a court consider each and every factor of RC 3113.31(E)(8)?

Yes. First, RC 33113.31(E)(8)(c) specifically directs a court to consider all relevant factors, including, but not limited to each of the factors set forth in the statute. In *Schneider v. Razek*,[81] the appellate court considered each of the factors addressed by the magistrate in weighing whether the trial court's grant of the motion to terminate CPO was made in error. In this case, the CPO was based on one incident of domestic violence, occurring nearly five years earlier. "While horrific, the incident arose out of what appear to have been fairly unique, emotionally charged circumstances in the history of the parties' relationship. RC 3113.31(E)(8)(c)(x), (xii)."[82] The court then determined that, at the time of hearing, Razek had appropriate deal-

[78]Dowhan v. Dowhan, 2012-Ohio-5830, ¶ 44, 2012 WL 6114935 (Ohio Ct. App. 11th Dist. Lake County 2012).

[79]Dowhan v. Dowhan, 2012-Ohio-5830, ¶ 44, 2012 WL 6114935 (Ohio Ct. App. 11th Dist. Lake County 2012).

[80]Dowhan v. Dowhan, 2012-Ohio-5830, ¶ 50, 2012 WL 6114935 (Ohio Ct. App. 11th Dist. Lake County 2012).

[81]Schneider v. Razek, 2015-Ohio-410, 28 N.E.3d 591 (Ohio Ct. App. 8th Dist. Cuyahoga County 2015); see also Allan v. Allan, 2014-Ohio-5039, 2014 WL 6065710 (Ohio Ct. App. 8th Dist. Cuyahoga County 2014) (court must consider the extensive list of factors in RC 3113.31(E)(8)(c) to ensure that petitioner and the protected parties under the order are safe).

[82]Schneider v. Razek, 2015-Ohio-410, 28 N.E.3d 591, ¶ 44 (Ohio Ct. App. 8th

ings with his children, with no evidence that he presented any safety concerns.

The appellate court reviewed the evidence presented to the trial court magistrate. While the trial court considered the fact that the ex wife did not consent to the CPO and that she presented evidence that she still feared him, the court focused on the fact that the domestic violence incident occurred five years earlier. R.C. 3113.31(E)(8)(c)(i), (ii).[83] Additionally, no evidence was presented at the hearing that the ex husband had threatened her or done anything to suggest that he posed a danger to her or the children.[84]

The court considered the other factors, noted that the ex husband primarily resided in Alaska, even though he still owned a home in Parma, (R.C. 3113.31(E)(8)(c)(iv)); that the parties had the ability to interact regarding their children, (R.C. 3113.31(E)(8)(c)(iii), (iv)); that he had undergone anger management counseling, (R.C. 3113.31(E)(8)(c)(ix)); that he had violated the terms of the CPO only once by increasing his interaction with his ex wife, (R.C. 3113.31(E)(8)(c)(v)); that he had not had continuing involvement with drugs or alcohol, (R.C. 3113.31(E)(8)(c)(vi)) that he had not been convicted on or plead guilty to any offense of violence or been the subject of any other protection orders, restraining orders or no contact orders, (R.C. 3113.31(E)(8)(c)(vii), (viii)) and that health and age of the ex husband were not relevant to the facts of the case.(R.C. 3113.31(E)(8)(c)(xi)).[85]

The appellate court acknowledged that the CPO is designed to provide the court with a tool in which "to bring about a cessation of domestic violence against the family or household members. RC 3113.31(E)(1). Protection orders are, therefore intended to prevent future domestic violence."[86] Since the court could find no evidence to suggest that the ex wife or the children continued to be in danger of physical harm and "Schneider has cited no cases in which it was found to be an abuse of discretion to terminate a protection order where, as here, there was no evidence of any continued threats or other incidents that would suggest that she or the children were in continued danger from Razek."[87] So too, there was substantial competent, credible evidence to support the magistrate's determination that the CPO was no longer needed.

Of significance is that the appellate court considered both "consent" and "fear," and determined that they were just two of the statutory factors that a court must consider in determining whether it was appropriate to terminate the order. However, these factors were not

---

Dist. Cuyahoga County 2015).

[83]Schneider v. Razek, 2015-Ohio-410, 28 N.E.3d 591, ¶ 46 (Ohio Ct. App. 8th Dist. Cuyahoga County 2015).

[84]Schneider v. Razek, 2015-Ohio-410, 28 N.E.3d 591, ¶ 46 (Ohio Ct. App. 8th Dist. Cuyahoga County 2015).

[85]Schneider v. Razek, 2015-Ohio-410, 28 N.E.3d 591, ¶ 46-50 (Ohio Ct. App. 8th Dist. Cuyahoga County 2015).

[86]Schneider v. Razek, 2015-Ohio-410, 28 N.E.3d 591, ¶ 51 (Ohio Ct. App. 8th Dist. Cuyahoga County 2015)., citing Felton v. Felton, 79 Ohio St. 3d 34, 41, 1997-Ohio-302, 679 N.E.2d 672 (1997).

[87]Schneider v. Razek, 2015-Ohio-410, 28 N.E.3d 591, ¶ 51 (Ohio Ct. App. 8th Dist. Cuyahoga County 2015).

given any extra weight. Additionally, Razek was not required to prove her fear "was no longer reasonable" in order to terminate the CPO.[88]

§ 12:26 Appeal of a civil protection order[1]

Ohio's statute specifically provides that the granting or denial of a civil protection order issued or a consent entry approved after a full hearing[2] is a final, appealable order.[3] The importance of this recent provision cannot be overstated. By way of historical context, there was no consistency regarding the protection order entered by the court after the full hearing. Most courts did not entertain an appeal "for the reason that it is not a final appealable order pursuant to RC 2505.02. By its own terms, this order was temporary, or provisional, in nature."[4]

Unlike ex parte protection orders, civil protection orders that are entered after the full hearing are not temporary in nature. They are final orders entered for a definite period of time. Additionally, they are the ultimate disposition of the controversy. This is true whether or not the orders are requested as a second count to a complaint for divorce. Most importantly, no other remedy exists that provides the same or similar relief.[5] Therefore, they can be appealed, as can other final orders or judgments.[6] However, a magistrate's grant or denial of a civil protection order may not be appealed. A judge may adopt,

---

[88]Schneider v. Razek, 2015-Ohio-410, 28 N.E.3d 591, ¶ 47 (Ohio Ct. App. 8th Dist. Cuyahoga County 2015).; but see Dowhan v. Dowhan, 2012-Ohio-5830, 2012 WL 6114935 (Ohio Ct. App. 11th Dist. Lake County 2012).

[Section 12:26]

[1]See also Basden v. Basden, 154 N.C. App. 520, 572 S.E.2d 442 (2002) (discussing whether an appeal from a protection order is moot because it is not heard until after the expiration of the protection order); Logsdon v. Boulais, 2001-Ohio-8689, 2001 WL 1256309 (Ohio Ct. App. 12th Dist. Clermont County 2001) (where appellate court stated that because the civil protection order issued had expired, the present appeal was moot, citing Saffold v. Saffold, 1999 WL 304310 (Ohio Ct. App. 8th Dist. Cuyahoga County 1999); VanMeter v. VanMeter, 2004-Ohio-3390, 2004 WL 1446055 (Ohio Ct. App. 10th Dist. Franklin County 2004) (court held that because this particular civil protection order is no longer in effect as a result of its expiration, the present appeal is moot).

[2]Or that modifies or terminates a protection order or consent agreement or that refuses to modify or terminate a protection order or consent agreement (Sub. S.B. 260, eff. 1-2-07).

[3]R.C. 3113.31(G); see also Martin v. Fisher, 2001 WL 370519 (Ohio Ct. App. 8th Dist. Cuyahoga County 2001); Stella v. Platz, 1999 WL 427672 (Ohio Ct. App. 4th Dist. Washington County 1999); Stickel v. Pryor, 2002-Ohio-3309, 2002 WL 1396077 (Ohio Ct. App. 2d Dist. Miami County 2002); Lamont v. Lamont, 2005-Ohio-2256, 2005 WL 1075613 (Ohio Ct. App. 11th Dist. Geauga County 2005); Daugherty v. Daugherty, 2012-Ohio-1520, 2012 WL 1139129 (Ohio Ct. App. 4th Dist. Hocking County 2012) (appellate court had jurisdiction to consider former husband's arguments challenging CPO, even though former wife's request for a protection order for son was still pending in the trial court, holding that under R.C. 3113.31(G), an order granting or denying a civil protection order, even if interlocutory, is immediately appealable).

[4]Haines v. Shiever, 1995 WL 348430, *2 (Ohio Ct. App. 8th Dist. Cuyahoga County 1995).

[5]See Felton v. Felton, 79 Ohio St. 3d 34, 1997-Ohio-302, 679 N.E.2d 672 (1997).

[6]See also Montecalvo v. Montecalvo, 126 Ohio App. 3d 377, 710 N.E.2d 379 (11th Dist. Trumbull County 1999); Yun v. Yun, 2003-Ohio-2644, 2003 WL 21185852 (Ohio

modify or reject the magistrate's grant or denial of the civil protection order.[7]

Pro se litigants and attorneys who file appeals should be aware that the movant has the duty to provide a transcript of the trial court proceedings, unless the transcript is unavailable or a statement of the evidence when no recording is made. This is reinforced in the Rules of Appellate Procedure as well as in several Supreme Court of Ohio decisions.[8] "When portions of the transcript necessary for resolution of assigned errors are omitted from the record, the reviewing court has nothing to pass upon and thus, as to those assigned errors, the court has no choice but to presume the validity of the lower court's proceedings, and affirm."[9]

Additionally, a litigant or attorney cannot attach copies of emails or texts to the brief in lieu of a transcript. Any exhibit attached to the appellate brief is not part of the record and may not be considered in determining the appeal.[10]

Q & A: What is the appropriate standard of review to be applied by an appellate court?

Appellate courts review judgments of a trial court by way of two different standards. A trial court decision may be challenged "as being against the manifest weight of the evidence" and/or "and abuse of discretion." Each standard involves different elements. The analysis of both legal standards has often encompassed broader legal constructs such as "sufficiency of" and "weight accorded to" the evidence, as well as the concept of "competent credible evidence." Moreover, some courts have even determined that the nature of the challenge will dictate the standard of review.

In addressing the issue of manifest weight of the evidence, the Ohio Supreme Court in, *C.E. Morris Co. v. Foley Const. Co.*,[11] stated that "[j]udgments going to all the essential elements of the case will not be reversed by a reviewing court as being against the manifest weight of the evidence."[12]

On the other hand, when applying an abuse of discretion standard, a decision will not be reversed unless such decision was unconsciona-

---

Ct. App. 5th Dist. Stark County 2003); Lamont v. Lamont, 2005-Ohio-2256, 2005 WL 1075613 (Ohio Ct. App. 11th Dist. Geauga County 2005).

[7]See Civ. R. 65.1(G); see also Text § 9:5; Text § 12:10, Magistrate's hearings.

[8]See App. R. 9.

[9]C.L. v. T.B., 2018-Ohio-1074, 2018 WL 1459874, ¶ 7 (Ohio Ct. App. 10th Dist. Franklin County 2018); quoting, Knapp v. Edwards Laboratories, 61 Ohio St. 2d 197, 199, 15 Ohio Op. 3d 218, 400 N.E.2d 384 (1980).

[10]C.L. v. T.B., 2018-Ohio-1074, ¶ 9, 2018 WL 1459874 (Ohio Ct. App. 10th Dist. Franklin County 2018); quoting, Kidane v. Gezahegn, 2015-Ohio-2662, ¶ 12, 2015 WL 3963956 (Ohio Ct. App. 10th Dist. Franklin County 2015) quoting, Cashlink, L.L.C. v. Mosin, Inc., 2012-Ohio-5906, ¶ 8, 2012 WL 6484299 (Ohio Ct. App. 10th Dist. Franklin County 2012).

[11]C. E. Morris Co. v. Foley Const. Co., 54 Ohio St. 2d 279, 8 Ohio Op. 3d 261, 376 N.E.2d 578 (1978).

[12]At *279. See also E.W. v. T.W., 2017-Ohio-8504, ¶ 13, 2017 WL 5192035 (Ohio Ct. App. 10th Dist. Franklin County 2017).

ble or unreasonable. For example, in *Blakemore v. Blakemore*,[13] the Supreme Court of Ohio determined that the term "abuse of discretion" connotes more than an error of law or judgment; it implies an unreasonable arbitrary or unconscionable attitude.[14]

Prior to 1999, appellate courts utilized inconsistent approaches when reviewing the grant or denial of a civil protection order.[15] Some courts reviewed the issuance of a civil protection order for an abuse of discretion.[16] Other courts considered whether the judgment was supported by some competent credible evidence going to all of the essential elements.[17] Still others applied a combination of the two.[18]

For example, in *Sroka v. Sroka*[19] the appellate court appeared to have considered a combination review by implying that the lower court abused its discretion by denying appellant's petition for civil protection order and then specifically stated that the denial was against the manifest weight of the evidence.

---

[13]Blakemore v. Blakemore, 5 Ohio St. 3d 217, 219, 450 N.E.2d 1140 (1983).

[14]At *1142. See also Kuhn v. Kuhn, 2013-Ohio-5807, 2013 WL 6869801 (Ohio Ct. App. 11th Dist. Lake County 2013) (defining "abuse of discretion," as in the Second Appellate District, as a failure to exercise sound, reasonable and legal decision-making and noting it is a term of art connoting judgment exercised by a court, which does not comport with reason or the record); Baltes v. Baltes, 2012-Ohio-4890, 2012 WL 5195824 (Ohio Ct. App. 11th Dist. Trumbull County 2012).

[15]See Wilburn v. Wilburn, 2006-Ohio-2553, 2006 WL 1409784 (Ohio Ct. App. 9th Dist. Lorain County 2006) (discussing the many standards of review on appeal existing presently); see also Abriani v. Abriani, 2007-Ohio-3534, 2007 WL 2008887 (Ohio Ct. App. 8th Dist. Cuyahoga County 2007).

[16]Strong v. Bauman, 1999 WL 317432 (Ohio Ct. App. 2d Dist. Montgomery County 1999); Woolum v. Woolum, 131 Ohio App. 3d 818, 723 N.E.2d 1135 (12th Dist. Preble County 1999); Thomas v. Thomas, 44 Ohio App. 3d 6, 540 N.E.2d 745 (10th Dist. Franklin County 1988); McWilliam v. Dickey, 2013-Ohio-4036, 2013 WL 5310439 (Ohio Ct. App. 8th Dist. Cuyahoga County 2013) (the decision whether or not to grant a CPO is within the discretion of the trial court and will not be reversed absent an abuse of discretion); Prater v. Mullins, 2013-Ohio-3981, 2013 WL 5230272 (Ohio Ct. App. 3d Dist. Auglaize County 2013); McMullen v. Baldwin, 2013-Ohio-2677, 2013 WL 3280031 (Ohio Ct. App. 5th Dist. Stark County 2013); Olson v. Olson, 2016-Ohio-149, 2016 WL 197117, ¶ 15 (Ohio Ct. App. 6th Dist. Wood County 2016) (utilizing an abuse of discretion standard to determine whether to reverse a trial court's decision regarding a CPO).

[17]Eastley v. Volkman, 132 Ohio St. 3d 328, 2012-Ohio-2179, 972 N.E.2d 517, ¶ 20 (2012); Eichenberger v. Eichenberger, 82 Ohio App. 3d 809, 613 N.E.2d 678 (10th Dist. Franklin County 1992); Still v. Still, 1999 WL 236049 (Ohio Ct. App. 2d Dist. Montgomery County 1999); Conkle v. Wolfe, 131 Ohio App. 3d 375, 722 N.E.2d 586 (4th Dist. Athens County 1998); Snyder v. Snyder, 1995 WL 493998 (Ohio Ct. App. 4th Dist. Ross County 1995); Kiedrowicz v. Kiedrowicz, 1999 WL 197793 (Ohio Ct. App. 6th Dist. Huron County 1999); Crawford v. Brandon, 2014-Ohio-3659, 2014 WL 4180286 (Ohio Ct. App. 12th Dist. Butler County 2014); Croone v. Arif, 2014-Ohio-5546, 2014 WL 7186677 (Ohio Ct. App. 8th Dist. Cuyahoga County 2014).

[18]Trent v. Trent, 1999 WL 298073 (Ohio Ct. App. 12th Dist. Preble County 1999); Siouffi v. Siouffi, 1998 WL 879255 (Ohio Ct. App. 2d Dist. Montgomery County 1998); Sitton v. Sitton, 1999 WL 55717 (Ohio Ct. App. 2d Dist. Montgomery County 1999); Stanzak v. Stanzak, 1990 WL 129456 (Ohio Ct. App. 12th Dist. Butler County 1990); Tischler v. Vahcic, 1995 WL 680928 (Ohio Ct. App. 8th Dist. Cuyahoga County 1995) (abrogated on other grounds by, Felton v. Felton, 79 Ohio St. 3d 34, 1997-Ohio-302, 679 N.E.2d 672 (1997)).

[19]Sroka v. Sroka, 121 Ohio App. 3d 728, 700 N.E.2d 916 (8th Dist. Cuyahoga County 1997).

Still other appellate districts even applied one standard of review in one case and a different standard in another case.[20]

In 1999, the Eighth District Court of Appeals, in *Reynolds v. White*[21] addressed the several standards of review and concluded that the standard of review for civil protection orders should depend on the *challenge* to the protection order. (Emphasis added)[22] "Because RC 3113.31 expressly authorizes the courts to craft protection orders that are tailored to the particular circumstances, it follows that the trial court has discretion in establishing the scope of a protection order and that judgment ought not be disturbed absent an abuse of discretion."[23] Thus, when challenging the scope of a civil protection order, the reviewing court must review the order for an abuse of discretion.

Conversely, if the issue is whether a protection order should have been issued at all, a petitioner must show by a preponderance of the evidence that the petitioner or the petitioner's family was in danger of domestic violence.[24] The *Reynolds* court applied the standard set forth in *Felton* and concluded that "[i]t is reasonable to infer from *Felton*

---

[20]See also Strong v. Bauman, 1999 WL 317432 (Ohio Ct. App. 2d Dist. Montgomery County 1999) (applying abuse of discretion); Still v. Still, 1999 WL 236049 (Ohio Ct. App. 2d Dist. Montgomery County 1999) (employing competent credible evidence standard); Siouffi v. Siouffi, 1998 WL 879255 (Ohio Ct. App. 2d Dist. Montgomery County 1998) (using a combined approach) or Eichenberger v. Eichenberger, 82 Ohio App. 3d 809, 613 N.E.2d 678 (10th Dist. Franklin County 1992) (employing competent credible evidence standard); Beach v. Beach, 1992 WL 328642 (Ohio Ct. App. 10th Dist. Franklin County 1992) (applying abuse of discretion).

[21]Reynolds v. White, 1999 WL 754496 (Ohio Ct. App. 8th Dist. Cuyahoga County 1999). See also Abuhamda-Sliman v. Sliman, 161 Ohio App. 3d 541, 544-545, 2005-Ohio-2836, 831 N.E.2d 453 (8th Dist. Cuyahoga County 2005) (observing that Ohio appellate courts have been quite inconsistent in reviewing CPOs and noting the three standards that have been applied: (1) abuse of discretion, (2) whether the judgment was supported by competent and credible evidence going to all essential elements, and (3) some combination of the two tests); Ferris v. Ferris, 2006-Ohio-878, 2006 WL 456811 (Ohio Ct. App. 12th Dist. Clermont County 2006); Tabor v. Palacio, 2008-Ohio-349, 2008 WL 282127 (Ohio Ct. App. 12th Dist. Butler County 2008); Allan v. Allan, 2014-Ohio-5039, 2014 WL 6065710 (Ohio Ct. App. 8th Dist. Cuyahoga County 2014); Corrao v. Corrao, 2016-Ohio-4862, 2016 WL 3632494 (Ohio Ct. App. 8th Dist. Cuyahoga County 2016).

[22]See also Young v. Young, 2006-Ohio-978, 2006 WL 515522 (Ohio Ct. App. 2d Dist. Greene County 2006) (discussing standard of review on appeal; the approach selected by the Eighth District has been followed by the Fourth and Tenth Districts and the Second District agreed to follow); Ferris v. Ferris, 2006-Ohio-878, 2006 WL 456811 (Ohio Ct. App. 12th Dist. Clermont County 2006); Williamson v. Williamson, 180 Ohio App. 3d 260, 2008-Ohio-6718, 905 N.E.2d 217 (2d Dist. Greene County 2008); Allan v. Allan, 2014-Ohio-5039, 2014 WL 6065710 (Ohio Ct. App. 8th Dist. Cuyahoga County 2014); Charles v. Peters, 2016-Ohio-1259, 2016 WL 1178776 (Ohio Ct. App. 2d Dist. Greene County 2016); Wootten v. Culp, 2017-Ohio-665, 85 N.E.3d 198 (Ohio Ct. App. 4th Dist. Adams County 2017).

[23]*Reynolds at *4*. Abuhamda-Sliman v. Sliman, 161 Ohio App. 3d 541, 2005-Ohio-2836, 831 N.E.2d 453, ¶ 9 (8th Dist. Cuyahoga County 2005); F.-S. v. Pacek, 2015-Ohio-4310, 2015 WL 6128507 (Ohio Ct. App. 9th Dist. Medina County 2015); Allan v. Allan, 2014-Ohio-5039, 2014 WL 6065710 (Ohio Ct. App. 8th Dist. Cuyahoga County 2014); Parker v. Parker, 2014-Ohio-5516, ¶ 17, 2014 WL 7177914 (Ohio Ct. App. 1st Dist. Hamilton County 2014); T.S. v. R.S., 2017-Ohio-281, 81 N.E.3d 932 (Ohio Ct. App. 9th Dist. Summit County 2017).

[24]Reynolds v. White, 1999 WL 754496 (Ohio Ct. App. 8th Dist. Cuyahoga County 1999); Birkhimer v. Dean, 2004-Ohio-2996, 2004 WL 1293250 (Ohio Ct. App. 4th Dist. Pike County 2004); Gooderham v. Patterson, 1999 WL 1034472 (Ohio Ct. App. 4th

that when a respondent contends that it was error to issue a protection order, the question on review is whether there was sufficient credible evidence to support a finding that the respondent had engaged in acts or threats of domestic violence."[25] In effect, the court determined that the *Felton* standard was essentially a manifest weight of the evidence review.[26] However, the appellate court also mentioned that *Felton* did not express any view as to whether the lower court also abused its discretion.[27]

Since *Reynolds*, courts have further refined these concepts and continued to apply different standards, independent of the challenge to the order, to different trial court decisions within the same appellate district and sometimes, within the same case.

For example, in *Birkhimer v. Dean*,[28] the appellate court utilized the standard set forth in *Felton* and articulated in *Reynolds* to reinforce the concept that when a party challenges the granting of a CPO, the standard on appeal is whether there is competent credible evidence to support the trial court's finding that the petitioner is in danger of domestic violence.[29] "Under this highly deferential standard of review, we do not decide whether we would have come to the same conclusion as the trial court. Rather, we are required to uphold the judgment so long as the record, as a whole, contains some evidence from which the trier of fact could have reached its ultimate factual conclusions. We are guided by the presumption that the trial court's factual findings are correct because of the knowledge that the trial court judge "is best able to view the witnesses and observe their demeanor, gestures and voice inflections, and use these observations in weighing the credibility of the proffered testimony.[30]

Additionally, the *Birkhimer* court utilized an abuse of discretion

---

Dist. Gallia County 1999); Gatt v. Gatt, 2002-Ohio-1749, 2002 WL 570389 (Ohio Ct. App. 9th Dist. Medina County 2002); Poth v. Poth, 2007-Ohio-5925, 2007 WL 3257367 (Ohio Ct. App. 10th Dist. Franklin County 2007), citing Abuhamda-Sliman v. Sliman, 161 Ohio App. 3d 541, 2005-Ohio-2836, 831 N.E.2d 453 (8th Dist. Cuyahoga County 2005); Rosine v. Rosine, 2010-Ohio-613, 2010 WL 598642 (Ohio Ct. App. 7th Dist. Mahoning County 2010).

[25]At *4, citing Felton v. Felton, 79 Ohio St. 3d 34, 43-44, 1997-Ohio-302, 679 N.E.2d 672 (1997).

[26]See Ritter v. Ritter, 2004-Ohio-2550, 2004 WL 1120824 (Ohio Ct. App. 8th Dist. Cuyahoga County 2004); Abuhamda-Sliman v. Sliman, 161 Ohio App. 3d 541, 2005-Ohio-2836, 831 N.E.2d 453 (8th Dist. Cuyahoga County 2005); McIntyre v. Johnson-Estes, 2011-Ohio-1696, 2011 WL 1327392 (Ohio Ct. App. 8th Dist. Cuyahoga County 2011).

[27]*Reynolds at *4.*

[28]Birkhimer v. Dean, 2004-Ohio-2996, 2004 WL 1293250 (Ohio Ct. App. 4th Dist. Pike County 2004). See also Bullard v. Alley, 2014-Ohio-1016, 2014 WL 1339719 (Ohio Ct. App. 4th Dist. Pike County 2014) (stressing that where Civ. R. 52 findings of fact and conclusions of law are not requested and a trial court fails to enter specific findings, appellate review of assignments of error is more limited); Walters v. Walters, 150 Ohio App. 3d 287, 2002-Ohio-6455, 780 N.E.2d 1032 (4th Dist. Gallia County 2002); Gooderham v. Patterson, 1999 WL 1034472 (Ohio Ct. App. 4th Dist. Gallia County 1999).

[29]At *3. See also Singhaus v. Zumbar, 2015-Ohio-4755, 2015 WL 7300195 (Ohio Ct. App. 5th Dist. Tuscarawas County 2015) (finding that the statutory criterion to determine whether or not to grant a CPO pursuant to RC 3113.31 is the existence or threatened existence of domestic violence and the potential danger to the child).

[30]At *3; quoting Seasons Coal Co., Inc. v. City of Cleveland, 10 Ohio St. 3d 77,

standard when the challenge was to the length or duration of the order.[31] While the Pike County Court of Appeals noted that a shorter term for the CPO may have been sufficient, "our role does not allow us to second guess or merely impose our judgment over the trial court. Given the court's findings that Dean's 'course of behavior continues to be threatening,' that Dean contacted Judge Blevins in connection with the situation and that Dean indicated he was capable of killing someone, we cannot say that the court's decision to grant Birkhimer a five-year protection order is unreasonable, unconscionable or arbitrary."[32]

Unfortunately, appellate courts continue to take multiple and inconsistent approaches when reviewing CPOs.[33] For example, some courts still review the grant or denial of civil protection orders under an abuse of discretion standard, particularly when the challenge is based on whether the order should have been issued at all.[34]

Other courts consider the manifest weight of the evidence standard-

---

79, 461 N.E.2d 1273, 38 U.C.C. Rep. Serv. 469 (1984); see also Walters v. Walters, 150 Ohio App. 3d 287, 2002-Ohio-6455, 780 N.E.2d 1032 (4th Dist. Gallia County 2002); Gooderham v. Patterson, 1999 WL 1034472 (Ohio Ct. App. 4th Dist. Gallia County 1999); Noah v. Brillhart, 2003-Ohio-2421, 2003 WL 21078077 (Ohio Ct. App. 9th Dist. Wayne County 2003); Carter v. Hooks, 2006-Ohio-5987, 2006 WL 3290733 (Ohio Ct. App. 12th Dist. Butler County 2006).

[31]See also Walters v. Walters, 150 Ohio App. 3d 287, 2002-Ohio-6455, 780 N.E.2d 1032 (4th Dist. Gallia County 2002).

[32]Birkhimer v. Dean, 2004-Ohio-2996, 2004 WL 1293250, *5 (Ohio Ct. App. 4th Dist. Pike County 2004).

[33]McBride v. McBride, 2012-Ohio-2146, ¶ 7, 971 N.E.2d 1007, 1009 (Ohio Ct. App. 12th Dist. Butler County 2012); Williams v. Hupp, 2011-Ohio-3403, 2011 WL 2670945 (Ohio Ct. App. 7th Dist. Mahoning County 2011).

[34]See, e.g., Bargar v. Kirby, 2011-Ohio-4904, 2011 WL 4436634 (Ohio Ct. App. 12th Dist. Butler County 2011); Hoyt v. Heindell, 191 Ohio App. 3d 373, 2010-Ohio-6058, 946 N.E.2d 258 (11th Dist. Lake County 2010); Smith v. Burroughs, 2010-Ohio-4806, 2010 WL 3861068 (Ohio Ct. App. 3d Dist. Wyandot County 2010); Baranack v. Rose, 2010-Ohio-2754, 2010 WL 2415385 (Ohio Ct. App. 5th Dist. Tuscarawas County 2010); Traut v. Leiby, 2010-Ohio-2563, 2010 WL 2298566 (Ohio Ct. App. 5th Dist. Richland County 2010); Snell v. Snell, 2010-Ohio-2245, 2010 WL 2010899 (Ohio Ct. App. 5th Dist. Richland County 2010) (noting that whether to grant a CPO is based on an abuse of discretion standard and if a finding of domestic violence, upon which a CPO is based, is challenged as against the manifest weight of the evidence, the court must determine whether there is competent credible evidence going to all the elements); Rangel v. Woodbury, 2009-Ohio-4407, 2009 WL 2679675 (Ohio Ct. App. 6th Dist. Lucas County 2009); Dennis v. Paulsen, 2009-Ohio-2916, 2009 WL 1719369 (Ohio Ct. App. 4th Dist. Hocking County 2009); Anderson v. Anderson, 2001-Ohio-3379, 2001 WL 1667875 (Ohio Ct. App. 7th Dist. Mahoning County 2001); Sroka v. Sroka, 121 Ohio App. 3d 728, 700 N.E.2d 916 (8th Dist. Cuyahoga County 1997) (holding that trial court's denial of petition for protection order was against the manifest weight of the evidence; though not specifically holding that trial court abused its discretion, it is implicit in court's conclusion); see also Reynolds v. Reynolds, 2001 WL 62552, *3 (Ohio Ct. App. 2d Dist. Montgomery County 2001) (appellate court stated that "[t]he standard of review of a trial court's decision to grant a civil protection order is abuse of discretion") (citing Strong v. Bauman, 1999 WL 317432 (Ohio Ct. App. 2d Dist. Montgomery County 1999)); Moore v. Guyton, 2013-Ohio-143, 2013 WL 221515 (Ohio Ct. App. 3d Dist. Paulding County 2013); Studer v. Studer, 2012-Ohio-2838, 2012 WL 2371452 (Ohio Ct. App. 3d Dist. Crawford County 2012); McElroy v. McElroy, 2016-Ohio-5148, 2016 WL 4039227 (Ohio Ct. App. 5th Dist. Guernsey County 2016) (determining that whether to grant a CPO lies within discretion of trial court and decision whether to grant a civil protection order should not be reversed absent an abuse of discretion); C.L. v. T.B., 2018-Ohio-1074, 2018 WL 1459874 (Ohio Ct. App. 10th Dist. Franklin County 2018); Dodds on behalf of S.S. v.

that is, whether the judgment was supported by competent, credible evidence going to all the essential elements of the CPO-when addressing whether the CPO should have been issued at all.[35]

"Under a manifest weight of the evidence challenge, the court weighs the evidence and all reasonable inferences, considers the credibility of witnesses and determines whether, in resolving conflicts in the evidence, the fact finder clearly lost its way and created such a manifest miscarriage of justice that the judgment must be reversed and a new trial ordered."[36]

According to the Ninth District Court of Appeals, in *Donovan v.*

Stamper, 2018-Ohio-193, ¶ 27, 2018 WL 481779 (Ohio Ct. App. 2d Dist. Champaign County 2018) (noting that when applying an abuse of discretion standard, most instances will result in decisions that are simply unreasonable, rather than decisions that are unconscionable or arbitrary and defining "unreasonable" as having "no sound reasoning process to support the decision. It is not enough that the reviewing court, were it deciding the issue *de novo,* would not have found that reasoning process to be persuasive, perhaps in view of countervailing reasoning processes that would support a contrary result.").

[35]See, e.g., Blocker v. Carron, 2011-Ohio-3673, 2011 WL 3198261 (Ohio Ct. App. 5th Dist. Tuscarawas County 2011); Jackson v. Jackson, 2011-Ohio-5529, 2011 WL 5135251 (Ohio Ct. App. 6th Dist. Lucas County 2011); Williams v. Hupp, 2011-Ohio-3403, 2011 WL 2670945 (Ohio Ct. App. 7th Dist. Mahoning County 2011); Rehfus v. Smith, 2015-Ohio-2145, 2015 WL 3498686 (Ohio Ct. App. 7th Dist. Carroll County 2015); Johnson v. Burke, 2016-Ohio-2947, 2016 WL 2757891 (Ohio Ct. App. 8th Dist. Cuyahoga County 2016); Smith v. Strong, 2017-Ohio-6918, 2017 WL 3098601 (Ohio Ct. App. 6th Dist. Lucas County 2017); J.R. v. E.H., 2017-Ohio-516, ¶ 10, 2017 WL 587314 (Ohio Ct. App. 10th Dist. Franklin County 2017); citing, Bradley v. Cox, 2004-Ohio-4840, ¶ 7–9, 2004 WL 2035318 (Ohio Ct. App. 10th Dist. Franklin County 2004); citing, C. E. Morris Co. v. Foley Const. Co., 54 Ohio St. 2d 279, 8 Ohio Op. 3d 261, 376 N.E.2d 578 (1978).

[36]Caramico v. Caramico, 2015-Ohio-4232, 2015 WL 5934194, ¶ 26 (Ohio Ct. App. 12th Dist. Clermont County 2015); citing Hyde v. Smith, 2015-Ohio-1701, 2015 WL 1976454, ¶ 13 (Ohio Ct. App. 12th Dist. Butler County 2015); C.Q. v. P.S., 2016-Ohio-4988, 2016 WL 3881115 (Ohio Ct. App. 9th Dist. Medina County 2016) (when the assignment of error was that petitioner's testimony was not credible, a manifest weight of the evidence standard is applicable); Cottrill v. Cottrill, 2017-Ohio-1422, 2017 WL 1376841 (Ohio Ct. App. 5th Dist. Fairfield County 2017); A.M. v. D.L., 2017-Ohio-5621, 2017 WL 2870214 (Ohio Ct. App. 9th Dist. Medina County 2017) ("[i]n determining whether a trial court's ruling is against the manifest weight of the evidence, the appellate court sits as a "thirteenth juror" to review the record, weigh the evidence and all reasonable inferences, consider the credibility of witnesses and determine whether the trier of fact "clearly lost its way and created a manifest miscarriage of justice."; [at ¶ 19; citing *J.K. v. M.K.*, [sic] 2015-Ohio-434, 2015 WL 557990 (Ohio Ct. App. Medina County 2015).] "In weighing the evidence, however, we are always mindful of the presumption in favor of the trial court's factual findings."" [At ¶ 19; quoting Lundin v. Niepsuj, 2017-Ohio-7153, ¶ 12, 2017 WL 3426957 (Ohio Ct. App. 9th Dist. Summit County 2017); Tredenary v. Fritz, 2017-Ohio-8632, 2017 WL 5569257 (Ohio Ct. App. 11th Dist. Lake County 2017); E.W. v. T.W., 2017-Ohio-8504, ¶ 13, 2017 WL 5192035 (Ohio Ct. App. 10th Dist. Franklin County 2017) (pointing out that whether the trial court applied the correct legal standard is a legal issue that an appellate court reviews *de novo*, indicating that an appellate review of question of law is *de novo* and further noting that applying the wrong legal standard or misapplying the correct legal standard may constitute an abuse of discretion citing Martin v. Martin, 2013-Ohio-5703, ¶ 6, 2013 WL 6843599 (Ohio Ct. App. 10th Dist. Franklin County 2013); Cornell v. Hatfield, 2018-Ohio-549, ¶ 9, 2018 WL 827136 (Ohio Ct. App. 12th Dist. Fayette County 2018) (the decision to grant or deny a DVCPO will not be reversed where such decision is supported by the manifest weight of the evidence); citing, Kohus v. Daly, 2016-Ohio-73, ¶ 43, 2016 WL 116121 (Ohio Ct. App. 12th Dist. Clermont County 2016).

Donovan, this standard encompasses both a "legal sufficiency" and "manifest weight" determination.[37] With respect to sufficiency of the evidence, " 'sufficiency' is a term of art meaning that legal standard which is applied to determine whether the case may go to a jury or whether the evidence is legally sufficient to support the jury verdict as a matter of law."[38] A sufficiency analysis requires a court to view the evidence in a light most favorable to the petitioner[39] "A sufficiency challenge tests the adequacy of the evidence."[40] "Weight tests the believability of the evidence offered and concerns the inclination of the greater amount of credible evidence, offered at trial, to support one side of the issue rather than the other."[41]

When assessing the sufficiency of the evidence in a civil protection order case, "we must determine whether, viewing the evidence in the light most favorable to [the petitioner], a reasonable trier of fact could find that the petitioner demonstrated by a preponderance of the evi-

---

[37]Donovan v. Donovan, 2012-Ohio-3521, ¶ 5, 2012 WL 3156462 (Ohio Ct. App. 9th Dist. Lorain County 2012), citing Eastley v. Volkman, 132 Ohio St. 3d 328, 2012-Ohio-2179, 972 N.E.2d 517 (2012), quoting State v. Thompkins, 78 Ohio St. 3d 380, 386–387, 1997-Ohio-52, 678 N.E.2d 541 (1997); R.C. v. J.G., 2013-Ohio-4265, 2013 WL 5437015 (Ohio Ct. App. 9th Dist. Medina County 2013); A.S. v. P.F., 2013-Ohio-4857, 2013 WL 5925968 (Ohio Ct. App. 9th Dist. Lorain County 2013); B.C. v. A.S., 2014-Ohio-1326, 2014 WL 1345260 (Ohio Ct. App. 9th Dist. Medina County 2014); M.K. v. J.K., 2015-Ohio-434, 2015 WL 557990 (Ohio Ct. App. 9th Dist. Medina County 2015); R.T. v. J.T., 2015-Ohio-4418, ¶ 19, 2015 WL 6449294 (Ohio Ct. App. 9th Dist. Medina County 2015); M.R. v. T.R., 2016-Ohio-3493, 2016 WL 3384940 (Ohio Ct. App. 9th Dist. Wayne County 2016).

[38]Donovan v. Donovan, 2012-Ohio-3521, ¶ 5, 2012 WL 3156462 (Ohio Ct. App. 9th Dist. Lorain County 2012), quoting State v. Thompkins, 78 Ohio St. 3d 380, 386, 1997-Ohio-52, 678 N.E.2d 541 (1997), quoting Black's Law Dictionary, 1433 (6th Ed. 1990). But see J.B. v. B.Y., 2016-Ohio-7918, ¶ 6, 2016 WL 6948078 (Ohio Ct. App. 9th Dist. Medina County 2016) (depending on the substance of the assignment of error, appellate court has discretion to determine whether to review under a sufficiency or a manifest weight of the evidence standard).

[39]R.C. v. J.G., 2013-Ohio-4265, 2013 WL 5437015 (Ohio Ct. App. 9th Dist. Medina County 2013); M.R. v. T.R., 2016-Ohio-3493, ¶ 12, 2016 WL 3384940 (Ohio Ct. App. 9th Dist. Wayne County 2016); M.J. v. L.P., 2016-Ohio-7080, 2016 WL 5723752 (Ohio Ct. App. 9th Dist. Medina County 2016); A.M. v. D.L., 2017-Ohio-5621, 2017 WL 2870214 (Ohio Ct. App. 9th Dist. Medina County 2017).

[40]M.H. v. J.H., 2015-Ohio-5178, 2015 WL 8553569, ¶ 5 (Ohio Ct. App. 9th Dist. Medina County 2015), citing Eastley v. Volkman, 132 Ohio St. 3d 328, ¶ 11, 2012-Ohio-2179, 972 N.E.2d 517 (2012) "In applying the sufficiency standard, 'we neither resolve evidence conflicts nor assess the credibility of witnesses, as both are functions reserved for the trial of fact.' " M.H. at ¶ 5, citing State v. Tucker, 2015-Ohio-3810, 2015 WL 5517839, ¶ 7 (Ohio Ct. App. 9th Dist. Medina County 2015), quoting State v. Jones, 2013-Ohio-4775, 2013 WL 5864591, ¶ 33 (Ohio Ct. App. 1st Dist. Hamilton County 2013).

[41]Donovan v. Donovan, 2012-Ohio-3521, ¶ 5, 2012 WL 3156462 (Ohio Ct. App. 9th Dist. Lorain County 2012), quoting State v. Thompkins, 78 Ohio St. 3d 380, 387, 1997-Ohio-52, 678 N.E.2d 541 (1997), quoting Black's Law Dictionary, 1594 (6th Ed. 1990); Serdy v. Serdy, 2013-Ohio-5532, 2013 WL 6670830 (Ohio Ct. App. 7th Dist. Noble County 2013) (noting that "[t]o reverse on weight of the evidence, the appellate court would have to find that the trier of fact clearly lost its way in resolving conflicts in the evidence and created a manifest miscarriage of justice" at ¶ 30); Bullard v. Alley, 2014-Ohio-1016, 2014 WL 1339719 (Ohio Ct. App. 4th Dist. Pike County 2014); A.M. v. S.M., 2018-Ohio-247, 2018 WL 542357 (Ohio Ct. App. 9th Dist. Summit County 2018) (the arguments regarding wife's "inconsistent" behavior and Husband's testimony that he never harmed-nor threatened to harm anyone, sound in weight, not sufficiency).

dence that a civil protection order should issue."[42] "In applying the sufficiency standard, 'we neither resolve evidence conflicts nor assess the credibility of witnesses, as both are functions reserved for the trier of fact.'"[43]

Conversely, in a manifest weight challenge, a reversal is only appropriate in the exceptional case where the evidence presented weights heavily in favor of the party seeking reversal.[44]

Some courts have even differentiated between standards to support a finding that respondent engaged in acts or threats of domestic violence[45] by applying a "sufficient credible evidence" standard or applying a "manifest weight of the evidence" standard, depending on the case before it.[46]

For example, in *A.M. v. D. L.*,[47] appellant argued that the trial court erred in finding that A.M. had a reasonable fear of imminent serious physical harm and raised this argument under both a "sufficiency of the evidence" and "manifest weight of the evidence" standard.[48]

The appellate court stated that "[w]hen reviewing such a finding, "the critical inquiry is 'whether a reasonable person would be placed

---

[42]A.M. v. D.L. at ¶ 11; quoting R.C. v. J.G., 2013-Ohio-4265, 2013 WL 5437015 (Ohio Ct. App. 9th Dist. Medina County 2013); citing Eastley v. Volkman, 132 Ohio St. 3d 328, 2012-Ohio-2179, ¶ 11, 972 N.E.2d 517 (2012), and State v. Jenks, 61 Ohio St. 3d 259, 574 N.E.2d 492 (1991) paragraph 2 of the syllabus.

[43]A.M. v. D.L. at ¶ 11.; citing State v. Tucker, 2015-Ohio-3810, ¶ 7, 2015 WL 5517839 (Ohio Ct. App. 9th Dist. Medina County 2015), quoting State v. Jones, 2013-Ohio-4775, ¶ 33, 2013 WL 5864591 (Ohio Ct. App. 1st Dist. Hamilton County 2013).

[44]M.R. v. T.R., 2016-Ohio-3493, ¶ 18, 2016 WL 3384940 (Ohio Ct. App. 9th Dist. Wayne County 2016), citing Collins v. Collins, 2015-Ohio-2618, ¶ 23, 2015 WL 4006005 (Ohio Ct. App. 9th Dist. Summit County 2015), quoting Boreman v. Boreman, 2002-Ohio-2320, ¶ 10, 2002 WL 1022990 (Ohio Ct. App. 9th Dist. Wayne County 2002); Martindale v. Martindale, 2017-Ohio-9266, ¶ 18, 102 N.E.3d 19 (Ohio Ct. App. 4th Dist. Athens County 2017).

[45]Abuhamda-Sliman v. Sliman, 161 Ohio App. 3d 541, 2005-Ohio-2836, 831 N.E.2d 453 (8th Dist. Cuyahoga County 2005); Gaydash v. Gaydash, 168 Ohio App. 3d 418, 2006-Ohio-4080, 860 N.E.2d 789 (9th Dist. Summit County 2006); Williamson v. Williamson, 180 Ohio App. 3d 260, 2008-Ohio-6718, 905 N.E.2d 217 (2d Dist. Greene County 2008); Hicks v. Barker, 2009-Ohio-2445, 2009 WL 1456532 (Ohio Ct. App. 12th Dist. Warren County 2009); Charles v. Peters, 2016-Ohio-1259, ¶ 19, 2016 WL 1178776 (Ohio Ct. App. 2d Dist. Greene County 2016); Majeed v. Majeed, 2016-Ohio-7243, 2016 WL 5887174 (Ohio Ct. App. 2d Dist. Montgomery County 2016); [J.R. v. E.H., 2017-Ohio-516, 2017 WL 587314 (Ohio Ct. App. 10th Dist. Franklin County 2017); E.W. v. T.W., 2017-Ohio-8504, ¶ 13, 2017 WL 5192035 (Ohio Ct. App. 10th Dist. Franklin County 2017).

[46]Hoff v. Brown, 2001 WL 876228 (Ohio Ct. App. 5th Dist. Stark County 2001); Williams v. Workman, 2005-Ohio-5388, 2005 WL 2514239 (Ohio Ct. App. 9th Dist. Summit County 2005) (holding that the standard for whether a CPO should have been granted is whether there is some competent credible evidence going to all the essential elements of the case); Rosen v. Chesler, 2009-Ohio-3163, 2009 WL 1900422 (Ohio Ct. App. 9th Dist. Lorain County 2009) (discussing the difference between manifest weight and sufficiency challenges); Morris v. Morris, 2009-Ohio-5164, 2009 WL 3119658 (Ohio Ct. App. 9th Dist. Summit County 2009) (Ohio Ct. App. 9th Dist. Summit County 2009) (applying a civil manifest weight of the evidence standard).

[47]A.M. v. D.L., 2017-Ohio-5621, 2017 WL 2870214 (Ohio Ct. App. 9th Dist. Medina County 2017).

[48]A.M. v. D.L., 2017-Ohio-5621, ¶ 8, 2017 WL 2870214 (Ohio Ct. App. 9th Dist. Medina County 2017).

in fear of imminent (in the sense of unconditional, non-contingent) serious physical harm.' "[49] "[E]ven with an established history of past abuse, there must be some competent, credible evidence that there is a present fear of harm."[50]

The court differentiated between the two standards and concluded that there was sufficient evidence presented at the hearing to indicate a threat of domestic violence based on the totality of the circumstances which included an alleged sexual assault four months prior to filing her petition, an alleged trespass one month prior and a history of violent behavior during the relationship. The court then pointed out that this was not "the exceptional case where the evidence presented weighs heavily in favor of the party seeking reversal. The trial court's determination that a domestic violence civil protection order should issue due to A.M.'s reasonable fear of imminent serious physical harm was not against the weight of the evidence."[51]

Still other courts apply a combination of the abuse of discretion standard and the manifest weight of the evidence standard.[52] And at least one court stated that a CPO must not be against the manifest weight of the evidence but also that the decision to grant a CPO is within the discretion of the trial court.[53]

Some appellate courts have determined that the focus of any review where there is a legal issue should be a *de novo* standard.[54] In *Martin v. Martin*,[55] appellant appealed the issuance of the CPO arguing that the trial court did not have the authority to issue the ex parte CPO, the continuance order or the authority to conduct the full hearing. The appellate court found that "[b]ased on these challenges, this ap-

---

[49]A.M. v. D.L., 2017-Ohio-5621, ¶ 9, 2017 WL 2870214 (Ohio Ct. App. 9th Dist. Medina County 2017).

[50]A.M. v. D.L., 2017-Ohio-5621, ¶ 10, 2017 WL 2870214 (Ohio Ct. App. 9th Dist. Medina County 2017), quoting McElroy v. McElroy, 2016-Ohio-5148, ¶ 38, 2016 WL 4039227 (Ohio Ct. App. 5th Dist. Guernsey County 2016).

[51]A.M. v. D.L., 2017-Ohio-5621, ¶ 25, 2017 WL 2870214 (Ohio Ct. App. 9th Dist. Medina County 2017).

[52]See e.g, Traut v. Leiby, 2010-Ohio-2563, 2010 WL 2298566 (Ohio Ct. App. 5th Dist. Richland County 2010); Schultz v. Schultz, 2010-Ohio-3665, 2010 WL 3075758 (Ohio Ct. App. 9th Dist. Medina County 2010); Tredenary v. Fritz, 2017-Ohio-8632, ¶ 31, 2017 WL 5569257 (Ohio Ct. App. 11th Dist. Lake County 2017) (focusing on manifest weight of the evidence analysis but also stating that "[b]ecause the record contains evidence, which, if believed, supported the court's denial of Antoinette's petition, the court's judgment was not an abuse of discretion.").

[53]McBride v. McBride, 2012-Ohio-2146, ¶ 7, 971 N.E.2d 1007, 1009 (Ohio Ct. App. 12th Dist. Butler County 2012); citing Trent v. Trent, 1999 WL 298073 (Ohio Ct. App. 12th Dist. Preble County 1999).

[54]E.W. v. T.W., 2017-Ohio-8504, 2017 WL 5192035 (Ohio Ct. App. 10th Dist. Franklin County 2017); [D.M.W.] v. [E.W.], 2018-Ohio-821, 2018 WL 1169656 (Ohio Ct. App. 10th Dist. Franklin County 2018) (applying a de novo standard when an appeal requires an analysis of the domestic violence statute).

[55]Martin v. Martin, 2013-Ohio-5703, 2013 WL 6843599 (Ohio Ct. App. 10th Dist. Franklin County 2013); E.W. v. T.W., 2017-Ohio-8504, ¶ 13, 2017 WL 5192035 (Ohio Ct. App. 10th Dist. Franklin County 2017) (pointing out that applying the wrong legal standard or misapplying the correct legal standard may constitute an abuse of discretion); Tredanary v. Fritz, 2018-Ohio-2374, n.2, 2018 WL 3045730 (Ohio Ct. App. 11th Dist. Lake County 2018) (noting that the standard of review employed when reviewing the imposition of sanctions for frivolous conduct varies but "we will apply a de novo standard of review when reviewing legal conclusions to the issue.").

peal requires analysis of R.C. 3113.31, the civil domestic violence statute; therefore, we apply a de novo standard."[56] The court relied on cases that stressed that when interpreting statutory authority and legislative enactments, the appellate court must apply a de novo standard of review.[57]

However, the Eighth District[58] and, more recently, others have taken a well-reasoned approach to appellate review that depends on the challenge to the order. All of these appellate courts agree that the issuance of a CPO shall be reviewed under the competent, credible evidence standard (manifest weight of the evidence) and that the scope of the order shall be subject to an abuse of discretion standard.[59] "These districts reasoned that the wording of RC 3113.31 dictates that the standard of review depend[s] on the nature of the challenge to the order."[60]

Of interest is that the Twelfth District Court of Appeals has stressed that there should be a consistent standard for the review of civil protection orders. In *McBride v. McBride*,[61] the dissent stated "I note that, as the majority has indicated, Ohio's appellate districts possess a conflict regarding the proper standard by which to review a trial

---

[56]Martin v. Martin, 2013-Ohio-5703, ¶ 6, 2013 WL 6843599 (Ohio Ct. App. 10th Dist. Franklin County 2013).

[57]Martin v. Martin, 2013-Ohio-5703, ¶ 6, 2013 WL 6843599 (Ohio Ct. App. 10th Dist. Franklin County 2013); Hope Academy v. Ohio Dept. of Edn., 2008-Ohio-4694, 2008 WL 4226106 (Ohio Ct. App. 10th Dist. Franklin County 2008); In re J.D., 172 Ohio App. 3d 288, 2007-Ohio-3279, 874 N.E.2d 858 (10th Dist. Franklin County 2007); [D.M.W.] v. [E.W.], 2018-Ohio-821, ¶ 11, 2018 WL 1169656 (Ohio Ct. App. 10th Dist. Franklin County 2018) ("[w]here an appeal requires an analysis of RC 3113.31, the civil domestic violence statute, we apply a *de novo* standard of review.").

[58]Corrao v. Corrao, 2016-Ohio-4862, 2016 WL 3632494 (Ohio Ct. App. 8th Dist. Cuyahoga County 2016). But see McWilliam v. Dickey, 2013-Ohio-4036, 2013 WL 5310439 (Ohio Ct. App. 8th Dist. Cuyahoga County 2013).

[59]See Abriani v. Abriani, 2007-Ohio-3534, 2007 WL 2008887 (Ohio Ct. App. 8th Dist. Cuyahoga County 2007); Holland v. Garner, 2010-Ohio-2963, 2010 WL 2573927 (Ohio Ct. App. 12th Dist. Butler County 2010); Martindale v. Martindale, 2017-Ohio-9266, ¶ 51, 102 N.E.3d 19 (Ohio Ct. App. 4th Dist. Athens County 2017); citing Wootten v. Culp, 2017-Ohio-665, 85 N.E.3d 198, ¶ 18 (Ohio Ct. App. 4th Dist. Adams County 2017), quoting Walters v. Walters, 150 Ohio App. 3d 287, 2002-Ohio-6455, 780 N.E.2d 1032, ¶ 19 (4th Dist. Gallia County 2002), citing Gooderham v. Patterson, 1999 WL 1034472 (Ohio Ct. App. 4th Dist. Gallia County 1999); see also Corrao v. Corrao, 2016-Ohio-4862, ¶ 16, 2016 WL 3632494 (Ohio Ct. App. 8th Dist. Cuyahoga County 2016).

[60]McBride v. McBride, 2012-Ohio-2146, 971 N.E.2d 1007 (Ohio Ct. App. 12th Dist. Butler County 2012); quoting Abuhamda-Sliman v. Sliman, 161 Ohio App. 3d 541, 2005-Ohio-2836, 831 N.E.2d 453, ¶ 9 (8th Dist. Cuyahoga County 2005); McGuire v. Sprinkle, 2007-Ohio-2705, 2007 WL 1585100 (Ohio Ct. App. 12th Dist. Warren County 2007); Young v. Young, 2006-Ohio-978, 2006 WL 515522 (Ohio Ct. App. 2d Dist. Greene County 2006); Williams v. Hupp, 2011-Ohio-3403, 2011 WL 2670945 (Ohio Ct. App. 7th Dist. Mahoning County 2011); Downs v. Strouse, 2006-Ohio-505, 2006 WL 280417 (Ohio Ct. App. 10th Dist. Franklin County 2006); Serdy v. Serdy, 2013-Ohio-5532, 2013 WL 6670830 (Ohio Ct. App. 7th Dist. Noble County 2013); Lundin v. Niepsuj, 2014-Ohio-1212, 2014 WL 1478284 (Ohio Ct. App. 9th Dist. Summit County 2014).

[61]McBride v. McBride, 2012-Ohio-2146, 971 N.E.2d 1007 (Ohio Ct. App. 12th Dist. Butler County 2012). See also Denney v. Sanders, 2016-Ohio-5113, 2016 WL 4063898 (Ohio Ct. App. 1st Dist. Hamilton County 2016) (discussing the different standards for appellate review).

court's decision when a CPO as been issued. This case may present an opportunity for the Supreme Court to speak definitively on this issue."[62]

In light of the rationale in *Felton*[63] and the reasoning of *Abuhamda-Sliman v. Sliman*,[64] and *McBride*,[65] it will be interesting to see whether more appellate courts continue to reverse trial court decisions denying or granting protection orders based on an abuse of discretion standard and/or elucidate when each standard should be used. Finally, it is hoped that the Supreme Court will determine the proper standard of review.

Q & A: Do any courts consider a trial court's decision to adopt a magistrate's decision when deciding the standard of review on appeal?

In *Friedlander v. Friedlander*,[66] the magistrate granted the CPO which was adopted and modified by the trial court to reinstate a supervised visitation order for appellant. Both parties objected to the trial court's *nunc pro tunc* entry. Appellant subsequently appealed, alleging that the trial court erred 1) in overruling his objections to the magistrate's decision and finding that he committed acts of domestic violence; 2) by permitting and considering testimony of alleged prior acts; and 3) by granting the CPO that included the minor children.[67]

The appellate court noted that the trial court had independently reviewed the decision of the magistrate.[68] In affirming the trial court decision, the Eighth District Court of Appeals determined that "[a] trial court's decision to adopt a magistrate's decision will not be reversed on appeal unless the decision amounts to an abuse of discretion."[69]

Q & A: What is the standard of review on appeal when the

---

[62]McBride v. McBride, 2012-Ohio-2146, ¶ 60, 971 N.E.2d 1007, 1021 (Ohio Ct. App. 12th Dist. Butler County 2012) (Piper, J., dissenting).

[63]Felton v. Felton, 79 Ohio St. 3d 34, 1997-Ohio-302, 679 N.E.2d 672 (1997). But see Young v. Young, 2006-Ohio-978, 2006 WL 515522, *3 (Ohio Ct. App. 2d Dist. Greene County 2006) (noting that "the *Felton* court held that there was 'sufficient, credible evidence to prove by a preponderance of the evidence that appellee had engaged in acts of domestic violence' . . . without expressing any view as to whether the lower court abused its discretion").

[64]Abuhamda-Sliman v. Sliman, 161 Ohio App. 3d 541, 2005-Ohio-2836, 831 N.E.2d 453 (8th Dist. Cuyahoga County 2005).

[65]McBride v. McBride, 2012-Ohio-2146, 971 N.E.2d 1007 (Ohio Ct. App. 12th Dist. Butler County 2012).

[66]Friedlander v. Friedlander, 2014-Ohio-2180, 2014 WL 2168238 (Ohio Ct. App. 8th Dist. Cuyahoga County 2014).

[67]Friedlander v. Friedlander, 2014-Ohio-2180, 2014 WL 2168238, ¶ 16 (Ohio Ct. App. 8th Dist. Cuyahoga County 2014).

[68]But see Civ. R. 65.1(F)(3)(c)(ii) which provides that a trial court reviews a magistrate's decision to determine if there are errors of law or defect on the face of the order.

[69]Friedlander v. Friedlander, 2014-Ohio-2180, 2014 WL 2168238, ¶ 16 (Ohio Ct. App. 8th Dist. Cuyahoga County 2014); Hynd v. Roesch, 2016-Ohio-7143, 2016 WL 5720642 (Ohio Ct. App. 11th Dist. Ashtabula County 2016) (stressing that an abuse of discretion standard was the appropriate standard on appeal when reviewing a trial court's adoption of a magistrate's decision, court also noted that where mother failed to object to the magistrate's decision, she waived her manifest weight of the evidence challenge on appeal where her only assignment of error was based on a challenge

trial court permits a party to reopen the case after resting to offer additional evidence?

According to the Third District Court of Appeals, the answer is an abuse of discretion. In *Nichols v. Young*,[70] appellant alleged that the trial court abused its discretion by allowing appellee to reopen the case to present additional testimony establishing a family or household member relationship between appellant and appellee in order to satisfy the statutory requirements of RC 3113.31.

The appellate court held that "[a] trial court has the discretion to permit a party to reopen her case after resting in rider to offer additional evidence and such decision will not be disturbed on appeal absent an abuse of discretion."[71]

Q & A: What is the appropriate standard of appellate review when the challenge to the trial court's decision involves a decision to terminate a civil protection order?

In *Schneider v. Razek*,[72] the ex wife appealed the trial court's decision to grant ex husband's motion to terminate the CPO. The appellate court advanced the appropriate standard of review when dealing with an appeal involving a motion to terminate a civil protection order. According to the Cuyahoga County Court of Appeals, "we believe, based on the permissive nature of the statute—i.e., a court 'may' modify or terminate a protection order—and the nature of the determinations involved—i.e., whether the protection order is 'no longer needed' or its terms 'are no longer appropriate'—the appropriate standard of review is abuse of discretion. See. e.g., *Twitty v. Bowe*, 10th Dist. Franklin No. 09AP-953, 2010-Ohio-1391, ¶ 6, citing *Jones v. Rose*, 4th Dist. Hocking No. 09CA7, 2009-Ohio-4347, ¶ 5."[73] Although the facts of the case involve a termination of a CPO, said analysis should also apply to a motion to modify a CPO.[74]

The court went on to point out that "even if the 'question on review' was whether there was sufficient credible evidence to support a finding that the civil protection order was no longer needed or its terms were no longer appropriate, i.e., a manifest weight standard of review, we would still find no error by the trial court, based on the record in this case."[75]

Q & A: What is the appellate standard for review for extending a protection order? For overruling a motion to extend a protection order?

---

father's credibility).

[70]Nichols v. Young, 2015-Ohio-1077, 2015 WL 1288148 (Ohio Ct. App. 3d Dist. Putnam County 2015).

[71]Nichols v. Young, 2015-Ohio-1077, 2015 WL 1288148, ¶ 26 (Ohio Ct. App. 3d Dist. Putnam County 2015), citing State v. Salaam, 2003-Ohio-1021, 2003 WL 832751 (Ohio Ct. App. 1st Dist. Hamilton County 2003), citing City of Columbus v. Grant, 1 Ohio App. 3d 96, 97, 439 N.E.2d 907 (10th Dist. Franklin County 1981).

[72]Schneider v. Razek, 2015-Ohio-410, 28 N.E.3d 591 (Ohio Ct. App. 8th Dist. Cuyahoga County 2015).

[73]Schneider v. Razek, 2015-Ohio-410, 28 N.E.3d 591, ¶ 40 (Ohio Ct. App. 8th Dist. Cuyahoga County 2015); Delaine v. Smith, 2016-Ohio-5250, 2016 WL 4141753 (Ohio Ct. App. 8th Dist. Cuyahoga County 2016).

[74]See also Text 9:5.

[75]Schneider v. Razek, 2015-Ohio-410, 28 N.E.3d 591, ¶ 40 (Ohio Ct. App. 8th Dist. Cuyahoga County 2015).

At least on Ohio appellate court has suggested a standard. In *Charles v. Peters,*[76] the appellate court addressed the various appellate standards for review regarding civil protection orders, acknowledging the challenge to the order-the scope or terms of the order or whether the order should be issued at all or extended.

"A protection order or an order extending a protection order requires sufficient evidence.[77] By contrast, no evidence is required to support an order overruling a motion for a protective order or a motion to extend a protection order. In a hypothetical proceeding on a motion to extend a protection order in which no evidence is presented, the trial court would be required to overrule the motion. We conclude, therefore, that in reviewing an order overruling a motion to extend a protection order, the standard of review is not whether there is sufficient evidence to support the order of the trial court overruling the motion (no quantum of evidence is required for that order), but whether that order is against the weight of the evidence."[78] Under the manifest weight standard, an appellate court must review, the record, weigh the evidence and all reasonable inferences, consider the credibility of witnesses ad determine whether in resolving conflicts in the evidence, the factfinder clearly lost its way and created a manifest miscarriage of justice.[79]

The Greene County Court of Appeals also determined that an abuse of discretion standard should be applied to review a trial court's decision to adopt, modify or vacate the order of the magistrate. It also indicated a preference for a trial court to conduct an independent *de novo* review when reviewing a magistrate's decision.

Q & A: How important is credibility to an appellate court review?

Credibility is extremely important because it is unlikely an appellate court will reverse the trial court decision if there is some credible evidence.[80] Under a manifest weight of the evidence challenge, the appellate court will not reverse as long as the judgment is supported by some competent credible evidence going to all the essential elements of the case.[81] Further, a reviewing court will presume that "the find-

---

[76]Charles v. Peters, 2016-Ohio-1259, 2016 WL 1178776 (Ohio Ct. App. 2d Dist. Greene County 2016).

[77]See also M.J. v. L.P., 2016-Ohio-7080, 2016 WL 5723752 (Ohio Ct. App. 9th Dist. Medina County 2016).

[78]Charles v. Peters, 2016-Ohio-1259, 2016 WL 1178776, ¶ 10 (Ohio Ct. App. 2d Dist. Greene County 2016).

[79]Charles v. Peters, 2016-Ohio-1259, 2016 WL 1178776, ¶ 10 (Ohio Ct. App. 2d Dist. Greene County 2016), citing Folck v. Redman, 2013-Ohio-3646, 2013 WL 4537103 (Ohio Ct. App. 2d Dist. Clark County 2013).

[80]A.M. v. S.M., 2018-Ohio-247, 2018 WL 542357 (Ohio Ct. App. 9th Dist. Summit County 2018).

[81]C. E. Morris Co. v. Foley Const. Co., 54 Ohio St. 2d 279, 8 Ohio Op. 3d 261, 376 N.E.2d 578 (1978) (syllabus); McKinney v. Brunney, 2014-Ohio-39, 2014 WL 80419 (Ohio Ct. App. 5th Dist. Fairfield County 2014). See also Crawford v. Brandon, 2014-Ohio-3659, 2014 WL 4180286 (Ohio Ct. App. 12th Dist. Butler County 2014) ("[i]t is not the role of the appellate court to substitute its own determination of credibility in place of the trial court." at¶ 15, quoting Weismuller v. Polston, 2012-Ohio-1476, 2012 WL 1107717, ¶ 24 (Ohio Ct. App. 12th Dist. Brown County 2012).)

ings of the trier of fact are correct."[82] "This presumption arises because the trier of fact has the best opportunity to 'view the witnesses and observe their demeanor, gestures and voice inflections and use these observations in weighing the credibility of the proffered testimony.' "[83]

Moreover, "[a] reviewing court should not reverse a decision simply because it holds a different opinion concerning the credibility of the witnesses and evidence submitted before the trial court."[84] Appellate courts can reverse on a finding of an error of law but not "a difference of opinion on credibility of witnesses and evidence."[85]

However, in *McBride v. Mc Bride*,[86] the dissent discussed the multiple factors for determining credibility and pointed out that "seeing and hearing testimony" are not the sole criteria for judging credibility.[87] The factors for analyzing credibility include "1) seeing and hearing firsthand the demeanor of the witness; 2) consistency of the witness on direct, cross and as compared with others testifying about the facts; 3) motive;[88] and 4) believability."[89] "Believability is fundamentally rooted in common sense as to whether or not the nature of circumstances as a whole are likely within the range of known probabilities. When put into the context of all the other circumstances, even testimony that is delivered with sincerity may not have 'believability.' "[90] The appellate court presumes that the findings of the trier of fact are correct because the trial court had the opportunity "to view the witnesses and observe their demeanor, gestures and voice inflections and use these observations in weighing the credibility of

---

[82] State v. Wilson, 113 Ohio St. 3d 382, 2007-Ohio-2202, 865 N.E.2d 1264, ¶ 24 (2007), citing Seasons Coal Co., Inc. v. City of Cleveland, 10 Ohio St. 3d 77, 80-81, 461 N.E.2d 1273, 38 U.C.C. Rep. Serv. 469 (1984). See also M.K. v. J.K., 2015-Ohio-434, 2015 WL 557990 (Ohio Ct. App. 9th Dist. Medina County 2015); Martindale v. Martindale, 2017-Ohio-9266, 102 N.E.3d 19 (Ohio Ct. App. 4th Dist. Athens County 2017).

[83] State v. Wilson, 113 Ohio St. 3d 382, 387, 2007-Ohio-2202, 865 N.E.2d 1264 (2007), citing Seasons Coal Co., Inc. v. City of Cleveland, 10 Ohio St. 3d 77, 80, 461 N.E.2d 1273, 38 U.C.C. Rep. Serv. 469 (1984); Baltes v. Baltes, 2012-Ohio-4890, 2012 WL 5195824 (Ohio Ct. App. 11th Dist. Trumbull County 2012); Bullard v. Alley, 2014-Ohio-1016, 2014 WL 1339719 (Ohio Ct. App. 4th Dist. Pike County 2014); Barrett v. Soltesz, 2015-Ohio-794, 2015 WL 995439 (Ohio Ct. App. 6th Dist. Erie County 2015); F.-S. v. Pacek, 2015-Ohio-4310, 2015 WL 6128507 (Ohio Ct. App. 9th Dist. Medina County 2015); Johnson v. Burke, 2016-Ohio-2947, 2016 WL 2757891 (Ohio Ct. App. 8th Dist. Cuyahoga County 2016).

[84] State v. Wilson, 113 Ohio St. 3d 382, 387, 2007-Ohio-2202, 865 N.E.2d 1264 (2007), citing Seasons Coal Co., Inc. v. City of Cleveland, 10 Ohio St. 3d 77, 81, 461 N.E.2d 1273, 38 U.C.C. Rep. Serv. 469 (1984); see also Crabtree v. Dinsmoor, 2013-Ohio-5797, 2013 WL 6869957 (Ohio Ct. App. 10th Dist. Franklin County 2013).

[85] State v. Wilson, 113 Ohio St. 3d 382, 387, 2007-Ohio-2202, 865 N.E.2d 1264 (2007).

[86] McBride v. McBride, 2012-Ohio-2146, 971 N.E.2d 1007 (Ohio Ct. App. 12th Dist. Butler County 2012).

[87] McBride v. McBride, 2012-Ohio-2146, ¶ 37, 971 N.E.2d 1007 (Ohio Ct. App. 12th Dist. Butler County 2012) (Piper, J., dissenting).

[88] Martin v. Hanood, 2009-Ohio-1501, 2009 WL 825766 (Ohio Ct. App. 7th Dist. Jefferson County 2009).

[89] McBride v. McBride, 2012-Ohio-2146, 971 N.E.2d 1007 (Ohio Ct. App. 12th Dist. Butler County 2012).

[90] McBride v. McBride, 2012-Ohio-2146, ¶ 37, 971 N.E.2d 1007 (Ohio Ct. App. 12th Dist. Butler County 2012).

the proffered testimony."[91] Each of these factors does not translate well on the written page, hence the need to defer to the trial court,who has the best opportunity to evaluate credibility.[92]

Of importance is that a trial court that issues or denies a CPO has determined the credibility of the petitioner and has concluded that there is or is not some competent credible evidence going to all the essential elements of the case. If a trial court indicates in its findings and conclusions that a petitioner's testimony is or is not credible, it is unlikely that an appellate court will reverse the trial court's decision.[93]

Q & A: Does the doctrine of mootness apply to appeals of civil protection orders?

Several appellate jurisdictions have weighed in on this issue. Some courts have held that once a civil protection order has expired, an appeal is moot.[94] The majority view, however, is that an appeal of a civil protection order is not moot even though it has expired, because the issues are capable of repetition, yet evade review,[95] or because potential adverse collateral consequences may occur from the expired order.[96]

---

[91]State v. Wilson, 113 Ohio St. 3d 382, 2007-Ohio-2202, 865 N.E.2d 1264 (2007), quoting Seasons Coal Co., Inc. v. City of Cleveland, 10 Ohio St. 3d 77, 461 N.E.2d 1273, 38 U.C.C. Rep. Serv. 469 (1984).

[92]See Dickson v. Miller, 2012-Ohio-2142, 2012 WL 1664012 (Ohio Ct. App. 5th Dist. Fairfield County 2012), quoting Davis v. Flickinger, 77 Ohio St. 3d 415, 418, 1997-Ohio-260, 674 N.E.2d 1159 (1997).

[93]For eg., Cable v. Cable, 2015-Ohio-4291, 2015 WL 6109531 (Ohio Ct. App. 2d Dist. Darke County 2015). See also Bressler v. Nunemaker, 2017-Ohio-5804, ¶ 9, 2017 WL 2964199 (Ohio Ct. App. 5th Dist. Licking County 2017) (finding that the trial court need not defer to the magistrate's determination regarding witness credibility and may reach its own conclusions).

[94]See, for example, Foster v. Foster, 2011-Ohio-6460, 2011 WL 6296722 (Ohio Ct. App. 10th Dist. Franklin County 2011), cause dismissed, 132 Ohio St. 3d 1467, 2012-Ohio-3141, 970 N.E.2d 968 (2012); Devine-Riley v. Clellan, 2011-Ohio-4367, 2011 WL 3841957 (Ohio Ct. App. 10th Dist. Franklin County 2011); Erbes v. Meyer, 2011-Ohio-3274, 2011 WL 2586349 (Ohio Ct. App. 2d Dist. Montgomery County 2011); Baldridge v. Baldridge, 2011-Ohio-2423, 2011 WL 1936056 (Ohio Ct. App. 2d Dist. Darke County 2011); VanMeter v. VanMeter, 2004-Ohio-3390, 2004 WL 1446055 (Ohio Ct. App. 10th Dist. Franklin County 2004); Hughes v. Hughes, 2007-Ohio-4774, 2007 WL 2696845 (Ohio Ct. App. 11th Dist. Lake County 2007) (overruled by, Fortney v. Willhoite, 2012-Ohio-3024, 2012 WL 2522835 (Ohio Ct. App. 11th Dist. Lake County 2012)); Cyran v. Cyran, 2016-Ohio-7323, 63 N.E.3d 187 (Ohio Ct. App. 2d Dist. Montgomery County 2016), motion to certify allowed, 148 Ohio St. 3d 1408, 2017-Ohio-573, 69 N.E.3d 749 (2017) and appeal allowed, 148 Ohio St. 3d 1409, 2017-Ohio-573, 69 N.E.3d 750 (2017) and judgment aff'd, 152 Ohio St. 3d 484, 2018-Ohio-24, 97 N.E.3d 487 (2018) (discussing mootness based on expiration of order and use of collateral consequences).

[95]Cauwenbergh v. Cauwenbergh, 2007-Ohio-1070, 2007 WL 726951 (Ohio Ct. App. 11th Dist. Ashtabula County 2007);Fortney v. Willhoite, 2012-Ohio-3024, 2012 WL 2522835 (Ohio Ct. App. 11th Dist. Lake County 2012).

[96]See Wilder v. Perna, 174 Ohio App. 3d 586, 592, 2007-Ohio-6635, 883 N.E.2d 1095 (8th Dist. Cuyahoga County 2007) (abrogated by, Cyran v. Cyran, 152 Ohio St. 3d 484, 2018-Ohio-24, 97 N.E.3d 487 (2018)); E.G. v. Ergh, 2014-Ohio-1332, 2014 WL 1345273 (Ohio Ct. App. 9th Dist. Lorain County 2014) (dismissing appeal as moot because appellant stated that he was not subject to any collateral consequences as a result of the CPO, but noting that the court would ordinarily address the issues raised on appeal notwithstanding the expiration of the CPO); D.R. v. J.R., 2013-Ohio-

For example, in *Daugherty v. Cross*,[97] the appellate court noted that although other jurisdictions have held that once the CPO has expired, any appeal is moot, it would decline to do so. Relying on the reasoning set forth in *Smith v. Smith*,[98] the court reasoned that a court may hear an otherwise moot case when the issues are capable of repetition, yet evade review. The court went on to say that "an exception to the mootness doctrine applies in exceptional circumstances when both: 1) the challenged action is too short in duration to be fully litigated before its cessation or expiration, and 2) there is a reasonable expectation that the same complaining party will be subject to the same action again."[99]

Similarly, the Eleventh District Court of Appeals framed the issue the same way in *Cauwenbergh v. Cauwenbergh*.[100] In that case, the duration of the CPO was four months, which was too short a period of time to be reviewed by the court of appeals. Additionally, the docket of the case in the trial court shows that appellee filed for an extension of the CPO, so that appellant would be subject to the same action again.[101]

The appellate court then relied on the Connecticut Supreme Court's finding that "the majority of states have held that such orders are not rendered moot by their expiration, either because of the collateral consequences caused by such orders, or because they are capable of

---

2987, 2013 WL 3486845, ¶ 9 (Ohio Ct. App. 9th Dist. Summit County 2013) (noting that collateral consequences include the effect on one's credit rating, the ability to drive certain vehicles, the ability to obtain a weapons permit and the ability to obtain employment and stating that "[d]ue to the possibility that adverse collateral consequences may occur, the expiration of a civil protection order does not render an error in the imposition of that order moot"); Olson v. Olson, 2016-Ohio-149, 2016 WL 197117 (Ohio Ct. App. 6th Dist. Wood County 2016); R.T. v. J.T., 2015-Ohio-4418, 2015 WL 6449294 (Ohio Ct. App. 9th Dist. Medina County 2015) (noting that collateral consequences can include the effect on one's credit rating, the ability to drive certain vehicles, the ability to obtain a weapons permit, and the ability to obtain employment).

[97] Daugherty v. Cross, 2006-Ohio-5545, 2006 WL 3020258 (Ohio Ct. App. 5th Dist. Richland County 2006).

[98] Smith v. Smith, 2001-Ohio-2139, 2001 WL 929375 (Ohio Ct. App. 3d Dist. Wyandot County 2001).

[99] Daugherty v. Cross, 2006-Ohio-5545, 2006 WL 3020258, *3 (Ohio Ct. App. 5th Dist. Richland County 2006), citing State ex rel. Calvary v. Upper Arlington, 89 Ohio St. 3d 229, 231, 2000-Ohio-142, 729 N.E.2d 1182 (2000). See also Detrick v. Preece, 2013-Ohio-2499, 2013 WL 3089090 (Ohio Ct. App. 3d Dist. Logan County 2013) (noting that, although the CPO had expired, the appeal was not moot because the issue (a CPO for both mother and child) is a factor to consider in any further custody proceedings).

[100] Cauwenbergh v. Cauwenbergh, 2007-Ohio-1070, 2007 WL 726951 (Ohio Ct. App. 11th Dist. Ashtabula County 2007). See also D.R. v. J.R., 2013-Ohio-2987, ¶ 9, 2013 WL 3486845 (Ohio Ct. App. 9th Dist. Summit County 2013) (Considering the collateral consequences to a respondent whose objections were not timely ruled on by the trial court and reversing judgment granting CPO on grounds that although the CPO had expired, it was improper for the trial court to have concluded that the objections were moot and holding that "this matter must be remanded to the trial court for a determination of whether, in light of J.R.'s objections, the protection order was properly granted in the first instance.").

[101] Cauwenbergh v. Cauwenbergh, 2007-Ohio-1070, 2007 WL 726951, *2 (Ohio Ct. App. 11th Dist. Ashtabula County 2007).

repetition, yet evading review."[102] The appellate court then went on to say that the collateral consequences can include the effect on one's credit rating, the ability to drive certain vehicles, the ability to obtain a weapons permit, the ability to obtain employment and the filing of the order in a national registry that is enforceable in 50 states.[103] There are also potential immigration consequences for persons who violate civil protection orders.[104]

On January 4, 2018, the Supreme Court of Ohio decided *Cyran v. Cyran*,[105] finally settling the issue of whether the collateral consequences exception to mootness applies to an appeal of an expired domestic violence civil protection order issued pursuant to RC 3113.31, in the absence of any collateral consequences at the time of the appeal.

In that case, the former wife filed a CPO against her former husband. The court granted the CPO, having found that petitioner was in danger of or had been a victim of domestic violence as defined by statute. The trial court dismissed the objections filed by respondent and adopted the magistrate's order granting the CPO.

Respondent appealed the decision, despite the fact that the CPO had expired two months before the filing of the appeal. Because the CPO had expired, the appellate court issued a "show-cause order asking the parties to explain why the case should not be dismissed as moot because the protection order had expired."[106] Appellant argued that he faced the possibility of collateral consequences with respect to his concealed carry permit and his credit report as well as his ability to obtain housing, drive certain vehicles and obtain future employment.[107] Additionally, he requested that the court adopt the decision of the Eighth District Court of Appeals in *Wilder v. Perna*,[108] in which the court found that "the possibility of collateral consequences

[102] Cauwenbergh v. Cauwenbergh, 2007-Ohio-1070, 2007 WL 726951, *2 (Ohio Ct. App. 11th Dist. Ashtabula County 2007), citing Putman v. Kennedy, 279 Conn. 162, 173-74, 900 A.2d 1256, 1263-64 (2006); see also Wilder v. Perna, 174 Ohio App. 3d 586, 2007-Ohio-6635, 883 N.E.2d 1095 (8th Dist. Cuyahoga County 2007) (abrogated by, Cyran v. Cyran, 152 Ohio St. 3d 484, 2018-Ohio-24, 97 N.E.3d 487 (2018)) (disagrees with the minority view that the expiration of a CPO renders an appeal moot and states, "We disagree with [the minority view] because a conclusion that the expiration of a domestic violence restraining order renders an appeal from that order moot ignores the gravity of these orders for the individuals involved, and is therefore, inconsistent with our developing collateral consequences jurisprudence."); but see Jagow v. Weinstein, 2011-Ohio-2683, 2011 WL 2174995 (Ohio Ct. App. 2d Dist. Montgomery County 2011) (noting that the court denied the appeal as moot after addressing both mootness exceptions and determining that neither applies).

[103] Cauwenbergh v. Cauwenbergh, 2007-Ohio-1070, 2007 WL 726951, *2 (Ohio Ct. App. 11th Dist. Ashtabula County 2007), citing Smith-Lawler v. Lawler, 97 Conn. App. 376, 381, 904 A.2d 1235, 1239 (2006).

[104] Saqr v. Naji, 2017-Ohio-8142, ¶ 22, 2017 WL 4538886 (Ohio Ct. App. 1st Dist. Hamilton County 2017); citing 8 U.S.C.A. § 1227(a)(2)(E)(ii).

[105] Cyran v. Cyran, 152 Ohio St. 3d 484, 2018-Ohio-24, 97 N.E.3d 487 (2018).

[106] Cyran v. Cyran, 152 Ohio St. 3d 484, 485, 2018-Ohio-24, ¶ 3, 97 N.E.3d 487 (2018).

[107] Cyran v. Cyran, 152 Ohio St. 3d 484, 485, 2018-Ohio-24, ¶ 3, 97 N.E.3d 487 (2018).

[108] Wilder v. Perna, 174 Ohio App. 3d 586, 2007-Ohio-6635, 883 N.E.2d 1095 (8th Dist. Cuyahoga County 2007) (abrogated by, Cyran v. Cyran, 152 Ohio St. 3d 484, 2018-Ohio-24, 97 N.E.3d 487 (2018)) (abrogating court finding absent a showing of

is sufficient to support appellate consideration of an expired domestic-violence civil protection order."[109] However, the appellate court dismissed the appeal as moot, having declined to apply the analysis of the Eighth appellate district.

On appeal to the Supreme Court, appellant asserted the following: 1) the collateral consequences exception to mootness applies to an appeal from an expired protection order when the appellant faces possible consequences that may not be ascertainable at the time of the appeal; and, 2) there is a rebuttable presumption that an appeal from an expired protection order is not moot.[110]

The Supreme Court of Ohio accepted the discretionary appeal and noted the conflicts between the appellate jurisdictions. The question presented was "Does the collateral consequences exception to mootness apply to an appeal from an expired protective order when the appellant faces possible collateral consequences that may not be ascertainable at the time of the appeal?"[111]

The Supreme Court held that "in the absence of demonstrated legal consequences, the collateral-consequences exception to the mootness doctrine does not apply to an expired domestic-violence civil protection order."[112] Comparing potential consequences to those imposed by law in traffic and criminal cases, the Supreme Court found that potential collateral consequences resulting from a CPO did not rise to the level of an exception to mootness because "[f]inding a reasonable possibility that a collateral consequence may occur calls for speculation,"[113] and "[s]peculation is insufficient to establish a legally cognizable interest for which a court can order relief using the collateral-consequences exception to the mootness doctrine."[114]

Moreover, the court declined to establish a rebuttable presumption that an appeal from an expired order is not moot based on the language of RC 3113.31 which does not authorize courts to hear appeals of expired orders. However, the court also noted that this was within the purview of the General Assembly, not the Supreme Court.

In her dissent, Justice Kennedy admonished the majority, stressing that proof of collateral consequences beyond a reasonable doubt is not required. Rather, "[c]ollateral consequences are measured by probability or certainty."[115]. Justice Kennedy agreed with appellant's argument that one possible consequence was that a trial court would consider a finding of domestic violence when deciding parental rights.

---

then-existing legal collateral consequences resulting from an expired domestic-violence civil protection order, an appeal of that order is moot).

[109]Cyran v. Cyran, 152 Ohio St. 3d 484, 485, 2018-Ohio-24, ¶ 3, 97 N.E.3d 487 (2018).

[110]Cyran v. Cyran, 152 Ohio St. 3d 484, 486, 2018-Ohio-24, ¶ 5, 97 N.E.3d 487 (2018).

[111]Cyran v. Cyran, 152 Ohio St. 3d 484, 486, 2018-Ohio-24, ¶ 6, 97 N.E.3d 487 (2018).

[112]Cyran v. Cyran, 152 Ohio St. 3d 484, 486, 2018-Ohio-24, ¶ 7, 97 N.E.3d 487 (2018).

[113]Cyran v. Cyran, 152 Ohio St. 3d 484, 488, 2018-Ohio-24, ¶ 11, 97 N.E.3d 487 (2018).

[114]Cyran v. Cyran, 152 Ohio St. 3d 484, 488, 2018-Ohio-24, ¶ 11, 97 N.E.3d 487 (2018).

[115]Cyran v. Cyran, 152 Ohio St. 3d 484, 489, 2018-Ohio-24, ¶ 15, 97 N.E.3d 487

Of significance is that Justice Kennedy focused her analysis on the inequities associated with a parent's inability to exercise his or her fundamental constitutional right to jointly parent children, if denied his or her day in court. "Today, the majority has given a weapon to those who would choose to manipulate parenting proceedings. Just as people race to the courthouse to use an ex parte CPO to get an advantage on residential parenting status before the filing of a divorce or custody action, they will use the majority' opinion to gain an advantage in an ongoing parenting dispute. Based on today's majority opinion, regardless of whether a full-hearing CPO expires or is dismissed, a respondent can never challenge on appeal the finding of domestic violence, and thereby, the respondent is branded forevermore with the taint of being a perpetrator of domestic violence."[116]

In a twist on the mootness argument, the First District Court of Appeals decided *Saqr v. Naji*,[117] where the appellate court differentiated between an appeal from the issuance of the CPO itself, and an appeal from a motion to terminate the CPO.

Relying on *Jagow v. Weinstein*,[118] the appellate court determined that even granting respondent the relief requested, would not eliminate any potential collateral consequences because the underlying protection order would still remain on his record. "In other words, terminating the CPO early would not 'void' it, only 'end' it, and the CPO would remain on the respondent's record even if he had been successful on appeal."[119] Thus, because appellant's challenge was to the motion to terminate, the court determined his assignment of error to be moot.

§ 12:27 Conflicting protection orders[1]

Recently, the Supreme Court of Ohio adopted Sup. R. 10.06, regarding Inter-Court Communication in Domestic Violence and Related Cases. This rule provides that a court issuing a protection order pursuant to RC 2919.26 or RC 3113.31 should make a reasonable effort to determine the existence and terms of any domestic violence civil protection orders, domestic violence temporary protection orders, and orders allocating parental rights and responsibilities issued by another court and involving the same parties. A court issuing an order allocating parental rights and responsibilities should make a reasonable effort to determine the existence and terms of any protection

---

(2018), citing Spencer v. Kemna, 523 U.S. 1, 14-16, 118 S. Ct. 978, 140 L. Ed. 2d 43 (1998).

[116]Cyran v. Cyran, 152 Ohio St. 3d 484, 494, 2018-Ohio-24, ¶ 34, 97 N.E.3d 487 (2018).

[117]Saqr v. Naji, 2017-Ohio-8142, 2017 WL 4538886 (Ohio Ct. App. 1st Dist. Hamilton County 2017).

[118]Jagow v. Weinstein, 2011-Ohio-2683, 2011 WL 2174995 (Ohio Ct. App. 2d Dist. Montgomery County 2011).

[119]Saqr v. Naji, 2017-Ohio-8142, ¶ 23, 2017 WL 4538886 (Ohio Ct. App. 1st Dist. Hamilton County 2017).

[Section 12:27]

[1]See generally, Jane H. Aiken and Jane C. Murphy, Evidence Issues in Domestic Violence Civil Cases, 34 Fam. L.Q. 43, 52 (2000). See also Text § 12:21, Remedies—Orders that grant other relief.

orders issued by another court pursuant to RC 2919.26 and RC 3113.31 and involving the same parties.[2]

To determine the existence and terms of other orders, a court may utilize the Ohio Courts Network, examine publicly available court records involving the same parties from other courts or use any other reasonable mechanism suitable for communicating and sharing public information.[3] A court need not make a record of any communication with another court for this purpose.[4]

If a court issuing such an order becomes aware that another court has issued a conflicting order, the court shall consider, if appropriate, revising its order to avoid conflict between the orders.[5]

A court shall consider and may adopt a local rule of court creating a procedure by which the court may revise its orders.[6]

Finally, this rule is not intended to change the procedures for the modification or termination of a domestic violence CPO pursuant to RC 3113.31(E)(8) or the procedures for filing an NCIC form pursuant to Rule 10 of the Rules of Superintendence.[7]

In many cases, a petitioner may consider several options to enhance his/her protection. Pursuant to RC 3113.31, the petitioner may file for a civil protection order. Additionally, the prosecutor may charge the same offender with the crime of domestic violence and issue the complainant a criminal protection order during the pendency of the criminal case.[8]

RC 3113.31(G) specifically permits a petitioner to utilize RC 3113.31 or any other available civil or criminal remedy. To that end, a petitioner is not foreclosed from utilizing the remedies contained in both the civil and criminal domestic violence statutes.

Q & A: Can a petitioner request both a civil protection order and a criminal protection order based on the same incident of domestic violence?

It depends on the order in which the protection orders are issued. If a petitioner is first granted a civil protection order, a subsequent criminal protection order should not invalidate the civil protection order. Nothing in the civil domestic violence statute suggests this possibility. If the legislature intended this, it would have specifically provided for it in the statute.

On the other hand, RC 2919.26(E) provides that a temporary protection order is effective until the disposition of the underlying criminal case or upon the issuance of a civil protection order or consent agreement, arising out of the same conduct that is the basis of the criminal complaint. Thus, if the criminal protection order was issued first, a

[2]Sup. R. 10.06(A)(1).

[3]Sup. R. 10.06(A)(2).

[4]Sup. R. 10.06(A)(3).

[5]Sup. R. 10.06(B)(1).

[6]Sup. R. 10.06(B)(2).

[7]Sup. R. 10.06(B)(3).

[8]See RC 2919.25, RC 2919.26.

civil protection order will effectively terminate the criminal order.[9] However, the underlying criminal action will remain undisturbed.

Disposition of the criminal case has been interpreted by the various courts to mean at the time of sentence or at the termination of probation. At least one Ohio court has addressed this issue. In *State v. Collins*,[10] the Meigs County Court of Appeals stated that a temporary protection order is effective only until disposition of the underlying criminal action. The court determined that "temporary protection orders issued pursuant to [RC 2919.26(E)] do not survive past the date of the judgment of conviction and sentence in the underlying criminal action."[11]

Of significance is that the *Collins* court also noted that a court may order a defendant to obey similar victim protection provisions as a condition of probation. Many courts have issued new protection orders that last through probation. Other courts have merely issued "no contact" orders as conditions of probation, which are not enforceable by the police. However, should the perpetrator violate these orders, probation may be revoked. According to the *Collins* court, a failure to obey the conditions of probation results in the imposition of the suspended sentence or a finding of contempt. In addition, if the violation of the terms of probation constitutes a new crime, the state may prosecute the defendant for the new crime.

Criminal protection orders issued in the underlying criminal action also terminate upon the issuance of a civil protection order under RC 3113.31 if the order arises out of the same incident.[12] The statute is silent as to whether that means upon the issuance of the ex parte order or the protection order issued after the full hearing. Because an ex parte order only remains effective until the full hearing (usually a period of seven to ten court days), it is probable that the legislative intent was for the criminal protection order to expire upon the issuance of a civil protection or the approval of a consent entry after the full hearing.

Of importance is that the Supreme Court standard forms provide that a petitioner requesting a civil protection order must notify the court of any pending or past civil or criminal cases.[13]

Q & A: A party requests a CPO under RC 3113.31 against her boyfriend. Unbeknownst to her, he sought a civil protection order against her based on the same facts under RC 2903.214? Can the courts consolidate the hearings in one court so as to avoid conflicting civil protection orders?

It is unclear whether the courts can consolidate the hearings into one case number and before one court. A CPO issued under RC 3113.31

[9]See also State v. Copp, 2003-Ohio-5399, 2003 WL 22318519 (Ohio Ct. App. 2d Dist. Montgomery County 2003).

[10]State v. Collins, 1997 WL 426150 (Ohio Ct. App. 4th Dist. Meigs County 1997).

[11]State v. Collins, 1997 WL 426150, *2 (Ohio Ct. App. 4th Dist. Meigs County 1997). See also Allan v. Allan, 2014-Ohio-5039, 2014 WL 6065710 (Ohio Ct. App. 8th Dist. Cuyahoga County 2014) (noting, in dicta, that a TPO is dissolved at the close of a criminal case, which in this case, occurred at the time of sentencing).

[12]See RC 2919.26(E).

[13]See Sup. R. Form 10.01-D.

is granted by the domestic relations court of the court of common pleas if the county has such a court; otherwise, the court is the court of common pleas if the county has no domestic relations division.[14] However, RC 2903.214 (A)(1) appears to be more restrictive, requiring that a petitioner file for a CPO in the court of common pleas of the county which the person to be protected resides.

Assuming that both family and non-family or household members are permitted to file the petitions under RC 2903.214, boyfriends/girlfriends (if cohabiting) may be permitted to seek protection in either court. Since the issues are the same and the parties are identical, it appears logical that one court should hear both cases. Since both statutes address mutual protection orders, it is likely that such provisions apply to the facts in this case, thus, permitting one of the courts to treat the later filed petition as a cross petition as is contemplated by RC 3113.31(E)(4) and RC 2903.214(E)(3).

A motion for one of the courts to relinquish jurisdiction over the action and the parties and transfer its case to the other court would be one way for this to be achieved.

Another way that this might be accomplished is to apply the jurisdictional priority rule which provides that "[a]s between [state] courts of concurrent jurisdiction, the tribunal whose power is first invoked by the institution of prior proceedings acquires jurisdiction, to the exclusion of all other tribunals, to adjudicate upon the whole issue and to settle the rights of the parties." * * * "In general, the jurisdictional priority rule applies when the causes of action are the same in both cases, and if the first case does not involve the same cause of action or the same parties as the second case, the first case will not prevent the second."[15]

Q & A: If both a criminal and a civil protection order are issued, which order controls when the terms of the orders conflict?

It depends. RC 2919.26(E) was written to avoid this type of conflict, and provides that a civil protection order issued after the issuance of a criminal protection order supercedes the criminal protection order. However, if the civil order is entered first, both the civil and criminal orders may be valid and possibly conflicting. For example, if the criminal protection order mandates no contact with all family or household members and the civil order indicates that the respondent is entitled to access with the children, conflicting orders exist. Law enforcement officials may be hesitant to enforce one or both or the orders. The court may be reluctant to hold the perpetrator in contempt for the violation of an order. The prosecutor may not charge the defendant for a violation under these circumstances.

Since the domestic violence statutes are silent regarding which protection order controls when the civil order is issued first, the provisions of the criminal order should control, unless the civil protection

[14] RC 3113.31(A)(2).

[15] Curington v. Moon, 2009-Ohio-3013, 2009 WL 1800373, *3 (Ohio Ct. App. 2d Dist. Montgomery County 2009); quoting State ex rel. Toledo Blade Co. v. Seneca Cty. Bd. of Commrs., 120 Ohio St. 3d 372, 376, 2008-Ohio-6253, 899 N.E.2d 961, 967, 37 Media L. Rep. (BNA) 1007 (2008).

order provisions are more restrictive and incorporate the criminal provisions.[16] However, most courts decide this on a case-by-case basis depending on which case is scheduled to be heard first, which order contains more restrictive provisions regarding safety issues, and whether the civil order temporarily resolves visitation and/or custody issues over which the criminal court does not have subject matter jurisdiction.[17]

Sometimes, there are strategic reasons for issuing both orders. Issuing a criminal protection order where there is already a civil order serves to:

> reinforce the criminal nature of the offense, and can give the criminal courts more leverage to protect the victim's safety. In addition, service of a criminal court order on the defendant may be easier than a civil order because the defendant is usually before the criminal court at the time of issuance.[18]

Although a victim may elect to pursue both civil and criminal remedies,[19] the victim must be informed of the differences between them. Civil and criminal orders differ in the nature of the relief available, the procedure for issuance, the length of time they are effective, and, most importantly, the court leverage over violations and the police enforcement of the orders.

To avoid potential conflicts in protection orders, the new Supreme Court standard forms require the petitioner filing for a civil protection order to indicate whether there are other past or present cases involving the petitioner, the respondent, and any of their family or household members.[20] This information will enable judges to craft orders that do not conflict with each other. Less ambiguity in the orders also enables police officers to better enforce the terms of current protection orders.

Q & A: What if a civil protection order conflicts with an earlier divorce and/or custody/visitation order issued by the domestic relations court/juvenile court?

It depends. It is clear that, with regard to safety issues, the civil protection order controls.[21] Likewise, the civil protection order should take precedence over custody/visitation orders until those orders are modified in the underlying divorce or custody action. However, it is important to notify the court of prior existing orders so that the court has the opportunity to make well-reasoned modifications and write

[16]See, e.g., In re William T., 172 Cal. App. 3d 790, 218 Cal. Rptr. 420 (5th Dist. 1985).

[17]See City of Rocky River v. Taylor, 2000 WL 193234 (Ohio Ct. App. 8th Dist. Cuyahoga County 2000).

[18]Janet Carter et al., Family Violence Prevention Fund, Domestic Violence: The Crucial Role of the Judge in Criminal Court Cases, A National Model for Judicial Education 85 (1992).

[19]See RC 3113.31(G).

[20]Sup. R. 10.01(B), Sup. R. Form 10.01-D.

[21]See In re Newsome, 2008-Ohio-2132, 2008 WL 1934428, *6 (Ohio Ct. App. 11th Dist. Ashtabula County 2008) (noting that if children visited father in jail, it would be a violation of the CPO and its not worth focusing on "something that can't happen unless a court says it can happen and not this court. The CPO court.").

them into any order entered.[22] If the police are given conflicting orders, they may choose to enforce neither order or enforce only the most recent order.

Of importance is that RC 3113.31 specifically states that the court may not make an award of support, custody, or visitation in a civil protection order if another court has already determined or is determining that issue.[23] Additionally, any order under RC 3113.31(E)(1)(d) or RC 3113.31(E)(1)(e) shall terminate on the date that a court in a divorce, dissolution of marriage, or legal separation brought by the petitioner or respondent issues a custody, visitation, or support order or on the date that a juvenile court issues such an order.[24]

Q & A: What if terms of a CPO conflict with a subsequently issued divorce decree?

A subsequent divorce entry must clarify whether the terms of a previously issued civil protection order are still in effect.[25] If this is not done by way of a modification of the protection order and a new 10-A form at the time of the divorce, a respondent may be exposed to prosecution for violating the civil protection order.[26]

Q & A: Does a criminal protection order take precedence over a domestic relations court's custody or visitation order?

No. At the outset, a municipal court is without jurisdiction to enter a custody or visitation order. Under RC 3105.65(B) and Civ.R. 75(I), the domestic relations court or common pleas court that originally rendered the divorce retains continuing jurisdiction over matters relating to the custody, care and support of children.[27] If a complainant files criminal domestic violence charges against his/her ex-spouse and the ex-spouse has visitation pursuant to a divorce decree, the criminal protection order issued by the court in the criminal case may not change the visitation award.[28]

However, the criminal protection order may contain a "no contact" provision.[29] The inclusion of such a provision where the minor child is

---

[22]See Sup. R. Form 10.01-D which authorizes a petitioner to so inform the court.

[23]See RC 3113.31(E)(1)(d), RC 3113.31(E)(1)(e); see also Text § 11:15, Ex parte protection orders—Available relief—Orders allocating parental rights and responsibilities; Text § 12:15, Remedies—Orders allocating parental rights and responsibilities. But cf. In re Salgado, 53 S.W.3d 752 (Tex. App. El Paso 2001).

[24]See RC 3113.31(E)(3)(b).

[25]See Devault v. Devault, 2004-Ohio-976, 2004 WL 397134 (Ohio Ct. App. 5th Dist. Ashland County 2004).

[26]See, e.g., State v. Dean, 2002-Ohio-3030, 2002 WL 1376032 (Ohio Ct. App. 7th Dist. Columbiana County 2002).

[27]See, e.g., Addams v. State ex rel. Hubbell, 104 Ohio St. 475, 135 N.E. 667 (1922), rev'd, 263 U.S. 64, 44 S. Ct. 86, 68 L. Ed. 165 (1923); Corbett v. Corbett, 123 Ohio St. 76, 9 Ohio L. Abs. 58, 174 N.E. 10 (1930); Van Divort v. Van Divort, 165 Ohio St. 141, 59 Ohio Op. 207, 134 N.E.2d 715, 62 A.L.R.2d 538 (1956).

[28]City of Rocky River v. Taylor, 2000 WL 193234 (Ohio Ct. App. 8th Dist. Cuyahoga County 2000) ("the General Assembly has not conferred upon the municipal courts jurisdiction to rule on matters of visitation").

[29]See, e.g., City of Columbus v. Kostrevski, 1993 WL 51127 (Ohio Ct. App. 10th Dist. Franklin County 1993) (court of appeals affirmed trial court despite fact that conflicting orders existed, where defendant had a domestic relations order permitting her to call children and a criminal protection order prohibiting contact with her

a protected party pursuant to the temporary protection order effectively restricts the parent from exercising his/her visitation rights. Counsel has a duty to inform the criminal court of a conflicting domestic relations court order. It may be necessary to specifically exclude a child subject to another court order from the restrictions of the criminal temporary protection order.

Q & A: What if a civil protection order includes a child as a protected family or household member and then awards the respondent visitation with that child?

This scenario also creates potentially conflicting concerns. Where the petitioner is granted a civil protection order that names the child as a protected person and then includes a provision that the respondent shall stay away from the family or household members named in the order, an award of visitation in a subsequent divorce action creates conflicting terms.[30]

An additional concern occurs when the subject of the protection order has a visitation order and is charged with a violation of the protection order where the alleged violation is a call to the home to arrange visitation. For example, in *City of Cleveland v. Rogers*,[31] the appellant was subject to a civil protection order that ordered him to refrain from abusing either mother or child and prohibited any contact with mother. Subsequently, a visitation order was granted him in juvenile court. A voicemail message to the mother of his child regarding visitation was the basis of a criminal prosecution for violating the civil protection order. The Cuyahoga County Court of Appeals reversed the trial court's conviction, and excluded any matters relating to the child by holding that the fact that the protection order stated that all issues of "custody, visitation, and support [of Christina] shall be addressed in Juvenile Court. That language, read in conjunction with the juvenile court order . . . lends itself to a reasonable interpretation by Rogers that visitation matters fell outside of the scope of the protection order and that the order authorized him to arrange visitations of

husband).

[30]See, e.g., Rush v. Rush, 1999 WL 1044482 (Ohio Ct. App. 8th Dist. Cuyahoga County 1999) (had petitioner's CPO been granted, lower court would have had discretion to order husband to stay away from family or household members named in the order, and order would have necessarily restricted visitation by implication); see also City of Toledo v. Eissa, 2003-Ohio-3425, 2003 WL 21489426 (Ohio Ct. App. 6th Dist. Lucas County 2003) (illustrates the conflict and consequences that exist); State v. Price, 118 Ohio St. 3d 144, 2008-Ohio-1974, 886 N.E.2d 852 (2008) (Supreme Court ruled that a divorce decree can modify a CPO beyond the sections of the CPO that concern parental rights and responsibilities); see also Text § 12:23, Duration of a civil protection order.

[31]City of Cleveland v. Rogers, 2002-Ohio-3547, 2002 WL 1501044 (Ohio Ct. App. 8th Dist. Cuyahoga County 2002); see also State v. Price, 2006-Ohio-3856, 2006 WL 2105855 (Ohio Ct. App. 2d Dist. Montgomery County 2006), judgment rev'd, 118 Ohio St. 3d 144, 2008-Ohio-1974, 886 N.E.2d 852 (2008) (appellant argued that he did not violate the CPO by having contact with petitioner and the son out of necessity, since the final divorce decree authorized him to have visitation and the divorce decree necessarily supersedes the no contact, previously the CPO. The court held that the decree authorized the defendant to respond to visitation arrangements authorized by Mrs. Price. It did not authorize other contacts unrelated to arranged visitation permitted at her discretion.).

Christina with Sharp."[32] To avoid such problems, it is important for counsel to either note in the protection order that the "no contact" provisions are subject to modifications as contained in the visitation provision or not name the child as a protected party.

Q & A: If a victim decides to pursue both a civil protection order action and a criminal action based on the same incident of domestic violence, does that raise either double jeopardy or collateral estoppel concerns?[33]

Nothing in the civil protection order statute precludes a petitioner from electing to pursue both civil and criminal remedies for the same incident of domestic violence.[34] In fact, "[s]ome judges recommend that victims of serious domestic violence consider pursuing their cases both civilly and criminally, at least in cases where there has been aggravated assault and battery or other felonious behavior."[35]

The Fifth Amendment to the United States Constitution precludes a criminal defendant from being placed in jeopardy by providing protection against a second prosecution for the same offense after an acquittal or conviction and against multiple punishments for the same offense.[36] A civil protection order proceeding is not a criminal proceeding, nor is the action of obtaining a civil protection order a criminal offense. The protections of the Double Jeopardy Clause are limited to criminal proceedings. Because civil protection order actions are civil in character and the relief available is remedial rather than punitive in nature and because all proceedings must be conducted in accordance with the Rules of Civil Procedure,[37] double jeopardy does not apply to a criminal proceeding arising from the same incident of violence.

The doctrine of collateral estoppel is contained within the constitutional guarantee against double jeopardy. Collateral estoppel means that "when an issue of ultimate fact has once been determined by a valid and final judgment, that issue cannot again be litigated between the same parties in any future proceeding."[38]

Additionally, the interest in preventing further injury to the victim in the civil context is distinct and separate from the state interest in

[32]City of Cleveland v. Rogers, 2002-Ohio-3547, 2002 WL 1501044, *3 (Ohio Ct. App. 8th Dist. Cuyahoga County 2002).

[33]See also Text § 13:13, Court enforcement of civil protection orders—Double jeopardy concerns.

[34]See RC 3113.31(G); see also Kitchen v. Kitchen, 2001 WL 279026 (Ohio Ct. App. 12th Dist. Madison County 2001); Hoff v. Brown, 2001 WL 876228, *4 (Ohio Ct. App. 5th Dist. Stark County 2001) (the court determined that the "wording of RC 3113.31(G) was intended in part to preclude alleged domestic violence perpetrators named in a C.P.O. petition from utilizing the doctrine of res judicata in this manner to defeat the legislative purpose of protecting domestic violence victims.").

[35]Peter Finn & Sarah Colson, National Institute of Justice, Civil Protection Orders: Legislation, Current Court Practice and Enforcement 3 (1990).

[36]See State v. Schultz, 1996 WL 71004 (Ohio Ct. App. 6th Dist. Wood County 1996); see also Ch 12 Court Enforcement of Civil Protection Orders and Related Issues.

[37]RC 3113.31(G).

[38]State v. Vanselow, 61 Ohio Misc. 2d 1, 5, 572 N.E.2d 269 (Mun. Ct. 1991).

prosecuting criminal acts.[39] Because a civil protection order proceeding is distinct from a criminal action, the theory of collateral estoppel is not applicable.[40]

The issue was raised in *State v. Petrusch*,[41] but the court noted that, because the defendant failed to raise the issue in the trial court, he was precluded from raising the issue on appeal. In that case, the petitioner obtained a civil protection order. At the full hearing, the respondent was found to have committed domestic violence. He was also prosecuted for domestic violence under RC 2919.25 based on the same incident. He appealed on the basis that the criminal prosecution in the municipal court, after previously being sanctioned in domestic relations court, was double jeopardy.

Collateral estoppel does not apply to that fact pattern because the parties are not the same in a criminal domestic violence action and a civil protection order proceeding. In the civil protection order action, the victim files for the protection order against the respondent. In the criminal action, it is the state or city charging the defendant. The victim becomes only a witness for the state or city.

The issue was also raised in *Cleveland v. Hogan*,[42] where the defendant moved to dismiss criminal domestic violence charges against him because his wife had failed to prevail in a civil protection order action in the domestic relations court. He argued that, since both actions arose from the same incident, his wife's unsuccessful civil domestic violence action precluded a prosecution under the doctrines of double jeopardy and collateral estoppel.

The trial court noted that the wife's civil protection order action was previously litigated and involved the same incident as the present criminal prosecution. However, the court first determined that double jeopardy, which applies only to proceedings which are essentially criminal in nature, did not attach in this case because, as is true in most civil actions, the civil proceeding did not carry criminal sanctions.[43]

The court then found that the doctrine of collateral estoppel did not apply to the fact pattern because there was no privity between the parties in both proceedings. The pivotal question to be answered was whether the complainant and the city of Cleveland were in privity with one another. The court held that "[f]or a nonparty to be considered in privity to a party in a prior proceeding, for collateral estoppel purposes, the rights of the party in the pending action must

[39] Jennifer Black, The Double Jeopardy Dilemma in Combating Domestic Violence: A Solution in United States v. Dixon, 33 U. Louisville J. Fam. L. 911, 925 (1995); see also Janet C. MacDonald, Ohio Revised Code Section 3113.31 and the Constitution: Ohio's Statutory Response to Domestic Violence and its Double Jeopardy Infirmity, 19 U. Dayton L. Rev. 317 (1993).

[40] See also Cleveland v. Hogan, 92 Ohio Misc. 2d 34, 699 N.E.2d 1020 (Mun. Ct. 1998).

[41] State v. Petrusch, 1995 WL 737509 (Ohio Ct. App. 2d Dist. Montgomery County 1995).

[42] Cleveland v. Hogan, 92 Ohio Misc. 2d 34, 699 N.E.2d 1020 (Mun. Ct. 1998); see also People v. Wouk, 317 Ill. App. 3d 33, 250 Ill. Dec. 603, 739 N.E.2d 64 (1st Dist. 2000).

[43] Cleveland v. Hogan, 92 Ohio Misc. 2d 34, 39, 699 N.E.2d 1020 (Mun. Ct. 1998).

have been presented and adjudicated in the prior proceeding or the nonparty must have controlled or participated in the litigation in the prior proceeding."[44] The court relied on the fact that the city of Cleveland could not have participated in the action in domestic relations court; did not have knowledge of the prior civil action; and even if the City was placed on notice of the existence of the civil protection order action, there was no action that it could take or was required to take.

Q & A: Does the doctrine of res judicata apply to civil protection order actions?[45]

Res judicata, or claim preclusion, is a doctrine that limits a litigant to one opportunity to litigate aspects of the case to prevent inconsistent results and multiplicity of suits and to promote finality and judicial economy. "The doctrine of res judicata acts to bar claims previously adjudicated in full (historically called estoppel by judgment in Ohio) as well as issues that have been previously adjudicated between the same parties (generally known as collateral estoppel)."[46]

Res judicata has come up in the context of civil protection orders. For example, in *Ruedele v. Kiefer*,[47] the plaintiff appealed the judgment of the trial court partitioning the parties' real property and awarding each party a sum of money for conversion and breach of contract. The appellant argued that the claims were barred by res judicata since the claims could have been raised in the civil protection order action. The appellate court stated that:

> In determining the civil protection action, the trial court was without authority to determine the claims raised by appellee in her counterclaim [in Common Pleas Court]. RC 3113.31(E)(1) specifies the types of relief a court may grant in making a civil protection order, and does not give the court the authority to award damages in a civil action for breach of contract or unjust enrichment, or to partition real estate. . . . Further, Subsection (G) specifically provides that the remedies provided by [section] 3113.31 of the Revised Code are in addition to any other available civil remedies.[48]

---

[44]Cleveland v. Hogan, 92 Ohio Misc. 2d 34, 42, 699 N.E.2d 1020 (Mun. Ct. 1998).

[45]See also Text § 13:13, Court enforcement of civil protection orders—Double jeopardy concerns; Rice v. Lewis, 2013-Ohio-5890, 2013 WL 6989772 (Ohio Ct. App. 4th Dist. Scioto County 2013) (discussion of res judicata relative to several dismissed SOOPOs and a custody action based on same underlying facts as the abuse and neglect complaint in juvenile court); see also Text 9:5.

[46]Walton v. Walton, 2004-Ohio-7151, 2004 WL 3017265, *2 (Ohio Ct. App. 6th Dist. Wood County 2004).

[47]Ruedele v. Kiefer, 1993 WL 438787 (Ohio Ct. App. 5th Dist. Licking County 1993), cause dismissed, 68 Ohio St. 3d 1444, 626 N.E.2d 686 (1994); but see Bumgardner v. Bumgardner, 2005-Ohio-3445, 2005 WL 1545790 (Ohio Ct. App. 12th Dist. Butler County 2005) (dismissal of CPO based on res judicata was warranted); see also Cleveland v. Hogan, 92 Ohio Misc. 2d 34, 699 N.E.2d 1020 (Mun. Ct. 1998) (noting that double jeopardy only applies in criminal proceedings and that most civil actions do not carry criminal sanctions).

[48]Ruedele v. Kiefer, 1993 WL 438787, *2 (Ohio Ct. App. 5th Dist. Licking County 1993), cause dismissed, 68 Ohio St. 3d 1444, 626 N.E.2d 686 (1994); see also Kitchen v. Kitchen, 2001 WL 279026, *1 (Ohio Ct. App. 12th Dist. Madison County 2001) ("[D]octrines of res judicata, estoppel by judgment and collateral estoppel do not preclude a party to a divorce from filing a petition for a civil domestic violence protec-

Similarly, in *Walton v. Walton*,[49] appellant appealed the issuance of a CPO for the wife. Appellant filed a complaint for divorce against appellee. Possession of the marital residence was addressed in a divorce motion prior to the issuance of the CPO.

On appeal, appellant asserted that the allegations raised in the petition for CPO had been previously litigated in the parties' pending domestic relations case. Appellant argued that, based on the doctrine of res judicata, the proceedings in the domestic relations case involved whether appellant had been abusive to appellee, thereby precluding the issue of abuse from being re-litigated in the CPO action.

The appellate court relied on the Supreme Court of Ohio's reasoning in *Felton v. Felton* to explain that a court is not precluded by statute from issuing a civil protection order even though the parties' underlying divorce action prohibited them from harassing each other. "While the facts in *Felton* differ slightly from those of this case, what is significant is the *Felton* court's holding that there are times when the general civil remedy available through a protection order issued pursuant to RC 3113.31 is necessary during the pendency of a divorce."[50] The domestic relations court's decision on the use of the residence was not res judicata precluding appellee from seeking a CPO even though issues of physical abuse had been raised in the domestic relations court.[51]

In *Hoff v. Brown*,[52] Brown filed a divorce against Hoff. They were divorced on Hoff's counterclaim after Brown dismissed his complaint. Subsequent to the divorce, Hoff filed for a CPO. Brown also filed a CPO. Both parties were granted CPOs against the other.

On appeal, Hoff argued that the allegations in Brown's petition for protection order against her were barred by the doctrine of res judicata, because they constituted counterclaims which should have been asserted by Brown in the divorce action. The appellate court disagreed.

The Stark County Court of Appeals noted that the action involved Ohio's domestic violence statute in which the remedies provided are specifically "in addition to and not in lieu of any other available civil or criminal remedies."[53] The court then held that "[o]ur analysis of Ohio's civil domestic violence statutory scheme leads us to conclude that the aforesaid wording of RC 3113.31(G) was intended in part to preclude alleged domestic violence perpetrators named in a C.P.O. pe-

tion order."); Walton v. Walton, 2004-Ohio-7151, 2004 WL 3017265, *2 (Ohio Ct. App. 6th Dist. Wood County 2004) (court held that the doctrine of res judicata does not apply as there are times when the general remedy available through a civil protection order is necessary during the pendency of a divorce), citing Felton v. Felton, 79 Ohio St. 3d 34, 1997-Ohio-302, 679 N.E.2d 672 (1997).

[49] Walton v. Walton, 2004-Ohio-7151, 2004 WL 3017265, *2 (Ohio Ct. App. 6th Dist. Wood County 2004).

[50] Walton v. Walton, 2004-Ohio-7151, 2004 WL 3017265, *2 (Ohio Ct. App. 6th Dist. Wood County 2004).

[51] Walton v. Walton, 2004-Ohio-7151, 2004 WL 3017265 (Ohio Ct. App. 6th Dist. Wood County 2004).

[52] Hoff v. Brown, 2001 WL 876228 (Ohio Ct. App. 5th Dist. Stark County 2001).

[53] Hoff v. Brown, 2001 WL 876228, *4 (Ohio Ct. App. 5th Dist. Stark County 2001), citing RC 3113.31(G).

tition from utilizing the doctrine of res judicata in this manner to defeat the legislative purpose of protecting domestic violence victims."[54] Even if, theoretically, the claims in a protection order petition could have been earlier raised, the reason for asserting them in the petition is not to seek unnecessary repeat judgments against the perpetrator, rather it is to ensure the safety of the victim. Thus, the trial court did not err in declining to find Brown's allegations in his petition for protective order barred by the doctrine of res judicata."[55]

These cases reinforce the position that the doctrine of res judicata should not apply to the issuing of orders under both the civil and criminal domestic violence statutes.[56] So long as the statute provides a petitioner with the option of utilizing various civil or criminal remedies, a petitioner's protection order action is not barred by either double jeopardy or collateral estoppel. Nor is a petitioner's civil action barred by res judicata.[57]

On the other hand, other courts have considered the doctrine of res judicata when one party requests a second civil protection order based on the same allegations set forth in the first petition after the first CPO was dismissed.[58]

Still other courts have considered the doctrine of res judicata as a bar to issues that were not raised in an appeal. For example, in *Parker v. Jamison*,[59] mother filed for a CPO against father. The trial court granted her CPO and then denied father's motion to vacate or modify the order. Father appealed the denial of his motion to vacate or modify the final CPO and argued that the trial court erred in issuing the CPO that allocated parental rights when the court had already allocated parental rights in the divorce proceeding.

The appellate court noted that father had failed to timely appeal the CPO. "If a final appealable order is not timely appealed, all matters that could have been reviewed had an appeal been taken become res judicata and are not reviewable in a related or subsequent proceeding or appeal."[60]

Finally, other courts have considered res judicata when a CPO was

[54]See also Skiles v. Dearth, 2000 WL 1838747 (Ohio Ct. App. 2d Dist. Clark County 2000) (discussing when not to apply res judicata); but see Tortorello v. Tortorello, 113 Haw. 432, 153 P.3d 1117 (2007).

[55]Hoff v. Brown, 2001 WL 876228, *4 (Ohio Ct. App. 5th Dist. Stark County 2001).

[56]See Cleveland v. Hogan, 92 Ohio Misc. 2d 34, 699 N.E.2d 1020 (Mun. Ct. 1998); see also Hoff v. Brown, 2001 WL 876228 (Ohio Ct. App. 5th Dist. Stark County 2001); Genari v. Genari, 2001-Ohio-1524, 2001 WL 848569 (Ohio Ct. App. 2d Dist. Greene County 2001) (appellant waived the defense of res judicata at the appellate level because he failed to plead it at the full hearing).

[57]See also Eichenberger v. Eichenberger, 1993 WL 460570 (Ohio Ct. App. 10th Dist. Franklin County 1993) (holding that the pendency of a divorce does not preclude the filing of a civil protection order).

[58]See Bumgardner v. Bumgardner, 2005-Ohio-3445, 2005 WL 1545790 (Ohio Ct. App. 12th Dist. Butler County 2005) (holding that the dismissal of the CPO based on res judicata was warranted.).

[59]Parker v. Jamison, 2003-Ohio-7295, 2003 WL 24135688 (Ohio Ct. App. 4th Dist. Scioto County 2003).

[60]Parker v. Jamison, 2003-Ohio-7295, 2003 WL 24135688, *3 (Ohio Ct. App. 4th Dist. Scioto County 2003), quoting Jeffers v. Jeffers, 2001 WL 118530, *3 (Ohio Ct.

granted ex parte but then dismissed and a CSPO was later filed by the same party raising the same issues and many of the same incidents.[61]

Q & A: Does res judicata apply where a party obtains a civil protection order in one county and the other party is denied a protection order from another county?

Venue concerns may create particular res judicata problems in domestic violence cases.[62] Besides cases in which one party relocates to a different county,[63] victims of domestic violence often leave the county in which they permanently reside in order to seek protection in a county in which they temporarily reside. Thus, courts may begin to see an increase in dismissals/appeals alleging that res judicata should be applied. Finally, the defense may also be raised as a way to limit forum shopping and conflicting orders.

For example, in *Sterling v. Sterling*,[64] the Fairfield County Court of Appeals remanded the matter to the trial court to rule on the issue of res judicata. Appellant challenged the issuance of a civil protection order entered on behalf of the ex-wife in Fairfield County against him because the issue had already been litigated in another county. The Muskingum County Common Pleas Court had previously issued appellant a protection order and at the full hearing "denied the parties' petitions for civil protection order . . . and found no basis for a civil protection order in Muskingum County."[65]

The appellate court noted that the record contained witness testimony that indicated that appellee's witnesses testified to the

App. 10th Dist. Franklin County 2001).

[61]See Irwin v. Murray, 2006-Ohio-1633, 2006 WL 832830 (Ohio Ct. App. 6th Dist. Lucas County 2006) (pointing out that actions brought under RC 3113.31 and RC 2903.214 are "separate tools in Ohio's comprehensive protection legislation and offer distinct forms of relief," at 2.); see also Moore v. Moore, 2003-Ohio-3789, 2003 WL 21658466 (Ohio Ct. App. 9th Dist. Wayne County 2003) (holding that res judicata did not preclude wife's CPO even though her previous petition for restraining order against husband in West Virginia had been denied. The Court based its decision on events occurring after the judgment in West Virginia had been entered); see also White v. Bain, 2008 SD 52, 752 N.W.2d 203 (S.D. 2008) (citing the reasoning in *Bumgardner*, but finding that res judicata did not bar the second petition because of subsequent acts that were also alleged in that petition.); Goldfuss v. Traxler, 2008-Ohio-6186, 2008 WL 5053451 (Ohio Ct. App. 3d Dist. Wyandot County 2008).

[62]See Civ.R. 3(B)(10); Text § 10:13, Jurisdiction and venue—In domestic violence cases.

[63]See Bach v. Crawford, 2003-Ohio-1255, 2003 WL 1193783 (Ohio Ct. App. 2d Dist. Montgomery County 2003).

[64]Sterling v. Sterling, 2002-Ohio-4997, 2002 WL 31111778 (Ohio Ct. App. 5th Dist. Fairfield County 2002); see also Wood v. Wood, 2003-Ohio-5587, 2003 WL 22389875 (Ohio Ct. App. 5th Dist. Coshocton County 2003); Duncan v. Duncan, 2010-Ohio-5334, 2010 WL 4345722 (Ohio Ct. App. 5th Dist. Muskingum County 2010) (despite appeal claiming that it was error to consider a particular incident in ruling on a petition for a CPO because the same evidence had been considered and dismissed in Licking County court, the appellate court noted that because appellee voluntarily dismissed the Licking County action prior to adjudication, *res judicata* did not apply; the court left open whether *res judicata* would have been a bar had the trial court dismissed the action).

[65]Sterling v. Sterling, 2002-Ohio-4997, 2002 WL 31111778, *3 (Ohio Ct. App. 5th Dist. Fairfield County 2002).

same issue as in the Muskingum County proceedings.[66] It stated that, under the doctrine of res judicata, "[a] valid, final judgment rendered upon the merits bars all subsequent actions based upon any claim arising out of the transaction or occurrence that was the subject matter of the previous action."[67]

In remanding the case to the trial court, the Fairfield County Court of Appeals determined that "[w]ithout the record of the Muskingum County proceedings before it, the trial court sub judice could not determine what the Muskingum County civil protection order petitions involved and what the Court of Common Pleas of Muskingum County heard in evidence in order to rule on appellant's motion to dismiss on the basis of res judicata."[68]

In this case, it is unclear whether the appellee also sought a protection order in Muskingum County or whether she only defended his petition against her. Unfortunately, the decision fails to address whether that issue influenced the court's analysis. Res judicata appears to apply to the facts of this case solely because similar issues had been previously litigated in another county.[69] Nothing in the decision suggests that the defense of res judicata can be raised only when the same party requesting the order is denied relief in one court and then goes to another court to attempt to obtain relief based on the same facts.[70]

Q & A: Where a party files a petition for civil protection order in one county which is denied and then files a second CPO in another county, is that CPO barred by res judicata?

In *Clagg v. Clagg*,[71] appellant filed a petition for civil protection order in Licking County. At the full hearing the petition was dismissed.

---

[66]Sterling v. Sterling, 2002-Ohio-4997, 2002 WL 31111778, *4 (Ohio Ct. App. 5th Dist. Fairfield County 2002).

[67]Sterling v. Sterling, 2002-Ohio-4997, 2002 WL 31111778, *3 (Ohio Ct. App. 5th Dist. Fairfield County 2002), quoting Grava v. Parkman Twp., 73 Ohio St. 3d 379, 1995-Ohio-331, 653 N.E.2d 226 (1995) (syl.); see also Wood v. Wood, 2003-Ohio-5587, 2003 WL 22389875, *2 (Ohio Ct. App. 5th Dist. Coshocton County 2003) (in which the appellate court discussed the doctrine of res judicata and noted that the "doctrine of res judicata requires a plaintiff to present every ground for relief in the first action, or be forever barred from asserting it"), citing National Amusements, Inc. v. City of Springdale, 53 Ohio St. 3d 60, 558 N.E.2d 1178 (1990).

[68]Sterling v. Sterling, 2002-Ohio-4997, 2002 WL 31111778, *4 (Ohio Ct. App. 5th Dist. Fairfield County 2002); see also Genari v. Genari, 2001-Ohio-1524, 2001 WL 848569 (Ohio Ct. App. 2d Dist. Greene County 2001) (appellant waived the defense of res judicata because he failed to plead it at the full hearing).

[69]See also RC 3113.31(E)(4), which provides guidance for the issuance of mutual civil protection orders in the same court.

[70]See also Bach v. Crawford, 2003-Ohio-1255, 2003 WL 1193783 (Ohio Ct. App. 2d Dist. Montgomery County 2003) (where appellant was denied a stalking CPO in Warren County and then filed for a domestic violence CPO in Montgomery County based on the same facts); Irwin v. Murray, 2006-Ohio-1633, 2006 WL 832830, *2 (Ohio Ct. App. 6th Dist. Lucas County 2006) (holding the doctrine of res judicata inapplicable in case where appellee obtained a CPO in domestic relations court and then obtained a stalking protection order in common pleas court; even if res judicata was application, it would not bar appellee's petition because additional allegations were made in common pleas court).

[71]Clagg v. Clagg, 2009-Ohio-328, 2009 WL 190049 (Ohio Ct. App. 10th Dist. Franklin County 2009).

Several months later, appellant filed another civil protection order in Franklin County. Appellee filed a motion to dismiss on the basis of res judicata and collateral estoppel and a motion for summary judgment. The trial court dismissed the petition, finding that the second CPO petition was based on the same facts as the Licking County petition.

On appeal, appellant argued that the second petition relied on different facts than her first petition and, therefore, neither res judicata nor collateral estoppel applied. While the parties were the same in both petitions, the facts were different. "The main event involved in the Licking County petition was a physical altercation in November 2007 and the main event in the Franklin County petition was two text messages in March 2008 indicating that appellee had seen appellant while she was on her balcony."[72] In reversing the trial court, the appellate court held that because the petitions did not rise out of the same transactions or occurrence, the doctrines of res judicata and collateral estoppal do not apply.[73]

Q & A: Does res judicata apply in cases where a party is denied a civil protection order and later requests another order?

In *Genari v. Genari*,[74] Mrs. Genari filed for a civil protection order on September 18, 2000. On September 26, 2000, Mrs. Genari appeared at the full hearing pro se, although Mr. Genari was represented by counsel. At the conclusion of the hearing, the magistrate denied her protection order. On October 5, 2000, Mr. Genari filed for a protection order based on the same altercation that had precipitated Mrs. Genari's earlier petition.[75] On October 6, 2000, Mrs. Genari again filed a protection order, which was denied at the ex parte hearing on the ground that her claim for relief was based on the same facts and circumstances that had supported her earlier petition.[76] At the full hearing on both parties' petitions, the court issued protection orders against both parties.

Apparently, the Second District Court of Appeals may have provided an exception for the application of the res judicata defense in civil protection order proceedings. The Greene County Court of Appeals noted that "[w]e cannot fault Mr. Genari for having failed to plead the defense of *res judicata*, because it appears from the record that he was never called upon to answer Mrs. Genari's petition with a responsive pleading."[77] There was no evidence in the record demonstrating that Mr. Genari had argued this issue in the trial court. Because he failed to raise the issue in the trial court, he waived the

[72] Clagg v. Clagg, 2009-Ohio-328, 2009 WL 190049, *4 (Ohio Ct. App. 10th Dist. Franklin County 2009).

[73] Clagg v. Clagg, 2009-Ohio-328, 2009 WL 190049, *4 (Ohio Ct. App. 10th Dist. Franklin County 2009).

[74] Genari v. Genari, 2001-Ohio-1524, 2001 WL 848569 (Ohio Ct. App. 2d Dist. Greene County 2001).

[75] Genari v. Genari, 2001-Ohio-1524, 2001 WL 848569, *1 (Ohio Ct. App. 2d Dist. Greene County 2001).

[76] Genari v. Genari, 2001-Ohio-1524, 2001 WL 848569, *1 (Ohio Ct. App. 2d Dist. Greene County 2001).

[77] Genari v. Genari, 2001-Ohio-1524, 2001 WL 848569, *3 (Ohio Ct. App. 2d Dist. Greene County 2001).

defense at the appellate level. However, it seems that the appellate court would have considered the defense had Mr. Genari "argued to the trial court that the adjudication of Mrs. Genari's previous petition should bar the claim for relief set forth in her current petition."[78]

Q & A: Does res judicata apply if an ex parte protection order was vacated in one state after a protection order was granted to petitioner in another state?

In *Barclay v. Haney*,[79] petitioner and respondent lived together in Ohio, during which time respondent made repeated phone calls and texts to her and spoofed her phone. Petitioner moved to Massachusetts for a short period during which she obtained a CPO. Upon her return to Ohio, she filed for a CPO. In her petition she alleged acts of repeated stalking, constant calling and texting. She also testified about her fear of respondent and how his behaviors caused her to change her routine. At the full hearing, respondent moved to dismiss the CPO on the grounds of res judicata. His motion was overruled because "there can't be two civil protection orders in effect."[80] Additionally, the magistrate noted that "the record is devoid of any evidence that a final, appealable order ever existed in the matter before the Gloucester District Court."[81] The trial court adopted the 2011 CPO as an order of the court and respondent appealed.

In respondent's assignment of error, he alleged that the trial court erred in failing to apply res judicata to the CPO claims. "Specifically, Mr. Haney contends that res judicata should bar Ms. Barclay's claims because nothing in the record indicates that the Gloucester District Court order was dismissed without prejudice."[82] The doctrine of res judicata "bars all subsequent action based on any claim arising out of a transaction or occurrence that was previously decided as a final and valid judgment in a prior action."[83]

While it is unclear whether the Gloucester District Court CPO was a temporary or ex parte protection order, it was nonetheless, vacated by the Gloucester District Court because there was a protection order

[78]Genari v. Genari, 2001-Ohio-1524, 2001 WL 848569, *3 (Ohio Ct. App. 2d Dist. Greene County 2001); see also Bumgardner v. Bumgardner, 2005-Ohio-3445, 2005 WL 1545790 (Ohio Ct. App. 12th Dist. Butler County 2005) (dismissal of wife's second CPO petition based on res judicata was warranted); M.K. v. J.K., 2015-Ohio-434, 2015 WL 557990 (Ohio Ct. App. 9th Dist. Medina County 2015) (suggesting that had appellant raised the issue, the court would have rejected the res judicata argument because he had introduced a copy of the petition as well as a copy of the prior court's decision and did not object when appellee testified about the prior incident).

[79]Barclay v. Haney, 2012-Ohio-5646, 2012 WL 6034070 (Ohio Ct. App. 9th Dist. Summit County 2012).

[80]Barclay v. Haney, 2012-Ohio-5646, ¶ 5, 2012 WL 6034070 (Ohio Ct. App. 9th Dist. Summit County 2012).

[81]Barclay v. Haney, 2012-Ohio-5646, ¶ 5, 2012 WL 6034070 (Ohio Ct. App. 9th Dist. Summit County 2012).

[82]Barclay v. Haney, 2012-Ohio-5646, ¶ 8, 2012 WL 6034070 (Ohio Ct. App. 9th Dist. Summit County 2012).

[83]Barclay v. Haney, 2012-Ohio-5646, ¶ 9, 2012 WL 6034070 (Ohio Ct. App. 9th Dist. Summit County 2012), quoting Moore v. Moore, 2003-Ohio-3789, 2003 WL 21658466 (Ohio Ct. App. 9th Dist. Wayne County 2003), citing Harris v. City of Lorain, 2003-Ohio-530, ¶ 15, 2003 WL 245737 (Ohio Ct. App. 9th Dist. Lorain County 2003).

in Ohio. Absent evidence that a final, appealable order ever existed with regard to Ms. Barclay's petition before the Gloucester District Court, the Summit County Court of Appeals determined that the CPO issued was a temporary order that was dismissed without prejudice. "Based on the record before us, we cannot say that the trial court erred by allowing Ms. Barclay's claims in her August 23, 2011, petition because there is no evidence that the dismissal without prejudice constituted a final and valid judgment in the Gloucester District Court."[84]

It is important to note that the Summit County appellate court did not consider the Civil Rules in its legal analysis. Pursuant to Civ. R. 41(A)(1), unless otherwise stated in the notice of dismissal or by stipulation, the dismissal is without prejudice, except that a notice of dismissal operates as an adjudication upon the merits of any claim that the plaintiff has once dismissed in any court. If the court dismisses the action after a notice of dismissal is filed, such dismissal is without prejudice and the action may be brought again by a petitioner. Civ. R. 41(A)(2) states that a court, on its own motion, may also dismiss an action upon such terms and conditions as the court deems proper. Unless otherwise specified in the order, a dismissal under division (A)(2) of this rule is without prejudice.[85]

A temporary or ex parte civil protection is not a final, appealable order; thus, it cannot be a final, valid judgment. One could logically assume that an ex parte or temporary CPO that is dismissed before a full hearing does not implicate the doctrine of res judicata or bar further filings based on the same facts.[86] However, it is less clear that this is so if a petitioner files and dismisses her action for a CPO more than once.[87]

Q & A: Where the domestic relations court denies a civil protection order, can the same party file a motion to modify custody based on the same incident of domestic violence?

Not according to the Lake County Court of Appeals in *Ventura v. Ventura*,[88] which determined that the doctrine of collateral estoppel was applicable to this fact situation. In that case, a mother filed a petition under the domestic violence statute claiming that her ex-husband had sexually abused her daughter. After a full hearing, the court denied the civil protection because the mother had failed to prove that the father had committed any act of domestic violence. The mother then filed a motion to modify custody and terminate joint custody of the child alleged to have been sexually abused.

The trial court dismissed the motion, stating that the appellant was attempting to relitigate the identical facts between the same parties after the matter had already been finally determined in the previous

[84]Barclay v. Haney, 2012-Ohio-5646, ¶ 10, 2012 WL 6034070 (Ohio Ct. App. 9th Dist. Summit County 2012).

[85]Civ. R. 41(A)(2).

[86]Barclay v. Haney, 2012-Ohio-5646, ¶ 10, 2012 WL 6034070 (Ohio Ct. App. 9th Dist. Summit County 2012).

[87]See Civ. R. 41(A)(1).

[88]Ventura v. Ventura, 1986 WL 10595 (Ohio Ct. App. 11th Dist. Lake County 1986).

domestic violence action. The Lake County Court of Appeals reasoned that, although RC 3113.31(G) provides that its remedies are in addition to, and not in lieu of, any other available civil or criminal remedies,

> a judgment rendered pursuant to the act is subject to the same "rules of conclusiveness" which generally apply to all judgments. Public policy dictates that those who have contested an issue shall be bound by the result of the contest, and that matters once tried shall be forever settled between the parties.[89]

The appellate court held that the doctrine of collateral estoppel did apply because the appellant's motion involved the same issue of child abuse which was previously litigated and decided between the same parties in the domestic violence action.[90] The court cautioned that to relitigate the issues in another case after an unsatisfactory outcome in the first action is not acceptable.

Q & A: Must the defense of res judicata be first raised in a responsive pleading?

According to the Second District Court of Appeals, the defense of res judicata does not need to be raised in a responsive pleading.[91] In *Bach v. Crawford*,[92] the appellate court applied the rationale set forth in *Genari* to overrule Bach's assignment of error that the trial court erred in holding that his claims were barred by res judicata. In that case, the boyfriend filed a petition for a CPO against his former girlfriend. The magistrate granted the petition, but the girlfriend objected. Subsequently, the trial court denied the petition and the boyfriend appealed.

On appeal, the boyfriend argued that the girlfriend waived the defense of res judicata because she failed to file the defense in a pleading. The appellate court relied on *Genari* and pointed out that "this court has previously stated that a respondent in a civil protection order action will not be faulted for the failure to plead the defense of res judicata where it appears from the record that the party was never called upon to answer the petition."[93] Crawford had previously argued in the trial court that much of the evidence argued at that

[89]Ventura v. Ventura, 1986 WL 10595, *1 (Ohio Ct. App. 11th Dist. Lake County 1986).

[90]See also Genari v. Genari, 2001-Ohio-1524, 2001 WL 848569 (Ohio Ct. App. 2d Dist. Greene County 2001) (where wife's petition for protection order was denied after a full hearing. Subsequently, she filed another civil protection order based on the same incidents, facts and circumstances that had supported her earlier petition. The husband also filed a petition for protection order. After a denial of her ex parte order, the trial court issued a civil protection order against both parties at the full hearing. Although the issue of res judicata was not raised by the husband (appellant), the appellate court indicated that had he raised the issue in the trial court, the appellate court may have considered a res judicata defense). But see Hoff v. Brown, 2001 WL 876228 (Ohio Ct. App. 5th Dist. Stark County 2001) (the appellate court stated that the doctrine of res judicata did not apply to civil protection order proceedings).

[91]See Text § 12:2, Full hearing—Scheduling and filing issues (discussing that there is no statutory requirement that a responsive pleading or answer be filed).

[92]Bach v. Crawford, 2003-Ohio-1255, 2003 WL 1193783 (Ohio Ct. App. 2d Dist. Montgomery County 2003).

[93]Bach v. Crawford, 2003-Ohio-1255, 2003 WL 1193783, *3 (Ohio Ct. App. 2d Dist. Montgomery County 2003).

hearing was previously argued before the Warren County court by Mr. Bach in his earlier attempt to obtain a CPO. The Second District Court of Appeals concluded that "[b]y arguing this to the magistrate at the hearing and in her objections to the trial court, Mrs. Crawford preserved the issue of res judicata for appeal."[94]

Q & A: Where the parties are involved in domestic relations litigation and one of them charges the other with domestic violence, does the criminal court have an obligation to permit cross-examination relative to motive, bias, or prejudice of the party on whose behalf the action is brought?[95]

This issue has been raised many times in Ohio. In *State v. Smith*,[96] the husband was charged with domestic violence against his soon-to-be ex-wife. He was found guilty of domestic violence and appealed on the ground that he was not able to explore on cross-examination the motive, intent, and interest of his wife who signed the complaint against him for domestic violence.

The Hamilton County Court of Appeals found that the trial court had noted the possible underlying motive of the wife when it stated "[y]ou have established that custody is an issue already. . . . The court understands that this is an issue."[97] The court then stated that the trial court did not abuse its discretion in excluding the testimony. The appellate court did not provide guidance as to whether a court is obligated to note a pending divorce or custody dispute for purposes of eliciting testimony regarding the underlying motive, intent, and interest in every criminal domestic violence case.

In *State v. Warren*,[98] the court found that the trial court did not commit reversible error by precluding cross-examination on the issue

---

[94]Bach v. Crawford, 2003-Ohio-1255, 2003 WL 1193783, *3 (Ohio Ct. App. 2d Dist. Montgomery County 2003).

[95]See also Text § 7:15, Case preparation—Client interview preparations; checklist.

[96]State v. Smith, 1985 WL 6801 (Ohio Ct. App. 1st Dist. Hamilton County 1985); see also State v. Day, 99 Ohio App. 3d 514, 651 N.E.2d 52 (12th Dist. Clermont County 1994).

[97]State v. Smith, 1985 WL 6801, *2 (Ohio Ct. App. 1st Dist. Hamilton County 1985). See also Spigos v. Spigos, 2004-Ohio-757, 2004 WL 308098, *4 (Ohio Ct. App. 10th Dist. Franklin County 2004) (court noted that the granting of a civil protection order offers a petitioner the potential for additional benefits not available under orders issued in the parties' divorce action (although the use of a protection order as a sword rather than a shield in an ongoing custody battle would not be one of the "additional benefits" intended by the legislature)); M.R. v. T.R., 2016-Ohio-3493, 2016 WL 3384940 (Ohio Ct. App. 9th Dist. Wayne County 2016) (supporting appellant's argument that wife filed her petition to obtain custody of the children and gain leverage in the divorce); Corrao v. Corrao, 2016-Ohio-4862, 2016 WL 3632494 (Ohio Ct. App. 8th Dist. Cuyahoga County 2016) (inferring that the CPO was used to gain leverage in the divorce); Vega v. Thomas, 2017-Ohio-298, 2017 WL 389911 (Ohio Ct. App. 8th Dist. Cuyahoga County 2017) (appellate court refused to take a position on appellee's motivation, noting that the trial court was in the best position to assess the credibility of the witnesses and declining to find that appellee had any motive for seeking CPO beyond the safety of her family. at ¶ 25).

[98]State v. Warren, 106 Ohio App. 3d 753, 667 N.E.2d 68 (1st Dist. Hamilton County 1995); see also State v. Sprow, 1997 WL 177703 (Ohio Ct. App. 6th Dist. Williams County 1997); State v. Younker, 2002-Ohio-5376, 2002 WL 31242238 (Ohio Ct. App. 2d Dist. Darke County 2002).

of bias, prejudice, or ulterior motive.[99] In that case, the appellant was denied the opportunity to cross-examine the victim in the criminal domestic violence case about the appellant's filing for custody. The appellate court noted that "the preclusion of the cross-examination of [the victim] concerning appellant's filing of the custody matter did not contribute to appellant's conviction. Therefore, we conclude that the limitation of the cross-examination of [the victim] was harmless error beyond a reasonable doubt."[100]

On the other hand, in *State v. Younker*,[101] the defendant challenged the trial court's refusal to allow him to cross-examine the victim regarding both the pending juvenile and domestic relations cases. He argued that a conviction for domestic violence would put the victim in a better position to gain custody in the divorce.

In sustaining defendant's first assignment of error, the Darke County Appellate Court reasoned that "Mrs. Younker has a pecuniary interest in the outcome of this prosecution and defendant wanted to cross-examine her about those matters to demonstrate her possible bias or prejudice."[102] The Court of Appeals held that because the inquiry defendant wished to make did not involve an irrelevant matter and did effect credibility, the trial court erred and abused its discretion and deprived defendant of his Sixth Amendment right to fully and effectively confront the witness about the pending divorce case.[103]

§ 12:28 Enforcement of civil protection orders[1]

Besides courts, law enforcement agencies are expected to enforce civil protection orders. RC 3113.31(F)(3) states that all civil protection orders issued within the state of Ohio are enforceable throughout the state. This is the case whether or not the petitioner has registered the protection order or consent agreement in the county in which the order was issued or in which the officer's agency has jurisdiction.[2] In fact, RC 3113.31(F)(3) also directs law enforcement agencies to remove respondents from the premises, if appropriate.

Q & A: Are out of state protection orders enforceable?

[99]But see State v. Fredrick, 2002-Ohio-1195, 2002 WL 360643 (Ohio Ct. App. 2d Dist. Montgomery County 2002) (reversed and held that preventing defendant from cross-examining the complainant on the subject of prior false accusations of domestic violence was an abuse of discretion).

[100]State v. Warren, 106 Ohio App. 3d 753, 759, 667 N.E.2d 68 (1st Dist. Hamilton County 1995).

[101]State v. Younker, 2002-Ohio-5376, 2002 WL 31242238 (Ohio Ct. App. 2d Dist. Darke County 2002).

[102]State v. Younker, 2002-Ohio-5376, 2002 WL 31242238, *1 (Ohio Ct. App. 2d Dist. Darke County 2002).

[103]State v. Younker, 2002-Ohio-5376, 2002 WL 31242238, *2 (Ohio Ct. App. 2d Dist. Darke County 2002).

[Section 12:28]

[1]See generally Text § 11:11, Ex parte protection orders—Service and notice provisions; Text § 12:8, Service of the protection order issued after the full hearing; Text § 14:16, Enforcement of protection orders issued by the courts of Ohio; Text § 14:17, Enforcement of out-of-state protection orders; Text § 18:9, Other remedies under VAWA.

[2]RC 3113.31(F)(3).

Yes. Ohio courts are authorized to enforce protection orders issued by courts of another state.[3] Additionally, law enforcement agencies are directed to enforce all protection orders issued by any court in this state and out-of-state protection orders, whether or not they are registered within this state.[4]

Q & A: What is the procedure to register a protection order issued by an Ohio court?

RC 3113.31(N) empowers a petitioner to register a protection order or consent agreement in a county other than the county in which the court that issued the order or consent agreement is located.[5]

A petitioner who obtains either a civil or criminal protection order may provide notice of the issuance or approval of the order to the judicial and law enforcement officials in any county other than the county issuing the order.[6] Registering the order or consent agreement in another county and filing a copy of the registered order with the law enforcement agency of that county are sufficient to provide notice to the judicial and law enforcement officials in that county.[7] A petitioner may also register and file a copy of a registered out-of-state protection order with the law enforcement agency in that county.[8]

A petitioner who wishes to register a protection order or consent agreement may do so by complying with RC 3113.31(N)(2), which provides that:

The petitioner shall obtain a certified copy of the order or agreement from the clerk of the court that issued the order;[9]

The petitioner shall present the certified copy of the order to the clerk of common pleas court for orders issued under RC 3113.31 or the clerk of the municipal court for orders issued under RC 2919.26 in the county in which the order is to be registered;[10] and

Upon accepting the certified copy of the order for registration, the clerk of court shall place an endorsement of registration on the order or agreement and give the petitioner a copy of the order or agreement that bears an endorsement of registration.[11]

The clerk of each common pleas and municipal court shall maintain a registry of certified copies of both civil and criminal protection orders and consent agreements that have been issued or approved by courts in other counties and have been registered with the clerk.[12]

---

[3]See Text § 14:17, Enforcement of out-of-state protection orders, Text § 18:9, Other remedies under VAWA; see also RC 2919.272(D).

[4]RC 3113.31(F)(3), RC 3113.31(N)(1), RC 2919.272.

[5]RC 3113.31(N)(2).

[6]RC 3113.31(N)(1).

[7]RC 3113.31(N)(1).

[8]RC 3113.31(N)(1), see also RC 2919.272.

[9]RC 3113.31(N)(2)(a).

[10]RC 3113.31(N)(2)(a).

[11]RC 3113.31(N)(2)(b).

[12]RC 3113.31(N)(3).

Q & A: Is the procedure the same for the registration of out of state protection orders?[13]

Yes. RC 2919.272(B) provides that a person who has obtained a protection order issued by a court of another state may provide notice of the issuance of the order to judicial and law enforcement officials in any county of this state by registering the order in that county and filing a copy of the registered order with the law enforcement agency in that county. The procedure for registering the order is the same as set forth above.[14] Both the clerk of courts and the law enforcement agency must maintain registries.[15]

Q & A: Are there any fees or costs associated with the registering and filing of protection orders?

No court or unit of state or local government shall charge a petitioner any fee, cost, deposit, or money in connection with the filing, issuance, registration, modification, enforcement, dismissal, withdrawal or service of a protection order or consent agreement or witness subpoena or for obtaining a certified copy of a protection order[16] including a protection order issued by a court of another state.[17] However, respondents may be assessed these costs.[18]

§ 12:29 Mutual protection orders

Perhaps the single most troubling aspect of enforcement of protection orders has been deciding whether to issue orders against both parties. Mutual protection orders make a big difference in the way police respond to domestic violence incidents and in the manner in which they enforce the protection orders.

In civil protection order proceedings, Ohio courts have always had the authority to issue civil protection orders on behalf of petitioners against respondents.[1] Unfortunately, courts have long utilized their judicial discretion to issue civil protection orders on behalf of respondents against petitioners in the same civil protection order proceeding. The enactment of the Violence Against Women Act of 1994[2] has all but reversed this trend.[3] Pursuant to RC 3113.31(E)(4), the authority of the Ohio courts to issue protection orders against both the petitioner and the respondent in the same proceeding has been sharply curtailed.

Q & A: What are mutual protection orders?

---

[13]See also Text § 14:16, Enforcement of protection orders issued by the courts of Ohio, and Text § 14:17, Enforcement of out-of-state protection orders.

[14]RC 2919.272(B), RC 3113.31(N)(2).

[15]RC 2919.272(C).

[16]R.C. 3113.31(J)(1), eff. 9/17/2014; R.C. 2903.214(J)(1), eff. 9/17/2014.

[17]See RC 3113.31(J). See also RC 2919.272(E), RC 2919.26(J).

[18]R.C. 3113.31(J)(2), eff. 9/17/2014; R.C. 2903.214(J)(2), eff. 9/17/2014.

[Section 12:29]

[1]See RC 3113.31.

[2]Codified in scattered sections of 18 U.S.C.A. and 42 U.S.C.A.

[3]See National Council of Juvenile & Family Court Judges, Family Violence Project, Family Violence: Improving Court Practice, Section II: Recommendations for the Courts (1990), reprinted in 41 Juv. & Fam. Ct. J. 17 (1990).

Mutual protection orders are most often civil protection orders that are entered against both parties and that arise out of one party's pleadings.[4] In any civil protection order action, the petitioner files a petition for protection order as set forth in RC 3113.31. If requested, an ex parte order is granted. At the full hearing, the respondent appears and agrees to be bound by the terms of the protection order. The only difference is that at this point the court may also issue a protection order against the petitioner. The court may do this on its own motion or at the request of the respondent.

A petitioner may agree to a mutual order of protection, or the court may issue one even if the evidence suggests that it is not warranted. The court may view this as an easy way to free the docket by settling the case while still issuing an order on behalf of the petitioner. Oftentimes, respondents agree to the terms of the civil protection order provided they too are awarded a protection order against the petitioner. In effect, the respondents are absolved from responsibility for the abuse by the additional language restraining both parties from further abuse.

Q & A: Why are mutual protection orders so problematic and potentially dangerous?

Mutual protection orders undermine the purpose of RC 3113.31 which is to protect the victim from violence and hold the perpetrator accountable for his/her actions. Too often, a mutual protection order places the victim at greater risk of injury. Police officers do not know what action to take. When police officers respond to a call and ascertain that the parties have mutual orders of protection, they usually either arrest both parties (even if there is no evidence of mutual abuse) or they arrest no one. Police officers are also less likely to utilize the primary physical aggressor factors to determine which party to arrest. These scenarios prejudice the victim who calls the police expecting enforcement of the protection order and create a significant disincentive to seek enforcement of the order from the police.[5] Notably, studies have repeatedly shown that a victim is less likely to call for help if a mutual protection order is in effect.[6]

A mutual protection order sends the wrong message to both the victim and the batterer. It tells the victim that he/she is equally responsible for the respondent's violent behavior. It reinforces the batterer's belief that his/her behavior is the result of factors not within his/her control.[7]

Respondents have benefitted from the issuance of mutual protection orders, at the expense of the true victim, in other types of subsequent evidentiary hearings such as divorce, custody, and various criminal

---

[4]But see Skiles v. Dearth, 2000 WL 1838747, *5 (Ohio Ct. App. 2d Dist. Clark County 2000) ("There is nothing inconsistent about one domestic partner obtaining a domestic violence protection order after the other has already obtained one.").

[5]Peter Finn & Sarah Colson, U.S. Department of Justice, Civil Protection Orders: Legislation, Current Court Practice and Enforcement 1, 47 (1990).

[6]Washington State Task Force on Gender and Justice in the Courts 30, 79 (1989).

[7]See Anne L. Ganley, Perpetrators of Domestic Violence: An Overview of Counseling the Court-Mandated Client, in Domestic Violence On Trial: Psychological and Legal Dimensions of Family Violence 3, 156–57 (D. Sonkin ed., 1986).

proceedings.[8] Batterers use the existence of mutual protection orders to illustrate to the court how abusive the victim has been as well. For the batterer, this levels the playing field and implies that the victim may not be the victim after all. Unfortunately, many courts fail to accurately discern which party has a history of committing domestic violence.

Mutual protection orders have also been used as a defense in criminal contempt proceedings as evidence that the victim is equally at fault.[9] Such cases are often dismissed because it cannot be proven beyond a reasonable doubt that the respondent violated the order.

Q & A: Are there the due process concerns with mutual protection orders?

Mutual protection orders violate the procedural due process rights of the petitioner concerning notice and an opportunity to be heard.[10] When a mutual order is granted to the respondent at the petitioner's full hearing on the ex parte order, the petitioner is not given notice of respondent's allegations, nor is the petitioner given an opportunity to be heard. Sometimes, no evidence of abuse is presented by the respondent. Since mutual protection orders are not sufficiently supported by the evidence, it is arguably a denial of due process to grant them. RC 3113.31(E)(4) codifies the procedure and addresses the due process concerns detailed in *Deacon v. Landers*.[11]

To demonstrate a denial of due process, it must first be shown that a liberty or property interest is involved.[12] Most case law regarding liberty interests applies to the interests of prisoners and mental patients.[13] However, "the liberty interest at stake for a battered woman is an interest in freedom of movement and travel and protection from the acts of her abuser."[14]

The trend is to recognize both liberty and property interests where the state has created a protected right.[15] To support this analysis, the Supreme Court, in *Paul v. Davis*,[16] held that:

> [T]here exists a variety of interests which are difficult of definition but

[8]Elizabeth Topliffe, Why Civil Protection Orders are Effective Remedies for Domestic Violence but Mutual Protective Orders are Not, 67 Ind. L.J. 1039, 1062 (1992).

[9]Washington State Task Force on Gender and Justice in the Courts 24 (1989).

[10]See Deacon v. Landers, 68 Ohio App. 3d 26, 587 N.E.2d 395 (4th Dist. Ross County 1990).

[11]Deacon v. Landers, 68 Ohio App. 3d 26, 587 N.E.2d 395 (4th Dist. Ross County 1990).

[12]See Vitek v. Jones, 445 U.S. 480, 100 S. Ct. 1254, 63 L. Ed. 2d 552 (1980).

[13]See Vitek v. Jones, 445 U.S. 480, 100 S. Ct. 1254, 63 L. Ed. 2d 552 (1980); see also Greenholtz v. Inmates of Nebraska Penal and Correctional Complex, 442 U.S. 1, 99 S. Ct. 2100, 60 L. Ed. 2d 668 (1979).

[14]Elizabeth Topliffe, Why Civil Protection Orders are Effective Remedies for Domestic Violence but Mutual Protective Orders are Not, 67 Ind. L.J. 1039, 1057 (1992).

[15]Vitek v. Jones, 445 U.S. 480, 100 S. Ct. 1254, 63 L. Ed. 2d 552 (1980); see also Siddle v. City of Cambridge, Ohio, 761 F. Supp. 503 (S.D. Ohio 1991).

[16]Paul v. Davis, 424 U.S. 693, 710–11, 96 S. Ct. 1155, 47 L. Ed. 2d 405, 1 I.E.R. Cas. (BNA) 1827 (1976); State v. Farmer, 2015-Ohio-5434, 2015 WL 9438270 (Ohio Ct. App. 5th Dist. Licking County 2015), appeal not allowed, 145 Ohio St. 3d 1459,

> are nevertheless comprehended within the meaning of either "liberty" or "property" as meant in the Due Process Clause. These interests attain this constitutional status by virtue of the fact that they have been initially recognized and protected by state law, and we have repeatedly ruled that the procedural guarantees of the Fourteenth Amendment apply whenever the State seeks to remove or significantly alter that protected status.

The Ohio legislature enacted protection order statutes in March of 1979 which have, in effect, created a liberty or property interest protected by state law.[17] The statutory language presumes that the petitioner is in jeopardy of continued injury or harm from the respondent.[18] It must be shown that the respondent has committed domestic violence and is capable of further violence against the petitioner.[19] The respondent must be afforded an evidentiary hearing. The respondent's "liberty interest" is protected by requiring that there be an evidentiary showing to support the petitioner's allegations before the respondent is restrained.[20]

The analysis set forth in *Paul v. Davis* clearly demonstrates that an evidentiary hearing before being restrained is an interest that cannot be taken away without due process.[21] Therefore, issuing a mutual protection order without affording the petitioner an opportunity to present evidence to contradict the respondent's allegations is a violation of the due process rights accorded every individual.

Q & A: Do other procedural problems exist with mutual protection orders?

All of the procedural issues arise from the due process safeguards accorded to each person. RC 3113.31 lists the procedure for courts to follow relative to mutual protection orders.[22] If a court issues a mutual restraining order without a separate petition, an affidavit, and a date for a full hearing at which the original petitioner has a right to face his/her accuser, the court has failed to comply with the statutory requirements of RC 3113.31. Since many courts still grant mutual protection orders as a matter of course, attorneys have an obligation to insist upon compliance with the statute.

Prior to the enactment of House Bill 335 in 1994, state courts had been conflicted in their approach towards the issuance of mutual protection orders. In *Deacon v. Landers*,[23] the Court of Appeals for Ross County determined that the trial court's issuance of a mutual protection order was improper because a full hearing was not afforded to the petitioner. The court found that

2016-Ohio-2807, 49 N.E.3d 321 (2016) (discussing the purposes of misdemeanor sentencing).

[17] See RC 3113.31, RC 2919.26.

[18] See RC 3113.31.

[19] See RC 3113.31(D).

[20] See Vitek v. Jones, 445 U.S. 480, 100 S. Ct. 1254, 63 L. Ed. 2d 552 (1980).

[21] See Deacon v. Landers, 68 Ohio App. 3d 26, 587 N.E.2d 395 (4th Dist. Ross County 1990); see also Marco v. Superior Court, 17 Ariz. App. 210, 496 P.2d 636 (Div. 2 1972).

[22] See RC 3113.31(C); see also RC 3113.31(E)(4).

[23] Deacon v. Landers, 68 Ohio App. 3d 26, 587 N.E.2d 395 (4th Dist. Ross County 1990).

> [i]t is manifestly clear from this exchange that appellant was denied an opportunity to cross-examine appellee and to present rebuttal evidence. Accordingly, we hold that appellant was neither given a "full hearing" under RC 3113.31, nor afforded an opportunity to be heard or defend herself consistent with due process of law.[24]

On the other hand, the Court of Appeals for Tuscarawas County utilized RC 3113.31(E)(1)(h) to sanction the granting of a mutual protection order. In *Clum v. Searcy*,[25] the court held that "the trial court has authority to issue mutual protective orders even though only one party seeks a unilateral protective order." The court relied on RC 3113.31(E)(1)(h) which provides, in part, that the court may grant other relief that the court considers equitable and fair. The court of appeals reasoned that RC 3113.31(E)(1)(h) grants "broad authority to the trial court to issue orders that best serve the parties involved in domestic violence."[26]

These conflicting cases emphasize the need for persuasive statutory authority to address and resolve the issues presented. The passage of VAWA was the catalyst for the enactment of Ohio's statutory provisions.[27]

Q & A: How has Ohio addressed these concerns regarding mutual protection orders?[28]

Under VAWA, the full faith and credit provision requires states and Indian tribes to enforce valid protection orders issued by foreign states and tribes as if the orders had been issued by the enforcing state or tribe.[29]

> A valid protection order is defined as a protection order that has been issued by a court which has jurisdiction over the parties and matter under the laws of such state or indian tribe and in circumstances where the defendant has been given reasonable notice and the opportunity to be heard sufficient to protect that person's right to due process.[30]

Under the mandates of VAWA, states stood to lose federal funding unless they had statutes in effect that specifically prohibited mutual protection orders unless the respondent filed a separate petition seeking such an order and the court made specific findings that the respondent, as well as the petitioner, was entitled to such an order.[31] To adequately address the issues presented and to comply with VAWA,

[24]Deacon v. Landers, 68 Ohio App. 3d 26, 31, 587 N.E.2d 395 (4th Dist. Ross County 1990).

[25]Clum v. Searcy, 1993 WL 535383, *2 (Ohio Ct. App. 5th Dist. Tuscarawas County 1993).

[26]Clum v. Searcy, 1993 WL 535383, *2 (Ohio Ct. App. 5th Dist. Tuscarawas County 1993).

[27]See 18 U.S.C.A. § 2265(c).

[28]See also Text Ch. 18, Federal Remedies.

[29]See 18 U.S.C.A. § 2265.

[30]American Bar Association, Stopping Violence Against Women: Using New Federal Laws, 29, American Bar Association (1996).

[31]See 18 U.S.C.A. § 2265.

the Ohio statute permits the issuance of mutual protection orders only under certain conditions.[32]

An Ohio court may issue an order of protection that requires a petitioner to do or refrain from doing an act that the court has already required a respondent to do or refrain from doing only if certain criteria are met.[33] To issue a mutual protection order, all of the following must occur:

(1) The respondent must file a separate petition for a protection order in accordance with RC 3113.31.[34]

(2) The petitioner must be given notice of the respondent's petition at least 48 hours before the court holds the hearing with respect to respondent's petition.[35] The petitioner may waive the right to receive this notice.[36]

(3) If the petitioner requested an ex parte order, the court must not delay the full hearing beyond the time specified in RC 3113.31(D) in order to consolidate the hearing with a hearing on the petition requested by the respondent.[37]

(4) At the full hearing, the respondent may present evidence in support of the request for the protection order. The petitioner is then afforded an opportunity to defend against that evidence.[38]

(5) The court must determine that the petitioner committed an act of domestic violence or violated a temporary protection order issued pursuant to RC 2919.26, that both the petitioner and the respondent acted primarily as aggressors, and that neither the petitioner nor the respondent acted in self-defense.[39]

It is clear from the statutory language that mutual orders of protec-

---

[32]See RC 3113.31(E)(4).

[33]RC 3113.31(E)(4).

[34]RC 3113.31(E)(4)(a); see also Wilkins v. Wilkins, 2004-Ohio-3139, 2004 WL 1366154 (Ohio Ct. App. 2d Dist. Champaign County 2004) (trial court lacked jurisdiction to order husband to refrain from having contact with wife as part of civil protection order issued upon husband's petition as wife did not file a separate petition for a civil protection order); Kovacs v. Kovacs, 2004-Ohio-2777, 2004 WL 1191103 (Ohio Ct. App. 6th Dist. Erie County 2004); Pringle v. Orth, 2011-Ohio-2177, 2011 WL 1782095 (Ohio Ct. App. 6th Dist. Lucas County 2011) (trial court committed error in issuing a civil protection order in favor of a respondent who did not file any petition for a protection order); Toledo v. Lewis, 2013-Ohio-3289, 2013 WL 3936455 (Ohio Ct. App. 6th Dist. Lucas County 2013) (applying *Smith* and holding that a conviction for violating a protection order does not lie under R.C. 2919.27 where the order was not validly issued in that no separate petition was filed and service was not perfected).

[35]Patterson v. Gooderham, 1999 WL 1001108 (Ohio Ct. App. 4th Dist. Gallia County 1999) (court reversed judgment granting civil protection order against first petitioner because respondent failed to serve petitioner with notice of respondent's petitioner at least 48 hours before the hearing on petitioner's petition).

[36]RC 3113.31(E)(4)(b).

[37]R.C. 3113.31(E)(4)(c). See also Gomez v. Kiner, 2012-Ohio-1019, 2012 WL 831460 (Ohio Ct. App. 10th Dist. Franklin County 2012) (noting trial court procedure for addressing mutual civil protection orders is to grant both ex parte CPOs and consolidate the petitions for the full hearings).

[38]RC 3113.31(E)(4)(d).

[39]RC 3113.31(E)(4)(d); see also State v. Wetherall, 2002-Ohio-1613, 2002 WL 440700, *1 (Ohio Ct. App. 1st Dist. Hamilton County 2002) (court held that the defense of self-defense may exonerate an accused's admitted use of force in a domestic violence case under RC 2919.25); Burke v. Melton, 2003-Ohio-7054, 2003 WL

tion should no longer be granted as a matter of course in the same proceeding. Due process protections must be afforded the petitioner. A respondent can never request a protection order at the full hearing on petitioner's case. However, it is not as clear whether the procedural mandates of RC 3113.31(E)(4) can be applied to other situations. For example, in some situations, the petitioner requests a civil protection order. After the ex parte hearing has been granted but before the full hearing is held, the respondent files for his/her own protection order. In such a case, there is no statutory direction regarding compliance with the procedural mandates of RC 3113.31(E)(4). Additionally, it is unclear whether the petitioner in the new protection order filing (the original respondent) may obtain an ex parte order. If the respondent in the original action has already been served with an ex parte protection order, he/she must note this fact on the standardized protection order forms.[40] This disclosure should eliminate an ex parte hearing. The new protection order action should be consolidated with the original protection order action, and a hearing for both actions should be scheduled on the same date and at the same time as the full hearing already scheduled on behalf of the original petitioner. Such an approach is designed to avoid the possibility of conflicting ex parte protection orders existing at the same time and is intended to reduce police confusion in the enforcement of a protection order.

Q & A: Can one of the parties waive the requirement of a separate petition?

The procedural mandates require that a separate petition be filed by the respondent. One Ohio court has recently addressed this issue. In *Wilkins v. Wilkins*,[41] the husband obtained a civil protection order. On the wife's objections, the trial court modified the order to require both parties to refrain from having contact with the other.

On appeal, the husband argued that the trial court was without jurisdiction to modify the magistrate's decision to issue a mutual protection order against the husband when the wife had not filed a separate petition. In reversing the trial court, the Second District Court of Appeals held that "the requirement that a respondent file a separate petition for protection order, as a prerequisite for the issuance of a protection order imposing restrictions upon a petitioner, is a jurisdictional limitation upon the special statutory power conferred by statute. Consequently, that limitation, being jurisdictional, cannot be waived."[42]

23009045 (Ohio Ct. App. 8th Dist. Cuyahoga County 2003); J.R. v. E.H., 2017-Ohio-516, 2017 WL 587314 (Ohio Ct. App. 10th Dist. Franklin County 2017) (discussion of self defense); Text 8:8.

[40]See Sup. R. Form 10.01-D.

[41]Wilkins v. Wilkins, 2004-Ohio-3139, 2004 WL 1366154 (Ohio Ct. App. 2d Dist. Champaign County 2004).

[42]Wilkins v. Wilkins, 2004-Ohio-3139, 2004 WL 1366154, *3 (Ohio Ct. App. 2d Dist. Champaign County 2004). But see N.S. v. S.B., 2017-Ohio-1556, ¶ 12, 2017 WL 1507322 (Ohio Ct. App. 8th Dist. Cuyahoga County 2017), as amended, (Aug. 22, 2017).

In dicta, the court added that the notice requirement of at least forty-eight hours contained in RC 3113.31(E)(4)(b) is expressly subject to the possibility of waiver.[43]

A hearing is only scheduled on the respondent's petition if the petitioner has been served with notice of the respondent's petition at least forty-eight hours before the court holds the hearing. If the petitioner requested an ex parte order, the court is required to hold the full hearing on petitioner's petition within the specified time limitations.[44] The court may not delay this hearing in order to consolidate both parties' hearings. It is implied that, if the petitioner has not been served with the respondent's petition 48 hours before the date set for the full hearing on her/his own petition, the court must set the hearing on the respondent's petition for a later date.

Ultimately, RC 3113.31(E)(4) places the burden on the court to assess the situation and determine whether the petitioner committed domestic violence as alleged in respondent's petition. RC 3113.31(E)(4) provides that the court consider certain basic principles to guide its decision. Unlike the police, the court is required to apply the primary physical aggressor factors to assist it in determining whether both parties acted as primary physical aggressors.[45]

For example, the court must investigate whether either party acted in self-defense.[46] According to *Black's Law Dictionary*, "self-defense" is defined as "the protection of one's person or property against some injury attempted by another" and as "an excuse for the use of force in resisting an attack on the person." *Black's Law Dictionary* refers to the Model Penal Code which provides that "a person is justified in the use of force against an aggressor when and to the extent it appears to him and he reasonably believes that such conduct is necessary to defend himself . . . against such aggressor's imminent use of unlawful force."[47] The court should carefully examine the parties' abusive re-

[43]Wilkins v. Wilkins, 2004-Ohio-3139, 2004 WL 1366154, *3 (Ohio Ct. App. 2d Dist. Champaign County 2004).

[44]RC 3113.31(D)(2)(a).

[45]See RC 2935.03(B)(3)(d).

[46]See RC 2935.03(B)(3)(d)(ii), Text § 8:8; see also State v. Wheatley, 2000 WL 145394 (Ohio Ct. App. 2d Dist. Montgomery County 2000) (relying on State v. Thomas, 77 Ohio St. 3d 323, 1997-Ohio-269, 673 N.E.2d 1339, 67 A.L.R.5th 775 (1997) for determining whether a party was acting in self defense); State v. Cornwell, 2015-Ohio-4617, 48 N.E.3d 169 (Ohio Ct. App. 9th Dist. Wayne County 2015) (the elements of self defense are cumulative such that a failure to prove any one of the elements of self defense demonstrates a failure to show that s/he acted in self defense); In re D.N., 195 Ohio App. 3d 552, 2011-Ohio-5494, 960 N.E.2d 1063 (8th Dist. Cuyahoga County 2011) (In cases of domestic violence, "the attacks are often repeated over time and escape from the home is rarely possible without the threat of great personal violence or death. The victims of such attacks have already retreated to the wall many times over and therefore should not be required as victims of domestic violence to attempt to flee to safety before being able to claim the affirmative defense of self defense," quoting *Thomas*, at 327–328); Gooden v. City of Brunswick, 2014 WL 1379528 (N.D. Ohio 2014); Text § 8:8; Text § 14:4. State v. Adams, 2018-Ohio-604, 2018 WL 920023 (Ohio Ct. App. 2d Dist. Champaign County 2018) (discussing the elements of self defense).

[47]Black's Law Dictionary (6th ed.) p 1359.

lationship to avoid punishing victims who are trying to protect themselves from further violence.[48]

The court should also consider the comparative severity of the injuries suffered by the persons involved,[49] any history of domestic violence or of violent acts by either person that can reasonably be ascertained,[50] each person's fear of physical harm resulting from the other person's threatened use of force or history of use of force, and the reasonableness of that fear.[51]

One way to identify the primary physical aggressor is to evaluate which party is afraid of being seriously hurt. "Usually only one party is afraid of the other. The primary aggressor usually is not concerned about being hurt but uses violence by the other party as a justification or explanation for his own actions."[52] Violence has been used as a method of intimidation.[53]

§ 12:30 Attorney representation

The petitioner's attorney has a responsibility to provide the court with the requisite evidence needed to substantiate the victim's claims.[1] Copies of prior convictions and the arrest record of the respondent are sufficient to demonstrate a violent criminal history. Describing the most recent domestic violence incident in detail can illustrate how a victim responded to the force directed at him/her by the perpetrator. It may also explain why the victim responded in a certain way to prevent injury or death. An expert in the area of domestic violence may be needed to explain the response of a particular victim to the perceived threat, strengthen the subjective belief of a particular victim regarding the threat or act of violence, and explore the mechanism of fear that surrounds the battering experience. It may also prove useful in explaining to the court why this particular victim does not fit the stereotypical model of a victim.

The attorney for the petitioner has a duty to educate the court that, in many cases when victims physically resist their batterers in self-defense, the batterer is most often the primary aggressor. Studies indicate that "women suffer more injuries during the assaults, are attacked much more frequently, with more aggressive actions during a single attack and that each attack is more severe than when women

[48]But see State v. Wetherall, 2002-Ohio-1613, 2002 WL 440700 (Ohio Ct. App. 1st Dist. Hamilton County 2002).

[49]See RC 2935.03(B)(3)(d)(iv).

[50]See RC 2935.03(B)(3)(d)(i).

[51]See RC 2935.03(B)(3)(d)(iv).

[52]Catherine F. Klein & Leslye E. Orloff, Providing Legal Protection for Battered Women: An Analysis of State Statutes and Case Law, 21 Hofstra L. Rev. 801, 1075 (1993).

[53]See Chieco v. Chieco, 170 A.D.2d 569, 566 N.Y.S.2d 345 (2d Dep't 1991).

[Section 12:30]

[1]See for example Maurer v. Cobb-Maurer, 994 N.E.2d 753 (Ind. Ct. App. 2013) (demonstrating the shortcomings of a hearing on domestic violence matters conducted without thorough presentation of the evidence and examination of the parties involved).

use force against their male batterers."[2] Therefore, violence between the parties should rarely be treated equally.

Police documentation by way of the incident report and hospital or emergency room records documenting the injuries inflicted upon either of the parties should help attorneys in preparing their case and presenting their evidence. Significantly, the police officers at the scene usually will have already made an initial determination of primary physical aggressor before making an arrest.

Since the enforcement of civil protection orders is crucial to the effectiveness of the process and since mutual protection orders create a significant disincentive to request police enforcement, mutual protection orders should only be used sparingly by courts. Compliance with the statutory mandates of RC 3113.31(E)(4) must be of the utmost concern for the practicing attorney. The benefits of the civil protection order will be lost unless compliance with the statutory procedure is strictly monitored and enforced.

Clearly, an attorney has a responsibility to understand the legal issues inherent in domestic violence cases. In a report from the American Bar Association's Commission on Domestic Violence, it states "Understanding domestic violence legal issues is a matter of professional competency."[3] The report also notes that "Law schools which fail to teach students about domestic violence legal issues may be exposing future attorneys to malpractice suits, disciplinary complaints or sanctions for ethical violations."[4]

This means that attorneys who represent victims of domestic violence in all areas of the legal spectrum must first screen all clients for domestic violence and then assess options so not to further endanger victims of domestic violence.[5] An attorney who fails to recognize and present evidence a pattern of domestic violence may jeopardize a client's custody case. An attorney who is unaware that his/her client is a victim of domestic violence may counsel a client to sign a separation agreement in a divorce case that may also contain a waiver or any tort claims. An attorney representing a client who is also a battered immigrant may jeopardize the client's immigration status.

---

[2]Angela Browne, Violence Against Women by Male Partners: Prevalence, Outcomes and Policy Implications, 48 Am. Psychol. 1077, 1078 (1993).

[3]Deborah Goelman and Roberta Valente, When Will They Ever Learn? Educating to End Domestic Violence: A Law School Report, American Bar Association Commission on Domestic Violence, 1997, p. 20. See also Saffren, Professional Responsibility in Civil Domestic Violence Matters, 24 Hastings Women's L.J. 3 (2013).

[4]Deborah Goelman and Roberta Valente, When Will They Ever Learn? Educating to End Domestic Violence: A Law School Report, American Bar Association Commission on Domestic Violence, 1997, p. 20.

[5]William T. Schemmel, Domestic Violence: An Attorney's Perspective, 46-OCT Res Gestae 39, 39 (2002).

Chapter 13

Court Enforcement of Civil Protection Orders and Related Issues

§ 13:1 Introduction

Civil protection orders are designed to prevent unlawful conduct between intimates. In fact, the Supreme Court, in *Felton v. Felton*,[1] stated: "The General Assembly enacted the domestic violence statutes specifically to criminalize those activities commonly known as domestic violence and to authorize a court to issue protection orders designed to ensure the safety and protection of a complainant in domestic violence cases."[2] "Accordingly, the primary purpose of such orders is

---

[Section 13:1]

[1]Felton v. Felton, 79 Ohio St. 3d 34, 1997-Ohio-302, 679 N.E.2d 672 (1997).

[2]Felton v. Felton, 79 Ohio St. 3d 34, 37, 1997-Ohio-302, 679 N.E.2d 672 (1997);

not to punish past conduct, but to prevent future harm."[3] The effectiveness of civil protection orders depends on how well they are enforced by both the judiciary and law enforcement agencies.[4] According to the National Institute of Justice,

> enforcement is the Achilles' heel of the civil protection order process, because an order without enforcement at best offers scant protection and at worst increases the victim's danger by creating a false sense of security. Offenders may routinely violate orders if they believe there is no real risk of being arrested.[5]

Unfortunately, a lack of consistent enforcement is still cited as a primary weakness of protection orders.[6]

Domestic relations court judges throughout the country are authorized by statute to enforce civil protection orders through contempt actions. Almost one-half of the states enforce civil protection orders through either civil or criminal contempt.[7] Many states enforce a civil protection order through either contempt or criminal prosecution as a misdemeanor.[8] The trend has been to expand the remedies available to petitioners by enforcing protection orders by contempt as well as criminal prosecution.

Ohio is one of a growing number of states to take advantage of both contempt and criminal sanctions for violations of civil protection orders.[9] The Ohio legislature recognized that the effectiveness of the civil protection order lies with its enforcement. Holding the offender accountable is a significant part of the enforcement process. Both contempt of court and criminal prosecution are viewed as deterrents to future criminal activity.[10] The major advantage of criminal prosecu-

---

see also Hershberger v. Hershberger, 2000-Ohio-1716, 2000 WL 1675568 (Ohio Ct. App. 3d Dist. Seneca County 2000). T.K. Logan, Robert Walker, William Hoyt and Teri Faragher, The Kentucky Civil Protective Order Study: A Rural and Urban Multiple Perspective Study of Protective Order Protection Consequences, Responses and Costs, NIJ (2009) and downloaded at www.ncjrs.gov/pdffiles1/nij/grants/228350.pdf.

[3]Hon. Hollis L. Webster, Enforcement in Domestic Violence Cases, 26 Loy. U. Chi. L.J. 663, 664 (1995).

[4]See Goodmark, Law is the Answer? Do We Know That for Sure?: Questioning the Efficacy of Legal Interventions for Battered Women, 23 St. Louis. U. Pub. L. Rev. 7 (2004).

[5]Peter Finn & Sarah Colson, National Institute of Justice, Civil Protection Orders: Legislation, Current Court Practice and Enforcement Ch. 5 at 49 (1990).

[6]David Zlotnick, Empowering the Battered Woman: The Use of Criminal Contempt Sanctions to Enforce Civil Protection Orders, 56 Ohio St. L.J. 1153, 1194 (1995).

[7]Catherine F. Klein & Leslye E. Orloff, Providing Legal Protection for Battered Women: An Analysis of State Statutes and Case Law, 21 Hofstra L. Rev. 801, 1095–96 (1993).

[8]Catherine F. Klein & Leslye E. Orloff, Providing Legal Protection for Battered Women: An Analysis of State Statutes and Case Law, 21 Hofstra L. Rev. 801, 1097 (1993); see also Hershberger v. Hershberger, 2000-Ohio-1716, 2000 WL 1675568 (Ohio Ct. App. 3d Dist. Seneca County 2000).

[9]RC 3113.31(L).

[10]See Margaret Martin Barry, Protective Order Enforcement: Another Pirouette, 6 Hastings Women's L.J. 339 (1995).

tion is that repeat violations of civil protection orders result in enhanced sanctions or penalties for the respondent.[11]

§ 13:2 Court enforcement of civil protection orders—Generally

"It is axiomatic that a court has the power to enforce its own orders and to punish violations of them. Our legislature enacted a series of statutes, both in Title 29, the criminal section, and in Title 31, the domestic relations section, in order to deal with this growing problem."[1]

Ohio's domestic violence statute allows for the enforcement of protection orders through either a misdemeanor or felony prosecution or contempt. RC 3113.31(L)(1) specifically provides that:

> [a] person who violates a protection order issued or a consent agreement approved under this section is subject to the following sanctions:
> (a) Criminal prosecution for a violation of section 2919.27 of the Revised Code, if the violation of the protection order or consent agreement constitutes a violation of that section;
> (b) Punishment for contempt of court.

Q & A: Do all civil protection order violations result in RC 2919.27 sanctions?

No. In the first instance, a petitioner chooses whether to pursue criminal prosecution or contempt.[2] Should the victim choose to pursue a contempt action, a motion is filed in domestic relations court.[3] Of course, RC 3113.31(L)(2) indicates that a petitioner may pursue both criminal prosecution and contempt of court proceedings for the same act in certain circumstances.

Should the petitioner wish to criminally pursue the violation, he/she must seek assistance from the prosecutor's office. However, many of the petitioners who contact the prosecutor's office are told that there is not enough evidence to bring a criminal prosecution. Others are told that the violation is intrinsically civil and should be addressed in domestic relations court.

RC 3113.31(L)(1) provides in part:

> A person who violates a protection order issued or a consent agreement approved under this section is subject to the following sanctions:
> (a) Criminal prosecution for a violation of section 2919.27 of the Revised Code, if the violation of the protection order or consent agreement constitutes a violation of that section;
> (b) Punishment for contempt of court.

It is noteworthy that RC 3113.31(L)(1)(a) provides for criminal prosecution for a violation only if the violation of the protection order constitutes a violation of RC 2919.27(B). This presumes that the violation

---

[11] See RC 2919.27.

[Section 13:2]

[1] City of Reynoldsburg v. Eichenberger, 1990 WL 52467, *2 (Ohio Ct. App. 5th Dist. Licking County 1990).

[2] RC 3113.31(L)(1).

[3] See Text § 13:8, Enforcement of civil protection orders; procedures for initiating contempt motions, for a discussion of the procedure for initiating a contempt motion.

is of the type that prohibits certain conduct or behavior. The term "recklessly" is the culpable mental state for the violation and assumes the actor intended the act but not the resulting harm.[4] The significance of this language suggests that the legislature contemplated that only certain violations should result in criminal prosecution.

Practically speaking, only serious infractions of a civil protection order result in RC 2919.27(A) sanctions.[5] Continued criminal acts of violence against the victim or other family or household members protected by the protection order, such as assaults or threats to kill or hurt, result in criminal prosecution. Sometimes, continued harassment[6] or stalking may result in criminal prosecution.[7] Although RC 2919.27(A) does not differentiate between actionable and nonactionable violations, it is arguable that only violations that rise to the level of a criminal offense result in RC 2919.27 sanctions.[8]

On the other hand, violations that do not result in bodily injury or threats to the petitioner or other family or household member have

---

[4]See State v. Patton, 106 Ohio App. 3d 736, 667 N.E.2d 57 (1st Dist. Hamilton County 1995).

[5]See, for example, State v. Evans, 2004-Ohio-318, 2004 WL 117613 (Ohio Ct. App. 5th Dist. Licking County 2004) (Defendant's unsuccessful attempt to purchase a rifle constituted a violation of the CPO; even though he could not have acquired the firearm because NCIC had denied his application is of no consequence. There was no evidence that he voluntarily contact the gun store to rescind his request to purchase the rifle before his application was denied.).

[6]See also State v. Rusu, 2005-Ohio-270, 2005 WL 156728 (Ohio Ct. App. 9th Dist. Summit County 2005); State v. Sullivan, 2015-Ohio-4845, 2015 WL 7573207 (Ohio Ct. App. 1st Dist. Hamilton County 2015) (contacting the victim while a TPO was in place pending a criminal domestic violence case was sufficient evidence to meet the elements of RC 2919.27; evidence supported by a screen shot of the telephone number as well as a return call to the number by the responding police officer).

[7]See City of Reynoldsburg v. Eichenberger, 1990 WL 52467 (Ohio Ct. App. 5th Dist. Licking County 1990); see also State v. Mustaine, 2000 WL 966387 (Ohio Ct. App. 2d Dist. Montgomery County 2000); State v. Pollis, 2000 WL 522431 (Ohio Ct. App. 11th Dist. Trumbull County 2000); State v. Havard, 2001 WL 1566932 (Ohio Ct. App. 12th Dist. Butler County 2001); State v. Frazier, 158 Ohio App. 3d 407, 2004-Ohio-4506, 815 N.E.2d 1155 (1st Dist. Hamilton County 2004) (affirming defendant's conviction for violating a criminal protection order based on sending a letter to petitioner in violation of the "no contact" provisions of the order. Even though the letter contained to overt threats and gave no indication that defendant planned to contact petitioner in person, the letter itself could have reasonable been deemed to attempt to defy the court's order and to cause petitioner and other family members emotional distress or psychological harm; see also the dissenting opinion.); State v. Zaciek, 2009-Ohio-383, 2009 WL 223910 (Ohio Ct. App. 6th Dist. Ottawa County 2009) (affirmed appellant's conviction for violating RC 2919.27(A) in case where CPO prohibited him from driving on a certain street where appellee's cottage was located but permitted contact to effect visitation).

[8]But see City of Columbus v. Kurtz, 1995 WL 723684 (Ohio Ct. App. 10th Dist. Franklin County 1995) (finding the defendant guilty of violating a protection order by coming to the petitioner's place of employment); State v. Havard, 2001 WL 1566932 (Ohio Ct. App. 12th Dist. Butler County 2001) (defendant contacted and followed his ex-wife and son in violation of the civil protection order); City of Kent v. Raymond, 2004-Ohio-527, 2004 WL 231515 (Ohio Ct. App. 11th Dist. Portage County 2004) (defendant's failure to depart public place within 500 feet of victim violated CPO); State v. Whelan, 2004-Ohio-5183, 2004 WL 2244485 (Ohio Ct. App. 9th Dist. Summit County 2004) (confirmed conviction for violating a protection order under RC 2912.27(A)(1) for failing to immediately depart in presence of protected party by being within 100 yards of protected person).

been enforced through a contempt action in domestic relations court. Failure to pay support and violations of orders related to custody and visitation are typically enforced through contempt.[9] Since these protection order violations do not rise to the level of a criminal offense, it is argued the penalty for the violation should not result in punishment but rather in securing future compliance with the court order. Unfortunately, "civil contempt proceedings provide ineffective immediate protection to a victim."[10]

Additionally, because violations of this type are intrinsically civil in scope, prosecutors often express a degree of discomfort in criminally prosecuting respondents/defendants. That discomfort is justified since the domestic relations courts have continuing jurisdiction over those issues.[11] However, this rationale may indicate a lack of understanding of the civil order itself.

Removal of the respondent from the premises has been enforced by both criminal prosecution and contempt, depending on the circumstances and the jurisdiction. The prosecutor may choose to bring charges where a respondent either refuses to vacate the residence or returns to the premises in violation of the civil protection order.[12] If the police arrest the respondent for violating the civil protection order,[13] the chances that the prosecutor will pursue charges are more likely.

Q & A: How are civil protection orders generally enforced?

A survey of some Ohio jurisdictions indicates that no official policy or procedure exists to articulate which civil protection order violations are enforced by civil contempt or criminal prosecution. It would appear that a review is made on an individual case-by-case basis. Further, few civil protection order violations are enforced either through a contempt action or by criminal prosecution.

Generally, municipal court prosecutors are more likely to bring charges against respondents whose violations result in bodily injury or threats thereof.[14] For example, in the City of Cleveland, municipal prosecutors are likely to prosecute violations of civil protection orders

---

[9]RC 3113.31(L)(1)(b); see also City of Columbus v. Patterson, 1982 WL 4556 (Ohio Ct. App. 10th Dist. Franklin County 1982); see also Margaret Martin Barry, Protective Enforcement: Another Pirouette, 6 Hastings Women's L.J. 339, 358 (1995) (arguing for criminal sanctions in failure to pay support cases).

[10]Hon. Hollis L. Webster, Enforcement in Domestic Violence Cases, 26 Loy. U. Chi. L.J. 663, 669 (1995) (footnote omitted).

[11]But see State v. Price, 2006-Ohio-3856, 2006 WL 2105855 (Ohio Ct. App. 2d Dist. Montgomery County 2006), judgment rev'd, 118 Ohio St. 3d 144, 2008-Ohio-1974, 886 N.E.2d 852 (2008) (where the defendant was convicted of violating CPO by calling and leaving harassing messages on answering machine, conviction reversed by Ohio Supreme Court because of intervening divorce decree).

[12]See Text § 13:2, Court enforcement of civil protection orders—Generally; see also State v. Bunch, 2001 WL 39599 (Ohio Ct. App. 9th Dist. Summit County 2001); State v. Salazar, 2007-Ohio-196, 2007 WL 126142 (Ohio Ct. App. 6th Dist. Sandusky County 2007); State v. Copp, 2003-Ohio-5399, 2003 WL 22318519 (Ohio Ct. App. 2d Dist. Montgomery County 2003) (upheld criminal conviction for violating CPO where appellant remained at a place within 500 yards of the residence of the protected parties).

[13]See RC 2935.03(B)(3)(b).

[14]See generally Margaret Martin Barry, Protective Enforcement: Another

pursuant to RC 2919.27 where there is a new incident of abuse. They also consider those cases in which the violation is a threat to hurt or kill.[15]

In contrast, inherently civil violations and technical violations are almost always referred to domestic relations courts for contempt actions.[16] These include custody or parenting time enforcement or support issues under RC 3113.31(E)(1)(d) and RC 3113.31(E)(1)(e) and violations regarding counseling[17] or property.[18]

Less clear are violations that do not result in actual abuse and are difficult to independently corroborate. For example, harassment,[19] threats,[20] a refusal to vacate the premises or a return to the premises are generally enforced as contempt[21] but may also be enforced through

---

Pirouette, 6 Hastings Women's L.J. 339, 357–58 (1995) (advocating criminal sanctions for violations due to failure to pay support as batterers often use money to manipulate and intimidate victims).

[15]See, e.g., City of Cleveland v. Serrano, 1999 WL 1024214 (Ohio Ct. App. 8th Dist. Cuyahoga County 1999) (trial court charged appellant with violating a civil protection order for attempting contact and threatening to kill his children at their school).

[16]See, for example, City of Springfield.

[17]RC 3113.31(E)(1)(f).

[18]RC 3113.31(E)(1)(h).

[19]Jeffers v. Jeffers, 2001 WL 118530 (Ohio Ct. App. 10th Dist. Franklin County 2001); State v. Price, 118 Ohio St. 3d 144, 2008-Ohio-1974, 886 N.E.2d 852 (2008) (where defendant was convicted of violating CPO by calling and leaving harassing messages on answering machine, conviction overturned by Ohio Supreme Court because of intervening divorce decree); State v. Putman-Albright, 2016-Ohio-319, 2016 WL 525863 (Ohio Ct. App. 2d Dist. Montgomery County 2016) (where CPO terms allowed respondent to have contact with the petitioner by phone, text or email and said communication only be regarding their child and respondent was subsequently convicted of violating the CPO, the court found that respondent was not permitted to speak to petitioner about matters beyond parental concerns; thus, affirming conviction under RC 2919.27); State v. Sims, 2016-Ohio-7341, 2016 WL 6069093 (Ohio Ct. App. 6th Dist. Wood County 2016); State v. Plummer, 2016-Ohio-7548, 2016 WL 6462544 (Ohio Ct. App. 12th Dist. Warren County 2016) (sending a series of text messages was grounds to convict for violating a CPO; proof that he was person who sent texts was established because the texts originated from his phone and included a pet name he called her during the relationship that only he knew).

[20]But see Com. v. Baker, 722 A.2d 718, 719, 721, (Pa. Super. Ct. 1998), order aff'd, 564 Pa. 192, 766 A.2d 328 (2001) (court noted that defendant's statement, "I'm going to kill this bitch," could not subject defendant to conviction for indirect contempt of a protection order which prohibited defendant from threatening plaintiff, where defendant made statement while incarcerated and where plaintiff was not aware of statement; interestingly, court stated that "an order underlying a contempt charge must be definite, clear, specific and leave no doubt or uncertainty as to what conduct is prohibited;" the court held "when a contempt conviction is based on a constitutionally protected activity of the fundamental nature of freedom of speech, the court must exercise restraint in prohibiting the activity so as to not destroy the right;" only true threats fall within that group of expressions which are not constitutionally protected; a true threat is one which "on its face and in the circumstances in which it is made is so unequivocal, unconditionally immediate and specific as to the person threatened, so as to convey a gravity of purpose and imminent prospect of execution," quoting U.S. v. Kelner, 534 F.2d 1020, 1027, 34 A.L.R. Fed. 767 (2d Cir. 1976)).

[21]See, e.g., State v. Higgins, 1996 WL 363543, *1 (Ohio Ct. App. 5th Dist. Licking County 1996) (discussing Higgins v. Higgins, No. 94-DR01488 RAS, where appellant's wife initiated a contempt action in domestic relations court, alleging appellant had

a criminal prosecution.[22] On the other hand, if the respondent refuses to vacate the premises and there is independent corroboration to support petitioner's allegation and the respondent has knowledge of the terms of the civil protection order, the respondent's mere presence at the premises may be sufficient to charge the respondent under RC 2919.27.[23]

Over the last two decades, more and more respondents have been criminally charged with a violation of a CPO under RC 2919.27 where the order required the respondent to have no contact with petitioner[24] or be about the residence, school, place of employment of any protected party or not be within 500 feet or another geographic distance of any protected person.

For example, in *State v. Stoner*,[25] Mr. Stoner was found guilty of violating a CPO for being within 500 feet of his estranged wife and a

---

violated the terms of the civil protection order by telephone harassment); see also Jeffers v. Jeffers, 2001 WL 118530 (Ohio Ct. App. 10th Dist. Franklin County 2001) (discussing the term harassment).

[22]See State v. Salazar, 2007-Ohio-196, 2007 WL 126142 (Ohio Ct. App. 6th Dist. Sandusky County 2007) (affirmed judgment of criminal violation of protection order for returning to the residence despite being barred from residence); see also State v. Boczek, 2006-Ohio-3767, 2006 WL 2042898, *5 (Ohio Ct. App. 11th Dist. Lake County 2006) (affirmed criminal conviction for violating a civil protection order based on numerous phone calls to appellee. "The fact that the evidence established that appellant received a copy and acknowledged receipt of the CPO one week before the incident. The record also shows that appellant was familiar with civil protection orders and had knowledge that he should not violate them."). See also State v. Havard, 2001 WL 1566932 (Ohio Ct. App. 12th Dist. Butler County 2001) (evidence that appellant followed his ex-wife to the residence, drove by 4 times, waving and honking his horn supported a conviction for violating the terms of the civil protection order which prohibited among other things, following, bothering, harassing and annoying); State v. Glascoe, 2013-Ohio-1368, 2013 WL 1390531 (Ohio Ct. App. 2d Dist. Montgomery County 2013) (affirmed conviction for reckless violation of protection order based on "contact" with protected party. Contact includes in-person communication by any means); but see State v. Calhoun, 2008-Ohio-265, 2008 WL 204674 (Ohio Ct. App. 2d Dist. Montgomery County 2008) (appeals court reversed conviction against appellant for violating CPO contact provisions. In this case, appellate court agreed that the calls made to the residence were for his son and son was not a protected person under CPO; note the dissent).

[23]See City of Columbus for a similar response. See also State v. Salazar, 2007-Ohio-196, 2007 WL 126142 (Ohio Ct. App. 6th Dist. Sandusky County 2007).

[24]State v. Ybarra, 2016-Ohio-5761, 2016 WL 4724354 (Ohio Ct. App. 5th Dist. Licking County 2016) (initiating contact with appellee via a third party by leaving an envelope at his ex wife's door was sufficient grounds to convict appellant for violating a protection order); State v. Sims, 2018-Ohio-769, 2018 WL 1136587 (Ohio Ct. App. 2d Dist. Clark County 2018) (violation of CSPO was upheld and not predicated on victim's permission where defendant resided on same street and within the 500 feet prohibited distance from victim); State v. Seibert, 2017-Ohio-9080, 2017 WL 6459890 (Ohio Ct. App. 9th Dist. Wayne County 2017) (where parties lived in same apartment building, defendant violated order as he knew he was within 500 feet of the victim).

[25]State v. Stoner, 2009-Ohio-2073, 2009 WL 1174942 (Ohio Ct. App. 2d Dist. Clark County 2009); see also State v. Bidlack, 2009-Ohio-4589, 2009 WL 2855732 (Ohio Ct. App. 6th Dist. Wood County 2009); State v. Shockey, 2013-Ohio-362, 2013 WL 457357 (Ohio Ct. App. 9th Dist. Summit County 2013) (upholding conviction for violating CPO because, although meeting was accidental, not departing immediately was the basis of the violation); State v. Weston, 2013-Ohio-791, 2013 WL 844379 (Ohio Ct. App. 5th Dist. Tuscarawas County 2013); State v. Hunter, 2013-Ohio-1469, 2013 WL 1501572 (Ohio Ct. App. 2d Dist. Montgomery County 2013); State v. Wisby, 2013-Ohio-1307, 2013 WL 1288202 (Ohio Ct. App. 12th Dist. Clermont County 2013);

protected party on the CPO. Stoner appealed the conviction on the ground that the State had failed to prove that he had acted recklessly and that he was within a 500-foot radius of his wife (Tristin).

The appellate court found that, based on aerial photographs and the testimony and measurements of police officers, it was reasonable for the court to conclude that Stoner was within that prohibited 500-foot radius. The Court also determined that "[a]lthough Stoner denied that he intended to violate the CPO or that he was aware that his presence at the Heriers' home violated the order, the trial court could reasonably infer from his conduct that Stoner, with heedless indifference to the consequences, perversely disregarded a known risk that his presence at the Heriers would place him within 500 feet of Tristin or a place where she was likely to be."[26] In upholding the conviction, the appellate court relied on Tristin's testimony that she could hear Stoner talking in a normal speaking voice and his own testimony that he could have called the Heriers to invite them to the party rather than drive to their home, two doors down from his wife.

§ 13:3 Court enforcement of civil protection orders—Criminal prosecution[1]

Under RC 2919.27(A), no person shall recklessly violate any terms[2] of a protection order issued or consent agreement approved pursuant to RC 2919.26 or RC 3113.31, a stalking protection order issued pursuant to RC 2903.213 or RC 2903.214[3], a juvenile civil protection order issued pursuant to RC 2151.34 or a protection order issued by a court of another state. In accordance with the statutory language set forth in RC 2919.27, the sanction for a civil protection order violation should apply to ex parte civil protection orders and ex parte stalking

---

State v. Reber, 2012-Ohio-2712, 2012 WL 2261119 (Ohio Ct. App. 5th Dist. Licking County 2012); State v. Tarver, 2012-Ohio-4335, 2012 WL 4344075 (Ohio Ct. App. 11th Dist. Portage County 2012) (to establish recklessness, the state was only required to prove that appellant disregarded a known risk that his conduct was likely to place him on the school grounds or within 500 ft. of B.K.); City of Lyndhurst v. Smith, 2015-Ohio-303, 2015 WL 405991 (Ohio Ct. App. 8th Dist. Cuyahoga County 2015).

[26]State v. Stoner, 2009-Ohio-2073, 2009 WL 1174942, *8 (Ohio Ct. App. 2d Dist. Clark County 2009); State v. Bardos, 2016-Ohio-8091, 2016 WL 7188532 (Ohio Ct. App. 9th Dist. Medina County 2016).

[Section 13:3]

[1]See also Text § 13:8, Enforcement of civil protection orders; procedures for initiating contempt motions; Text § 11:24, Ex parte protection orders—Violation of ex parte protection orders.

[2]See City of Strongsville v. N.D., 2016-Ohio-7484, 2016 WL 8453026 (Ohio Ct. App. 8th Dist. Cuyahoga County 2016) (in order to demonstrate that an offender had violated a term of the order pursuant to RC 2919.27, a court cannot take judicial notice of a prior proceeding in the court without introducing and admitting the TPO into evidence on the record); City of Cleveland v. Boone, 2018-Ohio-849, 2018 WL 1217716 (Ohio Ct. App. 8th Dist. Cuyahoga County 2018) (in appeal for violating a TPO, court reversed and rejected trial court's reliance on testimony that TPO existed on date in question and held that trial court could not take judicial notice of the content of TPO without having it be introduced as evidence and admitted as an exhibit or be stipulated to by appellant); see also Text § 12:21 on judicial notice.

[3]See State v. Headlee, 2009-Ohio-873, 2009 WL 478085 (Ohio Ct. App. 4th Dist. Washington County 2009); State v. Sims, 2018-Ohio-769, 2018 WL 1136587 (Ohio Ct. App. 2d Dist. Clark County 2018).

civil protection orders,[4] protection orders issued by the court after a full hearing, and consent agreements approved by the court after a full hearing.

A violation of any of the terms of the civil protection order subjects the violator to punishment under RC 2919.27(B), which requires that the respondent act "recklessly." One who recklessly violates a protection order does so when

> with heedless indifference to the consequences, he perversely disregards a known risk that his conduct is likely to cause a certain result or is likely to be of a certain nature. A person is reckless with respect to circumstances when, with heedless indifference to the consequences, he perversely disregards a known risk that such circumstances are likely to exist.[5]

The underlying purpose or intent of the perpetrator is irrelevant in determining whether he/she acted recklessly. The fact that he/she acted and that his/her conduct caused bodily injury to the victim is primary to any legal analysis.[6] A "reckless" violation does not necessarily mean that bodily injury must occur. In many cases, a defendant was the subject of a civil or criminal protection order. The violation may have been one in which the defendant remained within 500 feet of the petitioner for an extended period of time.[7]

Q & A: Can a respondent be criminally prosecuted for violating an ex parte civil protection order?[8]

Several courts have tangentially addressed whether criminal prosecution under RC 2919.27 may be considered by the court for the violation of an ex parte order.[9] In *State v. Myers*,[10] the defendant appealed the trial court's sentence which included a violation of the civil protec-

---

[4]See RC 2903.214.

[5]RC 2901.22(C).

[6]State v. Purvis, 1989 WL 126298 (Ohio Ct. App. 9th Dist. Medina County 1989).

[7]See for example, State v. Maupin, 2014-Ohio-5398, 2014 WL 6871008 (Ohio Ct. App. 12th Dist. Warren County 2014) (discussion of what behaviors can be considered "reckless"); City of Lyndhurst v. Smith, 2015-Ohio-303, 2015 WL 405991 (Ohio Ct. App. 8th Dist. Cuyahoga County 2015).

[8]See also Text § 11:11, Ex parte protection orders—Service and notice provisions; Text § 14:15, Potential police liability in the enforcement of protection orders; see Westlake v. Patrick, 2007-Ohio-1307, 2007 WL 853235 (Ohio Ct. App. 8th Dist. Cuyahoga County 2007) (concluding that the court could criminally punish a defendant for violating a facially valid ex parte order, even if the order is subsequently determined to be invalid after the violation occurred); see also Hunt v. Morrow County, Ohio, 2009-Ohio-4313, 2009 WL 2602204 (Ohio Ct. App. 5th Dist. Morrow County 2009) (noting that the CPO in the case, while not served, was a lawful, valid order); State v. Sutts, 2004-Ohio-3541, ¶ 2-3, ¶ 7, 2004 WL 1485909 (Ohio Ct. App. 12th Dist. Warren County 2004); State v. Hall, 2013-Ohio-660, ¶ 24, 30, 989 N.E.2d 111 (Ohio Ct. App. 5th Dist. Delaware County 2013), appeal allowed, cause remanded, 135 Ohio St. 3d 1456, 2013-Ohio-2285, 988 N.E.2d 576 (2013); State v. Hall, 2013-Ohio-5855, 2013 WL 6918874 (Ohio Ct. App. 5th Dist. Delaware County 2013).

[9]See also Text § 13:8, Enforcement of civil protection orders; procedures for initiating contempt motions. See also State v. Sutts, 2004-Ohio-3541, 2004 WL 1485909 (Ohio Ct. App. 12th Dist. Warren County 2004).

[10]State v. Myers, 2002-Ohio-253, 2002 WL 54753, *2 (Ohio Ct. App. 5th Dist. Perry County 2002); see also State v. Sanders, 327 N.J. Super. 385, 743 A.2d 385 (App. Div. 2000).

tion order because the civil protection order was an ex parte order that had expired at the time of the alleged offenses with which he was charged. The Perry Court of Appeals held that "the trial court could consider the ex parte order and the events which led up to it." Although the court did not address the service concerns,[11] it did state that the ex parte civil protection order did not violate appellant's due process rights.

Moreover, in *State v. Eschrich*,[12] the appellate court affirmed defendant's conviction for recklessly violating a protection order under R.C. 2919.27, despite the fact that the civil stalking protection order was later invalidated because the defendant never received actual notice of the final hearing of the CPO petition. The court held that the invalidity of a protection order is not a defense to a willful violation of the order. It should be mentioned that at the time defendant violated the order, it had not yet been declared invalid and thus, his reckless violation of the protection order was a crime.

Q & A: Is service of a civil protection order necessary in order to convict a defendant for its violation?[13]

Generally, in order to render a valid judgment against a party, a court must have personal jurisdiction over a party. A court may acquire personal jurisdiction[14] over a defendant by proper service of summons and a complaint, or the defendant must have entered an appearance in the underlying action and affirmatively waive service or otherwise voluntarily submit to the jurisdiction of the court.[15]

A trial court is without jurisdiction to render a judgment or make

[11]But see People v. Perez, 189 Misc. 2d 516, 734 N.Y.S.2d 398 (County Ct. 2001) (once "duly served," an individual violating a protection order may be prosecuted for criminal contempt; fax service outside of the state satisfies the requirements for service).

[12]State v. Eschrich, 2008-Ohio-2984, 2008 WL 2468572 (Ohio Ct. App. 6th Dist. Ottawa County 2008); State v. Schell, 2017-Ohio-2641, ¶ 51, 2017 WL 1748769 (Ohio Ct. App. 9th Dist. Summit County 2017); State v. Ybarra, 2016-Ohio-5761, 2016 WL 4724354 (Ohio Ct. App. 5th Dist. Licking County 2016) (relying on City of Reynoldsburg v. Eichenberger, 1990 WL 52467 (Ohio Ct. App. 5th Dist. Licking County 1990) (standing for the proposition that "[a]n order of the court must be obeyed unless and until a court finds it is invalid or rescinds it." At ¶ 12, quoting *Eichenberger*, citing In re Contempt of Court of White, 60 Ohio App. 2d 62, 65, 14 Ohio Op. 3d 34, 395 N.E.2d 499 (5th Dist. Stark County 1978); U.S. v. United Mine Workers of America, 330 U.S. 258, 293, 67 S. Ct. 677, 91 L. Ed. 884, 19 L.R.R.M. (BNA) 2346, 12 Lab. Cas. (CCH) P 51239 (1947)).

[13]See newly enacted RC 2919.27(D).

[14]See Text § 10:13, Jurisdiction and venue—In domestic violence cases; § 11:11, Ex parte protection orders—Service and notice provisions.

[15]Lucas v. Green, 1999 WL 961499 (Ohio Ct. App. 8th Dist. Cuyahoga County 1999), citing Maryhew v. Yova, 11 Ohio St. 3d 154, 464 N.E.2d 538 (1984); see also Smith v. Hensel, 2005-Ohio-3465, 2005 WL 1580810 (Ohio Ct. App. 5th Dist. Ashland County 2005) (noting that the appearance of the defendant, for any other reason than to object to jurisdiction, is deemed to be a voluntary submission to the jurisdiction of the court); see also Smith v. Hensel, 2005-Ohio-3465, 2005 WL 1580810 (Ohio Ct. App. 5th Dist. Ashland County 2005) (noting that the appearance of the defendant, for any other reason than to object to jurisdiction, is deemed to be a voluntary submission to the jurisdiction of the court, where appellant informed court that, had she known Smith and Riffle had filed petitions for CPO against her, she would have filed petitions against them, she consented to court jurisdiction; further, a determination of sufficiency of service of process is a matter within the trial court's sound discretion).

findings against a person not served with summons. Thus, when service of process has not been perfected, any judgment rendered or orders issued are void ab initio.[16] This would appear to include an unserved civil protection order.

While knowledge of the existence of the order had been sufficient to criminally violate a person for violating the civil protection order,[17] service of the order on the respondent is still necessary for a valid judgment. In effect, absent service of the civil protection, there can be no final CPO.

On the other hand, public policy dictates that perpetrators of domestic violence be held accountable for their actions. Since the purpose of a protection order is to provide legal protection from abusive acts and the enforcement provisions of these orders require accountability, statutes that grant ex parte protection orders must also confer criminal sanctions for violations of said orders.[18]

An ex parte protection order is granted to a complainant or petitioner without first providing either notice to the individual or an opportunity to be heard prior to its issuance. Constitutionally, procedural due process safeguards afford a defendant/respondent no-

---

Vance v. Nichols, 2007-Ohio-3819, 2007 WL 2164162 (Ohio Ct. App. 2d Dist. Darke County 2007); Text § 10:13, Jurisdiction and venue—In domestic violence cases; Text § 11:11, Ex parte protection orders—Service and notice provisions; Jones v. Jordan, 2007-Ohio-2519, 2007 WL 1508255 (Ohio Ct. App. 8th Dist. Cuyahoga County 2007). But see Gliozzo v. Univ. Urologists of Cleveland, Inc., 114 Ohio St. 3d 141, 2007-Ohio-3762, 870 N.E.2d 714 (2007) at syllabus (holding that when the affirmative defense of insufficiency of service is properly raised and preserved, a party's active participation in the litigation of cases does not constitute a waiver of that defense).

[16]Lucas v. Green, 1999 WL 961499, *5 (Ohio Ct. App. 8th Dist. Cuyahoga County 1999); State ex rel. Ballard v. O'Donnell, 50 Ohio St. 3d 182, 553 N.E.2d 650 (1990); see also State v. Eschrich, 2008-Ohio-2984, 2008 WL 2468572 (Ohio Ct. App. 6th Dist. Ottawa County 2008).

[17]See State v. Bunch, 2001 WL 39599 (Ohio Ct. App. 9th Dist. Summit County 2001) (RC 2919.27 does not require service of civil protection order be accomplished before respondent can be found to have violated it; prosecution must only prove beyond reasonable doubt that defendant acted in disregard of known risk that CPO was likely to have existed against him); see also City of Cleveland v. Serrano, 1999 WL 1024214 (Ohio Ct. App. 8th Dist. Cuyahoga County 1999) (appellant argued that he should not be found guilty of violating a temporary protection order where he was not served with the order; the appellate court affirmed the court decision without addressing the issue because the appellant had waived the requirement of the presentation of the evidence, and stipulated to a finding of guilt on a plea of no contest); MacDonald v. State, 997 P.2d 1187 (Alaska Ct. App. 2000) (ex parte protection order was binding on a defendant because he had actual knowledge of it); see also Midland Steel Prods. Co. v. U.A.W. Local 486, 61 Ohio St. 3d 121, 126, 573 N.E.2d 98 (1991) (determining that "[a] court's order is an 'order' only to the extent of its terms. To know an order, one must know its terms."); State v. Davidson, 2004-Ohio-6828, 2004 WL 2914137 (Ohio Ct. App. 4th Dist. Ross County 2004) (evidence presented by wife that husband had a copy of order and knew about order and testimony of deputy that husband was served in jail was sufficient to find that husband violated the protection order); State v. Hall, 2013-Ohio-660, 989 N.E.2d 111 (Ohio Ct. App. 5th Dist. Delaware County 2013), appeal allowed, cause remanded, 135 Ohio St. 3d 1456, 2013-Ohio-2285, 988 N.E.2d 576 (2013) (overruling State v. Mohabir); but see State v. Smith, 136 Ohio St. 3d 1, 2013-Ohio-1698, 989 N.E.2d 972 (2013) (state failed to prove that it served defendant with protection order before he allegedly violated it, and, thus, evidence was not sufficient for conviction).

[18]See Margaret Martin Barry, Protective Enforcement: Another Pirouette, 6 Hastings Women's L.J. 339, 357-58 (1995).

tice[19] and an opportunity for a hearing.[20] Since notice and an opportunity to be heard are cornerstones of due process, a predeprivation hearing is required unless there are extraordinary circumstances and additional safeguards are provided.[21] Therefore, both RC 3113.31 and RC 2919.26 mandate comparable procedural safeguards.

That said, the consensus of opinion from relevant appellate case law over the past 13 years, has demonstrated that service is not necessary for a criminal conviction under RC 2919.27(A) so long as the defendant/respondent has actual notice of the existence of the protection order. For example, in *State v. Bunch*, defendant was arrested for violating a civil protection order[22] issued pursuant to RC 3113.31 because he went to petitioner's house. Appealing his conviction, defendant argued that because he had not been served with a copy of the CPO, he could not have acted recklessly in violating the order. The evidence indicated that certified mail service of the CPO had been attempted but it was unclaimed and it was unclear whether service by ordinary mail was accomplished after certified mail was not perfected.

The appellate court specifically determined that service in not necessary in order to find an individual guilty of violating a CPO. The Summit County Court of Appeals held that "the Revised Code does not require that service of a CPO be accomplished upon the person against whom a CPO is issued before the person can be found to have violated the order. Rather, RC 2919.27 requires that the prosecution prove beyond a reasonable doubt that defendant acted in disregard of a known risk that a CPO was likely to have existed against him."[23] So long as the defendant had notice of the CPO, he/she can be convicted of violating the order.[24]

Since Bunch, other appellate districts have upheld judicial decisions supporting criminal convictions for violations of civil protection orders

[19]See Fahey v. Eschrich, 2006-Ohio-5619, 2006 WL 3041193 (Ohio Ct. App. 6th Dist. Ottawa County 2006) (CSPO invalidated because appellant did not receive actual notice of the final hearing of the protection order).

[20]See Mathews v. Eldridge, 424 U.S. 319, 96 S. Ct. 893, 47 L. Ed. 2d 18 (1976); see also Sniadach v. Family Finance Corp. of Bay View, 395 U.S. 337, 89 S. Ct. 1820, 23 L. Ed. 2d 349, 19 Wage & Hour Cas. (BNA) 5 (1969).

[21]See Blazel v. Bradley, 698 F. Supp. 756 (W.D. Wis. 1988); see also Fuentes v. Shevin, 407 U.S. 67, 92 S. Ct. 1983, 32 L. Ed. 2d 556, 10 U.C.C. Rep. Serv. 913 (1972); Boddie v. Connecticut, 401 U.S. 371, 91 S. Ct. 780, 28 L. Ed. 2d 113 (1971).

[22]RC 2919.27.

[23]State v. Bunch, 2001 WL 39599, *2 (Ohio Ct. App. 9th Dist. Summit County 2001). See also State v. Hoopingarner, 2011-Ohio-3040, 2011 WL 2464188 (Ohio Ct. App. 5th Dist. Tuscarawas County 2011); State v. Hall, 2013-Ohio-660, 989 N.E.2d 111 (Ohio Ct. App. 5th Dist. Delaware County 2013), appeal allowed, cause remanded, 135 Ohio St. 3d 1456, 2013-Ohio-2285, 988 N.E.2d 576 (2013) (overruling *State v. Mohabir*); but see State v. Thomas, 2012-Ohio-2430, 2012 WL 1970459 (Ohio Ct. App. 12th Dist. Warren County 2012); State v. Davidson, 2004-Ohio-6828, 2004 WL 2914137 (Ohio Ct. App. 4th Dist. Ross County 2004); State v. Bombardiere, 2007-Ohio-1537, 2007 WL 959895 (Ohio Ct. App. 3d Dist. Union County 2007).

[24]See also State v. Bombardiere, 2007-Ohio-1537, 2007 WL 959895 (Ohio Ct. App. 3d Dist. Union County 2007); MacDonald v. State, 997 P.2d 1187 (Alaska Ct. App. 2000) (ex parte protection order was binding on a defendant because he had actual knowledge of it); Murray City v. Culley, 1998 WL 1758314 (Utah Ct. App. 1998).

absent service of the order. In *State v. Rutherford*,[25] appellant claimed that because the state failed to present evidence that he was properly served with the protection order, he could not have recklessly violated the order because he could not have disregarded a known risk that the protection order existed. Expanding on the legal rationale set forth in Bunch, the appellate court determined that "RC 2919.27(A) does not make service of a civil protection order an element of the offense of violation of a civil protection order. Rather, that statute requires the State to prove beyond a reasonable doubt that defendant acted in disregard of a known risk that a protection order likely existed against him."[26] In this case, appellant had acknowledged in his appellate brief that he had notice of the protection order and that he was aware of both the order and its terms.[27]

Since a court has no authority to punish an individual for violating an ex parte civil protection order until the defendant has knowledge of its terms,[28] more appellate courts have found that actual notice is contingent upon a knowledge of the terms of the protection order, rather than on the existence of the order. In fact, the Supreme Court of Ohio determined that "[a] court's order is an 'order' only to the extent of its terms. To know an order, one must know its terms."[29] While Midland Steel applied to an ex parte temporary restraining order issued under Civ. R. 65, several courts have adopted a similar rationale in protection order cases.

For example, in *Toledo v. Lyphout*,[30] petitioner filed a police report alleging that her ex husband had violated the ex parte civil protection order. Defendant was charged and convicted of violating the protection order under RC 2919.27(A).

On appeal, defendant argued that the evidence was insufficient to show that he had acted with reckless disregard of a known risk that a civil protection order was likely to exist against him. The question was whether there was sufficient evidence that appellant knew of the

---

[25]State v. Rutherford, 2009-Ohio-2071, 2009 WL 1175050 (Ohio Ct. App. 2d Dist. Champaign County 2009). See also State v. Smith, 2011-Ohio-6730, 2011 WL 6916475, *5 (Ohio Ct. App. 10th Dist. Franklin County 2011), judgment rev'd, 136 Ohio St. 3d 1, 2013-Ohio-1698, 989 N.E.2d 972 (2013) (reversing court finding state failed to prove that it served defendant with protection order before he allegedly violated it and thus evidence insufficient for conviction).

[26]*Rutherford at *3*, citing *State v Bunch*; see also Toledo v. Lanier, 2009-Ohio-5191, 2009 WL 3132601 (Ohio Ct. App. 6th Dist. Lucas County 2009).

[27]But see State v. Williams, 2009-Ohio-3162, 2009 WL 1856743 (Ohio Ct. App. 9th Dist. Summit County 2009).

[28]See Toledo v. Lyphout, 2009-Ohio-4596, 2009 WL 2855714 (Ohio Ct. App. 6th Dist. Lucas County 2009); State v. Williams, 2009-Ohio-3162, 2009 WL 1856743 (Ohio Ct. App. 9th Dist. Summit County 2009) (pointing out that actual notice might have been accomplished if the law enforcement officer had advised the defendant of the existence of the order).

[29]Midland Steel Prods. Co. v. U.A.W. Local 486, 61 Ohio St. 3d 121, 126, 573 N.E.2d 98 (1991).

[30]Toledo v. Lyphout, 2009-Ohio-4596, 2009 WL 2855714 (Ohio Ct. App. 6th Dist. Lucas County 2009); State v. Williams, 2009-Ohio-3162, 2009 WL 1856743 (Ohio Ct. App. 9th Dist. Summit County 2009) (pointing out that actual notice might have been accomplished if the law enforcement officer had advised the defendant of the existence of the order); State v. Thomas, 2012-Ohio-2430, 2012 WL 1970459 (Ohio Ct. App. 12th Dist. Warren County 2012).

terms of the CPO. In relying on Midland Steel, the appellate court acknowledged that "actual notice requires more that general knowledge that an order has been issued."[31] Although the court reversed the conviction because it found that there was no actual notice of the prohibited behavior, the significance of this decision is that actual notice of the terms of the order is sufficient to find someone criminally liable of violating the terms of the protection order.[32] However, the Sixth District Court of Appeals also cautioned that absent proper service or actual notice of the prohibited behavior, the defendant could not be held criminally liable for disobedience of the order's terms.

Conversely, in *State v. Mohabir*,[33] appellant was arrested for violating a temporary protection order in violation of RC 2919.27. Appellant asserted that the protection order was not issued in compliance with the due process requirements of RC 2919.26(G)(1) which provides that "a copy of any protection order issued shall be issued by the court to the complainant, to the alleged victim, to the person who requested the order, to the defendant and to all law enforcement agencies that have jurisdiction to enforce the order. The court shall direct that a copy of the order be delivered to the defendant on the same day that the order is entered."

The evidence showed that there was no record that appellant was ever served with the order. The Fifth District court of Appeals noted that "the protection order statute makes criminal conduct that would otherwise be legal; therefore, the statute's requirements must be strictly construed in favor of the defendant and against the state. Previously, this Court has held the requirements of RC 2919.26 are mandatory to the issuance of a valid protection order. Therefore, the statute's due process requirements must be complied with prior to a trial court's finding a violation of a temporary protection order pursuant to RC 2919.27."[34]

The appellate court then held that the due process requirements of RC 2919.26 were not complied with in the issuance of the temporary protection order alleged to have been violated. The notation "via jail" was not sufficient to proof service and notice upon appellant. Since no evidence was provided to demonstrate actual service upon appellant in compliance with the statute, the conviction and sentence were reversed.

Q & A: So, what satisfies the requirements of service?[35]

According to the Supreme Court of Ohio, the answer is service. In

---

[31] At *3; citing Midland Steel.

[32] See also State v. Rutherford, 2009-Ohio-2071, 2009 WL 1175050 (Ohio Ct. App. 2d Dist. Champaign County 2009); State v. Williams, 2009-Ohio-3162, 2009 WL 1856743 (Ohio Ct. App. 9th Dist. Summit County 2009).

[33] State v. Mohabir, 2005-Ohio-78, 2005 WL 66484 (Ohio Ct. App. 5th Dist. Fairfield County 2005) (overruled by, State v. Hall, 2013-Ohio-660, 989 N.E.2d 111 (Ohio Ct. App. 5th Dist. Delaware County 2013)) (overruling court finding service of the temporary protection order on the defendant is not an element of the offense of violation of the protection order).

[34] State v. Mohabir, 2005-Ohio-78, 2005 WL 66484, *2 (Ohio Ct. App. 5th Dist. Fairfield County 2005) (overruled by, State v. Hall, 2013-Ohio-660, 989 N.E.2d 111 (Ohio Ct. App. 5th Dist. Delaware County 2013)) (citation omitted).

[35] But see RC 2919.27(D), enacted 9/27/2017, which superseded the holding in

State v. Smith,[36] defendant was charged with violating a civil protection order after breaking into the victim's home and attempting to strangle her. The victim had previously advised defendant that she had obtained a CSPO requiring him to stay at least 500 feet away from her. Defendant had not been served with the CSPO until after the incident occurred. The trial court found Smith guilty of violating the CSPO, which decision was affirmed by the Franklin County appellate court.

In his merit brief to the Ohio Supreme Court, Smith argued that he was not lawfully convicted of violating RC 2919.27 because he was never served with the order before the alleged offense. The State asserted that the plain language of RC 2919.27 requires only proof that the defendant recklessly violated a protection order issued pursuant to RC 2919.27, not proof of service. (RC 2919.27(A)(2) provides that no person shall recklessly violate the terms of a protection order issued pursuant to section * * * 2903.214 of the Revised Code). The State also claimed that protection orders are enforceable upon issuance, not service.

The majority stated that to prove a violation of RC 2919.27(A)(2), the state must prove, beyond a reasonable doubt, all requirements of RC 2903.214, including that the order be delivered to the defendant. That same element is also part of RC 3113.31. The pivotal question for any civil protection order is whether delivery implies service. According to the majority, "delivery" means that a court is mandated to bring about a transfer of possession of a copy of the protection order to the respondent. "The statute requires more than just the court's issuing the protection order and ordering its delivery to respondent. It requires that the order actually be delivered."[37] The only manner by which the court is able to fulfill this mandate is to serve the SSOOPO."[38]

In reversing the appellate court, the Supreme Court held that "service" and "delivery" are synonymous in this context and therefore, the State must establish beyond a reasonable doubt, that it served defendant with the order. Thus, when RC 2903.214(F)(1) requires "delivery" of the order, it is requiring "service" on the respondent.[39]

In its opinion, the majority also noted that the victim and the state have other recourse. "An offender who cannot be prosecuted for conduct that would have violated the protection order had it been properly served often commits other crimes during the same incident,

---

State v. Smith regarding violations of civil protection orders under RC 2919.27, so that unperfected service of a protection order or consent agreement does not preclude a prosecution for a violation of division (A) of that section.

[36]State v. Smith, 136 Ohio St. 3d 1, 2013-Ohio-1698, 989 N.E.2d 972 (2013).

[37]State v. Smith, 136 Ohio St. 3d 1, 2013-Ohio-1698, ¶ 19, 989 N.E.2d 972 (2013); State v. Ybarra, 2017-Ohio-9144, ¶ 23, 2017 WL 6508868 (Ohio Ct. App. 5th Dist. Licking County 2017) (evidence documenting that defendant was served with the CPO included fact that he had previously violated the same order which demonstrated that he had been served with the order).

[38]State v. Smith, 136 Ohio St. 3d 1, 2013-Ohio-1698, ¶ 28, 989 N.E.2d 972 (2013).

[39]State v. Smith, 136 Ohio St. 3d 1, 2013-Ohio-1698, ¶ 20, 989 N.E.2d 972 (2013).

such as burglary or assault, for which he may be punished to the full extent of the law."[40]

Of significance is that the opinion was divided 4-3. The dissent, written by Justice Lanzinger, found that proof of service or delivery is not needed for a conviction for violating the protection order. "The majority focuses on the technical service that is to take place after the order is issued."[41] "I disagree that this provision means that the crime of violating a protection order may not be charged unless a defendant has first been served with the order itself. The order has independent force, even apart from service. RC 2903.214(E)(2)(a) states that the protection order's validity dates from its issuance."[42] The dissent focused on the term "issuance," noting that a person may not be charged with the crime of violating a protection order under RC 2919.27 unless that order is "issued," but the statute is silent about "delivery" or "service."[43]

While service may be relevant in determining whether there was proof beyond a reasonable doubt that defendant acted recklessly, it is incumbent upon the State to prove a mens rea of recklessness-whether a defendant had knowledge of the order's existence and yet disregarded it.[44] "Here, however, Pickens gave testimony that, if believed, proved that she told Smith she had obtained an order and told him what it said. He ignored the protection order to stay away from Pickens and thereby violated it."[45] "I respectfully dissent and would hold that service of the protection order on the defendant is not an element of the crime of violating a protection order as defined in RC 2919.27(A)."[46]

So, we have learned from the Smith decision that "delivery" is synonymous with "service" and without proof of service, a conviction for violating RC 2919.27(A)(2) cannot stand.

However, the decision also raises many other concerns. Besides not being able to violate a defendant for a violation, the majority implies that a protection order not served on a respondent is unenforceable. If that is the case, can an unenforceable order still be valid? If neither valid nor enforceable, what is its purpose?

Civ. R. 65.1 also provides that an ex parte protection order signed by a magistrate becomes effective when signed by the magistrate and filed with the clerk. Civ. R. 65.1(F)(2)(b)(i). Similarly, a court's adoption, modification, or rejection of a magistrate's denial or granting or a protection order after a full hearing shall be effective when signed by the court and filed with the clerk. Civ. R. 65.1(F)(3)(c)(v). Finally, an order entered by the court under division (F)(3)(c) is a final appealable order. However, under *Smith*, if such an order is not served, it apparently lacks enforceability. If it also lacks validity because it has not been served, it cannot be a final appealable order. In any case, the majority opinion in Smith cannot be reconciled with Civ. R. 65.1.

---

[40] State v. Smith, 136 Ohio St. 3d 1, 2013-Ohio-1698, ¶ 27, 989 N.E.2d 972 (2013).

[41] State v. Smith, 136 Ohio St. 3d 1, 2013-Ohio-1698, ¶ 29, 989 N.E.2d 972 (2013); RC 2903.214(F)(1).

[42] State v. Smith, 136 Ohio St. 3d 1, 2013-Ohio-1698, ¶ 31, 989 N.E.2d 972 (2013).

[43] State v. Smith, 136 Ohio St. 3d 1, 2013-Ohio-1698, ¶ 32, 989 N.E.2d 972 (2013).

[44] State v. Smith, 136 Ohio St. 3d 1, 2013-Ohio-1698, ¶ 32, 989 N.E.2d 972 (2013)

[45] State v. Smith, 136 Ohio St. 3d 1, 2013-Ohio-1698, ¶ 33, 989 N.E.2d 972 (2013).

[46] State v. Smith, 136 Ohio St. 3d 1, 2013-Ohio-1698, ¶ 34, 989 N.E.2d 972 (2013).

Both RC 2903.214(F)(1) and RC 3113.13(F)(1) state that "the court shall cause a copy of any protection order that is issued under this section to the petitioner, to the respondent, and to all law enforcement agencies that have jurisdiction to enforce the order. The court shall direct that a copy of the order be delivered to the respondent on the same day that the order is entered." Since "service" is now synonymous with "delivery," it appears from the opinion that a civil protection order must be served on a respondent on the same day that the order is entered. That appears to mean personal service and only those orders personally served on the day the order is entered can form the basis of a conviction for a violation under RC 2919.27. If this is truly the Supreme Court's interpretation of the statutes, it apparently also means that a protection order not served on the day that the order is filed is invalid. Even if not invalid, can such an order be enforceable by law enforcement or the court?

Lastly, there was no introduction, either in the briefs or in the opinion, of the concept of "actual notice" or when, if ever, "actual notice" might be sufficient for a conviction for a violation of a protection order. Of interest is that the Staff notes to Civ. R. 65.1 affirm that "actual notice" was contemplated when the civil rule was adopted. In fact, the staff notes provide that "[a]lthough other methods of service are permitted in the event of failure of personal service, until the Respondent has actual notice (emphasis added) of a protection order, the order could not be enforced against that Respondent, nor could the respondent be prosecuted for violations occurring prior to such actual notice." (emphasis added) Division (C). That Civil Rule 65.1 acknowledges "actual notice," a concept that the majority in *State v. Smith* fails to consider in its legal reasoning, an apparent conflict between rule and judicial decision has been created.

Of interest is that *State v. Smith* was litigated before the adoption of Civ. R. 65.1. It is possible that the decision might have been decided differently had the Supreme Court the benefit of the 2012 civil rule. Maybe another case should be brought to test that hypothesis.

Since it is unclear whether this decision applies equally to both ex parte protection orders and protection orders issued after a full hearing, one wonders about the enforceability of a full hearing protection order not served pursuant to personal service and whether the Supreme Court meant to distinguish between the ex parte and full hearing CPO for purposes of a violation.[47]

If the majority's analysis applies equally to both ex parte and protection orders issued after a full hearing, then *Smith* implies service of all protection orders to be made on the same day that the order is entered and by extension of this logic, by personal service. This means that, after *Smith*, to prove a violation under RC 2919.27, the state must prove, "beyond a reasonable doubt," that the order was actually delivered or served to a respondent/defendant.

[47]But see State v. Hall, 2013-Ohio-660, 989 N.E.2d 111 (Ohio Ct. App. 5th Dist. Delaware County 2013), appeal allowed, cause remanded, 135 Ohio St. 3d 1456, 2013-Ohio-2285, 988 N.E.2d 576 (2013) (where appellate court upheld conviction for violating CPO, defendant appealed to the Supreme Court of Ohio on ground that he wasn't served with CPO issued after full hearing and Supreme Court remanded case to lower court ordering the court to comply with decision in *State v. Smith*).

However, such interpretation also implicates Civ. R. 65.1. Civ. R. 65.1(C)(2) provides that service of an ex parte protection order be made initially by personal service and if that fails, by alternate methods of service in accordance with Civ. R. 4 through 4.6.[48] A protection order issued after a full hearing is accomplished in accordance with Civ. R. 5(B), which is by ordinary mail.[49] The relevant civil rules indicate that service is complete upon mailing. Under Civ. R. 65.1, there is no proof beyond a reasonable doubt that a CPO issued after a full hearing has been delivered/served on a defendant/respondent. Rather, completion of service is presumed.

Even Justice Kennedy stressed the importance of adhering to the rules of civil procedure. She specifically made mention that a respondent must be served with the protection order and "[t]o fulfill this mandate the court must follow the requirements of the Rules of Civil Procedure. See RC 2903.214(G) ('Any proceeding under this section shall be conducted in accordance with the Rules of Civil Procedure* * *')."[50] Thus, she must also mean that Civ. R. 65.1 should be followed. If that is the case, Civ. R. 65.1 appears to have superseded the rationale she provided for the *Smith* decision.[51]

Q & A: Have any recent cases been decided that considered the legal rationale in *State v. Smith*?[52]

Although *Smith* applied to ex parte civil protection orders, the Supreme Court appeared to leave open whether the same legal analysis should also be applied to full hearing orders. In *State v. Hall*,[53] defendant appealed his conviction for violating a CPO to the Supreme Court of Ohio on the ground that he wasn't served with the CPO issued after the full hearing.

On remand from the Supreme Court of Ohio, the 5th District Court of Appeals was instructed to consider whether the previous appellate ruling in *Hall* should be modified in light of *State v. Smith*. In *State v. Hall*,[54] the appellate court reiterated the ruling in *Smith* that, in order to prove a violation of R.C. 2919.27(A)(2), the state must prove, beyond a reasonable doubt, all statutory requirements of the civil

[48] State v. Meinke, 2017-Ohio-7787, 97 N.E.3d 1184 (Ohio Ct. App. 9th Dist. Lorain County 2017) (that defendant's signature was on the protection order was evidence that he had accepted the order, suggesting that he was personally served with the CPO).

[49] Civ. R. 65.1(C)(3). State v. Sims, 2018-Ohio-769, 2018 WL 1136587 (Ohio Ct. App. 2d Dist. Clark County 2018).

[50] State v. Smith, 136 Ohio St. 3d, 2013-Ohio-1698, ¶ 21, 989 N.E.2d 972 (2013).

[51] See Staff Notes re: amendment to division (C) of Civ. R. 65.1 effective July 1, 2016, adopting the reasoning in *Smith* to support the Civil Rules of Procedure.

[52] State v. Meinke, 2017-Ohio-7787, 97 N.E.3d 1184 (Ohio Ct. App. 9th Dist. Lorain County 2017); State v. Sims, 2018-Ohio-769, 2018 WL 1136587 (Ohio Ct. App. 2d Dist. Clark County 2018); State v. Ybarra, 2017-Ohio-9144, ¶ 23, 2017 WL 6508868 (Ohio Ct. App. 5th Dist. Licking County 2017).

[53] State v. Hall, 2013-Ohio-660, 989 N.E.2d 111 (Ohio Ct. App. 5th Dist. Delaware County 2013), appeal allowed, cause remanded, 135 Ohio St. 3d 1456, 2013-Ohio-2285, 988 N.E.2d 576 (2013); State v. Verga, 2015-Ohio-2582, 2015 WL 3938069 (Ohio Ct. App. 12th Dist. Warren County 2015); State v. Ybarra, 2016-Ohio-5761, 2016 WL 4724354 (Ohio Ct. App. 5th Dist. Licking County 2016).

[54] State v. Hall, 2013-Ohio-5855, 2013 WL 6918874 (Ohio Ct. App. 5th Dist. Delaware County 2013).

protection order statutes, including the requirement that the order be delivered to the defendant. While the appellate court accepted that the term "delivery" was synonymous with "service," the court differentiated the facts of *Smith* from *Hall*. In *Smith*, the defendant was not served with the ex parte CPO before the incident that led to charges for the violation. In *Hall*, the defendant had been served with the ex parte CPO before the incident that resulted in the charges for violation.

Because Hall was served and did personally receive a copy of the ex parte CPO, he was or should have been aware that his conduct was prohibited by the CPO. "Whether that order was for the ex parte order or the subsequent order issued after full hearing is not germane to the issue in this case. He chose to disregard the obvious facts and continued to contact the victim."[55] While Hall argued that he did not receive notice that a final CPO had been issued, he was aware of the ex parte order and was never aware that the ex parte order ceased or was modified by the trial court. Therefore, the decision in *Smith* did not alter the resulting decision in *Hall*.

Of importance is that the expiration date of the ex parte order was July 26, 2013. Hall had acknowledged that a CPO was in effect at the time of some of the violations (July 29, 2011 and August 2, 2011) that occurred before the full hearing on August 8, 2011. Some of the violations occurred after the scheduled hearing on the full CPO. In that the ex parte order was served on defendant, it made no difference to the appellate court that he might not have been personally served with the full hearing CPO. Judge Hoffman dissented in part and explained that although he concurred with the majority regarding the convictions relating to conduct that occurred prior to the scheduled full hearing on August 8, 2011, he disagreed as to the validity of appellant's convictions for conduct occurring after that date.

The court focused on the fact that respondent/defendant had been served with the ex parte order, not the date on which respondent/defendant was served with the order issued after the full hearing. Implied in this statement is that because defendant was aware of the terms of the ex parte order, it was inconsequential that he might not have been served with the full hearing order. In this case, because the duration of the ex parte order was 2013, a protection order was in effect when it was violated.

Thus, it is important for practitioners to make sure that ex parte orders expire at least one year after their issuance. This time frame offers a rationale to a court who is asked to decide whether a defendant violated the terms of a CPO. It also provides practitioners and court with time to perfect service of a full hearing order. What is still unclear, however, is whether a violation occurring after the expiration of the ex parte order would be prosecutable if a defendant was not personally served with the full hearing order.

What was not a part of the court's legal analysis was a discussion of ORCP Civ. R. 65.1(C)(3) (due to the fact that Civ. R. 65.1 was not in effect at the time), which provides that service of a protection order is-

[55]State v. Hall, 2013-Ohio-5855, 2013 WL 6918874, ¶ 15 (Ohio Ct. App. 5th Dist. Delaware County 2013).

sued after a full hearing is accomplished in accordance with Civ. R. 5(B), which is by ordinary mail.[56] The relevant civil rules indicate that service of a full hearing civil protection order is complete upon mailing. Under Civ. R. 65.1, there is no "proof beyond a reasonable doubt" that a CPO issued after a full hearing has been delivered/served on a defendant/respondent. Rather, completion of service is presumed.

If the *Smith* analysis truly applies to both ex parte and full hearing civil protection orders, the real takeaway is that to prove a violation under RC 2919.27, the state must prove, beyond a reasonable doubt" that the order was served by personal service on a respondent/ defendant. Unfortunately, *Hall* does not provide detailed and specific guidance on this point.

Similarly, the 6th District Court of Appeals decided *State v. Johnson*,[57] in which the state did not prove that the full hearing CPO had been served before the violation occurred. In this case, petitioner obtained an ex parte domestic violence civil protection order on June 27, 2011, which by its terms expired on August 26, 2011, more than a year prior to the violations of the CPO. Appellant was served on August 4, 2011 and the trial court reset the full hearing date to August 26, 2011. On August 26, 2011, the court issued a full hearing order, extending it to August 24, 2016. On September 25, 2012, appellant was charged with violating a protection order pursuant to RC 2919.27. He argued that he had not been served with the full hearing order until December 2012, well after the alleged violation.

The appellate court relied on the reasoning of *Smith* which held that service must be perfected before the alleged violation and that service is an essential element which the state must prove beyond a reasonable doubt.[58] The court then determined that "the state had presented no testimony or documentary evidence that appellant received service of the full hearing order.[59] Indeed, the only evidence of service admitted was an affidavit of service from the Wood County Sheriff that averred a protection order from Lucas County was served on appellant on August 4, 2011. This was the ex parte order which, by its own terms, expired on August 26, 2011, more than a year prior to the violations of the orders that were alleged."[60] The court paid no heed to the state's argument that appellant was aware that there was

---

[56]State v. Sims, 2018-Ohio-769, 2018 WL 1136587 (Ohio Ct. App. 2d Dist. Clark County 2018).

[57]State v. Johnson, 2014-Ohio-2435, 2014 WL 2566260 (Ohio Ct. App. 6th Dist. Wood County 2014); State v. Terrell, 2014-Ohio-4344, 2014 WL 4823870 (Ohio Ct. App. 2d Dist. Clark County 2014) (where there was no evidence, beyond a reasonable doubt, that defendant had been served with the final order prior to his conduct that violated the protection order, the conviction was reversed); State v. Verga, 2015-Ohio-2582, 2015 WL 3938069 (Ohio Ct. App. 12th Dist. Warren County 2015).

[58]State v. Johnson, 2014-Ohio-2435, 2014 WL 2566260, ¶ 13 (Ohio Ct. App. 6th Dist. Wood County 2014). But see State v. Zobel, 2016-Ohio-5751, 2016 WL 4728100 (Ohio Ct. App. 5th Dist. Tuscarawas County 2016) (distinguishing *Smith* and noting that appellant was served with the order well before the conduct that gave rise to the charges occurred).

[59]State v. Meinke, 2017-Ohio-7787, 97 N.E.3d 1184 (Ohio Ct. App. 9th Dist. Lorain County 2017).

[60]State v. Johnson, 2014-Ohio-2435, 2014 WL 2566260, ¶ 14 (Ohio Ct. App. 6th Dist. Wood County 2014).

to be a full hearing on the ex parte protection order. Accordingly, awareness of a future full hearing was not sufficient to make appellant's subsequent acts a reckless violation under *Smith*.

It is unclear whether the ruling would have been different had the ex parte civil protection order still been in effect. The decision in *Hall* makes this a distinct possibility. However, such a reading of the *Hall* decision fails to contemplate whether an ex parte protection order expires, regardless of the date of expiration noted on the standardized Supreme Court forms, when the full hearing order is issued or whether the ex parte order remains in effect until the full hearing order is served.

Since *Hall*, the Hamilton County Court of Appeals decided *Cincinnati v. Phillips*.[61] In that case, appellant was convicted of violating a civil protection order. He asserted that there was insufficient evidence to demonstrate that the protection order had been served on him and that the trial court erred by admitting into evidence the city's exhibit entitled "County Writ Hamilton County Sheriff's Department." "This exhibit was meant to demonstrate that Phillips had been personally served with a copy of the protection order. We sustain the assignment of error because the exhibit was not properly authenticated prior to being admitted into evidence."[62]

While both sides agreed that the exhibit was a public record, the discussion focused on whether it had been properly authenticated per Evid. R. 1005. "Evid. R. 1005 provides that 'the contents of an official record * * * may be proved by copy, certified as correct in accordance with Rule 902, Civ. R. 44, Crim. R. 27 or be testified to by a witness who had compared in with the original.' "[63] "Although the print out copy bore a photocopied seal, the court has previously held that a photocopy of a seal will not suffice to self-authenticate a public record under the Rules of Evidence."[64]

The Court reversed appellant's conviction for violating the protection order, reasoning that because the "exhibit purporting to demonstrate that the protection order had been served upon Phillips was inadmissible, there is no evidence in the record to demonstrate that the Phillips had been served with the protection order. Consequently, there was no protection order issued in accordance with RC 3113. 31."[65]

Implicit in the appellate court's reasoning is that a certified copy of

---

[61]State v. Phillips, 2014-Ohio-2614, 2014 WL 2750667 (Ohio Ct. App. 1st Dist. Hamilton County 2014).

[62]State v. Phillips, 2014-Ohio-2614, 2014 WL 2750667, ¶ 2 (Ohio Ct. App. 1st Dist. Hamilton County 2014).

[63]State v. Phillips, 2014-Ohio-2614, 2014 WL 2750667, ¶ 3 (Ohio Ct. App. 1st Dist. Hamilton County 2014).

[64]State v. Phillips, 2014-Ohio-2614, 2014 WL 2750667, ¶ 4 (Ohio Ct. App. 1st Dist. Hamilton County 2014), citing State v. Skimmerhorn, 162 Ohio App. 3d 762, 2005-Ohio-4300, 835 N.E.2d 52 (1st Dist. Hamilton County 2005), appeal allowed, judgment rev'd on other grounds, 108 Ohio St. 3d 103, 2006-Ohio-164, 840 N.E.2d 1077 (2006).

[65]State v. Phillips, 2014-Ohio-2614, 2014 WL 2750667, ¶ 7 (Ohio Ct. App. 1st Dist. Hamilton County 2014). But see State v. Partlow, 2013-Ohio-2771, 2013 WL 3356575 (Ohio Ct. App. 10th Dist. Franklin County 2013) (upholding conviction and in dicta noted that introduction of time stamped CPO as an exhibit during trial

a service document is required to demonstrate service for purposes of a violation under R.C. 2919.27 in light of R.C. 3113.31(F)(1) which requires a court to direct that a copy of an order be delivered to the respondent on the same day that the order is entered. Of significance is that this court did not directly mention or consider the rationale of *Smith*. Rather, it focused on authentication in order to determine whether a CPO was adequately served on a respondent, such that he/she may be convicted for violating the CPO.[66] What was not discussed was whether authentication is necessary in order for the state to demonstrate the violation beyond a reasonable doubt or whether authentication is necessary to prove that service was perfected beyond a reasonable doubt or that the protection order was properly issued by the court beyond a reasonable doubt.[67]

In an interesting twist, the Sixth District Court of Appeals applied the reasoning in *Smith* to the proper issuance of a CPO in order to sustain a conviction for violating the protection order. In *Toledo v. Lewis*,[68] appellant, who was convicted of reckless violating a civil stalking protection order, appealed the conviction on the grounds that the underlying protection order was not issued in conformity with R.C. 2903.214.

Particularly, the facts of the case demonstrate that appellant had sought a civil stalking protection order under R.C. 2903.214, against Ms. Vargas. After the ex parte hearing, the court granted his ex parte CPO. At the full hearing, the court denied appellant's petition for CPO but then entered a protection order, *sua sponte*, against him on behalf of Vargas, prohibiting appellant from having any contact with Vargas. Subsequently, Vargas filed a criminal complaint alleging that appellant had violated the order.

The issue before the appellate court was whether appellant can be found guilty of violating the protection order that required the issuance of a valid court order pursuant to R.C. 2903.214 when, in fact, no valid order exists. Applying *Smith*, the state must prove beyond a rea-

---

important when considering whether sufficient evidence was introduced demonstrating that defendant violated the CPO under RC 2919.27); State v. Pesano, 2014-Ohio-5540, 2014 WL 7177311 (Ohio Ct. App. 5th Dist. Stark County 2014) (noting that while it would be better practice to enter the protection order into evidence, the record indicates that appellant repeatedly acknowledged the existence of the CPO; thus, conviction was not against manifest weight of the evidence; court found a reckless violation because appellant acknowledged the officer who served him with order told him to have no contact with victim, despite fact that paperwork regarding service of the order was excluded as being neither certified nor original).

[66]State v. Leason, 2011-Ohio-6591, 2011 WL 6740749 (Ohio Ct. App. 9th Dist. Summit County 2011) (discussion of what constitutes filing, where copy of CPO was not time stamped, for purposes of authenticating the order); State v. Meinke, 2017-Ohio-7787, 97 N.E.3d 1184 (Ohio Ct. App. 9th Dist. Lorain County 2017) (holding that documentary evidence of service is only one way to prove service of a civil protection order and that testimony can be used as well).

[67]See Toledo v. Lewis, 2013-Ohio-3289, 2013 WL 3936455 (Ohio Ct. App. 6th Dist. Lucas County 2013) (*Smith* stands for the proposition that the protection order must be properly issued in the first instance in compliance with all requirements of the statute and that this must be demonstrated beyond a reasonable doubt in order to sustain a conviction for violating the order).

[68]Toledo v. Lewis, 2013-Ohio-3289, 2013 WL 3936455 (Ohio Ct. App. 6th Dist. Lucas County 2013).

sonable doubt *all requirements* of R.C. 2903.214.[69] "Mindful of the importance of protection orders, the *Smith* court asserted that the violation of a *properly issued* protection order must not be countenanced."[70]

In this case, the problem was that the court did not comply with the provisions of R.C. 2903.214(E)(3) which set forth the procedure for filing mutual protection orders. In that the common pleas court failed to adhere to the provisions of R.C. 2903.214(E)(3) regarding protection orders and service, the order that was violated was not a properly issued order in the first instance. Because respondent Robin Vargas did not file a separate petition for protection order under R.C. 2903.214(E)(3)(a), appellant was not served with a copy of the petition as required by R.C. 2903.214(E)(3)(b). Thus, the civil stalking protection order was not a validly issued order and as such, a conviction for the crime of violating the order under R.C. 2919.27 cannot lie.

But, in *Hamper v. Dobrski*,[71] the question presented was whether the trial court erred when it found appellant in contempt for violating the ex parte CPO because he had not been served with the order. According to the appellate court, his reliance on *State v. Smith* was misplaced because Smith "concerned a criminal prosecution for violation of a protection order. In contrast, this case concerns the issue of whether Dobrski could be held in indirect civil contempt of the court's protection order, where the burden of proof is that of "clear and convincing evidence."[72]

Additionally, appellant had waited until he filed objections to the magistrate's decision to claim that he had not been served with the ex parte order at the time he turned off the utilities. Because he never indicated to the DR court that he lacked notice of the terms of the TPO, his claims were rejected.[73]

In *State v. Meinke*,[74] defendant disputed whether service of the protection order was perfected, and arguing that the State must provide satisfactory proof of the same.

Defendant first argued that witness testimony regarding the fact that service was perfected before the violations was inadmissible hearsay. One officer testified that dispatch verified service, that a paper copy was at the station with Defendant's signature on it and that he accepted it.

Additionally, he raised the issue that the state must prove that service was made in accordance with the civil rules and "a certified copy

[69]Toledo v. Lewis, 2013-Ohio-3289, 2013 WL 3936455, ¶ 7 (Ohio Ct. App. 6th Dist. Lucas County 2013).

[70]Toledo v. Lewis, 2013-Ohio-3289, 2013 WL 3936455, ¶ 9 (Ohio Ct. App. 6th Dist. Lucas County 2013),quoting *Smith* at ¶ 27.

[71]Hamper v. Dobrski, 2015-Ohio-1381, 2015 WL 1593249 (Ohio Ct. App. 8th Dist. Cuyahoga County 2015).

[72]Hamper v. Dobrski, 2015-Ohio-1381, 2015 WL 1593249, ¶ 15 (Ohio Ct. App. 8th Dist. Cuyahoga County 2015), citing Brown v. Executive 200, Inc., 64 Ohio St. 2d 250, 18 Ohio Op. 3d 446, 416 N.E.2d 610 (1980).

[73]Hamper v. Dobrski, 2015-Ohio-1381, 2015 WL 1593249, ¶ 19 (Ohio Ct. App. 8th Dist. Cuyahoga County 2015).

[74]State v. Meinke, 2017-Ohio-7787, 97 N.E.3d 1184 (Ohio Ct. App. 9th Dist. Lorain County 2017).

of the return would be irrefutable evidence of proper service and of this element."[75] The State responded that such an interpretation even went beyond the holding in *Smith*.

The appellate court found that the State was not required to prove irrefutable evidence. Additionally, the court also mentioned that service of a civil protection order is governed by Civ. R. 65.1(C). The appellate court held that "while documentary evidence may be one way to prove service, testimony may also be used."[76]

Finally, the court also made mention of the enactment of Senate Bill 7 in a footnote.

Of importance is that while noting the requirements of *Smith,* the court reasoned that service was perfected based on the requirements of Civ. R. 65.1 and acknowledged the use of testimony to prove that service was perfected.

Q & A: Is there any potential redress?

Yes. The Ohio General Assembly has recently enacted SB 7 which provides "[i]n a prosecution for a violation of this section, it is not necessary for the prosecution to prove that the protection order r consent agreement was served on the defendant if the prosecution proves that the defendant was *shown* the protection order or consent agreement or a copy of either or a judge, magistrate or law enforcement officer *informed* the defendant that a protection order or consent agreement had been issued, and proves that the defendant recklessly violated the terms of the order or agreement."[77]

Additionally the notes indicate that "[t]he amendments made by this act to division (D) of section 2919.27 of the Revised Code are intended to supersede the holding of the Ohio Supreme Court in *State v. Smith*, (2013), 136 Ohio St. 3d 1, so that unperfected service of a protection order or consent agreement does not preclude a prosecution for a violation of division (A) of that section."

However, it is important to note that a defendant must be shown an actual copy of the order or provided a copy of the order or law enforcement or a jurist must inform a defendant that the order was issued. This suggests that the petitioner/complainant/victim must show an actual copy of the order to the defendant unless this directive can be achieved via another person, a text or screen shot or another way can be found to eliminate contact between the parties. In this instance, testimony of the petitioner or another person who may have shown the copy to respondent would suffice in a prosecution for a violation.

If law enforcement is to inform the defendant of the issuance of the order, the statutory language does not state that a copy of the order must be provided to the defendant. However, under this framework, best practice would indicate that there must also be proof of service

---

[75]State v. Meinke, 2017-Ohio-7787, ¶ 12, 97 N.E.3d 1184, 1188 (Ohio Ct. App. 9th Dist. Lorain County 2017).

[76]State v. Meinke, 2017-Ohio-7787, ¶ 13, 97 N.E.3d 1184, 1188 (Ohio Ct. App. 9th Dist. Lorain County 2017).

[77]Emphasis added; RC 2919.27(D), eff. 9/27/2017.

provided to the clerk of courts to indicate a defendant has been so informed[78] or said officer or the jurist would be called upon to testify.

More importantly, the cases that have addressed "actual notice" may still be considered for their legal reasoning.

Q & A: How does one know when "actual notice" is ever sufficient for a conviction for a violation of a protection order?

In *Toledo v. Lyphout*,[79] that issue was specifically considered. In the case, the only testimony provided indicating that the defendant had any knowledge of the civil protection order was from the petitioner who testified as follows:

> A. The whole time, he's like, 'Bitch, everybody's going to know you're lying. Nobody's going to believe you. I'm going to make you pay for what you've done, you fucking bitch.' And he said-he said, I haven't been served yet, so you can't do shit.'
>
> Q. He said, 'I have not been served'?
>
> A. He said, 'I haven't been served yet, so you can't do shit.'[80]

While the focus of appellant's argument was that the trial court erred by not applying Civil Rule 4 (dealing with service of process), the appellee claimed that Civil Rule 65 governed. In determining whether actual notice was sufficient, the appellate court reviewed RC 3113.31(D)(2)(a), which provides that the issuing court "shall give the respondent notice of, and an opportunity to be heard at, the full hearing."[81]

The 6th District Court of Appeals agreed that Civil Rule 65 controlled. "It is a well-settled rule of construction that where a provision couched in general terms conflicts with a specific provision on the same subject, the latter must control."[82] The appellate court then held that because Civil Rule 65 deals with restraining orders and because a civil protection order is a variation of a restraining order, Civil R. 65 controls.[83]

The Court then pointed out that actual notice requires more than a general knowledge that an order has been issued.[84] In this case, the defendant admitted that he had not been served and no evidence was presented to demonstrate that he had more than a general knowledge of the terms of the civil protection order. In reversing the trial court's judgment, the appellate court held that he could not have received

---

[78]See also State v. Wills, 2006-Ohio-2295, 2006 WL 1256379 (Ohio Ct. App. 10th Dist. Franklin County 2006).

[79]Toledo v. Lyphout, 2009-Ohio-4596, 2009 WL 2855714 (Ohio Ct. App. 6th Dist. Lucas County 2009); see also State v. Williams, 2009-Ohio-3162, 2009 WL 1856743 (Ohio Ct. App. 9th Dist. Summit County 2009).

[80]*Toledo at *4*.

[81]At* 3.

[82]*Toledo at *3*; quoting State v. Taylor, 113 Ohio St. 3d 297, 300, 2007-Ohio-1950, 865 N.E.2d 37, 39 (2007); quoting Humphrys v. Winous Co., 165 Ohio St. 45, 48, 59 Ohio Op. 65, 133 N.E.2d 780 (1956).

[83]At *3; see also Toledo v. Lanier, 2009-Ohio-5191, 2009 WL 3132601 (Ohio Ct. App. 6th Dist. Lucas County 2009).

[84]At *3; citing, Midland Steel Prods. Co. v. U.A.W. Local 486, 61 Ohio St. 3d 121, 126, 573 N.E.2d 98 (1991).

actual notice o f the terms contained in the CPO. Therefore, he could not be criminally liable.[85]

Q & A: Besides notice/service of the order, what else must be proven for a violation under RC 2919.27?

In order to be found criminally liable for violating a protection order under RC 2919.27, the defendant/respondent must have the requisite degree of culpability.[86] For purposes of a criminal violation of a civil protection order under RC 2919.27, the requisite mental state is "reckless."[87] A person acts "recklessly" when, with heedless indifference to the consequences, he perversely disregards a known risk that his conduct is likely to cause a certain result or is likely to be of a certain nature.[88] Inherent in the definition is that the person has an awareness of the circumstances surrounding his/her actions. For example, in *State v. Patton*,[89] the Hamilton County Court of Appeals determined that the mental state of "recklessness" assumes that the defendant intends the act but not the harm.[90]

In *State v. Bunch*,[91] the defendant argued that the evidence was not sufficient to demonstrate that he acted recklessly in violating the civil protection order. Because he was never served with the CPO, he could not have disregarded a "known risk that [the CPO was] likely to exist."[92] But, the appellate court stated that RC 2919.27 only requires that "the prosecution prove beyond a reasonable doubt that defendant

---

[85]But see Toledo v. Lanier, 2009-Ohio-5191, 2009 WL 3132601 (Ohio Ct. App. 6th Dist. Lucas County 2009) (affirming trial court judgment and holding that actual notice was established).

[86]See generally RC 2901.21(A)(2); see also State v. Bunch, 2001 WL 39599 (Ohio Ct. App. 9th Dist. Summit County 2001); State v. Gordon, 2003-Ohio-6558, 2003 WL 22889573 (Ohio Ct. App. 10th Dist. Franklin County 2003) (holding that, even if defendant was unaware of CPO term prohibiting him from writing letters to his wife, knowing CPO restricted contact with his wife, defendant's letters in face of such knowledge indicated a perverse disregard of the risk that his conduct was likely to cause a violation).

[87]See RC 2901.22(C) for definition of "recklessly"; see also the definition of the term in the first paragraph of Text § 13:3, Court enforcement of civil protection orders—Criminal prosecution.

[88]See RC 2901.22(C); see, for example, State v. Worthy, 2008-Ohio-1448, 2008 WL 833995 (Ohio Ct. App. 9th Dist. Summit County 2008) (court upheld conviction for violating protection order under RC 2919.27 where parties had mutual restraining orders against the other. Both women ended up at the same restaurant, although only one was arrested for violating the other). See also State v. Headlee, 2009-Ohio-873, 2009 WL 478085 (Ohio Ct. App. 4th Dist. Washington County 2009).

[89]State v. Patton, 106 Ohio App. 3d 736, 667 N.E.2d 57 (1st Dist. Hamilton County 1995).

[90]See also West v. West, 1994 WL 680156 (Ohio Ct. App. 2d Dist. Montgomery County 1994) (determining that the violator must possess the requisite intent to defy the order. Thus, a respondent who is unaware of the terms of the order cannot violate it. Although the holding relates to a criminal contempt, the court analysis illustrates the constitutional dilemma. Since both a criminal contempt and a criminal prosecution are criminal in nature, constitutional safeguards must be considered.); Brown v. Executive 200, Inc., 64 Ohio St. 2d 250, 18 Ohio Op. 3d 446, 416 N.E.2d 610 (1980).

[91]State v. Bunch, 2001 WL 39599 (Ohio Ct. App. 9th Dist. Summit County 2001).

[92]State v. Bunch, 2001 WL 39599, *2 (Ohio Ct. App. 9th Dist. Summit County 2001); RC 2901.22(C).

acted in disregard of a known risk that a CPO was likely to have existed against him."[93]

The court relied on the victim's testimony to prove defendant's culpable mental state; she testified she had previously told the defendant that the order existed and, he responded, "I know." Additionally, the defendant admitted that a temporary protection order had previously been issued against him and that he had visited the child in violation of it. Despite a known risk that it was likely that the CPO was still in effect, he went to the victim's house.[94] Therefore, the elements of RC 2919.27(A)(1) were satisfied.[95]

Q & A: Can a respondent be found to have recklessly violated a CPO where he received notice of the order before he received an actual copy of the order and its terms?

In *State v. Gordon*,[96] the defendant argued that he was not given proper notice and an opportunity to be heard at a full hearing on the civil protection order (CPO). On June 6, 2002, defendant was served with notice of a full civil protection order hearing while incarcerated. On June 11, 2006, the full hearing was held but he was not present. He was served with a copy of the CPO on June 17, 2002. On November 22, 2002, he was charged with violating the terms of the CPO by mailing correspondence to his wife from jail between September and October 2002.

Although the CPO was forwarded to him at the correctional facility, he did not read it in detail. He admitted that he knew he could not phone or visit his wife but denied that he knew he could not write her. Thus, he could not have recklessly violated the terms of the CPO.

The appellate court noted that defendant's "assertions that he did not read the CPO 'in detail' does not provide any clue as to how he was able to extract the information about the telephonic and in-person prohibitions in the CPO but, for some reason, was not also able to extract the prohibitions on written correspondence."[97] Defendant knew that the CPO restricted contact with his wife. He should have known that letter writing indicated a perverse disregard of a risk that his conduct was likely to result in a RC 2919.27 violation. The Court held that "[a]ppellant's contact with his wife through writings, while being fully aware a CPO was in effect, demonstrated a heedless indifference to the consequences of his actions. Neither indifference, laziness, inat-

[93] State v. Bunch, 2001 WL 39599, *2 (Ohio Ct. App. 9th Dist. Summit County 2001); see also State v. Davidson, 2004-Ohio-6828, 2004 WL 2914137 (Ohio Ct. App. 4th Dist. Ross County 2004).

[94] State v. Bunch, 2001 WL 39599, *3 (Ohio Ct. App. 9th Dist. Summit County 2001).

[95] See also State v. Bombardiere, 2007-Ohio-1537, 2007 WL 959895 (Ohio Ct. App. 3d Dist. Union County 2007) (appellant admitted in testimony he knew of the terms of the CPO).

[96] State v. Gordon, 2003-Ohio-6558, 2003 WL 22889573 (Ohio Ct. App. 10th Dist. Franklin County 2003). See also Text § 13:8, Enforcement of civil protection orders; procedures for initiating contempt motions. See also Columbus v. Kiner, 2011-Ohio-4479, 2011 WL 3894387 (Ohio Ct. App. 10th Dist. Franklin County 2011).

[97] State v. Gordon, 2003-Ohio-6558, 2003 WL 22889573, *2 (Ohio Ct. App. 10th Dist. Franklin County 2003).

tention, nor anger constitutes an excuse for failing to read court orders and comply therewith."[98]

However, the court did not address the issue that service of the notice of the order appears to have preceded service of an actual copy of the order and the ramifications of that as fact.

Q & A: Is a return of service document evidence that a defendant had notice of the CPO?

At least one court addressed this issue. In *State v. Wills*,[99] appellant was charged with violating a CPO. The appellee presented the return of service document as evidence that appellant had notice of the CPO. The appellant objected arguing that the return of service document contained hearsay and could not be introduced to prove that he knew of the existence of the CPO. The document states that the deputy perfected service on appellant. The statement was signed by the deputy and included his badge number. The deputy sheriff who served the order was not doing so as a law enforcement officer but was doing so in lieu of the service bailiff by order of court.[100] The Tenth District Court of Appeals held that the return of service document was admissible as a public records exception set forth in Evid.R. 803(8).

Q & A: Can an individual be convicted for violating a protection order when another actually committed the act that led to the violation?

In *State v. Kersey*,[101] the appellate court reversed the conviction of a defendant for violating a CPO. The petitioner had received several calls from defendant's home telephone number, and which the number was indicated on petitioner's caller ID feature. As a result of the calls, petitioner filed a criminal complaint alleging that defendant had violated the CPO. In *Kersey*, the evidence demonstrated that defendant's wife had made the calls on behalf of his mother and that he had neither instructed his wife or mother to call nor had he encouraged nor discouraged this act.

The state argued that Kersey's failure to prevent his wife from making the calls rose to the level of recklessness. However, the Fourth District Court of Appeals reasoned that a violation of a CPO requires some action on the part of a defendant and the state had to prove that this defendant was somehow responsible for the calls. While the CPO in question prohibits Kersey from initiating contact or preventing oth-

[98]State v. Gordon, 2003-Ohio-6558, 2003 WL 22889573, *2 (Ohio Ct. App. 10th Dist. Franklin County 2003); see also State v. Cardinal, 2006-Ohio-5088, 2006 WL 2789903 (Ohio Ct. App. 10th Dist. Franklin County 2006).

[99]State v. Wills, 2006-Ohio-2295, 2006 WL 1256379 (Ohio Ct. App. 10th Dist. Franklin County 2006).

[100]State v. Wills, 2006-Ohio-2295, 2006 WL 1256379, *3 (Ohio Ct. App. 10th Dist. Franklin County 2006); but see State v. Mohabir, 2005-Ohio-78, 2005 WL 66484 (Ohio Ct. App. 5th Dist. Fairfield County 2005) (overruled by, State v. Hall, 2013-Ohio-660, 989 N.E.2d 111 (Ohio Ct. App. 5th Dist. Delaware County 2013)) (overruling court finding service of the temporary protection order on the defendant is not an element of the offense of violation of the protection order); State v. Phillips, 2014-Ohio-2614, 2014 WL 2750667 (Ohio Ct. App. 1st Dist. Hamilton County 2014) (holding that the non-authenticated return was not admissible as a public records exception).

[101]State v. Kersey, 2004-Ohio-274, 2004 WL 102845 (Ohio Ct. App. 4th Dist. Jackson County 2004).

ers from contacting the petitioner, it does not require him to prevent those around him from contacting her on their own initiative.[102] "Thus, Kersey's mere failure to prevent others from contacting Lyle (petitioner) does not result in his violating the protection order. It is only when those "others" are acting on Kersey's behalf or at his request, that Kersey violates the protection order."[103] Kersey's failure to advise his wife against calling petitioner does not constitute a violation, let alone a reckless violation.

Q & A: Can a person be convicted for violating a civil protection order when that person contacted the victim but the victim did not accept the calls?

According to *State v. Dinka*, the answer is yes. In *State v. Dinka*,[104] defendant was charged with violating a civil protection order. Pursuant to the CPO, defendant was not to initiate or have contact with the protected persons.

On appeal, defendant admitted that he made seven calls to petitioner but stated that he didn't violate the order because she did not accept the phone calls. In essence, he contends that he did not violate the terms of the CPO because he did not actually communicate with her.[105]

The 12th District appellate court found that appellant's repeated attempts to call Howard satisfied the contact term.[106] "As such, the state presented sufficient evidence from which the trier of fact could reasonably conclude that appellant was guilty of violating the CPO."[107]

Q & A: Can a person be convicted for violating a protection order where the protection order was subsequently determined to be invalid?

Yes, according to the Warren County Court of Appeals. In *State v. Sutts*,[108] the appellant was convicted of violating a criminal protection order pursuant to RC 2919.27. On appeal, he argued that he could not have violated a protection order that was invalid because the trial court failed to hold a full hearing on the matter with the time frame permitted under RC 2919.26.[109]

The Twelfth District Court of Appeals reviewed case law from other

---

[102] State v. Kersey, 2004-Ohio-274, 2004 WL 102845, *3 (Ohio Ct. App. 4th Dist. Jackson County 2004).

[103] State v. Kersey, 2004-Ohio-274, 2004 WL 102845, *3 (Ohio Ct. App. 4th Dist. Jackson County 2004).

[104] State v. Dinka, 2015-Ohio-63, 2015 WL 149026 (Ohio Ct. App. 12th Dist. Warren County 2015).

[105] State v. Dinka, 2015-Ohio-63, 2015 WL 149026, ¶ 14 (Ohio Ct. App. 12th Dist. Warren County 2015).

[106] See also State v. Leason, 2011-Ohio-6591, 2011 WL 6740749, ¶ 28 (Ohio Ct. App. 9th Dist. Summit County 2011) (defendant attempted to initiate contact with victim from the jail).

[107] State v. Dinka, 2015-Ohio-63, 2015 WL 149026, ¶ 15 (Ohio Ct. App. 12th Dist. Warren County 2015).

[108] State v. Sutts, 2004-Ohio-3541, 2004 WL 1485909 (Ohio Ct. App. 12th Dist. Warren County 2004); State v. Schell, 2017-Ohio-2641, ¶ 5, 12017 WL 1748769 (Ohio Ct. App. 9th Dist. Summit County 2017).

[109] See also City of Reynoldsburg v. Eichenberger, 1990 WL 52467 (Ohio Ct. App. 5th Dist. Licking County 1990) (stating that appellant cannot prevail on challenging

Ohio jurisdictions and held that a defendant cannot avoid prosecution for deliberately disobeying a protection order even if the order is subsequently determined to be invalid.[110] Relying on the reasoning set forth in *Board. of Educ. of Hamilton City School Dist. v. Hamilton Classroom Teachers Ass'n*[111] the appellate court held that "[a]ppellant's allegation that the protection order was invalid does not provide a defense to his willful violation of the order."[112] A trial court's failure to conduct an evidentiary hearing on a protection order was not an affirmative defense to a defendant's violations of the order.[113] That the appellant had knowledge of the existence of the order prior to the violations was crucial to the result.

Likewise, in *State v. Ybarra*,[114] appellant was convicted for violating a civil protection order by initiating contact with his ex wife via a neighbor who placed a letter sent by appellant at her door. In his assignment of error, appellant argued that, although the State proved he had been served with a copy of the CPO, the State did not prove that he received notice of the full hearing on the protection order as required by RC 3113.31(D)(2)(a) and therefore did not prove that the protection order was issued in accordance with the statute.

The appellate court relied on the analysis set forth in *City of Reynoldsburg v. Eichenberger*[115] in which appellant challenged his conviction for violating the protection order on the grounds that the order was void because the trial court failed to follow the statute in issuing the order. "We rejected his argument, holding that the appellant could not prevail after he deliberately disobeyed the order, even if we subsequently found the order to be invalid. 'An order of the court must be obeyed unless and until a court finds it invalid or rescinds it.'" City of Reynoldsburg v. Eichenberger, 1990 WL 52467 (Ohio Ct. App. 5th Dist. Licking County 1990), citing In re Contempt of Court of White, 60 Ohio App. 2d 62, 14 Ohio Op. 3d 34, 395 N.E.2d 499 (5th Dist. Stark County 1978); U.S. v. United Mine Workers of America, 330 U.S. 258, 67 S. Ct. 677, 91 L. Ed. 884, 19 L.R.R.M. (BNA) 2346, 12 Lab. Cas. (CCH) P 51239 (1947). We have further held that service of a temporary protection order is not an element of the offense as

TPO on ground it is void because he deliberately disobeyed the order. An order of the court must be obeyed unless and until a court finds it is invalid or rescinds it.).

[110] See also Westlake v. Patrick, 2007-Ohio-1307, 2007 WL 853235, *2 (Ohio Ct. App. 8th Dist. Cuyahoga County 2007) (holding that a party may be criminally punished for violating an order even though the order is determined to be invalid after the violation has occurred).

[111] Board of Educ. of Hamilton City School Dist. v. Hamilton Classroom Teachers Ass'n, 5 Ohio App. 3d 51, 53, 449 N.E.2d 26, 11 Ed. Law Rep. 277 (12th Dist. Butler County 1982), citing U.S. v. United Mine Workers of America, 330 U.S. 258, 293, 67 S. Ct. 677, 91 L. Ed. 884, 19 L.R.R.M. (BNA) 2346, 12 Lab. Cas. (CCH) P 51239 (1947).

[112] State v. Sutts, 2004-Ohio-3541, 2004 WL 1485909, *2 (Ohio Ct. App. 12th Dist. Warren County 2004); see also State v. Eschrich, 2008-Ohio-2984, 2008 WL 2468572 (Ohio Ct. App. 6th Dist. Ottawa County 2008).

[113] State v. Sutts, 2004-Ohio-3541, 2004 WL 1485909 (Ohio Ct. App. 12th Dist. Warren County 2004).

[114] State v. Ybarra, 2016-Ohio-5761, 2016 WL 4724354 (Ohio Ct. App. 5th Dist. Licking County 2016).

[115] City of Reynoldsburg v. Eichenberger, 1990 WL 52467 (Ohio Ct. App. 5th Dist. Licking County 1990).

defined by RC 2919.27(A), where the appellant was aware or should have been aware that his conduct was prohibited by a civil protection order, citing *Eichenberger*, supra. State v. Hall, 2013-Ohio-660, ¶ 23, 30-32, 989 N.E.2d 111 (Ohio Ct. App. 5th Dist. Delaware County 2013), appeal allowed, cause remanded, 135 Ohio St. 3d 1456, 2013-Ohio-2285, 988 N.E.2d 576 (2013).[116]

As such, this appellant could not disobey a protection order issued after a full hearing on the basis that he was not served with notice of the hearing. Since appellant had not addressed the underlying order, the CPO was valid and he was required to obey the law.

Q & A: When does a CPO become effective for purposes of a R.C. 2919.27 violation?

The Mahoning County Court of Appeals addressed this issue in *State v. Hamlett*.[117] In that case, defendant entered into a consent entry following a full hearing, which order prohibited him from coming within 500 feet of petitioner. The consent entry was entered into and signed by the parties on July 29, 2009, and journalized on August 5, 2009. On August 1, 2009, defendant violated the terms of the civil protection order.

It should be noted that the ex parte CPO had expired before the final CPO was granted; thus, the ex parte CPO could not serve as a basis for defendant's conviction for violating a CPO.

On appeal, defendant argued that the court erred in finding him guilty of the violation because the protection order had not been docketed or journalized at the time of the alleged offense. Defendant contended that the CPO was not effective on August 1, 2009, despite the fact that it was signed by the parties on July 29, 2009, "because valid court judgments require an indication that it was filed and on what date, and therefore the CPO was invalid until it was journalized on August 5."[118]

The appellate court framed the issue as whether the CPO was effective on the date the parties had notice of its terms and signed it, or when it was journalized.[119] It then defined journalization for purposes of a decision of the court and reasoned that a court speaks through its journal.[120] In reversing that part of the decision, the Ottawa County Court of Appeals held that since the CPO was not approved by the court and journalized until August 5, which was after the date of the offense, it was thus not effective until that date.[121]

Of importance is that attorneys must make certain to consider that

---

[116]City of Reynoldsburg v. Eichenberger, 1990 WL 52467, ¶ 12 (Ohio Ct. App. 5th Dist. Licking County 1990).

[117]State v. Hamlett, 191 Ohio App. 3d 397, 2010-Ohio-6605, 946 N.E.2d 277 (7th Dist. Mahoning County 2010).

[118]State v. Hamlett, 191 Ohio App. 3d 397, 2010-Ohio-6605, 946 N.E.2d 277, 280 (7th Dist. Mahoning County 2010).

[119]State v. Hamlett, 191 Ohio App. 3d 397, 2010-Ohio-6605, 946 N.E.2d 277, 280 (7th Dist. Mahoning County 2010).

[120]State v. Hamlett, 191 Ohio App. 3d 397, 2010-Ohio-6605, 946 N.E.2d 277, 280 (7th Dist. Mahoning County 2010); see also Civ. R. 58(A).

[121]State v. Hamlett, 191 Ohio App. 3d 397, 2010-Ohio-6605, 946 N.E.2d 277, 281 (7th Dist. Mahoning County 2010); see also Stickel v. Pryor, 2002-Ohio-3309, 2002 WL 1396077 (Ohio Ct. App. 2d Dist. Miami County 2002) (holding that the effective

the expiration date of an ex parte civil protection order be long enough to account for this concern, or periodically review the expiration date and extend it if needed.

Ina twist on the issue of perfected service, the Hamilton County Court of Appeals considered the issue of the type of proof needed to demonstrate that the civil protection order was in served and in effect at the time of the violation. In *State v. Brogden*,[122] appellant was charged with one count of violating an ex parte CSPO. Upon responding to the scene of an assault against the victim, the police officer discovered that Brogden had not been served and so he returned with a copy of the order and served him. Subsequently, the victim filed a complaint against him from which Brogden was found guilty.

On appeal, Brogden claimed that the conviction was based on insufficient evidence because the state failed to prove that the protection order was in effect on the date of the alleged offense. The appellate court held that "[t]o prove a violation of a civil protection order, the state is required to prove that the order was in effect on the date of the offense."[123]

Unfortunately, the entry indicating that the full hearing had been continued such that the order was in effect on the date of the offense had not been attached to the temporary order and the return of service upon respondent was left blank. Moreover, the entry was not certified, the entry was not identified by the officer and the officer did not testify that he had served Brogden with a copy of the entry continuing the temporary order. Because the state conceded that the entry was not properly admitted into evidence, there was insufficient evidence to convict Brogden.

This is yet another example of making sure that the expiration date of an ex parte civil protection order is one year after its issuance. If that date had been added to the order when issued, there might not have been a problem with whether the officer had served Brogden prior to the incident and whether that order was in effect on the date of the violation.

It is significant and clearly a best practice that the officer, upon discovering that Brogden had not yet been served, retrieved a copy of the order from the police station and returned to serve the order upon him.

Similarly, In *State v. Leason*,[124] Leason was convicted of violating a protection order and appealed. On appeal, he claimed that the absence of a time stamp on the protection order issued by the court meant that there was no evidence that the order was filed; thus, it was invalid. Appellant argued that a court speaks through its journal

---

date of a CPO is the date on which the court signed and filed the order).

[122]State v. Brogden, 2018-Ohio-735, 2018 WL 1136138 (Ohio Ct. App. 1st Dist. Hamilton County 2018).

[123]State v. Brogden, 2018-Ohio-735, ¶ 12, 2018 WL 1136138 (Ohio Ct. App. 1st Dist. Hamilton County 2018); citing State v. Frazier, 158 Ohio App. 3d 407, 2004-Ohio-4506, ¶ 9-10, 815 N.E.2d 1155 (1st Dist. Hamilton County 2004); State v. Collins, 1997 WL 426150 (Ohio Ct. App. 4th Dist. Meigs County 1997).

[124]State v. Leason, 2011-Ohio-6591, 2011 WL 6740749 (Ohio Ct. App. 9th Dist. Summit County 2011).

entries. "It is axiomatic that an order must be journalized, or "filed," before it may be considered valid."[125]

The appellate court relied on the reasoning of *Zanesville v. Rouse*[126] regarding the concepts of filing and certification of filing by the clerk. "A document has been filed as soon as it has been delivered in good faith to the proper officer of the clerk and received by the clerk to be kept in its proper place in the clerk's office."[127] "The Supreme Court clarified that, while "certification by a clerk on a document attests that it was indeed filed, such certification does not constitute filing but rather merely evidence of filing."[128] Other evidence of filing may be the entry of the document on the clerk's electronic docket and an affidavit by the clerk of courts; docketing of the case coupled with the deputy clerk's signature; electronic docketing of documents and events which were necessarily precipitated by the filing of the documents in question and the issuing judge's testimony that he/she issued the protection order; defendant's signature acknowledging receipt of the order and a signed certification by a deputy clerk that a certain document was a true copy of the protection order taken from the municipal court's records.[129]

The *Leason* appellate court determined that there was sufficient evidence to establish that the protection order had been filed. In the absence of a time stamped copy, the four copies of the protection order contained in the record bore the signature of the issuing judge and the date and one copy contained a certification by a deputy clerk that the document was a true copy of the original. Additionally, the NCIC form bore the time stamp of the clerk and the electronic docket of events for the case indicated that the protection order was filed.[130]

Although this applied to a protection order issued from a municipal court, the analysis is instructive for a civil attorney who is faced with the same type of challenge in a civil protection order case.

Q & A: For purposes of a violation, must the civil protection order have the signature of a judge before it can be considered a valid order?

According to *State v. Reeves*,[131] defendant, who appealed on the basis of ineffective assistance of trial counsel, argued that he did not

---

[125]State v. Leason, 2011-Ohio-6591, ¶ 8, 2011 WL 6740749 (Ohio Ct. App. 9th Dist. Summit County 2011).

[126]Zanesville v. Rouse, 126 Ohio St. 3d 1, 2010-Ohio-2218, 929 N.E.2d 1044 (2010), judgment vacated in part on reconsideration, 126 Ohio St. 3d 1227, 2010-Ohio-3754, 933 N.E.2d 260 (2010) (portion of judgment reinstating judgment of trial court vacated).

[127]State v. Leason, 2011-Ohio-6591, ¶ 10, 2011 WL 6740749 (Ohio Ct. App. 9th Dist. Summit County 2011), citing Zanesville v. Rouse, 126 Ohio St. 3d 1, 2010-Ohio-2218, ¶ 8, 929 N.E.2d 1044 (2010), judgment vacated in part on reconsideration, 126 Ohio St. 3d 1227, 2010-Ohio-3754, 933 N.E.2d 260 (2010).

[128]State v. Leason, 2011-Ohio-6591, ¶ 10, 2011 WL 6740749 (Ohio Ct. App. 9th Dist. Summit County 2011).

[129]State v. Leason, 2011-Ohio-6591, ¶ 10, 2011 WL 6740749 (Ohio Ct. App. 9th Dist. Summit County 2011).

[130]State v. Leason, 2011-Ohio-6591, ¶ 10, 2011 WL 6740749 (Ohio Ct. App. 9th Dist. Summit County 2011).

[131]State v. Reeves, 2015-Ohio-363, 2015 WL 420015 (Ohio Ct. App. 12th Dist.

violate a CPO because it was a void order because it wasn't signed by the judge. Rather, it was an ex parte CPO and the judge authorized the clerk to sign the order.

The appellate court differentiated between a full hearing CPO and an ex parte order. "For an ex parte civil protection order, the only requirement is that the order be 'issued' or 'approved.' See R.C. 3113. 31(F)(1). The statute does not prohibit the approval of the ex parte order when a clerk obtains authorization to sign the order per phone instructions of a judge. As such, Reeves trial counsel stipulating to the admission of the ex parte civil protection order approved by the judge did not fall below an objective standard of reasonableness."[132] However, had it been a full hearing CPO, a judge's signature would have been needed to make it a formal judgment entry that is final and appealable pursuant to Civ. R. 58.

Q & A: For purposes of a RC 2919.27 violation, must the prosecutor demonstrate that a defendant/respondent had the intent to violate the protection order or that the defendant committed an illegal act or both?

In the criminal context, several competing interests exist. In proving the crime, a prosecutor must show that a defendant committed the act. In proving the violation, a prosecutor must show that a defendant intended to defy the protection order by committing the act. The term "recklessly" as used in both RC 2919.25 and RC 2919.27 implies an intended act, but not necessarily the resulting harm.[133]

Where the violation of a civil protection order may also form the basis of an independent criminal offense, prosecutors should also consider charging a defendant with a new crime of domestic violence pursuant to RC 2919.25. The mere commission of the criminal act puts the perpetrator on notice that he/she may be subjected to criminal sanctions. Although a defendant may not have intended to violate a court order if the order was unknown to him/her, the defendant still intended to commit an illegal act. Therefore, where it may be difficult to demonstrate that a defendant knew of the issuance of a protection order or to prove that a defendant intended to violate the terms of an order, prosecutors should consider multiple charges.

Q & A: Can the violation of a civil protection order result in a new charge of domestic violence?

Absolutely. An offender may be charged with a new crime of domestic violence, violating a protection order, or both. In addition to the

Fayette County 2015).

[132]State v. Reeves, 2015-Ohio-363, ¶ 12, 2015 WL 420015 (Ohio Ct. App. 12th Dist. Fayette County 2015).

[133]State v. Patton, 106 Ohio App. 3d 736, 667 N.E.2d 57 (1st Dist. Hamilton County 1995); see also State v. Gordon, 2003-Ohio-6558, 2003 WL 22889573 (Ohio Ct. App. 10th Dist. Franklin County 2003); State v. LeValley, 2010-Ohio-288, 2010 WL 334984 (Ohio Ct. App. 2d Dist. Greene County 2010) (that the protection order was still in effect restraining defendant from entering the protected party's place of employment formed the basis of the violation and whether or not the protected party was still employed there was not a defense to the violation. The order did not state that a violation would occur only if defendant entered the job site while the protected party was present).

specific charge of violating a civil protection order,[134] a perpetrator can also be charged criminally for domestic violence under RC 2919.25. If the violation is one that is defined as an act of domestic violence under RC 2919.25(A) to RC 2919.25(C), a new charge can be filed against the offender.

Many Ohio courts having jurisdiction over criminal domestic violence cases will consolidate the violation and the new charge for trial purposes.[135] Consolidation is often advantageous to the efficient operation of the criminal justice system as the facts, witnesses, and information necessary for disposition will often be the same or similar.[136] Even though these offenses are consolidated for procedural purposes, they retain their individual character as to convictions and penalties. Each separate act carries its own penalty and generates its own punishment. Upon a finding of guilt, the court, in its discretion, can require the respondent/offender to serve the sentence in each case either concurrently or consecutively.[137]

Q & A: What are the advantages and disadvantages of criminal prosecution?

By making the violation of a civil protection order a crime itself, Ohio's statute grants law enforcement officials clear authority under their arrest powers to detain and arrest anyone who violates a civil protection order.[138] Law enforcement officers are also permitted to make an arrest without a warrant when they have reasonable cause to believe the respondent has violated the order.[139] Repeat violations are subject to increased penalties.[140]

In effect, criminal prosecution goes further in holding batterers accountable for their actions than other types of civil actions designed to force compliance rather than punish behavior.[141] Criminal prosecution evokes fear in the hearts of many respondents because it is more closely aligned with incarceration. If found guilty, a respondent is convicted of a crime.

Many victim advocates have asserted that the criminal justice system moves a case through the system faster than a contempt action moves through the domestic court. In any criminal case, there are specific time limits which must be followed.

---

[134]See RC 2919.27.

[135]See Crim.R. 8(A).

[136]It is the general practice of many of Ohio court systems, such as Cleveland Municipal Court and Springfield Municipal Court, to consolidate the charges for procedural efficacy but to consider them two separate crimes.

[137]See also State v. Fraley, 1999 WL 188156 (Ohio Ct. App. 12th Dist. Preble County 1999).

[138]See RC 2935.03.

[139]See RC 2935.03(B)(3)(b), RC 2935.03(B)(3)(g).

[140]RC 2919.27(B).

[141]See Margaret Martin Barry, Protective Enforcement: Another Pirouette, 6 Hastings Women's L.J. 339 (1995); see also Felton v. Felton, 79 Ohio St. 3d 34, 1997-Ohio-302, 679 N.E.2d 672 (1997).

In contrast, some have argued that the criminal procedure is slower than a contempt hearing.[142] Jury trials, which are commonplace in the criminal justice system, are likely to cause stress to a victim of domestic violence.[143]

Q & A: Who decides whether a petitioner should pursue a criminal prosecution under RC 2919.27?

Even though RC 3113.31(L)(1) permits a petitioner to pursue either criminal prosecution under RC 2919.27 or contempt for a violation of a civil protection order, the ultimate decision as to whether charges are filed against a respondent rests with the prosecutor. Although a petitioner may want to pursue criminal prosecution, it is within the prosecutor's discretion whether to bring criminal charges.

Q & A: How does a prosecutor decide to pursue a criminal prosecution?

If the respondent has recklessly violated the terms of the civil protection order, the defendant has been served or knows that a protection order has been issued against him or her,[144] and the prosecutor has probable cause to believe the crime of violating a protection order[145] has been committed by the respondent, the threshold test for criminal prosecution has been met. The prosecutor will then determine whether the violation is one that is intrinsically civil in scope.[146] Assuming the violation is not of the kind that should be addressed in domestic relations court, the prosecutor will determine whether any other independent evidence is necessary. Additional corroborating evidence, such as other witnesses, visible injuries, medical documentation, police intervention and/or arrest, or the observations of the officer on call, is often sought by the prosecutor in determining whether there is sufficient evidence to prevail at trial.

Q & A: What is the procedure for filing criminal charges for violating a protection order?

It depends. Generally, it is the petitioner/victim who will contact the prosecutor. Sometimes, however, the police officer contacts the prosecutor's office. In either case, the municipal prosecutor that is contacted is located in the city where the violation occurred.

The prosecutor must first review the evidence in order to determine whether there is enough evidence to file charges under RC 2919.27 and prevail at trial. Once the prosecutor decides to file charges and if an arrest was not made at the scene, a warrant is issued for the respondent's arrest. The respondent enters the criminal justice system

[142]David Zlotnick, Empowering the Battered Woman: The Use of Criminal Contempt Sanctions to Enforce Civil Protection Orders, 56 Ohio St. L.J. 1153, 1199 (1995).

[143]David Zlotnick, Empowering the Battered Woman: The Use of Criminal Contempt Sanctions to Enforce Civil Protection Orders, 56 Ohio St. L.J. 1153, 1201 (1995).

[144]See, for example, State v. Bunch, 2001 WL 39599 (Ohio Ct. App. 9th Dist. Summit County 2001). But see State v. Smith, 136 Ohio St. 3d 1, 2013-Ohio-1698, 989 N.E.2d 972 (2013).

[145]See RC 2919.27.

[146]See Text § 13:3, Court enforcement of civil protection orders—Criminal prosecution, for further discussion.

at the point of arrest. Within forty-eight hours, the respondent will appear in court to enter a plea or request additional time to obtain counsel.

In many situations, law enforcement officials will arrest the respondent for the violation of the protection order at the scene of the incident.[147] If the respondent is arrested, he/she will remain in jail until a prosecutor reviews the evidence, speaks with the police officer who made the arrest and/or the victim, and decides whether to pursue criminal prosecution. If charges are filed pursuant to RC 2919.27(A), bail will be set for the respondent.[148] An arraignment hearing is set for the next day on which the court is scheduled to conduct business. A plea is entered by the respondent at that time.

Depending on either the physical condition of the petitioner/victim or the reluctance of the victim to pursue criminal action, the police officer who was at the scene of the incident may initiate the request for the filing of charges. In some smaller cities, such as Springfield, the law enforcement agency routinely files the charges without first consulting the prosecutor.

Q & A: How does the aforementioned analysis apply to RC 3113.31(L)?

RC 3113.31(L)(1) provides that a person who violates a protection order or a consent agreement approved under this section is subject to the following sanctions: (a) criminal prosecution for a violation of RC 2919.27 if the violation of the protection order or consent agreement constitutes a violation of that section,[149] or (b) punishment for contempt of court. Because this section details both protection orders and consent agreements in the same sentence, it can be argued that the enforcement provisions apply only to protection orders issued after the full hearing.[150] Under this interpretation, it must be assumed that RC 3113.31(L) presumes that the protection order is not an ex parte order.

Q & A: What are the penalties for a violation of a civil protection order under RC 2919.27?[151]

Pursuant to RC 2919.27(B), whoever violates this section is guilty of violating a protection order or consent agreement issued per RC 2919.26 or RC 3113.31 or a stalking protection order issued per RC 2903.213 or RC 2903.214 or a juvenile protection order issued under RC 2151.34

---

[147]See RC 2935.03(B)(1), RC 2935.03(B)(3)(b).

[148]See RC 2919.251.

[149]But see Harris v. Miami Cty. Sheriff's Dept., 160 Ohio App. 3d 435, 2005-Ohio-1713, 827 N.E.2d 807 (2d Dist. Miami County 2005) (the appellate court affirmed the grant of the stalking civil protection order but said, "[t]he court would not have the authority to punish Harris for violating its order unless such authority had been specifically granted to it by RC 2903.214(K)." In *Harris*, there was no specific designation for a consent agreement. The court found a consent agreement was a civil protection order under RC 2903.214(E)(1) which allows a court to issue any protection order that is designed to protect the person named in the order.

[150]See People v. Stevens, 133 Misc. 2d 407, 506 N.Y.S.2d 995 (N.Y. City Ct. 1986) (discussing the meaning of the word "issued").

[151]See also Text § 13:15, Court enforcement of civil protection orders—Sentencing civil protection order violators; generally.

or a protection order issued by a court of another state.[152] If the offender violates a civil protection order and it is the first violation, the violation is a misdemeanor of the first degree.[153]

Violating a protection order is a fifth degree felony if the offender previously has been convicted of, pleaded guilty to or been adjudicated a delinquent child for a violation of a protection order or consent agreement approved under RC 2151.34, 2903.213, 2903.214,[154] 2919.26 or 3113.31 of the Revised Code;[155] two or more violations of section 2903.21 (aggravated menacing), 2903.211 (menacing by stalking), 2903.22(menacing) or 2911.211 (aggravated trespass) of the Revised Code or any combination of those offenses that that involve the same person who is the subject of the protection order[156] or one or more violations of this section.[157] If the offender violates a protection order or consent agreement while committing a felony offense, violating a protection order is a felony of the third degree.[158]

If the protection order violated * * * was an order issued pursuant to section 2151 or 2903.214 of the Revised Code that required electronic monitoring of the offender * * *, the court may require in addition to any other sentence imposed upon the offender that the offender by electronically monitored for a period not exceeding five years by a law enforcement agency designated by the court.[159]

The maximum sentence for a misdemeanor of the first degree is not more than six months in jail[160] and $1,000 in fines.[161] The penalty for a felony of the fifth degree is six, seven, eight, nine, ten, eleven, or twelve months[162] and up to $2,500 in fines.[163] The penalty for a felony of the third degree is one, two, three, four, or five years[164] and not more than a $10,000 fine.[165] The range of statutory prison terms for a felony of the fourth degree is between 6 to 18 months.[166]

Q & A: What factors does a court consider when sentencing protection order violators?

Although not specific to domestic violence cases, RC 2929.11 to RC 2929.13 provide the court with certain sentencing guidelines and

---

[152] RC 2919.27(B)(1).

[153] RC 2919.27(B)(2).

[154] State v. Headlee, 2009-Ohio-873, 2009 WL 478085 (Ohio Ct. App. 4th Dist. Washington County 2009).

[155] RC 2919.27(B)(3)(a).

[156] RC 2919.27(B)(3)(b).

[157] RC 2919.27(B)(3)(c).

[158] RC 2919.27(B)(4).

[159] RC 2919.27(B)(5).

[160] RC 2929.21(B)(1). See, for example State v. Wisby, 2013-Ohio-1307, 2013 WL 1288202 (Ohio Ct. App. 12th Dist. Clermont County 2013) (discussing statutory factors for imposition of sentence for a violation of a CPO).

[161] RC 2929.21(C)(1).

[162] RC 2929.14(A)(5); see also State v. Haamid, 2000 WL 45844 (Ohio Ct. App. 8th Dist. Cuyahoga County 2000).

[163] RC 2929.18(A)(3)(e).

[164] RC 2929.14(A)(3).

[165] RC 2929.18(A)(3)(c).

[166] R.C. 2929.14 (A)(4).

whether the offender previously served a prison term[187] or was previously subject to a community control sanction and then committed another offense while under the sanction.[188]

Assuming the sentencing court makes one of these findings, the court, after considering the factors contained in RC 2929.12, may find that a prison term is consistent with the purposes and principles of sentencing as set forth in RC 2929.11 and that the offender is not amenable to an available community control sanction.[189] At this point, the court shall impose a prison term on the offender.[190]

Reading RC 2929.13(B)(2)(a) in conjunction with RC 2929.13(F) suggests that mandatory prison terms may be imposed for violations of civil protection orders, if certain conditions are met.[191] Those violations that result in serious physical harm to the petitioner by the use of a deadly weapon, especially where the offender has previously been convicted of an offense that caused physical harm to the same victim, demonstrate both a propensity for violent conduct and a likelihood that the offender may commit future crimes.

Unfortunately, the presumption is against incarceration. Instead, monetary remuneration or various community service programs are most often considered by the courts in sentencing domestic violence offenders and violators. In light of RC 2929.11 to RC 2929.13 and recently enacted S.B. 50, eff. 1-8-04, however, the imposition of a prison term for certain domestic violence convictions is consistent with the principles and purposes of RC 2929.11 and the statutory guidelines provided in RC 2929.12 and RC 2929.13.

Q & A: Is a child's witnessing of domestic violence considered in sentencing the perpetrator?

Ohio law now requires a court to consider as an aggravating factor when sentencing an offender convicted of domestic violence, felonious assault, aggravated assault, or assault the fact that the offender committed the offense in the vicinity of the offender's or victim's child.[192] For an offense to be committed in the vicinity of a child, the offender must commit the offense within thirty feet of, or within the same residential unit as, a child who is under eighteen years of age, regardless of whether the offender knows the age of the child or whether the offender knows the offense is being committed within thirty feet of, or

10th Dist. Franklin County 1998).

[187]RC 2929.13(B)(1)(g).

[188]RC 2929.13(B)(1)(h).

[189]RC 2929.13(B)(2)(a).

[190]RC 2929.13(B)(2)(a); see also State v. Gonzalez, 1999-Ohio-826, 1999 WL 446441 (Ohio Ct. App. 3d Dist. Allen County 1999) (reversing defendant's sentence because the trial court failed to make the requisite statutory findings when it imposed the maximum sentence); State v. Smith, 1999 WL 417852 (Ohio Ct. App. 11th Dist. Portage County 1999) (discussing the procedure for the requisite statutory findings); City of Cleveland v. Serrano, 1999 WL 1024214 (Ohio Ct. App. 8th Dist. Cuyahoga County 1999).

[191]See also RC 2919.27 and RC 2919.27(B)(4).

[192]See RC 2929.12(B)(9).

within the same residential unit as, the child and regardless of whether the child actually views the commission of the offense.[193]

RC 2929.12(B)(9) states that a sentencing court shall consider all of the following that apply regarding the offender, the offense, or the victim, and any other relevant factors:

> If the offense is a violation of section 2919.25 or a violation of section 2903.11, 2903.12, or 2903.13 of the Revised Code involving a person who was a family or household member at the time of the violation, the offender committed the offense in the vicinity of one or more children who are not victims of the offense, and the offender or the victim of the offense is a parent, guardian, custodian, or person in loco parentis of one or more of those children.

By enacting such proactive legislation, the Ohio legislature has acknowledged that witnessing domestic violence has a detrimental impact on the children within the family relationship.[194]

If the offender commits domestic violence as set forth in RC 2929.12(B)(9), it is a requirement that the offender obtain counseling.[195] Moreover, the fact that the offender committed the crime as set forth in RC 2929.12(B)(9) shall be considered in favor of imposing imprisonment for a misdemeanor.[196] If the court has decided to impose a term of imprisonment on the offender, the factor listed in RC 2929.22(B)(1)(c) shall be considered in favor of imposing a longer term of imprisonment on the offender.[197]

§ 13:4 Court enforcement of civil protection orders—Contempt—Generally defined

Besides criminal prosecution under RC 2919.27, a violation of a civil protection order in Ohio may be enforced through a contempt proceeding against the respondent.[1] "The purpose of the law of contempt is to uphold and ensure the unimpeded and effective administration of justice, secure the dignity of the court and affirm the fundamental supremacy of the law."[2] Contempt may be classified as direct or indirect. Within these parameters, contempt is further grouped into either civil or criminal contempt. Ohio's domestic violence

---

[193] 1999 S.B. 9, eff. 3-8-00; RC 2929.01(NN).

[194] See also Text § 15:11, Impact of domestic violence on children.

[195] RC 2929.17(N).

[196] RC 2929.22(B)(1)(c).

[197] See RC 2929.22(B)(2); see also City of Cleveland v. Serrano, 1999 WL 1024214 (Ohio Ct. App. 8th Dist. Cuyahoga County 1999) (discussing factors favoring a shorter term of imprisonment under RC 2929.22(C) and (E)).

[Section 13:4]

[1] RC 3113.31(L)(1)(b). See also Text § 13:2, Court enforcement of civil protection orders—Generally; Text § 11:24, Ex parte protection orders—Violation of ex parte protection orders.

[2] In re Contemnor Caron, 110 Ohio Misc. 2d 58, 744 N.E.2d 787 (C.P. 2000) (syllabus at 58) (Judge Chinnock discusses the law of contempt in great detail); see generally William F. Chinnock and Mark P. Painter, The Law of Contempt in Ohio, 34 U. Tol. L. Rev. 309 (2003).

statute[3] is rather ambiguous in that it refers only to "contempt" without specifying whether a violation constitutes civil or criminal contempt or is considered direct or indirect contempt.

RC Ch. 2705 governs the contempt power of the court. RC 2705.02 provides in part: "A person guilty of any of the following acts may be punished as for a contempt: (A) Disobedience of, or resistance to, a lawful writ, process, order, rule, judgment, or command of a court or officer."

Contempt of court has been defined as disrespect for the authority of the court or disobedience of court orders.[4] Both statutory language and case law have illustrated that the primary interest involved in any contempt proceeding is the authority and proper functioning of the court.[5]

The power of contempt is essential to a court as it is necessary for the adequate performance of its judicial functions.[6] Certain fundamental principles regarding contempt are common to all courts. For example, a court possesses the power to determine what behavior constitutes contempt.[7] Although RC 2705.05 sets forth the statutory penalties for contempt, the Ohio Supreme Court has determined that a trial court possesses both statutory and inherent authority "to punish the disobedience of its orders with contempt proceedings."[8], a court has the authority to punish a contemnor for violating a court order "without regard to the statutory penalties."[9]

Q & A: What is the difference between direct and indirect contempt?[10]

Direct contempt is set forth in RC 2705.01, which provides "[a] court, or judge at chambers, may summarily punish a person guilty of misbehavior in the presence of or so near the court or judge as to obstruct the administration of justice."[11] Punishment may therefore be imposed summarily without the filing of a motion or the issuance of

[3] RC 3113.31(L)(1)(b).

[4] Denovchek v. Board of Trumbull County Com'rs, 36 Ohio St. 3d 14, 520 N.E.2d 1362 (1988); see also In re Contemnor Caron, 110 Ohio Misc. 2d 58, 744 N.E.2d 787 (C.P. 2000); Lyons v. Bowers, 2007-Ohio-1548, 2007 WL 959916 (Ohio Ct. App. 11th Dist. Lake County 2007); Hamper v. Dobrski, 2015-Ohio-1381, 2015 WL 1593249 (Ohio Ct. App. 8th Dist. Cuyahoga County 2015).

[5] Denovchek v. Board of Trumbull County Com'rs, 36 Ohio St. 3d 14, 520 N.E.2d 1362 (1988); see also Stewart v. Sydenstricker, 1996 WL 272948 (Ohio Ct. App. 4th Dist. Washington County 1996).

[6] See In re Contemnor Caron, 110 Ohio Misc. 2d 58, 744 N.E.2d 787 (C.P. 2000) (general discussion of contempt).

[7] See Beach v. Beach, 79 Ohio App. 397, 35 Ohio Op. 172, 74 N.E.2d 130 (3d Dist. Crawford County 1946).

[8] Zakany v. Zakany, 9 Ohio St. 3d 192, 192, 459 N.E.2d 870 (1984); see also State ex rel. Rice v. McGrath, 62 Ohio St. 3d 70, 577 N.E.2d 1100 (1991); Dombroski v. Dombroski, 1999 WL 783975 (Ohio Ct. App. 7th Dist. Harrison County 1999).

[9] McDaniel v. McDaniel, 74 Ohio App. 3d 577, 579, 599 N.E.2d 758 (8th Dist. Cuyahoga County 1991); see also Granger v. Granger, 2004-Ohio-5601, 2004 WL 2365905 (Ohio Ct. App. 8th Dist. Cuyahoga County 2004).

[10] See, for example, Rudduck v. Rudduck, 1999 WL 436818 (Ohio Ct. App. 5th Dist. Licking County 1999). See also Preston v. Shutway, 2013-Ohio-185, 986 N.E.2d 584 (Ohio Ct. App. 2d Dist. Champaign County 2013).

[11] See, for example, Heid v. Heid, 2002-Ohio-4271, 2002 WL 1922759 (Ohio Ct.

process. On the other hand, indirect contempt is defined as a failure to obey, or resistance to, a court order, writ, judgment, or command of a court or an officer.[12]

Direct contempt involves conduct that is in the presence of the court and which obstructs the administration of justice.[13] Such conduct requires no outside evidence and is punishable immediately following its occurrence.[14] Procedurally, no subsequent separate evidentiary hearing is required.[15]

In contrast, indirect contempt occurs outside the presence of the court.[16] Although the proscribed conduct is not immediately known to the court, it affects the administration of justice because the violation is a violation of a court order.[17] Procedurally, the contemnor is given notice of the particular charges, and a hearing is usually scheduled before the court in order to determine whether the contemnor committed the act alleged.[18]

For purposes of RC 3113.31(L), indirect contempt was contemplated by the Ohio legislature.[19] Violations of a civil protection order occur outside the presence of the court and are directed at the recipient of the court order. A court is only made aware of the contemnor's disobe-

---

App. 5th Dist. Stark County 2002).

[12]RC 2705.02(A); see also Dombroski v. Dombroski, 1999 WL 783975 (Ohio Ct. App. 7th Dist. Harrison County 1999) (discussing indirect and direct contempt).

[13]See McGill v. McGill, 3 Ohio App. 3d 455, 445 N.E.2d 1163 (2d Dist. Montgomery County 1982); State v. Treon, 91 Ohio L. Abs. 229, 188 N.E.2d 308 (Ct. App. 8th Dist. Cuyahoga County 1963); see also State Karnes v. Karnes, 1981 WL 5749 (Ohio Ct. App. 6th Dist. Wood County 1981) (wife found guilty of direct contempt for refusing to testify against her husband in his criminal domestic violence case).

[14]In re Purola, 73 Ohio App. 3d 306, 596 N.E.2d 1140 (3d Dist. Auglaize County 1991).

[15]In re Carroll, 28 Ohio App. 3d 6, 501 N.E.2d 1204 (8th Dist. Cuyahoga County 1985).

[16]In re Carroll, 28 Ohio App. 3d 6, 501 N.E.2d 1204 (8th Dist. Cuyahoga County 1985). See also Lyons v. Bowers, 2007-Ohio-1548, 2007 WL 959916 (Ohio Ct. App. 11th Dist. Lake County 2007) (noting that an indirect contempt is "one which is committed outside the presence of the court, but which also tends to obstruct the due and orderly administration of justice." Lyons v. Bowers, 2007-Ohio-1548, 2007 WL 959916, *2 (Ohio Ct. App. 11th Dist. Lake County 2007); Hamper v. Dobrski, 2015-Ohio-1381, 2015 WL 1593249 (Ohio Ct. App. 8th Dist. Cuyahoga County 2015); Austin v. Austin, 2016-Ohio-7900, 2016 WL 6908096 (Ohio Ct. App. 2d Dist. Montgomery County 2016) (finding that, at most, altering the CPO and giving the false impression that the order was still in effect could be considered indirect contempt but that no specific court order had been violated and that while she should not have altered the document, her actions did not rise to the level of contempt).

[17]State v. Local Union 5760, United Steelworkers of America, 172 Ohio St. 75, 15 Ohio Op. 2d 133, 173 N.E.2d 331 (1961).

[18]In re Carroll, 28 Ohio App. 3d 6, 501 N.E.2d 1204 (8th Dist. Cuyahoga County 1985).

[19]For the distinctions between direct and indirect contempt, see McGill v. McGill, 3 Ohio App. 3d 455, 445 N.E.2d 1163 (2d Dist. Montgomery County 1982); State v. Cline, 1989 WL 140159 (Ohio Ct. App. 11th Dist. Lake County 1989); State v. Persons, 1996 WL 384590 (Ohio Ct. App. 4th Dist. Meigs County 1996).

dience of the court order upon a filing of a contempt motion[20] or criminal prosecution.[21]

Q & A: What is the difference between civil and criminal contempt?

There is a significant, but often obscure, difference between criminal and civil contempt.[22] The primary difference is that in criminal contempt cases, the courts seek to punish the past violation of the order,[23] while in civil contempt cases, the court seeks to coerce future compliance with the order. Numerous courts repeatedly refer to this difference by suggesting that a civil contemnor has the "keys to the jailhouse door" in his pocket because he is free to leave as soon as he complies with the court's order.[24]

Expressed another way, "[c]ivil contempt exists when a party fails to do something ordered by the court for the benefit of the opposing party."[25] Although the court may impose a jail term as punishment for civil contempt, courts have stated that such punishment need not result in any imprisonment "if the contemnor would submit . . . to the lawful order of the court."[26] Civil contempt always allows the contemnor the opportunity to purge the contempt.

Criminal contempt, however, punishes the party who offends the court.[27] The sanctions imposed operate as punishment for the completed act of disobedience.[28] The punishment is for the act itself and is intended to penalize the party for violating the order of the court.

Although the distinction between civil and criminal contempt is often difficult to discern, it is crucial to determine whether a court's

---

[20]RC 3113.31(L)(1)(b).

[21]RC 3113.31(L)(1)(a).

[22]See State v. Yacovella, 1996 WL 38898 (Ohio Ct. App. 8th Dist. Cuyahoga County 1996).

[23]See, e.g., Jeffers v. Jeffers, 2001 WL 118530 (Ohio Ct. App. 10th Dist. Franklin County 2001) (discussing the difference between civil and criminal contempt); see also Boggs v. Boggs, 118 Ohio App. 3d 293, 692 N.E.2d 674 (5th Dist. Stark County 1997) (noting that criminal contempt operates as punishment for the completed act of disobedience); State v. Sandlin, 11 Ohio App. 3d 84, 463 N.E.2d 85 (6th Dist. Wood County 1983).

[24]See, e.g., In re Nevitt, 117 F. 448 (C.C.A. 8th Cir. 1902); State v. Christon, 68 Ohio App. 3d 471, 589 N.E.2d 53 (2d Dist. Montgomery County 1990); Denovchek v. Board of Trumbull County Com'rs, 36 Ohio St. 3d 14, 520 N.E.2d 1362 (1988).

[25]Stewart v. Sydenstricker, 1996 WL 272948, *2 (Ohio Ct. App. 4th Dist. Washington County 1996).

[26]Stewart v. Sydenstricker, 1996 WL 272948, *2 (Ohio Ct. App. 4th Dist. Washington County 1996).

[27]Brown v. Executive 200, Inc., 64 Ohio St. 2d 250, 18 Ohio Op. 3d 446, 416 N.E.2d 610 (1980). See also Robertson v. U.S. ex rel. Watson, 560 U.S. 272, 130 S. Ct. 2184, 176 L. Ed. 2d 1024 (2010) (originating from a challenge of ability of a private citizen to bring criminal contempt charges against someone else in a domestic violence case and in which Supreme Court of the United States dismissed writ of certiorari as improvidently granted, but in which case that was decided 5-4, there was a strongly worded dissent written by Chief Justice Roberts).

[28]Stewart v. Sydenstricker, 1996 WL 272948 (Ohio Ct. App. 4th Dist. Washington County 1996).

use of its contempt powers is civil or criminal in a given situation.[29] The use of civil versus criminal contempt directly impacts the constitutional rights of the individual accused of contempt.[30]

Q & A: How does one determine whether the contempt is criminal or civil?

The United States Supreme Court, in *Gompers v. Buck's Stove and Range Co.*,[31] established a test to determine whether contempt proceedings are civil or criminal. The court stated that the distinction between civil and criminal contempt lies in the "character and purpose" of the punishment.[32]

If the sanctions are designed primarily to benefit the complainant through remedial or coercive means, the contempt is civil.[33] In civil contempt proceedings, the sanction is always conditional. The punishment may be purged upon compliance with the underlying court order.[34]

In contrast, if the sanction is intended to punish a past act of disobedience, the contempt is criminal. In criminal contempt cases, the sanction is both punitive and unconditional.[35] Punishment for criminal contempt also serves to vindicate the authority of the court.[36]

In fact, the same act may constitute both civil and criminal

---

[29]See Denovchek v. Board of Trumbull County Com'rs, 36 Ohio St. 3d 14, 520 N.E.2d 1362 (1988); see also Robert J. Martineau, Contempt of Court: Eliminating the Confusion Between Civil & Criminal Contempt, 50 U.Cin. L. Rev. 677 (1981).

[30]See Dayton Women's Health Ctr. v. Enix, 68 Ohio App. 3d 579, 589 N.E.2d 121 (2d Dist. Montgomery County 1991).

[31]Gompers v. Buck's Stove & Range Co., 221 U.S. 418, 31 S. Ct. 492, 55 L. Ed. 797 (1911); see also In re Contemnor Caron, 110 Ohio Misc. 2d 58, 744 N.E.2d 787 (C.P. 2000).

[32]Gompers v. Buck's Stove & Range Co., 221 U.S. 418, 441, 31 S. Ct. 492, 55 L. Ed. 797 (1911); see also Brown v. Executive 200, Inc., 64 Ohio St. 2d 250, 18 Ohio Op. 3d 446, 416 N.E.2d 610 (1980); Lyons v. Bowers, 2007-Ohio-1548, 2007 WL 959916, *4 (Ohio Ct. App. 11th Dist. Lake County 2007) (stating that a key aspect of civil contempt as opposed to one that is purely criminal is the opportunity for the contemnor to purge himself of the contempt sanction and the discontinuation of the sanction once compliance is achieved, quoting In re Purola, 73 Ohio App. 3d 306, 312, 596 N.E.2d 1140 (3d Dist. Auglaize County 1991); Zemla v. Zemla, 2012-Ohio-2829, 2012 WL 2369394 (Ohio Ct. App. 9th Dist. Wayne County 2012).

[33]Stewart v. Sydenstricker, 1996 WL 272948 (Ohio Ct. App. 4th Dist. Washington County 1996); see also Denovchek v. Board of Trumbull County Com'rs, 36 Ohio St. 3d 14, 520 N.E.2d 1362 (1988); Lyons v. Bowers, 2007-Ohio-1548, 2007 WL 959916, *3 (Ohio Ct. App. 11th Dist. Lake County 2007) (civil contempt is a sanction to enforce compliance for losses or damages sustained by reason of noncompliance. Court held that because there were no damages or losses sustained by reason of noncompliance that are compensable, and because there is no practical opportunity for Defendant to purge or cure his contempt, his contempt was criminal in nature. Janet C. MacDonald, Ohio Revised Code Section 3113.31 and the Constitution: Ohio's Statutory Response to Domestic Violence and Its Double Jeopardy Infirmity, 19 U. Dayton L. Rev. 317, 337 (1993).

[34]Brown v. Executive 200, Inc., 64 Ohio St. 2d 250, 18 Ohio Op. 3d 446, 416 N.E.2d 610 (1980); see also ConTex, Inc. v. Consolidated Technologies, Inc., 40 Ohio App. 3d 94, 531 N.E.2d 1353 (1st Dist. Hamilton County 1988).

[35]Janet C. MacDonald, Ohio Revised Code Section 3113.31 and the Constitution: Ohio's Statutory Response to Domestic Violence and Its Double Jeopardy Infirmity, 19 U. Dayton L. Rev. 317, 337 (1993).

[36]Janet C. MacDonald, Ohio Revised Code Section 3113.31 and the Constitution:

contempt.[37] Both civil and criminal contempt may be considered by the court in the same hearing.[38] However, it must be cautioned "that a single trial for civil and criminal contempt can raise serious due process issues."[39]

Neither imprisonment nor fines are necessarily determining factors. Not all punishment can be designated criminal contempt, nor do all fines contemplate civil contempt. If the sentence is imprisonment, "it is remedial if 'the defendant stands committed unless and until he performs the affirmative act required by the court's order,' and is punitive if 'the sentence is limited to imprisonment for a definite period.' "[40] If the sentence is a fine, it is remedial when "it is paid to the complainant, and punitive when it is paid to the court, though a fine that would be payable to the court is also remedial when the defendant can avoid paying the fine simply by performing the affirmative act required by the court's order."[41]

Q & A: Is intent a necessary element of contempt?

It depends on whether the contempt is civil or criminal. If the contempt is civil, proof of intent is not a prerequisite to a finding of contempt.[42] Unlike civil contempt, the court must find proof of a purposeful, willing or intentional violation of a court order in criminal contempt because criminal contempt impinges on personal liberties.[43] A party's intent does not have to be proven by direct evidence since it is subjective.[44] Intent may be proven by circumstantial evidence.[45]

Ohio's Statutory Response to Domestic Violence and Its Double Jeopardy Infirmity, 19 U. Dayton L. Rev. 317, 441 (1993); see also Dayton Women's Health Ctr. v. Enix, 68 Ohio App. 3d 579, 589 N.E.2d 121 (2d Dist. Montgomery County 1991).

[37]Brown v. Executive 200, Inc., 64 Ohio St. 2d 250, 253, 18 Ohio Op. 3d 446, 416 N.E.2d 610 (1980).

[38]U.S. v. United Mine Workers of America, 330 U.S. 258, 299, 303-04, 67 S. Ct. 677, 91 L. Ed. 884, 19 L.R.R.M. (BNA) 2346, 12 Lab. Cas. (CCH) P 51239 (1947).

[39]See In re Contemnor Caron, 110 Ohio Misc. 2d 58, 99-100, 744 N.E.2d 787 (C.P. 2000); see also U.S. v. Rylander, 714 F.2d 996, 1004, 83-2 U.S. Tax Cas. (CCH) P 9574, 52 A.F.T.R.2d 83-5913 (9th Cir. 1983).

[40]Dayton Women's Health Ctr. v. Enix, 68 Ohio App. 3d 579, 591, 589 N.E.2d 121 (2d Dist. Montgomery County 1991); see also In re Cox, 1999 WL 1312688 (Ohio Ct. App. 11th Dist. Geauga County 1999) (noting that a sentence of 30 days is logically treated as a criminal contempt and the court was under no obligation to allow the appellant the opportunity to purge her contempt).

[41]Dayton Women's Health Ctr. v. Enix, 68 Ohio App. 3d 579, 591, 589 N.E.2d 121 (2d Dist. Montgomery County 1991); see also Ryder v. Ryder, 2002-Ohio-765, 2002 WL 258218 (Ohio Ct. App. 5th Dist. Stark County 2002) (holding that fines or prison sentences conditioned upon performance or non-performance of act are examples of civil contempt).

[42]See Pugh v. Pugh, 15 Ohio St. 3d 136, 472 N.E.2d 1085 (1984); see also Text § 13:8, Enforcement of civil protection orders; procedures for initiating contempt motions.

[43]See Brown v. Executive 200, Inc., 64 Ohio St. 2d 250, 18 Ohio Op. 3d 446, 416 N.E.2d 610 (1980); Midland Steel Prods. Co. v. U.A.W. Local 486, 61 Ohio St. 3d 121, 573 N.E.2d 98 (1991); West v. West, 1994 WL 680156 (Ohio Ct. App. 2d Dist. Montgomery County 1994).

[44]State v. Huffman, 131 Ohio St. 27, 5 Ohio Op. 325, 1 N.E.2d 313 (1936).

[45]See Midland Steel Prods. Co. v. U.A.W. Local 486, 61 Ohio St. 3d 121, 573 N.E.2d 98 (1991).

Q & A: Who determines whether the contempt is civil or criminal?

In most cases, the lower court does not differentiate between civil or criminal contempt. It is then up to the appellate court to determine whether the contempt is civil or criminal.[46] "[T]he appropriate standard for appellate review of contempt sentences is an inquiry into the primary purpose which the trial court sought to achieve by imposing such a sentence."[47] The relevant question, then, is whether the objective of the court was to coerce compliance with the court order or punish for past violations.[48]

A review of the court record is necessary to accomplish the review and determine the purpose of the sentence. The sentence itself is evidence of the objective, which the trial court sought to accomplish.[49] Usually, an appellate court will determine that a contempt is criminal on the basis that there is no action of any kind that could have purged a party of their fine or imprisonment.

It should be cautioned, however, that a trial court order may contain findings of both civil and criminal contempt.[50]

Q & A: May conditions be imposed to a sentence where the contempt is criminal?

It depends on whether the contempt is truly criminal. In criminal contempt, the sanction is both punitive and unconditional.[51] It also serves to vindicate the authority of the court.[52]

Sometimes, the unconditional element of criminal contempt is not so inflexible that the sanction may not provide for suspension conditioned upon future conduct[53] or earlier termination conditioned upon compliance with the court order.[54]

On the other hand, what may appear as criminal contempt, may, after legal analysis, be civil contempt. In *State v. Sandlin*,[55] the Sixth District Court of Appeals held that even if the contempt is criminal,

---

[46]See also Westlake v. Patrick, 2005-Ohio-4419, 2005 WL 2046415 (Ohio Ct. App. 8th Dist. Cuyahoga County 2005) (suggesting factors to be considered in determining whether a sanction amounts to either a civil remedy or a criminal penalty).

[47]State v. Sandlin, 11 Ohio App. 3d 84, 89, 463 N.E.2d 85 (6th Dist. Wood County 1983).

[48]Brown v. Executive 200, Inc., 64 Ohio St. 2d 250, 253-54, 18 Ohio Op. 3d 446, 416 N.E.2d 610 (1980).

[49]See State v. Sandlin, 11 Ohio App. 3d 84, 89, 463 N.E.2d 85 (6th Dist. Wood County 1983), citing State v. Kilbane, 61 Ohio St. 2d 201, 206, 15 Ohio Op. 3d 221, 400 N.E.2d 386 (1980).

[50]See, e.g., Boggs v. Boggs, 118 Ohio App. 3d 293, 692 N.E.2d 674 (5th Dist. Stark County 1997).

[51]See Rudduck v. Rudduck, 1999 WL 436818 (Ohio Ct. App. 5th Dist. Licking County 1999).

[52]William F. Chinnock and Mark P. Painter, The Law of Contempt in Ohio, 34 U. Tol. L. Rev. 309, 325-28 (2003).

[53]James v. James, 1999 WL 247320, *2 (Ohio Ct. App. 9th Dist. Wayne County 1999).

[54]State v. Kilbane, 61 Ohio St. 2d 201, 15 Ohio Op. 3d 221, 400 N.E.2d 386, 391 (1980); see also William F. Chinnock and Mark P. Painter, The Law of Contempt in Ohio, 34 U. Tol. L. Rev. 309, 328 (2003).

[55]State v. Sandlin, 11 Ohio App. 3d 84, 463 N.E.2d 85 (6th Dist. Wood County

conditions may be imposed to a definite sentence which allow for an earlier termination.[56] In this case, a Wood County prosecutor was found in contempt for failing to produce a photograph as ordered by the trial court. Since the refusal was a direct challenge to the court's authority, it was arguably criminal contempt. However, it was also a civil contempt because the prosecutor could purge her contempt upon the production of the photograph.

The appellate court held that "[i]n addition to its primary purpose having been coercive in nature, the contempt sanction was conditional and nondeterminative. Furthermore, the contemnor was provided an opportunity to purge herself of the contempt. As such, it becomes abundantly clear to this court that appellee, in finding appellant in contempt of court, proceeded under the trial court's civil contempt power."[57]

Q & A: May sentences for civil contempt ever become definite such that they resemble criminal contempt sentences?

According to "The Law of Contempt in Ohio," William Chinnock and Mark Painter suggest that "a suspended, indefinite civil sanction may become definite upon revocation of the suspension for further violations. Although historically suspended conditional sentences have been commonplace in criminal law, when applied to the law of contempt, such sentences give rise to the dilemma that their obvious purpose is not to vindicate the law as is the purpose of criminal contempt, but rather is coercive, as is the purpose of civil contempt."[58]

Q & A: May the same act constitute both civil and criminal contempt?

Yes. A civil sanction of an indefinite commitment until the ordered act is complied with may be combined with a criminal sanction of a definite fine and/or term of incarceration for the violation of the order.[59] It must be cautioned, however, that where the civil sanctions are used to coerce compliance and the criminal sanctions are used to punish past conduct, due process concerns may be raised if they are considered in the same trial.[60]

Q & A: Is a purge required in a contempt action?

Again it depends on whether the contempt is classified as civil or criminal. In a civil contempt, the sanction is always conditional. Therefore, the punishment must allow for a purge.[61] However, purge

1983).

[56]State v. Sandlin, 11 Ohio App. 3d 84, 86, 463 N.E.2d 85 (6th Dist. Wood County 1983), quoting State v. Kilbane, 61 Ohio St. 2d 201, 204-07, 15 Ohio Op. 3d 221, 400 N.E.2d 386 (1980).

[57]State v. Sandlin, 11 Ohio App. 3d 84, 87-88, 463 N.E.2d 85 (6th Dist. Wood County 1983).

[58]William F. Chinnock and Mark P. Painter, The Law of Contempt in Ohio, 34 U. Tol. L. Rev. 309, 328 (2003), footnotes omitted.

[59]William F. Chinnock and Mark P. Painter, The Law of Contempt in Ohio, 34 U. Tol. L. Rev. 309, 328 (2003); see also State v. Sandlin, 11 Ohio App. 3d 84, 463 N.E.2d 85 (6th Dist. Wood County 1983).

[60]See Text § 13:5, Court enforcement of civil protection orders—Contempt—Constitutional concerns.

[61]See State v. Sandlin, 11 Ohio App. 3d 84, 463 N.E.2d 85 (6th Dist. Wood County

conditions attached to the imposition of sanctions that seek to regulate future conduct are void.[62]

On the other hand, criminal contempt does not require the court to establish a purge.[63] Often a court will determine that the contempt is criminal on the basis that there is no action of any kind that could have purged a party of a fine or jail term.[64]

Q & A: Are there terms of a civil protection order that cannot be purged by a finding of civil contempt?

It has been argued that the "no contact" violation of a civil protection order cannot be purged by a finding of civil contempt. Since civil contempt must provide a purge mechanism and because there is no way to purge a past violation of a no-contact order, no-contact orders must be considered criminal contempt.

Several cases have discussed the issue of one party violating a no-contact provision of a court order. Although none of these cases have addressed a no-contact provision in a civil protection order, the court analysis relative to purges in contempt proceedings may be instructive. For example, in *Boggs v. Boggs*,[65] the appellant violated the court's no-contact order which prohibited appellant from having visitation in the presence of a certain adult. The trial court concluded that there was no way to purge the contempt of exposing the children to this person. In upholding the trial court decision, the appellate court held that "[b]ecause, as the court noted, there is no way to purge past violations of said order, we believe that the court did not err in failing to provide a purge mechanism for that aspect of the finding of contempt."[66] Therefore, since a no-contact violation does not provide a purge, the court must view the violation as a criminal contempt.[67]

1983).

[62]See Burchett v. Miller, 123 Ohio App. 3d 550, 552, 704 N.E.2d 636 (6th Dist. Erie County 1997).

[63]See Rudduck v. Rudduck, 1999 WL 436818 (Ohio Ct. App. 5th Dist. Licking County 1999); see also Heid v. Heid, 2002-Ohio-4271, 2002 WL 1922759 (Ohio Ct. App. 5th Dist. Stark County 2002).

[64]See State v. Christon, 68 Ohio App. 3d 471, 589 N.E.2d 53 (2d Dist. Montgomery County 1990) (in which the parties refused to go forward on the date set for hearing and requested a continuance. Despite a denial of a continuance, the parties still refused to go forward. The court found them in criminal contempt since there was no way to purge the contempt).

[65]Boggs v. Boggs, 118 Ohio App. 3d 293, 692 N.E.2d 674 (5th Dist. Stark County 1997); see also In re Howard, 2002-Ohio-5451, 2002 WL 31255755, *3 (Ohio Ct. App. 12th Dist. Butler County 2002); State v. Christon, 68 Ohio App. 3d 471, 478, 589 N.E.2d 53 (2d Dist. Montgomery County 1990).

[66]Boggs v. Boggs, 118 Ohio App. 3d 293, 299, 692 N.E.2d 674 (5th Dist. Stark County 1997).

[67]See also Lyons v. Bowers, 2007-Ohio-1548, 2007 WL 959916 (Ohio Ct. App. 11th Dist. Lake County 2007).

§ 13:5 Court enforcement of civil protection orders—Contempt—Constitutional concerns

The constitutional safeguards afforded a contemnor differ depending on whether the contempt is determined to be civil or criminal.[1] It is important that a family law practitioner understand this distinction because the constitutional rights accorded a contemnor flow from this distinction. The elements of criminal contempt are threefold: (1) that a valid court order covering respondent exists; (2) that respondent had notice of that order; and (3) that respondent intentionally violated the order. The elements of civil contempt are twofold: (1) that a valid order covering respondent exists; and (2) that respondent had notice of the order. There is no mandate that respondent intentionally violate the court order. It is unclear whether a defendant must only be aware that a CPO has been issued against him or her or be aware of its specific terms as well.

Q & A: What constitutional rights are afforded to a contemnor?[2]

" '[C]riminal contempt is a crime in every fundamental respect.' "[3] Most courts have agreed that the contemnor in a criminal contempt proceeding is entitled to the same due process rights as any criminal defendant. "The most important consequences arising from this classification of contempts is that many of the significant constitutional safeguards required in criminal trials are also required in criminal contempt proceedings."[4]

For example, due process considerations of notice and an opportunity to be heard are essential before one can be found guilty of criminal contempt. "[S]ince the punishment for criminal contempt impinges personal liberty, 'it must be shown that the alleged contemnor intended to defy the court.' "[5] Clearly, a respondent could not intend to defy the court unless he/she had actual notice of the terms of the order he/she was violating.[6] The Supreme Court, in *Midland Steel*,[7] reasoned that "actual notice of the TRO terms was nevertheless an essential element to his criminal contempt conviction."

On the other hand, if the contempt is civil, it has been argued that

---

[Section 13:5]

[1] See In re Contemnor Caron, 110 Ohio Misc. 2d 58, 744 N.E.2d 787 (C.P. 2000) (provides a general discussion of contemnor's due process rights).

[2] William F. Chinnock and Mark P. Painter, The Law of Contempt in Ohio, 34 U. Tol. L. Rev. 309 (2003).

[3] Brown v. Executive 200, Inc., 64 Ohio St. 2d 250, 252, 18 Ohio Op. 3d 446, 416 N.E.2d 610 (1980) (quoting Bloom v. State of Ill., 391 U.S. 194, 201, 88 S. Ct. 1477, 20 L. Ed. 2d 522 (1968)).

[4] State v. Kilbane, 61 Ohio St. 2d 201, 205, 15 Ohio Op. 3d 221, 400 N.E.2d 386 (1980); see also Brown v. Executive 200, Inc., 64 Ohio St. 2d 250, 18 Ohio Op. 3d 446, 416 N.E.2d 610 (1980).

[5] West v. West, 1994 WL 680156, *2 (Ohio Ct. App. 2d Dist. Montgomery County 1994) (quoting Midland Steel Prods. Co. v. U.A.W. Local 486, 61 Ohio St. 3d 121, 573 N.E.2d 98 (1991)).

[6] See Midland Steel Prods. Co. v. U.A.W. Local 486, 61 Ohio St. 3d 121, 573 N.E.2d 98 (1991).

[7] Midland Steel Prods. Co. v. U.A.W. Local 486, 61 Ohio St. 3d 121, 573 N.E.2d 98 (1991).

the contemnor is entitled only to those due process rights afforded in a civil action.[8] The Supreme Court in *Midland Steel* relied on its earlier decision in *Windham Bank v. Tomaszczyk*,[9] where the Supreme Court determined that, since the purpose of sanctions in a civil contempt is to coerce the contemnor into compliance with the lawful orders of the court, proof of intent is not required in civil contempt. Therefore, a lack of intent to defy the court is not a defense to a charge of civil contempt.[10] Since the Supreme Court in *Midland Steel* determined that, without actual notice of the terms of the order, a defendant could not have intended to defy the court and since the Supreme Court in *Windham Bank* stated that intent is not a material element in civil contempt, it can be inferred that actual notice of the terms of the order may not be a significant variable in civil contempt.[11]

Although Ohio courts differ in their interpretation of the constitutional safeguards accorded to each contemnor, some courts have gone so far as to suggest that the act of contempt itself, whether civil or criminal, mandates certain due process safeguards.[12] For example, many jurisdictions have found that contemnors are entitled to representation by counsel,[13] must be advised of the charges,[14] cannot be compelled to give evidence against themselves,[15] must be given a reasonable opportunity to defend or explain,[16] and be allowed to testify, examine witnesses, and secure witnesses on their behalf.[17]

Q & A: How does a court determine whether a respondent has the intent to defy a court order in a criminal contempt case?

At least one Ohio court set forth the standard for determining

[8]Schrader v. Huff, 8 Ohio App. 3d 111, 456 N.E.2d 587 (9th Dist. Summit County 1983).

[9]Windham Bank v. Tomaszczyk, 27 Ohio St. 2d 55, 56 Ohio Op. 2d 31, 271 N.E.2d 815, 54 A.L.R.3d 1235 (1971); see also Pournaras v. Pournaras, 1985 WL 4613 (Ohio Ct. App. 8th Dist. Cuyahoga County 1985).

[10]Midland Steel Prods. Co. v. U.A.W. Local 486, 61 Ohio St. 3d 121, 573 N.E.2d 98 (1991); see also In re Cox, 1999 WL 1312688 (Ohio Ct. App. 11th Dist. Geauga County 1999) (discussing when intent is an essential element).

[11]See McGill v. McGill, 3 Ohio App. 3d 455, 445 N.E.2d 1163 (2d Dist. Montgomery County 1982) (discussing the type of notice required in civil contempt proceedings).

[12]See, e.g., In re Contemnor Caron, 110 Ohio Misc. 2d 58, 744 N.E.2d 787 (C.P. 2000) (provides a thorough discussion of alleged contemnor's due process rights).

[13]See Risner v. Risner, 1993 WL 84591 (Ohio Ct. App. 3d Dist. Union County 1993); see also Margaret Martin Barry, Protective Enforcement: Another Pirouette, 6 Hastings Women's L.J. 339, 359 (1995).

[14]Risner v. Risner, 1993 WL 84591 (Ohio Ct. App. 3d Dist. Union County 1993).

[15]In re Appropriation for Juvenile and Probate Division for 1979, 62 Ohio St. 2d 99, 16 Ohio Op. 3d 104, 403 N.E.2d 974 (1980); see also In Matter of Contempt of Walker, 1986 WL 10934 (Ohio Ct. App. 4th Dist. Ross County 1986); Moran v. Colaner, 1999 WL 547958 (Ohio Ct. App. 5th Dist. Tuscarawas County 1999) (failing to advise a party of his Fifth Amendment right against self-incrimination is not a denial of his due process rights).

[16]Risner v. Risner, 1993 WL 84591 (Ohio Ct. App. 3d Dist. Union County 1993).

[17]Risner v. Risner, 1993 WL 84591 (Ohio Ct. App. 3d Dist. Union County 1993); see also McGill v. McGill, 3 Ohio App. 3d 455, 445 N.E.2d 1163 (2d Dist. Montgomery County 1982).

intent. In *West v. West*,[18] the Montgomery County Court of Appeals determined that the respondent had the intent to disobey a court order, and therefore, there was enough evidence to find the respondent guilty of criminal contempt beyond a reasonable doubt. In *West*, the respondent went to the day care center to visit the children over an hour before the petitioner arrived. The respondent claimed that he was not seeking a confrontation and did not intend to violate the protection order. However, the trial court found that, once the petitioner arrived at the day care center, the respondent used the opportunity to verbally abuse her. The appellate court relied on the petitioner's subjective belief of physical harm to conclude that "[i]f the Appellant's conduct may be construed as intending to cause the Appellant [sic] to believe that she would suffer physical harm at the hands of the Appellant, then there would be substantial evidence of [Appellant's] intent to disobey the protective order."[19]

The significance of this decision cannot be overstated. It permits a court to consider the subjective belief of the victim in determining whether certain conduct intentionally violates the statute. Additionally, "[a] court may admit evidence of prior 'crimes, wrongs, or acts' to prove intent."[20]

Q & A: Is a trial by jury an integral part of the contempt process?

Several Ohio cases have addressed the issue in the context of criminal contempt. For example, in *In re Appropriation for Juvenile and Probate Division for 1979*,[21] the Supreme Court determined that the appellants had no right to a trial by jury even in a criminal contempt, "for that right inheres only when the sentence for contempt exceeds six months' incarceration."

In the context of a civil action, it is clear that a trial by jury is not a due process right that is afforded to the litigant.[22] It has also been intimated by the Supreme Court of Ohio, in *In re Appropriation for Juvenile and Probate Division for 1979*, that a trial by jury is not a right accorded to a civil contemnor.[23] Most, if not all, sentences for civil contempt do not exceed 30 days.

However, other state courts have specifically addressed the issue of a trial by jury in a civil protection order contempt proceeding. For

---

[18]West v. West, 1994 WL 680156 (Ohio Ct. App. 2d Dist. Montgomery County 1994). But see Pugh v. Pugh, 15 Ohio St. 3d 136, 472 N.E.2d 1085 (1984) (holding that proof of intent to violate the order is not required for a finding of civil contempt); In re Cox, 1999 WL 1312688 (Ohio Ct. App. 11th Dist. Geauga County 1999) (intent is an essential element of indirect criminal contempt, but not a requirement of indirect civil contempt).

[19]West v. West, 1994 WL 680156, *3 (Ohio Ct. App. 2d Dist. Montgomery County 1994).

[20]West v. West, 1994 WL 680156, *4 (Ohio Ct. App. 2d Dist. Montgomery County 1994).

[21]In re Appropriation for Juvenile and Probate Division for 1979, 62 Ohio St. 2d 99, 101, 16 Ohio Op. 3d 104, 403 N.E.2d 974 (1980).

[22]See Text § 12:6, Full hearing—Evidentiary issues, for a discussion of the right to a jury in the full hearing on a civil protection order.

[23]See In re Appropriation for Juvenile and Probate Division for 1979, 62 Ohio St. 2d 99, 16 Ohio Op. 3d 104, 403 N.E.2d 974 (1980).

instance, in *Eichenlaub v. Eichenlaub*,[24] the Pennsylvania Court of Appeals determined that the purpose of the domestic violence statute was:

> to prevent continued abuse and deal with contempt situations in an expeditious manner lest the violation giving rise to the contempt become a criminal action for homicide. Faced with life and death situations, this Court must utilize its expertise in such matters to enforce its orders without the time delay involved in a jury trial.

The court held that "[t]o afford a jury trial in all instances of indirect criminal contempt for violation of a Protection From Abuse Act order would, in essence, wipe out the legislatively created remedy and enforcement under said Act."[25]

Similarly, the Oregon Supreme Court determined, in *State ex rel. Hathaway v. Hart*,[26] that "a party accused of the commission of a contempt is not entitled of right to a jury trial." The Supreme Court differentiated between criminal prosecution and criminal contempt, the former entitling the offender to a trial by jury. The court reasoned that, in a criminal contempt proceeding, it is the violation of the court's order that initiates the contempt; whereas, in a criminal prosecution, it is the nature of the act itself that initiates the prosecution. Although a contemnor may be accorded certain constitutional safeguards, such as the presumption of innocence, the requirement of proof beyond a reasonable doubt, and the right to confront one's accuser, because acts of contempt are punishable by a fine or imprisonment, the "defendant was not entitled to a jury trial, because this criminal contempt proceeding is not a criminal prosecution."[27]

At the very least, it is clear that a trial court has absolute discretion to determine which contempt proceedings necessitate a jury trial. Based on the foregoing analysis, a jury trial is not integral to either the civil or criminal contempt process.[28]

Q & A: Is a contemnor entitled to counsel?

According to *In re Contemnor Caron*,[29] the trial court determined that "an accused contemnor in criminal and civil contempt cases has the due process right to counsel, including court appointed counsel if

---

[24]Eichenlaub v. Eichenlaub, 340 Pa. Super. 552, 561, 490 A.2d 918 (1985).

[25]Eichenlaub v. Eichenlaub, 340 Pa. Super. 552, 561, 490 A.2d 918 (1985).

[26]State ex rel. Hathaway v. Hart, 70 Or. App. 541, 544, 690 P.2d 514 (1984), decision aff'd, 300 Or. 231, 708 P.2d 1137 (1985) (quoting State ex rel. Baker Lodge No. 47, AF & AM v. Sieber, 49 Or. 1, 11, 88 P. 313 (1907)).

[27]State ex rel. Hathaway v. Hart, 70 Or. App. 541, 544, 690 P.2d 514 (1984), decision aff'd, 300 Or. 231, 708 P.2d 1137 (1985); see also Cooke v. Naylor, 573 A.2d 376 (Me. 1990).

[28]See In re Contemnor Caron, 110 Ohio Misc. 2d 58, 118, 744 N.E.2d 787 (C.P. 2000) (court stated that "there is no statutory right to a jury trial in a contempt case in Ohio").

[29]In re Contemnor Caron, 110 Ohio Misc. 2d 58, 113, 744 N.E.2d 787 (C.P. 2000); see also Risner v. Risner, 1993 WL 84591 (Ohio Ct. App. 3d Dist. Union County 1993); Margaret Martin Barry, Protective Enforcement: Another Pirouette, 6 Hastings Women's L.J. 339 (1995).

indigent and incarceration is a possible sanction." The court relied on case law from Ohio and elsewhere to support its conclusion.[30]

Q & A: What is the appropriate venue in a criminal contempt action?

No Ohio court has addressed this issue. However, an Oregon Court of Appeals considered the issue in *Bachman v. Bachman*.[31] In that case, the defendant was found in criminal contempt for violating a restraining order (similar to Ohio's protection order). He was prosecuted in the county where the order was issued, not where the violation occurred. On appeal he argued that the prosecution for a criminal contempt should be in the county where the violation occurred and that prosecuting him in the other county violated his constitutional rights as a criminal defendant.

The appellate court narrowed the question to whether the legislature intended venue to be a statutory or constitutional protection afforded to a criminal defendant in a contempt proceeding where punitive sanctions are imposed. In rejecting the defendant's argument, the court held that "the legislature did not intend venue to be a statutory protection available to a contemnor when punitive sanctions are imposed. Moreover, Article I, section 11, does not apply because contempt is not a criminal prosecution. Contempt is violation of a court order, and the court that issued that order has the power to impose sanctions if that order is violated."[32]

Arguably, the same analysis can be applied to Ohio's protection order process.

§ 13:6 Civil or criminal contempt in the context of civil protection orders

Q & A: Does RC 3113.31 contemplate civil or criminal contempt?

The specific language of RC 3113.31 authorizes "[p]unishment for contempt of court."[1] Punishment is only authorized by the legislature after a respondent violates the civil protection order. "The statute first attempts to coerce acceptable behavior through the issuance of a protection order. If this fails, the statute punishes the unacceptable

[30]See, e.g., Lassiter v. Department of Social Services of Durham County, N. C., 452 U.S. 18, 101 S. Ct. 2153, 68 L. Ed. 2d 640 (1981); Schock v. Sheppard, 7 Ohio App. 3d 45, 453 N.E.2d 1292 (6th Dist. Lucas County 1982); Renshaw v. Renshaw, 2000 WL 1528635 (Ohio Ct. App. 5th Dist. Guernsey County 2000) (court found *Lassiter* modified *Calhoun* decision and even if criminal contempt, no right to counsel if the defendant is not deprived of his/her liberty); see also Zetty v. Piatt, 365 Md. 141, 776 A.2d 631 (2001) (where the Maryland Court of Appeals stated that in a civil protection order contempt action, an alleged contemnor was entitled to counsel if incarceration was being sought). But see In re Calhoun, 47 Ohio St. 2d 15, 1 Ohio Op. 3d 10, 350 N.E.2d 665 (1976) (overruling recognized by, Garfield Hts. v. Stefaniuk, 127 Ohio App. 3d 293, 712 N.E.2d 808 (8th Dist. Cuyahoga County 1998)) (the Ohio Supreme Court discussed when an indigent defendant did not have a right to counsel); Recco v. Recco, 1992 WL 89967 (Ohio Ct. App. 5th Dist. Tuscarawas County 1992).

[31]Bachman v. Bachman, 171 Or. App. 665, 16 P.3d 1185 (2000).

[32]Bachman v. Bachman, 171 Or. App. 665, 16 P.3d 1185, 1189 (2000).

[Section 13:6]

[1]RC 3113.31(L)(1)(b).

behavior. As contempt of court comes only after the coercion fails, it is punishment. Such contempt is clearly criminal in nature."[2]

While it seems logical to suggest that RC 3113.31(L)(1)(b) contemplates criminal contempt, it may be more reasonable to characterize the nature of contempt on a case-by-case basis. Applying the test set forth by the United States Supreme Court in *Gompers v. Buck's Stove & Range Co.*,[3] the "character and purpose" of the punishment imposed by the court will determine whether the contempt is civil or criminal.

From the relevant Ohio cases that have addressed the issue of contempt, it can be inferred that the courts determine the nature of contempt on a case-by-case basis. For example, in *Brown v. Executive 200, Inc.*,[4] the Supreme Court best illustrates this point.[5] In *Brown*, the Court questioned whether the contempt adjudications were civil or criminal in nature. The Court noted that "it is possible that the trial court imposed both types of sanctions to punish for both the civil and criminal contempt aspects of this cause."[6] The Court further noted that "to determine if the sanctions in the instant cause were criminal or civil in nature, it is necessary to determine the purpose behind each sanction: was it to coerce the appellees to obey the consent judgment decree, or was it to punish them for past violations?"[7], the appellate court, in *ConTex, Inc. v. Consolidated Technologies, Inc.*,[8] stated that "In determining the nature of a contempt decree, a reviewing court is not bound by the trial court's characterization of the decree as civil or criminal but must independently ascertain its nature."

There have been no reported Ohio cases that have held that, for purposes of a particular statute, the contempt is necessarily civil or criminal. Consequently, there have been no Ohio cases that specifically illustrate whether RC 3113.31(L)(1)(b) necessarily contemplates civil or criminal contempt in all cases.[9] In fact, no case illustrates the differences between civil and criminal contempt for purposes of RC 3113.31(L)(1)(b) and civil protection order violations. However, in *West v. West*,[10] the Montgomery County Court of Appeals discussed the unique nature of criminal contempt, analyzed the specific fact sce-

[2]Janet C. MacDonald, Ohio's Statutory Response to Domestic Violence and Its Double Jeopardy Infirmity, 19 U. Dayton L. Rev. 317, 344 (1993).

[3]Gompers v. Buck's Stove & Range Co., 221 U.S. 418, 441, 31 S. Ct. 492, 55 L. Ed. 797 (1911).

[4]Brown v. Executive 200, Inc., 64 Ohio St. 2d 250, 18 Ohio Op. 3d 446, 416 N.E.2d 610 (1980).

[5]See also ConTex, Inc. v. Consolidated Technologies, Inc., 40 Ohio App. 3d 94, 531 N.E.2d 1353 (1st Dist. Hamilton County 1988).

[6]Brown v. Executive 200, Inc., 64 Ohio St. 2d 250, 253, 18 Ohio Op. 3d 446, 416 N.E.2d 610 (1980).

[7]Brown v. Executive 200, Inc., 64 Ohio St. 2d 250, 254, 18 Ohio Op. 3d 446, 416 N.E.2d 610 (1980); see also Kennedy v. Mendoza-Martinez, 372 U.S. 144, 83 S. Ct. 554, 9 L. Ed. 2d 644 (1963).

[8]ConTex, Inc. v. Consolidated Technologies, Inc., 40 Ohio App. 3d 94, 95, 531 N.E.2d 1353 (1st Dist. Hamilton County 1988).

[9]But see Lyons v. Bowers, 2007-Ohio-1548, 2007 WL 959916 (Ohio Ct. App. 11th Dist. Lake County 2007) (discussing contempt in relation to RC 2903.214(K)); Westlake v. Patrick, 2005-Ohio-4419, 2005 WL 2046415 (Ohio Ct. App. 8th Dist. Cuyahoga County 2005).

[10]West v. West, 1994 WL 680156 (Ohio Ct. App. 2d Dist. Montgomery County

nario, and determined that there was enough evidence to uphold the conviction for criminal contempt for a civil protection order violation.

The approach taken by the *West* court suggests that, at least in that case, criminal contempt was contemplated by RC 3113.31(L)(1)(b).[11] The court relied on the arguments advanced by the Supreme Court in *Midland Steel* that, in cases of criminal contempt, it must be shown that the alleged contemnor intended to defy the court.[12]

Additionally, the *West* court found that "[i]t is fundamental to due process that an alleged contemnor have notice of the terms of the underlying order he is accused of violating."[13] Actual notice of the terms of a protection order is fundamental to a criminal contempt conviction.[14] It is noteworthy that the Supreme Court in *Midland* contrasted criminal contempt with civil contempt and that it relied on another Ohio Supreme Court opinion, *Windham Bank v. Tomaszczyk*,[15] to advance the argument that lack of intent is not a defense to a charge of civil contempt.[16]

Q & A: What civil protection order violations should be enforced through civil contempt?

In the vast majority of cases, criminal contempt should be considered by the domestic relations court when confronted with a civil protection order violation, as evidenced by the statutory language set forth in RC 3113.31(L).[17] However, certain violations may suggest that civil contempt be utilized. Since civil contempt is designed to coerce future compliance with the court order and can be purged by complying with the order,[18] violations that are inherently civil in nature are typically enforced by civil contempt.

In other domestic relations contexts, violations that are usually enforced by civil contempt have included failure to pay child support[19]

1994); see also Walker v. Bentley, 678 So. 2d 1265 (Fla. 1996) (deciding that courts may utilize either civil or criminal contempt when punishing violators of civil protection orders).

[11]See also Jeffers v. Jeffers, 2001 WL 118530 (Ohio Ct. App. 10th Dist. Franklin County 2001) (discussing the difference between civil and criminal contempt).

[12]See Midland Steel Prods. Co. v. U.A.W. Local 486, 61 Ohio St. 3d 121, 573 N.E.2d 98 (1991); see also In re Cox, 1999 WL 1312688 (Ohio Ct. App. 11th Dist. Geauga County 1999).

[13]West v. West, 1994 WL 680156, *4 (Ohio Ct. App. 2d Dist. Montgomery County 1994).

[14]See Midland Steel Prods. Co. v. U.A.W. Local 486, 61 Ohio St. 3d 121, 573 N.E.2d 98 (1991).

[15]Windham Bank v. Tomaszczyk, 27 Ohio St. 2d 55, 56 Ohio Op. 2d 31, 271 N.E.2d 815, 54 A.L.R.3d 1235 (1971).

[16]See also Text § 13:5, Court enforcement of civil protection orders—Contempt—Constitutional concerns.

[17]See, e.g., Jeffers v. Jeffers, 2001 WL 118530 (Ohio Ct. App. 10th Dist. Franklin County 2001).

[18]See, for example, Tucker v. Tucker, 10 Ohio App. 3d 251, 461 N.E.2d 1337, 1339 (10th Dist. Franklin County 1983).

[19]For a discussion on contempt in child support cases, see Morford v. Morford, 85 Ohio App. 3d 50, 619 N.E.2d 71 (4th Dist. Lawrence County 1993) (Stephenson, J., concurring). But see Margaret Martin Barry, Protective Enforcement: Another Pirouette, 6 Hastings Women's L.J. 339, 358 (1995).

or other monetary relief,[20] cancelling utilities,[21] failure to vacate a residence or turn over property,[22] and violations that involve an allocation of parental rights and responsibilities.[23] Arguably, these same actions may be the subject of protection order violations. If considered civil contempt in one context, it is likely that these same inherently civil violations would constitute civil contempt for purposes of a civil protection order violation.

It should be noted, however, that a failure to vacate the premises or a return to the premises during the time that the protection order is in effect are the types of civil protection order violations that have also been enforced by both civil and criminal contempt.[24] However, some Ohio courts that view this kind of action by a respondent as civil contempt expect that the removal of the respondent from the premises will accomplish the court's ultimate goal of securing future compliance with the protection order.

Other state courts have used the civil contempt remedy for a variety of violations. For example, in *Sanders v. Shephard*,[25] the court determined that the failure to return a minor child in accordance with the terms of the civil protection order was civil contempt because the incarceration was not punitive but rather effected to incur respondent's compliance. The purpose of the court's order was only to compel the production of the child rather than to punish respondent for his conduct. The court pointed out that the respondent could purge the contempt by returning the child. Placing the burden on the respondent to prove he was unable to produce the child through no fault of his own did not violate his due process rights in a civil contempt proceeding.

Q & A: What civil protection order violations have courts enforced through criminal contempt?

Ohio courts have held respondents in criminal contempt for a variety of assaultive behaviors including violent acts. *West v. West*[26] illustrates this point. In that case, the respondent was found in criminal contempt for violating a civil protection order granted to his wife. He had threatened his wife at the children's day care center. The nature of the threat was "You're going to get yours pretty quick now, liar."[27] The Franklin County Court of Appeals determined that there was sufficient evidence to sustain a finding of criminal contempt based upon the threats made by the respondent to his wife.

---

[20] See Pugh v. Pugh, 15 Ohio St. 3d 136, 472 N.E.2d 1085 (1984); Kurincic v. Kurincic, 2000 WL 1231551 (Ohio Ct. App. 8th Dist. Cuyahoga County 2000).

[21] Hamper v. Dobrski, 2015-Ohio-1381, 2015 WL 1593249 (Ohio Ct. App. 8th Dist. Cuyahoga County 2015).

[22] Pugh v. Pugh, 15 Ohio St. 3d 136, 472 N.E.2d 1085 (1984).

[23] See Stewart v. Sydenstricker, 1996 WL 272948 (Ohio Ct. App. 4th Dist. Washington County 1996); see also Shafer v. Shafer, 1993 WL 524958 (Ohio Ct. App. 4th Dist. Washington County 1993).

[24] See City of Columbus v. Patterson, 1982 WL 4556 (Ohio Ct. App. 10th Dist. Franklin County 1982).

[25] Sanders v. Shephard, 185 Ill. App. 3d 719, 133 Ill. Dec. 712, 541 N.E.2d 1150 (1st Dist. 1989).

[26] West v. West, 1994 WL 680156 (Ohio Ct. App. 2d Dist. Montgomery County 1994).

[27] West v. West, 1994 WL 680156, *1 (Ohio Ct. App. 2d Dist. Montgomery County

Courts around the country have also upheld findings of criminal contempt based on continued criminal acts against the victim by the respondent. These behaviors include threats to kill and threats to harm or hurt the petitioner,[28] the rape of the petitioner,[29] beatings,[30] or breaking into the petitioner's home,[31] violations of protection orders that are not in themselves a crime may also be enforced through criminal contempt. For example, continued harassment[32] by the respondent where he/she was ordered to have no contact with the petitioner,[33] where the respondent watched the petitioner and sent flowers to the petitioner,[34] and where the respondent continually telephoned and hung up on the petitioner[35] have been considered to be the types of behaviors for which a finding of criminal contempt would lie.

Other behaviors resulting in contempt have included contacting the petitioner and the minor child in violation of the civil protection order and damaging personal property.[36] Although no specific finding indicated that the contempt was criminal in that case, the appellant was sentenced to thirty days incarceration. This punishment was not intended to coerce compliance, nor was it remedial. Since the purpose of the punishment was punitive and designed to correct the already completed act of disobedience, the contempt was clearly criminal in nature.

At least one Ohio court determined that, in a protection order situation, the failure to vacate the premises was considered a criminal contempt.[37] In fact, depending on the specific court jurisdiction, a violation for a failure to vacate the premises or a return to the premises may also rise to the level of a criminal prosecution under RC 2919.27.

1994).

[28]See People v. Allen, 787 P.2d 174 (Colo. App. 1989); U.S. v. Dixon, 598 A.2d 724 (D.C. 1991), judgment aff'd in part, rev'd in part, 509 U.S. 688, 113 S. Ct. 2849, 125 L. Ed. 2d 556 (1993), cert. granted, U.S. v. Dixon, 503 U.S. 1004, 112 S. Ct. 1759, 118 L. Ed. 2d 422 (1992).

[29]See Cole v. Cole, 147 Misc. 2d 297, 556 N.Y.S.2d 217 (Fam. Ct. 1990).

[30]See People v. Townsend, 183 Ill. App. 3d 268, 131 Ill. Dec. 741, 538 N.E.2d 1297 (4th Dist. 1989).

[31]See People v. Allen, 787 P.2d 174 (Colo. App. 1989); Com. v. Gordon, 407 Mass. 340, 553 N.E.2d 915 (1990); distinguished by Com. v. Picariello, 40 Mass. App. Ct. 902, 660 N.E.2d 1102 (1996).

[32]See People v. Whitfield, 147 Ill. App. 3d 675, 101 Ill. Dec. 80, 498 N.E.2d 262 (4th Dist. 1986) (analyzing the term "harass" for purposes of a protection order violation). But see Jeffers v. Jeffers, 2001 WL 118530, *3 (Ohio Ct. App. 10th Dist. Franklin County 2001) (defining "harass" for purposes of a CPO violation and reversing the criminal contempt finding because appellant's actions did not legally constitute harassment).

[33]See State v. Higgins, 1996 WL 363543 (Ohio Ct. App. 5th Dist. Licking County 1996); In re Colaner, 2002-Ohio-3072, 2002 WL 1343261 (Ohio Ct. App. 5th Dist. Tuscarawas County 2002).

[34]See Saliterman v. State, 443 N.W.2d 841 (Minn. Ct. App. 1989).

[35]See Saliterman v. State, 443 N.W.2d 841 (Minn. Ct. App. 1989).

[36]See Petrak v. Petrak, 1994 WL 50386 (Ohio Ct. App. 12th Dist. Butler County 1994).

[37]See City of Columbus v. Patterson, 1982 WL 4556 (Ohio Ct. App. 10th Dist. Franklin County 1982).

Family law practitioners should advise their clients of the possibility of criminal prosecution for these kinds of violations, especially when the police have arrested the respondent for the violation. Only when the prosecutor declines to prosecute should a contempt action be considered.[38]

§ 13:7 Criminal and civil contempt; standards and burdens of proof

RC 3113.31 is silent regarding the proper standard of proof necessary to sustain a contempt sanction for the violation of a civil protection order. However, many Ohio courts have addressed this issue in the context of other civil proceedings, especially relative to criminal contempt.

Of importance is that the acts which rise to the level of a violation of a civil protection order do not necessarily result in physical harm or threats of continued bodily injury. For example, in *State v. Scott*,[1] the Supreme Court of South Dakota upheld the conviction of a defendant for violating a civil protection order where he repeatedly telephoned his wife. He appealed, arguing that he could not be convicted of anything other than the acts described in the statute. The Court rejected that argument, finding that, because the terms of the protection order prohibited telephone calls, the jury could properly find that he violated the order.[2]

Q & A: What standard of proof is necessary to establish criminal contempt?

The overwhelming majority of courts have cited *Brown v. Executive 200, Inc.*,[3] in which the Supreme Court of Ohio found that, to establish criminal contempt, the petitioner has the burden of proving beyond a reasonable doubt that the respondent violated the order.[4] The Supreme Court held that "the standard of proof required in criminal contempt proceedings is proof of guilt beyond a reasonable doubt and a contemnor cannot be given a criminal contempt sanction unless proven beyond a reasonable doubt."[5]

Several courts likened criminal contempt to other criminal proceedings. In doing so, these jurisdictions elevated the status of the criminal contempt proceeding and created a situation in which the contemnor is to be treated as a criminal defendant and accorded significant constitutional protections. "Because of its similarity to a crim-

---

[38]See Margaret Martin Barry, Protective Enforcement: Another Pirouette, 6 Hastings Women's L.J. 339 (1995); but see RC 3113.31(L)(2) (permitting both a criminal prosecution and contempt action).

[Section 13:7]

[1]State v. Scott, 1998 SD 2, 574 N.W.2d 595 (S.D. 1998).

[2]See also State v. Hoffman, 149 N.J. 564, 695 A.2d 236 (1997).

[3]Brown v. Executive 200, Inc., 64 Ohio St. 2d 250, 18 Ohio Op. 3d 446, 416 N.E.2d 610 (1980).

[4]See also In re Contemnor Caron, 110 Ohio Misc. 2d 58, 744 N.E.2d 787 (C.P. 2000) (discussion of the appropriate burden of proof).

[5]Brown v. Executive 200, Inc., 64 Ohio St. 2d 250, 252, 18 Ohio Op. 3d 446, 416 N.E.2d 610 (1980); see also Pugh v. Pugh, 15 Ohio St. 3d 136, 472 N.E.2d 1085 (1984); Jeffers v. Jeffers, 2001 WL 118530 (Ohio Ct. App. 10th Dist. Franklin County 2001).

inal proceeding, the standard of proof required for criminal contempt is 'proof of guilt beyond a reasonable doubt.' "[6]

Only one Ohio court specifically addressed the appropriate burden of proof as it relates to a violation of a civil protection order. In *West v. West*,[7] the Montgomery County Court of Appeals relied on *Brown v. Executive 200, Inc.* when it approved of the beyond a reasonable doubt standard to establish criminal contempt.

In *West*, the Montgomery County Court of Appeals first determined whether sufficient evidence existed for the trial court to find the appellant guilty beyond a reasonable doubt. The appellate court relied on *State v. Eskridge*[8] which noted that there must be "substantial evidence upon which the court could reasonably conclude that all the elements of an offense have been proven beyond a reasonable doubt." The *West* court concluded that "[i]f the Appellant's conduct may be construed as intending to cause the Appellant [sic] to believe that she would suffer physical harm at the hands of the Appellant, then there would be substantial evidence of [Appellant's] intent to disobey the protective order."[9]

The holding in *West* illustrates how petitioners may meet this burden of proof in criminal contempt proceedings. The petitioner's testimony may be enough to establish proof beyond a reasonable doubt. For example, the court sustained the criminal contempt sanction based on the petitioner's testimony that the respondent's comment "You're going to get yours pretty quick now, liar"[10] and his demeanor and tone of voice, coupled with prior threats that "all this pain and suffering will be taken care of later," "wait till you see what I have got planned," and that he would "make sure that she got everything she deserved,"[11] placed her in fear that he intended to carry out the threats of the past.

The court held that "'[i]t is sufficient if the offender knowingly causes the victim to believe that the offender will carry his threat into execution. Hence, it is the victim's subjective belief which becomes the focal point for determining whether certain conduct violates the statute.' "[12] Of significance is that, although the day care center employee also testified, it was the testimony of the petitioner and her belief that the appellant intended to cause her serious physical harm that provided the basis for the court to determine that she satisfied the burden of proof to sustain the criminal contempt sanction.

---

[6]Stewart v. Sydenstricker, 1996 WL 272948, *2 (Ohio Ct. App. 4th Dist. Washington County 1996) (quoting *Brown* at the syllabus).

[7]West v. West, 1994 WL 680156 (Ohio Ct. App. 2d Dist. Montgomery County 1994); see also Mabry v. Demery, 707 A.2d 49 (D.C. 1998).

[8]State v. Eskridge, 38 Ohio St. 3d 56, 59, 526 N.E.2d 304 (1988).

[9]West v. West, 1994 WL 680156, *3 (Ohio Ct. App. 2d Dist. Montgomery County 1994).

[10]West v. West, 1994 WL 680156, *1 (Ohio Ct. App. 2d Dist. Montgomery County 1994).

[11]West v. West, 1994 WL 680156, *3 (Ohio Ct. App. 2d Dist. Montgomery County 1994).

[12]West v. West, 1994 WL 680156, *3 (Ohio Ct. App. 2d Dist. Montgomery County 1994) (quoting City of Dayton v. Waugh, No. 6965, 2d Dist. Ct. App., Montgomery, 1-2-81).

Q & A: What standard of proof is necessary to establish civil contempt?

There is no case law indicating the level of proof necessary to find a respondent in civil contempt of a civil protection order. However, there is sufficient case law across the state of Ohio that has addressed this issue in the context of civil contempt in general.

If a violation is enforced through civil contempt, the standard of proof is less stringent than "beyond a reasonable doubt." Considerable authority in Ohio demonstrates that proof of civil contempt must be made by clear and convincing evidence.[13] In reaching their conclusions, each of the courts specifically examined the burden of proof characteristics inherent in both civil and criminal contempt. Even the Supreme Court in *Brown v. Executive 200, Inc.*[14] sanctioned the clear and convincing evidentiary standard for civil contempt.

Similarly, other court jurisdictions specifically discussed the differences between civil contempt proceedings and other civil proceedings. "The standard of proof differs from that of proof by a preponderance of the evidence found in wholly civil proceedings because even when civil contempt is charged the proceedings are quasi criminal in nature."[15]

On the other hand, some courts have determined that the appropriate standard of proof for civil contempt is a preponderance of the evidence.[16] Logic would support the use of this evidentiary standard. In light of the Ohio Supreme Court decision in *Felton v. Felton*,[17] it is arguable that the appropriate evidentiary standard in civil contempt proceedings for violations of civil protection orders is the preponderance of the evidence standard. In that case, the Court held that the preponderance of the evidence standard is to be applied when granting civil protection orders. For a court to place a stricter burden on the petitioner by applying a clear and convincing evidentiary standard to the violation of a civil protection order creates conflicting burdens of proof and serves no logical purpose.

§ 13:8 Enforcement of civil protection orders; procedures for initiating contempt motions

Generally, the process by which domestic relations courts enforce civil protection orders through contempt is much slower than the

[13]See Pugh v. Pugh, 15 Ohio St. 3d 136, 472 N.E.2d 1085 (1984); ConTex, Inc. v. Consolidated Technologies, Inc., 40 Ohio App. 3d 94, 531 N.E.2d 1353 (1st Dist. Hamilton County 1988); Stewart v. Sydenstricker, 1996 WL 272948 (Ohio Ct. App. 4th Dist. Washington County 1996); see also Kurincic v. Kurincic, 2000 WL 1231551 (Ohio Ct. App. 8th Dist. Cuyahoga County 2000).

[14]Brown v. Executive 200, Inc., 64 Ohio St. 2d 250, 18 Ohio Op. 3d 446, 416 N.E.2d 610 (1980). See also Hamper v. Dobrski, 2015-Ohio-1381, 2015 WL 1593249 (Ohio Ct. App. 8th Dist. Cuyahoga County 2015).

[15]Gruebel v. Gruebel, 1987 WL 14302, *9 (Ohio Ct. App. 4th Dist. Pickaway County 1987).

[16]See Iwanek v. Iwanek, 1991 WL 19307 (Ohio Ct. App. 9th Dist. Lorain County 1991); Conley v. Conley, 1991 WL 60687 (Ohio Ct. App. 9th Dist. Summit County 1991).

[17]Felton v. Felton, 79 Ohio St. 3d 34, 1997-Ohio-302, 679 N.E.2d 672 (1997).

criminal prosecution process.[1] The respondent may elude the process server or refuse to accept the pleadings. Even if adequately served, a respondent may continue the court hearing for any number of reasons.[2]

Family law practitioners should explain to their clients that a hearing will not be held until the respondent is served with the contempt motion. This is unfortunate because, by the time the case is set for hearing, time may have rendered the motion moot. There are no statutory procedures for filing a contempt motion for the violation of a civil protection order, particularly with regard to the time framework. Additionally, few courts have any mechanisms in place to expedite the hearing on a contempt motion.[3]

All courts should require speedy contempt hearings to effectuate the statutory objective of RC 3113.31, which is to protect a victim from further acts of domestic violence. "Granting a speedy hearing is essential because batterers are more likely to respond to a fast contempt mechanism . . ., because deterrence is generally more potent when a quick punishment follows an infraction."[4] Often, delays render the resultant legal action largely ineffective.[5]

As more attorneys become better educated about the enforcement remedies available, contempt may become a more widely used remedy in the future. Additionally, as more pro se litigants file their own protection orders, more litigants will demand that the court aid them in the enforcement of those orders.

Q & A: What is the procedure for initiating a contempt of court proceeding?

If the remedy for enforcement is contempt, a motion to show cause is filed by the petitioner in the domestic relations court.[6] This motion

[Section 13:8]

[1]But see David Zlotnick, Empowering the Battered Woman: The Use of Criminal Contempt Sanctions to Enforce Civil Protection Orders, 56 Ohio St. L.J. 1153, 1201 (1995).

[2]See, e.g., Thompson v. Thompson, 559 A.2d 311 (D.C. 1989) (holding that the trial court could not deny a continuance in a criminal contempt proceeding based on the respondent's failure to secure counsel prior to the hearing where the respondent was not notified until trial that he was entitled to court-appointed counsel or that the contempt charge would be treated as criminal rather than civil); see also State v. Christon, 68 Ohio App. 3d 471, 589 N.E.2d 53 (2d Dist. Montgomery County 1990) (general factors to consider in deciding to grant motion to continue).

[3]In Franklin County, the court has at least addressed the issue. Although there is no specific time frame within which a hearing must be scheduled or held, most contempt proceedings are brought before a hearing officer for disposition within two to four weeks.

[4]David Zlotnick, Empowering the Battered Woman: The Use of Criminal Contempt Sanctions to Enforce Civil Protection Orders, 56 Ohio St. L.J. 1153, 1201 (1995).

[5]See Margaret Martin Barry, Protective Enforcement: Another Pirouette, 6 Hastings Women's L.J. 339, 359 (1995).

[6]See Civ.R. 7(B); see also Kurincic v. Kurincic, 2000 WL 1231551 (Ohio Ct. App. 8th Dist. Cuyahoga County 2000) (service and notice of a contempt motion and finding of contempt).

is filed with the court and must be served upon the respondent. An alleged contemnor is entitled to notice of the charges against him/her.[7]

The statute is silent relative to the type of service/notice required. The Rules of Civil Procedure direct that service on motions filed subsequent to an original complaint be made by ordinary mail.[8] However, court practice suggests that service on a post-decree motion be made by certified mail. Because a motion to show cause (motion for contempt) is considered a new action and not part of the original proceeding and because one of the sanctions for contempt is incarceration, any motion to show cause for violating a civil protection order should be served on a respondent by certified mail.

The Civil Rules of Procedure have recently provided guidance to courts. The civil rules were amended to provide that "[s]ervice of a motion for modification, *contempt,* renewal or termination of a civil protection order issued after a full hearing or an approved consent agreement shall be made in the manner provided for service of process under Civ. R. 4 through 4.6."[9]

Pursuant to Civ. R. 65.1(C)(4)(b), "[a]fter service has been made in accordance with division (C)(4)(a) of this rule, any additional service required to be made on the Respondent, and, if applicable, on the parent, guardian, or legal custodian, shall be made in accordance with provisions of Civ. R. 5(B)."

Many courts have instituted local rules that provide additional procedures for the filing of court papers. For example, Cuyahoga County Domestic Relations Court Local Rule 15 provides that post-decree motions shall be served in the manner provided under Ohio Rules of Civil Procedure 4 to 4.6. In Cuyahoga County, a motion to show cause for violating a civil protection order is considered a post-decree motion. As such, service by certified mail is required.

For example, in *McGill v. McGill,*[10] the Court of Appeals for Montgomery County addressed the issue of service of the contempt motion, although not in connection with a violation of a protection order. The court found that

> an individual subject to contempt proceedings is entitled to adequate notice as well as an opportunity to be heard. Where the notice is sufficient to apprise a party of the charges against her, thereby enabling her to prepare her defense, such notice generally will withstand objections as to content. Further, notice which is reasonably calculated to reach the individual alleged to be in contempt also will withstand objection. Despite the potential for imprisonment there is no requirement that such notice must be personally served upon the individual.[11]

The court held that the service of a motion to show cause may be made by certified mail.

However, the very nature of a civil protection order and the

---

[7]RC 2705.03.

[8]See Civ.R. 5.

[9]Emphasis added; Civ. R. 65.1(C)(4)(a).

[10]McGill v. McGill, 3 Ohio App. 3d 455, 445 N.E.2d 1163 (2d Dist. Montgomery County 1982).

[11]McGill v. McGill, 3 Ohio App. 3d 455, 457, 445 N.E.2d 1163 (2d Dist. Montgomery County 1982).

extraordinary nature of the relief granted demands immediate and timely notice to the respondent of the motion to show cause. Although certified mail service may be used for other contempt motions, personal service is best able to effectuate the objective of immediate and timely notice. Without prompt service, the motion cannot be heard, the contemnor cannot be found guilty of the violation, there can be no punishment for the violation, and the purpose of the domestic violence statute as it relates to swift and certain enforcement of the protection order cannot be realized.

Additionally, the respondent must be given notice of the time and place of the adversarial hearing.[12] Some Ohio court jurisdictions send this notice by certified mail. Others require that notice of the hearing be attached to the original motion, and others send it out by ordinary mail. Some courts provide this notice by means of a second document at the time the alleged contemnor is served with the underlying motion. This document is often called an Order to Appear.

The purpose of the hearing is to evaluate the charge against the accused, hear testimony, and determine whether the accused has violated the civil protection order. If found guilty, a sanction is then imposed upon the contemnor by the court.[13]

Q & A: What happens if the respondent does not appear at the hearing on the contempt motion?

Should the respondent fail to appear at the contempt hearing after having been served with the motion as well as notified of the hearing, a citation will be issued for the respondent. A citation commands the respondent to appear for the specified hearing. If the respondent still fails to appear at this juncture, the court will issue a capias for the arrest of the respondent. A capias is a writ issued by the court to bring the person of the defendant before the court.

It is of great concern to the petitioner when the respondent fails to appear at the contempt hearing and the object of the hearing is to mandate compliance with the court order, such as returning the child to the petitioner or paying child support. Without the respondent present to submit to the court's authority, the issuance of an order, at this time, is rather ineffective. A citation or capias takes more time, and by the time the case is reset and the respondent appears, the reason for bringing the motion may have been rendered moot.

Q & A: Can a respondent be found in contempt for violating an ex parte protection order?[14]

It depends first on the nature of the violation and whether the contempt is deemed civil or criminal. A condition precedent to a finding of contempt is notice to the respondent of the underlying order

[12]See Vito v. Vito, 380 Pa. Super. 258, 551 A.2d 573 (1988). See Risner v. Risner, 1993 WL 84591 (Ohio Ct. App. 3d Dist. Union County 1993) for the constitutional due process procedural requirements necessary in contempt proceedings; see also Moran v. Colaner, 1999 WL 547958 (Ohio Ct. App. 5th Dist. Tuscarawas County 1999).

[13]See RC 2705.05.

[14]See also Text § 13:2, Court enforcement of civil protection orders—Generally, and Text § 13:3, Court enforcement of civil protection orders—Criminal prosecution.

against him/her.[15] It is unclear whether a contemnor must only have notice of the underlying order that prohibits him/her from doing something or must know of the specific terms of the order[16] before he/she can be found in contempt for violating the order. An ex parte protection order presupposes that the order was entered without the respondent having notice or an opportunity to be heard.

The same arguments that have been advanced to demonstrate why a court has no authority to punish a respondent for violating an ex parte protection order under RC 2919.27 can be applied to a charge of contempt for such a violation.[17] Service of process of the ex parte protection order on a respondent is evidence that the respondent has knowledge of the terms of the order. Without service of process and notice of the underlying terms of the order, it is unlikely that a respondent will be found in contempt.[18]

Of significance is that at least one Ohio court determined that punishing someone for the violation of an ex parte criminal protection order is a violation of due process. The appellant in *City of Columbus v. Patterson*[19] appealed his conviction for contempt on the grounds that, by making the violation of an ex parte protection order criminal conduct, the Columbus City Code denied him due process of law.[20] The appellate court stated:

> Here, the state law makes a violation of a temporary protection order a matter which is not criminal and is punishable by a civil contempt proceeding whereas the city has made the same act a crime. We conclude that a city cannot criminalize an act which is treated as being non-criminal by the state.[21]

Interestingly, the Cuyahoga County Court of Appeals upheld a finding that the husband had violated an ex parte protection order. In *Rush v. Rush*,[22] the husband violated an ex parte civil protection order by going to his wife's apartment. He appealed the trial court's ruling

---

[15]Midland Steel Prods. Co. v. U.A.W. Local 486, 61 Ohio St. 3d 121, 573 N.E.2d 98 (1991).

[16]See Text § 13:5, Court enforcement of civil protection orders—Contempt—Constitutional concerns, and Text § 13:6, Civil or criminal contempt in the context of civil protection orders.

[17]See also Text § 13:2, Court enforcement of civil protection orders—Generally, and Text § 13:3, Court enforcement of civil protection orders—Criminal prosecution.

[18]See People v. Perez, 189 Misc. 2d 516, 734 N.Y.S.2d 398 (County Ct. 2001) (discussion on what it means to be "duly served" for purposes of prosecution for violating a civil protection order).

[19]City of Columbus v. Patterson, 1982 WL 4556 (Ohio Ct. App. 10th Dist. Franklin County 1982); see also Rush v. Rush, 1999 WL 1044482 (Ohio Ct. App. 8th Dist. Cuyahoga County 1999); but see Westlake v. Patrick, 2007-Ohio-1307, 2007 WL 853235, *2 (Ohio Ct. App. 8th Dist. Cuyahoga County 2007) (concluding that the court could criminally punish a defendant for violating a facially valid ex parte order, even if the order is subsequently determined to be invalid after the violation occurred).

[20]But see State v. Myers, 2002-Ohio-253, 2002 WL 54753 (Ohio Ct. App. 5th Dist. Perry County 2002) (an ex parte protection order did not violate appellant's due process rights where the court admitted it into evidence and considered it as a sentencing factor).

[21]City of Columbus v. Patterson, 1982 WL 4556, *3 (Ohio Ct. App. 10th Dist. Franklin County 1982).

[22]Rush v. Rush, 1999 WL 1044482 (Ohio Ct. App. 8th Dist. Cuyahoga County

and argued that the court erred in finding him in indirect contempt because he was not accorded notice of the contempt charges.

The Eighth District Court of Appeals, noting the unambiguous warning page attached to the protection order, reasoned that the husband was aware of the ex parte protection order, because he had been served with a copy. Therefore, the trial court could have reasonably found that he violated the ex parte order. Additionally, the appellate court stated that because the trial court failed to impose a fine, the "[h]usband was not prejudiced by the court's cautionary finding."[23]

In a footnote, the court also stressed that a party may not negate the lawful effect of an ex parte order.[24] In calling attention to this fact, a respondent to a protection order proceeding is on notice not to defy that lawful order.

Q & A: What constitutes adequate notice of the underlying protection order for purposes of a contempt proceeding?[25]

Ohio and other states have considered the matter. In such cases, the record must reflect that the respondent was made aware of the terms of the underlying protection order.[26] For example, in *State v.*

1999).

[23]Rush v. Rush, 1999 WL 1044482, *7 (Ohio Ct. App. 8th Dist. Cuyahoga County 1999). But see Berry v. Patrick, 2005-Ohio-3708, 2005 WL 1707005 (Ohio Ct. App. 8th Dist. Cuyahoga County 2005) (holding that the trial court's failure to conduct a hearing and rule on a petition for a civil stalking protection order in a timely manner was an abuse of discretion and, thus, the court should not have found former boyfriend in contempt of court); see also Westlake v. Patrick, 2007-Ohio-1307, 2007 WL 853235, *2 (Ohio Ct. App. 8th Dist. Cuyahoga County 2007) (noting that a Court could criminally punish a defendant for violating an ex parte facially valid order even if the civil sanction for the same violation was reversed).

[24]Rush v. Rush, 1999 WL 1044482, *7 (Ohio Ct. App. 8th Dist. Cuyahoga County 1999); see also State v. Sanders, 327 N.J. Super. 385, 743 A.2d 385 (App. Div. 2000) (holding that it was irrelevant in a criminal contempt proceeding whether the order in effect at the time of the violation is later vacated or dismissed and no permanent order is granted by the court).

[25]See also In re Contemnor Caron, 110 Ohio Misc. 2d 58, 744 N.E.2d 787 (C.P. 2000) (general discussion of service and notice); see also Text § 13:3, Court enforcement of civil protection orders—Criminal prosecution. Hamper v. Dobrski, 2015-Ohio-1381, 2015 WL 1593249 (Ohio Ct. App. 8th Dist. Cuyahoga County 2015) (distinguishing case from *Smith* because Smith involved a criminal prosecution for violating a protection order and where he failed to inform court that he lacked notice of the terms of the order); but see State v. Smith, 136 Ohio St. 3d 1, 2013-Ohio-1698, 989 N.E.2d 972 (2013) (holding that service is a necessary prerequisite to a conviction for a violation of protection order under RC 2919.27.).

[26]See, e.g., People v. Stevens, 133 Misc. 2d 407, 506 N.Y.S.2d 995 (N.Y. City Ct. 1986); People v. Darnell, 190 Ill. App. 3d 587, 137 Ill. Dec. 844, 546 N.E.2d 789 (2d Dist. 1989) (overturning trial court's contempt conviction for violation of civil protection order because State failed to prove respondent had notice of order). But see People v. Hazelwonder, 138 Ill. App. 3d 213, 93 Ill. Dec. 1, 485 N.E.2d 1211 (4th Dist. 1985) (holding that there is no statutory requirement that notice of a protection order be given to the respondent in certain circumstances); MacDonald v. State, 997 P.2d 1187 (Alaska Ct. App. 2000) (where the ex parte protection order was binding on a defendant because he had actual knowledge of it); State v. Bunch, 2001 WL 39599 (Ohio Ct. App. 9th Dist. Summit County 2001); Olson v. State, 2001 WL 1007464 (Alaska Ct. App. 2001); Hamper v. Dobrski, 2015-Ohio-1381, 2015 WL 1593249 (Ohio Ct. App. 8th Dist. Cuyahoga County 2015) (appellant testified that he knew TPO forbade him from interfering with petitioner's possession of the home, including canceling utilities).

Bunch,[27] the Summit County Court of Appeals addressed the issue of service and notice where the defendant was found guilty of recklessly violating a civil protection order under RC 2919.27. In that case, the appellant had testified he had never been served with the CPO. Because he had not been served, he could not be said to have recklessly violated the CPO. The Summit County Court of Appeals stated that "the Revised Code does not require that service of a CPO be accomplished upon the person against whom a CPO is issued before the person can be found to have violated the order.[28] Rather, 2919.27 requires that the prosecution prove beyond a reasonable doubt that defendant acted in disregard of a known risk that a CPO was likely to have existed against him."[29] The evidence in this case demonstrated that the defendant knew that a CPO had been issued against him. He testified that he also knew of a prior temporary protection order, and his wife testified that she had previously advised him that a CPO had been issued and he responded, "I know."[30] Although this analysis applies to a criminal prosecution, the same reasoning may be used for a contempt violation where service has not been perfected but the respondent is aware of the terms of the CPO.[31]

In fact the Ohio Supreme Court, in *Midland Steel Products Co. v. Local 486*,[32] reasoned that actual notice of the terms of an ex parte order is essential to a finding of contempt. The majority also suggested

---

[27]State v. Bunch, 2001 WL 39599 (Ohio Ct. App. 9th Dist. Summit County 2001); see also Murray City v. Culley, 1998 WL 1758314, *1–2 (Utah Ct. App. 1998) (court noted that "service of a protective order probably establishes the requisite mens rea of intentionality, but it is not the only means of doing so, as demonstrated in this case"; "as long as a defendant who is subject to a protective order receives notice, either formally or informally, of the prohibited conduct, he may be convicted of violating that order"; notice is achieved by participating in the hearing, attending the hearing, or agreeing to the protective order). See also Text § 13:3.

[28]See, for example, State v. Rutherford, 2009-Ohio-2071, 2009 WL 1175050 (Ohio Ct. App. 2d Dist. Champaign County 2009).

[29]State v. Bunch, 2001 WL 39599, *2 (Ohio Ct. App. 9th Dist. Summit County 2001).

[30]See also State v. Bombardiere, 2007-Ohio-1537, 2007 WL 959895 (Ohio Ct. App. 3d Dist. Union County 2007) (Despite a lack of direct evidence that appellant was served with the CPO, he admitted in testimony that he knew the terms of the CPO. The Court concluded that he did have adequate notice of the terms and affirmed trial court decision convicting appellant of violating the CPO.); but see dissenting opinion in *State v. Bombardiere*, at *5, holding that "while Bombardiere was aware that a protection order may have been issued and had knowledge of an order's usual prohibitions, these also are not sufficient to prove service and notice upon him, which would give the order any lawful effect.").

[31]See State v. Chandler, 2004-Ohio-248, 2004 WL 102144, *3 (Ohio Ct. App. 1st Dist. Hamilton County 2004) ("To establish contempt, a party must prove not only that a party violated an existing order but also that the party had knowledge of the order." (citing Arthur Young & Co. v. Kelly, 68 Ohio App. 3d 287, 588 N.E.2d 233 (10th Dist. Franklin County 1990)).

[32]Midland Steel Prods. Co. v. U.A.W. Local 486, 61 Ohio St. 3d 121, 573 N.E.2d 98 (1991); see also State v. Bunch, 2001 WL 39599, *2 (Ohio Ct. App. 9th Dist. Summit County 2001) (appellant had not been served with the civil protection order; however, the appellate court affirmed the trial court decision and stated that RC 2919.27 requires that the prosecution prove beyond a reasonable doubt that the defendant acted in disregard of a known risk that a CPO was likely to have existed against him. The wife had testified that she had previously advised him that a CPO had been issued); Toledo v. Lyphout, 2009-Ohio-4596, 2009 WL 2855714 (Ohio Ct. App. 6th Dist.

that actual notice of the terms of the order may be effectuated by personal service, certified mail or ordinary mail, and that, for a non-party aider and abettor, "[i]t is clear that formal service of the order upon the alleged violators is not necessary prior to a contempt adjudication, as long as the parties had actual knowledge of the order."[33]

While service of process of the protection order on the respondent is sufficient evidence that the respondent has knowledge of the terms of an order,[34] a respondent may also be made aware of the terms of a protection order other than by service in accordance with Civil Rule 4 to Civil Rule 4.3 and Civil Rule 4.6. For example, a respondent may appear at the full hearing of the protection order without having been served with either the petition or the order.[35] In some cases, the court may inform the respondent of the terms of the order at the full hearing. If the court either notes this fact in the file or reads the terms into the court record, a respondent may have actual notice of the terms of the underlying order for purposes of a finding of contempt.[36]

Other times, the respondent may sign a consent entry at the full hearing thereby agreeing to abide by the terms of the protection order. If the respondent has not yet been served with the pleadings, the consent entry will detail that the respondent has accepted copies of the pleadings in open court and has agreed to waive any defects in service of process. Although the docket may reflect "no service," a perusal of the file will indicate that service was perfected at the hearing, and the consent entry should reflect this fact. For purposes of a contempt finding, this translates into actual notice of the terms of the order.

Q & A: Can a respondent be found in contempt when he/she did not intentionally violate an order of the court?

It depends on whether the contempt is civil or criminal.[37] It also depends on whether the state of mind of the contemnor can be established by circumstantial evidence.

Lucas County 2009).

[33]Midland Steel Prods. Co. v. U.A.W. Local 486, 61 Ohio St. 3d 121, 573 N.E.2d 98 (1991) (quoting Neshaminy Water Resources Authority v. Del-Aware Unlimited, Inc., 332 Pa. Super. 461, 470, 481 A.2d 879 (1984) (rejected by, In re Contempt of Dougherty, 429 Mich. 81, 413 N.W.2d 392, 81 A.L.R.4th 971 (1987))) (rejecting court stating that the court's analysis of this issue was incomplete, failing to recognize the limitations upon a court's power to impose a coercive sanction absent a present violation of the court's order).

[34]Evidence of notice may be found by reviewing the court docket regarding service of process.

[35]See Text § 12:3, Full hearing—Participation of the parties, for a more thorough discussion of this issue; see also Murray City v. Culley, 1998 WL 1758314 (Utah Ct. App. 1998).

[36]See State v. Bunch, 2001 WL 39599 (Ohio Ct. App. 9th Dist. Summit County 2001) (does not require service of a civil protection order be accomplished before respondent can be found to have violated it); see also People v. Stevens, 133 Misc. 2d 407, 506 N.Y.S.2d 995 (N.Y. City Ct. 1986).

[37]See, for example, In re Cox, 1999 WL 1312688 (Ohio Ct. App. 11th Dist. Geauga County 1999); see also Text § 13:4, Court enforcement of civil protection orders—Contempt—Generally defined.

Midland Steel Products Co. v. Local 486[38] has addressed these issues. In that case, it was disputed whether the contemnor had actual knowledge of the underlying order. The Ohio Supreme Court held that "in cases of criminal, indirect contempt, it must be shown that the alleged contemnor intended to defy the court."[39] Absent actual knowledge of the terms of the order, a contemnor is unable to form the intent to defy the court. Without intent, there can be no finding of contempt. The court also pointed out that "'proof of the elements of criminal contempt may be established by circumstantial evidence.' "[40]

In contrast, in civil contempt proceedings, "proof of purposeful, willing or intentional violation of a court order is not a prerequisite to a finding of contempt."[41] In *Pugh v. Pugh*,[42] the Supreme Court of Ohio determined that intent is not a crucial element of civil contempt. The Court relied on *Pedone v. Pedone*[43] when it stated that "[i]t is irrelevant that the transgressing party does not intend to violate the court order. If the dictates of the judicial decree are not followed, a contempt citation will result,"[44] the Supreme Court stressed that "'[a]n act does not cease to be a violation of a law and of a decree merely because it may have been done innocently.' "[45] In effect, the contemnor's state of mind is irrelevant in a civil contempt proceeding.

Q & A: Can a person violate a civil protection order by driving past the home or business of the petitioner when the protected party is not there at the time of the violation or when they see each other at a common place but the parties were coincidentally at the same place at the same time?

Not according to the Greene County appellate court in *Gevedon v. Gevedon*.[46] In that case, brothers obtained orders of protection against each other. One filed a motion to show cause and the magistrate found that neither brother was guilty of contempt. The evidence indicated that the parties were coincidentally at the same place at the same

---

[38]Midland Steel Prods. Co. v. U.A.W. Local 486, 61 Ohio St. 3d 121, 573 N.E.2d 98 (1991).

[39]Midland Steel Prods. Co. v. U.A.W. Local 486, 61 Ohio St. 3d 121, 127, 573 N.E.2d 98 (1991); see also West v. West, 1994 WL 680156 (Ohio Ct. App. 2d Dist. Montgomery County 1994).

[40]Midland Steel Prods. Co. v. U.A.W. Local 486, 61 Ohio St. 3d 121, 128, 573 N.E.2d 98 (1991) (quoting Walker v. City of Birmingham, 388 U.S. 307, 312, 87 S. Ct. 1824, 18 L. Ed. 2d 1210 (1967)).

[41]Pugh v. Pugh, 15 Ohio St. 3d 136, 140, 472 N.E.2d 1085 (1984); Windham Bank v. Tomaszczyk, 27 Ohio St. 2d 55, 56 Ohio Op. 2d 31, 271 N.E.2d 815, 54 A.L.R.3d 1235 (1971) (finding that, because the purpose of sanctions in a civil case is to coerce the contemnor to comply with the court orders, proof of intent is not required in civil contempt); see also Toth v. Toth, 1995 WL 502536 (Ohio Ct. App. 8th Dist. Cuyahoga County 1995); Rudduck v. Rudduck, 1999 WL 436818 (Ohio Ct. App. 5th Dist. Licking County 1999).

[42]Pugh v. Pugh, 15 Ohio St. 3d 136, 472 N.E.2d 1085 (1984).

[43]Pedone v. Pedone, 11 Ohio App. 3d 164, 165, 463 N.E.2d 656 (8th Dist. Cuyahoga County 1983).

[44]Pugh v. Pugh, 15 Ohio St. 3d 136, 140, 472 N.E.2d 1085 (1984).

[45]Pugh v. Pugh, 15 Ohio St. 3d 136, 472 N.E.2d 1085 (1984) (quoting McComb v. Jacksonville Paper Co., 336 U.S. 187, 191, 69 S. Ct. 497, 93 L. Ed. 599 (1949)).

[46]Gevedon v. Gevedon, 167 Ohio App. 3d 450, 2006-Ohio-3195, 855 N.E.2d 548 (2d Dist. Greene County 2006).

time so the respondent brother was not in contempt. The other brother was also found not to be in contempt because although he drove past his brother's businesses, the protected brother was not there at the time.[47] Additionally, the fact that the businesses were on a main thoroughfare where the brother would be expected to travel was important to the decision.

Q & A: In what court does one file a contempt motion for violating a civil protection order?

In Ohio, venue should not be a problem. Since civil protection orders are issued by the county domestic relations court or the common pleas court (if there is no domestic relations court in the county),[48] any contempt motion for the violation of a civil protection order must be filed in that court.

The common pleas courts are authorized to find persons in contempt under RC Ch. 2705. Both civil and criminal contempt are contemplated by statute.[49] Therefore, whether the nature of the violation constitutes civil or criminal contempt, the common pleas court in the county is the appropriate venue for a contempt proceeding.

Even if the violation occurred in a different county, the county that issued the order is the proper county to address its violation by a contempt motion. However, if criminal prosecution is contemplated pursuant to RC 3113.31(L), the proper venue is where the violation occurred.[50]

§ 13:9 Contempt—Penalty phase

Q & A: What are the penalties for contempt?[1]

Pursuant to RC Ch. 2705, a finding of contempt can result in penalties ranging from up to 30 days' incarceration and a fine of up to $250 for a first violation or both.[2] Increased penalties are provided for subsequent offenses of contempt. RC 2705.05(A)(2) mandates fines of not more than $500 and up to 60 days in jail or both for a second offense. RC 2705.05(A)(3) provides for a fine of not more than $1,000 or up to 90 days in jail or both for subsequent violations. Like RC 2919.27, RC Ch. 2705 authorizes the enhancement of penalties for subsequent violations.[3]

Q & A: Should multiple violations of a civil protection order against the same victim be punished separately?

---

[47]See also State v. Ball, 2006-Ohio-980, 2006 WL 515514 (Ohio Ct. App. 2d Dist. Montgomery County 2006) (discussing the standard forms and whether a person may violate a CPO for being around the premises even when the petitioner is not home).

[48]RC 3113.31(A)(2).

[49]See Text § 13:4, Court enforcement of civil protection orders—Contempt—Generally defined.

[50]See also Text § 13:6, Civil or criminal contempt in the context of civil protection orders; Bachman v. Bachman, 171 Or. App. 665, 16 P.3d 1185 (2000).

[Section 13:9]

[1]See also In re Contemnor Caron, 110 Ohio Misc. 2d 58, 744 N.E.2d 787, 820 (C.P. 2000).

[2]RC 2705.05(A)(1).

[3]See Pingue v. Pingue, 1995 WL 768535 (Ohio Ct. App. 5th Dist. Delaware County 1995) for a discussion of the application of the enhancement penalties of RC 2705.05.

No Ohio court has addressed whether each civil protection order violation should be punished separately in one contempt proceeding. When a respondent is alleged to have committed more than one violation of a civil protection order in a short period of time, generally the courts will consolidate the actions against the respondent. As with criminal violations, these violations are consolidated only for procedural purposes. "They retain their individual character as separated from each other by both time and circumstances."[4]

Various jurisdictions, however, have recognized the importance of punishing multiple protection order violations separately, especially where the violations involved violent acts. In *State v. Schackart*,[5] the defendant initially pulled a gun on his wife and ordered that she remove her clothing. Forty-five minutes later, he raped her. The court convicted him of both sexual assault and aggravated assault. He appealed his convictions on the grounds that he had been subjected to a double punishment for a single act which had continued over a period of time.

Even though this case involved criminal prosecution of violent acts, the same legal analysis can be applied to contempt proceedings. In *Schackart*, the Arizona Court of Appeals held that the defendant was correctly charged with both offenses since they were separate and distinct in time and nature. "[W]hen an act is punishable under different sections of the criminal code, punishment may be imposed under both; however, the sentences must be concurrent."[6]

For purposes of contempt violations, where individual acts are committed against another person and are separated by at least forty-five minutes in time, they should be punished separately, even where they are consolidated for trial purposes.[7] Substantively, they are distinct acts and should be treated accordingly.

A protocol that recognizes the uniqueness of each violent act upon the same victim and the impact each act has on the victim allows for a separate sentence for each violation and the enhancement of penalties for subsequent violations. It may also serve to deter a respondent from committing future violations.[8] It recognizes that each violation of the civil protection order is a "volitional act of criminal behavior"

---

[4]Catherine F. Klein & Leslye E. Orloff, Providing Legal Protection for Battered Women: An Analysis of State Statutes and Case Law, 21 Hofstra L. Rev. 801, 1106 (1993); see also Cable v. Clemmons, 36 S.W.3d 39 (Tenn. 2001).

[5]State v. Schackart, 153 Ariz. 422, 737 P.2d 398 (Ct. App. Div. 2 1987).

[6]State v. Schackart, 153 Ariz. 422, 424, 737 P.2d 398 (Ct. App. Div. 2 1987). But see Walker v. Walker, 86 N.Y.2d 624, 635 N.Y.S.2d 152, 658 N.E.2d 1025 (1995) (imposing maximum six-month jail term for each separate and distinct violation of protection order with sentences to be served consecutively); see also State v. Pickett, 628 So. 2d 1333 (La. Ct. App. 2d Cir. 1993), on reh'g, (Jan. 13, 1994) and writ denied, 637 So. 2d 476 (La. 1994) (noting the factors to be considered in ordering consecutive, rather than concurrent, sentences).

[7]Catherine F. Klein & Leslye E. Orloff, Providing Legal Protection for Battered Women: An Analysis of State Statutes and Case Law, 21 Hofstra L. Rev. 801, 1106–07 (1993).

[8]Catherine F. Klein & Leslye E. Orloff, Providing Legal Protection for Battered Women: An Analysis of State Statutes and Case Law, 21 Hofstra L. Rev. 801, 1107 (1993).

which subjects the victim of abuse to infringements on his/her freedom.[9]

Q & A: May a petitioner file a contempt motion alleging a course of conduct rather than seeking a separate finding and sentence for each individual violation?

A petitioner may be better served by filing a contempt motion alleging a continuous course of violent conduct rather than seeking a separate finding for each individual act. In many cases, a petitioner may be able to prove a course of conduct as opposed to individual acts of contempt. This can be of help in enabling petitioners to meet the "beyond a reasonable doubt" standard of proof.

Ohio's legislators have failed to address whether the acts proscribed by the domestic violence statutes contemplate a continuous course of conduct. However, several states have considered this issue. For example, in *People v. Thompson*,[10] a husband was charged and convicted of domestic violence after he raped, sodomized, and beat his wife. The California Appellate Court held that the prosecutor was not required to elect which act was the basis of the charge because domestic violence falls within the continuous course of conduct exception. The court determined that "the acts [were] so closely connected that they form[ed] part of one and the same transaction, and thus one offense."[11]

§ 13:10 Contempt—Other procedural issues[1]

Q & A: Do courts have continuing jurisdiction to enforce civil protection orders for violations occurring during the existence of the order even when brought after the order terminates?

Clearly, courts have jurisdiction to enforce civil protection orders for violations occurring during the existence of the order. The Ohio statutory scheme grants courts the authority to sanction contemnors.[2]

Public policy mandates that courts also have continuing jurisdiction to enforce orders for violations occurring during the existence of the order even though the petitioner does not bring the contempt action until after the order has expired.[3] Although RC 3113.31 is silent as to this issue, the major focus should be whether the order was in effect at the time of the violation. If the order was in effect when the violation occurred, it should not matter when the petitioner brings the

---

[9]James R. Thompson & Gary L. Starkman, Multiple Petty Contempts and the Guarantee of Trial by Jury, 61 Geo. L.J. 621, 642 (1973).

[10]People v. Thompson, 160 Cal. App. 3d 220, 206 Cal. Rptr. 516 (1st Dist. 1984).

[11]People v. Thompson, 160 Cal. App. 3d 220, 224, 206 Cal. Rptr. 516 (1st Dist. 1984).

[Section 13:10]

[1]See Text § 13:13, Court enforcement of civil protection orders—Double jeopardy concerns.

[2]See RC 3113.31(L).

[3]See also Torboli v. Torboli, 119 Md. App. 684, 705 A.2d 1186 (1998) (discussing when a court may enforce or otherwise address violations of an expired protection order).

contempt action. "Courts should enforce such orders post-termination to emphasize the importance of respect for court orders."[4]

At least one Ohio court addressed a similar issue. In *Petrak v. Petrak*,[5] the Butler County Appellate Court requested that the parties brief the following issue: "whether the trial court had jurisdiction to adjudge appellant guilty of contempt for violating the December 30 order where the order was entered prior to the divorce decree but the finding of contempt was issued after the divorce decree was entered."

In that case, the trial court issued a civil protection order to appellee in September 1992. At the full hearing in November 1992, the agreement provided that the protection order would continue until the divorce action was final. In December 1992, the court clarified the protection order. The divorce action was final on January 27, 1993. In April 1993, the court found the appellant in contempt for violating the December 1992 order. The contempt motion was filed after the order terminated and was based on conduct that occurred when the appellee vacated the premises pursuant to the divorce decree.

The Twelfth District Appellate Court determined that the protection order expired when the divorce was final. Because of this, there was no order upon which to find appellant in contempt. The court held that "the April 27, 1993 contempt judgment is void and a nullity because the trial court had no authority to make a contempt finding after the divorce decree was entered, and the trial court could not thereafter reinstate the temporary protection order upon which it found appellant in contempt."[6] The court relied exclusively on the fact that the divorce terminated the civil protection order, pursuant to the parties' agreement. The court in *Petrak* also made clear that, because the parties had filed separate divorce and protection order cases, a divorce decree entered in one case would have no effect on the validity of a temporary protection order issued in a separate case.[7]

What is less clear is whether the doctrine of merger applies when a civil protection order is filed as a second count to a divorce action. Pursuant to Civ.R. 75(G), a claim for a civil protection order based upon an allegation of domestic violence shall be a separate claim from a claim of divorce, dissolution of marriage, annulment or legal separation. Because it is a separate claim that is not entered pursuant to the divorce, it should survive the decree of divorce.

Courts in other states have ruled that a respondent may be held in contempt for refusing to obey the terms of a civil protection order that was subsequently vacated by a higher court.[8] The need for obedience to court orders and the safety and security of family and household members requires such a holding.

---

[4]Catherine F. Klein & Leslye E. Orloff, Providing Legal Protection for Battered Women: An Analysis of State Statutes and Case Law, 21 Hofstra L. Rev. 801, 1111 (1993).

[5]Petrak v. Petrak, 1994 WL 50386, *1 (Ohio Ct. App. 12th Dist. Butler County 1994).

[6]Petrak v. Petrak, 1994 WL 50386, *2 (Ohio Ct. App. 12th Dist. Butler County 1994).

[7]Petrak v. Petrak, 1994 WL 50386, *2 n.1 (Ohio Ct. App. 12th Dist. Butler County 1994). See also Text § 12:23, Duration of a civil protection order.

[8]See State v. Andrasko, 454 N.W.2d 648 (Minn. Ct. App. 1990); see also State v. Dahlen, 1999 WL 261847 (Minn. Ct. App. 1999); State v. Sanders, 327 N.J. Super.

Q & A: Can a court enforce a civil protection order to obtain a money judgment that becomes due during the existence of the order?

Under the aforementioned analysis, a petitioner should be able to enforce a protection order to obtain a monetary judgment that comes due during the life of the order even when the contempt motion is filed after the order expires. Again, so long as the order was in effect at the time of the alleged violation, a contempt action should be allowed.

However, a petitioner may not seek payment for expenses that accrued after the protection order expired. In *Drake v. Drake*,[9] the court of appeals dismissed a motion for contempt for failure to pay utilities ordered in a civil protection order where the petitioner sought payment for utilities used after the protection order had expired.

Q & A: Is the adjudication of a contempt motion a final appealable order?[10]

At least one Ohio court answered this in the negative. In *Grove v. Grove*,[11] the respondent appealed from a judgment finding him in contempt for failing to abide by the terms of a civil protection order. The trial court had found him in contempt for failing to enter into a lease agreement as previously ordered and again ordered him to enter into the lease agreement within thirty days or further sanctions would be imposed by the court.[12] The trial court then stayed execution of the judgment pending the appeal.

The Seneca County Court of Appeals determined that the entry appealed from was not a final appealable order because the trial court merely affirmed the former decree and did not impose a penalty. "Since the court did not address a penalty, one of the two essential components for a final order of contempt, this court lacks jurisdiction to review this matter and the appeal must be dismissed.[13] The court relied on the reasoning in *Cooper v. Cooper*.[14] The Cuyahoga County Court of Appeals held that "[i]n order for there to be a final order in contempt of court proceedings, there must be both a finding of contempt and the imposition of a sanction or penalty. The mere adjudication of contempt of court is not a final appealable order until a sanction or penalty is imposed."[15]

385, 743 A.2d 385 (App. Div. 2000).

[9]Drake v. Drake, 1985 WL 7861 (Ohio Ct. App. 2d Dist. Montgomery County 1985).

[10]See also Text § 13:13, Court enforcement of civil protection orders—Double jeopardy concerns.

[11]Grove v. Grove, 2001-Ohio-2109, 2001 WL 196496 (Ohio Ct. App. 3d Dist. Seneca County 2001).

[12]Grove v. Grove, 2001-Ohio-2109, 2001 WL 196496, *1 (Ohio Ct. App. 3d Dist. Seneca County 2001).

[13]Grove v. Grove, 2001-Ohio-2109, 2001 WL 196496, *1 (Ohio Ct. App. 3d Dist. Seneca County 2001).

[14]Cooper v. Cooper, 14 Ohio App. 3d 327, 471 N.E.2d 525 (8th Dist. Cuyahoga County 1984).

[15]Grove v. Grove, 2001-Ohio-2109, 2001 WL 196496, *1 (Ohio Ct. App. 3d Dist. Seneca County 2001), quoting Cooper v. Cooper, 14 Ohio App. 3d 327, 471 N.E.2d 525

§ 13:11 Court enforcement of civil protection orders—Related substantive concerns

Other state courts have addressed interesting contempt issues.

Q & A: Can a court enforce a civil protection order's property provisions despite a party's bankruptcy?

For example, at least one court determined that it could enforce a civil protection order's property provisions despite the party's bankruptcy. In *Rayan v. Dykeman*,[1] a California appellate court determined that the protection order provision transferring the real property did not involve a right to payment and, therefore, was not a debt dischargeable in bankruptcy. The court held that the civil protection order was not null and void due to the transferor's bankruptcy filing. Additionally, the trial court could impose sanctions for refusal to transfer real property as ordered in the civil protection order. The fact that the parties had stipulated to the provisions in the order was one of the factors considered by the court in its decision.

Q & A: Which court has jurisdiction to enforce a civil protection order against a minor?[2]

Juvenile courts have sole jurisdiction over juveniles under the age of 18 years.[3] It is important to note that juvenile courts may, by statute, retain jurisdiction over certain issues past the age of 18 years of age. In the context of protection orders, juvenile courts have jurisdiction to issue and enforce a protection order against a child until a date certain but not later than the date the respondent attains 19 years of age.[4]

The appropriate juvenile court to hear a petition for a civil protection order, to determine whether to issue a civil protection order, and to enforce a civil protection order against a juvenile respondent is in the county in which the person to be protected by the order resides.[5]

Additionally, the statute also provides that "[a]ny person who, while 18 years of age, violated (A)(1) or (2) of RC 2919.27 of the Revised Code by violating a protection order issued or consent agreement approved under RC 2151.34 or RC 3113.31 shall be considered a child for the purposes of that violation of section 2919.27 of the Revised Code."[6]

For purposes of enforcement for a civil protection order issued under RC 3113.31, RC 3113.31(L) applies to juvenile perpetrators as a basis for a delinquent child proceeding for a violation of RC 2919.27. The contempt provision of RC 3113.31(L)(1)(b) also applies to juvenile violators.[7]

(8th Dist. Cuyahoga County 1984).

[Section 13:11]

[1]Rayan v. Dykeman, 224 Cal. App. 3d 1629, 274 Cal. Rptr. 672 (4th Dist. 1990).

[2]See Text § 10:8; Text §§ 20:1 et seq.

[3]R.C. 2152.02(C).

[4]R.C. 2151.23(A)(16).

[5]R.C. 2151.34(A)(1); R.C. 3113.31(A)(2); Text § 20:06.

[6]R.C. 2152.02(C)(7).

[7]R.C. 2151.34(K)(1); R.C. 2152.02(C)(7); Text § 20:23.

Although no Ohio Court has specifically reviewed these jurisdictional provisions in the context of juvenile civil protection orders, other state courts have discussed these jurisdictional issues.

In *In re S.D.L.*,[8] the Iowa Supreme Court reached a similar conclusion. In that case, a seventeen-year-old boy lived with his teenaged girlfriend and their child. He subsequently abused his girlfriend and was charged in juvenile court with domestic abuse assault. The girlfriend obtained a no contact order. While these matters were pending, he violated the no contact order by abusing her again. The juvenile court heard the violations in the same juvenile proceeding with the assault charge. The juvenile court rejected the State's request to transfer the case to district court and the State's application for contempt, finding that such punitive measures were unauthorized under both the Juvenile Justice Act and the Domestic Abuse Act. The court held that the juvenile court had authority to hold the minor in contempt and detain him for domestic violence in violating the no contact order. The Supreme Court shared the juvenile court's view that the minor defendant should be rehabilitated but then stated, "We do not believe imposing a contempt sanction and promoting rehabilitation are mutually exclusive alternatives" under our juvenile code, as one underlying purpose of a contempt sanction is to modify the contemnor's behavior to conform to the terms required in the order.[9]

A similar issue was reviewed by the Ohio Attorney General in 1996. Pursuant to 1996 Ohio Op. Att'y. Gen. 96-061,[10] the basic issue raised was whether juvenile offenders are subject to the same procedures and enforcement provisions that apply to adult domestic violence offenders. That particular concern involved the criminal protection order statute.[11]

The attorney general analyzed the issue in the following manner: "A juvenile who violates a law that would be a crime if committed by an adult is classified as a 'delinquent child.' "[12] "A child who is alleged to be delinquent comes within the jurisdiction of the juvenile court and is not considered to be an alleged criminal."[13] The attorney general determined that RC 2919.25 applies to a juvenile "as a possible source of an allegation of delinquency in juvenile court, and not as part of any possible criminal proceeding."[14]

§ 13:12 Court enforcement of civil protection orders—Reunification concerns

Q & A: Does the reunification of parties prevent enforcement of the civil protection order by a petitioner?

Many state statutes provide that the validity of a civil protection or-

[8]In Interest of S.D.L., 568 N.W.2d 41 (Iowa 1997).

[9]In Interest of S.D.L., 568 N.W.2d 41, 43 (Iowa 1997).

[10]1996 Ohio Op. Att'y. Gen. No. 96-061, 1996 WL 708359.

[11]See RC 2919.25, RC 2919.26.

[12]1996 Ohio Op. Att'y. Gen. 96-061, 1996 WL 708359; see also RC 2151.02, RC 2151.011(B)(1).

[13]1996 Ohio Op. Att'y. Gen. 96-061, 1996 WL 708359; see RC 2151.23(A)(1).

[14]1996 Ohio Op. Att'y. Gen. 96-061, 1996 WL 708359.

der is not nullified and voided by the reunification of the parties.[1] Under RC 3113.31(E)(7)(a), a civil protection order is not waived or nullified by an invitation to the respondent from the petitioner to enter the residence, school, business, or place of employment. Additionally, every protection order shall state clearly that the protection order cannot be waived or nullified by an invitation to the respondent from the petitioner or other family or household member.[2]

The Ohio Supreme Court's standard forms, include a front warning page that is required to be attached to every protection order issued.[3] The warning states that "[o]nly the Court that issued this Protection Order can dismiss it. The Petitioner/Complainant cannot give you legal permission to violate this Protection Order. If you go near the Petitioner/Alleged Victim, even with the Petitioner/Alleged Victim's consent, you may be arrested."[4] Each protection order issued by any court within this state must also contain a Notice to Respondent that an invitation by the petitioner back to the home, school, or place of employment does not waive or nullify the protection order.[5]

The warning concerning the domestic violence protection order set forth in Superintendence Rule 10.01-G specifically advises a respondent that the protection order is between the respondent and the court. Absent another order designed to modify or terminate the terms of the original protection order, the original protection order will remain in effect for the designated statutory duration.[6] Any violations should be enforced against the respondent of the order.

Although the reunification of the parties may not be used by a respondent to justify nullifying or waiving a protection order, it may arguably be raised as a defense to a finding of contempt. The Ohio General Assembly noted that, just because a protection order cannot be waived or nullified by an invitation by the petitioner back to the residence, for example, that does not limit the court's discretion to determine that a respondent charged with a violation of RC 2919.27 or with contempt of court for violating a protection order issued or consent agreement did not commit the violation or was not in contempt of court.[7]

Q & A: How have the courts addressed the reunification of the parties after the issuance of a civil protection order?[8]

Courts in Ohio and other states have enforced protection orders

---

[Section 13:12]

[1]See Text § 12:22, Remedies—Miscellaneous issues.

[2]RC 3113.31(E)(7)(a).

[3]Sup. R. 10.01.

[4]Sup. R. Form 10.01-G.

[5]Sup. R. Form 10.01-H to Sup. R. Form 10.01-J.

[6]See RC 3113.31(E)(3).

[7]RC 3113.31(E)(7)(b). But see State v. Dejarlais, 136 Wash. 2d 939, 969 P.2d 90 (1998); State v. Bombardiere, 2007-Ohio-1537, 2007 WL 959895 (Ohio Ct. App. 3d Dist. Union County 2007) (on the other hand, court relied on legal reasoning of *State v. Lucas* to uphold the constitutionality of RC 2919.27 despite appellant's argument that RC 2919.27 was unconstitutional as applied to him because he was criminally punished because the victim manipulated him into violating the CPO).

[8]See Text § 12:22, Remedies—Miscellaneous issues.

where the violation of the order occurred following a reunification of the parties. *Cole v. Cole*[9] suggests that the reunification of the parties following the issuance of a civil protection order is not a defense to contempt where the action causing the new violation resulted in further physical harm to the petitioner. The Licking County Court of Appeals in *City of Reynoldsburg v. Eichenberger*[10] implied that it is the continued presence of the defendant in violation of the terms of the protection order which mandates a finding of contempt, rather than continued harm to the petitioner. It is important to note that Eichenberger was decided in 1990, and it is unclear whether newly enacted RC 3113.31(E)(7)(b) would have had any effect on the court's analysis.

In *Cole v. Cole*,[11] the court held that reunification of the parties after the issuance of a protection order did not waive the petitioner's right to enforce the civil protection order. In that case, the parties proceeded to live together again after the court entered a civil protection order prohibiting the husband from harassing, assaulting, or recklessly endangering the petitioner. After the parties separated, the respondent entered the petitioner's home without her consent and raped her. The court held that:

> The validity of the court's order was in no way impaired, affected, nor nullified, by the petitioner's consensual cohabitation with the respondent after entry of the order. As stated in the order itself, the order remains in full force and effect until such time, if at all, as the order is modified or terminated by a future order of a court having competent jurisdiction.[12]

The New York Family Court further reasoned that:

> acquiescence by a petitioner in cohabitation by a respondent after an order of protection is issued does not constitute a waiver by the petitioner of the right to be free from intrusions by the respondent after cohabitation terminates, upon either the rights of safety or the rights of privacy secured by the order. A victim of domestic violence who has procured an order of protection is entitled to the court's protection from further violence throughout the duration of an order of protection, even if the victim is desirous of pursuing a goal of voluntary reconciliation with the offender. . . . The law does not impair an individual's choice to pursue a relationship with one whose prior conduct has evinced a need for judicial limits upon destructive behavior.[13]

The court decision in *Cole* clearly illustrates the public policy reasons underlying the need to enforce an existing civil protection order despite the parties' reunification.

---

[9]Cole v. Cole, 147 Misc. 2d 297, 556 N.Y.S.2d 217 (Fam. Ct. 1990).

[10]City of Reynoldsburg v. Eichenberger, 1990 WL 52467 (Ohio Ct. App. 5th Dist. Licking County 1990).

[11]Cole v. Cole, 147 Misc. 2d 297, 556 N.Y.S.2d 217 (Fam. Ct. 1990).

[12]Cole v. Cole, 147 Misc. 2d 297, 300, 556 N.Y.S.2d 217 (Fam. Ct. 1990); see also A.B. v. L.M., 289 N.J. Super. 125, 672 A.2d 1296 (App. Div. 1996) (determining that a protection order should not be set aside based on the parties' reconciliation or mutual violation of its terms without careful consideration by the court of the need for continued protection).

[13]Cole v. Cole, 147 Misc. 2d 297, 300-01, 556 N.Y.S.2d 217 (Fam. Ct. 1990).

The Franklin County Court of Appeals applied a similar analysis in *City of Reynoldsburg v. Eichenberger*.[14] In that case, the court of appeals found the defendant in contempt for violating a protection order. The defendant argued that the attempt to reconcile negated the protection order. Although the appellate court did not address the issue of whether or not the appellee waived her right to enforce the order as to past violations, the court held that "[i]t was irrelevant whether appellant's wife gave her consent or not [to have him come home], because only the trial court could give . . . permission."[15]

Additionally, the court refused to dismiss the contempt charge despite the wife's request since the purpose of the "proceedings [was] to punish appellant . . . for purposely violating an order of the court."[16] The court further explained that "[a]n order of the court must be obeyed unless and until a court finds it is invalid or rescinds it."[17] These judicial statements emphasize the essential purpose of criminal contempt proceedings.

Q & A: Does a victim's initiation of contact with the abuser waive the victim's right to enforce the civil protection order?

At least one Ohio trial court answered this in the affirmative. In *Ferguson v. Ferguson*,[18] the victim obtained a civil protection order against her husband. Several months later, she filed a contempt motion, alleging that her husband violated the protection order by physically assaulting her and threatening to kill her. The trial court dismissed her contempt motion on the grounds that, by agreeing to meet her husband to exchange their possessions, she put him in a position of having to disobey the protection order. The trial court concluded that she waived her right to enforce the protection order against her husband for the beating. After requesting and receiving findings of fact and conclusions of law, the victim appealed the trial court's decision.[19]

However, the Fifth District Court of Appeals reversed the trial court's decision on the grounds that the trial court failed to provide findings of fact and conclusions of law. The court noted that findings of fact and conclusions of law are unnecessary in regards to motions for contempt. Because Civ.R. 52 does not preclude such findings and because the trial court chose to provide findings, it was required to do so pursuant to the civil rule.

---

[14]City of Reynoldsburg v. Eichenberger, 1990 WL 52467 (Ohio Ct. App. 5th Dist. Licking County 1990).

[15]City of Reynoldsburg v. Eichenberger, 1990 WL 52467, *2 (Ohio Ct. App. 5th Dist. Licking County 1990); see also State v. Lucas, 100 Ohio St. 3d 1, 2003-Ohio-4778, 795 N.E.2d 642, 648 (2003) (Supreme Court stated that the issue of an invitation is irrelevant as to the culpability of a respondent's violation of a protection order.).

[16]City of Reynoldsburg v. Eichenberger, 1990 WL 52467, *4 (Ohio Ct. App. 5th Dist. Licking County 1990).

[17]City of Reynoldsburg v. Eichenberger, 1990 WL 52467, *4 (Ohio Ct. App. 5th Dist. Licking County 1990).

[18]Ferguson v. Ferguson, 2000 WL 1724294 (Ohio Ct. App. 5th Dist. Knox County 2000).

[19]Ferguson v. Ferguson, 2000 WL 1724294 (Ohio Ct. App. 5th Dist. Knox County 2000).

In the instant case, the trial court merely adopted the findings of the prevailing party. In doing so, it failed to address the alleged violations of the civil protection order. Because the findings failed to address all claims presented, the decision was reversed with instructions to state all findings of fact and conclusions of law as to each of the allegations of contempt.

The appellate court then declined to rule on the appellant's other assignments of error.

Punishing the victim for having contact with the perpetrator and effectively blaming the victim for violating the order are clearly inconsistent with the statutory prohibitions against mutual protection orders, the anti-nullification and anti-waiver language of RC 3113.31, legislative intent, and public policy. These cases of first impression should reinforce that a petitioner's consent or invitation to the respondent is irrelevant to the determination of whether the respondent violated the protection order.[20]

Q & A: Can a petitioner be found in contempt or criminally prosecuted for violating his/her own protection order?[21]

No Ohio court has addressed whether a petitioner may be found in contempt for violating his/her protection order, when he/she reestablishes contact with his/her partner.[22] However, Ohio's standard forms do suggest that a petitioner cannot be held in contempt for violating a civil protection order granted on his/her behalf.[23] The warning provides that "[o]nly the Court can change this order. The Petitioner/Alleged Victim cannot give you legal permission to change this order. If you go near the Petitioner/Alleged Victim, even with the Petitioner's /Alleged Victim's consent, you may be arrested."[24] Nothing in the warning or the actual orders indicates or implies that the petitioner may be sanctioned for contacting the respondent.[25]

However, in *State v. Lucas*,[26] the Supreme Court of Ohio recently held that a victim may not be criminally prosecuted for violating a protection order issued on their behalf. The Supreme Court of Ohio accepted certification because of the conflicting law in two Ohio appellate districts.

---

[20]But see Henley v. Iowa Dist. Court for Emmet County, 533 N.W.2d 199, 203 (Iowa 1995) (finding victim in contempt for violating "no contact" order directed against her male companion and holding that the evidence was sufficient to establish that she willfully aided and abetted her companion's knowing and intentional violation of the order and concluding that "[a]lthough we are sympathetic to Henley's plight as a victim, her willful disregard for her own safety cannot deter us from upholding an enforceable order for her protection").

[21]See Text § 12:22, Remedies—Miscellaneous issues; Text § 11:12, Ex parte protection orders—Available relief; see generally, Leigh Goodmark, Law is the Answer? Do We Know for Sure? Questioning the Efficacy of Legal Interventions for Battered Women, 23 St. Louis U. Pub. L. Rev. (2004).

[22]But see Henley v. Iowa Dist. Court for Emmet County, 533 N.W.2d 199 (Iowa 1995); Hutcheson v. Iowa Dist. Court for Lee County, 480 N.W.2d 260 (Iowa 1992).

[23]See Sup. R. Form 10.01-G to Sup. R. Form 10.01-J.

[24]Sup. R. Form10.01-G.

[25]See Sup. R. Form 10.01-G to Sup. R. Form 10.01-J; see also RC 3113.31(E)(7). See also State v. Youngpeter, 2005-Ohio-329, 2005 WL 196754 (Ohio Ct. App. 3d Dist. Van Wert County 2005).

[26]State v. Lucas, 100 Ohio St. 3d 1, 2003-Ohio-4778, 795 N.E.2d 642 (2003).

In *North Olmsted v. Bullington*,[27] the city prosecutor charged the victim, who had a criminal protection order issued on her behalf, with willfully aiding and abetting the intentional violation of her own order. The victim had been seen in a vehicle with her husband, the subject of the criminal order. On appeal, the City of North Olmsted challenged the trial court's dismissal of the complicity charges brought against the original victim. The Eighth District Court of Appeals held that, as a matter of law, the trial court's decision to dismiss the complicity charges against the victim was proper. The appellate court considered whether "a victim of a crime in a protected class of a criminal law may be punished for its criminal violation."[28] The court relied on legislative intent and noted that the law "focused absolutely on the behavior of the offender with intent to punish the offender's behavior and not the behavior of the victim, whom the order is designed to protect."[29]

However, the Licking County Court of Appeals concluded the opposite. In *State v. Lucas*,[30] the original victim was charged and convicted of complicity to aid and abet in the violation of her own protection order. In rejecting the reasoning in *North Olmsted v. Bullington*, the Licking County Court of Appeals relied on the literal language of RC 2919.27(A)(1) which provides that "no person shall recklessly violate the terms of a protection order issued pursuant to RC 2919.26 or RC 3113.31."[31] The appellate court held that ". . .we find that appellant's mental state went beyond "reckless" to the point of intentional. Unlike the victim of a statutory rape, who is automatically protected as a result of his or her age, the victim of a protection order asks for the protection. A victim is not a protected person under the laws authorizing the issuance of protective orders merely by his or her existence, but rather the status is achieved through a formal request to the trial court. We cannot agree with the *Bullington* court's public policy rational[e], as it becomes overreaching when the victim, such as appellant herein, requested the protection order and then recklessly exposed herself to the offender from whom she had sought protection."[32]

In a unanimous decision, the Ohio Supreme Court held that "an individual who is the protected subject of a temporary protection order may not be prosecuted for aiding and abetting the restrainee under

---

[27]N. Olmsted v. Bullington, 139 Ohio App. 3d 565, 744 N.E.2d 1225 (8th Dist. Cuyahoga County 2000).

[28]N. Olmsted v. Bullington, 139 Ohio App. 3d 565, 568, 744 N.E.2d 1225 (8th Dist. Cuyahoga County 2000).

[29]N. Olmsted v. Bullington, 139 Ohio App. 3d 565, 568, 744 N.E.2d 1225 (8th Dist. Cuyahoga County 2000).

[30]State v. Lucas, 147 Ohio App. 3d 297, 2002-Ohio-2514, 770 N.E.2d 114 (5th Dist. Licking County 2002), judgment rev'd, 100 Ohio St. 3d 1, 2003-Ohio-4778, 795 N.E.2d 642 (2003) (reversing court finding defendant, as protected subject of order, was immune from prosecution for complicity).

[31]State v. Lucas, 147 Ohio App. 3d 297, 300, 2002-Ohio-2514, 770 N.E.2d 114 (5th Dist. Licking County 2002), judgment rev'd, 100 Ohio St. 3d 1, 2003-Ohio-4778, 795 N.E.2d 642 (2003).

[32]State v. Lucas, 147 Ohio App. 3d 297, 301, 2002-Ohio-2514, 770 N.E.2d 114 (5th Dist. Licking County 2002), judgment rev'd, 100 Ohio St. 3d 1, 2003-Ohio-4778, 795 N.E.2d 642 (2003).

the protection order in violating said order."[33] The court considered legislative intent, the warning page of the protection order forms and the instructive analysis of *Gebardi v. United States* relating to the Mann Act.[34]

While courts continue to harbor concerns over possible misuse of domestic violence complaints by parties seeking to gain unfair advantage in ongoing domestic disputes, this concern must be balanced by considering the articulated legislative intent of assuring that victims of domestic violence are provided the maximum protection from abuse that the law can provide.[35] Any decision by the appellate court to punish the victim of domestic violence defies reality. Unlike other crimes, it is clear that the parties have a relationship. It is the abuse they want stopped. Victims look to the justice system to stop the abuse. If that is achieved, they often want to return to their partners. "Victims come from a variety of circumstances, but the optimism that often underlies their forgiveness of their abusers should not deny them the protection of the law."[36]

Q & A: If a respondent is found in contempt of court for violating the terms of a protection order, may the petitioner be awarded attorney fees?

One Ohio court has answered this in the affirmative. In *Patterson v. Loveless*,[37] the court of appeals determined that a court has the authority to punish a violation of a civil protection order as contempt under RC 3113.31(L)(1)(b). The court then held that "attorney fees may be awarded as costs of the action to a party who successfully prosecutes charges in contempt."[38] The court relied on *McDaniel v. McDaniel*.[39] However, the court cautioned that the fees must be incurred and must be reasonable in amount.[40]

Similarly, in *Granger v. Granger*,[41] the Eighth District Court of Appeals reversed a trial court decision denying an award of attorney fees. Appellant requested attorney fees from her former husband after

---

[33]State v. Lucas, 147 Ohio App. 3d 297, 2002-Ohio-2514, 770 N.E.2d 114 (5th Dist. Licking County 2002), judgment rev'd, 100 Ohio St. 3d 1, 2003-Ohio-4778, 795 N.E.2d 642 (2003); State v. Youngpeter, 2005-Ohio-329, 2005 WL 196754 (Ohio Ct. App. 3d Dist. Van Wert County 2005) (appellant argued the warning on the protection order form advising a petitioner that only a court could change the terms of the order was sufficient to notify a petitioner that defying the court's warning could be a crime. Green County appeals court relied on the reasoning in *State v. Lucas* to support its reversal of the trial court decision.).

[34]Gebardi v. U.S., 287 U.S. 112, 53 S. Ct. 35, 77 L. Ed. 206, 84 A.L.R. 370 (1932).

[35]See A.B. v. L.M., 289 N.J. Super. 125, 130, 672 A.2d 1296 (App. Div. 1996).

[36]See A.B. v. L.M., 289 N.J. Super. 125, 131, 672 A.2d 1296 (App. Div. 1996).

[37]Patterson v. Loveless, 2001 WL 524372 (Ohio Ct. App. 2d Dist. Montgomery County 2001).

[38]Patterson v. Loveless, 2001 WL 524372, *3 (Ohio Ct. App. 2d Dist. Montgomery County 2001).

[39]McDaniel v. McDaniel, 74 Ohio App. 3d 577, 599 N.E.2d 758 (8th Dist. Cuyahoga County 1991); see also Fry v. Fry, 64 Ohio App. 3d 519, 582 N.E.2d 11 (3d Dist. Paulding County 1989).

[40]Patterson v. Loveless, 2001 WL 524372, *3 (Ohio Ct. App. 2d Dist. Montgomery County 2001).

[41]Granger v. Granger, 2004-Ohio-5601, 2004 WL 2365905 (Ohio Ct. App. 8th Dist. Cuyahoga County 2004).

he was found in contempt for violating the terms of a civil protection order by failing to obtain a psychological evaluation. The trial court adopted the magistrate's finding of contempt, but reversed an award of attorney fees because "[t]he Court lack statutory authority to award attorney fees on a show cause for domestic violence order except as authorized in Ohio Revised Code Section 3113.31(K)."[42]

On appeal, the appellant argued that the trial court erred, as a matter of law, in determining that it lacked statutory authority to award attorney fees for civil contempt of a CPO pursuant to RC 3113.31. The appellate court relied on *McDaniel v. McDaniel*[43] when it reasoned that "[p]ursuant to RC 3113.31(L)(1)(b), a person who violates a domestic violence protection order may be subject to a finding of contempt. A trial court may exercise its discretion to impose any sanction that is reasonable in light of the contemptuous conduct."[44]

§ 13:13 Court enforcement of civil protection orders—Double jeopardy concerns[1]

Q & A: What is double jeopardy?

Double jeopardy refers to an enigmatic legal doctrine set forth in both the Fifth Amendment to the United States Constitution and Article I, Section 10, of the Ohio Constitution. The Fifth Amendment to the United States Constitution provides, in part, "nor shall any person be subject for the same offence [sic] to be twice put in jeopardy of life or limb."[2] The principles of double jeopardy, as set forth in case law, originate from this statement.[3]

The double jeopardy provisions are designed to protect criminal defendants from being punished twice for the same offense. Additionally, the Double Jeopardy Clause protects against a second prosecution for the same offense following an acquittal and a second prosecution for the same offense following a conviction.[4]

The Double Jeopardy Clause prohibits only multiple criminal punishments and prosecutions for the same offense;[5] aggregate punishment is permissible. "Cumulative sanctions are allowable

---

[42]Granger v. Granger, 2004-Ohio-5601, 2004 WL 2365905, *1 (Ohio Ct. App. 8th Dist. Cuyahoga County 2004).

[43]McDaniel v. McDaniel, 74 Ohio App. 3d 577, 579, 599 N.E.2d 758 (8th Dist. Cuyahoga County 1991).

[44]Granger v. Granger, 2004-Ohio-5601, 2004 WL 2365905, *1 (Ohio Ct. App. 8th Dist. Cuyahoga County 2004).

[Section 13:13]

[1]See also Text § 12:27, Conflicting protection orders.

[2]See State v. Tolbert, 60 Ohio St. 3d 89, 573 N.E.2d 617 (1991).

[3]For a detailed discussion of the Double Jeopardy Clause, see 2 Katz and Giannelli, Baldwin's Ohio Practice, Criminal Law, Chs 72–74.

[4]See Janet C. MacDonald, Ohio Revised Code Section 3113.31 and the Constitution: Ohio's Statutory Response to Domestic Violence and Its Double Jeopardy Infirmity, 19 U. Dayton L. Rev. 317, 324 (1993); see also State v. Lugli, 1995 WL 458671 (Ohio Ct. App. 6th Dist. Huron County 1995); State v. James, 1997 WL 269139 (Ohio Ct. App. 11th Dist. Portage County 1997).

[5]See Helvering v. Mitchell, 1938-1 C.B. 317, 303 U.S. 391, 399, 58 S. Ct. 630, 82 L. Ed. 917, 38-1 U.S. Tax Cas. (CCH) P 9152, 20 A.F.T.R. (P-H) P 796 (1938).

because they punish separate and distinct crimes."[6] A state may prosecute a person for two separate offenses arising out of the same conduct, provided that each offense requires proof of an element that the other offense does not.[7]

In *Blockburger v. United States*,[8] the United States Supreme Court established the "same elements" test to decide which acts may be separately punished and which acts may not under the double jeopardy provisions. To survive a constitutional challenge on double jeopardy grounds, a court must first determine whether the legislature intended to impose cumulative punishment. The court must then analyze the nature and elements of the specific crime. The Supreme Court stated that "[t]he applicable rule is that, where the same act or transaction constitutes a violation of two distinct statutory provisions, the test to be applied to determine whether there are two offenses or only one is whether each provision requires proof of an additional fact which the other does not."[9] If it is concluded that there are two distinct and separate acts, the punishments are cumulative and the imposition of the punishments survives a constitutional challenge on double jeopardy grounds.

Ohio has repeatedly applied the directives of *Blockburger* to determine whether multiple prosecutions and multiple punishments are precluded on double jeopardy grounds.[10] Although the ruling set forth in *Blockburger* was later modified by other significant United States Supreme Court decisions,[11] recent Ohio cases addressing double jeopardy issues usually begin with the *Blockburger* analysis.[12]

---

[6]Janet C. MacDonald, Ohio Revised Code Section 3113.31 and the Constitution: Ohio's Statutory Response to Domestic Violence and Its Double Jeopardy Infirmity, 19 U. Dayton L. Rev. 317, 324 (1993).

[7]Jennifer Black, The Double Jeopardy Dilemma in Combatting Domestic Violence: A Solution in United States vs. Dixon, 33 U. Louisville J. Fam. L. 911, 913 (1995); see also State v. Morton, 292 N.J. Super. 92, 678 A.2d 308 (App. Div. 1996) (Where a $250,000 judgment was entered against the defendant in a proceeding under the domestic violence act and he was later convicted of aggravated assault, double jeopardy did not preclude criminal prosecution, even though the judgment arose out of the same incident.).

[8]Blockburger v. U.S., 284 U.S. 299, 52 S. Ct. 180, 76 L. Ed. 306 (1932); see also People v. Wood, 260 A.D.2d 102, 698 N.Y.S.2d 122 (4th Dep't 1999), aff'd, 95 N.Y.2d 509, 719 N.Y.S.2d 639, 742 N.E.2d 114 (2000) (discussing *Blockburger* analysis in domestic violence context).

[9]Blockburger v. U.S., 284 U.S. 299, 304, 52 S. Ct. 180, 76 L. Ed. 306 (1932).

[10]See State v. Bowling, 36 Ohio App. 3d 74, 520 N.E.2d 1387 (1st Dist. Hamilton County 1987); State v. Kimbler, 31 Ohio App. 3d 147, 509 N.E.2d 99 (10th Dist. Franklin County 1986); see also State v. Schultz, 1996 WL 71004 (Ohio Ct. App. 6th Dist. Wood County 1996); Cable v. Clemmons, 36 S.W.3d 39 (Tenn. 2001) (addressing whether multiple convictions for contempt for violating a protection order constitute punishment for the same offense in violation of double jeopardy principles).

[11]See Ashe v. Swenson, 397 U.S. 436, 90 S. Ct. 1189, 25 L. Ed. 2d 469 (1970) (addressing the issue of collateral estoppel); Grady v. Corbin, 495 U.S. 508, 110 S. Ct. 2084, 109 L. Ed. 2d 548 (1990) (overruled by, U.S. v. Dixon, 509 U.S. 688, 113 S. Ct. 2849, 125 L. Ed. 2d 556 (1993)) (expanding the *Blockburger* "same elements" test to include "same conduct" test whereby state has to establish, as an essential element of subsequent offense, conduct that constitutes an offense for which defendant has already been prosecuted); U.S. v. Dixon, 598 A.2d 724 (D.C. 1991), judgment aff'd in part, rev'd in part, 509 U.S. 688, 113 S. Ct. 2849, 125 L. Ed. 2d 556 (1993) (overruling

Unfortunately, few Ohio courts have specifically addressed double jeopardy in the context of civil protection order violations.[13] The issue was considered in the context of whether a finding of contempt for a violation of a civil protection order precludes a subsequent conviction for domestic violence under RC 2919.25.[14]

Applying the *Blockburger* analysis to domestic violence cases, a prosecution and punishment for domestic violence may either follow or precede a finding and punishment for contempt for a violation of a civil protection order. Utilizing the "same elements" test, the elements of contempt are (1) knowledge of the civil protection order and (2) a willful violation of one of its conditions. The elements of domestic violence require proof of both the requisite mental state and physical harm or fear of such harm. The primary question is whether each offense contains an element not contained in the other; if not, they are the same offense, and separate punishment is prohibited by double jeopardy. An incident of domestic violence contains different elements from a contempt violation. Since each statutory provision requires proof of a fact which the other does not, they should survive the *Blockburger* analysis and withstand a double jeopardy challenge.[15]

In *United States v. Dixon*,[16] the United States Supreme Court ruled that double jeopardy does not necessarily bar a petitioner from enforc-

---

Grady and returning to the *Blockburger* analysis). But see Shipley v. State, 620 N.E.2d 710, 717 (Ind. Ct. App. 1993) (stating that, in addition to *Blockburger* analysis, courts must also look at the manner in which the offenses are charged and not merely the statutory definitions of the offenses); Scott Storper, Double Jeopardy's Door Revolves Again in United States vs. Dixon: The Untimely Death of the "Same Conduct" Standard, 49 U. Miami L.Rev. 881 (1995).

[12]See State v. Tolbert, 1990 WL 37785 (Ohio Ct. App. 1st Dist. Hamilton County 1990), judgment rev'd, 60 Ohio St. 3d 89, 573 N.E.2d 617 (1991) (reversing court finding conviction on lesser included offense pursuant to plea of no contest did not prevent state from later prosecuting defendant on greater offense); State v. Vanselow, 61 Ohio Misc. 2d 1, 572 N.E.2d 269 (Mun. Ct. 1991); State v. Lugli, 1995 WL 458671 (Ohio Ct. App. 6th Dist. Huron County 1995); State v. Higgins, 1996 WL 363543 (Ohio Ct. App. 5th Dist. Licking County 1996).

[13]See Westlake v. Patrick, 2005-Ohio-4419, 2005 WL 2046415 (Ohio Ct. App. 8th Dist. Cuyahoga County 2005) (holding that double jeopardy did not bar subsequent criminal prosecution for protection order violation in light of prior civil contempt proceeding involving violation of protection order where contempt proceeding did not require proof of a mens rea and the criminal prosecution required the city to show that defendant acted recklessly). See also Walker v. Walker, 2011-Ohio-3933, 2011 WL 3452362 (Ohio Ct. App. 5th Dist. Stark County 2011) (applying Westlake and determined that double jeopardy prohibitions do not apply to CSPO proceedings because they are civil in nature).

[14]See State v. Harding, 1985 WL 6477, *1 (Ohio Ct. App. 5th Dist. Tuscarawas County 1985) (The trial court dismissed a domestic violence charge under RC 2919. 25, finding that the conduct of which defendant was accused in the criminal action was the same conduct for which he was found in contempt in a civil action. The appellate court reversed, holding that "we are of the opinion that although the conduct is identical, it is not the 'same offense' within the meaning of the former jeopardy clauses of the state and federal constitutions. The criminal offense is an offense against the person of the wife alleged to have been assaulted and the contempt sentence was for an indirect affront to the authority of the court.").

[15]See also In re Contemnor Caron, 110 Ohio Misc. 2d 58, 744 N.E.2d 787 (C.P. 2000). But see State v. Gilley, 135 N.C. App. 519, 522 S.E.2d 111 (1999).

[16]U.S. v. Dixon, 598 A.2d 724 (D.C. 1991), judgment aff'd in part, rev'd in part, 509 U.S. 688, 113 S. Ct. 2849, 125 L. Ed. 2d 556 (1993), cert. granted, U.S. v. Dixon,

ing her civil protection order through criminal contempt while the state proceeds against the offender criminally for his crime. The Court determined that the contempt proceeding and several of the subsequent criminal prosecutions were separate and distinct offenses because each required proof of additional elements under the *Blockburger* "same elements" test. Thus, the petitioner was allowed to proceed with the two actions.

Dixon illustrates that a petitioner need not be forced to choose between contempt under RC 3113.31 and new criminal charges. The Supreme Court "cleared the way for victims of domestic violence to bring contempt actions against their batterers to obtain swift enforcement of civil protection orders and thereby secure their immediate safety without jeopardizing the state's ability to vindicate society's interests in prosecuting the batterer."[17]

However, it must be cautioned that various state courts have interpreted the principles set forth in *Dixon* to examine and redefine how and whether subsequent prosecutions of criminal offenses differ from criminal contempt convictions in civil protection order violation cases. One such court concluded that,

> In determining whether the Double Jeopardy Clause precludes a subsequent prosecution for a substantive criminal offense following an adjudication of criminal contempt based upon violation of a court order forbidding such criminal act, the test involves comparison of the elements of the offense actually deemed to have been violated in the contempt proceeding against the elements of the substantive criminal offense(s), rather than comparison of the general literal elements of contempt with the elements of the subsequent substantive criminal offense.[18]

The focus has moved to the offense for which the defendant was actually held in contempt. Under this analysis, a subsequent prosecution for assault for violating the protection order is barred on double jeopardy grounds because simple assault does not include any element not contained in the contempt violation. Because criminal contempt is a crime in the ordinary sense, it is important to analyze whether a subsequent prosecution for an offense of domestic violence or a related crime after a contempt conviction may be prohibited on double jeopardy grounds.

Q & A: How does this relate to Ohio's statutory scheme?

It must be stressed that Ohio's civil protection order statute clearly provides for both civil and criminal remedies. RC 3113.31(G) states that the remedies and procedures provided in this section are in addition to, and not in lieu of, any other available civil and criminal remedies. It is clear that the legislature contemplated situations whereby both civil and criminal remedies would be employed.

503 U.S. 1004, 112 S. Ct. 1759, 118 L. Ed. 2d 422 (1992); see also Blockburger v. U.S., 284 U.S. 299, 52 S. Ct. 180, 76 L. Ed. 306 (1932).

[17]Catherine F. Klein & Leslye E. Orloff, Providing Legal Protection for Battered Women: An Analysis of State Statutes and Case Law, 21 Hofstra L. Rev. 801, 1126 (1993).

[18]State v. Gilley, 135 N.C. App. 519, 522 S.E.2d 111, 116 (1999); see also Com. v. Decker, 445 Pa. Super. 101, 664 A.2d 1028 (1995); State v. Dye, 139 N.C. App. 148, 532 S.E.2d 574 (2000).

On public policy grounds, it is difficult to believe that a violator of a protection order cannot be found guilty of criminal contempt and subsequently prosecuted for domestic violence or other criminal conduct because of double jeopardy.[19] Such an outcome would defeat the main purpose of the protection order which is to provide protection for victims.[20]

Q & A: Do double jeopardy concerns arise where a victim files for a civil protection order and criminal charges are filed for domestic violence under RC 2919.25?

Several Ohio courts have addressed some form of this issue. For example, in *City of Cleveland v. Hogan*,[21] the Cleveland Municipal Court discussed double jeopardy in a case where a defendant was charged with domestic violence under RC 2919.25. He moved to dismiss the criminal case on double jeopardy and collateral estoppel grounds after his wife's petition for civil protection order under RC 3113.31 was denied.

The Cleveland Municipal Court noted that double jeopardy applies only to criminal proceedings, and not to civil actions unless the penalties are imposed for the purpose of punishment.[22] The court determined that "[b]y definition, the civil protection that the complainant herein sought from the domestic relations division was remedial, and not punitive, in nature."[23]

Q & A: Does the mere issuance of a civil protection order bar a subsequent prosecution and conviction for domestic violence under RC 2919.25?

At least one Ohio jurisdiction found that double jeopardy does not apply in this fact situation. In *State v. Ohm*,[24] the victim sought a civil protection order and filed a complaint alleging domestic violence under RC 2919.25. The defendant moved to dismiss the criminal case on the basis that the filing of a criminal charge of domestic violence while he

[19]See, for example, State v. Weaver, 2002 SD 76, 648 N.W.2d 355 (S.D. 2002) (Supreme Court of South Dakota affirmed convictions for multiple punishments of defendant for assault in one county and violation of a protection order in the other; court held convictions did not violate double jeopardy although they involved same conduct; court noted protection order statute provides that "any proceeding under this chapter is in addition to other civil or criminal remedies"; as such, legislature intended to impose multiple punishments for same conduct; said statute is similar to RC 3113. 31(G)).

[20]See Com. v. Burge, 947 S.W.2d 805 (Ky. 1996); see also Com. v. Decker, 445 Pa. Super. 101, 664 A.2d 1028 (1995) (disagreeing with the holding in *Allen* in light of *Dixon*).

[21]Cleveland v. Hogan, 92 Ohio Misc. 2d 34, 699 N.E.2d 1020 (Mun. Ct. 1998); see also Westlake v. Patrick, 2005-Ohio-4419, 2005 WL 2046415 (Ohio Ct. App. 8th Dist. Cuyahoga County 2005). See State v. Davis, 2008-Ohio-5281, 2008 WL 4531895 (Ohio Ct. App. 1st Dist. Hamilton County 2008) (in a twist on this theme, court held that where defendant is acquitted of the CPO violation, his conviction for domestic violence was upheld and where the trial court erred by not finding him in contempt, defendant cannot be retried for the CPO violation charge due to double jeopardy principles).

[22]Cleveland v. Hogan, 92 Ohio Misc. 2d 34, 39, 699 N.E.2d 1020 (Mun. Ct. 1998).

[23]Cleveland v. Hogan, 92 Ohio Misc. 2d 34, 39, 699 N.E.2d 1020 (Mun. Ct. 1998).

[24]State v. Ohm, 107 Ohio Misc. 2d 19, 736 N.E.2d 121 (Mun. Ct. 2000); see also State v. Petrusch, 1995 WL 737509 (Ohio Ct. App. 2d Dist. Montgomery County 1995) (declining to consider defendant's double jeopardy argument where issue was raised for first time on appeal).

was subject to a civil protection order violated his constitutional rights on double jeopardy grounds.

The Akron Municipal Court analyzed the concept of double jeopardy as applied to this fact pattern and determined that "[t]here is a substantial difference between being convicted of contempt for violating the protection order and being subject to its terms and conditions."[25] The court then reasoned that, under a *Blockburger*[26] analysis, the defendant's argument would fail because there is a difference between establishing the need for a protection order and proving that a defendant has committed the offense in question. The court found that the issuance of a civil protection order is not a finding that the defendant committed a criminal offense.

What is important is that the Akron Municipal Court noted the inherent unfairness in making a victim of domestic violence choose between two remedies. The court stated that "[t]his choice frustrates the purpose of the civil protection order, which is to prevent further contact between the complainant and the alleged offender until further disposition by the domestic relations court. Thus, the legislature clearly designed a system in which civil protection orders supplement, but do not supplant, criminal charges for various domestic violence crimes."[27]

Q & A: Does the issuance of a civil protection order based on an incident for which the abuser was acquitted of criminal charges violate the Double Jeopardy Clause?

Although there is no reported Ohio case specifically addressing this issue, a persuasive argument can be made that the issuance of a civil protection order under these circumstances would not violate the double jeopardy provisions. Of importance is that the remedy of a civil protection order is in addition to, and not in lieu of, any other civil or criminal remedy.[28] The civil statute specifically sanctions the use of both criminal and civil remedies.

At least one court determined that the issuance of a civil protection order did not violate double jeopardy where the defendant was acquitted of criminal charges based on the same incident. In *Donley v. Donley*,[29] the Vermont Supreme Court stated that, "[w]hile there are criminal consequences for violating relief-from-abuse orders, the abuse-prevention proceeding itself is unquestionably civil and remedial rather than punitive in nature."[30]

The *Donley* Court's legal analysis is applicable to cases in Ohio as well as those in Vermont. The Court determined that the issue revolves around whether the court action is properly categorized as remedial or as deterring and retributive. The Court reasoned that, because the legislature intended a civil protection order action to be a

[25]State v. Ohm, 107 Ohio Misc. 2d 19, 23, 736 N.E.2d 121 (Mun. Ct. 2000).

[26]Blockburger v. U.S., 284 U.S. 299, 52 S. Ct. 180, 76 L. Ed. 306 (1932).

[27]State v. Ohm, 107 Ohio Misc. 2d 19, 24, 736 N.E.2d 121 (Mun. Ct. 2000); see also RC 3113.31(G); see also State v. Brown, 394 N.J. Super. 492, 927 A.2d 569 (App. Div. 2007) (citing *Ohm* at 578).

[28]See RC 3113.31(G).

[29]Donley v. Donley, 165 Vt. 619, 686 A.2d 943 (1996).

[30]Donley v. Donley, 165 Vt. 619, 620, 686 A.2d 943 (1996) (citation omitted).

civil proceeding, the rules of civil procedure and the civil evidentiary standard of proof apply. Further, the civil domestic violence statute is civil in nature, thereby precluding the application of double jeopardy.[31]

Q & A: Does a finding of guilt under RC 2919.27 preclude a subsequent finding of contempt under RC 3113.31 for the exact same act?

For purposes of enforcement of a civil protection order, when an individual is prosecuted criminally for a violation of a protection order under RC 2919.27, a subsequent punishment for contempt for a violation of the same order fails the *Blockburger*[32] analysis. Under these circumstances, the offense of violating a civil protection order is considered the same offense for purposes of contempt of court and criminal prosecution under RC 3113.31(L).[33] The criminal offense of violation of a court order requires proof of a court order and its intentional violation. Contempt of court also requires proof of a court order and its intentional violation (at least in a criminal contempt). As they are considered offenses having the same elements under *Blockburger*, the subsequent contempt is barred by the Double Jeopardy Clause.

Additionally, Ohio's legislators recognized the double jeopardy concerns inherent in the statute. RC 3113.31(L)(2)[34] specifically prevents a subsequent punishment for contempt following a criminal conviction for a violation of a civil protection order.[35]

Q & A: Does it really matter whether the respondent is criminally prosecuted before he/she is found in contempt?

Under Ohio's statute, yes. RC 3113.31(L)(2)[36] is worded in such a way as to permit both a contempt action and a criminal prosecution for the same violation. The statute suggests that whether a particular respondent can be found in contempt and criminally prosecuted for the same action that constitutes a violation depends on whether the contempt action precedes the criminal prosecution. These statutory

[31]See also Cleveland v. Hogan, 92 Ohio Misc. 2d 34, 699 N.E.2d 1020 (Mun. Ct. 1998) (determining that the civil protection order is remedial, and not punitive, in nature).

[32]Blockburger v. U.S., 284 U.S. 299, 52 S. Ct. 180, 76 L. Ed. 306 (1932).(implied overruling recognized by, State v. Ayala, 129 Idaho 911, 935 P.2d 174 (Ct. App. 1996))

[33]See also Hudson v. U.S., 522 U.S. 93, 118 S. Ct. 488, 494, 139 L. Ed. 2d 450, 162 A.L.R. Fed. 737 (1997) (rejecting *Halper* analysis, stating "[w]e have since recognized that all civil penalties have some deterrent effect") (citations omitted).

[34]See also RC 2903.214(K)(2).

[35]See Hudson v. U.S., 522 U.S. 93, 118 S. Ct. 488, 496, 139 L. Ed. 2d 450, 162 A.L.R. Fed. 737 (1997) ("To hold that the mere presence of a deterrent purpose renders such sanctions 'criminal' for double jeopardy purposes would severely undermine the Government's ability to engage in effective regulation."), abrogating U.S. v. Halper, 490 U.S. 435, 109 S. Ct. 1892, 104 L. Ed. 2d 487 (1989) (abrogated by, Hudson v. U.S., 522 U.S. 93, 118 S. Ct. 488, 139 L. Ed. 2d 450, 162 A.L.R. Fed. 737 (1997)), overruling recognized by Lanni v. Engler, 994 F. Supp. 849 (E.D. Mich. 1998) (largely disavowing the *Halper* analysis, which may, in effect, invalidate *Vaneslow*); State v. Yacovella, 1996 WL 38898 (Ohio Ct. App. 8th Dist. Cuyahoga County 1996).

[36]See also RC 2903.214(K).

requirements are an effort to avoid the perceived implications associated with double jeopardy.[37]

RC 3113.31(L)(2) precludes a contempt action following a criminal conviction for the same activity. In contrast, the statute provides that "[t]he punishment of a person for contempt of court for violation of a protection order issued or a consent agreement approved under this section does not bar criminal prosecution of the person for a violation of [RC] 2919.27."[38] The only caveat is that "a person punished for contempt of court is entitled to credit for the punishment imposed upon conviction of a violation of that section."[39] In such a case, a respondent may be punished for contempt and then convicted of an RC 2919.27 violation for violating the same protection order for the same activity.[40] Again, it must be noted that the punishment for contempt must be credited against the criminal punishment.

However, the Hamilton County Municipal Court rejected this approach. In *State v. Vanselow*,[41] the court stated that "[t]he fact that the civil sanction preceded the criminal, rather than vice versa, would seem of no great importance. In a double jeopardy inquiry which case came first is determined only to negate the subsequent prosecution."

Q & A: Is RC 3113.31(L) unconstitutional?

At least one Ohio case is in conflict with the state statute. In *State v. Vanselow*,[42] the Hamilton County Municipal Court determined that RC 3113.31(L) is unconstitutional. In that case, the defendant was found guilty of contempt under RC 3113.31 for violating a civil protection order issued by the domestic relations court. Subsequently, the defendant was convicted of violating a protection order under RC 2919.27 for the same activity. The question presented to the court was

---

[37]See Janet C. MacDonald, Ohio Revised Code Section 3113.31 and the Constitution: Ohio's Statutory Response to Domestic Violence and Its Double Jeopardy Infirmity, 19 U. Dayton L. Rev. 317, 323–24 (1993).

[38]RC 3113.31(L)(2); see also People v. Kelley, 52 Cal. App. 4th 568, 60 Cal. Rptr. 2d 653 (4th Dist. 1997), as modified (Feb. 11, 1997) (prosecution for stalking after defendant was convicted of contempt for violating restraining order did not violate the constitutional prohibition against double jeopardy since the statutory provisions relating to violation of restraining order create a punishment enhancement but do not define a crime and thus do not count for double jeopardy analysis).

[39]RC 3113.31(L)(2).

[40]See also Harvard Law Review Association, Double Jeopardy—Substantive Criminal Charges following a Finding of Criminal Contempt, 107 Harv. L.Rev. 144 (1993); Westlake v. Patrick, 2005-Ohio-4419, 2005 WL 2046415 (Ohio Ct. App. 8th Dist. Cuyahoga County 2005) (holding that double jeopardy did not bar the criminal prosecution after a contempt finding, arising from the same incident).

[41]State v. Vanselow, 61 Ohio Misc. 2d 1, 8, 572 N.E.2d 269 (Mun. Ct. 1991). But see Westlake v. Patrick, 2005-Ohio-4419, 2005 WL 2046415 (Ohio Ct. App. 8th Dist. Cuyahoga County 2005) (holding that jeopardy did not attach to an earlier contempt proceeding involving violation of civil stalking protection order when there was a subsequent criminal prosecution for violating the same protection order); State v. Gonzales, 123 N.M. 337, 1997-NMCA-039, 940 P.2d 185 (Ct. App. 1997) (holding that double jeopardy does not bar prosecution for domestic violence after a finding of contempt for the same behavior in civil court); see also Hudson v. U.S., 522 U.S. 93, 118 S. Ct. 488, 139 L. Ed. 2d 450, 162 A.L.R. Fed. 737 (1997).

[42]State v. Vanselow, 61 Ohio Misc. 2d 1, 572 N.E.2d 269 (Mun. Ct. 1991), distinguished by Mahoney v. Com., 415 Mass. 278, 612 N.E.2d 1175 (1993); see also Mary Elizabeth Collins, Mahoney v. Commonwealth: A Response to Domestic Violence, 29 New Eng. L. Rev. 981 (1995).

whether the finding of contempt under RC 3113.31 barred the state from prosecuting the same defendant for the same activity under RC 2919.27.

The court held:

> A defendant, having been found guilty of contempt of court for violating a temporary protection order under RC 3113.31, may not subsequently be prosecuted under RC 2919.27 for the exact same act, as such prosecution would violate the Double Jeopardy Clause of the Fifth Amendment to the United States Constitution, and Section 10, Article I of the Ohio Constitution.[43]

The court added that "RC 3113.31(L)(1), insofar as it purports to allow criminal prosecutions for the same acts that have already been adjudicated in a contempt proceeding, is unconstitutional."[44] The court noted that the credit provision of RC 3113.31(L)(2) "does not save the otherwise unconstitutional prosecution."[45]

Of significance is that the court in *Vanselow* relied on *Grady v. Corbin*[46] to buttress its position. However, the United States Supreme Court overruled the *Grady* "conduct" test in *United States v. Dixon*[47] in 1993. It can be argued that *Vanselow* would have been decided differently if considered by the court today.

Q & A: Under what circumstances does a civil penalty constitute punishment for double jeopardy purposes?

The protections of the Double Jeopardy Clause apply only to criminal proceedings.[48] The distinction between civil and criminal penalties and proceedings becomes important when considering that contempt of court plays an essential role in the enforcement of Ohio's civil protection orders.[49]

Since criminal contempt appears to be contemplated by the Ohio

---

[43]State v. Vanselow, 61 Ohio Misc. 2d 1, 2, 572 N.E.2d 269 (Mun. Ct. 1991).

[44]State v. Vanselow, 61 Ohio Misc. 2d 1, 2, 572 N.E.2d 269 (Mun. Ct. 1991); see also Janet C. MacDonald, Ohio Revised Code Section 3113.31 and the Constitution: Ohio's Statutory Response to Domestic Violence and Its Double Jeopardy Infirmity, 19 U. Dayton L. Rev. 317 (1993).

[45]State v. Vanselow, 61 Ohio Misc. 2d 1, 8, 572 N.E.2d 269 (Mun. Ct. 1991).

[46]Grady v. Corbin, 495 U.S. 508, 110 S. Ct. 2084, 109 L. Ed. 2d 548 (1990) (overruled by, U.S. v. Dixon, 509 U.S. 688, 113 S. Ct. 2849, 125 L. Ed. 2d 556 (1993)).

[47]U.S. v. Dixon, 598 A.2d 724 (D.C. 1991), judgment aff'd in part, rev'd in part, 509 U.S. 688, 113 S. Ct. 2849, 125 L. Ed. 2d 556 (1993).

[48]See Patton v. Patton, 2010-Ohio-2096, 2010 WL 1918793 (Ohio Ct. App. 5th Dist. Muskingum County 2010) (constitutional rights to counsel and against double jeopardy do not attach); Butcher v. Stevens, 182 Ohio App. 3d 77, 2009-Ohio-1754, 911 N.E.2d 928 (4th Dist. Athens County 2009) (Motions for civil protection orders are civil in nature); Westlake v. Patrick, 2005-Ohio-4419, 2005 WL 2046415 (Ohio Ct. App. 8th Dist. Cuyahoga County 2005).

[49]See RC 3113.31(L); see also In re Contemnor Caron, 110 Ohio Misc. 2d 58, 744 N.E.2d 787 (C.P. 2000) (discussion of double jeopardy concerns); Westlake v. Patrick, 2005-Ohio-4419, 2005 WL 2046415 (Ohio Ct. App. 8th Dist. Cuyahoga County 2005) (discussing contempt of court, double jeopardy, and RC 2903.214); see also Cheh, Constitutional Limits on Using Civil Remedies to Achieve Criminal Law Objectives: Understanding & Transcending the Civil-Criminal Law Distinction, 42 Hastings L.J. 1325, 1405 (1991) (contempt sanctions for violations of protective orders are criminal in nature).

legislature,[50] it is essential that the court determine whether the relief sought is remedial or punitive.[51] If the contempt were only considered civil and the relief remedial, the Double Jeopardy Clause would not be involved, and the issue of multiple punishment would not have been addressed by the statute.[52] Because criminal contempt is also considered by RC 3113.31(L), the punitive nature of the punishment subjects a subsequent prosecution to a potential double jeopardy challenge.[53]

However, the court in *State v. Vanselow*[54] addressed this issue and determined that the classification of a proceeding as a "civil matter" is of little consequence. The court concluded that the thirty-day sanction for a violation of a civil protection order was clearly punishment. The court relied on *United States v. Halper*,[55] where the United States Supreme Court framed the issue as "whether a civil sanction, in application, may be so divorced from any remedial goal that it constitutes 'punishment' for the purpose of double jeopardy analysis." The *Vanselow* court applied the test set forth in *Halper* that when "determining whether a particular civil sanction constitutes criminal punishment, it is the purposes actually served by the sanction in question, not the underlying nature of the proceeding giving rise to the sanction, that must be evaluated."[56]

The *Vanselow* court agreed with the ill-founded opinion in *Halper* that "under the Double Jeopardy Clause a defendant who already has been punished in a criminal prosecution may not be subjected to an additional civil sanction to the extent that the second sanction may

---

[50]See Text § 13:4, Court enforcement of civil protection orders—Contempt—Generally defined, to Text § 13:10, Contempt—Other procedural issues, for a detailed analysis of contempt; but see Lyons v. Bowers, 2007-Ohio-1548, 2007 WL 959916, *2 (Ohio Ct. App. 11th Dist. Lake County 2007) (holding that it is well settled that contempt proceedings are considered sui generis, in that they are neither purely civil nor criminal. However, courts have found it necessary to classify contempt proceedings either civil or criminal in nature) (citing Brown v. Executive 200, Inc., 64 Ohio St. 2d 250, 253, 18 Ohio Op. 3d 446, 416 N.E.2d 610 (1980)).

[51]See for example, Westlake v. Patrick, 2007-Ohio-1307, 2007 WL 853235, *2 (Ohio Ct. App. 8th Dist. Cuyahoga County 2007) (in a footnote the Court stated that "in the prior appeal in this matter, this court determined that the prosecution here did not implicate double jeopardy because the award of attorney's fees upon a finding of contempt in the civil case was a civil sanction, not a punitive criminal sanction." No fine was imposed.).

[52]See RC 3113.31(L)(2); see also Cleveland v. Hogan, 92 Ohio Misc. 2d 34, 699 N.E.2d 1020 (Mun. Ct. 1998).

[53]See Hudson v. U.S., 522 U.S. 93, 118 S. Ct. 488, 496, 139 L. Ed. 2d 450, 162 A.L.R. Fed. 737 (1997) ("To hold that the mere presence of a deterrent purpose renders such sanctions 'criminal' for double jeopardy purposes would severely undermine the Government's ability to engage in effective regulation."); see also Com. v. Decker, 445 Pa. Super. 101, 664 A.2d 1028 (1995).

[54]State v. Vanselow, 61 Ohio Misc. 2d 1, 572 N.E.2d 269 (Mun. Ct. 1991).

[55]U.S. v. Halper, 490 U.S. 435, 447 n.7, 109 S. Ct. 1892, 104 L. Ed. 2d 487 (1989) (abrogated by, Hudson v. U.S., 522 U.S. 93, 118 S. Ct. 488, 139 L. Ed. 2d 450, 162 A.L.R. Fed. 737 (1997)).

[56]U.S. v. Halper, 490 U.S. 435, 447 n.7, 109 S. Ct. 1892, 104 L. Ed. 2d 487 (1989) (abrogated by, Hudson v. U.S., 522 U.S. 93, 118 S. Ct. 488, 139 L. Ed. 2d 450, 162 A.L.R. Fed. 737 (1997)) (largely disavowing the *Halper* analysis, which may, in effect, invalidate *Vanselow*); see also State v. Yacovella, 1996 WL 38898 (Ohio Ct. App. 8th Dist. Cuyahoga County 1996).

not fairly be characterized as remedial, but only as a deterrent or retribution."[57]

Q & A: Can a defendant be punished criminally for a violation of a protection order, even though the protection order was later determined to be invalid?

According to *Westlake v. Patrick*,[58] the answer is in the affirmative. In an earlier case, being *Westlake v. Patrick*,[59] appellee was charged with recklessly violating a civil protection order in violation of RC 2919.27. The trial court dismissed the charge on the grounds that double jeopardy precluded the subsequent prosecution because he had already been punished by a contempt finding in an earlier civil contempt proceeding. In the earlier case, the appellate court reversed the trial court decision finding that "the statutory scheme (of RC 2903.214) is not so punitive in purpose or effect so as to transform what was clearly intended to be a civil remedy into a criminal penalty."[60] Thus, double jeopardy did not bar the subsequent criminal prosecution.

On remand from the earlier case, appellee renewed his motion to dismiss informing the court that, on appeal in the civil case in which the protection order was issued, this court had concluded that appellee should not have been found in contempt because the hearing on the protection order was not conducted or concluded in a timely manner.[61] Appellee contended that the ruling was *res judicata* and collateral estoppel. The municipal court reasoned that although res judicata and collateral estoppel did not apply, the protection order appellee was alleged to have violated was invalid, so the state could not prove that he violated it. The City of Westlake then appealed the order dismissing the charge against appellee for violating the protection order.

In the instant case, the Eighth District Court of Appeals noted that there was no inconsistency in its determination that that appellee may be punished criminally even though the civil sanction for the same violation was reversed. "A civil sanction is remedial in nature. 'The right to remedial relief falls with an injunction which events prove was erroneously issued.' "[62] On the other hand, criminal punishment is intended to vindicate the court's authority which had been

---

[57]State v. Vanselow, 61 Ohio Misc. 2d 1, 8, 572 N.E.2d 269 (Mun. Ct. 1991) (quoting *Halper* at 448–49). But see Hudson v. U.S., 522 U.S. 93, 118 S. Ct. 488, 139 L. Ed. 2d 450, 162 A.L.R. Fed. 737 (1997); Westlake v. Patrick, 2005-Ohio-4419, 2005 WL 2046415 (Ohio Ct. App. 8th Dist. Cuyahoga County 2005).

[58]Westlake v. Patrick, 2007-Ohio-1307, 2007 WL 853235 (Ohio Ct. App. 8th Dist. Cuyahoga County 2007).

[59]Westlake v. Patrick, 2005-Ohio-4419, 2005 WL 2046415, *3 (Ohio Ct. App. 8th Dist. Cuyahoga County 2005). See also Stickel v. Pryor, 2002-Ohio-3309, 2002 WL 1396077 (Ohio Ct. App. 2d Dist. Miami County 2002).

[60]Westlake v. Patrick, 2005-Ohio-4419, 2005 WL 2046415, *3 (Ohio Ct. App. 8th Dist. Cuyahoga County 2005).

[61]See Berry v. Patrick, 2005-Ohio-3708, 2005 WL 1707005 (Ohio Ct. App. 8th Dist. Cuyahoga County 2005).

[62]Westlake v. Patrick, 2005-Ohio-4419, 2005 WL 2046415, *2 (Ohio Ct. App. 8th Dist. Cuyahoga County 2005), quoting U.S. v. United Mine Workers of America, 330 U.S. 258, 295, 67 S. Ct. 677, 91 L. Ed. 884, 19 L.R.R.M. (BNA) 2346, 12 Lab. Cas. (CCH) P 51239 (1947).

equally flouted whether or not the command was right."[63] Thus, a party may be punished for violating an order even though the order is determined to be invalid after the violation has occurred.[64] However, if a person is acquitted on a CPO violation charge, even based on erroneous reasoning, that person may not be retried for the same charge, based on double jeopardy principles.[65]

Q & A: Is an award of attorney's fees and/or a fine imposed in a contempt finding a civil sanction for purposes of double jeopardy?

It depends. In *Westlake v. Patrick*,[66] defendant was charged with violating a civil protection order under RC 2903.214 and which was the subject of a motion to show cause. The Rocky River Municipal Court dismissed the criminal case on double jeopardy grounds. On appeal, the City argued that jeopardy did not attach as the statutory scheme of RC 2903.214 establishes a civil penalty, rather that a criminal penalty. The City also argued that in a criminal matter it must prove that the defendant acted with the requisite intent and a contempt proceeding did not require proof of mens rea.

The appellate court noted that "courts must look "to the statute on its face" and only the clearest of proof" will take what the legislature intended as a civil remedy and make it a criminal penalty. The factors include: (1) "whether the sanction involves an affirmative disability or restraint; (2) whether it has historically been regarded as a punishment; (3) whether it comes into play only on a finding of scienter; (4) whether its operation will promote the traditional aims of punishment-retribution and deterrence; (5) whether the behavior to which it applies is already a crime; (6) whether an alternative purpose to which it may rationally be connected is assignable for it; and (7) whether it appears excessive in relation to the alternative purposes assigned."[67]

In applying the factors, the Eighth District Court of Appeals reasoned that double jeopardy claims generally apply only where the contempt finding is criminal. RC 2903.214 appears, on its face, to provide for a civil sanction and is civil in nature. The statute shows a legislative intent designed to ensure the "safety and protection" of the complainant. The court then went on to point out that an analysis of the other factors does not provide clear proof that the statute provides

---

[63] Westlake v. Patrick, 2005-Ohio-4419, 2005 WL 2046415, *2 (Ohio Ct. App. 8th Dist. Cuyahoga County 2005), quoting Salvage Process Corporation v. Acme Tank Cleaning Process Corporation, 86 F.2d 727, 32 U.S.P.Q. 103 (C.C.A. 2d Cir. 1936).

[64] Westlake v. Patrick, 2005-Ohio-4419, 2005 WL 2046415, *2 (Ohio Ct. App. 8th Dist. Cuyahoga County 2005); State v. Helser, 2009-Ohio-3155, 2009 WL 1845232 (Ohio Ct. App. 3d Dist. Allen County 2009) (holding that double jeopardy does not attach to a criminal violation of a CPO, even if the court that granted the CPO did not make a finding that defendant had stalked or harassed in violation of the ex parte CPO).

[65] See State v. Davis, 2008-Ohio-5281, 2008 WL 4531895 (Ohio Ct. App. 1st Dist. Hamilton County 2008).

[66] Westlake v. Patrick, 2005-Ohio-4419, 2005 WL 2046415 (Ohio Ct. App. 8th Dist. Cuyahoga County 2005).

[67] Westlake v. Patrick, 2005-Ohio-4419, 2005 WL 2046415, *2 (Ohio Ct. App. 8th Dist. Cuyahoga County 2005), quoting Hudson v. U.S., 522 U.S. 93, 99, 118 S. Ct. 488, 139 L. Ed. 2d 450, 162 A.L.R. Fed. 737 (1997), citing Kennedy v. Mendoza-Martinez, 372 U.S. 144, 83 S. Ct. 554, 9 L. Ed. 2d 644 (1963).

a criminal penalty.[68] In reversing the trial court, the court held that double jeopardy did not apply and bar a subsequent criminal prosecution.

The defendant-appellee also argued that there was a punitive sanction because the trial court fined the defendant $500.00 and awarded attorney's fees. Since no fine was found in a journalized entry, the court would not address whether a fine imposed by the court in the contempt action was a criminal penalty.

Regarding the attorney's fees, the appellate court held that a trial court may, in its discretion, include attorney fees as part of the costs taxable to a defendant found guilty of civil contempt.[69]

The Court further noted that even assuming double jeopardy was implicated in the instant case, defendant's argument would not survive the analysis set forth in *Blockburger v. United States*.[70] The prior contempt action did not require proof of a mens rea and a criminal proceeding under RC 2919.27 requires the city to show that the defendant acted recklessly.[71]

Q & A: Does double jeopardy bar a subsequent criminal prosecution for a violation of a different provision of the civil protection order from that which formed the basis for the criminal contempt finding?

No. In *State v. Higgins*,[72] the respondent violated the civil protection order by telephone harassment, and his wife initiated a contempt action in domestic relations court. Subsequently, the respondent violated the protection order by running the petitioner off the road. The respondent was criminally prosecuted under RC 2919.27 for the alleged violation. The defendant moved to dismiss the criminal prosecution on double jeopardy grounds. The trial court denied his motion, finding that the conduct giving rise to the State's complaint arose after the contempt action was commenced. The court also noted that no record of the hearing on the contempt was made.

The Licking County Court of Appeals utilized the *Blockburger*[73] analysis to determine whether multiple prosecutions violated the Double Jeopardy Clause. The court determined that "there are two separate and independent acts in this case, either or both of which . . . constitute independent and separate violations. Thus, we agree with the trial court the principle of double jeopardy does not bar prosecution of the criminal case."[74]

---

[68]Westlake v. Patrick, 2005-Ohio-4419, 2005 WL 2046415, *2 (Ohio Ct. App. 8th Dist. Cuyahoga County 2005).

[69]Westlake v. Patrick, 2005-Ohio-4419, 2005 WL 2046415, *3 (Ohio Ct. App. 8th Dist. Cuyahoga County 2005), citing Planned Parenthood Ass'n of Cincinnati, Inc. v. Project Jericho, 52 Ohio St. 3d 56, 67, 556 N.E.2d 157, 165 (1990).

[70]Blockburger v. U.S., 284 U.S. 299, 52 S. Ct. 180, 76 L. Ed. 306 (1932).

[71]Westlake v. Patrick, 2005-Ohio-4419, 2005 WL 2046415, *4 (Ohio Ct. App. 8th Dist. Cuyahoga County 2005).

[72]State v. Higgins, 1996 WL 363543 (Ohio Ct. App. 5th Dist. Licking County 1996).

[73]Blockburger v. U.S., 284 U.S. 299, 52 S. Ct. 180, 76 L. Ed. 306 (1932).

[74]State v. Higgins, 1996 WL 363543, *1 (Ohio Ct. App. 5th Dist. Licking County

§ 13:14 Court enforcement of civil protection orders—Collateral estoppel concerns[1]

At the outset, it is important to note that double jeopardy applies only to proceedings that are essentially criminal.[2] Therefore, since most civil actions do not result in criminal sanctions, double jeopardy generally does not attach. However, those civil actions that impose penalties to punish, rather than to coerce compliance, may be considered criminal in nature.[3]

In addition, the Double Jeopardy Clause contains at least one ancillary protection. Principles of collateral estoppel, also known as "issue preclusion," are "embodied in the Fifth Amendment guarantee against double jeopardy."[4]

Where the application of the double jeopardy provisions bars the entire prosecution, then a court need not consider whether particular issues are precluded from relitigation. Collateral estoppel is applicable to criminal cases only when double jeopardy is not.[5] In effect, double jeopardy prohibits the prosecution of the crime itself, whereas collateral estoppel forbids the government from relitigating certain facts in order to establish the fact of the crime.[6]

In deciding whether to bar a prosecution on the basis of collateral estoppel, a court must consider the following:

(1) Whether a final judgment has been rendered in the first proceeding;
(2) Whether there are issues present in both proceedings which are sufficiently similar and sufficiently material;
(3) Whether, after an examination of the record of the initial proceedings, the issues were actually litigated in the first case;
(4) Whether, after an examination of the record of the first proceeding, the issues were necessarily decided in the first case; and
(5) Whether there is privity between the parties in both proceedings.[7]

Q & A: Both parties file motions for civil protection orders against each other. One party prevails on the petition while

---

1996); see also State v. Winningham, 958 S.W.2d 740 (Tenn. 1997).

[Section 13:14]

[1]See also Text § 12:27, Conflicting protection orders; Tortorello v. Tortorello, 113 Haw. 432, 153 P.3d 1117 (2007) (discussing domestic violence and res judicata).

[2]Breed v. Jones, 421 U.S. 519, 95 S. Ct. 1779, 44 L. Ed. 2d 346 (1975); see also Helvering v. Mitchell, 1938-1 C.B. 317, 303 U.S. 391, 58 S. Ct. 630, 82 L. Ed. 917, 38-1 U.S. Tax Cas. (CCH) P 9152, 20 A.F.T.R. (P-H) P 796 (1938).

[3]See U.S. v. Halper, 490 U.S. 435, 109 S. Ct. 1892, 104 L. Ed. 2d 487 (1989) (abrogated by, Hudson v. U.S., 522 U.S. 93, 118 S. Ct. 488, 139 L. Ed. 2d 450, 162 A.L.R. Fed. 737 (1997)).

[4]Ashe v. Swenson, 397 U.S. 436, 436, 90 S. Ct. 1189, 25 L. Ed. 2d 469 (1970); see also U.S. v. Bailin, 977 F.2d 270 (7th Cir. 1992).

[5]See U.S. v. Bailin, 977 F.2d 270 (7th Cir. 1992).

[6]U.S. v. Rogers, 960 F.2d 1501, Fed. Sec. L. Rep. (CCH) P 97735 (10th Cir. 1992) (citing U.S. v. Mock, 604 F.2d 341, 343–44, 80-1 U.S. Tax Cas. (CCH) P 9184, 45 A.F.T. R.2d 80-549 (5th Cir. 1979)).

[7]See Goodson v. McDonough Power Equipment, Inc., 2 Ohio St. 3d 193, 443 N.E.2d 978 (1983).

the other party's motion is denied. That party also filed a criminal complaint for domestic violence. Does that criminal action constitute double jeopardy?

In *Pennsylvania v. Allen*,[8] both parties sought civil protection orders against the other. The girlfriend obtained a civil protection order. The boyfriend failed to meet his burden of proof, and his petition was denied at the full hearing. He also attempted to pursue a criminal complaint against his partner after his request for a civil protection order, based on the same set of facts, had been denied. Although the boyfriend filed the criminal complaint before he requested his civil protection order, the parties' motions for protection orders were heard before the criminal complaint was to be heard. The girlfriend argued that prosecution of the criminal complaint was barred on double jeopardy grounds and by the doctrine of collateral estoppel.

The *Allen* court found that a party was unable to bring a criminal complaint where the petition for civil protection order had already been denied after extensive testimony. The court reasoned that, rather than constituting double jeopardy, such an action was barred by collateral estoppel. The boyfriend's criminal complaint was based on facts that had already been adjudicated against him in the civil protection order action. When issues have been decided by a valid final judgment, those issues cannot be relitigated between the same parties.

It is not clear whether the result would be the same if litigated by the courts in Ohio. In the *Allen* case, the court determined that the parties were the same. Pennsylvania law provides that an individual citizen may file what is known as a "private criminal complaint." The court stated, "Accordingly, given the complainant's personal interest and role in the matter at hand, this Court is satisfied that there is mutuality of the parties in both proceedings, despite the fact that the Commonwealth is the named party in the latter proceeding."[9]

Ohio's criminal domestic violence statute[10] does not allow the filing of private criminal complaints. The prosecutor files a complaint on behalf of the state or city. The interest of the state in enforcing the law is decidedly different from the interest of the complainant in protecting himself/herself from further abuse. While the goals of the complainant and the city are likely to be congruent, they are just as likely to be mutually exclusive in that the city or state is unable to call or cross-examine witnesses in the civil protection order action. Nor could the state have directed the complainant or required the complainant to undertake a certain course of action. Nor could the state appeal an adverse ruling.

---

[8]Commonwealth of Pennsylvania v. Gloria J. Allen, 17 Phila. Co. Rptr. 137, 1988 WL 679778 (Pa. C.P. 1988); see also Cleveland v. Hogan, 92 Ohio Misc. 2d 34, 699 N.E.2d 1020 (Mun. Ct. 1998).

[9]Commonwealth of Pennsylvania v. Gloria J. Allen, 17 Phila. Co. Rptr. 137, 1988 WL 679778 (Pa. C.P. 1988). But see Cleveland v. Hogan, 92 Ohio Misc. 2d 34, 43, 699 N.E.2d 1020 (Mun. Ct. 1998) (distinguishing *Pennsylvania v. Allen* from the case at bar, noting that the *Allen* court found privity between the complainant and the state of Pennsylvania because Pennsylvania law provides that an individual citizen may file a private criminal complaint).

[10]RC 2919.25.

Therefore, under Ohio law, there is no privity of the parties.[11] To that end, both parties may file simultaneous civil and criminal domestic violence actions.[12] Even if one party's protection order is denied, that party may still prevail on a criminal complaint alleging domestic violence.

Conversely, in *Cleveland v. Hogan*[13] defendant's wife filed for a civil protection order which was denied by the domestic relations court. Subsequently, the defendant was charged with domestic violence under RC 2919.25 based on the same acts that were set forth in the CPO. Defendant filed a motion to dismiss arguing that the criminal prosecution was barred under the doctrines of double jeopardy and collateral estoppel.

The issue before the trial court was whether the City and the complainant were in privity with one another. The trial court relied on the Supreme Court which has held that "privity, for collateral estoppel purposes, exists whenever the relationship between the party to the prior action and another party is close enough to include that other party within res judicata."[14] The court reasoned that the City of Cleveland was not a party to the prior civil protection order litigation between the defendant and the complainant and therefore, defendant's motion to dismiss was denied.

Q & A: Should the doctrine of collateral estoppel be applied to violations of civil protection orders?[15]

"Collateral estoppel" means that "when an issue of ultimate fact has once been determined by a valid and final judgment, that issue cannot again be litigated between the same parties in any future

---

[11]See Cleveland v. Hogan, 92 Ohio Misc. 2d 34, 699 N.E.2d 1020 (Mun. Ct. 1998) (prosecution of defendant for violating RC 2919.25 is not precluded on collateral estoppel grounds even though domestic relations court found for defendant following hearing on merits of a civil protection order involving the same issues); see also People v. Krstic, 292 Ill. App. 3d 720, 226 Ill. Dec. 909, 686 N.E.2d 692 (1st Dist. 1997) (holding that the state may not be collaterally estopped from pursuing subsequent criminal prosecution when State was not a party to the initial proceeding); State v. Brown, 394 N.J. Super. 492, 927 A.2d 569 (App. Div. 2007).

[12]See RC 3113.31(G). See also Walton v. Walton, 2004-Ohio-7151, 2004 WL 3017265 (Ohio Ct. App. 6th Dist. Wood County 2004) (court may issue a CPO even though a domestic relations court had litigated some of the issues in a divorce action between the same parties).

[13]Cleveland v. Hogan, 92 Ohio Misc. 2d 34, 699 N.E.2d 1020 (Mun. Ct. 1998); see also State v. Brown, 394 N.J. Super. 492, 927 A.2d 569 (App. Div. 2007) (the issue was whether a subsequent criminal prosecution can be dismissed on the ground of collateral estoppel where a family court had previously dismissed the final restraining order on the ground that petitioner failed to prove that defendant committed acts of domestic violence).

[14]Cleveland v. Hogan, 92 Ohio Misc. 2d 34, 699 N.E.2d 1020, *41 (Mun. Ct. 1998), citing Thompson v. Wing, 70 Ohio St. 3d 176, 1994-Ohio-358, 637 N.E.2d 917 (1994).

[15]See Text § 12:27, Conflicting protection orders. See also Wood v. Wood, 2003-Ohio-5587, 2003 WL 22389875 (Ohio Ct. App. 5th Dist. Coshocton County 2003); Folmar v. Griffin, 2008-Ohio-2941, 2008 WL 2573279 (Ohio Ct. App. 5th Dist. Delaware County 2008).

lawsuit."[16] Collateral estoppel is applicable in criminal cases only when double jeopardy is not.[17]

In *Ashe v. Swenson*,[18] the United States Supreme Court established collateral estoppel as a constitutional component of the Fifth Amendment guarantee against double jeopardy. The doctrine of collateral estoppel seeks to prevent relitigation of a finally litigated issue in a subsequent proceeding between the same parties, whether the same or different evidence is to be introduced. If collateral estoppel is applicable, the issue in question is deemed foreclosed and, therefore, cannot be relitigated.

The principles embodied in the doctrine of collateral estoppel as defined in *Ashe v. Swenson* may be applied to criminal cases[19] and civil protection order violations.[20]

In the context of civil protection orders, the *Vanselow* court framed the issue as whether the respondent violated the civil protection order by the acts alleged. If the respondent had previously been found guilty of contempt of court for having violated a protection order under RC 3113.31, the same respondent may not subsequently be prosecuted under RC 2919.27. The *Vanselow* court determined that, because the respondent had previously been found guilty of contempt, the issue of whether the respondent had violated the civil protection order had already been decided. The court then found that the State could not relitigate the issue in another forum.

It is notable, however, that the Hamilton County Municipal Court applied *Ashe v. Swenson* and *Grady v. Corbin*[21] to justify its holding that a finding of contempt in domestic relations court barred a subsequent criminal prosecution for the same acts of abuse. However, the *Grady* conduct test, on which the *Vanselow* court relied, was rejected in *United States v. Dixon*.[22]

To that end, the United States Supreme Court has still not clarified whether the theory of collateral estoppel specifically precludes criminal prosecution for the same incident of abuse after the respondent has already been found guilty of contempt in civil court. The majority rationale set forth in *Dixon* appears to reject collateral estoppel as a bar to subsequent criminal proceedings.[23] The reason for this may be that the parties are different in the contempt hearing (victim/

[16] Ashe v. Swenson, 397 U.S. 436, 442, 90 S. Ct. 1189, 25 L. Ed. 2d 469 (1970); see also U.S. v. Bailin, 977 F.2d 270 (7th Cir. 1992).

[17] U.S. v. Bailin, 977 F.2d 270 (7th Cir. 1992); see also Cleveland v. Hogan, 92 Ohio Misc. 2d 34, 699 N.E.2d 1020 (Mun. Ct. 1998).

[18] Ashe v. Swenson, 397 U.S. 436, 90 S. Ct. 1189, 25 L. Ed. 2d 469 (1970); see also State v. Tolbert, 1990 WL 37785 (Ohio Ct. App. 1st Dist. Hamilton County 1990), judgment rev'd, 60 Ohio St. 3d 89, 573 N.E.2d 617 (1991).

[19] See State v. Schultz, 1996 WL 71004 (Ohio Ct. App. 6th Dist. Wood County 1996).

[20] See State v. Vanselow, 61 Ohio Misc. 2d 1, 572 N.E.2d 269 (Mun. Ct. 1991).

[21] Grady v. Corbin, 495 U.S. 508, 110 S. Ct. 2084, 109 L. Ed. 2d 548 (1990) (overruled by, U.S. v. Dixon, 509 U.S. 688, 113 S. Ct. 2849, 125 L. Ed. 2d 556 (1993)).

[22] U.S. v. Dixon, 598 A.2d 724 (D.C. 1991), judgment aff'd in part, rev'd in part, 509 U.S. 688, 113 S. Ct. 2849, 125 L. Ed. 2d 556 (1993).

[23] But see U.S. v. Dixon, 598 A.2d 724 (D.C. 1991), judgment aff'd in part, rev'd in part, 509 U.S. 688, 113 S. Ct. 2849, 125 L. Ed. 2d 556 (1993).

petitioner and abuser/respondent) than in the criminal prosecution (State and alleged abuser).[24]

Q & A: A party filed a petition for CPO in one county. When it was dismissed in that county, the same party filed another CPO in another county. Was the second CPO barred by the doctrines of res judicata and collateral estoppel?

In *Clagg v. Clagg*,[25] appellant appealed the trial court's decision granting summary judgment to appellee on the grounds that because her petition for CPO was barred by res judicata and collateral estoppel.

In this case, appellant sought a CPO in Licking County. At the full hearing, the court dismissed the petition. Several days later, she filed another petition for CPO in Franklin County. The trial court dismissed that petition because it was based on the same facts as the earlier petition in Licking County.

In reversing the trial court, the appellate court determined that, although the parties were the same, the facts were different for each petition. The ground for the first petition was a physical altercation; the ground for the second was two text messages. Neither the doctrines of collateral estoppel or res judicata applied to the facts in this case.

Additionally, the trial court had indicated that the petitioner should have contacted the police to report any violations of the order rather than file for another CPO in another county. However, the appellate court emphasized that "Ohio law does not require a certain sequence of remedies and appellant did not have only one 'appropriate remedy' as the trial court found. While it may be a preferable remedy, there is no requirement that appellant call the police before seeking a protection order."[26]

Q & A: The residential parent filed a request for the reallocation of parental rights and responsibilities claiming that her ex-husband should now have supervised visitation of the children. While the motion was pending in Washington County, residential parent filed and was granted a CPO in Franklin County based on the same facts alleged in her earlier motion. After a hearing on the first motion, father's visitation rights were reinstated. Was the Washington County determination reinstating father's visitation barred by the doctrine of collateral estoppel?

In *Yannitell v. Oaks*,[27] the appellant appealed the denial of her motion to reallocate parental rights in Washington County claiming that

---

[24]Jennifer Black, The Double Jeopardy Dilemma in Combating Domestic Violence: A Solution in United States v. Dixon, 33 U. Louisville J. Fam. L. 91, 925 (1995) (determining that criminal contempt proceedings that follow contempt findings do not fall within the *Ashe* definition of collateral estoppel relative to the same parties).

[25]Clagg v. Clagg, 2009-Ohio-328, 2009 WL 190049 (Ohio Ct. App. 10th Dist. Franklin County 2009).

[26]Clagg v. Clagg, 2009-Ohio-328, 2009 WL 190049, *4 (Ohio Ct. App. 10th Dist. Franklin County 2009).

[27]Yannitell v. Oaks, 2008-Ohio-6271, 2008 WL 5077646 (Ohio Ct. App. 4th Dist. Washington County 2008).

the same issues were already litigated in the CPO hearing in Franklin County and thus barred by the doctrine of collateral estoppel and res judicata.

In affirming the trial court decision, the appellate court pointed out that RC 3113.31 contemplates that orders allocating parental rights and responsibilities in a CPO are temporary under RC 3113.31(E)(1)(d). While the statute permits a court to issue temporary orders in order to stop domestic violence, *"it does not vest the court with authority to modify the allocation of parental rights and responsibilities in a CPO proceeding."*[28] Because there was a pending motion to reallocate parental rights and responsibilities in Washington County at the time the CPO was filed in Franklin County, the Franklin County had no jurisdiction to consider the CPO relative to the children's issues. In finding that there was no valid final judgment with which to apply the doctrine of collateral estoppel, the court also indicated that the CPO should have been filed in Washington County and consolidated with the pending motion to reallocate or modify parenting time.[29]

This makes sense because courts have held that collateral estoppel cannot be applied unless the identical issue was 1) actually litigated, 2) directly determined, and 3) essential to the prior judgment.[30]

Q & A: May the petitioner appeal a finding of not guilty of criminal contempt for the violation of a civil protection order?

No. Criminal contempt is a crime in every fundamental respect. The criminal safeguards of the double jeopardy provisions apply in the criminal contempt proceeding. Case law has taken the approach that, where a respondent is found not guilty of criminal contempt for the violation of a civil protection order, the petitioner cannot appeal the court decision.

At least one jurisdiction relied on the double jeopardy provisions inherent in the constitution. The court, in *Denovchek v. Board of Trumbull County Commissioners*,[31] held that:

> no appeal lies to review an acquittal from or dismissal on the merits of a charge of criminal contempt of court. To allow an appeal from an acquittal on the merits of a criminal contempt charge poses a threat to the contemnor's right not to be placed twice in jeopardy for the same offense.

On appeal, the Supreme Court of Ohio held that "[t]here is no right of appeal from the dismissal of a contempt motion when the party making the motion is not prejudiced by the dismissal."[32] The Supreme

[28]Yannitell v. Oaks, 2008-Ohio-6271, 2008 WL 5077646, *8 (Ohio Ct. App. 4th Dist. Washington County 2008).

[29]Yannitell v. Oaks, 2008-Ohio-6271, 2008 WL 5077646, *8 (Ohio Ct. App. 4th Dist. Washington County 2008).

[30]See Folmar v. Griffin, 2008-Ohio-2941, 2008 WL 2573279 (Ohio Ct. App. 5th Dist. Delaware County 2008).

[31]Denovchek v. Board of Trumbull County Com'rs, 1987 WL 5981, *2 (Ohio Ct. App. 11th Dist. Trumbull County 1987), judgment aff'd, 36 Ohio St. 3d 14, 520 N.E.2d 1362 (1988); see also Cipolla v. Cipolla, 264 Pa. Super. 53, 398 A.2d 1053 (1979) (holding that double jeopardy attaches in the criminal contempt proceeding and an adjudication on the merits of not guilty of indirect criminal contempt is an absolute bar to appellate review).

[32]Denovchek v. Board of Trumbull County Com'rs, 36 Ohio St. 3d 14, 14, 520

Court, however, did not base its decision on double jeopardy grounds and, in fact, noted that there is a special category of domestic relations contempt cases in which appeals have been allowed.

However, a criminal contempt conviction is a separate final judgment from which an immediate appeal may be taken regardless of the status of the underlying case.[33] A civil contempt finding against a party is not a final appealable order until and is reviewable only upon appeal of the underlying case.[34] In any case, to constitute a final appealable order there must be both a finding of contempt and imposition of a sanction.[35]

Q & A: A parent was charged with domestic violence for abusing his/her child. At the time charges were filed, the parent had already agreed to a case plan in juvenile court. Is the subsequent domestic violence prosecution barred by double jeopardy?

At least one Ohio Court is apparently ready to address this issue. In *Lyndhurst v. Dumas*,[36] the defendant committed an act of domestic violence against his son. He was charged in municipal court, but he alleged in motions to dismiss that he had already agreed to a case plan in juvenile court. Since the actions in both courts arose from the same incident of domestic violence, it is his contention that he was put in double jeopardy by having to answer the domestic violence charges in Lyndhurst Municipal Court.

The trial court denied his motion to dismiss the complaint, ruling that "[t]he juvenile matter did not put defendant in such jeopardy as would prohibit this court from going forward on the charge of domestic violence. Therefore, this court holds that these two charges do not constitute the same offense."[37] On appeal, the Eighth District Court of Appeals reversed and remanded for a full hearing on the double jeopardy claim contained in the motion to dismiss.

The appellate court relied on the *Blockburger* "same elements" test and concluded that the appellant misapplied the standard to be used. "Rather than looking at the conduct of the accused, this court must

---

N.E.2d 1362 (1988).

[33]In re Christensen Engineering Co., 194 U.S. 458, 24 S. Ct. 729, 48 L. Ed. 1072 (1904).

[34]See Doyle v. London Guarantee & Accident Co., 204 U.S. 599, 608, 27 S. Ct. 313, 316, 51 L. Ed. 641, 645 (1907); Fox v. Capital Co., 299 U.S. 105, 107, 57 S. Ct. 57, 58-59, 81 L. Ed. 67, 68-69 (1936).

[35]See In re Contemnor Caron, 110 Ohio Misc. 2d 58, 744 N.E.2d 787, 836 (C.P. 2000); see also Cooper v. Cooper, 14 Ohio App. 3d 327, 471 N.E.2d 525 (8th Dist. Cuyahoga County 1984); Grove v. Grove, 2001-Ohio-2109, 2001 WL 196496 (Ohio Ct. App. 3d Dist. Seneca County 2001); see also Text § 13:10, Contempt—Other procedural issues.

[36]City of Lyndhurst v. Dumas, 2000 WL 45854 (Ohio Ct. App. 8th Dist. Cuyahoga County 2000); see also State v. Hoff, 1999 WL 668804 (Ohio Ct. App. 5th Dist. Perry County 1999) (prior adjudication in juvenile court did not prohibit subsequent prosecution for domestic violence; double jeopardy did not attach).

[37]City of Lyndhurst v. Dumas, 2000 WL 45854, *1 (Ohio Ct. App. 8th Dist. Cuyahoga County 2000).

review the elements of the crime for which he is being charged."[38] Since the appellate court was unable to deduce the nature of the juvenile court proceedings from the record, it was unable to determine whether the defendant was ever put in double jeopardy. Of significance is that the appellate court framed the question in terms of whether the defendant was charged with a criminal offense in juvenile court. If the defendant was charged in juvenile court, then a subsequent criminal prosecution is barred on double jeopardy grounds. On the other hand, if juvenile court is considered a civil court and if no criminal charges were filed, double jeopardy does not attach to the criminal prosecution in Lyndhurst.

§ 13:15 Court enforcement of civil protection orders—Sentencing civil protection order violators; generally

Consistent enforcement of civil protection orders is the key to their effectiveness. Without swift and consistent judicial sentencing for violations of civil protection orders, they will become ineffective mechanisms for reducing recidivism in domestic violence cases. The National Institute of Justice found that "for civil protection orders to deter batterers from further abusing their partners, respondents must believe that the judge will impose a meaningful penalty for any violation."[1]

One commentator has written, "Domestic violence is repeated because it works and is covertly and inadvertently reinforced by society's institutions."[2] Since battering is learned behavior, courts can provide batterers with motivation for change. "Battering stops when batterers are held accountable and choose to stop."[3]

Therefore, the primary objectives for any sentencing judge should be the same in all domestic violence cases: to stop the violence, protect the victim and other family and household members, and hold the batterer accountable for his/her behavior.[4] This should be the underlying principle whether sentencing follows a contempt sanction pursuant to RC 3113.31 or a criminal prosecution under RC 2919.27. No court can effectively sentence a batterer without addressing those issues which are common to both the victim and the batterer. Underlying these goals is the legislative intention to treat domestic violence

---

[38]City of Lyndhurst v. Dumas, 2000 WL 45854, *2 (Ohio Ct. App. 8th Dist. Cuyahoga County 2000).

[Section 13:15]

[1]Peter Finn & Sarah Colson, National Institute of Justice, Civil Protection Orders: Legislation, Current Court Practice and Enforcement 4, 57 (1990); see also Arthur L. Burnett, Sr., Dispensing Justice in Domestic Violence Cases: Pretrial Release and Sentencing of Offenders, 9-WTR Crim. Just. 8 (1995).

[2]Anne L. Ganley, Domestic Violence, The What, Why and Who, as Relevant to Civil Court Cases, in Domestic Violence in Civil Court Cases: A National Model for Judicial Education 20, 30 (Jacqueline A. Agtuca et al. eds. 1992).

[3]Anne L. Ganley, Domestic Violence, The What, Why and Who, as Relevant to Civil Court Cases, in Domestic Violence in Civil Court Cases: A National Model for Judicial Education 20, 40 (Jacqueline A. Agtuca et al. eds. 1992).

[4]See State v. Lee, 73 Ohio Misc. 2d 9, 20, 657 N.E.2d 604 (Mun. Ct. 1995) (noting that the defendant's sentence for domestic violence was in line with "the primary ends of promoting the victim's safety and holding the batterer accountable").

as a serious crime.[5] Effective sentencing for perpetrators of domestic violence depends on the individual to be sentenced, the nature of the relationship of the parties, and the sentencing scheme designed by the court.

The United States Attorney General's Task Force on Family Violence, Final Report stated in part:

> The imposition of a just sentence is the desired culmination of any criminal judicial proceeding. The sanction rendered is not only punishment for the offender but also an indication of the seriousness of the criminal conduct and a method of providing protection and support to the victim. Too often in family violence cases, the sentence fails on all three accounts . . ..
>
> In all cases when the victim has suffered serious injury, the convicted abuser should be sentenced to a term of incarceration. In cases involving a history of repeated abusive behavior or when there is a significant threat of continued harm, incarceration is also the preferred disposition. In serious incidents of violence, incarceration is the punishment necessary to hold the abuser accountable for his crime. It also clearly signals the seriousness with which the offense is viewed by the community and provides secure protection to the victim.
>
> Judges and the sentences they impose can strongly re-enforce the message that violence is a serious criminal matter for which the abuser will be held accountable. Judges should not underestimate their ability to influence the defendant's behavior. Even a stern admonition from the bench can help to deter the defendant from future violence.[6]

The National Council of Juvenile and Family Court Judges has recommended significant court system improvements in an effort to reduce the incidence of domestic violence.[7] In order for a sentencing judge to effectively impose a meaningful sentence, the judge must have a substantial amount of information available to him/her about the perpetrator and the crime. Additionally, the National Council of Juvenile and Family Court Judges specifically advocated that every sentence imposed by a judge in a domestic violence case should "a) hold the batterer accountable; b) order offender involvement in activities specifically designed to reduce further violence; c) require an alcohol and drug evaluation where appropriate, mandate successful completion of treatment, and provide for mandatory chemical testing; and d) provide for formal supervision and monitoring of compliance."[8] Such conditions are more likely to secure the protection of the victim from future harm.

Accountability may be accomplished by supervised probation, restitution to the victim, and jail time. Treatment programs should

---

[5]See Felton v. Felton, 79 Ohio St. 3d 34, 37, 1997-Ohio-302, 679 N.E.2d 672 (1997) (noting that the "General Assembly enacted the domestic violence statutes specifically to criminalize those activities commonly known as domestic violence and to authorize a court to issue protection orders designed to ensure the safety and protection of a complainant in a domestic violence case").

[6]The U.S. Attorney General's Task Force on Family Violence, Final Report, U.S. Dep't of Justice, Washington, D.C., 1984 at 34–36.

[7]See Family Violence Project, National Council of Juvenile and Family Court Judges, Family Violence: Improving Court Practice 19 (1990).

[8]Family Violence Project, National Council of Juvenile and Family Court Judges, Family Violence: Improving Court Practice 20 (1990).

specifically address issues of domestic violence and violent behavior.[9] "Individual counseling or couples counseling does not address these issues or remediate the problems of violence, power or control."[10], drug and alcohol testing should be considered by every judge at sentencing, if appropriate. Although drugs and alcohol do not cause domestic violence, these substances often act as a trigger or excuse for violence.[11]

Q & A: What specific factors should courts consider at the time of sentencing?

Several factors have been considered by courts at the time of sentencing.[12] The presence of these factors may be used to enhance a batterer's sentence, especially where the batterer is criminally prosecuted for the violation under RC 2919.27. Even in a contempt proceeding, these factors should be seen as a red flag that a particular contemnor is more likely to disregard court orders in the future. They include:

(1) offender's prior criminal history;[13]
(2) nature of victim's injuries;[14]
(3) use of a weapon;[15]
(4) current terms of probation, if any;
(5) pattern of offender's abusive behavior;[16]
(6) threats made by offender to harm self, victim, or others;[17]
(7) previous violations of court orders;
(8) presence of children in home who may be affected by abuse;
(9) drug, alcohol, and/or mental health evaluations, where appropriate;[18]

---

[9]See Anne L. Ganley, Perpetrators of Domestic Violence: An Overview of Counseling the Court-Mandated Client, in Domestic Violence on Trial: Psychological and Legal Dimensions of Family Violence (D. Sonkin ed., 1986).

[10]Family Violence Project, National Council of Juvenile and Family Court Judges, Family Violence: Improving Court Practice 20 (1990).

[11]The Urban Institute: A Guide to Research, Courts and Communities: Confronting Violence in the Family, State Justice Institute Conference, San Francisco, CA: March 25–28, 1993, at 17.

[12]See also RC 2929.11 to 2929.13; see also State v. Mitchell, 2007-Ohio-167, 2007 WL 118001 (Ohio Ct. App. 10th Dist. Franklin County 2007) (discussing the types of findings sufficient to satisfy *Foster*); State v. Toma, 2014-Ohio-2256, 2014 WL 2459663 (Ohio Ct. App. 7th Dist. Columbiana County 2014) (discussion of the seriousness or recidivism factors in RC 2929.12); State v. Farmer, 2015-Ohio-5434, 2015 WL 9438270 (Ohio Ct. App. 5th Dist. Licking County 2015), appeal not allowed, 145 Ohio St. 3d 1459, 2016-Ohio-2807, 49 N.E.3d 321 (2016) (discussing the purposes of misdemeanor sentencing).

[13]State v. Trammell, 2002-Ohio-2935, 2002 WL 1332713 (Ohio Ct. App. 2d Dist. Montgomery County 2002). See State v. Pickett, 628 So. 2d 1333 (La. Ct. App. 2d Cir. 1993), on reh'g, (Jan. 13, 1994) and writ denied, 637 So. 2d 476 (La. 1994).

[14]State v. Morton, 292 N.J. Super. 92, 678 A.2d 308 (App. Div. 1996).

[15]People v. Campbell, 199 Ill. App. 3d 775, 145 Ill. Dec. 786, 557 N.E.2d 556 (1st Dist. 1990).

[16]State v. Williams, 655 So. 2d 552 (La. Ct. App. 2d Cir. 1995).

[17]State v. Olson, 119 Idaho 370, 806 P.2d 963 (Ct. App. 1991).

[18]People v. Riederer, 217 Cal. App. 3d 829, 266 Cal. Rptr. 355 (3d Dist. 1990).

(10) vulnerability of victims (elderly, children, handicapped);[19]
(11) victim impact statement;[20] and
(12) prior treatment for domestic violence.[21]

A court should know which of the above factors apply to a particular batterer before sentencing.[22] As stated earlier, each sentence imposed by a judge should seek to enforce the sentencing goals in domestic violence cases which are to hold the batterer accountable for his/her actions and protect the victim. The existence of any of the first nine factors indicates an increased likelihood that the respondent will continue to abuse his/her partner and will fail to abide by the terms of an existing protection order. If several of the factors apply to a particular respondent, a court should consider imposing a term of incarceration.

Should a respondent continue to violate a protection order, increased sanctions should result. Taking into account the sentencing guidelines set forth in RC Chapter 2929,[23] a court may consider increased fines, additional jail time,[24] a greater probationary period, longer community service, and/or restitution for the victim.[25]

For example, a longer probationary period allows for greater monitoring. Violations of civil protection orders may be more readily identified, and strict monitoring of violators may yield greater compliance with the terms of the existing protection orders.

Revocation of probation should always be considered if the violator commits subsequent offenses against the same individual.[26] The behavior of a respondent who continually violates a protection order demonstrates either an inability to comply with court orders or a pathological desire to further injure that victim. In any case, caution dictates the imposition of a greater penalty.

Additionally, courts should retain jurisdiction over cases in order to

[19] State v. Wentz, 805 P.2d 962 (Alaska 1991).

[20] See State v. Trubee, 2005-Ohio-552, 2005 WL 335833, *12 (Ohio Ct. App. 3d Dist. Marion County 2005) (abrogated on other grounds by, State v. Foster, 109 Ohio St. 3d 1, 2006-Ohio-856, 845 N.E.2d 470 (2006)) (holding that information contained in victim impact statement could be used to assist trial court in sentencing a defendant within the statutory range).

[21] Janet Carter et al., Domestic Violence: The Crucial Role of the Judge in Criminal Court Cases: A National Model for Judicial Education 138–40 (1991). See also State v. Manzanares, 19 Kan. App. 2d 214, 866 P.2d 1083 (1994) (disapproved of by, State v. Guebara, 24 Kan. App. 2d 260, 944 P.2d 164 (1997)); State v. Kidwell, 1995 WL 68164 (Ohio Ct. App. 10th Dist. Franklin County 1995); State v. Trammell, 2002-Ohio-2935, 2002 WL 1332713 (Ohio Ct. App. 2d Dist. Montgomery County 2002).

[22] State v. Henry, 2015-Ohio-4145, 2015 WL 5813874 (Ohio Ct. App. 7th Dist. Belmont County 2015).

[23] See also Text § 13:3, Court enforcement of civil protection orders—Criminal prosecution.

[24] State v. Stamper, 2016-Ohio-433, 2016 WL 525818 (Ohio Ct. App. 2d Dist. Champaign County 2016); R.C. 2929.19(B)(4).

[25] See State v. Toler, 174 Ohio App. 3d 335, 2007-Ohio-6967, 882 N.E.2d 28 (3d Dist. Hardin County 2007) (restitution is limited to economic losses suffered by victim that stemmed from the domestic violence); see also RC 2929.18.

[26] See People v. Whitfield, 147 Ill. App. 3d 675, 101 Ill. Dec. 80, 498 N.E.2d 262 (4th Dist. 1986).

evaluate a defendant for rehabilitation, including his/her potential and suitability for probation. Should the court subsequently discover that a defendant is not suitable for probation, the court has an obligation to revoke probation and impose a term of incarceration.

Q & A: What types of sentences have been upheld for violations of civil protection orders?

The type of sentence for a violation of a civil protection order often depends on whether the violation is brought as a criminal prosecution under RC 2919.27 or as a contempt under RC 3113.31(L)(1)(b). It also depends on whether the contempt is treated as criminal or civil contempt.[27]

A national survey reveals that several types of sentences have been imposed by the courts for violations of civil protection orders.[28] They include incarceration,[29] community service, monetary sanctions, bond, probation,[30] batterer intervention programs,[31] and enhanced protection orders. However, there is no consistent formula by which a court decides which sentence to impose for which acts with either contempt or criminal prosecution.

If a respondent is criminally prosecuted for a violation of a civil protection order, possible jail time may be imposed by the court.[32] More often, the court will suspend the jail time and order probation for a period of years.[33] Generally, jail time is not imposed for first-time protection order violators. However, under RC 2919.27, additional violations will result in enhanced penalties.[34] Although a respondent who is found guilty of criminal contempt may be ordered to jail, it is much more likely that a suspended sentence and probation will be the result.

Unfortunately, suspended sentences and probation should not be considered unless the court has a clear policy in place to both monitor the probation of domestic violence violators and ensure compliance with the civil protection order. Absent a structured formal policy,

---

[27]See, for example, Burchett v. Miller, 123 Ohio App. 3d 550, 552, 704 N.E.2d 636 (6th Dist. Erie County 1997) (holding that "trial court abuses its discretion in ordering purge conditions with respect to imposition of sanctions for civil contempt which are unreasonable or where compliance is impossible").

[28]See, e.g., City of Cleveland v. Serrano, 1999 WL 1024214 (Ohio Ct. App. 8th Dist. Cuyahoga County 1999).

[29]See City of Columbus v. Kurtz, 1995 WL 723684 (Ohio Ct. App. 10th Dist. Franklin County 1995); see also State v. Olson, 119 Idaho 370, 806 P.2d 963 (Ct. App. 1991).

[30]See City of Columbus v. Kurtz, 1995 WL 723684 (Ohio Ct. App. 10th Dist. Franklin County 1995); see also State v. Rickert, 164 Vt. 602, 665 A.2d 887 (1995); State v. Butler, 122 Idaho 776, 839 P.2d 43 (Ct. App. 1992).

[31]See State v. Rickert, 164 Vt. 602, 665 A.2d 887 (1995); see also State v. Trammell, 2002-Ohio-2935, 2002 WL 1332713 (Ohio Ct. App. 2d Dist. Montgomery County 2002) (defendant's previous conviction resulted in completion of an anger management program, but court sentenced him to a term of incarceration for second offense as his violence increased since his previous incident).

[32]See City of Columbus v. Kurtz, 1995 WL 723684 (Ohio Ct. App. 10th Dist. Franklin County 1995).

[33]See City of Columbus v. Kurtz, 1995 WL 723684 (Ohio Ct. App. 10th Dist. Franklin County 1995).

[34]See RC 2919.27(B)(1)(b).

victims will lack the protections necessary to secure their safety, and respondents will continue to violate court orders if they believe nothing will happen to them.

Most courts consider the imposition of a fine for both contempt and criminal prosecution. Community service may also be imposed as a sentence in lieu of jail.[35] Sometimes a bond is required of the respondent to ensure compliance with the order. Where the offender has to pay money to the court to secure compliance with the court order, this action may serve as a deterrent to future violations.[36] A court may even revise a civil protection order to increase the victim's protection by further limiting the access of the offender.

Restitution[37] is also considered a favorable sentencing option, whether in terms of medical care, property damage, lost wages, costs of counseling, etc. In domestic violence cases, restitution may include ambulance and emergency room fees, replacement of locks, transportation expenses to escape the violence, costs of staying at a shelter or hotel, and moving expenses. Restitution to the victim should be the first priority of the offender and should supersede the repayment of other costs, including attorney fees and costs of probation.

Some statutes have specifically listed terms for victim restitution which include: cost of shelter, lost earnings, emergency housing, out-of-pocket expenses for injuries, moving expenses, cost of obtaining an unlisted telephone number, and reasonable attorney fees.[38] Placing financial responsibilities upon a batterer at the time of sentencing helps to hold a batterer responsible for his/her actions.

While this may be the first time the offender has violated the protection order, it is important to remember that it is the second time the offender has committed domestic violence towards the victim.[39] Furthermore, the threat of new court involvement becomes a strong deterrent to future violence.[40]

Incarceration should always be contemplated by the court when the violation causes new or continued physical harm to the victim or when there is a significant threat of continued harm.[41], courts should order a contemnor to jail where the severity of the domestic violence justifies a prison sentence to prevent future abuse or where there is a history of prior contempt findings. In the latter instance, it should not matter whether the contemnor is found guilty of criminal contempt or criminally prosecuted.

Q & A: How have Ohio's domestic relations courts sentenced contemnors?

---

[35]See RC 2951.02(F).

[36]See, e.g., City of Cleveland v. Serrano, 1999 WL 1024214 (Ohio Ct. App. 8th Dist. Cuyahoga County 1999).

[37]See RC 2951.02(C)(1)(a).

[38]See Mass. Gen. Laws Ann. ch. 209A, § 7 (West 1992); see also RC 2951.02(C).

[39]See Jeffrey Edleson & Maryann Sayers, Relative Effectiveness of Group Treatments for Men Who Batter, 26 Soc. Work Res. & Abstracts 10, 10-17 (1990).

[40]See Jeffrey Edleson & Maryann Sayers, Relative Effectiveness of Group Treatments for Men Who Batter, 26 Soc. Work Res. & Abstracts 10, 10-17 (1990).

[41]See Attorney General's Task Force on Family Violence, U.S. Department of Justice, Final Report 35 (1984); see also Peter Finn & Sarah Colson, National Institute of Justice, Civil Protection Orders: Legislation, Current Court Practice and Enforcement 4, 58 (1990).

Rarely do Ohio courts hold violators of civil protection orders in contempt of court. It is unclear whether the reason for this is because few victims bring contempt actions, believing that such actions provide an ineffective sanction, or because it is a remedy that is discouraged by the courts themselves. Each attorney has an obligation to inform the client that contempt actions may be filed should the respondent violate the protection order.

When contempt has been considered, however, Ohio courts have approached the sentencing of civil protection order violators with little consistency. Since the language of RC 3113.31(L)(1)(b) is ambiguous in that it fails to indicate whether a violation of a civil protection order constitutes civil or criminal contempt, few reported cases specifically state whether the contempt is criminal or civil.[42] It is even difficult to find consensus around the state regarding the type of sanction imposed for any specific violation.

Where contempt has been considered by the court for a civil protection order violation, it is important to resolve whether a specific violation rises to the level of criminal or civil contempt. It is equally important to discern the specific intent of the court in sentencing the contemnor.

For example, violations such as failing to pay support or turn over property or issues relating to the allocation of parental rights and responsibilities are most often considered civil contempt.[43] If treated as civil contempt, the goal of the court is to obtain compliance with the order. Jail time, if ordered at all, will most likely be suspended. Community service may or may not be considered. Even if a period of incarceration or community service is contemplated by the court, a respondent may purge the contempt by complying with the underlying court order.

Continued criminal acts against the victim which include assaults, threats, or destruction of property should be treated as criminal contempt. Additionally, certain violations of protection orders that may not themselves rise to the level of criminal behavior, such as telephoning, harassing, and following or watching the victim, should be considered criminal contempt.

At least one trial court determined that damage to the residence and to personal property on vacating the marital residence deserved thirty days' incarceration. Although the court, in *Petrak v. Petrak*,[44] did not specifically state whether the contempt was criminal or civil, the fact that the contempt was not remedial in nature suggests that the purpose of the sanction was to punish the contemnor for his behavior in damaging the property.

---

[42]See Petrak v. Petrak, 1994 WL 50386 (Ohio Ct. App. 12th Dist. Butler County 1994) (failing to indicate whether contempt was civil or criminal). But see West v. West, 1994 WL 680156 (Ohio Ct. App. 2d Dist. Montgomery County 1994) (specifically addressing this issue); see also In re Contemnor Caron, 110 Ohio Misc. 2d 58, 744 N.E.2d 787 (C.P. 2000) (generally, for a discussion of sanctions).

[43]See West v. West, 1994 WL 680156 (Ohio Ct. App. 2d Dist. Montgomery County 1994); but see In re Contemnor Caron, 110 Ohio Misc. 2d 58, 744 N.E.2d 787 (C.P. 2000).

[44]Petrak v. Petrak, 1994 WL 50386 (Ohio Ct. App. 12th Dist. Butler County 1994).

If treated as criminal contempt, most courts will sentence the contemnor to a term of incarceration, suspend the sentence and impose a fine, and order probation as punishment for a first violation. Subsequent violations may result in jail time, although the period of incarceration is not uniform around the state.

Where the violation results in serious physical harm to the victim or where there is continued violence and periodic violations, criminal prosecution under RC 2919.27 should be encouraged. However, if a contempt proceeding is brought and the contempt is treated as criminal, a court is less likely to suspend the sentence and order probation for the contemnor in these instances. A period of incarceration is often imposed.

Of significance is that certain violations have been treated either as civil or criminal contempt. Depending on the court jurisdiction and the particular situation between the parties, violations in which a respondent refuses to vacate the premises, re-enters the premises of the victim, or harasses or threatens the victim have been considered both civil and criminal contempt.

For example, in *West v. West*,[45] the Montgomery County Domestic Relations Court sentenced the respondent to a period of incarceration for violating a civil protection order. In that case, the trial court found the respondent in criminal contempt for threatening the petitioner/victim. The trial court imposed a thirty-day jail sentence and permitted the contemnor to serve his sentence on weekends so as not to interfere with his employment. Although no fine was imposed in *West*, such a penalty is allowable pursuant to RC 2705.05(A)(1). The sentence imposed by the *West* trial court was upheld on appeal as comporting with statutory guidelines.

Q & A: What sentences have Ohio courts imposed for respondents who have been criminally prosecuted under RC 2919.27?[46]

Even if criminal prosecution is sought pursuant to RC 2919.27, most Ohio jurisdictions will often suspend jail sentences and impose a fine and a one- or two-year probation for a first violation. However, if the respondent committed serious injury to the victim and the violence occurred during the time the civil protection order was in effect, prison terms of thirty days to six months have not been considered unreasonable for an offender.[47] Because the statute contemplates increased

[45]West v. West, 1994 WL 680156 (Ohio Ct. App. 2d Dist. Montgomery County 1994).

[46]State v. Stamper, 2016-Ohio-433, 2016 WL 525818 (Ohio Ct. App. 2d Dist. Champaign County 2016) (In a novel sentencing, trial court ordered respondent to reside at a certain address and not move from that address without written permission from the court and ordered him not to travel to or be present in the county where the victims resided).

[47]See also State v. Salazar, 2007-Ohio-196, 2007 WL 126142, *2 (Ohio Ct. App. 6th Dist. Sandusky County 2007) (9 months incarceration not unreasonable where appellant previously violated the order 1 year earlier and which should have served as an effective reminder of the validity of the protection order between the parties.)

penalties for subsequent violations, these violations often result in jail time for the offender.[48]

Q & A: What types of alternative sentencing approaches should courts examine when a finding of contempt is made?

Ohio courts should heed the recommendations of the National Council of Juvenile and Family Court Judges. In *Improving Court Practice*, it is suggested that courts

> should develop, publicize and monitor a clear, formal policy regarding violations [of protection orders]. This might include follow up hearings, promoting the arrest of violators, incremental sanctions for violations, treating violations as criminal contempt, and establishment of procedures for modification of orders. In addition, courts can establish procedures for monitoring offenders for compliance.[49]

Whenever a case results in a finding of contempt, the court should retain the case on its docket in order to monitor compliance. This is true whether the contempt is treated as civil or criminal. Court social services, community services programs, or specific probation agencies should be employed to actively monitor the case. If violations occur, these agencies should immediately notify the court, and the respondent should immediately be brought before the court.

Courts should schedule review hearings periodically to monitor compliance with the present order and with the underlying protection order. Review hearings are designed to provide information regarding a respondent's failure to obey the protection order and the terms of his/her sentence. Sometimes, new or revised orders may be entered by the court. Additionally, review hearings subject the respondent to repeated court appearances, which tends to enforce compliance.

Q & A: What types of alternative sentences have been considered by the courts?

In some jurisdictions, contempt sentences have been delayed pending subsequent civil protection order violations.[50] These conditional delays are contingent upon the respondent's compliance with all previous court orders, including counseling. At the point that a violation occurs, the respondent is required to appear for sentencing.[51]

The advantages of this method cannot be overstated. Knowing that the sentence may still be imposed if the respondent commits a future violation may compel the respondent to become involved in a batterers' program or inspire him/her to seek ways to change his/her behavior. On the other hand,

> if the deterrent is ineffective, a judge will be asked to impose a sentence on the first violation at a time when the respondent has already demonstrated his unwillingness to stop the violence and comply with the civil

[48] RC 2919.27.

[49] National Council of Juvenile & Family Court Judges, Family Violence: Improving Court Practice 23 (1990).

[50] See Rush v. Rush, 1999 WL 1044482 (Ohio Ct. App. 8th Dist. Cuyahoga County 1999).

[51] See People v. Lucas, 170 Ill. App. 3d 164, 120 Ill. Dec. 481, 524 N.E.2d 246 (3d Dist. 1988); People v. Whitfield, 147 Ill. App. 3d 675, 101 Ill. Dec. 80, 498 N.E.2d 262 (4th Dist. 1986).

protection order. Under these circumstances, even judges sympathetic to batterers will be more likely to impose longer sentences upon batterers, one that is more akin to those given in all other criminal actions.[52]

Q & A: Have contempt sentences been overturned?

Yes, courts have overturned contempt sentences in domestic violence cases. Many courts have overturned sentences because of procedural errors.[53] Other courts have overturned sentences because the lower court failed to include the mandatory minimum jail terms, failed to order batterers' treatment, imposed too light a sentence where there were no mitigating circumstances, or imposed too severe a sentence.[54]

In *West v. West*,[55] the Montgomery County Court of Appeals overturned the contempt sanction as it related to the trial court's modification of visitation. In that case, the appellate court held that the trial court was without jurisdiction to modify the visitation schedule of the respondent:

> Although the trial court is imbued with broad discretion in its imposition of contempt sanctions, it must impose only those sanctions which it has the jurisdiction to issue. If the court imposes sanctions which are not specified by statute nor are within its inherent power, it exceeds its authority. Modification of visitation is not an available statutory sanction for criminal contempt.[56]

Finally, at least one court overturned the criminal contempt finding because the appellant's actions did not constitute harassment. In *Jeffers v. Jeffers*,[57] the appellant argued that the finding of contempt was against the manifest weight of the evidence. In *Jeffers*, the ex-wife was found in contempt for appearing at her ex-husband's party and harassing him. The appellate court considered the legal definition of harassment, and the testimony of the parties and witnesses, and held that the trial court erred in finding appellant guilty of criminal contempt because her actions did not legally constitute harassment.

[52]Catherine F. Klein & Leslye E. Orloff, Providing Legal Protection for Battered Women: An Analysis of State Statutes and Case Law, 21 Hofstra L. Rev. 801, 1135 (1993).

[53]See Petrak v. Petrak, 1994 WL 50386 (Ohio Ct. App. 12th Dist. Butler County 1994) (holding that contempt judgment is void because the underlying order expired on the issuance of the divorce decree); see also People v. Horton, 250 Ill. App. 3d 944, 189 Ill. Dec. 469, 620 N.E.2d 437 (4th Dist. 1993) (holding that the sentence was erroneous where the court failed to inform the defendant about the procedural steps necessary to perfect an appeal).

[54]See State v. J.F., 262 N.J. Super. 539, 543, 621 A.2d 520, 522 (App. Div. 1993) (vacating the part of the sentence that banished the defendant from the state because banishment is not among the remedies authorized by the Prevention of Domestic Violence Act and stating, "[a]uthority existing elsewhere generally holds that, as a matter of state law, orders banishing defendant from a state may not be issued in the absence of legislative authorization").

[55]West v. West, 1994 WL 680156 (Ohio Ct. App. 2d Dist. Montgomery County 1994).

[56]West v. West, 1994 WL 680156, *5 (Ohio Ct. App. 2d Dist. Montgomery County 1994).

[57]Jeffers v. Jeffers, 2001 WL 118530, *3 (Ohio Ct. App. 10th Dist. Franklin County 2001).

Q & A: When can sealing the record be considered by the court?[58]

If an offender is convicted of domestic violence[59] or of violating a civil or criminal protection order under RC 2919.27, sealing of the record may be considered by the court. Ohio's criminal statute contains a provision that allows the court to seal a convicted person's record under certain circumstances.[60] RC 2953.32(A)(1) provides in pertinent part:

> a first offender may apply to the sentencing court if convicted in this state, or to a court of common pleas if convicted in another state or in a federal court, for the sealing of the conviction record. Application may be made at the expiration of three years after the offender's final discharge if convicted of a felony, or at the expiration of one year after the offender's final discharge if convicted of a misdemeanor.

The sealing of the record may also be considered for a first offender[61] who was arrested for any misdemeanor offense.[62]

For domestic violence purposes, an offender may seek to have the record of his/her domestic violence conviction, if charged as a misdemeanor offense, sealed at the expiration of one year after his/her final discharge. If the offender/respondent has been convicted of violating a protection order and it is charged as a misdemeanor, the same holds true.

Of great significance is that, effective March 23, 2000, RC 2953.36 was amended[63] to preclude the sealing of certain records, which include convictions of an offense of violence when the offense is a misdemeanor of the first degree or a felony.[64] Pursuant to the Supreme Court in *State v. LaSalle*,[65] "[t]he statutory law in effect at the time of the filing of an R.C. 2953.32 application to seal a record of conviction is controlling."

---

[58]See §§ 20:1 et seq.; Text § 12:23; see generally, State v. Vanzandt, 142 Ohio St. 3d 223, 2015-Ohio-236, 28 N.E.3d 1267 (2015); see also State v. Ninness, 2013-Ohio-974, 2013 WL 1093008 (Ohio Ct. App. 6th Dist. Ottawa County 2013); State v. Radcliff, 142 Ohio St. 3d 78, 2015-Ohio-235, 28 N.E.3d 69 (2015); State v. Grillo, 2015-Ohio-308, 27 N.E.3d 951 (Ohio Ct. App. 5th Dist. Richland County 2015) (discussing the difference between sealing and expungement).

[59]See RC 2919.25.

[60]See RC 2953.32 et seq.; see also State v. Simon, 87 Ohio St. 3d 531, 2000-Ohio-474, 721 N.E.2d 1041 (2000).

[61]See State v. Johnson, 2008-Ohio-1183, 2008 WL 697721 (Ohio Ct. App. 7th Dist. Mahoning County 2008) (defines a first offender and differentiates between sealing a record and judicial expungement).

[62]RC 2953.32(A)(2).

[63]1999 S.B. 13, eff. 3-23-00.

[64]RC 2953.36(C); see State v. Powers, 2002-Ohio-6672, 2002 WL 31730985 (Ohio Ct. App. 5th Dist. Fairfield County 2002); State v. LaSalle, 96 Ohio St. 3d 178, 2002-Ohio-4009, 772 N.E.2d 1172 (2002) (holding that absent a clear pronouncement by the general assembly that a statute is to be applied retrospectively, a statute may be applied prospectively only). See also State v. Lawson, 2013-Ohio-2111, 2013 WL 2296318 (Ohio Ct. App. 10th Dist. Franklin County 2013) (denying application to expunge or seal felony and misdemeanor stalking convictions because menacing by stalking is an "offense of violence" as defined in RC 2901.01(A)(9) and excluded under RC 2953.36(C)).

[65]State v. LaSalle, 96 Ohio St. 3d 178, 2002-Ohio-4009, 772 N.E.2d 1172, 1172–1173 (2002).

Since the great majority of domestic violence offenses are charged as misdemeanors under RC 2919.25, and because the term "offense of violence" includes RC 2919.25,[66] it follows that those offenders who are convicted pursuant to RC 2919.25(A) and RC 2919.25(B) are subject to these restrictive provisions.[67]

For those offenders convicted under the threat provision of the criminal domestic violence statute, RC 2919.25(C), or for a violation of either a civil or criminal protection order,[68] a request may be made to seal their records.

Q & A: What is the procedure for sealing or expunging criminal records?

Before a record of conviction can be sealed, the court must determine whether the offender wishing to seal his/her records has been rehabilitated to the satisfaction of the court.[69] The court must weigh the interests of the offender in having the records sealed against the legitimate needs, if any, of the government to maintain those records.[70] The prosecutor may file objections and request that the court consider the reasons against granting the offender's application.[71]

If an offender's record is sealed, the court shall order all official records pertaining to the case sealed, including all index records.[72] The proceedings in the case shall be considered not to have occurred; and the conviction of the offender shall be sealed except that, upon a conviction of a subsequent offense, the sealed record of the prior conviction may be considered by the court in determining the sentence or other appropriate disposition.[73] In effect, even if the offender's records are sealed, the court may still consider the sealed record to increase the sentence to a felony on the offender's subsequent offense.

By way of public policy, it has been said that expungement or sealing of records is not suitable in domestic violence cases.[74] Sealing records of domestic violence perpetrators only serves to reduce the seriousness of the crime in the mind of the batterer. Additionally, "if a

[66]See RC 2901.01(A)(9)(a).

[67]See Cleveland v. Hang, 110 Ohio Misc. 2d 47, 743 N.E.2d 1004 (Mun. Ct. 2000); see also State v. Muqdady, 110 Ohio Misc. 2d 51, 744 N.E.2d 278 (Mun. Ct. 2000) (defendant raised question whether amendment to RC 2953.36 regarding prohibition against sealing records of violent misdemeanors is ex post factor law).

[68]See RC 2919.27(A).

[69]See RC 2953.32(C)(1)(c); State v. J.S., 2017-Ohio-7613, 97 N.E.3d 790 (Ohio Ct. App. 10th Dist. Franklin County 2017).

[70]See RC 2953.32(C)(1)(e). See State v. Radcliff, 142 Ohio St. 3d 78, 2015-Ohio-235, 28 N.E.3d 69 (2015) (discussing City of *Pepper Pike v. Doe* and the codification of the balancing test into RC 2953.52(B)(2)(d)).

[71]See RC 2953.32(C)(1)(d). See also State v. J.S., 2017-Ohio-7613, 97 N.E.3d 790 (Ohio Ct. App. 10th Dist. Franklin County 2017) (court reversed based on the highly hypothetical and speculative nature of the prosecutor's reasoning).

[72]See RC 2953.32(C)(2); Vaccaro v. Vaccaro, 425 Mass. 153, 680 N.E.2d 55 (1997) (discussion of expungement of name from a protection order record keeping data base).

[73]RC 2953.32(C)(2).

[74]See also State v. Tyler, 2002-Ohio-4300, 2002 WL 1934995 (Ohio Ct. App. 10th Dist. Franklin County 2002); Rieger v. Rieger, 165 Ohio App. 3d 454, 2006-Ohio-482, 847 N.E.2d 9 (2d Dist. Montgomery County 2006).

batterer's record is expunged, it may destroy the one means the public has of assessing the danger the offender presents to society and other potential victims."[75] That the offender has not committed another act of violence in the year after his/her conviction or the expiration of his/her probationary term does not necessarily mean that the batterer's violence has ceased. In most instances, a batterer will continue to batter multiple partners over time.[76]

By its recent amendment to the statute, the Ohio legislature has recognized that it is necessary to treat violence against intimate partners as seriously as other criminal behavior.

Q & A: Can a court expunge a CPO or seal the record of a CPO proceeding?[77]

It depends.[78] It is clear that the granting of a civil protection order is not a conviction or a criminal offense. No charges are filed, and if the CPO is granted, a respondent is not found guilty of a crime. The grant of a civil protection order is not the same as a conviction for the crime of domestic violence. Therefore, it is arguable that there is nothing to expunge or seal.[79] On the other hand, appellate courts have focused their legal reasoning on the statutory and judicial authority of a court to seal the record of a civil protection order proceeding and using a balancing test to weigh the interests of individual privacy

[75]Catherine F. Klein & Leslye E. Orloff, Providing Legal Protection for Battered Women: An Analysis of State Statutes and Case Law, 21 Hofstra L. Rev. 801, 1136 (1993).

[76]See Lenore E. Walker, Terrifying Love 72 (1989); see also Lenore E. Walker & Angela Browne, Gender and Victimization by Intimates, 53 J. Personality 177 (1985).

[77]See Text 12:23, HB 49, eff. 9/29/2017, newly enacted RC 3113.31 (G)(2) provides that "an order issued under this section, other than an ex parte order, refuses to grant a protection order, the court, on its own motion, shall order that the ex parte order issued under this section and all of the records pertaining to that ex parte order be expunged after either of the following occurs: a) the period of the notice of appeal from the order that refuses to grant a protection order has expired or b) the order that refuses to grant the protection order is appealed and an appellate court to which the last appeal of that order is taken affirms the order."

[78]See also Vaccaro v. Vaccaro, 425 Mass. 153, 680 N.E.2d 55 (1997) (court held that trial court had no statutory authority to direct expungement of husband's record from statewide domestic violence record-keeping system); Rieger v. Montgomery Cty. Clerk of Courts, 2009-Ohio-426, 2009 WL 242668 (Ohio Ct. App. 2d Dist. Montgomery County 2009); but see R.C. 2151.358(D); permitting the sealing of protection orders issued against juvenile respondents, pursuant to; but see RC 2151.358(D), permitting the sealing of protection orders issued against juvenile respondents; Text 20:24.

[79]See R.C. 2953.32(C)(2); see also Rieger v. Montgomery Cty. Clerk of Courts, 2009-Ohio-426, 2009 WL 242668 (Ohio Ct. App. 2d Dist. Montgomery County 2009) (holding that there was no compelling or extraordinary reason to justify sealing the consensual order); Vaccaro v. Vaccaro, 425 Mass. 153, 680 N.E.2d 55 (1997); but see P.E.S. v. K.L., 720 A.2d 487 (Pa. Super. Ct. 1998) (a victim filed for a protection order but failed to appear at the full hearing, and the trial court considered the case "open" in its computer system; the court expanded the concept of expungement to cases where a respondent seeks to protect his/her reputation; where the domestic violence petition was dismissed, there was no compelling reason to allow the record to stand, and all documents in the computer system identifying the matter were to be expunged; expungement of the documents was warranted given the potential harm to the respondent's livelihood and reputation, and given the fact that the petitioner failed to pursue the action for protection order)).

against legitimate government need to maintain the records.[80] In *Rieger v. Rieger*,[81] appellant agreed to be bound by the terms of a consent entry civil protection order. One year after its expiration, appellant sought to have the CPO sealed on the ground that Internet availability prevented him from obtaining a better job. The trial court denied his motion and he appealed.

While noting that the legislature was the proper vehicle to provide such a remedy, the court of appeals concluded that the trial court erred in finding that it required statutory authorization to seal records of a CPO proceeding. In applying the doctrine of judicial expungement[82] to a motion to seal the record of a CPO, the appellate court reversed and remanded the case to the trial court, instructing the lower court to engage in weighing the various interests involved to determine whether the circumstances were unusual and exceptional such that sealing the record was required.[83] On remand, the court of appeals again found that Rieger failed to demonstrate any direct connection between the CPO record and his alleged difficulty in finding employment.[84]

In *Schussheim v. Schussheim*,[85] respondent appealed the trial court's decision denying his motion to expunge and seal the record of an ex parte CPO issued by the trial court against him and later dismissed by the petitioner. The trial court found that respondent failed to present evidence that his employment had been directly affected or directly harmed by the record of the CPO and/or would be hindered or terminated under company policy as a result.

On appeal, respondent/appellant argued that the trial court had the authority to expunge and seal, both under the constitution and the Ohio Supreme Court's *Pepper Pike* decision.[86] The appellate court stressed that there is no statutory or judicial authority to expunge

[80]Bemis v. Oblak, 2006-Ohio-403, 2006 WL 234862, *2 (Ohio Ct. App. 2d Dist. Champaign County 2006) (holding that, under other circumstances, court may consider sealing pursuant to its common law powers to seal the records of a proceeding); Rieger v. Rieger, 165 Ohio App. 3d 454, 2006-Ohio-482, 847 N.E.2d 9 (2d Dist. Montgomery County 2006) (noting that the magistrate did not need statutory authority to seal the record of a CPO); but see dissenting opinion in Rieger (noting that, although the protection order was issued pursuant to RC 3113.31, "an allegation of domestic violence and a finding that domestic violence occurred are necessary predicates to the issuance of a protective order. And domestic violence is a criminal offense. Therefore, under the extraordinary-circumstances standard of Pepper Pike v. Doe, [66 Ohio St.2d 374, 421 NE2d 1303 (1981)] expungement of the protection order and sealing of the record of the proceeding in which it was issued may be proper." At 463).

[81]Rieger v. Rieger, 165 Ohio App. 3d 454, 2006-Ohio-482, 847 N.E.2d 9 (2d Dist. Montgomery County 2006).

[82]City of Pepper Pike v. Doe, 66 Ohio St. 2d 374, 20 Ohio Op. 3d 334, 421 N.E.2d 1303 (1981).

[83]Rieger v. Rieger, 165 Ohio App. 3d 454, ¶ 47, 2006-Ohio-482, 847 N.E.2d 9 (2d Dist. Montgomery County 2006).

[84]Rieger v. Rieger, 2007-Ohio-2366, 2007 WL 1430191 (Ohio Ct. App. 2d Dist. Montgomery County 2007).

[85]Schussheim v. Schussheim, 2012-Ohio-2573, 2012 WL 2087406 (Ohio Ct. App. 12th Dist. Warren County 2012), judgment rev'd, 137 Ohio St. 3d 133, 2013-Ohio-4529, 998 N.E.2d 446 (2013).

[86]City of Pepper Pike v. Doe, 66 Ohio St. 2d 374, 20 Ohio Op. 3d 334, 421 N.E.2d 1303 (1981). See State v. Vanzandt, 2013-Ohio-2290, 990 N.E.2d 692 (Ohio Ct. App.

and seal the records of a CPO,[87] and declined to extend the *Pepper Pike* holding (*Pepper Pike* dealt with whether a criminal defendant charged but not convicted had the right to judicial expungement) to include non-criminal cases or proceedings.[88]

Of significance is the dissenting opinion in *Schussheim*, in which Judge Piper noted that "[s]ociety does not condone violence in general and violence within the family unit is particularly disturbing. Therefore, ex parte proceedings make it easy and convenient for "victims" to present criminal domestic violence accusations. There is no denying that the stigma of such allegations can be damaging and onerous."[89]

The dissent then pointed out that while the majority opinion acknowledged the holding in *Pepper Pike* which established that a judge has the authority to expunge, absent statutory authority, once a balancing test is performed to determine whether the individual's privacy interest outweighs the government's legitimate need to maintain the records, it erroneously found that because *Pepper Pike* was a criminal proceeding, such judicial authority is not applicable to a civil proceeding.[90]

In finding that judicial expungement should apply, the dissenting judge concluded that the allegation in this case is one of domestic violence, which is a criminal accusation, regardless of whether the proceeding is labeled criminal, civil or quasi-criminal. Therefore, a judicial remedy springing from constitutional principles should be applicable to a CPO. "The accused in an ex parte civil protection order which is dismissed, or unsubstantiated, should at least have the due process of having his privacy interest weighed by the court, particularly where the allegations arose from a domestic quarrel where the parties subsequently divorced and are currently raising their children together and the party who originally initiated the ex parte proceedings supports the sealing of the records. The inherent authority of the trial court to administer justice should be permitted to operate, particularly where the legislature has failed to act."[91]

However, if a respondent violates the terms of a civil protection order issued pursuant to RC 3113.31, he or she may be charged with

1st Dist. Hamilton County 2013), judgment rev'd, 142 Ohio St. 3d 223, 2015-Ohio-236, 28 N.E.3d 1267 (2015) (discussing expungement and sealing of records and when a court may seal or unseal records).

[87]But see Rieger v. Rieger, 165 Ohio App. 3d 454, ¶ 47, 2006-Ohio-482, 847 N.E.2d 9 (2d Dist. Montgomery County 2006) (noting that the magistrate did not need statutory authority to seal the record of a CPO).

[88]Schussheim v. Schussheim, 2012-Ohio-2573, 2012 WL 2087406, *4 (Ohio Ct. App. 12th Dist. Warren County 2012), judgment rev'd, 137 Ohio St. 3d 133, 2013-Ohio-4529, 998 N.E.2d 446 (2013); see also R.C. 2953.32; R.C. 2953.52.

[89]Schussheim v. Schussheim, 2012-Ohio-2573, 2012 WL 2087406, *5 (Ohio Ct. App. 12th Dist. Warren County 2012), judgment rev'd, 137 Ohio St. 3d 133, 2013-Ohio-4529, 998 N.E.2d 446 (2013) (Piper,J., dissenting).

[90]Schussheim v. Schussheim, 2012-Ohio-2573, 2012 WL 2087406, *5 (Ohio Ct. App. 12th Dist. Warren County 2012), judgment rev'd, 137 Ohio St. 3d 133, 2013-Ohio-4529, 998 N.E.2d 446 (2013) (Piper,J., dissenting).

[91]Schussheim v. Schussheim, 2012-Ohio-2573, 2012 WL 2087406, *7 (Ohio Ct. App. 12th Dist. Warren County 2012), judgment rev'd, 137 Ohio St. 3d 133, 2013-Ohio-4529, 998 N.E.2d 446 (2013) (Piper,J., dissenting).

the crime of violating a protection order, a criminal offense under RC 2919.27. If convicted, RC 2953.32 may apply depending on the nature of the act and whether it is a first offense.

Subsequent to the appellate decision, appellant appealed the decision to the Supreme Court of Ohio. Of note is that no brief by appellee was filed. On October 16, 2013, the Supreme Court of Ohio issued an opinion.[92] Justice O'Donnell wrote the opinion for the majority which held that a "court has inherent authority to order expungement and sealing of records that relate to a dissolved civil protection order in an adult proceeding when 'unusual and exceptional circumstances' exist."[93] To determine whether "unusual and exceptional circumstances" exist that would grant a court the inherent authority to order the sealing and expungement of records would depend on a balancing test-whether the interest of the accused in his/her right to be free from unwarranted punishment outweighs the legitimate need of government to maintain the records. "Where there is no compelling state interest to retain the records, the expungement applicant is entitled to his remedy."[94] Of note is that the majority relied on the reasoning set forth in *Pepper Pike v. Doe* to support its decision.

The majority explained that the fact that the original complainant who petitioned for the CPO in the first instance moved to dissolve the CPO and provided an affidavit stating that she believed the expungement to be in the best interests of the minor children provided the "unusual and exceptional circumstances" in this case. Additionally, the Supreme Court stressed that the trial court, on remand, should consider that no related criminal charges were filed.

However, the Chief Justice issued a separate dissent in which she noted her concern for the majority's "disturbing judicial activism."[95] She reasoned that "[b]y asserting that there is no statute that precludes sealing of records in adult proceedings and therefore the court may rule to allow it, the majority fails to acknowledge the significance of the General Assembly's enactment of a comprehensive statutory scheme that permits the sealing of records related to CPOs but limits the applicability of the sealing provision to juvenile proceedings. If the legislature had wanted to afford adults the same sealing provision, it would have done so."[96]

The dissent also admonished the majority for expanding the holding in *Pepper Pike v. Doe*, noting that the case at hand was not a criminal case, a fact that distinguished it from *Pepper Pike*. While the right to expunge and seal, in *Pepper Pike*, was based on the fact that the case

[92]Schussheim v. Schussheim, 137 Ohio St. 3d 133, 2013-Ohio-4529, 998 N.E.2d 446 (2013).

[93]Schussheim v. Schussheim, 137 Ohio St. 3d 133, 2013-Ohio-4529, ¶ 14, 998 N.E.2d 446 (2013).

[94]Schussheim v. Schussheim, 137 Ohio St. 3d 133, 2013-Ohio-4529, ¶ 14, 998 N.E.2d 446 (2013).

[95]Schussheim v. Schussheim, 137 Ohio St. 3d 133, 2013-Ohio-4529, ¶ 18, 998 N.E.2d 446 (2013).

[96]Schussheim v. Schussheim, 137 Ohio St. 3d 133, 2013-Ohio-4529, ¶ 20, 998 N.E.2d 446 (2013).

arose from "a person's use of the court as a vindictive tool to harass,"[97] the contrary was true in *Schussheim*. In *Schussheim*, the fact that Henneman requested that the CPO be dismissed did not change the fact that she needed the CPO in the first instance. "And that she shortly thereafter notified the court that the CPO should be dissolved gives rise to the inference that she had responsibly, rather than vindictively, used the courts to secure only that protection that she needed for only that time that she needed it."[98] In that Henneman never claimed the domestic violence allegations were untrue when she requested that the CPO be dissolved, this case is ordinary and usual; there is nothing to indicate that this CPO was not issued for valid reasons.[99] A balancing test would demonstrate only that the underlying CPO was dismissed, there were no further acts of domestic violence and no criminal charges pending and Schussheim's fear that the record could inhibit future employment. Nothing in the record provides the requisite "unusual and exceptional circumstances."

Concluding that the majority extended *Pepper Pike*, redefined "unusual and exceptional circumstances" and legislated from the bench, the Chief Justice found that, with the limited information presented to the court, "we cannot know whether the majority's new law is good public policy for Ohio. As a practical matter, there is great potential for unintended consequences in the majority's decision. Most obviously, it increases the risk that respondents will use fear, intimidation, false promises, or threats to procure favorable affidavits from domestic violence victims."[100]

In *Henneman v. Schussheim*,[101] the case was remanded to the trial court to again address appellant's request of expungement. The trial court again denied the request finding that "there was a legitimate need of the government to maintain its record of the CPO, at least until the parties' minor child was emancipated."[102]

On appeal, the appellate court first noted that there had been another incident between father and daughter and that the mother, in light of the recent incident, no longer approved of the expungement. The court then found the evidence relevant despite no criminal charges being filed and reiterated the trial court's statement that the state had interest in maintaining the record where there were repeated acts of conduct.[103] In affirming the original judgment, the court held that "[w]hile we recognize that the Ohio Supreme Court

[97]Schussheim v. Schussheim, 137 Ohio St. 3d 133, 2013-Ohio-4529, ¶ 34, 998 N.E.2d 446 (2013).

[98]Schussheim v. Schussheim, 137 Ohio St. 3d 133, 2013-Ohio-4529, ¶ 42, 998 N.E.2d 446 (2013).

[99]Schussheim v. Schussheim, 137 Ohio St. 3d 133, 2013-Ohio-4529, ¶ 41, 998 N.E.2d 446 (2013).

[100]Schussheim v. Schussheim, 137 Ohio St. 3d 133, 2013-Ohio-4529, ¶ 60, 998 N.E.2d 446 (2013).

[101]Henneman v. Schussheim, 2015-Ohio-829, 2015 WL 1005340, *3 (Ohio Ct. App. 12th Dist. Warren County 2015).

[102]Henneman v. Schussheim, 2015-Ohio-829, 2015 WL 1005340, ¶ 7 (Ohio Ct. App. 12th Dist. Warren County 2015).

[103]Henneman v. Schussheim, 2015-Ohio-829, 2015 WL 1005340, ¶ 18 (Ohio Ct. App. 12th Dist. Warren County 2015).

has found that unusual and exceptional circumstances may exist in the present case, we cannot find that the trial court abused its discretion in determining that the state's interest in maintaining the record outweighs appellant's interest in 'clearing his name.' "[104]

Q & A: Has the Ohio General Assembly considered the issue of expunging or sealing protection orders?

Yes, effective September 2017, the Ohio legislature enacted legislation in all the protection order statutes, to wit: RC 3113.31, RC 2903.214, RC 2919.26 and RC 2903.213 directing a court to expunge certain protection order proceedings under certain circumstances.

According to RC 3113.31(G)(2), if a court refuses to grant a protection order, other than an ex parte protection order, the court, on its own motion, shall order that the ex parte order issued under this section and all of the records pertaining to that ex parte order be expunged after either of the following:

a) The period of the notice of appeal from the order that refuses to grant a protection order has expired.
b) The order that refuses to grant the protection order is appealed and an appellate court to which the last appeal of that order is taken affirms the order.

Of significance is that the legislature chose not to follow the test set forth in *Schussheim,* relative to "unusual and exceptional circumstances." It is noteworthy that the legislature spoke in terms of expungement, not sealing. Moreover, the language of the statute mandated that the court automatically expunge the records, rather than on a motion filed by either party.

In the criminal context, RC 2919.26(D)(2)(b) and RC 2903.213(D)(2)(b) both provide that if at a hearing under division (D)(2)(a) of this section, the court determines that an ex parte order should be revoked, the court on its own motion, shall revoke the ex parte CPO and order all of the records pertaining to that ex parte order expunged.

Finally, the juvenile protection order statute contains an apparent internal inconsistency between the provision in the newly enacted law mandating expungement and the law as written before the enactment of the new language which directs a court to seal such records.[105]

At the time of the publishing of this book, courts are in the process of developing procedures and processes for the expungement of these records.

§ 13:16 Probation for violations of protection orders

Ohio's contempt statute fails to address whether probation is

[104] Henneman v. Schussheim, 2015-Ohio-829, 2015 WL 1005340, ¶ 20 (Ohio Ct. App. 12th Dist. Warren County 2015); see also Ward v. Balsley, 2014-Ohio-4050, 2014 WL 4629607 (Ohio Ct. App. 5th Dist. Muskingum County 2014) (and its companion cases); Wetz v. Pomeroy, 2014-Ohio-5085, 2014 WL 6158910 (Ohio Ct. App. 12th Dist. Warren County 2014) (no unusual and exceptional circumstances to expunge and seal such that respondent's interest in clearing his name from "scandalous accusations" was outweighed by state's interest in maintaining public records, despite petitioner having filed and dismissed repeated petitions).

[105] See R.C. 2151.358; R.C. 2151.34(G)(2); R.C. 2151.34(6); Chapter 20:24.

contemplated when a defendant is found guilty of contempt.[1] The probation statute is silent as well.[2] Although probation is not a usual sanction for contempt, it is arguable that any sanction that may result in imprisonment should allow for probation. Courts, as an alternative to jail, often utilize probation when sentencing defendants for domestic violence[3] or for violations of protection orders that result in criminal prosecution under RC 2919.27.[4]

At the very least, attorneys should consider the types of probationary sanctions that have been imposed by courts for violations of protection orders so that specific examples may be articulated when considering an appropriate sentence for either a criminal or civil contempt.[5]

Q & A: What approaches have courts taken relative to probation?

Violations of protection orders have also encouraged creative probation techniques such as restricting the batterer's movement as it relates to the victim. For example, in *State v. Sutley*,[6] the court of appeals upheld the trial court's probation order which required the respondent to remain outside one section of his home county and to stay away from the victim and her family. The court held that such restrictions were both proper and reasonable as they were directly related to the crime and helped to insure the prevention of future criminal behavior.

Q & A: How does a court determine the conditions for probation?

RC 2951.02(C)(1)(a) sets forth the conditions for a misdemeanant's probation. Many of the conditions are mandatory, such as requiring a defendant to abide by the law.[7] A trial court has discretion to impose additional requirements[8] designed to promote the interests of doing justice, rehabilitate the offender and ensure the offender's good behavior.[9] In order for a condition to be validly imposed, the condition must (1) be reasonably related to rehabilitating the offender, (2) have some relationship to the crime for which the offender was convicted,

---

[Section 13:16]

[1]See RC Ch. 2705.

[2]See RC 2951.02.

[3]See RC 2919.25.

[4]See also RC 3113.31(L).

[5]See, e.g., State v. Sutley, 1990 WL 208811 (Ohio Ct. App. 11th Dist. Ashtabula County 1990); see also State v. Conkle, 129 Ohio App. 3d 177, 717 N.E.2d 411 (9th Dist. Wayne County 1998).

[6]State v. Sutley, 1990 WL 208811 (Ohio Ct. App. 11th Dist. Ashtabula County 1990).

[7]State v. Conkle, 129 Ohio App. 3d 177, 717 N.E.2d 411 (9th Dist. Wayne County 1998).

[8]See RC 2951.02(C)(1)(a).

[9]See City of North Olmsted v. Morgan, 1998 WL 518156, *5 (Ohio Ct. App. 8th Dist. Cuyahoga County 1998).

and (3) relate to conduct which is criminal or reasonably related to future criminality and serves the statutory ends of probation.[10]

Q & A: What are examples of valid and invalid conditions imposed on probation?[11]

Under the factors enumerated in *State v. Conkle*, a requirement that a defendant who has been convicted of domestic violence have no contact with his/her spouse/partner or that person's residence or property is a valid condition of probation. In *State v. Conkle*,[12] the Wayne County Court of Appeals determined that the conditions of probation imposed by the trial court met the test.[13]

Similarly, in *State v. Mueller*,[14] a condition of probation requiring the defendant to vacate the jointly owned house was permissible.[15]

Conversely, in *State v. Brillhart*,[16] the Wayne County Court of Appeals reversed the trial court's decision denying a defendant access to his children as a condition of probation for a domestic violence conviction.[17] The court reiterated the three factors for valid probation conditions and found that a "no contact" order with the children for a

---

[10]State v. Conkle, 129 Ohio App. 3d 177, 717 N.E.2d 411 (9th Dist. Wayne County 1998); see also State v. Jones, 49 Ohio St. 3d 51, 550 N.E.2d 469 (1990); see also City of North Olmsted v. Morgan, 1998 WL 518156 (Ohio Ct. App. 8th Dist. Cuyahoga County 1998); State v. Farmer, 2017-Ohio-2995, 2017 WL 2293048 (Ohio Ct. App. 5th Dist. Licking County 2017) (even though restrictions could not be reviewed, the disputed probationary restrictions included firearms prohibition, order to gain employment, receive a mental health evaluation, submit to random urinalysis, submit to warrantless searches of home and property and that he be subjected to a Single Validated Risk Assessment pursuant to RC 5120.114).

[11]See also text § 12:22 (discussing nexus between the restrictions in CPO and the conduct the court is trying to prevent when determining conditions for probation).

[12]State v. Conkle, 129 Ohio App. 3d 177, 717 N.E.2d 411 (9th Dist. Wayne County 1998).

[13]See also State v. Stewart, 1995 WL 136489 (Ohio Ct. App. 6th Dist. Wood County 1995) (affirming the trial court's ordering of the defendant into a batterers' program as a condition of probation, finding, in light of the *Conkle* factors, that successful participation in such a program was a valid condition of probation); City of North Olmsted v. Morgan, 1998 WL 518156 (Ohio Ct. App. 8th Dist. Cuyahoga County 1998) (relinquishing gun during probation after conviction for domestic violence is a valid condition of probation).

[14]State v. Mueller, 122 Ohio App. 3d 483, 702 N.E.2d 139 (1st Dist. Hamilton County 1997).

[15]See also State v. Kidwell, 1995 WL 68164 (Ohio Ct. App. 10th Dist. Franklin County 1995); State v. Sutley, 1990 WL 208811 (Ohio Ct. App. 11th Dist. Ashtabula County 1990).

[16]State v. Brillhart, 129 Ohio App. 3d 180, 717 N.E.2d 413 (9th Dist. Wayne County 1998); see also In re Miller, 82 Ohio App. 3d 81, 611 N.E.2d 451 (6th Dist. Lucas County 1992) (holding that prohibitions against going to specified place of business, associating with specified person, and dressing as a female were invalid conditions of juvenile's probation); State v. Krug, 89 Ohio App. 3d 595, 626 N.E.2d 984 (1st Dist. Hamilton County 1993) (holding that suspension of defendant's driving privileges was invalid condition of probation).

[17]See also Mabry v. Demery, 707 A.2d 49 (D.C. 1998) (holding that respondent could not be ordered to appear at a child support hearing as a condition of his probation); see also State v. Sturgeon, 138 Ohio App. 3d 882, 742 N.E.2d 730 (1st Dist. Hamilton County 2000) (four-year no contact order as condition of probation effectively terminated defendants' parental rights and is not constitutionally or statutorily permitted).

period of two years was too long.[18] In fact, the court stated that witnessing the abuse was insufficient to justify the imposition of a condition that would completely separate a father from his children for two years.[19] However, the court noted that a lesser time restriction placed on the visitation arrangement may be permissible.

Q & A: What is a no-contact order?

A no-contact order is an order directing one party to stay away from the other party. In domestic violence cases, no-contact orders are issued by a judge, most often in municipal court, when a criminal case is filed, when a motion for TPO is filed or at arraignment/first appearance or any point during the pendency of the case. It is also granted as a pretrial condition of release from jail or in lieu of a TPO.

Further, a no-contact order can be issued at sentencing as a term of probation and, if issued, will remain in effect until probation is completed or at such other time as the court requires.

A violation of a no-contact order is a probation violation but is not the basis of a motion to show cause or a criminal charge under RC 2919.27. If a violation is suspected, a call is made to either the offender's probation officer or to the court for further proceedings. If said violation is found to have occurred, the court may order the offender to jail to serve out the remainder of the sentence.

Unlike the domestic violence statutes, there is no statutory duty to arrest.[20] However, under RC 2951.08, a law enforcement officer may arrest a person in violation of a community control sanction without an arrest warrant. A no-contact order is one such a community control sanction of probation.

Under RC 2951.08(A), "[d]uring a period of community control, any peace officer may arrest the person under a community control sanction without a warrant, if the peace officer has reasonable ground to believe that the person has violated or is violating any of the following that is a condition of the person's community control sanction." Subsection (A) of the aforementioned statute also lists the types of conditions found in community control sanctions for which a violation would allow an arrest. These conditions include, for example:

(1) a condition that prohibits ownership, possession, or use of a firearm, deadly weapon, ammunition or dangerous ordnance;[21]

(2) a condition that prohibits the person form being within a specified structure or geographic area;[22]

(3) a condition that prohibits the person form contacting or communicating with any specified individual;[23]

---

[18]See People v. Jungers, 127 Cal. App. 4th 698, 25 Cal. Rptr. 3d 873 (4th Dist. 2005) (where court discussed invalid conditions of probation as being arbitrary, capricious, or exceeding the bounds of reason under the circumstances).

[19]State v. Brillhart, 129 Ohio App. 3d 180, 186, 717 N.E.2d 413 (9th Dist. Wayne County 1998).

[20]See R.C. 2935.03.

[21]R.C. 29051.08(A)(1).

[22]R.C. 2951.08(A)(2).

[23]R.C. 2951.08(A)(4).

(4) a condition that prohibit the person from associating with a specified individual.[24]

Since a no-contact order is a type of community control sanction, violators of these sanctions may be arrested without a warrant.

In fact, the Ohio Attorney General issued an opinion in September 2017 indicating that no contact orders are community control sanctions for which a police officer may arrest the offender, even if the alleged victim consents to the contact or communication and provided that the peace officer has reasonable ground to believe that the person has violated or is violating the condition of the person's community control sanction. The AG also defined "reasonable ground" as probable cause which may be found upon a peace officer's own observation of the violation of a condition of a community control sanction or based upon any other information received by a peace officer, including any other reasonably trustworthy information given to the officer by the alleged victim or witness.[25]

Q & A: Can a no-contact order be entered into LEADS for dissemination to NCIC?

Yes, so long as there is an actual form. Pursuant to NCIC, a no-contact order is included in the definition of a protection order for purposes of entry into NCIC. It meets the criteria as it is "an injunction or restraining order or any other order issued by a civil or criminal court for the purpose of preventing violence or contact or communication with, or physical proximity to another person."[26] As of the date of the book release, the Supreme Court of Ohio is considering the development of forms for this purpose.

Q & A: What happens after the officer makes the arrest?

Within three business days after making an arrest under this section, the arresting field officer, probation officer, or peace officer or the department or agency of the arresting officer shall notify the chief probation officer or the chief probation officer's designee that the person has been arrested. Within 30 days of being notified that a field officer, probation officer, or peace officer has made an arrest under this section, the chief probation officer or designee, or another probation officer designated by the chief probation officer, promptly shall bring the person who was arrested before the judge or magistrate before whom the cause was pending.[27]

Q & A: If an officer arrests the person in one jurisdiction and the sentencing court is in another, which law enforcement agency would hold him and which probation officer or court should be contacted?

Based on the reading of the statute, no matter where the violation occurred, the probation officer or department in the sentencing court should be informed that the offender is being held in the other jurisdiction. As soon as practicable, a request should be made to the issuing court to pick up and transport the offender to a holding cell in the sentencing court's jurisdiction.

---

[24] R.C. 2951.08(A)(5).

[25] 2017 Ohio Op. Att'y Gen. No. 2017-031, 2017 WL 4466515.

[26] 18 U.S.C.A. § 2266.

[27] See R.C. 2951.08(B).

§ 13:17 Victim impact statement

A victim impact statement is a statement made before sentencing which is read during sentencing in a criminal trial to inform the court of the impact the offense or violation had on the victim and the family or household members.[1] Under RC 2947.051(A), victim impact statements are required in all cases in which a person is convicted of or pleads guilty to a felony offense.[2] The court shall consider the victim impact statement in determining the sentence to be imposed on the offender.[3] RC 2947.051(B) requires the victim impact statement to include statements that refer to economic loss, physical injury, the seriousness and permanence of that injury,[4] any change in the victim's personal welfare or familial relationships, and any psychological impact experienced by the victim or the victim's family.[5]

Pursuant to R.C. 2930.13, a victim impact statement may include the following: (1) an explanation of the nature and extent of any physical, psychological, or emotional harm suffered by the victim as a result of the crime; (2) an explanation of the extent of any property damage or other economic loss suffered by the victim as a result of that crime; (3) an opinion regarding the extent to which, if any, the victim needs restitution for harm caused by the defendant as a result of that crime; (4) the victim's recommendation for an appropriate sanction or disposition for the defendant or alleged juvenile offender regarding that crime or specified delinquent act.[6]

The purpose of the victim impact statement is best expressed in the 1982 Report for the President's Task Force on Victims of Crime:

> Judges should allow for, and give appropriate weight to, input at sentenc-

---

[Section 13:17]

[1]See State v. Ridenour, 128 Ohio App. 3d 134, 713 N.E.2d 1140 (9th Dist. Summit County 1998); State v. Williams, 2002-Ohio-2941, 2002 WL 1370436 (Ohio Ct. App. 2d Dist. Greene County 2002); State v. Thompson, 2003-Ohio-4432, 2003 WL 21995316 (Ohio Ct. App. 2d Dist. Champaign County 2003); see also Payne v. Tennessee, 501 U.S. 808, 821, 111 S. Ct. 2597, 115 L. Ed. 2d 720 (1991); State v. Fautenberry, 72 Ohio St. 3d 435, 1995-Ohio-209, 650 N.E.2d 878 (1995); State v. Fraley, 1999 WL 188156 (Ohio Ct. App. 12th Dist. Preble County 1999).

[2]See also R.C. 2930.14; State v. Hendking, 2000 WL 126733 (Ohio Ct. App. 8th Dist. Cuyahoga County 2000) (determining that victim impact statement may not be necessary where court has information about effect of the crime on the victim and where the victim impact statement added little to the proceedings); see also State v. Thompson, 1991 WL 299492 (Ohio Ct. App. 5th Dist. Holmes County 1991); State v. Sturgeon, 138 Ohio App. 3d 882, 742 N.E.2d 730 (1st Dist. Hamilton County 2000) concurring opinion.

[3]RC 2947.051(A); see also RC 2929.13(B); see also State v. Clevenger, 2007-Ohio-7034, 2007 WL 4554023 (Ohio Ct. App. 9th Dist. Lorain County 2007) (holding that a reliance on victim impact statement as a basis for imposing a prison term is not an abuse of discretion); State v. Henry, 2015-Ohio-4145, 2015 WL 5813874 (Ohio Ct. App. 7th Dist. Belmont County 2015).

[4]State v. Ayers, 1997 WL 271486 (Ohio Ct. App. 2d Dist. Montgomery County 1997).

[5]See In re Contempt of Morris, 110 Ohio App. 3d 475, 674 N.E.2d 761 (8th Dist. Cuyahoga County 1996); see also State v. Williams, 2002-Ohio-2941, 2002 WL 1370436 (Ohio Ct. App. 2d Dist. Greene County 2002); State v. Thompson, 2003-Ohio-4432, 2003 WL 21995316 (Ohio Ct. App. 2d Dist. Champaign County 2003).

[6]N. Olmsted v. Rieck, 2011-Ohio-1557, 2011 WL 1167755 (Ohio Ct. App. 8th Dist. Cuyahoga County 2011).

ing for victims of violent crime. . . . Every victim must be allowed to speak at the time of sentencing. The victim, no less than the defendant, comes to court seeking justice. . . . Defendants speak and are spoken for often at great length, before sentence is imposed. It is outrageous that the system should contend it is too busy to hear from the victim.[7]

Q & A: When should a court consider the use of a victim impact statement?

Public policy dictates that a victim impact statement should, at the very least, be encouraged for use in the sentencing phase of a civil protection order violation where the respondent is criminally prosecuted under RC 2919.27. Victim impact statements should especially be considered where the violation caused serious physical injury to the victim or another family member or where the offender has previously been convicted of violating a protection order under RC 2919. 27(B)(1)(b).

Although the victim impact statement is not specifically required in a misdemeanor offense, many municipal courts have, in practice, received these statements for use in determining the offender's sentence in domestic violence cases.[8]

In fact, this approach is sanctioned by the National Council of Juvenile and Family Court Judges and adopted by their Model Code. The Model Code states that victims should be present at the time of sentencing and address the court. Specifically, Section 214 of the Model Code provides that a victim of domestic violence is entitled to provide the court with a victim impact statement, victim opinion statement, and an assessment of the risk of further harm. The rationale for this is that victims of domestic violence are entitled to all the rights accorded other victims of violent crime.[9]

Because Ohio case law likens the rights of defendants in criminal contempt cases to those of defendants in other criminal cases,[10] it is equally logical to compare the rights of victims in criminal contempt cases with those of victims in other criminal cases. Applying the rationale expressed by the National Council of Juvenile and Family Court Judges to contempt cases, victims in criminal contempt cases should be permitted the same opportunity to provide the court with a victim impact statement.

Q & A: If a victim impact statement is submitted to the court, what due process rights are accorded to the defendant or respondent?

If a victim impact statement is presented to the court, certain due process rights are accorded to the defendant. The court must balance the dictates of due process with the legitimate interests of the victim. Unfortunately, the Ohio statute does not address the procedure by which victims may be heard. The due process rights of the defendant

---

[7]1982 Report for the President's Task Force on Victims of Crime #252.

[8]For example, certain judges in the Cleveland Municipal Court have adopted this method.

[9]National Council of Juvenile and Family Court Judges, Family Violence: A Model State Code, Section 214, Commentary at 14 (1994).

[10]See, e.g., Brown v. Executive 200, Inc., 64 Ohio St. 2d 250, 18 Ohio Op. 3d 446, 416 N.E.2d 610 (1980).

are not violated by the use of the impact statement so long as the statements are made under oath. The defendant must have notice that the witness offering the impact statement will be testifying, or will be available, so that the defendant may cross-examine the victim.[11] However, it should be cautioned that oath-taking and cross-examination of the victim regarding the impact statement may give the victim the feeling that he/she is on trial and, in effect, nullify the reasons for permitting the statement. To avoid this undesirable result, the court might frame the victim's statement by requesting remarks on the impact of the crime on the victim's life and the victim's perspective on the need for restitution. However, the respondent is not entitled to have his victim speak at his sentencing on a charge of domestic violence.[12]

Q & A: How do victim impact statements aid the court in sentencing respondents for civil protection order violations?[13]

Somehow, the impact of the violation on the victim of domestic violence should be made known to the court and should be accorded significant weight. In most cases, there are no witnesses to the crime. The impact statement can articulate the abuse suffered by the victim at the hands of the batterer and the impact of that abuse on the victim. Additionally, it may also educate the court about the victim's financial circumstances. Judges will need information relative to the economic consequences of sentencing a particular respondent so that the victim will not become economically disadvantaged. Judges may structure sentences so that a respondent may be granted work release or weekend incarceration to continue to provide the economic support on which many victims are dependent.

Even in cases where a victim impact statement is not required by statute or utilized by a court, the court has always had latitude to consider a wide range of sentencing options.[14] In sentencing a defendant or respondent, both the guilt of the defendant and the harm caused by his/her acts are an important factor in the exercise of the court's sentencing discretion. The harm caused by the crime of domestic violence or the violation of the civil protection order relates to the seriousness of the offense and provides a standard for determining the magnitude of the sentence.

Absent the statutory authority to submit victim impact statements to the courts, a court should order the department of probation to make inquiries and prepare presentence investigation reports concerning the defendant/respondent.[15] Many of the same factors set forth in RC 2947.051(B) should be noted in the presentence investigation

[11]State v. Kinley, 1993 WL 224496 (Ohio Ct. App. 2d Dist. Clark County 1993), judgment aff'd, 72 Ohio St. 3d 491, 1995-Ohio-279, 651 N.E.2d 419 (1995), reh'g granted, opinion recalled, 75 Ohio St. 3d 1442, 663 N.E.2d 324 (1996).

[12]State v. Williams, 2002-Ohio-2941, 2002 WL 1370436 (Ohio Ct. App. 2d Dist. Greene County 2002).

[13]See also Text § 13:15, Court enforcement of civil protection orders—Sentencing civil protection order violators; generally.

[14]See, e.g., State v. Trubee, 2005-Ohio-552, 2005 WL 335833, *12 (Ohio Ct. App. 3d Dist. Marion County 2005) (abrogated by, State v. Foster, 109 Ohio St. 3d 1, 2006-Ohio-856, 845 N.E.2d 470 (2006)).

[15]Crim.R. 32.2; see also RC 2951.02.

report. This information is crucial in administering appropriate sentences that take into account the impact of the crime on a particular victim.

Q & A: Does a court's failure to grant a victim permission to make a victim impact statement afford the defendant any grounds for relief?

This issue was addressed by the Summit County Court of Appeals in *State v. Ridenour*.[16] In that case, the defendant was convicted for domestic violence. At sentencing, the defendant's counsel indicated that the victim wished to address the court.[17] Since the court had previously received a victim impact statement as part of the presentence report, the trial court denied the request. The defendant appealed, stating that the court had abused its discretion in failing to allow the victim to address the court at sentencing.

Relying on RC 2930.14(A), the defendant argued that the victim had a mandatory right to make a statement before sentencing. The appellate court noted that "[t]he victim impact statement 'is not for the benefit of the defendant but rather to be sure the court considers the impact of causing physical harm upon the victim when the court imposes . . . sentence.' "[18] The Summit County Court of Appeals held that "[t]he failure of a trial court to allow a victim impact statement does not afford a defendant any grounds for relief."[19]

Of importance in this case is that the defendant's counsel requested that the victim be allowed to make a statement. In most cases, it is the prosecutor who makes the request on behalf of the victim. It is possible that the court denied the request solely because it was made by defendant's counsel and was likely to be conciliatory toward the defendant.

If courts consider victim impact statements in civil protection order hearings or in hearings on violations of civil protection orders, the legal issues raised in *Ridenour* may be applied to the civil arena. Where the abuse inflicted on a victim is severe, a court may be more likely to allow a victim to make a statement.

---

[16]State v. Ridenour, 128 Ohio App. 3d 134, 713 N.E.2d 1140 (9th Dist. Summit County 1998); see also State v. Chandler, 1998 WL 791826 (Ohio Ct. App. 9th Dist. Summit County 1998); State v. Williams, 2002-Ohio-2941, 2002 WL 1370436 (Ohio Ct. App. 2d Dist. Greene County 2002); Lewis v. Office of Prosecuting Atty. of Columbiana Cty., 2006-Ohio-4685, 2006 WL 2590561, *3 (Ohio Ct. App. 7th Dist. Columbiana County 2006) (Court also stated that Ridenior did not hold that RC 2930.01 et seq. provides a cause of action for victims of domestic violence.).

[17]See City of Cleveland v. Serrano, 1999 WL 1024214 (Ohio Ct. App. 8th Dist. Cuyahoga County 1999) (trial court judge heard the victim's concerns as well as the opinion of the victim advocate).

[18]State v. Ridenour, 128 Ohio App. 3d 134, 713 N.E.2d 1140 (9th Dist. Summit County 1998) (quoting State v. Johnson, 1985 WL 4654, *9 (Ohio Ct. App. 9th Dist. Summit County 1985)); State v. Williams, 2002-Ohio-2941, 2002 WL 1370436 (Ohio Ct. App. 2d Dist. Greene County 2002).

[19]State v. Ridenour, 128 Ohio App. 3d 134, 713 N.E.2d 1140 (9th Dist. Summit County 1998); see also RC 2930.19(C). See also State v. Flekel, 2002-Ohio-2963, 2002 WL 1307430 (Ohio Ct. App. 8th Dist. Cuyahoga County 2002) (holding that the absence of a victim impact statement or records regarding victim's injuries in presentence report did not prejudice defendant and would not have mitigated sentence).

§ 13:18 Ohio Domestic Violence Network; victim impact statement; form[1]

OHIO DOMESTIC VIOLENCE NETWORK

◊ Victim Impact Statement

(adapted from the National Victim Center's Victim Impact Statement)

If you need more space to answer any of the following questions, please feel free to use as much paper as you need, and simply attach those sheets to this impact statement.

Your Name____

Defendant's Name____________________________________

1. How has this crime affected you and those close to you? Please feel free to discuss your feelings about what has happened and how it has affected your general well being. Has this crime affected your relationship with any family members, friends, co-workers, and other people? As a result of this crime, if you or others close to you have sought any type of victim services, such as counseling by either a licensed professional, member of the clergy, or a community-sponsored support group, you may wish to mention this.

2. What physical injuries or symptoms have you or others close to you suffered as a result of this crime? You may want to write about how long the injuries lasted, how long they are expected to last, and if you sought medical treatment for these injuries. You may also want to discuss what changes you have made in your life as a result of these injuries.

3. Has this crime affected your ability to perform your work, make a living, run a household, go to school or enjoy any other activities you previously performed or enjoyed? If so, please explain how these activities have been affected by this crime.

INFORMATION IS POWER!

[Section 13:18]

[1]This form is reprinted with permission from the Ohio Domestic Violence Network.

Chapter 14

Police Enforcement of Protection Orders and Other Relevant Issues

§ 14:1 Introduction

Law enforcement officials are the "gatekeepers" in domestic violence actions. They are often the first persons victims of domestic violence contact for protection from the abuse in their lives. Pursuant to Ohio law, law enforcement officials are mandated to enforce civil and criminal protection orders.[1] Unfortunately, an inadequate response from law enforcement renders a civil protection order useless. Worse, it grants undesirable power to the abuser who begins to believe that the justice system is either unable or unwilling to hold him/her responsible for his/her actions.

Consistent police enforcement of civil protection orders is critical to

---

[Section 14:1]

[1]RC 3113.31(F)(1), RC 3113.31(F)(3); see also RC 2919.26(G)(1).

an orderly protection order process. If law enforcement officials fail to regularly enforce civil protection orders in a uniform manner, the process becomes flawed. "In the absence of aggressive law enforcement, judges are rendered virtually powerless to effectively administer and uphold the law in protection order cases."[2]

§ 14:2 Ohio statutory procedure

Ohio's civil and criminal protection order statute is replete with procedural mandates for law enforcement.[1] Each of these procedures is designed to both enable victims to secure adequate protection from their abusers and enhance law enforcement response.

For example, RC 3113.31(F)(1) specifically directs that "[a] copy of any protection order, or consent agreement, that is issued or approved . . . shall be issued by the court . . . to all law enforcement agencies that have jurisdiction to enforce the order or agreement." Both the ex parte civil protection order as well as the order issued after the full hearing are to be forwarded to the local law enforcement agency with the power to enforce the order.[2] In most jurisdictions, copies of the protection order are forwarded to the agency in the geographic area in which the petitioner resides or is employed and to those agencies which the petitioner regularly visits.

The importance of this provision cannot be overstated. Once a local law enforcement agency receives a copy of a protection order, there is no doubt that the agency and its officers are on notice that a civil protection order is in effect for a named individual.[3] The police officers of the local enforcement agency are then required to enforce the protection order in accordance with its terms. A failure to enforce the order may subject the law enforcement official and agency to sanctions[4] or potential civil liability.[5]

Q & A: What is the procedure by which a local law enforcement agency receives a copy of a protection order?

It depends on the county and whether the order is the ex parte protection order or the protection order issued after the full hearing. RC 3113.31 states only that a copy of a protection order or consent agreement shall be issued by a court to all law enforcement agencies

---

[2]Peter Finn & Sarah Colson, National Institute of Justice, Civil Protection Orders: Legislation, Current Court Practice and Enforcement 4, 58 (1990).

[Section 14:2]

[1]RC 3113.31(F)(1) to RC 3113.31(F)(3), RC 3113.31(N), RC 2919.26(G)(1), RC 2919.26(G)(4).

[2]See RC 3113.31(F)(1); see also RC 2935.03(A), RC 2935.03(B), RC 2919.26(G)(1).

[3]See Campbell v. Campbell, 294 N.J. Super. 18, 22, 682 A.2d 272 (Law Div. 1996) ("Whether or not the police officers had actual knowledge of the restraining order is irrelevant. Inherent in the mandate of the statute that a restraining order must be sent to the police department is the proposition that the police are charged with knowledge of that order.").

[4]RC 2935.032(A)(3).

[5]See Text § 14:7, Police liability for failing to protect victims of domestic violence—Introduction, for a discussion. See also Campbell v. Campbell, 294 N.J. Super. 18, 682 A.2d 272 (Law Div. 1996).

that have jurisdiction to enforce the order or agreement.[6] A 10-A Form is also required to be provided to law enforcement for entry into the National Crime Information Center (NCIC) database.[7]

A survey of Ohio's 88 counties demonstrates that law enforcement agencies receive copies of civil protection orders by various methods. There is little consistency regarding procedure. In some counties, local rules dictate procedure. In other counties, local practice determines policy.

Many domestic relations courts direct the county sheriff's department to personally serve the local law enforcement agency with a copy of the protection order. In other jurisdictions, court personnel or clerks of courts mail copies of protection orders to the local law enforcement agencies. Since RC 3113.31(F)(1)[8] fails to definitively state whether law enforcement agencies are to be served or noticed,[9] it is no wonder that police departments receive copies of protection orders by different methods.

For purposes of procedure, some court jurisdictions also differentiate between the ex parte order and the order issued after the full hearing. For example, Cuyahoga County Domestic Relations Court Local Rule 26(B)(4) provides that the ex parte order, as well as the order resulting from the full hearing, be served on the appropriate local law enforcement agency in accordance with RC 3113.31(F)(1).

However, the local rule does not specifically address how the local law enforcement agency is to receive copies of the orders. Since the local rule uses the term "served," it is arguable that, at least in Cuyahoga County, the county sheriff is to personally serve the local police department. On the other hand, court practice suggests otherwise. While the ex parte protection order is personally served, the order issued after the full hearing is mailed to a respondent by either certified or ordinary mail.

Court practice reveals that a petitioner's attorney is responsible to facilitate or effectuate service of the ex parte order in many counties.[10] Absent specific written procedure to effectuate service of process, the county sheriff's department usually serves the local law enforcement agency with the ex parte order by personal service pursuant to service instructions supplied by the petitioner's attorney. Additionally, in some local police jurisdictions, an identification form detailing specific

[6]RC 3113.31(F)(1).

[7]Sup.R. 10, Sup.R. Form 10-A. (Note that the requirement is based on an unwritten policy between The Ohio Highway Patrol that administers LEADS, courts and local law enforcement agencies and the mandates of the Supreme Court Rule of Superintendence.)

[8]See also RC 2919.26(G)(1).

[9]See also Text § 11:11, Ex parte protection orders—Service and notice provisions, Text § 13:3, Court enforcement of civil protection orders—Criminal prosecution.

[10]See also Neb. Op. Att'y Gen. No. 00018 (3-6-00), 2000 WL 263818 (determining that law enforcement officers could legally detain person for reasonable amount of time (45 to 60 minutes) in order to effectuate service of protection order; reasoning that, if unserved order is found in computer database, decision to detain alleged perpetrator in order to notify process server is reasonable; relying on fact of potential future violence if order not served and difficulty of relocating respondent who is released without being served).

identifying characteristics of the respondent is served along with the order.[11] An attorney always has the option of appointing a private process server pursuant to Civil Rule 4.1(B). Where it is known that the respondent may be difficult to serve, the attorney may request the appointment of a private process server to accomplish service over both the respondent and the local law enforcement agency.

Generally, so long as the local law enforcement agency receives a copy of the order, it does not matter how this mandate is effected. The only caveat is that the ex parte order be received by the police without delay because the turnaround time for the full hearing is only seven or ten court days.[12]

There is little consistency regarding how the protection order that results from the full hearing is forwarded to the local law enforcement agency. Some attorneys utilize the sheriff's department to serve a copy of the order; others manually deliver a copy to the local police department or request that the client do so. Others mail a copy to the police department themselves and still others do nothing at all.

For example, in Franklin County, the attorney for the petitioner is responsible for hand delivering a copy of all civil protection orders to the central police station and the county sheriff's department. The client is told to obtain several certified copies of the protection order in order to hand deliver copies to surrounding police districts. In Cuyahoga County, local rule directs the petitioner or counsel to serve a copy of any protection order issued after the full hearing on the local law enforcement agency.[13]

In other jurisdictions, the clerks of court mail a copy of the order to the local police department. Several jurisdictions rely on the domestic relations court personnel to mail copies of the protection orders to the local law enforcement agency.[14]

Because there are few specific written procedures around the state that detail the manner of service, the vehicle for service, or the time frame in which the local law enforcement agency must be served, in many instances the law enforcement agency fails to receive a copy of the final protection order. Without a copy of the final protection order, law enforcement agencies may be without the crucial knowledge necessary to enhance victim safety. They may not know which terms to enforce. They may not know whether the terms of the ex parte order have been modified or whether the order has been terminated by the court. Since the duration of a civil protection order is now five years,[15] this knowledge is essential for efficient and accurate enforcement.

Q & A: May law enforcement officers legally detain an individual for any period of time in order to effect service of the protection order upon that individual?

There is no case law on point in this state. However, the Nebraska

[11]The Cleveland Police Department requires an identification form.

[12]RC 3113.31(D)(2)(a).

[13]See Cuy. D.R. R. 26(B)(4).

[14]Noble and Washington counties are among the jurisdictions utilizing this approach.

[15]RC 3113.31(E)(3)(a).

Attorney General recently issued an opinion dealing with this issue.[16] In its request, the captain of the Douglas County Sheriff's Department indicated that many respondents need to be served with protection orders. Since the respondent may be at the scene of the incident when the police arrive, the police are in a position to serve the protection order.

In its opinion, the Nebraska Attorney General determined that the nature of domestic violence and the potential for future violence makes service of a protection order a matter of immediacy. "There is compelling public policy supporting the authorization of law enforcement officers to detain an individual who is the respondent to an unserved protection order. This legitimate concern for the safety of the potential victim of domestic violence would appear to provide further support for the detention of an individual. . ."[17]

The Attorney General also noted that if the individual subject to an unserved protection order is released before service is perfected, he or she is aware of the order and may attempt to avoid service in the future. Forty-five minutes to an hour is a reasonable period of time to detain a respondent for this purpose.

Q & A: Can the law enforcement agency ever be liable for failing to enforce the protection order or consent agreement?[18]

Where the statute authorizes that a law enforcement agency receive a copy of a protection order or consent agreement,[19] a civil rights action against the officer and the law enforcement agency may lie for a failure to protect a victim of domestic violence. If the law enforcement agency does, in fact, receive a copy of the order, it is put on notice regarding the existence and terms of the order. A failure to enforce the order may result in liability.[20]

For example, in *Campbell v. Campbell*,[21] a New Jersey court held that a restraining order and the knowledge of its existence create a special relationship between the police and the protected party. The New Jersey law mandates that police be sent copies of restraining orders. Once received, the police have knowledge of the order restraining a particular individual. Therefore, where an officer failed to make an arrest where there was probable cause to suspect that the order was being violated, the officer could not claim immunity.[22]

However, the converse may also be true. Should a law enforcement official fail to receive a copy of the protection order issued after the

[16]Neb. Op. Att'y Gen. 00018 (3-9-00), 2000 WL 263818.

[17]Neb. Op. Att'y Gen. 00018 (3-9-00), 2000 WL 263818, at *3.

[18]See text §§ 14:8 to 14:14.

[19]RC 3113.31(F)(1).

[20]See Text § 14:8 to § 14:14; see also R.C. 737.11 which provides that police officers have the duty to enforce all protection orders issued pursuant to R.C. 2903.213 or 2903.214.

[21]Campbell v. Campbell, 294 N.J. Super. 18, 682 A.2d 272 (Law Div. 1996).

[22]But see Semple v. City of Moundsville, 963 F. Supp. 1416 (N.D. W. Va. 1997), judgment aff'd, 195 F.3d 708 (4th Cir. 1999) (finding that the existence of a protection order did not give rise to a special relationship such that the failure to protect was actionable). See also Town of Castle Rock, Colo. v. Gonzales, 545 U.S. 748, 125 S. Ct. 2796, 162 L. Ed. 2d 658 (2005).

full hearing, the agency and its officials may argue that they are not required to enforce the order. Officers may use this argument to limit liability in civil rights actions.[23]

Q & A: Must a law enforcement agency actually receive a copy of the protection order to be able to enforce the order?

Absolutely not. Ohio's domestic violence statute has always contemplated that civil and criminal protection orders were enforceable by more than one law enforcement agency.[24] Historically, local law enforcement agencies had interpreted the statute to mean that civil protection orders are enforceable only within the jurisdictional boundaries of the law enforcement agency or the county court. Some jurisdictions further limited the enforcement potential of the civil protection order by requiring that the local police department receive an actual copy of the order before it can be enforced.

In 1994, the enforcement capability of civil protection orders was again clarified.[25] The jurisdiction of the civil protection order for purposes of police enforcement was established as statewide. All law enforcement agencies were specifically authorized to enforce protection orders issued by a court in another county of Ohio.[26] A registration procedure was also adopted in order to provide notice of the order to judicial and law enforcement officials in other counties.[27]

Additionally, in 1994, the United States Congress enacted the federal Violence Against Women Act, which provides for nationwide enforcement of both civil and criminal protection orders.[28] VAWA requires all state and indian tribal courts to give full faith and credit to an order of protection issued by any other state or tribal court and requires that the order be enforced as if it was the order of the enforcing state or tribe.[29]

Nothing in the statutory language contained in either RC 3113.31(F)(1) or RC 3113.31(F)(3) requires that an actual copy of the order be delivered to the law enforcement agency prior to police enforcement of a civil protection order.[30] On the contrary, both RC 3113.31(F)(1) and RC 3113.31(F)(3) suggest that law enforcement agencies with jurisdiction to enforce the order have access to a copy of the order but that enforcement of the order is not contingent on an actual copy of the order being delivered to the law enforcement agency.

RC 3113.31(F)(1) is limited in scope and apparently applies only to those local law enforcement agencies to which a copy of the order can easily be delivered. It is noteworthy that RC 3113.31 does not provide a specific time limitation within which a law enforcement agency must receive a copy of a protection order. The absence of any time frame validates the limited scope of RC 3113.31(F)(1) and strengthens

[23]But see the following Q & A: for a more thorough discussion.

[24]See RC 3113.31(F)(1); see also RC 2919.26(G)(1).

[25]See 1994 H.B. 335, eff. 12-9-94.

[26]RC 3113.31(F)(3); see also RC 2919.26(G)(3) and RC 2919.26(G)(4).

[27]See RC 3113.31(N); see also RC 2919.26(G)(3) referring to RC 3113.31(N).

[28]18 U.S.C.A. § 2266.

[29]See 18 U.S.C.A. § 2265(a).

[30]See also RC 2919.26(G)(1) and (G)(4).

the assertion that police enforcement is not contingent on the receipt of an actual copy of the order.[31]

At the same time, RC 3113.31(F)(3)[32] is clearly more expansive in its directives and far-reaching in its consequences. It instructs all law enforcement agencies to enforce all protection orders issued by the courts in Ohio. This mandate exists whether or not a petitioner has registered the protection order in a county in which the officer's agency has jurisdiction.[33]

That the statute permits a law enforcement agency to enforce an order issued by any county in Ohio without mandating that the order be registered in the other county[34] implies that an actual copy of the order is not a prerequisite to enforcement. The statutory language creates an inference that every law enforcement official is charged with at least constructive knowledge of the existence of any civil protection order issued by any court in this state. This is especially true now that all protection orders are required to be entered into the National Crime Information Center (NCIC) database.[35]

These statutory provisions qualify the jurisdictional boundaries for the enforcement of a civil protection order. Local law enforcement officials are expected to enforce a civil protection order according to its terms.[36] The statute is replete with references reflecting this sentiment. For example, RC 3113.31(F)(3) specifically requires that any officer of a law enforcement agency shall enforce a protection order issued or consent agreement approved in this state in accordance with the provisions of the order or agreement, including removing the respondent from the premises, if appropriate.[37] This is the directive whether or not the petitioner has registered the order in the county in which the officer's agency has jurisdiction.[38]

The introduction of Form 10-A[39] as a way to supply relevant protection order information to a database which can then be accessed by law enforcement agencies within the state and around the country bolsters the position that law enforcement officials are obligated to enforce a civil protection order even though they have not received an

[31]See also Collins v. Clancy, 2014 WL 1653103 (S.D. Ohio 2014) (noting that a police officer need only confirm the existence and specifics of the CPO by way of the computer system which is standard procedure).

[32]See also RC 2919.26(G)(4).

[33]RC 3113.31(F)(3).

[34]See RC 3113.31(F)(3), RC 3113.31(N).

[35]See also David M. Fine, The Violence Against Women Act of 1994: The Proper Federal Role in Policing Domestic Violence, 84 Cornell L. Rev. 252, 294 (1998).

[36]See Text § 11:11, Ex parte protection orders—Service and notice provisions, Text § 12:4, Full hearing—Continuances; Text § 13:8, Enforcement of civil protection orders; procedures for initiating contempt motions.

[37]See Md. Op. Att'y Gen. 99-012 (8-10-99), 1999 WL 636670 (finding that trial court in domestic relations action may have authority to order law enforcement officers to return a minor child to custodial parent by use of force and noting that force must be reasonable under specific circumstances of case and that officer would be immune from liability under 42 U.S.C.A. § 1983).

[38]See RC 3113.31(F)(3); see also RC 3113.31(N); RC 2919.26(G)(4).

[39]Protection Order Notice to National Crime Information Center (NCIC).

actual copy of the order.[40] The National Crime Information Center (NCIC) database provides police officers with an effective method of obtaining information without a copy of the order.

However, entering this information into the NCIC database only provides an officer with notice that a civil protection order was, at some time, in existence. Although a presumption is created that the protection order is still in effect, an officer of a law enforcement agency may need to inquire further to determine whether the protection order is valid and should be enforced.[41]

Q & A: Does Ohio's domestic violence statute offer guidance to police officers regarding methods of enforcing protection orders?

There are two specific statutory provisions that suggest that arrest of an individual suspected of violating a protection order is the desired method of police enforcement. RC 2935.03(B)(3)(b) provides the preferred method of police enforcement. If the police officer has reasonable grounds to believe that the offense of violating a protection order has been committed and reasonable cause to believe that a particular person is guilty of committing the offense, it is the preferred course of action in this state for the officer to arrest and detain that person pursuant to RC 2935.03(B)(1) until a warrant can be obtained.[42]

Additionally, RC 2935.032(F) indicates that a police officer who arrests a respondent on the basis of a protection order or consent agreement violation is immune from liability in a civil action for damages for injury, death, or loss to person or property that allegedly was caused by or related to the arrest for enforcing a protection order that appears to be valid "on its face."[43] The statutory intent is to enforce a protection order whether or not it can be independently verified and whether or not a copy of the order has previously been served on the officer's agency.

Q & A: What is the purpose of the National Crime Information Center?

The National Crime Information Center (NCIC) is a nationwide computerized information system dedicated to serving local, state, and federal criminal justice agencies by providing criminal information concerning certain individuals.[44] Recently, the Federal Bureau of Investigation established a new NCIC file for the entry, storage, and retrieval of civil and criminal protection orders. The FBI's objectives are to provide timely and accurate information to courts and police officers who need to verify orders, to notify law enforcement agencies nationwide of the existence and terms of protection orders, and to support the identification of persons who are subject to protection

---

[40] Sup. R. 10.

[41] See also Text Ch. 11, Issuance of a Civil Protection Order, to Text Ch. 13, Court Enforcement of Civil Protection Orders and Related Issues.

[42] See also RC 2935.032.

[43] Note that this provision is to be considered in accordance with RC 9.86 and RC 2744.03.

[44] See David M. Fine, The Violence Against Women Act of 1994: The Proper Federal Role in Policing Domestic Violence, 84 Cornell L. Rev. 252, 294 (1998).

orders and, therefore, prohibited from purchasing, receiving, or possessing firearms under federal law.[45]

Q & A: What is the purpose of Form 10-A?

The Ohio Supreme Court promulgated a specific rule to enhance the response of Ohio's courts to changes in the domestic violence law. Rule 10 of the Rules of Superintendence for the Courts of Ohio states:

> Upon issuance of a civil or criminal protection order by a court pursuant to section 2919.26(E)(2) or 3113.31 of the Revised Code, the court shall complete Form 10-A. Form 10-A and a copy of the order shall be filed by the court with the local law enforcement agency for entry in the National Crime Information Center database and nationwide dissemination.

Entering protection order information into NCIC is intended to create a national clearinghouse for all protection orders issued by courts within the country to provide law enforcement agencies anywhere in the nation with the tools necessary to effectuate enforcement, including determining whether a particular protection order exists against a named individual. Each Form 10-A delineates the subject's name and address; any identifying characteristics, such as race, gender, height, weight, eye and hair color, date of birth, and social security number; whether the order is a civil or criminal domestic violence protection order or an anti-stalking protection order; the case number; whether the subject is Brady disqualified;[46] the duration of the order; the issuing judge; the terms of the order; the protected party or parties; and the date of birth of the protected party or parties. This information is then entered in the NCIC database.[47]

Historically, LEADS[48] was both the entering and disseminating agency. In October 1997, LEADS indicated that NCIC would become the disseminating agency for protection orders, effective January 1, 1998. As the federal crime information database, NCIC is the logical entry point for this data. Under the mandates of VAWA, the only way to provide law enforcement agencies around the country with the ability to enforce protection orders nationwide was to include them in a national database.[49] However, LEADS remains the conduit by which protection orders are entered into the national database.

Because NCIC was designated as the vehicle by which this information is circulated to law enforcement agencies nationwide and since the statute requires all law enforcement agencies to enforce all protec-

---

[45]See also Text § 18:11, Firearm offenses under VAWA; Donaldson v. City of Seattle, 65 Wash. App. 661, 831 P.2d 1098 (Div. 1 1992), opinion corrected (July 1, 1992) (upheld trial court's preventing jury in negligence action from considering city's failure to enter protection order on State Criminal Information System, resulting in failure of police to arrest boyfriend for violating order).

[46]See Text § 18:11, Firearm offenses under VAWA; see also Printz v. U.S., 521 U.S. 898, 117 S. Ct. 2365, 138 L. Ed. 2d 914 (1997) (discussing the application and constitutionality of portions of the Brady Bill).

[47]See Text § 14:5, False arrest, warrantless arrests and searches, and weapons confiscation.

[48]Law Enforcement Automation Data System.

[49]See 18 U.S.C.A. § 2265(a).

tion orders issued in Ohio,[50] implicit in RC 3113.31(F)(3) is that all law enforcement agencies are charged with knowledge of the existence of all civil protection orders issued by the courts of Ohio. If an officer is uncertain about particular terms, the officer must still enforce an order that appears valid on its face.[51] Additionally, the officer can contact the issuing court to validate and/or clarify the terms of the order.

Although the primary reason for filing protection orders and 10-A forms with the local law enforcement agency is for nationwide dissemination of protection orders rather than to establish a procedure for serving local police departments with copies of the orders, this has become an unintended result. Since Superintendence Rule 10 directs the issuing court to file a copy of the order and the 10-A form with the local law enforcement agency, the implication is that the local law enforcement agency has received a copy of the order. The law enforcement agency is then directed to enter the requisite information into the NCIC database.[52] Receipt of the protection order by way of an actual copy or through accessing NCIC puts a local law enforcement agency on notice that a protection order is in existence and charges the local agency with knowledge of its terms.

Compliance with Superintendence Rule 10 has significant and far-reaching ramifications. It puts the officer on notice that a protection order exists against a specific individual. Should an officer, in reliance on the entry in NCIC and on the facially valid protection order, arrest an individual, the officer is immune from liability resulting from the arrest.[53] On the other hand, a failure to enforce an order according to its terms could subject the officer and the law enforcement agency to civil liability for a failure to protect the victim of domestic violence, especially where the statute indicates that arrest is the preferred course of action in the state, a protection order is in effect, or the law enforcement agency has knowledge of the order.[54]

Moreover, entering this data into NCIC suggests a growing awareness that all protection orders are to be enforced nationwide. Creating a nationwide database ensures the victim that the order follows the person not the place, taking into account that the victim often relocates to escape the violence. More importantly, local law enforcement agencies are on notice that a protection order issued anywhere in the country is enforceable by the law enforcement agencies and courts of Ohio.

Q & A: How often is a court required to update the NCIC form?

---

[50]See RC 3113.31(F)(3); see also RC 2919.26(G)(4).

[51]See RC 2935.032(F).

[52]Sup. R. 10, eff. 3-24-98; see also Donaldson v. City of Seattle, 65 Wash. App. 661, 662, 677, 831 P.2d 1098 (Div. 1 1992), opinion corrected (July 1, 1992) (appellate court affirmed trial court's decision preventing jury from considering city's failure to enter a protection order on the Washington Criminal Information System Database because the testimony indicated that "it was impossible to enter such orders on the state controlled system without the proper information"; "Likewise, if the order was not on the computer system and Leola could not provide the police with a copy, the police could not be expected to make an arrest.").

[53]See RC 2935.032(F).

[54]See Campbell v. Campbell, 294 N.J. Super. 18, 682 A.2d 272 (Law Div. 1996).

The NCIC form should be generated when a victim first obtains a protection order.[55] A notation should be made in Terms and Conditions, provision 8, that the subject has not yet been served with the protection order. Additionally, the NCIC form should reflect that the respondent is not Brady disqualified because he/she has not yet been served. When service is perfected, another NCIC form should be generated by the court noting the date and time of service in provision 8. A new form should be generated after the full hearing, detailing any changes in the terms or conditions. If a continuance is granted after the respondent was served and had the opportunity to appear at the full hearing, a new NCIC form should be generated that prohibits that individual from purchasing or possessing a handgun under the Brady prohibitions.[56] Finally, any other subsequent orders issued by a domestic relations court, juvenile court, or criminal court should necessitate a new NCIC form noting the change.

Once that individual is Brady disqualified, both state and federal remedies attach and the federal authorities should be notified if a violation occurs.[57]

Q & A: Can law enforcement enter a protection order issued after a full hearing into LEADS and then into NCIC before the order is served?

Yes, but the entering agency should not enter the protection order in a manner different than provided to the agency by the court. That is, an ETO code should never be used for a full hearing protection order or consent agreement protection order simply because the order has not been served. The lack of service does not transform the order into an ex parte order. It is still a valid protection order and should be entered without delay when sent over by the trial court.

Q & A: What procedures have the various domestic relations courts established to effect the mandates of Superintendence Rule 10?

There are no written procedures in place that detail how the issuing domestic relations court is to file a copy of a civil protection order and 10-A form with the local law enforcement agency. Most jurisdictions, however, have established unwritten policies. Nearly all of the jurisdictions have adopted the 10-A form set forth in the rule. The county sheriff's department has been empowered to both receive the copies of the orders and forms and enter the information into the NCIC database in many of the metropolitan counties.

For example, the Cuyahoga County Domestic Relations Court has established an internal procedure to facilitate the mandate of the Supreme Court. Each civil protection order issued and accompanying 10-A form must be served upon the sheriff's department for entry into the NCIC database.[58] The county sheriff's department is the law enforcement agency authorized by the court to enter this data. Local police departments are expected to access the NCIC database for information pertaining to a particular person.

---

[55] Sup. R. 10-A. See also Text § 18:11, Firearm offenses under VAWA, Text § 14:2, Ohio statutory procedure.

[56] 18 U.S.C.A. § 922(t).

[57] See also Text § 18:11, Firearm offenses under VAWA.

[58] See Cuy. Cty. Local R. 26(B)(4).

Q & A: Does RC 3113.31 require the police to establish an index?

Yes. RC 3113.31(F)(2) requires all law enforcement agencies to establish and maintain an index for the protection orders and consent agreements that are delivered to the agencies as set forth in RC 3113.31(F)(1).[59] This includes the ex parte order and the order or consent agreement issued after the full hearing.[60] The rationale behind this provision is to both document receipt of a particular protection order and create a local database that sets forth all protection orders issued within a particular jurisdiction.

This index is used to compile information such as the date and time that the agency received the protection order or consent agreement. The date and time that an officer receives a protection order is crucial in light of the trend in this country toward imposing liability for failing to protect victims of domestic violence.[61] A victim may need this information to prove that a particular police department knew of the civil protection order and failed to enforce it. For example, the date and time an order was received by the agency demonstrates that the law enforcement agency had direct knowledge of the existence of the order. Failure to respond to a domestic violence call or failure to investigate a domestic violence incident when the agency or officer had knowledge of a civil protection order may subject the agency or officer to civil liability. On the other hand, the date and time a protection order is received may provide evidence in support of an officer in a police liability case brought against him or her.

Additionally, RC 3113.32(A) directs the chief of the law enforcement agency to keep a separate record of domestic violence disputes and domestic violence problems on a specific form which is submitted to the Bureau of Criminal Investigation. The information compiled through the maintenance of an index[62] will aid the law enforcement agency in complying with the requirements of RC 3113.32(A).

Q & A: Do law enforcement officials require specific domestic violence training?

Yes. According to RC 109.744, the attorney general of the state of Ohio is required to adopt rules overseeing the training of law enforcement officials in the handling of domestic violence incidents and protection orders issued under RC 2919.26 or RC 3113.31. These rules must include:

(A) fifteen or more hours of training;

(B) training in the following:

(1) recent amendments to the domestic violence-related laws;

(2) notifying a victim of domestic violence of his/her rights;

---

[59]See also RC 2919.26(G)(2).

[60]RC 3113.31(F)(2).

[61]See Text § 14:7, Police liability for failing to protect victims of domestic violence—Introduction.

[62]See RC 3113.31(F)(2).

(3) processing protection orders under RC 3113.31 or RC 2919.26.[63]

Q & A: Are State Highway Patrol troopers considered "peace officers" for purposes of the domestic violence statutes?

The Ohio Attorney General issued an opinion on that issue in 1996.[64] The Attorney General determined that troopers of the State Highway Patrol are not peace officers as defined in RC 2935.03(B)(1). The troopers are, therefore, not subject to the domestic violence arrest provisions detailed in RC 2935.03(B)(3). The State Highway Patrol is also not required to adopt domestic violence policies and procedures pursuant to RC 2935.032.

Q & A: Are law enforcement agencies prohibited from investigating and maintaining domestic violence reports of perpetrators?

No Ohio court has addressed this issue, but recently a New York appellate court tackled the question. In *Groves v. State of New York at Albany*,[65] a defendant in a criminal domestic violence proceeding sought to have the court issue an order prohibiting law enforcement agencies from investigating and maintaining a record of reports of defendant's domestic violence against his girlfriend.

In this case, the defendant and his girlfriend were involved in a dating relationship. The focus of defendant's argument was that he and the victim were not members of the same household. The court determined that ". . . the fact that such protections are available only to a specific subset of victims of domestic violence that, at present, does not include individuals who are dating, does not mean that . . . law enforcement agencies do not have a legitimate interest in investigating and maintaining reports of domestic violence between such individuals."[66] In affirming the lower court decision, the appellate court concluded that although some statutes limit the class of victims entitled to certain relief, they do not limit a law enforcement agency's authority to investigate and maintain reports of domestic violence occurring between individuals who may not be members of the same family or household.[67] Because the victim is permitted to report the domestic violence to law enforcement agencies, the law enforcement agency is not precluded from investigating or maintaining a record of it. The court left open the question of whether the defendant could have had the reports sealed and expunged.

Of significance is that Ohio has a similar statutory framework to New York. Under RC 3113.32(A), the chief of a law enforcement agency is directed to keep a record of domestic violence disputes and domestic violence problems on a specific form, which is then submitted to the Bureau of Criminal Identification. Nothing in this provision

---

[63] RC 109.744.

[64] 1996 Ohio Op. Att'y Gen. No. 96-014, 1996 WL 118256.

[65] Groves v. State University of New York at Albany, 265 A.D.2d 141, 707 N.Y.S.2d 261 (3d Dep't 2000).

[66] Groves v. State University of New York at Albany, 265 A.D.2d 141, 144, 707 N.Y.S.2d 261 (3d Dep't 2000).

[67] Groves v. State University of New York at Albany, 265 A.D.2d 141, 144, 707 N.Y.S.2d 261 (3d Dep't 2000).

precludes the filing of a report if the victim is not of the protected class of individuals protected by the Ohio's Domestic Violence Act. Likewise, nothing in the statute limits a law enforcement agency's authority to investigate and maintain records of all reports of domestic violence.

§ 14:3 Arrest of the perpetrator[1]

Q & A: Are the police expected to arrest a respondent for violating a civil protection order or committing an act of domestic violence?

It depends.[2] Although Ohio's arrest statute does not mandate that an arrest be made in every instance, arrest is the preferred course of action in the state of Ohio if a police officer has reasonable grounds to believe that the offense of domestic violence or of violating a protection order or consent agreement has been committed and reasonable cause to believe that a particular person is guilty of committing the offense.[3] Ohio's preferred arrest policy applies to the offense of domestic violence as defined under RC 2919.25[4] and a violation of a civil or criminal protection order or consent agreement under RC 2919.27. Since civil protection order violations are encompassed in RC 2919.27, police are empowered to arrest domestic violence perpetrators for these violations.

The statutory language of the preferred arrest policy gives police the discretion not to arrest but sets forth certain parameters within which police must act. For example, if there are reasonable grounds to

---

[Section 14:3]

[1]See Christopher D. Maxwell, Joel H. Garner & Jeffrey A. Fagan, The Effects of Arrest on Intimate Partner Violence: New Evidence from the Spouse Assault Replication Program, National Institute of Justice, June 2001; Cheryl Hanna, The Paradox of Hope: The Crime and Punishment of Domestic Violence, 39 Wm. & Mary L. Rev. 1505 (1998); see also City of Warren v. Culver, 2004-Ohio-333, 2004 WL 144227 (Ohio Ct. App. 11th Dist. Trumbull County 2004) (discussion of arrest, generally).

[2]See also Eve S. Buzawa & Thomas Austin, Determining Police Response to Domestic Violence Victims: The Role of Victim Preference, 36 Am. Behav. Scientist 610 (1993).

[3]RC 2935.03(B)(3)(b); see also Akron v. Sutton, 106 Ohio Misc. 2d 46, 733 N.E.2d 690 (Mun. Ct. 2000); Scott v. City of Bexley, 11 Fed. Appx. 514 (6th Cir. 2001) (dissent found that whether probable cause existed at time of arrest is different from the reasonable grounds of Ohio's preferred arrest policy and that allowing preferred arrest policy to be considered when determining whether probable cause exists is improper under the law); Andrea D. Lyon, Be Careful What You Wish For: An Examination of Arrest & Prosecution Patterns of Domestic Violence Cases in Two Cities in Michigan, 5 Mich. J. Gender & L. 253 (1999); see also City of Cleveland v. Morales, 2002-Ohio-5862, 2002 WL 31402003 (Ohio Ct. App. 8th Dist. Cuyahoga County 2002); State v. O'Neill, 2015-Ohio-815, 29 N.E.3d 365 (Ohio Ct. App. 3d Dist. Allen County 2015); State v. DeLong, 2007-Ohio-2330, 2007 WL 1413394, *2 (Ohio Ct. App. 4th Dist. Ross County 2007) (emphasizing that "RC 2935.03 does not give law enforcement carte blanche authority to disregard constitutional principles"); Alagha v. Cameron, 2009-Ohio-4886, 2009 WL 2974892 (Ohio Ct. App. 1st Dist. Hamilton County 2009).

[4]See State v. Hardges, 2011-Ohio-61, 2011 WL 181344 (Ohio Ct. App. 9th Dist. Summit County 2011) (noting that Ohio's preferred arrest policy applies to those in relationships, live-in relationships, those who have children in common or who are married); see also Soltesz v. City of Sandusky, 138 F. Supp. 2d 932 (N.D. Ohio 2001), judgment aff'd, 49 Fed. Appx. 522 (6th Cir. 2002) (holding that officers had no probable cause to arrest, under RC 2919.25, a person not related by affinity).

believe that domestic violence occurred or that there was a violation of a protection order, police should arrest the individual.[5] Additionally, the statute requires police to explain in a mandatory incident report that is to be written by officers at the scene and submitted to the law enforcement agency why they chose not to arrest a certain individual, "when [arrest] is the preferred course of action in this state."[6] Every law enforcement agency's written policy must include examples of reasons an officer may consider for not arresting the individual.[7]

Each of these conditions has increased the likelihood that a law enforcement agency may be exposed to civil liability for its officer's failure to arrest. In effect, if there are reasonable grounds to believe that the offense of violating a civil protection order occurred and reasonable cause to believe a certain individual committed the act, a failure to arrest that individual may be considered a violation of the state's preferred arrest policy.[8] The fact that an officer also has to document his/her reasons for not arresting in a written incident report may make it easier to prove officer and agency liability.[9] Some reasons for not arresting an individual may be unacceptable in light of the state's preferred arrest policy.

Q & A: Must a police officer obtain a warrant prior to arresting a domestic violence suspect when the suspect is not present at the scene?

Not according to R.C. 2935.03(B)(3)(b) which provides that it is the preferred course of action to arrest and detain an individual who the officer believes to be guilty until a warrant can be obtained when that individual has left the scene. The officer must then promptly seek a warrant.[10]

Likewise, the Allen County appellate court considered a similar issue in *State v. O'Neill*,[11] In that case, the victim contacted the police after defendant threw a beer can at her and attempted to drag her around the house by her hair. The defendant had left the scene in a car by the time the officers arrived. The officers testified at trial that they had observed the scene and corroborated the victim's statement. One of the officers later discovered defendant at a bar and arrested him for domestic violence. Of importance is that the victim also signed a written statement. The officer also searched his auto and found cocaine and he was arrested for this as well. Although the trial court acquitted him on the domestic violence charge, he pled no contest and was found guilty of possession of cocaine. At the time of trial, his motion to suppress was overruled as the arresting officer complied with RC 2935.03 and thus, defendant's warrantless arrest was constitutionally permissible.

---

[5]See RC 2935.03(B)(3)(a)(i) to RC 2935.03(B)(3)(a)(iii); see, e.g., Morales v. County of Nassau, 256 A.D.2d 608, 683 N.Y.S.2d 127 (2d Dep't 1998), aff'd, 94 N.Y.2d 218, 703 N.Y.S.2d 61, 724 N.E.2d 756 (1999).

[6]See RC 2935.032(D).

[7]RC 2935.032(A)(4).

[8]RC 2935.03(B)(3)(b).

[9]RC 2935.03(B)(3)(c); see also RC 2935.032(A)(4), RC 2935.032(D).

[10]R.C. 2935.03(B)(3)(g).

[11]State v. O'Neill, 2015-Ohio-815, 29 N.E.3d 365 (Ohio Ct. App. 3d Dist. Allen County 2015).

On appeal, defendant claimed that the arresting officer was not authorized to arrest him without first obtaining a warrant and that the officer was prohibited from making a warrantless arrest under RC 2935.03 (B)(3)(g) because he was not at the scene when law enforcement arrived. The appellate court reviewed the statutory schema relative to RC 2935.03(B)(3)(b) and its application to domestic violence which provided that "[i]f * * *a peace officer has reasonable grounds to believe that the offense of domestic violence * * *has been committed and reasonable cause to believe that a particular person is guilty of committing the offense, *it is the preferred course of action in this state that the officer arrest and detain that person* * * *until a warrant can be obtained.*"[12]

The court acknowledged the Revised Code and determined that "O'Neill's contention that his arrest was constitutionally infirm rests upon the effect of RC 2935.03(B)(3)(g) on an officer's authority to make a warrantless arrest of a domestic violence suspect."[13] RC 2935.03(B)(3)(g) provides that "[i]f a peace officer* * *intends pursuant to division (B)(3)(a) to (g) of this section to arrest a person pursuant to division (B)(1) of this section and if the officer is unable to do so because the person is not present, the officer promptly shall seek a warrant for the arrest of the person."[14] Defendant argued that (B)(3)(g) mandates that a police officer obtain a warrant before arresting a domestic violence suspect when the suspect is not present at the scene.

Relying on statutory construction, the appellate court rejected his argument and held that "[w]e conclude that RC 2935.03(B)(3)(g) does not operate to revoke an officer's legal authority to make a warrantless arrest in cases involving domestic violence. To the contrary, we find that when viewed in context with the related provisions in RC 2935.03(B) and (D), the language 'promptly shall seek a warrant for the arrest of the person' is far more reasonably construed to compel an officer to *expediently continue* the investigation and *not postpone or delay* the pursuit, detention and arrest of a domestic violence suspect simply because the suspect recently left the scene prior to law enforcement's arrival. We conclude that this interpretation is more consistent with the overall statutory scheme articulated by the legislature in RC 2935.03 and decline to adopt O'Neill's position on appeal."[15]

Q & A: Does an arrest made in accordance with Ohio's preferred arrest policy generate a duty to conduct a follow-up investigation by searching for the absent violator?

Ohio law is silent. The only guidance provided is found in RC 2935.03(G)(3)(g) which states that if a peace officer intends to arrest a person pursuant to RC 2935.03(B)(1) and if the officer is unable to do so because the person is not present, the officer shall promptly seek a warrant for the arrest of that person.

---

[12]State v. O'Neill, 2015-Ohio-815, 29 N.E.3d 365, ¶ 24 (Ohio Ct. App. 3d Dist. Allen County 2015).

[13]State v. O'Neill, 2015-Ohio-815, 29 N.E.3d 365, ¶ 25 (Ohio Ct. App. 3d Dist. Allen County 2015).

[14]State v. O'Neill, 2015-Ohio-815, 29 N.E.3d 365, ¶ 25 (Ohio Ct. App. 3d Dist. Allen County 2015).

[15]State v. O'Neill, 2015-Ohio-815, 29 N.E.3d 365, ¶ 33 (Ohio Ct. App. 3d Dist. Allen County 2015).

Interestingly, a similar issue was raised in *Donaldson v. City of Seattle*.[16] In that case it was alleged that police negligence caused the death of the girlfriend who was attacked by her boyfriend. The question presented was whether a mandatory duty to arrest generated a mandatory duty to conduct a follow-up investigation by searching for the perpetrator.[17]

The Court held that nothing in Washington's Domestic Violence Act directs the police to conduct follow-up investigations after the initial response. "Liability for negligent investigation would be a substantial change in the law and is certainly not required as a necessary inference from the duty to make a mandatory duty to arrest."[18] Such a broad interpretation would render the duty to investigate open-ended as to priority, duration and intensity.[19]

Q & A: Is the arrest of an individual for committing domestic violence or for violating a protection order made pursuant to a warrant?

No. RC 2935.03(B)(1) provides that, where there is reasonable ground to believe that an offense of domestic violence has occurred, the officer may arrest and detain until a warrant can be obtained any person whom the officer has reasonable cause to believe is guilty of the violation.[20] The offense of domestic violence as defined in RC 2919. 25, the offense of violating a protection order as defined in RC 2919. 27, the offense of menacing by stalking as defined in RC 2903.21, and the offense of aggravated trespass as defined in RC 2911.211 are included offenses for which warrantless arrests may be effected.[21]

Q & A: What constitutes reasonable grounds to believe that the offense of domestic violence or violating a protection order has been committed and reasonable cause to believe that a particular person is guilty of committing the offense?[22]

According to RC 2935.03, reasonable grounds exist if the following occurs:

---

[16] Donaldson v. City of Seattle, 65 Wash. App. 661, 831 P.2d 1098 (Div. 1 1992), opinion corrected (July 1, 1992).

[17] Donaldson v. City of Seattle, 65 Wash. App. 661, 671, 831 P.2d 1098 (Div. 1 1992), opinion corrected (July 1, 1992).

[18] Donaldson v. City of Seattle, 65 Wash. App. 661, 671, 831 P.2d 1098 (Div. 1 1992), opinion corrected (July 1, 1992).

[19] Donaldson v. City of Seattle, 65 Wash. App. 661, 671, 831 P.2d 1098 (Div. 1 1992), opinion corrected (July 1, 1992).

[20] See Alley v. Bettencourt, 134 Ohio App. 3d 303, 730 N.E.2d 1067 (4th Dist. Pike County 1999).

[21] See Beck v. State of Ohio, 379 U.S. 89, 85 S. Ct. 223, 13 L. Ed. 2d 142 (1964); see also State v. Heston, 29 Ohio St. 2d 152, 58 Ohio Op. 2d 349, 280 N.E.2d 376 (1972); State v. Andrews, 57 Ohio St. 3d 86, 565 N.E.2d 1271 (1991); State v. Farrow, 919 P.2d 50 (Utah Ct. App. 1996) (discussing whether warrantless arrests are limited to emergency situations), for a discussion of warrantless arrests and probable cause to arrest; but see Soltesz v. City of Sandusky, 138 F. Supp. 2d 932 (N.D. Ohio 2001), judgment aff'd, 49 Fed. Appx. 522 (6th Cir. 2002) (holding that officers did not have probable cause to arrest a person not related by affinity pursuant to RC 2919.25).

[22] See State v. DeLong, 2007-Ohio-2330, 2007 WL 1413394 (Ohio Ct. App. 4th Dist. Ross County 2007). See also Lappin v. Gabel, 2016 WL 1258588 (N.D. Ohio 2016) (addressing what is probable cause to arrest in domestic violence situations).

(1) A person executes a written statement alleging that the person in question has committed the offense.[23]

(2) No written statement is executed, but the police officer, based upon his/her own knowledge and observation of the facts and circumstances of the alleged incident or based upon any other information, including but not limited to, any reasonably trustworthy information given to the officer by the alleged victim or any witness of the alleged incident, concludes that the offense of domestic violence or violating a protection order has been committed and has reasonable cause to believe that the person in question is guilty of committing the offense.[24]

(3) No written statement is executed, but the police officer witnessed the person in question commit the offense.[25]

In short, if the police officer has reason to believe that the offense was committed by a particular person, the police officer should arrest that individual.[26] Conversely, if there exists no reasonable grounds to make this determination, the officer at the scene should not arrest.

Q & A: If the police officer chooses not to arrest the alleged perpetrator, what are the responsibilities of the officer and the agency?[27]

At that point, the individual police officer has two primary obligations. The police officer is required to state his/her reasons for not arresting the alleged perpetrator.[28] This must be done in writing in the mandatory report made of the incident.[29]

Additionally, Ohio law enforcement agencies are required to adopt policies that provide examples of reasons that a police officer may

---

[23]RC 2935.03(B)(3)(a)(i); but see also RC 2935.03(B)(3)(e)(i). See also White v. Roch, 2005-Ohio-1127, 2005 WL 602684 (Ohio Ct. App. 9th Dist. Summit County 2005) (discussing both probable cause to arrest and probable cause to institute a criminal prosecution); State v. Christian, 2005-Ohio-1440, 2005 WL 704866 (Ohio Ct. App. 7th Dist. Mahoning County 2005) (domestic violence complaint executed by defendant's girlfriend was sufficient to justify defendant's warrantless arrest and detention for that offense); State v. O'Neill, 2015-Ohio-815, 29 N.E.3d 365 (Ohio Ct. App. 3d Dist. Allen County 2015).

[24]RC 2935.03(B)(3)(a)(ii); see also Wildoner v. Borough of Ramsey, 162 N.J. 375, 744 A.2d 1146 (2000) (probable cause for arrest was provided by a witness and police officers' observation).

[25]RC 2935.03(B)(3)(a)(iii).

[26]See, e.g., Fletcher v. Town of Clinton, 196 F.3d 41 (1st Cir. 1999) (ruling that, where police saw man in home from which he was barred by domestic violence restraining order, they could reasonably believe resident of home was in danger and, thus, their entry to protect resident was reasonable; court also ruled that officers were entitled to qualified immunity from civil rights action, stressing that officers must be given wide latitude where domestic violence is involved); Adams v. Township of Champion, OH, 68 F. Supp. 2d 906 (N.D. Ohio 1999); but see Latiolais v. Guillory, 747 So. 2d 675 (La. Ct. App. 3d Cir. 1999), writ denied, 753 So. 2d 832 (La. 2000) and writ denied, 753 So. 2d 833 (La. 2000) (affirmed decision that sheriffs did not breach their duty to victim stating that arresting the abuser is discretionary by law enforcement officials if there is no cause to believe there is impending danger).

[27]See also Ardoin v. City of Mamou, 685 So. 2d 294 (La. Ct. App. 3d Cir. 1996) (discussing when a police officer has a duty to arrest for violating a temporary restraining order). 2001 Ohio Op. Att'y Gen. No. 01–039

[28]See RC 2935.032(D); see also RC 2935.03(B)(3)(c).

[29]See RC 2935.032(D).

consider for not arresting a person who allegedly committed the offense of domestic violence or violated a protection order when arrest of the alleged offender is the preferred course of action in this state.[30] Although this clause was intended to empower the agency and give the officer the discretion not to arrest under certain circumstances articulated by the particular agency, a law enforcement agency's failure to include such a provision in its written procedures may subject the agency to liability for failing to protect victims of domestic violence. Since RC 2935.032 provides for sanctions to be imposed on an officer by a law enforcement agency should he/she fail to comply with the state's preferred arrest policy,[31] the absence of satisfactory reasons not to arrest exposes both the agency and the officer to liability for not complying with the state policy.

Q & A: Can a law enforcement agency adopt a mandatory arrest policy?[32]

Absolutely.[33] Nothing in RC 2935.03 precludes a law enforcement agency from requiring its police officers to arrest a particular offender if there is reasonable cause to believe that the person committed the offense of domestic violence or violated a protection order.[34] Several law enforcement agencies around the state have adopted mandatory arrest policies. For example, Cleveland's police department has adopted a "shall arrest" policy for the crime of domestic violence when the offense is committed in the officer's presence or if the officer has probable cause to believe the offense of domestic violence has been committed by a primary physical aggressor.[35] Cleveland's policy mandates that an arrest be made if there is probable cause.

Q & A: Can a law enforcement agency adopt a less restrictive policy than the preferred arrest policy?

No. RC 2935.032(B)(1)(b) provides that a law enforcement agency is not precluded from including in its policies and procedures a provision that does not require its officers to arrest alleged offenders but that grants the officer less discretion in those circumstances in deciding whether to arrest the alleged offender than is given to officers by RC 2935.03(B)(1) and RC 2935.03(B)(3).[36] RC 2935.03(B)(1) and RC 2935.03(B)(3) allow for a warrantless arrest in domestic violence cases

---

[30]RC 2935.032(A)(4).

[31]RC 2953.032(A)(3).

[32]But see G. Kristian Miccio, A House Divided: Mandatory Arrest, Domestic Violence, and the Conservatization of the Battered Women's Movement, 42 Hous. L.Rev. 237 (2005) (discussing mandatory arrest and contrasting policies among domestic violence advocates).

[33]See, for example, State v. Lampe, 2003-Ohio-3059, 2003 WL 21360725 (Ohio Ct. App. 1st Dist. Hamilton County 2003) (sheriff's mandatory arrest policy was not unconstitutional as applied to defendant).

[34]RC 2935.032(B)(1)(a); see also Dennis Saccuzzo, How Should the Police Respond to Domestic Violence: A Therapeutic Jurisprudence Analysis of Mandatory Arrest, 39 Santa Clara L. Rev. 765 (1999); Donna M. Welch, Mandatory Arrest of Domestic Violence: Panacea or Perpetuation of the Problem of Abuse? 43 De Paul L. Rev. 1133 (1994).

[35]General Police Order, Cleveland Police Department, Domestic Violence Arrest and Reporting Procedures, 7-12-95; see also Cincinnati Police Department which also has a domestic violence mandatory arrest policy in effect.

[36]RC 2935.032(B)(1)(b).

and encourage arrest as the preferred course of action in the state. In effect, RC 2935.032(B)(1)(b) permits a law enforcement agency to adopt a policy that is more restrictive than preferred arrest, but it may not adopt a less restrictive arrest policy.

RC 2935.032(B) also provides that, if a law enforcement agency adopts an arrest policy described in either RC 2935.032(B)(1)(a) or RC 2935.032(B)(1)(b), the police officers within that particular law enforcement agency are required to comply with RC 2935.03(B)(1) as it relates to making arrests. RC 2935.03(B)(1) discusses reasonable grounds to arrest for certain offenses. Violations of civil protection orders are encompassed within RC 2935.03(B)(1), as they are violations of protection orders as defined in RC 2919.27.

The Trumbull County Court of Appeals, in *State v. Carbone*,[37] advanced a balancing test between arresting of an alleged perpetrator of domestic violence and protecting the rights of the accused. The court noted that the state has a strong interest in protecting the health, welfare, and safety of household residents. "The state advances this interest by requiring the arrest of the accused as soon as possible after the probable cause determination is made. By requiring a preliminary probable cause determination, both RC 2935.03 and 2935.032 protect the accused's constitutional rights, while simultaneously advancing the legislative purpose of preempting household violence before it escalates further."[38]

In effect, the Eleventh District Court of Appeals has validated Ohio's statutory framework vis-a-vis the United States Constitution for purposes of warrantless arrests in the case of misdemeanors and felonies.

Q & A: Do the terms "probable cause," "reasonable grounds," and "reasonable cause" mean the same thing, or do they create different standards?

Within the Ohio statute, "reasonable cause," "probable cause," and "reasonable grounds" are used interchangeably when referring to the arrest of an offender alleged to have committed the offense of domestic violence or violating a protection order.[39] For example, RC 2935.03 permits a law enforcement official to arrest and detain until a warrant can be obtained any person whom the officer has reasonable cause to believe is guilty of a violation.[40] In domestic violence situations, RC 2935.03 also enumerates circumstances which constitute reasonable grounds to believe that domestic violence has been committed.[41]

Case law has applied the term "probable cause" in creating the

---

[37]State v. Carbone, 1997 WL 799557 (Ohio Ct. App. 11th Dist. Trumbull County 1997); see also State v. Lampe, 2003-Ohio-3059, 2003 WL 21360725 (Ohio Ct. App. 1st Dist. Hamilton County 2003).

[38]State v. Carbone, 1997 WL 799557, *7 (Ohio Ct. App. 11th Dist. Trumbull County 1997).

[39]See RC 2935.03.

[40]RC 2935.03(B)(1); see also State v. Carbone, 1997 WL 799557, *5–6 (Ohio Ct. App. 11th Dist. Trumbull County 1997).

[41]RC 2935.03(B)(3)(a). But see State v. DeLong, 2007-Ohio-2330, 2007 WL 1413394 (Ohio Ct. App. 4th Dist. Ross County 2007) (reliance on RC 2935.03(B)(1) and (3) did not justify warrantless entry).

standard by which officers may arrest a certain individual.[42] For example, in *Beck v. Ohio*,[43] the United States Supreme Court found that a warrantless arrest is constitutionally valid if, "at the moment the arrest was made, the officers had probable cause to make it." The Court defined probable cause as "whether at that moment the facts and circumstances within their knowledge and of which they had reasonably trustworthy information were sufficient to warrant a prudent man in believing that the petitioner had committed or was committing an offense."[44]

In resolving the differences in the terminology employed by the statute and the case law, the courts generally incorporate the word "reasonable" in the definition of probable cause. *Black's Law Dictionary* defines "reasonable cause" as a basis for arrest without a warrant as "such state of facts as would lead man of ordinary care and prudence to believe . . . that person sought to be arrested is guilty of committing a crime."[45] "Reasonable grounds" is defined "within statute authorizing arrest without warrant . . . [as] substantially probable cause."[46] "Probable cause" is defined as "[r]easonable grounds for belief that a person should be arrested."[47]

Because each term references the other, it is clear that one term may be substituted for the other. In creating a standard for arresting an alleged offender of domestic violence, the terms are substantially equivalent.

Q & A: Can a law enforcement officer arrest a person for violating a no-contact order issued by a judge?[48]

A no-contact order is an order directing one party to stay away from

---

[42]See State v. Carbone, 1997 WL 799557, *6 (Ohio Ct. App. 11th Dist. Trumbull County 1997). See also State v. Martindale, 2005-Ohio-6437, 2005 WL 3293762 (Ohio Ct. App. 5th Dist. Fairfield County 2005); Alagha v. Cameron, 2009-Ohio-4886, 2009 WL 2974892 (Ohio Ct. App. 1st Dist. Hamilton County 2009).

[43]Beck v. State of Ohio, 379 U.S. 89, 91, 85 S. Ct. 223, 13 L. Ed. 2d 142 (1964); see also State v. Cowdin, 25 Kan. App. 2d 176, 959 P.2d 929 (1998) (holding that a victim's affidavit was sufficient for a magistrate to find probable cause to issue a search warrant); State v. Galloway, 2001 WL 81257 (Ohio Ct. App. 9th Dist. Summit County 2001); Hunt v. Morrow County, Ohio, 2009-Ohio-4313, 2009 WL 2602204 (Ohio Ct. App. 5th Dist. Morrow County 2009).

[44]Beck v. State of Ohio, 379 U.S. 89, 91, 85 S. Ct. 223, 13 L. Ed. 2d 142 (1964); see also State v. Heston, 29 Ohio St. 2d 152, 58 Ohio Op. 2d 349, 280 N.E.2d 376 (1972); State v. Cowdin, 25 Kan. App. 2d 176, 959 P.2d 929 (1998) (discussing the standard of review for whether a warrant for arrest or search may be issued). See also State v. Martindale, 2005-Ohio-6437, 2005 WL 3293762 (Ohio Ct. App. 5th Dist. Fairfield County 2005) (in which a warrantless entry did not give rise to a warrantless arrest where victim was not present at scene when defendant was arrested and when she appeared subsequent to the arrest, she denied any domestic violence occurred); Collins v. Clancy, 2014 WL 1653103 (S.D. Ohio 2014). But see Ornelas v. U.S., 517 U.S. 690, 696, 116 S. Ct. 1657, 134 L. Ed. 2d 911 (1996) (a police officer has reasonable or probable cause to arrest when the events leading up to the arrest, "viewed from the standpoint of an objectively reasonable police officer, amounts to" probable cause); State v. O'Neill, 2015-Ohio-815, 29 N.E.3d 365 (Ohio Ct. App. 3d Dist. Allen County 2015); State v. DeLong, 2007-Ohio-2330, 2007 WL 1413394 (Ohio Ct. App. 4th Dist. Ross County 2007).

[45]Black's Law Dictionary (6th ed.) p 1265.

[46]Black's Law Dictionary (6th ed.) p 1266.

[47]Black's Law Dictionary (6th ed.) p 1201.

[48]See also § 13:16.

the other party. In domestic violence cases, no-contact orders are issued by a judge, most often in municipal court, when a criminal case is filed, when a motion for TPO is filed or at arraignment/first appearance or any point during the pendency of the case. No-contact orders are also granted as a pretrial condition of release from jail or in lieu of a TPO.

Further, a no-contact order can be issued at sentencing as a term of probation and will remain in effect until probation is completed or at such other time as the court requires.

A violation of a no-contact order is a probation violation and does not form the basis of a motion to show cause or a criminal charge under RC 2919.27. If a violation is suspected, a call is made to either the offender's probation officer or to the court for further proceedings. If said violation is found to have occurred, the court may order the offender to jail to serve out the remainder of the sentence.

Unlike protection orders, there is no statutory duty to arrest because no-contact orders are orders of a court, and are not issued by statute.[49] However, under RC 2951.08, a law enforcement officer may arrest a person in violation of a community control sanction without an arrest warrant. A no-contact order is one example of a community control sanction of probation.

Under RC 2951.08(A), "[d]uring a period of community control, any peace officer may arrest the person under a community control sanction without a warrant, if the peace officer has reasonable ground to believe that the person has violated or is violating any of the following that is a condition of the person's community control sanction." Subsection (A) of the aforementioned statute also lists the types of conditions found in community control sanctions for which a violation would allow an arrest. These conditions include, for example:

(1) a condition that prohibits ownership, possession, or use of a firearm, deadly weapon, ammunition or dangerous ordnance;[50]

(2) a condition that prohibits the person form being within a specified structure or geographic area;[51]

(3) a condition that prohibits the person form contacting or communicating with any specified individual;[52]

(4) a condition that prohibit the person from associating with a specified individual.[53]

Since a no-contact order is a type of community control sanction, violators of these sanctions may be arrested without a warrant.

In fact, the Ohio Attorney General issued an opinion in September 2017 indicating that these orders are community control sanctions for which a police officer may arrest the offender, even if the alleged victim consents to the contact or communication provided that the peace officer has reasonable ground to believe that the person has violated or is violating the condition of the person's community control

---

[49]See R.C. 2935.03.

[50]R.C. 29051.08(A)(1).

[51]R.C. 2951.08(A)(2).

[52]R.C. 2951.08(A)(4).

[53]R.C. 2951.08(A)(5).

sanction. The AG also defined "reasonable ground" as probable cause and may be found upon a peace officer's own observation of the violation of a condition of a community control sanction or based upon any other information received by a peace officer, including any other reasonably trustworthy information given to the officer by the alleged victim or witness.[54]

Q & A: Can a no-contact order be entered into LEADS for dissemination to NCIC?

Yes, so long as there is an actual form. Pursuant to NCIC, a no-contact order is included in the definition of a protection order for purposes of entry into NCIC. It meets the criteria as it is "an injunction or restraining order or any other order issued by a civil or criminal court for the purpose of preventing violence or contact or communication with, or physical proximity to another person."[55]

§ 14:4 Determination of primary physical aggressor[1]

Q & A: Is it the preferred course of action in this state to arrest both parties?

No. However, this issue only arises in those cases where both parties have allegedly committed domestic violence and the officer must determine which party is the primary physical aggressor.[2] RC 2935.03(B)(3)(b) provides that:

> [i]f . . . a peace officer has reasonable grounds to believe that the offense of domestic violence or the offense of violating a protection order has been committed and reasonable cause to believe that family or household members have committed the offense against each other, it is the preferred course of action . . . that the officer . . . arrest . . . the family or household member who committed the offense and whom the officer has reasonable cause to believe is the primary physical aggressor.

The "preferred arrest" provision of RC 2935.03(B)(3)(b) only applies to that family or household member who committed the offense and who the officer has reasonable cause to believe is the primary physical aggressor. The preferred arrest policy does not apply to the other family or household member who may have committed the offense but who the officer does not have reasonable cause to believe is the primary physical aggressor. However, under RC 2935.03(B)(3)(b), an officer still has the discretion to arrest, pursuant to RC 2935.03(B)(1), the individual considered to be the nonprimary physical aggressor if

---

[54] 2017 Ohio Op. Att'y Gen. No. 2017-031, 2017 WL 4466515.

[55] 18 U.S.C.A. § 2266.

[Section 14:4]

[1] See, e.g., State v. Boldin, 2008-Ohio-6408, 2008 WL 5147450, *9 (Ohio Ct. App. 11th Dist. Geauga County 2008) (stressing that the issue of the identity of the primary physical aggressor in an altercation is not an element of domestic violence; rather, it relates to officer response; at most it is relevant to a claim of self defense); Cleveland v. Reese, 2016-Ohio-296, 2016 WL 515907 (Ohio Ct. App. 8th Dist. Cuyahoga County 2016).

See also Text § 8:8; Text § 12:29.

[2] But see Daniel G. Saunders, The Tendency to Arrest Victims of Domestic Violence: A Preliminary Analysis of Officer Characteristics, 10 J. Interpersonal Violence 147 (1995).

that person has committed an offense of domestic violence or violating a protection order.[3] This presupposes that the officer has determined that one of the parties is the primary physical aggressor and has first arrested that party.

It is equally possible, however, that the officer will choose not to arrest the other family or household member. Where the officer is unsure which party is the primary physical aggressor, the officer should follow the dictates of RC 2935.03(B)(3)(d) in order to determine which party is the primary physical aggressor.

Of significance is that the statute authorizes an officer to provide a clear statement articulating why he/she chose not to arrest a particular individual who the officer has reasonable cause to believe committed the offense of domestic violence or violating a protection order only when it is the preferred course of action in this state to arrest.[4] Since there is no preferred course of action to arrest a person who committed the offense but who is not the primary physical aggressor,[5] there is no comparable statutory requirement for an officer to articulate reasons for not arresting the nonprimary physical aggressor.[6]

Q & A: How does a police officer determine who is the primary physical aggressor?

Where the police officer has determined that family or household members have committed domestic violence against each other, RC 2935.03(B)(3)(d) sets forth four factors to aid the officer in determining who is the primary physical aggressor.[7] In addition to any other relevant circumstances, the officer should consider the following:

(1) any history of domestic violence or any other violent acts by either person involved in the alleged offense that the officer reasonably can ascertain;[8]

(2) if violence is alleged, whether the alleged violence was caused by a person acting in self-defense;[9]

(3) each person's fear of physical harm, if any, resulting from the

[3] See State v. Johnson, 1989 WL 43040 (Ohio Ct. App. 2d Dist. Greene County 1989) (whether both parties in a domestic violence altercation may be guilty of domestic violence).

[4] RC 2935.03(B)(3)(c).

[5] See RC 2935.03(B)(3)(b).

[6] See RC 2935.03(B)(3)(c).

[7] See State v. Powell, 2006-Ohio-1778, 2006 WL 903596 (Ohio Ct. App. 3d Dist. Allen County 2006). See also Revision of Patrol Guide Procedure 110–38, "Family Offenses/Domestic Violence," in Handling the Domestic Violence Case, 271 PLI/Est. 379 (Practising Law Inst. 1998); Marion Wanless, Mandatory Arrest: A Step Toward Eradicating Domestic Violence, But Is it Enough? 1996 U. Ill. L. Rev. 533 (1996); Stewart v. Stewart, 2001 WL 274097 (Tenn. Ct. App. 2001) (discussing primary physical aggressor and whether the police must make a determination that the "victim" is not the primary physical aggressor before obtaining a protection order).

[8] RC 2935.03(B)(3)(d)(i).

[9] RC 2935.03(B)(3)(d)(ii); see also Gooden v. City of Brunswick, 2014 WL 1379528 (N.D. Ohio 2014) (discussion of self defense); State v. Wheatley, 2000 WL 145394 (Ohio Ct. App. 2d Dist. Montgomery County 2000); State v. Johnson, 1989 WL 43040 (Ohio Ct. App. 2d Dist. Greene County 1989); State v. Caudill, 2007-Ohio-1557, 2008 WL 852626 (Ohio Ct. App. 6th Dist. Wood County 2008) (discussing what is needed to establish self-defense). See also Text § 12:29. See also § 8:8; Text § 12:29 (before *State v. Wheatley*).

other person's threatened use, or history of the use, of force against any person and the reasonableness of that fear;[10] and

(4) the comparative severity of any injuries suffered by the persons involved in the alleged offense.[11]

It is noteworthy that a police officer is not required to consider the aforementioned factors but is merely encouraged to examine these factors in determining whom to arrest.[12] However, the four factors, when considered by the officer, provide direction in certain ambiguous situations.

The first and last factors depend on objective evidence and, therefore, are more readily documented by an officer. For example, an officer may radio dispatch to retrieve information regarding each person's criminal history.[13] Documentation by way of an arrest record, conviction, or presence of a protection order or police report is usually sufficient to demonstrate a criminal history. This includes both the reported and unreported criminal history. Additionally, an officer can objectively examine the parties and observe their injuries and demeanor.[14] Oftentimes, the officer is able to assess who is more seriously injured by comparing the nature of the injuries inflicted.[15] These factors can aid the officer in making the appropriate decision.

Q & A: Is the decision to arrest one or both of the parties always an obvious determination for a police officer?[16]

Unfortunately, it is not always obvious which person is the primary physical aggressor. Under certain circumstances, one party may indeed be more seriously injured, but that party may also be the primary physical aggressor. Consider the scenario where one party chokes the other party. To stop the continued act of choking, the other party may grab a knife, fork, or scissors and stab the first party. When the police arrive, they objectively view the evidence. One party has choke marks around the neck. The other party has been stabbed by the utensil. Are the police obligated to arrest the party who caused the stab wound simply because the injury appears more serious?

It depends. In order to assess who is truly the primary physical aggressor, each of the four factors should be considered concurrently. Initially, the police should explore the criminal history of the parties[17] and the comparative nature of the injuries inflicted by them.[18] Careful fact-finding by the officer at this stage will enable him/her to begin accurately piecing together what happened.

---

[10]RC 2935.03(B)(3)(d)(iii).

[11]RC 2935.03(B)(3)(d)(iv).

[12]See, e.g., State v. Lampe, 2003-Ohio-3059, 2003 WL 21360725 (Ohio Ct. App. 1st Dist. Hamilton County 2003) (discussion of on what officer based his determination of primary physical aggressor).

[13]See RC 2935.03(B)(3)(d)(i).

[14]See Siouffi v. Siouffi, 1998 WL 879255 (Ohio Ct. App. 2d Dist. Montgomery County 1998) (officer's notation and testimony regarding the victim's demeanor helped convict the perpetrator).

[15]See RC 2935.03(B)(1)(d)(iv).

[16]See also Text § 12:29, Mutual protection orders.

[17]RC 2935.03(B)(3)(d)(i).

[18]RC 2935.03(B)(3)(d)(iv).

In determining the primary physical aggressor, officers must always separate the parties and interview all witnesses separately. Officers should interview all children who can speak. Officers should note the height and weight of the parties. Officers should examine the injuries and note if they appear offensive or defensive. Officers should review the physical demeanor of the parties and note their physical conditions and whether there is evidence of injury including marks, abrasions or redness. They should note whether either or both appear intoxicated or on drugs. They should note any spontaneous declarations. Finally, officers should note if either party exhibits fear. This may be demonstrated by crying, shaking, or sometimes anger. Calm usually defines the perpetrator.

The officer is also encouraged to consider whether the alleged violence was caused by a person acting in self-defense[19] and each person's fear of physical harm and the reasonableness of that fear.[20] Since these factors are much more subjective, this type of an evaluation may place the officer in the position of both judge and jury. The officer must, in a split second, determine whether to arrest one or both of the parties. Depending on the outcome of this assessment, the officer will determine which party is the primary physical aggressor. The officer should then arrest the primary physical aggressor, but the officer may arrest both parties.

The officer may decide that one party stabbed the other in self-defense. After weighing the four factors, the officer may determine that the person stabbed was, in fact, the primary physical aggressor. If it can be demonstrated that the primary aggressor caused the incident or created the situation causing the victim to respond or be injured, the officer should arrest the primary aggressor. The officer should also note in the police report whether the victim was in fear of the primary aggressor and whether the fear was reasonable in light of the facts presented by the parties.

On the other hand, the officer may choose to arrest both parties. The officer may determine that both parties were primary physical aggressors. The officer may decide that the party who stabbed the other indeed committed a crime and should be arrested as well.

In some instances, the police officer may reject a claim of self-defense and conclude that the person who stabbed his/her partner was the primary aggressor. This is more likely to occur when a victim has no visible injuries to substantiate the explanation given or when the injury allegedly inflicted in self-defense is sufficiently serious to require hospitalization or treatment.

The primary physical aggressor factors should always be considered conjointly by a police officer because they are instrumental in substantiating the officer's decision to arrest. It is also imperative that a police officer note in the mandatory incident report which person was arrested and why. Although not required by statute, it is crucial for an officer to articulate reasons for both arresting and not

[19] RC 2935.03(B)(3)(d)(ii).

[20] RC 2935.03(B)(3)(d)(iii).

arresting. Besides complying with the statute,[21] an incident report detailing whether or not a party was arrested and why may insulate an officer from potential liability should there be a subsequent lawsuit alleging police liability for the failure to protect victims of domestic violence.

RC 2935.032(A)(1) may also provide some direction for the officer who does not have a clear picture of the situation. RC 2935.032(A) directs each law enforcement agency to adopt policies that include a provision requiring the officer to arrest an individual who commits a felonious or aggravated assault provided that the person has first been determined to be the primary physical aggressor as set forth in RC 2935.03(B)(3)(d).[22] Consideration of the primary physical aggressor factors does not appear to be discretionary. Although there is no requirement that the police officer arrest the person who perpetrated the stabbing even though the injury was serious, once the officer decides that the individual was the primary physical aggressor, the officer must then arrest that individual for felonious or aggravated assault.[23]

Q & A: What questions should a police officer ask to determine which party is the primary physical aggressor?

Across the country, more and more law enforcement officials are arresting both parties. This trend suggests that police officers either cannot adequately determine who the primary physical aggressor is or find it more expedient to arrest both parties and allow the prosecutors to sort things out.

When making a determination about whom to arrest, officers should consider asking the following:

(1) Who in the relationship poses the most danger to the other?

(2) Who is most at risk of future harm/injury?

(3) Was the amount of force used appropriate and reasonable under the circumstances of the case?

(4) What is the relative severity of the injuries inflicted on each person?

(5) What is the likelihood of future harm?

(6) Have there been prior complaints of domestic violence with the same parties?[24]

Officers who investigate the scene of the incident must always remember to document their observations as to whether the victim appears to be in fear of physical harm. Officers should document this by noting the victim's response by way of his/her emotional state, de-

---

[21]See RC 2935.03(B)(3)(c); see also RC 2935.032(A)(4), RC 2935.032(D); see also Cleveland v. Williams, 2003-Ohio-31, 2003 WL 60989 (Ohio Ct. App. 8th Dist. Cuyahoga County 2003).

[22]RC 2935.032(A)(1)(a)(ii).

[23]RC 2935.032(A)(1)(a), RC 2935.032(A)(1)(b).

[24]Domestic Violence Arrest Training Project, Primary Aggressor Curriculum, Section II(B). For copy, contact California Alliance Against Domestic Violence at 1-800-524-4765.

meanor, and words. It is important for the officer to ask about the victim's belief that harm or injury was both serious and imminent.[25]

Q & A: Can an officer testify as to which party was the primary physical aggressor?

According to the Stark County Court of Appeals, the answer is in the affirmative. In *State v. Grieg*,[26] appellant claimed that the trial court erred in permitting a deputy to testify that he believed the appellant was the primary physical aggressor. Appellant contended that the deputy testified as an expert on domestic violence and because of this, he should not have opined about who was the primary physical aggressor.

However, the court found that the officer was not offered as an expert; rather, he was a an investigator who followed up on domestic violence reports and trained on domestic violence issues regarding investigations, psychological effects of domestic violence and legal updates.[27] "In cases in which both parties have injuries and one argues self-defense,[28] such as the instant case, the investigator must determine who was the primary physical aggressor to seek an arrest warrant."[29]

The appellate court went on to point out that, as explained in *State v. Boldin*,[30] "[t]he issue of who the primary aggressor is in an altercation is not an element of domestic violence. Rather, it relates to the proper procedure a police officer should follow when making an arrest in a domestic violence case."[31] "The Court notes RC 2935.03 requires police departments to seek an arrest warrant for the party they have reason to believe is the primary physical aggressor."[32] The issue of primary physical aggressor may become relevant at trial when a defendant asserts self defense but "* * *a determination of the identity of the primary physical aggressor is not an element of the of-

[25]See also Text § 6:13, Trial presentation—Physical evidence.

[26]State v. Greig, 2014-Ohio-4063, 2014 WL 4638838 (Ohio Ct. App. 5th Dist. Stark County 2014).

[27]State v. Greig, 2014-Ohio-4063, 2014 WL 4638838, ¶ 22 (Ohio Ct. App. 5th Dist. Stark County 2014).

[28]See also State v. Batie, 2015-Ohio-762, 2015 WL 929478 (Ohio Ct. App. 8th Dist. Cuyahoga County 2015) (noting that while the primary physical aggressor is not necessarily the same as the initial aggressor, the primary aggressor question can undermine a claim of self defense, where the officer's testimony goes beyond that inquiry and treads on the realm of who initiated the altercation, at ¶ 8); State v. Adams, 2018-Ohio-604, 2018 WL 920023 (Ohio Ct. App. 2d Dist. Champaign County 2018).

[29]State v. Greig, 2014-Ohio-4063, 2014 WL 4638838, ¶ 22 (Ohio Ct. App. 5th Dist. Stark County 2014).; State v. Boldin, 2008-Ohio-6408, 2008 WL 5147450, *9 (Ohio Ct. App. 11th Dist. Geauga County 2008) (stressing that the issue of the identity of the primary physical aggressor in an altercation is not an element of domestic violence; rather, it relates to officer response, at most it is relevant to a claim of self defense).

[30]State v. Boldin, 2008-Ohio-6408, 2008 WL 5147450 (Ohio Ct. App. 11th Dist. Geauga County 2008).

[31]State v. Greig, 2014-Ohio-4063, 2014 WL 4638838, ¶ 23 (Ohio Ct. App. 5th Dist. Stark County 2014), quoting *Boldin* at ¶ 78.

[32]State v. Greig, 2014-Ohio-4063, 2014 WL 4638838, ¶ 23 (Ohio Ct. App. 5th Dist. Stark County 2014), quoting *Boldin* ¶ 79.

fense of domestic violence."[33] "An officer's testimony regarding the primary physical aggressor does not invade the province of the factfinder because the officer is not opining on the ultimate issue in the case."[34] Thus, the appellate court overruled appellant's sole assignment of error.

§ 14:5 False arrest, warrantless arrests and searches, and weapons confiscation[1]

Q & A: When a police officer arrests a person for domestic violence or for violating a protection order, can the police officer be sued for false arrest?

Obviously, anyone can be sued. The more important question is whether the person who sues for false arrest will prevail.[2] Since officers are encouraged to arrest when there are reasonable grounds to do so, they are also at a greater risk of being sued. To avoid this type of frivolous suit, RC 2935.032(D) mandates that officers prepare written incident reports. The reasons why an officer arrested an individual will be documented by the officer as part of the evidence gathering.[3]

Additionally, probable cause to arrest is a defense to false arrest.[4] Therefore, in any false arrest case, it is important to determine whether it was objectively reasonable for the officers to believe that probable cause existed at the time of the arrest.[5]

Moreover, a specific good faith immunity provision has been

---

[33]State v. Greig, 2014-Ohio-4063, 2014 WL 4638838, ¶ 23 (Ohio Ct. App. 5th Dist. Stark County 2014), quoting Boldin at ¶ 81.

[34]State v. Greig, 2014-Ohio-4063, 2014 WL 4638838, ¶ 23 (Ohio Ct. App. 5th Dist. Stark County 2014).

[Section 14:5]

[1]See also Text § 18:11, Firearm offenses under VAWA; Text § 12:22, Remedies—Miscellaneous issues; Text § 14:15, Potential police liability in the enforcement of protection orders. U.S. v. Gatson, 776 F.3d 405 (6th Cir. 2015) (Firearms conviction under 18 U.S.C.A. 922(g)(9) affirmed since police stop was not an illegal search and seizure).

[2]See, e.g., Faulkner v. Faulkner, 2000 WL 5910 (Ohio Ct. App. 6th Dist. Sandusky County 2000); see also Klein v. Long, 275 F.3d 544, 2001 FED App. 0434P (6th Cir. 2001); Gooden v. City of Brunswick, 2014 WL 1379528 (N.D. Ohio 2014); Meekins v. City of Oberlin, 2018-Ohio-1308, 2018 WL 1640059 (Ohio Ct. App. 8th Dist. Cuyahoga County 2018) (discussion of false arrest claim for violating a CPO and political subdivision immunity under RC 2744).

[3]See for example, White v. Roch, 2005-Ohio-1127, 2005 WL 602684 (Ohio Ct. App. 9th Dist. Summit County 2005) (where officers had probable cause to arrest mother for domestic violence and that there was a written statement by son alleging mother hit son on his arm hard enough to make him cry).

[4]See, e.g., Wolford v. Sanchez, 2005-Ohio-6992, 2005 WL 3556681 (Ohio Ct. App. 9th Dist. Lorain County 2005). See also Scott v. City of Bexley, 11 Fed. Appx. 514 (6th Cir. 2001).

[5]See Beck v. State of Ohio, 379 U.S. 89, 85 S. Ct. 223, 13 L. Ed. 2d 142 (1964); see also Wildoner v. Borough of Ramsey, 162 N.J. 375, 744 A.2d 1146 (2000); Donovan v. Briggs, 250 F. Supp. 2d 242 (W.D. N.Y. 2003); Beier v. City of Lewiston, 354 F.3d 1058 (9th Cir. 2004); Alagha v. Cameron, 2009-Ohio-4886, 2009 WL 2974892 (Ohio Ct. App. 1st Dist. Hamilton County 2009); Collins v. Clancy, 2014 WL 1653103 (S.D. Ohio 2014); Gooden v. City of Brunswick, 2014 WL 1379528 (N.D. Ohio 2014) (discussion about probable cause determinations to arrest); Al-Lamadani v. Lang, 624 Fed. Appx. 405 (6th Cir. 2015) (finding that a jury could reasonably infer that the officer lacked

included in the law. Law enforcement officials who arrest an offender for an incident of domestic violence or violating a protection order are immune in any civil action for damages for injury, death, or loss to person or property that arises from, or is related to, the arrest.[6] Likewise, if an officer arrests an individual based on a protection order, the officer is immune from civil liability where the protection order appears valid on its face.[7] These provisions go far in insulating an officer from liability.[8]

Q & A: Does a warrantless arrest automatically give rise to a warrantless search?[9]

The Fourth Amendment prohibits all unreasonable searches and seizures.[10] However, it is silent on the critical issue of when a warrant is required. Case law has provided the exceptions to the warrant requirement.[11]

In the domestic violence arena, the issue often arises in situations where a search of the residence is incidental to an arrest or where an officer had probable cause to believe that someone at the premises had committed an act of domestic violence. For example, in *State v. Michael*,[12] the Third District Court of Appeals reversed a trial court decision to suppress evidence found during an arrest for domestic violence. The court of appeals stated that, in the course of a lawful arrest, police officers may search the offender for weapons and other

---

probable cause to detain the appellee); Fields v. City of Salem Police Dept., 2015 WL 461887 (D.N.J. 2015).

[6]RC 2935.03(B)(4). See for eg., Perez v. City of Fremont, 2015 WL 833680 (Cal. App. 1st Dist. 2015), unpublished/noncitable (appellate court found that officer's conduct in shooting suspect was reasonable under extremely dangerous exigent circumstances).

[7]RC 2935.032(F).

[8]See Lisa Lerman, Expansion of Arrest Power: A Key to Effective Intervention, 7 Vt. L. Rev. 59 (1982). But see Al-Lamadani v. Lang, 624 Fed. Appx. 405 (6th Cir. 2015) (where the officer should have known that suspect had not been served, it is arguable that the officer did not have probable cause to detain him on the night of the incident; thus affirming denial of qualified immunity).

[9]See State v. Sharpe, 174 Ohio App. 3d 498, 2008-Ohio-267, 882 N.E.2d 960 (2d Dist. Clark County 2008) (warrantless search of house was not justified by exigent circumstances to retrieve weapon police believed to be there); see also State v. Martindale, 2005-Ohio-6437, 2005 WL 3293762 (Ohio Ct. App. 5th Dist. Fairfield County 2005) (discussing exceptions to the warrant requirement); Amanda Jane Proctor, Breaking Into the Marital Home to Break Up Domestic Violence: Fourth Amendment Analysis of "Disputed Permission," 170 American University Journal of Gender, Social Policy & the Law 139 (2009).

[10]See State v. Perkins, 358 N.J. Super. 151, 817 A.2d 364 (App. Div. 2003); U.S. v. Baker, 254 F. Supp. 2d 768 (S.D. Ohio 2003).

[11]See State v. Jenkins, 104 Ohio App. 3d 265, 269 n.5, 661 N.E.2d 806 (1st Dist. Hamilton County 1995) ("'[T]he police bear a heavy burden when attempting to demonstrate an urgent need that might justify warrantless searches or arrests.'") (quoting Welsh v. Wisconsin, 466 U.S. 740, 749, 104 S. Ct. 2091, 80 L. Ed. 2d 732 (1984)). See also William A. Alford III, Does Domestic Violence Constitute an Exigency Justifying a Warrantless Search? 37 Washburn L. J. 763 (1998)

.

[12]State v. Michael, 1997 WL 335527 (Ohio Ct. App. 3d Dist. Crawford County 1997); see also State v. Howard, 2007-Ohio-3170, 2007 WL 1806077 (Ohio Ct. App. 7th Dist. Mahoning County 2007).

dangerous criminal products.[13] The appellate court determined that the arrest of the defendant was constitutional because the officer (1) had obtained information from the defendant's wife regarding domestic violence and (2) had seen the wife's injuries. Such information provided sufficient evidence of probable cause to arrest for domestic violence.[14]

In contrast, in *State v. Samarghandi*,[15] police officers responded to a 911 call. Upon their arrival, they spoke with Mrs. Samarghandi who was outside and who informed them that there was no violence or weapons, that she only wanted her husband to return her car keys, and that her second call to 911 was to cancel the first call. The police entered the residence even though neither party consented to the entry.[16] Both parties were arrested for resisting arrest. The court found that an argument by the defendants and the husband's refusal to part with the car keys did not constitute criminal behavior, especially domestic violence.

The Hamilton County Municipal Court determined that there was no probable cause to arrest both the husband and wife where the officers did not have a valid basis to obtain consent to enter and remain in the defendants' home,[17] that no exigent circumstances existed, and that no official duty existed to investigate the domestic situation. The court pointed out that "[it] does not find that a radio run for a domestic 'situation' is tantamount to a domestic violence situation."[18]

The Supreme Court of Ohio considered this issue in *State v. Applegate*.[19] In this case, the victim called 911 from a convenience store, stating that she and her husband were involved in an altercation and that she wanted him removed from the house. Officers were dispatched to the home on a call of domestic violence and, upon their arrival, they heard an angry male yelling and arguing and bumping noises suggesting furniture being overturned. Believing the persons inside could be in danger, the officers entered the common entryway and announced themselves as officers as they went upstairs. The of-

[13] See for e.g.; United States v. Jones, 861 F.3d 638 (7th Cir. 2017), as amended, (June 30, 2017).

[14] See also City of Alliance v. Hawkins, 1997 WL 116915 (Ohio Ct. App. 5th Dist. Stark County 1997).

[15] State v. Samarghandi, 84 Ohio Misc. 2d 6, 680 N.E.2d 738 (Mun. Ct. 1997); see also U.S. v. Baker, 254 F. Supp. 2d 768 (S.D. Ohio 2003).

[16] But see State v. Semenchuk, 2002-Ohio-674, 2002 WL 253876 (Ohio Ct. App. 8th Dist. Cuyahoga County 2002) (when daughter consented to police entry into home).

[17] See U.S. v. Baker, 254 F. Supp. 2d 768 (S.D. Ohio 2003) (where federal district court discussed whether officers had a valid basis to enter residence).

[18] State v. Samarghandi, 84 Ohio Misc. 2d 6, 9, 680 N.E.2d 738 (Mun. Ct. 1997); see also City of East Palestine, Ohio v. Adrian, 1997 WL 321623 (Ohio Ct. App. 7th Dist. Columbiana County 1997).

[19] State v. Applegate, 68 Ohio St. 3d 348, 1994-Ohio-356, 626 N.E.2d 942 (1994); see also State v. Byerly, 1998 WL 637689 (Ohio Ct. App. 11th Dist. Portage County 1998); State v. Schroeder, 2001 WL 1308002 (Ohio Ct. App. 6th Dist. Wood County 2001). But see State v. DeLong, 2007-Ohio-2330, 2007 WL 1413394, *2 (Ohio Ct. App. 4th Dist. Ross County 2007) (RC 2935.03(B)(1) and (3) did not give law enforcement justification for warrantless entry; see also dissenting opinion at *4); State v. Fisher, 2014-Ohio-3029, 2014 WL 3372484 (Ohio Ct. App. 5th Dist. Fairfield County 2014).

ficers confronted the defendant, ordered him to put down the bottle and arrested him when he refused to comply. When he was later searched, as part of the custodial booking, cocaine was found.

The trial court found him guilty, but the appellate court reversed the conviction, stating that the warrantless entry was not justified by sufficient evidence of exigent circumstances.[20]

The Ohio Supreme Court reversed the court of appeals stating that the officers' warrantless entry into Applegate's home was justified by exigent circumstances. The Supreme Court reasoned that "[e]xigent circumstances justify a warrantless entry into a residence by police when police are at the residence pursuant to an emergency call reporting domestic violence and where the officers hear sounds from inside the residence which are indicative of violence."[21] The court then noted that the officers' actions were conservative, prudent and reasonable.[22]

Other state decisions have found that police response to a domestic violence call qualifies as an "exigent circumstance" for warrantless entry into a defendant's residence.[23] For example, in *State v. Greene*,[24] the Arizona Supreme Court recognized that domestic violence calls involve extreme danger where the immediate presence of the police officer is essential:

> The call itself creates a sufficient indication that an exigency exists allowing the officer to enter a dwelling if no circumstance indicates that entry is unnecessary. Once the officer entered the apartment pursuant to the exigency, he could lawfully take steps "reasonably related to the routine investigation of the offense and the identification of the perpetrator."

Additionally, the Supreme Court allowed evidence obtained from the defendant's apartment where such evidence was related to a different crime for which the defendant was not being investigated.

---

[20]State v. Applegate, 68 Ohio St. 3d 348, 1994-Ohio-356, 626 N.E.2d 942, 943 (1994).

[21]State v. Applegate, 68 Ohio St. 3d 348, 1994-Ohio-356, 626 N.E.2d 942, 942–943 (1994); see also U.S. v. Lawrence, 236 F. Supp. 2d 953 (D. Neb. 2002); State v. Gooden, 2008-Ohio-178, 2008 WL 186646 (Ohio Ct. App. 9th Dist. Summit County 2008); State v. Gooden, 2008-Ohio-178, 2008 WL 186646 (Ohio Ct. App. 9th Dist. Summit County 2008) (the emergency aid exception allows officers to enter a dwelling without a warrant and without probable cause when the reasonably believe, based on specific and articulable facts, that a person within the dwelling is in need of immediate aid); State v. Fisher, 2014-Ohio-3029, 2014 WL 3372484 (Ohio Ct. App. 5th Dist. Fairfield County 2014) (answering the question of whether any exigent circumstances extinguished the need for a search warrant in a domestic violence case, finding that facts of case do not support any exception to the warrant requirement justifying warrantless entry).

[22]State v. Applegate, 68 Ohio St. 3d 348, 1994-Ohio-356, 626 N.E.2d 942, 944 (1994).

[23]See also Com. v. Morrison, 429 Mass. 511, 710 N.E.2d 584 (1999); State v. Chiampo, 2003-Ohio-2422, 2003 WL 21078082 (Ohio Ct. App. 9th Dist. Wayne County 2003); People v. Mascarenas, 972 P.2d 717 (Colo. App. 1998). But see Com. v. Midi, 46 Mass. App. Ct. 591, 708 N.E.2d 124 (1999).

[24]State v. Greene, 162 Ariz. 431, 433, 784 P.2d 257 (1989) (quoting State v. Fleischman, 157 Ariz. 11, 15, 754 P.2d 340 (Ct. App. Div. 2 1988)) (citations omitted); see also Fletcher v. Town of Clinton, 196 F.3d 41 (1st Cir. 1999); Joyce v. Town of Tewksbury, Mass., 112 F.3d 19, 21–22 (1st Cir. 1997); Anderson v. City of West Bend Police Dept., 774 F. Supp. 2d 925 (E.D. Wis. 2011); but see U.S. v. Davis, 290 F.3d 1239 (10th Cir. 2002) (discussing when exigent circumstances exist).

Q & A: Are police officers allowed to make warrantless entries based on reports of alleged domestic violence at the premises?[25]

In *City of Dayton v. Johnson*,[26] the officers responded to a call alleging domestic violence at the premises. On arriving, the officers knocked and requested to speak to the persons inside. The male told them to leave. The officers heard a female voice in the apartment and requested that the female come outside so that they could verify her safety. When she did not respond, the officers' superior gave them permission to enter the premises. The male was subsequently arrested and found guilty of obstruction of official business. On appeal, the defendant argued that the officers were not conducting lawful duties when they attempted to enter his apartment without a search warrant.

The Montgomery County Court of Appeals relied on the United States Supreme Court's holding in *Mincey v. Arizona*,[27] where the Court acknowledged "the need to protect or preserve life or avoid serious injury is justification for what would be otherwise illegal absent an exigency or emergency."[28] The appellate court held that "[t]he exigent circumstances exception to the warrant requirement applies when the police have a reasonable basis to believe someone inside the premises requires immediate aid."[29] The anonymous telephone call reporting fighting in the apartment and the defendant's refusal to

[25]See also Thacker v. City of Columbus, 328 F.3d 244, 2003 FED App. 0127P (6th Cir. 2003) (exigent circumstances justified police officers' warrantless entry into caller's home); City of Brooklyn v. Muniz, 2008-Ohio-54, 2008 WL 98200 (Ohio Ct. App. 8th Dist. Cuyahoga County 2008) (officers could enter premises where they had a complaint of domestic violence, a complainant who corroborated the claim and who expressed a fear that her daughter might be in danger and thus the officers were under a duty to investigate. Thus, a sweep of the premises was warranted.). But see U.S. v. Tatman, 615 F. Supp. 2d 664 (S.D. Ohio 2008), aff'd, 397 Fed. Appx. 152 (6th Cir. 2010); Lappin v. Gabel, 2016 WL 1258588 (N.D. Ohio 2016) (addressing what is probable cause to arrest in domestic violence situations).

[26]City of Dayton v. Johnson, 1999 WL 55705 (Ohio Ct. App. 2d Dist. Montgomery County 1999); see also State v. Applegate, 68 Ohio St. 3d 348, 1994-Ohio-356, 626 N.E.2d 942 (1994); State v. Chiampo, 2003-Ohio-2422, 2003 WL 21078082 (Ohio Ct. App. 9th Dist. Wayne County 2003); State v. Martindale, 2005-Ohio-6437, 2005 WL 3293762 (Ohio Ct. App. 5th Dist. Fairfield County 2005).

[27]Mincey v. Arizona, 437 U.S. 385, 392–93, 98 S. Ct. 2408, 57 L. Ed. 2d 290 (1978); see also Tierney v. Davidson, 133 F.3d 189 (2d Cir. 1998) (holding that police officers are entitled to qualified immunity from civil rights claims arising from their response to a domestic dispute, including warrantless entry and search of couple's home, and setting forth considerations used in determining whether use of force violates due process); State v. Gooden, 2008-Ohio-178, 2008 WL 186646 (Ohio Ct. App. 9th Dist. Summit County 2008); State v. Fisher, 2014-Ohio-3029, 2014 WL 3372484 (Ohio Ct. App. 5th Dist. Fairfield County 2014) (noting that since *Applegate*, courts of appeals have found application of the emergency aid exception requires an officer to have a "reasonable belief that it was necessary to investigate an emergency threatening life and limb." At ¶ 40, quoting *Gooden*, at ¶ 7, citing *Applegate* at 350).

[28]City of Dayton v. Johnson, 1999 WL 55705, *3 (Ohio Ct. App. 2d Dist. Montgomery County 1999) (quoting *Mincey*); see also State v. Comer, 2002 UT App 219, 51 P.3d 55 (Utah Ct. App. 2002).

[29]City of Dayton v. Johnson, 1999 WL 55705, *3 (Ohio Ct. App. 2d Dist. Montgomery County 1999); Thacker v. City of Columbus, 328 F.3d 244, 2003 FED App. 0127P (6th Cir. 2003). But see Fletcher v. Town of Clinton, 196 F.3d 41, 50 (1st Cir. 1999) (noting that "victims of domestic violence do not give up their constitutional

permit the officers to speak with the female occupant provided a reasonable basis for the police to believe that the female was at risk of injury.[30]

Q & A: Can the police officer confiscate a weapon used in the domestic violence incident or violation of a protection order?

Yes. Not only must the law enforcement officer seize a weapon[31] used, threatened, or brandished during the incident,[32] the same officer is immune from liability for the seizure.[33] RC 2935.03(B)(3)(h) provides in part:

> If a peace officer . . . responds to a report of an alleged incident of . . . domestic violence or . . . violating a protection order [or consent agreement] and if the circumstances . . . involved the use or threatened use of a deadly weapon or any person . . . brandished a deadly weapon during or in relation to the incident, the deadly weapon . . . constitutes contraband, and, to the extent possible, the officer shall seize the deadly weapon.[34]

Q & A: Can the police confiscate a weapon that has not been used, brandished, or threatened with use in relation to the incident?[35]

It is unclear whether police officials responding to an incident of domestic violence or violating a protection order may seize all weapons discovered at the premises. Nothing in the domestic violence statute confers immunity on a police officer who confiscates a weapon that has not been used, threatened with use, or brandished during or in relation to the incident of domestic violence or violating a protection order.

However, several jurisdictions have examined a similar issue and held that, where a spouse voluntarily consents to a search and seizure of weapons in the home, it is not necessary that they be in plain view

rights or the sanctity of their homes as the price for obtaining a restraining order against an abuser").

[30]But see City of Brooklyn v. Muniz, 2008-Ohio-54, 2008 WL 98200, *5 (Ohio Ct. App. 8th Dist. Cuyahoga County 2008) (dissent stated that city failed to prove that defendant's conduct gave rise to a substantial safety risk to his daughter).

[31]See RC 2903.11(A) for a definition of "deadly weapon." See also State v. Taylor, 2003-Ohio-2025, 2003 WL 1916787 (Ohio Ct. App. 9th Dist. Summit County 2003) (holding that a pitchfork was a deadly weapon); Melanie L. Mecka, Seizing the Ammunition from Domestic Violence: Prohibiting the Ownership of Firearms to Abusers, 29 Rutgers L.J. 607 (1998); Emily J. Sack, Confronting the Issue of Gun Seizure in Domestic Violence Cases, 6 J. Center for Families, Child. & Cts. 3 (2003).

[32]See RC 2935.03(B)(3)(h).

[33]See RC 2935.03(B)(4).

[34]See also State v. Majka, 2002-Ohio-1378, 2002 WL 462858 (Ohio Ct. App. 9th Dist. Summit County 2002) (firearms and ammunition seized during an investigation for domestic violence, where the defendant pled no contest to an amended charge of disorderly conduct, is contraband and as such the trial court properly denied the return of his property); City of Cleveland v. Carpenter, 2003-Ohio-6923, 2003 WL 22976619, *3 (Ohio Ct. App. 8th Dist. Cuyahoga County 2003) (relied on reasoning of *State v. Majka* to affirm decision concluding that misdemeanor crimes of violence such as simple assault need not have a domestic violence relationship element in order to disqualify misdemeanant from possessing firearms).

[35]See also Text § 12:22, Remedies—Miscellaneous issues.

in order for the police to seize them.[36] In *State v. Piccus*,[37] the wife contacted the police alleging domestic violence and then invited them into the house and led them to her husband's guns. The Eighth District Court of Appeals found that she had voluntarily consented to the search. The court of appeals relied on the well-established principle that "a wife may consent to a search of a marital residence as long as the search is limited to areas of common control."[38] The court concluded that "[s]ince we hold that his wife voluntarily consented to the search and seizure of the weapons, reliance on the plain view exception to the warrant requirement is not necessary."[39]

The Fourth Amendment to the United States Constitution provides that the people have a right to be free from unreasonable searches and seizures.[40] The plain view exception to the warrant requirement "extend[s] to nonpublic places such as the home, where searches and seizures without a warrant are presumptively unreasonable, the police's longstanding authority to make warrantless seizures in public places of such objects as weapons and contraband."[41] The justification for this extension is the desirability of sparing the police the inconvenience and potential risk of getting a search warrant to seize objects that are already in plain view of the officer in the course of a lawful search.[42]

In the area of consent searches, it is well settled that certain third parties may voluntarily consent to searches, which will allow for the admission of seized evidence confiscated during or in relation to the search.[43] Most of the third party consent cases involve the husband-wife relationship, and the predominant view is that, when spouses jointly own or occupy the premises in question, either spouse may

---

[36]See State v. Piccus, 1988 WL 32145 (Ohio Ct. App. 8th Dist. Cuyahoga County 1988); see also State v. McCarthy, 26 Ohio St. 2d 87, 55 Ohio Op. 2d 161, 269 N.E.2d 424 (1971); State v. Esparza, 1990 WL 7966 (Ohio Ct. App. 3d Dist. Defiance County 1990); State v. Masten, 1989 WL 111983 (Ohio Ct. App. 3d Dist. Hancock County 1989).

[37]State v. Piccus, 1988 WL 32145 (Ohio Ct. App. 8th Dist. Cuyahoga County 1988).

[38]State v. Piccus, 1988 WL 32145, *2 (Ohio Ct. App. 8th Dist. Cuyahoga County 1988).

[39]State v. Piccus, 1988 WL 32145, *2 (Ohio Ct. App. 8th Dist. Cuyahoga County 1988).

[40]See, e.g., State v. Perkins, 358 N.J. Super. 151, 817 A.2d 364 (App. Div. 2003) (Superior Court concluded that searches and seizures conducted pursuant to Domestic Violence Act do not turn afoul of the Fourth Amendment guarantees because they are undertaken to promote legitimate state interests unrelated to the acquisition of evidence of criminality or in furtherance of a criminal prosecution); see also U.S. v. Baker, 254 F. Supp. 2d 768 (S.D. Ohio 2003).

[41]Arizona v. Hicks, 480 U.S. 321, 326–27, 107 S. Ct. 1149, 94 L. Ed. 2d 347 (1987) (citing Payton v. New York, 445 U.S. 573, 100 S. Ct. 1371, 63 L. Ed. 2d 639 (1980)); see also Coolidge v. New Hampshire, 403 U.S. 443, 91 S. Ct. 2022, 29 L. Ed. 2d 564 (1971).

[42]Arizona v. Hicks, 480 U.S. 321, 107 S. Ct. 1149, 94 L. Ed. 2d 347 (1987).

[43]See, e.g., State v. Beougher, 2003-Ohio-3591, 2003 WL 21537459 (Ohio Ct. App. 9th Dist. Summit County 2003) (domestic violence victim's consent to search residence she and defendant shared was voluntary, and thus, weapon police removed from residence was admissible during prosecution for domestic violence; victim asked office to remove weapon and voluntarily showed officer where weapon was located).

consent to a search for incriminating items which may subsequently be used against one of the parties.[44]

Q & A: Does the court have the authority, pursuant to a protection order, to order the search of a non-party's residence (without that party's consent) and seize all weapons found, including those belonging to the non-party?

Although no Ohio case has addressed this,[45] a Pennsylvania appellate court discussed some of the relevant considerations in *Kelly v. Mueller*.[46] The trial court had granted an ex-girlfriend a protection order due to threats by the defendant to kill her with a loaded shotgun, and which required the defendant to turn over to police all weapons used or threatened to be used by him. When the police went to defendant's residence to collect the weapons listed in the order, his son stated there were no weapons. Because Plaintiff had testified she had previously seen the weapons at that location, the court issued a Supplemental Order directing the sheriff to search both the residence of the father and the son and the family's cabin.

On appeal, the father argued that the trial court exceeded its authority by issuing orders to search his residence and the hunting cabin and to seize all weapons found, regardless of ownership. In Pennsylvania as in Ohio, the court may grant any protection order to bring about the cessation of domestic violence.[47]

While both statutes grant the court the authority to require the abuser to relinquish all weapons, it does not specifically grant the court the authority to search the abuser's residence or other property to seize weapons. In *Kelly*, the Pennsylvania appeals court reframed the issue to whether the trial court exceeded its authority and abused its discretion in choosing between remedies afforded by their domestic violence statute (PFA Act) and whether other available options were as efficacious under the circumstances and would achieve the required result, protection of appellee from possible death or serious injury.[48] Under this analysis, the search and seizure of a defendant is apparently within the intent of the domestic abuse act, even though it was not expressly included in the list of available remedies contained therein.

In affirming the trial court, the appellate court reasoned that the facts warranted a finding that appellee was in serious danger due to

---

[44]See U.S. v. Matlock, 415 U.S. 164, 94 S. Ct. 988, 39 L. Ed. 2d 242 (1974); see also State v. Stoken, 1987 WL 28162 (Ohio Ct. App. 1st Dist. Hamilton County 1987).

[45]See State v. Elschlager, 2017-Ohio-5545, 2017 WL 2806352, ¶ 36 (Ohio Ct. App. 5th Dist. Delaware County 2017) (where law enforcement obtained search warrant to recover stolen items in a stalking case (where a CPO/TPO was not issued), the confiscation of a gun when the warrant didn't specifically mention firearms did not fall within the parameters of the good faith exception).

[46]Kelly v. Mueller, 2004 PA Super 425, 861 A.2d 984 (2004), decision vacated, 590 Pa. 91, 912 A.2d 202 (2006)

[47]See also RC 3113.31(E)(1); Sup. R. Form 10.01-H to Sup. R. Form 10.01-J include a provision ordering a respondent to refrain from possessing, using, carrying, or obtaining a deadly weapon and ordering a respondent to turn over all deadly weapons in his/her possession to the law enforcement officer who serves respondent with the Order.

[48]Kelly v. Mueller, 2004 PA Super 425, 861 A.2d 984, 992 (2004), decision vacated, 590 Pa. 91, 912 A.2d 202 (2006).

the defendant's threats to use one of several weapons which could result in death or serious injury. The law "is sufficiently explicit and broad to deal with weapons, once adequately described under oath, to the same degree that an affidavit of probable cause would have been permissible to authorize a search and seizure."[49] "Exigent circumstances required that no further hearings be initiated at that time. The fact that father was not a party did not exempt his home, cottage and automobile from search for identified weapons which his live-in son would have had available to carry out his threats. If a court cannot reach weapons located wherever an abuser resides, it nullifies the preventive thrust of the most critical section of the Act, that is, to disarm the abuser. Every person in close proximity to the abuser would be in danger, including his father, the police, and appellee. Permitting son to remain in the house with father without surrender of the weapons based upon father's claim of privacy, would be irresponsible."[50]

However, the Supreme Court of Pennsylvania vacated the Superior Court decision and reinstated the trial court order finding that the issue of whether the Protection from Abuse (PFA) Act authorized courts to order search and seizure without offending the protections of the Fourth Amendment and its counterpart under Commonwealth Constitution was not properly challenged in the common pleas court or raised in the statement of matters complained of filed by the boyfriend and his father and, thus, was waived and should not have been decided by the Superior Court on appeal.[51]

Q & A: Are police officers permitted to confiscate the weapons of individuals subject to protection orders?

A police officer may confiscate a deadly weapon or firearm without a warrant in accordance with RC 2935.03(B)(3)(h) which states that if a peace officer responds to a report of an alleged offense of domestic violence or an alleged incident of the offense of violating a protection order and if the circumstances of the incident involved the use or threatened use of a deadly weapon or any person involved in the incident brandished a deadly weapon during or in relation to the incident, the deadly weapon that was used, threatened to be used or brandished constitutes contraband and, to the extent possible, the officer shall seize the deadly weapon as contraband pursuant to Chapter 2981.

Neither domestic violence statute permits law enforcement to specifically confiscate weapons.[52] However, both civil and criminal protection orders routinely contain provisions that authorize law enforcement agencies to receive and store any and all weapons belonging to a certain individual that are surrendered by that individual. In issuing civil protection orders, courts rely on the statutory language contained in RC 3113.31(E)(1) for legal authority. Courts that grant

[49]Kelly v. Mueller, 2004 PA Super 425, 861 A.2d 984, 993 (2004), decision vacated, 590 Pa. 91, 912 A.2d 202 (2006).

[50]Kelly v. Mueller, 2004 PA Super 425, 861 A.2d 984, 993 (2004), decision vacated, 590 Pa. 91, 912 A.2d 202 (2006).

[51]Kelley v. Mueller, 590 Pa. 91, 912 A.2d 202 (2006).

[52]R.C. 3113.31; R.C. 2919.25.

such orders indicate that they are needed to "bring about a cessation of domestic violence against the family or household members."[53] The statute also contains a catch-all provision that provides that the court may "grant other relief that the court considers equitable and fair***."[54]

When issuing a criminal protection order, a court may include terms designed to ensure the safety of and protection of the complainant or family or household member.[55]

The standardized protection order forms also provide guidance. In fact, the forms facilitate the court's use of the catch-all authority to address firearms, noting that "a respondent shall not possess, use, carry or obtain any deadly weapon at any time while this Order remain in effect unless Respondent is excepted for official use pursuant to 18 U.S.C. 925(a)(1).

Additionally, a respondent shall turn over all deadly weapons and concealed carry weapon license in Respondent's possession to the law enforcement agency that serves Respondent with this order.

Finally, any law enforcement agency is authorized to take possession of deadly weapons pursuant to this paragraph and hold them in protective custody until further Court order. The forms also advise that upon expiration of this Order, any deadly weapons, including firearms and ammunition, held in protective custody by law enforcement pursuant to this Order shall be disposed of as unclaimed property pursuant to RC 2981.12 unless the Respondent files a motion for return with this Court within 30 days before the expiration of this Order.

Courts do have the discretion to incorporate into protection orders the federal remedy provided by Congress under the Gun Control Act of 1968. Specifically, 18 U.S.C.A. § 922(g)(8)[56] provides that it is a federal crime to possess a firearm/ammunition while subject to a qualifying protection order.[57]

Currently, federal law has not been codified into Ohio state law and there are no statutory processes in place regarding domestic violence and the surrender,[58] storage or return of weapons.

---

[53]RC 3113.31(E)(1).

[54]R.C. 3113.31(E)(1)(h).

[55]RC 2919.26(C)(1); but see State v. Conkle, 2003-Ohio-2410, 2003 WL 21060822 (Ohio Ct. App. 5th Dist. Knox County 2003) (where the person who requested the order failed to appear at the hearing on the motion for the protection order pursuant to RC 2919.26(C)(1)).

[56]See also U.S. v. Wilson, 159 F.3d 280 (7th Cir. 1998) (rejecting a constitutional challenge to 18 U.S.C.A. § 922(g)(8)); U.S. v. Smith, 964 F. Supp. 286 (N.D. Iowa 1997), judgment aff'd, 171 F.3d 617 (8th Cir. 1999) (upholding federal firearms prohibition upon a domestic violence conviction); State v. S.A., 290 N.J. Super. 240, 249, 675 A.2d 678 (App. Div. 1996); U.S. v. Meade, 986 F. Supp. 66 (D. Mass. 1997), aff'd, 175 F.3d 215 (1st Cir. 1999).

[57]See Woolum v. Woolum, 131 Ohio App. 3d 818, 723 N.E.2d 1135 (12th Dist. Preble County 1999) (relying on RC 3113.31(E)(1)(h) for authority to include such a provision); Conkle v. Wolfe, 131 Ohio App. 3d 375, 722 N.E.2d 586 (4th Dist. Athens County 1998) (noting that a court may issue a protection order that includes other relief that the court considers equitable and fair). See also Text § 12:22; Text § 18:13.

[58]Weisberg, State Firearm Surrender Laws Lower Risk of Death, 23 Domestic

Q & A: If a party is prohibited from obtaining or possessing a firearm under the standardized protection order forms and pursuant to state law, is that party subject to the federal restrictions under 18 U.S.C.A. § 922(g)(8)?[59]

It depends. A protection order issued under RC 3113.31 or RC 2919.25 may contain certain prohibitions. Pursuant to Ohio's standardized domestic violence forms and RC 3113.31(E)(1) and RC 3113.31(E)(1)(h),[60] a court may prohibit a person from possessing, obtaining, carrying or using any deadly weapon. Should a respondent have a weapon in his possession, he or she is required to turn over the weapon to the local law enforcement agency. After a respondent is served with the protection order, he or she is on notice of the prohibition and a failure to turn over the firearm to the law enforcement agency is a violation of the protection order.[61] Obtaining a firearm while subject to the protection order is also prohibited.

Any law enforcement agency that receives weapons in this manner is authorized to retain possession of the weapons until further order of court. When the protection order is terminated by operation of law, unless earlier modified or dismissed, the weapons should be returned to the respondent/offender.

On the other hand, a party is subject to the federal firearms prohibition only if certain elements are met. Federal law prohibits an abuser subject to a *qualifying* protection order from possessing firearms or ammunition. Pursuant to 18 U.S.C.A. § 922(g)(8), a qualifying protection order meets the following conditions:

i. the protected party must be a spouse, present or former cohabitant with the respondent, parent of a common child, or a child of the respondent;

ii. the order must have been entered after a hearing of which the respondent had notice and an opportunity to appear; and

iii. the order must include a finding that the respondent represents a credible threat to the protected party or must include an express prohibition against harassment, stalking or the use of force that would reasonably be expected to cause injury.

Unless all conditions are met, an abuser is not subject to the federal prohibition nor is that person Brady disqualified pursuant to Sup. R. 10.[62] In effect, only certain family and household members are subject to the federal prohibition. Children of the victim and others related by consanguinity or affinity, such as grandchildren, are not protected parties for purposes of the federal ban. Therefore, an abuser related to the above would not be subject to Brady disqualification or the federal firearms prohibition. Additionally, until a protection order is served and the abuser has had a hearing, he or she is not subject to

Violence Report 24 (Dec. /Jan. 2018).

[59]See also Text § 18:11, Firearm offenses under VAWA; Text § 18:12, Firearm offenses under VAWA; significant cases. Text § 12:22, remedies, miscellaneous issues; Text § 18:11, firearm offenses under VAWA, Text § 18:13, domestic violence and firearm protection.

[60]Sup. R. 10.01-H, Sup. R. 10.01-I to 10.01-J, and Sup. R. 10.02-A.

[61]See RC 3113.31(L); see also RC 2919.27.

[62]See also Text § 18:11, Firearm offenses under VAWA.

the prohibition. If the abuser has been served and fails to appear at the second hearing or if the abuser continues the hearing,[63] he or she may be Brady disqualified and subject to the federal ban under 18 U.S.C.A. § 922(d)(8). Finally, the entry must state that the respondent represents a credible threat to the protected party or must include a prohibition such as exists in Ohio's standardized forms.[64]

Q & A: Can the person subject to the protection order ever retrieve his/her weapons?

Yes, when the protection order expires or terminates. 18 U.S.C.A. § 922 (g)(8) states that it is unlawful for a person to possess any firearms when that person is subject to a protection order. Implicit in that statement is that when the protection order is dismissed or terminated, the firearms are to be returned.[65]

Similarly, the standardized domestic violence forms prohibit possessing or obtaining a weapon or firearm for the duration of the protection order. However, when the protection order terminates, a party is no longer subject to such a provision.

The new Supreme Court forms provide that "[u]pon the expiration of this Order, any deadly weapons, including firearms and ammunition, held in protective custody by law enforcement pursuant to this Order shall be disposed of as unclaimed property pursuant to RC 2981.12 unless the Respondent files a motion for return with this Court within 30 days before expiration of this Order."[66] In that the full hearing forms require a motion being filed 30 days before expiration of the Order, the court has jurisdiction to address the issue.

Q & A: What is the procedure for the return of firearms?[67]

There are no federal cases that have addressed this issue.

However, the issue was recently raised in Ohio. In *Golden v. Bay Village Police Department*,[68] the defendant was the subject of a criminal protection order issued in connection with an allegation of domestic violence. The police confiscated several guns from Golden's home pursuant to the order. Subsequently, the charge of domestic violence was dismissed[69] and the protection order was dissolved.

Mr. Golden requested the return of his guns and he was advised

---

[63]See RC 3113.31(D)(2).

[64]See Sup. R. 10.01-H to 10.01-J, Sup. R. 10.02-A; see also Text § 18:11, Firearm offenses under VAWA.

[65]See also Text § 18:11, Firearm offenses under VAWA; see also Text § 12:22, Remedies—Miscellaneous issues.

[66]See Sup. R. Form 10.01-I and 10.01-J.

[67]See Sup. R. Form 10.01-I and 10.01-J. Text § 18:11; Text § 12:22; see also Wysocki v. Oberlin Police Dept., 2014-Ohio-2869, 2014 WL 2957713 (Ohio Ct. App. 9th Dist. Lorain County 2014).

[68]Golden v. Bay Village Police Dept., 2002-Ohio-673, 2002 WL 253878 (Ohio Ct. App. 8th Dist. Cuyahoga County 2002); see also Kise v. Barber, 2005-Ohio-6438, 2005 WL 3293763 (Ohio Ct. App. 5th Dist. Knox County 2005) (discussing subject matter jurisdiction to entertain such a motion); Emily J. Sack, Confronting the Issue of Gun Seizure in Domestic Violence Cases, 6 J. Center for Families, Child. & Cts. 3 (2003).

[69]But see Matter of J.W.D., 149 N.J. 108, 693 A.2d 92 (1997) (defendant not entitled to return of weapons if trial court, after dismissing domestic violence complaint, finds the defendant poses threat to public health, safety or welfare); see also In re Seizure of Weapons Belonging to Smilovic, 2006 WL 3543104 (N.J. Super. Ct.

that he would need a court order for the release of the weapons and further advised to file a replevin action. Mr. Golden was then informed that if he failed to secure a replevin order, the weapons would be destroyed. After receiving the replevin order, he then requested attorney fees. From the denial of fees, he appealed.

The Eighth District Court of Appeals stated that the trial court did not err in denying Golden's request for fees. The court reasoned that since the police confiscated the weapons pursuant to a court order, the defendant was on notice that it would take a court order to release his weapons.[70]

The appellate court then noted that "[t]he fact that the protection order was dissolved is of no consequence. The police department confiscated the weapons pursuant to court order; thus, it was reasonable for the police not to return the property unless instructed to do so by the court."[71]

The court then held that the police recommendation of a replevin action[72] was reasonable in light of the fact that the defendant failed to request the return of his property when the charges against him were dismissed and because of the several months delay. Therefore, the police did not exercise bad faith, necessitating an award of attorney fees.

Q & A: Can a person who has been convicted of domestic violence possess a firearm or request the return of a firearm confiscated during an investigation for domestic violence?

No. Pursuant to 18 U.S.C.A. § 922(g)(9), it is unlawful for any person who has been convicted in any court of a misdemeanor crime or domestic violence to possess any firearm.[73] Therefore, that person may not request the return of any firearm seized during the investigation.[74] It is also true that if the charge is amended to disorderly conduct, the same person would not be permitted the return of his firearms or the possessing of firearms in the future.[75] However, if the underlying criminal case is dismissed, the firearms should be returned.[76]

Q & A: Is a defendant prohibited from possessing firearms or ammunition and precluded from the return of his/her weapons where he/she is convicted of a threat of domestic violence?

App. Div. 2006).

[70]See Sup. R. 10.01-H to 10.01-J and Sup. R. 10.02-A; note that Ohio's standardized forms provide that law enforcement agencies shall hold weapons in protective custody until further court order.

[71]Golden v. Bay Village Police Dept., 2002-Ohio-673, 2002 WL 253878, *2 (Ohio Ct. App. 8th Dist. Cuyahoga County 2002). But see State v. Solomon, 262 N.J. Super. 618, 621 A.2d 559 (Ch. Div. 1993).

[72]See Wilhoit v. N. Olmsted, 151 Ohio Misc. 2d 21, 2009-Ohio-1702, 905 N.E.2d 723 (Mun. Ct. 2009).

[73]See also City Of North Ridgeville v. Kingsboro, 2002-Ohio-30, 2002 WL 5682 (Ohio Ct. App. 9th Dist. Lorain County 2002); Blackburn v. Jansen, 241 F. Supp. 2d 1047 (D. Neb. 2003).

[74]See, for example, City of Cleveland v. Carpenter, 2003-Ohio-6923, 2003 WL 22976619 (Ohio Ct. App. 8th Dist. Cuyahoga County 2003).

[75]See State v. Majka, 2002-Ohio-1378, 2002 WL 462858 (Ohio Ct. App. 9th Dist. Summit County 2002); see also City of Cleveland v. Carpenter, 2003-Ohio-6923, 2003 WL 22976619 (Ohio Ct. App. 8th Dist. Cuyahoga County 2003).

[76]See State v. Solomon, 262 N.J. Super. 618, 621 A.2d 559 (Ch. Div. 1993); see also State v. S.A., 290 N.J. Super. 240, 675 A.2d 678 (App. Div. 1996).

Not according to the Rocky River Municipal Court. In *Wilhoit v. North Olmsted*,[77] the defendant was charged with domestic violence against his spouse. Pursuant to the TPO, he was ordered to surrender his firearms to the North Olmsted Police Department. Although he was charged with domestic violence, he pled no contest to a fourth degree threat of domestic violence under RC 2919.25(C). After his motion for the return of his firearms was denied, he filed a civil petition in replevin.

The court reasoned that 1) federal law prescribes the possession of firearms for those who are convicted of an offense of domestic violence pursuant to 18 U.S.C.A § 922(g)(9); 2) 18 U.S.C.A. § 921(a)(33)(A)(ii) provides that a "misdemeanor crime of domestic violence" is one that has, as an element, the use or attempted use of physical force, or the threatened use of a deadly weapon, committed by a former or current spouse; 3) domestic violence is defined under RC 2919.25(C) as committing an act "by threat of force"; and 4) defendant was charged with domestic violence but plead and was convicted of a reduced charge of threat of domestic violence under RC 2919.25(C).

The court then held that, although his conviction of threat of domestic violence is a misdemeanor crime of domestic violence for state law purposes, because it includes a "threat of force," it is not a crime of domestic violence as defined in the federal code, which has as an element the "threatened use of a deadly weapon."[78] Because his conviction for domestic violence is not a crime of domestic violence as set forth in 18 U.S.C., he is not prohibited from possessing any firearms.[79] Therefore, his weapons are subject to return.

Q & A: Can police search a car belonging to a party arrested for domestic violence and confiscate a baseball bat and knife from the car?

At least one Ohio court has answered this in the affirmative. In *City of North Olmsted v. Szucs*,[80] the defendant was arrested for domestic violence against his wife. Since she did not want his car to remain on the premises, the police impounded the car. As the police inventoried the contents of the automobile, they seized a bat and knife. Defendant argued that the seizure of the bat and knife from his car were not subject to a warrantless search as incident to the arrest. The city contended that it was not required to obtain a warrant to search the car as they were taking an inventory of the vehicle prior to its being towed.

The Eighth District Court of Appeals affirmed the trial court's decision in favor of the city and held that "it is clear that Szucs' car was impounded as a result of his arrest on the domestic violence charge,

---

[77]See Wilhoit v. N. Olmsted, 151 Ohio Misc. 2d 21, 2009-Ohio-1702, 905 N.E.2d 723 (Mun. Ct. 2009).

[78]See Wilhoit v. N. Olmsted, 151 Ohio Misc. 2d 21, 2009-Ohio-1702, 905 N.E.2d 723 (Mun. Ct. 2009).

[79]But see Joshua M. Jones, 18 USC 922(g)(9) and the Circuit Split: The Case for a Broad Definition of Domestic Violence, 45 No. 1 Crim. Law Bull. 3 (2009) (taking the position that a broader definition of crime of domestic violence is sound public policy).

[80]City of North Olmsted v. Szucs, 2000 WL 574372 (Ohio Ct. App. 8th Dist. Cuyahoga County 2000).

because Mrs. Szucs did not want his car to remain on the property, and because Szucs did not give permission to release his car to anyone.[81] Hence, the North Olmsted Police Department was within the ambit of its authority to impound the car and follow the department procedure to inventory its contents. As such, the search was not unreasonable under the circumstances.

Q & A: When an officer investigates an incident of domestic violence, must the officer Mirandize the alleged defendant?

At least two Ohio courts have addressed this issue. In *City of Akron v. Sutton*,[82] the defendant was charged with domestic violence based on the officer's conversation with the defendant as well as conversations with the victim and neighbors. In his appeal, defendant argued that he was entitled to a reading of his *Miranda* rights before making any statements to the police, because under the preferred arrest policies of the Ohio Revised Code, he was in custody from the time the officer entered the home.[83]

The Akron Municipal Court determined that, ". . . under the Ohio and Akron Police policies regarding domestic violence, the officer's questions were intended to investigate the alleged incident, not to extract a coerced confession from defendant, the prevention of which is the policy underlying the *Miranda* requirements."[84] To Mirandize each party involved in a domestic violence encounter would frustrate the purposes of the preferred arrest statute because police officers would be forced to restructure and formalize their investigative process by "'Mirandizing' every person to whom they intended to speak, potentially including the victim, since he or she may also be arrested under the statute. The primary purpose of these statutes is to ensure adequate police response to domestic violence situations and to ensure that a potentially negative or even dangerous situation is averted."[85]

In contrast, the Eighth District Court of Appeals reached the opposite conclusion. In *City of Cleveland v. Morales*,[86] the officers placed the appellant in handcuffs and ordered him to remain on the bed. Although they questioned him concerning the events, they failed to inform him of his Miranda rights. The defendant appealed the trial court decision, arguing that he was not informed of his Miranda warnings.

The State justified its actions by focusing on Ohio's preferred arrest policy in domestic violence cases pursuant to RC 2935.03(B)(3). Because an officer should arrest and detain the person whom it has reasonable cause to believe is the perpetrator of the crime and because

---

[81] City of North Olmsted v. Szucs, 2000 WL 574372, *3 (Ohio Ct. App. 8th Dist. Cuyahoga County 2000).

[82] Akron v. Sutton, 106 Ohio Misc. 2d 46, 733 N.E.2d 690 (Mun. Ct. 2000).

[83] Akron v. Sutton, 106 Ohio Misc. 2d 46, 733 N.E.2d 690, 692 (Mun. Ct. 2000).

[84] Akron v. Sutton, 106 Ohio Misc. 2d 46, 733 N.E.2d 690, 693 (Mun. Ct. 2000).

[85] Akron v. Sutton, 106 Ohio Misc. 2d 46, 733 N.E.2d 690, 692–93 (Mun. Ct. 2000).

[86] City of Cleveland v. Morales, 2002-Ohio-5862, 2002 WL 31402003 (Ohio Ct. App. 8th Dist. Cuyahoga County 2002); see also State v. Dillon, 2005-Ohio-1016, 2005 WL 563978 (Ohio Ct. App. 8th Dist. Cuyahoga County 2005) (discussing when an officer can arrest).

an officer must determine the primary physical aggressor[87] and prepare a mandatory incident report,[88] an officer should be able to fully investigate the incident. Since the officers were not coercing a confession, there was no need to Mirandize the appellant.

The Cuyahoga County Court of Appeals reversed the trial court and distinguished its decision from *Akron v. Sutton*. 'Unlike the trial court in *Sutton*, we do not believe that the statute entitles an investigating officer carte blanche freedom in questioning anyone involved in a domestic violence dispute without regard to applicable *Miranda* warnings. In giving RC 2935.03(B)(3)(b) plain and ordinary reading, there is simply no directive which would permit an officer to freely question any individual involved in a domestic dispute without regard to the applicable *Miranda* warnings . . . . In no manner does the statute permit the investigating officer free rein in determining the guilty party without first recognizing the constitutional protections afforded to a defendant. To allow such a course of action would, for all intents and purposes, extinguish the protections afforded a suspect by *Miranda* in domestic violence cases.' "[89]

Additionally, the *Morales* appellate court noted that the appellant was handcuffed and told to remain seated on the bed. "Unlike *Sutton*, the appellant's freedom of movement was clearly severely restrained due to the actions of the officers."[90] The court reasoned that, by restricting the defendant's freedom of movement, the officers created a custodial interrogation, justifying the need to inform him of his *Miranda* rights.

§ 14:6 Law enforcement policies and procedures

Q & A: Do all Ohio law enforcement agencies have written policies in place regarding the appropriate response to domestic violence cases?

Each law enforcement agency in Ohio was required to adopt written policies and procedures for the implementation of Ohio's preferred arrest policy by March 9, 1995.[1] The purpose of these policies and procedures was to commit a law enforcement agency to describing in writing its appropriate responses to an incident of domestic violence or violating a protection order. There is, unfortunately, no way to

---

[87] See RC 2935.03(B)(3)(b).

[88] RC 2935.032(D).

[89] City of Cleveland v. Morales, 2002-Ohio-5862, 2002 WL 31402003 (Ohio Ct. App. 8th Dist. Cuyahoga County 2002); see also State v. DeLong, 2007-Ohio-2330, 2007 WL 1413394 (Ohio Ct. App. 4th Dist. Ross County 2007).

[90] City of Cleveland v. Morales, 2002-Ohio-5862, 2002 WL 31402003, *3 (Ohio Ct. App. 8th Dist. Cuyahoga County 2002).

[Section 14:6]

[1] 1994 H.B. 335, eff. 12-9-94; see RC 2935.032; see also State v. DeLong, 2007-Ohio-2330, 2007 WL 1413394, *2 (Ohio Ct. App. 4th Dist. Ross County 2007) (noting that RC 2935.032 "involves law enforcement agency 'arrest polices,' not specific duties on the part of law enforcement officers").

monitor this process; and, at present, it is unclear how many of Ohio's law enforcement agencies have adopted written policies.[2]

All police policies were to include certain provisions that stressed the appropriate response to domestic violence. Police officers in the state of Ohio were and are required to comply as follows:

(1) to respond without undue delay to a report of an alleged incident of the offense of domestic violence or violation of a protection order or consent agreement;[3]

(2) if the alleged offender has been granted pretrial release from custody on a prior charge of domestic violence or violating a protection order and has violated one or more conditions of that pretrial release, the officer must document the facts and circumstances of the violation in the mandatory incident report;[4]

(3) to separate the victim of the offense and the alleged offender, conduct separate interviews with the victim and the alleged offender[5] in separate locations, and take a written statement from the victim that indicates:

  (a) the frequency and severity of any prior incidents of physical abuse of the victim by the alleged offender;

  (b) the number of times the victim has called police officers for assistance;

  (c) the disposition of those calls, if known.[6]

(4) that all law enforcement agencies comply with Ohio's preferred arrest policies.[7]

These provisions were intended to buttress the police officer's response to domestic violence by focusing on certain aspects of the battering experience vis-a-vis the justice system and modifying the way police approach the situation. Prior to this requirement, it was not unheard of for victims to wait for hours for officers to respond, if they responded at all. Police officers are now required under RC 2935.032(A)(2)(a) to make domestic violence calls a priority and respond quickly when a call is made. No longer can domestic violence calls receive a lower priority than less serious personal or property crimes.

---

[2]See Akron v. Sutton, 106 Ohio Misc. 2d 46, 733 N.E.2d 690 (Mun. Ct. 2000) (Akron Municipal Court noted Akron's compliance); see also City of Cleveland v. Morales, 2002-Ohio-5862, 2002 WL 31402003 (Ohio Ct. App. 8th Dist. Cuyahoga County 2002).

[3]RC 2935.032(A)(2)(a).

[4]RC 2935.032(A)(2)(b).

[5]See State v. Samarghandi, 84 Ohio Misc. 2d 6, 680 N.E.2d 738 (Mun. Ct. 1997) (court determined that, to conduct separate interviews under RC 2935.032(A)(2)(c), the officer has to have a reasonable basis to believe that domestic violence has occurred); but see State v. DeLong, 2007-Ohio-2330, 2007 WL 1413394 (Ohio Ct. App. 4th Dist. Ross County 2007) (separating a domestic violence victim from the perpetrator and conducting separate interviews under RC 2935.032(A)(2)(c) does not give the deputies the authority to enter the home to talk to appellee).

[6]RC 2935.032(A)(2)(c).

[7]RC 2935.032(A)(2)(d).

Law enforcement officers who respond to a domestic violence call can no longer interview the parties together.[8] Joint interviews failed to provide accurate information and often prejudiced the victim.[9] Since abuse is about power and control,[10] interviewing the batterer and the victim together only strengthens the perceived power of the abuser and restricts the ability of the police to fully investigate the crime. Moreover, it impedes the factual determination of which party was the primary physical aggressor. Separating the victim and the alleged offender reduces the risk of harm to the victim and enables the officers to thoroughly investigate the incident.[11]

The police officer must also consider the number of times a victim has called the police and the results of the contact. Including these factors in the written incident report may strengthen the prosecutor's case against an alleged perpetrator and puts the justice system on notice that a particular individual is potentially more lethal and may be more likely to disobey court orders.

In order to stress the importance of compliance with the preferred arrest and mandatory incident report policies, the Ohio legislature required all law enforcement agencies to comply with these provisions.[12] Additionally, each law enforcement agency was authorized to provide its own sanctions for noncompliance which are to be incorporated into the agency's written policies.[13] Officers who fail to comply with either the state's arrest policy or the law enforcement agency's arrest policy and the provisions regarding the mandatory incident report will be subject to specific sanctions.[14]

Moreover, an officer who investigates a report of an incident of domestic violence or violating a protection order is also required do all of the following:

(1) complete a domestic violence report;[15]

(2) advise the victim of the availability of a temporary protection order under RC 2919.26 or RC 3113.31;[16]

(3) give the victim the officer's name and badge number, the report number of the incident, if available, a telephone number the victim can call for information about the case, the telephone

[8]RC 2935.032(A)(2)(c).

[9]Mashburn v. Mashburn, 2000-Ohio-2606, 2000 WL 1726517 (Ohio Ct. App. 7th Dist. Mahoning County 2000).

[10]Anne L. Ganley, Domestic Violence: The What, Why and Who, as Relevant to Civil Court Cases in Domestic Violence in Civil Court Cases: A National Model For Judicial Education 23, 33 (Jacqueline A. Agtuca et al. eds., 1992).

[11]See Smith v. City of Elyria, 857 F. Supp. 1203 (N.D. Ohio 1994), for a discussion of why it is necessary to separate the parties.

[12]See RC 2935.032(A)(2)(d).

[13]See RC 2935.032(A)(3).

[14]See RC 2935.032(A)(3).

[15]RC 2935.032(C)(1); see also State v. Wright, 1998 WL 542697 (Ohio Ct. App. 10th Dist. Franklin County 1998).

[16]RC 2935.032(C)(2). See also Brown v. Grabowski, 922 F.2d 1097 (3d Cir. 1990) (Police officers did not violate a victim's due process rights by failing to advise her of her right to a restraining order in civil court as required by statute since the act did not create or exacerbate the danger or constrain her freedom to seek an order on her own.).

number of a domestic violence shelter in the area, and information on any local victim advocate program.[17]

Each of these provisions is specifically designed to enhance victim safety and hold perpetrators accountable for their actions.[18] The victim is given an opportunity to document the pattern of abuse and explain the battering experience. These provisions also send a clear message to both the victim and the abuser that domestic violence will not be tolerated and that resources are available to assist victims. Most victims have no knowledge of the resources available to them until someone tells them. Since police officers are often the first persons called when there is abuse, police now have a duty to provide this information.[19] Most officers in Ohio distribute information sheets or cards to victims of domestic violence.[20]

Regardless of whether an officer actually arrests a party in connection with an alleged incident of domestic violence, he or she must make a written report of the incident.[21] Even if there is no arrest, a report must be prepared. In that case, the report must include a clear statement of the officer's reasons for not arresting the alleged perpetrator.

Q & A: Must the mandatory incident report contain any specific details?

According to RC 2935.032(D), the mandatory incident report must contain certain details which support a thorough police investigation and an effective prosecution. These details include the following:

(1) the officer's observations of the victim and the alleged offender;[22]
(2) any visible injuries of the victim or alleged offender;
(3) any weapons found at the scene;
(4) the actions of the alleged offender;
(5) any statements made by the victim or witnesses; and
(6) any other significant facts and circumstances.[23]

The incident report aids the victim by providing documentation of the abuse for the future. The report documents the history of abuse and may be used to show that the victim has undergone the pattern of abuse that is often the battering experience.

Each of these law enforcement requirements contained in RC 2935.032 serves the primary goals of reducing the incidence of domes-

[17]RC 2935.032(C)(3).

[18]See for e.g., Wilson v. Town of Mamou, 972 So. 2d 461 (La. Ct. App. 3d Cir. 2007), writ denied, 978 So. 2d 307 (La. 2008) (where statutory language similar to RC 2935.03 and RC 2935.032(C), police department found negligent in failing to protect victim of domestic violence where police had a duty to comply with the statute as to arrest, arranging for transportation to shelter, advising victim of right to other civil or criminal actions).

[19]RC 2935.032(C).

[20]See RC 2935.032(C). Contact the Ohio Domestic Violence Network or the Action Ohio Domestic Violence Coalition for sample brochures and information cards.

[21]RC 2935.032(D).

[22]See, e.g., State v. Dent, 2002-Ohio-4522, 2002 WL 2008423 (Ohio Ct. App. 9th Dist. Summit County 2002).

[23]RC 2935.032(D).

tic violence and protecting the victim. Law enforcement officials play a critical role by arresting offenders who violate protection orders and investigating and gathering evidence at the scene. Further, they have a responsibility to provide victims with information about the availability of protection orders.[24] Requiring officers to provide victims with information regarding protection orders gives victims the opportunity to seek court remedies before the situation escalates in frequency and severity.[25]

Q & A: How is a written incident report of a domestic violence incident useful to a prosecutor or an attorney?[26]

A well-written incident report, containing sufficient details of the incident as set forth in RC 2935.032(D), is a useful tool to the prosecutor in prosecuting a criminal domestic violence case, with or without the testimony of the victim.

A written report serves to preserve evidence of the victim's physical and emotional condition, including details such as torn clothing, physical injuries, marks and redness, crying, fear, anger, etc.; the condition of the crime scene, such as disarray of furniture, damaged property, blood, or other physical evidence; the condition of the suspect; and any spontaneous declarations[27] or excited utterances of the victim.[28] An incident report detailing the officer's observations and the victim's statements as to the cause of the assault may be admitted to substantiate the officer's testimony at trial, to impeach a witness,[29] or to refresh a witness's recollection.[30] Furthermore, it establishes a complete picture of the crime scene, which, if used in conjunction with the officer's testimony at trial, offers substantial evidence to support a criminal conviction without the testimony of the victim.

A written police report may be admitted under the business records exception to the Hearsay Rule[31] to provide the court with documentation that a report of the incident was made. In such a case, the testimony of the victim should precede any report, and a records custodian for the police department would be required to authenticate

[24] See RC 2935.032(C); see also RC 3113.31(I).

[25] Anne L. Ganley, Domestic Violence: The What, Why and Who, as Relevant to Civil Court Cases in Domestic Violence in Civil Court Cases: A National Model for Judicial Education 25 (Jacqueline A. Agtuca et al. eds., 1992).

[26] See Text Ch. 16, Domestic Violence Case Strategy and Evidentiary Considerations.

[27] See State v. Jackson, 2002-Ohio-1202, 2002 WL 398655 (Ohio Ct. App. 2d Dist. Montgomery County 2002); Cleveland v. Thomas, 2003-Ohio-30, 2003 WL 60981 (Ohio Ct. App. 8th Dist. Cuyahoga County 2003).

[28] See Evid.R. 803(2), Evid.R. 803(3); see also Text Ch. 5, Domestic Violence Prosecution—Initiation and Initial Case Preparation; see also Text Ch. 16, Domestic Violence Case Strategy and Evidentiary Considerations; Douglas E. Beloof and Joel Shapiro, Let the Truth Be Told: Proposed Hearsay Exceptions To Admit Domestic Violence Victims' Out of Court Statements as Substantive Evidence, 11 Colum. J. Gender & L. 1 (2002).

[29] See State v. Suarez, 2002-Ohio-4890, 2002 WL 31087432 (Ohio Ct. App. 8th Dist. Cuyahoga County 2002).

[30] See Evid.R. 612; see also State v. Murphy, 65 Ohio St. 3d 554, 605 N.E.2d 884 (1992) (citing Weis v. Weis, 147 Ohio St. 416, 34 Ohio Op. 350, 72 N.E.2d 245, 169 A.L.R. 668 (1947)).

[31] See Evid.R. 803(6), Evid.R. 803(8), Evid.R. 901(B)(7), Evid.R. 902(4).

the report. However, where the victim is reluctant to testify, the officer's testimony is necessary in order for the prosecutor to proceed without the victim.[32]

In a civil protection order action, the petitioner may offer evidence of the report as a way of demonstrating a pattern of abuse and documenting the abusive incident in question. However, the testimony of the officer at the scene, who investigated the incident, wrote the report, and arrested the respondent, provides admissible, probative, and relevant evidence. The written incident report validates the officer's testimony. Without the testimony from the officer, the report may or may not be admitted into evidence.

Because victims in domestic violence cases are often reluctant to testify at trial (especially in criminal cases), the officer responding to the call must investigate and assemble admissible and probative evidence.[33] This evidence must be gathered with the knowledge that the victim may not be available as a witness for the prosecution at the time of trial. A police report, a signed complaint by the victim providing reasonable cause to make the arrest,[34] the 911 tape, and photographs of the victim taken at the scene are examples of the types of evidence that aid the prosecutor in proceeding with the case, with or without the cooperation of the victim, by providing necessary independent evidence to convict a perpetrator.[35]

Q & A: Why should the police officer testify at trial?[36]

The officer's testimony is crucial to the prosecutor who needs to make a case without the benefit of the victim's testimony.[37] It may be sufficient evidence to convict the perpetrator. In *State v. Justice*,[38] the victim refused to testify against her husband at trial. The sheriff's testimony regarding the victim's oral statement implicating the defendant provided sufficient evidence to support a criminal conviction.

---

[32]See State v. Justice, 92 Ohio App. 3d 740, 637 N.E.2d 85 (9th Dist. Wayne County 1994).

[33]See State v. Lee, 73 Ohio Misc. 2d 9, 657 N.E.2d 604 (Mun. Ct. 1995); Text Ch. 5, Domestic Violence Prosecution—Initiation and Initial Case Preparation; see also Text Ch. 16, Domestic Violence Case Strategy and Evidentiary Considerations; Douglas E. Beloof and Joel Shapiro, Let the Truth Be Told: Proposed Hearsay Exceptions To Admit Domestic Violence Victims' Out of Court Statements as Substantive Evidence, 11 Colum. J. Gender & L. 1 (2002).

[34]See RC 2935.03(B)(3)(a)(i); see also RC 2935.03(B)(3)(b).

[35]See State v. Lee, 73 Ohio Misc. 2d 9, 657 N.E.2d 604 (Mun. Ct. 1995); State v. Turner, 1996 WL 348016 (Ohio Ct. App. 1st Dist. Hamilton County 1996); City of Cleveland v. Botson, 1991 WL 95069 (Ohio Ct. App. 8th Dist. Cuyahoga County 1991); City of Cleveland Heights v. Reed, 1995 WL 601126 (Ohio Ct. App. 8th Dist. Cuyahoga County 1995).

[36]See Text Ch. 16, Domestic Violence Case Strategy and Evidentiary Considerations, for a further discussion of the Rules of Evidence and the importance of police officer testimony.

[37]See, e.g., State v. Johnson, 2003-Ohio-1699, 2003 WL 1735250 (Ohio Ct. App. 5th Dist. Stark County 2003); see also State v. Smith, 2002-Ohio-3402, 2002 WL 1461627 (Ohio Ct. App. 4th Dist. Highland County 2002); State v. Brown, 1998 WL 227182 (Ohio Ct. App. 3d Dist. Allen County 1998).

[38]State v. Justice, 92 Ohio App. 3d 740, 637 N.E.2d 85 (9th Dist. Wayne County 1994).

In some cases, the police officer's testimony and the testimony of another witness provide the necessary evidence needed to support a conviction.[39] For example, in *Cleveland Heights v. Brewer*,[40] there was an altercation between a husband and wife which was heard by the downstairs neighbor. An officer responded to the scene, heard the wife screaming, and arrested the defendant. The wife made a voluntary statement detailing the incident. At trial, the wife recanted portions of her written statement. However, the officer and the neighbor both testified to what they had seen and heard. The Cuyahoga County Court of Appeals concluded that the prosecutor could rely on the testimony of a witness who did not actually observe the incident but whose presence in the vicinity allowed her to hear noises indicative of physical violence. The court found no error in the trial court's judgment and determined that the wife's written statement corresponded so closely with the testimony of the police officer and the neighbor that the wife's recantation should be afforded little weight.[41]

Similarly, in *Siouffi v. Siouffi*,[42] the police officers' testimony that the victim seemed upset and shaken helped support a finding that the defendant's conduct placed the victim in fear of imminent serious physical harm under RC 3113.31(A)(1)(b). That testimony coupled with the victim's expression of fear provided credible evidence to justify granting a civil protection order.[43]

Sometimes, an officer's testimony will support an element of the offense. For example, in *State v. Ball*,[44] the police officer testified as to the proximity of the defendant to the building in which the complainant lived. The distance in yards was in dispute and the officer's testimony was crucial to showing that defendant violated the terms of the ex-parte civil protection order. The appellate court held that the trial court did not err in utilizing the testimony of two officers, that the distance between the parties was 100 yards, within the civil protection order's prohibition.

---

[39]See, e.g., State v. Seitz, 2003-Ohio-1879, 2003 WL 1871039 (Ohio Ct. App. 11th Dist. Portage County 2003); State v. Taylor, 2003-Ohio-2025, 2003 WL 1916787 (Ohio Ct. App. 9th Dist. Summit County 2003).

[40]Cleveland Hts. v. Brewer, 109 Ohio App. 3d 838, 673 N.E.2d 215 (8th Dist. Cuyahoga County 1996); see also State v. Taylor, 2003-Ohio-2025, 2003 WL 1916787 (Ohio Ct. App. 9th Dist. Summit County 2003).

[41]See State v. Vance, 2000 WL 1028547 (Ohio Ct. App. 5th Dist. Stark County 2000); see also State v. Saade, 2002-Ohio-5564, 2002 WL 31320312 (Ohio Ct. App. 8th Dist. Cuyahoga County 2002). But see State v. Attaway, 111 Ohio App. 3d 488, 676 N.E.2d 600 (1st Dist. Hamilton County 1996), wherein the officer testified that, on responding to the scene, he had observed the victim's bloody lip and scratches to her neck. The defendant testified and disputed the officer's account. The victim testified that she had lied to the officer. The First District Court of Appeals concluded that there was no other extrinsic corroborating evidence from which to conclude that the statement to the arresting officer was more credible than the victim's recantation under oath and reversed the trial court.

[42]Siouffi v. Siouffi, 1998 WL 879255 (Ohio Ct. App. 2d Dist. Montgomery County 1998); see also State v. Parks, 2000 WL 221968 (Ohio Ct. App. 5th Dist. Licking County 2000); Mashburn v. Mashburn, 2000-Ohio-2606, 2000 WL 1726517 (Ohio Ct. App. 7th Dist. Mahoning County 2000).

[43]See also City of Hamilton v. Roberson, 1998 WL 842754 (Ohio Ct. App. 12th Dist. Butler County 1998).

[44]State v. Ball, 2001 WL 468383 (Ohio Ct. App. 2d Dist. Montgomery County 2001).

Q & A: Does Ohio's statute provide direction in cases where the victim fails to cooperate?[45]

Yes, within the criminal context. RC 2935.03(B)(3)(e)(ii) provides that:

> If a person is arrested for or charged with committing the offense of domestic violence . . . and if the victim of the offense does not cooperate with the involved law enforcement or prosecuting authorities in the prosecution of the offense . . . or does not wish the prosecution of the offense to continue or wishes to drop charges, . . . the involved prosecuting authorities, in determining whether to continue with the prosecution of the offense or whether to dismiss charges . . . and notwithstanding the victim's failure to cooperate or the victim's wishes, shall consider all facts and circumstances that are relevant to the offense, including, but not limited to, the statements and observations of the peace officers who responded to the incident that resulted in the arrest or filing of the charges and of all witnesses to that incident.

This section emphasizes the statutory intention to encourage prosecutors to prove a domestic violence case without the participation of the victim. Because it is widely recognized that victims of domestic violence are frequently unwilling to testify,[46] the legislative directive sanctions this approach and provides for an offender-focused investigation to move the case beyond the victim's testimony. Reframing the approach to prosecution removes the burden from the victim and creates a societal environment for holding the abuser accountable.[47]

In contrast, the entire scope of RC 3113.31 is victim driven. No comparable requirement is authorized in RC 3113.31. Unlike a criminal case, there is no underlying crime. The victim does not become a witness for the city or state. Generally, it is the victim who requests the order, and it is the victim who must testify about the incidents justifying the order. It is highly unlikely that the victim will not participate. Of course, it is possible that another adult family or household member may file the petition for a civil protection order on the victim's behalf.[48] If a victim files for the protection order and the victim fails to appear, the court will dismiss the case on the grounds that the victim failed to prosecute the action.[49]

---

[45]See also Text § 16:13, Hearsay exceptions; *Crawford* concerns.

[46]See also Paula Finley Mangum, Reconceptualizing Battered Woman Syndrome Evidence: Prosecution Use of Expert Testimony on Battering, 19 B.C. Third World L.J. 593 (1999); Anna Farber Conrad, The Use of Victim Advocates and Expert Witnesses in Battered Women Cases, 30-Dec Colo. Law 43 (2001).

[47]Robert C. Davis, Barbara E. Smith & Heather J. Davies, Effects of No-Drop Prosecution of Domestic Violence Upon Conviction Rates, Justice Research and Policy Vol. 3, No. 2 (Fall 2001); Cheryl Hanna, No Right to Choose: Mandated Victim Participation in Domestic Violence Prosecutions, 109 Harv. L. Rev. 1849 (1996); Cathleen A. Booth, No-Drop Policies: Effective Legislation or Protectionist Attitude? 30 U. Tol. L. Rev. 621 (1999); Kalyani Robbins, No Drop Prosecution of Domestic Violence: Just Good Policy or Equal Protection Mandate? 52 Stan. L. Rev. 205 (1999).

[48]RC 3113.31(C); see also Carney v. Pankey, 1988 WL 34644 (Ohio Ct. App. 7th Dist. Mahoning County 1988).

[49]See Civ.R. 41(B).

Q & A: Does the judge have the authority to dismiss the case against the defendant where the victim wants the case to be dismissed?[50]

The tendency in Ohio had been for appellate courts to conclude that a trial court, over the objections of the prosecutor, is without discretion to dismiss a domestic violence action against the offender on the request of the victim witness who does not wish to proceed. The justification behind this principle is that, because the victim is a witness for the state, his/her interest is incidental to the principal controversy between the defendant and the state. "The duty of a judge is to hear and determine controversies, not to refuse to hear them, for whatever reason."[51]

The Supreme Court rejected these arguments, however, in *State v. Busch*[52] in September 1996. The Supreme Court resolved the issue by permitting a court to dismiss a domestic violence case over the objections of the prosecutor in certain circumstances. *Busch* merely gives a trial court permission to dismiss; it does not require a court to do so. In *Busch*, the trial court dismissed the case because the victim did not wish to proceed. The Franklin County Court of Appeals reversed the dismissal, and the case proceeded to the Ohio Supreme Court. In reaching its decision, the majority wrote, "We do not suggest that in every domestic violence case where the victim refuses to testify a trial judge has the unfettered power to dismiss the case."[53] The Court then proceeded to cite five factors that a lower court should consider before granting a dismissal: (1) the seriousness of the injuries, (2) the presence of independent witnesses, (3) the status of counseling, (4) whether the complainant's refusal to testify is coerced, and (5) whether the offender is a first-time offender.

Subsequent to *Busch*, courts have decided similar issues based on their interpretation of the mandates and the factors contained in *Busch*.[54] Of great significance is that the Ohio General Assembly recently enacted 1997 Senate Bill 98,[55] which overturns *Busch* and limits a court's ability to dismiss a case under certain circumstances. It provides that "a court cannot dismiss criminal charges when the

---

[50]See also Text § 16:8, Documenting evidence of domestic violence.

[51]State v. Wise, 99 Ohio App. 3d 239, 242, 650 N.E.2d 191 (10th Dist. Franklin County 1994) (quoting Dayton v. Thomas, No. 6567 (2d Dist. Ct. App., Montgomery, 4-18-80) (slip opinion)); Lakewood v. Pfeifer, 61 Ohio Misc. 2d 704, 583 N.E.2d 1133 (Mun. Ct. 1991), judgment aff'd, 83 Ohio App. 3d 47, 613 N.E.2d 1079 (8th Dist. Cuyahoga County 1992).

[52]State v. Busch, 76 Ohio St. 3d 613, 1996-Ohio-82, 669 N.E.2d 1125 (1996).

[53]State v. Busch, 76 Ohio St. 3d 613, 616, 1996-Ohio-82, 669 N.E.2d 1125 (1996). But see *Busch* dissent rejecting the majority opinion and utilizing the same legal rationale articulated in State v. Wise, 99 Ohio App. 3d 239, 650 N.E.2d 191 (10th Dist. Franklin County 1994).

[54]See, e.g., State v. Lewis, 125 Ohio App. 3d 352, 708 N.E.2d 745 (9th Dist. Lorain County 1998) (distinguishing Busch and reversing the trial court decision); see also State v. Clipner, 1999 WL 715891 (Ohio Ct. App. 10th Dist. Franklin County 1999) (factors provided in *Busch* provide valuable guidelines).

[55]1997 S.B. 98, eff. 3-17-98. See RC 1901.20(A)(2); see also Akron v. Hockman, 144 Ohio App. 3d 262, 759 N.E.2d 1286 (9th Dist. Summit County 2001).

only reason for dismissal is the request of the complaining witness and the prosecutor objects to the dismissal."[56]

In contrast, in the civil arena, where the victim is an adult and another adult files on behalf of the victim who does not wish to proceed, the legal reasoning used to justify proving the case without an available victim does not apply. Unlike the criminal arena, it is the victim who chooses to file an action to obtain a civil protection order.[57] There is no underlying crime, nor is there a prosecutor to decide whether to file charges. As such, the victim is the only focus. If another adult files the petition and the victim does not want to participate or chooses not to proceed, it is likely that the court would honor the victim's request and dismiss the action.

Q & A: Can the court hold a witness in contempt for refusing to testify?[58]

Yes, it is within the trial court's discretion to hold the complaining witness in criminal contempt for failing to testify at her husband's domestic violence trial. In *State v. Adams*,[59] the appellant wife refused to testify at the trial of her husband who had been charged with domestic violence against her. Appealing the contempt verdict, the appellant argued that Ohio's immunity statute does not provide protection against compelled self-incrimination to the same extent as the Fifth Amendment. Her main concern was that the prosecutor would attempt to charge her with perjury if she failed to give the answers the prosecutor wanted or expected, especially because the case was based almost entirely on her testimony. Because Ohio's immunity statute does not differentiate between perjury that occurred before the immunity was granted and the perjury that occurred after the immunity was granted, the statute did not protect her from any type of perjury prosecution.

In affirming the trial court, the Harrison County Court of Appeals reasoned that while the prosecutor may compel appellant to testify by granting her immunity under RC 2945.44, she cannot be prosecuted

[56]1997 S.B. 98, eff. 3-17-98. See RC 1901.20(A)(2); see also State v. Cox, 2001-Ohio-3213, 2001 WL 301429 (Ohio Ct. App. 7th Dist. Belmont County 2001); but see State v. Noland, 2001 WL 710160 (Ohio Ct. App. 10th Dist. Franklin County 2001); State v. Lowe, 2001 WL 682292 (Ohio Ct. App. 10th Dist. Franklin County 2001); State v. Taylor, 2001 WL 951728 (Ohio Ct. App. 10th Dist. Franklin County 2001); State v. Watkins, 2003-Ohio-668, 2003 WL 321541, *3 (Ohio Ct. App. 10th Dist. Franklin County 2003) (in which the appellate court stated that RC 1901.20(A)(2) does not apply to the case because the complaining witness, the officer, did not request the dismissal; it noted that RC 1901.20(A)(2) does not address the situation here in which an alleged victim, who is not the complaining witness, does not wish to proceed; additionally, it held that "[w]hile *Busch* has essentially been legislatively superseded, this court has previously held that 'the factors provided in *Busch* still provide valuable guidelines which a court should consider before dismissing a charge in a domestic case' "; the court also noted that these factors should be articulated in the record).

[57]RC 3113.31.

[58]See also Text § 16:21, "Other acts" testimony.

[59]State v. Adams, 153 Ohio App. 3d 134, 2003-Ohio-3086, 791 N.E.2d 1045 (7th Dist. Harrison County 2003); but see State v. Smith, 2003-Ohio-5461, 2003 WL 22336098, *2 (Ohio Ct. App. 3d Dist. Seneca County 2003) (court held that the trial court did not abuse its discretion in finding that the grant of immunity to Lisa would further the administration of justice).

for perjury she may have committed prior to the grant of immunity.[60] However, the state is not precluded, under the Fifth Amendment, from prosecuting an immunized witness for any perjury committed during the immunized testimony or afterward. In doing so, the state may not use prior inconsistent statements against her, except those inconsistencies in testimony given after the grant of immunity.[61]

Q & A: If the victim of the domestic violence is a child, can the victim testify in court?[62]

Where the victim is the child, it is expected that a parent will file the petition for a civil protection order on the child's behalf.[63] RC 3113.31(A)(1) specifically includes a provision regarding an act of domestic violence committed against a child as grounds for obtaining a civil protection order. Under RC 3113.31(A)(1)(c), domestic violence includes "[c]ommitting any act with respect to a child that would result in the child being an abused child, as defined in [RC] 2151.031." Physical abuse of a child and child sexual abuse are acts that require the filing of a civil protection order.

In many cases, the parent files the petition, and the affidavit supporting the need for the order details an abusive incident by one of the parents against the child. In many instances, the court will grant the civil protection order without requiring the child to testify. If raised at all, the issue of whether the child must testify will be raised at the full hearing. The court will decide whether the child is both competent to testify[64] and a credible witness.[65]

Most jurisdictions permit a parent to testify on the child's behalf relative to the abusive or violent incident, utilizing various exceptions to the hearsay rule,[66] including: (1) the excited utterance exception,[67]

---

[60]State v. Adams, 153 Ohio App. 3d 134, 2003-Ohio-3086, 791 N.E.2d 1045 (7th Dist. Harrison County 2003).

[61]State v. Adams, 153 Ohio App. 3d 134, 2003-Ohio-3086, 791 N.E.2d 1045 (7th Dist. Harrison County 2003).

[62]See Text § 16:8, Documenting evidence of domestic violence.

[63]See RC 3113.31(C).

[64]See Brandt v. Brandt, 2006-Ohio-883, 2006 WL 456716 (Ohio Ct. App. 3d Dist. Auglaize County 2006) (discussing competency of child to testify at CPO hearing); see also State v. Muttart, 116 Ohio St. 3d 5, 2007-Ohio-5267, 875 N.E.2d 944 (2007).

[65]See RC 2317.01; Evid.R. 601(A); see also State v. Frazier, 61 Ohio St. 3d 247, 574 N.E.2d 483 (1991); Schulte v. Schulte, 71 Ohio St. 3d 41, 1994-Ohio-459, 641 N.E.2d 719 (1994); State v. Wallace, 37 Ohio St. 3d 87, 524 N.E.2d 466 (1988) (regarding determination of competency of child who was under ten at the time of event about which child is to testify).

[66]See Text Ch. 5, Domestic Violence Prosecution—Initiation and Initial Case Preparation; Text Ch. 16, Domestic Violence Case Strategy and Evidentiary Considerations; see also In re Morrill, 147 N.H. 116, 784 A.2d 690 (2001) (Supreme Court of New Hampshire held that exclusion of children's testimony did not violate husband's right to due process).

[67]See State v. Lee, 73 Ohio Misc. 2d 9, 657 N.E.2d 604 (Mun. Ct. 1995); Evid.R. 803(2); see also State v. Storch, 66 Ohio St. 3d 280, 1993-Ohio-38, 612 N.E.2d 305 (1993); City of Cleveland v. Marek, 1997 WL 47651 (Ohio Ct. App. 8th Dist. Cuyahoga County 1997); Ross v. Ross, 2006-Ohio-5274, 2006 WL 2846327 (Ohio Ct. App. 4th Dist. Ross County 2006).

(2) the child's statements in abuse cases,[68] and (3) the present sense impression exception.[69]

In those cases where the parent is not permitted to testify, the rationale is that the parent does not have personal knowledge of the abusive incident and that there is no independent evidence of the incident. The parent's statements to the court are considered hearsay and do not fit within any hearsay exception.[70] However, a written incident report may be admitted into evidence to provide corroborating evidence of a child's statements made at the scene.

Q & A: When should police officers treat the offense of domestic violence or violating a protection order as a felonious assault?

RC 2935.032(A)(1) directs each law enforcement policy to specifically state that, if police officers determine that there are reasonable grounds to believe that a person knowingly caused serious physical harm to another or knowingly caused or attempted to cause physical harm to another by means of a deadly weapon, the officer shall treat the offense as felonious assault.[71] In that instance, the statute directs the police officer to arrest the offender for felonious assault.[72] *Black's Law Dictionary* provides that "the term 'shall' is a word of command, and one which has always or which must be given a compulsory meaning . . . and is inconsistent with a concept of discretion."[73]

Additionally, the officer must consider the primary physical aggressor factors in determining whom to arrest in "dual violence" cases.[74] Once the police officer determines the primary physical aggressor, the officer is required to arrest that individual.[75] The officer may also arrest the other offending party but is not required to do so.[76]

Q & A: When should an officer treat domestic violence or violating a protection order as aggravated assault?

If the officer determines that there are reasonable grounds to believe that a person, while under the influence of sudden passion or in a sudden fit of rage brought on by serious provocation by the victim that is reasonably sufficient to incite the person into using deadly force, knowingly caused serious physical harm to another or knowingly caused or attempted to cause physical harm to another by the use of a deadly weapon, the officer shall treat the offense as aggravated assault[77] and arrest the individual for aggravated assault.[78]

---

[68]See Evid.R. 807; Ross v. Ross, 2006-Ohio-5274, 2006 WL 2846327 (Ohio Ct. App. 4th Dist. Ross County 2006).

[69]See Evid.R. 803(1).

[70]See Text Ch. 5, Domestic Violence Prosecution—Initiation and Initial Case Preparation, for a more complete discussion of various evidentiary issues.

[71]See RC 2935.032(A)(1)(a).

[72]RC 2935.032(A)(1)(a)(i).

[73]Black's Law Dictionary (6th ed.) p 1375.

[74]See RC 2935.032(A)(1)(a)(ii).

[75]RC 2935.032(A)(1)(a)(ii).

[76]See RC 2935.032(A)(1)(a)(ii).

[77]RC 2935.032(A)(1)(b).

[78]See RC 2935.032(A)(1)(b)(i).

Similarly, law enforcement policies must contain provisions indicating that an officer faced with such a situation would arrest the offender for aggravated assault.[79] As with felonious assault, the officer must consider the primary physical aggressor factors in determining which individual to arrest in "dual violence" cases.[80]

§ 14:7 Police liability for failing to protect victims of domestic violence—Introduction

One of the most dramatic trends existing in the country today is the imposition of police liability for the failure to protect victims of domestic violence.[1] Police liability has long been associated with use of excessive force in, for example, an arrest. But does liability attach to the officer who neglects to act where the victim is injured as a result of that lack of action? Until recently, courts have been reluctant to impose liability for an officer's failure to act.[2] It appears, however, from recent case law that courts have begun to recognize that the police have a duty to aid victims of domestic violence and must be held accountable for their failure to act under certain circumstances.[3] In fact, there have been an increased number of successful damage suits against local governments under 42 U.S.C.A. § 1983 of the federal civil rights law charging police failure to protect victims of domestic violence.[4] This trend has serious implications for police policy in domestic violence cases. An arrest avoidance policy or a lack of a formal policy as to appropriate police response to domestic violence may be the basis for recovery when a victim is injured after police fail to assist.

§ 14:8 Police liability for failing to protect victims of domestic violence—Legal theories for recovery

Before deciding on a legal theory, plaintiffs must first choose a forum. The main advantage of selecting federal court is that sovereign immunity issues do not exist. Even after a plaintiff decides where to bring an action, he/she must demonstrate that he/she is a member of a class of individuals requiring special protection.

Additionally, the plaintiff must survive a common legal strategy, the motion for summary judgment.[1] Before a claim will warrant a trial on the merits of the case, the plaintiff must state sufficient facts

---

[79]RC 2935.032(A)(1)(b).

[80]See RC 2935.032(A)(1)(b)(ii).

[Section 14:7]

[1]See Kapila Juthani, Police Treatment of Domestic Violence and Sexual Abuse: Affirmative Duty to Protect vs. Fourth Amendment Privacy, 59 N.Y.U. Ann. Surv. Am. L. 51 (2002) (discussing the conflicting principles of police protection and privacy interests).

[2]Frank Carrington, Avoiding Liability for Police Failure to Protect, The Police Chief (Sept. 1989).

[3]See, e.g., Thurman v. City of Torrington, 595 F. Supp. 1521 (D. Conn. 1984).

[4]See John R. Williams, Representing Plaintiffs in Civil Rights Litigation Under Section 1983, 666 PLI/Lit. 273, 590 (2001).

[Section 14:8]

[1]See, e.g., Watson v. City of Kansas City, Kan., 857 F.2d 690 (10th Cir. 1988)

to state a claim for relief. Most motions to dismiss have been made by defendants alleging qualified immunity.[2] The test of qualified immunity for police officers sued under 42 U.S.C.A. § 1983 is whether, in performing discretionary functions, they have engaged in conduct that violates " 'clearly established constitutional rights of which a reasonable person would have known.' "[3] Qualified immunity is an affirmative defense. The burden rests with the defendants to raise the defense in their answer and to establish the defense on a motion for summary judgment or at trial.[4] Finally, if summary judgment is denied and the case is allowed to proceed, the plaintiff must still be able to prove his/her claim with sufficient evidence to recover damages. It is important to note that qualified immunity is the norm and protects all but those who are either incompetent or who knowingly violate the law.

Q & A: Under what legal theory would an aggrieved party sue a police officer for failing to act?

Legal opinions throughout the country have advanced several theories on which a legal claim against the police for failing to protect a victim of domestic violence may be based.[5] The cases that have received the most scrutiny have arisen under the United States Constitution under 42 U.S.C.A. § 1983.[6] 42 U.S.C.A. § 1983 states:

> Every person who, under color of any statute, ordinance, regulation, custom, or usage, of any State or Territory or the District of Columbia, subjects, or causes to be subjected, any citizen of the United States or other person within the jurisdiction thereof to the deprivation of any rights, privileges, or immunities secured by the Constitution and laws, shall be liable to the party injured in an action at law, suit in equity, or other proper proceeding for redress.

To sustain a constitutional claim, a plaintiff must show that (1) the conduct complained of was committed by a person or entity acting under color of state law and (2) the conduct deprived the plaintiff/victim of a constitutional right. Potential civil liability originates from a landmark decision by the United States Supreme Court. In *Monell v. Department of Social Services*,[7] the Supreme Court held that a local government or municipality may be sued for damages under 42

(reversing a district court's granting of summary judgment in favor of the city); Thurman v. City of Torrington, 595 F. Supp. 1521 (D. Conn. 1984) (denying a motion to dismiss).

[2]See, e.g., Mitchell v. Forsyth, 472 U.S. 511, 528, 105 S. Ct. 2806, 86 L. Ed. 2d 411, 2 Fed. R. Serv. 3d 221 (1985); see also Didzerekis v. Stewart, 41 F. Supp. 2d 840 (N.D. Ill. 1999) (holding that the defendant officers were not entitled to dismissal of the action on the basis of qualified immunity).

[3]Hunter v. Bryant, 502 U.S. 224, 112 S. Ct. 534, 116 L. Ed. 2d 589 (1991); see also May v. Franklin County Bd. of Com'rs, 59 Fed. Appx. 786 (6th Cir. 2003).

[4]See In re State Police Litigation, 88 F.3d 111, 123 (2d Cir. 1996).

[5]See, for example, Lewis v. City of Lake Charles, 2007 WL 4622780 (W.D. La. 2007) (discussing the most common theories for recovery).

[6]See generally Rahul Patel & Ann N. Sagerson, Procedural Means of Enforcement Under 42 U.S.C. 1983, 89 Geo. L.J. 1938 (2001).

[7]Monell v. Department of Social Services of City of New York, 436 U.S. 658, 694, 98 S. Ct. 2018, 56 L. Ed. 2d 611, 17 Fair Empl. Prac. Cas. (BNA) 873, 16 Empl. Prac. Dec. (CCH) P 8345 (1978); see also Culberson v. Doan, 65 F. Supp. 2d 701, 715 (S.D. Ohio 1999) (denying defendants' motions to dismiss, holding that plaintiff's complaint sufficiently alleges a violation of 42 U.S.C.A. § 1983 and reasoning that "a municipality is only liable under § 1983 when the injury is caused by the execution of its policy

U.S.C.A. § 1983 for the acts of its employees "when execution of a government's policy or custom, whether made by its lawmakers or by those whose edicts or acts may fairly be said to represent official policy, inflicts the injury [in violation of a citizen's constitutional rights]."[8]

Victims of domestic violence have brought three kinds of constitutional claims against police which derive from the Fourteenth Amendment of the United States Constitution.[9] First, under a substantive due process theory, victims of domestic violence have sued the law enforcement agency and the municipality alleging that a special relationship was created between themselves and the police. They have also alleged a denial of their right to liberty without due process of law. Second, they have sued alleging a denial of equal protection under the law. Third, they have sued under a procedural due process theory, alleging a denial of a protected property interest.

§ 14:9 Police liability for failing to protect victims of domestic violence—Legal theories for recovery—Substantive due process

Under a substantive due process theory, an individual must show that he/she was injured by an action or inaction taken in accordance with a municipal policy or custom. The gist of the argument is that a state (or municipality) or its officials creates an affirmative duty to protect an individual from physical harm. This duty arises because of a special relationship created between the state and the individual. A duty may also be created because of a capricious and willful governmental policy of inaction toward certain citizens which constitutes state action. The key issue in these cases is whether the plaintiff can prove a violation of the plaintiff's right to due process.

Generally, under the "public duty rule," police officers owe a duty to the public in general, but they owe no duty to specific individuals unless a "special relationship" has been created between the law enforcement agency and the victim. Some of the earlier cases suggested that the special relationship existed because the police had knowledge of the violence inflicted on the victim and that a protection order placed an affirmative duty on the police to protect the victim.[1]

In 1988, the Ninth Circuit Court of Appeals decided that more than

---

or custom. 'A "custom" for the purposes of Monell liability must "be so permanent and well settled as to constitute a custom or usage with the force of law.' " (citations omitted)); see also Kelley v. City of Wake Village, Texas, 264 Fed. Appx. 437 (5th Cir. 2008) ("In order for municipal liability to be imposed under § 1983, three elements must be proven: a policy maker, an official policy and a violation of constitutional rights whose 'moving force' is the policy of custom."), citing *Monell*. See also Okin v. Village of Cornwall-On-Hudson Police Dept., 577 F.3d 415 (2d Cir. 2009) (addressing municipal liability).

[8]See generally Hon. David T. Hamilton, The Importance and Overuse of Policy and Custom Claims: A View from the Bench, 48 DePaul L. Rev. 723 (Spring 1999).

[9]See for example, Knight v. Chattanooga Police Dept., 2008 WL 2704458 (E.D. Tenn. 2008).

[Section 14:9]

[1]See Dudosh v. City of Allentown, 629 F. Supp. 849 (E.D. Pa. 1985); see also Sherrell By and Through Wooden v. City of Longview, 683 F. Supp. 1108 (E.D. Tex. 1987) (finding that police awareness of the victim's situation created the special

state awareness was needed to create a special relationship. In *Balistreri v. Pacifica Police Department*,[2] the court established four factors for determining a special relationship in domestic violence failure to protect cases: (1) whether the state created or assumed a custodial relationship toward the plaintiff; (2) whether the state was aware of a specific risk of harm to the plaintiff; (3) whether the state affirmatively placed the plaintiff in a position of danger; and (4) whether the state affirmatively committed itself to the protection of the plaintiff. The court held that "the restraining order together with the defendants' repeated notice of [the victim's] plight, as alleged in the complaint, are sufficient to state a claim that the defendants owed [her] a duty to take reasonable measures to protect [the victim] from her estranged husband."[3] However, the court later affirmed the dismissal of the plaintiff's due process claim based on a narrow reading of the Supreme Court's holding in *DeShaney v. Winnebago County Department of Social Services*,[4] stating that the due process clause did not impose on the government an affirmative duty to protect, even though the government was aware of the victim's plight and took some steps to protect plaintiff.[5]

Another pre-*DeShaney* case, and the principal case in Ohio concerning the special relationship exception to the public duty rule, is *Sawicki v. Village of Ottawa Hills*.[6] That case held that, for a plaintiff to demonstrate a special relationship to avoid the immunity provided by the public duty rule, the plaintiff must show: (1) an assumption by the municipality, through promises or actions, of an affirmative duty to act on behalf of the party who was injured; (2) knowledge on the part of the municipality's agents that inaction could lead to harm; (3) some form of direct contact between the municipality's agents and the injured party; and (4) that party's justifiable reliance on the municipality's affirmative undertaking.

However, the United States Supreme Court, in *DeShaney*, appears to have narrowed the circumstances under which a special relationship may arise.[7] In that case, a child who was beaten and permanently brain damaged by his father claimed a due process violation because

relationship).

[2]Balistreri v. Pacifica Police Dept., 855 F.2d 1421 (9th Cir. 1988), opinion amended and superseded, 901 F.2d 696 (9th Cir. 1988).

[3]Balistreri v. Pacifica Police Dept., 855 F.2d 1421, 1426 (9th Cir. 1988), opinion amended and superseded, 901 F.2d 696 (9th Cir. 1988).

[4]DeShaney v. Winnebago County Dept. of Social Services, 489 U.S. 189, 109 S. Ct. 998, 103 L. Ed. 2d 249 (1989).

[5]See also Pinder v. Commissioners of Cambridge in City of Cambridge, 821 F. Supp. 376 (D. Md. 1993), judgment aff'd, 33 F.3d 368 (4th Cir. 1994), reh'g granted and opinion vacated, (Oct. 14, 1994) and on reh'g, 54 F.3d 1169 (4th Cir. 1995) and judgment rev'd, 54 F.3d 1169 (4th Cir. 1995) (examining *Balistreri* holding and noting that the government's awareness of the victim's plight is but one of the factors that determines the existence of a special relationship).

[6]Sawicki v. Village of Ottawa Hills, 37 Ohio St. 3d 222, 525 N.E.2d 468 (1988). But see Boggs v. Hughes, 1994 WL 28635 (Ohio Ct. App. 2d Dist. Greene County 1994) (holding that RC Ch. 2744 supersedes the public duty rule); Sudnik v. Crimi, 117 Ohio App. 3d 394, 690 N.E.2d 925 (8th Dist. Cuyahoga County 1997) (same).

[7]See also Stevens v. Trumbull County Sheriffs' Dept., 63 F. Supp. 2d 851 (N.D. Ohio 1999) (law enforcement agency had no affirmative duty to protect domestic

local officials knew of the abuse but did not act to remove him from his father's custody.

The Supreme Court concluded that the state had no constitutional duty to protect the child and that the Due Process Clause does not confer an affirmative duty on the government to protect an individual from private violence.[8] The Court rejected the claim that a special relationship existed because the child was not in the custody of the social services agency at the time he was injured by his father. In effect, the Court rejected the argument that police knowledge that a person faces a special danger and knowledge of the threatening party's identity creates a special relationship between the police and the victim. Without a special relationship, there is no basis on which a claim can be brought. The Supreme Court held:

> The affirmative duty to protect arises . . . from the limitation which it has imposed on his freedom to act in his own behalf. . . . In the substantive due process analysis, it is the State's affirmative act of restraining the individual's freedom to act on his own behalf—through incarceration, institutionalization, or other similar restraint of personal liberty—which is the "deprivation of liberty" triggering the protections of the Due Process Clause, not its failure to act to protect his liberty interests against harms inflicted by other means.[9]

Some courts have opined that the *DeShaney* holding is limited to situations in which the state is not involved in the harm, as either a custodian or an actor.[10] These courts have examined the possibility that *DeShaney* leaves open the question of whether liability may still attach in other situations and under other theories. For example, in *Horton v. Flenory*,[11] the Third Circuit interpreted the *DeShaney* decision to suggest that policies demonstrating a deliberate indifference to victims of domestic violence may not shield the police from liability. The court noted that *DeShaney* stands for the proposition that the Fourteenth Amendment imposes no obligation on the government to

---

violence victim from ex-boyfriend due to the fact that 911 dispatcher told victim that someone would come to her house and did not violate her substantive due process rights by not immediately dispatching officers to the house because she did not indicate she was in imminent danger; had the victim indicated the danger was imminent, the failure to dispatch officers to the home may have resulted in a violation of her substantive due process rights); but see Muthukumarana v. Montgomery County, 370 Md. 447, 805 A.2d 372 (2002) (where the 911 operator who was sued in negligence prevailed in summary judgment action); see also May v. Franklin County Bd. of Com'rs, 59 Fed. Appx. 786 (6th Cir. 2003) (in 3 calls to 911 made by decedent, officers were told the calls were not a priority; officers went to her apartment, knocked on door but left when no one answered; the officer was entitled to qualified immunity because administrator had not alleged a constitutional violation based upon either a custodial-type setting or a situation in which the police displaced other means of help or protection; the administration sufficiently pled that officer had a duty to protect her after emboldening her ex-boyfriend by going to her apartment, knocking and then leaving, although she was restrained inside; however, the officer was not sufficiently culpable to be liable under a substantive due process theory as his actions were reasonable and did not shock the conscience). David Basil, A Primer on the Public Duty Doctrine as Applied to Police Protection, 37 Urb. Law. 403 (2005).

[8] See also Garrett v. Gilless, 47 F.3d 1168 (6th Cir. 1995).

[9] DeShaney v. Winnebago County Dept. of Social Services, 489 U.S. 189, 200, 109 S. Ct. 998, 103 L. Ed. 2d 249 (1989).

[10] See, e.g., Horton v. Flenory, 889 F.2d 454 (3d Cir. 1989).

[11] Horton v. Flenory, 889 F.2d 454 (3d Cir. 1989).

prevent harm to a private person, even though it is aware that the third party is in imminent danger.

Similarly, in *Freeman v. Ferguson*,[12] the police chief was sued under 42 U.S.C.A. § 1983 for the death of a woman and her daughter by the woman's estranged husband. The allegation was that the police chief failed to perform his duties because of his close personal relationship with the estranged husband, which caused him to direct his officers not to enforce the restraining order. The Eighth Circuit Court of Appeals stated that *DeShaney* considers the possibility of police liability where police conduct actually interferes with the resources offering protection within the community. In effect, the constitutional duty to protect can arise where law enforcement action actually increases the individual's danger of, or vulnerability to, domestic violence beyond the level it would have been absent the police action.

In distinguishing its holding from *DeShaney*, the *Freeman* court stated that the violence was not limited to private violence between the victims and the estranged husband but rather was the result of the police chief's interference. The court also acknowledged that it was not clear how large a role the police must play in creating the danger before a constitutional duty to protect arises, but "that at some point such actions do create such a duty."[13]

Of significance is that the *DeShaney* Court favored state action rather than state inaction.[14] Even in its discussion limiting a state's duty to protect to custodial relationships, the Court preferred the concept of state action as a basis for an actionable due process claim. It is arguable that a municipal policy of nonenforcement of domestic violence laws or a decision not to provide protection to victims of domestic violence, if such decision results from a city's policy, is, in fact, state action; and a violation of the due process clause. However, the inaction must deprive an individual of the fundamental right to bodily integrity.[15]

There are two exceptions to the general rule that a failure to protect an individual against private violence does not constitute a violation of the Due Process Clause. First, when the state takes a person into

[12]Freeman v. Ferguson, 911 F.2d 52 (8th Cir. 1990); see also Sadrud-Din v. City of Chicago, 883 F. Supp. 270 (N.D. Ill. 1995) (plaintiff presented sufficient evidence to establish a special relationship; the city knew of its employees' failure to properly investigate complaints of domestic violence).

[13]Freeman v. Ferguson, 911 F.2d 52, 55 (8th Cir. 1990); see also Dudosh v. City of Allentown, 722 F. Supp. 1233 (E.D. Pa. 1989) (holding that police liability may attach if police escort or remove victims to and from locations that increase their risk of danger).

[14]See, e.g., Stevens v. Trumbull County Sheriffs' Dept., 63 F. Supp. 2d 851, 854 (N.D. Ohio 1999) (relying on *DeShaney* and, quoting Perry v. Wildes, 149 F.3d 1184 (6th Cir. 1998), stating "'we are unwilling to say that police response to a citizen's call for assistance subjects the officers to potential liability for creating a "special danger" premised upon a heightened sense of security. It does not follow from police presence and opinions about the potential for danger that a constitutional violation has occurred' ").

[15]See Ingraham v. Wright, 430 U.S. 651, 97 S. Ct. 1401, 51 L. Ed. 2d 711 (1977); see also Lauren McFarlane, Domestic Violence Victims v. Municipalities: Who Pays When the Police Will Not Respond? 41 Case W. Res. L. Rev. 929, 963 (1991) (stating that "Section 1983 was created to address not only arbitrary enforcement of the laws, but also their nonenforcement").

custody, the Constitution imposes some responsibility for that person's safety and well-being. Second, when state officials affirmatively place an individual in a dangerous situation, there can be a constitutional violation.[16]

To make out a claim under a state-created danger theory, "a plaintiff must demonstrate that (1) the charged state entity and the charged individual actors created the danger or increased plaintiff's vulnerability to the danger in some way; (2) plaintiff was a member of a limited and specifically definable group; (3) defendants' conduct put plaintiff at substantial risk of serious, immediate, and proximate harm; (4) the risk was obvious or known; (5) defendants acted recklessly in conscious disregard of that risk; and (6) such conduct, when viewed in total, is conscience shocking."[17] However, the *DeShaney* Supreme Court did not specify what actions of a state would render one of its citizens more vulnerable to danger or how much more vulnerable to danger a state must make a person before that person's due process rights are violated.[18]

In *Kallstrom v. City of Columbus*,[19] the Tenth Circuit Court of Appeals determined that liability is based on "affirmative acts by the state, which either create or increase the risk that an individual will be exposed to private acts of violence."[20] In effect, the officer's affirmative actions would have to increase the vulnerability of an individual to private acts of violence beyond the level it would have been had

[16]DeShaney v. Winnebago County Dept. of Social Services, 489 U.S. 189, 200-01, 109 S. Ct. 998, 103 L. Ed. 2d 249 (1989); see also Huffman v. County of Los Angeles, 147 F.3d 1054 (9th Cir. 1998); May v. Franklin County Bd. of Com'rs, 59 Fed. Appx. 786 (6th Cir. 2003); Kallstrom v. City of Columbus, 136 F.3d 1055, 13 I.E.R. Cas. (BNA) 1202, 26 Media L. Rep. (BNA) 1353, 1998 FED App. 0055P (6th Cir. 1998); Gonzales v. City of Castle Rock, 307 F.3d 1258 (10th Cir. 2002), on reh'g en banc, 366 F.3d 1093 (10th Cir. 2004), rev'd on other grounds, 545 U.S. 748, 125 S. Ct. 2796, 162 L. Ed. 2d 658 (2005); Smith v. Town of East Haven, 2005 WL 677284 (D. Conn. 2005) (discussing state created danger); Text § 14:14, Significant cases involving police officer action or inaction.

[17]Gonzales v. City of Castle Rock, 307 F.3d 1258, 1263 (10th Cir. 2002), on reh'g en banc, 366 F.3d 1093 (10th Cir. 2004), rev'd, 545 U.S. 748, 125 S. Ct. 2796, 162 L. Ed. 2d 658 (2005), quoting Currier v. Doran, 242 F.3d 905, 918 (10th Cir. 2001), citing Armijo By and Through Chavez v. Wagon Mound Public Schools, 159 F.3d 1253, 1262-63, 130 Ed. Law Rep. 496 (10th Cir. 1998).

[18]May v. Franklin County Bd. of Com'rs, 59 Fed. Appx. 786 (6th Cir. 2003), quoting Gazette v. City of Pontiac, 41 F.3d 1061, 1065, 1994 FED App. 0405P (6th Cir. 1994); Burella v. City of Philadelphia, 501 F.3d 134 (3d Cir. 2007) (discussing affirmatively acting v. a failure to act).

[19]Kallstrom v. City of Columbus, 136 F.3d 1055, 13 I.E.R. Cas. (BNA) 1202, 26 Media L. Rep. (BNA) 1353, 1998 FED App. 0055P (6th Cir. 1998); but see Brooks v. Knapp, 221 Fed. Appx. 402, 2007 FED App. 0812N (6th Cir. 2007) (failure to act as opposed to affirmative conduct, does not cause a "state-created danger"); Morrow v. Stoner, 2014 WL 4403436 (N.D. Ohio 2014) (dismissing the § 1983 claim against two judicial officers on the grounds that there was no state created danger, relying on *DeShaney v. Winnebago)*.

[20]Kallstrom v. City of Columbus, 136 F.3d 1055, 1066, 13 I.E.R. Cas. (BNA) 1202, 26 Media L. Rep. (BNA) 1353, 1998 FED App. 0055P (6th Cir. 1998); see also Davis v. Brady, 143 F.3d 1021, 1025, 1998 FED App. 0137P (6th Cir. 1998); May v. Franklin County Bd. of Com'rs, 59 Fed. Appx. 786 (6th Cir. 2003). See also Okin v. Village of Cornwall-On-Hudson Police Dept., 577 F.3d 415 (2d Cir. 2009) (addressing state created danger theory).

there been no state action[21] and must be differentiated from "a failure to act that merely does not decrease or eliminate a pre-existing danger."[22]

For example, in *May v. Franklin County Board of Commissioners*,[23] the decedent made three calls to 911 from her apartment. In each, screaming and crying could be heard. The officers were not told that the call was a priority by the dispatcher. Upon arrival, they knocked, looked in the windows, and because they could not see or hear anything, they left. The administrator of the estate of the deceased woman argued that a special relationship was created when she placed her 911 calls.

The Sixth Circuit Court of Appeals found that there was no special relationship because there was no custodial restraint on the decedent's liberty or on her ability to protect herself. However, the court noted that the theory of state created danger could apply if the administrator could show that the officer increased the decedent's vulnerability to harm. The administrator argued that the officer's arrival, minimal investigation and subsequent departure were affirmative acts that emboldened the boyfriend to hurt the decedent, whereas the officer stated that his failure to enter the premises was an omission.

The Circuit Court held that the officer did not create the danger, put the decedent in danger or make her more vulnerable to harm. The officer responded to the call and took reasonable measures to enter the premises. Because the administrator has not shown the requisite culpability on the officer's part to make out a violation of the decedent's constitutional rights, the officer is therefore entitled to qualified immunity and the substantive due process claim is reversed. In a concurring opinion, Justice Ryan stated "[e]ven if Ratliff 'emboldened' Moss, Ratliff did not create the danger; Moss did that. At most, Ratliff failed to rescue Kirk. At the very least, he did not violate the law by breaking down the door."[24]

Of significance is that the majority noted that if the officer had known what the decedent had said to the 911 operator "and the way in which the calls were terminated, this might be a different case, but there is nothing in the record to indicate that he had been told either the specific content or even their general nature. There is also nothing in the record to establish that Franklin Township had any standards setting out the appropriate response to a domestic violence 911 call."[25] It appears that, at the very least, the court was concerned with the policies or lack thereof within the dispatcher's office. Had the officer been told and then ignored a known risk, liability might lie. Had the administrator sued the 911 dispatcher or the municipality based on a failure to train the dispatchers, liability might have attached as well.

[21]May v. Franklin County Bd. of Com'rs, 59 Fed. Appx. 786 (6th Cir. 2003).

[22]Gonzales v. City of Castle Rock, 307 F.3d 1258, 1263 (10th Cir. 2002), on reh'g en banc, 366 F.3d 1093 (10th Cir. 2004), rev'd, 545 U.S. 748, 125 S. Ct. 2796, 162 L. Ed. 2d 658 (2005).

[23]May v. Franklin County Bd. of Com'rs, 59 Fed. Appx. 786 (6th Cir. 2003).

[24]May v. Franklin County Bd. of Com'rs, 59 Fed. Appx. 786, 795-96 (6th Cir. 2003).

[25]May v. Franklin County Bd. of Com'rs, 59 Fed. Appx. 786, 794 (6th Cir. 2003).

§ 14:10 Police liability for failing to protect victims of domestic violence—Legal theories for recovery—Equal protection

Despite the uncertainty of prevailing under a substantive due process theory after *DeShaney*, a victim of domestic violence may still have a remedy under the Equal Protection Clause of the Fourteenth Amendment of the United States Constitution.[1] The Equal Protection Clause provides that no state shall deny to any person equal protection of the laws. Under this theory, a plaintiff must prove that the police intentionally discriminated against the plaintiff on the basis of the plaintiff's sex or status as a victim of domestic (versus nondomestic) violence.[2]

In failure-to-protect cases, in order to prove a deprivation of equal protection under 42 U.S.C.A. § 1983, a plaintiff must show that: (1) a municipal policy or custom existed at the time of the injury, (2) the policy discriminated against a group of which he/she was a member, and (3) the injury was causally linked to the policy.[3] For example, in *Watson v. City of Kansas City*,[4] the plaintiff alleged that the defendant's policy or custom of providing less protection to domestic violence victims than other victims of assault deprived her of her equal protection guarantees. The Tenth Circuit Court reiterated that, in equal protection cases, the plaintiff has the burden of demonstrating discriminatory intent. The court stated that "[i]t is not necessary to demonstrate that the challenged action was taken solely for discriminatory purposes; it is necessary only to prove that a discriminatory purpose was a motivating factor."[5]

The relevant case law in the area provides numerous requirements necessary to prevail on an equal protection claim. For instance, the discriminatory acts of law enforcement must derive from a municipal policy, either a formal written policy or law or an informal, unwritten policy or custom.[6] Evidence of a written policy may include a statement in a general police order or police handbook of police procedure. It may be contained in a local ordinance. It may be based on a

---

[Section 14:10]

[1]See McKee v. City of Rockwall, Tex., 877 F.2d 409 (5th Cir. 1989).

[2]See, e.g., Thurman v. City of Torrington, 595 F. Supp. 1521 (D. Conn. 1984) (concluding that police who have notice of the possibility that women may be attacked more often in domestic relationships are under a duty to take reasonable measures to protect them and that the failure to perform this duty would constitute a denial of equal protection).

[3]See Watson v. City of Kansas City, Kan., 857 F.2d 690 (10th Cir. 1988).

[4]Watson v. City of Kansas City, Kan., 857 F.2d 690 (10th Cir. 1988).

[5]Watson v. City of Kansas City, Kan., 857 F.2d 690, 694 (10th Cir. 1988); see also Semple v. City of Moundsville, 963 F. Supp. 1416 (N.D. W. Va. 1997), judgment aff'd, 195 F.3d 708 (4th Cir. 1999) (finding that the city had not discriminated in violation of the Equal Protection Clause); Soto v. Flores, 103 F.3d 1056 (1st Cir. 1997) (adopting standard set forth in *Watson*).

[6]But see Kelley v. City of Wake Village, Texas, 264 Fed. Appx. 437 (5th Cir. 2008) (focusing on the policy maker rather than the officer; as officer was not a policy maker, liability could not be imposed in his official capacity).

discriminatory policy that gives lower priority to 911 domestic violence calls than to 911 nondomestic violence calls.[7]

Absent a clearly defined written policy evidencing discrimination, discrimination may be demonstrated where the plaintiff can show that the police denied assistance to victims of domestic violence. "To establish the existence of an informal policy, two types of evidence have emerged: facts showing a 'pattern or practice' of discrimination and facts suggesting that the municipality condoned or approved of the discrimination."[8]

Evidence of an unwritten policy may be shown in the policy of assigning a lower priority to domestic violence calls or sending fewer officers to the scene of a domestic incident. It may be found in training materials or in a city policy that fails to take reasonable steps to adequately train its officers in the handling of domestic violence.[9] It may also be proven by statistical data showing the number of nondomestic arrests versus the number of domestic arrests for assaults.[10]

Besides proving that a policy or custom exists, a plaintiff must prove that the policy or custom is discriminatory on its face. Such a policy must be, at the very least, covertly based on gender and must raise an inference of discriminatory purpose.[11] Evidence of adverse

[7]See Fajardo v. County of Los Angeles, 179 F.3d 698 (9th Cir. 1999) (reversing district court ruling that it did not need to decide whether a custom or policy existed because it had "'previously found that such a [policy] meets the rational basis test' "); see also Navarro v. Block, 72 F.3d 712 (9th Cir. 1995), as amended on denial of reh'g, (Jan. 12, 1996) (remanding case to determine whether city had discriminatory policy or custom and, if so, whether it had a rational basis).

[8]Lauren McFarlane, Domestic Violence Victims v. Municipalities: Who Pays When the Police Will Not Respond? 41 Case W. Res. L. Rev. 929, 936 (1991); see also Thurman v. City of Torrington, 595 F. Supp. 1521 (D. Conn. 1984); Watson v. City of Kansas City, Kan., 857 F.2d 690 (10th Cir. 1988); Soto v. Carrasquillo, 878 F. Supp. 324, 329 (D.P.R. 1995), aff'd, 103 F.3d 1056 (1st Cir. 1997) (while single incident by itself is generally an insufficient basis for inferring the existence of a policy or custom, the "evidence of a plaintiff's own case may be sufficient if these facts indicate an ongoing pattern of police indifference which raises an inference of a policy or custom" or "if there is proof that supervisors or decision-makers have approved or authorized the discriminatory conduct") (citations omitted).

[9]But see Cossio v. City and County of Denver, Colo., 986 F. Supp. 1340 (D. Colo. 1997), judgment aff'd, 139 F.3d 911 (10th Cir. 1998) (distinguishing case from *Sadrud* and finding that the evidence did not establish an equal protection violation for police failure to arrest a domestic abuse assailant where there was no evidence regarding training of police officers, or that the victim had a history of domestic violence and summoning of the police); Ford v. Town of Grafton, 44 Mass. App. Ct. 715, 693 N.E.2d 1047 (1998) (detailing standard for prevailing on an equal protection claim based on law enforcement authority's different treatment of domestic abuse and non-domestic abuse cases, relying on *Soto v. Flores*); see also McClure v. Town of East Brookfield, 1999 WL 1323628 (Mass. Super. Ct. 1999).

[10]See Watson v. City of Kansas City, Kan., 857 F.2d 690 (10th Cir. 1988); Cellini v. City of Sterling Heights, 856 F. Supp. 1215 (E.D. Mich. 1994) (plaintiff was entitled to access, subject to appropriate protective order, to police records necessary to perform statistical study to support the equal protection claim).

[11]See Personnel Adm'r of Massachusetts v. Feeney, 442 U.S. 256, 99 S. Ct. 2282, 60 L. Ed. 2d 870, 19 Fair Empl. Prac. Cas. (BNA) 1377, 19 Empl. Prac. Dec. (CCH) P 9240 (1979); see also Watson v. City of Kansas City, Kan., 857 F.2d 690 (10th Cir. 1988); Soto v. Flores, 103 F.3d 1056 (1st Cir. 1997); Eckert v. Town of Silverthorne, 25

impact may also be used to prove that the policy or custom was discriminatory.

The *Watson* Court determined that a plaintiff must demonstrate both a pattern of deliberate indifference on the part of the police department and that, because of her membership in a certain class, she was treated differently by the police. In *Watson*, the evidence proffered by the plaintiff, her version of the events, accumulated statistical evidence,[12] and the type of training police officers received in handling domestic violence situations, demonstrated a pattern sufficient to constitute a policy or custom.

Many courts have distinguished between two distinct types of discrimination that may be alleged under an equal protection claim. In *Watson*, the court differentiated between the plaintiff's allegations of class-based discrimination based on her status as a victim of domestic violence and her allegations of class-based discrimination based on her sex.[13]

The *Watson* Court, citing *Personnel Administrator v. Feeney*,[14] proposed a twofold analysis for addressing a plaintiff's sex-based claim: (1) whether the classification is indeed neutral in the sense that it is not gender-based and (2) if not, whether the adverse effect reflects invidious gender-based discrimination.[15] The Court found that the evidence presented by the plaintiff of a policy which discriminates against victims of domestic violence must also address adverse impact. The *Watson* plaintiff failed to present any evidence of adverse impact. Additionally, under the *Feeney* rule, a plaintiff must show that the classification was adopted to purposely discriminate against women. Absent evidence of adverse impact or discriminatory purpose, a

---

Fed. Appx. 679 (10th Cir. 2001) (court stated that a plaintiff has the burden of showing discriminatory intent and though the discriminatory purpose need not be the only purpose, it must be a motivating factor in the decision).

[12]But see Eckert v. Town of Silverthorne, 25 Fed. Appx. 679 (10th Cir. 2001) (district court discussed *Watson* and statistical evidence).

[13]See also Thurman v. City of Torrington, 595 F. Supp. 1521 (D. Conn. 1984). But see Hynson By and Through Hynson v. City of Chester Legal Dept., 864 F.2d 1026 (3d Cir. 1988) (appearing not to distinguish between discrimination of domestic violence victims based on status and based on sex).

[14]Personnel Adm'r of Massachusetts v. Feeney, 442 U.S. 256, 99 S. Ct. 2282, 60 L. Ed. 2d 870, 19 Fair Empl. Prac. Cas. (BNA) 1377, 19 Empl. Prac. Dec. (CCH) P 9240 (1979).

[15]Watson v. City of Kansas City, Kan., 857 F.2d 690 (10th Cir. 1988); Personnel Adm'r of Massachusetts v. Feeney, 442 U.S. 256, 99 S. Ct. 2282, 60 L. Ed. 2d 870, 19 Fair Empl. Prac. Cas. (BNA) 1377, 19 Empl. Prac. Dec. (CCH) P 9240 (1979) (articulating a rule directing a plaintiff to show that the municipality carried out or approved a particular cause of action, in part, because of its adverse impact on women). Under the *Feeney* analysis, the policy must be motivated by a specific discriminatory purpose to harm women. See also Amy Eppler, Battered Women and the Equal Protection Clause: Will the Constitution Help Them When the Police Won't? 95 Yale L.J. 788 (1986); Carolyne R. Hathaway, Comment, Gender Based Discrimination in Police Reluctance to Respond to Domestic Assault Complaints, 75 Geo. L.J. 667 (1986). But see 42 U.S.C.A. § 13981, wherein the federal Violence Against Women Act of 1994 creates a civil rights remedy for gender-motivated violence for victims who have been denied that right. The Act's express inclusion of persons acting under "color of state law" brings within this provision the plethora of case law already developed under 42 U.S.C.A. § 1983.

plaintiff has failed to state a prima facie case of sex-based discrimination.[16]

In adequately demonstrating that a municipality has a policy that discriminates against domestic violence victims, proof of adverse impact may be found by showing that the failure to enforce domestic violence laws disproportionately harms women since most reported victims of domestic violence are female.[17] It is arguable that, if a plaintiff is able to demonstrate that the police do not arrest offenders in domestic violence cases because they believe it is acceptable to batter women, the standard articulated in *Feeney* may be met. However, documented evidence of a blatantly discriminatory policy is often difficult to unearth, and a plaintiff may be unable to present evidence of a discriminatory intent by the municipality sufficient to state a prima facie case for sex-based discrimination.[18]

The cases have shown that, where police classifications reflect and perpetrate negative myths and stereotypes about women, even if manifested in gender-neutral terms, they often result in disparate treatment of domestic violence victims.[19] If a plaintiff is able to demonstrate disparate treatment, the burden of proof shifts to the governmental defendant to show a gender-neutral purpose. For example, offering less police protection to victims of domestic violence does nothing to further important governmental interests and reflects discriminatory police policies that violate victims' constitutional rights under the Equal Protection Clause.[20]

If a plaintiff is able to prove that the discriminatory purpose is gender-based, the governmental defendant must show that "the classification serves 'important governmental objectives and that the discriminatory means employed' are 'substantially related to the achievement of those objectives.' "[21] It is important to note that the Supreme Court has used an intermediate level of scrutiny for claims of sex-based discrimination.

Many lower courts have applied the "rational basis" test to claims

---

[16]See also Soto v. Flores, 103 F.3d 1056 (1st Cir. 1997).

[17]See U.S. Dep't of Justice, Bureau of Justice Statistics, Domestic Violence: Violence Between Intimates, Pub. No. NCJ-149259 (1994). See also McDonald v. City of Chicago, 1994 WL 732865, *3 (N.D. Ill. 1994) (treating domestic violence abuse reports from women with less priority than other crimes not involving women reporting domestic violence abuse is tantamount to a gender-based administrative classification and clearly states a claim for Equal Protection violations).

[18]See, e.g., Soto v. Flores, 103 F.3d 1056 (1st Cir. 1997).

[19]See, e.g., Williams v. City of Montgomery, 21 F. Supp. 2d 1360 (M.D. Ala. 1998), aff'd, 200 F.3d 821 (11th Cir. 1999) (holding that "disparate impact" claim, which could not be brought under 42 U.S.C.A. § 1983, could be recast and maintained as a "disparate treatment" claim).

[20]See e.g. Hynson By and Through Hynson v. City of Chester Legal Dept., 864 F.2d 1026 (3d Cir. 1988) (adopting a three-pronged test to demonstrate that a facially neutral policy is executed in a discriminatory manner if: (1) a reasonable police officer would know that the policy had a discriminatory impact on women, (2) bias against women was a motivating factor behind the adoption of the policy, and (3) there was no important public interest served by the adoption of the policy).

[21]Mississippi University for Women v. Hogan, 458 U.S. 718, 724, 102 S. Ct. 3331, 73 L. Ed. 2d 1090, 5 Ed. Law Rep. 103, 29 Empl. Prac. Dec. (CCH) P 32868 (1982) (quoting Wengler v. Druggists Mut. Ins. Co., 446 U.S. 142, 150, 100 S. Ct. 1540, 64 L. Ed. 2d 107, 22 Empl. Prac. Dec. (CCH) P 30856 (1980)).

of discrimination against victims of domestic violence.[22] Under that test, the plaintiff must show that the policy at issue is not rationally related to a legitimate governmental interest. In domestic violence cases, a governmental interest is not legitimate if an irrational prejudice or antipathy against victims of domestic violence motivates the policy at issue. Where the policy is not rationally related to the purpose articulated by the governmental defendant, because it does not serve that purpose or is tenuously linked to that purpose, it fails the "rational basis" test.

Besides a discriminatory policy or practice, a plaintiff must also prove that the injuries were caused by the policy or custom. For example, in *Thurman v. City of Torrington*,[23] the court stated that "a complaint . . . will survive dismissal if it alleges a policy or custom of condoning police misconduct that violates constitutional rights and alleges 'that the City's pattern of inaction caused the plaintiffs any compensable injury.' "[24]

§ 14:11 Police liability for failing to protect victims of domestic violence—Legal theories for recovery—Procedural due process

Several court jurisdictions have also permitted recovery under a procedural due process theory where the right to protection is grounded in state law, rather than the Due Process Clause of the Constitution. Under this theory, a victim's right to police protection is based on a property interest created by a state statute or protection order. Even the holding in *DeShaney* does not preclude consideration of a procedural due process violation under *Board of Regents v. Roth*.[1] In *Roth*, the United States Supreme Court held that a property interest created by state law was protected by the Due Process Clause of the United States Constitution. For a protected property right to exist, a person "must have more than a unilateral expectation of it. He must, instead, have a legitimate claim of entitlement to it."[2] The Court also pointed out that, with respect to property interests, they are "defined by existing rules or understandings that stem from an in-

[22]See, e.g., Watson v. City of Kansas City, Kan., 857 F.2d 690 (10th Cir. 1988); Siddle v. City of Cambridge, Ohio, 761 F. Supp. 503 (S.D. Ohio 1991).

[23]Thurman v. City of Torrington, 595 F. Supp. 1521, 1530 (D. Conn. 1984) (quoting Batista v. Rodriguez, 702 F.2d 393, 397 (2d Cir. 1983)).

[24]But see Bartalone v. Berrien County, 643 F. Supp. 574 (W.D. Mich. 1986) (dismissing case because the plaintiff failed to demonstrate that her injury was the result of municipal policy or custom).

[Section 14:11]

[1]Board of Regents of State Colleges v. Roth, 408 U.S. 564, 92 S. Ct. 2701, 33 L. Ed. 2d 548, 1 I.E.R. Cas. (BNA) 23 (1972).

[2]Board of Regents of State Colleges v. Roth, 408 U.S. 564, 577, 92 S. Ct. 2701, 33 L. Ed. 2d 548, 1 I.E.R. Cas. (BNA) 23 (1972); see also Burella v. City of Philadelphia, 501 F.3d 134, 152 (3d Cir. 2007) (see concurring opinion discussing whether the Pa statute's intent to mandate arrest can get around "the deeply rooted nature of law enforcement and discretion, even in the presence of seemingly mandatory legislative commands").

dependent source such as state law."[3] Procedural due process protections apply whenever the state decides to eliminate or change the protected status that surrounds the individual.

Victims of domestic violence may raise a viable procedural due process claim if the state in which the violence occurred created an enforceable statutory right to protection from domestic violence.[4] For example, in *Coffman v. Wilson Police Department*,[5] the victim alleged that the police failed to arrest her husband in spite of a valid protection order. The federal district court determined that it was not the domestic violence statute, but the protection order, that conferred the property right on the protected individual. "Nowhere [in the statute] does it state that the police must protect those who allege that they are abused. The . . . language does not itself entitle the plaintiff to police protection."[6] In Ohio, as in other states, the legislature has recognized a domestic violence victim's need for protection through the passage of laws that create these entitlements.

However, several federal courts have summarily dismissed these arguments, stating that such statutes and procedures were not enacted pursuant to a substantive constitutional obligation. For example, in *Semple v. City of Moundsville*,[7] the federal district court applied the rationale set forth in *DeShaney v. Winnebago County Department of Social Services*[8] in not finding a special relationship.

While the district court agreed with the United States Supreme Court's analysis in *Board of Regents v. Roth*,[9] it noted:

> While it is clear that a state law may create a liberty or property interest that cannot be taken away without due process of law, it is also true that state laws mandating that certain procedures be followed in certain situations do not automatically create a protected entitlement. Rather, in order to raise a meritorious procedural due process claim based on a

[3] Board of Regents of State Colleges v. Roth, 408 U.S. 564, 577, 92 S. Ct. 2701, 33 L. Ed. 2d 548, 1 I.E.R. Cas. (BNA) 23 (1972); see also Estate of Brown ex rel. Brown v. Woodham, 840 So. 2d 1105 (Fla. 1st DCA 2003) (in which court found special duty created by domestic violence statute).

[4] See Lauren McFarlane, Domestic Violence Victims v. Municipalities: Who Pays When the Police Will Not Respond? 41 Case W. Res. L. Rev. 929 (1991).

[5] Coffman v. Wilson Police Dept., 739 F. Supp. 257 (E.D. Pa. 1990). See also Calloway v. Kinkelaar, 168 Ill. 2d 312, 213 Ill. Dec. 675, 659 N.E.2d 1322 (1995) (finding that the plaintiff was entitled to special protection because her protection order created a statutory duty to protect her by reasonable means); Gonzales v. City of Castle Rock, 307 F.3d 1258 (10th Cir. 2002), on reh'g en banc, 366 F.3d 1093 (10th Cir. 2004), rev'd on other grounds, 545 U.S. 748, 125 S. Ct. 2796, 162 L. Ed. 2d 658 (2005) (court reversed dismissal for failure to state a claim, and held that complaint stated a cause of action for deprivation of procedural due process rights stemming from Colorado statute requiring officers to use reasonable means to enforce restraining order and imposing duty to arrest based on belief that restrained person had violated the order).

[6] Coffman v. Wilson Police Dept., 739 F. Supp. 257, 264 (E.D. Pa. 1990).

[7] Semple v. City of Moundsville, 963 F. Supp. 1416, 1428–29 (N.D. W. Va. 1997), judgment aff'd, 195 F.3d 708 (4th Cir. 1999); see also Ford v. Town of Grafton, 44 Mass. App. Ct. 715, 693 N.E.2d 1047 (1998).

[8] DeShaney v. Winnebago County Dept. of Social Services, 489 U.S. 189, 109 S. Ct. 998, 103 L. Ed. 2d 249 (1989).

[9] Board of Regents of State Colleges v. Roth, 408 U.S. 564, 92 S. Ct. 2701, 33 L. Ed. 2d 548, 1 I.E.R. Cas. (BNA) 23 (1972).

liberty or property interest created by a state law, a plaintiff must "show that the procedures that [were not followed] were enacted pursuant to a substantive constitutional obligation."[10]

The *Semple* court found that the plaintiffs' procedural due process claims were merely *DeShaney* claims couched in the language of procedural due process. The court pointed out that, although a statute may prescribe and codify certain procedures for dealing with domestic violence, such as requiring police to inform a victim of available assistance or remedies or training police officers on domestic violence,[11] the statute does not automatically give rise to a constitutionally protected entitlement that can be enforced by individuals.[12] Since, absent a custodial relationship, there is no independent, substantive constitutional interest on which the procedures in the statutes are based, the plaintiffs' claims failed.[13] Under a *Semple* analysis, similar police procedures codified in Ohio's statutes may fail to provide victims of domestic violence with a right to protection.

In *Coffman v. Wilson Police Department*,[14] the court decided that the threshold question was whether the orders of a court create a property interest in police enforcement. The court found that "a court order may create a property right. . . . It is clear that a court may issue a protective order under the [statute]. Moreover, this order must be issued to the police department that has jurisdiction to enforce it."[15] The court concluded that the protection order itself created the special relationship if, pursuant to that act, a provision details that the police department is required to enforce the order. This creates a constitutionally enforceable property right to police protection.[16]

---

[10]Semple v. City of Moundsville, 963 F. Supp. 1416, 1430 (N.D. W. Va. 1997), judgment aff'd, 195 F.3d 708 (4th Cir. 1999) (citation omitted) (quoting Doe by Fein v. District of Columbia, 93 F.3d 861, 868 (D.C. Cir. 1996), certified question answered, 697 A.2d 23 (D.C. 1997)).

[11]See also City of Canton, Ohio v. Harris, 489 U.S. 378, 109 S. Ct. 1197, 103 L. Ed. 2d 412 (1989) (substantive due process claim may be converted to a procedural due process claim if there is a statutory duty to train police officers in domestic violence situations).

[12]Semple v. City of Moundsville, 963 F. Supp. 1416, 1431 (N.D. W. Va. 1997), judgment aff'd, 195 F.3d 708 (4th Cir. 1999).

[13]Semple v. City of Moundsville, 963 F. Supp. 1416, 1431 (N.D. W. Va. 1997), judgment aff'd, 195 F.3d 708 (4th Cir. 1999).

[14]Coffman v. Wilson Police Dept., 739 F. Supp. 257 (E.D. Pa. 1990).

[15]Coffman v. Wilson Police Dept., 739 F. Supp. 257, 264 (E.D. Pa. 1990). But see Ford v. Town of Grapton, 427 Mass. 1108, 700 N.E.2d 268 (1998) (questioning whether a protective order properly served on the police creates a Roth property interest that is secured by due process of law and declining to decide whether a protective order creates a special relationship between the police and a domestic violence victim and, thereby, provides a constitutionally protected "property interest"); see also Semple v. City of Moundsville, 963 F. Supp. 1416 (N.D. W. Va. 1997), judgment aff'd, 195 F.3d 708 (4th Cir. 1999).

[16]But see Doe by Nelson v. Milwaukee County, 903 F.2d 499 (7th Cir. 1990) (court was reluctant to adopt the rationale of *Coffman*); Hynson v. City of Chester, 731 F. Supp. 1236 (E.D. Pa. 1990) (same).

Besides demonstrating an entitlement to protection, a plaintiff must show a deprivation of due process.[17] The evidence must also establish that the governmental defendant acted with deliberate indifference or willful, wanton, or reckless conduct. Negligent acts resulting in unintended loss or injury do not demonstrate a deprivation of due process.[18]

Additionally, the *Coffman* court cautioned that its ruling was not to be mistaken for "a litigant's bonanza."[19] The court stated that the scope of the *Roth* property interest was limited to those cases in which it can be demonstrated that the deprivation of the property right by the police caused the victim's injuries. The court also limited a victim's property right to reasonable police response.[20]

§ 14:12 Police liability for failing to protect victims of domestic violence—Legal theories for recovery—State duty to protect

Finally, lawsuits against the police for a failure to protect have been brought under a state-created duty to protect. Assuming the plaintiff can overcome the state tort immunity,[1] recovery is possible based on the duty created by the special relationship that arises from the state statute or ordinance.[2] For example, in *Sorichetti v. City of New York*,[3] the court found a special relationship between the police and the mother and daughter sufficient to support a negligence judgment in light of the fact that the police knew of the existence of a protection order, the father's violent nature, his threats against both mother and child when he picked up the child for weekend visits, and the mother's plea for assistance and failed to act after assuring the mother they would.

Ohio's domestic violence laws contain provisions that may create certain protections for victims of domestic violence. For example, a police official's duty to respond without delay to reported incidents of domestic violence,[4] the duty to provide a victim of domestic violence with information or assistance in domestic violence situations,[5] and a law enforcement agency's duty to adopt domestic violence policies and procedures,[6] provide officer training in the handling of domestic

[17] See Coffman v. Wilson Police Dept., 739 F. Supp. 257 (E.D. Pa. 1990).

[18] See Daniels v. Williams, 474 U.S. 327, 106 S. Ct. 662, 88 L. Ed. 2d 662 (1986).

[19] Coffman v. Wilson Police Dept., 739 F. Supp. 257, 266 (E.D. Pa. 1990).

[20] See also Siddle v. City of Cambridge, Ohio, 761 F. Supp. 503 (S.D. Ohio 1991) (applying a similar test but reaching a contrary conclusion).

[Section 14:12]

[1] See R.C. 2744.

[2] See Sorichetti by Sorichetti v. City of New York, 65 N.Y.2d 461, 492 N.Y.S.2d 591, 482 N.E.2d 70 (1985);Sachanowski v. Wyoming County Sheriff's Dept., 244 A.D.2d 908, 665 N.Y.S.2d 197 (4th Dep't 1997).

[3] Sorichetti by Sorichetti v. City of New York, 65 N.Y.2d 461, 492 N.Y.S.2d 591, 482 N.E.2d 70 (1985).

[4] RC 2935.032(A)(2).

[5] RC 3113.31(I), RC 2935.032(C)(3).

[6] RC 2935.032, RC 2935.03.

violence offenses,[7] and maintain an index of protection orders[8] may create entitlements to protection. The state's preferred arrest policy for domestic violence offenses or violations of protection orders may also create a right to be protected.[9]

Historically, the concept of sovereign immunity created an almost absolute defense to a state's or municipality's liability for its employees' negligent acts in providing, for example, police services.[10] Additionally, police have, under the public duty doctrine, a general duty to protect all citizens and a specific duty to protect no one in particular.[11]

However, where the police have been negligent in their protection and the plaintiff can demonstrate a special relationship between herself and the police, liability may still attach provided the elements of negligence are met.[12] In this context, a special relationship exception to the public duty rule exists where the government offers greater protection to one individual. Accordingly, a statute or ordinance indicates a clear legislative intent on the part of the government to protect a specific and identifiable class of individuals of which the plaintiff is a member.[13] Where the governmental entity with whom the injured party has had direct contact has given that party assur-

---

[7]See RC 109.744; see also City of Canton, Ohio v. Harris, 489 U.S. 378, 109 S. Ct. 1197, 103 L. Ed. 2d 412 (1989) (substantive due process claim may be converted to a procedural due process claim if there is a statutory duty to train police officers in domestic violence situations); Kalina v. City of Waterbury, 7 Conn. L. Rptr. 106, 1992 WL 175093, *2–3 (Conn. Super. Ct. 1992).

[8]RC 3113.31(F), RC 2919.26(G)(2).

[9]See RC 2935.03(B)(3)(b); Simpson v. City of Miami, 700 So. 2d 87 (Fla. 3d DCA 1997). But see Eckert v. Town of Silverthorne, 25 Fed. Appx. 679 (10th Cir. 2001) (circuit court held that summary judgment decision of district court was proper, even though Colorado had a mandatory arrest statute, police standards, and protocol in effect); Town of Castle Rock, Colo. v. Gonzales, 545 U.S. 748, 125 S. Ct. 2796, 162 L. Ed. 2d 658 (2005); Burella v. City of Philadelphia, 501 F.3d 134 (3d Cir. 2007).

[10]See generally, Barbara E. Armacost, Affirmative Duties, Systemic Harms and the Due Process Clause, 94 Michigan L. Rev. 982, 1001 (1996). See also Lee v. City of Oakland, 2006 WL 2046011 (Cal. App. 1st Dist. 2006), unpublished/noncitable (holding that the complaint was sufficient to state a claim under the doctrine of vicarious liability as the city stipulated it had a duty to place defendant in custody and that it breached its statutory duty).

[11]See Sawicki v. Village of Ottawa Hills, 37 Ohio St. 3d 222, 525 N.E.2d 468 (1988) (holding that the public duty rule and the special relationship exception comprise an independent doctrine that survives the abrogation of sovereign immunity). But see Amborski v. Toledo, 67 Ohio App. 3d 47, 585 N.E.2d 974 (6th Dist. Lucas County 1990) (stating that the intent of RC Ch. 2744 was to codify the concept of sovereign immunity and, therefore, to abrogate the public duty rule and special relationship exception theory of municipal liability); Boggs v. Hughes, 1994 WL 28635 (Ohio Ct. App. 2d Dist. Greene County 1994) (holding that RC Ch. 2744 supersedes the public duty rule).

[12]See, e.g., Simpson v. City of Miami, 700 So. 2d 87 (Fla. 3d DCA 1997); see also Nichole Galvin, Williams vs. Mayor of Baltimore: A Police Officer May Lose Immunity from Civil Liability where Special Relationship Exists, 31 U. Balt.L.F. 84 (2000).

[13]See Sorichetti by Sorichetti v. City of New York, 65 N.Y.2d 461, 492 N.Y.S.2d 591, 482 N.E.2d 70 (1985).

ances of protection and the party has relied on either the express or implied assurances to assist, a special relationship may be created.[14]

It has been argued that a traditional tort analysis should be applied to state law failure-to-protect cases, whether or not a special relationship exception can be found.[15] An ordinary negligence standard would neither impose complete immunity from liability nor an absolute duty on a municipality's police department to protect its citizens and enforce its laws. Police departments would be held to a standard of reasonable, due care, and liability would be limited by proximate cause and foreseeability.[16]

The general rule of negligence is that, where a person can reasonably foresee that his/her action or failure to take action involves an unreasonable risk of harm to another, there is a duty to avoid such harm. Tort law requires that a plaintiff must establish a duty owed, a breach of that duty, causation, and actual injury. An example of a breach of duty is where the municipality or its agents fails in the performance of its duties and violates formal professional standards.[17]

Additionally, in police failure-to-protect cases, the police and the victim must have a special relationship. Under this standard, police officers may be insulated from liability because liability is contingent on a police officer's breach of a duty to provide protection to citizens and proof that police inaction was the proximate cause of the injuries.

In order to prevail under a state negligence claim or a claim based

[14]See Sawicki v. Village of Ottawa Hills, 37 Ohio St. 3d 222, 525 N.E.2d 468 (1988); Mastroianni v. County of Suffolk, 91 N.Y.2d 198, 668 N.Y.S.2d 542, 691 N.E.2d 613 (1997) (summary judgment was precluded because special relationship had arisen between the officers and the decedent and whether officers acted reasonably was a fact question, relying on Cuffy v. City of New York, 69 N.Y.2d 255, 260, 513 N.Y.S.2d 372, 505 N.E.2d 937 (1987), and defining the elements of a special relationship/special duty). But see Boggs v. Hughes, 1994 WL 28635 (Ohio Ct. App. 2d Dist. Greene County 1994) (holding that RC Ch. 2744 supersedes the public duty rule).

[15]See Gerald P. Krause, Comment, Municipal Liability: The Failure to Provide Adequate Police Protection—The Special Duty Doctrine Should Be Discarded, 1984 Wis. L. Rev. 499, 522 (1984) (noting the inequitable results of limiting the liability analysis to the special duty rule and finding that the majority of courts go to great lengths to protect a municipality from liability, even where the employees fall short in the performance of their assigned duties). See also Smith v. Town of East Haven, 2005 WL 677284 (D. Conn. 2005) (holding that Smith's state law negligence claim should survive summary judgment motion where the officers knew that the offender had threatened to kill the victim, he had guns, the victim had made previous reports of domestic abuse, there was a restraining order in place, and the offender had been arrested for violating the order).

[16]Gerald P. Krause, Comment, Municipal Liability: The Failure to Provide Adequate Police Protection—The Special Duty Doctrine Should Be Discarded, 1984 Wis. L. Rev. 499, 524 (1984); see Ellsworth v. County of Orange, 2001 WL 1515802 (Cal. App. 4th Dist. 2001), unpublished/noncitable, (Nov. 28, 2001) (where Appellate Court affirmed the lower court's decision to grant defendant police officers' motion for summary judgment where the decedent did not have a restraining order, there was no duty of care owed to Ellsworth; thus, no special relationship existed).

[17]Gerald P. Krause, Comment, Municipal Liability: The Failure to Provide Adequate Police Protection—The Special Duty Doctrine Should Be Discarded, 1984 Wis. L. Rev. 499, 525 (1984). See also Williams v. City of Montgomery, 21 F. Supp. 2d 1360 (M.D. Ala. 1998), aff'd, 200 F.3d 821 (11th Cir. 1999) (finding that municipality could be held liable under state law for negligent acts of its police detective in not responding properly to a domestic violence complaint of a woman ultimately killed by her ex-husband).

on state law, there must be (1) an assumption by the municipality, through promises or actions, of an affirmative duty to act on behalf of the party who was injured, (2) knowledge on the part of the municipality's agents that inaction could lead to harm, (3) some form of direct contact between the municipality's agents and the injured party, and (4) justifiable reliance by the injured party on the municipality's affirmative undertaking.[18]

A review of pertinent case law[19] in this area indicates that the existence of a protection order and communication between the plaintiff and the police establishes a special relationship between the plaintiff and the police and a duty to protect. A protection order issued pursuant to a special statutory proceeding should satisfy the first prong of this test. The court order, itself, and the police charged with enforcement of the order provide the promise to act and the plaintiff's justifiable reliance on the agency's affirmative undertaking. Additionally, the requirement that protection orders be served on law enforcement officials and entered into NCIC reinforces the fact that the agency is on notice of the existence of the order.[20] A history of prior incidents of domestic violence of which the police are aware demonstrates knowledge on the part of the police that inaction could lead to harm. Where the plaintiff has objected to the perpetrator's presence in the home or other protected place, and has communicated this to the law enforcement agency, the plaintiff has sufficiently complied with the factors.

Campbell v. Campbell[21] is an example of a failure-to-protect case that successfully applied the elements of negligence in its legal analysis and decisionmaking process. In that case, the plaintiff alleged that the police department was negligent in failing to arrest her estranged husband and that its negligence was the proximate cause of her being shot. The plaintiff argued that the police had actual knowledge of her restraining order and that this created the duty to arrest her estranged husband.

The plaintiff relied on New Jersey's Prevention of Domestic Violence Act[22] which directs the court to send copies of restraining orders to the appropriate police departments. The defendants moved for summary

[18]See Sawicki v. Village of Ottawa Hills, 37 Ohio St. 3d 222, 525 N.E.2d 468 (1988); see also Mastroianni v. County of Suffolk, 91 N.Y.2d 198, 668 N.Y.S.2d 542, 691 N.E.2d 613 (1997) (discussing the common elements of special duty rule); but see Finch v. County of Saratoga, 305 A.D.2d 771, 758 N.Y.S.2d 220 (3d Dep't 2003) (where victim failed to demonstrate she justifiably relied on county sheriff to protect her from stalker).

[19]See, e.g., Campbell v. Campbell, 294 N.J. Super. 18, 682 A.2d 272 (Law Div. 1996).

[20]See RC 3113.31(F), RC 2919.26(G); Sup. R. 10, eff. 3-24-98.

[21]Campbell v. Campbell, 294 N.J. Super. 18, 682 A.2d 272 (Law Div. 1996); see also Calloway v. Kinkelaar, 168 Ill. 2d 312, 213 Ill. Dec. 675, 659 N.E.2d 1322 (1995) (recognizing a cause of action because the police officers' statutory duty to enforce a protection order was breached by the willful or wanton acts or omissions of law enforcement officers which caused injury to plaintiff); Sneed v. Howell, 306 Ill. App. 3d 1149, 240 Ill. Dec. 203, 716 N.E.2d 336 (5th Dist. 1999) (utilizing the rationale set forth in *Calloway v. Kinkelaar* to reverse dismissal of amended complaint brought by administrator of decedent's estate against the husband, the city and the county state's attorney); Moore v. Green, 219 Ill. 2d 470, 302 Ill. Dec. 451, 848 N.E.2d 1015 (2006), citing *Calloway*.

[22]N.J. Stat. Ann. § 2C:25-17.

judgment, claiming that they were not negligent in the performance of their duties because they were not told of the order, had no knowledge of it, and, therefore, had no basis for arresting the plaintiff's husband and, further, because they were immune from liability under the state Tort Claims Act.[23]

The Superior Court of New Jersey first found that the police department had, at the very least, constructive notice of the order prior to the incident because the Prevention of Domestic Violence Act provided explicit directions for notification to police of domestic violence orders.[24] Next, the New Jersey court determined that, because the police were sued under a negligence theory and not for governmental failure to provide police protection, the immunity afforded under the Tort Claims Act was not applicable.[25]

The court also stated that the restraining order established a special relationship between the plaintiff and the police. The court found that "by virtue of the court order, the police, as the officers charged with its enforcement, promised to protect the plaintiff and that that promise created a special relationship between the plaintiff and the police officers which exempts it from the immunity statute."[26]

The court noted that the immunity statute appeared to be in direct conflict with the domestic violence statute, which requires a police officer to make an arrest when there is probable cause to believe that a domestic violence order has been violated. The court stressed that "the Legislature has made it clear that a police officer must enforce a domestic violence order and all other laws which protect domestic violence victims."[27]

The *Campbell* court concluded that the police officers were not immune from liability for failing to make an arrest under a domestic violence order. The court held that the existence of the domestic violence order, the officers' actual or constructive knowledge of the order, the history of prior incidents of domestic violence, and the plaintiff's objections to the presence of the defendant at the premises "demonstrate that a high risk situation was presented, which required the police officers to enforce the arrest provision of the Prevention of Domestic Violence Act."[28]

Since Ohio has a similar arrest statute,[29] the same legal analysis may be applied to similar police failure-to-protect cases in Ohio where the police have failed to arrest a defendant who has violated a protection order.

---

[23]N.J. Stat. Ann. §§ 59:1-1 to 59:10A-6.

[24]For similar Ohio provisions, see RC 3113.31(F) (notification of law enforcement), RC 2919.26(G) (temporary protection orders).

[25]Campbell v. Campbell, 294 N.J. Super. 18, 682 A.2d 272 (Law Div. 1996).

[26]Campbell v. Campbell, 294 N.J. Super. 18, 26, 682 A.2d 272 (Law Div. 1996).

[27]Campbell v. Campbell, 294 N.J. Super. 18, 24, 682 A.2d 272 (Law Div. 1996); see also Simpson v. City of Miami, 700 So. 2d 87 (Fla. 3d DCA 1997).

[28]Campbell v. Campbell, 294 N.J. Super. 18, 28, 682 A.2d 272 (Law Div. 1996).

[29]See RC 2935.03.

§ 14:13 Civil rights remedies for gender-motivated violence

The federal Violence Against Women Act of 1994[1] created civil rights remedies for gender-motivated violence for victims[2] who have been denied the right to bring civil rights lawsuits.[3] Federal civil rights laws have been ineffective in scope and have failed to reach the majority of victims of gender-motivated violence, and state laws have systematically failed to provide adequate redress. Under 42 U.S.C.A. § 13981, a provable cause of action may result in compensatory and punitive damages,[4] injunctive[5] and declaratory relief, and other appropriate relief, including attorney fees.[6] against any person, including a person acting "under color of state law," who commits a crime of violence motivated by gender.[7]

In *Brzonkala v. Virginia Polytechnic Institute and State University*, the Fourth Circuit Court of Appeals, sitting en banc, found the civil cause of action under VAWA for victims of gender-motivated violent crimes to be unconstitutional. The *Brzonkala* court relied on the reasoning in *United States v. Lopez*.[8] It read *Lopez* as holding that a valid enactment under the Commerce Clause must either regulate an economic activity or include a "jurisdictional element" demarcating its outer limits. VAWA meets neither requirement. *Brzonkala* was appealed to the Supreme Court on the issue of whether the civil liability provision of VAWA might be sustained under the Commerce Clause or Section 5 of the Fourteenth Amendment. In cases consolidated

---

[Section 14:13]

[1]Also known as the Gender-Motivated Violence Act. See 42 U.S.C.A. § 13981 (1994).

[2]See Ziegler v. Ziegler, 28 F. Supp. 2d 601 (E.D. Wash. 1998) (holding that VAWA applies to both men and women and allowing ex-husband to file counterclaim against ex-wife in federal suit in which she alleges ten years of domestic violence and psychological abuse); Schwenk v. Hartford, 204 F.3d 1187 (9th Cir. 2000). See also Renee Jarasinsky, Gender Difference in Perceiving Violence and Its Implication for the VAWA's Civil Rights Remedy, 27 Fordham Urb. L.J. 965, 1000 (2000).

[3]But see Brzonkala v. Virginia Polytechnic Institute and State University, 169 F.3d 820, 136 Ed. Law Rep. 15 (4th Cir. 1999), judgment aff'd, 529 U.S. 598, 120 S. Ct. 1740, 146 L. Ed. 2d 658, 144 Ed. Law Rep. 28, 82 Fair Empl. Prac. Cas. (BNA) 1313, 77 Empl. Prac. Dec. (CCH) P 46376 (2000) (en banc opinion finding unconstitutional the civil cause of action under VAWA for victims of gender-motivated violent crimes). See also Stacey L. McKinley, The Violence Against Women Act After United States v. Lopez: Will Domestic Violence Jurisdiction Be Returned to the States, 44 Clev. St. L. Rev. 345 (1996); Charis Mincavage, Title III of the Violence Against Women Act: Can it Survive a Commerce Clause Challenge in the Wake of United States v. Lopez, 102 Dick. L. Rev. 441 (1998); see also Text § 18:5, The Violence Against Women Act.

[4]See Doe v. Doe, 929 F. Supp. 608, 611 (D. Conn. 1996).

[5]Doe v. Doe, 929 F. Supp. 608, 611 (D. Conn. 1996).

[6]See U.S. v. Hayes, 135 F.3d 133 (2d Cir. 1998) (determining that the victim was entitled to the full amount of her losses and finding that restitution under VAWA (18 U.S.C.A. § 2264) includes medical expenses, temporary housing costs, lost income, school expenses, child care, and attorney fees).

[7]See also Ericson v. Syracuse University, 45 F. Supp. 2d 344 (S.D. N.Y. 1999).

[8]U.S. v. Lopez, 2 F.3d 1342, 85 Ed. Law Rep. 647 (5th Cir. 1993), judgment aff'd, 514 U.S. 549, 115 S. Ct. 1624, 131 L. Ed. 2d 626, 99 Ed. Law Rep. 24 (1995).

under *United States v. Morrison*,[9] the United States Supreme Court considered whether gender-motivated acts of violence against women have substantial effects on interstate commerce. The plaintiffs argued that gender-motivated crimes affect interstate commerce by imposing medical and legal costs on victims; impeding travel, work, and business transactions of those who fear such violence; and inhibiting the productivity of actual and potential victims. The respondents argued that Congress lacks the authority under the Commerce Clause to regulate non-economic conduct and that VAWA is outside Congress's enforcement power under Section 5 of the Fourteenth Amendment because it regulates purely private conduct rather than state action.

On May 15, 2000, the Supreme Court rendered its opinion, striking down the civil remedy provision under VAWA in a five-to-four decision. The decision affirmed the federal appeals court ruling dismissing the suit and finding that 42 U.S.C.A. § 13981 cannot be sustained under the Commerce Clause. The majority of the Court determined that gender-motivated crimes of violence are not economic activity, effectively placing it outside Congress's enforcement power.[10]

The Supreme Court's invalidation of the civil rights remedy limits a domestic violence victim's right to redress for gender-motivated crimes of violence.[11] Moreover, it has effectively curtailed Congress's ability to determine what is an important national interest and enact appropriate legislation.[12]

However, victims of gender-motivated crimes of violence may still seek damages from their abusers in state court under state tort laws or pursuant to state legislation whose provisions are analogous to the federal remedies.[13] Legislation has recently been introduced in Ohio permitting victims to pursue redress in state court for crimes of gender-motivated violence.[14] Ohio's legislation does not expand recovery against governmental defendants.

As stated above, civil rights lawsuits alleging gender-based violence may be brought in both state and federal court.[15] However, VAWA's legislative history suggests that Congress contemplated federal court

[9]U.S. v. Morrison, 527 U.S. 1068, 120 S. Ct. 11, 144 L. Ed. 2d 842, 140 Ed. Law Rep. 20 (1999).

[10]See U.S. v. Morrison, 529 U.S. 598, 120 S. Ct. 1740, 146 L. Ed. 2d 658, 144 Ed. Law Rep. 28, 82 Fair Empl. Prac. Cas. (BNA) 1313, 77 Empl. Prac. Dec. (CCH) P 46376 (2000); see also Julie Goldscheid, United States v. Morrison and the Civil Rights Remedy of the Violence Against Women Act: A Civil Rights Law Struck Down in the Name of Federalism, 86 Cornell L. Rev. 109 (November 2000); Marianne Moody Jennings, United States v. Morrison: Where the Commerce Clause meets Civil Rights and Reasonable Minds Part Ways: A Point and Counterpoint from a Constitutional and Social Perspective, 35 New. Eng. L. Rev. 23 (2000); Julie Goldscheid and Lisa E. Kaufman, Seeking Redress for Gender-Based Bias Crimes—Charting New Ground In Familiar Legal Territory, 16 Mich. J. Race & L. 265 (2001).

[11]Julie Goldscheid, The Civil Rights Remedy of the 1994 Violence Against Women Act: Struck Down but not Ruled Out, 39 Fam. L. Q. 157 (2005).

[12]NOW LDEF, U.S. Supreme Court Strikes Down VAWA Civil Rights Remedy: *U.S. v. Morrison*, 5 Domestic Violence Report 81 (Aug./Sept. 2000).

[13]See, e.g., New York City's Gender-Motivated Violence Protection Act, passed by New York City Council in December 2000.

[14]See 2003 H.B. 141, introduced 3-25-03.

[15]42 U.S.C.A. § 13981(e)(3). See also David M. Fine, Note, The Violence Against

as the primary forum.[16] When deciding on a forum, practitioners should consider both the procedural and evidentiary differences between state and federal court, including the applicable procedural and evidentiary rules, a court's responsiveness to civil rights claims, and the time delay for trial in each court.[17]

A plaintiff must prove that the defendant committed a crime of violence[18] and that the crime was motivated by gender as defined in 42 U.S.C.A. § 13981(d)(1). This provision includes offenses that involve the actual use, attempted use, or threatened use of physical force against a person or property. By its plain language, the VAWA does not require either a criminal prosecution or a conviction to support a civil rights claim.[19]

Only gender-motivated violent acts may form the basis for recovery under 42 U.S.C.A. § 13981. Violence committed by strangers or other random acts of violence do not fall within the purview of the law.[20] In order to prove gender-based motivation, the totality of the circumstances must be evaluated for both circumstantial and direct evidence of gender-based bias, including patterns of behavior and statements evincing bias.[21]

The federal statute enumerates a two-pronged analysis. First, the plaintiff must proved that the violent act was committed "because of gender or on the basis of gender."[22] Second, the plaintiff must prove that the violent act was "due, at least in part, to an animus based on the victim's gender."[23] As with other recently enacted statutes, only litigation will determine the significance of the term "animus" and whether the use of this term requires additional evidence to prove gender motivation. Additionally, attorneys should look to existing civil rights law and cases brought under 42 U.S.C.A. § 1983, as well as the legislative history of the VAWA, to prove such a claim. Victims should be advised that they retain the right to litigate these actions while pursuing other criminal remedies, civil protection orders, or divorce actions against their abusers.

Women Act of 1994: The Proper Federal Role in Policing Domestic Violence, 84 Cornell L. Rev. 252, 283 (1998).

[16]Stopping Violence Against Women Using New Federal Laws Study Guide, American Bar Association VideoLaw Seminars 65 (1996).

[17]Stopping Violence Against Women Using New Federal Laws Study Guide, American Bar Association VideoLaw Seminars 65 (1996); David M. Fine, Note, The Violence Against Women Act of 1994: The Proper Federal Role in Policing Domestic Violence, 84 Cornell L. Rev. 252, 284–88 (1998).

[18]See 42 U.S.C.A. § 13981(d)(2)(A); see also Julie Goldscheid, Proving Gender Motivation in Civil Rights Remedy Claims Under the Violence Against Women Act, Clearinghouse Rev. (Mar/April 1999).

[19]42 U.S.C.A. § 13981(e)(2); see also Stopping Violence Against Women Using New Federal Laws Study Guide, American Bar Association VideoLaw Seminars 53 (1996).

[20]42 U.S.C.A. § 13981(e)(1).

[21]Stopping Violence Against Women Using New Federal Laws Study Guide, American Bar Association VideoLaw Seminars 54 (1996).

[22]42 U.S.C.A. § 13981(d)(1).

[23]42 U.S.C.A. § 13981(d)(1); see also Stopping Violence Against Women Using New Federal Laws Study Guide, American Bar Association VideoLaw Seminars 54–55 (1996).

Future litigation will also determine whether civil recovery under VAWA will be interpreted to permit suits against governmental defendants, including municipalities, states, and their officials.[24] The VAWA's express inclusion of "persons acting under color of state law" suggests that governmental officials are to be included. The legislative history provides that claims against governmental entities will be permitted where a governmental entity could be sued under 42 U.S.C.A. § 1983. However, some domestic violence experts have suggested that many of the limitations on 42 U.S.C.A. § 1983 claims do not apply to VAWA claims.[25] Nonetheless, attorneys should refer to 42 U.S.C.A. § 1983 cases for guidance and interpretation because both federal and state courts have explored the circumstances under which governmental officials may be liable for civil rights violations.

Generally, municipalities have been granted immunity from suit unless the civil rights violation resulted from a government agent following an official policy, ordinance, or custom.[26] Although punitive damages are permitted to a victim,[27] it is unclear whether a municipality would be subject to the punitive damage provision.[28]

§ 14:14 Significant cases involving police officer action or inaction

Q & A: What types of officer action or inaction impose potential liability for a failure to protect victims of domestic violence?

Several court decisions from around the country have advanced persuasive legal arguments that, in domestic violence situations, police must respond to calls for assistance, arrest or restrain the persons who are committing or about to commit violent crimes, especially where a protection order is in effect,[1] and investigate alleged domestic violence. A failure to act in these circumstances imposes potential liability for an officer's inaction.[2] However, the most common cases where liability has been found are cases involving 911 calls and cases where the officers failed to make arrests where an arrest was required under state mandatory or preferred arrest laws.[3]

---

[24]See Goldscheid, The Civil Rights Remedy of the 1994 Violence Against Women Act: Struck Down but not Ruled Out, 39(1) Fam. L. Q. 157 (Spring 2005).

[25]See, e.g., Stopping Violence Against Women Using New Federal Laws Study Guide, American Bar Association VideoLaw Seminars 61 (1996) ("VAWA contains no provisions concerning the liability of governmental entities.").

[26]Stopping Violence Against Women Using New Federal Laws Study Guide, American Bar Association VideoLaw Seminars 61 (1996); see also Text § 14:7, Police liability for failing to protect victims of domestic violence—Introduction.

[27]See 42 U.S.C.A. § 13981(c).

[28]Stopping Violence Against Women Using New Federal Laws Study Guide, American Bar Association VideoLaw Seminars 61 (1996).

[Section 14:14]

[1]See, e.g., Sneed v. Howell, 306 Ill. App. 3d 1149, 240 Ill. Dec. 203, 716 N.E.2d 336 (5th Dist. 1999).

[2]But see Brooks v. Knapp, 221 Fed. Appx. 402, 2007 FED App. 0812N (6th Cir. 2007).

[3]See Robert A. Shapiro, Personal Liability of Policeman, Sheriff, or Similar

The landmark case is that of Thurman v. City of Torrington.[4] In that case, the officers failed to act to protect the victim of domestic violence who had obtained a protection order. The officer allegedly stood by and watched as the victim's husband beat her and even as she lay on the ground with a stab wound. The victim sued and argued that the police officers and the municipality denied her equal protection under the law. The court determined that police officers may not afford victims of domestic violence lesser protection than victims of stranger assaults simply because of the domestic relationship between the parties.[5] The court held that "[p]olice action is subject to the equal protection clause and section 1983 whether in the form of commission of violative acts or omission to perform required acts pursuant to the police officer's duty to protect."[6]

Several state court rulings have also demonstrated that police officers have a specific duty to enforce protection orders. For example, in *Baker v. City of New York*,[7] an appeals court held that the police department owed a special duty to an individual who obtained a protection order because "[t]he order of protection was issued by the court pursuant to statute . . . and the certificate with which plaintiff was furnished constituted authority to a peace officer, when presented by the plaintiff, to arrest the husband when charged with a violation of the terms of the order."

Similarly, in *Nearing v. Weaver*,[8] the Oregon Supreme Court determined that a peace officer had a duty to arrest a person without a warrant "when the officer has probable cause to believe that an order . . . has been served and filed and that the person has violated the order." The court held that police officers who failed to arrest the offender could be subjected to liability for their failure to protect the victim of domestic violence. The existence of the restraining order created the special relationship between the plaintiff and the officer, and officers who knowingly fail to enforce such orders are potentially liable for the resulting emotional and physical harm to the intended beneficiaries of the judicial order.[9] In *Nearing*, the legal right arose independently of the ordinary tort elements of a negligence action.

However, in *Sorichetti v. City of New York*,[10] the court instructed the jury not to base the special duty on the order of protection alone

---

Peace Officer for Injury Suffered as a Result of Failure to Enforce Law or Arrest Law Breaker, 41 A.L.R.3d 700 (1999).

[4]Thurman v. City of Torrington, 595 F. Supp. 1521 (D. Conn. 1984); see also Didzerekis v. Stewart, 41 F. Supp. 2d 840 (N.D. Ill. 1999) (police officers were liable for delaying entrance into victim's home although they were aware that the victim was being abused by her husband).

[5]Thurman v. City of Torrington, 595 F. Supp. 1521 (D. Conn. 1984).

[6]Thurman v. City of Torrington, 595 F. Supp. 1521, 1527 (D. Conn. 1984).

[7]Baker v. City of New York, 25 A.D.2d 770, 771, 269 N.Y.S.2d 515 (2d Dep't 1966); see also Morales v. County of Nassau, 256 A.D.2d 608, 683 N.Y.S.2d 127 (2d Dep't 1998), aff'd, 94 N.Y.2d 218, 703 N.Y.S.2d 61, 724 N.E.2d 756 (1999).

[8]Nearing v. Weaver, 295 Or. 702, 709, 670 P.2d 137 (1983); see also Danielle Lynn Lordi, Police Liability Under State Tort Law for Failure to Enforce Protection Orders: The Last Demand for Accountability, 85 Or. L. Rev. 325 (2006).

[9]Nearing v. Weaver, 295 Or. 702, 670 P.2d 137 (1983).

[10]Sorichetti by Sorichetti v. City of New York, 65 N.Y.2d 461, 492 N.Y.S.2d 591,

but rather on the order in combination with the police officer's knowledge of the defendant's violent propensity and the police officer's conduct relative to the alleged violation of the order. In that case, a statute existed to protect victims of domestic violence. The plaintiff obtained a protection order on behalf of herself and her infant child. The police were well aware of the violence inflicted by the husband toward his wife throughout the marriage.

The New York Court of Appeals attached liability to the police officers because it determined that the presence of the domestic violence statute and the protection order created a special relationship. The court reasoned that

> [t]he [protection] order evinces a preincident legislative and judicial determination that its holder should be accorded a reasonable degree of protection from a particular individual. It is presumptive evidence that the individual whose conduct is proscribed has already been found by a court to be a dangerous or violent person and that violations of the order's terms should be treated seriously.[11]

The specific factors used by the court to establish this special relationship were "(1) the order of protection; (2) the police department's knowledge of [the ex-husband's] violent history . . .; (3) its response to [the individual's] pleas for assistance on the day of the assault; and (4) [the individual's] reasonable expectation of police protection."[12]

Of significance is that the court specifically noted the police response to the wife's plea to have her ex-husband arrested. The police officers repeatedly told her they would investigate if he failed to return the child within a reasonable period of time. The court found her reliance on the police officers' statements was reasonable and provided "a critical factor in the creation of a special duty of protection."[13]

Q & A: Under which legal theories have Ohio courts imposed liability for police failure to protect victims of domestic violence?

The principal case in Ohio concerning the special relationship exception to the general duty rule is *Sawicki v. Village of Ottawa Hills*.[14] The "general duty rule" creates a duty for law enforcement officials to protect the public in general, but it does not create a duty to protect any specific individual. In that case, a woman freed herself from an attempted rape and, while her boyfriend struggled to control the rapist, contacted the local police dispatcher. While waiting for assistance, a family member came to the rescue of the woman and her boyfriend and was killed by the rapist. The suit was brought alleging that the police failed to respond to the call for help.

482 N.E.2d 70 (1985); see also Raucci v. Town of Rotterdam, 902 F.2d 1050 (2d Cir. 1990) (finding that the special duty imposed by that relationship is recognized in only a narrow class of cases).

[11]Sorichetti by Sorichetti v. City of New York, 65 N.Y.2d 461, 469–70, 492 N.Y.S.2d 591, 482 N.E.2d 70 (1985); see also Calloway v. Kinkelaar, 168 Ill. 2d 312, 213 Ill. Dec. 675, 659 N.E.2d 1322 (1995).

[12]Sorichetti by Sorichetti v. City of New York, 65 N.Y.2d 461, 469, 492 N.Y.S.2d 591, 482 N.E.2d 70 (1985).

[13]Sorichetti by Sorichetti v. City of New York, 65 N.Y.2d 461, 470, 492 N.Y.S.2d 591, 482 N.E.2d 70 (1985).

[14]Sawicki v. Village of Ottawa Hills, 37 Ohio St. 3d 222, 525 N.E.2d 468 (1988).

The Supreme Court of Ohio determined that for a plaintiff to demonstrate a special duty or relationship required under the special duty exception to the public duty rule, the plaintiff must show: (1) an assumption by the municipality, through promises or actions, of an affirmative duty to act on behalf of the party who was injured; (2) knowledge on the part of the municipality's agents that inaction could lead to harm; (3) some form of direct contact between the municipality's agents and the injured party; and (4) that party's justifiable reliance on the municipality's affirmative undertaking.[15] The court cited *Sorichetti* as a case that applied an exception to the general duty rule.

The Supreme Court concluded, however, that no liability could attach to a municipality that had "no statutory obligation and, in fact, was legislatively forbidden to answer . . . calls for assistance originating beyond its jurisdictional boundaries."[16] Another factor that directly affected the court's ruling was that the person killed was the rescuer and not the person raped. The rescuer did not justifiably rely upon the actions of the police department, nor did the department make any promises to the rescuer. It is unclear whether the court's decision would have been different had the victim been killed and the police failed to respond to the victim's call for assistance.

Unfortunately, the court in *Sawicki* also pointed out that the facts of the case occurred before the effective date of RC 2744.02 regarding the liability of political subdivisions for injury, death, or loss. Under RC 2744.02, municipalities appear to be protected from liability deriving from the actions of their employees. Several subsequent court decisions expand the legal analysis set forth in *Sawicki* and advance the argument that sovereign immunity was codified under RC 2744.02, thereby abrogating the public duty/special relationship theory of municipal liability.[17]

In *City of Canton v. Harris*,[18] the respondent was arrested by officers of the Canton police department. She was brought to the police

---

[15]Sawicki v. Village of Ottawa Hills, 37 Ohio St. 3d 222, 525 N.E.2d 468 (1988).

[16]Sawicki v. Village of Ottawa Hills, 37 Ohio St. 3d 222, 232, 525 N.E.2d 468 (1988).

[17]See Colbert v. Cleveland, 99 Ohio St. 3d 215, 2003-Ohio-3319, 790 N.E.2d 781 (2003) (discussion of the three tier analysis for reviewing claims of political subdivision immunity under R.C. 2744); see also Maddox v. E. Cleveland, 2012-Ohio-9, 2012 WL 20134 (Ohio Ct. App. 8th Dist. Cuyahoga County 2012); see also Grothouse v. Ohio Dept. of Health, 80 Ohio App. 3d 258, 608 N.E.2d 1183 (10th Dist. Franklin County 1992) (holding that RC 2744.02 effectively abrogated the public duty/special relationship theory of municipal liability); see also Amborski v. Toledo, 67 Ohio App. 3d 47, 585 N.E.2d 974 (6th Dist. Lucas County 1990) (same); Smith v. Minnick, 68 Ohio App. 3d 619, 589 N.E.2d 409 (6th Dist. Lucas County 1990); Lewis v. Cleveland, 89 Ohio App. 3d 136, 623 N.E.2d 1233 (8th Dist. Cuyahoga County 1993) (upholding the constitutionality of RC 2744.02(B)(1)(b) and finding that the *Sawicki* test does not apply to causes of action arising after the effective date of RC Ch. 2744); Boggs v. Hughes, 1994 WL 28635 (Ohio Ct. App. 2d Dist. Greene County 1994).

[18]City of Canton, Ohio v. Harris, 489 U.S. 378, 109 S. Ct. 1197, 103 L. Ed. 2d 412 (1989); see also Culberson v. Doan, 65 F. Supp. 2d 701 (S.D. Ohio 1999) (relying on *Harris*); Brown v. Shaner, 172 F.3d 927, 931, 43 Fed. R. Serv. 3d 441, 1999 FED App. 0139P (6th Cir. 1999) (liability possible where the city fails to act (disciplining officers) in response to repeated claims of constitutional violations by the officers); Pearce v. Estate of Longo, 766 F. Supp. 2d 367 (N.D. N.Y. 2011), aff'd in part, rev'd in part on other grounds, 473 Fed. Appx. 16 (2d Cir. 2012).

station and was later found sitting on the floor. She was asked if she needed medical attention, and she responded incoherently. No medical attention was administered. After her release from custody, she was hospitalized. Subsequently, she filed suit, alleging both state law claims and constitutional violations under 42 U.S.C.A. § 1983.

The *Canton* Court has provided a promising new legal option for victims of domestic violence. The circuit court of appeals held that "a municipality is liable for failure to train its police force, where the plaintiff proves that the municipality acted recklessly, intentionally, or with gross negligence, and that the lack of training was so reckless or grossly negligent that deprivation of persons' constitutional rights was substantially certain."[19]

The Supreme Court considered the failure-to-train claim and held that "[t]he inadequacy of police training may serve as the basis for section 1983 liability only where the failure to train . . . amounts to deliberate indifference to the constitutional rights of persons with whom the police come into contact."[20] The issue is whether the training program is adequate and, if it is not, whether such inadequate training can justifiably be said to represent city policy for which liability can be imposed.[21]

The Supreme Court determined that, where the need for more training is obvious and the inadequacy so likely to result in the violation of constitutional rights, a party must show that the city policymakers were deliberately indifferent to the need for more training in light of the duties assigned to specific officers. The Court then stated that, for liability to attach, the identified deficiency in the city's training program must be closely related to the ultimate injury and must have caused the police officers' deliberate indifference to the needs of the victim.

Victims of domestic violence may be able to apply this theory of liability to argue that, where a municipality maintains or persists in following a written policy or practice that offers lesser protection to victims of domestic violence with a deliberate indifference to the policy's impact on women, potential liability exists.

> Because this theory circumvents the special relationship doctrine, a battered woman could still claim a liberty deprivation under the due process clause. A battered woman might also assert a "failure to train" claim if she could proffer evidence that a city's inadequate police train-

---

[19]City of Canton, Ohio v. Harris, 489 U.S. 378, 378, 109 S. Ct. 1197, 103 L. Ed. 2d 412 (1989). See also Okin v. Village of Cornwall-On-Hudson Police Dept., 577 F.3d 415 (2d Cir. 2009) (extending the *Monell* theory of liability to a municipality that fails to train, or that sanctions discriminatory policies and customs and reversing district court's dismissal of petitioner's municipal liability claims).

[20]City of Canton, Ohio v. Harris, 489 U.S. 378, 379, 109 S. Ct. 1197, 103 L. Ed. 2d 412 (1989); Al-Lamadani v. Lang, 624 Fed. Appx. 405 (6th Cir. 2015) (Circuit court stated that to prevail under a failure to train theory, the plaintiff must show 1) the training was inadequate for the tasks preformed; 2) the inadequacy was the result of the municipality's deliberate indifference; and 3) the inadequacy was closely related to or actually caused the injury. At *415).

[21]But see Smith v. Town of East Haven, 2005 WL 677284 (D. Conn. 2005) (discussing *Moxell* liability based on a municipality's failure to train U.S. officers).

ing regarding domestic violence calls amounted to deliberate indifference to the need for heightened protection for these victims.[22]

It is surprising that the Supreme Court, which decided *Canton* and *DeShaney* only five days apart, did not address the special relationship exception and its implications after *DeShaney*, nor did it even mention *DeShaney* in its *Canton* opinion. Clearly, the facts in *Canton* indicate a custodial relationship between the police and the victim. Instead, the Supreme Court appears to have developed a separate actionable substantive due process claim under the "failure to train" theory of municipal liability.[23]

Siddle v. City of Cambridge[24] suggests that the existence of a civil protection order pursuant to a state statute creates a protected property interest. In *Siddle*, the plaintiff brought substantive and procedural due process claims as well as an equal protection claim against the Cambridge Police Department. Initially, the United States District Court rejected the substantive due process claim of special relationship under the holding espoused in *DeShaney*. The plaintiff relied on *Board of Regents v. Roth*[25] in advancing a procedural due process argument that RC 3113.31 creates a property interest that is protected by the Due Process Clause. The plaintiff's obtaining of a civil protection order created the property interest, which then created a duty on the part of government. The rationale for a procedural due process claim is that, once such a property right is found to exist, the government's failure to adequately protect that right constitutes a denial of a right to procedural due process.

The United States District Court advanced the test of "reasonable protection" for determining whether a protection order under RC 3113.31 creates a property interest that confers on those individuals greater rights to protection than other citizens. Similar standards of "reasonable protection" have been considered by other jurisdictions to deny both substantive due process and equal protection claims.[26]

The *Siddle* court stated:

> Even under Ohio law, absent some exception, Plaintiff is not entitled to protection as an individual. Moreover, at all times, it is important to remember the primary duty of the government is to protect the public. This duty is of paramount importance and is the springboard from which the scope of the duty the government owes to the bearer of the protective order should be determined.[27]

Applying the test of reasonable protection, the *Siddle* court found

---

[22]Laura S. Harper, Note, Battered Women Suing Police for Failure to Intervene: Viable Legal Avenues after DeShaney v. Winnebago County Department of Social Services, 75 Cornell L. Rev. 1393, 1417 (1990); see also Smith v. City of Elyria, 857 F. Supp. 1203 (N.D. Ohio 1994).

[23]But see Smith v. Town of East Haven, 2005 WL 677284 (D. Conn. 2005).

[24]Siddle v. City of Cambridge, Ohio, 761 F. Supp. 503 (S.D. Ohio 1991); see also Gonzales v. City of Castle Rock, 307 F.3d 1258 (10th Cir. 2002), on reh'g en banc, 366 F.3d 1093 (10th Cir. 2004), rev'd on other grounds, 545 U.S. 748, 125 S. Ct. 2796, 162 L. Ed. 2d 658 (2005).

[25]Board of Regents of State Colleges v. Roth, 408 U.S. 564, 92 S. Ct. 2701, 33 L. Ed. 2d 548, 1 I.E.R. Cas. (BNA) 23 (1972).

[26]See, e.g., Coffman v. Wilson Police Dept., 739 F. Supp. 257 (E.D. Pa. 1990).

[27]Siddle v. City of Cambridge, Ohio, 761 F. Supp. 503, 509 (S.D. Ohio 1991).

that it was unreasonable to require the police to commit all of their time and resources to the protection of a single citizen, whether that person possesses a valid court order or not. However, the court also stressed that a police department which owed an individual a duty to protect could not completely ignore that duty. The court determined:

> A police department must be reasonable in its efforts to protect the individual's safety. Likewise, the individual can expect only reasonable protection from the police given their time, resources and personnel. . . . Beyond that level of protection, an individual must take legal steps to protect himself or herself, just as the rest of the public is obligated to do.[28]

The court concluded that the police acted reasonably toward the plaintiff, both toward her individually and by way of their police policy, creating neither a viable procedural due process nor equal protection claim.

The importance of the *Siddle* decision cannot be overstated. The federal court applied the test of reasonable protection to determine the level of protection afforded to individuals who have protection orders. However, it also reinforced the rationale articulated in *Board of Regents v. Roth*[29] by conceding that a protection order creates a duty to protect an individual, thus leaving open the possibility of a successful procedural due process claim.[30]

More recent Ohio cases have relied on a mixture of the various legal theories to conclude that no special relationship exists. For example, in *Blankenship v. City of Cleveland*,[31] the plaintiff argued that a special relationship arose because the police placed her in a position of danger by not arresting the perpetrator. However, the plaintiff did not seek a protection order.

The federal court determined, in its ruling on the City's motion for summary judgment, that there was no special relationship and no established constitutional right to protection. The court held that:

> the police decided not to arrest [], drove him around the corner, and let him go. Despite [plaintiff's] arguments, this Court cannot find that this behavior created or exacerbated the danger in any way. [Plaintiff] was certainly no worse off than if the police had never responded. Therefore, this Court concludes that the police did not create or exacerbate the danger, and no special relationship was created. . . . The [Sixth C]ircuit has now ruled at least three times that exacerbating or contributing to

---

[28]Siddle v. City of Cambridge, Ohio, 761 F. Supp. 503, 509 (S.D. Ohio 1991).

[29]Board of Regents of State Colleges v. Roth, 408 U.S. 564, 92 S. Ct. 2701, 33 L. Ed. 2d 548, 1 I.E.R. Cas. (BNA) 23 (1972).

[30]See, e.g., Gonzales v. City of Castle Rock, 307 F.3d 1258 (10th Cir. 2002), on reh'g en banc, 366 F.3d 1093 (10th Cir. 2004), rev'd on other grounds, 545 U.S. 748, 125 S. Ct. 2796, 162 L. Ed. 2d 658 (2005) (where the Tenth Circuit Court of Appeals reversed the dismissal of a 1983 action brought by the mother on behalf of her deceased children against the city and police officers; the Tenth Circuit Court of Appeals held that mother had stated a cause of action for deprivation of procedural due process rights stemming from Colorado statute imposing duty to arrest based on belief that restrained person has violated the restraining order); but see Town of Castle Rock, Colo. v. Gonzales, 545 U.S. 748, 125 S. Ct. 2796, 162 L. Ed. 2d 658 (2005).

[31]Blankenship v. City of Cleveland, No. 1:95CV0556, at 10 (N.D. Ohio, 4-2-96).

the danger does not create a special relationship which would give rise to an affirmative duty.[32]

The federal court, however, denied summary judgment relative to plaintiff's equal protection claims. The court relied on *Thurman v. City of Torrington*,[33] *Watson v. City of Kansas City*,[34] *McKee v. City of Rockwall*,[35] *Freeman v. Ferguson*,[36] and *Balistreri v. Pacifica Police Department*[37] to advance the rationale that treating victims of domestic violence differently from victims of other felonious assaults violates the Equal Protection Clause.

The federal court also stressed that the above-mentioned circuit court decisions relied on direct legal authority. For example, *McKee* and *Freeman* relied on the Supreme Court's note in *DeShaney* that the state may not deny its protective services to certain disavowed minorities. Many courts relied on earlier race discrimination cases such as *Smith v. Ross*.[38] After noting that the circuit courts considered women and victims of domestic violence as disavowed minorities and extended the rationale of *Ross* to gender discrimination, the federal district court determined that the defendants were not entitled to qualified immunity on these claims. The defendants appealed the denial of qualified immunity.

On appeal, the circuit court reversed the federal district court and held that the defendant police officers were entitled to qualified immunity. The court noted that the plaintiff acknowledged that she had the burden of demonstrating that the defendants acted with a discriminatory purpose, which meant that she had to prove that the defendants' failure to arrest her former boyfriend was an intentional act of discrimination on the basis of her gender or status as a victim of domestic violence. "If she was unable to do that, then defendants could not have violated her constitutionally guaranteed right to equal protection of the laws. And, if they did not violate a constitutional right, they were entitled to qualified immunity."[39]

The court reasoned that the examples given by Ms. Blankenship to support a discriminatory purpose (which included the fact that they failed to act when told that an arrest warrant was outstanding and failed to prepare a written police report of the incident until more than three months had elapsed) only demonstrated "sloppy police work"[40] and did not raise an inference of discriminatory purpose.

Reliance was placed on the fact that:

> Plaintiff failed to proffer evidence that on other occasions defendants arrested the perpetrators of violent felonious conduct in (1) situations involving similarly situated male victims and (2) situations not involving

---

[32] Blankenship v. City of Cleveland, No. 1:95CV0556, at 10 (N.D. Ohio, 4-2-96).

[33] Thurman v. City of Torrington, 595 F. Supp. 1521 (D. Conn. 1984).

[34] Watson v. City of Kansas City, Kan., 857 F.2d 690 (10th Cir. 1988).

[35] McKee v. City of Rockwall, Tex., 877 F.2d 409 (5th Cir. 1989).

[36] Freeman v. Ferguson, 911 F.2d 52 (8th Cir. 1990).

[37] Balistreri v. Pacifica Police Dept., 901 F.2d 696 (9th Cir. 1988).

[38] Smith v. Ross, 482 F.2d 33 (6th Cir. 1973) (per curiam).

[39] Blankenship v. City of Cleveland, 145 F.3d 1330 (6th Cir. 1998) (per curiam).

[40] Blankenship v. City of Cleveland, 145 F.3d 1330 (6th Cir. 1998) (per curiam).

victims of domestic violence. Also missing is any evidence that the conduct of police responding to instances of domestic violence should be substantially similar to their response to other kinds of violent felonious conduct.[41]

Finally, the court held that, where there is no evidence that the situation confronted by the officers was substantially similar to other violent felonious episodes and should be treated the same and where the plaintiff failed to demonstrate a pattern of conduct by the defendants in dealing with violent episodes, one single episode cannot support an equal protection claim. The court also noted that, because police have discretion to arrest or not to arrest in any given situation, "we decline to assume that what is unexplained is invidious."[42]

The *Blankenship* case is significant for two reasons. First, the federal district court effectively combined many of the legal theories advanced by the courts of other jurisdictions relative to both equal protection and substantive due process claims. For example, it determined that exacerbating or contributing to the danger does not create a special relationship. In noting that the police officer's failure to arrest the plaintiff's estranged boyfriend was a result of both types of discrimination, the court chose not to distinguish between the specific requirements and elements of discrimination based on gender and on status as a domestic violence victim.

In effect, the court's legal analysis strengthened the plaintiff's equal protection arguments. By not separating the two types of discrimination, the court circumvented the need to provide specific evidence supporting each type of discrimination and the restrictive rule articulated in *Personnel Administrator v. Feeney*.[43] Finally, the court rejected the legal standard articulated in *Hynson v. City of Chester Legal Department*[44] in stating that, "In 1993, given all the authority discussed above, no reasonable police officer could think that intentional discrimination against women or victims of domestic violence comported with the requirements of the equal protection clause of the fourteenth amendment. Therefore, the police officers are not entitled to qualified immunity."[45]

It is also noteworthy that the *Blankenship* court relied on legal authority from jurisdictions that held that the conduct at issue and treating domestic violence victims differently does constitute a violation of the Equal Protection Clause.[46] At no point did the court retreat from this position and limit its focus only to decisions that granted qualified immunity.

---

[41]Blankenship v. City of Cleveland, 145 F.3d 1330 (6th Cir. 1998) (per curiam).

[42]Blankenship v. City of Cleveland, 145 F.3d 1330 (6th Cir. 1998) (per curiam).

[43]Personnel Adm'r of Massachusetts v. Feeney, 442 U.S. 256, 99 S. Ct. 2282, 60 L. Ed. 2d 870, 19 Fair Empl. Prac. Cas. (BNA) 1377, 19 Empl. Prac. Dec. (CCH) P 9240 (1979).

[44]Hynson By and Through Hynson v. City of Chester Legal Dept., 864 F.2d 1026 (3d Cir. 1988).

[45]Blankenship v. City of Cleveland, No. 1:95CV0556, at 21 (N.D. Ohio, 4-2-96).

[46]See, e.g., McKee v. City of Rockwall, Tex., 877 F.2d 409 (5th Cir. 1989); Brown v. Grabowski, 922 F.2d 1097 (3d Cir. 1990) (determining that discrimination against women victims of domestic violence as opposed to other crimes of gender is a valid cause of action under the Equal Protection Clause and that police failure to inform the plaintiff of the right to a restraining order in civil court did not rise to a

Even the circuit court's reversal is important because the court did not summarily rule out a favorable decision based on evidence of a pattern or course of conduct. Where a victim can establish both a pattern of conduct and that other similarly situated individuals were treated differently than the victim, a favorable ruling may result. Nor did the court rely on the stringent analysis set forth in *Feeney*.

The facts of this case indicate that the incident took place prior to the statutory modifications that made arrest the preferred course of action in the state of Ohio.[47] Given the court's reliance on the fact that the police have discretion to arrest or not arrest in any given situation, it is unclear whether the court's ruling would have been affected by the statutory enactments of December 1994. Unfortunately, there are no cases that have determined whether the wording of Ohio's preferred arrest statute effectively and severely limits police discretion to arrest in domestic violence situations.

The absence of a civil protection order in *Blankenship* probably influenced the result. It is unlikely that this part of the case would have been decided in this way had the plaintiff obtained a civil protection order that entitled her to greater protection under the law.

Another Ohio case that addressed the failure of the police to protect victims of domestic violence is *Smith v. City of Elyria*.[48] In that case, the victim was stabbed and killed by her ex-husband. During the marriage, her husband was convicted of domestic violence. At the time of the incident in question, the victim's then ex-husband failed to leave her residence. The fact that the victim had invited him back to her residence was the reason given for the officer's failure to respond immediately. The victim's family sued the Elyria Police Department alleging 42 U.S.C.A. § 1983 violations.

In reliance on the reasoning of *DeShaney*, the court determined that

> [t]he mere fact that the State is aware that a person is in danger does not create a duty to protect, even if the State expresses willingness to protect the victim. The State must take some action which places the victim in a dangerous position, or increases the potential danger, or deprives the victim of his or her ability to use self-help.[49]

The *Smith* court found that the specific facts of the case supported a claim that the officers' acts created or increased the victim's danger which prevented summary judgment on plaintiffs' substantive due process claim. "The police officers did not merely fail to perform their duties; they told [him] that he did not have to leave, and advised him to go back if [the victim] tried to throw him out."[50]

However, the court did not indicate that this affirmative duty to act on the victim's behalf created a special relationship. In fact, a special relationship was not the condition precedent to recovery under the theory of substantive due process. Rather, the court addressed the

---

constitutional violation).

[47] RC 2935.03.

[48] Smith v. City of Elyria, 857 F. Supp. 1203 (N.D. Ohio 1994).

[49] Smith v. City of Elyria, 857 F. Supp. 1203, 1209 (N.D. Ohio 1994) (citation omitted); see also Collins v. City of Harker Heights, Tex., 503 U.S. 115, 112 S. Ct. 1061, 117 L. Ed. 2d 261, 7 I.E.R. Cas. (BNA) 233, 15 O.S.H. Cas. (BNA) 1513 (1992).

[50] Smith v. City of Elyria, 857 F. Supp. 1203, 1210 (N.D. Ohio 1994).

special relationship doctrine under the plaintiffs' procedural due process claim.

The plaintiffs alleged that the Ohio dereliction of duty statute, RC 2921.44(A)(2), created a constitutionally protected property interest rather than RC 3113.31, which created the property interest in *Siddle*. However, the court found that the special relationship doctrine had been negated by the enactment of the sovereign immunity statute, RC 2744.02. The court held that "the special relationship doctrine does not provide plaintiff with a protected property interest under Ohio law."[51] Absent a protected property interest, there cannot be a claim alleging procedural due process violations.

Plaintiffs also asserted equal protection claims, alleging, among other things, that the victim was discriminated against because she was a woman. The court held that the facts demonstrate a discriminatory intent "because they reveal a sexually discriminatory assumption that [the victim's ex-husband] had a right to exercise dominion and control over his ex-wife and her home."[52]

Additionally, the plaintiffs presented evidence to suggest disparate treatment because of her status as a victim of domestic, versus nondomestic, violence. Although the court distinguished between the two types of discrimination, the court determined that the same evidence supported both a sex discrimination claim and a claim based on status as a victim of domestic violence.

The court subsequently denied summary judgment on plaintiffs' equal protection claims because there was enough evidence to suggest that the police officers treated the victim differently because of her sex and status as a victim of domestic violence. "There is also evidence that the police officers affirmatively created or increased the danger to [the victim] and limited her ability to use self-help, then failed to protect her. If plaintiffs prove these constitutional violations, the City has admitted that the violations were caused by City policies."[53]

The plaintiffs then alleged that the city had failed to train its officers in the appropriate response to domestic violence and had failed to supervise the officers by allowing them to apply the law in an unequal manner. The court relied on the Supreme Court's holding in *City of Canton v. Harris*[54] to uphold the plaintiffs' due process claims. However, the *Smith* court narrowed the issues to "(1) was the training

[51]Smith v. City of Elyria, 857 F. Supp. 1203, 1211 (N.D. Ohio 1994).

[52]Smith v. City of Elyria, 857 F. Supp. 1203, 1212 (N.D. Ohio 1994).

[53]Smith v. City of Elyria, 857 F. Supp. 1203, 1213 (N.D. Ohio 1994).

[54]City of Canton, Ohio v. Harris, 489 U.S. 378, 388, 109 S. Ct. 1197, 103 L. Ed. 2d 412 (1989) (holding that "the inadequacy of police training may serve as the basis for section 1983 liability only where the failure to train amounts to deliberate indifference to the rights of persons with whom the police come into contact"); see also Culberson v. Doan, 65 F. Supp. 2d 701, 715 (S.D. Ohio 1999) (relying on *Harris* when it stated that "a 'custom' for the purposes of Monell liability must 'be so permanent and well settled as to constitute a custom or usage with the force of law' "); Collins v. City of Harker Heights, Tex., 503 U.S. 115, 112 S. Ct. 1061, 117 L. Ed. 2d 261, 7 I.E.R. Cas. (BNA) 233, 15 O.S.H. Cas. (BNA) 1513 (1992). But see Eckert v. Town of Silverthorne, 25 Fed. Appx. 679 (10th Cir. 2001); Smith v. Town of East Haven, 2005 WL 677284 (D. Conn. 2005).

given to the Elyria police officers adequate, and if not, (2) can the inadequate training justifiably be said to represent city policy."[55] The court acknowledged that the plaintiffs did not articulate any particular deficiencies in the training, but that inadequate training may be shown by the officers' behavior and the fact that they were not able to remember the content of the program. The court found that "[a]lthough there is no evidence in the record that the police officers were inadequately trained, there is evidence that the violation of plaintiffs' constitutional rights was caused by a City policy or custom."[56]

Of significance is that the court provided another reason why the officers acted as they did, which, in effect, appears to expand the holding of *City of Canton v. Harris*. The court focused on whether the officers failed to apply the training they received, rather than on whether the officers were given proper training, the former representing a city policy or custom. This expansion suggests an additional avenue for a plaintiff to recover damages in failure-to-protect cases.

A short time after this decision was rendered, the parties settled their claims. Significantly, the court readily found evidence of discriminatory intent on the part of the municipality because of its domestic disputes policy. The court relied on the written police policy as well as the manner in which the officers actually responded to this particular incident as clear evidence that the policy had a discriminatory impact against victims of domestic violence, which are more frequently women.

The court's rationale suggests that the court may have applied a less stringent test to determine discriminatory intent than did the United States Supreme Court in *Personnel Administrator v. Feeney*.[57] In *Feeney*, the Supreme Court indicated that discriminatory purpose was the operative phrase and stressed that, for a neutral law that disproportionately adversely affects a given class of individuals to be unconstitutional as a violation of the Equal Protection Clause, the disproportionate impact must be traced to a discriminatory purpose. The Supreme Court held:

> "[D]iscriminatory purpose," however, implies more than intent as volition or intent as awareness of consequences. It implies that the decisionmaker, in this case a state legislature, selected or reaffirmed a particular course of action at least in part "because of," not merely "in spite of," its adverse effects upon an identifiable group.[58]

The holding in *Smith* also suggests a relaxation of the standard established by *Feeney*. However, it should be noted that the court in *Smith* interpreted the holding in *Feeney* to conclude that "[t]o succeed on this [discrimination] claim, plaintiffs must demonstrate that the policy applied was either discriminatory on its face, or had a disproportionately adverse impact on women and was motivated by

[55]Smith v. City of Elyria, 857 F. Supp. 1203, 1213 (N.D. Ohio 1994).

[56]Smith v. City of Elyria, 857 F. Supp. 1203, 1213 (N.D. Ohio 1994).

[57]Personnel Adm'r of Massachusetts v. Feeney, 442 U.S. 256, 99 S. Ct. 2282, 60 L. Ed. 2d 870, 19 Fair Empl. Prac. Cas. (BNA) 1377, 19 Empl. Prac. Dec. (CCH) P 9240 (1979).

[58]Personnel Adm'r of Massachusetts v. Feeney, 442 U.S. 256, 279, 99 S. Ct. 2282, 60 L. Ed. 2d 870, 19 Fair Empl. Prac. Cas. (BNA) 1377, 19 Empl. Prac. Dec. (CCH) P 9240 (1979).

discriminatory intent."[59] In any case, lawyers should consider bringing equal protection claims in light of the legal analysis espoused by the court in *Smith*.

Q & A: In recent court actions, under which theories of liability have plaintiffs successfully prevailed?

DeShaney has influenced legal opinion regarding the efficacy of alleging substantive due process claims under 42 U.S.C.A. § 1983 in failure-to-protect cases. The overriding principle expressed by the Supreme Court in *DeShaney* is that, as a general rule, police do not have a constitutionally imposed duty to protect victims of domestic violence.[60] The court, however, held that the fact that El Paso had a contract with the El Paso Shelter for Battered Women to provide transportation to the shelter did not create a dangerous situation.[61]

However, the Maryland District Court, in *Pinder v. Commissioners of Cambridge*,[62] interpreted *DeShaney* to apply substantive due process to government inaction outside of the custodial context. The defendants in *Pinder* relied on *DeShaney* to support their argument that "outside of a custodial context, such as for prisoners, the state has no obligation to protect an individual from acts of private violence."[63] However, the *Pinder* court reasoned that the public should have the same right as state prisoners to be free from the arbitrary exercise of governmental authority.

The court suggested another way to approach the perceived limitations imposed by *DeShaney*. For example, the court stated that the *DeShaney* Court was ambivalent over whether a substantive due process right based on a failure to act can exist outside of a strictly custodial context.[64] The court also provided a standard by which future courts should view *DeShaney*. The district court relied on the factors enumerated in *Jensen v. Conrad*[65] to establish a special relationship and an affirmative duty to act and then focused on the burdens imposed by the *DeShaney* decision to "require[] an analysis of whether a state acted to create the duty such that the corresponding failure to

[59]Smith v. City of Elyria, 857 F. Supp. 1203, 1211 (N.D. Ohio 1994).

[60]See Leavitt v. City of El Paso, 2000 WL 33348224, *6 (W.D. Tex. 2000), aff'd, 264 F.3d 1140 (5th Cir. 2001) (the district court noted that "although the Fifth Circuit has never recognized a due process claim based on state-created danger, it also has not eliminated the possibility of such a claim."); Smith v. Town of East Haven, 2005 WL 677284 (D. Conn. 2005) (discussing state-created danger claim and *Moxell* claim for purposes of liability).

[61]Leavitt v. City of El Paso, 2000 WL 33348224, *7 (W.D. Tex. 2000), aff'd, 264 F.3d 1140 (5th Cir. 2001).

[62]Pinder v. Commissioners of Cambridge in City of Cambridge, 821 F. Supp. 376 (D. Md. 1993), judgment aff'd, 33 F.3d 368 (4th Cir. 1994), reh'g granted and opinion vacated, (Oct. 14, 1994) and on reh'g, 54 F.3d 1169 (4th Cir. 1995) and judgment rev'd, 54 F.3d 1169 (4th Cir. 1995) (judgment of district court denying qualified immunity to police officer reversed).

[63]Pinder v. Commissioners of Cambridge in City of Cambridge, 821 F. Supp. 376, 387 (D. Md. 1993), judgment aff'd, 33 F.3d 368 (4th Cir. 1994), reh'g granted and opinion vacated, (Oct. 14, 1994) and on reh'g, 54 F.3d 1169 (4th Cir. 1995) and judgment rev'd, 54 F.3d 1169 (4th Cir. 1995).

[64]See also Freeman v. Ferguson, 911 F.2d 52 (8th Cir. 1990).

[65]Jensen v. Conrad, 747 F.2d 185 (4th Cir. 1984).

act is arbitrary."[66] Based on the legal analysis set forth under *Pinder* and the plethora of cases on which it relies, it is definitely possible to prevail on a substantive due process claim in post-DeShaney failure-to-protect cases.[67]

In the Tenth Circuit decision, *Gonzales v. City of Castle Rock*,[68] the eleven-judge en banc panel affirmed the three-judge Tenth Circuit's decision reversing the U.S. District Court's dismissal of Ms. Gonzales' procedural due process claim. The Circuit Court was asked to consider whether a court-issued domestic restraining order, whose enforcement is mandated by a state statute, creates a property interest protected by the due process clause of the Fourteenth Amendment. The main concern of the defendants was that a court decision that allowed a protected property right in the enforcement of the restraining order would "'carve out an exception contrary to *DeShaney* and the general rule that the state does not have an affirmative duty to protect individuals from private third parties.' "[69]

In this case, Ms. Gonzales had a restraining order, which excluded her husband from the family home and prevented him access to the children, except for the exercise of specific visitation. Mr. Gonzales kidnapped the three daughters from the front of Ms. Gonzales' home. When she discovered the children missing, she contacted the Castle Rock police department and requested that they enforce the restraining order, which they refused to do. He later murdered the three children.

---

[66]Pinder v. Commissioners of Cambridge in City of Cambridge, 821 F. Supp. 376, 394 (D. Md. 1993), judgment aff'd, 33 F.3d 368 (4th Cir. 1994), reh'g granted and opinion vacated, (Oct. 14, 1994) and on reh'g, 54 F.3d 1169 (4th Cir. 1995) and judgment rev'd, 54 F.3d 1169 (4th Cir. 1995); see also Kallstrom v. City of Columbus, 136 F.3d 1055, 13 I.E.R. Cas. (BNA) 1202, 26 Media L. Rep. (BNA) 1353, 1998 FED App. 0055P (6th Cir. 1998); May v. Franklin County Bd. of Com'rs, 59 Fed. Appx. 786 (6th Cir. 2003); Gazette v. City of Pontiac, 41 F.3d 1061, 1994 FED App. 0405P (6th Cir. 1994); Gonzales v. City of Castle Rock, 307 F.3d 1258 (10th Cir. 2002), on reh'g en banc, 366 F.3d 1093 (10th Cir. 2004), rev'd on other grounds, 545 U.S. 748, 125 S. Ct. 2796, 162 L. Ed. 2d 658 (2005).

[67]But see Eckert v. Town of Silverthorne, 25 Fed. Appx. 679 (10th Cir. 2001) (Circuit court stated the special relationship theory another way: the theory of danger creation means that "a state actor who creates a substantial risk and then fails to protect a citizen 'is as much an active tortfeasor as if [they] had thrown him into a snake pit.' " To prevail, a plaintiff must show "(1) the charged state entity and the charged individual actors created the danger or increased plaintiff's vulnerability to the danger in some way; (2) plaintiff was a member of a limited and specifically definable group; (3) defendants' conduct put plaintiff at substantial risk of serious, immediate, and proximate harm; (4) the risk was obvious or known; (5) defendants acted recklessly in conscious disregard of that risk; and (6) such conduct, when viewed in total, is conscious shocking." Circuit court held no evidence suggested that the acts of appellees increased appellants' exposure to harm.); see also Gonzales v. City of Castle Rock, 307 F.3d 1258 (10th Cir. 2002), on reh'g en banc, 366 F.3d 1093 (10th Cir. 2004), rev'd, 545 U.S. 748, 125 S. Ct. 2796, 162 L. Ed. 2d 658 (2005) (reversed on grounds that Mrs. Gonzales had no protected right to police enforcement of her restraining order); Text § 14:9, Police liability for failing to protect victims of domestic violence—Legal theories for recovery—Substantive due process.

[68]Gonzales v. City of Castle Rock, 366 F.3d 1093 (10th Cir. 2004), rev'd, 545 U.S. 748, 125 S. Ct. 2796, 162 L. Ed. 2d 658 (2005).

[69]Gonzales v. City of Castle Rock, 366 F.3d 1093, 1099 (10th Cir. 2004), rev'd, 545 U.S. 748, 125 S. Ct. 2796, 162 L. Ed. 2d 658 (2005), quoting from Appellee's brief to the court.

Ms. Gonzales sued the City of Castle Rock and the Castle Rock Police Department under a federal 1983 claim alleging both substantive and procedural due process claims by failing to enforce the restraining order. She relied on the language of the Colorado statute, which defined the crime of violating a restraining order and the duties of peace officers in that regard. Under that provision, officers "*shall* use every reasonable means to enforce a restraining order" and "shall arrest, or, if an arrest is impractical under the circumstances, seek a warrant for the arrest of a restrained person when the peace officer has information amounting to probable cause that . . . [t]he restrained person has violated or attempted to violate any provision of the restraining order."[70] The plaintiffs relied on the holding in *Siddle v. City of Cambridge*,[71] which concluded that "a protective order obtained pursuant to state law 'creates a property right which incurs a duty on the part of the government.' "[72] Ohio's statute provides that "any officer of a law enforcement agency shall enforce a protection order issued . . . by any court in this state in accordance with the provisions of the order."[73] The *Siddle* court noted that "holders of protective orders are entitled to greater rights than other citizens and that such an order 'would have no valid purpose unless a means to enforce it exists.' "[74] Ohio's statute also imposes a duty on a police officer to arrest the person whom the officer has reasonable grounds to believe has committed the offense of domestic violence or violating a protection order.[75]

In distinguishing *DeShaney*, the Tenth Circuit Court of Appeals stated that "DeShaney makes clear that all individuals do not possess a substantive right to protection by the state from the harm of third parties . . . But such a ruling does not foreclose a state from creating through its own laws an entitlement for particular citizens in having their court-issued restraining order enforced. Our opinion is therefore not contrary to DeShaney . . . [w]e are persuaded Ms. Gonzales' complaint states a claim that she possessed a protected property interest in the enforcement of the terms of her restraining order and that the officers' arbitrary denial of that entitlement violated her procedural due process rights."[76] Therefore Ms. Gonzales may proceed with her procedural due process claim against the City of Castle Rock.

Following the Tenth Circuit Court decision, the city of Castle Rock appealed to the United States Supreme Court and was granted certiorari. Attorneys for Castle Rock argued that a previous Supreme Court ruling in *DeShaney v. Winnebago County Department of Social*

[70]Gonzales v. City of Castle Rock, 366 F.3d 1093, 1104 (10th Cir. 2004), rev'd, 545 U.S. 748, 125 S. Ct. 2796, 162 L. Ed. 2d 658 (2005).

[71]Siddle v. City of Cambridge, Ohio, 761 F. Supp. 503 (S.D. Ohio 1991).

[72]Gonzales v. City of Castle Rock, 366 F.3d 1093, 1109 (10th Cir. 2004), rev'd, 545 U.S. 748, 125 S. Ct. 2796, 162 L. Ed. 2d 658 (2005), quoting Siddle, at 509.

[73]RC 3113.31(F)(3).

[74]Gonzales v. City of Castle Rock, 366 F.3d 1093, 1109 (10th Cir. 2004), rev'd, 545 U.S. 748, 125 S. Ct. 2796, 162 L. Ed. 2d 658 (2005), quoting Siddle, at 509.

[75]RC 2935.03(B)(3)(b).

[76]Gonzales v. City of Castle Rock, 366 F.3d 1093, 1100 (10th Cir. 2004), rev'd, 545 U.S. 748, 125 S. Ct. 2796, 162 L. Ed. 2d 658 (2005), quoting Siddle, at 509.

Services[77] established that the Due Process Clause of the Constitution does not require law enforcement to protect persons from harm inflicted by third parties.

On the other hand, attorneys for Mrs. Gonzales and the Amici Curiae responded that *DeShaney* was a substantive due process claim whereas Mrs. Gonzales makes a procedural due process argument; thus, the *DeShaney* analysis does not apply. While acknowledging that *DeShaney* rejected the argument that the Due Process Clause imposes a special duty on government actors to protect the life, liberty and property of specific citizens from the actions of third parties, attorneys for Mrs. Gonzales stressed that the *DeShaney* Court failed to consider the Gonzales's situation. In *Gonzales*, a court issued a specific restraining order requiring that a specific person be protected from further harm from another specific person. In issuing the order, the court determined that one specific individual was at risk of danger from another specific person.

Q & A: Has the Supreme Court issued any rulings in this area?

On June 27, 2005, the U.S. Supreme Court issued its decision[78] and reversed the Tenth Circuit Court. The Court did not accept the Circuit Court of Appeals conclusion that Colorado gave Mrs. Gonzales a right to police enforcement of a restraining order.[79] Nor did Colorado law, through its domestic violence and mandatory arrest statutes, create a personal entitlement to police enforcement of restraining orders. Accordingly, Mrs. Gonzales did not have a protected property right in police enforcement of her restraining order.

The Supreme Court noted that *DeShaney v. Winnebago County Department of Social Services*,[80] acknowledged that substantive due process does not require the State to protect the life, liberty and property of its citizens, but left unanswered the question of whether a person has a procedural due process right to receive protection from the State under its statutes.

The Court reasoned that the procedural Due Process Clause of the U.S. Constitution does not protect everything that might be described as a benefit. "To have a property interest in a benefit, a person clearly must have more than an abstract need or desire" and "more that a unilateral expectation of it. He must, instead, have a legitimate claim of entitlement to it."[81] Additionally, entitlements are created, not by

---

[77]DeShaney v. Winnebago County Dept. of Social Services, 489 U.S. 189, 109 S. Ct. 998, 103 L. Ed. 2d 249 (1989).

[78]Town of Castle Rock, Colo. v. Gonzales, 545 U.S. 748, 125 S. Ct. 2796, 162 L. Ed. 2d 658 (2005).

[79]Town of Castle Rock, Colo. v. Gonzales, 545 U.S. 748, 125 S. Ct. 2796, 162 L. Ed. 2d 658 (2005) at syl See also Kathleen K. Curtis, The Supreme Court's Attack on Domestic Violence Legislation—Discretion, Entitlement, and Due Process in *Town of Castle Rock v. Gonzales*, 32 Wm. Mitchell L. Rev. 1181 (2006).

[80]DeShaney v. Winnebago County Dept. of Social Services, 489 U.S. 189, 109 S. Ct. 998, 103 L. Ed. 2d 249 (1989).

[81]Town of Castle Rock, Colo. v. Gonzales, 545 U.S. 748, 125 S. Ct. 2796, 2803, 162 L. Ed. 2d 658 (2005), quoting Board of Regents of State Colleges v. Roth, 408 U.S. 564, 577, 92 S. Ct. 2701, 33 L. Ed. 2d 548, 1 I.E.R. Cas. (BNA) 23 (1972).

the Constitution, but rather by existing rules that stem from a source such as state law.[82]

In deciding whether a benefit is a protected entitlement, the Court found that where governmental officials have the discretion to grant or deny it, there is no entitlement. The Court was unpersuaded by the reasoning advanced by the Tenth Circuit Court which found that Colorado law created an entitlement to enforcement of the restraining order because the court-issued order dictated that its terms must be enforced and the state statute required such enforcement.[83] Rather, the Court found that if enforcement means either an arrest or an arrest warrant, depending on whether the defendant is at the scene, the duty to enforce is not mandatory. This exercise of discretion by law enforcement does not create the sort of entitlement out of which a property interest is created.

The United States Supreme Court then held that "the benefit that a third party may receive from having someone else arrested for a crime generally does not trigger protections under the Due Process Clause, neither in its procedural[84] nor in its "substantive" manifestations. This result reflects our continuing reluctance to treat the Fourteenth Amendment as " 'a font of tort law,'[85] but it does not mean States are powerless to provide victims with personally enforceable remedies. Although the framers of the Fourteenth Amendment and the Civil Rights Act of 1871, 17 Stat. 13 (the original source of Section 1983), did not create a system by which police departments are generally held financially accountable for crimes that better policing might have prevented, the people of Colorado are free to craft such a system under state law."[86]

In reviewing Colorado law, the Court noted that statutory tort immunity does not apply to a willful or wanton act or omission. Additionally, the court acknowledged that "[t]he state cases cited by the dissent that afford a cause of action for police failure to enforce restraining orders, vindicate state common-law or statutory tort

[82]Town of Castle Rock, Colo. v. Gonzales, 545 U.S. 748, 125 S. Ct. 2796, 2803, 162 L. Ed. 2d 658 (2005); see also Howard ex rel. Estate of Howard v. Bayes, 457 F.3d 568, 2006 FED App. 0285P (6th Cir. 2006) (holding no constitutional violation in the 1983 action for wrongful death; absent a restraining order or evidence of domestic violence, it is not surprising that liability toward law enforcement for failing to arrest was not found).

[83]Town of Castle Rock, Colo. v. Gonzales, 545 U.S. 748, 125 S. Ct. 2796, 162 L. Ed. 2d 658 (2005).

[84]See Tritia L. Yuen, No Relief: Understanding the Supreme Courts' Decision in Town of Castle Rock v. Gonzales Through the Rights/Remedies Framework, 55 Am. U. L. Rev. 1843 (2006).

[85]Town of Castle Rock, Colo. v. Gonzales, 545 U.S. 748, 125 S. Ct. 2796, 2810, 162 L. Ed. 2d 658 (2005), citing, Parratt v. Taylor, 451 U.S. 527, 544, 101 S. Ct. 1908, 68 L. Ed. 2d 420 (1981) (overruled by, Daniels v. Williams, 474 U.S. 327, 106 S. Ct. 662, 88 L. Ed. 2d 662 (1986)) (quoting Paul v. Davis, 424 U.S. 693, 701, 96 S. Ct. 1155, 47 L. Ed. 2d 405, 1 I.E.R. Cas. (BNA) 1827 (1976) (overruling court finding mere lack of due care by a state official does not deprive an individual of life, liberty or property under Fourteenth Amendment).

[86]Town of Castle Rock, Colo. v. Gonzales, 545 U.S. 748, 125 S. Ct. 2796, 2810, 162 L. Ed. 2d 658 (2005).

claims-not procedural due process claims under the Federal Constitution."[87]

Although Colorado law mandates that police officers "shall use every reasonable means to enforce" a restraining order, the Supreme Court concluded that the legislative intent of Colorado law was to permit officer discretion. "A well established tradition of police discretion has long co-existed with apparently mandatory arrest statutes."[88]

However, Justice Stevens argued in his dissent that the primary goal of requiring specific action was to remove the option of officer inaction. Stevens noted that "the crucial point is that, under the statute, the police were *required* to provide enforcement; *they lacked the discretion to do nothing*."[89]

Q & A: Since *Gonzales*, how have states addressed the issue?

The Supreme Court's failure to recognize a legal and constitutional policy basis for police enforcement of protection orders is a setback for victims of domestic violence because they lose a federal right to sue if their local governments fail to protect them.[90] Without financial consequences for a police failure to enforce, and hence, protect victims of domestic violence, law enforcement agencies may no longer have the incentive to enforce protection orders according to law.

The true impact of *Gonzales* may not be known for several years. Clearly, it is now up to the states to enact laws that hold law enforcement officials accountable for violating the laws of the state.[91] Montana, Tennessee and Pennsylvania[92] have legislation that imposes on law enforcement an affirmative duty to protect certain individuals.

For example, Tennessee has crafted exceptions into its Tort Immunity Laws.[93] Additionally, Tennessee's arrest laws provide that a law enforcement officer is statutorily obligated to make an arrest

---

[87]Town of Castle Rock, Colo. v. Gonzales, 545 U.S. 748, 125 S. Ct. 2796, 2810, 162 L. Ed. 2d 658 (2005); but see RC 2744.09(E), which provides that the immunity conferred by RC 2744.02 does not extend to claims alleging violations of federal statutes or the United States Constitution.

[88]Town of Castle Rock, Colo. v. Gonzales, 545 U.S. 748, 125 S. Ct. 2796, 2805, 162 L. Ed. 2d 658 (2005).

[89]Town of Castle Rock, Colo. v. Gonzales, 545 U.S. 748, 125 S. Ct. 2796, 162 L. Ed. 2d 658 (2005) (Stevens, J. dissenting) (emphasis added).

[90]See Lynn A. Combs, Between a Rock and a Hard Place: The Legacy of *Castle Rock v. Gonzales*, 58 Hastings L.J. 387 (2006); Nicole M. Quesler, Refusing To Remove an Obstacle to the Remedy: The Supreme Courts Decision in *Town of Castle Rock v. Gonzales* continues to Deny Domestic Violence Victims Meaningful Recourse, 40 Akron L. Rev. 391 (2007).

[91]See also Emily J. Martin & Caroline Bettinger-Lopez, *Castle Rock v. Gonzales* and the Future of Police Protection of Victims of Domestic Violence, 11(1) DVR 1 (Oct./Nov. 2005); Gorn Zorza, Things We Can Do After the *Castle Rock v. Gonzales* Decision, 11(1) DVR 1 (Oct./Nov. 2005); Danielle Lynn Lordi, Police Liability under State Tort Law for Failure to Enforce Protection Orders: The Last Demand for Accountability, 85 Or. L. Rev. 325 (2006); G. Kristian Miccio, A Cruel Deception: *Castle Rock*, Constitutional Protection and Conceptions of State Accountability, 10 Georgetown Journal of Gender and the Law 87 (2009).

[92]But see Burella v. City of Philadelphia, 501 F.3d 134 (3d Cir. 2007) (although Pa statute provides that a police officer "shall arrest" a defendant for violating a domestic abuse restraining order, the statute was silent as to whether a victim could demand an arrest).

[93]T.C.A. 29-20-201 et seq. (providing that negligent act or omission is operational

when the officer has probable cause to believe an individual has violated an order of protection; in all other cases, an officer has discretion to make an arrest.[94]

Additionally, the Supreme Court of Tennessee decided *Matthews v. Pickett County*,[95] In that case, the court answered the question of whether a protection order could create a special duty. The Supreme Court held that the deputies' failure to arrest husband upon reasonable cause to believe that he had violated a protection order was operational in nature so that deputies were not entitled to immunity under GTLA and the special duty exception negated public duty doctrine immunity and allowed the wife to pursue a negligence action for damage.[96]

Finally, domestic violence experts around the country should encourage their states to revisit mandatory/preferred arrest statutes as well as police policies, protocols and procedures that dictate how officers respond to domestic violence calls. If victims of domestic violence cannot count on law enforcement for protection, the protection orders issued on their behalf are essentially meaningless.

Q & A: What other trends exist?

Although recent trends suggest a greater likelihood of prevailing in state courts under a state-created duty to protect[97] rather than under a substantive due process claim, a special relationship claim may also be affected by state tort laws which may have abrogated the special relationship theory of municipal liability.[98] Additionally, over the past five years, there has been an increase in the probability of succeeding on the merits of the case where plaintiffs bring equal protection claims under 42 U.S.C.A. § 1983.[99]

In recent years, both the federal and state court decisions have split on whether civil liability attaches to the police and the municipality

---

in nature and subject to the GTLA when the act or omission occurs in the absence of a formulated policy guiding the conduct or omission or when the conduct deviates from an established plan or policy).

[94]Op. Att'y Gen. 01-119 (2001); interpreting T.C.A. 36-3-611.

[95]Matthews v. Pickett County, 996 S.W.2d 162 (Tenn. 1999).

[96]Matthews v. Pickett County, 996 S.W.2d 162 (Tenn. 1999).

[97]See David Pruessner, The Forgotten Foundation of State Created Danger Claims, 20 Rev. Litig. 357 (2001); see also Jeremy Daniel Kernodle, Policing the Police: Clarifying the Test For Holding the Government Liable under 42 U.S.C. 1983 and the State Created Danger Theory, 54 Vand. L. Rev. 165 (2001); see also Kallstrom v. City of Columbus, 136 F.3d 1055, 13 I.E.R. Cas. (BNA) 1202, 26 Media L. Rep. (BNA) 1353, 1998 FED App. 0055P (6th Cir. 1998); but see May v. Franklin County Bd. of Com'rs, 59 Fed. Appx. 786 (6th Cir. 2003); Brooks v. Knapp, 221 Fed. Appx. 402, 2007 FED App. 0812N (6th Cir. 2007) (neither officers' assurances to wife of additional patrols nor failure to do anything other than to detain husband briefly on the night before he killed her caused a state created danger actionable under § 1983).

[98]See, e.g., Smith v. City of Elyria, 857 F. Supp. 1203 (N.D. Ohio 1994). But see Sawicki v. Village of Ottawa Hills, 37 Ohio St. 3d 222, 525 N.E.2d 468 (1988); see also RC Ch. 2744.

[99]But see Morrow v. Stoner, 2014 WL 4403436 (N.D. Ohio 2014) (dismissing the 1983 claim against two judicial officers on the grounds that there was no state created danger, relying on *DeShaney v. Winnebago,* declining to exercise jurisdiction over the state claims but dismissing them without prejudice).

for their failure to protect victims of domestic violence.[100] Similarly, the evidence necessary to trigger liability under any of the theories is not uniform. For example, in *Hakken v. Washtenaw County*,[101] the plaintiff alleged that the county sheriff's department had failed to respond to her calls involving her ex-husband's abusive conduct. The plaintiff claimed that the county had a policy or custom of affording less protection to domestic violence victims. Although the court granted the defendant's summary judgment motion to dismiss the state tort claims and ruled that the plaintiff had failed to establish a policy or custom of deliberate indifference in domestic violence situations, the court granted the plaintiff leave to present statistical data sufficient to demonstrate that crimes against women in domestic violence cases are treated differently that other crimes. In effect, the Michigan District Court permitted the plaintiff an opportunity to present evidence of a pattern of unequal treatment toward victims of domestic violence and time to prove that the pattern represents a custom in the sheriff's department.

Similarly, in *Navarro v. Block*,[102] the relatives of a deceased domestic violence victim brought a claim under 42 U.S.C.A. § 1983 and an equal protection claim because a 911 dispatcher failed to dispatch the police which allegedly resulted in the victim's death. The relatives claimed that it was the custom and policy of the sheriff's department not to provide emergency assistance in domestic violence situations and that the sheriff's department failed to train its dispatchers in the proper handling of 911 domestic violence calls. The Ninth Circuit overturned the decision of the district court and held that summary judgment was inappropriate in that the county's policy or custom of according lower priority to domestic violence calls may be an actionable 42 U.S.C.A. § 1983 claim. Although the court determined that the plaintiffs failed to present evidence of an "invidious intent or motive"[103] and failed to demonstrate a deliberate indifference to the rights of domestic violence victims arising from a failure to train dispatchers, the court left open the possibility of an equal protection violation where the county has a policy or custom of not classifying domestic violence 911 calls as emergencies.[104]

In *Fajardo v. County of Los Angeles*,[105] the Ninth Circuit Court of Appeals reversed the district court ruling and remanded the case to

[100]See, for example, Kelley v. City of Wake Village, Texas, 264 Fed. Appx. 437 (5th Cir. 2008) (both discussing when municipal liability can attach); see also Text § 14:13, Civil rights remedies for gender-motivated violence.

[101]Hakken v. Washtenaw County, 901 F. Supp. 1245 (E.D. Mich. 1995).

[102]Navarro v. Block, 72 F.3d 712 (9th Cir. 1995), as amended on denial of reh'g, (Jan. 12, 1996).

[103]Navarro v. Block, 72 F.3d 712, 717 (9th Cir. 1995), as amended on denial of reh'g, (Jan. 12, 1996).

[104]Villanueva v. City of Scottsbluff, 779 F.3d 507 (8th Cir. 2015). But see Ricketts v. City of Columbia, Mo., 36 F.3d 775 (8th Cir. 1994) (evidence failed to demonstrate that the police custom of disparate treatment caused the injury nor did it establish that the city intentionally discriminated against women in providing less protection for victims of domestic violence).

[105]Fajardo v. County of Los Angeles, 179 F.3d 698 (9th Cir. 1999). But see Lunini v. Grayeb, 395 F.3d 761 (7th Cir. 2005), as amended on denial of reh'g and reh'g en banc, (Mar. 4, 2005) (reversing district court decision holding that plaintiff had a

determine whether the county has a discriminatory policy or custom of giving lower priority to domestic violence calls and, if so, whether the policy or custom has a rational basis. Since the district court erred by equating domestic violence calls with not-in-progress calls and by assuming that domestic violence crimes were less injurious than nondomestic violence crimes, the court also erred in concluding as a matter of law that the county's classification was rational and reasonable under an "equal protection" analysis. The court went on to state that survivors of domestic violence victims could maintain an equal protection claim against a sheriff and county under 42 U.S.C.A. § 1983 based on allegations that the county had a policy or custom[106] that discriminated against victims domestic violence by giving their 911 calls less priority.[107]

In *Estate of Macias v. Ihde*,[108] the estate of a woman murdered by her husband after the husband had committed several violations of a protection order, sued the Sheriff of Sonoma County. Under an Equal Protection claim, the estate said the sheriff had violated her constitutional right to non-discriminatory police services by failing to take reports, ignoring evidence, discouraging her from calling, and otherwise failing to take proper action in response to her complaints. The federal district court dismissed her case. On appeal, the Ninth Circuit Court of Appeals reversed, stating:

> It is well established that "there is no constitutional right to be protected by the state against being murdered by criminals or madmen." [Quoting] *Bowers v. DeVito*.[109] There is a constitutional right, however, to have police services administered in a nondiscriminatory manner—a right that is violated when a state actor denies such protection to disfavored persons. See Navarro v. Block.[110] (recognizing a cause of action under § 1983 based upon the discriminatory denial of police services); *Balistreri v. Pacifica Police Dep't*.[111] (same). . . . The alleged constitutional deprivation in this matter was the alleged denial of equal police protection to Mrs. Macias.[112]

On the other hand, the failure of a 911 operator to promptly dispatch police to the scene of a domestic dispute that resulted in a double murder did not render the city liable to the victim's family. In *Beltran*

right to be free from deliberate withdrawal of police protection and remanding case with instructions to enter summary judgment in favor of defendants).

[106] Estate of Soberal v. City of Jersey City, 529 F. Supp. 2d 477 (D.N.J. 2007), order vacated in part on other grounds, 334 Fed. Appx. 492 (3d Cir. 2009) (defining policy and custom).

[107] Fajardo v. County of Los Angeles, 179 F.3d 698, 698 (9th Cir. 1999).

[108] Estate of Macias v. Ihde, 219 F.3d 1018 (9th Cir. 2000); see also Jamie Zengler, Estate of Macias v. Ihde: Do Police Officers Have a Duty to Protect Victims of Domestic Violence? 3 J.L. & Fam. Stud. 97 (2001).

[109] Bowers v. DeVito, 686 F.2d 616, 618 (7th Cir. 1982).

[110] Navarro v. Block, 72 F.3d 712, 715-17 (9th Cir. 1995), as amended on denial of reh'g, (Jan. 12, 1996).

[111] Balistreri v. Pacifica Police Dept., 901 F.2d 696, 700-01 (9th Cir. 1988).

[112] Estate of Macias v. Ihde, 219 F.3d 1018, 1028 (9th Cir. 2000); see also Jamie Zenger, Estate of Macias vs. Ihde: Do Police Officers Have a Duty to Protect Victims of Domestic Violence? 3 J.L. & Fam. Stud. 97, 99 (2001).

v. City of El Paso,[113] a murdered woman's family filed a Section 1983 lawsuit against the 911 dispatch operator and the City of El Paso, alleging that classifying the 911 call a level 4 priority rather than a level priority 3 call was an equal protection violation under the 14th Amendment. Following a denial of summary judgment, the City appealed.

The 5th Circuit Court of Appeals reversed and remanded the case with instructions that it be dismissed. At the outset, the court noted that, under DeShaney's, the "due process clause does not require a state to provide its citizens with particular protective services. Therefore, a state's failure to protect an individual against private violence does not violate the due process clause. . ."[114] However, the court acknowledged *DeShaney's* warning that a state may not selectively deny its protective services to certain disfavored minorities without violating the equal protection clause.[115]

Regarding the due process claim, the court found that no evidence was presented by the family sufficient to establish a special relationship between the 911 operator and the decedent such that the city had a duty to protect the decedent. Although the family argued that by encouraging the victim to stay in the bathroom and telling her that the police were on the way, the 911 operator became the custodian of her safety. However, the operator offered advice but had not affirmatively placed the victim in custody by restraining her in the bathroom. Nor did the operator's statement that the police were on the way in conjunction with advice to remain in the bathroom create a dangerous situation for which the city must be held responsible.

The 5th Circuit held that "Beltran must show that Amador acted with 'deliberate indifference' to Sonye Herrera's situation . . . Deliberate indifference requires that the state actor both knew of and disregarded an excessive risk to the victim's health and safety . . . The only facts presented by Beltran that even remotely suggest misfeasance are 1) Amador's failure to record the previous Herrera family injury to a child incident in the dispatch report; 2) her statement to Sonye Herrera that the police were on their way; 3) the advice Amador provided to Sonye Herrera to stay in the bathroom; and 4) Amador's disconnecting of the telephone call. Given Amador's understanding that 1) a radio call was going out to patrol cars based on her report; 2) the locked bathroom was a relatvely safe place; and 3) Armando Herrera was leaving the scene, she did not display deliberate indifference to Sonye Herrera's situation. She had no reason to know that Sonye Herrera's life was in immediate danger. Moreover, rather than disregard the threat, it appears that Amador was doing what she could to keep Sonye Herrera safe. Her errors constitute negligence, not deliberate indifference."[116]

The *Beltran* court also pointed out that certain intentionally

---

[113]Beltran v. City of El Paso, 367 F.3d 299 (5th Cir. 2004).

[114]Beltran v. City of El Paso, 367 F.3d 299, 304 (5th Cir. 2004), quoting, DeShaney v. Winnebago County Dept. of Social Services, 489 U.S. 189, 197, 109 S. Ct. 998, 103 L. Ed. 2d 249 (1989).

[115]Beltran v. City of El Paso, 367 F.3d 299, 304 (5th Cir. 2004).

[116]Beltran v. City of El Paso, 367 F.3d 299, 308 (5th Cir. 2004).

discriminatory policies, practices and customs of law enforcement with regard to domestic violence might violate the equal protection clause. To prevail on a gender based equal protection claim, a plaintiff must show (1) the existence of a policy, practice or custom of law enforcement to provide less protection to victims of domestic assault than to victims of other assaults; (2) that discrimination against women was a motivating fact; and (3) that the plaintiff was injured by the policy, custom or practice.[117]

In rejecting Beltran's claim, the court concluded that she had failed to present evidence demonstrating that discrimination against women motivated El Paso's handling of the 911 call. She did not demonstrate that El Paso assigns a lower level priority to family violence calls as a result of an effort to discriminate against women. The only evidence that could have been considered is that Amador questioned Sonye Herrera about the nature of the relationship between her and her male assailant. "Amador's question regarding the nature of the relationship between Sonye Herrera and her assailant is better understood as an eminently reasonable question that an emergency operator might ask to assess the situation at hand, rather than an attempt to discriminate against Sonye Herrera or her mother based on their relationship to the attacker."[118]

Finally, the Court determined that even if *Beltran* had established a valid constitutional claim under the theories of Equal Protection or Due Process, the 911 operator's "conduct was objectively reasonable in light of the clearly established legal rules at the time of the incident and qualified immunity protects her from any civil liability."[119]

Several recent court opinions addressing municipal liability have refined the analysis for bringing suit against a municipality in the context of domestic violence.[120] In differentiating between the municipality and the officer, liability against a municipality may not lie, although specific officers may be found liable.

For example, in *Estate of Soberal v. City of Jersey City,*[121] a woman was killed by her boyfriend, a city police officer. Her estate sued the

[117]See also Shipp v. McMahon, 234 F.3d 907, 914 (5th Cir. 2000) (overruled on other grounds by, McClendon v. City of Columbia, 305 F.3d 314 (5th Cir. 2002)).

[118]Beltran v. City of El Paso, 367 F.3d 299, 306 (5th Cir. 2004).

[119]Beltran v. City of El Paso, 367 F.3d 299, 308 (5th Cir. 2004).

[120]See also Text § 14:12, Police liability for failing to protect victims of domestic violence—Legal theories for recovery—State duty to protect. See also Lee v. City of Oakland, 2006 WL 2046011 (Cal. App. 1st Dist. 2006), unpublished/noncitable (holding that the complaint was sufficient to state a claim under the doctrine of vicarious liability as the city stipulated it had a duty to place defendant in custody and that it breached its statutory duty); Pearce v. Estate of Longo, 766 F. Supp. 2d 367, 374-75 (N.D. N.Y. 2011), aff'd in part, rev'd in part on other grounds, 473 Fed. Appx. 16 (2d Cir. 2012) (a municipality can be found to have a custom that causes a constitutional violation when it is "faced with a pattern of misconduct and does nothing, compelling the conclusion that [it] has acquiesced in or tacitly authorized its subordinates' unlawful actions"; quoting Reynolds v. Giuliani, 506 F.3d 183, 192 (2d Cir. 2007)).

[121]Estate of Soberal v. City of Jersey City, 529 F. Supp. 2d 477 (D.N.J. 2007), order vacated in part, 334 Fed. Appx. 492 (3d Cir. 2009) (vacating court finding district court erred in denying summary judgment based on qualified immunity for police lieutenant, inspector and sergeant); see also Kelley v. City of Wake Village, Texas, 264 Fed. Appx. 437 (5th Cir. 2008).

city, police department and individual officers alleging a violation of section 1983, municipal liability and state law tort claims. The New Jersey District Court determined that "a municipality cannot be held liable under section 1983 based on the theory of *respondeat superior;* however, a municipality can be sued directly under section 1983 if the action that caused a constitutional tort was based on a municipal custom or policy."[122] "Municipal liability will attach only when the decision-maker possesses final authority to establish the municipal policy with respect to the action ordered."[123]

Not only must there be a specific policy or custom, there must also be a nexus between the policy or custom and the constitutional violation that occurred. Further, the municipality is not liable unless it is clear that the municipality or its officials possessed the final authority to establish the municipal policy or custom. "The fact that a particular officer, even a policymaking official, has discretion in the exercise of particular functions does not, without more, give rise to municipal liability based on an exercise of that discretion."[124]

The Court also considered the definitions of a "policy" and a "custom." "A 'policy' is made when a 'statement, ordinance, regulation, or decision' is 'officially adopted and promulgated by that body's officers.' "[125] "A 'custom' is 'a given course of conduct, although not specifically endorsed or authorized by law . . . so well-settled and permanent as virtually to constitute law.' "[126]

There have also been another line of state law cases in which the state domestic violence laws have overridden the state tort immunity laws. For example, in *Lacey v Village of Palatine*,[127] family members brought suit against the municipality and the officers when a victim was killed by her former boyfriend. The appellate court noted that the Illinois Domestic Violence Act imposed a duty on law enforcement officials to "promptly undertake all reasonable steps to assist a person protected under the Act, when they learn of threatening conduct and

[122]Estate of Soberal v. City of Jersey City, 529 F. Supp. 2d 477, 490 (D.N.J. 2007), order vacated in part, 334 Fed. Appx. 492 (3d Cir. 2009), citing Monell v. Department of Social Services of City of New York, 436 U.S. 658, 98 S. Ct. 2018, 56 L. Ed. 2d 611, 17 Fair Empl. Prac. Cas. (BNA) 873, 16 Empl. Prac. Dec. (CCH) P 8345 (1978). See also Hernandez v. City of Napa, 781 F. Supp. 2d 975 (N.D. Cal. 2011).

[123]Estate of Soberal v. City of Jersey City, 529 F. Supp. 2d 477, 490 (D.N.J. 2007), order vacated in part, 334 Fed. Appx. 492 (3d Cir. 2009), quoting Pembaur v. City of Cincinnati, 475 U.S. 469, 481, 106 S. Ct. 1292, 89 L. Ed. 2d 452 (1986).

[124]Estate of Soberal v. City of Jersey City, 529 F. Supp. 2d 477 (D.N.J. 2007), order vacated in part, 334 Fed. Appx. 492 (3d Cir. 2009), at syllabus.

[125]Estate of Soberal v. City of Jersey City, 529 F. Supp. 2d 477, 490 (D.N.J. 2007), order vacated in part, 334 Fed. Appx. 492 (3d Cir. 2009), quoting Monell v. Department of Social Services of City of New York, 436 U.S. 658, 690, 98 S. Ct. 2018, 56 L. Ed. 2d 611, 17 Fair Empl. Prac. Cas. (BNA) 873, 16 Empl. Prac. Dec. (CCH) P 8345 (1978).

[126]Estate of Soberal v. City of Jersey City, 529 F. Supp. 2d 477, 490 (D.N.J. 2007), order vacated in part, 334 Fed. Appx. 492 (3d Cir. 2009), quoting Bielevicz v. Dubinon, 915 F.2d 845, 850 (3d Cir. 1990).

[127]Lacey v. Village of Palatine, 379 Ill. App. 3d 62, 318 Ill. Dec. 64, 882 N.E.2d 1187 (1st Dist. 2008), decision rev'd, 232 Ill. 2d 349, 328 Ill. Dec. 256, 904 N.E.2d 18 (2009).

an ongoing violation of a protection order."[128] The court reversed the trial court decision to grant the officers' motion to dismiss and stated that whether the defendants breached a legal duty by willful and wanton conduct is a question of fact for the jury to decide. Of significance is that the *Lacey* court held that the provisions in the Domestic Violence Act override the Tort Immunity Act when determining whether police officers are entitled to absolute immunity where there are allegations that the officers engaged in willful and wanton conduct by failing to aid a victim of domestic violence.

Some state law decisions have even upheld an officer's duty to protect in domestic violence cases on a state law claim. For example, in *Calloway v. Kinkelaar*,[129] the plaintiff based her claim for relief on the protection order she had obtained and on the sheriff's awareness of that order. She premised her argument on the fact that she was entitled to special protection because her protection order created a statutory duty to protect her by reasonable means. As in *Smith v. City of Elyria*,[130] the court recognized a cause of action where the statutory duties were breached by the willful or wanton acts or omissions of law enforcement officers which caused injury to the plaintiff. To the extent that the sheriff and county willfully and wantonly failed to protect her, to investigate, and to arrest her husband, the court held that she had stated valid causes of action.

Q & A: What can law enforcement agencies do to insulate themselves from liability?

Several law enforcement commentators have suggested a threefold approach for law enforcement agencies in light of recent court decisions. Pursuant to RC 2935.032(A), law enforcement agencies must have written policies in place that set forth the extent of their discretion in making arrests. The policies should also detail their investigatory procedures and officer and 911 dispatcher response to domestic violence calls.[131] Law enforcement agencies must examine any unwritten practices or customs in responding to victims of domestic violence. All policies and practices must be evaluated to ensure that they do not reflect a deliberate indifference on the part of the agency toward domestic violence victims. Since plaintiffs try to use department policies or protocols as evidence to demonstrate that victims of domestic violence are treated less seriously than other crimes, particularly in federal equal protection lawsuits, the importance of drafting and enforcing good policies cannot be understated.

---

[128] Lacey v. Village of Palatine, 379 Ill. App. 3d 62, 318 Ill. Dec. 64, 882 N.E.2d 1187, 1196 (1st Dist. 2008), decision rev'd, 232 Ill. 2d 349, 328 Ill. Dec. 256, 904 N.E.2d 18 (2009), Calloway v. Kinkelaar, 168 Ill. 2d 312, 213 Ill. Dec. 675, 659 N.E.2d 1322 (1995).

[129] Calloway v. Kinkelaar, 168 Ill. 2d 312, 213 Ill. Dec. 675, 659 N.E.2d 1322 (1995).

[130] Smith v. City of Elyria, 857 F. Supp. 1203 (N.D. Ohio 1994).

[131] See, e.g., May v. Franklin County Bd. of Com'rs, 59 Fed. Appx. 786 (6th Cir. 2003).

Police departments should also document the training officers receive in handling domestic violence situations[132] and review the training manuals to ensure that they do not discourage arrests in domestic violence cases or rationalize different treatment for domestic violence victims. Law enforcement agencies must verify that officers are aware of the community resources available to assist victims of domestic violence.[133]

Finally, agencies must validate their own statistical data to certify that any discrepancies in the arrest rate[134] between domestic and nondomestic assaults are not the result of a bias against women or victims of domestic violence. Any disparity in these rates must be evaluated to see whether it can be explained in terms of legitimate law enforcement interests.

Legislative enactment is the most effective way to combat the problem of police inaction.[135] A failure to comply with the statutory requirements may result in civil liability.[136] Statutorily defined duties on police officers, particularly in terms of arrest procedures, will enable courts to establish the causal connection between the police officer's failure to act and the victim's injury.[137]

For example, where the state statute provides for the issuance of protection orders to victims of domestic violence, it necessarily suggests that the victim should be afforded a greater right to protection. Where the state statute requires that protection orders be sent to police, as in Ohio, the police are put on notice of the existence of the order.[138] The police officer may have a greater duty to protect the individual, and the failure to do so may subject the law enforcement agency, its officers, and the municipality to liability. Additionally, where the "statute specifically imposes upon the police officer a duty to arrest and remove the perpetrator, and the police officer fails to do so, then any further injury inflicted upon a woman may be directly attributed to the officer's failure to act."[139]

Q & A: Can a police officer be found liable for failing to file an incident report?

---

[132]See RC 109.744.

[133]See RC 2935.032(C).

[134]And any policy of giving lower priority to 911 domestic violence calls than to 911 non-domestic violence calls.

[135]See, for example, Estate of Soberal v. City of Jersey City, 529 F. Supp. 2d 477 (D.N.J. 2007), order vacated in part on other grounds, 334 Fed. Appx. 492 (3d Cir. 2009) (differentiating between failure to affirmatively act versus the failure to act).

[136]But see Burella v. City of Philadelphia, 501 F.3d 134 (3d Cir. 2007); Town of Castle Rock, Colo. v. Gonzales, 545 U.S. 748, 125 S. Ct. 2796, 162 L. Ed. 2d 658 (2005).

[137]See Robert A. Shapiro, Personal Liability of Policeman, Sheriff, or Similar Peace Officer for Injury Suffered as a Result of Failure to Enforce Law or Arrest Law Breaker, 41 A.L.R.3d 700 (1999); see also Ardoin v. City of Mamou, 685 So. 2d 294 (La. Ct. App. 3d Cir. 1996) (discussing when the police have a duty to arrest for violation of a restraining order).

[138]See Campbell v. Campbell, 294 N.J. Super. 18, 682 A.2d 272 (Law Div. 1996) (state law requires that a restraining order be sent to the police, the police are on notice of the existence of the order and, thus, cannot claim immunity for failing to make an arrest where there is probable cause to believe the order was violated; a failure to enforce such an order according to its terms may result in liability.).

[139]Gary M. Bishop, Section 1983 and Domestic Violence: A Solution to the Problem

At least one court answered this in the affirmative. In *Huff v. Rock Island County Sheriff's Merit Commission*,[140] the deputy failed to file a mandated domestic violence report[141] because the aggressor was a county corrections officer. An Illinois appellate court determined that a discharge of the deputy was too severe, but upheld a demotion and a 216-day suspension.

Q & A: Can a law enforcement agency be found liable for failing to adequately serve a protection order?

The Supreme Court of Washington, in *Washburn v. City of Federal Way*[142] considered a similar issue. In that case, the Federal Way Police Department served an antiharassment order on Kim forbidding him to contact the deceased. The deceased's family sued the City, alleging that the officer negligently served the order which resulted in Roznowski's death. The City claimed it had no duty under the public duty doctrine and foreclosing any tort liability such that its motion for summary judgment should have been granted. The Supreme Court disagreed with the City's argument and found that the City had a duty to serve the antiharassment order on Kim and because it had a duty to act, it had a duty to act with reasonable care in serving the order.

In serving the order, the officer confirmed Kim's identity, handed him the order, informed him he needed to appear in court and left. Despite the fact that he saw Roznowski, he did not inquire as to her safety, nor did he advise Kim that she had restrained him from contacting her and that he needed to vacate the home. However, the former police chief testified that he had a duty to minimize the danger to Roznowski and that proper service of the order required 1) reading the petition, and the order and the LEIS form which detailed how the recipient would likely react to service to prepare for violence; 2) ensuring that the recipient understood the contents and effect of the order which might have required the officer to bring a translator; 3) contacting petitioner to verify his or her safety and health as part of effective service; and 4) enforcing the antiharassment order, which, in this case, required at a minimum that Hensing inform Kim that Kim had to leave.[143] Additionally, Roznowski's daughter presented testimony that the Hensing's improper service of the order led to her mother's death.

The Supreme Court upheld the lower court's denial of the City's motion for summary judgment and decision against the City because it found that as a part of Hensing's duty to act reasonably, he owed Roznowski a duty to guard against the criminal conduct of Kim. He should have known he was serving Kim at Roznowski's house, he should have known how Kim would react to the order when served, and in not doing so, he created a new and real risk to Roznowksi.

of Police Officers' Inaction, 30 B.C. L. Rev. 1357, 1388 (1989).

[140] Huff v. Rock Island County Sheriff's Merit Com'n, 294 Ill. App. 3d 477, 228 Ill. Dec. 738, 689 N.E.2d 1159 (3d Dist. 1998), as modified on denial of reh'g, (Feb. 19, 1998).

[141] See RC 2935.032(C)(1), RC 2935.032(A)(2)(b), RC 2935.032(A)(3).

[142] Washburn v. City of Federal Way, 178 Wash. 2d 732, 310 P.3d 1275 (2013).

[143] Washburn v. City of Federal Way, 178 Wash. 2d 732, 741–742, 310 P.3d 1275, 1281 (2013).

In that the legislature has acted and required police officers to serve antiharassment orders as the default means of service, the municipality owes a duty to specific individuals and that this duty most not be discharged negligently. The City had a duty to act and this duty required the City to act in a reasonable manner. Hensing knew or should have known that Roznowski and Kim were both present in the home and that his service of the antiharassment order might trigger Kim to act violently.[144]

Of significance to Ohio and its statutory schema, police officers, or at the very least, sheriff deputies are entrusted with serving civil protection orders. Ohio's statutory schema also directs police officers to enforce the orders, including removal of the respondent from the premises. Should an officer or deputy who is designated to serve the order fails to remove the respondent from the premises and the petitioner is injured or killed, liability might attach.

§ 14:15 Potential police liability in the enforcement of protection orders

Q & A: Can a police officer arrest a defendant/respondent for violating a protection order, absent service of that order on the defendant/respondent? The Supreme Court decided one part of this concern. In *State v. Smith*,[1] the Court held that the state must prove, beyond a reasonable doubt, that a protection order has been served on a respondent in order to prove a criminal violation under RC 2919.27. However, *Smith* applies to an ex parte civil protection order and the enforceability of a civil protection order by police was arguably not contemplated.

In the domestic violence context, service on a respondent and the enforcement of a protection order become competing concerns that must be evaluated. On the one hand, an ex parte protection order must be served on a respondent before that respondent is weapons banned, before a full hearing on a CPO may be held and of course, before a court may convict a respondent for its violation.

In fact, due process dictates that a respondent be given notice and an opportunity to be heard before a full hearing order can be entered against him/her. A failure to serve the respondent results in a contin-

---

[144]Washburn v. City of Federal Way, 178 Wash. 2d 732, 762, 310 P.3d 1275, 1291 (2013).

[Section 14:15]

[1]State v. Smith, 136 Ohio St. 3d 1, 2013-Ohio-1698, 989 N.E.2d 972 (2013); see also Text § 13:3; Al-Lamadani v. Lang, 624 Fed. Appx. 405 (6th Cir. 2015) (noting that an individual cannot be in violation of a civil protection order when he has not yet been served with the order and that "service of process is fundamental to any procedural imposition on a named defendant" and where there is a question as to whether officer was aware that suspect had not yet been served with wife's protection order, "we conclude that there is evidence in the record upon which a reasonable jury could find that officer Lang lacked probable cause to seize Mr. Al-Lamadani." At *411; Murphy Bros., Inc. v. Michetti Pipe Stringing, Inc., 526 U.S. 344, 350, 119 S. Ct. 1322, 143 L. Ed. 2d 448, 43 Fed. R. Serv. 3d 1 (1999); citing Mayo v. Macomb County, 183 F.3d 554, 557, 1999 FED App. 0245P (6th Cir. 1999); Wiley v. Oberlin Police Dept., 330 Fed. Appx. 524, 528-29 (6th Cir. 2009) (both cases stand for the proposition that a "valid" protection order is one in which suspect had been previously served with the order; thus there was probable cause to arrest suspect).

uance of the full hearing, even though the ex parte order remains in effect. A failure to serve a respondent will eventually result in a dismissal of the CPO.[2]

On the other hand, a failure to enforce a protection order may subject a victim to future harm. The enforcement provisions of a protection order are designed to effectuate compliance with the terms of the order and to hold the abuser accountable for their actions should they not comply. To condition police enforcement of an ex parte protection order on service of the documents on a respondent frustrates the intent and purposes of the domestic violence statutes[3] which is to provide immediate legal protections from abusive acts.

A police officer may enforce an ex parte protection order by arresting the individual without having to first verify service of that order. For example, in *Alagha v. Cameron*,[4] the wife was granted a CPO which she showed to the officer when that officer was called to the scene. She informed the officer that her husband had violated the order. The officer called the sheriff's department to verify the validity of the protection order. After confirming its validity, the officer signed a complaint against appellant for violating the order. Thereafter, the officer obtained a written statement from the wife and subsequently arrested the husband.

Among appellant's arguments, he claimed that the officer never attempted to determine if the protection order had been served on him. Besides having probable cause to arrest, the appellate court noted that "[p]roof of service of the order is not essential in every case to obtain a conviction for violating the protection order under RC 2919. 27. Therefore, Officer Cameron did not have to verify that the order was served on *Alagha* to have probable cause to believe that he committed the offense."[5]

While the *Smith* holding provides that service is an essential element for a conviction for violating the order under RC 2919.27, it should not be a barrier to police enforcement.

Q & A: Is *State v. Smith* still applicable in light of the amendments to RC 2919.27?

Recently, the Ohio General Assembly enacted SB 7, effective September 27, 2017 which provides in part, "[i]n a prosecution for a violation of this section, it is not necessary for the prosecution to prove that the protection order or consent agreement was served on the defendant if the prosecution proves that the defendant was shown the protection order or consent agreement or a copy of either or a

[2]See Text § 11:11.

[3]RC 2919.26; RC 3113.31.

[4]Alagha v. Cameron, 2009-Ohio-4886, 2009 WL 2974892 (Ohio Ct. App. 1st Dist. Hamilton County 2009); see also Hunt v. Morrow County, Ohio, 2009-Ohio-4313, 2009 WL 2602204 (Ohio Ct. App. 5th Dist. Morrow County 2009) (where law enforcement officer attempted to verify service by contacting the prosecutor and the sheriff, and even though CPO had not been served on the appellant, officer exercised due care and appellant's claims for false arrest would not lie).

[5]But see State v. Smith, 136 Ohio St. 3d 1, 2013-Ohio-1698, 989 N.E.2d 972 (2013) (holding that the state must prove, beyond a reasonable doubt, that the CPO has been served on a respondent in order to prove a violation under RC 2919.27); Text § 13:3; Al-Lamadani v. Lang, 624 Fed. Appx. 405 (6th Cir. 2015).

judge, magistrate or law enforcement officer informed the defendant that a protection order or consent agreement had been issued, and proves that the defendant recklessly violated the terms of the order or consent agreement."[6]

Additionally, the notes indicate that "[t]he amendments made by this act to division (D) of section 2919.27 of the Revised Code are intended to supersede the holding of the Ohio Supreme Court in State v. Smith, 136 Ohio St. 3d 1, 2013-Ohio-1698, 989 N.E.2d 972 (2013), so that unperfected service of a protection order or consent agreement does not preclude a prosecution for a violation of division (A) of that section."

If law enforcement is to inform a defendant of the issuance of the order, the statute does not state that a copy of the order be provided to the defendant. However, under this framework, best practice would suggest that there must also be proof of service provided to the clerk of courts to indicate that a defendant has been so informed or said officer would be called upon to testify to this fact.

Q & A: What are the public policy concerns for officers who have to arrest offenders who have violated protection orders?

Law enforcement officials around the state have been reluctant to enforce protection orders that they are unable to specifically validate.[7] Law enforcement officers are fearful that they may be subject to false arrest and malicious prosecution claims even if they have a copy of a protection order that appears to be valid. This is of particular concern for officers who are called upon to enforce ex parte protection orders.

On June 26, 1997, the Ohio General Assembly passed 1997 Senate Bill 1, effective October 21, 1997. In order to reduce the reluctance of individual officers to enforce protection orders, RC 2935.032(F) now provides that

> a peace officer who [in good faith] arrests an offender for the offense of violating a protection order with respect to a protection order or consent agreement of this state or another state that on its face is valid is immune from liability in a civil action for damages for injury, death, or loss to person or property that allegedly was caused by or related to the arrest.

The adoption of RC 2935.032(F), the immunity provision for police officers in this state who enforce a facially valid protection order, should eliminate any reasons an officer might have for not enforcing the protection order. The legislature expects police officers to enforce all protection orders. To carry out the legislative intent, immunity was granted to officers who enforce facially valid orders of this or any other state.[8] No reciprocal immunity is accorded to officers who refuse to enforce protection orders no matter what the reason.

In effect, RC 2935.032(F) permits an officer who visually inspects a copy of a protection order to make an on-the-spot determination that the order is still valid for purposes of enforcement. If a police officer arrests an alleged respondent for a violation of a facially valid order,

---

[6]R.C. 2919.27(D).

[7]See, e.g., State v. Blaylock, 2000 WL 706797 (Ohio Ct. App. 2d Dist. Montgomery County 2000).

[8]See RC 2935.032(F).

the officer will enjoy good faith immunity even if the order is later found to be invalid.

A facially valid order is one that appears valid by looking at it. It may have the judge's signature affixed to it. It may or may not be a certified copy. A certified copy is signed by the judge and is stamped as an official order by the clerk of court. Unfortunately, RC 2935.032 fails to specifically define a "facially valid order." It is unclear from the statute whether the officer needs to see a certified copy or whether a copy of the order without the judge's signature is acceptable. Additionally, the statute is silent regarding whether an attempt to validate is a prerequisite to reliance on the immunity provision of RC 2935.032(F).

RC 2935.032(F) is important because it enables an officer to respond to an incident of domestic violence and/or a violation of a protection order and rely on the facially valid order for enforcement purposes. It is always preferable for the victim or the attorney to provide the law enforcement agency or the individual officer with a certified copy of the order. A certified copy of the protection order takes the guesswork out of the process and facilitates the officer's ready enforcement of the terms of the protection order.

Q & A: Does Ohio's statute contain any provisions that limit an officer's liability for arresting an alleged offender in a given situation?

Ohio's statute contains a provision permitting a police officer to arrest an offender if the officer is presented with a "facially valid" protection order.[9] There is no prerequisite that the protection order be served on the respondent before an officer may enforce it.[10] Inclusion of this provision in the statute reinforces the importance of police enforcement of a protection order, whether or not the order has been served on the respondent. Based on the recent statutory amendments, it is logical for police officials to enforce an ex parte protection order that appears facially valid or of which the officer knows the respondent has knowledge.

Inherent in this analysis is, however, a word of caution. The same legal reasoning that has been used to conclude that a respondent cannot be found guilty under RC 2919.27 or found in contempt under RC Chapter 2705 for violating an ex parte protection order of which he/she has no knowledge may be applied to police enforcement of a protection order.[11] Absent either notice or service of the ex parte order, a respondent presumably has no knowledge of its terms. It is arguably a

[9]RC 2935.032(F); see also State v. Blaylock, 2000 WL 706797, *3 (Ohio Ct. App. 2d Dist. Montgomery County 2000) (court "recognized that police departments that are required to enforce protection orders must be able to rely upon their validity until they are found otherwise by a court of law," quoting City of Xenia v. Berry, 1994 WL 12494 (Ohio Ct. App. 2d Dist. Greene County 1994)).

[10]See Alagha v. Cameron, 2009-Ohio-4886, 2009 WL 2974892 (Ohio Ct. App. 1st Dist. Hamilton County 2009) (holding that a police officer need not verify with defendant that the order was served to have probable cause to believe that he had committed the offense of violating the protection order), citing State v. Rutherford, 2009-Ohio-2071, 2009 WL 1175050 (Ohio Ct. App. 2d Dist. Champaign County 2009) (stressing that RC 2919.27 does not make service of a civil protection order an element of the offense of violating the protection order).

[11]See Text Ch. 13, Court Enforcement of Civil Protection Orders and Related Is-

denial of due process for police to arrest a person who has no knowledge of the proscribed conduct and no intent to defy the order.

Unfortunately, there are no reported cases that have addressed the specific issue of whether a police officer would enjoy qualified immunity for either failing to enforce an ex parte protection order or arresting a respondent when the officer knows the respondent is not aware of the terms of the order. It is probable that a court would not find an officer liable for failing to enforce an ex parte protection order where it can be demonstrated that the officer knew that the respondent was unaware of the terms of the order.[12]

Similarly, it is doubtful that an officer would be found liable for enforcing an ex parte civil protection order where the officer was unable to verify service on the respondent.[13] This is especially true where the officer attempts to verify the existence of the protection order pursuant to standard procedure before making an arrest.[14]

However, if it can be shown that the officer had specific knowledge that the respondent did not know of the terms of the order and intentionally arrested the respondent, such conduct may suggest that the officer's actions were outside the scope of his/her employment. In that situation, an officer's actions may provide a legal basis for concluding that the officer acted in bad faith or performed his/her duties in a reckless manner.[15]

Q & A: What is proper police procedure for enforcement of an ex parte protection order?

Both the legislature, in enacting RC 3113.31 and RC 2919.25, and the Ohio Supreme Court, in its holding in *Felton v. Felton*,[16] sanctioned the use of ex parte protection orders to protect victims of domestic violence and offer them immediate relief. The *Felton* Court cited the immediacy and severity of the consequences for violating the order. For example, the police are authorized to immediately arrest a violator of a protection order without a warrant.[17] Criminal prosecution may be brought against the perpetrator. Finally, the police have the ability to provide twenty-four-hour enforcement of the order. Each of these examples reinforces a policy of enforcement on the issuance of the order.

Because the domestic violence statutes are silent and there is no reported Ohio case law that details when the police may arrest for a violation of a protection order, police have pursued various courses of

---

sues, for a discussion of court enforcement of protection orders; see also Text Ch. 11, Issuance of a Civil Protection Order; see also Midland Steel Prods. Co. v. U.A.W. Local 486, 61 Ohio St. 3d 121, 573 N.E.2d 98 (1991).

[12]But see State v. Palacios, 1995 WL 434379 (Ohio Ct. App. 9th Dist. Lorain County 1995) (police enforced a protection order and arrested the defendant in spite of the uncertain existence of the protection order).

[13]See RC 2935.032(F).

[14]See Allen v. McCoy, 1991 WL 54189 (Ohio Ct. App. 10th Dist. Franklin County 1991).

[15]See Allen v. McCoy, 1991 WL 54189 (Ohio Ct. App. 10th Dist. Franklin County 1991).

[16]Felton v. Felton, 79 Ohio St. 3d 34, 1997-Ohio-302, 679 N.E.2d 672 (1997).

[17]RC 2935.03.

action. In *Allen v. McCoy*,[18] the police officer attempted to verify the validity of the protection order with the court clerk before enforcement. In *City of Xenia v. Berry*,[19] the officer asked the offender if she had knowledge of the order prior to the arrest.

In any case, the officers responding to a call or incident of domestic violence or violating a protection order may still enforce the order after notifying the respondent of the order and handing him/her a copy of the order. In some jurisdictions, this has been considered adequate service of process.[20] In most Ohio jurisdictions, such notice does not comport with Civil Rule 4 service requirements. However, even in Ohio, some courts provide the petitioner with several copies of the civil protection order specifically so that the police can provide the respondent with a copy.[21] At the very least, it puts the respondent on notice that there is a civil protection order in existence and sets forth the terms of the order. Although no arrest may be made at this point, the police, after handing the respondent a copy of the order or posting it on the door, can enforce the order according to its terms (including arrest) should the respondent persist in disobeying the protection order.[22]

Q & A: What, if any, guidance do the civil and criminal rules of procedure provide?

Because RC 2919.26 and RC 3113.31 fail to offer a satisfactory answer regarding when to enforce a protection order, "the rules for criminal and civil procedure regarding notice, arrest and temporary restraining orders may shed additional light on constructing these limits."[23] In a criminal context, a person may be arrested if there is probable cause.[24] Neither service nor notice is a condition precedent to an arrest. In fact, a perpetrator may be arrested based on evidence presented to the court by a victim at an ex parte hearing.[25] If there is probable cause to make the arrest, the arrest should be a valid act of law enforcement.[26]

Under the legal analysis of *Midland Steel Products Co. v. Local*

[18]Allen v. McCoy, 1991 WL 54189 (Ohio Ct. App. 10th Dist. Franklin County 1991).

[19]City of Xenia v. Berry, 1994 WL 12494 (Ohio Ct. App. 2d Dist. Greene County 1994).

[20]Peter Finn & Sarah Colson, National Institute of Justice, Civil Protection Orders: Legislation, Current Court Practice and Enforcement 60 (1990).

[21]Such a procedure is followed in Montgomery County.

[22]See also Alagha v. Cameron, 2009-Ohio-4886, 2009 WL 2974892 (Ohio Ct. App. 1st Dist. Hamilton County 2009) (where police officer had probable cause to believe that an offense of violating the CPO was committed, the arrest of the defendant was correct procedure, even though verification of service of the order on the defendant was not made before the arrest took place).

[23]Laing P. Akers, Supreme Court Memorandum on Protection Orders (June 19, 1998).

[24]See RC 2935.03.

[25]See RC 2919.25; Laing P. Akers, Supreme Court Memorandum on Protection Orders (June 19, 1998).

[26]Laing P. Akers, Supreme Court Memorandum on Protection Orders (June 19, 1998).

486,[27] the Rules of Civil Procedure provide that temporary restraining orders may be issued ex parte if there is a risk of immediate loss/damage to property or injury to persons.[28] Pursuant to the Civil Rules, however, notice is a necessary precedent to enforcement.[29]

In domestic violence cases, immediacy of enforcement is often crucial to the outcome. It is arguable that, in light of the public policy concerns addressed in *Felton*, and because RC 3113.31(L) provides that a violation of a civil protection order may be a criminal act, a police officer should be permitted to arrest a violator of a civil protection order who does not have notice of the order.[30]

Q & A: Does the failure of a law enforcement agency to serve an ex parte protection order within 10 days of its issuance create a federal 1983 claim?

Not according to the Sixth Circuit Court of Appeals. In *Jones v. Union County, Tennessee*,[31] the ex-wife sued the county and sheriff's department under § 1983, alleging that her constitutional rights were violated when she was shot by her ex-husband after the sheriff's department failed to serve him with an ex parte order of protection. The district court granted summary judgment to the defendants and wife appealed.

The Sixth Circuit Court of Appeals affirmed the lower court and held that "[b]ecause DeShaney controls in this case, it is unnecessary to reach plaintiff's arguments about whether Union county exhibited deliberate indifference to the risk that Plaintiff would be harmed if the ex parte order of protection were not served before the rescheduled date of the hearing or whether its failure to serve the ex parte order caused her injuries. In any case, it is a matter of speculation as to whether timely service of the ex parte order of protection would have deterred Plaintiff's ex-husband, inasmuch as he was not deterred by the prospect of being charged with committing murder or attempted murder. As *DeShaney* clearly held, the state, as a general rule, cannot be held liable under the Due Process Clause for private acts of violence. Thus, echoing the sentiment expressed by the Supreme Court in *DeShaney* while we are moved by the natural desire not to leave Plaintiff without a legal remedy for her injuries, we regrettably conclude that the Constitution cannot provide her with any relief."[32]

The court held that, because she only complained that the sheriff's department failed to serve the ex parte protection order on her ex-

[27]Midland Steel Prods. Co. v. U.A.W. Local 486, 61 Ohio St. 3d 121, 573 N.E.2d 98 (1991).

[28]See Civ.R. 65; see also Laing P. Akers, Supreme Court Memorandum on Protection Orders (June 19, 1998).

[29]See also MacDonald v. State, 997 P.2d 1187 (Alaska Ct. App. 2000); Rush v. Rush, 1999 WL 1044482 (Ohio Ct. App. 8th Dist. Cuyahoga County 1999).

[30]See Laing P. Akers, Supreme Court Memorandum on Protection Orders (June 19, 1998). But see Rush v. Rush, 1999 WL 1044482 (Ohio Ct. App. 8th Dist. Cuyahoga County 1999); City of Columbus v. Patterson, 1982 WL 4556 (Ohio Ct. App. 10th Dist. Franklin County 1982).

[31]Jones v. Union County, TN, 296 F.3d 417, 2002 FED App. 0235P (6th Cir. 2002).

[32]Jones v. Union County, TN, 296 F.3d 417, 430-431, 2002 FED App. 0235P (6th Cir. 2002) (internal citations omitted).

husband in a timely manner, no special relationship was created and she was not denied her right to substantive due process. The court also reasoned that she had already obtained her order and was awaiting a hearing on the order when her ex-husband shot her. Therefore, the failure to serve that order did not deny her effective and meaningful access to the courts.

Q & A: Does the Smith holding apply to protection orders issued after a full hearing?

Unfortunately, it is unclear at this time. While Smith applied to an ex parte CPO, the Supreme Court of Ohio subsequently remanded *State v. Hall*[33] to the appellate court and instructed to address the issue of service of a full hearing CPO in light of the *Smith* analysis. The appellate court determined that the decision in *Smith* did not alter the previous decision in *Hall*.

What was not a part of either court's legal analysis was a discussion of Civ. R. 65.1(C)(3) (due to the fact that Civ. R. 65.1 was not in effect at that time), which provides that service of a protection order issued after a full hearing is accomplished in accordance with Civ. R. 5(B), which is by ordinary mail. The relevant civil rules indicate that service of a full hearing CPO is complete upon mailing. Completion of service is presumed when there is no return to the clerk of courts.

Q & A: Are police officers obligated to enforce a protection order resulting from a full hearing where the respondent has not been served of where the officer cannot verify service?

In the context of a full hearing CPO, the respondent already has adequate knowledge of the terms of a protection order that results from a full hearing. From that standpoint, the order issued after the full should be enforced by the police whether or not the order has been served and whether or not the police can verify service of the order. There is no question that the order is valid. The respondent has already been served with the ex parte order. In fact, the situation is similar to an uncontested divorce. The divorce is no less final and the terms of the divorce are no less enforceable because a defendant was not sent a copy of the final papers.

Another approach to this problem may be a recognition that a failure to enforce may result in the injury or death of the victim. Because victims depend on law enforcement for help, the failure to provide this help may cause significant damage to the individual victim and society at large.

Additionally, Civ. R. 65.1(C)(3) requires that "[a]fter service has been made in accordance with division (C)(2) of this rule, any additional service required to be made during the course of the proceedings on Respondent and, if applicable, on the parent, guardian, or legal custodian of Respondent, shall be made in accordance with the provisions of Civ.R. 5(B)," which provides that service is complete upon mailing and which is considered perfected by ordinary mail.

In that a respondent had already been served with the ex parte CPO, was aware of the date and time for the full hearing and may have participated in the hearing, the respondent should have known

[33]State v. Hall, 135 Ohio St. 3d 1456, 2013-Ohio-2285, 988 N.E.2d 576 (2013); see also Text § 13:3.

that a CPO could be issued against him or her and therefore, police officers should always enforce a CPO issued after a full hearing even if that officer might not be absolutely certain of proof of service of the full hearing order on respondent.

Q & A: How is police enforcement of a protection order affected by modification or termination of the order at the full hearing?

Whenever a protection order is modified or terminated[34] at the full hearing, it is important that the existence of the new order and its terms be communicated to the respondent. Since any new terms were not previously known to the respondent, a copy of the order should be served on the respondent. At the very least, a respondent should have knowledge of the new terms. Additionally, each time a protection order is modified, a new NCIC form must be generated detailing new terms or changes. It is important to note any new terms in field 8 of the NCIC form and comment when necessary to explain any modifications.[35]

An officer who chooses not to enforce an order after noting that the respondent was not served with the modified protection order would probably not be found liable for refusing to enforce it. However, the officer may put the respondent on notice of the terms of the order. At that point, any subsequent violations may result in the arrest of the respondent. Additionally, an officer may also enforce a modified protection order against a respondent without verifying service if the order is facially valid.[36] The officer should not be found liable for enforcing the order.[37]

If the protection order is dissolved or terminated after the full hearing, an entry detailing the dismissal should also be served on the respondent. A new NCIC form should be completed detailing that the protection order has been terminated or dismissed.[38] Should an officer enforce the order, he/she should not be found liable even if the order is later discovered to have been dismissed.[39] An officer should be able to rely on RC 2935.032(F) as a defense to enforcing a protection order that is later found to be invalid.

Q & A: An officer arrests an individual for violating a protection order, having first verified the existence of the order. The order is later determined to have been dismissed at the time of the arrest. Can the officer be found liable for false arrest?[40]

The Franklin County Court of Appeals considered this issue in *Allen v. McCoy*.[41] In that case, one of the parties obtained a civil protection order. Because the protection order was not served, the

---

[34]See RC 3113.31(E)(8).

[35]See also Text § 14:2, Ohio statutory procedure.

[36]See RC 2935.032(F).

[37]See RC 2935.032(F).

[38]See also Text § 14:2, Ohio statutory procedure, for further discussion.

[39]See Allen v. McCoy, 1991 WL 54189 (Ohio Ct. App. 10th Dist. Franklin County 1991).

[40]See also Text § 14:5, False arrest, warrantless arrests and searches, and weapons confiscation.

[41]Allen v. McCoy, 1991 WL 54189 (Ohio Ct. App. 10th Dist. Franklin County

court dismissed the order against the appellant. Another incident ensued, and the police were called out to enforce the protection order and remove the appellant from the home. The officers contacted the clerk of courts to verify the existence of the civil protection order. They were told that the protection order was valid. The appellant was subsequently arrested for refusing to vacate the premises. The charges against the appellant were dropped when it was discovered that the civil protection order had been dismissed prior to the arrest. The appellant filed an action against the officers alleging claims of false arrest and unlawful imprisonment.

The court of appeals reasoned that "[t]he officers on the scene viewed a signed Civil Protection Order and called to verify that it was still valid. Once learning that it was still valid, the officers proceeded to enforce the order. Thus, the officers' actions were based upon probable cause."[42] The court held that, even if their actions were negligent, sovereign immunity insulated the officers from liability.

It has been asserted by many that an officer has a duty to protect a person who perceives that his/her life is in danger and that the state has an interest in protecting its citizens from abuse. This reasoning illustrates why a court is reluctant to find the officer and the law enforcement agency liable for false arrest. Although an individual can always bring a civil action against a law enforcement agency, its officers, and the city alleging false arrest, *Allen* implies that an officer, acting in good faith and within the scope of his/her employment, would likely prevail in that type of lawsuit.

Q & A: Prior to enforcing a civil protection order, an officer contacts the clerk's office to validate the existence of the order. In reliance upon the clerk, the officer arrests the individual. The order is later found to be invalid. Can the clerk of courts be found liable for false arrest?

Not according to *Allen v. McCoy*.[43] In that case, the officers responded to a call requesting that the defendant be removed from the premises. The officers were told that defendant was in violation of a civil protection order. In compliance with standard procedure, the officers contacted the clerk of courts to verify the validity of the civil protection order. It was later discovered that the protection order had been dismissed prior to the defendant's arrest. The officers were sued for false arrest.

The Franklin County Court of Appeals determined that the clerk of courts either failed to properly record the dismissal or negligently informed the officer that the protection order was still valid. Although the clerk of courts was not sued, the court's legal analysis is of importance. The court reasoned that

> [t]here are no facts that allege that the actions of the clerk or the officers were outside the scope of their employment or that their actions support

---

1991); see also Alagha v. Cameron, 2009-Ohio-4886, 2009 WL 2974892 (Ohio Ct. App. 1st Dist. Hamilton County 2009).

[42] Allen v. McCoy, 1991 WL 54189, *1 (Ohio Ct. App. 10th Dist. Franklin County 1991).

[43] Allen v. McCoy, 1991 WL 54189 (Ohio Ct. App. 10th Dist. Franklin County 1991).

a legal basis for malicious purpose, bad faith, or performance of their duties in a wanton or reckless manner. Consequently, even if their actions were negligent, they are protected under the guise of sovereign immunity.[44]

This case illustrates the wide range of immunity afforded to municipalities and their employees. The language also reinforces the legal rationale in the body of law developed in failure-to-protect cases, pursuant to which courts have explored the circumstances under which governmental entities may be liable for civil rights violations.

§ 14:16 Enforcement of protection orders issued by the courts of Ohio[1]

Q & A: Must law enforcement agencies enforce all protection orders issued in the state even if the order is not registered in the county in which it is to be enforced?

Yes. RC 3113.31 specifically states that all civil protection orders issued within the state are enforceable throughout the state of Ohio.[2] Additionally, the statute provides for enforcement regardless of whether the petitioner has registered the protection order or consent agreement in the county in which the officer's agency has jurisdiction.[3]

Only out-of-county civil protection orders issued under RC 3113.31 and criminal protection orders issued under RC 2919.26 and out-of-state protection orders are subject to the statute's registration procedures.[4] RC 3113.31 does not contemplate the registration of protection orders issued by different municipalities within a single county. However, the Ohio legislature has clearly manifested its intent for law enforcement agencies to enforce all protection orders issued by any court in this state.[5]

Q & A: What is the procedure for registering protection orders issued by an Ohio court?

RC 3113.31(N) empowers a petitioner to register a protection order or consent agreement in a county other than the county in which the court that issued the order or approved the agreement is located.[6]

A petitioner who obtains either a civil or criminal protection order may provide notice of the issuance or approval of the order or the termination or modification of the order[7] to the judicial and law enforcement officials in any county other than the county issuing the order or in which the order or agreement is modified or terminated

---

[44]Allen v. McCoy, 1991 WL 54189, *1 (Ohio Ct. App. 10th Dist. Franklin County 1991).

[Section 14:16]

[1]See generally Text § 12:28, Enforcement of civil protection orders. See also R.C. 3113.31(J), eff. 9/17/2014 (providing that no fees or costs may be assessed to a petitioner for the enforcement of a CPO).

[2]RC 3113.31(F)(3).

[3]RC 3113.31(F)(3).

[4]See RC 3113.31(N), RC 2919.272.

[5]RC 3113.31(F)(3), RC 2919.26.

[6]RC 3113.31(N)(2).

[7]RC 3113.31(E)(8)(d).

under RC 3113.31(E)(8)(d).[8] Registering the order or consent agreement in the other county and filing a copy of the registered order with a law enforcement agency in that county are sufficient to provide notice to the judicial and law enforcement officials in that county.[9] The petitioner may also file a copy of the registered order or consent agreement with a law enforcement agency of the other county.[10]

A petitioner who wishes to register a protection order or consent agreement may do so by complying with RC 3113.31(N)(2) which provides that:

(1) The petitioner is required to obtain a certified copy of the order from the clerk of the court that issued the order.[11]

(2) The petitioner is to present the certified copy of the order to the clerk of common pleas court for orders issued under RC 3113.31 or the clerk of the municipal court for orders issued under RC 2919.26 in the county in which the order is to be registered.[12]

(3) Upon accepting the certified copy of the order or agreement for registration, the clerk of court shall place an endorsement of registration on the order or agreement and give the petitioner a copy of the order or agreement that bears an endorsement of registration.[13]

(4) The clerk of each common pleas and municipal court shall maintain a registry of certified copies of protection orders and consent agreements that have been issued or approved by courts in other counties and have been registered with the clerk.[14]

It has been suggested that the underlying purpose for the registration of a protection order in another county is to make it easier for police officials to accurately determine whether an order is in existence in any given jurisdiction in order to enforce it. The endorsement of registration is convincing evidence of the existence of the order at a certain date and time. The actual order provides the law enforcement agency with the terms to be enforced.

Police officials are more likely to enforce a protection order that bears an endorsement of registration from the local county even when they are unable to verify the validity of the order. Since county and municipal clerks are required to maintain an index of registered orders[15] and since all orders accepted for registration have arguably been verified by the clerk, it is more likely than not that a police call to the local clerk of court will yield accurate information if the order has been registered.

Q & A: Do all Ohio jurisdictions utilize the same procedures for the registration of protection orders?

There are no mandated statutory procedures for the registration of

[8] RC 3113.31(N)(1).

[9] RC 3113.31(N)(1).

[10] RC 3113.31(N)(1).

[11] RC 3113.31(N)(2)(a).

[12] RC 3113.31(N)(2)(a).

[13] RC 3113.31(N)(2)(b).

[14] RC 3113.31(N)(3).

[15] RC 3113.31(N)(3).

orders issued within a specific county. The procedures for the registration of civil protection orders issued by different municipalities within a single county are as diverse as the various court jurisdictions. However, many counties utilize a system similar to that set forth in the statute for the registration of out-of-county protection orders.[16]

Some local jurisdictions have developed procedures to both register and verify the validity of the orders. For example, Hamilton County Domestic Relations Court utilizes the Central Warrant Unit to index and register all civil protection orders issued within the county. This process enables police officers to verify orders twenty-four hours a day.

On the other hand, Cuyahoga County has no procedures to register civil protection orders that are issued by courts within the county. Nor does Cuyahoga County have a countywide system in place for law enforcement officials to verify the validity of civil protection orders on a twenty-four-hour basis. However, the city of Cleveland has a Central Warrant Unit which indexes all criminal orders issued within the city limits.

Until there exists either a statewide or countywide protection order registry that enables law enforcement officials to verify the existence and validity of orders twenty-four hours a day and the clerks of court to input and delete information relative to protection orders, police officials will remain uncertain about the validity of the orders they are called upon to enforce.

Q & A: What happens if the petitioner who wishes to register the order is indigent and cannot afford the cost of the certified copies?

RC 3113.31(N)(4) was recently repealed by 2003 H.B. 548, effective on March 31, 2003.

The clerk of courts is now directed to waive any fees associated with the registration of the protection order or consent agreement. Whether a petitioner is indigent or not, no court or unit of government including the Clerk of Courts shall charge any fee, cost, deposit or money in connection with the filing of a petition or in connection with the filing, issuance, registration, modification, enforcement, dismissal, withdrawal or service of a protection order or consent agreement or a witness subpoena or for obtaining a certified copy of a protection order or consent agreement.[17] No longer must a petitioner prove indigency.

§ 14:17 Enforcement of out-of-state protection orders[1]

Q & A: Are Ohio law enforcement agencies and courts

[16]RC 3113.31(N)(1) to RC 3113.31(N)(3); RC 3113.31(N)(4) was repealed by 2002 H 548, eff. 3-31-03; see also amended RC 3113.31(J).

[17]RC 3113.31(J)(1), eff. 9/17/2014.

[Section 14:17]

[1]See Text § 12:28, Enforcement of civil protection orders; Text § 18:9, Other remedies under VAWA; see also Md. Op. Att'y Gen. 00-009 (4-11-00), 2000 WL 472838 ; State v. Haney, 197 Ohio App. 3d 152, 2011-Ohio-6023, 966 N.E.2d 921 (12th Dist. Clinton County 2011) (a person in Ohio may commit a violation of a Kentucky civil protection order if the protection order actually contained terms prohibiting firearms possession; warning and precatory language are not sufficient to demonstrate that the ban was incorporated into the protection order itself).

required to enforce protection orders issued by the courts of other states?

Yes. All state and Indian tribal courts must afford full faith and credit to orders of protection issued by all other state and tribal courts and must enforce those orders as if they were the order of the enforcing state or tribe.[2] The full faith and credit mandate applies to both civil and criminal protection orders.[3]

Ohio's domestic violence statutes were recently amended to establish procedures for putting into effect the mandate of VAWA. Protection orders issued by another state are accorded full faith and credit in Ohio and are to be enforced by courts and police officers in accordance with the terms of the orders.[4]

An out-of-state protection order shall be recognized and enforced by all courts and law enforcement agencies in Ohio[5] if the courts and law enforcement agencies have first ascertained that the following due process requirements have been met:

(1) The issuing state or tribal court has jurisdiction over the parties and the subject matter under the laws of that state or tribe.[6]

(2) Reasonable notice and an opportunity to be heard was given to the party against whom the order was sought in the issuing court's jurisdiction sufficient to protect that person's due process rights.[7]

(3) In the case of an ex parte protection order, notice and an opportunity to be heard was provided within the time required by the law of the issuing court's jurisdiction and, in any event, within a reasonable time after the order was issued sufficient to protect the person's due process rights.[8]

(4) In the case of a mutual protection order, there is interstate enforcement only if a counterpetition seeking a protection order was filed and resulted in specific findings by the court that each party was entitled to such an order.[9]

---

[2]See 18 U.S.C.A. § 2265(a); see also People v. Hadley, 172 Misc. 2d 697, 658 N.Y.S.2d 814 (N.Y. City Crim. Ct. 1997) (ruling that New York must use its own penal law to charge a man with criminal contempt for violating a New Jersey protection order in New York).

[3]18 U.S.C.A. § 2266; see also RC 2919.27(D) for a definition of "protection order issued by a court of another state."

[4]See RC 2919.27(A)(3); see also RC 2919.272(D).

[5]See RC 1901.18(A)(9), RC 1901.19(A)(6), RC 2919.272(D) for authority to enforce out-of-state protection orders.

[6]18 U.S.C.A. § 2265(b)(1).

[7]18 U.S.C.A. § 2265(b)(2); see also People v. Hadley, 172 Misc. 2d 697, 658 N.Y.S.2d 814 (N.Y. City Crim. Ct. 1997) (determining that to accord out-of-state protection order full faith and credit in enforcing state, party seeking to enforce order must establish that defendant was afforded due process before the order was issued and was given reasonable opportunity to be heard in conformity with law of issuing state and consistent with due process).

[8]18 U.S.C.A. § 2265(b)(2).

[9]18 U.S.C.A. § 2265(c); see also Text § 12:29, Mutual protection orders, for an in-depth discussion of mutual protection orders.

Q & A: What procedures are in place for the registration of out-of-state protection orders?[10]

Pursuant to RC 2919.272, a person who obtains a protection order issued by a court of another state may register the order in any county of this state. RC 2919.27(D) defines an out-of-state protection order as a civil or criminal protection order similar to those issued under RC 3113.31 and RC 2919.26 respectively.

The person who intends to register an out-of-state protection order must first obtain a certified copy of the out-of-state order and present it to the clerk of the municipal court or common pleas court in the Ohio county in which the order is to be registered. The clerk is required to place an endorsement of registration on the order. A copy of the registered order is then given to the person, and the person may then file the order with a law enforcement agency in that county.[11]

The clerk of courts is required to maintain a registry of certified copies of out-of-state protection orders.[12] Additionally, the local law enforcement agency is expected to maintain a registry for protection orders delivered to that agency.[13] The local law enforcement agency is to note in the registry the date and time that the agency received the order.[14]

The law enforcement agency that is called upon to enforce an out-of-state protection order is required to enforce the order according to its terms. A law enforcement officer shall enforce a foreign order, regardless of whether the order is registered in the county in which the officer's agency has jurisdiction.[15]

RC 3113.31(N)(1) specifies that notice of an out-of-state protection order may be provided to the judicial and law enforcement officials in any county in this state by registering the order in that county in accordance with RC 2919.272. The provisions for the registration of out-of-state protection orders mirror the registration procedures for the registration of protection orders issued in counties within the state.[16]

Q & A: Under which state's laws should a protection order be enforced?[17]

It depends on the nature of the provision of the protection order. The material provisions of the out-of-state protection order must be enforced as defined in the protection order, even if the enforcing court's protection order statute does not contain the same provisions. A material provision is one that relates to the substance of the order and its

[10]See also Text § 11:11, Ex parte protection orders—Service and notice provisions; Text § 12:28, Enforcement of civil protection orders. See Smith v. Smith, 2013-Ohio-3551, 2013 WL 4401326 (Ohio Ct. App. 5th Dist. Muskingum County 2013) (registering a foreign petition for domestic violence and ex parte civil protection order as a foreign judgment).

[11]RC 2919.272(B).

[12]RC 2919.272(C).

[13]RC 2919.272(C).

[14]RC 2919.272(C).

[15]RC 2919.272(D).

[16]See RC 3113.31(N).

[17]See also Tim Lininger, Evidentiary Issues in Federal Prosecutions of Violence Against Women, 36 Ind. L. Rev. 687 (2003).

terms, rather than to its form. For example, a foreign protection order is in force for the time period specified by the issuing state.[18] If the out-of-state order is effective for one year in the issuing state, Ohio courts and law enforcement agencies can only enforce the order during the one-year period even though an Ohio protection order may be effective for five years.

Additionally, the enforcing court must enforce an out-of-state protection order even if the persons protected by the order would not qualify for relief under the laws of the enforcing state or the type of relief provided would not be available under the enforcing state's laws. For example, some states have statutes that protect persons who are dating or who have an intimate relationship. Even though these classes of individuals are not included under RC 2919.25 or RC 3113.31, Ohio courts and police officers must enforce such out-of-state orders according to their terms. Similarly, if an out-of-state protection order grants the use of an automobile and that remedy is not available in the enforcing court, the enforcing court must still enforce the out-of-state protection order according to its terms. An Ohio court may not expand an out-of-state order to include remedies available in Ohio but not in the issuing state.

On the other hand, the law of the enforcing court's jurisdiction determines the applicable procedures and remedies if the out-of-state order is violated.[19] "For example, if mandatory arrest provisions and penalties apply to violations of protection orders issued in the enforcing jurisdiction, then mandatory arrest must occur if a foreign protection order is violated in the enforcing jurisdiction, regardless of whether or not the issuing jurisdiction has a comparable mandatory arrest law."[20]

Q & A: Should Ohio's law enforcement officials ever notify federal officials when there is a violation of a protection order?

Pursuant to RC 2935.032(G), each Ohio law enforcement agency or official that arrests an offender for an alleged incident of domestic violence or violating a protection order (either criminal or civil) is required to consider referring the case to federal authorities for prosecution under federal law if the incident constitutes a violation of VAWA.

Q & A: Should law enforcement officials enforce an out-of-state protection order even though they are unable to verify whether the order has been served on the respondent or whether the order is still in existence?

The American Bar Association has recommended that the issuing court provide an official form certifying compliance with service

---

[18]Barbara J. Hart, Lecture on Full Faith and Credit for Protection Orders and Federal Domestic Violence Crimes, National Conference on Domestic Violence, National College of District Attorneys 3 (October 9, 1995).

[19]See also People v. Hadley, 172 Misc. 2d 697, 658 N.Y.S.2d 814 (N.Y. City Crim. Ct. 1997) (ruling that New York must use its own penal law to charge a man with criminal contempt for violating a New Jersey protection order in New York).

[20]Stopping Violence Against Women Using New Federal Laws Study Guide, American Bar Association VideoLaw Seminars 27 (1996).

requirements.[21] Even without this certification, Ohio's law enforcement officials are immune from liability for enforcing a protection order that appears valid on its face.[22] This provision applies to out-of-state protection orders as well as to those issued by Ohio courts.

---

[21]Stopping Violence Against Women Using New Federal Laws Study Guide, American Bar Association VideoLaw Seminars 27 (1996).

[22]See RC 2935.032(F).

Chapter 15

Domestic Violence and Custody and Visitation Issues

KeyCite®: Cases and other legal materials listed in KeyCite Scope can be researched through the KeyCite service on Westlaw®. Use KeyCite to check citations for form, parallel references, prior and later history, and comprehensive citator information, including citations to other decisions and secondary materials.

§ 15:1 Introduction

Over the past decade, domestic violence and the increased frequency and severity of the violent acts of perpetrators against victims,[1] espe-

---

[Section 15:1]

[1]Mildred D. Pagelow, Justice for Victims of Spouse Abuse in Divorce and Child Custody Cases, 8 Violence and Victims 1, 69 (1993); Donald Dutton and Susan Painter, The Battered Women Syndrome: Effects of Severity & Intermittency of Abuse, 63

cially after separation,[2] have received increased public attention. Public awareness and community response have been focused primarily on preventing violence towards victims by enhancing victim safety and holding perpetrators of domestic violence accountable for their actions. This is evidenced by the nature and extent of the domestic violence laws enacted in Ohio and throughout the country.

Only recently have the children living within these violent families been considered to be victims of domestic violence. Children living in families where domestic violence occurs are victimized by being physically or sexually abused by the perpetrator[3] and/or by witnessing the abuse between their parents.[4] "Shelters for battered women and researchers across North America have tried to change these children's status from 'forgotten' to high risk children in need of protection and specialized support services."[5]

Understanding the interrelationship of custody and visitation issues within the context of domestic violence requires an in-depth understanding of the domestic violence laws. Civil protection orders may be requested for safety reasons.[6] Criminal domestic violence

---

American Journal of Orthopsychiatry 614, 614-622 (1993).

[2]See National Crime Statistics, U.S. Department of Justice, report on the Nation of Crime and Justice: The Data, Washington, D.C.: Government Printing Office (1983) (finding that, in almost 75% of reported spousal domestic violence cases, the partners were either divorced or separated); see also Martha R. Mahoney, Legal Images of Battered Women: Redefining the Issue of Separation, 90 Mich. L. Rev. 1 (1991); Heck v. Reed, 529 N.W.2d 155, 36 A.L.R.5th 849 (N.D. 1995) (incorporating the findings that domestic violence increases after separation). See also Barbara J. Hart, The Legal Road to Freedom (1991), available at http://www.mincava.umn.edu/hart/legalro.htm; Julie Kence Field, Screening for Domestic Violence: Meeting the Challenge of Identifying Domestic Relations Cases Involving Domestic Violence and Developing Strategies for Those Cases, Vol. 39, Issue 2, Court Rev. 4 (2002); Maureen Sheeran & Scott Hampton, Supervised Visitation in Cases of Domestic Violence, 50 Juv. & Fam. Ct. J. 13, 13-21 (1999) (explaining that abusers tend to escalate the violence to another, more dangerous level after the victim separates from the abuser).

[3]See Debra Whitcomb, Prosecutors, Kids, and Domestic Violence Cases, 36-OCT Prosecutor 32, 33 (2002) (noting that violence against women and children often coexist in families and that the rate of child abuse increases as the abuse towards the mother escalates in both frequency and severity); C. McGee, Childhood Experiences of Domestic Violence, 15.

[4]See Mildred D. Pagelow, Effects of Domestic Violence on Children and Their Consequences for Custody and Visitation Agreements, 7 Mediation Q. 348 (1990); see also Lee H. Bowker et al., On the Relationship Between Wife Beating and Child Abuse, in Feminist Perspectives on Wife Abuse 158, 164 (Kersti Yllo & Michelle Bograd eds., 1988); see also Lenore E. Walker, The Battered Woman Syndrome (1984).

[5]Peter G. Jaffe, Children of Domestic Violence: Special Challenges in Custody and Visitation Disputes, in Domestic Violence: Resolving Custody and Visitation Disputes, A National Judicial Curriculum 20 (1995) (citation omitted); Kernic, et al., Children in the Crossfire: Child Custody Determinations Among Couples with a History of Intimate Partner Violence, 11 Violence Against Women 991 (2005).

[6]See Text Ch. 11, Issuance of a Civil Protection Order; Text Ch. 12, Full Hearing on Civil Protection Orders, for a thorough discussion of civil protection orders; see also Victoria Holt, et al., Civil Protection Orders and Risk of Subsequent Police-Reported Violence, 288 J. Am. Med. Ass'n. 589 (August 7, 2002); Allie Meiers, Civil Orders of Protection: A Tool to Keep Children Safe, 19 J. Am. Acad. Matrim. Law. 373 (2005).

charges may be filed against the abuser because of an act of domestic violence.[7] Each of these legal actions impacts the familial relationship.

The complexities inherent in familial relationships also create competing policies for lawyers and judges and for parents.[8] Balancing these competing considerations becomes especially complicated in domestic violence cases in which there are also custody and visitation issues. For example, the victim of domestic violence may request that the abuser exercise only supervised visitation rights because of the presence of domestic violence in the family. The abuser, on the other hand, may demand custody or shared parenting as a way of maintaining control over the abused party, especially where there is sufficient evidence that he/she did not abuse the children[9]

§ 15:2 Custody and visitation issues; background information

Child custody and visitation statutes have undergone a complete metamorphosis over the past several decades.[1] The battle has been presented as a need to focus on the rights of children.[2] The premise that children should not be considered extensions of their parents is reflected in a change of terminology from "custody" and "visitation," which suggest ownership and privilege, to an "allocation of parental rights and responsibilities," which indicates a shift from possessing a child to parenting a child. It is also an attempt to remove any stigma attached to the noncustodial parent which can influence the resulting parenting roles.

No longer is either parent granted an automatic preference for custody. Maximization of parenting time with both parents is perceived as the most beneficial parenting arrangement for children. Recent court decisions across the country reflect these rather simple statutory modifications. Increasingly, fathers who petition the court for custody are being awarded full custody or joint custody.[3] More

---

[7]See Text Ch. 2, Criminal Domestic Violence in Ohio.

[8]See Clare Dalton, When Paradigms Collide: Protecting Battered Parents and their Children in the Family Court System, 37 Fam. & Conciliation Courts Rev. 273 (1999); see also Ellen K. Solender, Report on Miscommunication Problems Between the Family Courts & Domestic Violence Victims, 19 Women's Rts. L. Rep. 155 (1998).

[9]See, e.g., Julie Kunce Field & Karen Gulberg Cook, "But He Never Hit The Kids": Domestic Violence as Family Abuse, 73 Mich. B. J. 922 (1994).

[Section 15:2]

[1]See RC 3109.04, RC 3109.051. See also National Council of Juvenile and Family Court Judges, Family Violence in Child Custody Statutes: An Analysis of State Courts and Legal Practices, 29 Fam. L.Q. 197 (1995); Nancy Lemon, Custody and Visitation Trends in the United States in Domestic Violence Cases, 3 J. of Aggression, Maltreatment & Trauma 329-343 (2000).

[2]See, e.g., Angela C. Robinson, Protecting Children's Rights in Domestic Violence Cases, in Trial 20 (Family Law) August 1997; Leigh Goodmark, From Property to Personhood: What the Legal System Should Do for Children in Family Violence Cases, 102 W. Va. L. Rev. 237 (1999).

[3]See Ruth I. Abrams & John M. Greaney, Supreme Judicial Court of Massachusetts, Report of the Gender Bias Study of the Supreme Judicial Court 62–63 (1989) (citing similar findings from the entire United States); Lenore J. Weitzman & Ruth B. Dixon, Child Custody Awards: Legal Standards and Empirical Patterns for Child Custody, Support and Visitation After Divorce, 12 U.C. Davis L. Rev. 471,

court decisions are favoring parenting plans that maximize contact with both parents.[4]

Unfortunately, children do not hire lawyers, pay attorney fees, or lobby legislators. Vocal parents' rights groups have reframed the issues to be consistent with their own agendas. Increasingly, state and federal legislators have enacted legislation that is parents'-rights oriented rather than children's-rights oriented. Even the best-intentioned courts can only do so much for children given the focus of the laws with which they must work.

Q & A: What standard do courts use to make custody and visitation determinations?

In child custody awards, the primary objective of the court has been to grant both the possession of the child and the decisionmaking responsibilities to one or both of the parents by developing a parenting structure suitable for all involved. One of the parents can be awarded sole custody, or both parents may be awarded joint custody (now called shared parenting). Each state has incorporated a specific standard into its statutory scheme. This standard, often with a list of accompanying factors, is to be applied by the state's domestic relations courts in making custody determinations.

Over time, the "best interest of the child" standard has emerged as the foundation on which most parenting arrangements are designed.[5] However, the standard is vague. There is wide variation in court interpretations of this language, and even the statutory factors do not always provide guidance concerning the meaning of "best interest."

"The best interests of the child custody standard is crafted in gender-neutral terms to reflect demands for equal treatment made by feminists and fathers' groups."[6] In theory, this standard was adopted to demonstrate a deliberate shift from factors that automatically favor the parents to those that reflect the best interests of the child. In applying this standard, many state custody statutes have added other criteria to the best-interest test, such as more neutral factors like financial resources, a preference for joint custody, or a preference for a parent who is most likely to allow the child access to the other parent. Unfortunately, the relationship between the parents has

---

502–04 (1979); Joan Zorza, Protecting the Children in Custody Disputes When One Parent Abuses the Other, 29 Clearinghouse Rev. 1113 (1996); Nancy Polikoff, Why are Mothers Losing: A Brief Analysis of Criteria Used in Child Custody Determinations, 7 Women's Rts. L. Rep. 235, 236 (1983); see also Phyllis Chesler, Mothers on Trial: The Battle for Children and Custody (1986).

[4]Michael J. Voris, Civil Orders of Protection: Do They Protect Children, the Tag-along Victims of Domestic Violence? 17 Ohio N.U. L. Rev. 599, 608 (1991).

[5]See Lenore J. Weitzman & Ruth B. Dixon, Child Custody Awards: Legal Standards and Empirical Patterns for Child Custody, Support and Visitation After Divorce, 12 U.C. Davis L. Rev. 471, 503, 506, 509 (1979); see also Katherine Hunt Federle, Looking for Rights in All the Wrong Places: Resolving Custody Disputes in Divorce Proceedings, 15 Cardozo L. Rev. 1523 (1994); Phyllis T. Bookspan, From a Tender Years Presumption to a Primary Parent Presumption: Has Anything Really Changed? . . . Should It? 8 BYU J. Pub. L. 75 (1994).

[6]Developments in the Law: Legal Responses to Domestic Violence, 106 Harv. L. Rev. 1498, 1599 (1993).

become increasingly irrelevant.[7] Where the violent behavior of the parents has occurred outside the direct presence of the child or is unknown to the child, the parents' interaction is seldom even mentioned by the courts.[8]

Q & A: What factors are the most relevant in determining the best interest of the child?

Neither the courts nor the state legislatures are in agreement regarding which factors are the most relevant in determining "best interest" for an award of custody and visitation.[9] Clearly, the best-interest standard presupposes that the most significant and relevant factors are those that directly impact the child.[10] Obviously, the relationship between the child's parents affects the relationship the child has with each parent. Where the parents' relationship is abusive, it necessarily affects the child's relationship with his/her parents, each parent's relationship with the child, and the parents' relationship with each other.[11] Unlike many of the best-interest factors that only peripherally affect the child, domestic violence is one factor that directly impacts the child of the parties.[12] This is true whether the violence was directed at the child or at the other parent.[13] Since battering within the family affects the entire family unit, regardless of whether the violence occurred in the presence of the child, domestic violence is relevant to custody and visitation determinations.[14]

---

[7]Naomi R. Cahn, Civil Images of Battered Women: The Impact of Domestic Violence on Child Custody Decisions, 44 Vand. L. Rev. 1041, 1043, 1060 (1991).

[8]Developments in the Law: Legal Responses to Domestic Violence, 106 Harv. L. Rev. 1498, 1600 (1993).

[9]Amy B. Levin, Comment, Child Witnesses of Domestic Violence: How Should Judges Apply the Best Interests of the Child Standard in Custody and Visitation Cases Involving Domestic Violence? 47 UCLA L. Rev. 813 (2000).

[10]Naomi R. Cahn, Civil Images of Battered Women: The Impact of Domestic Violence on Child Custody Decisions, 44 Vand. L. Rev. 1041, 1042 (1991); see also Leslie D. Johnson, Caught in the Crossfire: Examining Legislation and Judicial Responses to the Forgotten Victims of Domestic Violence, 22 Law & Psych. Rev. — (1998).

[11]Naomi R. Cahn, Civil Images of Battered Women: The Impact of Domestic Violence on Child Custody Decisions, 44 Vand. L. Rev. 1041, 1049–58 (1991); see also Michael J. Voris, Civil Orders of Protection: Do They Protect Children, the Tag-along Victims of Domestic Violence? 17 Ohio N.U. L. Rev. 599, 605 (1991); Bonnie E. Rabin, Violence Against Mothers Equals Violence Against Children: Understanding the Connections, 58 Alb. L. Rev. 1109 (1995).

[12]See Howard A. Davidson, American Bar Association, A Report to the President of the American Bar Association, The Impact of Domestic Violence on Children (1994); see also Michael J. Voris, Civil Orders of Protection: Do They Protect Children, the Tag-along Victims of Domestic Violence? 17 Ohio N.U. L. Rev. 599, 605 (1991); Janice A. Drye, Symposium, The Silent Victims of Domestic Violence: Children Forgotten By the Judicial System, 34 Gonz. L. Rev. 229 (1998–99).

[13]Naomi R. Cahn, Civil Images of Battered Women: The Impact of Domestic Violence on Child Custody Decisions, 44 Vand. L. Rev. 1041 (1991); Peter G. Jaffe et al., Children of Battered Women (1990).

[14]See Massachusetts Continuing Legal Education, Child Custody and Domestic Violence: Strategy for Advocacy When Children Witness Violence (97-10.02) Library of Congress Card No. 96-77980; see also Mildred D. Pagelow, Children in Violent Families: Direct and Indirect Victims, in Young Children and Their Families (Shirley Hill & B.J. Barnes eds., 1982); Janet Johnston & Linda E.G. Campbell, Parent-Child

Therefore, evidence of domestic violence within the family should influence all custody and visitation decisions issued by the court.[15]

Statutory language adding domestic violence as a factor in custody and visitation determinations is still evolving. The impact of the recent statutes is difficult to assess because the legal system has been slow to recognize the detrimental impact of domestic violence on children. As more courts begin to both recognize the severity of the problem and consider domestic violence as a substantial best interest factor, there is an increased likelihood that credible evidence of domestic violence will be admitted at trial; and, since "[j]udicial opinions both reflect and advance social policies[, t]he court [and] the legal system can eventually make inroads against the social forces that condone abuse."[16]

§ 15:3 Battering; public policy considerations

The late 1980s saw a shift in the way society viewed battering and its effects on children. This change in focus was a direct result of an increased public awareness of violence in the home which led to a greater understanding of the battering experience and its impact on the child.[1] Breaking the cycle of violence is the ultimate societal goal. Integrating evidence of domestic violence into custody and visitation decision-making is the way to achieve this goal.

State legislatures and judges are being persuaded to conclude that domestic violence has a detrimental impact on the child.[2] Federal public policy statements have been issued directing state legislatures and state and local courts to both recognize the damaging effects of battering on children and prescribe ways to break the cycle of violence within the home.[3]

For example, in 1990, the United States House of Representatives and the United States Senate unanimously passed a joint resolution which provides in part: "It is the sense of the Congress that, for

---

Relationships in Domestic Violence Families Disputing Custody, 31 Fam. & Conciliation Cts. Rev. 285 (1993); Jack, Child Custody and Domestic Violence Allegations: New York's Approach to Custody Proceedings involving Intimate Partner Abuse, 5 Alb. Gov't. L. Rev. 885 (2012).

[15]Naomi R. Cahn, Civil Images of Battered Women: The Impact of Domestic Violence on Child Custody Decisions, 44 Vand. L. Rev. 1041, 1087–92 (1991); see also Philip C. Crosby, Custody of Vaughn: Emphasizing the Importance of Domestic Violence in Child Custody Cases, 72 B.U. L. Rev. 483 (1997).

[16]Michael J. Voris, Civil Orders of Protection: Do They Protect Children, the Tag-along Victims of Domestic Violence? 17 Ohio N.U. L. Rev. 599, 609 (1991).

[Section 15:3]

[1]See, e.g., Alan Tomkins et al., The Plight of Children Who Witness Women Battering: Psychological Knowledge & Policy Implications, 18 L. & Psychol. Rev. 137 (1994); Bancroft and Silverman, The Batterer as Parent: Addressing the Impact of Domestic Violence on Family Dynamics (Sage Publications 2002); see also Bailey, A Review of "The Batterer as a Parent" by Lundy Bancroft & Jay G. Silverman and "Why Does He Do That?" by Lundy Bancroft, 39 Fam. L. Q. 221 (Spring 2005).

[2]See also Pauline Quirion et al., Protecting Children Exposed to Domestic Violence in Contested Custody & Visitation Litigation, 6 B. U. Pub. Int. L. J. 501 (1997).

[3]See Susan L. Kerlitz, Domestic Violence & Child Custody Disputes: A Resource Handbook for Judges & Court Managers (Nat'l Ctr. for State Cts. 1997).

purposes of determining child custody, credible evidence of physical abuse of a spouse should create a statutory presumption that it is detrimental to the child to be placed in the custody of the abusive spouse."[4]

The United States Congress relied on certain fundamental principles advanced by domestic violence experts during the past decade to support its resolution. These include:

> that physical abuse of a spouse is relevant to child abuse in child custody disputes; that violent tendencies may be passed on from one generation to the next; that the effects of physical abuse of a spouse on children include actual and potential emotional and physical harm; that children are emotionally traumatized by witnessing physical abuse of a parent; that state courts have often failed to recognize the detrimental effects of having as a custodial parent an individual who physically abuses his or her spouse, insofar as the courts do not hear or weigh evidence of domestic violence in child custody litigation.[5]

Additionally, Congress noted that few states have recognized the interrelated nature of child custody and battering and have enacted legislation that allows or requires courts to consider evidence of physical abuse of a spouse in child custody cases.[6] Based on these principles, Congress determined that domestic violence has a detrimental impact on children.[7]

In the early 1990s, the National Council of Juvenile and Family Court Judges, with the assistance of legislators, the ABA, the AMA, and both prosecutors and defense counsel, developed a Model State Code on Domestic Violence ("Model Code"). The underlying purpose of the Model Code was to reduce family violence and ensure the safety of the victim and the children. The Model Code set forth certain presumptions concerning custody. Section 401 of the Model Code provides:

> In every proceeding where there is at issue a dispute as to the custody of a child, a determination by the court that domestic or family violence has occurred raises a rebuttable presumption that it is detrimental to the child and not in the best interest of the child to be placed in sole custody, joint custody or joint physical custody with the perpetrator of family violence.[8]

The commentary to this section indicates that this directive is applicable to civil protection order actions, divorces, and child protection cases.[9]

Similar provisions relating to visitation issues were addressed in both the Model Code and House Resolution 172 public policy

---

[4] H.R. Con. Res. 172 (1990), authored by Rep. Constance Morella.

[5] H.R. Con. Res. 172 §§ A-1, A-2.

[6] H.R. Con. Res. 172 § A-3.

[7] H.R. Con. Res. 172 § A-3.

[8] National Council of Juvenile & Family Court Judges, Model Code on Domestic and Family Violence, § 401 at 33 (1994); see also Lynne R. Kurtz, Protecting New York's Children: An Argument for the Creation of a Rebuttable Presumption Against Awarding a Spouse Abuser Custody of a Child, 60 Alb. L. Rev. 1345 (1997).

[9] National Council of Juvenile & Family Court Judges, Model Code on Domestic and Family Violence, § 401 at 33 (1994).

statements. For example, House Resolution 172 indicated that "this resolution was not intended to encourage states to prohibit supervised visitation." Inherent in that statement is that visitation between the abuser and the children should be supervised.[10]

The Model Code only provides that domestic violence must be considered in visitation determinations.[11] This provision neither directs a judge to summarily restrict an abuser's visitation nor limits a court's discretion in awarding visitation. The goal of a domestic relations court should be to analyze the evidence of domestic violence in the relationship and determine its impact on the parties' children.

In response to the growing awareness of the detrimental effect domestic violence has on children, policymakers and practitioners have begun designing interventions sufficient to address the nature and extent of the problem.[12] "Through cross-agency collaboration, innovative pilot programs are being implemented at various sites throughout the country to offer mental health services to children exposed to domestic violence and improve law enforcement responses to domestic violence incidences in which children are present."[13]

§ 15:4 General statutory and court trends

Prior to 1990, both legislatures and courts were reluctant to require that domestic violence influence child custody decisions.[1] Few statutes required courts to consider evidence of domestic violence. If considered at all, the weight accorded to evidence of domestic violence by the courts was insignificant. This was reflected in court records devoid of evidence of domestic violence. Even the process by which courts assessed domestic violence and its impact on children was inconsistent at best. Consequently, the violence perpetrated within the familial relationship was never regarded by the courts as a basis for preventing a parent from being granted custody or for awarding only supervised visitation to that parent.[2]

However, over the past 15 years, every state has enacted statutes

---

[10]H.R. Con. Res. 172 § A-3 (1990).

[11]National Council of Juvenile & Family Court Judges, Model Code on Domestic and Family Violence, § 402 at 33.

[12]Nancy Ver Steegh, The Silent Victims: Children and Domestic Violence, 26 Wm. Mitchell L. Rev. 775 (2000); Peter Jaffe & Robert Geffner, Child Custody Disputes and Domestic Violence: Critical Issues for Mental Health, Social Service and Legal Professionals in Children Exposed to Marital Violence: Theory, Research, and Applied Issues (George W. Holden, et al., eds. 1998); Laura McCloskey, et al., The Effects of Systemic Family Violence on Children's Mental Health, 66 Child Development 1239 (1995).

[13]Lucy Salcido Carter et al., Domestic Violence and Children: Analysis and Recommendations, 9 Future of Children 4, 5 (1999); see also Jeffrey Edleson & Susan Schechtor, Effective Intervention in Domestic Violence & Child Maltreatment Cases: Guidelines for Policy and Practice, Recommendations from the National Council of Juvenile & Family Court Judges Family Violence Dep't (1999); Lois A. Weithorn, Protecting Children from Exposure to Domestic Violence: The Use and Abuse of Child Maltreatment, 53 Hastings L.J. 1 (2001).

[Section 15:4]

[1]See Naomi R. Cahn, Civil Images of Battered Women: The Impact of Domestic Violence on Child Custody Decisions, 44 Vand. L. Rev. 1041, 1044 (1991).

[2]Amy B. Levin, Child Witnesses of Domestic Violence: How Should Judges

that specifically direct courts to evaluate evidence of domestic violence in the family before making custody or visitation decisions.[3] Domestic violence has emerged as one of the "best interest" factors in various state statutes.[4] The inclusion of domestic violence in state custody and visitation statutes has forced courts to recognize the detrimental impact of domestic violence on children[5] and consider this evidence at trial.[6]

Many state legislatures also require courts to include specific findings of fact in their decisions awarding custody or visitation to an abusive parent.[7] Some court decisions even require findings of fact detailing the effect of domestic violence on the child, as well as the appropriateness of the custody award.[8] These findings are essential to an appeal,[9] especially when credible evidence of domestic violence was presented to the court. Written findings of fact are often indicative of whether a judge considered and weighed the domestic violence in the relationship.

Although it is the responsibility of the court to make written, detailed, and specific findings of fact pursuant to RC 3109.04(C), the parties obviously have an interest in ensuring that they are accurate. If the findings appear to be deficient, the prevailing party should request that the court revise or supplement its findings. Because the prevailing party will have to defend these findings on appeal, it is

---

Apply the Best Interests of the Child Standard in Custody & Visitation Cases Involving Domestic Violence?, 47 UCLA L. Rev. 813 (2000); S. Doyne, et al., Custody Disputes Involving Domestic Violence: Making Children's Needs a Priority, 50 Juvenile and Family Court Journal 1, 1-12 (1999).

[3]See National Council of Juvenile and Family Court Judges, 10(1) Synergy 1, 10 (2006) (noting that every state now includes domestic violence as a factor or consideration for the court to consider in determining appropriated child custody arrangements). See also National Council of Juvenile & Family Court Judges, Family Violence in Child Custody Statutes: An Analysis of State Codes & Legal Practice, 29 Fam. L. Q. 197–225 (1995).

[4]See also Frederica Lehrman, Factoring Domestic Violence into Custody Cases, 32 Trial 34 (1996); Amy B. Levin, Child Witnesses of Domestic Violence: How Should Judges Apply the Best Interests of the Child Standard in Custody & Visitation Cases Involving Domestic Violence?, 47 UCLA L. Rev. 813 (2000).

[5]See generally, Amy B. Levin, Child Witnesses of Domestic Violence: How Should Judges Apply the Best Interests of the Child Standard in Custody & Visitation Cases Involving Domestic Violence?, 47 UCLA L. Rev. 813 (2000).

[6]See Naomi R. Cahn, Civil Images of Battered Women: The Impact of Domestic Violence on Child Custody Decisions, 44 Vand. L. Rev. 1041 (1991); see also Daniel G. Saunders, Child Custody Decisions in Families Experiencing Woman Abuse, 39 Social Work 51 (1994); C. Dalton, When Paradigms Collide: Protecting Battered Parents & Their Children in the Family Court System, 37 Fam. & Conciliation Cts. Rev. 273–90 (1999).

[7]See, e.g., RC 3109.04(C).

[8]See Custody of Vaughn, 422 Mass. 590, 664 N.E.2d 434 (1996); see also Newman v. Newman, 1996 WL 753202 (Ohio Ct. App. 5th Dist. Perry County 1996); In re Adoption of Zak, 87 Mass. App. Ct. 540, 32 N.E.3d 361 (2015) (it is well documented that witnessing domestic violence, as well as being one of the victims, has a profound impact on children).

[9]Newman v. Newman, 1996 WL 753202 (Ohio Ct. App. 5th Dist. Perry County 1996) (noting that the purpose of specific written findings of fact is to facilitate a reviewing court's consideration on appeal); see also Smith v. Smith, 2001 WL 542317 (Ohio Ct. App. 9th Dist. Wayne County 2001).

important that the findings comport with the factual basis of the case and are fully developed.

Q & A: Why should domestic violence be considered by the courts when making determinations of custody and/or visitation?

Very simply, because children are affected by the violence in their homes, even when it is not directed at them.[10] The detrimental impact on children exposed to domestic violence is significant whether the children are abused themselves or whether they witness the violence between their parents.[11] Lenore E. Walker, recognized by both academicians and the judicial system as a leading expert in the area of domestic violence, stated it well:

> children who live in a battering relationship experience the most insidious form of child abuse. Whether or not they are physically abused by either parent is less important than the psychological scars they bear from watching their fathers beat their mothers. They learn to become part of a dishonest conspiracy of silence. They learn to lie to prevent inappropriate behavior, and they learn to suspend fulfillment of their needs rather than risk another confrontation. . . . They do expend a lot of energy avoiding problems. They live in a world of make-believe.[12]

When children come from homes where domestic violence exists, they experience increased rates of school dropout, delinquency, teen crime, and teen suicide.[13]

In addition, the long-term effect of living with violence in the home is that the violence is often repeated by the children when they become

---

[10]Michael J. Voris, Civil Orders of Protection: Do They Protect Children, the Tag-along Victims of Domestic Violence? 17 Ohio N.U. L. Rev. 599, 609 (1991); see also Leslie D. Johnson, Caught in the Crossfire: Examining Legislative and Judicial Response to the Forgotten Victims of Domestic Violence, 22 Law & Psychol. Rev. 271 (1998); Marlene Rapkin, The Impact of Domestic Violence on Child Custody Decisions, 19 J. Juv. L. 404, 406 (1998) (asserting that children are harmed even if they didn't witness the violence).

[11]See National Center on Women and Family Law, The Effects of Woman Abuse on Children: Psychological and Legal Authority (1994); see also Peter G. Jaffe et al., Children of Battered Women (1990); Maura O'Keefe, Predictors of Child Abuse in Maritally Violent Families, 10 J. Interpersonal Violence 1, 3 (1995); Susan Schechter et al., Domestic Violence and Children: What Should the Courts Consider? 1 Juv. & Fam. Justice Today 4, 10 (1993).

[12]Lenore E. Walker, The Battered Woman 149–50 (1979); see also Jeffrey L. Edleson, Children's Witnessing of Adult Domestic Violence, 14 J. of Interpersonal Violence 839–70 (1999); Janis Wolak & David Finkelhor, Children Exposed to Partner Violence, in Partner Violence: A Comprehensive Review of 20 Years of Research (Sage Publications 1998).

[13]Commonwealth of Massachusetts, Department of Youth Services, Delinquent Youth and Family Violence: A Study of Abuse and Neglect in Homes of Serious Juvenile Offenders 17–18 (1985); see also Nechama Masliansky, Child Custody and Visitation Determinations When Domestic Violence Has Occurred, 30 Clearinghouse Rev. 275 (1996); Robert K. Ross, County of San Diego, Department of Health Services, Office of Violence and Injury Prevention, Report of the Suicide Homicide Audit Committee (1996) (finding the following risk factors: use of alcohol and other drugs, chronic school truancy, access to firearms, unhealthy interpersonal relationships, domestic violence, low self esteem, academic failure, poor school attachment, and poor family management).

adults.[14] These adults are much more likely to become violent with their own partners and children.[15] The cycle of violence continues for these children into adulthood because, the more they lived with violence as children, the more violence they will tolerate as adults.[16] Some studies even suggest that boys are more likely than girls to become violent as adults in their own homes.[17]

The fact that both adult domestic violence victims and perpetrators learned the behavior in their own homes of origin suggests that the perpetuation of domestic violence from generation to generation can only be stopped by societal action, especially by the judicial system. "The judge must take care to fashion a disposition which will protect all the family or household members."[18] The safety of the victim and other family members, particularly the children, should be one of the court's primary concerns. A judge who fails to consider the impact of domestic violence in all judicial rulings guarantees the continuation of the cycle of violence in the next generation.

As more statistical and empirical data is amassed by researchers regarding the adverse impact of domestic violence on children,[19] the relevance of domestic violence as a factor in the context of custody and visitation should become evident to courts.[20] The current research suggests "the urgent need for judges to become increasingly alert, forward looking, and involved, in order to break the cycle of violence

[14]See Ellen C. Herrenkohl et al., Perspectives on the Intergenerational Transmission of Abuse, in The Dark Side of Families: Current Family Violence Research 305, 306–16 (David Finkelhor & R. J. Gelles eds., 1983); see also M. A. Straus et al., Behind Closed Doors: Violence in the American Family (1980); D. Kalmuss, The Intergenerational Transmission of Marital Aggression, 46 J. Marriage & Fam. 11–19 (1984); Byron Egeland, A History of Abuse is a Major Risk Factor for Abusing the Next Generation, Current Controversies on Family Violence 197-208 (Richard J. Gelles, et al., eds. 1993).

[15]Del Martin, Battered Wives 23 (1976).

[16]Lenore E. Walker, The Battered Woman 146–47 (1979); see also Helen S. Pan et al., Predicting Mild & Severe Husband-to-Wife Physical Aggression, 62 J. Consulting Clin. Psychol. 975 (1994); Jennifer Langhinrichsen-Rohling et al., The Relationship Behavior Networks of Young Adults: A Test of the Intergenerational Transmission of Violence Hypothesis, 19 J. Fam. Violence 139 (2004).

[17]M. A. Straus et al., Behind Closed Doors: Violence in the American Family 16 (1980); see also Mildred D. Pagelow, Violence in Families: Is There an Intergenerational Transmission? (paper presented at annual meeting of Society for the Study of Social Problems 1982); Mildred D. Pagelow, The Cycle of Violence in Families: Fact or Fiction? (paper presented at Tenth World Congress of the Int'l Sociological Ass'n 1982).

[18]National Council of Juvenile & Family Court Judges, Family Violence: Improving Court Practice 19 (1990); see also G. Miller, Violence By & Against America's Children, 17 J. Juv. Just. 6 (1989) (noting that the most significant difference between delinquent and non-delinquent youth was the history of family violence or abuse).

[19]See, e.g., Ending the Cycle of Violence: Community Responses to Children of Battered Women (Einat Peled et al. eds., Sage Publications 1995); Janis Wolak & David Finkelhor, Children Exposed to Partner Violence, in Partner Violence: A Comprehensive Review of 20 Years of Research (Sage Publications 1998).

[20]See Marjory D. Fields, The Impact of Spouse Abuse on Children and Its Relevance in Custody and Visitation Decisions in New York State, 3 Cornell J.L. & Pub. Pol'y 221–52 (1994); see also Marlene Rapkin, Note: The Impact of Domestic Violence on Child Custody Decisions, 19 J. Juv. J. 404 (1998) (citing Domestic Violence Statistics, Pac. Bus. News, Nov. 17, 1997 (available in 1997 WL 15021813)).

and to protect the present and future welfare of the children."[21] Over the next decade, credible evidence of domestic violence and its effects on children should advance judicial decisions that prohibit an award of custody and shared parenting to abusers and craft visitation awards that reflect the safety of the children.[22] Moreover, judicial decisions should be written to demonstrate that violence in the home is not acceptable behavior.[23]

§ 15:5 Ohio's legislative response to domestic violence

Ohio is one of approximately thirty-four states to recently modify its custody and visitation statutes.[1] In April 1991, the Ohio legislature altered both the terminology and substance of the custody and visitation statutes.[2] For example, the terms "custody" and "visitation" were changed to "allocation of parental rights and responsibilities." The "custodial parent" became the "residential parent and legal custodian,"[3] and the "noncustod ial parent" became the "nonresidential parent."[4] Additionally, the term "shared parenting" replaced "joint custody." However, the enactment of 1990 Senate Bill 3 did not amend the Revised Code with regard to custody issues in juvenile court.[5] Juvenile courts still refer to awards of custody. For purposes of this treatise, the words "custody" and "visitation" shall be used because of their universal recognition by all professions.

The Ohio General Assembly expanded the "best interest" factors to include evidence of domestic violence.[6] In doing so, the legislature requires courts to consider evidence of domestic violence before awarding custody, visitation, or shared parenting.

Q & A: What specific evidence of domestic violence is required by the statute?

The evidence of domestic violence that the statute requires courts to consider when awarding custody and visitation is rather specific.

---

[21] Michael J. Voris, Civil Orders of Protection: Do They Protect Children, the Tag-along Victims of Domestic Violence? 17 Ohio N.U. L. Rev. 599, 607 (1991); see also Audrey E. Slone & Rebecca J. Fialk, Harvard Women's Law Journal: Criminalizing the Exposure of Children to Family Violence: Breaking the Cycle of Abuse, 33 PLI/NY 331 (1997).

[22] Naomi R. Cahn, Civil Images of Battered Women: The Impact of Domestic Violence on Child Custody Decisions, 44 Vand. L. Rev. 1041 (1991); see also Mildred D. Pagelow, Justice for Victims of Spouse Abuse in Divorce and Child Custody Cases, 8 Violence and Victims 69 (1993).

[23] Michael J. Voris, Civil Orders of Protection: Do They Protect Children, the Tag-along Victims of Domestic Violence? 17 Ohio N.U. L. Rev. 599, 609 (1991); see also Felton v. Felton, 79 Ohio St. 3d 34, 1997-Ohio-302, 679 N.E.2d 672 (1997).

[Section 15:5]

[1] See Merry Hofford et al., Family Violence in Child Custody Statutes: An Analysis of State Codes and Legal Practice, 29 Fam. L.Q. 2 (1995); see also RC 3109.04, RC 3109.051.

[2] See 1990 S.B. 3, eff. 4-11-91; see also RC 3109.04, RC 3109.051.

[3] See RC 3109.04(K)(1), RC 3109.04(K)(2).

[4] See RC 3109.04(K)(3), RC 3109.04(K)(4).

[5] See RC 2151.23.

[6] See RC 3109.04(F)(1)(h); see also RC 3109.04(F)(2)(c), RC 3109.051(D)(12); Am. Sub. 2007 S.B. 260, eff. 1-2-07.

Courts are mandated to consider only evidence of a conviction for domestic violence or another offense that causes physical harm to a family member.[7]

Specifically, the Ohio Revised Code provides that a conviction or plea of guilty by a parent for domestic violence under RC 2919.25, or for any offense involving a victim who was a member of the same family or household that is the subject of the current action if the victim was physically harmed in the commission of the offense,[8] is a factor that the courts are required to consider when determining the best interest of the child in an award of custody[9] or visitation.[10] Similarly, a court is required to consider evidence of a conviction for domestic violence when a modification of a child custody award is requested by one of the parties.[11]

When shared parenting is requested by one of the parties, the Ohio legislature has both permitted and required courts to consider evidence of domestic violence.[12] The legislature directs a court to consider all of the best-interest factors enumerated in RC 3109.04(F)(1), as well as those factors set forth in RC 3109.04(F)(2), including "any history of or potential for, child abuse, spouse abuse, other domestic violence, or parental kidnapping by either parent."[13] Evidence of a history or pattern of domestic violence is in addition to evidence of any conviction and must be considered by the courts, whether or not the parent was convicted of domestic violence pursuant to RC 2919.25.

In an effort to further reinforce that domestic violence has a detrimental impact on Ohio's children, the Ohio legislature recently amended several criminal statutes, including provisions of the sentencing statutes[14] to require the court to consider as an aggravating factor in determining the sentence of an offender convicted of domestic violence, felonious assault, aggravated assault, or assault that the offender committed the offense in the vicinity of the offender's or victim's child. Pursuant to amended RC 2929.01(NN), an offense is committed in the vicinity of a child if:

> the offender commits the offense within thirty feet of or within the same residential unit as a child who is under eighteen years of age, regardless of whether the offender knows the age of the child or whether the of-

[7]See RC 3109.04(F)(1)(h); see also RC 3109.051(D)(12).

[8]See Text Ch. 2, Criminal Domestic Violence in Ohio, for a discussion of acts that constitute domestic violence.

[9]RC 3109.04(F)(1)(h).

[10]See RC 3109.051(D)(12).

[11]See RC 3109.04(F)(1).

[12]RC 3109.04(F)(2).

[13]RC 3109.04(F)(2)(c). See also In re Marriage of C.M.C., 87 Wash. App. 84, 940 P.2d 669 (Div. 1 1997), reconsideration filed, (Aug. 11, 1997) and decision aff'd, 136 Wash. 2d 800, 966 P.2d 1247 (1998) (holding that joint parental decision-making is statutorily precluded upon finding a history of acts of domestic violence by one parent, regardless of whether those acts caused grievous bodily harm or fear of such harm).

[14]RC 2903.15(A), RC 2929.01, RC 2929.12, RC 2929.17, RC 2929.17(N), RC 2929. 22; see also Audrey E. Slone & Rebecca J. Fialk, Harvard Women's Law Journal: Criminalizing the Exposure of Children to Family Violence: Breaking the Cycle of Abuse, 33 PLI/NY 331 (1997).

fender knows the offense is being committed within thirty feet of or within the same residential unit as the child and regardless of whether the child actually views the commission of the offense.

The court should consider as a factor in felony sentencing whether the offender committed domestic violence or assault against a family or household member in the vicinity of one or more children who are not victims of the offense and the offender or victim is a parent, guardian, or person in loco parentis of one or more of the children.[15] When considering whether to impose a longer prison term against a misdemeanor offender, the court shall consider this factor in favor of imposing a longer term of imprisonment.[16]

If an offender is convicted of either felony or misdemeanor domestic violence or assault against a family or household member and there is a child in the vicinity, RC 2929.17(N) requires that the offender obtain counseling.[17]

In effect, committing domestic violence within sight or sound of one's children dictates whether the court is to consider the additional sentencing factors. It is hoped that the General Assembly will introduce legislation of similar importance directing domestic relations courts to consider whether domestic violence was committed in the presence of children and providing that witnessing domestic violence has a detrimental impact on children.[18]

§ 15:6 Ohio's judicial response to domestic violence

During the last 10 years, Ohio's courts have considered evidence of domestic violence in resolving both custody and visitation disputes. Besides evidence of a criminal conviction for domestic violence or another related offense, a court is not required to consider any other evidence of domestic violence in its custody and visitation determinations.[1] Neither a history or pattern of domestic violence nor the testimony of the victim, even when corroborated by police reports, medical records, or witnesses, are enumerated "best interest" factors that must be accorded weight by the courts. Nor is a court mandated to consider them before awarding custody or visitation.

However, RC 3109.04(F)(1) provides that a court may consider any and all relevant factors in determining the best interest of the child, which may include a history or pattern of domestic violence or the testimony of the victim, whether or not supported by other documentary evidence. Because the legislature did not limit the best-interest factors to those enumerated in RC 3109.04(F)(1), a court is permitted to consider any other relevant factors, including a history or pattern

---

[15] RC 2929.12(B)(9); see also RC 2929.22(B)(1)(c) for misdemeanor sentencing.

[16] See RC 2929.22(B)(2).

[17] See also RC 2951.02(C)(1)(ii) for misdemeanor sentencing.

[18] See also Howard Davidson, Child Protection Policy & Practice at Century's End, 33 Fam. L.Q. 777 (1999); J. Kolbo, et al., Children Who Witness Domestic Violence: A Review of Empirical Literature, 11 Journal of Interpersonal Violence 281 (1996).

[Section 15:6]

[1] See RC 3109.04(F)(1)(h); see also RC 3109.051(D)(12).

of domestic violence.[2] Therefore, the victim's attorney should always introduce credible evidence of domestic violence for the courts to consider in determining both custody and visitation matters. This should include evidence that the children saw, heard, or otherwise knew about the domestic violence.[3]

Q & A: What weight should courts accord to evidence of domestic violence for purposes of making a custody or visitation decision?[4]

Courts in Ohio[5] and elsewhere have discretion to decide what weight to accord to each best-interest factor, including domestic violence.[6] The absence of a set standard within which a court must evaluate the impact of a specific factor has created extreme differences in the way courts have handled evidence of domestic violence. "While it is important for trial courts to retain discretion to decide cases on the facts presented, there needs to be a standard indicating how domestic violence should affect the decision."[7]

Ohio's statutory scheme only provides that domestic violence be considered along with several other best-interest factors. Unfortunately, the statute fails to assign a specific weight to evidence of domestic violence.[8] No legislative guidance is provided to the courts for evaluating the relevant evidence, nor does a standard exist so that there is consistency in court decisions.

Various state court decisions reflect significant inconsistencies in the weight a court accords to evidence of domestic violence. For example, some courts have determined that domestic violence is not particularly relevant to custody and visitation matters and do not give it serious consideration.[9] Other courts have noted the domestic violence in their opinions but have based their decisions on various

[2]See also RC 3109.051(D)(15). See Rodriguez v. Rodriguez, 1999-Ohio-854, 1999 WL 692425 (Ohio Ct. App. 3d Dist. Hancock County 1999) (affirming denial of father's request for custody even though mother's boyfriend had two domestic violence convictions, noting that the evidence established that the incidents did not occur in the relationship with the mother).

[3]See Katherine M. Reihing, Protecting Victims of Domestic Violence & Their Children After Divorce: The American Law Institute's Model, 37 Fam. & Conciliation Cts. Rev. 393 (1999).

[4]See also Text § 15:12, Consideration of domestic violence as a best-interest factor—In custody decisions; recent case law.

[5]See, e.g., Holbrook v. Smith, 1999 WL 699876 (Ohio Ct. App. 12th Dist. Clermont County 1999) (according domestic violence significant weight in a modification of custody determination).

[6]See also Kim Susser, Weighing the Domestic Violence Factors in Custody Cases: Tipping the Scales in Favor of Protecting Victims & Their Children, 27 Fordham Urb. L. J. 875 (2000); Marlene Rapkin, The Impact of Domestic Violence on Child Custody Decisions, 19 J. Juv. L. 40 (1998).

[7]Naomi R. Cahn, Civil Images of Battered Women: The Impact of Domestic Violence on Child Custody Decisions, 44 Vand. L. Rev. 1041, 1072 (1991).

[8]See Seeling v. Seeling, 1999 WL 1270980 (Ohio Ct. App. 12th Dist. Warren County 1999).

[9]See, e.g., Collinsworth v. O'Connell, 508 So. 2d 744 (Fla. 1st DCA 1987).

other factors.[10] Still other courts have dismissed the domestic violence conviction as an "isolated act."[11]

Conversely, in other cases, domestic violence is accorded substantial weight and becomes the major factor in the court's decision.[12] Some courts even link evidence of domestic violence with creating an environment that endangers the child's physical health and mental, moral, or emotional development.[13] In still others cases, once domestic violence has been found, it is the controlling factor in determining the award of custody.[14] Some courts are even likely to advance social policy in their opinions.[15]

Generally, courts that have considered domestic violence have been influenced by a pattern or history of violence.[16] Where a history or pattern of domestic violence has been demonstrated and corroborated by independent evidence, courts are more likely to award custody to the nonabusive parent[17] and supervised visitation to the abusive parent.[18] Courts have also been influenced by the frequency and sever-

---

[10]See, e.g., Marshall v. Marshall, 117 Ohio App. 3d 182, 690 N.E.2d 68 (3d Dist. Allen County 1997); see also Horning v. Wolff, 2006-Ohio-6397, 2006 WL 3505864 (Ohio Ct. App. 5th Dist. Stark County 2006).

[11]See Boling v. Valecko, 2002-Ohio-449, 2002 WL 185182 (Ohio Ct. App. 9th Dist. Summit County 2002) (trial court dismissed the conviction for domestic violence as an isolated act without admitting evidence related to appellee's difficulty managing his anger and a history of an inability to control his anger with a former wife); see also Bland v. Bland, 2003-Ohio-828, 2003 WL 470180 (Ohio Ct. App. 9th Dist. Summit County 2003); Rodriguez v. Rodriguez, 1999-Ohio-854, 1999 WL 692425 (Ohio Ct. App. 3d Dist. Hancock County 1999) (noting that the convictions for domestic violence against mother's boyfriend did not occur in the relationship with the mother and thus, the court approved the denial of father's custody request).

[12]See, e.g., Alexander v. Oiler, 1997 WL 7166 (Ohio Ct. App. 2d Dist. Clark County 1997); see also Dodd v. Dodd, 2001 WL 812244 (Ohio Ct. App. 6th Dist. Lucas County 2001).

[13]See, e.g., Lee v. Lee, 1988 WL 85102 (Ohio Ct. App. 4th Dist. Washington County 1988); Bertram v. Kilian, 133 Wis. 2d 202, 394 N.W.2d 773 (Ct. App. 1986); see also Holbrook v. Smith, 1999 WL 699876 (Ohio Ct. App. 12th Dist. Clermont County 1999); Louderback v. Louderback, 1999 WL 94902 (Ohio Ct. App. 2d Dist. Montgomery County 1999) (appellant objected to the fact that trial court considered a domestic violence conviction as a factor in assessing the parties' mental health); Boling v. Valecko, 2002-Ohio-449, 2002 WL 185182 (Ohio Ct. App. 9th Dist. Summit County 2002) (trial court excluded evidence related to the appellant's conviction for domestic violence and mental state).

[14]See, e.g., Heck v. Reed, 529 N.W.2d 155, 36 A.L.R.5th 849 (N.D. 1995) (finding a statutory rebuttable presumption against awarding custody to the abuser).

[15]See, e.g., R.H. v. B.F., 39 Mass. App. Ct. 29, 653 N.E.2d 195 (1995), aff'd, 422 Mass. 590, 664 N.E.2d 434 (1996).

[16]See, e.g., Michelli v. Michelli, 655 So. 2d 1342, 1351 (La. Ct. App. 1st Cir. 1995) (defining a history of violence as "the consummation of more than one isolated act of anger") (Fitzsimmons, J., concurring); see also Huesers v. Huesers, 1998 ND 54, 574 N.W.2d 880 (N.D. 1998) (considering three incidents to constitute a pattern of domestic violence). But see Hamilton v. Hamilton, 886 S.W.2d 711 (Mo. Ct. App. W.D. 1994) (holding that two incidents of assault do not constitute a pattern of domestic violence). See also Text § 11:10, Ex parte protection orders—Legal standard for issuance, Text § 12:11, Standard of proof, and Text § 16:8, Documenting evidence of domestic violence.

[17]See, e.g., Dodd v. Dodd, 2001 WL 812244 (Ohio Ct. App. 6th Dist. Lucas County 2001).

[18]But see Neff v. Neff, 1998 WL 433846 (Ohio Ct. App. 8th Dist. Cuyahoga County

ity of the violence in the relationship[19] and the likelihood of future violence.[20]

Q & A: Does a conviction for domestic violence carry more weight than evidence of a history of violence in the relationship?

It depends. In some cases, a conviction for domestic violence is accorded as much or as little weight as the other factors under RC 3109.04(F)(1).[21]

More often, however, a conviction for domestic violence does influence a court's decision. This is especially important because the Revised Code specifically requires courts to consider whether a parent, or any member of the household of either parent has been convicted for domestic violence, or any sexually oriented offense or any other crime that has resulted in domestic violence against a family or household member.[22] For example, the Wayne County Court of Appeals determined that the trial court did not abuse its discretion in awarding a mother custody of the parties' children where the father had been convicted of domestic violence. In *Butzer v. Butzer*,[23] the trial court designated the mother as the residential parent and legal

1998) (according little weight to a history of domestic violence in a modification of visitation determination because of mutual allegations of abuse and because the violence was not committed against the children); see Bland v. Bland, 2003-Ohio-828, 2003 WL 470180,*12 (Ohio Ct. App. 9th Dist. Summit County 2003) (in which the Summit County appellate court affirmed the award of custody to the father even though he was charged once with domestic violence. "Although we believe that such an offense is intolerable, a single offense does not constitute a 'history' of domestic violence. In any event, the record reveals that the trial court considered father's domestic violence charge in determining whether a modification of the prior custody order was in the best interest of the children. The trial court explained that the domestic violence charge was in the past, and it was an isolated event that appeared to have been resolved."); Baker v. Baker, 2007-Ohio-7172, 2007 WL 4615953 (Ohio Ct. App. 4th Dist. Washington County 2007).

[19]See, e.g., In re Marriage of Forbes, 570 N.W.2d 757 (Iowa 1997); see also Joan Zorza, Protecting the Children in Custody Disputes When One Parent Abuses the Other, 29 Clearinghouse Rev. 1113, 1115 (1996).

[20]See, e.g., Brown v. Brown, 1993 OK CIV APP 142, 867 P.2d 477 (Ct. App. Div. 1 1993); see also Carla Garrity & Mitchell Baris, Custody and Visitation: Is it Safe? 17 Fam. Advoc. 40, 43 (1995); Holbrook v. Smith, 1999 WL 699876 (Ohio Ct. App. 12th Dist. Clermont County 1999) (upholding finding that man with whom appellant was living ha propensity for violence and that his behavior adversely impacted the children). But see Couch v. Couch, 978 S.W.2d 505 (Mo. Ct. App. W.D. 1998) (holding that husband's alleged propensity toward violence did not require court to enter written findings of fact and law).

[21]See State ex rel. Thompson v. Spon, 83 Ohio St. 3d 551, 1998-Ohio-298, 700 N.E.2d 1281 (1998) (upholding an award of custody to the parent convicted of domestic violence); Smith v. Smith, 2002-Ohio-223, 2002 WL 57973 (Ohio Ct. App. 9th Dist. Wayne County 2002); Hussein v. Hussein, 2005-Ohio-6399, 2005 WL 3249490 (Ohio Ct. App. 5th Dist. Morrow County 2005) (holding that trial court did not abuse its discretion in not using father's two-year-old domestic violence conviction as a determining factor in the custody determination). But see Morris v. Morris, 2000 WL 222025 (Ohio Ct. App. 5th Dist. Stark County 2000) (according substantial weight to father's domestic violence conviction and determining that, although he may be less likely to deny visitation, he was more likely to cause friction during exchanges of the child).

[22]See RC 3109.04(F)(1)(h). See also Am. Sub. 2007 S.B. 260, eff. 1-2-07.

[23]Butzer v. Butzer, 1998 WL 34615 (Ohio Ct. App. 9th Dist. Wayne County 1998).

custodian. On appeal, the father argued that the trial court had accorded too much weight to his one domestic violence conviction.

The appellate court provided a record replete with evidence justifying the trial court's decision and, therefore, found no abuse of discretion. The appeals court noted that, besides the conviction for domestic violence, the father had been convicted for disorderly conduct, which charge had been pled down from domestic violence.[24] These convictions, coupled with other evidence suggesting that the mother was the better parent, formed the basis of the trial court's conclusion.

While acknowledging that the trial court placed much importance on the domestic violence convictions, the Wayne County Court of Appeals did not indicate that domestic violence should be accorded more weight than the other "best interest" factors.[25] Evidence of both convictions and the fact that the assault had taken place in front of the children were crucial to the court's decision.[26]

Q & A: Is the court prohibited from awarding custody or shared parenting to a parent who has been convicted of domestic violence pursuant to RC 3109.04(F)(1)?

No. The statute explicitly permits an award of custody to an abuser, even if the evidence demonstrates that the parent was convicted of domestic violence or any other offense that caused physical harm to a family or household member.[27] When the court awards custody or visitation or determines whether to grant shared parenting in any proceeding, it must consider whether either parent or any member of the household of either parent[28] has been convicted of or pleaded guilty to a violation of RC 2919.25 or any sexually oriented offense,[29] or any other offense involving a victim who was a member of the family or household that is the subject of the proceeding and caused physical harm to the victim in the commission of the offense.[30] The court may designate that parent as the custodial parent and/or issue a shared parenting decree *only if* it determines that it is in the best interest of the child *and* it makes specific written findings of fact to support its determination.[31]

---

[24]But see Prusia v. Prusia, 2003-Ohio-2000, 2003 WL 1904410 (Ohio Ct. App. 6th Dist. Lucas County 2003) (father's plea to disorderly conduct did not bar his designation as residential parent and legal custodian).

[25]See RC 3109.04(F)(1).

[26]But see Schmidt v. Schmidt, 1999 WL 225157 (Ohio Ct. App. 12th Dist. Clermont County 1999) (affirming shared parenting and finding that, although appellee pleaded no contest to domestic violence charge involving appellant, there was no evidence that he presented a physical threat to the children); Smith v. Smith, 2002-Ohio-223, 2002 WL 57973 (Ohio Ct. App. 9th Dist. Wayne County 2002).

[27]See RC 3109.04(F)(1)(h); see also RC 3109.04(C), RC 3109.04(F)(2)(c); State ex rel. Thompson v. Spon, 83 Ohio St. 3d 551, 1998-Ohio-298, 700 N.E.2d 1281 (1998) (upholding award of custody to parent convicted of domestic violence); Schmidt v. Schmidt, 1999 WL 225157 (Ohio Ct. App. 12th Dist. Clermont County 1999). But see Moneypenny v. Moneypenny, 2001 WL 39602 (Ohio Ct. App. 9th Dist. Medina County 2001).

[28]Am. Sub. 2007 S.B. 260, eff. 1-2-07.

[29]Am. Sub. 2007 S.B. 260, eff. 1-2-07.

[30]RC 3109.04(C).

[31]RC 3109.04(C).

These requirements are reinforced by the term "shall" which has been defined as "establish[ing] a mandatory duty, absent a clear and unequivocal intent that it receive a construction other than its ordinary meaning."[32] Similarly, the use of the condition precedent "only if" clearly requires that, before it awards custody to a convicted abuser, a court must determine that it is in the best interest of the child and make written findings of fact to support its determination.

Where RC 3109.04(F)(1)(h) sets forth the best-interest factors, including a conviction for domestic violence or any sexually oriented offense,[33] RC 3109.04(C) provides procedures with which the court must comply if it determines that a parent has been convicted of or pleaded guilty to domestic violence. The burden is placed on the court to justify its decision. If the court's decision to award the abuser custody or shared parenting is not supported by some credible evidence, it is likely that the court will be reversed on appeal.

Q & A: Where a parent has been convicted of or pleaded guilty to domestic violence, must the victim's attorney request written findings of fact?

The statutory language contained in RC 3109.04(C) indicates that the court shall first consider whether either parent or any member of the household of either parent[34] has been convicted of or pleaded guilty to domestic violence or a sexually oriented offense.[35] If the court determines that one of the parents has been convicted of or pleaded guilty to domestic violence and further decides to award custody or shared parenting to that parent, the obligation is on the court to issue specific findings of fact to support its determination.[36] RC 3109.04(C) uses the term "only if," which indicates a clear intent on the part of the legislature to require that courts issue these findings whether or not they are requested.[37] Further, the findings of fact, justifying why an award of custody or shared parenting to the abuser is in the best interest of the child, must be written into the court's original custody or shared parenting decision.[38] The mandate is on the court to provide the findings in support of its decision. The statutory language sug-

---

[32]State ex rel. Plain Dealer Pub. Co. v. Barnes, 38 Ohio St. 3d 165, 167, 527 N.E.2d 807, 15 Media L. Rep. (BNA) 2083 (1988).

[33]Am. Sub. 2007 S.B. 260, eff. 1-2-07.

[34]Am. Sub. 2007 S.B. 260, eff. 1-2-07.

[35]Am. Sub. 2007 S.B. 260, eff. 1-2-07.

[36]See Smith v. Smith, 2001 WL 542317 (Ohio Ct. App. 9th Dist. Wayne County 2001). See also Morrison v. Morrison, 2014-Ohio-2254, 2014 WL 2443912 (Ohio Ct. App. 9th Dist. Summit County 2014).

[37]But see Moneypenny v. Moneypenny, 2001 WL 39602 (Ohio Ct. App. 9th Dist. Medina County 2001) (The appellate court upheld the decision to award custody to the parent who was convicted of domestic violence without issuing express findings as to the conclusion that such an award was in the best interest of the children. The appellate court noted that "Civ.R. 52 states that a trial court's judgment entry may be general unless one of the parties requests separate 'findings of fact.' ").

[38]See also Text § 15:13, Consideration of domestic violence as a best-interest factor—Findings of fact that support a court decision.

gests that a court may not designate the abuser the custodial parent without first making specific findings of fact to justify its decision.[39]

Where the court fails to support its decision with findings of fact, the victim's attorney should request that the court issue specific findings of fact, particularly when the court's decision contradicts the evidence of domestic violence or when the evidence of domestic violence appears to be discounted by the court as irrelevant to the best interest of the child. A court may be less likely to ignore evidence of domestic violence if it knows that the attorney will request written findings of fact if they are not provided in the decision. Ultimately, a court's failure to justify its decision, or its refusal to issue findings of fact, should provide the legal basis for an appeal.[40]

Q & A: What weight should be accorded domestic violence in a custody or visitation determination where it is argued that the violence was mutual?

In cases where both parents allege spouse abuse,[41] the court may have to determine which parent is the primary physical aggressor.[42] The court should be encouraged to consider the history of abusive conduct by the parties (not necessarily against each other), the comparative severity of the parties' injuries, whether either party acted in self-defense, the fear of each party, and the reasonableness of that fear. Reports from law enforcement agencies and medical facilities provide crucial evidence for determining which party is the primary physical aggressor. A court that articulates the primary-aggressor factors[43] to substantiate its decision has accorded significant weight to the evidence of domestic violence.

The North Dakota Supreme Court used another approach to determine which parent should be awarded custody where there were allegations of mutual domestic violence. In *Owan v. Owan*,[44] the Supreme Court held that the trial court must determine whether the

[39]See, e.g., Schmidt v. Schmidt, 1999 WL 225157 (Ohio Ct. App. 12th Dist. Clermont County 1999) (remanding case for specific written findings of fact); see also Smith v. Smith, 2001 WL 542317 (Ohio Ct. App. 9th Dist. Wayne County 2001) (Remanding the case for the trial court to provide specific written findings of fact. The Wayne County Court of Appeals determined that although the magistrate made extensive findings of fact, the trial court did not make any such findings as mandated by RC 3109.04(C).).

[40]See Newman v. Newman, 1996 WL 753202 (Ohio Ct. App. 5th Dist. Perry County 1996); Smith v. Smith, 2001 WL 542317 (Ohio Ct. App. 9th Dist. Wayne County 2001).

[41]See, e.g., Huesers v. Huesers, 1998 ND 54, 574 N.W.2d 880 (N.D. 1998) (considering the extent of the domestic violence committed by each party against the other).

[42]See, e.g., Dodd v. Dodd, 2001 WL 812244 (Ohio Ct. App. 6th Dist. Lucas County 2001); see also William G. Austin, Assessing Credibility in Allegations of Marital Violence in the High-Conflict Child Custody Case, 38 Fam. & Conciliation Courts Rev. 462 (2000).

[43]See RC 2935.03(B)(3)(d).

[44]Owan v. Owan, 1997 ND 50, 560 N.W.2d 900 (N.D. 1997); see also Zimmerman v. Zimmerman, 1997 ND 182, 569 N.W.2d 277 (N.D. 1997).

domestic violence inflicted by one party was significantly greater than that inflicted by the other.[45]

The Cuyahoga County Court of Appeals, in *Neff v. Neff*,[46] upheld the trial court's award of overnight visitation to the child's father, noting that

> [w]hile each parent has accused the other of engaging in domestic violence against her or him, neither has been convicted nor pled guilty to domestic violence pursuant to RC 2919.15. We find the fact that there has been an alleged history of spousal abuse and violent behavior between the two parties in the past is not grounds, in and of itself, to deny visitation rights.

While this case speaks to visitation rather than custody, it is likely than a domestic violence conviction will be accorded more weight that a history of domestic violence.

Q & A: Must findings of fact be issued in temporary custody proceedings?

RC 3109.04(C) does not specifically address this issue. However, findings of fact are required in "any proceeding" in which there is a custody or shared parenting matter and a conviction for domestic violence. *Black's Law Dictionary* defines "proceeding" as "the form and manner of conducting juridical business before a court . . . including all possible steps in an action from its commencement to the execution of judgment."[47] Because a temporary custody hearing is a proceeding pursuant to RC 3109.04(C), the court should be mandated to issue findings of fact to support its determination if it awards temporary custody to the convicted abuser.

From a public policy standpoint, it is crucial for courts to carefully consider and assess a parent's criminal record of domestic violence at all stages of a custody proceeding.[48] If a parent's criminal history is relevant to determining the best interest of the child at the final custody hearing and post-decree hearings, it is just as relevant to determining the best interest of the child at the temporary custody hearing. The safety of the child and the abused parent should be of great concern at the temporary custody hearing since the violence may escalate during the months after the parties separate.[49]

If the requirements of RC 3109.04(C) are to serve the legislative purpose of protecting children from domestic violence and its consequences, the statute must apply to temporary as well as permanent custody hearings. That purpose is clearly frustrated when courts fail to issue the statutorily required findings of fact in temporary custody orders.

Unfortunately, the Ohio Supreme Court rejected these public policy

---

[45]See also Findings on Domestic Violence, Case Development Custody/Visitation, 17 Fair Share 13 (1997).

[46]Neff v. Neff, 1998 WL 433846,*2 (Ohio Ct. App. 8th Dist. Cuyahoga County 1998).

[47]Black's Law Dictionary (6th ed.) p 1204.

[48]But see Baker v. Baker, 494 N.W.2d 282 (Minn. 1992).

[49]See Martha R. Mahoney, Legal Images of Battered Women: Redefining the Issue of Separation, 90 Mich. L. Rev. 1 (1991).

arguments in *State ex rel. Thompson v. Spon*.[50] In that case, the couple was married and had two children. The husband was convicted of domestic violence. The wife obtained a civil protection order from the domestic relations court that designated her the residential parent and legal custodian of the minor children. Subsequently, the husband filed a divorce action against the wife, who had relocated to Georgia. The trial court issued an ex parte order in the divorce naming the husband the temporary residential parent and legal custodian of the children. After a full hearing, the magistrate continued the ex parte temporary custody order in effect during the pendency of the divorce. The wife then requested findings of fact and conclusions of law. The judge denied the request, noting that the order was issued as a pretrial order pursuant to Civil Rule 75(M). The court found that "[p]retrial orders are by necessity interlocutory in nature and may be entered by a magistrate 'without judicial approval,' and magistrates may, but are not required by the civil rules to enter findings of fact and conclusions of law in support of pretrial orders."[51] The wife then filed a writ of mandamus to compel Judge Spon to require the magistrate to issue findings of fact and conclusions of law. The writ was dismissed, and the wife appealed to the Ohio Supreme Court.

In a per curiam opinion, the Supreme Court upheld the decision of the Richland County Court of Appeals and determined that the RC 3109.04(C) requirement of findings of fact and conclusions of law applies to final decrees allocating parental rights and responsibilities or subsequent modifications of final decrees rather than to temporary orders. The Court also noted that such a conclusion is consistent with the applicable rules of civil procedure, to wit, Civil Rule 53(C) and Civil Rule 75(M).

Two justices dissented from the opinion and, in a written dissent, favored reversing the court of appeals decision and issuing the writ. The dissent noted that the RC 3109.04(C) requirement of written findings of fact applies to pretrial proceedings under Civil Rule 53(C)(3)(a) and Civil Rule 75(M) and stressed that "[t]he phrase 'any proceeding' is not limited to proceedings involving a permanent allocation of parental rights and responsibilities for the care of children. Courts are not free to delete or insert words in interpreting an unambiguous statute."[52] The dissent pointed out that an appeal is not an adequate remedy for a magistrate's pretrial orders and stated that, where a statute's written findings requirement conflicts with civil rules of procedure, the statute is controlling "because the findings requirement is substantive rather than procedural."[53]

More importantly, the dissent acknowledged the public policy considerations advanced by appellant and reinforced by the Ohio legislature relative to domestic violence cases:

---

[50]State ex rel. Thompson v. Spon, 83 Ohio St. 3d 551, 1998-Ohio-298, 700 N.E.2d 1281 (1998).

[51]State ex rel. Thompson v. Spon, 83 Ohio St. 3d 551, 552, 1998-Ohio-298, 700 N.E.2d 1281 (1998).

[52]State ex rel. Thompson v. Spon, 83 Ohio St. 3d 551, 556-57, 1998-Ohio-298, 700 N.E.2d 1281 (1998) (Stratton, J., dissenting) (citation omitted).

[53]State ex rel. Thompson v. Spon, 83 Ohio St. 3d 551, 557, 1998-Ohio-298, 700 N.E.2d 1281 (1998) (Stratton, J., dissenting).

There are potentially harmful effects from the placement of these children in the custody of a convicted abuser. Every day that a child spends with a convicted abuser is critical and may cause irreversible damage. As of May 1998, when the briefs in this case were filed, the court had yet to conduct a final hearing on the matter and the temporary order of November 1997 remained in effect. Unfortunately, the reality is that a final hearing in these types of cases may not take place for months or even years. For these reasons, I believe the General Assembly intended the words "any proceeding" in RC 3109.04(C) also to apply to temporary orders.[54]

§ 15:7 Presenting evidence of domestic violence in custody and visitation proceedings; practice pointers

Credible evidence of domestic violence[1] should always be presented to the court whenever shared parenting, custody, and/or visitation become issues in the case. This is true whether or not the abuser has been convicted of domestic violence or any other offense involving a family or household member.[2]

A lack of a conviction for domestic violence or any other offense should not detract from the real issue—that domestic violence occurred. In some cases, the victim may have decided not to prosecute, or the prosecutor may have determined that there was insufficient evidence to charge the perpetrator or prevail at trial. The standard of proof in a criminal case may be a major obstacle to prevailing in court.[3] Often, victims of domestic violence are reluctant to prosecute or are likely to recant if the case proceeds to trial. As one commentator explained, "[o]nce the battering begins, remaining with her batterer and supporting his behavior may be her only means of survival."[4]

Family law practitioners should always examine the parties' relationship and look for a pattern or history of domestic violence.[5] Most statutes direct courts to consider a history of abuse before making complex custody/visitation or shared parenting decisions.[6] However, a

[54]State ex rel. Thompson v. Spon, 83 Ohio St. 3d 551, 558, 1998-Ohio-298, 700 N.E.2d 1281 (1998) (Stratton, J., dissenting).

[Section 15:7]

[1]See generally William G. Austin, Assessing Credibility in Allegations of Marital Violence in the High-Conflict Child Custody Case, 38 Fam. & Conciliation Courts Rev. 462 (2000); see also Leigh Goodmark, From Property to Personhood: What the Legal System Should Do for Children in Family Violence Cases, 102 W. Va. L. Rev. 237 (1999).

[2]See RC 3109.04(F)(1)(h).

[3]See RC 2901.05.

[4]Roberta L. Valente, Addressing Domestic Violence: The Role of the Family Law Practitioner, 29 Fam. L.Q. 187, 190 (1995) (citation omitted); see also Pauline Quirion, Why Attorneys Should Routinely Screen Clients for Domestic Violence, 42 Boston B. J. 12 (1998).

[5]See, e.g., Dodd v. Dodd, 2001 WL 812244 (Ohio Ct. App. 6th Dist. Lucas County 2001); see also Wissink v. Wissink, 301 A.D.2d 36, 749 N.Y.S.2d 550 (2d Dep't 2002) (requiring a complete psychological evaluation of the parties in light of an extensive domestic violence history).

[6]RC 3109.04(F)(2)(c); see also Jane H. Aiken and Jane C. Murphy, Dealing with Complex Evidence of Domestic Violence: A Primer for the Civil Bench, 39 (2) Court

history of violence in the parties' relationship should always be contemplated whenever domestic violence is alleged.

A history of domestic violence demonstrates a significant probability of continued abuse in the future.[7] Research demonstrates that children of victims of domestic violence are more likely to experience abuse and continued abuse in the future than those whose mothers have not been battered.[8] In addition, the more severe the abuse of the mother, the worse the child abuse.[9] Significantly, several studies have found that women who were abused are more likely to abuse their children than women who were not abused.[10]

The frequency and severity of the abuse may be an important evidentiary consideration.[11] In fact, the more serious the prior abuse, the more serious the future violations. A detailed history of domestic violence in the relationship should assist the court in determining whether the abuse has escalated in both frequency and severity over time and, especially, since the parties' separation.[12] Such escalation should be seen as a red flag, and the victim's attorney should stress to the court the need for added protection for the victim and the children.

Q & A: How is evidence of a history of abuse presented in court?[13]

The victim is, in many domestic violence cases, the only witness to the abusive act and is often in the best position to demonstrate a pattern and history of domestic violence within the relationship. Often, he/she is the only person who can testify about the acts of violence suffered at the hands of the abuser. A history of domestic violence is best shown simply by asking the victim to recount several incidents of

Rev. 12, 20 (2002).

[7]See Carla Garrity & Mitchell Baris, Custody and Visitation: Is it Safe? 17 Fam. Advoc. 40, 43 (1995); see also G. Miller, Violence By and Against America's Children, 17 J. Juv. Just. 6 (1989).

[8]See Liane V. Davis & Bonnie E. Carlson, Observations of Spouse Abuse: What Happens to the Children? 2 J. Interpersonal Violence 278 (1987); see also Evan Stark & Anne Flitcraft, Woman-Battering, Child Abuse and Social Heredity: What is the Relationship? in Marital Violence 147, 165 (N. Johnson ed., 1985); Lavita Nad Karni and Barbara Zeek Shaw, Making a Difference: Tools to Help Judges Support the Healing of Children Exposed to Domestic Violence, 39(2) Court Rev. 24 (2002).

[9]See Lee H. Bowker et al., On the Relationship Between Wife Beating and Child Abuse, in Feminist Perspectives on Wife Abuse 158, 164 (Kersti Yllo & Michelle Bograd eds., 1988).

[10]See, e.g., Murray A. Straus et al., Behind Closed Doors: Violence in the American Family 216–17 (1980); see also Joan Zorza, Protecting the Children in Custody Disputes When One Parent Abuses the Other, 29 Clearinghouse Rev. 1113, 1116 (1996).

[11]Mary Ann Dutton & Catherine L. Waltz, Domestic Violence: Understanding Why It Happens and How To Recognize It, 17 Fam. Advoc. 14 (1995); see also Peter Jaffe et al., Children of Battered Women (1990); Howard Davidson, Report to the President of the American Bar Assoc., The Impact of Domestic Violence on Children 1 (1994); Daniel G. Saunders, Child Custody Decisions in Families Experiencing Woman Abuse, 39 Soc. Work 51 (1994).

[12]See also Debra Whitcomb, Prosecutors, Kids and Domestic Violence Cases, 36-OCT Prosecutor 32, 33 (2002).

[13]See Text § 16:21, "Other acts" testimony; see also Text § 8:4, Statutory elements of domestic violence under RC 3113.31(A)(1)(b); Text § 11:10, Ex parte protection orders—Legal standard for issuance.

abuse, specific to both time and place.[14] These incidents may be of actual or attempted physical abuse or threats to harm or kill.[15] Attorneys must be cautioned, however, that one or two isolated or minor incidents of domestic violence may not provide the court with sufficient evidence of a pattern or history of abuse in custody cases.[16]

It must be stressed to the court that the victim's testimony should not be ignored or discounted simply because there is no other independent corroboration.[17] In fact, the Ohio Supreme Court, in *Felton v. Felton*,[18] noted that "[o]ften the only evidence of domestic violence is the testimony of the victim."

Other evidence corroborating the victim's testimony may be that he/she sought refuge at a shelter for victims of domestic violence or that the victim attended various counseling sessions because of the abuse. It may be the victim's testimony adduced at a civil protection order hearing or at a criminal domestic violence trial that was transcribed by a court reporter. It may be the testimony of the victim advocate or another witness who saw the visible signs of the battering. It may be the testimony of an advocate or expert that the victim's behaviors are consistent with having been abused. It may be a finding from another court of competent jurisdiction, child protective service's records, domestic violence shelter records, and/or school records.

In still other cases, the victim's testimony may be corroborated by independent documentation of the acts of violence.[19] Police reports, medical records, photographs, and certified copies of criminal convictions provide the court with the best documentation. Because these documents are introduced into evidence most often, courts have come to expect that all incidents should be independently documented. It should be cautioned, however, that a history of domestic violence may not be adequately reflected in the criminal record.[20]

Unfortunately, the victim will not have the type of extrinsic documentation desired by the court and argued for by opposing counsel. The victim may not have reported the incident to the police. The victim may have told the doctor or medical staff that the injuries were caused by something other than an abusive act.

On the other hand, the victim may have reported the incident, but the police may not have prepared a written report. The victim may have disclosed the abuse to medical personnel, but it was not noted on the victim's record.

---

[14]See Hoffman v. Hoffman, 1998 WL 469876 (Ohio Ct. App. 9th Dist. Summit County 1998).

[15]See RC 3113.31(A)(1) for acts that constitute domestic violence.

[16]See Simmons v. Simmons, 649 So. 2d 799 (La. Ct. App. 2d Cir. 1995); In re Marriage of Forbes, 570 N.W.2d 757 (Iowa 1997); see also Huesers v. Huesers, 1998 ND 54, 574 N.W.2d 880 (N.D. 1998). But see Hamilton v. Hamilton, 886 S.W.2d 711 (Mo. Ct. App. W.D. 1994).

[17]See also Text § 16:8, Documenting evidence of domestic violence; Hoffman v. Hoffman, 1998 WL 469876 (Ohio Ct. App. 9th Dist. Summit County 1998); Yoel v. Yoel, 1998 WL 1051779 (Ohio Ct. App. 11th Dist. Lake County 1998).

[18]Felton v. Felton, 79 Ohio St. 3d 34, 44, 1997-Ohio-302, 679 N.E.2d 672 (1997).

[19]See also Text Ch. 16, Domestic Violence Case Strategy and Evidentiary Considerations.

[20]National Council of Juvenile & Family Court Judges, Family Violence: Improving Court Practice 19 (1990).

Family law practitioners must, especially in contested custody and visitation cases, be prepared to present the case without the benefit of other independent documentation. Attorneys must continue to stress to the court the value and importance of the victim's testimony.

Q & A: How does evidence of a history of abuse demonstrate a detrimental impact on the children?

The importance of demonstrating a history of domestic violence cannot be overstated.[21] Besides illustrating the abusive nature of the relationship and the probability of continuing violence in the future,[22] a history of domestic violence in the relationship directly and detrimentally impacts the children.[23] Even though the primary victim of the domestic violence may be the spouse, the attorney should explore the detrimental impact on the children of witnessing domestic violence[24] and living within a family structure where abuse is perceived as the norm. The fact that one parent has committed acts of domestic violence against the other is indicative of that parent's poor parenting skills and inability to function as a parent.[25] In light of the findings, any attorney who fails to demonstrate this connection is not adequately representing his/her client.

An expert who can provide general testimony about the detrimental impact of domestic violence on children can help establish that needed link.[26] An expert who has examined the children involved in the litigation can provide credible evidence of the specific effects of domestic violence on those particular children.

Q & A: How important is a history of domestic violence in custody determinations?

The Iowa Court of Appeals, in *In re Marriage of Brainard*,[27] held that, though he had been a generally good parent, the father's history

---

[21]M. A. Straus et al., Behind Closed Doors: Violence in the American Family 16 (1980); see also Wissink v. Wissink, 301 A.D.2d 36, 749 N.Y.S.2d 550 (2d Dep't 2002).

[22]See Daniel G. Saunders, Child Custody Decisions in Families Experiencing Woman Abuse, 39 Soc. Work 51 (1994).

[23]National Center on Women and Family Law, Inc., The Effects of Woman Abuse on Children: Psychological and Legal Authority (1994); see also Leslie D. Johnson, Caught in the Crossfire: Examining Legislation and Judicial Responses to the Forgotten Victims of Domestic Violence, 22 Law & Psych. Rev. — (1998).

[24]See Peter Jaffe et al., Children of Battered Women (1990); Howard Davidson, Report to the President of the American Bar Assoc., The Impact of Domestic Violence on Children (1994); Daniel G. Saunders, Child Custody Decisions in Families Experiencing Woman Abuse, 39 Soc. Work 51 (1994); Leigh Goodmark, From Property to Personhood: What the Legal System Should do for Children in Family Violence Cases, 102 W. Va. L. Rev. 237 (1999).

[25]Mildred D. Pagelow, Justice for Victims of Spouse Abuse in Divorce and Child Custody Cases, 8 Violence and Victims 76 (1993); see also Linda Keenan, Domestic Violence and Custody Litigation: The Need for Statutory Reform, 13 Hofstra L. Rev. 407 (1985); Lundy Bancroft, The Parenting of Men Who Batter, 39(2) Court Rev. 44 (2002).

[26]See Naomi R. Cahn, Civil Images of Battered Women: The Impact of Domestic Violence on Child Custody Decisions, 44 Vand. L. Rev. 1041, 1086–87 (1991); see also Myra Sun & Elizabeth Thomas, Custody Litigation on Behalf of Battered Women, 21 Clearinghouse Rev. 563 (1987).

[27]In re Marriage of Brainard, 523 N.W.2d 611 (Iowa Ct. App. 1994); see also Michelli v. Michelli, 655 So. 2d 1342 (La. Ct. App. 1st Cir. 1995); Wissink v. Wissink, 301 A.D.2d 36, 749 N.Y.S.2d 550 (2d Dep't 2002).

of domestic violence was the major factor in denying him custody because of the negative impact on children raised in homes touched by domestic abuse. In this case, the history of abusive acts was the primary consideration of the court. However, the court did not define what or how many incidents constitutes a history of domestic violence.

Conversely, in *Simmons v. Simmons*,[28] the Louisiana Court of Appeals upheld a joint custody award with father as the primary parent, finding that a single past act of family violence, justified by the wife's adulterous acts, did not constitute a "history of perpetrating family violence."

Other state legislatures have recently added domestic violence considerations to a determination of child custody, with the presumption against awarding custody to the abusive parent.[29] An Oklahoma Court of Appeals interpreted "ongoing domestic abuse" that creates a presumption against the abusive parent having custody as "abuse which is still occurring, or has occurred with sufficient frequency and recency to give rise to some expectation that it will continue or will recur."[30]

Q & A: What evidence is necessary to demonstrate a "potential for abuse" as used in RC 3109.04(F)(2)(c)?

A "potential for abuse" is set forth as a factor to be considered in determining whether shared parenting is in the best interest of the child.[31] However, a "potential for abuse" must be explored whenever domestic violence is alleged.

Sometimes, the incidents a victim relates rise only to the level of a "potential for abuse." In those situations, there is no actual physical violence. The victim is able to articulate a pattern of threatening conduct or verbal harassment that has created a fear of potential future harm. Evidence of a "potential for abuse" may be predicated on acts by the abuser such as the following: (1) a pattern of threatening conduct, such as threats to hurt, maim, or kill, (2) a pattern of following or stalking behavior, (3) a past history of actual physical abuse directed either at the victim or another intimate partner, (4) past suicide attempts or threats of suicide by the abuser, (5) destructive

---

[28]Simmons v. Simmons, 649 So. 2d 799, 800 (La. Ct. App. 2d Cir. 1995); see also Hamilton v. Hamilton, 886 S.W.2d 711 (Mo. Ct. App. W.D. 1994) (finding that two incidents of abuse did not constitute a pattern of domestic violence); In re Marriage of Forbes, 570 N.W.2d 757 (Iowa 1997) (finding that judge must weigh evidence of domestic violence, including its nature, severity, frequency, and at whom directed, not simply count the number of incidents).

[29]See, e.g., Fla Stat § 61.13(2)(b); N.D. Cent. Code § 14-09-06.2(1)(j). See also RC 3109.04(F)(2)(c).

[30]Brown v. Brown, 1993 OK CIV APP 142, 867 P.2d 477, 479 (Ct. App. Div. 1 1993); In re Joshua C., 2007-Ohio-3953, 2007 WL 2216969 (Ohio Ct. App. 6th Dist. Lucas County 2007) (severe and ongoing domestic violence would be detrimental to the health and safety of the children); but see Reaper v. James, 2009-Ohio-151, 2009 WL 104613, *3 (Ohio Ct. App. 4th Dist. Lawrence County 2009) (affirming award of custody to father despite his history of domestic violence, noting that the evidence did not indicate that the father would subject his children to domestic violence nor that he subjected any of his other children to domestic violence; however, the court was mindful "of the impact and detriment that can occur as a result of a child being subjected to or as a witness to domestic violence, physical or mental").

[31]See RC 3109.04(F)(2)(c).

behavior such as throwing and damaging personal property, especially items that are meaningful to the victim, (6) violence towards neighbors, co-workers, or family members, (7) a history of alcohol and/or drug abuse, (8) familiarity with and use of weapons, and (9) torturing or killing of animals. Any of these behaviors is a likely predictor of a potential for physical abuse of a victim.

Significantly, several of these factors may increase the risk that the abuser will kill the victim. Although the lethality of a batterer cannot be predicted with any certainty, the greater the number of lethality factors and the greater the intensity with which a batterer pursues the victim, the more likely it is that the batterer will engage in life-threatening behaviors.[32] Attorneys should always assess the dangerousness in the relationship, especially in light of research that demonstrates that separation increases the risk of future abuse and even death.[33] "Violence is often triggered by the anger aroused by threatened loss and excessive feelings of dependency—making separation an extremely dangerous period."[34] Thus, violence is the abuser's way of reestablishing power and exercising control.

A lethality assessment attempts to identify when a batterer is most dangerous by evaluating the batterer's beliefs and patterns of violence, coercion, and control. An attorney should routinely question his/her client about whether any of the above-mentioned factors exist in the parties' relationship. Once the potential for violence is assessed, a safety plan for the victim and children should be formulated.[35] It may be advisable for the client to go into hiding if an assessment indicates that the potential for future violence is great.

Q & A: How do you prove a "potential for abuse"?

The behaviors listed in the previous answer indicate a "potential for abuse" by illustrating a past history of physical abuse and the victim's fear of the abuser. This is not an objective fear based on what a reasonable person may believe. Rather, it is the subjective fear of the particular victim due to the past and present behavior of the abuser.

Several Ohio court jurisdictions have espoused this subjective approach. For example, in *Eichenberger v. Eichenberger*,[36] the evidence presented to the court indicated that the victim feared the defendant. The victim testified "'You have grabbed my arm, and you have threatened to kill me. That you would do away with me. That you would silence me. Those were your words. I remember that

[32] Barbara J. Hart, Beyond the "Duty to Warn": A Therapist's "Duty to Protect" Battered Women and Children, in Feminist Perspectives on Wife Abuse 234, 242 (Kersti Yllo & Michelle Bograd eds., 1988).

[33] See Assessing Dangerousness: Violence by Sexual Offenders, Batterers, and Child Abusers (Jacquelyn C. Campbell ed., 1995); Evan Stark & Anne H. Flitcraft, Women and Children at Risk: A Feminist Perspective on Child Abuse, 18 Int'l J. Health Servs. 97–118 (1988); see also Patsy A. Klaus & Michael R. Rand, Bureau of Justice Statistics, U.S. Dep't of Justice, Special Report: Family Violence 4 (1984).

[34] Adele Harrell, A Guide to Research on Family Violence 24 (1993).

[35] See Text § 16:5, Preventing domestic violence; Safety plans and provisions, for a discussion of safety planning.

[36] Eichenberger v. Eichenberger, 82 Ohio App. 3d 809, 613 N.E.2d 678 (10th Dist. Franklin County 1992). See also Text § 12:11.

vividly.' "[37] The Franklin County Court of Appeals determined that the victim's testimony about the defendant's threats constituted competent, credible evidence. The court held that "[the victim's] state of mind could very well have been the product, in part at least, of her past interactions with appellant. The fear she claimed to have felt and the reasonableness of that fear could and should be determined with reference to her history with appellant."[38] In *Snyder v. Snyder*,[39] the appellee testified that she heard the appellant tell his son that he "might end up in the jail cell beside him because he might do the same thing," where the son was in jail for allegedly murdering his wife. She further testified that she knew that the appellant kept loaded guns in the bedroom. The Ross County Court of Appeals upheld the trial court's issuance of a civil protection order, finding that "appellee's testimony constitutes sufficient competent, credible evidence to support a finding that appellant placed appellee by threat of force in fear of imminent serious physical harm."[40]

These cases illustrate the utilization by some courts of a subjective standard to determine fear and a past history of violent interactions. The abuser's present behaviors provide a basis for the victim's fear that the abuser might harm the victim in the future. These behaviors are indicative of potential future physical violence and, hence, the "potential for abuse."

Besides providing evidence of a "potential for abuse," many of the behaviors listed in the previous answer support a victim's fear of imminent serious physical harm as defined in RC 3113.31(A)(1)(b). The use of the term "imminent" must be differentiated from the term "immediate," and both courts and attorneys should be careful not to confuse the terms. "Imminent" is broader in scope than "immediate" and includes "more of the facts and circumstances of the woman's experience in the relationship."[41] The victim's attorney should elicit descriptive evidence of the most recent incident of violence against the victim, the past history of violent behavior, providing that it is specific to time and place, and the conduct of the defendant that triggered the victim's fear. Threats alone may be enough to substantiate a victim's fear. Other acts, such as torturing animals, stalking, and suicide/homicide threats, may also provide credible evidence to support a victim's fear of the abuser. It should also be noted that the event that triggers the prosecution for domestic violence or the request

[37]Eichenberger v. Eichenberger, 82 Ohio App. 3d 809, 816, 613 N.E.2d 678 (10th Dist. Franklin County 1992).

[38]Eichenberger v. Eichenberger, 82 Ohio App. 3d 809, 816, 613 N.E.2d 678 (10th Dist. Franklin County 1992).

[39]Snyder v. Snyder, 1995 WL 493998, *2 (Ohio Ct. App. 4th Dist. Ross County 1995).

[40]Snyder v. Snyder, 1995 WL 493998, *5 (Ohio Ct. App. 4th Dist. Ross County 1995).

[41]Martha R. Mahoney, Legal Images of Battered Women: Redefining the Issue of Separation, 90 Mich. L. Rev. 1, 84 (1991) (footnote omitted); see also Text § 8:4, Statutory elements of domestic violence under RC 3113.31(A)(1)(b).

for a protection order or divorce is often a culmination of a series of events and is not always the most serious conduct.[42]

Q & A: How is "other acts" evidence presented?[43]

The admission of "other acts" evidence[44] and the use of a subjective belief, rather than an objective reasonable person belief, that a threat would cause imminent harm reflect a recognition on the part of courts regarding the unique nature of domestic violence cases. They also serve to promote the dual goals of ensuring the victim's safety and holding the abuser accountable.

In *State v. Collie*,[45] the Hamilton County Court of Appeals set forth a test to be used in domestic violence cases where the gravamen of the offense is a threat. The court held:

> because of our recognition of the unique nature of domestic violence cases, and our concern for the victims thereof, we today announce a test which the state shall be permitted to use in the future in cases brought under RC 2919.25(C). We hold that in order to prove the element of the belief of a family member that the offender will cause imminent physical harm, evidence of "other acts" against the same victim will be admissible with appropriate safeguards as herein set forth.[46]

The court further explained that the other acts must have been against the same victim and must be specific as to time and place.

Similarly, in *State v. Taylor*,[47] the Hamilton County Municipal Court determined that:

> A close analysis of the law, however, does not establish an absolute requirement that to sustain a domestic violence threat conviction, the state must prove the accused's ability to carry out the threat imminently and/or movement toward carrying it out. Instead, the critical inquiry is whether or not the proof fully evidences a reasonable belief by the victim that the accused will cause imminent physical harm.

Although the *Collie* and *Taylor* holdings are in the context of criminal domestic violence under RC 2919.25, the courts' reasoning can easily be applied to any domestic violence case where the attorney has

---

[42]See State v. Bolds, 1993 WL 35578 (Ohio Ct. App. 5th Dist. Stark County 1993); see also State v. Collie, 108 Ohio App. 3d 580, 671 N.E.2d 338 (1st Dist. Hamilton County 1996).

[43]See Text § 16:21, "Other acts" testimony.

[44]See also Jane H. Aiken and Jane C. Murphy, Dealing with Complex Evidence of Domestic Violence: A Primer for the Civil Bench, 39(2) Court Rev. 12, 20 (2002).

[45]State v. Collie, 108 Ohio App. 3d 580, 671 N.E.2d 338 (1st Dist. Hamilton County 1996).

[46]State v. Collie, 108 Ohio App. 3d 580, 583-84, 671 N.E.2d 338 (1st Dist. Hamilton County 1996); see also Visnich v. Visnich, 1999 WL 1299300, *3 (Ohio Ct. App. 11th Dist. Trumbull County 1999) (determining that "[t]he language used in defining 'domestic violence' clearly contemplates prior acts being used as evidence to support a CPO" and relying on Evid.R. 404(B) in support of its position); State v. Schweitzer, 2015-Ohio-925, 30 N.E.3d 190 (Ohio Ct. App. 3d Dist. Auglaize County 2015) (evidence of prior physical abuse can be used to establish the basis of the victim's belief that the offender is about to cause imminent physical harm).

[47]State v. Taylor, 79 Ohio Misc. 2d 82, 85, 671 N.E.2d 343 (Mun. Ct. 1996) (citations omitted).

to prove a threat of harm.[48] Of significance is that, in the civil domestic violence statute, the threat must be sufficient to put the victim in fear of imminent serious physical harm whereas, in the criminal context, the threat must place the victim in fear of imminent physical harm. Because the standard of proof in a criminal case is "beyond a reasonable doubt" and because the prosecution must prove each element of the crime beyond a reasonable doubt, the conduct that constitutes a threat for purposes of criminal domestic violence is less offensive than that required in the civil context. Since, in the civil context, the standard of proof is "by a preponderance of the evidence," the conduct complained of must be of a more serious nature.

In the context of custody and visitation,[49] the family law practitioner may need to demonstrate that threatening behavior towards the victim is adequate justification for not awarding custody or shared parenting to the abuser. Threatening behavior often foreshadows future abuse, and it may be crucial to demonstrate a past history of domestic violence. The legal analyses articulated in *Collie*[50] and *Taylor*[51] provide the method by which attorneys can demonstrate whether a recent threat rises to the level of domestic violence. A threat that creates a subjective belief of imminent physical harm, and can be demonstrated by other past acts of domestic violence, establishes both a history of domestic violence and a potential for further abuse. This provides the court with credible evidence for determining whether awarding custody, shared parenting, and/or visitation to the abuser is in the best interest of the child.

It must be stressed, however, that proof of prior domestic violence is not necessary to establish the right to a civil protection order. A civil protection order is aimed at deterring prospective violence while criminal domestic violence prosecution is aimed at punishing past violence. Raising the requirement for a civil protection order to proof of prior violence would be an adoption of the "one free bite" rule for domestic violence victims—only if the victim is hurt could he/she get an order to prevent him/her from being hurt. Such logic thwarts the true intent of the domestic violence statute. Past acts of domestic violence only permit attorneys to demonstrate a history where one exists and to justify the victim's fear that the recent threat may cause future abuse.

Q & A: According to RC 3109.04(F)(1)(h), what is meant by "any other offense"?[52]

Trespass,[53] aggravated trespass,[54] menacing,[55] aggravated menacing,[56] menacing by stalking,[57] disorderly conduct,[58] criminal mischief,[59]

---

[48]See RC 3113.31(A)(1)(b). See also Text § 8:4, Statutory elements of domestic violence under RC 3113.31(A)(1)(b); Text § 11:10, Ex parte protection orders—Legal standard for issuance.

[49]See RC 3109.04(F)(1), RC 3109.04(F)(2).

[50]State v. Collie, 108 Ohio App. 3d 580, 671 N.E.2d 338 (1st Dist. Hamilton County 1996); see also Siouffi v. Siouffi, 1998 WL 879255 (Ohio Ct. App. 2d Dist. Montgomery County 1998).

[51]State v. Taylor, 79 Ohio Misc. 2d 82, 671 N.E.2d 343 (Mun. Ct. 1996).

[52]See also RC 2901.01(A)(9) for a definition of an "offense of violence."

[53]RC 2911.21.

[54]RC 2911.211.

assault,[60] aggravated assault,[61] burglary,[62] criminal damaging,[63] breaking and entering,[64] aggravated arson,[65] and a violation of either a civil or criminal protection order under RC 2919.27 have been used by various court systems as examples of "other offenses"[66] for purposes of RC 3109.04(F)(1)(h). So long as any of these offenses has been committed by the abuser, provided the victim of the offense was a member of the family or household that is the subject of the current custody or visitation proceeding, and provided the victim was physically harmed in the commission of the crime, the statutory mandates are satisfied.

In many criminal cases, the perpetrator is charged with domestic violence. Where there is not enough evidence to prevail at trial, the prosecutor may reduce the charge to a lesser offense rather than risk an outright acquittal.[67] It should be noted that this action does not lessen the fact that a crime of violence was committed against an intimate partner.[68]

In other cases, there may not be enough evidence to support each of the elements of the crime of domestic violence. The prosecutor may either charge under domestic violence, and then give a jury instruction on the lesser included offense such as disorderly conduct, or charge the perpetrator under another criminal code section rather than decline to charge at all.[69] In this way, the perpetrator may still be held accountable for committing a crime of violence. So long as the offense was committed against the same individual and the perpetrator caused physical harm to that individual in the commission of the offense, a conviction for this type of an offense must be considered by the courts before awarding custody or visitation.

---

[55]RC 2903.22.

[56]RC 2903.21.

[57]RC 2903.211.

[58]RC 2917.11; see also Butzer v. Butzer, 1998 WL 34615 (Ohio Ct. App. 9th Dist. Wayne County 1998). But see Prusia v. Prusia, 2003-Ohio-2000, 2003 WL 1904410 (Ohio Ct. App. 6th Dist. Lucas County 2003) (disorderly conduct was not an offense of violence; rather it is a crime against the public place).

[59]RC 2909.07.

[60]RC 2903.13.

[61]RC 2903.12.

[62]RC 2911.12.

[63]RC 2909.06.

[64]RC 2911.13.

[65]RC 2909.02.

[66]See also RC 2901.01(A)(9) for the list of "offenses of violence."

[67]See State v. Kidder, 32 Ohio St. 3d 279, 513 N.E.2d 311 (1987).

[68]But see Prusia v. Prusia, 2003-Ohio-2000, 2003 WL 1904410 (Ohio Ct. App. 6th Dist. Lucas County 2003) (in which the father's conviction for disorderly conduct did not bar his designation as residential parent and legal custodian and is not an offense of violence such that it fits within the parameters of RC 3109.04(F)(1)(h)).

[69]See City of Bucyrus v. Fawley, 50 Ohio App. 3d 25, 552 N.E.2d 676 (3d Dist. Crawford County 1988); see also State v. Hunt, 1996 WL 132268 (Ohio Ct. App. 5th Dist. Stark County 1996).

Family law attorneys should never underestimate the significance of protection orders in custody and visitation litigation.[70] Violations of civil protection orders that result in convictions under RC 2919.27 are "other offenses" which courts are required to consider before awarding custody and visitation. Depending on the nature of the violation, it may provide independent evidence of domestic violence which must be accorded sufficient weight by the court. Moreover, if the violation is pursued as criminal conduct,[71] there is an enhancement of penalties for a subsequent violation.[72]

Q & A: Why is it important to request a finding of domestic violence in the protection order issued after the full hearing?[73]

A specific finding of domestic violence in a civil protection order is important for two reasons. First, it may be useful to enhance and support a pattern or history of domestic violence, which can then form the basis for a specific parenting plan in a custody or visitation proceeding, whether or not shared parenting is requested.[74] Second, a court is less likely to ignore evidence of domestic violence where there is some documentation of the abuse.[75] Since courts are likely to accord more weight to evidence of domestic violence in a relationship if the violence is documented, a finding that the other parent committed domestic violence provides documented and, therefore, credible evidence.

Attorneys for the victim often fail to request findings of domestic violence or negotiate them away because so many protection orders are entered by agreement of the parties. Rather than risk trial and an uncertain outcome, attorneys often negotiate an agreement. This consent agreement, suggested either by the court or one of the parties, indicates only that the perpetrator be bound by the terms of the order. A finding that the respondent committed an act of domestic violence is lacking. Further, the attorney for the respondent may request a finding that explains that the respondent's signature on the consent entry in no way indicates an admission of guilt.

Because the absence of a specific finding of domestic violence may alter the course of future custody, visitation, or even criminal proceedings, it is important for family law attorneys to understand the implications of negotiating away findings of domestic violence. The attorney should consider whether there are other pending cases or issues before presenting the domestic violence case to the court.

---

[70]See Peter Finn, Civil Protection Orders: A Flawed Opportunity for Intervention, in Women Battering: Policy Responses 155–89 (M. Steinman ed., Univ. of Neb. Press 1991); Allie Meiers, Civil Orders of Protection: A Tool to Keep Children Safe, 19 J. Am. Acad. Matrim. Law. 373 (2005).

[71]See Text Ch. 14, Police Enforcement of Protection Orders and Other Relevant Issues, for a discussion of civil protection order violations that rise to the level of criminal conduct.

[72]See R.C. 2919.27(B); RC 3113.31(L)(1); see also Text Ch. 14, Police Enforcement of Protection Orders and Other Relevant Issues.

[73]See Leslye Orloff, Jason Knott & Alicia Carra, Creating a Jurisdictionally Sound Protection Order, Legal Momentum 2006 (discussing that a protection order issued by a court without subject matter jurisdiction is invalid for purposes of full faith and credit. Consent orders without findings of abuse may not be valid in other states because there is no subject matter jurisdiction).

[74]RC 3109.04(F)(2)(c).

[75]But see Felton v. Felton, 79 Ohio St. 3d 34, 1997-Ohio-302, 679 N.E.2d 672 (1997).

For example, a finding of domestic violence in a civil protection order may be a specific source of independent documentation of the history of abuse for custody and visitation purposes. Without such a finding, the attorney who prepares the custody/visitation case may have a more difficult time demonstrating to the court that certain instances of conduct rose to the level of domestic violence. In addition, a court may view the absence of a finding of domestic violence in a consent entry as evidence that domestic violence did not occur or was insignificant and that the protection order was only maintained in order to keep the parties apart. In either case, the protection order would not be considered credible evidence of domestic violence for purposes of a relevant best-interest factor.

Moreover, if there is a pending criminal domestic violence action, the defendant may argue for a dismissal of the criminal case because the prior consent agreement did not include a finding that the respondent committed an act of domestic violence. The defendant may also argue that the absence of a finding is a clear indication that the petitioner does not believe the defendant is guilty of any crime.

In many cases, however, a specific finding of domestic violence is inconsequential. So long as the terms remain intact and that the respondent agrees to abide by the terms of the protection order, most victims would more readily sign the consent entry than risk a full hearing. The victim is more concerned with whether the protection order is effective for a certain period of time and enforceable by both the courts and the law enforcement agencies.

It should also be noted that a finding of domestic violence is not a condition precedent to charging a respondent with violating a civil protection order under RC 2919.27. The act of violating the terms of the protection order is the necessary element and is evidence of a continuing act of domestic violence.

Q & A: What is meant by "other domestic violence" in RC 3109.04(F)(2)(c)?

RC 3109.04(F)(2)(c) includes "other domestic violence" as a factor that the court must consider in determining whether shared parenting is in the best interest of the children. No Ohio cases have addressed this particular issue. However, one possibility is that the Ohio legislature intended to include domestic violence occurring against persons other than spouses or children. Since RC 3113.31(A)(3) encompasses over twenty-seven categories of persons covered,[76] domestic violence against spouses and children represents only a small percentage of the covered individuals.

Attorneys should always ask whether the abuser has committed domestic violence against another family or household member, even where the victim is not a member of the current household. Many researchers have found that batterers tend to move from one victim to another.[77] Where domestic violence has occurred against another person or member of the victim's or perpetrator's household, such as a

---

[76]See Text Ch. 10, Nature of the Domestic Violence Relationship, for a discussion of the various family and household member classifications covered under RC 3113. 31.

[77]National Council of Juvenile & Family Court Judges, Family Violence: A Guide

former spouse, parent, grandparent, in-law, or other relative, the likelihood of future domestic violence against a current partner or member of the household is increased.[78] Of significance is that past domestic violence against an intimate partner is likely to be an indicator of domestic violence towards a current partner.[79]

Although "other domestic violence" must be specifically considered in making a shared parenting determination under RC 3109.04(F)(2)(c), it should also be considered by an attorney whenever domestic violence has been alleged. It should also be brought to the court's attention as relevant to any custody and visitation proceeding because of the risk of continued violence in the future.

Q & A: Can a child's exposure to domestic violence between his parents be enough to demonstrate a "potential for abuse"?[80]

Studies indicate that there is a high correlation between spouse abuse and child abuse.[81] One study found that in forty-five percent of selected maritally violent couples, one of the children was being abused.[82] In fact, other studies suggest that domestic violence to children occurs in over seventy percent of the homes where spousal abuse occurs.

The abuse may be physical, sexual, and/or emotional.[83] Since studies have demonstrated that exposure to domestic violence causes, at the very least, emotional harm to the children,[84] it may also be considered a "potential for abuse" of these children. Children who observe violence within their family believe the violence could happen

---

to Research, in Courts and Communities: Confronting Violence in the Family (1993); see also Daniel G. Saunders, Child Custody Decisions in Families Experiencing Woman Abuse, 39 Soc. Work 51, 53 (1994).

[78]Daniel G. Saunders, Child Custody Decisions in Families Experiencing Woman Abuse, 39 Soc. Work 51 (1994).

[79]Daniel G. Saunders, Child Custody Decisions in Families Experiencing Woman Abuse, 39 Soc. Work 51, 53 (1994); see also Joan Zorza, Protecting the Children in Custody Disputes When One Parent Abuses the Other, 29 Clearinghouse Rev. 1113, 1114 (1996); Irwin v. Schmidt, 236 A.D.2d 401, 653 N.Y.S.2d 627 (2d Dep't 1997) (denying defendant custody due to his domestic violence against his current wife).

[80]See generally Lavita Nad Karni and Barbara Zeek Shaw, Making a Difference: Tools to Help Judges Support the Healing of Children Exposed to Domestic Violence, 39(2) Court Rev. 24 (2002).

[81]See Howard Davidson, Child Abuse & Domestic Violence: Legal Connections & Controversies, 29 Fam. L.Q. 357 (1995); see also Jeffrey L. Edleson, Intervention & Issues in the Co-Occurrence of Child Abuse & Domestic Violence, 4 Child Maltreatment 2 (1999); Murray Strauss, Ordinary Violence, Child Abuse & Wife-Beating: What Do They Have in Common? in The Dark Side of Families: Current Family Violence Research 213, 218–19 (David Finklehor et al. eds., Sage Publications 1983).

[82]Alan Rosenbaum & K. Daniel O'Leary, Children: The Unintended Victims of Marital Violence, 51 Am. J. Orthopsychiatry 692, 693 (1981); see also Michael J. Voris, Civil Orders of Protection: Do They Protect Children, the Tag-along Victims of Domestic Violence? 17 Ohio N.U. L. Rev. 599, 606 (1991).

[83]See Suzanne H. Jackson, Child Abuse, in The Impact of Domestic Violence on Your Legal Practice, A Lawyer's Handbook 5-17, ABA Commission on Domestic Violence (1996).

[84]Joel S. Milner & Ruth G. Gold, Screening Spouse Abusers for Child Abuse Potential, J. Clin. Psychol. 161 (1986); see also 9 The Future of Children Number 3 (The David & Lucille Packard Found. 1999); Ending the Cycle of Violence: Community Responses to Children of Battered Women (Einat Peled et al. eds., Sage Publications 1995); Text § 15:11, Impact of domestic violence on children.

to them. They also internalize a subjective fear and belief that a threat directed at the other parent or even at them could cause them physical harm or injury in the future.[85]

Family law practitioners should consider presenting evidence to the court demonstrating that the children witnessed some or all of the abusive incidents.[86] Expert testimony should also be elicited to show the court that witnessing domestic violence is child abuse or, at the very least, provides clear documentation of a potential for future abuse.[87]

§ 15:8 Safety concerns of the victim

Although evidence of domestic violence is now considered and admitted in custody and visitation proceedings, courts do not routinely include provisions in their orders to safeguard the victims and their children.[1] In custody and/or visitation cases involving domestic violence, it is up to the family law attorney to make sure that the safety of victims and their children is never discounted or ignored by the court.[2]

Research indicates that up to seventy-five percent of reported domestic assaults may occur after separation or divorce.[3] In fact, studies indicate that separated and divorced women are fourteen times more likely than married women to report having been the victim of domestic violence by a spouse or ex-spouse.[4] Moreover, women are more likely to be murdered when they attempt to separate from their partners or report abuse.[5] Consequently, victims of domestic violence are at a greater risk for further abuse during court-mandated interac-

---

[85]See Custody of Vaughn, 422 Mass. 590, 664 N.E.2d 434 (1996).

[86]Nancy K.D. Lemon, The Legal System's Response to Children Exposed to Domestic Violence, 9 Future of Children 67 (1999); see also Wissink v. Wissink, 301 A.D.2d 36, 749 N.Y.S.2d 550 (2d Dep't 2002) (reversing an award of custody to father and requiring a complete psychological evaluation of all parties in light of an extensive history of domestic violence).

[87]See Evan Stark & Anne Flitcraft, Woman-Battering, Child Abuse and Social Heredity: What is the Relationship? in Marital Violence (N. Johnson ed., 1985); see also Nancy K.D. Lemon, The Legal Response to Children Exposed to Domestic Violence, 9 Future of Children 67 (1999).

[Section 15:8]

[1]National Council of Juvenile & Family Court Judges, Family Violence in Child Custody Statutes: An Analysis of State Codes and Legal Practice, 29 Fam. L.Q. 2, 221 (1995); see also Text § 16:7, Ohio Domestic Violence Network—Escape plan for children; form.

[2]See Alan J. Tomkins et al., The Plight of Children Who Witness Woman Battering: Psychological Knowledge & Policy Implications, 18 Law & Psychol. Rev. 137, 185 (1994); see also Cartalin Glass, Tamara Kuenner & Sharon Lopez, Custody and Visitation: Considerations for Every Attorney Retained by a Survivor of Domestic Violence, 36 Clearinghouse Review 529 (2003); Jill Davies & Eleanor Lyon, Safety Planning with Battered Women, Complexities/Difficult Choices (Claire M. Renzetti & Jeffery L. Edleson eds. 1998).

[3]Barbara J. Hart, State Codes on Domestic Violence: Analysis, Commentary and Recommendations, 43 Juv. & Fam. Ct. J. 1, 34 (No. 4, 1992).

[4]Caroline W. Harlow, U.S. Dep't of Justice, Female Victims of Violent Crime 5, 13 (1991).

[5]Martha R. Mahoney, Legal Images of Battered Women: Redefining the Issue of

tion such as unsupervised visitation, transfers from one parent to the other, or shared parenting arrangements where contact and communication are unavoidable.[6]

Q & A: Can the safety of the abused parent ever be assured?

The short answer is that, in many cases, the safety of the victim cannot be adequately assured. "Perhaps at no point in a domestic violence case is the potential for further violence and harassment greater than when the domestic violence perpetrator has continuing access to the abused party and the children through a custody or visitation order."[7]

The safety of victims and other family members must be considered at all stages of custody and visitation proceedings by both the courts and the attorneys for the victims. Courts must begin to routinely include protective conditions in all parenting plans to safeguard the nonabusive parent and the children.[8] Safe visitation arrangements and the confidentiality of the victim's address must be considered in designing each and every court order.[9]

Attorneys must aid their clients in assessing the clients' safety under any court-ordered custody or visitation plan. Additionally, safety plans for the victim and children should be created.[10] Victim advocates can also act as a useful resource for attorneys and victims and can develop a safety plan with the victim or update and revise such plans as needed.

Unfortunately, in many cases, a victim may not feel comfortable or even safe admitting to domestic violence. Victims' reasons for not disclosing abuse are multifaceted.[11] They range from a mistrust of the legal system, which has failed to offer support to the victims, to a fear that the abuser will make good on the promise that the victim will never have custody of the children. Victims can never be sure that resources are available to prevent the abuser from continuing the violence.

Separation, 90 Mich. L. Rev. 1, 58–59 (1991).

[6]See Linda R. Keenan, Note, Domestic Violence and Custody Litigation: The Need for Statutory Reform, 13 Hofstra L. Rev. 407, 424 (1985); Julie Kunce Field, Screening for Domestic Violence: Meeting the Challenge of Identifying Domestic Relations Cases Involving Domestic Violence and Developing Strategies for Those Cases, 39(2) Court Rev. 4 (2002).

[7]Nancy K.D. Lemon, Custody and Visitation, in Domestic Violence in Civil Court Cases: A National Model for Judicial Education 200 (Jacqueline Agtuca et al. eds., 1992); see also Michael R. Voris, Civil Orders of Protection: Do They Protect Children, the Tag-Along Victims of Domestic Violence? 17 Ohio N.U. L. Rev. 599 (1991).

[8]See Clare Dalton, When Paradigms Collide: Protecting Battered Parents and Their Children in the Family Court System, 37 Fam. & Concil. Cts. Rev. 273 (July 1999).

[9]See Joan Zorza, Recognizing and Protecting the Privacy and Confidentiality Needs of Battered Women, 29 Fam. L.Q. 273 (1995).

[10]See Deborah M. Goelman, Safety Planning, in The Impact of Domestic Violence on Your Legal Practice: A Lawyer's Handbook 2-11 (1996); Roberta L. Valente, Addressing Domestic Violence: The Role of the Family Law Practitioner, 29 Fam. L.Q. No. 2, 187 (1995).

[11]Mildred D. Pagelow, Justice for Victims of Spouse Abuse in Divorce and Child Custody Cases, 8 Violence and Victims 1 (1993).

§ 15:9 Confidentiality

Separation is a time of increased violence for victims of domestic violence. In fact, the National Crime Statistics demonstrate that "in almost 75% of reported spousal assaults, the partners were divorced or separated."[1]

Q & A: What can be done to protect the confidentiality needs of victims of domestic violence?[2]

In certain situations, keeping the victim's address confidential is essential to maintaining the safety of both the victim and the children. If the victim moved to escape the domestic violence, it is imperative that the victim's address and telephone number be kept confidential, especially where it is evident that the abuse may continue in the future or where the victim believes that he/she is in danger of future abuse.

Ohio has no statutory provisions either restricting or discouraging disclosure of a victim's address during the pendency of a divorce action, even when domestic violence is an issue in a custody dispute. This is not to be confused with notices of intent to relocate, which restrict access to the victim's address after a visitation or parenting order is entered by the court.[3] As a matter of court practice or general policy, most courts require disclosure of all addresses and telephone numbers when children are involved in order to permit unrestricted access to children for the other parent at all times.[4] A few counties permit the victim to keep his/her address confidential during the pendency of the divorce action. After visitation and custody issues are resolved, the courts decide whether to invoke the restrictions of RC 3109.051(G).

Obviously, courts may prohibit disclosure at every stage of the divorce proceeding if the facts of the case warrant such restrictions. This is considered by a court where the abuse directed at the other parent is both frequent and severe, where the child is a victim of child

---

[Section 15:9]

[1]Anne L. Ganley, Domestic Violence: The What, Why and Who, as Relevant to Civil Court Cases, in Domestic Violence in Civil Court Cases, A National Model for Judicial Education 43 (Jacqueline Agtuca et al. eds., 1992) (citation omitted); see also Martha R. Mahoney, Legal Images of Battered Women: Redefining the Issues of Separation, 90 Mich. L. Rev. 1 (1991); Heck v. Reed, 529 N.W.2d 155, 36 A.L.R.5th 849 (N.D. 1995); Jennifer Hardesty, Separation Assault in the Context of Post Divorce Parenting, 8 Violence Against Women 597 (May 2002).

[2]See also Text § 17:4, Confidentiality and liability concerns, Text § 18:2, Batterer access to the victim—Limiting access to victim information; Sacharow v. Sacharow, 177 N.J. 62, 826 A.2d 710, 711 (2003) (discussing New Jersey Address Confidentiality Program Act and whether a court is an "agency under the government"). See also Civ. R. 65.1(B)(4).

[3]See RC 3109.051(G).

[4]Sacharow v. Sacharow, 826 A.2d 710, 711 (N. J. Supreme Ct. 2003) (in assessing the best interests of a child in the context of a parent's request for address confidentiality in custody proceedings, a court should take into account: (1) the good faith of the parties; (2) the prior history of dealings between them; (3) the relationship between each parent and the child; (4) any efforts by either party to alienate the child from the other parent; (5) the effect that address confidentiality has or will have on those relationships and on the child; (6) any special needs of the child; and (7) any other matter that bears on the best interests of the child).

abuse, or where the abuser has a history of stalking and locating the victim and the children even after frequent moves.

Where court practices and policies permit confidentiality of the victim's address, it is essential that all court pleadings include a confidentiality provision. For family law practitioners, it is imperative that even the parenting affidavit[5] reflect the confidential address. Since the purpose of the parenting affidavit is to provide addresses of the children outside of the county or state within the past five years, it is sufficient for the affiant to note that the confidential address is within the state of Ohio or within the forum jurisdiction.

Q & A: After custody has been determined, can the court mandate that the residential parent disclose his/her address to the other parent?

It depends. Ohio's statute details a procedure for parents who intend to move to another location after custody/visitation has been determined. RC 3109.051(G)(1) requires that a residential parent who intends to move to another residence file a Notice of Intent to Relocate with the court. This is the case even if the nonresidential parent has been convicted of domestic violence.[6] The notice must be filed whether the residential parent is moving across the street or to another state, and the notice must be filed prior to the actual move.[7]

Unless the court previously determined that the nonresidential parent has been convicted of domestic violence, the court must order a copy of the notice sent to the nonresidential parent.[8] On a motion by that parent or the court, a hearing may be scheduled to determine whether it is in the best interest of the child to revise the visitation schedule.[9]

If the court determines that the nonresidential parent has been convicted of domestic violence, the court must issue an order that the nonresidential parent not be given a copy of any notice of relocation.[10] However, in spite of the conviction for domestic violence, the court may still order that a notice of relocation be sent if the court, at the time of the original hearing, found that it was in the best interest of the child to give the nonresidential parent a copy of the relocation notice. The court must issue an order that, should the residential parent plan to move, the nonresidential parent must be given a copy of any notice of relocation, and the court must support its decision by specific findings of fact and conclusions of law.[11]

In cases where visitation was established prior to April 11, 1991, the effective date of the statutory amendment detailing the notice of relocation, the statute requires the court to follow a similar

[5]See RC 3109.27.

[6]RC 3109.051(G)(1).

[7]See RC 3109.051(G)(1).

[8]RC 3109.051(G)(1).

[9]See RC 3109.051(G)(1).

[10]RC 3109.051(G)(2).

[11]RC 3109.051(G)(2).

procedure.[12] Additionally, RC 3109.051(G)(4) provides a notice and hearing procedure for a residential parent who does not want the nonresidential parent to receive a notice of intent to relocate because of a later conviction for domestic violence. If the court determines that the nonresidential parent has been convicted of domestic violence, a copy of the relocation notice will no longer be given to that parent unless the court determines that it is in the best interest of the child and supports its decision with specific written findings of fact.[13]

Q & A: If the parent's address was confidential at the time of the divorce hearing, does that parent still have to notify the court and the other parent of the intent to relocate?

It depends. If the victim's address had been confidential because of the other parent's conviction for domestic violence, the victim does not have to provide notice of his/her intent to relocate.[14] However, RC 3109.051(G) does not address whether a notice must be given to the other parent where the residential parent's address was already confidential at the time of the divorce but there was no conviction for domestic violence. It must be stressed that a notice of intent to relocate must always be filed with the court. The only question is whether the notice should be sent to the other parent.

Because RC 3109.051(G) is silent on whether notice of intent to relocate must be given to the abusive parent where the residential parent's address has been confidential because of the fear of continued abuse, the attorney for the residential parent should not ignore this issue. In order to effectively protect the victim, the issue must be considered in the divorce judgment entry that sets forth the obligation of the victim to provide notice of relocation. A finding or order should be included in the entry that restricts or prevents disclosure of the residential parent's address to the nonresidential parent even if the residential parent moves. A provision such as this should insure confidentiality of the victim's address into the future. It will also provide the victim with peace of mind.

Q & A: What types of protections can be ordered by a court?

It is noteworthy that the National Council of Juvenile and Family Court Judges drafted the Model Code on Domestic and Family Violence ("Model Code") with the primary objective focusing on "1. The protection and safety of all victims of domestic or family violence in a fair, prompt and effective manner; and 2. The prevention of future violence in all families."[15] These statements enhance the importance of according safety and protection to each and every victim of domestic violence and his/her children and, each provision of the Model Code is built on this premise.

Attorneys practicing in this area should become familiar with the Model Code. The Model Code may be useful in educating courts that the safety of both the victim and the children must be the paramount concern in custody/visitation disputes. Courts may discover a useful

---

[12] See RC 3109.051(G)(3).

[13] RC 3109.051(G)(4).

[14] RC 3109.051(G)(2).

[15] National Council of Juvenile & Family Court Judges, Model Code on Domestic and Family Violence, § 101 at 1 (1994).

ally in the Model Code, and its precepts may be included in judicial opinions.

Realistically, however, the court's primary goal in crafting parenting plans is to to maximize parental involvement and contact with both parents. It is difficult to provide safety, confidentiality, and privacy for the victim where access and contact to the children is the expectation of the court.

For the parties, the goals are conflicting as well. The victim does not want the batterer to know where he/she lives. However, the batterer wants to know where the children live. In some situations, the abused parent and the children only want the abuse to stop; they do not want to lose contact with the abusive parent.[16] Protection orders may give victims the opportunity to accomplish the dual goals of restricting the batterer's access to the victim and permitting contact with the child.

Protection orders are crucial for victims of domestic violence.[17] They should be requested in all cases where the victim meets the elements of RC 3113.31 and seeks restraints on the abuser. Protection orders can address the following issues:

(1) the safety of the victim at home, school, and place of employment;
(2) custody and visitation arrangements;
(3) removal of the batterer from the home;
(4) financial provisions for the victim and children;
(5) the surrender of any weapons in the home or in the batterer's possession; and
(6) domestic violence counseling.

The court can also fashion specific remedies in order to stop the violence and deter the batterer from continued manipulation. For example, the court can suspend the batterer's visitation rights until domestic violence counseling is completed.[18]

Protection orders that have specific and restrictive terms place the batterer on notice that he/she is restrained from continuing the abusive conduct. In the standard protection order forms that were recently adopted by the Ohio Supreme Court for dissemination in January 1998, there is a specific warning that informs the respondent of the penalties for violating the order.[19]

Besides law enforcement agencies, which are served with protection orders so that they may be called on to offer protection if a violation of the order occurs, other entities may be peripherally mentioned in the

---

[16]See Robert B. Straus, Supervised Visitation and Family Violence, 29 Fam. L.Q. 229, 239 (1995).

[17]See Text § 8:1, Introduction; see also Victoria Holt, et al., Civil Protection Orders and Risk of Subsequent Police-Reported Violence, 288 J. Am. Med. Ass'n 589 (August 2002); Lavita Nad Karni and Barbara Zeek Shaw, Making a Difference: Tools to Help Judges Support the Healing of Children Exposed to Domestic Violence, 39(2) Court Rev. 24 (2002); Allie Meiers, Civil Orders of Protection: A Tool to Keep Children Safe, 19 J. Am. Acad. Matrim. Law. 373 (2005); National Council of Juvenile and Family Court Judges, A Guide for Effective Issuance and Enforcement of Placement Orders (2006).

[18]See Sup. R. Form 10.01-H to Sup. R. Form 10.01-J.

[19]Sup. R. Form 10.01-G.

protection order to further protect the victim. Since schools, day care centers, doctors, dentists, hospitals and clinics, businesses, utility companies, and banks and credit card companies, and the like are places that the victim and/or the children frequent and since they are familiar with the victim's address, they should be considered for inclusion in any protection order.[20]

Any establishment might disclose the whereabouts of the victim to the batterer should be included in the protection order. Only when they have been joined as a party to the order do they have an obligation to obey the terms of the order and restrict the abuser's contact to the victim and the children.

Even if disclosure is not the concern, it may be necessary to join the entity as a party so that its employees abide by the terms of an order that restricts the abuser's access, for example, to the children's day care center. If the entity is not a party, it has no legal responsibility to comply with the terms of the protection order. Sanctions cannot attach to an entity that is not joined as a party, unless otherwise provided by statute.

Depending on the circumstances of the case, the nonresidential parent may or may not be permitted access to certain medical, school, and day care records of the children.[21] In such cases, a recordkeeper may be subject to contempt for failing to abide by the terms of a court order. A recordkeeper of an agency does not have to be joined as a party in order to be sanctioned.

The availability of civil protection orders in any court jurisdiction and the development of individual and creative remedies are essential for the victim. Court enforcement of protection orders can also be of great assistance to the victim, if done swiftly and punitively.[22]

§ 15:10 Batterer access to the victim and children[1]

Even when the court does not send a copy of the notice of intent to relocate to the abusive parent, the batterer uses other legal or even illegal avenues to gain access to the victim and children. If a batterer is unable to locate the victim's address from court documents, the batterer may try to locate the victim through either child support re-

[20]See Joan Zorza, Confidentiality, American Bar Assoc. Comm'n on Domestic Violence, The Impact of Domestic Violence on Your Legal Practice: A Lawyer's Handbook 2-17 (1996).

[21]See RC 3109.051(H) to RC 3109.051(J).

[22]See Text Ch. 12, Court Enforcement of Civil Protection Orders and Related Issues.

[Section 15:10]

[1]Katherine M. Reiking, Domestic Violence: Protecting Victims of Domestic Violence and their Children After Divorce: The American Law Institute's Model, 37 Fam. & Conciliation Courts Rev. 393 (1999); Bancroft and Silverman, The Batterer as Parent: Addressing the Impact of Domestic Violence on Family Dynamics (Sage Publications 2002); see also Text § 18:16, Battered immigrant provisions of the Violence Against Women Act 2000—VAWA self-petitions; Text § 18:18, Battered immigrant provisions of the Violence Against Women Act 2000—Those eligible to file a VAWA self-petition for lawful permanent resident status.

cords[2] or the children's medical or school records. CSEA records are a valuable source of location information since the victim will keep that information updated in order to keep receiving support checks. The Ohio legislature has provided both parents with equal access to the children's medical and school records.[3] Unfortunately, the very records that provide for continued access to the children often create a dangerous situation for the victim. In many situations, victims should provide a trusted relative's address rather than their own.

The attorney or victim advocate should assist the victim in completing a safety plan in the event that the victim's whereabouts are made known to the batterer. Although various community resources may help provide a confidential location,[4] there is no guarantee that disclosure of a confidential location and future injury will be prevented.

Q & A: If, during divorce or post-decree custody proceedings, the abusive parent alleges that the other parent's living accommodations are inadequate for the children, must the court permit the parent to inspect the children's residence?

Not necessarily. Where the victim wishes to maintain a confidential address and it can be demonstrated that the parent requesting the inspection has committed domestic violence or that there is risk for future violence, the victim's attorney should explore the use of less risky alternatives. To controvert the abuser's argument that the housing and living accommodations are inadequate for the children and that the abuser must view them himself/herself, the victim's attorney must argue that a better alternative is to have the court's investigative personnel visit the home and make a report to the court. A guardian ad litem may also be used to inspect the home. Providing that the accommodations are satisfactory, there should be no further need for the abusive parent to personally inspect the other parent's residence.

Q & A: How does the statute address the issues of equal access to records?

RC 3109.051(H)(1) requires that parents have equal access to the child's school records. The nonresidential parent is granted equal access to the child's records unless the court finds that it is in the child's best interest to restrict the nonresidential parent's access. If access is restricted, the court must specify the terms, if any, under which the parent is to have access and must enter its written findings of fact and opinion in the journal.[5] If access is not restricted, nothing need be noted in the parenting decree.

"Records" are defined in RC 3109.051(N)(2) as "any record, document, file, or other material that contains information directly related

[2]But see RC 3111.51, RC 3111.13(H) (CSEA prohibits use of social security numbers and addresses in administrative orders where the agency has reason to believe that a person named in the order is a potential victim of domestic violence).

[3]But see RC 3313.672, RC 3319.321(F) (if the parent and child are in a shelter, the record keeper of the school the child is temporarily attending may not release to the other parent any information about the location of the school).

[4]See Developments in the Law: Legal Responses to Domestic Violence, 106 Harv. L. Rev. 1498, 1507–09 (1993).

[5]See RC 3109.051(H)(1).

to a child, including, but not limited to" records maintained by public and private school, day care facilities or preschools, hospitals or other facilities for the treatment of the child, or agencies, departments, instrumentalities, or other entities of the state or political subdivision of the state, except the child support enforcement agency.

Every parenting decree must contain a notice that the keeper of a record who knowingly fails to comply with the court order is in contempt of court.[6] Thus, a recordkeeper who fails to permit the nonresidential parent access to records may be found in contempt.[7] A copy of any order restricting the access of the nonresidential parent to the children's records must be presented to the recordkeeper by the residential parent.[8] If the recordkeeper is given a copy of the order that restricts access to the nonresidential parent and then knowingly permits access, the recordkeeper may also be found in contempt of court.[9]

The abused residential parent should be cautioned that, unless the nonresidential parent's access is specifically restricted by the court order, he/she may not unilaterally authorize a recordkeeper to disregard the law and withhold the records if they are requested by the abusive nonresidential parent. However, a civil protection order, detailing that some agencies not disclose certain information, may provide immediate protection to the victim, unless and until the court orders otherwise.

The court may eliminate any conditions or restrictions that minimize parental contact in parenting plans issued pursuant to a divorce or modification of custody and/or visitation. For this reason, the attorney for the abused residential parent must review the terms of any existing protection order. A protection order that restricts access to records may conflict with a subsequent or prior parenting plan. The client's attorney has a responsibility to inform the court of the existence and terms of the protection order. Any restrictions regarding access should be allowed to remain in full force and effect for the duration of the protection order. Any subsequent parenting decree should reflect the court's continuing legal authority for such restrictions.[10]

Q & A: Would a CPO supersede R.C. 3109.051(H)(1) and render a parent's access to school records null?

Not unless the civil protection order specifically addressed school records. The purpose of a CPO is not to prevent access to information; rather, it is designed to restrict contact between persons, either directly or indirectly. While a CPO may contain specific restrictions, these are not automatic. Since the provisions of R.C. 3109.051(H) apply only to records access, it is unlikely that the mere issuance of a CPO would negate the mandate of R.C. 3109.051(H).

Q & A: Does the statute address the issue of equal access to the child's day care facility?

Yes. RC 3109.051(I) requires a court to determine whether the

[6]RC 3109.051(H)(1).

[7]See RC 3109.051(H)(1), RC 3109.051(H)(2).

[8]RC 3109.051(H)(2); see also RC 3313.672, RC 3319.321(F).

[9]RC 3109.051(H)(1), RC 3109.051(H)(2).

[10]See RC 3113.31(E)(1).

nonresidential parent should have equal access to any day care facility that is or that, in the future, may be attended by the child. If access is to be restricted, the court must articulate the terms and conditions under which the nonresidential parent is to have access. The court is required to note its findings of fact and opinions in the journal entry and must include the terms and conditions in the parenting decree.[11]

Significantly, the General Assembly specifically articulated that the nonresidential parent may not have more access than that provided to the residential parent. Additionally, the court need not include in its parenting decree any terms that reflect an award of equal access. If nothing is mentioned in the parenting decree, equal access is presumed.

If access is restricted by an existing protection order, the restrictive conditions must be either included in the parenting decree or specifically modified. It is critical that conflicting court orders are not entered on the court docket. Compliance from the day care facility and enforcement by the police will be compromised if the parenting decree and the protection order conflict.

Q & A: Does the statute address the issue of equal access to the child's school activities?

Yes. RC 3109.051(J) provides that both parents are granted equal access to the child's school activities unless the activity is one to which the residential parent is not legally entitled to access or unless such access is not in the child's best interest. If access to the child's activities is to be restricted, the court must enter written findings of fact in its journal entry and issue an order detailing the restrictive terms and conditions. As with access to records, the court is also required to include in its order that any school official or employee who knowingly fails to comply with such an order is in contempt of court.[12]

Access to student activities must be permitted unless the residential parent presents the school official or employee, the board of education, or the governing body of a private school with a copy of the order limiting the nonresidential parent's access.[13] If, after presentment of the order, the school official or employee permits the nonresidential parent unauthorized access, that employee or official is in contempt of court.[14]

Q & A: What parenting plan options are available to victims of domestic violence?

In crafting adequate parenting plans that balance parental contact with the safety concerns of the parties, courts should strive to protect the confidentiality of the victim's work, home, and school addresses. For example, the court may preserve the confidentiality of the victim's address by providing for the exchange of the children through a third

[11] RC 3109.051(I).

[12] RC 3109.051(J)(1).

[13] See RC 3109.051(J)(1), RC 3109.051(J)(2).

[14] See RC 3109.051(J)(1), RC 3109.051(J)(2).

party.[15] Supervised visitation centers may also provide this service. At present, several Ohio counties[16] are in the process of establishing such centers through grants provided pursuant to the Violence Against Women Act. Additionally, courts may be able to craft plans that permit access to the child at school or day care. Such orders should require the school or day care center to note on the child's file that the nonresidential parent is restricted from inspecting any portion of the file containing the victim's address.

Courts generally require hospitals to release medical records pursuant to a subpoena duces tecum or court order. However, it is often the abusive parent's request for the records that creates the dilemma. Courts should restrict an abuser's access to the victim's address. The court may request that the records be turned over to the court so that the court can block out the victim's address and telephone number before handing the information over to the requesting party.

In some court jurisdictions, victims are also permitted to provide a relative's address and telephone number in court documents rather than their own so that confidentiality can be assured while still permitting access to the children. So long as the victim can receive mail at the address provided and the other parent can call the children at specific times, this should be an acceptable alternative.

§ 15:11 Impact of domestic violence on children[1]

Violence directed at one of the parents by the other is always harmful to the children of the relationship.[2] This is true whether or not the violence is also directed at the children, whether the children only

[15]Robert B. Straus, Supervised Visitation and Family Violence, 27 Fam. L.Q. 229 (1994).

[16]Cuyahoga, Marietta, and Washington counties are among the counties beginning such programs.

[Section 15:11]

[1]See Geffner, Igelmen, and Zellner, The Effects of Intimate Partner Violence in Children (Haworth Maltreatment & Trauma Press 2003). See also Text § 15:7, Presenting evidence of domestic violence in custody and visitation proceedings; practice pointers; Marjory D. Fields, The Impact of Spousal Abuse on Children and its Relevance in Custody and Visitation Decisions in New York States, 3 Cornell J. L. & Pub. Policy 221, 228 (1994); Lundy Bancroft, The Parenting of Men Who Batter, 39(2) Court Review (Summer 2002); Sherry Hamby, David Finkelhor & Heather Turner, Intervention Following Family Violence: Best Practices and Helpseeking Obstacles in a Nationally Representative Sample of Families with Children, Psychology of Violence 1 (2014).

[2]Naomi R. Cahn, Civil Images of Battered Women: The Impact of Domestic Violence on Child Custody Decisions, 5 Vand. L. Rev. 1041 (1991); see also Peter G. Jaffe et al., Children of Battered Women (1990); Lucy Salcido Carter et al., Domestic Violence and Children: Analysis and Recommendations, 9 Future of Children 4, 5 (1999); Jeffrey Edleson & Susan Schechtor, Effective Intervention in Domestic Violence & Child Maltreatment Cases: Guidelines for Policy and Practice, Recommendations from the National Council of Juvenile & Family Court Judges Family Violence Dep't (1999); Alan J. Tomkins et al., The Plight of Children Who Witness Woman Battering: Psychological Knowledge and Policy Implications, 18 Law and Psychol. Rev. 137 (1994); Mary Kenning, et al., "Research on the Effects of Witnessing Parental Battering: Clinical and Legal Policy Implications" in M. Steinman, ed., Women Battering: Policy Responses, 237, Cincinnati: Anderson Publishing.

witness the abuse,[3] or whether the children do not directly witness the abuse but suffer its consequences.[4]

General Indications of Trauma to Children

The most consistent trauma to children of all ages is the constant disruption of their daily lives.[5] The nonabusive parent is often forced to relocate to avoid the abuse. The children are removed from their school, friends, and home to hide from the abusive parent. Sometimes, a child is even removed from the nonabusive parent by the children's services agency who is accused of failing to protect the child.[6]

The effect on the child is significant,[7] even where the child only hears the sounds of his/her parent fighting—screams and threats, glass breaking, or furniture smashing.[8] This is true even if the child did not see or hear the actual fight. Children who are exposed to domestic violence often see the results of the battering incident—the bruising, the blood, the torn clothes, the holes in the wall, or the overturned furniture.

Many parents minimize the effects of the violence on their children. The excuses given by parents are that the children were either in their rooms, sleeping, or not at home when the violence occurred.

---

[3]See Alan J. Tomkins et al., The Plight of Children Who Witness Woman Battering: Psychological Knowledge and Policy Implications, 18 Law & Psychol. Rev. 137, 185 (1994); J. Kolbo, E. Blakely & D. Engleman, Children Who Witness Violence: A Review of Empirical Literature, 11(2) Journal of Interpersonal Violence 281-93 (1996); E.M. Cummings, Children Exposed to Marital Conflict and Violence: Conceptual and Theoretical Directions, Children Exposed to Marital Violence: Theory, Research, and Applied Issues, 55-93 (G.W. Holden, R. Geffner, & E.N. Jouriles, eds., APA, Washington D.C. (1998)); Allison Turkel & Christina Shaw, Strategies for Handling Cases Where Children Witness Domestic Violence, Update National Center for Prosecution of Child Abuse, Vol. 16 No. 2 (2003).

[4]J. Kashani et al., Family Violence: Impact on Children, 31 J. Am. Acad. Child Adolesc. Psychiatry 181 (1992); see also Howard A. Davidson, A Report to the President of the American Bar Association, The Impact of Domestic Violence on Children (1994); Children Exposed to Marital Violence (G. W. Holden et al., eds., Am. Psychol. Ass'n 1998); Honore M. Hughes et al., Witnessing Spouse Abuse and Experiencing Physical Abuse: "A Double Whammy"? 4 J. Fam. Violence 197 (1989); John W. Fantazzo & Wanda K. Mohr, Prevalence and Effects of Child Exposure to Domestic Violence, 9 Future of Children 21 (1999).

[5]See Myra Sun & Elizabeth Thomas, Custody Litigation on Behalf of Battered Women, 21 Clearinghouse Rev. 563 (1987); see also Joan Zorza, Protecting the Children in Custody Disputes When One Parent Abuses the Other, 29 Clearinghouse Rev. 1113, 1116 (1996).

[6]Howard A. Davidson, A Report to the President of the American Bar Association, The Impact of Domestic Violence on Children (1994); G. Kristian Miccio, Reasonable Battered Mother? Redefining, Reconstructing, & Recreating the Battered Mother in Child Protective Proceedings, 22 Harv. Women's L.J. 89 (1999); G. Kristian Miccio, In The Name of Mothers & Children: Deconstructing the Myth of the Passive Battered Mother & the "Protected Child" in Child Neglect Proceedings, 58 Alb. L. Rev. 1087 (1995).

[7]Teresa Meuer and Kathryn Webster, Effects of Domestic Abuse on Child Witnesses, 1997 Wiley Family Law Update 201 (1997).

[8]See Lenore E. Walker, The Battered Woman Syndrome (1984); see also Mildred D. Pagelow, Children in Violent Families: Direct and Indirect Victims, in Young Children and Their Families 55 (Shirley Hill & B. J. Barnes eds., 1982).

However, these same children are often able to provide accurate and detailed accounts of their parents' abuse to counselors.[9]

Unfortunately, many of the children who witness the abuse are also directly affected by the violence at home. For example, the children may be abused just by being in physical proximity to the parents. They may be harmed by flying objects aimed at the other parent.[10] They may be harmed by the abuser simply as a way of further abusing the other parent.[11] Children may also intervene to protect a parent and be injured in the crossfire.[12] Sometimes, the child is physically or sexually abused by the abusive parent as well.[13]

Perhaps the most significant long-term effect of domestic violence in the family is that the cycle of violence will repeat itself in successive generations.[14] This intergenerational transmission of violence often manifests itself later in life when the child becomes an adult.[15]

Recent research suggests that "people who, as children, had observed their parents engaging in physical violence were more likely to engage in the same sort of activity with their own spouses than those who never saw their parents fight."[16] Although the studies fail to definitively demonstrate cause and effect between observing parental abuse and becoming violent as adults, significant correlations exist to suggest that witnessing parental violence as a child is an identifiable factor associated with adult violence and adult victimization.[17]

There are also relatively short-term effects of domestic violence on

---

[9]Peter G. Jaffe et al., Children of Battered Women 21 (1990).

[10]Maria Roy, Children in the Crossfire 92 (1988).

[11]National Center on Women and Family Law, Inc., The Effects of Woman Abuse on Children: Psychological and Legal Authority 2 (1994); see also Joan Zorza, Protecting the Children in Custody Disputes When One Parent Abuses the Other, 29 Clearinghouse Rev. 1113 (1996); Jerry Von Talge, Victimization Dynamics: The Psycho-Social and Legal Implications of Family Violence Directed Toward Women and the Impact on Child Witnesses, 27 W. St. U.L. Rev. 111 (1999-2000).

[12]Maria Roy, Children in the Crossfire 89–90 (1988).

[13]Lenore E. Walker, The Battered Woman Syndrome 59 (1984); see also Lee H. Bowker et al., On the Relationship Between Wife Beating and Child Abuse, in Feminist Perspectives on Wife Abuse 158, 164 (Kersti Yllo & Michelle Bograd eds., 1988); see also Honore M. Hughes et al., Witnessing Spouse Abuse and Experiencing Physical Abuse: "A Double Whammy"? 4 J. Fam. Violence 197 (1989).

[14]R. Herrenkohl & L. Toedler, Perspective on the Intergenerational Transmission of Abuse, in The Dark Side of Families: Current Family Violence Research 306–16 (David Finkelhor et al. eds., 1983); see also Debra Kalmuss, The Intergenerational Transmission of Marital Aggression, 46 J. Marriage & Fam. 11 (1984); but see Cathy Spatz Widom, Does Violence Beget Violence? A Critical Examination of the Literature, 106 Psychol. Bull. 3, 3-28 (1989); Joan Kaufman and Edward Zigler, Do Abused Children Become Abusive Parents?, 57 Am. J. Orthopsychiatry 186 (1987).

[15]See M.A. Straus et al., Behind Closed Doors: Violence in the American Family 101 (1980); see also Judith Wallerstein & Sandra Blakeslee, Second Chances 121 (1989); Fred Markowitz, Attitudes and Family Violence: Linking Intergenerational and Cultural Theories, 16 Journal of Family Violence 205, 205-18 (2001).

[16]Del Martin, Battered Wives 23 (1976).

[17]National Center on Women and Family Law, Inc., The Effects of Woman Abuse on Children: Psychological and Legal Authority 10 (1994); see also David Wolfe et al., A Multivariate Investigation of Children's Adjustment to Family Violence, in Family Abuse and its Consequences 228–43 (Gerald Hotaling et al. eds., 1988); John W.

children.[18] They often experience shock, fear, and guilt and also suffer from a variety of physical and behavioral complaints.[19] For example, children may be damaged by way of delayed social development.[20]

Researchers have found that preschool-aged children often resist going to bed, associating nighttime with violence.[21] They present with intense fear and screaming.[22] Their physical complaints include sleep difficulties, such as insomnia, bedwetting, nightmares, and sleepwalking.[23]

As the children mature and their awareness grows, they feel guilty because they are unable to stop the violence or protect the abused parent. Often, they lose respect for and become angry with the parent who is abused.[24]

The types of behavioral problems often differ depending on the child's gender. Some of the literature suggests that both sexes suffer from domestic violence but that its effects are demonstrated in different ways at different ages.[25] Generally, boys become aggressive and disruptive toward family members and schoolmates, and girls become withdrawn, passive, and anxious.[26] Other studies suggest that older girls score high on "all measures of physical and behavioral problems,

---

Fantuzzo & Carol U. Lindquist, The Effects of Observing Conjugal Violence on Children: A Review and Analysis of Research Methodology, 4 J. Fam. Violence 77–94 (1989); Melissa A. Trepiccione, At the Crossroads of Law and Social Science: Is Charging a Battered Mother With Failure to Protect Her Child an Acceptable Solution When the Child Witnesses Domestic Violence?, 69 Fordham L. Rev. 1487 (2001).

[18]National Center on Women and Family Law, Inc., The Effects of Woman Abuse on Children: Psychological and Legal Authority 5 (1994); see also J. D. Osofsky, Children Who Witness Domestic Violence: The Invisible Victims, 9 Soc. Pol'y Rep. 11 (Soc'y for Research in Child Dev. 1995).

[19]Mildred D. Pagelow, Children in Violent Families: Direct and Indirect Victims, in Young Children and Their Families 47, 60 (Shirley Hill & B. J. Barnes eds., 1982); Myra Sun & Elizabeth Thomas, Custody Litigation on Behalf of Battered Women, 21 Clearinghouse Rev. 563, 564 (1987); Laura McCloskey et al., The Effects of Systemic Family Violence on Children's Mental Health, 66 Child Development 1239 (1995).

[20]Myra Sun & Elizabeth Thomas, Custody Litigation on Behalf of Battered Women, 21 Clearinghouse Rev. 563 (1987); see also Mildred D. Pagelow, Effects of Domestic Violence on Children and Their Consequences for Custody and Visitation Agreements, 7 Mediation Q. 348 (1990).

[21]Myra Sun & Elizabeth Thomas, Custody Litigation on Behalf of Battered Women, 21 Clearinghouse Rev. 563 (1987).

[22]Myra Sun & Elizabeth Thomas, Custody Litigation on Behalf of Battered Women, 21 Clearinghouse Rev. 563 (1987); see also Mildred D. Pagelow, Effects of Domestic Violence on Children and Their Consequences for Custody and Visitation Agreements, 7 Mediation Q. 348 (1990).

[23]Mildred D. Pagelow, Effects of Domestic Violence on Children and Their Consequences for Custody and Visitation Agreements, 7 Mediation Q. 348 (1990).

[24]Myra Sun & Elizabeth Thomas, Custody Litigation on Behalf of Battered Women, 21 Clearinghouse Rev. 563 (1987); see also Terry Davidson, Conjugal Crime: Understanding and Changing the Wifebeating Pattern (1978).

[25]Mildred D. Pagelow, Effects of Domestic Violence on Children and Their Consequences for Custody and Visitation Agreements, 7 Mediation Q. 348, 351 (1990).

[26]Barbara J. Hart, State Codes on Domestic Violence: Analysis, Commentary, and Recommendations, 43 Juv. & Fam. Ct. J. 29, 33 (1992); see also Peter Jaffe et al., Similarities in Behavioral and Social Maladjustment Among Child Victims and Witnesses to Family Violence, 56 Am. J. Orthopsychiatry 142–6 (1986).

including aggression, and lower in social competence."[27] Both sexes suffer delays in speech development and motor and cognitive skills, and their school performance also suffers.[28]

Children of all ages also present with various somatic complaints ranging from stomach aches and diarrhea to insomnia.[29] These children also report higher rates of abdominal distress, asthma, headaches, colds, sore throats, and bedwetting.[30]

Q & A: Does the age of the child influence how the child responds to domestic violence?

Yes. Age matters in relation to a child's needs, his/her gender, and the differing roles that manifest themselves at each stage in the child's cognitive and social development.[31] A child's response appears to be related to both gender and age.[32]

For example, forming strong emotional bonds is crucial for an infant's healthy emotional development.[33] Domestic violence, at this stage in the child's development, interferes with the child's feeding, sleeping, and nurturing.[34] Infants are likely to have eating, sleeping, weight, or responsiveness problems.[35] Toddlers show signs of terror and even suffer from mood and interaction disorders.[36] Additionally, the child may emotionally distance himself/herself from his/her parents because of the fear and anger created by the abusive relationship.[37]

As the child ages, role modeling and emulating the same-sex parent is fundamental to emotional growth.[38] For the pre-adolescent child, role modeling may be impaired and influenced by the domestic violence within the relationship. Girls have a tendency to withdraw,

---

[27]Mildred D. Pagelow, Effects of Domestic Violence on Children and Their Consequences for Custody and Visitation Agreements, 7 Mediation Q. 348, 351 (1990).

[28]Myra Sun & Elizabeth Thomas, Custody Litigation on Behalf of Battered Women, 21 Clearinghouse Rev. 563 (1987); see also Mindy S. Rosenberg, Children of Battered Women: The Effects of Witnessing Violence on Their Social Problem-Solving Abilities, 10 Behavior Therapist 85 (1987).

[29]See Elaine Hilberman & Kit Munson, Sixty Battered Women, 2 Victimology: Am. Int'l J. 463 (1977–78).

[30]See Elaine Hilberman & Kit Munson, Sixty Battered Women, 2 Victimology: Am. Int'l J. 463 (1977–78); see also Myra Sun & Elizabeth Thomas, Custody Litigation on Behalf of Battered Women, 21 Clearinghouse Rev. 563 (1987).

[31]See generally Peter G. Jaffe et al., Children of Battered Women (1990); see also James O. Palmer, The Psychological Assessment of Children (1970); S. Graham-Bermann, "The Impact of Woman Abuse on Children's Social Development: Research and Theoretical Perspectives," Children Exposed to Marital Violence: Theory, Research, and Applied Issues 21-54 (G.W. Holden, R. Geffner & E.N. Jouriles, eds., APA, Washington, D.C. (1998)).

[32]Liane V. Davis & Bonnie E. Carlson, Observations of Spouse Abuse: What Happens to the Children? 2 J. Interpersonal Violence 278, 279 (1987).

[33]James O. Palmer, The Psychological Assessment of Children 46–47 (1970).

[34]Peter G. Jaffe et al., Children of Battered Women 40 (1990).

[35]Peter G. Jaffe et al., Children of Battered Women 40 (1990).

[36]Peter G. Jaffe et al., Children of Battered Women 40 (1990).

[37]National Center on Women and Family Law, Inc., The Effects of Woman Abuse on Children: Psychological and Legal Authority (1994).

[38]Liane V. Davis & Bonnie E. Carlson, Observations of Spouse Abuse: What Happens to the Children? 2 J. Interpersonal Violence 278, 279 (1987).

and boys are more likely to act out violently to resolve conflicts with peers.[39]

In addition, these children may lack confidence or have a dismal outlook on life in general. They often blame themselves for the violence existing within their families.[40] They often feel conflicted if forced to choose sides in parental violence, especially when they love the parent whose battering they hate and the parent whose helplessness they also hate.[41]

Because teenagers seek independence, they are also at great risk from witnessing domestic violence.[42] They risk imitating the same abusive parental patterns in their dating relationships.[43] Teen boys may begin to threaten their mothers and act out violent roles in dating. Girls may begin to accept threats, violence, and controlling behavior in their dating relationships.

Worse, a small group of teenagers separate from their parents by disconnecting emotionally—living in a make-believe world, acting delinquently, running away, or committing suicide. Each are escapist routes, but each provides a way for children to leave the violence within their homes.[44]

Q & A: Can witnessing an isolated incident of violence be damaging to a child?

It depends.[45] The impact on a particular child may vary with the child's age, the stage of development, and response to traumatic events. Only time will tell whether one incident of violence will affect a child emotionally. However, the effects of a one-time incident must never be minimized or underestimated. Even a one-time incident may

[39]Liane V. Davis & Bonnie E. Carlson, Observations of Spouse Abuse: What Happens to the Children? 2 J. Interpersonal Violence 278, 279 (1987); see also National Center on Women and Family Law, Inc., The Effects of Woman Abuse on Children: Psychological and Legal Authority 25, 27–30 (1994).

[40]National Center on Women and Family Law, Inc., The Effects of Woman Abuse on Children: Psychological and Legal Authority 7, 28 (1994); see also Peter G. Jaffe et al., Children of Battered Women 42 (1990).

[41]Carla Garrity & Mitchell A. Baris, Custody & Visitation: Is It Safe? 17 Fam. Advoc. 40, 42 (1995); see also Laura Crites & Donna Coker, What Therapists See That Judges May Miss: A Unique Guide to Custody Decisions When Spouse Abuse is Charged, 27 Judges' J. 8 (1988); see also Jann Jackson, Intervention with Children Who Have Witnessed Abuse 4 (1990).

[42]National Center on Women and Family Law, Inc., The Effects of Woman Abuse on Children: Psychological and Legal Authority 33 (1994); see also Barbara Forsstrom-Cohen & Alan Rosenbaum, The Effects of Parental Marital Violence on Young Adults: An Exploratory Investigation, 47 J. Marriage & Fam. 467 (1985).

[43]See Troubled Family Legacies and Resilience, 16(2) ABA Child Law Practice 24–29 (1997) for additional information on the intergenerational transmission of domestic violence.

[44]Peter G. Jaffe et al., Children of Battered Women 41 (1990).

[45]But see Nancy E. Johnson, Domestic Violence Research: The Year in Review 55, 56 (1998) (describing a psychological study suggesting "all [domestic violence] has the potential to induce trauma in the child witness regardless of intensity or frequency").

be part of a pattern of abuse that is likely to escalate in both frequency and severity over time.[46]

Q & A: Can behavior such as threatening the other parent, throwing and breaking objects, punching holes in the wall, pulling phones out of the wall, and restraining a parent cause emotional damage to a child?

"Children who live in a world of violence, even if directed at things, may have difficulty determining what is normal behavior."[47] The child's age, stage of development, and coping mechanisms are significant variables in determining the effects of the violent behavior on the child.[48]

Each of the above-described acts may be categorized as violent behavior. All of these behaviors are consistent with the potential for future abuse. These acts may be perceived as threats of violence. The batterer may act in such a way as to send an implied threat that something or someone the child loves may soon be on the receiving end of the batterer's rage.

Although the particular act may be directed at the spouse, the children may be given the message that it can also happen to them. Over time, cues in the voice or facial expressions may portend impending physical violence.[49] Of necessity, children of domestic violence begin to recognize these cues and will modify their own behaviors accordingly.

Q & A: Can the use of alcohol contribute to domestic violence?

Research has demonstrated that violent persons are more likely to abuse alcohol than nonviolent persons.[50]

Drinking is linked to violence in several complex ways:

(1) chronic alcohol abuse creates stress in families,

(2) heavy drinking can lessen inhibitions, and

(3) alcohol can be the trigger for violence.[51]

It should be stressed, however, that alcohol use is a variable, and not the cause, of battering. Battering must be considered a separate problem that must be addressed. Treating the alcohol does not necessarily stop the abuse. In custody determinations, alcohol must be considered an aggravating, not a mitigating, factor in assessing the violent party's parental fitness. Treatment through a batterer's program may be delayed until the alcohol addiction is addressed, but it should not be replaced by alcohol treatment.

---

[46]See K. Rose & J. Goss, Domestic Violence Statistics, National Criminal Justice Reference Service, Bureau of Justice Statistics 12 (1989).

[47]Faith Enyeart, Domestic Violence and Parenting Plans, in Domestic Violence Curriculum 213 (1991).

[48]See, e.g., Wissink v. Wissink, 301 A.D.2d 36, 749 N.Y.S.2d 550 (2d Dep't 2002).

[49]The Dark Side of Families: Current Family Violence Research (David Finkelhor & R. J. Gelles eds., 1983).

[50]R. M. Tolman & L. W. Bennett, A Review of Quantitative Research on Men Who Batter, 5 J. Interpersonal Violence 87–110 (1990); see also Deborah C. Richardson & Jennifer L. Campbell, Alcohol and Wife Abuse: The Effect of Alcohol on Attributions of Blame for Wife Abuse, 6 Personality & Soc. Psychol. Bull. 468–76 (1980).

[51]Adele Harrell, National Council of Juvenile & Family Court Judges, A Guide to Research on Family Violence 17 (1993).

Q & A: What characteristics exist to determine whether a child is affected by witnessing the abuse between the parents?

The markers of witnessed violence are not always apparent to persons not trained in the area of domestic violence. Children who witness domestic violence may present as perfectly normal, even happy and well-adjusted. Professionals suggest that courts should look for the following signs in children:

(1) eating/sleeping disorders,
(2) mood-related disorders,
(3) emotional neediness,
(4) overcompliance, clinginess, or withdrawal,
(5) aggression or destructive behavior,
(6) detachment, avoidance, or fantasy family life,
(7) somatic complaints, fingernail biting, restlessness, or stuttering,
(8) school problems from distraction to disruption, and
(9) suicidal ideation.[52]

Q & A: What does the research demonstrate?

The research on children who witness violence is relatively recent, and the empirical research lacks the methodological structure, scope, and focus of research findings available in other areas.[53] Few empirical studies exist, and many researchers have relied on clinical samples that may not be representative of the population at large.[54] Most of the research on children's responses to domestic violence is based on the observation of children who lived in battered women's shelters.[55] Samples that relied on only the mother's report of the child's adjustment may also be faulty because the mother's perceptions may have been skewed due to the domestic violence. Moreover, about one-third of these studies separated exposed children from those who were also direct victims of abuse, thus failing to separate the unique impact on children who have been exposed to domestic violence from those who have directly suffered its effects.[56]

Overall, existing studies reveal that some children exposed to adult domestic violence exhibit more difficulties than those not so exposed. But not all children exposed to domestic violence show evidence of greater problems than other children. The studies only suggest trends,

---

[52]See generally National Center on Women and Family Law, Inc., The Effects of Woman Abuse on Children: Psychological and Legal Authority (1994); see also Domestic Violence and Parenting Plans § 191 at 213.

[53]See Wanda K. Mohr, Making the Invisible Victims of Domestic Violence Visible, 2 Domestic Violence Report 1, No. 6 (1997). But see Lundy Bancroft, Assessing Risk to Children From Contact with Batterers, 7 Domestic Violence Report 4, 49 (April/May 2002).

[54]Honore M. Hughes, Impact of Spouse Abuse on Children of Battered Women, 2 Violence Update 1, 3 (1992).

[55]Honore M. Hughes & Susan J. Barad, Psychological Functioning of Children in a Battered Women's Shelter: A Preliminary Investigation, 53 Amer. J. Orthopsychiatry 525 (1983).

[56]Jeffrey L. Edleson, Should Childhood Exposure to Adult Domestic Violence be Defined as Child Maltreatment under the Law?, Presented at the workshop on "Children and Domestic Violence" (2000).

which may or may not indicate an individual child's experiences. In fact, recent research demonstrates only the degree of variability in children's experiences and the impact of those experiences on a particular child. Variables include the level of violence within a particular family, the degree to which each child is exposed to that violence, other stressors to which a child may be exposed, the harm it produces for a particular child, the unique individual coping skills each child brings to the situation, and other protective factors in a child's life.[57]

Clearly, more empirical data must be collected on the developmental impact of witnessed abuse on children.[58] The studies must also consider other environmental variables that may influence outcomes.[59] The development of children who remain in the home must also be tracked. Additionally, more empirical data is needed to establish a clear and definitive detrimental impact of witnessing domestic violence on children.[60]

Despite their methodological flaws,[61] the published studies do demonstrate that children's behavior problems are linked to the domestic violence in their lives and that regular exposure to parental violence adversely affects the children of the relationship.[62]

§ 15:12 Consideration of domestic violence as a best-interest factor—In custody decisions; recent case law

In every custody action, courts should consider credible evidence of domestic violence before awarding custody to either parent.[1] Since do-

[57]Jeffrey L. Edleson, Should Childhood Exposure to Adult Domestic Violence be Defined as Child Maltreatment under the Law?, Presented at the workshop on "Children and Domestic Violence" at 3-4 (2000); see also Melissa A. Trepiccione, At the Crossroads of Law and Social Science: Is Charging a Battered Mother with Failure to Protect her Child an Acceptable Solution When her Child Witnesses Domestic Violence?, 69 Fordham L. Rev. 1487 (2001).

[58]Honore M. Hughes, Impact of Spouse Abuse on Children of Battered Women, 2 Violence Update 1 (1992).

[59]Honore M. Hughes, Impact of Spouse Abuse on Children of Battered Women, 2 Violence Update 1, 3 (1992).

[60]Liane V. Davis & Bonnie E. Carlson, Observations of Spouse Abuse: What Happens to the Children? 2 J. Interpersonal Violence 278 (1987).

[61]Melissa A. Trepiccione, At the Crossroads of Law and Social Science: Is Charging a Battered Mother With Failure to Protect Her Child an Acceptable Solution When the Child Witnesses Domestic Violence?, 69 Fordham L. Rev. 1487 (2001).

[62]See Liane V. Davis & Bonnie E. Carlson, Observations of Spouse Abuse: What Happens to the Children? 2 Journal of Interpersonal Violence 278–91 (1987).

[Section 15:12]

[1]See Henry v. Johnson, 192 W. Va. 82, 450 S.E.2d 779 (1994). See also J.D. v. N.D., 170 Misc. 2d 877, 882, 652 N.Y.S.2d 468 (Fam. Ct. 1996) (Domestic violence as a custody factor is not limited to overt acts of violence causing physical injury but includes "an unmistakable pattern of power and control" exerted by one party over the other. The husband's pattern of psychological, sexual, and economic abuse, plus his threats and intimidation, showed that it is in the child's best interest to be in the custody of their mother); Clark v. Clark, 2004-Ohio-1577, 2004 WL 615708 (Ohio Ct. App. 7th Dist. Noble County 2004) (affirmed awarding custody to father because mother's violent behavior in the presence of child was not appropriate); Barry v. Barry, 169 Ohio App. 3d 129, 133, 2006-Ohio-5008, 862 N.E.2d 143 (8th Dist. Cuyahoga County 2006) (court held that "We cannot conceive how domestic violence

mestic violence detrimentally affects the children of the parties,[2] courts have an obligation to consider, not only whether domestic violence occurred in the relationship, but the effect of the domestic violence on the particular children involved.[3]

Q & A: What weight do courts accord to domestic violence when making custody and visitation determinations?[4]

Unfortunately, the courts are inconsistent in the weight accorded to domestic violence as a best-interest factor. It is clear, however, that some Ohio courts are of the opinion that domestic violence should be accorded as much weight as the other best-interest factors[5] such as honoring and facilitating visitation[6] and the mental health of the parents.[7]

Q & A: Is domestic violence considered in relocation cases?[8]

---

by one spouse against the other could not be relevant in a determination of an allocation of parental rights and responsibilities regarding their children. The fact that the domestic violence was previously litigated within the confines of this case is of no import, the hearing was not held before the judge who presided over the trial and the wife had the right to present the evidence in the context of its effect upon the children" and reversed that part of the decision.).

[2]See Text § 15:11, Impact of domestic violence on children; see also Wissink v. Wissink, 301 A.D.2d 36, 40, 749 N.Y.S.2d 550 (2d Dep't 2002) (in reversing the custody award to father in light of extensive domestic violence, appellate court stated that "there is overwhelming authority that a child living in a home where there has been abuse between the adults becomes a secondary victim and is likely to suffer psychological injury.").

[3]See Amy B. Levin, Child Witnesses of Domestic Violence: How Should Judges Apply the Best Interests of the Child Standard in Custody & Visitation Cases Involving Domestic Violence?, 47 UCLA L. Rev. 813 (2000). See also Wheeler v. Wheeler, 2015-Ohio-4206, 2015 WL 5918030 (Ohio Ct. App. 4th Dist. Scioto County 2015) (where minor witnessed some of the abuse, the appellate court indicated that the trial court did not have to wait for the divorce case to proceed to the point of allocating parental rights and responsibilities before taking steps to protect the wife and children. at ¶ 5).

[4]See also Text § 15:6, Ohio's judicial response to domestic violence.

[5]See, e.g., Dodd v. Dodd, 2001 WL 812244, *7 (Ohio Ct. App. 6th Dist. Lucas County 2001) (in which the appellate court affirmed the trial court's designation of the non-offending parent as the residential parent and legal custodian, over the recommendations of the court appointed psychologist and the guardian ad litem. The appellate court focused on the repeated pattern of domestic violence in the relationship while noting that the psychological report stressed that appellant recognized his proclivity to violence. The court was concerned that "his inability to control his anger is very much in question."); Baker v. Baker, 2004-Ohio-469, 2004 WL 226092 (Ohio Ct. App. 6th Dist. Lucas County 2004) (affirmed trial court's award of designating mother the residential parent in spite of fact that she was the subject of a one-year CPO; the trial court judge state that he did not feel that domestic violence was an ongoing problem in the parties' marriage).

[6]See, e.g., Holbrook v. Smith, 1999 WL 699876 (Ohio Ct. App. 12th Dist. Clermont County 1999).

[7]See Boling v. Valecko, 2002-Ohio-449, 2002 WL 185182 (Ohio Ct. App. 9th Dist. Summit County 2002) (court viewed father's conviction for domestic violence as an isolated incident and placed little weight on his domestic violence); see also Smith v. Smith, 2001 WL 542317 (Ohio Ct. App. 9th Dist. Wayne County 2001); Louderback v. Louderback, 1999 WL 94902 (Ohio Ct. App. 2d Dist. Montgomery County 1999).

[8]See also Paul S. Haberman, Before Death, We Must Part: Relocation and Protection for Domestic Violence Victims in Volatile Divorce and Custody Situations, 43 Fam. Ct. Rev. 149 (2005).

In *Marshall v. Marshall*,[9] the wife left Ohio with the children several months prior to the filing of the parties' divorce action in Ohio. The testimony indicates that she left because of spouse abuse which apparently took place in front of the children. While the trial court acknowledged that the husband's five acts of domestic violence "'could result in the finding of the commission of an offense of Domestic Violence,'" it focused on the fact that the wife left the state and did not return as ordered by the court and awarded custody to the husband.[10] The trial court concluded:

> This must be considered by the Court when examining the likelihood of each of the parties to honor and facilitate visitation. Also, the mere fact of the Defendant leaving the area in the manner in which she did impacts on the Courts [sic] Decision and this Court would find that the Plaintiff would be more likely to honor and facilitate those rights.[11]

The Allen County Court of Appeals reversed and remanded the case with instructions to award custody of the children to the wife. The court found that the trial court abused its discretion in awarding custody to the husband. The appellate court gave more credence to the issue of domestic violence as a reason for the wife's relocation and suggested that nonresidence alone should not deprive a parent of custody.[12]

It is significant that the Allen County Court of Appeals determined that relocation alone should not be a reason to award custody to one of the parents.[13] This court considered several best-interest factors, including domestic violence and which parent had primary caregiver status.[14] In effect, the appellate court indicated that the domestic violence in the relationship provided ample justification for the wife's relocation to North Carolina and her failure to abide by the trial court's order to return to Ohio. Moreover, the facts of this case indicate that the husband was not denied access to the children.

Q & A: Must the court consider the best interest of the children before awarding custody of them to one parent over the other pursuant to a civil protection order?

---

[9]Marshall v. Marshall, 117 Ohio App. 3d 182, 690 N.E.2d 68 (3d Dist. Allen County 1997). See also Janet M. Bowermaster, Relocation Custody Disputes Involving Domestic Violence, 46 U. Kan. L. Rev. 433 (1998). But see Schmidt v. Schmidt, 1999 WL 225157 (Ohio Ct. App. 12th Dist. Clermont County 1999).

[10]Marshall v. Marshall, 117 Ohio App. 3d 182, 185, 690 N.E.2d 68 (3d Dist. Allen County 1997).

[11]Marshall v. Marshall, 117 Ohio App. 3d 182, 185, 690 N.E.2d 68 (3d Dist. Allen County 1997).

[12]See also Gruber v. Gruber, 400 Pa. Super. 174, 583 A.2d 434 (1990); Desmond v. Desmond, 134 Misc. 2d 62, 509 N.Y.S.2d 979 (Fam. Ct. 1986). These cases are examples of an emerging body of case law which permits the removal of children from the home state by the abused custodial parent, especially where the primary motivation of the relocation is not to thwart visitation and where there are supportive services in the other state for the victim. See also Austin, Relocation Law and the Threshold of Harm: Integrating Legal and Behavioral Perspectives, 34 Fam. L.Q. 63 (2000).

[13]See Janet M. Bowermaster, Relocation Custody Disputes Involving Domestic Violence, 46 U. Kan. L. Rev. 433 (1998).

[14]See also Eddington v. McCabe, 98 A.D.3d 613, 949 N.Y.S.2d 734 (2d Dep't 2012).

Not according to the Clermont County Court of Appeals in *Couch v. Harrison*.[15] In that case, the parties were divorced and had a shared parenting arrangement. The appellant-mother's new husband hit the child, while appellant stood by. The father obtained a civil protection order on behalf of his daughters to protect them from future domestic violence. On appeal, the mother argued that the trial court failed to consider the best interests of the children before awarding custody of them to the father in that he failed to present evidence to show that such a placement was in the best interest of the children under RC 3109.04.

The Twelfth District Court of Appeals noted that the court had jurisdiction to temporarily provide for the care of minor children pursuant to RC 3113.31(E)(1)(d). The appellate court held that "[a]lthough placement of minor children under RC 3113.31(E)(1)(d) necessarily involves considerations of the best interest of the children, the statute does not specifically require the trial court to consider the 'best interest factors' used for creating or modifying a shared parenting plan, or determining companionship rights."[16] Because a court is not free to add words to a statute, the fact that the legislature did not include a mandate for trial courts to weigh the best interest factors in RC 3109.04(F)(1) before allocating parental rights and responsibilities in a civil protection order indicates that it did not mean to do so. The court then noted that ". . . RC 3113.31 demonstrates a clear and unambiguous legislative intent to enable the trial court to immediately provide for the temporary safety and protection of minor children. Where, as in this case, a minor child is the victim of domestic violence by a parent, it is patently obvious that it is in the child's best interest to be removed from an abusive situation."[17]

It is significant that the court noted in a footnote that the abuse of minor children and incidents of domestic violence are factors for determining the best interest of the child under RC 3109.04(F)(2)(g).

Q & A: Is a no contest plea a conviction for purposes of RC 3109.04(F)(1)(h)?

Clearly, courts must consider evidence of a conviction for or plea of guilty to the crime of domestic violence under RC 2919.25 before awarding custody to either parent.[18] No Ohio cases have addressed the issue of whether a "no contest" plea is a conviction for purposes of RC 3109.04(F)(1)(h).[19] Black's Law Dictionary defines "conviction" as "the result of a criminal trial which ends in a judgment or sentence

[15]Couch v. Harrison, 2001-Ohio-4199, 2001 WL 121108 (Ohio Ct. App. 12th Dist. Clermont County 2001).

[16]Couch v. Harrison, 2001-Ohio-4199, 2001 WL 121108 (Ohio Ct. App. 12th Dist. Clermont County 2001); see also Parker v. Jamison, 2003-Ohio-7295, 2003 WL 24135688 (Ohio Ct. App. 4th Dist. Scioto County 2003).

[17]Couch v. Harrison, 2001-Ohio-4199, 2001 WL 121108 (Ohio Ct. App. 12th Dist. Clermont County 2001).

[18]See RC 3109.04(C); see also RC 3109.04(F)(1)(h), RC 3109.04(F)(2)(c).

[19]But see Schmidt v. Schmidt, 1999 WL 225157 (Ohio Ct. App. 12th Dist. Clermont County 1999) (choosing not to distinguish between the effect of a "no contest" plea versus a conviction for purposes of RC 3109.04(F)(1)(h)); see also Morris v. Morris, 2000 WL 222025 (Ohio Ct. App. 5th Dist. Stark County 2000); Smith v. Smith, 2002-Ohio-223, 2002 WL 57973 (Ohio Ct. App. 9th Dist. Wayne County 2002).

that the accused is guilty as charged. The final judgment on a verdict or finding of guilty, a plea of guilty, or a plea of nolo contendere."[20] "Nolo contendere" is defined as "a plea in a criminal case which has a similar legal effect as pleading guilty."[21]

It would appear that a conviction is a conviction is a conviction. If there was a trial and the defendant was found guilty before a judge or jury, the defendant would be convicted. If the defendant pleads guilty to the crime, he/she will be convicted. If the defendant pleads no contest, the defendant is convicted when the court finds the defendant guilty and pronounces sentence.

It is likely that the Ohio legislature provided that a conviction by way of a "no contest" plea has the same effect as any other criminal conviction for domestic violence in determining whether a parent should be awarded custody.[22] That is, as a conviction that must be considered admissible evidence to prove domestic violence. Since a "no contest" plea translates into a finding of guilt for purposes of a criminal conviction, the nature of the plea itself is irrelevant to the issue of admissibility in the context of custody.

Even if a "no contest" plea is inadmissible,[23] a conviction entered on that plea is admissible when such conviction is authorized pursuant to statute.[24] For purposes of custody, the legislature requires the courts to consider evidence of a prior conviction for purposes of establishing domestic violence.[25]

Q & A: Does a defendant's entry into a diversion program change how the courts should interpret RC 3109.04(F)(1)(h)?

At least one Ohio appellate court responded in the affirmative. In *Moore v. Moore*,[26] the Licking County Appellate Court determined that the entry into a diversion program is different from a conviction or guilty plea. In *Moore*, a mother appealed, arguing that the trial court erred in designating her ex-husband as residential parent after he admitted to committing domestic violence. The court of appeals first determined that a conviction or guilty plea is a relevant best-interest factor under RC 3109.04(F)(1)(h). The court then held that, where the defendant had entered into a diversion program provided

[20]Black's Law Dictionary (6th ed.) p 333.

[21]Black's Law Dictionary (6th ed.) p 1048.

[22]See Morris v. Morris, 2000 WL 222025 (Ohio Ct. App. 5th Dist. Stark County 2000); see also Grimm v. Grimm, 2002-Ohio-3208, 2002 WL 1396799 (Ohio Ct. App. 7th Dist. Jefferson County 2002); but see Schmidt v. Schmidt, 1999 WL 225157 (Ohio Ct. App. 12th Dist. Clermont County 1999).

[23]See Evid.R. 410, Evid.R. 609, Evid.R. 803(21).

[24]See Mapes v. Ohio, 498 U.S. 977, 111 S. Ct. 504, 112 L. Ed. 2d 433 (1990) (making an analogous argument regarding the Rules of Criminal Procedure and Evidence and determining that the rules "prohibit only the admission of a no contest plea. These rules do not prohibit the admission of a conviction entered upon that plea when such conviction is made relevant by statute").

[25]See RC 3109.04(C), RC 3109.04(F)(1)(h), which was recently amended to include whether either parent or any member of the household of either parent previously has been convicted of or pleaded guilty to a violation of RC 2919.25 or a sexually oriented offense, see also Sub. Am. 2007 S.B. 260, eff. 1-2-07.

[26]Moore v. Moore, 1994 WL 370005 (Ohio Ct. App. 5th Dist. Licking County 1994).

by the trial court, there was no conviction. Since there was no conviction, there was no need for the court to make specific findings to support its decision. Thus, there was no violation of RC 3109.04(C) which requires a court to prepare written findings of fact to support its award of custody to a parent who was convicted of or pleaded guilty to domestic violence.

Although entering into a diversion program does not equate to a conviction for purposes of issuing findings of fact according to RC 3109.04(C), evidence that one of the parents committed domestic violence should be considered by the court before awarding custody. An entry into a diversion program should not negate the fact that domestic violence occurred.

Q & A: Should the court consider a domestic violence charge which was dismissed?[27]

At least one Ohio court addressed this issue. From a procedural standpoint, completion of a selective intervention program negates the underlying domestic violence charge, thereby preventing a conviction in the action.

In *Cahill v. Cahill*,[28] the domestic violence charge was dismissed after the appellant completed a selective intervention program developed for first-time offenders. The appellant argued that the court committed prejudicial error in considering the domestic violence charge, which was ultimately dismissed, in determining custody and visitation. The Cuyahoga County Court of Appeals concluded:

> A review of the record indicates not only that the referee was informed the domestic violence charge was dismissed pursuant to appellant's completion of the selective intervention program, but also that the domestic violence charge was not a substantial factor in the referee's report and recommendation. In light of the evidence supporting the referee's decision, the single mischaracterization of the domestic violence charge as a conviction did not prejudice appellant and constitutes, at most, harmless error.[29]

It is clear that, while the referee accorded little weight to the domestic violence charge in its determination, it did consider evidence of domestic violence by way of the introduction of the temporary protection order and testimony regarding a physical altercation between the parents. Ohio courts should follow the lead of the Cuyahoga County Domestic Relations Court in considering other independent evidence of domestic violence before rendering their decisions, whether or not the act of domestic violence results in a conviction.

---

[27]See Meaney v. Meaney, 2010-Ohio-1969, 2010 WL 1782486 (Ohio Ct. App. 11th Dist. Lake County 2010) (upholding trial court and finding that domestic violence charges were simply that-charges, and appellee was not convicted of domestic violence in the past. Absent conviction, this factor does not rise to the same weight as some of the other factors).

[28]Cahill v. Cahill, 1994 WL 284996 (Ohio Ct. App. 8th Dist. Cuyahoga County 1994). But see Holbrook v. Smith, 1999 WL 699876 (Ohio Ct. App. 12th Dist. Clermont County 1999) (appellant's boyfriend's extensive criminal record, including a domestic violence complaint being filed against him and a propensity for violence, was significant factor in custody modification).

[29]Cahill v. Cahill, 1994 WL 284996, *3 (Ohio Ct. App. 8th Dist. Cuyahoga County 1994).

Q & A: Does a misdemeanor disorderly conduct conviction bar a parent from being designated residential parent and legal custodian pursuant to RC 3109.04(C) or RC 3109.04(F)(1)(h)?

The Lucas County Court of Appeals has answered this in the negative. In *Prusia v. Prusia*,[30] the appellee (father) was designated the residential parent and legal custodian of the child, despite the fact that he had been charged with domestic violence against the appellant (mother). On appeal, appellant argued that the father should not have been so designated pursuant to RC 3109.04(C) and RC 3109.04(F)(1)(h). Under these provisions, a parent that has been convicted of or pleaded guilty to domestic violence or other offense that caused harm may only be designated as the residential parent of a child if the court finds it is in the best interest of the child and it makes specific findings of fact to support its determination.

In this case, the appellate court determined that the father did not plead guilty to an offense of violence involving a household member. Rather, he pled guilty to disorderly conduct under RC 2917.11. The court reasoned that disorderly conduct is not specifically defined as an offense of violence under RC 2901.01(A)(9); rather it is a crime against the public peace. "Although Caroline argues that Gregory was guilty of domestic violence, he was not convicted of anything other than disorderly conduct. Since the trial court was not required to consider RC 3109.04(C) or RC 3109.04(F)(1)(h), it did not abuse its discretion in choosing to overlook the misdemeanor."[31]

The Sixth District Court of Appeals focused on the part of the statute that provides as follows ". . . any other offense involving a victim who at the time of the commission of the offense was a member of the family or household that is the subject of the proceeding and caused physical harm to victim in the commission of the offense . . ."[32] The court clearly presumed that "any other offense" meant an "offense of violence" as defined in RC 2901.01(A)(9). Since disorderly conduct does not appear in the list of violent offenses, it is not contemplated by RC 3109.04(C) or RC 3109.04(F)(1)(h). Thus, the court was not required to follow its statutory mandates.

However, the statutory language does not speak in terms of "offense of violence." Thus, other jurisdictions may decide that a plea to disorderly conduct is the type of offense contemplated by statute.

Q & A: Should domestic violence be a relevant factor in a modification of a custody award?

In *Alexander v. Oiler*,[33] the Clark County Court of Appeals decided the question in the affirmative. In that case, the court of appeals ac-

---

[30]Prusia v. Prusia, 2003-Ohio-2000, 2003 WL 1904410 (Ohio Ct. App. 6th Dist. Lucas County 2003).

[31]Prusia v. Prusia, 2003-Ohio-2000, 2003 WL 1904410 (Ohio Ct. App. 6th Dist. Lucas County 2003).

[32]RC 3109.04.

[33]Alexander v. Oiler, 1997 WL 7166 (Ohio Ct. App. 2d Dist. Clark County 1997); see also Meade v. Meade, 2000-Ohio-1912, 2000 WL 1532872 (Ohio Ct. App. 3d Dist. Marion County 2000) (the court considered evidence of domestic violence in its decision); Holbrook v. Smith, 1999 WL 699876 (Ohio Ct. App. 12th Dist. Clermont County 1999); Clark v. Clark, 1997 WL 170298 (Ohio Ct. App. 10th Dist. Franklin County

complished two things. First, relying on RC 3109.04(F)(1), it affirmed that domestic violence is a factor to be considered by the court when modifying custody. The appellate court researched the record and concluded that there was overwhelming evidence to support a substantial change of circumstances. Second, the court made a broad public policy statement that "[a]s a general proposition, the manifestation of violence in the home is a substantial change in circumstances that raises serious questions as to the child's safety and well-being."[34] The trial court had also considered evidence that Oiler had twice been arrested for domestic violence and that one of the incidents resulted in a conviction.

Q & A: Does the trial court have jurisdiction to modify the terms of the allocation of parental rights and responsibilities under a civil protection order?

Not according to the Eighth District Court of Appeals in *Signer v. Signer*.[35] In *Signer*, the plaintiff-appellant appealed the trial court's modification of the allocation of parental rights and responsibilities in a CPO. She argued that the court lacked jurisdiction to amend the CPO because the expiration date on the order was not until 2007 and because the statute did not provide for an amendment.[36]

The appellate court determined that modifying a protection order is controlled by RC 3113.31(E)(3)(b) which limits any modifications to those expressly set forth in statute. The statute provides that a protection order shall be valid for a date certain but not to exceed five years[37] and that any order under (E)(1)(d) such as custody, visitation and support, "shall terminate on the date that a court in an action for

1997) (trial court designated appellee as the residential parent despite evidence of domestic violence in her new home. The trial court noted that further domestic violence would be grounds to support a motion to modify parental rights and responsibilities); Hostetter v. Cotton, 2004-Ohio-3524, 2004 WL 1486264 (Ohio Ct. App. 5th Dist. Licking County 2004) (incidents of domestic violence and subsequent probation was a change of circumstances); Sallee v. Sallee, 142 Ohio App. 3d 366, 755 N.E.2d 941 (12th Dist. Warren County 2001); Coe v. Schneider, 2006-Ohio-440, 2006 WL 242597 (Ohio Ct. App. 4th Dist. Washington County 2006) (holding that domestic violence between mother and her girlfriend in vicinity of child negatively affected the child and supported the trial court's finding that the environment in mother's house was not safe and nurturing, thus a change of circumstances warranting a change in custody occurred); Sheppeard v. Brown, 2008-Ohio-203, 2008 WL 186670 (Ohio Ct. App. 2d Dist. Clark County 2008) (Custodial parent's testimony that she continued her relationship with the perpetrator after his arrest for domestic violence against her demonstrates that she minimizes the domestic violence and there is no domestic violence in father's home. The court affirmed trial court judgment upholding change of custody.); Brocklehurst v. Paul, 2012-Ohio-4356, 2012 WL 4351901 (Ohio Ct. App. 5th Dist. Muskingum County 2012) (as some of the domestic violence occurred in the presence of the children, the appellate court upheld the trial court decision that this was a change in circumstances).

[34] Alexander v. Oiler, 1997 WL 7166, *4 (Ohio Ct. App. 2d Dist. Clark County 1997).

[35] Signer v. Signer, 2006-Ohio-3580, 2006 WL 1918115 (Ohio Ct. App. 8th Dist. Cuyahoga County 2006).

[36] Signer v. Signer, 2006-Ohio-3580, 2006 WL 1918115 (Ohio Ct. App. 8th Dist. Cuyahoga County 2006).

[37] RC 3113.31(E)(3)(a).

divorce . . . brought by the petitioner or respondent issues an order allocation parental responsibilities for the care of children . . . ."[38]

In light of this analysis, the Cuyahoga County Court of Appeals found that the trial court erred in modifying the civil protection order. It held that the domestic violence statute does not vest any authority in the court to modify the terms of the allocation of parental rights and responsibilities under the civil protection order.[39] The appellate court acknowledged that the trial court could have modified the allocation of parental rights and responsibilities under a CPO if it did so in the underlying divorce and in compliance with Civ.R. 75(N).

Of note is that Sub. S.B. 260 was enacted in December 2006 and became effective on January 2, 2007. RC 3113.31 was amended to permit courts to modify and terminate civil protection orders issued after the full hearing subject to certain conditions.[40]

Q & A: Does the trial court also lack jurisdiction to modify a CPO to permit the father to exercise visitation?

The Athens County Court of Appeals addressed a similar issue in *Yazdani-Isfehani v. Yazdani-Isfehani*.[41] In that case, the mother requested and was granted an ex parte CPO. At the full hearing, the magistrate recommended that mother should have a CPO for five years, designated her residential parent and legal custodian and suspended father's visitation.

Subsequently, mother filed a divorce complaint against father. Father then moved the court to modify the visitation order in the CPO, but did not request such a modification in the "companion" divorce action. The magistrate denied his request, which was then upheld by the trial court.

On appeal, father argued that the trial court erred in finding that it had no jurisdiction to modify the CPO to permit him to exercise visitation. Further, he asserted that "public policy mandates that the court maintain continuing jurisdiction over custody and visitation matters in the context of a CPO proceeding in order to uphold the state's fundamental interest in children's welfare."[42]

The appellate court acknowledged that the issuance of a CPO after a full hearing was a final appealable order. As such, a court may grant a party relief from a final judgment pursuant to Civ.R. 60. Since this was not done and "in the absence of any statutory grant of continuing jurisdiction that would permit the modification of the allocation of parental rights and responsibilities once a CPO has issued,

[38]Signer v. Signer, 2006-Ohio-3580, 2006 WL 1918115, *5 (Ohio Ct. App. 8th Dist. Cuyahoga County 2006); RC 3113.31(E)(3)(b); State v. Price, 118 Ohio St. 3d 144, 2008-Ohio-1974, 886 N.E.2d 852 (2008) (Supreme Court held that a divorce decree can modify a CPO beyond the CPO's sections concerning parental rights and responsibilities).

[39]Signer v. Signer, 2006-Ohio-3580, 2006 WL 1918115, *5 (Ohio Ct. App. 8th Dist. Cuyahoga County 2006).

[40]RC 3113.31(E)(8); see also Text § 12:25, Modification and termination of civil protection orders.

[41]Yazdani-Isfehani v. Yazdani-Isfehani, 170 Ohio App. 3d 1, 2006-Ohio-7105, 865 N.E.2d 924 (4th Dist. Athens County 2006).

[42]Yazdani-Isfehani v. Yazdani-Isfehani, 170 Ohio App. 3d 1, 2, 2006-Ohio-7105, 865 N.E.2d 924 (4th Dist. Athens County 2006).

and in light of the General Assembly's express intention that a domestic court have the authority to modify such orders in the context of a later divorce, dissolution or legal separation proceeding, we find that the trial court properly found that it lacked the requisite jurisdiction to modify visitation in the context of the CPO proceeding."[43]

It is important to note that recently amended RC 3113.31(E)(8) permits both the modification and termination of CPOs consistent with the enumerated factors set forth in the statutory provision.[44] The enactment of this provision permits the modification of the allocation of parental rights and responsibilities in a CPO proceeding.

Q & A: Does a domestic relations court lose jurisdiction to address abuse towards a child because the juvenile court has previously issued an order allocating parental rights and responsibilities?[45]

Although no court has yet specifically addressed this issue, the Butler County Court of Appeals has commented on this. In *Hyde v. Smith*,[46] petitioner sought a protection order on behalf of herself and named her parents and son as protected parties on the order. On appeal, appellant claimed that the domestic relations courts erred by designating appellee as sole residential parent and legal custodian and awarding him supervised visitation when his motion for legal custody was pending in juvenile court. He also asserted that appellee's parent should be removed from the protection order as they were not family or household members as defined in RC 3113.31(A)(3). Appellee conceded that her parents should be removed from the CPO because no evidence was presented that they were family or household members.

The appellate court explained that RC 3113.31(E)(1)(d) provides that a domestic relations court, including divisions of the same county court, has no jurisdiction to make a custody award if another court has determined or is determining parental rights and responsibilities.[47] "That statute, however, has been limited to allow a domestic relations court 'to make emergency decision, on an interim basis, to protect children from imminently dangerous situations.' That is exactly what the domestic relations court did here."[48]

The court reasoned that the trial court stated that the CPO was to remain in effect for a date certain and that appellant's supervised visitation "was to continue * * * *until further order of court but not to

---

[43]Yazdani-Isfehani v. Yazdani-Isfehani, 170 Ohio App. 3d 1, 2, 2006-Ohio-7105, 865 N.E.2d 924 (4th Dist. Athens County 2006); see also Signer v. Signer, 2006-Ohio-3580, 2006 WL 1918115 (Ohio Ct. App. 8th Dist. Cuyahoga County 2006).

[44]Am. Sub. S.B. 260, eff. 1-2-07.

[45]see Text § 12:15; Text § 12:16.

[46]Hyde v. Smith, 2015-Ohio-1701, 2015 WL 1976454 (Ohio Ct. App. 12th Dist. Butler County 2015).

[47]Hyde v. Smith, 2015-Ohio-1701, 2015 WL 1976454, ¶ 36 (Ohio Ct. App. 12th Dist. Butler County 2015), quoting Couch v. Harrison, 2001-Ohio-4199, 2001 WL 121108 (Ohio Ct. App. 12th Dist. Clermont County 2001).

[48]Hyde v. Smith, 2015-Ohio-1701, 2015 WL 1976454, ¶ 36 (Ohio Ct. App. 12th Dist. Butler County 2015), quoting Hoyt v. Heindell, 191 Ohio App. 3d 373, 2010-Ohio-6058, ¶ 31, 946 N.E.2d 258 (11th Dist. Lake County 2010).

extend past the Final CPO expiration date."[49] The court also noted that, "in ruling on Smith's objections to the magistrate's decision, the domestic relations court found it was 'not prohibited from making parenting orders at least until such time that the Juvenile Court initiates orders concerning [the child.]' "[50]

In that there were recent threats to break in and burn down the house in which appellee resided with her son, the trial court's decision was not unreasonable. In fact, the court also pointed out that appellant had only recently filed his motion in juvenile court and the court had yet to hold a hearing on the matter and questioned whether the "juvenile court was even in the process of 'determining the allocation' of such rights and responsibilities as that phrase is used in RC 3113. 31(E)(1)(d)."[51]

"Regardless, as the Ohio Supreme Court previously stated, the domestic relations court has extensive authority under RC 3113.31(E) 'to tailor the domestic violence protection order to the exact situation before it at the time' in order to carry out the legislative goals of protecting victims of domestic violence."[52] In overruling the assignment of error, the appellate court held that, based on the facts and circumstances of this case, the appellate court found no error in the domestic relations court's decision to temporarily provide for the care of the parties' son until the juvenile court could initiate its own orders concerning the child.[53]

Of interest is that the appellate court did not set a specific expiration to be at the end of the five year period. Rather, the trial court determined that the CPO "was to continue* * *until further order of court, but not to extend past the Final CPO expiration date."[54]

Although the court in *Hyde* had not previously made a parenting determination, the reasoning of the Butler County Court of Appeals is instructive. Where there is a finding that that the child 's safety is at risk by having been abused by the other parent, a domestic relations court should be able to temporarily provide for the care of the child until the juvenile court initiates its own orders. That should be interpreted to mean until juvenile court actually issues emergency orders addressing the underlying issues in the CPO relative to the child, whether or not the juvenile court has previously issued permanent orders. To do otherwise would thwart the intents and purposes of the domestic violence statute.

It would be wise for courts to adopt policies that address the

---

[49] Hyde v. Smith, 2015-Ohio-1701, 2015 WL 1976454, ¶ 37 (Ohio Ct. App. 12th Dist. Butler County 2015).

[50] Hyde v. Smith, 2015-Ohio-1701, 2015 WL 1976454, ¶ 37 (Ohio Ct. App. 12th Dist. Butler County 2015).

[51] Hyde v. Smith, 2015-Ohio-1701, 2015 WL 1976454, ¶ 38 (Ohio Ct. App. 12th Dist. Butler County 2015).

[52] Hyde v. Smith, 2015-Ohio-1701, 2015 WL 1976454, ¶ 39 (Ohio Ct. App. 12th Dist. Butler County 2015), citing Felton v. Felton, 79 Ohio St. 3d 34, 38, 44-45, 1997-Ohio-302, 679 N.E.2d 672 (1997).

[53] Hyde v. Smith, 2015-Ohio-1701, 2015 WL 1976454, ¶ 39 (Ohio Ct. App. 12th Dist. Butler County 2015).

[54] Hyde v. Smith, 2015-Ohio-1701, 2015 WL 1976454, ¶ 42 (Ohio Ct. App. 12th Dist. Butler County 2015).

interplay between domestic violence civil protection orders and the allocation of parental rights and responsibilities. When the two courts work together, policies can be developed to address how the courts are made aware of subsequent or conflicting orders and how long a CPO relative to a child should remain in effect *vis-a-vis* a subsequent order of the court.[55]

Q & A: Can a trial court adjudicate a motion to modify visitation based on the outcome of a related proceeding to establish a CPO?[56]

In *Dowhan v. Dowhan*,[57] the Lake County Domestic Relations Court granted the parties a divorce and ordered that defendant-father have no parenting time until further order of court or upon a motion to modify filed by defendant. At the time of the divorce, defendant was incarcerated. Two years later and while defendant was still incarcerated, plaintiff filed a petition for CPO after receiving a threatening letter from defendant. Before the full hearing, defendant was released from prison. Petitioner was then granted a full hearing CPO which ordered respondent to maintain a distance of 1000 feet from her and the children. Subsequently, respondent filed a Motion to Modify Custody and Establish Visitation and a Motion to Modify the CPO by removing the children as protected parties, which motion to modify the CPO was denied. The court then denied his Motion to Modify Custody and Establish Visitation. In its opinion, the court noted that, after a day of trial on respondent's Motion to Modify CPO, it (the same court) had found petitioner and children in fear of imminent serious physical harm from respondent.

On appeal, respondent claimed that the domestic relations court's refusal to consider his Motion to Modify Custody based on the civil protection order proceeding violated his due process rights and the statutory provisions of R.C. 3113.31 which provided that a CPO may temporarily allocate parental rights and responsibilities if no other court has determined or is determining the allocation pursuant to R.C. 3113.31(E)(1)(d). Such an order shall terminate when a domestic relations court, in a divorce, issues another order allocating parental rights and responsibilities. R.C. 3113.31(E)(3)(b). " '[W]hile the statute permits a court to issue temporary orders allocating parental rights and responsibilities in order to stop domestic violence, it does not vest the court with authority to modify the allocation of parental rights and responsibilities in the CPO proceeding.' "[58]

The appellate court found that the reasoning of *Yazdani-Isfehani* was wrongly applied to the instant case. Noting that the statute and case law contemplates the situation where a protection order is issued pending the final allocation of parental rights and responsibilities in a divorce, this case is one in which parental rights and responsibilities

[55]See, for e.g., Sup.R. 10.06.

[56]See also Text 12:15.

[57]Dowhan v. Dowhan, 2013-Ohio-4097, 2013 WL 5346465 (Ohio Ct. App. 11th Dist. Lake County 2013).

[58]Dowhan v. Dowhan, 2013-Ohio-4097, 2013 WL 5346465, ¶ 14 (Ohio Ct. App. 11th Dist. Lake County 2013), quoting Yazdani-Isfehani v. Yazdani-Isfehani, 170 Ohio App. 3d 1, 2006-Ohio-7105, 865 N.E.2d 924, ¶ 23 (4th Dist. Athens County 2006).

was already decided. "The subsequent protection order, preventing Terrance from coming within 1000 feet of Sharon or the children, is wholly consistent with the allocation of parental rights and responsibilities set forth in the divorce decree."[59] In fact, because Terrance could not come within 1000 feet of the children, it rendered a hearing on his Motion to Modify unnecessary. "We need not notice the underlying factual basis for the protection order, since it is the fact of the protection order and its terms which preclude the possibility of Terrance exercising visitation with his children. The failure to hold a hearing on the Motion to Modify did not deprive Terrance of the opportunity to be heard, as Terrance had fully exercised that right in the proceeding to modify the protection order and the appeal thereof. In affirming the trial court's decision, the appellate court held that "[m]odification of the protection order is a necessary prerequisite to the establishment of parenting time with the children."[60]

However, the dissenting judge found that "the trial court's denial of appellant's motion to modify custody and establish visitation is predicated upon its review of testimony and evidence which had been presented in a separate action."[61] Because the CPO was not admitted into evidence in the underlying Motion to Modify Custody, the trial court relied on improper evidence.

Of interest is that the same trial judge conducted the CPO modification hearing and the Motion to Modify Custody. The trial court affirmed the terms of the original protection order that prohibited Terrance from coming within 1000 feet of mother and children and also found that his wish to visit with his children did not overcome Mother's testimony as to the violence suffered by the children along with the present fear of future violence.

Q & A: Whether the allocation of parental rights and responsibilities set forth in a divorce decree can modify a previously issued CPO beyond the scope of the CPO provisions concerning the parental rights and responsibilities?

The Ohio Supreme Court answered this question in the affirmative in *State v. Price*.[62] In that case, the parties separated and the mother obtained a CPO, which order listed her and the minor child as protected parties, granted her temporary custody and suspended the father's visitation rights until he engages in counseling for his bipolar disorder and takes his medication.

A year later, mother filed and was granted a divorce by the same

[59]Dowhan v. Dowhan, 2013-Ohio-4097, 2013 WL 5346465, ¶ 15 (Ohio Ct. App. 11th Dist. Lake County 2013).

[60]Dowhan v. Dowhan, 2013-Ohio-4097, 2013 WL 5346465, ¶ 19 (Ohio Ct. App. 11th Dist. Lake County 2013).

[61]Dowhan v. Dowhan, 2013-Ohio-4097, 2013 WL 5346465, ¶ 26 (Ohio Ct. App. 11th Dist. Lake County 2013).

[62]State v. Price, 118 Ohio St. 3d 144, 2008-Ohio-1974, 886 N.E.2d 852 (2008). But see In re K.C., 2014-Ohio-372, 2014 WL 467476 (Ohio Ct. App. 9th Dist. Summit County 2014) (finding that, although the trial court (juvenile court) believed that communication and contact was necessary to effectuate visitation, it had no ability to modify the CPO to allow the parties to communicate as that authority was vested solely with the domestic relations court and implying that only the same court is able to modify the CPO).

court that granted her CPO. The decree provided that mother was awarded full custody and that visitation was to be at her discretion until he provided proof that he completed the parenting seminar. At that time, he could petition the court for visitation.

For the next three years, father was given regular visits with the minor child. She then suspended visitation alleging the child was displaying violent tendencies after returning from visiting his father. Father also pleaded guilty to violating the CPO based on telephone calls made to mother. Several months later, father again made calls to mother who contacted the police claiming he violated the CPO. Father was again found guilty of violating the CPO and sentenced to five years of community control. The appellate court upheld father's conviction and he appealed to the Supreme Court of Ohio.

At the outset, the Court noted that "RC 3113.31(E)(3)(b) provides that any sections of a CPO involving the allocation of parental rights and responsibilities and support "shall terminate on the date that a court in an action for divorce* * *issues an order for the care of children* * *."[63] It also pointed out that the CPO itself followed the statute stating that "except for paragraphs 11, 12, 13, 14, and 15 above, this order survives a divorce, dissolution of marriage or legal separation." Based on the statute and the CPO form, the Court articulated that a divorce decree overrides the paragraphs of the CPO regarding custody and visitation. The Court also noted that paragraph 20 of the CPO states that "any part of the CPO can be modified by an order of the court."

The Court also noted that paragraph 20 of the CPO states that "any part of the CPO can be modified by an order of the court." "The same court that imposed the CPO modified it in this case through the divorce decree. The court had the power to allow contact between the parties and we find that it exercised that power in the divorce decree by allowing some contact for purposes of effectuating visitation. The CPO remained in effect in all instances to prevent any *abuse* by Jeffrey, including harassing telephonic contact." Of significance is that the Supreme Court indicated that the same court may modify the CPO in a different action when the issue is related to the custody/visitation issues.

Thus, the Court found that "as an order from the same court that issued the CPO, a divorce decree may modify the terms of a CPO.[64] Depending upon how a divorce decree allocates parental rights and responsibilities, it may modify multiple aspects of the CPO beyond the paragraphs dealing with parental rights and responsibilities."[65]

The Court went on to address three categories of contact that were forbidden by the CPO: 1) abuse of the protected parties; 2) physical proximity; and 3) indirect contact, including the telephone. While it acknowledged that the abuse provision cannot be modified by a subsequent allocation of parental rights because there is no instance

---

[63]State v. Price, 118 Ohio St. 3d 144, 147, 2008-Ohio-1974, 886 N.E.2d 852 (2008).

[64]See also Text § 12:15, Remedies—Orders allocating parental rights and responsibilities.

[65]State v. Price, 118 Ohio St. 3d 144, 147, 2008-Ohio-1974, 886 N.E.2d 852 (2008).

where abuse would be necessary to achieve visitation,[66] "the very nature of visitation must necessarily yield a temporary relaxation of the type of contact forbidden in the CPO."[67]

The Court then discussed whether the terms of the divorce decree were precise or imprecise. Since the decree stated that visitation was to be at mother's discretion, it is clear that the decree implies that father must contact her in order to seek visitation. "At stake is whether Jeffrey can be convicted of a felony for so asking."[68]

"If we were to affirm Jeffrey's conviction, we would be giving this court's imprimatur to Item V of the divorce decree, which sets forth that "visitation shall be at the discretion of the mother," and we would encourage its use in future cases where a divorce is granted while a CPO is still active. We cannot. The divorce decree in this case left the protected parties and the respondent without clear boundaries regarding nonabusive contact."[69]

Therefore, the Supreme Court of Ohio reversed the appellate court and held that the divorce decree, permitting visitation at the discretion of the mother, created a limited exception to the no-contact provision of the CPO.

Had the decree of divorce been drafted more concisely and less ambiguously relative to appellant's access to visitation, the Court probably would not have accepted certiorari. However, in light of the seemingly contradictory provisions between the CPO and the subsequent decree of divorce and because a criminal conviction for violating the CPO was involved, the Court felt compelled to address this apparent contradiction. In doing so, the Court reiterated a concept that should be noted by advocates and scholars alike: "a defendant cannot be convicted of violating an order that does not alert him specifically as to what conduct is allowed."[70]

Additionally, the Supreme Court addressed a gap in Ohio's domestic violence laws that has created conflicting orders problems for respondents. It is clear that any custody or visitation order issued in a CPO under RC 3113.31 terminates by operation of law upon the issuance of an order allocating parental rights and responsibilities in a subsequent divorce proceeding.[71] While the divorce decree modifies the terms of the CPO as relating to parental rights and responsibilities, the statute is silent as to whether the contact provisions are also modified. If they are not, provisions regarding parental access in a subsequently issued divorce decree have no effect if the parent is not able to have contact with his/her child.

Q & A: Whether the allocation of parental rights in a CPO action pursuant to RC 3113.31(E)(3)(b) is regarded as a custody proceeding?[72]

[66]State v. Price, 118 Ohio St. 3d 144, 147, 2008-Ohio-1974, 886 N.E.2d 852 (2008).

[67]State v. Price, 118 Ohio St. 3d 144, 148, 2008-Ohio-1974, 886 N.E.2d 852 (2008).

[68]State v. Price, 118 Ohio St. 3d 144, 149, 2008-Ohio-1974, 886 N.E.2d 852 (2008).

[69]State v. Price, 118 Ohio St. 3d 144, 150, 2008-Ohio-1974, 886 N.E.2d 852 (2008).

[70]State v. Price, 118 Ohio St. 3d 144, 2008-Ohio-1974, 886 N.E.2d 852 (2008).

[71]RC 3113.31(E)(3)(b).

[72]See also Text § 12:16, Remedies—Protected party concerns.

Not according to the Noble County Court of Appeals in *Tabler v. Myers*.[73] In *Tabler*, appellant mother and father were the unmarried parents of two children. Appellee is the father's mother and the paternal grandmother of the minor children.

In 2001 and prior to the birth of the second daughter, appellant obtained a CPO whereby the appellee (grandmother) was designated residential parent and legal custodian of the older child. In 2006, father filed a complaint in Juvenile Court to establish an allocation of parental rights and visitation of the children and requesting that he be designated legal custodian. Appellant filed a counterclaim requesting that she be designated the legal custodian. The trial court used the change of circumstances standard, determined that no modification was necessary to serve the best interests of the children and named the appellee the residential parent and legal custodian of the older child and named appellant the residential parent and legal custodian of the younger child.

On appeal, the appellant argued that the trial court erred when it applied a change of circumstances standard based on an expired CPO, rather than treat the juvenile court action as an initial custody proceeding.

The importance of this case for domestic violence purposes is in its holding that an award of custody in a CPO is a temporary order and that any custody order issued in a subsequent divorce or juvenile court action is to be considered an initial custody determination and thus, governed by the best interest standard. *Tabler* is one of several recent appellate court decisions that has determined that a CPO is not regarded as a custody proceeding. "Rather, a CPO that deals with the custody of a minor child is only a temporary order that lasts until the issue is litigated in a domestic relations or juvenile court."[74]

In reversing the trial court decision, the Noble County appellate court reasoned that the appellee's award of custody, arising from the CPO, was merely a temporary order and not an initial custody determination. Because this was a juvenile court case involving a non-parent, a parental suitability standard must be used.[75]

Similarly, in *Boling v. Valecko*,[76] the Summit County appellate court also determined that a custody order issued in a CPO is a temporary order. The court reasoned that a subsequent divorce proceeding requesting an allocation of parental rights and responsibilities is an initial custody determination subject to the best interest standard.

In neither *Tabler* nor *Boling* was the subsequent divorce or juvenile

---

[73]Tabler v. Myers, 173 Ohio App. 3d 657, 2007-Ohio-6219, 880 N.E.2d 103 (7th Dist. Noble County 2007).

[74]Tabler v. Myers, 173 Ohio App. 3d 657, 660, 2007-Ohio-6219, 880 N.E.2d 103 (7th Dist. Noble County 2007), citing Boling v. Valecko, 2002-Ohio-449, 2002 WL 185182 (Ohio Ct. App. 9th Dist. Summit County 2002); see also McCue v. Marlin, 187 Ohio App. 3d 1, 2010-Ohio-1298, 930 N.E.2d 855 (7th Dist. Mahoning County 2010); citing, Couch v. Harrison, 2001-Ohio-4199, 2001 WL 121108 (Ohio Ct. App. 12th Dist. Clermont County 2001).

[75]Tabler v. Myers, 173 Ohio App. 3d 657, 663, 2007-Ohio-6219, 880 N.E.2d 103 (7th Dist. Noble County 2007).

[76]Boling v. Valecko, 2002-Ohio-449, 2002 WL 185182 (Ohio Ct. App. 9th Dist. Summit County 2002).

court proceeding considered a modification of a prior custody award subject to a change of circumstances standard.[77]

Q & A: Can a trial court refuse to hear evidence of spousal abuse?

Unfortunately, no Ohio court has directly examined this specific issue. In some cases, courts have not considered evidence of domestic violence or have found the evidence unpersuasive.[78] However, several appellate courts across the country have reversed decisions where the trial court refused to hear evidence of one parent's abuse of the other.[79] For example, in *Bertram v. Kilian*,[80] the Wisconsin Court of Appeals held that parent violence and abuse affects the interaction and interrelationship of the child with the parent and may affect the mental and physical health of the children. In *Marchant v. Marchant*,[81] the appellate court reversed a custody award to a batterer because the trial court attempted to justify the husband's rape and abuse of his wife. The court stated that the "most serious aspect of [domestic violence] is the proven tendency of family violence to be passed down to successive generations. While children may not be immediate victims, they certainly are the victims and perpetrators of such violence in the future."[82]

Finally, in *Henry v. Johnson*,[83] the West Virginia Supreme Court of Appeals held that domestic violence should be taken into account when making an award of temporary custody. In that case, the Court took an important step by writing a strong public policy syllabus, providing that "Children are often physically assaulted or witness violence against one of their parents and may suffer deep and lasting emotional harm from victimization and from exposure to family violence; consequently, a family law master should take domestic violence into account when making an award of temporary custody."[84]

Q & A: Should a statute that permits the consideration of domestic violence as a factor in custody determinations always automatically award custody to the nonabusive spouse?

Statutes that provide for domestic violence as a factor in determining the best interest of the child should not be interpreted to mean that custody should automatically be awarded to the parent just

[77]See Couch v. Harrison, 2001-Ohio-4199, 2001 WL 121108 (Ohio Ct. App. 12th Dist. Clermont County 2001).

[78]See, e.g., Kennedy v. Kennedy, 517 So. 2d 621 (Ala. Civ. App. 1987); Hall v. Hall, 571 So. 2d 1176 (Ala. Civ. App. 1990).

[79]See, e.g., In re Marriage of Brainard, 523 N.W.2d 611 (Iowa Ct. App. 1994); Bruner v. Hager, 534 N.W.2d 825 (N.D. 1995).

[80]Bertram v. Kilian, 133 Wis. 2d 202, 394 N.W.2d 773 (Ct. App. 1986).

[81]Marchant v. Marchant, 743 P.2d 199 (Utah Ct. App. 1987).

[82]Marchant v. Marchant, 743 P.2d 199, 204 (Utah Ct. App. 1987).

[83]Henry v. Johnson, 192 W. Va. 82, 450 S.E.2d 779 (1994).

[84]Henry v. Johnson, 192 W. Va. 82, 83, 450 S.E.2d 779 (1994). But see Patricia Ann S. v. James Daniel S., 190 W. Va. 6, 435 S.E.2d 6 (1993) (declining to find error where trial court failed to consider father's abuse of the mother and children as a factor weighing against him).

because he/she is the nonabusive parent.[85] For example, in *Gehring v. Gehring*,[86] the trial court named the father as the residential parent of the three minor children in spite of the fact that he was the subject of a CPO in which the mother had been granted temporary custody. In affirming the decision of the trial court, the Warren County Court of Appeals noted that the lower court had acknowledged that the father had exhibited abusive behavior towards the mother. However, in weighing the best interests of the children, the trial court balanced the father's abuse towards the mother against the mother's failure to care for the children. In reviewing the record, the appellate court relied on the trial court's notation, which stated that "though the Court is reluctant to give any abusive man custody of small children such as here, the Court must focus solely on what is the best for the children."[87] It found that "[h]ere, the scale tips slightly towards" the father as the residential parent.[88]

However, parental fitness is extremely important in custody determinations; and, in abusive relationships, the batterer is often less fit to parent the children.[89] Evidence of spousal abuse should be considered as a factor that weighs heavily against the abusive parent.[90] However, it must be stressed that domestic violence is just one of the

[85]See Randy F. Kandel, Squabbling in the Shadows: What the Law Can Learn from the Way Divorcing Couples Use Protective Orders as Bargaining Chips in Domestic Spats and Child Custody Mediation, 48 S.C. L. Rev. 441, 467 (1997). But see Daniel G. Saunders, Child Custody Decisions in Families Experiencing Woman Abuse, 39 Soc. Work 51 (1994). See also Mildred D. Pagelow, Justice for Victims of Spouse Abuse in Divorce and Child Custody Cases, 8 Violence and Victims 1, 16 (1993).

[86]Gehring v. Gehring, 2004-Ohio-95, 2004 WL 47688 (Ohio Ct. App. 12th Dist. Warren County 2004); see also Carr v. Carr, 2001-Ohio-2466, 2001 WL 569296 (Ohio Ct. App. 4th Dist. Washington County 2001); Moneypenny v. Moneypenny, 2001 WL 39602 (Ohio Ct. App. 9th Dist. Medina County 2001); Smith v. Smith, 2002-Ohio-223, 2002 WL 57973 (Ohio Ct. App. 9th Dist. Wayne County 2002); Hussein v. Hussein, 2005-Ohio-6399, 2005 WL 3249490 (Ohio Ct. App. 5th Dist. Morrow County 2005) (court upheld trial court finding that domestic violence is not an automatic reason to deny residential parenting rights to the guilty party).

[87]Gehring v. Gehring, 2004-Ohio-95, 2004 WL 47688, *4 (Ohio Ct. App. 12th Dist. Warren County 2004).

[88]Gehring v. Gehring, 2004-Ohio-95, 2004 WL 47688, *4 (Ohio Ct. App. 12th Dist. Warren County 2004).

[89]Developments in the Law—Legal Responses to Domestic Violence, 106 Harv. L. Rev. 1498, 1608, 1620 (1993); but see D.O.H. v. T.L.H., 799 So. 2d 714 (La. Ct. App. 3d Cir. 2001), writ not considered, 805 So. 2d 1190 (La. 2002) (where court awarded custody of two children to father after a psychologist testified he knew he was treating father for spousal abuse and his treatment consisted of helping him learn anger management).

[90]Laura Crites & Donna Coker, What Therapists See That Judges May Miss: A Unique Guide to Custody Decisions When Spouse Abuse is Charged, 27 Judges' J. 8 (1988); see also Naomi R. Cahn, Civil Images of Battered Women: The Impact of Domestic Violence on Child Custody Decisions, 44 Vand. L. Rev. 1041, 1089 (1991); Ricci v. Delehanty, 1998 ME 231, 719 A.2d 518 (Me. 1998) (awarding father custody of a child he had previously abused and noting that he had addressed his anger and violence problems in therapy); Wissink v. Wissink, 301 A.D.2d 36, 749 N.Y.S.2d 550 (2d Dep't 2002) (reversing the order awarding custody to the father and requiring a new custody hearing after completion of a comprehensive psychological evaluation of the parties and child, in light of an extensive history of domestic violence perpetrated by the father against the mother).

relevant best interest factors and must be considered along with those other factors.[91]

Q & A: Are formerly battered spouses unfit parents because of the domestic violence perpetrated on them?[92]

Recent case law rejects the notion that formerly battered spouses are per se unfit parents. In *Lewelling v. Lewelling*,[93] the Texas Supreme Court held that "evidence that a parent is a victim of spousal abuse, by itself, is no evidence that awarding custody to that parent would significantly impair the child." The court further emphasized that in a custody dispute:

> [E]vidence of spousal abuse [is] to be considered only as a factor that weighs heavily against the abusive parent. . . While expressing continued concern for the best interest of the child, the Legislature has also determined that removing a child from a parent simply because she has suffered physical abuse at the hands of her spouse is not in the best interest of our state.[94]

Conversely, evidence of domestic violence perpetrated on one of the parents demonstrates a disregard for the child. Recent case law has revealed that evidence of domestic violence may indicate a finding of parental unfitness on the part of the abusive parent.

For example, in *Odom v. Odom*,[95] the Louisiana Court of Appeals determined that the father was an unfit parent in light of his long history of domestic violence against his former wife. This proposition was furthered in *Crabtree v. Crabtree*[96] wherein the Missouri Court of Appeals held that the father's long history of physical abuse of the mother was one factor which reflected negatively on his ability to serve as custodial parent.

Q & A: When is a child's witnessing of domestic violence a reason not to award custody to the abusive parent?

There is nothing in Ohio's custody statute[97] that establishes a presumption that abuse to the nonabusive parent is per se abuse to the child. Rather, the abuse to the child must be real, or there must be a significant risk of abuse to the child. Thus, a parent may be

---

[91]But see Couch v. Couch, 978 S.W.2d 505 (Mo. Ct. App. W.D. 1998) (upholding trial court's findings that, although there had been domestic violence against appellant, there was no evidence of domestic violence directed at the children); see also Reaper v. James, 2009-Ohio-151, 2009 WL 104613 (Ohio Ct. App. 4th Dist. Lawrence County 2009) (affirming award of custody to father despite his history of domestic violence, noting that the evidence did not indicate that the father would subject his children to domestic violence nor that he subjected any of his other children to domestic violence).

[92]See G. Holden, J. Stein, K. Ritchie, S. Harris & E. Jouriles, "Parenting Behaviors and Beliefs of Battered Women," Children Exposed to Marital Violence: Theory, Research and Applied Issues 289-331 (G.W. Holden, R. Geffner & E.N. Jouriles, eds., APA, Washington, D.C. (1998)).

[93]Lewelling v. Lewelling, 796 S.W.2d 164, 167 (Tex. 1990).

[94]Lewelling v. Lewelling, 796 S.W.2d 164, 168 (Tex. 1990).

[95]Odom v. Odom, 606 So. 2d 862 (La. Ct. App. 2d Cir. 1992), writ denied, 608 So. 2d 153 (La. 1992).

[96]Crabtree v. Crabtree, 802 S.W.2d 567 (Mo. Ct. App. W.D. 1991); see also Knock v. Knock, 224 Conn. 776, 621 A.2d 267 (1993).

[97]RC 3109.04.

considered a risk to the child where the abuse inflicted on the other parent indicates that the abusive parent will be a danger to the child or where the child suffers emotionally or psychologically as a consequence of witnessing domestic violence between the parents. Several court cases from around the country advance this proposition.

In *Custody of Vaughn*,[98] the Massachusetts high court indicated its support of the proposition that

> physical force within the family is both intolerable and too readily tolerated, and that a child who has been either the victim or the spectator of such abuse suffers a distinctly grievous kind of harm[, particularly when the abuse is] inflicted on those who are weaker and less able to defend themselves—almost invariably a child or a woman.

In A.F. v. N.F.,[99] the appellate court specifically held that domestic violence, when it occurs in the presence of the child, directly relates to the parties' parenting and custodial abilities. Similarly, in *In re Custody of Williams*,[100] the trial court properly considered evidence of domestic violence in its custody determination even though the child was too young to comprehend the father's attack on the mother.

§ 15:13 Consideration of domestic violence as a best-interest factor—Findings of fact that support a court decision[1]

Few Ohio appellate courts have either examined or interpreted those provisions of the statute that relate to domestic violence as a best-interest factor.[2] The reason for this appears to arise from the inherent power of the trial court to decide a case and the reluctance of appellate courts to reverse trial court decisions. Few appellate courts will substitute their judgment for that of the trial court.[3] A trial court's judgment relating to custody will not be reversed by the reviewing

---

[98]Custody of Vaughn, 422 Mass. 590, 595, 664 N.E.2d 434 (1996); see also Heck v. Reed, 529 N.W.2d 155, 36 A.L.R.5th 849 (N.D. 1995); Philip C. Crosby, Custody of Vaughn: Emphasizing the Importance of Domestic Violence in Child Custody Cases, 77 B. U. L. Rev. 483 (1997); Phyllis E. Federico & Robert Kinscherff, Custody of Vaughn: Impact of Domestic Violence on Child Custody—Children Are No Longer the Forgotten Victims, 40 Boston Bar J. 8 (1996).

[99]A.F. v. N.F., 156 A.D.2d 750, 549 N.Y.S.2d 511 (2d Dep't 1989); see also Engh v. Jensen, 547 N.W.2d 922 (N.D. 1996) (determining that a lack of violence toward the children does not negate a statutory presumption against granting custody to the parent who committed violence on the other parent).

[100]In re Custody of Williams, 104 Ill. App. 3d 16, 59 Ill. Dec. 791, 432 N.E.2d 375 (3d Dist. 1982).

[Section 15:13]

[1]See also Text § 15:6, Ohio's judicial response to domestic violence.

[2]See RC 3109.04(F)(1)(h) which was recently amended to include whether either parent or any member of the household of either parent has previously been convicted of or pleaded guilty to a violation of RC 2919.25 or a sexually oriented offense. See also Sub. Am. 2007 S.B. 260, eff. 1-2-07). See also RC 3109.04(F)(2)(c), RC 3109.04(C). See also Leslie D. Johnson, Caught in the Crossfire: Examining Legislative & Judicial Response to the Forgotten Victims of Domestic Violence, 22 Law & Psychol. Rev. 271 (1998); Smith v. Smith, 2002-Ohio-223, 2002 WL 57973 (Ohio Ct. App. 9th Dist. Wayne County 2002) (the appellate court independently reviewed the record and considered the factors set forth in RC 3109.04(F)(1)).

[3]See Bazzoli v. Bazzoli, 1993 WL 274329 (Ohio Ct. App. 5th Dist. Knox County 1993); see also Louderback v. Louderback, 1999 WL 94902 (Ohio Ct. App. 2d Dist.

court as against the manifest weight of the evidence when it is supported by a substantial amount of competent, credible evidence.[4] For a judgment to be reversed on abuse of discretion grounds, the court's attitude must be found to be "unreasonable, arbitrary or unconscionable."[5] The overwhelming effect is to make difficult prevailing on an appeal on the basis that the trial court failed to specifically address domestic violence as a factor in its decision.[6]

For example, in *Whiteman v. Whiteman*,[7] the Wood County Court of Appeals determined that "[o]ur job as reviewing court in this case is not to substitute our judgment for that of the trial court. Where there is competent, credible evidence to support the decision made by the trial court, we will not reverse its decision merely because we would have decided differently." Similarly, in *Burik v. Johnson*,[8] the court reluctantly decided not to overturn the ruling of the trial court. It relied on *Seasons Coal Co. v. City of Cleveland*[9] wherein the court found that "'[t]he underlying rationale of giving deference to the findings of the trial court rests with the knowledge that the trial judge is best able to view the witnesses and observe their demeanor, gestures and voice inflections, and use these observations in weighing the credibility of the proffered testimony.' "[10]

On the other hand, the trial court must provide findings of fact where one of the parents has committed domestic violence and requests custody, visitation or shared parenting.[11]

Q & A: Should courts issue public policy decisions, either as part of the syllabus or as part of the findings of fact, to support their conclusions?

Unfortunately, an appellate court's reluctance to review a trial court decision also deters that appellate court from using its own judgment to promote public policy in this area. After determining that it was unable to overturn the trial court decision because the record

Montgomery County 1999).

[4]See Marshall v. Marshall, 117 Ohio App. 3d 182, 690 N.E.2d 68 (3d Dist. Allen County 1997); see also Bechtol v. Bechtol, 49 Ohio St. 3d 21, 550 N.E.2d 178 (1990), opinion corrected, 51 Ohio St. 3d 701, 554 N.E.2d 899 (1990); Moneypenny v. Moneypenny, 2001 WL 39602 (Ohio Ct. App. 9th Dist. Medina County 2001).

[5]Blakemore v. Blakemore, 5 Ohio St. 3d 217, 219, 450 N.E.2d 1140 (1983); see also Marshall v. Marshall, 117 Ohio App. 3d 182, 186, 690 N.E.2d 68 (3d Dist. Allen County 1997) (explaining that "'one of the essentials, in order for the action of the court below to constitute reversible error, is that its action must plainly appear to effect an injustice to one of the parties' ") (quoting Ohio Jur. 3d, § 163).

[6]See Schmidt v. Schmidt, 1999 WL 225157 (Ohio Ct. App. 12th Dist. Clermont County 1999) (remanding case for specific findings of fact because it was undisputed that appellee had pleaded guilty to a domestic violence offense); see also Smith v. Smith, 2001 WL 542317 (Ohio Ct. App. 9th Dist. Wayne County 2001).

[7]Whiteman v. Whiteman, 1995 WL 29536, *2 (Ohio Ct. App. 6th Dist. Wood County 1995).

[8]Burik v. Johnson, 1997 WL 66762 (Ohio Ct. App. 4th Dist. Pike County 1997).

[9]Seasons Coal Co., Inc. v. City of Cleveland, 10 Ohio St. 3d 77, 461 N.E.2d 1273, 38 U.C.C. Rep. Serv. 469 (1984).

[10]Burik v. Johnson, 1997 WL 66762, *4 (Ohio Ct. App. 4th Dist. Pike County 1997).

[11]See RC 3109.04(C), RC 3109.04(F)(1)(h), RC 3109.04(F)(2)(c), RC 3109.051(D)(9), RC 3109.051(D)(12).

contained sufficient, credible evidence, the *Burik* court then expressed its opinion:

> At this juncture, we note that the incidents that appellant alleges to have occurred are troublesome. We note that the purpose of visitation with a parent is to foster and encourage the formation of a strong parent-child relationship. . . . If, however, a parent creates or permits the creation of circumstances that expose a child to a significant risk of serious physical or emotional harm, the court may restrict or deny that parent's visitation rights. A parent's right to visitation with his or her child is not absolute. If visitation with a parent presents a risk of serious physical or emotional harm, the court, acting in the best interest of the child, should restrict or deny visitation.[12]

Conversely, many reviewing courts elsewhere in the country have reversed trial court decisions based on the public policy implications of domestic violence on child custody decisions. In *R. H. v. B. F.*,[13] the Massachusetts Appellate Court concluded that

> in cases where, as here, there is credible evidence of physical abuse to a household member by a person seeking custody of or visitation with a child, a trial judge must make detailed and precise findings of fact which demonstrate that the effects of the domestic violence on the child have been evaluated and, in the event physical or legal custody is awarded to the perpetrator of the abuse, how such an award advances the best interests of the child.

Upon granting a review of the *R. H. v. B. F.* appellate decision, the Supreme Judicial Court held that the probate court "failed to consider the special risks to the child in awarding custody to a father who had committed acts of violence against the mother. It is well documented that witnessing domestic violence, as well as being one of its victims, has a profound impact on children."[14] The Supreme Judicial Court further concluded that: "We agree with the Appeals Court that the judge below 'fail[ed] to make detailed and comprehensive findings of fact on the issues of domestic violence and its effect upon the child as well as upon the father's parenting ability.' "[15]

The Supreme Judicial Court went on to admonish the trial court, stating that:

> Domestic violence is an issue too fundamental and frequently recurring to be dealt with only by implication. The very frequency of domestic violence in disputes about child custody may have the effect of inuring courts to it and thus minimizing its significance. Requiring the courts to make explicit findings about the effect of the violence on the child and the appropriateness of the custody award in light of that effect will serve to keep these matters well in the foreground of the judges' thinking.[16]

---

[12]Burik v. Johnson, 1997 WL 66762, *5 (Ohio Ct. App. 4th Dist. Pike County 1997).

[13]R.H. v. B.F., 39 Mass. App. Ct. 29, 41, 653 N.E.2d 195 (1995), aff'd, 422 Mass. 590, 664 N.E.2d 434 (1996).

[14]Custody of Vaughn, 422 Mass. 590, 599, 664 N.E.2d 434 (1996) (This is the review of *R.H. v. B.F.* The Supreme Judicial Court assigned a fictitious name to the case.).

[15]Custody of Vaughn, 422 Mass. 590, 599, 664 N.E.2d 434 (1996).

[16]Custody of Vaughn, 422 Mass. 590, 599–600, 664 N.E.2d 434 (1996).

Similarly, in *Gant v. Gant*,[17] the trial court failed to enter any findings of fact regarding the existence of domestic violence or explain why the allege abuser was given custody of the children. In reversing the trial court decision, the Missouri Court of Appeals held that

> [it is inappropriate] to assume, based merely on the court's silence, . . . that the court did not believe that domestic violence . . . had occurred. . . . [G]iven the gravity of this issue, the overarching concern for domestic violence expressed by the legislature, and the evidence of domestic violence in this case, it was mandatory for the trial court to indicate on the record whether or not the court believed that domestic violence had occurred.[18]

The court further clarified that a finding of domestic violence requires the entry of findings of fact and conclusions of law as to the basis for the award of custody and visitation decisions, regardless of who is given primary custody.

The most notable effect of opinions of this kind are their broad-based ability to influence other judges to consider domestic violence as a factor when making a parenting award.[19] Additionally, these cases issue a directive to trial courts to detail their findings in all custody and visitation determinations where, despite evidence of domestic violence, they decide to award custody to the batterer.

Q & A: Should courts issue findings of fact where there is credible evidence of domestic violence?

Pursuant to RC 3109.04(C), the trial court must enter specific written findings of fact if it awards custody to a parent convicted of domestic violence under RC 2919.25. In *Newman v. Newman*,[20] the Perry County Court of Appeals determined that "the purpose of specific written findings of fact is to facilitate a reviewing court's consideration on appeal." Without written findings of fact, an appellate court would be unable to determine whether the trial court abused its discretion or whether its decision was against the manifest weight of the evidence.

In *Newman*, the trial court awarded custody to the abusive parent and failed to enter findings of fact to support its decision in accordance with RC 3109.04(C). The appellee had admitted that he was convicted of domestic violence involving his son. The trial court found that "in the case at hand, the court finds that it is in the children's best interest to designate the Plaintiff as their residential parent and

[17]Gant v. Gant, 892 S.W.2d 342 (Mo. Ct. App. W.D. 1995). But see Mund v. Mund, 1999 WL 86680 (Mo. Ct. App. E.D. 1999), transferred to Mo. S. Ct., 7 S.W.3d 401 (Mo. 1999) (Dowd, J., dissenting).

[18]Gant v. Gant, 892 S.W.2d 342, 346 (Mo. Ct. App. W.D. 1995).

[19]See also Michael J. Voris, Civil Orders of Protection: Do They Protect the Children, the Tag-along Victims of Domestic Violence? 17 Ohio N.U. L. Rev. 599, 609 (1991).

[20]Newman v. Newman, 1996 WL 753202, *2 (Ohio Ct. App. 5th Dist. Perry County 1996); see also Schmidt v. Schmidt, 1999 WL 225157 (Ohio Ct. App. 12th Dist. Clermont County 1999) (remanding for specific findings regarding domestic violence conviction); Smith v. Smith, 2001 WL 542317 (Ohio Ct. App. 9th Dist. Wayne County 2001) (the failure to make such a finding is reversible error); see Morrison v. Morrison, 2014-Ohio-2254, 2014 WL 2443912 (Ohio Ct. App. 9th Dist. Summit County 2014) (sustaining wife's third assignment of error and remanding to trial court).

legal custodian and that the Defendant have liberal and frequent visitation with the children."[21] The court relied on the fact that the children wished to reside with their father and that both parents were suitable custodians. Concluding that the trial court's findings were not in conformity with the meaning of RC 3109.04(C), the appellate court reversed and remanded the case.

Likewise, in *Helbling v. Helbling*,[22] the North Dakota Supreme Court reversed and remanded the trial court's custody award to the father because the court failed to make detailed findings of fact about alleged physical and mental abuse to both the mother and child. Because North Dakota has, by statute,[23] a rebuttable presumption against awarding custody to the abuser, the Supreme Court determined that it was important for the court to provide specific findings to justify awarding custody to the abuser despite the statutory presumption. In order for the presumption to be triggered in any given case, some evidence of domestic violence must be indicated.[24] Findings of fact regarding credible evidence of domestic violence demonstrate both the amount and extent of the evidence required to raise the presumption.[25]

Q & A: What type of findings of fact must be made where the evidence indicates that each parent committed domestic violence against the other during the marriage?

The North Dakota Supreme Court addressed this issue in *Owan v. Owan*.[26] In that case, there was evidence that each parent committed acts of domestic violence against the other during their relationship. The Court ruled that the trial court is required to make specific written findings on the amount and extent of the evidence and determine whether the domestic violence inflicted by one party is significantly greater than that inflicted by the other and whether that finding requires any change in the award of custody.

§ 15:14 Shared parenting considerations

Joint custody, or "shared parenting"[1] as it is now termed in Ohio, has enjoyed increasing prominence over the past ten years. Since 1991, there has been an increasing movement toward awarding shared

---

[21]Newman v. Newman, 1996 WL 753202, *2 (Ohio Ct. App. 5th Dist. Perry County 1996).

[22]Helbling v. Helbling, 532 N.W.2d 650 (N.D. 1995); see also Heck v. Reed, 529 N.W.2d 155, 36 A.L.R.5th 849 (N.D. 1995).

[23]N.D. Cent. Code § 14-09-06.2(1)(j).

[24]See Merry Hofford et al., Family Violence in Child Custody Statutes: An Analysis of State Codes and Legal Practice, 29 Fam. L.Q. 197, 225 (1995) (discussing the type of evidence that triggers the presumption).

[25]See Krank v. Krank, 529 N.W.2d 844, 51 A.L.R.5th 785 (N.D. 1995).

[26]Owan v. Owan, 1997 ND 50, 560 N.W.2d 900 (N.D. 1997); see also Huesers v. Huesers, 1998 ND 54, 574 N.W.2d 880 (N.D. 1998).

[Section 15:14]

[1]See D. Lee Khachaturian, Comment, Domestic Violence & Shared Parental Responsibility: Dangerous Bedfellows, 44 Wayne L. Rev. 1745 (1999); Judith G. Greenburg, Domestic Violence and the Danger of Joint Custody Presumptions, 25 N. Ill. U. L. Rev. 403 (2005); Gabrielle Davis et al., The Dangers of Presumptive Joint Physical Custody, The Battered Women's Justice Project, (May 2010).

parenting, even over the objection of one of the parents. While this concept fails to rise to the level of a presumption in favor of shared parenting, it comes remarkably close. A conviction by one of the parties for domestic violence[2] and a history of domestic violence[3] are factors that a court must consider before awarding shared parenting to one of the parties.[4]

The premise of shared parenting is that the parents can amicably resolve their differences or put them aside for the benefit of the children. In short, the parties must agree to agree. Unfortunately, where there is continuing violence by one party to the other, this underlying premise fails.[5] This is primarily because domestic violence is predicated on one party's use of power to control the other party and force that party to submit to his/her will.[6]

For example, in *Kelly-Doley v. Doley*,[7] the Eleventh District Court of Appeals upheld the trial court's decision against awarding shared parenting. In that case, appellant downplayed the relevance of the arguments between the parties because they had nothing to do with the minor child.

The trial court ruled that shared parenting would not be in the best interests of the child and stated that "[U]pon review of the evidence presented, both to the Magistrate and to this court, it is abundantly clear that these parties could never communicate sufficiently for a shared parenting order to work. [Appellant's] uncontrolled temper, his use of vile and obscene language, and his threats, both veiled and overt, do not lend themselves to a civil relationship with [appellee].

---

[2]RC 3109.04(F)(1)(h); see also Am. Sub. 2007 S.B. 260, eff. 1-2-07.

[3]RC 3109.04(F)(2). See also Kelly-Doley v. Doley, 1999 WL 262165 (Ohio Ct. App. 11th Dist. Lake County 1999) (upholding decision against award of shared parenting based on a history of violence in the relationship); In re Marriage of C.M.C., 87 Wash. App. 84, 940 P.2d 669 (Div. 1 1997), reconsideration filed, (Aug. 11, 1997) and decision aff'd, 136 Wash. 2d 800, 966 P.2d 1247 (1998) (holding that joint parental decision-making is statutorily precluded upon finding a history of acts of domestic violence by one parent, regardless of whether those acts caused grievous bodily harm or fear of such harm).

[4]See also Text § 15:5, Ohio's legislative response to domestic violence; Text § 15:6, Ohio's judicial response to domestic violence.

[5]See Joanne Schulman & Valerie Pitt, Second Thoughts on Joint Child Custody: Analysis of Legislation and Its Implications for Women and Children, 12 Golden Gate U. L. Rev. 538, 554–56 (1982); see also Daniel G. Saunders, Child Custody Decisions in Families Experiencing Woman Abuse, 39 Soc. Work 51, 55 (1994); Laura Crites & Donna Coker, What Therapists See That Judges May Miss: A Unique Guide to Custody Decisions When Spouse Abuse is Charged, 27 Judges' J. 8 (1988); Mildred D. Pagelow, Justice for Victims of Spouse Abuse in Divorce and Child Custody Cases, 8 Violence and Victims 1, 74 (1993); D. Lee Khachaturian, Comment, Domestic Violence and Shared Parental Responsibility: Dangerous Bedfellows, 44 Wayne L. Rev. 1745 (Winter 1999); Conner, Back to the Drawing Board: Barriers to Joint Decision-Making in Custody Cases Involving Intimate Partner Violence, 18 Duke J. Gender L. & Pol'y 223 (2011).

[6]See Joan Zorza, Protecting the Children in Custody Disputes When One Parent Abuses the Other, 29 Clearinghouse Rev. 1113 (1996); see also Linda R. Keenan, Domestic Violence and Custody Litigation: The Need for Statutory Reform, 13 Hofstra L. Rev. 407, 431 (1985); T. Grillo, The Mediation Alternative: Process Dangers for Women, 100 Yale L.J. 1545 (1991).

[7]Kelly-Doley v. Doley, 1999 WL 262165 (Ohio Ct. App. 11th Dist. Lake County 1999).

This Court is of the opinion that to place this child in a shared parenting situation between these two parents so filled with hatred would be devastating to the child."[8] The appellate court noted that the trial court was required to consider spousal abuse pursuant to RC 3109.04(F)(2). It relied on the history of abusive conduct between the parties, much of which was witnessed by the children.

Of significance is that the court did not need to find a conviction for domestic violence to support its decision. Consideration of the parties' testimony, a police report and the fact that some of the violence occurred in the presence of the child was sufficient evidence to support a finding against an award of shared parenting.

Moreover, the Eleventh District Court of Appeals decision relied on appellant's infliction of emotional abuse towards appellee. For example, appellant publicly used degrading language towards her in order to embarrass her at the child's school dance recital. He also deliberately took the child as a tax exemption, making it difficult for the appellee to try to claim the child.[9]

The National Council of Juvenile and Family Court Judges cautions that "Court Orders which force victims to share custody with their abusers place both victims and children in danger."[10] Additionally, the Council points out that "continued aggression and violence between divorced spouses with joint custody has the most adverse consequences for children of any custody option."[11] The Council relies on the studies of Judith Wallerstein set forth in her book, Second Chances: Men, Women and Children a Decade After Divorce.[12]

Additionally, House Congressional Resolution 172, adopted in 1990, warns that "joint custody guarantees the batterer continued access and control over the battered spouse's life through the children."[13] Against this background, many judicial authorities strongly urge against an award of shared parenting where domestic violence is an issue.

Q & A: In cases where shared parenting is requested, what best-interest factors are courts required to consider in determining whether to award it?

In cases where shared parenting is requested by one of the parties, the court is required to consider all the best interest factors contained in both RC 3109.04(F)(1) and RC 3109.04(F)(2).[14] A conviction or plea of guilty for domestic violence or another offense that caused physical

[8]Kelly-Doley v. Doley, 1999 WL 262165, *7 (Ohio Ct. App. 11th Dist. Lake County 1999).

[9]Kelly-Doley v. Doley, 1999 WL 262165, *8 (Ohio Ct. App. 11th Dist. Lake County 1999).

[10]National Council of Juvenile & Family Court Judges, Family Violence: Improving Court Practice 26 (1990).

[11]National Council of Juvenile & Family Court Judges, Family Violence: Improving Court Practice 26 (1990).

[12]Judith S. Wallerstein & Sandra Blakeslee, Second Chances: Men, Women and Children a Decade After Divorce (1989).

[13]H.R. Con. Res. 172, 101st Cong., 2d sess. (1990).

[14]See MacFarlane v. MacFarlane, 2006-Ohio-3155, 2006 WL 1704531 (Ohio Ct. App. 8th Dist. Cuyahoga County 2006) (noting that court considered 3109.04(F)(1) and (F)(2) factors in determining child's best interest); see also Schmidt v. Schmidt,

harm to a member of the victim's household is among the factors that the court must evaluate before rendering its decision.[15] Besides that and other relevant factors, the court must consider "[a]ny history of, or potential for, child abuse, spouse abuse, other domestic violence, or parental kidnapping by either parent."[16] Thus, an exploration into that history must be made whether or not the parent was convicted of domestic violence.[17]

The court could have considered a "history of or potential for spouse abuse" without a legislative mandate. What is significant is that Ohio's legislature established this mandate for courts to follow prior to awarding shared parenting to the parties.

Unlike sole custody and/or visitation, shared parenting encourages continued contact between the parents. Since shared parenting presupposes that the parents participate jointly in decision-making regarding the children, it creates a situation where the batterer is provided legally required opportunities to continue the abuse. Because the risks are greater for victims in shared parenting arrangements, victims must be permitted to present additional, and often undocumented, evidence of domestic violence. It is often easier to prove a "history of or potential for" spouse abuse or "other" domestic violence than it is to prevail at a criminal domestic violence trial.

Q & A: What special problems does shared parenting pose for the domestic violence victim and/or the family law practitioner?

Where the court orders shared parenting or where the parties agree to a shared parenting plan, it may be more difficult to achieve the goal of allowing access to the children while protecting the abused parent from future harm.[18] Since a shared parenting plan presupposes that the parents can resolve issues relative to their children amicably,[19] there may appear to be no reason to restrict a parent's access to records, activities, or the victim's address.

1999 WL 225157, *2 (Ohio Ct. App. 12th Dist. Clermont County 1999) ("[A]lthough appellee had pleaded no contest to a domestic violence charge involving appellant, there was no evidence that he presented a physical threat to the children.").

[15]RC 3109.04(F)(1)(h).

[16]RC 3109.04(F)(2)(c); Taylor v. Taylor, 1995 WL 507446, *3 (Ohio Ct. App. 5th Dist. Richland County 1995) (noting that RC 3109.04(F)(1) mandates the "best interest of a child" determination should include both (F)(1) and (F)(2) factors"). See also Mund v. Mund, 1999 WL 86680 (Mo. Ct. App. E.D. 1999), transferred to Mo. S. Ct., 7 S.W.3d 401 (Mo. 1999) (stating that, where trial court finds pattern of domestic violence, it must make specific findings as to why custody was given to abusive parent).

[17]See Kelly-Doley v. Doley, 1999 WL 262165 (Ohio Ct. App. 11th Dist. Lake County 1999); see also Text § 15:7, Presenting evidence of domestic violence in custody and visitation proceedings; practice pointers.

[18]See Robert D. Felner & Lisa Terre, Child Custody Dispositions and Children's Adaptation Following Divorce, in Psychology and Child Custody Dispositions 106 (Lois A. Weithorn et al. eds., Univ. of Nebraska Press 1987).

[19]See also N. Polikoff, Joint Custody: Only By Agreement of the Parties, 8 Women's Advocate 1, 3 (1987).

Often the abusive parent desires shared parenting and files a plan in accordance with the statute.[20] Sometimes, the abusive parent may request shared parenting for no other reason than to allow him/her to continue to abuse the victim. If no counter proposal is filed, the court has the authority to adopt the abuser's shared parenting plan. The court may also order the abused parent to file a shared parenting plan. The court has the discretion to adopt the abuser's plan, over the objection of the abused parent,[21] or to craft its own plan.

Victims of domestic violence may agree to shared parenting for many reasons.[22] They may be afraid that they will lose custody altogether if the case goes to trial. Sometimes, they only desire to avoid the stress of a trial. Sometimes, they may lack evidence of a conviction for domestic violence or documentation of a history of abuse[23] that may be necessary to prevail at trial.

Many commentators and researchers suggest that shared parenting not be awarded by the courts where there is a history of domestic violence.[24] Two psychologists proposed a risk assessment for determining whether to award shared parenting: "Before determining a shared parenting plan, evaluate the endangering parent for (1) ability to maintain impulse control; (2) capacity to empathize with the child; (3) ability to change problem-solving style; and (4) capacity to create and maintain a safe environment for the child."[25] An abuser who is not able to modify behavior suggests a high risk situation for the children. Where the relationship is highly conflicted, the safety of the child must become the paramount concern.

In cases where the victim wants to maintain a confidential address, it is important for the practitioner to present evidence of the history and pattern of violence within the marriage[26] before the parenting plan is crafted and becomes a court order. A pattern or history of domestic violence may be a convincing reason to restrict access to the victim, especially where it can be demonstrated that the abuse is likely to continue. It may also serve as a significant reason to deny an abuser's request for shared parenting.[27] A conviction for domestic

[20]See RC 3109.04(D)(1)(a)(i) to RC 3109.04(D)(1)(a)(iii), RC 3109.04(G).

[21]See Schmidt v. Schmidt, 1999 WL 225157 (Ohio Ct. App. 12th Dist. Clermont County 1999).

[22]Lenore E. Walker & Glenace E. Edwall, Domestic Violence and Determination of Visitation and Custody in Divorce, in Domestic Violence on Trial 127, 130–31 (D. Sonkin ed., 1987).

[23]See Text § 15:7, Presenting evidence of domestic violence in custody and visitation proceedings; practice pointers.

[24]See, e.g., Daniel G. Saunders, Child Custody Decisions in Families Experiencing Woman Abuse, 39 Soc. Work 51 (1994).

[25]Carla Garrity & Mitchell A. Baris, Custody & Visitation: Is it Safe? 17 Fam. Advoc. 40, 43 (1995).

[26]See RC 3109.04(F)(2). See also Text § 15:7, Presenting evidence of domestic violence in custody and visitation proceedings; practice pointers, Text § 15:9, Confidentiality, Text § 15:10, Batterer access to the victim and children. Text § 15:11, Impact of domestic violence on children.

[27]RC 3109.04(F)(2)(c).

violence may serve as a justification for either avoiding shared parenting altogether or, at the very least, limiting or restricting access.[28]

Where it can be demonstrated that the child is also the victim of domestic violence or could be harmed from continuing exposure to parental domestic violence,[29] it is unlikely that a court will order shared parenting. If ordered, however, specific restrictions regarding access to records, day care facilities, and activities must be included in the court order.

The equal access provisions contained in RC 3109.051(H) to RC 3109.051(J) apply to all orders that allocate parental rights and responsibilities, including shared parenting plans. The victim should be cautioned that, absent specific written restrictions curtailing access, the other parent is automatically entitled to equal access.

Q & A: Should shared parenting be considered by the courts when there is a history of domestic violence in the parents' relationship?[30]

Many state courts have determined that a finding of a history of domestic violence is a significant factor against an award of joint custody. For example, in *Ouellette v. Ouellette*,[31] the Connecticut Court of Appeals held that joint custody is not a viable solution in a divorce agreement where the marriage had a history of violence, restraining orders, calls to the police, and loud arguments. In *In re Marriage of Heilmann*,[32] the Kansas Court of Appeals determined that, given the history of violence by the father and threats to take the mother's life, the trial court did not abuse its discretion in awarding sole custody to the mother despite father's request for joint custody.

These cases illustrate the importance of presenting to the court the history of domestic violence in a relationship. The common thread found in cases that have denied a request for joint custody is a history of violence against one of the parties. RC 3109.04(F)(2)(c) mirrors the legal reasoning set forth in these cases.

However, despite a history of violence, courts have awarded joint custody over the objection of one of the parties where the children express a preference for an abusive parent and the parties are able to agree on major decisions involving the children such as religion and education.[33]

Q & A: Can a court issue a civil protection order against a parent even where the parties have shared parenting?

---

[28]See RC 3109.04(F)(1)(h), RC 3109.04(F)(2).

[29]See also Text § 15:9, Confidentiality, Text § 15:10, Batterer access to the victim and children. Text § 15:11, Impact of domestic violence on children.

[30]See also Text § 15:7, Presenting evidence of domestic violence in custody and visitation proceedings; practice pointers.

[31]Ouellette v. Ouellette, 1993 WL 360442 (Conn. Super. Ct. 1993); see also In re Marriage of C.M.C., 87 Wash. App. 84, 940 P.2d 669 (Div. 1 1997), reconsideration filed, (Aug. 11, 1997) and decision aff'd, 136 Wash. 2d 800, 966 P.2d 1247 (1998).

[32]Matter of Marriage of Heilmann, 771 P.2d 948 (Kan. Ct. App. 1989); see also Caven v. Caven, 136 Wash. 2d 800, 966 P.2d 1247 (1998) (holding that state statute prohibits joint decision-making upon a finding of a history of acts of domestic violence regardless of whether those acts caused grievous bodily harm); In re Marriage of C.M.C., 87 Wash. App. 84, 940 P.2d 669 (Div. 1 1997), reconsideration filed, (Aug. 11, 1997) and decision aff'd, 136 Wash. 2d 800, 966 P.2d 1247 (1998).

[33]See, e.g., In re Marriage of Dempster, 809 S.W.2d 450 (Mo. Ct. App. S.D. 1991);

At least one court has addressed this particular issue. In *Ellibee v. Ellibee*,[34] the court granted the mother a protection order on behalf of the children against the father because he had administered severe spankings to his son during parenting time. The court determined that the granting of a ninety-day protection order was proper, especially given the intent of the state's domestic violence statute. This result was appropriate regardless of the fact that the parents had joint custody of the children. The court's only objective was to provide safety to the children while in their father's care.

§ 15:15 Domestic violence and visitation issues

Visitation decisions are equally difficult for courts to make in light of the competing interests of permitting the noncustodial parent frequent access to the children and protecting the abused parent from further harm. While it is apparent that children need access to both parents, they need to feel safe; and continued conflict between the parents adversely impacts the children.[1] As two commentators explained:

> A parent's "right to visitation" cannot take precedence over a child's exposure to a high-risk environment. Visitation is designed to build supportive relationships and to allow a child to feel loved and cared for by a parent who will promote the child's continuing development. Unfortunately, relationships do not grow and flourish in an environment of fear.[2]

The National Council of Juvenile and Family Court Judges has expressed its opinion that "the propensity for continued violence remains after the divorce or separation and frequently recurs during unsupervised visitation or joint custody."[3] A National Institute of Justice study found that "nowhere is the potential for renewed violence greater than during visitation."[4]

These studies suggest that the periods during separation or after

---

Collinsworth v. O'Connell, 508 So. 2d 744 (Fla. 1st DCA 1987); O.J.G. v. G.W.G., 770 S.W.2d 372 (Mo. Ct. App. E.D. 1989).

[34]See Text § 12:15, Remedies—Orders allocating parental rights and responsibilities. See also Ellibee v. Ellibee, 121 Idaho 501, 826 P.2d 462 (1992); but see Couch v. Harrison, 2001-Ohio-4199, 2001 WL 121108 (Ohio Ct. App. 12th Dist. Clermont County 2001) (where court of appeals held that, while a civil protection order could not permanently allocation parental rights and responsibilities, it may do so on a temporary basis); Schottenstein v. Schottenstein, 2003-Ohio-5032, 2003 WL 22176786 (Ohio Ct. App. 10th Dist. Franklin County 2003) (relying on *Couch v. Harrison*); Kitchen v. Kitchen, 2001 WL 279026 (Ohio Ct. App. 12th Dist. Madison County 2001); but see Kiedrowicz v. Kiedrowicz, 1999 WL 197793 (Ohio Ct. App. 6th Dist. Huron County 1999).

[Section 15:15]

[1]See Michael J. Voris, Civil Orders of Protection: Do They Protect Children, the Tag-along Victims of Domestic Violence? 17 Ohio N.U. L. Rev. 599 (1991); see also Laura Crites & Donna Coker, What Therapists See That Judges May Miss: A Unique Guide to Custody Decisions When Spouse Abuse is Charged, 27 Judges' J. 8, 42 (1988).

[2]Carla Garrity & Mitchell Baris, Custody and Visitation: Is it Safe? 17 Fam. Advoc. 40, 43 (1995).

[3]National Council of Juvenile & Family Court Judges, Family Violence: Improving Court Practice 26 (1987).

[4]Peter Finn & Sarah Colson, Civil Protection Orders: Legislation, Current

divorce are the most threatening for the victim of domestic violence.[5] The victim is more likely to be assaulted or even killed during these times.[6] Even the children are at greater risk of violence directed at them during these particular times.[7]

Notwithstanding these studies, visitation and continued access with the abusive parent are still considered to be in the best interest of the child;[8] and thus, some visitation is likely to be awarded.[9] In most court jurisdictions, restricting visitation requires evidence that visitation with the abusive parent will endanger a child's physical, mental, or emotional health.[10] Evidence that demonstrates this particular point is often difficult to obtain. Oftentimes, there is some history of abuse toward one of the parents, but being able to show that it causes injury or harm to the child's physical, mental, or emotional health is more difficult. Absent a showing of direct impact, however, few courts are likely to restrict an abuser's access to the children.[11]

Practice and Enforcement 43 (1990).

[5]See also J.L. Hardesty, Separation assault in the context of post divorce parenting, Violence Against Women, 8, 597–625 (Sage Publications 2002); R.E. Fleury, C.M. Sullivan & D.I. Bybee, When ending the relationship does not end the violence, Violence Against Women, 6, 1363–83 (Sage Publications 2000).

[6]Joan Zorza, Protecting the Children in Custody Disputes When One Parent Abuses the Other, 29 Clearinghouse Rev. 1113, 1115 (1996).

[7]Joan Zorza, Protecting the Children in Custody Disputes When One Parent Abuses the Other, 29 Clearinghouse Rev. 1113, 1115–16 (1996); see also National Council on Family & Juvenile Court Judges, Family Violence: A Guide to Research 27 (1993).

[8]See Shafor v. Shafor, 2009-Ohio-191, 2009 WL 119853, *2 (Ohio Ct. App. 12th Dist. Warren County 2009) (in discussing the best interest of a child in the context of visitation, the court stated that "the trial court has the discretion to limit or restrict visitation rights"); citing Anderson v. Anderson, 147 Ohio App. 3d 513, 2002-Ohio-1156, 771 N.E.2d 303 (7th Dist. Carroll County 2002) ("This includes the power to restrict the time and place of visitation, to determine the conditions under which visitation will take place and to deny visitation rights altogether if visitation would not be in the best interests of the child."); quoting Jannetti v. Nichol, 2000 WL 652540, *3 (Ohio Ct. App. 7th Dist. Mahoning County 2000).

[9]See Morris v. Morris, 2000 WL 222025 (Ohio Ct. App. 5th Dist. Stark County 2000) (noting that, although appellant (abuser) may be less likely to deny visitation, he was more likely to cause friction during exchanges of the child).

[10]See, e.g., Bodine v. Bodine, 38 Ohio App. 3d 173, 175, 528 N.E.2d 973 (10th Dist. Franklin County 1988) (holding that "when there is clear and convincing evidence that a proposed visitation arrangement will be harmful to the welfare of the children, a trial court abuses its discretion in failing to impose sufficient restrictions to ensure the children's well being"); People v. Hazelwonder, 138 Ill. App. 3d 213, 93 Ill. Dec. 1, 485 N.E.2d 1211 (4th Dist. 1985); see also Lawrence v. Delkamp, 2000 ND 214, 620 N.W.2d 151 (N.D. 2000).

[11]But see Hall v. Hall, 408 N.W.2d 626, 629 (Minn. Ct. App. 1987) (no error in imposing supervised visitation although there was no domestic violence directed toward the children where the purpose of the relief was to minimize the risk of additional danger to the victim-mother); see also Dodd v. Dodd, 2001 WL 812244, *10 (Ohio Ct. App. 6th Dist. Lucas County 2001) (where the appellate court stated that when allocating parental rights and issuing visitation orders, courts should seek to avoid conflict; "The Court finds that Plaintiff [appellant] was the aggressor in most of the cases of domestic violence and that he has verbally abused Defendant in front of the children. To avoid further incidents, a strict visitation schedule must be imposed"; the court recognized that the parties in this case would never be able to agree to a visitation schedule).

Q & A: What factors should the court consider where it orders supervised or restricted visitation?

According to *Shaughnessy v. Shaughnessy*,[12] a trial court must consider all the factors set forth in RC 3109.051(C) and RC 3109.051(D). In this case, the appellant was awarded restricted and supervised access to her children. Her said visitation was supervised and limited to two and one half hours per week. On appeal, she argued that she was precluded from presenting evidence relative to the allocation and responsibilities and that restricted and supervised visitation at the appellee's house was unreasonable, arbitrary and unconscionable.

The Seventh District Court of Appeals found that the trial court's decision with respect to visitation was unreasonable and arbitrary because the court had failed to consider the various factors enumerated in the statute. The appellate court indicated that a trial court must consider the factors set forth in RC 3109.051(D) when awarding visitation, especially where visitation is restricted in a given case. Where the trial court does not consider the factors or fails to support its decision with findings, an appeals court must reverse the decision as arbitrary and unreasonable. In this case, the failure to consider all relevant factors was tantamount to punishing the party and mandated reversal in order to conduct an evidentiary hearing to determine appropriate terms and conditions for visitation.[13]

Significantly, the appellate court only summarily addressed the domestic violence issues. Clearly, it failed to give any specific weight to domestic violence when considering the factors, in spite of the fact that appellee conceded filing a domestic violence complaint against her husband.

Q & A: What is the effect of an abused spouse restricting the abuser's visitation with the parties' minor children?

It is not uncommon for difficulties to arise in visitation where the evidence demonstrates a pattern of domestic violence. The trouble is compounded when a court attempts to balance the nonabusive parent's reluctance to permit visitation or restricted visitation with the abusive parent's right to visit the children. Often, the court perceives a parent's reluctance as a violation rather than as a justifiable response to fear of an abusive spouse.[14]

In fact, a client should think twice before restricting the other parent's visitation, even if the client is pursuing criminal charges for domestic violence and has a criminal protection order. For example, in *Van Dyke v. Spencer*,[15] the Montgomery County Appellate Court upheld a contempt order against the custodial mother for violating visita-

[12]Shaughnessy v. Shaughnessy, 1999 WL 159211 (Ohio Ct. App. 7th Dist. Mahoning County 1999).

[13]Shaughnessy v. Shaughnessy, 1999 WL 159211, *12 (Ohio Ct. App. 7th Dist. Mahoning County 1999).

[14]But see McClead v. McClead, 2007-Ohio-4624, 2007 WL 2570735 (Ohio Ct. App. 4th Dist. Washington County 2007) (affirmed trial court decision declining to find appellee in contempt due to concern for her child's safety as basis for denying him visitation).

[15]Van Dyke v. Spencer, 1998 WL 896540 (Ohio Ct. App. 2d Dist. Montgomery County 1998). See also Morris v. Morris, 2000 WL 222025 (Ohio Ct. App. 5th Dist.

tion orders. The trial court found that the difficulty with the implementation of visitation was the mother's filing of domestic violence charges against the father as well as her obtaining a temporary protection order. According to the defendant, because of the protection order, he lost over thirty-three days of scheduled visitation.

The trial court found, and the appellate court agreed, that a domestic violence charge and protection order constituted contempt of visitation, noting that the plaintiff had "apparently falsely obtain[ed] a temporary protection order. Plaintiff never demonstrated a reasonable basis for obtaining the protection order."[16] That, coupled with the fact that the plaintiff went to the pediatrician to check for signs of sexual abuse, demonstrated an inability to facilitate visitation. The court also found that she had manipulated the system to obtain a temporary protection order.

The Montgomery County Court of Appeals rejected the mother's argument that, in filing charges and seeking the criminal protection order, she did not intend to deny the father visitation. The court held that "[t]he clear consequence of her volitionary act of gaining a protective order was to deny visitation, in fact, to the father. She is deemed in law to have intended the natural and probable consequence of her voluntary acts."[17]

This decision highlights a parent's obligation to facilitate visitation[18] even where criminal charges have been filed and the other parent is subject to a criminal protection order. It also serves to instruct clients not to summarily restrict or terminate visitation in reliance on a pending criminal action and protection order. Under such circumstances, a protection order may create a false sense of security for the alleged victim. Of course, it is unclear from the appellate decision whether its holding is restricted to the facts of the case in which the criminal domestic violence case was dismissed because the plaintiff failed to appear at trial.

Stark County 2000) (affirming grant of custody to mother although she denied father access to the child); In re Marriage of Daniels, 568 N.W.2d 51, 56 (Iowa Ct. App. 1997) (determining that, while mother's eleven-month denial of visitation was unjustified, it does not justify award of custody to father and finding "the detrimental effects of family violence to be the more compelling factor when considering which custodial award would be in the best interest of the children").

[16]Van Dyke v. Spencer, 1998 WL 896540, *1 (Ohio Ct. App. 2d Dist. Montgomery County 1998).

[17]Van Dyke v. Spencer, 1998 WL 896540, *2 (Ohio Ct. App. 2d Dist. Montgomery County 1998); see also Campbell v. Campbell, 604 A.2d 33, 36 (Me. 1992) (Under similar facts, a Maine appellate court remanded, requiring the trial court to find by clear and convincing evidence that the parent misused the protection order process. The court further held that a parent's questionable litigation tactic in filing for a protection order where there was little credible evidence is relevant to custody only if (1) the parent willfully misused the protection order process to gain a tactical advantage in the divorce proceeding and (2) there is a nexus between the misuse of the protection process at the time of the ongoing divorce litigation and the children's best interest after the divorce litigation is concluded. The court further stated that the willful misuse must demonstrate that the parent will, after the divorce, have a lessened ability and willingness to work with the other parent.).

[18]See also Ford v. Ford, 700 So. 2d 191 (Fla. 4th DCA 1997). But see In re Marriage of Daniels, 568 N.W.2d 51 (Iowa Ct. App. 1997).

Q & A: Do courts look at a history of domestic violence when determining the type of visitation to be accorded the nonresidential parent?

Most courts look at the history of domestic violence when determining custody.[19] Because a history and pattern of domestic violence in the relationship may lead to potential future violence against the other parent and possibly the child, courts should request evidence of a history of abuse in the parties' relationship.[20] This is especially true when the abusive parent begins to physically discipline the child in an aggressive manner, similar in style to that abuse inflicted on the other parent.

Sometimes, courts will consider the past history of the domestic violence, the history of violating court orders, and a present inability to control one's anger in restricting visitation orders. For example, in *Dodd v. Dodd*,[21] the Lucas County Court of Appeals upheld the trial court's decision to restrict the appellant's visitation in order to prevent contact between the parties. The court eliminated the weekday evening, structured the exchange of the children at the Toledo Police Station, and struck the language that said "other times as the parties' may agree," observing that "[o]bviously, given the nature of these people, they will never agree." The court relied on evidence of appellant's violations of the restraining order, the pattern of domestic violence, and the fact that the appellant was the aggressor in most of the domestic violence incidents in designating the non-offending parent as the residential parent and legal custodian and restricting the visitation in order to avoid further incidents.

Sometimes, the court may discount a history and pattern of abuse in the relationship, especially where the abuse took place in the past.

---

[19]See Text § 15:7, Presenting evidence of domestic violence in custody and visitation proceedings; practice pointers; see also Kahn v. Kahn, 236 A.D.2d 612, 654 N.Y.S.2d 34 (2d Dep't 1997) (reversing award of custody to father because of his prior history of violence toward the mother and because he had relocated outside the United States, making abduction of the child a strong possibility); but see Fordham v. Fordham, 2009-Ohio-1915, 2009 WL 1110796 (Ohio Ct. App. 3d Dist. Logan County 2009) (court wouldn't reverse trial court decision that expanded ex husband's visitation in spite of numerous violations of CPO and conviction for domestic violence. Although appellate court may had reached a different conclusion regarding the expansive visitation, court reluctant to find that trial court had abused its discretion).

[20]But see Neff v. Neff, 1998 WL 433846,*2 (Ohio Ct. App. 8th Dist. Cuyahoga County 1998) (upholding award of overnight visitation to father and finding that, even "assuming arguendo defendant-appellee had episodes of 'uncontrollable rage' in the past, there has been no evidence presented which would suggest that these incidents would be more likely to occur during an overnight visit as opposed to a full day visit to which plaintiff-appellant does not object").

[21]Dodd v. Dodd, 2001 WL 812244 (Ohio Ct. App. 6th Dist. Lucas County 2001); see also Bodine v. Bodine, 38 Ohio App. 3d 173, 175, 528 N.E.2d 973 (10th Dist. Franklin County 1988) (noting that defendant had a violent temper; that this violence was occasionally directed at wife, with the children as unintended victims and that defendant sought couseling to control his anger); but see Baker v. Baker, 2007-Ohio-7172, 2007 WL 4615953, *4 (Ohio Ct. App. 4th Dist. Washington County 2007) (Distinguishing *Bodine* and stating that in *Bodine*, there was a long history of occasional physical violence towards mother. Here by the mother's own admission, there was only one incident of physical violence directed toward the mother, and it occurred near the end of the marriage. Thus, it was not an abuse of discretion to allow father to have unsupervised visitation.).

For example, in *Neff v. Neff*,[22] the Eighth District Court of Appeals decided that "an alleged history of spousal abuse and violent behavior between the two parties in the past is not grounds, in and of itself, to deny visitation rights." The court relied on the magistrate's findings which noted that, although there was undisputed evidence of the violent nature of the relationship, there was no evidence establishing any physical violence directed at the children. The court also pointed out that the record supports the fact that the children had a good relationship with both parents.

Neff illustrates the maxim that a parent's right to visit with his/her child is a natural right and "should be denied only under extraordinary circumstances, such as unfitness of the noncustodial parent or a showing that visitation with the noncustodial parent would cause harm to the children."[23] The *Neff* court noted that such circumstances must be demonstrated by clear and convincing evidence and the burden of proof is on the party contesting the court's issuance of visitation privileges.

Unfortunately, the Eighth District Court of Appeals sought evidence of a domestic violence conviction under RC 2919.25 in order to support a party's allegations of violence by the other.[24] However, the court left open the possibility of considering a documented history of past violence where the child witnessed the violence between the parents or where a parent had been previously convicted of domestic violence.

For reasons stated throughout this text, domestic violence between the parents has a detrimental effect on the children.[25] However, several courts adhere to the old maxim that domestic violence not directed at the children has no effect on the children. For example, in *Neff v. Neff*,[26] the appeals court affirmed the trial court's award of overnight visitation to the father. The Cuyahoga County Court of Appeals reiterated the magistrate's finding that "there is no evidence establishing any physical violence directed at the children" to support its decision.[27] It is unfortunate that the court failed to recognize the negative impact of violence on children who witness the abuse between their parents. The fact that neither the trial court nor the appellate court made mention of this indicates the importance of continued judicial education in this area.

---

[22]Neff v. Neff, 1998 WL 433846,*2 (Ohio Ct. App. 8th Dist. Cuyahoga County 1998).

[23]Neff v. Neff, 1998 WL 433846,*2 (Ohio Ct. App. 8th Dist. Cuyahoga County 1998).

[24]Neff v. Neff, 1998 WL 433846,*2 (Ohio Ct. App. 8th Dist. Cuyahoga County 1998) ("While each parent has accused the other of engaging in domestic violence against her or him, neither has been convicted nor pled guilty to domestic violence pursuant to RC 2919.15.").

[25]See Text § 15:5, Ohio's legislative response to domestic violence.

[26]Neff v. Neff, 1998 WL 433846 (Ohio Ct. App. 8th Dist. Cuyahoga County 1998).

[27]Neff v. Neff, 1998 WL 433846,*2 (Ohio Ct. App. 8th Dist. Cuyahoga County 1998).

Q & A: What factors should a court consider in crafting a visitation plan where domestic violence is an issue?[28]

Whatever the ultimate court decision, the type of visitation schedule arranged must be drafted to protect the victim's safety.[29] Protective arrangements should be detailed to meet a client's individual needs. These may include:

(1) specifying the hours and days of visitation and prohibiting contact at other times, liberal or open-ended visitation should be discouraged by the courts;

(2) conditioning visitation on participation in batterer's intervention and/or substance abuse treatment program;

(3) utilizing a third party to provide transportation and serve as an intermediary between the parents;

(4) using a third party to supervise visits when there is a danger of child abuse or abduction;

(5) transferring the children in a neutral location such as a library, police station,[30] store, or restaurant; and

(6) restraining the abuser from exercising visitation while under the influence of drugs and/or alcohol.[31]

Even if the visitation is not supervised, certain safeguards, such as neutral pick-up and drop-off points and designated hours and days of access, should be adopted in all cases in which domestic violence is present.

Q & A: How have the courts addressed the issue of supervised visitation?

Supervised visitation should be considered the preferred method of resolution in disputed visitation cases in order to reduce the risk of further violence between the parties.[32] At the very least, supervised access should be awarded until a professional has fully completed an

---

[28]See generally Lavita Nad Karni and Barbara Zeek Shaw, Making a Difference: Tools to Help Judges Support the Healing of Children Exposed to Domestic Violence, 39(2) Court Rev. 24 (2002).

[29]See Consideration in Visitation Decisions: A Checklist, in Domestic Violence and Children: Resolving Custody and Visitation Disputes, A National Judicial Curriculum 148 (Janet Carter et al. eds., 1995); see also Joseph C. McGill, Robin M. Deutsch & Robert A. Zibbell, Visitation and Domestic Violence: A Clinical Model of Family Assessment & Access Planning, 37 Fam. & Conciliation Courts Rev. 315 (1999); see for example, Dodd v. Dodd, 2001 WL 812244 (Ohio Ct. App. 6th Dist. Lucas County 2001) (in which the trial court's decision to restrict visitation because the evidence demonstrated the parties would never agree was affirmed by the appellate court).

[30]Shimman v. Germano, 2008-Ohio-717, 2008 WL 466787 (Ohio Ct. App. 6th Dist. Lucas County 2008).

[31]Myra Sun & Elizabeth Thomas, Custody Litigation on Behalf of Battered Women, 21 Clearinghouse Rev. 563, 576 (1987); see also National Council of Juvenile & Family Court Judges, Model Code on Domestic and Family Violence § 405 (1994).

[32]See Robert Straus, Supervised Visitation & Family Violence, 29 Fam. L. Q. 229 (1995); see also Robert Straus & Eve Alda, Supervised Child Access: The Evolution of Social Service, 32 Fam. & Conciliation Cts. Rev. 230–46 (1994); Martha Bailey, Supervised Access: A Long-Term Solution? 37 Fam. & Conciliation Courts Rev. 478 (Oct. 1999). See also Lang v. Lang, 2004-Ohio-2035, 2004 WL 869367 (Ohio Ct. App. 2d Dist. Miami County 2004) (appellate court affirmed lower court decision to issue a CPO that requires supervised visitation unless a contrary order is entered by the court in the divorce as the domestic relations court is in the best position to assess visitation in this situation; the inclusion of the child within the scope of the CPO does

assessment and the batterer has successfully completed a domestic violence treatment program.

Several courts have recognized the danger posed by unsupervised visitation when domestic violence is an issue.[33] For these courts, imposing a supervised visitation schedule in protection order hearings or in custody disputes is the norm. Many of these judges either award supervised visitation or suspend visitation for a period of time until other professionals are able to determine the impact of the violence on the children.

In *Eichenberger v. Eichenberger*,[34] the Franklin County Court of Appeals suspended the respondent's visitation rights until a guardian ad litem had an opportunity to investigate and make a recommendation as to the appropriate type of visitation. Such a judicial response stresses the importance of caution in this area. Other court jurisdictions have concluded that supervised visitation should be awarded pending the outcome of a risk assessment.[35]

Other courts, however, have imposed specific supervised visitation schedules where domestic violence exists without making the supervised visitation conditional. For example, in *Katz v. Katz*,[36] where the defendant abused his wife in the presence of the child, the court ordered supervised visitation under carefully controlled circumstances.[37]

In other cases, a court may award supervised visitation for a set term of years. For example, in *Zamonski v. Wan*,[38] the appellate court upheld the trial court's decision ordering supervised visitation for a period of three years and completion of a batterer's program. The court relied on the fact that the appellee had previously been granted a civil protection order and noted that there was testimony that ap-

---

not constitute plain error).

[33]See, e.g., Van Horn v. Van Horn, 1996 WL 735581, *3(Ohio Ct. App. 7th Dist. Mahoning County 1996) (affirming trial court's award of only supervised visitation to father because of his two domestic violence convictions, his instances of violence toward his children, and his dangerous propensities); see also Brown v. Brown, 2000 WL 271769 (Ohio Ct. App. 10th Dist. Franklin County 2000) in which the Court of Appeals (overruled respondent's objections to the inclusion of supervised visitation in the CPO of one year's duration; supervised visitation did not violate the respondent's due process rights or the legislature's intent regarding RC 3113.31).

[34]Eichenberger v. Eichenberger, 82 Ohio App. 3d 809, 613 N.E.2d 678 (10th Dist. Franklin County 1992).

[35]See, e.g., Cosme v. Figueroa, 258 N.J. Super. 333, 609 A.2d 523 (Ch. Div. 1992).

[36]Katz v. Katz, 97 A.D.2d 398, 467 N.Y.S.2d 223 (2d Dep't 1983); see also Lufft v. Lufft, 188 W. Va. 339, 424 S.E.2d 266, 270 (1992). But see In re Whaley, 86 Ohio App. 3d 304, 620 N.E.2d 954 (4th Dist. Athens County 1993) (finding no abuse of discretion where trial court granted father unsupervised visitation with the child where there was evidence of violence against two girlfriends, but no evidence that it occurred in the child's presence).

[37]See also Roof v. Roof, 298 S.C. 58, 378 S.E.2d 251 (1989); Finch v. Finch, 479 So. 2d 473 (La. Ct. App. 1st Cir. 1985); Edelen v. Edelen, 457 So. 2d 171 (La. Ct. App. 2d Cir. 1984).

[38]Zamonski v. Wan, 2003-Ohio-780, 2003 WL 366756 (Ohio Ct. App. 2d Dist. Montgomery County 2003).

pellant "would take their daughter to China and that she would have no recourse to have the child returned to her."[39]

These cases illustrate that a court is more likely to award supervised visitation where the violence toward the spouse or partner was witnessed by the child. Many courts also limit or suspend visitation until an evaluation of the abusive parent's violent tendencies is completed. Still other courts require evidence that the abusive parent is no longer violent before granting an award of unsupervised visitation.[40]

Q & A: Is the suspension of visitation preferred in custody/visitation disputes involving domestic violence?

Not always. Most courts believe that children need to have access to both parents and that suspended visitation is an extreme sanction reserved only for the greatest emergencies.[41] Without actual acts of physical or sexual abuse directed at the children, some courts are unlikely to suspend the abuser's visitation rights.[42]

The court's overriding concern should be breaking the cycle of violence. If the visitation places the children at an increased risk of harm, the court has a responsibility to protect the children. Judge Voris states:

> If the court is unable to devise adequate safeguards for the protection of the children, then its only alternative is to terminate visitation. Where there is clear and convincing evidence that a proposed visitation arrangement will be harmful to the welfare of the children, a trial court abuses its discretion in failing to impose restrictions to ensure the children's well-being.[43]

However, some states have empowered their courts with statutory grants of authority to suspend visitation "to guard the safety of the victim and the children."[44] Physical or sexual abuse of the children or other family members has been found to constitute sufficient grounds for suspending visitation for a period of time.[45]

Q & A: How else have courts restricted abusers' visitation rights?

At least one court restricted the respondent's visitation by condition-

---

[39]Zamonski v. Wan, 2003-Ohio-780, 2003 WL 366756, *3 (Ohio Ct. App. 2d Dist. Montgomery County 2003).

[40]See Lufft v. Lufft, 188 W. Va. 339, 424 S.E.2d 266 (1992).

[41]But see Yazdani-Isfehani v. Yazdani-Isfehani, 170 Ohio App. 3d 1, 2006-Ohio-7105, 865 N.E.2d 924 (4th Dist. Athens County 2006) (wherein the court suspended father's visitation based in part on children's testimony that they feared him and did not wish to see him, even under supervised visitation, pending the appointment of a GAL and further investigation regarding children's best interest).

[42]See Michael J. Voris, Civil Orders of Protection: Do They Protect the Children, the Tag-along Victims of Domestic Violence? 17 Ohio N.U. L. Rev. 599 (1991).

[43]Michael J. Voris, Civil Orders of Protection: Do They Protect Children, the Tag-along Victims of Domestic Violence? 17 Ohio N.U. L. Rev. 599, 609 (1991).

[44]See Minn. Stat. Ann. § 518B.01.6(a)(4).

[45]See Ellibee v. Ellibee, 121 Idaho 501, 826 P.2d 462 (1992); see also Stuckey v. Stuckey, 768 P.2d 694 (Colo. 1989); see also State v. Price, 118 Ohio St. 3d 144, 2008-Ohio-1974, 886 N.E.2d 852 (2008) (where CPO suspended defendant's visitation rights until he engages in regular counseling for his bipolar disorder and takes his medication).

ing the visitation on the respondent's completion of domestic violence counseling. In *Mary Ann McG. v. William R. P.*,[46] the West Virginia Supreme Court of Appeals overruled the appellant's objection and affirmed the trial court's ruling that child visitation and reconciliation counseling were not to occur until the appellant's husband completed individual treatment for domestic violence.[47]

However, the Ninth District Court of Appeals rejected a probation condition prohibiting a domestic violence defendant from having any contact with his children for two years. In *State v. Brillhart*,[48] the court concluded that a defendant should not have been denied access to his own children following his domestic violence conviction for assaulting the children's mother. While acknowledging that one of the children had witnessed the abuse, the court said that this was insufficient to justify imposing a condition that would completely separate a father and his children for two years. One justice dissented, noting that there was evidence presented at trial that indicated a past history of abuse toward the children.

The Wayne County Appellate Court stated "[s]uch a condition places a substantial burden on [the defendant's] constitutional privacy interest in his children without a comparable benefit."[49] The court further noted that "[t]he condition is not reasonably related to future criminality nor does it serve the statutory ends of probation, which are justice, rehabilitation, and ensuring the offender's good behavior."[50]

The court then indicated specific factors for valid probation conditions. These include (1) that the condition of probation be reasonably related to rehabilitating the offender, (2) that it have some relationship to the crime for which the offender was convicted, and (3) that it relate to conduct that is criminal or reasonably related to future criminality and serves the statutory ends of probation.[51] Witnessing the abuse was insufficient to justify the imposition of a condition that would completely separate a father and his children for two years.[52] However, placing a lesser restriction on the visitation arrangement was acceptable to the court.

---

[46]Mary Ann McG. v. William R.P., 201 W. Va. 584, 499 S.E.2d 313 (1997).

[47]See also Irwin v. Schmidt, 236 A.D.2d 401, 653 N.Y.S.2d 627 (2d Dep't 1997); see also Heckel v. Heckel, 2000 WL 1279171 (Ohio Ct. App. 12th Dist. Butler County 2000) (upholding a restriction that the Hamilton Police Department was an appropriate pick up and drop off exchange point).

[48]State v. Brillhart, 129 Ohio App. 3d 180, 717 N.E.2d 413 (9th Dist. Wayne County 1998); see also State v. Sturgeon, 138 Ohio App. 3d 882, 742 N.E.2d 730 (1st Dist. Hamilton County 2000) (four year no contact order against the victim or children as a condition of probation was not reasonably related to the violation in light of the fact that he did not abuse his children; such a restriction effectively terminated his parental rights without affording him procedural guarantees of notice and an opportunity to be heard per RC Ch. 2151).

[49]State v. Brillhart, 129 Ohio App. 3d 180, 186, 717 N.E.2d 413 (9th Dist. Wayne County 1998).

[50]State v. Brillhart, 129 Ohio App. 3d 180, 186, 717 N.E.2d 413 (9th Dist. Wayne County 1998).

[51]State v. Brillhart, 129 Ohio App. 3d 180, 186, 717 N.E.2d 413 (9th Dist. Wayne County 1998).

[52]State v. Brillhart, 129 Ohio App. 3d 180, 186, 717 N.E.2d 413 (9th Dist. Wayne County 1998).

It is important to note that the appellate court did acknowledge that the father should not have unlimited access to his children and discussed the fact that there may be other means which place less restriction on the father's relationship with his children. It is equally significant that the court noted that the father had not been convicted of abusing the children, which effectively lessened the detrimental impact of a child's witnessing the violence between his/her parents.

Q & A: How have courts responded to violations of visitation restrictions in domestic violence and custody/visitation disputes?

Recently, courts have begun to respond more effectively to violations of visitation restrictions provided for in protection orders.[53] Courts that recognize and understand that defendants often seek visitation to get closer to their victims will punish the violation more severely. A failure to exact swift punishment against an abuser who violates a visitation order, creates a situation where the abuser is not held accountable for his/her actions. Such a response is likely to exacerbate an already tense situation and foster a lack of protection for the victim.

§ 15:16 Presenting evidence of domestic violence—Use of experts; generally

Expert testimony is appropriate in child custody litigation.[1] In determining custody, the court is typically required to consider the mental health of both the parents and the children.[2] The court also has the authority to order the parties to undergo physical and/or mental examinations.[3] Since independent experts as well as treating professionals may testify at trial, family law practitioners should use their expertise to educate the court about the effects of domestic violence on children and the psychological dynamics of abuse.

Evidence Rule 702 requires that three conditions be met before expert testimony is admitted:

(1) that the testimony relates to matters beyond the knowledge or experience possessed by laypersons or dispels a misconception common among laypersons;

(2) that the expert must be qualified; and

(3) that the testimony be based on reliable scientific, technical, or other specialized information.

---

[53]See City of Toledo v. Eissa, 2003-Ohio-3425, 2003 WL 21489426 (Ohio Ct. App. 6th Dist. Lucas County 2003); see also State v. Carver, 113 Wash. 2d 591, 781 P.2d 1308 (1989), opinion amended, 113 Wash. 2d 591, 789 P.2d 306 (1990) and opinion amended on reconsideration, (Apr. 13, 1990) (reversing trial court's modification of custody as penalty for noncustodial parent's contempt for violation of visitation conditions, finding that sanction exceeded court's authority).

[Section 15:16]

[1]See also Jane H. Aiken and Jane C. Murphy, Dealing with Complex Evidence of Domestic Violence: A Primer for the Civil Bench, 39(2) Court Rev. 12, 20 (2002).

[2]See RC 3109.04(C).

[3]Civ.R. 35; see also RC 3109.04(C).

The usual test for whether expert testimony would be helpful in a given case is whether the subject matter is "beyond the ken of the average lay person."[4] In the custody arena,

> useful psychological evidence in all child custody and visitation cases concern aspects of parents' and children's personalities that are not readily apparent. These may include the personality adjustment of the parents (emotional stability, intellectual functioning, responsibility and self-control); their capacity to work cooperatively for the benefit of the children; identification of the children's emotional, developmental and educational needs; identification of the parents' motives in seeking custody and the quality of the parent-child relationship.[5]

The dynamics of domestic violence, including personality traits and responses of both batterers and victims, are beyond the knowledge of the layperson.[6] More importantly, the effect of domestic violence on children is not a matter of common knowledge.[7]

§ 15:17 Presenting evidence of domestic violence—Use of domestic violence experts[1]

Experts are often used to explain the battered women's responses to violence in criminal cases where battered women kill their partners.[2] Ohio's courts including the Supreme Court of Ohio have agreed that they need the help of experts to explain the battered woman's experiences.[3] Both the court and the jury need to be educated as to why a victim stays in a battering relationship, why a victim remains

[4]State v. Thomas, 66 Ohio St. 2d 518, 521, 20 Ohio Op. 3d 424, 423 N.E.2d 137 (1981) (overruled by, State v. Koss, 49 Ohio St. 3d 213, 551 N.E.2d 970 (1990)) (overruled to the extent that Thomas holds that expert testimony concerning battered women syndrome may not be admitted to support the affirmative defense of self-defense); State v. Myers, 2014-Ohio-3759, 2014 WL 4269104 (Ohio Ct. App. 6th Dist. Wood County 2014), appeal not allowed, 144 Ohio St. 3d 1507, 2016-Ohio-652, 45 N.E.3d 1051 (2016) and appeal not allowed, 145 Ohio St. 3d 1447, 2016-Ohio-1596, 48 N.E.3d 585 (2016).

[5]Myra Sun & Elizabeth Thomas, Custody Litigation on Behalf of Battered Women, 21 Clearinghouse Rev. 563, 566 (1987).

[6]Developments in the Law: Legal Responses to Domestic Violence, 106 Harv. L. Rev. 1498, 1574–86 (1993).

[7]Developments in the Law: Legal Responses to Domestic Violence, 106 Harv. L. Rev. 1498, 1574–86 (1993).

[Section 15:17]

[1]See also Yanni, Experts as Final Arbiters: State Law and Problematic Expert Testimony on Domestic Violence in Child Custody Cases, 116 Colum. L. Rev. 533 (2016).

[2]See Alana Bowman, A Matter of Justice: Overcoming Juror Bias in Prosecutions of Batterers Through Expert Witness Testimony of the Common Experiences of Battered Women, 2 S. Cal. Rev. L. & Women's Stud. 219, 229 (1992); see also Martha R. Mahoney, Legal Images of Battered Women: Redefining the Issue of Separation, 9 Mich. L. Rev. 1 (1991). See also Text § 16:23, Civil domestic violence case strategy.

[3]See State v. Haines, 112 Ohio St. 3d 393, 2006-Ohio-6711, 860 N.E.2d 91 (2006); State v. Koss, 49 Ohio St. 3d 213, 551 N.E.2d 970 (1990) (overruling recognized by, Bechtel v. State, 1992 OK CR 55, 840 P.2d 1 (Okla. Crim. App. 1992)); see also State v. Dyson, 2000 WL 1597952 (Ohio Ct. App. 2d Dist. Champaign County 2000); State v. Thomas, 2003-Ohio-5746, 2003 WL 22429536 (Ohio Ct. App. 2d Dist. Montgomery County 2003); State v. Myers, 2014-Ohio-3759, 2014 WL 4269104 (Ohio Ct. App. 6th Dist. Wood County 2014), appeal not allowed, 144 Ohio St. 3d 1507, 2016-Ohio-652,

in a violent situation, and why a victim often tells no one about the abuse.[4] Since the fear of future abuse, which is likely to escalate in both frequency and severity when the victim does leave, reluctance of the victim to leave, and the victim's silence about the violence often become issues in custody litigation involving battered women, analogies must be drawn to criminal cases and expert testimony regarding "battered woman syndrome" must become part of a custody trial.[5]

The knowledge of "battered woman syndrome" is becoming highly advanced. Expert testimony has been used to support a claim of self-defense or temporary insanity.[6] In fact, battered woman syndrome, an aspect of posttraumatic stress disorder, has been recognized as a diagnostic category in the American Psychiatric Association's book, The Diagnostic and Statistical Manual (DSM III), since 1980.

Expert testimony can also respond to a number of judicial misconceptions and attitudinal issues that may alter the outcome of the case.[7] The expert may address the batterer's attacks on the victim's emotional stability. Courts rarely comprehend the extreme fear, sense of helplessness, and dependence that prevents victims of domestic violence from leaving the battering relationships.[8]

The expert can also address the problems inherent in a joint custody or shared parenting arrangement where domestic violence is involved. The expert can assess the prospects for successful shared parenting, given the dynamics within the individual family. Experts may also be useful in countering the argument that the victim, by denying visitation, is unwilling to foster a healthy relationship between the children and the other parent. The expert should be able to explain the fear that causes a victim's reluctance to allow visitation.[9] Finally, an expert may be vague in explaining the results of the MMPI or other psychological test administered to the victim of domestic violence.[10]

Q & A: Who qualifies as a domestic violence expert?

Experts must be qualified before they are able to render opinions on the battered woman's experiences generally or in a particular case. In domestic violence cases, the expert witness should:

---

45 N.E.3d 1051 (2016) and appeal not allowed, 145 Ohio St. 3d 1447, 2016-Ohio-1596, 48 N.E.3d 585 (2016).

[4]See State v. Haines, 112 Ohio St. 3d 393, 2006-Ohio-6711, 860 N.E.2d 91 (2006).

[5]Myra Sun & Elizabeth Thomas, Custody Litigation on Behalf of Battered Women, 21 Clearinghouse Rev. 563, 567 (1987).

[6]See RC 2901.06, RC 2945.39, RC 2945.392.

[7]Myra Sun & Elizabeth Thomas, Custody Litigation on Behalf of Battered Women, 21 Clearinghouse Rev. 563, 567 (1987); see also Naomi R. Cahn, Civil Images of Battered Women: The Impact of Domestic Violence on Child Custody Decisions, 44 Vand. L. Rev. 1041, 1086–87 (1991).

[8]Myra Sun & Elizabeth Thomas, Custody Litigation on Behalf of Battered Women, 21 Clearinghouse Rev. 563, 567 (1987).

[9]Myra Sun & Elizabeth Thomas, Custody Litigation on Behalf of Battered Women, 21 Clearinghouse Rev. 563, 567 (1987).

[10]See for example, Harley v. Harley, 2003-Ohio-232, 2003 WL 146014 (Ohio Ct. App. 4th Dist. Athens County 2003) (where trial court declined to qualify Dr. McClanahan as an expert concerning a correlation between deviant MMPI scores and domestic violence. However, the error was harmless because there was no evidence that the former wife was a victim of domestic violence).

(1) have a broad-based knowledge relative to the effects of domestic violence on children;

(2) be able to address the reasons why a batterer fails to be an appropriate parent;

(3) be able to explain the stress of the victim that may affect the victim's ability to parent;

(4) have an intimate understanding of the battered woman's experiences;

(5) have special training in the area of domestic violence by way of academic background and training;

(6) provide the court with his/her credentials, including the length of time spent in the field, the number of custody evaluations performed, a list of his/her published or unpublished works on the subject, participation in professional seminars, conferences, or other continuing education programs, and any professional licenses.[11]

Experts should be familiar with the fact pattern of the particular case. Attorneys should also use experts to provide opinions as to the fitness of each parent. The expert may be able to provide the court with general research on domestic violence and its relation to the facts of the case. In both capacities, experts are useful and often necessary to an effective presentation.

Additionally, testimony from a domestic violence expert can assist the court in evaluating the following:

(1) the impact of witnessing violence on children;

(2) the risk of child abuse by the perpetrator of domestic violence;

(3) the likelihood that the abuser will continue to be violent in the future;

(4) the effect of abuse on the adult victim's parenting;

(5) whether the abused parent can adequately parent once protected from ongoing violence;

(6) effective remedies to mitigate long-term consequences of past violence to ensure the post-separation adjustment of the child and the abused parent;

(7) the usefulness of batterer intervention services and parenting education for domestic violence perpetrators;

(8) protective measures essential to safeguarding the child and abused parent; and

(9) the child's wishes in light of the domestic violence.[12]

Q & A: Can a victim advocate testify as to what the minor child told to her?

Clearly, that is hearsay and inadmissible under the evidentiary rules. However, if there is other independent evidence corroborating the testimony, the admission of the advocate's statement, while hearsay, is not reversible error. For example, in *Lang v. Lang*,[13] the appellant appealed the trial court's decision arguing that the CPO

[11]Myra Sun & Elizabeth Thomas, Custody Litigation on Behalf of Battered Women, 21 Clearinghouse Rev. 563, 567–68 (1987).

[12]Domestic Violence and Children: Resolving Custody and Visitation Disputes, A National Judicial Curriculum 81–82 (Janet Carter et al. eds., 1995).

[13]Lang v. Lang, 2004-Ohio-2035, 2004 WL 869367 (Ohio Ct. App. 2d Dist. Miami County 2004).

should not have included the child where there was no admissible evidence to establish that the child had been a victim of domestic violence. The appellate court affirmed the trial court decision even though the advocate had testified that the minor child told her that "daddy told me to tell my mommy that he was going to cut her up and put her in the river."[14]

The Miami County Court of Appeals held that the admission of the advocate's testimony concerning the statement made by the child, even if erroneous, was not an obvious defect in the proceeding. The magistrate's conclusion that the statement was not hearsay because it was admitted into evidence not to prove that appellant had made the statement, but to prove the mental state of the child resulting from the threats made against his mother may have been an erroneous analysis of the rule.[15] However, it is not so clearly erroneous as to constitute plain error.

§ 15:18 Presenting evidence of domestic violence—Use of mental health professionals and other experts[1]

The widespread implementation of the "best interest of the child" standard for resolving custody and visitation disputes has put more power in the hands of professionals such as clinical social workers, therapists, and caseworkers who are appointed by the court or even the parties to evaluate which parent is best suited to have custody of the children.[2] Judges often follow the recommendations and evaluations of these professionals in determining custody and visitation.[3] Unfortunately, this reliance by the courts on the recommendations of

---

[14]Lang v. Lang, 2004-Ohio-2035, 2004 WL 869367, *3 (Ohio Ct. App. 2d Dist. Miami County 2004).

[15]Lang v. Lang, 2004-Ohio-2035, 2004 WL 869367, *3 (Ohio Ct. App. 2d Dist. Miami County 2004).

[Section 15:18]

[1]Peter Jaffe and Richard Geffner, Child Custody Disputes and Domestic Violence: Critical Issues for Mental Health, Social Service, and Legal Professionals (G.W. Holden, R. Geffner, & E.N. Jouriles, Eds., 1998); K.A. LaFortune & B.N. Carpenter, Custody Evaluations: A Survey of Mental Health Professionals, 16 Behavioral Science and the law 207 (1998). Joyanna Silberg, PHD, Elizabeth Samson, and the DVLEAP Custody and Abuse Technical Assistance Project, Preparing DV Survivors for a Custody Evaluation, 18 Domestic Violence Report 49, 54 (April/May 2013); Sanchez v. Sanchez, 2016-Ohio-4933, 2016 WL 3745699 (Ohio Ct. App. 1st Dist. Hamilton County 2016) (discussing the use of expert testimony per Evid. R. 702, regarding whether the children's statements were consistent with sexual abuse in a DVCPO case). Stephen J. Yanni, Experts as Final Arbiters: State Law and Problematic Expert Testimony on Domestic Violence in Child Custody Cases, 116 Colum. L. Rev. 533 (2016) (discussing use of mental health experts, state evidentiary rules and previous judgments, admissibility of expert testimony in custody cases, reconciling scientific limitations with the prevalence of domestic violence and rethinking the role of the expert).

[2]See Martha Fineman, Dominant Discourse, Professional Language and Legal Change in Child Custody Decisionmaking, 101 Harv. L. Rev. 727, 740–44 (1988); see also William G. Austin, Partner Violence and Risk Assessment in Child Custody Evaluations, 39 Fam. Ct. Rev. 483 (2001); J.N. Bow & P. Bower, Assessing Allegations of Domestic Violence in Child Custody Evaluations, 18 J. of Interpersonal Violence 1394 (2003).

[3]See Myra Sun & Elizabeth Thomas, Custody Litigation on Behalf of Battered Women, 21 Clearinghouse Rev. 563, 573 (1987); see also Rita Smith & Pamela Coukos,

mental health professionals has created problems for victims of domestic violence and their children.[4] Unlike experts who have developed an expertise and understanding on the battering experiences and the effect of domestic violence on children, these professionals lack specific knowledge and uniform training regarding domestic violence issues.[5]

Sometimes, each parent alleges that the other has been abusive or that, at the very least, the relationship was one in which there was reciprocal violence. Because such a high percentage of parents in contested custody cases report being abused in the marriage, mental health professionals must also evaluate the credibility of the parents in ascertaining the credibility of the domestic violence allegations.[6]

Many court-appointed mental health professionals ignore the realities of abuse within the family structure.[7] In a desire to project an air of evenhandedness with both parents, therapists have been known to justify the batterer's abusive actions during counseling sessions or break confidentiality to inform the batterer of the allegations of violence.[8] They fail to understand why the victim does not want the abuser to have visitation with the children. Unfortunately, the victim's unwillingness to compromise with regard to the batterer's access to the children is perceived as an inability to foster and encourage a relationship with that parent, another best interest factor.[9]

Mental health therapists or family court services staff may provide valuable information to a court. It is unfortunate, however, that few

---

Fairness & Accuracy in Evaluations of Domestic Violence & Child Abuse in Custody Determinations, 36 Judges' J. 38 (1997). But see Wiederholt v. Fischer, 169 Wis. 2d 524, 485 N.W.2d 442 (Ct. App. 1992) (finding that the court is not required to accept the expert opinion of the court evaluator but must only consider the evaluator's opinions and independently determine what is in the best interest of the children); Baker v. Baker, 2004-Ohio-469, 2004 WL 226092 (Ohio Ct. App. 6th Dist. Lucas County 2004); Evans v. Evans, 2001 WL 1098065 (Ohio Ct. App. 10th Dist. Franklin County 2001), cause dismissed, 93 Ohio St. 3d 1465, 756 N.E.2d 1240 (2001) and cause dismissed, 93 Ohio St. 3d 1478, 757 N.E.2d 775 (2001).

[4]Annette M. Gonzalez & Linda M. Rio Reichmann, Representing Children in Civil Cases Involving Domestic Violence, 39 Fam. L. Q. 197, 216-18 (ABA Section of Family Law, Spring 2005); 11 Violence Against Women No. 8 (Aug. 2005) (reports of 4 NIJ funded empirical studies of court orders in custody and visitation cases with histories of interpersonal violence).

[5]See Nancy S. Erickson, Problems With Custody Evaluations, Domestic Violence Report, Vol. 11, No. 5 Pg. 67 (June/July 2006).

[6]See William G. Austin, Assessing Credibility in Allegations of Marital Violence in the High-Conflict Child Custody Case, 38 Fam. & Conciliation Courts Rev. 462 (2000).

[7]Lenore E. Walker & Glenace E. Edwall, Domestic Violence and Determination of Visitation and Custody in Divorce, in Domestic Violence on Trial: Psychological and Legal Dimensions of Family Violence 55, 141 (Daniel J. Sonkin ed., 1987); see also Dodd v. Dodd, 2001 WL 812244 (Ohio Ct. App. 6th Dist. Lucas County 2001) (in which the mental health experts' report and testimony was discounted for downplaying the pattern of domestic violence in the case).

[8]See Rita Smith & Pamela Coukos, Fairness and Accuracy in Evaluations of Domestic Violence and Child Abuse in Custody Determinations, 36 Judges' J. 38 (1997).

[9]RC 3109.04(F)(1)(f), RC 3109.04(F)(2)(b); see Dodd v. Dodd, 2001 WL 812244 (Ohio Ct. App. 6th Dist. Lucas County 2001) (discussing the issue of which parent is likely to foster and encourage access to the other parent).

therapists, evaluators, or court-appointed clinical psychologists have been trained in, or are knowledgeable about, domestic violence.[10] In fact, the studies of therapists' knowledge and understanding of domestic violence demonstrate that, as professionals, they are sadly lacking in knowledge and that the average mental health professional has incorporated some misconceptions about battered women into his/her belief systems.[11] Such misconceptions include the belief that women often exaggerate the violence and that they can easily leave the battering situation.[12] Even the Report of the American Psychological Association Presidential Task Force on Violence and the Family, which was released in 1996, concludes that many therapists lack adequate training to identify or assess family violence.[13] More importantly, many therapists who administer the MMPI and other psychological tests fail to address the correlation between deviant test scores and domestic violence.[14] Therefore, it is crucial to find experts who can aid the trier of fact in determining whether a specific victim's deviant score on the MMPI was related to a history of spousal abuse by the other party.[15]

As further evidence of therapists' inadequate training are the results of a 1996 survey of psychologists. In Child Custody Evaluation Practices: A 1996 Survey of Psychologists, Mark and Melissa Ackerman surveyed psychologists from around the country to determine what criteria is used to make custody recommendations.[16] In spite of the fact that most states now have statutes requiring judges to consider domestic violence in custody determinations, domestic violence was not considered a factor in custody recommendations

[10] See D. J. Hurley & P. G. Jaffe, Children's Observations of Violence II: Clerical Implications for Children's Mental Health Professionals, 35 Canadian J. of Psychiatry 471–76 (1990); but see Dodd v. Dodd, 2001 WL 812244 (Ohio Ct. App. 6th Dist. Lucas County 2001) (where the appellate court affirmed the trial court in naming the non-offending parent the residential parent and legal custodian of the children in spite of the guardian ad litem's recommendation and over the report and testimony of the court appointed psychologist; instead, the court relied on the testimony of the court counselor who noted the repeated pattern of domestic violence).

[11] Therapist Perceptions of Family Violence, Battering and Family Therapy: A Feminist Perspective 42 (Marsali Hansen & Michele Harway eds., 1993).

[12] See also Laura Crites & Donna Coker, What Therapists See That Judges May Miss: A Unique Guide to Custody Decisions When Spouse Abuse is Charged, 27 Judges' J. 8 (1988).

[13] American Psychological Assocation, Violence and the Family: Report of the American Psychological Association Presidential Task Force on Violence and the Family, Wash. D.C. (1996). See also J.N. Bow & F.A. Quinnell, Psychologists' Current Practices and Procedures in Child Custody Evaluations: Five Years After American Psychological Association Guidelines, 32 Professional Psychology: Research and Practice (2001); M.J. Ackerman & M.C. Ackerman, Child Custody Evaluation Practices: A 1996 Survey of Psychologists, 30 Fam. L.Q. 565 (1996).

[14] Erickson, Use of the MMPI-2 in Child Custody Evaluations Involving Battered Woman: What Does Psychological Research Tell Us?, 39 Fam. L. Q. 87 (Spring 2005).

[15] See Harley v. Harley, 2003-Ohio-232, 2003 WL 146014 (Ohio Ct. App. 4th Dist. Athens County 2003).

[16] Joan Zorza, Domestic Violence Seldom Considered in Psychologist's Child Custody Recommendations, 2 Domestic Violence Report 65 (1997).

except perhaps as a rationalization for not recommending joint custody or shared parenting.[17]

Because courts rely on the opinions of mental health professionals in determining custody and visitation issues,[18] it is crucial that family law practitioners enlist therapists that can assess domestic violence and dispel the stereotypes so engrained in the system.[19]

Q & A: Should the court allow expert testimony of battered woman syndrome in child custody cases?

Ohio has not specifically addressed this issue. At least one state court did address this issue. In *Knock v. Knock*,[20] a Connecticut Court of Appeals found that the presence of battering in the household had, at a minimum, some effect on the parenting skills of both spouses and the child's response to the parent's even after their separation. The court then concluded that an expert's testimony concerning the battered woman syndrome was relevant to the best interest of the child in determining custody. However, the appellate court noted that the trial court also considered corroborating evidence, police and medical reports, in deciding that the spouse was a battered woman.

Q & A: Should courts consider expert testimony regarding the damaging effects of domestic violence on children?

At least one Ohio court has considered expert testimony concerning the harmful effects of domestic violence on the children. In *In re Orwell*,[21] the Montgomery County Court of Appeals reviewed the record and found that the psychological testimony regarding the harmful effects of domestic violence on the children provided clear and convincing evidence of emotional abuse by the parents towards their children, sufficient enough to uphold the trial court's decision awarding permanent custody to the Montgomery County Children's Services Board.

---

[17]See Mark J. & Melissa C. Ackerman, Child Custody Evaluation Practices: A 1996 Survey of Psychologists, 30(3) Fam. L.Q. 565 (1996); see also Erickson & Zorza, Evaluating the Handling of Domestic Violence Cases by Custody Evaluators, 10 Domestic Violence Report 49 (2005).

[18]See Navigating Custody & Visitation Evaluations in Cases with Domestic Violence: A Judge's Guide, State Justice Institute, National Council of Juvenile & Family Court Judges (2004).

[19]See Martha R. Mahoney, Legal Images of Battered Women: Redefining the Issue of Separation, 90 Mich. L. Rev. 1, 43–49 (1991); see also Mary Ann Dutton, The Dynamics of Domestic Violence: Understanding the Response from Battered Women, 68 Fla. B.J. 24 (1994); Mary Ann Dutton, Understanding Women's Responses to Domestic Violence: A Redefinition of Battered Woman Syndrome, 21 Hofstra L. Rev. 1191 (1993); Laura Crites & Donna Coker, What Therapists See that Judges May Miss: A Unique Guide to Custody Decisions When Spouse Abuse is Charged, 27 Judges' J. 8 (1988).

[20]Knock v. Knock, 224 Conn. 776, 621 A.2d 267 (1993); see also Hamilton v. Hamilton, 93 N.C. App. 639, 379 S.E.2d 93 (1989) (awarding custody to nonabusive parent in part due to testimony of expert witness regarding domestic violence); Jane H. Aiken & Jane C. Murphy, Evidence Issues in Domestic Violence Civil Cases, 34 Fam. L.Q. 43 (2000).

[21]In re Orwell, 1993 WL 531958 (Ohio Ct. App. 2d Dist. Montgomery County 1993); see also Laura Crites & Donna Coker, What Therapists See That Judges May Miss: A Unique Guide to Custody Decisions When Spouse Abuse is Charged, 27 Judges' J. 8 (1988).

In *Orwell*, the appellate court considered the testimony of the psychologist from the transcript and included it in its decision. The transcript provided:

> Research shows that children are profoundly effected [sic] by chaos and arguments and physical violence, or emotional, verbal violence and abuse that goes on in the home. Specifically what happens is that, well, because children identify typically with the same-sex parent little girls grow up to be victims and little boys grow up to be abusers because they model, they learn to model that kind of behavior that they observe at home. And children do not have to be directly abused in the sense of their being physically hit. They only have to witness that.[22]

It is important for a court to include in its opinion evidence of the detrimental effects of domestic violence on children.[23] Judicial opinions that advance social policy send a powerful message to the public that domestic violence detrimentally affects children.

Q & A: Should expert opinions be sought on the issue of visitation?

Several courts have relied on the opinions of experts to educate them on the issue of visitation and domestic violence. For example, in *Hall v. Hall*,[24] the Minnesota Court of Appeals upheld the decision of the trial court where the court relied, in part, on a social worker's recommendation of supervised visitation to support its order.

Experts well versed in the area of domestic violence will be able to provide the court with much-needed information and can educate the court as to why domestic violence harms the children. With the expert's testimony, a court may be more likely to understand that abuse of one parent by the other instills within the children a sense of fear that they too will become the victims of an act of domestic violence.

If the detrimental effects of domestic violence on and the danger it poses to the children cannot be communicated by expert testimony, courts will continue to consider domestic violence largely irrelevant to custody decisions. Courts will likely conclude that parents who are violent toward their partners may, nonetheless, be very good parents, that domestic violence has little effect on the children, or that, even if the parent was violent during the time the parties lived together, the violence will cease upon separation. An expert in the area of domestic violence should be able to contradict these conclusions.

§ 15:19 Presenting evidence of domestic violence—Use of a guardian ad litem[1]

RC 3109.04(B)(2)(a) requires the appointment of a guardian ad

[22]In re Orwell, 1993 WL 531958, *3 (Ohio Ct. App. 2d Dist. Montgomery County 1993).

[23]See for example, Wissink v. Wissink, 301 A.D.2d 36, 749 N.Y.S.2d 550 (2d Dep't 2002).

[24]Hall v. Hall, 408 N.W.2d 626 (Minn. Ct. App. 1987).

[Section 15:19]

[1]See generally Leigh Goodmark, From Property to Personhood: What the Legal System Should Do for Children in Family Violence Cases, 102 W. Va. L.Rev. 237 (1999); see also Grams, Guardians ad Litem and the Cycle of Domestic Violence: How

litem upon the motion of either party where the court interviews the child. Besides the requirement to appoint a guardian as set forth by statute, a guardian ad litem may be appointed for other reasons if the court finds that it is necessary to protect the interest of a child.[2]

In the absence of a statutory requirement, the court should consider appointing a guardian ad litem in a contested custody case involving domestic violence.[3] This is true even where the child only witnesses the violence. A child may be as traumatized by witnessing abuse as by being physically abused. Appointing a guardian for the child during court proceedings can greatly assist the child, the parents, and the court.[4]

In Ohio,[5] the recommendation of the guardian ad litem can greatly influence the court's decision in awarding custody and visitation.[6] Unfortunately, many guardians are heavily influenced by the policies that encourage contact with the abusive parent, often with a lack of understanding of the risks to the children from that contact.

If the guardian ad litem appears to have minimized the significance of the abuse toward the other parent and the children and if the children are fearful of the abuser, it is possible for the court to order that an attorney be appointed for the children, separate and apart from the guardian ad litem.[7]

Recently, the Supreme Court of Ohio adopted Superintendence Rule 48, effective March 1, 2009, which addresses the appointment and responsibilities of a guardian ad litem. The Rule also provides for the training requirements for guardians ad litem.

Q & A: Who does the guardian ad litem represent?

It is important to clarify whether the child's guardian represents the child or the best interest of the child because those roles can sometimes conflict. An attorney who serves as both the child's legal counsel and guardian ad litem occupies two potentially conflicting roles.[8] Often the child's stated wishes conflict with the guardian's opinion of what is in the best interest of the child.[9]

---

the Recommendations Turn, 22 Law & Ineq. 105 (2004); Gonzalez & Reichmann, Representing Children in Civil Cases Involving Domestic Violence, 39 Fam. L. Q. 197 (Spring 2005).

[2]Sup. R. 48. See, e.g., Cuy. D.R. R. 35(A); see also Gotwald v. Gotwald, 768 S.W.2d 689 (Tenn. Ct. App. 1988) (approving the appointment of a child advocate in a spousal abuse case).

[3]See Hon. Sheila M. Murphy, Guardian ad Litem: The Guardian Angels of Our Children in Domestic Violence Court, 30 Loy. U. Chi. L. J. 281 (1999); see also Hastings, Letting Down Their Guard: What Guardians ad Litem Should Know about Domestic Violence in Child Custody Disputers, 24 B.C. Third World L.J. 283 (2004).

[4]See generally, Hon. Sheila M. Murphy, Guardians Ad Litem: The Guardian Angels of our Children in Domestic Violence Court, 30 Loy. U. Chi. L.J. 281 (1999).

[5]See generally, Karen E. Elliott, The Guardian ad Litem in Ohio's Domestic Relations Courts: The Square Peg Fits, 27 Ohio N.U. L. Rev. 267 (2001).

[6]See, e.g., Dodd v. Dodd, 2001 WL 812244 (Ohio Ct. App. 6th Dist. Lucas County 2001) (in which the court noted the influence of an experienced guardian ad litem, but still awarded custody to the other parent based upon the repeated pattern of domestic violence).

[7]See, e.g., Cuyahoga D.R. R. 35(E).

[8]Ilana Horowitz Ratner, The Child's Advocate, 7 Domestic Relations J. of Ohio 1

Where a conflict arises, Ohio law has found that an attorney cannot fulfill both roles. *In re Baby Girl Baxter*[10] and *Bawidamann v. Bawidamann*[11] suggest that it is the duty of the guardian ad litem/attorney to petition the court to withdraw as the guardian, but continue as the attorney, as soon the conflict is discovered. "The difficulty with this mandate is that the child is then represented by an attorney who the child knows disagrees with his or her position, and whom the child may no longer trust. No adult client would choose to continue with such 'zealous' representation, and no child client should be compelled to do so."[12]

Conversely, in *Gallimore v. Gallimore*,[13] the Miami County Court of Appeals found that the attorney should withdraw as the child's legal counsel but remain the guardian ad litem. The court held that "[t]here is, however, no reason why the conflict of interest cannot be resolved as the court did here; allowing the attorney to withdraw as legal counsel and appointing another attorney as counsel who is not subject to the conflict."[14]

In custody and visitation cases where domestic violence is an issue, an attorney is wise to recognize the potential conflict and request that the court order the guardian ad litem to withdraw as counsel for the child where the child has expressed a fear of the abuser and the guardian intends to recommend an award of custody to that parent, despite the child's concerns.

Superintendence Rule 48 directs a guardian ad litem to represent the best interest of the child.[15] The Rule acknowledges that conflicts may arise and that the representation of the best interest may be inconsistent with the wishes of the child.[16] In cases where there is a conflict between a child's best interest and the child's wishes, the Rule directs a guardian to, at the earliest practical time, request in writing

(1995). See also In re Kenneth R., 1998 WL 833569, *2 (Ohio Ct. App. 6th Dist. Lucas County 1998) (relying on another appellate court's interpretation of when a guardian ad litem may also be considered an attorney for the child and holding that "in the absence of an express dual appointment, courts should not presume a dual appointment when the appointed guardian ad litem is also an attorney"); see also Sup. R. 48(D)(7), (D)(8).

[9]Ilana Horowitz Ratner, The Child's Advocate, 7 Domestic Relations J. of Ohio 1, 2 (1995).

[10]See In re Baby Girl Baxter, 17 Ohio St. 3d 229, 479 N.E.2d 257 (1985).

[11]Bawidamann v. Bawidamann, 63 Ohio App. 3d 691, 580 N.E.2d 15 (2d Dist. Montgomery County 1989).

[12]Ilana Horowitz Ratner, The Child's Advocate, 7 Domestic Relations J. of Ohio 3 (1995).

[13]Gallimore v. Gallimore, 1989 WL 33112 (Ohio Ct. App. 2d Dist. Miami County 1989). See also In re Janie M., 131 Ohio App. 3d 637, 723 N.E.2d 191 (6th Dist. Lucas County 1999).

[14]Gallimore v. Gallimore, 1989 WL 33112, *3 (Ohio Ct. App. 2d Dist. Miami County 1989). But see Am. Sub. S.B. 238, eff. 9-21-06 (requesting Supreme Court of Ohio to adopt rules regarding the standards, qualifications, and service of guardians ad litem and makes the appointment and service of guardians ad litem subject to those rules; the bill maintains current law regarding a person's dual role as attorney and guardian ad litem until the Supreme Court adjusts rules regulating the conflict between the roles).

[15]Sup. R. 48(D)(1).

[16]Sup. R. 48(D)(1).

that the court promptly resolve the conflict by entering appropriate orders.[17] Unfortunately, the Rule is silent as to whether the guardian ad litem is to continue in the role of the guardian and another be appointed as an attorney for the child as set for in *Gallimore*, or whether the guardian must resign as the guardian and another be appointed to fulfill that role as set forth in *In re Baby Girl Baxter* and *Bawidamann*.

Q & A: Does RC 3113.31 authorize the appointment of a guardian ad litem?

Not according to the Cuyahoga County Court of Appeals in *Jackson v. Jackson*.[18] In that case, the appellant alleged that the trial court erred by not appointing a guardian ad litem for the minor child. The appellant stated that such an appointment was mandatory under RC 3113.31. The Cuyahoga County Court of Appeals found that RC 3113.31 does not mandate that the trail court appoint a guardian ad litem for a minor child who might be the subject of a domestic violence complaint rather that its purpose is to provide protection from domestic violence. The court held that "[i]t is, therefore, within the discretion of the trial court to appoint a guardian ad litem in a domestic violence allegation pursuant to RC 3113.31 if the court considers it necessary."[19]

§ 15:20 Presenting evidence of domestic violence—Role of the attorney[1]

It is imperative that the victim's attorney introduces relevant evidence[2] of the domestic violence in the custody or visitation case. Attorneys should always strive to collect and save documentary evidence, including civil and criminal protection orders, 911 tapes, voice mail tapes, police reports, medical records, criminal histories, copies of arrests and convictions, letters written by the perpetrator, journals kept by the victim or the children detailing the abuse, and pictures of the abused victim and children. Victims should be encouraged to assist in the information gathering.

---

[17] Sup. R. 48(D)(8).

[18] Jackson v. Jackson, 1993 WL 526704 (Ohio Ct. App. 8th Dist. Cuyahoga County 1993).

[19] Jackson v. Jackson, 1993 WL 526704, *3 (Ohio Ct. App. 8th Dist. Cuyahoga County 1993); but see Hassebroek v. Hassebroek, 2000 WL 665694 (Minn. Ct. App., 2000) (discussing when an appointment of a guardian ad litem is required).

[Section 15:20]

[1] See generally, Cartlin Glass, Tamara Kaennen & Sharon Lopez, Custody and Visitation: Considerations for Every Attorney Retained by a Survivor of Domestic Violence, 36 Clearinghouse Review 529 (2003); Robert L. Valente, Addressing Domestic Violence: The Role of the Family Law Practictioner, 29 Fam. L. W. 187 (1995); Julie Kunce Field, Screening for Domestic Violence: Meeting the Challenge of Identifying Domestic Relations Cases Involving Domestic Violence and Developing Strategies for Those Cases, 39(2) Court Rev. 4 (2002); Kathleen Waits, Critical Issues: Battered Women and Family Lawyers: The Need for an Identification Protocol, 58 Alb. L. Rev. 1027 (Spring 1995).

[2] See Litigating Domestic Violence Cases: Effective Use of the Rules of Evidence (outline of a Continuing Legal Education teleconference conducted October 16, 2002, through the ABA Commission on Domestic Violence), available at www.abanet.org/domviol.; Jane H. Aiken & Gail C. Murphy, Evidence Issues in Domestic Violence Cases, 34 Fam. Law Q. 43 (2000).

Interviewing and deposing witnesses who saw the abuse or the results of the violence must be done early in the case. This is crucial to preserving evidence and may even enhance negotiations with the batterer's attorney.

Attorneys have an obligation to call experts who understand the dynamics of domestic violence. More importantly, a familiarity with children's development and the detrimental effects of battering on children is also necessary to explain why an award of custody or unsupervised visitation to a batterer may not be in the best interest of the child.

Attorneys have to learn to assess the potential relevance of domestic violence to their particular case. The family law practitioner must prepare the expert to conduct an evaluation in three areas: the history of the domestic violence, the strategies used by the victim for resisting that violence, and the psychological effects of the violence on the victim and the children.[3] Such an evaluation should explain the victim's response to the violence. It may also challenge preconceived beliefs held by the court. Additionally, the effective use of expert testimony requires a focus on the link between those areas and the legal elements of the particular case (e.g., self defense, duress, failure to protect).[4]

The practitioner must also have a working knowledge of the criminal domestic violence statute[5] and an understanding of the criminal procedure. Since there is a significant interrelationship between custody and a criminal conviction for domestic violence, a familiarity with the criminal statute will enhance the quality of the victim's legal representation.

Should the court refer the case to a court-appointed evaluator for a custody/visitation evaluation, the attorney should prepare the client for the evaluation. The client must articulate the reasons for wanting custody or for restricting visitation. The client should bring any evidence of the violence to the evaluator. "Useful evidence of violence includes photographs showing injuries, medical records, police reports, copies of past orders of protection, records of the batterer's criminal convictions, or references to witnesses in a criminal case."[6]

Counsel should inform the evaluator of the need to separate the parties for the interview and to adequately safeguard the victim from further abuse before, during, or immediately after the appointment. Additionally, the attorney should make the evaluator aware of the violence so that the client does not simply appear vindictive or too rigid to facilitate access where the client wants to limit the abuser's visitation.[7]

---

[3]See Mary Ann Dutton & Catherine L. Waltz, Domestic Violence: Understanding Why It Happens and How to Recognize It, 17 Fam. Advoc. 14, 18 (1995).

[4]Mary Ann Dutton & Catherine L. Waltz, Domestic Violence: Understanding Why It Happens and How to Recognize It, 17 Fam. Advoc. 14, 18 (1995).

[5]See RC 2919.25 to RC 2919.27.

[6]Myra Sun & Elizabeth Thomas, Custody Litigation on Behalf of Battered Women, 21 Clearinghouse Rev. 563, 574 (1987).

[7]Myra Sun & Elizabeth Thomas, Custody Litigation on Behalf of Battered

§ 15:21 Presenting evidence of domestic violence—Role of the attorney—Strategies for court

Victims of domestic violence are likely to be perceived by opposing counsel as unstable,[1] homeless, and manipulative individuals whose allegations of violence are unfounded and are a ploy to obtain custody.[2] Experts are needed to address these common weaknesses in the client's case.

A solid argument can be made that spending time at a shelter may actually benefit the children and the victim of violence. Rather than being seen as evidence of instability, it may be argued that flight to a shelter demonstrates a determination on the victim's part to restore stability to the children and protect them from future harm.

An effective way to address testimony about exaggerated claims of violence is to present expert testimony on the dynamics of domestic violence. A practitioner who anticipates such a claim can respond effectively by conducting a thorough investigation of the studies that address the responses of the victim to the domestic violence.

It must be cautioned that the expert witness may have to respond to adverse expert testimony, such as from social workers and court-appointed mental health professionals, by showing that the evidence they presented has no scientific basis, that the scope of the investigation was too narrow, and that the theories used are not widely accepted. However, the use of an expert is fraught with concern. The same learned helplessness that makes an individual a victim can be used to disparage that individual's parenting ability.[3]

In most cases, the attorney should anticipate psychological evaluations of the parties. Unfortunately, the batterer may have normal

---

Women, 21 Clearinghouse Rev. 563, 574 (1987); see also Laura Crites & Donna Coker, What Therapists See That Judges May Miss: A Unique Guide to Custody Decisions When Spouse Abuse is Charged, 27 Judges' J. 8 (1988) (discussing psychological evaluations and the importance of requesting an evaluator with an understanding of spouse abuse); Joan Zorza, Domestic Violence Seldom Considered in Psychologists' Child Custody Recommendations, 2 DVR 65 (1997); Wissink v. Wissink, 301 A.D.2d 36, 40, 749 N.Y.S.2d 550 (2d Dep't 2002) (reversing the trial court decision awarding custody to the father in light of the documented history of domestic violence by the father against the mother and directing the court to hold a new custody hearing after a comprehensive forensic psychological evaluation including clinical evaluation, psychological testing, review of records and information from collateral sources and the evaluator must consider: the nature of the psychopathology of the victim and abuser, whether the child might be in danger of becoming a future victim or a witness to the abuse of some other victim, the child's developmental needs given the fact that she had lived with the abuse all of her life and the remedial efforts that should be undertaken in regard to all parties concerned).

[Section 15:21]

[1]Rebecca D. Cornia, Current Use of Batteren Women Syndrome: Institutionalization of Negative Stereotypes About Women, 8 UCLA Women's L. J. 99 (1997).

[2]See Joan S. Meier, Understanding Judicial Resistance and Imagining Solutions, 11 Am. U. J. Gender Soc. Pol'y & L. 657 (2003); May E. Becker, Double Binds Facing Mothers in Abusive Families: Social Support Systems, Custody Outcomes and Liability for Acts of Others, 2 U. Chi. L. Sch. Roundtable 13 (2005) (judges and mental health professionals often see mothers either as saints or as demonic women who are indifferent or intentional want to hurt them).

[3]Myra Sun & Elizabeth Thomas, Custody Litigation on Behalf of Battered Women, 21 Clearinghouse Rev. 563, 569 (1987).

scores on objectively scored psychological tests such as the Minnesota Multiphasic Personality Inventory (MMPI), which is widely used in custody evaluations.[4] The batterer may make a better impression in interviews with the evaluator than the victim. The court may treat the evaluator's report as objective evidence that the domestic violence did not impair the batterer's parenting ability. On the other hand, if the victim performs poorly, the court may treat him/her as functioning less effectively because of the domestic violence.[5]

The family law practitioner should contact his/her own expert who can address the inherent problems and validity of such "objective" tests. Perhaps, another psychologist with an understanding of the dynamics of violence can reinterpret the results of the test. If an expert is testifying on the victim's behalf, it may be useful to request clarification of the relationship of MMPI test results to domestic violence issues.[6]

When reports are inaccurate, whether from a mental health evaluator, guardian ad litem or mediator, family lawyers should consider objecting to the report, request an examination of the maker of the report and lay the foundation for an appeal.[7] "The makers of the report should be questioned about their qualifications to be expert witnesses; the theoretical bases for their conclusions and recommendations; the scholarly literature upon which they rely; the sources of their information; their reliance on self-report by the parties or collateral sources and multi-level hearsay; their views of the credibility of the parties; and their consideration of other pending court cases between the parties, prior court orders or criminal convictions."[8] It is important to remember that some of these evaluators would not be qualified as expert witnesses.[9]

§ 15:22 Presenting evidence of domestic violence—Role of the attorney—Specific trial concerns

Nothing is more important than adequate trial preparation. Prepar-

[4]Jean M. Baker & Rachel Burkholder, Testing's Role in Custody Disputes, 10 Fam. Advoc. 21, 24 (1988); Nancy S. Erickson, Use of the MMPI-2 in Child Custody Evaluations Involving Battered Women: What Does Psychological Research Tell Us?, 39 Fam. L.Q. 87, 88 (Spring 2005).

[5]See Laura Crites & Donna Coker, What Therapists See That Judges May Miss: A Unique Guide to Custody Decisions When Spouse Abuse is Charged, 27 Judges' J. 8, 41 (1988).

[6]See Jean M. Baker & Rachel Burkholder, Testing's Role in Custody Disputes, 10 Fam. Advoc. 21 (1988); Erickson, Use of the MMPI-Z in Child Custody Evaluations Involving Battered Women: What Does the Psychological Research Tell Us?, 39 Fam. L. Q. 87 (2005); see also Harley v. Harley, 2003-Ohio-232, 2003 WL 146014 (Ohio Ct. App. 4th Dist. Athens County 2003).

[7]Judge Marjorie D. Fields, Lawyer Skills Training for DV Representation: Tips from a Retired Judge, Domestic Violence Report, Vol. 12, No.1, Page 1 (October/November 2006).

[8]Judge Marjorie D. Fields, Lawyer Skills Training for DV Representation: Tips from a Retired Judge, Domestic Violence Report, Vol. 12, No.1, Page 1 (October/November 2006).

[9]Judge Marjorie D. Fields, Lawyer Skills Training for DV Representation: Tips from a Retired Judge, Domestic Violence Report, Vol. 12, No.1, Page 1 (October/November 2006).

ing the client for trial necessitates involving the client in gathering the evidence, such as obtaining police and hospital reports and talking to witnesses. The children should be evaluated and treated if they are suffering any psychological or physical problems. The victim must keep a journal detailing the abuse and prepare a chronology of past incidents of abuse. If there is any new violence, it must be reported to and documented by the police. Adequate trial preparation also includes preparing the client and other witnesses to accurately illustrate the abusive nature of the parties' relationship.

Because victims of domestic violence often become reluctant to proceed with the legal action, counseling with other victims is often a positive experience. Parenting classes also strengthen the victim's position in court. Counseling and group therapy demonstrate the victim's desire to break the pattern of violence and a growing maturity and healing.[1]

If the client wishes to dismiss the case, counsel should propose that the case be continued for a period of time.[2] If the case is dismissed, the client must be informed that any temporary orders such as temporary custody or restraining orders will terminate.

It is important that the client feel protected at all court hearings. This may be the first time a victim faces the batterer since separation. Each look and touch may appear very threatening to a victim. Counsel should advise the client that a victim advocate can also accompany him/her to all stages of the proceeding.[3] Advocates are helpful in explaining the justice system to the client, obtaining shelter and financial assistance for the victim, explaining the legal options to the client, and providing transportation to and from court. Each type of assistance makes it a little easier for the victim to get on with his/her life.

It is also important for attorneys to advise clients that certain actions may have unintended consequences. For example, RC 3109.04(E)(1) limits a court's power to alter a prior decree which allocated parental rights and responsibilities. Practically, this means that if a domestic violence victim fails to raise the issue of domestic violence at the time of the final divorce hearing, she/he will not be able to modify the allocation of parental rights and responsibilities without new evidence of domestic violence occurring since the prior divorce decree. At the very least, she/he must be able to demonstrate a present detrimental impact of the violence by the other parent towards the child.

While it may be important for victims of domestic violence to seek mental health counseling, attorneys should inform their clients that the opposing party may subpoena psychological treatment records. As a general rule, medical records from a psychiatrist are protected by the physician-patient privilege under RC 2317.02(B)(1) and as such,

[Section 15:22]

[1]Myra Sun & Elizabeth Thomas, Custody Litigation on Behalf of Battered Women, 21 Clearinghouse Rev. 563, 574 (1987).

[2]Myra Sun & Elizabeth Thomas, Custody Litigation on Behalf of Battered Women, 21 Clearinghouse Rev. 563, 574 (1987).

[3]See RC 3113.31(M); see also Text Ch. 17, Role of the Victim Advocate.

any communication made to a physician by a patient is privilege and a physician may not testify as to the communications.

However, as an exception to the rule, either parent, in a custody proceeding, has put his or her mental and physical health in issue. RC 3109.04(F)(1)(e) provides that in determining the best interest of a child, the court shall consider the mental and physical health of all persons involved in the situation. Thus, once in issue, the physician-patient privilege does not apply.[4]

§ 15:23 Mediation in domestic violence cases[1]

Mediation is the process by which litigants attempt to resolve their disputes through face-to-face interaction facilitated by a neutral third party.[2] The desired result is that the parents may be able to enhance their capacities to fully participate in raising their children. Inherent in the mediation process is the presumption that the parties negotiate in good faith and have equality in their ability to bargain and compromise. For the mediation to be successful, it must occur only when both parties have relatively equivalent bargaining power.

"The domestic violence relationship is inherently unbalanced as to power, therefore making mediation inappropriate."[3] The inequality of power between the abuser and the abused[4] renders the process and the product ineffectual and creates a situation where the participation is neither voluntary or consensual. As commentator Barbara Hart explained:

> [T]he battered woman is not free to choose. She is not free to elect or reject mediation if the batterer prefers it, not free to identify and advocate for components essential for her autonomy and safety and that of her children, not free to terminate mediation when she concludes it is not working. She is ultimately not free to agree or disagree with the language of the agreement. Her apparent consent is under duress.[5]

Before ordering the parties into custody/visitation mediation where

---

[4]See Gill v. Gill, 2003-Ohio-180, 2003 WL 132447 (Ohio Ct. App. 8th Dist. Cuyahoga County 2003); see also Signer v. Signer, 2006-Ohio-3580, 2006 WL 1918115 (Ohio Ct. App. 8th Dist. Cuyahoga County 2006).

[Section 15:23]

[1]See also Sup. R. 16.

[2]See also Joanne Fuller & Rose Mary Lyons, Domestic Violence Symposium Issue, Mediation Guidelines, 33 Willamette L. Rev. 905 (1997).

[3]Howard A. Davidson, A Report to the President of the American Bar Assoc., The Impact of Domestic Violence on Children 15 (1994); see also Gail Godkasian, Confronting Domestic Violence: A Guide for Criminal Justice Agencies 61 (1986); National Council of Juvenile & Family Court Judges, Family Violence: Improving Court Practice 28 (1990).

[4]A.M. Davis & R. Salem, Dealing with Power Imbalances in the Mediation of Interpersonal Disputes, 6 Mediation Q. 17–26 (1984); Penelope Bryan, Killing Us Softly: Divorce Mediation and the Politics of Power, 40 Buff. L. Rev. 44 (1992); L. Newark, A. Harrell, & P. Salem, Domestic Violence and Empowerment in Custody and Visitation Cases, 33 Fam. & Conciliation Ct. Rev. 30 (1995).

[5]Barbara J. Hart, Gentle Jeopardy: The Further Endangerment of Battered Women and Children in Custody Mediation, 7 Mediation Q. 317, 321 (1990); Susan L. Pollet, Mediating Domestic Violence, 77 Sep. N.Y. St. B.J. 42 (2005).

there is evidence of domestic violence, Ohio courts[6] must determine that it is in the best interest of the parties and make specific written findings of fact to support their determinations.[7] The statutory language requires that mediation[8] may be considered if the parents fail to agree on a suitable parenting plan, on which parent should be awarded custody, or on the type of visitation the noncustodial parent should receive.[9]

The statutory provisions in the mediation statute regarding domestic violence mirror the custody/visitation best-interest factors of RC 3109.04(F)(1)(h) and RC 3109.051(D)(12) and the obligation on the court to enter findings if the abuser is to be awarded custody in spite of a conviction for domestic violence or another offense.[10] RC 3109.052(A) requires the court to determine whether either parent has been convicted of domestic violence or another offense. If the court determines that one of the parents has been convicted, the court may still order the parties into mediation. However, the court may only order mediation if the court determines that it is in the best interest of the parties to order mediation and then makes specific written findings of fact to support its determination.[11]

The pros and cons of mediation in domestic violence cases is a topic worthy of debate.[12] Some mediators suggest that mediation is helpful to domestic violence victims because it results in the empowerment of the victim and an opportunity to end the violence.[13] Conversely, advocates for domestic violence victims argue that the unequal bargaining power between the parties, and the fact that even the most skillful mediators find it difficult to reduce the differences in power, hinders the parties' ability to engage in effective mediation.[14] More and more, policymakers in states with experience in mediating custody disputes are beginning to conclude that mediation of custody issues must not occur in families where there has been domestic

[6]See RC 2701.01 et seq. (Ohio's Uniform Mediation Act, adopted by the General Assembly in 2004 and eff. 4-25-05); Sup. R. 16.

[7]See RC 3109.052(A).

[8]See, e.g., Jennifer P. Maxwell, Mandatory Mediation of Custody in the Face of Domestic Violence: Suggestions for Courts & Mediators, 37 Fam. & Conciliation Cts. Rev. 335 (1999).

[9]See RC 3109.052(A).

[10]See RC 3109.04(C).

[11]RC 3109.052(A).

[12]Nancy Van Ver Steegh, Yes, No, and Maybe: Informed Decision-making about Divorce Mediation in the Presence of Domestic Violence, 9 Wm. & Mary J. Women & L. 145 (2003); Brenda V. Smith, Battering, Forgiveness, and Redemption, 11 Am. U. J. Gender Soc. Pol'y & L. 921 (2003).

[13]See, e.g., Dennis Marthaler, Successful Mediation with Abusive Couples, 24 Mediation Q. 53, 53–65 (1989); Peter Salem & Ann L. Milne, Making Mediation Work in a Domestic Violence Case, 17 Fam. Advoc. 34 (1995).

[14]See, e.g., Barbara J. Hart, Gentle Jeopardy: The Further Endangerment of Battered Women and Children in Custody Mediation, 7 Mediation Q. 317, 317–330 (1990); Mildred D. Pagelow, Justice for Victims of Spouse Abuse in Divorce and Child Custody Cases, 8 Violence and Victims 1 (1993).

violence[15] or, if it is to occur at all, that specific procedures be included.[16]

Q & A: What specific concerns should be addressed by the victim's attorney before mediation?

Where the court orders mediation or where the victim of domestic violence agrees to mediate, the attorney for the victim should describe and discuss the mediation process to him/her.[17] In addition, the attorney should inform the client of the issues that are appropriate to mediate.[18]

Regarding any agreement that may be entered into by the parties, the attorney should tell the client that he/she should not feel compelled to reach an agreement and that the client should not sign any agreement until the attorney has reviewed it. Although the court may order the parties into mediation, the court cannot order the parties to reach an agreement.

Finally, attorneys should caution their clients about providing to the mediator during the mediation previously undisclosed information or information unknown to the abuser.[19] Since mediators often raise issues concerning relocation, daycare, and employment, the abuser will report this information to his/her attorney.[20] Any admission made by a party in mediation may be the subject of subsequent discovery prior to trial.

§ 15:24 Other issues that impact custody and visitation awards

Q & A: Is proof of domestic violence towards one child enough to base the issuance of a civil protection order to protect another sibling?

---

[15]See, e.g., Barbara J. Hart, Gentle Jeopardy: The Further Endangerment of Battered Women and Children in Custody Mediation, 7 Mediation Q. 317, 317–330 (1990); Sara Krieger, The Dangers of Mediation in Domestic Violence Cases, 8 Cardozo Women's L. J. 235 (2002).

[16]See National Council of Juvenile & Family Court Judges, Model Code on Domestic and Family Violence § 407 (1994) (suggesting that the mediator has a duty to screen for domestic violence, assess the danger posed by the batterer, recognize that victims are at a heightened risk of future violence as they attempt to end the relationship, and utilize the legal system to gain essential safeguards); see also Jessica Pearson, Mediating When Domestic Violence Is a Factor: Policies & Practices in Court-Based Divorce Mediation Programs, 14 Mediation Q. 319 (1997); Zylstra, Mediation and Domestic Violence: A Practical Screening Method for Mediators & Mediation Program Administrators, 2001 J. Disp. Resol. 253 (2001); Maxwell, Mandatory Mediation of Custody in the Face of Domestic Violence: Suggestions for Courts and Mediators, 37 Fam. & Conciliation Cts. Rev. 335 (1999); Murphy & Rubinson, Domestic Violence and Mediation: Responding to the Challenges of Crafting Effective Screens, 39 Fam. L. Q. 53 (Spring 2005).

[17]Margaret Drew, Lawyer Malpractice and Domestic Violence: Are We Revictimizing Our Clients?, 39 Fam. L.Q. 7, 19 (2005).

[18]See RC 3109.052(A).

[19]Myra Sun & Elizabeth Thomas, Custody Litigation on Behalf of Battered Women, 21 Clearinghouse Rev. 563, 572–73 (1987); see also Rimelspach, Mediating Family Disputes in a World with Domestic Violence: How to Devise a Safe and Effective Court-Connected Mediation Program, 17 Ohio St. J. on Disp. Resol. 95 (2001).

[20]Myra Sun & Elizabeth Thomas, Custody Litigation on Behalf of Battered Women, 21 Clearinghouse Rev. 563, 573 (1987).

At least two appellate courts have recently addressed this specific issue. In *Parrish v. Parrish*,[1] the appellant had requested the issuance of a civil protection order on behalf of her child because respondent had previously beaten his child. Appellant argued that evidence of abuse towards one child of a family is sufficient to support the grant of a civil protection order to protect another child. In this case, appellant had no relationship with appellee's child, the child was not living with her and the violence allegedly committed by appellee towards his child occurred a year prior to the hearing at issue.[2]

The appellant based her request on the fact that domestic violence in the home has a detrimental impact on children. Moreover, his pattern of abuse of his child at an earlier time demonstrated his predilection for corporal punishment. In effect, the totality of appellee's actions was sufficient to satisfy the requirements of the civil protection order statute.

The Fourth District Court of Appeals upheld the trial court's dismissal of the civil protection order. It reasoned that appellant failed to ". . . support her claims with evidence of either injuries or attempts to injure either her children or herself, in order to meet the requirements of this portion of the statute."[3] At the very least, Mrs. Parrish had to establish that she believed her husband would physically harm her or her children. The court then addressed the appellant's concern that "the trial court 'erroneously assumed children can be unaffected by domestic violence in their home' " by explaining that the trial court was obligated to follow the requirements of the statute in determining the existence of domestic violence.[4]

Because the incident towards appellee's child took place more than a year before trial and because the evidence failed to show that appellee directed his anger towards appellant or her children, the court declined to reverse the trial court decision. Recently, the Ohio Supreme Court has decided to hear the case.[5]

This case raises some interesting issues. For example, the appellant chose to file a civil protection order on behalf of the minor child. Therefore, she was mandated to prove the existence of domestic violence against that child.[6] Had she been able to file for a civil protection order because of abuse directed at her, she could have listed her child as a protected party on her civil protection order. The appellate

[Section 15:24]

[1]Parrish v. Parrish, 146 Ohio App. 3d 640, 2000-Ohio-2693, 767 N.E.2d 1182 (4th Dist. Ross County 2000).

[2]See Fugate v. Fugate, 2008-Ohio-737, 2008 WL 483251 (Ohio Ct. App. 3d Dist. Auglaize County 2008); but see Kurincic v. Kurincic, 2000 WL 217808 (Ohio Ct. App. 8th Dist. Cuyahoga County 2000) (social worker noted it was in one child's best interests to keep father away from her because of allegations he abused another child).

[3]Parrish v. Parrish, 146 Ohio App. 3d 640, 644, 2000-Ohio-2693, 767 N.E.2d 1182 (4th Dist. Ross County 2000).

[4]Parrish v. Parrish, 146 Ohio App. 3d 640, 647, 2000-Ohio-2693, 767 N.E.2d 1182 (4th Dist. Ross County 2000).

[5]Parrish v. Parrish, 91 Ohio St. 3d 1447, 742 N.E.2d 145 (2001).

[6]Parrish v. Parrish, 146 Ohio App. 3d 640, 644, 2000-Ohio-2693, 767 N.E.2d 1182 (4th Dist. Ross County 2000).

court also stated that proof of "immediate and present danger of domestic violence to the family or household member" is "required not only by RC 3113.31(D) for the issuance of an ex parte CPO, but also by RC 3113.31(A)(1)(b), to support the grant of a CPO after hearing."[7] However, it is unclear whether an immediate and present danger is required to support the issuance of a CPO after a full hearing.[8]

Parrish was dismissed sua sponte by the Ohio Supreme Court as having been improvidently allowed.[9] However, Justices Resnick and Stratton issued a dissenting opinion that addressed some of the underlying concerns raised in the appeal. First, the dissent noted that the burden of proof was by a preponderance of the evidence as set forth in *Felton v. Felton*,[10] and that the record in the underlying case was unclear at best.[11] The dissent stated that "[w]hen granting a protection order, the trial court must find that the petitioner has shown, *by a preponderance of the evidence that the petitioner or the petitioner's family or household members are in danger of domestic violence*."[12]

Second, the dissent found that the excluded evidence of appellee's physical abuse of his son was indeed relevant under RC 3113.31. The dissent determined that appellee's son was a "family or household member" as defined in RC 3113.31 because he was a child of appellee. The dissent concluded that in civil protection proceedings, "a trial court must consider evidence that respondent abused family or household members other than those for whom the protection order is sought."[13]

Third, the dissent addressed the "totality of the circumstances" argument advanced by appellant. Disagreeing with the court of appeals that the evidence presented by appellant consisted of events mostly remote in time to the petition and did not support a finding that appellee threatened her or her children,[14] the dissent stated:

> Courts cannot look at incidents of domestic violence in a vacuum. Domestic violence is almost always a series of incidents that gradually

[7]Parrish v. Parrish, 146 Ohio App. 3d 640, 647, 2000-Ohio-2693, 767 N.E.2d 1182 (4th Dist. Ross County 2000).

[8]See, e.g., Felton v. Felton, 79 Ohio St. 3d 34, 1997-Ohio-302, 679 N.E.2d 672 (1997); see also Siouffi v. Siouffi, 1998 WL 879255 (Ohio Ct. App. 2d Dist. Montgomery County 1998); Text § 8:4, Statutory elements of domestic violence under RC 3113. 31(A)(1)(b); Text § 11:10, Ex parte protection orders—Legal standard for issuance; Text § 12:11, Standard of proof.

[9]Parrish v. Parrish, 146 Ohio App. 3d 640, 2000-Ohio-2693, 767 N.E.2d 1182 (4th Dist. Ross County 2000).

[10]Felton v. Felton, 79 Ohio St. 3d 34, 1997-Ohio-302, 679 N.E.2d 672 (1997).

[11]Parrish v. Parrish, 95 Ohio St. 3d 1201, 1205, 2002-Ohio-1623, 765 N.E.2d 359, 362 (2002); see also Felton v. Felton, 79 Ohio St. 3d 34, 1997-Ohio-302, 679 N.E.2d 672 (1997).

[12]Parrish v. Parrish, 95 Ohio St. 3d 1201, 1204, 2002-Ohio-1623, 765 N.E.2d 359, 362 (2002) (citing Felton v. Felton, 79 Ohio St. 3d 34, 1997-Ohio-302, 679 N.E.2d 672 (1997), paragraph 2 of syllabus, citing RC 3113.31(D)).

[13]Parrish v. Parrish, 95 Ohio St. 3d 1201, 1206, 2002-Ohio-1623, 765 N.E.2d 359, 363 (2002).

[14]Parrish v. Parrish, 95 Ohio St. 3d 1201, 1207, 2002-Ohio-1623, 765 N.E.2d 359, 364 (2002).

escalate into increasing acts of brutality, repeating themselves in cycles. Thus, in a petition for a civil protection order, evidence of respondent's prior acts of violence toward the petitioner or the respondent's family or other household members should be admissible to prove by a preponderance of the evidence that petitioner and her children are in danger of domestic violence.[15]

Next, the dissent relied on *Eichenberger v. Eichenberger*,[16] to reinforce its position that a history of past domestic violence is useful in determining danger of future domestic violence and that the reasonableness of fear should correlate with that history. The dissent noted that "in determining whether a petitioner is in danger of domestic violence, threats of violence, whether physical or verbal, should be considered."[17]

Further, the dissent admonished the lower courts, noting that there was a delay of three years from the time the case was first filed and stating that "a delay of this magnitude is unacceptable."[18] Quoting *Felton*, the dissent then reiterated the importance of judges in communicating that domestic violence is unacceptable, in understanding the reality of domestic violence and the need to break the cycle of violence and in implementing legislative initiatives.[19]

In conclusion, the dissent would have reversed the appellate court and remanded the case to the trial court for rehearing. Of importance is that the dissent mentioned that this case contained an issue "in which I believe guidance is greatly needed."[20]

The primary importance of the dissent in *Parrish* is the recognition that courts must not preclude evidence at a protection order hearing that a respondent abused other family or household members than those for whom the protection order is sought. Relevant evidence may include a history of abuse directed toward another family or household member as defined in RC 3113.31(A)(3). Finding that appellant's testimony of appellee's abuse toward his own son was relevant and permissible under RC 3113.31(A)(1), the dissent followed the principles set forth in *Felton* that, for a petitioner to prevail, she must only demonstrate that she and her children are in danger of domestic violence.

Equally important is that the dissent would consider the totality of the abusive actions rather than a specific act to support the issuance of a civil protection order. For example, the dissent considered evi-

---

[15]Parrish v. Parrish, 95 Ohio St. 3d 1201, 1207, 2002-Ohio-1623, 765 N.E.2d 359, 364 (2002).

[16]Eichenberger v. Eichenberger, 82 Ohio App. 3d 809, 613 N.E.2d 678 (10th Dist. Franklin County 1992).

[17]Parrish v. Parrish, 95 Ohio St. 3d 1201, 1208, 2002-Ohio-1623, 765 N.E.2d 359, 365 (2002).

[18]Parrish v. Parrish, 95 Ohio St. 3d 1201, 1208, 2002-Ohio-1623, 765 N.E.2d 359, 365 (2002).

[19]Parrish v. Parrish, 95 Ohio St. 3d 1201, 1208, 2002-Ohio-1623, 765 N.E.2d 359, 365 (2002); see also Felton v. Felton, 79 Ohio St. 3d 34, 45, 1997-Ohio-302, 679 N.E.2d 672 (1997) (quoting Michael Voris, The Domestic Violence Civil Protection Order and the Role of the Court, 24 Akron L. Rev. 423, 432 (1990)).

[20]Parrish v. Parrish, 95 Ohio St. 3d 1201, 1210, 2002-Ohio-1623, 765 N.E.2d 359, 366 (2002) (Stratton, J., dissenting).

dence that appellee tended to throw, slam and otherwise damage objects in the home, as well as damage the walls and door of the couple's home.[21] In permitting such evidence, the dissent acknowledged that a petitioner need not demonstrate danger only through verbal threats in order to prevail under RC 3113.31(A)(1)(b). The destruction of personal property, whether or not the specific physical act was directed at petitioner, may put her in fear of imminent serious physical harm.

Although the dissenting opinion failed to specifically address these concerns, permitting relevant evidence of abuse toward another family or household member and demonstrating fear of future abuse and danger to the petitioner and protected parties based on this seems sufficient to prevail at a civil protection order hearing. It would appear that the dissent did not feel that independent proof as to the existence of domestic violence towards appellant's son was necessary.

In contrast, the Eleventh District Court of Appeals recently issued a decision in *Carpeno v. Carpeno*.[22] In that case, the mother petitioned for a CPO for her four children based on allegations that her husband had abused the children. At the full hearing, she presented evidence that there was an ongoing criminal investigation for alleged physical and sexual abuse of the children. The mother testified that three of her children told her that their father had sexually abused them from young ages until age 12. She further stated that he fondled them, rubbed his body parts and body fluids on the girls and that her son witnessed these events.[23]

The oldest girl testified that her father had been touching her from the time she was three years old until seventh grade. The second daughter testified that she had informed her mother that her father was not only a physical abuser, but that he was also a sexual abuser.[24] Both girls stated that they did not feel safe spending time with him.

Although the magistrate issued a civil protection order for all four children, the father objected and another hearing was held. The trial court then issued an order adopting part of the Magistrate's Decision to issue a CPO for the oldest daughter, but overruled the recommendation to issue the CPO for the other three children. The court found that the oldest daughter testified with specificity as to when and what actions occurred. The second daughter did not meet her burden of proof by a preponderance of the evidence and no evidence was presented as to the basis for a CPO for the other two children.

The mother appealed the denial of a CPO for the three other children and the Eleventh District Court of Appeals held that the "trial court erred in requiring each named protected party to demonstrate an independent act of abuse when the evidence established sexual

[21] Parrish v. Parrish, 95 Ohio St. 3d 1201, 1207, 2002-Ohio-1623, 765 N.E.2d 359, 364 (2002).

[22] Carpeno v. Carpeno, 2005-Ohio-7046, 2005 WL 3610425 (Ohio Ct. App. 11th Dist. Lake County 2005).

[23] Carpeno v. Carpeno, 2005-Ohio-7046, 2005 WL 3610425 (Ohio Ct. App. 11th Dist. Lake County 2005).

[24] Carpeno v. Carpeno, 2005-Ohio-7046, 2005 WL 3610425, *1 (Ohio Ct. App. 11th Dist. Lake County 2005).

abuse toward another protected party and risk to the remaining siblings."[25] The court reversed the trial court decision as being against the manifest weight of the evidence and an abuse of discretion.[26] The appellate court pointed out that there was an ongoing criminal investigation of the allegations of sexual abuse of two of the minor children. In that the trial court had found that Elise was a victim of domestic violence and granted a CPO, "it follows that any remaining children of the family would also properly fall within the ambit of the CPO."[27]

Q & A: My client has custody pursuant to RC 3109.042. Must the Court apply the best interest test of RC 3109.04(F) in designating which parent should be awarded custody?

RC 3109.042 provides that "an unmarried female who gives birth to a child is the sole residential parent and legal custodian of the child until a court of competent jurisdiction issues an order designating another person as the residential parent and legal custodian. A court designating the residential parent and legal custodian of a child described in this section shall treat the mother and father as standing upon an equality when making the designation."

According to *Horning v. Wolff*,[28] the answer is yes. In that case, the biological parents were never married, but lived together until after the child's birth. The father was charged with domestic violence and pled to disorderly conduct. Subsequently, the father filed a Motion to Establish Custody and the Allocation of Parental Rights and Responsibilities.

The trial court stated that the "best interest of the child" test applies when making such a determination. On appeal, the appellant-mother asserted that the trial court erred in applying the best interest test rather than the change of circumstances test in naming a parent the residential parent and legal custodian. In the instant case, mother has custody pursuant to RC 3109.042.

The appellate court first noted that the courts must resolve custody disputes between unmarried parents. The court then stated that "RC 3109.042 confers a default status on [the mother] as the residential parent until an order is issued by the trial court designating the residential parent and legal guardian. It is not, in and of itself, a decree allocating parental rights and responsibilities."[29] Based on this analysis, the Stark County Court of Appeals held that such an initial

[25] Carpeno v. Carpeno, 2005-Ohio-7046, 2005 WL 3610425 (Ohio Ct. App. 11th Dist. Lake County 2005). See also Albers v. Albers, 2012-Ohio-3838, 2012 WL 3637366 (Ohio Ct. App. 2d Dist. Greene County 2012).

[26] Carpeno v. Carpeno, 2005-Ohio-7046, 2005 WL 3610425, *2 (Ohio Ct. App. 11th Dist. Lake County 2005).

[27] Carpeno v. Carpeno, 2005-Ohio-7046, 2005 WL 3610425, *2 (Ohio Ct. App. 11th Dist. Lake County 2005); relying on Felton v. Felton, 79 Ohio St. 3d 34, 1997-Ohio-302, 679 N.E.2d 672 (1997) (to support its reasoning, noting that "the intent of the domestic violence statute as contained in RC 3113.31 is to protect the victims of domestic violence and that this protection extends to siblings.").

[28] Horning v. Wolff, 2006-Ohio-6397, 2006 WL 3505864 (Ohio Ct. App. 5th Dist. Stark County 2006).

[29] Horning v. Wolff, 2006-Ohio-6397, 2006 WL 3505864, *3 (Ohio Ct. App. 5th Dist. Stark County 2006).

custody determination need only be based on the best interests of the child according to RC 3109.04(B)(1) rather than the requirements set forth under RC 3109.04(E)(1)(a).

Of importance is that attorneys representing unmarried victims of domestic violence must inform their clients that a custody determination under RC 3109.042 exists as such until a court issues an order designating one of the parties the residential parent and legal custodian of a child.

Q & A: What is the connection between parental kidnapping and domestic violence?

Evidence of either parent's abduction of the children is relevant to a custody determination.[30] Parental kidnapping is also present with some degree of regularity in domestic violence cases.[31] Pursuant to RC 3109.04(F)(2)(c), it is a best interest factor that a court must consider in an award of shared parenting.

In many instances, batterers abduct the children as a way of continuing to terrorize the victim. Once the battered spouse leaves the abuser, the batterer directs hostility toward the children. Childsnatching is a prime example of this behavior, for which court-ordered shared parenting or visitation provides the access and opportunity.[32]

In some cases, the battered spouse may flee the jurisdiction to escape further abuse,[33] causing that spouse to be in violation of criminal custodial interference laws.

As the attorney for a parent who flees the jurisdiction with the children, it is important to advise the client of the potential civil and criminal penalties for detaining or concealing a child in violation of custody or visitation orders. The attorney for the victim should advise his/her client to seek alternative provisions for safety.

In 1980, the Parental Kidnapping Prevention Act (PKPA) was enacted to deter child abductions.[34] Custody orders issued in compliance with PKPA are accorded full faith and credit in other states.[35]

---

[30] See, e.g., Khan v. Khan, 236 A.D.2d 612, 654 N.Y.S.2d 34 (1997); see also Geoffrey Greif & Rebecca Hagar, Abduction of Children by their Parents: A Survey of the Problem in Social Work (1991).

[31] Janet M. Bowermaster, Relocation Custody Disputes Involving Domestic Violence, 46 U. Kan. L. Rev. 433 (1998).

[32] See Linda K. Girdner & Patricia M. Hoff, Parental Abduction, in The Impact of Domestic Violence on Your Legal Practice 5–11 (1996).

[33] See, e.g., Carter v. Carter, 940 S.W.2d 12 (Mo. Ct. App. W.D. 1997) (affirming decision to allow mother to move out of state with the child because the arrangement best protected the mother and child from potential harm); see also Jacoby v. Carter, 167 A.D.2d 786, 563 N.Y.S.2d 344 (3d Dep't 1990).

[34] 28 U.S.C.A. § 1738A; see also Patricia M. Hoff, Parental Kidnapping: Prevention and Remedies, (parts 1 & 2) 13 Juv. & Child Welfare L. Rptr. 173 (1995), (parts 3 & 4) 14 Juv. & Child Welfare L. Rptr. 12 (1995); Ch 17, Federal Remedies.

[35] See 28 U.S.C.A. § 1738A; see also Linda Keenan, Domestic Violence and Custody Litigation: The Need for Statutory Reform, 13 Hofstra L. Rev. 407 (1985); In re Custody of Thorensen, 46 Wash. App. 493, 730 P.2d 1380 (Div. 1 1987).

Similarly, the Uniform Child Custody Jurisdiction Act may be useful in retrieving an abducted child.[36]

Q & A: Can a parent lose custody where the parent's live-in companion is the perpetrator of domestic violence?

According to several state court decisions, the answer is "yes." For example, in *Kraft v. Kraft*,[37] the North Dakota Supreme Court held that domestic violence by a parent's live-in companion may be imputed to the parent, thus depriving the parent of custody.

Q & A: May a domestic relations court bar a parent from future contact with an abusive companion?

Yes, if the evidence is compelling that the parent's conduct is adversely affecting the child's welfare. In *Sills v. Irelan*,[38] the Indiana Court of Appeals determined that a parent's freedom of association, while constitutionally protected, is not absolute. The court found that the mother's association with her boyfriend presented a clear and present danger to her child's welfare, thereby implicating the state's important interest in protecting the child from physical and emotional harm. The appellate court upheld the lower court's decision barring the mother from having contact with her boyfriend if she wished to retain custody of her child.

Q & A: Is a temporary custodial parent's flight from the state with the children pending a divorce and refusal to return them reason to award custody to the other parent?

Not according to the Allen County Court of Appeals. In *Marshall v. Marshall*,[39] the mother was awarded temporary custody pending the parties' divorce. Subsequently, the mother left the state of Ohio with the children. When she refused to return the children from North Carolina to Ohio in spite of a court order, the trial court awarded the father permanent custody in the divorce.

The appellate court reversed the trial court's decision, relying on evidence that the father had physically abused the mother in front of the children. Additionally, the evidence demonstrated that the mother was the children's primary caregiver, the father did not exercise his visitation, and he worked long hours. At least this appellate court determined that the physical abuse and primary caregiver evidence was more important to the custody determination than the fact that the mother had fled the state.

Q & A: Are victims of domestic violence ever blamed for failing to protect their children?

More and more frequently, victims of domestic violence with chil-

[36]See RC 3109.21; see also Coleman v. Coleman, 493 N.W.2d 133 (Minn. Ct. App. 1992) (victim's flight with the children is not considered to be an abduction under the UCCJA); Text Ch. 18, Federal Remedies.

[37]Kraft v. Kraft, 554 N.W.2d 657 (N.D. 1996); see also Joan Zorza, The UCCJA: Why Do We Have It and How Does It Help Battered Women in Custody Disputes? 5 Domestic Violence Rep. 1 (1999).

[38]Sills v. Irelan, 663 N.E.2d 1210 (Ind. Ct. App. 1996).

[39]Marshall v. Marshall, 117 Ohio App. 3d 182, 690 N.E.2d 68 (3d Dist. Allen County 1997); see also In re Marriage of Marconi, 584 N.W.2d 331 (Iowa 1998) (ruling that the wife's flight from the state with her children because of abuse was sufficient grounds to require the trial court to vacate the default judgment of divorce taken against her); O'Neill v. Stone, 721 So. 2d 393 (Fla. 2d DCA 1998).

dren are faced with untenable choices.[40] They have to calculate how to protect themselves and their children from future violence from an abusive partner. If they decide to leave, they often do so without an adequate means of financial support. If they stay, they risk further harm, to both themselves and their children.

Unfortunately, victims of domestic violence are all too often blamed for their failure to leave the home with their children.[41] "Unwarranted litigation may be based on conclusions that a parent neglected her children by not doing enough to protect them from violence in the home, or that fleeing with her children from an abuser was irresponsible."[42]

Most states have mandated that their courts consider domestic violence in determining custody disputes between parents.[43] As courts acknowledge the detrimental impact of domestic violence on children and the negative impact of the child witnessing abuse between his/her parents, many state courts have determined that the victim of domestic violence has neglected the child by not leaving the abusive situation. The child protective service agency may remove the child and place him/her in foster care and charge the victim with neglect or abuse.[44]

For example, in *Couch v. Harrison*,[45] the appellee requested a civil protection order on behalf of his daughters to protect them from domestic violence committed by the appellant's present husband. In this case, the appellant mother failed to protect the girls from abuse.

The girls' mother challenged the finding of domestic violence and

[40]Audrey E. Stone & Rebecca J. Fialk, Criminalizing the Exposure of Children to Family Violence: Breaking the Cycle of Abuse, 20 Harv. Women's L.J. 205 (1997); see also Linda J. Panko, Legal Backlash: The Expanding Liability of Women who Fail to Protect their Children from their Male Partner's Abuse, 6 Hastings Women's L.J. 67 (1995).

[41]The "Failure to Protect" Working Group, Charging Battered Mothers with "Failure to Protect": Still Blaming the Victim, 27 Fordham Urb. L. J. 849 (Winter 2000); see also Stark, A Failure to Protect: Unraveling the Battered Mother's Dilemma, 27 Wash. St. U. L. Rev. 29 (2000).

[42]Howard A. Davidson, American Bar Association, A Report to the President of the American Bar Association, The Impact of Domestic Violence on Children 17 (1994).

[43]Amy R. Melner, Rights of Abused Mothers vs. Best Interest of Abused Children: Courts' Termination of Battered Women's Parental Rights Due to Failure to Protect their Children from Abuse, 7 S. Cal. Rev. L. & Women's Stud. 299 (1998).

[44]See, e.g., In re Lonell J., 242 A.D.2d 58, 673 N.Y.S.2d 116 (1st Dep't 1998) (holding that domestic violence committed in the presence of the child was sufficient to establish neglect per se, even to the victim of the abuse); see also Matter of Theresa CC, 178 A.D.2d 687, 576 N.Y.S.2d 937, 938 (3d Dep't 1991) (where department of social services petitioned to adjudicate children neglected because of domestic violence, appellate court reversed trial court's dismissal of application, holding that the evidence overwhelmingly demonstrated serious impairment of the children's emotional health resulting from the parents' domestic violence against each other and finding both parents responsible for the emotional abuse of their children); Evan Stark, A Failure to Protect: Unravelling "The Battered Mother's Dilemma," 27 W. St. U. L. Rev. 29 (1999-2000). But see Matter of Michael M., 156 Misc. 2d 98, 591 N.Y.S.2d 681 (Fam. Ct. 1992) (determining that only the father was neglectful because of the domestic violence he perpetrated against the mother).

[45]Couch v. Harrison, 2001-Ohio-4199, 2001 WL 121108 (Ohio Ct. App. 12th Dist. Clermont County 2001).

argued that she did not commit an affirmative act resulting in the abuse of her children. The appeals court overruled her assignment of error, relying on the principle embodied in RC 2919.22 "that parents and guardians have a legal duty to protect their children from harm."[46] An inexcusable failure to discharge that affirmative duty constitutes an act under RC 2919.22.[47] Therefore, the appellant's standing by while her husband repeatedly struck her daughter was an "act" that resulted in the abuse of her child.[48]

Recently, several state legislatures have enacted similar legislation which makes it possible to charge a victim of abuse with a crime for failing to protect the children from abuse.[49] Generally, it is the mother (as the victim of domestic violence) who is charged under these laws.[50] In these instances, the abusive parent also abuses the child. The parent charged with failing to protect is charged because he/she was present when the abuse took place but did nothing to prevent the abuse from happening;[51] the parent left the child alone with the abuser, knowing the abuser had abused the child in the past; or after discovering the abuse, the parent failed to seek medical attention for the child.[52]

Ohio enacted similar legislation in August 1999. Pursuant to RC 2903.15(A):

> No parent, guardian, custodian, or person having custody of a child under eighteen years of age or of a mentally or physically handicapped child under twenty-one years of age shall cause serious physical harm to the child, or the death of the child, as a proximate result of permitting the child to be abused, to be tortured, to be administered corporal punish-

---

[46]Couch v. Harrison, 2001-Ohio-4199, 2001 WL 121108, *2 (Ohio Ct. App. 12th Dist. Clermont County 2001); see also Schottenstein v. Schottenstein, 2003-Ohio-5032, 2003 WL 22176786 (Ohio Ct. App. 10th Dist. Franklin County 2003).

[47]Couch v. Harrison, 2001-Ohio-4199, 2001 WL 121108, *2 (Ohio Ct. App. 12th Dist. Clermont County 2001).

[48]See also Kurincic v. Kurincic, 2000 WL 217808 (Ohio Ct. App. 8th Dist. Cuyahoga County 2000).

[49]See Laurel A. Kent, Addressing the Impact of Domestic Violence on Children: Alternatives to Laws Criminalizing the Commission of Domestic Violence in the Presence of a Child, 2001 Wisc. L. Rev. 1337 (2001); Melissa A. Trepiccione, At the Crossroads of Law & Social Science: Is Charging a Battered Mother with Failure to Protect Her Child an Acceptable Solution When Her Child Witnesses Domestic Violence?, 69 Fordham L. Rev. 1487 (2001); Audrey E. Stone & Rebecca J. Fialk, Criminalizing the Exposure of Children to Family Violence: Breaking the Cycle of Abuse, 20 Harv. Women's L.J. 205 (1997); Lois A. Weithorn, Protecting Children From Exposure to Domestic Violence: The Use & Abuse of Child Maltreatment, 53 Hastings L.J. 1 (2001).

[50]Suzanne D'Amico, Inherently Female Cases of Child Abuse and Neglect: A Gender-Neutral Analysis, 28 Fordham Urb. L.J. 855 (2001); Jeanne A. Fugate, Who's Failing Whom? A Critical Look at Failure-to-Protect Laws, 76 N.Y.U. L. Rev. 272 (2001).

[51]See Couch v. Harrison, 2001-Ohio-4199, 2001 WL 121108 (Ohio Ct. App. 12th Dist. Clermont County 2001); see also Kurincic v. Kurincic, 2000 WL 217808 (Ohio Ct. App. 8th Dist. Cuyahoga County 2000).

[52]See also Linda J. Panko, Legal Backlash: The Expanding Liability of Women Who Fail to Protect Their Children from Their Partner's Abuse, 6 Hastings Women's L.J. 67 (1995); V. Puliani Enos, Prosecuting Battered Mothers: State Laws' Failure to Protect Battered Women and Abused Children, 19 Harv. Women's L.J. 229 (1996).

ment or other physical disciplinary measure, or to be physically restrained in a cruel manner or for a prolonged period.

Under such "failure to protect" statutes, a prosecutor must prove that there was a legal duty to protect the child, that the passive parent had actual or constructive notice of the forseeability of abuse, that the child was injured by the abuse, and that the passive parent failed to prevent the abuse from occurring.[53]

Unfortunately, battering cases should not fall into the generalized "failure to protect" cases. If a battered woman is not able to protect herself from violence from an abusive partner, how is she able to protect her children from the violence she was unable to escape?[54] Advocates critical of the statutory scheme set forth by "failure to protect" statutes are most concerned by a strict liability standard applied by the prosecutor and the court. By imposing strict liability, maternal harm, rather than maternal conduct, becomes the basis for a conviction and removal of the children.[55]

Unlike many other state statutes, Ohio's RC 2903.15 has an affirmative defense built into the statutory scheme. RC 2903.15(B) provides, "It is an affirmative defense to a charge under this section that the defendant did not have readily available a means to prevent the harm to the child or the death of the child and that the defendant took timely and reasonable steps to summon aid."[56]

Even with the affirmative defense, there is an increased likelihood that battered women who seek protection orders will later be charged with failure to protect if there are allegations of child abuse in the affidavit in support of the petition for a civil protection order.[57] As more courts charge victims of domestic violence with failure to protect their children from abuse, the battered parent will have the sole responsibility to prevent such abuse. The battered parent will be blamed for not being able to control the circumstances that caused the battering in the first place and punished for not being able to change the situation.

Q & A: Have there been any cases that address the constitutionality of removing children from the battered parent?

In a case of first impression, the United States District Court for

---

[53]Linda J. Panko, Legal Backlash: The Expanding Liability of Women Who Fail to Protect Their Children from Their Partner's Abuse, 6 Hastings Women's L.J. 67, 68 (1995); see also Text § 8:7, Parents and children.

[54]Lesley E. Daigle, Empowering Women to Protect: Improving Intervention with Victims of Domestic Violence in Cases of Child Abuse and Neglect; A Study of Travis County, Texas, 7 Tex. J. Women & L. 287, 289–90 (1998). See also Justine A. Dunlap, The "Pitiless Double Abuse" of Battered Mothers, 11 Am. U. J. Gender Soc. Pol'y & L. 523 (2003).

[55]G. Kristian Miccio, Reasonable Battered Mother? Redefining, Reconstructing, & Recreating the Battered Mother in Child Protective Proceedings, 22 Harv. Women's L.J. 89, 93 (1999).

[56]See also G. Kristian Miccio, Reasonable Battered Mother? Redefining, Reconstructing, & Recreating the Battered Mother in Child Protective Proceedings, 22 Harv. Women's L.J. 89 (1999).

[57]Deborah Epstein, Effective Intervention in Domestic Violence Cases: Rethinking the Roles of Prosecutors, Judges and the Court System, 11 Yale J. L. & Feminism 3, 5 (1999). See also Amanda J. Jackson, Nicholson v. Scoppetta: Providing a Conceptual Framework for Non-Criminalization of Battered Mothers and Alternatives to Removal of Their Children From the Home, 33 Cap. U. L. Rev. 821 (2005).

the Eastern District of New York issued a preliminary injunction prohibiting the Administration for Children's Services from removing children from battered mothers not otherwise deemed to be unfit. In *In re Nicholson*,[58] a class action suit was filed in federal district court on behalf of women who were battered and who, through no fault of their own, had their children removed by the children's services agency[59] The judge focused his concern on the agency's practice of removing children of battered mothers for the reason that the mothers "engaged in" domestic violence by being victims of such violence and that the children had been witnesses. By granting the injunction, the court validated the plaintiffs' claim that this policy violated the constitutional right of parents and children not to be separated by the government unless the parent is unfit to care for the child. Additionally, the court required the children's services agency to improve its response to domestic violence in families.[60]

The Second Circuit court of Appeals certified certain questions of state law to the New York State Court of Appeals.[61] Of the questions asked, the most important public policy concern focuses on whether there must be particularized harm to a child in order to justify removal of a child by the child protection agency. While removal may be an appropriate remedy where the abuse has been directed at the child, it is not necessarily the appropriate remedy when the child has been exposed to parental domestic violence. In light of the flaws in current research,[62] routine removal of children who are exposed to domestic violence is neither an appropriate nor a necessary response.[63] While it is clear from existing literature that children exposed to

[58]In re Nicholson, 181 F. Supp. 2d 182 (E.D. N.Y. 2002), opinion supplemented, 203 F. Supp. 2d 153 (E.D. N.Y. 2002) and modified and superseded, 294 F. Supp. 2d 369 (E.D. N.Y. 2003) and modified and supplemented, 2004 WL 1304055 (E.D. N.Y. 2004); see also Nicholson v. Scoppetta, 3 N.Y.3d 357, 787 N.Y.S.2d 196, 820 N.E.2d 840 (2004)(there is no blanket presumption favoring removal of a child who witnesses domestic violence, instead, particularized evidence must exist to justify removal); In re T.B., 2015-Ohio-2580, 2015 WL 3937950 (Ohio Ct. App. 12th Dist. Fayette County 2015) (children determined to be neglected based on mother's inability to ensure their safety because of domestic violence perpetrated on mother and one other child by her boyfriend).

[59]See Stark, The Battered Mother in the Child Protective Services Caseload: Developing an Appropriate Response, 23 Women's Rts. L. Rep. 107 (2002); Maureen K. Collins, Nicholson v. Williams: Who is Failing to Protect Whom? Collaborating the Agendas of Child Welfare Agencies and Domestic Violence Services to Better Protect and Support Battered Mothers and Their Children, 38 N. Eng. L. Rev. 725 (2004).

[60]See for example, Luara M. Fernandez, Domestic Violence and the Child Welfare System, 189 PLI/Crim. 55 (2002); see also Elaine Chill, Confronting the Agency in Battered Mothers, 74 S. Cal. L. Rev. 1223 (2001); Allison Turkel & Christina Shaw, Update, Strategies for Handling Cases Where Children Witness Domestic Violence, Natural Center for Prosecution of Child Abuse, Vol. 16, No. 2 (2003).

[61]Nicholson v. Scoppetta, 344 F.3d 154 (2d Cir. 2003), certified question accepted, 1 N.Y.3d 538, 775 N.Y.S.2d 233, 807 N.E.2d 283 (2003) and certified question answered, 3 N.Y.3d 357, 787 N.Y.S.2d 196, 820 N.E.2d 840 (2004).

[62]See Text § 15:11, Impact of domestic violence on children; see also Shima Baradaran-Robison, Tipping the Balance in Favor of Justice: Due Process and the Thirteenth and Nineteenth Amendments in Child Removal from Battered Mothers, 2003 B.Y.U. L. Rev. 227 (2003).

[63]Jeffrey L. Edleson, Should Childhood Exposure to Adult Domestic Violence be defined as Child Maltreatment under the Law?, presented at the workshop on

violence are sometimes at risk for developing a series of behavioral, emotional and cognitive problems that may persist into adulthood, the extent of harm to a particular child is difficult to ascertain.

In October 2004, the New York Court of Appeals ruled that "exposing a child to domestic violence is not presumptively neglectful. Not every child exposed to domestic violence is at risk of impairment. A fortiori, exposure of a child to violence is not presumptively grounds for removal, and in many instances removal may do more harm to the child than good."[64] Therefore, a child welfare agency cannot remove a child from the battered mother's home merely because the child has been exposed to domestic violence. Further the agency must, except in rare circumstances, obtain a court order if it wants to remove a child from the battered mother's home because she has "allowed" the child to witness domestic violence. Finally, the judge cannot order removal of the child from the care or custody of the battered mother unless there is a risk of serious harm to the child. A court "must balance that risk against the harm removal might bring, and it must examine factually which course is in the child's best interest."[65] The court of appeals rejected the notion that placement in foster care is the safer course of action, warning that the term "should not be used to mask a dearth of evidence or as a watered-down impermissible presumption."[66]

After the state court issued its decision, *Nicholson* returned to federal court. After realizing that they may not be able to extend the original injunction, the plaintiffs entered into a settlement whereby the City of New York specifically acknowledged the applicable law and stated that it intended to comply with the law. Until September 1, 2005, the case will remain on the court's "suspense" docket where the child protection agency will be monitored for compliance. If there are any problems, the plaintiffs can return to court.

Therefore, any policy that encourages removal of a child from a parent without first assessing the degree of harm to that particular child is not in the best interests of that child. Such a blanket policy does not, over the long-term, protect children from future abuse.[67]

Q & A: If a victim of domestic violence flees the state with his/her children, what protections does he/she have?[68]

The Violence Against Women Act of 1994 contains full-faith-and-

---

"Children and Domestic Violence" (2000).

[64]Nicholson v. Scoppetta, 3 N.Y.3d 357, 787 N.Y.S.2d 196, 205, 820 N.E.2d 840, 849 (2004); see also New Jersey Div. of Youth and Family Services v. S.S., 372 N.J. Super. 13, 855 A.2d 8 (App. Div. 2004).

[65]Nicholson v. Scoppetta, 3 N.Y.3d 357, 787 N.Y.S.2d 196, 205, 820 N.E.2d 840, 852 (2004).

[66]Nicholson v. Scoppetta, 3 N.Y.3d 357, 787 N.Y.S.2d 196, 205, 820 N.E.2d 840, 853 (2004).

[67]Lois A. Weithorn, Protecting Children From Exposure to Domestic Violence: The Use and Abuse of Child Maltreatment, 53 Hastings L.J. 1 (2001); Evan Stark, The Battered Mother in the Child Protective Service Caseload: Developing an Appropriate Response, 23 Women's Rights L. Rep. 107 (2002).

[68]See generally, Linda K. Girdner & Patricia Hoff, Parental Abduction, in The Impact of Domestic Violence on Your Legal Practice (ABA 1996); Deborah M. Goelman, Shelter From the Storm: Using Jurisdictional Statutes to Protect Victims of Domestic Violence After the Violence Against Women Act of 2000, 13 Colum. J. Gender & L. 101 (2004); Janet M. Bowermaster, Relocation Child Custody Disputes Involving Domestic

credit provisions which require states, tribes, and territories to enforce valid protection orders issued by courts in other jurisdictions.[69] VAWA's full-faith-and-credit provisions require the second state to enforce the first state's protection order. Even ex parte protection orders are entitled to full faith and credit if the respondent has been served.

This mandate should ensure that victims who are forced to flee across state lines because of domestic violence can retain the legal protections of pre-existing protection orders, including those awarding custody.

Under VAWA,[70] as amended in 2005, the term protection order includes:

(1) any injunction, restraining order or any other order issued by a civil or criminal court for the purpose of preventing violent or threatening acts or harassment against sexual violence or contact or communication with or physical proximity to, another person, including any temporary or final orders issued by civil or criminal courts whether obtained by filing an independent action as a pendente lite order in another proceeding so long as any civil order was issued in response to a complaint, petition, or motion filed by or on behalf of a person seeking protection; and

(2) any support, child custody or visitation provision, orders, remedies or relief issued as part of a protection order, restraining order, or stay away injunction pursuant to State, tribal, territorial, or local law authorizing the issuance of protection orders, restraining orders, or injunctions for the protection of victims of domestic violence, dating violence, sexual violence or stalking.

Full faith and credit should always be accorded to valid protection orders awarding victims of domestic violence, sexual assault and stalking custody, visitation and support.[71] Thus, victims who flee their home states with their children and have previously obtained protection orders from the issuing states should be able to enforce custody, visitation and support provisions within civil protection orders.[72] Accordingly, these provisions within civil protection orders should be entitled to full faith and credit when issued for the safety and protection of either parent or child and provided the orders comply with the

---

Violence, 46 U. Kan. L. Rev. 433 (1998); Klein, Orloff & Sarangapani, Border Crossings: Understanding the Civil, Criminal, and Immigration Implications for Battered Women Fleeing Across State Lines with Their Children, 39 Fam. L. Q. 109 (Spring 2005); Jessica Miles, We Are Never Getting Back Together: Domestic Violence Victims, Defendants and Due Process, 35 Cardozo L. Rev. 141 (2013); see also Legal Resource Center on Violence Against Women at http://www.lrcvaw.org for information on interstate custody cases involving domestic violence.

[69]See 18 U.S.C.A. § 2265 to 18 U.S.C.A. § 2266. See also Text § 18:9, Other remedies under VAWA.

[70]See amended 18 U.S.C.A. § 2266. See also RC 2919.27(D), which has not been amended since 3-31-03.

[71]See amended 18 U.S.C.A. §§ 2265 to 2266; see also Text § 18:9, Other remedies under VAWA.

[72]See 18 U.S.C.A. § 2265; see also Text § 18:9, Other remedies under VAWA.

Uniform Child Custody Jurisdictional Act (UCCJA),[73] the Parental Kidnapping and Prevention Act[74] and Uniform Child Custody Jurisdiction and Enforcement Act (UCCJEA).[75]

Attorneys and advocates should still advise clients of the potential problems that may arise. Where there exists a previously issued custody, visitation or support order in a divorce, an enforcing court may be reluctant to enforce a protection order containing conflicting custody, visitation or support terms. Clients who leave their home states should be aware that courts in their new states may refuse to enforce conflicting orders even if granted pursuant to a protection order.

VAWA does not permit the enforcement of custody and support orders issued pursuant to state divorce and child custody laws.[76] Custody, visitation and support orders issued pursuant to state divorce and child custody laws are still entitled to full faith and credit under other federal law and provided certain conditions are met.[77]

Q & A: What are these "other Federal laws"?[78]

The issue of whether custody awards in protection orders are entitled to interstate enforcement turns on three laws: the Violence Against Women Act (VAWA);[79] the Uniform Child Custody Jurisdiction Act (UCCJA);[80] and the Parental Kidnapping and Prevention Act (PKPA)[81] and the recently adopted Uniform Child Custody Jurisdiction and Enforcement Act (UCCJEA).[82]

For a protection order to be enforceable under the UCCJA and the PKPA, the parties must be given reasonable notice and an opportunity to be heard. Ex parte protection orders grant relief because of the immediacy of the danger to the victim and/or child. Until the party is served with the order, an ex parte protection order does not comply with the notice requirements of the UCCJA and the PKPA. Besides notice, custody provisions within protection orders must meet the jurisdictional requirements of the UCCJA[83] and the PKPA. Otherwise, it will be almost impossible to obtain interstate enforcement.

---

[73]RC 3109.21 et seq.

[74]28 U.S.C.A. § 1738A.

[75]See RC 3127.01 et seq.

[76]See Susan B. Carbone et al., Enforcing Domestic Violence Protection Orders Throughout the Country: New Frontiers of Protection for Victims of Domestic Violence, 50 Juv. & Fam. Ct. 2, 40 (1999).

[77]RC 3109.21 et seq.; 28 U.S.C.A. § 1738A. See RC 3127.01 et seq.

[78]See generally, Joan Zorza, Guide to Interstate Custody: A Manual for Domestic Violence Advocates, Center on Women and Family Law (1995); Deborah M. Goelman, Shelter From the Storm: Using Jurisdictional Statutes to Protect Victims of Domestic Violence After the Violence Against Women Act of 2000, 13 Colum. J. Gender & L. 101 (2004); Kathleen A. Hogan, Custody Jurisdiction, 26-WTR Fam. Advoc. 22 (2004).

[79]18 U.S.C.A. Rule 2261 et seq.

[80]See RC 3109.21 et seq. (for Ohio's version).

[81]18 U.S.C.A. § 1738A; see also Patricia Hoff, Parental Kidnapping: Prevention and Remedies (parts 1 & 2), 13 Juv. & Child Welfare L. Rep. 173 (1995), (parts 3 & 4) 14 Juv. & Child Welfare L. Rep. 12 (1995).

[82]S.B. 185, eff. 4-10-05, and repealing the UCCJA in Ohio.

[83]See Ryan v. Ryan, 784 So. 2d 1215 (Fla. 2d DCA 2001) (where former husband failed to file a UCCJA affidavit in conjunction with the petition).

Every state has adopted its own version of the UCCJA into state law. Under Ohio's version of the UCCJA, there are four ways for a state to assert jurisdiction in a custody matter.[84] First, "home state" jurisdiction is where a child has lived for six consecutive months immediately preceding the filing of the proceeding.[85] Second, jurisdiction may be asserted in the state if one of the parents has "significant connections" with that state.[86] Significant connections include substantial evidence of the child's present or future care, protection, training, and personal relationships. This may only be invoked if it is in the best interests of the child. The third way is "emergency jurisdiction," where the child is physically present in the new state and the child is in need of protection from abuse or mistreatment,[87] is threatened with abuse or is otherwise neglected or dependent. This is usually done on a temporary basis and only to protect endangered children.[88] Finally, the fourth basis for jurisdiction is where the child is physically present and no other state has jurisdiction.

The PKPA is federal law, preempting the UCCJA in cases where there is a conflict between the laws of the issuing state and the enforcing state. The PKPA applies to all interstate child custody cases and requires states to honor other states' custody and visitation orders, provided the orders are in compliance with PKPA's provisions.[89] The PKPA provides the same four grounds for asserting jurisdiction as the UCCJA except that "home state" is given the highest priority. Moreover, no state may assert jurisdiction when another state has continuing jurisdiction pursuant to the PKPA.[90]

Q & A: What is the UCCJEA?

Ohio has recently replaced the UCCJA with the Uniform Child Custody Jurisdiction and Enforcement Act (UCCJEA).[91] The primary goal of the UCCJEA is to establish uniform criteria for jurisdiction in interstate custody cases to avoid competition and promote cooperation among states.[92] Under the UCCJEA, Ohio courts must give full faith

---

[84]See RC 3109.22.

[85]See for example, Stewart v. Stewart, 708 N.E.2d 903 (Ind. Ct. App. 1999); In re Holbert, 1997 WL 566191 (Ohio Ct. App. 10th Dist. Franklin County 1997); Giambrone v. Giambrone, 32 Mass. App. Ct. 118, 586 N.E.2d 23 (1992).

[86]See State ex rel. In Interest of R.P. v. Rosen, 966 S.W.2d 292 (Mo. Ct. App. W.D. 1998).

[87]Michael v. Michael, 1999 WL 1212820 (Ohio Ct. App. 12th Dist. Preble County 1999).

[88]Powers v. Powers, 95 Ohio App. 3d 352, 642 N.E.2d 451 (3d Dist. Crawford County 1994); Wren v. Wren, 2001 WL 1647297 (Neb. Ct. App. 2001). But see UCCJEA, adopted by Ohio in RC 3127.18 and 28 U.S.C.A. § 1738A(c)(1).

[89]See, e.g., Snowberger v. Wesley, 2006-Ohio-3343, 2006 WL 1791177 (Ohio Ct. App. 9th Dist. Summit County 2006) (discussing PKPA); see also In re Parentage, Parenting, and Support of A.R.K.-K., 142 Wash. App. 297, 174 P.3d 160 (Div. 1 2007).

[90]See also Schuyler v. Ashcraft, 293 N.J. Super. 261, 680 A.2d 765 (App. Div. 1996); In re Jorgensen, 627 N.W.2d 550 (Iowa 2001).

[91]Sub S.B. 185, eff. 4-10-2005. See also Pearson v. Pearson, 2005-Ohio-4909, 2005 WL 2268207 (Ohio Ct. App. 4th Dist. Meigs County 2005) (where motions were filed before the effective date of UCCJEA, the court determined that the statutory scheme did not expressly state that it is to be applied retroactively).

[92]Application of the Uniform Child Custody Jurisdiction and Enforcement Act

and credit to valid child custody determinations of sister states.[93] For an initial custody determination of a court to be valid and entitled to full faith and credit, the court must have jurisdiction over the matter.[94] In any interstate custody case, "home state" jurisdiction is now superior to other jurisdictional grounds,[95] unless the other state's court declines to exercise jurisdiction.[96]

Under the UCCJEA, a court must decline jurisdiction (except in temporary jurisdiction cases) where the person seeking to invoke the provision has engaged in unjustifiable conduct unless the parents and all persons acting as parents have agreed to the exercise of jurisdiction, the court having jurisdiction determines that Ohio is a more appropriate forum or no court of any other state would have jurisdiction.[97] Unjustifiable conduct is defined as conduct by a parent or that parent's surrogate that attempts to create jurisdiction in Ohio by removing the child from the child's home state, secreting the child, retaining the child, or restraining or otherwise preventing the child from returning to the child's home state in order to prevent the other parent from commencing a parenting proceeding in the child's home state.[98]

If an Ohio court declines jurisdiction, it may still craft an appropriate remedy to ensure the safety of the child and prevent a repetition of the unjustifiable conduct, including staying the proceeding until a child custody proceeding is commenced in a court having jurisdiction.

Q & A: Can a state exercise temporary emergency custody jurisdiction under the UCCJEA?

Yes. The UCCJEA authorizes temporary emergency jurisdiction in cases where the parent and child flee their home state due to threats of mistreatment and abuse, against either.[99] A court of this state has temporary emergency jurisdiction where the child has been abandoned

---

(UCCJEA) in Recent Domestic Violence Cases, 9 DVR 5 (Oct./Nov. 2003); see also Full Faith and Credit for Custody Orders: Improvements Brought by the UCCJEA and VAWA II, 7 DVR 1 (Oct./Nov. 2001); Zorza, The UCCJEA: What is it and How Does it Affect Battered Women in Child Custody Disputes, 27 Fordham Urb. L. J. 909 (2000); Patricia M. Hoff, The ABC's of the UCCJEA: Interstate Child-Custody Practice Under the New Act, 32 Fam. L.Q. 267 (Summer 1998); Kelly Gaines Stoner, The Uniform Child Custody Jurisdiction and Enforcement Act (UCCJEA)—A Metamorphosis of the Uniform Child Custody Jurisdiction Act (UCCJA), 75 N.D.L.Rev. 301 (1999).

[93] RC 3127.33(A); 28 U.S.C.A. § 1738(A)(a); see also Ashburn v. Roth, 2007-Ohio-2995, 2007 WL 1731426 (Ohio Ct. App. 12th Dist. Butler County 2007).

[94] Ashburn v. Roth, 2007-Ohio-2995, 2007 WL 1731426 (Ohio Ct. App. 12th Dist. Butler County 2007); see also RC 3127.15; 28 U.S.C.A. § 1738(A)(c)(2).

[95] RC 3127.15(A)(1); see also Rosen v. Celebrezze, 117 Ohio St. 3d 241, 2008-Ohio-853, 883 N.E.2d 420 (2008) (discusses home state and subject matter jurisdiction in a case of first impression for Ohio); In re R.M.S.N., 2017-Ohio-9007, 2017 WL 6389095 (Ohio Ct. App. 7th Dist. Belmont County 2017) (thorough discussion of the UCCJEA; where CPO issued by Ohio court suspended appellant's parenting time, court concluded that Ohio was not an appropriate forum for the custody matters as none of the parties resided in Ohio).

[96] RC 3127.15(A)(2); RC 3127.21 and RC 3127.22.

[97] RC 3127.22.

[98] RC 3127.22(D).

[99] RC 3127.18. See also Susan B. Carbone et al., Enforcing Domestic Violence Protection Orders Throughout the Country: New Frontiers of Protection for Victims of Domestic Violence, 50 Juv. & Fam. Ct. 2, 40 (1999). Note that many states have now adopted the Uniform Child Custody Jurisdiction and Enforcement Act (UCCJEA),

or it is necessary in an emergency to protect the child because the child, or a sibling or parent of the child, is subjected to or threatened with mistreatment or abuse.[100] The temporary emergency order remains in effect until a custody order is issued by another state and becomes permanent if no other order is issued by another state within six months.[101] Clearly, under this provision, the safety and protection of both the child and the battered parent are paramount considerations.

For example, in *Martindale v. Martindale,*[102] the Fourth District Court of Appeals, in a narrow decision limited to the facts of the case, agreed with mother that Ohio had obtained emergency custody jurisdiction over the children when it granted mother an ex parte CPO against the father who was residing in Pennsylvania.[103]

In this case, the parties were living in Ohio when father, who was a military service member, was transferred to Pennsylvania. Approximately one year later, mother and children had returned to Ohio wherein she requested a CPO, claiming that father posed a threat to her and the children. She also filed a complaint for legal separation in Ohio, requesting custody of the children. Subsequently, mother was granted a five year ex parte CPO, after which the trial court also granted her motion for temporary custody. Father filed for a divorce in Pennsylvania and asked the Ohio court to dismiss mother's complaint for legal separation. The trial court issued an emergency custody order but then vacated it (in light of communication between the courts) pending resolution of the jurisdictional issues and/or the mother's abuse action.[104]

The Ohio magistrate recommended that the legal separation be dismissed because the parties were Pennsylvania residents, Pennsylvania was the children's home state and mother could counterclaim for legal separation in the Pennsylvania divorce action. The court then adopted the magistrate's decision.

On appeal, mother argued that the trial court erred when it dismissed her legal separation without first determining which state had custody jurisdiction. Father then argued that Ohio lacked custody jurisdiction and that mother was using the legal separation to circumvent the UCCJEA.[105]

While noting that the trial court did not possess jurisdictional

---

including Ohio. See RC 3127.01 et seq. Under the UCCJEA, abuse against the child's parent is a basis for exercising emergency jurisdiction; see for example, Arnold v. Arnold, 2001 WL 1205284 (Iowa Ct. App. 2001); Martindale v. Martindale, 2016-Ohio-524, 2016 WL 562864 (Ohio Ct. App. 4th Dist. Athens County 2016) (trial court erred for failing to consider the factors provided for determining whether a court is an inconvenient forum per UCCJEA).

[100]RC 3127.18(A)(1) to RC 3127.18(A)(2).

[101]RC 3127.18(B).

[102]Martindale v. Martindale, 2016-Ohio-524, 2016 WL 562864 (Ohio Ct. App. 4th Dist. Athens County 2016).

[103]Martindale v. Martindale, 2016-Ohio-524, 2016 WL 562864, ¶ 32 (Ohio Ct. App. 4th Dist. Athens County 2016) (see decision for a discussion about timing).

[104]Martindale v. Martindale, 2016-Ohio-524, 2016 WL 562864, ¶ 7 (Ohio Ct. App. 4th Dist. Athens County 2016).

[105]Martindale v. Martindale, 2016-Ohio-524, 2016 WL 562864, ¶ 25 (Ohio Ct. App.

grounds to make an initial determination in a child custody proceeding under the UCCJEA, the court acknowledged that the UCCJEA also provides that Ohio has temporary emergency jurisdiction if the child is present in Ohio and "is subjected to or threatened with mistreatment or abuse."[106] Emergency jurisdiction attached because mother was granted a CPO which terms were still in effect.

"Consequently, we find that the trial court in this case-which is the same court as the one that dealt with the domestic violence civil protection order issues-continues to have jurisdiction to hear the custody and child support issues through the domestic violence civil protection order case."[107]

Of note is that the ex parte CPO was granted on December 20, 2013, effective until December 20, 2018. The magistrate issued a recommendation denying the full hearing CPO on October 31, 2014 which was neither adopted nor rejected by the trial court judge, which meant that the ex parte CPO was still in effect. Thus, the appellate court found that "the trial court did have subject matter jurisdiction to hear and decide the emergency custody issues set forth in the petition for the domestic violence civil protection order. And since the trial court has not resolved the civil protection order case, it would have subject matter jurisdiction to hear the custody issues."[108]

In stressing that the above finding was "limited to this exceptional set of circumstances,"[109] the appellate court, in a footnote, stated that "[t]his finding is not meant to encourage litigants, who otherwise would not be able to avail themselves of the jurisdiction of a court, to then use the emergency mechanisms of the domestic violence civil protection order statutes to then obtain jurisdiction."[110]

Q & A: What are the other provisions of the UCCJEA?

Where one state is made aware that another jurisdiction is subsequently or simultaneously asked to adjudicate the same custodial issues, that court shall immediately communicate with the court of the other state to resolve the jurisdictional conflict.[111] The UCCJEA also permits attorneys to participate in the required conference calls between judges of the two states when custody actions have been filed in more than one state.[112]

4th Dist. Athens County 2016).

[106] R.C. 3127.18(A).

[107] Martindale v. Martindale, 2016-Ohio-524, 2016 WL 562864, ¶ 32 (Ohio Ct. App. 4th Dist. Athens County 2016).

[108] Martindale v. Martindale, 2016-Ohio-524, 2016 WL 562864, ¶ 34 (Ohio Ct. App. 4th Dist. Athens County 2016).

[109] Martindale v. Martindale, 2016-Ohio-524, 2016 WL 562864, ¶ 32 (Ohio Ct. App. 4th Dist. Athens County 2016).

[110] RC 3127.11.

[111] RC 3127.18; see also In re Marriage of Vanlaarhoven, 2002 MT 222, 311 Mont. 368, 55 P.3d 942 (2002); but see McNabb ex rel. Foshee v. McNabb, 31 Kan. App. 2d 398, 65 P.3d 1068 (2003).

[112] RC 3127.09.

Unlike the UCCJA, the UCCJEA contains more detailed evidentiary procedures.[113] Finally, the UCCJEA also includes domestic violence as a mandatory factor for courts to consider in determining which court is the more appropriate forum to hear the case.[114]

While the UCCJEA is a significant improvement, there are still challenges for battered women and their children. The battered parent must rely on the court to determine whether an emergency exists. If the batterer commences litigation in the other state before the battered parent has been gone for the six-month period, that parent must return to the other state to defend the action.

Q & A: How does the UCCJEA deal with confidentiality?

Under the UCCJEA, identifying information will be sealed and not disclosed to the other party or the public if a party alleges in an affidavit or pleading under oath that the health, safety or liberty of a party or child would be jeopardized by the disclosure of the identifying information.[115] It is up to the state to develop adequate procedures to protect the confidentiality of the battered parent.

Additionally, in cases of temporary emergency jurisdiction, the name and address of the parent seeking protection and who is designated the child's residential parent does not have to be disclosed.

Amended 18 U.S.C.A. § 2266 has clarified that full faith and credit given to protection orders includes custody, support and visitation provisions issued as part of a protection order, restraining order, or stay-away injunction.[116] Therefore, if a victim flees with her children across state lines, it is now possible that any pre-existing protection orders awarding her custody will be accorded full faith and credit and enforceable in the new state. It is also likely that a victim of domestic violence may be able to obtain a civil protection order in the new state, which order may provide protection to and custody of her children.[117] However, unlike VAWA's full faith and credit provisions, which do not require giving notice a second time in order to register a protection order in another jurisdiction, the UCCJEA requires that notice be given to the opposing parent before a custody decree can be registered (and enforced).[118]

Q & A: What protections does a victim of domestic violence have if he/she flees across state lines with the children *before* a custody order has been issued?

Because ongoing domestic violence may leave a victim no choice but to leave the jurisdiction, victims with children are often faced with the dilemma of escaping the battering situation or remaining in the jurisdiction because custody and visitation laws favor maximum contacts with the children. For example, the UCCJA, the PKPA, and

[113]RC 3127.11.

[114]RC 3127.21(B)(1).

[115]RC 3127.23.

[116]Under the UCCJEA, abuse against the child's parent is a basis for exercising emergency jurisdiction; see for example, Arnold v. Arnold, 2001 WL 1205284 (Iowa Ct. App. 2001).

[117]See Ashburn v. Roth, 2007-Ohio-2995, 2007 WL 1731426 (Ohio Ct. App. 12th Dist. Butler County 2007).

[118]RC 3127.19, RC 3127.35(B), and RC 3127.35(C).

the UCCJEA were designed to limit parental abductions and reduce jurisdictional conflict.[119] The focus has been on "home state" jurisdiction.[120] If a party flees the state, that state still is considered the home state of the child. The abuser can thus file for custody in his/her own state, litigate the case there, and possibly obtain custody even though the victim may be in hiding in another state.

The abuser may be able to serve the victim by publication service if he/she cannot locate the victim.[121] Obviously, if the victim is unaware of the action, he/she will not be able to litigate. Without the victim's participation, the court will likely grant custody to the abusive parent. Often, the victim will be forced to choose between safety and litigating the custody case.

On the other hand, interstate jurisdictional laws do contain provisions that protect victims of domestic violence in interstate cases. Such provisions include the emergency jurisdiction clause, the inconvenient forum clause,[122] and the requirement that courts communicate[123] before a child is returned to the home state.[124]

On the other hand, these interstate jurisdictional laws, including Ohio's adoption of the UCCJEA, do contain provisions that protect domestic violence victims in interstate cases. Such provisions include the emergency jurisdiction provisions,[125] the inconvenient forum clause,[126] and communication between the courts,[127] before a child is returned to the home state.[128]

More and more state laws have been enacted to include domestic violence against a parent as a reason to exercise emergency jurisdiction.[129] Additionally, courts are rendering opinions that support exercising emergency jurisdiction because of domestic violence.[130]

---

[119]See Eva L. Klain, Parental Kidnapping and Domestic Violence and Child Abuse: Changing Legal Responses to Related Violence (Am. Prosecutors Research Inst. 1995); Zorza, Full Faith & Credit for Custody Orders: Improvements Brought by the UCCJEA and VAWA II, 7 Dom. Violence Rep. 10 (Oct./Nov. 2001); Billie Lee Dunford-Jackson, The Uniform Child Custody Jurisdiction and Enforcement Act: Affording Protection for Victims of Domestic Violence and Their Children, 50 Juv. & Fam. Ct. J. 55 (1999).

[120]See RC 3109.22(A)(1) and RC 3127.01 et seq.; see also In Interest of E.A., 552 N.W.2d 135 (Iowa 1996); Boeckmann v. Baker, 2003-Ohio-456, 2003 WL 203579 (Ohio Ct. App. 2d Dist. Greene County 2003).

[121]See RC 3109.23.

[122]Jeanne E.M. v. Lindey M.M., 189 Misc. 2d 669, 734 N.Y.S.2d 837 (Fam. Ct. 2001); Stoneman v. Drollinger, 2003 MT 25, 314 Mont. 139, 64 P.3d 997 (2003) (safety of victims of domestic violence should be given priority when considering jurisdictional issues under UCCJEA).

[123]In re Simons, 118 Ohio App. 3d 622, 693 N.E.2d 1111 (2d Dist. Montgomery County 1997).

[124]See RC 3109.21 et seq., replaced by RC 3127.01 et seq.

[125]See RC 3127.18(A)(2), which includes abuse towards a parent of the child.

[126]See also RC 3127.21(B)(1), which mandates that domestic violence is a factor to be considered.

[127]RC 3127.18(D).

[128]RC 3127.01 et seq.

[129]See, e.g., Cal. Fam. Code § 3424.

[130]See, e.g., Powers v. Powers, 95 Ohio App. 3d 352, 642 N.E.2d 451 (3d Dist.

Q & A: What are the consequences of an abuser taking his/her child out of state?[131]

If an abuser leaves the state with the child, the victim should file for custody if no custody order has been issued. Often the court will award the victim custody even if the child is not present. If the victim does not know the whereabouts of the child, parent locator services are available to attempt to locate the absent parent.[132]

If the victim does not file for custody, the state in which the child now resides with the abuser may become the child's home state after six months. If the abuser then files for custody in the new state, the court may correctly exercise jurisdiction over the case. On the other hand, the court may decline to exercise jurisdiction based on the "unclean hands" of the abuser[133] or the alleged victim.[134]

If the victim already has a custody order, the victim should contact the local prosecutor to press charges for child stealing or should return to the court that issued the custody order.

Q & A: What if a victim flees the state in violation of an already-existing custody or visitation order?

How the court deals with the offending party in this case will often depend on whether the court believes that the safety of the victim and child may be impaired. Courts must weigh the safety needs of the victim and child against the need for litigants to obey lawful court orders.

A victim who flees the state with the children in violation of a custody order may be charged with abduction,[135] interference with custody,[136] child stealing, kidnapping,[137] or contempt of court.[138] Victims should consider using evidence of their history of domestic violence as a defense to such charges.[139]

Crawford County 1994); see also Squires v. Squires, 12 Ohio App. 3d 138, 468 N.E.2d 73 (12th Dist. Preble County 1983); Trader v. Darrow, 630 A.2d 634 (Del. 1993).

[131]See also Katare v. Katare, 175 Wash. 2d 23, 283 P.3d 546 (2012) (discussion of risk factors for child abduction when a parent wishes to take the child out of the country).

[132]See 42 U.S.C.A. § 663.

[133]See RC 3109.26.

[134]See, e.g., Dymitro v. Dymitro, 129 Idaho 527, 927 P.2d 917 (Ct. App. 1996).

[135]RC 2905.02.

[136]See Vachon v. Pugliese, 931 P.2d 371 (Alaska 1996).

[137]RC 2905.01 to RC 2905.03.

[138]But see Ashburn v. Roth, 2007-Ohio-2995, 2007 WL 1731426 (Ohio Ct. App. 12th Dist. Butler County 2007) (affirming trial court decision holding that the Ohio Domestic relations court did not abuse its discretion in exercising jurisdiction over the matter and in issuing the initial CPO:

> The mere existence of visitation orders in another state does not form the basis upon which to deny a CPO when the petitioner is subject to the threat of violence.

Ashburn v. Roth, 2007-Ohio-2995, 2007 WL 1731426, *3 (Ohio Ct. App. 12th Dist. Butler County 2007).

[139]Joan Zorza, Guide To Interstate Custody: A Manual For Domestic Violence Advocates (Nat'l Ctr. for Women & Fam. Law, 2d ed. 1995).

§ 15:25 Relocation legal issues for attorneys and advocates

RELOCATION CHECKLIST[1]

Intake questions for victim advocates[2]

Survivor's goals and fears

What is the survivor's primary goal?

What is the survivor's biggest concern?

What specific questions does the survivor have regarding her potential relocation with her child?

Existing court orders

Are there any previous court orders regarding the child (including as part of a protection order, paternity, child protection, child support or custody case)?

If so, when were they entered?

From which state or tribal court?

What do the existing orders say about custody and visitation?

Has the survivor or the perpetrator ever violated a court order?

Is the survivor aware of any other court proceeding involving the child?

Jurisdictional issues

Where has the child been living since birth (including dates and the parent with whom the child has been living)?

Where have each of the parents been living since the child's birth (including dates)?

What connections does the family have with each of the locations, including where is there evidence of the child's care, protection, training, and personal relationships (e.g., with caregivers, medical professionals, teachers, relatives, etc.)?

---

[1] The Legal Resource Center is supported by Grant No. 2004-WT-AX-K079 awarded by the Office on Violence Against Women, U.S. Department of Justice. The opinions, findings, conclusions, and recommendations expressed in this document are those of the authors and do not necessarily reflect the views of the Department of Justice, Office on Violence Against Women.

[2] These questions are designed to help a victim advocate gather information relevant to a survivor's decision to relocate. With this factual information, an attorney may assess the interstate issues and provide the survivor with her legal options.

If the survivor has left the state in which the perpetrator lives, has she checked regularly with the domestic relations court in the county she left to determine if the perpetrator has filed for custody?

If the survivor has relocated, what type of contact does the perpetrator have with the new state (e.g., business dealings, family, previously lived there, stalked the survivor there, made threats by phone or e-mail)?

Has any court ever been asked to consider if it had jurisdiction over the child or a party?

If so, which court and what was the outcome?

History of abuse

What was the most recent physical threat or violent act against the survivor?

What was the most recent physical threat or violent act against the child?

What is the history of abuse against the survivor and the child?

What type of visitation, if any, does the survivor think is appropriate for the child to have with the perpetrator?

What evidence is available to document the abuse (e.g., previous protection orders, convictions, police reports, medical records, or witnesses)?

Relocation

Does the survivor want to move to a different location?

Where?

Why?

Does the perpetrator know where the survivor is living?

If not, does the survivor want to keep her location confidential (if possible)?

Does the perpetrator have special expertise or access to equipment that would make it possible to locate or stalk the survivor in a new state? (E.g., is he a law enforcement officer?)

How might relocation affect the children?

Does the survivor have the ability to travel between the two locations?

Would the perpetrator have any difficulty traveling between the two locations?_

Additional concerns

Does the survivor have immigration concerns?

Does the survivor have financial concerns?

Would she have better employment opportunities in the new location?

Is there a difference in the availability of child care in the two locations?

Will the survivor have somewhere to live in the new jurisdiction (e.g., are there family members with whom she could stay, or is there a shelter or transitional housing program there?)

Would the survivor qualify for free legal assistance?

For training or information on interstate issues involving custody and domestic violence, please contact the Legal Resource Center on Violence Against Women at 301-270-1550, www.lrcvaw.org.

RELOCATION CHECKLIST[1]

For attorneys representing domestic violence survivors

Legal Issues

Pre-existing court orders

1. *Has a custody order been entered previously, including as part of a protection order?*

- ☐ Will leaving the state with her children violate the existing custody order or visitation schedule, exposing the survivor to contempt charges?

- ☐ Will leaving the state violate a criminal law, such as the state parental kidnapping law?[2]

  - Is there a domestic violence exemption that would prevent her from being charged with parental kidnapping?

  - Is there a domestic violence defense that she could assert if charged?

  - Is there a child protection defense that she could assert if charged?

  - Does she have the evidence necessary to utilize these legal protections?

- ☐ Will leaving the state with her children violate the state relocation law?

  - Under the relocation law, are there steps she needs to take prior to leaving the state, such as requesting permission from the court to relocate or notifying the other parent?

  - If there is no relocation statute, does case law establish criteria she must meet before leaving?

---

[1] The Legal Resource Center is supported by Grant No. 2004-WT-AX-K079 awarded by the Office on Violence Against Women, U.S. Department of Justice. The opinions, findings, conclusions, and recommendations expressed in this document are those of the authors and do not necessarily reflect the views of the Department of Justice, Office on Violence Against Women.

[2] In some states, this may be known as a child concealment, parental abduction or custodial interference law.

- Are there any domestic violence exceptions to the relocation standards?

☐ Will the state from which she is fleeing have continuing exclusive jurisdiction over custody and visitation matters?

- Have all the parties and the child left the state?
- If someone continues to live in the issuing state, has the state made a determination that the child no longer has a connection with the state?

Protection orders

2. *Should she file for a protection order before she leaves the state?*

☐ Is she eligible for a protection order in this state?

☐ If she seeks a protection order, is the court likely to grant one?

☐ Is the perpetrator likely to obey an order?

☐ Is the new state likely to enforce the order?

☐ Is temporary custody available as part of a protection order?

☐ If temporary custody is likely to be awarded, is visitation likely to be granted to the perpetrator?

☐ If she seeks a protection order and receives one, will she be able to leave the state with her children (see issues above regarding an existing custody order)?

☐ If she does not seek a protection order, is there other evidence that proves the history of domestic violence, such as previous protection orders, criminal convictions, police reports, medical records, or adult witnesses?

3. *Should she file for a protection order in the new state?*

☐ Will she be eligible for a protection order in the new state?

- Can she meet the statutory requirements for issuance of a protection order in the new state (e.g., does the abuse meet the statutory definition)?

- ☐ Will the court in the new state have personal jurisdiction over the perpetrator?
    - Does the perpetrator have minimum contacts with the new state, sufficient to satisfy due process?
    - How have the new state's courts interpreted personal jurisdiction in the protection order context?
- ☐ If she seeks a protection order, is the court likely to grant one?
- ☐ Is the perpetrator likely to obey an order from the new state?
- ☐ Will it be necessary to disclose her new location in order to obtain a protection order?
    - Is it safe to do so?

Custody orders

4. *Should she file for a custody order in domestic relations court before she leaves the state?*

- ☐ Has the state adopted a version of the Uniform Child Custody Jurisdiction and Enforcement Act (UCCJEA)?
- ☐ Is the state from which she is fleeing the child's home state?
    - If so, is the perpetrator likely to file for custody within six months after she leaves?
    - Can an attorney or an advocate in the home state check with the family court to be sure that the perpetrator has not filed for custody?
- ☐ If it is not the home state, does the court have another basis for exercising jurisdiction?
    - Does it have a significant connection to the family, including substantial evidence of the child's care, protection, training, and relationships?
- ☐ Is the state from which she is fleeing likely to decline jurisdiction in favor of the refuge state, based on inconvenient forum?

- Will she have an attorney available to make the jurisdictional argument?
- Is the court likely to accept the inconvenient forum argument based on the history of domestic violence and the other seven statutory factors?
- If the state retains jurisdiction, is the judge likely to penalize her in the underlying custody case for having requested the change in jurisdiction?

□ Can the new state exercise emergency jurisdiction?

- Has there been abuse or mistreatment of the child or the parent or a sibling (in UCCJEA states)?
- Is the new state likely to exercise emergency jurisdiction?
- Would it be helpful for the judge in the new state to communicate with the judge in the original state, as mandated by the UCCJEA?

□ Will the child custody jurisdictional laws or judicial practice require her to return to the original state to litigate the custody case?

5. *Would one state's custody laws provide greater protection for the survivor and her children?*

□ Is domestic violence a factor in custody determinations or is there a rebuttable presumption against awarding custody to perpetrators?

□ Does she have the evidence necessary to assert the legal protections in these laws?

□ Is a court likely to view her flight to another state as forum shopping or an attempt to deprive the perpetrator of contact with the children?

□ In practice, are courts likely to award joint custody or unsupervised visitation to the perpetrator?

Other legal considerations

6. *Are there other legal protections that could keep her safer in one state versus the other?*

- ☐ Are there confidentiality laws that would permit her to keep her address confidential?

- ☐ Do the rules of evidence differ such that one state is more likely to permit the evidence of domestic violence to be introduced?

7. *If she leaves the original state, will she be liable for breaking contracts?*

- ☐ Will she be liable for a mortgage or a lease?

- ☐ Could she be charged with stealing the perpetrator's vehicle?

8. *Are there immigration-related consequences to leaving the state?*

- ☐ Will it be more difficult to obtain benefits in another state?

- ☐ Will her acts be charged criminally, leading to a deportable offense?

- ☐ In the new state, will she be able to gather the evidence necessary to seek domestic violence-related immigration relief?

9. *Will it be more difficult to seek child support if she leaves?*

- ☐ Will the new state have personal jurisdiction over the perpetrator?

10. *Will it be more difficult to file for divorce in the new state?*

<u>Non-Legal Issues</u>

1. *Will the refuge state be a safer place for her?*

- ☐ Will the violence increase if she leaves?

- ☐ Will the perpetrator know where she is going?

- ☐ How lethal is the perpetrator?

- ☐ Is the perpetrator likely to stalk her in the new state?

- ☐ Is the perpetrator likely to harm other family members if she leaves?

- ☐ Does she have family support in the new state?

- ☐ Are there domestic violence resources in the new state?

- ☐ How does law enforcement respond to domestic violence, including protection order enforcement?
- ☐ How do the courts respond to domestic violence?
- ☐ Does the perpetrator have special expertise or access to equipment that would make it possible to locate or stalk the survivor in a new state? (E.g., Is he a law enforcement officer? Is he employed by a cell phone company?)

2. *Will she be able to survive economically?*
   - ☐ Will she have a place to live with her children?
   - ☐ Will she have a job?
   - ☐ Will she have childcare?
   - ☐ Will she have health insurance?
   - ☐ Will she be eligible for public benefits?
   - ☐ Will she be eligible for unemployment if she leaves a job?

3. *How will relocation affect the children?*
   - ☐ If she leaves, is the perpetrator likely to file for and receive custody or unsupervised visitation with the children?
   - ☐ Will her shelter in the refuge state be safe for the children?
   - ☐ Do the children have special medical or other needs that can be met in the new state?
   - ☐ How will the children adjust to a complete change in their environment?

4. *How will she be able to get to the refuge state or back?*
   - ☐ Does she have a vehicle or the funds to travel?
   - ☐ Does she have a medical condition that may impede her travel?
   - ☐ If she needs to return to the home state for custody litigation, how will she be able to return?

5. *What should she bring with her?*

- ☐ Money, credit cards, ATM cards, checkbooks, saleable items (e.g., jewelry)
- ☐ Clothing, medicine, and toiletries for her and children
- ☐ Court orders and pleadings (for protection order, divorce, custody, paternity, immigration, criminal and other cases)
- ☐ Identification (social security, driver's license, birth certificates, public assistance or state ID)
- ☐ Children's school records, medical records (including vaccinations), and passports
- ☐ Work permits, green cards, and other immigration papers
- ☐ Health insurance cards
- ☐ Insurance papers
- ☐ Telephone/address books
- ☐ Ownership documents for car/house (title, registration, deed)
- ☐ Copy of lease or rental agreement, mortgage payment book
- ☐ Car/house/office keys
- ☐ Family photographs, other sentimental items perpetrator may destroy
- ☐ Address book and contact information for anyone who may have evidence of the abuse (e.g., police officers, neighbors, doctors, social services' providers, shelters, county registry of protection orders, clerk of court, schools)
- ☐ Toys, sentimental items

> For training or information on interstate issues involving custody and domestic violence, please contact the Legal Resource Center on Violence Against Women at 301-270-1550, www.lrcvaw.org.

Chapter 16

Domestic Violence Case Strategy and Evidentiary Considerations

§ 16:1 Introduction[1]

Any attorney litigating a case involving domestic violence must be

[Section 16:1]

[1]See generally Julie Kunce Field, Screening for Domestic Violence: Meeting the Challenge of Identifying Domestic Relations Cases Involving Domestic Violence and Developing Strategies for Those Cases, 39(2) Court Rev. 4 (2002); Standards of Practice for Lawyers Representing Victims of Domestic Violence, Sexual Assault and Stalking in Civil Protection Order Cases, American Bar Association, Commission on

certain that he or she understand the issues that frame the case.[2] Misconceptions about domestic violence abound, and both fact-finders and attorneys may hold prejudices and biases that need to be addressed.[3] For example, judges may be hesitant to grant protection orders to victims who are unable to document the incidents of violence. Others may believe that domestic violence is not significant enough to break up a marriage. Attorneys who do not understand the profile of both the victim and the batterer and the dynamic of the violent relationship may be inclined to re-victimize the abused.[4]

Any client who comes to a family practitioner may be a victim of domestic violence.[5] Sometimes, a client may come to an attorney because of violence in the home and request a divorce, protection order, or custody. Other times, having come to an attorney for another family law problem, the client does not disclose the violence. Asking the right questions and identifying the signs of domestic violence in a relationship will aid in the representation of the client.[6]

Obviously, an attorney may also be called on to represent the alleged perpetrator of domestic violence.[7] In that instance, the attorney must be prepared to defend against the victim's allegations.

Thorough preparation of any case entails an inquiry into, and an analysis of, both the factual and legal issues. This may include assessing whether domestic violence is a factor. Once domestic violence is identified, individual legal options must be explored. Additionally, the safety of the victim must be considered at this point in the case.[8] Failure to address domestic violence in a relationship will shortchange a client who may be in need of specific legal services.[9]

Q & A: Does an attorney have a legal and ethical obligation

Domestic Violence (2007); Jane H. Aiken and Jane C. Murphy, Dealing with Complex Evidence of Domestic Violence: A Primer for the Civil Bench, 39(2) Court Rev. 12 (2002); Tom Lininger, Evidentiary Issues in Federal Prosecutions of Violence Against Women, 36 Ind. L. Rev. 687 (2003).

[2]Linda G. Mills, On the Other Side of Silence: Effective Lawyering for Intimate Abuse, 81 Cornell L. Rev. 1225 (1996); see also Ann Shalleck, Theory & Experience in Constructing the Relationship between Lawyer & Client: Representing Women Who Have Been Abused, 64 Tenn. L. Rev. 1019 (1997).

[3]See, e.g., Jo Ann Merica, The Lawyer's Basic Guide to Domestic Violence, 62 Tex. Bar J. 915 (1999).

[4]See, e.g., Jo Ann Merica, The Lawyer's Basic Guide to Domestic Violence, 62 Tex. Bar J. 915 (1999); see also Drew, Lawyer Malpractice and Domestic Violence: Are We Revictimizing Our Clients?, 39 Fam. L. Q. (Spring 2005).

[5]See Attorney Screening for Victims of Domestic Violence (Ohio Domestic Violence Network, 1999); see also Pauline Quirion, Why Attorneys Should Routinely Screen Clients for Domestic Violence, 42 Boston Bar J. 12 (1998); John M. Burman, Lawyers and Domestic Violence: Part II, 24-DEC Wyo. Law 37 (2001).

[6]See Attorney Screening for Victims of Domestic Violence (Ohio Domestic Violence Network, 1999).

[7]See Barbara Salomon, Guilty Until Proven Innocent: Representing the Alleged Abuser, 17 Fam. Advoc. 30 (1995); see also Myrna S. Raeder, The Better Way: The Role of Batterers' Profiles & Expert "Social Framework" Background in Cases Implicating Domestic Violence, 68 U. Colo. L. Rev. 147 (1997).

[8]See Text § 16:6, Ohio Domestic Violence Network—Strategies for dealing with domestic violence; safety planning; form.

[9]See Attorney Screening for Victims of Domestic Violence (Ohio Domestic Violence Network, 1999).

in the representation of clients who are victims or perpetrators of domestic violence?

Yes. As domestic violence becomes more visible to the legal profession and the community at large, it may become increasingly difficult for an attorney to argue that he or she has neither a legal or ethical responsibility to understand the dynamics of domestic violence nor an obligation to take reasonable precautions to minimize the potential harm to a client who is a victim of that violence.[10] Additionally, lawyers who represent batterers also need to be aware of their responsibility to warn others or take steps to minimize the potential harm.[11] The failure to ask the right questions, develop the correct strategies or refer clients to supportive services may lead to malpractice suits or further endanger the victim and children.

The first step in effectively representing either a victim or batterer starts with an understanding of the dynamics of domestic violence including why a victim stays with an abuser who continues to batters. This is critical since a batterer's reason for an a victim's reaction to domestic violence often appears counter-intuitive, making traditional approaches ineffective at best and harmful at worst.[12] Her reaction may appear illogical and unstable. However, what appears like crazy behavior may be a normal approach to a crazy situation.

Both victims and perpetrators of domestic violence have a wide range of legal problems which may include family law, criminal, bankruptcy, immigration, probate, tax and property issues. For example, in allocating parental rights and responsibilities, courts in Ohio consider domestic violence as one of the best in interest factors.[13] An attorney who fails to recognize and present evidence of domestic violence might jeopardize a client's case. Family law practitioners need to understand the dynamics of domestic violence and its effects on children so that they can craft appropriate custody and visitation arrangements.[14]

Tort law provides another example. An attorney who has failed to identify a client as a victim of domestic violence may advise the client to sign a separation agreement in a divorce that contains a boilerplate waiver of all claims. This may result in the client waiving claims against the batterer for intentional torts such as assault, battery, infliction of emotional distress, property torts, trespass, wrongful

---

[10]John M. Burman, Lawyers and Domestic Violence, 24-OCT Wyo. Law. 36 (2001); see also Dana Harrington Conner, To Protect or To Serve: Confidentiality, Client Protection and Domestic Violence, 79 Temp. L. Rev. 877 (2006) (discussing decision making, ethical issues and how an attorney's actions can affect victim safety).

[11]Burman, Lawyers and Domestic Violence at 37; see also Sarah Buel and Margaret Drew, Do Ask and Do Tell: Rethinking the Lawyer's Duty to Warn in Domestic Violence Cases, 75 U. Cin. L. Rev. 447 (2006).

[12]John M. Burman, Lawyers and Domestic Violence, 24-OCT Wyo. Law. 38 (2001).

[13]RC 3109.04(F); see also Text Ch. 15, Domestic Violence and Custody and Visitation Issues.

[14]William T. Schemmel, Domestic Violence: An Attorney's Perspective, 46-OCT Res Gestae 46 (2002).

death and economic torts including tortious interference with contractual relations and fraudulent transfer.[15]

Similarly, an attorney representing an immigrant client who is unaware his or her client is a victim of domestic violence may compromise the client's immigration status. If the attorney files a divorce action rather than pursuing available remedies under VAWA, he or she might impair the client's ability to file for certain immigration benefits without the batterer's participation.[16]

Likewise, estate and tax attorneys may represent clients whose choices are unduly influenced by abusive partners. Employment or labor lawyers may need to advise employees about personnel or workplace violence and safety issues and represent victims who are terminated for reasons related to the abuse. Education attorneys or lawyers representing children involved in delinquency cases who understand that children living in violent homes may be negatively impacted by the abuse are in better positions to represent them in disciplinary actions or help them obtain necessary services to heal from the abuse. Landlord tenant cases involving noisy tenants may be resolved without eviction if the victim obtains a civil protection order.[17]

Finally, defense lawyers may represent victims as perpetrators of domestic violence or other crimes of violence. Domestic violence issues such as battered women's syndrome and self-defense may be a major aspect of a criminal defense. A lawyer who does not understand battering and its effects may also harm his/her clients.[18] So too, prosecutors may need to help a jury understand why a victim who has been abused repeatedly continues to remain in an abusive relationship and why doing so is not a defense to additional criminal charges.

Attorneys for victims seeking civil protection orders need to understand the pros and cons of obtaining these orders. For example, an attorney who represents a client requesting a CPO must become familiar both with the dynamics and laws regarding domestic violence. One of the more important issues to discuss with a client is whether obtaining the CPO will actually protect the client or endanger her further by angering the batterer.

So too, attorneys for batterers must understand the potential consequences for their clients of having protection orders issued against them (firearms restrictions, deportation concerns).

Q & A: What are an attorney's legal and ethical obligations in this area?

Pursuant to the Ohio Rules of Professional Conduct, R. 1.1, a lawyer shall provide *competent* representation to a client. Competent representation requires the legal knowledge, skill, thoroughness and prepa-

[15]William T. Schemmel, Domestic Violence: An Attorney's Perspective, 46-OCT Res Gestae 39 (2002).

[16]William T. Schemmel, Domestic Violence: An Attorney's Perspective, 46-OCT Res Gestae 40 (2002).

[17]Pauline Quirion, Why Attorneys Should Routinely Screen Clients for Domestic Violence, 42-OCT B. B.J. 12 (1998) (detailing the intersection between law practice specialties and domestic violence clients).

[18]Pauline Quirion, Why Attorneys Should Routinely Screen Clients for Domestic Violence, 42-OCT B. B.J. 12 at 27 (1998).

ration *reasonably* necessary for the representation. Competency means determining if there are barriers to representing your client. A critical element of competence is proper factual investigation. Competency avoids malpractice lawsuits. As an effective advisor for the client, doing nothing is not competent lawyering. Thus, screening every client for domestic violence is competent lawyering.[19]

Every attorney has both a legal and ethical duty to act as a reasonable lawyer under the circumstances. The questions to ask are (1) what should a reasonable lawyer know about domestic violence; (2) what should a reasonable lawyer do to determine if the client is either a victim or batterer; and (3) what should a reasonable lawyer do if she/he discovers that the client is either a victim or a batterer.[20]

In order to fulfill the responsibility to act reasonably, a lawyer should screen all prospective clients to determine if they are either victims or perpetrators of domestic violence.[21] Only with that information can an attorney competently represent a client effectively or refer them to an attorney who can.

Proper screening also includes assessing the risk of future harm and advising them of additional steps to ensure their safety. This may include referrals to advocates to assist in safety planning. Safety planning includes changing locks, planning escape routes, neighborhood watch, cell phone 911 calls, varying predictable routines and easy document retrieval.

Finally, an attorney may need to take precautions when contacting victims, as this communication may increase the possibility of violence or providing confidential addresses when preparing court documents. Likewise, the attorney may need to provide victims with advance notice of court dates, service of documents, and discovery dates. As the attorney for a victim, courthouse security should be addressed as well.[22]

Q & A: What if the client denies the battering, but you suspect it?

A lawyer should confront the client if the explanations to certain questions do not make sense or match the physical or circumstantial evidence suggesting abuse. The attorney "should be sensitive to certain behaviors that may indicate abuse such as (1) when a client seems fearful of her partner; (2) when a client suddenly moves without adequate explanation; (3) when a client has limited access to money especially money she has earned; (4) when there are repeated reconciliations followed by separations; and (5) when her partner is

---

[19]Tools for Attorneys to Screen for Domestic Violence, American Bar Association, Commission on Domestic Violence (2005).

[20]John M. Burman, Lawyers and Domestic Violence: Part 1, 24-OCT Wyo. Law. 36, 39 (2001).

[21]See Kathleen Waits, Battered Women and Family Lawyers: The Need for an Identification Protocol, 58 Alb. L. Rev. 1027 (1995); John M. Burman, Lawyers and Domestic Violence: Raising the Standard of Practice, 9 Mich. J. Gender & L. 207 (2003).

[22]Burman, Lawyers and Domestic Violence: Raising the Standard of Practice, 9 Mich. J. Gender & L. 207, 240-243 (2003).

unwilling to grant her a divorce even though she has insisted that the relationship is over."[23]

§ 16:2 Identifying domestic violence—Interviewing the parties[1]

Interviewing a victim of domestic violence is often quite challenging. The victim often denies or minimizes the violence. The victim may be afraid to divulge the truth because the batterer has threatened to kill the victim if he/she tells. The batterer may have told the victim that no one would believe him/her if he/she spoke about the violence. Because domestic violence is rarely an isolated or individual event, many victims of domestic violence begin to believe that these incidents represent normal behavior.[2] "The more successful a perpetrator has been in isolating the abused party, the more they control what the abused party believes."[3] It must be reinforced to the client that the law does not support such behavior.

Interviewing the perpetrator of domestic violence may be just as challenging. He/she may also deny or minimize the violence,[4] but for different reasons. The batterer may honestly believe he/she did nothing wrong, that either the victim provoked him/her or the victim actually caused the abuse. In either case, the perpetrator fails to take responsibility for his/her actions.

It must be stressed that domestic violence is more than physical abuse.[5] It also includes financial, emotional, and psychological abuse.[6] The physical signs of domestic violence are just the most obvious indicator that domestic violence exists within the relationship.

A lawyer interviewing either the victim[7] or the alleged perpetrator[8]

---

[23]Pauline Quirion, Kathleen Waits, Battered Women and Family Lawyers: The Need for Identification Protocol, 58 Alb. L. Rev. 1027, 1057 (1995).

[Section 16:2]

[1]See, generally, Kathleen Walts, Battered Women and Family Lawyers: The Need for an Identification Protocol, 58 Alb. L. Rev. 1027 (1995).

[2]Judith Armatta, Getting Beyond the Law's Complicity in Intimate Violence Against Women, 33 Willamette L. Rev. 773, 817 (1997).

[3]Anne L. Ganley, Domestic Violence: The What, Why and Who, as Relevant to Civil Court Cases, in Domestic Violence in Civil Court Cases, A National Model for Judicial Education 43 (Jacqueline Agtuca et al. eds., 1992).

[4]Anne L. Ganley, Domestic Violence: The What, Why and Who, as Relevant to Civil Court Cases, in Domestic Violence in Civil Court Cases, A National Model for Judicial Education 36 (Jacqueline Agtuca et al. eds., 1992); see also John M. Burman, Lawyers and Domestic Violence: Part II, 24-DEC Wyo. Law 37 (2001) (discussing responsibilities of lawyers who represent batterers).

[5]Anne L. Ganley, Domestic Violence: The What, Why and Who, as Relevant to Civil Court Cases, in Domestic Violence in Civil Court Cases, A National Model for Judicial Education 22 (Jacqueline Agtuca et al. eds., 1992).

[6]See Mary Ann Dutton & Catherine L. Waltz, Domestic Violence: Understanding Why It Happens and How to Recognize It, 17 Fam. Advoc. 14 (1995).

[7]See Fredrica L. Lehrman, Client Interview, in The Impact of Domestic Violence on Your Legal Practice: A Lawyer's Handbook 2-7 (Deborah M. Goelman et al. eds., 1996).

[8]See Barbara Salomon, Guilty Until Proven Innocent: Representing the Alleged Abuser, 17 Fam. Advoc. 30 (1995) (discussing representation issues).

must be aware that there are certain interviewing techniques that will more readily yield reliable factual information. If the attorney fails to inquire about the domestic violence in the relationship, it is unlikely a court will be given this information. If the court is unaware of the violence and custody and visitation are issues in the case, the children of the relationship will remain at risk, and the cycle of violence will continue unbroken.

Q & A: What types of questions can be asked of a client who does not disclose abuse at the interview?

For the attorney who interviews a client that fails to disclose any domestic violence in the relationship, the following questions may be asked as a way of opening the door:

(1) If there are injuries, comment "When I see injuries, I ask whether there is violence at home."

(2) If there are bruises or other visible signs of injury, say "Abuse is such a common problem; is it happening to you?"

(3) If the client appears afraid, say "You seem frightened and anxious. Are you afraid of your partner?" "Has he/she ever hurt you?"

(4) If you, the attorney, are concerned, say "I am concerned for your safety. Is there a chance that you are in an abusive relationship now?"

(5) As the attorney you may also ask rather general questions such as "Have there been times during your relationship when you had physical fights?" or "Has your partner ever hurt you?" or "Have you ever been in a relationship where you have been hit, punched, kicked or hurt in any way? Are you in such a relationship now?"

(6) Sometimes, the client may talk about the children in the relationship. If this has been disclosed, ask "Does your partner lose his/her temper with the children? Does he/she lose his/her temper with you? Does he/she become abusive when he/she loses his/her temper?"

(7) Sometimes the issue of drugs or alcohol comes up in the interview. Ask "Does your spouse use drugs or alcohol? How does your spouse act when drinking or on drugs?"

(8) Sometimes, the client may say that he/she does not know what his/her partner earns, that the partner does not share this information with him/her, and that the partner care of all the finances. Ask "Is he/she overprotective of you. Does your partner want to take care of you? Does he/she let you have friends? Is he/she ever jealous of you and your friends? If he/she is as jealous and controlling as you describe, he/she may react strongly and use physical force? Is this happening to you?"

In many cases, questions such as these encourage the client to speak frankly about the relationship with his/her partner. If you sense abuse in the relationship and the client will not disclose if asked a specific and pointed question about physical violence in the home, the above-listed questions may produce the desired result in a less direct manner. These questions will act as red flags that there is abuse in the parties' relationship.

Q & A: If the client discloses the domestic violence in an interview with his/her attorney, will the client necessarily be a good witness?

No. Attorneys should understand that a victim's behavior in court is consistent with being traumatized by violence. In fact, how the victim acts in court is often in direct response to what the perpetrator did prior to the court appearance or what the perpetrator is doing during the proceeding.

Sometimes, the victim will appear weak, reticent, or hysterical in court,[9] while the batterer tends to be calm and organized. The victim may minimize or even deny the violence directed against him/her. Since the batterer is accustomed to exerting power and control in the relationship, this behavior often extends into the courtroom. The victim, in contrast, is accustomed to compromising his/her needs and giving in to that control.[10] "Rather than viewing the abused party's behavior as either masochistic or crazy or as indicating that there really was no violence, it should be viewed as a normal response to violence and as contributing to the abused party's survival and the survival of the children."[11]

Sometimes, however, a victim may appear determined and empowered. This may be the result of a victim advocate or victim counselor who instills in the victim a sense of self esteem. It may also be the result of time and healing.

§ 16:3 Identifying domestic violence—Client intake questionnaire—Victim

Attorneys should include several questions in their intake interview that are often red flags or warning signs that the relationship is abusive.

A. Does your partner:

	Yes	No
(1) embarrass you in front of others?	____	____
(2) belittle your accomplishments?	____	____
(3) make you feel unworthy?	____	____
(4) constantly contradict himself/herself to confuse you?	____	____
(5) isolate you from the people you care about?	____	____
(6) make you feel ashamed a lot of the time?	____	____
(7) use intimidation to make you do what he/she wants?	____	____
(8) control finances?	____	____
(9) make you feel like you are crazy?	____	____
(10) lose control when drunk?	____	____
(11) get angry, without an apparent reason?	____	____
(12) use physical force to get you to do something?	____	____

---

[9]Mildred D. Pagelow, Justice for Victims of Spouse Abuse in Divorce and Child Custody Cases, 8 Violence and Victims 1 (1993).

[10]Catherine F. Klein & Leslye E. Orloff, Representing a Victim of Domestic Violence, 17 Fam. Advoc. 24 (1995).

[11]Anne L. Ganley, Domestic Violence: The What, Why and Who, as Relevant to Civil Court Cases, in Domestic Violence in Civil Court Cases, A National Model for Judicial Education 46 (Jacqueline Agtuca et al. eds., 1992).

(13) threaten you verbally?	____	____
(14) grab, pinch, shove, slap, or kick you?	____	____
(15) attack you while you were pregnant?	____	____
(16) punch, hit, or choke you?	____	____
(17) force you to have sex?	____	____
(18) threaten you with a weapon?	____	____
(19) threaten to kill you and/or himself?	____	____
(20) hurt pets?	____	____
(21) destroy property?	____	____

"Yes" answers to questions (A)(1) to (A)(9) indicate that there are some power and control issues in the relationship.[1] Attorneys should be alert to these signs because they are an indication that domestic violence may be occurring. "Yes" answers to questions (A)(10) to (A)(17) indicate that the partner's behavior is abusive and that he/she uses force to achieve goals and get what he/she wants out of the relationship. "Yes" answers to questions (A)(18) to (A)(21) are a predictor of lethality or future abuse. The attorney should explain to the client that "yes" answers suggest that the level of danger is heightened and that a safety plan should be completed by the victim.

It is crucial to ask if any of these acts were committed in the presence of the children. If the answer is "yes," the attorney must ask follow-up questions that may indicate child abuse. The risk of child abuse is significantly higher when there is domestic violence between the parents.[2] Even if the children are not abused physically by the parent, they suffer psychologically from witnessing the violence between their parents. "Children from violent families can provide clinicians with detailed accounts of abusive incidents their parents never realized they had witnessed."[3]

B. Do you:

	Yes	No
(1) believe you can help or change your partner's abusive behavior?	____	____
(2) change yourself to make your partner less angry?	____	____
(3) find that not making your partner angry has become a large part of your life?	____	____
(4) stay with your partner out of fear?	____	____

[Section 16:3]

[1]National Council of Juvenile & Family Court Judges, Family Violence: A Guide to Research, in Courts and Communities: Confronting Violence in the Family 24 (1993).

[2]See Gerald T. Hotaling & Murray A. Straus, Intrafamily Violence and Crime Outside the Family, in Cessation of Family Violence: Deterrence and Dissuasion 315–76 (Lloyd Ohlin & Michael Tonry eds., 1989).

[3]National Council of Juvenile & Family Court Judges, Family Violence: A Guide to Research, in Courts and Communities: Confronting Violence in the Family 27 (1993) (citation omitted).

C. Does your partner:

	Yes	No
(1) tell you that you cannot do anything right?	____	____
(2) lose his/her temper easily and frequently?	____	____
(3) abuse alcohol or drugs?	____	____
(4) constantly need to prove himself/herself?	____	____
(5) have an erratic work attendance record?	____	____
(6) act jealous even when you go out with friends?	____	____

Did your partner:

(7) grow up in an abusive family?	____	____
(8) have a prison or jail record?	____	____
(9) blame his/her problems on you and others?	____	____

Sections (B) and (C) explore the psychological dynamics of the parties involved in the relationship. "Yes" answers to these questions indicate the risk factors specific to the victim and the perpetrator.

D. Have you:

	Yes	No
(1) called the police to intervene?	____	____
(2) Has anyone else called the police?	____	____
(3) sought assistance from a hospital or emergency room?	____	____
(4) done these things to or in front of the children?	____	____

Section (D) details the level of outside intervention. "Yes" answers to these questions indicate that independent documentation of specific incidents of violence directed at the victim may exist. "No" answers suggest that there is no other corroboration of the incidents.

The answers to these questions should assist the attorney in deciding how to best prepare the victim for court. If the attorney's only witness is the victim, thorough client preparation is essential in order to provide the court with competent, credible evidence of domestic violence and to communicate to the court the details surrounding the violence and the relevance to the best interest of the children.

An affirmative response to some or most of these questions should indicate that the client is in an abusive relationship and that legal intervention and protection may be necessary.

Even if the victim is still unwilling to admit that domestic violence is part of the relationship, the questionnaire should place the attorney on notice that abuse may be present. An attorney who has an accurate understanding of the psychological dynamics of battering is more likely to deduce violence in a relationship and exact an appropriate response to the questionnaire from the client.

§ 16:4 Identifying domestic violence—Client intake questionnaire—Perpetrator

Interviewing a perpetrator[1] of domestic violence, either by way of a deposition or during trial, involves asking questions that establish the pattern of violence while not permitting the perpetrator to shift the blame for the violence to the victim. For example, the victim's attorney should ask the perpetrator the following:

(1) What happens when you get angry?
(2) How do you react when you fight?
(3) Did you ever hit [the victim]?
(4) How do you and your spouse/partner handle finances?
(5) Do you mind if your spouse/partner works?
(6) Do you insist on accompanying your spouse/partner to his/her appointments?

It is extremely important to ask the perpetrator direct, candid questions. The batterer will try to take advantage of any vagueness on the attorney's part by giving ambiguous answers that avoid taking responsibility for the violence.[2]

The attorney must decide how to define domestic violence and actually define it for the perpetrator. The batterer may not consider that his/her actions rise to the level of domestic violence. "Tell the batterer that violence is any action or statement that makes the abused person feel afraid or coerces the abused person to do something that he or she does not want to do."[3]

There are no excuses for violence. Drugs, alcohol, and stress do not cause the violence.[4] If the stress is removed, the violence still exists. It is important that attorneys hold the perpetrator accountable for the choices he/she makes.

In fact, alcohol and drugs are the most frequently used defenses in criminal domestic violence cases and civil protection order cases despite the fact that the legal system long ago rejected alcohol as a legal excuse for the commission of a crime.

§ 16:5 Preventing domestic violence; safety plans and provisions

Because a victim of domestic violence is at an increased risk of being further assaulted or even killed when he/she attempts to leave the

[Section 16:4]

[1]See also Barbara Salomon, Guilty Until Proven Innocent: Representing the Alleged Abuser, 17 Fam. Advoc. 30 (1995).

[2]American Bar Assoc. Comm'n on Domestic Violence, The Client, in The Impact of Domestic Violence on Your Legal Practice, A Lawyer's Handbook 2-9 (1996).

[3]American Bar Assoc. Comm'n on Domestic Violence, The Client, in The Impact of Domestic Violence on Your Legal Practice, A Lawyer's Handbook 2-9 (1996) (citation omitted).

[4]National Council of Juvenile & Family Court Judges, Family Violence: A Guide to Research, in Courts and Communities: Confronting Violence in the Family 17 (1993).

batterer,[1] safety planning with the victim is crucial to protect the victim from further harm. A personalized safety plan is a document that addresses safety at home, at work, and at court and is designed to meet the needs of the victim given his/her particular circumstances. Many victim advocates and shelters for victims of domestic violence have written safety plans available for victims. Family law practitioners should consider preparing safety plans with victims that address their safety concerns.[2]

Q & A: What types of provisions should safety plans include?

Personalized safety plans should address safety at home, at work, and at court. Safety plans at home should include: (1) changing locks, adding deadbolts, and obtaining an apartment that is not on the first floor, (2) keeping a telephone in a safe place, (3) keeping in a hidden place a packed suitcase, containing: clothing; diapers; court papers; passports; identification items such as a social security card, birth certificate, driver's license, or welfare card; school and medical records; credit cards; checkbooks; insurance papers; bank books; address book; keys; and money for telephone calls, transportation, and one month's expenses, (3) making copies of protection orders and other court documents and serving copies of the orders on appropriate law enforcement agencies, schools, day care centers, and baby sitters, (4) showing neighbors a picture of the batterer and developing signals for neighbors and/or relatives to call the police, (5) obtaining an unlisted telephone number, and (6) developing an escape route.[3]

Safety plans at work should include (1) providing security guards with the license plate number, the type of vehicle, and a picture of the batterer, (2) developing signals with co-workers for them to call the police, (3) keeping a copy of protection orders at work, and (4) traveling to and from work with another person.[4]

Safety plans at court should include provisions for attorneys representing victims of domestic violence. The victim's attorney should consider arriving in court before the client or with the client so that the client is not alone with the batterer. In addition, the attorney should strategically place himself/herself between the client and the batterer and restrict contact between the client and batterer. Finally, the attorney should assess safety when the victim exits the courthouse.[5]

Safety plans are also available for children of the victim. Victim

---

[Section 16:5]

[1]See Ronet Bachman & Linda E. Saltzman, U.S. Dep't of Justice, National Crime Victimization Survey, Violence Against Women: Estimates from the Redesigned Survey 4 (1995); see also Barbara J. Hart, State Codes on Domestic Violence: Analysis, Commentary, and Recommendations, 43 Juv. & Fam. Ct. J. 34 (1992).

[2]See Text § 16:6, Ohio Domestic Violence Network—Strategies for dealing with domestic violence; safety planning; form.

[3]American Bar Assoc. Comm'n on Domestic Violence, Safety Planning, in The Impact of Domestic Violence on Your Legal Practice: A Lawyer's Handbook 2-11 to 2-14 (Deborah M. Goelman et al. eds., 1996).

[4]American Bar Assoc. Comm'n on Domestic Violence, Safety Planning, in The Impact of Domestic Violence on Your Legal Practice: A Lawyer's Handbook 2-14 (Deborah M. Goelman et al. eds., 1996).

[5]American Bar Assoc. Comm'n on Domestic Violence, Safety Planning, in The

advocates and domestic violence shelter advocates and counselors are in the best position to aid both parent and child in crafting appropriate child safety plans. Such plans should detail an escape route, include telephone numbers of family and friends or neighbors, and teach the child how to call 911 for assistance.

Impact of Domestic Violence on Your Legal Practice: A Lawyer's Handbook 2-14 (Deborah M. Goelman et al. eds., 1996).

§ 16:6 Ohio Domestic Violence Network—Strategies for dealing with domestic violence; safety planning; form[1]

OHIO DOMESTIC VIOLENCE NETWORK

◊ Strategies for Dealing With Domestic Violence:

Safety Planning

It may help you and your children stay safer if you develop a plan for your safety ahead of time. If you need some help working out your personal safety plan, you may want to ask a trusted friend, another survivor of abuse, or call a domestic violence hotline. The design of a safety plan is an ongoing process. It is a good idea to review it periodically, so you will be prepared to use it. Keep it in a safe place where your abuser is not likely to find it.

Name: ______________________

Date: ______________________

Review Dates: ______________________

____

____

◊ Personalized Safety Plan

The following steps represent my plan for increasing my safety and preparing in advance for the possibility of further violence. Although I do not have control over my partner's violence, I do have a choice about how to respond to my partner and how to best get myself and my children to safety.

STEP 1: SAFETY DURING A VIOLENT INCIDENT. Women cannot always avoid violent incidents. In order to increase safety, abused women may use a variety of strategies.

I can use some or all of the following strategies:

A. If I decide to leave, I will______________________. (Practice how to get out safely. What doors, windows, elevators, stairwells or fire escapes would you use?)

B. I can keep my purse and car keys ready and put them (place) ______________ ______________________in order to leave quickly.

C. I can tell ____________________ about the violence and request they call the police if they hear suspicious noises coming from my house.

D. I can teach my children how to call 911 or 0 to contact the police and the fire department.

E. I will use ____________________ as my code word with my children or my friends so they can call for help.

INFORMATION IS POWER! 31

[Section 16:6]

[1]This form is reprinted with permission from the Ohio Domestic Violence Network.

F. If I have to leave my home, I will go to ______________________.
(Decide this even if you don't think there will be a next time).
If I cannot go to the location above, then I can go to ______________
or ______________________.

G. I can also teach some of these strategies to some/all of my children.

H. When I expect we are going to have an argument, I will try to move to a space that is lowest risk, such as ______________________. (Try to avoid the bathroom, garage, kitchen, other rooms with weapons, or rooms without access to an outside door.)

I. I will use my judgment and intuition. If the situation is very serious, I can give my partner what is necessary to calm down. I have to protect myself until I/we are out of danger.

STEP 2: SAFETY WHEN PREPARING TO LEAVE. Abused women frequently leave the residence they share with the abusive partner. Leaving must be done strategically in order to increase safety. Abusers often strike back when they believe their partner is leaving the relationship.

I can use some or all of the following safety strategies:

A. I will leave money and an extra set of keys with ______________________ so I can leave quickly.

B. I will keep copies of important documents or keys at ______________.

C. I will open a savings account by (date) ______________ to increase my independence.
I will have statements of the account go to ______________________.

D. Other things I can do to increase my independence include: ______________
____
____
____
____

E. The domestic violence program's hotline number is ______________________.

F. I can keep change for phone calls on me at all times. I understand that if I use my telephone credit card, the next month's bill will tell my abuser those numbers I called after I left. To keep my telephone communications confidential, I must either use coins or I might get a friend to let me use their telephone credit card for a limited time when I first leave.

G. I will check with ______________ and ______________ to see who would be able to let me stay with them or lend me some money.

H. I can leave extra clothes with ______________________.

I. I will sit down and review my safety plan every ______________ in order to plan the safest way to leave the residence. ______________ (domestic violence advocate or friend) has agreed to help me review this plan.

J. I will rehearse my escape plan and, as appropriate, practice it with my children.

STEP 3: SAFETY IN MY OWN RESIDENCE. There are many things a woman can do to increase her safety in her own residence. It may be impossible to do everything at once, but safety measures can be added step by step.

Safety measures I can use include:

A. I can change the locks on my doors and windows as soon as possible.

B. I can replace wooden doors with steel/metal doors.

C. I can install security systems including additional locks, window bars, poles to wedge against doors, an electronic system, etc.
I can change the code on my old security system, or I can periodically change the code on my new one so my abuser does not learn it.

D. I can install a new garage door opener.

E. I can purchase rope ladders to be used to escape from second floor windows.

F. I can install smoke detectors and purchase fire extinguishers for each floor in my house/apartment.

G. I can install an outside lighting system that lights up when a person is coming close to my house.

H. I will teach my children how to use the telephone to make a collect call to me and to ____________________ (friend/minister/family/other) in the event that my partner abducts the children.

I. I will tell people who take care of my children who has permission to pick up my children and that my partner is not permitted to do so. The people I will inform about pick-up permission include:

School ____________________

Day Care Staff ____________________

Baby-sitter ____________________

Sunday School Teacher ____________________

Others ____________________

J. I can inform (neighbor) ____________________, (pastor) ____________________ and (friend) ____________________ that my partner no longer resides with me, and they should call the police if he is seen near my residence.

STEP 4: SAFETY WITH A PROTECTION ORDER. Many abusers obey protection orders, but one can never be sure which violent partner will obey and which will violate protection orders. I recognize that I may need to ask the police and the courts to enforce my protection order.

The following are some steps I can take to enforce my protection order:

A. I will keep my protection order ____________________ (location). (Always keep it on or near your person. If you change purses, that's the first thing that should go in).

B. I will give my protection order to police departments in the community where I work, in those communities where I usually visit family or friends, and in the community where I live.

C. I can call the local domestic violence program if I am not sure about B above or if I have some problem with my protection order.

D. I will inform my employer, my minister, my closest friend, and ____________ ____________ and ______________________ that I have a protection order in effect.

E. If my partner destroys my protection order, I can get another certified copy from the courthouse by going to the Clerk of Courts located at ______________.

F. If my partner violates the protection order, I can call the police and report a violation, contact my attorney, and/or advise the court of the violation.

G. If the police do not help, I can contact my advocate or attorney and file a complaint with the chief of police.

H. I can also file a criminal complaint with the prosecutor in the jurisdiction where the violation occurred. I can charge my abusive partner with a violation of the protection order and all the crimes committed in violating the order. I can call the domestic violence advocate to help me with this.

STEP 5: SAFETY ON THE JOB AND IN PUBLIC. Each abused woman must decide if and when she will tell others that her partner has abused her and that she may be at continued risk. Friends, family, and co-workers can help protect you. Each woman should carefully consider which people to ask to help her secure safety.

I might do any or all of the following:

A. I can inform my boss, the security supervisor and ______________________ at work of my situation.

B. I can ask ____________________ to help screen my phone calls at work.

C. When leaving work, I can ______________________________________.

D. When driving home, if problems occur I can ______________________.

E. If I use public transit, I can ____________________________________.

F. I can use different grocery stores and shopping malls to conduct my business, and I can shop at different hours than I did when living with my abuser.

G. I can also ____.

STEP 6: SAFETY AND DRUG OR ALCOHOL CONSUMPTION. Most people in this culture consume alcohol. Many consume mood-altering drugs. Much of this consumption is legal, and some is not. The legal ramifications of using illegal drugs can be very hard on an abused woman, may hurt her relationship with her children, and may put her at a

disadvantage in other legal actions with her abusive partner. Therefore, women should carefully consider the potential cost of the use of illegal drugs. But beyond this, the use of any alcohol or other drugs can reduce a woman's awareness and ability to act quickly to protect herself from her abuser. Furthermore, the abuser may use alcohol or drug consumption as an excuse to be violent. Therefore, in the context of drug or alcohol use, a woman needs to make specific safety plans.

If drug or alcohol consumption has occurred in my relationship with my abuser, I can enhance my safety with some or all of the following:

A. If I am going to consume, I can do so in a safe place and with people who understand the risk of violence and are committed to my safety.
B. I can also ____________________.
C. If my partner is consuming, I can ____________________.
D. I might also ____________________.
E. To safeguard my children, I might ____________________ and ____________________.

STEP 7: SAFETY AND MY EMOTIONAL HEALTH. The experience of being abused and verbally degraded by partners is usually exhausting and emotionally draining. The process of building a new life for myself takes much courage and incredible energy.

To conserve my emotional energy and resources and to avoid hard emotional times, I can do some of the following:

A. If I feel down and ready to return to a potentially abusive situation, I can ____________________.
B. When I have to communicate with my partner in person or by telephone, I can ____________________.
C. I can try to use "I can..." statements with myself and to be assertive with others.
D. I can tell myself "____________________" whenever I feel others are trying to control or abuse me.
E. I can read ____________________ to help me feel stronger.
F. I can call ____________________ and ____________________ as other resources to be of support to me.
G. Other things I can do to help me feel stronger are ____________________.
H. I can attend workshops and support groups at the domestic violence program, or I can ____________________ or ____________________ to gain support and strengthen my relationships with other people.

STEP 8: ITEMS TO TAKE WHEN LEAVING. When women leave partners, it is important to take certain items with them. Beyond this, women sometimes give an extra copy of papers and an extra set of clothing to a friend just in case they have to leave quickly.

Items with asterisks (*) on the following list are the most important to take. If there is time, the other items might be taken or stored outside the home.

These items might be best placed in one location so that if we have to leave in a hurry, I can grab them quickly.

When I leave, I should try to take:

- *• Identification
- *• Children's birth certificates
- *• My birth certificate
- *• Social security cards
- *• Abuser's social security and license plate numbers
- *• School and vaccination records
- *• Money
- *• Checkbook, ATM card
- *• Credit cards
- *• Keys--house/car/office
- *• Driver's license and registration
- *• Medications
- *• Work permits
- *• Green Card

- • Welfare identification
- • Passport(s)
- • Divorce/Custody Papers
- • Medical records--for all family members
- • Lease/rental agreement, house deed, mortgage payment book
- • Bank books
- • Insurance papers
- • Small objects I could sell
- • Address book
- • Pictures
- • Jewelry
- • Children's favorite toys and/or blankets
- • Items of special sentimental value

TELEPHONE NUMBERS I NEED TO KNOW:

Police department (home) ____________________

Police department (school) ____________________

Police department (work) ____________________

Domestic Violence Hotline ____________________

Legal Advocate ____________________

County registry of protection orders ____________________

Work number ____________________

Supervisor's home number ____________________

Spiritual Advisor ____________________

Other ____________________

§ 16:7 Ohio Domestic Violence Network—Escape plan for children; form[1]

OHIO DOMESTIC VIOLENCE NETWORK

◊ Escape Plan for Children

You have the right to feel safe. Home can sometimes be a place that is not safe because someone is using their body and/or words to hurt the people in your home. This is a safety plan for you to follow when someone in your home becomes violent, and you feel scared.

My Escape Plan

I will know how to call 911 or 0 for help.

I can tell a family member or a friend.

I can talk with my schoolteacher or counselor.

I can save money for a phone call at a pay phone.

If I have a house key, I will keep it in a safe place.

I will keep a few of my favorite things together in case we have to leave suddenly.

INFORMATION IS POWER!

[Section 16:7]

[1]This form is reprinted with permission from the Ohio Domestic Violence Network.

§ 16:8 Documenting evidence of domestic violence

Because domestic violence is most often an act between intimate partners, without witnesses, the abuse may be difficult to document.[1] In some cases, the secrecy of the domestic violence may be so encompassing that no one other than the parties (and their children) has any knowledge of the violence.[2] The violence may have occurred behind closed doors so that no medical records or police reports are available.[3] Family and friends may deny that domestic violence exists because they were shielded from the abuse, or clothing or dark glasses may have hidden the victim's bruises. In such cases, the isolation surrounding the domestic violence can compound its detrimental effect. Sometimes, it is difficult for the victim's attorney to even link the occurrence of the domestic violence to the legal elements of the case.

In deciding how best to present a domestic violence case to the court, the victim's attorney must consider both the pattern and history of abuse in the relationship.[4] A history of domestic violence in the relationship demonstrates a significant probability of continued abuse in the future. A history of abuse in the relationship also demonstrates why a particular victim may have a subjective belief at the time of the presenting incident that the perpetrator may cause imminent serious physical harm. The frequency and severity of the domestic violence often describes a pattern that may be useful evidence. In fact, the more serious the prior abuse, the more serious the future abusive conduct is likely to be.

§ 16:9 Victim Testimony

A domestic violence victim may either present testimony by narrative or by being asked relevant questions, specific to time and place. The court will attempt to determine the credibility of a victim by observing demeanor and the ability to recollect the incidents of abuse with specificity.

Q & A: How is evidence of domestic violence presented to the court?

The victim is often in the best position to demonstrate both the current abusive act and a history of domestic violence within the relationship.[1] A history of domestic violence is best shown simply by asking the victim to recount several incidents of abuse, specific to

---

[Section 16:8]

[1]See Marie DeSanctis, Bridging the Gap between the Rules of Evidence & Justice for Victims of Domestic Violence, 8 Yale J. L. & Feminism 359 (1996); see also Judge David M. Gersten, Evidentiary Trends in Domestic Violence, 72 Fla. Bar J. 65 (1998); see also Tom Lininger, Evidentiary Issues in Federal Prosecutions of Violence Against Women, 36 Ind. L. Rev. 687 (2003).

[2]See Mildred D. Pagelow, Justice for Victims of Spouse Abuse in Divorce and Child Custody Cases, 8 Violence and Victims 1 (1993).

[3]Felton v. Felton, 79 Ohio St. 3d 34, 44, 1997-Ohio-302, 679 N.E.2d 672 (1997).

[4]Judith Armatta, Getting Beyond the Law's Complicity in Intimate Violence Against Women, 33 Willamette L. Rev. 773, 817 (1997).

[Section 16:9]

[1]See Hoffman v. Hoffman, 1998 WL 469876 (Ohio Ct. App. 9th Dist. Summit County 1998).

both time and place.[2] These incidents may be of actual or attempted physical abuse, threats to harm or kill, or stalking behavior.[3] If believed, these acts, singularly and collectively, may demonstrate a lengthy pattern of abuse, insult, threat, or verbal intimidation. Attorneys must be cautioned, however, that one or two isolated or minor incidents of domestic violence may not provide the court with sufficient evidence of a pattern or history of abuse.[4]

It must be stressed to the court that a victim's testimony should not be ignored or discounted simply because there is no other independent corroboration. In fact, the Ohio Supreme Court, in *Felton v. Felton*,[5] noted that "[o]ften the only evidence of domestic violence is the testimony of the victim."[6] In fact, the *Felton* Court clearly indicated that the statute does not require any corroboration of the petitioner's testimony as long as the preponderance of the evidence test is met.[7]

Similarly, in *Hoffman v. Hoffman*,[8] the victim obtained a civil protection order. The defendant appealed on the ground that the plaintiff's evidence was not reliable because there was no corroborating evidence. The court relied on the legal reasoning of *Felton* to uphold the trial court's decision, noting that the victim's testimony is often the only evidence on which to rely as justification for the issuance of a civil protection order.

Where a threat is the alleged act of domestic violence, the petitioner must present some evidence that she/he believed the respondent would cause her/him imminent serious physical harm at the time the incident took place.[9] This can be shown by either the victim's statements or from other evidence in which it could be inferred that the

---

[2]See State v. Collie, 108 Ohio App. 3d 580, 671 N.E.2d 338 (1st Dist. Hamilton County 1996).

[3]See RC 3113.31(A)(1) for acts which constitute domestic violence.

[4]See Simmons v. Simmons, 649 So. 2d 799 (La. Ct. App. 2d Cir. 1995); In re Marriage of Forbes, 570 N.W.2d 757 (Iowa 1997).

[5]Felton v. Felton, 79 Ohio St. 3d 34, 44, 1997-Ohio-302, 679 N.E.2d 672 (1997).

[6]See A.M. v. S.M., 2018-Ohio-247, 2018 WL 542357 (Ohio Ct. App. 9th Dist. Summit County 2018).

[7]Felton v. Felton, 79 Ohio St. 3d 34, 1997-Ohio-302, 679 N.E.2d 672 (1997); see also Yoel v. Yoel, 1998 WL 1051779 (Ohio Ct. App. 11th Dist. Lake County 1998); Cunningham v. Morgan, 2004-Ohio-6007, 2004 WL 2578873 (Ohio Ct. App. 8th Dist. Cuyahoga County 2004); Terrell v. Terrell, 2003-Ohio-150, 2003 WL 125013 (Ohio Ct. App. 8th Dist. Cuyahoga County 2003); Kabeer v. Purakaloth, 2006-Ohio-3584, 2006 WL 1932333 (Ohio Ct. App. 10th Dist. Franklin County 2006); Crawford v. Brandon, 2014-Ohio-3659, 2014 WL 4180286 (Ohio Ct. App. 12th Dist. Butler County 2014) (pointing out that Ohio Supreme Court, in *Felton*, rejected the contention that corroborating eyewitness testimony or medical evidence must be presented to establish domestic violence by a preponderance of the evidence.). But see M.R. v. T.R., 2016-Ohio-3493, 2016 WL 3384940 (Ohio Ct. App. 9th Dist. Wayne County 2016) (Court noted that wife's testimony was not sufficient to support her petition because of contradictory evidence and without corroboration of her injuries, either through the police or another and because she never informed the police officer of the acts of physical abuse and because she never called any of the other officers as witnesses and because she waited over 10 days to file the petition, it was arguable that she filed the petition as a way to secure custody in the underlying divorce case).

[8]Hoffman v. Hoffman, 1998 WL 469876 (Ohio Ct. App. 9th Dist. Summit County 1998).

[9]See Eichenberger v. Eichenberger, 82 Ohio App. 3d 809, 613 N.E.2d 678 (10th

victim believed the respondent would cause imminent serious physical harm.[10]

Q & A: The victim gave conflicting accounts of the cause of her injuries. Does that make her a less credible witness?

It depends on the facts of the case. For example, in *State v. Pruiett*,[11] appellant asserted that his conviction for domestic violence should be overturned because his girlfriend gave conflicting accounts of the cause of her injuries.

The victim informed the police that appellant had caused her eye injury and had burned her the month before. She then told the police that she had informed the hospital personnel that her nephew had accidentally kicked her causing her eye injury. She also admitted that she did not come forward sooner out of fear of appellant. However, she had informed other relatives of the cause of her injuries who also testified.

The Summit County Court of Appeals affirmed the conviction and noted that [w]e are not in a position to speculate on the reasons for which the victim may not have sought medical treatment for the burns immediately, but a reasonable juror could find D.H.s reasons for providing different explanations for her injuries credible and probable. We do note that many times in domestic violence and assault cases, the victims are hesitant to act against their attacker, out of fear.[12]

§ 16:10 Independent documentation of domestic violence[1]

Sometimes, a victim's testimony may be corroborated by extrinsic, independent documentation. Police reports, medical records, photographs, 911 calls and even certified copies of criminal convictions may provide a court with sufficient documentation of the abuse suffered. It must be cautioned, however, that the history and pattern of domestic

---

Dist. Franklin County 1992); Ankenbruck v. Ankenbruck, 2000 WL 1804360 (Ohio Ct. App. 11th Dist. Trumbull County 2000).

[10]See also State v. Brown, 2003-Ohio-710, 2003 WL 352460 (Ohio Ct. App. 12th Dist. Butler County 2003), quoting Hamilton v. Cameron, 121 Ohio App. 3d 445, 700 N.E.2d 336 (12th Dist. Butler County 1997).

[11]State v. Pruiett, 2004-Ohio-4321, 2004 WL 1837036 (Ohio Ct. App. 9th Dist. Summit County 2004). See also Kabeer v. Purakaloth, 2006-Ohio-3584, 2006 WL 1932333 (Ohio Ct. App. 10th Dist. Franklin County 2006); Hunter v. Hunter, 2006-Ohio-6307, 2006 WL 3462139 (Ohio Ct. App. 2d Dist. Montgomery County 2006) (any factual inconsistency regarding the exact time of the confrontation between the parties is a trivial fact and has no bearing upon the truth of Mrs. Hunter's assertions nor the reasonableness of her fear); Johnson v. Auls, 2008-Ohio-6123, 2008 WL 5049751, *5 (Ohio Ct. App. 10th Dist. Franklin County 2008) (stressing that a petitioner's testimony alone can be sufficient to meet the preponderance of the evidence standard and that to the extent that limited inconsistencies in the evidence were resolved in favor of appellee does not mandate a reversal of the trial court judgment in favor of the appellee).

[12]State v. Pruiett, 2004-Ohio-4321, 2004 WL 1837036, *4 (Ohio Ct. App. 9th Dist. Summit County 2004); citing, City of Cleveland Heights v. Reed, 1995 WL 601126 (Ohio Ct. App. 8th Dist. Cuyahoga County 1995).

[Section 16:10]

[1]Deirdre Bialo-Padin, JD and Richard R. Peterson, PHD, A Race against Time: Evidence Collection in Domestic Violence Cases, 18 Domestic Violence Report 49, 51 (April/May 2013).

violence against a specific victim may not be adequately reflected in the records or reports.

Q & A: How difficult is it to obtain independent documentation?

Unfortunately, it is unusual for victims to have adequate extrinsic documentation of the domestic violence inflicted upon them.[2] Sometimes, victims do not report the domestic violence incident to the police or prosecutor's office. Other times, they do not seek medical assistance.[3] "Generally, the victim will not photograph bruises or share these episodes of abuse with others."[4]

On the other hand, the victim may have gone to the police and reported the incident and/or sought medical assistance. It should also be pointed out to the court that records and reports do not tell the whole story. The absence of any notation of known or suspected abuse in the victim's medical record or the absence of a police report does not necessarily mean that the abuse did not occur. It may mean only that the victim-patient did not disclose the abuse and the hospital personnel failed to ask about domestic violence. It may mean only that the police failed to make a report or that the victim failed to request that a report of the incident be made. Only when these documents are needed as evidence in a subsequent court hearing does the victim discover that no police report of the incident was made and that the medical records do not mention the victim's injuries or that the injuries were the result of domestic violence.

Sometimes, the medical records and police reports fail to accurately detail either the domestic violence incident or the perpetrator. If the records or reports do not accurately reflect the nature of the incident, it may be difficult to use them to demonstrate a pattern or history of domestic violence.

Occasionally, the victim may specifically mislead the recorder by stating that he/she fell down the stairs, took sedatives, cut himself/herself with a knife, or other similar excuses for the injuries. In these instances, it is likely that the victim will finally admit the truth in court and testify that the "fall down the stairs" was actually committed by the victim's partner.

Q & A: How does counsel view this apparent lack of documentation?

---

[2]See Mildred D. Pagelow, Justice for Victims of Spouse Abuse in Divorce and Child Custody Cases, 8 Violence and Victims 1, 71 (1993); see also Rielinger v. Rielinger, 2009-Ohio-1236, 2009 WL 714185 (Ohio Ct. App. 8th Dist. Cuyahoga County 2009) (finding that appellant failed to demonstrate that documentation is required for a finding of domestic violence).

[3]See State v. Gatson, 2009-Ohio-120, 2009 WL 94596 (Ohio Ct. App. 8th Dist. Cuyahoga County 2009) (noting that the fact that appellee did not seek medical treatment at a hospital for the injuries did not negate the unlawful conduct of appellant). See also State v. Trefney, 2012-Ohio-869, 2012 WL 691630, *4 (Ohio Ct. App. 11th Dist. Portage County 2012) (pointing out that there is no case law authority requiring the state to produce expert medical testimony to establish causation in a domestic violence matter, citing State v. McClure, 1993 WL 211663 (Ohio Ct. App. 2d Dist. Greene County 1993) and stating that "[i]n many domestic violence cases, medical evidence is absent, and often the only evidence is the testimony of the victim"). In fact, the essential element in the statute is that the state must prove, beyond a reasonable doubt, that defendant caused the physical harm.

[4]Felton v. Felton, 79 Ohio St. 3d 34, 44, 1997-Ohio-302, 679 N.E.2d 672 (1997).

Opposing counsel may take advantage of this misinformation and be quick to use it against the victim. If there is no documentation by way of a police report or medical records, then the abuser's attorney will claim that the abuse did not really occur. Moreover, the abuser's attorney may comment that the alleged violence could not have been as bad as the victim claims since the victim did not leave the relationship earlier or since there was no medical intervention. Further, if the information provided in the report or record is different from that provided by the victim in court, counsel may attempt to impeach the witness and contend that he/she is not to be believed.

Family law practitioners should educate the court that the experiences surrounding the victimization caused by domestic violence encourage victim responses such as failing to divulge the incident and/or the source of the domestic violence. A court should not penalize a victim who only begins to articulate the incidents of abuse suffered at the hands of the batterer in later court proceedings.[5]

§ 16:11 Legal responsibilities of law enforcement and medical personnel

In December 1994, the Ohio legislature enacted 1994 House Bill 335 to address some of the problems characteristic of existing police response to victims of domestic violence. Prior to the enactment of this legislation, law enforcement agencies generally failed to record incidents of domestic violence in their police reports. A great lack of detail permeated those reports that even considered the issue. This failure reflected an inadequacy in the way domestic violence calls were being handled. Additionally, medical intervention specific to the needs of domestic violence victims did not exist.

Q & A: What are the legal responsibilities of law enforcement agencies regarding the documentation of domestic violence?

In an effort to reinforce the seriousness of the crime of domestic violence and to provide documentation and substantiation of a history of abuse for a victim's future, law enforcement agencies are now required to direct their officers to prepare mandatory incident reports each time they are contacted regarding an incident of domestic violence or a violation of a civil or criminal protection order, whether or not an arrest is made.[1] Law enforcement officers must also separate the parties when responding to a call and conduct separate interviews.[2] They are required to take a written statement from the victim that indicates the frequency and severity of any prior incidents of physical abuse of the victim by the alleged offender, the number of times the victim has called the police for assistance and the disposition of the calls, if known.[3]

Each police report shall document the officer's observations of the

---

[5]See Myra Sun & Elizabeth Thomas, Custody Litigation on Behalf of Battered Women, 21 Clearinghouse Rev. 563 (1987).

[Section 16:11]

[1]See RC 2935.032(C), RC 2935.032(D).

[2]RC 2935.032(A)(2)(c).

[3]RC 2935.032(A)(2)(c).

parties, any visible injuries of the victim and the alleged offender, any weapons at the scene, the actions of the alleged offender, any statements made by the victim or witnesses and any other significant facts or circumstances.[4]

Q & A: What are the legal responsibilities of medical personnel regarding documenting incidents of domestic violence?

Likewise, medical personnel were directed to adopt new procedures.[5] RC 2921.22(F)(1) now requires doctors, nurses, psychologists, social workers, and counselors who know or have reasonable cause to believe that their patient or client has been the victim of domestic violence, as defined in RC 3113.31, to note on the patient's or client's record known or suspected abuse and the basis for the belief.[6] To comply with the statute, medical personnel need only indicate that the patient's injuries are inconsistent with the explanation given and that the person suspects that the cause of the injury is or may be domestic violence.[7]

In an effort to address the medical profession's failure to adequately identify and evaluate domestic violence within the family, the statute specifically requires that hospitals adopt protocols "for conducting an interview with the patient, for conducting one or more interviews, separate and apart from the interview with the patient, with any family or household member present, and for creating whenever possible a photographic record of the patient's injuries" in situations where a doctor, intern, resident, or nurse knows or has reasonable cause to believe that the patient has been the victim of domestic violence.[8]

Q & A: Whether there is a specific duty not to discharge a patient to the care of the suspected abuser?

At least one Indiana appellate court reversed summary judgment in favor of the hospital and considered whether a hospital has a statutory duty of care to report suspected abuse of "endangered adults" to law enforcement or a social services agency. In *McSwane v. Bloomington Hospital and Health Care System*,[9] the parties were married for 1 year. He took her to Bloomington hospital to be treated for lacerations

---

[4]RC 2935.032(D).

[5]See also Improving the Health Care Response to Domestic Violence: A Resource Manual for Health Care Providers (Carol Warshaw & Anne Ganley eds., Fam. Violence Prevention Fund 1995); Wendy G. Goldberg & Michael C. Tomlane-Vich, Domestic Violence Victims in the Emergency Room, 251 JAMA 3259 (1984).

[6]See James T.R. Jones, Battered Spouse's Damage Actions Against Non-Reporting Physicians, 45 De Paul L. Rev. 191 (1996). But see Ariella Hyman et al., Laws Mandating Reporting of Domestic Violence: Do They Promote Patient Well-Being? 273 JAMA 1781 (1987).

[7]See Jennifer Robertson, Symposium on Reconceptualizing Violence Against Women by Intimate Partners: Critical Issues, Domestic Violence & Health Care: An Ongoing Dilemma, 58 Alb. L. Rev. 1193 (1995); see also Council on Scientific Affairs Am. Med. Ass'n., Violence Against Women: Relevance for Medical Practitioners, 267 JAMA 3184 (1992). See State v. Pruiett, 2004-Ohio-4321, 2004 WL 1837036, *4 (Ohio Ct. App. 9th Dist. Summit County 2004) (victim did not seek immediate medical treatment for burns and did not mention burns or their cause to medical personnel; court noted that many times in domestic violence and assault cases, the victims are hesitant to act against their attacker out of fear).

[8]RC 3727.08.

[9]McSwane v. Bloomington Hosp. and Healthcare System, 882 N.E.2d 244 (Ind.

she said she received from a fall from a horse. The nurse noted that he wouldn't let anyone get too close to Malia. He answered for her. Hospital policy required that suspicions of domestic violence be conveyed to attending physicians. Concern mounted when a nurse noted she wasn't dirty. She then pointed at a domestic violence brochure and Malia nodded her head, suggesting she was a victim of domestic violence. Subsequently, her mother told the staff that he had beaten her with a poker. Security was contacted. Malia advised them she wanted to leave. Security accompanied her out of hospital, although she was advised she could remain in hospital if she wanted. She was discharged to her husband who killed her on their way home. Her mother then sued the hospital and the doctor who treated Malia.

The question raised in the *McSwane* case was whether there is a specific duty not to discharge a patient to the care of the suspected abuser. In a case of first impression, the appellate court held ". . . that such a duty might sometimes be included in a hospital's general duty of care toward a patient, or in the alternative might arise by virtue of statutory requirements to report certain abuse of certain endangered adults."[10] The court also concluded that 1) hospitals have a duty to exercise reasonable care in rendering hospital services including a duty to safeguard the welfare of patients from harm inflicted by third persons; and 2) hospitals have a duty to protect patients from external circumstances peculiarly within the hospital's control. The issue of first impression was whether that duty may also extend to the discharge of a person into the custody of a person who allegedly inflicted the injuries that necessitated the patient's hospitalization. The court also determined that "a hospital's duty of reasonable care requires consideration of evidence that the patient is a victim of domestic abuse."[11]

In his dissent, the Chief Justice disagreed with the majority holding as being too broad and based on flawed reasoning. He concluded that the hospital had no duty to prevent the patient from leaving with her husband.

The Supreme Court of Indiana vacated the opinion of the court of appeals in *McSwane v. Bloomington Hosp. and Healthcare System*,[12] and affirmed the summary judgment granted to the hospital. While the Supreme Court agreed that "a hospital's duty of care to a patient who presents observable signs of domestic abuse includes some reasonable measures to address the patient's risk," it concluded that Bloomington did meet its duty. The attempt to ask the patient about the abuse outside the earshot of the abuser, the security examinations of the abuser, facilitating the telephone calls to law enforcement and

---

Ct. App. 2008), transfer granted, opinion vacated, IN RAP 58(A), 898 N.E.2d 1217 (Ind. 2008) and opinion vacated, 916 N.E.2d 906 (Ind. 2009).

[10]McSwane v. Bloomington Hosp. and Healthcare System, 882 N.E.2d 244, 249 (Ind. Ct. App. 2008), transfer granted, opinion vacated, IN RAP 58(A), 898 N.E.2d 1217 (Ind. 2008) and opinion vacated, 916 N.E.2d 906 (Ind. 2009).

[11]McSwane v. Bloomington Hosp. and Healthcare System, 882 N.E.2d 244, 252 (Ind. Ct. App. 2008), transfer granted, opinion vacated, IN RAP 58(A), 898 N.E.2d 1217 (Ind. 2008) and opinion vacated, 916 N.E.2d 906 (Ind. 2009).

[12]McSwane v. Bloomington Hosp. and Healthcare System, 916 N.E.2d 906 (Ind. 2009).

declarations that the patient did not have to leave the hospital with her abuser were all actions indicating that Bloomington had exercised its duty of care to the patient.[13] The Supreme Court held that a hospital's duty of care of a patient does not extend to off-premises activities; that Bloomington Hospital did not breach its duty of care and that the patient in this case was contributorily negligent as a matter of law.[14]

The dissent found that a breach of the hospital's duty of care was a matter for the trial court to decide and not subject to summary judgment. Further, such a determination could not be made by the Supreme Court as a matter of law. That the emergency room charge nurse did not inform the treating physician of the suspected abuse is an indication that the emergency room staff failed to follow the hospital's adopted domestic violence policies which requires such communication from staff to the treating physician. "This concern is amplified because the attending physician was able to spend time alone with Malia before she was heavily medicated and while the "husband" was out of the exam room. Thus the doctor, had he been properly informed, could have asked appropriate questions regarding domestic abuse during that period, which could have given the patient a reasonable opportunity to seek refuge."[15]

As to the issue of the patient's contributory negligence, the dissent also found that the determination could not be made by a summary disposition. In that the patient was highly medicated, that she underwent surgery to repair her injuries and that she was discharged within 90 minutes after her surgery, ". . . it leaves open the likelihood that she had not fully recovered from the general anesthesia and was thus mentally and/or physically incapable of reasonable decision making or self-protection, when allowed to leave the hospital."[16] The dissenting opinion indicates its opposition to the majority holding and finds that the trial court should be reversed.

Unlike Indiana's endangered adult statute, an Ohio victim of domestic violence is not commonly considered an endangered adult. Ohio's statutes require mandatory reporting to Adult Protective Services of certain abused, neglected or exploited adults[17] and children.[18] Ohio statutes require the reporting of certain injuries suspected to be caused by offenses of violence to law enforcement[19] and the mandatory recording of known or suspected abuse by medical personnel, social workers and counselors.[20]

All Ohio hospitals have been required to adopt protocols dealing with domestic violence.[21] What is clear from the decision is that hospitals should review and modify those policies periodically, if needed.

---

[13]*Bloomington at 910.*

[14]*Bloomington* at Synopsis.

[15]*Bloomington at 912.*

[16]*Bloomington at 913.*

[17]RC 5101.61.

[18]RC 2151.421.

[19]RC 2921.22(B).

[20]RC 2921.22(F)(1).

[21]RC 3727.08.

§ 16:12 Evidentiary considerations involving independent documentation

Q & A: Are witness accounts helpful in establishing a history or pattern of domestic violence?

Absolutely. The testimony of other witnesses may help establish that the defendant did in fact abuse the victim.[1] Police testimony is especially useful to corroborate the victim's testimony regarding the extent of the injuries[2] and, in the absence of the victim's testimony, to show that the victim suffered physical injury. Witness testimony may also document a victim's condition and demeanor at the time of the incident.[3]

Sometimes, eyewitness testimony may prove useful in the identification of the individual who committed the act of abuse against the victim. For example, it may prove to be crucial where the abuser testifies that he/she did not strike the victim or that he/she was not at home at the time of the incident. It may also be useful to identify the weapon used and tie the weapon to the perpetrator.[4]

Sometimes the only testimony is from someone who has only witnessed the consequences of the altercation, such as bruises or broken bones, not the altercation itself.[5] Even this type of corroboration is sufficient for the issuance of a civil protection order.[6]

Q & A: What is the value of a police report?[7]

Police reports often provide the court with the most reliable evi-

[Section 16:12]

[1]See, e.g., Cleveland Hts. v. Brewer, 109 Ohio App. 3d 838, 673 N.E.2d 215 (8th Dist. Cuyahoga County 1996); see also Evid.R. 701; State v. King, 2000 WL 330048 (Ohio Ct. App. 5th Dist. Stark County 2000); State v. Clifford, 2002-Ohio-4531, 2002 WL 2010639 (Ohio Ct. App. 9th Dist. Summit County 2002) (holding that evidence supported by finding that statements made by witness to a police officer where witness was present during an altercation and personally observed argument, was an excited utterance and exception to hearsay rules).

[2]See State v. Warren, 106 Ohio App. 3d 753, 667 N.E.2d 68 (1st Dist. Hamilton County 1995). See also State v. Trefney, 2012-Ohio-869, 2012 WL 691630 (Ohio Ct. App. 11th Dist. Portage County 2012) (indicating that the deputy's opinion testimony as an officer about the cause of the injuries to victim was proper under Evid. R. 701; Evid. R. 702.).

[3]See Cleveland Hts. v. Brewer, 109 Ohio App. 3d 838, 673 N.E.2d 215 (8th Dist. Cuyahoga County 1996); Siouffi v. Siouffi, 1998 WL 879255 (Ohio Ct. App. 2d Dist. Montgomery County 1998); see also State v. Taylor, 2003-Ohio-2025, 2003 WL 1916787 (Ohio Ct. App. 9th Dist. Summit County 2003).

[4]See State v. Taylor, 2003-Ohio-2025, 2003 WL 1916787 (Ohio Ct. App. 9th Dist. Summit County 2003).

[5]See, for example, State v. Hunt, 2007-Ohio-3281, 2007 WL 1847660 (Ohio Ct. App. 10th Dist. Franklin County 2007) (witnessing bruises and marks shortly after incident provides circumstantial evidence that abuse occurred); see also Rosine v. Rosine, 2010-Ohio-613, 2010 WL 598642 (Ohio Ct. App. 7th Dist. Mahoning County 2010) (determining that a witness's testimony of what he/she actually observed (a bruise) is not hearsay); Eckstein v. Colian, 2012-Ohio-4038, 2012 WL 3834883 (Ohio Ct. App. 7th Dist. Columbiana County 2012) (testimony from witnesses describing the side effects of a concussion from the incident).

[6]Hoffman v. Hoffman, 1998 WL 469876 (Ohio Ct. App. 9th Dist. Summit County 1998).

[7]See also Text § 14:6, Law enforcement policies and procedures.

dence documenting the abuse. It must be cautioned, however, that the history and pattern of abuse may not be adequately reflected in these reports.[8]

Police officers who respond to the scene of a domestic violence incident are in the best position to collect reliable evidence regarding the violence. The evidence must be documented in a mandatory incident report that the officer must prepare for each incident of domestic violence or violation of either a civil or criminal protection order.[9]

In order to collect the most reliable evidence, the General Assembly has directed that law enforcement agencies comply with certain mandates. For example, the officer must separate the parties in order to conduct separate interviews in separate locations.[10] A written statement must be taken from the victim that includes the frequency and severity of any prior incidents of physical abuse of the victim by the offender and the number of times the victim has called the police and the disposition of those calls, if known.[11]

Additionally the mandatory incident report must contain the following information:

(1) the officer's observations of the victim and the alleged offender;
(2) any visible injuries of the victim or alleged offender;
(3) any weapons found at the scene;
(4) the actions of the alleged offender;
(5) any statements made by the victim or witnesses; and
(6) any other significant facts and circumstances.[12]

There is no doubt that the incident report aids the victim by providing reliable documentation of the abuse. Because the report often documents a history of abuse, it may be useful in demonstrating that the victim suffers from a pattern of abuse typical of the battering experience.

A well written report serves to preserve evidence of the victim's physical and emotional condition including details such as torn clothing; physical injuries; marks and redness; the victim's emotional condition including, crying shaking, fear, anger, etc.; and the condition of the incident scene, such as disarray of furniture, damaged property, holes in the wall, blood or other physical evidence. It may also document the condition and demeanor of the suspect and may document any spontaneous declarations or excited utterances of either the victim, witnesses, or the suspect.[13]

A written police report is admitted into evidence under the business records exception to the hearsay rule.[14] The testimony of the victim

[8]See Text § 14:4, Determination of primary physical aggressor, for a further discussion.

[9]See RC 2935.032(C), RC 2935.032(D).

[10]See RC 2935.032(A)(2)(b).

[11]See RC 2935.032(A)(2)(c).

[12]See RC 2935.032(D).

[13]See Evid.R. 803(2), Evid.R. 803(3).

[14]See Evid.R. 803(6), Evid.R. 803(8), Evid.R. 901(B)(7), Evid.R. 902(4). But see

should precede any report, if possible, and the records custodian for the law enforcement agency (or the officer who wrote the report) is required to authenticate the report.

Q & A: How is the testimony of the officer used in court?[15]

While an incident report establishes a complete picture of the crime scene if used in conjunction with the officer's testimony at a hearing or trial, it also offers substantial evidence to support the issuance of a civil protection order or a criminal conviction even without the testimony of the victim.[16] The police officer who responded to the scene or who investigated the incident, wrote the report and arrested the respondent can provide admissible, probative, and relevant evidence to the court.[17] The report validates the officer's testimony and preserves evidence for later use in court.

Police officer testimony may provide documentation regarding the nature and extent of the victim's injuries.[18] Such testimony may corroborate the victim's testimony that he/she believed the abuser's actions would cause imminent serious physical harm[19] or the victim's emotional condition at the time of the incident.[20]

Sometimes, a victim may not want to testify at the hearing or the court does not find the victim credible because of lapses[21] or inconsis-

State v. Conkle, 2003-Ohio-2410, 2003 WL 21060822 (Ohio Ct. App. 5th Dist. Knox County 2003) (state attempted to argue that officer's report was a narrative of the incident, that it was not hearsay because the investigative report was used to provide information only).

[15]State v. Clark, 2018-Ohio-521, ¶ 30, 2018 WL 798385 (Ohio Ct. App. 6th Dist. Lucas County 2018) (police detective testified that victims of domestic violence fail to call the police about the abusive behavior or call 911 when injured; stay with their perpetrators for many years and return to the relationship after leaving and lied about the cause of injuries).

[16]See State v. Lynch, 1999 WL 11244 (Ohio Ct. App. 9th Dist. Lorain County 1999). But see State v. Wright, 1998 WL 542697, *4 (Ohio Ct. App. 10th Dist. Franklin County 1998) (defendant argued that officer testimony was improper to show whether defendant violated protection order; officer was merely attempting to describe a police procedure as applied to the circumstances of the case); State v. Lewis, 1998 WL 310747 (Ohio Ct. App. 2d Dist. Montgomery County 1998) (police testimony was unable to demonstrate current cohabitation or cohabitation within the year prior to the offense).

[17]See State v. Lee, 73 Ohio Misc. 2d 9, 657 N.E.2d 604 (Mun. Ct. 1995); see also State v. Seitz, 2003-Ohio-1879, 2003 WL 1871039 (Ohio Ct. App. 11th Dist. Portage County 2003).

[18]See State v. Warren, 106 Ohio App. 3d 753, 667 N.E.2d 68 (1st Dist. Hamilton County 1995); see also State v. Mount, 2000 WL 1028511 (Ohio Ct. App. 5th Dist. Stark County 2000); State v. Trefney, 2012-Ohio-869, 2012 WL 691630 (Ohio Ct. App. 11th Dist. Portage County 2012).

[19]See Siouffi v. Siouffi, 1998 WL 879255 (Ohio Ct. App. 2d Dist. Montgomery County 1998).

[20]Siouffi v. Siouffi, 1998 WL 879255 (Ohio Ct. App. 2d Dist. Montgomery County 1998); see also Sitton v. Sitton, 1999 WL 55717 (Ohio Ct. App. 2d Dist. Montgomery County 1999).

[21]See Cleveland v. Thomas, 2003-Ohio-30, 2003 WL 60981 (Ohio Ct. App. 8th Dist. Cuyahoga County 2003) (where an elderly female testified at trial that she did not recall precisely how she had fallen. She had previously told an officer who had responded to the 9-1-1 call that her daughter had pushed her down. The officer testified as to the victim's demeanor and as to the victim's statement regarding the

tencies in his/her story.[22] In this instance, the officer's testimony may be crucial to prove that domestic violence occurred,[23] or another material element of the offense of domestic violence.[24]

Sometimes, a police officer's observations are used to support the issuance of the protection order, especially when the incident is a "he said/she said." For example, in *Cable v. Cable,*[25] appellant hit appellee in the face with his fist breaking her glasses. After striking her, he drove away. She called the police approximately an hour after the incident, after she called her mother and another. When the police arrived, the responding officer observed that the area around appellee's eye was red and beginning to swell and had what appeared to be knuckle indentations.[26] She told the police about the argument and that he had struck her twice. Subsequently, she sought a CPO.

At the full hearing, appellant denied striking her or being present at her residence. Both parties testified as to the approximate timeline. In fact, appellant testified, as did his girlfriend's mother, that appellant was at the girlfriend's house to watch her children at the time alleged by appellee. Appellant argued that the timeline he presented demonstrated that he was not at appellee's residence when she alleged he struck her and therefore, the incident never happened.[27]

The trial court determined that appellee's testimony regarding the

---

perpetrator and the nature of the act of violence made at the time of the incident).

[22]See Angela Corsilles, Note, No-Drop Policies in the Prosecution of Domestic Violence Cases: Guarantee to Action or Dangerous Solution? 63 Fordham L. Rev. 853 (1994); Joel Shapiro, Let the Truth Be Told: Proposed Hearsay Exceptions to Admit Domestic Violence Victims' Out of Court Statements as Substantive Evidence, 11 Colum. J. Gender & L. 1 (2002); see also State v. Payne, 2000 WL 1010969 (Ohio Ct. App. 8th Dist. Cuyahoga County 2000); State v. Coleman, 1999 WL 958479 (Ohio Ct. App. 2d Dist. Montgomery County 1999); State v. Washington, 2001 WL 460888 (Ohio Ct. App. 10th Dist. Franklin County 2001); State v. Brown, 1998 WL 227182 (Ohio Ct. App. 3d Dist. Allen County 1998) (both neighbor and police testimony as well as hospital records of injury sufficient to sustain conviction). But see State v. Travis, 165 Ohio App. 3d 626, 2006-Ohio-787, 847 N.E.2d 1237 (2d Dist. Montgomery County 2006) (trial court's error in permitting police officer to comment on credibility of alleged victim prejudiced defendant and warranted reversal of his conviction for domestic violence).

[23]See State v. Justice, 92 Ohio App. 3d 740, 637 N.E.2d 85 (9th Dist. Wayne County 1994); see also Cleveland Hts. v. Brewer, 109 Ohio App. 3d 838, 673 N.E.2d 215 (8th Dist. Cuyahoga County 1996). But see State v. Attaway, 111 Ohio App. 3d 488, 676 N.E.2d 600 (1st Dist. Hamilton County 1996); State v. Hermann, 1999 WL 744178 (Ohio Ct. App. 5th Dist. Stark County 1999); City of Akron v. Taylor, 2001-Ohio-1947, 2001 WL 1626941 (Ohio Ct. App. 9th Dist. Summit County 2001). But see M.R. v. T.R., 2016-Ohio-3493, 2016 WL 3384940 (Ohio Ct. App. 9th Dist. Wayne County 2016) (where petitioner failed to inform responding officer about the physical abuse and officer thought the altercation was only verbal; at hearing, the incident was construed as not having occurred and provided the appellate court with a record that indicated insufficient evidence that respondent knowingly caused physical harm).

[24]See State v. Cox, 2001-Ohio-3213, 2001 WL 301429 (Ohio Ct. App. 7th Dist. Belmont County 2001) (officer testified as to the parties' relationship). But see State v. Lewis, 1998 WL 310747 (Ohio Ct. App. 2d Dist. Montgomery County 1998).

[25]Cable v. Cable, 2015-Ohio-4291, 2015 WL 6109531 (Ohio Ct. App. 2d Dist. Darke County 2015).

[26]Cable v. Cable, 2015-Ohio-4291, 2015 WL 6109531, ¶ 4 (Ohio Ct. App. 2d Dist. Darke County 2015).

[27]Cable v. Cable, 2015-Ohio-4291, 2015 WL 6109531, ¶ 7 (Ohio Ct. App. 2d Dist.

events was more credible. Particularly, the trial court properly considered the testimony of the responding officer that appellee's injuries did not appear self-inflicted. He also testified that, "based on his investigation, Kyle would have had time to travel to Tawni's residence and strike her after he left the restaurant but before he arrived at Melissa's house to watch her children. When he interviewed Kyle, Deputy Joseph observed that he did not have any scrapes or bruises on his hands. Deputy Joseph testified, however, that it is not uncommon for a perpetrator to have no marks on his hands after striking someone. Additionally, Deputy Joseph testified that in his experience, it was not at all uncommon for a victim of domestic violence to wait hours, or even days, before involving the police and making a report."[28] He also testified that the injuries observed on appellee were not self inflicted.

The appellate court found that there was sufficient credible evidence to support finding that appellant committed domestic violence, thus overruling his objection.

Q & A: Can the officer's testimony be used when the victim recants her testimony in court?[29]

A police officer's testimony may be admitted under the "excited utterance" exception to the hearsay rule when the officer testifies as to the out-of-court statements of the victim.[30] This is often the case when a victim recants her testimony in court. For example, in *State v. Louk*,[31] the Delaware Court of Appeals affirmed the trial court decision to admit the deputy's testimony as to statements made by the victim at the scene of a domestic violence incident. As the deputy arrived within three to four minutes of receiving the call and the victim was holding the telephone when he arrived at the scene, the court found "the facts regarding the complained of testimony as being close in time and immediately after the incident to qualify as an excited utterance."[32] The court of appeals noted that "[t]he controlling factor in determining whether a statement is an excited utterance is whether the statement was made under such circumstances as would reason-

Darke County 2015).

[28]Cable v. Cable, 2015-Ohio-4291, 2015 WL 6109531, ¶ 8 (Ohio Ct. App. 2d Dist. Darke County 2015).

[29]See also Text § 16:21, "Other acts" testimony; Text § 14:6, Law enforcement policies and procedures; Text § 16:13, Hearsay exceptions; *Crawford* concerns. Text § 16:14; Text § 16:22; State v. Payne, 2000 WL 1010969 (Ohio Ct. App. 8th Dist. Cuyahoga County 2000); State v. Mack, 2015-Ohio-5214, 2015 WL 8607454 (Ohio Ct. App. 11th Dist. Ashtabula County 2015); State v. Tracy, 2016-Ohio-4652, 2016 WL 3522546 (Ohio Ct. App. 7th Dist. Belmont County 2016).

[30]See State v. Whitfield, 2002-Ohio-5984, 2002 WL 31431840 (Ohio Ct. App. 1st Dist. Hamilton County 2002) (police officer's hearsay testimony relating domestic violence victim's statements made upon arrival of officer at scene was excited utterance).

[31]State v. Louk, 2002-Ohio-988, 2002 WL 358639 (Ohio Ct. App. 5th Dist. Delaware County 2002).

[32]State v. Louk, 2002-Ohio-988, 2002 WL 358639, *2 (Ohio Ct. App. 5th Dist. Delaware County 2002); see also City of Shaker Heights v. Al-Gureshi, 1998 WL 183818 (Ohio Ct. App. 8th Dist. Cuyahoga County 1998); see also State v. Manzell, 2007-Ohio-4076, 2007 WL 2283550 (Ohio Ct. App. 5th Dist. Stark County 2007).

ably show that it resulted from impulse rather than reason and reflection."[33]

Additionally, police officers may provide expert testimony. The testimony may be used to explain that some persons who file domestic violence complaints later recant their claims. In *State v. Wright*,[34] the appellate court affirmed the trial court's decision and supported its finding that the complaining victim's prior recantations were the products of fear and pressure from the defendant and his family.

Sometimes, police officers may even provide opinion testimony. In *State v. Plott,*[35] appellant argued that the State improperly introduced expert testimony which the appellate court determined involved victims' recantation of their statements. After examining the record, the appellate court found that "there is no indication that Lieutenant Windsor was offering an expert opinion on this issue and thus we cannot find it was erroneous. Lieutenant Windsor was simply offering an opinion based on his nineteen years of experience as a police officer and his interactions with domestic violence victims as to why he was not surprised that Mele was uncooperative with the investigation."[36] Additionally, based on his interactions with victims of domestic violence and because he was not offering an ultimate opinion as to whether domestic violence did or did not happen, he was able to provide an opinion as to why victims recant.[37]

Q & A: Is the officer's testimony ever used in lieu of the complaining witness?[38]

Yes. One of the peculiar realities of the domestic violence case is that, because of the nature of the relationship, some victims do not want their intimate partners prosecuted. During the 1990's, many states, including Ohio, passed preferred or mandatory arrest policies. Next, statutes were amended to permit prosecutors the ability to continue with the prosecution, despite the wishes of the victim to drop the case or the failure to cooperate. In Ohio, prosecutors were directed to consider all facts and circumstances relevant to the offense, including the statements and observations of the police officer that responded to the incident and other witnesses to the incident. Evidence-based prosecution signals a shift away from the focus on victim testimony.

---

[33]State v. Louk, 2002-Ohio-988, 2002 WL 358639, *2 (Ohio Ct. App. 5th Dist. Delaware County 2002), citing State v. Smith, 34 Ohio App. 3d 180, 190, 517 N.E.2d 933 (5th Dist. Richland County 1986).

[34]State v. Wright, 2008-Ohio-3678, 2008 WL 2833649 (Ohio Ct. App. 8th Dist. Cuyahoga County 2008).

[35]State v. Plott, 2017-Ohio-38, 80 N.E.3d 1108 (Ohio Ct. App. 3d Dist. Seneca County 2017), appeal not allowed, 150 Ohio St. 3d 1452, 2017-Ohio-8136, 83 N.E.3d 938 (2017).

[36]State v. Plott, 2017-Ohio-38, ¶ 92, 80 N.E.3d 1108 (Ohio Ct. App. 3d Dist. Seneca County 2017), appeal not allowed, 150 Ohio St. 3d 1452, 2017-Ohio-8136, 83 N.E.3d 938 (2017).

[37]State v. Plott, 2017-Ohio-38, ¶ 93, 80 N.E.3d 1108 (Ohio Ct. App. 3d Dist. Seneca County 2017), appeal not allowed, 150 Ohio St. 3d 1452, 2017-Ohio-8136, 83 N.E.3d 938 (2017).

[38]See also Text § 16:13 regarding *Crawford* concerns. See also Text §§ 16:14, 16:22.

As this approach has become the norm in some jurisdictions and the ideal in others, advocates and prosecutors have spent less time attempting to convince unwilling and reluctant victims.[39] Rather, police officers often testify about their observations and the statements made by victims.[40] 911 tapes and police reports often corroborate that testimony. More and more, convictions result without the testimony of the victim. Clearly, proceeding without the victim is far better than forcing these witnesses to testify.[41]

Q & A: What can medical evidence demonstrate to the court?

Proof of physical injury or of serious physical injury is not required in order to prevail in a domestic violence action.[42] Medical evidence is, therefore, not necessary. Nonetheless, medical evidence may be admissible[43] to prove the nature of the injury sustained by the victim. It may also be useful in corroborating the victim's testimony that abuse occurred.[44] Medical evidence may support an inference that the pain was intense. It may corroborate the victim's testimony as to the manner in which an injury was inflicted.[45] It may even corroborate or establish that the victim was subjected to a pattern of physical abuse over a period of time. For example, documentation of scars or unhealed fractures may be sufficient evidence to demonstrate a pattern of physical abuse.

Medical records include records from an emergency room, office or clinic appointment, counselling or social work session, and surgery or operative reports. All related documents, such as radiology, lab reports or pathology reports, may be part of a record.

Because it is the business of hospitals to diagnose and treat patients' injuries, entries made in medical records which are relevant to diagnosis and treatment qualify for admission under the business records

[39]See State v. Justice, 92 Ohio App. 3d 740, 637 N.E.2d 85 (9th Dist. Wayne County 1994); State v. Lee, 73 Ohio Misc. 2d 9, 657 N.E.2d 604 (Mun. Ct. 1995); but see Text § 16:13, Hearsay exceptions; *Crawford* concerns.

[40]State v. Stephens, 2008-Ohio-890, 2008 WL 583789 (Ohio Ct. App. 9th Dist. Summit County 2008).

[41]See also Text § 16:22.

[42]See State v. Nielsen, 66 Ohio App. 3d 609, 585 N.E.2d 906 (6th Dist. Huron County 1990); see also Text § 8:4, Statutory elements of domestic violence under RC 3113.31(A)(1)(b); State v. Warfield, 2003-Ohio-2366, 2003 WL 21054785 (Ohio Ct. App. 11th Dist. Trumbull County 2003) (affirming trial court decision noting that the fact that there were no visible injuries or that no one else witnessed the assault does not somehow negate her testimony; police failed to observe any visible injuries).

[43]See Evid.R. 803(6). But see State v. Henderson, 1999 WL 689736 (Ohio Ct. App. 11th Dist. Trumbull County 1999).

[44]See State v. Patterson, 1998 WL 655388 (Ohio Ct. App. 10th Dist. Franklin County 1998); State v. Zembower, 1998 WL 156858 (Ohio Ct. App. 11th Dist. Lake County 1998); see also State v. Taylor, 2003-Ohio-2025, 2003 WL 1916787 (Ohio Ct. App. 9th Dist. Summit County 2003) (Emergency room physician testified that victim was upset and crying and that she stated that her boyfriend struck her with a pitch fork and that her injuries could have been inflicted by a pitch fork.); State v. Dartt, 2008-Ohio-373, 2008 WL 303135 (Ohio Ct. App. 6th Dist. Lucas County 2008).

[45]See State v. Rohrer, 1998 WL 400768 (Ohio Ct. App. 5th Dist. Fairfield County 1998).

exception to the hearsay rule.[46] These records may also be used to show the serious nature of a victim's injuries as evidenced by a lengthy course of rehabilitation.[47]

As discussed earlier, medical personnel, including doctors, nurses, psychologists, counselors, and social workers, are required to document known or suspected abuse in a patient's medical record.[48] In effect, those professionals are required to determine whether the patient's explanation of the injuries is consistent with their clinical observations. Additionally, medical personnel are required to create a photographic record of the patient's injuries in situations where a doctor, intern, resident, or nurse knows or has reasonable cause to believe that the patient has been the victim of domestic violence.[49] Medical staff should be subpoenaed to testify about their own observations where needed.[50] Testimony may be useful in this instance to corroborate a victim's story of how the abuse occurred.

Medical records may be admitted into evidence[51] in lieu of a physician's testimony,[52] and anything contained in those records about which the physician could testify may be received into evidence. For example, the physician's observations of the patient's physical and emotional condition (as noted in the patient's chart), the medical opinion as to the cause of the injury and as germane to treatment, and the diagnosis and prognosis may be admitted into evidence.[53] However, all records must be authenticated through a records custodian.[54]

Because medical personnel are often the first people that victims of domestic violence go to for help, it is important that these professionals do the following:

(1) interview the patient alone;[55]
(2) report any unusual circumstances surrounding the visit;
(3) record events in as much detail as possible;

---

[46]Evid.R. 803(4), Evid.R. 803(6); see also State v. Grooms, 1998 WL 487087 (Ohio Ct. App. 9th Dist. Summit County 1998); State v. Henderson, 1999 WL 689736 (Ohio Ct. App. 11th Dist. Trumbull County 1999).

[47]See RC 2901.01(A)(3) for the definition of "physical harm"; see also RC 2901.01(A)(5) for the definition of "serious physical harm."

[48]RC 2921.22(F)(1).

[49]RC 3727.08.

[50]See Evid.R. 702 for qualifications of an expert; see also State v. Kraus, 2007-Ohio-6027, 2007 WL 3348426 (Ohio Ct. App. 12th Dist. Warren County 2007).

[51]See Evid.R. 803(6).

[52]See Evid.R. 702 for the qualifications of an expert witness.

[53]Evid.R. 803(4); but see, e.g., State v. Todd, 24 Kan. App. 2d 796, 954 P.2d 1 (1998); State v. Daniels, 2004-Ohio-828, 2004 WL 344128 (Ohio Ct. App. 9th Dist. Lorain County 2004) (where evidence that appellant was the person who caused the victim's injuries was admitted into evidence in contravention of Evid.R. 803; defendant failed to cite Evid.R. 803 as the basis of his objection, thus the trial court did not err when the evidence was admitted).

[54]See Evid.R. 901(B)(10), Evid.R. 902; but see State v. Caudill, 2007-Ohio-1557, 2008 WL 852626 (Ohio Ct. App. 6th Dist. Wood County 2008) (hospital record self authenticating in accordance with RC 2317.422).

[55]RC 3727.08.

(4) document all statements made by the victim as these statements may be admitted into evidence as exceptions to the hearsay rule;[56]

(5) describe in detail the patient's physical injuries, emotional condition, and behavior;

(6) supplement the written description with photographs or life-like drawings;

(7) save bloodied or torn clothing; and

(8) note prognosis and future appointments.

Q & A: Why should photographs be used as evidence of domestic violence?

Photographs, like eyewitness description of the injuries, may provide corroboration of the degree of injury and even that an injury occurred.[57] Photographic evidence of the victim's injuries is properly admissible if it tends to prove or disprove a material fact, to illustrate or articulate other relevant evidence, or to corroborate or disprove other evidence in the case.[58]

So long as a photograph is properly authenticated, it may be admitted into evidence.[59] "A photograph is not objectionable if it is properly identified, is relevant and competent, and is an accurate representation of the scene which it portrays. A proper foundation is required on which there must be testimony that the photograph is a fair and accurate representation of that which it represents."[60] Victims may authenticate photographs taken by their friends, family, or the police by nothing that the photographs were taken after the altercation with the perpetrator, by whom, and that they represent a fair and accurate depiction of the appearance of the victim after the alleged fight.[61] However, it should be noted that the court has the discretion to

---

[56]Evid.R. 803(3); see also Text § 5:14 to Text § 5:21, Case preparation—Hearsay exceptions; see State v. Daniels, 2004-Ohio-828, 2004 WL 344128 (Ohio Ct. App. 9th Dist. Lorain County 2004).

[57]See, e.g., State v. Parks, 2000 WL 221968 (Ohio Ct. App. 5th Dist. Licking County 2000); see also State v. Ward, 2002-Ohio-3779, 2002 WL 1724242 (Ohio Ct. App. 10th Dist. Franklin County 2002) (where photographs taken by officer were used to reinforce victim's testimony that domestic violence had occurred).

[58]Evid.R. 1001, Evid.R. 1002; see also State v. Poling, 1998 WL 255574 (Ohio Ct. App. 3d Dist. Shelby County 1998); State v. Slavens, 1999 WL 4895 (Ohio Ct. App. 4th Dist. Vinton County 1998).

[59]See Evid.R. 901, Evid.R. 1002; see also State v. Poling, 1998 WL 255574 (Ohio Ct. App. 3d Dist. Shelby County 1998); State v. Slavens, 1999 WL 4895 (Ohio Ct. App. 4th Dist. Vinton County 1998); State v. S.M., 2015-Ohio-1916, 2015 WL 2376057 (Ohio Ct. App. 10th Dist. Franklin County 2015) (Evid. R. 901(A) does not require time-stamping on a photograph for it to be admissible).

[60]Kubiszak v. Rini's Supermarket, 77 Ohio App. 3d 679, 603 N.E.2d 308 (8th Dist. Cuyahoga County 1991).

[61]See State v. Clemence, 2003-Ohio-3660, 2003 WL 21545745 (Ohio Ct. App. 8th Dist. Cuyahoga County 2003). See also State v. Peine, 1982 WL 5837 (Ohio Ct. App. 11th Dist. Lake County 1982) (discussing Evid. R. 901(B)(1)); Croone v. Arif, 2014-Ohio-5546, 2014 WL 7186677, ¶ 26 (Ohio Ct. App. 8th Dist. Cuyahoga County 2014) (it is unnecessary to show who took the picture or when it was taken so long as testimony is provided that the photo is a fair and accurate representation of what it represents); State v. Miller, 2015-Ohio-956, 2015 WL 1142955, ¶ 22 (Ohio Ct. App. 11th Dist. Trumbull County 2015) (noting the difference between admissibility of the photos and credibility of the testimony of the foundational witness; finding that ap-

exclude photographs that may arouse emotions or unfairly prejudice the defendant[62] or where the photographs are demonstrated to be merely cumulative.[63]

Generally, photographs will demonstrate the severity of the victim's injuries[64] and may assist the court in determining the degree of physical injury actually inflicted as well as the defendant's intent.[65] For example, photographs depicting the nature and location of the injuries on the victim's body may demonstrate the abuser's intent to cause serious physical harm rather than a lesser degree of harm.[66] Obviously, this is an important consideration in a domestic violence case where the degree of physical harm is either an element of the offense or is crucial to the presentation of the case. Without any other corroboration, photographs that document serious physical harm are likely to provide credible and reliable evidence that domestic violence occurred.

Photographs may also corroborate a victim's testimony of experiencing protracted pain. For example, a series of photographs that show the existence of the injury over time or one photograph depicting the victim's emotional trauma is sufficient. They may also be useful in aiding the court in understanding the medical evidence presented. Sometimes photographs may even aid the court in determining which party was the primary physical aggressor.[67] Photographs taken by the police that document the suspect's injuries or lack of injuries may help determine the primary physical aggressor.

Sometimes, photographs may corroborate testimony of a history of injury that may be relevant to show a pattern of abuse. For example, scars from prior injuries may enable an attorney to document past abusive acts.

Finally, photographs may be used to support the state's case where the victim is reluctant or unwilling to testify or where the victim minimizes the abuse to the court.[68] For example, it is not unusual for a victim of domestic violence to claim that he/she received the injuries from a fall rather than from an abusive act. Photographs taken at or

---

pellant's challenges to the photos go to the weight rather that the admissibility of the photos and court was free to disbelieve the testimony of the foundational witness; proper foundation for authentication was laid by testimony of victim that she and her mother took the photos that accurately depicted the condition of her back and arm on the morning after she was injured).

[62]See State v. Flowers, 2000 WL 296081 (Ohio Ct. App. 9th Dist. Summit County 2000).

[63]See Croone v. Arif, 2014-Ohio-5546, 2014 WL 7186677 (Ohio Ct. App. 8th Dist. Cuyahoga County 2014).

[64]See City of Cleveland v. Botson, 1991 WL 95069 (Ohio Ct. App. 8th Dist. Cuyahoga County 1991).

[65]See State v. Slavens, 1999 WL 4895 (Ohio Ct. App. 4th Dist. Vinton County 1998).

[66]See RC 2901.01(A)(3), RC 2901.01(A)(5).

[67]See Text § 14:3, Arrest of the perpetrator. But see State v. Wood, 1998 WL 468813 (Ohio Ct. App. 12th Dist. Brown County 1998).

[68]See, e.g., State v. Ragland, 2001 WL 888753 (Ohio Ct. App. 9th Dist. Summit County 2001); State v. Hughes, 2015-Ohio-1173, 2015 WL 1403276 (Ohio Ct. App. 5th Dist. Tuscarawas County 2015).

around the time of the incident may be useful in demonstrating otherwise.

Victims' attorneys must understand, however, that many photographs may be needed to demonstrate the nature of the injury. It is often the case that the victim does not bruise initially and the medical evidence may be insufficient to detail the extent of the injuries inflicted. A photograph taken immediately after the incident may not explicitly demonstrate the significance of the injury. Several photographs taken at various intervals after the incident may be needed to demonstrate the severity of the abuse inflicted.

In addition to photographs of the victim's injuries, photographs of the crime scene may also be helpful in demonstrating that an altercation occurred. Where the victim testifies that domestic violence occurred, photographs showing overturned furniture or holes in the wall may add credibility to that testimony.

Q & A: How are photographs authenticated?

According to Evid. R. 901(A), "[t]he requirement of authentication or identification as a condition precedent to admissibility is satisfied by evidence sufficient to support a finding that the matter in question is what the proponent claims."[69] Evidence of verification of the date and time taken is not necessary for admissibility.[70] Time-stamping on a photograph is not necessary for it to be admissible. Rather, a photograph is admissible if it is shown to be an accurate representation of what it purports to represent.[71] "Thus it is unnecessary to show who took the photograph or when it was taken, provided that there is testimony that the photograph is a fair and accurate representation of what it represents."[72]

Q & A: Can one spouse testify against the other?

Under Evid. R. 601(B)(1), a spouse is a competent witness to testify against the other spouse who is charged with a crime, only when the crime is against the testifying spouse or a child of either spouse or the testifying spouse elects to testify.

---

[69]State v. S.M., 2015-Ohio-1916, 2015 WL 2376057, ¶ 24 (Ohio Ct. App. 10th Dist. Franklin County 2015).

[70]State v. S.M., 2015-Ohio-1916, 2015 WL 2376057, ¶ 24 (Ohio Ct. App. 10th Dist. Franklin County 2015).

[71]State v. S.M., 2015-Ohio-1916, 2015 WL 2376057, ¶ 24 (Ohio Ct. App. 10th Dist. Franklin County 2015), citing State v. Hannah, 54 Ohio St. 2d 84, 88, 8 Ohio Op. 3d 84, 374 N.E.2d 1359 (1978).

[72]State v. S.M., 2015-Ohio-1916, 2015 WL 2376057, ¶ 24 (Ohio Ct. App. 10th Dist. Franklin County 2015); see also Croone v. Arif, 2014-Ohio-5546, 2014 WL 7186677, ¶ 26 (Ohio Ct. App. 8th Dist. Cuyahoga County 2014) (it is unnecessary to show who took the picture or when it was taken so long as testimony is provided that the photo is a fair and accurate representation of what it represents); State v. Miller, 2015-Ohio-956, 2015 WL 1142955, ¶ 22 (Ohio Ct. App. 11th Dist. Trumbull County 2015) (noting the difference between admissibility of the photos and credibility of the testimony of the foundational witness; finding that appellant's challenges to the photos go to the weight rather that the admissibility of the photos and court was free to disbelieve the testimony of the foundational witness; proper foundation for authentication was laid by testimony of victim that she and her mother took the photos that accurately depicted the condition of her back and arm on the morning after she was injured. ¶ 23); State v. Garrison, 2018-Ohio-463, 2018 WL 704129 (Ohio Ct. App. 5th Dist. Muskingum County 2018), appeal denied, 153 Ohio St. 3d 1429, 2018-Ohio-2418, 100 N.E.3d 445 (2018).

For example, in *State v. Kelly*,[73] appellant argued on appeal that the judgment convicting him of domestic violence should be overturned because the trial court permitted an incompetent witness to testify. In this case, appellant was charged with domestic violence against his 10 year old stepson.

In his appeal, appellant claimed that his wife was incompetent to testify because the requirements of Evid.R. 601(B)(2) were not met and permitting her to testify constituted plain error. Because the trial court had failed to instruct the wife regarding spousal competency or make a finding on the record that she had voluntarily elected to testify, she was incompetent to testify. "Pursuant to the Evid. R. 601(B)(1) exception, Wanda was a competent witness because the crime charged was against her son, i.e., 'a crime against * * * a child of either spouse.' Thus it was not necessary, pursuant to Evid. R. 601(B)(2), for the trial court to instruct Wanda of her right to choose not to testify or for Wanda to elect to testify on the record. See, eg., *State v. Wilson*, 3d Dist. Putnam No. 12-05-20, 2006-Ohio 2000, ¶ 10 (emphasis sic.) (because the crime charged * * * was against Wilson's daughter, [his wife] was unquestionably *competent* to testify"). Accordingly, the admission of Wanda's testimony does not amount to plain error."[74]

Q & A: May children testify about the abuse inflicted by one parent against the other?[75]

The children are often the only witnesses to abuse that occurs at home.[76] Should the court require additional or corroborative evidence of the domestic violence, a victim's attorney can file a motion to permit a child to testify. Most courts require that the attorney file such motion. Many courts will also appoint a guardian ad litem for the child who will be there when the court interviews the child.[77] Before the child is permitted to testify, the trier of fact will seek to qualify the child as competent to testify.[78]

---

[73]State v. Kelly, 2013-Ohio-4755, 2013 WL 5783710 (Ohio Ct. App. 11th Dist. Ashtabula County 2013).

[74]State v. Kelly, 2013-Ohio-4755, 2013 WL 5783710, ¶ 16 (Ohio Ct. App. 11th Dist. Ashtabula County 2013).

[75]See generally, Leigh Goodmark, Family Violence Litigation: Protecting the Child and Preparing Your Case, Vol 21, No. 11 Child Law Practice 170; see also Leigh Goodmark, From Property to Personhood: What the Legal System Should Do for Children in Family Violence Cases, 102 W. Va. L. Rev. 237 (1999).

[76]But see, e.g., In re Morrill, 147 N.H. 116, 784 A.2d 690 (2001) (New Hampshire Supreme Court excluded testimony of couple's children in proceedings on wife's petition for domestic violence restraining order as cumulative of their handwritten statements and held that such action did not violate husband's right to due process where husband was given opportunity to cross-examine other witnesses and examine children's handwritten statements given to police and read by court.).

[77]See, e.g., RC 3109.04(B)(2).

[78]See RC 2317.01; Evid.R. 601(A); see also State v. Frazier, 61 Ohio St. 3d 247, 574 N.E.2d 483 (1991); State v. Wallace, 37 Ohio St. 3d 87, 524 N.E.2d 466 (1988) (regarding determination of competency of child who was under ten at time of event about which child is to testify); State v. Williams, 2000 WL 1161997 (Ohio Ct. App. 1st Dist. Hamilton County 2000); In re Pollitt, 2000 WL 1528669 (Ohio Ct. App. 4th Dist. Adams County 2000); Brandt v. Brandt, 2006-Ohio-883, 2006 WL 456716 (Ohio Ct. App. 3d Dist. Auglaize County 2006) (discussing competency of child to testify at CPO

For example, in *Brandt v. Brandt*,[79] the trial court granted the CPO but refused to permit the child to testify at the hearing. Appellant argued that the ruling materially prejudiced him by preventing him from presenting testimony of the parties' minor child and by not conducting an in camera interview with the child.[80]

The appellate court first considered Evid.R. 601(A) which states that every person is competent to be a witness except children under the age of ten. The court then relied on the Supreme Court of Ohio's decision in *State v. Frazier*,[81] which held that it is the duty of the trial court to conduct a voir dire examination of a child less than ten years of age to determine the child's competency. In determining whether a child under the age of ten is competent to testify, the trial court must consider (1) the child's ability to perceive accurate impressions of fact or to observe acts about which he or she will testify, (2) the child's ability to recall those impressions or observations, (3) the child's ability to convey what was observed, (4) the child's knowledge of truth and falsity, and (5) the child's appreciation of responsibility to be truthful.[82]

In the instant case, the trial court failed to conduct the preliminary examination as to competency of the child. Rather, the court relied on a public policy determination to exclude the testimony of a minor child. The Third District Court of Appeals then held that "where the child is the only eyewitness to the central incident of the hearing besides the parties themselves, it seems to us that the need for calling the child to testify is sufficiently imperative to either request a competency hearing or permit the testimony."[83]

The victim's attorney should instruct the court of the standard of proof in civil domestic violence cases. A preponderance of the evidence

---

hearing); Ross v. Ross, 2006-Ohio-5274, 2006 WL 2846327 (Ohio Ct. App. 4th Dist. Ross County 2006) (holding that where the child did not testify at trial and the child's statements were admitted through the mother, grandmother, babysitter and social worker, the trial court need not determine the child's competency); L.N.Y v. Breh, 2016-Ohio-966, 2016 WL 936854 (Ohio Ct. App. 2d Dist. Montgomery County 2016).

[79]Brandt v. Brandt, 2006-Ohio-883, 2006 WL 456716 (Ohio Ct. App. 3d Dist. Auglaize County 2006).

[80]Brandt v. Brandt, 2006-Ohio-883, 2006 WL 456716, *2 (Ohio Ct. App. 3d Dist. Auglaize County 2006).

[81]State v. Frazier, 61 Ohio St. 3d 247, 250-51, 574 N.E.2d 483 (1991). See also Jones v. Jones, 2011-Ohio-4393, 2011 WL 3847339 (Ohio Ct. App. 9th Dist. Summit County 2011) (children's testimony was proffered, but because the testimony of both children failed to address any fact in issue and was not relevant to the determination of the issuance of a CPO, it was not admitted into evidence and therefore trial court was not obligated to conduct a voir dire examination of the children to determine whether they were competent to testify); State v. Rivera, 2013-Ohio-3244, 2013 WL 3877817 (Ohio Ct. App. 8th Dist. Cuyahoga County 2013) (finding that five year old child competent to testify where he could not remember how to spell his name, the city in which he resided or the alphabet, but he knew the difference between a lie and the truth, his age and birthday, the color of his home and the judge's robe as well as being able to recall details about his birthday parties); Evid. R. 601.

[82]Brandt v. Brandt, 2006-Ohio-883, 2006 WL 456716, *2 (Ohio Ct. App. 3d Dist. Auglaize County 2006), citing State v. Frazier, 61 Ohio St. 3d 247, 251, 574 N.E.2d 483 (1991). See also Prado v. Elsayed, 2012-Ohio-290, 2012 WL 259573 (Ohio Ct. App. 2d Dist. Montgomery County 2012).

[83]Brandt v. Brandt, 2006-Ohio-883, 2006 WL 456716, *3 (Ohio Ct. App. 3d Dist. Auglaize County 2006).

standard requires nothing more than the testimony of the victim.[84] However, where the court requires more and the victim has no other independent or extrinsic evidence or documentation, child witnesses may be crucial to the case.

A child witness's prior statements made to the police as part of a 911 recording, for example, may be admissible under the excited utterance exception to the hearsay rule.[85] In that case, the child may not need to testify in court.

Generally, there is a trend toward more liberal requirements for the "excited utterance" exception when applied to young children, even where the child is the victim of domestic violence[86] and not merely a witness to the violence inflicted on one parent by the other.[87]

Q & A: Before admitting into evidence a statement made by a child that qualifies as an excited utterance exception to hearsay, must the court determine competency?

Not according to *Ross v. Ross*.[88] In this case, appellant argued that before admitting into evidence the statements made by his child which qualified as excited utterances, the court was required to determine the child's competency. Since the court failed to determine competency, the statements should have been inadmissible.

Appellant relied on the Ohio Supreme Court's decision in *State v. Said*[89] for the proposition that a child must be found competent at the time the statement was made before the statement can qualify under any hearsay exception.[90] However, the Ross County appellate court relied on the holding in *State v. Street* which relied on the reasoning

---

[84]See Felton v. Felton, 79 Ohio St. 3d 34, 1997-Ohio-302, 679 N.E.2d 672 (1997).

[85]See Evid.R. 803(2); see also State v. Lee, 73 Ohio Misc. 2d 9, 657 N.E.2d 604 (Mun. Ct. 1995); Buchanan v. Buchanan, 1999 WL 619049, *2 (Ohio Ct. App. 12th Dist. Clermont County 1999) (finding the statement "Mommy hit me in the teeth" to be admissible as an excited utterance and finding the fact that the child made the statement to her father later when she returned home to be inconsequential in light of the liberal requirements for the hearsay exception when applied to young children).

[86]See Ross v. Ross, 2006-Ohio-5274, 2006 WL 2846327, *4 (Ohio Ct. App. 4th Dist. Ross County 2006) (appellant argued that it was error for the trial court to terminate father's parenting time and grant a CPO based on four hearsay statements made by the child and entered into evidence through the child's mother); see also Evid.R. 807 (providing that "an out of court statement made by a child who is under 12 years of age at the time of trial or hearing, describing any sexual act performed by, with or on the child * * * is not excluded as hearsay under Evid.R. 802 if certain conditions apply.").

[87]See Buchanan v. Buchanan, 1999 WL 619049 (Ohio Ct. App. 12th Dist. Clermont County 1999). But see Rush v. Rush, 1999 WL 1044482 (Ohio Ct. App. 8th Dist. Cuyahoga County 1999) (statements made by a child recounting acts of abuse are inadmissible hearsay that do not fall within the excited utterance exception when repeated by an intake worker from the Department of Human Services).

[88]Ross v. Ross, 2006-Ohio-5274, 2006 WL 2846327 (Ohio Ct. App. 4th Dist. Ross County 2006).

[89]State v. Said, 71 Ohio St. 3d 473, 477, 1994-Ohio-402, 644 N.E.2d 337 (1994).

[90]But see State v. Silverman, 121 Ohio St. 3d 581, 2009-Ohio-1576, 906 N.E.2d 427 (2009), clarification granted, 123 Ohio St. 3d 1521, 2009-Ohio-6487, 918 N.E.2d 524 (2009) (holding that a hearsay statement of a child declarant can be admitted under Evid. R. 807 without a determination of the child's competence to testify).

in *Said* to exclude excited utterances from the general rule.[91] The *Street* court noted that "while *State v. Said* held that a child must be found competent at the time the statement is made before the statement can qualify under any hearsay exception, the court excepted excited utterances from this general rule."[92]

The Ross County Court of Appeals appellate court found appellant's assignment of error without merit but would not delve deeper into the circumstances surrounding the statements because he had failed to object to the admission of the statement at the trial court level. However, "had the trial court determined that the statements would have been admissible as excited utterances, based upon the reasoning of *Said*, there would have been no requirement that the child be determined competent."[93]

Q & A: Can a parent testify on behalf of a minor child about abuse inflicted on the minor child?

It depends. In *Buchanan v. Buchanan*,[94] appellant appealed the trial court's decision finding that she had committed domestic violence against her daughter. After her visitation with the minor child, appellant informed her ex-husband and father of the child that the child had sustained a bruise to her cheek. When he inquired as to the cause, the child replied that "Mommy hit me in the teeth." Appellee sought a CPO. The order was granted by the trial court, based in part, on the testimony of appellee that his daughter had told him that "Mommy hit me in the teeth."

The trial court admitted the testimony as an excited utterance, an exception to hearsay under Evid. R. 803(2). "In admitting Joanna's statement to her father, the magistrate correctly noted that the courts have liberalized the requirements for the hearsay exceptions when applied to young children."[95] "Joanna was upset and crying when she greeted her father after visitation with appellant. These circumstances indicate impulse rather than reflection."[96] In affirming the judgment of the trial court, the appellate court held that "[a]n appellate court should allow wide discretion to determine whether in fact a declarant was, at the time of an offered statement, still under the influence of

[91]Ross v. Ross, 2006-Ohio-5274, 2006 WL 2846327, *7 (Ohio Ct. App. 4th Dist. Ross County 2006), quoting State v. Street, 122 Ohio App. 3d 79, 85-86, 701 N.E.2d 50 (9th Dist. Lorain County 1997).

[92]State v. Street, 122 Ohio App. 3d 79, 85-86, 701 N.E.2d 50 (9th Dist. Lorain County 1997) citing State v. Said, 71 Ohio St. 3d 473, 477, 1994-Ohio-402, 644 N.E.2d 337 (1994), quoting State v. Wallace, 37 Ohio St. 3d 87, 94-95, 524 N.E.2d 466, 473 (1988) (which stated that "as we noted in *State v. Wallace*, the circumstances involving an excited utterance make that exception *sui generis* with respect to requiring competency of a child declarant.").

[93]Ross v. Ross, 2006-Ohio-5274, 2006 WL 2846327, *7 (Ohio Ct. App. 4th Dist. Ross County 2006).

[94]Buchanan v. Buchanan, 1999 WL 619049 (Ohio Ct. App. 12th Dist. Clermont County 1999).

[95]Buchanan v. Buchanan, 1999 WL 619049, *2 (Ohio Ct. App. 12th Dist. Clermont County 1999), citing State v. Storch, 66 Ohio St. 3d 280, 1993-Ohio-38, 612 N.E.2d 305 (1993).

[96]Buchanan v. Buchanan, 1999 WL 619049, *2 (Ohio Ct. App. 12th Dist. Clermont County 1999).

an exciting event."[97] The most important take away from this case is that under the right circumstances, the trial court should permit a parent to testify about what the child said. Of note is that, in this case, there was also independent proof of a physical act of violence in that appellee had also reported the suspected abuse to children's services and the child received medical treatment.

In *State v. Storch*,[98] the Supreme Court addressed this issue in light of Evid. R. 807 which allows for child statements in sexual and physical violence cases under certain circumstances. The Supreme Court stressed that:

> [C]ircumstances may exist where the evidence clearly indicates that a child may suffer significant emotional harm by being forced to testify in the actual presence of a person he or she is accusing of abuse. In such circumstances, the child may be considered unavailable for purposes of the Rules of Evidence and the out-of-court statements admitted without doing violence to Section 10, Article 1, assuming Evid. R. 807 is otherwise satisfied. However, the presumption mandated by Section 10, Article 1 is that a child will be required in most circumstances to testify "face to face" with the individual being accused. This presumption is especially strong in cases where the trial court is on notice of situations which increase the risk that a child may be telling of abuse without the abuse having occurred or when the child would be under significant pressure to name one party as opposed to another as the source of established abuse. Such situations include on-going domestic relations disputes (see, e.g., the facts in State v. Boston, 46 Ohio St. 3d 108, 545 N.E.2d 1220 (1989)) and extreme animosity between adults in households where a child spends significant periods of time.[99]

The Supreme Court of Ohio held that "the determination of a child declarant's availability is best made at a pretrial proceeding. Evid. R. 807 contemplates that a pretrial hearing will be conducted at which time the ability of the child to testify should be addressed and an initial determination as to the admissibility of the child's statements should be made."[100]

Although the Supreme Court affirmed the appellate court and reversed the conviction of Storch, it clearly stated that "we are not unmindful of the fact that a requirement that a child testify at trial is an additional stress upon a child whose mental and emotional health may be fragile already. We believe, however, that Evid. R. 807 provides the proper balance for the legitimate concerns of all whose interests the court must consider while still complying with the requirements of Section 10 Article I."[101]

Q & A: What does Evidence Rule 807 state?

Evid. R. 807 permits a proponent to introduce an out-of-court statement (1) made by a child under 12, and (2) describing a sexual act or act of physical violence. Although competency of the child need not be

---

[97]Buchanan v. Buchanan, 1999 WL 619049, *2 (Ohio Ct. App. 12th Dist. Clermont County 1999), citing State v. Wagner, 30 Ohio App. 3d 261, 263, 508 N.E.2d 164 (8th Dist. Cuyahoga County 1986).

[98]State v. Storch, 66 Ohio St. 3d 280, 1993-Ohio-38, 612 N.E.2d 305 (1993)

[99]State v. Storch, 66 Ohio St. 3d 280, 293, 1993-Ohio-38, 612 N.E.2d 305 (1993).

[100]State v. Storch, 66 Ohio St. 3d 280, 293, 1993-Ohio-38, 612 N.E.2d 305 (1993).

[101]State v. Storch, 66 Ohio St. 3d 280, 295, 1993-Ohio-38, 612 N.E.2d 305 (1993).

established,[102] several conditions must be met before a child's out of court statement regarding the abuse can be admitted. The court must find that: (1) "the totality of the circumstances surrounding the making of the statement provides particularized guarantees of trustworthiness that make the statement at least reliable as statements admitted pursuant to Evid. R. 803 and 804****"; (2) the child's testimony "is not reasonably obtainable"; (3) there exists "independent proof of the sexual act or act of physical violence"; and (4) the defendant was given notice, at least 10 days before trial or hearing, of the content of the statement and the circumstances surrounding it.

The Rule also addresses what "is not reasonably obtainable by the proponent of the statement" means.

For example, in *State v. Meyerson*,[103] the child's mother left the child in the care of Mr. Meyerson, the man with whom she was in a relationship. Upon her return home, she found the child unresponsive and took him to the hospital. After an examination during which other signs of abuse were discovered, Mr. Meyerson was questioned and arrested in connection with the incident.

Statements made by the child in the presence of his therapist and grandmother were admitted, over objection by Mr. Meyerson.

On appeal, Mr. Meyerson argued that the trial court erred in admitting the statements which was hearsay. The appellate court found that the statements made by the child to his therapist were determined to be admissible under Evid. R. 803(4) in that they were made for the primary purpose of medical diagnosis or treatment.

As to the statements made by the child to his grandmother, the trial court admitted them pursuant to Evid. R. 807. The appellate court reasoned that the trial court did not abuse its discretion in admitting these statements and even if they were inadmissible, they would be considered harmless error because grandmother's statements were cumulative.

§ 16:13 Hearsay exceptions; *Crawford* concerns[1]

Until recently, victim testimony has provided the primary focus of any domestic violence hearing. Officer testimony has been permitted regarding their observations of the crime scene and the offender and

---

[102]State v. Meyerson, 2017-Ohio-8726, ¶ 19, 2017 WL 5907415 (Ohio Ct. App. 9th Dist. Summit County 2017), cause dismissed, 151 Ohio St. 3d 1469, 2017-Ohio-9106, 87 N.E.3d 1268 (2017) and appeal not allowed, 152 Ohio St. 3d 1448, 2018-Ohio-1600, 96 N.E.3d 301 (2018).

[103]State v. Meyerson, 2017-Ohio-8726, 2017 WL 5907415 (Ohio Ct. App. 9th Dist. Summit County 2017), cause dismissed, 151 Ohio St. 3d 1469, 2017-Ohio-9106, 87 N.E.3d 1268 (2017) and appeal not allowed, 152 Ohio St. 3d 1448, 2018-Ohio-1600, 96 N.E.3d 301 (2018).

[Section 16:13]

[1]Joel Shapiro, Let the Truth be Told: Proposed Hearsay Exceptions to Admit Domestic Violence Victims' Out of Court Statements as Substantive Evidence, 11 Colum. J. Gender and L. 1 (2002); Kristine Soule, The Prosecution's Choice: Admitting a Non-Testifying Domestic Violence Victim's Statements under *Crawford v. Washington*, 12 Tex. Wesleyan L.R. 689 (2006); see also Text Ch. 5, Domestic Violence Prosecution—Initiation and Initial Case Preparation. Bailey, The Aftermath of Crawford and Davis: Deconstructing the Sound of Silence, 2009 BYU L. Rev. 1 (2009).

victim's demeanor. However, this testimony was often admitted only if the officer noted something out of the ordinary in his/her report.

Evidence-based prosecution has created the shift from the victim to other relevant evidence. The new focus is on the identification, collection and presentation of all relevant evidence capable of convincing a trier of fact that the respondent or offender committed the act, regardless of the origin of the evidence. The extensive use of certain exceptions to the hearsay rule often appears as the mainstay of any aggressive trial preparation.[2]

While this relatively recent focus appears to conflict with the Confrontation Clause of the Sixth Amendment to the United States Constitution, which provides in part that "in all criminal prosecutions, the accused shall enjoy the right . . . to be confronted with the witnesses against him,"[3] the United States Supreme Court has clearly sanctioned the admissibility of some hearsay statements made by unavailable declarants.[4] Such statements do not infringe on a defendant's right of confrontation if the proponent of the statement made a good faith effort to secure the declarant's attendance at trial and if the proposed out-of-court statement met the test of reliability. The statement had to either (1) fall within a firmly rooted hearsay exception, or (2) bear particularized guarantees of trustworthiness.[5]

However, *Crawford v. Washington*[6] appears to have substantially altered the law with respect to the various rules of evidence regarding hearsay and hearsay exceptions. The United States Supreme Court reversed the Washington Supreme Court and the assault conviction of Michael Crawford who was sentenced to four and a half years for stabbing a man who he believed raped his wife.

In a rather confusing opinion, immersed in historical nuance and reference, Justice Scalia held that the Sixth Amendment's guarantee of the right of an accused to be "confronted with the witnesses against him" meant just that.[7]

The majority dismissed the Roberts rule, calling it "amorphous,

---

[2]See Text § 5:14, Case preparation—Hearsay exceptions—Generally.

[3]U.S. Const. Amend. 6. See also Tom Lininger, Yes, Virginia, There is a Confrontation Clause, 71 Brook. L. Rev. 401 (2005).

[4]See, e.g., White v. Illinois, 502 U.S. 346, 112 S. Ct. 736, 116 L. Ed. 2d 848, 33 Fed. R. Evid. Serv. 881 (1992).

[5]Ohio v. Roberts, 448 U.S. 56, 100 S. Ct. 2531, 65 L. Ed. 2d 597, 7 Fed. R. Evid. Serv. 1 (1980) (abrogated by, Crawford v. Washington, 541 U.S. 36, 124 S. Ct. 1354, 158 L. Ed. 2d 177, 63 Fed. R. Evid. Serv. 1077 (2004)); see also City of Lakewood v. Reese, 1997 WL 127182 (Ohio Ct. App. 8th Dist. Cuyahoga County 1997); State v. Allen, 2004-Ohio-3111, 2004 WL 1353169 (Ohio Ct. App. 8th Dist. Cuyahoga County 2004) (discussing *Roberts* and *Crawford* and their application in Ohio).

[6]Crawford v. Washington, 541 U.S. 36, 62, 124 S. Ct. 1354, 158 L. Ed. 2d 177, 63 Fed. R. Evid. Serv. 1077 (2004). See also Lininger, Prosecuting Batterers after *Crawford*, 91 Va. L. Rev. 747 (2005); Amber Allred Furbee, Legal Crossroads: The Hearsay Rule Meets the Sixth Amendment Confrontation Clause in *Crawford v. Washington*, 38 Creighton L. Rev. 999 (2005); Jeanine Percival, The Price of Silence: The Prosecution of Domestic Violence Cases in Light of *Crawford v. Washington*, 79 S. Cal. L. Rev. 213 (2005); James C. Latimer, Confrontation After *Crawford*: The Decision's Impact on How Hearsay is Analyzed Under the Confrontation Clause, 36 Seton Hall L. Rev. 327 (2006).

[7]See David Fiege, The Supreme Court kills evidence-based prosecution, posted at http://www.dvmen.org/dv-57.htm. But see Bloom, Utter Excitement About Nothing:

subjective and unpredictable." It noted that "some courts wind up attaching the same significance to opposite facts."[8] "By replacing categorical constitutional guarantees with open-ended balancing tests, we do violence to their design. Vague standards are manipulable, and, while that might be a small concern in run-of-the-mill assault prosecutions like this one, the Framers had an eye toward politically charged cases . . . great state trials where the impartiality of even those at the highest levels of the judiciary might not be so clear. It is difficult to imagine Roberts' [sic] providing any meaningful protection in those circumstances."[9] "Dispensing with confrontation because testimony is obviously reliable is akin to dispensing with jury trial because a defendant is obviously guilty. This is not what the Sixth Amendment prescribes."[10]

The *Crawford* decision, by insisting on the right of an accused to confront the witness, rather than just a tape recording or police report, appears to eliminate a judge's ability to admit this evidence without the actual witness being subject to cross-examination.[11] As a result, domestic violence prosecutors who have been either unable or unwilling to arrest and jail reluctant witnesses may no longer be able to convict a defendant without the victim's testimony.[12]

Under *Crawford*, the legal analysis appears to turn on the definition of a "testimonial statement" without specifically defining or distinguishing them from other types of statements. Instead, the Court concluded "[w]e leave for another day any effort to spell out a comprehensive definition of 'testimonial.' Whatever else the term covers, it applies at a minimum to prior testimony at a preliminary hearing, before a grand jury, or a former trial; and to police interrogations."[13]

Under *Crawford*, if a statement is testimonial and offered against an accuser to prove the truth of what it asserts, it cannot be admitted unless the accused has an opportunity to cross-examine the maker of

---

Why Domestic Violence Evidence-Based Prosecution Will Survive *Crawford v. Washington*, 36 St. Marys L.J. 717 (2005); King-Ries, Crawford v. Washington: The End of Victimless Prosecution?, 28 Seattle U. L.Rev. 301 (2005).

[8]Crawford v. Washington, 541 U.S. 36, 62, 124 S. Ct. 1354, 158 L. Ed. 2d 177, 63 Fed. R. Evid. Serv. 1077 (2004).

[9]Crawford v. Washington, 541 U.S. 36, 62, 124 S. Ct. 1354, 158 L. Ed. 2d 177, 63 Fed. R. Evid. Serv. 1077 (2004).

[10]Crawford v. Washington, 541 U.S. 36, 62, 124 S. Ct. 1354, 158 L. Ed. 2d 177, 63 Fed. R. Evid. Serv. 1077 (2004).

[11]See David Fiege, The Supreme Court kills evidence-based prosecution, posted at http://www.dvmen.org/dv-57.htm.

[12]Lawrence B. Usching, Rethinking Strategies for Prosecution of Domestic Violence in the Wake of *Crawford*, 71 Brook. L. Rev. 391 (2005).

[13]Crawford v. Washington, 541 U.S. 36, 62, 124 S. Ct. 1354, 158 L. Ed. 2d 177, 63 Fed. R. Evid. Serv. 1077 (2004). See also Carol A. Chase, Is *Crawford* a "Get Out of Jail Free" Card for Batterers and Abusers? An Argument for a Narrow Definition of "Testimonial," 84 Or. L. Rev. 1093 (2005); Adam Silberlight, Confronting a Testimonial Definition in a Post-*Crawford* Era, 29 Am. J. Trial Advoc. 65 (2005); Melissa Moody, A Blow to Domestic Violence Victims: Applying the "Testimonial Statements" Test in *Crawford v. Washington*, 11 Wm. & Mary J. Women & L. 387 (2005). See also State v. Byrd, 160 Ohio App. 3d 538, 2005-Ohio-1902, 828 N.E.2d 133 (2d Dist. Montgomery County 2005); State v. Primo, 2005-Ohio-3903, 2005 WL 1799314 (Ohio Ct. App. 12th Dist. Butler County 2005).

the statement. Under *Roberts*, hearsay could usually be admitted against an accuser if it was deemed reliable and reliability could be found if the statement fit within a firmly rooted hearsay exception or it was deemed to have particularized guarantees of trustworthiness. If a statement is testimonial, *Crawford* establishes the requirement of cross-examination. If it is not testimonial, the ban does not apply.

In effect, *Crawford* demands a two-pronged inquiry. If the statement is testimonial, then the witness must testify or other-than admissible hearsay may be introduced. If the witness is unavailable, then he/she must have been subject to cross-examination at a prior time. Reliability and trustworthiness are not issues under *Crawford*.

Another way to consider the same issue is whether the witness is available. If the witness is available, then the *Crawford* analysis is unnecessary. If the witness is unavailable, then there must be a further inquiry as to whether the statement is testimonial. If the statement is not testimonial, a *Crawford* analysis is not conducted. Traditional hearsay analysis and the reliability test are applied as usual.

If the statement is testimonial, then it may not be admitted if the alleged accuser is unable to confront the declarant of the statement. There is no question that the statement may be admissible under traditional hearsay analysis. The real question is whether the statement, once admitted, is a testimonial statement subject to the Confrontation Clause.

In the domestic violence context, the victim often makes the statements to a nurse, doctor, or the police. These out-of-court statements have been admissible hearsay exceptions for purposes of medical treatment, diagnosis, excited utterances, and present sense exceptions.

If not testimonial, the statements are often made to a non-governmental agent, made under the stress of the event, initiated by the declarant and informally questioned, made for the purpose of seeking aid or treatment, or made spontaneously.

If testimonial, such statements are often made in anticipation of future litigation, made during structured questioning, initiated by the listener, memorialized by way of an affidavit, or made to a governmental agent.

It appears that, for purposes of statements, the term testimonial[14] means one of the following:

(1) In-court testimony or its equivalent such as affidavits, custodial examinations, or prior testimony that the defendant was unable to cross-examine;

(2) Formalized extrajudicial statements contained in formalized testimonial materials such as affidavits, depositions, prior testimony or confessions; or

(3) Statements made under circumstances that would lead an objective witness to reasonably believe the statement would be used for trial.

In admonishing the majority, Chief Justice Rehnquist's concurring

[14]See also State v. Davis, 2005-Ohio-6224, 2005 WL 3117198 (Ohio Ct. App. 8th Dist. Summit County 2005).

opinion criticized them for grandly declaring that the definition of a testimonial statement must wait for another day.[15] He pointed out that thousands of prosecutors need answers as to what beyond the specific kinds of testimony the court lists is covered by the new rule. "They need them [answers] now, not months or years from now. Rules of criminal evidence are applied every day in courts throughout the country, and parties should not be left in the dark.[16]

Experts generally seem confident that *Crawford* only ruled unconstitutional a very small area of hearsay statements.[17] For domestic violence purposes,[18] this means that testimonial hearsay as described by the courts after *Crawford* means only those statements that are formal and made for the purpose of proving or establishing facts in judicial proceedings as opposed to business or personal purposes.[19] They will be made to a government actor, such as a law enforcement official, not someone who is not associated with governmental activity, such as the victims friend.[20]

Over time, it has become clear that the firmly rooted exceptions to hearsay have survived after Crawford.[21] Only testimonial hearsay statements must be scrutinized to determine whether witness unavailability creates a confrontation clause dilemma.[22] If the statement at

---

[15]Crawford v. Washington, 541 U.S. 36, 62, 124 S. Ct. 1354, 158 L. Ed. 2d 177, 63 Fed. R. Evid. Serv. 1077 (2004).

[16]Crawford v. Washington, 541 U.S. 36, 62, 124 S. Ct. 1354, 158 L. Ed. 2d 177, 63 Fed. R. Evid. Serv. 1077 (2004).

[17]See, e.g., U.S. v. Cromer, 389 F.3d 662, 65 Fed. R. Evid. Serv. 1151, 2004 FED App. 0412P (6th Cir. 2004) (Sixth Circuit Court of Appeals, relying on the reasoning of *Crawford*, reversed the defendants conviction and held that statements of a confidential informant are testimonial in nature and may not be offered to establish the guilt of an accused absent the opportunity for the accused to cross examine; additionally, the court provided guidance on developing a more comprehensive definition for the term "testimonial."); U.S. v. Pugh, 405 F.3d 390, 67 Fed. R. Evid. Serv. 172, 2005 FED App. 0204P (6th Cir. 2005) (holding that the proper inquiry in deciding whether a statement is testimonial for evidentiary purposes is "whether a reasonable person in the declarant's position would anticipate his statement being used against the accused in investigating and prosecuting the crime"); Donna D. Bloom, "Utter Excitement" About Nothing: Why Domestic Violence Evidence-Based Prosecution Will Survive *Crawford v. Washington*, 36 St. Mary's L. J. 717 (2005).

[18]See Myrna S. Raeder, Remember the Ladies and the Children, Too, 71 Brook. L. Rev. 311 (2005); Myrna S. Raeder, Domestic Violence, Child Abuse and Trustworthiness Exceptions After *Crawford*, 20-SUM Crim. Just. 24 (2005). See also Simon, Confrontation and Domestic Violence Post-*Davis*: Is There and Should There Be a Doctrinal Exception?, 17 Mich. J. Gender & L. 175 (2011).

[19]See State v. Wills, 2006-Ohio-2295, 2006 WL 1256379, *3 (Ohio Ct. App. 10th Dist. Franklin County 2006) (the admission of the return of service document did not deprive appellant of his rights to confront and cross-examine witnesses against him; "Rather, the return of service document was prepared as part of an everyday business activity and clearly is not the type of testimonial evidence which the Supreme Court was concerned about in *Crawford*. Thus, we find that because the return of service document in this case before us is a non-testimonial public record, its admission did not violate appellant's constitutional rights to confront and cross-examine witnesses against him.").

[20]See also U.S. v. Dorman, 108 Fed. Appx. 228 (6th Cir. 2004).

[21]But see Robert P. Mosteller, *Crawford's* Impact on Hearsay Statements in Domestic Violence & Child Abuse Cases, 71 Brook. L. Rev. 411 (2005).

[22]See State v. Byrd, 160 Ohio App. 3d 538, 2005-Ohio-1902, 828 N.E.2d 133 (2d

issue is non-testimonial[23]; and even if it is not otherwise the type of hearsay that fits within a well-established exception such as excited utterance[24] or medical records statements,[25] the hearsay may still be admitted under the old *Roberts* rule provided that it contains sufficient indicia of reliability.[26]

Since *Crawford*, the Supreme Court of the United States has issued other decisions, clarifying and redefining its legal analysis. For example, in *Michigan v. Bryant*,[27] the United States Supreme Court further expounded on the "primary purpose test." In that case, the issued involved the statements made by a dying victim to law enforcement about his assailant.

The Supreme Court emphasized the importance of considering all relevant circumstances. Relying on its previous opinion in *Davis v. Washington*,[28] where the primary purpose of an interrogation is to respond to an ongoing emergency, its purpose is not to create a record for trial and thus is not within the scope of the Confrontation Clause. At the same time, there may be other circumstances, aside from ongoing emergencies, when a statement is not obtained with a primary purpose of creating an out-of-court substitute for trial testimony.[29] "The existence *vel non* of an ongoing emergency is not the touchstone of the testimonial inquiry."[30] Instead, "whether an ongoing emergency exists is simply one factor . . . that informs the ultimate inquiry regarding the primary purpose of the interrogation."[31]

The Court then addressed the informality of the situation and the

---

Dist. Montgomery County 2005) (court held that the admission of statements that a victim made to a police officer were testimonial and violated defendant's confrontation rights, effectively barring the officer from testifying as to those hearsay statements made by the alleged victim).

[23]State v. Cannaday, 2005-Ohio-1513, 2005 WL 736583, *6 (Ohio Ct. App. 10th Dist. Franklin County 2005) (affirming conviction and holding that *Crawford* only applies to statements that are, in fact, hearsay, and that are not subject to common-law exceptions to the hearsay rule, such as excited utterances. Because we have previously determined that Thompsons statement was admissible as an excited utterance, we find appellants reliance upon *Crawford* is misplaced.).

[24]See State v. Byrd, 160 Ohio App. 3d 538, 2005-Ohio-1902, 828 N.E.2d 133 (2d Dist. Montgomery County 2005); Demons v. State, 277 Ga. 724, 595 S.E.2d 76, 80 (2004).

[25]Evans v. Luebbers, 371 F.3d 438 (8th Cir. 2004). See also State v. Nix, 2004-Ohio-5502, 2004 WL 2315035 (Ohio Ct. App. 1st Dist. Hamilton County 2004) (statements made to a police officer by the victim in a hospital shortly before he died were not testimonial).

[26]People v. Compan, 100 P.3d 533 (Colo. App. 2004), judgment aff'd, 121 P.3d 876 (Colo. 2005) (overruled by, Nicholls v. People, 2017 CO 71, 396 P.3d 675 (Colo. 2017)) (overruling court finding nontestimonial statements do not implicate a defendant's right to confrontation under the Colorado Constitution).

[27]Michigan v. Bryant, 562 U.S. 344, 131 S. Ct. 1143, 179 L. Ed. 2d 93, 84 Fed. R. Evid. Serv. 1033 (2011).

[28]Davis v. Washington, 547 U.S. 813, 126 S. Ct. 2266, 165 L. Ed. 2d 224, 70 Fed. R. Evid. Serv. 472, 30 A.L.R.6th 599 (2006).

[29]Michigan v. Bryant, 562 U.S. 344, 358, 131 S. Ct. 1143, 179 L. Ed. 2d 93, 84 Fed. R. Evid. Serv. 1033 (2011).

[30]Michigan v. Bryant, 562 U.S. 344, 374, 131 S. Ct. 1143, 179 L. Ed. 2d 93, 84 Fed. R. Evid. Serv. 1033 (2011).

[31]Michigan v. Bryant, 562 U.S. 344, 374, 131 S. Ct. 1143, 179 L. Ed. 2d 93, 84

interrogation. Unlike *Crawford* where the interrogation was at the police station and more likely to provoke testimonial statements, less formal questioning is less likely to reflect a primary purpose aimed at obtaining testimonial evidence against the accused.

The real question is whether, in light of all the circumstances, and viewed objectively, the primary purpose of the conversation was to create an out-of-court substitute for trial testimony. Applying the principles, the Court held that the statements made by a dying victim about his murderer were not testimonial because the circumstances objectively indicated that the conversation was primarily aimed at meeting the emergency, not establishing evidence for trial (even where the relevant statements were made to law enforcement).[32]

Q & A: Has the Supreme Court of Ohio addressed the Confrontation Clause issue in light of *Crawford*?

Most of the Supreme Court of Ohio decisions that have addressed *Crawford* have done so in the context of the rape of either an adult or child. For example, in *State v. Stahl*,[33] the Ohio Supreme Court considered whether an adult rape victim had made testimonial statements to a nurse practitioner during an emergency room medical exam at a hospital DOVE unit specializing in health care for victims of rape and domestic violence. The victim died from unrelated causes prior to trial.

Defendant advanced an argument that the statement made to the nurse practitioner was testimonial and inadmissible at trial because it could be reasonably expected that her statement made to the nurse would be used in a future prosecution. Additionally, defendant argued that because the victim signed a consent form prior to the exam authorizing the release of evidence and information in the investigation and prosecution of the crime, she reasonably expected her statement to be used by the prosecution. Finally, Stahl argued that DOVE's mission statement sets forth that the primary purpose is to assist law enforcement. The prosecution responded that the statement was made in connection with her medical examination for purposes of medical diagnosis and therefore, there was no reason to believe that it would be used at a later prosecution.[34]

The Supreme Court adopted an "objective witness" test for Ohio. For Confrontation Clause purposes, a testimonial statement includes one made "under circumstances, which would lead an objective witness reasonably to believe that the statement would be available for use at a later trial."[35] "In determining whether a statement is testimonial for Confrontation Clause purposes, courts should focus on the expectation of the declarant at the time of making the statement;

Fed. R. Evid. Serv. 1033 (2011).

[32]Michigan v. Bryant, 562 U.S. 344, 131 S. Ct. 1143, 179 L. Ed. 2d 93, 84 Fed. R. Evid. Serv. 1033 (2011).

[33]State v. Stahl, 111 Ohio St. 3d 186, 2006-Ohio-5482, 855 N.E.2d 834 (2006). See also State v. Thomas, 2015-Ohio-5247, 54 N.E.3d 732 (Ohio Ct. App. 9th Dist. Summit County 2015).

[34]State v. Stahl, 111 Ohio St. 3d 186, 189, 2006-Ohio-5482, 855 N.E.2d 834 (2006).

[35]State v. Stahl, 111 Ohio St. 3d 186, 196, 2006-Ohio-5482, 855 N.E.2d 834 (2006), quoting Crawford v. Washington, 541 U.S. 36, 52, 124 S. Ct. 1354, 158 L. Ed. 2d 177, 63 Fed. R. Evid. Serv. 1077 (2004).

the intent of the questioner is relevant only if it could affect a reasonable declarant's expectations. This test conforms to *Crawford* and is supported by both state and federal authority. This definition also prevents trampling on other portions of hearsay law that Crawford expressly states do not implicate the right to confront witnesses."[36] Under that test, the mission statement is irrelevant to the issue of the victim's reasonable expectation when giving the account of the event.[37]

In light of the fact that the victim had previously given a statement to a police officer which included the identity of the defendant, it was reasonable for the victim to believe that the statement made to the nurse practitioner about the identity of the defendant would be used primarily for health care purposes. "While Stahl correctly argues that the DOVE unit, like other emergency rooms, partly serves a prosecutorial function by collecting evidence, this function is at best secondary to the DOVE unit's primary motivation, the care of its patients."[38] Thus, the majority held that the statement was nontestimonial in nature.[39]

In her dissent, Justice Lanzinger noted that the nurse practitioner was also the coordinator for victim services at the DOVE unit and had elicited statements from the victim about the crime and identity of the perpetrator; thus, making the statements testimonial because the nurse's activities were primarily to collect evidence for use in the prosecution of the case.[40]

In *State v. Siler*,[41] the Supreme Court of Ohio set forth a test for courts to apply when faced with a Confrontation Clause challenge to statements made by a child declarant in response to police interrogation. The Court adopted the "primary purpose test"[42] rather than the "objective witness test" for deciding whether a statement is testimonial or non-testimonial and noting that it should apply when the government actor is a law enforcement interrogator.

The Court also found that the child's age had nothing to do with the analysis and could find no cases in which "a court concluded that a declarant's age rendered statements to police non-testimonial. Rather, courts have held that children's statements to police and police agents are testimonial in circumstances that indicate no on-going emergency

[36]State v. Stahl, 111 Ohio St. 3d 186, 196, 2006-Ohio-5482, 855 N.E.2d 834 (2006).

[37]State v. Stahl, 111 Ohio St. 3d 186, 197, 2006-Ohio-5482, 855 N.E.2d 834 (2006).

[38]Stahl, 111 Ohio St. 3d 186 at 196-197.

[39]In a written dissent, some of the justices found that it was reasonable to suppose that the victim expected her statements, and physical evidence collected would be used in the prosecution of her case, Thus, the nurse's primary purpose was forensic—no actual medical treatment was provided in the DOVE unit.

[40]State v. Stahl, 111 Ohio St. 3d 186, 200, 2006-Ohio-5482, 855 N.E.2d 834 (2006).

[41]State v. Siler, 116 Ohio St. 3d 39, 2007-Ohio-5637, 876 N.E.2d 534 (2007); State v. Little, 2016-Ohio-8398, 78 N.E.3d 323 (Ohio Ct. App. 3d Dist. Allen County 2016).

[42]See also Monica Vozakis, Constitutional Law-The Confrontation Clause and the New "Primary Purpose Test" in Domestic Violence Cases, 7 WYLR 605 (2007); State v. Jones, 135 Ohio St. 3d 10, 2012-Ohio-5677, ¶ 145, 984 N.E.2d 948 (2012); State v. Williams, 2013-Ohio-726, 987 N.E.2d 322 (Ohio Ct. App. 6th Dist. Lucas County 2013) (focusing on the Ohio Supreme Court's primary purpose test to determine whether statements are testimonial); State v. King, 2013-Ohio-1694, 2013 WL 1798337 (Ohio Ct. App. 2d Dist. Montgomery County 2013).

existed and that the primary purpose of the interrogation was to establish past events potentially related to later criminal prosecution."[43]

In concurrence, one of the justices remarked that "it was still an open question whether children, by virtue of their reasoning abilities, should be subject to the objective witness standard as expressed in *Stahl* when they are questioned by those other than police officers. We should hesitate to express dicta on this issue when the ramifications on any ruling regarding testimonial statements can be so great, particularly where the child is the victim as well as the witness, in, for example, sexual abuse cases."[44]

Moreover, in *State v. Muttart*,[45] defendant was convicted of raping a child. Besides addressing competency issues in light of the child's out-of-court statements made to medical personnel, the Supreme Court tackled the issue of whether the admission of those hearsay statements violated appellant's Sixth Amendment rights of confrontation under *Crawford*.

The Supreme Court, in determining whether a child's statements are admissible under the hearsay rule, should consider whether the child was questioned in a leading or suggestive manner; whether there is a motive to fabricate (such as a pending legal proceeding) and whether the child understood the need to tell the truth.[46] In determining whether the same statements are made for purposes of medical diagnosis or treatment, the trial court may be guided by the age of the child making the statements, which might suggest the absence or presence of an ability to fabricate and the consistency of those declarations.[47]

In affirming the conviction, the Supreme Court of Ohio held that the victim's statements made for purposes of medical diagnosis and treatment were exceptions to the hearsay rule, were nontestimonial in nature and did not violate defendant's Sixth Amendment right of confrontation.[48]

Finally, in *State v. Arnold*,[49] the Supreme Court of Ohio was again faced with the question of whether statements made by a child victim to interviewers at a child advocacy center were testimonial such that they violated defendant's right to confrontation.

In that case, the child victim made statements to a social worker for the child advocacy center, who served both as a forensic interviewer collecting information for use by the police and as a medical

[43] State v. Siler, 116 Ohio St. 3d 39, 49, 2007-Ohio-5637, 876 N.E.2d 534 (2007).

[44] State v. Siler, 116 Ohio St. 3d 39, 52, 2007-Ohio-5637, 876 N.E.2d 534 (2007).

[45] State v. Muttart, 116 Ohio St. 3d 5, 2007-Ohio-5267, 875 N.E.2d 944 (2007).

[46] State v. Muttart, 116 Ohio St. 3d 5, 2007-Ohio-5267, 875 N.E.2d 944, 954 (2007).

[47] State v. Muttart, 116 Ohio St. 3d 5, 2007-Ohio-5267, 875 N.E.2d 944, 955 (2007).

[48] See also State v. Thomas, 2015-Ohio-5247, 54 N.E.3d 732 (Ohio Ct. App. 9th Dist. Summit County 2015); State v. Durham, 2017-Ohio-954, 2017 WL 1034560 (Ohio Ct. App. 8th Dist. Cuyahoga County 2017), appeal not allowed, 149 Ohio St. 3d 1435, 2017-Ohio-4396, 76 N.E.3d 1209 (2017) and cert. denied, 138 S. Ct. 743, 199 L. Ed. 2d 611 (2018).

[49] State v. Arnold, 126 Ohio St. 3d 290, 2010-Ohio-2742, 933 N.E.2d 775 (2010).

interviewer eliciting information for diagnosis and treatment. Some of the statements made to the interviewer described defendant's acts, such as that he touched her "pee-pee," that his "pee-pee" went inside her "pee-pee," that his "pee-pee" touched her "butt," and that his mouth touched her "pee-pee." Other statements related to the facts that defendant locked the door before raping her and that he removed her underpants.

The Supreme Court held that the descriptive statements made by the child to the interviewer were necessary for medical diagnosis and treatment, were nontestimonial,[50] and did not violate defendant's right of confrontation.

The Court then employed the primary-purpose test to determine whether the primary purpose of that portion of the interview regarding statements made by the child about the locked door, removal of underwear and what defendant's "pee-pee" looked like was to enable police assistance to meet an ongoing emergency.[51] In finding that these statements were not made to meet an ongoing emergency, the Court noted that the statements involved a description of past events, that a reasonable observer would not perceive an ongoing emergency at the time of questioning and that the questioning was not objectively necessary to resolve an emergency because there was no ongoing emergency.[52] "Finally, the interview was rather formal, more akin to the videotaped planned interview of *Crawford* than to the frantic 9-1-1 call or the sequestered but spur-of-the-moment interview recounted in *Davis*."[53] Because these particular statements related primarily to the state's investigation and not to meet an ongoing emergency, they were testimonial in nature and inadmissible pursuant to *Crawford*.

Interestingly, the dissent in this case determined that the interviewer could not be both acting as an agent for law enforcement and acting as an agent for medical professionals. One of the dissenting judges admonished the majority for charting "a course different from the Confrontation Clause jurisprudence of the Supreme Court of the United States and adopt[ing] its own dual-capacity test in which the interrogation is examined on a question-by-question basis to determine whether the interviewer acted as an agent of law enforcement or as an agent of some other entity when eliciting a particular statement. Applying this test, it finds that testimonial and non-testimonial statements are interspersed throughout Marshall's interview and that Marshall acted variously as an agent of law enforcement and as a medical examiner. This analysis is contrary to United States Supreme

---

[50]See also State v. Muttart, 116 Ohio St. 3d 5, 2007-Ohio-5267, 875 N.E.2d 944 (2007).

[51]State v. Arnold, 126 Ohio St. 3d 290, 2010-Ohio-2742, 933 N.E.2d 775, 783-84 (2010), quoting State v. Siler, 116 Ohio St. 3d 39, 2007-Ohio-5637, 876 N.E.2d 534 (2007), at paragraph one of the syllabus (in turn quoting Davis v. Washington, 547 U.S. 813, 822, 126 S. Ct. 2266, 165 L. Ed. 2d 224, 70 Fed. R. Evid. Serv. 472, 30 A.L.R.6th 599 (2006)).

[52]State v. Arnold, 126 Ohio St. 3d 290, 2010-Ohio-2742, 933 N.E.2d 775, 784 (2010).

[53]State v. Arnold, 126 Ohio St. 3d 290, 2010-Ohio-2742, 933 N.E.2d 775, 784 (2010).

Court jurisprudence, which directs that we should look to the primary purpose of the interrogation, not the secondary or tertiary purpose."[54]

Q & A: What about the Supreme Court of the United States?

In still another confrontation clause decision relating to abuse of children, the Supreme Court of the United States reversed the judgment of the Ohio Supreme Court in a case entitled *Ohio v. Clark.*[55] In *Clark*, the minor child responded to teacher questioning that Clark physically abused him. Clark was subsequently tried and convicted. The State introduced the child's statements to his teachers as evidence of Clark's guilt but the minor child did not testify. The trial court denied Clark's motion to exclude the statements under the Confrontation Clause. On appeal, the appellate court reversed the conviction on Confrontation Clause grounds and the Supreme Court of Ohio affirmed.

The Ohio Supreme Court found that the primary purpose of the teacher's questioning was "not to deal with an ongoing emergency, but rather to gather evidence potentially relevant to a subsequent criminal prosecution."[56] In that Ohio's mandatory reporting law required certain professionals including preschool teachers to report suspected child abuse to governmental authorities, the teachers acted as agents of the State by eliciting statements that are " 'functionally identical to live, in-court testimony, doing precisely what a witness does on direct examination.' "[57]

The question presented to the Supreme Court of the United States was whether the minor child's statements made to persons other than law enforcement officers are subject to the Confrontation Clause. The Supreme Court once again refined its decision in *Crawford* and explained that the Confrontation Clause "generally prohibits the introduction of "testimonial" statements by a nontestifying witness, unless the witness is "unavailable to testify, and the defendant had had a prior opportunity for cross examination."[58]

Referencing the definition of "primary purpose" in *Michigan v. Bryant*,[59] the *Bryant* court reiterated that in making a "primary purpose" determination, courts must consider "all of the relevant

---

[54]State v. Arnold, 126 Ohio St. 3d 290, 2010-Ohio-2742, 933 N.E.2d 775, 797 (2010) (O'Donnell, J. dissenting).

[55]State v. Clark, 137 Ohio St. 3d 346, 2013-Ohio-4731, 999 N.E.2d 592 (2013), rev'd and remanded, 135 S. Ct. 2173, 192 L. Ed. 2d 306 (2015).

[56]Ohio v. Clark, 135 S. Ct. 2173, 2178, 192 L. Ed. 2d 306 (2015), citing State v. Clark, 137 Ohio St. 3d 346, 350, 2013-Ohio-4731, 999 N.E.2d 592, 597 (2013), rev'd and remanded, 135 S. Ct. 2173, 192 L. Ed. 2d 306 (2015).

[57]Ohio v. Clark, 135 S. Ct. 2173, 2179, 192 L. Ed. 2d 306 (2015), citing *Clark*, 355, quoting Melendez-Diaz v. Massachusetts, 557 U.S. 305, 310–311, 129 S. Ct. 2527, 174 L. Ed. 2d 314 (2009).

[58]Ohio v. Clark, 135 S. Ct. 2173, 2179, 192 L. Ed. 2d 306 (2015), quoting, Crawford v. Washington, 541 U.S. 36, 54, 124 S. Ct. 1354, 158 L. Ed. 2d 177, 63 Fed. R. Evid. Serv. 1077 (2004).

[59]Michigan v. Bryant, 562 U.S. 344, 131 S. Ct. 1143, 179 L. Ed. 2d 93, 84 Fed. R. Evid. Serv. 1033 (2011); Cleveland v. Merritt, 2016-Ohio-4693, 69 N.E.3d 102 (Ohio Ct. App. 8th Dist. Cuyahoga County 2016), appeal not allowed, 147 Ohio St. 3d 1506, 2017-Ohio-261, 67 N.E.3d 824 (2017) (focused on whether an ongoing emergency can exist during the time the victim is temporarily separated from the later-identified abuser); State v. Conyer, 2017-Ohio-7506, 2017 WL 3971689 (Ohio Ct. App. 7th Dist.

circumstances."[60] "A statement qualifies as testimonial if the 'primary purpose' of the conversation was 'to creat[e] an out-of-court substitute for trial testimony.' "[61] "Where no such primary purpose exists, the admissibility of a statement is the concern of the state and federal rules of evidence, not the Confrontation Clause."[62]

The Supreme Court, in *Clark,* stressed that the Confrontation Clause does not bar every statement that satisfies the primary purpose test. "The Court has recognized that the Confrontation Clause does not prohibit the introduction of out-of-court statements that would have been admissible in a criminal case at the time of founding. See *Giles v. California*, 554 U.S. 353, 358-359, 128 S. Ct. 2678, 171 L. Ed. 2d 488; *Crawford*, 541 U.S. at 56 n. 6, 62, 124 S.Ct. 1354. Thus, the primary purpose test is a necessary, but not always sufficient, condition for the exclusion of out-of-court statements under the Confrontation Clause."[63]

In the case at hand, the Supreme Court narrowed the question to whether statements made to individuals who are not law enforcement officers could raise confrontation concerns and found that, considering all relevant circumstances, the child's statements were not testimonial as they were not made with the primary purpose of creating evidence for Clark's prosecution.[64] Rather, they "occurred in the context of an ongoing emergency involving suspected child abuse" and the teachers questions were aimed at identifying and ending a threat. At no point did they inform the child that his answers would be used to arrest or punish his abuser, nor did the child indicate that he intended his statements to be used by police or prosecutors. Further, the conversation was both informal and spontaneous.[65]

In striking a balance with *Crawford*, the *Clark* court focused on the age of the child and the persons to whom the answers to the questions were addressed. L.P.'s age further confirms that the statements in question were not testimonial because "[s]tatements made by very young children will rarely, if ever, implicate the Confrontation Clause."[66] As a historical matter, moreover, there is strong evidence that statements made in circumstances like these were regularly admitted at common law. Finally, although statements to individuals other than law enforcement officers are not categorically outside the Sixth Amendment's reach, the fact that L.P. was speaking to his teach-

---

Mahoning County 2017), appeal not allowed, 152 Ohio St. 3d 1478, 2018-Ohio-1990, 98 N.E.3d 294 (2018).

[60]Ohio v. Clark, 135 S. Ct. 2173, 2180, 192 L. Ed. 2d 306 (2015), citing *Bryant* at 369. State v. Grabe, 2017-Ohio-1017, 2017 WL 1058827 (Ohio Ct. App. 7th Dist. Mahoning County 2017).

[61]Ohio v. Clark, 135 S. Ct. 2173, 2180, 192 L. Ed. 2d 306 (2015), citing *Bryant* at 369.

[62]Michigan v. Bryant, 562 U.S. 344, 359, 131 S. Ct. 1143, 179 L. Ed. 2d 93, 84 Fed. R. Evid. Serv. 1033 (2011).

[63]Ohio v. Clark, 135 S. Ct. 2173, 2180–81, 192 L. Ed. 2d 306 (2015).

[64]Ohio v. Clark, 135 S. Ct. 2173, 2181, 192 L. Ed. 2d 306 (2015).

[65]Ohio v. Clark, 135 S. Ct. 2173, 2181, 192 L. Ed. 2d 306 (2015).

[66]Ohio v. Clark, 135 S. Ct. 2173, 2182, 192 L. Ed. 2d 306 (2015); see also State v. Saltz, 2015-Ohio-3097, 2015 WL 4610972 (Ohio Ct. App. 3d Dist. Hancock County 2015).

ers is highly relevant. Statements to individuals who are not "principally charged with uncovering and prosecuting criminal behavior are significantly less likely to be testimonial that those given to law enforcement."[67]

Relying on its decision in *Bryant*, the Supreme Court of the United States reversed the Supreme Court of Ohio and held that the test is not whether a jury would view the statements as the equivalent of in-court testimony; rather, the test is whether a statement was given with the "primary purpose of creating an out-of-court substitute for trial testimony."[68] Therefore, the child's statements to his teachers were not testimonial and the decision in *Clark* was reversed and remanded.

Of importance is that not all out-of-court statements that support the prosecution's case are barred by the Confrontation Clause. In effect, many statements made by children to teachers, caregivers or medical personnel may admissible in a criminal case and not barred by the Sixth Amendment.

Q & A: Does a complainant's reading a prior statement made to police into the record violate the Confrontation Clause when that complainant invokes the 5th Amendment right against incrimination?

In *State v. Arnold*,[69] the complainant refused to answer questions at trial and denied any memory of giving a statement to the police alleging that his son caused him physical harm. The prosecutor had him read the statement he made to police into the record which was objected to by the defense. On appeal, Arnold contended that allowing complainant to read his prior statements in to the record violated the Confrontation Clause.

The appellate court first noted that Confrontation Clause violations are subject to harmless error analysis. It then stated that "[w]e would note that it is unclear, how inclusion of this evidence violates Arnold's Confrontation Clause rights when the witness, Lester Arnold, was present in open court to be confronted regarding his testimonial statement. 'The Court in *Crawford* was explicit: "when the declarant appears for cross-examination at trial, the Confrontation Clause places no constraints at all on the use of his prior testimonial statements."' "[70]

[67] Ohio v. Clark, 135 S. Ct. 2173, 2182, 192 L. Ed. 2d 306 (2015).

[68] Ohio v. Clark, 135 S. Ct. 2173, 2177, 192 L. Ed. 2d 306 (2015); quoting *Bryant, supra*, at 358. See also Cleveland v. Merritt, 2016-Ohio-4693, 69 N.E.3d 102 (Ohio Ct. App. 8th Dist. Cuyahoga County 2016), appeal not allowed, 147 Ohio St. 3d 1506, 2017-Ohio-261, 67 N.E.3d 824 (2017).

[69] State v. Arnold, 2014-Ohio-1134, 2014 WL 1339806 (Ohio Ct. App. 3d Dist. Seneca County 2014), judgment aff'd, 147 Ohio St. 3d 138, 2016-Ohio-1595, 62 N.E.3d 153 (2016).

[70] State v. Arnold, 2014-Ohio-1134, 2014 WL 1339806, ¶ 37 (Ohio Ct. App. 3d Dist. Seneca County 2014), judgment aff'd, 147 Ohio St. 3d 138, 2016-Ohio-1595, 62 N.E.3d 153 (2016), quoting State v. Knauff, 2011-Ohio-2725, 2011 WL 2225022, ¶ 43 (Ohio Ct. App. 4th Dist. Adams County 2011), quoting *Crawford*, at 59.

On appeal to the Supreme Court of Ohio, defendant sought discretionary review. In *State v. Arnold,*[71] the Supreme Court affirmed Arnold's conviction. The majority first determined that Arnold "lacked standing to raise any supposed violation of the Fifth Amendment privilege against self-incrimination of the prosecution witness."[72] Additionally, neither Arnold nor the complaining witness ever demonstrated that the information of the witness sought by the State would violate the right against incrimination. In fact, the burden on the one claiming the privilege must assert something more than "chimerical fears."[73] Without a basis for the privilege being offered, any error was harmless. Lastly, Arnold's right to cross examine a witness who was allowed to read into evidence his prior statement to police did not violate Arnold's confrontation clause rights.[74]

In *State v. Goshade,*[75] the complainant also invoked the Fifth Amendment right against self-incrimination. Her 911 calls were admitted into evidence, which calls contained her cry for help and appellant's conversation. On appeal, appellant contended that the 911 tapes were inadmissible testimonial hearsay and the evidence of the statements made to police violated the Confrontation Clause. The complainant's statement had been admitted as an excited utterance exception to hearsay in the trial court and the appellate court had to analyze whether the statement was testimonial or not, noting that a testimonial statement is one that would be later used at trial as part of the investigation of a crime and the information sought was about past events.

The appellate court noted that the complaining witness had invoked her 5th Amendment right against self-incrimination and because she did so, she was unavailable to testify. "The mere fact that she was called to the stand and answered a few questions does not serve to safeguard Goshade's right to confrontation."[76] Because the complaining witness did not testify and because Goshade had no opportunity for cross examination, the admission of her statement to the officer by way of a 911 call violated Goshade's right to confrontation, unless that statement is not testimonial. "In assessing whether a statement is testimonial, the court must 'objectively evaluate the circumstances in which the encounter occur[red] and the statements and actions of the parties.' "[77] "The focus is not on the subjective or actual purpose or intent of the interrogator or the declarant, but on 'the purpose that

---

[71]State v. Arnold, 147 Ohio St. 3d 138, 2016-Ohio-1595, 62 N.E.3d 153 (2016).

[72]State v. Arnold, 147 Ohio St. 3d 138, 2016-Ohio-1595, 62 N.E.3d 153 (2016) (at syllabus).

[73]State v. Arnold, 147 Ohio St. 3d 138, 148, 2016-Ohio-1595, 62 N.E.3d 153 (2016).

[74]But see the three dissenting opinions.

[75]State v. Goshade, 2013-Ohio-4457, 2013 WL 5577906 (Ohio Ct. App. 1st Dist. Hamilton County 2013).

[76]State v. Goshade, 2013-Ohio-4457, 2013 WL 5577906, ¶ 11 (Ohio Ct. App. 1st Dist. Hamilton County 2013), citing State v. Osman, 2011-Ohio-4626, 2011 WL 4064473 (Ohio Ct. App. 4th Dist. Athens County 2011).

[77]State v. Goshade, 2013-Ohio-4457, 2013 WL 5577906, ¶ 15 (Ohio Ct. App. 1st Dist. Hamilton County 2013), quoting State v. Jones, 135 Ohio St. 3d 10, 2012-Ohio-5677, 984 N.E.2d 948, ¶ 150 (2012).

reasonable participants would have had' under the same circumstances."[78] "The focus must be on the parties at the time of the interrogation and not based on hindsight."[79] As the officer was responding to an ongoing emergency situation, said statements were correctly admitted into evidence under the excited utterance exception to hearsay. Considering the totality of the circumstances, the court held that her statements were not testimonial.

Unlike *Arnold* in which the appellate court ignored the complaining witness's invoking his Fifth Amendment right against incrimination because he had appeared at the trial and read his police statement into the record, the *Goshade* court found the witness to be unavailable; thus, her 911 call was subject to the analysis in *Crawford*.

Q & A: How have other courts addressed statements made to 911 operators or officers responding to the scene of the incident?

Simply put, a statement made to a 911 operator[80] or an officer at the scene[81] are statements made under the aura of excitement and are not calculated for use at a future criminal trial. Such statements are neither a solemn declaration nor a conscious account of the crime made with an eye towards trial.[82] A victim of domestic violence, answering questions about an abusive incident is not a witness

[78]State v. Goshade, 2013-Ohio-4457, 2013 WL 5577906, ¶ 15 (Ohio Ct. App. 1st Dist. Hamilton County 2013), quoting State v. Jones, 135 Ohio St. 3d 10, 2012-Ohio-5677, 984 N.E.2d 948, ¶ 150 (2012).

[79]State v. Goshade, 2013-Ohio-4457, 2013 WL 5577906, ¶ 15 (Ohio Ct. App. 1st Dist. Hamilton County 2013).

[80]See State v. Byrd, 160 Ohio App. 3d 538, 2005-Ohio-1902, 828 N.E.2d 133 (2d Dist. Montgomery County 2005); see also State v. Newell, 2005-Ohio-2848, 2005 WL 1364937 (Ohio Ct. App. 5th Dist. Stark County 2005), citing State v. Dunivant, 2005-Ohio-1497, 2005 WL 840357 (Ohio Ct. App. 9th Dist. 2005); People v. Conyers, 4 Misc. 3d 346, 777 N.Y.S.2d 274 (Sup 2004); State v. Mills, 2005-Ohio-2128, 2006 WL 1132543 (Ohio Ct. App. 2d Dist. Montgomery County 2006); State v. McDaniel, 2011-Ohio-6326, 2011 WL 6153697 (Ohio Ct. App. 2d Dist. Montgomery County 2011); State v. Williams, 2013-Ohio-726, 987 N.E.2d 322 (Ohio Ct. App. 6th Dist. Lucas County 2013) (statements in neighbor's audio call, reporting domestic violence between defendant and his wife were non- testimonial and not subject to confrontation clause) (syllabus); State v. Norris, 2015-Ohio-624, 2015 WL 753346, ¶ 17 (Ohio Ct. App. 2d Dist. Montgomery County 2015) (*Byrd* does not compel a broad conclusion that all statements to the police by a victim are testimonial in nature); State v. Kerr, 2016-Ohio-965, 2016 WL 936844 (Ohio Ct. App. 2d Dist. Montgomery County 2016).

[81]Akron v. Hutton, 2005-Ohio-3300, 2005 WL 1523880 (Ohio Ct. App. 9th Dist. Summit County 2005); State v. Mack, 2015-Ohio-5214, 2015 WL 8607454 (Ohio Ct. App. 11th Dist. Ashtabula County 2015); Cleveland v. Merritt, 2016-Ohio-4693, 69 N.E.3d 102 (Ohio Ct. App. 8th Dist. Cuyahoga County 2016), appeal not allowed, 147 Ohio St. 3d 1506, 2017-Ohio-261, 67 N.E.3d 824 (2017) (finding that the ongoing emergency did not cease merely because police officers arrive, or the victim is not currently being abused or is temporarily separated from later-identified abuser. At ¶ 18); State v. Conyer, 2017-Ohio-7506, 2017 WL 3971689 (Ohio Ct. App. 7th Dist. Mahoning County 2017), appeal not allowed, 152 Ohio St. 3d 1478, 2018-Ohio-1990, 98 N.E.3d 294 (2018) (finding anonymous call non-testimonial despite fact that caller appeared calm on call and used past tense to indicate that that it was not an emergency; term "just" happened meant drive-by shooting happened in close proximity in time to when 911 call made and it posed ongoing threat to public).

[82]Crawford v. Washington, 541 U.S. 36, 124 S. Ct. 1354, 1367 n.7, 158 L. Ed. 2d 177, 63 Fed. R. Evid. Serv. 1077 (2004). See also State v. Nix, 2004-Ohio-5502, 2004 WL 2315035 (Ohio Ct. App. 1st Dist. Hamilton County 2004) (statements made to a

against her attacker within the meaning of *Crawford*. For example, in *People v. Moscat*,[83] the defendant moved to exclude a 911 tape made by the complaining witness in a domestic abuse case. Both sides anticipated that the complainant would refuse to testify. Defendant argued that the 911 call is hearsay and that its admission would violate his Sixth Amendment right to confront the witness. The state argued that the 911 call was an excited utterance exception to the hearsay rule and that its admission would not violate the Sixth Amendment. Without the admission of this evidence, the state would be unable to proceed to trial.

The court focused its legal analysis on whether a 911 call is testimonial in nature and concluded it wasn't.[84] "A 911 call is typically initiated not by the police, but by the victim of a crime. It is generated not by the desire of the prosecution or the police to seek evidence against a particular suspect; rather, the 911 call has its genesis in the urgent desire of a citizen to be rescued from immediate peril. . . Moreover, a 911 call can usually be seen as part of the criminal incident itself, rather than as part of the prosecution that follows."[85] A 911 call is not testimonial in nature, rather it qualifies as an excited utterance exception to the hearsay rule, because there has been no opportunity for the called to reflect and falsify her (or his) account of the events.[86] As recognized in *Moscat* and other similar cases, including *Byrd*, these statements are excited utterances and are not testimonial in nature under *Crawford*.[87]

Recently, the U.S. Supreme Court issued opinions in two cases that clarified the scope and definition of a testimonial statement. Both *Washington v. Davis*,[88] and *Hammon v. Indiana*,[89] were argued before the United States Supreme Court in March 2006.

---

police officer by the victim in a hospital shortly before he died were not testimonial); Michigan v. Bryant, 562 U.S. 344, 131 S. Ct. 1143, 179 L. Ed. 2d 93, 84 Fed. R. Evid. Serv. 1033 (2011) (dying declaration in context of an ongoing emergency is nontestimonial).

[83]People v. Moscat, 3 Misc. 3d 739, 777 N.Y.S.2d 875 (N.Y. City Crim. Ct. 2004); State v. Mizenko, 2006 MT 11, 330 Mont. 299, 127 P.3d 458 (2006).

[84]See also State v. Davis, 116 Wash. App. 81, 64 P.3d 661 (Div. 1 2003), aff'd, 154 Wash. 2d 291, 111 P.3d 844 (2005), aff'd, 547 U.S. 813, 126 S. Ct. 2266, 165 L. Ed. 2d 224, 70 Fed. R. Evid. Serv. 472, 30 A.L.R.6th 599 (2006) (Supreme Court of Washington held that emergency 911 calls should be assessed on a case by case basis and that the statements made should be individually evaluated for admissibility in light of the confrontation clause).

[85]People v. Moscat, 3 Misc. 3d 739, 777 N.Y.S.2d 875 (N.Y. City Crim. Ct. 2004).

[86]People v. Moscat, 3 Misc. 3d 739, 777 N.Y.S.2d 875 (N.Y. City Crim. Ct. 2004).

[87]People v. Moscat, 3 Misc. 3d 739, 777 N.Y.S.2d 875 (N.Y. City Crim. Ct. 2004); State v. Nelson, 2004-Ohio-6153, 2004 WL 2626817 (Ohio Ct. App. 1st Dist. Hamilton County 2004); State v. Naugler, 2005-Ohio-6274, 2005 WL 3148081 (Ohio Ct. App. 12th Dist. Madison County 2005), judgment aff'd, 111 Ohio St. 3d 130, 2006-Ohio-5340, 855 N.E.2d 456 (2006); State v. Russo, 2006-Ohio-2172, 2006 WL 1163750 (Ohio Ct. App. 9th Dist. Summit County 2006); State v. Mills, 2005-Ohio-2128, 2006 WL 1132543 (Ohio Ct. App. 2d Dist. Montgomery County 2006) (a 911 emergency call made by an assault victim is not testimonial hearsay for purposes of *Crawford*), citing State v. Byrd, 160 Ohio App. 3d 538, 2005-Ohio-1902, 828 N.E.2d 133 (2d Dist. Montgomery County 2005), quoting People v. Moscat, 3 Misc. 3d 739, 777 N.Y.S.2d 875 (N.Y. City Crim. Ct. 2004); State v. Williams, 2009-Ohio-6967, 2009 WL 5174155 (Ohio Ct. App. 6th Dist. Lucas County 2009).

[88]State v. Davis, 154 Wash. 2d 291, 111 P.3d 844 (2005), aff'd, 547 U.S. 813, 126

In *Davis*, the victim made statements in a 911 call to the police stating that her former boyfriend hit her with his fists. The trial court allowed into evidence the 911 call made by the alleged victim even though she failed to appear at trial. Both the appellate court and the Washington Supreme Court upheld the lower court decision that a 911 call is an utterance and an exception to hearsay.

At oral argument, Davis claimed that the Confrontation Clause applied to 911 calls because it was understood that the Clause applied to immediate reports of crime to governmental agents, such as to police dispatchers. The state responded that the purpose of the Confrontation Clause would not be served by Davis's interpretation since 911 operators were not likely to solicit testimony in preparation of a trial.

In *Hammon*, the victim told the police, who responded to a domestic violence call, that her husband had hit, shoved and had thrown her down. The officer had her fill out and sign a "battery affidavit" describing her husband's violent conduct. She did not testify at trial but had memorialized her statement in the affidavit. The trial court admitted her statements as excited utterances. The Supreme Court of Indiana reversed the lower courts and determined that admissibility of a statement under a hearsay exception did not end the inquiry after *Crawford*, but the court had to look to whether the victim's statements were testimonial, in which case they should have been excluded as violative of the Confrontation Clause.

The Indiana Supreme Court held that the victim's purpose in making the statement could be considered, but that the officer's motivation in questioning was more important. Under that analysis, the initial statements were not considered for future use at trial, but only to find out what was going on. The affidavit, however, was testimonial as it was taken to preserve the victim's account for a future use.

The U. S. Supreme Court consolidated the decisions, which allowed it to address the issues before it and expand the parameters of *Crawford*. In Davis, the U.S. Supreme Court held that the woman's excited utterances made in a 911 call to police officers amounted to "an ongoing emergency" and thus, were nontestimonial.[90] In *Hammon*, the Court determined that the statements and the affidavit were testimonial and could not be introduced in the felony prosecution of her husband.

S. Ct. 2266, 165 L. Ed. 2d 224, 70 Fed. R. Evid. Serv. 472, 30 A.L.R.6th 599 (2006).

[89]Hammon v. State, 829 N.E.2d 444 (Ind. 2005), rev'd and remanded, 547 U.S. 813, 126 S. Ct. 2266, 165 L. Ed. 2d 224, 70 Fed. R. Evid. Serv. 472, 30 A.L.R.6th 599 (2006).

[90]See Colon v. Taskey, 414 Fed. Appx. 735 (6th Cir. 2010) (upholding state appellate court's finding that domestic violence victim's statements to a police officer at the scene were made during an ongoing emergency and therefore were nontestimonial and not a violation of the Confrontation Clause); Cleveland v. Merritt, 2016-Ohio-4693, 69 N.E.3d 102 (Ohio Ct. App. 8th Dist. Cuyahoga County 2016), appeal not allowed, 147 Ohio St. 3d 1506, 2017-Ohio-261, 67 N.E.3d 824 (2017); State v. Martin, 2016-Ohio-225, 57 N.E.3d 411 (Ohio Ct. App. 5th Dist. Tuscarawas County 2016); State v. Heard, 2017-Ohio-8796, ¶ 15, 2017 WL 5988500 (Ohio Ct. App. 12th Dist. Warren County 2017) (although 911 caller victim did not speak to dispatcher, it was sufficient that a voice was heard in the background telling another "to get away, to get off and to leave me alone" and the dispatcher listened to determine what was *currently happening* and because 911 call was used to address ongoing emergency, it was non-testimonial).

In *Crawford*, Scalia declined to define testimonial statements. In *Davis* and *Hammon*, the Court established the rule that "statements are nontestimonial when made in the course of police interrogation under circumstances objectively indicating that the primary purpose of interrogation is to enable police assistance to meet an ongoing emergency.[91] They are testimonial when the circumstances objectively indicate that there is no such ongoing emergency, and that the primary purpose of the interrogation is to establish or prove past events potentially relevant to later criminal prosecution."[92] The Court also differentiated *Davis* from *Crawford* by pointing out that a 911 call is ordinarily designed primarily to describe current circumstances requiring police assistance, whereas in *Crawford*, the interrogation took place at a police station and was directed solely at establishing a past crime.[93]

Applying this standard to *Davis*, Justice Scalia reasoned that the 911 call was part of an ongoing emergency[94] and that the victim was not acting as a witness or testifying. In applying the standard to *Hammon*, Justice Scalia noted that there was no emergency in progress.[95] When the officer arrived, the victim told him things were fine and that there was no immediate threat to her person. "When the officer questioned Amy for the second time, and elicited the challenged statements, he was not seeking to determine (as in *Davis*) 'what is happening' but rather 'what happened.' Objectively viewed, the primary, if not indeed the sole, purpose of the interrogation was to investigate a possible crime-which is, of course, precisely what the officer *should* have done."[96]

Of note is that Justice Scalia responded to criticism expressed by the prosecuting attorney for the State of Washington and several amici that the decision could hinder the prosecution of domestic

---

[91]See State v. Naugler, 111 Ohio St. 3d 130, 2006-Ohio-5340, 855 N.E.2d 456 (2006); see also State v. McKenzie, 2006-Ohio-5725, 2006 WL 3095671 (Ohio Ct. App. 8th Dist. Cuyahoga County 2006) (testimony from police officer that the victim said, "that's him, that's him. He's the one that just hit me" was not testimonial in nature. Statements victim made to police officer after defendant was secured in the police car were testimonial. The Court also stated the facts in *McKenzie* were similar to *Davis*; State v. Hunneman, 2006-Ohio-7023, 2006 WL 3833897 (Ohio Ct. App. 12th Dist. Clermont County 2006).

[92]Davis v. Washington, 547 U.S. 813, 126 S. Ct. 2266, 2268–69, 165 L. Ed. 2d 224, 70 Fed. R. Evid. Serv. 472, 30 A.L.R.6th 599 (2006).

[93]State v. Davis, 154 Wash. 2d 291, 111 P.3d 844 (2005), aff'd, 547 U.S. 813, 126 S. Ct. 2266, 165 L. Ed. 2d 224, 70 Fed. R. Evid. Serv. 472, 30 A.L.R.6th 599 (2006).

[94]See also State v. Mitchell, 171 Ohio App. 3d 225, 2007-Ohio-1696, 870 N.E.2d 228 (8th Dist. Cuyahoga County 2007).

[95]See also Toledo v. Loggins, 2007-Ohio-5887, 2007 WL 3227385 (Ohio Ct. App. 6th Dist. Lucas County 2007); State v. Heard, 2017-Ohio-8796, ¶ 13, 2017 WL 5988500 (Ohio Ct. App. 12th Dist. Warren County 2017) (where officer asked victim what *had happened* was not an ongoing emergency; rather questioning was designed to establish past events, with those events potentially relevant to a later prosecution and thus, testimonial in nature).

[96]Davis v. Washington, 547 U.S. 813, 126 S. Ct. 2266, 2278, 165 L. Ed. 2d 224, 70 Fed. R. Evid. Serv. 472, 30 A.L.R.6th 599 (2006); see also Cleveland v. Colon, 2007-Ohio-269, 2007 WL 179082 (Ohio Ct. App. 8th Dist. Cuyahoga County 2007) (noting that a Confrontation Clause analysis cannot be avoided in instances where a testimonial statement falls within a firmly rooted hearsay exception).

violence cases in which victims later refuse to testify. The Court stated that, on remand, the Indiana courts could determine whether a claim for forfeiture by wrongdoing might be raised. Forfeiture by wrongdoing is when a person obtains the witness's absence by wrongdoing and forfeits the constitutional right to confrontation.[97]

Justice Scalia stated that "[t]his particular type of crime is notoriously susceptible to intimidation or coercion of the victim to ensure that she does not testify at trial. When this occurs, the Confrontation Clause gives the criminal a windfall. We may not, however, vitiate constitutional guarantees when they have the effect of allowing the guilty to go free. But when defendants seek to undermine the judicial process by procuring or coercing silence from witnesses and victims, the Sixth Amendment does not require courts to acquiesce. While defendants have no duty to assist the State in proving their guilt, they *do* have the duty to refrain from acting in ways that destroy the integrity of the criminal-trial system. We reiterate what we said in *Crawford*: that 'the rule of forfeiture by wrongdoing. . .extinguishes confrontation claims on essentially equitable grounds.' "[98]

Q & A: What is forfeiture by wrongdoing?[99]

Unfortunately, the U.S. Supreme Court in *Giles v. California*[100] held that the California Supreme Court's theory of "forfeiture by wrongdoing" was not an exception to the Sixth Amendment confrontation requirement because it was not established at the time of the founding of the Bill of Rights or in American jurisprudence since that time. In remanding the matter back to the California Supreme Court, the Court held that appellant did not forfeit his right to confront the victim's statements unless he killed her with the intent to prevent her from testifying.[101]

The U.S. Supreme Court's majority appears to impose a two-tiered

---

[97]State v. Davis, 154 Wash. 2d 291, 111 P.3d 844 (2005), aff'd, 547 U.S. 813, 126 S. Ct. 2266, 165 L. Ed. 2d 224, 70 Fed. R. Evid. Serv. 472, 30 A.L.R.6th 599 (2006); see also Evid. R 804(A)(6); Allie Phillips, Weathering the Storm after *Crawford v. Washington*, Update Vol. 17, Number 6 (2004) (view article at http://www.ndaa-apri.org).

[98]Davis v. Washington, 547 U.S. 813, 126 S. Ct. 2266, 2279–80, 165 L. Ed. 2d 224, 70 Fed. R. Evid. Serv. 472, 30 A.L.R.6th 599 (2006), quoting Crawford v. Washington, 541 U.S. 36, 62, 124 S. Ct. 1354, 158 L. Ed. 2d 177, 63 Fed. R. Evid. Serv. 1077 (2004).

[99]Amanda L. Stubson, *Giving Victims a Voice: The Doctrine of Forfeiture by Wrongdoing as a Remedy to the Silencing Effect of Crawford*, 32 Hamline L. Rev. 265 (2009); Sarah M. Buel, Putting Forfeiture to Work, 43 U.C. Davis L. Rev. 1295 (2013); Sarah M. Buel, De Facto Witness Tampering, 29 Berkeley J. Gender L. & Just. 72 (2014).

[100]Giles v. California, 554 U.S. 353, 128 S. Ct. 2678, 171 L. Ed. 2d 488 (2008). See also Tanner, Herb, Jr., Forfeiture by Wrongdoing in a Post-*Giles* World, 42 *Prosecutor, Journal of the National District Attorneys Association* 34 (Oct-Dec 2008); Deborah Tuerkheimer, *Forfeiture After Giles: The Relevance of "Domestic Violence Context"*; 13 Lewis & Clark L. rev. 711 (fall 2009); but see State v. McLaughlin, 272 S.W.3d 506 (Mo. Ct. App. E.D. 2008) (in *en banc* decision, evidence was admitted under forfeiture by wrongdoing doctrine and judgment was affirmed).

[101]Giles v. California, 554 U.S. 353, 128 S. Ct. 2678, 2679, 171 L. Ed. 2d 488 (2008). See also State v. Fry, 125 Ohio St. 3d 163, 2010-Ohio-1017, 926 N.E.2d 1239 (2010) (where Supreme Court of Ohio found that defendant forfeited his confrontation rights by killing his victim, where her murder was designed to prevent her testimony against him in the criminal proceeding).

analysis in domestic violence cases: prosecutors must show defendant's wrongdoing against the victim and show that the wrongdoing was committed with the intent to prevent the victim from testifying.

In his dissent, Justice Breyer stressed that "[e]ven the majority appears to recognize the problem with its 'purpose' requirement, for it ends its opinion by creating a kind of presumption that will transform *purpose* into *knowledge-based intent*—at least where domestic violence is at issue; and that is the area where the problem is most likely to arise."[102]

The dissent also pointed out that in *Davis v. Washington*,[103] the Court "recognized that 'domestic violence' cases are 'notoriously susceptible to intimidation or coercion of the victim to ensure that she does not testify at trial.' We noted the concern that '[w]hen this occurs, the Confrontation Clause gives the criminal a windfall.' "[104] The Court "replied to that concern by stating that 'one who obtains the absence of a witness by wrongdoing forfeits the constitutional right to confrontation.' "[105] To the extent that it insists upon an additional showing of purpose, the Court, according to the dissent, breaks the promise implicit in those words and, in doing so, grants the defendant not fair treatment, but a windfall. "I can find no history, no underlying purpose, no administrative consideration, and no constitutional principle that requires this result."[106]

The Supreme Court remanded the case back to the Court of Appeals for the Second District with instructions to vacate its previous decision in light of the Supreme Court's decision. In reversing its opinion, the Court of Appeals held that, in light of the reasoning set forth in *Giles v. California*, the prosecutor presented no evidence demonstrating that the defendant killed the victim with the intent to prevent her from testifying.[107]

Of concern to domestic violence experts is that 911 calls that describe completed events are likely to be testimonial as are statements made to responding officers.

Therefore, 911 calls should be made when the domestic violence is still in progress and the dispatcher should be advised that an ongoing emergency is in progress. If victims describe "what is happening," rather than "what happened" to the 911 operators and advise if any weapons are involved or present on the premises, it is likely that the statement is non-testimonial and admissible.

---

[102]Giles v. California, 554 U.S. 353, 128 S. Ct. 2678, 2708, 171 L. Ed. 2d 488 (2008).

[103]Davis v. Washington, 547 U.S. 813, 126 S. Ct. 2266, 165 L. Ed. 2d 224, 70 Fed. R. Evid. Serv. 472, 30 A.L.R.6th 599 (2006).

[104]Giles v. California, 554 U.S. 353, 128 S. Ct. 2678, 2709, 171 L. Ed. 2d 488 (2008), quoting Davis v. Washington, 547 U.S. 813, 832–33, 126 S. Ct. 2266, 165 L. Ed. 2d 224, 70 Fed. R. Evid. Serv. 472, 30 A.L.R.6th 599 (2006).

[105]Giles v. California, 554 U.S. 353, 128 S. Ct. 2678, 2709, 171 L. Ed. 2d 488 (2008), quoting Davis v. Washington, 547 U.S. 813, 833, 126 S. Ct. 2266, 165 L. Ed. 2d 224, 70 Fed. R. Evid. Serv. 472, 30 A.L.R.6th 599 (2006).

[106]Giles v. California, 554 U.S. 353, 128 S. Ct. 2678, 2709, 171 L. Ed. 2d 488 (2008).

[107]People v. Giles, 2009 WL 457832 (Cal. App. 2d Dist. 2009), unpublished/noncitable and unpublished/noncitable and unpublished/noncitable.

Q & A: When are cell phone records considered non-testimonial for Confrontation Clause purposes?

Although not factually on point, the Supreme Court of Ohio's decision in *State v. Hood*[108] offers judicial guidance in domestic violence and stalking cases in which the issue is the admissibility of cell phone records. In *Hood*, appellant was one of several men who allegedly burst into a Cleveland home and robbed a group of people. One of the co-conspirators was shot and killed during the commission of the robbery. Hood was charged with murder, aggravated burglary, and aggravated robbery. As part of the proof to establish Hood's involvement in the crimes, the state introduced cell phone records to demonstrate his communication with the other co-conspirators and his whereabouts during the time in question.[109] The question presented to the Supreme Court was whether, in general, cell phone records produced by a cell phone company constitute testimonial evidence that implicate a defendant's right to cross examine a witness under the Confrontation Clause of the U.S. Constitution.[110]

At trial, the state introduced the records arguing that the records fell within the business records exception to the hearsay rule and that one of the co-conspirators could even verify the records based on his own knowledge. The defense objected to their use, arguing that they had not been authenticated as a business record, had not been identified by any phone company and that the alleged subpoenas to the cell phone companies were not in the file. The cell phone records were admitted into evidence.

On appeal, one of the issues raised was whether the trial court erred "by allowing cell phone records to be admitted into evidence without being properly authenticated in violation of the Confrontation Clause."[111] The appellate court held that "[a]ssuming arguendo that these records were inadmissible and violative of appellant's right to confront the witnesses against him, any error on the part of the trial court in this regard was harmless."[112] Because the admission of the cell phone records did not contribute to Hood's conviction, the trial court's judgment was affirmed.

On a discretionary appeal to the Supreme Court of Ohio, Hood states the following proposition of law: "[c]ell phone records are not admissible as business records without proper authentication. The admission of unauthenticated cell phone records under the business records

[108] State v. Hood, 135 Ohio St. 3d 137, 2012-Ohio-6208, 984 N.E.2d 1057 (2012).

[109] State v. Hood, 135 Ohio St. 3d 137, ¶ 5, 2012-Ohio-6208, 984 N.E.2d 1057 (2012).

[110] State v. Hood, 135 Ohio St. 3d 137, ¶ 4, 2012-Ohio-6208, 984 N.E.2d 1057 (2012).

[111] State v. Hood, 135 Ohio St. 3d 137, ¶ 29, 2012-Ohio-6208, 984 N.E.2d 1057 (2012).

[112] State v. Hood, 135 Ohio St. 3d 137, ¶ 29, 2012-Ohio-6208, 984 N.E.2d 1057 (2012), quoting State v. Hood, 2010-Ohio-5477, ¶ 27, 2010 WL 4522416 (Ohio Ct. App. 8th Dist. Cuyahoga County 2010), decision aff'd, 135 Ohio St. 3d 137, 2012-Ohio-6208, 984 N.E.2d 1057 (2012).

exception violates the Confrontation Clause of the Sixth Amendment to the United State Constitution."[113]

The Supreme Court of Ohio first determined that generally, cell phone records are business records that are not prepared for litigation, are non-testimonial and thus, the Confrontation Clause does not affect their admissibility.[114] But in *Hood*, there is no assurance that the cell phone records are business records under Evidence Rule 803(6) because there was no foundation laid by a custodian of the record or by any other qualified witness.[115] Nor was a certification or affidavit authenticating them attached. Had they been authenticated, "we could be sure that they were not testimonial, that is, that they were not prepared for use at trial."[116] In that the records were not authenticated as business records, the Supreme Court was unable to discern whether they were prepared for use at trial or prepared in the ordinary course of business and thus, whether they were testimonial in nature. Therefore, the admission of the records was constitutional error.[117] However, because the admission of the records in Hood was harmless in that there was overwhelming evidence of his guilt, the judgment of the appellate court was affirmed.

§ 16:14 Hearsay exceptions—Excited Utterances[1]

Statements made by a witness contemporaneous with or soon after a startling or exciting event[2] are afforded a high degree of credibility.[3]

---

[113]State v. Hood, 135 Ohio St. 3d 137, ¶ 31, 2012-Ohio-6208, 984 N.E.2d 1057 (2012).

[114]State v. Hood, 135 Ohio St. 3d 137, ¶ 39, 2012-Ohio-6208, 984 N.E.2d 1057 (2012); State v. Craig, 110 Ohio St. 3d 306, 2006-Ohio-4571, 853 N.E.2d 621, ¶ 82 (2006); State v. Davis, 116 Ohio St. 3d 404, 2008-Ohio-2, 880 N.E.2d 31, ¶ 171 (2008) (discussing elements of a business record exception under Evid. R. 803(6); State v. Edwards, 2017-Ohio-7231, 96 N.E.3d 890 (Ohio Ct. App. 9th Dist. Summit County 2017), appeal not allowed, 152 Ohio St. 3d 1409, 2018-Ohio-723, 92 N.E.3d 880 (2018).

[115]State v. Hood, 135 Ohio St. 3d 137, ¶ 40, 2012-Ohio-6208, 984 N.E.2d 1057 (2012).

[116]State v. Hood, 135 Ohio St. 3d 137, ¶ 42, 2012-Ohio-6208, 984 N.E.2d 1057 (2012).

[117]State v. Hood, 135 Ohio St. 3d 137, ¶ 42, 2012-Ohio-6208, 984 N.E.2d 1057 (2012).

[Section 16:14]

[1]See State v. Wallace, 37 Ohio St. 3d 87, 88, 524 N.E.2d 466 (1988); see also State v. Shelton, 2002-Ohio-5157, 2002 WL 31160564 (Ohio Ct. App. 11th Dist. Portage County 2002) (discussing the foundation necessary before introducing testimony as an excited utterance exception to the hearsay rule); State v. Lampe, 2003-Ohio-3059, 2003 WL 21360725 (Ohio Ct. App. 1st Dist. Hamilton County 2003); State v. Gough, 2004-Ohio-4550, 2004 WL 1925700 (Ohio Ct. App. 5th Dist. Licking County 2004); see also Text § 5:15, Case preparation—Hearsay exceptions—Excited utterance; Celeste E. Byron, The Use of the Excited Utterance Hearsay Exception in the Prosecution of Domestic Violence Cases After *Crawford v. Washington*, 24 Rev. Litig. 409 (2005).

[2]See, e.g., State v. Smith, 2002-Ohio-3402, 2002 WL 1461627 (Ohio Ct. App. 4th Dist. Highland County 2002), quoting State v. Taylor, 66 Ohio St. 3d 295, 303, 612 N.E.2d 316 (1993) (discussing time considerations after which a statement can no longer be an excited utterance; "[t]herefore the amount of time between the statement and the event is relevant but not dispositive of the question."); State v. Walker, 2001

In domestic violence cases, there may be several excited utterances because of the highly charged and emotional nature of the event.

To qualify as an excited utterance under Evid.R. 803(2),[4] a statement must meet the following test:

- There must be a startling or exciting occurrence;[5]
- The statement must be made while the one making it is still under the stress caused by the excitement of the event or condition;[6]
- The declaration or statement must concern the startling or exciting occurrence; and
- The one making the statement must have first-hand knowledge of the event.[7]

WL 1782885 (Ohio Ct. App. 5th Dist. Stark County 2001).

[3]See State v. Cornell, 129 Ohio App. 3d 106, 717 N.E.2d 361 (10th Dist. Franklin County 1998); see also State v. Griffitts, 2002-Ohio-921, 2002 WL 252786 (Ohio Ct. App. 2d Dist. Montgomery County 2002) (discussing whether there is a time limit to determine whether a domestic violence victim is making a statement under the stress of a startling occurrence in order to admit the statement as an excited utterance); State v. Justice, 92 Ohio App. 3d 740, 746, 637 N.E.2d 85 (9th Dist. Wayne County 1994); State v. Shelton, 2002-Ohio-5157, 2002 WL 31160564 (Ohio Ct. App. 11th Dist. Portage County 2002) (discussing the factors necessary to decide whether a statement is an excited utterance). But see State v. Turner, 1996 WL 348016 (Ohio Ct. App. 1st Dist. Hamilton County 1996) (victim's statements to police made three days after incident did not qualify as excited utterance and were not admissible); State v. Mack, 2015-Ohio-5214, 2015 WL 8607454 (Ohio Ct. App. 11th Dist. Ashtabula County 2015) (note dissent which argues that if complainant "lied" about the events in question, she could not be under stress due to a startling event).

[4]See City of Shaker Heights v. Al-Gureshi, 1998 WL 183818 (Ohio Ct. App. 8th Dist. Cuyahoga County 1998), quoting State v. Taylor, 66 Ohio St. 3d 295, 300, 612 N.E.2d 316 (1993), relying on the syllabus of Potter v. Baker, 162 Ohio St. 488, 55 Ohio Op. 389, 124 N.E.2d 140, 53 A.L.R.2d 1234 (1955) (detailing a four-part test for determining admissibility of an excited utterance); State v. Cornell, 129 Ohio App. 3d 106, 717 N.E.2d 361 (10th Dist. Franklin County 1998); State v. Crowley, 2009-Ohio-6689, 2009 WL 4893283 (Ohio Ct. App. 2d Dist. Clark County 2009); State v. Mauldin, 2010-Ohio-4192, 2010 WL 3482689 (Ohio Ct. App. 7th Dist. Mahoning County 2010) (an abuse of discretion standard of review applies to a determination of whether a declaration should be admissible under the excited utterance exception to the hearsay rule); State v. Mack, 2015-Ohio-5214, 2015 WL 8607454 (Ohio Ct. App. 11th Dist. Ashtabula County 2015); State v. Boss, 2017-Ohio-697, 85 N.E.3d 529 (Ohio Ct. App. 5th Dist. Ashland County 2017).

[5]See also State v. Bunch, 2010-Ohio-515, 2010 WL 547402 (Ohio Ct. App. 8th Dist. Cuyahoga County 2010) (Evid. R. 803(1) and (2) contemplate that statements made by witnesses who personally observe startling events may be admissible even though they are introduced as hearsay).

[6]See State v. Stover, 2014-Ohio-2572, 2014 WL 2701213 (Ohio Ct. App. 9th Dist. Wayne County 2014) (discussing conditions necessary to qualify as an excited utterance and determining statement not an excited utterance); State v. Little, 2016-Ohio-8398, 78 N.E.3d 323 (Ohio Ct. App. 3d Dist. Allen County 2016) (officer's testimony that victim told him that defendant "grabbed her by the hair and slammed her head into a glass table" was admissible as an excited utterance and did not violate *Crawford*. at syllabus).

[7]See State v. Lee, 73 Ohio Misc. 2d 9, 657 N.E.2d 604 (Mun. Ct. 1995); State v. Brown, 2006-Ohio-6267, 2006 WL 3446238 (Ohio Ct. App. 8th Dist. Cuyahoga County 2006), aff'd on other grounds, 119 Ohio St. 3d 447, 2008-Ohio-4569, 895 N.E.2d 149 (2008) (holding that victim's on-the-scene statements to officer were nontestimonial); State v. Rohrer, 1998 WL 400768 (Ohio Ct. App. 5th Dist. Fairfield County 1998); State v. Ewers, 1999 WL 502152 (Ohio Ct. App. 6th Dist. Erie County 1999). See also

Q & A: Are 911 calls considered excited utterances?

Yes. Because 911 calls often record statements made by a victim under "excited circumstances," 911 tapes or transcripts may be admitted into evidence as excited utterances under Evid.R. 803(2).[8] Sometimes this is the single most important piece of evidence presented because it may capture the fear and anxiety of the victim or other witness, and even the violence as it is unfolding.

It should be noted that 911 tapes may also contain statements made by the alleged defendant/respondent. These statements are generally not hearsay and may be admissible as admissions of a party.[9]

Q & A: Is there a certain amount of time after which a statement can no longer be considered an excited utterance?

No. In *State v. Taylor*,[10] the Ohio Supreme Court noted that "[t]here is no per se amount of time after which a statement can no longer be considered to be an excited utterance. The central requirements are that the statement must be made while the declarant is still under the stress of the event and the statement may not be the result of reflective thought."[11]

Text § 5:15, Case preparation—Hearsay exceptions—Excited utterance. But see State v. Labombarbe, 1997 WL 640587 (Ohio Ct. App. 6th Dist. Wood County 1997) (discussing when a statement should not be admitted); Mayfield v. Cuccarese, 2008-Ohio-1812, 2008 WL 1747439 (Ohio Ct. App. 8th Dist. Cuyahoga County 2008).

[8]State v. Jorden, 134 Ohio App. 3d 131, 730 N.E.2d 447 (1st Dist. Hamilton County 1999); State v. Yun, 2001 WL 1082354 (Ohio Ct. App. 5th Dist. Stark County 2001); see also Text § 5:15, Case preparation—Hearsay exceptions—Excited utterance; City of Shaker Heights v. Al-Gureshi, 1998 WL 183818 (Ohio Ct. App. 8th Dist. Cuyahoga County 1998) (discussing when a police officer's statement may be admitted as an excited utterance exception to the hearsay rule); State v. Louk, 2002-Ohio-988, 2002 WL 358639 (Ohio Ct. App. 5th Dist. Delaware County 2002); U.S. v. Cruz, 156 F.3d 22, 50 Fed. R. Evid. Serv. 212 (1st Cir. 1998) (affirming lower court decision to admit statements made to staff of battered women's shelter into evidence as excited utterance); State v. Williams, 2013-Ohio-726, 987 N.E.2d 322 (Ohio Ct. App. 6th Dist. Lucas County 2013) (audio recording and printed transcript of neighbor's 911 call was excited utterance) (syllabus); State v. Kerr, 2016-Ohio-965, 2016 WL 936844 (Ohio Ct. App. 2d Dist. Montgomery County 2016); State v. Boss, 2017-Ohio-697, 85 N.E.3d 529 (Ohio Ct. App. 5th Dist. Ashland County 2017); State v. Martin, 2016-Ohio-225, 57 N.E.3d 411 (Ohio Ct. App. 5th Dist. Tuscarawas County 2016).

[9]See Evid.R. 801(D); see also State v. Lee, 73 Ohio Misc. 2d 9, 17, 657 N.E.2d 604 (Mun. Ct. 1995).

[10]State v. Taylor, 66 Ohio St. 3d 295, 612 N.E.2d 316 (1993). See also State v. Jeffries, 2006-Ohio-828, 2006 WL 438701 (Ohio Ct. App. 5th Dist. Stark County 2006).

[11]State v. Taylor, 66 Ohio St. 3d 295, 303, 612 N.E.2d 316 (1993); see also State v. Walker, 2001 WL 1782885 (Ohio Ct. App. 5th Dist. Stark County 2001) (discussing whether a thirty minute time frame is too long); State v. Cornell, 129 Ohio App. 3d 106, 717 N.E.2d 361 (10th Dist. Franklin County 1998) (statements made by victim to police within ten minutes after incident qualified as excited utterances); State v. Ducey, 2004-Ohio-3833, 2004 WL 1607310 (Ohio Ct. App. 10th Dist. Franklin County 2004); State v. Travis, 165 Ohio App. 3d 626, 2006-Ohio-787, 847 N.E.2d 1237 (2d Dist. Montgomery County 2006) (statement made to police within first hour of offense an excited utterance); State v. Williams, 2009-Ohio-6967, 2009 WL 5174155 (Ohio Ct. App. 6th Dist. Lucas County 2009); State v. Bennett, 1998 WL 820517 (Ohio Ct. App. 5th Dist. Tuscarawas County 1998) (where there is no intervening circumstance, statements made to police after victim walked three blocks to call police from a pay phone fell within the excited utterance hearsay exception); Cleveland v. Amoroso, 2015-Ohio-95, 2015 WL 178418 (Ohio Ct. App. 8th Dist. Cuyahoga County 2015);

Q & A: How and when does a victim's attorney present tape-recorded evidence?

Tape-recorded calls may be admitted into evidence under certain circumstances.[12] For example, 911 emergency calls may corroborate a victim's testimony that he/she was abused by a specific individual or that he/she was fearful and emotional at the time of the call. A transcript of the victim's statements may also be admitted to prove that domestic violence occurred, even absent the testimony and/or presence of the victim at trial[13] or when the victim recants her testimony in court.[14]

Attorneys and prosecutors should assure that these 911 tapes and transcripts are preserved for future use. Attorneys have an obligation to request and examine the evidence contained in these items, determine whether a child witness is on the tape, and analyze the nature of the recorded conversation.

Q & A: How is a 911 tape authenticated so that it may be admitted into evidence?[15]

An attorney wishing to present this evidence must comply with the evidentiary rules that govern the admission of audio recordings.[16] A witness may authenticate a 911 tape by identifying the voice of the individual on the tape, based on having heard the voice in question at any time under circumstances connecting the voice to the speaker. It is immaterial whether the person identifying the voice originally heard

---

State v. Mack, 2015-Ohio-5214, 2015 WL 8607454 (Ohio Ct. App. 11th Dist. Ashtabula County 2015); but see State v. Harris, 163 Ohio App. 3d 286, 2005-Ohio-4696, 837 N.E.2d 830 (1st Dist. Hamilton County 2005) (statements made to police at police station after victim calmed down were the result of reflective thought); State v. Manzell, 2007-Ohio-4076, 2007 WL 2283550 (Ohio Ct. App. 5th Dist. Stark County 2007); Toledo v. Murray, 2014-Ohio-3625, 2014 WL 4161247 (Ohio Ct. App. 6th Dist. Lucas County 2014).

[12] State v. Newell, 1998 WL 667651 (Ohio Ct. App. 5th Dist. Stark County 1998) (discussing the requirements for authentication of a tape recording). But see Basista v. Basista, 2000 WL 777005 (Ohio Ct. App. 8th Dist. Cuyahoga County 2000) (court denied the CPO, based on evidence presented in the audiotape).

[13] See State v. Lee, 73 Ohio Misc. 2d 9, 657 N.E.2d 604 (Mun. Ct. 1995); see also State v. Newell, 1998 WL 667651 (Ohio Ct. App. 5th Dist. Stark County 1998); State v. Cox, 2001-Ohio-3213, 2001 WL 301429 (Ohio Ct. App. 7th Dist. Belmont County 2001) (specifically footnote reference on page 2 wherein the appellate court noted that the Ohio legislature has taken steps to encourage prosecutors to continue with the prosecution of cases even where the victim fails to appear or wishes to withdraw her complaint); State v. Ragland, 2001 WL 888753 (Ohio Ct. App. 9th Dist. Summit County 2001); State v. Semenchuk, 2002-Ohio-674, 2002 WL 253876 (Ohio Ct. App. 8th Dist. Cuyahoga County 2002).

[14] State v. Washington, 2001 WL 460888 (Ohio Ct. App. 10th Dist. Franklin County 2001).

[15] See also Text § 6:14, Trial presentation—911 tapes and transcripts (providing some questions asked to the custodian of the records for admission). But see State v. Boss, 2017-Ohio-697, 85 N.E.3d 529 (Ohio Ct. App. 5th Dist. Ashland County 2017) (finding that trial court error, if any, in admitting an audiotape of the victim's call for emergency assistance under the business records exception to the hearsay rule was harmless, during prosecution for domestic violence; the audiotape was admissible under the excited utterance expectation to the hearsay rule. At syllabus; ¶ 17).

[16] Evid.R. 901(B)(5); Evid.R. 901(B)(6).

it firsthand or through a mechanical or electronic transmission or recording.[17]

Where the item to be authenticated is a telephone conversation, evidence that the call was made from the number that the telephone company assigned to a particular person at the time in question will authenticate the conversation. Additionally, evidence that the call was made to a number that the telephone company assigned to the business (law enforcement agency) at the time in question will authenticate the conversation.[18] In the case of a person, the circumstances presented by the proponent at the hearing where the evidence is sought to be admitted must show that the person who received the call or engaged in the telephone conversation is the person that the proponent seeks to identify.[19]

For example in *State v. Norris*,[20] the 911 call indicating that Norris had hit her was admitted into evidence. On appeal, he challenged the admission of the 911 call. The appellate court first noted that 911 calls are usually admissible under the excited utterance or present sense exception of the hearsay rule so long as "the declaration was made under such circumstances as would reasonably show that it resulted from impulse rather than reason and reflection."[21] Additionally, such statements may not run afoul of the Confrontation Clause.

Once it was determined that the statements made were exceptions to the hearsay rule and did not violate the Confrontation Clause, it became necessary to determine whether they were properly authenticated. Per Evid. R. 901(A), "[t]he requirement of authentication or identification as a condition precedent to admissibility is satisfied by evidence sufficient to support a finding that the material in question is what its proponent claims." In this case, the police officer testified that the CD he produced contained the call from the address in question on the date and time in question. Another officer testified that, upon responding to the residence, he found the victim bleeding and crying and her description of the incident matched what was said in the 911 call.[22]

The appellate court found that "[t]hese statements leave little doubt that Battle was, in fact, the 911 caller. Moreover, we have held that 911 recordings are sufficiently authenticated when the keeper of such records testifies that he or she keeps such records, about how such records are recorded and stored and transferred to CDs and about how

[17]Text § 5:12, Case preparation—Physical evidence.

[18]See also State v. Mitchell, 171 Ohio App. 3d 225, 2007-Ohio-1696, 870 N.E.2d 228 (8th Dist. Cuyahoga County 2007).

[19]Text § 5:12, Case preparation—Physical evidence; see also State v. Newell, 1998 WL 667651 (Ohio Ct. App. 5th Dist. Stark County 1998).

[20]State v. Norris, 2015-Ohio-624, 2015 WL 753346 (Ohio Ct. App. 2d Dist. Montgomery County 2015).

[21]State v. Norris, 2015-Ohio-624, 2015 WL 753346, ¶ 12 (Ohio Ct. App. 2d Dist. Montgomery County 2015), quoting State v. Travis, 165 Ohio App. 3d 626, 2006-Ohio-787, 847 N.E.2d 1237 (2d Dist. Montgomery County 2006); citing, State v. Humphries, 79 Ohio App. 3d 589, 598, 607 N.E.2d 921 (12th Dist. Clermont County 1992).

[22]State v. Norris, 2015-Ohio-624, 2015 WL 753346, ¶ 23 (Ohio Ct. App. 2d Dist. Montgomery County 2015).

they are retrieved from the system."[23] "The threshold standard for authenticating evidence pursuant to Evid. R. 901(A) is low; it does not require conclusive proof of authenticity, but only sufficient foundational evidence for the trier of fact to conclude that the evidence is what its proponent claims it to be."[24] Therefore, the appellate court overruled appellant's assignment of error.

§ 16:15 Hearsay exceptions—Present sense impressions[1]

A present sense impression is a statement describing or explaining an event or condition made while the declarant was perceiving the event or condition or immediately thereafter.[2] Present sense impressions often bear a high degree of trustworthiness because the declarant described the event and/or uttered a statement about the event in close temporal proximity to the event.[3] The spontaneity of the statement is the key to its trustworthiness.[4]

The present sense impression exception is based on verification, and since it is usually made to a third party, that third party subsequently testifies to it.[5] The third party is usually present at the time of the declarant's observation, has an opportunity to observe the situation and provides an independent check on the accuracy of the declarant's observation.[6]

If the third party who offers the testimony about another's present sense impression was not present at the time the declarant made the statement, the statement may lack credibility and the validity of the statement is suspect. However, the third party's presence is not an

---

[23]State v. Norris, 2015-Ohio-624, 2015 WL 753346, ¶ 24 (Ohio Ct. App. 2d Dist. Montgomery County 2015); State v. Kerr, 2016-Ohio-965, 2016 WL 936844 (Ohio Ct. App. 2d Dist. Montgomery County 2016).

[24]State v. Norris, 2015-Ohio-624, 2015 WL 753346, ¶ 24 (Ohio Ct. App. 2d Dist. Montgomery County 2015).

[Section 16:15]

[1]See also Text § 5:17, Case preparation—Hearsay exceptions—Present sense impression.

[2]Evid.R. 803(1).

[3]See State v. Wages, 87 Ohio App. 3d 780, 623 N.E.2d 193 (8th Dist. Cuyahoga County 1993); see also State v. Jackson, 2002-Ohio-1202, 2002 WL 398655 (Ohio Ct. App. 2d Dist. Montgomery County 2002); Text § 5:17, Case preparation—Hearsay exceptions—Present sense impression.

[4]See Cox v. Oliver Machinery Co., 41 Ohio App. 3d 28, 534 N.E.2d 855 (12th Dist. Butler County 1987).

[5]See, e.g., State v. Jackson, 2002-Ohio-1202, 2002 WL 398655 (Ohio Ct. App. 2d Dist. Montgomery County 2002) (discussing third party testimony in which witness testified that her daughter was "hysterical" and "'really upset' when she placed the call and that her emotions were in response to Appellant's striking their child"); State v. Little, 2016-Ohio-8398, 78 N.E.3d 323 (Ohio Ct. App. 3d Dist. Allen County 2016) (testimony of victim's neighbor regarding what victim's children told her was admissible under the present sense exception to hearsay rule and did not violate *Crawford*).

[6]See State v. Wages, 87 Ohio App. 3d 780, 623 N.E.2d 193 (8th Dist. Cuyahoga County 1993). See also State v. Travis, 165 Ohio App. 3d 626, 2006-Ohio-787, 847 N.E.2d 1237 (2d Dist. Montgomery County 2006) (oral statement made to police constituted a present sense exception).

absolute prerequisite to the admission of the statement[7] and the trial court has the discretion to determine whether to admit the statement into evidence.[8]

Q & A: Can a 911 call ever qualify as a present sense impression?[9]

Yes. Sometimes a 911 tape contains statements made by an anonymous eyewitness or the witness who called to report the incident.[10] Statements such as these may qualify as present sense impressions, especially where there is independent corroboration.[11] For example, the police officer that responds to the call may often corroborate the description of the event or even the identity of the abuser.

§ 16:16 Hearsay exceptions—Then-existing mental, physical, or emotional condition

Under Evid.R. 803(3), testimony regarding the then-existing mental, physical, or emotional condition of the victim may be admitted into evidence under certain circumstances. Wherever the bodily or mental feelings of an individual are material, the usual expressions of those feelings are original and competent evidence.[1] To qualify as a hearsay exception, the statement:

- Must relate to the declarant's intent, motive, design, mental feeling, pain or bodily health;
- Generally may not refer to a statement of memory or belief to prove the fact remembered or believed;
- Must be directed toward the future and not the past;[2]
- Must not include any explanation of why the declarant was of a certain state of mind;[3] and
- Must be relevant to a material issue in the case.

Witnesses may relate out of court statements that reflect any then-existing mental or emotional condition that the victim/declarant experienced, such as fear or anxiety. For example, a victim's state-

---

[7]State v. Wages, 87 Ohio App. 3d 780, 623 N.E.2d 193 (8th Dist. Cuyahoga County 1993).

[8]State v. Martin, 2000 WL 1145465 (Ohio Ct. App. 12th Dist. Brown County 2000).

[9]See also State v. Crowley, 2009-Ohio-6689, 2009 WL 4893283 (Ohio Ct. App. 2d Dist. Clark County 2009). See also State v. Norris, 2015-Ohio-624, 2015 WL 753346 (Ohio Ct. App. 2d Dist. Montgomery County 2015) (no differentiation between present sense impressions and excited utterances).

[10]See State v. Naugler, 2005-Ohio-6274, 2005 WL 3148081 (Ohio Ct. App. 12th Dist. Madison County 2005), judgment aff'd, 111 Ohio St. 3d 130, 2006-Ohio-5340, 855 N.E.2d 456 (2006) (holding that audio recordings of 911 calls admissible as present sense impressions).

[11]See Evid.R. 803(1); see also Text § 5:17, Case preparation—Hearsay exceptions—Present sense impression.

[Section 16:16]

[1]Mutual Life Ins. Co. of New York v. Hillmon, 145 U.S. 285, 12 S. Ct. 909, 36 L. Ed. 706 (1892).

[2]State v. Stewart, 75 Ohio App. 3d 141, 598 N.E.2d 1275 (11th Dist. Ashtabula County 1991).

[3]State v. Stewart, 75 Ohio App. 3d 141, 598 N.E.2d 1275 (11th Dist. Ashtabula County 1991).

ments made to a police officer two days before the attack is admissible as evidence of the victim's fear that the respondent would cause her/him serious physical injury.[4]

§ 16:17 Hearsay exceptions—Medical diagnosis or treatment

Under Evid. R. 803(4), statements made for purposes of medical diagnosis or treatment and describing medical history or past or present symptoms, pain, or sensations, or the inception or general character of the cause or external source thereof insofar as reasonably pertinent to diagnosis or treatment is admissible as a hearsay exception.[1] In *State v. Dever*,[2] the Ohio Supreme Court held that "statements made by a child during a medical examination identifying the perpetrator of sexual abuse, if made for the purpose of diagnosis or treatment are admissible pursuant to Evid. R. 803(4), when such statements are made for the purposes enumerated in that rule."

In *State v. Dartt*,[3] appellant challenged the admission of statements by a minor child to the emergency room doctor regarding the identity of the perpetrator. In this case, appellant stepfather hit the child in the eye. When asked by the emergency room doctor what happened, the child responded, "Dad hit me last night."

On appeal, the Lucas County Court of Appeals held that the testimony of the doctor was admissible under Evid. R. 803(4) and determined that "[w]e have no doubt that Dr. Hercher, a qualified, experienced medical doctor could treat the boy's bruising without ever exchanging a word with him. Common sense, however, dictates that when a doctor can determine the cause of one's injuries from the mouth of the injured one, this is preferable as it facilitates and expedites a patient's diagnosis and recovery. Dr. Hercher's purpose in asking the boy "what happened" was for medical diagnosis and treatment. Thus, her testimony regarding the boy's answer was properly admitted pursuant to Evid. R. 803(4)."[4]

---

[4]See State v. Sherrell, 1995 WL 497590 (Ohio Ct. App. 5th Dist. Tuscarawas County 1995); see also State v. Apanovitch, 33 Ohio St. 3d 19, 514 N.E.2d 394 (1987); State v. Wages, 87 Ohio App. 3d 780, 623 N.E.2d 193 (8th Dist. Cuyahoga County 1993).

[Section 16:17]

[1]See also State v. Vanderhorst, 2010-Ohio-1856, 2010 WL 1712246 (Ohio Ct. App. 8th Dist. Cuyahoga County 2010); State v. Muttart, 116 Ohio St. 3d 5, 2007-Ohio-5267, 875 N.E.2d 944 (2007).

[2]State v. Dever, 64 Ohio St. 3d 401, 1992-Ohio-41, 596 N.E.2d 436 (1992); see also State v. Sopko, 2009-Ohio-140, 2009 WL 97705 (Ohio Ct. App. 8th Dist. Cuyahoga County 2009).

[3]State v. Dartt, 2008-Ohio-373, 2008 WL 303135 (Ohio Ct. App. 6th Dist. Lucas County 2008).

[4]State v. Dartt, 2008-Ohio-373, 2008 WL 303135, *2 (Ohio Ct. App. 6th Dist. Lucas County 2008); see also State v. Muttart, 116 Ohio St. 3d 5, 2007-Ohio-5267, 875 N.E.2d 944 (2007) (discussing competency of a child to testify in order to have child's statement admitted as a hearsay exception pursuant to Evid. R. 803(4); State v. Meyerson, 2017-Ohio-8726, 2017 WL 5907415 (Ohio Ct. App. 9th Dist. Summit County 2017), cause dismissed, 151 Ohio St. 3d 1469, 2017-Ohio-9106, 87 N.E.3d 1268 (2017) and appeal not allowed, 152 Ohio St. 3d 1448, 2018-Ohio-1600, 96 N.E.3d 301 (2018).

§ 16:18 Hearsay exceptions—Recorded Recollection

Under Evid.R. 803(5), this exception requires that the evidence be:

- a memorandum or record;
- concerning a matter that the declarant once had knowledge of, but now has trouble accurately recalling during testimony; and
- which, the witness's other testimony established, was made or adopted by the witness when the matter was fresh and which accurately reflects the witness's prior knowledge.

This exception is utilized when a witness has testified that his/her present recollection is either absent or incomplete, but that his/her recollection was complete at the time the memorandum or recording sought to be introduced was made and that his/her recollection was accurately recorded at that time.[1]

Q & A: What happens if the victim takes the stand to testify and forgets what happened?

Once on the stand and facing his/her abuser, it is not unusual for a victim of domestic violence to forget what happened. The attorney may wish to refresh the victim's recollection of the events in question.[2] Sometimes the victim may forget when the incident occurred. For example, in *State v. Burd*,[3] the victim could not remember the exact date of the incident. The defendant appealed, arguing that her inability to remember the events witnessed constituted reversible error. Because the victim was consistent in her testimony as to what happened and because she believed defendant would cause her imminent physical harm, the Mercer County Court of Appeals determined that there was sufficient evidence to support the conviction.

Although the witness may read the memorandum into the court record, the document itself cannot be admitted into evidence unless the party against whom it was offered proffers it.[4]

Examples of such memoranda or records include police reports, affidavits in support of protection orders, victim's tape-recorded statements[5] or journals or diaries of the abusive incidents.[6]

[Section 16:18]

[1]State v. Woods, 48 Ohio App. 3d 1, 548 N.E.2d 954 (1st Dist. Hamilton County 1988), cause dismissed, 38 Ohio St. 3d 715, 533 N.E.2d 783 (1988).

[2]See Evid.R. 612, Evid.R. 803(5).

[3]State v. Burd, 1994 WL 265894 (Ohio Ct. App. 3d Dist. Mercer County 1994); see also State v. Widder, 2003-Ohio-3925, 2003 WL 21697868 (Ohio Ct. App. 9th Dist. Summit County 2003) (discussing when to use these statements; alleged victim's prior written statement to refresh victim's recollection could not serve as substantive evidence).

[4]See State v. Aiken, 1993 WL 204646 (Ohio Ct. App. 8th Dist. Cuyahoga County 1993).

[5]See State v. Marcy, 165 Vt. 89, 680 A.2d 76 (1996) (rejected by, State v. Spaulding, 197 Vt. 378, 2014 VT 91, 103 A.3d 487 (2014)) (rejecting court returning to rule that a specific avowal of the reliability of the recorded recollection from the declarant herself is necessary for admissibility).

[6]See also State v. Sochor, 1999 WL 547927 (Ohio Ct. App. 5th Dist. Stark County 1999).

§ 16:19 Hearsay exceptions—Judgment of previous conviction

Sometimes, convictions of prior crimes, such as convictions for domestic violence against the same or another victim or other violent crimes, may be useful to demonstrate a history or pattern of violent deeds or a subjective belief that the abuser will hurt the victim in the future.[1] Under Evid.R. 803(21), evidence of a previous conviction is admissible as a hearsay exception if:

- it is evidence of a final judgment, entered after trial or on any plea other than a no contest or equivalent plea;[2]
- it finds a person guilty of a crime punishable by death or imprisonment in excess of one year;
- it must be offered to prove any fact essential to sustain a judgment; and
- it must not be used by the government in a criminal prosecution, for purposes other than impeachment against persons other than the accused.[3]

Only certified copies of convictions may be offered into evidence.[4]

In civil protection order proceedings, admitting the actual conviction into evidence is not often necessary. If the objective is to impeach

[Section 16:19]

[1]See, e.g., State v. Thompson, 2000 WL 235535 (Ohio Ct. App. 9th Dist. Lorain County 2000); see also State v. Moissis, 2002-Ohio-4955, 2002 WL 31101605 (Ohio Ct. App. 11th Dist. Lake County 2002). But see State v. Semenchuk, 2002-Ohio-674, 2002 WL 253876 (Ohio Ct. App. 8th Dist. Cuyahoga County 2002).

[2]See State v. Stout, 1996 WL 556903 (Ohio Ct. App. 9th Dist. Wayne County 1996) (discussing when a prior conviction may be admitted into evidence pursuant to Evid.R. 609); see also State v. Kraus, 2007-Ohio-6027, 2007 WL 3348426 (Ohio Ct. App. 12th Dist. Warren County 2007) (discussing Evid.R. 609).

[3]See Evid.R. 803(21).

[4]See RC 2945.75(B); Evid.R. 803(8); see also State v. Gwen, 134 Ohio St. 3d 284, 2012-Ohio-5046, 982 N.E.2d 626 (2012) (addressing method of proving prior conviction for purposes of enhancing offense under RC 2919.25(D)(4)); State v. Shaw, 2017-Ohio-1259, 2017 WL 1231741 (Ohio Ct. App. 7th Dist. Belmont County 2017) (no requirement that a defendant stipulate to prior offenses); State v. Tate, 138 Ohio St. 3d 139, 2014-Ohio-44, 4 N.E.3d 1016 (2014) (holding that there is more than one way to provide sufficient proof of a prior conviction; a stipulation will suffice); State v. Russell, 2013-Ohio-1381, 2013 WL 1438000 (Ohio Ct. App. 12th Dist. Butler County 2013); State v. King, 2000 WL 330048, *4 (Ohio Ct. App. 5th Dist. Stark County 2000) (noting "additional evidence beyond a certified copy of a conviction must be offered to prove appellant's prior conviction"); State v. Moissis, 2002-Ohio-4955, 2002 WL 31101605 (Ohio Ct. App. 11th Dist. Lake County 2002); State v. Estep, 2004-Ohio-1747, 2004 WL 728913 (Ohio Ct. App. 4th Dist. Gallia County 2004) (facsimile copy of a certified copy of the judgment entry of defendant's prior conviction was admitted into evidence without objection); State v. Wilson, 1997 WL 666159 (Ohio Ct. App. 2d Dist. Champaign County 1997), citing State v. McCoy, 89 Ohio App. 3d 479, 624 N.E.2d 1102 (10th Dist. Franklin County 1993); State v. Krouskoupf, 2017-Ohio-7971, 2017 WL 4329771 (Ohio Ct. App. 5th Dist. Muskingum County 2017) (when proving a prior conviction, state must have a certified copy of judgment entry of conviction and sufficient evidence to prove identity of defendant with person named in the order); City of Cleveland v. Boone, 2018-Ohio-849, 2018 WL 1217716 (Ohio Ct. App. 8th Dist. Cuyahoga County 2018) (in order to show that appellant had violated TPO, a certified copy of TPO was required for proper authentication and admission into evidence; Evid. R. 902(4)).

the credibility of the witness,[5] an attorney may not need to admit a certified copy of the conviction into evidence. The attorney needs only to ask the abuser whether he/she was convicted for *specified crime* on *[specific date]*. If he/she denies the conviction, the respondent is shown a copy of the conviction. Once again, the abuser should be asked whether he/she was convicted of the crime set forth in the conviction. This line of questioning may be all that is needed to get a perpetrator to admit that he has been convicted before or to impeach his credibility.

Evid.R. 803(21) is particularly pertinent in felony domestic violence prosecutions.[6]

Q & A: Is a LEADS printout admissible under Evid. R. 803(8)?

It depends on the jurisdiction. Evid. R. 803(8) provides that "records, reports, statements or data compilations, in any form, of public offices or agencies, setting forth (a) the activities of the office or agency, or b) matters observed pursuant to a duty imposed by law as to which matters there was a duty to report, excluding, however, in "criminal cases matters observed by police officers and other law enforcement personnel, unless offered by defendant, unless the sources of information or other circumstances indicate a lack of trustworthiness." Such records may be considered exceptions and not excluded by the hearsay rule, even though the declarant is available as a witness.

At least one appellate district has found that a LEADS printout is not admissible under Evid. R. 803(8) because they are exempt from disclosure under the Ohio Public Records Act.[7] Other districts have held that LEADS reports can fall under the public records exception, if properly authenticated.[8]

In *State v. Castillo,*[9] the officer's testimony as to the identity of the victim regarding a violation of a protection order was based on his recollection of undocumented computer generated information obtained from an ambiguous database.[10] Although the source of the information was either the LEADS database or NCIC because protection orders must be entered into LEADS for entry into NCIC, no information was presented as to which database was used to glean the information. "Perhaps the computer printout would have qualified as an exception to the hearsay rule under Evid. R. 803(8), but the State

---

[5]See also Andrew J. Glendon, Battling Domestic Violence Through the Admission of Character Evidence, 28 Pac. L. J. 789 (1997).

[6]See Text § 5:21, Case preparation—Hearsay exceptions—Judgment of previous conviction.

[7]State v. Straits, 1999 WL 976212 (Ohio Ct. App. 5th Dist. Fairfield County 1999).

[8]State v. Lett, 2009-Ohio-5268, 2009 WL 3165550, ¶ 22 (Ohio Ct. App. 7th Dist. Mahoning County 2009); State v. Papusha, 2007-Ohio-3966, 2007 WL 2229579, ¶ 13, ¶ 16 (Ohio Ct. App. 12th Dist. Preble County 2007); Middleburg Hts. v. D'Ettorre, 138 Ohio App. 3d 700, 707-708, 742 N.E.2d 196 (8th Dist. Cuyahoga County 2000).

[9]State v. Castillo, 2015-Ohio-2738, 2015 WL 4070122 (Ohio Ct. App. 3d Dist. Henry County 2015).

[10]State v. Castillo, 2015-Ohio-2738, 2015 WL 4070122, ¶ 30 (Ohio Ct. App. 3d Dist. Henry County 2015).

chose not to offer the printout into evidence or lay the proper foundation."[11]

§ 16:20 Other statements that may be admitted into evidence[1]

Under Evid.R. 801(D), certain statements are not considered hearsay. For example, a statement is not hearsay if the declarant testifies at the hearing and is subject to cross-examination concerning the statement and the statement is (a) inconsistent with his/her testimony and was given under oath subject to cross-examination by the party against whom the statement is offered and subject to the penalty of perjury at trial, hearing, or other proceeding or in deposition, or (b) consistent with his/her testimony and is offered to rebut an express or implied charge against him of recent fabrication or improper influence or motive,[2] or (c) one of identification of a person soon after perceiving him, if the circumstances demonstrate the reliability of the prior identification.[3] Additionally, a prior written statement is usually not hearsay where it is merely cumulative and where the author is available for cross examination.[4]

For example, where a victim changes his/her testimony regarding the facts, the prior inconsistent statement is not hearsay and may be admitted into evidence under Evid.R. 801(D)(1)(a).[5] The testimony is then available to the defendant for purposes of impeachment.[6]

Similarly, a statement is not hearsay if the statement is offered

---

[11]State v. Castillo, 2015-Ohio-2738, 2015 WL 4070122, ¶ 30 (Ohio Ct. App. 3d Dist. Henry County 2015).

[Section 16:20]

[1]See Pamela Vartabedian, The Need to Hold Batterers Accountable: Admitting Prior Acts of Abuse in Cases of Domestic Violence, 47 Santa Clara L.Rev. 157 (2008).

[2]See also State v. Musgrove, 2008-Ohio-494, 2008 WL 344144 (Ohio Ct. App. 2d Dist. Montgomery County 2008).

[3]Evid.R. 801(D)(1); but see Evid.R. 607(A). But see State v. Castillo, 2015-Ohio-2738, 2015 WL 4070122 (Ohio Ct. App. 3d Dist. Henry County 2015) (finding that the identification of the victim was based on inadmissible hearsay because there was no personal knowledge of the victim's identity apart from the undocumented computer generated information-the photograph of the driver was depicted on the computer as that of the victim).

[4]See for example, Cornell v. Hatfield, 2018-Ohio-549, 2018 WL 827136 (Ohio Ct. App. 12th Dist. Fayette County 2018).

[5]But see Evid.R. 607(A) and Evid.R. 613; State v. Sullens, 2017-Ohio-4081, 2017 WL 2376766 (Ohio Ct. App. 10th Dist. 2017) (discussion of Evid. R. 613 and conditions that must be met before admitting a witness's prior inconsistent statement); State v. Kraus, 2007-Ohio-6027, 2007 WL 3348426 (Ohio Ct. App. 12th Dist. Warren County 2007); State v. Hill, 2004-Ohio-2048, 2004 WL 870439 (Ohio Ct. App. 2d Dist. Montgomery County 2004) (victims prior inconsistent written statement to police was inadmissible at trial where victim admitted making statement to officer that was inconsistent with her trial testimony); State v. Parsons, 2004-Ohio-2216, 2004 WL 937287 (Ohio Ct. App. 6th Dist. Wood County 2004). See also State v. Trefney, 2012-Ohio-869, 2012 WL 691630 (Ohio Ct. App. 11th Dist. Portage County 2012); State v. Abernathy, 2015-Ohio-1363, 2015 WL 1530810 (Ohio Ct. App. 5th Dist. Stark County 2015) (discussion of Evid. R. 613, how to introduce extrinsic evidence and that the court, on its own motion, may call the (recanting) victim as a witness under Evid. R. 614).

[6]See also State v. Walker, 2001 WL 1782885 (Ohio Ct. App. 5th Dist. Stark County 2001); State v. Hancock, 2004-Ohio-1492, 2004 WL 596103 (Ohio Ct. App. 1st Dist. Hamilton County 2004) (discussing that prior inconsistent statements offered

against a party and is (a) his/her own statement, in either his/her individual or a representative capacity, or (b) a statement of which he/she has manifested his adoption or belief in its truth, or (c) a statement by a person authorized by him/her to make a statement concerning the subject.[7]

Under Evid.R. 801(D)(2), a criminal defendant's own out-of-court statement may be offered against that defendant.[8] It does not require that the statement be introduced to contradict the defendant's position. Rather, it only requires that the statement be offered against the defendant's interest, and in support of the state's case.

For example, in *State v. King*,[9] the Stark County Court of Appeals held that the neighbor's testimony as to what the defendant said to her was admissible under Evid.R. 801(D)(2), which provides that a statement of a party offered against that party, is not hearsay.[10]

Q & A: When can a statement made by a child be considered an utterance that is not hearsay?

In *State v. Humbert*,[11] appellant and his mother had been living together and on the date in question, appellant had yelled and punched her. Said incident was witnessed by his nephew who screamed, "Uncle Craig. Stop, Uncle Craig." *Humbert* appealed his conviction.

On appeal, appellant argued that the trial court erred in admitting hearsay testimony from his mother, who testified that during the altercation her grandson had said, "Uncle Craig. Stop, Uncle Craig." However, the appellate court held that:

> [T]he contested utterance as described by the witness is similar to the non-verbal act of physically intervening in an attempt to stop a fight. Although in the context of Ms. Humbert-Williams's testimony, the child's statement to Mr. Humbert to "[s]top" includes an implied assertion that Mr. Humbert was attacking Ms. Humbert-Williams, the child did not intend it to be an assertion. That is, the child did not intend to "say that something is so, eg., that an event happened or that a condition existed." State v. Carter, 72 Ohio St. 3d 545, 549, 1995-Ohio-104, 651 N.E.2d 965 (1995) (quoting 2 McCormick, Evidence, Section 246, at 98 (4 Ed. 1992)). Thus, the child's utterance is not a "statement" as defined by Evidence

---

for purpose of impeachment may only be considered as substantive evidence if the prior inconsistent statement is not inadmissible as hearsay); but see Evid.R. 607; State v. Stover, 2014-Ohio-2572, 2014 WL 2701213 (Ohio Ct. App. 9th Dist. Wayne County 2014); State v. Abernathy, 2015-Ohio-1363, 2015 WL 1530810 (Ohio Ct. App. 5th Dist. Stark County 2015).

[7]Evid.R. 801(D)(2).

[8]See State v. Thompson, 87 Ohio App. 3d 570, 622 N.E.2d 735 (9th Dist. Medina County 1993); State v. Johnson, 2003-Ohio-2540, 2003 WL 21142519 (Ohio Ct. App. 12th Dist. Butler County 2003).

[9]State v. King, 2000 WL 330048 (Ohio Ct. App. 5th Dist. Stark County 2000).

[10]See also State v. Beeson, 2002-Ohio-4341, 2002 WL 1943752 (Ohio Ct. App. 2d Dist. Montgomery County 2002); State v. Amos, 2012-Ohio-2964, 2012 WL 2499444 (Ohio Ct. App. 2d Dist. Clark County 2012).

[11]State v. Humbert, 2012-Ohio-5870, 2012 WL 6206770 (Ohio Ct. App. 9th Dist. Summit County 2012).

Rule 801(A) because it was not intended as an assertion. Therefore, the utterance is excluded from the definition of hearsay.[12]

Q & A: Can a defendant use his own statements to prove self-defense in a domestic violence case?

It depends on the trustworthiness of the statement. For example, in *State v. Bunch*,[13] the defendant committed an act of violence against his stepfather (victim). He argued that he pushed the victim down the stairs because the victim came at him with a knife. In the instant case, the defendant chose not to testify but wanted his statement to police admitted into evidence to support his claim of self-defense. The trial court ruled the statement inadmissible evidence.

On appeal, defendant argued that the trial court erred when it ruled that the arresting officer's testimony about what defendant had told him about the incident was inadmissible. The appellate court affirmed the trial court and first noted that because self defense is an affirmative defense, it require proof by a preponderance of the evidence and it is the defendant who must offer the evidence that established that defense, including the use of the defendant's own statements.[14] The court then found that ". . . in the instant case, the nature of, and circumstances surrounding, the defendant's statements to the police "indicate lack of trustworthiness" and undermine the purpose of the rule against hearsay."[15]

Q & A: Can evidence of an anonymous letter and anonymous telephone call be admissible as an exception to the hearsay rule?

According to the Montgomery County Court of Appeals, the answer is yes. In *Bryant v. Spear-Hardy*,[16] appellant appealed the granting of a CSPO and argued that that trial court erred when it admitted an anonymous letter and telephone call into evidence.

The appellate court first explained that hearsay is defined as a "statement other that one made by a declarant while testifying at the trial or hearing, offered to prove the truth of the matter asserted." Evid. R. 801(C) "A "statement" as included in the definition of hearsay is an oral or written assertion or nonverbal conduct of a person if that conduct is intended by him as an assertion." Evid. R. 801(A). The court then opined that one reason for appellant's appeal was her belief that the evidence was insufficient for the trial court to conclude that she, rather than another, made the telephone call and sent the letter.

In affirming the trial court decision, the appellate court then concluded that so long as the anonymous letter and the telephone call were the types of verbal acts offered to establish that accusations and

[12]State v. Humbert, 2012-Ohio-5870, ¶ 15, 2012 WL 6206770 (Ohio Ct. App. 9th Dist. Summit County 2012).

[13]State v. Bunch, 2010-Ohio-515, 2010 WL 547402 (Ohio Ct. App. 8th Dist. Cuyahoga County 2010).

[14]*Bunch at *2*; quoting State v. Seliskar, 35 Ohio St. 2d 95, 96, 64 Ohio Op. 2d 58, 298 N.E.2d 582 (1973).

[15]*Bunch at *3*.

[16]Bryant v. Spear-Hardy, 2010-Ohio-1903, 2010 WL 1731763 (Ohio Ct. App. 2d Dist. Montgomery County 2010).

threats were made and not that the statements were true, they may be admitted into evidence.[17] Both the letter and call were admitted as statements of a party opponent under Evid. R. 801(D)(2)(a). Moreover, the greater weight of the evidence supports the finding that no one other than the appellant made the telephone call or sent the letter.[18]

Q & A: How does one authenticate or identify a writing such that it may be admitted into evidence?

Under the evidentiary rules, the requirement of authentication or identification as a condition precedent to admissibility is satisfied by evidence sufficient to support a finding that the matter in question is what the proponent claims.[19] The general purpose behind the requirement that a document is authenticated prior to admission is to prove that the writing is what the proponent claims it to be.[20]

The rule then provides the following examples of authentication or identification which include distinctive characteristics and the like: appearance, contents, substance, internal patterns, or other distinctive characteristics taken in conjunction with circumstances connecting it with the alleged speaker.[21]

For example, in *Kuhn v. Kuhn*[22] respondent appealed the granting of a CPO on, among other grounds, that the trial court erred in adopting the magistrate's decision in that the magistrate used impermissible hearsay to support the finding of domestic violence and specifically, that respondent objected to the admission of a suicide note because there was no direct evidence that he was the author. In this case, an officer testified that respondent's condition, the note and the loaded shotgun caused the officer to be concerned for appellee's safety.

The appellate court upheld the trial court and found that respondent was the author of the note based on the circumstances surrounding the unsigned note admitted in this case which included that 1) the note was found in his motel room; 2) the note specifically mentions respondent's wife and daughter by name; 3) the note alludes to a difficult marital situation; 4) the note appears to have blood on it and respondent was bleeding when the police arrived; 5) the note was written on the inside of a cardboard beer case; 6) the motel room was strewn with empty beer cans; 7) the note has all the indicia of a suicide note; 8) there were packages of over-the-counter sleeping pills in the room; and, 9) respondent was found in a disassociated state and

[17]*Bryant at *6.*

[18]See also Kuhn v. Kuhn, 2013-Ohio-5807, 2013 WL 6869801 (Ohio Ct. App. 11th Dist. Lake County 2013) (applying to an unsigned note allegedly written by respondent and found in his hotel room).

[19]Evid. R. 901(A).

[20]Rehfus v. Smith, 2015-Ohio-2145, 2015 WL 3498686 (Ohio Ct. App. 7th Dist. Carroll County 2015) (discussing how an evaluation can be authenticated).

[21]Evid. R. 901(B)(4).

[22]Kuhn v. Kuhn, 2013-Ohio-5807, 2013 WL 6869801 (Ohio Ct. App. 11th Dist. Lake County 2013). See also J.R. v. E.H., 2017-Ohio-516, 2017 WL 587314 (Ohio Ct. App. 10th Dist. Franklin County 2017) (audiotape, that was listened to by the court in chambers, admitted into evidence and authenticated by petitioner who identified voices of both her and respondent and because respondent did not deny that it was his voice on cell).

unresponsive.[23] Additionally, respondent had testified that the handwriting was definitely similar to his printing. "The totality of the facts and circumstances surrounding the note and its contents establish distinctive characteristics sufficient to authenticate it. As there was sufficient evidence to establish that the note was written by Mr. Kuhn, it was admissible under Evid. R. 801(D)(2)."[24] In this case, the appellate court concluded there was ample evidence that respondent wrote the suicide letter.

Q & A: How is an internet conversation authenticated so that it may be admitted into evidence?

In *State v. Craycraft*,[25] appellant argued that the admission of the IM/email should have been excluded as hearsay. A witness testified that the email was a printout of an online conversation he had with a person he believed to be appellant. The Butler County Court of Appeals reviewed applicable case law and determined that "[t]o establish the documents, namely computer printouts of conversations between the victim and appellant, the 'proponent need not prove beyond any doubt that the evidence is what it purports to be.'[26] Instead, the proponent must only demonstrate a 'reasonable likelihood' that the evidence is authentic.[27] Such evidence may be supplied by the testimony of a witness with knowledge."[28] After considering the other provisions of the rule, the court determined that appellant was the speaker of the conversation and concluded that the totality of the facts and circumstances surrounding the IM/email conversation were sufficient to authenticate the IM/email conversation.[29]

Once it was established that appellant was the speaker of the conversation for authentication purposes, the appellate court could reasonably conclude that the same fact (that appellant was the speaker) that authenticated the IM/email conversation also rendered it non-hearsay. Therefore, appellant's statements in the IM/email

[23]Kuhn v. Kuhn, 2013-Ohio-5807, 2013 WL 6869801, ¶ 44 (Ohio Ct. App. 11th Dist. Lake County 2013).

[24]Kuhn v. Kuhn, 2013-Ohio-5807, 2013 WL 6869801, ¶ 54 (Ohio Ct. App. 11th Dist. Lake County 2013).

[25]State v. Craycraft, 2010-Ohio-596, 2010 WL 610601 (Ohio Ct. App. 12th Dist. Clermont County 2010), judgment rev'd on other grounds by, 128 Ohio St. 3d 337, 2010-Ohio-6332, 944 N.E.2d 220 (2010).

[26]Quoting State v. Bell, 2009-Ohio-2335, 2009 WL 1395857 (Ohio Ct. App. 12th Dist. Clermont County 2009), quoting State v. Aliff, 2000 WL 378370 (Ohio Ct. App. 4th Dist. Lawrence County 2000).

[27]Quoting State v. Bell, 2009-Ohio-2335, 2009 WL 1395857 (Ohio Ct. App. 12th Dist. Clermont County 2009), quoting State v. Aliff, 2000 WL 378370 (Ohio Ct. App. 4th Dist. Lawrence County 2000). But see State v. Thomas, 2012-Ohio-2430, 2012 WL 1970459 (Ohio Ct. App. 12th Dist. Warren County 2012) (holding that a customer of a cell phone cannot authenticate the bill and thus, the phone bill should not have been admitted because it was not properly authenticated, but that such error did not amount to plain error nor did it prejudice defendant).

[28]*Craycraft at *6*, quoting, State v. Bell, 2009-Ohio-2335, 2009 WL 1395857 (Ohio Ct. App. 12th Dist. Clermont County 2009), quoting State v. Brantley, 2008-Ohio-281, 2008 WL 217513, *34 (Ohio Ct. App. 12th Dist. Butler County 2008); Evid. R. 901(B)(1).

[29]*Craycraft at *8*; Evid. R. 901(B)(4).

conversations were admissible as admissions by a party-opponent in that they were appellant's own statements.[30]

Q & A: Must cell phone records be authenticated before they can be admitted into evidence?

According to *State v. Hood*,[31] cell phone records, if properly authenticated, are business records. In order to be a business record under Evid. R. 803(6), the record must manifest the following: 1) the record must be one regularly recorded in a regularly conducted activity; 2) it must have been entered by a person with knowledge of the act, event or condition; 3) it must have been recorded at or near the time of the transaction; and 4) a foundation must be laid by the custodian of the record or by some other qualified witness.[32]

Additionally, cell phone records must be authenticated before they can be admitted into evidence. Authentication may only be provided by a custodian or other witness who is qualified to testify that the records were kept in the ordinary course of a regularly conducted business.[33] If not properly authenticated by the custodian of the records or other qualified witness, the records do not qualify as business records. As such, the records do not fall within an exception to the hearsay rule and cannot be admitted into evidence.[34]

Q & A: How are jail telephone calls authenticated for purposes of a domestic violence conviction?

This issue was addressed by the 1st District Appellate Court. In *State v. Salaam,*[35] defendant appealed his domestic violence conviction on the grounds that the admission of testimony regarding his re-

---

[30]*Craycraft at *8*; Evid. R. 801(D)(2)(a). But see State v. Abernathy, 2015-Ohio-1363, 2015 WL 1530810 (Ohio Ct. App. 5th Dist. Stark County 2015) (noting that screen shots of text messages recanting victim sent to her father may be hearsay but could be admissible for impeachment purposes).

[31]State v. Hood, 135 Ohio St. 3d 137, 2012-Ohio-6208, 984 N.E.2d 1057 (2012). See also State v. Clark, 2018-Ohio-521, 2018 WL 798385 (Ohio Ct. App. 6th Dist. Lucas County 2018) (discussing spoofing and "phone dump" and when and how to collect data from a work cell phone and when preserving text messages in photographs and subpoenaing phone records would be sufficient evidence).

[32]State v. Hood, 135 Ohio St. 3d 137, ¶ 39, 2012-Ohio-6208, 984 N.E.2d 1057 (2012); State v. Edwards, 2017-Ohio-7231, 96 N.E.3d 890 (Ohio Ct. App. 9th Dist. Summit County 2017), appeal not allowed, 152 Ohio St. 3d 1409, 2018-Ohio-723, 92 N.E.3d 880 (2018); quoting, State v. Davis, 116 Ohio St. 3d 404, 2008-Ohio-2, 880 N.E.2d 31, ¶ 171 (2008).

[33]State v. Hood, 135 Ohio St. 3d 137, 2012-Ohio-6208, 984 N.E.2d 1057 (2012) (syllabus); State v. Edwards, 2017-Ohio-7231, ¶ 25, 96 N.E.3d 890 (Ohio Ct. App. 9th Dist. Summit County 2017), appeal not allowed, 152 Ohio St. 3d 1409, 2018-Ohio-723, 92 N.E.3d 880 (2018); quoting State v. Baker, 2003-Ohio-4637, ¶ 11, 2003 WL 22047697 (Ohio Ct. App. 9th Dist. Summit County 2003) (discussing that witness whose testimony establishes foundation for a business record exception need not have personal knowledge of the exact circumstances of preparation and production of the document, but needs to be familiar with the operation of the business and the circumstances of the preparation, maintenance and retrieval of the record in order to reasonably testify that the record is what it purports to be and was made in the ordinary course of business).

[34]See also State v. Thomas, 2012-Ohio-2430, 2012 WL 1970459 (Ohio Ct. App. 12th Dist. Warren County 2012) (a customer of a cellular telephone service does not possess knowledge to authenticate his or her own bill).

[35]State v. Salaam, 2015-Ohio-4552, 47 N.E.3d 495 (Ohio Ct. App. 1st Dist. Hamilton County 2015).

corded jail house call was in error. The state offered rebuttal testimony from a police officer who had monitored calls defendant had made to the complainant in the case while incarcerated. However, the officer had not been responsible for the actual recording of the conversations; rather, the calls had been recorded by Global Tel Network that automatically records all jail house conversations and were requested by the officer. The requested discs had been generated by an employee of the Hamilton County Sheriff's Office.[36]

At trial and over objection, the officer testified about the content of the calls wherein defendant stated that he had smacked the victim because she had "burned" him and that he would harm her if she appeared in court and testified against him and that he would kill her if he had to serve prison time. "Although the trial court allowed Officer Kowalski to testify about the content of the telephone calls, it sustained Salaam's objection and did not allow the state to admit the discs containing the recorded calls into evidence. The court determined that the discs were a business record that had not been appropriately authenticated by the person who maintained the record."[37]

On appeal, Salaam argued the trial court admitted the officer's testimony about the recorded jail-house calls in violation of Evid. R. 1002. He asserted that the original recorded conversations should have been introduced into evidence to prove the content of the conversations.

Evid. R. 1002 provides that "[t]o prove the content of a writing, recording or photograph, the original writing, recording or photograph is required, except as otherwise provided in these rules or by statute enacted by the General Assembly * * *" Evid. R. 1004 contains exceptions to this rule requiring the original to be introduced into evidence and provides that an original is not necessary to prove the content of a writing, recording or photograph if the original has been lost or destroyed, the original cannot be obtained, the original is in the possession of an opponent who will not produce it or if the original concerns collateral matters and is not closely related to a controlling issue.[38]

Since none of the exceptions contained in Evid. R. 1004 were present, Officer Kowalski's testimony of the content of the calls violated Evid. R. 1002, requiring that an original recording of the telephone calls be introduced into evidence to prove the content of the calls.

However, the appellate court also determined that because there was other evidence to establish that Salaam had committed domestic violence, the admission of the calls constituted harmless error.

Q & A: Can a court admit testimony to prove the contents of an email, without introducing the email into evidence and does such an admission violate Evid. R. 1002?

---

[36]State v. Salaam, 2015-Ohio-4552, ¶ 3, 47 N.E.3d 495 (Ohio Ct. App. 1st Dist. Hamilton County 2015).

[37]State v. Salaam, 2015-Ohio-4552, ¶ 4, 47 N.E.3d 495 (Ohio Ct. App. 1st Dist. Hamilton County 2015).

[38]State v. Salaam, 2015-Ohio-4552, ¶ 7, 47 N.E.3d 495 (Ohio Ct. App. 1st Dist. Hamilton County 2015); Evid. R. 1004.

This issue was addressed in *Bartells v. Bertel*,[39] where the trial court granted a civil stalking protection order to ex-wife's boyfriend against her ex-husband. At the full hearing, the trial court refused to admit certain social media posts by ex-wife into evidence, which ex-husband argued showed that ex-wife was using her boyfriend's CSPO as a means to keep ex-husband away from their children and as a motive to lie in support of her boyfriend. Additionally, the trial court permitted the ex-wife to identify one of the posts but would not allow the ex-husband to cross examine ex-wife as to whether she lied in her deposition.

After the trial court overruled ex-husband's objections, the ex-husband appealed the issuance of the CSPO, claiming that the court erred in excluding evidence of the ex-wife's bias and character for untruthfulness. He argued that the Facebook post (he was not permitted to admit into evidence) was admissible under Evid. R. 608(B) and 616(A) to show her bias, prejudice and motive against him. The court's failure to permit him cross examination to show that she lied was also an error.

The appellate court examined Evid. R. 608(B) which states that "specific instances of the conduct of a witness, for the purpose of attacking* * *the witness's character for truthfulness may not be proved by extrinsic evidence."[40] Evid. 616 governs methods of impeachment and provides that "[b]ias, prejudice, interest or motive to misrepresent may be shown to impeach the witness either by examination of the witness or by extrinsic evidence."[41]

The appellate court found no abuse of discretion regarding the Facebook post. "Respondent sought to introduce and admit the Facebook post to show that Patricia was unhappy with the domestic relations court's failure to favorably rule in her parenting time dispute with respondent and that she was searching for other ways to protect her children from Respondent. While the post itself was not admitted into evidence, the testimony about the post was not stricken and remained of record. ***Hence, while the trial court limited Respondent's questioning, it nevertheless allowed him to challenge Patricia's credibility and show she was inconsistent between her deposition and her testimony at the CPO hearing."[42]

Relying on Evid. R. 611(A), the court found that the trial court did not abuse its discretion in not allowing respondent to cross-examine Patricia as to whether she lied in her deposition as a trial court has discretion to manage the presentation of evidence.[43]

In assignment of error two, ex-husband asserted that the trial court erred in admitting the testimony to prove the contents of an email, in

[39]Bartells v. Bertel, 2018-Ohio-21, 2018 WL 265509 (Ohio Ct. App. 12th Dist. Butler County 2018).

[40]Bartells v. Bertel, 2018-Ohio-21, ¶ 22-23, 2018 WL 265509 (Ohio Ct. App. 12th Dist. Butler County 2018).

[41]Bartells v. Bertel, 2018-Ohio-21, ¶ 23, 2018 WL 265509 (Ohio Ct. App. 12th Dist. Butler County 2018); Evid. R. 616(A).

[42]Bartells v. Bertel, 2018-Ohio-21, ¶ 26, 2018 WL 265509 (Ohio Ct. App. 12th Dist. Butler County 2018).

[43]Bartells v. Bertel, 2018-Ohio-21, ¶ 27, ¶ 28, 2018 WL 265509 (Ohio Ct. App. 12th Dist. Butler County 2018).

contravention of the "Best Evidence Rule." The basis of his claim was that the email should have been introduced into evidence. Pursuant to Evid. R. 1002, "[t]o prove the contents of a writing, recording or photograph, the original writing, recording or photograph is required, except as otherwise provided* * *," suggesting that the original writing is more reliable, complete and accurate as to its contents and meaning.

The court went on to discuss Evid. R. 1004 which provided exceptions to the original writing and admitting other evidence of the contents of the writing if, "[a]t the time when an original was under the control of the party whom offered, that party was put on notice, by the pleadings or otherwise, that the contents would be subject of proof at the hearing and that party does not produce the original at the hearing."[44] Thus, " 'the best evidence rule does not exclude all but the primary evidence of fact; it requires only that the best evidence available be produced, whether it be primary or secondary.' "[45] Because both parties testified as to the contents of the email and because ex-husband, on cross examination, admitted to sending it and because he had a copy of the original email in his phone and was on notice that the email would be an issue at trial, "Petitioner satisfied all of the requirements of Evid. R. 1004(3) and was thus relieved from the burden of presenting the email at the hearing;"[46] thus, the trial court did not err in permitting Petitioner to prove the existence and contents of the email through oral testimony.[47]

Q & A: When can social networking media posts from Facebook, Twitter, LinkedIn and MySpace, etc.) be used as evidence in a case? What social media may be used as evidence? How are these posts authenticated? Are they considered inadmissible hearsay?

Social media is often defined as "forms of electronic communications (as websites for social networking and microblogging) through which users create online communities to share information, ideas, personal messages and other content (as videos). Social media allows individuals and organizations to use the Internet to create and exchange "User Generated Content" that is "continuously modified by all users in a participatory and collaborative fashion."[48] "Content is user generated if it 1) is published either on a publicly accessible website or on a social media networking site accessible to a selected group of people, as opposed to e-mailed; 2) shows a certain amount of creative effort, rising above republication of existing content; and 3) is created outside

[44]Bartells v. Bertel, 2018-Ohio-21, ¶ 34, 2018 WL 265509 (Ohio Ct. App. 12th Dist. Butler County 2018).

[45]Bartells v. Bertel, 2018-Ohio-21, ¶ 34, 2018 WL 265509 (Ohio Ct. App. 12th Dist. Butler County 2018); quoting, State v. Sims, 2009-Ohio-550, ¶ 26, 2009 WL 295402 (Ohio Ct. App. 12th Dist. Butler County 2009).

[46]Bartells v. Bertel, 2018-Ohio-21, ¶ 36, 2018 WL 265509 (Ohio Ct. App. 12th Dist. Butler County 2018).

[47]Bartells v. Bertel, 2018-Ohio-21, ¶ 36, 2018 WL 265509 (Ohio Ct. App. 12th Dist. Butler County 2018).

[48]Honorable Paul W. Grimm, Lisa Yurwit Bergstrom & Melissa M. O'Toole-Loureiro, Authentication of Social Media Evidence, 36 Am. J. Trial Advoc. 433, 434 (2013).

of professional routines and practices such that it was not intended for a commercial market."[49]

Because social media is often stored on remote servers, is accessed through unique interfaces, can be dynamic and collaborative in nature and is uniquely susceptible to alteration and fabrication, evidentiary standards must begin to understand and comport with the unique nature of these electronic communications.[50]

Generally, a person wanting to authenticate social media evidence must comport with Evid. R. 901(a) which requires that the person lay a foundation of evidence sufficient to support a finding that the matter in question is what its proponent claims. Such evidence might be authenticated by 1) someone with personal knowledge who testifies that a matter is what it is claimed to be; 2) use of an expert, when shown a posting to have been made by person A, compares it to another of unknown authenticity; 3) opinion testimony by an expert who understands how social media was created; 4) distinctive circumstances or characteristics, such as appearance, contents, substance, internal patterns, or other distinctive characteristics, taken in conjunction with circumstances; and 5) official publications such as newspapers or periodicals which are often self-authenticating.[51]

Where a party offers into evidence printouts of Facebook messages received from another, testimony of the person receiving the messages may be used to authenticate the printouts by 1) evidence indicating that the person downloaded and printed the exchange of messages from own computer; 2) evidence demonstrating a recognition of the user's name as belonging to the other party; and 3) the other party's profile contained photos and other entries identifying the other party as the holder of the account. The need to authenticate is crucial because the user could generate the same information to others besides the named sender.[52]

In deciding how best to be prepare to authenticate printouts of posts on social media sites, it is important to inquire of the purported creator if s/he has indeed created the profile and if s/he added the posting in question. It might also be prudent to hire a computer expert to search the computer of the person who created the profile and posting and examine the internet history and hard drive to determine if it was used to originate the profile or post. Finally, obtaining information directly from the social networking website in an effort to link the establishment of the profile to the person who allegedly created it

---

[49]Honorable Paul W. Grimm, Lisa Yurwit Bergstrom & Melissa M. O'Toole-Loureiro, Authentication of Social Media Evidence, 36 Am. J. Trial Advoc. 433, 434 (2013).

[50]See Boehning and Toal, Authenticating Social Media Evidence, N.Y.L.J., Vol. 248-No. 65, October 2012. www.NYLJ.com; Heather L. Griffith, Understanding and Authenticating Evidence From Social Networking Sites, 7 Wash.J. L. Tech. & Arts, 209 (2012).

[51]See also Evid. R. 901(B); Griffith, Understanding and Authenticating Evidence From Social Networking Sites, 7 Wash. J. L. Tech. & Arts, 209 (2012); Grimm, Lisa Yurwit Bergstrom & Melissa M. O'Toole-Loureiro, Authentication of Social Media Evidence, 36 Am. J. Trial Advoc. 433, 468 (2013).

[52]Grimm, Lisa Yurwit Bergstrom & Melissa M. O'Toole-Loureiro, Authentication of Social Media Evidence, 36 Am. J. Trial Advoc. 433, 447 (2013).

and the posting sought to be introduced to the person who initiated it is crucial.[53] A word of caution to counsel that he/she may need to use different authentication methods depending on the type of communication involved. (such as email, chats, photographs, or video from social networking sites).[54]

For example, in *State v. Gibson,*[55] appellant appealed his convictions, arguing that printouts from Facebook and an audio recording downloaded from SoundCloud were admitted into evidence without establishing a proper foundation as to relevance, authenticity and authorship.[56] One of appellant's arguments was that the detectives did not have personal knowledge about the ownership and control of the Facebook profile pages. In a case of first impression, the appellate court was asked to rule on whether the printouts and images which identified appellant as the perpetrator and demonstrated appellant's association with known gang members should have been admitted into evidence, even though the police were not completely certain that appellant had posted the information.

At trial, the state presented exhibit evidence purporting to represent printouts from appellant's Facebook profile page as well as printouts from public Facebook profile pages belonging to others. In its decision, the Lucas County appellate court first determined that the printouts were relevant to the charge under Evid. R. 401 and 104(B) The Court then determined that those printouts were sufficiently authenticated under Evid. R. 901(A) and 104(A).[57] "We believe that a combination of both personal knowledge of the appearance and substance of the public Facebook profile pages, taken in conjunction with direct and circumstantial evidence was sufficient to meet the threshold admissibility requirement set forth in Evid. R. 901(B)(1)."[58]

In making its ruling, the appellate court discussed the definitions and uses of both Facebook and SoundCloud, acknowledged the hurdles of admitting electronically stored information, and reviewed various federal and state cases, including *Lorraine v. Markel American Insurance Co.,*[59] which have evaluated the admissibility from evidence from social media networking sites. The Court relied on the Honorable Paul W. Grimm, the author of the *Lorraine* decision as well as the author of several articles discussing the admissibility of social media evidence and explaining that, in recent years, two lines of cases have emerged. "One line of cases sets an unnecessarily high bar for the

[53]Griffith, Understanding and Authenticating Evidence From Social Networking Sites, 7 Wash. J. L. Tech. & Arts, 209, 216 (2012).

[54]See Griffith, Understanding and Authenticating Evidence From Social Networking Sites, 7 Wash. J. L. Tech. & Arts, 209 (2012) (for a discussion of the different types of authentication methods).

[55]State v. Gibson, 2015-Ohio-1679, 2015 WL 1962850 (Ohio Ct. App. 6th Dist. Lucas County 2015).

[56]State v. Gibson, 2015-Ohio-1679, 2015 WL 1962850, ¶ 32 (Ohio Ct. App. 6th Dist. Lucas County 2015).

[57]State v. Gibson, 2015-Ohio-1679, 2015 WL 1962850, ¶ 33 (Ohio Ct. App. 6th Dist. Lucas County 2015).

[58]State v. Gibson, 2015-Ohio-1679, 2015 WL 1962850, ¶ 49 (Ohio Ct. App. 6th Dist. Lucas County 2015).

[59]Lorraine v. Markel American Insurance Co.241 F.R.D. 534 (D. Md. 2007).

admissibility of social media evidence by not admitting the exhibits unless the court definitely determines that the evidence is authentic."[60] "Another line of cases take a different tact, determining the admissibility of social media evidence based on whether there was sufficient evidence of authenticity for a reasonable jury to conclude that the evidence was authentic."[61] In the article, *Authentication of Social Media Evidence* by Honorable Paul W. Grimm, Lisa Yurwit Bergstrom & Melissa M. O'Toole-Loureiro, the authors suggested that the second line of cases offered a more reasonable approach because it considered the rules of evidence.[62] "It is clear that the best approach for authenticating and admitting social media evidence is to follow Rules 104(a) and (b). Following such an approach, courts consider evidence from all sources (even if not from a live witness)-including documents, whether electronic or hard copy-on a continuum. That is, clearly authentic evidence is admitted, clearly inauthentic evidence is excluded and everything in between is conditionally relevant and admitted for the jury to make the final determination of authenticity."[63]

The appellate court then addressed the Ohio Rules of Evidence, to wit: Evid. R. 104 and 901 as well as relevant Ohio cases.[64] After reviewing the evidence in the case, the Court affirmed the trial court and concluded that there was substantial evidence submitted, to wit: unique street names, gang terminology, photos, artwork and gang signs utilized on the subject Facebook profile pictures indicating the owners' gang affiliation by which a jury could conclude the profile pages were those of the appellant and thus, the trial court did not abuse its discretion in the admission of this evidence.[65] The Court also determined that because the SoundCloud soundtrack was hearsay, it should not have been admitted and because the state failed to present substantial evidence that the song was attributable to a member of the gang in question, it was not sufficiently authenticated. However, any error was harmless as inclusion of the song would not have changed the outcome of the trial.[66]

In effect, the Lucas County Court of Appeals suggested that Ohio is also leaning towards a lower standard to allow admission of social media as evidence, leaving it up to juries to decide whether such posts/printouts are legitimate based on the facts presented.

Since Gibson, several other cases have addressed this issue. For

---

[60]State v. Gibson, 2015-Ohio-1679, 2015 WL 1962850, ¶ 41 (Ohio Ct. App. 6th Dist. Lucas County 2015).

[61]State v. Gibson, 2015-Ohio-1679, 2015 WL 1962850, ¶ 41 (Ohio Ct. App. 6th Dist. Lucas County 2015).

[62]Grimm, Lisa Yurwit Bergstrom & Melissa M. O'Toole-Loureiro, Authentication of Social Media Evidence, 36 Am. J. Trial Advoc. 433, 433 (2013).

[63]State v. Gibson, 2015-Ohio-1679, 2015 WL 1962850, ¶ 4 (Ohio Ct. App. 6th Dist. Lucas County 2015), quoting Grimm at 465.

[64]See Hartford Insurance Company v. Parker, 1982 WL 6662 (Ohio Ct. App. 6th Dist. Lucas County 1982) (suggesting a low bar to offer evidence as being authentic).

[65]State v. Gibson, 2015-Ohio-1679, 2015 WL 1962850, ¶ 70 (Ohio Ct. App. 6th Dist. Lucas County 2015).

[66]State v. Gibson, 2015-Ohio-1679, 2015 WL 1962850, ¶ 77 (Ohio Ct. App. 6th Dist. Lucas County 2015).

example, in *State v. Inkton,*[67] appellant appealed his conviction, arguing that the trial court had improperly admitted unauthenticated hearsay evidence, to wit: Facebook posts.

The appellate court first discussed concerns addressed by Facebook which included printouts, noting that anyone could create a fictitious name or masquerade under another's name or access another's account by obtaining the user's name and password.[68] In finding that there was no evidence presented suggesting that another made the posts or modified privacy settings, the court held that the Facebook post was admissible as a statement by a party opponent and not inadmissible hearsay.[69]

In the civil protection order context, several trial courts have upheld the issuance of a civil protection order based on Facebook posts and data transmitted via Facebook and found that such posts provide evidence of mental distress and threatening conduct.[70]

The Supreme Court standardized protection order forms were written to restrain a respondent from having any contact with the petitioner or protected parties which includes contact by landline, cordless, cellular or digital telephone, text, instant messaging, fax, e-mail, voice mail, delivery service, social networking media, blogging, writing, electronic communications or communications by any means directly or through another person.[71] In fact, Cuyahoga County has added the following provisions to its protection order forms:

> **It is further ordered** that respondent shall not post any photos, videos, or other images of Petitioner or minor child(ren), shall not refer to Petitioner or the minor child(ren) on any form of social media and shall not use any form of surveillance on Petitioner or minor child(ren).

---

[67] State v. Inkton, 2016-Ohio-693, 60 N.E.3d 616 (Ohio Ct. App. 8th Dist. Cuyahoga County 2016).

[68] State v. Inkton, 2016-Ohio-693, ¶ 86–87, 60 N.E.3d 616, 631 (Ohio Ct. App. 8th Dist. Cuyahoga County 2016).

[69] State v. Inkton, 2016-Ohio-693, ¶ 90, 60 N.E.3d 616, 632 (Ohio Ct. App. 8th Dist. Cuyahoga County 2016).

[70] Frenchko v. Frenchko-Nagy, 2015-Ohio-4546, 42 N.E.3d 829 (Ohio Ct. App. 11th Dist. Trumbull County 2015) (not against the weight of the evidence for the magistrate to conclude that the act of posting links to the profile of a man with a known criminal record, who was ultimately discovered to have made the offensive phone call, when petitioner had requested no contact with respondent, could cause her mental distress); Partin v. Morrison, 2015-Ohio-4740, 2015 WL 7293332 (Ohio Ct. App. 12th Dist. Brown County 2015) (noting the importance of introducing texts and Facebook posts to demonstrate mental distress); Barton v. Barton, 2015-Ohio-3869, 2015 WL 5691887 (Ohio Ct. App. 2d Dist. Greene County 2015) (while Facebook posting was distasteful, it was not transmitted to Ms. Barton and does not indicate any explicit threat of force, at ¶ 20); Wulf v. Opp, 2015-Ohio-3285, 2015 WL 4878495 (Ohio Ct. App. 12th Dist. Clermont County 2015); Caramico v. Caramico, 2015-Ohio-4232, 2015 WL 5934194 (Ohio Ct. App. 12th Dist. Clermont County 2015).

[71] See Sup. R. 10.01-10.05.

§ 16:21 "Other acts" testimony[1]

The admission of "other acts" evidence[2] is an issue attorneys frequently address in domestic violence proceedings due to the nature of domestic violence. Because domestic violence often has tragic and irreversible consequences, it is imperative for courts to have as much relevant information as is available.[3]

Generally, evidence of previous or subsequent criminal acts, independent of the offense for which the defendant is charged, is not admissible in criminal cases. It is ordinarily inadmissible to show that a defendant acted in conformity with that misconduct on a given occasion.[4]

[Section 16:21]

[1]See State v. Williams, 134 Ohio St. 3d 521, 2012-Ohio-5695, 983 N.E.2d 1278 (2012); State v. Sargent, 2015-Ohio-704, 29 N.E.3d 331 (Ohio Ct. App. 6th Dist. Lucas County 2015) (discussing the admissibility of other acts evidence and the recent case law).

[2]See also State v. Broom, 40 Ohio St. 3d 277, 533 N.E.2d 682 (1988); State v. Sims, 191 Ohio App. 3d 622, 2010-Ohio-6228, 947 N.E.2d 227 (2d Dist. Greene County 2010).

[3]See State v. Bone, 2006-Ohio-3809, 2006 WL 2053398 (Ohio Ct. App. 10th Dist. Franklin County 2006) (Court found that evidence of prior acts and behavior is particularly important to prove the crime of menacing by stalking. Stalking may require examination of the offender's past conduct involving the victim to assist a jury in understanding the context of what otherwise might appear to be an innocent act. A defendant's otherwise innocent appearing acts, when put into the context of previous contacts he has had with the victim may be knowing attempts to cause mental distress.). See also State v. Taylor, 2013-Ohio-4588, 2013 WL 5657956 (Ohio Ct. App. 5th Dist. Richland County 2013) (finding that trial court did not err in the admission of state's evidence of appellant's prior criminal background, divorce filings and subsequent dismissals thereof, civil protection orders issued on behalf of victim, numerous photos depicting injuries sustained by victim and victim's thoughts of suicide); State v. Kinsworthy, 2014-Ohio-1584, 2014 WL 1489250 (Ohio Ct. App. 12th Dist. Warren County 2014) (prior bad acts of violence between the victim and defendant are relevant in establishing the victim's belief of impending serious harm and are particularly important in proving the crime of menacing by stalking and can assist the jury in understanding that a defendant's otherwise innocent appearing acts, when put into the context of previous contacts he has had with the victim, may be knowing attempts to cause mental distress, at ¶ 19, quoting State v. Hart, 2009-Ohio-997, 2009 WL 580808 (Ohio Ct. App. 12th Dist. Warren County 2009)).

[4]See for example, State v. Russell, 2013-Ohio-1381, 2013 WL 1438000 (Ohio Ct. App. 12th Dist. Butler County 2013). See State v. Cornwell, 2015-Ohio-4617, 48 N.E.3d 169 (Ohio Ct. App. 9th Dist. Wayne County 2015) (where police officer's testimony regarding defendant's violent past with victim should have been excluded as inadmissible "other bad acts" in defendant's domestic violence trial, defendant was not materially prejudiced by its admission and as such the admission was harmless error.). City of Cleveland v. Reynolds, 2018-Ohio-97, ¶ 12, 2018 WL 386657 (Ohio Ct. App. 8th Dist. Cuyahoga County 2018) (while Evid. R. 404(B) prohibits the introduction of evidence of other crimes or acts "to prove the character of a person in order to show action in conformity therewith," where the victim's subjective belief that the offender will cause the victim physical harm is an element of the offense, such as in aggravated menacing cases, "evidence of a defendant's violent character is admissible to prove that the victim believed the defendant would cause physical harm." Citing, Cleveland v. McCoy, 2016-Ohio-3451, ¶ 4, 2016 WL 3348404 (Ohio Ct. App. 8th Dist. Cuyahoga County 2016).

However, "other acts" evidence is admissible in certain cases under Evid.R. 404(B) to establish motive,[5] opportunity, intent,[6] preparation, plan,[7] knowledge, identity,[8] or absences of mistake or accident.

Such evidence is admissible provided that the probative value of the evidence outweighs the prejudicial value of its admission.[9] It is not admissible solely to show the defendant's propensity to commit the crime in question.[10]

The threshold question in determining the admissibility of "other acts" evidence under Evid.R. 404(B) is whether any of the matters of

---

[5]See State v. King, 2000 WL 330048 (Ohio Ct. App. 5th Dist. Stark County 2000); State v. Weatherholtz, 2003-Ohio-3633, 2003 WL 21543813 (Ohio Ct. App. 3d Dist. Wyandot County 2003); State v. Partlow, 2013-Ohio-2771, 2013 WL 3356575 (Ohio Ct. App. 10th Dist. Franklin County 2013) (noting that the details of the facts involved in appellant's prior domestic violence convictions may be admissible if relevant to non-character issues such as a possible motive or identity, at ¶ 27); R.C. 2945. 59.

[6]See State v. Stephens, 2008-Ohio-890, 2008 WL 583789 (Ohio Ct. App. 9th Dist. Summit County 2008); State v. Sieng, 2003-Ohio-7246, 2004 WL 67836 (Ohio Ct. App. 2d Dist. Clark County 2003); see also State v. Thompson, 2003-Ohio-3939, 2003 WL 21710623 (Ohio Ct. App. 8th Dist. Cuyahoga County 2003); State v. Blonski, 125 Ohio App. 3d 103, 707 N.E.2d 1168 (9th Dist. Medina County 1997); State v. Johnson, 73 Ohio Misc. 2d 1, 657 N.E.2d 383 (Mun. Ct. 1994); State v. Clay, 181 Ohio App. 3d 563, 2009-Ohio-1235, 910 N.E.2d 14 (8th Dist. Cuyahoga County 2009); State v. Williams, 2011-Ohio-2702, 2011 WL 2175078, *4 (Ohio Ct. App. 6th Dist. Lucas County 2011) (as to the admission of other acts of domestic violence, prior acts against the same victim are admissible in a domestic violence prosecution to prove the defendant's intent, so long as the current act and the other acts must have occurred reasonably near to each other and a similar scheme or plan must have been utilized to commit the offense at issue and the other offenses); State v. Machuca, 2016-Ohio-254, 2016 WL 363448 (Ohio Ct. App. 3d Dist. Allen County 2016), appeal not allowed, 145 Ohio St. 3d 1472, 2016-Ohio-3028, 49 N.E.3d 1314 (2016).

[7]See Evid.R. 404(B); see State v. Yun, 2001 WL 1082354 (Ohio Ct. App. 5th Dist. Stark County 2001); see also State v. Thompson, 2000 WL 235535 (Ohio Ct. App. 9th Dist. Lorain County 2000) (Lorain County Appellate Court "[a]dmitted the details of Mr. Thompson's prior conviction as it was evidence that tends to show Ms. Olah's state of mind during the current incident"; but see State v. Deyling, 1998 WL 46753 (Ohio Ct. App. 9th Dist. Medina County 1998).

[8]State v. Thompson, 2003-Ohio-3939, 2003 WL 21710623 (Ohio Ct. App. 8th Dist. Cuyahoga County 2003); State v. Griffin, 2003-Ohio-3196, 2003 WL 21414664 (Ohio Ct. App. 1st Dist. Hamilton County 2003); see State v. Richardson, 2010-Ohio-471, 2010 WL 497343 (Ohio Ct. App. 6th Dist. Lucas County 2010) (other acts testimony "may be used to establish a "behavioral blueprint" which "can be used to identify the perpetrator* * *through the characteristics of acts rather than through a person's character." at *10, quoting State v. Lowe, 69 Ohio St. 3d 527, 531, 1994-Ohio-345, 634 N.E.2d 616 (1994)); State v. Sargent, 2015-Ohio-704, 29 N.E.3d 331 (Ohio Ct. App. 6th Dist. Lucas County 2015).

[9]See State v. Smith, 49 Ohio St. 3d 137, 551 N.E.2d 190 (1990). See also State v. Sines, 2006-Ohio-1956, 2006 WL 1044445 (Ohio Ct. App. 5th Dist. Stark County 2006); State v. Vandyne, 2017-Ohio-584, 2017 WL 777746 (Ohio Ct. App. 5th Dist. Guernsey County 2017) (where appellant's argument that victim's characterization of appellant as a violent, bad tempered person was unfair prejudice, court found that comments about appellant's temperament did not contribute to his conviction).

[10]State v. Wright, 2001-Ohio-2473, 2001 WL 1627643 (Ohio Ct. App. 4th Dist. Washington County 2001); State v. Sims, 2018-Ohio-769, 2018 WL 1136587 (Ohio Ct. App. 2d Dist. Clark County 2018).

proof (motive, opportunity, scheme, etc.) are at issue in the case. If not, then "other acts" evidence is inadmissible.[11]

In fact, the Supreme Court of Ohio set forth a three factor analysis for the admission of "other acts" evidence, to wit: 1) whether the other act evidence is relevant under Evid. R. 401; 2) whether the evidence is presented to prove a permissible purpose, such as those listed in Evid. R. 404(B), or whether it is presented to prove the character of the accused to show conformity therewith; and 3) whether the danger of unfair prejudice under Evid. R. 403 substantially outweighs the probative value of the other acts evidence.[12]

Several Ohio courts have expanded the evidence standard to include "other acts" in cases involving threats of domestic violence. For example, in *State v. Collie*,[13] the Hamilton County Court of Appeals articulated the test for admitting prior bad acts regarding the same victim.[14] The court held that prior acts are admissible to prove the element of belief in the imminence of physical harm if such evidence is specific to time and place.[15]

Moreover, some Ohio courts have even determined that "other acts evidence" can be useful in prosecutions for menacing by stalking because it can form the foundation of engaging in a pattern of conduct[16] as well as provide information that would demonstrate mental distress.[17] In effect, ". . .it can assist the jury in understanding that a defendant's otherwise innocent appearing acts, when put into the

[11]See State v. Richardson, 2010-Ohio-471, 2010 WL 497343 (Ohio Ct. App. 6th Dist. Lucas County 2010).

[12]State v. Lipkins, 2017-Ohio-4085, ¶ 19, 92 N.E.3d 82 (Ohio Ct. App. 10th Dist. Franklin County 2017); citing, State v. Williams, 134 Ohio St. 3d 521, 2012-Ohio-5695, 983 N.E.2d 1278, ¶ 20 (2012).

[13]State v. Collie, 108 Ohio App. 3d 580, 671 N.E.2d 338 (1st Dist. Hamilton County 1996); see also State v. Kent, 1999 WL 689222 (Ohio Ct. App. 7th Dist. Mahoning County 1999); Jane H. Aiken & Jane C. Murphy, Evidence Issues in Domestic Violence Civil Cases, 34 Fam. L.Q. 43 (2000).

[14]See also State v. Remley, 1999 WL 4168 (Ohio Ct. App. 5th Dist. Stark County 1998) (discussing that evidence of other acts is admissible if there is substantial proof that the alleged other acts were committed by the defendant and the evidence tends to prove motive, opportunity, intent, preparation, plan, knowledge, identity, or absence of mistake or accident).

[15]See also State v. Kneisley, 1999 WL 12730 (Ohio Ct. App. 2d Dist. Montgomery County 1999); State v. Muncey, 1999 WL 59675 (Ohio Ct. App. 12th Dist. Madison County 1999); State v. Blonski, 125 Ohio App. 3d 103, 707 N.E.2d 1168 (9th Dist. Medina County 1997); State v. Grubb, 111 Ohio App. 3d 277, 675 N.E.2d 1353 (2d Dist. Montgomery County 1996); State v. Newell, 1998 WL 667651 (Ohio Ct. App. 5th Dist. Stark County 1998); State v. Drake, 135 Ohio App. 3d 507, 734 N.E.2d 865 (12th Dist. Butler County 1999) (prior acts were admissible to show victim's state of mind); see also State v. Crowley, 2009-Ohio-6689, 2009 WL 4893283 (Ohio Ct. App. 2d Dist. Clark County 2009) (evidence of defendant's prior domestic violence was not used to prove his bad character; rather, it was used to explain why the victim contacted the police in response to his calls to her and to prove that she had a reasonable basis to fear that he would harm her as he had done so in the past); State v. Bunch, 2010-Ohio-515, 2010 WL 547402 (Ohio Ct. App. 8th Dist. Cuyahoga County 2010); Evid. R. 404(B); City of Cleveland v. Reynolds, 2018-Ohio-97, 2018 WL 386657 (Ohio Ct. App. 8th Dist. Cuyahoga County 2018).

[16]State v. Kronenberg, 2018-Ohio-1962, ¶ 33, 2018 WL 2277773 (Ohio Ct. App. 8th Dist. Cuyahoga County 2018).

[17]State v. Granakis, 2017-Ohio-8428, ¶ 20, 2017 WL 5146115 (Ohio Ct. App. 9th

context of previous contacts he has had with the victim, may be knowing attempts to cause mental distress."[18]

Q & A: Is "other acts" evidence addressed in the civil domestic violence context?

Similarly, many Ohio courts have held that RC 3113.31 contemplates prior acts being used as evidence in support of a CPO. For example, in *Visnich v. Visnich*,[19] the court specifically determined that "[t]he language used in defining 'domestic violence' clearly contemplates prior acts being used as evidence to support a CPO. Otherwise, it would be unnecessary to specify that multiple acts may be considered when an application for a CPO has been filed."[20] The court then stated that Evid.R. 404(B) permits the introduction of evidence concerning other crimes, wrongs, or acts if offered for the limited purpose of demonstrating 'motive, opportunity, intent, preparation, plan, knowledge, identity or absences of mistake or accident.' "[21] The court then reasoned that the defendant's prior use of firearms was admissible to support the victim's fear of imminent serious physical harm.

Q & A: Why is a history of domestic violence important to the case?

It is crucial that the attorney elicit information regarding the history of abuse in the relationship.[22] "Due to the cyclical nature of domestic violence, introduction of evidence of the relationship's history of abuse. . . is vital in allowing a court to fully comprehend the risk posed to a particular petitioner."[23] A history of abuse provides the court with additional evidence that may be relevant in assessing the seriousness of the abuse in the relationship necessary to support the issuance of the order and in crafting appropriate remedies.

Dist. Wayne County 2017).

[18]State v. Granakis, 2017-Ohio-8428, ¶ 21, 2017 WL 5146115 (Ohio Ct. App. 9th Dist. Wayne County 2017); citing State v. Halgrimson, 2000 WL 1675051 (Ohio Ct. App. 9th Dist. Lorain County 2000); quoting, State v. Tichon, 102 Ohio App. 3d 758, 768, 658 N.E.2d 16 (9th Dist. Summit County 1995); quoting, State v. Bilder, 99 Ohio App. 3d 653, 658, 651 N.E.2d 502 (9th Dist. Summit County 1994); State v. Phillips, 2018 SD 2, 906 N.W.2d 411 (S.D. 2018) (evidence of prior acts of domestic violence relevant to show motive, provide context, and show nature of parties' relationship).

[19]Visnich v. Visnich, 1999 WL 1299300 (Ohio Ct. App. 11th Dist. Trumbull County 1999).

[20]Visnich v. Visnich, 1999 WL 1299300 (Ohio Ct. App. 11th Dist. Trumbull County 1999).

[21]Visnich v. Visnich, 1999 WL 1299300 (Ohio Ct. App. 11th Dist. Trumbull County 1999); see also State v. Buchanan, 1999 WL 326195 (Ohio Ct. App. 12th Dist. Clermont County 1999) (testimony at trial concerning a magistrate's prior finding of civil domestic violence was admissible to show the lack of accident).

[22]Lisa A. Linsky, Use of Domestic Violence History Evidence in the Criminal Prosecution: A Common Sense Approach, 16 Pace L. Rev. 73, 74 (1995).

[23]Catherine F. Klein & Leslye E. Orloff, Symposium on Domestic Violence, Providing Legal Protection for Battered Women: An Analysis of State Statutes and Case Law, 21 Hofstra L. Rev. 801, 900 (1993).

A history of abuse usually implies that there is a stronger likelihood of future violence. A defendant's past conduct is important evidence in predicting probable future abusive conduct.[24]

Domestic violence almost always takes the form of a pattern of behavior, rather than a single incident. Prior incidents of abuse tend to demonstrate that pattern of abuse.

Providing the court with a history of the abuser's violence permits the court to understand the parties' relationship and can negate the defense that the victim's injuries were accidental or unintentional. Such evidence may also aid the fact finder in understanding why the victim may be reluctant to testify or why he/she did not disclose the abuse sooner. It may also demonstrate why a victim believes that he/she is in danger of imminent serious physical harm.

A history of abuse enables an attorney to prove the case where the allegation of domestic violence is in the nature of a threat. For example, in *Bruns v. Bruns*,[25] the defendant pinned the victim to the wall and pushed his elbow into her breast. He also threw silverware past her head and threw plates at her, causing her to duck to avoid being hit. At the hearing, the victim testified that she truly feared for her safety and that there had been prior incidents of abuse. The defendant argued that there were no visible injuries,[26] and thus, there was no evidence to support a finding of domestic violence under RC 3113.31(A)(1)(a). The appellate court affirmed the trial court decision that the victim was fearful of imminent physical harm and stated that the defendant had attempted to cause bodily injury in that the elbow to the breast caused the victim pain. The court reasoned that "threats of violence constitute domestic violence if the fear resulting from those threats is reasonable."[27] The reasonableness of the fear depends on the petitioner's history with the respondent.[28]

Similarly, the Trumbull County Court of Appeals noted that the court may look at a past history when considering whether to grant a civil protection order. In *Visnich v. Visnich*,[29] the court held that "testimony regarding appellant's past use of firearms in the context of

[24]See Cruz-Foster v. Foster, 597 A.2d 927 (D.C. 1991).

[25]Bruns v. Bruns, 1999 WL 819344 (Ohio Ct. App. 6th Dist. Erie County 1999); see also Sitton v. Sitton, 1999 WL 55717 (Ohio Ct. App. 2d Dist. Montgomery County 1999); State v. Brown, 2003-Ohio-710, 2003 WL 352460 (Ohio Ct. App. 12th Dist. Butler County 2003); Text § 11:10, Ex parte protection orders—Legal standard for issuance.

[26]See also State v. Warfield, 2003-Ohio-2366, 2003 WL 21054785 (Ohio Ct. App. 11th Dist. Trumbull County 2003).

[27]Bruns v. Bruns, 1999 WL 819344, *3 (Ohio Ct. App. 6th Dist. Erie County 1999), quoting Eichenberger v. Eichenberger, 82 Ohio App. 3d 809, 613 N.E.2d 678 (10th Dist. Franklin County 1992); see also Conkle v. Wolfe, 131 Ohio App. 3d 375, 383, 722 N.E.2d 586 (4th Dist. Athens County 1998).

[28]Bruns v. Bruns, 1999 WL 819344, *3 (Ohio Ct. App. 6th Dist. Erie County 1999); see also Reynolds v. Reynolds, 2001 WL 62552 (Ohio Ct. App. 2d Dist. Montgomery County 2001); Rhodes v. Gunter, 2003-Ohio-2342, 2003 WL 21040724, *3 (Ohio Ct. App. 9th Dist. Lorain County 2003).

[29]Visnich v. Visnich, 1999 WL 1299300, *3 (Ohio Ct. App. 11th Dist. Trumbull County 1999); see also Trent v. Trent, 1999 WL 298073 (Ohio Ct. App. 12th Dist. Preble County 1999); Ankenbruck v. Ankenbruck, 2000 WL 1804360 (Ohio Ct. App. 11th Dist. Trumbull County 2000).

domestic violence was clearly admissible to prove that appellee was justified in her fear of 'imminent serious physical harm.' "[30]

Q & A: How does one elicit such evidence?

Asking the victim to simply recount several incidents of abuse, specific to time and place, best shows a history of domestic violence.[31] Where the victim is either unable or unwilling to describe with specificity the exact nature and extent of the violence as required by RC 3113.31(C)(1), the court may question the credibility of the victim or wonder whether there is truly an emergency need for the order.

Q & A: What kind of evidence is sufficient?

The incidents of past abuse may be of actual or attempted physical abuse or threats to harm or kill. If believed, these acts, either singularly or collectively, may demonstrate a lengthy pattern of abuse, threats, and intimidation. It must be cautioned, however, that one or two isolated incidents of domestic violence may not provide the court with sufficient evidence of a pattern or history of the abuse.[32]

Courts that treat each incident of abuse in isolation minimize the effect and seriousness of the abuse on the victim and the family.[33] Excluding evidence of past abuse violates the fundamental purpose of Ohio's domestic violence statute, which is to prevent future abusive conduct.

Q & A: Is character evidence admissible to prove other conduct?

Generally, evidence of a person's character is not admissible to prove that he/she acted in conformity therewith on a particular occasion.[34] However, in *State v. Clemence*,[35] the defendant testified on direct that he had previously pled guilty to a prior act of domestic violence.[36] He also testified that he would never lay a hand on the victim. In putting his peaceful character in issue, he opened the door to testimony concerning his prior acts of domestic violence.

Q & A: What is demeanor evidence?

---

[30]See also State v. Seitz, 2003-Ohio-1879, 2003 WL 1871039 (Ohio Ct. App. 11th Dist. Portage County 2003).

[31]But see Rush v. Rush, 1999 WL 1044482 (Ohio Ct. App. 8th Dist. Cuyahoga County 1999) (noting that "[w]hile a victim's history with the perpetrator may cause the victim to experience reasonable fear of the perpetrator's threats of domestic violence, . . . [the] wife's evidence here was vague and wholly lacking in specific details"). See also Bruner v. Bruner, 2000-Ohio-2554, 2000 WL 1486452 (Ohio Ct. App. 7th Dist. Mahoning County 2000).

[32]See Simmons v. Simmons, 649 So. 2d 799 (La. Ct. App. 2d Cir. 1995); see also Rhodes v. Gunter, 2003-Ohio-2342, 2003 WL 21040724 (Ohio Ct. App. 9th Dist. Lorain County 2003). But see State v. Ornellas, 79 Haw. 418, 903 P.2d 723 (Ct. App. 1995).

[33]Jane H. Aiken and Jane C. Murphy, Dealing with Complex Evidence of Domestic Violence: A Primer for the Civil Bench, 39(2) Court Rev. 12 (2002).

[34]Evid.R. 404(A); but see Evid.R. 404(A)(1) and (2) for the exceptions. State v. Stark, 2017-Ohio-873, 2017 WL 962916 (Ohio Ct. App. 9th Dist. Wayne County 2017) (noting that character of victim is seldom relevant in a criminal prosecution and finding that violent character of victim not relevant unless accused shows he acted in self-defense or out of extreme emotional distress from reasonable provocation).

[35]State v. Clemence, 2003-Ohio-3660, 2003 WL 21545745 (Ohio Ct. App. 8th Dist. Cuyahoga County 2003).

[36]See also State v. Granakis, 2017-Ohio-8428, 2017 WL 5146115 (Ohio Ct. App. 9th Dist. Wayne County 2017).

Demeanor evidence is the way someone acts during the proceeding. Generally, appellate courts do not overturn a lower court decision. As the Supreme Court of Ohio observed in *Seasons Coal Co. v. Cleveland*,[37] "[t]he underlying rationale of giving deference to the findings of the trial court rests with the knowledge that the trial judge is best able to view the witnesses and observe their demeanor, gestures, and voice inflections, and use these observations in weighing the credibility of the proffered testimony."[38] "Such deference is particularly important in light of research that indicates that as much as 'ninety percent of the total meaning of testimony is interpreted through non-verbal behavior, such as voice inflection, hand gestures, and the overall visual demeanor of the witness. The witness' choice of words accounts for only ten percent of the meaning of their testimony.' "[39]

It is important for the attorney to ask the victim to describe what he/she is seeing as the respondent answers questions. While it is not wise to interpret the respondent's demeanor for the court, it is proper to ask the court to "let the record reflect" the attorney's observations. In this way, the behavior is on the record. It may also be proper for the victim or another witness to testify as to what they saw.

Generally speaking, if a victim recants his/her testimony, the prosecutor can impeach her/him with prior statements, medical records, a 911 tape, or other hearsay exceptions. However, if the victim does not testify, certain evidence still must be elicited including evidence of the parties' relationship, the identity of the perpetrator, evidence of the act and be able to rebut a defendant's self-defense claim.

§ 16:22 The reluctant or recanting witness[1]

It is not unusual for victims to become reluctant to proceed with their domestic violence cases, particularly with the passage of time.[2] If the victim does not appear at the hearing, the case in chief depends primarily on evidence derived from exceptions to the hearsay rule.[3] Where the victim testifies but is either a hostile witness or changes her/his story, the case in chief depends on both the exceptions to the

---

[37]Seasons Coal Co., Inc. v. City of Cleveland, 10 Ohio St. 3d 77, 461 N.E.2d 1273, 38 U.C.C. Rep. Serv. 469 (1984).

[38]Seasons Coal Co., Inc. v. City of Cleveland, 10 Ohio St. 3d 77, 80, 461 N.E.2d 1273, 38 U.C.C. Rep. Serv. 469 (1984). See also Johnson v. Auls, 2008-Ohio-6123, 2008 WL 5049751 (Ohio Ct. App. 10th Dist. Franklin County 2008).

[39]State v. Venters, 2003-Ohio-2831, 2003 WL 21267278 (Ohio Ct. App. 2d Dist. Montgomery County 2003), quoting State v. Evans, 67 Ohio St. 3d 405, 410-411, 1993-Ohio-186, 618 N.E.2d 162 (1993) (holding modified by, State v. Lozada, 92 Ohio St. 3d 74, 2001-Ohio-149, 748 N.E.2d 520 (2001)).

[Section 16:22]

[1]See also Text § 14:6, Law enforcement policies and procedures; Text § 16:12, Evidentiary considerations involving independent documentation. Njeri Mathes Rutledge, Turning a Blind Eye: Perjury in Domestic Violence Cases, 39 N.M. L.Rev. 149 (2009). See also Bonomi, Martin, Ganganna and Grabmeier, New Insights on the Process of Victim Recantation, 18 Domestic Violence Report 49 (April/May 2013).

[2]See Cheryl Hanna, No Right to Choose, Mandated Victim Participation in Domestic Violence Prosecutions, 109 Harv. L. Rev. 1849 (1996).

[3]But see Crawford v. Washington, 541 U.S. 36, 124 S. Ct. 1354, 158 L. Ed. 2d 177, 63 Fed. R. Evid. Serv. 1077 (2004); see also Text § 16:13, Hearsay exceptions: *Crawford* concerns.

hearsay rule and whether the defendant was sufficiently able to discredit the victim's testimony.[4]

Q & A: How are the elements of domestic violence proven without the presence or testimony of the victim?[5]

Testimony of the police[6] who responded to the call and other witness testimony may help a prosecutor prove a crime was committed. The excited utterance of the victim is often used when testified to by others.[7] In *State v. Cox*,[8] the appellate court noted that the admission of an excited utterance does not require independent proof or corroboration. In this case, the testimony by the officer that the victim was appellant's former girlfriend and that appellant had told police he felt his children were being abused by his ex-girlfriend was sufficient evidence to prove the element of family or household member.[9]

Another way that Courts have dealt with the perils of victimless prosecution after *Crawford* is to firmly encourage victims to attend their trials by employing more persuasive means.

Q & A: Have victims of domestic violence who recant their statements of abuse be criminally charged with a crime or be compelled to testify?[10]

For example, in *State v. Manzell*,[11] the victim told the Sheriff that defendant struck her in the leg. Prior to the preliminary hearing, the victim signed a notarized statement recanting her allegations against defendant. She was charged and convicted of filing a false police report

---

[4]See State v. Clay, 181 Ohio App. 3d 563, 2009-Ohio-1235, 910 N.E.2d 14 (8th Dist. Cuyahoga County 2009) (discussing when prosecutor may impeach own recanting witness under Evid. R. 607(A)).

[5]See generally, Tonya McCormick, Convicting Domestic Violence Abusers when the Victim Remains Silent, 13 BYU J. Pub. L. 427 (1999). See also Text § 16:12 to 16:14; State v. Mack, 2015-Ohio-5214, 2015 WL 8607454 (Ohio Ct. App. 11th Dist. Ashtabula County 2015) (finding that recanting victim's statements to officer were excited utterances and admissible under Potter v. Baker, 162 Ohio St. 488, 55 Ohio Op. 389, 124 N.E.2d 140, 53 A.L.R.2d 1234 (1955).

[6]See, e.g., State v. Suarez, 2002-Ohio-4890, 2002 WL 31087432 (Ohio Ct. App. 8th Dist. Cuyahoga County 2002) (discussing the recantation of the victim); see also State v. Taylor, 2003-Ohio-2025, 2003 WL 1916787 (Ohio Ct. App. 9th Dist. Summit County 2003). But see State v. Dotson, 2006-Ohio-1093, 2006 WL 562029 (Ohio Ct. App. 7th Dist. Columbiana County 2006) (judgment of conviction for domestic violence reversed where only evidence was offered by the officer who did not actually witness incident, but rather took the written statement of the victim and victim recanted on the stand).

[7]See, e.g., City of Shaker Heights v. Al-Gureshi, 1998 WL 183818 (Ohio Ct. App. 8th Dist. Cuyahoga County 1998); see also State v. Jackson, 2002-Ohio-1202, 2002 WL 398655 (Ohio Ct. App. 2d Dist. Montgomery County 2002).

[8]State v. Cox, 2001-Ohio-3213, 2001 WL 301429, *2 (Ohio Ct. App. 7th Dist. Belmont County 2001); State v. Jorden, 134 Ohio App. 3d 131, 730 N.E.2d 447 (1st Dist. Hamilton County 1999); see also Text § 5:15, Case preparation—Hearsay exceptions—Excited utterance.

[9]State v. Cox, 2001-Ohio-3213, 2001 WL 301429, *3 (Ohio Ct. App. 7th Dist. Belmont County 2001); see also State v. Jorden, 134 Ohio App. 3d 131, 137, 730 N.E.2d 447 (1st Dist. Hamilton County 1999) (evidence of officers that victim was mother of defendant's child was sufficient where victim did not testify).

[10]See also Text § 14:6, Law enforcement policies and procedures.

[11]State v. Manzell, 2007-Ohio-4076, 2007 WL 2283550 (Ohio Ct. App. 5th Dist. Stark County 2007).

and jailed for 30 days. At the subsequent trial, victim testified for the state that defendant had abused her.

On appellant's claim that he was denied a fair trial, the court noted that "it is aware of the troubling phenomenon of recantation of testimony by persons involved in domestic violence situations."[12]

In *State v. Smith*,[13] the trial court compelled the victim to testify. On appeal, the appellant argued that the trial corut erred when it forced the victim to testify. The appellate court explained the reasoning for compelling a victim to testify when it stated that "we are aware that in domestic violence cases it is not uncommon for the complaining witness to change her story, "forget" details or recant for anyone of a variety of reasons including threats of reprisal or genuine reconciliation.[14] It is, therefore, the purpose of the domestic violence statute to impose criminal sanctions upon assaultive behavior even though the relationship may be marked by cyclical periods of fighting and harmony."[15] In this case, Lisa was the primary witness and the case was based almost entirely on her testimony. "Had the trial court not compelled her testimony, the act of domestic violence may have gone unpunished. In a domestic violence case, the "wrongdoer not only injures his spouse but he also injures the public* * *"[16] "The testimony of the injured spouse is necessary for the truth to be known as far as possible to enable the law to provide justice."[17]

According to domestic violence expert Barbara Hart, victims of domestic violence might have additional options of resisting compulsion to testify against their batterers. These methods include educating the prosecutor about the dynamics of "resistance." For example, advocates or civil attorneys might discuss the danger of retaliation, costs of testifying and the chilling effect of coercion. Additional methods include identification of victim statements and other evidence sufficient to prove a case without the victim. Other ideas might be to charge the defendant with witness tampering or intimidation or asserting options for the admission of hearsay victim statements for a forfeiture by wrongdoing action.[18] Still other options might include filing of Motions to Quash Subpoena or motions for injunctive relief against contempt or incarceration of the victim.

[12]State v. Manzell, 2007-Ohio-4076, 2007 WL 2283550, *3 (Ohio Ct. App. 5th Dist. Stark County 2007).

[13]State v. Smith, 2003-Ohio-5461, 2003 WL 22336098 (Ohio Ct. App. 3d Dist. Seneca County 2003).

[14]State v. Smith, 2003-Ohio-5461, 2003 WL 22336098 (Ohio Ct. App. 3d Dist. Seneca County 2003), citing State v. Attaway, 111 Ohio App. 3d 488, 676 N.E.2d 600 (1st Dist. Hamilton County 1996); State v. Brown (May 8, 1998), Allen App. No. 1-97-74.

[15]State v. Smith, 2003-Ohio-5461, 2003 WL 22336098, *2 (Ohio Ct. App. 3d Dist. Seneca County 2003), citing State v. Attaway, 111 Ohio App. 3d 488, 676 N.E.2d 600 (1st Dist. Hamilton County 1996).

[16]State v. Smith, 2003-Ohio-5461, 2003 WL 22336098, *2 (Ohio Ct. App. 3d Dist. Seneca County 2003), quoting State v. Antill, 176 Ohio St. 61, 26 Ohio Op. 2d 366, 197 N.E.2d 548 (1964).

[17]State v. Smith, 2003-Ohio-5461, 2003 WL 22336098, *2 (Ohio Ct. App. 3d Dist. Seneca County 2003)at *2, quoting State v. Antill, 176 Ohio St. 61, 26 Ohio Op. 2d 366, 197 N.E.2d 548 (1964)

[18]See also Text § 16:13.

§ 16:23 Civil domestic violence case strategy[1]

In a civil domestic violence case, the attorney will have several opportunities to present the case to the fact-finder.[2] The victim's attorney should begin by requesting an opening statement so that he/she can address any misconceptions regarding domestic violence. In that opening statement, the attorney should discuss the dynamics of the abusive relationship and stress that it may not be possible for a victim to leave the relationship. The attorney should also advise the court that the evidentiary standard is a preponderance of the evidence.

Victims of domestic violence can be very challenging witnesses for even the most seasoned attorneys.[3] They may forget what transpired, or they may be unable to speak of the abusive incident in front of the abuser. They may minimize the violent acts inflicted on them. Should the victim be unable to remember certain information about the acts of violence, the attorney should ask the court for permission to refresh the witness's recollection. Diaries, journals, or other documents may jog the victim's memory. If the client still cannot remember but the information is in writing, the attorney should offer the writing into evidence.[4]

During the case-in-chief, the victim's attorney should use visual aids such as photographs and timelines detailing the abuse. These may be effective in explaining the case and may reinforce the nature of the abusive incident to the court. The attorney should also bring in any extrinsic evidence, including third-party witnesses and medical and police reports, if available. Demonstrative evidence such as this may provide a method of presenting the same testimony twice. It also reinforces the victim's testimony.

"A trial court's determination as to the admissibility of evidence is generally a matter within the sound discretion of the trial court."[5] Sometimes, however, it may be in the client's interest for the attorney to proffer testimony. Proffering testimony might become necessary should the trier of fact determine that certain evidence is not relevant or, if not considered by the court in its decision, might prejudice the rights of the moving party. The purpose of a proffer is to assist the reviewing court in determining whether the trial court's exclusion of evidence affected the moving party's substantial rights.

Should the trial court deny a petitioner's request to permit a party

---

[Section 16:23]

[1]See generally Jane H. Aiken and Jane C. Murphy, Dealing with Complex Evidence of Domestic Violence: A Primer for the Civil Bench, 39(2) Court Rev. 12 (2002).

[2]See generally, Cartlin Glass, Tamara Kuennen & Sharon Lopez, Custody & Visitation: Considerations for Every Attorney Retained by a Survivor of Domestic Violence, 36 Clearinghouse Rev. 529 (2003).

[3]See, generally, State v. Cressel, 2004-Ohio-68, 2004 WL 41724 (Ohio Ct. App. 2d Dist. Montgomery County 2004) (holding that minor inconsistencies in victim's testimony as to when she called her mother and where defendant stood when he choked her did not render conviction against manifest weight of the evidence).

[4]See Evid.R. 612, Evid.R. 803(5).

[5]Tarini v. Tarini, 2012-Ohio-6165, 2012 WL 6738317 (Ohio Ct. App. 10th Dist. Franklin County 2012), quoting Davis v. Killing, 171 Ohio App. 3d 400, 2007-Ohio-2303, 870 N.E.2d 1209 (11th Dist. Trumbull County 2007).

to testify, such as allowing children who might have witnessed a domestic violence incident,[6] an attorney for the petitioner might request that the testimony be proffered. In effect, proffered testimony is what a party would have testified to if permitted to testify. Such testimony is on the record and is preserved for an appeal.

§ 16:24 Use of expert witnesses[1]

In 1990, Ohio became one of a majority of states that recognized the use of expert testimony relative to "battered woman's syndrome." Pursuant to RC 2901.06, "battered woman's syndrome" is a matter of commonly accepted scientific knowledge not within the general understanding or experience of the general population.[2]

Over the past two decades, expert testimony has been used to explain to a jury why and how a victim of domestic violence believed her life was in danger and why there was no escape short of killing her abuser. Expert testimony can demonstrate that a person is a battered woman and how that affected perceptions and conduct. An expert can be used to establish self-defense, that a particular person had a belief of imminent danger of death or great bodily harm necessary to justify the use of force in question[3] or to explain a battered woman's plea of not guilty by reason of insanity. In that case, testimony would be used as evidence to establish the requisite impairment of the person's reason such that she did not know the wrongfulness of her act.

Recently, in *State v. Haines*,[4] the Supreme Court of Ohio held that when the credibility of an alleged victim of domestic violence has been challenged on cross-examination during the State's case-in-chief, the State may introduce limited expert testimony regarding the "battered woman syndrome" to aid the judge or jury in determining the victim's

[6]See, e.g., Jones v. Jones, 2011-Ohio-4393, 2011 WL 3847339 (Ohio Ct. App. 9th Dist. Summit County 2011).

[Section 16:24]

[1]Conrad, The Use of Victim Advocates and Expert Witnesses in Battered Women Cases, 30-Dec. Colo. Law 43 (2001);Admissibility of expert testimony concerning domestic-violence syndromes to assist jury in evaluating victim's testimony or behavior, 57 A.L.R.5th 315.

[2]See State v. Koss, 49 Ohio St. 3d 213, 551 N.E.2d 970 (1990); RC 2901.26; RC 2945.392; see also State v. Caudill, 2007-Ohio-1557, 2008 WL 852626, *8 (Ohio Ct. App. 6th Dist. Wood County 2008) (the Court held that expert testimony is permitted in cases other that those charging domestic violence and is not limited to married couples, parties who live together or who share familial or financial responsibilities); citing *State v. Haines* at 57).

[3]See State v. Goff, 128 Ohio St. 3d 169, 2010-Ohio-6317, 942 N.E.2d 1075 (2010) (court order compelling a defendant to submit to a psychiatric exam conducted by a state expert in response to defendant's raising defense of self defense supported by expert testimony on battered woman syndrome does not violate defendant's right of self-incrimination, but testimony must be limited to information related to battered woman syndrome and whether defendant's actions were affected by the syndrome).

[4]State v. Haines, 112 Ohio St. 3d 393, 2006-Ohio-6711, 860 N.E.2d 91 (2006). See also State v. Myers, 2014-Ohio-3759, 2014 WL 4269104 (Ohio Ct. App. 6th Dist. Wood County 2014), appeal not allowed, 144 Ohio St. 3d 1507, 2016-Ohio-652, 45 N.E.3d 1051 (2016) and appeal not allowed, 145 Ohio St. 3d 1447, 2016-Ohio-1596, 48 N.E.3d 585 (2016).

state of mind in returning to or remaining in a relationship with the defendant despite the abuse.

The Supreme Court first put the issue into historical context by discussing its prior holding in *State v. Koss*[5] and noting that it first recognized the admissibility of expert testimony regarding battered woman syndrome. In that case, the defendant killed her husband and testimony regarding battered woman syndrome was offered to demonstrate self-defense. The Court found that " '[e]xpert testimony regarding the battered woman syndrome can be admitted to help the jury not only understand the battered woman syndrome but also to determine whether defendant had reasonable grounds for an honest belief that she was in imminent danger when considering the issue of self-defense.' "[6] The *Koss* court then concluded that expert testimony on battered woman syndrome is admissible pursuant to Evid.R. 702 "where the evidence establishes that the woman is a battered woman, and when an expert is qualified to testify about the battered woman syndrome, expert testimony concerning the battered woman syndrome may be admitted to assist the trier of fact in determining whether the defendant acted in self-defense."[7] In that same year, the General Assembly enacted RC 2901.06, which recognized the value of battered woman syndrome testimony.

Because the instant case involved the use of such testimony in the State's case-in-chief, the Court then acknowledged that neither *Koss* nor RC 2901.26 nor RC 2945.392 limits the use of such testimony to self-defense or insanity cases; thus, admissibility of such testimony does not end with Evid.R. 702.

The Court relied on cases from other jurisdictions to illustrate the need to present this testimony, when relevant, as rehabilitative evidence during the State's case-in-chief. Additionally, expert testimony could be introduced to explain a victim's behavior, but it may only be considered relevant if there is some evidentiary foundation that the victim is a battered woman. Evid.R. 401. The Court then noted that the *Koss* court held that "in order to be classified as a battered woman, the couple must go through the battering cycle at least twice."[8] The Court concluded that while testimony describing the battered woman syndrome may be prejudicial to defendants charged with domestic violence, trial courts may admit limited and carefully tailored testimony on the general characteristics of a victim's suffering from

[5]State v. Koss, 49 Ohio St. 3d 213, 551 N.E.2d 970 (1990).

[6]State v. Haines, 112 Ohio St. 3d 393, 399, 2006-Ohio-6711, 860 N.E.2d 91 (2006), quoting State v. Koss, 49 Ohio St. 3d 213, 215, 551 N.E.2d 970 (1990).

[7]State v. Haines, 112 Ohio St. 3d 393, 400, 2006-Ohio-6711, 860 N.E.2d 91 (2006), quoting State v. Koss, 49 Ohio St. 3d 213, 218, 551 N.E.2d 970 (1990).

[8]State v. Haines, 112 Ohio St. 3d 393, 402, 2006-Ohio-6711, 860 N.E.2d 91 (2006), quoting State v. Koss, 49 Ohio St. 3d 213, 216, 551 N.E.2d 970 (1990); see also State v. Caudill, 2007-Ohio-1557, 2008 WL 852626 (Ohio Ct. App. 6th Dist. Wood County 2008); State v. Drew, 2008-Ohio-2797, 2008 WL 2349649 (Ohio Ct. App. 10th Dist. Franklin County 2008); State v. Long, 2011-Ohio-1050, 2011 WL 806839 (Ohio Ct. App. 9th Dist. Summit County 2011); State v. Sorah, 2007-Ohio-5898, 2007 WL 3243536 (Ohio Ct. App. 12th Dist. Clermont County 2007).

the battered woman syndrome.[9] However, an expert cannot opine that the alleged victim in the case was a battered woman, may not testify that the defendant was a batterer or that he is guilty of the crime and cannot comment on the victim's truthfulness.[10]

In her dissent, Justice Lanzinger admonished the majority for permitting prosecutor to utilize an expert to present evidence of the battered woman syndrome. She then stated that "I believe we should follow precedent as it stands and the statute as written. I would hold that the state may not introduce evidence of battered woman syndrome to demonstrate the victim's state of mind, ie. to explain why she returned to the defendant despite his aggressions towards her, when her credibility is challenged upon cross-examination. To do otherwise is to transform a shield for the defense into a sword for the prosecution."[11]

Q & A: Who qualifies as an expert?[12]

As more prosecutors abandon evidence-based prosecution for a victim's appearance in court, it is important to know who qualifies as an expert. Most often, experts have testified about why victims recant or change their stories, why they minimize the violence inflicted against them, and the dynamics of battering.

For example, in *State v. Dyson*,[13] the expert was the executive director of Choices, a program for victims of domestic violence and where she had been employed for over 15 years. She was also had a Master's in Social Work. She had contact with clients, had provided training on domestic violence issues to police and other organizations and had published articles on the issue. She was familiar with the common patterns of behavior in violent relationships. Clearly, she had demonstrated a specialized knowledge about domestic violence. In *State v. Thomas*,[14] the expert was a certified instructor with OPOTA, was a law enforcement officer involved in training officers on domestic

[9]See also State v. Long, 2011-Ohio-1050, 2011 WL 806839 (Ohio Ct. App. 9th Dist. Summit County 2011); State v. Baughman, 2014-Ohio-1821, 2014 WL 1759189 (Ohio Ct. App. 5th Dist. Fairfield County 2014) (testifying on why a victim might recant criminal allegations in light of the cycle of violence).

[10]See Hawes, Removing the Roadblocks to Successful Domestic Violence Prosecutions: Prosecutorial Use of Expert testimony on the Battered Woman Syndrome in Ohio, 53 Clev. St. L. Rev. 133 (2005–2006).

[11]State v. Haines, 112 Ohio St. 3d 393, 408, 2006-Ohio-6711, 860 N.E.2d 91 (2006).

[12]See also Evid. R. 702.

[13]State v. Dyson, 2000 WL 1597952 (Ohio Ct. App. 2d Dist. Champaign County 2000); State v. Frazier, 2012-Ohio-790, 2012 WL 642765 (Ohio Ct. App. 9th Dist. Summit County 2012) (in which the expert was a licensed social worker who was employed as the director of services at the Battered Women's Shelter and testified as an expert on the dynamics of battered women's syndrome which included victim's returning to their abuser after the abuse).

[14]State v. Thomas, 2003-Ohio-5746, 2003 WL 22429536 (Ohio Ct. App. 2d Dist. Montgomery County 2003); see also State v. Musgrove, 2008-Ohio-494, 2008 WL 344144 (Ohio Ct. App. 2d Dist. Montgomery County 2008) (where the expert was a retired supervisor from a police department domestic violence unit and a certified instructor who testified about the high rate of victims who refuse to testify); State v. Clark, 2018-Ohio-521, ¶ 30, 2018 WL 798385 (Ohio Ct. App. 6th Dist. Lucas County 2018) (police detective testified that victims of domestic violence fail to call the police about the abusive behavior or call 911 when injured; stay with their perpetrators for

violence, was on the local domestic violence task force and wrote grants for domestic violence programs.

Finally, in *State v. Kraus*,[15] the expert had a degree in social work and crisis counseling. According to the appellate decision, she was a state registered advocate with advanced status and close to 200 hours of specific training in victimization, domestic violence, child abuse and sexual assault. She had dealt with several thousand victims of domestic violence over her career. The Warren County appellate court determined that while not the best witness to testify about domestic violence and its impact on victims, it is well settled that the expert on the subject need not be the best expert on the subject in order for his or her testimony to be admissible.[16] "Instead, 'the test is whether a particular witness offered as an expert will aid the trier of fact in the search for the truth.' "[17] Of importance is that the Court also noted that the expert was not qualified to make any diagnosis or an opinion as to whether domestic violence actually occurred in the case at hand but that her testimony was helpful in understanding the victim's motives for wanting to minimize the abuser's actions and to recant her prior accusations.[18]

Q & A: What could an expert testify about in the civil domestic violence context?

A victim's attorney should also consider using expert witnesses in civil protection order hearings and in various family law cases.[19] An expert may testify about the dynamics of an abusive relationship.[20] An expert may dispel myths and educate the court about the effects of do-

---

many years and return to the relationship after leaving and lied about the cause of injuries).

[15]State v. Kraus, 2007-Ohio-6027, 2007 WL 3348426 (Ohio Ct. App. 12th Dist. Warren County 2007). See also State v. Horton, 2012-Ohio-3340, 2012 WL 3027221 (Ohio Ct. App. 9th Dist. Summit County 2012).

[16]State v. Kraus, 2007-Ohio-6027, 2007 WL 3348426, *5 (Ohio Ct. App. 12th Dist. Warren County 2007).

[17]State v. Kraus, 2007-Ohio-6027, 2007 WL 3348426, *5 (Ohio Ct. App. 12th Dist. Warren County 2007), quoting Alexander v. Mt. Carmel Medical Center, 56 Ohio St. 2d 155, 159, 10 Ohio Op. 3d 332, 383 N.E.2d 564 (1978).

[18]State v. Kraus, 2007-Ohio-6027, 2007 WL 3348426, *6 (Ohio Ct. App. 12th Dist. Warren County 2007).

[19]See Text § 15:17, Presenting evidence of domestic violence—Use of experts; generally, and Text § 15:18, Presenting evidence of domestic violence—Use of mental health professionals and other experts, for a general discussion of expert witnesses; see also Evid.R. 702; Paula Finley Mangum, Reconceptualizing Battered Women Syndrome Evidence: Prosecution Use of Expert Testimony on Battering, 19 B.C. Third World L.J. 593 (1999); Hawes, Removing the Roadblocks to Successful Domestic Violence Prosecutions: Prosecutorial Use of Expert Testimony on the Battered Woman Syndrome in Ohio, 53 Cleve. St. L.R. 133 (2005); Jane H. Aiken & Jane C. Murphy, Evidence Issues in Domestic Violence Civil Cases, 34 Fam. L.Q. 43 (2000); U.S. v. Young, 316 F.3d 649, 59 Fed. R. Evid. Serv. 1332 (7th Cir. 2002) (discussing admissibility of expert testimony on domestic violence).

[20]State v. Dyson, 2000 WL 1597952 (Ohio Ct. App. 2d Dist. Champaign County 2000). See also State v. Thomas, 2003-Ohio-5746, 2003 WL 22429536 (Ohio Ct. App. 2d Dist. Montgomery County 2003) (where appellate court concerned that the holding in State v. Dyson may be read too broadly as permitting statistical evidence of guilt or innocence of the accused; "In Dyson, we approved the use of expert testimony about the "behavioral characteristics" of victims of domestic violence to explain why they sometimes recant their prior accusations against their abusers"); State v. Kraus,

mestic violence on the abused. The expert may also be able to explain why the victim stays with the batterer, why his/her testimony may minimize the violence, why the victim may recant her testimony,[21] and the effects of the violence over time. The expert may be able to testify about the battered person's experiences. This information may be crucial to the court's ability to understand the evidence presented. It may also explain a victim's mental state in seeking the civil protection order or why a victim has a subjective belief that his/her abuser would cause him/her imminent harm.[22]

For civil domestic violence purposes, family law attorneys should be sure that the expert has, at a minimum, counseled or advocated for battered persons.[23] If the expert has written articles on the subject, he or she may have more credibility with the court. If the expert has previously testified, he/she may be a more reliable witness. Where the expert is asked to determine whether a particular victim suffers from "battered woman syndrome"[24] or post-traumatic stress disorder,[25] a psychologist or psychiatrist may be a necessary investment for the case.

Sometimes an attorney may want to use an expert who can testify about the batterer.[26] This may be instrumental in providing the court with the framework in which to judge the batterer's credibility. For example, an expert can testify about the excuses that a batterer often gives to justify his/her behavior. This testimony may offer the court an educated way to evaluate the batterer's testimony.

2007-Ohio-6027, 2007 WL 3348426 (Ohio Ct. App. 12th Dist. Warren County 2007).

[21]See, e.g., State v. Clark, 83 Haw. 289, 926 P.2d 194 (1996); People v. Salinas, 131 Cal. Rptr. 2d 313 (App. 5th Dist. 2003), as modified, (Mar. 18, 2003) and review granted and opinion superseded, 134 Cal. Rptr. 2d 222, 68 P.3d 1190 (Cal. 2003) and review dismissed, cause remanded, 20 Cal. Rptr. 3d 175, 99 P.3d 499 (Cal. 2004); State v. Thomas, 2003-Ohio-5746, 2003 WL 22429536 (Ohio Ct. App. 2d Dist. Montgomery County 2003) (holding that the behavioral characteristics of victims of abuse is permissible; testimony is relevant to show the dynamics of abusive relationships and to explain why a victim might recant her accusation or be uncooperative with authorities).

[22]See, e.g., Stark v. Stark, 2002-Ohio-90, 2002 WL 109281 (Ohio Ct. App. 5th Dist. Delaware County 2002); see also State v. Bosse, 1997 WL 219130 (Ohio Ct. App. 5th Dist. Delaware County 1997) (use of a psychological report was admitted into evidence to prove the state of mind of the parties).

[23]See State v. Dyson, 2000 WL 1597952 (Ohio Ct. App. 2d Dist. Champaign County 2000) (regarding the expert's specialized knowledge in the field); see also Evid.R. 702; Stark v. Stark, 2002-Ohio-90, 2002 WL 109281 (Ohio Ct. App. 5th Dist. Delaware County 2002); State v. Musgrove, 2008-Ohio-494, 2008 WL 344144 (Ohio Ct. App. 2d Dist. Montgomery County 2008).

[24]See Mary Ann Dutton, Understanding Women's Responses to Domestic Violence: A Redefinition of Battered Woman's Syndrome, 21 Hofstra L. Rev. 1191 (1993).

[25]See American Psychiatric Association, Diagnostic and Statistical Manual of Mental Disorders (DSM-IV) 427–29 (1994).

[26]See Stark v. Stark, 2002-Ohio-90, 2002 WL 109281 (Ohio Ct. App. 5th Dist. Delaware County 2002) (husband's court-ordered counselor telling the wife that she should be careful around him was not considered to be hearsay).

Finally, an expert may be useful in demonstrating that a protected party, such as a child, is in need of protection.[27] In *Stark v. Stark*,[28] the wife was granted a civil protection order for herself. The minor child of the parties was a protected party. The respondent appealed the trial court decision, arguing that the appellee failed to establish by a preponderance of the evidence that the respondent committed acts of domestic violence against the persons to be protected by the order. A social worker[29] for the child testified that the child feared having visitation with his father. The child suffered from anxiety and panic attacks, uncontrollable crying, nightmares, and hallucinations prior to visiting his father. The appellate court noted that from these factors, the court could conclude that the minor child "[w]as in danger of commission of domestic violence, as defined by statute."[30]

Since the closing argument is the last chance to inform the court about the theory of the case, the attorney should use the closing argument to tie the evidence together. In the closing, the attorney should draw reasonable inferences from the evidence presented and suggest that certain evidence implies a logical and reliable conclusion. This is also the time to address any weaknesses in the case. Where possible, an attorney should use expert testimony to turn these perceived weaknesses to his/her advantage. For example, the expert can explain that a victim's weak testimony, such as denial or forgetfulness, is actually typical victim behavior and supports a finding of domestic violence. Finally, using supportive case law such as the *Felton*[31] decision can appeal to the court's reason and buttress the attorney's argument and theory of the case.

§ 16:25 Cross-examination of the victim[1]

Q & A: Is a defendant permitted to cross-examine a victim about prior false accusations of domestic violence?

It is within the court's discretion whether such a question may be permitted on cross-examination. In *State v. Husseln*,[2] the trial court refused to admit evidence that the victim had previously filed five false domestic violence charges against the defendant that resulted in either dismissals or acquittals. The First District Court of Appeals reversed, stating that "[u]nder Evid.R. 608(B), a defendant is permitted, in the court's discretion, to cross examine a victim about prior false

[27]See also Lang v. Lang, 2004-Ohio-2035, 2004 WL 869367 (Ohio Ct. App. 2d Dist. Miami County 2004).

[28]Stark v. Stark, 2002-Ohio-90, 2002 WL 109281 (Ohio Ct. App. 5th Dist. Delaware County 2002).

[29]See generally, Fran S. Davis, The Criminalization of Domestic Violence: What Social Workers Need to Know, Vol. 48 No. 2 Social Worker 237 (2003).

[30]Stark v. Stark, 2002-Ohio-90, 2002 WL 109281 (Ohio Ct. App. 5th Dist. Delaware County 2002).

[31]Felton v. Felton, 79 Ohio St. 3d 34, 1997-Ohio-302, 679 N.E.2d 672 (1997).

[Section 16:25]

[1]See also § 12:26.

[2]State v. Husseln, 152 Ohio App. 3d 67, 2003-Ohio-1369, 786 N.E.2d 536 (1st Dist. Hamilton County 2003); see also State v. Younker, 2002-Ohio-5376, 2002 WL 31242238 (Ohio Ct. App. 2d Dist. Darke County 2002).

accusations if they are clearly probative of truthfulness or untruthfulness."[3] Relying on the reasoning of *State v. Fredrick*, the Hamilton County Court of Appeals reversed the trial court decision and stated that if it could be shown that the victim made false allegations of domestic violence in the past, it would have been highly probative of the victim's truthfulness or untruthfulness with respect to the present charge of domestic violence. The court also noted that the evidence of the victim's prior false allegations was admissible under Evid.R. 616(A) to show a victim's bias, prejudice, interest or motive for misrepresentation.[4] Here, the prior false charges were highly probative of whether the victim was telling the truth in this instance.

Q & A: Is a defendant/respondent allowed to cross-examine a victim about other pending cases?

It depends. For example, the Hamilton County Court of Appeals found that the lower court did not commit reversible error by precluding cross-examination on the issue of bias, prejudice, or ulterior motive. In *State v. Warren*,[5] the appellant was denied the opportunity to cross-examine the victim in the criminal domestic violence case about the appellant's filing of a custody motion in another court. The appellate court noted that "the preclusion of the cross-examination of *[the victim]* concerning appellant's filing of the custody matter did not contribute to appellant's conviction. Therefore, we conclude that the limitation of the cross-examination of *[the victim]* was harmless error beyond a reasonable doubt."[6]

On the other hand, the Second District Court of Appeals determined that the trial court abused its discretion by refusing to permit the defendant to cross-examine the victim regarding both pending juvenile and domestic relations cases. In *State v. Younkers*,[7] the defendant argued on appeal that a conviction for domestic violence would put the victim in a better position to gain custody in the pending divorce action.

In sustaining defendant's first assignment of error, the Darke County appellate court reasoned that ". . . Mrs. Younker has a

[3]State v. Husseln, 152 Ohio App. 3d 67, 69, 2003-Ohio-1369, 786 N.E.2d 536 (1st Dist. Hamilton County 2003), citing State v. Boggs, 63 Ohio St. 3d 418, 588 N.E.2d 813 (1992) and State v. Fredrick, 2002-Ohio-1195, 2002 WL 360643 (Ohio Ct. App. 2d Dist. Montgomery County 2002); see also State v. Wright, 2008-Ohio-3678, 2008 WL 2833649 (Ohio Ct. App. 8th Dist. Cuyahoga County 2008) (upholding trial court's finding that the prior recantations documented by notarized statements were the products of fear and pressure from defendant and his family); State v. Hunt, 2014-Ohio-3839, 2014 WL 4384140 (Ohio Ct. App. 2d Dist. Greene County 2014).

[4]See also State v. Vanderpool, 2014-Ohio-1364, 2014 WL 1350197 (Ohio Ct. App. 11th Dist. Portage County 2014) (Evid. R. 616(A) discussing impeachment of a witness by a showing of bias or establishing a motive to misrepresent via either examination or extrinsic evidence, so long as the impeachment evidence is relevant). See also Bartells v. Bertel, 2018-Ohio-21, 2018 WL 265509 (Ohio Ct. App. 12th Dist. Butler County 2018).

[5]State v. Warren, 106 Ohio App. 3d 753, 667 N.E.2d 68 (1st Dist. Hamilton County 1995); see also State v. Smith, 1985 WL 6801 (Ohio Ct. App. 1st Dist. Hamilton County 1985).

[6]State v. Warren, 106 Ohio App. 3d 753, 756, 667 N.E.2d 68 (1st Dist. Hamilton County 1995).

[7]State v. Younker, 2002-Ohio-5376, 2002 WL 31242238 (Ohio Ct. App. 2d Dist. Darke County 2002).

pecuniary interest in the outcome of this prosecution, and Defendant wanted to cross-examine her about those matters to demonstrate her possible bias or prejudice."[8] The Court of Appeals held that, because the inquiry Defendant wished to make did not involve an irrelevant matter and did affect credibility, the trial court erred and abused its discretion and deprived Defendant of his Sixth Amendment right to fully and effectively confront the witness about the pending divorce case.[9]

---

[8]State v. Younker, 2002-Ohio-5376, 2002 WL 31242238 (Ohio Ct. App. 2d Dist. Darke County 2002).

[9]State v. Younker, 2002-Ohio-5376, 2002 WL 31242238 (Ohio Ct. App. 2d Dist. Darke County 2002).

Chapter 17

Role of the Victim Advocate

§ 17:1 What is a victim advocate

A victim advocate is loosely defined as a person who provides support and assistance to a victim of domestic violence. Pursuant to RC 3113.31(A)(5), a victim advocate is one "who provides support and assistance for a person who files a petition under this section."[1]

RC 3113.31(M) provides that "[i]n all stages of a proceeding under this section, a petitioner may be accompanied by a victim advocate." This means that a victim advocate is permitted to accompany a petitioner to the hearing for either the ex parte protection order or the order issued after the full hearing.[2]

Advocates may include social workers,[3] counselors, domestic violence shelter workers, volunteers, and witness victim personnel. Each individual is effective in creating access to the justice system and breaking down barriers to legal remedies.[4]

§ 17:2 The role of the victim advocate[1]

Victim advocates are to provide both *support* and *assistance* to the

---

[Section 17:1]

[1]See also RC 2919.26(K); Conrad, The Use of Victim Advocates and Expert Witnesses in Battered Women Cases, 30-Dec. Colo. Law 43 (2001).

[2]See also RC 2919.26(A)(2).

[3]See generally, Fran S. Davis, The Criminalization of Domestic Violence: What Social Workers Need to Know, Vol. 48 No. 2 Social Work 237 (2003).

[4]National Council of Juvenile & Family Court Judges, A Guide to Research on Family Violence, Urban Institute 43 (1996).

[Section 17:2]

[1]See THEMIS: A Manual for Legal Advocates; for information contact the Ohio

victims of domestic violence and their families.[2] They can effectively monitor the justice system's reaction and response to the victim. Because the primary concern of the advocate is to ensure that the victim's needs are met, the advocate's role is to provide information regarding the victim's legal and nonlegal options, including giving the victim adequate available resources. Additionally, victim advocates provide information designed to assist victims in weighing their options, such as information about various legal interventions, possible outcomes, and information about safety plans and protection orders.

A victim advocate may help a victim express his/her account of the events to the court. Helping the victim create a chronology regarding the incidents of violence, specific to time and place, and gathering relevant evidence about these events is essential. Advocates may also help victims identify witnesses. In doing so, a victim advocate provides needed assistance to a victim while, at the same time, acting as a liaison with the victim's attorney. By providing support to the victim, both within and outside the justice system, the victim advocate increases the likelihood that the victim will cooperate with the system.

Effective intervention must be premised on a clear understanding of the dynamics of domestic violence combined with a realistic assessment of the options available to the victim. "Effective intervention only works when there is consideration given to both the victim's perspective and the legal system's perspective."[3]

Many victims of domestic violence may be distraught and their lives in disarray at the time they request assistance from the justice system. Yet, the situations in which victims of domestic violence find themselves often demand immediate attention. A specially trained victim advocate is in the best position to understand the psychological impact of domestic violence. The advocate helps the victim sift through the numerous decisions he/she has to make and aids him/her in making both the decision and the legal forum less intimidating.

On the other hand, victim advocates do not have the right to make decisions for victims. "An advocate's role is to understand the woman's perspectives and choices and give her information that is relevant and helps her to get what she needs from the court system or any other system."[4] The advocate has a duty to help a victim make his/her own choices by providing accurate information about the justice system. Making decisions for the victim fails to understand that effective advocacy values a victim's right to make his/her own decisions. In fact, making decisions for a victim is an ineffective way to plan for his/her safety. It may actually increase the danger to the victim or his/her children.[5]

Because the victim advocate may be in a good position to facilitate

---

Domestic Violence Network, 1-800-934-9840.

[2]See Hon. Hollis L. Webster, Enforcement in Domestic Violence Cases, 26 Loy. U. Chi. L.J. 663, 667 (1995).

[3]Leslie Landis, Policy Issues for Advocacy Programs, at 4 (Nat'l College of Dist. Attorneys 1995).

[4]Jill Davies, Planning for Safety: An Approach to Advocacy for Connecticut's Family Violence Victim Advocates, Legal Advocacy Project (Conn. Coalition Against Domestic Violence, Inc. 1992).

[5]Jill Davies, Planning for Safety: An Approach to Advocacy for Connecticut's

the court process for the victim, he/she may aid the court and the attorney who represents the victim. Victim advocates can assist courts with domestic violence cases by working with the attorneys. Advocates can provide crucial help to domestic relations courts and attorneys by doing the following:

(1) helping victims locate and complete forms and explaining the court process to them;

(2) collecting evidence through victim interviews, criminal history records, police records, medical records, and contacts with witnesses;

(3) notifying victims of hearings, case status, and the release of the offender from jail, if applicable;

(4) accompanying the victim to court and arranging for safe waiting places; and

(5) providing the victim assistance and referral services as victims often need shelter, day care, bus fare, public benefits information, and/or transportation while waiting for court hearings.[6]

Q & A: What specifically does a victim advocate do for the victim?

Because victims face many daunting decisions as they enter the justice system, victim advocates are needed to help victims decide whether to seek protection from the justice system and whether to contact the police or the hospital in order to document the domestic violence and create a history of the violence for the victim's future.[7] The advocate should explain to the victim the options available to him/her, including whether to file for a civil protection order, file charges in municipal court, or both. Additionally, the advocate may also help the victim decide whether to seek possession of the residence, whether to ask for support, and what to do about custody/visitation issues.

Accompanying the victim to court is significant for the victim of domestic violence.[8] Since victims of domestic violence are often afraid to face their abusers in court, especially at the second hearing, they may fail to show up. A victim advocate's presence and escort are crucial and provide needed encouragement to follow through with the court process.[9]

Family Violence Victim Advocates, Legal Advocacy Project 2 (Conn. Coalition Against Domestic Violence, Inc. 1992).

[6]Jill Davies, Planning for Safety: An Approach to Advocacy for Connecticut's Family Violence Victim Advocates, Legal Advocacy Project 42 (Conn. Coalition Against Domestic Violence, Inc. 1992).

[7]See Donald A. Griesmann, Mahoning County's Response to Domestic Violence: Voluntary Advocacy Legal Unit, 9 Ohio Lawyer 8 (1995).

[8]But see City of Warren v. Culver, 2004-Ohio-333, 2004 WL 144227 (Ohio Ct. App. 11th Dist. Trumbull County 2004) (where appellate court upheld trial court's decision to declare a mistrial where domestic violence advocate, who sat at prosecutor's table during trial, was seen conversing with juror after closing arguments but before jury was instructed; mistrial was based on appearance of impropriety).

[9]See Domestic Violence Victim's Advocation without Engaging in the Unauthorized Practice of Law (Americorps & Southeastern Ohio Legal Servs. 4-15-99).

Q & A: What can a victim advocate do for the prosecutor or attorney?[10]

Often times, counsel has the same misconceptions about domestic violence as the public.[11] Victim advocates may help the attorney and/or prosecutor in understanding the dynamics of domestic violence. Where victims recant their stories, or fail to appear in court, victim advocates may help explain the experiences of the battered victim. As more victims are charged with domestic violence or other related crimes, such knowledge is even more crucial for both defense counsel and the prosecutor.

Q & A: Can a victim advocate attend the initial interview between attorney and client without waiving the attorney-client privilege?[12]

The Ohio Code of Professional Responsibility requires that all confidences and secrets remain confidential.[13] A confidence refers to information protected by the attorney-client privilege[14] and a secret is other information gained in the professional relationship, the disclosure of which could hurt or embarrass the client, or which the client requests not to be disclosed.[15]

An attorney has a duty to protect both kinds of information, until and unless the court, at trial, or the opposing party through discovery, demands the information. In order to protect information even upon court or party demand, therefore, it must be a confidence meaning that it is within the attorney-client privilege. Information received by a lawyer or communicated by the lawyer to the client or prospective client in meetings or intake interviews is presumptively within the privilege.[16]

Obviously, third parties may be present at an intake interview or at a meeting between an attorney and client when they act to facilitate the communication between the attorney and client.[17] For example, a language translator can be present without waiving the privilege. Similarly, a secretarial assistant who records the intake interview or

---

[10]See also Jeanine Percival, The Price of Silence: The Prosecution of Domestic Violence Cases in Light of *Crawford v. Washington*, 79 S. Cal. L. Rev. 213 (2005).

[11]See, e.g., Anna Farber Conrad, The Use of Victim Advocates & Expert Witnesses in Battered Women Cases, 30-Dec Colo. Law 43 (2001).

[12]RC 2317.02(A); see generally, Caruso, Exploring Exceptions to Attorney-Client Privilege, 19 (3) Ohio Lawyer (13) (2005).

[13]Code of Professional Responsibility, Canon 4; The revisions to Canon 4 (which are to be released in 2005), an example of how an attorney should act in preserving the evidentiary privilege includes avoiding professional discussions in the presence of persons to whom the privilege does not extend, DR 4-101.

[14]Code of Professional Responsibility DR 4-101(A).

[15]Code of Professional Responsibility DR 4-101(A).

[16]See generally, Applicability of Attorney-Client Privilege to Communications Made in Presence of or Solely to or by Family Members or Companion, Confidant, or Friend of Attorneys or Client or Attesting Witnesses for Client's Will, 67 A.L.R.6th 341. State v. Shipley, 94 Ohio App. 3d 771, 641 N.E.2d 822 (5th Dist. Licking County 1994)(presence of client's brother during some, if not all, of the client's communications with attorney did not waive attorney-client privilege protecting communications).

[17]See also State v. McDermott, 72 Ohio St. 3d 570, 1995-Ohio-80, 651 N.E.2d 985 (1995); Stroh v. General Motors Corp., 213 A.D.2d 267, 623 N.Y.S.2d 873 (1st Dep't 1995).

attends the meeting for the attorney, an investigator who will assist in the case and who needs to hear the statements made by the client, an accountant, a doctor, or forensic expert who is present at the interview or who will be consulted later by the attorney can all be present without waiving the attorney-client privilege. It is arguable that each of the above individuals is necessary to an attorney who is to provide effective representation of the client.[18]

On the other hand, if a victim of domestic violence requests the presence of a friend, family member or advocate, that request may cause the privilege to be waived.[19] If the reason for the request is to assist a victim in more effectively communicating her story to counsel and this need can be proven to the satisfaction of the court, the privilege will probably not be waived. It must be demonstrated, however, that the need for the presence of the third party is necessary for the effective communication necessary for the representation of the client and is more than to provide the victim with moral support.

The importance of psychological support after an abusive incident may be used to show the need for a third party. A psychotherapist's expert opinion may also demonstrate why the support of an advocate is necessary after such a traumatic experience. Demonstrating the clients fear of the other party due to the domestic violence may also prove why a third party may be necessary.

Lacking adequate proof, the attorney-client privilege may be waived and any information provided to the attorney in front of a third party may be disclosed to the opposing side.

§ 17:3 The unauthorized practice of law[1]

As victim advocates enter the justice system on behalf of and while assisting victims of domestic violence, they need to be concerned about the unauthorized practice of law. It is important to remember that victim advocates are not lawyers, and they must not act in a legal capacity while assisting victims.[2]

Q & A: What is the unauthorized practice of law?

---

[18]See also Weis v. Weis, 147 Ohio St. 416, 34 Ohio Op. 350, 72 N.E.2d 245, 169 A.L.R. 668 (1947).

[19]But see Newman v. State, 384 Md. 285, 863 A.2d 321 (2004) (where court placed importance on the fact that attorney requested defendants friend to accompany defendant in hopes of maintaining order during the meetings).

[Section 17:3]

[1]See ABA Commission on Nonlawyer Practice, Nonlawyer Activity in Law-Related Situations: A Report with Recommendations, 75-80 (1995); Kristine C. Lizdas & Sandra L. Murphy, Domestic Violence Advocates and the Unauthorized Practice of Law, The Battered Women's Justice Project (2009).

[2]See John Greacen, "The Distinction Between Legal Information & Legal Advice: Developments since 1995," Management Information Exchange Journal (Summer 2000); see also John Greacen, "No Legal Advice from Court Personnel What Does that Mean?" 34 Judges Journal (American Bar Association Winter 1995); Margaret F. Brown, Domestic Violence Advocates' Exposure to Liability for Engaging in the Unauthorized Practice of Law, 34 Colum. J.L. & Soc. Probs. 279 (2001). See also Francis v. Francis, 2014 ND 111, 847 N.W.2d 131 (N.D. 2014) (in which the North Dakota Supreme Court held that that trial court's error of allowing domestic violence advocate to object on wife's behalf and conduct direct and redirect examination of wife such that the advocate participated like attorney warranted reversal of the protection

Since the unauthorized practice of law is defined and interpreted in many ways, it is necessary to define what constitutes the practice of law.[3] According to Ethical Consideration 3-5 of the Code of Professional Responsibility, "[f]unctionally, the practice of law relates to the rendition of services for others that call for the professional judgment of a lawyer. The essence of the professional judgment of the lawyer is his educated ability to relate the general body and philosophy of law to a specific legal problem of a client."

Generally, the practice of law includes (1) accepting cases from clients, (2) offering legal advice to clients, (3) charging fees for services, (4) rendering independent judgment on behalf of a client, (5) drafting and/or signing legal documents, and (6) appearing in a representative capacity before a court or other tribunal.[4]

Ethical Consideration 3-1 specifically provides:

> The prohibition against the practice of law by a layman is grounded in the need of the public for integrity and competence of those who undertake to render legal services. Because of the fiduciary and personal character of the lawyer-client relationship and the inherently complex nature of our legal system, the public can better be assured of the requisite responsibility and competence if the practice of law is confined to those who are subject to the requirements and regulations imposed upon members of the legal profession.

When a nonlawyer engages in any of the activities which affect the legal rights and obligations of clients, this is considered the unauthorized practice of law.[5] The Ohio Supreme Court created a Board of Commissioners on the Unauthorized Practice of Law to oversee and monitor complaints regarding the unauthorized practice of law.[6]

Victim advocates are among the class of individuals who might unwittingly engage in the unauthorized practice of law.[7] They may convey information to a victim that may be construed as providing legal advice. They may help clients prepare legal documents that may be construed as providing a legal opinion. Substituting the words of the advocate for the words of the victim may be considered the unauthorized practice of law. Determining whether there is sufficient evidence to file a civil protection order is a legal conclusion that the advocate is not in a position to make.

Q & A: Is this a particular problem for advocates dealing with pro se litigants?

Absolutely. Where a client enters the justice system without counsel,

---

order and remand for new hearing).

[3]See, e.g., Wolfman, Modern Legal Ethics (1986); Task Force on the Model Definition of the Practice of Law, ABA Challenge Statement: Model Definition of the Practice of Law, available at http://www.abanet.org/cpr/model_def_challenge.html.

[4]Unauthorized Practice of Law (Nat'l Federation of Paralegal Ass'ns 1998); see also Code of Professional Responsibility.

[5]Unauthorized Practice of Law (Nat'l Federation of Paralegal Ass'ns 1998). But see Schmitz, Whats the Harm? Rethinking the Role of Domestic Violence Advocates and the Unauthorized Practice of Law, 10 Wm. & Mary J. Women & Law 295 (Winter 2004).

[6]See Gov. Bar R. VII.

[7]See, e.g., State v. Errington, 310 N.W.2d 681 (Minn. 1981); see also Margaret F. Brown, Domestic Violence Advocates' Exposure to Liability for Engaging in the Unauthorized Practice of Law, 34 Colum. J.L. & Soc. Probs. 279 (2001).

a victim advocate may commit the unauthorized practice of law in responding to questions presented by the pro se litigant. The process of getting the domestic violence forms, completing them properly, filing them, and appearing at the hearing may be confusing for the pro se victim.

A victim advocate is advised not to go beyond providing general information. Suggesting what a client should write or advising him/her how to write it may be perceived as the unauthorized practice of law.

In 1998, the Cuyahoga County Bar Association raised the issue of what information a lay advocate may impart to a litigant without it being considered the unauthorized practice of law. The bar association requested an opinion from the Supreme Court Board of Commissioners on the Unauthorized Practice of Law regarding the unauthorized practice of law by victim advocates and clerks of court who aid victims in filling out the standard domestic violence forms. Although the Board failed to provide an advisory opinion, it provided the County Bar Association with a copy of a Maryland Attorney General Opinion.[8]

The Maryland Attorney General determined that the following constitutes the unauthorized practice of law by a lay advocate:

(1) providing any advice relating to a victim's rights or remedies, including whether a victim's particular circumstances suggest that he/she should pursue a particular remedy;

(2) providing information about the legal aspects of judicial proceedings, such as how to present a case, call witnesses, introduce evidence, and the like;

(3) using the advocate's own language in preparing or filling out form pleadings or other legal documents; or

(4) engaging in advocacy before any governmental representative on behalf of an individual action.[9]

The Maryland Attorney General Opinion provides that a lay advocate may do the following without engaging in the authorized practice of law:

(1) provide victims with basic information about the existence of legal rights and remedies;

(2) provide victims with basic information about the manner in which judicial proceedings are conducted;

(3) assist victims in preparing legal pleadings or other legal document on their own behalf by defining unfamiliar terms on a form, explaining where on the form the victim is to provide certain information, and if necessary transcribing or otherwise recording a victim's own words verbatim;

(4) sit with a victim at the trial table, if permitted by the court; and

(5) engage in the general advocacy of the rights of victims of battering as a group.[10]

Providing general information about legal rights does not constitute

---

[8]Md. Op. Att'y Gen. 95-056 (12-19-95), 1995 WL 783587, at *1.

[9]Md. Op. Att'y Gen. 95-056 (12-19-95), 1995 WL 783587, at *1.

[10]Md. Op. Att'y Gen. 95-056 (12-19-95), 1995 WL 783587, at *1.

the unauthorized practice of law. However, a nonlawyer's offering of specific legal advice relative to these rights to a particular victim falls within the unauthorized practice of law. For example, advising a victim as to whether a particular individual fits within the definition of family or household member under RC 3113.31 is giving legal advice. Suggesting that a client get continuances to obtain counsel is not legal advice; however, preparing the pleading is clearly unacceptable and rises to the level of applying facts to the law in preparation of a legal document. Helping the client describe the incidents necessitating the protection order is legal advice. Advising a particular client to bring specific witness or documents may also be considered the unauthorized practice of law.

Q & A: How does a non lawyer in Ohio know when and how to help a victim of domestic violence?

Nonlawyer Victim Advocates Roles and Activities[11]

This chart should assist nonlawyer domestic violence victim advocates by providing guidelines for determining in most situations whether engaging in certain activities constitutes the unauthorized practice of law. This chart is based on Ohio case law research; a 1995 Opinion of the Maryland Attorney General; Ohio Supreme Court Rules of Superintendence 10.01, 10.02, and 10.03; and the January 2004 Report of the Ohio State Bar Associations (OSBAs) Unauthorized Practice of Law Committee on various issues pertaining to domestic violence and the unauthorized practice of law by nonlawyer victim advocates. This chart may not answer all your questions regarding unauthorized practice of law for every conceivable case or situation. If you have further questions or want a more definitive legal opinion, you should contact an attorney.

CAN	CANNOT
Provide information contained in docket reports, case files, indexes, and other reports	Disclose the outcome of a matter submitted to a judge for decision until the outcome is reflected in a journal entry
Answer questions concerning court rules, procedures, ordinary practices, and the types of legal actions that DV victims can pursue. Such questions often contain the words "Can I" or "How do I"	Answer questions regarding the merits of a persons case or regarding the types of legal actions that the person's should pursue based on their particular circumstances
Provide examples of forms or pleadings for the guidance of parties or victims	Draft or prepare forms or pleadings for parties or victims (other than assisting in the preparation of CPO forms)
Explain the CPO process and how cases generally are managed	Give an opinion as to what will happen if you go to court
Explain requirements to have CPO or TPO case considered by court	Tell someone whether or not to bring action or recommend specific course of conduct

[11]By Michael Smalz, senior statewide attorney with Ohio State Legal Services Association.

CAN	CANNOT
Provide legal definitions	Give legal interpretations
Provide procedural definitions	Give procedural advice
Provide guidance on how to compute due dates and deadlines	Speculate as to when a judge will make a decision on a particular matter
Identify which court forms might meet a persons needs (warning: no guarantees and should seek attorney's assistance)	Suggest that a person must use a particular form, unless it is a court-approved form (e.g., the standard DV protection order forms)
Assist the petitioner in the preparation of the Supreme Court-mandated forms, including but not limited to, answering questions about the forms, reading or explaining the questions or relevant portions of the forms, defining unfamiliar terms, explaining where on the form the person is to provide certain information, and filling out the blanks on a court form with the information provided by the person	Tell people what specific answers they should give to fill in the blanks on a court form or interpret the meaning of court rules, laws, or cases
Read court or lawyer-approved forms and instructions to a person	Modify the forms or instructions and give or read the modified forms or instructions to a person
Suggest that a person contact a lawyer and provide them with info about legal aid and referral resources	
Provide copies of requested statutes, rules, ordinances, and cases or show or tell people where copies of rules, laws, ordinances or cases may be found	Interpret the meaning of those statutes, rules, ordinance or cases for a party, victim, or other person
Educate yourself by researching domestic violence statutes, ordinances, and rules, and generally explain these statutes, ordinances, and rules to a person	Interpret the meaning of particular statutes, ordinances, or rules for another person
Give someone the statutory definition of domestic violence or family or household members	Advise someone as to whether s/he falls within the definitions of a "family" or "household member" or whether certain conduct falls within the definition of "domestic violence"
Tell a party how the judge hearing the victim's case has rules in past cases	Advise a party or victim what the judge will do in the client's case
Educate oneself on domestic violence law by researching and reading case law	Interpret the meaning of particular cases for a party, victim, or other person

CAN	CANNOT
Do community education, operate a website, or otherwise provide general legal information on domestic violence law and remedies to DV victims, the general public, etc.	Give legal advice to a specific person that is tailored to that person's needs
Provide people with basic information about the existence of legal rights and remedies	Provide any advice relating to a specific person's rights or remedies
Provide people with basic information about court procedures (e.g., the right to question the opposing witnesses) and the availability of witness subpoenas	Provide advice as to how to present a case, call witnesses, introduce evidence, and the like
Accompany the victim to court (victim advocates)	Present oral or written arguments to the court
Sit with victim at the trial table, if permitted by the court	Sit with the victim at the trial table without the permission of the court
Accompany and sit with the victim during a mediation session, provide requested factual information to the mediator, and answer the mediator's questions	Advocate or negotiate on behalf of the victim or any other party during the mediation session
Engage in the general advocacy of the rights of battered women as a group	Engage in advocacy before any court or governmental representative on behalf of a specific person

Don't tell parties what to do, tell them *how* to do it.

Q & A: Can an advocate advise a client to answer all required questions?

Nothing in the law suggests that an advocate should not inform a petitioner to answer each question set forth in a petition or any accompanying pleading completely. This is especially true for the petition[12] and the parenting proceeding affidavit.[13]

In fact, Sup. R Form 10.01-C stresses that a petitioner fill out the petition as completely and accurately as possible. Sup. R. 10.01-E provides that a petitioner list their criminal background and members of the household. Additionally, petitioners are on notice that they have a duty to notify the court of any custody, visitation, parenting time, divorce dissolution, separation, neglect, abuse, dependency, guardianship, parentage, termination of parental rights, or domestic

[12] Sup. R. Form 10.01-D.

[13] Sup. R. Form 10.01-F.

violence cases concerning the children that are the subject of pending case.[14]

Petitioners who fail to or wrongly answer questions on any court form regarding other relevant court cases, including both current and pertinent past cases run a risk that their petitions will be denied. They may even find themselves charged with perjury.

For example, in *State v. Rodriguez*,[15] appellant appealed her third degree felony conviction. In this case, appellant had sought a civil protection order against the father of her child, alleging that the father, who had legal custody, had abused the child.

When appellant appeared at the domestic relations court, she was instructed to fill out the documents. After completing the papers without the assistance of court personnel or any attorney, the court staff member notarized her affidavits. She obtained an ex parte order and the minor child was removed from her father's custody and placed in the custody of appellant. Subsequently, she was charged with perjury for providing false statements on her petition for CPO, when it was discovered that there was a previously closed custody case in juvenile court in which the father was awarded legal custody after the child was adjudicated neglected by appellant and a pending child support case.

The statements alleged to be false included appellant's responses on her parenting proceeding affidavit regarding other known litigation, past or present which concerns the custody of the child and whether she had been a party to a civil or criminal case or investigation concerning child abuse, child neglect or domestic violence.

The applicable statute is RC 2921.11(A) which provides that [n]o person, in any official proceeding, shall knowingly make a false statement under oath or affirmation, or knowingly swear or affirm the truth of a false statement previously made, when either statement is material. RC 2921.11(B) states that a falsification is material, regardless of its admissibility in evidence, if it can affect the course or outcome of the proceeding. It is no defense to a charge under this section that the offender mistakenly believed a falsification to be immaterial.

In affirming the trial court, the appellate court relied on the testimony of Judge Kessler, the domestic relations court judge who granted the ex parte CPO and whose deposition was sufficient to support a finding that appellant's false statement was material under RC 2921.11. "Judge Kessler indicated that it is very important that a petitioner is truthful in completing the petition and affidavit, due to the ex parte nature of the proceedings during which the other party is not present or able to respond to allegations. Judge Kessler indicated that she relied upon appellant's parenting affidavit in granting the ex parte order in this case, and would have asked appellant additional questions during the hearing had appellant disclosed to her the information at issue. She further testified that had she been aware there was a pending court order in juvenile court, she would have contacted

[14]Sup. R. Form 10.01-E.

[15]State v. Rodriguez, 2009-Ohio-549, 2009 WL 295403 (Ohio Ct. App. 12th Dist. Butler County 2009).

the juvenile court and asked for a copy of its orders before granting the ex parte order."[16]

Additionally, it was significant that the court staff member testified that she had provided the petitioner with the document packet and had instructed her to disclose any criminal or civil cases that might pertain to the order.

The importance of this case cannot be overstated. Domestic violence victims who seek protection orders cannot argue that they did not "knowingly" provide false information or that they did not understand the questions on the form. Moreover, petitioners who answer questions with "NO" when the answer is "YES" or "NO pending cases" when there are pending cases or who fail to answer a question may find themselves charged with a crime.[17]

Finally, victim advocates should be able to provide this advice to petitioners without worrying that their warning amounts to the unauthorized practice of law.

§ 17:4 Confidentiality and privilege

Confidentiality[1] and privilege are critical components for keeping victims of domestic violence safe. In fact, confidentiality often means safety for a victim. Understanding the laws governing confidentiality and privileged communications is essential for effective advocacy.

Q & A: What are confidentiality and privilege?

A **confidential communication** is a statement made under circumstances demonstrating that the person making the statement intends for their words to be heard only by the one she/he is addressing.

A **privileged communication** is a statement made by a certain person within a recognized, protected relationship which the law protects from forced disclosure. Privileges can be created by statute, regulations or case law.

A confidential communication may be privileged, depending on the relationship between the parties and the circumstances in which the statement is made.

The Violence Against Women Act is the most relevant authority on

---

[16]State v. Rodriguez, 2009-Ohio-549, 2009 WL 295403, *3 (Ohio Ct. App. 12th Dist. Butler County 2009).

[17]See also State v. Blanton, 2015-Ohio-4620, 48 N.E.3d 1018 (Ohio Ct. App. 3d Dist. Marion County 2015), cause dismissed, 145 Ohio St. 3d 1420, 2016-Ohio-1173, 47 N.E.3d 165 (2016) (holding that the victim/complainant in a criminal domestic violence case can be charged and convicted of obstructing justice for harboring or concealing the defendant who was charged with a domestic violence felony when police asked whether Defendant was in her residence and she stated that he was not); R.C. 2921.32(A)(1).

[Section 17:4]

[1]See, e.g., Leslie A. Hagen & Kim Morden Rattet, Communications and Violence Against Women: Michigan Law on Privilege, Confidentiality, and Mandatory Reporting, 17 T.M. Cooley L. Rev. 183 (2000). Joan Zorza, Recognizing and Protecting the Privacy and Confidentiality Needs of Battered Women, 29 Fam. L.Q. 273, 281 (1995); Rachel Callanan, My Lips are Sealed: The Need for a Testimonial Privilege and Confidentiality for Victim Advocates, 18 Hamline J. Pub. L. & Policy 226 (1996).

the issue of confidentiality. It regulates the steps all VAWA-funded programs must take to preserve confidentiality for those persons receiving the services. Generally, VAWA provides the following:

1) mandates the protection of confidentiality and privacy of those receiving victim services;
2) mandates that disclosure of personally identifying individual information collected in connection with the services is prohibited;[2]
3) mandates that revealing individual client information without the consent of the client whose information is being sought is prohibited;
4) mandates that the client's consent must be sought and must be in an informed, written and reasonably time limited release;
5) absent a release, the information may be released only when compelled by a court or other statutory mandate.[3]

Q & A: Does Ohio have an advocate/victim privilege?

No. Unlike other states, no privilege exists between a victim and advocate[4] so that an advocate can effectively frustrate subpoenas requiring information about the victim.[5] With that in mind, it is important for advocates to warn victims of possible disclosures before they are asked to make statements of a sensitive nature.[6] "[P]rogram staff must have clear understandings of the procedures to be followed in the event of a request for information about a battered woman, including receipt of a subpoena or a request to serve a resident of the shelter."[7] Shelter clients and all victims who utilize domestic violence programs must sign detailed releases articulating when and to whom certain information may be disclosed.

Information regarding a victim may be released under certain circumstances which include victim consent, if the conversation to the advocate was made in front of a third part or shared with another outside of the confidential relationship, if the testimonial privilege is waived by the filing of criminal charges, or if ordered pursuant to

---

[2]See also 42 U.S.C.A. § 13925(a)(18).

[3]See 42 U.S.C.A. § 13925(b)(2)(A) to (D).

[4]See Rachel Callanan, My Lips are Sealed: The Need for a Testimonial Privilege and Confidentiality for Victim-Advocates, 18 Hamline J. Pub. L. & Policy 226 (1996); Michael Bressman & Fernando R. Laguarda, Jaffee v. Redmond: Towards Recognition of a Federal Counselor-Battered Woman Privilege, 30 Creighton L.Rev. 319 (1997). See also, People v. Turner, 109 P.3d 639 (Colo. 2005) (Supreme Court of Colorado determined the scope of the victim-advocate privilege set forth in Colorados statute and held that records of assistance provided to a client by the domestic violence agency are within the scope of the statutory privilege).

[5]See Com. v. Tripolone, 425 Mass. 487, 681 N.E.2d 1216 (1997); see also People v. Ramsey, 174 Misc. 2d 304, 307, 665 N.Y.S.2d 501 (Sup 1997); V.B.T. v. Family Services of Western Pennsylvania, 705 A.2d 1325 (Pa. Super. Ct. 1998), order aff'd, 556 Pa. 430, 728 A.2d 953 (1999) (discussion of Pennsylvania's statutory privileges protecting confidential communications between a domestic violence counselor/advocate and a victim of domestic violence); see also State v. Lizotte, 200 Conn. 734, 517 A.2d 610 (1986).

[6]See Loretta Frederick, Advocacy: Issues Regarding Confidentiality (Nat'l College of District Attorneys 1998).

[7]See Loretta Frederick, presentation on Advocacy: Issues Regarding Confidentiality at 5 (Nat'l College of District Attorneys 1998).

subpoena and a Motion to Quash or Motion for Protective Order has been denied.

Confidentiality and privilege limits occur if there is a duty to warn, suspected child abuse or neglect, a communication was made in presence of others, a law suit against the program by the privilege holder, per FOIA requests, court cases where the court orders *in camera* review of records or if waived by the privilege holder.

Q & A: What arguments can be made to justify that information provided by a victim to an advocate is privileged communications?

Although there is no specific statute or rule in Ohio that provides all advocates with privilege, some domestic violence programs have attempted to claim a privilege between advocate and victims. In fact, some program advocates have even faced contempt rather that divulge information.

Privileged communications stems from the common law and has been outlined by Professor Henry Wigmore as containing the following criteria: 1) the communication originates in confidence that it will not be disclosed; 2) confidentiality must be essential to the full and satisfactory maintenance of the relationship between the parties; 3) the relationship must be one which, in the opinion of the community, ought to be diligently fostered; and 4) the injury that would inure to the relationship by the disclosure of the communication must be greater than the benefit thereby gained for the correct disposal of the litigation.[8]

In regards to domestic violence, advocates can and should make the argument that all communications with domestic violence service providers are privileged. The rationale for this is the following: 1) the communication of a victim and an advocate originates in confidence that it will not be disclosed; 2) to effectively review options, make safety plans, and maintain the relationship with the advocate, confidentiality is an essential element; 3) the community has, through legislation and public policy, stated that the relationship between victim and advocate needs to be protected; and 4) the injury to the victim of domestic violence can be serious.[9]

Q & A: What should a domestic violence program consider before drafting a confidentiality policy?[10]

In drafting and implementing policies regarding confidentiality in domestic violence cases, an advocacy program must:

(1) determine the purpose for collecting any information about the victim;

(2) determine the harm that could come to the victim or his/her family if the information was disclosed to the abuser or the abuser's attorney;

(3) determine whether, in light of this risk, the information should be recorded at all; and

[8] Ohio Domestic Violence Network, Advanced Justice System Advocacy: Working in the Civil Legal System (2007).

[9] Ohio Domestic Violence Network, Advanced Justice System Advocacy: Working in the Civil Legal System (2007).

[10] Julie Kunce Field, presentation on Communicating Privileged Communications: Model Policy on Confidentiality, at 1 (Ohio Domestic Violence Network 2002).

(4) if the information is recorded, determine the best format to use for the record and how detailed the record should be.[11]

Q & A: What other Ohio statutes address the confidentiality concerns of victims of domestic violence?

Several other Ohio statutes touch on the issue of confidentiality and victims of domestic violence temporarily residing in a shelter. For example, a shelter for victims of domestic violence, in order to qualify for funding, must require persons employed by or volunteering services to the shelter to maintain the *confidentiality* of any information that would identify individuals served by the shelter.[12]

Moreover, Ohio's statutory scheme limits public access to school records concerning pupils. Under RC 3313.672(C), if, at the time of a pupil's initial entry to a public or nonpublic school, the pupil is under the care of a shelter for victims of domestic violence, the pupil or his parent shall notify the school and the school shall inform the school from which it requests records of that fact. Furthermore, if a student transfers schools and is under the care of a shelter for victims of domestic violence, "no person shall release to a parent of a student who is not the student's residential parent or permit any other person to have access to, any information about the location of the. . . school to which a student has transferred or information that would enable the parent who is not the student's residential parent or the other person to determine the location of that. . . school."[13]

Where child support enforcement agencies issue administrative support orders finding the existence of a parent and child relationship, the order shall contain the full names, addresses, and social security numbers of the mother and father of the child who is the subject of the order and the full name and address of the child, except where the agency has reason to believe that a person named in the order is a potential victim of domestic violence.[14]

Many of Ohio's governmental and state agencies recognize the need to maintain the confidentiality of victims residing in domestic violence shelters. Clearly, public policy suggests a legislative commitment to protect the victims and children of domestic violence who seek emergency shelter. On balance, the safety of the victim and children is considered just as or more important than the public's right to know.

§ 17:5 Liability and disclosure concerns

Q & A: What can be done to insulate the advocacy program from liability or disclosure?

No matter whether the advocacy program is an external program, meaning that it functions independently from a governmental agency, or whether it is staffed as part of a governmental agency, it is

[11]See Loretta Frederick, presentation on Advocacy: Issues Regarding Confidentiality at 7 (Nat'l College of District Attorneys 1998); see also Rachel Callanan, My Lips are Sealed: The Need for a Testimonial Privilege and Confidentiality for Victim-Advocates, 18 Hamline J. Pub. L. & Policy 226 (1996). But see RC 2317.02(G)(1)(g).

[12]RC 3113.36(A)(5).

[13]RC 3319.321(F).

[14]RC 3111.51; see also RC 3111.13(H).

important to have a policy in place that addresses confidentiality. Domestic violence programs should have strong confidentiality policies and all employees should have an understanding of the process to be followed in case they are issued a subpoena, warrants or service of process requests for a shelter resident, or are required to provide testimony at trial.[1]

In any case, victims must be informed of any potential disclosures to persons outside of the shelter, before they are asked to make potentially incriminating or sensitive statements.[2]

Victim advocacy programs that are housed in governmental agencies such as police departments or prosecutors' offices must have a policy regarding the evidence gathering functions of its advocates. Victims should be informed of the potential for disclosure before the victim is encouraged to make any statement.

All victim advocates, whether housed in governmental agencies or a shelter, should inform victims of Ohio's requirements concerning mandatory reporting of child abuse.[3] Victims should be made aware of these requirements before providing sensitive information to an advocate.

Q & A: Do Ohio domestic violence shelters have any statutory immunity from liability?

Yes. RC 2305.236 to RC 2305.239[4] confers immunity from liability upon a shelter and its directors, owners, trustees, officers, employees, victim advocates and volunteers for harm that family or household members cause to victims of domestic violence or other persons on the shelter's premises, or on premises other than the shelter's premises under specified circumstances.[5]

As defined, a shelter client includes one who utilizes either the services or the facility of a shelter.[6] It appears that the immunity would extend to clients who are residents of the shelter facility as well as clients who use other services or programs operated by a shelter even if the programs are located in other agencies and even if the clients are not a residents of the shelter. Immunity also extends to victim advocates who provide support and assistance for a victim of a crime and are housed in a crime victim service organization.[7] On the other hand, under the definition of shelter as defined in RC 3113.33, the im-

---

[Section 17:5]

[1]See, e.g., People v. Ramsey, 174 Misc. 2d 304, 665 N.Y.S.2d 501 (Sup 1997); see also Julie Kunce Field, presentation on Communicating Privileged Communications: How to Respond to Subpoenas, Warrants and Service of Process (Ohio Domestic Violence Network 2002).

[2]See Kristine Lizdas, presentation on Data Privacy and Confidentiality Issues for Advocacy Programs (Nat'l College of District Attorneys 2001).

[3]See RC 2151.421; see also Julie Kunce Field, presentation on Communicating Privileged Communications: Child Abuse and Neglect Reporting Checklist (Ohio Domestic Violence Network 2002) (discussing model policy on child abuse and neglect reporting).

[4]2002 S.B. 131, eff. 8-14-02.

[5]RC 2305.236, RC 2305.237(A).

[6]RC 2305.236(H).

[7]RC 2305.236(I).

munity does not seem to extend to those domestic violence programs that do not have a temporary residential facility.

Immunity from liability is conferred upon a shelter where the perpetrator causes harm to the shelter client or other person who is on the shelter premises.[8] RC 2305.238(A) also extends immunity to the shelter if the tortious act occurs on premises other than the shelter premises provided that the shelter staff is acting within its official capacity and the staff is providing assistance to a shelter client including, but not limited to, accompanying the client to a health care practitioner's or an attorney's office.[9] It would appear that harm to another shelter resident or a staff member or volunteer or even a passer-by would be covered.

RC 2305.238 lists the conditions under which immunity would exist if the incident were committed on premises other than the shelter premises. Since the statute anticipates harm to either a shelter client or other person and because it applies to both shelter premises and premises other than the shelter premises, it follows that immunity should extend to the shelter in other circumstances than a health practitioner's office or an attorney's office. The term *including but not limited to. . .*, as provided in RC 2305.238, presupposes more than accompanying the client to the doctor's or lawyer's office. It could include the client who is harmed while returning from a shelter service, the client who is shot in her car outside of the shelter premises, or the client who is shot at an independent agency such as welfare or family court.

Of significance is that a shelter and its staff, etc., would not be immune from liability if the harm sustained by the shelter client or other person and the act or omission involved a malicious purpose, bad faith, or wanton or reckless conduct.[10] *"Reckless conduct" would include the release of confidential information that pertains to a shelter client.*

Q & A: When can an external domestic violence program be sued or prosecuted for failing to disclose the whereabouts of a victim of domestic violence who is or who has been a shelter resident?

Even with strong confidentiality policies, an external domestic violence program may be ordered to disclose certain information about a victim. In In re Grand Jury Supoena Duces Tecum Directed to Keeper of Records of My Sister's Place,[11] the government requested from the shelter any information it had regarding the whereabouts of a certain victim of domestic violence (the prosecutor needed the victim's address in order to aid its prosecution of the victim's assault case against her boyfriend. The director of My Sister's Place filed a motion to quash subpoena on the grounds that the requested informa-

---

[8] RC 2305.237(A).

[9] RC 2305.238(A)(1).

[10] See proposed RC 2305.238.

[11] In re Grand Jury Subpoena, 2001 WL 1914310 (Ohio C.P. 2001), aff'd in part, 2002-Ohio-5600, 2002 WL 31341083 (Ohio Ct. App. 4th Dist. Athens County 2002). See also State ex rel. Hope House, Inc. v. Merrigan, 133 S.W.3d 44 (Mo. 2004) (discussing domestic violence and confidentiality); People v. Turner, 109 P.3d 639 (Colo. 2005).

tion was protected by the counselor/client privilege; that because the program receives federal funding, it is bound by certain duties of confidentiality and that the release of this information would have a chilling effect on the agency's ability to carry out its mission, and that it is against public policy.

On November 5, 2001, the court denied the motion to quash. In its opinion, the judge recognized effective counseling of battered women as equally important as investigating and prosecuting those who batter women. Since neither policy was found to be more important than the other, the court denied the motion. However, on reconsideration, the court reversed its earlier ruling and ordered the subpoena quashed, relying on the statutory language contained in RC 3113.40. The statute provides that "[w]hen a shelter for victims of domestic violence provides accommodations to a person, the shelter, on admitting the person shall determine, if possible, the person's last known residential address and county of residence. The information concerning the address and county of residence is confidential and may be released only to a public children services agency pursuant to section 2151.422 of the Revised Code."[12]

The court held that the "statute appears to be a legislative statement of public policy. It provides the interests of individuals who choose to seek shelter in a shelter for victims of domestic violence take precedence even over the public's right to have individuals prosecuted for acts of violence against victims and society as a whole."[13]

On appeal, the Fourth District Appellate Court upheld the trial court decision. In rejecting the state's "law enforcement" public policy exception to confidentiality under RC 3113.40, the court held that "[b]oth interests, the need for criminal prosecutions and the need for confidentiality of domestic violence victims, are important interests to protect. Nevertheless, in this instance, it is clear that the Ohio General Assembly's intent is to elevate the interests of confidentiality for victims of domestic violence over the need for criminal prosecutions."[14]

Q & A: When can a shelter worker be arrested for refusing to admit a police officer into a domestic violence shelter?

In *Brooks v. Rothe*,[15] a domestic violence shelter worked called 911 when one of the residents showed signs of a drug overdose. "But, adhering literally to the shelter's policy of not admitting law enforcement personnel without a search warrant, Brooks repeatedly refused to admit or provide information to the officer who responded to the call."[16] After warning her several times, "to secure a potential crime scene," and that she would be arrested if she failed to comply, the officer arrested her. She was charged with resisting arrest and obstructing a police officer. Although the charges against Brooks were later

[12]RC 3113.40.

[13]In re Grand Jury Subpoena, 2001 WL 1914310 (Ohio C.P. 2001), aff'd in part, 2002-Ohio-5600, 2002 WL 31341083 (Ohio Ct. App. 4th Dist. Athens County 2002).

[14]In re Grand Jury Subpoena Duces Tecum Directed to Keeper of Records of My Sister's Place, 2002-Ohio-5600, 2002 WL 31341083, *6 (Ohio Ct. App. 4th Dist. Athens County 2002).

[15]Brooks v. Rothe, 577 F.3d 701 (6th Cir. 2009).

[16]Brooks v. Rothe, 577 F.3d 701, 702 (6th Cir. 2009).

dropped, she sued the officer and the municipality per a section 1983 action for wrongful imprisonment and excessive force and state law claims of assault and battery and false arrest.

The district court granted summary judgment to defendants holding that "the officer was justified in his warrantless entry into the shelter because of exigent circumstances-specifically a concern about the imminent destruction of evidence."[17] Because no constitutional violations occurred, Brook's claims against the municipalities were dismissed and the individual officers were granted qualified immunity. The decision was affirmed by the Circuit Court of Appeals.

In its analysis, the court addressed probable cause to arrest, exigent circumstances, search warrants and warrantless arrests. Unfortunately, such a decision should also serve as a warning to domestic violence shelter workers who refuse to admit a law enforcement officer into the shelter.

Of interest is that, in the dissenting opinion, the judge found that Brooks was resisting an unlawful command as the officers did not have a search warrant. "Taking the facts in the light most favorable to Brooks, I would hold that the government has not met its burden of establishing exigent circumstances."[18] Moreover, the order that Brooks permit Rothe entry into the shelter was not a lawful order because it was not supported by a warrant or exigent circumstances.

Q & A: What federal mandates exist to protect domestic violence victims from disclosure?

Congress has enacted legislation that has enhanced the safety of victims of domestic violence. Many of these legislative enactments include compliance restrictions on those agencies requesting funds. The expectation of confidentiality and privacy permeates existing law. Victims of domestic violence should expect confidentiality as to their whereabouts from batterers who spend much time discovering their locations, monitoring them and harassing them.

To combat batterer methods used to access victims, such as postal records, driver's license, motor vehicle records, voting records and the Freedom of Information Act,[19] Congress enacted the Family Violence Prevention and Services Act[20] and the Victims of Crimes Act (hereinafter called VOCA)[21] In order for shelter agencies to qualify for federal funding,[22] these Acts direct shelter programs to implement policies and procedures to assure the confidentiality of records of any individual provided service.[23] Moreover, domestic violence shelter programs that are granted VOCA funds are required to follow the regulations set forth in 28 CFR Part 22, which prohibit disclosure of identifying information of shelter clients, require programs to certify that they will do so and mandate that the programs will assure clients that

[17] Brooks v. Rothe, 577 F.3d 701, 702 (6th Cir. 2009).

[18] Brooks v. Rothe, 577 F.3d 701, 710 (6th Cir. 2009).

[19] See 42 U.S.C.A. § 552.

[20] 42 U.S.C.A. §§ 10401 to 10413.

[21] 42 U.S.C.A. §§ 10601 to 10607.

[22] 42 U.S.C.A. § 10402(f).

[23] 42 U.S.C.A. § 10402(a)(2)(E); 42 U.S.C.A. § 10604(a).

their individual identifying information will not be revealed. Shelters that fail to comply with these federal funding directives risk losing the very money necessary to operate their programs and provide the services necessary to help victims of domestic violence.

Similarly, Congress enacted the Violence Against Women Act (hereinafter called VAWA),[24] which earmarked monies for services to combat violence against women by, among other things, supporting shelters and programming for victims of domestic violence and restricting batterer access. For example, VAWA directed the United States Postal Service to implement new regulations to "secure the confidentiality of domestic violence shelters and abused persons' addresses."[25] The Social Security Administration changed its procedure to make it easier for domestic violence victims to change their social security numbers to avoid being located.[26] Additionally, the Driver's Privacy Protection Act was enacted to stop the widespread practice of motor vehicle registries from selling or giving out information about licensed drivers.[27]

Of particular significance is that VAWA mandated the U.S. Attorney General to conduct a study detailing the means by which an abuser obtains information concerning a victim's whereabouts. The purpose of this study was to explore the feasibility of creating an effective means of protecting the confidentiality of the victim, while preserving the public's right to access such records for legitimate purposes.[28] The Department of Justice Report concluded, "there are persuasive policy arguments supporting the protection of victim-counselor communications."[29]

VAWA permits the release of information in only three circumstances: with the informed, written, reasonably time limited consent of the person, statutory mandates such as mandatory reporting statutes or court mandate. It is unclear if a subpoena is such a mandate.

Identifying information, whether the survivor is in shelter and why, records of client/advocate while in shelter, communications between client and advocate and testimony in court or before other entities is confidential so long as there is a client/advocate privilege. Although such a privilege does not exist in Ohio, VAWA 2013,[30] FVPSA,[31] VOCA[32] and other federal laws such as The Clery Act[33] have mandated that confidentiality is a grant condition in that grantees and sub-grantees

[24]42 U.S.C.A. § 40281.

[25]42 U.S.C.A. § 13951.

[26]Social Security Administration, Social Security Number, Policy & General Procedures Manuel, PAMS RM 00205.045.

[27]18 U.S.C.A. §§ 2721 to 2725.

[28]See 42 U.S.C.A. § 14014; see also 42 U.S.C.A. § 40508.

[29]Report to Congress: The Confidentiality of Communications between Sexual Assault or Domestic Violence Victims and Their Counselors, Findings and Model Legislation, 42 U.S.C.A. § 13942, at 16, December 1995.

[30]42 U.S.C.A. § 13925.

[31]42 U.S.C.A. § 10406(c)(5)(B)(ii).

[32]42 U.S.C.A. §§ 10610 *et seq.*

[33]42 U.S.C.A. § 1092(f).

are required to protect the confidentiality and privacy of persons receiving shelter services. In effect, grantees may not disclose, reveal or release personally identifying information or individual information in connection with services requested, utilized or denied through grantees' or sub-grantees' programs, regardless of whether the information has been encoded, encrypted, hashed or otherwise protected.

§ 17:6 Record keeping and information-sharing

Maintaining and handling client records[1] and collecting information from and about victims of domestic violence is a critical function of any victim advocacy program.[2] Improper handling of victims' records can cause great harm to the victims.[3]

For example, a disclosure of information about a victim's residence or location can make the victim accessible to the abuser from whom he/she is hiding.[4] Information about the victim and his/her children may provide ammunition to the abuser seeking to punish the victim through child custody battles or child protection complaints. Disclosing certain information to the abuser may even hinder an underlying criminal case, thereby placing the victim in greater danger.

Because counselors and social workers have a duty to note in a client's record known or suspected abuse and the basis for that belief,[5] disclosure and confidentiality issues are of greater concern than ever before.

Q & A: What are the potential problems with putting notations in a victim's file?

Over the past 10 years, victim advocates have been encouraged to note the abuse in the record in order to preserve the history of the violence for the victim's future. Because any record may end up in the wrong hands, "the contents of the record may be misinterpreted, inaccurate, embarrassing or twisted in a way that the thoughts and feelings of the victim may be used against her."[6] Therefore, it is important to consider the purpose of the notation. Extraneous background information, information suggesting she is unstable, descriptive information about her day-to-day activities, or judgmental inferences are examples of notations that should be avoided.

Q & A: Does it make a difference if the advocate works for the local prosecutor's office?

[Section 17:6]

[1]See also Pepe v. Pepe, 258 N.J. Super. 157, 609 A.2d 127, 20 Media L. Rep. (BNA) 1515 (Ch. Div. 1992).

[2]See Loretta Frederick, presentation on Advocacy: Issues Regarding Confidentiality (Nat'l College of District Attorneys 1998).

[3]See Catherine F. Klein & Leslye E. Orloff, Providing Legal Protection for Battered Women: An Analysis of State Statutes and Case Law, 21 Hofstra L. Rev. 801, 1054 (1993); see also Text § 12:5, Full hearing—Discovery issues. See also 1992 Iowa Op. Att'y Gen. 92-3-3, 1992 WL 470341.

[4]See Waliser v. Tada, 1990 WL 20080 (Ohio Ct. App. 10th Dist. Franklin County 1990), cause dismissed, 61 Ohio St. 3d 1405, 573 N.E.2d 1097 (1991).

[5]See RC 2921.22(F)(1), RC 2317.02(G)(1)(g).

[6]Julie Kunce Field, presentation on Communicating Privileged Communications: Notes in Client Files: Problems and Issues (Ohio Domestic Violence Network 2002).

It depends. If the victim advocate works for the prosecutor's office or a law enforcement agency, the victim advocate should be aware that any information obtained by the advocate about the victim may be disclosed.[7] The prosecutor has an obligation to disclose certain information to the defense attorney including exculpatory evidence (which may include recantations of the victim). Exculpatory evidence is generally evidence that is favorable to an accused and material to guilt or to punishment.[8] Prosecutors have a duty to disclose other relevant evidence such as names and addresses of witnesses, statements of defendants, and past criminal records of the witnesses, unless the evidence is not relevant.[9]

It is important that neither the prosecutor nor the advocate hand over the records to the defendant or his attorney without requesting that the court perform an in camera review of the record to determine whether there is a need to breach confidentiality by disclosing the records.[10]

On the other hand, the prosecutor's work product is protected from disclosure to the defense under the principles that hold an attorney's legal research opinions, conclusions and impressions are not generally discoverable by the other party to the litigation.

Q & A: What information are shelter employees or advocates mandated to provide children services agencies?[11]

There is specific statutory language regarding the role of the children services agency when a report is made pursuant to RC 2151.421. If the victim and children are living in a domestic violence or homeless shelter in one county and were brought to the shelter pursuant to an agreement with the shelter in the other county, the agencies are required to communicate with each other about the information contained in the report. Additionally, the agency of the county from which the children were brought shall conduct an investigation and provide services to or take custody of the children if needed.[12] Otherwise, the children services agency that received the report is to conduct the investigation required pursuant to RC 2151.421.

Of importance is that both children services agencies may ask the shelter in which the children are living to provide information concerning the children's residence address and county of residence to the

[7]See Com. v. Bing Sial Liang, 434 Mass. 131, 747 N.E.2d 112 (2001) (discussing when a victim advocate's notes are subject to a discovery order and when they are nondiscoverable due to the work product doctrine). See also Wendy J. Murphy, Minimizing the Likelihood of Discovery of Victims' Counseling Records and Other Personal Information in Criminal Cases: Massachusetts Gives the Nod to a Constitutional Right to Confidentiality, 32 N. Eng. L.Rev. 983, 1016 (1998).

[8]See, e.g., Brady v. Maryland, 373 U.S. 83, 83 S. Ct. 1194, 10 L. Ed. 2d 215 (1963); see also U.S. v. Bagley, 473 U.S. 667, 105 S. Ct. 3375, 87 L. Ed. 2d 481 (1985).

[9]See RC 2945.04 which permits protection orders to crime victim or witnesses if it is found likely that intimidation or domestic violence will occur.

[10]See, e.g., U.S. v. Lowe, 948 F. Supp. 97, 46 Fed. R. Evid. Serv. 347 (D. Mass. 1996).

[11]See, e.g., State ex rel. Hope House, Inc. v. Merrigan, 133 S.W.3d 44 (Mo. 2004).

[12]See RC 2151.422(B) and RC 2151.422(C).

agencies.[13] Under RC 3113.40, the shelter providing services to victims of domestic violence shall inquire of the resident, her last known residential address and county of residence. Such information may be released only to a public children services agency.

Except for disclosure to the children services agency pursuant to RC 2151.421, the address of the resident and the children shall remain confidential.[14]

§ 17:7 Subpoenas and warrants

Q & A: How should an advocate or a shelter program deal with a subpoena requesting records or other documents?

Because the disclosure of records and communications may endanger a victim of domestic violence, it is important to have policies in place to address record- keeping and responding to subpoenas.

Every program should adopt record-keeping practices that protect the confidentiality of the client and balances the need for information sharing.[1]

When someone other than the victim requests records, the program should not confirm that records about the victim exist or that the victim has ever received services.

However, sometimes advocates and records are subpoenaed in a variety of legal matters. A subpoena may be issued where the victim is a witness in a criminal prosecution brought against the batterer, where the victim is a party in a divorce, child custody action or child support action, or where a prosecutor or defense attorney seeks information. In any case, the business office of the shelter or program is not required to accept the subpoena for someone who is not there. A subpoena must be delivered in person, read to them or left at the person's usual place of business or put in a sealed envelope and mailed by certified or express mail, return receipt requested.[2]

There are two types of subpoenas. A subpoena of the person requires a specific person to attend a court proceeding and provide testimony. A subpoena duces tecum requires a person or program to produce specific records, documents or other physical evidence. Often a subpoena requires both a specific person to testify and produce specific records.

Advocates should never reveal information to anyone serving a subpoena. Programs must develop procedures for responding to subpoenas and inform all staff. Programs should also designate one person, either the custodian of the records or the Executive Director to accept subpoenas.

Procedures should address the following: 1) what to do when a process server comes to the door with a subpoena; 2) who should accept the subpoena; 3) whether program attorneys will be contacted; 4) who

---

[13] RC 2151.422(B).

[14] RC 3113.40.

[Section 17:7]

[1] See generally, Ohio Domestic Violence Network, Advanced Justice System Advocacy: Working in the Civil Legal System (2007).

[2] Civ. R. 45(B).

will discuss the subpoena with the victim; and 5) other circumstances under which specific records might be released.

In criminal cases, a program's records or advocates might be subpoenaed for information regarding the alleged crime. In these cases, the program attorney might want to file a Motion to Quash the subpoena. The grounds for this might be a defect with the subpoena, it is used as a form of harassment, it causes undo hardship to the person required to appear or that the information sought is confidential.

For example, under RC 2317.02(G)(1), ". . . a person licensed under Chapter 4757 of the Revised Code as a professional clinical counselor, professional counselor, social worker or independent social worker shall not testify concerning a confidential communication received from a client."

Additionally, under RC 2930.07(A), if the prosecutor in a case determines that there are reasonable grounds for a victim in a case to be apprehensive regarding acts or threats of violence or intimidation by the alleged defendant ". . . the prosecutor may file a motion with the court requesting that the court issue an order specifying that the victim . . . not be compelled . . . to give testimony that would disclose the victim's or the victim's representative's address, place of employment or similar identifying fact without the victim's or victim's representative's consent."

In civil cases, a program's records or advocate might be subpoenaed to provide information for a family law case, a domestic violence civil protection order action, or a tort suit. Subpoenas may be used at a deposition or at trial.

Q & A: What types of warrants may be used?

A search warrant is a written order, issued by a judge or magistrate in the name of the state, directed to law enforcement, allowing them to search a specific person or place for evidence specified in the warrant. For a search warrant to be valid, it must 1) identify the property and name or describe the person or place to be searched; 2) the warrant must state the grounds for its issuance; 3) the warrant must be properly dated and signed by a judicial officer; 4) the officer must identify himself/herself and announce the purpose of the visit prior to entering; 5) the officer must present a copy of the warrant, any supporting affidavits and receipt for any property to be taken; and 6) the search may not go beyond the property described in the warrant. If a search warrant is served upon the domestic violence program it would probably be for physical evidence, such as clothing or other items associated with a crime or for children.

It is unlikely that a search warrant would be issued for a victim's records or that a judge would approve a search warrant for such records, as they are not often considered evidence of a crime. However, it is good practice that names of clients not be written on case folders.

An arrest warrant is a written order, issued by a judge or magistrate in the name of the state, directed to law enforcement, permitting them to arrest a specified person for a crime for which there is probable cause. An arrest warrant does not give law enforcement authority to search the premises. Therefore, while the agency must comply with the arrest warrant, law enforcement is not necessarily allowed on site.

A bench warrant is an order from the court allowing the police to seize a person and is used to 1) compel attendance before the court; 2) compel an answer to a charge of contempt; or 3) produce a witness who failed to respond to a subpoena that had been duly served.

§ 17:8 Miscellaneous

Q & A: What is the difference between a fact witness and an expert witness?

A **fact witness** is a person whose testimony is limited to giving facts. They testify to what they saw, heard or know. They have personal knowledge of either the incident that underlies the lawsuit or the persons involved. The fact witness is an individual who knows facts about the case. Fact witness testimony consists of a recitation of the facts/events as opposed to an expert witness whose testimony consists of the presentation of an opinion, diagnosis etc. A fact witness may give opinion testimony only if the opinions are rationally based on the actual perceptions of the witness and helpful to a clear understanding of the witness' testimony or the determination of a fact in issue.

Advocates may give fact testimony only if they have information from their own personal knowledge to impart. That means that an advocate may provide factual information that they themselves know or have witnessed, observed or heard.

On the other hand, an **expert witness** is allowed to give his/her professional opinion. Experts must be qualified before they can render opinions on battered women's experiences generally or in a particular case.[1]

Q & A: How is an expert witness used in trial?

Evidence R. 702 requires that three conditions be met before expert testimony is admitted at trial:

1) That the testimony relates to matters beyond the knowledge or experience possessed by lay persons, or dispels a misconception common among lay persons;
2) That the expert must be qualified; and
3) That the testimony must be based on reliable, scientific, technical or other specialized information.

Generally, expert testimony as to domestic violence is appropriate in criminal cases.[2] In the criminal context, R.C. 2901.06. states that Battered Woman Syndrome is a matter of commonly accepted scientific knowledge, and not within the general understanding or experiences of the general population.[3] For example, experts have been used to explain a battered woman's responses to violence in criminal cases where battered women kill their partners, why she believed her life was in danger and why there was no escape short of killing their batterers, and how being a victim affected her perceptions and conduct.

[Section 17:8]

[1]See Text § § 15:17, 16.24.

[2]See generally, Text § § 15:17, 16.24; see also R.C. 2901.06; R.C. 2945.392.

[3]R.C. 2945.392.

Expert testimony is also useful in child custody litigation. In determining custody, the court is typically required to consider the mental health of both parents and the children.[4] The court also has the authority to order the parties to undergo physical or mental examinations.[5] Additionally, experts have been helpful in educating the court about the effects of domestic violence on children as the effect of domestic violence on children is not a matter of common knowledge.[6]

Finally, expert testimony is useful in both the civil and criminal context in enabling a court or jury to understand the psychological dynamics of abuse. The fear of future abuse, reluctance to leave and the silence about the violence often become issues in a divorce or civil protection order proceeding, or a criminal case. The dynamics of domestic violence, including personality traits and the responses of the parties are beyond the knowledge of the layperson.

Q & A: What is the context for experts being used by Ohio's courts to address issues relating to victims of domestic violence?

Over time, Ohio's courts, including the Supreme Court of Ohio, have agreed that the use of experts is necessary to explain the battered woman's experiences. Both the court and the jury need to be educated as to why a victim stays in a battering relationship, why she remains in a violent situation, why she recants and why she often tells no one about the abuse.

In *State v.Haines*,[7] the Supreme Court of Ohio held that when the credibility of an alleged victim of domestic violence has been challenged on cross-examination during the prosecutor's case in chief, the state may introduce limited expert testimony regarding the battered woman syndrome to aid the judge and jury in determining the victim's state of mind in returning to or remaining in a relationship with the defendant despite the abuse. Additionally, expert testimony can be introduced to explain the victim's behavior, but it may be only considered relevant if there is some evidentiary foundation that the victim is a battered woman (going through the battering cycle at least twice, which establishes a pattern).[8] The Supreme Court held that trial courts may admit limited and carefully tailored testimony on the general characteristics of a victim suffering from BWS.[9] However, an expert cannot opine that the alleged victim in the case was a battered woman, may not testify that the defendant was a batterer or that he is guilty of the crime, and cannot comment on the victim's truthfulness.[10]

---

[4]R.C. 3109.04(F)(1)(e).

[5]Civ. R. 35.

[6]See also Text § § 15:16, 15.17.

[7]State v. Haines, 112 Ohio St. 3d 393, 2006-Ohio-6711, 860 N.E.2d 91 (2006).

[8]State v. Haines, 112 Ohio St. 3d 393, 402, 2006-Ohio-6711, 860 N.E.2d 91 (2006).

[9]State v. Haines, 112 Ohio St. 3d 393, 404, 2006-Ohio-6711, 860 N.E.2d 91 (2006).

[10]State v. Haines, 112 Ohio St. 3d 393, 404, 2006-Ohio-6711, 860 N.E.2d 91

Q & A: Have there been cases in which advocates have been used as experts?

Yes. For example, in *State v. Dyson*,[11] the expert was the executive director of Choices, a shelter for victims of domestic violence, where she had worked for over fifteen years. She also held a master's degree in social work, had contact with clients, provided training to police and other organizations and published articles on the issues. She was familiar with the patterns of behaviors in violent relationships. Clearly, she had demonstrated a specialized knowledge about domestic violence.

Similarly, in *State v. Thomas*,[12] the expert was a certified instructor with the Ohio Police Officers Training Academy, was a law enforcement officer involved in training officers on domestic violence, was on the local domestic violence task force, and wrote grants for domestic violence programs.

Finally, in *State v. Kraus*,[13] the expert had a degree in social work and crisis counseling. According to the appellate court, she was a state registered advocate with advanced status and close to 200 hours of specific training in victimization, domestic violence, child abuse, sexual assault. She had dealt with several thousand victims of domestic violence over her career.

The Warren County appellate court determined that while the expert in question was not the best witness to testify about domestic violence and its impact on victims, it is well settled that an expert on a subject need not be the best expert on the subject in order for his or her testimony to be admissible.[14] "Instead, the test is whether a particular witness offered as an expert will aid the trier of fact in the search for the truth."[15] Of importance is that the Court also noted that the expert was not qualified to make diagnoses or give an opinion as to whether domestic violence actually occurred in the case at hand, but that her testimony was helpful in understanding the victim's motives for wanting to minimize the abuser's actions and to recant her prior accusations.[16]

Q & A: What can an advocate as expert testify to in a civil case?

In civil domestic violence cases, experts might be used to testify about the dynamics of an abusive relationship and to dispel myths

(2006).

[11]State v. Dyson, 2000 WL 1597952 (Ohio Ct. App. 2d Dist. Champaign County 2000).

[12]State v. Thomas, 2003-Ohio-5746, 2003 WL 22429536 (Ohio Ct. App. 2d Dist. Montgomery County 2003); see also State v. Musgrove, 2008-Ohio-494, 2008 WL 344144 (Ohio Ct. App. 2d Dist. Montgomery County 2008).

[13]State v. Kraus, 2007-Ohio-6027, 2007 WL 3348426 (Ohio Ct. App. 12th Dist. Warren County 2007).

[14]State v. Kraus, 2007-Ohio-6027, 2007 WL 3348426, *5 (Ohio Ct. App. 12th Dist. Warren County 2007).

[15]State v. Kraus, 2007-Ohio-6027, 2007 WL 3348426, *5 (Ohio Ct. App. 12th Dist. Warren County 2007), quoting Alexander v. Mt. Carmel Medical Center, 56 Ohio St. 2d 155, 10 Ohio Op. 3d 332, 383 N.E.2d 564 (1978).

[16]State v. Kraus, 2007-Ohio-6027, 2007 WL 3348426, *6 (Ohio Ct. App. 12th Dist. Warren County 2007).

and educate the court about the effects on the abused and the effects of battering over time. They might also explain why the victim stays, why the victim might minimize the violence or why the victim might recant her testimony. They might also explain a victim's mental state or why a victim has a subjective belief that his/her abuser would cause him/her imminent harm.

Expert testimony can be used to respond to a number of judicial misconceptions and attitudes that may alter the outcome of the case. It may address the batterers' attacks on the victim's emotional stability. It may help courts comprehend the extreme fear, sense of helplessness and dependence that prevent victims from leaving the batterer. It may be used to turn a victim's weakness into a strength—testimony such as denial or forgetfulness is actually typical victim behavior.

In the context of custody, an expert can assess the prospects for successful shared parenting, given the dynamics within the family. Experts may also be useful in countering arguments that the victim, by denying visitation, is unwilling to foster a healthy relationship between the children and their father. The expert can often explain the fear that causes a victim's reluctance to allow visitation.

Some experts may be needed to testify about the batterer. This may be instrumental in providing the court with the framework in which to judge the batterer's credibility regarding excuses given to justify his behavior.

Q & A: In this context, what are expert qualifications?

At a minimum, the expert must have counseled or advocated for battered persons. If the expert has a degree or published in the area, he or she may have more credibility. If she/he has previously testified, she may be a more reliable witness. Where an expert is asked to determine whether a particular victim suffers from BWS, or PTSD, a psychologist or psychiatrist should be considered.

Q & A: What should an advocate know if she or he intends to become an expert witness in a custody case/civil case?

In a custody or civil case, advocates as experts should:

1) Have a broad based knowledge regarding the dynamics of domestic violence and the effects of domestic violence on children;
2) Be able to address the reasons why a batterer fails to be an appropriate parent;
3) Be able to explain the stress of the victim that might affect her ability to parent;
4) Have an intimate understanding of the battered victim's experiences including an understanding of why victims remain with their abusers, why they minimize the violence and why they might recant;
5) Have some special training in the area of domestic violence by way of academic background and training;

Q & A: How can an advocate qualify as an expert witness in a domestic violence case?

The following is a list of factors that may qualify an advocate as an expert witness in a court:

1) Work at a domestic violence shelter;
2) Work as a victim system advocate;
3) Providing legal advocacy for victims (as a justice system advocate);
4) Work in a program funded by the DOJ Office on Violence Against Women;
5) Participation in a community domestic violence task force and/or other domestic violence related coalitions;
6) Assisted in drafting domestic violence laws, court forms, law enforcement/hospital protocols etc.;
7) Training or presenting on domestic violence in schools, community colleges, universities, or other professional groups, etc.;
8) Attending trainings, conferences, and workshops;
9) Writing articles on domestic violence for newsletters, local newspapers, and other publications;
10) Having education and degrees (eg., AA, BA, MS LSW, certified counselor);
11) Appear on television or radio presenting information on domestic violence.[17]

Q & A: What should be included in a resume or curriculum vitae?

Besides contact information such as name, address, and telephone number and email address, advocates should list their current employment and relevant past employment including dates of employ. They should detail their education, including name of school, name of degree and date of degree. They should articulate their domestic violence trainings and certificates including conferences, workshops, in-house trainings, in-service, seminars etc. as well as name and date of training and type of certificate received. They should include any organizational affiliations and task forces and as well as the name of the organization, any positions held and dates of service.

Publications should be listed, including articles written for newspapers, newsletters, professional journals, brochures and academic publications. Any presentations made, whether conference-based, community or in-service should be documented in the curriculum vitae, as well as any awards.

Finally, if the prospective witness has testified before as an expert, he or she should be sure to list the name of the court, year of testimony, the party for which he or she testified, and the type of case.

Q & A: Can a domestic violence shelter and/or shelter personnel be sued for the intentional interference with a parents custodial rights?

While no Ohio court has addressed this issue, it was addressed in *Casivant v. Greene County Community Action Agency, Inc.*[18] In that case, the mother entered a domestic violence shelter because the

---

[17]Hallie Bongar White & Jane Larrington, Becoming an Expert Witness & Developing Your Curriculum Vitae or Resume, Southwest Center for Law and Policy & Office on Violence Against Women, U.S. Department of Justice (2005).

[18]Casivant v. Greene County Community Action Agency, Inc., 234 A.D.2d 818,

father had allegedly abused her. She then requested that the shelter coordinator help her remove the children from their fathers home after the father was arrested for domestic violence. Subsequently, the father filed a lawsuit against the mother, the domestic violence shelter and the domestic violence coordinator for the intentional interference of his custodial rights.

The appellate court reversed the trial courts denial of the shelter and the coordinators motion for summary judgment and held that as a matter of law, the mother, coordinator and shelter did not willfully disobey a court custody order.[19] The court found that the father could not prove that the shelter and shelter coordinator intentionally interfered with his custodial rights when the mother and shelter coordinator removed the children from the fathers home.

The court relied on the narrow definition of a tortious intentional interference with a parents custodial rights, which includes violent abduction, willful disobedience of a court order and wrongful detention. The shelter coordinator had no knowledge the father had a custody order awarding him sole custody of the children. She had consulted with her supervisor and an attorney from the Department of Childrens Services before assisting in the removal. She was advised that if the father was to be arrested and the children left alone, they needed to be removed.[20]

This case is important because victim advocates may be asked to help a shelter resident in gaining possession of children. Advocates must review all court orders and should never assist clients unless they are very clear that their actions will not give rise to a lawsuit in tort.

§ 17:9 Conclusion

Unfortunately, federal and state laws create conflicting concerns for shelter programs and their employees, volunteers and victim advocates who are caught between the interests of the victim, whose safety is often contingent on the assurance of confidentiality and the system that is dependent on information in order to function. Such policies that require shelters or advocates to divulge the very information that will keep victims safe ignores the realities of domestic violence and sends conflicting messages to entities that provide protection to victims of domestic violence. In the end, without the assurance of absolute confidentiality, many domestic violence victims will choose not to seek help from a shelter or domestic violence program.

In the future, Ohio's lawmakers will have no choice but to clearly define that information which is to be considered "confidential." Others will have to work within the boundaries of that definition in order

---

652 N.Y.S.2d 115 (3d Dep't 1996), aff'd, 90 N.Y.2d 969, 665 N.Y.S.2d 952, 688 N.E.2d 1034 (1997).

[19] Casivant v. Greene County Community Action Agency, Inc., 234 A.D.2d 818, 652 N.Y.S.2d 115 (3d Dep't 1996), aff'd, 90 N.Y.2d 969, 665 N.Y.S.2d 952, 688 N.E.2d 1034 (1997).

[20] Casivant v. Greene County Community Action Agency, Inc., 234 A.D.2d 818, 820, 652 N.Y.S.2d 115 (3d Dep't 1996), aff'd, 90 N.Y.2d 969, 665 N.Y.S.2d 952, 688 N.E.2d 1034 (1997).

to effectively provide services for victims and prepare cases for court.[1] Exceptions should be narrowly drawn so as not to further endanger domestic violence victims and their children.

[Section 17:9]

[1]See, e.g., RC 2317.02(G)(1)(g), which states that licensed social workers and counselors may be ordered to reveal communications with their patients in testimony where the testimony is sought in a civil action and concerns court-ordered treatment or services received by the patient as part of a case plan under RC 2151.412 or the court-ordered treatment or services are necessary or relevant to dependency, neglect or abuse of permanent custody proceedings under RC Ch. 2151.

Chapter 18

Federal Remedies

§ 18:1 Federal government's involvement in domestic violence; introduction

Victims of domestic violence must be able to keep their whereabouts confidential from batterers who spend much time discovering their locations, monitoring them, and harassing them.

Although much has been done on a statewide level to combat domestic violence, existing legal remedies have not gone far enough in eradicating this age-old epidemic. During the early 1990s, the federal government became increasingly concerned about the negative impact of domestic violence on society. The enactment of the Violence Against Women Act (VAWA) has done much to recognize and protect the confidentiality needs of victims of domestic violence.

§ 18:2 Batterer access to the victim—Limiting access to victim information[1]

Q & A: What is being done at the national level to prohibit batterers from discovering the whereabouts of their victims and children?

Batterers have been able to obtain access to their victims by a variety of methods, including accessing postal records, driver's license and motor vehicles records, and voting records. The Violence Against Women Act (VAWA) recently mandated that the United States Attorney General conduct a study detailing the means by which an abuser obtains information concerning a victim's whereabouts. The purpose of the study is to explore the feasibility of creating an effective means of protecting the confidentiality of the abused while preserving the public's right to access such records for legitimate purposes.[2] The results of this study, when completed, should provide sufficient documentation regarding the need for confidentiality and nondisclosure to assist state legislatures who may be willing to enact legislation.

The Violence Against Women Act restricts the ways in which batterers can obtain access to victims of domestic violence. For example, the Freedom of Information Act[3] allows a person to request the forwarding address of anyone who recently moved or the name and address of anyone who rented a post office box. As enacted, VAWA directs the U.S. Postal Service to change its policy and prohibit access by the public to residential addresses of domestic violence victims upon the presentation of a valid protection order.[4] Addresses for domestic violence shelters are also afforded confidentiality upon verification by the state domestic violence coalition that the organization or shelter is a domestic violence shelter.[5]

The Driver's Privacy Protection Act,[6] another section of the Violence Against Women Act, was recently passed to stop the widespread practice of motor vehicle registries giving out or selling information about individual or all licensed drivers or owners of registered motor vehicles. Under the new law, states will no longer be able to release

---

[Section 18:2]

[1]See also Kristen M. Driskell, Identity Confidentiality for Women Fleeing Domestic Violence, 20 Hastings Women's L. J. 129 (2009).

[2]See 42 U.S.C.A. § 14014, 42 U.S.C.A. § 40508.

[3]5 U.S.C.A. § 552.

[4]See 42 U.S.C.A. § 40281.

[5]See 42 U.S.C.A. § 40281, 42 U.S.C.A. § 13951; for more information on Ohio's statewide coalitions, call Ohio Domestic Violence Network at 1-800-934-9840 or A.C.T.I.O.N. Ohio at (614) 221-1255.

[6]18 U.S.C.A. § 2721 to 18 U.S.C.A. § 2725; see also Reno v. Condon, 528 U.S. 141, 120 S. Ct. 666, 145 L. Ed. 2d 587, 28 Media L. Rep. (BNA) 1281 (2000) (as to the constitutionality of statute).

an "individual's photograph, social security number, driver identification number, name, address . . ., telephone number, and medical or disability information."[7]

Since access to voting records also permits batterers to gain access to victims, some states have allowed victims of domestic violence to vote without revealing their addresses.[8] In New Jersey, for example, a victim of domestic violence who has obtained a protection order can register to vote without listing the street address on the registration form.[9] The registrant need only attach a copy of the order, a note indicating that he/she fears further abuse, and another address, including a post office box, where he/she can receive mail.[10] Ohio now permits a program applicant to its address confidentiality program who is eligible to vote to apply to the board of elections of the county in which the program participant resides to request that the registration record be confidential.[11]

Q & A: What has been done on the state level?

Recently Sub. HB 359 was enacted by the Ohio General Assembly which act created an address confidentiality program for victims of domestic violence, menacing by stalking, human trafficking, trafficking in persons, rape or sexual battery and to allow wireless service account transfer in a domestic violence situation. The law authorized the Secretary of State to establish this program.[12]

To qualify, an adult survivor of any of the aforementioned crimes or a parent or guardian acting on behalf of a minor, incompetent or ward, when changing residence may apply to the secretary of state with the assistance of an application assistant to have an address designated by the secretary of state serve as the person's address.[13]

The application shall be made on a form prescribed by the secretary of state and shall be filed with the secretary of state that contains the following: 1) a notarized statement by the applicant that the applicant fears for the safety of the applicant, a member of the applicant's household or the minor, incompetent or ward on whose behalf the application is made because the applicant is a victim of any one of the offenses provided above; 2) a knowing or voluntary designation of the secretary of state as the agent for purposes of receiving service of process and the receipt of mail; 3) the mailing address and telephone number at which the secretary of state may contact the applicant; 4) the address of the applicant's residence, school, institution of higher education, business or place of employment that the applicant requests

---

[7]18 U.S.C.A. § 2725; see also 18 U.S.C.A. § 2721; see http://www.gazetteextra.com/mezera021507.asp for case in which a jury awarded $25,000 under Driver's Privacy Protection Act suit.

[8]See, e.g., N.J. Stat. Ann. § 2C:25-26(c). See also Arizona, Florida, Illinois, Nevada, New York, and Rhode Island which all have legislation that allows for a type of address confidentiality program.

[9]N.J. Stat. Ann. § 19:31-3.2.

[10]N.J. Stat. Ann. § 19:31-3.2.

[11]R.C. 111.44(A).

[12]See also Falconi v. Secretary of State, 129 Nev. 260, 299 P.3d 378, 129 Nev. Adv. Op. No. 28 (2013).

[13]R.C. 111.42.

not be disclosed for the reason that disclosure will increase the risk that the applicant or another in the household on whose behalf the application is made will be threatened or physically harmed by another person; 5) the signature of the applicant and the date on which the applicant and the application assistant signed the application.[14] Neither a report to law enforcement nor the issuance of a civil protection order is necessary.

In effect the enactment of this law authorizes the Ohio Secretary of State to provide the program participant with a substitute mailing address and the Secretary of State would be responsible for forwarding mail to the participant.[15]

RC 3113.31 was also amended to authorize a court, after an ex parte or full CPO hearing, to issue an order directing a wireless service provider or reseller to transfer the rights to, and billing responsibility for, the wireless service number or numbers in use by a petitioner or any minor children in the care of the petitioner when the petitioner is not the account holder.[16]

§ 18:3 Batterer access to the victim—Changing a Social Security number

Recently, the federal government made it easier for victims of domestic violence to change their social security numbers to avoid being located. Because the social security number has become a major part of everyone's identity, it is a useful way to track an individual. Unfortunately, it can become a way for abusers to locate their victims.

The Social Security Administration has changed its procedures to help victims of domestic violence secure new numbers.[1] An individual needing to change his/her social security number must apply in person at any Social Security office. Evidence documenting the abuse or harassment must be presented along with a current social security number and original documents establishing U.S. citizenship or immigration status, age, identity and evidence of a legal name change if name was changed. Prior to this procedure, victims of domestic violence had to prove not only that they were abused but that their abusers had misused their social security numbers.

The best evidence of abuse comes from third parties, such as police or medical professional, and describes the nature and extent of the harassment, abuse of life endangerment. Other evidence may include court restraining or protection orders, and letters from shelters, family members, friends, counselors or others who have knowledge of the domestic violence or abuse.[2]

Providing new social security numbers is designed to help victims of domestic violence establish new identities in order to reduce their risk of future violence.

[14] R.C.111.42(A).

[15] R.C. 111.43.

[16] R.C. 3113.31.45-459.

[Section 18:3]

[1] See also Social Security Administration, Social Security Number, Policy & General Procedures Manual, PAMS RM § 00205.045 (Nov. 1998).

[2] See SSA Publication No. 05-10093 (October 2006); www.socialsecurity.gov.

§ 18:4 Batterer access to the victim—Name change

Victims of domestic violence may choose to change their names. If a victim is considering a name change, it should be done before the social security number change so that "an abuser cannot use the victim's new social security number to connect the victim with her former name."[1]

There are two ways to change one's name. A victim can apply to the probate court to request a judicial name change. Ohio law has been amended to permit a person to submit, along with the application for name change, a waiver form that requires a person to detail why the publication of the notice would jeopardize the applicant's personal safety.[2] If satisfactory proof is presented, the court shall waive the notice requirement[3] and shall order all records of the change of name proceeding to be sealed and opened only by order of the court for good cause shown or at the request of the applicant for any reason.[4]

Ohio's new probate forms will allow a person to request that probate court waive the requirement that the information be published in a newspaper of general circulation. Victims of domestic violence and those under protection orders will be eligible for the waiver. The application to waive the publication requirement and seal file will be granted where the applicant can demonstrate that publication of notice in a newspaper of general circulation will jeopardize the applicant's personal safety.[5]

Should a victim choose to apply to the court for a name change, documentation regarding the abuse can demonstrate to the court the danger to the victim.[6] For example, a protection order, medical records and photographs following a beating, police reports, a letter from the prosecutor or a domestic violence shelter, and copies of any official court documents, such as a conviction or divorce decree, may provide useful information.

When a victim of domestic violence has children, it becomes more difficult. The court must then notify the other parent of the requested name change. It can be argued that, in cases where the abuser has used the child to find the abused parent, a name change should be permitted without notice to the other parent.

It is important to remember that a name change does not modify the abuser's access to the children. A failure to adequately address custody/visitation issues may lead to contempt motions or, worse, a modification of custody to the abusive parent.[7]

Before going into hiding, it is imperative that victims of domestic

---

[Section 18:4]

[1]Sharon Knope, United States Attorneys' Bulletin 47 (January 1999).

[2]R.C. 2717.01(A)(4).

[3]R.C. 2717.01(A)(4)(a).

[4]R.C. 2717.01(A)(4)(b).

[5]Sup. R. Form 21.6; RC 2717.01(A)(4).

[6]Sharon Knope, United States Attorneys' Bulletin 47 January 1999.

[7]See Sharon Knope, United States Attorneys' Bulletin 48–50 January 1999 (discussing other problems that victims of domestic violence may encounter should they desire to change their names).

violence seek assistance from their local domestic violence organization and/or an attorney who specializes in family law in the state the victim is leaving and the state in which the victim desires to reside. Remember, relocation alone—even with a new social security number and name change—may not be enough, especially where there are children.

Alternatively, a victim/survivor may simply adopt a new name and hold himself/herself out to everyone by that name. Usage is the key to this type of name change. However, this type of name change is not recommended if a legal name change can be done safely.

§ 18:5 The Violence Against Women Act

Q & A: What is the Violence Against Women Act?

On September 13, 1994, President Clinton signed into law the Violence Against Women Act (VAWA). This legislation has enabled the federal government to become an active participant in the fight against domestic violence by granting it jurisdiction over certain domestic violence crimes.[1] It has recognized that "violence against women is a crime with far-reaching, harmful consequences for families, children and society."[2]

Under VAWA, there now exist new federal crimes of domestic violence stalking, and violating a protection order, as well as increased penalties for crimes against women. However, the federal crimes do not extinguish state criminal actions for the same conduct.[3] The Gun Control Act was also amended to include domestic violence related crimes. In effect, VAWA provides victims of domestic violence greater protection and recourse nationwide.

Under VAWA, victims were provided civil rights remedies for gender-motivated crimes against women.[4] Unfortunately, in 2000, the United States Supreme Court struck down the civil remedy provision in VAWA. In *U.S. v. Morrison*,[5] the United States Supreme Court considered whether gender-motivated acts of violence against women have substantial effects on interstate commerce. The Supreme Court

---

[Section 18:5]

[1]Elizabeth M. Schneider, Symposium: The Violence Against Women Act of 1994: A Promise Waiting to be Fulfilled, Introduction: The Promise of the Violence Against Women Act of 1994, 4 J.L. & Pol'y 371 (1996); see Carolyn Peri Weiss, Recent Development, Title 111 of the Violence Against Women Act: Constitutionally Safe and Sound, 75 Wash. U. L. Q. 723 (1997) (discussing extensive legislative history of VAWA).

[2]Margaret S. Groban, Enforcement of the Federal Domestic Violence Laws, United States Attorneys' Bulletin, January 1999, quoting Domestic and Sexual Violence Data Collection: A Report to Congress under the Violence Against Women Act, 1 (NIJ Research Report 1996).

[3]See Pamela A. Paziotopoulos, Violence Against Women Act: Federal Relief for State Prosecutors, 30-June Prosecutors 20 (1996) (discussing issues for prosecutors to consider).

[4]See 42 U.S.C.A. § 13981; but see Sally F. Goldfarb, The Supreme Court, The Violence Against Women Act, and the Use and Abuse of Federalism, 71 Fordham L. Rev. 57 (2002).

[5]U.S. v. Morrison, 529 U.S. 598, 120 S. Ct. 1740, 146 L. Ed. 2d 658, 144 Ed. Law Rep. 28, 82 Fair Empl. Prac. Cas. (BNA) 1313, 77 Empl. Prac. Dec. (CCH) P 46376 (2000).

concluded that gender-motivated crimes of violence are not economic activity, effectively placing it outside Congress's enforcement powers.[6]

§ 18:6 Interstate domestic violence and stalking under VAWA[1]

It is a federal crime for a person who travels in interstate or foreign commerce or enters or leaves Indian country or is present within the special maritime and territorial jurisdiction of the United States with the intent to kill, injure, harass, or intimidate that person's spouse, intimate partner, or dating partner and who, in the course of or as a result of such travel or presence, commits or attempts to commit a crime of violence against that spouse, intimate partner, or dating partner.[2] Under this provision of VAWA, there must be a specific intent to kill, injure, harass or intimidate the spouse, intimate partner, or dating partner at the time of the interstate travel.

It is also a federal crime for a person who causes a spouse or intimate partner, or dating partner to travel in interstate or foreign commerce or enter or leave Indian country by force, coercion, duress, or fraud, and who, in the course of, as a result of, or to facilitate such conduct or travel, commits or attempts to commit a crime of violence against that spouse or intimate partner.[3] Although this subsection of VAWA does not require a showing of specific intent to cause an intimate partner or spouse to travel interstate, it does require proof that the interstate travel resulted from force, coercion, duress, or fraud. A dating partner is defined as a person who is or has been in a social relationship of a romantic or intimate nature with the abuser. The existence of such a relationship is based on a consideration of the length of the relationship, the type of relationship and the frequency of interaction between the persons involved in the relationship.[4]

Under amended 18 U.S.C.A. § 2261(a)(1) and 18 U.S.C.A. § 2261(a)(2), there is no longer the requirement of a completed crime of violence. Additionally, the term "bodily injury" has been removed from the statute. Kidnapping with no resulting physical injuries would appear to fall under the purview of the amended statute.

The statute, as amended, has also changed the interstate nexus

---

[6]See Text § 14:13, Civil rights remedies for gender-motivated violence; see also Julie Goldsheid, United States v. Morrison and the Civil Rights Remedy of the Violence Against Women Act: A Civil Rights Law Struck Down in the Name of Federalism, 86 Cornell L. Rev. 109 (2000); Jennifer R. Hagan, Can We Lose the Battle and Still Win the War? The Fight Against Domestic Violence After the Death of Title III of the Violence Against Women Act, 50 DePaul L. Rev. 919 (2001); Sally F. Goldfarb, "No Civilized System of Justice": The Fate of the Violence Against Women Act, 102 W. Va. L. Rev. 499 (2000).

[Section 18:6]

[1]Leonard Karp and Laura C. Belleau, Federal Law and Domestic Violence: The Legacy of the Violence Against Women Act, 16 J. Am. Acad. Matrim. Law 173 (1999); see generally, Tom Lininger, Evidentiary Issues in Federal Prosecutions of Violence Against Women, 36 Ind. L.R. 687 (2003); see also U.S. v. Ruggles, 210 F.3d 373 (6th Cir. 2000) (discussing the admission of "other acts" evidence under Fed. R. Evid. 404(b) and concluding that prior acts of domestic violence are admissible to show intent, an element of the offense of interstate travel to commit domestic violence).

[2]Amended 18 U.S.C.A. § 2261(a)(1).

[3]Amended 18 U.S.C.A. § 2261(a)(2).

[4]18 U.S.C.A. § 2266(10).

language and has clarified the interstate domestic violence to cover assault before travel.

The term "spouse or intimate partner" refers to a spouse, former spouse,[5] a person who shares a child in common with the abuser, or a person who cohabits or has cohabited as a spouse with the abuser.[6] It also includes a person who is or has been in a social relationship of a romantic or intimate nature with the abuser, as determined by the length of the relationship, the type of relationship and the frequency of interaction between the persons involved in the relationship.[7] This section presupposes the spouse or intimate partner resides or has resided with the abuser. It also includes any other person similarly situated to a spouse who is protected by the domestic or family violence laws of the state in which the injury occurred or where the victim resides.[8] "State" includes "a State of the United States, the District of Columbia, a commonwealth, territory, or possession of the United States."[9]

Q & A: When is stalking[10] a federal crime?

Under 18 U.S.C.A. § 2261A(1), it is a federal crime to travel in interstate or foreign commerce or within the special maritime and territorial jurisdiction of the United States with the intent to kill, injure, harass or place under surveillance with the intent to kill, injure, harass or intimidate another person, and in the course of, or as a result of such travel or presence, the abuser places that person in reasonable fear of death of, or serious bodily injury to, or causes or attempts to cause or would reasonably be expected to cause substantial emotional distress to that person, a member of the immediate family of that person or the spouse or intimate partner of that person.

Under 18 U.S.C.A. § 2261A(2)(A), it is a federal crime to use the mail, any interactive computer service, electronic communication service, or electronic communication system or any facility of interstate or foreign commerce to engage in a course of conduct that causes substantial emotional distress with the intent to kill, injure, harass, or place under surveillance with intent to kill, injure, harass, or in-

---

[5]See U.S. v. Larsen, 2008 WL 5781437 (E.D. Wis. 2008), aff'd, 615 F.3d 780 (7th Cir. 2010).

[6]18 U.S.C.A. § 2266(7)(A)(i)(1); see also U.S. v. Barnette, 211 F.3d 803, 53 Fed. R. Evid. Serv. 1346, 195 A.L.R. Fed. 721 (4th Cir. 2000) (discussion of the term "intimate partner").

[7]18 U.S.C.A. § 2266(7)(A)(i)(11).

[8]18 U.S.C.A. § 2266(7)(B).

[9]18 U.S.C.A. § 2266(8).

[10]See, e.g., U.S. v. Crawford, 2001 WL 185140 (D. Me. 2001) (upholding 18 U.S.C.A. § 2261A); U.S. v. Al-Zubaidy, 283 F.3d 804, 2002 FED App. 0098P (6th Cir. 2002); see also U.S. v. Vollmer, 1 Fed. Appx. 573 (8th Cir. 2001); U.S. v. Young, 202 F.3d 262 (4th Cir. 1999); U.S. v. Wills, 346 F.3d 476 (4th Cir. 2003); U.S. v. Bowker, 372 F.3d 365, 2004 FED App. 0178P (6th Cir. 2004), cert. granted, judgment vacated on other grounds, 543 U.S. 1182, 125 S. Ct. 1420, 161 L. Ed. 2d 181 (2005); U.S. v. Cross, 308 F.3d 308 (3d Cir. 2002) (discussing elements of enhanced penalty under 18 U.S.C. 2261(b)); United States v. Matusiewicz, 165 F. Supp. 3d 166 (D. Del. 2015); United States v. Matusiewicz, 165 F. Supp. 3d 166 (D. Del. 2015) (where prosecutors had to prove that defendants' cyberstalking proximately caused death of victim such that enhanced penalties could be applied under 18 U.S.C. § 2261(b); see also 18 U.S.C.A. § 2261A(2)(A)).

timidate, or cause substantial emotional distress to a person in another State or tribal jurisdiction or within the special maritime and territorial jurisdiction of the United States It is also a federal crime to use the mail, any interactive computer service or any facility of interstate or foreign commerce to engage in a course of conduct that causes substantial emotional distress with the intent to place a person in another State tribal jurisdiction or within the special maritime and territorial jurisdiction of the United States, in reasonable fear of the death of, or serious bodily injury to (i) that person; (ii) a member of the immediate family of that person;[11] or (iii) a spouse or intimate partner of that person.[12]

Section 2261A(1) addresses situations involving stalking while travelling in interstate or foreign commerce. Section 2261A(2) applies to acts of stalking through the use of the mail or other computer service or facility committed by a person in one state against a person in another state.

Section 2261A(1) requires specific intent to "stalk" another at the time of interstate travel and section 2261(A)(2) requires specific intent of the abuser in one state to "stalk" another who is in another state through the use of the mail or other computer service.[13] Section 2261(A)(2)(B) further refines the mandate by requiring specific intent to place another including that person's immediate family or a spouse or intimate partner of that person in reasonable fear of death or serious bodily injury.

Both sections 2261A(1) and (2) contemplate acts committed by and against strangers[14] as well as family and intimate partners. "Immediate family" is defined as a spouse, parent, sibling, child or any other person living in the same household and related by blood or marriage.[15] A "spouse or intimate partner" includes a spouse, former spouse of the target of the stalking, a person who shares a child in common with the target of the stalking, or a person who cohabits or has cohabited as a spouse with the target of the stalking.[16] An "intimate partner" also includes a person who is or who has been in a social relationship of a romantic or intimate nature.[17]

Q & A: Is cyberstalking a crime?[18]

Yes. Under amended U.S.C.A. § 2261A(2), cyberstalking is a federal

---

[11]See for example, U.S. v. Jordan, 591 F. Supp. 2d 686 (S.D. N.Y. 2008).

[12]18 U.S.C.A. § 2261A(2)(B).

[13]See, for example, U.S. v. Shrader, 675 F.3d 300 (4th Cir. 2012) (discussing specific intent).

[14]See for example, U.S. v. Fullmer, 584 F.3d 132, 50 A.L.R. Fed. 2d 659 (3d Cir. 2009) (applying the statute to stalking by an animal rights organization).

[15]18 U.S.C.A. § 115.

[16]18 U.S.C.A. § 2266(7)(A)(ii).

[17]18 U.S.C.A. § 2266(7)(A)((ii)(11).

[18]U.S. v. Bowker, 372 F.3d 365, 2004 FED App. 0178P (6th Cir. 2004), cert. granted, judgment vacated on other grounds, 543 U.S. 1182, 125 S. Ct. 1420, 161 L. Ed. 2d 181 (2005). But see Elonis v. U.S., 135 S. Ct. 2001, 192 L. Ed. 2d 1, 43 Media L. Rep. (BNA) 1749 (2015) (finding that the crime of making threatening communications based on comments posted on a social networking website required a showing that defendant intended to issue threats or knew that the communications would be used as threats, even where the statute by its terms does not contain scienter

crime if a person uses the mail, any interactive computer service, or any facility of interstate or foreign commerce to engage in a course of conduct[19] that causes substantial emotional distress to that person or places that person in reasonable fear of the death of, or serious bodily injury,[20] to any of the persons described in clauses (i) through (iii) of subparagraph (B). These persons include that person, a member of the immediate family of that person, or a spouse or intimate partner of that person.[21] Pursuant to this section, there must be the intent to act.

Additionally, the Communications Act of 1934 was amended to expand the definition of a telecommunications devise-in regard to the current prohibition against anonymous communications with the intent to annoy, abuse, threaten or harass the recipient-to include "any devise or software that can be used to originate telecommunications or other types of communications that are transmitted in whole or in part by the internet."[22] This amendment is designed to strengthen federal stalking prosecution tools.

Q & A: What other terms should be defined?

For purposes of 18 U.S.C.A. § 2261, to "travel in interstate or foreign commerce' does not include travel from one state to another by an individual who is a member of an Indian tribe and who remains at all times in the territory of the Indian tribe of which the individual is a member."[23] A "course of conduct" is a pattern of conduct composed of two or more acts, evidencing a continuity of purpose.[24] "Bodily injury" means any act, except one done in self-defense, which results in physical injury or sexual abuse.[25] Additionally, "serious bodily injury" has the same meaning as in 18 U.S.C.A. § 2119(2).[26]

Q & A: What is the venue for federal prosecutions for traveling across state lines and committing a crime of violence?

According to the Fourth Circuit Court of Appeals, the venue lies in any district where travel occurred. In *U.S. v. Barnette*,[27] the defendant traveled from North Carolina to Virginia to firebomb his former girlfriend's apartment. He later drove from North Carolina to Virginia to murder her and was convicted in federal district court in North Carolina for traveling across state lines and committing a crime of violence in violation of 18 U.S.C.A. § 2261(a). He argued that venue was proper only in Virginia where the crimes of violence occurred.

The court noted that because VAWA does not have its own venue

---

requirements).

[19] 18 U.S.C.A. § 2266(2) (definition of course of conduct as a pattern of conduct composed of two or more acts, evidencing a continuity of purpose).

[20] 18 U.S.C.A. § 2261A(2)(A) and (B); see also 18 U.S.C.A. § 115 (definition of immediate family); 18 U.S.C.A. § 2266(7)(A)(ii); 18 U.S.C.A. § 2266(6).

[21] 18 U.S.C.A. § 2261(A)(2)(B).

[22] 47 U.S.C.A. § 223(h)(1).

[23] 18 U.S.C.A. § 2266(9).

[24] 18 U.S.C.A. § 2266(2).

[25] 18 U.S.C.A. § 2266(1).

[26] See also 18 U.S.C.A. § 1365(g)(3).

[27] U.S. v. Barnette, 211 F.3d 803, 53 Fed. R. Evid. Serv. 1346, 195 A.L.R. Fed. 721 (4th Cir. 2000).

provision, it could rely on 18 U.S.C.A. § 3237(a), which provides that an offense begun in one district and completed in another may be prosecuted in any district where the offense was begun, continued or completed.[28] It then held that because a violation of 18 U.S.C.A. § 2261 consists of both traveling and committing a violent act, and because the travel occurred in both states, venue was proper in the courts of North Carolina.

§ 18:7 Interstate violation of a protection order under VAWA

It is a federal crime for a person to travel in interstate or foreign commerce or enter or leave Indian country or is present within the special maritime and territorial jurisdiction of the United States, with the intent to engage in conduct that violates the portion of a protection order that prohibits or provides protection against violence, threats, or harassment against, or contact or communications with or physical proximity to, another person or that would violate such portion of a protection order in the jurisdiction in which the order was issued and subsequently engages in such conduct.[1] This subsection prohibits interstate travel with the intent to engage in conduct that either violates a valid protection order that forbids violence, threats of violence, harassment, or contact, communication with, or physical proximity to, the victim or that would violate the statute if the conduct occurred in the jurisdiction in which the order was issued. To establish a violation, the government must demonstrate that the person who violated the order had the specific intent to violate the protection order at the time of interstate travel and that a violation actually occurred.[2]

It is also a federal crime to cause another person to travel in interstate or foreign commerce or to enter or leave Indian Country by force, coercion, duress or fraud and in the course of, as a result of, or to facilitate such conduct or travel engages in conduct that violates the portion of a protection order that prohibits or provides protection against violence, threats, or harassment against, contact or communication with or physical proximity to, another person or that would violate such a portion of a protection order in the jurisdiction in which the order was issued.[3] Although this subsection does not require a showing of specific intent to cause a victim to travel interstate or foreign commerce, it does require proof that the travel resulted from force, coercion, duress, or fraud. There must also be proof that the person engaged in conduct in violation of the protection order during the course of or as a result of the forced or coerced travel.

Under amended 18 U.S.C.A. § 2262, the intimate partner requirement was eliminated. Additionally, that conduct deemed prohibited

---

[28] U.S. v. Barnette, 211 F.3d 803, 813, 53 Fed. R. Evid. Serv. 1346, 195 A.L.R. Fed. 721 (4th Cir. 2000).

[Section 18:7]

[1] 18 U.S.C.A. § 2262(a)(1).

[2] U.S. v. Wright, 128 F.3d 1274 (8th Cir. 1997) (court determined Congress had authority under commerce clause to enact provision of Violence Against Women Act 18 U.S.C.A. § 2262(a)(1) because statute requires cross of state line).

[3] 18 U.S.C.A. § 2262(a)(2).

was broadened in scope. Moreover, the prohibited conduct need not have injured the victim.

Protection orders include both civil and criminal domestic violence orders and anti-stalking protection orders. Such orders are defined as:

(1) any injunction, restraining order or any other order issued by a civil or criminal court for the purpose of preventing violent or threatening acts or harassment against sexual violence or contact or communication with or physical proximity to, another person, including any temporary or final orders issued by civil or criminal courts whether obtained by filing an independent action as a *pendente lite* order in another proceeding so long as any civil order was issued in response to a complaint, petition, or motion filed by or on behalf of a person seeking protection; and

(2) any support, child custody or visitation provision, orders, remedies or relief issued as part of a protection order, restraining order, or stay away injunction pursuant to State, tribal, territorial, or local law authorizing the issuance of protection orders, restraining orders, or injunctions for the protection of victims of domestic violence, dating violence, sexual violence or stalking.[4]

Q & A: What are the penalties for violating 18 U.S.C.A. § 2261, 18 U.S.C.A. § 2261A, and 18 U.S.C.A. § 2262?

Penalties for violations of subsections 18 U.S.C.A. § 2261 (interstate domestic violence), 18 U.S.C.A. § 2261A (interstate stalking and cyberstalking), and 18 U.S.C.A. § 2262 (interstate violation of protection order) vary depending on the extent of the bodily injury to the victim. Maximum terms of imprisonment range from five years for bodily injury to life in prison if death results.[5] If the victim is permanently disfigured or suffers life-threatening bodily injury, the term of imprisonment is not more than 20 years. If serious bodily injury results or if the abuser uses a dangerous weapon during the offense, the term of imprisonment is not more than 10 years.[6] Fines may also be part of the sentence.

8 U.S.C.A. § 2265A was added to permit doubling the maximum penalty for repeat federal domestic violence offenders or stalkers-a sentencing consequence already permitted for repeat federal sexual assault offenders.[7]

§ 18:8 Significant cases brought under VAWA[1]

Since 1994, there have been several cases brought under VAWA. Many of those cases have challenged the constitutionality of the inter-

---

[4]18 U.S.C.A. § 2262(d)(5) ("protection order" defined); 28 U.S.C.A. § 534(e)(3)(B).

[5]18 U.S.C.A. § 2261(b), 18 U.S.C.A. § 2262(b); United States v. Matusiewicz, 165 F. Supp. 3d 166 (D. Del. 2015).

[6]18 U.S.C.A. § 2261(b), 18 U.S.C.A. § 2262(b).

[7]American Bar Association Commission on Domestic Violence in VAWA 2005 Guide for Attorneys and can be found at http://www.abanet.org/domviol.

[Section 18:8]

[1]Derek W. Kelley, A Survey of Federal Cases Involving the Constitutionality of the Violence Against Women Act, 9 B.U. Pub. Int. L.J. 133 (1999).

state travel provisions. In those cases, the primary question presented to the courts is whether, in light of *United States v. Lopez*,[2] Congress's Commerce Clause power includes the authority to create the national crime of interstate domestic violence as contained in VAWA.[3]

The first person prosecuted under VAWA was Christopher Bailey. In *United States v. Bailey*,[4] the defendant was charged with interstate domestic violence in violation of 18 U.S.C.A. § 2261(a)(2) and one count of kidnapping after beating his wife in West Virginia and, over a six-day period, driving back and forth between Kentucky, Ohio, and West Virginia with his wife tied up in the trunk of the car. He finally brought his wife to an emergency room claiming that she fell and hit her head. He was charged and convicted on both counts and sentenced to life imprisonment for kidnapping and twenty years for interstate domestic violence.

The Fourth Circuit Court of Appeals rejected the argument that, under the Supreme Court's decision in *United States v. Lopez*,[5] the conduct regulated by the statute at issue here must directly affect interstate commerce in order for the statute to be a valid exercise of Congress's Commerce Clause power. Instead, it found Supreme Court case law upholding federal statutes that forbid the transportation of a woman or girl in interstate commerce for prostitution or other immoral purposes to be controlling. Since the interstate domestic violence law requires the crossing of a state line, the statute places the relevant transaction squarely in interstate commerce. The *Bailey* court reasoned that the statute's requirement of the commission of a crime of violence resulting in bodily injury is no different from the immoral purposes forbidden by the statutes previously upheld by the Supreme Court. The court held that the statute at issue did not exceed congressional authority.

Several cases were prosecuted under 18 U.S.C.A. § 2261(a)(1), the interstate domestic violence statute. For example, in *United States v. Gluzman*,[6] the defendant was convicted of interstate domestic violence for traveling from New Jersey to New York to murder her estranged husband. The defendant brought the ax and hatchet used to commit the murder with her from New Jersey to New York. The Second Circuit affirmed the trial court decision, adopting its holding and analysis. In *Gluzman*, the court found that Congress had a reasonable basis for concluding that domestic violence has an impact on inter-

---

[2]U.S. v. Lopez, 514 U.S. 549, 115 S. Ct. 1624, 131 L. Ed. 2d 626, 99 Ed. Law Rep. 24 (1995); see also Stacey L. McKinley, The Violence Against Women Act After United States v. Lopez: Will Domestic Violence Jurisdiction Be Returned to the States, 44 Clev. St. L. Rev. 345 (1996).

[3]See 18 U.S.C.A. § 2261; see also U.S. v. Crawford, 2001 WL 185140 (D. Me. 2001) (upholding constitutionality of the interstate stalking statute); U.S. v. Al-Zubaidy, 283 F.3d 804, 2002 FED App. 0098P (6th Cir. 2002) (statute setting forth offense of interstate stalking was within Congress's authority under the Commerce Clause); 18 U.S.C.A. § 2261A.

[4]U.S. v. Bailey, 112 F.3d 758 (4th Cir. 1997).

[5]U.S. v. Lopez, 514 U.S. 549, 115 S. Ct. 1624, 131 L. Ed. 2d 626, 99 Ed. Law Rep. 24 (1995); U.S. v. Helem, 186 F.3d 449 (4th Cir. 1999); see also U.S. v. Sensmeier, 2 Fed. Appx. 473 (6th Cir. 2001).

[6]U.S. v. Gluzman, 154 F.3d 49 (2d Cir. 1998); see also U.S. v. Jacobs, 244 F.3d 503 (6th Cir. 2001).

state commerce and that the statute was sustainable as a regulation of the channels of interstate commerce.

Similarly, in *United States v. Lankford*,[7] the Fifth Circuit Court of Appeals held that the interstate domestic violence provision[8] was constitutionally sound. The court found that the statute properly fell within one of the three broad categories of activity articulated by the Supreme Court in *United States v. Lopez*. It reasoned that the interstate domestic violence provision is encompassed within the first of the *Lopez* categories as a regulation of the use of channels of interstate commerce and noted that Congress may forbid or punish the use of channels of interstate commerce to promote immorality to persons in other states. The *Lankford* court then determined that it need not address whether domestic violence substantially affects interstate commerce, noting that whether "violence against a spouse is a private or noncommercial activity is of no moment."[9] Other courts have similarly rebuffed challenges to this provision of VAWA by finding that it is a valid exercise of congressional authority under the first *Lopez* category.[10]

Q & A: What does "during or as a result of interstate travel" mean for purposes of 18 U.S.C.A. § 2261?

The Sixth Circuit Court of Appeals was the first appeals court to address the scope of the interstate provisions of VAWA. In *United States v. Page*,[11] the defendant brutally beat and injured his girlfriend in Columbus, Ohio, and then traveled to Washington, Pennsylvania, where he left her for treatment at a hospital. Although the beating took place in Ohio, the prosecution presented evidence that the injuries worsened during the trip to Pennsylvania. The defendant argued that the words "that conduct" refer to the narrow act of interstate travel, not the episode of battering which occurred inside the defendant's condominium in Ohio.

The en banc Sixth Circuit divided evenly on the issue. The majority concluded that the beating that took place inside the defendant's condominium and that the use of a stun gun and mace was precisely what enabled him to force the victim to travel across state lines. "To assume that Congress intended to criminalize only those beatings occurring precisely during travel but not those occurring inside a home that are integrally related to forcible interstate travel would be to suggest that Congress somehow missed the boat."[12]

The dissent in *Page*, on the other hand, concluded that Congress intended 18 U.S.C.A. § 2261(a)(2), together with 18 U.S.C.A. § 2261(a)(1), to impose federal liability on domestic violence only when it occurs during or after interstate travel and that beatings that occur prior to a forced interstate trip are not within the scope of 18 U.S.C.A. § 2261(a)(2).

---

[7]U.S. v. Lankford, 196 F.3d 563 (5th Cir. 1999).

[8]18 U.S.C.A. § 2261(a)(1).

[9]U.S. v. Lankford, 196 F.3d 563, 571 (5th Cir. 1999).

[10]See, e.g., U.S. v. Wright, 128 F.3d 1274 (8th Cir. 1997).

[11]U.S. v. Page, 167 F.3d 325, 1999 FED App. 0066P (6th Cir. 1999); see also U.S. v. Ruggles, 210 F.3d 373 (6th Cir. 2000).

[12]U.S. v. Page, 167 F.3d 325, 329, 1999 FED App. 0066P (6th Cir. 1999).

The *Page* majority then construed the phrases "crime of violence" and "causes bodily injury" to include oral threats that cause a victim to fail to get medical treatment which results in the aggravation of the injuries inflicted prior to the interstate travel.[13] The court then concluded that, "[b]y any definition, the painful swelling and loss of blood that [the victim] suffered as a result of being unable to seek prompt medical attention constituted 'bodily injury.' "[14]

The court upheld the constitutionality of 18 U.S.C.A. § 2261(a)(2)[15] and rejected the defendant's claim that a victim can only have one intimate partner and that proof that someone other than the defendant fits the definition of that term precludes a conviction under the statute.

Other cases considered prosecutions under 18 U.S.C.A. § 2262, interstate violation of a protection order.[16] *United States v. Casciano*[17] was the first case dealing with an interstate violation of a protection order under 18 U.S.C.A. § 2262. In *Casciano*, the Second Circuit had to decide whether Massachusetts, the issuing state, had issued a valid protection order.[18]

After determining that the validity of the protection order should be determined by the judge rather than the jury, the Second District reiterated that due process requires that the Massachusetts trial court to have obtained personal jurisdiction over the defendant by service of process, giving him notice and an opportunity to be heard. While the court noted that service on the defendant was imperfect in that it was left at his last place of residence, it concluded that "Massachusetts cases reveal that imperfect service does not automatically invalidate a judicial order or decision when the defendant has had actual notice of the pending legal action, and no prejudice has accrued."[19] Because the evidence clearly demonstrated that the defendant had actual notice of the protection order well in advance of the hearing date, the court held that the protection order was valid and that Casciano's conduct was in violation of a valid protection order.

Casciano is important because it articulates that imperfectly perfected service does not automatically invalidate a judicial order. Once again, the distinction between notice and service is blurred. In this instance, it leaves open the question of whether personal service is necessary for the enforcement of an out-of-state protection order.[20]

---

[13]U.S. v. Page, 167 F.3d 325, 330, 1999 FED App. 0066P (6th Cir. 1999).

[14]U.S. v. Page, 167 F.3d 325, 334, 1999 FED App. 0066P (6th Cir. 1999).

[15]See U.S. v. Larsen, 2008 WL 5781437 (E.D. Wis. 2008), aff'd, 615 F.3d 780 (7th Cir. 2010).

[16]See, e.g., U.S. v. Romines, 139 F.3d 895 (4th Cir. 1998); see also U.S. v. Young, 208 F.3d 216 (6th Cir. 2000).

[17]U.S. v. Casciano, 124 F.3d 106 (2d Cir. 1997); see also U.S. v. Von Foelkel, 136 F.3d 339 (2d Cir. 1998) (upholding the constitutionality of 18 U.S.C.A. § 2262(a)(1)).

[18]See also David M. Fine, The Violence Against Women Act of 1994: The Proper Federal Role in Policing Domestic Violence, 84 Cornell L. Rev. 252 (1998).

[19]U.S. v. Casciano, 124 F.3d 106, 112 (2d Cir. 1997) (citation omitted).

[20]See Text § 11:11, Ex parte protection orders—Service and notice provisions, for a discussion of the problems of service and notice.

§ 18:9 Other remedies under VAWA[1]

The Violence Against Women Act directs states to grant full faith and credit to civil and criminal protection orders issued in every state or tribal court in order to safeguard victims of domestic violence from continuing violence.[2]

Q & A: What is "full faith and credit"?

Pursuant to the United States Constitution, full faith and credit is given to most final court decisions issued by another court.[3] That means that the parties who litigated an issue in a court are bound by that court's decision. Courts of another state must then treat the matter as one that has been decided by the other court. To that end, the courts of the new state must honor and enforce the decision of the issuing court as if it were the order of the enforcing state.

Under VAWA, all state and Indian tribal courts must afford full faith and credit to protection orders issued by all other state and tribal courts and must enforce those orders as if they were the orders of the enforcing state or tribe.[4] The full faith and credit mandate applies to both civil and criminal protection orders.[5]

Ohio's domestic violence statutes were amended to establish procedures for implementing the mandates of VAWA. To that end, protection orders issued by any other state are to be accorded full faith and credit in Ohio and are to be enforced by courts and law enforcement agencies in accordance with the terms of the order.[6]

Q & A: What is a valid protection order?

A "valid" protection order is defined as an order of protection that has been issued by a court which has jurisdiction over the parties and subject matter under that state's laws, and in circumstances where the defendant has been given reasonable notice and the opportunity to be heard sufficient to comply with due process.

Q & A: How is compliance with VAWA effected?

An out-of-state protection order shall be recognized and enforced by all courts and law enforcement agencies in Ohio[7] if the courts and law enforcement agencies have first ascertained that the following due process requirements have been met:

[Section 18:9]

[1]See also Text § 14:7, Police liability for failing to protect victims of domestic violence—Introduction.

[2]18 U.S.C.A. § 2265(a).

[3]U.S. Const. Art. IV § 1.

[4]See 18 U.S.C.A. § 2265(a); see also People v. Hadley, 172 Misc. 2d 697, 658 N.Y.S.2d 814 (N.Y. City Crim. Ct. 1997) (ruling that New York must use its own penal law to charge a man with criminal contempt for violating a New Jersey protection order in New York); Catherine F. Klein, Full Faith and Credit: Interstate Enforcement of Protection Orders under the Violence Against Women Act, 29 Fam. L.Q. 253 (1995); Emily J. Sack, Domestic Violence Across State Lines: The Full Faith and Credit Clause, Congressional Power and Interstate Enforcement of Protection Orders, 98 Nw. U. L.Rev. 927 (2004).

[5]18 U.S.C.A. § 2266(5); see also RC 2919.27(D) for a definition of "protection order issued by a court of another state."

[6]See RC 2919.27(A)(3), RC 2919.272(D), RC 3113.31(N)(1); see also Text § 14:17, Enforcement of out-of-state protection orders.

[7]See RC 1901.18(A)(9), RC 1901.19(A)(6), RC 2919.272(D) for authority to

(1) The issuing state or tribal court has jurisdiction over the parties and the subject matter under the laws of that state or tribe.[8]

(2) Reasonable notice and an opportunity to be heard was given to the party against whom the order was sought in the issuing court's jurisdiction sufficient to protect that person's due process rights.[9]

(3) In the case of an ex parte protection order, notice and an opportunity to be heard was provided within the time required by the law of the issuing court's jurisdiction and, in any event, within a reasonable time after the order was issued sufficient to protect the person's due process rights.[10]

(4) In the case of a mutual protection order, there is interstate enforcement only if a counterpetition seeking a protection order was filed and resulted in specific findings by the court that each party was entitled to such an order.[11]

Q & A: Are consent protection orders considered valid protection orders under VAWA?

It is unclear whether a protection order issued without a finding of domestic violence is an order issued by a court with subject matter jurisdiction. Consent protection orders are based on an agreement between the parties that the respondent agrees to be bound by the terms of the order.[12] In fact, the Supreme Court's standard Consent Agreement and Domestic Violence Civil Protection Order form does not include space for findings of fact, suggesting that when the parties agree to the terms of the order, there is no reason for findings that a respondent did or did not do something.[13]

Sometimes, consent civil protection orders are granted with a notation of "no findings" or "this is not an admission that domestic violence was committed." Inscribing "no findings" on the protection order form may cause the order to be considered invalid. Protection orders issues without findings may violate VAWA provisions making them unenforceable across state lines.

To be considered a valid protection order under VAWA for full faith and credit purposes, the issuing court must have jurisdiction over the parties and subject matter jurisdiction under that state's laws.[14] A court's subject matter jurisdiction for issuing a protection order

---

enforce out-of-state protection orders.

[8]18 U.S.C.A. § 2265(b)(1).

[9]18 U.S.C.A. § 2265(b)(2); see also People v. Hadley, 172 Misc. 2d 697, 658 N.Y.S.2d 814 (N.Y. City Crim. Ct. 1997) (determining that to accord out-of-state protection order full faith and credit in enforcing state, party seeking to enforce order must establish that defendant was afforded due process before the order was issued and was given reasonable opportunity to be heard in conformity with law of issuing state and consistent with due process).

[10]18 U.S.C.A. § 2265(b)(2).

[11]18 U.S.C.A. § 2265(c); see also Text § 12:29, Mutual protection orders, for an in-depth discussion of mutual protection orders; also note that antistalking protection orders issued in compliance with RC 2903.213 and RC 2903.214 are accorded full faith and credit.

[12]RC 3113.31.

[13]Sup. R. 10.01-J.

[14]See 18 U.S.C.A. § 2265(b)(1).

depends on the court having subject matter jurisdiction. Subject matter jurisdiction is based on the occurrence of an act of domestic violence or acts of stalking or threats. Absent a finding of domestic violence, the order may be unenforceable because the court does not have the subject matter jurisdiction to issue the order.

Validity does not mean that the court must hold a full hearing. Consent to the issuance of the order by the respondent may avoid a full hearing on the subject of the domestic violence. Some experts in the filed of domestic violence and VAWA have stated that in consenting, there must be some finding of domestic violence which may be the admission of one incident of abuse or a general agreement to the issuance of a finding coupled with an uncontested pleading by the petitioner alleging domestic violence.[15]

The affidavit filed by the petitioner may also form the basis of a valid protection order. When the abuser does not contest the issuance of the protection order and the protection order petition alleges facts sufficient to constitute domestic violence under state law, it is arguable that protection orders across the country have subject matter jurisdiction to issue valid consent protection orders. Not filing a responsive pleading to the petition may satisfy this requirement.[16]

In order to reduce the potential for problems in Ohio, all protection orders issued should be issued on the standardized Supreme Court form that contains: a statement that the court has found that it has subject matter jurisdiction to issue the order; a citation to the Ohio Revised Code defining domestic violence for purposes of issuing the protection order; and a statement that the court finds that the petitioner is entitled to a protection order under Ohio's statutes.[17]

Q & A: What types of protection orders are accorded full faith and credit?

The full faith and credit provision of VAWA was updated under VAWA 2005 and applies to:

(1) any injunction, restraining order or any other order issued by a civil or criminal court for the purpose of preventing violent or threatening acts or harassment against sexual violence or contact or communication with or physical proximity to, another person, including any temporary or final orders issued by civil or criminal courts whether obtained by filing an independent action as a *pendente lite* order in another proceeding so long as any civil order was issued in response to a complaint, petition, or motion filed by or on behalf of a person seeking protection; and

(2) any support, child custody or visitation provision, orders, remedies or relief issued as part of a protection order, restraining order, or stay away injunction pursuant to State, tribal, territorial, or local law authorizing the issuance of protection orders,

---

[15]See Leslye Orloff, Jason Knott and Alicia Carra, Creating a Jurisdictionally Sound Protection Order, Legal Momentum 2006.

[16]Orloff at 7.

[17]Sup. R. 10.01-J; see also Orloff at 8.

restraining orders, or injunctions for the protection of victims of domestic violence, dating violence, sexual violence or stalking.[18]

In other words, temporary and final orders and civil and criminal protection orders are accorded full faith and credit under VAWA. Moreover, many other protection provisions issued by courts such as restraining orders and no contact orders and which are not in protection orders may now be considered protection orders so long as their purpose is to provide safety and protection for victims of domestic violence.

Q & A: Are ex parte orders contemplated by VAWA?

Yes, provided that notice and the opportunity to be heard are provided within the time required by the issuing state or tribal law and, in any event, within a reasonable time after the order is issued, sufficient to protect the respondent's due process rights. In effect, if the respondent has been served with the protection order in the issuing state, the enforcing state has the authority to enforce the order.

Q & A: Are custody, support, and visitation orders issued pursuant to a protection order contemplated under VAWA?[19]

Full faith and credit should always be accorded to valid protection orders awarding victims of domestic violence, sexual assault and stalking custody, visitation and support.[20] VAWA 2005 bolsters existing federal provisions requiring enforcement of protection orders issued in a foreign state by explicitly stating that custody, visitation and support provisions included in a protection order and issued under the state's protection order statutes must also receive full faith and credit and thus are enforceable across state lines.[21] Law enforcement and courts are required to enforce these orders.[22] Thus, victims who flee their home states with their children and have previously obtained protection orders from the issuing states should be able to enforce custody, visitation and support provisions within civil protection orders.[23] Accordingly, these provisions within civil protection orders should be entitled to full faith and credit when issued for the safety and protection of either parent or child and provided the orders comply with the Uniform Child Custody Jurisdictional Act (UCCJA) [recently replaced by the UCCJEA in Ohio], the Parental Kidnapping and

---

[18] 18 U.S.C.A. § 2266(d)(5) ("protection order" defined); 28 U.S.C.A. § 534(e)(3)(B).

[19] See Goelman, Shelter from the Storm: Using the Jurisdictional Statutes to Protect Victims of Domestic Violence After the Violence Against Women Act of 2000, 13 Colum. J. Gender & L. 101 (2004).

[20] See amended 18 U.S.C.A. §§ 2265 to 2266. See, e.g. Zorza, Full Faith and Credit for Custody Orders: Improvements Brought by the UCCJEA and VAWA II, 7 Domestic Violence Rep. 10 (Oct./Nov. 2001); Goelman, Shelter from the Storm: Using the Jurisdictional Statutes to Protect Victims of Domestic Violence After the Violence Against Women Act of 2000, 13 Colum. J. Gender & L. 101, 155 (2004).

[21] See 18 U.S.C.A. § 2266(d)(5).

[22] See 18 U.S.C.A. § 2265(a).

[23] See 18 U.S.C.A. § 2266(d)(5); see also Text § 15:24, Other issues that impact custody and visitation awards.

Prevention Act[24] and Uniform Child Custody Jurisdiction and Enforcement Act (UCCJEA).[25]

Attorneys and advocates should still advise clients of the potential problems that may arise. Where there exists a previously issued custody, visitation or support order in a divorce, an enforcing court may be reluctant to enforce a protection order containing conflicting custody, visitation or support terms. Clients who leave their home states should be aware that courts in their new states may refuse to enforce conflicting orders even if granted pursuant to a protection order.

VAWA does not permit the enforcement of custody and support orders issued pursuant to state divorce and child custody laws.[26] However, custody, visitation and support orders issued pursuant to state divorce and child custody laws are still entitled to full faith and credit under other federal law and provided certain conditions are met.[27]

Q & A: What are these other federal laws?[28]

The issue of whether custody awards in protection orders are entitled to interstate enforcement turns on several laws: the Violence Against Women Act (VAWA);[29] the Uniform Child Custody Jurisdiction Act (UCCJA);[30] the recently adopted Uniform Child Custody Jurisdiction and Enforcement Act (UCCJEA);[31] and the Parental Kidnapping and Prevention Act (PKPA).[32] Custody provisions within protection orders are entitled to interstate enforcement if they meet the jurisdictional requirements of the UCCJA and the PKPA. Otherwise it will be almost impossible to obtain interstate enforcement.

Every state has adopted its own version of the UCCJA into state law. Under the UCCJA, there are four ways for a state to assert jurisdiction in a custody matter. First, "home state" jurisdiction is where a child has lived for six consecutive months, immediately preceding the filing of the proceeding. Second, jurisdiction may be asserted in the state if one of the parents has "significant connections" with that state. Significant connections include substantial evidence of the child's present or future care, protection, training, and personal relationships. This may only be invoked if it is in the best interests of the child. The third way is "emergency jurisdiction" where the child is

[24]28 U.S.C.A. § 1738A.

[25]See RC 3127.01 et seq.

[26]See amended 18 U.S.C.A. § 2266; see also Judge Susan B. Carbon et al., Enforcing Domestic Violence Protection Orders throughout the Country: New Frontiers of Protection for Victims of Domestic Violence, 50 Juv. & Fam. Ct. 2, 40 (1999).

[27]28 U.S.C.A. § 1738A; RC 3127.01 et seq.

[28]See generally, Joan Zorza, Guide to Interstate Custody: A Manual for Domestic Violence Advocates, Center on Women and Family Law (1995).

[29]18 U.S.C.A. § 2266(d)(5).

[30]As adopted by Ohio in RC 3109.21 et seq. Recently adopted Sub. S.B. 185 replaces the UCCJA with the Uniform Child Custody Jurisdiction and Enforcement Act (UCCJEA), as adopted by Ohio in RC 3127.01 et seq.

[31]Sub. S.B. 185, eff. 4-10-05, and repeals the UCCJA in Ohio.

[32]28 U.S.C.A. § 1738A.

physically present in the new state and the child is in need of protection from abuse or mistreatment or is threatened with abuse or is otherwise neglected or dependent. This is usually done on a temporary basis and only to protect endangered children. Finally, the fourth basis for jurisdiction is where the child is physically present and no other state has jurisdiction.

Ohio has recently replaced the UCCJA with the Uniform Child Custody Jurisdiction and Enforcement Act (UCCJEA).[33] The primary goal of the UCCJEA is to establish uniform criteria for jurisdiction in interstate custody cases to avoid competition and to promote cooperation among states.[34] In any interstate custody case, home state jurisdiction is now superior to other jurisdictional grounds,[35] unless the other states court declines to exercise jurisdiction.[36]

Under the UCCJEA, a court must decline jurisdiction (except in temporary jurisdiction cases) where the person seeking to invoke the provision has engaged in unjustifiable conduct unless the parents and all persons acting as parents have agreed to the exercise of jurisdiction, the court having jurisdiction determines that Ohio is a more appropriate forum or no court of any other state would have jurisdiction.[37] Unjustifiable conduct is defined as conduct by a parent or that parents surrogate that attempts to create jurisdiction in Ohio by removing the child from the childs home state, secreting the child, retaining the child, or restraining or otherwise preventing the child from returning to the childs home state in order to prevent the other parent from commencing a parenting proceeding in the childs home state.[38]

If an Ohio court declines jurisdiction, it may still craft an appropriate remedy to ensure the safety of the child and prevent a repetition of the unjustifiable conduct, including staying the proceeding until a child custody proceeding is commenced in a court having jurisdiction.

The UCCJEA authorizes temporary emergency jurisdiction in cases where the parent and child flee their home state due to threats of mistreatment and abuse against either.[39] A court of this state has temporary emergency jurisdiction where the child has been abandoned or it is necessary in an emergency to protect the child because the child, or a sibling or parent of the child, is subjected to or threatened with mistreatment or abuse.[40] The temporary emergency order remains in effect until a custody order is issued by another state and becomes permanent if no other order is issued by another state within

---

[33]Sub. S.B. 185, eff. 4-10-05.

[34]See Hoff, The ABCs of the UCCJEA: Interstate Child-Custody Practice Under the New Act, 32 Fam. L. Q. 267 (Summer 1998); see also Zorza, The UCCJEA: Why Do We Have It and How Does It Help Battered Women in Custody Disputes? Vol. 5, No. 1 Domestic Violence Report October/November 1999.

[35]RC 3127.15(A)(1).

[36]RC 3127.15(A)(2); RC 3127.21 and RC 3127.22.

[37]RC 3127.22.

[38]RC 3127.22(D).

[39]RC 3127.18.

[40]RC 3127.18(A)(1) to RC 3127.18(A)(2).

six months.[41] Clearly, under this provision, the safety and protection of both the child and the battered parent are paramount considerations.

Where one state is made aware that another jurisdiction is subsequently or simultaneously asked to adjudicate the same custodial issues, that court shall immediately communicate with the court of the other state to resolve the jurisdictional conflict.[42] The UCCJEA also permits attorneys to participate in the required conference calls between judges of the two states when custody actions have been filed in more than one state.[43]

Unlike the UCCJA, the UCCJEA contains more detailed evidentiary procedures.[44] Finally, the UCCJEA also includes domestic violence as a mandatory factor for courts to consider in determining which court is the more appropriate forum to hear the case.[45]

While the UCCJEA is a significant improvement, there are still challenges for battered women and their children. The battered parent must rely on the court to determine whether an emergency exists. If the batterer commences litigation in the other state before the battered parent has been gone for the six-month period, that parent must return to the other state to defend the action.

However, unlike VAWAs full faith and credit provisions, which do not require giving notice a second time to register a protection order in another jurisdiction, the UCCJEA requires that notice be given to the opposing parent before a custody decree can be registered (and enforced).[46]

The PKPA is federal law, preempting the UCCJA in cases where there is a conflict between the laws of the issuing state and the enforcing state. It applies to all interstate child custody cases and requires states to honor another state's custody and visitation orders, provided they comply with the Act. The PKPA provides the same four grounds for asserting jurisdiction as the UCCJA except that "home state" is given the highest priority. Moreover, no other state may assert jurisdiction when another state has continuing jurisdiction pursuant to the PKPA.

Amended 18 U.S.C.A. § 2266(d)(5) has clarified that full faith and credit given to protection orders may include custody, support and visitation provisions issued under state divorce and child custody laws provided the order is entitled to full faith and credit under other federal law including the UCCJA and the PKPA.[47]

Q & A: How does the UCCJEA deal with address confidentiality?

---

[41]RC 3127.18(B).

[42]RC 3127.18; see also Text § 15:24, Other issues that impact custody and visitation awards.

[43]RC 3127.09.

[44]RC 3127.11.

[45]RC 3127.21(B)(1).

[46]RC 3127.19, RC 3127.35(B) and RC 3127.35(C).

[47]See Judge Susan B. Carbon et al., Enforcing Domestic Violence Protection Orders throughout the Country: New Frontiers of Protection for Victims of Domestic Violence, 50 Juv. & Fam. Ct. 2, 40 (1999). Note: Many states have adopted the Uniform Child Custody Jurisdiction and Enforcement Act (UCCJEA), including Ohio. Under

Under the UCCJEA, identifying information will be sealed and not disclosed to the other party or the public if a party alleges in an affidavit or pleading under oath that the health, safety or liberty of a party or child would be jeopardized by the disclosure of the identifying information.[48] It is up to the state to develop adequate procedures to protect the confidentiality of the battered parent.

Additionally, in cases of temporary emergency jurisdiction, the name and address of the parent seeking protection and who is designated the childs residential parent does not have to be disclosed.

Q & A: Are provisions in a protection order pertaining to payment of court costs or attorney fees enforceable under VAWA?

It should be argued that all provisions or terms of a protection order that relate to the safety and protection of the victim and family or other household members are to be accorded full force and credit and enforced according to the terms of the order.

If attorney fees are ordered, the enforcing court should honor the terms of the protection order as written. On the other hand, VAWA 2000 explicitly provides that all states by way of the courts and all units of local government must certify that its laws, policies and practices do not require that in connection with the filing, issuance, registration or service of a protection order or a petition for a protection order to protect a victim of domestic violence, stalking or sexual assault, that the victim bear the costs associated with the filing, issuance, registration or service of a protection order, whether issued inside or outside the state.[49] Based on this language, if the victim is assessed court costs, the enforcing court need not honor that provision of the order.

Q & A: What if a victim seeks to have her protection order registered in the new state?

According to VAWA 2000, victims should not be assessed a fee for registering their protection orders.[50]

Q & A: Are mutual orders of protection accorded full faith and credit?

Mutual protection orders are those entered against both the petitioner and the respondent. Usually, mutual protection orders are issued by the court at the request of the respondent (during the petitioner's case against the respondent) without according the petitioner the same due process protections of reasonable notice and an opportunity to be heard as to the respondent's allegations.[51]

Under VAWA, only certain mutual protection orders are accorded full faith and credit. Unless the respondent filed a cross- or counter-petition seeking a protection order and the court made specific findings that each party was entitled to a protection order, only the order

---

the UCCJEA, abuse against the child's parent is a basis for exercising emergency jurisdiction.

[48]RC 3127.23.

[49]VAWA 2000, 42 U.S.C.A. § 3766(hh)(4).

[50]See VAWA 2000, 42 U.S.C.A. § 3766hh(4).

[51]See Text § 12:29, Mutual protection orders.

in favor of the petitioner is entitled to full faith and credit.[52] The Ohio General Assembly addressed these concerns by enacting RC 3113.31(E)(4) and RC 2919.26(I)(2).

Victims' attorneys should inform their clients that it is unwise to agree to mutual orders, even those entered by consent, that include findings of fact that the respondent is entitled to a protection order. In effect, the victim of domestic violence would be admitting that he/she also inflicted acts of abuse against the respondent.

Q & A: What if the due process requirements of VAWA have not been complied with and the defendant has already been charged?

Ohio includes certain procedural safeguards in the domestic violence statute.[53] For example, Ohio law provides an out-of-state defendant with an affirmative defense: It is an affirmative defense to a charge of violating an out-of-state protection order under RC 2919.27(A)(3) that the out-of-state protection order does not comply with the requirements set forth in 18 U.S.C.A. § 2265(b).[54] An affirmative defense in a pleading is defined as a "matter asserted by defendant which, assuming the complaint to be true, constitutes a defense to it" or as "[a] response to a plaintiff's claim which attacks the plaintiff's *legal* right to bring an action, as opposed to attacking the truth of claim."[55]

If an individual is charged with violating an out-of-state protection order and the due process requirements of 18 U.S.C.A. § 2265 have not been met, he/she may argue in his/her defense that the protection order from the issuing state is not valid and should not be accorded full faith and credit by a court in this state.[56] A defendant so charged should not be found guilty of violating the out-of-state protection order.

Q & A: Under which state laws should a protection order be enforced?[57]

It depends on the nature of the protection order. The material provisions of the out-of-state protection order must be enforced as defined in the protection order, even if the enforcing court's protection order statute does not contain the same provisions. A material provision is one that relates to the substance of the order and its terms, rather than to its form.

For example, a foreign protection order is in force for the time pe-

---

[52]See 18 U.S.C.A. § 2265(b)(2).

[53]RC 2919.27, RC 2919.272.

[54]RC 2919.27(C).

[55]Black's Law Dictionary (6th ed.) p 60.

[56]See also U.S. v. Casciano, 124 F.3d 106, 112 (2d Cir. 1997) (upholding defendant's conviction under VAWA for travelling out of state to violate Massachusetts protection order, rejecting defendant's claim that his due process rights were violated and that the order was invalid because it was not served in accordance with Massachusetts law, noting "imperfect service does not automatically invalidate a judicial order or decision when the defendant has had actual notice of the pending legal action, and no prejudice has accrued").

[57]Celia Guzaldo Gamrath, Enforcing Orders of Protection Across State Lines, 88 Ill. B.J. 452 (Aug. 2000); Emily J. Sack, Domestic Violence Across State Lines: The Full Faith and Credit Clause, Congressional Power, and Interstate Enforcement of Protection Orders, 98 N.W.U. L. Rev. 827 (2004).

riod specified by the issuing state.[58] If the out-of-state order is effective for one year or twenty years in the issuing state, Ohio courts and law enforcement agencies can only enforce the order during either the one- or twenty-year time frame, even though a protection order in Ohio is effective for five years.

Additionally, the enforcing court must enforce an out-of-state protection order even if the persons protected by the order would not qualify for relief under the laws of the enforcing state or if the type of relief provided would not be available under the enforcing state's laws. For example, some states have statutes that cover all dating relationships. Even though these classes of individuals are not included under RC 2919.25 or RC 3113.31, Ohio courts and police officers must enforce such out-of-state protection orders according to their terms. Similarly, if an out-of-state protection order grants the use of an automobile and that remedy is not available in the enforcing court's jurisdiction, the enforcing court must still enforce the out-of-state protection order according to its terms. Likewise, an order prohibiting an abuser from being around the victim's place of employment or school is enforceable even if the enforcing court does not have the authority to issue a similar order.

Although an Ohio court may not expand an out-of-state protection order to include remedies available in Ohio but not in the issuing state, nothing prevents a state from granting broader coverage under its laws than the federal law requires.[59] For example, a state could decide that all support provisions (e.g., spousal support or child support) contained in protection orders must be granted full faith and credit as part of the state's law honoring other states' protection orders, even though the state is not required to do so under VAWA.[60]

On the other hand, the Maryland Attorney General focuses its analysis on criminal enforcement. Where the out-of-state order awards temporary use of the automobile to the petitioner and the respondent fails to abide by that part of the order, a law enforcement official would not be authorized to arrest the respondent nor would criminal prosecution lie because violation of a similar term in a Maryland order would not constitute a criminal offense.[61] Following this rationale, a respondent may be arrested and criminally prosecuted under Ohio law for violating an out-of-state protection order only to the extent tat the violation implicates the sort of relief that could be granted under Ohio law.[62]

Q & A: Which state's enforcement remedies would apply to the violation of an out-of-state protection order?[63]

---

[58]Barbara J. Hart, Lecture on Full Faith and Credit for Protection Orders and Federal Domestic Violence Crimes, National Conference on Domestic Violence, National College of District Attorneys 3 (October 9, 1995).

[59]Joan Zorza, The Implications of Full Faith and Credit for Protective Orders, 2 Domestic Violence Rep. 19, 30 (1996).

[60]Joan Zorza, The Implications of Full Faith and Credit for Protective Orders, 2 Domestic Violence Rep. 19, 30 (1996).

[61]Md. Op. Att'y Gen.00–009, (4-11-00), 2000 WL 472838, at *9.

[62]See Md. Op. Att'y Gen.00–009, (4-11-00), 2000 WL 472838, at *9, for analogy.

[63]See Md. Op. Att'y Gen.00–009, (4-11-00), 2000 WL 472838.

The law of the enforcing court's jurisdiction determines the applicable procedures and remedies when an out-of-state protection order is violated.[64] "For example, if mandatory arrest provisions and penalties apply to violations of protection orders issued in the enforcing jurisdiction, then mandatory arrest must occur if a foreign protection order is violated in the enforcing jurisdiction, regardless of whether or not the issuing jurisdiction has a comparable mandatory arrest law."[65]

Similarly, if the enforcing state's law includes the confiscation of a weapon that would not have been seized in the issuing state, the abuser can be arrested in the enforcing state in conformity with its laws. Moreover, the same violation may be a felony in the enforcing state that would be a misdemeanor or punished by contempt in the issuing state. Even if a particular sentence might not have been possible in the issuing state, the violator might be subject to restitution, attorney fees, or a fine in the enforcing state.[66]

Q & A: Can a defendant be charged with a violation of a protection order issued by a court (of another state), merely because of his possession of firearms in the new state?

Apparently yes, but only if the protection order actually prohibits the possession of firearms. In *State v. Haney*,[67] a Kentucky district court had granted a domestic violence protection order restricting defendant from committing acts of abuse and requiring him to surrender his license to carry a concealed firearms. The order also stated that federal law may prohibit an person subject to a protection order from possessing a firearm pursuant to 18 U.S.C.A. § 922(g)(8).

In this case, the defendant was observed at a gun show in Ohio sitting on the vendor's side of a table containing multiple guns, and was subsequently arrested for violating the protection order, in accordance with RC 2919.27(A)(3) (prohibiting violation of a protection order issued by a court of another state). Defendant appealed his conviction, arguing that the prohibition on the possession of firearms was not part of the terms of the Kentucky protection order. The state asserted that § 922(g)(8) outlines the conditions necessary to prohibit the possession of firearms under federal law and that because the Kentucky protection order satisfied the conditions of the federal statute, the prohibition was therefore incorporated into the Kentucky protection order as well.

Although the Clinton County appellate court agreed that the Kentucky protection order satisfied the conditions in § 922(g)(8), the protection order did not actually contain a specific provision prohibiting the possession of firearms as contained in the federal statute. In determining whether the Kentucky protection order expressly

[64]See also People v. Hadley, 172 Misc. 2d 697, 658 N.Y.S.2d 814 (N.Y. City Crim. Ct. 1997).

[65]Stopping Violence Against Women Using New Federal Laws Study Guide, American Bar Association VideoLaw Seminars 27 (1996).

[66]Joan Zorza, The Implications of Full Faith and Credit for Protective Orders, 2 Domestic Violence Rep. 16, 30 (1996).

[67]State v. Haney, 197 Ohio App. 3d 152, 2011-Ohio-6023, 966 N.E.2d 921 (12th Dist. Clinton County 2011).

incorporated the firearm prohibition into the order as a term, the appellate court reviewed the order and its references to any restrictions on firearm possession.

The court found that the first reference to any restriction was noted in the Warning Page of the order, where the appellant was warned that because he was subject to a state domestic violence protection order, he could be subjected to federal penalties relating to the possession of firearms. Such restriction was not placed into the body of the actual order. "Therefore, unless the court expressly prohibits the possession of firearms or the state legislature enacts the equivalent of Section 922(g)(8), there is no state authority prohibiting the possession of firearms merely because a state civil protection order has been issued."[68]

The second reference was found near the conclusion of the order, which provided that "[p]ursuant to 18 USC 922(g)(8), it may be a federal violation to purchase, receive or possess a firearm or ammunition while subject to this order."[69] However, that language provided only notice to appellant that it might be a violation of federal law for him to possess firearms. "A reference to the existence of federal law that may apply to appellant due to his status as a person subject to a protection order does not inherently make a subsequent violation of that federal law also a violation of the state protection order. The prohibitions contained in the federal law remain separate and distinct from a state protection order unless the state protection order clearly and expressly articulates otherwise."[70]

Therefore, the trial court erred in deciding that the prohibition against firearms was incorporated into the Kentucky protection order. While appellant might have possessed firearms, he did not violate any terms of the actual Kentucky order.

This decision seems to suggest that absent specific prohibitions contained in a state protection order, a state court cannot depend on federal prohibitions when charging a defendant with a violation of the order. Query whether a defendant could be charged with a violation of a state protection order by a federal prosecutor in a federal court.

Q & A: Can the abuser also be charged with federal domestic violence?

As stated above, it is likely that the enforcing jurisdiction will charge the violator with violating the protection order. It is equally possible for the United States Attorney to charge the violator with crossing state lines in order to pursue the victim, either with the intent to cause physical harm or to stalk the victim[71] or to violate a protection order.[72]

Q & A: Can the abuser be charged in both federal court and the enforcing state court for the violation?

---

[68]State v. Haney, 197 Ohio App. 3d 152, 2011-Ohio-6023, 966 N.E.2d 921 (12th Dist. Clinton County 2011).

[69]State v. Haney, 197 Ohio App. 3d 152, 2011-Ohio-6023, 966 N.E.2d 921 (12th Dist. Clinton County 2011).

[70]State v. Haney, 197 Ohio App. 3d 152, 2011-Ohio-6023, 966 N.E.2d 921 (12th Dist. Clinton County 2011).

[71]18 U.S.C.A. § 2261(a)(1), 18 U.S.C.A. § 2261A.

[72]18 U.S.C.A. § 2261(a)(2).

Yes. An abuser may be charged in both state and federal court for the violation of the protection order.[73] The elements of the crimes are not identical because the federal domestic violence claim requires the crossing of state lines, an element that is not involved in a state domestic violence violation.[74] To that end, an abuser should not be able to successfully raise a challenge on double jeopardy grounds.

Q & A: How should foreign protection orders be authenticated?

At present, the federal government has not instituted rules for authenticating foreign protection orders. However, the Maryland Attorney General has recently offered guidance on authenticating out-of-state protection orders. In an opinion issued on April 11, 2000,[75] the Maryland Attorney General provided guidance to police officers regarding the authentication of out-of-state orders. At the outset, the opinion stressed that the officer's task is to make a good faith evaluation of the authenticity of the order. The officer must first determine from the face of the order the identity of the respondent and whether the order is still in effect. The officer should then assess whether there is probable cause to believe that the respondent has violated the order and if so, whether a similar violation of a Maryland protection order could furnish the basis for a criminal prosecution.[76]

The attorney general then cautioned officers to authenticate the order before making an arrest. The opinion states that, under federal law, a copy of an order that contains or is accompanied by an attestation of the clerk of the issuing court, the court seal (if any) and a certification by the court is properly authenticated.[77] Additionally, the law of the jurisdiction in which the order was entered may also permit other forms of authentication. Finally, the opinion then addresses those instances where the officer is not presented with a copy of the order.

Q & A: Must a respondent be notified when a protection order is to be registered or filed in another state?

No. In fact, 18 U.S.C.A. § 2265(d)(1) was recently amended to prohibit the notification to a respondent that the protection order has been registered or filed in the enforcing state, unless requested to do so by the victim or the party protected under such order. If children are involved, the UCCJEA may require notification.

Some states have statutes and procedures in place that require service and notice to a defendant before a court will adopt a foreign decree. Because of the safety concerns inherent in any protection order proceedings, VAWA 2000 has mandated that defendants not be notified of the registration of a protection order in another state, except when requested by the victim.

Additionally, 18 U.S.C.A. § 2265(d) was amended to provide

[73]See, e.g., Md. Op. Att'y Gen.00–009, (4-11-00), 2000 WL 472838.

[74]See Joan Zorza, The Implications of Full Faith and Credit for Protective Orders, 2 Domestic Violence Rep. 19, 30 (1996); see also RC 3113.31(L), RC 2919.27.

[75]Md. Op. Att'y Gen.00–009, (4-11-00), 2000 WL 472838.

[76]Md. Op. Att'y Gen.00–009, (4-11-00), 2000 WL 472838, at *9–10.

[77]Md. Op. Att'y Gen.00–009, (4-11-00), 2000 WL 472838, at *10; see also 28 U.S.C.A. § 1738.

increased internet security and confidentiality for victims by prohibiting courts from publishing information regarding the registration or filing of a protection order, restraining order or injunction on the internet. For example no internet posting or information or evidence contained in the court's file can be published.[78]

Q & A: Is registration of the order a prerequisite for enforcement of the order?

No. Any valid protection order shall be accorded full faith and credit even though it has not been registered or filed in the enforcing state. Therefore, it shall be enforced in the enforcing state according to its terms by both the courts and law enforcement officials.[79]

Q & A: How is it determined whether the criminal or civil court handles the out-of-state protection orders for enforcement purposes?

"[VAWA] is silent with respect to which particular forum, civil or criminal, must afford full faith and credit to an order issued outside of the jurisdiction."[80] The American Bar Association has suggested that the nature of the violation determines the forum. For example, if the violation is one which falls within RC 2919.27, the municipal court has jurisdiction. On the other hand, if the violation is inherently civil, the domestic relations court would have jurisdiction to enforce the terms of the out-of-state order.

Q & A: Should Ohio's law enforcement officials ever notify federal officials when there is a violation of a protection order?

Yes. Before VAWA was enacted, only local law enforcement officials and prosecutors investigated domestic violence incidents or violations of protection orders. Since VAWA federalized the crimes of domestic violence and violating a protection order, and because Ohio is authorized to enforce out-of-state protection orders, both the FBI and the U.S. attorney may now investigate and prosecute these crimes. Pursuant to RC 2935.032(G), each Ohio law enforcement agency or official that arrests an offender for an alleged incident of domestic violence or violating a protection order (either criminal or civil) is required to consider referring the case to federal authorities for prosecution under federal law if the incident constitutes a violation of VAWA.

Q & A: Should law enforcement officials enforce an out-of-state protection order even though they are unable to verify whether the order has been served on the respondent or whether the order is still in existence?

The American Bar Association has recommended that the issuing court provide an official form certifying compliance with service requirements.[81] Even without this certification, Ohio's law enforcement officials are immune from liability for enforcing a protection or-

[78]American Bar Association Commission on Domestic Violence in VAWA 2005 Guide for Attorneys and can be found at http://www.abanet.org/domviol.

[79]18 U.S.C.A. § 2265(d)(2).

[80]Stopping Violence Against Women Using New Federal Laws Study Guide, American Bar Association VideoLaw Seminars 27 (1996).

[81]Stopping Violence Against Women Using New Federal Laws Study Guide, American Bar Association VideoLaw Seminars 27 (1996).

der that appears valid on its face.[82] This provision applies to out-of-state protection orders as well as to those issued by Ohio courts.

Q & A: Should clients be assessed fees or costs for service of process of out-of-state protection orders?

No. The mandates of VAWA require that all protection orders issued anywhere in the country be enforced by the courts and law enforcement agencies of each state. States boundaries may no longer prohibit enforcement. Additionally, victims of domestic violence are able to file for protection orders where they temporarily reside. That victims are so readily encouraged to travel across state lines to file for their protection orders and because these orders are enforceable everywhere, it is reasonable to assume that the legal proceedings are not cost prohibitive.

Clients who are unable to afford the fees should not be forced to choose between not filing for a protection order or filing for an order that may be dismissed for lack of service or determined to be invalid and unenforceable because the abuser has not been given adequate due process protections under VAWA.[83] Several experts have suggested that "victims of domestic violence not be charged any fees for filing of petitions for orders of protection or the service of process on those charged with committing acts of domestic violence."[84] In 2000, VAWA was amended to provide this relief.

Pursuant to VAWA 2000, all states were required to "certify that their laws, policies and practices do not require, in connection with the prosecution of any misdemeanor or felony domestic violence offense or in connection with the filing, issuance, registration, or service of a protection order, or a petition for a protection order, to protect a victim of domestic violence, stalking or sexual assault that the victim bear the costs associated with the filing of criminal charges against the offender or the costs associated with the filing, issuance, registration or service of a warrant, protection order, petition for a protection order or witness subpoena, whether issued inside or outside the State, tribal or local jurisdiction."[85] All Ohio courts and all units of local government were mandated to comply. By implication, the clerks of courts and all law enforcement agencies are included. Any charges for the prosecution of a domestic violence case as well as all costs associated with a stalking or domestic violence protection order are prohibited under VAWA. Ohio's laws were amended by 2002 H.B. 548, effective on March 31, 2003.[86]

In addition to prohibiting filing fees and costs for protection orders,[87] Ohio statutes were amended to prohibit costs to victims for the

---

[82]See RC 2935.032(F).

[83]See 18 U.S.C.A. § 2265(b)(2).

[84]Judge Susan B. Carbon et al., Enforcing Domestic Violence Protection Orders throughout the Country: New Frontiers of Protection for Victims of Domestic Violence, 50 Juv. & Fam. Ct. 2, 41 (1999).

[85]VAWA 2000, 42 U.S.C.A. § 3796hh-1(c)(1)(B)(4).

[86]See RC 3113.31(J), RC 2919.26(J), RC 2903.214(J), RC 2903.213(I); see also Text § 11:3, Filing issues.

[87]See R.C. 3113.31(J), 2919.26(J), 2903.214(J), 2903.213(I).

registration of protection orders[88] and language, substantially similar to the federal prohibition was included regarding service of process, service of warrants, and criminal charges for the prosecution of domestic violence cases. Additionally, Ohio law prohibits charging a fee for certified copies of a protection order.

Effective 9/17/2014, RC 311.31(J) and RC 2903.214(J) were again amended to prohibit a court from assessing costs and fees to a petitioner for the modification, enforcement, dismissal and withdrawal of a protection order or consent agreement as well as for witness subpoenas.[89] Hopefully, this amendment will eliminate costs and fees to a petitioner who withdraws a protection order or whose protection order is denied. However, under the recent amendment to RC 3113.31(J), a court may assess costs and fees to a respondent.[90]

Unfortunately, costs have been taxed to petitioners who file an appeal of the denial of a CPO or against petitioners who fail to prevail in their appeal.[91]

§ 18:10 Military Protection orders (MPO)[1]

Q & A: What is a military protection order (MPO)?

A Military Protection Order (MPO) is issued by a military commander to ensure the safety of service-members and family members from the threat of domestic violence. It is issued to preserve good order and discipline.[2] A MPO is a direct order to service-members to have no contact with a victim or designated places. It may also enjoin a service-member from doing certain things or require a service-member to move into government quarters. It may also require a service-member to provide support to other family members.[3]

A family member is eligible to file a MPO against any active duty member of the military if the commander agrees to it. The active duty member does not have to be a spouse or intimate partner but does have to be a service member.

If the abuser is a civilian spouse, the military commander can issue an order barring the spouse from the base.

Q & A: How are MPOs enforced?

---

[88]See RC 2919.272, RC 3113.31(N), RC 2919.26(G)(3), RC 2903.214(M).

[89]RC 3113.31(J)(1), eff. 9/17/2014; RC 2903.214(J)(1), eff. 9/17/2014.

[90]RC 3113.31(J)(2).

[91]See, for example, D.R. v. J.R., 2013-Ohio-2987, 2013 WL 3486845 (Ohio Ct. App. 9th Dist. Summit County 2013).

[Section 18:10]

[1]Representing Victims of intimate Partner Violence Connected with the Military, A Handbook for Civil Attorneys, Ellen C. Schell, J.D. The Battered Women's Justice Project (2013). See also Church, The Servicemembers Civil Relief Act: Protecting Victims of Domestic Violence in Protection Order Cases Involving the Military, 12 T.M. Cooley J. Prac. & Clinical L. 335 (2010).

[2]See Christine Hansen, A Considerable Service: An Advocate's Introduction to Domestic Violence and the Military, Vol.6(4) Domestic Violence Report (April/May 2001).

[3]Christine Hansen, A Considerable Service: An Advocate's Introduction to Domestic Violence and the Military, Vol.6(4) Domestic Violence Report (April/May 2001).

MPOs are enforceable by the military and are exclusively military responsibility. They are not enforceable by a civilian court. Local law enforcement agencies are prohibited from enforcing MPOs. They may, however, notify military police for incidents occurring off base and involving a service member.

An MPO is only enforceable while the service-member is attached to the commander that issued the order. If the service-member is transferred or discharged, the order is no longer valid. The commander has the authority to modify or terminate the MPO at any time.

A violation of a MPO constitutes a violation of a direct and lawful order and may subject the service member to prosecution under the Uniform Code of Military Justice. Apprehension and arrest are not mandatory. Possible sanctions include confinement to quarters, imposition of other sanctions, such as treatment or non-judicial punishment.[4]

Q & A: Can spouses obtain civil protection orders against military abusers?

Yes. A victim of domestic violence should obtain a civil protection order, if possible, because the military order may not protect her off base and will not result in an arrest if her military abuser violates it.[5] MPOs are not a substitute for a CPO which is judicially enforced.

In fact, obtaining both a MPO and a CPO can enhance victim safety and should be requested by victims so long as they contain consistent provisions.[6]

Q & A: Are civil protection orders enforceable on military bases?

Yes. Civil protection orders may be enforced on any military installation.[7]

Pursuant to the Armed Forces Domestic Security Act enacted in 2002, civilian protection orders are enforceable on military bases. Under 10 U.S.C.A. § 1561a "a civilian order of protection shall have the same force and effect on a military installation as such order has within the jurisdiction of the court that issued such order." A civilian order of protection has the same meaning as set forth in 18 U.S.C.A. § 2266(d)(5).[8]

Q & A: Are MPOs and CPOs accorded full faith and credit?

The Full Faith and Credit provisions of VAWA do not apply to MPOs

[4]Christine Hansen, A Considerable Service: An Advocate's Introduction to Domestic Violence and the Military, Vol.6(4) Domestic Violence Report (April/May 2001).

[5]Christine Hansen, A Considerable Service: An Advocate's Introduction to Domestic Violence and the Military, Vol.6(4) Domestic Violence Report (April/May 2001).

[6]See Judith Beals, (updated by Patricia Erwin) Understanding the Military Response to Domestic Violence: Tools for Civilian Advocates, Battered Women's Justice Project (2007).

[7]See V.A. Davidian, Domestic Violence Remedies, 28-FALL Fam. Advoc. 17 (2005); Jennifer Heintz, Safe at Home Base? A Look At The Military's New Approach To Dealing with Domestic Violence on Military Installations, 48 St. Louis U. L.J. 277 (2003).

[8]See also Text § 18:6, Federal crimes under VAWA.

for several reasons. A military installation is not included in the definition of state, territory or tribal land. A military abuser is not afforded due process; there is no requirement of reasonable notice and a hearing before a MPO is issued. MPOs are not court orders; they are administrative orders initiated and issued by the service member's military commander.[9]

On the other hand, a CPO is accorded full faith and credit.[10] However, service of the CPO and arrest of a service member is dependent on the relationship between the military command and local law enforcement.[11]

§ 18:11 Firearm offenses under VAWA[1]

Implicit in the domestic violence context is a threat or the reality of bodily injury. Because firearms provide a vehicle by which to make such a threat a reality, Congress has enacted legislation restricting possession of firearms by certain classes of persons when one of the parties has perpetrated domestic violence.[2]

Q & A: Is it a federal crime to possess a firearm while subject to a protection order?

It is a federal crime to possess a firearm and/or ammunition while subject to a valid or qualifying protection order.[3] Under 18 U.S.C.A. § 922(g)(8), only certain persons are protected parties. These intimate partners include spouses, former spouses, present or former cohabitants, a parent of a common child, or a child of the respondent.[4]

Dating relationships and persons who have never cohabited nor had

---

[9]Christine Hansen, A Considerable Service: An Advocate's Introduction to Domestic Violence and the Military, Vol.6(4) Domestic Violence Report (April/May 2001).

[10]See Text § 18:9, Other remedies under VAWA.

[11]See Text § 18:9, Other remedies under VAWA.

[Section 18:11]

[1]Kerri Fredheim, Closing the Loopholes in Domestic Violence Laws: The Constitutionality of 18 U.S.C. 922(g)(9), 19 Pace L. Rev. 445 (1999); see also Jodi L. Nelson, The Lautenberg Amendment: An Essential Tool for Combatting Domestic Violence, 75 N.D. L. Rev. 365 (1999). See also U.S. v. Napier, 233 F.3d 394, 2000 FED App. 0397P (6th Cir. 2000) (holding that 922(g)(8) does not violate due process, or the commerce clause, or the Second Amendment); U.S. v. Baker, 197 F.3d 211, 1999 FED App. 0392P (6th Cir. 1999). See also Text § 12:22, Remedies—Miscellaneous issues.

[2]See Susan Carbon, Peter MacDonald & Seema Zeya, Enforcing Domestic Violence Protection Orders Throughout the Country: New Frontiers of Protection for Victims of Domestic Violence (Part II), 50 Juv. and Fam. Ct. Journal 2, 43–48 (1999). See also Alison J. Nathan, At the Intersection of Domestic Violence and Guns: The Public Interest Exception and the Lauter-Berg Amendment, 85 Cornell L. Rev. 822 (2000); Darren Mitchell and Susan B. Carbon, Firearms and Domestic Violence: A Primer for Judges, 39(2) Court Rev. 32 (2002).

[3]18 U.S.C.A. § 922(g)(8). See U.S. v. Pierson, 139 F.3d 501 (5th Cir. 1998) (upholding the constitutionality of 18 U.S.C.A. § 922(g)(8)); U.S. v. Bostic, 168 F.3d 718 (4th Cir. 1999); U.S. v. Napier, 233 F.3d 394, 2000 FED App. 0397P (6th Cir. 2000); U.S. v. Henson, 55 F. Supp. 2d 528 (S.D. W. Va. 1999); U.S. v. Bunnell, 106 F. Supp. 2d 60 (D. Me. 2000); People v. Adams, 193 Misc. 2d 78, 747 N.Y.S.2d 909 (Sup 2002) (discussing elements of 18 U.S.C.A. § 922(g)(8)); United States v. Crespo, 2017 WL 685572 (S.D. N.Y. 2017) (slip opinion).

[4]See 18 U.S.C.A. § 921(a)(32).

a child with the respondent are not protected parties.[5] These individuals may still utilize various state law remedies that address firearm possession.[6]

Q & A: What is the relationship between state and federal law?

The constitutionality of the federal law has been upheld in *Conkle v. Wolfe*.[7] While State firearm laws need not be identical to federal laws, federal prohibitions apply regardless of whether they are consistent with state laws.

It is well within the authority of Ohio courts to recognize the federal restrictions contained in 18 U.S.C.A § 922(g)(8) and 18 U.S.C.A. § 922(g)(9) by explicitly restraining an individual subject to a protection order from possessing weapons or firearms. Ohios standardized protection order forms specifically permit an Ohio court to restrain a respondent from possessing, using, carrying, or obtaining a deadly weapon and further require a respondent to surrender all such weapons to law enforcement to be held in protective custody for the duration of the civil protection order or until further order of court.

Such restraints appear in the body of a protection order[8] as well as on the Warning Page[9] which advises respondents/defendants that they may be subject to federal penalties for possessing, transporting or accepting a firearm. In addition, the NCIC form[10] contains Brady Handgun Disqualifier information that is entered into the national law enforcement database.

Additionally, law enforcement officers are required to seize as contraband any deadly weapon used, threatened to be used or brandished in any incident of alleged domestic violence or violation of any protection order.[11]

Q & A: Why would a person want to rely on state rather than federal law?

Generally, a case brought pursuant to state law usually proceeds more quickly through the process. The federal process may be hindered by a lack of federal resources and time constraints. On the other hand, federal penalties and detention policies provide more protection for victims of domestic violence.

Q & A: What is the state courts role with respect to federal firearm law?

Both state and federal law address the issue of firearms but differ significantly in their approach. For example, under federal law, a person who is the subject of a qualifying protection order is not permitted to possess a firearm while the order is in effect. In contrast, state

[5]See 18 U.S.C.A. § 921(a)(32) for a definition of intimate partner.

[6]See, e.g., Sup. R. Form 10.01-H to Sup. R. Form 10.01-J; see also Text § 12:22, Remedies—Miscellaneous issues; Sup. R. Form 10.02-A.

[7]Conkle v. Wolfe, 131 Ohio App. 3d 375, 722 N.E.2d 586 (4th Dist. Athens County 1998).

[8]See Sup. R. Forms 10.01-H to 10.01-J.

[9]See Sup. R. Form 10.01-G.

[10]Sup. R. Form 10-A.

[11]RC 2935.03(B)(3)(h).

law imposes such a ban only when the court exercises its discretion to prohibit firearm possession as part of a protection order.

Q & A: Can a respondent legally possess a firearm when the protection order does not include a state law firearm prohibition yet otherwise satisfy the federal Gun Control Act requirements?

No. The issue raised here has more to do with the Supremacy Clause of the U.S. Constitution which, in certain situations, preempts or supercedes state law. This case would not trigger the Supremacy Clause; however, state courts would not be able to set aside federal firearm laws. Rather, both laws remain in force and would apply to the aforementioned situation. Although a respondent would not be subject to a state firearm prohibition in that the state court did not prohibit gun possession, the respondent would still be subject to federal prosecution under the federal firearms law, because the federal law is independent of state law.[12]

Q & A: What is the state courts role in the enforcement of the federal prohibition when it is the state court protection order that triggers the federal law?

Sometimes, a state court judge or magistrate may fail to check the NCIC box to inform that a certain respondent is Brady Disqualified, or omit checking the box that restrains the respondent from possessing firearms in the actual order. Further, a court may omit checking the NCIC box and interlineate that federal law does not apply against a certain respondent, believing that an omission would override the operation of 18 U.S.C.A. § 922(g)(8).

However, 18 U.S.C.A. § 922(g)(8) does not rely upon state law definitions or standards to determine whether a person is prohibited from possessing a firearm. Rather, the question of whether a protection order issued by a state court triggers the federal prohibition is determined solely by reference to the specific requirements of the federal statute.[13] In practice, this means that the particular findings and terms of the protection order must be assessed against the federal requirements and inquiry must be made into whether the federal notice and hearing requirements were satisfied.[14]

Thus, an otherwise qualifying protection order will still trigger the federal prohibition even if the issuing state court rules that the respondent is entitled to possess a firearm under state law or if the court fails to note on the order or NCIC form that the federal prohibition would apply. Simply put, state court judges do not determine the applicability of federal law.[15]

It is the nature of the conduct proscribed by the protection order

---

[12]Mitchell and Carbone, Firearms and Domestic Violence: A Primer for Judges, 39 Ct. Rev. 32 (Summer 2003).

[13]Mitchell and Carbone, Firearms and Domestic Violence: A Primer for Judges, 39 Ct. Rev. 32 (Summer 2003).

[14]Mitchell and Carbone, Firearms and Domestic Violence: A Primer for Judges, 39 Ct. Rev. 32 (Summer 2003).

[15]Mitchell and Carbone, Firearms and Domestic Violence: A Primer for Judges, 39 Ct. Rev. 32 (Summer 2003); but see State v. Haney, 197 Ohio App. 3d 152, 2011-Ohio-6023, 966 N.E.2d 921 (12th Dist. Clinton County 2011).

and/or the findings of fact included therein that determines whether federal law applies.[16] For example, protection orders that contain either the requisite findings (finding that a respondent engaged in acts of domestic violence) or prohibitory language (prohibiting a respondent from abusing or threatening a petitioner) or both would clearly trigger the subsequent enforcement of federal firearms law.

Q & A: What types of restraints must be ordered for a protection order to be a qualifying order?

The protection order must expressly restrain the defendant-respondent from harassing, stalking, or threatening an intimate partner or it must restrain the defendant-respondent from engaging in other conduct that would place an intimate partner in reasonable fear of bodily injury to that partner or his/her child.[17]

Q & A: Is an ex parte protection order a qualifying order for purposes of the federal firearm prohibition?

A reading of the statute suggests that the protection order must have been issued following an evidentiary hearing for which the defendant-respondent had notice of and an opportunity to participate.[18] Until the defendant-respondent has been served and has actual notice of the allegations against him/her,[19] he/she is not prohibited from possessing a firearm.[20] Thus, ex parte protection orders that have not been served on the defendant-respondent do not comply with the requirements of VAWA.[21]

Q & A: What specific findings must be included in a qualifying protection order?

The protection order must include a specific finding that the defendant represents a credible threat to the physical safety of the victim,[22] or must include an explicit[23] prohibition against the use, attempted use or threatened use of physical force against such intimate partner or child that would reasonable be expected to cause bodily injury.[24] Implicit in this is that the fear is based on a subjective belief

---

[16]Mitchell and Carbone, Firearms and Domestic Violence: A Primer for Judges, 39 Ct. Rev. 32 (Summer 2003).

[17]18 U.S.C.A. § 922(g)(8)(B); Sup. R. Form 10.01-H to Sup. R. Form 10.01-J.

[18]18 U.S.C.A. § 922(g)(8)(A). See U.S. v. Wilson, 159 F.3d 280 (7th Cir. 1998) (underlying hearing must provide minimum due process protections; defendant was provided advance notice of the action when he was served with the initial emergency order).

[19]See, e.g., U.S. v. Kafka, 222 F.3d 1129 (9th Cir. 2000).

[20]See Sup. R. Form 10-A.

[21]Darren Mitchell and Susan B. Carbon, Firearms and Domestic Violence: A Primer for Judges, 39(2) Court Rev. 32 (2002); see U.S. v. Calor, 340 F.3d 428, 2003 FED App. 0291P (6th Cir. 2003) (discussing at what point an ex parte order may provide actual notice).

[22]18 U.S.C.A. § 922(g)(8)(C)(i).

[23]See Magoon v. Thoroughgood, 148 N.H. 139, 803 A.2d 1070 (2002) (defining term "explicitly" as used in 18 U.S.C.A. § 922; see also U.S. v. Sanchez, 639 F.3d 1201 (9th Cir. 2011) (defining the term "explicit").

[24]18 U.S.C.A. § 922(g)(8)(C)(ii); see also Sup. R. Form 10-A. See, for example, U.S. v. Sanchez, 639 F.3d 1201 (9th Cir. 2011) (discussion of the requirements contained in 18 U.S.C.A. § 922(g)(8)(C) regarding explicit prohibitions on the use, at-

by the victim that the defendant would harm him/her. An objective component does not appear necessary.

Q & A: Is there an "official use" exception for police officers[25] or military personnel who are subject to a civil protection order?

Although the experts believe this to be true, there are no cases on point.[26] Pursuant to the Gun Control Act, as amended in 1994, 18 U.S.C.A. § 922(g)(8) covers persons subject to a qualifying protection order. Under federal law, persons subject to a qualifying protection order are generally prohibited from possessing any firearm or ammunition in or affecting commerce (or shipping or transporting any firearm or ammunition in interstate or foreign commerce, or receiving any such firearm or ammunition).

18 U.S.C.A. § 925(a)(1) is the so-called "Government Exception" or the "Official Use Exception" and provides a limited exception or relief from disability. This exception exempts government employees from certain federal firearm restrictions that infringe on their governmental duties. The exception "frees members of the armed forces and law enforcement agencies who might otherwise be prohibited from carrying firearms to do so in connection with their public responsibilities."[27]

Under § 925(a)(1), government employees subject to qualifying protection orders appear to be excluded from the firearm restrictions to the extent they use or possess government-issued firearms in their official capacities. In short, law enforcement officers, military members and other local, state, and federal employees are exempted from the firearms disabilities imposed by § 922(g)(8).

Q & A: How should attorneys representing victims of domestic violence respond to this apparent ambiguity?

Attorneys representing victims of domestic violence have a duty to assess and request firearm restrictions in civil protection orders whenever a client expresses concerns over weapons, even if the respondent is a law enforcement official or member of the military. At both the ex parte and full hearings, an independent inquiry should be made to assess whether a respondent owns or is in possession of weapons. If re-

---

tempted use or threatened use of physical force against an intimate partner or child that would reasonably be expected to cause bodily injury, which were not met by a no-contact order). But see U.S. v. Emerson, 270 F.3d 203, 263 (5th Cir. 2001) (noting that the fact that state law might not require express or explicit findings to that effect is not a fatal flaw); U.S. v. Bostic, 168 F.3d 718 (4th Cir. 1999); U.S. v. Larson, 843 F. Supp. 2d 641 (W.D. Va. 2012), aff'd, 502 Fed. Appx. 336 (4th Cir. 2013) (holding that a state court "no contact" order was contemplated by the mandates contained in 18 U.S.C.A. § 922(g)(8)).

[25]See Sup. R. Form 10.0-H, 10-01-I and 10.01-J providing that "Respondent shall not possess, use, carry or obtain any deadly weapon at any time while the Order remains in effect *unless Respondent is excepted for official use pursuant to 18 U.S.C. 925(a)(1).*" (emphasis added).

[26]See Darren Mitchell and Susan Carbon, Firearms and Domestic Violence: A Primer for Judges, 39(2) Court Rev. 32, 35 (2002).

[27]Lisa D. May, The Backfiring of the Domestic Violence Firearm Bans, 14 Colum. J. Gender & L. 1, 7 (2005), quoting U.S. v. Lewitzke, 176 F.3d 1022, 1027 n.4 (7th Cir. 1999). See also McBride v. McBride, 2012-Ohio-2146, 971 N.E.2d 1007 (Ohio Ct. App. 12th Dist. Butler County 2012) (noting that the *Brady* prohibition has exceptions for police officers regarding protection orders).

spondent owns or possesses weapons, the attorney has a duty to safely plan with a client and advocate for protection orders that require relinquishment, removal, or confiscation of these weapons.

However, attorneys must also advise their clients that some judges may consider the Government Exception set forth in 18 U.S.C.A. § 925(A)(1) and refuse to prohibit governmental employees from using or possessing their weapons in their official capacities. However, governmental employees are still prohibited from owning or possessing personal weapons.[28]

Additionally, it is also important to discuss financial issues with a client who depends on a police officer or member of the military as the sole breadwinner. If these governmental officials are prohibited from possessing weapons in their official capacities, they may lose their ability to earn a living.

Q & A: How do the federal mandates affect respondents?

Attorneys who represent respondents/defendants have a duty to inform their clients that if the federal mandates are satisfied, he or she may be prosecuted for mere possession of a weapon even if the defendant has not otherwise violated the protection order.[29]

Since some courts will refuse to acknowledge the exception for governmental officials, it is wise to address the potential for loss of employment with your client.

Q & A: Must the state protection order provide a notice or warning about the federal consequences under the Gun Control Act?

Yes. Prior to VAWA 2005, a state court was not required to provide notice of the existence or consequences of violating the federal firearms prohibition imposed by 18 U.S.C.A. § 922(g)(8) resulting from the issuance of a protection order. In fact, 18 U.S.C.A § 922(g)(8) had withstood several Fifth Amendment due process challenges relating to a lack of notice.[30]

VAWA 2005 directed all states who received federal STOP monies to certify that their local courts have judicial administrative policies and practices to provide notification to domestic violence offenders regarding federal, state or local laws addressing firearms and domestic violence regarding the requirements delineated in 18 U.S.C.A. § 922(g)(8) and (g)(9).

The Ohio General Assembly[31] enacted several provisions in order to effectuate compliance with the federal mandate. RC 3113.31(F)(2) was added to state that "upon the issuance of a protection order or the approval of a consent agreement under this section, the court shall provide the parties to the order or agreement with the following notice orally or by form:

---

[28]See Darren Mitchell and Susan Carbon, Firearms and Domestic Violence: A Primer for Judges, 39(2) Court Rev. 32, 35 (2002).

[29]See U.S. v. Wilson, 159 F.3d 280 (7th Cir. 1998).

[30]Fanny L. Haslebacher, Presentation on Firearms and Domestic Violence: Important Considerations for Judges, presented to National College of District Attorneys Thirteenth Annual National Conference on Domestic Violence (2002); see e.g. U.S. v. Kafka, 222 F.3d 1129 (9th Cir. 2000); U.S. v. Reddick, 203 F.3d 767 (10th Cir. 2000); U.S. v. Bostic, 168 F.3d 718 (4th Cir. 1999).

[31]Am. Sub. H. B. 562, eff. 7/1/2008.

NOTICE

As a result of this order or consent agreement, it may be unlawful for you to possess or purchase a firearm, including a rifle, pistol, or revolver, or ammunition pursuant to federal law under 18 USCA 922(g)(8) for the duration of the order. If you have any questions whether this law makes it illegal for you to possess or purchase a firearm or ammunition, you should consult an attorney.

This provision was also added to RC 2903.214(F)(2). Additionally, the notice requirement is necessary only when there is a domestic relationship between the petitioner and the respondent or the complainant and the defendant.[32]

Similar provisions were added to RC 2903.213(G)(2) and RC 2919.26(G)(2). Furthermore, in the criminal context the notice requirement applies both to protection orders and convictions for misdemeanor crimes involving violence.

However, it must be noted that for purposes of the federal firearms ban, only intimate partners are covered. Under RC 2903.213, only non-family or household members are covered. Because an "intimate partner" is defined as a spouse, former spouse or person who cohabits or has cohabited[33] with that person or a parent or child under 18 U.S.C.A. § 921(a)(32), dating relationships or strangers are not covered and therefore, the federal Notice provisions do not apply and should be deleted from the statute.

Q & A: What is the Brady Act and when is the subject of a protection order Brady disqualified for NCIC purposes?

The Brady Act[34] attempts to restrict certain groups of persons from obtaining handguns. Prior to NCIC, there was no centralized mechanism for firearms background checks and the Brady Act relied on the willingness of local sheriffs and other state law enforcement to conduct the checks. Since 1998, all background checks are conducted through NCIC before a firearm is transferred.[35]

In order to be Brady disqualified from possessing a firearm for NCIC purposes,[36] the respondent/offender must be subject to a qualifying protection order[37] or convicted of a misdemeanor crime of domestic violence.[38]

For purposes of a qualifying protection order, a respondent/offender must be an intimate partner.[39] Because the underlying protection order must protect an intimate partner or child of an intimate partner, other family or household members are not subject to the Brady

[32]See also RC 2943.033.

[33]Mann v. Helmig, 2007 WL 1035015 (E.D. Ky. 2007), aff'd, 289 Fed. Appx. 845 (6th Cir. 2008) (noting that the District Court has stated that cohabitates implies a sexual relationship).

[34]18 U.S.C.A. § 922(t).

[35]Barbara J. Hart, Mary B. Maleft, & Darren B. Mitchell, presentation on Firearms and Domestic Violence: State and Federal Crimes, for the National College of District Attorneys, 2001.

[36]Sup. R. Form 10-A.

[37]18 U.S.C.A. § 922(g)(8).

[38]18 U.S.C.A. § 922(g)(9).

[39]See 18 U.S.C.A. § 921(a)(32).

prohibitions. Additionally, a "qualifying protection order" is one that is issued after a hearing with notice[40] to the respondent/offender who is provided a right to participate.[41] Finally, there must be a specific finding that the respondent either presents a credible threat to the victim or prohibits the use of physical force.[42]

Q & A: On the NCIC form, the judge did not mark that I was Brady disqualified. How is it that the NCIC database still determined that I was Brady disqualified?

The determination of whether a protection order subjects an individual to federal firearms prohibitions is one made solely with reference to the criteria set forth in 18 U.S.C.A. § 922(g)(8) and is independent from a decision made by a state court. Nothing in the federal statute affects the applicability of state law or usurps a state court's jurisdiction under state law. Similarly, a state court does not have the authority to abrogate the federal Gun Control Act through findings that an individual may possess firearms under state law.[43] Section 922(g)(8) does not require that an otherwise qualified protection order contain findings restricting state or federal firearm possession. Likewise, an otherwise qualifying protection order does not fail simply because a state court rules, under state law, that an individual may possess firearms or is silent as to firearm rights. An omission in the NCIC form does not override federal law. Section 922(g)(8) has withstood repeated constitutional Commerce Clause and Tenth Amendment challenges.[44]

Q & A: Does it matter if the resolution of the protection order proceeding resulted in a consent agreement?[45]

It depends. First of all, this issue would only be raised in a civil protection order proceeding because consent agreements are an available remedy only in the civil context.[46]

All protection orders provide a restraint from harassing, stalking, or threatening or engaging in other conduct that would place an intimate partner in reasonable fear of bodily injury.[47] However, the

---

[40]U.S. v. Elkins, 2011 WL 1642271 (W.D. Va. 2011) (noting that the government will be required to prove beyond a reasonable doubt that Elkins knew of the existence of the domestic protective order, but it will not have to prove that he knew that he was prohibited from possessing a firearm, since ignorance of the law is not a defense in this case).

[41]See 18 U.S.C.A § 922(g)(8)(A); see also U.S. v. Bena, 2010 WL 1418389 (N.D. Iowa 2010), aff'd, 664 F.3d 1180 (8th Cir. 2011) (discussion of "notice").

[42]See 18 U.S.C.A. § 922(g)(8)(C).

[43]See Weissenburger v. Iowa Dist. Court for Warren County, 740 N.W.2d 431 (Iowa 2007).

[44]Fanny L Haslebacher, presentation on Firearms and Domestic Violence: Important Considerations for Judges, presented to the National College of District Attorneys Thirteenth Annual National Conference on Domestic Violence (2002); see also U.S. v. Emerson, 270 F.3d 203 (5th Cir. 2001); U.S. v. Napier, 233 F.3d 394, 2000 FED App. 0397P (6th Cir. 2000); U.S. v. Jones, 231 F.3d 508 (9th Cir. 2000); U.S. v. Meade, 175 F.3d 215 (1st Cir. 1999).

[45]See U.S. v. Wilson, 159 F.3d 280 (7th Cir. 1998); but see U.S. v. Spruill, 292 F.3d 207 (5th Cir. 2002). See also Text § 18:9, Other remedies under VAWA.

[46]See RC 3113.31(E)(3).

[47]See Sup. R. Forms 10.01-I and 10.01-J.

standardized consent entry order does not provide for specific findings,[48] and in fact, states that the parties agree to waive their right to request findings of fact and conclusions of law.[49]

To facilitate enforcement of the federal arms restrictions and to comply with Brady requirements, all civil protection orders issued by way of a consent agreement should include a specific finding that the respondent represents a credible threat to the physical safety of the victim.[50] However, if a consent order does prohibit the respondent from using physical force, it can be argued that such a restraint provides compliance.

Q & A: If a full hearing was scheduled and the respondent continues the hearing, does that make the protection order a non-qualifying order?

Not necessarily. Pursuant to 18 U.S.C.A. § 922(g)(8), a qualifying order is one that was issued after a hearing with notice. The statute is silent as to whether a hearing must be held or just provided to a respondent.

So long as the respondent was served with the order, was made aware of the allegations against him/her and was noticed with a full hearing date at which time he would have the right to participate, the protection order should be a "qualifying protection order." Any continuance filed that moves the date of the full hearing to another date should not change the status of the order. If, however, the respondent objects to the continuance, the protection order may no longer be considered a qualifying order as the respondent would lose his right to participate on a specific day.

Q & A: Does 18 U.S.C.A. § 922(g)(8) apply when a protection order was issued by consent and without a hearing?

In cases in which the court signs a consent agreement entered into between the parties, the fact that the parties and/or their attorneys met with the court constitutes a hearing, regardless of whether testimony was taken. Although the Gun Control Act fails to define the term, a "hearing" has been interpreted as "an opportunity to be heard, to present one's side of a case."[51]

Q & A: Does a court appearance wherein the court grants a continuance of the full hearing constitute a "hearing" under 18 U.S.C.A. § 922(g)(8)?

---

[48]See U.S. v. Emerson, 270 F.3d 203, 263 (5th Cir. 2001) (Fifth Circuit Court of Appeals noted that the fact that state law might not require express or explicit findings to that effect is not a fatal flaw); see also U.S. v. Bostic, 168 F.3d 718 (4th Cir. 1999). But see U.S. v. Sanchez, 639 F.3d 1201 (9th Cir. 2011).

[49]See Sup. R. Form 10.01-J.

[50]See 18 U.S.C.A. § 922(g)(8).

[51]See U.S. v. Wilson, 159 F.3d 280 (7th Cir. 1998); but see U.S. v. Spruill, 292 F.3d 207 (5th Cir. 2002) (holding that 922(g)(8) says that actual notice of the hearing means the hearing must have been set for a particular time and place and the defendant must have received notice of that and thereafter the hearing must have been held at that time and place and an agreement between the parties without an actual hearing fails to comply with 922(g)(8); because the parties' agreement was made pursuant to a special procedure, Spruill did not receive process and no hearing date was set).

This issue was raised in *United States v. Calor*.[52] In that case, the wife obtained an ex parte protection order, which was served on Mr. Calor by personal service. The order provided that Mr. Calor not possess any firearms and that all firearms in his possession were to be turned in to the local sheriff department. The hearing on the final order was continued for Mr. Calor to obtain counsel. He subsequently violated the protection order by returning to the marital residence. The responding officers searched his vehicle and found four handguns. Mr. Calor was indicted on one count of possessing a firearm in violation of 18 U.S.C.A. § 922(g)(8).

Appealing his conviction, Mr. Calor asserts that there was no hearing as required by the terms of 18 U.S.C.A. 922(g)(8). The Sixth Circuit Court of Appeals reasoned that "[w]hile we agree that the term has not been given a consistent meaning in federal law and its construction has been context dependent, the term is not ambiguous in this context. In order for a court proceeding to be the predicate hearing for a court order that triggers the 922(g)(8) firearm disability, the statute straightforwardly requires that the subject of the court order be given actual notice of the proceeding and an opportunity to participate.[53] The Court then held that the actual notice requirement is satisfied by the summons written into the ex parte protection order that was served on Calor and the opportunity to participate requirement is satisfied because Calor could have presented reasons why the court should not enter an order finding that he posed a credible threat to the safety of his wife or child.[54] Waiving his opportunity to be heard and to participate does not alter his status under 922(g)(8).[55]

Q & A: Does an ex parte protection order constitute a valid warrant for the search and seizure of weapons under the Fourth Amendment?

The Sixth Circuit Court of Appeals considered this question in *U.S. v. Calor*.[56] The Sixth Circuit noted that the lower court reasoned that the ex parte protection order included the authority for the sheriff to enter a residence to enforce the seizure of weapons and thus, the sheriffs were acting pursuant to a valid search warrant when they seized the firearm.[57] However, the Sixth Circuit reasoned that had Mr. Calor not given permission to enter his residence to conduct a search and the sheriffs had relied only on the ex parte order, "we would have a basis for considering whether an EPO, which requires

[52]U.S. v. Calor, 340 F.3d 428, 431, 2003 FED App. 0291P (6th Cir. 2003); but see U.S. v. Spruill, 292 F.3d 207 (5th Cir. 2002) (holding that a hearing is just that-an actual hearing; Calor's reliance on *Spruill* was misplaced because the domestic violence order was entered by agreement of the parties, but without the parties appearing before a judge at a noticed hearing).

[53]U.S. v. Calor, 340 F.3d 428, 431, 2003 FED App. 0291P (6th Cir. 2003); U.S. v. Wilson, 159 F.3d 280 (7th Cir. 1998); but see U.S. v. Collins, 2008 WL 817089 (E.D. Ky. 2008) (discussing actual notice and an opportunity to participate and distinguishing facts from those in *Calor* and *Wilson*).

[54]U.S. v. Calor, 340 F.3d 428, 431, 2003 FED App. 0291P (6th Cir. 2003).

[55]U.S. v. Calor, 340 F.3d 428, 431, 2003 FED App. 0291P (6th Cir. 2003); citing U.S. v. Wilson, 159 F.3d 280 (7th Cir. 1998).

[56]U.S. v. Calor, 340 F.3d 428, 2003 FED App. 0291P (6th Cir. 2003).

[57]U.S. v. Calor, 340 F.3d 428, 432, 2003 FED App. 0291P (6th Cir. 2003).

the removal of an alleged domestic abuser and his firearms from the home, is a valid search warrant under the Fourth Amendment."[58]

Q & A: If a client has a protection order obtained in a state court, does that person have state remedies related to firearm possession available to them?

Where there is a prohibition against firearms in the protection order, the victim is entitled to state law enforcement in addition to federal enforcement.[59] However, if the prohibition does not appear in the protection order and the victim meets the requirements of the federal statute, the victim will only be entitled to federal law enforcement.[60] Attorneys should be cautioned that, because it is often difficult to enforce this provision in federal court, it is important to include a firearms prohibition in the protection order.[61] Additionally, because individual states have also enacted restrictions concerning firearms which may be included in state court orders, these restrictions must be given full faith and credit by enforcing jurisdictions, just like any portions of a protection order.[62]

Q & A: What remedies are provided a non-qualifying victim?

Any victim granted a civil or criminal protection order may also utilize the state law remedies, provided the remedy is set forth in the protection order. Pursuant to Ohio's standardized forms, a court may order a respondent not to possess, use, carry or obtain any deadly weapon.[63] Respondents are ordered to turn over all deadly weapons in their possession to the law enforcement agencies who serve respondent with the order. Additionally, any law enforcement agency receiving deadly weapons shall hold them in protective custody until further court order.[64]

If a victim does not qualify as an intimate partner, state law is the only remedy open to a victim or other family or household member. If a victim is issued an ex parte protection order, the state law remedies apply until service is perfected and a hearing is provided. If a consent entry is considered a non-qualifying protection order, a victim may only utilize state law remedies.

The disadvantage of the state remedy is that all protection orders that comply with the federal statute are now entered into the NCIC database. All law enforcement agencies have access to the database and respondents/offenders may be deterred from possessing firearms

---

[58]U.S. v. Calor, 340 F.3d 428, 432, 2003 FED App. 0291P (6th Cir. 2003).

[59]See U.S. v. Bostic, 168 F.3d 718 (4th Cir. 1999) (court held that 18 U.S.C.A. § 922(g)(8) does not interfere with states' domestic relations laws); see also U.S. v. Visnich, 109 F. Supp. 2d 757 (N.D. Ohio 2000) (district court held that 18 U.S.C.A. § 922(g)(8) is constitutional and firearm possession can be regulated by Congress).

[60]Judge Susan B. Carbon et al., Enforcing Domestic Violence Protection Orders throughout the Country: New Frontiers of Protection for Victims of Domestic Violence, 50 Juv. & Fam. Ct. 2, 45 (1999).

[61]Sup. R. Form 10.01-H to Sup. R. Form 10.01-J.

[62]See, e.g., Conkle v. Wolfe, 131 Ohio App. 3d 375, 722 N.E.2d 586 (4th Dist. Athens County 1998); Woolum v. Woolum, 131 Ohio App. 3d 818, 723 N.E.2d 1135 (12th Dist. Preble County 1999).

[63]See Sup. R. Form 10.01-H to Sup. R. Form 10.01-J, Sup. R. Form 10.02-A.

[64]See Sup. R. Form 10.01-H to Sup. R. Form 10.01-J, Sup. R. Form 10.02-A.

if they knew they were prohibited from doing so. At least background checks enable gun dealers to discover this information before transferring a firearm to a person subject to a qualifying protection order or convicted of a misdemeanor crime of domestic violence.

Q & A: Can any charges be filed against the gun dealer or another who sells a firearm to the respondent/offender?

Yes. Under 18 U.S.C.A. § 922(d)(8), it is now a federal crime to knowingly transfer or sell a firearm to a person subject to a valid protection order. Law enforcement officers are exempt from this provision if the intended use of the firearm is professional.

Q & A: If a defendant was convicted for the crime of domestic violence, is he/she also prohibited from possessing a firearm?[65]

Under 18 U.S.C.A. § 922(g)(9),[66] it is now a federal crime to possess a firearm and/or ammunition after a conviction for a misdemeanor crime of domestic violence.[67] This provision applies to convictions both before and after September 30, 1996.[68]

A qualifying domestic violence crime must be committed by an intimate partner. The Gun Control Act defines an intimate partner as a current or former spouse, parent of a child in common or a current or past cohabitant.[69] The qualifying crime must be committed by a current or former spouse, parent or guardian of the victim, by a person

[65]See U.S. v. Tooley, 717 F. Supp. 2d 580 (S.D. W. Va. 2010), aff'd, 468 Fed. Appx. 357 (4th Cir. 2012) (holding that the statute prohibiting those convicted of misdemeanor crimes of domestic violence from possessing a firearm does not violate the Second Amendment); see also Harvard Law Review Association, Constitutional Law—Second Amendment—En Banc Seventh Circuit Holds Prohibition on Firearm Possession by Domestic Violence Misdemeanants to be Constitutional.—United States v. Skoien, 614 F.3d 638 (7th Cir. 2010) (en banc), 124 Harv. L. Rev. 1074 (2011) (noting that the Seventh Circuit Court of Appeals found a substantial relationship between the goal of reducing domestic violence and a lifetime ban on firearm possession by domestic violence misdemeanants); John Wilkinson and Toolsi Gowin Meisner, Domestic Violence and Firearms: A Deadly Combination, 3 Strategies 2011.

[66]See Kerri Fredheim, Closing the Loopholes in Domestic Violence Laws: The Constitutionality of 18 U.S.C. 922(g)(9), 19 Pace L. Rev. 445 (Spring 1999). See also Tom Lininger, A Better Way to Disarm Batterers, 54 Hastings L.J. 525 (2003); Melanie L. Mecka, Seizing the Ammunition From Domestic Violence: Prohibiting the Ownership of Firearms by Abusers, 29 Rutgers L.J. 607 (1998). But see Lisa D. May, The Backfiring of the Domestic Violence Firearms Ban, 14 Colum. J. Gender & L. 1 (2005).

[67]18 U.S.C.A. § 921(a)(33). See U.S. v. Smith, 964 F. Supp. 286 (N.D. Iowa 1997), judgment aff'd, 171 F.3d 617 (8th Cir. 1999); see also U.S. v. Meade, 986 F. Supp. 66 (D. Mass. 1997), aff'd, 175 F.3d 215 (1st Cir. 1999); U.S. v. Boyd, 52 F. Supp. 2d 1233 (D. Kan. 1999), aff'd, 211 F.3d 1279 (10th Cir. 2000); U.S. v. Costigan, 2000 WL 898455 (D. Me. 2000), judgment aff'd, 18 Fed. Appx. 2 (1st Cir. 2001); U.S. v. Kavoukian, 315 F.3d 139 (2d Cir. 2002) (recognizing that several circuits have determined that any ambiguity was cleared by legislative history). But see U.S. v. Finnell, 27 Fed. Appx. 166 (4th Cir. 2001) (holding that a conviction for a misdemeanor crime of domestic violence under 18 U.S.C.A. § 922(g)(9) does not violate either the Second Amendment or the Full Faith and Credit Clause of the U.S. Constitution.); U.S. v. Nason, 9 F.3d 155, 39 Fed. R. Evid. Serv. 1294 (1st Cir. 1993); U.S. v. White, 258 F.3d 374 (5th Cir. 2001) (the predicate offenses were not misdemeanor crimes of domestic violence).

[68]U.S. v. Lewitzke, 176 F.3d 1022 (7th Cir. 1999); see also National Ass'n of Government Employees, Inc. v. Barrett, 968 F. Supp. 1564 (N.D. Ga. 1997), aff'd, 155 F.3d 1276 (11th Cir. 1998); U.S. v. Hicks, 992 F. Supp. 1244 (D. Kan. 1997).

[69]18 U.S.C.A. § 921(a)(32); but see U.S. v. Shelton, 325 F.3d 553 (5th Cir. 2003)

with whom the victim shares a child in common, by a person who is cohabiting with or has cohabited with the victim as a spouse, parent or guardian or by a person similarly situated to a spouse, parent or guardian of the victim.[70]

A qualifying domestic violence crime must have as an element of the crime the use or attempted use of physical force or the threatened use of a deadly weapon.[71] It must be a misdemeanor under federal or state law. However, at least one court has stated that what constitutes a conviction of a misdemeanor crime must be defined by federal law.

In *United States v. Cadden*,[72] the defendant pled no contest to a misdemeanor crime of domestic violence and completed a term of probation. He was later charged with possession of firearms. The question presented was whether his no-contest plea to the domestic violence misdemeanor in Rhode Island is a misdemeanor conviction under federal firearms statutes.

The Rhode Island District Court noted that 18 U.S.C.A. § 922(g)(9) prohibits the possession of a firearm by anyone previously convicted of a misdemeanor crime of domestic violence. The court then reasoned that "the omission of any reference to state law was Congress's clear message to the courts that the determination of whether or not a conviction is a conviction for purposes of 18 U.S.C.A. § 922(g)(9) must be decided as a matter of federal, not state law."[73]

Q & A: How is "use or attempted use of physical force"

(holding that domestic relationship required for conviction for federal offense was not required to be contained as element of predicate state offense); U.S. v. Watkins, 407 F. Supp. 2d 825 (E.D. Ky. 2006).

[70] 18 U.S.C.A. § 921(a)(33); see U.S. v. Cuervo, 354 F.3d 969, 63 Fed. R. Evid. Serv. 567 (8th Cir. 2004), cert. granted, judgment vacated on other grounds, 543 U.S. 1099, 125 S. Ct. 1050, 160 L. Ed. 2d 994 (2005) (discussing the term "similarly situated to a spouse"; statute prohibiting possession of firearm by an ineligible person was not unconstitutionally vague as applied to defendant who had been convicted of a misdemeanor crime of domestic violence perpetrated against his secretary with whom he had an affair); U.S. v. Shelton, 325 F.3d 553 (5th Cir. 2003) (defendant's live-in girlfriend of two months was considered similarly situated to a spouse for purposes of federal offense). See also U.S. v. England, 2014 WL 4988149 (S.D. Ohio 2014) (case law suggests that victim need not have lived with defendant so long as they shared an intimate personal relationship).

[71] See People v. Adams, 193 Misc. 2d 78, 747 N.Y.S.2d 909, 917 (Sup 2002) (discussing what is necessary to establish the "use or attempted use of physical force" element; court held all that is necessary is that the individual "be convicted of a crime containing an element of an act which was intended to cause pain or injury to another, coupled with the apparent ability to execute such act"), quoting U.S. v. Smith, 171 F.3d 617, 621 (8th Cir. 1999); see also U.S. v. Huntley, 2007 WL 581622 (N.D. Iowa 2007), report and recommendation adopted, 2007 WL 778403 (N.D. Iowa 2007).

[72] U.S. v. Cadden, 98 F. Supp. 2d 193 (D.R.I. 2000).

[73] U.S. v. Cadden, 98 F. Supp. 2d 193, 197 (D.R.I. 2000); see also U.S. v. Nobriga, 474 F.3d 561 (9th Cir. 2006) (abrogated by, Voisine v. U.S., 136 S. Ct. 2272, 195 L. Ed. 2d 736 (2016)) (abrogating court finding reckless domestic assault qualifies as a misdemeanor crime of domestic violence under statute prohibiting possession of a firearm by person convicted of a misdemeanor crime of domestic violence); U.S. v. Hayes, 482 F.3d 749 (4th Cir. 2007), rev'd and remanded, 555 U.S. 415, 129 S. Ct. 1079, 172 L. Ed. 2d 816, 50 A.L.R. Fed. 2d 639 (2009) (reversing court holding domestic relationship need not be a defining element of the predicate offense to support a conviction for possession of a firearm by a person convicted of misdemeanor crime of domestic violence).

defined for purposes of 18 U.S.C.A. § 922(g)(9) and 18 U.S.C.A. § 921(a)(33)(A)(ii)?

18 U.S.C.A. § 922(g)(9) provides that "[i]t shall be unlawful for any person who has been convicted in any court of a misdemeanor crime of domestic violence, to ship or transport in interstate or foreign commerce, or to possess in or affecting commerce, any firearm or ammunition; or to receive any firearm or ammunition which has been shipped or transported in interstate or foreign commerce." "A misdemeanor crime of domestic violence has, as an element of the offense, the use or attempted use of physical force or the threatened use of a deadly weapon, committed by a person having a domestic relationship with the victim."[74]

The circuit courts appear to be split over how much physical force is necessary for the gun bans.[75] Many of the circuit courts have held that the predicate offense merely needs an element of offensive contact such as simple battery or assault.[76] Other courts have determined that the predicate offense must be more than mere contact; rather, it must be violent in nature.[77]

For example and of special interest to Ohio legal experts is the case of *U. S. v. Castleman.*[78] The Sixth Circuit Court of Appeals had advanced a standard to be applied when determining whether a conviction qualifies as a predicate offense for possession of a firearm by a person convicted of a misdemeanor crime of domestic violence.

In this case, Castleman pleaded guilty to misdemeanor domestic assault. To be convicted under Tennessee law, a person is guilty of assault if that person intentionally, knowingly or recklessly causes bodily injury to another or intentionally or knowingly causes another to reasonably fear imminent bodily injury or intentionally or knowingly causes physical contact with another and a reasonable person would regard the contact as extremely offensive or provocative.[79] Several years later, federal agents discovered that Castlemen and his wife were buying firearms and selling them on the black market and Castleman was indicted on two counts of possession of a firearm after

[74]18 U.S.C.A. § 921(a)(33)(A)(ii).

[75]See Joshua M. Jones, 18 U.S.C. § 922(g)(9) and the Circuit Split: The Case for a Broad Definition of Domestic Violence, 45 No. 1 Crim. Law. Bull. 3 (2009) (noting that the federal gun bans do not include threats unless they are made with a deadly weapon); see also Wilhoit v. N. Olmsted, 151 Ohio Misc. 2d 21, 2009-Ohio-1702, 905 N.E.2d 723 (Mun. Ct. 2009); Com. v. Gorassi, 432 Mass. 244, 733 N.E.2d 106 (2000).

[76]See U.S. v. Griffith, 455 F.3d 1339 (11th Cir. 2006); see also U.S. v. Smith, 171 F.3d 617 (8th Cir. 1999).

[77]U.S. v. Belless, 338 F.3d 1063 (9th Cir. 2003) (abrogated by, U.S. v. Castleman, 572 U.S. 157, 134 S. Ct. 1405, 188 L. Ed. 2d 426 (2014)) (abrogating court finding common law meaning of force applied to meaning of force in definition of misdemeanor crime of domestic violence); but see Joshua M. Jones, 18 U.S.C.A. § 922(g)(9) and the Circuit Split: The Case for a Broad Definition of Domestic Violence, 45 No. 1 Crim. Law Bull. 3 (2009) (arguing for a broad definition of 18 U.S.C.A. § 922(g)(9)).

[78]U.S. v. Castleman, 695 F.3d 582 (6th Cir. 2012), rev'd and remanded, 572 U.S. 157, 134 S. Ct. 1405, 188 L. Ed. 2d 426 (2014).

[79]U.S. v. Castleman, 695 F.3d 582, 584 (6th Cir. 2012), rev'd and remanded, 572 U.S. 157, 134 S. Ct. 1405, 188 L. Ed. 2d 426 (2014); Tenn. Code Ann. § 39-13-101.

being convicted of misdemeanor domestic violence which is defined as having as an element, the use or attempted use of physical force.[80]

The U.S. District Court for the Western District of Tennessee dismissed the counts reasoning that the misdemeanor domestic assault conviction did not qualify as a domestic violence crime requiring the use or attempted use of physical force as defined in 18 U.S.C.A. § 921(a)(33)(A)(ii). "Drawing upon cases from some of our sister circuits, the district court read § 921(a)(33)(A)(ii) to require 'force in the sense of violent contact' instead of merely 'force as a scientific concept relating to the movement of matter.'(Order 5, R. 108) In adopting the construction of § 922(g)(9), the district court rejected the construction adopted by other circuits and urged by the government, under which a domestic assault conviction resulting from 'subtle and indirect uses of physical force' would permit liability under § 922(g)(9). (Gov't Br. 18.) Reasoning that Tennessee Code § 39-13-111(b)(1) would permit a conviction for assaultive conduct not involving physical contact, the court concluded that Castleman's conviction did not qualify as a predicate offense for purposes of § 922(g)(9)."[81]

In order to determine whether a conviction qualifies as a predicate offense for possession of a firearm by a person convicted of a misdemeanor crime of domestic violence, a federal appellate court must first determine the degree of force necessary for a misdemeanor domestic battery offense to qualify as a misdemeanor crime of domestic violence.[82] Once that is decided, a court applies the "categorical approach" in which a court looks to the statutory definition of the offense and not the particular facts underlying the conviction. "If a defendant can violate the statute in a manner that involves the use or attempted use of physical force and in a manner that does not, [a court] 'may consider the indictment, guilty plea or similar documents to determine whether they necessarily establish the nature of the prior conviction.' "[83]

"The touchstone of the government's argument is that § 922(g)(9)'s reference to misdemeanor domestic violence crimes triggers § 922(g)(9) liability for a defendant convicted of any generic, common-law assault and battery offense that involves no more than slight physical touching."[84] However, the Castleman court relied on the reasoning of

---

[80]U.S. v. Castleman, 695 F.3d 582, 584 (6th Cir. 2012), rev'd and remanded, 572 U.S. 157, 134 S. Ct. 1405, 188 L. Ed. 2d 426 (2014).

[81]U.S. v. Castleman, 695 F.3d 582, 584-85 (6th Cir. 2012), rev'd and remanded, 572 U.S. 157, 134 S. Ct. 1405, 188 L. Ed. 2d 426 (2014).

[82]U.S. v. Castleman, 695 F.3d 582, 585 (6th Cir. 2012), rev'd and remanded, 572 U.S. 157, 134 S. Ct. 1405, 188 L. Ed. 2d 426 (2014). See also U.S. v. Gatson, 776 F.3d 405 (6th Cir. 2015) (the 6th Circuit Court found that the holding in *Castleman* does not support defendant's argument in which he infers that every act of domestic violence would be considered nonviolent in a nondomestic context, where his convictions satisfied the definition of a violent felony); United States v. Williams, 655 Fed. Appx. 419 (6th Cir. 2016).

[83]U.S. v. Castleman, 695 F.3d 582, 585 (6th Cir. 2012), rev'd and remanded, 572 U.S. 157, 134 S. Ct. 1405, 188 L. Ed. 2d 426 (2014), quoting U.S. v. Hays, 526 F.3d 674, 679 (10th Cir. 2008), citing Shepard v. U.S., 544 U.S. 13, 26, 125 S. Ct. 1254, 161 L. Ed. 2d 205 (2005).

[84]U.S. v. Castleman, 695 F.3d 582, 585 (6th Cir. 2012), rev'd and remanded, 572

United States v. Anderson,[85] in which the Sixth Circuit decided that a defendant's aggravated assault conviction qualified as a violent felony under § 924(e)(2)(B) because the underlying Ohio statute required the defendant to knowingly cause "serious physical harm to another."

> Undertaking a categorical analysis of the Ohio statute, we concluded that "only by knowingly using force capable of causing physical pain or injury, *i.e.*, violent physical force," can a defendant cause serious physical injury to a victim. [*Anderson*] at 32. And reasoning that "the degree of injury has a 'logical relation to the use of physical force,'" our ruling was grounded in the fact that proof of a "serious" physical injury was required to obtain a conviction and, in turn, to qualify the conviction as a violent felony. *Id.* at 34 (quoting De Leon Castellanos v. Holder, 652 F.3d 762, 766 (7th Cir. 2011).
>
> In this case, by contrast, the [Tennessee] statute does not require proof of a serious physical injury. Rather, it requires proof of just some physical injury, regardless of how slight.[86]

Thus, Castleman's conviction under Tennessee law in which he caused an unspecified bodily injury is not a misdemeanor crime of domestic violence. Because Castleman's indictment adopts the language of the statute but does not specify the type or severity of the injury he caused, the Circuit court was unable to conclude that his domestic violence assault conviction entailed violent physical force.[87]

On March 26, 2014, the United States Supreme Court issued its opinion in *Castleman*.[88] In reversing and remanding the case back to the lower court, Justice Sotomayor focused on the dynamics of domestic violence when considering how much force is necessary for the federal gun ban. She noted that "because perpetrators of domestic violence are routinely prosecuted under applicable assault or battery laws, it makes sense for Congress to have classified as a 'misdemeanor crime of domestic violence' the type of conduct that supports a common-law battery conviction."[89] Therefore, it was logical that Congress meant to incorporate that misdemeanor-specific definition of "force" in defining "misdemeanor crime of domestic violence."[90] Thus, the physical force requirement of § 922(g)(9) is satisfied by the degree of force that supports a common law battery conviction, namely offensive touching.[91]

Justice Sotomayor reasoned that where the word "violent" or

U.S. 157, 134 S. Ct. 1405, 188 L. Ed. 2d 426 (2014).

[85]U.S. v. Anderson, 695 F.3d 390 (6th Cir. 2012).

[86]U.S. v. Castleman, 695 F.3d 582, 590 (6th Cir. 2012), rev'd and remanded, 572 U.S. 157, 134 S. Ct. 1405, 188 L. Ed. 2d 426 (2014).

[87]U.S. v. Castleman, 695 F.3d 582, 591 (6th Cir. 2012), rev'd and remanded, 572 U.S. 157, 134 S. Ct. 1405, 188 L. Ed. 2d 426 (2014).

[88]U.S. v. Castleman, 572 U.S. 157, 134 S. Ct. 1405, 188 L. Ed. 2d 426 (2014).

[89]U.S. v. Castleman, 572 U.S. 157, 134 S. Ct. 1405, 1411, 188 L. Ed. 2d 426 (2014).

[90]U.S. v. Castleman, 572 U.S. 157, 134 S. Ct. 1405, 1411, 188 L. Ed. 2d 426 (2014).

[91]U.S. v. Vinson, 794 F.3d 418 (4th Cir. 2015), on reh'g, 805 F.3d 120 (4th Cir. 2015). But see Wysocki v. Oberlin Police Dept., 2014-Ohio-2869, 2014 WL 2957713 (Ohio Ct. App. 9th Dist. Lorain County 2014) (applying *Castleman* and finding that the elements of the crime for which defendant was convicted (criminal mischief after a plea even though he was charged with domestic violence) did not contain the

"violence" standing alone "would connote a substantial degree of force,"[92] that is not true of domestic violence. " 'Domestic violence' is not merely a type of 'violence'; it is a term of art encompassing acts that one might not characterize as 'violent' in a nondomestic violence context."[93] She relied heavily on the amicus brief of NNEDV which stressed the dynamic of domestic violence and that acts of hitting, slapping, shoving, grabbing, pinching, biting and hair pulling are considered domestic violence. "Indeed, 'most physical assaults committed against women and men by intimates are relatively minor and consist of pushing, grabbing, shoving, slapping and hitting.' "[94] Justice Sotomayor added that minor uses of force, accumulated over time, can subject one intimate partner to the other's control. "If a seemingly minor act like this (squeezing of the arm) draws the attention of the authorities and leads to a successful prosecution for a misdemeanor offense, it does not offend common sense or the English language to characterize the resulting conviction as a 'misdemeanor crime of domestic violence.' "[95] Of interest is that Justice Scalia concurred in the judgment but admonished the majority for ignoring the authorities and instead, basing its definition on an amicus brief.[96]

The importance of this decision cannot be overstated. First, the Court decided on a low threshold for the "physical force" necessary to apply the federal forearms prohibition. Additionally, trial courts will not be forced to structure their judgment entries so as to include a provision indicating specific findings of fact that a defendant committed some objective violent physical injury as well as a description of that injury.

Q & A: Whether a misdemeanor crime of domestic violence includes the "reckless" use of force for purposes of 18 U.S.C. 922(g)(9)?

In light of the *Castleman* decision, the United States Supreme Court, in *Armstrong v. United States*,[97] remanded and ordered the First Circuit Court of Appeals to reconsider its decisions in *U.S. v. Armstrong*,[98] and *U.S. v. Voisine*.[99] In consolidated cases, the First

---

requisite element of physical force necessary for his conviction to be considered a misdemeanor crime of domestic violence).

[92]U.S. v. Castleman, 572 U.S. 157, 134 S. Ct. 1405, 1411, 188 L. Ed. 2d 426 (2014), quoting Johnson v. U.S., 559 U.S. 133, 140, 130 S. Ct. 1265, 176 L. Ed. 2d 1 (2010).

[93]U.S. v. Castleman, 572 U.S. 157, 134 S. Ct. 1405, 1411, 188 L. Ed. 2d 426 (2014), citing Brief for National Network to End Domestic Violence et al. as Amicus Curiae 4-9; DOJ Office on Violence Against Women, online at http://www.ovw.usdoj.gov/domviolence.

[94]U.S. v. Castleman, 572 U.S. 157, 134 S. Ct. 1405, 1411, 188 L. Ed. 2d 426 (2014), quoting DOJ, P. Tjaden & N. Thoennes, Extent, Nature and Consequences of Intimate Partner Violence 11 (2000).

[95]U.S. v. Castleman, 572 U.S. 157, 134 S. Ct. 1405, 1412, 188 L. Ed. 2d 426 (2014).

[96]U.S. v. Castleman, 572 U.S. 157, 134 S. Ct. 1405, 1420–21, 188 L. Ed. 2d 426 (2014).

[97]Armstrong v. U.S., 572 U.S. 1032, 134 S. Ct. 1759, 188 L. Ed. 2d 590 (2014).

[98]U.S. v. Armstrong, 706 F.3d 1 (1st Cir. 2013), cert. granted, judgment vacated, 572 U.S. 1032, 134 S. Ct. 1759, 188 L. Ed. 2d 590 (2014).

Circuit issued its opinion on January 30, 2015, in *U.S. v. Voisine.*[100] Both Voisine and Armstrong had been convicted under state law misdemeanor crimes of domestic violence as defined in 18 U.S.C. 921(a)(33)(A), and which statutes allowed convictions based on a recklessness *mens rea*. Subsequently, both had been federally charged for possessing firearms in violation of 18 U.S.C. 922(g)(9). Both filed motions to dismiss the charges, arguing that their indictments did not charge a federal offense and that § 922(g)(9) violated the Constitution. The district court denied the motions and both defendants entered guilty pleas conditioned on the right to appeal. The cases were appealed to the U.S. Supreme Court who vacated the judgments and remanded the cases back to the Circuit Court of Appeals.

The predicate offenses in these cases were convictions under Maine assault statutes which provides that "[a] person is guilty of assault if [t]he person intentionally, knowingly or recklessly causes bodily injury or offensive physical contact to another person."[101] The question presented was whether Maine's definition of recklessness fits within § 921(a)(33)(A)'s "use of physical force" language.

In affirming the judgments of guilt, the majority determined that "[t]he question before us is a narrow one. We are asked to decide whether a conviction for reckless assault against a person in a domestic relationship in Maine constitutes a federal 'misdemeanor crime of domestic violence.' Congress in passing the Lautenberg Amendment recognized that guns and domestic violence are a lethal combination, and singled out firearm possession by those convicted of domestic violence offenses from firearm possession in other contexts. *Castleman* recognizes as much."[102] Therefore, reckless assault in Maine can be considered a "use of force" requirement within the meaning of a "misdemeanor crime of domestic violence" for purposes of ¶ 922(g)(9) because it includes an element of intentionality and specificity.

Interestingly, the dissent in *Voisine* stressed that the majority erroneously framed the question and failed to resolve the seminal issue of "whether a Maine conviction for the 'reckless' causation of an 'offensive physical contact' necessarily involves the 'use or attempted use of physical force' as required to establish a 'misdemeanor crime of domestic violence' for purposes of 18 U.S.C. ¶ 922(g)(9). The majority fails to persuasively explain why, *in all cases*, the merely reckless causation of offensive physical contact categorically must involve the 'use or attempted use of physical force,' 18 U.S.C. ¶ 921(a)(33)(A), particularly in light of the host of cases that strongly suggest otherwise. As explained herein, these cases hold that the 'use' of phys-

[99]U.S. v. Voisine, 495 Fed. Appx. 101 (1st Cir. 2013), cert. granted, judgment vacated, 572 U.S. 1032, 134 S. Ct. 1759, 188 L. Ed. 2d 590 (2014).

[100]U.S. v. Voisine, 778 F.3d 176 (1st Cir. 2015), aff'd, 136 S. Ct. 2272, 195 L. Ed. 2d 736 (2016).

[101]U.S. v. Voisine, 778 F.3d 176, 178 (1st Cir. 2015), aff'd, 136 S. Ct. 2272, 195 L. Ed. 2d 736 (2016).

[102]U.S. v. Voisine, 778 F.3d 176, 187 (1st Cir. 2015), aff'd, 136 S. Ct. 2272, 195 L. Ed. 2d 736 (2016).

ical force requires the active or intentional employment of force, which cannot be satisfied by merely reckless conduct."[103]

Of significance is that the majority of the court specifically stressed that the decision was "informed by congressional recognition in § 922(g)(9) of the special risks posed by firearm possession by domestic abusers. 'Domestic violence often escalates in severity over time. . .and the presence of a firearm increases the likelihood that it will escalate to a homicide . . ..' *Castleman*, 134 S.Ct. at 1408." The Court also pointed out that the federal sentencing scheme should consider each state's choice as to how to define its own crimes, through statutory text and judicial decision.[104]

Additionally, the Court recognized the importance of the *Castleman* rationale to "ensure that individuals who engage in the 'seemingly minor act[s]' that actually constitute domestic violence, like squeezing or shoving, may not possess a firearm. Castleman, 134 S.Ct. at 1412. This range of predicate acts is broader than that found in other federal prohibitions involving the use of physical force."[105]

The *Voisine* case went back up to the Supreme Court and a decision was rendered on June 27, 2016.[106] Once again the question to be decided was a narrow one-whether state misdemeanor assault convictions for reckless (contrasted to knowing or intentional) conduct trigger the statutory firearms ban.[107]

Both Voisine and Armstrong argued that a federal statute that prohibited them from owning firearms because of misdemeanor domestic violence convictions[108] violated their civil rights. The majority opinion first presented the statutory structure and addressed the federal firearms ban language which states that the misdemeanor offense of domestic violence must have, "as an element, the use or attempted use of physical force." It is important to note that many states have enacted domestic violence assault misdemeanor statutes that have extended their reach to anyone "intentionally, knowingly or recklessly" causing offensive physical contact.

The Court began its analysis by adopting the Model Penal Code's definition of *mens rea*-the mental states required for criminal convictions. "Statutory text and background alike leads us to conclude that a reckless domestic assault qualifies as a misdemeanor crime of domestic violence under 922(g)(9)."[109] "Because fully two-thirds of such state laws extend to recklessness, construing 922(g)(9) to exclude

---

[103]U.S. v. Voisine, 778 F.3d 176, 188 (1st Cir. 2015), aff'd, 136 S. Ct. 2272, 195 L. Ed. 2d 736 (2016).

[104]U.S. v. Voisine, 778 F.3d 176, 177 (1st Cir. 2015), aff'd, 136 S. Ct. 2272, 195 L. Ed. 2d 736 (2016).

[105]U.S. v. Voisine, 778 F.3d 176, 177 (1st Cir. 2015), aff'd, 136 S. Ct. 2272, 195 L. Ed. 2d 736 (2016).

[106]Voisine v. U.S., 136 S. Ct. 2272, 195 L. Ed. 2d 736 (2016).

[107]Voisine v. U.S., 136 S. Ct. 2272, 2276, 195 L. Ed. 2d 736 (2016); United States v. Howell, 838 F.3d 489 (5th Cir. 2016), cert. denied, 137 S. Ct. 1108, 197 L. Ed. 2d 212 (2017).

[108]U.S.C. § 922(g)(9).

[109]Voisine v. U.S., 136 S. Ct. 2272, 2278, 195 L. Ed. 2d 736 (2016).

crimes committed with that state of mind would substantially undermine the provision's design."[110]

The Court focused on the term "use," suggesting that it requires volitional" use of force as opposed to an accident. Thus, "the word 'use' does not exclude from 922(g)(9)'s compass an act of force carried out in conscious disregard of its substantial risk of causing harm."[111] The harm such conduct causes is the result of a deliberate decision to endanger another. "A person who assaults another recklessly 'uses' force, no less than one who carries out the same action knowingly or intentionally."[112]

Acknowledging that Congress enacted the firearms ban to take guns away from abusers convicted under misdemeanor assault and domestic violence laws, the Court held that the federal firearms ban applies to any person with a prior misdemeanor conviction for the use of physical force against another in a domestic relationship.

Conversely, the dissent written by Justice Thomas and joined by Justice Sotomayor (author of *Castleman*) argued that reckless conduct does not qualify as it does not have as an element, "the use or attempted use of physical force." Noting that the Supreme Court has previously defined "use" as intentional conduct, Thomas found that reckless conduct does not involve the "use or attempted use of physical force." Because the Maine statute criminalizes all reckless conduct, both Thomas and Sotomayor expressed concerns that conduct such as recklessly injuring another while texting resulting in a car crash would be considered in the definition of "reckless" for purposes of the gun ban. "[T]he use of physical force is narrower than most state assault statutes which punish anyone who recklessly causes physical injury."[113] Arguing that the majority conflates "volitional" conduct with "intentional" conduct, Justice Thomas stressed that the "use" of force requires the intent to cause harm and that the majority's definition is overbroad. Since "volitional" conduct includes conduct that is not intended to cause harm, the majority overlooks the critical distinction between intentional conduct and that conduct that is not intentional, but still reckless or accidental. The "use" of force has a well-understood meaning applying only to intentional acts designed to cause harm.

While Sotomayor found, in *Castleman,* that the physical force requirement of 922(g)(9) is satisfied by the degree of force that supports a common law battery conviction and that even minor uses of force are domestic violence when they accumulate over time, she declined to broaden that decision to include volitional acts that might employ force but are not intended to harm another.

Q & A: Does U.S.C. § 922(g)(9) violate a person's second amendment rights to bear arms?[[114]

[110]Voisine v. U.S., 136 S. Ct. 2272, 2278, 195 L. Ed. 2d 736 (2016).

[111]Voisine v. U.S., 136 S. Ct. 2272, 2279, 195 L. Ed. 2d 736 (2016).

[112]Voisine v. U.S., 136 S. Ct. 2272, 2280, 195 L. Ed. 2d 736 (2016).

[113]Voisine v. U.S., 136 S. Ct. 2272, 2285, 195 L. Ed. 2d 736 (2016).

[114]See also District of Columbia v. Heller, 554 U.S. 570, 128 S. Ct. 2783, 171 L. Ed. 2d 637 (2008); U.S. v. White, 593 F.3d 1199 (11th Cir. 2010); Binderup v. Attorney

According to *Stimmel v. Sessions*,[115] the Sixth Circuit Court of Appeals addressed a much too often mantra of gun advocates: that 922(g)(9) violated an individual's second amendment rights. In that case, the court held that a statute disqualifying misdemeanants from possessing firearms by virtue of a domestic violence conviction did not violate rights protected by the Second Amendment.

"On the government's evidence, . . .it is reasonable to conclude that domestic abusers have high recidivism rates, pose a continued risk to their families, as well as law enforcement, are more likely to kill their victims when armed, and should therefore be disarmed. In accord with the unanimous view of those circuits that have addressed the question, we conclude the fit here is, at least, reasonable. Section § 922(g)(9) survives intermediate scrutiny."[116]

Q & A: If a defendant is convicted of domestic violence threat under RC 2919.25(C), is he/she prohibited from possessing guns under 18 U.S.C.A. § 922(g)(9)?

The Rocky River Municipal Court recently addressed this issue in the context of a return of firearms. In *Wilhoit v. North Olmsted*,[117] the defendant was charged with domestic violence against his spouse. Pursuant to the TPO, he was ordered to surrender his firearms to the North Olmsted Police Department. He pled from a first degree domestic violence to a fourth degree threat of domestic violence under RC 2919.25(C). His motion for the return of his firearms was denied and he subsequently filed a civil replevin action for the return.

The trial court reviewed the issue to determine whether a defendant who is convicted of a threat of domestic violence is precluded from possessing firearms or ammunition. The court considered the following factors: 1) federal law prescribes the possession of firearms for those who are convicted of an offense of domestic violence pursuant to 18 U.S.C.A. § 922(g)(9); 2) 18 U.S.C.A. § 921(a)(33)(A)(ii) provides that a "misdemeanor crime of domestic violence" is one that has, as an element, the use or attempted use of physical force, or the threatened use of a deadly weapon, committed by a former or current spouse; 3) domestic violence is defined under RC 2919.25(C) as committing an act "by threat of force"; and 4) the defendant was charged with domestic violence but pled and was convicted of the reduced charge of threat of domestic violence under RC 2919.25(C).

The court then held that, although his conviction of threat of domestic violence was a misdemeanor crime of domestic violence, because it included a "threat of force," it was not a crime of domestic violence as defined in the federal code, which has as an element the "threatened use of a deadly weapon."[118] Because his conviction for do-

General United States of America, 836 F.3d 336 (3d Cir. 2016), cert. denied, 137 S. Ct. 2323, 198 L. Ed. 2d 746 (2017) and cert. denied, 137 S. Ct. 2323, 198 L. Ed. 2d 746 (2017); Cee v. Stone, 2017-Ohio-8687, 2017 WL 5664759 (Ohio Ct. App. 3d Dist. Union County 2017).

[115] Stimmel v. Sessions, 879 F.3d 198 (6th Cir. 2018).

[116] Stimmel v. Sessions, 879 F.3d 198, 211 (6th Cir. 2018).

[117] Wilhoit v. N. Olmsted, 151 Ohio Misc. 2d 21, 2009-Ohio-1702, 905 N.E.2d 723 (Mun. Ct. 2009).

[118] Wilhoit v. N. Olmsted, 151 Ohio Misc. 2d 21, 2009-Ohio-1702, 905 N.E.2d 723

mestic violence was not a crime of domestic violence as set forth in Title 18 of the U.S. Code, the defendant was not prohibited from possessing any firearms.

Q & A: The defendant pled guilty to assault, not domestic violence, in order to keep his guns. The judge didn't even ask who the victim was. Can his guns still be taken from him?

The definition of "misdemeanor crime of domestic violence"[119] includes all misdemeanors under federal or state law that involve the use or attempted use of physical force (simple assault, assault and battery, disorderly conduct[120] are all examples), if separate inquiry reveals that the offense was committed by a federally-defined qualifying person.[121] This is true whether or not the convicting statute specifically defines or classifies the offense as a domestic violence misdemeanor and whether or not the convicting statute has a relationship element. The federal courts have uniformly held that the singular term "element" modifies the phrase "the use or attempted use of physical force or the threatened use of a deadly weapon."[122] While 18 U.S.C.A. § 921(a)(33) requires proof of a domestic violence relationship, the predicate misdemeanor must have only one element: the use or attempted use of physical force or the threatened use of a deadly weapon on the convicting statute and does not refer to the relationship requirement.[123]

For example, in *City of Cleveland v. Carpenter*,[124] defendant was arrested for domestic violence and his weapons were seized at the time of his arrest. He pled no contest to misdemeanor assault. Subsequently, he filed a motion for the return of his weapons, which motion was denied by the municipal court judge.

On appeal, appellant contended that the court erred by denying his motion to return the weapons. The appellate court noted that other federal and state courts have held that state misdemeanor crimes of violence such as simple assault need not have a domestic violence relationship element in order to disqualify a misdemeanant from possessing firearms.[125] While the federal law requires proof of a domestic relationship, the predicate misdemeanor need only have one element:

(Mun. Ct. 2009).

[119]18 U.S.C.A. § 921(a)(33); see also RC 2901.01(A)(9)(a) for the definition of an offense of violence; U.S. v. Jenkins, 2007 WL 542899 (E.D. Tenn. 2007).

[120]See U.S. v. Smith, 56 M.J. 711 (A.F.C.C.A. 2001) (finding that disorderly conduct satisfies the requirement that the offense have as an element the use or attempted use of physical force). See also State v. Majka, 2002-Ohio-1378, 2002 WL 462858 (Ohio Ct. App. 9th Dist. Summit County 2002); but see Wysocki v. Oberlin Police Dept., 2014-Ohio-2869, 2014 WL 2957713 (Ohio Ct. App. 9th Dist. Lorain County 2014).

[121]City of Cleveland v. Cleveland Police Patrolman's Ass'n, 2000 WL 573195 (Ohio Ct. App. 8th Dist. Cuyahoga County 2000).

[122]Fanny L Haslebacher, Firearms and Domestic Violence: Important Considerations for Judges, presented at the National College of District Attorneys Thirteenth Annual National Conference on Domestic Violence (2002).

[123]See e.g., U.S. v. Shelton, 325 F.3d 553 (5th Cir. 2003); U.S. v. Meade, 175 F.3d 215 (1st Cir. 1999); U.S. v. Smith, 171 F.3d 617 (8th Cir. 1999).

[124]City of Cleveland v. Carpenter, 2003-Ohio-6923, 2003 WL 22976619 (Ohio Ct. App. 8th Dist. Cuyahoga County 2003).

[125]City of Cleveland v. Carpenter, 2003-Ohio-6923, 2003 WL 22976619, *3 (Ohio

the use or attempted use of physical force.[126] In affirming the trial court, the Cuyahoga County Court of Appeals held that the City of Cleveland has a legal basis to withhold appellants firearms; that is, appellant was convicted of assault, which constitutes a misdemeanor crime of violence pursuant to Section 922(g), Title 18, U.S. Code and precludes appellants right to possess any firearms.[127]

Q & A: Does the federal Gun Ban for Individuals Convicted of a Misdemeanor Crime of Domestic Violence under 18 U.S.C.A. § 922(g)(9) require that the underlying misdemeanor offense specifically include a domestic relationship between the offender and the victim?

While the cases set forth in the preceding Q & A indicate that a misdemeanor crime of violence involves the use of or attempted use of physical force, no case specifically addressed whether the underlying crime must have a domestic relationship element. That issue was specifically raised in *U.S. v. Hayes*.[128] In *Hayes*, the defendant, following a conditional guilty plea, was convicted of possession of a firearm after having previously been convicted of a qualifying misdemeanor crime of domestic violence in violation of 18 U.S.C.A. § 922(g)(9) that prohibits people convicted of a misdemeanor crime of domestic violence from purchasing or possessing firearms or ammunition.

The Fourth Circuit Court reversed the district court decision, dismissed the indictment and held that defendant's conviction for battery was based on a crime that did not specifically include a domestic relationship between the offender and the victim. In doing so, the Fourth Circuit contradicted the holdings of nine other circuits that previously addressed the same issue.

The U.S. Supreme Court, in a 7-2 decision, reversed the Fourth Circuit and held that a domestic relationship need not be a defining

---

Ct. App. 8th Dist. Cuyahoga County 2003); see also State v. Majka, 2002-Ohio-1378, 2002 WL 462858 (Ohio Ct. App. 9th Dist. Summit County 2002).

[126]City of Cleveland v. Carpenter, 2003-Ohio-6923, 2003 WL 22976619, *3 (Ohio Ct. App. 8th Dist. Cuyahoga County 2003) citing, U.S. v. Smith, 171 F.3d 617, 620 (8th Cir. 1999).

[127]City of Cleveland v. Carpenter, 2003-Ohio-6923, 2003 WL 22976619, *4 (Ohio Ct. App. 8th Dist. Cuyahoga County 2003).

[128]U.S. v. Hayes, 482 F.3d 749 (4th Cir. 2007), rev'd and remanded, 555 U.S. 415, 129 S. Ct. 1079, 172 L. Ed. 2d 816, 50 A.L.R. Fed. 2d 639 (2009); see also Koll v. Department of Justice, 2009 WI App 74, 317 Wis. 2d 753, 769 N.W.2d 69, 2009 (Ct. App. 2009) (disorderly conduct is a crime of domestic violence for purposes of the federal gun ban, after *Hayes* decision); but see Descamps v. U.S., 570 U.S. 254, 133 S. Ct. 2276, 186 L. Ed. 2d 438 (2013) (defendants in *Voisine* argued that *Hayes* was implicitly overruled because *Descamps* limited the extent to which courts can look at the facts underlying the predicate conviction to determine whether they fit the subsequent conviction, under the modified categorical approach.

U.S. v. Voisine, 778 F.3d 176, 187 (1st Cir. 2015), aff'd, 136 S. Ct. 2272, 195 L. Ed. 2d 736 (2016), citing *Descamps* at 2281-82. Rejecting the argument, the *Voisine* majority found that "[w]hether the predicate conviction involved a domestic relationship is not a fact about the predicate conviction discerned through application of the modified categorical approach, in violation of *Decamps*; rather, it is an element proved anew in the § 922(g)(9) proceeding."

U.S. v. Voisine, 778 F.3d 176, 177 (1st Cir. 2015), aff'd, 136 S. Ct. 2272, 195 L. Ed. 2d 736 (2016).

element of the predicate offense.[129] The Court determined that the definition of a "misdemeanor crime of domestic violence" imposed two requirements—that the crime must have "as an element, the use or attempted use of physical force, or the threatened use of a deadly weapon" and that it must be "committed by" a person who has a specified domestic relationship with the victim. The definition does not, however, require the predicate-offense to include, as an element, the existence of that domestic relationship. Instead, it suffices for the Government to charge and prove a prior conviction that was, in fact, for "an offense . . . committed by" the defendant against a spouse or other domestic victim."[130]

The Court went on to say that "[t]he text, context, purpose, and what little there is of drafting history all point in the same direction: Congress defined "misdemeanor crime of domestic violence" to include an offense "committed by" a person who has a specified domestic relationship with the victim, whether or not the misdemeanor statute itself designates the domestic relationship as an element of the crime."[131] Therefore, a conviction under a state assault statute is a misdemeanor crime of domestic violence for purposes of the federal gun ban under 18 U.S.C.A. § 922(g)(9).

Q & A: Does 18 U.S.C.A. 922(g)(9) apply to law enforcement officers?

It does apply to law enforcement officers.[132] In effect, that means that law enforcement officers who have been convicted of a qualifying domestic violence misdemeanor will not be able to possess or receive firearms for any purpose, including the performance of official duties.[133] This provision forever precludes defendants from possessing firearms or ammunition following a conviction, regardless of when the conviction occurred.[134]

Q & A: What due process requirements exist in the statute?

Additionally, the statutory provision contains due process requirements to ensure that the qualifying conviction was obtained with

[129] U.S. v. Hayes, 555 U.S. 415, 129 S. Ct. 1079, 172 L. Ed. 2d 816, 50 A.L.R. Fed. 2d 639 (2009).

[130] U.S. v. Hayes, 555 U.S. 415, 129 S. Ct. 1079, 172 L. Ed. 2d 816, 50 A.L.R. Fed. 2d 639 (2009) (at syllabus). See also U.S. v. England, 2014 WL 4988149 (S.D. Ohio 2014).

[131] U.S. v. Hayes, 555 U.S. 415, 129 S. Ct. 1079, 1082, 172 L. Ed. 2d 816, 50 A.L.R. Fed. 2d 639 (2009).

[132] 18 U.S.C.A. § 925; see also Fraternal Order of Police v. U.S., 173 F.3d 898 (D.C. Cir. 1999); Gillespie v. City of Indianapolis, 185 F.3d 693, 15 I.E.R. Cas. (BNA) 520 (7th Cir. 1999). See also Alison J. Nathan, At the Intersection of Domestic Violence and Guns: The Public Interest Exception and the Lautenberg Amendment, 85 Cornell L. Rev. 822 (2000). See Sup. R. Form 10.0-H, 10-01-I and 10.01-J providing that "Respondent shall not possess, use, carry or obtain any deadly weapon at any time while the Order remains in effect *unless Respondent is excepted for official use pursuant to 18 U.S.C. 925(a)(1)."* (emphasis added).

[133] See City of Cleveland v. Cleveland Police Patrolman's Ass'n, 2000 WL 573195 (Ohio Ct. App. 8th Dist. Cuyahoga County 2000).

[134] Judge Susan B. Carbon et al., Enforcing Domestic Violence Protection Orders throughout the Country: New Frontiers of Protection for Victims of Domestic Violence, 50 Juv. & Fam. Ct. 2, 45 (1999).

advice of counsel and with notice of a right to a jury trial.[135] A failure to comply with these due process requirements means that the conviction will not qualify as a domestic violence conviction under 18 U.S.C.A. § 922(g)(9). Persons convicted under RC 2919.25(A) and RC 2919.25(B) or substantially similar municipal ordinances will generally be prohibited from possessing firearms under 18 U.S.C.A. § 922(g)(9). On the other hand, persons convicted under RC 2919.25(C) may or may not be under a federal firearm prohibition as a result of such a conviction.

Additionally, the Ohio General Assembly enacted several provisions in order to effectuate compliance with VAWA 2005. RC 2919.26(G)(2) was added to state that "upon the issuance of a protection order under this section, the court shall provide the parties to the order with the following notice orally or by form:

NOTICE

If you are convicted of a misdemeanor crime involving violence in which you are or were a spouse, intimate partner, parent, or guardian of the victim or are or were involved in another, similar relationship with the victim, it may be unlawful for you to possess or purchase a firearm, including a rifle, pistol, or revolver, or ammunition pursuant to federal law under 18 U.S.C.A. 922(g)(9). If you have any questions whether this law makes it illegal for you to possess or purchase a firearm or ammunition, you should consult an attorney."

Similar provisions were included in RC 2903.213(G)(2). RC 2943.033 was added to define those domestic relationships covered. Moreover, RC 2943.033(C) states: "Prior to accepting a guilty plea or plea of no contest to an indictment, information, or complaint that charges a person with a misdemeanor offense of violence, the court shall inform the defendant either personally or in writing that under 18 U.S.C.A. § 922(G)(9) it may be unlawful for the person to ship, transport, purchase, or possess a firearm or ammunition as a result of any conviction for a misdemeanor offense of violence. The plea may not be vacated based on a failure to inform the person so charged regarding the restrictions under 18 U.S.C.A. § 922(g)(9).

Q & A: Is an individual who has been pardoned or whose conviction was expunged or set aside or whose civil rights have been restored, considered convicted of a misdemeanor crime of domestic violence?

The conviction will not qualify if the conviction has been expunged, unless the expungement provides that the person is still under a firearms disability.[136] Additionally, a conviction will not qualify if the person has been pardoned or has had his/her civil rights restored.

It is important for courts to advise convicted defendants that a conviction will bar them from legally acquiring or possessing firearms

[135]See U.S. v. Jackson, 213 F.3d 644 (9th Cir. 2000) (upholding conviction in spite of defendant's challenge that he did not knowingly and intelligently waive his right to a jury trial); see also U.S. v. Smith, 171 F.3d 617 (8th Cir. 1999); U.S. v. Akins, 243 F.3d 1199 (9th Cir. 2001), opinion amended and superseded on other grounds on denial of reh'g, 276 F.3d 1141 (9th Cir. 2002).

[136]See 18 U.S.C.A. § 921(a)(33).

and ammunition under federal law.[137] Appropriate waivers of the right to counsel and a jury trial should also be noted.

Of significance is that the victim need not have obtained a civil protection order for the abuser to be subject to the ramifications of 18 U.S.C.A. § 922(g)(9). So long as the defendant has been convicted of a misdemeanor crime of domestic violence, the mandates of VAWA attach.[138]

Q & A: Is a person who received a deferred judgment/ adjudication subject to the firearms disability?

What is a conviction is determined by the law of the jurisdiction in which the proceedings were held. If the State law where the proceedings were held does not consider a deferred judgment or adjudication to be a conviction, the person would not be subject to the disability.[139]

Q & A: Are local criminal ordinances misdemeanors under State law for purposes of section 922(g)(9)?

Yes, assuming a violation of the ordinance meets the definition of a "misdemeanor crime of domestic violence" in all other respects.

Q & A: What should an individual do if he/she has been convicted of a misdemeanor crime of domestic violence?

Individuals subject to a firearms disability should immediately dispose of their firearms and ammunition. ATF recommends that such persons transfer their firearms and ammunition to a third party who may lawfully receive and possess them such as a local police agency or a federal firearms dealer. The continued possession of firearms and ammunition by persons under this disability is a violation of law and may subject the possessor to criminal penalties. In addition, such firearms and ammunition are subject to seizure and forfeiture.[140]

Q & A: What if a person sold a firearm to someone convicted of a misdemeanor crime of domestic violence?

It is also a federal crime to knowingly transfer or sell a firearm to a person convicted of a misdemeanor crime of domestic violence.[141] The violation under 18 U.S.C.A. § 922(d)(9) must be "knowing." Therefore, the prosecutor must demonstrate that the transferor knew the defendant/purchaser was prohibited from possessing a weapon. To assist the gun dealer or other transferor, the purchaser of a firearm is required to state that he/she has not been convicted of a misdemeanor crime of domestic violence.

<u>Miscellaneous Firearm Provisions</u>

Q & A: Must a state court notify a defendant about the federal law or its application to him or her?

---

[137]See City of Cleveland v. Cleveland Police Patrolman's Ass'n, 2000 WL 573195 (Ohio Ct. App. 8th Dist. Cuyahoga County 2000) ("[T]he statutory prohibition against the possession of firearms is not permanent but can be removed if the conviction is expunged or set aside or the defendant is pardoned.").

[138]See City of Cleveland v. Cleveland Police Patrolman's Ass'n, 2000 WL 573195 (Ohio Ct. App. 8th Dist. Cuyahoga County 2000) (prohibition against possession of a firearm does not automatically bar the defendant from employment as a police officer).

[139]18 U.S.C.A. § 921(a)(33); 27 C.F.R. § 478.11.

[140]18 U.S.C.A. §§ 922(g)(9), (d)(1).

[141]See 18 U.S.C.A. § 922(d)(9).

Under federal law, a state court is not required to provide a defendant notice of federal consequences of a state court conviction. If a defendant is federally charged with violating 18 U.S.C.A. § 922(g)(9), the federal government is not required to prove that the defendant knew possessing a firearm was illegal, the government must only prove that the defendant knowingly possessed a firearm.[142]

18 U.S.C. 922(g)(9) has withstood several constitutional challenges on the basis that it violated the notice requirement of the Fifth Amendment's Due process Clause. For example, in *U.S. v. Hancock*,[143] the defendant argued that the government was required to prove that he had actual knowledge of the mandates of 18 U.S.C.A. § 922(g)(9). The circuit court of appeals rejected this argument and held that the requirement of "knowing" conduct refers to knowledge of the firearm possession and not knowledge of the legal consequences of the possession.[144] In fact, ignorance of the law is no excuse.

Q & A: What is the penalty for violating 18 U.S.C.A. § 922(d)(8), 18 U.S.C.A. § 922(g)(8), or 18 U.S.C.A. § 922(d)(9), or 18 U.S.C.A. § 922(g)(9)?

The penalty for a violation of 18 U.S.C.A. § 922(d)(8), 922(g)(8), 922(d)(9) and 922(g)(9) is a ten-year term of imprisonment. For misdemeanor crime violations, an optional additional fine of $250,000 is also permitted. The Bureau of Alcohol, Tobacco and Firearms has jurisdiction to investigate.

Q & A: When may the firearms be returned to a respondent/offender?[145]

The federal firearms restrictions remain in effect for the duration of the qualifying protection order.[146] When the order terminates by operation of law or is dismissed, the prohibition is removed and the respondent should be permitted to retrieve his firearms.

---

[142]Fanny L. Haslebacher, Firearms and Domestic Violence: Important Considerations for Judges, presented to the National College of District Attorneys Thirteenth Annual National Conference on Domestic Violence (2002); see also U.S. v. Mitchell, 209 F.3d 319 (4th Cir. 2000), cert. denied, 531 U.S. 849, 121 S. Ct. 123, 148 L. Ed. 2d 78 (2000); U.S. v. Beavers, 206 F.3d 706, 2000 FED App. 0058P (6th Cir. 2000), cert. denied, 529 U.S. 1121, 120 S. Ct. 1989, 146 L. Ed. 2d 815 (2000); U.S. v. Hutzell, 217 F.3d 966 (8th Cir. 2000); U.S. v. Hancock, 231 F.3d 557 (9th Cir. 2000), cert. denied, 532 U.S. 989, 121 S. Ct. 1641, 149 L. Ed. 2d 500 (2001).

[143]U.S. v. Hancock, 231 F.3d 557 (9th Cir. 2000), cert. denied, 532 U.S. 989, 121 S. Ct. 1641, 149 L. Ed. 2d 500 (2001); see also U.S. v. Shelton, 325 F.3d 553 (5th Cir. 2003).

[144]See U.S. v. Beavers, 206 F.3d 706, 2000 FED App. 0058P (6th Cir. 2000), cert. denied, 529 U.S. 1121, 120 S. Ct. 1989, 146 L. Ed. 2d 815 (2000); U.S. v. Hutzell, 217 F.3d 966 (8th Cir. 2000); U.S. v. Mitchell, 209 F.3d 319 (4th Cir. 2000), cert. denied, 531 U.S. 849, 121 S. Ct. 123, 148 L. Ed. 2d 78 (2000); see also Brian E. Sobczyk, 18 U.S.C. § 922(g)(9) and the Lambert Due Process Exception Requiring Actual Knowledge of the Law: U.S. v. Hutzell, 217 F.3d 966 (8th Cir. 2000), 80 Neb. L. Rev. 103 (2001).

[145]See also Text § 12:22.

[146]See, for example, State v. S.A., 290 N.J. Super. 240, 675 A.2d 678 (App. Div. 1996).

If the respondent is restricted from possessing firearms pursuant to state law remedies, weapons held must be returned when the protection order expires.[147]

If a defendant is charged with domestic violence but the charges are subsequently dismissed, the defendant may petition the court for the return of his/her firearms. In *Kise v. Barber*,[148] the defendant sought the return of his weapons after dismissal of the domestic violence charge. He argued that his complaint for return of his weapons should not have been dismissed for lack of subject matter jurisdiction by a Civ. R. 12(B)(6) motion just because a new indictment was filed against him. In reversing the trial court, the appellate court noted that the city/municipal court is entitled to defend against the return of the firearms under RC 2923.13(A) or argue that the gun is contraband.[149]

Q & A: What is the procedure for the return of firearms?[150]

The Ohio Supreme Court forms provide that "[u]pon the expiration of this Order, any deadly weapons, including firearms and ammunition, held in protective custody by law enforcement pursuant to this Order shall be disposed of as unclaimed property pursuant to RC 2981.12 unless the Respondent files a motion for return with this Court within 30 days before expiration of this Order."[151] In that the full hearing forms require a motion being filed 30 days before expiration of the Order, the court has jurisdiction to address the issue.

The issue has been raised in Ohio. In *Golden v. Bay Village Police Department*,[152] the defendant was the subject of a criminal protection order issued in connection with an allegation of domestic violence. The police confiscated several guns from Golden's home pursuant to the order. Subsequently, the charge of domestic violence was dismissed and the protection order was dissolved.

Mr. Golden requested the return of his guns and he was advised

---

[147]See Caron v. U.S., 524 U.S. 308, 118 S. Ct. 2007, 141 L. Ed. 2d 303 (1998) (in returning weapons, a court cannot return some firearms but restrict the right to carry others).

[148]Kise v. Barber, 2005-Ohio-6438, 2005 WL 3293763 (Ohio Ct. App. 5th Dist. Knox County 2005).

[149]Kise v. Barber, 2005-Ohio-6438, 2005 WL 3293763, *2 (Ohio Ct. App. 5th Dist. Knox County 2005).

[150]See also Aloi v. Nassau County Sheriff's Dept., 9 Misc. 3d 1050, 800 N.Y.S.2d 873 (Sup 2005); Fisher v. Kealoha, 2012 WL 2526923 (D. Haw. 2012); Furda v. State, 193 Md. App. 371, 997 A.2d 856 (2010); Matter of J.W.D., 149 N.J. 108, 693 A.2d 92 (1997). See Henderson v. U.S., 135 S. Ct. 1780, 191 L. Ed. 2d 874 (2015) (Supreme Court granted certiorari to address property rights to certain surrendered firearms not involved in the underlying criminal case when the individual is a prohibited person under 18 U.S.C. 922(g) which almost certainly will have consequences in domestic violence firearm surrender cases; Court held that a court could approve proposed transfer to third persons for purchase of firearms, if, but only if, such disposition prevented felon form later exercising control over firearms); see also Weisberg, Kelly, U.S. Supreme Court to Decide Henderson Case: Scope of Felon's Ownership Rights to Firearms, 20 Domestic Violence Reports 49 (April/May 2015); Text 12:22; Text 14:5.

[151]See Super. R. Form 10.01-I and 10.01-J.

[152]Golden v. Bay Village Police Dept., 2002-Ohio-673, 2002 WL 253878 (Ohio Ct. App. 8th Dist. Cuyahoga County 2002); see Wilhoit v. N. Olmsted, 151 Ohio Misc. 2d 21, 2009-Ohio-1702, 905 N.E.2d 723 (Mun. Ct. 2009).

that he would need a court order for the release of the weapons and was further advised to file a replevin action.[153] He was then informed that if he failed to secure a replevin order, the weapons would be destroyed. After receiving the replevin order, Mr. Golden then requested attorney fees. From the denial of fees, he appealed.

The Eighth District Court of Appeals stated that the trial court did not err in denying Golden's request for fees. The court reasoned that since the police confiscated the weapons pursuant to a court order, the defendant was on notice that it would take a court order to release his weapons.[154]

The appellate court then noted that "[t]he fact that the protection order was dissolved is of no consequence. The police department confiscated the weapons pursuant to court order; thus it was reasonable for the police not to return the property unless instructed to do so by the court."[155]

The court then held that the police recommendation of a replevin action was reasonable in light of the fact that the defendant failed to request the return of his property when the charges against him were dismissed and because of the several months delay. Therefore, the police did not exercise the bad faith necessary for an award of attorney fees.

Q & A: Are there any double jeopardy implications of enforcing 922(g)(8) provisions?

Since persons constrained by protection orders prohibiting firearm possession may be subject to state prosecution for violating the protection orders, as well as federal efforts to enforce section 922(g)(8), double jeopardy concerns may arise in the context of a subsequent federal prosecution. It can be argued that an abuser would not be barred by double jeopardy because an element of the federal firearms offenses is the interstate commerce nexus, which is not an element of a state crime.

To date, only one court has articulated the potential effect of double jeopardy on federal and state prosecution. In *U.S. v. Jacobs*,[156] the Sixth Circuit Court of Appeals held that prosecution of the defendant on federal charges of interstate domestic violence, possession of a firearm while subject to a court order, and use of a deadly weapon during a crime of violence, which arose from the same incident involving alleged abduction of his estranged wife that had given rise to a state court abduction charge he had previously pleaded guilty to, did not violate the defendant's double jeopardy rights.

---

[153]See also Wysocki v. Oberlin Police Dept., 2014-Ohio-2869, 2014 WL 2957713 (Ohio Ct. App. 9th Dist. Lorain County 2014).

[154]See Sup. R. Form 10.01-H to Sup. R. Form 10.01-J and 10.02-A. Note that Ohio's standardized forms provide that law enforcement agencies shall hold weapons in protective custody until further court order.

[155]Golden v. Bay Village Police Dept., 2002-Ohio-673, 2002 WL 253878, *2 (Ohio Ct. App. 8th Dist. Cuyahoga County 2002). But see State v. Solomon, 262 N.J. Super. 618, 621 A.2d 559 (Ch. Div. 1993).

[156]U.S. v. Jacobs, 244 F.3d 503 (6th Cir. 2001), syllabus at 503.

§ 18:12 Firearm offenses under VAWA; significant cases

In *United States v. Wilson*,[1] the defendant was arrested for an outstanding arrest warrant and, as the state trooper was executing the warrant, the trooper discovered several firearms in the defendant's truck. Because the defendant was also subject to a protection order obtained by his wife, he was convicted of possessing a firearm under 18 U.S.C.A. § 922(g)(8).

The defendant in *Wilson* argued that he did not know that there existed a statute that restricted his ability to possess a firearm while subject to a protection order. Since the statute required that any violation of 18 U.S.C.A. § 922(g)(8) be committed knowingly, he arguably did not have the intent to commit the crime.

The Seventh Circuit Court of Appeals rejected this argument, holding that, because a recent U.S. Supreme Court decision defined "knowingly" as "factual knowledge," not knowledge of the law, a defendant's ignorance of the law is no defense in this context.[2] The court then upheld the constitutionality of 18 U.S.C.A. § 922(g)(8), stating that the statutory language did not exceed the authority of Congress under the Commerce Clause.[3]

However, the U.S. District Court for the Northern District of Texas found that the statute that makes it a federal crime to possess a firearm while subject to a domestic violence protection order unconstitutionally infringes upon due process rights. In *United States v. Emerson*,[4] the wife filed for divorce and obtained a protection order restraining her husband from threatening her. The court issued the order without first finding that the defendant represents a credible threat. The defendant owned a gun and was charged with violating the order pursuant to 18 U.S.C.A. § 922(g)(8). The pro se husband challenged 18 U.S.C.A. § 922(g)(8) as being unconstitutional because it violated his Second and Fifth Amendment rights. The court relied on the reasoning set forth in *United States v. Pierson*[5] and summarily dismissed his Commerce Clause challenge.

The district court initially addressed whether the Second Amendment guarantees an individual a personal right to bear arms. Relying on an "individual right" interpretation, the *Emerson* court held that 18 U.S.C.A. § 922(g)(8) was unconstitutional because it allowed "a state court divorce proceeding, without particularized findings of the threat of future violence, to automatically deprive a citizen of his

[Section 18:12]

[1]U.S. v. Wilson, 159 F.3d 280 (7th Cir. 1998); see also U.S. v. Napier, 233 F.3d 394, 2000 FED App. 0397P (6th Cir. 2000) (18 U.S.C.A. § 922(g)(8) does not require that the defendant have actual knowledge of the firearms restrictions); U.S. v. Reddick, 203 F.3d 767 (10th Cir. 2000).

[2]See U.S. v. Baker, 197 F.3d 211, 1999 FED App. 0392P (6th Cir. 1999); see also U.S. v. Meade, 175 F.3d 215 (1st Cir. 1999); U.S. v. Napier, 233 F.3d 394, 2000 FED App. 0397P (6th Cir. 2000); U.S. v. Hutzell, 217 F.3d 966 (8th Cir. 2000).

[3]See also U.S. v. Pierson, 139 F.3d 501 (5th Cir. 1998).

[4]U.S. v. Emerson, 46 F. Supp. 2d 598 (N.D. Tex. 1999), rev'd and remanded, 270 F.3d 203 (5th Cir. 2001).

[5]U.S. v. Pierson, 139 F.3d 501 (5th Cir. 1998).

Second Amendment rights."[6] The court left open the possibility that had the trial court issued findings regarding future violence and advised the defendant regarding the statute, he may not have been able to challenge the statute successfully.

Moreover, the court then held that 18 U.S.C.A. § 922(g)(8) was also unconstitutional on due process grounds under the Fifth Amendment. The court reasoned that the long tradition of firearm ownership in this country compels a finding of a protected liberty interest in the possession of a firearm. Because the defendant was never personally informed that the divorce court's order would require him to relinquish ownership of his gun, the court determined that the statute violated his Fifth Amendment rights. "Because § 922(g)(8) is an obscure, highly technical statute with no *mens rea* requirement, it violates Emerson's Fifth Amendment due process rights to be subject to prosecution without proof of knowledge that he was violating the statute."[7]

On appeal, the United States Court of Appeals for the Fifth Circuit reversed and remanded the case and held that while finding that the Second Amendment protects the right of individuals to keep and bear arms, the federal statute did not violate that right. The *Emerson* court reasoned that "[a]lthough, as we have held, the Second Amendment *does* protect individual rights, that does not mean that those rights may never be made subject to any limited, narrowly tailored specific exceptions or restrictions for particular cases that are reasonable and not inconsistent with the right of Americans generally to individually keep and bear their private arms as historically understood in this country."[8]

Several federal cases have also upheld the constitutionality of 18 U.S.C.A. § 922(g)(9).[9] For example, in *U.S. v. Boyd*,[10] the defendant argued that 18 U.S.C.A. § 922(g)(9) was unconstitutional because it violated the fair notice requirement of the Due Process Clause of the Fifth Amendment and it constitutes an impermissible exercise of federal congressional power under the Commerce Clause. The Tenth Circuit Court of Appeals held that since ignorance of the law is no excuse, the defendant's constitutional challenge on the basis of fair

[6] U.S. v. Emerson, 46 F. Supp. 2d 598, 610 (N.D. Tex. 1999), rev'd and remanded, 270 F.3d 203 (5th Cir. 2001).

[7] U.S. v. Emerson, 46 F. Supp. 2d 598, 613 (N.D. Tex. 1999), rev'd and remanded, 270 F.3d 203 (5th Cir. 2001); see also U.S. v. Shelton, 325 F.3d 553 (5th Cir. 2003).

[8] U.S. v. Emerson, 270 F.3d 203, 261 (5th Cir. 2001).

[9] See Blackburn v. Jansen, 241 F. Supp. 2d 1047 (D. Neb. 2003) (holding that 18 U.S.C.A. § 922(g)(9) is not unconstitutional because persons who are convicted of a domestic violence misdemeanor crime lose their right to carry a gun while persons convicted of other misdemeanor crimes do not). See also U.S. v. Tooley, 717 F. Supp. 2d 580 (S.D. W. Va. 2010), aff'd, 468 Fed. Appx. 357 (4th Cir. 2012) (holding that the statute prohibiting those convicted of misdemeanor crimes of domestic violence from possessing a firearm does not violate the second Amendment); see also Harvard Law Review Association, Constitutional Law—Second Amendment—En Banc Seventh Circuit Holds Prohibition on Firearm Possession by Domestic Violence Misdemeanants to be Constitutional.—United States v. Skoien, 614 F.3d 638 (7th Cir. 2010) (En Banc), 124 Harv. L. Rev. 1074 (2011) (noting that there is a relationship between the goal of reducing domestic violence and a lifetime ban on firearm possession by domestic violence misdemeanants).

[10] U.S. v. Boyd, 211 F.3d 1279 (10th Cir. 2000).

notice is rejected. The court then stated that the statute does not exceed Congress' jurisdiction under the Commerce Clause.[11]

§ 18:13 Domestic violence and firearm prohibition[1]

Federal authority

The 2005 Reauthorization of the Violence Against Women Act (VAWA) requires all jurisdictions receiving VAWA monies to certify that judicial administrative policies and practices include notification to domestic violence offenders of the requirements delineated in 18 U.S.C.A. § 922(g). Failure to certify could result in non-eligibility to receive these monies.

Specifically, 18 U.S.C.A. § 922(g) identifies two instances when the firearms prohibition is triggered due to domestic violence. Pursuant to 18 U.S.C.A. § 922(g)(8), a person subject to a qualifying protection order is prohibited from shipping, transporting, possessing or purchasing any firearm, when the protected party is the person's intimate partner or child of such intimate partner or person. This prohibition stays in place for the duration of the qualifying protection order. The other instance is cited under 18 U.S.C.A. § 922(g)(9), which prohibits a person convicted of a misdemeanor crime of domestic violence from shipping, transporting, possessing or purchasing any firearm or ammunition for life.

For the purpose of clarifying who is an intimate partner in the context of firearms disability, 18 U.S.C.A. § 921(a)(32) defines an "intimate partner," with respect to a person, as any of the following:

- A spouse of the person;
- A former spouse of the person;
- An individual who is a parent of a child of the person; or
- An individual who cohabitates or has cohabited with the person.

A "misdemeanor crime of domestic violence" is defined in 18 U.S.C.A. § 921(a)(33)(A) and includes two critical components. First, the crime must be a recognizable "misdemeanor under federal, state, or tribal law."[2] This component recognizes that most criminal acts of intimate partner violence are not charged as felonies, but most often are charged as misdemeanors. Further, Congress acknowledged in this statute that intimate partner violence escalates in frequency and severity and access to firearms increases the possibility of lethality. The other critical and controversial component is the description of a "crime of domestic violence." The federal code states that the misdemeanor crime of domestic violence has, as an element, the use or at-

---

[11]See also U.S. v. Willbern, 2000 WL 554134 (D. Kan. 2000); U.S. v. Meade, 175 F.3d 215 (1st Cir. 1999); National Ass'n of Government Employees, Inc. v. Barrett, 968 F. Supp. 1564 (N.D. Ga. 1997), aff'd, 155 F.3d 1276 (11th Cir. 1998); U.S. v. Hancock, 231 F.3d 557 (9th Cir. 2000).

[Section 18:13]

[1]The authors would like to thank Diana L. Ramos-Reardon, Esq., of the Ohio Supreme Court's Domestic Violence Program for providing the following article, which was published by the Court in July 2009 and is available from the Court's website at www.supremecourt.ohio/domviol.

[2]18 U.S.C.A. § 921(a)(33)(A)(i).

tempted use of physical force, or the threatened use of a deadly weapon, committed by a current or former spouse, parent, or guardian of the victim, by a person with whom the victim shares a child in common, by a person who is cohabiting with or has cohabited with the victim as a spouse, parent, or guardian, or by a person similarly situated to a spouse, parent, or guardian of the victim.[3]

Clearly, this component has two aspects: a violent act involving "the use or attempted use of physical force or the threatened use of a deadly weapon" and the commission of the violent act by a person who has a specified domestic relationship with the victim. The U.S. Supreme Court in U.S. v. Hayes, 555 U.S. 415, 129 S. Ct. 1079, 172 L. Ed. 2d 816, 50 A.L.R. Fed. 2d 639 (2009), examined the question whether the predicate offense must include as a specific element the existence of a domestic relationship between the offender and victim so that the firearm disability under 18 U.S.C.A. § 922(g)(9) would apply. The Court held that the predicate offense need not specify the domestic relationship as a discrete element of the offense for the firearm disability to apply under 18 U.S.C.A. § 922(g)(9).[4] In other word, all the prosecution must prove is the occurrence of a violent offense where there is a specified domestic relationship between the offender and victim.[5]

Applicability to state law

To determine whether the firearms disability applies to a particular case, there must exist a qualified domestic relationship between the parties—defendant/respondent and victim/petitioner. In Ohio, the relevant domestic relationships are found under the umbrella of "family or household member" as defined in §§ 2919.25 and 3113.31 of the Ohio Revised Code. As defined by statute, "family or household member" means:

- A spouse, a person living as a spouse, or a former spouse of the offender;
- A parent or a child of the offender, or another person related by consanguinity or affinity to the offender;
- A parent or a child of a spouse, person living as a spouse, or former spouse of the offender, or another person related by consanguinity or affinity to a spouse, person living as a spouse, or former spouse of the offender; or
- The natural parent of any child of whom the offender is the other natural parent or is the putative other natural parent.

Although Ohio's concept of "family or household member" has been well-litigated to clarify the relationships and nuances in this term of art, it does not align easily with much of the terminology used in the federal code in the context of domestic violence and firearms disability. For example, the federal code includes such relationships as: an intimate partner; a guardian of the victim; a person with whom the

[3] 18 U.S.C.A. § 921(a)(33)(A)(ii).

[4] U.S. v. Hayes, 555 U.S. 415, 129 S. Ct. 1079, 1087, 172 L. Ed. 2d 816, 50 A.L.R. Fed. 2d 639 (2009).

[5] U.S. v. Hayes, 555 U.S. 415, 129 S. Ct. 1079, 1087, 172 L. Ed. 2d 816, 50 A.L.R. Fed. 2d 639 (2009).

victim shares a child in common; a person who is cohabiting with or has cohabited with the victim as a spouse, parent, or guardian; and a person similarly situated to a spouse, parent, or guardian of the victim. These terms have no legal significance in Ohio.

Thus, in reconciling state and federal laws for the purpose of providing appropriate notice to persons subject to the firearms disability, the notice requirement applies only in those cases where the victim is related to the offender as follows:

- A spouse, former spouse, or person living as a spouse of the offender;
- A child of the offender;
- A child of a spouse, person living as a spouse, or former spouse of the offender; or
- The natural parent of any child of whom the offender is the other natural parent or the putative natural parent.

Clearly excluded from the qualifying family or household member relationships are instances where the offender is the child (adult or minor) of the victim or other family or household relationships, not described above, asserted by affinity or consanguinity.

What is a qualifying protection order?

In Ohio, three types of protection may be qualifying protection orders for the purposes of firearms disability within the context of domestic violence. These are domestic violence temporary protection orders,[6] domestic violence civil protection orders,[7] and in some instances civil stalking and sexually oriented offenses protection orders.[8] *Ex parte* protection orders are not qualifying protection orders, because notice was not provided to the offender, nor did the offender have an opportunity to be heard.

Civil stalking or sexually oriented offenses protection orders, pursuant to RC 2903.214, are qualifying protection orders for the purpose of judicial notice regarding firearms disability only in those cases where a qualifying family or household member relationship is established. A person subject to a protection order under this section where the person is not family or a household member is not firearms disqualified due to domestic violence.

Judicial notice of firearms disability

To apply federal law to Ohio's proceedings, the Ohio Revised Code requires courts to provide oral *or* written notice about firearms disability to offenders in two instances—those who are subject to a qualifying protection order and those who may be convicted of a misdemeanor offense of violence against a qualifying family or household member.

The Supreme Court of Ohio included the firearms disability notice in the warning pages—Sup. R. Forms 10.01-G and 10.03-H—to be attached to the corresponding protection order. The judicial notice of

[6]RC 2919.26.

[7]RC 3113.31.

[8]RC 2903.214.

firearms disability requirement is separate and distinct to the court's assessment and determination whether the offender must surrender any deadly weapons, including firearms, to the designated law enforcement agency. Even in those instances where the relationship of the offender is not one of a qualifying family or household member, the court may determine that the safety of the protected party and community are at risk by the offender's continued possession of a deadly weapon. In such instances, the court is in its right to order any firearms to be surrendered to law enforcement.

In criminal proceedings, state law appears to suggest that the firearms disability notice must be provided during arraignment.[9] However, federal law is silent on this particular point. The Supreme Court of Ohio has promulgated Sup. R. Form 10.04-A to provide written notice regarding firearms disability to a person facing a possible conviction of a misdemeanor offense of violence against a qualifying family or household member. This form is applicable and relevant in those instances where the court does not provide oral notice.

Although the Ohio Revised Code and Rules of Superintendence are clear that notice must be provided to defendants facing a misdemeanor conviction due to an offense of violence against a qualifying family or household member, failure to provide said notice is not a defense to vacate the defendant's plea.[10]

The U.S. Supreme Court's decision in *Hayes* clarified the meaning of "crime of domestic violence." For the purpose of firearms disqualification, a crime of domestic violence would appear not to be limited to a charge of domestic violence under RC 2919.25, but it indeed refers to any misdemeanor offense of violence[11] against a qualifying family or household member. Furthermore, RC 2943.033, which directs criminal courts to provide judicial firearms disability notices in relevant cases, makes reference to "offenses of violence" in line with the *Hayes* decision. If the offender's and victim's relationship is not evident, this may require the court to inquire about the existence of relevant relationships to assess the appropriateness of providing the judicial notice.

Lastly, because federal and state law requires notice must be given on two separate instances—upon the issuance of a qualifying protection order and prior to conviction of a misdemeanor crime of domestic violence—a criminal court issuing a domestic violence temporary protection order at arraignment cannot substitute the notice required for the issuance of a protection order for the one to be provided prior to the a conviction of a misdemeanor offense of violence.[12] Although the net effect of both notices is to advise the defendant about the federal firearms disability, the relative impact of each notice on a person's life is distinct. Therefore, the notices must be treated and given individually.

Implications for courts

Courts have a duty to provide notice to offenders regarding their

---

[9]RC 2943.033(C).

[10]RC 2943.033(C).

[11]RC 2901.01(A)(9).

[12]RC 2943.033(C); 18 U.S.C.A. § 922(g)(8) to (9).

possible firearms disability.[13] This duty does not extend to conferring with the offender about possible applicable exception nor does it include explaining the implications of the notice to the offender. Although the enforcement of the firearms disability falls squarely on the FBI, the court's involvement in providing due notice to domestic violence offenders can have a significant impact in the community's safety.

Upon the expiration of the protection order, a person who has been subject to a protection order may motion the court to return any firearm confiscated as a result of the protection order. The court is well-advised to require law enforcement to conduct a thorough background check to ascertain no impediments exist to grant such an order. Law enforcement's background check should not be limited to ascertaining convictions under RC 2919.25 or other intuitive prohibition, but also include checks on convictions for an offense of violence where the qualifying family or household member relationship is established.[14] Because the latter is an important part of the background check to determine the person's eligibility to have any firearms returned, the court should consider instituting local procedures to make readily identifiable the existence of the qualifying family or household member relationship in the judgment entry or other court documents consulted in the process of a background check.

§ 18:14 Immigration and domestic violence; an overview[1]

Domestic violence presents intractable issues under any circumstances. However, when that violence is compounded by the immigration status of either the abuser or the abused, the problems presented are considerably more complicated. An abused spouse, for instance, is unlikely to seek assistance from the authorities if there is a legitimate fear that obtaining help might have the unintended consequence of causing the deportation of an abuser who provides the sole support for the family unit.[2] The legitimacy of this threat is apparent in light of the fact that under current provisions of immigra-

[13]RC 2943.033(C), 2903.214(F)(2), 3113.31(F)(2).

[14]See U.S. v. Hayes, 555 U.S. 415, 129 S. Ct. 1079, 1087, 172 L. Ed. 2d 816, 50 A.L.R. Fed. 2d 639 (2009).

[Section 18:14]

[1]The authors would like to thank Ann Benson, Esq., Directing Attorney with the State of Washington's Defender Association's Immigration Project, for her review of the materials dealing with immigrants/resident aliens and domestic violence. See also Leslye E. Orloff, Deeana Jang and Catherine F. Klein, With No Place to Turn: Improving Legal Advocacy for Battered Immigrant Women, 29 Fam. L. Q. 313 (1995); Maurice Goldman, The Violence Against Women Act: Meeting its Goal in Protecting Battered Immigrant Women?, 37 Fam. & Conciliation Courts Rev. 375 (1999); Rogerson, Unintended and Unavoidable: The Failure to Protect Rule and Its Consequences for Undocumented Parents and Their Children, 50 Fam. Ct. Rev. 580 (2012); Liebmann, Ethical Advocacy for Immigrant Survivors of Family Crisis, 50 Fam. Ct. Rev. 650 (2012).

[2]See Felicia E. Franco, Unconditional Safety for Conditional Immigrant Women, 11 Berkeley Women's L.J. 99 (1996); Leslye E. Orloff, Mary Ann Dutton, and Giselle Aguilar, Haas v. Nawal Ammar: Battered Immigrant Women's Willingness to Call for Help and Police Response, 13 UCLA Women's L.J. 43 (2003); Chacón, Tensions and Trade-Offs: Protecting Trafficking Victims in the Era of Immigration Enforcement,

tion law, noncitizen abusers will be subject to deportation upon conviction for conduct that falls technically under Ohio's domestic violence and other laws, but in reality involves relatively minor infractions.[3]

Additionally, an abused spouse who lacks legal immigration status may be subjected to the added fear that her U.S. citizen abuser will turn her over to the Bureau of Immigration & Customs Enforcement (BICE, formerly INS) for deportation. Such fears are often compounded by the likelihood that this would result in permanent separation from her children. The very real threat of deportation is an additional complicating factor in the lives of immigrant families contending with domestic violence.

A basic understanding of recent changes in our country's immigration laws, as well as other laws that affect those not entitled to full-citizenship protections, is essential for anyone assisting those noncitizens who are involved in abusive relationships.[4] Therefore, anyone seeking to help, and not hinder, immigrant families contending with domestic violence issues must familiarize themselves with the answers to the threshold questions that those issues present.[5]

All of the information that exists about the rights and perils surrounding immigrants embroiled in violent interpersonal relationships

---

158 U. Pa. L. Rev. 1609, 1653 (2010); Chacón, Overcriminalizing Immigration, 102 J. Crim. L. & Criminology 613 (2012); Olivares, Battered by Law: The Political Subordination of Immigrant Women, 64 Am. U. L. Rev. 231, 238 (2014) ("Finally, cultural constraints and dictates, which teach obedience to one's husband and against leaving a marriage under any circumstance, may operate against a battered immigrant's attempts to escape abusive relationships.").

[3]See e.g., Cespedes v. Lynch, 805 F.3d 1274 (10th Cir. 2015) (holding that a conditional lawful permanent resident's violation of a no contact provision of a state issued protection order fell within the INA's removability statute); 8 U.S.C.A. § 1227(a)(2)(E)(ii); Garcia-Hernandez v. Boente, 847 F.3d 869, 872–73 (7th Cir. 2017) (In this case, the immigration judge looked at documents in the record of conviction to determine the portions of the protection order that Garcia-Hernandez was charged with and convicted of violating. The state court determined that Garcia–Hernandez violated the "stay away" portion of the protection order by going to Talavera's residence and confronting her. The immigration judge thus found that Garcia–Hernandez, by violating the protection order's "stay-away" provision, engaged in conduct that violated portions of the protection order that "involve[d] protection against credible threats of violence, repeated harassment, or bodily injury." 8 U.S.C.A. § 1227(a)(2)(E)(ii).).

[4]Virginia P. Coto, Lucha, The Struggle for Life: Legal Services for Battered Immigrant Women, 53 U. Miami L. Rev. 749 (1999).

[5]Leslye E. Orloff and Janice V. Kaguyutan, Offering a Helping Hand: Legal Protections For Battered Immigrant Women: A History of Legislative Responses, 10 Am. U. J. Gender Soc. Pol'y & L. 95 (2001). *Criminal Defense: Assault and Battery Cases*, 92 Am. Jur. Trials 1; Foreign Wives, Domestic Violence: US Law Stigmatizes and Fails to Protect Mail-Order Brides, 22 Hastings Women's L.J. 81, 111 (2011); Horowitz, Giving Battered Immigrant Fiancées a Way Out of Abusive Relationships: Proposed Amendments to the Immigration and Nationality Act, 78 Brook. L. Rev. 123 (2012); James A. Kushner, *Alienage—Federal Legislation*, Government Discrimination: Equal Protection Law and Litigation § 5:7; James A. Kushner, *Gender*, Government Discrimination: Equal Protection Law and Litigation § 5:11; James A. Kushner, *Privacy and Family—Marriage and Children*, Government Discrimination: Equal Protection Law and Litigation § 6:24; § 28:51. Victims of domestic violence, 3 Religious Organizations and the Law § 28:51 (March 2017 Update) (Another important service rendered by some churches is representation of victims of domestic violence. This area of legal services is complicated because the laws intended to protect these victims, most of whom are women, are often difficult to utilize.).

could easily fill a book of its own. The information in the sections that follow is provided to the practitioner in an effort to identify seminal issues that need to be considered when either the alleged victim, the alleged batterer, their children or all of the above are not citizens of the United States. This is by no means a complete compendium of all of the considerations that a thoughtful domestic violence practitioner is likely to contemplate while representing a client with immigration problems. This review should raise primary questions for further legal research on the specific constructs encountered in the individual case. More in-depth analysis and practical guidance may be found by consulting the domestic violence link at the website of the National Immigration Project: http://www.nationalimmigrationproject.org.

§ 18:15 Applicable federal statutory scheme

The current laws that apply to this problem are an amalgam of statutes and recent amendments to those statutes. The primary statute governing immigration law is the Immigration and Nationality Act (INA) contained at Title 8 of the United States Code Annotated (U.S.C.A.).

Over the years, Congress has attempted to "fix" perceived problems with the country's immigration policy with piecemeal amendments to the INA. The past 15 years have witnessed enormous changes to the INA, in particular to the immigration laws relevant to the confluence of immigration law and domestic violence. The pertinent federal legislation containing provisions that impact the rights of non-citizens who are parties to abusive relationships includes:

- 1986 Immigration Marriage Fraud Amendments to Title 8, U.S.C.A.—Immigration and Nationality Act of 1952[1]
- Title 6, U.S.C.A.
- Immigration Act of 1990[2]
- Violence Against Women Act of 1994—Part of the Violence Crime Control and Law Enforcement Act of 1994[3]
- Personal Responsibility and Work Opportunity and Reconciliation Act of 1996[4]
- Illegal Immigration Reform and Immigrant Responsibility Act of 1996[5]
- Victims of Trafficking and Violence Protection Act of 2000.[6]

[Section 18:15]

[1]Pub. L. No. 99-639, 100 Stat. 3537.

[2]Pub. L. No. 101-649, 104 Stat. 4978 (1990).

[3]Pub. L. No. 103-322, 108 Stat. 1796 (1994), amended by the Violence Against Women Reauthorization Act of 2013, Pub. L. No. 113-4, 127 Stat. 54 (2013). The original Violence Against Women Act of 1994 (VAWA). 42 U.S.C.A. § 14043, was repealed in 2013.

[4]Pub. L. No. 104-193, 110 Stat. 2105 (1996), *U and T Visas*, Law of Asylum in the United States § 1:16; Anker, Law of Asylum in the United States § 1:15 (2018 ed.) (discusses "U" and "T" visas, both of which visa categories condition lawful permanent resident (LPR) status on cooperation with law enforcement).

[5]Pub. L. No. 104-208, 110 Stat. 3009 (1996).

[6]Pub. L. No. 106-386, 114 Stat. 1464 (2000).

§ 18:16 Battered immigrant provisions of the Violence Against Women Act 2000—General provisions

Prior to the passage of the original Violence Against Women Act of 1994 (VAWA),[1] Congress heard from many battered women's advocates about significant problems encountered by immigrant women trapped in abusive relationships due in significant part to the fact that under existing immigration laws, their abusive spouses had control over whether to petition for their lawful immigration status (greencards). As a result, Congress amended provisions of the immigration law to allow for immigrant survivors of domestic violence, and their children, to obtain lawful status without relying on abusive partners or parents. The two primary avenues for doing this, outlined below, are known as the "self-petition" and "VAWA cancellation of removal."[2]

Congress further addressed the plight of domestic violence and immigrants in the Victims of Trafficking and Violence Protection Act of 2000, also known as VAWA 2000.[3] In passing theses provisions, Congress thought of the fact that immigrant women and children are often targeted as victims of crimes in the United States and needed help to be enabled to fully participate in the investigation of the crimes committed against them and the prosecution of the perpetrators of those crimes.

One of the most significant barriers immigrant victims of crime face is their fear of deportation due to their unlawful status. Congress recognized that the self-petitioning process and the VAWA cancellation of removal process as it existed before VAWA 2000 did not fully address this issue, in large part due to the fact that the legal remedies were only available to immigrant survivors whose partners were U.S. citizens or lawful permanent residents (LPRs or greencard holders). Immigrant crime victims whose perpetrators' status was unknown, or who were not LPRs or U.S. citizens, remained in fear of deportation. The precarious nature of their legal status inhibited their meaningful participation in the necessary investigation of the crimes committed against them. Congress moved to remedy this situation in VAWA 2000 by creating a new visa category for immigrant victims of crimes known as the U visa. Additionally, to address the ever-increasing problem of immigrants trafficked into the United States each year by illegal trafficking networks for illicit purposes, Congress also established the T Visa to allow the victims of such offenses the ability to seek relief from such exploitation.

In creating the U and the T Visas, Congress intended to strengthen the ability of law enforcement to detect, investigate and prosecute cases of domestic violence, sexual assault, trafficking and a wide variety of other crimes and to increase the level of safety and protection afforded to these vulnerable populations.[4]

[Section 18:16]

[1] 42 U.S.C.A. § 14043.

[2] VAWA 2005 amends 8 U.S.C.A. § 1229C(d) by exempting victims of domestic abuse, sexual assault or trafficking from sanctions for failing to voluntarily depart.

[3] 22 U.S.C.A. § 7101.

[4] The Violence Against Women Act of 2000, Section-by-Section Summary, Vol.

VAWA 2005 eliminates some of the major obstacles immigrant crime victims face in achieving safety and legal immigration status. Most of these amendments are to portions of the Immigration and Nationality Act and many are technical in nature, but are very powerful in their impact.[5]

§ 18:17 General screening questions to ask

"There are several ways a survivor may be eligible to attain legal immigration status without the abuser's knowledge, cooperation or control. The type of immigration relief may depend on:

Who is the perpetrator of the abuse

Whether the perpetrator is the victim's spouse, or former spouse

Whether the perpetrator is the victim's parent, step-parent, or son or daughter over age 21

Whether victim's child has been abused

The immigration status of the abuser

If the victim's spouse or parent has ever filed immigration papers for victim

If the victim came to U.S. on a fiancé visa

Whether the victim has filed a police report, or is willing to cooperate with police, prosecutors, or other government officials (e.g. EEOC, child protective services, adult protective services, judges or magistrates)."[1]

§ 18:18 Battered immigrant provisions of the Violence Against Women Act 2000—Those eligible to file a VAWA self-petition for lawful permanent resident status

Federal immigration law sets forth limited categories of non-citizens who are eligible to file a self-petition as a result of their abuse at the hands of their U.S. citizen or lawful permanent resident partners.[1] Those individuals include:

146, No. 126 Congressional Record, 106th Congress Second Session, Wednesday October 11, 2000, S10196. See also Greta D. Stoltz, The U Visa: Another Remedy for Battered Immigrant Women, 7 Scholar 127 (2004).

[5]American Bar Association Commission on Domestic Violence in VAWA 2005 Guide for Attorneys and can be found at: http://www.icadvinc.org/wp-content/uploads/2018/01/Standards-of-Practice-for-Lawyers-Representing-Victims-of-Domestic-Violence-Sexual-Assault-and-Stalking-in-Civil-Protection-Order-Cases.pdf.

[Section 18:17]

[1]*Identifying Forms of Immigration Relief Available for Battered Immigrant Victims*, 9 Family & Intimate Partner Violence Quarterly, Number 2, Civil Research Institute (2017).

[Section 18:18]

[1]VAWA 2005 amends 8 U.S.C.A. § 1154(a)(1)(D) to permit children who were eligible to self-petition before they turned 21 but did not and are now over 21, to self-petition up to age 25 if they can show the abuse was "at least one central reason" for the filing delay. This only applies to children of U.S. citizens. VAWA 2005 amends 8 U.S.C.A. § 1154(a)(1)(A) to expand VAWA self-petitioning to abuse victims who have been battered or subjected to extreme cruelty by their adult U.S. citizen son or daughter. See also http://apps.americanbar.org/humanrights/docs/project_docs/DV_Trafficking.pdf.

- Abused spouses or former spouses who are married or were married (within the past two years) to U.S. citizens or lawful permanent residents, on behalf of themselves.
- Abused spouses or former spouses who are or were married to U.S. citizens or lawful permanent residents, on behalf of their children under the age of 21 years (regardless of whether the children were abused or were the children of the U.S. citizen or lawful permanent resident).[2]
- Abused children of U.S. citizens or lawful permanent resident aliens, and for their children (regardless of whether there is an allegation that their children are abused).[3]
- Unabused spouses or former spouses of U.S. citizens or lawful permanent resident aliens, who are the immigrant parents of children abused by those U.S. citizens or lawful resident spouses or former spouses.[4]

Thus, in order to succeed on a VAWA self-petition, the petitioner must be able to prove that he or she:

(1) Is or was married to a U.S. citizen or lawful permanent resident or, in the case of a self-petitioning child, that the abuser is the child's natural parent, stepparent, or adoptive parent,[5] and that the spouse or partner subjected the petitioner to battery or extreme cruelty.[6]
The inclusion of the term "extreme cruelty" in the definition of battering contained in the immigration provisions of VAWA makes its reach much broader than the definition of assaultive behavior found in Ohio state law.[7] Thus, battering and extreme cruelty are defined in the federal regulations so as to encompass

[2] Immigration and Nationality Act § 204(a)(1)(A)(iii), Gallagher and Dizon, Immigration Law Service 2d § 7:164 (IMMLS2d updated May 2018); 8 U.S.C.A. § 1154(a)(1)(A)(iv), (B)(ii), amended by the Violence Against Women Reauthorization Act of 2013, Pub. L. No. 113-4, 127 Stat. 54 (2013).

[3] Immigration and Nationality Act § 204(a)(1)(A)(iv), Gallagher and Dizon, Immigration Law Service 2d § 7:177; 8 U.S.C.A. § 1154(a)(1)(A)(iv), (B)(ii), amended by the Violence Against Women Reauthorization Act of 2013, Pub. L. No. 113-4, 127 Stat. 54 (2013) (updated May 2018).

[4] Immigration and Nationality Act § 204(a)(1)(A)(iii), Gallagher and Dizon, Immigration Law Service 2d § 7:177; 8 U.S.C.A. § 1154(a)(1)(A)(iii), (B)(ii), amended by the Violence Against Women Reauthorization Act of 2013, Pub. L. No. 113-4, 127 Stat. 54 (2013).

[5] Immigration and Nationality Act § 204(a)(1)(A)(iv), Gallagher and Dizon, Immigration Law Service 2d § 7:164; 8 U.S.C.A. § 1154(a)(1)(A)(iv), (B)(ii), amended by the Violence Against Women Reauthorization Act of 2013, Pub. L. No. 113-4, 127 Stat. 54 (2013).

[6] Immigration and Nationality Act § 204(a)(1)(A)(iv), Gallagher and Dizon, Immigration Law Service 2d § 7:164; 8 U.S.C.A. § 1154(a)(1)(A)(iv), (B)(ii), amended by the Violence Against Women Reauthorization Act of 2013, Pub. L. No. 113-4, 127 Stat. 54 (2013), Lazaro v. Holder, 390 Fed. Appx. 319 (5th Cir. 2010); Uppal v. Holder, 605 F.3d 712 (9th Cir. 2010); Morales-Garcia v. Holder, 567 F.3d 1058, 09 (9th Cir. 2009).

[7] See RC 2919.25(A) to RC 2919.25(C); 8 C.F.R. 204.2(c)(1)(vi), 8 C.F.R. 204.2(e)(1)(vi). Morales-Garcia v. Holder, 567 F.3d 1058 (9th Cir. 2009); Aragon Trinidad v. Holder, 367 Fed. Appx. 749 (9th Cir. 2010); Vasquez-Hernandez v. Holder, 590 F.3d 1053 (9th Cir. 2010); Orea-Barbosa v. Holder, 402 Fed. Appx. 296, 297 (9th Cir. 2010).

not only causing or attempting to cause physical, mental, psychological and sexual injuries or abuse, but also other, more innocuous, conduct that on its surface may not appear to the casual observer to reflect violent behavior.[8] If the petitioner is able to show that certain non-violent actions of the alleged abusive spouse or partner nonetheless fit into an overall pattern of psychological violence, such evidence may be considered by the immigration authorities in determining whether the petition should be granted.[9]

Decisions of the state courts of Ohio provide guidance as to what actions other than physical abuse constitute extreme cruelty. For instance, the Fifth District Court of Appeals found that, where an abusive husband called a former girlfriend several times a week during his marriage to the petitioner, trying to get the former girlfriend to go to bed with him, isolated the wife from her family, limited her phone calls to 20 minutes, would not provide necessary medical care when she was gravely ill with cancer, refused to allow her to talk to her friends, made her feel incompetent, would start arguments with her and not speak to her for several days afterwards, and caused her to discover stained sheets and a mattress pad in the laundry basket upon her unexpected return from the hospital, there was sufficient evidence to sustain a trial court's conclusion that the husband had subjected the wife to "extreme cruelty."[10]

(2) Is a current resident of the United States, unless his or her situation fits into one of the categories exempted from this requirement. Such exemptions include instances where the abusive spouse or partner is an employee of the U.S. government or is a member of the U.S. uniformed services, or has subjected the petitioner to battery or extreme cruelty *in* the United States.[11]

(3) Either currently resides or once resided with the abuser.[12]

(4) Is of good moral character, and has been for the three years immediately preceding the filing of the petition.[13]

The statute does not provide a definition for "good moral character." The Immigration and Nationality Act does provide,

---

[8]See 8 C.F.R. 204.2(c)(1)(vi), 8 C.F.R. 204.2(e)(1)(vi) (1998).

[9]See 8 C.F.R. 204.2(c)(1)(vi), 8 C.F.R. 204.2(e)(1)(vi) (1998).

[10]Harshbarger v. Harshbarger, 1993 WL 221269 (Ohio Ct. App. 5th Dist. Licking County 1993); see also Conner v. Conner, 1981 WL 6290 (Ohio Ct. App. 5th Dist. Richland County 1981); Dickson v. Dickson, 1982 WL 5380 (Ohio Ct. App. 8th Dist. Cuyahoga County 1982).

[11]8 U.S.C.A. § 1154(a)(1)(A), (B), amended by the Violence Against Women Reauthorization Act of 2013, Pub. L. No. 113-4, 127 Stat. 54 (2013).

[12]8 U.S.C.A. § 1154(a)(1)(A), (B), amended by the Violence Against Women Reauthorization Act of 2013, Pub. L. No. 113-4, 127 Stat. 54 (2013).

[13]8 U.S.C.A. § 1154(a)(1)(A), (B), amended by the Violence Against Women Reauthorization Act of 2013, Pub. L. No. 113-4, 127 Stat. 54 (2013); 8 C.F.R. § 204.02(c)(2)(v).

however, statutory bars that will prevent a petitioner from establishing good moral character.[14] As a result:

- A habitual drunkard,
- A habitual gambler or anyone who has been convicted of two or more gambling offenses,
- Anyone who has engaged in prostitution within 10 years of the application for a visa, admission or adjustment of status,
- Anyone who was involved in smuggling a person into the United States,
- Anyone who is or has practiced polygamy,
- Anyone who has been convicted of any crime relating to a controlled substance,
- Anyone who has been convicted of any crime involving moral turpitude (except for petty or juvenile offenses),
- Anyone who has been convicted of two or more offenses for which the aggregate sentence actually imposed was five years or more,
- Anyone who has been confined to a penal institution for an aggregate period of 180 days or more,
- Anyone who has been convicted of an aggravated felony,

is an individual who cannot establish "good moral character" under the law.[15]

(5) That the petitioner married the abusive partner in good faith, which is construed under immigration law to mean not solely for an immigration benefit.[16]

"Screening questions might include:

Is the victim married or formerly married to a U.S. citizen or lawful permanent resident, or

Is the victim the parent of an adult, over 21 year old U.S. citizen son or daughter?

Has the victim or victim's under 21 year old child been battered or subjected to extreme cruelty?

Is or was the perpetrator of the battering or extreme cruelty the victim's U.S. citizen spouse, former spouse, parent, step-parent or over 21 year old son or daughter?

Did the victim live with the perpetrator for some period of time?

Did any of the abuse occur in the U.S.?")."[17]

---

[14] 8 U.S.C.A. § 1101(f) (1999), amended by the Violence Against Women Reauthorization Act of 2013, Pub. L. No. 113-4, 127 Stat. 54 (2013).

[15] 8 U.S.C.A. §§ 1101(f), 1182, 1254(a)(1), repealed in September 1996 by Pub. L. No. 104-208, 110 Stat. 3009-615.

[16] Gallagher and Dizon, Immigration Law Service 2d § 7:224, updated Feb. 2013, 8 U.S.C.A. § 1154(a)(1)(A), (B), amended by the Violence Against Women Reauthorization Act of 2013, Pub. L. No. 113-4, 127 Stat. 54 (2013) (Updated May 2018).

[17] *Identifying Forms of Immigration Relief Available for Battered Immigrant Victims*, 9 Family & Intimate Partner Violence Quarterly, Number 2, Civil Research Institute (2016).

§ 18:19 Battered immigrant provisions of the Violence Against Women Act 2000—U Visas eligibility[1]

U Visas (so named because of where they are found in the subsection of the U.S.C.A.)[2] cover the situations of non-citizens who are victims of crime and who have suffered substantial abuse, either mental or physical, as a result of that criminal activity. An applicant qualifies to obtain a U Visa if they have been the victim of one of the crimes enumerated in the Victims of Trafficking and Violence Protection Act[3]or if they are the victim's spouse or the victim's child or the parent of an alien child victim.

The types of criminal activity that U Visas cover include virtually all varieties of crimes against persons, obstructions of justice, blackmail, extortion, and unlawful restraints of persons and specifically include domestic violence and sexual assault, regardless of whether the violation was of any qualifying federal or state law.[4]

To qualify for a U Visa, applicants must first meet five criteria. They are:

(1) That the applicant suffered substantial physical or mental abuse as a result of being a victim of one or more of the criminal activities listed in the Victims of Trafficking and Violence Protection Act;[5]

(2) That they must possess information concerning the criminal activity;[6]

(3) That they must be helpful or be likely to be helpful to a federal, state, or local investigation or prosecution of criminal activity listed in the statute;[7]

(4) That they must obtain a certification from a law enforcement official, prosecutor, judge, BCIS official, or other federal or state

[Section 18:19]

[1]See generally Rena Cutlip-Mason, Natalie Nanasi and Joan Zorga, The U Visa: A Tool for Some Non-Citizen Battered Women, Vol. 13(3) Domestic Violence Report 33 (Feb./March 2008); see also Jean Bruggman & Elizabeth Keyes, Meeting the Legal Needs of Human Trafficking Victims: An Introduction for Domestic Violence Attorneys and Advocates, American Bar Association (2008); Eva Klein & Amanda Kloer, Meeting the Legal Needs of Child Trafficking Victims: An introduction for Children's Attorneys and Advocates, American Bar Association (2008); http://apps.americanbar.org/humanrights/docs/project_docs/DV_Trafficking.pdf.

[2]8 U.S.C.A. § 1101(a)(15)(U), amended by the Violence Against Women Reauthorization Act of 2013, Pub. L. No. 113-4, 127 Stat. 54 (2013).

[3]8 U.S.C.A. § 1101(a)(15)(U)(i), amended by the Violence Against Women Reauthorization Act of 2013, Pub. L. No. 113-4, 127 Stat. 54 (2013); 8 U.S.C.A. § 1101(a)(15)(U)(ii), amended by the Violence Against Women Reauthorization Act of 2013, Pub. L. No. 113-4, 127 Stat. 54 (2013).

[4]8 U.S.C.A. § 1101(a)(15)(U)(iii), amended by the Violence Against Women Reauthorization Act of 2013, Pub. L. No. 113-4, 127 Stat. 54 (2013).

[5]8 U.S.C.A. § 1101(a)(15)(U)(i)(I), amended by the Violence Against Women Reauthorization Act of 2013, Pub. L. No. 113-4, 127 Stat. 54 (2013).

[6]8 U.S.C.A. § 1101(a)(15)(U)(i)(II), amended by the Violence Against Women Reauthorization Act of 2013, Pub. L. No. 113-4, 127 Stat. 54 (2013).

[7]8 U.S.C.A. § 1101(a)(15)(U)(i)(III), amended by the Violence Against Women Reauthorization Act of 2013, Pub. L. No. 113-4, 127 Stat. 54 (2013).

authorities investigating or prosecuting any of the criminal activities defined in the statute;[8] and

(5) That the criminal activities investigated or prosecuted violated the laws of the United States or occurred in the United States or the territories or possessions of the United States.[9]

Filing an application for a U Visa is appropriate when:

(1) The victim's abuser is not a U.S. citizen or lawful permanent resident;
(2) The victim's abuser is not a spouse or parent;
(3) The violence used against the victim falls outside the definition of domestic violence, but is a crime or form of sexual violence covered by the statute;
(4) A battered immigrant was divorced from the citizen or lawful permanent resident more than two years ago;
(5) A battered immigrant is seeking a waiver of inadmissibility, since such waivers are broader for those seeking a U Visa than those waivers provided in cases where the battered immigrant is pursuing a self-petition for legal resident status.[10]

"Screening questions might include:

Is the victim a victim of any of the following criminal activities: attempts, conspiracy and solicitation to commit any of the following: rape, torture, human trafficking, incest, domestic violence, sexual assault, prostitution, sexual exploitation, female genital mutilation, being held hostage, slave trade, involuntary servitude, stalking, fraud in foreign labor contracting, kidnapping, false imprisonment, perjury or any similar activity?

Did the criminal activity occur in the U.S.; if not, was it a violation of U.S. law?

Does the victim have information that has been, is being or is likely to be helpful in the detection, investigation, prosecution, conviction or sentencing of the perpetrator?

Did the victim or is the victim willing to: call the police, make a police report, speak to the police or prosecutors, or participate in a hearing or trial?[11]

§ 18:20 Battered immigrant provisions of the Violence Against Women Act 2000—T Visas eligibility

Victims of "severe forms of trafficking" are eligible for relief.[1] Severe forms of trafficking are defined as:

---

[8] 8 U.S.C.A. § 1184(p)(1), amended by the Violence Against Women Reauthorization Act of 2013, Pub. L. No. 113-4, 127 Stat. 54 (2013).

[9] 8 U.S.C.A. § 1101(a)(15)(U)(i)(IV), amended by the Violence Against Women Reauthorization Act of 2013, Pub. L. No. 113-4, 127 Stat. 54 (2013).

[10] 8 U.S.C.A. § 1101(a)(15)(U), amended by the Violence Against Women Reauthorization Act of 2013, Pub. L. No. 113-4, 127 Stat. 54 (2013).

[11] *Identifying Forms of Immigration Relief Available for Battered Immigrant Victims*, 9 Family & Intimate Partner Violence Quarterly, Number 2, Civil Research Institute (2016).

[Section 18:20]

[1] 22 U.S.C.A. § 7105, amended by the Violence Against Women Reauthorization

(1) Sex trafficking in which a commercial sex act is induced by force, fraud, or coercion, or in which the person induced to perform such act has not attained the age of 18 years;[2]

(2) The recruitment, harboring, transportation, provision, or obtaining of a person for labor or service through the use of force, fraud, or coercion for the purpose of subjugation to involuntary servitude, peonage, debt bondage, or slavery.[3]

Additional criteria for a successful application include:

(1) Proof that the applicant is physically present in the United States, American Samoa (AS), or the Northern Mariana Islands (NMI) because of being a victim of trafficking. Such proof must establish that the victim is currently being held in a trafficking situation in the US, AS or NMI, was recently liberated from a trafficking situation in one of those locations, or was previously trafficked and remained in one of those locations for reasons directly related to the trafficking. Such reasons include that the victim was liberated by law enforcement and is continuing to assist, escaped before law enforcement became involved and had no clear chance to leave the location in the interim, and, in the case of those who were previously trafficked, left the location and then returned as a result of continued victimization at the hands of the traffickers or as a result of a new incident. Others who leave the location voluntarily, are presumed to be ineligible to obtain a T Visa.[4]

(2) Proof that the applicant has complied with any reasonable request for assistance in the investigation of a law enforcement agency or is under the age of 18 years old.[5]

(3) Proof that the applicant will suffer extreme hardship involving unusual and severe harm if removed from the country.[6]

(4) Proof that the applicant is admissible to the United States, or if inadmissible, grounds to have the ineligibility waived.[7]

(5) For victims whose last day of victimization occurred before October 28, 2000, filing of the application for the T Visa before January 31, 2002, or if the victim was under 21 years of age, then either within one year of the victim's twenty-first birthday, or within one year of January 31, 2002 (whichever is later).

Act of 2013, Pub. L. No. 113-4, 127 Stat. 54 (2013).

[2]22 U.S.C.A. § 7102(9)(A), amended by the Violence Against Women Reauthorization Act of 2013, Pub. L. No. 113-4, 127 Stat. 54 (2013).

[3]22 U.S.C.A. § 7102(9)(B), amended by the Violence Against Women Reauthorization Act of 2013, Pub. L. No. 113-4, 127 Stat. 54 (2013).

[4]8 C.F.R. § 214.11(b)(2). Gallagher, Dizon, and Wettstein, Immigration Law Service 2d § 6:309, updated May 2018.

[5]8 C.F.R. & 214.11(b)(3). Gallagher and Dizon, Immigration Law Service 2d § 6:309, updated Feb. 2013.

[6]8 C.F.R. & 214.11(b)(4). Gallagher and Dizon, Immigration Law Service 2d § 6:309, updated May 2018; Morales-Garcia v. Holder, 567 F.3d 1058 (9th Cir. 2009); Jean-Louis v. Attorney General of U.S., 582 F.3d 462 (3d Cir. 2009).

[7]8 C.F.R. & 214.11(b). But see Rivas-Banos v. Holder, 344 Fed. Appx. 30 (5th Cir. 2009); Luna-Arevalo v. Holder, 341 Fed. Appx. 290 (9th Cir. 2009); Vasquez-Hernandez v. Holder, 590 F.3d 1053 (9th Cir. 2010).

Waivers of the deadline requirement may be granted under extraordinary circumstances.[8]

(6) For victims whose last day of victimization occurred after October 28, 2002, there is no deadline for filling of the application for the T Visa.

"Screening questions might include:

Was the victim involved in a commercial sex act induced by force, fraud or coercion?

Was the victim induced to perform a commercial sex act when under age 18?

Was the victim subjected to involuntary servitude, peonage, debt bondage or slavery by force, fraud or coercion?

Was the victim kidnapped, coerced, or recruited to migrate to the U.S.?

Does the victim have control over her own identity documents?

Has the victim's movement been restricted since arriving in the U.S.?

Is the victim under 18 years of age or has the victim done or is the victim willing to do the following: make a police report, speak to police or prosecutors, participate in a trial or hearing or willing to assist in an investigation or prosecution of the traffickers?"[9]

§ 18:21 Battered immigrant provisions of the Violence Against Women Act 2000—Cancellation of removal

The Violence Against Women Act provisions that address "cancellation of removal" (formerly known as suspension of deportation) created a very complex process through which the immigration courts waive the grounds for the applicant's removal from the United States.[1] This process should not be undertaken without the assistance of an attorney who is extremely well-versed in immigration law. Cancellation of removal can only be undertaken once a removal proceeding is pending before an immigration judge.[2] Therefore, a potential applicant who has not yet been the subject of a removal complaint must first surrender to the authorities before a request for cancellation of removal will be entertained.[3] If an application for cancellation of re-

---

[8] 8 C.F.R. § 214.11(d)(4).

[9] *Identifying Forms of Immigration Relief Available for Battered Immigrant Victims*, 9 Family & Intimate Partner Violence Quarterly, Number 2, Civil Research Institute (2016).

[Section 18:21]

[1] Gallagher, Dizon, and Wettstein, Immigration Law Service 2d § 13:225, updated May 2018. See also INA § 240A(b)(2)(A)(i); 8 C.F.R. § 1240.11(a)(1).

[2] INA § 240A(b)(2)(A)(i)(II); Gallagher and Dizon, Immigration Law Service 2d § 13:228, updated May 2018. But see In re Marriage of Meredith, 148 Wash. App. 887, 201 P.3d 1056 (Div. 2 2009).

[3] INA § 240A(b)(2)(A)(i)(I); Gallagher and Dizon, Immigration Law Service 2d § 13:228, updated May 2018; Foster v. Foster, 654 F. Supp. 2d 348 (W.D. Pa. 2009); Krefter v. Wills, 623 F. Supp. 2d 125 (D. Mass. 2009).

moval is granted, the removal process can be ended and an applicant can receive legal permanent residence status.[4]

§ 18:22 Battered immigrant provisions of the Violence Against Women Act 2000—Those eligible to seek cancellation of removal

Cancellation of removal is a remedy available only to a victim who is in removal proceedings who can show extreme hardship if she were to be removed and has been in the U.S. for three years of continued presence.[1] Those individuals who are eligible to seek cancellation of removal include:

(1) Abused spouses, former spouses and intended spouses of U.S. citizens and lawful permanent residents of the United States;[2]
(2) Abused children of U.S. citizens and lawful permanent residents of the United States for themselves and their children;[3] and
(3) Parents of children abused by a U.S. citizen or lawful permanent resident.[4]

For individuals who have not yet entered the removal process, but who wish to be placed in removal proceedings to avail themselves of cancellation of removal, they may surrender to the U.S. Department of Homeland Security. At that time, DHS may issue an NTA, thus initiating removal proceedings, which are conducted before an immigration judge. Also, contact National Immigrant Women's Advocacy Project (NIWAP) at 202-274-4457 or e-mail at mailto:info@niwap.org.[5]

Interestingly, it is not just those who are abused who can avail themselves of the cancellation of removal process.[6] An alien's commission of an offense of domestic violence may be considered a crime of moral turpitude and is, therefore, deportable.[7] However, an individual convicted of domestic violence, either as a first, second or fourth degree

---

[4]See INA § 240A(b)(2)(A).

[Section 18:22]

[1]*Identifying Forms of Immigration Relief Available for Battered Immigrant Victims*, 9 Family & Intimate Partner Violence Quarterly, Number 2, Civil Research Institute (2017).

[2]Gallagher and Dizon, Immigration Law Service 2d § 13:225, updated May 2018. See also INA § 240A(b)(2)(A)(i)(I).

[3]Gallagher and Dizon, Immigration Law Service 2d § 13:225. See also INA § 240A(b)(2)(A)(i)(II).

[4]Gallagher and Dizon, Immigration Law Service 2d § 13:225; Lozano v. Montoya Alvarez, 572 U.S. 1, 134 S. Ct. 1224, 1237-38, 188 L. Ed. 2d 200 (2014).

[5]8 C.F.R. § 274a.12(c)(10); Gallagher and Dizon, Immigration Law Service 2d § 13:228.

[6]Immigration and Nationality Act § 240A(b)(1)(C), or §§ 240A(b)(1)(B) and 101(f)(3), Gallagher and Dizon, Immigration Law Service 2d § 13:222.

[7]In re Tran, 21 I. & N. Dec. 291, 1996 WL 170083 (B.I.A. 1996); Morales-Garcia v. Holder, 567 F.3d 1058 (9th Cir. 2009); Jean-Louis v. Attorney General of U.S., 582 F.3d 462 (3d Cir. 2009), Gallagher and Dizon, Immigration Law Service 2d § 13:88; Aldape-Garcia v. Holder, 472 Fed. Appx. 304 (5th Cir. 2012); U.S. v. Ramos-Perez, 2011 WL 5513234 (S.D. Cal. 2011), aff'd, 533 Fed. Appx. 737 (9th Cir. 2013), opinion amended and superseded, 572 Fed. Appx. 465 (9th Cir. 2014) and aff'd, 572 Fed. Appx. 465 (9th Cir. 2014); U.S. v. Villavicencio, 2011 WL 4345161 (N.D. Cal. 2011); Prudencio v. Holder, 669 F.3d 472 (4th Cir. 2012); Narayan v. Holder, 501 Fed. Appx.

misdemeanor, may still apply for cancellation of removal, if removal proceedings are commenced.[8] That is because the "description" of the category of offenses encompassing crimes involving moral turpitude in the law also includes an exception.

Accordingly, because a misdemeanor offense that carries a maximum sentence of no more than 1 year in prison is a "petty offense" under the act,[9] it does not bar a defendant, on the basis of the misdemeanor conviction alone, from establishing good moral character under the immigration law. A defendant who has such a conviction retains eligibility for cancellation of removal.[10] In a Fifth Circuit case, the court held that an alien's prior Texas misdemeanor assault conviction was not for a crime involving moral turpitude, and thus did not preclude his eligibility for cancellation of removal.[11]

Employing the same reasoning, an alien convicted of a petty offense involving moral turpitude is not ineligible for voluntary departure, either.[12] Additionally, even if an alien accumulates more than one domestic violence misdemeanor conviction, that fact, in and of itself, will not prevent eligibility to file an application for cancellation of removal.[13] Only convictions of two or more felony crimes of moral turpitude not arising out of a single scheme of criminal misconduct, rendering an alien inadmissible under the immigration law, would prevent eligibility to file an application for cancellation of removal.[14]

"Screening questions might include:

Has the victim had an order of deportation or removal issued against her?

Is the victim currently in removal proceedings?

Is the victim a spouse, former spouse (may file beyond the two year limitation), child or step-child of a U.S. citizen or lawful permanent resident?

Was the victim's child abused by the child's other parent who is a U.S. citizen or lawful permanent resident?

Did the victim or victim's child suffer battering or extreme cruelty perpetrated by a person described above?

675 (9th Cir. 2012). But see Alonzo v. Lynch, 821 F.3d 951 (8th Cir. 2016); Palapa-Cabrerra v. Sessions, 727 Fed. Appx. 315 (9th Cir. 2018).

[8]Immigration and Nationality Act § 240A(b)(1)(C), or §§ 240A(b)(1)(B) and 101(f)(3)—INA § 101 amended by the Violence Against Women Reauthorization Act of 2013, Pub. L. No. 113-4, 127 Stat. 54 (2013). See In re Garcia-Hernandez, 23 I. & N. Dec. 590, 2003 WL 21043271 (B.I.A. 2003). But see Rivas-Banos v. Holder, 344 Fed. Appx. 30 (5th Cir. 2009); Luna-Arevalo v. Holder, 341 Fed. Appx. 290 (9th Cir. 2009); Vasquez-Hernandez v. Holder, 590 F.3d 1053 (9th Cir. 2010), Gallagher and Dizon, Immigration Law Service 2d § 13:88, updated Feb. 2013; Lopez Ayala v. Holder, 452 Fed. Appx. 749 (9th Cir. 2011).

[9]Immigration and Nationality Act § 212(a)(2), amended by the Violence Against Women Reauthorization Act of 2013, Pub. L. No. 113-4, 127 Stat. 54 (2013).

[10]Immigration and Nationality Act § 240A(b)(1)(B), amended by the Violence Against Women Reauthorization Act of 2013, Pub. L. No. 113-4, 127 Stat. 54 (2013).

[11]Gomez-Perez v. Lynch, 829 F.3d 323 (5th Cir. 2016).

[12]Matter of Urpi-Sancho, 13 I. & N. Dec. 641, 1970 WL 18758 (B.I.A. 1970).

[13]In re Garcia-Hernandez, 23 I. & N. Dec. 590, 2003 WL 21043271 (B.I.A. 2003).

[14]INA § 240A(b)(1)(C), or §§ 240A(b)(1)(B) and 101(f)(3), INA § 101 amended by the Violence Against Women Reauthorization Act of 2013, Pub. L. No. 113-4, 127 Stat. 54 (2013). See In re Garcia-Hernandez, 23 I. & N. Dec. 590, 2003 WL 21043271 (B.I.A. 2003).

Has the victim lived in the U.S. continually for at least three years?[15]

How did the victim enter the U.S.?"[16]

§ 18:23 Other remedies available to battered immigrants

There are two other forms of immigrant relief. The first is the battered spouse waiver which "helps battered spouses of U.S. citizens who have filed immigration applications and attained conditional permanent residence for the foreign born spouse; the victim will have a lawful permanent residency card that expires two years after it was issued."[1]

Finally, "immigrants who are granted a work visa are often allowed to obtain immigration visas for their spouses and children. However, these visas of work visa holders do not include legal work authorization. It is often the case that the abused spouse cannot flee the batterer. VAWA 2005 remedied this situation by allowing abused immigrant spouses to obtain work authorization in order to be able to leave the abuser and sustain themselves and their children apart from the abuser."[2]

§ 18:24 Battered immigrants and civil protection orders

Q & A: Are battered immigrants able to obtain civil protection orders?

Yes. Civil protection orders are granted by the courts of each of the states and a CPO, once granted, is enforceable throughout the country. Because a CPO is civil in nature and victim initiated, there is no criminal justice system involvement. Granting a CPO is not dependent on immigration status and the issuance of a CPO has no immigration consequences for either party, unless violated.

There is no federal or state requirement for police, prosecutors or the courts to ask about the immigration status of a victim of domestic violence. Further, there is no federal or state mandate for police, prosecutors or the courts to report the immigration status of a victim to immigration services.[1]

As in most states, consent civil protection orders are permissible in Ohio. Some experts advise caution when entering into a consent

---

[15]See INA section 240(A)(b)(2)(B) for allowance of limited absences.

[16]*Identifying Forms of Immigration Relief Available for Battered Immigrant Victims*, 9 Family & Intimate Partner Violence Quarterly, Number 2, Civil Research Institute (2017).

[Section 18:23]

[1]*Identifying Forms of Immigration Relief Available for Battered Immigrant Victims*, 9 Family & Intimate Partner Violence Quarterly, Number 2, Civil Research Institute (2017).

[2]*Identifying Forms of Immigration Relief Available for Battered Immigrant Victims*, 9 Family & Intimate Partner Violence Quarterly, Number 2, Civil Research Institute (2017); see also Section 106 of the Immigration and Nationality Act.

[Section 18:24]

[1]See NOW Legal Momentum, Immigrant Women Program at 212-925-6635 ext. 650 or email at help@legalmomentum.org.

protection order because it is unclear whether a consent protection order is jurisdictionally sound. "For a protection order to be legally binding, the court must have subject matter jurisdiction to issue the order. Absent subject matter jurisdiction, these protection orders are not enforceable under VAWA's full faith and credit provisions (across state lines)."[2] Therefore, it is possible that that a protection order issued without a finding could be vacated for a lack of jurisdiction.

To remedy this potential problem, all Ohio protection orders contain a statement that the court has found that it has jurisdiction over the parties and subject matter and that Respondent will be provided with reasonable notice and opportunity to be heard within the time required by Ohio law. All protection orders contain a provision that provides that "[t]he above named Respondent is restrained from committing acts of abuse or threats of abuse against the Petitioner and other protected persons named in this order as set forth below. Additional terms of this Order are set forth below."[3]

Q & A: Besides the usual remedies available to victims of domestic violence, are there other remedies that may help immigrant victims of domestic violence?

Yes. In Ohio, RC 3113.31(E)(1) contains a catch-all that provides, "after an ex parte hearing or full hearing, the court may grant any protection order, with or without bond, or approve any consent agreement to bring about a cessation of domestic violence against the family or household members." Additionally, RC 3113.31(E)(1)(h) provides that the court can grant other relief that it deems equitable and fair.

Among the remedies that should be provided include child support and spousal support. Such awards are critical for low income battered immigrants who may not be able to work and are not eligible to receive government benefits.[4]

Besides support, other forms of economic relief are available to battered immigrants including rent, mortgage and utility payments, possession of the residence or vehicle, or child care expenses.[5]

Finally, it is important that attorneys consider immigration affidavits of support as evidence of the ability to pay child support and/or spousal support. In the affidavit of support, the U.S. citizen or LPR agrees to sponsor the immigrant by way of a sworn statement so that the immigrant does not end up as a public charge.[6] "Among the many

[2] *Seeking Protection Orders for Immigrant Victims*, 9 Family & Intimate Partner Violence Quarterly, Number 2, Civil Research Institute (2017). see also 18:9.

[3] Sup. R. 10.01-H-J.

[4] *Providing Economic Relief for Immigrant Victims: Child Support and Spousal Support*, 9 Family & Intimate Partner Violence Quarterly, Number 3, Civil Research Institute (2017).

[5] *Providing Economic Relief for Immigrant Victims: Child Support and Spousal Support*, 9 Family & Intimate Partner Violence Quarterly, Number 3, Civil Research Institute (2017).

[6] Form I-864; see also In re Marriage of Kumar, 13 Cal. App. 5th 1072, 220 Cal. Rptr. 3d 863 (1st Dist. 2017), review denied, (Oct. 18, 2017)(holding that a victim of domestic violence who was brought to the U.S. through an I-864 Affidavit of Support may seek to enforce financial support obligations in family/domestic relations court as set forth in the I-864 Affidavit rather than in state or federal court).

requirements to qualify as a sponsor, the petitioner must demonstrate an annual income of at least 125 % of federal poverty guidelines."[7]

Divorce does not terminate the obligation.

These two provisions give a court the statutory authority to consider some of the following remedies. For example, an immigrant victim may also have a pending immigration case or is in the process of filing an application. The respondent may be ordered to provide the petitioner with access to or copies of any documents related to the petitioner's immigration application, including work permit, social security card, alien registration card and passport. Sometimes, a petitioner may need to prove the respondent's immigration status and may need certain documents which may include a passport, work permit, certificate of naturalization or citizenship paper, birth certificate, etc.

A respondent may be ordered not to withdraw an application for permanent residency that he has filed on petitioner's behalf and may even be ordered to take all necessary action to ensure that the petitioner's application is not denied. Finally, a respondent may be enjoined from communication with any government agency including ICE or the Department of Homeland Security or a particular Embassy or Consulate about the petitioner.[8]

Q & A: Can the CPO include provisions regarding children?

Yes. Child issues usually arise when a non-citizen respondent is thought to want to return with the children to his/her country of residence. Clients should be asked certain questions which may aid the attorney in evaluating whether specific provisions should be included in the CPO. For example, does the respondent have family living abroad? Does he/she have the financial means to travel abroad? Has the respondent taken any recent trips abroad to visit family or friends? Is the respondent's country of origin a signatory to the Hague Convention?[9] Has the respondent made threats to kidnap the children or prevent the petitioner from seeing them? Has the respondent recently lost a job?

---

[7] *Providing Economic Relief for Immigrant Victims: Child Support and Spousal Support*, 9 Family & Intimate Partner Violence Quarterly, Number 3, Civil Research Institute (2017). See also In re Marriage of Kumar, 13 Cal. App. 5th 1072, 220 Cal. Rptr. 3d 863 (1st Dist. 2017), review denied, (Oct. 18, 2017) (court held that an immigrant spouse has standing to enforce the support obligation created by an I-864 affidavit in *state* court (emphasis added) and that an immigrant spouse has not duty to mitigate damages and find work).

[8] And see In re Marriage of Meredith, 148 Wash. App. 887, 201 P.3d 1056 (Div. 2 2009) (holding that a domestic violence protection order, which prohibited a husband from contacting any agency regarding his wife's immigration status, violated husband's right to free speech and violated his right to petition government). To the same point, see also In re Marriage of Guthrie, 188 Wash. App. 1057, 2015 WL 4400535 (Div. 1 2015), review denied, 185 Wash. 2d 1005, 366 P.3d 1245 (2016).

[9] See https://www.hcch.net/en/states/hcch-members for an updated list of signatories; see also Simcox v. Simcox, 511 F.3d 594, 2007 FED App. 0502P (6th Cir. 2007) (reversing the district court's order requiring a U.S. citizen (mother) to return to Mexico with two of her children who were living with her in Ohio. The district court found that the children's return was required by the Hague Convention. The case was remanded with instructions to the district court to determine appropriate conditions to ensure the children's safety when they returned to Mexico.); Foster v. Foster, 654 F. Supp. 2d 348 (W.D. Pa. 2009); Krefter v. Wills, 623 F. Supp. 2d 125 (D. Mass. 2009). See also Rial v. Rijo, 2010 WL 1643995 (S.D. N.Y. 2010); In re Filipczak,

In some cases, a respondent may be specifically prohibited from removing children from the U.S. or obtaining passports for them.

The petitioner shall provide a certified copy of the protection order to the Office of Passport Services with a written request that a passport shall not be issued for the child. The order must include a provision that names her/him residential parent and legal custodian of the child(ren).

Since the Department of State may not revoke a passport that has already been issued to the child and because there is no way to track the use of a passport once it has been issued, it is important to request that the court or the attorney hold the passport, if a parent believes that the other parent would abduct the child from the United States.

If the child is a dual national and the custodial parent fears abduction, that parent should request that a foreign embassy or consulate in the U.S. not issue a passport to the child. Such a request must be in writing and include a certified copy of all relevant orders including that the parent is the sole custodial parent and that he/she is not permitted to travel outside of the United States. On the other hand, if the child is only a U.S. citizen, the parent should request that no visas for that country be issued in the child's U.S. passport. Unfortunately, no international law mandates compliance with that request, although some countries may voluntarily comply.

Further, the petitioner should also request in writing that the U.S. Department of State's Children's Passport Issuance Alert Program inform her or him if the other parent or guardian requests a passport in the name of a minor child.[10] It is not necessary for a parent to have any custodial rights to the child in order to request entry into CPIAP.

Respondents may also be enjoined from removing children from the court's jurisdiction or relinquishing children's passports.[11]

Q & A: What type of documentation may be needed for a battered immigrant victim of domestic violence?

It depends. If a victim files a divorce, she or he may need to obtain a marriage certificate or license, wedding or family photos, family event photos, and love letters in order to prove that a valid marriage existed.

If a victim wants to self-petition under VAWA, she or he needs to show she or he was married or formerly married to the abuser. She or he also needs to show she or he resided with the abuser, insurance

838 F. Supp. 2d 174 (S.D. N.Y. 2011), judgment aff'd, 513 Fed. Appx. 16 (2d Cir. 2013); In re Lozano, 809 F. Supp. 2d 197 (S.D. N.Y. 2011), aff'd, 697 F.3d 41, 86 A.L.R. Fed. 2d 619 (2d Cir. 2012), aff'd, 572 U.S. 1, 134 S. Ct. 1224, 188 L. Ed. 2d 200 (2014); Aly v. Aden, 2013 WL 593420 (D. Minn. 2013); Taglieri v. Monasky, 876 F.3d 868, 875, (6th Cir. 2017), reh'g en banc granted, opinion vacated, (Mar. 2, 2018) and on reh'g en banc, 2018 WL 5023787 (6th Cir. 2018); Orellana v. Cartagena, 2017 WL 5586374, *8 (E.D. Tenn. 2017); Luis Ischiu v. Gomez Garcia, 274 F. Supp. 3d 339, 350 (D. Md. 2017); Soonhee Kim v. Ferdinand, 287 F. Supp. 3d 607, 627 (E.D. La. 2018).

[10]Children's Passport Alert Issuance Program (CPIAP), U.S. Department of State Overseas Citizen Services, Office of Children's Issues at 1-888-407-4747 or https://travel.state.gov/content/travel/en/International-Parental-Child-Abduction/prevention/passport-issuance-alert-program.html.

[11]See for example, Owais v. Costandinidis, 2008-Ohio-1615, 2008 WL 867726 (Ohio Ct. App. 2d Dist. Greene County 2008).

policies with spouse as beneficiary, mail addressed to both, joint bank accounts and/or copies of joint leases and bills will demonstrate that. She or he will also need evidence of the violence and police, medical, or other court documents relative to the relationship may provide sufficient proof. Finally, she or he will need to document the abuser's status as a citizen or lawful permanent resident. A birth certificate, copy of the abuser's passport or green card may provide needed evidence when appearing before an immigration official.

Q & A: What exceptions to the Hague Convention's requirement that a child must be returned to the country of habitual residence may be invoked in order to protect a child who is likely to be abused by the parent seeking repatriation?

The Hague Convention, a multilateral treaty, is designed to protect children internationally from the harmful effects of their wrongful removal by establishing procedures to ensure their prompt return to the State of their habitual residence, so that the rights of custody and of access under the law of one Contracting State are effectively respected in the other Contracting States.[12]

The removal of a child under the Convention is deemed wrongful when it is in breach of rights of custody attributed to a person under the law of the State in which the child was habitually resident immediately before the removal.[13] Under the Convention, when a parent wrongfully removes a child from one contracting state which is the child's country of habitual residence to another contracting state, the other parent may initiate a proceeding to repatriate the child to the first state. In the United States, the petitioning party bears the burden of proving that the child was wrongfully removed.[14] Once the petitioner establishes that removal was wrongful, the child must be returned unless the respondent can establish one of four defenses.[15]

Under Article 13(b) of the Hague Convention, one of the defenses is that repatriation would constitute a grave risk of harm to the child. A grave risk of harm from repatriation arises in two situations: "(1) where returning the child means sending him to a zone of war, famine, or disease; or (2) in cases of serious abuse or neglect, or extraordinary emotional dependence, when the court in the country of habitual residence, for whatever reason, may be incapable or unwilling to give the child adequate protection."[16] The potential harm to the child must be severe, and the the level of risk and danger required to

---

[12]Abbott v. Abbott, 560 U.S. 1, 130 S. Ct. 1983, 2002, 176 L. Ed. 2d 789, 7 A.L.R. Int'l 749 (2010); Luis Ischiu v. Gomez Garcia, 274 F. Supp. 3d 339, 350 (D. Md. 2017); Soonhee Kim v. Ferdinand, 287 F. Supp. 3d 607, 627 (E.D. La. 2018); Campomanes Flores v. Elias-Arata, 2018 WL 3495865, *3 (M.D. Fla. 2018).

[13]Abbott v. Abbott, 560 U.S. 1, 130 S. Ct. 1983, 2002, n.6, 176 L. Ed. 2d 789, 7 A.L.R. Int'l 749 (2010); Luis Ischiu v. Gomez Garcia, 274 F. Supp. 3d 339, 350 (D. Md. 2017); Soonhee Kim v. Ferdinand, 287 F. Supp. 3d 607, 627 (E.D. La. 2018); Campomanes Flores v. Elias-Arata, 2018 WL 3495865, *3 (M.D. Fla. 2018).

[14]22 U.S.C.A. § 9003.

[15]Blondin v. Dubois, 189 F.3d 240, 246 (2d Cir. 1999). See also, Oliver A. v. Diana Pina B., 151 A.D.3d 485, 56 N.Y.S.3d 311 (1st Dep't 2017), leave to appeal denied, 29 N.Y.3d 917, 64 N.Y.S.3d 667, 86 N.E.3d 559 (2017).

[16]Blondin v. Dubois, 238 F.3d 153, 162 (2d Cir. 2001). See also, Luis Ischiu v. Gomez Garcia, 274 F. Supp. 3d 339, 350 (D. Md. 2017)

trigger this exception has consistently been held to be very high.[17] The grave risk involves not only the magnitude of the potential harm but also the probability that the harm will materialize.[18]

This " 'grave risk' exception is to be interpreted narrowly, lest it swallow the rule.[19]

---

[17]Norden-Powers v. Beveridge, 125 F. Supp. 2d 634, 640 (E.D. N.Y. 2000).

[18]Van De Sande v. Van De Sande, 431 F.3d 567, 570 (7th Cir. 2005); de Freitas Pinto v. Barone, 2017 WL 2779700, *3 (S.D. Cal. 2017); Luis Ischiu v. Gomez Garcia, 274 F. Supp. 3d 339, 350 (D. Md. 2017).

[19]Simcox v. Simcox, 511 F.3d 594, 604, 2007 FED App. 0502P (6th Cir. 2007); see Souratgar v. Lee, 720 F.3d 96 (2d Cir. 2013), citing an earlier opinion that held permissive invocation of the affirmative defenses would lead to the collapse of the whole structure of the Convention by depriving it of the spirit of mutual confidence which is its inspiration, i.e., Blondin v. Dubois, 189 F.3d 240, 246 (2d Cir. 1999). See also, Acosta v. Acosta, 725 F.3d 868, 92 Fed. R. Evid. Serv. 68 (8th Cir. 2013); Vilen-Burch v. Burch, 2013 WL 1909472 (S.D. Ind. 2013); Selo v. Selo, 929 F. Supp. 2d 718 (E.D. Mich. 2013); Panteleris v. Panteleris, 30 F. Supp. 3d 674 (N.D. Ohio 2014), aff'd, 601 Fed. Appx. 345 (6th Cir. 2015); Culculoglu v. Culculoglu, 2013 WL 4045905 (D. Nev. 2013); Taglieri v. Monasky, 876 F.3d 868, 875 (6th Cir. 2017), reh'g en banc granted, opinion vacated, (Mar. 2, 2018) and on reh'g en banc, 2018 WL 5023787 (6th Cir. 2018); Orellana v. Cartagena, 2017 WL 5586374, *8 (E.D. Tenn. 2017); Luis Ischiu v. Gomez Garcia, 274 F. Supp. 3d 339, 350 (D. Md. 2017); Soonhee Kim v. Ferdinand, 287 F. Supp. 3d 607, 627 (E.D. La. 2018); Oliver A. v. Diana Pina B., 151 A.D.3d 485, 56 N.Y.S.3d 311 (1st Dep't 2017), leave to appeal denied, 29 N.Y.3d 917, 64 N.Y.S.3d 667, 86 N.E.3d 559 (2017); de Freitas Pinto v. Barone, 2017 WL 2779700, *3 (S.D. Cal. 2017).

Chapter 19

Tort Remedies Available

Written by Dana Goldstein

§ 19:1 General concerns[1]

The elimination of spousal immunity[2] as a defense to a tort has enabled family members, particularly spouses, to initiate personal injury actions in order to redress injuries they sustained during an abusive relationship.[3] The specific goal of these personal injury lawsuits is to make the victim whole by providing compensation for medical bills, psychiatric bills, loss of wages, physical disfigurement, permanent physical injury, pain and suffering, property loss, and punitive damages in the case of intentional torts.

Pursuing tort claims is important because it is the only vehicle that

---

[Section 19:1]

[1]See, generally, Leonard Karp and Cheryl L. Karp, Domestic Torts: Family Violence, Conflict, and Sexual Abuse (1989 & Supp. 1999); Fredrica L. Lehrman, Elements of Interpersonal Domestic Violence Torts: Traditional Actions, Domestic Violence Report, 3 (Dec./Jan. 1996); Rhonda L. Kohler, The Battered Woman and Tort Law: A New Approach to Fighting Domestic Violence, 25 Loy. L.A. L. Rev. 1025 (1992); Heather Tonsing, Battered Women Syndrome as a Tort Cause of Action, 12 J.L. & Health 407 (1998).

[2]Carl Tobias, Interspousal Tort Immunity in America, 23 Ga. L. Rev. 359 (1989).

[3]In Shearer v. Shearer, 18 Ohio St. 3d 94, 480 N.E.2d 388 (1985), the Ohio Supreme Court abolished both interspousal immunity and parental immunity.

provides victims with a means of recovering monetary damages for the pain and suffering they endured. In a domestic violence scenario the injuries and damages are often uncompensated when a divorce action is pursued. In a divorce, the court is interested in making an equitable distribution of property[4] and an equitable award of alimony.[5] It is not the court's responsibility to compensate an injured victim. Similarly, in granting civil protection orders, the court is more interested in protecting a victim of domestic violence, enhancing her safety and holding the perpetrator accountable. The hearing officer rarely addresses the issue of compensating victims for sustained injuries.[6]

Civil litigation is also important because it provides victims of domestic violence with an important opportunity to vindicate his or her individual rights and in doing so provides empowerment. In contrast to criminal cases where the prosecutor ultimately makes the final decision about charges and pleas, in civil cases, the victims of domestic violence decide whether and under which terms they are willing to settle.[7] In civil cases, the victim controls essential decisions affecting the case against the perpetrator.[8]

Successful civil suits also have an important deterrent effect. These suits let perpetrators know that crime does not pay and that they must account to those whom they have victimized. Large verdicts reinforce the concept that victims of domestic violence have suffered important injuries and that perpetrators must pay for them.[9] It also validates the battered victim's experiences.

When deciding whether to pursue a personal injury action, one must also consider the disadvantages to bringing such an action. There are overriding costs to pursue litigation such as deposition fees, expert fees, and attorney fees, which may make the initiation of a lawsuit unreasonable unless the actual monetary damages are extensive or the behavior so outrageous as to likely invoke a sizeable punitive award. If there are no assets, no home, or any other likely means to recover, the initiation of a lawsuit to obtain monetary

---

[4]RC 3105.17.1 addresses the issue of dividing property. Under RC 3105.17.1(C)(1), the Court is directed to make an equal division of all marital property except in cases where equal division is inequitable, then the Court shall divide the property in an equitable fashion.

[5]See RC 3105.18 (C)(1)(a) to (C)(1)(k), which list the express factors a Court is to consider when awarding spousal support. None of the factors address whether a party is a victim of domestic violence. The Court is interested in making an equitable distribution of assets and income assuming each party contributed equally to the production of marital income.

[6]See RC 3113.31, which lists the remedies available in a Civil Protection Order. None of the remedies are intended to compensate or redress victims of violence with monetary awards.

[7]U.S. Department of Justice, Office of Justice Programs, OVC Bulletin, December 1992.

[8]U.S. Department of Justice, Office of Justice Programs, OVC Bulletin, December 1992.

[9]U.S. Department of Justice, Office of Justice Programs, OVC Bulletin, December 1992.

compensation is fruitless and most attorneys will not pursue the case.[10] There is also the obvious reason of not pursuing a case, which is that if the case is not a strong case on liability grounds, there is the possibility of not only a defense verdict but also a win for the perpetrator.

Q & A: Are tort actions available to married as well as unmarried individuals?

Yes, tort actions are available to both married and unmarried individuals. For unmarried individuals, the cases are frequently simpler since there are no issues of whether to bring a divorce action contemporaneously with a tort action.

§ 19:2 Types of intentional torts available to victims of domestic violence[1]

Generally in domestic violence cases, perpetrators have intentionally, as opposed to negligently, committed acts of violence against the victim. The most common types of intentional torts arising in a domestic violence situation are assault, battery, intentional infliction of emotional distress, tortious infliction of sexually transmitted diseases, and battery for rape. Perpetrators may also perpetrate other less commonly pursued torts such as fraud, conversion, trespass, and false imprisonment during the course of inflicting the violence.

The most common intentional torts are assault, battery, intentional infliction of emotional distress, intentional infliction of sexually transmitted diseases, and battery arising from a rape.

§ 19:3 Elements of an assault

A perpetrator commits an assault when he makes an intentional or willful threat or attempts to harm or touch another offensively, which threat or attempt reasonably places the other in fear of such contact.[1] An assault may also occur merely with an intentional threat; there is no need for actual contact with the victim as long as the intended threat would place a reasonable person in immediate fear of harmful contact. An essential element of an assault is that the perpetrator knows with substantial certainty that his act will bring about fear or harmful or offensive contact.[2] A perpetrator may commit an assault even though the perpetrator has no ability to complete the contemplated injury.

---

[10]But see Jennifer Wriggins, Domestic Violence Torts, 75 S. Cal. L. Rev. 121 (2001) (discussing the possibility of civil liability for domestic violence torts through insurance reform).

[Section 19:2]

[1]See also Jennifer Wriggins, Domestic Violence Torts, 75 S. Cal. L. Rev. 121 (2001); Clare Dalton, Domestic Violence, Domestic Torts, and Divorce: Constraints and Possibilities, 21 New Eng. L. Rev. 319 (1997); Linda K. Meier & Brian K. Zoeller, Taking Abusers to Court; Civil Remedies for Domestic Violence Victims, Trial Magazine (1995).

[Section 19:3]

[1]Alexander v. Haymon, 254 F. Supp. 2d 820 (S.D. Ohio 2003); see also Schweller v. Schweller, 1997 WL 793106 (Ohio Ct. App. 1st Dist. Hamilton County 1997) (discussing assault and battery in a domestic violence case).

[2]See Smith v. John Deere Co., 83 Ohio App. 3d 398, 614 N.E.2d 1148 (10th Dist. Franklin County 1993), citing Scott v. Perkins, 1975 WL 181780 (Ohio Ct. App. 10th

For example, if the perpetrator threatens to kill the victim and aims a gun at the victim, an assault is committed even if the gun is unloaded as long as the victim believed the gun to be loaded.[3] When there is nothing in the act that would cause reasonable fear of immediate harmful contact, there is no assault,[4] nor is there an assault when the victim is not afraid or in fear of imminent harm.[5]

The most common types of behaviors in a domestic violence action that would constitute an assault are the threats of death along with some accompanying conduct that is threatening but that does not result in contact. Examples of these behaviors are when a perpetrator threatens to kill a victim and gets a gun, when a perpetrator threatens to kill a victim while holding a knife, or when a perpetrator threatens to kill a victim while holding his hands behind his back inferring that he has a weapon of some sort.

In Ohio, there are very few reported cases of civil assault arising from domestic violence. In the case of *Stokes v. Meimaris*,[6] a woman sued her ex-husband based on actions that occurred after the marriage. One of her causes of action was for an assault when her ex-husband intentionally swung a baseball bat at her causing her to fear for her physical safety. The ex-wife was awarded $2,000 for injuries and the Court stated that proof of physical injury was not necessary as injuries were presumed in an assault and battery action.

§ 19:4 Elements of a battery

The definition of a battery is an intentional harmful or offensive touching of another person.[1] In order to constitute a battery there must be some positive and intended act. The traditional notion of domestic violence where a perpetrator hits a victim, or shoves a victim into a wall, or shoves a victim down the stairs, or pulls the victim's hair would all constitute a battery. The test for a battery is what would be considered harmful or offensive to a reasonable person, not an unduly sensitive individual.[2]

In *Schmidt v. Schmidt*,[3] a wife brought criminal charges against her former husband for domestic violence. The husband was acquitted and filed civil malicious prosecution charges against his former wife

---

Dist. Franklin County 1975).

[3] 6 O. Jur 3d Assault—Civil Aspects, Section 3. See also State v. Tate, 54 Ohio St. 2d 444, 8 Ohio Op. 3d 441, 377 N.E.2d 778 (1978). See also Schweller v. Schweller, 1997 WL 793106 (Ohio Ct. App. 1st Dist. Hamilton County 1997).

[4] 6 O. Jur 3d Assault—Civil Aspects, Section 3, citing Rice v. Reed, 66 Ohio L. Abs. 385, 117 N.E.2d 183 (Ct. App. 2d Dist. Montgomery County 1951).

[5] Smith v. John Deere Co., 83 Ohio App. 3d 398, 614 N.E.2d 1148 (10th Dist. Franklin County 1993).

[6] Stokes v. Meimaris, 111 Ohio App. 3d 176, 675 N.E.2d 1289 (8th Dist. Cuyahoga County 1996).

[Section 19:4]

[1] See 6 O. Jur 3d Assault—Civil Assault, Section 2, citing Love v. City of Port Clinton, 37 Ohio St. 3d 98, 524 N.E.2d 166 (1988).

[2] Restatement of the Law (Torts), § 19.

[3] Schmidt v. Schmidt, 2000 WL 895264 (Ohio Ct. App. 12th Dist. Clermont County 2000).

and the former wife countered with assault and battery charges arising from the acts of the former husband when he entered the marital home broke down a bedroom door, ripped the phone out of wife's hands and threw it against the wall, tore a nightshirt from her, threw her against the wall, and disabled her vehicle. The former husband during the course of discovery failed to respond to requests for admissions thereby admitting that $132.50 was fair and reasonable to pay for repair of former wife's vehicle, that $6,043.46 was a fair and reasonable amount for attorney fees, that former wife was entitled to a nominal compensatory damages, and that former wife was entitled to receive ten times actual damages of $61,759.60 as and for punitive damages.[4] The perpetrator further admitted at trial that hatred, ill will, or a spirit of revenge motivated his conduct toward his former wife. Based on the requests for admissions that went unanswered, and the admissions of the perpetrator, the court of appeals affirmed the amount of damages including the amount of punitive damages.

§ 19:5 Intentional infliction of emotional distress[1]

In 1983, the Ohio Supreme Court first recognized the tort of intentional infliction of emotional distress. In *Yeager v. Local Union 20*,[2] the Supreme Court stated that, in order to prevail in this type of intentional tort, it is not enough that the perpetrator act with an intent which is tortious or even criminal, or that he intended to inflict emotional distress, or even that his conduct has been characterized by malice. Liability arises only where the conduct has been so outrageous, and so extreme in degree, as to go beyond all possible bounds of decency and be regarded as atrocious and utterly intolerable in civilized society.[3] The Court set such high standards because they

---

[4]In 2005 a new tort reform law was passed that limits the amount one can recover for punitive damages though there is an exception where a tort action seeks damages from conduct that also constitutes a felony and the perpetrator was convicted of the felony. See RC 2315.21, which states the circumstances in which punitive damages are limited. See also Ernst, Baldwin's Ohio Practice, Tort Law, Chs. 18 to 20, 22, and 23.

[Section 19:5]

[1]See Leonard Karp & Cheryl L. Karp, Beyond the Normal Ebb and Flow: Infliction of Emotional Distress in Domestic Violence Cases, 28 Fam. L. Q. 389 (1994); see also Ira M. Ellman & Stephen D. Sugarman, Spousal Emotional Abuse as a Tort?, 55 Md. L. Rev. 1268 (1996).

[2]Yeager v. Local Union 20, Teamsters, Chauffeurs, Warehousemen, & Helpers of America, 6 Ohio St. 3d 369, 453 N.E.2d 666, 116 Lab. Cas. (CCH) P 56408 (1983) (abrogated on other grounds by, Welling v. Weinfeld, 113 Ohio St. 3d 464, 2007-Ohio-2451, 866 N.E.2d 1051, 35 Media L. Rep. (BNA) 1979 (2007)); see Stockdale v. Baba, 153 Ohio App. 3d 712, 2003-Ohio-4366, 795 N.E.2d 727 (10th Dist. Franklin County 2003) (discussing intentional and negligent infliction of emotional distress in a stalking case and discusses "seriousness" of the emotional distress); Nicolazzo v. Yoingco, 149 Ohio Misc. 2d 44, 2007-Ohio-7269, 898 N.E.2d 94 (C.P. 2007).

[3]Yeager v. Local Union 20, Teamsters, Chauffeurs, Warehousemen, & Helpers of America, 6 Ohio St. 3d 369, 453 N.E.2d 666, 116 Lab. Cas. (CCH) P 56408 (1983) (abrogated on other grounds by, Welling v. Weinfeld, 113 Ohio St. 3d 464, 2007-Ohio-2451, 866 N.E.2d 1051, 35 Media L. Rep. (BNA) 1979 (2007)), citing Restatement of the Law 2d (Torts) 71, § 46 (1965).

were worried that things such as name-calling might invoke litigation.[4] The Court in *Yeager*, stated: "Against a large part of the frictions and irritations and clashing of temperaments incident to participation in a community life, a certain toughening of the mental hide is a better protection than the law could ever be."[5] While recognizing that compensation is certainly not warranted when someone's feelings are hurt, there is still a need to be protected from such intentional infliction of emotional distress that is so outrageous in nature.

The elements of an intentional infliction of emotional distress are:

1) that the actor either intended to cause emotional distress or knew or should have known that actions taken would result in serious emotional distress to the plaintiff;
2) that the actor's conduct was so extreme and outrageous as to go 'beyond all possible bounds of decency' and was such that it can be considered as 'utterly intolerable in a civilized community';
3) that the actor's actions were the proximate cause of plaintiff's psychic injury;
4) that the mental anguish suffered by plaintiff is serious and of a nature that 'no reasonable [person] could be expected to endure it'. (citations omitted)[6]

Most of the victims of domestic violence who claim intentional infliction of emotional distress are also in situations where they have been a victim of assault and battery as well.[7] Common examples of intentional infliction of emotional distress are killing the pet to which the victim has a strong emotional attachment and threatening the victim with a gun, which would also constitute a battery.

There is a dearth of case law in Ohio for intentional infliction of emotional distress arising out of domestic violence altercations. However, in New Mexico, in *Hakkila v. Hakkila*, the Court held that insults and yelling over ten years did not constitute intentional infliction of emotional distress and did not rise to the level of extreme, out-

[4]See Darden v. Fambrough, 2013-Ohio-5583, 5 N.E.3d 712, 37 I.E.R. Cas. (BNA) 730 (Ohio Ct. App. 8th Dist. Cuyahoga County 2013) (noting that "liability clearly does not extend to mere insults, indignities, threats, annoyances, petty oppressions, or other trivialities" and that persons "must necessarily be expected and required to be hardened to a certain amount of rough language, and to occasional acts that are definitely inconsiderate and unkind" at ¶ 22, quoting *Yeager* at 372).

[5]Yeager v. Local Union 20, Teamsters, Chauffeurs, Warehousemen, & Helpers of America, 6 Ohio St. 3d 369, 453 N.E.2d 666, 116 Lab. Cas. (CCH) P 56408 (1983) (abrogated by, Welling v. Weinfeld, 113 Ohio St. 3d 464, 2007-Ohio-2451, 866 N.E.2d 1051, 35 Media L. Rep. (BNA) 1979 (2007)), citing Prosser, Law of Torts, § 12 (4th Ed. 1971) (abrogating court recognizing tort of false-light invasion of privacy).

[6]Irvine v. Akron Beacon Journal, 2002-Ohio-3191, 30 Media L. Rep. (BNA) 2008, 2002 WL 1371184 (Ohio Ct. App. 9th Dist. Summit County 2002), citing Pyle v. Pyle, 11 Ohio App. 3d 31, 463 N.E.2d 98 (8th Dist. Cuyahoga County 1983) and Yeager v. Local Union 20, Teamsters, Chauffeurs, Warehousemen, & Helpers of America, 6 Ohio St. 3d 369, 453 N.E.2d 666, 116 Lab. Cas. (CCH) P 56408 (1983) (abrogated on other grounds by, Welling v. Weinfeld, 113 Ohio St. 3d 464, 2007-Ohio-2451, 866 N.E.2d 1051, 35 Media L. Rep. (BNA) 1979 (2007)) (other citations omitted).

[7]See for example, Pournaras v. Pournaras, 1985 WL 4613 (Ohio Ct. App. 8th Dist. Cuyahoga County 1985).

rageous and intolerable.[8] In Maine, the Maine Supreme Judicial Court in *Henriksen v. Henriksen*, held that where a husband chased a wife throughout the house threatening physical violence and rape, such behavior did constitute an intentional infliction of emotional distress and affirmed a $75,000 award for compensatory damages and $40,000 award for punitive damages.[9]

§ 19:6 Intentional infliction of sexually transmitted diseases

In 1989, the Ohio Supreme Court recognized a lawsuit for transmitting sexual diseases. In *Mussivand v. David*, the Court held that "[a] person who knows, or should know, that he or she is infected with a venereal disease has the duty to abstain from sexual conduct or, at a minimum, to warn those persons with whom he or she expects to have sexual relations of his or her condition."[1] The Court, in support of its position of recognizing a duty to either abstain or warn others of venereal disease, relied on RC 3701.81(A) which requires someone who knows that they have a contagious disease to take reasonable steps to prevent exposure to others. While the Court talked about this tort in terms of negligently transmitting sexual diseases (i.e. having a duty to abstain from sexual conduct or having a duty of warning people with whom you have sexual contact of your venereal disease), another lower court recognized this tort of transmitting sexual disease and stated that, in addition to a fraud or negligence cause of action, one might have a cause of action for either a negligent or intentional infliction of emotional distress.[2]

If pursuing the aforementioned cases as an intentional tort, the cases would be developed as an intentional battery where there was an intentional offensive or harmful contact with the offensive or unwanted contact being the contraction of the venereal disease. One could also pursue these cases in the context of intentionally inflicting emotional distress.

If pursuing this type of case as a negligence tort, one would have to show: (1) a duty or obligation; (2) a breach of that duty; (3) harm that is closely causally connected to the breach of duty; and (4) damages.[3] In this case, the duty to abstain from sex or disclose your venereal disease would be imposed by case law and by statute. The failure to comply with this duty of abstention or at the least the failure to disclose to your sexual partner the nature of your venereal disease would constitute the breach and if the sexual partner, having never been notified of the venereal disease, then contracted the venereal disease within the time period expected after having sexual contact (and presumably did not have sex with another from whom they could have contracted the disease), then the victim could pursue a cause of action

[8] Hakkila v. Hakkila, 112 N.M. 172, 1991-NMCA-029, 812 P.2d 1320 (Ct. App. 1991).

[9] Henriksen v. Cameron, 622 A.2d 1135 (Me. 1993).

[Section 19:6]

[1] Mussivand v. David, 45 Ohio St. 3d 314, 544 N.E.2d 265 (1989).

[2] See Watts v. Watts, 1992 WL 318944 (Ohio Ct. App. 6th Dist. Lucas County 1992).

[3] Prosser, Law of Torts, Elements of Cause of Action, § 30.

for negligence. The benefit of pursuing a cause of action for negligence as opposed to an intentional tort is the extended statute of limitations period, which is two years from the date of the negligent conduct.

§ 19:7 Rape

Under common law, rape was specifically defined to exclude situations of marriage.[1] There was an irrevocable implied consent by married women to sexual intercourse with their husbands so that husbands could not be found guilty in a criminal trial for rape.[2]

Ohio courts have joined a majority of jurisdictions and permitted the prosecution of rape among spouses. In *Ohio v. Rittenhour*, an Ohio court of appeals expressly held that a spouse could be criminally prosecuted for rape.[3] The Court held that, "[t]he state is not regulating consensual sex between married couples in RC 2907.12(A)(2) or RC 2907.02(A)(2). Rather, appellant's conduct is unlawful because it was compelled by force against another person."[4] Most criminal courts that have addressed this issue have held that the institution of marriage does not strip a person of his or her right to personal safety nor does marriage strip a person of his or her right to bodily integrity.[5] Other courts in Ohio have also upheld the criminal prosecution of rape between husband and wife[6] and when doing so have, in essence, provided precedent for a civil cause of action for battery arising from rape. While a battery action arising from rape has not been brought in Ohio, presumably the courts in Ohio would recognize such an action especially in light of these criminal prosecutions for rape between spouses. Pursuing a cause of action for rape would constitute a battery where the perpetrator commits an intentional harmful or offensive touching of another.[7]

Q & A: What other tort actions can a victim of domestic violence bring?

Other suits against batterers may include the intentional interference with custody, parental kidnapping, libel, slander, defamation and invasion of privacy.

Domestic violence is not limited to physical abuse. In an abusive re-

---

[Section 19:7]

[1]Leonard Karp and Cheryl L. Karp, Domestic Torts: Family Violence, Conflict and Sexual Abuse, Family Law Series (Shepard's/McGraw-Hill, Inc. 1989), citing People v. Liberta, 64 N.Y.2d 152, 485 N.Y.S.2d 207, 474 N.E.2d 567 (1984).

[2]Leonard Karp and Cheryl L. Karp, Domestic Torts: Family Violence, Conflict and Sexual Abuse, Family Law Series (Shepard's/McGraw-Hill, Inc. 1989).

[3]State v. Rittenhour, 112 Ohio App. 3d 219, 221, 678 N.E.2d 293 (3d Dist. Crawford County 1996).

[4]State v. Rittenhour, 112 Ohio App. 3d 219, 221, 678 N.E.2d 293 (3d Dist. Crawford County 1996).

[5]State v. Hardy, 2004-Ohio-56, 2004 WL 35941 (Ohio Ct. App. 8th Dist. Cuyahoga County 2004).

[6]See, e.g., State v. Lee, 2005-Ohio-996, 2005 WL 544837 (Ohio Ct. App. 9th Dist. Summit County 2005), judgment aff'd, 111 Ohio St. 3d 361, 2006-Ohio-5849, 856 N.E.2d 921 (2006).

[7]For more information on pursuing a battery see Text § 19:4, Elements of a battery.

lationship, a victim may also suffer both economic and property injuries. Potential economic tort actions may include fraud, fraudulent transfer or concealment, breach of a fiduciary duty and tortious interference with contractual relations.[8] "Property torts may include: interference with property interest by exclusion, conversion, trespass to chattels, replevin and destruction of property."[9]

Q & A: Does a domestic relations court have subject matter jurisdiction to find that a party converted money belonging to the other and whether the court can award damages in the sum owed?

In *Howard v. Pharis-Rine*,[10] that exact issue was raised by appellant who argued that the domestic relations court did not have subject matter jurisdiction to litigate a tort claim for conversion and to award damages to appellee for conversion.[11]

Appellee was granted a CPO. The trial court granted the protection order and also awarded her a judgment for funds that appellant improperly withdrew from her bank account and converted for her own use and benefit. In awarding such relief, the trial court relied on both RC 3113.31(E)(1)(h) which provided that the court could grant relief that the court considered fair and equitable including apportionment of household and personal property and on RC 3105.011 which discusses the court's equitable powers.

The appellate court first reasoned that a domestic relations court is generally not the proper forum in which to litigate a tort claim.[12] It reviewed RC 3105.011 which provides that a domestic relations court has full equity power and jurisdiction appropriate to the determination of all domestic relations matters. It also considered the appellate court reasoning in *Gibson v. Gibson*,[13] in which the appellate court concluded that "RC 3105.011 gave the domestic relations court the equitable power to divide property and to consider the damage done to the vehicle in the court's property division, but not the power to grant damages. The court held, therefore, that entering a judgment for damages was beyond the authority of the domestic relations court."[14]

The Licking County Court of Appeals concluded that neither statute grants a domestic relations court this power and held that the trial court had no authority to litigate the tort claim and award damages to appellee.

---

[8]Barbara J. Hart and Erika A. Sussman, Civil Tort Suits and Economic Justice for Battered Women, Victim Advocate 6-7 (2004).

[9]Barbara J. Hart and Erika A. Sussman, Civil Tort Suits and Economic Justice for Battered Women, Victim Advocate 7 (2004).

[10]Howard v. Pharis-Rine, 2009-Ohio-3981, 2009 WL 2457775 (Ohio Ct. App. 5th Dist. Licking County 2009).

[11]*Howard at *2.*

[12]*Howard at *2*; quoting Koepke v. Koepke, 52 Ohio App. 3d 47, 49, 556 N.E.2d 1198 (6th Dist. Wood County 1989) (stating that to combine intentional tort claims with divorce actions is inconsistent with the goals of each, since a party to a divorce cannot recover damages and the collection of monetary damages is the primary objective of a tort claim).

[13]Gibson v. Gibson, 87 Ohio App. 3d 426, 622 N.E.2d 425 (4th Dist. Scioto County 1993).

[14]*Howard at 83*, quoting *Gibson at *3*.

Besides suits against an individual batterer, torts may also be brought against third parties, either because of their acts or their omissions. For example, employers may be sued for failing to protect victims who have protection orders or if they are aware of abuse by a co-worker. Landlords may be sued if they let an intimate partner into the premises or permit them to remain. Retailers may be sued for selling guns to batterers. Police officers may be sued for failing to protect victims of domestic violence.[15]

Q & A: Can a party file a tort action alleging an improper disclosure of records?

Recently, the Ohio Supreme Court addressed the right to privacy as a tort and its applicability in the domestic violence context. In *Hageman v. Southwest General Health Center*,[16] the Supreme Court of Ohio granted the ex-wife's attorney's discretionary appeal. In this case, husband began therapy and admitted having homicidal thoughts about his wife. Soon after, the wife filed for a divorce. While the divorce was pending, husband assaulted his wife and was charged with domestic violence. Wife subsequently obtained a civil protection order. In preparation for her CPO full hearing, wife's attorney subpoenaed the medical (mental health) records of the husband. Her attorney had believed that the husband had waived his privilege to those records by filing a counterclaim in the divorce action.

On the day scheduled for the full hearing on the CPO, the prosecutor in the pending criminal case against husband appeared and wife's attorney gave the prosecutor the subpoenaed mental health records. The parties subsequently entered into an agreement and the records were not admitted into evidence, nor were the records admitted into evidence in the criminal case.

Husband then sued wife's attorney, his ex-wife, the therapist, and Southwest General Health Center alleging that each entity had improperly disclosed his medical records without his permission. The trial court granted summary judgment to all defendants; on appeal, summary judgment to all defendants was affirmed, except as to wife's attorney. In reversing the trial court, the Eighth District Court of Appeals held that the wife's attorney "had overstepped her bounds as [the ex-wife's] divorce attorney when she disseminated information regarding [Hageman's] psychiatric condition to the prosecution."[17]

The Supreme Court relied on the reasoning set forth in a case decided about 18 years earlier by the Court. In Biddle v. Warren Gen. Hosp.,[18] the Supreme Court of Ohio determined that the unauthorized disclosure of medical information obtained through a physician-

[15]See Text § 14:9, Police liability for failing to protect victims of domestic violence—Legal theories for recovery—Substantive due process.

[16]Hageman v. Southwest Gen. Health Ctr., 119 Ohio St. 3d 185, 2008-Ohio-3343, 893 N.E.2d 153 (2008).

[17]Hageman v. Southwest Gen. Health Ctr., 119 Ohio St. 3d 185, 187, 2008-Ohio-3343, 893 N.E.2d 153 (2008), quoting Hageman v. Southwest Gen. Health Ctr., 2006-Ohio-6765, 2006 WL 3743095 (Ohio Ct. App. 8th Dist. Cuyahoga County 2006), judgment aff'd and remanded, 119 Ohio St. 3d 185, 2008-Ohio-3343, 893 N.E.2d 153 (2008).

[18]Biddle v. Warren Gen. Hosp., 86 Ohio St. 3d 395, 1999-Ohio-115, 715 N.E.2d 518 (1999).

patient relationship is a breach of confidentiality and a palpable wrong.[19] In *Biddle*, the Supreme Court held that, because such an injury was difficult to remedy, a separate tort for breach of confidentiality was introduced.

In affirming the Court of Appeals, the Supreme Court of Ohio reasoned that "[a]llowing attorneys with such information obtained through discovery to treat the information as public would violate the policy of maintaining the confidentiality of individual medical records. We therefore recognize that waiver of medical confidentiality for litigation purposes is limited to the specific case for which the records are sought and an attorney who violates this limited waiver by disclosing the records to a third party unconnected to the litigation may be held liable for these actions."[20]

In his dissent, Justice O'Donnell pointed out that the majority created a new duty upon attorneys to protect the confidentiality of an adversary's medical records obtained in the course of litigation and imposed liability for their unauthorized disclosure even if the disclosure is relevant and favorable to their client in a separate proceeding.[21]

It does not appear that the attorney raised the issue of a lawyer's duty to warn, which may have been expanded in this case as a way to protect the ex-wife from future injury. Some experts in the domestic violence arena have indicated that the time has come to broaden the duty to warn beyond the physician-patient relationship.[22]

§ 19:8 Miscellaneous questions

Q & A: Can I bring a personal injury action for assault and battery and seek monetary damages if criminal charges for assault and battery (or domestic violence) were already brought against the perpetrator?

Yes, domestic violence may be prosecuted both criminally and pursued as a basis for a personal injury action. In a criminal action, the state brings the case and seeks remedies that are intended to deter and punish the perpetrator. Remedies that the state imposes are generally fines or incarceration. While the criminal claim is intended to punish and deter conduct, the tort claim is intended to provide specific financial compensation to the victim for the sustained injuries. While both cases may be brought simultaneously, timing of the cases may be important. For example, if the trial in the personal injury action precedes the trial in the criminal case the defendant may invoke the Fifth Amendment privilege against self-incrimination and refuse to testify in the personal injury action. If the criminal case precedes the personal injury action and the perpetrator is found guilty in the criminal case, one could file summary judgment and possibly win on

[19]Hageman v. Southwest General Health Center, 119 Ohio St. 3d at 188.

[20]Hageman v. Southwest General Health Center, 119 Ohio St. 3d at 191.

[21]Hageman v. Southwest General Health Center, 119 Ohio St. 3d at 195–96.

[22]See, e.g., Buel & Drew, "Symposium: The Future of 'The Duty to Protect': Scientific and Legal Perspectives on Tarasoff's Thirtieth Anniversary–Do Ask and Do Tell: Rethinking the Lawyer's Duty to Warn in Domestic Violence Cases," 75 U. Cin. L. Rev. 447 (Winter 2006).

the issue of liability based on the legal principle of collateral estoppel in the civil case.[1] Since the standard of proof is higher in a criminal case ("guilty beyond a reasonable doubt")[2] than in a civil case where one needs to find the perpetrator liable only by a slight majority of the evidence (51% or a "preponderance of the evidence"),[3] a guilty finding can establish that a tort has been committed in the civil case. On the other hand, if the criminal case precedes the civil case and the defendant is found not guilty, that should not have any bearing on the civil case because of the different standard of proof elements in a criminal case and a civil case.[4]

Q & A: What if I hit back during an incident of domestic violence, can I still bring a personal injury action?

Yes, the fact that you hit back in self-defense or even caused some injury to the perpetrator may not be considered by a jury to reduce your damages if you are bringing a claim for an intentional tort, though it may be considered by the jury when determining who is at fault and whether an intentional tort occurred. The concept of comparative negligence where your conduct would act to reduce the amount of recovery is not a defense or considered as a factor to reduce compensation in an intentional tort claim.

§ 19:9 Statute of limitations

Under the Ohio Revised Code, the time for bringing a cause of action for an assault/battery is one year from when the assault/battery occurred.[1] This same statute of limitations of one year would apply to the intentional tort of rape and to the intentional transmission of sexually transmitted diseases. In causes of action where one is alleging the intentional infliction of emotional distress, the time period for bringing a law suit is four years.[2] If, however, the intentional infliction of emotional distress arises from an assault/battery, then the time period for bringing the lawsuit is one year, the same as for an assault/battery, as this is considered a "parasitic" claim.[3] The statute of limitations for bringing a negligence action is two years.[4] One might bring a cause of action for negligence for the negligent infliction of sexually transmitted diseases.

One particular difficulty for victims of domestic violence is that they

---

[Section 19:8]

[1]The issue of collateral estoppel is addressed in more detail in Text § 19:10, Issues of joining a divorce and personal injury action.

[2]State v. Jenks, 61 Ohio St. 3d 259, 574 N.E.2d 492 (1991).

[3]See 44 O. Jur. 3d, "Evidence & Witnesses" Section 950, citing Lewistown Foundry & Machine Co. v. Hartford Stone Co., 92 Ohio St. 76, 110 N.E. 515 (1915).

[4]Schweller v. Schweller, 1997 WL 793106 (Ohio Ct. App. 1st Dist. Hamilton County 1997).

[Section 19:9]

[1]See RC 2305.111.

[2]RC 2305.09.

[3]See Manin v. Diloreti, 94 Ohio App. 3d 777, 641 N.E.2d 826 (9th Dist. Summit County 1994).

[4]RC 2305.10.

are frequently intimidated and are often unable to pursue their cause of action against their perpetrator because of the fear created by the perpetrator. The second unique problem facing some victims of domestic violence is that, even if they have the courage to bring the cause of action, they may have to return to the very same household where the perpetrator resides. Domestic violence cases are different from typical non-domestic violence assault and battery cases because, in typical assault/battery cases, the victim and perpetrator don't live in the same household. In domestic violence, the assault frequently continues (the fear of imminent bodily harm continues) as long as the parties reside together. Therefore, one could argue that the statute of limitations should not start until after the assault is removed (i.e. at least until the domestic violence stops or the parties separate).

Calculating the time period in which a victim can bring a cause of action in a domestic violence scenario is also complicated by the fact that in domestic violence the intentional torts are frequently repeated throughout the entire marriage. "Because each act of abuse is but 'one moment' in a larger picture of coercive control, focusing upon any single act alone will fail to convey and quantify the harm caused."[5] The critical question is whether the statute of limitations should run when each of these acts of violence is committed or whether the statute should begin running when the "assault is removed" and the parties separate/divorce.

Six states have held that the statute of limitations for interspousal torts is tolled during the marriage.[6] The reasoning in these old cases was based on the outdated doctrine of interspousal immunity, which provides that marital discord would occur if spouses were required to race to the courthouse to file their tort claim in order to prevent the running of the statute of limitations. These states have held that the time period for filing claims does not begin to run until after the marriage is dissolved.

Five states have held that, with the elimination of interspousal immunity, the statute of limitations is no longer tolled during the marriage.[7] States adhering to strict enforcement of the statute of limitations assert that tolling the statute of limitations would sanction the return of interspousal immunity through the back door. Courts strictly enforcing the statute of limitations have held that it is only fair and equal that tort litigation between spouses should be treated in the same manner as any other tort action. These states have also held that allowing the tolling of the statute of limitations during mar-

[5]Barbara J. Hart and Erika A. Sussman, Civil Tort Suits and Economic Justice for Battered Women, Victim Advocate at 7 (2004).

[6]These states are Colorado, Indiana, Kentucky, Oregon, Pennsylvania, and Wisconsin. See Linker v. Linker, 28 Colo. App. 131, 470 P.2d 921 (App. 1970)); Parrett v. Palmer, 8 Ind. App. 356, 35 N.E. 713 (1893); Anheier v. De Long, 164 Ky. 694, 176 S.W. 195 (1915); Cary v. Cary, 159 Or. 578, 80 P.2d 886, 121 A.L.R. 1371 (1938); Morrish v. Morrish, 262 Pa. 192, 105 A. 83 (1918); Charmley v. Charmley, 125 Wis. 297, 103 N.W. 1106 (1905).

[7]These states are Idaho, Kansas, New Jersey, Oklahoma, and Washington. See Kilgrow v. Kilgrow, 4th Judicial Dist. Case No. 74760; In re Crawford's Estate, 155 Kan. 388, 125 P.2d 354 (1942); Tevis v. Tevis, 79 N.J. 422, 400 A.2d 1189 (1979); Catron v. First Nat. Bank & Trust Co. of Tulsa, 1967 OK 107, 434 P.2d 263 (Okla. 1967); Stephens v. Stephens, 85 Wash. 2d 290, 534 P.2d 571 (1975).

riage would be prejudicial to the defendant because of problems related to recollection of witnesses and preservation of evidence during the tolling of the statute.[8]

When adhering to this strict statute of limitations and comparing domestic violence to other cases, courts often fail to consider that domestic violence scenarios between spouses are completely dissimilar to traditional torts in that the fear of the "assault" continues as long as the parties continue to reside together. In domestic violence, the perpetrator and victim are forced to reside together, oftentimes in continuous disharmony and violence, which is in marked contrast to the traditional assault and battery situations where the victim and the perpetrator do not reside together and may have only limited contact with each other.

Another way to look at the statute of limitations bar as it applies to domestic violence is to consider it a "continuing tort." Under this theory, the abuse is a cumulative injury rather than a single occurrence. Therefore, the statute of limitations begins to run only when the abuse stops.[9]

An example of the type of case that would present a good issue for an appeal is when a victim/spouse continues to hear threats such as, "If you leave, I will kill you", which presumably controlled the victim/ spouse and kept the victim in the marriage and kept the victim from filing any personal injury action. Arguably, the beginning period for calculating the statute of limitations could be extended until the victim actually left, separated, and freed themselves from the continuing threats/ "assaults" of the perpetrator.

One Ohio case addressed the statute of limitations issue and, in that case, the court adhered to the strict enforcement of the one year statute though it is unclear whether it was even argued that the statute of limitations should be tolled until the cycle of violence was broken or the parties separated/divorced. In *Owens v. Owens*,[10] the court strictly adhered to the one year statute of limitations barring a wife's claim against her husband when her husband drove his vehicle with his spouse partially out of the car, dragging her down the roadway, and causing a rear tire to pass over her right arm. The incident occurred on April 3, 1978, while the parties were husband and wife. The wife waited until after the divorce was final, which occurred in February of 1979, to file the personal injury action. The wife filed the personal injury action on December 4, 1979, more than a year after the incident, and the court dismissed her action as barred by the statute of limitations.[11]

---

[8]See Kilgrow v. Kilgrow, 4th Judicial Dist. Case No. 74760; In re Crawford's Estate, 155 Kan. 388, 125 P.2d 354 (1942); Tevis v. Tevis, 79 N.J. 422, 400 A.2d 1189 (1979); Catron v. First Nat. Bank & Trust Co. of Tulsa, 1967 OK 107, 434 P.2d 263 (Okla. 1967); Stephens v. Stephens, 85 Wash. 2d 290, 534 P.2d 571 (1975).

[9]Barbara J. Hart and Erika A. Sussman, Civil Tort Suits and Economic Justice for Battered Women, Victim Advocate at 7 (2004).

[10]Owens v. Owens (Ohio Ct. App. 1st Dist. Hamilton County 1984).

[11]The *Owens* case was filed prior to the elimination of interspousal immunity, which occurred in 1985. It is interesting to note that in the Owens case the victim apparently never argued that the statute of limitations is tolled until the divorce is final

§ 19:10 Miscellaneous Issues

Q & A: Does RC 3113.31 create a tort remedy?

In *Oliver v. Johnson*,[1] the respondent appealed the dismissal of her petition for CPO. In this case, the parties were spouses. Upon his release from prison for raping and kidnapping her, the wife filed for a CPO. The husband filed a motion to dismiss claiming that the CPO action was barred by a four year statute of limitations for certain torts found in RC 2305.09(D) which provides "for an injury to the right of Plaintiff not arising on contract . . . ." The trial court agreed with the respondent husband and dismissed the petition.

The appellate court reversed the trial court decision and determined that there is no statute of limitations for filing a CPO. In fact, there are no time limitations in the language of RC 3113.31(D). Absent express time limitations in the statute, the trial court looked to the time limitations set forth in RC 2305 and concluded that RC 2305.09(D) covered protection orders.

In reviewing the trial court decision, the Court of Appeals had to decide whether RC 3113.31 created a "civil action" because the time limitations of RC 2305 apply to "civil actions." The court relied on RC 2703.01 which defines an action as "an ordinary proceeding in a court of justice . . . ."[2] "Because an action/civil action is an "ordinary proceeding," it is distinguishable from "special proceedings" which are actions created by statute. "Where the law confers a right and authorizes a special application to a court to enforce it, the proceeding is special as opposed to ordinary."[3]

RC 3113.31 meets the definition of a special statutory proceeding and the time limitations of RC 2305 cannot act as a bar to the filing of a CPO. The only time frame is that the petitioner must demonstrate that he/she is in fear of imminent serious physical harm.

Q & A: Can a respondent raise other civil tort claims such as malicious prosecution, abuse of process, intentional or negligent infliction of emotional distress, libel or slander,[4] defamation and frivolous conduct[5] after a dismissal of a civil protection order or as part of a civil protection order proceeding?[6]

---

as parties were unable to pursue lawsuits between each other until they were divorced. Had that argument been made, the victim may have been able to pursue her cause of action.

[Section 19:10]

[1]Oliver v. Johnson, 2007-Ohio-5880, 2007 WL 3227668 (Ohio Ct. App. 4th Dist. Jackson County 2007).

[2]Oliver v. Johnson, 2007-Ohio-5880, 2007 WL 3227668 (Ohio Ct. App. 4th Dist. Jackson County 2007).

[3]Oliver v. Johnson, 2007-Ohio-5880, 2007 WL 3227668 (Ohio Ct. App. 4th Dist. Jackson County 2007).

[4]See also Boddie v. Landers, 2016-Ohio-1410, 2016 WL 1290780 (Ohio Ct. App. 10th Dist. Franklin County 2016), appeal not allowed, 146 Ohio St. 3d 1492, 2016, 2016-Ohio-5585, 57 N.E.3d 1171 (2016) (case against victim for libel and slander and defamation was brought because of a news story regarding a Columbus program to help victims of domestic violence in which the violence inflicted against the victim by Boddie was discussed).

[5]Guerrieri v. Brys, 2014-Ohio-1178, 2014 WL 1326098 (Ohio Ct. App. 7th Dist.

Of course such claims have been filed but, to date, few, if any respondents have prevailed on these claims.

For example, in *Malone v. Lowry*,[7] Lowry was granted an ex parte civil stalking protection order under RC 2903.214. At the full hearing, the parties entered into a settlement agreement, entitled "Agreed Judgment Entry and Order" and the CSPO was dismissed. Five months later Malone filed a complaint alleging abuse of process,[8] malicious prosecution,[9] intentional and negligent infliction of emotional distress, libel and slander. According to Malone, these claims were based on the conduct of Lowry in relation to and subsequent to the filing for the civil protection order. Lowry filed a motion for summary judgment which was granted.

On appeal, Malone argued that the trial court erred when it ruled that other civil claims were precluded by the parties' settlement agreement. He also stated that RC 2903.214 is limited to orders of protection from menacing and stalking. Thus, he was unable to file his claims in the underlying stalking case and the remedies he sought were unavailable in the stalking case.

The Greene County Appellate Court noted that "[a]lthough the specified remedy under RC 2903.214 is an ex parte protection order followed possibly by a permanent order, the Lowrys argue that there is nothing within the statute that precluded Malone from filing other claims. As support, they point to this case and the claims brought forth by Malone as evidence. Furthermore, the Lowrys contend that the trial court's basis for dismissing the claims was not the settlement agreement, but because the claims lacked merit."[10]

While pointing out the Lowrys' position in the opinion, the appellate court did not specifically state whether it affirmed the trial court's grant of summary judgment on this ground. However, in its analysis, the court noted that there was no genuine issue of material fact of any of Malone's claims.

Mahoning County 2014) (defining the term "frivolous conduct" in a case where respondent filed a suit against petitioner for misusing CSPO process and alleging frivolous conduct and requesting expenses pursuant to R.C. 2323.51).

[6]See for example, Moore v. Petty, 2013 WL 12149772 (Ohio C.P. 2013) (discussing the elements of the intentional infliction of emotional distress, abuse of process and wrongful eviction); Rogers v. Olt, 2018-Ohio-2110, 2018 WL 2465131 (Ohio Ct. App. 2d Dist. Miami County 2018) (thorough discussion of the elements of abuse of process, malicious prosecution, intentional infliction of emotional distress, frivolous conduct and vexatious litigator).

[7]Malone v. Lowry, 2007-Ohio-5665, 2007 WL 3076599 (Ohio Ct. App. 2d Dist. Greene County 2007).

[8]See also Walsh v. Walsh, 2008-Ohio-5701, 2008 WL 4787566 (Ohio Ct. App. 4th Dist. Lawrence County 2008) (affirming trial court's decision to grant summary judgment in favor of wife, where appellant filed an abuse of process claim against his wife after he was found not guilty of violating the CPO alleging that the reported violations were an abuse of the judicial system which she used "as a tool to cause delay and obtain strategic advantages in the divorce proceeding").

[9]Binkley v. Schuster, 2018 WL 2933859 (N.D. Ohio 2018) (filing of a federal § 1983 claim).

[10]Malone v. Lowry, 2007-Ohio-5665, 2007 WL 3076599, *3 (Ohio Ct. App. 2d Dist. Greene County 2007).

In *Cantrell v. Deitz*,[11] Cantrell filed a claim of abuse of process and intentional infliction of emotional distress against Deitz, after Deitz failed to appear at the full hearing on his civil protection order against Cantrell and the court dismissed the petition for want of prosecution. Cantrell alleged that Deitz filed the petition for CPO without probable cause and by asserting false claims against him. He also claimed that the proceedings initiated by Deitz were perverted in an attempt "to accomplish an improper purpose for which it was not designed."[12] He further claimed that as a direct and proximate result of the wrongful use of the process, he sustained direct damage in defending himself in the original petition.[13] The trial court dismissed his claims after Deitz filed a motion for summary judgment.

The appellate court noted that appellant had mixed the elements of the tort of "abuse of process" and the tort of "malicious civil prosecution" and that the Supreme Court had previously recognized each tort as a distinct tort in its own right.[14]

The Court then discussed the elements of each tort. In order to establish a claim of abuse of process, three elements must be satisfied: 1) a legal proceeding has been set in motion in proper form and with probable cause, 2) the proceeding has been perverted to attempt to accomplish an ulterior purpose for which it was not designed and 3) direct damage has resulted from the wrongful use of process.[15]

In order to establish a claim of malicious prosecution, four elements must be satisfied: 1) malicious institution of prior proceedings by the defendant against the plaintiff, 2) a lack of probable cause to file the prior lawsuit, 3) termination of the prior proceedings in favor of the plaintiff,[16] and 4) seizure of the plaintiff's person or property during the prior proceedings.[17]

" '[A]buse of process' differs from 'malicious prosecution' in that the former connotes the use of process properly initiated for improper

---

[11]Cantrell v. Deitz, 2013-Ohio-1204, 2013 WL 1286661 (Ohio Ct. App. 10th Dist. Franklin County 2013)).

[12]Cantrell v. Deitz, 2013-Ohio-1204, ¶ 6, 2013 WL 1286661 (Ohio Ct. App. 10th Dist. Franklin County 2013).

[13]Cantrell v. Deitz, 2013-Ohio-1204, ¶ 6, 2013 WL 1286661 (Ohio Ct. App. 10th Dist. Franklin County 2013).

[14]Cantrell v. Deitz, 2013-Ohio-1204, ¶ 18, 2013 WL 1286661 (Ohio Ct. App. 10th Dist. Franklin County 2013), quoting Yaklevich v. Kemp, Schaeffer & Rowe Co., L.P.A., 68 Ohio St. 3d 294, 298, 1994-Ohio-503, 626 N.E.2d 115 (1994).

[15]Cantrell v. Deitz, 2013-Ohio-1204, ¶ 15, 2013 WL 1286661 (Ohio Ct. App. 10th Dist. Franklin County 2013), citing Hershey v. Edelman, 187 Ohio App. 3d 400, 2010-Ohio-1992, 932 N.E.2d 386 (10th Dist. Franklin County 2010).

[16]See also Jones v. Nichols, 2012-Ohio-4344, 2012 WL 4351313 (Ohio Ct. App. 12th Dist. Warren County 2012) (voluntary dismissal of a CPO by wife against former husband is not a termination of the proceedings in plaintiff's favor for purposes of a malicious prosecution claim).

[17]Jones v. Nichols, 2012-Ohio-4344, ¶ 17, 2012 WL 4351313 (Ohio Ct. App. 12th Dist. Warren County 2012) at citing Robb v. Chagrin Lagoons Yacht Club, Inc., 75 Ohio St. 3d 264, 1996-Ohio-189, 662 N.E.2d 9 (1996) (syllabus); Fox v. Askren, 2014 WL 6606330 (Ohio C.P. 2014)(trial order).

purposes, while the latter relates to the malicious initiation of a lawsuit which one has no reasonable chance of winning."[18]

After reviewing the case in light of the various elements of abuse of process and malicious prosecution and noting that appellant had failed to put forth any argument regarding the emotional distress claim, the appellate court found that the trial court had properly granted the summary judgment motion.[19]

Similarly, in *Mettke v. Mouser*,[20] appellant filed a defamation action against appellee after her petition for CPO was denied at the ex parte stage and dismissed for want of prosecution. Appellant asserted that he was defamed by her statements set forth in the petition for protection order explaining the need for protection. After each party moved for summary judgment, the trial court granted appellee's motion, finding that "appellee's statements in the affidavit in support of the petition for a civil protection order were covered by an absolute privilege from civil liability."[21]

Appellant appealed the trial court decision arguing that the trial court erred by concluding that appellee's statements were covered by absolute privilege and granting summary judgment in her favor. Initially, the appellate court explored when summary judgment is appropriate which is "where the moving party demonstrates that 1) there is no genuine issue of material fact, 2) the moving party is entitled to judgment as a matter of law, and 3) reasonable minds can come to but one conclusion, and that conclusion is adverse to the party against whom the motion for summary judgment is made."[22]

The court went on to discuss the concept of "absolute privilege" and that "absolute privilege" "applies in a limited number of circumstances, including 'judicial proceedings in established courts of justice.' "[23] In a case of first impression by the Tenth District, the Court noted that it has not previously addressed whether absolute privilege applies to an affidavit in support of a petition for CPO but that two other appellate courts had addressed the application of

[18]Jones v. Nichols, 2012-Ohio-4344, ¶ 20, 2012 WL 4351313 (Ohio Ct. App. 12th Dist. Warren County 2012), quoting Clermont Environmental Reclamation Co. v. Hancock, 16 Ohio App. 3d 9, 11, 474 N.E.2d 357 (12th Dist. Clermont County 1984); Rogers v. Olt, 2018-Ohio-2110, ¶ 25, 2018 WL 2465131 (Ohio Ct. App. 2d Dist. Miami County 2018) (a voluntary dismissal of a complaint (including a civil protection order) is not a termination of the proceedings in a party's favor for purposes of a malicious prosecution claim).

[19]See also Herb v. Loughlin, 2012-Ohio-4351, 2012 WL 4340722 (Ohio Ct. App. 5th Dist. Licking County 2012).

[20]Mettke v. Mouser, 2013-Ohio-2781, 2013 WL 3356583 (Ohio Ct. App. 10th Dist. Franklin County 2013).

[21]Mettke v. Mouser, 2013-Ohio-2781, ¶ 3, 2013 WL 3356583 (Ohio Ct. App. 10th Dist. Franklin County 2013).

[22]Mettke v. Mouser, 2013-Ohio-2781, ¶ 5, 2013 WL 3356583 (Ohio Ct. App. 10th Dist. Franklin County 2013), quoting Capella III, L.L.C. v. Wilcox, 190 Ohio App. 3d 133, 2010-Ohio-4746, 940 N.E.2d 1026 (10th Dist. Franklin County 2010), citing Gilbert v. Summit County, 104 Ohio St. 3d 660, 2004-Ohio-7108, 821 N.E.2d 564 (2004).

[23]Mettke v. Mouser, 2013-Ohio-2781, ¶ 6, 2013 WL 3356583 (Ohio Ct. App. 10th Dist. Franklin County 2013), quoting M.J. DiCorpo, Inc. v. Sweeney, 69 Ohio St. 3d 497, 1994-Ohio-316, 634 N.E.2d 203 (1994).

absolute privilege in similar cases.[24] In each case, the courts concluded that because the statements were made in relation to a judicial proceeding and were reasonably related to that proceeding, the statements were covered by absolute privilege.[25]

Relying on the reasoning of the aforementioned cases and in support of its own application of the doctrine of absolute privilege in other cases in the Tenth District, the Franklin County Court of Appeals held that "a petitioner's statements in a petition for a civil protection order are covered by an absolute privilege from civil liability when the statements bear a reasonable relation to the subject of the petition. Absolute privilege applies because such statements are made as part of a judicial proceeding in an established court of justice. In this case, appellee's statements in her petition for a civil protection order were reasonably related to the need for a civil protection order. Therefore, appellee was entitled to judgment as a matter of law and the trial court did not err by granting summary judgment."[26]

Finally, there is a notation in the opinion that addressed appellant's assertion that appellee's handwritten statement in the petition did not claim appellant engaged in specific acts of domestic violence. However, the court determined that the petition itself referred to appellant engaging in such acts and thus, those references were part of the standard language on the petition form.[27]

It is hoped that other appellate courts follow the reasoning advanced by the Franklin County Court of Appeals to deter future filings of intentional torts by respondents, especially when alleging defamation.

Q & A: Can one spouse prevail on a claim of malicious prosecution[28] where the other spouse records or tapes their conversation?

Pursuant to federal[29] and state[30] wiretapping laws, a person is legally permitted to record and tape a conversation of his/her spouse only if the person doing the taping is a party to the conversation. However, a person cannot secretly tape his/her spouse while the spouse is talking to another person, such as a lover or paramour.[31]

Of interest is that there is a growing trend for the perpetrator to sue the victim of sexual or domestic violence in tort on the basis of

[24]Mettke v. Mouser, 2013-Ohio-2781, ¶ 8, 2013 WL 3356583 (Ohio Ct. App. 10th Dist. Franklin County 2013), citing Hiddens v. Leibold, 2007-Ohio-6688, 2007 WL 4372970 (Ohio Ct. App. 2d Dist. Montgomery County 2007); Lasater v. Vidahl, 2012-Ohio-4918, 979 N.E.2d 828 (Ohio Ct. App. 9th Dist. Summit County 2012).

[25]Mettke v. Mouser, 2013-Ohio-2781, ¶ 8, 2013 WL 3356583 (Ohio Ct. App. 10th Dist. Franklin County 2013), citing *Hiddens* at ¶ 44.

[26]Mettke v. Mouser, 2013-Ohio-2781, ¶ 10, 2013 WL 3356583 (Ohio Ct. App. 10th Dist. Franklin County 2013).

[27]Mettke v. Mouser, 2013-Ohio-2781, ¶ 10, 2013 WL 3356583 (Ohio Ct. App. 10th Dist. Franklin County 2013).

[28]See Wallace v. Noel, 2009-Ohio-6984, 2009 WL 5174175 (Ohio Ct. App. 6th Dist. Wood County 2009) (discussing elements of a malicious prosecution claim).

[29]18 U.S.C.A. §§ 2510 et seq.

[30]RC 2933.51 to 2933.66.

[31]See Hodges v. Hodges, 175 Ohio App. 3d 121, 2008-Ohio-601, 885 N.E.2d 307 (6th Dist. Lucas County 2008) (appellate court upheld wife's malicious prosecution claim).

malicious prosecution. This usually arises when the underlying criminal case is dismissed against the perpetrator.[32]

Q & A: Once the civil protection order was adjudicated and the protection order denied, can that party file civil claims (based on the same facts giving rise to the protection order) against the other person?

According to the Ninth District Court of Appeals, the answer is yes. *In J.P. v. T.H.*,[33] J.P. was denied a civil stalking protection order after a full hearing on the matter. While the case was still being litigated, J.P. also filed a complaint for money damages for assault, battery, invasion of privacy and defamation stemming from the same incident that was the basis for the civil protection order.[34] After a series of motions, the trial court entered summary judgment for T.H. on the basis that all of J.P.'s claims were barred by the doctrine of res judicata "since these matters have been resolved as a result of earlier litigation."[35]

On appeal J.P. assigned as error the trial court's grant of summary judgment for T.H. J.P. contends that the trial court erred by holding that the doctrine of res judicata barred his civil tort claims against T.H.

The appellate court began its analysis by reviewing the doctrine of res judicata and noting that the trial court determined that J.P.'s civil claims against T.H. involved matters that were resolved by the earlier CSPO litigation, namely J.P.'s failed effort to secure a permanent CSPO."[36] It mused that the trial court found that "since the underlying facts in the tort case were previously litigated at the CSPO hearing, no genuine issues of material fact remained to be litigated and T.H. was entitled to judgment as a matter of law."[37]

However, the appellate court relied on RC 2903.214(G), which provides that the remedies available in a CSPO case are in addition to, and not in lieu of, any other available civil and criminal remedies. Thus, the failure to allege tort claims contemporaneously with the CSPO petition did not preclude J.P. from subsequently bringing a civil action against T.H.[38] "To hold otherwise would punish petitioners seeking protection orders by forever depriving them of all legal reme-

---

[32]See Wallace v. Noel, 2009-Ohio-6984, 2009 WL 5174175 (Ohio Ct. App. 6th Dist. Wood County 2009) (discussing when a criminal case is terminated in favor of the accused).

[33]J.P. v. T.H., 2017-Ohio-233, 2017 WL 277518 (Ohio Ct. App. 9th Dist. Lorain County 2017).

[34]J.P. v. T.H., 2017-Ohio-233, ¶ 3, 2017 WL 277518 (Ohio Ct. App. 9th Dist. Lorain County 2017).

[35]J.P. v. T.H., 2017-Ohio-233, ¶ 5, 2017 WL 277518 (Ohio Ct. App. 9th Dist. Lorain County 2017).

[36]J.P. v. T.H., 2017-Ohio-233, ¶ 27, 2017 WL 277518 (Ohio Ct. App. 9th Dist. Lorain County 2017).

[37]J.P. v. T.H., 2017-Ohio-233, ¶ 27, 2017 WL 277518 (Ohio Ct. App. 9th Dist. Lorain County 2017).

[38]J.P. v. T.H., 2017-Ohio-233, ¶ 28, 2017 WL 277518 (Ohio Ct. App. 9th Dist. Lorain County 2017).

dies simply for prioritizing their own physical safety and/or the physical safety of their family members over their pecuniary damages."[39]

The court also mentioned that while a CSPO is designed to prevent future conduct, a civil tort claim is designed to consider past conduct. Therefore, the appellate court concluded that the trial court erred. The two cases involved facts that were neither directly at issue in the other litigation nor fully litigated in the previous CSPO case, J.P.'s civil claims are not barred by res judicata.[40]

§ 19:11 Issues of joining a divorce and personal injury action

One of the main legal issues when representing an injured spouse is whether to bring a divorce and a personal injury action in the same case or whether to file a divorce in Domestic Relations Court and a separate personal injury action in Common Pleas Court. This is a complicated legal issue with no clear answers. The advantage to bringing separate claims is that the injuries sustained in the personal injury action will be separately considered, evaluated, and compensated. If one joins a divorce and personal injury claim, it is possible that compensation for the personal injury action may be subsumed by the divorce action without proper compensation for the pain and suffering sustained by the victim. For example, if the cases are joined, the court may make a ruling on the property and spousal support issues (impaired earning capacity due to the violence) that does not fully compensate for pain and suffering where there are no concrete dollar values assigned to pain and suffering. In a separate personal injury action, pain and suffering would be evaluated and fully compensated. Another advantage to filing separate claims for individuals in higher tax brackets is that personal injury actions are generally not taxed,[1] whereas adjustments to spousal support in order to compensate for injuries is taxed.[2]

If one decides to separate the claims for divorce and the personal injury action, then a disadvantage to filing separate claims is the possible defense of res judicata (claim preclusion) and collateral estoppel (issue preclusion). Res judicata, or claim preclusion, states that all claims arising out of the same incidents must be brought at the same time or the cause of action is lost or prevented. Res judicata would operate to prevent the litigation in the second proceeding of all matters, legal and factual, that were or could have been adjudicated in the first proceeding. Most courts have rejected the application of res judicata to a subsequently filed tort action and have stated that the cause of action for a divorce is not the same as or identical to a tort or personal injury cause of action.[3] The purpose of a divorce is not to

---

[39] J.P. v. T.H., 2017-Ohio-233, ¶ 28, 2017 WL 277518 (Ohio Ct. App. 9th Dist. Lorain County 2017).

[40] J.P. v. T.H., 2017-Ohio-233, ¶ 29, 2017 WL 277518 (Ohio Ct. App. 9th Dist. Lorain County 2017).

[Section 19:11]

[1] See 26 U.S.C.A. § 104(a).

[2] See 26 U.S.C.A. § 71.

[3] See Folmar v. Griffin, 2008-Ohio-2941, 2008 WL 2573279 (Ohio Ct. App. 5th

compensate for personal injuries[4] and personal injury damages cannot be granted as part of a divorce. Similarly, in personal injury actions, the court is not attempting to distribute assets and end a marriage. Finally, the evidentiary issues in a divorce and personal injury action are completely different. In a divorce, particularly in a no-fault divorce,[5] the Court is not concerned with determining fault whereas in a personal injury action determining fault is the cornerstone of the case.[6]

The majority of states seem to hold that tort claims brought subsequent to a divorce judgment are permissible and not barred by res judicata.[7]

A few states have reached the opposite conclusion and have held that a tort and a divorce action must be joined in one case. For example, a Tennessee Court of Appeals held that, because the husband had been required by the divorce decree to pay the wife's past and future medical bills as well as lost wages due to tortious injuries the husband inflicted on the wife, the subsequent tort action was barred by res judicata because the claim had already been adjudicated. The states of Alabama[8], New Jersey[9], Texas[10], and New York[11] have all barred subsequent personal injury claims after a divorce has been settled or concluded.

Ohio seems to follow the majority of states and has held that a subsequent filing of a personal injury action is not barred by the filing

Dist. Delaware County 2008) (addressing issue preclusion).

[4]See R.C. 3105.171 and R.C. 3105.18. See also Leonard Karp and Cheryl L. Karp, Domestic Torts: Family Violence, Conflict and Sexual Abuse, Family Law Series (Shepard's/McGraw-Hill, Inc. 1989).

[5]In order to preclude defenses of res judicata, one may consider filing divorce under general grounds of incompatibility or living separate and apart for a year, though that would create statute of limitation problems for the personal injury action.

[6]Leonard Karp and Cheryl L. Karp, Domestic Torts: Family Violence, Conflict and Sexual Abuse, Family Law Series (Shepard's/McGraw-Hill Inc. 1989).

[7]See Simmons v. Simmons, 773 P.2d 602 (Colo. App. 1988) (wife's claim for intentional infliction of emotional distress was not barred by res judicata); Waite v. Waite, 593 So. 2d 222 (Fla. 3d DCA 1991), decision approved, 618 So. 2d 1360 (Fla. 1993) (wife's claim for assault and battery was not precluded by a previous divorce); McCoy v. Cooke, 165 Mich. App. 662, 419 N.W.2d 44 (1988) (an assault and battery and intentional infliction of emotional distress were not barred even after divorce court divided marital assets based on fault); Aubert v. Aubert, 129 N.H. 422, 529 A.2d 909 (1987) (a husband's claim for assault and battery not barred even though the divorce was granted on the underlying basis of the assault and battery where the wife shot the husband in the face); Noble v. Noble, 761 P.2d 1369 (Utah 1988) (the intentional infliction of emotional distress claim was not barred even after a divorce judgment); Henriksen v. Cameron, 622 A.2d 1135 (Me. 1993) (the state's divorce proceeding is not intended to determine tortious conduct; therefore, intentional torts are not barred by preceding divorce); Ward v. Ward, 155 Vt. 242, 583 A.2d 577, 4 A.L.R.5th 1152 (1990) (the wife's assault and battery claim against husband could not be properly joined with a divorce and had to be conducted as a separate action in part because a tort is a claim at law while divorce is equitable in nature).

[8]Jackson v. Hall, 460 So. 2d 1290 (Ala. 1984).

[9]Brown v. Brown, 208 N.J. Super. 372, 506 A.2d 29 (App. Div. 1986).

[10]Brinkman v. Brinkman, 966 S.W.2d 780 (Tex. App. San Antonio 1998).

[11]Vasquez v. Vasquez, 175 Misc. 2d 847, 670 N.Y.S.2d 740 (Sup 1998).

of a prior divorce.[12] In *Koepke v. Koepke*,[13] the Wood County Court of Appeals held that a tort action for intentional infliction of emotional distress should be considered separately from a divorce proceeding. The court went on to state that while there is a strong interest in judicial economy and joinder of claims, that concern for judicial economy, "does not outweigh the fact that a domestic relations forum is not the proper forum in which to litigate a tort claim."[14] The Court went on to state that it is inconsistent to combine an intentional tort with a divorce since in the divorce a party cannot recover damages.[15]

There are several other Ohio cases that set the precedent and permit intentional tort actions to be brought subsequent to a divorce proceeding but these were all decided when the doctrine of spousal immunity applied and therefore the parties had to be divorced before they could initiate a lawsuit amongst themselves.[16] Since these cases were decided before spousal tort immunity was abolished, it is unclear what precedent-setting effect they would have. Nevertheless, the Court in *Kobe v. Kobe* did state that a spouse should have the same remedies for injuries inflicted by the other spouse that the court would give them against another person.[17]

Q & A: Where should one file a cause of action if joining a divorce and personal injury action?

The Court of Common Pleas has jurisdiction to hear a divorce action as stated in RC 3105.01.1 and a personal injury action pursuant to RC 2305.01. Frequently, the Division of Domestic Relations as part of the Common Pleas Court assumes jurisdiction over divorces.[18] While there is no case law on this issue, the General Common Pleas Court Division should have jurisdiction to hear both the personal injury claim and the divorce.

Q & A: Where do I file if I want to separate the filing of the divorce with the filing of a personal injury action?

While there are no clear answers nor reported decisions on this matter, it appears that if one wants to have these issues separately

[12]But see Barton v. Barton, 2016-Ohio-5264, 2016 WL 4168857 (Ohio Ct. App. 2d Dist. Greene County 2016), appeal not allowed, 148 Ohio St. 3d 1411, 2017-Ohio-573, 69 N.E.3d 751 (2017) (finding that "Barton's claim of fraud against his ex wife could have been raised in the prior to appeal from his domestic violence civil protection order or in the appeal of his final divorce decree, which Barton failed to prosecute. Accordingly, those claims are barred by res judicata.¶ 23, citing Bank of Am., N.A. v. Kuchta, 141 Ohio St. 3d 75, 2014-Ohio-4275, 21 N.E.3d 1040, ¶ 15-16 (2014)).

[13]Koepke v. Koepke, 52 Ohio App. 3d 47, 556 N.E.2d 1198 (6th Dist. Wood County 1989).

[14]Koepke v. Koepke, 52 Ohio App. 3d 47, 49, 556 N.E.2d 1198 (6th Dist. Wood County 1989).

[15]Koepke v. Koepke, 52 Ohio App. 3d 47, 48, 556 N.E.2d 1198 (6th Dist. Wood County 1989); see also Howard v. Pharis-Rine, 2009-Ohio-3981, 2009 WL 2457775 (Ohio Ct. App. 5th Dist. Licking County 2009).

[16]See Kobe v. Kobe, 61 Ohio App. 2d 67, 15 Ohio Op. 3d 86, 399 N.E.2d 124 (8th Dist. Cuyahoga County 1978); Green v. Green, 4 Ohio App. 3d 133, 446 N.E.2d 837 (6th Dist. Lucas County 1982).

[17]Kobe v. Kobe, 61 Ohio App. 2d 67, 71, 15 Ohio Op. 3d 86, 399 N.E.2d 124 (8th Dist. Cuyahoga County 1978).

[18]See R.C. 3105.91 and 1 Ohio Family Law, Section 22.1 "Jurisdiction" (Anderson Pub. Co. 2003).

considered, presumably one would first file either the personal injury action in Common Pleas then later file the divorce in the Domestic Relations Division of the Common Pleas Court, or vice-versa. In the personal injury action, one would want to make a jury demand in order to buttress the argument that the actions should be separated and that juries are not available in the Domestic Relations Division of the Common Pleas Court. If the value of the case and the expected outcome of the personal injury action is less than $15,000.00, one could consider filing in Municipal Court as opposed to Common Pleas Court. If the value of the case exceeds $15,000.00 then one would need to file in Common Pleas Court as the jurisdiction of Municipal Court is only up to $15,000.00.[19]

§ 19:12 Remedies

Compensatory damages are intended to compensate the victim for all injuries sustained. The compensation is intended to make the victim whole. Compensation for such things as medical bills and hospital bills, future medical expenses, loss of wages, loss due to the permanency of the injury, compensation for disfigurement, and any amount of pain and suffering are all permissible as damages.[1] While these damages are compensable, under the tort reform law passed in 2005, the amount that can be awarded for non-economic loss such as pain and suffering is limited. RC 2315.18 sets forth the limitations for recovery of non-economic loss. The tort reform law withstood a constitutional challenge in 2007, when the Supreme Court of Ohio upheld its constitutionality in *Arbino v. Johnson & Johnson*.[2]

In addition to compensatory damages, a victim may pursue punitive damages intended to punish the wrongdoer, but these damages are available only when actual malice has been proven.[3] Actual malice is present where the perpetrator possessed either the state of mind which is characterized by hatred, ill will or a spirit of revenge or a serious disregard for the rights and safety of other persons that has a great probability of causing harm.[4]

The tort reform legislation that was enacted by the state legislature also limited the amount of punitive damages that can be awarded; however, these limitations may not apply in cases where the perpetrator was previously convicted of a felony that is the basis of the tort action. RC 2315.21 outlines these limitations and caps on punitive damage awards. If pursuing a claim for punitive damages one should consult this law to make sure how and if it applies.

In domestic violence scenarios, post-traumatic stress disorders and battered women's syndrome inflicted by the intentional infliction of

---

[19]See RC 1901.17; RC 1901.22; RC 2305.01.

[Section 19:12]

[1]Fantozzi v. Sandusky Cement Prod. Co., 64 Ohio St. 3d 601, 1992-Ohio-138, 597 N.E.2d 474 (1992).

[2]Arbino v. Johnson & Johnson, 116 Ohio St. 3d 468, 2007-Ohio-6948, 880 N.E.2d 420 (2007).

[3]Cabe v. Lunich, 70 Ohio St. 3d 598, 1994-Ohio-4, 640 N.E.2d 159, 33 A.L.R.5th 825 (1994).

[4]Preston v. Murty, 32 Ohio St. 3d 334, 512 N.E.2d 1174 (1987).

emotional distress commonly occurs. Employing a mental health expert is essential in proving claims for post traumatic stress disorder and/or battered women's syndrome. Counsel must prove not only that an emotionally traumatic event took place but that it was the proximate cause of the emotional distress. A mental health professional's testimony can establish a causal relationship between emotional abuse and post traumatic stress disorder or battered women's syndrome.

A thorough direct examination of the expert psychologist and of the expert's assessment of all pertinent sources will take the jury on a trip into the mind of the victim. Counsel should urge the expert to interview sympathetic friends, family and clergy to buttress their opinions.

Q & A: Can I recover for the cost of my medical bills even if my health insurance has paid for some or all of the hospital/medical bill?

Yes, even though insurance may have paid for the medical bill, one is still entitled to receive full compensation for the entire amount of the medical bill even if insurance paid for the bill and the victim actually incurred no costs.[5] The collateral benefit rule states that a plaintiff's recovery of the reasonable value of her medical treatment is not limited to the amount paid by the insurance.[6] The rationale for the decision is that the wrongdoer should not get the benefit of payments that come to the victim from an outside source.[7] In addition, the victim may have to reimburse the insurance company for a portion of the bill that was paid. Frequently attorneys can negotiate with the insurance company so that there is not a dollar-for-dollar recovery sought by the insurance company on bills paid.

---

[5] The collateral source rule was impacted by the tort reform law passed in 2005. While the collateral source rule remains in effect, under RC 2315.20 a perpetrator may introduce evidence of any benefit or collateral source that was received by the victim as a result of the inflicted damages.

[6] Ferrell v. Summa Health Sys., 165 Ohio App. 3d 110, 2005-Ohio-5944, 844 N.E.2d 1233 (9th Dist. Summit County 2005), judgment aff'd, 112 Ohio St. 3d 84, 2006-Ohio-6503, 858 N.E.2d 351 (2006).

[7] Pryor v. Webber, 23 Ohio St. 2d 104, 52 Ohio Op. 2d 395, 263 N.E.2d 235 (1970), overturned due to legislative action in 2002 Ohio Laws File 250.

Chapter 20

Juvenile Protection Orders*

KeyCite®: Cases and other legal materials listed in KeyCite Scope can be researched through the KeyCite service on Westlaw®. Use KeyCite to check citations for form, parallel references, prior and later history, and comprehensive citator information, including citations to other decisions and secondary materials.

*The author would like to thank Diana Ramos Reardon, Domestic Violence Program manager for the Supreme Court of Ohio for her thoughtful collaboration and comments regarding the following questions and answers.

§ 20:1 Generally

R.C. 2151.34 Juvenile Civil Protection Orders
Bench Guide for Ohio Courts

R.C. 2151.34 Offenses

▶JCPO can be requested and granted based on allegations of behavioral components of these crimes and without a delinquency finding (C)(2)(a).

- Felonious assault (R.C. 2903.11)
- Aggravated assault (R.C. 2903.12)
- Assault (R.C. 2903.13)
- Aggravated menacing (R.C. 2903.21)
- Menacing (R.C. 2903.22)
- Menacing by stalking (R.C. 2903.211)
- Any sexually oriented offense (R.C. 2950.01)
- Aggravated trespass (R.C. 2911.211)

Petitioner can file for a JCPO when elements of these crimes are met, but no criminal charges have been filed.

Relief Granted by JCPOs

▶Respondent shall not:

- Harm, attempt to harm, threaten, follow, stalk, harass, force sexual relations upon, or commit sexually oriented offenses upon protected person(s)
- Enter residence, school, business, or place of employment or other specific locations
- Remove, damage, hide, or dispose of property or pets
- Initiate or have contact with protected person(s)
- Cause or encourage any other person to do any act prohibited by JCPO

▶Respondent shall:

- Stay away from protected person(s)

▶Respondent may:

- Be electronically monitored

▶Respondent shall not:

- Possess, use, carry, or obtain any deadly weapon (F)(2)

Jurisdiction

▶Juvenile division of the Court of Common Pleas in the county in which the person to be protected by the order resides (A)(1).

Standard of Proof

▶Ex parte hearing (D)(1):

- Court may issue an ex parte order upon showing of good cause
- Court may issue an ex parte order upon showing of immediate and present danger

▶Full hearing:

- Preponderance of the evidence (G)
- If petitioner requests electronic monitoring, clear and convincing burden of proof much be used, solely for the purpose of determining the appropriateness of ordering electronic monitoring (E)(1)(b)

Contents of a Petition

▶Petition contains (C)(2):

- Allegation of offense
- Request for relief
- Request for electronic monitoring
- Notification to respondent and respondent's parent/guardian (D)(2)(a)
- Notification to petitioner's parent/guardian at the discretion of the court (C)(3)

▶Supreme Court of Ohio has developed Juvenile Civil Protection Order forms

- http://www.supremecourt.ohio.gov/

▶No costs are associated with the filing of a JCPO petition (J)

Relief

▶Persons to Seek Relief (C)(1):
- Person on his or her own behalf
- Any parent or adult family/household member on behalf of any family/household member
- Any person determined by the court in its discretion as an appropriate person to seek relief on behalf of any child

Appointment of Counsel

▶Any party to a JCPO may be represented by counsel.
▶Court appointment of counsel at the discretion of the court, only for juvenile respondents
▶No mention is made about court appointed counsel for the petitioner

In all stages of proceedings, a petitioner may be accompanied by a victim advocate (L).

Ex Parte Hearing and Ex Parte Order

▶If ex parte JCPO is requested by the petitioner (D)(1):
- Court must conduct a hearing as soon as possible after the petition is filed
- Hearing scheduled no later than the next day after court is in session after petition is filed

▶Court must find good cause that order is necessary for safety and protection of the petitioner (D)(1)
▶Immediate and present danger constitutes good cause and includes, but is not limited to (D)(1):
- Situations in which respondent has threatened petitioner with bodily harm
- Situations in which respondent has been adjudicated a delinquent child for committing any offenses alleged in petition

▶If court does not grant ex parte order (D)(3):
- Court shall schedule a full hearing
- Court can proceed as in normal civil action

▶If petitioner does not file for ex parte order (D)(3):
- Court shall schedule full hearing
- Court can proceed as in normal civil action

Full Hearing and Order Issued After Full Hearing

▶Court shall schedule full hearing for a date that is within 10 court days after ex parte hearing (D)(2)(a)
▶Court shall give the respondent notice of, and opportunity to be heard at, full hearing (D)(2)(a)
▶Full hearing will be held on date scheduled unless court grants a continuance (D)(2)(a)
▶Standard of proof is preponderance of the evidence (Ohio Rules of Civil Procedure)

Good practice to put the expiration date in the juvenile protection order forms at least six months from ex parte hearing date to ensure that ex parte order will not expire until after the full hearing has been heard.

The court issues its ruling at the full hearing. Issuance of JCPO is not in lieu of any other civil or criminal remedies (G).

Continuances

▶Continuances can be granted when (D)(2)(a)(i-iv):
- Lack of service to the respondent
- Parties agree to continuance
- Continuance is needed to allow party to obtain counsel
- Other good cause

▶Ex parte JCPO does not expire because court grants a continuance (D)(2)(b)

Consent Agreements

▶Statute does not provide for a consent agreement protection order:
- Parties can agree to the terms of the order prior to court date or on court date
- Court may adopt those terms and enter JCPO agreed to by parties
- Court should indicate no full hearing was held
- Court should ask respondent if s/he knowingly waived his/her right to hearing

Service and Notice

▶A copy of any protection order must be delivered to the respondent and his/her parent/guardian/custodian on the same day the order is issued(F)(1)

▶Ex parte order does not expire because of a failure to serve notice of the full hearing upon the respondent before the date set for the full hearing or because the court grants a continuance (D)(2)(b)

Duration of JCPO

▶Duration (E)(2)(a):

- Date certain
- Cannot be extended beyond when respondent turns 19 years old
- Expiration date may be respondent's 19th birthday

Reciprocal JCPOs

▶Mutual JCPOs are not permitted

▶A court may not issue a protection order that requires a petitioner to do or to refrain from doing an act that the court may require a respondent to do or refrain from doing unless all the following apply (E)(3):

- Respondent must file a separate petition and fulfill the same statutory requirements as the petitioner
- This petition must be served on the petitioner at least 48 hours before the hearing, unless waived by the petitioner
- After a full hearing where both parties present evidence, the court may grant respondent the JCPO
- If original petitioner requested an ex parte JCPO, the court should not delay any hearing on that request in order to consolidate a hearing on respondent's request for JCPO

Renewal, Modification and Termination of JCPOs

▶JCPO may be renewed in the same manner as original order was issued (E)(2)(b)

▶JCPO cannot be waived or nullified by invitation or consent of the protected person(s) (E)(5)(a):

- Petitioner's invitation or consent to the respondent's violation may be an affirmative defense to the violation

▶Statute is silent regarding modification and termination of the protection order

Enforcement and Registration of JCPO

▶Any officer of a law enforcement agency shall enforce a protection order issued, including removing respondent from the premises (F)(4)

▶Person who obtains a protection order issued by a court of another state may provide notice of the issuance of the order to the judicial and law enforcement officials in any county of this state (M)(1)

▶Petitioner may register a protection order issued in a county other than the county in which the court that issued the order is located (M)(2)

Sealing of Records

▶If JCPO not granted:

- All records of proceedings are automatically sealed R.C. 2151.358 (D)(2)

▶If JCPO granted:

- All records of proceeding are automatically sealed when respondent attains 19 years of age if in compliance of terms (E)(6)

▶If non compliance of terms:

- Court or juvenile, on motion to seal records, may seal records 2 years after JCPO expiration date R.C. 2151.358(D)(3)(a)
- Notice and opportunity to respond, within 30 days, must be given to petitioner/petitioner's attorney R.C. 2151.358(D)(3)(b)(iii)
- Hearing must be held within 30 days after receipt of response R.C. 2151.358(D)(3)(b)(iii)
- Even without response, court has discretion to hold a hearing R.C. 2151.358(D)(3)(b)(iii)

▶If records are sealed:

- They still may be subject to inspection under certain circumstances set forth in R.C. 2151.358(D)(4)

Violation of JCPOs

▶Juvenile Court retains jurisdiction for adjudicating violations including while respondent is 18 years old (B)

▶If respondent violates the JCPO (K)(1):

- Subject to prosecution as a delinquent under R.C. 2919.27
- May be found in contempt of court
- Punishment for contempt of court does not bar prosecution for violating the order, but credit must be given for the punishment imposed upon the adjudication as a delinquent child
- Juvenile adjudicated as a delinquent child shall not be subsequently punished for contempt of court out of the same activity

Electronic Monitoring

▶Electronic monitoring may be granted if there is clear and convincing evidence that (E) (1)(b):

- The petitioner reasonably believes that the respondent's conduct at any time preceding the filing of the petition endangered the health, welfare, or safety of the protected person(s)
- The respondent presents a continuing danger to the protected person
- Clear and convincing burden only pertains to the determination of the appropriateness of the electronic monitoring

▶Direct sheriff to install device & monitor respondent (N)

▶Respondent required to pay for device (N)

- If indigent, monitor is paid for from State Crime Victim Reparation Fund

Civil Rule 65.1 applies to all proceedings under this statute.

This document was created by Kathleen Vogtsberger, M.S.S.A., LSW, and Timothy Boehnlein, M.A., Domestic Violence & Child Advocacy Center and Alexandria Ruden, Esq., Legal Aid Society of Cleveland, in collaboration with Bellefaire JCB and Cuyahoga County Juvenile Court.

The content of this document was created in Cuyahoga County, Ohio and applies to Ohio Revised Code 2151.34, granting minors access to Juvenile Civil Protection Orders. This Bench Guide can be used throughout the state of Ohio.

This project was supported by Grant No. 2010-WY-AX-K019 awarded by the Office on Violence Against Women, U.S. Department of Justice. The opinions, findings, conclusions, and recommendations expressed in this publication/program/exhibition are those of the author(s) and do not necessarily reflect the views of the Department of Justice, Office on Violence Against Women.

Recently, the Ohio General Assembly enacted 2010 Ohio H.B. 10 (NS). This law authorizes juvenile courts to hear a petition for protection order against a child under R.C. 2151.34 and 3113.31, to determine whether a civil protection order should issue against a juvenile respondent and to enforce a protection order issued, or consent agreement approved, under either section against a juvenile respondent until a date certain, but not later than the date the respondent attains 19 years of age.[1]

Persons seeking protection against juvenile respondents are now permitted to file for civil protection orders in the juvenile division of the common pleas court.[2] Parents may seek relief from abusive children.[3] A person who has a child in common with another person who is under 18 years of age may seek relief against that juvenile respondent.[4] Parents or adult family or household members, or any person who is determined by the court in its discretion as an appropriate person, may seek relief on behalf of minors against juvenile respondents.[5] Additionally, minors may seek protection orders for themselves against juvenile respondents without parental consent or approval.[6]

Although a juvenile petitioner may seek protection on his or her own, the juvenile court has discretion to determine whether to notify the parent of the minor or another appropriate person.[7] Of concern is that there is no guidance regarding who is "an appropriate person."

Q & A: What is the most significant aspect of the new juvenile protection order law?

It is arguable that the age of the parties is the most important aspect of this new law. For example, a minor petitioner may file on his or her own behalf in juvenile court against a juvenile respondent. But once that juvenile turns 18 years of age, that same minor petitioner must seek his or her civil protection order in Common Pleas Court under R.C. 2903.214. This may act as a deterrent for a minor petitioner who is hesitant to file in an adult court.

There may also be times when the same parties are forced to try their cases in different courts at the same time. This is of particular concern when dealing with mutual civil protection orders and two courts are involved. A petitioner over the age of 18 years must file for a civil protection order against a juvenile respondent in juvenile court. On the other hand, that same juvenile must file his or her own protection order against an adult petitioner in common pleas court.

The fact that the statute did not contemplate this scenario is problematic and instructive. Clearly, where protection orders are filed in different courts based on the same activities, the statutory provi-

[Section 20:1]

[1]R.C. 2151.23(A)(16).

[2]See R.C. 2151.34, 3113.31(A)(2).

[3]R.C. 3113.31(A)(2).

[4]R.C. 3113.31(A)(3)(b).

[5]R.C. 2151.34(C), 3113.31(C).

[6]R.C. 2151.34(C).

[7]R.C. 2151.34(A)(3).

sions cannot be adhered to, and it is arguable that mutual and often conflicting protection orders will result.

Q & A: Is the new juvenile protection order a civil order?

Yes, the juvenile protection order is a civil proceeding. Because the determination whether to grant a protection order is civil, it is not the equivalent of finding that the person against whom the order is granted has committed a criminal offense.[8]

§ 20:2 Types of orders

According to the law, there are two types of protection orders against a minor. Under R.C. 3113.31(A)(1), the respondent must be under the age of 18 years of age. The respondent must be a family or household member of the person to be protected. The petitioner must allege that the juvenile respondent engaged in domestic violence against the person to be protected as defined in R.C. 3113.31(A)(1).

Under R.C. 2151.34, the respondent must be under the age of 18 years of age. The petitioner must allege that the respondent engaged in a violation of one of the assault crimes, menacing crimes, aggravated trespass or a sexually oriented offense.

Q & A: Does it really matter whether a civil protection order is requested pursuant to R.C. 2151.34 or 3113.31?

Yes. Each statute addresses specific relationships and prohibited behaviors. Where the protection order is requested for a family or household member, specific relationships are mandated. Additionally, domestic violence is the prohibited behavior.

On the other hand, where a protection order is issued pursuant to R.C. 2151.34, no relationship is necessary and the prohibited behaviors include the menacing and assault crimes, as well as aggravated trespass and the sexually oriented offense crimes.

§ 20:3 Behaviors justifying issuance of order

Q & A: What are the prohibited behaviors?

Besides domestic violence as defined in R.C. 3113.31, the covered offenses are set forth in R.C. 2151.34(A)(2) and include—

— felonious assault[1]
— aggravated assault[2]
— assault[3]

---

[8]Insani v. Federici, 2011-Ohio-6322, 2011 WL 6153649, *2 n.1 (Ohio Ct. App. 2d Dist. Greene County 2011); see also In re D.L., 189 Ohio App. 3d 154, 2010-Ohio-1888, 937 N.E.2d 1042 (6th Dist. Ottawa County 2010); but see J.L. v. M.D., 2011-Ohio-6208, 2011 WL 6016950, *7 (Ohio Ct. App. 11th Dist. Lake County 2011) (erroneously stating that the issuance of a protection after a full hearing is a separate, final *criminal* protection order premised upon the alleged criminal conduct prompting the underlying petition; emphasis added).

[Section 20:3]

[1]R.C. 2903.11.

[2]R.C. 2903.12.

[3]R.C. 2903.13.

— aggravated menacing[4]
— menacing by stalking[5]
— menacing[6]
— aggravated trespass[7]
— any sexually oriented offense as defined in R.C. 2950.01

These behaviors are consistent with bullying, harassment, teen dating violence[8] and other types of juvenile violence.

§ 20:4 Criminal charge or conviction as prerequisite for order

Q & A: Is a criminal charge or conviction necessary to file for or obtain a juvenile civil protection order?

Neither R.C. 2151.34 nor 3113.31 requires a criminal complaint, criminal charge, arrest or conviction.[1] While not precluded, a charge or conviction does not trigger the civil protection order process.

§ 20:5 Persons who may seek orders

Q & A: Who may seek relief?

Only certain persons may obtain a juvenile civil protection order. They include: any person filing on behalf of that person,[1] any parent or adult family or household member on behalf of any other family or household member[2] or any person who is determined by the court in its discretion as an appropriate person to seek relief under this section on behalf of any child.[3]

It is important to note that the statute does not mandate a minimum age for the person who files a petition in juvenile court. In effect, a petitioner can be 12, 25 or 65 years of age and will still have to file for the juvenile civil protection order in juvenile court so long as the respondent is a person under the age of 18 years of age.

Where a parent or another adult family or household member files on behalf of a minor, that person need not be a petitioner nor does that parent have to be listed as a protected party in the petition, unless appropriate.

---

[4]R.C. 2903.21.

[5]R.C. 2903.211; J.H. v. S.P., 2013-Ohio-3833, 2013 WL 4779047 (Ohio Ct. App. 10th Dist. Franklin County 2013).

[6]R.C. 2903.22.

[7]R.C. 2911.211.

[8]First Study of Protection Orders for Teen Victims of Dating Violence, 18 Domestic Violence Report 49, 57 (April/May 2013); also in National Criminal Justice Reference Service, An Exploratory Study of Juvenile Orders of Protection as a Remedy for Dating Violence, https://www.ncjrs.gov/.

[Section 20:4]

[1]But see J.L. v. M.D., 2011-Ohio-6208, 2011 WL 6016950 (Ohio Ct. App. 11th Dist. Lake County 2011).

[Section 20:5]

[1]R.C. 2151.34(C)(1)(a), 3113.31(C).

[2]R.C. 2151.34(C)(1)(b), 3113.31(C).

[3]R.C. 2151.34(C)(1)(c).

Where a minor files on his or her own behalf, the court may want to appoint a guardian ad litem for the petitioner if he or she is a child.

Q & A: Who are these "appropriate" persons?

These persons are not parents or other family or household members and may include a guardian ad litem, teacher, counselor, DCFS worker or even a police officer. They may also be another person as determined by the juvenile court.

Of significance is that the statute is silent as to who those appropriate persons can be and also with regard to the procedure by which a person is determined to be an appropriate person.

Q & A: Can a merchant file for a protection order against an individual?

The intent of the statute was to prevent juvenile violence committed by children under the age of 18 years. It was designed to protect individuals from domestic violence, assault, stalking, bullying and dating violence, to name a few undesirable behaviors.

The prohibited behaviors also include aggravated trespass, which is defined "enter[ing] or remain[ing] on the land or premises of another with purpose to commit on that land or those premises a misdemeanor, the elements of which involve causing physical harm to another person or causing another person to believe that the offender will cause physical harm to him."[4] That said, it is clear that a merchant may believe a juvenile who trespasses on his premises or land or business will cause physical harm to him or her.

Whether the statutory rationale should be expanded to include store merchants in the legislative schema is unclear. That the statute is silent as to this concern gives credence to the fact that its breadth is expansive enough to cover this scenario.

Of significance is that the FBI's National Criminal Identification Center (NCIC) database may not accept a civil protection order where the petitioner is a merchant or corporation. Since NCIC uses the Violence Against Women Act's definition of "person," which is not dependent on age, NCIC would not accept a corporation order, such as orders brought by Wal-Mart, Dairy Queen or Sears.[5]

Q & A: JH, by and through her mother, filed a juvenile civil protection order against respondent. At the full hearing, only the minor child appeared to testify against respondent. Can the court issue a juvenile civil protection order for the minor without the petitioner mother appearing and testifying at the full hearing?

This is the issue that the Franklin County Court of Appeals tackled in *J.H. v. S.P.*[6] J.H.'s mother filed a petition for civil protection order on behalf of her minor daughter because of appellant's threatening telephone, text and twitter messages towards her. After the trial court issued the JCPO, appellant, by and through her mother, ap-

[4]R.C. 29011.211.

[5]See 18 U.S.C.A. § 2266(5)(A). But see HB 129, eff. 9-17-2014, in which employers, corporations, associations may seek protection orders on behalf of the corporation.

[6]J.H. v. S.P., 2013-Ohio-3833, 2013 WL 4779047 (Ohio Ct. App. 10th Dist. Franklin County 2013).

pealed the decision on the grounds that, because appellee's mother did not appear at the full hearing, she was denied due process as she was not able to confront her accuser . . . . appellee's mother. Appellant argued that the mother was required to prove the allegations because she was the petitioner who actually filed the petition. "Appellant seems to suggest that S.H. had to prove that she believed that appellant would cause physical harm or mental distress to S.H., as she was the petitioner."[7]

Besides the fact the court noted that appellant failed to raise this issue before the trial court, the appellate court did discuss the merits of the issue. Noting that CPOs are civil in nature, the right to confront one's accuser applies to criminal trials. "Thus, the Confrontation Clauses of the U.S. and Ohio Constitutions apply only to criminal matters."[8] So too, there is no legal requirement in a civil case that the moving party be personally in the courtroom during trial because both she and her daughter were represented by counsel, no subpoena was issued by either counsel requiring her presence and R.C. 2151.34(C)(1)(b) permits a parent to file a civil protection on behalf of another family or household member. "Thus, although S.H. was technically the petitioner, she was clearly seeking relief on behalf of appellee, (her daughter) as indicated in the heading of the petition. Therefore, the real 'accuser' appellant needed to confront was appellee, not appellee's mother. Appellee appeared at the full hearing and was cross-examined by appellant's counsel. For all of these reasons, we find appellant's due process rights were not violated by S.H.'s absence at the full hearing * * *."[9]

§ 20:6 Jurisdiction and venue

Q & A: Which court has jurisdiction and where is venue proper?

Pursuant to R.C. 2151.34(A)(1), the Juvenile Division of the Court of Common Pleas of the county in which the person to be protected by the protection order resides has jurisdiction to issue and enforce a civil protection order against a person under the age of 18 years of age.[1]

Consistent with Civ. R. 3(B)(10), venue for filing juvenile civil protection orders is proper in the county in which the person to be protected resides.

In an interesting twist, a California appellate court determined that where a petitioner obtained a DV restraining order (civil protection order) from juvenile court and the juvenile court issued an order relinquishing and transferring the case to a domestic relations court,

[7] J.H. v. S.P., 2013-Ohio-3833, 2013 WL 4779047, ¶ 21 (Ohio Ct. App. 10th Dist. Franklin County 2013).

[8] J.H. v. S.P., 2013-Ohio-3833, 2013 WL 4779047, ¶ 23 (Ohio Ct. App. 10th Dist. Franklin County 2013), citing State v. Hayden, 96 Ohio St. 3d 211, 2002-Ohio-4169, ¶ 4, 773 N.E.2d 502 (2002).

[9] J.H. v. S.P., 2013-Ohio-3833, ¶ 25, 2013 WL 4779047 (Ohio Ct. App. 10th Dist. Franklin County 2013).

[Section 20:6]

[1] R.C. 2151.34(A)(1), 3113.31(A)(2).

that petitioner was able to renew the protection order in the domestic relations court. In *Priscila N. v. Leonardo G.*,[2] a protection order was issued in the juvenile court which ordered Leonardo not to have contact with appellant or the children. Juvenile court terminated jurisdiction over the children and transferred the case to family court where dissolution proceedings were ongoing. The protection order was attached to the orders.

After the parties' divorce was finalized, Leonardo continued to violate the protection order necessitating the need for enforcement of the order. Prior to the expiration of the protection order, Priscila filed a motion to renew the order which was denied because the family court found that it had no authority to renew a protection order issued by a juvenile court. Moreover, there was no statutory mechanism to request a permanent renewal of the order because the permanent renewal mechanism was only available under the Domestic Violence Prevention Act (wherein DV restraining orders were only issued and renewed in family court). Although the trial court did suggest that Priscila apply again for an initial order, she declined and appealed the denial of her motion.

The appellate court reversed and remanded and concluded that "the legislative history of the Family Code and the Welfare and Institutions Code indicates the Legislature intended juvenile and family courts to work together to protect victims of domestic violence. In order to effectuate this intent, we construe both statutes broadly, avoiding a formalistic reading that would require domestic violence victims who receive a DVRO from the juvenile court to repeat the process in family court."[3].

While it is clear that Ohio's rules and statutes differ from those in California, the California appellate court decision is instructive for its insightful analysis relative to effectuating legislative intent. In fact, the appellate court focused on the "legislative goal of preventing retraumatization of victims who would have been required to apply twice for what was essentially the same order."[4] In effect, this opinion extends protections for victims, clarifying that all domestic violence restraining orders are to be treated the same.

Even though Ohio courts might not permit juvenile courts to relinquish and transfer jurisdiction over the children to the domestic relations and family courts even if a juvenile court terminated jurisdiction over a case, this structural analysis may assist counsel in preparing supporting arguments should a similar issue arise.

§ 20:7 Procedure for seeking order

Q & A: What is the procedure for filing a civil protection order against a juvenile respondent?

---

[2]Priscila N. v. Leonardo G., 17 Cal. App. 5th 1208, 226 Cal. Rptr. 3d 221 (2d Dist. 2017); see also Garcia v. Escobar, 17 Cal. App. 5th 267, 225 Cal. Rptr. 3d 300 (2d Dist. 2017).

[3]Priscila N. v. Leonardo G., 17 Cal. App. 5th 1208, 1210, 226 Cal. Rptr. 3d 221, 222 (2d Dist. 2017).

[4]Priscila N. v. Leonardo G., 17 Cal. App. 5th 1208, 1214, 226 Cal. Rptr. 3d 221 (2d Dist. 2017).

The statutory language is similar to that contained in R.C. 2903.214 and 3113.31. If an ex parte civil protection order is requested, the court shall hold an ex parte hearing as soon as possible after the petition is filed, but not later than the next day after the court is in session after the petition is filed. If the petition is for a juvenile domestic violence civil protection order, the court shall hold an ex parte hearing on the same day that the petition is filed.[1]

The court, for good cause shown at the ex parte hearing, may enter any temporary orders, with or without bond, that the court finds necessary for the safety and protection of the person to be protected by the order.[2] Immediate and present danger constitutes good cause and includes, but is not limited to, situations in which the respondent has threatened the person to be protected with bodily harm or in which the respondent previously has been convicted of or pleaded guilty to, or been adjudicated a delinquent child for, committing a violation of the offenses described above.[3]

If an ex parte order has been granted, there shall be a full hearing set for a date within 10 court days after the ex parte hearing.[4] If the petitioner is a family or household member and the request is for the juvenile respondent to vacate the premises, a full hearing will be set within seven court days after the ex parte hearing.[5] For any other reason, the full hearing will be scheduled within 10 court days.[6]

§ 20:8 Petition

Q & A: What must be contained in the petition?

The petition for a civil protection order must include an allegation that the juvenile respondent (1) engaged in a violation of the Revised Code sections pertaining to assault crimes, menacing crimes, or aggravated trespass; (2) committed a sexually oriented offense; or (3) violated a municipal ordinance substantially equivalent to any of those offenses against the person to be protected by the protection order, including a description of the nature and extent of the violation.[1]

Where the parties are family or household members, the petition must contain an allegation that the juvenile respondent engaged in

---

[Section 20:7]

[1]R.C. 2151.34(D)(1), 3113.31(D)(1).

[2]R.C. 2151.34(D)(1), 3113.31(D)(1) (stating specifically that temporary orders include those set forth in R.C. 3113.31(E)(1)).

[3]R.C. 2151.34(D)(1), 3113.31(D)(1).

[4]R.C. 2151.34(D)(2).

[5]R.C. 3113.31(D)(2)(a).

[6]R.C. 3113.31(D)(2)(a).

[Section 20:8]

[1]R.C. 2151.34(C)(2)(a); see also In re E.P., 2011-Ohio-5829, 2011 WL 5507221 (Ohio Ct. App. 8th Dist. Cuyahoga County 2011) (noting that because petitioner failed to allege any facts in the petition, respondent could not have a meaningful opportunity to be heard without knowing the allegations against him prior to the hearing).

domestic violence, including a description of the nature and extent of the domestic violence.[2]

The domestic violence statute also requires that the petition contain a provision setting forth the nature of the relationship between the petitioner and the respondent.[3]

The allegation of violence and the nature and extent of the violence may be set forth in the either the form petition promulgated by the Supreme Court of Ohio or in an attached affidavit.[4]

A petition must also include a request for relief.[5]

If a petition is requested pursuant to R.C. 2151.34, the petitioner may also seek relief in the form of electronic monitoring of the respondent.[6] If this is sought, the petitioner must (1) allege that at any time preceding the filing of the petition, the respondent engaged in conduct that would cause a reasonable person to believe that the health, welfare or safety of the person to be protected was at risk; (2) describe of the nature and extent of that conduct; and (3) allege that the respondent presents a continuing danger to the person to be protected.[7]

§ 20:9 Notice of petition, hearing, and order

Q & A: Who receives notice of the filing of the petition and request for civil protection order?

Pursuant to R.C. 2151.34(D)(2)(a), the court shall provide notice of, and an opportunity to be heard at, the full hearing to the respondent and the parent, guardian or legal custodian of the respondent.

Q & A: Are parents entitled to notice of the juvenile protection order procedure?

If a minor petitioner files a petition for civil protection order under R.C. 2151.34, notice of the proceeding may be given to a parent of the child petitioner or any person who is determined by the court to be an appropriate person to receive notice of the filing of the petition.[1]

On the other hand, the statute clearly states that a copy of the petition and the ex parte protection order shall be delivered to the respondent on the same day the order is entered and to the parent, guardian or legal custodian of the respondent on the same day the order is entered.[2]

No such notification requirements are imposed on a juvenile court under R.C. 3113.31.

Q & A: Who else must be notified of the protection order?

Besides the petitioner, a copy of a civil protection order issued pur-

---

[2]R.C. 3113.31(C)(1).

[3]R.C. 3113.31(C)(2).

[4]Sup. R. 10.05(C); see also Sup. R. Forms 10.05-B to 10.05-F.

[5]R.C. 2151.34(C)(2)(c), 3113.31(C)(3).

[6]R.C. 2151.34(C)(2)(b).

[7]R.C. 2151.34(C)(2)(b).

[Section 20:9]

[1]R.C. 2151.34(C)(3)(a), (b).

[2]R.C. 2151.34(F)(1).

suant to R.C. 2151.34(F)(1) or 3113.31(F)(1) must be delivered to all law enforcement agencies that have jurisdiction to enforce the order.

Q & A: Are schools entitled to notice of a juvenile civil protection order?

The statutes are silent and provide no guidance regarding schools and whether they should be notified of the issuance of a civil protection order, or whether they are obligated to enforce a civil protection order.

Unfortunately, the statutes do not address issues relating to juveniles who attend the same school district or school, or are even in the same class. In light of state[3] and federal law indicating that juveniles cannot be denied an education or be excluded from public schools absent very limited circumstances, schools should adopt policies detailing how to comply with these court orders.

While it is highly improbable that a juvenile court would grant a protection order excluding a student from school, it is likely that an order will restrict a juvenile respondent's access in and around school grounds and during activities. Therefore, juvenile courts should adopt policies regarding notification to school districts.

The juvenile civil protection order forms provide for optional notice to a petitioner's and/or respondent's school(s).[4]

Besides the concerns set forth above, the statute does not address the extent to which schools must accommodate the juvenile civil protection order provisions. Nor do the statutes address the liability of a school that fails to enforce the terms of the juvenile civil protection order.

§ 20:10 Hearing

Q & A: Will the full hearing[1] always go forward on the date set in an ex parte civil protection order?

The full hearing will go forward on the scheduled date unless the court grants a continuance for a lack of service, the parties consent to a continuance, the continuance is needed to allow a party to obtain counsel, or for other good cause.[2]

Q & A: Are juvenile civil protection order proceedings open to the public?

It depends. According to the Ohio Rules of Juvenile Procedure, the juvenile court may exclude the general public from any hearing.[3] This also means that the juvenile court has the discretion to permit access to the public. The Ohio Rules of Civil Procedure do not address public access to a hearing.

Since a juvenile civil protection order proceeding must be conducted

---

[3]R.C. 3313.66.

[4]See http://www.sconet.state.oh.us/JCS/domesticViolence/protection_forms/juvenileForms/default.asp.

[Section 20:10]

[1]See also §§ 12:1 et seq.

[2]R.C. 2151.34(D)(2)(a)(i) to (iv), 3113.319(D)(2)(a)(i) to (iv).

[3]Juv. Proc. R. 27.

in accordance with the Rules of Civil Procedure,[4] it is likely that public access would be permitted at a hearing for a civil protection order in juvenile court.

§ 20:11 Hearing—Standard of proof

Q & A: What is the standard of proof in a juvenile protection order proceeding?

The statute is silent. However, based on the legal analysis in *Felton v. Felton*,[1] the Supreme Court of Ohio determined that the correct standard of proof in civil domestic violence proceedings is a preponderance of the evidence. This same analysis and result has been applied to the civil stalking protection orders proceedings issued pursuant to R.C. 2903.214.

Consistent with domestic violence and other civil protection order proceedings, the evidentiary standard of proof for a juvenile civil protection order is the preponderance of the evidence standard.[2]

Of significance is that where the petitioner requests electronic monitoring for the juvenile respondent, the court must then apply an additional and higher standard of proof—a clear and convincing evidence standard—solely for the purpose of determining the appropriateness of ordering electronic monitoring. Therefore, any time a petition includes an allegation that the respondent engaged in conduct that would cause a reasonable person to believe that the health, welfare or safety of the person to be protected was at risk,[3] the court, at the full hearing, must find, by clear and convincing evidence, that the petitioner reasonably believed that the respondent's conduct, at any time preceding the filing of the petition, endangered the health, welfare or safety of the person to be protected and that the respondent presents a continuing danger to the person to be protected.[4]

Q & A: Does the grant of a juvenile civil protection order depend on a danger of future violence?

It appears that appellate jurisdictions considering this question have determined that when granting a civil protection order after a full hearing, the trial court must find that a petitioner has shown, by a preponderance of the evidence, that petitioner or petitioner's family

---

[4]R.C. 2151.34(G).

[Section 20:11]

[1]Felton v. Felton, 79 Ohio St. 3d 34, 1997-Ohio-302, 679 N.E.2d 672 (1997); see also In re E.P., 2011-Ohio-5829, 2011 WL 5507221 (Ohio Ct. App. 8th Dist. Cuyahoga County 2011) (noting that the Rules of Civil Procedure apply to juvenile civil protection orders and commenting that these rules do permit discovery).

[2]See In re E.P., 2011-Ohio-5829, 2011 WL 5507221, *3 (Ohio Ct. App. 8th Dist. Cuyahoga County 2011) (applying the legal analysis of *Felton v. Felton,* and stating that "[l]ike the statute in *Felton*, RC 2151.34 simply requires proof by a preponderance of the evidence that the petitioner is in danger of one of the enumerated offenses in RC 2151.34(C)(2) if the juvenile civil protection is not granted"); see also Insani v. Federici, 2011-Ohio-6322, 2011 WL 6153649 (Ohio Ct. App. 2d Dist. Greene County 2011); J.H. v. S.P., 2013-Ohio-3833, 2013 WL 4779047 (Ohio Ct. App. 10th Dist. Franklin County 2013).

[3]R.C. 2151.34(C)(2)(b).

[4]R.C. 2151.34(E)(1)(b).

or household members are in danger of a new violation of one of the enumerated offenses contained in RC 2151.34(A)(2).[5]

Q & A: Is that the same standard as for the issuance of an ex parte juvenile civil protection order?

No. The standard of proof for the issuance of an ex parte juvenile civil protection order appears to be either "good cause" or "immediate and present danger."[6] The statute provides that "[t]he court may issue temporary orders upon a showing of good cause."[7] If an ex parte civil protection order is requested, the court must find good cause that the order is necessary for the safety and protection of the petitioner.[8] The statute also provides that "[i]mmediate and present danger to the person to be protected by the protection order constitutes good cause" and includes situations in which the respondent has been convicted of or pleaded guilty or been adjudicated a delinquent child for committing any one of the offenses alleged in the petition or situations in which respondent has threatened the petitioner with bodily harm.[9]

That good cause is the apparent standard is derived from both domestic violence and stalking case law and the similarities among the civil statutes.

Q & A: Is the full hearing order a continuation of the ex parte order?

No. In *J.L. v M.D.*,[10] the trial court issued a juvenile civil protection order for a juvenile female with ADHD against a juvenile male with autism. On appeal, appellant challenged the issuance of the order contending that appellee was required to demonstrate that she was in immediate and present danger to her person at the full hearing.

The appellate court indicated that the immediate and present danger standard applied to the ex parte hearing and that once a protection order is issued after the full hearing, that protection order cannot be deemed a "continuation of the original ex parte order.[11] Since the court may issue another protection order at the conclusion of the full hearing, the new order would not be considered a continuation of the ex parte juvenile civil protection order. The court then pointed out that appellee was required to establish appellant had engaged in conduct constituting menacing by stalking in violation of RC 2903.211. (It is interesting to note that the Lake County Court of Appeals did not address the danger of future harm.)

---

[5]In re E.P., 2011-Ohio-5829, 2011 WL 5507221 (Ohio Ct. App. 8th Dist. Cuyahoga County 2011); citing Felton v. Felton, 79 Ohio St. 3d 34, 1997-Ohio-302, 679 N.E.2d 672 (1997); see also Insani v. Federici, 2011-Ohio-6322, 2011 WL 6153649 (Ohio Ct. App. 2d Dist. Greene County 2011); J.H. v. S.P., 2013-Ohio-3833, 2013 WL 4779047 (Ohio Ct. App. 10th Dist. Franklin County 2013).

[6]See, for example, J.L. v. M.D., 2011-Ohio-6208, 2011 WL 6016950 (Ohio Ct. App. 11th Dist. Lake County 2011).

[7]R.C. 2151.34(D)(1).

[8]R.C. 2151.34(D)(1).

[9]R.C. 2151.34(D)(1).

[10]J.L. v. M.D., 2011-Ohio-6208, 2011 WL 6016950 (Ohio Ct. App. 11th Dist. Lake County 2011).

[11]J.L. v. M.D., 2011-Ohio-6208, 2011 WL 6016950, *7 (Ohio Ct. App. 11th Dist. Lake County 2011).

§ 20:12 Applicability of Rules of Juvenile Procedure

Q & A: Do the Rules of Juvenile Procedure apply to juvenile civil protection orders?

No. The Rules of Civil Procedure apply to both juvenile civil protection order proceedings and domestic violence civil protection order proceedings.[1]

§ 20:13 Discovery issues

Q & A: Is discovery permitted in a civil protection order proceeding?

Yes. RC 3113.31(G) provides that civil domestic violence actions "shall be conducted in accordance with the Rules of Civil Procedure. Recently adopted Civ. R. 65.1 applies only to civil protection order proceedings and specifically provides for a procedure for discovery.[1]

Q & A: What is the procedure for discovery under Civ. R. 65. 1(D)?

First and foremost, a civil protection order proceeding is a special statutory proceeding.[2] Under Civ. R. 65.1(D)(2), whether to grant discovery in a particular civil protection order action is within the discretion of the court and may be had only upon entry of an order, which shall contain the following to the extent applicable:

(1) The time and place of the discovery;[3]

(2) The identities of the persons permitted to be present, which shall include any victim advocate;[4]

(3) Such terms and conditions deemed by the court to be necessary to assure the safety of the Petitioner, including if applicable, maintaining the confidentiality of the Petitioner's address.[5]

Finally, any discovery under the rule must be completed prior to the time set for the full hearing.[6] Although the rule does not contemplate a continuance process in order to address meaningful discovery, the Staff Notes of the Rule indicate that, because there is a shortened time frame between the ex parte order and the full hearing, a statutory request for a continuance might be appropriate.

§ 20:14 Counsel

Q & A: When a civil protection order is issued against a juvenile respondent, must counsel be appointed for that juvenile respondent?

No. According to R.C. 2151.34(O), appointment of counsel for the re-

---

[Section 20:12]

[1]R.C. 2151.34(G), 3113.31(G).

[Section 20:13]

[1]Civ. R. 65.1(D).

[2]Civ. R. 65.1(A).

[3]Civ. R. 65.1(D)(2)(a).

[4]Civ. R. 65.1(D)(2)(b).

[5]Civ. R. 65.1(D)(2)(c).

[6]Civ. R. 65.1(D)(1).

spondent is within the discretion of the court.[1] Of interest is that R.C. 3113.31 does not even mention appointment of counsel.

Q & A: Is a petitioner entitled to counsel?

Of course either party may hire an attorney to represent him or her in a juvenile civil protection order proceeding. However, the statute is silent as to whether counsel may be appointed for a petitioner.

Q & A: Have there been any cases that have addressed this issue?

The 6th District appellate court, in *In re D.L.*,[2] has provided cogent arguments in favor of mandatory court-appointed counsel for juvenile respondents in juvenile civil protection order proceedings.

In *In re D.L.*, the trial court issued a civil protection order against a 13-year-old minor on behalf of a minor victim. The minor respondent was not provided with court-appointed counsel. In fact, the trial court permitted both fathers to cross-examine the minor children.

On appeal, the minor respondent claimed that he was not provided the due process protections established by Civ. R. 17(B). First, the appellate court reviewed Rule 17(B), which provides that "[w]henever a minor or incompetent person has a representative, such as a guardian or other like fiduciary, the representative may sue or defend on behalf of the minor." The court concluded that it was proper for the father of the juvenile petitioner to file for the civil protection order on behalf of his child in the first instance.

However, that same representative, unless he or she is a licensed attorney, does not have the right to act as counsel for the minor. The *In re D.L.* court relied on the reasoning set forth in a Cuyahoga County appellate court case, *In re Unauthorized Practice of Law in Cuyahoga County*,[3] which concluded that no one, other than an attorney, may appear in court as a representative of another. *In dicta*, the *In re D.L.* court also admonished the trial court, stating that "[j]udges have an ethical duty to prevent the unauthorized practice of law."[4] "Therefore, although Civ. R. 17(B) permits a parent to act 'on behalf of' his or her minor child, it does not permit a non-attorney parent to act as a lawyer for that child."[5]

Therefore, the parents in this case were not in any position to act as their children's legal representatives in a court of law.

The court then went on to say that "[t]his case also illustrates the troublesome issues inherent with juvenile civil protection orders which the Ohio Legislature has addressed under the newly enacted Shynerra

---

[Section 20:14]

[1]See also Civ. R. 65.1(E) which provides that in a special statutory proceeding under R.C. 2151.34, the court, in its discretion, may determine if the respondent is entitled to court-appointed counsel at the full hearing.

[2]In re D.L., 189 Ohio App. 3d 154, 2010-Ohio-1888, 937 N.E.2d 1042 (6th Dist. Ottawa County 2010).

[3]In re Unauthorized Practice of Law in Cuyahoga County, 175 Ohio St. 149, 151, 23 Ohio Op. 2d 445, 192 N.E.2d 54, 2 A.L.R.3d 712 (1963).

[4]In re D.L., 189 Ohio App. 3d 154, 158, 2010-Ohio-1888, 937 N.E.2d 1042 (6th Dist. Ottawa County 2010).

[5]In re D.L., 189 Ohio App. 3d 154, 158, 2010-Ohio-1888, 937 N.E.2d 1042 (6th Dist. Ottawa County 2010).

Grant Law."[6] The court reasoned that, while the issuance of a civil protection order is not a crime, violation of the order is a crime which may possibly result in incarceration. Noting that certain constitutional protections are not afforded to a defendant during the initial grant of the civil protection order, the court then explained that there are certain civil actions, including contempt proceedings, in which a defendant is accorded due process protections. Therefore, a juvenile respondent should be entitled to these same protections because the violation of the civil protection order may lead to criminal consequences.[7]

Finally, the appellate court also found that it was improper for the father of the juvenile respondent to have agreed to proceed without a lawyer for the child. At the very least, the child was entitled to advice of counsel which is both "warranted and necessary to protect a juvenile respondent in a civil protection order proceeding."[8]

In reversing the trial court, the appellate court determined that the parent's waiver of counsel for his child was invalid and that the trial court erred by not appointing counsel to protect the child's due process rights.[9] Moreover, the court expressed hope that the new law will provide the judiciary with guidance. However, it is unclear whether the law, over time, will provide answers or only more questions. Hopefully, a balance can be reached between appointing counsel for a juvenile in a civil protection order proceeding and permitting a parent to actively present the claim of his or her child without engaging in the unauthorized practice of law.

On the other hand, the Greene County Court of Appeals addressed this issue as well. In *Insani v. Frederici*,[10] respondent failed to attend the full hearing and claimed his rights were violated because he was not represented by counsel and because the trial court did not inquire as to his reasons for or understanding of his waiver of his right to counsel.

The Greene County appellate court clarified that "[g]enerally, a child, the child's parents or custodian, or any other person in loco parentis of the child is entitled to representation by legal counsel at all stages of the proceeding in the juvenile court; if, as an indigent person, a party is unable to employ counsel, the party is entitled to have counsel provided for him."[11] However, the court also stated that counsel must be provided for a child not represented by the child's

---

[6]In re D.L., 189 Ohio App. 3d 154, 158, 2010-Ohio-1888, 937 N.E.2d 1042 (6th Dist. Ottawa County 2010).

[7]In re D.L., 189 Ohio App. 3d 154, 159-60, 2010-Ohio-1888, 937 N.E.2d 1042 (6th Dist. Ottawa County 2010).

[8]In re D.L., 189 Ohio App. 3d 154, 161, 2010-Ohio-1888, 937 N.E.2d 1042 (6th Dist. Ottawa County 2010).

[9]In re D.L., 189 Ohio App. 3d 154, 161, 2010-Ohio-1888, 937 N.E.2d 1042 (6th Dist. Ottawa County 2010).

[10]Insani v. Federici, 2011-Ohio-6322, 2011 WL 6153649 (Ohio Ct. App. 2d Dist. Greene County 2011); see also Juv. R. 3.

[11]Insani v. Federici, 2011-Ohio-6322, 2011 WL 6153649, *2 (Ohio Ct. App. 2d Dist. Greene County 2011), citing R.C. 2151.352: "If a party appears without counsel, the court shall ascertain whether the party knows of the party's right to counsel and of the party's right to be provided with counsel if the party is an indigent person.

parent, guardian or custodian. If the interests of two or more such parties conflict, separate counsel shall be provided for each of them.[12] Inherent in such a statement by the court is the suggestion that the parents of the child may act as legal counsel for their child.

Q & A: How can a court determine whether a juvenile has validly waived his right to counsel?

The court in *Insani v. Frederici*,[13] addressed the factors for assessing for a waiver of the right to counsel. In making this determination, courts must consider the totality of the circumstances, including the child's age, intelligence and education; the child's background and experience generally and in the court system; the presence or absence of the juvenile's parent, guardian or custodian; the language used by the court in describing the juvenile's rights; the juvenile's conduct; the juvenile's emotional stability and the complexity of the proceedings. The degree to which the juvenile's parent is capable of assisting and willing to assist the juvenile in the waiver analysis is also a factor.[14]

The Greene County Court of Appeals overruled the assignment of error and concluded that because respondent failed to appear at the hearing, the court had no obligation to inquire about his rights.

§ 20:15 Service of order

Q & A: What type of service is proper for a juvenile protection order?

A copy of any protection order must be delivered to the respondent on the same day the order is entered.[1] As with the other civil protection orders, the statutory language suggests personal service on the respondent because it is the only method of service that fulfills the statutory mandate.

Recently, the Supreme Court of Ohio adopted a new rule of civil procedure that applies to the service of a juvenile civil protection order. Civ. R. 65.1(C)(1) specifically addresses service of civil protection orders. The clerk of courts shall cause service to be made of a copy of the petition and all other documents required by the applicable protection order statute to be served on the respondent and, if applicable, on the parent, guardian or legal custodian of the Respondent.

Q & A: What type of service is contemplated by Civ. R. 65.1?

Because Ohio's juvenile protection order statute fails to clearly state that personal service is required[2] or address the methods of alternative service, Civ. R. 65.1 was needed to address this problem. Civ. R. 65.1(C)(2) provides that initial service and service of any ex

---

[12] Insani v. Federici, 2011-Ohio-6322, 2011 WL 6153649, *2 (Ohio Ct. App. 2d Dist. Greene County 2011).

[13] Insani v. Federici, 2011-Ohio-6322, 2011 WL 6153649 (Ohio Ct. App. 2d Dist. Greene County 2011).

[14] Insani v. Federici, 2011-Ohio-6322, 2011 WL 6153649, *2 (Ohio Ct. App. 2d Dist. Greene County 2011), citing In re Anderson, 92 Ohio St. 3d 63, 66, 2001-Ohio-131, 748 N.E.2d 67 (2001).

[Section 20:15]

[1] R.C. 2151.34(F)(1); R.C. 3113.31(F)(1); see also Text § 11:11.

[2] R.C. 2151.34(F).

parte protection order that is entered shall be made in accordance with the provisions for personal service of process within the state under Civ. R. 4.1(B) or outside the state under Civ. R. 4.3(B)(2). Upon failure of such personal service, or in addition to such personal service, service may be made in accordance with any applicable provision of Civ. R. 4 through Civ. R. 4.6.

Q & A: Does this mean certified mail, ordinary mail and service by publication?

Yes. Certified mail service,[3] ordinary mail service,[4] and service by publication[5] are adequate alternative methods of service for serving civil protection orders, should personal service fail.

Recent amendments to Civ. R. 4.4 permit the use of publication by posting service of process as an appropriate method of service in Civ. R. 65.1 civil protection order proceedings. A petitioner who is proceeding in *forma pauperis* (indigent) and who requests posting service of process must file an affidavit with the court pursuant to the requirements of Civ.R. 4.4(A)(2).

Civ. R. 4.4(A)(2) allows for publication by a clerk in a conspicuous place in the courthouse. Per the language of the Civil Rules, posting appears to be reserved for persons with limited resources.

According to the Staff Notes, "Division (A)(2) of this rule is amended to provide that publication by posting service of process is an appropriate method of service in Civ. R. 65.1 civil protection order proceedings under the conditions described in that division of the rule. As stated in division (A)(2) of the rule, a petitioner who is proceeding in forma pauperis and who requests publication by posting service of process must file an affidavit with the court containing the same averments required by division (A)(1) of the rule, ie., that service of summons cannot be made because the residence of the defendant is unknown to the affiant, all of the efforts made on behalf of the party to ascertain the residence of the defendant, and that the residence of the defendant cannot be ascertained with reasonable diligence.

The service of process by publication by posting of a civil protection order shall not impact the prompt entry of such an order into the protection order file of the National Crime Information Center, it is to be noted that the alternative method of posting in the website of the clerk of courts is not available for service of protection orders issued pursuant to Civ. R. 65.1."

Q & A: What is the proper method of serving a juvenile protection order issued after a full hearing?

Generally, Civ. R. 5 applies to the service of papers other than process and specifically applies to every order required by its terms to be served, including civil protection orders issued after a full hearing. Service by mail is complete upon mailing.[6]

Civ. R. 65.1(C)(3) provides that after service has been made in ac-

[3]Civ. R. 4.1(A).

[4]Civ. R. 4.6(D).

[5]Civ. R. 4.4.

[6]Civ. R. 5(B).

cordance with division (C)(2) of this rule, any additional service required to be made during the course of the proceedings on Respondent and, if applicable, on the parent, guardian or legal custodian of Respondent, shall be made in accordance with the provisions of Civ. R. 5(B). Since the civil protection order issued after a full hearing is neither a writ nor a summons, it is not process. Hence, its service is governed by Civ. R. 5(B).

Q & A: Must the juvenile protection order be served on a parent, legal custodian or guardian of the respondent?

Yes. Civ. R. 65.1 provides the procedure for service to these individuals.[7]

§ 20:16 Ex parte orders

Q & A: Must a petitioner request an ex parte juvenile civil protection order? What if the court denies my request for an ex parte civil protection order?

No. The statutes permit a petitioner to file for a protection order but a petitioner does not have to request an ex parte order. Sometimes, the court may not issue an ex parte order, even if an ex parte order is requested. In either case, the court shall proceed as in a normal civil action and grant the full hearing on the matter.[1]

Of note is that any proceeding under either statute shall be conducted in accordance with the Rules of Civil Procedure.[2]

§ 20:17 Relief provided by order

Q & A: What relief is available?

That depends on the nature of the civil protection order. If it is granted pursuant to R.C. 2151.34(E)(1)(a), the court may issue any protection order, with or without bond, that contains terms designed to ensure the safety and protection of the person to be protected by the protection order. Pursuant to a recent legislative amendment to RC 2151, "the court may include within a protection order issued under this section a term requiring that the respondent not remove, damage, hide, harm or dispose of any companion animal owned or possessed by the person to be protected by the order, and may include with the order a term authorizing the person to be protected by the order to remove a companion animal owned by the person to be protected by the order from the possession of the respondent."[1]

After a full hearing, if the petition contains a request for electronic monitoring of the respondent, or the court, upon its own motion, finds by clear and convincing evidence that the petitioner reasonably believed that the respondent's conduct at any time preceding the filing of the petition endangered the health, welfare or safety of the

---

[7]See also R.C. 2151.34(F)(1).

[Section 20:16]

[1]R.C. 2151.34(D)(3), 3113.31(D)(3); § 11:22.

[2]R.C. 2151.34(G), 3113.31(G).

[Section 20:17]

[1]See R.C. 2151.34(E)(1)(a).

person to be protected and the respondent presents a continuing danger to the person to be protected, the court may order the respondent to be electronically monitored for a period of time and under terms and conditions that the court determines are appropriate. Electronic monitoring shall be in addition to any other relief granted to the petitioner.[2]

Of significance, electronic monitoring is applicable only to those protection orders issued under R.C. 2151.34.

If a protection order is issued under R.C. 3113.31, the court may grant any protection order with or without bond to bring about the cessation of domestic violence. R.C. 3113.31(E)(1) details the nature of relief, which may include—

— directing a respondent to refrain from abusing, threatening or committing a sexually oriented offense.

— granting possession of, or ordering respondent to vacate, the residence of the petitioner.

— temporarily allocating parental rights and responsibilities of children if no other court has jurisdiction.

— requiring a respondent to maintain support.

— requiring any of the parties to seek counseling.

— requiring the respondent to refrain from entering the residence, school, business or place of employment of the petitioner or the protected parties.

— apportioning personal property or awarding use of an automobile.

— granting other relief as is equitable and fair.

Q & A: Can a juvenile respondent be removed from his or her residence through a juvenile civil protection order?

Yes. Under R.C. 3113.31(E)(1), the court may grant any protection order to bring about a cessation of domestic violence against a family or household member. R.C. 3113.31(E)(1)(b) specifically includes a provision ordering the respondent to vacate the premises or awarding exclusive possession of the premises to the petitioner. Under R.C. 2151.34(E)(1)(a), a court may issue any protection order that contains terms designed to ensure the safety and protection of the person to be protected by the protection order.

The removal of a juvenile respondent will most likely occur in actions between parents and children, or between siblings. Therefore, a juvenile respondent may be removed from his or her home through a juvenile protection order.

The more important issue is where a juvenile respondent would go—to a detention home or another type of juvenile facility? Would the court return the child to the home over the objections of the parent? The statute fails to address these concerns.

---

[2]R.C. 2151.34(E)(1)(b).

§ 20:18 Mutual orders

Q & A: Can a court issue mutual juvenile civil protection orders?[1]

Mutual protection orders are entered against both parties and arise out of one party's filing of a petition for civil protection order. A petitioner may agree to a mutual order of protection; courts have also been known to issue such orders *sua sponte*.

Since 1994, both state and federal law clearly mandate that a court cannot issue a mutual civil protection order against a party where no petition for such an order has been filed.[2]

Specifically, Ohio courts may issue an order of protection that requires a petitioner to do or refrain from doing an act only if certain criteria are met.[3] For purposes of juvenile protection orders:

(1) the juvenile respondent must file a separate petition against the petitioner, alleging the nature and extent of the specific behavior;[4]

(2) the petitioner must be served with notice of the respondent's petition at least 48 hours before the court holds a hearing with respect to the respondent's petition, unless the petitioner waives the right to receive that notice;[5]

(3) if the petitioner has requested an ex parte order pursuant to R.C. 2151.34(D), the court must not delay any hearing required by that statute beyond the time specified therein in order to consolidate the hearing with a hearing on the petition filed by the respondent;[6] and

(4) after a full hearing at which the respondent presents evidence in support of the request for a protection order and the petitioner is afforded an opportunity to defend against the evidence, the court must determine that the petitioner has committed (a) a violation of R.C. 2903.11, 2903.12, 2903.13, 2903.21, 2903.211, 2903.22, or 2911.211; (b) a sexually oriented offense; or (c) a violation of a protection order issued pursuant to R.C. 2903.213.[7]

In effect, the court must find that the petitioner's behavior is equivalent to the respondent's behavior.

If the petitioner and respondent are family or household members, the court must also find that both the petitioner and respondent acted

[Section 20:18]

[1]See also § 12:29.

[2]R.C. 2903.214(E)(3), 3113.31(E)(4); see also the federal Violence Against Women Act of 1994, codified in scattered sections of Titles 18 and 42 of the United States Code; § 12:29, supra.

[3]R.C. 2151.34(E)(3), 2903.214(E)(3), 3113.31(E)(4).

[4]R.C. 2151.34(E)(3)(a).

[5]R.C. 2151.34(E)(3)(b).

[6]R.C. 2151.34(E)(3)(c).

[7]R.C. 2151.34(E)(3)(d); see also R.C. 3113.31(E)(4).

primarily as aggressors and that neither petitioner nor respondent acted in self-defense.[8]

§ 20:19 Consent agreements

Q & A: Can the court grant a juvenile civil protection order by way of a consent agreement?

No. While R.C. 2151.34 does not provide for a consent agreement protection order, a civil protection order issued under R.C. 3113.31 does permit such orders. Consent agreements presuppose that both parties voluntarily enter into such agreements and that they waive their rights to a full hearing. More importantly, there are no findings that the respondent committed the prohibited behaviors.

Sometimes, however, the parties do agree to the terms of a protection order. Upon review, the court may decide to adopt those terms and enter the protection order agreed to by the parties. If the court does accept the terms of a civil protection order entered by agreement, the juvenile court should indicate that no full hearing was held and that the juvenile respondent knowingly and voluntarily waived his or her right to a full hearing. Of importance is notifying the juvenile respondent that a violation of such an order carries the same penalties, both civil and criminal, as a protection order issued after a full hearing. This is even more important should a court not permit the appointment of counsel.

§ 20:20 Duration of order; renewal; modification

Q & A: How long does a juvenile protection order last?

R.C. 2151.34(E)(2)(a) states that a protection order issued shall be valid until a date certain, but not later than the date the respondent attains 19 years of age.

R.C. 3113.31(E)(3)(a) provides that any protection order issued or consent agreement approved shall be valid until a date certain, but not later than five years from the date of its issuance or approval or not later than the date a respondent who is less than 18 years of age attains 19 years of age, unless modified or terminated as provided in R.C. 3113.31(E)(8).

No matter whether the civil protection order is issued against a family or household member or not, the duration of the order is until the juvenile respondent attains 19 years of age. That could also mean that a juvenile civil protection order may remain in effect for a longer period than five years. This might occur where a petitioner obtains a civil protection against a juvenile respondent of 10 or 13 years of age. Technically, such an order can remain in effect until age 19 years, which is longer than the five-year duration.

On the other hand, the duration of a civil protection order issued against a juvenile respondent pursuant to R.C. 3113.31 is five years from the date of its issuance, or not later than the date a respondent who is less than 18 years of age attains 19 years of age. Because the length of any protection order issued under R.C. 3113.31 is limited to five years or attainment of age 19, it is apparently more time-restrictive.

[8]R.C. 3113.31(E)(4)(d).

Additionally, only civil protection orders issued pursuant to R.C. 3113.31 may be modified or terminated under R.C. 3113.31(E)(8).

Q & A: Can juvenile protection orders be renewed?

Yes. They can be renewed in the same manner as the original order was issued.[1]

Q & A: If a juvenile court grants a juvenile civil protection order until the respondent's 19th birthday, how is such an order renewed? By which court? Does the juvenile court lose jurisdiction over the case when that juvenile respondent turns 19 years of age?

Both R.C. 2151.34 and 3113.31 contain provisions that permit a juvenile court to renew a juvenile civil protection order "in the same matter as the original order was issued."[2] Besides a lack of clarity regarding the procedure for such a renewal, this particular provision is fraught with ambiguity.

First, the juvenile court has jurisdiction over juveniles under the age of 18 years.[3] However, juvenile courts may, by statute, retain jurisdiction over certain issues past the age of 18 years of age. In the context of protection orders, juvenile courts have jurisdiction to issue and enforce a protection order against a child not later than the date the child attains 19 years.[4] Additionally, the statute also provides that "[a]ny person who, while eighteen years of age, violates (A)(1) or (2) of section 2919.27 of the Revised Code by violating a protection order issued or consent agreement approved under section 2151.34 or 3113.31 of the Revised Code, shall be considered a child for the purposes of that violation of section 2919.27 of the Revised Code."[5]

The issue is whether the juvenile court retains jurisdiction to renew the civil protection order against a juvenile respondent well after that respondent turns 19 years of age. If juvenile court retains jurisdiction over the renewal of a protection order of a child turned adult, it is arguably contrary to the intents and purposes of the statute. If, on the other hand, the juvenile court no longer retains jurisdiction, then a renewal must be brought in the general division of the common pleas court. Will the common pleas court accept jurisdiction to address a renewal when it didn't issue the original civil protection order? This begs the question of what evidence is needed to prevail on a renewal action or whether a renewal brought in the common pleas court general division becomes a proceeding *de novo*.

Obviously, the legislature did not consider the impact of this provision when it crafted the legislation.

Q & A: Can a juvenile civil protection order be modified?

R.C. 3113.31(E)(8) details a process by which a court may modify and terminate a domestic violence civil protection order. This section of the Revised Code should also apply to juvenile civil protection orders issued under R.C. 3113.31.

[Section 20:20]

[1]R.C. 2151.34(E)(2)(b), 3113.31(E)(3)(c); see also § 12:24.

[2]R.C. 2151.34(E)(2)(b), 3113.31(E)(3)(c).

[3]R.C. 2152.02(C).

[4]R.C. 2151.23(A)(16).

[5]R.C. 2152.02(C)(7).

On the other hand, R.C. 2151.34 is silent regarding modification or termination of a juvenile civil protection order issued pursuant to that section.

§ 20:21 Fees and costs

Q & A: Can juvenile courts assess fees or costs related to the filing of a juvenile civil protection order?

No. Consistent with Ohio's civil protection order schema and federal law, no fees or costs can be assessed to a petitioner or the person to be protected for the filing, issuance, registration, modification, enforcement, dismissal or withdrawal or service of a protection order or a witness subpoena or for obtaining a certified copy of a protection order.[1] However, courts may assess these fees or costs to a respondent.[2]

§ 20:22 Delinquency adjudication and civil protection order

Q & A: Can a juvenile respondent be the subject of a juvenile civil protection order for the same incident that the juvenile has been adjudicated delinquent?

Yes. According to R.C. 2151.34(G), the remedies and procedures provided in R.C. 2151.34 are in addition to, and not in lieu of, any other available civil or criminal remedies or other available remedies under Chapter 2151 or 2152 of the Revised Code.[1]

§ 20:23 Penalties for violation of order

Q & A: What are the penalties for violating a juvenile civil protection order?

A violation of a juvenile civil protection order may entail civil and/or criminal penalties.[1]

If a juvenile violates a juvenile civil protection order, he or she is subject to prosecution as a delinquent under R.C. 2919.27 or to being held in contempt of court. The punishment for contempt does not bar prosecution for violating the order under R.C. 2919.27, but credit must be given for any punishment imposed upon conviction or adjudication as a delinquent child.

A juvenile convicted or adjudicated as a delinquent child shall not be subsequently punished for contempt of court out of the same activity.

A juvenile court retains jurisdiction for adjudicating violations while the respondent is 18 years old.[2]

[Section 20:21]

[1]R.C. 2151.34(J)(1); 42 U.S.C.A. § 3796gg-5.

[2]R.C. 2151.34(J)(2).

[Section 20:22]

[1]See also R.C. 3113.31(G).

[Section 20:23]

[1]R.C. 2151.34(K)(1), (2), 2919.27, 3113.31(L)(1), (2).

[2]R.C. 2152.02(C)(7).

§ 20:24 Confidentiality of orders; sealing or expungement

Q & A: Are juvenile civil protection orders confidential from the public or are they subject to a public records exception?

Generally, juvenile court records are not permitted for any public use except in the course of an appeal or as authorized by order of the court.[1] However, there is nothing in R.C. 2151.34 that limits public access of juvenile civil protection orders, juvenile civil protection order proceedings, or records.

In fact, juvenile civil protection orders, once issued, are subject to inclusion in the FBI's National Criminal Identification Center (NCIC) database. The FBI requires the entry of the respondent's full name, address and identifying characteristics as well as the full name of the petitioner and one numerical identifier.[2]

Q & A: Can juvenile civil protection orders be sealed and/or expunged?

Juvenile civil protection orders may be sealed under certain circumstances and it does not matter whether the protection order was issued under R.C. 2151.34 or 3113.31.

If a court does not issue a protection order after a full hearing, the court shall automatically seal all of the records in that proceeding.[3] That would include any ex parte protection order.

If a full hearing or consent agreement juvenile civil protection order is granted, all records shall be sealed on the day the respondent attains 19 years of age. This is the case unless the petitioner provides evidence of noncompliance. To ensure that the civil protection order is sealed in a timely manner, the actual order must specify the date of the respondent's 19th birthday as the date of the expiration of the order.[4]

If the juvenile court does not seal the juvenile civil protection order records due to the respondent's noncompliance with the terms of the order, the court may, *sua sponte* or per the respondent's petition, have the record sealed at any time after two years after the expiration of the protection order or consent agreement.[5]

In making a determination whether to seal records of a noncompliant respondent, the court may require the person filing an application to submit relevant documentation to support the application.[6] The court shall promptly notify the victim or the victim's attorney of any proceedings to seal records initiated.[7]

The victim or the victim's attorney may file a response with the court within 30 days of receiving notice of the sealing proceeding. If the victim does not file a response with the court, or if a response is

[Section 20:24]

[1]Juv. Proc. R. 37(B); see also R.C. 149.43.

[2]Sup. R. 10; Sup. R. Form 10-A; Sup. R. 10-B.

[3]R.C. 2151.358(D)(2).

[4]R.C. 2151.358(D)(1), 2151.34(E)(6), 3113.31(E)(9).

[5]R.C. 2151.358(D)(3)(a).

[6]R.C. 2151.358(D)(3)(b)(i).

[7]R.C. 2151.358(D)(3)(b)(ii).

filed and no objections to the sealing are noted, the court may order the records sealed without conducting a hearing on the application. The court may also, in its discretion, conduct a hearing. If the court exercises its discretion to hold a hearing, it shall do so within 30 days of making the decision and shall give notice by regular mail to the victim, his or her attorney and to the person who is subject of the records under consideration. If the victim files a responsive pleading objecting to the sealing, the court shall conduct a hearing on the application within 30 days after the court receives the response and shall provide all parties with notice of the hearing by regular mail.[8] After conducting the hearing, the court may order the records sealed.[9]

R.C. 2151.358(D)(4) details who may inspect sealed records.

It is unclear whether sealed juvenile protection order records may also be expunged. Nothing in the relevant statutes indicate whether expungement is permissible or mandated; however, the placement of the requirements for sealing a juvenile civil protection order in the expungement section of the Revised Code may be indicative of the legislative thought process.

However, there seems to be an inconsistency between the new language and the already existing statutory language. Under recently enacted RC 2151.34(G)(2), "If as provided in division (G)(1) of this section an order issued under this section, other than an ex parte order, refuses to grant a protection order, the court, on its own motion, shall order that the ex parte order issued under this section and all of the records pertaining to the ex parte order be expunged after either of the following occurs:

(a) The period of the notice of appeal from the order that refuses to grant a protection order has expired.

(b) The order that refuses to grant the protection order is appealed and an appellate court to which the last appeal of the order is taken affirms the order."

However, the Juvenile Code also provides that: "Any protection order issued pursuant to this section shall include a provision that the court will automatically seal all of the records of the proceeding in which the order is issued on the date the respondent attains the age of nineteen years unless the petitioner provides the court with evidence that the respondent has not complied with all of the terms of the protection order. The protection order shall specify the date when the respondent attains the age of nineteen years."[10]

Apparently, the legislature must determine whether sealing or expunging is the appropriate method to address the issue of removing documents from a court file.

§ 20:25 Firearms limitations arising from order

Q & A: Are juvenile respondents subject to firearms limitations?

A juvenile who is subject to a juvenile civil protection order must be

[8]R.C. 2151.358(D)(3)(b)(iii).

[9]R.C. 2151.358(D)(3)(b)(iv).

[10]R.C. 2151.34(6).

given a statutorily prescribed notice that it may be unlawful for him or her to possess or purchase a firearm or ammunition pursuant to federal law[1] The notice advises him or her to consult an attorney for further advice.[2]

Although federal law creates a firearms disability when an act of violence is committed against an intimate partner, it is unlikely that this statute actually applies to most juvenile respondents. An "intimate partner," for purposes of the firearms disability, includes spouses, former spouses, the parent of a child of the respondent, or an individual who cohabits or has cohabited with the respondent.[3] Because dating relationships, or stranger or friend relationships, are not contemplated by federal statute, the disability language contained in the state notice would not apply in most cases of juvenile violence.

§ 20:26 Forms used by court

Q & A: Must a juvenile court use the standard civil protection order forms?

Yes. In every case in which a court of common pleas that has juvenile jurisdiction issues an order pursuant to R.C. 2151.34 or 3113.31, it shall use the applicable juvenile protection order forms or forms that are substantially similar to those forms.[1]

§ 20:27 Appeal of order

Q & A: Is the granting of a juvenile civil protection order a final, appealable order?

Yes. According to R.C. 2151.34(G), any order issued under R.C. 2151.34, other than an ex parte order, that grants a protection order or that refuses to grant a protection order, is a final, appealable order.[1]

Q & A: What is the standard for reviewing juvenile civil protection orders?

As stated in *In re E.P.*,[2] "[t]he petitioner's burden of proof in obtaining a juvenile civil protection order and the standard for reviewing such orders come from analogous case law addressing adult civil protection orders."[3] As with adult domestic violence protection orders, there appear to be two standards of review that may be applied depending on the challenge to the protection order.

[Section 20:25]

[1]R.C. 2151.34(F)(2), citing 18 U.S.C.A. § 922(g)(8).

[2]R.C. 2151.34(F)(2).

[3]18 U.S.C.A. § 921(a)(32).

[Section 20:26]

[1]See Sup. R. 10.05(C); see also Sup. R. Forms 10.05-B to 10.05-F.

[Section 20:27]

[1]See also R.C. 3113.31(G); see J.L. v. M.D., 2011-Ohio-6208, 2011 WL 6016950 (Ohio Ct. App. 11th Dist. Lake County 2011) (ex parte civil protection order is not a final appealable order).

[2]In re E.P., 2011-Ohio-5829, 2011 WL 5507221 (Ohio Ct. App. 8th Dist. Cuyahoga County 2011).

[3]In re E.P., 2011-Ohio-5829, 2011 WL 5507221, *2 (Ohio Ct. App. 8th Dist. Cuyahoga County 2011); see also Text § 12:26.

Where the challenge involves the scope of the protection order, the reviewing court must review the order for an abuse of discretion.[4] However, when an appellant challenges whether the protection should have been issued at all, the standard of review is whether the trial court's decision was supported by sufficient competent, credible evidence, essentially a manifest weight of the evidence standard.[5]

§ 20:28 Recent cases

Appellate courts have begun to interpret the new juvenile protection order statute. Both procedurally and substantively, the courts have begun to understand the parameters of this new law and its similarity to the domestic violence and stalking protection order statutes.

Q & A: What actions rise to the level needed to obtain a juvenile civil protection order?

In *Insani v. Frederici*,[1] the respondent and petitioner, both under 18, dated each other and attended the same school. The parents of Lindsay, who were unhappy with the arrangement, filed a protection order against Alex alleging that when confronting Alex who climbed into Lindsay's window, Alex acted in a threatening manner and clenched his hands into fists. Lindsay's father testified that Alex's conduct made him feel threatened for his safety as well as the safety of his wife and child. In addition, Alex refused to leave a classroom when told to do so, and the school principal testified that Lindsay was afraid to come to school. A few days later, Alex's parents filed a juvenile protection order against Lindsay, claiming that she continued to contact Alex after she had filed her petition, thus making it more difficult for Alex to avoid her.

The appellate court noted that to obtain a juvenile protection order, a petitioner must allege a violation of one of the offenses set forth in RC 2151.34(C)(2)[2] and that menacing is one of the listed offenses and the one on which the parents' relied. Menacing is defined as "knowingly caus[ing] another to believe that the offender will cause physical harm to the person or property of the other person, the other person's unborn or a member of the other person's immediate family."[3]

In light of the incidents alleged, the appellate court found that "the trial court could have concluded, by a preponderance of the evidence,

---

[4]See § 12:26.

[5]See § 12:26; see also In re E.P., 2011-Ohio-5829, 2011 WL 5507221 (Ohio Ct. App. 8th Dist. Cuyahoga County 2011); Insani v. Federici, 2011-Ohio-6322, 2011 WL 6153649 (Ohio Ct. App. 2d Dist. Greene County 2011); J.L. v. M.D., 2011-Ohio-6208, 2011 WL 6016950 (Ohio Ct. App. 11th Dist. Lake County 2011); J.H. v. S.P., 2013-Ohio-3833, 2013 WL 4779047 (Ohio Ct. App. 10th Dist. Franklin County 2013).

[Section 20:28]

[1]Insani v. Federici, 2011-Ohio-6322, 2011 WL 6153649 (Ohio Ct. App. 2d Dist. Greene County 2011).

[2]J.L. v. M.D., 2011-Ohio-6208, 2011 WL 6016950 (Ohio Ct. App. 11th Dist. Lake County 2011) (discussing procedure for a JCPO (incorrectly naming it a "criminal protection order") and the evidence necessary to satisfy a menacing by stalking claim).

[3]Insani v. Federici, 2011-Ohio-6322, 2011 WL 6153649, *3 (Ohio Ct. App. 2d Dist. Greene County 2011).

that if a juvenile civil protection order were not granted, the Insanis were in danger of physical harm. The trial court's conclusion was not against the manifest weight of the evidence."[4]

Q & A: How is it determined whether a petitioner is in danger of future harm?

As with the recent cases that have interpreted the juvenile protection order statute, each has analogized the statute to existing domestic violence and adult civil stalking protection order statutes and cases.

For example, in *In re E.P.*[5] two sixth-grade boys got into a fight on the school bus. The mother of the 11-year-old filed for a protection order against the 12-year-old. The respondent had broken the petitioner's nose. The trial court granted the juvenile protection order and respondent appealed, alleging that the trial court applied an incorrect standard of proof when granting the protection order and that the protection order was against the manifest weight of the evidence.

The Cuyahoga County Court of Appeals examined the appropriate standard for a court to apply when determining whether to issue a civil protection order after a full hearing. The appellate court disputed respondent's claim that the correct standard of proof was "an immediate and present danger" stating that an immediate and present danger standard is to be applied to an ex parte juvenile civil protection order.[6] In light of existing case law, the correct standard to be applied when obtaining a juvenile civil protection order after a full hearing is whether the petitioner is in danger of future harm.[7] The court noted that the juvenile protection order statute is similar to the civil domestic violence statute, in that both are designed to protect a petitioner from *future* harm.

The court then pointed out that to determine whether a petitioner is in danger of future harm in the domestic violence context, courts routinely look to the past histories of the parties relative to violent acts.[8] The appellate court reasoned that since the children were not friends and did not "hang out," there was no evidence of a pattern of conduct and no further threats had been made since the bus incident,

---

[4]Insani v. Federici, 2011-Ohio-6322, 2011 WL 6153649, *4 (Ohio Ct. App. 2d Dist. Greene County 2011).

[5]In re E.P., 2011-Ohio-5829, 2011 WL 5507221 (Ohio Ct. App. 8th Dist. Cuyahoga County 2011).

[6]See J.L. v. M.D., 2011-Ohio-6208, 2011 WL 6016950 (Ohio Ct. App. 11th Dist. Lake County 2011) (immediate and present danger finding necessary to support issuance of ex parte order which was not subject to an appeal).

[7]In re E.P., 2011-Ohio-5829, 2011 WL 5507221, *4 (Ohio Ct. App. 8th Dist. Cuyahoga County 2011), citing Felton v. Felton, 79 Ohio St. 3d 34, 1997-Ohio-302, 679 N.E.2d 672 (1997). See also Wetterman v. B.C., 2013-Ohio-57, 2013 WL 141752 (Ohio Ct. App. 9th Dist. Medina County 2013) (finding that a civil protection order is designed to protect petitioner from future violence and that proof of past acts of violence is not enough to demonstrate future risk). But see J.L. v. M.D., 2011-Ohio-6208, 2011 WL 6016950 (Ohio Ct. App. 11th Dist. Lake County 2011) (overruling appellant's assignment of error and finding that appellee did not have to prove fear of danger for purposes of the full hearing order, only that the *mens rea* for and elements of an act of menacing by stalking be met).

[8]In re E.P., 2011-Ohio-5829, 2011 WL 5507221, *5 (Ohio Ct. App. 8th Dist. Cuyahoga County 2011).

there was no evidence that the petitioner was in danger of future harm from the respondent. "One incident resulting in a broken nose does not equate with a danger of future harm."[9] "This court does not believe that the legislature intended for every child who gets into a fight at school to be able to obtain a juvenile civil protection order. The potential ramifications of such a holding would be far reaching. This could not have been what the legislature intended when it passed H.B. 10."[10]

Thus, the assignments of error were sustained and the judgment granting the juvenile civil protection order was reversed and the protection order vacated.

In *Wetterman v. B.C.*,[11] Wetterman sought a JCPO for his minor son against the son's half-sibling. After the JCPO was denied, the father appealed.

In its decision, the majority focused on a danger of future harm in order to find that the evidence was insufficient to support the issuance of a juvenile civil protection order. The appellate court noted that the civil protection order is designed to provide the court with a tool in which to bring about an end to the violence and intended to prevent further violence.[12] Evidence of past abuse is relevant in determining whether there is a reasonable fear of further violence. However, even with past acts, there must be some competent evidence that there is a present fear of harm.[13] "Having reviewed RC 2151.34 and the purpose of civil protection orders, we conclude that the petitioner must establish that he or she (or the person the petitioner is seeking relief on behalf of) is in danger of further domestic violence before a protection order may be issued under RC 2151.34."[14]

In holding that the there was insufficient evidence for granting the protection order because there was no present risk of domestic violence, the court relied on the fact that Wetterman never testified that he feared B.C. would commit further offenses against J.W. or that J.W. was at risk of further abuse from B.C.

The dissent agreed with Wetterman's attorney that "the danger to the child was inherent in the act that was committed against him" and would have reversed the denial of the JCPO.[15] "While appellant has not explicitly set forth a current threat, I agree with him that the danger is inherent based on the child's youth. The majority stresses that no harm has come to J.W. by the hand of B.C. over the past

---

[9]In re E.P., 2011-Ohio-5829, 2011 WL 5507221, *7 (Ohio Ct. App. 8th Dist. Cuyahoga County 2011).

[10]In re E.P., 2011-Ohio-5829, 2011 WL 5507221, *7 (Ohio Ct. App. 8th Dist. Cuyahoga County 2011).

[11]Wetterman v. B.C., 2013-Ohio-57, 2013 WL 141752 (Ohio Ct. App. 9th Dist. Medina County 2013).

[12]Wetterman v. B.C., 2013-Ohio-57, 2013 WL 141752, ¶ 9-10 (Ohio Ct. App. 9th Dist. Medina County 2013)

[13]Wetterman v. B.C., 2013-Ohio-57, 2013 WL 141752, ¶ 12 (Ohio Ct. App. 9th Dist. Medina County 2013).

[14]Wetterman v. B.C., 2013-Ohio-57, 2013 WL 141752, ¶ 13 (Ohio Ct. App. 9th Dist. Medina County 2013).

[15]Wetterman v. B.C., 2013-Ohio-57, 2013 WL 141752, ¶ 16 (Ohio Ct. App. 9th Dist. Medina County 2013).

couple of years. However Father testified to the changes in J.W.'s affect after visits with Mother when B.C. was present. Further, the absence of any recent harm or danger may lie in the fact as stated by the majority that '[c]ontact between the children has been restricted and closely supervised * * * since [the sexual assault].' "[16]

Of significance is that the dissent found each of the cases cited in support of the majority decision to be inapposite to the case at hand. In each of the cited cases, the victim was an adult who was capable of assessing impending danger, seeking protection and reporting abuse to authorities. Conversely, J.W. was only four years old at the time of the hearing and lacked the ability to advocate for himself or to protect himself or process what he was experiencing.[17]

In *J.H. v. S.P.*[18] J.H.'s mother filed a petition for civil protection order on behalf of her minor daughter because of appellant's threatening telephone, text and twitter messages towards her. Among the grounds on appeal, appellant alleged that the trial court erred when it determined that appellant engaged in menacing by stalking as there was no evidence to establish the legal elements necessary to support a finding that appellant engaged in menacing by stalking.

Noting that R.C. 2151.34 is similar to the civil domestic violence statute, both statutes were designed to prevent future violence. In that the complained acts revolved around threats by telephone and social media and that the stalking statute provides that "No person, through the use of any electronic method of remotely transferring information, including but not limited to, any computer, computer network, computer program, or computer system, shall post a message with the purpose to urge or incite another to commit a violation of division (A)(1) of this section" and the definition of "pattern of conduct" is defined in a similar manner, the appellate court found that "[a]ppellant's repeated text messages and tweets threatening to beat appellee up can be characterized as nothing less than knowing attempts to cause appellee to believe appellant would cause her physical harm."[19] Of importance is that appellee did not have to provide evidence that appellant actually carried out her threats of physical violence. It was enough that appellant knowingly cause appellee to believe she would cause her physical harm or mental distress.

---

[16]Wetterman v. B.C., 2013-Ohio-57, 2013 WL 141752, ¶ 26 (Ohio Ct. App. 9th Dist. Medina County 2013).

[17]Wetterman v. B.C., 2013-Ohio-57, 2013 WL 141752, ¶ 24 (Ohio Ct. App. 9th Dist. Medina County 2013).

[18]J.H. v. S.P., 2013-Ohio-3833, 2013 WL 4779047 (Ohio Ct. App. 10th Dist. Franklin County 2013).

[19]J.H. v. S.P., 2013-Ohio-3833, 2013 WL 4779047, ¶ 19 (Ohio Ct. App. 10th Dist. Franklin County 2013).

APPENDICES

APPENDIX A

Ohio Revised Code (Selected Provisions)

The Supreme Court *of* Ohio

PROTECTION ORDERS OVERVIEW CARD

TYPE OF ORDER	FOR WHOM?	JURISDICTION, VENUE & STANDARD OF PROOF	LENGTH OF ORDER, OBJECTIONS & VIOLATION
DV Civil Protection Order (DV CPO) **DV Juvenile Civil Protection Order (DV JCPO)** **R.C. 3113.31**	• Domestic violence, menacing by stalking, aggravated trespass, child abuse or sexually oriented offense committed by an adult or juvenile who is a household member • Criminal charges not required • Custody and support issues may be addressed • Person may seek relief on the person's own behalf • Any parent or adult household member may seek relief on behalf of any other family or household member	• Common Pleas Court Juvenile division if respondent is under 18 years old • Common Pleas Court Domestic Relations division if respondent is 18 years or older • *Ex Parte* order may be solely signed by a magistrate per Civ.R. 65.1 • Hearing within 7 or 10 court days if *Ex Parte* order issued, depending if respondent is ordered to vacate or is evicted from residence • Normal civil action if no *Ex Parte* order is issued or requested • Venue: Where petitioner currently or temporarily resides • Standard of proof: Preponderance of the evidence	• In effect for a specified time up to 5 years and may be renewed • In effect for a specified time not to exceed the respondent's 19th birthday, if respondent is a minor at the time of issuance • Objections may be filed after issuance of final appealable order per Civ.R. 65.1 • Criminal violation under R.C. 2919.27 • Contempt of court under R.C. 3113.31 • Adjudicated a delinquent child under R.C. 2919.27
Juvenile Civil Protection Order (JCPO) **R.C. 2151.34**	• Felonious assault, aggravated assault, assault, aggravated menacing, menacing by stalking, menacing, aggravated trespass, and sexually oriented offense committed by a juvenile • Criminal charges not required • Any person on behalf of that person • Any parent or adult family or household member may seek relief on behalf of any other family or household member • Any person who the court deems as an appropriate person may seek relief on behalf of a child	• Common Pleas Court Juvenile Division if respondent is under 18 years old • *Ex Parte* order may be solely signed by a magistrate per Civ.R. 65.1 • Hearing within 10 court days if *Ex Parte* order issued • Normal civil action if no *Ex Parte* order is issued or requested • Venue: Where petitioner resides • Standard of proof: Preponderance of the evidence; clear and convincing for electronic monitoring requests	• In effect for a specified time not to exceed the respondent's 19th birthday • Objections may be filed after issuance of final appealable order per Civ.R. 65.1 • Criminal violation under R.C. 2919.27 • Contempt of court under R.C. 2151.34 • Adjudicated a delinquent child under R.C. 2919.27

PROTECTION ORDERS OVERVIEW CARD

TYPE OF ORDER	FOR WHOM?	JURISDICTION, VENUE & STANDARD OF PROOF	LENGTH OF ORDER & VIOLATION
Civil Stalking Protection Order **or** **Civil Sexually Oriented Offense Protection Order (CSPO or CSOOPO)** **R.C. 2903.214**	• Menacing by stalking or victims of a sexually oriented offense • Criminal charges not required • Person may seek relief on the person's own behalf • Any parent or adult household member may seek relief on behalf of any other family or household member	• Common Pleas Court if respondent is 18 years or older • *Ex Parte* order may be solely signed by a magistrate per Civ.R. 65.1 • Hearing within 10 court days if *Ex Parte* order is issued • Normal civil action if no *Ex Parte* order is issued or requested • Venue: Where petitioner resides	• In effect for a specified time up to 5 years and may be renewed • Objections may be filed after issuance of final appealable order per Civ.R. 65.1 • Criminal violation under R.C. 2919.27 • Contempt of court under R.C. 2903.214
DV Temporary Protection Order (DV TPO) **R.C. 2919.26**	• Criminal charges of domestic violence, stalking, criminal damaging or endangering, criminal mischief, burglary, aggravated trespass, sexually oriented offense or any offense of violence (R.C. 2901.01) against a family or household member • Either misdemeanor or felony charge	• Municipal or County Court (generally) or Common Pleas Court General division • Venue: Court that has jurisdiction over criminal case	• In effect for the duration of criminal case or until a DV CPO (R.C. 3113.31) is issued arising out of the same activities • Criminal violation under R.C. 2919.27
Criminal Protection Order (CrPO) **R.C. 2903.213**	• Criminal charges of felonious assault, aggravated assault, assault, aggravated menacing, menacing by stalking, aggravated trespass, menacing or sexually oriented offense against someone who is NOT a family or household member • Excludes DV and offenses of violence against family or household member • Either misdemeanor or felony charge	• Municipal or County Court (generally) or Common Pleas Court General division • Venue: Court that has jurisdiction over criminal case	• In effect for the duration of criminal case or until CSPO or CSOOPO (R.C. 2903.214) is issued arising out of the same activities • Criminal violation under R.C. 2919.27

Protection Order Forms: For technical assistance on protection order forms and related matters, contact the Domestic Violence Program at 614.387.9408. Forms may be found at: sc.ohio.gov/JCS/domesticViolence/default.asp

This project was supported by Subgrant No. 2009-RA-E01-2224 awarded by the Office of Justice Programs through the State of Ohio, Office of Criminal Justice Services. The opinions, findings, and conclusions or recommendations expressed in this publication are those of the authors and do not necessarily reflect the views of the Supreme Court of Ohio, Department of Justice, or the State of Ohio, Office of Criminal Justice Services.

Published 8/2014

Current through File 105 of the 132nd General Assembly (2017-2018).

BALDWIN'S OHIO REVISED CODE ANNOTATED

CHAPTER 2903 HOMICIDE AND ASSAULT

ASSAULT

ASSAULT

2903.11. Felonious assault

(A) No person shall knowingly do either of the following:

(1) Cause serious physical harm to another or to another's unborn;

(2) Cause or attempt to cause physical harm to another or to another's unborn by means of a deadly weapon or dangerous ordnance.

(B) No person, with knowledge that the person has tested positive as a carrier of a virus that causes acquired immunodeficiency syndrome, shall knowingly do any of the following:

(1) Engage in sexual conduct with another person without disclosing that knowledge to the other person prior to engaging in the sexual conduct;

(2) Engage in sexual conduct with a person whom the offender knows or has reasonable cause to believe lacks the mental capacity to appreciate the significance of the knowledge that the offender has tested positive as a carrier of a virus that causes acquired immunodeficiency syndrome;

(3) Engage in sexual conduct with a person under eighteen years of age who is not the spouse of the offender.

(C) The prosecution of a person under this section does not preclude prosecution of that person under section 2907.02 of the Revised Code.

(D) (1) (a) Whoever violates this section is guilty of felonious assault. Except as otherwise provided in this division or division (D)(1)(b) of this section, felonious assault is a felony of the second degree. If the victim of a violation of division (A) of this section is a peace officer or an investigator of the bureau of criminal identification and investigation, felonious assault is a felony of the first degree.

(b) Regardless of whether the felonious assault is a felony of the first or second degree under division (D)(1)(a) of this section, if the offender also is convicted of or pleads guilty to a specification as described in section 2941.1423 of the Revised Code that was included in the indictment, count in the indictment, or information charging the offense, except as otherwise provided in this division or unless a longer prison term is required under any other provision of law, the court shall sentence the offender to a mandatory prison term as provided in division (B)(8) of section 2929.14 of the Revised Code. If the victim of the offense is a peace officer or an investigator of the bureau of criminal identification and investigation, and if the victim suffered serious physical harm as a result of the commission of the offense, felonious assault is a felony of the first degree, and the court, pursuant to division (F) of section 2929.13 of the Revised Code, shall impose as a mandatory prison term one of the prison terms prescribed for a felony of the first degree.

(2) In addition to any other sanctions imposed pursuant to division (D)(1) of this section for felonious assault committed in violation of division (A)(1) or (2) of this section, if the offender also is convicted of or pleads guilty to a specification of the type described in section 2941.1425 of the Revised Code that was included in the indictment, count in the indictment, or information charging the offense, the court shall sentence the offender to a mandatory prison term under division (B)(9) of section 2929.14 of the Revised Code.

(3) In addition to any other sanctions imposed pursuant to division (D)(1) of this section for felonious assault committed in violation of division (A)(2) of this section, if the deadly weapon used in the commission of the violation is a motor vehicle, the court shall impose upon the offender a class two suspension of the offender's driver's license, commercial driver's license, temporary instruction permit, probationary license, or nonresident operating privilege as specified in division (A)(2) of section 4510.02 of the Revised Code.

(E) As used in this section:

(1) "Deadly weapon" and "dangerous ordnance" have the same meanings as in section 2923.11 of the Revised Code.

(2) "Motor vehicle" has the same meaning as in section 4501.01 of the Revised Code.

(3) "Peace officer" has the same meaning as in section 2935.01 of the Revised Code.

(4) "Sexual conduct" has the same meaning as in section 2907.01 of the Revised Code, except that, as used in this section, it does not include the insertion of an instrument, apparatus, or other object that is not a part of the body into the vaginal or anal opening of another, unless the offender knew at the time of the insertion that the instrument, apparatus, or other object carried the offender's bodily fluid.

(5) "Investigator of the bureau of criminal identification and investigation" means an investigator of the bureau of criminal identification and investigation who is commissioned by the superintendent of the bureau as a special agent for the purpose of assisting law enforcement officers or providing emergency assistance to peace officers pursuant to authority granted under section 109.541 of the Revised Code.

(6) "Investigator" has the same meaning as in section 109.541 of the Revised Code.

(F) The provisions of division (D)(2) of this section and of division (F)(20) of section 2929.13, divisions (B)(9) and (C)(6) of section 2929.14, and section 2941.1425 of the Revised Code shall be known as "Judy's Law."

(2017 H 63, eff. 10-17-17; 2011 H 86, eff. 9-30-11; 2008 H 280, eff. 4-7-09; 2006 H 461, eff. 4-4-07; 2006 H 347, eff. 3-14-07; 2006 H 95, eff. 8-3-06; 1999 H 100, eff. 3-23-00; 1999 S 142, eff. 2-3-00; 1996 S 239, eff. 9-6-96; 1995 S 2, eff. 7-1-96; 1983 S 210, eff. 7-1-83; 1982 H 269, S 199; 1972 H 511)

2903.12. Aggravated assault

(A) No person, while under the influence of sudden passion or in a sudden fit of rage, either of which is brought on by serious provocation occasioned by the victim that is reasonably sufficient to incite the person into using deadly force, shall knowingly:

(1) Cause serious physical harm to another or to another's unborn;

(2) Cause or attempt to cause physical harm to another or to another's unborn by means of a deadly weapon or dangerous ordnance, as defined in section 2923.11 of the Revised Code.

(B) Whoever violates this section is guilty of aggravated assault. Except as otherwise provided in this division, aggravated assault is a felony of the fourth degree. If the victim of the offense is a peace officer or an investigator of the bureau of criminal identification and investigation, aggravated assault is a felony of the third degree. Regardless of whether the offense is a felony of the third or fourth degree under this division, if the offender also is convicted of or pleads guilty to a specification as described in section 2941.1423 of the Revised Code that was included in the indictment, count in the indictment, or information charging the offense, except as otherwise provided in this division, the court shall sentence the offender to a mandatory prison term as provided in division (B)(8) of section 2929.14 of the Revised Code. If the victim of the offense is a peace officer or an investigator of the bureau of criminal identification and investigation, and if the victim suffered serious physical harm as a result of the commission of the offense, aggravated assault is a felony of the third degree, and the court, pursuant to division (F) of section 2929.13 of the Revised Code, shall impose as a mandatory prison term one of the prison terms prescribed for a felony of the third degree.

(C) As used in this section:

(1) "Investigator of the bureau of criminal identification and investigation" has the same meaning as in section 2903.11 of the Revised Code.

(2) "Peace officer" has the same meaning as in section 2935.01 of the Revised Code.

(2011 H 86, eff. 9-30-11; 2008 H 280, eff. 4-7-09; 2006 H 347, eff. 3-14-07; 1999 S 142, eff. 2-3-00; 1996 S 239, eff. 9-6-96; 1984 H 37, eff. 6-22-84; 1983 S 210; 1982 H 269, S 199, H 103; 1972 H 511)

2903.13. Assault

(A) No person shall knowingly cause or attempt to cause physical harm to another or to another's unborn.

(B) No person shall recklessly cause serious physical harm to another or to another's unborn.

(C) (1) Whoever violates this section is guilty of assault, and the court shall sentence the offender as provided in this division and divisions (C)(1), (2), (3), (4), (5), (6), (7), (8), (9), and (10) of this section. Except as otherwise provided in division (C)(2), (3), (4), (5), (6), (7), (8), or (9) of this section, assault is a misdemeanor of the first degree.

(2) Except as otherwise provided in this division, if the offense is committed by a caretaker against a functionally impaired person under the caretaker's care, assault is a felony of the fourth degree. If the offense is committed by a caretaker against a functionally impaired person under the caretaker's care, if the offender previously has been convicted of or pleaded guilty to a violation of this section or section 2903.11 or 2903.16 of the Revised Code, and if in relation to the previous conviction the offender was a caretaker and the victim was a functionally impaired person under the offender's care, assault is a felony of the third degree.

(3) If the offense occurs in or on the grounds of a state correctional institution or an institution of the department of youth services, the victim of the offense is an employee of the department of rehabilitation and correction or the department of youth services, and the offense is committed by a person incarcerated in the state correctional institution or by a person institutionalized in the department of youth services institution pursuant to a commitment to the department of youth services, assault is a felony of the third degree.

(4) If the offense is committed in any of the following circumstances, assault is a felony of the fifth degree:

(a) The offense occurs in or on the grounds of a local correctional facility, the victim of the offense is an employee of the local correctional facility or a probation department or is on the premises of the facility for business purposes or as a visitor, and the offense is committed by a person who is under custody in the facility subsequent to the person's arrest for any crime or delinquent act, subsequent to the person's being charged with or convicted of any crime, or subsequent to the person's being alleged to be or adjudicated a delinquent child.

(b) The offense occurs off the grounds of a state correctional institution and off the grounds of an institution of the department of youth services, the victim of the offense is an employee of the department of rehabilitation and correction, the department of youth services, or a probation department, the offense occurs during the employee's official work hours and while the employee is engaged in official work responsibilities, and the offense is committed by a person incarcerated in a state correctional institution or institutionalized in the department of youth services who temporarily is outside of the institution for any purpose, by a parolee, by an offender under transitional control, under a community control sanction, or on an escorted visit, by a person under post-release control, or by an offender under any other type of supervision by a government agency.

(c) The offense occurs off the grounds of a local correctional facility, the victim of the offense is an employee of the local correctional facility or a probation department, the offense occurs during the employee's official work hours and while the employee is engaged in official work responsibilities, and the offense is committed by a person who is under custody in the facility subsequent to the person's arrest for any crime or delinquent act, subsequent to the person being charged with or convicted of any crime, or subsequent to the person being alleged to be or adjudicated a delinquent child and who temporarily is outside of the facility for any purpose or by a parolee, by an offender under transitional control, under a community control sanction, or on an escorted visit, by a person under post-release control, or by an offender under any other type of supervision by a government agency.

(d) The victim of the offense is a school teacher or administrator or a school bus operator, and the offense occurs in a school, on school premises, in a school building, on a school bus, or while the victim is outside of school premises or a school bus and is engaged in duties or official responsibilities associated with the victim's employment or position as a school teacher or administrator or a school bus operator, including, but not limited to, driving, accompanying, or chaperoning students at or on class or field trips, athletic events, or other school extracurricular activities or functions outside of school premises.

(5) If the victim of the offense is a peace officer or an investigator of the bureau of criminal identification and investigation, a firefighter, or a person performing emergency medical service, while in the performance of their official duties, assault is a felony of the fourth degree.

(6) If the victim of the offense is a peace officer or an investigator of the bureau of criminal identification and investigation and if the victim suffered serious physical harm as a result of the commission of the offense, assault is a felony of the fourth degree, and the court, pursuant to division (F) of section 2929.13 of the Revised Code, shall impose as a mandatory prison term one of the prison terms prescribed for a felony of the fourth degree that is at least twelve months in duration.

(7) If the victim of the offense is an officer or employee of a public children services agency or a private child placing agency and the offense relates to the officer's or employee's performance or anticipated performance of official responsibilities or duties, assault is either a felony of the fifth degree or, if the offender previously has been convicted of or pleaded guilty to an offense of violence, the victim of that prior offense was an officer or employee of a public children services agency or private child placing agency, and that prior offense related to the officer's or employee's performance or anticipated performance of official responsibilities or duties, a felony of the fourth degree.

(8) If the victim of the offense is a health care professional of a hospital, a health care worker of a hospital, or a security officer of a hospital whom the offender knows or has reasonable cause to know is a health care professional of a hospital, a health care worker of a hospital, or a security officer of a hospital, if the victim is engaged in the performance of the victim's duties, and if the hospital offers de-escalation or crisis intervention training for such professionals, workers, or officers, assault is one of the following:

(a) Except as otherwise provided in division (C)(8)(b) of this section, assault committed in the specified circumstances is a misdemeanor of the first degree. Notwithstanding the fine specified in division (A)(2)(b) of section 2929.28 of the Revised Code for a misdemeanor of the first degree, in sentencing the offender under this division and if the court decides to impose a fine, the court may impose upon the offender a fine of not more than five thousand dollars.

(b) If the offender previously has been convicted of or pleaded guilty to one or more assault or homicide offenses committed against hospital personnel, assault committed in the specified circumstances is a felony of the fifth degree.

(9) If the victim of the offense is a judge, magistrate, prosecutor, or court official or employee whom the offender knows or has reasonable cause to know is a judge, magistrate, prosecutor, or court official or employee, and if the victim is engaged in the performance of the victim's duties, assault is one of the following:

(a) Except as otherwise provided in division (C)(8)(b) of this section, assault committed in the specified circumstances is a misdemeanor of the first degree. In sentencing the offender under this division, if the court decides to impose a fine, notwithstanding the fine specified in division (A)(2)(b) of section 2929.28 of the Revised Code for a misdemeanor of the first degree, the court may impose upon the offender a fine of not more than five thousand dollars.

(b) If the offender previously has been convicted of or pleaded guilty to one or more assault or homicide offenses committed against justice system personnel, assault committed in the specified circumstances is a felony of the fifth degree.

(10) If an offender who is convicted of or pleads guilty to assault when it is a misdemeanor also is convicted of or pleads guilty to a specification as described in section 2941.1423 of the Revised Code that was included in the indictment, count in the indictment, or information charging the offense, the court shall sentence the offender to a mandatory jail term as provided in division (G) of section 2929.24 of the Revised Code.

If an offender who is convicted of or pleads guilty to assault when it is a felony also is convicted of or pleads guilty to a specification as described in section 2941.1423 of the Revised Code that was included in the indictment, count in the indictment, or information charging the offense, except as otherwise provided in division (C)(6) of this section, the court shall sentence the offender to a mandatory prison term as provided in division (B)(8) of section 2929.14 of the Revised Code.

(D) As used in this section:

(1) "Peace officer" has the same meaning as in section 2935.01 of the Revised Code.

(2) "Firefighter" has the same meaning as in section 3937.41 of the Revised Code.

(3) "Emergency medical service" has the same meaning as in section 4765.01 of the Revised Code.

(4) "Local correctional facility" means a county, multicounty, municipal, municipal-county, or multicounty-municipal jail or workhouse, a minimum security jail established under section 341.23 or 753.21 of the Revised Code, or another county, multicounty, municipal, municipal-county, or multicounty-municipal facility used for the custody of persons arrested for any crime or delinquent act, persons charged with or convicted of any crime, or persons alleged to be or adjudicated a delinquent child.

(5) "Employee of a local correctional facility" means a person who is an employee of the political subdivision or of one or more of the affiliated political subdivisions that operates the local correctional facility and who operates or assists in the operation of the facility.

(6) "School teacher or administrator" means either of the following:

(a) A person who is employed in the public schools of the state under a contract described in section 3311.77 or 3319.08 of the Revised Code in a position in which the person is required to have a certificate issued pursuant to sections 3319.22 to 3319.311 of the Revised Code.

(b) A person who is employed by a nonpublic school for which the state board of education prescribes minimum standards under section 3301.07 of the Revised Code and who is certificated in accordance with section 3301.071 of the Revised Code.

(7) "Community control sanction" has the same meaning as in section 2929.01 of the Revised Code.

(8) "Escorted visit" means an escorted visit granted under section 2967.27 of the Revised Code.

(9) "Post-release control" and "transitional control" have the same meanings as in section 2967.01 of the Revised Code.

(10) "Investigator of the bureau of criminal identification and investigation" has the same meaning as in section 2903.11 of the Revised Code.

(11) "Health care professional" and "health care worker" have the same meanings as in section 2305.234 of the Revised Code.

(12) "Assault or homicide offense committed against hospital personnel" means a violation of this section or of section 2903.01, 2903.02, 2903.03, 2903.04, 2903.041, 2903.11, 2903.12, or 2903.14 of the Revised Code committed in circumstances in which all of the following apply:

(a) The victim of the offense was a health care professional of a hospital, a health care worker of a hospital, or a security officer of a hospital.

(b) The offender knew or had reasonable cause to know that the victim was a health care professional of a hospital, a health care worker of a hospital, or a security officer of a hospital.

(c) The victim was engaged in the performance of the victim's duties.

(d) The hospital offered de-escalation or crisis intervention training for such professionals, workers, or officers.

(13) "De-escalation or crisis intervention training" means de-escalation or crisis intervention training for health care professionals of a hospital, health care workers of a hospital, and security officers of a hospital to facilitate interaction with patients, members of a patient's family, and visitors, including those with mental impairments.

(14) "Assault or homicide offense committed against justice system personnel" means a violation of this section or of section 2903.01, 2903.02, 2903.03, 2903.04, 2903.041, 2903.11, 2903.12, or 2903.14 of the Revised Code committed in circumstances in which the victim of the offense was a judge, magistrate, prosecutor, or court official or employee whom the offender knew or had reasonable cause to know was a judge, magistrate, prosecutor, or court official or employee, and the victim was engaged in the performance of the victim's duties.

(15) "Court official or employee" means any official or employee of a court created under the constitution or statutes of this state or of a United States court located in this state.

(16) "Judge" means a judge of a court created under the constitution or statutes of this state or of a United States court located in this state.

(17) "Magistrate" means an individual who is appointed by a court of record of this state and who has the powers and may perform the functions specified in Civil Rule 53, Criminal Rule 19, or Juvenile Rule 40, or an individual who is appointed by a United States court located in this state who has similar powers and functions.

(18) "Prosecutor" has the same meaning as in section 2935.01 of the Revised Code.

(19) (a) "Hospital" means, subject to division (D)(19)(b) of this section, an institution classified as a hospital under section 3701.01 of the Revised Code in which are provided to patients diagnostic, medical, surgical, obstetrical, psychiatric, or rehabilitation care or a hospital operated by a health maintenance organization.

(b) "Hospital" does not include any of the following:

(i) A facility licensed under Chapter 3721. of the Revised Code, a health care facility operated by the department of mental health or the department of developmental disabilities, a health maintenance organization that does not operate a hospital, or the office of any private, licensed health care professional, whether organized for individual or group practice;

(ii) An institution for the sick that is operated exclusively for patients who use spiritual means for healing and for whom the acceptance of medical care is inconsistent with their religious beliefs, accredited by a national accrediting organization, exempt from federal income taxation under section 501 of the "Internal Revenue Code of 1986," 100 Stat. 2085, 26 U.S.C. 1, as amended, and providing twenty-four-hour nursing care pursuant to the exemption in division (E) of section 4723.32 of the Revised Code from the licensing requirements of Chapter 4723. of the Revised Code.

(20) "Health maintenance organization" has the same meaning as in section 3727.01 of the Revised Code.

(2013 H 59, eff. 9-29-13; 2012 H 62, eff. 3-22-13; 2012 H 525, eff. 10-1-12; 2011 H 86, eff. 9-30-11; 2008 H 280, eff. 4-7-09; 2006 H 347, eff. 3-14-07; 2002 H 490, eff. 1-1-04; 2000 H 412, eff. 4-10-01; 1999 S 142, eff. 2-3-00; 1999 S 1, eff. 8-6-99; 1997 S 111, eff. 3-17-98; 1997 H 106, eff. 11-21-97; 1996 H 480, eff. 10-16-96; 1996 S 239, eff. 9-6-96; 1995 S 2, eff. 7-1-96; 1994 H 571, eff. 10-6-94; 1994 S 116, eff. 9-29-94; 1992 H 561, eff. 4-9-93; 1988 H 642; 1972 H 511)

2903.14. Negligent assault

(A) No person shall negligently, by means of a deadly weapon or dangerous ordnance as defined in section 2923.11 of the Revised Code, cause physical harm to another or to another's unborn.

(B) Whoever violates this section is guilty of negligent assault, a misdemeanor of the third degree.

(1996 S 239, eff. 9-6-96; 1972 H 511, eff. 1-1-74)

MENACING; STALKING

2903.21. Aggravated menacing

(A) No person shall knowingly cause another to believe that the offender will cause serious physical harm to the person or property of the other person, the other person's unborn, or a member of the other person's immediate family. In addition to any other basis for the other person's belief that the offender will cause serious physical harm to the person or property of the other person, the other person's unborn, or a member of the other person's immediate family, the other person's belief may be based on words or conduct of the offender that are directed at or identify a corporation, association, or other organization that employs the other person or to which the other person belongs.

(B) Whoever violates this section is guilty of aggravated menacing. Except as otherwise provided in this division, aggravated menacing is a misdemeanor of the first degree. If the victim of the offense is an officer or employee of a public children services agency or a private child placing agency and the offense relates to the officer's or employee's performance or anticipated performance of official responsibilities or duties, aggravated menacing is a felony of the fifth degree or, if the offender previously has been convicted of or pleaded guilty to an offense of violence, the victim of that prior offense was an officer or employee of a public children services agency or private child placing agency, and that prior offense related to the officer's or employee's performance or anticipated performance of official responsibilities or duties, a felony of the fourth degree.

(C) As used in this section, "organization" includes an entity that is a governmental employer.

(2014 H 129, eff. 9-17-14; 2000 H 412, eff. 4-10-01; 1996 S 239, eff. 9-6-96; 1972 H 511, eff. 1-1-74)

2903.211. Menacing by stalking

(A) (1) No person by engaging in a pattern of conduct shall knowingly cause another to believe that the offender will cause physical harm to the other person or a family or household member of the other person or cause mental distress to the other person or a family or household member of the other person. In addition to any other basis for the other person's belief that the offender will cause physical harm to the other person or the other person's family or household member or mental distress to the other person or the other person's family or household member, the other person's belief or mental distress may be based on words or conduct of the offender that are directed at or identify a corporation, association, or other organization that employs the other person or to which the other person belongs.

(2) No person, through the use of any form of written communication or any electronic method of remotely transferring information, including, but not limited to, any computer, computer network, computer program, computer system, or telecommunication device shall post a message or use any intentionally written or verbal graphic gesture with purpose to do either of the following:

(a) Violate division (A)(1) of this section;

(b) Urge or incite another to commit a violation of division (A)(1) of this section.

(3) No person, with a sexual motivation, shall violate division (A)(1) or (2) of this section.

(B) Whoever violates this section is guilty of menacing by stalking.

(1) Except as otherwise provided in divisions (B)(2) and (3) of this section, menacing by stalking is a misdemeanor of the first degree.

(2) Menacing by stalking is a felony of the fourth degree if any of the following applies:

(a) The offender previously has been convicted of or pleaded guilty to a violation of this section or a violation of section 2911.211 of the Revised Code.

(b) In committing the offense under division (A)(1), (2), or (3) of this section, the offender made a threat of physical harm to or against the victim, or as a result of an offense committed under division (A)(2) or (3) of this section, a third person induced by the offender's posted message made a threat of physical harm to or against the victim.

(c) In committing the offense under division (A)(1), (2), or (3) of this section, the offender trespassed on the land or premises where the victim lives, is employed, or attends school, or as a result of an offense committed under division (A)(2) or (3) of this section, a third person induced by the offender's posted message trespassed on the land or premises where the victim lives, is employed, or attends school.

(d) The victim of the offense is a minor.

(e) The offender has a history of violence toward the victim or any other person or a history of other violent acts toward the victim or any other person.

(f) While committing the offense under division (A)(1) of this section or a violation of division (A)(3) of this section based on conduct in violation of division (A)(1) of this section, the offender had a deadly weapon on or about the offender's person or under the offender's control. Division (B)(2)(f) of this section does not apply in determining the penalty for a violation of division (A)(2) of this section or a violation of division (A)(3) of this section based on conduct in violation of division (A)(2) of this section.

(g) At the time of the commission of the offense, the offender was the subject of a protection order issued under section 2903.213 or 2903.214 of the Revised Code, regardless of whether the person to be protected under the order is the victim of the offense or another person.

(h) In committing the offense under division (A)(1), (2), or (3) of this section, the offender caused serious physical harm to the premises at which the victim resides, to the real property on which that premises is located, or to any personal property located on that premises, or, as a result of an offense committed under division (A)(2) of this section or an offense committed under division (A)(3) of this section based on a violation of division (A)(2) of this section, a third person induced by the offender's posted message caused serious physical harm to that premises, that real property, or any personal property on that premises.

(i) Prior to committing the offense, the offender had been determined to represent a substantial risk of physical harm to others as manifested by evidence of then-recent homicidal or other violent behavior, evidence of then-recent threats that placed another in reasonable fear of violent behavior and serious physical harm, or other evidence of then-present dangerousness.

(3) If the victim of the offense is an officer or employee of a public children services agency or a private child placing agency and the offense relates to the officer's or employee's performance or anticipated performance of official responsibilities or duties, menacing by stalking is either a felony of the fifth degree or, if the offender previously has been convicted of or pleaded guilty to an offense of violence, the victim of that prior offense was an officer or employee of a public children services agency or private child placing agency, and that prior offense related to the officer's or employee's performance or anticipated performance of official responsibilities or duties, a felony of the fourth degree.

(C) Section 2919.271 of the Revised Code applies in relation to a defendant charged with a violation of this section.

(D) As used in this section:

(1) "Pattern of conduct" means two or more actions or incidents closely related in time, whether or not there has been a prior conviction based on any of those actions or incidents, or two or more actions or incidents closely related in time, whether or not there has been a prior conviction based on any of those actions or incidents, directed at one or more persons employed by or belonging to the same corporation, association, or other organization. Actions or incidents that prevent,

obstruct, or delay the performance by a public official, firefighter, rescuer, emergency medical services person, or emergency facility person of any authorized act within the public official's, firefighter's, rescuer's, emergency medical services person's, or emergency facility person's official capacity, or the posting of messages, use of intentionally written or verbal graphic gestures, or receipt of information or data through the use of any form of written communication or an electronic method of remotely transferring information, including, but not limited to, a computer, computer network, computer program, computer system, or telecommunications device, may constitute a "pattern of conduct."

(2) "Mental distress" means any of the following:

(a) Any mental illness or condition that involves some temporary substantial incapacity;

(b) Any mental illness or condition that would normally require psychiatric treatment, psychological treatment, or other mental health services, whether or not any person requested or received psychiatric treatment, psychological treatment, or other mental health services.

(3) "Emergency medical services person" is the singular of "emergency medical services personnel" as defined in section 2133.21 of the Revised Code.

(4) "Emergency facility person" is the singular of "emergency facility personnel" as defined in section 2909.04 of the Revised Code.

(5) "Public official" has the same meaning as in section 2921.01 of the Revised Code.

(6) "Computer," "computer network," "computer program," "computer system," and "telecommunications device" have the same meanings as in section 2913.01 of the Revised Code.

(7) "Post a message" means transferring, sending, posting, publishing, disseminating, or otherwise communicating, or attempting to transfer, send, post, publish, disseminate, or otherwise communicate, any message or information, whether truthful or untruthful, about an individual, and whether done under one's own name, under the name of another, or while impersonating another.

(8) "Third person" means, in relation to conduct as described in division (A)(2) of this section, an individual who is neither the offender nor the victim of the conduct.

(9) "Sexual motivation" has the same meaning as in section 2971.01 of the Revised Code.

(10) "Organization" includes an entity that is a governmental employer.

(11) "Family or household member" means any of the following:

(a) Any of the following who is residing or has resided with the person against whom the act prohibited in division (A)(1) of this section is committed:

(i) A spouse, a person living as a spouse, or a former spouse of the person;

(ii) A parent, a foster parent, or a child of the person, or another person related by consanguinity or affinity to the person;

(iii) A parent or a child of a spouse, person living as a spouse, or former spouse of the person, or another person related by consanguinity or affinity to a spouse, person living as a spouse, or former spouse of the person.

(b) The natural parent of any child of whom the person against whom the act prohibited in division (A)(1) of this section is committed is the other natural parent or is the putative other natural parent.

(12) "Person living as a spouse" means a person who is living or has lived with the person against whom the act prohibited in division (A)(1) of this section is committed in a common law marital relationship, who otherwise is cohabiting with that person, or who otherwise has cohabited with the person within five years prior to the date of the alleged commission of the act in question.

(E) The state does not need to prove in a prosecution under this section that a person requested or received psychiatric treatment, psychological treatment, or other mental health services in order to show that the person was caused mental distress as described in division (D)(2)(b) of this section.

(F) (1) This section does not apply to a person solely because the person provided access or connection to or from an electronic method of remotely transferring information not under that person's control, including having provided capabilities that are incidental to providing access or connection to or from the electronic method of remotely transferring the information, and that do not include the creation of the content of the material that is the subject of the access or connection. In addition, any person providing access or connection to or from an electronic method of remotely transferring information not under that person's control shall not be liable for any action voluntarily taken in good faith to block the receipt or transmission through its service of any information that it believes is, or will be sent, in violation of this section.

(2) Division (F)(1) of this section does not create an affirmative duty for any person providing access or connection to or from an electronic method of remotely transferring information not under that person's control to block the receipt or transmission through its service of any information that it believes is, or will be sent, in violation of this section except as otherwise provided by law.

(3) Division (F)(1) of this section does not apply to a person who conspires with a person actively involved in the creation or knowing distribution of material in violation of this section or who knowingly advertises the availability of material of that nature.

(2016 H 151, eff. 8-16-16; 2014 H 129, eff. 9-17-14; 2007 S 10, eff. 1-1-08; 2003 S 8, eff. 8-29-03; 2001 S 40, eff. 1-25-02; 2000 H 412, eff. 4-10-01; 1999 H 202, § 3, eff. 3-10-00; 1999 H 137, eff. 3-10-00; 1998 S 215, eff. 3-30-99; 1995 S 2, eff. 7-1-96; 1992 H 536, eff. 11-5-92)

2903.212. Bail

(A) Except when the complaint involves a person who is a family or household member as defined in section 2919.25 of the Revised Code, if a person is charged with a violation of section 2903.21, 2903.211, 2903.22, or 2911.211 of the Revised Code, a violation of a municipal ordinance that is substantially similar to one of those sections, or a sexually oriented offense and if the person, at the time of the alleged violation, was subject to the terms of any order issued pursuant to section 2903.213, 2933.08, or 2945.04 of the Revised Code or previously had been convicted of or pleaded guilty to a violation of section 2903.21, 2903.211, 2903.22, or 2911.211 of the Revised Code that involves the same complainant, a violation of a municipal ordinance that is substantially similar to one of those sections and that involves the same complainant, or a sexually oriented offense that involves the same complainant, the court shall consider all of the following, in addition to any other circumstances considered by the court and notwithstanding any provisions to the contrary contained in Criminal Rule 46, before setting the amount and conditions of the bail for the person:

(1) Whether the person has a history of violence toward the complainant or a history of other violent acts;

(2) The mental health of the person;

(3) Whether the person has a history of violating the orders of any court or governmental entity;

(4) Whether the person is potentially a threat to any other person;

(5) Whether setting bail at a high level will interfere with any treatment or counseling that the person is undergoing.

(B) Any court that has jurisdiction over violations of section 2903.21, 2903.211, 2903.22, or 2911.211 of the Revised Code, violations of a municipal ordinance that is substantially similar to one of those sections, or sexually oriented offenses may set a schedule for bail to be used in cases involving those violations. The schedule shall require that a judge consider all of the factors listed in division (A) of this section and may require judges to set bail at a certain level or impose other reasonable conditions related to a release on bail or on recognizance if the history of the alleged offender or the circumstances of the alleged offense meet certain criteria in the schedule.

(C) As used in this section, "sexually oriented offense" has the same meaning as in section 2950.01 of the Revised Code.

(2006 S 260, eff. 1-2-07; 1992 H 536, eff. 11-5-92)

2903.213. Protection order as pretrial condition of release

(A) Except when the complaint involves a person who is a family or household member as defined in section 2919.25 of the Revised Code, upon the filing of a complaint that alleges a violation of section 2903.11, 2903.12, 2903.13, 2903.21, 2903.211, 2903.22, or 2911.211 of the Revised Code, a violation of a municipal ordinance substantially similar to section 2903.13, 2903.21, 2903.211, 2903.22, or 2911.211 of the Revised Code, or the commission of a sexually oriented offense, the complainant, the alleged victim, or a family or household member of an alleged victim may file a motion that requests the issuance of a protection order as a pretrial condition of release of the alleged offender, in addition to any bail set under Criminal Rule 46. The motion shall be filed with the clerk of the court that has jurisdiction of the case at any time after the filing of the complaint. If the complaint involves a person who is a family or household member, the complainant, the alleged victim, or the family or household member may file a motion for a temporary protection order pursuant to section 2919.26 of the Revised Code.

(B) A motion for a protection order under this section shall be prepared on a form that is provided by the clerk of the court, and the form shall be substantially as follows:

"Motion for Protection Order

....

Name and address of court

State of Ohio

v. No. ....

....

Name of Defendant

(Name of person), moves the court to issue a protection order containing terms designed to ensure the safety and protection of the complainant or the alleged victim in the above-captioned case, in relation to the named defendant, pursuant to its authority to issue a protection order under section 2903.213 of the Revised Code.

A complaint, a copy of which has been attached to this motion, has been filed in this court charging the named defendant with a violation of section 2903.11, 2903.12, 2903.13, 2903.21, 2903.211, 2903.22, or 2911.211 of the Revised Code, a violation of a municipal ordinance substantially similar to section 2903.13, 2903.21, 2903.211, 2903.22, or 2911.211 of the Revised Code, or the commission of a sexually oriented offense.

I understand that I must appear before the court, at a time set by the court not later than the next day that the court is in session after the filing of this motion, for a hearing on the motion, and that any protection order granted pursuant to this motion is a pretrial condition of release and is effective only until the disposition of the criminal proceeding arising out of the attached complaint or until the issuance under section 2903.214 of the Revised Code of a protection order arising out of the same activities as those that were the basis of the attached complaint.

....

Signature of person

....

Address of person"

(C) (1) As soon as possible after the filing of a motion that requests the issuance of a protection order under this section, but not later than the next day that the court is in session after the filing of the motion, the court shall conduct a hearing to determine whether to issue the order. The person who requested the order shall appear before the court and provide the court with the information that it requests concerning the basis of the motion. If the court finds that the safety and protection of the complainant or the alleged victim may be impaired by the continued presence of the alleged offender, the court may issue a protection order under this section, as a pretrial condition of release, that contains terms designed to ensure the safety and protection of the complainant or the alleged victim, including a requirement that the alleged offender refrain from entering the residence, school, business, or place of employment of the complainant or the alleged victim. The court may include within a protection order issued under this section a term requiring that the alleged offender not remove, damage, hide, harm, or dispose of any companion animal owned or possessed by the complainant or the alleged victim, and may include within the order a term authorizing the complainant or the alleged victim to remove a companion animal owned by the complainant or the alleged victim from the possession of the alleged offender.

(2) (a) If the court issues a protection order under this section that includes a requirement that the alleged offender refrain from entering the residence, school, business, or place of employment of the complainant or the alleged victim, the order shall clearly state that the order cannot be waived or nullified by an invitation to the alleged offender from the complainant, the alleged victim, or a family or household member to enter the residence, school, business, or place of employment or by the alleged offender's entry into one of those places otherwise upon the consent of the complainant, the alleged victim, or a family or household member.

(b) Division (C)(2)(a) of this section does not limit any discretion of a court to determine that an alleged offender charged with a violation of section 2919.27 of the Revised Code, with a violation of a municipal ordinance substantially equivalent to that section, or with contempt of court, which charge is based on an alleged violation of a protection order issued under this section, did not commit the violation or was not in contempt of court.

(D) (1) Except when the complaint involves a person who is a family or household member as defined in section 2919.25 of the Revised Code, upon the filing of a complaint that alleges a violation specified in division (A) of this section, the court, upon its own motion, may issue a protection order under this section as a pretrial condition of release of the alleged offender if it finds that the safety and protection of the complainant or the alleged victim may be impaired by the continued presence of the alleged offender.

(2) (a) If the court issues a protection order under this section as an ex parte order, it shall conduct, as soon as possible after the issuance of the order but not later than the next day that the court is in session after its issuance, a hearing to determine whether the order should remain in effect, be modified, or be revoked. The hearing shall be conducted under the standards set forth in division (C) of this section.

(b) If at a hearing conducted under division (D)(2)(a) of this section the court determines that the ex parte order that the court issued should be revoked, the court, on its own motion, shall order that the ex parte order that is revoked and all of the records pertaining to that ex parte order be expunged.

(3) If a municipal court or a county court issues a protection order under this section and if, subsequent to the issuance of the order, the alleged offender who is the subject of the order is bound over to the court of common pleas for prosecution of a felony arising out of the same activities as those that were the basis of the complaint upon which the order is based, notwithstanding the fact that the order was issued by a municipal court or county court, the order shall remain in effect, as though it were an order of the court of common pleas, while the charges against the alleged offender are pending in the court of common pleas, for the period of time described in division (E)(2) of this section, and the court of common pleas has exclusive jurisdiction to modify the order issued by the municipal court or county court. This division applies when the alleged offender is bound over to the court of common pleas as a result of the person waiving a preliminary hearing on the felony charge, as a result of the municipal court or county court having determined at a preliminary hearing that there is probable cause to believe that the felony has been committed and that the alleged offender committed it, as a result of the alleged offender having been indicted for the felony, or in any other manner.

(E) A protection order that is issued as a pretrial condition of release under this section:

(1) Is in addition to, but shall not be construed as a part of, any bail set under Criminal Rule 46;

(2) Is effective only until the disposition, by the court that issued the order or, in the circumstances described in division (D)(3) of this section, by the court of common pleas to which the alleged offender is bound over for prosecution, of the criminal proceeding arising out of the complaint upon which the order is based or until the issuance under section 2903.214 of the Revised Code of a protection order arising out of the same activities as those that were the basis of the complaint filed under this section;

(3) Shall not be construed as a finding that the alleged offender committed the alleged offense and shall not be introduced as evidence of the commission of the offense at the trial of the alleged offender on the complaint upon which the order is based.

(F) A person who meets the criteria for bail under Criminal Rule 46 and who, if required to do so pursuant to that rule, executes or posts bond or deposits cash or securities as bail, shall not be held in custody pending a hearing before the court on a motion requesting a protection order under this section.

(G) (1) A copy of a protection order that is issued under this section shall be issued by the court to the complainant, to the alleged victim, to the person who requested the order, to the defendant, and to all law enforcement agencies that have jurisdiction to enforce the order. The court shall direct that a copy of the order be delivered to the defendant on the same day that the order is entered. If a municipal court or a county court issues a protection order under this section and if, subsequent to the issuance of the order, the defendant who is the subject of the order is bound over to the court of common pleas for prosecution as described in division (D)(3) of this section, the municipal court or county court shall direct that a copy of the order be delivered to the court of common pleas to which the defendant is bound over.

(2) All law enforcement agencies shall establish and maintain an index for the protection orders delivered to the agencies pursuant to division (G)(1) of this section. With respect to each order delivered, each agency shall note on the index the date and time of the agency's receipt of the order.

(3) Regardless of whether the petitioner has registered the protection order in the county in which the officer's agency has jurisdiction, any officer of a law enforcement agency shall enforce a protection order issued pursuant to this section in accordance with the provisions of the order.

(H) Upon a violation of a protection order issued pursuant to this section, the court may issue another protection order under this section, as a pretrial condition of release, that modifies the terms of the order that was violated.

(I) (1) Subject to division (I)(2) of this section and regardless of whether a protection order is issued or a consent agreement is approved by a court of another county or by a court of another state, no court or unit of state or local government shall charge the movant any fee, cost, deposit, or money in connection with the filing of a motion pursuant to this section, in connection with the filing, issuance, registration, modification, enforcement, dismissal, withdrawal, or service of a protection order, consent agreement, or witness subpoena or for obtaining certified copies of a protection order or consent agreement.

(2) Regardless of whether a protection order is issued or a consent agreement is approved pursuant to this section, if the defendant is convicted the court may assess costs against the defendant in connection with the filing, issuance, registration, modification, enforcement, dismissal, withdrawal, or service of a protection order, consent agreement, or witness subpoena or for obtaining a certified copy of a protection order or consent agreement.

(J) As used in this section:

(1) "Sexually oriented offense" has the same meaning as in section 2950.01 of the Revised Code.

(2) "Companion animal" has the same meaning as in section 959.131 of the Revised Code.

(3) "Expunge" means to destroy, delete, and erase a record, as appropriate for the record's physical or electronic form or characteristic, so that the record is permanently irretrievable.

(2017 H 49, eff. 9-29-17; 2014 S 177, eff. 3-23-15; 2014 H 309, eff. 9-17-14; 2010 H 238, eff. 9-8-10; 2008 H 562, eff. 6-24-08; 2006 S 260, eff. 1-2-07; 2002 H 548, eff. 3-31-03; 1999 H 137, eff. 3-10-00; 1998 H 302, eff. 7-29-98; 1997 S 98, eff. 3-17-98; 1997 H 93, eff. 12-31-97; 1993 S 31, eff. 9-27-93; 1992 H 536)

2903.214. Protection orders and electronic monitoring; persons who may seek relief; ex parte

(A) As used in this section:

(1) "Court" means the court of common pleas of the county in which the person to be protected by the protection order resides.

(2) "Victim advocate" means a person who provides support and assistance for a person who files a petition under this section.

(3) "Family or household member" has the same meaning as in section 3113.31 of the Revised Code.

(4) "Protection order issued by a court of another state" has the same meaning as in section 2919.27 of the Revised Code.

(5) "Sexually oriented offense" has the same meaning as in section 2950.01 of the Revised Code.

(6) "Electronic monitoring" has the same meaning as in section 2929.01 of the Revised Code.

(7) "Companion animal" has the same meaning as in section 959.131 of the Revised Code.

(8) "Expunge" has the same meaning as in section 2903.213 of the Revised Code.

(B) The court has jurisdiction over all proceedings under this section.

(C) A person may seek relief under this section for the person, or any parent or adult household member may seek relief under this section on behalf of any other family or household member, by filing a petition with the court. The petition shall contain or state all of the following:

(1) An allegation that the respondent is eighteen years of age or older and engaged in a violation of section 2903.211 of the Revised Code against the person to be protected by the protection order or committed a sexually oriented offense against the person to be protected by the protection order, including a description of the nature and extent of the violation;

(2) If the petitioner seeks relief in the form of electronic monitoring of the respondent, an allegation that at any time preceding the filing of the petition the respondent engaged in conduct that would cause a reasonable person to believe that the health, welfare, or safety of the person to be protected was at risk, a description of the nature and extent of that conduct, and an allegation that the respondent presents a continuing danger to the person to be protected;

(3) A request for relief under this section.

(D) (1) If a person who files a petition pursuant to this section requests an ex parte order, the court shall hold an ex parte hearing as soon as possible after the petition is filed, but not later than the next day that the court is in session after the petition is filed. The court, for good cause shown at the ex parte hearing, may enter any temporary orders, with or without bond, that the court finds necessary for the safety and protection of the person to be protected by the order. Immediate and present danger to the person to be protected by the protection order constitutes good cause for purposes of this section. Immediate and present danger includes, but is not limited to, situations in which the respondent has threatened the person to be protected by the protection order with bodily harm or in which the respondent previously has been convicted of or pleaded guilty to a violation of section 2903.211 of the Revised Code or a sexually oriented offense against the person to be protected by the protection order.

(2) (a) If the court, after an ex parte hearing, issues a protection order described in division (E) of this section, the court shall schedule a full hearing for a date that is within ten court days after the ex parte hearing. The court shall give the respondent notice of, and an opportunity to be heard at, the full hearing. The court shall hold the full hearing on the date scheduled under this division unless the court grants a continuance of the hearing in accordance with this division. Under any of the following circumstances or for any of the following reasons, the court may grant a continuance of the full hearing to a reasonable time determined by the court:

(i) Prior to the date scheduled for the full hearing under this division, the respondent has not been served with the petition filed pursuant to this section and notice of the full hearing.

(ii) The parties consent to the continuance.

(iii) The continuance is needed to allow a party to obtain counsel.

(iv) The continuance is needed for other good cause.

(b) An ex parte order issued under this section does not expire because of a failure to serve notice of the full hearing upon the respondent before the date set for the full hearing under division (D)(2)(a) of this section or because the court grants a continuance under that division.

(3) If a person who files a petition pursuant to this section does not request an ex parte order, or if a person requests an ex parte order but the court does not issue an ex parte order after an ex parte hearing, the court shall proceed as in a normal civil action and grant a full hearing on the matter.

(E) (1) (a) After an ex parte or full hearing, the court may issue any protection order, with or without bond, that contains terms designed to ensure the safety and protection of the person to be protected by the protection order, including, but not limited to, a requirement that the respondent refrain from entering the residence, school, business, or place of employment of the petitioner or family or household member. If the court includes a requirement that the respondent refrain from entering the residence, school, business, or place of employment of the petitioner or family or household member in the order, it also shall include in the order provisions of the type described in division (E)(5) of this section. The court may include within a protection order issued under this section a term requiring that the respondent not remove, damage, hide, harm, or dispose of any companion animal owned or possessed by the person to be protected by the order, and may include within the order a term authorizing the person to be protected by the order to remove a companion animal owned by the person to be protected by the order from the possession of the respondent.

(b) After a full hearing, if the court considering a petition that includes an allegation of the type described in division (C)(2) of this section, or the court upon its own motion, finds upon clear and convincing evidence that the petitioner reasonably believed that the respondent's conduct at any time preceding the filing of the petition endangered the health, welfare, or safety of the person to be protected and that the respondent presents a continuing danger to the person to be protected, the court may order that the respondent be electronically monitored for a period of time and under the terms and conditions that the court determines are appropriate. Electronic monitoring shall be in addition to any other relief granted to the petitioner.

(2) (a) Any protection order issued pursuant to this section shall be valid until a date certain but not later than five years from the date of its issuance.

(b) Any protection order issued pursuant to this section may be renewed in the same manner as the original order was issued.

(3) A court may not issue a protection order that requires a petitioner to do or to refrain from doing an act that the court may require a respondent to do or to refrain from doing under division (E)(1) of this section unless all of the following apply:

(a) The respondent files a separate petition for a protection order in accordance with this section.

(b) The petitioner is served with notice of the respondent's petition at least forty-eight hours before the court holds a hearing with respect to the respondent's petition, or the petitioner waives the right to receive this notice.

(c) If the petitioner has requested an ex parte order pursuant to division (D) of this section, the court does not delay any hearing required by that division beyond the time specified in that division in order to consolidate the hearing with a hearing on the petition filed by the respondent.

(d) After a full hearing at which the respondent presents evidence in support of the request for a protection order and the petitioner is afforded an opportunity to defend against that evidence, the court determines that the petitioner has committed a violation of section 2903.211 of the Revised Code against the person to be protected by the protection order issued pursuant to division (E)(3) of this section, has committed a sexually oriented offense against the person to be protected by the protection order issued pursuant to division (E)(3) of this section, or has violated a protection order issued pursuant to section 2903.213 of the Revised Code relative to the person to be protected by the protection order issued pursuant to division (E)(3) of this section.

(4) No protection order issued pursuant to this section shall in any manner affect title to any real property.

(5) (a) If the court issues a protection order under this section that includes a requirement that the alleged offender refrain from entering the residence, school, business, or place of employment of the petitioner or a family or household member, the order shall clearly state that the order cannot be waived

or nullified by an invitation to the alleged offender from the complainant to enter the residence, school, business, or place of employment or by the alleged offender's entry into one of those places otherwise upon the consent of the petitioner or family or household member.

(b) Division (E)(5)(a) of this section does not limit any discretion of a court to determine that an alleged offender charged with a violation of section 2919.27 of the Revised Code, with a violation of a municipal ordinance substantially equivalent to that section, or with contempt of court, which charge is based on an alleged violation of a protection order issued under this section, did not commit the violation or was not in contempt of court.

(F) (1) The court shall cause the delivery of a copy of any protection order that is issued under this section to the petitioner, to the respondent, and to all law enforcement agencies that have jurisdiction to enforce the order. The court shall direct that a copy of the order be delivered to the respondent on the same day that the order is entered.

(2) Upon the issuance of a protection order under this section, the court shall provide the parties to the order with the following notice orally or by form:

"NOTICE

As a result of this order, it may be unlawful for you to possess or purchase a firearm, including a rifle, pistol, or revolver, or ammunition pursuant to federal law under 18 U.S.C. 922(g)(8) for the duration of this order. If you have any questions whether this law makes it illegal for you to possess or purchase a firearm or ammunition, you should consult an attorney."

(3) All law enforcement agencies shall establish and maintain an index for the protection orders delivered to the agencies pursuant to division (F)(1) of this section. With respect to each order delivered, each agency shall note on the index the date and time that it received the order.

(4) Regardless of whether the petitioner has registered the protection order in the county in which the officer's agency has jurisdiction pursuant to division (M) of this section, any officer of a law enforcement agency shall enforce a protection order issued pursuant to this section by any court in this state in accordance with the provisions of the order, including removing the respondent from the premises, if appropriate.

(G) (1) Any proceeding under this section shall be conducted in accordance with the Rules of Civil Procedure, except that a protection order may be obtained under this section with or without bond. An order issued under this section, other than an ex parte order, that grants a protection order, or that refuses to grant a protection order, is a final, appealable order. The remedies and procedures provided in this section are in addition to, and not in lieu of, any other available civil or criminal remedies.

(2) If as provided in division (G)(1) of this section an order issued under this section, other than an ex parte order, refuses to grant a protection order, the court, on its own motion, shall order that the ex parte order issued under this section and all of the records pertaining to that ex parte order be expunged after either of the following occurs:

(a) The period of the notice of appeal from the order that refuses to grant a protection order has expired.

(b) The order that refuses to grant the protection order is appealed and an appellate court to which the last appeal of that order is taken affirms the order.

(H) The filing of proceedings under this section does not excuse a person from filing any report or giving any notice required by section 2151.421 of the Revised Code or by any other law.

(I) Any law enforcement agency that investigates an alleged violation of section 2903.211 of the Revised Code or an alleged commission of a sexually oriented offense shall provide information to the victim and the family or household members of the victim regarding the relief available under this section and section 2903.213 of the Revised Code.

(J) (1) Subject to division (J)(2) of this section and regardless of whether a protection order is issued or a consent agreement is approved by a court of another county or by a court of another state, no court or unit of state or local government shall charge the petitioner any fee, cost, deposit, or money in connection with the filing of a petition pursuant to this section, in connection with the filing, issuance, registration, modification, enforcement, dismissal, withdrawal, or service of a protection order, consent agreement, or witness subpoena or for obtaining a certified copy of a protection order or consent agreement.

(2) Regardless of whether a protection order is issued or a consent agreement is approved pursuant to this section, the court may assess costs against the respondent in connection with the filing, issuance, registration, modification, enforcement, dismissal, withdrawal, or service of a protection order, consent agreement, or witness subpoena or for obtaining a certified copy of a protection order or consent agreement.

(K) (1) A person who violates a protection order issued under this section is subject to the following sanctions:

(a) Criminal prosecution for a violation of section 2919.27 of the Revised Code, if the violation of the protection order constitutes a violation of that section;

(b) Punishment for contempt of court.

(2) The punishment of a person for contempt of court for violation of a protection order issued under this section does not bar criminal prosecution of the person for a violation of section 2919.27 of the Revised Code. However, a person punished for contempt of court is entitled to credit for the punishment imposed upon conviction of a violation of that section, and a person convicted of a violation of that section shall not subsequently be punished for contempt of court arising out of the same activity.

(L) In all stages of a proceeding under this section, a petitioner may be accompanied by a victim advocate.

(M) (1) A petitioner who obtains a protection order under this section or a protection order under section 2903.213 of the Revised Code may provide notice of the issuance or approval of the order to the judicial and law enforcement officials in any county other than the county in which the order is issued by registering that order in the other county pursuant to division (M)(2) of this section and filing a copy of the registered order with a law enforcement agency in the other county in accordance with that division. A person who obtains a protection order issued by a court of another state may provide notice of the issuance of the order to the judicial and law enforcement officials in any county of this state by registering the order in that county pursuant to section 2919.272 of the Revised Code and filing a copy of the registered order with a law enforcement agency in that county.

(2) A petitioner may register a protection order issued pursuant to this section or section 2903.213 of the Revised Code in a county other than the county in which the court that issued the order is located in the following manner:

(a) The petitioner shall obtain a certified copy of the order from the clerk of the court that issued the order and present that certified copy to the clerk of the court of common pleas or the clerk of a municipal court or county court in the county in which the order is to be registered.

(b) Upon accepting the certified copy of the order for registration, the clerk of the court of common pleas, municipal court, or county court shall place an endorsement of registration on the order and give the petitioner a copy of the order that bears that proof of registration.

(3) The clerk of each court of common pleas, municipal court, or county court shall maintain a registry of certified copies of protection orders that have been issued by courts in other counties pursuant to this section or section 2903.213 of the Revised Code and that have been registered with the clerk.

(N) (1) If the court orders electronic monitoring of the respondent under this section, the court shall direct the sheriff's office or any other appropriate law enforcement agency to install the electronic monitoring device and to monitor the respondent. Unless the court determines that the respondent is indigent, the court shall order the respondent to pay the cost of the installation and monitoring of the electronic monitoring device. If the court determines that the respondent is indigent and subject to the maximum amount allowable to be paid in any year from the fund and the rules promulgated by the attorney general under division (N)(2) of this section, the cost of the installation and monitoring of the electronic monitoring device may be paid out of funds from the reparations fund created pursuant to section 2743.191 of the Revised Code. The total amount of costs for the installation and monitoring of electronic monitoring devices paid pursuant to this division and sections 2151.34 and 2919.27 of the Revised Code from the reparations fund shall not exceed three hundred thousand dollars per year.

(2) The attorney general may promulgate rules pursuant to section 111.15 of the Revised Code to govern payments made from the reparations fund pursuant to this division and sections 2151.34 and 2919.27 of the Revised Code. The rules may include reasonable limits on the total cost paid pursuant to this division and sections 2151.34 and 2919.27 of the Revised Code per respondent, the amount of the three hundred thousand dollars allocated to each county, and how invoices may be submitted by a county, court, or other entity.

(2018 H 1, eff. 7-6-18; 2017 H 49, eff. 9-29-17; 2014 S 177, eff. 3-23-15; 2014 H 309, eff. 9-17-14; 2010 H 10, eff. 6-17-10; 2009 H 1, eff. 10-16-09; 2008 H 471, eff. 4-7-09; 2008 H 562, eff. 6-24-08; 2006 S 260, eff. 1-2-07; 2002 H 548, eff. 3-31-03; 1998 H 302, eff. 7-29-98)

2903.22. Menacing

(A) No person shall knowingly cause another to believe that the offender will cause physical harm to the person or property of the other person, the other person's unborn, or a member of the other person's immediate family. In addition to any other basis for the other person's belief that the offender will cause physical harm to the person or property of the other person, the other person's unborn, or a member of the other person's immediate family, the other person's belief may be based on words or conduct of the offender that are directed at or identify a corporation, association, or other organization that employs the other person or to which the other person belongs.

(B) Whoever violates this section is guilty of menacing. Except as otherwise provided in this division, menacing is a misdemeanor of the fourth degree. If the victim of the offense is an officer or employee of a public children services agency or a private child placing agency and the offense relates to the officer's or employee's performance or anticipated performance of official responsibilities or duties, menacing is a misdemeanor of the first degree or, if the offender previously has been convicted of or pleaded guilty to an offense of violence, the victim of that prior offense was an officer or employee of a public children services agency or private child placing agency, and that prior offense related to the officer's or employee's performance or anticipated performance of official responsibilities or duties, a felony of the fourth degree.

(C) As used in this section, "organization" includes an entity that is a governmental employer.

(2014 H 129, eff. 9-17-14; 2000 H 412, eff. 4-10-01; 1996 S 239, eff. 9-6-96; 1972 H 511, eff. 1-1-74)

CHAPTER 2911 ROBBERY, BURGLARY, AND TRESPASS

Section

2911.211. Aggravated trespass

(A) No person shall enter or remain on the land or premises of another with purpose to commit on that land or those premises a misdemeanor, the elements of which involve causing physical harm to another person or causing another person to believe that the offender will cause physical harm to him.

(B) Whoever violates this section is guilty of aggravated trespass, a misdemeanor of the first degree.

(1992 H 536, eff. 11-5-92)

CHAPTER 2919 OFFENSES AGAINST THE FAMILY

NONSUPPORT; CHILD ENDANGERING; RELATED OFFENSES

Section

DOMESTIC VIOLENCE

NONSUPPORT; CHILD ENDANGERING; RELATED OFFENSES

2919.22. Endangering children

(A) No person, who is the parent, guardian, custodian, person having custody or control, or person in loco parentis of a child under eighteen years of age or a mentally or physically handicapped child under twenty-one years of age, shall create a substantial risk to the health or safety of the child, by violating a duty of care, protection, or support. It is not a violation of a duty of care, protection, or support under this division when the parent, guardian, custodian, or person having custody or control of a child treats the physical or mental illness or defect of the child by spiritual means through prayer alone, in accordance with the tenets of a recognized religious body.

(B) No person shall do any of the following to a child under eighteen years of age or a mentally or physically handicapped child under twenty-one years of age:

(1) Abuse the child;

(2) Torture or cruelly abuse the child;

(3) Administer corporal punishment or other physical disciplinary measure, or physically restrain the child in a cruel manner or for a prolonged period, which punishment, discipline, or restraint is excessive under the circumstances and creates a substantial risk of serious physical harm to the child;

(4) Repeatedly administer unwarranted disciplinary measures to the child, when there is a substantial risk that such conduct, if continued, will seriously impair or retard the child's mental health or development;

(5) Entice, coerce, permit, encourage, compel, hire, employ, use, or allow the child to act, model, or in any other way participate in, or be photographed for, the production, presentation, dissemination, or advertisement of any material or performance that the offender knows or reasonably should know is obscene, is sexually oriented matter, or is nudity-oriented matter;

(6) Allow the child to be on the same parcel of real property and within one hundred feet of, or, in the case of more than one housing unit on the same parcel of real property, in the same housing unit and within one hundred feet of, any act in violation of section 2925.04 or 2925.041 of the Revised Code when the person knows that the act is occurring, whether or not any person is prosecuted for or convicted of the violation of section 2925.04 or 2925.041 of the Revised Code that is the basis of the violation of this division.

(C) (1) No person shall operate a vehicle, streetcar, or trackless trolley within this state in violation of division (A) of section 4511.19 of the Revised Code when one or more children under eighteen years of age are in the vehicle, streetcar, or trackless trolley. Notwithstanding any other provision of law, a person may be convicted at the same trial or proceeding of a violation of this division and a violation of division (A) of section 4511.19 of the Revised Code that constitutes the basis of the charge of the violation of this division. For purposes of sections 4511.191 to 4511.197 of the Revised Code and all related provisions of law, a person arrested for a violation of this division shall be considered to be under arrest for operating a vehicle while under the influence of alcohol, a drug of abuse, or a combination of them or for operating a vehicle with a prohibited concentration of alcohol, a controlled substance, or a metabolite of a controlled substance in the whole blood, blood serum or plasma, breath, or urine.

(2) As used in division (C)(1) of this section:

(a) "Controlled substance" has the same meaning as in section 3719.01 of the Revised Code.

(b) "Vehicle," "streetcar," and "trackless trolley" have the same meanings as in section 4511.01 of the Revised Code.

(D) (1) Division (B)(5) of this section does not apply to any material or performance that is produced, presented, or disseminated for a bona fide medical, scientific, educational, religious, governmental, judicial, or other proper purpose, by or to a physician, psychologist, sociologist, scientist, teacher, person pursuing bona fide studies or research, librarian, member of the clergy, prosecutor, judge, or other person having a proper interest in the material or performance.

(2) Mistake of age is not a defense to a charge under division (B)(5) of this section.

(3) In a prosecution under division (B)(5) of this section, the trier of fact may infer that an actor, model, or participant in the material or performance involved is a juvenile if the material or performance, through its title, text, visual representation, or otherwise, represents or depicts the actor, model, or participant as a juvenile.

(4) As used in this division and division (B)(5) of this section:

(a) "Material," "performance," "obscene," and "sexual activity" have the same meanings as in section 2907.01 of the Revised Code.

(b) "Nudity-oriented matter" means any material or performance that shows a minor in a state of nudity and that, taken as a whole by the average person applying contemporary community standards, appeals to prurient interest.

(c) "Sexually oriented matter" means any material or performance that shows a minor participating or engaging in sexual activity, masturbation, or bestiality.

(E) (1) Whoever violates this section is guilty of endangering children.

(2) If the offender violates division (A) or (B)(1) of this section, endangering children is one of the following, and, in the circumstances described in division (E)(2)(e) of this section, that division applies:

(a) Except as otherwise provided in division (E)(2)(b), (c), or (d) of this section, a misdemeanor of the first degree;

(b) If the offender previously has been convicted of an offense under this section or of any offense involving neglect, abandonment, contributing to the delinquency of, or physical abuse of a child, except as otherwise provided in division (E)(2)(c) or (d) of this section, a felony of the fourth degree;

(c) If the violation is a violation of division (A) of this section and results in serious physical harm to the child involved, a felony of the third degree;

(d) If the violation is a violation of division (B)(1) of this section and results in serious physical harm to the child involved, a felony of the second degree.

(e) If the violation is a felony violation of division (B)(1) of this section and the offender also is convicted of or pleads guilty to a specification as described in section 2941.1422 of the Revised Code that was included in the indictment, count in the indictment, or information charging the offense, the court shall sentence the offender to a mandatory prison term as provided in division (B)(7) of section 2929.14 of the Revised Code and shall order the offender to make restitution as provided in division (B)(8) of section 2929.18 of the Revised Code.

(3) If the offender violates division (B)(2), (3), (4), or (6) of this section, except as otherwise provided in this division, endangering children is a felony of the third degree. If the violation results in serious physical harm to the child involved, or if the offender previously has been convicted of an offense under this section or of any offense involving neglect, abandonment, contributing to the delinquency of, or physical abuse of a child, endangering children is a felony of the second degree. If the offender violates division (B)(2), (3), or (4) of this section and the offender also is convicted of or pleads guilty to a specification as described in section 2941.1422 of the Revised Code that was included in the indictment, count in the indictment, or information charging the offense, the court shall sentence the offender to a mandatory prison term as provided in division (B)(7) of section 2929.14 of the Revised Code and shall order the offender to make restitution as

provided in division (B)(8) of section 2929.18 of the Revised Code. If the offender violates division (B)(6) of this section and the drug involved is methamphetamine, the court shall impose a mandatory prison term on the offender as follows:

(a) If the violation is a violation of division (B)(6) of this section that is a felony of the third degree under division (E)(3) of this section and the drug involved is methamphetamine, except as otherwise provided in this division, the court shall impose as a mandatory prison term one of the prison terms prescribed for a felony of the third degree that is not less than two years. If the violation is a violation of division (B)(6) of this section that is a felony of the third degree under division (E)(3) of this section, if the drug involved is methamphetamine, and if the offender previously has been convicted of or pleaded guilty to a violation of division (B)(6) of this section, a violation of division (A) of section 2925.04 of the Revised Code, or a violation of division (A) of section 2925.041 of the Revised Code, the court shall impose as a mandatory prison term one of the prison terms prescribed for a felony of the third degree that is not less than five years.

(b) If the violation is a violation of division (B)(6) of this section that is a felony of the second degree under division (E)(3) of this section and the drug involved is methamphetamine, except as otherwise provided in this division, the court shall impose as a mandatory prison term one of the prison terms prescribed for a felony of the second degree that is not less than three years. If the violation is a violation of division (B)(6) of this section that is a felony of the second degree under division (E)(3) of this section, if the drug involved is methamphetamine, and if the offender previously has been convicted of or pleaded guilty to a violation of division (B)(6) of this section, a violation of division (A) of section 2925.04 of the Revised Code, or a violation of division (A) of section 2925.041 of the Revised Code, the court shall impose as a mandatory prison term one of the prison terms prescribed for a felony of the second degree that is not less than five years.

(4) If the offender violates division (B)(5) of this section, endangering children is a felony of the second degree. If the offender also is convicted of or pleads guilty to a specification as described in section 2941.1422 of the Revised Code that was included in the indictment, count in the indictment, or information charging the offense, the court shall sentence the offender to a mandatory prison term as provided in division (B)(7) of section 2929.14 of the Revised Code and shall order the offender to make restitution as provided in division (B)(8) of section 2929.18 of the Revised Code.

(5) If the offender violates division (C) of this section, the offender shall be punished as follows:

(a) Except as otherwise provided in division (E)(5)(b) or (c) of this section, endangering children in violation of division (C) of this section is a misdemeanor of the first degree.

(b) If the violation results in serious physical harm to the child involved or the offender previously has been convicted of an offense under this section or any offense involving neglect, abandonment, contributing to the delinquency of, or physical abuse of a child, except as otherwise provided in division (E)(5)(c) of this section, endangering children in violation of division (C) of this section is a felony of the fifth degree.

(c) If the violation results in serious physical harm to the child involved and if the offender previously has been convicted of a violation of division (C) of this section, section 2903.06 or 2903.08 of the Revised Code, section 2903.07 of the Revised Code as it existed prior to March 23, 2000, or section 2903.04 of the Revised Code in a case in which the offender was subject to the sanctions described in division (D) of that section, endangering children in violation of division (C) of this section is a felony of the fourth degree.

(d) In addition to any term of imprisonment, fine, or other sentence, penalty, or sanction it imposes upon the offender pursuant to division (E)(5)(a), (b), or (c) of this section or pursuant to any other provision of law and in addition to any suspension of the offender's driver's or commercial driver's license or permit or nonresident operating privilege under Chapter 4506., 4509., 4510., or 4511. of the Revised Code or under any other provision of law, the court also may impose upon the offender a class seven suspension of the offender's driver's or commercial driver's license or permit or nonresident operating privilege from the range specified in division (A)(7) of section 4510.02 of the Revised Code.

(e) In addition to any term of imprisonment, fine, or other sentence, penalty, or sanction imposed upon the offender pursuant to division (E)(5)(a), (b), (c), or (d) of this section or pursuant to any other provision of law for the violation of division (C) of this section, if as part of the same trial or proceeding the offender also is convicted of or pleads guilty to a separate charge charging the violation of division (A) of section 4511.19 of the Revised Code that was the basis of the charge of the violation of division (C) of this section, the offender also shall be sentenced in accordance with section 4511.19 of the Revised Code for that violation of division (A) of section 4511.19 of the Revised Code.

(F) (1) (a) A court may require an offender to perform not more than two hundred hours of supervised community service work under the authority of an agency, subdivision, or charitable organization. The requirement shall be part of the community control sanction or sentence of the offender, and the court shall impose the community service in accordance with and subject to divisions (F)(1)(a) and (b) of this section. The court may require an offender whom it requires to perform supervised community service work as part of the offender's community control sanction or sentence to pay the court a reasonable fee to cover the costs of the offender's participation in the work, including, but not limited to, the costs of procuring a policy or policies of liability insurance to cover the period during which the offender will perform the work. If the court requires the offender to perform supervised community service work as part of the offender's community control sanction or sentence, the court shall do so in accordance with the following limitations and criteria:

(i) The court shall require that the community service work be performed after completion of the term of imprisonment or jail term imposed upon the offender for the violation of division (C) of this section, if applicable.

(ii) The supervised community service work shall be subject to the limitations set forth in divisions (B)(1), (2), and (3) of section 2951.02 of the Revised Code.

(iii) The community service work shall be supervised in the manner described in division (B)(4) of section 2951.02 of the Revised Code by an official or person with the qualifications described in that division. The official or person periodically shall report in writing to the court concerning the conduct of the offender in performing the work.

(iv) The court shall inform the offender in writing that if the offender does not adequately perform, as determined by the court, all of the required community service work, the court may order that the offender be committed to a jail or workhouse for a period of time that does not exceed the term of imprisonment that the court could have imposed upon the offender for the violation of division (C) of this section, reduced by the total amount of time that the offender actually was imprisoned under the sentence or term that was imposed upon the offender for that violation and by the total amount of time that the offender was confined for any reason arising out of the offense for which the offender was convicted and sentenced as described in sections 2949.08 and 2967.191 of the Revised Code, and that, if the court orders that the offender be so committed, the court is authorized, but not required, to grant the offender credit upon the period of the commitment for the community service work that the offender adequately performed.

(b) If a court, pursuant to division (F)(1)(a) of this section, orders an offender to perform community service work as part of the offender's community control sanction or sentence and if the offender does not adequately perform all of the required community service work, as determined by the court, the court may order that the offender be committed to a jail or workhouse for a period of time that does not exceed the term of imprisonment that the court could have imposed upon the offender for the violation of division (C) of this section, reduced by the total amount of time that the offender actually was imprisoned under the sentence or term that was imposed upon the offender for that violation and by the total amount of time that the offender was confined for any reason arising out of the offense for which the offender was convicted and sentenced as described in sections 2949.08 and 2967.191 of the Revised Code. The court may order that a person committed pursuant to this division shall receive hour-for-hour credit upon the period of the commitment for the community service work that the offender adequately performed. No commitment pursuant to this division shall exceed the period of the term of imprisonment that the sentencing court could have imposed upon the offender for the violation of division (C) of this section, reduced by the total amount of time that the offender actually was imprisoned under that sentence or term and by the total amount of time that the offender was confined for any reason arising out of the offense for which the offender was convicted and sentenced as described in sections 2949.08 and 2967.191 of the Revised Code.

(2) Division (F)(1) of this section does not limit or affect the authority of the court to suspend the sentence imposed upon a misdemeanor offender and place the offender under a community control sanction pursuant to section 2929.25 of the Revised Code, to require a misdemeanor or felony offender to perform supervised community service work in accordance with division (B) of section 2951.02 of the Revised Code, or to place a felony offender under a community control sanction.

(G) (1) If a court suspends an offender's driver's or commercial driver's license or permit or nonresident operating privilege under division (E)(5)(d) of this section, the period of the suspension shall be consecutive to, and commence after, the period of suspension of the offender's driver's or commercial driver's license or permit or nonresident operating privilege that is imposed under Chapter 4506., 4509., 4510., or 4511. of the Revised Code or under any other provision of law in relation to the violation of division (C) of this section that is the basis of the suspension under division (E)(5)(d) of this section or in relation to the violation of division (A) of section 4511.19 of the Revised Code that is the basis for that violation of division (C) of this section.

(2) An offender is not entitled to request, and the court shall not grant to the offender, limited driving privileges if the offender's license, permit, or privilege has been suspended under division (E)(5)(d) of this section and the offender, within the preceding six years, has been convicted of or pleaded guilty to three or more violations of one or more of the following:

(a) Division (C) of this section;

(b) Any equivalent offense, as defined in section 4511.181 of the Revised Code.

(H) (1) If a person violates division (C) of this section and if, at the time of the violation, there were two or more children under eighteen years of age in the motor vehicle involved in the violation, the offender may be convicted of a violation of division (C) of this section for each of the children, but the court may sentence the offender for only one of the violations.

(2) (a) If a person is convicted of or pleads guilty to a violation of division (C) of this section but the person is not also convicted of and does not also plead guilty to a separate charge charging the violation of division (A) of section 4511.19 of the Revised Code that was the basis of the charge of the violation of division (C) of this section, both of the following apply:

(i) For purposes of the provisions of section 4511.19 of the Revised Code that set forth the penalties and sanctions for a violation of division (A) of section 4511.19 of the Revised Code, the conviction of or plea of guilty to the violation of division (C) of this section shall not constitute a violation of division (A) of section 4511.19 of the Revised Code;

(ii) For purposes of any provision of law that refers to a conviction of or plea of guilty to a violation of division (A) of section 4511.19 of the Revised Code and that is not described in division (H)(2)(a)(i) of this section, the conviction of or plea of guilty to the violation of division (C) of this section shall constitute a conviction of or plea of guilty to a violation of division (A) of section 4511.19 of the Revised Code.

(b) If a person is convicted of or pleads guilty to a violation of division (C) of this section and the person also is convicted of or pleads guilty to a separate charge charging the violation of division (A) of section 4511.19 of the Revised Code that was the basis of the charge of the violation of division (C) of this section, the conviction of or plea of guilty to the violation of division (C) of this section shall not constitute, for purposes of any provision of law that refers to a conviction of or plea of guilty to a violation of division (A) of section 4511.19 of the Revised Code, a conviction of or plea of guilty to a violation of division (A) of section 4511.19 of the Revised Code.

(I) As used in this section:

(1) "Community control sanction" has the same meaning as in section 2929.01 of the Revised Code;

(2) "Limited driving privileges" has the same meaning as in section 4501.01 of the Revised Code;

(3) "Methamphetamine" has the same meaning as in section 2925.01 of the Revised Code.

(2011 H 86, eff. 9-30-11; 2008 H 280, eff. 4-7-09; 2006 S 8, eff. 8-17-06; 2006 S 53, eff. 5-17-06; 2004 S 58, eff. 8-11-04; 2002 H 490, eff. 1-1-04; 2002 S 123, eff. 1-1-04; 2000 S 180, eff. 3-22-01; 1999 S 107, eff. 3-23-00; 1999 H 162, eff. 8-25-99; 1997 S 60, eff. 10-21-97; 1996 S 269, § 8, eff. 5-15-97; 1996 S 269, § 1, eff. 7-1-96; 1996 H 353, § 4, eff. 5-15-97; 1996 H 353, § 1, eff. 9-17-96; 1995 H 167, eff. 5-15-97; 1995 S 2, eff. 7-1-96; 1994 H 236, eff. 9-29-94; 1988 H 51, eff. 3-17-89; 1985 H 349; 1984 S 321, H 44; 1977 S 243; 1972 H 511)

DOMESTIC VIOLENCE

2919.25. Domestic violence

(A) No person shall knowingly cause or attempt to cause physical harm to a family or household member.

(B) No person shall recklessly cause serious physical harm to a family or household member.

(C) No person, by threat of force, shall knowingly cause a family or household member to believe that the offender will cause imminent physical harm to the family or household member.

(D) (1) Whoever violates this section is guilty of domestic violence, and the court shall sentence the offender as provided in divisions (D)(2) to (6) of this section.

(2) Except as otherwise provided in divisions (D)(3) to (5) of this section, a violation of division (C) of this section is a misdemeanor of the fourth degree, and a violation of division (A) or (B) of this section is a misdemeanor of the first degree.

(3) Except as otherwise provided in division (D)(4) of this section, if the offender previously has pleaded guilty to or been convicted of domestic violence, a violation of an existing or former municipal ordinance or law of this or any other state or the United States that is substantially similar to domestic violence, a violation of section 2903.14, 2909.06, 2909.07, 2911.12, 2911.211, or 2919.22 of the Revised Code if the victim of the violation was a family or household member at the time of the violation, a violation of an existing or former municipal ordinance or law of this or any other state or the United States that is substantially similar to any of those sections if the victim of the violation was a family or household member at the time of the commission of the violation, or any offense of violence if the victim of the offense was a family or household member at the time of the commission of the offense, a violation of division (A) or (B) of this section is a felony of the fourth degree, and, if the offender knew that the victim of the violation was pregnant at the time of the violation, the court shall impose a mandatory prison term on the offender pursuant to division (D)(6) of this section, and a violation of division (C) of this section is a misdemeanor of the second degree.

(4) If the offender previously has pleaded guilty to or been convicted of two or more offenses of domestic violence or two or more violations or offenses of the type described in division (D)(3) of this section involving a person who was a family or household member at the time of the violations or offenses, a violation of division (A) or (B) of this section is a felony of the third degree, and, if the offender knew that the victim of the violation was pregnant at the time of the violation, the court shall impose a mandatory prison term on the offender pursuant to division (D)(6) of this section, and a violation of division (C) of this section is a misdemeanor of the first degree.

(5) Except as otherwise provided in division (D)(3) or (4) of this section, if the offender knew that the victim of the violation was pregnant at the time of the violation, a violation of division (A) or (B) of this section is a felony of the fifth degree, and the court shall impose a mandatory prison term on the offender pursuant to division (D)(6) of this section, and a violation of division (C) of this section is a misdemeanor of the third degree.

(6) If division (D)(3), (4), or (5) of this section requires the court that sentences

an offender for a violation of division (A) or (B) of this section to impose a mandatory prison term on the offender pursuant to this division, the court shall impose the mandatory prison term as follows:

(a) If the violation of division (A) or (B) of this section is a felony of the fourth or fifth degree, except as otherwise provided in division (D)(6)(b) or (c) of this section, the court shall impose a mandatory prison term on the offender of at least six months.

(b) If the violation of division (A) or (B) of this section is a felony of the fifth degree and the offender, in committing the violation, caused serious physical harm to the pregnant woman's unborn or caused the termination of the pregnant woman's pregnancy, the court shall impose a mandatory prison term on the offender of twelve months.

(c) If the violation of division (A) or (B) of this section is a felony of the fourth degree and the offender, in committing the violation, caused serious physical harm to the pregnant woman's unborn or caused the termination of the pregnant woman's pregnancy, the court shall impose a mandatory prison term on the offender of at least twelve months.

(d) If the violation of division (A) or (B) of this section is a felony of the third degree, except as otherwise provided in division (D)(6)(e) of this section and notwithstanding the range of prison terms prescribed in section 2929.14 of the Revised Code for a felony of the third degree, the court shall impose a mandatory prison term on the offender of either a definite term of six months or one of the prison terms prescribed in section 2929.14 of the Revised Code for felonies of the third degree.

(e) If the violation of division (A) or (B) of this section is a felony of the third degree and the offender, in committing the violation, caused serious physical harm to the pregnant woman's unborn or caused the termination of the pregnant woman's pregnancy, notwithstanding the range of prison terms prescribed in section 2929.14 of the Revised Code for a felony of the third degree, the court shall impose a mandatory prison term on the offender of either a definite term of one year or one of the prison terms prescribed in section 2929.14 of the Revised Code for felonies of the third degree.

(E) Notwithstanding any provision of law to the contrary, no court or unit of state or local government shall charge any fee, cost, deposit, or money in connection with the filing of charges against a person alleging that the person violated this section or a municipal ordinance substantially similar to this section or in connection with the prosecution of any charges so filed.

(F) As used in this section and sections 2919.251 and 2919.26 of the Revised Code:

(1) "Family or household member" means any of the following:

(a) Any of the following who is residing or has resided with the offender:

(i) A spouse, a person living as a spouse, or a former spouse of the offender;

(ii) A parent, a foster parent, or a child of the offender, or another person related by consanguinity or affinity to the offender;

(iii) A parent or a child of a spouse, person living as a spouse, or former spouse of the offender, or another person related by consanguinity or affinity to a spouse, person living as a spouse, or former spouse of the offender.

(b) The natural parent of any child of whom the offender is the other natural parent or is the putative other natural parent.

(2) "Person living as a spouse" means a person who is living or has lived with the offender in a common law marital relationship, who otherwise is cohabiting with the offender, or who otherwise has cohabited with the offender within five years prior to the date of the alleged commission of the act in question.

(3) "Pregnant woman's unborn" has the same meaning as "such other person's unborn," as set forth in section 2903.09 of the Revised Code, as it relates to the pregnant woman. Division (C) of that section applies regarding the use of the term in this section, except that the second and third sentences of division (C)(1) of that section shall be construed for purposes of this section as if they included a reference to this section in the listing of Revised Code sections they contain.

(4) "Termination of the pregnant woman's pregnancy" has the same meaning

as "unlawful termination of another's pregnancy," as set forth in section 2903.09 of the Revised Code, as it relates to the pregnant woman. Division (C) of that section applies regarding the use of the term in this section, except that the second and third sentences of division (C)(1) of that section shall be construed for purposes of this section as if they included a reference to this section in the listing of Revised Code sections they contain.

(2010 S 58, eff. 9-17-10; 2010 H 10, eff. 6-17-10; 2008 H 280, eff. 4-7-09; 2003 S 50, eff. 1-8-04; 2002 H 548, eff. 3-31-03; 2002 H 327, eff. 7-8-02; 1997 H 238, eff. 11-5-97; 1997 S 1, eff. 10-21-97; 1995 S 2, eff. 7-1-96; 1994 H 335, eff. 12-9-94; 1992 H 536, eff. 11-5-92; 1990 S 3; 1988 H 172; 1987 S 6; 1984 H 587; 1980 H 920; 1978 H 835)

2919.251. Factors to be considered when setting bail; bail schedule; appearance by video conferencing equipment

(A) Subject to division (D) of this section, a person who is charged with the commission of any offense of violence shall appear before the court for the setting of bail if the alleged victim of the offense charged was a family or household member at the time of the offense and if any of the following applies:

(1) The person charged, at the time of the alleged offense, was subject to the terms of a protection order issued or consent agreement approved pursuant to section 2919.26 or 3113.31 of the Revised Code or previously was convicted of or pleaded guilty to a violation of section 2919.25 of the Revised Code or a violation of section 2919.27 of the Revised Code involving a protection order or consent agreement of that type, a violation of an existing or former municipal ordinance or law of this or any other state or the United States that is substantially similar to either section, a violation of section 2909.06, 2909.07, 2911.12, or 2911.211 of the Revised Code if the victim of the violation was a family or household member at the time of the violation a violation of an existing or former municipal ordinance or law of this or any other state or the United States that is substantially similar to any of those sections if the victim of the violation was a family or household member at the time of the commission of the violation, or any offense of violence if the victim of the offense was a family or household member at the time of the offense;

(2) The arresting officer indicates in a police report or other document accompanying the complaint any of the following:

(a) That the arresting officer observed on the alleged victim objective manifestations of physical harm that the arresting officer reasonably believes are a result of the alleged offense;

(b) That the arresting officer reasonably believes that the person had on the person's person at the time of the alleged offense a deadly weapon or dangerous ordnance;

(c) That the arresting officer reasonably believes that the person presents a credible threat of serious physical harm to the alleged victim or to any other person if released on bail before trial.

(B) To the extent that information about any of the following is available to the court, the court shall consider all of the following, in addition to any other circumstances considered by the court and notwithstanding any provisions to the contrary contained in Criminal Rule 46, before setting bail for a person who appears before the court pursuant to division (A) of this section:

(1) Whether the person has a history of domestic violence or a history of other violent acts;

(2) The mental health of the person;

(3) Whether the person has a history of violating the orders of any court or governmental entity;

(4) Whether the person is potentially a threat to any other person;

(5) Whether the person has access to deadly weapons or a history of using deadly weapons;

(6) Whether the person has a history of abusing alcohol or any controlled substance;

(7) The severity of the alleged violence that is the basis of the offense, including but not limited to, the duration of the alleged violent incident, and whether the alleged violent incident involved serious physical injury, sexual assault,

strangulation, abuse during the alleged victim's pregnancy, abuse of pets, or forcible entry to gain access to the alleged victim;

(8) Whether a separation of the person from the alleged victim or a termination of the relationship between the person and the alleged victim has recently occurred or is pending;

(9) Whether the person has exhibited obsessive or controlling behaviors toward the alleged victim, including but not limited to, stalking, surveillance, or isolation of the alleged victim;

(10) Whether the person has expressed suicidal or homicidal ideations;

(11) Any information contained in the complaint and any police reports, affidavits, or other documents accompanying the complaint.

(C) Any court that has jurisdiction over charges alleging the commission of an offense of violence in circumstances in which the alleged victim of the offense was a family or household member at the time of the offense may set a schedule for bail to be used in cases involving those offenses. The schedule shall require that a judge consider all of the factors listed in division (B) of this section and may require judges to set bail at a certain level if the history of the alleged offender or the circumstances of the alleged offense meet certain criteria in the schedule.

(D) (1) Upon the court's own motion or the motion of a party and upon any terms that the court may direct, a court may permit a person who is required to appear before it by division (A) of this section to appear by video conferencing equipment.

(2) If in the opinion of the court the appearance in person or by video conferencing equipment of a person who is charged with a misdemeanor and who is required to appear before the court by division (A) of this section is not practicable, the court may waive the appearance and release the person on bail in accordance with the court's schedule for bail set under division (C) of this section or, if the court has not set a schedule for bail under that division, on one or both of the following types of bail in an amount set by the court:

(a) A bail bond secured by a deposit of ten per cent of the amount of the bond in cash;

(b) A surety bond, a bond secured by real estate or securities as allowed by law, or the deposit of cash, at the option of the person.

(3) Division (A) of this section does not create a right in a person to appear before the court for the setting of bail or prohibit a court from requiring any person charged with an offense of violence who is not described in that division from appearing before the court for the setting of bail.

(E) As used in this section:

(1) "Controlled substance" has the same meaning as in section 3719.01 of the Revised Code.

(2) "Dangerous ordnance" and "deadly weapon" have the same meanings as in section 2923.11 of the Revised Code.

(2005 H 29, eff. 8-26-05; 2003 S 50, eff. 1-8-04; 1995 S 2, eff. 7-1-96; 1992 H 536, eff. 11-5-92; 1990 S 3; 1985 H 475)

2919.26. Temporary protection orders

(A) (1) Upon the filing of a complaint that alleges a violation of section 2909.06, 2909.07, 2911.12, or 2911.211 of the Revised Code if the alleged victim of the violation was a family or household member at the time of the violation, a violation of a municipal ordinance that is substantially similar to any of those sections if the alleged victim of the violation was a family or household member at the time of the violation, any offense of violence if the alleged victim of the offense was a family or household member at the time of the commission of the offense, or any sexually oriented offense if the alleged victim of the offense was a family or household member at the time of the commission of the offense, the complainant, the alleged victim, or a family or household member of an alleged victim may file, or, if in an emergency the alleged victim is unable to file, a person who made an arrest for the alleged violation or offense under section 2935.03 of the Revised Code may file on behalf of the alleged victim, a motion that requests the issuance of a temporary protection order as a pretrial condition of release of the alleged offender, in addition to any bail set under Criminal Rule 46. The motion shall be filed with the clerk of the court that has jurisdiction of the case at any time after the filing of the complaint.

(2) For purposes of section 2930.09 of the Revised Code, all stages of a proceeding arising out of a complaint alleging the commission of a violation, offense of violence, or sexually oriented offense described in division (A)(1) of this section, including all proceedings on a motion for a temporary protection order, are critical stages of the case, and a victim may be accompanied by a victim advocate or another person to provide support to the victim as provided in that section.

(B) The motion shall be prepared on a form that is provided by the clerk of the court, which form shall be substantially as follows:

"MOTION FOR TEMPORARY PROTECTION ORDER
.... Court
Name and address of court

State of Ohio
v. No.
....
....
Name of Defendant

(name of person), moves the court to issue a temporary protection order containing terms designed to ensure the safety and protection of the complainant, alleged victim, and other family or household members, in relation to the named defendant, pursuant to its authority to issue such an order under section 2919.26 of the Revised Code.

A complaint, a copy of which has been attached to this motion, has been filed in this court charging the named defendant with .... (name of the specified violation, the offense of violence, or sexually oriented offense charged) in circumstances in which the victim was a family or household member in violation of (section of the Revised Code designating the specified violation, offense of violence, or sexually oriented offense charged), or charging the named defendant with a violation of a municipal ordinance that is substantially similar to .... (section of the Revised Code designating the specified violation, offense of violence, or sexually oriented offense charged) involving a family or household member.

I understand that I must appear before the court, at a time set by the court within twenty-four hours after the filing of this motion, for a hearing on the motion or that, if I am unable to appear because of hospitalization or a medical condition resulting from the offense alleged in the complaint, a person who can provide information about my need for a temporary protection order must appear before the court in lieu of my appearing in court. I understand that any temporary protection order granted pursuant to this motion is a pretrial condition of release and is effective only until the disposition of the criminal proceeding arising out of the attached complaint, or the issuance of a civil protection order or the approval of a consent agreement, arising out of the same activities as those that were the basis of the complaint, under section 3113.31 of the Revised Code.

....
Signature of person
(or signature of the arresting officer who filed the motion on behalf of the alleged victim)

....
Address of person (or office address of the arresting officer who filed the motion on behalf of the alleged victim)"

(C) (1) As soon as possible after the filing of a motion that requests the issuance of a temporary protection order, but not later than twenty-four hours after the filing of the motion, the court shall conduct a hearing to determine whether to issue the order. The person who requested the order shall appear before the court and provide the court with the information that it requests concerning the basis of the motion. If the person who requested the order is unable to appear and if the court finds that the failure to appear is because of the person's hospitalization or medical condition resulting from the offense alleged in the complaint, another person who is able to provide the court with the information it requests may appear in lieu of the person who requested the order. If the court finds that the safety and protection of the complainant, alleged victim, or any other family or household member of the alleged victim may be impaired by the continued presence of the alleged offender, the court may issue a temporary protection order, as a pretrial condition of release, that contains terms designed to ensure the safety and protection of the complainant, alleged victim, or the family or household member, including a requirement that the alleged offender refrain from entering the residence, school, business, or place of employment of the complainant, alleged victim, or the family or household member. The court may include within a protection order issued under this section a term requiring that the alleged offender not remove, damage, hide, harm, or dispose of any companion animal owned or possessed by the complainant, alleged victim, or any other family or household member of the alleged victim, and may include within the order a term authorizing the complainant, alleged victim, or other family or household member of the alleged victim to remove a companion animal owned by the complainant, alleged victim, or other family or household member from the possession of the alleged offender.

(2) (a) If the court issues a temporary protection order that includes a requirement that the alleged offender refrain from entering the residence, school, business, or place of employment of the complainant, the alleged victim, or the family or household member, the order shall state clearly that the order cannot be waived or nullified by an invitation to the alleged offender from the complainant, alleged victim, or family or household member to enter the residence, school, business, or place of employment or by the alleged offender's entry into one of those places otherwise upon the consent of the complainant, alleged victim, or family or household member.

(b) Division (C)(2)(a) of this section does not limit any discretion of a court to determine that an alleged offender charged with a violation of section 2919.27 of the Revised Code, with a violation of a municipal ordinance substantially equivalent to that section, or with contempt of court, which charge is based on an alleged violation of a temporary protection order issued under this section, did not commit the violation or was not in contempt of court.

(D) (1) Upon the filing of a complaint that alleges a violation of section 2909.06, 2909.07, 2911.12, or 2911.211 of the Revised Code if the alleged victim of the violation was a family or household member at the time of the violation, a violation of a municipal ordinance that is substantially similar to any of those sections if the alleged victim of the violation was a family or household member at the time of the violation, any offense of violence if the alleged victim of the offense was a family or household member at the time of the commission of the offense, or any sexually oriented offense if the alleged victim of the offense was a family or household member at the time of the commission of the offense, the court, upon its own motion, may issue a temporary protection order as a pretrial condition of release if it finds that the safety and protection of the complainant, alleged victim, or other family or household member of the alleged offender may be impaired by the continued presence of the alleged offender.

(2) (a) If the court issues a temporary protection order under this section as an ex parte order, it shall conduct, as soon as possible after the issuance of the order, a hearing in the presence of the alleged offender not later than the next day on which the court is scheduled to conduct business after the day on which the alleged offender was arrested or at the time of the appearance of the alleged offender pursuant to summons to determine whether the order should remain in effect, be modified, or be revoked. The hearing shall be conducted under the standards set forth in division (C) of this section.

(b) If at a hearing conducted under division (D)(2)(a) of this section the court determines that the ex parte order that the court issued should be revoked, the court, on its own motion, shall order that the ex parte order that is revoked and all of the records pertaining to that ex parte order be expunged.

(3) An order issued under this section shall contain only those terms authorized in orders issued under division (C) of this section.

(4) If a municipal court or a county court issues a temporary protection order under this section and if, subsequent to the issuance of the order, the alleged offender who is the subject of the order is bound over to the court of common pleas

for prosecution of a felony arising out of the same activities as those that were the basis of the complaint upon which the order is based, notwithstanding the fact that the order was issued by a municipal court or county court, the order shall remain in effect, as though it were an order of the court of common pleas, while the charges against the alleged offender are pending in the court of common pleas, for the period of time described in division (E)(2) of this section, and the court of common pleas has exclusive jurisdiction to modify the order issued by the municipal court or county court. This division applies when the alleged offender is bound over to the court of common pleas as a result of the person waiving a preliminary hearing on the felony charge, as a result of the municipal court or county court having determined at a preliminary hearing that there is probable cause to believe that the felony has been committed and that the alleged offender committed it, as a result of the alleged offender having been indicted for the felony, or in any other manner.

(E) A temporary protection order that is issued as a pretrial condition of release under this section:

(1) Is in addition to, but shall not be construed as a part of, any bail set under Criminal Rule 46;

(2) Is effective only until the occurrence of either of the following:

(a) The disposition, by the court that issued the order or, in the circumstances described in division (D)(4) of this section, by the court of common pleas to which the alleged offender is bound over for prosecution, of the criminal proceeding arising out of the complaint upon which the order is based;

(b) The issuance of a protection order or the approval of a consent agreement, arising out of the same activities as those that were the basis of the complaint upon which the order is based, under section 3113.31 of the Revised Code.

(3) Shall not be construed as a finding that the alleged offender committed the alleged offense, and shall not be introduced as evidence of the commission of the offense at the trial of the alleged offender on the complaint upon which the order is based.

(F) A person who meets the criteria for bail under Criminal Rule 46 and who, if required to do so pursuant to that rule, executes or posts bond or deposits cash or securities as bail, shall not be held in custody pending a hearing before the court on a motion requesting a temporary protection order.

(G) (1) A copy of any temporary protection order that is issued under this section shall be issued by the court to the complainant, to the alleged victim, to the person who requested the order, to the defendant, and to all law enforcement agencies that have jurisdiction to enforce the order. The court shall direct that a copy of the order be delivered to the defendant on the same day that the order is entered. If a municipal court or a county court issues a temporary protection order under this section and if, subsequent to the issuance of the order, the defendant who is the subject of the order is bound over to the court of common pleas for prosecution as described in division (D)(4) of this section, the municipal court or county court shall direct that a copy of the order be delivered to the court of common pleas to which the defendant is bound over.

(2) Upon the issuance of a protection order under this section, the court shall provide the parties to the order with the following notice orally or by form:

"NOTICE

As a result of this protection order, it may be unlawful for you to possess or purchase a firearm, including a rifle, pistol, or revolver, or ammunition pursuant to federal law under 18 U.S.C. 922(g)(8) for the duration of this order. If you have any questions whether this law makes it illegal for you to possess or purchase a firearm or ammunition, you should consult an attorney."

(3) All law enforcement agencies shall establish and maintain an index for the temporary protection orders delivered to the agencies pursuant to division (G)(1) of this section. With respect to each order delivered, each agency shall note on the index, the date and time of the receipt of the order by the agency.

(4) A complainant, alleged victim, or other person who obtains a temporary protection order under this section may provide notice of the issuance of the temporary protection order to the judicial and law enforcement officials in any

county other than the county in which the order is issued by registering that order in the other county in accordance with division (N) of section 3113.31 of the Revised Code and filing a copy of the registered protection order with a law enforcement agency in the other county in accordance with that division.

(5) Any officer of a law enforcement agency shall enforce a temporary protection order issued by any court in this state in accordance with the provisions of the order, including removing the defendant from the premises, regardless of whether the order is registered in the county in which the officer's agency has jurisdiction as authorized by division (G)(4) of this section.

(H) Upon a violation of a temporary protection order, the court may issue another temporary protection order, as a pretrial condition of release, that modifies the terms of the order that was violated.

(I) (1) As used in divisions (I)(1) and (2) of this section, "defendant" means a person who is alleged in a complaint to have committed a violation, offense of violence, or sexually oriented offense of the type described in division (A) of this section.

(2) If a complaint is filed that alleges that a person committed a violation, offense of violence, or sexually oriented offense of the type described in division (A) of this section, the court may not issue a temporary protection order under this section that requires the complainant, the alleged victim, or another family or household member of the defendant to do or refrain from doing an act that the court may require the defendant to do or refrain from doing under a temporary protection order unless both of the following apply:

(a) The defendant has filed a separate complaint that alleges that the complainant, alleged victim, or other family or household member in question who would be required under the order to do or refrain from doing the act committed a violation or offense of violence of the type described in division (A) of this section.

(b) The court determines that both the complainant, alleged victim, or other family or household member in question who would be required under the order to do or refrain from doing the act and the defendant acted primarily as aggressors, that neither the complainant, alleged victim, or other family or household member in question who would be required under the order to do or refrain from doing the act nor the defendant acted primarily in self-defense, and, in accordance with the standards and criteria of this section as applied in relation to the separate complaint filed by the defendant, that it should issue the order to require the complainant, alleged victim, or other family or household member in question to do or refrain from doing the act.

(J) (1) Subject to division (J)(2) of this section and regardless of whether a protection order is issued or a consent agreement is approved by a court of another county or a court of another state, no court or unit of state or local government shall charge the movant any fee, cost, deposit, or money in connection with the filing of a motion pursuant to this section, in connection with the filing, issuance, registration, modification, enforcement, dismissal, withdrawal, or service of a protection order, consent agreement, or witness subpoena or for obtaining a certified copy of a protection order or consent agreement.

(2) Regardless of whether a protection order is issued or a consent agreement is approved pursuant to this section, if the defendant is convicted the court may assess costs against the defendant in connection with the filing, issuance, registration, modification, enforcement, dismissal, withdrawal, or service of a protection order, consent agreement, or witness subpoena or for obtaining a certified copy of a protection order or consent agreement.

(K) As used in this section:

(1) "Companion animal" has the same meaning as in section 959.131 of the Revised Code.

(2) "Sexually oriented offense" has the same meaning as in section 2950.01 of the Revised Code.

(3) "Victim advocate" means a person who provides support and assistance for a victim of an offense during court proceedings.

(4) "Expunge" has the same meaning as in section 2903.213 of the Revised Code.

(2018 H 1, eff. 7-6-18; 2017 H 49, eff. 9-29-17; 2014 S 177, eff. 3-23-15; 2014 H 309, eff. 9-17-

14; 2010 H 238, eff. 9-8-10; 2008 H 562, eff. 6-24-08; 2006 S 260, eff. 1-2-07; 2006 S 17, eff. 8-3-06; 2006 H 95, eff. 8-3-06; 2003 S 50, eff. 1-8-04; 2002 H 548, eff. 3-31-03; 1999 H 137, eff. 3-10-00; 1997 S 98, eff. 3-17-98; 1997 S 1, eff. 10-21-97; 1994 H 335, eff. 12-9-94; 1992 H 536, eff. 11-5-92; 1990 S 3; 1984 H 587; 1980 H 920; 1978 H 835)

2919.27. Violating a protection order, consent agreement, or anti-stalking protection order; protection order issued by court of another state

(A) No person shall recklessly violate the terms of any of the following:

(1) A protection order issued or consent agreement approved pursuant to section 2919.26 or 3113.31 of the Revised Code;

(2) A protection order issued pursuant to section 2151.34, 2903.213, or 2903.214 of the Revised Code;

(3) A protection order issued by a court of another state.

(B) (1) Whoever violates this section is guilty of violating a protection order.

(2) Except as otherwise provided in division (B)(3) or (4) of this section, violating a protection order is a misdemeanor of the first degree.

(3) Violating a protection order is a felony of the fifth degree if the offender previously has been convicted of, pleaded guilty to, or been adjudicated a delinquent child for any of the following:

(a) A violation of a protection order issued or consent agreement approved pursuant to section 2151.34, 2903.213, 2903.214, 2919.26, or 3113.31 of the Revised Code;

(b) Two or more violations of section 2903.21, 2903.211, 2903.22, or 2911.211 of the Revised Code, or any combination of those offenses, that involved the same person who is the subject of the protection order or consent agreement;

(c) One or more violations of this section.

(4) If the offender violates a protection order or consent agreement while committing a felony offense, violating a protection order is a felony of the third degree.

(5) If the protection order violated by the offender was an order issued pursuant to section 2151.34 or 2903.214 of the Revised Code that required electronic monitoring of the offender pursuant to that section, the court may require in addition to any other sentence imposed upon the offender that the offender be electronically monitored for a period not exceeding five years by a law enforcement agency designated by the court. If the court requires under this division that the offender be electronically monitored, unless the court determines that the offender is indigent, the court shall order that the offender pay the costs of the installation of the electronic monitoring device and the cost of monitoring the electronic monitoring device. If the court determines that the offender is indigent and subject to the maximum amount allowable and the rules promulgated by the attorney general under section 2903.214 of the Revised Code, the costs of the installation of the electronic monitoring device and the cost of monitoring the electronic monitoring device may be paid out of funds from the reparations fund created pursuant to section 2743.191 of the Revised Code. The total amount paid from the reparations fund created pursuant to section 2743.191 of the Revised Code for electronic monitoring under this section and sections 2151.34 and 2903.214 of the Revised Code shall not exceed three hundred thousand dollars per year.

(C) It is an affirmative defense to a charge under division (A)(3) of this section that the protection order issued by a court of another state does not comply with the requirements specified in 18 U.S.C. 2265(b) for a protection order that must be accorded full faith and credit by a court of this state or that it is not entitled to full faith and credit under 18 U.S.C. 2265(c).

(D) In a prosecution for a violation of this section, it is not necessary for the prosecution to prove that the protection order or consent agreement was served on the defendant if the prosecution proves that the defendant was shown the protection order or consent agreement or a copy of either or a judge, magistrate, or law enforcement officer informed the defendant that a protection order or consent agreement had been issued, and proves that the defendant recklessly violated the terms of the order or agreement.

(E) As used in this section, "protection order issued by a court of another state" means an injunction or another order issued by a criminal court of another state for the purpose of preventing violent or threatening acts or harassment against, contact or communication with, or physical proximity to another person, including a temporary order, and means an injunction or order of that nature issued by a civil court of another state, including a temporary order and a final order issued in an independent action or as a pendente lite order in a proceeding for other relief, if the court issued it in response to a complaint, petition, or motion filed by or on behalf of a person seeking protection. "Protection order issued by a court of another state" does not include an order for support or for custody of a child issued pursuant to the divorce and child custody laws of another state, except to the extent that the order for support or for custody of a child is entitled to full faith and credit under the laws of the United States.

(2017 S 7, eff. 9-27-17; 2010 H 10, eff. 6-17-10; 2008 H 471, eff. 4-7-09; 2003 S 50, eff. 1-8-04; 2002 H 548, eff. 3-31-03; 1998 H 302, eff. 7-29-98; 1997 S 1, eff. 10-21-97; 1995 S 2, eff. 7-1-96; 1994 H 335, eff. 12-9-94; 1992 H 536, eff. 11-5-92; 1985 H 475; 1984 H 587)

2919.271. Mental condition evaluations

(A) (1) (a) If a defendant is charged with a violation of section 2919.27 of the Revised Code or of a municipal ordinance that is substantially similar to that section, the court may order an evaluation of the mental condition of the defendant if the court determines that either of the following criteria apply:

(i) If the alleged violation is a violation of a protection order issued or consent agreement approved pursuant to section 2919.26 or 3113.31 of the Revised Code, that the violation allegedly involves conduct by the defendant that caused physical harm to the person or property of a family or household member covered by the order or agreement, or conduct by the defendant that caused a family or household member to believe that the defendant would cause physical harm to that member or that member's property.

(ii) If the alleged violation is a violation of a protection order issued pursuant to section 2903.213 or 2903.214 of the Revised Code or a protection order issued by a court of another state, that the violation allegedly involves conduct by the defendant that caused physical harm to the person or property of the person covered by the order, or conduct by the defendant that caused the person covered by the order to believe that the defendant would cause physical harm to that person or that person's property.

(b) If a defendant is charged with a violation of section 2903.211 of the Revised Code or of a municipal ordinance that is substantially similar to that section, the court may order an evaluation of the mental condition of the defendant.

(2) An evaluation ordered under division (A)(1) of this section shall be completed no later than thirty days from the date the order is entered pursuant to that division. In that order, the court shall do either of the following:

(a) Order that the evaluation of the mental condition of the defendant be preceded by an examination conducted either by a forensic center that is designated by the department of mental health and addiction services to conduct examinations and make evaluations of defendants charged with violations of section 2903.211 or 2919.27 of the Revised Code or of substantially similar municipal ordinances in the area in which the court is located, or by any other program or facility that is designated by the department of mental health and addiction services or the department of developmental disabilities to conduct examinations and make evaluations of defendants charged with violations of section 2903.211 or 2919.27 of the Revised Code or of substantially similar municipal ordinances, and that is operated by either department or is certified by either department as being in compliance with the standards established under division (B)(7) of section 5119.10 of the Revised Code or division (C) of section 5123.04 of the Revised Code.

(b) Designate a center, program, or facility other than one designated by the department of mental health and addiction services or the department of developmental disabilities, as described in division (A)(2)(a) of this section, to conduct the evaluation and preceding examination of the mental condition of the defendant.

Whether the court acts pursuant to division (A)(2)(a) or (b) of this section, the court may designate examiners other than the personnel of the center, program, facility, or department involved to make the evaluation and preceding examination of the mental condition of the defendant.

(B) If the court considers that additional evaluations of the mental condition of a defendant are necessary following the evaluation authorized by division (A) of this section, the court may order up to two additional similar evaluations. These evaluations shall be completed no later than thirty days from the date the applicable court order is entered. If more than one evaluation of the mental condition of the defendant is ordered under this division, the prosecutor and the defendant may recommend to the court an examiner whom each prefers to perform one of the evaluations and preceding examinations.

(C) (1) The court may order a defendant who has been released on bail to submit to an examination under division (A) or (B) of this section. The examination shall be conducted either at the detention facility in which the defendant would have been confined if the defendant had not been released on bail, or, if so specified by the center, program, facility, or examiners involved, at the premises of the center, program, or facility. Additionally, the examination shall be conducted at the times established by the examiners involved. If such a defendant refuses to submit to an examination or a complete examination as required by the court or the center, program, facility, or examiners involved, the court may amend the conditions of the bail of the defendant and order the sheriff to take the defendant into custody and deliver the defendant to the detention facility in which the defendant would have been confined if the defendant had not been released on bail, or, if so specified by the center, program, facility, or examiners involved, to the premises of the center, program, or facility, for purposes of the examination.

(2) A defendant who has not been released on bail shall be examined at the detention facility in which the defendant is confined or, if so specified by the center, program, facility, or examiners involved, at the premises of the center, program, or facility.

(D) The examiner of the mental condition of a defendant under division (A) or (B) of this section shall file a written report with the court within thirty days after the entry of an order for the evaluation of the mental condition of the defendant. The report shall contain the findings of the examiner; the facts in reasonable detail on which the findings are based; the opinion of the examiner as to the mental condition of the defendant; the opinion of the examiner as to whether the defendant represents a substantial risk of physical harm to other persons as manifested by evidence of recent homicidal or other violent behavior, evidence of recent threats that placed other persons in reasonable fear of violent behavior and serious physical harm, or evidence of present dangerousness; and the opinion of the examiner as to the types of treatment or counseling that the defendant needs. The court shall provide copies of the report to the prosecutor and defense counsel.

(E) The costs of any evaluation and preceding examination of a defendant that is ordered pursuant to division (A) or (B) of this section shall be taxed as court costs in the criminal case.

(F) If the examiner considers it necessary in order to make an accurate evaluation of the mental condition of a defendant, an examiner under division (A) or (B) of this section may request any family or household member of the defendant to provide the examiner with information. A family or household member may, but is not required to, provide information to the examiner upon receipt of the request.

(G) As used in this section:

(1) "Bail" includes a recognizance.

(2) "Examiner" means a psychiatrist, a licensed independent social worker who is employed by a forensic center that is certified as being in compliance with the standards established under division (B)(7) of section 5119.10 or division (C) of section 5123.04 of the Revised Code, a licensed professional clinical counselor who is employed at a forensic center that is certified as being in compliance with such standards, or a licensed clinical psychologist, except that in order to be an examiner, a licensed clinical psychologist shall meet the criteria of division (I) of section 5122.01 of the Revised Code or be employed to conduct examinations by the department of mental health and addiction services or by a forensic center certified as being in compliance with the standards established under division (B)(7) of section 5119.10 or division (C) of section 5123.04 of the Revised Code that is designated by the department of mental health and addiction services.

(3) "Family or household member" has the same meaning as in section 2919.25 of the Revised Code.

(4) "Prosecutor" has the same meaning as in section 2935.01 of the Revised Code.

(5) "Psychiatrist" and "licensed clinical psychologist" have the same meanings as in section 5122.01 of the Revised Code.

(6) "Protection order issued by a court of another state" has the same meaning as in section 2919.27 of the Revised Code.

(2013 H 83, eff. 3-20-14; 2013 H 59, eff. 9-29-13; 2011 H 153, eff. 9-29-11; 2009 S 79, eff. 10-6-09; 2001 H 94, eff. 9-5-01; 1999 H 202, eff. 2-9-00; 1998 H 302, eff. 7-29-98; 1997 S 1, eff. 10-21-97; 1996 S 223, eff. 3-18-97; 1995 S 2, eff. 7-1-96; 1985 H 475, eff. 3-7-86)

2919.272. Protection order issued by court of another state; procedure for registration in Ohio; registry of orders by law enforcement agencies

(A) As used in this section, "protection order issued by a court of another state" has the same meaning as in section 2919.27 of the Revised Code.

(B) A person who has obtained a protection order issued by a court of another state may provide notice of the issuance of the order to judicial and law enforcement officials in any county of this state by registering the order in that county and filing a copy of the registered order with a law enforcement agency in that county. To register the order, the person shall obtain a certified copy of the order from the clerk of the court that issued the order and present that certified copy to the clerk of the court of common pleas or the clerk of a municipal court or county court in the county in which the order is to be registered. Upon accepting the certified copy of the order for registration, the clerk shall place an endorsement of registration on the order and give the person a copy of the order that bears proof of registration. The person then may file with a law enforcement agency in that county a copy of the order that bears proof of registration.

(C) The clerk of each court of common pleas and the clerk of each municipal court and county court shall maintain a registry of certified copies of protection orders issued by courts of another state that have been registered with the clerk. Each law enforcement agency shall establish and maintain a registry for protection orders delivered to the agency pursuant to this section. The agency shall note in the registry the date and time that the agency received an order.

(D) An officer of a law enforcement agency shall enforce a protection order issued by a court of another state in accordance with the provisions of the order, including removing the person allegedly violating the order from the premises, regardless of whether the order is registered as authorized by division (B) of this section in the county in which the officer's agency has jurisdiction.

(E) (1) Subject to division (E)(2) of this section and regardless of whether a protection order is issued or a consent agreement is approved by a court of another county or a court of another state, no court or unit of state or local government shall charge a person who registers and files an order any fee, cost, deposit, or money in connection with the filing, issuance, registration, modification, enforcement, dismissal, withdrawal, or service of a protection order, consent agreement, or witness subpoena or for obtaining a certified copy of a protection order or consent agreement, including a protection order issued by a court of another state.

(2) Regardless of whether a protection order is issued or a consent agreement is approved pursuant to this section, the court may assess costs against the person who is subject to a registered and filed order in connection with the filing, issuance, registration, modification, enforcement, dismissal, withdrawal, or service of a protection order, consent agreement, or witness subpoena or for obtaining a certified copy of a protection order or consent agreement.

(2014 H 309, eff. 9-17-14; 2002 H 548, eff. 3-31-03; 1997 S 1, eff. 10-21-97)

CHAPTER 2935 ARREST, CITATION, AND DISPOSITION ALTERNATIVES

Section

2935.03. Arrest and detention until warrant can be obtained

(A) (1) A sheriff, deputy sheriff, marshal, deputy marshal, municipal police officer, township constable, police officer of a township or joint police district, member of a police force employed by a metropolitan housing authority under division (D) of section 3735.31 of the Revised Code, member of a police force employed by a regional transit authority under division (Y) of section 306.35 of the Revised Code, state university law enforcement officer appointed under section 3345.04 of the Revised Code, veterans' home police officer appointed under section 5907.02 of the Revised Code, special police officer employed by a port authority under section 4582.04 or 4582.28 of the Revised Code, or a special police officer employed by a municipal corporation at a municipal airport, or other municipal air navigation facility, that has scheduled operations, as defined in section 119.3 of Title 14 of the Code of Federal Regulations, 14 C.F.R. 119.3, as amended, and that is required to be under a security program and is governed by aviation security rules of the transportation security administration of the United States department of transportation as provided in Parts 1542. and 1544. of Title 49 of the Code of Federal Regulations, as amended, shall arrest and detain, until a warrant can be obtained, a person found violating, within the limits of the political subdivision, metropolitan housing authority housing project, regional transit authority facilities or areas of a municipal corporation that have been agreed to by a regional transit authority and a municipal corporation located within its territorial jurisdiction, college, university, veterans' home operated under Chapter 5907. of the Revised Code, port authority, or municipal airport or other municipal air navigation facility, in which the peace officer is appointed, employed, or elected, a law of this state, an ordinance of a municipal corporation, or a resolution of a township.

(2) A peace officer of the department of natural resources, a state fire marshal law enforcement officer described in division (A)(23) of section 109.71 of the Revised Code, or an individual designated to perform law enforcement duties under section 511.232, 1545.13, or 6101.75 of the Revised Code shall arrest and detain, until a warrant can be obtained, a person found violating, within the limits of the peace officer's, state fire marshal law enforcement officer's, or individual's territorial jurisdiction, a law of this state.

(3) The house sergeant at arms, if the house sergeant at arms has arrest authority pursuant to division (E)(1) of section 101.311 of the Revised Code, and an assistant house sergeant at arms shall arrest and detain, until a warrant can be obtained, a person found violating, within the limits of the sergeant at arms's or assistant sergeant at arms's territorial jurisdiction specified in division (D)(1)(a) of section 101.311 of the Revised Code or while providing security pursuant to division (D)(1)(f) of section 101.311 of the Revised Code, a law of this state, an ordinance of a municipal corporation, or a resolution of a township.

(4) The senate sergeant at arms and an assistant senate sergeant at arms shall arrest and detain, until a warrant can be obtained, a person found violating, within the limits of the sergeant at arms's or assistant sergeant at arms's territorial jurisdiction specified in division (B) of section 101.312 of the Revised Code, a law of this state, an ordinance of a municipal corporation, or a resolution of a township.

(B) (1) When there is reasonable ground to believe that an offense of violence, the offense of criminal child enticement as defined in section 2905.05 of the Revised Code, the offense of public indecency as defined in section 2907.09 of the Revised Code, the offense of domestic violence as defined in section 2919.25 of the Revised Code, the offense of violating a protection order as defined in section 2919.27 of the Revised Code, the offense of menacing by stalking as defined in section 2903.211 of the Revised Code, the offense of aggravated trespass as defined in section 2911.211 of the Revised Code, a theft offense as defined in section 2913.01 of the Revised Code, or a felony drug abuse offense as defined in section 2925.01 of the Revised Code, has been committed within the limits of the political subdivision, metropolitan housing authority housing project, regional transit authority facilities or those areas of a municipal corporation that have been agreed to by a regional transit authority and a municipal corporation located within its territorial jurisdiction, college, university, veterans' home operated under Chapter 5907. of the Revised Code, port authority, or municipal airport or other municipal air navigation facility, in which the peace officer is appointed, employed, or elected or within the limits of the territorial jurisdiction of the peace officer, a peace officer described in division (A) of this section may arrest and detain until a warrant can be obtained any person who the peace officer has reasonable cause to believe is guilty of the violation.

(2) For purposes of division (B)(1) of this section, the execution of any of the following constitutes reasonable ground to believe that the offense alleged in the statement was committed and reasonable cause to believe that the person alleged in the statement to have committed the offense is guilty of the violation:

(a) A written statement by a person alleging that an alleged offender has committed the offense of menacing by stalking or aggravated trespass;

(b) A written statement by the administrator of the interstate compact on mental health appointed under section 5119.71 of the Revised Code alleging that a person who had been hospitalized, institutionalized, or confined in any facility under an order made pursuant to or under authority of section 2945.37, 2945.371, 2945.38, 2945.39, 2945.40, 2945.401, or 2945.402 of the Revised Code has escaped from the facility, from confinement in a vehicle for transportation to or from the facility, or from supervision by an employee of the facility that is incidental to hospitalization, institutionalization, or confinement in the facility and that occurs outside of the facility, in violation of section 2921.34 of the Revised Code;

(c) A written statement by the administrator of any facility in which a person has been hospitalized, institutionalized, or confined under an order made pursuant to or under authority of section 2945.37, 2945.371, 2945.38, 2945.39, 2945.40, 2945.401, or 2945.402 of the Revised Code alleging that the person has escaped from the facility, from confinement in a vehicle for transportation to or from the facility, or from supervision by an employee of the facility that is incidental to hospitalization, institutionalization, or confinement in the facility and that occurs outside of the facility, in violation of section 2921.34 of the Revised Code.

(3) (a) For purposes of division (B)(1) of this section, a peace officer described in division (A) of this section has reasonable grounds to believe that the offense of domestic violence or the offense of violating a protection order has been committed and reasonable cause to believe that a particular person is guilty of committing the offense if any of the following occurs:

(i) A person executes a written statement alleging that the person in question has committed the offense of domestic violence or the offense of violating a protection order against the person who executes the statement or against a child of the person who executes the statement.

(ii) No written statement of the type described in division (B)(3)(a)(i) of this section is executed, but the peace officer, based upon the peace officer's own knowledge and observation of the facts and circumstances of the alleged incident of the offense of domestic violence or the alleged incident of the offense of violating a protection order or based upon any other information, including, but not limited to, any reasonably trustworthy information given to the peace officer by the alleged victim of the alleged incident of the offense or any witness of the alleged incident of the offense, concludes that there are reasonable grounds to believe that the offense of domestic violence or the offense of violating a protection order has been committed and reasonable cause to believe that the person in question is guilty of committing the offense.

(iii) No written statement of the type described in division (B)(3)(a)(i) of this section is executed, but the peace officer witnessed the person in question commit the offense of domestic violence or the offense of violating a protection order.

(b) If pursuant to division (B)(3)(a) of this section a peace officer has reasonable grounds to believe that the offense of domestic violence or the offense of violating a protection order has been committed and reasonable cause to believe that a particular person is guilty of committing the offense, it is the preferred course of action in this state that the officer arrest and detain that person pursuant to division (B)(1) of this section until a warrant can be obtained.

If pursuant to division (B)(3)(a) of this section a peace officer has reasonable grounds to believe that the offense of domestic violence or the offense of violating a protection order has been committed and reasonable cause to believe that family or household members have committed the offense against each other, it is the preferred course of action in this state that the officer, pursuant to division (B)(1) of this section, arrest and detain until a warrant can be obtained the family or household member who committed the offense and whom the officer has reasonable cause to believe is the primary physical aggressor. There is no preferred course of action in this state regarding any other family or household member who committed the offense and whom the officer does not have reasonable cause to believe is the primary physical aggressor, but, pursuant to division (B)(1) of this section, the peace officer may arrest and detain until a warrant can be obtained any other family or household member who committed the offense and whom the officer does not have reasonable cause to believe is the primary physical aggressor.

(c) If a peace officer described in division (A) of this section does not arrest and detain a person whom the officer has reasonable cause to believe committed the offense of domestic violence or the offense of violating a protection order when it is the preferred course of action in this state pursuant to division (B)(3)(b) of this section that the officer arrest that person, the officer shall articulate in the written report of the incident required by section 2935.032 of the Revised Code a clear statement of the officer's reasons for not arresting and detaining that person until a warrant can be obtained.

(d) In determining for purposes of division (B)(3)(b) of this section which family or household member is the primary physical aggressor in a situation in which family or household members have committed the offense of domestic violence or the offense of violating a protection order against each other, a peace officer described in division (A) of this section, in addition to any other relevant circumstances, should consider all of the following:

(i) Any history of domestic violence or of any other violent acts by either person involved in the alleged offense that the officer reasonably can ascertain;

(ii) If violence is alleged, whether the alleged violence was caused by a person acting in self-defense;

(iii) Each person's fear of physical harm, if any, resulting from the other person's threatened use of force against any person or resulting from the other person's use or history of the use of force against any person, and the reasonableness of that fear;

(iv) The comparative severity of any injuries suffered by the persons involved in the alleged offense.

(e) (i) A peace officer described in division (A) of this section shall not require, as a prerequisite to arresting or charging a person who has committed the offense of domestic violence or the offense of violating a protection order, that the victim of the offense specifically consent to the filing of charges against the person who has committed the offense or sign a complaint against the person who has committed the offense.

(ii) If a person is arrested for or charged with committing the offense of domestic violence or the offense of violating a protection order and if the victim of the offense does not cooperate with the involved law enforcement or prosecuting authorities in the prosecution of the offense or, subsequent to the arrest or the filing of the charges, informs the involved law enforcement or prosecuting authorities that the victim does not wish the prosecution of the offense to continue or wishes to drop charges against the alleged offender relative to the offense, the involved prosecuting authorities, in determining whether to continue with the prosecution of the offense or whether to dismiss charges against the alleged offender relative to the offense and notwithstanding the victim's failure to cooperate or the victim's wishes, shall consider all facts and circumstances that are relevant to the offense, including, but not limited to, the statements and observations of the peace officers who responded to the incident that resulted in the arrest or filing of the charges and of all witnesses to that incident.

(f) In determining pursuant to divisions (B)(3)(a) to (g) of this section whether to arrest a person pursuant to division (B)(1) of this section, a peace officer described in division (A) of this section shall not consider as a factor any possible shortage of cell space at the detention facility to which the person will be taken subsequent to the person's arrest or any possibility that the person's arrest might cause, contribute to, or exacerbate overcrowding at that detention facility or at any other detention facility.

(g) If a peace officer described in division (A) of this section intends pursuant to divisions (B)(3)(a) to (g) of this section to arrest a person pursuant to division (B)(1) of this section and if the officer is unable to do so because the person is not present, the officer promptly shall seek a warrant for the arrest of the person.

(h) If a peace officer described in division (A) of this section responds to a report of an alleged incident of the offense of domestic violence or an alleged incident of the offense of violating a protection order and if the circumstances of the incident involved the use or threatened use of a deadly weapon or any person involved in the incident brandished a deadly weapon during or in relation to the incident, the deadly weapon that was used, threatened to be used, or brandished constitutes contraband, and, to the extent possible, the officer shall seize the deadly weapon as contraband pursuant to Chapter 2981. of the Revised Code. Upon the seizure of a deadly weapon pursuant to division (B)(3)(h) of this section, section 2981.12 of the Revised Code shall apply regarding the treatment and disposition of the deadly weapon. For purposes of that section, the "underlying criminal offense" that was the basis of the seizure of a deadly weapon under division (B)(3)(h) of this section and to which the deadly weapon had a relationship is any of the following that is applicable:

(i) The alleged incident of the offense of domestic violence or the alleged incident of the offense of violating a protection order to which the officer who seized the deadly weapon responded;

(ii) Any offense that arose out of the same facts and circumstances as the report of the alleged incident of the offense of domestic violence or the alleged incident of the offense of violating a protection order to which the officer who seized the deadly weapon responded.

(4) If, in the circumstances described in divisions (B)(3)(a) to (g) of this section, a peace officer described in division (A) of this section arrests and detains a person pursuant to division (B)(1) of this section, or if, pursuant to division (B)(3)(h) of this section, a peace officer described in division (A) of this section seizes a deadly weapon, the officer, to the extent described in and in accordance with section 9.86 or 2744.03 of the Revised Code, is immune in any civil action for damages for injury, death, or loss to person or property that arises from or is related to the arrest and detention or the seizure.

(C) When there is reasonable ground to believe that a violation of division (A)(1), (2), (3), (4), or (5) of section 4506.15 or a violation of section 4511.19 of the Revised Code has been committed by a person operating a motor vehicle subject to regulation by the public utilities commission of Ohio under Title XLIX of the Revised Code, a peace officer with authority to enforce that provision of law may stop or detain the person whom the officer has reasonable cause to believe was operating the motor vehicle in violation of the division or section and, after investigating the circumstances surrounding the operation of the vehicle, may arrest and detain the person.

(D) If a sheriff, deputy sheriff, marshal, deputy marshal, municipal police officer, member of a police force employed by a metropolitan housing authority under division (D) of section 3735.31 of the Revised Code, member of a police force employed by a regional transit authority under division (Y) of section 306.35 of the Revised Code, special police officer employed by a port authority under section 4582.04 or 4582.28 of the Revised Code, special police officer employed by a municipal corporation at a municipal airport or other municipal air navigation facility described in division (A) of this section, township constable, police officer of a township or joint police district, state university law enforcement officer appointed under section 3345.04 of the Revised Code, peace officer of the department of natural resources, individual designated to perform law enforcement duties under section 511.232, 1545.13, or 6101.75 of the Revised Code, the house sergeant at arms if the house sergeant at arms has arrest authority pursuant to division (E)(1) of section 101.311 of the Revised Code, or an assistant house sergeant at arms is authorized by division (A) or (B) of this section to arrest and detain, within the limits of the political subdivision, metropolitan housing authority housing project, regional transit authority facilities or those areas of a municipal corporation that have been agreed to by a regional transit authority and a municipal corporation located within its territorial jurisdiction, port authority, municipal airport or other municipal air navigation facility, college, or university in which the officer is appointed, employed, or elected or within the limits of the territorial jurisdiction of the peace officer, a person until a warrant can be obtained, the peace officer, outside the limits of that territory, may pursue, arrest, and detain that person until a warrant can be obtained if all of the following apply:

(1) The pursuit takes place without unreasonable delay after the offense is committed;

(2) The pursuit is initiated within the limits of the political subdivision, metropolitan housing authority housing project, regional transit authority facilities or those areas of a municipal corporation that have been agreed to by a regional transit authority and a municipal corporation located within its territorial jurisdiction, port authority, municipal airport or other municipal air navigation facility, college, or university in which the peace officer is appointed, employed, or elected or within the limits of the territorial jurisdiction of the peace officer;

(3) The offense involved is a felony, a misdemeanor of the first degree or a substantially equivalent municipal ordinance, a misdemeanor of the second degree or a substantially equivalent municipal ordinance, or any offense for which points are chargeable pursuant to section 4510.036 of the Revised Code.

(E) In addition to the authority granted under division (A) or (B) of this section:

(1) A sheriff or deputy sheriff may arrest and detain, until a warrant can be obtained, any person found violating section 4503.11, 4503.21, or 4549.01, sections 4549.08 to 4549.12, section 4549.62, or Chapter 4511. or 4513. of the Revised Code on the portion of any street or highway that is located immediately adjacent to the boundaries of the county in which the sheriff or deputy sheriff is elected or appointed.

(2) A member of the police force of a township police district created under section 505.48 of the Revised Code, a member of the police force of a joint police district created under section 505.482 of the Revised Code, or a township constable appointed in accordance with section 509.01 of the Revised Code, who has received a certificate from the Ohio peace officer training commission under section 109.75 of the Revised Code, may arrest and detain, until a warrant can be obtained, any person found violating any section or chapter of the Revised Code listed in division (E)(1) of this section, other than sections 4513.33 and 4513.34 of the Revised Code, on the portion of any street or highway that is located immediately adjacent to the boundaries of the township police district or joint police district, in the case of a member of a township police district or joint police district police force, or the unincorporated territory of the township, in the case of a township constable. However, if the population of the township that created the township police district served by the member's police force, or the townships and municipal corporations that created the joint police district served by the member's police force, or the township that is served by the township constable, is sixty thousand or less, the member of the township police district or joint police district police force or the township constable may not make an arrest under division (E)(2) of this section on a state highway that is included as part of the interstate system.

(3) A police officer or village marshal appointed, elected, or employed by a municipal corporation may arrest and detain, until a warrant can be obtained, any person found violating any section or chapter of the Revised Code listed in division (E)(1) of this section on the portion of any street or highway that is located immediately adjacent to the boundaries of the municipal corporation in which the police officer or village marshal is appointed, elected, or employed.

(4) A peace officer of the department of natural resources, a state fire marshal law enforcement officer described in division (A)(23) of section 109.71 of the Revised Code, or an individual designated to perform law enforcement duties under section 511.232, 1545.13, or 6101.75 of the Revised Code may arrest and detain, until a warrant can be obtained, any person found violating any section or chapter of the Revised Code listed in division (E)(1) of this section, other than sections 4513.33 and 4513.34 of the Revised Code, on the portion of any street or

highway that is located immediately adjacent to the boundaries of the lands and waters that constitute the territorial jurisdiction of the peace officer or state fire marshal law enforcement officer.

(F) (1) A department of mental health and addiction services special police officer or a department of developmental disabilities special police officer may arrest without a warrant and detain until a warrant can be obtained any person found committing on the premises of any institution under the jurisdiction of the particular department a misdemeanor under a law of the state.

A department of mental health and addiction services special police officer or a department of developmental disabilities special police officer may arrest without a warrant and detain until a warrant can be obtained any person who has been hospitalized, institutionalized, or confined in an institution under the jurisdiction of the particular department pursuant to or under authority of section 2945.37, 2945.371, 2945.38, 2945.39, 2945.40, 2945.401, or 2945.402 of the Revised Code and who is found committing on the premises of any institution under the jurisdiction of the particular department a violation of section 2921.34 of the Revised Code that involves an escape from the premises of the institution.

(2) (a) If a department of mental health and addiction services special police officer or a department of developmental disabilities special police officer finds any person who has been hospitalized, institutionalized, or confined in an institution under the jurisdiction of the particular department pursuant to or under authority of section 2945.37, 2945.371, 2945.38, 2945.39, 2945.40, 2945.401, or 2945.402 of the Revised Code committing a violation of section 2921.34 of the Revised Code that involves an escape from the premises of the institution, or if there is reasonable ground to believe that a violation of section 2921.34 of the Revised Code has been committed that involves an escape from the premises of an institution under the jurisdiction of the department of mental health and addiction services or the department of developmental disabilities and if a department of mental health and addiction services special police officer or a department of developmental disabilities special police officer has reasonable cause to believe that a particular person who has been hospitalized, institutionalized, or confined in the institution pursuant to or under authority of section 2945.37, 2945.371, 2945.38, 2945.39, 2945.40, 2945.401, or 2945.402 of the Revised Code is guilty of the violation, the special police officer, outside of the premises of the institution, may pursue, arrest, and detain that person for that violation of section 2921.34 of the Revised Code, until a warrant can be obtained, if both of the following apply:

(i) The pursuit takes place without unreasonable delay after the offense is committed;

(ii) The pursuit is initiated within the premises of the institution from which the violation of section 2921.34 of the Revised Code occurred.

(b) For purposes of division (F)(2)(a) of this section, the execution of a written statement by the administrator of the institution in which a person had been hospitalized, institutionalized, or confined pursuant to or under authority of section 2945.37, 2945.371, 2945.38, 2945.39, 2945.40, 2945.401, or 2945.402 of the Revised Code alleging that the person has escaped from the premises of the institution in violation of section 2921.34 of the Revised Code constitutes reasonable ground to believe that the violation was committed and reasonable cause to believe that the person alleged in the statement to have committed the offense is guilty of the violation.

(G) As used in this section:

(1) A "department of mental health and addiction services special police officer" means a special police officer of the department of mental health and addiction services designated under section 5119.08 of the Revised Code who is certified by the Ohio peace officer training commission under section 109.77 of the Revised Code as having successfully completed an approved peace officer basic training program.

(2) A "department of developmental disabilities special police officer" means a special police officer of the department of developmental disabilities designated under section 5123.13 of the Revised Code who is certified by the Ohio peace officer training council under section 109.77 of the Revised Code as having successfully completed an approved peace officer basic training program.

(3) "Deadly weapon" has the same meaning as in section 2923.11 of the Revised Code.

(4) "Family or household member" has the same meaning as in section 2919.25 of the Revised Code.

(5) "Street" or "highway" has the same meaning as in section 4511.01 of the Revised Code.

(6) "Interstate system" has the same meaning as in section 5516.01 of the Revised Code.

(7) "Peace officer of the department of natural resources" means an employee of the department of natural resources who is a natural resources law enforcement staff officer designated pursuant to section 1501.013 of the Revised Code, a forest-fire investigator appointed pursuant to section 1503.09 of the Revised Code, a natural resources officer appointed pursuant to section 1501.24 of the Revised Code, or a wildlife officer designated pursuant to section 1531.13 of the Revised Code.

(8) "Portion of any street or highway" means all lanes of the street or highway irrespective of direction of travel, including designated turn lanes, and any berm, median, or shoulder.

(2016 S 293, eff. 9-14-16; 2013 H 59, eff. 9-29-13; 2012 H 487, eff. 9-10-12; 2011 H 153, eff. 9-29-11; 2009 S 79, eff. 10-6-09; 2008 H 562, eff. 9-23-08; 2007 H 119, eff. 9-29-07; 2006 H 241, eff. 7-1-07; 2005 H 68, eff. 6-29-05; 2002 H 675, § 1.04, eff. 1-1-04; 2002 H 675, § 1.01, eff. 3-14-03; 2002 H 545, eff. 3-19-03; 2002 S 123, eff. 1-1-04; 2000 S 317, eff. 3-22-01; 2000 S 137, eff. 5-17-00; 1998 S 187, eff. 3-18-99; 1997 S 1, eff. 10-21-97; 1996 S 285, eff. 7-1-97; 1996 H 670, eff. 12-2-96; 1996 S 269, eff. 7-1-96; 1995 S 2, eff. 7-1-96; 1994 H 335, eff. 12-9-94; 1994 S 82, eff. 5-4-94; 1993 H 42, eff. 2-9-94; 1992 H 536; 1991 H 77; 1990 H 669, H 88; 1988 H 708, § 1)

2935.032. Domestic violence arrest policies

(A) Not later than ninety days after the effective date of this amendment, each agency, instrumentality, or political subdivision that is served by any peace officer described in division (B)(1) of section 2935.03 of the Revised Code shall adopt, in accordance with division (E) of this section, written policies, written procedures implementing the policies, and other written procedures for the peace officers who serve it to follow in implementing division (B)(3) of section 2935.03 of the Revised Code and for their appropriate response to each report of an alleged incident of the offense of domestic violence or an alleged incident of the offense of violating a protection order. The policies and procedures shall conform to and be consistent with the provisions of divisions (B)(1) and (B)(3) of section 2935.03 of the Revised Code and divisions (B) to (D) of this section. Each policy adopted under this division shall include, but not be limited to, all of the following:

(1) Provisions specifying that, if a peace officer who serves the agency, instrumentality, or political subdivision responds to an alleged incident of the offense of domestic violence, an alleged incident of the offense of violating a protection order, or an alleged incident of any other offense, both of the following apply:

(a) If the officer determines that there are reasonable grounds to believe that a person knowingly caused serious physical harm to another or to another's unborn or knowingly caused or attempted to cause physical harm to another or to another's unborn by means of a deadly weapon or dangerous ordnance, then, regardless of whether the victim of the offense was a family or household member of the offender, the officer shall treat the incident as felonious assault, shall consider the offender to have committed and the victim to have been the victim of felonious assault, shall consider the offense that was committed to have been felonious assault in determining the manner in which the offender should be treated, and shall comply with whichever of the following is applicable:

(i) Unless the officer has reasonable cause to believe that, during the incident, the offender who committed the felonious assault and one or more other persons committed offenses against each other, the officer shall arrest the offender who committed the felonious assault pursuant to section 2935.03 of the Revised Code and shall detain that offender pursuant to that section until a warrant can be obtained, and the arrest shall be for felonious assault.

(ii) If the officer has reasonable cause to believe that, during the incident, the offender who committed the felonious assault and one or more other persons committed offenses against each other, the officer shall determine in accordance with division (B)(3)(d) of section 2935.03 of the Revised Code which of those persons is the primary physical aggressor. If the offender who committed the felonious assault is the primary physical aggressor, the officer shall arrest that offender for felonious assault pursuant to section 2935.03 of the Revised Code and shall detain that offender pursuant to that section until a warrant can be obtained, and the officer is not required to arrest but may arrest pursuant to section 2935.03 of the Revised Code any other person who committed an offense but who is not the primary physical aggressor. If the offender who committed the felonious assault is not the primary physical aggressor, the officer is not required to arrest that offender or any other person who committed an offense during the incident but may arrest any of them pursuant to section 2935.03 of the Revised Code and detain them pursuant to that section until a warrant can be obtained.

(b) If the officer determines that there are reasonable grounds to believe that a person, while under the influence of sudden passion or in a sudden fit of rage, either of which is brought on by serious provocation occasioned by the victim that is reasonably sufficient to incite the person into using deadly force, knowingly caused serious physical harm to another or to another's unborn or knowingly caused or attempted to cause physical harm to another or to another's unborn by means of a deadly weapon or dangerous ordnance, then, regardless of whether the victim of the offense was a family or household member of the offender, the officer shall treat the incident as aggravated assault, shall consider the offender to have committed and the victim to have been the victim of aggravated assault, shall consider the offense that was committed to have been aggravated assault in determining the manner in which the offender should be treated, and shall comply with whichever of the following is applicable:

(i) Unless the officer has reasonable cause to believe that, during the incident, the offender who committed the aggravated assault and one or more other persons committed offenses against each other, the officer shall arrest the offender who committed the aggravated assault pursuant to section 2935.03 of the Revised Code and shall detain that offender pursuant to that section until a warrant can be obtained, and the arrest shall be for aggravated assault.

(ii) If the officer has reasonable cause to believe that, during the incident, the offender who committed the aggravated assault and one or more other persons committed offenses against each other, the officer shall determine in accordance with division (B)(3)(d) of section 2935.03 of the Revised Code which of those persons is the primary physical aggressor. If the offender who committed the aggravated assault is the primary physical aggressor, the officer shall arrest that offender for aggravated assault pursuant to section 2935.03 of the Revised Code and shall detain that offender pursuant to that section until a warrant can be obtained, and the officer is not required to arrest but may arrest pursuant to section 2935.03 of the Revised Code any other person who committed an offense but who is not the primary physical aggressor. If the offender who committed the aggravated assault is not the primary physical aggressor, the officer is not required to arrest that offender or any other person who committed an offense during the incident but may arrest any of them pursuant to section 2935.03 of the Revised Code and detain them pursuant to that section until a warrant can be obtained.

(2) Provisions requiring the peace officers who serve the agency, instrumentality, or political subdivision to do all of the following:

(a) Respond without undue delay to a report of an alleged incident of the offense of domestic violence or the offense of violating a protection order;

(b) If the alleged offender has been granted pretrial release from custody on a prior charge of the offense of domestic violence or the offense of violating a protection order and has violated one or more conditions of that pretrial release, document the facts and circumstances of the violation in the report to the law enforcement agency that the peace officer makes pursuant to division (D) of this section;

(c) Separate the victim of the offense of domestic violence or the offense of violating a protection order and the alleged offender, conduct separate interviews with the victim and the alleged offender in separate locations, and take a written statement from the victim that indicates the frequency and severity of any prior incidents of physical abuse of the victim by the alleged offender, the number of times the victim has called peace officers for assistance, and the disposition of those calls, if known;

(d) Comply with divisions (B)(1) and (B)(3) of section 2935.03 of the Revised Code and with divisions (B), (C), and (D) of this section.

(3) Sanctions to be imposed upon a peace officer who serves the agency, instrumentality, or political subdivision and who fails to comply with any provision in the policy or with division (B)(1) or (B)(3) of section 2935.03 of the Revised Code or division (B), (C), or (D) of this section.

(4) Examples of reasons that a peace officer may consider for not arresting and detaining until a warrant can be obtained a person who allegedly committed the offense of domestic violence or the offense of violating a protection order when it is the preferred course of action in this state that the officer arrest the alleged offender, as described in division (B)(3)(b) of section 2935.03 of the Revised Code.

(B) (1) Nothing in this section or in division (B)(1) or (B)(3) of section 2935.03 of the Revised Code precludes an agency, instrumentality, or political subdivision that is served by any peace officer described in division (B)(1) of section 2935.03 of the Revised Code from including in the policy it adopts under division (A) of this section either of the following types of provisions:

(a) A provision that requires the peace officers who serve it, if they have reasonable grounds to believe that the offense of domestic violence or the offense of violating a protection order has been committed within the limits of the jurisdiction of the agency, instrumentality, or political subdivision and reasonable cause to believe that a particular person committed the offense, to arrest the alleged offender;

(b) A provision that does not require the peace officers who serve it, if they have reasonable grounds to believe that the offense of domestic violence or the offense of violating a protection order has been committed within the limits of the jurisdiction of the agency, instrumentality, or political subdivision and reasonable cause to believe that a particular person committed the offense, to arrest the alleged offender, but that grants the officers less discretion in those circumstances in deciding whether to arrest the alleged offender than peace officers are granted by divisions (B)(1) and (B)(3) of section 2935.03 of the Revised Code.

(2) If an agency, instrumentality, or political subdivision that is served by any peace officer described in division (B)(1) of section 2935.03 of the Revised Code includes in the policy it adopts under division (A) of this section a provision of the type described in division (B)(1)(a) or (b) of this section, the peace officers who serve the agency, instrumentality, or political subdivision shall comply with the provision in making arrests authorized under division (B)(1) of section 2935.03 of the Revised Code.

(C) When a peace officer described in division (B)(1) of section 2935.03 of the Revised Code investigates a report of an alleged incident of the offense of domestic violence or an alleged incident of the offense of violating a protection order, the officer shall do all of the following:

(1) Complete a domestic violence report in accordance with division (D) of this section;

(2) Advise the victim of the availability of a temporary protection order pursuant to section 2919.26 of the Revised Code or a protection order or consent agreement pursuant to section 3113.31 of the Revised Code;

(3) Give the victim the officer's name, the officer's badge number if the officer has a badge and the badge has a number, the report number for the incident if a report number is available at the time of the officer's investigation, a telephone number that the victim can call for information about the case, the telephone number of a domestic violence shelter in the area, and information on any local victim advocate program.

(D) A peace officer who investigates a report of an alleged incident of the offense of domestic violence or an alleged incident of the offense of violating a protection order shall make a written report of the incident whether or not an arrest is made.

The report shall document the officer's observations of the victim and the alleged offender, any visible injuries of the victim or alleged offender, any weapons at the scene, the actions of the alleged offender, any statements made by the victim or witnesses, and any other significant facts or circumstances. If the officer does not arrest and detain until a warrant can be obtained a person who allegedly committed the offense of domestic violence or the offense of violating a protection order when it is the preferred course of action in this state pursuant to division (B)(3)(b) of section 2935.03 of the Revised Code that the alleged offender be arrested, the officer must articulate in the report a clear statement of the officer's reasons for not arresting and detaining that alleged offender until a warrant can be obtained. The officer shall submit the written report to the law enforcement agency to which the officer has been appointed, employed, or elected.

(E) Each agency, instrumentality, or political subdivision that is required to adopt policies and procedures under division (A) of this section shall adopt those policies and procedures in conjunction and consultation with shelters in the community for victims of domestic violence and private organizations, law enforcement agencies, and other public agencies in the community that have expertise in the recognition and handling of domestic violence cases.

(F) To the extent described in and in accordance with section 9.86 or 2744.03 of the Revised Code, a peace officer who arrests an offender for the offense of violating a protection order with respect to a protection order or consent agreement of this state or another state that on its face is valid is immune from liability in a civil action for damages for injury, death, or loss to person or property that allegedly was caused by or related to the arrest.

(G) Each agency, instrumentality, or political subdivision described in division (A) of this section that arrests an offender for an alleged incident of the offense of domestic violence or an alleged incident of the offense of violating a protection order shall consider referring the case to federal authorities for prosecution under 18 U.S.C. 2261 if the incident constitutes a violation of federal law.

(H) As used in this section:

(1) "Another's unborn" has the same meaning as in section 2903.09 of the Revised Code.

(2) "Dangerous ordnance" and "deadly weapon" have the same meanings as in section 2923.11 of the Revised Code.

(3) "The offense of violating a protection order" includes the former offense of violating a protection order or consent agreement or anti-stalking protection order as set forth in section 2919.27 of the Revised Code as it existed prior to the effective date of this amendment.

(1997 S 1, eff. 10-21-97; 1994 H 335, eff. 12-9-94)

2935.033. Peace officer may assist federal law enforcement with arrest authority under USA Patriot Act

(A) Any peace officer may render assistance to any federal law enforcement officer who has arrest authority under the "Uniting and Strengthening America by Providing Appropriate Tools Required to Intercept and Obstruct Terrorism (USA Patriot Act) Act of 2001," Pub. L. No. 107-056, 115 Stat. 272, as amended, if both of the following apply:

(1) There is a threat of imminent physical danger to the federal law enforcement officer, a threat of physical harm to another person, or any other serious emergency situation present.

(2) Either the federal law enforcement officer requests emergency assistance or it appears that the federal law enforcement officer is unable to request assistance, and the circumstances reasonably indicate that assistance is appropriate.

(B) "Federal law enforcement officer" has the same meaning as in section 9.88 of the Revised Code.

(2005 S 9, eff. 4-14-06)

CHAPTER 3109 CHILDREN

PARENTAL RIGHTS AND RESPONSIBILITIES

Section

PARENTAL RIGHTS AND RESPONSIBILITIES

3109.04. Court awarding parental rights and responsibilities; shared parenting; modifications; best interests of child; child's wishes

(A) In any divorce, legal separation, or annulment proceeding and in any proceeding pertaining to the allocation of parental rights and responsibilities for the care of a child, upon hearing the testimony of either or both parents and considering any mediation report filed pursuant to section 3109.052 of the Revised Code and in accordance with sections 3127.01 to 3127.53 of the Revised Code, the court shall allocate the parental rights and responsibilities for the care of the minor children of the marriage. Subject to division (D)(2) of this section, the court may allocate the parental rights and responsibilities for the care of the children in either of the following ways:

(1) If neither parent files a pleading or motion in accordance with division (G) of this section, if at least one parent files a pleading or motion under that division but no parent who filed a pleading or motion under that division also files a plan for shared parenting, or if at least one parent files both a pleading or motion and a shared parenting plan under that division but no plan for shared parenting is in the best interest of the children, the court, in a manner consistent with the best interest of the children, shall allocate the parental rights and responsibilities for the care of the children primarily to one of the parents, designate that parent as the residential parent and the legal custodian of the child, and divide between the parents the other rights and responsibilities for the care of the children, including, but not limited to, the responsibility to provide support for the children and the right of the parent who is not the residential parent to have continuing contact with the children.

(2) If at least one parent files a pleading or motion in accordance with division (G) of this section and a plan for shared parenting pursuant to that division and if a plan for shared parenting is in the best interest of the children and is approved by the court in accordance with division (D)(1) of this section, the court may allocate the parental rights and responsibilities for the care of the children to both parents and issue a shared parenting order requiring the parents to share all or some of the aspects of the physical and legal care of the children in accordance with the approved plan for shared parenting. If the court issues a shared parenting order under this division and it is necessary for the purpose of receiving public assistance, the court shall designate which one of the parents' residences is to serve as the child's home. The child support obligations of the parents under a shared parenting order issued under this division shall be determined in accordance with Chapters 3119., 3121., 3123., and 3125. of the Revised Code.

(B) (1) When making the allocation of the parental rights and responsibilities for the care of the children under this section in an original proceeding or in any proceeding for modification of a prior order of the court making the allocation, the court shall take into account that which would be in the best interest of the children. In determining the child's best interest for purposes of making its allocation of the parental rights and responsibilities for the care of the child and for purposes of resolving any issues related to the making of that allocation, the court, in its discretion, may and, upon the request of either party, shall interview in chambers any or all of the involved children regarding their wishes and concerns with respect to the allocation.

(2) If the court interviews any child pursuant to division (B)(1) of this section, all of the following apply:

(a) The court, in its discretion, may and, upon the motion of either parent, shall appoint a guardian ad litem for the child.

(b) The court first shall determine the reasoning ability of the child. If the court determines that the child does not have sufficient reasoning ability to express the child's wishes and concern with respect to the allocation of parental rights and responsibilities for the care of the child, it shall not determine the child's wishes and concerns with respect to the allocation. If the court determines that the child has sufficient reasoning ability to express the child's wishes or concerns with respect to the allocation, it then shall determine whether, because of special circumstances, it would not be in the best interest of the child to determine the child's wishes and concerns with respect to the allocation. If the court determines that, because of special circumstances, it would not be in the best interest of the child to determine the child's wishes and concerns with respect to the allocation, it shall not determine the child's wishes and concerns with respect to the allocation and shall enter its written findings of fact and opinion in the journal. If the court determines that it would be in the best interests of the child to determine the child's wishes and concerns with respect to the allocation, it shall proceed to make that determination.

(c) The interview shall be conducted in chambers, and no person other than the child, the child's attorney, the judge, any necessary court personnel, and, in the judge's discretion, the attorney of each parent shall be permitted to be present in the chambers during the interview.

(3) No person shall obtain or attempt to obtain from a child a written or recorded statement or affidavit setting forth the child's wishes and concerns regarding the allocation of parental rights and responsibilities concerning the child. No

court, in determining the child's best interest for purposes of making its allocation of the parental rights and responsibilities for the care of the child or for purposes of resolving any issues related to the making of that allocation, shall accept or consider a written or recorded statement or affidavit that purports to set forth the child's wishes and concerns regarding those matters.

(C) Prior to trial, the court may cause an investigation to be made as to the character, family relations, past conduct, earning ability, and financial worth of each parent and may order the parents and their minor children to submit to medical, psychological, and psychiatric examinations. The report of the investigation and examinations shall be made available to either parent or the parent's counsel of record not less than five days before trial, upon written request. The report shall be signed by the investigator, and the investigator shall be subject to cross-examination by either parent concerning the contents of the report. The court may tax as costs all or any part of the expenses for each investigation.

If the court determines that either parent previously has been convicted of or pleaded guilty to any criminal offense involving any act that resulted in a child being a neglected child, that either parent previously has been determined to be the perpetrator of the neglectful act that is the basis of an adjudication that a child is a neglected child, or that there is reason to believe that either parent has acted in a manner resulting in a child being a neglected child, the court shall consider that fact against naming that parent the residential parent and against granting a shared parenting decree. When the court allocates parental rights and responsibilities for the care of children or determines whether to grant shared parenting in any proceeding, it shall consider whether either parent or any member of the household of either parent has been convicted of or pleaded guilty to a violation of section 2919.25 of the Revised Code or a sexually oriented offense involving a victim who at the time of the commission of the offense was a member of the family or household that is the subject of the proceeding, has been convicted of or pleaded guilty to any sexually oriented offense or other offense involving a victim who at the time of the commission of the offense was a member of the family or household that is the subject of the proceeding and caused physical harm to the victim in the commission of the offense, or has been determined to be the perpetrator of the abusive act that is the basis of an adjudication that a child is an abused child. If the court determines that either parent has been convicted of or pleaded guilty to a violation of section 2919.25 of the Revised Code or a sexually oriented offense involving a victim who at the time of the commission of the offense was a member of the family or household that is the subject of the proceeding, has been convicted of or pleaded guilty to any sexually oriented offense or other offense involving a victim who at the time of the commission of the offense was a member of the family or household that is the subject of the proceeding and caused physical harm to the victim in the commission of the offense, or has been determined to be the perpetrator of the abusive act that is the basis of an adjudication that a child is an abused child, it may designate that parent as the residential parent and may issue a shared parenting decree or order only if it determines that it is in the best interest of the child to name that parent the residential parent or to issue a shared parenting decree or order and it makes specific written findings of fact to support its determination.

(D) (1) (a) Upon the filing of a pleading or motion by either parent or both parents, in accordance with division (G) of this section, requesting shared parenting and the filing of a shared parenting plan in accordance with that division, the court shall comply with division (D)(1)(a)(i), (ii), or (iii) of this section, whichever is applicable:

(i) If both parents jointly make the request in their pleadings or jointly file the motion and also jointly file the plan, the court shall review the parents' plan to determine if it is in the best interest of the children. If the court determines that the plan is in the best interest of the children, the court shall approve it. If the court determines that the plan or any part of the plan is not in the best interest of the children, the court shall require the parents to make appropriate changes to the plan to meet the court's objections to it. If changes to the plan are made to meet the court's objections, and if the new plan is in the best interest of the children, the court shall approve the plan. If changes to the plan are not made to meet the court's objections, or if the parents attempt to make changes to the plan to meet the court's objections, but the court determines that the new plan or any part of the new plan still is not in the best interest of the children, the court may reject the portion of the parents' pleadings or deny their motion requesting shared parenting of the children and proceed as if the request in the pleadings or the motion had not been made. The court shall not approve a plan under this division unless it determines that the plan is in the best interest of the children.

(ii) If each parent makes a request in the parent's pleadings or files a motion and each also files a separate plan, the court shall review each plan filed to determine if either is in the best interest of the children. If the court determines that one of the filed plans is in the best interest of the children, the court may approve the plan. If the court determines that neither filed plan is in the best interest of the children, the court may order each parent to submit appropriate changes to the parent's plan or both of the filed plans to meet the court's objections, or may select one of the filed plans and order each parent to submit appropriate changes to the selected plan to meet the court's objections. If changes to the plan or plans are submitted to meet the court's objections, and if any of the filed plans with the changes is in the best interest of the children, the court may approve the plan with the changes. If changes to the plan or plans are not submitted to meet the court's objections, or if the parents submit changes to the plan or plans to meet the court's objections but the court determines that none of the filed plans with the submitted changes is in the best interest of the children, the court may reject the portion of the parents' pleadings or deny their motions requesting shared parenting of the children and proceed as if the requests in the pleadings or the motions had not been made. If the court approves a plan under this division, either as originally filed or with submitted changes, or if the court rejects the portion of the parents' pleadings or denies their motions requesting shared parenting under this division and proceeds as if the requests in the pleadings or the motions had not been made, the court shall enter in the record of the case findings of fact and conclusions of law as to the reasons for the approval or the rejection or denial. Division (D)(1)(b) of this section applies in relation to the approval or disapproval of a plan under this division.

(iii) If each parent makes a request in the parent's pleadings or files a motion but only one parent files a plan, or if only one parent makes a request in the parent's pleadings or files a motion and also files a plan, the court in the best interest of the children may order the other parent to file a plan for shared parenting in accordance with division (G) of this section. The court shall review each plan filed to determine if any plan is in the best interest of the children. If the court determines that one of the filed plans is in the best interest of the children, the court may approve the plan. If the court determines that no filed plan is in the best interest of the children, the court may order each parent to submit appropriate changes to the parent's plan or both of the filed plans to meet the court's objections or may select one filed plan and order each parent to submit appropriate changes to the selected plan to meet the court's objections. If changes to the plan or plans are submitted to meet the court's objections, and if any of the filed plans with the changes is in the best interest of the children, the court may approve the plan with the changes. If changes to the plan or plans are not submitted to meet the court's objections, or if the parents submit changes to the plan or plans to meet the court's objections but the court determines that none of the filed plans with the submitted changes is in the best interest of the children, the court may reject the portion of the parents' pleadings or deny the parents' motion or reject the portion of the parents' pleadings or deny their motions requesting shared parenting of the children and proceed as if the request or requests or the motion or motions had not been made. If the court approves a plan under this division, either as originally filed or with submitted changes, or if the court rejects the portion of the pleadings or denies the motion or motions requesting shared parenting under this division and proceeds as if the request or requests or the motion or motions had not been made, the court shall enter in the record of the case findings of fact and conclusions of law as to the reasons for the approval or the rejection or denial. Division (D)(1)(b) of this section applies in relation to the approval or disapproval of a plan under this division.

(b) The approval of a plan under division (D)(1)(a)(ii) or (iii) of this section is discretionary with the court. The court shall not approve more than one plan under either division and shall not approve a plan under either division unless it determines that the plan is in the best interest of the children. If the court, under either division, does not determine that any filed plan or any filed plan with submitted changes is in the best interest of the children, the court shall not approve any plan.

(c) Whenever possible, the court shall require that a shared parenting plan approved under division (D)(1)(a)(i), (ii), or (iii) of this section ensure the opportunity for both parents to have frequent and continuing contact with the child, unless frequent and continuing contact with any parent would not be in the best interest of the child.

(d) If a court approves a shared parenting plan under division (D)(1)(a)(i), (ii), or (iii) of this section, the approved plan shall be incorporated into a final shared parenting decree granting the parents the shared parenting of the children. Any final shared parenting decree shall be issued at the same time as and shall be appended to the final decree of dissolution, divorce, annulment, or legal separation arising out of the action out of which the question of the allocation of parental rights and responsibilities for the care of the children arose.

No provisional shared parenting decree shall be issued in relation to any shared parenting plan approved under division (D)(1)(a)(i), (ii), or (iii) of this section. A final shared parenting decree issued under this division has immediate effect as a final decree on the date of its issuance, subject to modification or termination as authorized by this section.

(2) If the court finds, with respect to any child under eighteen years of age, that it is in the best interest of the child for neither parent to be designated the residential parent and legal custodian of the child, it may commit the child to a relative of the child or certify a copy of its findings, together with as much of the record and the further information, in narrative form or otherwise, that it considers necessary or as the juvenile court requests, to the juvenile court for further proceedings, and, upon the certification, the juvenile court has exclusive jurisdiction.

(E) (1) (a) The court shall not modify a prior decree allocating parental rights and responsibilities for the care of children unless it finds, based on facts that have arisen since the prior decree or that were unknown to the court at the time of the prior decree, that a change has occurred in the circumstances of the child, the child's residential parent, or either of the parents subject to a shared parenting decree, and that the modification is necessary to serve the best interest of the child. In applying these standards, the court shall retain the residential parent designated by the prior decree or the prior shared parenting decree, unless a modification is in the best interest of the child and one of the following applies:

(i) The residential parent agrees to a change in the residential parent or both parents under a shared parenting decree agree to a change in the designation of residential parent.

(ii) The child, with the consent of the residential parent or of both parents under a shared parenting decree, has been integrated into the family of the person seeking to become the residential parent.

(iii) The harm likely to be caused by a change of environment is outweighed by the advantages of the change of environment to the child.

(b) One or both of the parents under a prior decree allocating parental rights and responsibilities for the care of children that is not a shared parenting decree may file a motion requesting that the prior decree be modified to give both parents shared rights and responsibilities for the care of the children. The motion shall include both a request for modification of the prior decree and a request for a shared parenting order that complies with division (G) of this section. Upon the filing of the motion, if the court determines that a modification of the prior decree is authorized under division (E)(1)(a) of this section, the court may modify the prior decree to grant a shared parenting order, provided that the court shall not modify the prior decree to grant a shared parenting order unless the court complies with divisions (A) and (D)(1) of this section and, in accordance with those divisions, approves the submitted shared parenting plan and determines that shared parenting would be in the best interest of the children.

(2) In addition to a modification authorized under division (E)(1) of this section:

(a) Both parents under a shared parenting decree jointly may modify the terms of the plan for shared parenting approved by the court and incorporated by it into the shared parenting decree. Modifications under this division may be made at any time. The modifications to the plan shall be filed jointly by both parents with the court, and the court shall include them in the plan, unless they are not in the best interest of the children. If the modifications are not in the best interests of the children, the court, in its discretion, may reject the modifications or make modifications to the proposed modifications or the plan that are in the best interest of the children. Modifications jointly submitted by both parents under a shared parenting decree shall be effective, either as originally filed or as modified by the court, upon their inclusion by the court in the plan. Modifications to the plan made by the court shall be effective upon their inclusion by the court in the plan.

(b) The court may modify the terms of the plan for shared parenting approved by the court and incorporated by it into the shared parenting decree upon its own motion at any time if the court determines that the modifications are in the best interest of the children or upon the request of one or both of the parents under the decree. Modifications under this division may be made at any time. The court shall not make any modification to the plan under this division, unless the modification is in the best interest of the children.

(c) The court may terminate a prior final shared parenting decree that includes a shared parenting plan approved under division (D)(1)(a)(i) of this section upon the request of one or both of the parents or whenever it determines that shared parenting is not in the best interest of the children. The court may terminate a prior final shared parenting decree that includes a shared parenting plan approved under division (D)(1)(a)(ii) or (iii) of this section if it determines, upon its own motion or upon the request of one or both parents, that shared parenting is not in the best interest of the children. If modification of the terms of the plan for shared parenting approved by the court and incorporated by it into the final shared parenting decree is attempted under division (E)(2)(a) of this section and the court rejects the modifications, it may terminate the final shared parenting decree if it determines that shared parenting is not in the best interest of the children.

(d) Upon the termination of a prior final shared parenting decree under division (E)(2)(c) of this section, the court shall proceed and issue a modified decree for the allocation of parental rights and responsibilities for the care of the children under the standards applicable under divisions (A), (B), and (C) of this section as if no decree for shared parenting had been granted and as if no request for shared parenting ever had been made.

(F) (1) In determining the best interest of a child pursuant to this section, whether on an original decree allocating parental rights and responsibilities for the care of children or a modification of a decree allocating those rights and responsibilities, the court shall consider all relevant factors, including, but not limited to:

(a) The wishes of the child's parents regarding the child's care;

(b) If the court has interviewed the child in chambers pursuant to division (B) of this section regarding the child's wishes and concerns as to the allocation of parental rights and responsibilities concerning the child, the wishes and concerns of the child, as expressed to the court;

(c) The child's interaction and interrelationship with the child's parents, siblings, and any other person who may significantly affect the child's best interest;

(d) The child's adjustment to the child's home, school, and community;

(e) The mental and physical health of all persons involved in the situation;

(f) The parent more likely to honor and facilitate court-approved parenting time rights or visitation and companionship rights;

(g) Whether either parent has failed to make all child support payments, including all arrearages, that are required of that parent pursuant to a child support order under which that parent is an obligor;

(h) Whether either parent or any member of the household of either parent previously has been convicted of or pleaded guilty to any criminal offense involving any act that resulted in a child being an abused child or a neglected child; whether either parent, in a case in which a child has been adjudicated an abused child or a neglected child, previously has been determined to be the perpetrator of the abusive or neglectful act that is the basis of an adjudication; whether either parent or any member of the household of either parent previously has been convicted of or pleaded guilty to a violation of section 2919.25 of the Revised Code or a sexually oriented offense involving a victim who at the time of the commission of the offense was a member of the family or household that is the subject of the current proceeding; whether either parent or any member of the household of either parent previously has been convicted of or pleaded guilty to any offense involving a victim who at the time of the commission of the offense was a member of the family or household that is the subject of the current proceeding and caused physical harm to the victim in the commission of the offense; and whether there is reason to believe that either parent has acted in a manner resulting in a child being an abused child or a neglected child;

(i) Whether the residential parent or one of the parents subject to a shared parenting decree has continuously and willfully denied the other parent's right to parenting time in accordance with an order of the court;

(j) Whether either parent has established a residence, or is planning to establish a residence, outside this state.

(2) In determining whether shared parenting is in the best interest of the children, the court shall consider all relevant factors, including, but not limited to, the factors enumerated in division (F)(1) of this section, the factors enumerated in section 3119.23 of the Revised Code, and all of the following factors:

(a) The ability of the parents to cooperate and make decisions jointly, with respect to the children;

(b) The ability of each parent to encourage the sharing of love, affection, and contact between the child and the other parent;

(c) Any history of, or potential for, child abuse, spouse abuse, other domestic violence, or parental kidnapping by either parent;

(d) The geographic proximity of the parents to each other, as the proximity relates to the practical considerations of shared parenting;

(e) The recommendation of the guardian ad litem of the child, if the child has a guardian ad litem.

(3) When allocating parental rights and responsibilities for the care of children, the court shall not give preference to a parent because of that parent's financial status or condition.

(G) Either parent or both parents of any children may file a pleading or motion with the court requesting the court to grant both parents shared parental rights and responsibilities for the care of the children in a proceeding held pursuant to division (A) of this section. If a pleading or motion requesting shared parenting is filed, the parent or parents filing the pleading or motion also shall file with the court a plan for the exercise of shared parenting by both parents. If each parent files a pleading or motion requesting shared parenting but only one parent files a plan or if only one parent files a pleading or motion requesting shared parenting and also files a plan, the other parent as ordered by the court shall file with the court a plan for the exercise of shared parenting by both parents. The plan for shared parenting shall be filed with the petition for dissolution of marriage, if the question of parental rights and responsibilities for the care of the children arises out of an action for dissolution of marriage, or, in other cases, at a time at least thirty days prior to the hearing on the issue of the parental rights and responsibilities for the care of the children. A plan for shared parenting shall include provisions covering all factors that are relevant to the care of the children, including, but not limited to, provisions covering factors such as physical living arrangements, child support obligations, provision for the children's medical and dental care, school placement, and the parent with which the children will be physically located during legal holidays, school holidays, and other days of special importance.

(H) If an appeal is taken from a decision of a court that grants or modifies a decree allocating parental rights and responsibilities for the care of children, the court of appeals shall give the case calendar priority and handle it expeditiously.

(I) (1) Upon receipt of an order for active military service in the uniformed services, a parent who is subject to an order allocating parental rights and responsibilities or in relation to whom an action to allocate parental rights and responsibilities is pending and who is ordered for active military service shall notify the other parent who is subject to the order or in relation to whom the case is pending of the order for active military service within three days of receiving the military service order.

(2) On receipt of the notice described in division (I)(1) of this section, either parent may apply to the court for a hearing to expedite an allocation or modification proceeding so that the court can issue an order before the parent's active military service begins. The application shall include the date on which the active military service begins.

The court shall schedule a hearing upon receipt of the application and hold the hearing not later than thirty days after receipt of the application, except that the court shall give the case calendar priority and handle the case expeditiously if exigent circumstances exist in the case.

The court shall not modify a prior decree allocating parental rights and responsibilities unless the court determines that there has been a change in circumstances of the child, the child's residential parent, or either of the parents subject to a shared parenting decree, and that modification is necessary to serve the best interest of the child. The court shall not find past, present, or possible future active military service in the uniformed services to constitute a change in circumstances justifying modification of a prior decree pursuant to division (E) of this section. The court shall make specific written findings of fact to support any modification under this division.

(3) Nothing in division (I) of this section shall prevent a court from issuing a temporary order allocating or modifying parental rights and responsibilities for the duration of the parent's active military service. A temporary order shall specify whether the parent's active military service is the basis of the order and shall provide for termination of the temporary order and resumption of the prior order within ten days after receipt of notice pursuant to division (I)(5) of this section, unless the other parent demonstrates that resumption of the prior order is not in the child's best interest.

(4) At the request of a parent who is ordered for active military service in the uniformed services and who is a subject of a proceeding pertaining to a temporary order for the allocation or modification of parental rights and responsibilities, the court shall permit the parent to participate in the proceeding and present evidence by electronic means, including communication by telephone, video, or internet to the extent permitted by the rules of the supreme court of Ohio.

(5) A parent who is ordered for active military service in the uniformed services and who is a subject of a proceeding pertaining to the allocation or modification of parental rights and responsibilities shall provide written notice to the court, child support enforcement agency, and the other parent of the date of termination of the parent's active military service not later than thirty days after the date on which the service ends.

(J) As used in this section:

(1) "Abused child" has the same meaning as in section 2151.031 of the Revised Code.

(2) "Active military service" means service by a member of the uniformed services in compliance with military orders to report for combat operations, contingency operations, peacekeeping operations, a remote tour of duty, or other active service for which the member is required to report unaccompanied by any family member, including any period of illness, recovery from injury, leave, or other lawful absence during that operation, duty, or service.

(3) "Neglected child" has the same meaning as in section 2151.03 of the Revised Code.

(4) "Sexually oriented offense" has the same meaning as in section 2950.01 of the Revised Code.

(5) "Uniformed services" means the United States armed forces, the army national guard, and the air national guard or any reserve component thereof, or the commissioned corps of the United States public health service.

(K) As used in the Revised Code, "shared parenting" means that the parents share, in the manner set forth in the plan for shared parenting that is approved by the court under division (D)(1) and described in division (L)(6) of this section, all or some of the aspects of physical and legal care of their children.

(L) For purposes of the Revised Code:

(1) A parent who is granted the care, custody, and control of a child under an order that was issued pursuant to this section prior to April 11, 1991, and that does not provide for shared parenting has "custody of the child" and "care, custody, and control of the child" under the order, and is the "residential parent," the "residential parent and legal custodian," or the "custodial parent" of the child under the order.

(2) A parent who primarily is allocated the parental rights and responsibilities for the care of a child and who is designated as the residential parent and legal custodian of the child under an order that is issued pursuant to this section on or after April 11, 1991, and that does not provide for shared parenting has "custody of the child" and "care, custody, and control of the child" under the order, and is the "residential parent," the "residential parent and legal custodian," or the "custodial parent" of the child under the order.

(3) A parent who is not granted custody of a child under an order that was issued pursuant to this section prior to April 11, 1991, and that does not provide for shared parenting is the "parent who is not the residential parent," the "parent who is not the residential parent and legal custodian," or the "noncustodial parent" of the child under the order.

(4) A parent who is not primarily allocated the parental rights and responsibilities for the care of a child and who is not designated as the residential parent and legal custodian of the child under an order that is issued pursuant to this section on or after April 11, 1991, and that does not provide for shared parenting is the "parent who is not the residential parent," the "parent who is not the residential parent and legal custodian," or the "noncustodial parent" of the child under the order.

(5) Unless the context clearly requires otherwise, if an order is issued by a court pursuant to this section and the order provides for shared parenting of a child, both parents have "custody of the child" or "care, custody, and control of the child" under the order, to the extent and in the manner specified in the order.

(6) Unless the context clearly requires otherwise and except as otherwise provided in the order, if an order is issued by a court pursuant to this section and the order provides for shared parenting of a child, each parent, regardless of where the child is physically located or with whom the child is residing at a particular point in time, as specified in the order, is the "residential parent," the "residential parent and legal custodian," or the "custodial parent" of the child.

(7) Unless the context clearly requires otherwise and except as otherwise provided in the order, a designation in the order of a parent as the residential parent for the purpose of determining the school the child attends, as the custodial parent for purposes of claiming the child as a dependent pursuant to section 152(e) of the "Internal Revenue Code of 1986," 100 Stat. 2085, 26 U.S.C.A. 1, as amended, or as the residential parent for purposes of receiving public assistance pursuant to division (A)(2) of this section, does not affect the designation pursuant to division (L)(6) of this section of each parent as the "residential parent," the "residential parent and legal custodian," or the "custodial parent" of the child.

(M) The court shall require each parent of a child to file an affidavit attesting as to whether the parent, and the members of the parent's household, have been convicted of or pleaded guilty to any of the offenses identified in divisions (C) and (F)(1)(h) of this section.

(2011 H 121, eff. 6-9-11; 2007 H 119, eff. 6-30-07; 2006 S 260, eff. 1-2-07; 2004 S 185, eff. 4-11-05; 2000 S 180, eff. 3-22-01; 1994 H 415, eff. 11-9-94; 1993 S 115, eff. 10-12-93; 1990 S 3, H 514, H 591; 1983 H 93; 1981 S 39, H 71; 1977 S 135; 1975 H 370, H 1; 1974 H 740, H 233; 131 v H 745; 1953 H 1; GC 8005-4; Source—GC 8033)

3109.043. Temporary order regarding allocation of parental rights and responsibilities while action pending

In any proceeding pertaining to the allocation of parental rights and responsibilities for the care of a child, when requested in the complaint, answer, or counterclaim, or by motion served with the pleading, upon satisfactory proof by affidavit duly filed with the clerk of the court, the court, without oral hearing and for good cause shown, may make a temporary order regarding the allocation of parental rights and responsibilities for the care of the child while the action is pending.

If a parent and child relationship has not already been established pursuant to section 3111.02 of the Revised Code, the court may take into consideration when determining whether to award parenting time, visitation rights, or temporary custody to a putative father that the putative father is named on the birth record of the child, the child has the putative father's surname, or a clear pattern of a parent and child relationship between the child and the putative father exists.

(2006 H 136, eff. 5-17-06)

3109.051. Parenting time rights

(A) If a divorce, dissolution, legal separation, or annulment proceeding involves a child and if the court has not issued a shared parenting decree, the court shall consider any mediation report filed pursuant to section 3109.052 of the Revised Code and, in accordance with division (C) of this section, shall make a just and reasonable order or decree permitting each parent who is not the residential parent to have parenting time with the child at the time and under the conditions that the court directs, unless the court determines that it would not be in the best interest of the child to permit that parent to have parenting time with the child and includes in the journal its findings of fact and conclusions of law. Whenever possible, the order or decree permitting the parenting time shall ensure the opportunity for both parents to have frequent and continuing contact with the child, unless frequent and continuing contact by either parent with the child would not be in the best interest of the child. The court shall include in its final decree a specific schedule of parenting time for that parent. Except as provided in division (E)(6) of section 3113.31 of the Revised Code, if the court, pursuant to this section, grants parenting time to a parent or companionship or visitation rights to any other person with respect to any child, it shall not require the public children services agency to provide supervision of or other services related to that parent's exercise of parenting time or that person's exercise of companionship or visitation rights with respect to the child. This section does not limit the power of a juvenile court pursuant to Chapter 2151. of the Revised Code to issue orders with respect to children who are alleged to be abused, neglected, or dependent children or to make dispositions of children who are adjudicated abused, neglected, or dependent children or of a common pleas court to issue orders pursuant to section 3113.31 of the Revised Code.

(B) (1) In a divorce, dissolution of marriage, legal separation, annulment, or child support proceeding that involves a child, the court may grant reasonable companionship or visitation rights to any grandparent, any person related to the child by consanguinity or affinity, or any other person other than a parent, if all of the following apply:

(a) The grandparent, relative, or other person files a motion with the court seeking companionship or visitation rights.

(b) The court determines that the grandparent, relative, or other person has an interest in the welfare of the child.

(c) The court determines that the granting of the companionship or visitation rights is in the best interest of the child.

(2) A motion may be filed under division (B)(1) of this section during the pendency of the divorce, dissolution of marriage, legal separation, annulment, or child support proceeding or, if a motion was not filed at that time or was filed at that time and the circumstances in the case have changed, at any time after a decree or final order is issued in the case.

(C) When determining whether to grant parenting time rights to a parent pursuant to this section or section 3109.12 of the Revised Code or to grant companionship or visitation rights to a grandparent, relative, or other person pursuant to this section or section 3109.11 or 3109.12 of the Revised Code, when establishing a specific parenting time or visitation schedule, and when determining other parenting time matters under this section or section 3109.12 of the Revised Code or visitation matters under this section or section 3109.11 or 3109.12 of the Revised Code, the court shall consider any mediation report that is filed pursuant to section 3109.052 of the Revised Code and shall consider all other relevant factors, including, but not limited to, all of the factors listed in division (D) of this section. In considering the factors listed in division (D) of this section for purposes of determining whether to grant parenting time or visitation rights, establishing a specific parenting time or visitation schedule, determining other parenting time matters under this section or section 3109.12 of the Revised Code or visitation matters under this section or under section 3109.11 or 3109.12 of the Revised Code, and resolving any issues related to the making of any determination with respect to parenting time or visitation rights or the establishment of any specific parenting time or visitation schedule, the court, in its discretion, may interview in chambers any or all involved children regarding their wishes and concerns. If the court interviews any child concerning the child's wishes and concerns regarding those parenting time or visitation matters, the interview shall be conducted in chambers, and no person other than the child, the child's attorney, the judge, any necessary court personnel, and, in the judge's discretion, the attorney of each parent shall be permitted to be present in the chambers during the interview. No person shall obtain or attempt to obtain from a child a written or recorded statement or affidavit setting forth the wishes and concerns of the child regarding those parenting time or visitation matters. A court, in considering the factors listed in division (D) of this section for purposes of determining whether to grant any parenting time or visitation rights, establishing a parenting time or visitation schedule, determining other parenting time matters under this section or section 3109.12 of the Revised Code or visitation matters under this section or under section 3109.11 or 3109.12 of the Revised Code, or resolving any issues related to the making of any determination with respect to parenting time or visitation rights or the establishment of any specific parenting time or visitation schedule, shall not accept or consider a written or recorded statement or affidavit that purports to set forth the child's wishes or concerns regarding those parenting time or visitation matters.

(D) In determining whether to grant parenting time to a parent pursuant to this section or section 3109.12 of the Revised Code or companionship or visitation rights to a grandparent, relative, or other person pursuant to this section or section 3109.11 or 3109.12 of the Revised Code, in establishing a specific parenting time or visitation schedule, and in determining other parenting time matters under this section or section 3109.12 of the Revised Code or visitation matters under this section or section 3109.11 or 3109.12 of the Revised Code, the court shall consider all of the following factors:

(1) The prior interaction and interrelationships of the child with the child's parents, siblings, and other persons related by consanguinity or affinity, and with the person who requested companionship or visitation if that person is not a parent, sibling, or relative of the child;

(2) The geographical location of the residence of each parent and the distance between those residences, and if the person is not a parent, the geographical location of that person's residence and the distance between that person's residence and the child's residence;

(3) The child's and parents' available time, including, but not limited to, each parent's employment schedule, the child's school schedule, and the child's and the parents' holiday and vacation schedule;

(4) The age of the child;

(5) The child's adjustment to home, school, and community;

(6) If the court has interviewed the child in chambers, pursuant to division (C) of this section, regarding the wishes and concerns of the child as to parenting time by the parent who is not the residential parent or companionship or visitation by the grandparent, relative, or other person who requested companionship or visitation, as to a specific parenting time or visitation schedule, or as to other parenting time or visitation matters, the wishes and concerns of the child, as expressed to the court;

(7) The health and safety of the child;

(8) The amount of time that will be available for the child to spend with siblings;

(9) The mental and physical health of all parties;

(10) Each parent's willingness to reschedule missed parenting time and to facilitate the other parent's parenting time rights, and with respect to a person who requested companionship or visitation, the willingness of that person to reschedule missed visitation;

(11) In relation to parenting time, whether either parent previously has been convicted of or pleaded guilty to any criminal offense involving any act that

resulted in a child being an abused child or a neglected child; whether either parent, in a case in which a child has been adjudicated an abused child or a neglected child, previously has been determined to be the perpetrator of the abusive or neglectful act that is the basis of the adjudication; and whether there is reason to believe that either parent has acted in a manner resulting in a child being an abused child or a neglected child;

(12) In relation to requested companionship or visitation by a person other than a parent, whether the person previously has been convicted of or pleaded guilty to any criminal offense involving any act that resulted in a child being an abused child or a neglected child; whether the person, in a case in which a child has been adjudicated an abused child or a neglected child, previously has been determined to be the perpetrator of the abusive or neglectful act that is the basis of the adjudication; whether either parent previously has been convicted of or pleaded guilty to a violation of section 2919.25 of the Revised Code involving a victim who at the time of the commission of the offense was a member of the family or household that is the subject of the current proceeding; whether either parent previously has been convicted of an offense involving a victim who at the time of the commission of the offense was a member of the family or household that is the subject of the current proceeding and caused physical harm to the victim in the commission of the offense; and whether there is reason to believe that the person has acted in a manner resulting in a child being an abused child or a neglected child;

(13) Whether the residential parent or one of the parents subject to a shared parenting decree has continuously and willfully denied the other parent's right to parenting time in accordance with an order of the court;

(14) Whether either parent has established a residence or is planning to establish a residence outside this state;

(15) In relation to requested companionship or visitation by a person other than a parent, the wishes and concerns of the child's parents, as expressed by them to the court;

(16) Any other factor in the best interest of the child.

(E) The remarriage of a residential parent of a child does not affect the authority of a court under this section to grant parenting time rights with respect to the child to the parent who is not the residential parent or to grant reasonable companionship or visitation rights with respect to the child to any grandparent, any person related by consanguinity or affinity, or any other person.

(F) (1) If the court, pursuant to division (A) of this section, denies parenting time to a parent who is not the residential parent or denies a motion for reasonable companionship or visitation rights filed under division (B) of this section and the parent or movant files a written request for findings of fact and conclusions of law, the court shall state in writing its findings of fact and conclusions of law in accordance with Civil Rule 52.

(2) On or before July 1, 1991, each court of common pleas, by rule, shall adopt standard parenting time guidelines. A court shall have discretion to deviate from its standard parenting time guidelines based upon factors set forth in division (D) of this section.

(G) (1) If the residential parent intends to move to a residence other than the residence specified in the parenting time order or decree of the court, the parent shall file a notice of intent to relocate with the court that issued the order or decree. Except as provided in divisions (G)(2), (3), and (4) of this section, the court shall send a copy of the notice to the parent who is not the residential parent. Upon receipt of the notice, the court, on its own motion or the motion of the parent who is not the residential parent, may schedule a hearing with notice to both parents to determine whether it is in the best interest of the child to revise the parenting time schedule for the child.

(2) When a court grants parenting time rights to a parent who is not the residential parent, the court shall determine whether that parent has been convicted of or pleaded guilty to a violation of section 2919.25 of the Revised Code involving a victim who at the time of the commission of the offense was a member of the family or household that is the subject of the proceeding, has been convicted of or pleaded guilty to any other offense involving a victim who at the time of the commission of the offense was a member of the family or household that is the subject

of the proceeding and caused physical harm to the victim in the commission of the offense, or has been determined to be the perpetrator of the abusive act that is the basis of an adjudication that a child is an abused child. If the court determines that that parent has not been so convicted and has not been determined to be the perpetrator of an abusive act that is the basis of a child abuse adjudication, the court shall issue an order stating that a copy of any notice of relocation that is filed with the court pursuant to division (G)(1) of this section will be sent to the parent who is given the parenting time rights in accordance with division (G)(1) of this section.

If the court determines that the parent who is granted the parenting time rights has been convicted of or pleaded guilty to a violation of section 2919.25 of the Revised Code involving a victim who at the time of the commission of the offense was a member of the family or household that is the subject of the proceeding, has been convicted of or pleaded guilty to any other offense involving a victim who at the time of the commission of the offense was a member of the family or household that is the subject of the proceeding and caused physical harm to the victim in the commission of the offense, or has been determined to be the perpetrator of the abusive act that is the basis of an adjudication that a child is an abused child, it shall issue an order stating that that parent will not be given a copy of any notice of relocation that is filed with the court pursuant to division (G)(1) of this section unless the court determines that it is in the best interest of the children to give that parent a copy of the notice of relocation, issues an order stating that that parent will be given a copy of any notice of relocation filed pursuant to division (G)(1) of this section, and issues specific written findings of fact in support of its determination.

(3) If a court, prior to April 11, 1991, issued an order granting parenting time rights to a parent who is not the residential parent and did not require the residential parent in that order to give the parent who is granted the parenting time rights notice of any change of address and if the residential parent files a notice of relocation pursuant to division (G)(1) of this section, the court shall determine if the parent who is granted the parenting time rights has been convicted of or pleaded guilty to a violation of section 2919.25 of the Revised Code involving a victim who at the time of the commission of the offense was a member of the family or household that is the subject of the proceeding, has been convicted of or pleaded guilty to any other offense involving a victim who at the time of the commission of the offense was a member of the family or household that is the subject of the proceeding and caused physical harm to the victim in the commission of the offense, or has been determined to be the perpetrator of the abusive act that is the basis of an adjudication that a child is an abused child. If the court determines that the parent who is granted the parenting time rights has not been so convicted and has not been determined to be the perpetrator of an abusive act that is the basis of a child abuse adjudication, the court shall issue an order stating that a copy of any notice of relocation that is filed with the court pursuant to division (G)(1) of this section will be sent to the parent who is granted parenting time rights in accordance with division (G)(1) of this section.

If the court determines that the parent who is granted the parenting time rights has been convicted of or pleaded guilty to a violation of section 2919.25 of the Revised Code involving a victim who at the time of the commission of the offense was a member of the family or household that is the subject of the proceeding, has been convicted of or pleaded guilty to any other offense involving a victim who at the time of the commission of the offense was a member of the family or household that is the subject of the proceeding and caused physical harm to the victim in the commission of the offense, or has been determined to be the perpetrator of the abusive act that is the basis of an adjudication that a child is an abused child, it shall issue an order stating that that parent will not be given a copy of any notice of relocation that is filed with the court pursuant to division (G)(1) of this section unless the court determines that it is in the best interest of the children to give that parent a copy of the notice of relocation, issues an order stating that that parent will be given a copy of any notice of relocation filed pursuant to division (G)(1) of this section, and issues specific written findings of fact in support of its determination.

(4) If a parent who is granted parenting time rights pursuant to this section or

any other section of the Revised Code is authorized by an order issued pursuant to this section or any other court order to receive a copy of any notice of relocation that is filed pursuant to division (G)(1) of this section or pursuant to court order, if the residential parent intends to move to a residence other than the residence address specified in the parenting time order, and if the residential parent does not want the parent who is granted the parenting time rights to receive a copy of the relocation notice because the parent with parenting time rights has been convicted of or pleaded guilty to a violation of section 2919.25 of the Revised Code involving a victim who at the time of the commission of the offense was a member of the family or household that is the subject of the proceeding, has been convicted of or pleaded guilty to any other offense involving a victim who at the time of the commission of the offense was a member of the family or household that is the subject of the proceeding and caused physical harm to the victim in the commission of the offense, or has been determined to be the perpetrator of the abusive act that is the basis of an adjudication that a child is an abused child, the residential parent may file a motion with the court requesting that the parent who is granted the parenting time rights not receive a copy of any notice of relocation. Upon the filing of the motion, the court shall schedule a hearing on the motion and give both parents notice of the date, time, and location of the hearing. If the court determines that the parent who is granted the parenting time rights has been so convicted or has been determined to be the perpetrator of an abusive act that is the basis of a child abuse adjudication, the court shall issue an order stating that the parent who is granted the parenting time rights will not be given a copy of any notice of relocation that is filed with the court pursuant to division (G)(1) of this section or that the residential parent is no longer required to give that parent a copy of any notice of relocation unless the court determines that it is in the best interest of the children to give that parent a copy of the notice of relocation, issues an order stating that that parent will be given a copy of any notice of relocation filed pursuant to division (G)(1) of this section, and issues specific written findings of fact in support of its determination. If it does not so find, it shall dismiss the motion.

(H) (1) Subject to section 3125.16 and division (F) of section 3319.321 of the Revised Code, a parent of a child who is not the residential parent of the child is entitled to access, under the same terms and conditions under which access is provided to the residential parent, to any record that is related to the child and to which the residential parent of the child legally is provided access, unless the court determines that it would not be in the best interest of the child for the parent who is not the residential parent to have access to the records under those same terms and conditions. If the court determines that the parent of a child who is not the residential parent should not have access to records related to the child under the same terms and conditions as provided for the residential parent, the court shall specify the terms and conditions under which the parent who is not the residential parent is to have access to those records, shall enter its written findings of facts and opinion in the journal, and shall issue an order containing the terms and conditions to both the residential parent and the parent of the child who is not the residential parent. The court shall include in every order issued pursuant to this division notice that any keeper of a record who knowingly fails to comply with the order or division (H) of this section is in contempt of court.

(2) Subject to section 3125.16 and division (F) of section 3319.321 of the Revised Code, subsequent to the issuance of an order under division (H)(1) of this section, the keeper of any record that is related to a particular child and to which the residential parent legally is provided access shall permit the parent of the child who is not the residential parent to have access to the record under the same terms and conditions under which access is provided to the residential parent, unless the residential parent has presented the keeper of the record with a copy of an order issued under division (H)(1) of this section that limits the terms and conditions under which the parent who is not the residential parent is to have access to records pertaining to the child and the order pertains to the record in question. If the residential parent presents the keeper of the record with a copy of that type of order, the keeper of the record shall permit the parent who is not the residential parent to have access to the record only in accordance with the most recent order that has been issued pursuant to division (H)(1) of this sec-

tion and presented to the keeper by the residential parent or the parent who is not the residential parent. Any keeper of any record who knowingly fails to comply with division (H) of this section or with any order issued pursuant to division (H)(1) of this section is in contempt of court.

(3) The prosecuting attorney of any county may file a complaint with the court of common pleas of that county requesting the court to issue a protective order preventing the disclosure pursuant to division (H)(1) or (2) of this section of any confidential law enforcement investigatory record. The court shall schedule a hearing on the motion and give notice of the date, time, and location of the hearing to all parties.

(I) A court that issues a parenting time order or decree pursuant to this section or section 3109.12 of the Revised Code shall determine whether the parent granted the right of parenting time is to be permitted access, in accordance with section 5104.039 of the Revised Code, to any child day-care center that is, or that in the future may be, attended by the children with whom the right of parenting time is granted. Unless the court determines that the parent who is not the residential parent should not have access to the center to the same extent that the residential parent is granted access to the center, the parent who is not the residential parent and who is granted parenting time rights is entitled to access to the center to the same extent that the residential parent is granted access to the center. If the court determines that the parent who is not the residential parent should not have access to the center to the same extent that the residential parent is granted such access under section 5104.039 of the Revised Code, the court shall specify the terms and conditions under which the parent who is not the residential parent is to have access to the center, provided that the access shall not be greater than the access that is provided to the residential parent under section 5104.039 of the Revised Code, the court shall enter its written findings of fact and opinions in the journal, and the court shall include the terms and conditions of access in the parenting time order or decree.

(J) (1) Subject to division (F) of section 3319.321 of the Revised Code, when a court issues an order or decree allocating parental rights and responsibilities for the care of a child, the parent of the child who is not the residential parent of the child is entitled to access, under the same terms and conditions under which access is provided to the residential parent, to any student activity that is related to the child and to which the residential parent of the child legally is provided access, unless the court determines that it would not be in the best interest of the child to grant the parent who is not the residential parent access to the student activities under those same terms and conditions. If the court determines that the parent of the child who is not the residential parent should not have access to any student activity that is related to the child under the same terms and conditions as provided for the residential parent, the court shall specify the terms and conditions under which the parent who is not the residential parent is to have access to those student activities, shall enter its written findings of facts and opinion in the journal, and shall issue an order containing the terms and conditions to both the residential parent and the parent of the child who is not the residential parent. The court shall include in every order issued pursuant to this division notice that any school official or employee who knowingly fails to comply with the order or division (J) of this section is in contempt of court.

(2) Subject to division (F) of section 3319.321 of the Revised Code, subsequent to the issuance of an order under division (J)(1) of this section, all school officials and employees shall permit the parent of the child who is not the residential parent to have access to any student activity under the same terms and conditions under which access is provided to the residential parent of the child, unless the residential parent has presented the school official or employee, the board of education of the school, or the governing body of the chartered nonpublic school with a copy of an order issued under division (J)(1) of this section that limits the terms and conditions under which the parent who is not the residential parent is to have access to student activities related to the child and the order pertains to the student activity in question. If the residential parent presents the school official or employee, the board of education of the school, or the governing body of the chartered nonpublic school with a copy of that type of order, the school official or employee shall permit the parent who is not the residential parent to have access to the student activity only in accordance with the most recent order that

has been issued pursuant to division (J)(1) of this section and presented to the school official or employee, the board of education of the school, or the governing body of the chartered nonpublic school by the residential parent or the parent who is not the residential parent. Any school official or employee who knowingly fails to comply with division (J) of this section or with any order issued pursuant to division (J)(1) of this section is in contempt of court.

(K) If any person is found in contempt of court for failing to comply with or interfering with any order or decree granting parenting time rights issued pursuant to this section or section 3109.12 of the Revised Code or companionship or visitation rights issued pursuant to this section, section 3109.11 or 3109.12 of the Revised Code, or any other provision of the Revised Code, the court that makes the finding, in addition to any other penalty or remedy imposed, shall assess all court costs arising out of the contempt proceeding against the person and require the person to pay any reasonable attorney's fees of any adverse party, as determined by the court, that arose in relation to the act of contempt, and may award reasonable compensatory parenting time or visitation to the person whose right of parenting time or visitation was affected by the failure or interference if such compensatory parenting time or visitation is in the best interest of the child. Any compensatory parenting time or visitation awarded under this division shall be included in an order issued by the court and, to the extent possible, shall be governed by the same terms and conditions as was the parenting time or visitation that was affected by the failure or interference.

(L) Any parent who requests reasonable parenting time rights with respect to a child under this section or section 3109.12 of the Revised Code or any person who requests reasonable companionship or visitation rights with respect to a child under this section, section 3109.11 or 3109.12 of the Revised Code, or any other provision of the Revised Code may file a motion with the court requesting that it waive all or any part of the costs that may accrue in the proceedings. If the court determines that the movant is indigent and that the waiver is in the best interest of the child, the court, in its discretion, may waive payment of all or any part of the costs of those proceedings.

(M) (1) A parent who receives an order for active military service in the uniformed services and who is subject to a parenting time order may apply to the court for any of the following temporary orders for the period extending from the date of the parent's departure to the date of return:

(a) An order delegating all or part of the parent's parenting time with the child to a relative or to another person who has a close and substantial relationship with the child if the delegation is in the child's best interest;

(b) An order that the other parent make the child reasonably available for parenting time with the parent when the parent is on leave from active military service;

(c) An order that the other parent facilitate contact, including telephone and electronic contact, between the parent and child while the parent is on active military service.

(2) (a) Upon receipt of an order for active military service, a parent who is subject to a parenting time order and seeks an order under division (M)(1) of this section shall notify the other parent who is subject to the parenting time order and apply to the court as soon as reasonably possible after receipt of the order for active military service. The application shall include the date on which the active military service begins.

(b) The court shall schedule a hearing upon receipt of an application under division (M) of this section and hold the hearing not later than thirty days after its receipt, except that the court shall give the case calendar priority and handle the case expeditiously if exigent circumstances exist in the case. No hearing shall be required if both parents agree to the terms of the requested temporary order and the court determines that the order is in the child's best interest.

(c) In determining whether a delegation under division (M)(1)(a) of this section is in the child's best interest, the court shall consider all relevant factors, including the factors set forth in division (D) of this section.

(d) An order delegating all or part of the parent's parenting time pursuant to division (M)(1)(a) of this section does not create standing on behalf of the person to whom parenting time is delegated to assert visitation or companionship rights independent of the order.

(3) At the request of a parent who is ordered for active military service in the uniformed services and who is a subject of a proceeding pertaining to a parenting time order or pertaining to a request for companionship rights or visitation with a child, the court shall permit the parent to participate in the proceeding and present evidence by electronic means, including communication by telephone, video, or internet to the extent permitted by rules of the supreme court of Ohio.

(N) The juvenile court has exclusive jurisdiction to enter the orders in any case certified to it from another court.

(O) As used in this section:

(1) "Abused child" has the same meaning as in section 2151.031 of the Revised Code, and "neglected child" has the same meaning as in section 2151.03 of the Revised Code.

(2) "Active military service" and "uniformed services" have the same meanings as in section 3109.04 of the Revised Code.

(3) "Confidential law enforcement investigatory record" has the same meaning as in section 149.43 of the Revised Code.

(4) "Parenting time order" means an order establishing the amount of time that a child spends with the parent who is not the residential parent or the amount of time that the child is to be physically located with a parent under a shared parenting order.

(5) "Record" means any record, document, file, or other material that contains information directly related to a child, including, but not limited to, any of the following:

(a) Records maintained by public and nonpublic schools;

(b) Records maintained by facilities that provide child care, as defined in section 5104.01 of the Revised Code, publicly funded child care, as defined in section 5104.01 of the Revised Code, or pre-school services operated by or under the supervision of a school district board of education or a nonpublic school;

(c) Records maintained by hospitals, other facilities, or persons providing medical or surgical care or treatment for the child;

(d) Records maintained by agencies, departments, instrumentalities, or other entities of the state or any political subdivision of the state, other than a child support enforcement agency. Access to records maintained by a child support enforcement agency is governed by section 3125.16 of the Revised Code.

(2012 S 316, § 120.01, eff. 1-1-14; 2011 H 121, eff. 6-9-11; 2004 H 11, eff. 5-18-05; 2000 S 180, eff. 3-22-01; 1997 H 408, eff. 10-1-97; 1996 H 274, eff. 8-8-96; 1991 H 155, eff. 7-22-91; 1990 S 3, H 15)

3109.052. Mediation order; report

(A) If a proceeding for divorce, dissolution, legal separation, annulment, or the allocation of parental rights and responsibilities for the care of a child involves one or more children, if the parents of the children do not agree upon an appropriate allocation of parental rights and responsibilities for the care of their children or do not agree upon a specific schedule of parenting time for their children, the court may order the parents to mediate their differences on those matters in accordance with mediation procedures adopted by the court by local rule. When the court determines whether mediation is appropriate in any proceeding, it shall consider whether either parent previously has been convicted of or pleaded guilty to a violation of section 2919.25 of the Revised Code involving a victim who at the time of the commission of the offense was a member of the family or household that is the subject of the proceeding, whether either parent previously has been convicted of or pleaded guilty to an offense involving a victim who at the time of the commission of the offense was a member of the family or household that is the subject of the proceeding and caused physical harm to the victim in the commission of the offense, and whether either parent has been determined to be the perpetrator of the abusive act that is the basis of an adjudication that a child is an abused child. If either parent has been convicted of or pleaded guilty to a violation of section 2919.25 of the Revised Code involving a victim who at the time of the commission of the offense was a member of the family or household that is the subject of the proceeding, has been convicted of or pleaded guilty to any other offense involving a victim who at the time of the commission of the offense was a member of the family or household that is the subject of the proceeding and caused physical harm to the victim in the commission of the offense, or has been determined to be the perpetrator of the abusive act that is the basis of an adjudication that a child is an abused child, the court may order mediation only if the court determines that it is in the best interests of the parties to order mediation and makes specific written findings of fact to support its determination.

If a court issues an order pursuant to this division requiring mediation, it also may order the parents to file a mediation report within a specified period of time and order the parents to pay the cost of mediation, unless either or both of the parents file a motion requesting that the court waive that requirement. Upon the filing of a motion requesting the waiver of that requirement, the court, for good cause shown, may waive the requirement that either or both parents pay the cost of mediation or may require one of the parents to pay the entire cost of mediation. Any mediation procedures adopted by local court rule for use under this division shall include, but are not limited to, provisions establishing qualifications for mediators who may be employed or used and provisions establishing standards for the conduct of the mediation.

(B) If a mediation order is issued under division (A) of this section and the order requires the parents to file a mediation report, the mediator and each parent who takes part in mediation in accordance with the order jointly shall file a report of the results of the mediation process with the court that issued the order under that division. A mediation report shall indicate only whether agreement has been reached on any of the issues that were the subject of the mediation, and, if agreement has been reached, the content and details of the agreement. No mediation report shall contain any background information concerning the mediation process or any information discussed or presented in the process. The court shall consider the mediation report when it allocates parental rights and responsibilities for the care of children under section 3109.04 of the Revised Code and when it establishes a specific schedule of parenting time under section 3109.051 of the Revised Code. The court is not bound by the mediation report and shall consider the best interest of the children when making that allocation or establishing the parenting time schedule.

(C) If a mediation order is issued under division (A) of this section, the mediator shall not be made a party to, and shall not be called as a witness or testify in, any action or proceeding, other than a criminal, delinquency, child abuse, child neglect, or dependent child action or proceeding, that is brought by or against either parent and that pertains to the mediation process, to any information discussed or presented in the mediation process, to the allocation of parental rights and responsibilities for the care of the parents' children, or to the awarding of parenting time rights in relation to their children. The mediator shall not be made a party to, or be called as a witness or testify in, such an action or proceeding even if both parents give their prior consent to the mediator being made a party to or being called as a witness or to testify in the action or proceeding.

(D) Division (A) of this section does not apply to either of the following:

(1) Any proceeding, or the use of mediation in any proceeding that is not a proceeding for divorce, dissolution, legal separation, annulment, or the allocation of parental rights and responsibilities for the care of a child;

(2) The use of mediation in any proceeding for divorce, dissolution, legal separation, annulment, or the allocation of parental rights and responsibilities for the care of a child, in relation to issues other than the appropriate allocation of parental rights and responsibilities for the care of the parents' children and other than a specific parenting time schedule for the parents' children.

(2000 S 180, eff. 3-22-01; 1990 S 3, eff. 4-11-91)

3109.06. Certification to juvenile court

Except as provided in division (K) of section 2301.03 of the Revised Code, any court, other than a juvenile court, that has jurisdiction in any case respecting the allocation of parental rights and responsibilities for the care of a child under eighteen years of age and the designation of the child's place of residence and legal custodian or in any case respecting the support of a child under eighteen years of age, may, on its own motion or on motion of any interested party, with the consent of the juvenile court, certify the record in the case or so much of the record and such further information, in narrative form or otherwise, as the court deems necessary or the juvenile court requests, to the juvenile court for further proceedings; upon the certification, the juvenile court shall have exclusive jurisdiction.

In cases in which the court of common pleas finds the parents unsuitable to have the parental rights and responsibilities for the care of the child or children and unsuitable to provide the place of residence and to be the legal custodian of the child or children, consent of the juvenile court shall not be required to such certification. This section applies to actions pending on August 28, 1951.

In any case in which a court of common pleas, or other court having jurisdiction, has issued an order that allocates parental rights and responsibilities for the care of minor children and designates their place of residence and legal custodian of minor children, has made an order for support of minor children, or has done both, the jurisdiction of the court shall not abate upon the death of the person awarded custody but shall continue for all purposes during the minority of the children. The court, upon its own motion or the motion of either parent or of any interested person acting on behalf of the children, may proceed to make further disposition of the case in the best interests of the children and subject to sections 3109.42 to 3109.48 of the Revised Code. If the children are under eighteen years of age, it may certify them, pursuant to this section, to the juvenile court of any county for further proceedings. After certification to a juvenile court, the jurisdiction of the court of common pleas, or other court, shall cease, except as to any payments of spousal support due for the spouse and support payments due and unpaid for the children at the time of the certification.

Any disposition made pursuant to this section, whether by a juvenile court after a case is certified to it, or by any court upon the death of a person awarded custody of a child, shall be made in accordance with sections 3109.04 and 3109.42 to 3109.48 of the Revised Code. If an appeal is taken from a decision made pursuant to this section that allocates parental rights and responsibilities for the care of a minor child and designates the child's place of residence and legal custodian, the court of appeals shall give the case calendar priority and handle it expeditiously.

(2010 H 10, eff. 6-17-10; 1999 H 191, eff. 10-20-99; 1990 S 3, eff. 4-11-91; 1990 H 514; 1983 H 93; 1953 H 1; GC 8005-6; Source—GC 8034-1)

3109.07. Appeal to the court of appeals

An appeal to the court of appeals may be had pursuant to the Rules of Appellate Procedure and, to the extent not in conflict with those rules, Chapter 2505. of the Revised Code.

(1986 H 412, eff. 3-17-87; 129 v 291; 1953 H 1; GC 8005-7; Source—GC 8035)

VISITATION RIGHTS OF RELATIVES

3109.11. Visitation rights of grandparents and other relatives when parent deceased

If either the father or mother of an unmarried minor child is deceased, the court of common pleas of the county in which the minor child resides may grant the parents and other relatives of the deceased father or mother reasonable companionship or visitation rights with respect to the minor child during the child's minority if the parent or other relative files a complaint requesting reasonable companionship or visitation rights and if the court determines that the granting of the companionship or visitation rights is in the best interest of the minor child. In determining whether to grant any person reasonable companionship or visitation rights with respect to any child, the court shall consider all relevant factors, including, but not limited to, the factors set forth in division (D) of section 3109.051 of the Revised Code. Divisions (C), (K), and (L) of section 3109.051 of the Revised Code apply to the determination of reasonable companionship or visitation rights under this section and to any order granting any such rights that is issued under this section.

The remarriage of the surviving parent of the child or the adoption of the child by the spouse of the surviving parent of the child does not affect the authority of the court under this section to grant reasonable companionship or visitation rights with respect to the child to a parent or other relative of the child's deceased father or mother.

If the court denies a request for reasonable companionship or visitation rights made pursuant to this section and the complainant files a written request for findings of fact and conclusions of law, the court shall state in writing its findings of fact and conclusions of law in accordance with Civil Rule 52.

Except as provided in division (E)(6) of section 3113.31 of the Revised Code, if the court, pursuant to this section, grants any person companionship or visitation rights with respect to any child, it shall not require the public children services agency to provide supervision of or other services related to that person's exercise of companionship or visitation rights with respect to the child. This section does not limit the power of a juvenile court pursuant to Chapter 2151. of the Revised Code to issue orders with respect to children who are alleged to be abused, neglected, or dependent children or to make dispositions of children who are adjudicated abused, neglected, or dependent children or of a common pleas court to issue orders pursuant to section 3113.31 of the Revised Code.

(2000 S 180, eff. 3-22-01; 1996 H 274, eff. 8-8-96; 1990 S 3, eff. 4-11-91; 1990 H 15; 1971 H 163)

PARENT CONVICTED OF KILLING OTHER PARENT

3109.41. Definitions

As used in sections 3109.41 to 3109.48 of the Revised Code:

(A) A person is "convicted of killing" if the person has been convicted of or pleaded guilty to a violation of section 2903.01, 2903.02, or 2903.03 of the Revised Code.

(B) "Custody order" means an order designating a person as the residential parent and legal custodian of a child under section 3109.04 of the Revised Code or any order determining custody of a child under section 2151.23, 2151.33, 2151.353, 2151.354, 2151.415, 2151.417, 2152.16, 2152.17, 2152.19, 2152.21, or 3113.31 of the Revised Code.

(C) "Visitation order" means an order issued under division (B)(1)(c) of section 2151.33 or under section 2151.412, 3109.051, 3109.12, or 3113.31 of the Revised Code.

(2000 S 179, § 3, eff. 1-1-02; 1999 H 191, eff. 10-20-99)

3109.42. Unavailability of custody for parent convicted of killing other parent

Except as provided in section 3109.47 of the Revised Code, if a parent is convicted of killing the other parent of a child, no court shall issue a custody order designating the parent as the residential parent and legal custodian of the child or granting custody of the child to the parent.

(1999 H 191, eff. 10-20-99)

3109.43. Unavailability of visitation rights for parent convicted of killing other parent

Except as provided in section 3109.47 of the Revised Code, if a parent is convicted of killing the other parent of a child, no court shall issue a visitation order granting the parent visitation rights with the child.

(1999 H 191, eff. 10-20-99)

3109.44. Notice of conviction

Upon receipt of notice that a visitation order is pending or has been issued granting a parent visitation rights with a child or a custody order is pending or has been issued designating a parent as the residential parent and legal custodian of a child or granting custody of a child to a parent prior to that parent being convicted of killing the other parent of the child, the court in which the parent is convicted of killing the other parent shall immediately notify the court that issued the visitation or custody order of the conviction.

(1999 H 191, eff. 10-20-99)

3109.45. Termination of visitation order upon receipt of notice of conviction

On receipt of notice under section 3109.44 of the Revised Code, a court that issued a visitation order described in that section shall terminate the order.

(1999 H 191, eff. 10-20-99)

3109.46. Termination of custody order upon receipt of notice of conviction; deemed new complaint for custody

If the court to which notice is sent under section 3109.44 of the Revised Code is a juvenile court that issued a custody order described in that section, the court shall retain jurisdiction over the order. If the court to which notice is sent is not a juvenile court but the court issued a custody order described in that section, the court shall transfer jurisdiction over the custody order to the juvenile court of the county in which the child has a residence or legal settlement.

On receipt of the notice in cases in which the custody order was issued by a juvenile court or after jurisdiction is transferred, the juvenile court with jurisdiction shall terminate the custody order.

The termination order shall be treated as a complaint filed under section 2151.27 of the Revised Code alleging the child subject of the custody order to be a dependent child. If a juvenile court issued the terminated custody order under a prior juvenile proceeding under Chapter 2151. of the Revised Code in which the child was adjudicated an abused, neglected, dependent, unruly, or delinquent child or a juvenile traffic offender, the court shall treat the termination order as a new complaint.

(1999 H 191, eff. 10-20-99)

3109.47. Custody or visitation order when in best interest of child

(A) A court may do one of the following with respect to a parent convicted of killing the other parent of a child if the court determines, by clear and convincing evidence, that it is in the best interest of the child and the child consents:

(1) Issue a custody order designating the parent as the residential parent and legal custodian of the child or granting custody of the child to that parent;

(2) Issue a visitation order granting that parent visitation rights with the child.

(B) When considering the ability of a child to consent and the validity of a child's consent under this section, the court shall consider the wishes of the child, as expressed directly by the child or through the child's guardian ad litem, with due regard for the maturity of the child.

(1999 H 191, eff. 10-20-99)

3109.48. Court order and consent of custodian required for visitation

No person, with the child of the parent present, shall visit the parent who has been convicted of killing the child's other parent unless a court has issued an order granting the parent visitation rights with the child and the child's custodian or legal guardian consents to the visit.

(1999 H 191, eff. 10-20-99)

PARENTAL RIGHTS OF RAPE OR SEXUAL BATTERY OFFENDERS

3109.50. Definitions

As used in sections 3109.501 to 3109.507 of the Revised Code:

(A) "Parental rights" means parental rights and responsibilities, parenting time, or any other similar right established by the laws of this state with respect to a child. "Parental rights" does not include the parental duty of support for a child.

(B) "Rape" means a violation of section 2907.02 of the Revised Code or similar law of another state.

(C) "Sexual battery" means a violation of section 2907.03 of the Revised Code or similar law of another state.

(2014 S 207, eff. 3-23-15)

3109.501. Action by victim to establish offender as parent of child conceived as result of offense

(A) Except as provided in division (C) and subject to division (D) of this section, a person who is the victim of rape or sexual battery for which a child was conceived as a result may bring an action to declare the person who was convicted of or pleaded guilty to the offense to be the parent of the child conceived as a result of rape or sexual battery committed by the other person.

(B) In an action seeking a declaration described in division (A) of this section, a court may issue an order declaring that the other person is the parent of a child conceived as a result of rape or sexual battery committed by the other person if all of the following are established by clear and convincing evidence:

(1) The other person was convicted of or pleaded guilty to the rape or sexual battery.

(2) The person bringing the action was the victim of the rape or sexual battery.

(3) The child was conceived as a result of the rape or sexual battery.

(4) Both persons are the parents of the child established pursuant to genetic testing conducted in different places or at different times or as provided in Chapter 3111. of the Revised Code.

(C) A person to whom the following apply may seek a declaration described in division (A) of this section only pursuant to a proceeding for divorce, dissolution, legal separation, or annulment:

(1) The person is the victim of a rape or sexual battery for which a child was conceived as a result.

(2) The person is married to the person who was convicted of or pleaded guilty to the rape or sexual battery.

(D) An action seeking a declaration under division (A) of this section shall be filed in a court with jurisdiction over juvenile matters if the parents of the child are not married and in a court with jurisdiction over domestic relations matters, pursuant to a proceeding for divorce, dissolution, legal separation, or annulment, if the parents of the child are married.

(2014 S 207, eff. 3-23-15)

3109.502. Action to be continued until issuance of judgment and exhaustion of appeals

An action under section 3109.501 of the Revised Code shall be continued until the court renders a judgment and all appeals have been exhausted in the criminal proceedings regarding the charge of rape or sexual battery that is the basis of the action. On the final disposition of the criminal proceedings, the court shall do one of the following:

(A) Proceed with the action if the person was convicted of or pleaded guilty to rape or sexual battery;

(B) Dismiss the action if the person was acquitted of the charge of rape or sexual battery.

(2014 S 207, eff. 3-23-15)

3109.503. Notices

(A) A person who brings an action under division (A) of section 3109.501 of the Revised Code seeking a declaration that another person is the parent of a child conceived as a result of rape or sexual battery committed by the other person shall notify the court in which the action is brought of any order previously issued by any court that grants the other person parental rights with respect to that child. The notice shall include the name of the court that issued the order, the date of issuance of the order, the name and number of the case in which the order was issued, the parental rights granted under the order, and the name of the person to whom the parental rights were granted.

(B) A court that issues an order under section 3109.501 of the Revised Code declaring a person to be the parent of a child conceived as a result of rape or sexual battery committed by the person shall notify any court that has issued an order granting the person parental rights with respect to that child and that was identified in accordance with division (A) of this section by the person who brought the action.

(2014 S 207, eff. 3-23-15)

3109.504. Prohibition against order granting parental rights to offender; termination of order upon notice

(A) No court shall issue an order granting parental rights with respect to a child to a person who has been convicted of or pleaded guilty to rape or sexual battery and has been declared, in an action or proceeding under section 3109.501 or 3109.505 of the Revised Code regarding that child, to be the parent of a child conceived as a result of rape or sexual battery committed by the person.

(B) On receipt of a notice under section 3109.503 of the Revised Code, a court that has issued an order granting parental rights regarding the person and child addressed in the notice shall terminate the order.

(2014 S 207, eff. 3-23-15)

3109.505. Consolidation of actions

Any action described in section 3109.501 of the Revised Code may be consolidated with any action or proceeding for parental rights regarding a child conceived as a result of rape or sexual battery.

(2014 S 207, eff. 3-23-15)

3109.506. Relative of offender may be granted only those rights consented to by other parent

A relative of a person whose parental rights with that person's child have been terminated, denied, or limited pursuant to sections 3109.50 to 3109.505 of the Revised Code may be granted only those rights consented to by the other parent of the child.

(2014 S 207, eff. 3-23-15)

3109.507. Order concerning offender's parental rights may only be revoked or modified upon motion of victim; limitation of parental rights does not relieve debts

(A) If a court issues an order under section 3109.501 of the Revised Code declaring a person to be the parent of a child conceived as a result of rape or sexual battery committed by the person, no court shall revoke or modify the order or the resulting denial, termination, or limitation of the person's parental rights and the person's relatives' rights under sections 3109.50 to 3109.506 of the Revised Code, except upon motion of the victim of the rape or sexual battery requesting the revocation or modification. The motion shall be made in the court that issued the order under section 3109.501 of the Revised Code.

(B) The denial, termination, or limitation of parental rights under sections 3109.50 to 3109.506 of the Revised Code does not relieve the person of any debts owed to the other parent or the child prior to the denial, termination, or limitation.

(2014 S 207, eff. 3-23-15)

CHAPTER 3113 NEGLECT, ABANDONMENT, OR DOMESTIC VIOLENCE

Section

3113.31. Petitions; protection orders concerning domestic violence or sexually oriented offense; support orders; sanctions for violations; notification of law enforcement agencies and courts

(A) As used in this section:

(1) "Domestic violence" means any of the following:

(a) The occurrence of one or more of the following acts against a family or household member:

(i) Attempting to cause or recklessly causing bodily injury;

(ii) Placing another person by the threat of force in fear of imminent serious physical harm or committing a violation of section 2903.211 of the Revised Code or section 2911.211 of the Revised Code;

(iii) Committing any act with respect to a child that would result in the child being an abused child, as defined in section 2151.031 of the Revised Code;

(iv) Committing a sexually oriented offense.

(b) The occurrence of one or more of the acts identified in divisions (A)(1)(a)(i) to (iv) of this section against a person with whom the respondent is or was in a dating relationship.

(2) "Court" means the domestic relations division of the court of common pleas in counties that have a domestic relations division and the court of common pleas in counties that do not have a domestic relations division, or the juvenile division of the court of common pleas of the county in which the person to be protected by a protection order issued or a consent agreement approved under this section resides if the respondent is less than eighteen years of age.

(3) "Family or household member" means any of the following:

(a) Any of the following who is residing with or has resided with the respondent:

(i) A spouse, a person living as a spouse, or a former spouse of the respondent;

(ii) A parent, a foster parent, or a child of the respondent, or another person related by consanguinity or affinity to the respondent;

(iii) A parent or a child of a spouse, person living as a spouse, or former spouse of the respondent, or another person related by consanguinity or affinity to a spouse, person living as a spouse, or former spouse of the respondent.

(b) The natural parent of any child of whom the respondent is the other natural parent or is the putative other natural parent.

(4) "Person living as a spouse" means a person who is living or has lived with the respondent in a common law marital relationship, who otherwise is cohabiting with the respondent, or who otherwise has cohabited with the respondent within five years prior to the date of the alleged occurrence of the act in question.

(5) "Victim advocate" means a person who provides support and assistance for a person who files a petition under this section.

(6) "Sexually oriented offense" has the same meaning as in section 2950.01 of the Revised Code.

(7) "Companion animal" has the same meaning as in section 959.131 of the Revised Code.

(8) "Dating relationship" means a relationship between individuals who have, or have had, a relationship of a romantic or intimate nature. "Dating relationship" does not include a casual acquaintanceship or ordinary fraternization in a business or social context.

(9) "Person with whom the respondent is or was in a dating relationship" means an adult who, at the time of the conduct in question, is in a dating relationship with the respondent who also is an adult or who, within the twelve months preceding the conduct in question, has had a dating relationship with the respondent who also is an adult.

(10) [1]"Expunge" has the same meaning as in section 2903.213 of the Revised Code.

(B) The court has jurisdiction over all proceedings under this section. The petitioner's right to relief under this section is not affected by the petitioner's leaving the residence or household to avoid further domestic violence.

(C) A person may seek relief under this section on the person's own behalf, or any parent or adult household member may seek relief under this section on behalf of any other family or household member, by filing a petition with the court. The petition shall contain or state:

(1) An allegation that the respondent engaged in domestic violence against a family or household member of the respondent or against a person with whom the respondent is or was in a dating relationship, including a description of the nature and extent of the domestic violence;

(2) The relationship of the respondent to the petitioner, and to the victim if other than the petitioner;

(3) If the petition is for protection of a person with whom the respondent is or was in a dating relationship, the facts upon which the court may conclude that a dating relationship existed between the person to be protected and the respondent;

(4) A request for relief under this section.

(D) (1) If a person who files a petition pursuant to this section requests an ex parte order, the court shall hold an ex parte hearing on the same day that the petition is filed. The court, for good cause shown at the ex parte hearing, may enter any temporary orders, with or without bond, including, but not limited to, an order described in division (E)(1)(a), (b), or (c) of this section, that the court finds necessary to protect the family or household member or the person with whom the respondent is or was in a dating relationship from domestic violence. Immediate and present danger of domestic violence to the family or household member

[1]Division designation is as a result of harmonization of 2017 H 49 and 2018 H 1.

or to the person with whom the respondent is or was in a dating relationship constitutes good cause for purposes of this section. Immediate and present danger includes, but is not limited to, situations in which the respondent has threatened the family or household member or person with whom the respondent is or was in a dating relationship with bodily harm, in which the respondent has threatened the family or household member or person with whom the respondent is or was in a dating relationship with a sexually oriented offense, or in which the respondent previously has been convicted of, pleaded guilty to, or been adjudicated a delinquent child for an offense that constitutes domestic violence against the family or household member or person with whom the respondent is or was in a dating relationship.

(2) (a) If the court, after an ex parte hearing, issues an order described in division (E)(1)(b) or (c) of this section, the court shall schedule a full hearing for a date that is within seven court days after the ex parte hearing. If any other type of protection order that is authorized under division (E) of this section is issued by the court after an ex parte hearing, the court shall schedule a full hearing for a date that is within ten court days after the ex parte hearing. The court shall give the respondent notice of, and an opportunity to be heard at, the full hearing. The court shall hold the full hearing on the date scheduled under this division unless the court grants a continuance of the hearing in accordance with this division. Under any of the following circumstances or for any of the following reasons, the court may grant a continuance of the full hearing to a reasonable time determined by the court:

(i) Prior to the date scheduled for the full hearing under this division, the respondent has not been served with the petition filed pursuant to this section and notice of the full hearing.

(ii) The parties consent to the continuance.

(iii) The continuance is needed to allow a party to obtain counsel.

(iv) The continuance is needed for other good cause.

(b) An ex parte order issued under this section does not expire because of a failure to serve notice of the full hearing upon the respondent before the date set for the full hearing under division (D)(2)(a) of this section or because the court grants a continuance under that division.

(3) If a person who files a petition pursuant to this section does not request an ex parte order, or if a person requests an ex parte order but the court does not issue an ex parte order after an ex parte hearing, the court shall proceed as in a normal civil action and grant a full hearing on the matter.

(E) (1) After an ex parte or full hearing, the court may grant any protection order, with or without bond, or approve any consent agreement to bring about a cessation of domestic violence against the family or household members or persons with whom the respondent is or was in a dating relationship. The order or agreement may:

(a) Direct the respondent to refrain from abusing or from committing sexually oriented offenses against the family or household members or persons with whom the respondent is or was in a dating relationship;

(b) With respect to a petition involving family or household members, grant possession of the residence or household to the petitioner or other family or household member, to the exclusion of the respondent, by evicting the respondent, when the residence or household is owned or leased solely by the petitioner or other family or household member, or by ordering the respondent to vacate the premises, when the residence or household is jointly owned or leased by the respondent, and the petitioner or other family or household member;

(c) With respect to a petition involving family or household members, when the respondent has a duty to support the petitioner or other family or household member living in the residence or household and the respondent is the sole owner or lessee of the residence or household, grant possession of the residence or household to the petitioner or other family or household member, to the exclusion of the respondent, by ordering the respondent to vacate the premises, or, in the case of a consent agreement, allow the respondent to provide suitable, alternative housing;

(d) With respect to a petition involving family or household members, temporarily allocate parental rights and responsibilities for the care of, or establish temporary parenting time rights with regard to, minor children, if no other court has determined, or is determining, the allocation of parental rights and responsibilities for the minor children or parenting time rights;

(e) With respect to a petition involving family or household members, require the respondent to maintain support, if the respondent customarily provides for or contributes to the support of the family or household member, or if the respondent has a duty to support the petitioner or family or household member;

(f) Require the respondent, petitioner, victim of domestic violence, or any combination of those persons, to seek counseling;

(g) Require the respondent to refrain from entering the residence, school, business, or place of employment of the petitioner or, with respect to a petition involving family or household members, a family or household member;

(h) Grant other relief that the court considers equitable and fair, including, but not limited to, ordering the respondent to permit the use of a motor vehicle by the petitioner or, with respect to a petition involving family or household members, other family or household members and the apportionment of household and family personal property;

(i) Require that the respondent not remove, damage, hide, harm, or dispose of any companion animal owned or possessed by the petitioner;

(j) Authorize the petitioner to remove a companion animal owned by the petitioner from the possession of the respondent;

(k) Require a wireless service transfer in accordance with sections 3113.45 to 3113.459 of the Revised Code.

(2) If a protection order has been issued pursuant to this section in a prior action involving the respondent and the petitioner or, with respect to a petition involving family or household members, one or more of the family or household members or victims, the court may include in a protection order that it issues a prohibition against the respondent returning to the residence or household. If it includes a prohibition against the respondent returning to the residence or household in the order, it also shall include in the order provisions of the type described in division (E)(7) of this section. This division does not preclude the court from including in a protection order or consent agreement, in circumstances other than those described in this division, a requirement that the respondent be evicted from or vacate the residence or household or refrain from entering the residence, school, business, or place of employment of the petitioner or, with respect to a petition involving family or household members, a family or household member, and, if the court includes any requirement of that type in an order or agreement, the court also shall include in the order provisions of the type described in division (E)(7) of this section.

(3) (a) Any protection order issued or consent agreement approved under this section shall be valid until a date certain, but not later than five years from the date of its issuance or approval, or not later than the date a respondent who is less than eighteen years of age attains nineteen years of age, unless modified or terminated as provided in division (E)(8) of this section.

(b) With respect to an order involving family or household members, subject to the limitation on the duration of an order or agreement set forth in division (E)(3)(a) of this section, any order under division (E)(1)(d) of this section shall terminate on the date that a court in an action for divorce, dissolution of marriage, or legal separation brought by the petitioner or respondent issues an order allocating parental rights and responsibilities for the care of children or on the date that a juvenile court in an action brought by the petitioner or respondent issues an order awarding legal custody of minor children. Subject to the limitation on the duration of an order or agreement set forth in division (E)(3)(a) of this section, any order under division (E)(1)(e) of this section shall terminate on the date that a court in an action for divorce, dissolution of marriage, or legal separation brought by the petitioner or respondent issues a support order or on the date that a juvenile court in an action brought by the petitioner or respondent issues a support order.

(c) Any protection order issued or consent agreement approved pursuant to this section may be renewed in the same manner as the original order or agreement was issued or approved.

(4) A court may not issue a protection order that requires a petitioner to do or

to refrain from doing an act that the court may require a respondent to do or to refrain from doing under division (E)(1)(a), (b), (c), (d), (e), (g), or (h) of this section unless all of the following apply:

(a) The respondent files a separate petition for a protection order in accordance with this section.

(b) The petitioner is served notice of the respondent's petition at least forty-eight hours before the court holds a hearing with respect to the respondent's petition, or the petitioner waives the right to receive this notice.

(c) If the petitioner has requested an ex parte order pursuant to division (D) of this section, the court does not delay any hearing required by that division beyond the time specified in that division in order to consolidate the hearing with a hearing on the petition filed by the respondent.

(d) After a full hearing at which the respondent presents evidence in support of the request for a protection order and the petitioner is afforded an opportunity to defend against that evidence, the court determines that the petitioner has committed an act of domestic violence or has violated a temporary protection order issued pursuant to section 2919.26 of the Revised Code, that both the petitioner and the respondent acted primarily as aggressors, and that neither the petitioner nor the respondent acted primarily in self-defense.

(5) No protection order issued or consent agreement approved under this section shall in any manner affect title to any real property.

(6) (a) With respect to an order involving family or household members, if a petitioner, or the child of a petitioner, who obtains a protection order or consent agreement pursuant to division (E)(1) of this section or a temporary protection order pursuant to section 2919.26 of the Revised Code and is the subject of a parenting time order issued pursuant to section 3109.051 or 3109.12 of the Revised Code or a visitation or companionship order issued pursuant to section 3109.051, 3109.11, or 3109.12 of the Revised Code or division (E)(1)(d) of this section granting parenting time rights to the respondent, the court may require the public children services agency of the county in which the court is located to provide supervision of the respondent's exercise of parenting time or visitation or companionship rights with respect to the child for a period not to exceed nine months, if the court makes the following findings of fact:

(i) The child is in danger from the respondent;

(ii) No other person or agency is available to provide the supervision.

(b) A court that requires an agency to provide supervision pursuant to division (E)(6)(a) of this section shall order the respondent to reimburse the agency for the cost of providing the supervision, if it determines that the respondent has sufficient income or resources to pay that cost.

(7) (a) If a protection order issued or consent agreement approved under this section includes a requirement that the respondent be evicted from or vacate the residence or household or refrain from entering the residence, school, business, or place of employment of the petitioner or, with respect to a petition involving family or household members, a family or household member, the order or agreement shall state clearly that the order or agreement cannot be waived or nullified by an invitation to the respondent from the petitioner or other family or household member to enter the residence, school, business, or place of employment or by the respondent's entry into one of those places otherwise upon the consent of the petitioner or other family or household member.

(b) Division (E)(7)(a) of this section does not limit any discretion of a court to determine that a respondent charged with a violation of section 2919.27 of the Revised Code, with a violation of a municipal ordinance substantially equivalent to that section, or with contempt of court, which charge is based on an alleged violation of a protection order issued or consent agreement approved under this section, did not commit the violation or was not in contempt of court.

(8) (a) The court may modify or terminate as provided in division (E)(8) of this section a protection order or consent agreement that was issued after a full hearing under this section. The court that issued the protection order or ap-

proved the consent agreement shall hear a motion for modification or termination of the protection order or consent agreement pursuant to division (E)(8) of this section.

(b) Either the petitioner or the respondent of the original protection order or consent agreement may bring a motion for modification or termination of a protection order or consent agreement that was issued or approved after a full hearing. The court shall require notice of the motion to be made as provided by the Rules of Civil Procedure. If the petitioner for the original protection order or consent agreement has requested that the petitioner's address be kept confidential, the court shall not disclose the address to the respondent of the original protection order or consent agreement or any other person, except as otherwise required by law. The moving party has the burden of proof to show, by a preponderance of the evidence, that modification or termination of the protection order or consent agreement is appropriate because either the protection order or consent agreement is no longer needed or because the terms of the original protection order or consent agreement are no longer appropriate.

(c) In considering whether to modify or terminate a protection order or consent agreement issued or approved under this section, the court shall consider all relevant factors, including, but not limited to, the following:

(i) Whether the petitioner consents to modification or termination of the protection order or consent agreement;

(ii) Whether the petitioner fears the respondent;

(iii) The current nature of the relationship between the petitioner and the respondent;

(iv) The circumstances of the petitioner and respondent, including the relative proximity of the petitioner's and respondent's workplaces and residences and whether the petitioner and respondent have minor children together;

(v) Whether the respondent has complied with the terms and conditions of the original protection order or consent agreement;

(vi) Whether the respondent has a continuing involvement with illegal drugs or alcohol;

(vii) Whether the respondent has been convicted of, pleaded guilty to, or been adjudicated a delinquent child for an offense of violence since the issuance of the protection order or approval of the consent agreement;

(viii) Whether any other protection orders, consent agreements, restraining orders, or no contact orders have been issued against the respondent pursuant to this section, section 2919.26 of the Revised Code, any other provision of state law, or the law of any other state;

(ix) Whether the respondent has participated in any domestic violence treatment, intervention program, or other counseling addressing domestic violence and whether the respondent has completed the treatment, program, or counseling;

(x) The time that has elapsed since the protection order was issued or since the consent agreement was approved;

(xi) The age and health of the respondent;

(xii) When the last incident of abuse, threat of harm, or commission of a sexually oriented offense occurred or other relevant information concerning the safety and protection of the petitioner or other protected parties.

(d) If a protection order or consent agreement is modified or terminated as provided in division (E)(8) of this section, the court shall issue copies of the modified or terminated order or agreement as provided in division (F) of this section. A petitioner may also provide notice of the modification or termination to the judicial and law enforcement officials in any county other than the county in which the order or agreement is modified or terminated as provided in division (N) of this section.

(e) If the respondent moves for modification or termination of a protection order or consent agreement pursuant to this section and the court denies the motion, the court may assess costs against the respondent for the filing of the motion.

(9) Any protection order issued or any consent agreement approved pursuant

to this section shall include a provision that the court will automatically seal all of the records of the proceeding in which the order is issued or agreement approved on the date the respondent attains the age of nineteen years unless the petitioner provides the court with evidence that the respondent has not complied with all of the terms of the protection order or consent agreement. The protection order or consent agreement shall specify the date when the respondent attains the age of nineteen years.

(F) (1) A copy of any protection order, or consent agreement, that is issued, approved, modified, or terminated under this section shall be issued by the court to the petitioner, to the respondent, and to all law enforcement agencies that have jurisdiction to enforce the order or agreement. The court shall direct that a copy of an order be delivered to the respondent on the same day that the order is entered.

(2) Upon the issuance of a protection order or the approval of a consent agreement under this section, the court shall provide the parties to the order or agreement with the following notice orally or by form:

"NOTICE

As a result of this order or consent agreement, it may be unlawful for you to possess or purchase a firearm, including a rifle, pistol, or revolver, or ammunition pursuant to federal law under 18 U.S.C. 922(g)(8) for the duration of this order or consent agreement. If you have any questions whether this law makes it illegal for you to possess or purchase a firearm or ammunition, you should consult an attorney."

(3) All law enforcement agencies shall establish and maintain an index for the protection orders and the approved consent agreements delivered to the agencies pursuant to division (F)(1) of this section. With respect to each order and consent agreement delivered, each agency shall note on the index the date and time that it received the order or consent agreement.

(4) Regardless of whether the petitioner has registered the order or agreement in the county in which the officer's agency has jurisdiction pursuant to division (N) of this section, any officer of a law enforcement agency shall enforce a protection order issued or consent agreement approved by any court in this state in accordance with the provisions of the order or agreement, including removing the respondent from the premises, if appropriate.

(G) (1) Any proceeding under this section shall be conducted in accordance with the Rules of Civil Procedure, except that an order under this section may be obtained with or without bond. An order issued under this section, other than an ex parte order, that grants a protection order or approves a consent agreement, that refuses to grant a protection order or approve a consent agreement that modifies or terminates a protection order or consent agreement, or that refuses to modify or terminate a protection order or consent agreement, is a final, appealable order. The remedies and procedures provided in this section are in addition to, and not in lieu of, any other available civil or criminal remedies.

(2) If as provided in division (G)(1) of this section an order issued under this section, other than an ex parte order, refuses to grant a protection order, the court, on its own motion, shall order that the ex parte order issued under this section and all of the records pertaining to that ex parte order be expunged after either of the following occurs:

(a) The period of the notice of appeal from the order that refuses to grant a protection order has expired.

(b) The order that refuses to grant the protection order is appealed and an appellate court to which the last appeal of that order is taken affirms the order.

(H) The filing of proceedings under this section does not excuse a person from filing any report or giving any notice required by section 2151.421 of the Revised Code or by any other law. When a petition under this section alleges domestic violence against minor children, the court shall report the fact, or cause reports to be made, to a county, township, or municipal peace officer under section 2151.421 of the Revised Code.

(I) Any law enforcement agency that investigates a domestic dispute shall provide information to the family or household members involved, or the persons in the dating relationship who are involved, whichever is applicable regarding the relief available under this section and, for family or household members, section 2919.26 of the Revised Code.

(J) (1) Subject to divisions (E)(8)(e) and (J)(2) of this section and regardless of whether a protection order is issued or a consent agreement is approved by a court of another county or a court of another state, no court or unit of state or local government shall charge the petitioner any fee, cost, deposit, or money in connection with the filing of a petition pursuant to this section or in connection with the filing, issuance, registration, modification, enforcement, dismissal, withdrawal, or service of a protection order, consent agreement, or witness subpoena or for obtaining a certified copy of a protection order or consent agreement.

(2) Regardless of whether a protection order is issued or a consent agreement is approved pursuant to this section, the court may assess costs against the respondent in connection with the filing, issuance, registration, modification, enforcement, dismissal, withdrawal, or service of a protection order, consent agreement, or witness subpoena or for obtaining a certified copy of a protection order or consent agreement.

(K) (1) The court shall comply with Chapters 3119., 3121., 3123., and 3125. of the Revised Code when it makes or modifies an order for child support under this section.

(2) If any person required to pay child support under an order made under this section on or after April 15, 1985, or modified under this section on or after December 31, 1986, is found in contempt of court for failure to make support payments under the order, the court that makes the finding, in addition to any other penalty or remedy imposed, shall assess all court costs arising out of the contempt proceeding against the person and require the person to pay any reasonable attorney's fees of any adverse party, as determined by the court, that arose in relation to the act of contempt.

(L) (1) A person who violates a protection order issued or a consent agreement approved under this section is subject to the following sanctions:

(a) Criminal prosecution or a delinquent child proceeding for a violation of section 2919.27 of the Revised Code, if the violation of the protection order or consent agreement constitutes a violation of that section;

(b) Punishment for contempt of court.

(2) The punishment of a person for contempt of court for violation of a protection order issued or a consent agreement approved under this section does not bar criminal prosecution of the person or a delinquent child proceeding concerning the person for a violation of section 2919.27 of the Revised Code. However, a person punished for contempt of court is entitled to credit for the punishment imposed upon conviction of or adjudication as a delinquent child for a violation of that section, and a person convicted of or adjudicated a delinquent child for a violation of that section shall not subsequently be punished for contempt of court arising out of the same activity.

(M) In all stages of a proceeding under this section, a petitioner may be accompanied by a victim advocate.

(N) (1) A petitioner who obtains a protection order or consent agreement under this section or a temporary protection order under section 2919.26 of the Revised Code may provide notice of the issuance or approval of the order or agreement to the judicial and law enforcement officials in any county other than the county in which the order is issued or the agreement is approved by registering that order or agreement in the other county pursuant to division (N)(2) of this section and filing a copy of the registered order or registered agreement with a law enforcement agency in the other county in accordance with that division. A person who obtains a protection order issued by a court of another state may provide notice of the issuance of the order to the judicial and law enforcement officials in any county of this state by registering the order in that county pursuant to section 2919.272 of the Revised Code and filing a copy of the registered order with a law enforcement agency in that county.

(2) A petitioner may register a temporary protection order, protection order, or consent agreement in a county other than the county in which the court that issued the order or approved the agreement is located in the following manner:

(a) The petitioner shall obtain a certified copy of the order or agreement from the clerk of the court that issued the order or approved the agreement and present that certified copy to the clerk of the court of common pleas or the clerk of a municipal court or county court in the county in which the order or agreement is to be registered.

(b) Upon accepting the certified copy of the order or agreement for registration, the clerk of the court of common pleas, municipal court, or county court shall place an endorsement of registration on the order or agreement and give the petitioner a copy of the order or agreement that bears that proof of registration.

(3) The clerk of each court of common pleas, the clerk of each municipal court, and the clerk of each county court shall maintain a registry of certified copies of temporary protection orders, protection orders, or consent agreements that have been issued or approved by courts in other counties and that have been registered with the clerk.

(O) Nothing in this section prohibits the domestic relations division of a court of common pleas in counties that have a domestic relations division or a court of common pleas in counties that do not have a domestic relations division from designating a minor child as a protected party on a protection order or consent agreement.

(2018 H 1, eff. 7-6-18; 2017 H 49, eff. 9-29-17; 2016 H 359, eff. 9-8-16; 2014 S 177, eff. 3-23-15; 2014 H 309, eff. 9-17-14; 2010 H 10, eff. 6-17-10; 2008 H 562, eff. 6-24-08; 2006 S 260, eff. 1-2-07; 2006 S 17, eff. 8-3-06; 2006 H 95, eff. 8-3-06; 2002 H 548, eff. 3-31-03; 2000 S 180, eff. 3-22-01; 1997 H 352, eff. 1-1-98; 1997 S 1, eff. 10-21-97; 1996 H 438, eff. 7-1-97; 1996 H 274, eff. 8-8-96; 1994 H 335, eff. 12-9-94; 1993 H 173, eff. 12-31-93; 1992 H 536, S 10; 1990 S 3, H 591; 1988 H 172, H 708; 1987 H 231; 1986 H 428, H 509; 1984 H 113, H 614, H 587; 1980 H 920; 1978 H 835)

CHAPTER 3127 UNIFORM CHILD CUSTODY JURISDICTION AND ENFORCEMENT ACT

Section

3127.01. Definitions

(A) As used in the Revised Code, "uniform child custody jurisdiction and enforcement act" means the act addressing interstate recognition and enforcement of child custody orders adopted in 1997 by the national conference of commissioners on uniform state laws or any law substantially similar to the act adopted by another state.

(B) As used in sections 3127.01 to 3127.53 of the Revised Code:

(1) "Abandoned" means the parents of a child have failed to visit or maintain contact with the child for more than ninety days, regardless of whether the parents resume contact with the child after that ninety-day period.

(2) "Child" means an individual who has not attained eighteen years of age.

(3) "Child custody determination" means a judgment, decree, or other order of a court that provides for legal custody, physical custody, parenting time, or visitation with respect to a child. "Child custody determination" includes an order that allocates parental rights and responsibilities. "Child custody determination" includes permanent, temporary, initial, and modification orders. "Child custody determination" does not include an order or the portion of an order relating to child support or other monetary obligations of an individual.

(4) "Child custody proceeding" means a proceeding in which legal custody, physical custody, parenting time, or visitation with respect to a child is an issue. "Child custody proceeding" may include a proceeding for divorce, separation, neglect, abuse, dependency, guardianship, parentage, termination of parental rights, or protection from domestic violence. "Child custody proceeding" does not include a proceeding regarding juvenile delinquency, contractual emancipation, or enforcement pursuant to sections 3127.31 to 3127.47 of the Revised Code.

(5) "Commencement" means the filing of the first pleading in a proceeding.

(6) "Court" means an entity authorized under the law of a state to establish, enforce, or modify a child custody determination.

(7) "Home state" means the state in which a child lived with a parent or a person acting as a parent for at least six consecutive months immediately preceding the commencement of a child custody proceeding and, if a child is less than six months old, the state in which the child lived from birth with any of them. A period of temporary absence of any of them is counted as part of the six-month or other period.

(8) "Initial determination" means the first child custody determination concerning a particular child.

(9) "Issuing court" means the court that makes a child custody determination for which enforcement is sought under sections 3127.01 to 3127.53 of the Revised Code.

(10) "Issuing state" means the state in which a child custody determination is made.

(11) "Modification" means a child custody determination that changes, replaces, supersedes, or is otherwise made after a determination concerning the same child, whether or not it is made by the court that made the previous determination.

(12) "Person" means an individual; corporation; business trust; estate; trust; partnership; limited liability company; association; joint venture; government; governmental subdivision, agency, or instrumentality; public corporation; or any other legal or commercial entity.

(13) "Person acting as a parent" means a person, other than the child's parent, who meets both of the following criteria:

(a) The person has physical custody of the child or has had physical custody for a period of six consecutive months, including any temporary absence from the child, within one year immediately before the commencement of a child custody proceeding; and

(b) The person has been awarded legal custody by a court or claims a right to legal custody under the law of this state.

(14) "Physical custody" means the physical care and supervision of a child.

(15) "State" means a state of the United States, the District of Columbia, Puerto Rico, the United States Virgin Islands, or any territory or insular possession subject to the jurisdiction of the United States.

(16) "Tribe" means an Indian tribe or Alaskan Native village that is recognized by federal or state law.

(17) "Warrant" means an order issued by a court authorizing law enforcement officers to take physical custody of a child.

(2004 S 185, eff. 4-11-05)

3127.02. Exception for certain proceedings

Sections 3127.01 to 3127.53 of the Revised Code do not govern adoption proceedings or proceedings pertaining to the authorization of emergency medical care for a child.

(2004 S 185, eff. 4-11-05)

3127.03. Applicability to children of Indian descent

(A) A child custody proceeding that pertains to an Indian child as defined in the Indian Child Welfare Act, 25 U.S.C. 1901 et seq., is not subject to sections 3127.01 to 3127.53 of the Revised Code to the extent that the proceeding is governed by the Indian Child Welfare Act.

(B) A court of this state shall treat a tribe as if it were a state of the United States for the purpose of applying sections 3127.01 to 3127.53 of the Revised Code.

(C) A child custody determination made by a tribe under factual circumstances in substantial conformity with the jurisdictional standards of sections 3127.01 to 3127.53 of the Revised Code shall be recognized and enforced under sections 3127.31 to 3127.47 of the Revised Code.

(2004 S 185, eff. 4-11-05)

3127.04. Applicability to foreign countries and custody determinations made in foreign countries

(A) A court of this state shall treat a foreign country as if it were a state of the United States for the purpose of applying sections 3127.01 to 3127.24 of the Revised Code.

(B) Except as otherwise provided in division (C) of this section, a child custody determination made in a foreign country under factual circumstances in substantial conformity with the jurisdictional standards of sections 3127.01 to 3127.53 of the Revised Code shall be recognized and enforced under sections 3127.31 to 3127.47 of the Revised Code.

(C) A court of this state need not apply sections 3127.01 to 3127.53 of the Revised Code if the law governing child custody determinations of a foreign country violates fundamental principles of human rights.

(2004 S 185, eff. 4-11-05)

3127.05. Parties bound by custody determinations

A child custody determination made by a court of this state with jurisdiction under sections 3127.01 to 3127.53 of the Revised Code binds all persons who have been served in accordance with the laws of this state, notified in accordance with section 3127.07 of the Revised Code, or who have submitted to the jurisdiction of the court, and who have been given an opportunity to be heard. As to those persons, the determination is conclusive as to all decided issues of law and fact except to the extent the determination is modified.

(2004 S 185, eff. 4-11-05)

3127.06. Priority of handling of jurisdictional challenge

Upon the request of a party to a child custody proceeding that raises a question of existence or exercise of jurisdiction under sections 3127.01 to 3127.53 of the Revised Code, the question shall be given calendar priority and handled expeditiously.

(2004 S 185, eff. 4-11-05)

3127.07. Notice required for jurisdiction over person outside state; proof of service

(A) Notice required for the exercise of jurisdiction over a person outside this state may be given in a manner prescribed by the Rules of Civil Procedure, or the Rules of Juvenile Procedure, as appropriate, for service of process or by the law of the state in which the service is made. Notice shall be given in a manner reasonably calculated to give actual notice but may be by publication if other means are not effective.

(B) Proof of service may be made in the manner prescribed by the Rules of Civil Procedure, or the Rules of Juvenile Procedure, as appropriate, or by the law of the state in which the service is made.

(C) Notice is not required if the person submits to the jurisdiction of the court.

(2004 S 185, eff. 4-11-05)

3127.08. Immunity from personal jurisdiction and service of process

(A) A party to a child custody proceeding, including a modification proceeding, or a petitioner or respondent in a proceeding to enforce or register a child custody determination, is not subject to personal jurisdiction in this state for another proceeding or purpose solely by reason of having participated, or of having been physically present for the purpose of participating, in the child custody proceeding.

(B) A person who is subject to personal jurisdiction in this state on a basis other than physical presence is not immune from service of process in this state. A party present in this state who is subject to the jurisdiction of another state is not immune from service of process allowable under the laws of that state.

(C) The immunity granted by division (A) of this section does not extend to civil litigation based on acts unrelated to the participation in a proceeding under sections 3127.01 to 3127.53 of the Revised Code that are committed by an individual while present in this state.

(2004 S 185, eff. 4-11-05)

3127.09. Communication between courts

(A) A court of this state may communicate with a court in another state concerning a proceeding arising under sections 3127.01 to 3127.53 of the Revised Code.

(B) The court may give the parties the opportunity to participate in the communication. If the parties are not able to participate in the communication, they shall be given the opportunity to present facts and legal arguments before a decision concerning jurisdiction is made.

(C) Communication between courts concerning scheduling, calendars, court records, and similar matters may occur without informing the parties. A record need not be made of the communication.

(D) Except as otherwise provided in division (C) of this section, a record shall be made of a communication under this section. The parties shall be informed promptly of the communication and granted access to the record.

(E) For the purposes of this section, "record" means information that is inscribed on a tangible medium or that is stored in an electronic or other medium and is retrievable in perceivable form.

(2004 S 185, eff. 4-11-05)

3127.10. Testimony of out-of-state witnesses

(A) In addition to other procedures available to a party, a party to a child custody proceeding may offer testimony of witnesses who are located in another state, including testimony of the parties and the child, by deposition or other means allowable in this state for testimony taken in another state. The court on its own motion may order that the testimony of a person be taken in another state and may prescribe the manner in which and the terms upon which the testimony is taken.

(B) A court of this state may permit an individual residing in another state to be deposed or to testify by telephone, audiovisual means, or other electronic means before a designated court or at another location in that state. A court of this state shall cooperate with courts of other states in designating an appropriate location for the deposition or testimony.

(C) Documentary evidence transmitted from another state to a court of this state by technological means that do not produce an original writing may not be excluded from evidence on an objection based on the means of transmission.

(2004 S 185, eff. 4-11-05)

3127.11. Requests made on other courts

(A) A court of this state may request the appropriate court of another state to do any of the following:

(1) Hold an evidentiary hearing;

(2) Order a person to produce or give evidence pursuant to procedures of that state;

(3) Order that an evaluation be made concerning the allocation of parental rights and responsibilities for the care of a child involved in a pending proceeding with respect to the designation of a parent as the residential parent and legal custodian of the child and with respect to the custody of the child in any other person;

(4) Forward to the court of this state a certified copy of the transcript of the record of the hearing, the evidence otherwise presented, and any evaluation prepared in compliance with the request;

(5) Order a party to a child custody proceeding or any person having physical custody of the child to appear in the proceeding with or without the child.

(B) Upon request of a court of another state, a court of this state may hold a hearing or enter an order described in division (A) of this section.

(C) The court may assess travel and other necessary and reasonable expenses incurred under divisions (A) and (B) of this section against the parties according to the law of this state.

(D) Upon appropriate request by a court or law enforcement official of another state, a court of this state shall forward a certified copy of the pleadings, orders, decrees, records of hearings, evaluations, and other pertinent records with respect to a child custody proceeding to the court or law enforcement official of the other state.

(2004 S 185, eff. 4-11-05)

3127.15. Jurisdiction to make initial determination

(A) Except as otherwise provided in section 3127.18 of the Revised Code, a court of this state has jurisdiction to make an initial determination in a child custody proceeding only if one of the following applies:

(1) This state is the home state of the child on the date of the commencement of the proceeding, or was the home state of the child within six months before the commencement of the proceeding and the child is absent from this state but a parent or person acting as a parent continues to live in this state.

(2) A court of another state does not have jurisdiction under division (A)(1) of this section or a court of the home state of the child has declined to exercise jurisdiction on the basis that this state is the more appropriate forum under section 3127.21 or 3127.22 of the Revised Code, or a similar statute of the other state, and both of the following are the case:

(a) The child and the child's parents, or the child and at least one parent or a person acting as a parent, have a significant connection with this state other than mere physical presence.

(b) Substantial evidence is available in this state concerning the child's care, protection, training, and personal relationships.

(3) All courts having jurisdiction under division (A)(1) or (2) of this section have declined to exercise jurisdiction on the ground that a court of this state is the more appropriate forum to determine the custody of the child under section 3127.21 or 3127.22 of the Revised Code or a similar statute enacted by another state.

(4) No court of any other state would have jurisdiction under the criteria specified in division (A)(1), (2), or (3) of this section.

(B) Division (A) of this section is the exclusive jurisdictional basis for making a child custody determination by a court of this state.

(C) Physical presence of, or personal jurisdiction over, a party or a child is not necessary or sufficient to make a child custody determination.

(2004 S 185, eff. 4-11-05)

3127.16. Exclusive continuing jurisdiction

Except as otherwise provided in section 3127.18 of the Revised Code, a court of this state that has made a child custody determination consistent with section 3127.15 or 3127.17 of the Revised Code has exclusive, continuing jurisdiction over the determination until the court or a court of another state determines that the child, the child's parents, and any person acting as a parent do not presently reside in this state.

(2004 S 185, eff. 4-11-05)

3127.17. Modification of custody determination by court of another state

Except as otherwise provided in section 3127.18 of the Revised Code, a court of this state may not modify a child custody determination made by a court of another state unless the court of this state has jurisdiction to make an initial determination under division (A)(1) or (2) of section 3127.15 of the Revised Code and one of the following applies:

(A) The court of the other state determines that it no longer has exclusive, continuing jurisdiction under section 3127.16 of the Revised Code or a similar statute of the other state or that a court of this state would be a more convenient forum under section 3127.21 of the Revised Code or a similar statute of the other state.

(B) The court of this state or a court of the other state determines that the child, the child's parents, and any person acting as a parent do not presently reside in the other state.

(2004 S 185, eff. 4-11-05)

3127.18. Temporary emergency jurisdiction

(A) A court of this state has temporary emergency jurisdiction if a child is present in this state and either of the following applies:

(1) The child has been abandoned.

(2) It is necessary in an emergency to protect the child because the child, or a sibling or parent of the child, is subjected to or threatened with mistreatment or abuse.

(B) If there is no previous child custody determination that is entitled to be enforced under this chapter and a child custody proceeding has not been commenced in a court of a state having jurisdiction under sections 3127.15 to 3127.17 of the Revised Code or a similar statute of another state, a child custody determination made under this section remains in effect until an order is obtained from a court of a state having jurisdiction under sections 3127.15 to 3127.17 of the Revised Code or a similar statute of another state. If a child custody proceeding has not been or is not commenced in a court of a state having jurisdiction under sections 3127.15 to 3127.17 of the Revised Code or a similar statute of another state, a child custody determination made under this section becomes a final determination, if it so provides and this state becomes the home state of the child.

(C) If there is a previous child custody determination that is entitled to be enforced under this chapter, or a child custody proceeding has been commenced in a court of a state having jurisdiction under sections 3127.15 to 3127.17 of the Revised Code or a similar statute of another state, any order issued by a court of this state under this section must specify in the order a period that the court considers adequate to allow the person seeking an order to obtain an order from the state having jurisdiction under sections 3127.15 to 3127.17 of the Revised Code or a similar statute of another state. The order issued in this state remains in effect until an order is obtained from the other state within the period specified or until the period expires.

(D) A court of this state that has been asked to make a child custody determination under this section, upon being informed that a child custody proceeding has been commenced in or a child custody determination has been made by a court of a state having jurisdiction under sections 3127.15 to 3127.17 of the Revised Code or a similar statute of another state, shall immediately communicate with the other court. A court of this state that is exercising jurisdiction pursuant to sections 3127.15 to 3127.17 of the Revised Code, upon being informed that a child custody proceeding has been commenced in or a child custody determination has been made by a court of another state under a statute similar to this section, shall immediately communicate with the court of that state to resolve the emergency, protect the safety of the parties and the child, and determine a period for the duration of the temporary order.

(2004 S 185, eff. 4-11-05)

3127.19. Notice and opportunity to be heard prior to custody determination

(A) Before a child custody determination is made under this chapter, notice and an opportunity to be heard in accordance with the standards set forth in section 3127.07 of the Revised Code shall be given to all persons entitled to notice under the law of this state as in child custody proceedings between residents of this state, any parent whose parental rights have not been previously terminated, and any person having physical custody of the child.

(B) This chapter does not govern the enforceability of a child custody determination made without notice or an opportunity to be heard.

(C) The obligation to join a party and the right to intervene as a party in a child custody proceeding under this chapter shall be governed by the law of this state as in child custody proceedings between residents of this state.

(2004 S 185, eff. 4-11-05)

3127.20. Pendency of proceedings in another state

(A) Except as otherwise provided in section 3127.18 of the Revised Code, a court of this state may not exercise its jurisdiction under sections 3127.15 to 3127.17 of the Revised Code if, at the time of the commencement of the proceeding, a child custody proceeding concerning the child is pending in a court of another state having jurisdiction substantially in conformity with this chapter, unless the proceeding has been terminated or is stayed by the court of the other state because a court of this state is a more convenient forum under section 3127.21 of the Revised Code or a similar statute of the other state.

(B) Except as otherwise provided in section 3127.18 of the Revised Code, a court of this state, before hearing a child custody proceeding, shall examine the court documents and other information supplied by the parties pursuant to section 3127.23 of the Revised Code. If the court determines that a child custody proceeding is pending in a court in another state having jurisdiction substantially in accordance with this chapter, the court of this state shall stay its proceeding and communicate with the court of the other state. If the court of the state having jurisdiction substantially in accordance with this chapter does not determine that the court of this state is a more appropriate forum, the court of this state shall dismiss the proceeding.

(C) In a proceeding to modify a child custody determination, a court of this state shall determine whether a proceeding to enforce the determination has been commenced in another state. If a proceeding to enforce a child custody determination has been commenced in another state, the court may do any of the following:

(1) Stay the proceeding for modification pending the entry of an order of a court of the other state enforcing, staying, denying, or dismissing the proceeding for enforcement;

(2) Enjoin the parties from continuing with the proceeding for enforcement;

(3) Upon the demonstration of an emergency, proceed with the modification under conditions the court considers appropriate.

(2004 S 185, eff. 4-11-05)

3127.21. Inconvenient forum; more appropriate forum

(A) A court of this state that has jurisdiction under this chapter to make a child custody determination may decline to exercise its jurisdiction at any time if it determines that it is an inconvenient forum under the circumstances and that a court of another state is a more convenient forum. The issue of inconvenient forum may be raised upon motion of a party, the court's own motion, or at the request of another court.

(B) Before determining whether it is an inconvenient forum, a court of this state shall consider whether it is appropriate for a court of another state to exercise jurisdiction. For this purpose, the court shall allow the parties to submit information and shall consider all relevant factors, including the following:

(1) Whether domestic violence has occurred and is likely to continue in the future and which state could best protect the parties and the child;

(2) The length of time the child has resided outside this state;

(3) The distance between the court in this state and the court in the state that would assume jurisdiction;

(4) The relative financial circumstances of the parties;

(5) Any agreement of the parties as to which state should assume jurisdiction;

(6) The nature and location of the evidence required to resolve the pending litigation, including the testimony of the child;

(7) The ability of the court of each state to decide the issue expeditiously and the procedures necessary to present the evidence;

(8) The familiarity of the court of each state with the facts and issues in the pending litigation.

(C) If a court of this state determines that it is an inconvenient forum and that a court of another state is a more appropriate forum, it shall stay the proceedings upon condition that a child custody proceeding be promptly commenced in another designated state and may impose any other condition the court considers just and proper.

(D) A court of this state may decline to exercise its jurisdiction under this chapter if a child custody determination is incidental to an action for divorce or another proceeding while still retaining jurisdiction over the divorce or other proceeding.

(2004 S 185, eff. 4-11-05)

3127.22. Unjustifiable conduct; expenses

(A) Except as otherwise provided in section 3127.18 of the Revised Code or another law of this state, if a court of this state has jurisdiction under this chapter because a person seeking to invoke its jurisdiction has engaged in unjustifiable conduct, the court shall decline to exercise its jurisdiction unless one of the following applies:

(1) The parents and all persons acting as parents have agreed to the exercise of jurisdiction.

(2) A court of the state otherwise having jurisdiction under sections 3127.15 to 3127.17 of the Revised Code determines that this state is a more appropriate forum under section 3127.21 of the Revised Code or a similar statute of the state.

(3) No court of any other state would have jurisdiction under the criteria specified in sections 3127.15 to 3127.17 of the Revised Code.

(B) If a court of this state declines to exercise its jurisdiction pursuant to division (A) of this section, it may fashion an appropriate remedy to ensure the safety of the child and prevent a repetition of the unjustifiable conduct, including staying the proceeding until a child custody proceeding is commenced in a court having jurisdiction under sections 3127.15 to 3127.17 of the Revised Code or a similar statute of another state.

(C) If a court dismisses a petition or stays a proceeding because it declines to exercise its jurisdiction pursuant to division (A) of this section, it shall assess against the party seeking to invoke its jurisdiction necessary and reasonable expenses including costs, communication expenses, attorney's fees, investigative fees, expenses for witnesses, travel expenses, and child care during the course of the proceedings, unless the party from whom fees are sought establishes that the assessment would be clearly inappropriate. The court may not assess fees, costs, or expenses against this state or a political subdivision of this state unless authorized by law other than this chapter.

(D) As used in this section, "unjustifiable conduct" means conduct by a parent or that parent's surrogate that attempts to create jurisdiction in this state by removing the child from the child's home state, secreting the child, retaining the child, or restraining or otherwise preventing the child from returning to the child's home state in order to prevent the other parent from commencing a child custody proceeding in the child's home state.

(2004 S 185, eff. 4-11-05)

3127.23. Facts to be pleaded

(A) Each party in a child custody proceeding, in the party's first pleading or in an affidavit attached to that pleading, shall give information if reasonably ascertainable under oath as to the child's present address or whereabouts, the places where the child has lived within the last five years, and the name and present address of each person with whom the child has lived during that period. In this pleading or affidavit, each party also shall include all of the following information:

(1) Whether the party has participated as a party, a witness, or in any other capacity in any other proceeding concerning the allocation, between the parents of the same child, of parental rights and responsibilities for the care of the child including any designation of parenting time rights and the designation of the residential parent and legal custodian of the child or that otherwise concerned the custody of or visitation with the same child and, if so, the court, case number and the date of the child custody determination, if any;

(2) Whether the party knows of any proceedings that could affect the current proceeding, including proceedings for enforcement of child custody determinations, proceedings relating to domestic violence or protection orders, proceedings to adjudicate the child as an abused, neglected, or dependent child, proceedings seeking termination of parental rights, and adoptions, and, if so, the court, the case number, and the nature of the proceeding;

(3) Whether the party knows of any person who is not a party to the proceeding and has physical custody of the child or claims to be a parent of the child who is designated the residential parent and legal custodian of the child or to have parenting time rights with respect to the child or to be a person other than a parent of the child who has custody or visitation rights with respect to the child and, if so, the names and addresses of those persons.

(B) If the declaration under division (A)(1), (2), or (3) of this section is in the affirmative, the declarant shall give additional information as required by the court. The court may examine the parties under oath as to details of the information furnished and as to other matters pertinent to the court's jurisdiction and the disposition of the case.

(C) Each party has a continuing duty to inform the court of any child custody proceeding concerning the child in this or any other state that could affect the current proceeding.

(D) If a party alleges in an affidavit or a pleading under oath that the health, safety, or liberty of a party or child would be jeopardized by the disclosure of identifying information, the information shall be sealed and may not be disclosed to the other party or the public unless the court orders the disclosure to be made after a hearing in which the court takes into consideration the health, safety, and liberty of the party or child and determines that the disclosure is in the interests of justice.

(E) A public children services agency, acting pursuant to a complaint or an action on a complaint filed under section 2151.27 of the Revised Code, is not subject to the requirements of this section.

(F) As used in this section, "abused child" has the same meaning as in section 2151.031 of the Revised Code, "neglected child" has the same meaning as in section 2151.03 of the Revised Code, and "dependent child" has the same meaning as in section 2151.04 of the Revised Code.

(2004 S 185, eff. 4-11-05)

3127.24. Personal appearance of parties may be required

(A) The court may order any party to a child custody proceeding who is in this state to appear personally before the court with or without the child. The court may order any person who is in this state and who has physical custody or control of the child to appear personally with the child.

(B) If a party to a child custody proceeding whose presence is desired by the court is outside this state with or without the child, the court may order that the notice given under section 3127.07 of the Revised Code include a statement directing that party to appear personally with or without the child and informing the party that failure to appear may result in a decision adverse to that party.

(C) The court may enter any orders necessary to ensure the safety of the child and of any person ordered to appear under this section.

(D) If a party to a child custody proceeding who is outside this state is directed to appear under division (B) of this section or desires to appear personally before the court with or without the child, the court may require another party to pay reasonable and necessary travel and other expenses for the appearance of the party and the child.

(2004 S 185, eff. 4-11-05)

3127.31. Definitions

As used in sections 3127.31 to 3127.47 of the Revised Code:

(A) "Petitioner" means a person who seeks enforcement of an order for return of a child under the Hague Convention on the Civil Aspects of International Child Abduction or enforcement of a child custody determination.

(B) "Respondent" means a person against whom a proceeding has been commenced for enforcement of an order for return of a child under the Hague Convention on the Civil Aspects of International Child Abduction or enforcement of a child custody determination.

(2004 S 185, eff. 4-11-05)

3127.32. Enforcement of order relating to abducted child

Under this chapter, and subject to sections 2101.022 and 2301.03 of the Revised Code, a juvenile court or other court with appropriate jurisdiction may enforce an order for the return of a child made under the Hague Convention on the Civil Aspects of International Child Abduction as if it were a child custody determination.

(2004 S 185, eff. 4-11-05)

3127.33. Enforcement of custody determination of court of another state

(A) A court of this state shall recognize and enforce a child custody determination of a court of another state if that state exercised jurisdiction in substantial conformity with this chapter or the determination was made under factual circumstances meeting the jurisdictional standards of this chapter and the determination has not been modified in accordance with this chapter.

(B) A court of this state may use any remedy available under other law of this state to enforce a child custody determination made by a court of another state. The remedies provided in sections 3127.31 to 3127.47 of the Revised Code are cumulative and do not affect the availability of other remedies to enforce a child custody determination.

(2004 S 185, eff. 4-11-05)

3127.34. Court without jurisdiction may issue temporary order enforcing certain provisions

(A) A court of this state that does not have jurisdiction to modify a child custody determination may issue a temporary order enforcing either of the following:

(1) A parenting time or visitation schedule made by a court of another state;

(2) The parenting time or visitation provisions of a child custody determination of another state that does not provide for a specific parenting time or visitation schedule.

(B) If a court of this state makes an order under division (A)(2) of this section, it shall specify in the order a period that it considers adequate to allow the petitioner to obtain an order from a court having jurisdiction under the criteria specified in sections 3127.15 to 3127.24 of the Revised Code. The order shall remain in effect until an order is obtained from the other court or until the period expires.

(2004 S 185, eff. 4-11-05)

3127.35. Registration of out-of-state child custody determination; contest of determination

(A) Subject to sections 2101.022 and 2301.03 of the Revised Code, the clerk of a juvenile court or other court with appropriate jurisdiction may register a child custody determination issued by a court of another state, with or without a simultaneous request for enforcement, on receipt of all of the following:

(1) A letter or other document requesting that the child custody determination be registered;

(2) Two copies, including one certified copy, of the determination sought to be registered, and a statement under penalty of perjury that, to the best of the knowledge and belief of the person seeking registration, the order has not been modified;

(3) Except as otherwise provided in section 3127.23 of the Revised Code, the name and address of the person seeking registration and any parent who is designated the residential parent and legal custodian of the child or to have parenting time with respect to the child or any person acting as a parent who has been awarded custody or visitation in the child custody determination sought to be registered;

(4) An advance deposit or fee established by the court.

(B) On receipt of the documents and information required by division (A) of this section, the registering court shall do both of the following:

(1) Cause the child custody determination to be filed as a foreign judgment together with one copy of any accompanying documents and information, regardless of their form;

(2) Serve notice of the registration request on the persons named pursuant to division (A)(3) of this section, and provide them with an opportunity to contest the registration in accordance with this section.

(C) The notice required by division (B)(2) of this section shall state all of the following:

(1) That the registered child custody determination is enforceable as of the date of the registration in the same manner as a child custody determination issued by a court of this state;

(2) That a hearing to contest the validity of the registered determination must be requested within thirty days after service of notice;

(3) That failure to contest the registration shall result in confirmation of the child custody determination and preclude further contest of that determination with respect to any matter that could have been asserted.

(D) A person seeking to contest the validity of a registered order shall request a hearing within thirty days after service of the notice. At that hearing, the court shall confirm the registered order unless the person contesting registration establishes one of the following circumstances:

(1) The issuing court did not have jurisdiction under sections 3127.15 to 3127.24 of the Revised Code or a similar statute of another state.

(2) The child custody determination sought to be registered has been vacated, stayed, or modified by a court having jurisdiction to do so under sections 3127.15 to 3127.24 of the Revised Code or a similar statute of another state.

(3) The person contesting registration was entitled to notice of the child custody proceeding for which registration is sought, but notice was not given in accordance with the standards of section 3127.07 of the Revised Code or a similar statute of another state.

(E) If a timely request for a hearing to contest the validity of the registration is not made, the registration is confirmed as a matter of law and the person requesting registration and all persons served in accordance with division (B)(2) of this section must be notified of the confirmation.

(F) Confirmation of a registered child custody determination, whether by operation of law or after notice and hearing, precludes further contest of the determination with respect to any matter that could have been asserted at the time of registration.

(2004 S 185, eff. 4-11-05)

3127.36. Enforcement of out-of-state registered child custody determination

(A) Subject to sections 2101.022 and 2301.03 of the Revised Code, a juvenile court or other court of this state may grant any relief normally available under the law of this state to enforce a registered child custody determination made by a court of another state.

(B) Subject to sections 2101.022 and 2301.03 of the Revised Code, a juvenile court and each other court of this state shall recognize and enforce, but may not modify except in accordance with sections 3127.15 to 3127.24 of the Revised Code, a registered child custody determination of a court of another state.

(2004 S 185, eff. 4-11-05)

3127.37. Communication between enforcing and modifying court; effect of out-of-state pending modification order on enforcement order

Subject to sections 2101.022 and 2301.03 of the Revised Code, if a proceeding for enforcement under sections 3127.31 to 3127.46 of the Revised Code is commenced in a juvenile court or other court of this state with appropriate jurisdiction and the court determines that a proceeding to modify the determination is pending in a court of another state having jurisdiction to modify the determination under sections 3127.15 to 3127.24 of the Revised Code or a similar statute of another state, the enforcing court shall immediately communicate with the modifying court. The proceeding for enforcement shall continue unless the enforcing court, after consultation with the modifying court, stays or dismisses the proceeding.

(2004 S 185, eff. 4-11-05)

3127.38. Verification of enforcement orders

(A) A petition for enforcement pursuant to sections 3127.31 to 3127.46 of the Revised Code must be verified. All orders sought to be enforced and any order confirming registration must be attached to the petition. The orders attached to the petition shall be the original or a certified copy, whichever a court requires.

(B) A petition for enforcement of a child custody determination shall state all of the following:

(1) Whether the court that issued the child custody determination identified the jurisdictional basis it relied upon in exercising jurisdiction and, if so, what the basis was;

(2) Whether the determination for which enforcement is sought has been vacated, stayed, or modified by a court whose decision must be enforced under this chapter and, if so, identify the court, the case number, and the nature of the proceeding;

(3) Whether any proceeding has been commenced that could affect the current proceeding, including proceedings for enforcement of child custody determinations, proceedings relating to domestic violence or protection orders, proceedings to adjudicate the child as an abused, neglected, or dependent child, proceedings seeking termination of parental rights, and adoptions, and, if so, the court, the case number, and the nature of the proceeding;

(4) The present physical address of the child and the respondent, if known;

(5) Whether relief in addition to the immediate physical custody of the child and attorney's fees is sought, including a request for assistance from law enforcement officials and, if so, the relief sought;

(6) If the child custody determination has been registered and confirmed under section 3127.35 of the Revised Code, the date and place of registration.

(C) Upon the filing of a petition, the court shall issue an order directing the respondent to appear in person with or without the child at a hearing and may enter any order necessary to ensure the safety of the parties and the child. If possible, the hearing must be held on the next judicial day after service of the order. If holding the hearing on that date is impossible, the court shall hold the hearing on the first judicial day possible. The court may extend the date of the hearing at the request of the petitioner.

(D) An order issued under division (C) of this section shall state the time and place of the hearing and advise the respondent that at the hearing the court will order that the petitioner may take immediate physical custody of the child and that the respondent pay fees, costs, and expenses under section 3127.42 of the Revised

Code and may schedule a hearing to determine whether further relief is appropriate, unless the respondent appears and establishes either of the following:

(1) That the child custody determination has not been registered and confirmed under section 3127.35 of the Revised Code and that one of the following circumstances applies:

(a) The issuing court did not have jurisdiction under sections 3127.15 to 3127.24 of the Revised Code or a similar statute of another state.

(b) The child custody determination for which enforcement is sought has been vacated, stayed, or modified by a court having jurisdiction to do so under sections 3127.15 to 3127.24 of the Revised Code or a similar statute of another state.

(c) The respondent was entitled to notice of the child custody proceeding for which enforcement is sought, but notice was not given in accordance with the standards of section 3127.07 of the Revised Code or a similar statute of another state.

(2) That the child custody determination for which enforcement is sought was registered and confirmed under section 3127.35 of the Revised Code but has been vacated, stayed, or modified by a court of a state having jurisdiction to do so under sections 3127.15 to 3127.24 of the Revised Code or a similar statute of another state.

(2004 S 185, eff. 4-11-05)

3127.39. Service of process

Except as otherwise provided in section 3127.41 of the Revised Code, the petition and order shall be served by any method authorized by the Rules of Civil Procedure upon respondent and any person who has physical custody of the child.

(2004 S 185, eff. 4-11-05)

3127.40. Petitioner to take immediate physical custody; exceptions; fees and expenses; refusal to testify; privileges

(A) Unless the court issues a temporary emergency order pursuant to section 3127.18 of the Revised Code, upon a finding that a petitioner is entitled to immediate physical custody of the child, the court shall order that the petitioner may take immediate physical custody of the child unless the respondent establishes either of the following:

(1) That the child custody determination has not been registered and confirmed under section 3127.35 of the Revised Code and that one of the following circumstances applies:

(a) The issuing court did not have jurisdiction under sections 3127.15 to 3127.24 of the Revised Code or a similar statute of another state.

(b) The child custody determination for which enforcement is sought has been vacated, stayed, or modified by a court of a state having jurisdiction to do so under sections 3127.15 to 3127.24 of the Revised Code or a similar statute of another state.

(c) The respondent was entitled to notice of the child custody proceeding for which enforcement is sought, but notice was not given in accordance with the standards of section 3127.07 of the Revised Code or a similar statute of another state.

(2) That the child custody determination for which enforcement is sought was registered and confirmed under section 3127.35 of the Revised Code but has been vacated, stayed, or modified by a court of a state having jurisdiction to do so under sections 3127.15 to 3127.24 of the Revised Code or a similar statute of another state.

(B) The court shall award the fees, costs, and expenses authorized under section 3127.42 of the Revised Code, and may grant additional relief, including a request for the assistance of law enforcement officials, and shall set a further hearing to determine whether the additional relief is appropriate.

(C) If a party called to testify in a proceeding to enforce a child custody determination refuses to answer on the basis that the testimony may be self-incriminating, the court may draw an adverse inference from the refusal.

(D) A privilege against disclosure of communications between spouses and a defense of immunity based on the relationship of husband and wife or parent and child may not be invoked in a proceeding under this chapter.

(2004 S 185, eff. 4-11-05)

3127.41. Warrant to take physical custody

(A) Upon the filing of a petition seeking enforcement of a child custody determination, the petitioner may file a verified application for the issuance of a warrant to take physical custody of the child if the child is imminently likely to suffer serious physical harm or be removed from this state.

(B) If the court, upon the testimony of the petitioner or another witness, finds that the child is imminently likely to suffer serious physical harm or be removed from this state, it may issue a warrant to take physical custody of the child. If possible, the court shall hear the petition on the next judicial day after the warrant is executed. If it is impossible to hold a hearing on that date, the court shall hold the hearing on the first judicial day possible. The application for the warrant shall include the statements required by division (B) of section 3127.38 of the Revised Code.

(C) A warrant to take physical custody of a child shall do all of the following:

(1) Specify the facts upon which a conclusion of imminent serious physical harm or removal from the jurisdiction is based;

(2) Direct law enforcement officers to take physical custody of the child immediately;

(3) Provide for the placement of the child pending final relief.

(D) The respondent shall be served with the petition, warrant, and order immediately after the child is taken into physical custody.

(E) A warrant to take physical custody of a child is enforceable throughout this state. If the court finds on the basis of the testimony of the petitioner or another witness that a less intrusive remedy is not effective, it may authorize law enforcement officers to enter private property to take physical custody of the child. If required by exigent circumstances of the case, the court may authorize law enforcement officers to make a forcible entry at any hour.

(F) The court may impose conditions upon the placement of a child to ensure the appearance of the child and the child's custodian.

(2004 S 185, eff. 4-11-05)

3127.42. Award of fees and expenses

(A) A court shall award the prevailing party in an action to enforce a child custody determination, including a state, necessary and reasonable expenses incurred by or on behalf of the party, including costs, communication expenses, attorney's fees, investigative fees, expenses for witnesses, travel expenses, and child care during the course of the proceedings, unless the party from whom fees or expenses are sought establishes that the award would be clearly inappropriate.

(B) The court shall not assess fees, costs, or expenses against a state or a political subdivision of a state unless authorized by law other than this chapter.

(2004 S 185, eff. 4-11-05)

3127.43. Full faith and credit by court

A court of this state shall accord full faith and credit to an order issued by another state consistent with this chapter that enforces a child custody determination by a court of another state unless the order has been vacated, stayed, or modified by a court having jurisdiction to do so under sections 3127.15 to 3127.24 of the Revised Code or a similar statute of another state.

(2004 S 185, eff. 4-11-05)

3127.44. Appeal from final order; expedited review

An appeal may be taken from a final order in a proceeding under sections 3127.31 to 3127.47 of the Revised Code. The supreme court of this state shall, by rule, provide for expedited appellate review of cases appealed under this section. Unless the court enters a temporary emergency order under section 3127.18 of the Revised Code, the enforcing court may not stay an order enforcing a child custody determination pending appeal.

(2004 S 185, eff. 4-11-05)

3127.45. Permissible action by prosecutor

(A) In a case arising under this chapter or involving the Hague Convention on the Civil Aspects in International Child Abduction, the prosecutor may take any lawful action, including resort to a proceeding under sections 3127.31 to 3127.47 of the Revised Code or any other available civil proceeding, to locate a child, obtain the return of a child, or enforce a child custody determination if there is any of the following:

(1) An existing child custody determination;

(2) A request to locate a child, obtain the return of a child, or enforce a child custody determination from a court in a pending child custody proceeding;

(3) A reasonable belief that a criminal statute has been violated;

(4) A reasonable belief that the child has been wrongfully removed or retained in violation of the Hague Convention on the Civil Aspects of International Child Abduction.

(B) A prosecutor acting under this section acts on behalf of the court and may not represent any party.

(2004 S 185, eff. 4-11-05)

3127.46. Permissible action by law enforcement officer

At the request of a prosecutor or other appropriate public official acting under section 3127.45 of the Revised Code, a law enforcement officer may take any lawful action reasonably necessary to locate a child or a party and assist the prosecutor or appropriate public official with responsibilities under section 3127.45 of the Revised Code.

(2004 S 185, eff. 4-11-05)

3127.47. Non-prevailing respondent; assessment of expenses and costs

If the respondent is not the prevailing party, the court may assess against the respondent all direct expenses and costs incurred by the prosecutor or other appropriate public official and law enforcement officers under section 3127.45 or 3127.46 of the Revised Code.

(2004 S 185, eff. 4-11-05)

3127.51. Uniformity of application and construction

In applying and construing sections 3127.01 to 3127.53 of the Revised Code, consideration shall be given to the need to promote uniformity of law with respect to its subject matter among states that enact a uniform child custody jurisdiction and enforcement act.

(2004 S 185, eff. 4-11-05)

3127.52. Severability

If any provision of this chapter or its application to any person or circumstance is held invalid, the invalidity does not affect other provisions or applications of this chapter that can be given effect without the invalid provision or application, and to this end the provisions of this chapter are severable.

(2004 S 185, eff. 4-11-05)

3127.53. Retroactivity of laws

A motion or other request for relief made in a parenting or child custody proceeding or to enforce a parenting or child custody determination that was commenced before the effective date of this section is governed by the law in effect at the time the motion or other request was made.

(2004 S 185, eff. 4-11-05)

APPENDIX B

Rules of Superintendence for the Courts of Ohio

Current through August 1, 2018

RULES OF SUPERINTENDENCE FOR THE COURTS OF OHIO

Sup R Form 10.03-A	Motion for criminal protection order (CRPO)—Repealed
Sup R Form 10.03-B	Criminal protection order (CRPO) (R.C. 2903.213)
Sup R Form 10.03-D	Petition for civil stalking protection order or civil sexually oriented offense protection order
Sup R Form 10.03-E	Civil stalking protection order or civil sexually oriented offense protection order *ex parte*
Sup R Form 10.03-F	Civil stalking protection order or civil sexually oriented offense protection order full hearing
Sup R Form 10.03-G	How to obtain a civil stalking protection order or civil sexually oriented offense protection order
Sup R Form 10.03-H	Warning concerning the attached protection order
Sup R 10.04	Standard notice concerning possession or purchase of a firearm
Sup R Form 10.04-A	Notice concerning possession or purchase of firearms
Sup R 10.05	Standard civil protection order forms in Juvenile Division of the Court of Common Pleas
Sup R Form 10.05-A	How to obtain a petition for a juvenile civil protection order or a juvenile domestic violence civil protection order
Sup R Form 10.05-B	Petition for juvenile civil protection order and juvenile domestic violence protection order
Sup R Form 10.05-C	Juvenile civil protection order or juvenile domestic violence civil protection order *ex parte*
Sup R Form 10.05-D	Juvenile civil protection order full hearing
Sup R Form 10.05-E	Juvenile domestic violence civil protection order and consent agreement civil protection order
Sup R Form 10.05-F	Warning concerning the attached juvenile civil protection order or juvenile domestic violence civil protection order
Sup R 10.06	Inter-court communication in domestic violence and related cases

The full text of the matters covered by the Superintendence Rules relating to Ohio domestic violence, stalking, sexual violence and juvenile protection order forms, notices, warnings, petitions, motions, completion instruction, and more may be found on the Supreme Court of Ohio's website at http://www.supremecourt.ohio.gov.

Table of Laws and Rules

UNITED STATES CONSTITUTION

IMMIGRATION AND NATIONALITY ACT

UNITED STATES CODE ANNOTATED

UNITED STATES CODE ANNOTATED—Continued

UNITED STATES CODE ANNOTATED—Continued

42 U.S.C.A. Sec.	Sec.
10604(a)	17:5
10610	17:5
13701	4:7
13925	17:5
13925(a)(18)	17:4
13925(b)(2)(A) to (D)	17:4
13942	17:5
13951	17:5, 18:2
13981	14:10, 14:13, 18:5
13981(c)	14:13
13981(d)(1)	14:13
13981(d)(2)(A)	14:13
13981(e)(1)	14:13
13981(e)(2)	14:13
13981(e)(3)	14:13
14014	17:5, 18:2
14043	18:15, 18:16
40281	11:6, 17:5, 18:2
40508	17:5, 18:2

47 U.S.C.A. Sec.	Sec.
223(h)(1)	18:6
332(d)	12:20

UNITED STATES PUBLIC LAWS

Pub. L. No.	Sec.
99-639	18:15
101-649	18:15
103-322	18:15
104-193	18:15
104-208	18:15, 18:18
106-386	18:15
113-4 (2013)	18:15, 18:18, 18:19, 18:20, 18:22

TREASURY REGULATIONS

Reg.	Sec.
214.11(d)(4)	18:20

CODE OF FEDERAL REGULATIONS

8 C.F.R. Sec.	Sec.
204.2(c)(1)(vi)	18:18
204.02(c)(2)(v)	18:18
204.2(e)(1)(vi)	18:18
214.11(b)	18:20
214.11(b)(2)	18:20
214.11(b)(3)	18:20
214.11(b)(4)	18:20
274a.12(c)(10)	18:22
1240.11(a)(1)	18:21

27 C.F.R. Sec.	Sec.
478.11	18:11

47 C.F.R. Sec.	Sec.
20.3	12:20

FEDERAL RULES OF EVIDENCE

Rule	Sec.
403	5:21

HOUSE OF REPRESENTATIVES BILLS

No.	Sec.
32	2:5, 10:9
129	9:5, 20:5
137	3:6
151	9:4
162	8:7
172	15:3, 15:14
335	5:1, 5:14, 11:3, 12:29, 14:2, 14:6
359	18:2
484	7:24
494	12:22
4142	12:22

SENATE BILLS

No.	Sec.
1	10:7, 11:12, 11:20, 11:21, 12:4, 14:15
3	15:5
9	12:15, 13:3
13	13:15
47	11:3
98	4:9, 5:3, 14:6

ARIZONA STATUTES

Sec.	Sec.
13-3602B.4	11:6

ARKANSAS ATTORNEY GENERAL OPINIONS

	Sec.
97-392	10:4

CALIFORNIA EVIDENCE CODE

Sec.	Sec.
912(b)	12:5
1037 to 1037.7	12:5

CALIFORNIA FAMILY CODE

Sec.	Sec.
3424	15:24
6304	12:22
6389	12:22

FLORIDA STATUTES

Sec.	Sec.
61.13(2)(b)	15:7
741.30(2)(b)	11:6

IOWA ATTORNEY GENERAL OPINIONS

MARYLAND ATTORNEY GENERAL OPINIONS

MASSACHUSETTS GENERAL LAWS

MINNESOTA STATUTES

MISSOURI STATUTES

NEBRASKA ATTORNEY GENERAL OPINIONS

NEW JERSEY STATUTES

NEW YORK FAMILY COURT ACT

NORTH DAKOTA CENTURY CODE

OHIO CONSTITUTION

OHIO REVISED CODE

OHIO REVISED CODE—Continued

OHIO REVISED CODE—Continued

OHIO REVISED CODE—Continued

OHIO REVISED CODE—Continued

OHIO REVISED CODE—Continued

OHIO REVISED CODE—Continued

OHIO REVISED CODE—Continued

OHIO REVISED CODE—Continued

OHIO REVISED CODE—Continued

OHIO REVISED CODE—Continued

OHIO LAWS

OHIO RULES OF APPELLATE PROCEDURE

OHIO RULES OF CIVIL PROCEDURE

Rule	Sec.
2	12:21
3	10:13
3(A)	11:4, 11:21, 12:4
3(B)	10:13
3(B)(1)	10:13
3(B)(6)	10:13
3(B)(10)	9:5, 10:13, 12:27, 20:6
3(D)	10:13
4 to 4.6	11:6, 11:11, 13:3, 13:8
4	11:11, 12:8, 12:24, 12:25, 13:3, 13:8, 14:15, 20:15
4(E)	11:4, 11:21, 12:4
4.1	11:22, 12:1, 12:25
4.1(A) to (C)	11:11
4.1(A)	11:11, 20:15
4.1(B)	9:5, 11:11, 14:2, 20:15
4.1(C)	11:11
4.3	10:13
4.3(A)(3)	10:13
4.3(A)(9)	10:13
4.3(A)(10)	10:13
4.3(B)(2)	11:11, 20:15
4.4	11:11, 11:22, 12:1, 20:15
4.4(A)(2)	11:11, 11:21, 20:15
4.4(A)(2)(b)	11:11, 11:21
4.4(A)(2)(d)	11:11, 11:21
4.6	11:11, 11:22, 12:1, 12:24, 12:25, 13:8, 20:15
4.6(D)	11:11, 12:8, 20:15
5	11:11, 12:8, 12:25, 13:8, 20:15
5(A)	11:11
5(B)	11:6, 11:11, 12:8, 12:24, 12:25, 13:3, 13:8, 20:15
5(D)	12:8
6	11:20
6(B)	12:2
6(D)	11:11
7(B)	13:8
7(B)(2)	11:9
11	9:9, 12:8, 12:21
12(B)(6)	12:2, 18:11
13(A)	12:1
15	8:4, 11:2, 12:2
15(B)	12:2
17(B)	20:14
18	10:9
18(A)	11:3
19	10:9
26(B)(1)	12:5
26(C)	12:5
30	12:5
33	12:5
34	12:5
35	15:16
41	9:5, 12:7

Rule	Sec.
41(A)	9:5, 12:7
41(A)(1)	12:27
41(A)(1)(a)	12:7
41(A)(2)	12:7, 12:27
41(B)	12:25, 14:6
41(B)(1)	12:7, 12:25
41(B)(2)	12:7
41(B)(3)	12:7
44	13:3
45(B)	17:7
50(A)	12:7
50(A)(1)	12:7
50(A)(4)	12:7
52	12:7, 12:10, 13:12, 15:6
53	9:5, 12:9, 12:10, 12:25
53(C)	15:6
53(C)(3)(a)	15:6
53(D)(2) or (3)	9:5
53(D)(2)	9:5, 11:9, 12:10
53(D)(2)(b)	11:9
53(D)(3)	9:5, 11:9, 12:10
53(D)(3)(a)(ii)	9:5, 12:10
53(D)(4)	12:10
53(D)(4)(3)	11:9
53(D)(4)(d)	12:10
53(D)(4)(e)	9:5, 12:10
53(D)(6)	9:5
53(E)(4)(a)	12:9
53(E)(4)(c)	12:9
58	12:9, 13:3
58(A)	12:9, 13:3
59	9:5, 12:6, 12:10
59(A)(8	12:6
60	12:25, 15:12
60(A)	12:16, 12:23, 12:25
60(B)	9:3, 9:5, 9:6, 9:7, 12:25
60(B)(2)	9:5, 12:10, 12:25
60(B)(4)	9:5, 12:25
60(B)(5)	9:5
65	13:3, 14:15
65(C)	11:1
65(D)	2:7, 12:5
65(F)(3)(d)	12:10
65(G)	12:10
65.1	9:5, 11:9, 11:11, 11:21, 11:23, 12:5, 12:6, 12:7, 12:8, 12:10, 12:25, 13:3, 20:13, 20:15
65.1(A)	9:5, 12:5, 12:10, 12:25, 20:13
65.1(B)(4)	11:6, 15:9
65.1(C)	9:5, 11:11, 12:8, 13:3
65.1(C)(1)	11:11, 20:15
65.1(C)(2)	11:11, 11:21, 13:3, 20:15
65.1(C)(3)	12:8, 13:3, 14:15, 20:15
65.1(C)(4)	11:11
65.1(C)(4)(a)	12:24, 12:25, 13:8

OHIO RULES OF CIVIL PROCEDURE—Continued

OHIO RULES OF CRIMINAL PROCEDURE

OHIO RULES OF EVIDENCE

OHIO RULES OF EVIDENCE—Continued

OHIO RULES OF PRACTICE OF THE SUPREME COURT

CUYAHOGA COUNTY, OHIO RULES

OHIO CODE OF PROFESSIONAL RESPONSIBILITY

OHIO RULES OF PROFESSIONAL CONDUCT

OHIO JUVENILE PROCEDURE

OHIO RULES OF SUPERINTENDENCE

SUMMIT COUNTY, OHIO RULES

OHIO ATTORNEY GENERAL OPINIONS

OHIO HOUSE OF REPRESENTATIVES BILLS

OHIO SENATE BILLS

PENNSYLVANIA STATUTES ANNOTATED

TENNESSEE CODE

TEXAS FAMILY CODE ANNOTATED

Sec.	Sec.	Sec.	Sec.
84.003	11:21	84.003(b)	12:4

TEXAS ATTORNEY GENERAL OPINION

	Sec.
JC-0289	12:19

Table of Cases

A

Alley v. Bettencourt, 134 Ohio App. 3d 303, 730 N.E.2d 1067 (4th Dist. Pike County 1999)—14:3

Alliance, City of v. Hawkins, 1997 WL 116915 (Ohio Ct. App. 5th Dist. Stark County 1997)—14:5

Aloi v. Nassau County Sheriff's Dept., 9 Misc. 3d 1050, 800 N.Y.S.2d 873 (Sup 2005)—18:11

Alonzo v. Lynch, 821 F.3d 951 (8th Cir. 2016)—18:22

Alpha Benefits Agency, Inc. v. King Ins. Agency, Inc., 134 Ohio App. 3d 673, 731 N.E.2d 1209 (8th Dist. Cuyahoga County 1999)—12:5

Alston v. Voorhies, 2010 WL 3895069 (N.D. Ohio 2010)—5:21

Aly v. Aden, 2013 WL 593420 (D. Minn. 2013)—18:24

A.M. v. D.L., 2017-Ohio-5621, 2017 WL 2870214 (Ohio Ct. App. 9th Dist. Medina County 2017)—2:4, 8:4, 8:5, 9:7, 12:26

A.M. v. S.M., 2018-Ohio-247, 2018 WL 542357 (Ohio Ct. App. 9th Dist. Summit County 2018)—8:4, 8:5, 12:11, 12:26, 16:9

A.M., In re, 2010-Ohio-948, 2010 WL 890940 (Ohio Ct. App. 2d Dist. Greene County 2010)—12:10

Amalgamated Clothing Workers of America v. Richman Bros., 348 U.S. 511, 75 S. Ct. 452, 99 L. Ed. 600, 71 Ohio L. Abs. 177 (1955)—11:23

Amborski v. Toledo, 67 Ohio App. 3d 47, 585 N.E.2d 974 (6th Dist. Lucas County 1990)—14:12, 14:14

Amendment of the Commission's Rules Regarding the 37.0-38.6 GHz and 38.6-40.0 GHz Bands, In the Matter of, 11 F.C.C.R. 4930, 1995 WL 783585 (F.C.C. 1995)—11:3

Anderson v. Anderson, 147 Ohio App. 3d 513, 2002-Ohio-1156, 771 N.E.2d 303 (7th Dist. Carroll County 2002)—15:15

Anderson v. Anderson, 2001-Ohio-3379, 2001 WL 1667875 (Ohio Ct. App. 7th Dist. Mahoning County 2001)—8:4, 8:8, 11:2, 11:10, 12:11, 12:24, 12:26

Anderson v. Deas, 273 Ga. App. 770, 615 S.E.2d 859 (2005)—10:13

Anderson v. City of West Bend Police Dept., 774 F. Supp. 2d 925 (E.D. Wis. 2011)—14:5

Anderson, In re, 92 Ohio St. 3d 63, 2001-Ohio-131, 748 N.E.2d 67 (2001)—20:14

Andrews v. Rutherford, 363 N.J. Super. 252, 832 A.2d 379 (Ch. Div. 2003)—10:9

Anheier v. De Long, 164 Ky. 694, 176 S.W. 195 (1915)—19:9

Ankenbruck v. Ankenbruck, 2000 WL 1804360 (Ohio Ct. App. 11th Dist. Trumbull County 2000)—8:4, 8:5, 11:10, 12:11, 16:9, 16:21

Anthony T. v. Anthony J., 134 Misc. 2d 375, 510 N.Y.S.2d 810 (Fam. Ct. 1986)—10:13

Apprendi v. New Jersey, 530 U.S. 466, 120 S. Ct. 2348, 147 L. Ed. 2d 435 (2000)—2:7

Appropriation for Juvenile and Probate Division for 1979, In re, 62 Ohio St. 2d 99, 16 Ohio Op. 3d 104, 403 N.E.2d 974 (1980)—13:5

A.R. v. M.R., 351 N.J. Super. 512, 799 A.2d 27 (App. Div. 2002)—10:13

Aragon Trinidad v. Holder, 367 Fed. Appx. 749 (9th Cir. 2010)—18:18

Arbino v. Johnson & Johnson, 116 Ohio St. 3d 468, 2007-Ohio-6948, 880 N.E.2d 420 (2007)—19:12

Ardoin v. City of Mamou, 685 So. 2d 294 (La. Ct. App. 3d Cir. 1996)—14:3, 14:14

Argersinger v. Hamlin, 407 U.S. 25, 92 S. Ct. 2006, 32 L. Ed. 2d 530 (1972)—3:2, 7:9

Arizona v. Hicks, 480 U.S. 321, 107 S. Ct. 1149, 94 L. Ed. 2d 347 (1987)—14:5

Armijo By and Through Chavez v. Wagon Mound Public Schools, 159 F.3d 1253, 130 Ed. Law Rep. 496 (10th Cir. 1998)—14:9

Armstrong v. U.S., 572 U.S. 1032, 134 S. Ct. 1759, 188 L. Ed. 2d 590 (2014)—18:11

Arnold v. Arnold, 2001 WL 1205284 (Iowa Ct. App. 2001)—15:24

Arruda v. Farmer, 2015-Ohio-5511, 55 N.E.3d 604 (Ohio Ct. App. 5th Dist. Licking County 2015)—9:2, 9:8, 9:9

Arthur Young & Co. v. Kelly, 68 Ohio App. 3d 287, 588 N.E.2d 233 (10th Dist. Franklin County 1990)—13:8

88 S. Ct. 1477, 20 L. Ed. 2d 522 (1968)—13:5

Bloom v. Macbeth, 2008-Ohio-4564, 2008 WL 4151319 (Ohio Ct. App. 5th Dist. Ashland County 2008)—9:2, 9:4, 9:8

Boals v. Miller, 2011-Ohio-1470, 2011 WL 1118464 (Ohio Ct. App. 5th Dist. Ashland County 2011)—8:4, 9:9, 12:21, 12:22

Board of Educ. of Hamilton City School Dist. v. Hamilton Classroom Teachers Ass'n, 5 Ohio App. 3d 51, 449 N.E.2d 26, 11 Ed. Law Rep. 277 (12th Dist. Butler County 1982)—13:3

Board of Regents of State Colleges v. Roth, 408 U.S. 564, 92 S. Ct. 2701, 33 L. Ed. 2d 548 (1972)—14:11, 14:14

Boddie v. Connecticut, 401 U.S. 371, 91 S. Ct. 780, 28 L. Ed. 2d 113 (1971)—13:3

Boddie v. Landers, 2016-Ohio-1410, 2016 WL 1290780 (Ohio Ct. App. 10th Dist. Franklin County 2016)—19:10

Bodine v. Bodine, 38 Ohio App. 3d 173, 528 N.E.2d 973 (10th Dist. Franklin County 1988)—15:15

Boeckmann v. Baker, 2003-Ohio-456, 2003 WL 203579 (Ohio Ct. App. 2d Dist. Greene County 2003)—15:24

Boggs v. Boggs, 118 Ohio App. 3d 293, 692 N.E.2d 674 (5th Dist. Stark County 1997)—13:4

Boggs v. Hughes, 1994 WL 28635 (Ohio Ct. App. 2d Dist. Greene County 1994)—14:9, 14:12, 14:14

Boldt v. Boldt, 155 Or. App. 244, 963 P.2d 719 (1998)—8:8

Boling v. Valecko, 2002-Ohio-449, 2002 WL 185182 (Ohio Ct. App. 9th Dist. Summit County 2002)—15:6, 15:12

Bond v. Heebsh, 1982 WL 6579 (Ohio Ct. App. 6th Dist. Lucas County 1982)—10:6

Boniek v. Boniek, 443 N.W.2d 196 (Minn. Ct. App. 1989)—8:3

Bordenkircher v. Hayes, 434 U.S. 357, 98 S. Ct. 663, 54 L. Ed. 2d 604 (1978)—5:3

Boreman v. Boreman, 2002-Ohio-2320, 2002 WL 1022990 (Ohio Ct. App. 9th Dist. Wayne County 2002)—12:26

Bower v. Long, 2013-Ohio-5467, 2013 WL 6579075 (Ohio Ct. App. 6th Dist. Lucas County 2013)—9:2, 9:3, 9:8

Bowers v. DeVito, 686 F.2d 616 (7th Cir. 1982)—14:14

Bowman v. Bowman, 2014-Ohio-2851, 2014 WL 2957475 (Ohio Ct. App. 9th Dist. Medina County 2014)—8:4, 8:6, 8:7, 9:7

Bowman v. Leisz, 2014-Ohio-4763, 2014 WL 5422556 (Ohio Ct. App. 12th Dist. Warren County 2014)—9:5, 12:25

Boyd v. Essin, 170 Or. App. 509, 12 P.3d 1003 (2000)—9:2

Boykin v. Alabama, 395 U.S. 238, 89 S. Ct. 1709, 23 L. Ed. 2d 274 (1969)—3:2

Boyle v. Boyle, 12 Pa. D. & C.3d 767, 1979 WL 764 (C.P. 1979)—11:14

Bradley v. Cox, 2004-Ohio-4840, 2004 WL 2035318 (Ohio Ct. App. 10th Dist. Franklin County 2004)—8:4, 12:6, 12:11, 12:26

Brady v. Maryland, 373 U.S. 83, 83 S. Ct. 1194, 10 L. Ed. 2d 215 (1963)—17:6

Brainard, In re Marriage of, 523 N.W.2d 611 (Iowa Ct. App. 1994)—15:7, 15:12

Brandt v. Brandt, 2006-Ohio-883, 2006 WL 456716 (Ohio Ct. App. 3d Dist. Auglaize County 2006)—14:6, 16:12

Breed v. Jones, 421 U.S. 519, 95 S. Ct. 1779, 44 L. Ed. 2d 346 (1975)—13:14

Bressler v. Nunemaker, 2017-Ohio-5804, 2017 WL 2964199 (Ohio Ct. App. 5th Dist. Licking County 2017)—12:10, 12:26

Bright v. Lane, 2003-Ohio-225, 2003 WL 139755 (Ohio Ct. App. 5th Dist. Ashland County 2003)—9:2, 9:4

Brinkley v. Houk, 866 F. Supp. 2d 747 (N.D. Ohio 2011)—5:17

Brinkman v. Brinkman, 966 S.W.2d 780 (Tex. App. San Antonio 1998)—19:11

Brocklehurst v. Paul, 2012-Ohio-4356, 2012 WL 4351901 (Ohio Ct. App. 5th Dist. Muskingum County 2012)—15:12

Brooklyn v. Perna, 2012-Ohio-265, 2012 WL 253314 (Ohio Ct. App.

8th Dist. Cuyahoga County 2012)—8:7

Brooklyn, City of v. Muniz, 2008-Ohio-54, 2008 WL 98200 (Ohio Ct. App. 8th Dist. Cuyahoga County 2008)—8:6, 14:5

Brooks v. Knapp, 221 Fed. Appx. 402, 2007 FED App. 0812N (6th Cir. 2007)—14:9, 14:14

Brooks v. Rothe, 577 F.3d 701 (6th Cir. 2009)—17:5

Brown v. Brown, 2000 WL 271769 (Ohio Ct. App. 10th Dist. Franklin County 2000)—12:15, 12:17, 15:15

Brown v. Brown, 1993 OK CIV APP 142, 867 P.2d 477 (Ct. App. Div. 1 1993)—15:6, 15:7

Brown v. Brown, 208 N.J. Super. 372, 506 A.2d 29 (App. Div. 1986)—19:11

Brown v. Executive 200, Inc., 64 Ohio St. 2d 250, 18 Ohio Op. 3d 446, 416 N.E.2d 610 (1980)—3:10, 9:7, 13:3, 13:4, 13:5, 13:6, 13:7, 13:13, 13:17

Brown v. Grabowski, 922 F.2d 1097 (3d Cir. 1990)—14:6, 14:14

Brown v. Grauman, 2013-Ohio-4814, 2013 WL 5914961 (Ohio Ct. App. 2d Dist. Champaign County 2013)—9:5, 9:7

Brown v. Naff, 2012-Ohio-1770, 2012 WL 1383262 (Ohio Ct. App. 2d Dist. Miami County 2012)—12:25

Brown ex rel. Brown, Estate of v. Woodham, 840 So. 2d 1105 (Fla. 1st DCA 2003)—14:11

Brubaker v. Farr, 2006-Ohio-2001, 2006 WL 1062102 (Ohio Ct. App. 3d Dist. Shelby County 2006)—8:6, 12:11

Bruner v. Bruner, 2000-Ohio-2554, 2000 WL 1486452 (Ohio Ct. App. 7th Dist. Mahoning County 2000)—8:4, 8:8, 11:2, 11:10, 12:11, 12:24, 16:21

Bruner v. Hager, 534 N.W.2d 825 (N.D. 1995)—15:12

Bruns v. Bruns, 1999 WL 819344 (Ohio Ct. App. 6th Dist. Erie County 1999)—8:3, 8:4, 8:5, 8:8, 11:10, 11:25, 12:11, 16:21

Bryant v. Spear-Hardy, 2010-Ohio-1903, 2010 WL 1731763 (Ohio Ct. App. 2d Dist. Montgomery County 2010)—9:8, 16:20

Brzonkala v. Virginia Polytechnic Institute and State University, 169 F.3d 820, 136 Ed. Law Rep. 15 (4th Cir. 1999)—14:13

Buchanan v. Buchanan, 1999 WL 619049 (Ohio Ct. App. 12th Dist. Clermont County 1999)—16:12

Buchert v. Newman, 90 Ohio App. 3d 382, 629 N.E.2d 489 (1st Dist. Hamilton County 1993)—2:5

Bucksbaum v. Mitchell, 2004-Ohio-2233, 2004 WL 943865 (Ohio Ct. App. 5th Dist. Richland County 2004)—9:4, 9:7, 9:8

Bucyrus, City of v. Fawley, 50 Ohio App. 3d 25, 552 N.E.2d 676 (3d Dist. Crawford County 1988)—15:7

Bugh v. Mitchell, 329 F.3d 496, 61 Fed. R. Evid. Serv. 399, 2003 FED App. 0138P (6th Cir. 2003)—5:14

Bullard v. Alley, 2014-Ohio-1016, 2014 WL 1339719 (Ohio Ct. App. 4th Dist. Pike County 2014)—8:4, 8:6, 8:7, 8:8, 9:7, 12:10, 12:26

Bullcoming v. New Mexico, 564 U.S. 647, 131 S. Ct. 2705, 180 L. Ed. 2d 610 (2011)—5:16, 7:22

Bumgardner v. Bumgardner, 2005-Ohio-3445, 2005 WL 1545790 (Ohio Ct. App. 12th Dist. Butler County 2005)—12:27

Burchett v. Miller, 123 Ohio App. 3d 550, 704 N.E.2d 636 (6th Dist. Erie County 1997)—13:4, 13:15

Burella v. City of Philadelphia, 501 F.3d 134 (3d Cir. 2007)—14:9, 14:11, 14:12, 14:14

Burger King Corp. v. Rudzewicz, 471 U.S. 462, 105 S. Ct. 2174, 85 L. Ed. 2d 528 (1985)—10:13

Burik v. Johnson, 1997 WL 66762 (Ohio Ct. App. 4th Dist. Pike County 1997)—15:13

Burke v. Melton, 2003-Ohio-7054, 2003 WL 23009045 (Ohio Ct. App. 8th Dist. Cuyahoga County 2003)—8:3, 8:8, 12:29

Burkholder v. Carter, 2008-Ohio-4644, 2008 WL 4193260 (Ohio Ct. App. 3d Dist. Allen County 2008)—12:11

Burnett v. Burnett, 2012-Ohio-2673, 2012 WL 2196336 (Ohio Ct. App. 6th Dist. Sandusky County 2012)—8:4, 9:5, 10:13, 12:1

Burns v. Adams, 2014-Ohio-1917, 2014 WL 1853038 (Ohio Ct. App. 4th Dist. Scioto County 2014)—12:6

Bush v. Bush, 2015-Ohio-2017, 2015 WL 3385649 (Ohio Ct. App. 5th Dist. Licking County 2015)—12:11, 12:16

Bush v. Rauch, 38 F.3d 842, 1994 FED App. 0362P (6th Cir. 1994)—4:7

Butcher v. Stevens, 182 Ohio App. 3d 77, 2009-Ohio-1754, 911 N.E.2d 928 (4th Dist. Athens County 2009)—11:3, 12:1, 12:3, 12:4, 12:7, 12:22, 13:13

Butler, State ex rel. v. Demis, 66 Ohio St. 2d 123, 20 Ohio Op. 3d 121, 420 N.E.2d 116 (1981)—12:6

Butram v. Butram, 2005-Ohio-5469, 2005 WL 2622797 (Ohio Ct. App. 5th Dist. Ashland County 2005)—9:5

Butzer v. Butzer, 1998 WL 34615 (Ohio Ct. App. 9th Dist. Wayne County 1998)—15:6, 15:7

Byron v. Byron, 2012-Ohio-1632, 2012 WL 1264486 (Ohio Ct. App. 1st Dist. Hamilton County 2012)—8:4

C

Caban v. Ransome, 2009-Ohio-1034, 2009 WL 582761 (Ohio Ct. App. 7th Dist. Mahoning County 2009)—9:2, 9:3, 9:5, 9:7, 9:8, 12:2

Cabe v. Lunich, 70 Ohio St. 3d 598, 1994-Ohio-4, 640 N.E.2d 159, 33 A.L.R.5th 825 (1994)—19:12

Cable v. Cable, 2015-Ohio-4291, 2015 WL 6109531 (Ohio Ct. App. 2d Dist. Darke County 2015)—8:4, 12:26, 16:12

Cable v. Clemmons, 36 S.W.3d 39 (Tenn. 2001)—13:9, 13:13

Cahill v. Cahill, 1994 WL 284996 (Ohio Ct. App. 8th Dist. Cuyahoga County 1994)—15:12

Caito v. Zucallo, 2001-Ohio-8881, 2001 WL 1388377 (Ohio Ct. App. 11th Dist. Portage County 2001)—12:5

Calhoun, In re, 47 Ohio St. 2d 15, 1 Ohio Op. 3d 10, 350 N.E.2d 665 (1976)—13:5

Calicoat v. Calicoat, 2009-Ohio-5869, 2009 WL 3683665 (Ohio Ct. App. 2d Dist. Miami County 2009)—8:2, 8:4, 9:5, 9:9, 12:2, 12:14

California v. Green, 399 U.S. 149, 90 S. Ct. 1930, 26 L. Ed. 2d 489 (1970)—5:16

Callahan v. Akron Gen. Med. Ctr., 2009-Ohio-5148, 2009 WL 3119626 (Ohio Ct. App. 9th Dist. Summit County 2009)—12:21

Calloway v. Kinkelaar, 168 Ill. 2d 312, 213 Ill. Dec. 675, 659 N.E.2d 1322 (1995)—14:11, 14:12, 14:14

Calvary, State ex rel. v. Upper Arlington, 89 Ohio St. 3d 229, 2000-Ohio-142, 729 N.E.2d 1182 (2000)—12:26

Calzo v. Lynch, 2012-Ohio-1353, 2012 WL 1067921 (Ohio Ct. App. 5th Dist. Richland County 2012)—11:2, 12:10

Campbell v. Campbell, 294 N.J. Super. 18, 682 A.2d 272 (Law Div. 1996)—14:2, 14:12, 14:14

Campbell v. Campbell, 604 A.2d 33 (Me. 1992)—15:15

Campbell v. Campbell, 584 So. 2d 125 (Fla. 4th DCA 1991)—12:15

Campomanes Flores v. Elias-Arata, 2018 WL 3495865 (M.D. Fla. 2018)—18:24

Canton, Ohio, City of v. Harris, 489 U.S. 378, 109 S. Ct. 1197, 103 L. Ed. 2d 412 (1989)—14:11, 14:12, 14:14

Cantrell v. Deitz, 2013-Ohio-1204, 2013 WL 1286661 (Ohio Ct. App. 10th Dist. Franklin County 2013)—19:10

Capella III, L.L.C. v. Wilcox, 190 Ohio App. 3d 133, 2010-Ohio-4746, 940 N.E.2d 1026 (10th Dist. Franklin County 2010)—19:10

Capital One Bank, USA, N.A. v. Essex, 2014-Ohio-4247, 2014 WL 4792583 (Ohio Ct. App. 2d Dist. Montgomery County 2014)—12:23

Caplan v. Donovan, 450 Mass. 463, 879 N.E.2d 117 (2008)—10:13

Capps v. Capps, 715 S.W.2d 547 (Mo. Ct. App. E.D. 1986)—12:24

Caramico v. Caramico, 2015-Ohio-4232, 2015 WL 5934194 (Ohio Ct. App. 12th Dist. Clermont County 2015)—8:5, 12:1, 12:4, 12:7, 12:26, 16:20

2018 WL 827136 (Ohio Ct. App. 12th Dist. Fayette County 2018)—10:4, 12:16, 12:26, 16:20
Corrao v. Corrao, 2016-Ohio-4862, 2016 WL 3632494 (Ohio Ct. App. 8th Dist. Cuyahoga County 2016)—9:7, 12:26, 12:27
Cosme v. Figueroa, 258 N.J. Super. 333, 609 A.2d 523 (Ch. Div. 1992)—12:15, 12:18, 15:15
Cossio v. City and County of Denver, Colo., 986 F. Supp. 1340 (D. Colo. 1997)—14:10
Cottrill v. Cottrill, 2017-Ohio-1422, 2017 WL 1376841 (Ohio Ct. App. 5th Dist. Fairfield County 2017)—8:4, 11:2, 12:10, 12:11, 12:26
Couch v. Couch, 978 S.W.2d 505 (Mo. Ct. App. W.D. 1998)—15:6, 15:12
Couch v. Harrison, 2001-Ohio-4199, 2001 WL 121108 (Ohio Ct. App. 12th Dist. Clermont County 2001)—8:6, 8:7, 12:15, 12:16, 15:12, 15:14, 15:24
Coughlin v. Lancione, 1992 WL 40557 (Ohio Ct. App. 10th Dist. Franklin County 1992)—8:4, 11:10, 12:11
Court of White, In re Contempt of, 60 Ohio App. 2d 62, 14 Ohio Op. 3d 34, 395 N.E.2d 499 (5th Dist. Stark County 1978)—4:6, 13:3
Coverdell v. Department of Social and Health Services, State of Wash., 834 F.2d 758, 10 Fed. R. Serv. 3d 143 (9th Cir. 1987)—4:7
Cowans v. Bagley, 624 F. Supp. 2d 709 (S.D. Ohio 2008)—5:16
Cox v. Oliver Machinery Co., 41 Ohio App. 3d 28, 534 N.E.2d 855 (12th Dist. Butler County 1987)—5:17, 16:15
Cox, In re, 1999 WL 1312688 (Ohio Ct. App. 11th Dist. Geauga County 1999)—13:4, 13:5, 13:6, 13:8
C.Q. v. P.S., 2016-Ohio-4988, 2016 WL 3881115 (Ohio Ct. App. 9th Dist. Medina County 2016)—9:5, 12:6, 12:10, 12:26
Crabtree v. Crabtree, 802 S.W.2d 567 (Mo. Ct. App. W.D. 1991)—15:12
Crabtree v. Dinsmoor, 2013-Ohio-5797, 2013 WL 6869957 (Ohio Ct. App. 10th Dist. Franklin County 2013)—8:4, 11:2, 12:11, 12:26
Crager v. Ohio, 557 U.S. 930, 129 S. Ct. 2856, 174 L. Ed. 2d 598 (2009)—5:14
Crawford v. Brandon, 2014-Ohio-3659, 2014 WL 4180286 (Ohio Ct. App. 12th Dist. Butler County 2014)—12:5, 12:26, 16:9
Crawford v. Mack, 929 A.2d 250 (Pa. Super. Ct. 2007)—12:7
Crawford v. Washington, 541 U.S. 36, 124 S. Ct. 1354, 158 L. Ed. 2d 177, 63 Fed. R. Evid. Serv. 1077 (2004)—5:14, 5:15, 5:16, 5:26, 7:22, 16:13, 16:22
Crawford's Estate, In re, 155 Kan. 388, 125 P.2d 354 (1942)—19:9
Croone v. Arif, 2014-Ohio-5546, 2014 WL 7186677 (Ohio Ct. App. 8th Dist. Cuyahoga County 2014)—12:26, 16:12
Cross v. Ledford, 161 Ohio St. 469, 53 Ohio Op. 361, 120 N.E.2d 118 (1954)—12:11
Croswell v. Shenouda, 275 N.J. Super. 614, 646 A.2d 1140 (Ch. Div. 1994)—10:7
Cruz-Foster v. Foster, 597 A.2d 927 (D.C. 1991)—12:24, 16:21
C.S., In re, 2012-Ohio-2988, 2012 WL 2523966 (Ohio Ct. App. 10th Dist. Franklin County 2012)—6:14
C.T., In re, 2013-Ohio-2458, 991 N.E.2d 1171 (Ohio Ct. App. 8th Dist. Cuyahoga County 2013)—2:7
Cuffy v. City of New York, 69 N.Y.2d 255, 513 N.Y.S.2d 372, 505 N.E.2d 937 (1987)—14:12
Culberson v. Doan, 65 F. Supp. 2d 701 (S.D. Ohio 1999)—14:8, 14:14
Culculoglu v. Culculoglu, 2013 WL 4045905 (D. Nev. 2013)—18:24
Cunningham v. Morgan, 2004-Ohio-6007, 2004 WL 2578873 (Ohio Ct. App. 8th Dist. Cuyahoga County 2004)—12:11, 16:9
Curington v. Moon, 2009-Ohio-3013, 2009 WL 1800373 (Ohio Ct. App. 2d Dist. Montgomery County 2009)—7:24, 9:2, 9:3, 12:27
Currier v. Doran, 242 F.3d 905 (10th Cir. 2001)—14:9
Curry v. State, 811 So. 2d 736 (Fla. 4th DCA 2002)—9:2
Custis v. U.S., 511 U.S. 485, 114 S. Ct. 1732, 128 L. Ed. 2d 517 (1994)—2:7, 3:2

2008 WL 5124388 (Ohio Ct. App. 5th Dist. Fairfield County 2008)—12:15, 12:23, 12:25

Demons v. State, 277 Ga. 724, 595 S.E.2d 76 (2004)—16:13

Dempster, In re Marriage of, 809 S.W.2d 450 (Mo. Ct. App. S.D. 1991)—15:14

Denney v. Sanders, 2016-Ohio-5113, 2016 WL 4063898 (Ohio Ct. App. 1st Dist. Hamilton County 2016)—9:7, 10:11, 12:26

Dennis v. Paulsen, 2009-Ohio-2916, 2009 WL 1719369 (Ohio Ct. App. 4th Dist. Hocking County 2009)—9:5, 12:24, 12:26

Denovchek v. Board of Trumbull County Com'rs, 36 Ohio St. 3d 14, 520 N.E.2d 1362 (1988)—13:4, 13:14

Denovchek v. Board of Trumbull County Com'rs, 1987 WL 5981 (Ohio Ct. App. 11th Dist. Trumbull County 1987)—13:14

Depos v. Depos, 307 N.J. Super. 396, 704 A.2d 1049 (Ch. Div. 1997)—12:5

Derolph v. Cirillo, 2004-Ohio-5564, 2004 WL 2348509 (Ohio Ct. App. 5th Dist. Licking County 2004)—9:7, 9:8

Descamps v. U.S., 570 U.S. 254, 133 S. Ct. 2276, 186 L. Ed. 2d 438 (2013)—18:11

DeShaney v. Winnebago County Dept. of Social Services, 489 U.S. 189, 109 S. Ct. 998, 103 L. Ed. 2d 249 (1989)—14:9, 14:11, 14:14

Desmond v. Desmond, 134 Misc. 2d 62, 509 N.Y.S.2d 979 (Fam. Ct. 1986)—15:12

Detrick v. Preece, 2013-Ohio-2499, 2013 WL 3089090 (Ohio Ct. App. 3d Dist. Logan County 2013)—8:4, 12:26

Devault v. Devault, 2004-Ohio-976, 2004 WL 397134 (Ohio Ct. App. 5th Dist. Ashland County 2004)—8:2, 11:1, 11:7, 12:14, 12:27

Devine-Riley v. Clellan, 2011-Ohio-4367, 2011 WL 3841957 (Ohio Ct. App. 10th Dist. Franklin County 2011)—12:26

Dewey v. Olson, 2000 WL 1434138 (Ohio Ct. App. 6th Dist. Lucas County 2000)—5:19

Diaz v. U.S., 223 U.S. 442, 32 S. Ct. 250, 56 L. Ed. 500 (1912)—2:7

Dickerson v. Dickerson, 87 Ohio App. 3d 848, 623 N.E.2d 237 (6th Dist. Lucas County 1993)—4:1

Dickson v. Ball, 2006-Ohio-3436, 2006 WL 1817265 (Ohio Ct. App. 10th Dist. Franklin County 2006)—9:5, 12:25

Dickson v. Dickson, 1982 WL 5380 (Ohio Ct. App. 8th Dist. Cuyahoga County 1982)—18:18

Dickson v. Miller, 2012-Ohio-2142, 2012 WL 1664012 (Ohio Ct. App. 5th Dist. Fairfield County 2012)—8:5, 12:26

Didonato v. Stewart, 2015-Ohio-270, 2015 WL 329507 (Ohio Ct. App. 5th Dist. Tuscarawas County 2015)—9:7

Didzerekis v. Stewart, 41 F. Supp. 2d 840 (N.D. Ill. 1999)—14:8, 14:14

Dilley v. Dilley, 2011-Ohio-2093, 2011 WL 1662359 (Ohio Ct. App. 11th Dist. Geauga County 2011)—12:17

Disciplinary Counsel v. Campbell, 126 Ohio St. 3d 150, 2010-Ohio-3265, 931 N.E.2d 558 (2010)—4:6

District of Columbia v. Heller, 554 U.S. 570, 128 S. Ct. 2783, 171 L. Ed. 2d 637 (2008)—9:9, 18:11

Dixon v. U.S., 548 U.S. 1, 126 S. Ct. 2437, 165 L. Ed. 2d 299 (2006)—7:25

D.L., In re, 189 Ohio App. 3d 154, 2010-Ohio-1888, 937 N.E.2d 1042 (6th Dist. Ottawa County 2010)—20:1, 20:14

D.M.H. by Hefel v. Thompson, 577 N.W.2d 643 (Iowa 1998)—10:11

D.N. v. K.M., 216 N.J. 587, 83 A.3d 825 (2014)—11:3, 12:4, 12:7

D.N., In re, 195 Ohio App. 3d 552, 2011-Ohio-5494, 960 N.E.2d 1063 (8th Dist. Cuyahoga County 2011)—8:8, 12:29

Dobos v. Dobos, 179 Ohio App. 3d 173, 2008-Ohio-5665, 901 N.E.2d 248 (12th Dist. Clermont County 2008)—10:13

Dodd v. Dodd, 2001 WL 812244 (Ohio Ct. App. 6th Dist. Lucas County 2001)—15:6, 15:7, 15:12, 15:15, 15:18, 15:19

Dodds on behalf of S.S. v. Stamper, 2018-Ohio-193, 2018 WL 481779 (Ohio Ct. App. 2d Dist. Cham-

Dupal v. Sommer, 2009-Ohio-5791, 2009 WL 3600358 (Ohio Ct. App. 5th Dist. Stark County 2009)—9:4, 9:5, 9:8

Durrah v. Durrah, 2006-Ohio-2138, 2006 WL 1132851 (Ohio Ct. App. 12th Dist. Butler County 2006)—10:12, 10:13

Durrstein v. Cox, 2003-Ohio-4585, 2003 WL 22026056 (Ohio Ct. App. 2d Dist. Montgomery County 2003)—12:9

Dustin, In re, 1999 WL 956880 (Ohio Ct. App. 11th Dist. Lake County 1999)—5:14

Dutton v. Evans, 400 U.S. 74, 91 S. Ct. 210, 27 L. Ed. 2d 213 (1970)—5:26

Dybo v. Dybo, 1999 WL 1073781 (Ohio Ct. App. 11th Dist. Geauga County 1999)—8:7, 12:11

Dyke v. Price, 2000 WL 1546555 (Ohio Ct. App. 2d Dist. Montgomery County 2000)—2:5, 10:6, 11:3, 12:4

Dymitro v. Dymitro, 129 Idaho 527, 927 P.2d 917 (Ct. App. 1996)—15:24

E

E-Z Loader Boat Trailers, Inc. v. Travelers Indem. Co., 106 Wash. 2d 901, 726 P.2d 439 (1986)—8:3

E.A., In Interest of, 552 N.W.2d 135 (Iowa 1996)—15:24

Eastley v. Volkman, 132 Ohio St. 3d 328, 2012-Ohio-2179, 972 N.E.2d 517 (2012)—9:7, 12:26

East Palestine, Ohio, City of v. Adrian, 1997 WL 321623 (Ohio Ct. App. 7th Dist. Columbiana County 1997)—14:5

Eastwood v. Eastwood, 2010-Ohio-6492, 2010 WL 5550706 (Ohio Ct. App. 9th Dist. Summit County 2010)—12:21

Eatmon v. Safferman, 157 N.C. App. 141, 578 S.E.2d 328 (2003)—8:4

Eble v. Emery, 2007-Ohio-4857, 2007 WL 2729462 (Ohio Ct. App. 10th Dist. Franklin County 2007)—12:25

Echemann v. Echemann, 2016-Ohio-3212, 2016 WL 3057979 (Ohio Ct. App. 3d Dist. Shelby County 2016)—3:6, 9:5, 9:7, 9:8

Eckert v. Town of Silverthorne, 25 Fed. Appx. 679 (10th Cir. 2001)—14:10, 14:12, 14:14

Eckliff v. Walters, 168 Ohio App. 3d 727, 2006-Ohio-4817, 861 N.E.2d 843 (11th Dist. Lake County 2006)—12:9

Eckstein v. Colian, 2012-Ohio-4038, 2012 WL 3834883 (Ohio Ct. App. 7th Dist. Columbiana County 2012)—11:10, 12:11, 16:12

E. Cleveland v. Perkins, 2009-Ohio-2131, 2009 WL 1244154 (Ohio Ct. App. 8th Dist. Cuyahoga County 2009)—2:4, 2:5, 7:3, 8:4, 10:8

Eddington v. McCabe, 98 A.D.3d 613, 949 N.Y.S.2d 734 (2d Dep't 2012)—15:12

Edelen v. Edelen, 457 So. 2d 171 (La. Ct. App. 2d Cir. 1984)—15:15

Edwards v. Reser, 2007-Ohio-6520, 2007 WL 4277861 (Ohio Ct. App. 6th Dist. Ottawa County 2007)—2:5, 10:6, 12:7

E.G. v. Ergh, 2014-Ohio-1332, 2014 WL 1345273 (Ohio Ct. App. 9th Dist. Lorain County 2014)—12:26

E.H. v. T.S., 2015-Ohio-5444, 2015 WL 9461788 (Ohio Ct. App. 3d Dist. Hardin County 2015)—12:7

Eichenberger v. Eichenberger, 1993 WL 460570 (Ohio Ct. App. 10th Dist. Franklin County 1993)—11:7, 11:10, 12:14, 12:15, 12:27

Eichenberger v. Eichenberger, 82 Ohio App. 3d 809, 613 N.E.2d 678 (10th Dist. Franklin County 1992)—8:3, 8:4, 11:2, 11:9, 11:10, 11:21, 11:25, 12:2, 12:4, 12:11, 12:26, 15:7, 15:15, 15:24, 16:9, 16:21

Eichenlaub v. Eichenlaub, 340 Pa. Super. 552, 490 A.2d 918 (1985)—13:5

Elkins v. Elkins, 1992 WL 180118 (Ohio Ct. App. 10th Dist. Franklin County 1992)—11:4, 11:7, 12:7, 12:15, 12:21

Elkins v. Manley, 2016-Ohio-8307, 2016 WL 7427267 (Ohio Ct. App. 8th Dist. Cuyahoga County 2016)—9:2, 9:7, 9:8

Elkins v. Reed, 2014-Ohio-1217, 2014 WL 1350806 (Ohio Ct. App. 5th Dist. Stark County 2014)—9:7, 9:8, 9:9

Ellet v. Falk, 2010-Ohio-6219, 2010 WL 5269870 (Ohio Ct. App. 6th

F

Gaydash v. Gaydash, 168 Ohio App. 3d 418, 2006-Ohio-4080, 860 N.E.2d 789 (9th Dist. Summit County 2006)—8:1, 8:4, 8:5, 11:10, 12:21, 12:22, 12:26
Gazette v. City of Pontiac, 41 F.3d 1061, 1994 FED App. 0405P (6th Cir. 1994)—14:9, 14:14
Gebardi v. U.S., 287 U.S. 112, 53 S. Ct. 35, 77 L. Ed. 206, 84 A.L.R. 370 (1932)—4:6, 12:22, 13:12
Gehring v. Gehring, 2004-Ohio-95, 2004 WL 47688 (Ohio Ct. App. 12th Dist. Warren County 2004)—15:12
Geigep v. Progressive Preferred Ins. Co., 2008 WL 5325462 (Ohio C.P. 2008)—10:5
Genari v. Genari, 2001-Ohio-1524, 2001 WL 848569 (Ohio Ct. App. 2d Dist. Greene County 2001)—11:10, 11:11, 11:22, 12:1, 12:7, 12:27
Gevedon v. Gevedon, 167 Ohio App. 3d 450, 2006-Ohio-3195, 855 N.E.2d 548 (2d Dist. Greene County 2006)—12:19, 13:8
Giambrone v. Giambrone, 32 Mass. App. Ct. 118, 586 N.E.2d 23 (1992)—15:24
Gibson v. Gibson, 2006-Ohio-2880, 2006 WL 1555935 (Ohio Ct. App. 4th Dist. Washington County 2006)—11:3, 12:3
Gibson v. Gibson, 87 Ohio App. 3d 426, 622 N.E.2d 425 (4th Dist. Scioto County 1993)—19:7
Gibson v. Redman, 2001-Ohio-3449, 2001 WL 1497085 (Ohio Ct. App. 7th Dist. Jefferson County 2001)—12:9
Gibson v. Redman—12:9
Gideon v. Wainwright, 372 U.S. 335, 83 S. Ct. 792, 9 L. Ed. 2d 799, 93 A.L.R.2d 733 (1963)—3:2, 7:9
Gilbert v. Summit County, 104 Ohio St. 3d 660, 2004-Ohio-7108, 821 N.E.2d 564 (2004)—19:10
Giles v. California, 554 U.S. 353, 128 S. Ct. 2678, 171 L. Ed. 2d 488 (2008)—5:14, 5:15, 16:13
Gill v. Gill, 2003-Ohio-180, 2003 WL 132447 (Ohio Ct. App. 8th Dist. Cuyahoga County 2003)—15:22
Gillespie v. City of Indianapolis, 185 F.3d 693 (7th Cir. 1999)—18:11
Gilreath v. Kinderdine, 2004-Ohio-868, 2004 WL 362335 (Ohio Ct. App. 2d Dist. Miami County 2004)—9:1, 9:2, 9:4, 9:8
Gina C v. Stephen F, 150 Misc. 2d 459, 576 N.Y.S.2d 776 (Fam. Ct. 1991)—10:7
Glancy v. Spradley, 2012-Ohio-4224, 2012 WL 4074986 (Ohio Ct. App. 12th Dist. Butler County 2012)—8:6, 10:8
Glenn v. Glenn, 2009-Ohio-1345, 2009 WL 765480 (Ohio Ct. App. 5th Dist. Stark County 2009)—12:2, 12:25
Gliozzo v. Univ. Urologists of Cleveland, Inc., 114 Ohio St. 3d 141, 2007-Ohio-3762, 870 N.E.2d 714 (2007)—13:3
Gloria C. v. William C., 124 Misc. 2d 313, 476 N.Y.S.2d 991 (Fam. Ct. 1984)—10:7
Goe v. Goe, 2007-Ohio-6767, 2007 WL 4395135 (Ohio Ct. App. 5th Dist. Stark County 2007)—3:10
Goldade v. State, 674 P.2d 721 (Wyo. 1983)—5:19
Goldberg v. Kelly, 397 U.S. 254, 90 S. Ct. 1011, 25 L. Ed. 2d 287 (1970)—9:3
Golden v. Bay Village Police Dept., 2002-Ohio-673, 2002 WL 253878 (Ohio Ct. App. 8th Dist. Cuyahoga County 2002)—12:22, 14:5, 18:11
Goldfuss v. Davidson, 79 Ohio St. 3d 116, 1997-Ohio-401, 679 N.E.2d 1099 (1997)—12:16
Goldfuss v. Traxler, 2008-Ohio-6186, 2008 WL 5053451 (Ohio Ct. App. 3d Dist. Wyandot County 2008)—9:5, 12:27
Gomez v. Dyer, 2008-Ohio-1523, 2008 WL 850127 (Ohio Ct. App. 7th Dist. Noble County 2008)—8:7, 12:3, 12:4, 12:7
Gomez v. Kiner, 2012-Ohio-1019, 2012 WL 831460 (Ohio Ct. App. 10th Dist. Franklin County 2012)—12:29
Gompers v. Buck's Stove & Range Co., 221 U.S. 418, 31 S. Ct. 492, 55 L. Ed. 797 (1911)—13:4, 13:6
Gonzales v. City of Castle Rock, 366 F.3d 1093 (10th Cir. 2004)—14:14
Gonzales v. City of Castle Rock, 307 F.3d 1258 (10th Cir. 2002)—14:9, 14:11, 14:14
Goode v. Goode, 89 Ohio App. 3d 405,

Guthrie, In re Marriage of, 188 Wash. App. 1057, 2015 WL 4400535 (Div. 1 2015)—18:24

H

Haas v. Semrad, 2007-Ohio-2828, 2007 WL 1653032 (Ohio Ct. App. 6th Dist. Lucas County 2007)—10:13

Hagaman, In re Marriage of, 123 Ill. App. 3d 549, 78 Ill. Dec. 922, 462 N.E.2d 1276 (4th Dist. 1984)—12:11

Hagany v. Cohnen, 29 Ohio St. 82, 1876 WL 44 (1876)—12:7

Hageman v. Southwest General Health Center, 119 Ohio St. 3d—19:7

Hageman v. Southwest Gen. Health Ctr., 119 Ohio St. 3d 185, 2008-Ohio-3343, 893 N.E.2d 153 (2008)—19:7

Hageman v. Southwest Gen. Health Ctr., 2006-Ohio-6765, 2006 WL 3743095 (Ohio Ct. App. 8th Dist. Cuyahoga County 2006)—19:7

Haines v. Shiever, 1995 WL 348430 (Ohio Ct. App. 8th Dist. Cuyahoga County 1995)—12:26

Hakken v. Washtenaw County, 901 F. Supp. 1245 (E.D. Mich. 1995)—14:14

Hakkila v. Hakkila, 112 N.M. 172, 1991-NMCA-029, 812 P.2d 1320 (Ct. App. 1991)—19:5

Hall v. Hall, 571 So. 2d 1176 (Ala. Civ. App. 1990)—15:12

Hall v. Hall, 408 N.W.2d 626 (Minn. Ct. App. 1987)—15:15, 15:18

Halley v. Ashley, 1997 WL 760662 (Ohio Ct. App. 9th Dist. Summit County 1997)—8:5, 8:6, 11:2, 11:5, 11:10, 11:16, 11:25, 12:17

Halton v. Crossley, 2012-Ohio-550, 2012 WL 440724 (Ohio Ct. App. 5th Dist. Coshocton County 2012)—9:8

Hamilton v. Ali, 350 N.J. Super. 479, 795 A.2d 929 (Ch. Div. 2001)—10:9

Hamilton v. Cameron, 121 Ohio App. 3d 445, 700 N.E.2d 336 (12th Dist. Butler County 1997)—2:4, 8:4, 16:9

Hamilton v. Hamilton, 886 S.W.2d 711 (Mo. Ct. App. W.D. 1994)—15:6, 15:7

Hamilton v. Hamilton, 93 N.C. App. 639, 379 S.E.2d 93 (1989)—15:18

Hamilton, City of v. Roberson, 1998 WL 842754 (Ohio Ct. App. 12th Dist. Butler County 1998)—8:8, 14:6

Hamlin-Scanlon v. Taylor, 2008-Ohio-411, 2008 WL 315458 (Ohio Ct. App. 9th Dist. Summit County 2008)—9:3, 9:4

Hammon v. State, 829 N.E.2d 444 (Ind. 2005)—16:13

Hamper v. Dobrski, 2015-Ohio-1381, 2015 WL 1593249 (Ohio Ct. App. 8th Dist. Cuyahoga County 2015)—3:10, 11:10, 11:11, 12:1, 12:17, 13:3, 13:4, 13:6, 13:7, 13:8

Hangen v. McCaleb, 2006-Ohio-776, 2006 WL 400134 (Ohio Ct. App. 2d Dist. Greene County 2006)—9:2

Hanna v. Keszei, 2009-Ohio-4136, 2009 WL 2490035 (Ohio Ct. App. 12th Dist. Clermont County 2009)—11:23, 12:15

Hanson v. Denckla, 357 U.S. 235, 78 S. Ct. 1228, 2 L. Ed. 2d 1283 (1958)—10:13

Harbaugh v. Jarrell, 2005-Ohio-1753, 2005 WL 856927 (Ohio Ct. App. 5th Dist. Ashland County 2005)—8:8, 11:10

Harkai v. Scherba Industries, Inc., 136 Ohio App. 3d 211, 736 N.E.2d 101 (9th Dist. Medina County 2000)—12:10

Harlett v. Harlett, 1996 WL 629510 (Ohio Ct. App. 2d Dist. Montgomery County 1996)—12:23, 12:24, 12:25

Harley v. Harley, 2003-Ohio-232, 2003 WL 146014 (Ohio Ct. App. 4th Dist. Athens County 2003)—15:17, 15:18, 15:21

Harper v. Neal, 2016-Ohio-7179, 2016 WL 5874628 (Ohio Ct. App. 4th Dist. Hocking County 2016)—12:10

Harrell v. Harrell, 1996 WL 170379 (Ohio Ct. App. 9th Dist. Lorain County 1996)—4:1

Harris v. City of Lorain, 2003-Ohio-530, 2003 WL 245737 (Ohio Ct. App. 9th Dist. Lorain County 2003)—12:27

Harris v. Miami Cty. Sheriff's Dept., 160 Ohio App. 3d 435, 2005-Ohio-

K

Kneisley v. Lattimer-Stevens Co., 40 Ohio St. 3d 354, 533 N.E.2d 743 (1988)—7:26
Knight v. Chattanooga Police Dept., 2008 WL 2704458 (E.D. Tenn. 2008)—14:8
Knock v. Knock, 224 Conn. 776, 621 A.2d 267 (1993)—15:12, 15:18
Knuth v. Knuth, 1992 WL 145387 (Minn. Ct. App. 1992)—12:24
Kobe v. Kobe, 61 Ohio App. 2d 67, 15 Ohio Op. 3d 86, 399 N.E.2d 124 (8th Dist. Cuyahoga County 1978)—19:11
Koepke v. Koepke, 52 Ohio App. 3d 47, 556 N.E.2d 1198 (6th Dist. Wood County 1989)—19:7, 19:11
Kohus v. Daly, 2016-Ohio-73, 2016 WL 116121 (Ohio Ct. App. 12th Dist. Clermont County 2016)—8:6, 12:4, 12:26
Koll v. Department of Justice, 2009 WI App 74, 317 Wis. 2d 753, 769 N.W.2d 69 (Ct. App. 2009)—18:11
Kovacs v. Kovacs, 2004-Ohio-2777, 2004 WL 1191103 (Ohio Ct. App. 6th Dist. Erie County 2004)—12:29
K.R. v. T.B., 2017-Ohio-8647, 2017 WL 5608198 (Ohio Ct. App. 10th Dist. Franklin County 2017)—9:5, 12:10
Kraft v. Kraft, 554 N.W.2d 657 (N.D. 1996)—15:24
Kramer v. Kramer, 2002-Ohio-4383, 2002 WL 1967104 (Ohio Ct. App. 3d Dist. Seneca County 2002)—9:2, 9:8
Kranek v. Richards, 2011-Ohio-6374, 2011 WL 6164727 (Ohio Ct. App. 7th Dist. Jefferson County 2011)—9:4, 9:8, 12:15
Krank v. Krank, 529 N.W.2d 844, 51 A.L.R.5th 785 (N.D. 1995)—15:13
Krassnoski v. Rosey, 454 Pa. Super. 78, 684 A.2d 635 (1996)—12:21
Krefter v. Wills, 623 F. Supp. 2d 125 (D. Mass. 2009)—18:21, 18:24
Kreuzer v. Kreuzer, 2002-Ohio-105, 2002 WL 27392 (Ohio Ct. App. 2d Dist. Greene County 2002)—8:4
Kreuzer v. Kreuzer, 144 Ohio App. 3d 610, 2001-Ohio-1542, 761 N.E.2d 77 (2d Dist. Greene County 2001)—9:2, 9:3
Kristen V., In re, 2008-Ohio-2994, 2008 WL 2468839 (Ohio Ct. App. 6th Dist. Ottawa County 2008)—2:2
Krlich v. Clemente, 2017-Ohio-7945, 98 N.E.3d 752 (Ohio Ct. App. 11th Dist. Trumbull County 2017)—9:4
Kruszynski v. Kruszynski, 2013-Ohio-3355, 2013 WL 3965465 (Ohio Ct. App. 5th Dist. Fairfield County 2013)—9:7, 9:8
Krzystan v. Bauer, 2017-Ohio-858, 2017 WL 945183 (Ohio Ct. App. 6th Dist. Ottawa County 2017)—9:2, 9:7, 9:8
K.U. v. M.S., 2017-Ohio-8029, 2017 WL 4350999 (Ohio Ct. App. 7th Dist. Mahoning County 2017)—9:5, 12:10
Kubiszak v. Rini's Supermarket, 77 Ohio App. 3d 679, 603 N.E.2d 308 (8th Dist. Cuyahoga County 1991)—16:12
Kuehn v. Kuehn, 55 Ohio App. 3d 245, 564 N.E.2d 97 (12th Dist. Clinton County 1988)—12:25
Kuhn v. Kuhn, 2013-Ohio-5807, 2013 WL 6869801 (Ohio Ct. App. 11th Dist. Lake County 2013)—8:4, 8:5, 8:8, 12:26, 16:20
Kumar, In re Marriage of, 13 Cal. App. 5th 1072, 220 Cal. Rptr. 3d 863 (1st Dist. 2017)—18:24
Kuptz v. Youngstown City School Dist. Bd. of Edn., 175 Ohio App. 3d 738, 2008-Ohio-1676, 889 N.E.2d 166, 233 Ed. Law Rep. 895 (7th Dist. Mahoning County 2008)—12:25
Kurincic v. Kurincic, 2000 WL 1231551 (Ohio Ct. App. 8th Dist. Cuyahoga County 2000)—13:6, 13:7, 13:8
Kurincic v. Kurincic, 2000 WL 217808 (Ohio Ct. App. 8th Dist. Cuyahoga County 2000)—8:3, 8:7, 12:15, 15:24
Kvasne v. Collins, 2010 WL 3210949 (N.D. Ohio 2010)—2:5

L

Lacey v. Village of Palatine, 379 Ill. App. 3d 62, 318 Ill. Dec. 64, 882 N.E.2d 1187 (1st Dist. 2008)—14:14
Lain v. Ververis, 1999 WL 893611 (Ohio Ct. App. 12th Dist. Preble

Lewis v. Cleveland, 89 Ohio App. 3d 136, 623 N.E.2d 1233 (8th Dist. Cuyahoga County 1993)—14:14

Lewis v. Gravely, 2016-Ohio-1502, 2016 WL 1404159 (Ohio Ct. App. 4th Dist. Adams County 2016)—2:4, 2:7, 8:4, 11:2

Lewis v. Jacobs, 2013-Ohio-3461, 2013 WL 4041333 (Ohio Ct. App. 2d Dist. Montgomery County 2013)—9:8

Lewis v. City of Lake Charles, 2007 WL 4622780 (W.D. La. 2007)—14:8

Lewis v. Office of Prosecuting Atty. of Columbiana Cty., 2006-Ohio-4685, 2006 WL 2590561 (Ohio Ct. App. 7th Dist. Columbiana County 2006)—13:17

Lewistown Foundry & Machine Co. v. Hartford Stone Co., 92 Ohio St. 76, 110 N.E. 515 (1915)—19:8

Lias v. Beekman, 2007-Ohio-5737, 2007 WL 3108899 (Ohio Ct. App. 10th Dist. Franklin County 2007)—3:6, 9:7, 9:8, 12:3

Lightner v. Pennsylvania Co., 17 Phila. 137 (Pa. C.P. 1884)—13:14

Liles v. Keith, 2009-Ohio-6874, 2009 WL 5064577 (Ohio Ct. App. 3d Dist. Auglaize County 2009)—9:8

Lillard v. Allen, 2008-Ohio-3664, 2008 WL 2836879 (Ohio Ct. App. 8th Dist. Cuyahoga County 2008)—12:16

Liming v. Damos, 2011-Ohio-2726, 2011 WL 2225067 (Ohio Ct. App. 4th Dist. Athens County 2011)—3:10

Linda D. v. Peter D., 152 Misc. 2d 564, 577 N.Y.S.2d 354 (Fam. Ct. 1991)—12:21

Linda N. on behalf of Rebecca N. v. William N., 289 Neb. 607, 856 N.W.2d 436 (2014)—8:5

Lindsay v. Jackson, 2000 WL 1268810 (Ohio Ct. App. 1st Dist. Hamilton County 2000)—9:3, 9:5, 9:8, 12:1, 12:6, 12:9

Linker v. Linker, 28 Colo. App. 131, 470 P.2d 921 (App. 1970)—19:9

Little v. Little, 2011-Ohio-318, 2011 WL 303823 (Ohio Ct. App. 10th Dist. Franklin County 2011)—12:24

Livingood v. Negrete, 547 N.W.2d 196 (Iowa 1996)—10:9

L.L. v. R.B., 2017-Ohio-7553, 2017 WL 3980553 (Ohio Ct. App. 5th Dist. Guernsey County 2017)—8:5, 9:5, 9:8, 12:10

L.L.L. v. Junies, 2014-Ohio-141, 2014 WL 201640 (Ohio Ct. App. 2d Dist. Greene County 2014)—9:3

Lloyd v. Thornsbery, 2018-Ohio-2893, 2018 WL 3536755 (Ohio Ct. App. 11th Dist. Portage County 2018)—9:5, 9:7

L.N.Y v. Breh, 2016-Ohio-966, 2016 WL 936854 (Ohio Ct. App. 2d Dist. Montgomery County 2016)—16:12

Loeffler v. Loeffler, 1995 WL 628239 (Ohio Ct. App. 6th Dist. Lucas County 1995)—8:7

Loewen v. Newsome, 2012-Ohio-566, 2012 WL 473850 (Ohio Ct. App. 9th Dist. Summit County 2012)—12:6

Logsdon v. Boulais, 2001-Ohio-8689, 2001 WL 1256309 (Ohio Ct. App. 12th Dist. Clermont County 2001)—12:26

Londrico v. Delores C. Knowlton, Inc., 88 Ohio App. 3d 282, 623 N.E.2d 723 (9th Dist. Summit County 1993)—12:25

Lonell J., In re, 242 A.D.2d 58, 673 N.Y.S.2d 116 (1st Dep't 1998)—8:7, 15:24

Long v. Sloan, 2017 WL 3088038 (N.D. Ohio 2017)—2:8

Lopez Ayala v. Holder, 452 Fed. Appx. 749 (9th Cir. 2011)—18:22

Lorain, City of v. Prudoff, 1994 WL 709667 (Ohio Ct. App. 9th Dist. Lorain County 1994)—8:7

Losey v. Diersing, 2013-Ohio-1108, 2013 WL 1196674 (Ohio Ct. App. 12th Dist. Clermont County 2013)—9:5, 9:7, 11:20

Louderback v. Louderback, 1999 WL 94902 (Ohio Ct. App. 2d Dist. Montgomery County 1999)—15:6, 15:12, 15:13

Lovcik v. Ellingson, 1997 ND 201, 569 N.W.2d 697 (N.D. 1997)—8:8

Love v. City of Port Clinton, 37 Ohio St. 3d 98, 524 N.E.2d 166 (1988)—19:4

Lovell, In re, 226 Mich. App. 84, 572 N.W.2d 44 (1997)—10:8, 10:9

Lozada v. Lozada, 2014-Ohio-5700, 2014 WL 7357285 (Ohio Ct. App.

M

8901, 2001 WL 1401978 (Ohio Ct. App. 11th Dist. Portage County 2001)—8:4, 10:4, 10:5, 10:6, 10:8, 10:11, 12:11
Maglionico v. Maglionico—10:4
Magoon v. Thoroughgood, 148 N.H. 139, 803 A.2d 1070 (2002)—18:11
Mahoney v. Com., 415 Mass. 278, 612 N.E.2d 1175 (1993)—13:13
Mahoney v. Shaker Square Beverages, 46 Ohio Op. 250, 64 Ohio L. Abs. 200, 102 N.E.2d 281 (C.P. 1951)—10:3
Majeed v. Majeed, 2016-Ohio-7243, 2016 WL 5887174 (Ohio Ct. App. 2d Dist. Montgomery County 2016)—8:3, 8:5, 12:11, 12:26
M.A.L., In re, 2007-Ohio-2426, 2007 WL 1454164 (Ohio Ct. App. 2d Dist. Miami County 2007)—3:2
Mallin v. Mallin, 44 Ohio App. 3d 53, 541 N.E.2d 116 (8th Dist. Cuyahoga County 1988)—11:12, 11:14, 12:14, 12:22
Malone v. Lowry, 2007-Ohio-5665, 2007 WL 3076599 (Ohio Ct. App. 2d Dist. Greene County 2007)—9:3, 19:10
Malwitz, In re Marriage of, 99 P.3d 56 (Colo. 2004)—10:13
Malwitz, In re Marriage of, 81 P.3d 1076 (Colo. App. 2003)—10:13
Mancino v. City of Lakewood, 36 Ohio App. 3d 219, 523 N.E.2d 332 (8th Dist. Cuyahoga County 1987)—12:7
Manin v. Diloreti, 94 Ohio App. 3d 777, 641 N.E.2d 826 (9th Dist. Summit County 1994)—19:9
Mann v. Helmig, 2007 WL 1035015 (E.D. Ky. 2007)—18:11
Mann v. Sumser, 2002-Ohio-5103, 2002 WL 31151164 (Ohio Ct. App. 5th Dist. Stark County 2002)—9:7, 9:9, 12:21, 12:22
Mansaray v. Sankoh, 2005-Ohio-1451, 2005 WL 704856 (Ohio Ct. App. 10th Dist. Franklin County 2005)—10:4, 10:5
Mapes v. Ohio, 498 U.S. 977, 111 S. Ct. 504, 112 L. Ed. 2d 433 (1990)—15:12
Maple Heights, City of v. Spearman, 1998 WL 355850 (Ohio Ct. App. 8th Dist. Cuyahoga County 1998)—2:7
Marchant v. Marchant, 743 P.2d 199 (Utah Ct. App. 1987)—15:12
Marco v. Superior Court, 17 Ariz. App. 210, 496 P.2d 636 (Div. 2 1972)—12:29
Marconi, In re Marriage of, 584 N.W.2d 331 (Iowa 1998)—15:24
Marker v. Grimm, 65 Ohio St. 3d 139, 601 N.E.2d 496 (1992)—11:16
Markowitz v. Markowitz, 2006-Ohio-5932, 2006 WL 3234010 (Ohio Ct. App. 8th Dist. Cuyahoga County 2006)—8:4, 11:10, 12:19, 12:22
Marquette v. Marquette, 1984 OK CIV APP 25, 686 P.2d 990 (Ct. App. Div. 1 1984)—12:11
Marriage of Heilmann, Matter of, 771 P.2d 948 (Kan. Ct. App. 1989)—15:14
Marshall v. Marshall, 2016-Ohio-3405, 2016 WL 3384312 (Ohio Ct. App. 11th Dist. Portage County 2016)—12:21
Marshall v. Marshall, 117 Ohio App. 3d 182, 690 N.E.2d 68 (3d Dist. Allen County 1997)—15:6, 15:12, 15:13, 15:24
Martauz v. Martauz, 2009-Ohio-2642, 2009 WL 1581185 (Ohio Ct. App. 7th Dist. Mahoning County 2009)—8:4, 8:8, 11:2, 11:10, 12:11
Martin v. Dockter, 2018-Ohio-858, 2018 WL 1216633 (Ohio Ct. App. 10th Dist. Franklin County 2018)—9:5, 12:10
Martin v. Fisher, 2001 WL 370519 (Ohio Ct. App. 8th Dist. Cuyahoga County 2001)—10:11, 12:26
Martin v. Hanood, 2009-Ohio-1501, 2009 WL 825766 (Ohio Ct. App. 7th Dist. Jefferson County 2009)—8:4, 8:7, 11:10, 12:11, 12:26
Martin v. Martin, 2013-Ohio-5703, 2013 WL 6843599 (Ohio Ct. App. 10th Dist. Franklin County 2013)—8:1, 12:4, 12:10, 12:24, 12:26
Martin v. Popson, 2013-Ohio-3956, 2013 WL 5211329 (Ohio Ct. App. 6th Dist. Ottawa County 2013)—9:8
Martin v. Wills, 2017-Ohio-9382, 2017 WL 6804072 (Ohio Ct. App. 7th Dist. Mahoning County 2017)—9:4
Martindale v. Martindale, 2017-Ohio-9266, 102 N.E.3d 19 (Ohio Ct.

McGill v. McGill, 3 Ohio App. 3d 455, 445 N.E.2d 1163 (2d Dist. Montgomery County 1982)—13:4, 13:5, 13:8

McGuire v. Sprinkle, 2007-Ohio-2705, 2007 WL 1585100 (Ohio Ct. App. 12th Dist. Warren County 2007)—8:4, 9:5, 11:2, 11:25, 12:2, 12:26

McIntyre v. Johnson-Estes, 2011-Ohio-1696, 2011 WL 1327392 (Ohio Ct. App. 8th Dist. Cuyahoga County 2011)—12:2, 12:6, 12:26

McKee v. City of Rockwall, Tex., 877 F.2d 409 (5th Cir. 1989)—14:10, 14:14

McKinley v. Kuhn, 2011-Ohio-134, 2011 WL 281135 (Ohio Ct. App. 4th Dist. Hocking County 2011)—9:2, 9:8

McKinney v. Brunney, 2014-Ohio-39, 2014 WL 80419 (Ohio Ct. App. 5th Dist. Fairfield County 2014)—12:26

McKinnie v. Roadway Express, Inc., 341 F.3d 554, 2003 FED App. 0294P (6th Cir. 2003)—11:21

McKitrick v. Smith, 2009 WL 1067321 (N.D. Ohio 2009)—2:7

McKnight v. Scott, 665 A.2d 973 (D.C. 1995)—10:12

McMullen v. Baldwin, 2013-Ohio-2677, 2013 WL 3280031 (Ohio Ct. App. 5th Dist. Stark County 2013)—9:4, 12:26

McNabb ex rel. Foshee v. McNabb, 31 Kan. App. 2d 398, 65 P.3d 1068 (2003)—15:24

McNair v. McNair, 151 N.H. 343, 856 A.2d 5 (2004)—10:13

McNaughton v. Cochenour, 2015-Ohio-4648, 2015 WL 6953983 (Ohio Ct. App. 4th Dist. Ross County 2015)—9:2, 9:7, 9:8

McQueen v. Goldey, 20 Ohio App. 3d 41, 484 N.E.2d 712 (12th Dist. Butler County 1984)—5:19

McSwane v. Bloomington Hosp. and Healthcare System, 916 N.E.2d 906 (Ind. 2009)—16:11

McSwane v. Bloomington Hosp. and Healthcare System, 882 N.E.2d 244 (Ind. Ct. App. 2008)—16:11

McWilliam v. Dickey, 2013-Ohio-4036, 2013 WL 5310439 (Ohio Ct. App. 8th Dist. Cuyahoga County 2013)—9:5, 9:8, 12:26

Meade v. Meade, 2000-Ohio-1912, 2000 WL 1532872 (Ohio Ct. App. 3d Dist. Marion County 2000)—15:12

Meaney v. Meaney, 2010-Ohio-1969, 2010 WL 1782486 (Ohio Ct. App. 11th Dist. Lake County 2010)—15:12

Meaney v. U.S., 112 F.2d 538, 130 A.L.R. 973 (C.C.A. 2d Cir. 1940)—5:19

Mechtel v. Mechtel, 528 N.W.2d 916 (Minn. Ct. App. 1995)—12:1, 12:6, 12:7

Meekins v. City of Oberlin, 2018-Ohio-1308, 2018 WL 1640059 (Ohio Ct. App. 8th Dist. Cuyahoga County 2018)—14:5

Meeks v. Papadopulos, 62 Ohio St. 2d 187, 16 Ohio Op. 3d 212, 404 N.E.2d 159 (1980)—9:8

Melendez-Diaz v. Massachusetts, 557 U.S. 305, 129 S. Ct. 2527, 174 L. Ed. 2d 314 (2009)—5:14, 7:22, 16:13

Meredith, In re Marriage of, 148 Wash. App. 887, 201 P.3d 1056 (Div. 2 2009)—18:21, 18:24

Merola v. Merola, 146 A.D.2d 611, 536 N.Y.S.2d 842 (2d Dep't 1989)—8:3

Mettke v. Mouser, 2013-Ohio-2781, 2013 WL 3356583 (Ohio Ct. App. 10th Dist. Franklin County 2013)—19:10

Meyers v. First Nat. Bank of Cincinnati, 3 Ohio App. 3d 209, 444 N.E.2d 412 (1st Dist. Hamilton County 1981)—11:3

Meyers v. Sparrow, 2009-Ohio-945, 2009 WL 533057 (Ohio Ct. App. 5th Dist. Ashland County 2009)—9:4, 9:8

Meyers v. Wimer, 2005-Ohio-3753, 2005 WL 1714194 (Ohio Ct. App. 2d Dist. Montgomery County 2005)—8:4, 11:10

M.H. v. J.H., 2017-Ohio-8679, 2017 WL 5706128 (Ohio Ct. App. 9th Dist. Medina County 2017)—12:10

M.H. v. J.H., 2015-Ohio-5178, 2015 WL 8553569 (Ohio Ct. App. 9th Dist. Medina County 2015)—8:4, 8:5, 12:24, 12:26

M.H. v. J.P., 2017-Ohio-33, 2017 WL 74862 (Ohio Ct. App. 9th Dist. Lorain County 2017)—9:5

Moore v. City of East Cleveland, Ohio, 431 U.S. 494, 97 S. Ct. 1932, 52 L. Ed. 2d 531 (1977)—10:3, 10:9
Moore v. Green, 219 Ill. 2d 470, 302 Ill. Dec. 451, 848 N.E.2d 1015 (2006)—14:12
Moore v. Guyton, 2013-Ohio-143, 2013 WL 221515 (Ohio Ct. App. 3d Dist. Paulding County 2013)—8:4, 12:16, 12:26
Moore v. Higgins, 2015-Ohio-1751, 2015 WL 2169232 (Ohio Ct. App. 2d Dist. Montgomery County 2015)—12:25
Moore v. Moore, 2003-Ohio-3789, 2003 WL 21658466 (Ohio Ct. App. 9th Dist. Wayne County 2003)—12:7, 12:27
Moore v. Moore, 2003-Ohio-1382, 2003 WL 1422447 (Ohio Ct. App. 5th Dist. Licking County 2003)—12:7
Moore v. Moore, 1994 WL 370005 (Ohio Ct. App. 5th Dist. Licking County 1994)—15:12
Moore v. Petty, 2013 WL 12149772 (Ohio C.P. 2013)—19:10
Morales-Garcia v. Holder, 567 F.3d 1058 (9th Cir. 2009)—18:18, 18:20, 18:22
Morales v. County of Nassau, 256 A.D.2d 608, 683 N.Y.S.2d 127 (2d Dep't 1998)—14:3, 14:14
Moran v. Colaner, 1999 WL 547958 (Ohio Ct. App. 5th Dist. Tuscarawas County 1999)—13:5, 13:8
Morehart v. Snider, 2009-Ohio-5674, 2009 WL 3465746 (Ohio Ct. App. 9th Dist. Summit County 2009)—3:10
Morford v. Morford, 85 Ohio App. 3d 50, 619 N.E.2d 71 (4th Dist. Lawrence County 1993)—13:6
Morgan v. Partridge, No. 02-1848 (C.P., Montgomery, 2-25-03)—9:3, 11:8
Morgan v. U.S., 304 U.S. 1, 58 S. Ct. 773, 82 L. Ed. 1129, 1 Lab. Cas. (CCH) P 17033, 1 Lab. Cas. (CCH) P 17037 (1938)—12:1
Mormile, State ex rel. v. Garfield Hts. Mun. Court, 79 Ohio App. 3d 539, 607 N.E.2d 890 (8th Dist. Cuyahoga County 1992)—4:1
Morrill, In re, 147 N.H. 116, 784 A.2d 690 (2001)—14:6, 16:12
Morris v. McQuillen, 2009-Ohio-2848, 2009 WL 1677848 (Ohio Ct. App. 5th Dist. Richland County 2009)—9:3, 9:4
Morris v. Morris, 2009-Ohio-5164, 2009 WL 3119658 (Ohio Ct. App. 9th Dist. Summit County 2009)—2:4, 8:4, 11:10, 12:26
Morris v. Morris, 2000 WL 222025 (Ohio Ct. App. 5th Dist. Stark County 2000)—15:6, 15:12, 15:15
Morris v. Stonewall, 1999 WL 1037507 (Ohio Ct. App. 12th Dist. Clinton County 1999)—8:5, 11:10, 11:25, 12:24
Morris, In re Contempt of, 110 Ohio App. 3d 475, 674 N.E.2d 761 (8th Dist. Cuyahoga County 1996)—13:17
Morrish v. Morrish, 262 Pa. 192, 105 A. 83 (1918)—19:9
Morrison v. Morrison, 2014-Ohio-2254, 2014 WL 2443912 (Ohio Ct. App. 9th Dist. Summit County 2014)—15:6, 15:13
Morrison v. Warden, Ross Correctional Inst., 2011 WL 2945838 (S.D. Ohio 2011)—3:2
Morrow v. Stoner, 2014 WL 4403436 (N.D. Ohio 2014)—14:9, 14:14
Morton v. Pyles, 2012-Ohio-5343, 2012 WL 5842789 (Ohio Ct. App. 7th Dist. Mahoning County 2012)—9:4, 9:8
Moser v. Moser, 72 Ohio App. 3d 575, 595 N.E.2d 518 (3d Dist. Allen County 1991)—12:2
Motes v. U.S., 178 U.S. 458, 20 S. Ct. 993, 44 L. Ed. 1150 (1900)—5:15
Mottice v. Kirkpatrick, 2001-Ohio-7042, 2001 WL 1673733 (Ohio Ct. App. 5th Dist. Stark County 2001)—9:3, 9:4, 12:7
M.R. v. T.R., 2016-Ohio-3493, 2016 WL 3384940 (Ohio Ct. App. 9th Dist. Wayne County 2016)—2:4, 8:4, 12:11, 12:26, 12:27, 16:9, 16:12
Mugan v. Mugan, 231 N.J. Super. 31, 555 A.2d 2 (App. Div. 1989)—12:17
Mugrage v. Mugrage, 335 N.J. Super. 653, 763 A.2d 347 (Ch. Div. 2000)—12:5
Mullane v. Central Hanover Bank & Trust Co., 339 U.S. 306, 70 S. Ct. 652, 94 L. Ed. 865 (1950)—9:5
Mullen v. Hobbs, 2012-Ohio-6098,

O

P

Q

R

Reaper v. James, 2009-Ohio-151, 2009 WL 104613 (Ohio Ct. App. 4th Dist. Lawrence County 2009)—15:7, 15:12

Recco v. Recco, 1992 WL 89967 (Ohio Ct. App. 5th Dist. Tuscarawas County 1992)—13:5

Reese v. Reese, 1997 WL 272368 (Ohio Ct. App. 8th Dist. Cuyahoga County 1997)—10:13, 12:15

Rehfus v. Smith, 2015-Ohio-2145, 2015 WL 3498686 (Ohio Ct. App. 7th Dist. Carroll County 2015)—8:8, 9:3, 9:7, 11:2, 12:10, 12:26, 16:20

Reich v. Reich, 239 A.D.2d 246, 657 N.Y.S.2d 671 (1st Dep't 1997)—12:22

Reichard v. Nationwide Mut. Fire Ins. Co., 1992 WL 361829 (Ohio Ct. App. 2d Dist. Montgomery County 1992)—8:3

Reising v. Reising, 2017-Ohio-2859, 2017 WL 2241670 (Ohio Ct. App. 8th Dist. Cuyahoga County 2017)—9:5, 9:7

Renee v. Sanders, 160 Ohio St. 279, 52 Ohio Op. 175, 116 N.E.2d 420 (1953)—12:7

Reno v. Condon, 528 U.S. 141, 120 S. Ct. 666, 145 L. Ed. 2d 587 (2000)—18:2

Renshaw v. Renshaw, 2000 WL 1528635 (Ohio Ct. App. 5th Dist. Guernsey County 2000)—13:5

Retterer v. Little, 2012-Ohio-131, 2012 WL 134305 (Ohio Ct. App. 3d Dist. Marion County 2012)—3:6, 9:2, 9:4, 9:8

Reynolds v. Giuliani, 506 F.3d 183 (2d Cir. 2007)—14:14

Reynolds v. Reynolds, 2001 WL 62552 (Ohio Ct. App. 2d Dist. Montgomery County 2001)—8:4, 9:2, 11:10, 11:13, 12:11, 12:26, 16:21

Reynolds v. U.S., 98 U.S. 145, 25 L. Ed. 244, 1878 WL 18416 (1878)—5:15

Reynolds v. White, 1999 WL 754496 (Ohio Ct. App. 8th Dist. Cuyahoga County 1999)—8:5, 8:6, 8:7, 11:10, 11:12, 12:11, 12:26

Reynolds v. Whitney, 2004-Ohio-1628, 2004 WL 626872 (Ohio Ct. App. 10th Dist. Franklin County 2004)—9:5, 10:13

Reynoldsburg, City of v. Eichenberger, 1990 WL 52467 (Ohio Ct. App. 5th Dist. Licking County 1990)—4:6, 13:2, 13:3, 13:12

R.G. v. R.M., 2017-Ohio-8918, 88 N.E.3d 1027 (Ohio Ct. App. 7th Dist. Mahoning County 2017)—9:2, 9:5, 9:7, 9:8, 11:10, 12:10

R.G. v. T.D., 448 Pa. Super. 525, 672 A.2d 341, 107 Ed. Law Rep. 876 (1996)—8:3

R.H. v. B.F., 39 Mass. App. Ct. 29, 653 N.E.2d 195 (1995)—15:6, 15:13

Rhodes v. Gunter, 2003-Ohio-2342, 2003 WL 21040724 (Ohio Ct. App. 9th Dist. Lorain County 2003)—8:4, 8:8, 9:2, 11:10, 11:13, 11:25, 12:11, 16:21

Rial v. Rijo, 2010 WL 1643995 (S.D. N.Y. 2010)—18:24

Ricci v. Delehanty, 1998 ME 231, 719 A.2d 518 (Me. 1998)—15:12

Rice v. Lewis, 2013-Ohio-5890, 2013 WL 6989772 (Ohio Ct. App. 4th Dist. Scioto County 2013)—8:8, 9:5, 12:27

Rice v. Reed, 66 Ohio L. Abs. 385, 117 N.E.2d 183 (Ct. App. 2d Dist. Montgomery County 1951)—19:3

Rice, State ex rel. v. McGrath, 62 Ohio St. 3d 70, 577 N.E.2d 1100 (1991)—13:4

Richardson v. Smith, 2012 WL 5903986 (N.D. Ohio 2012)—5:21

Richter v. Richter, 2009-Ohio-3828, 2009 WL 2371882 (Ohio Ct. App. 12th Dist. Butler County 2009)—8:4, 11:10

Ricketts v. City of Columbia, Mo., 36 F.3d 775 (8th Cir. 1994)—14:14

Riddle v. Riddle, 1988 WL 94005 (Ohio Ct. App. 5th Dist. Richland County 1988)—10:6

Rieger v. Marsh, 2011-Ohio-6808, 2011 WL 6930159 (Ohio Ct. App. 2d Dist. Montgomery County 2011)—5:3

Rieger v. Montgomery Cty., 2009-Ohio-4125, 2009 WL 2489855 (Ohio Ct. App. 2d Dist. Montgomery County 2009)—7:13

Rieger v. Montgomery Cty. Clerk of Courts, 2009-Ohio-426, 2009 WL 242668 (Ohio Ct. App. 2d Dist. Montgomery County 2009)—12:23, 13:15

Rudduck v. Rudduck, 1999 WL 436818 (Ohio Ct. App. 5th Dist. Licking County 1999)—13:4, 13:8
Ruedele v. Kiefer, 1993 WL 438787 (Ohio Ct. App. 5th Dist. Licking County 1993)—11:14, 12:14, 12:17, 12:27
Rufener v. Hutson, 2012-Ohio-5061, 2012 WL 5364703 (Ohio Ct. App. 8th Dist. Cuyahoga County 2012)—9:2, 9:5, 9:7, 9:8
Runions v. Burchett, 2018-Ohio-2754, 2018 WL 3414235 (Ohio Ct. App. 2d Dist. Clark County 2018)—12:22
Rush v. Rush, 1999 WL 1044482 (Ohio Ct. App. 8th Dist. Cuyahoga County 1999)—8:8, 11:24, 12:13, 12:15, 12:16, 12:27, 13:8, 13:15, 14:15, 16:12, 16:21
Rush v. Rush—11:24
Ryan v. Ryan, 784 So. 2d 1215 (Fla. 2d DCA 2001)—15:24
Rybolt v. Riley, 20 Cal. App. 5th 864, 229 Cal. Rptr. 3d 576 (3d Dist. 2018)—12:24
Ryder v. Ryder, 2002-Ohio-765, 2002 WL 258218 (Ohio Ct. App. 5th Dist. Stark County 2002)—13:4

S

Saari v. Saari, 2000 WL 1729455 (Ohio Ct. App. 9th Dist. Lorain County 2000)—9:2, 9:3, 12:11, 12:24
Sabrina J. v. Robbin C., 2001 WL 85157 (Ohio Ct. App. 6th Dist. Lucas County 2001)—12:10
Sabur v. El-Zant, 1999 WL 652042 (Ohio Ct. App. 8th Dist. Cuyahoga County 1999)—12:15
Sachanowski v. Wyoming County Sheriff's Dept., 244 A.D.2d 908, 665 N.Y.S.2d 197 (4th Dep't 1997)—14:12
Sacharow v. Sacharow, 177 N.J. 62, 826 A.2d 710 (2003)—11:6, 15:9
Sadrud-Din v. City of Chicago, 883 F. Supp. 270 (N.D. Ill. 1995)—14:9
Saffold v. Saffold, 1999 WL 304310 (Ohio Ct. App. 8th Dist. Cuyahoga County 1999)—12:26
Salgado v. Montgomery Cty. Sheriff, 2015-Ohio-3387, 2015 WL 5000131 (Ohio Ct. App. 2d Dist. Montgomery County 2015)—12:22
Salgado, In re, 53 S.W.3d 752 (Tex. App. El Paso 2001)—12:27
Saliterman v. State, 443 N.W.2d 841 (Minn. Ct. App. 1989)—13:6
Sallee v. Sallee, 142 Ohio App. 3d 366, 755 N.E.2d 941 (12th Dist. Warren County 2001)—15:12
Salvage Process Corporation v. Acme Tank Cleaning Process Corporation, 86 F.2d 727 (C.C.A. 2d Cir. 1936)—13:13
Samples v. Cruz, 2001 WL 534165 (Ohio Ct. App. 8th Dist. Cuyahoga County 2001)—8:7
Sanchez v. Sanchez, 2016-Ohio-4933, 2016 WL 3745699 (Ohio Ct. App. 1st Dist. Hamilton County 2016)—8:6, 8:8, 12:15, 15:18
Sanders v. Shephard, 185 Ill. App. 3d 719, 133 Ill. Dec. 712, 541 N.E.2d 1150 (1st Dist. 1989)—8:2, 11:10, 13:6
San Filipo v. San Filipo, 81 Ohio App. 3d 111, 610 N.E.2d 493 (9th Dist. Summit County 1991)—12:9
Sanitary Commercial Services, Inc. v. Shank, 57 Ohio St. 3d 178, 566 N.E.2d 1215 (1991)—9:5
Santosky v. Kramer, 455 U.S. 745, 102 S. Ct. 1388, 71 L. Ed. 2d 599 (1982)—8:7
Saqr v. Naji, 2017-Ohio-8142, 2017 WL 4538886 (Ohio Ct. App. 1st Dist. Hamilton County 2017)—12:10, 12:25, 12:26
Saunders, State ex rel. v. Court of Common Pleas of Allen County, 34 Ohio St. 3d 15, 516 N.E.2d 232 (1987)—10:13
Saur v. Robinson, 2014 WL 1922848 (S.D. Ohio 2014)—7:11
Sawicki v. Village of Ottawa Hills, 37 Ohio St. 3d 222, 525 N.E.2d 468 (1988)—14:9, 14:12, 14:14
Sawyer, State ex rel. v. O'Connor, 54 Ohio St. 2d 380, 8 Ohio Op. 3d 393, 377 N.E.2d 494 (1978)—2:7
Saxton v. Warden, Trumbull Correctional Institution, 2018 WL 1014920 (S.D. Ohio 2018)—2:7
Scheib v. Crosby, 160 Wash. App. 345, 249 P.3d 184 (Div. 3 2011)—12:5
Schenley v. Kauth, 160 Ohio St. 109, 51 Ohio Op. 30, 113 N.E.2d 625 (1953)—12:9
Schindler v. Schindler, 1998 WL 46764 (Ohio Ct. App. 9th Dist.

Shafer v. Shafer, 1993 WL 524958 (Ohio Ct. App. 4th Dist. Washington County 1993)—13:6
Shafor v. Shafor, 2009-Ohio-191, 2009 WL 119853 (Ohio Ct. App. 12th Dist. Warren County 2009)—15:15
Shah v. Shah, 184 N.J. 125, 875 A.2d 931 (2005)—10:13
Shah v. Shah, 373 N.J. Super. 47, 860 A.2d 940 (App. Div. 2004)—10:13
Shaker Heights, City of v. Al-Gureshi, 1998 WL 183818 (Ohio Ct. App. 8th Dist. Cuyahoga County 1998)—16:12, 16:14, 16:22
Shaker Heights, City of v. Mosely, 2005-Ohio-5433, 2005 WL 2562915 (Ohio Ct. App. 8th Dist. Cuyahoga County 2005)—2:5, 2:8
Shaker Hts. v. Mosely, 113 Ohio St. 3d 329, 2007-Ohio-2072, 865 N.E.2d 859 (2007)—2:8
Sharpe v. Sharpe, 695 So. 2d 1302 (Fla. 5th DCA 1997)—10:4
Shaughnessy v. Shaughnessy, 1999 WL 159211 (Ohio Ct. App. 7th Dist. Mahoning County 1999)—12:3, 15:15
Shearer v. Shearer, 18 Ohio St. 3d 94, 480 N.E.2d 388 (1985)—19:1
Shepard v. U.S., 544 U.S. 13, 125 S. Ct. 1254, 161 L. Ed. 2d 205 (2005)—18:11
Sheppeard v. Brown, 2008-Ohio-203, 2008 WL 186670 (Ohio Ct. App. 2d Dist. Clark County 2008)—15:12
Sherlock v. Myers, 2004-Ohio-5178, 2004 WL 2244102 (Ohio Ct. App. 9th Dist. Summit County 2004)—9:5
Sherman v. Sherman, 2013-Ohio-3501, 2013 WL 4106674 (Ohio Ct. App. 1st Dist. Hamilton County 2013)—12:22
Sherrell By and Through Wooden v. City of Longview, 683 F. Supp. 1108 (E.D. Tex. 1987)—14:9
Sherry S., In re, 2008-Ohio-6401, 2008 WL 5147442 (Ohio Ct. App. 6th Dist. Erie County 2008)—5:20
Shields v. Fry, 301 Ill. App. 3d 570, 234 Ill. Dec. 821, 703 N.E.2d 921 (4th Dist. 1998)—8:5
Shillitani v. U.S., 384 U.S. 364, 86 S. Ct. 1531, 16 L. Ed. 2d 622 (1966)—3:10
Shimman v. Germano, 2008-Ohio-717, 2008 WL 466787 (Ohio Ct. App. 6th Dist. Lucas County 2008)—8:8, 12:15, 15:15
Shipley v. State, 620 N.E.2d 710 (Ind. Ct. App. 1993)—13:13
Shipp v. McMahon, 234 F.3d 907 (5th Cir. 2000)—14:14
Shockey v. Shockey, 2008-Ohio-6797, 2008 WL 5340554 (Ohio Ct. App. 5th Dist. Delaware County 2008)—9:2, 9:5, 9:8, 12:2
Short v. Walker, 2001 WL 32808 (Ohio Ct. App. 12th Dist. Preble County 2001)—9:2, 9:3, 9:4, 9:8
Shutway v. Shutway, 2000 WL 146533 (Ohio Ct. App. 8th Dist. Cuyahoga County 2000)—12:7
Siddle v. City of Cambridge, Ohio, 761 F. Supp. 503 (S.D. Ohio 1991)—12:29, 14:10, 14:11, 14:14
Sigler v. Arvay, 2002-Ohio-6762, 2002 WL 31761478 (Ohio Ct. App. 9th Dist. Summit County 2002)—11:21, 12:2, 12:4, 12:7
Signer v. Signer, 2006-Ohio-3580, 2006 WL 1918115 (Ohio Ct. App. 8th Dist. Cuyahoga County 2006)—9:5, 11:4, 11:7, 12:15, 12:25, 15:12, 15:22
Sills v. Irelan, 663 N.E.2d 1210 (Ind. Ct. App. 1996)—15:24
Simcox v. Simcox, 511 F.3d 594, 2007 FED App. 0502P (6th Cir. 2007)—18:24
Simmons v. Simmons, 649 So. 2d 799 (La. Ct. App. 2d Cir. 1995)—15:7, 16:9, 16:21
Simmons v. Simmons, 773 P.2d 602 (Colo. App. 1988)—19:11
Simons, In re, 118 Ohio App. 3d 622, 693 N.E.2d 1111 (2d Dist. Montgomery County 1997)—15:24
Simpson v. City of Miami, 700 So. 2d 87 (Fla. 3d DCA 1997)—14:12
Sinclair v. Sinclair, 182 Ohio App. 3d 691, 2009-Ohio-3106, 914 N.E.2d 1084 (4th Dist. Athens County 2009)—12:23
Sinclair v. Sinclair, Nos. 08CA16, 08CA25 (Ohio Ct. App. 4th Dist. Athens County May 18, 2009)—12:23
Sindel v. Sindel, 1975 WL 181946 (Ohio Ct. App. 10th Dist. Franklin County 1975)—4:1, 10:6
Singh v. Ashcroft, 386 F.3d 1228 (9th Cir. 2004)—7:11

2012 WL 2128013 (Ohio Ct. App. 9th Dist. Summit County 2012)—2:8

State v. Bridgeman, 55 Ohio St. 2d 261, 9 Ohio Op. 3d 401, 381 N.E.2d 184 (1978)—2:2

State v. Bridges, 2015-Ohio-4480, 2015 WL 6522860 (Ohio Ct. App. 10th Dist. Franklin County 2015)—2:8, 3:10

State v. Brillhart, 129 Ohio App. 3d 180, 717 N.E.2d 413 (9th Dist. Wayne County 1998)—12:15, 13:16, 15:15

State v. Brinkley, 105 Ohio St. 3d 231, 2005-Ohio-1507, 824 N.E.2d 959 (2005)—5:17

State v. Brogden, 2018-Ohio-735, 2018 WL 1136138 (Ohio Ct. App. 1st Dist. Hamilton County 2018)—13:3

State v. Brooke, 113 Ohio St. 3d 199, 2007-Ohio-1533, 863 N.E.2d 1024 (2007)—2:7, 3:2, 5:22

State v. Brooke, 165 Ohio App. 3d 409, 2005-Ohio-6161, 846 N.E.2d 897 (11th Dist. Lake County 2005)—3:2

State v. Brooks, 2008-Ohio-6600, 2008 WL 5228438 (Ohio Ct. App. 7th Dist. Mahoning County 2008)—5:21

State v. Brooks, 44 Ohio St. 3d 185, 542 N.E.2d 636 (1989)—8:3

State v. Broom, 40 Ohio St. 3d 277, 533 N.E.2d 682 (1988)—5:24, 16:21

State v. Broughton, 51 Ohio App. 3d 10, 553 N.E.2d 1380 (12th Dist. Clermont County 1988)—2:8

State v. Brown, 2017-Ohio-9259, 103 N.E.3d 32 (Ohio Ct. App. 11th Dist. Ashtabula County 2017)—2:8

State v. Brown, 2015-Ohio-950, 2015 WL 1138651 (Ohio Ct. App. 11th Dist. Lake County 2015)—2:5, 2:8, 4:1, 7:3, 10:6, 10:9

State v. Brown, 2009-Ohio-5390, 2009 WL 3236206 (Ohio Ct. App. 4th Dist. Athens County 2009)—6:13

State v. Brown, 119 Ohio St. 3d 447, 2008-Ohio-4569, 895 N.E.2d 149 (2008)—2:5, 2:8

State v. Brown, 394 N.J. Super. 492, 927 A.2d 569 (App. Div. 2007)—13:13, 13:14

State v. Brown, 2006-Ohio-6267, 2006 WL 3446238 (Ohio Ct. App. 8th Dist. Cuyahoga County 2006)—4:1, 5:14, 8:4, 8:5, 16:14

State v. Brown, 166 Ohio App. 3d 32, 2006-Ohio-1181, 849 N.E.2d 44 (5th Dist. Stark County 2006)—2:5, 4:1

State v. Brown, 2003-Ohio-710, 2003 WL 352460 (Ohio Ct. App. 12th Dist. Butler County 2003)—2:4, 11:10, 12:11, 16:9, 16:21

State v. Brown, 2002-Ohio-277, 2002 WL 91088 (Ohio Ct. App. 2d Dist. Montgomery County 2002)—3:3

State v. Brown, 1998 WL 227182 (Ohio Ct. App. 3d Dist. Allen County 1998)—14:6, 16:12

State v. Brown, 1983 WL 6945 (Ohio Ct. App. 6th Dist. Lucas County 1983)—5:26

State v. Brown, 1982 WL 5220 (Ohio Ct. App. 8th Dist. Cuyahoga County 1982)—3:3, 3:4

State v. Brown (May 8, 1998), Allen App. No. 1-97-74—16:22

State v. Bruce, 2018-Ohio-2478, 2018 WL 3147965 (Ohio Ct. App. 7th Dist. Jefferson County 2018)—13:3

State v. Brumley, 2017-Ohio-8803, 2017 WL 5997928 (Ohio Ct. App. 11th Dist. Portage County 2017)—2:8

State v. Bryant, 2008-Ohio-3078, 2008 WL 2487253 (Ohio Ct. App. 12th Dist. Warren County 2008)—5:14

State v. Buchanan, 1999 WL 326195 (Ohio Ct. App. 12th Dist. Clermont County 1999)—16:21

State v. Bulger, 2011-Ohio-3828, 2011 WL 3359861 (Ohio Ct. App. 8th Dist. Cuyahoga County 2011)—6:14

State v. Bump, 2016-Ohio-4717, 2016 WL 3573174 (Ohio Ct. App. 2d Dist. Champaign County 2016)—10:6

State v. Bunch, 2010-Ohio-515, 2010 WL 547402 (Ohio Ct. App. 8th Dist. Cuyahoga County 2010)—7:24, 16:14, 16:20, 16:21

State v. Bunch, 2001 WL 39599 (Ohio Ct. App. 9th Dist. Summit County 2001)—4:5, 11:11, 12:25, 13:2, 13:3, 13:8

State v. Conyer, 2017-Ohio-7506, 2017 WL 3971689 (Ohio Ct. App. 7th Dist. Mahoning County 2017)—2:8, 16:13
State v. Cook, 2005-Ohio-1550, 2005 WL 736671 (Ohio Ct. App. 6th Dist. Wood County 2005)—5:14
State v. Cooper, 163 Ohio Misc. 2d 27, 2010-Ohio-6697, 950 N.E.2d 248 (Mun. Ct. 2010)—4:5
State v. Copp, 2003-Ohio-5399, 2003 WL 22318519 (Ohio Ct. App. 2d Dist. Montgomery County 2003)—11:5, 12:27, 13:2
State v. Corbin, 194 Ohio App. 3d 720, 2011-Ohio-3491, 957 N.E.2d 849 (6th Dist. Wood County 2011)—2:5
State v. Cordle, 2010-Ohio-5919, 2010 WL 4926590 (Ohio Ct. App. 5th Dist. Delaware County 2010)—2:2
State v. Cornell, 129 Ohio App. 3d 106, 717 N.E.2d 361 (10th Dist. Franklin County 1998)—5:15, 16:14
State v. Cornwell, 2015-Ohio-4617, 48 N.E.3d 169 (Ohio Ct. App. 9th Dist. Wayne County 2015)—2:5, 7:3, 7:24, 8:8, 10:6, 12:29, 16:21
State v. Corpening, 2011-Ohio-6002, 2011 WL 5829679 (Ohio Ct. App. 11th Dist. Ashtabula County 2011)—3:2
State v. Corrill, 133 Ohio App. 3d 550, 729 N.E.2d 403 (12th Dist. Butler County 1999)—2:8
State v. Cosme, 2007-Ohio-1454, 2007 WL 926357 (Ohio Ct. App. 8th Dist. Cuyahoga County 2007)—5:14
State v. Costell, 2016-Ohio-3386, 2016 WL 3223905 (Ohio Ct. App. 3d Dist. Union County 2016)—2:2, 5:21, 6:13
State v. Cotton, 2010-Ohio-804, 2010 WL 746756 (Ohio Ct. App. 6th Dist. Lucas County 2010)—7:22
State v. Coulter, 75 Ohio App. 3d 219, 598 N.E.2d 1324 (12th Dist. Warren County 1992)—7:24
State v. Cowdin, 25 Kan. App. 2d 176, 959 P.2d 929 (1998)—14:3
State v. Cox, 2003-Ohio-1935, 2003 WL 1889479 (Ohio Ct. App. 4th Dist. Adams County 2003)—3:3
State v. Cox, 2001-Ohio-3213, 2001 WL 301429 (Ohio Ct. App. 7th Dist. Belmont County 2001)—14:6, 16:12, 16:14, 16:22
State v. Crager, 116 Ohio St. 3d 369, 2007-Ohio-6840, 879 N.E.2d 745 (2007)—5:14
State v. Crager, 164 Ohio App. 3d 816, 2005-Ohio-6868, 844 N.E.2d 390 (3d Dist. Marion County 2005)—5:14
State v. Craig, 2017-Ohio-4342, 2017 WL 2616900 (Ohio Ct. App. 4th Dist. Athens County 2017)—2:8, 3:3
State v. Craig, 2010-Ohio-1857, 2010 WL 1712253 (Ohio Ct. App. 8th Dist. Cuyahoga County 2010)—5:24
State v. Craig, 110 Ohio St. 3d 306, 2006-Ohio-4571, 853 N.E.2d 621 (2006)—16:13
State v. Craun, 158 Ohio App. 3d 389, 2004-Ohio-4403, 815 N.E.2d 1141 (3d Dist. Shelby County 2004)—2:2, 8:7
State v. Crawford, 2007-Ohio-2254, 2007 WL 1378390 (Ohio Ct. App. 6th Dist. Fulton County 2007)—10:7
State v. Crawley, 2014-Ohio-1949, 2014 WL 1877544 (Ohio Ct. App. 8th Dist. Cuyahoga County 2014)—2:7
State v. Craycraft, 193 Ohio App. 3d 594, 2011-Ohio-413, 953 N.E.2d 337 (12th Dist. Clermont County 2011)—2:8
State v. Craycraft, 2010-Ohio-596, 2010 WL 610601 (Ohio Ct. App. 12th Dist. Clermont County 2010)—16:20
State v. Creech, 150 Ohio St. 3d 540, 2016-Ohio-8440, 84 N.E.3d 981 (2016)—7:21
State v. Cremeans, 5 Ohio App. 3d 8, 448 N.E.2d 837 (4th Dist. Meigs County 1982)—4:7
State v. Cressel, 2004-Ohio-68, 2004 WL 41724 (Ohio Ct. App. 2d Dist. Montgomery County 2004)—16:23
State v. Crosby, 2012-Ohio-4130, 2012 WL 3939970 (Ohio Ct. App. 10th Dist. Franklin County 2012)—3:2
State v. Crosby, 186 Ohio App. 3d 453, 2010-Ohio-1584, 928 N.E.2d

Ct. App. 9th Dist. Summit County 1997)—13:3
State v. Daws, 104 Ohio App. 3d 448, 662 N.E.2d 805 (2d Dist. Montgomery County 1994)—7:24
State v. Dawson, 2001-Ohio-3977, 2001 WL 1568406 (Ohio Ct. App. 10th Dist. Franklin County 2001)—5:15
State v. Dawson, 1979 WL 209389 (Ohio Ct. App. 10th Dist. Franklin County 1979)—11:10
State v. Day, 99 Ohio App. 3d 514, 651 N.E.2d 52 (12th Dist. Clermont County 1994)—2:7, 5:21, 12:27
State v. Dean, 2018-Ohio-1740, 2018 WL 2085103 (Ohio Ct. App. 6th Dist. Lucas County 2018)—2:8
State v. Dean, 2016-Ohio-8422, 2016 WL 7626242 (Ohio Ct. App. 11th Dist. Trumbull County 2016)—3:2
State v. Dean, 2002-Ohio-3030, 2002 WL 1376032 (Ohio Ct. App. 7th Dist. Columbiana County 2002)—12:27
State v. Deanda, 136 Ohio St. 3d 18, 2013-Ohio-1722, 989 N.E.2d 986 (2013)—2:8, 3:3
State v. Deem, 40 Ohio St. 3d 205, 533 N.E.2d 294 (1988)—2:8, 3:3, 3:4
State v. Dejarlais, 136 Wash. 2d 939, 969 P.2d 90 (1998)—11:12, 12:22, 13:12
State v. DeJesus, 2015-Ohio-4111, 2015 WL 5782347 (Ohio Ct. App. 2d Dist. Greene County 2015)—3:2, 7:11
State v. DeLong, 2007-Ohio-2330, 2007 WL 1413394 (Ohio Ct. App. 4th Dist. Ross County 2007)—14:3, 14:5, 14:6
State v. Demiduk, 1998 WL 355864 (Ohio Ct. App. 7th Dist. Columbiana County 1998)—5:19
State v. Demint, 2018-Ohio-2091, 2018 WL 2437253 (Ohio Ct. App. 4th Dist. Ross County 2018)—8:8
State v. Dengg, 2009-Ohio-4101, 2009 WL 2488048 (Ohio Ct. App. 11th Dist. Portage County 2009)—3:8, 4:7
State v. Denis, 117 Ohio App. 3d 442, 690 N.E.2d 955 (6th Dist. Ottawa County 1997)—2:4
State v. Dent, 2002-Ohio-4522, 2002 WL 2008423 (Ohio Ct. App. 9th Dist. Summit County 2002)—14:6
State v. Dever, 64 Ohio St. 3d 401, 1992-Ohio-41, 596 N.E.2d 436 (1992)—5:14, 5:26, 16:17
State v. Deyling, 1998 WL 46753 (Ohio Ct. App. 9th Dist. Medina County 1998)—5:21, 5:24, 16:21
State v. Dial, 2013-Ohio-3980, 998 N.E.2d 821 (Ohio Ct. App. 3d Dist. Allen County 2013)—7:22
State v. Dickson, 1993 WL 437738 (Ohio Ct. App. 5th Dist. Holmes County 1993)—8:7
State v. Diggle, 2012-Ohio-1583, 2012 WL 1187970 (Ohio Ct. App. 3d Dist. Auglaize County 2012)—5:15, 7:22
State v. Diles, 2004-Ohio-6368, 2004 WL 2715626 (Ohio Ct. App. 5th Dist. Morrow County 2004)—3:3
State v. Dillard, 2006-Ohio-3524, 2006 WL 1868318 (Ohio Ct. App. 7th Dist. Jefferson County 2006)—5:16
State v. Dillon, 2005-Ohio-1016, 2005 WL 563978 (Ohio Ct. App. 8th Dist. Cuyahoga County 2005)—14:5
State v. Dinka, 2015-Ohio-63, 2015 WL 149026 (Ohio Ct. App. 12th Dist. Warren County 2015)—13:3
State v. Dinka, 2013-Ohio-4646, 2013 WL 5741499 (Ohio Ct. App. 12th Dist. Warren County 2013)—7:9
State v. Dirmeyer, 2014-Ohio-759, 9 N.E.3d 464 (Ohio Ct. App. 3d Dist. Seneca County 2014)—2:2
State v. Diroll, 2007-Ohio-6930, 2007 WL 4481430 (Ohio Ct. App. 11th Dist. Portage County 2007)—2:4
State v. Dixon, 2013-Ohio-4149, 2013 WL 5407478 (Ohio Ct. App. 5th Dist. Stark County 2013)—7:12
State v. Dixon, 2005 WL 1940110 (Ohio C.P. 2005)—10:10
State v. Dixon, 152 Ohio App. 3d 760, 2003-Ohio-2550, 790 N.E.2d 349 (3d Dist. Logan County 2003)—5:17
State v. Dixon, 14 Ohio App. 3d 396, 471 N.E.2d 864 (8th Dist. Cuyahoga County 1984)—5:3
State v. Dobson, 2014-Ohio-3710, 2014 WL 4245968 (Ohio Ct. App.

5th Dist. Stark County 2005)—2:5

State v. Edwards, 83 Ohio App. 3d 357, 614 N.E.2d 1123 (10th Dist. Franklin County 1992)—8:3, 8:4

State v. Eicholtz, 2013-Ohio-302, 2013 WL 425820 (Ohio Ct. App. 2d Dist. Clark County 2013)—5:14, 5:15, 6:14, 7:22

State v. Elijah, 2000 WL 968781 (Ohio Ct. App. 2d Dist. Montgomery County 2000)—7:25

State v. Elliott, 104 Ohio App. 3d 812, 663 N.E.2d 412 (10th Dist. Franklin County 1995)—8:4, 8:6

State v. Elschlager, 2017-Ohio-5545, 2017 WL 2806352 (Ohio Ct. App. 5th Dist. Delaware County 2017)—14:5

State v. Encarnacion, 168 Ohio App. 3d 577, 2006-Ohio-4425, 861 N.E.2d 152 (12th Dist. Butler County 2006)—7:11

State v. English, 2014-Ohio-89, 2014 WL 117396 (Ohio Ct. App. 10th Dist. Franklin County 2014)—3:3

State v. Erdman, 2017-Ohio-1092, 2017 WL 1131929 (Ohio Ct. App. 12th Dist. Butler County 2017)—3:2

State v. Errington, 310 N.W.2d 681 (Minn. 1981)—17:3

State v. Eschrich, 2008-Ohio-2984, 2008 WL 2468572 (Ohio Ct. App. 6th Dist. Ottawa County 2008)—4:6, 9:5, 13:3

State v. Eskridge, 38 Ohio St. 3d 56, 526 N.E.2d 304 (1988)—13:7

State v. Esner, 2008-Ohio-6654, 2008 WL 5259725 (Ohio Ct. App. 8th Dist. Cuyahoga County 2008)—2:7, 5:22

State v. Esparza, 1999 WL 155955 (Ohio Ct. App. 3d Dist. Defiance County 1999)—6:14, 8:7

State v. Esparza, 1990 WL 7966 (Ohio Ct. App. 3d Dist. Defiance County 1990)—14:5

State v. Estep, 2004-Ohio-1747, 2004 WL 728913 (Ohio Ct. App. 4th Dist. Gallia County 2004)—16:19

State v. Estepp, 1989 WL 2293 (Ohio Ct. App. 1st Dist. Hamilton County 1989)—5:26

State v. Euton, 2007-Ohio-6704, 2007 WL 4374293 (Ohio Ct. App. 3d Dist. Auglaize County 2007)—2:2

State v. Evans, 122 Ohio St. 3d 381, 2009-Ohio-2974, 911 N.E.2d 889 (2009)—2:8, 3:4

State v. Evans, 2004-Ohio-318, 2004 WL 117613 (Ohio Ct. App. 5th Dist. Licking County 2004)—13:2

State v. Evans, 153 Ohio App. 3d 226, 2003-Ohio-3475, 792 N.E.2d 757 (7th Dist. Jefferson County 2003)—2:8

State v. Evans, 67 Ohio St. 3d 405, 1993-Ohio-186, 618 N.E.2d 162 (1993)—16:21

State v. Evans, 1987 WL 10358 (Ohio Ct. App. 12th Dist. Butler County 1987)—5:19

State v. Ewers, 1999 WL 502152 (Ohio Ct. App. 6th Dist. Erie County 1999)—16:14

State v. Fabritz, 276 Md. 416, 348 A.2d 275 (1975)—8:3

State v. Fagan, 2009-Ohio-3760, 2009 WL 2351753 (Ohio Ct. App. 2d Dist. Clark County 2009)—7:24

State v. Fairbanks, 117 Ohio St. 3d 543, 2008-Ohio-1470, 885 N.E.2d 888 (2008)—2:7

State v. Farmer, 2017-Ohio-2995, 2017 WL 2293048 (Ohio Ct. App. 5th Dist. Licking County 2017)—13:16

State v. Farmer, 2015-Ohio-5434, 2015 WL 9438270 (Ohio Ct. App. 5th Dist. Licking County 2015)—9:2, 12:29, 13:15

State v. Farrow, 919 P.2d 50 (Utah Ct. App. 1996)—14:3

State v. Fautenberry, 72 Ohio St. 3d 435, 1995-Ohio-209, 650 N.E.2d 878 (1995)—13:17

State v. Feckley, 2003-Ohio-3667, 2003 WL 21555109 (Ohio Ct. App. 8th Dist. Cuyahoga County 2003)—3:2

State v. Feldman, 2009-Ohio-5765, 2009 WL 3526249 (Ohio Ct. App. 11th Dist. Lake County 2009)—7:11

State v. Ferguson, 2003-Ohio-665, 2003 WL 321532 (Ohio Ct. App. 10th Dist. Franklin County 2003)—5:3

State v. Fernandez, 2012-Ohio-2538, 2012 WL 2061589 (Ohio Ct. App. 2d Dist. Montgomery County 2012)—2:5, 7:3

State v. Finley, 146 Ohio App. 3d 548,

State v. Fry, 125 Ohio St. 3d 163, 2010-Ohio-1017, 926 N.E.2d 1239 (2010)—6:14, 16:13

State v. Fuller, 2015-Ohio-1325, 2015 WL 1512371 (Ohio Ct. App. 2d Dist. Greene County 2015)—7:12

State v. Furr, 2018-Ohio-2205, 2018 WL 2937866 (Ohio Ct. App. 1st Dist. Hamilton County 2018)—3:2

State v. Galdamez, 2015-Ohio-3681, 41 N.E.3d 467 (Ohio Ct. App. 10th Dist. Franklin County 2015)—7:11

State v. Gallegos-Martinez, 2010-Ohio-6463, 2010 WL 5550237 (Ohio Ct. App. 5th Dist. Delaware County 2010)—7:12

State v. Galloway, 2001 WL 81257 (Ohio Ct. App. 9th Dist. Summit County 2001)—14:3

State v. Ganelli, 2005-Ohio-770, 2005 WL 433439 (Ohio Ct. App. 8th Dist. Cuyahoga County 2005)—2:7

State v. Garmendia, 2003-Ohio-3769, 2003 WL 21658528 (Ohio Ct. App. 2d Dist. Montgomery County 2003)—7:11

State v. Garrett, 2003-Ohio-5000, 2003 WL 22170186 (Ohio Ct. App. 12th Dist. Butler County 2003)—2:8

State v. Garrison, 2018-Ohio-1048, 2018 WL 1433184 (Ohio Ct. App. 5th Dist. Muskingum County 2018)—2:8

State v. Garrison, 2018-Ohio-463, 2018 WL 704129 (Ohio Ct. App. 5th Dist. Muskingum County 2018)—2:8, 13:3, 16:12

State v. Gatson, 2009-Ohio-120, 2009 WL 94596 (Ohio Ct. App. 8th Dist. Cuyahoga County 2009)—8:3, 16:10

State v. Gay, 2015-Ohio-1832, 2015 WL 2254985 (Ohio Ct. App. 8th Dist. Cuyahoga County 2015)—2:8

State v. Gearig, 2010-Ohio-939, 2010 WL 877575 (Ohio Ct. App. 6th Dist. Williams County 2010)—7:11

State v. Gee, 2000-Ohio-1963, 2000 WL 33226303 (Ohio Ct. App. 4th Dist. Scioto County 2000)—10:2

State v. Gerwin, 69 Ohio St. 2d 488, 23 Ohio Op. 3d 420, 432 N.E.2d 828 (1982)—2:7, 3:2

State v. Getsy, 84 Ohio St. 3d 180, 1998-Ohio-533, 702 N.E.2d 866 (1998)—7:25

State v. Gibson, 2015-Ohio-1679, 2015 WL 1962850 (Ohio Ct. App. 6th Dist. Lucas County 2015)—16:20

State v. Gibson, 2009-Ohio-4984, 2009 WL 3043980 (Ohio Ct. App. 8th Dist. Cuyahoga County 2009)—2:8

State v. Gibson, 2005-Ohio-1495, 2005 WL 730059 (Ohio Ct. App. 8th Dist. Cuyahoga County 2005)—2:5, 7:3, 10:8

State v. Gibson, 34 Ohio App. 3d 146, 517 N.E.2d 990 (8th Dist. Cuyahoga County 1986)—3:2

State v. Gibson, 45 Ohio St. 2d 366, 74 Ohio Op. 2d 525, 345 N.E.2d 399 (1976)—7:9

State v. Gilfillan, 2009-Ohio-1104, 2009 WL 638264 (Ohio Ct. App. 10th Dist. Franklin County 2009)—5:14

State v. Gilley, 135 N.C. App. 519, 522 S.E.2d 111 (1999)—13:13

State v. Gillispie, 2012-Ohio-2942, 985 N.E.2d 145 (Ohio Ct. App. 2d Dist. Montgomery County 2012)—5:24

State v. Gipson, 2016-Ohio-994, 2016 WL 962400 (Ohio Ct. App. 3d Dist. Allen County 2016)—2:5, 2:7, 7:3

State v. Glascoe, 2013-Ohio-1368, 2013 WL 1390531 (Ohio Ct. App. 2d Dist. Montgomery County 2013)—13:2

State v. Godbolt, 1999 WL 254370 (Ohio Ct. App. 5th Dist. Licking County 1999)—5:21

State v. Goff, 128 Ohio St. 3d 169, 2010-Ohio-6317, 942 N.E.2d 1075 (2010)—7:24, 16:24

State v. Goins, 2001-Ohio-8647, 2001 WL 1525298 (Ohio Ct. App. 12th Dist. Butler County 2001)—6:15

State v. Golding, 2009-Ohio-1437, 2009 WL 806915 (Ohio Ct. App. 11th Dist. Lake County 2009)—2:8

State v. Gomez, 2011-Ohio-5475, 2011 WL 5067230 (Ohio Ct. App. 9th Dist. Summit County 2011)—2:5, 4:1, 10:6, 10:7

State v. Griffin, 142 Ohio App. 3d 65, 753 N.E.2d 967 (1st Dist. Hamilton County 2001)—5:24

State v. Griffith, 2010-Ohio-5556, 2010 WL 4632607 (Ohio Ct. App. 10th Dist. Franklin County 2010)—3:2

State v. Griffitts, 2002-Ohio-921, 2002 WL 252786 (Ohio Ct. App. 2d Dist. Montgomery County 2002)—5:15, 16:14

State v. Grillo, 2015-Ohio-308, 27 N.E.3d 951 (Ohio Ct. App. 5th Dist. Richland County 2015)—13:15

State v. Grimes, 2006-Ohio-4262, 2006 WL 2373382 (Ohio Ct. App. 8th Dist. Cuyahoga County 2006)—5:14

State v. Grinnell, 112 Ohio App. 3d 124, 678 N.E.2d 231 (10th Dist. Franklin County 1996)—7:25

State v. Grooms, 1998 WL 487087 (Ohio Ct. App. 9th Dist. Summit County 1998)—16:12

State v. Grossniklaus, 2012-Ohio-2560, 2012 WL 2087401 (Ohio Ct. App. 9th Dist. Wayne County 2012)—6:13

State v. Grubb, 111 Ohio App. 3d 277, 675 N.E.2d 1353 (2d Dist. Montgomery County 1996)—5:24, 8:8, 16:21

State v. Grundy, 2006-Ohio-521, 2006 WL 288114 (Ohio Ct. App. 9th Dist. Summit County 2006)—5:3

State v. Guerriero, 2012-Ohio-5990, 2012 WL 6619273 (Ohio Ct. App. 7th Dist. Mahoning County 2012)—3:2

State v. Gulley, 2011-Ohio-4123, 2011 WL 3652761 (Ohio Ct. App. 8th Dist. Cuyahoga County 2011)—2:8

State v. Gwen, 134 Ohio St. 3d 284, 2012-Ohio-5046, 982 N.E.2d 626 (2012)—16:19

State v. Gwen, 2011-Ohio-1512, 2011 WL 1226763 (Ohio Ct. App. 9th Dist. Summit County 2011)—5:15

State v. Haamid, 2000 WL 45844 (Ohio Ct. App. 8th Dist. Cuyahoga County 2000)—13:3

State v. Haas, 2010-Ohio-6249, 2010 WL 5289198 (Ohio Ct. App. 11th Dist. Portage County 2010)—3:2

State v. Habo, 2013-Ohio-2142, 2013 WL 2308483 (Ohio Ct. App. 11th Dist. Portage County 2013)—2:2, 2:4, 7:12, 8:7

State v. Hadinger, 61 Ohio App. 3d 820, 573 N.E.2d 1191 (10th Dist. Franklin County 1991)—2:5, 10:6, 10:10

State v. Haines, 112 Ohio St. 3d 393, 2006-Ohio-6711, 860 N.E.2d 91 (2006)—7:24, 15:17, 16:24, 17:8

State v. Haines, 2005-Ohio-1692, 2005 WL 820539 (Ohio Ct. App. 11th Dist. Lake County 2005)—7:24

State v. Hairston, 2009-Ohio-2346, 2009 WL 1396434 (Ohio Ct. App. 10th Dist. Franklin County 2009)—5:23

State v. Hairston, 2008-Ohio-891, 2008 WL 583787 (Ohio Ct. App. 9th Dist. Summit County 2008)—5:21

State v. Halgrimson, 2000 WL 1675051 (Ohio Ct. App. 9th Dist. Lorain County 2000)—16:21

State v. Hall, 2018-Ohio-1676, 2018 WL 2028318 (Ohio Ct. App. 11th Dist. Trumbull County 2018)—2:8

State v. Hall, 2014-Ohio-2959, 2014 WL 2984992 (Ohio Ct. App. 4th Dist. Ross County 2014)—7:24, 7:25

State v. Hall, 2014-Ohio-416, 2014 WL 523072 (Ohio Ct. App. 2d Dist. Montgomery County 2014)—7:12

State v. Hall, 2013-Ohio-5856, 2013 WL 6918863 (Ohio Ct. App. 5th Dist. Delaware County 2013)—4:4

State v. Hall, 2013-Ohio-5855, 2013 WL 6918874 (Ohio Ct. App. 5th Dist. Delaware County 2013)—4:6, 11:21, 12:8, 13:3

State v. Hall, 2013-Ohio-660, 989 N.E.2d 111 (Ohio Ct. App. 5th Dist. Delaware County 2013)—4:5, 4:6, 12:8, 13:3

State v. Hall, 135 Ohio St. 3d 1456, 2013-Ohio-2285, 988 N.E.2d 576 (2013)—14:15

State v. Hall, 2012-Ohio-266, 2012 WL 253317 (Ohio Ct. App. 8th Dist. Cuyahoga County 2012)—5:15, 6:14, 7:22

State v. Hall, 2006-Ohio-1446, 2006

State v. Hawkins, 2012-Ohio-4622, 2012 WL 4762031 (Ohio Ct. App. 2d Dist. Montgomery County 2012)—2:5, 7:3, 10:6

State v. Hawn, 138 Ohio App. 3d 449, 741 N.E.2d 594 (2d Dist. Montgomery County 2000)—5:17, 5:24

State v. Hayden, 96 Ohio St. 3d 211, 2002-Ohio-4169, 773 N.E.2d 502 (2002)—20:5

State v. Hazel, 2018-Ohio-766, 2018 WL 1136978 (Ohio Ct. App. 2d Dist. Clark County 2018)—10:7

State v. Hazel, 2012-Ohio-835, 2012 WL 690312 (Ohio Ct. App. 2d Dist. Clark County 2012)—2:5, 4:1, 5:19

State v. Headlee, 2009-Ohio-873, 2009 WL 478085 (Ohio Ct. App. 4th Dist. Washington County 2009)—13:3

State v. Headley, 6 Ohio St. 3d 475, 453 N.E.2d 716 (1983)—3:8, 4:7

State v. Heard, 2017-Ohio-8796, 2017 WL 5988500 (Ohio Ct. App. 12th Dist. Warren County 2017)—7:22, 16:13

State v. Heaton, 108 Ohio App. 3d 38, 669 N.E.2d 885 (12th Dist. Clermont County 1995)—7:26

State v. Heffley, 2007-Ohio-904, 2007 WL 638453 (Ohio Ct. App. 3d Dist. Allen County 2007)—2:7

State v. Helm, 2016-Ohio-500, 56 N.E.3d 436 (Ohio Ct. App. 1st Dist. Hamilton County 2016)—2:7

State v. Helser, 2009-Ohio-3155, 2009 WL 1845232 (Ohio Ct. App. 3d Dist. Allen County 2009)—13:13

State v. Henderson, 1999 WL 689736 (Ohio Ct. App. 11th Dist. Trumbull County 1999)—16:12

State v. Henderson, 58 Ohio St. 2d 171, 12 Ohio Op. 3d 177, 389 N.E.2d 494 (1979)—2:7

State v. Hendking, 2000 WL 126733 (Ohio Ct. App. 8th Dist. Cuyahoga County 2000)—13:17

State v. Henry, 2015-Ohio-4145, 2015 WL 5813874 (Ohio Ct. App. 7th Dist. Belmont County 2015)—13:15, 13:17

State v. Henton, 121 Ohio App. 3d 501, 700 N.E.2d 371 (11th Dist. Ashtabula County 1997)—5:21

State v. Herder, 65 Ohio App. 2d 70, 19 Ohio Op. 3d 47, 415 N.E.2d 1000 (10th Dist. Franklin County 1979)—2:7

State v. Hergesheimer, 2014 WL 4725365 (Idaho Ct. App. 2014)—5:6

State v. Hermann, 1999 WL 744178 (Ohio Ct. App. 5th Dist. Stark County 1999)—16:12

State v. Hernandez, 2017-Ohio-4157, 2017 WL 2442980 (Ohio Ct. App. 7th Dist. Belmont County 2017)—5:22

State v. Hernandez, 2009-Ohio-386, 2009 WL 223882 (Ohio Ct. App. 6th Dist. Lucas County 2009)—5:24

State v. Hersh, 2012-Ohio-3807, 974 N.E.2d 161 (Ohio Ct. App. 8th Dist. Cuyahoga County 2012)—3:6

State v. Hess, 2004-Ohio-534, 2004 WL 231481 (Ohio Ct. App. 3d Dist. Seneca County 2004)—10:7

State v. Heston, 29 Ohio St. 2d 152, 58 Ohio Op. 2d 349, 280 N.E.2d 376 (1972)—14:3

State v. Hicks, 1995 WL 768588 (Ohio Ct. App. 5th Dist. Richland County 1995)—3:6

State v. Hicks, 88 Ohio App. 3d 515, 624 N.E.2d 332 (10th Dist. Franklin County 1993)—2:2, 8:7

State v. Higgins, 1996 WL 363543 (Ohio Ct. App. 5th Dist. Licking County 1996)—3:10, 13:2, 13:6, 13:13

State v. Higgs, 123 Ohio App. 3d 400, 704 N.E.2d 308 (11th Dist. Trumbull County 1997)—3:2

State v. Hight, 2011-Ohio-5013, 2011 WL 4529356 (Ohio Ct. App. 5th Dist. Licking County 2011)—2:8

State v. Hiles, 2009-Ohio-6602, 2009 WL 4827654 (Ohio Ct. App. 4th Dist. Ross County 2009)—5:22, 5:23

State v. Hill, 2018-Ohio-1345, 2018 WL 1721859 (Ohio Ct. App. 3d Dist. Henry County 2018)—3:2

State v. Hill, 2016-Ohio-7524, 2016 WL 6393146 (Ohio Ct. App. 6th Dist. Wood County 2016)—3:2

State v. Hill, 2011-Ohio-5810, 2011 WL 5452038 (Ohio Ct. App. 2d Dist. Montgomery County 2011)—6:14

State v. Hughes, 2018-Ohio-1237, 2018 WL 1578822 (Ohio Ct. App. 6th Dist. Wood County 2018)—2:2

State v. Hughes, 2015-Ohio-1173, 2015 WL 1403276 (Ohio Ct. App. 5th Dist. Tuscarawas County 2015)—2:5, 4:1, 7:3, 10:6, 10:9, 16:12

State v. Hull, 2003-Ohio-5306, 2003 WL 22284065 (Ohio Ct. App. 7th Dist. Mahoning County 2003)—3:2

State v. Humbarger, 149 Ohio App. 3d 30, 2002-Ohio-4160, 775 N.E.2d 585 (3d Dist. Van Wert County 2002)—10:6, 10:9

State v. Humbert, 2012-Ohio-5870, 2012 WL 6206770 (Ohio Ct. App. 9th Dist. Summit County 2012)—16:20

State v. Humphries, 79 Ohio App. 3d 589, 607 N.E.2d 921 (12th Dist. Clermont County 1992)—16:14

State v. Hunneman, 2006-Ohio-7023, 2006 WL 3833897 (Ohio Ct. App. 12th Dist. Clermont County 2006)—16:13

State v. Hunt, 2014-Ohio-3839, 2014 WL 4384140 (Ohio Ct. App. 2d Dist. Greene County 2014)—16:25

State v. Hunt, 2007-Ohio-3281, 2007 WL 1847660 (Ohio Ct. App. 10th Dist. Franklin County 2007)—16:12

State v. Hunt, 1996 WL 132268 (Ohio Ct. App. 5th Dist. Stark County 1996)—10:6, 15:7

State v. Hunter, 2013-Ohio-1469, 2013 WL 1501572 (Ohio Ct. App. 2d Dist. Montgomery County 2013)—13:2

State v. Hunter, 2012-Ohio-1121, 2012 WL 929696 (Ohio Ct. App. 9th Dist. Lorain County 2012)—2:5

State v. Hupp, 2009-Ohio-1441, 2009 WL 806901 (Ohio Ct. App. 11th Dist. Lake County 2009)—2:7

State v. Husseln, 152 Ohio App. 3d 67, 2003-Ohio-1369, 786 N.E.2d 536 (1st Dist. Hamilton County 2003)—16:25

State v. Ikharo, 2011-Ohio-2746, 2011 WL 2201193 (Ohio Ct. App. 10th Dist. Franklin County 2011)—7:11

State v. Ikharo, 2005-Ohio-6616, 2005 WL 3416177 (Ohio Ct. App. 10th Dist. Franklin County 2005)—7:11

State v. Imondi, 2015-Ohio-2605, 2015 WL 3964244 (Ohio Ct. App. 11th Dist. Lake County 2015)—7:24, 8:8

State v. Inkton, 2016-Ohio-693, 60 N.E.3d 616 (Ohio Ct. App. 8th Dist. Cuyahoga County 2016)—16:20

State v. Inman, 2014-Ohio-3538, 2014 WL 4057720 (Ohio Ct. App. 9th Dist. Medina County 2014)—5:21, 5:24, 6:14

State v. Ireson, 72 Ohio App. 3d 235, 594 N.E.2d 165 (4th Dist. Ross County 1991)—2:7

State v. Irwin, 2007-Ohio-4996, 2007 WL 2758606 (Ohio Ct. App. 7th Dist. Mahoning County 2007)—8:4

State v. Issa, 1998 WL 80301 (Ohio Ct. App. 1st Dist. Hamilton County 1998)—6:14

State v. Ivey, 98 Ohio App. 3d 249, 648 N.E.2d 519 (8th Dist. Cuyahoga County 1994)—2:2, 8:6, 8:7

State v. Jackman, 2008-Ohio-1944, 2008 WL 1822391 (Ohio Ct. App. 8th Dist. Cuyahoga County 2008)—5:22

State v. Jackson, 2015-Ohio-1694, 2015 WL 1966236 (Ohio Ct. App. 3d Dist. Seneca County 2015)—3:2

State v. Jackson, 2013-Ohio-1390, 990 N.E.2d 184 (Ohio Ct. App. 3d Dist. Hancock County 2013)—7:12

State v. Jackson, 2011-Ohio-3079, 2011 WL 2519512 (Ohio Ct. App. 10th Dist. Franklin County 2011)—3:3

State v. Jackson, 2002-Ohio-1202, 2002 WL 398655 (Ohio Ct. App. 2d Dist. Montgomery County 2002)—14:6, 16:15, 16:22

State v. Jalowiec, 91 Ohio St. 3d 220, 2001-Ohio-26, 744 N.E.2d 163 (2001)—6:13

State v. James, 2009-Ohio-4392, 2009 WL 2625838 (Ohio Ct. App. 7th Dist. Columbiana County 2009)—2:7

State v. Koons, 2007-Ohio-5242, 2007 WL 2851882 (Ohio Ct. App. 7th Dist. Columbiana County 2007)—2:5, 4:1

State v. Koslowski, 166 Wash. 2d 409, 209 P.3d 479 (2009)—5:16

State v. Koss, 49 Ohio St. 3d 213, 551 N.E.2d 970 (1990)—7:24, 15:17, 16:24

State v. Kraus, 2007-Ohio-6027, 2007 WL 3348426 (Ohio Ct. App. 12th Dist. Warren County 2007)—7:24, 16:12, 16:19, 16:20, 16:24, 17:8

State v. Kronenberg, 2018-Ohio-1962, 2018 WL 2277773 (Ohio Ct. App. 8th Dist. Cuyahoga County 2018)—16:21

State v. Krouskoupf, 2017-Ohio-7971, 2017 WL 4329771 (Ohio Ct. App. 5th Dist. Muskingum County 2017)—16:19

State v. Krug, 89 Ohio App. 3d 595, 626 N.E.2d 984 (1st Dist. Hamilton County 1993)—13:16

State v. Kurle, 390 N.W.2d 48 (N.D. 1986)—8:4

State v. Kutnar, 1999 WL 960943 (Ohio Ct. App. 11th Dist. Lake County 1999)—2:8

State v. Kvasne, 169 Ohio App. 3d 167, 2006-Ohio-5235, 862 N.E.2d 171 (8th Dist. Cuyahoga County 2006)—2:5, 2:8, 7:3

State v. Labombarbe, 1997 WL 640587 (Ohio Ct. App. 6th Dist. Wood County 1997)—16:14

State v. Lahmann, 2007-Ohio-1795, 2007 WL 1121472 (Ohio Ct. App. 12th Dist. Butler County 2007)—3:8, 4:7

State v. Lampe, 2003-Ohio-3059, 2003 WL 21360725 (Ohio Ct. App. 1st Dist. Hamilton County 2003)—14:3, 14:4, 16:14

State v. Land, 1995 WL 1049591 (Ohio Ct. App. 11th Dist. Lake County 1995)—2:8

State v. Landers, 188 Ohio App. 3d 786, 2010-Ohio-3709, 936 N.E.2d 1026 (4th Dist. Meigs County 2010)—5:3, 5:4

State v. Langford, 2003-Ohio-159, 2003 WL 125069 (Ohio Ct. App. 8th Dist. Cuyahoga County 2003)—2:7

State v. LaPrairie, 2011-Ohio-2184, 2011 WL 1753195 (Ohio Ct. App. 2d Dist. Greene County 2011)—2:8

State v. LaSalle, 96 Ohio St. 3d 178, 2002-Ohio-4009, 772 N.E.2d 1172 (2002)—7:26, 13:15

State v. Lawrence, 2008-Ohio-1354, 2008 WL 757529 (Ohio Ct. App. 12th Dist. Butler County 2008)—2:5, 2:8

State v. Lawson, 2014-Ohio-879, 2014 WL 1325751 (Ohio Ct. App. 7th Dist. Mahoning County 2014)—7:9

State v. Lawson, 2013-Ohio-2111, 2013 WL 2296318 (Ohio Ct. App. 10th Dist. Franklin County 2013)—13:15

State v. Lawson, 2012-Ohio-1050, 2012 WL 907913 (Ohio Ct. App. 8th Dist. Cuyahoga County 2012)—2:8

State v. Lawson, 2007-Ohio-2656, 2007 WL 1560266 (Ohio Ct. App. 10th Dist. Franklin County 2007)—9:2, 9:8

State v. Leason, 2011-Ohio-6591, 2011 WL 6740749 (Ohio Ct. App. 9th Dist. Summit County 2011)—13:3

State v. Leasure, 2015-Ohio-5327, 43 N.E.3d 477 (Ohio Ct. App. 4th Dist. Ross County 2015)—2:7

State v. Ledbetter, 1989 WL 114314 (Ohio Ct. App. 12th Dist. Clermont County 1989)—5:15

State v. Lee, 190 Ohio App. 3d 581, 2010-Ohio-5672, 943 N.E.2d 602 (3d Dist. Crawford County 2010)—3:3

State v. Lee, 2005-Ohio-996, 2005 WL 544837 (Ohio Ct. App. 9th Dist. Summit County 2005)—5:16, 19:7

State v. Lee, 73 Ohio Misc. 2d 9, 657 N.E.2d 604 (Mun. Ct. 1995)—5:15, 5:26, 8:4, 8:5, 13:15, 14:6, 16:12, 16:14

State v. LeGrant, 2014-Ohio-5803, 2014 WL 7463132 (Ohio Ct. App. 2d Dist. Miami County 2014)—2:8

State v. Lemmons, 2011-Ohio-3322, 2011 WL 2586486 (Ohio Ct. App. 5th Dist. Delaware County 2011)—3:3

State v. Lenoir, 2003-Ohio-2820, 2003 WL 21267227 (Ohio Ct. App. 2d Dist. Montgomery County 2003)—5:15

State v. Lucente, 2005-Ohio-1657, 2005 WL 775886 (Ohio Ct. App. 7th Dist. Mahoning County 2005)—7:11

State v. Lugli, 1995 WL 458671 (Ohio Ct. App. 6th Dist. Huron County 1995)—3:10, 13:13

State v. Luke, 2011-Ohio-4330, 2011 WL 3813588 (Ohio Ct. App. 3d Dist. Union County 2011)—2:2, 8:7

State v. Lundberg, 2002-Ohio-1811, 2002 WL 506439 (Ohio Ct. App. 2d Dist. Montgomery County 2002)—12:19

State v. Lundgren, 1994 WL 171657 (Ohio Ct. App. 11th Dist. Lake County 1994)—7:24

State v. Lynch, 1999 WL 11244 (Ohio Ct. App. 9th Dist. Lorain County 1999)—2:7, 5:21, 10:7, 16:12

State v. Mabry, 1996 WL 577701 (Ohio Ct. App. 9th Dist. Medina County 1996)—8:3, 10:7

State v. Machuca, 2016-Ohio-254, 2016 WL 363448 (Ohio Ct. App. 3d Dist. Allen County 2016)—5:24, 16:21

State v. Mack, 2015-Ohio-5214, 2015 WL 8607454 (Ohio Ct. App. 11th Dist. Ashtabula County 2015)—5:15, 16:12, 16:13, 16:14, 16:22

State v. Maggard, 2011-Ohio-4233, 2011 WL 3765523 (Ohio Ct. App. 1st Dist. Hamilton County 2011)—3:2

State v. Majka, 2002-Ohio-1378, 2002 WL 462858 (Ohio Ct. App. 9th Dist. Summit County 2002)—12:22, 14:5, 18:11

State v. Malone, 2012-Ohio-449, 2012 WL 382801 (Ohio Ct. App. 4th Dist. Hocking County 2012)—6:14

State v. Malott, 2015-Ohio-2968, 2015 WL 4507537 (Ohio Ct. App. 2d Dist. Montgomery County 2015)—8:8

State v. Manley, 2004-Ohio-4930, 2004 WL 2245114 (Ohio Ct. App. 2d Dist. Montgomery County 2004)—5:17

State v. Manning, 2008-Ohio-3801, 2008 WL 2931593 (Ohio Ct. App. 8th Dist. Cuyahoga County 2008)—6:15

State v. Manning, 74 Ohio App. 3d 19, 598 N.E.2d 25 (9th Dist. Lorain County 1991)—7:24

State v. Mansour, 2011-Ohio-5438, 2011 WL 5028611 (Ohio Ct. App. 11th Dist. Trumbull County 2011)—8:3, 8:5

State v. Manzanares, 19 Kan. App. 2d 214, 866 P.2d 1083 (1994)—13:15

State v. Manzell, 2007-Ohio-4076, 2007 WL 2283550 (Ohio Ct. App. 5th Dist. Stark County 2007)—16:12, 16:14, 16:22

State v. Maple, 2011-Ohio-1516, 2011 WL 1138387 (Ohio Ct. App. 9th Dist. Summit County 2011)—2:2, 2:5, 10:6, 10:7

State v. Marcum, 2013-Ohio-2447, 994 N.E.2d 1 (Ohio Ct. App. 4th Dist. Hocking County 2013)—7:11, 7:12

State v. Marcum, 2006-Ohio-7068, 2006 WL 3849861 (Ohio Ct. App. 7th Dist. Columbiana County 2006)—5:12

State v. Marcy, 165 Vt. 89, 680 A.2d 76 (1996)—16:18

State v. Mariana, 1999 WL 1271022 (Ohio Ct. App. 12th Dist. Butler County 1999)—7:24

State v. Mariano, 2009-Ohio-5426, 2009 WL 3255304 (Ohio Ct. App. 11th Dist. Lake County 2009)—2:7

State v. Marquez, 2008-Ohio-5324, 2008 WL 4561147 (Ohio Ct. App. 11th Dist. Ashtabula County 2008)—11:3

State v. Marrero, 2011-Ohio-1390, 2011 WL 1049294 (Ohio Ct. App. 10th Dist. Franklin County 2011)—3:3, 5:12, 6:14, 7:22

State v. Martin, 2016-Ohio-225, 57 N.E.3d 411 (Ohio Ct. App. 5th Dist. Tuscarawas County 2016)—2:5, 4:1, 5:14, 5:15, 6:13, 7:22, 10:6, 16:13, 16:14

State v. Martin, 2015-Ohio-1106, 2015 WL 1331818 (Ohio Ct. App. 5th Dist. Delaware County 2015)—7:12

State v. Martin, 2011-Ohio-1213, 2011 WL 899553 (Ohio Ct. App. 9th Dist. Summit County 2011)—5:12

State v. Martin, 2010-Ohio-244, 2010 WL 320475 (Ohio Ct. App. 8th

(Ohio Ct. App. 11th Dist. Lake County 2000)—5:20

State v. McLean, 87 Ohio App. 3d 392, 622 N.E.2d 402 (1st Dist. Hamilton County 1993)—7:9

State v. McNeal, 2002-Ohio-2981, 2002 WL 1376177 (Ohio Ct. App. 3d Dist. Allen County 2002)—5:17

State v. McNeil, 2016-Ohio-4669, 2016 WL 3573123 (Ohio Ct. App. 9th Dist. Summit County 2016)—2:4

State v. McNichols, 2002-Ohio-6253, 2002 WL 31538788 (Ohio Ct. App. 4th Dist. Hocking County 2002)—8:7

State v. McQueen, 2009-Ohio-6272, 2009 WL 4308654 (Ohio Ct. App. 10th Dist. Franklin County 2009)—2:5

State v. McQuirt, 2016-Ohio-1095, 2016 WL 1071464 (Ohio Ct. App. 2d Dist. Montgomery County 2016)—3:2, 7:11

State v. Meadows, 2001-Ohio-2510, 2001 WL 803822 (Ohio Ct. App. 4th Dist. Scioto County 2001)—6:15

State v. Meeks, 2015-Ohio-1527, 34 N.E.3d 382 (Ohio Ct. App. 5th Dist. Stark County 2015)—5:21, 5:24

State v. Meeks, 1995 WL 1036642 (Ohio Ct. App. 11th Dist. Lake County 1995)—9:10

State v. Meinke, 2017-Ohio-7787, 97 N.E.3d 1184 (Ohio Ct. App. 9th Dist. Lorain County 2017)—2:5, 4:4, 4:7, 13:3

State v. Mernar, 345 N.J. Super. 591, 786 A.2d 141 (App. Div. 2001)—11:11

State v. Messenger, 2010-Ohio-479, 2010 WL 530087 (Ohio Ct. App. 3d Dist. Marion County 2010)—2:5, 10:6

State v. Meyerson, 2017-Ohio-8726, 2017 WL 5907415 (Ohio Ct. App. 9th Dist. Summit County 2017)—16:12, 16:17

State v. Michael, 1997 WL 335527 (Ohio Ct. App. 3d Dist. Crawford County 1997)—14:5

State v. Middleton, 85 Ohio App. 3d 403, 619 N.E.2d 1113 (4th Dist. Vinton County 1993)—2:7

State v. Milano-Tavella, 1999 WL 668562 (Ohio Ct. App. 5th Dist. Delaware County 1999)—2:8

State v. Miles, 2012-Ohio-2607, 2012 WL 2128035 (Ohio Ct. App. 9th Dist. Summit County 2012)—2:4

State v. Miller, 2015-Ohio-956, 2015 WL 1142955 (Ohio Ct. App. 11th Dist. Trumbull County 2015)—16:12

State v. Miller, 2013-Ohio-1651, 2013 WL 1787565 (Ohio Ct. App. 8th Dist. Cuyahoga County 2013)—8:4

State v. Miller, 2012-Ohio-6115, 2012 WL 6726698 (Ohio Ct. App. 3d Dist. Henry County 2012)—2:2

State v. Miller, 2012-Ohio-997, 2012 WL 764907 (Ohio Ct. App. 12th Dist. Warren County 2012)—2:7

State v. Miller, 96 Ohio St. 3d 384, 2002-Ohio-4931, 775 N.E.2d 498 (2002)—5:17

State v. Miller, 134 Ohio App. 3d 649, 731 N.E.2d 1192 (1st Dist. Hamilton County 1999)—8:6, 8:7

State v. Miller, 105 Ohio App. 3d 679, 664 N.E.2d 1309 (4th Dist. Washington County 1995)—2:5, 10:6

State v. Miller, 91 Ohio App. 3d 270, 632 N.E.2d 569 (3d Dist. Logan County 1993)—3:7

State v. Mills, 2005-Ohio-2128, 2006 WL 1132543 (Ohio Ct. App. 2d Dist. Montgomery County 2006)—5:16, 10:7, 16:13

State v. Mills, 1997 WL 133430 (Ohio Ct. App. 1st Dist. Hamilton County 1997)—2:2, 8:3, 8:7

State v. Mink, 2004-Ohio-2042, 2004 WL 869523 (Ohio Ct. App. 2d Dist. Montgomery County 2004)—8:7

State v. Mitchell, 2011-Ohio-2465, 2011 WL 2112619 (Ohio Ct. App. 12th Dist. Butler County 2011)—2:8

State v. Mitchell, 2007-Ohio-167, 2007 WL 118001 (Ohio Ct. App. 10th Dist. Franklin County 2007)—8:5, 13:15

State v. Mitchell, 171 Ohio App. 3d 225, 2007-Ohio-1696, 870 N.E.2d 228 (8th Dist. Cuyahoga County 2007)—5:14, 5:16, 16:13, 16:14

State v. Mitchell, 1996 WL 695665 (Ohio Ct. App. 8th Dist. Cuyahoga County 1996)—5:21

State v. Mizenko, 2006 MT 11, 330 Mont. 299, 127 P.3d 458 (2006)—16:13

State v. Mohabir, 2005-Ohio-78, 2005 WL 66484 (Ohio Ct. App. 5th Dist. Fairfield County 2005)—13:3

State v. Moissis, 2002-Ohio-4955, 2002 WL 31101605 (Ohio Ct. App. 11th Dist. Lake County 2002)—16:19

State v. Molen, 2008-Ohio-6237, 2008 WL 5064887 (Ohio Ct. App. 2d Dist. Montgomery County 2008)—6:15

State v. Monroe, 2011-Ohio-3045, 2011 WL 2476280 (Ohio Ct. App. 8th Dist. Cuyahoga County 2011)—5:17

State v. Monroe, 2000 WL 807228 (Ohio Ct. App. 4th Dist. Pike County 2000)—5:3

State v. Montgomery, 148 Ohio St. 3d 347, 2016-Ohio-5487, 71 N.E.3d 180 (2016)—3:2

State v. Montgomery, 2014-Ohio-1789, 2014 WL 1692762 (Ohio Ct. App. 3d Dist. Putnam County 2014)—3:2

State v. Montgomery, 2010-Ohio-4555, 2010 WL 3733844 (Ohio Ct. App. 11th Dist. Ashtabula County 2010)—7:9, 7:11

State v. Montgomery, 159 Ohio App. 3d 752, 2005-Ohio-1018, 825 N.E.2d 250 (1st Dist. Hamilton County 2005)—2:9

State v. Montgomery, 1986 WL 15250 (Ohio Ct. App. 8th Dist. Cuyahoga County 1986)—5:26

State v. Montiel, 185 Ohio App. 3d 362, 2009-Ohio-6589, 924 N.E.2d 375 (2d Dist. Montgomery County 2009)—5:3

State v. Moore, 2017-Ohio-8483, 2017 WL 5197255 (Ohio Ct. App. 8th Dist. Cuyahoga County 2017)—3:2

State v. Moore, 2015-Ohio-4182, 2015 WL 5864786 (Ohio Ct. App. 8th Dist. Cuyahoga County 2015)—7:11

State v. Moore, 2010-Ohio-509, 2010 WL 547707 (Ohio Ct. App. 8th Dist. Cuyahoga County 2010)—2:2, 2:5, 7:3

State v. Moore, 2008-Ohio-1477, 2008 WL 835621 (Ohio Ct. App. 12th Dist. Butler County 2008)—13:3

State v. Moorer, 2009-Ohio-1494, 2009 WL 818945 (Ohio Ct. App. 9th Dist. Summit County 2009)—5:12, 5:15, 5:16, 7:22

State v. Morales, 2014-Ohio-362, 2014 WL 467331 (Ohio Ct. App. 1st Dist. Hamilton County 2014)—5:14

State v. Moran, 1998 WL 831570 (Ohio Ct. App. 9th Dist. Lorain County 1998)—5:3

State v. Morgan, 100 Ohio St. 66, 125 N.E. 109 (1919)—7:24

State v. Morris, 141 Ohio St. 3d 399, 2014-Ohio-5052, 24 N.E.3d 1153 (2014)—5:24

State v. Morris, 2012-Ohio-6151, 985 N.E.2d 274 (Ohio Ct. App. 9th Dist. Medina County 2012)—5:21

State v. Morrow, 2008-Ohio-3958, 2008 WL 3009683 (Ohio Ct. App. 9th Dist. Summit County 2008)—5:24

State v. Morton, 292 N.J. Super. 92, 678 A.2d 308 (App. Div. 1996)—13:13, 13:15

State v. Morton, 1994 WL 49941 (Ohio Ct. App. 3d Dist. Seneca County 1994)—10:4, 10:5, 10:6

State v. Moser, 1999 WL 550272 (Ohio Ct. App. 6th Dist. Wood County 1999)—8:7

State v. Mossbarger, 2000 WL 303140 (Ohio Ct. App. 4th Dist. Pike County 2000)—8:3

State v. Mount, 2000 WL 1028511 (Ohio Ct. App. 5th Dist. Stark County 2000)—16:12

State v. Mrus, 71 Ohio App. 3d 828, 595 N.E.2d 460 (11th Dist. Trumbull County 1991)—7:3, 10:4, 10:6, 10:8

State v. Mueller, 122 Ohio App. 3d 483, 702 N.E.2d 139 (1st Dist. Hamilton County 1997)—12:14, 13:16

State v. Muhumed, 2012-Ohio-6155, 2012 WL 6738337 (Ohio Ct. App. 10th Dist. Franklin County 2012)—7:11

State v. Mullins, 1999 WL 668812 (Ohio Ct. App. 5th Dist. Richland County 1999)—2:7, 8:3, 10:9, 13:3

State v. Muncey, 1999 WL 59675 (Ohio Ct. App. 12th Dist. Madison County 1999)—5:15, 16:21

State v. Noble, 2007-Ohio-7051, 2007 WL 4554247 (Ohio Ct. App. 9th Dist. Lorain County 2007)—3:2

State v. Noggle, 67 Ohio St. 3d 31, 1993-Ohio-189, 615 N.E.2d 1040, 83 Ed. Law Rep. 720 (1993)—10:8

State v. Noland, 2001 WL 710160 (Ohio Ct. App. 10th Dist. Franklin County 2001)—5:3, 14:6

State v. Nolton, 19 Ohio St. 2d 133, 48 Ohio Op. 2d 119, 249 N.E.2d 797 (1969)—2:8

State v. Nordstrom, 2015-Ohio-1454, 2015 WL 1737857 (Ohio Ct. App. 8th Dist. Cuyahoga County 2015)—3:2

State v. Norris, 2016-Ohio-5381, 2016 WL 4362859 (Ohio Ct. App. 5th Dist. Licking County 2016)—3:3

State v. Norris, 2015-Ohio-624, 2015 WL 753346 (Ohio Ct. App. 2d Dist. Montgomery County 2015)—5:14, 5:15, 5:16, 6:14, 7:22, 16:13, 16:14, 16:15

State v. Novel, 1986 WL 11348 (Ohio Ct. App. 5th Dist. Licking County 1986)—3:8, 4:7

State v. Nunez, 2017-Ohio-4295, 92 N.E.3d 294 (Ohio Ct. App. 8th Dist. Cuyahoga County 2017)—5:24, 7:21

State v. O'Brien, 30 Ohio St. 3d 122, 508 N.E.2d 144 (1987)—8:6

State v. Ocasio, 2003-Ohio-6240, 2003 WL 22764145 (Ohio Ct. App. 2d Dist. Montgomery County 2003)—2:8, 3:2, 3:3

State v. Ohm, 107 Ohio Misc. 2d 19, 736 N.E.2d 121 (Mun. Ct. 2000)—3:10, 13:13

State v. Olson, 119 Idaho 370, 806 P.2d 963 (Ct. App. 1991)—13:15

State v. Oluoch, 2007-Ohio-5560, 2007 WL 3027074 (Ohio Ct. App. 10th Dist. Franklin County 2007)—7:11

State v. O'Neal, 87 Ohio St. 3d 402, 2000-Ohio-449, 721 N.E.2d 73 (2000)—8:8, 9:10

State v. O'Neal, 1997 WL 770162 (Ohio Ct. App. 1st Dist. Hamilton County 1997)—2:7

State v. O'Neill, 2015-Ohio-815, 29 N.E.3d 365 (Ohio Ct. App. 3d Dist. Allen County 2015)—14:3

State v. O'Neill, 140 Ohio App. 3d 48, 2000-Ohio-2656, 746 N.E.2d 654 (7th Dist. Jefferson County 2000)—2:7, 3:2

State v. Ornellas, 79 Haw. 418, 903 P.2d 723 (Ct. App. 1995)—8:4, 16:21

State v. O'Rourke, 2015-Ohio-670, 2015 WL 782623 (Ohio Ct. App. 4th Dist. Athens County 2015)—3:2

State v. Osborne, 2016-Ohio-282, 2016 WL 515404 (Ohio Ct. App. 9th Dist. Summit County 2016)—7:24

State v. Osman, 2011-Ohio-4626, 2011 WL 4064473 (Ohio Ct. App. 4th Dist. Athens County 2011)—16:13

State v. Osterhaus, 2000 WL 1006573 (Ohio Ct. App. 2d Dist. Montgomery County 2000)—8:4

State v. Ott, 2017-Ohio-521, 2017 WL 659374 (Ohio Ct. App. 9th Dist. Summit County 2017)—2:7, 7:9

State v. Ouch, 2006-Ohio-6949, 2006 WL 3805676 (Ohio Ct. App. 10th Dist. Franklin County 2006)—7:11

State v. Overton, 2011-Ohio-4204, 2011 WL 3669374 (Ohio Ct. App. 10th Dist. Franklin County 2011)—3:3

State v. Page, 2005-Ohio-1493, 2005 WL 730057 (Ohio Ct. App. 8th Dist. Cuyahoga County 2005)—5:21

State v. Palacios, 1995 WL 434379 (Ohio Ct. App. 9th Dist. Lorain County 1995)—14:15

State v. Pallai, 2008-Ohio-6635, 2008 WL 5245576 (Ohio Ct. App. 7th Dist. Mahoning County 2008)—4:1

State v. Palmer, 148 Ohio App. 3d 246, 2002-Ohio-3536, 772 N.E.2d 726 (1st Dist. Hamilton County 2002)—3:3

State v. Palmer, 2000 WL 311916 (Ohio Ct. App. 10th Dist. Franklin County 2000)—7:24

State v. Papusha, 2007-Ohio-3966, 2007 WL 2229579 (Ohio Ct. App. 12th Dist. Preble County 2007)—16:19

State v. Parish, 2014-Ohio-1410, 2014 WL 1350961 (Ohio Ct. App. 5th Dist. Stark County 2014)—10:7

State v. Pertee, 1995 WL 688800 (Ohio Ct. App. 9th Dist. Wayne County 1995)—2:5, 10:9

State v. Pesano, 2014-Ohio-5540, 2014 WL 7177311 (Ohio Ct. App. 5th Dist. Stark County 2014)—13:3

State v. Pessetto, 160 N.H. 813, 8 A.3d 75 (2010)—12:22

State v. Petaway, 2009-Ohio-1304, 2009 WL 737772 (Ohio Ct. App. 3d Dist. Logan County 2009)—6:15

State v. Petrusch, 1995 WL 737509 (Ohio Ct. App. 2d Dist. Montgomery County 1995)—12:27, 13:13

State v. Phillips, 2018 SD 2, 906 N.W.2d 411 (S.D. 2018)—16:21

State v. Phillips, 2016-Ohio-4687, 69 N.E.3d 80 (Ohio Ct. App. 9th Dist. Summit County 2016)—3:2

State v. Phillips, 2016-Ohio-1216, 2016 WL 1176067 (Ohio Ct. App. 5th Dist. Licking County 2016)—5:14, 5:25

State v. Phillips, 2014-Ohio-2614, 2014 WL 2750667 (Ohio Ct. App. 1st Dist. Hamilton County 2014)—13:3

State v. Phillips, 2012-Ohio-6023, 2012 WL 6651822 (Ohio Ct. App. 10th Dist. Franklin County 2012)—2:2, 2:4, 8:7

State v. Phillips, 2010-Ohio-1941, 2010 WL 1757943 (Ohio Ct. App. 12th Dist. Butler County 2010)—2:7

State v. Phillips, 1991 WL 2018 (Ohio Ct. App. 9th Dist. Lorain County 1991)—3:2

State v. Piccus, 1988 WL 32145 (Ohio Ct. App. 8th Dist. Cuyahoga County 1988)—14:5

State v. Pichardo-Reyes, 2017-Ohio-8534, 2017 WL 5290871 (Ohio Ct. App. 12th Dist. Butler County 2017)—2:8

State v. Pickens, 141 Ohio St. 3d 462, 2014-Ohio-5445, 25 N.E.3d 1023 (2014)—5:15

State v. Pickett, 628 So. 2d 1333 (La. Ct. App. 2d Cir. 1993)—13:9, 13:15

State v. Pigge, 2010-Ohio-6541, 2010 WL 5621533 (Ohio Ct. App. 4th Dist. Ross County 2010)—3:2

State v. Pina, 49 Ohio App. 2d 394, 3 Ohio Op. 3d 457, 361 N.E.2d 262 (2d Dist. Clark County 1975)—11:3

State v. Pineda, 2005-Ohio-6386, 2005 WL 3219708 (Ohio Ct. App. 8th Dist. Cuyahoga County 2005)—7:11

State v. Pittman, 2013-Ohio-962, 2013 WL 1092420 (Ohio Ct. App. 2d Dist. Montgomery County 2013)—7:12

State v. Plas, 1995 WL 500110 (Ohio Ct. App. 9th Dist. Lorain County 1995)—5:21

State v. Plott, 2017-Ohio-38, 80 N.E.3d 1108 (Ohio Ct. App. 3d Dist. Seneca County 2017)—4:1, 7:3, 10:6, 16:12

State v. Plummer, 2016-Ohio-7548, 2016 WL 6462544 (Ohio Ct. App. 12th Dist. Warren County 2016)—13:2

State v. Poling, 1998 WL 255574 (Ohio Ct. App. 3d Dist. Shelby County 1998)—5:12, 6:13, 10:8, 16:12

State v. Poling, 1991 WL 84229 (Ohio Ct. App. 11th Dist. Trumbull County 1991)—7:23, 7:24

State v. Pollard, 21 Ohio St. 2d 171, 50 Ohio Op. 2d 394, 256 N.E.2d 620 (1970)—5:24

State v. Pollis, 2000 WL 522431 (Ohio Ct. App. 11th Dist. Trumbull County 2000)—13:2

State v. Poppe, 2006-Ohio-1994, 2006 WL 1062023 (Ohio Ct. App. 3d Dist. Auglaize County 2006)—2:8, 8:3

State v. Povroznik, 2018-Ohio-1516, 2018 WL 1882896 (Ohio Ct. App. 8th Dist. Cuyahoga County 2018)—2:8

State v. Powell, 2017-Ohio-5629, 2017 WL 2857221 (Ohio Ct. App. 9th Dist. Summit County 2017)—2:8

State v. Powell, 2006-Ohio-1778, 2006 WL 903596 (Ohio Ct. App. 3d Dist. Allen County 2006)—14:4

State v. Powell, 49 Ohio St. 3d 255, 552 N.E.2d 191 (1990)—2:2

State v. Powers, 2002-Ohio-6672, 2002 WL 31730985 (Ohio Ct. App. 5th Dist. Fairfield County 2002)—13:15

State v. Presley, 2003-Ohio-6069, 2003 WL 22681425 (Ohio Ct.

State v. Renner, 125 Ohio App. 3d 383, 708 N.E.2d 765 (2d Dist. Montgomery County 1998)—8:4

State v. Rexroad, 2005-Ohio-6790, 2005 WL 3489726 (Ohio Ct. App. 7th Dist. Columbiana County 2005)—2:5, 4:1

State v. Reyes, 172 N.J. 154, 796 A.2d 879 (2002)—10:13

State v. Reynolds, 80 Ohio St. 3d 670, 1998-Ohio-171, 687 N.E.2d 1358 (1998)—5:17

State v. Reynolds, 25 Ohio App. 3d 59, 495 N.E.2d 971 (1st Dist. Hamilton County 1985)—2:8

State v. Rhoads, 2013-Ohio-152, 2013 WL 221512 (Ohio Ct. App. 12th Dist. Clermont County 2013)—2:4, 8:4, 8:5

State v. Richard, 2005-Ohio-6494, 2005 WL 3315308 (Ohio Ct. App. 8th Dist. Cuyahoga County 2005)—9:5

State v. Richardson, 2010-Ohio-471, 2010 WL 497343 (Ohio Ct. App. 6th Dist. Lucas County 2010)—5:21, 5:24, 7:22, 7:24, 16:21

State v. Rickert, 164 Vt. 602, 665 A.2d 887 (1995)—13:15

State v. Ridenour, 128 Ohio App. 3d 134, 713 N.E.2d 1140 (9th Dist. Summit County 1998)—13:17

State v. Ridley, 2013-Ohio-1268, 2013 WL 1289533 (Ohio Ct. App. 6th Dist. Lucas County 2013)—5:19, 5:21

State v. Riedel, 2017-Ohio-8865, 100 N.E.3d 1155 (Ohio Ct. App. 8th Dist. Cuyahoga County 2017)—2:5, 4:1, 7:3

State v. Rieves, 2018-Ohio-955, 109 N.E.3d 190 (Ohio Ct. App. 8th Dist. Cuyahoga County 2018)—3:2

State v. Rihm, 101 Ohio App. 3d 626, 656 N.E.2d 372 (2d Dist. Clark County 1995)—2:8, 3:3

State v. Riley, 2007-Ohio-879, 2007 WL 625898 (Ohio Ct. App. 6th Dist. Wood County 2007)—7:22

State v. Rinehart, 2002-Ohio-6143, 2002 WL 31520346 (Ohio Ct. App. 4th Dist. Ross County 2002)—2:5, 7:3, 10:6

State v. Rittenhour, 112 Ohio App. 3d 219, 678 N.E.2d 293 (3d Dist. Crawford County 1996)—19:7

State v. Rittenhouse, 1999 WL 1271026 (Ohio Ct. App. 12th Dist. Fayette County 1999)—13:3

State v. Rivera, 2013-Ohio-3244, 2013 WL 3877817 (Ohio Ct. App. 8th Dist. Cuyahoga County 2013)—7:3, 10:9, 16:12

State v. Robb, 88 Ohio St. 3d 59, 2000-Ohio-275, 723 N.E.2d 1019 (2000)—5:14

State v. Roberson, 2018-Ohio-1955, 2018 WL 2277130 (Ohio Ct. App. 6th Dist. Lucas County 2018)—2:8

State v. Roberts, 2015-Ohio-5044, 2015 WL 8154018 (Ohio Ct. App. 9th Dist. Wayne County 2015)—2:5, 4:1, 10:6

State v. Robinette, 118 Ohio App. 3d 450, 693 N.E.2d 305 (4th Dist. Jackson County 1997)—8:4

State v. Robinson, 2009-Ohio-2921, 2009 WL 1719359 (Ohio Ct. App. 6th Dist. Erie County 2009)—3:2

State v. Robinson, 1998 WL 404216 (Ohio Ct. App. 7th Dist. Mahoning County 1998)—5:23

State v. Robinson, 656 A.2d 744 (Me. 1995)—9:10

State v. Rockburn, 2003-Ohio-3537, 2003 WL 21513054 (Ohio Ct. App. 8th Dist. Cuyahoga County 2003)—7:9

State v. Rocker, 1996 WL 490687 (Ohio Ct. App. 5th Dist. Guernsey County 1996)—5:15

State v. Rodgers, 166 Ohio App. 3d 218, 2006-Ohio-1528, 850 N.E.2d 90 (10th Dist. Franklin County 2006)—2:5, 4:1, 10:10

State v. Rodgers, 131 Ohio Misc. 2d 1, 2005-Ohio-1730, 827 N.E.2d 872 (C.P. 2005)—2:5, 4:1, 10:10

State v. Rodriguez, 2014-Ohio-911, 2014 WL 1345415 (Ohio Ct. App. 9th Dist. Summit County 2014)—5:21

State v. Rodriguez, 2009-Ohio-549, 2009 WL 295403 (Ohio Ct. App. 12th Dist. Butler County 2009)—11:2, 11:3, 12:3, 17:3

State v. Rodriguez, 2006-Ohio-3378, 2006 WL 1793688 (Ohio Ct. App. 6th Dist. Huron County 2006)—2:5, 4:1, 7:3

State v. Rodriguez, 2002-Ohio-3978, 2002 WL 1791115 (Ohio Ct. App.

Dist. Sandusky County 2007)—13:2, 13:15
State v. Sallie, 81 Ohio St. 3d 673, 1998-Ohio-343, 693 N.E.2d 267 (1998)—7:24
State v. Saltsman, 1997 WL 779119 (Ohio Ct. App. 2d Dist. Montgomery County 1997)—10:4, 10:8
State v. Saltz, 2015-Ohio-3097, 2015 WL 4610972 (Ohio Ct. App. 3d Dist. Hancock County 2015)—16:13
State v. Samarghandi, 84 Ohio Misc. 2d 6, 680 N.E.2d 738 (Mun. Ct. 1997)—2:4, 14:5, 14:6
State v. Sanchez, 2010-Ohio-6153, 2010 WL 5235932 (Ohio Ct. App. 8th Dist. Cuyahoga County 2010)—2:7, 5:5, 5:15, 6:14, 7:22
State v. Sanchez, 1994 WL 619796 (Ohio Ct. App. 9th Dist. Medina County 1994)—8:5
State v. Sanders, 2013-Ohio-5220, 3 N.E.3d 749 (Ohio Ct. App. 7th Dist. Columbiana County 2013)—5:3
State v. Sanders, 327 N.J. Super. 385, 743 A.2d 385 (App. Div. 2000)—13:3, 13:8, 13:10
State v. Sandlin, 11 Ohio App. 3d 84, 463 N.E.2d 85 (6th Dist. Wood County 1983)—13:4
State v. Sandridge, 2006-Ohio-5243, 2006 WL 2831024 (Ohio Ct. App. 8th Dist. Cuyahoga County 2006)—2:8
State v. Santiago, 2002-Ohio-1114, 2002 WL 388901 (Ohio Ct. App. 9th Dist. Lorain County 2002)—6:13
State v. Sappienza, 84 Ohio St. 63, 95 N.E. 381 (1911)—7:25
State v. Sargent, 2015-Ohio-704, 29 N.E.3d 331 (Ohio Ct. App. 6th Dist. Lucas County 2015)—5:21, 5:24, 7:21, 16:21
State v. Sartain, 2008-Ohio-2124, 2008 WL 1933447 (Ohio Ct. App. 11th Dist. Lake County 2008)—2:7
State v. Sayres, 1997 WL 142361 (Ohio Ct. App. 4th Dist. Washington County 1997)—8:4, 8:8
State v. Schackart, 153 Ariz. 422, 737 P.2d 398 (Ct. App. Div. 2 1987)—13:9
State v. Schaefer, 2000 WL 492094 (Ohio Ct. App. 2d Dist. Greene County 2000)—2:8
State v. Schauer, 2000 WL 670304 (Ohio Ct. App. 4th Dist. Pickaway County 2000)—5:19
State v. Schell, 2017-Ohio-2641, 2017 WL 1748769 (Ohio Ct. App. 9th Dist. Summit County 2017)—13:3
State v. Schlaf, 2008-Ohio-6151, 2008 WL 5049959 (Ohio Ct. App. 8th Dist. Cuyahoga County 2008)—7:11
State v. Schlee, 117 Ohio St. 3d 153, 2008-Ohio-545, 882 N.E.2d 431 (2008)—12:25
State v. Schmidt, 2010-Ohio-4809, 2010 WL 3836161 (Ohio Ct. App. 3d Dist. Mercer County 2010)—7:12
State v. Schoeneman, 2012-Ohio-4710, 2012 WL 4831655 (Ohio Ct. App. 5th Dist. Stark County 2012)—9:8
State v. Schroeder, 2001 WL 1308002 (Ohio Ct. App. 6th Dist. Wood County 2001)—14:5
State v. Schultz, 1996 WL 71004 (Ohio Ct. App. 6th Dist. Wood County 1996)—12:27, 13:13, 13:14
State v. Schwab, 119 Ohio App. 3d 463, 695 N.E.2d 801 (12th Dist. Butler County 1997)—9:2, 9:3, 9:8
State v. Schwartz, 77 Ohio App. 3d 484, 602 N.E.2d 671 (12th Dist. Butler County 1991)—2:4, 8:4
State v. Schweitzer, 2015-Ohio-925, 30 N.E.3d 190 (Ohio Ct. App. 3d Dist. Auglaize County 2015)—2:4, 8:4, 8:8, 15:7
State v. Scott, 2015-Ohio-5397, 2015 WL 9435159 (Ohio Ct. App. 5th Dist. Fairfield County 2015)—5:21
State v. Scott, 1999 WL 126933 (Ohio Ct. App. 7th Dist. Belmont County 1999)—5:24, 10:4, 10:5, 10:6, 10:8
State v. Scott, 1998 SD 2, 574 N.W.2d 595 (S.D. 1998)—12:13, 13:7
State v. Scott, 31 Ohio St. 2d 1, 60 Ohio Op. 2d 1, 285 N.E.2d 344 (1972)—5:20
State v. Scruggs, 136 Ohio App. 3d 631, 737 N.E.2d 574 (2d Dist. Montgomery County 2000)—9:1, 9:2, 9:8

WL 937754 (Ohio Ct. App. 3d Dist. Marion County 2013)—5:14, 5:15

State v. Sprow, 1997 WL 177703 (Ohio Ct. App. 6th Dist. Williams County 1997)—12:27

State v. S.R., 63 Ohio St. 3d 590, 589 N.E.2d 1319 (1992)—8:4

State v. S.S., 2014 WL 6851969 (Ohio Ct. App. 10th Dist. Franklin County 2014)—3:3

State v. Stage, 2012-Ohio-3300, 2012 WL 2979331 (Ohio Ct. App. 9th Dist. Medina County 2012)—6:14

State v. Stahl, 111 Ohio St. 3d 186, 2006-Ohio-5482, 855 N.E.2d 834 (2006)—5:14, 6:14, 7:22, 16:13

State v. Stamper, 2016-Ohio-433, 2016 WL 525818 (Ohio Ct. App. 2d Dist. Champaign County 2016)—13:15

State v. Starett, 2009-Ohio-744, 2009 WL 405908 (Ohio Ct. App. 4th Dist. Athens County 2009)—2:7, 3:2, 5:22

State v. Stark, 2017-Ohio-873, 2017 WL 962916 (Ohio Ct. App. 9th Dist. Wayne County 2017)—16:21

State v. Starkey, 1998 WL 753257 (Ohio Ct. App. 5th Dist. Stark County 1998)—3:6

State v. Steed, 140 N.H. 153, 665 A.2d 1072 (1995)—9:10

State v. Stephens, 2008-Ohio-890, 2008 WL 583789 (Ohio Ct. App. 9th Dist. Summit County 2008)—5:24, 16:12, 16:21

State v. Sterling, 1998 WL 517867 (Ohio Ct. App. 5th Dist. Tuscarawas County 1998)—8:2

State v. Stevenson, 1996 WL 596452 (Ohio Ct. App. 8th Dist. Cuyahoga County 1996)—2:7

State v. Stewart, 2003-Ohio-214, 2003 WL 139971 (Ohio Ct. App. 2d Dist. Montgomery County 2003)—2:8

State v. Stewart, 1995 WL 136489 (Ohio Ct. App. 6th Dist. Wood County 1995)—13:16

State v. Stewart, 75 Ohio App. 3d 141, 598 N.E.2d 1275 (11th Dist. Ashtabula County 1991)—5:15, 5:18, 16:16

State v. Stewart, 51 Ohio St. 2d 86, 5 Ohio Op. 3d 52, 364 N.E.2d 1163 (1977)—3:2

State v. Stocker, 90 Haw. 85, 976 P.2d 399 (1999)—8:7

State v. Stoken, 1987 WL 28162 (Ohio Ct. App. 1st Dist. Hamilton County 1987)—14:5

State v. Stoneham, 2017 WL 2644320 (Ariz. Ct. App. Div. 1 2017)—5:14

State v. Stoner, 2009-Ohio-2073, 2009 WL 1174942 (Ohio Ct. App. 2d Dist. Clark County 2009)—12:19, 13:2

State v. Storch, 66 Ohio St. 3d 280, 1993-Ohio-38, 612 N.E.2d 305 (1993)—5:14, 5:15, 5:26, 14:6, 16:12

State v. Stout, 1996 WL 556903 (Ohio Ct. App. 9th Dist. Wayne County 1996)—16:19

State v. Stover, 2014-Ohio-2572, 2014 WL 2701213 (Ohio Ct. App. 9th Dist. Wayne County 2014)—5:15, 16:14, 16:20

State v. Stowers, 81 Ohio St. 3d 260, 1998-Ohio-632, 690 N.E.2d 881 (1998)—7:24

State v. Straits, 1999 WL 976212 (Ohio Ct. App. 5th Dist. Fairfield County 1999)—16:19

State v. Street, 122 Ohio App. 3d 79, 701 N.E.2d 50 (9th Dist. Lorain County 1997)—16:12

State v. Streight, 2002-Ohio-672, 2002 WL 235445 (Ohio Ct. App. 3d Dist. Auglaize County 2002)—8:8

State v. Strimpel, 2018-Ohio-1628, 2018 WL 1975769 (Ohio Ct. App. 8th Dist. Cuyahoga County 2018)—3:2

State v. Stringfield, 124 Ohio App. 3d 665, 707 N.E.2d 43 (9th Dist. Medina County 1998)—2:5, 10:2, 10:7

State v. Strunk, 1999 WL 12743 (Ohio Ct. App. 1st Dist. Hamilton County 1999)—2:4, 3:8, 8:4, 8:5

State v. Stuber, 71 Ohio App. 3d 86, 593 N.E.2d 48 (3d Dist. Allen County 1990)—2:8

State v. Studgions, 2016-Ohio-5236, 2016 WL 4141347 (Ohio Ct. App. 8th Dist. Cuyahoga County 2016)—2:8

State v. Studgions, 2016-Ohio-4701, 2016 WL 3571261 (Ohio Ct. App. 8th Dist. Cuyahoga County 2016)—3:2, 7:11

State v. Stump, 2016-Ohio-2723, 2016

2014-Ohio-44, 4 N.E.3d 1016 (2014)—7:21, 16:19

State v. Tate, 54 Ohio St. 2d 444, 8 Ohio Op. 3d 441, 377 N.E.2d 778 (1978)—19:3

State v. Tatum, 2009-Ohio-453, 2009 WL 252361 (Ohio Ct. App. 5th Dist. Stark County 2009)—7:21

State v. Taylor, 2017-Ohio-1405, 2017 WL 1376829 (Ohio Ct. App. 12th Dist. Butler County 2017)—13:3

State v. Taylor, 2016-Ohio-5912, 2016 WL 5118653 (Ohio Ct. App. 5th Dist. Richland County 2016)—3:3

State v. Taylor, 2014-Ohio-3820, 2014 WL 4362406 (Ohio Ct. App. 8th Dist. Cuyahoga County 2014)—5:17

State v. Taylor, 2014-Ohio-3647, 2014 WL 4176135 (Ohio Ct. App. 2d Dist. Montgomery County 2014)—2:8

State v. Taylor, 2013-Ohio-4588, 2013 WL 5657956 (Ohio Ct. App. 5th Dist. Richland County 2013)—7:3, 10:6, 16:21

State v. Taylor, 2013-Ohio-1300, 2013 WL 1288668 (Ohio Ct. App. 3d Dist. Seneca County 2013)—7:9

State v. Taylor, 2008-Ohio-1462, 2008 WL 834437 (Ohio Ct. App. 9th Dist. Lorain County 2008)—6:14, 7:22

State v. Taylor, 113 Ohio St. 3d 297, 2007-Ohio-1950, 865 N.E.2d 37 (2007)—13:3

State v. Taylor, 2003-Ohio-2025, 2003 WL 1916787 (Ohio Ct. App. 9th Dist. Summit County 2003)—8:3, 12:22, 14:5, 14:6, 16:12, 16:22

State v. Taylor, 2001 WL 951728 (Ohio Ct. App. 10th Dist. Franklin County 2001)—5:3, 14:6

State v. Taylor, 79 Ohio Misc. 2d 82, 671 N.E.2d 343 (Mun. Ct. 1996)—2:4, 8:4, 8:8, 11:10, 15:7

State v. Taylor, 66 Ohio St. 3d 295, 612 N.E.2d 316 (1993)—5:15, 5:26, 16:14

State v. Tebelman, 2010-Ohio-481, 2010 WL 529496 (Ohio Ct. App. 3d Dist. Putnam County 2010)—6:15

State v. Terrell, 2014-Ohio-4344, 2014 WL 4823870 (Ohio Ct. App. 2d Dist. Clark County 2014)—4:4, 13:3

State v. Terrell, 2008-Ohio-1863, 2008 WL 1759095 (Ohio Ct. App. 2d Dist. Montgomery County 2008)—8:3

State v. Terry, 2006-Ohio-4320, 2006 WL 2390284 (Ohio Ct. App. 3d Dist. Crawford County 2006)—2:5

State v. Thayer, 2009-Ohio-5198, 2009 WL 3132946 (Ohio Ct. App. 6th Dist. Erie County 2009)—3:2

State v. Thomas, 2015-Ohio-5247, 54 N.E.3d 732 (Ohio Ct. App. 9th Dist. Summit County 2015)—16:13

State v. Thomas, 2015-Ohio-2152, 2015 WL 3540469 (Ohio Ct. App. 8th Dist. Cuyahoga County 2015)—3:2

State v. Thomas, 2014-Ohio-2666, 2014 WL 2810643 (Ohio Ct. App. 2d Dist. Darke County 2014)—2:8

State v. Thomas, 2013-Ohio-5386, 2013 WL 6535216 (Ohio Ct. App. 1st Dist. Hamilton County 2013)—5:24

State v. Thomas, 2012-Ohio-2430, 2012 WL 1970459 (Ohio Ct. App. 12th Dist. Warren County 2012)—2:7, 13:3, 16:20

State v. Thomas, 2011-Ohio-1629, 2011 WL 1233310 (Ohio Ct. App. 9th Dist. Lorain County 2011)—5:21

State v. Thomas, 2011-Ohio-1191, 2011 WL 882644 (Ohio Ct. App. 10th Dist. Franklin County 2011)—2:8

State v. Thomas, 2009-Ohio-1784, 2009 WL 1019855 (Ohio Ct. App. 8th Dist. Cuyahoga County 2009)—5:21

State v. Thomas, 2003-Ohio-5746, 2003 WL 22429536 (Ohio Ct. App. 2d Dist. Montgomery County 2003)—15:17, 16:24, 17:8

State v. Thomas, 77 Ohio St. 3d 323, 1997-Ohio-269, 673 N.E.2d 1339, 67 A.L.R.5th 775 (1997)—7:24, 12:29

State v. Thomas, 1989 WL 147652 (Ohio Ct. App. 8th Dist. Cuyahoga County 1989)—2:8, 3:3, 3:4

State v. Thomas, 66 Ohio St. 2d 518, 20 Ohio Op. 3d 424, 423 N.E.2d 137 (1981)—7:24, 15:16

State v. Treon, 91 Ohio L. Abs. 229, 188 N.E.2d 308 (Ct. App. 8th Dist. Cuyahoga County 1963)—13:4

State v. Tribble, 2017-Ohio-4425, 2017 WL 2665145 (Ohio Ct. App. 7th Dist. Mahoning County 2017)—3:2

State v. Trimble, 122 Ohio St. 3d 297, 2009-Ohio-2961, 911 N.E.2d 242 (2009)—3:3

State v. Troyer, 2016-Ohio-3090, 2016 WL 2944812 (Ohio Ct. App. 5th Dist. Holmes County 2016)—2:7, 3:2, 5:22

State v. Trubee, 2005-Ohio-552, 2005 WL 335833 (Ohio Ct. App. 3d Dist. Marion County 2005)—13:15, 13:17

State v. Truitt, 2011-Ohio-2271, 2011 WL 1842247 (Ohio Ct. App. 10th Dist. Franklin County 2011)—3:2

State v. Tucker, 2015-Ohio-3810, 2015 WL 5517839 (Ohio Ct. App. 9th Dist. Medina County 2015)—12:26

State v. Turks, 2010-Ohio-5944, 2010 WL 5050549 (Ohio Ct. App. 3d Dist. Allen County 2010)—2:8, 5:14, 5:15

State v. Turner, 2016-Ohio-813, 2016 WL 860301 (Ohio Ct. App. 8th Dist. Cuyahoga County 2016)—2:5, 7:3

State v. Turner, 2004-Ohio-6489, 2004 WL 2785954 (Ohio Ct. App. 3d Dist. Marion County 2004)—7:24

State v. Turner, 1996 WL 348016 (Ohio Ct. App. 1st Dist. Hamilton County 1996)—14:6, 16:14

State v. Tvaroch, 2012-Ohio-5836, 982 N.E.2d 751 (Ohio Ct. App. 11th Dist. Trumbull County 2012)—5:25

State v. Twyford, 94 Ohio St. 3d 340, 2002-Ohio-894, 763 N.E.2d 122 (2002)—5:21

State v. Tyler, 2002-Ohio-4300, 2002 WL 1934995 (Ohio Ct. App. 10th Dist. Franklin County 2002)—13:15

State v. Tymcio, 42 Ohio St. 2d 39, 71 Ohio Op. 2d 22, 325 N.E.2d 556 (1975)—7:9

State v. Underwood, 124 Ohio St. 3d 365, 2010-Ohio-1, 922 N.E.2d 923 (2010)—3:3

State v. Unger, 67 Ohio St. 2d 65, 21 Ohio Op. 3d 41, 423 N.E.2d 1078 (1981)—9:5, 11:21, 12:2, 12:4

State v. Valdez, 2017-Ohio-4260, 2017 WL 2569810 (Ohio Ct. App. 1st Dist. Hamilton County 2017)—7:11, 7:12

State v. Vales, 2000 WL 217802 (Ohio Ct. App. 8th Dist. Cuyahoga County 2000)—2:7, 3:2, 5:22

State v. Vance, 2000 WL 1028547 (Ohio Ct. App. 5th Dist. Stark County 2000)—14:6

State v. Vandergriff, 2001-Ohio-4327, 2001 WL 1117182 (Ohio Ct. App. 11th Dist. Ashtabula County 2001)—2:2, 8:7

State v. Vanderhorst, 2010-Ohio-1856, 2010 WL 1712246 (Ohio Ct. App. 8th Dist. Cuyahoga County 2010)—5:5, 6:14, 7:22, 10:9, 16:17

State v. Vanderpool, 2014-Ohio-1364, 2014 WL 1350197 (Ohio Ct. App. 11th Dist. Portage County 2014)—16:25

State v. Vandyne, 2017-Ohio-584, 2017 WL 777746 (Ohio Ct. App. 5th Dist. Guernsey County 2017)—16:21

State v. Van Hoose, 1993 WL 386314 (Ohio Ct. App. 2d Dist. Clark County 1993)—2:5, 10:6

State v. Vanselow, 61 Ohio Misc. 2d 1, 572 N.E.2d 269 (Mun. Ct. 1991)—3:10, 12:27, 13:13, 13:14

State v. Vanzandt, 142 Ohio St. 3d 223, 2015-Ohio-236, 28 N.E.3d 1267 (2015)—13:15

State v. Vanzandt, 2013-Ohio-2290, 990 N.E.2d 692 (Ohio Ct. App. 1st Dist. Hamilton County 2013)—13:15

State v. Varney, 2005-Ohio-1752, 2005 WL 859493 (Ohio Ct. App. 5th Dist. Ashland County 2005)—8:8

State v. Vaughn, 2003-Ohio-7023, 2003 WL 22999297 (Ohio Ct. App. 7th Dist. Carroll County 2003)—7:24

State v. Velazquez, 2016-Ohio-875, 2016 WL 868890 (Ohio Ct. App. 12th Dist. Butler County 2016)—7:11

State v. Veney, 120 Ohio St. 3d 176, 2008-Ohio-5200, 897 N.E.2d 621 (2008)—3:2

State v. Venters, 2003-Ohio-2831, 2003 WL 21267278 (Ohio Ct. App. 2d Dist. Montgomery County 2003)—16:21

State v. Verga, 2015-Ohio-2582, 2015 WL 3938069 (Ohio Ct. App. 12th Dist. Warren County 2015)—4:4, 13:3

State v. Villafuerte, 2008-Ohio-5587, 2008 WL 4750347 (Ohio Ct. App. 8th Dist. Cuyahoga County 2008)—7:11

State v. Villavicencio, 2014-Ohio-1522, 2014 WL 1408291 (Ohio Ct. App. 8th Dist. Cuyahoga County 2014)—7:11

State v. Vinson, 2008-Ohio-2523, 2008 WL 2192819 (Ohio Ct. App. 9th Dist. Summit County 2008)—5:24

State v. Voland, 99 Ohio Misc. 2d 61, 716 N.E.2d 299 (C.P. 1999)—8:6

State v. Volpe, 2008-Ohio-1678, 2008 WL 928342 (Ohio Ct. App. 10th Dist. Franklin County 2008)—2:7, 5:22

State v. Voskoboynikov, 2009-Ohio-4882, 2009 WL 2964369 (Ohio Ct. App. 8th Dist. Cuyahoga County 2009)—7:11

State v. Waddy, 1989 WL 133508 (Ohio Ct. App. 10th Dist. Franklin County 1989)—6:13

State v. Wagers, 2010-Ohio-2311, 2010 WL 2026779 (Ohio Ct. App. 12th Dist. Preble County 2010)—2:7

State v. Wages, 87 Ohio App. 3d 780, 623 N.E.2d 193 (8th Dist. Cuyahoga County 1993)—5:17, 5:18, 16:15, 16:16

State v. Wagner, 2015-Ohio-5183, 2015 WL 8571092 (Ohio Ct. App. 3d Dist. Seneca County 2015)—8:8

State v. Wagner, 1993 WL 303255 (Ohio Ct. App. 9th Dist. Medina County 1993)—2:5, 10:9

State v. Wagner, 30 Ohio App. 3d 261, 508 N.E.2d 164 (8th Dist. Cuyahoga County 1986)—16:12

State v. Wagster, 1996 WL 134538 (Ohio Ct. App. 1st Dist. Hamilton County 1996)—8:7

State v. Waheed, 2016-Ohio-2951, 2016 WL 2841926 (Ohio Ct. App. 1st Dist. Hamilton County 2016)—2:7, 3:2, 5:21, 5:22, 7:21

State v. Walburg, 2011-Ohio-4762, 2011 WL 4362748 (Ohio Ct. App. 10th Dist. Franklin County 2011)—2:5, 4:1, 10:6

State v. Walenciej, 2009-Ohio-936, 2009 WL 501251 (Ohio Ct. App. 7th Dist. Jefferson County 2009)—5:23

State v. Walker, 2017-Ohio-511, 78 N.E.3d 922 (Ohio Ct. App. 10th Dist. Franklin County 2017)—7:11

State v. Walker, 2016-Ohio-398, 2016 WL 529920 (Ohio Ct. App. 8th Dist. Cuyahoga County 2016)—4:1, 7:3

State v. Walker, 2007-Ohio-4047, 2007 WL 2269467 (Ohio Ct. App. 8th Dist. Cuyahoga County 2007)—2:4

State v. Walker, 2006-Ohio-917, 2006 WL 475789 (Ohio Ct. App. 9th Dist. Summit County 2006)—5:3

State v. Walker, 2005-Ohio-6365, 2005 WL 3220217 (Ohio Ct. App. 10th Dist. Franklin County 2005)—7:24

State v. Walker, 2001 WL 1782885 (Ohio Ct. App. 5th Dist. Stark County 2001)—16:14, 16:20

State v. Wallace, 2006-Ohio-5819, 2006 WL 3183386 (Ohio Ct. App. 9th Dist. Lorain County 2006)—2:5, 10:6, 10:7

State v. Wallace, 37 Ohio St. 3d 87, 524 N.E.2d 466 (1988)—5:15, 14:6, 16:12, 16:14

State v. Walton, 2014-Ohio-618, 2014 WL 705418 (Ohio Ct. App. 4th Dist. Washington County 2014)—7:11

State v. Waltzer, 2011-Ohio-5147, 2011 WL 4599828 (Ohio Ct. App. 8th Dist. Cuyahoga County 2011)—2:8

State v. Waltzer, 2011-Ohio-594, 2011 WL 486945 (Ohio Ct. App. 8th Dist. Cuyahoga County 2011)—5:14

State v. Wang, 1984 WL 13997 (Ohio Ct. App. 1st Dist. Hamilton County 1984)—2:7, 3:2

State v. Ward, 2010-Ohio-4614, 2010 WL 3782643 (Ohio Ct. App. 10th Dist. Franklin County 2010)—2:5, 2:7, 10:6

State v. Ward, 2009-Ohio-3145, 2009

WL 1844486 (Ohio Ct. App. 11th Dist. Geauga County 2009)—2:8, 8:3, 8:5

State v. Ward, 166 Ohio App. 3d 188, 2006-Ohio-1407, 849 N.E.2d 1076 (2d Dist. Greene County 2006)—3:2, 4:1, 10:10

State v. Ward, 2002-Ohio-3779, 2002 WL 1724242 (Ohio Ct. App. 10th Dist. Franklin County 2002)—16:12

State v. Ward, 2000 WL 33231613 (Ohio Ct. App. 10th Dist. Franklin County 2000)—10:6

State v. Warfield, 2003-Ohio-2366, 2003 WL 21054785 (Ohio Ct. App. 11th Dist. Trumbull County 2003)—16:12, 16:21

State v. Warren, 2015-Ohio-604, 2015 WL 759145 (Ohio Ct. App. 8th Dist. Cuyahoga County 2015)—2:8

State v. Warren, 106 Ohio App. 3d 753, 667 N.E.2d 68 (1st Dist. Hamilton County 1995)—12:27, 16:12, 16:25

State v. Washington, 2001 WL 460888 (Ohio Ct. App. 10th Dist. Franklin County 2001)—16:12, 16:14

State v. Washington, 319 N.J. Super. 681, 726 A.2d 326 (Law Div. 1998)—12:22

State v. Watkins, 2003-Ohio-668, 2003 WL 321541 (Ohio Ct. App. 10th Dist. Franklin County 2003)—5:3, 14:6

State v. Watkins, 99 Ohio St. 3d 12, 2003-Ohio-2419, 788 N.E.2d 635 (2003)—3:2

State v. Watson, 2005-Ohio-1729, 2005 WL 845228 (Ohio Ct. App. 5th Dist. Stark County 2005)—2:5, 2:8

State v. Watson, 28 Ohio St. 2d 15, 57 Ohio Op. 2d 95, 275 N.E.2d 153 (1971)—5:24

State v. Watts, 1998 WL 906745 (Ohio Ct. App. 2d Dist. Montgomery County 1998)—5:17, 5:18

State v. Weatherholtz, 2003-Ohio-3633, 2003 WL 21543813 (Ohio Ct. App. 3d Dist. Wyandot County 2003)—16:21

State v. Weathers, 2013-Ohio-1104, 988 N.E.2d 16 (Ohio Ct. App. 12th Dist. Butler County 2013)—7:12

State v. Weathers, 2011-Ohio-6793, 2011 WL 6921088 (Ohio Ct. App. 12th Dist. Butler County 2011)—2:8

State v. Weaver, 2002 SD 76, 648 N.W.2d 355 (S.D. 2002)—13:13

State v. Webb, 64 Wash. App. 480, 824 P.2d 1257 (Div. 1 1992)—8:8

State v. Weber, 125 Ohio App. 3d 120, 707 N.E.2d 1178 (10th Dist. Franklin County 1997)—7:11

State v. Webley, 2013-Ohio-4598, 2013 WL 5676267 (Ohio Ct. App. 8th Dist. Cuyahoga County 2013)—9:5

State v. Welch, 2017-Ohio-314, 81 N.E.3d 997 (Ohio Ct. App. 2d Dist. Clark County 2017)—3:2

State v. Wellman, 37 Ohio St. 2d 162, 66 Ohio Op. 2d 353, 309 N.E.2d 915 (1974)—3:2, 5:22, 7:9

State v. Wells, 2009-Ohio-6803, 2009 WL 4984066 (Ohio Ct. App. 7th Dist. Belmont County 2009)—5:22

State v. Wenger, 58 Ohio St. 2d 336, 12 Ohio Op. 3d 309, 390 N.E.2d 801 (1979)—8:3

State v. Wenker, 2011-Ohio-786, 2011 WL 646376 (Ohio Ct. App. 9th Dist. Summit County 2011)—2:2

State v. Wentz, 805 P.2d 962 (Alaska 1991)—13:15

State v. Werfel, 2003-Ohio-6958, 2003 WL 22994981 (Ohio Ct. App. 11th Dist. Lake County 2003)—5:21, 7:24, 9:2

State v. Wesley, 2002-Ohio-4429, 2002 WL 1986545 (Ohio Ct. App. 8th Dist. Cuyahoga County 2002)—2:7, 5:21

State v. Weston, 2013-Ohio-791, 2013 WL 844379 (Ohio Ct. App. 5th Dist. Tuscarawas County 2013)—13:2

State v. Wetherall, 2002-Ohio-1613, 2002 WL 440700 (Ohio Ct. App. 1st Dist. Hamilton County 2002)—8:8, 12:29

State v. Wheatley, 2000 WL 145394 (Ohio Ct. App. 2d Dist. Montgomery County 2000)—12:29, 14:4

State v. Whelan, 2004-Ohio-5183, 2004 WL 2244485 (Ohio Ct. App. 9th Dist. Summit County 2004)—13:2

State v. White, 2014-Ohio-1446, 2014

2011 WL 6382541 (Ohio Ct. App. 12th Dist. Warren County 2011)—2:2, 8:7
State v. Zima, 102 Ohio St. 3d 61, 2004-Ohio-1807, 806 N.E.2d 542 (2004)—2:8, 3:3
State v. Zobel, 2016-Ohio-5751, 2016 WL 4728100 (Ohio Ct. App. 5th Dist. Tuscarawas County 2016)—13:3
State v. Zuber, 2001-Ohio-2427, 2001 WL 301408 (Ohio Ct. App. 4th Dist. Hocking County 2001)—8:3, 8:5
State v. Zuniga, 2005-Ohio-2078, 2005 WL 1007173 (Ohio Ct. App. 11th Dist. Lake County 2005)—7:11
State/City of Akron v. McGlaughlin, 1998 WL 801930 (Ohio Ct. App. 9th Dist. Summit County 1998)—8:7
State /City of Toledo v. Kinnebrew, 2018-Ohio-129, 2018 WL 388852 (Ohio Ct. App. 6th Dist. Lucas County 2018)—2:2
State /City of Toledo v. Lear, 2018-Ohio-1874, 2018 WL 2174378 (Ohio Ct. App. 6th Dist. Lucas County 2018)—2:7, 5:3
State , City of Twinsburg v. Milano, 2018-Ohio-1367, 2018 WL 1750475 (Ohio Ct. App. 9th Dist. Summit County 2018)—3:2
State Dept. of Human Services v. Northern, 563 S.W.2d 197 (Tenn. Ct. App. 1978)—8:4
State Farm Fire & Cas. Co. v. Davidson, 87 Ohio App. 3d 101, 621 N.E.2d 887 (2d Dist. Montgomery County 1993)—10:3
State Farm Fire & Cas. Co. v. Hiermer, 720 F. Supp. 1310 (S.D. Ohio 1988)—8:3
State Karnes v. Karnes, 1981 WL 5749 (Ohio Ct. App. 6th Dist. Wood County 1981)—13:4
State Police Litigation, In re, 88 F.3d 111 (2d Cir. 1996)—14:8
Steckler v. Steckler, 492 N.W.2d 76 (N.D. 1992)—8:4, 8:8, 12:15
Steen v. Goad, 2001-Ohio-1771, 2001 WL 1421527 (Ohio Ct. App. 9th Dist. Wayne County 2001)—8:4, 11:13
Stella v. Platz, 1999 WL 427672 (Ohio Ct. App. 4th Dist. Washington County 1999)—12:15, 12:16, 12:21, 12:22, 12:23, 12:26
Stephens v. Stephens, 85 Wash. 2d 290, 534 P.2d 571 (1975)—19:9
Sterling v. Sterling, 2002-Ohio-4997, 2002 WL 31111778 (Ohio Ct. App. 5th Dist. Fairfield County 2002)—12:2, 12:4, 12:7, 12:25, 12:27
Stevens v. Provitt, 2003-Ohio-7226, 2003 WL 23097088 (Ohio Ct. App. 11th Dist. Trumbull County 2003)—5:12
Stevens v. Trumbull County Sheriffs' Dept., 63 F. Supp. 2d 851 (N.D. Ohio 1999)—14:9
Stevenson v. Stevenson, 314 N.J. Super. 350, 714 A.2d 986 (Ch. Div. 1998)—8:4, 12:25
Stewart v. State, 1 Ohio St. 66, 1852 WL 10 (1852)—7:24
Stewart v. Stewart, 2001 WL 274097 (Tenn. Ct. App. 2001)—14:4
Stewart v. Stewart, 708 N.E.2d 903 (Ind. Ct. App. 1999)—15:24
Stewart v. Sydenstricker, 1996 WL 272948 (Ohio Ct. App. 4th Dist. Washington County 1996)—13:4, 13:6, 13:7
Stickel v. Pryor, 2002-Ohio-3309, 2002 WL 1396077 (Ohio Ct. App. 2d Dist. Miami County 2002)—11:11, 12:9, 12:23, 12:26, 13:3, 13:13
Still v. Still, 1999 WL 236049 (Ohio Ct. App. 2d Dist. Montgomery County 1999)—9:2, 9:8, 11:13, 12:26
Stimmel v. Sessions, 879 F.3d 198 (6th Cir. 2018)—18:11
Stockdale v. Baba, 153 Ohio App. 3d 712, 2003-Ohio-4366, 795 N.E.2d 727 (10th Dist. Franklin County 2003)—19:5
Stokes v. Meimaris, 111 Ohio App. 3d 176, 675 N.E.2d 1289 (8th Dist. Cuyahoga County 1996)—19:3
Stoneman v. Drollinger, 2003 MT 25, 314 Mont. 139, 64 P.3d 997 (2003)—15:24
Storch v. Sauerhoff, 334 N.J. Super. 226, 757 A.2d 836 (Ch. Div. 2000)—10:2
Stout v. Bushong, 2008-Ohio-2223, 2008 WL 1991613 (Ohio Ct. App. 4th Dist. Adams County 2008)—9:8
Strassell v. Chapman, 2010-Ohio-

T

2003 WL 125013 (Ohio Ct. App. 8th Dist. Cuyahoga County 2003)—12:1, 12:6, 12:11, 16:9

Tevis v. Tevis, 79 N.J. 422, 400 A.2d 1189 (1979)—19:9

Thacker v. City of Columbus, 328 F.3d 244, 2003 FED App. 0127P (6th Cir. 2003)—14:5

Theibert v. Anderson, 2017-Ohio-1029, 2017 WL 1075534 (Ohio Ct. App. 5th Dist. Knox County 2017)—9:7, 9:8

Theresa CC, Matter of, 178 A.D.2d 687, 576 N.Y.S.2d 937 (3d Dep't 1991)—15:24

The V Cos., State ex rel. v. Marshall, 81 Ohio St. 3d 467, 1998-Ohio-329, 692 N.E.2d 198 (1998)—12:4

Thom v. Mulvin, 2009-Ohio-3797, 2009 WL 2365996 (Ohio Ct. App. 6th Dist. Erie County 2009)—8:4, 11:2, 11:10, 12:11, 12:22

Thomas v. Thomas, 44 Ohio App. 3d 6, 540 N.E.2d 745 (10th Dist. Franklin County 1988)—8:3, 10:13, 11:5, 11:7, 11:10, 11:13, 11:22, 12:11, 12:14, 12:17, 12:24, 12:26

Thompson v. Koontz, 2000 WL 1739291 (Ohio Ct. App. 8th Dist. Cuyahoga County 2000)—8:7

Thompson v. Thompson, 559 A.2d 311 (D.C. 1989)—13:8

Thompson v. Warden, Warren Correctional Inst., 2014 WL 2515317 (S.D. Ohio 2014)—5:16

Thompson v. Wing, 70 Ohio St. 3d 176, 1994-Ohio-358, 637 N.E.2d 917 (1994)—13:14

Thompson, State ex rel. v. Spon, 83 Ohio St. 3d 551, 1998-Ohio-298, 700 N.E.2d 1281 (1998)—12:15, 15:6

Thorensen, In re Custody of, 46 Wash. App. 493, 730 P.2d 1380 (Div. 1 1987)—15:24

Thurman v. City of Torrington, 595 F. Supp. 1521 (D. Conn. 1984)—14:7, 14:8, 14:10, 14:14

Tierney v. Davidson, 133 F.3d 189 (2d Cir. 1998)—14:5

Tighe v. Kaiser, 2016-Ohio-1400, 2016 WL 1297407 (Ohio Ct. App. 6th Dist. Ottawa County 2016)—8:5, 9:2, 9:8

Tischler v. Vahcic, 1995 WL 680928 (Ohio Ct. App. 8th Dist. Cuyahoga County 1995)—8:7, 11:10, 12:11, 12:15, 12:16, 12:26

T.L., In re, 2011-Ohio-4709, 2011 WL 4346334 (Ohio Ct. App. 9th Dist. Medina County 2011)—6:14

Todd v. Todd, 772 S.W.2d 14 (Mo. Ct. App. E.D. 1989)—12:21

Tokatly v. Ashcroft, 371 F.3d 613 (9th Cir. 2004)—7:11

Toledo v. Green, 2015-Ohio-1864, 33 N.E.3d 581 (Ohio Ct. App. 6th Dist. Lucas County 2015)—5:14, 5:15, 5:16, 6:14, 7:22

Toledo v. Green, 2015-Ohio-386, 27 N.E.3d 1015 (Ohio Ct. App. 6th Dist. Lucas County 2015)—6:14

Toledo v. Huggins, 2013-Ohio-3467, 2013 WL 4041572 (Ohio Ct. App. 6th Dist. Lucas County 2013)—5:15

Toledo v. Jenkins, 2015-Ohio-1270, 2015 WL 1510849 (Ohio Ct. App. 6th Dist. Lucas County 2015)—6:14, 7:22

Toledo v. Lanier, 2009-Ohio-5191, 2009 WL 3132601 (Ohio Ct. App. 6th Dist. Lucas County 2009)—11:11, 13:3

Toledo v. Lewis, 2013-Ohio-3289, 2013 WL 3936455 (Ohio Ct. App. 6th Dist. Lucas County 2013)—4:4, 9:5, 12:29, 13:3

Toledo v. Loggins, 2007-Ohio-5887, 2007 WL 3227385 (Ohio Ct. App. 6th Dist. Lucas County 2007)—7:22, 16:13

Toledo v. Lyphout, 2009-Ohio-4596, 2009 WL 2855714 (Ohio Ct. App. 6th Dist. Lucas County 2009)—2:7, 9:5, 11:11, 13:3, 13:8

Toledo v. Murray, 2014-Ohio-3625, 2014 WL 4161247 (Ohio Ct. App. 6th Dist. Lucas County 2014)—16:14

Toledo v. Sailes, 180 Ohio App. 3d 56, 2008-Ohio-6400, 904 N.E.2d 543 (6th Dist. Lucas County 2008)—5:12, 5:15, 5:16, 7:22

Toledo v. Wells, 2014-Ohio-4636, 2014 WL 5332877 (Ohio Ct. App. 6th Dist. Lucas County 2014)—9:10

Toledo, City of v. Eissa, 2003-Ohio-3425, 2003 WL 21489426 (Ohio Ct. App. 6th Dist. Lucas County 2003)—12:19, 12:27, 15:15

Toledo, City of v. Emery, 2000 WL 864305 (Ohio Ct. App. 6th Dist. Lucas County 2000)—3:6, 9:2, 9:8

Toledo, City of v. Montgomery, 2002-

U

V

W

Waite v. Waite, 593 So. 2d 222 (Fla. 3d DCA 1991)—19:11

Waldmann v. Waldmann, 48 Ohio St. 2d 176, 2 Ohio Op. 3d 373, 358 N.E.2d 521 (1976)—11:6

Waliser v. Tada, 1990 WL 20080 (Ohio Ct. App. 10th Dist. Franklin County 1990)—11:6, 12:5, 17:6

Walker v. Bentley, 678 So. 2d 1265 (Fla. 1996)—13:6

Walker v. City of Birmingham, 388 U.S. 307, 87 S. Ct. 1824, 18 L. Ed. 2d 1210 (1967)—13:8

Walker v. Edgington, 2008-Ohio-3478, 2008 WL 2699430 (Ohio Ct. App. 2d Dist. Clark County 2008)—3:6, 9:2, 9:8

Walker v. Lees, 2001 WL 197853 (Ohio Ct. App. 5th Dist. Licking County 2001)—8:4, 8:5, 12:15

Walker v. State Medical Bd. of Ohio, 2002-Ohio-682, 2002 WL 243318 (Ohio Ct. App. 10th Dist. Franklin County 2002)—9:5

Walker v. Walker, 2011-Ohio-3933, 2011 WL 3452362 (Ohio Ct. App. 5th Dist. Stark County 2011)—7:9, 9:5, 13:13

Walker v. Walker, 86 N.Y.2d 624, 635 N.Y.S.2d 152, 658 N.E.2d 1025 (1995)—13:9

Wallace v. Masten, 2003-Ohio-1081, 2003 WL 927600 (Ohio Ct. App. 4th Dist. Hocking County 2003)—9:4, 9:9

Wallace v. Noel, 2009-Ohio-6984, 2009 WL 5174175 (Ohio Ct. App. 6th Dist. Wood County 2009)—19:10

Walsh v. Walsh, 2008-Ohio-5701, 2008 WL 4787566 (Ohio Ct. App. 4th Dist. Lawrence County 2008)—19:10

Walters v. Walters, 150 Ohio App. 3d 287, 2002-Ohio-6455, 780 N.E.2d 1032 (4th Dist. Gallia County 2002)—12:23, 12:26

Walton v. Walton, 2004-Ohio-7151, 2004 WL 3017265 (Ohio Ct. App. 6th Dist. Wood County 2004)—12:9, 12:27, 13:14

Ward v. Balsley, 2014-Ohio-4050, 2014 WL 4629607 (Ohio Ct. App. 5th Dist. Muskingum County 2014)—12:23, 13:15

Ward v. Ward, 155 Vt. 242, 583 A.2d 577, 4 A.L.R.5th 1152 (1990)—19:11

Wardeh v. Altabchi, 158 Ohio App. 3d 325, 2004-Ohio-4423, 815 N.E.2d 712 (10th Dist. Franklin County 2004)—8:7, 11:10, 12:15, 12:25

Wardeh v. Altabchi—12:15

Warnecke v. Whitaker, 2011-Ohio-5442, 2011 WL 5028789 (Ohio Ct. App. 3d Dist. Putnam County 2011)—9:8

Warren, City of v. Culver, 2004-Ohio-333, 2004 WL 144227 (Ohio Ct. App. 11th Dist. Trumbull County 2004)—8:3, 14:3, 17:2

Washburn v. City of Federal Way, 178 Wash. 2d 732, 310 P.3d 1275 (2013)—14:14

Waters v. Lattany, 2007-Ohio-1047, 2007 WL 707519 (Ohio Ct. App. 6th Dist. Lucas County 2007)—9:5, 12:7, 12:15

Watson v. City of Kansas City, Kan., 857 F.2d 690 (10th Cir. 1988)—14:8, 14:10, 14:14

Watts v. Watts, 2014-Ohio-1901, 2014 WL 1836326 (Ohio Ct. App. 5th Dist. Fairfield County 2014)—8:4

Watts v. Watts, 1992 WL 318944 (Ohio Ct. App. 6th Dist. Lucas County 1992)—19:6

Wayte v. U.S., 470 U.S. 598, 105 S. Ct. 1524, 84 L. Ed. 2d 547 (1985)—5:3

Webb v. Greene County Sheriff's Office, 494 F. Supp. 2d 779 (S.D. Ohio 2007)—4:7

Weber v. Forinash, 2015-Ohio-3187, 2015 WL 4720532 (Ohio Ct. App. 6th Dist. Sandusky County 2015)—8:4, 11:2, 12:10

Weber v. Weber, 2011-Ohio-2980, 2011 WL 2436963 (Ohio Ct. App. 2d Dist. Greene County 2011)—8:4, 11:2, 11:10, 12:11, 12:24

Weis v. Weis, 147 Ohio St. 416, 34 Ohio Op. 350, 72 N.E.2d 245, 169 A.L.R. 668 (1947)—14:6, 17:2

Weismuller v. Polston, 2012-Ohio-1476, 2012 WL 1107717 (Ohio Ct. App. 12th Dist. Brown County 2012)—9:5, 9:7, 12:26

Weissenburger v. Iowa Dist. Court for Warren County, 740 N.W.2d 431 (Iowa 2007)—12:22, 18:11

Welborn-Harlow v. Fuller, 2013-Ohio-54, 2013 WL 139592 (Ohio Ct. App. 6th Dist. Wood County 2013)—9:5, 9:8

Index

ORC	Ohio Revised Code
Sup	Superintendance Rules
T	Text

Cross References to another main heading are in CAPITAL LETTERS.